# TRAVELING WITH YOUR PET
## THE AAA PET BOOK®

The AAA guide to more than 13,000
pet-friendly, AAA-RATED® lodgings
and 400 campgrounds
across the United States and Canada

8th Edition

AAA PUBLISHING

| | |
|---|---|
| President & CEO | **Robert Darbelnet** |
| Executive Vice President, Publishing & Administration | **Rick Rinner** |
| Managing Director, Travel Information | **Bob Hopkins** |
| | |
| Director, Product Development & Sales | **Bill Wood** |
| Director, Publishing Marketing | **Patty Wight** |
| Director, Manufacturing & Quality | **Susan Sears** |
| Director, Tourism Information Development (TID) | **Michael Petrone** |
| Director, Publishing Operations/Travel Information | **Jeff Zimmerman** |
| Director, Publishing/GIS Systems & Development | **Ramin Kalhor** |
| Director, GIS/Cartography | **Jan Coyne** |
| Director, Purchasing & Corporate Services | **Becky Barrett** |
| Director, Business Development | **Gary Sisco** |
| | |
| Product Manager | **Marquita Dudley** |
| Manager, Public Relations | **Justin McNaull** |
| Buyer | **Bob Bailes** |
| TID Regional Managers | **Lisa Brenneman, Todd Cronson, Michel Mousseau, Stacy Brunick, Patrick Schardin** |
| TID Field Operations Manager | **Laurie DiMinico** |
| Manager, Travel Information Operations | **Brenda Daniels** |
| Publishing Business Manager | **Linda Indolfi** |
| Manager, Electronic Media Design | **Mike McCrary** |
| Manager, Pre-Press/Photo Services & Product Support | **Tim Johnson** |
| Manager, Graphic Communication Services | **Yvonne Macklin** |
| Manager, Application Development | **Scott Chrisien** |
| | |
| Development Editor | **Alison Lockwood** |
| Art Director and Cover Design | **Barbra Natali** |
| Photo Research | **Denise Campbell** |
| Quality Services | **Terry Lane, Andrea Payne-Lecky** |
| Paginator | **Christine Carter** |
| Technical Specialist | **Roland Levett** |
| System Analyst | **Samuel Allen** |
| Programmer | **James Cothrine** |
| Data Processors | **Lucy Berger, Connie Delle Donne, Dawn Garrison, Kelly Giewont, Jennifer Lopresti, Carolyn Shackelford, Andrea Tlumacki, Susan Trapp** |
| Proofreader | **Janet D'Amico** |

AAA wishes to acknowledge the following for their assistance: Dogpark.com®

### Cover Photos

| | |
|---|---|
| Couple running on beach | **IT International Ltd/eStock Photo** |
| Mackenzie, a.k.a. "Kenzie" amid a field of Texas Bluebonnets | **Photo Contest winner Genie Ketterl** |
| Addison, a.k.a. "Addy" hiking in White Mountain National Forest | **Photo Contest winners Michael Gibson and Diana Perry** |

Published by AAA Publishing
1000 AAA Drive, Heathrow, Florida 32746

Eighth Edition Copyright © 2006 AAA Publishing. All rights reserved.
ISBN 10: 1-59508-093-7 ISBN 13: 978-1-59508-093-6 Stock Number 552206
Printed in the USA by Dickinson Press

# Traveling with Your Pet Photo Contest Entry Form

The next time you go on vacation with your pet, be sure to take along your camera.

The winning entry in AAA's PetBook Photo Contest will appear on the cover of the 9th edition of **Traveling With Your Pet: The AAA PetBook®**. The winner also will receive $100, five complimentary copies of the book as well as a year's supply of Milk-bone® dog snacks.

**MILK-BONE**

Please print

**Name:** _____

**Address:** _____

**City:** _____ **State:** ____ **Zip code:** _____

**Daytime phone:** _____ **Evening phone:** _____

**Pet's name/gender:** _____ **Animal breed:** _____

**Photo taken:** _____

Please answer the following questions:

*1. Why do you travel with your pet? _____

_____

*2. What is your favorite place or city to take your pet, and why? _____

_____

3. Tell us about an adventure you had while traveling with your pet. _____

_____

**\*Required answer**

**Traveling with Your Pet: The AAA PetBook® Photo Contest Official Rules**

1. Email one digital photo to Petbookcontest@national.aaa.com. Please send the photo as a .jpeg file attachment no larger than 2 MB, and include the information requested on the entry form in the body of the email. The digital photo **must** have a minimum resolution of 1200 pixels by 1600 pixels. The entry form information (name, address, phone, pet's name/gender, animal breed and answers to questions) **must** be included in the email for contest consideration. Minor digital enhancement for cropping, red-eye removal, filters and correction functions are permitted, but images that are determined to be significantly altered will be disqualified. Photographers are not permitted to place borders or frames around their image or to place a watermark, signature, date or copyright notices on the image.

**OR**

2. Send printed color 8" x 10" unmounted photo that is in focus, along with the completed entry form to:

> **PetBook Photo Contest**
> **AAA**
> **1000 AAA Drive, MS 64**
> **Heathrow, FL 32746**

Official Rules *continued*

3. Photos must be postmarked by Nov. 22, 2006, and received by Nov. 30, 2006, to be eligible for the contest.

4. Photo must feature at least one pet and have a travel theme.

5. Only **one** photo may be entered per household.

6. The entrant must be the person who took the photo and who has full rights to the photo.

7. The entrant must obtain full consent from all models or persons appearing in the photo for full use of the photo, including use and publishing in this contest and the other uses stated herein.

8. All photos entered in the contest, including the prize-winning photo(s), along with all rights of every kind therein, become the sole and exclusive property of AAA and will not be returned.

9. A panel of judges will choose the winning photo based on the following qualities: impact, lighting, composition and effectively conveying the idea that *Traveling With Your Pet: The AAA PetBook* is about traveling on vacation with your pet. Posed or studio photographs will be disqualified.

10. The winner will be notified **by mail** by Dec. 22, 2006.

**Disclaimer**

By participating, entrants agree that: (i) these rules and the decisions of AAA shall be final in all respects, and (ii) AAA may put the winner's photo on the front or back cover or spine of the 9th edition of *Traveling With Your Pet: The AAA PetBook.* The winner grants AAA the right to use his or her name, likeness, portrait, picture, photo, answers on entry form and/or prize information for advertising, publicity and promotional purposes relating to the book, *Traveling With Your Pet: The AAA PetBook*, and the contest without compensation or permission (unless prohibited by law). The winner agrees to hold harmless and release AAA from any injuries, losses or damages of any kind that may result from taking a photo intended to be submitted. The pet travel accessories prize will be selected at the sole discretion of AAA. The winner agrees to hold harmless and release AAA from use of the pet travel accessories. AAA is not responsible for late, lost or misdirected entries or mail; for technical, hardware or software malfunctions, lost or unavailable network connections, or failed, incorrect, inaccurate, incomplete, garbled or delayed electronic communications, whether caused by the sender or by any of the equipment or programming associated with or utilized in this promotion, or by any human error that may occur in the processing of entries; or for loss of or damage to any entries. AAA retains the right to not award the prize should no acceptable photos be received.

**Eligibility**

No purchase is necessary to enter the contest or claim the prize. Open to U.S. or Canadian residents 18 years or older except for employees of AAA, CAA and their clubs.

By submitting an entry I agree that I have read the Contest Rules, assent thereto, and submit the enclosed photo in accordance therewith; I attest that I own all rights to the photo and it has not been published or accepted for publication in any medium; and f the photo portrays any living person or persons, I have secured a model release or releases. I further agree that should my entry be chosen as the winning entry I will execute all necessary paperwork/releases as requested by AAA.

# ABOUT THIS BOOK

Welcome to the 8th edition of **Traveling With Your Pet — The AAA PetBook**®. *Traveling With Your Pet* is a must for the traveler who's also an animal lover. This comprehensive book provides all the information you need to know about taking a four-legged friend on the road. Will Spot be a good car passenger? Is it safe to take Snowball on a plane? What are the important rules of pet etiquette? Is pet insurance a good idea? *Traveling With Your Pet* answers all of these questions and more. Here are just some of the features covered:

- Dog parks where you and your furry friends can play, exercise or just relax.

- An extensive listing of animal clinics compiled by the Veterinary Emergency & Critical Care Society. Names, addresses and phone numbers provide valuable information for unexpected or emergency situations, both en route and at your destination.

- A roundup of pet-friendly attractions.

- National public lands in the United States and Canada that allow pets, along with recreation information.

- Border crossing procedures and tips for travelers — both entering Canada from the United States and vice versa.

- Policies pertaining to service animals.

*Traveling With Your Pet* lists more than 13,000 AAA-RATED® lodgings. And the listings show AAA's trustworthy diamond ratings, the traveler's assurance of quality. Other handy features include:

- Informative highway directions.

- Specific information about lodgings' pet policies: deposits and fees (rounded to the nearest dollar), housekeeping service, designated rooms and other stipulations relating to travelers with pets.

- Additional details about the lodgings themselves, including icons for amenities, recreation, dining and accessibility.

- Icons designating AAA's member discount programs.

- Listings for AAA's highest rated campgrounds, including rate and pet policy information and service/amenity icons.

All of this valuable information is packaged in a contemporary, easy-to-read format, making *Traveling With Your Pet — The AAA PetBook* as indispensable an on-the-road companion as Spot's water dish or Snowball's litter box. Don't leave home without it, and remember: It always pays to *Travel With Someone You Trust*®.

# TABLE OF CONTENTS

## Traveling With Pets

## Pet-Friendly Places in the U.S. and Canada

## Pet-Friendly Lodgings

## U.S. Lodgings

## Canadian Lodgings

## Pet-Friendly Campgrounds

Many people view their pets as full-fledged members of the family. Spot and Snowball often have their own beds, premium-quality foods, a basketful of toys and a special place in their humans' hearts.

Until it's time to go on vacation, that is. Then the family dog or cat is consigned to "watching the fort" at home while everyone else experiences the joy of traveling. Many animal lovers hesitate to take their pet with them because they don't think they'll be able to find accommodations that accept four-legged guests. Others aren't sure how — or if — their furry friends will adapt.

The truth is, including a pet in the family vacation is fairly easy, so long as you plan ahead. Most pets respond well to travel, a fact that isn't lost on the tourism industry. More than 13,000 AAA-RATED® hotels and motels from coast to coast are pet-friendly, and airline bookings for pet passengers are on the rise. Great companions at home, pets are earning their stripes on the road, too.

So if you've been longing to hit the trail with a canine or feline companion, read the tips on the following pages. You may find that a getaway can be far more enjoyable with than without your pet.

## Should Your Pet Travel?

Before you make reservations, determine if your pet is able to travel. Most animals can and do make the most of the experience, but a small percentage simply are not cut out for traveling. Illness, physical condition and temperament are important factors, as is your pet's ability to adjust to such stresses as changes to his environment and routine. When in doubt, check with your veterinarian. If you feel your pet isn't up to the trip, it's better for everyone if he stays home.

❧ **Rule 1: Pets who are very young, very old, pregnant, sick, injured, prone to biting or excessive vocalizing, or who cannot follow basic obedience commands should not travel.**

Even if Spot and Snowball are seasoned travelers, take into account the type of vacation and activities you have planned. No pet is going to be happy (or safe) cooped up in a car or hotel room. Likewise, the family dog may love camping and hiking, but the family cat may not. Putting a little thought toward your animal's needs and safety will pay off in a more enjoyable vacation for everyone.

❧ **Rule 2: If your pet can't actively participate in the trip, she should stay home.**

Most of the information in this book pertains to cats and dogs. If you own a bird, hamster, pig, ferret, lizard or other exotic creature, remember that unusual animals are not always accepted as readily as more conventional pets. Always specify the type of pet you have when making arrangements.

Also check states' animal policies. **Hawaii** imposes 120-day or 5-days-or-less quarantines for all imported dogs, cats and other carnivores to prevent the importation of rabies. Guide dogs and other service animals are exempt from the quarantine provided they have: a standard health certificate; a current rabies vaccination with documentation of the product name, lot number and lot expiration date; and an electronic identification microchip implanted and operational. Upon arrival, guide dogs still must be examined for external parasites and undergo serum antibody testing and a microchip scan. For additional details, obtain the Hawaii Rabies Quarantine Information Brochure from the Hawaii Department of Agriculture, Animal Quarantine Station, 99-951 Halawa Valley St., Aiea, HI 96701-5602; phone (808) 483-7151, fax (808) 483-7161. The Web site address is www.hawaiiag.org/hdoa/ai_aqs_info.htm.

**North Carolina** has stringent restrictions regarding pets in lodgings. Make certain you understand an accommodation's specific policies before making reservations.

❧ **Rule 3: Be specific when making travel plans that include your pet. Nobody wants unpleasant surprises on vacation.**

If Spot and Snowball stay behind, leave them in good hands while you're gone. **Family, friends and neighbors** make good sitters (provided they're willing), especially if they know your pet and can care for him in your home. Provide detailed instructions for feeding, exercise and medication, as well as phone numbers for your destination, your veterinarian and your local animal emergency clinic.

**Professional pet sitters** offer a range of services, from feeding and walking your pet daily to full-time house sitting while you are gone. Interview several candidates, and always check credentials and references. For additional information, contact the National Association of Professional Pet Sitters or Pet Sitters International. *(See sidebars on p. 8 and p. 9.)*

**Kennels** board many animals simultaneously and generally are run by professionals who will provide food and exercise according to your instructions. Pets usually are kept in a run (dogs) or cage (cats and small dogs) and may not get the same level of human interaction as at home. **Veterinary clinics** also board pets and may be the best choice if yours is sick, injured or needs special medical care. For further information on how to select a kennel, contact the American Boarding Kennels Association.

Veterinarians, fellow pet owners and professional associations are a good source of referrals for sitters and kennels.

❧ **Rule 4: Never leave your pet with someone you don't trust.**

# Travelers Who Have Disabilities

Individuals with disabilities who own service animals to assist them with everyday activities undoubtedly face challenges, but traveling should not be one of them. Service animals (the accepted term for animals trained to help people with disabilities) are not pets and thus are not subject to many of the laws or policies pertaining to pets.

The Americans With Disabilities Act (ADA) defines a service animal as "any guide dog, signal dog or other animal individually trained to provide assistance to an individual with a disability." ADA regulations stipulate that public accommodations are required to modify policies, practices and procedures to permit the use of a service animal by an individual with a disability.

The purpose of these regulations is to provide equal access opportunities for people with disabilities and to ensure that they are not separated from their service animals. A tow truck operator, for example, must allow a service animal to ride in the truck with her owner rather than in the towed vehicle.

Public accommodations may charge a fee or deposit to an individual who has a disability — provided that fee or deposit is required of all customers — but no fees or deposits may be charged for the service animal, even those normally charged for pets.

The handler/owner is responsible for the animal's care and behavior; if the dog creates an altercation or poses a direct threat, the handler may be required to remove it from the premises and pay for any resulting damages.

## CHOOSING A PET SITTER

**Before hiring a pet sitter, ask:**
- Is he or she insured (for commercial liability) and bonded?
- What is included in the fee?
- Does the sitter require that your pet have a current vaccination?
- What kind of animals does the sitter typically care for?
- How will a medical, weather or home emergency be handled?
- Does he or she fully understand your pet's medical or dietary needs?
- How much time will be spent with your pet?

**The pet sitter should:**
- Have a polished, professional attitude.
- Provide references.
- Have a standard contract outlining terms of service.
- Have experience in caring for animals.
- Insist on current vaccinations.
- Ask about your pet's health, temperament, schedule and needs.
- Visit and interact with your pet before you leave.
- Devote time and attention to your pet.
- Be affiliated with pet care organizations.

**Be sure you:**
- Explain your pet's personality — favorite toys, good and bad habits, hiding spots, general health, etc.
- Leave care instructions, keys, food and water dishes, extra supplies (food, medication, etc.), and phone numbers for your veterinarian and an emergency contact.
- Bring pets inside before leaving.

## CHOOSING A KENNEL

**Before reserving a kennel, ask:**
- What is included in the fee?
- Are current vaccinations required?
- What kind of animals do they board?
- How will a medical or weather emergency be handled?
- Will your pet be kept in a cage or run?
- Will your pet receive daily exercise?
- Does the kennel fully understand your pet's medical or dietary needs?
- How and how often will staff interact with your pet?

**The kennel should:**
- Require proof of current vaccinations.
- Be clean, well-ventilated and offer adequate protection from the elements.
- Have separate areas for dogs, cats and other animals, with secure fencing and caging.
- Clean and disinfect facilities daily.
- Give your pet his regular food on his regular schedule.
- Provide soft bedding in runs/cages.
- Understand your pet's medical needs.
- Provide or obtain veterinary care if necessary.
- Offer sufficient supervision.
- Have a friendly, animal-loving staff.

**Be sure you:**
- Notify staff of behavior quirks (dislike of other animals, children, etc.).
- Provide food and medication.
- Leave a familiar object with your pet.
- Leave phone numbers for your veterinarian and an emergency contact.
- Spend time with your pet before boarding him.

The **Delta Society,** an organization devoted to companion and service animals, has information about laws that affect people and service animals in public accommodations. Phone (425) 226-7357 for a catalog, or visit www.deltasociety.org.

# Preparing Your Pet for Travel

Happily, many vacations can be planned to include fun activities for pets. Trips to parks, nature trails, the ocean or lakes offer exposure to the world beyond the window or fence at home, as well as the chance to explore new sights and sounds. Even the streets of an unfamiliar city can provide a smorgasbord of discoveries for your animal friend to enjoy.

Once you decide Spot and Snowball are ready to hit the road, plan accordingly:

❧ **Get a clean bill of health from the veterinarian.** Update your pet's vaccinations, check his general physical condition and obtain a health certificate showing proof of up-to-date inoculations, particularly rabies, distemper and kennel cough. Such documentation will be necessary if you cross state or country lines, and also may come in handy in the unlikely event your pet gets lost and must be retrieved from the local shelter. Don't forget to ask the doctor about potential health risks at your destination (Lyme disease, heartworm infection) and the necessary preventive measures.

If your pet is taking prescribed medicine, pack a sufficient supply plus a few days' extra. Also take the prescription in case you need a refill. Be prepared for emergencies by getting the names and numbers of clinics or doctors at your destination from your veterinarian or the American Animal Hospital Association. **Hint:** Obtain these references before you leave and keep them handy throughout the trip.

Make sure your pet is in good physical shape overall, especially if you are planning an active vacation. If your animal is primarily sedentary or overweight, he may not be up to lengthy hikes through the woods.

**Note:** Some owners believe a sedated animal will travel more easily than one that is fully aware, but this is rarely the case. In fact, tranquilizing an animal can make travel much more stressful. Always consult a veterinarian about what is best for your pet, and administer sedatives only under the doctor's direction. In addition, never give an animal medication that is specifically prescribed for humans. The dosage may be too high for an animal's much smaller body mass, or may cause dangerous side effects.

❧ **Acclimate your pet to car travel.** Even if you're flying, your pet will have to ride in the car to get to the airport or terminal, and you don't want any unpleasant surprises before departure.

## CONTACT INFORMATION

The following organizations offer information, tips, brochures and other travel materials designed to help you and your pet enjoy a happy and safe vacation.

**American Animal Hospital Association**
12575 W. Bayaud Ave., Lakewood, CO 80228
(303) 986-2800 — www.healthypet.com

**American Boarding Kennels Association**
1702 East Pikes Peak Ave.
Colorado Springs, CO 80909
(719) 667-1600 — www.abka.com

**American Society for the Prevention of Cruelty to Animals**
424 E. 92nd St., New York, NY 10128-6804
(212) 876-7700 — www.aspca.org

**American Veterinary Medical Association**
1931 N. Meacham Rd., Suite 100
Schaumburg, IL 60173
(847) 925-8070 — www.avma.org

**Dogpark.com**®
716 Fourth St., San Rafael, CA 94901
www.dogpark.com

**Humane Society of the United States**
2100 L St. NW, Washington, DC 20037
(202) 452-1100 — www.hsus.org

**National Association of Professional Pet Sitters**
15000 Commerce Pkwy., Suite C
Mt. Laurel, NJ 08054
(856) 439-0324 — www.petsitters.org

**PetGroomer.com**
P.O. Box 2489
Yelm, WA 98597
(360) 446-5348 — www.petgroomer.com

**Pet Sitters International**
201 E. King St., King, NC 27021
(336) 983-9222 — www.petsit.com

**USDA-APHIS**
USDA-APHIS-Animal Care
4700 River Rd., Unit 84
Riverdale, MD 20737-1234
(301) 734-7833 — www.aphis.usda.gov/ac

Some animals are used to riding in the car and even enjoy it. But most associate the inside of the carrier or the car with one thing only: the annual visit to the V-E-T. Considering that these visits usually end with a jab from a sharp needle, it's no wonder that some pets forget their training and act up in the car. If this is your situation, you will have to re-train your animal to view a drive as a reward, not a punishment.

Begin by allowing your pet to become used to the car without actually going anywhere. Then take short trips to places that are fun for animals, such as the park or the drive-through window at a fast-food restaurant. (Keep those indulgent snacks to a minimum!) Be sure to praise her for good behavior with words, petting and healthy treats. It shouldn't take long before you and your furry friend are enjoying leisurely drives without incident. (See Traveling by Car, p. 12.)

❧ **Brush up on behavior.** Will Snowball make a good travel companion? Or will he be an absolute terror on the road? Don't wait until the vacation is already under way to find out; review general behavioral guidelines with respect to your animal, keeping in mind that the unfamiliarity of travel situations may test the temperament of even the most well-behaved pet.

It's a good idea to socialize Spot by exposing her to other people and animals (especially if she normally stays inside). You're likely to encounter both on your trip, and it is important that she learns to behave properly in the company of strangers. Make her introduction to the outside world gradual, such as a walk in a new neighborhood or taking her along while you run errands. Exposure to new situations will help reduce fear of the unknown and result in more socially acceptable behavior.

Is your pet housebroken? How is he around children? Does he obey vocal commands? Be honest about your animal's ability to cope in unfamiliar surroundings. Depending on the length and nature of the trip and your pet's level of command response, an obedience refresher course might be a good idea.

❧ **Learn about your destination.** Check into quarantines or other restrictions well in advance, and make follow-up calls as your departure date approaches. Find out what types of documentation will be required — not just en route, but on the way home as well.

Be aware of potential safety or health risks where you're going, and plan accordingly. For example, the southeastern United States — particularly Florida — is home to alligators and heartworm-carrying mosquitoes, and many mountainous and wooded areas may harbor ticks that transmit Lyme disease.

Confirm all travel plans within a few days of your departure, especially with lodgings and airlines; their policies may have changed after you made the reservations. If you plan to visit state parks or attractions that accept pets on the premises, obtain their animal regulations in advance.

## What To Take

- ❑ Carrier or crate. (See Selecting a Carrier or Crate, p. 11, for specifications.)
- ❑ Nylon or leather collar or harness, license tag, ID tag(s) and leash. All should be sturdy and should fit your pet properly.
- ❑ Food and water dishes.
- ❑ Can opener and spoon (for canned food).
- ❑ An ample supply of food, plus a few days' extra.
- ❑ Bottled water from home. (Many animals are finicky about their drinking water.)
- ❑ Cooler with ice.
- ❑ Healthy treats.
- ❑ Medications, if necessary.
- ❑ Health certificate and other required documents.
- ❑ A blanket or other bedding. (If your pet is used to sleeping on the furniture, bring an old blanket or sheet to place on top of the hotel's bedding.)
- ❑ Litter supplies (for cats or other small animals), a scooper and plastic bags (for dogs).
- ❑ Favorite toys.
- ❑ Carpet deodorizer.
- ❑ Chewing preventative.

- ❑ A recent photograph and a written description including name, breed, gender, height, weight, coloring and distinctive markings.
- ❑ Grooming supplies:
  comb/brush
  nail clippers
  shampoo
  cloth and paper towels
  cotton balls/tissues
- ❑ First-aid kit:
  gauze, bandages and adhesive tape
  hydrogen peroxide
  rubbing alcohol
  ointment
  muzzle
  scissors
  tweezers (for removing ticks, burrs, splinters, etc.)
  local emergency phone numbers
  first-aid guide (such as Pet First Aid: Cats & Dogs, published by The Humane Society of the United States and the American Red Cross)

❧ **Determine the best mode of transportation.** Most people traveling with pets drive. Many airlines do accept animals in the passenger cabin or cargo hold, and as more people choose to fly with their pets airlines are becoming more pet-conscious. Restrictions vary as to the type and number of pets an airline will carry, however, so inquire about animal shipping and welfare policies before making reservations. If your pet must travel in the cargo hold, heed the cautionary advice in the Traveling by Air section. *(See p. 13.)*

Flying is really the only major option to car travel. Amtrak, as well as Greyhound and other interstate bus lines, do not accept pets. **Note:** Seeing-eye dogs and other service animals are exempt from the regulations prohibiting pets on Amtrak and interstate bus lines. Local rail and bus companies may allow pets in small carriers, but this is an exception rather than a rule.

The only cruise ship that currently permits pets is the Cunard Line's *Queen Elizabeth 2* (on trans-Atlantic crossings); kennels are provided, but animals are accepted on a very limited basis. Some charter and sightseeing boat companies permit pets onboard, however.

A word of advice: Never try to sneak your pet onto any mode of public transportation where she is not permitted. You may face legal action or fines, and the animal may be confiscated if discovered.

❧ **Pack as carefully for your pet as you do for yourself.** *(See What To Take, p. 10.)* Make sure she has a collar with a license tag and ID tag(s) listing her name and yours, along with your address and phone number. As an added precaution, some owners outfit their dog with a second tag listing the name and number of a contact person at home. Popular backup identification methods are to have your animal tattooed with an ID number (usually a social security number) or to implant a microchip under her skin.

If your pet requires medication, make sure that is specified on his tag. This helps others understand your animal's needs and also may prevent people from keeping a found pet or from stealing one to sell.

**Note:** Choke chains, collars that tighten when they are pulled, may be useful during training sessions, but they do not make good full-time collars. If the chain catches on something, your pet could choke herself trying to pull free. For regular wear, use a harness or a conventional collar made of nylon or leather.

# Selecting a Carrier or Crate

This is one of the most important steps in ensuring your pet's safety when traveling. A good-quality carrier not only contains your pet during transit, it also gives him a safe, reassuring place to stay when confinement is necessary at your destination. Acclimate the animal before the trip so he views the crate as a cozy den, not a place of exile.

If you plan to travel by car, a carrier will confine your pet en route, and also may come in handy if Spot or Snowball must stay in the room unsupervised. A secured crate will prevent your pet from escaping from the room when the cleaning staff arrives, or at night if camping in the open. *(See At Your Destination, p. 16.)*

Some airlines allow small pets to travel in the passenger cabin as carry-on luggage. There are no laws dictating the type of carrier to use, but remember that it must be small enough to fit under a standard airplane seat and should not exceed 45 linear inches (length + width + height), or roughly **23 by 13 by 9 inches.** If your pet will be flying in the cargo hold, you must use a carrier that meets U.S. Department of Agriculture Animal and Plant Health Inspection Service (USDA-APHIS) specifications. *(See Traveling by Air, p. 13.)*

Crates are available at pet supply stores; some airlines also sell carriers. Soft-sided travel bags are handy for flyers with small pets. Before you make the investment, make sure your carrier is airline-approved.

Even if you never take to the skies, these common-sense guidelines provide a good rule of thumb in selecting a crate for other uses. USDA-APHIS rules stipulate the following:

❧ The crate must be enclosed, but with ventilation openings occupying at least 14 percent of total wall space, at least one-third of which must be located on the top half of the kennel. A three-quarter-inch lip or rim must surround the exterior to prevent air holes from being blocked.

❧ The crate must open easily, but must be sufficiently strong to hold up during normal cargo transit procedures (loading, unloading, etc.).

❧ The floor must be solid and leakproof, and must be covered with an absorbent lining or material (such as an old towel or litter).

**Ventilation openings**

**Live animal label**

**Spacer bar**

**Name and address label**

**Food and water dishes**

# HEATSTROKE
## AND
# HYPOTHERMIA

The best way to treat heatstroke or hypothermia is to prevent it. Do not leave pets unattended in a car, even if only for a few minutes. Also heed airlines' restrictions on pet travel, and carefully investigate animal welfare policies to make certain the airline has safeguards to protect your pet from both conditions.

Other preventive measures are to avoid strenuous exercise — including such activities as hiking and "fetch" — when the sun is strongest (10 a.m.-2 p.m.), and to provide your pet access to clean, fresh drinking water at all times.

Following are the warning signs and basic first aid for heatstroke and hypothermia. Always be alert to your pet's physical condition and watch for symptoms — immediate attention to the situation may mean the difference between life and death. If your pet is struck with either disorder, take him to an animal hospital or veterinarian as fast as safely possible.

### HEATSTROKE

**Symptoms**
- rapid, shallow breathing
- excessive salivation
- heavy panting
- hot to the touch
- glazed eyes
- unsteadiness, dizziness
- deep red or purple tongue or gums
- vomiting
- body temperature of 104 F or higher

**First Aid**
- place pet in the shade
- quickly dampen with cool water, especially on the head and neck
- give small amounts of water

### HYPOTHERMIA

**Symptoms**
- shivering
- weakness
- lethargy
- cold to the touch
- body temperature of 95 F or lower

**First Aid**
- place in a warm area
- wrap in towels or a blanket
- quickly warm by gently massaging the head, chest and extremities

❧ The crate must be just large enough to allow the animal to turn freely while standing, and to have a full range of normal movement while standing or lying down.

❧ The crate must offer exterior grips or handles so that handlers do not have to place their hands or fingers inside.

❧ Food and water dishes must be securely attached and accessible without opening the kennel.

❧ If the carrier has wheels, they must be removed or immobilized prior to loading.

❧ One-inch lettering stating "Live Animal" or "Wild Animal" must be placed visibly on the exterior, and must be accompanied by directional arrows showing the crate's proper orientation. It also is a good idea to label the crate with your name, home address and home phone number, as well as an address and phone number where you can be reached during the trip. (Hint: Use an adhesive label or an indelible marker and write directly on the crate, as paper may be ripped off accidentally in transit.)

❧ Attach a list of care instructions (feeding, watering, etc.) for a 24-hour period to the exterior of the carrier. This will help airport workers care for your pet if he is sent to the wrong destination.

❧ If you are traveling with multiple pets, note that crates may contain only one animal whose weight exceeds 20 pounds. Smaller animals may travel together under the following guidelines: one species to a crate, except compatible dogs and cats of similar size; two puppies or kittens under 6 months of age; 15 guinea pigs or rabbits; 50 hamsters. **Note:** These are federal limits; airlines may impose more stringent regulations.

# Traveling by Car

The first step in ensuring your pet's well-being during a vacation is to train her to ride in the car. For safety reasons, pets should be confined to the back seat, either in a carrier or a harness attached to the car's seat belt. This keeps the animal from interfering with or distracting the driver, and also may save her life in the event of an accident. And a restrained animal will not be able to break free and run away the second the car door is opened.

To help prevent car sickness, feed your pet a light meal four to six hours before departing. Do not give an animal food or water in a moving vehicle.

Never allow your pet to ride in the bed of a pickup truck. It's illegal in some states; he also can jump out or be thrown, endangering himself and others on the road. Harnessing or leashing him to the truck bed is not advisable either: If he tries to jump out, he could be dragged along the road or the restraint could become a noose. Avoid placing animals in campers or trailers as well. **If your pet cannot ride in the car with you, leave him at home.**

Don't let your dog stick her head out the window, no matter how enjoyable it seems. Road debris and other flying objects can injure delicate eyes and ears, and the animal is at greater risk for severe injury if the vehicle should stop suddenly or be struck. If it is hot outside, run the air conditioner instead of opening the windows, and be sure that the air flow is reaching your pet.

AAA recommends that drivers stop every two hours to stretch their legs and take a quick break from driving. Your pet will appreciate the same break. Plan to visit a rest stop every four hours or so to let him have a drink and a chance to answer the call of nature. (Cat owners should bring along a litter box; dog owners should clean up afterward.)

Be sure your pet is leashed before opening the car door. This is not merely a courtesy to fellow travelers; it will prevent her from unexpectedly breaking free and running away. Keep in mind that even the most obedient pet may become disoriented during travel or in strange places and set off for home. **Hint:** If your pet is not used to traveling, use a harness instead of a collar; it is more difficult for an animal to wriggle out of a harness.

**NEVER** leave an animal in a parked car, even if the windows are partially open. Even on pleasant days the temperature inside a car can soar to well over 100 degrees in less than 10 minutes, placing your pet at risk for heatstroke and possibly death. On very cold days, hypothermia is a risk. Also, animals left unattended in parked cars frequently are stolen.

# Traveling by Air

*(Service animals are normally exempt from most of the regulations and fees specified in this section. Check policies with the airline when making reservations.)*

Opinion is divided as to whether air travel is truly safe for pets. Statistically, it is less dangerous than being a passenger in a car, but some experts warn of potentially deadly conditions for animals. The truth lies somewhere in between: Most pets arrive at their destination in fine condition, but death or injury is always a possibility. Before you decide to fly, know the risk factors and the necessary precautions to keep your pet safe.

❧ **Determine whether your pet is fit to fly.** The Animal Welfare Act (AWA), administered by USDA-APHIS, specifies that dogs and cats must be at least 8 weeks old and weaned at least 5 days before air travel. Animals that are very young, very old, pregnant, ill or injured should not fly at all. Cats, snub-nosed dogs (pugs, boxers, etc.) and long-nosed dogs (shelties, collies, etc.) are prone to severe respiratory difficulties in an airplane's poorly ventilated cargo hold and should travel only in the passenger cabin (if size allows) with their owner. Some airlines will not accept snub-nosed breeds if the temperature exceeds 70 degrees anywhere in the routing.

❧ **Decide where your pet will fly.** Most animals fly in the hold as checked baggage when traveling with their owners, or as cargo when they are unaccompanied. The AWA was enacted to ensure animals traveling in this manner are treated humanely and are not subjected to dangerous or life-threatening conditions. For specific requirements pertaining to your animal, check with the airline in advance, as policies vary. Some airlines will not ship dogs as checked baggage, and others will only accept dogs shipped as cargo from "known shippers"; i.e., commercial shippers or licensed pet breeders. Except for service animals, Southwest accepts no pets in the cabin or cargo department.

Items classified as "dangerous goods" (dry ice or toxic chemicals, for example) must be transported in a different part of the hold from where live animals are carried. Some planes are designed to have separate hold areas,

---

## AIRLINE CONTACT INFORMATION

Following is a list of the major North American airlines and their toll-free reservation numbers.

Web site addresses include information about flying with animals. Hint: Look under links for baggage, cargo or special services, or do a site search for "pets."

**Air Canada** . . . . . . . . . . . . . . . (888) 247-2262
www.aircanada.ca

**Alaska Airlines** . . . . . . . . . . . . (800) 252-7522
www.alaskaair.com

**America West Airlines** . . . . . . . (800) 235-9292
www.americawest.com

**American Airlines** . . . . . . . . . . (800) 433-7300
www.aa.com

**Continental Airlines** . . . . . . . . (800) 523-3273
www.continental.com

**Delta Airlines**. . . . . . . . . . . . . . (800) 221-1212
www.delta.com

**Northwest Airlines** . . . . . . . . . . (800) 225-2525
www.nwa.com

**Southwest Airlines** . . . . . . . . . . (800) 435-9792
www.iflyswa.com (accepts service animals only)

**United Airlines** . . . . . . . . . . . . . (800) 864-8331
www.ual.com

**US Airways** . . . . . . . . . . . . . . . . (800) 428-4322
www.usair.com

but so-called "people mover" airlines that are primarily interested in getting human passengers from one point to another as quickly as possible may not give priority to this feature. Check your airline's specific baggage policies so you know exactly where in the hold your pet will be traveling.

Small pets may be taken into the passenger cabin with you as carry-on luggage. This places the animal's welfare squarely in your hands but is feasible only if he is very well-behaved and fits comfortably in a container that meets standard carry-on regulations. *(See Selecting a Carrier or Crate, p. 11.)* Keep in mind that the carrier — with the animal inside — must be kept under the seat in front of you throughout the flight. **Note:** AWA regulations do not apply to animals traveling in the cabin.

❉ **Do your homework.** Investigate the airline's animal transport and welfare policies, especially if you are flying with a small or commuter airline. All airlines are subject to basic AWA regulations, but specific standards of care vary greatly from one company to another. Do your research well in advance and confirm the information 24-48 hours before departing.

The more information an airline provides, the better care your pet is likely to receive. Beware of companies that have vague animal welfare guidelines, or none at all. All major airlines provide information about pet transport on

## Pet Insurance

Just like their owners, pets can experience major medical problems at some point in their lifetime— even those that live indoors. And if illness strikes while you're on the road, it may be necessary to obtain care quickly. As a result, more and more people who travel with their devoted companion are considering pet health insurance.

Insurance plans run the gamut from basic coverage and routine care for illness and injury to comprehensive health maintenance, vaccinations and exams. Annual premiums range from less than $100 to more than $350, depending on the type of pet and plan. When choosing your plan, consider the following:

- What are the enrollment guidelines (age, breed, specific restrictions, etc.)?
- Which expenses are covered and which are excluded?
- What is the plan's policy concerning existing health problems?
- Does the plan allow you to use your own veterinarian?
- How are veterinary fees paid?
- Is a multiple pet discount offered?

their Web sites. Also talk to fellow travelers and pet owners about their experiences. Finally, keep in mind that airlines are not required to transport live animals and can refuse to carry them for any reason.

❉ **Protect your investment.** Most people think of their pets as part of the family, but the legal system assigns them the same value as a piece of luggage. Inquire about insurance — an airline that won't insure animals in its care may not be the right one for your pet. (Always read the fine print before purchasing any insurance policy.) Also ask if the airline's workers are trained to handle animals. Few are, but it doesn't hurt to check. Remember, it's up to you to choose an airline that values pets and will treat yours with care.

❉ **Understand the potential hazards.** Because a plane's cargo hold is neither cooled nor heated until takeoff, the most dangerous time for your pet is that spent on the ground in this unventilated compartment. In summer the space absorbs heat while the plane sits on the tarmac; the reverse is true in winter, when it is no warmer inside the hold than outside. Both instances expose pets to the possibility of serious injury or death from heatstroke or hypothermia. **Note:** The latter also may be a concern during flight if the hold's heater is disabled or turned off, allowing the temperature to drop to nearfreezing levels.

To minimize these risks, USDA-APHIS rules prohibit animals from being kept in the hold or on the tarmac for more than 45 minutes when temperatures are above 85 F or below 45 F. Some airlines impose even tighter temperature restrictions and may not permit animals to fly on planes going to cities where the ground temperatures may exceed these limits. Delta, for example, does not carry animals in the cargo hold May 15 through Sept. 15. (Exceptions may be made for animals whose veterinarians certify they are acclimated to colder temperatures, but never warmer.)

❉ **Make stress-free travel arrangements.** Once you decide to fly, reserve space for Spot or Snowball when you arrange your own tickets, preferably well in advance of your travel date. Airlines accept only a limited number of animals per flight — usually two to four in the passenger cabin and one pet per passenger — on a first-come, first-served basis. More animals are generally allowed in the cargo hold.

Prepare to pay an additional fee, about $75-$100 each way; the cost is often greater for large animals traveling on a flight without their owner. (Unfortunately, pets are not eligible for frequent flyer miles.) Always reconfirm your reservations and flight information 24-48 hours before departure.

If your pet will be flying in the hold, travel on the same plane and reserve a nonstop flight. This not only reduces the danger of heatstroke or hypothermia during layovers, it also eliminates the possibility that she will be placed on the wrong connecting flight. In summer, fly during the early morning or late evening when temperatures are cooler. Because of large crowds and the chance of heavy air traffic causing delays, avoid holiday travel whenever possible.

Additional precautions may be necessary when traveling outside the United States and Canada. Other countries may impose lengthy quarantines, and airline workers outside North America may not be bound by animal welfare laws. *(See International Travel, p. 18.)*

❧ **Play an active role in your pet's well-being.** Flying safely with your pet requires careful planning and attention to his welfare. See the veterinarian within 10 days of departure for a health certificate (required by most airlines) and a pre-flight check-up.

Address any concerns you have about your pet traveling by air, especially if you are considering tranquilization. Sedation usually is not recommended for cats and dogs, regardless of whether they fly in the cabin or in the hold. Exposure to increased altitude pressure can create respiratory and cardiovascular problems; animals with short, wide heads are particularly susceptible to disorientation and possible injury. Sedation should never be administered without your veterinarian's approval.

Obtain an airline-approved carrier and acclimate your pet to its presence by leaving it open with a familiar object inside. A sturdy, well-ventilated crate adds an additional measure of protection.

Because animals are classified as luggage, they may be loaded on the plane via conveyor belt. If the crate falls off the belt, your pet could be injured or released. Ask that she be hand-carried on and off the plane, and that you be permitted to watch both procedures. Also ask about "counter-to-counter" shipping, in which the animal is loaded immediately before departure and unloaded immediately after arrival. There usually is an additional fee for this service.

Make sure you will have access to your pet if there is a lengthy layover or delay. Think twice about flying on an airline that won't allow you to check on your animal under such circumstances.

❧ **Prepare for the flight.** Keep in mind that traveling with an animal will require additional pre-flight time and preparation on your part. Exercise your pet before the flight, and arrive at least two but not more than four hours before departure. If he is traveling as carry-on luggage, check-in is normally at the passenger terminal; if he is traveling as checked baggage or as cargo in the cargo hold, proceed to the airline's cargo terminal, which is often in a different location. Find this out when making reservations and again when confirming flight information.

Make sure your animal's crate is properly labeled and secured, but do not lock it in case airline personnel have to provide emergency care. Include an ice pack for extra comfort on a hot day or a hot water bottle on a cold day. **Hint:** Wrap in a towel to prevent leaking.

Do not feed your pet less than four hours before departure, but provide water up until boarding. **Hint:** Freeze water in the bowl so that it melts throughout the trip, providing a constant drinking source.

Spot or Snowball should wear a sturdy collar (breakaway collars are recommended for cats) and two identification tags marked with your name, home address and phone number, and travel address and phone number. It's also a good idea to clip your pet's nails before departure so they won't accidentally get caught on any part of the carrier.

**Note:** You may be required to take your pet out of the carrier as you pass through security on your way to the gate. Make sure the animal is wearing a collar and leash or harness.

Attach food and water dishes inside the carrier so that airline workers can reach them without opening the door. If the trip will take longer than 12 hours, also attach a plastic bag with at least one meal's worth of dry food. Animals under 16 weeks of age must be fed every 12 hours, adult animals every 24 hours. Water must be provided at least every 12 hours, regardless of the animal's age.

Allow your pet to answer the call of nature before boarding, but do not take her out of the carrier while in the terminal. As a courtesy, wait until you are outside and away from fellow travelers. Keep her leash with you — do not leave it inside or attached to the kennel.

If your pet is traveling as carry-on luggage, let the passenger sitting next to you know. Someone with allergies may want to change seats.

Perhaps the most important precaution is to alert the flight crew and the captain that your pet is aboard. The pilot must activate the heater for the cargo hold; make sure this is done once you are in the air. If there are layovers or delays, ask the flight crew to be sure your pet has adequate shelter and/or ventilation; better yet, ask them to allow you to check in person.

If you have arranged to watch your pet being unloaded, ask a flight attendant to call the baggage handlers and let them know you are on the way. Above all, do not hesitate to voice any concerns you have for your pet's welfare — it is your responsibility to do so.

❧ **Be prepared for emergencies.** In the unlikely event your pet gets lost en route, contact the airline, local humane shelters, animal control agencies or USDA-APHIS. Many airlines can trace a pet that was transferred to the wrong flight. If your pet is injured in transit, proceed to the nearest animal hospital; register any complaints with USDA-APHIS. **Hint:** Carry a list of emergency contact numbers and a current photograph of your pet in your wallet or purse, just in case.

# At Your Destination

How well you and your companion behave on the road directly affects the way future furry travelers will be treated. Always clean up after your pet and keep him under your control. This is not only a courtesy to fellow human travelers; it's the surest way to enjoy a safe and happy vacation.

Inquire about pet policies before making lodging reservations. Properties may impose restrictions on the type or size of pet allowed, or they may designate only certain rooms, such as smoking rooms, for travelers with animals. If you have a dog, get a room on the first floor with direct access outside, preferably near a walking area; keep her leashed on any excursion.

Lodgings may have supervision policies requiring that pets be crated when unattended or that they may not be left alone at all. Allow your pet only in designated exercise or animal-approved areas; never take him into such off-limits places as the lobby, pool area, patio or restaurant. Prepare to receive limited housekeeping service, or none at all.

Expect to pay some type of additional charge, which may be per room or per pet and may include any of the following: refundable deposit, non-refundable deposit, daily fee, weekly fee.

If staying with friends or relatives, make certain your pet is a welcome guest. Know and respect their "house rules," especially if they have small children or pets of their own.

Once in the room, check for such hazards as chemically treated toilet water, hiding spaces and electrical cords before freeing your pet. Give her time to adjust to her new surroundings under your supervision.

Above all, practice good "petiquette":

🐾 Try not to leave your pet alone, but if you must, crate or otherwise confine her.

🐾 Crate at night as well.

🐾 To keep your pet and the housekeeper from having an unexpected encounter, leave the "Do Not Disturb" sign on the door when you go out without him.

🐾 Barking dogs make poor hotel neighbors — keep your pet quiet.

🐾 Don't allow your pet on the furniture. If she insists on sleeping on the bed, bring a bedspread or sheet from home and place that on top of the hotel bedding.

🐾 Clean up after your pet immediately — inside the room and out — and leave no trace of him behind when checking out.

🐾 Dispose of litter and other "accidents" properly — check with housekeeping.

🐾 Notify the management immediately if something is damaged, and be ready to pay for repairs.

🐾 Add a little extra to the housekeeping tip.

🐾 When you take your pet out of the room, keep her leashed, especially in wilderness areas and around small children. No matter how obedient she is at home, new stimuli and distractions may cause her to forget or ignore vocal commands. Know and obey animal policies at parks, beaches and other public areas. Check before arriving to make certain animals still are welcome, even if you've been there before — the rules may have changed.

🐾 Look for outdoor cafes when selecting restaurants. For health reasons, pets are not permitted inside eating establishments, but many restaurants allow animals to sit quietly with their owners at outdoor tables. Drive-through restaurants are another alternative.

# In Case of Emergency

Be prepared for any turn of events by knowing how to get to the nearest animal hospital. *(See Animal Clinics, p. 49.)* Also have the name and number of a local animal shelter and a local veterinarian handy — ask your veterinarian for a recommendation. Take first-aid supplies with you and know how to use them. An animal in pain may become aggressive, so exercise caution at all times.

Emergency evacuation shelters do not accept pets, and domesticated animals do not fare well if left to weather an emergency on their own, especially when far from home. Avert a potential tragedy by planning in advance where you will go with your pet in case of evacuation. Use the listings in this book to find other lodgings willing to take you and your pet. Above all, don't wait for disaster to strike. Leave as soon as the evacuation order is announced, and take your animal with you.

# The Great Outdoors

Travelers planning an active or camping vacation should make some additional preparations. Check in advance to be sure your pet is permitted at campgrounds, parks, beaches, trails and anywhere else you will be visiting. If there are restrictions — and there usually are — follow them. Remember that pets other than service animals usually are not allowed in public buildings.

**Note:** It is not advisable to take animals other than dogs into wilderness areas. For example, bringing a pet is not recommended at some national parks in Alaska. Also keep in mind that rural areas often have few veterinarians and even fewer boarding kennels.

Use common sense. Clean up after your pet, do not allow excessive vocalizing and keep her under your control. If the property requires your pet to be leashed or crated at all times, do so. Few parks or natural areas will allow a pet to be unattended, even when chained — the risk of disagreeable encounters with other travelers or wildlife is too great. The National Park Service may confiscate pets that harm wildlife or other visitors.

If camping, crate your pet at night to protect him from the elements and predators. (Chaining confines the animal but won't keep him from becoming a midnight snack.)

When hiking, stick to the trail and keep your pet on a short leash. It is all too easy for an unleashed pet to wander off and get lost or fall prey to a larger animal. Keep an eye out for such wildlife as alligators, bears, big cats, porcupines and skunks, and avoid other dogs and small children. Be aware of indigenous poisonous plants, such as English ivy and oleander, or those causing physical injury, such as cactus, poison ivy or stinging nettle. Your veterinarian or local poison control center should be able to give you a full list of hazardous flora.

Before setting out on the trail, make sure both of you are in good physical shape. An animal that rarely exercises at home will not suddenly be ready for a 10-mile trek across uneven terrain. Plan a hike well within the limits of your pet's endurance and don't push — remember, if Spot gets too tired to make it back on her own, you'll have to carry her.

Carry basic first-aid supplies, including a first-aid guide. *(See What to Take, p. 10.)* Also carry fresh drinking water for both of you — "found" water may contain harmful germs or toxins. Drink often, not just when thirst strikes, and have your pet do the same. Watch for signs of dehydration, leg or foot injuries, heat exhaustion or heatstroke. Stop immediately and return home or to camp if any of these occur.

**Note:** Dogs can carry their own backpacks (check your local pet store for specially designed packs), but should never carry more than one-third of their body weight. Train the dog to accept the pack beforehand, and only use it with a strong, healthy animal in excellent physical condition.

No matter where or how you spend your vacation, visit the veterinarian when you return home to check for injuries, parasites and general health.

**Note:** Most campgrounds accept pets. The AAA CampBook guides are an excellent source for obtaining detailed information regarding pet policies, restrictions and extra charges for campgrounds in the United States and Canada. AAA members may obtain complimentary copies of the CampBook guides at their local AAA club.

# Traveling Between the United States and Canada

Traveling across the international border with your pet — either from the United States into Canada or from Canada into the United States — should prove largely hassle-free, although some basic regulations need to be kept in mind.

Effective Dec. 31, 2006, the Western Hemisphere Travel Initiative will require all travelers — including U.S. citizens — to have a passport for air and sea travel to and from Canada. The requirement will be extended to land border crossings at the end of 2007. Visit the U.S. State Department's travel Web site at www.travel.state.gov, or phone (877) 4882-778 for more information.

U.S. Customs grants returning U.S. citizens who stay in Canada more than 48 hours an individual $800 duty-free exemption (if not used within the prior 30 days). Any amount over the $800 exemption is subject to duty.

The exemption is based on fair retail value and applies to goods acquired for personal or household use or as gifts but not intended for sale. All items for which the exemption is claimed must accompany you upon return.

A 7 percent Goods and Service Tax (GST) is levied on most items sold and most services rendered in Canada. In New Brunswick, Nova Scotia or Newfoundland and Labrador, a Harmonized Sales Tax (HST) of 15 percent (which includes the GST) is charged on goods and services. Rebates can be claimed on some items. Brochures that explain the GST and contain a rebate form are available at tourist information centers, customs offices and duty free shops at the border and in airports.

U.S. citizens taking pet cats and dogs three months of age and older into Canada must carry a health certificate signed by a licensed veterinarian that describes the animal and provides proof of rabies vaccination within the past 12 or 36 months, depending on the type of vaccine. Collar tags are not sufficient proof of immunization. The certificate also is needed to bring a pet back into the United States; make sure the vaccination doesn't expire while you're in Canada. **Note:** Pit bulls are not permitted into Ontario.

Service animals are exempt from import restrictions. Also exempt are up to two puppies or kittens under three months old; obtain a certificate of health from your veterinarian indicating that the animal is too young to vaccinate. **Note:** For details on pet imports, contact the Canadian Embassy; 501 Pennsylvania Ave. N.W., Washington, DC 20001; phone (202) 682-1740. The Web site address is www.canadianembassy.org.

The Canadian Food Inspection Agency (CFIA) provides additional pet information; phone (613) 225-2342 or visit the Web site at www.inspection.gc.ca. If you need assistance while in Canada, contact the U.S. Embassy, 490 Sussex Dr., Ottawa, ON, Canada K1N 1G8; phone (613) 238-5335.

Canadian Customs allows Canadian citizens to bring back from the United States, duty and tax free, goods valued up to $200 any number of times per year, provided the visit is 48 hours or more. A $50 exemption, excluding alcoholic beverages and tobacco products, may be claimed if the visit is 24 hours or more and no other exemption is being used. If returning from a visit of 7 days or more (not counting the day of departure from Canada), the exemption goes up to $750.

Canadian travelers may take pet cats and dogs into the United States with no restrictions, but U.S. Customs requires that dogs have proof of rabies vaccination no less than 30 days before arrival. For additional information on U.S. regulations, contact the Animal and Veterinary Services department of the USDA-APHIS National Center for Import and Export, (301) 734-3277.

# International Travel

If you plan to travel abroad with Spot or Snowball, prepare for a lengthy flight and at least a short quarantine period. Be aware that airline and animal workers in other countries may not be bound by the same animal welfare laws that exist in the United States and Canada. Contact the embassy or consulate at your destination for information about documentation and quarantine requirements, animal control laws and animal welfare regulations.

As with any trip, have your pet checked by your regular veterinarian within 10 days of departure to obtain a health certificate showing proof of rabies and other inoculations. If you are traveling with an animal other than a domesticated dog or cat, check with USDA-APHIS for restrictions or additional documentation required.

The booklet "Pets and Wildlife: Licensing and Health Requirements" has general information about traveling abroad with animals; write U.S. Customs & Border Protection, 1300 Pennsylvania Ave. N.W., Washington, D.C. 20229; phone (202) 354-1000, or visit www.customs.gov.

**Note:** Island nations such as Australia and the United Kingdom, which are rabies-free, have adopted the Pet Travel Scheme (PETS) to allow entry for dogs and cats from the U.S. and Canada without the usual 6-month quarantine. Pets must be tested and vaccinated for rabies at least 6 months prior to travel, be implanted with microchip identification and receive a certificate of treatment from an official government veterinarian. For information, visit the U.K. Web site for the Department for Environment, Food and Rural Affairs (DEFRA) at www.defra.gov.uk. Hawaii, which has a standard 120-day quarantine for all imported animals except guide dogs, has adopted a similar expedited program of 5 days or less; a pet must have been vaccinated at least *twice* for rabies in its lifetime.

# Loss Prevention Tips

Searching the woods or an unfamiliar town for a missing pet is easily prevented by following these helpful tips:

- ❧ Have your pet wear a sturdy nylon or leather collar with current ID and rabies tags firmly attached. Be

sure the ID tag includes the phone number of an emergency contact. Consider having your pet implanted with microchip identification; it's a simple procedure similar to a vaccination.

- ❧ Keep your pet on a leash or harness. Even trained animals can become agitated or disoriented in unfamiliar surroundings and fail to obey vocal commands.

- ❧ Attach the leash or harness while your pet is still inside the closed car or crate.

- ❧ Do not leave your pet unattended at any time, anywhere. A stolen pet is extremely difficult to recover.

- ❧ Escape-proof your hotel room by crating your pet and asking hotel management to make certain no one enters your room while you are gone. (Inform the property that you're traveling with an animal when making reservations.)

- ❧ Take along a recent picture and a detailed written description of your pet.

If your pet gets lost these steps will improve your chances of recovery:

- ❧ If your pet is lost in transit, contact the airline immediately. Ask to trace the animal via the airline's automated baggage tracking system.

- ❧ Contact local police, animal control, animal shelters, humane organizations and veterinary clinics with a description and a recent photograph. Stay in contact until your pet is found, and provide your home and destination phone numbers.

- ❧ Post signs and place an ad in the local newspaper so that anyone who comes across your pet knows she is lost and how to reach you.

# The Last Word

You are ultimately responsible for your pet's welfare and behavior while traveling. Since animals cannot speak for themselves, it is up to you to focus on your pet's well-being every step of the way. It also is important to make sure he conducts himself properly so that other pets will be welcome visitors in the future. Following the common-sense information in this book will help ensure that both you and your animal companion have a safe and happy trip.

# PET-FRIENDLY PLACES

IN THE **U.S.** AND **CANADA**

Dog Parks
Attractions
National Public Lands
Animal Clinics

# DOG PARKS

**A** dog park is a place where people and their dogs can play together. These places offer dogs an area to play, exercise and socialize with other dogs while their owners enjoy the park-like setting. Dog park size and features vary greatly from location to location, from several hundred square feet in urban areas to several hundred acres in the suburbs and rural locations. Dog owners should remember to always keep their animal leashed until they reach the dog park entrance, to maintain voice control of their animal at all times, to bring their own supply of bags for picking up after their pet (and to be diligent in doing so), and to always have fresh water available for their dog. Please observe all dog park rules.

This list of dog parks in the United States and Canada is provided by Dogpark.com®. Dogpark.com is all about dogs — all breeds, all mixes of breeds, and all shapes, sizes and dispositions. It provides articles and information about dogs and their care, health and play. Online, visit www.dogpark.com.

The dog parks listed here welcome people who travel with their dogs; private parks or parks requiring local residency are not included. **Note:** Fence types and heights vary, and some areas have no fencing at all, requiring that the dog be under firm voice control.

## United States

### ARIZONA

**Chaparral Park - Scottsdale**
5401 N. Hayden Rd. (at the southeast corner of McDonald Drive and Hayden Road)
Daily dawn-9 p.m.
Fenced, 2.2 acres, benches, shade, restroom, water, separate areas for large and small dogs.

**Horizon Park - Scottsdale**
15444 N. 100th St. (Thompson Peak Parkway and 100th Street, east of SR 101 off Frank Lloyd Wright Boulevard)
Daily dawn-10:30 p.m.
Fenced, lighted, benches, little shade, tables, disposal bags, trash cans, parking, phones, restrooms; bring your own water.

**Vista del Camino Park - Scottsdale**
7700 East Pierce St. (take Pierce Street heading west from Hayden Road)
Daily dawn-10:30 p.m.
Fenced, lighted, 1 acre, grass turf, benches, restrooms nearby, dog and people water fountains, mutt mitt stations.

**Creamery Park - Tempe**
tempe.gov/pkrec/parkfacil/offleash.htm
8th Street and Una Avenue (just south of University near Rural)
Daily 6 a.m.-midnight
Fenced, lighted, benches, disposal bags, trash cans, parking, water.

**Jaycee Park - Tempe**
tempe.gov/pkrec/parkfacil/offleash.htm
5th Street and Hardy Drive
Daily 6 a.m.-midnight
Fenced, lighted, trees, benches, disposal bags, trash cans, parking, water. Access for the disabled.

**Mitchell Park - Tempe**
tempe.gov/pkrec/parkfacil/offleash.htm
Mitchell Drive and 9th Street
Daily 6 a.m.-midnight
Fenced, lighted, trees, benches, disposal bags, trash cans, parking, water. Access for the disabled.

**Papago Park - Tempe**
tempe.gov/pkrec/parkfacil/offleash.htm
Curry Road and College Avenue
Daily 6 a.m.-midnight.
Fenced, lighted, trees, disposal bags, trash cans, parking, water.

**Tempe Sports Complex - Tempe**
tempe.gov/pkrec/parkfacil/offleash.htm
Warner Road and Hardy Drive
Daily 6 a.m.-midnight
Fenced, lighted, trees, disposal bags, trash cans, parking, water.

### CALIFORNIA

**Calabasas Bark Park - Calabasas**
cityofcalabasas.com/recreation/barkpark.html
or send comments and questions to mai@cmbarkpark.org
4232 Las Virgenes Rd., south of the Las Virgenes Municipal Water District (approximately 2 miles west of US 101 on the south side)
Daily 5 a.m.-9 p.m.
Fenced, lighted, trees, benches, scoops, trash cans, paved parking, dog water fountain, separate areas for large and small dogs.

**Costa Mesa Bark Park - Costa Mesa**
cmbarkpark.org, hotline (949) 733-4101
Arlington Drive and Newport Boulevard, across from the Orange County Fairgrounds Equestrian Center
Wed.-Mon. dawn-dusk; phone ahead in rainy conditions
Fenced, 2.1 acres, grass turf, trees, benches, tables, disposal bags, trash cans, parking, restrooms, water. Access for the disabled.

**Elizabeth Anne Perrone Dog Park - Glen Ellen**
sonoma-county.org/PARKS/foundation/
perrone_dog_park.htm
13630 Sonoma Hwy. in Sonoma Valley Regional Park (SR 12 between Arnold Drive and Madrone Road)
Daily dawn-dusk. Parking fee $4.
Fenced, 1 acre, double-gated entry, covered gazebo, shade trees, dog water fountain.

# CALIFORNIA (CONT'D)

**Huntington Dog Beach - Huntington Beach**
dogbeach.org
Pacific Coast Highway between 21st and Seapoint streets
Daily 5 a.m.-10 p.m.; parking lot closes at 8 p.m.
Unfenced, benches and tables on the bluffs above the beach, disposal bags, trash cans, metered parking, restrooms. Dogs may be off leash anywhere on the beach while under an owner's supervision. Access for the disabled to the sand.

**Laguna Niguel Pooch Park - Laguna Niguel**
ci.laguna-niguel.ca.us/index.asp?SID=481
31461 Golden Lantern near Chapparosa Park
Tues.-Thurs. and Sat. 7 a.m.-dusk, Sun. 8 a.m.-dusk, Mon. and Fri. noon-dusk
Fenced, 1.1 acres, landscaped, water.

**Long Beach Recreation Dog Park - Long Beach**
geocities.com/lbdogpark
5201 East 7th St. at Park
Daily dawn-10 p.m.
Fenced, lighted, trees, crushed-granite surface, benches, tables, disposal bags, trash cans, parking, water, separate fenced area for small dogs. Access for the disabled.

**Palm Springs Dog Park - Palm Springs**
ci.palm-springs.ca.us/dogpark.html
3200 E Tahquitz Canyon Way, behind City Hall
Daily dawn-10 p.m.
Fenced, lighted, double-gated entry, trees, benches, tables, shelter, disposal bags, trash cans, parking, phones, dual-level drinking fountains, separate areas for large and small dogs, antique fire hydrants. Unusual iron fence created by sculptor Phill Evans. Access for the disabled.

**Redondo Beach Dog Park - Redondo Beach**
rbdogpark.com
Southeast corner of 190th Street and Flagler Lane
Daily dawn-dusk; closed Wed. dawn-noon for maintenance
Fenced, trees, benches, disposal bags, trash cans, parking, phones, water, separate fenced area for small dogs. Access for the disabled.

**Granite Dog Park - Sacramento**
cityofsacramento.org/parksandrecreation/parks/dogpark1.htm
Ramona Avenue off Power Inn Road in Granite Regional Park
Daily dawn-10 p.m.
Fenced, 2 acres, bench, disposal bags, trash cans, water spigot for dogs. Access for the disabled.

**Partner Park - Sacramento**
cityofsacramento.org/parksandrecreation/parks/dogpark1.htm
5699 South Land Park Dr. at Fruitridge Road, behind Belle Cooledge Community Center
Daily dawn-10 p.m.
Fenced, lighted, 2 acres landscaped with turf and mature trees, bench, disposal bags, trash cans, water spigot for dogs. Access for the disabled.

**Balboa Park - San Diego**
sandiego.gov/park-and-recreation/general-info/dogs.shtml
Two off-leash areas:
(1) Nate's Point at El Prado, on the southwest side of Cabrillo Bridge
(2) Morley Field, northwest of the tennis courts
Daily 24 hours
Unfenced, large field.

**Cadman Community Park - San Diego**
sandiego.gov/park-and-recreation/general-info/dogs.shtml
4280 Avati Dr.
Phone (858) 581-9929 for specific hours
Unfenced.

**Capehart Park (Pacific Beach) - San Diego**
sandiego.gov/park-and-recreation/general-info/dogs.shtml
Soledad Mountain Road and Feldspar Street
Daily 24 hours
Fenced, 1 acre, picnic tables, benches, parking, separate grass-turf areas for large and small dogs, areas to provide water for dogs, drinking fountain.

**Dog Beach - San Diego**
sandiego.gov/park-and-recreation/general-info/dogs.shtml
Voltaire Street in Ocean Beach; enter the parking lot at the west end of Voltaire
Daily 24 hours
Unfenced, disposal bags, trash cans, water, restrooms nearby. Access for the disabled.

**Fiesta Island - San Diego**
sandiego.gov/park-and-recreation/general-info/dogs.shtml
Mission Bay Park; this island allows dogs anywhere outside the fenced areas.
Daily 6 a.m.-10 p.m.

**Grape Street Park - San Diego**
sandiego.gov/park-and-recreation/general-info/dogs.shtml
Grape Street and Granada Avenue
Mon.-Fri. 7:30 a.m.-9 p.m.; Sat.-Sun. and holidays 9-9
Unfenced, 5 acres, lighted, trees, benches, tables, trash cans, parking, restrooms, water.

**Alamo Square Park - San Francisco**
sfgov.org/site/recpark_index.asp?id=1448
Scott Street between Hayes and Fulton streets in the western half of the park
Daily 6 a.m.-10 p.m.
Unfenced; dogs must be under firm voice control.

**Alta Plaza Park - San Francisco**
sfgov.org/site/recpark_index.asp?id=1448
Clay Street between Scott and Steiner streets, on the second terrace of the park
Daily 6 a.m.-10 p.m.
Unfenced; dogs must be under firm voice control.

**Bernal Heights - San Francisco**
sfgov.org/site/recpark_index.asp?id=1448
Bernal Heights Boulevard at the top of the hill
Daily 6 a.m.-10 p.m.
Unfenced; dogs must be under firm voice control.

# CALIFORNIA (CONT'D)

### Brotherhood Mini Park - San Francisco
*sfgov.org/site/recpark_index.asp?id=1448*
Head Street and Brotherhood Way on Department of
Public Works property, improved by Recreation and Parks
Dept.
Daily 6 a.m.-10 p.m.
Unfenced; dogs must be under firm voice control.

### Buena Vista Park - San Francisco
*sfgov.org/site/recpark_index.asp?id=1448*
Buena Vista West at Central Avenue
Daily 6 a.m.-10 p.m.
Unfenced; dogs must be under firm voice control.

### Corona Heights - San Francisco
*sfgov.org/site/recpark_index.asp?id=1448*
Roosevelt Way and Museum Way in the field next to
Randall Museum
Daily 6 a.m.-10 p.m.
Fenced.

### Crocker Amazon Playground - San Francisco
*sfgov.org/site/recpark_index.asp?id=1448*
Between LaGrande and Dublin streets in the northern
portion of park, adjacent to community garden
Daily 6 a.m.-10 p.m.
Unfenced; dogs must be under firm voice control.

### Dolores Park - San Francisco
*sfgov.org/site/recpark_index.asp?id=1448*
Between Church and Dolores streets, south of tennis
courts and soccer field to central lawn
Daily 6 a.m.-10 p.m.
Unfenced; dogs must be under firm voice control.

### Douglass Park - San Francisco
*sfgov.org/site/recpark_index.asp?id=1448*
27th and Douglass streets, upper field
Daily 6 a.m.-10 p.m.
Unfenced; dogs must be under firm voice control.

### Eureka Valley Recreation Center - San Francisco
*sfgov.org/site/recpark_index.asp?id=1448*
Collingwood Street, adjacent to the tennis courts, east of
baseball diamond
Daily 6 a.m.-10 p.m.
Fenced.

### Golden Gate Park - San Francisco
*sfgov.org/site/recpark_index.asp?id=1448*
Four off-leash areas:
(1) Southeast section bounded by Lincoln Way, King Drive
and 2nd and 7th avenues
(2) Northeast section at Fulton and Willard streets
(3) South-central area bounded by Martin Luther King Jr.
Drive, Middle Drive and 34th and 38th avenues
(4) Fenced dog-training area near 38th Avenue and Fulton
Street

### Jefferson Park - San Francisco
*sfgov.org/site/recpark_index.asp?id=1448*
Eddy and Laguna Streets at the northwest end of the park
Daily 6 a.m.-10 p.m.
Unfenced; dogs must be under firm voice control.

### Lafayette Park - San Francisco
*sfgov.org/site/recpark_index.asp?id=1448*
Near Sacramento Street between Octavia and Gough
streets
Daily 6 a.m.-10 p.m.
Unfenced; dogs must be under firm voice control.

### Lake Merced - San Francisco
*sfgov.org/site/recpark_index.asp?id=1448*
Lake Merced Boulevard and Middlefield Drive, northern
lake area
Daily 6 a.m.-10 p.m.
Unfenced; dogs must be under firm voice control.

### McKinley Square - San Francisco
*sfgov.org/site/recpark_index.asp?id=1448*
San Bruno Avenue and 20th Street, on the west slope
Daily 6 a.m.-10 p.m.
Unfenced; dogs must be under firm voice control.

### McLaren Park - San Francisco
*sfgov.org/site/recpark_index.asp?id=1448*
Two off-leash areas:
(1) A 59-acre hilltop bounded by Shelly Drive with trails,
open areas, reservoir and fence at roadway. Includes
natural area, excludes group picnic facilities, children's play
area and custodian housing. Leash restrictions during
performances at amphitheater.
(2) South entrance at 1600 block of Geneva adjacent to
natural area with open area fenced on roadway
Daily 6 a.m.-10 p.m.

### Mountain Lake Park - San Francisco
*sfgov.org/site/recpark_index.asp?id=1448*
North of Lake Street at 8th Avenue, east end of park
Daily 6 a.m.-10 p.m.
Unfenced; dogs must be under firm voice control.

### Pine Lake Park - San Francisco
*sfgov.org/site/recpark_index.asp?id=1448*
Crestlake and Vale streets, west of and contiguous to
Stern Grove and adjacent to the parking lot
Daily 6 a.m.-10 p.m.
Unfenced; dogs must be under firm voice control.

### Potrero Hill Mini Park - San Francisco
*sfgov.org/site/recpark_index.asp?id=1448*
22nd Street between Arkansas and Connecticut streets
Daily 6 a.m.-10 p.m.
Unfenced; dogs must be under firm voice control.

### St. Mary's Recreation Center - San Francisco
*sfgov.org/site/recpark_index.asp?id=1448*
Justin and Benton Streets, lower terrace of the park
Daily 6 a.m.-10 p.m.
Fenced.

### Stern Grove - San Francisco
*sfgov.org/site/recpark_index.asp?id=1448*
Wawona Street between 21st and 23rd avenues, north
side
Daily 6 a.m.-10 p.m.
Unfenced; dogs must be under firm voice control.

### Upper Noe Recreation Center - San Francisco
*sfgov.org/site/recpark_index.asp?id=1448*
30th Street between Church and Sanchez streets, behind
and along the baseball field
Daily 6 a.m.-10 p.m.
Fenced.

# CALIFORNIA (CONT'D)

### Walter Haas Playground - San Francisco
sfgov.org/site/recpark_index.asp?id=1448
Diamond Heights Boulevard on upper terrace of the park
Daily 6 a.m.-10 p.m.
Unfenced; dogs must be under firm voice control.

### Field of Dogs - San Rafael
fieldofdogs.org
3540 Civic Center Dr. near the intersection of US 101 and
North San Pedro Road
Daily dawn-dusk
Fenced, double-gated entry, trees, benches, tables, shelter,
disposal bags, trash cans, parking, water. Access for the
disabled.

### DeTurk Roundbarn Park - Santa Rosa
ci.santa-rosa.ca.us/rp/
819 Donahue St. between West 8th and 9th streets
Daily dawn-dusk
Fenced, water (small neighborhood park).

### Doyle Park Dog Park - Santa Rosa
ci.santa-rosa.ca.us/rp/
700 Hoen Ave. within Doyle Park (go west on Sonoma
Avenue, turn left on Hoen and then turn right into the
parking lot; the fenced dog park is behind the stadium)
Daily dawn-dusk
Fenced, 3/4 acre, bench, disposal bags, water.

### Galvin Dog Park - Santa Rosa
ci.santa-rosa.ca.us/rp/
3330 Yulupa Ave. in Don Galvin Park, next to Bennet
Valley Golf Course
Daily dawn-dusk
Fenced, double-gated entry, trees, trash cans, parking,
water. Access for the disabled.

### Northwest Community Dog Park - Santa Rosa
ci.santa-rosa.ca.us/rp/
2620 W. Steele Lane in Northwest Community Park (go
west on Gurneville Road, turn right on Marlow and then
turn right at the first traffic light into the park's parking lot;
walk east along the path to the dog park on the left)
Daily dawn-dusk
Fenced, 1 acre, benches, disposal bags, trash cans,
restrooms nearby, water, separate area for small dogs.

### Rincon Valley Dog Park - Santa Rosa
ci.santa-rosa.ca.us/rp/
5108 Badger Rd. in Rincon Valley Community Park
Daily dawn-dusk
Fenced, 1/2 acre, trees, benches, tables, disposal bags,
trash cans, parking, phones, restrooms, water, separate
fenced areas for large and small dogs (large-dog area
closed during the winter), fenced pond area for dogs
(open year-round). Monitors are present during peak hours
to enforce rules. Access for the disabled.

**Off-leash, unfenced, under voice control areas:**

### 700 Doyle Park Drive - Santa Rosa
ci.santa-rosa.ca.us/rp/
700 Doyle Park Dr. (go west on Sonoma, turn left on
Hoen and then turn right into the parking lot; the
unfenced, off-leash area is to the right of the fenced dog
park)
Daily 6-9 a.m., early Apr.-late Oct.

### Doyle Park - Santa Rosa
ci.santa-rosa.ca.us/rp/
700 Hoen Ave. (the fenced dog park is behind the
stadium)
Mon.-Fri. 6-9 a.m.
Dogs may be off leash within the park, but must be kept
on leash from the parking lot to the park entrance.

### Franklin Park - Santa Rosa
ci.santa-rosa.ca.us/rp/
2095 Franklin Ave.
Daily 6-8 a.m.

### Southwest Community - Santa Rosa
ci.santa-rosa.ca.us/rp/
1698 Hearn Ave.
Daily 6-8 a.m.

### Youth Community - Santa Rosa
ci.santa-rosa.ca.us/rp/
1725 Fulton Rd.
Daily 6-8 a.m.

### Remington Dog Park - Sausalito
dogpark-sausalito.com
Ebbtide at Bridgeway
Mon.-Fri. 7-7, Sat.-Sun. 8-7
Fully fenced, lighted, safety-gated entry, picnic tables,
benches, tents for shelter, scoops and scooper cleaning
station, trash cans, parking, water, tennis balls and
racquets provided.

### Sierra Madre Dog Park - Sierra Madre
ci.sierra-madre.ca.us/departments/administrative_services/
licenses_detail.asp?ID=279
611 East Sierra Madre Blvd. in Sierra Vista Park, south of
the tennis courts
Daily 6 a.m.-10 p.m. Permit required; daily permit $5. Daily
and annual permits are available at City Hall; the Sierra
Madre Police Department, 242 W. Sierra Madre Blvd.; or
the Sierra Madre Community Recreation Center, 611 E.
Sierra Madre Blvd.
Fenced, lighted, double-gated entry, trees, benches,
disposal bags, trash cans, parking, phones, restrooms,
water, separate fenced areas for large/active dogs and
"special needs" dogs. Access for the disabled.

# COLORADO

### Grandview Off-Leash Dog Park - Aurora
For additional information phone (303) 739-7160
17900 E. Quincy Ave., west of Quincy Reservoir and just
east of Pitkin Street
Daily dawn-dusk
Fenced, trash cans, parking, water.

### East Boulder Community - Boulder City
ci.boulder.co.us/parks-recreation/PARKS/
dog_parks_main.htm
5660 Sioux Dr.
Daily dawn-dusk
Fenced, disposal bags, trash cans, parking, water,
fenced-off swimming area. Access for the disabled.

# COLORADO (CONT'D)

### Foothills Community Park - Boulder City
*ci.boulder.co.us/parks-recreation/PARKS/
dog_parks_main.htm*
Locust Avenue and Lee Hill Road, west of Broadway
Daily dawn-dusk
Fenced, disposal bags, trash cans, parking, water. Access for the disabled.

### Howard H. Hueston Park - Boulder City
*ci.boulder.co.us/parks-recreation/PARKS/
dog_parks_main.htm*
34th Street near O'Neal Parkway
Daily dawn-dusk
Unfenced, trees, benches, tables, trash cans, parking.
Dogs must be under voice and sight control. Access for the disabled.

### Valmont Dog Park - Boulder City
*ci.boulder.co.us/parks-recreation/PARKS/
dog_parks_main.htm*
Valmont and Airport roads
Daily dawn-dusk
Fenced, disposal bags, trash cans, parking, water. Access for the disabled.

### Palmer Park - Colorado Springs
*http://www.springsgov.com/Page.asp?NavID=5109*
Maizeland Road and Academy Boulevard
Daily 5 a.m.-11 p.m., May-Oct.; 5 a.m.-9 p.m., rest of year
Fenced, benches, tables, disposal bags, trash cans, parking, restrooms, water. Access for the disabled.

### Rampart Dog Park - Colorado Springs
*http://www.springsgov.com/Page.asp?NavID=5109*
8270 Lexington Dr. (from the intersection of Lexington Drive and N. Union Boulevard, go north on Lexington, then turn left into the park entrance)
Daily 5 a.m.-11 p.m., May-Oct.; 5 a.m.-9 p.m., rest of year
Fenced, trees, benches, disposal bags, trash cans, parking, water. Access for the disabled.

### Barnum Park - Denver
*www.denvergov.org/PRdogsoffleash/ or Dogs-off-leash
hotline: (303) 964-1006*
Hooker and West 5th
Daily 5:00 a.m.-11:00 p.m
Natural barriers (turf with split-rail fencing to delineate boundaries), 3 acres, trees, trash bags and cans, parking, restroom, bulletin board.

### Berkeley Park - Denver
*www.denvergov.org/PRdogsoffleash/ or Dogs-off-leash
hotline: (303) 964-1006*
Sheridan and West 46th
Daily 5:00 a.m.-11:00 p.m.
Fenced, 2 acres, turf, double-gate entry, trees, trash bags and cans, parking, bulletin board.

### Denver Off-Leash Dog Park - Denver
*denvergov.org or email kelledl@ci.denver.co.us for
additional information*
678 South Jason St. behind the Denver Municipal Animal Shelter
Daily dawn-dusk
Fenced, grass turf, parking, toys. Access for the disabled.

### Fuller Park - Denver
*www.denvergov.org/PRdogsoffleash/ or Dogs-off-leash
hotline: (303) 964-1006*
Franklin and East 29th
Daily 5:00 a.m.-11:00 p.m.
Fenced, 1 acre, turf, double-gate entry, trash bags and cans, bulletin board, on-street neighborhood parking only.

### Green Valley Ranch East Park - Denver
*www.denvergov.org/PRdogsoffleash/ or Dogs-off-leash
hotline: (303) 964-1006*
Jebel and East 45th
Daily 5:00 a.m.-11:00 p.m.
Natural barriers (native vegetation and split-rail fencing to delineate boundaries), 2 acres, trash bags and cans, parking.

### Kennedy Park - Denver
*www.denvergov.org/PRdogsoffleash/ or Dogs-off-leash
hotline: (303) 964-1006*
Hampden and South Dayton
Daily 5:00 a.m.-11:00 p.m.
Natural barriers (native vegetation and split-rail fencing to delineate boundaries), 3 acres, trash bags and cans, bulletin board, very limited parking.

# FLORIDA

### Happy Tails Canine Park - Bradenton
51st Street West at G.T. Bray Park, about halfway between Manatee Avenue and Cortez Road
Daily dawn-dusk
Eight-foot fence, 3 acres, trees, benches, tables, disposal bags, trash cans, parking (including handicapped spaces), restrooms nearby, water.

### Dr. Paul's Pet Care Center Dog Park - Coral Springs
*TopPetCare.com*
Sportsplex Drive in the Sportsplex Regional Park Complex (park off Sportsplex Drive at the west pedestrian entrance)
Daily 7:30 a.m.-9:30 p.m.
Enclosed, lighted, trees, shaded area, paved running path, picnic table, gazebo, disposal bag dispensers, trash cans, indoor restroom, separate areas for large and small dogs, dog and people water fountains, dog shower, dog statues, weatherproof dog agility equipment.

### The Dog Park in Lake Ida Park - Delray Beach
*http://www.co.palm-beach.fl.us/parks/specfac/dog_park/
index.htm*
2929 Lake Ida Rd. (take the Atlantic Avenue West exit off I-95, proceed west to Congress Avenue, go north on Congress for 1 mile, turn right onto Lake Ida Road and proceed east under I-95; park entrance is on the left)
Daily dawn-dusk; closed Thurs. noon-3 for maintenance
Fenced, 2.5 acres, partial paved pathway, eight shaded sitting areas, disposal bag dispensers and receptacles, restrooms and parking nearby, separate fenced areas for large and small dogs, two canine drinking stations, dog washing area, information kiosk.

# FLORIDA (CONT'D)

## Pooch Pines Dog Park at Okeeheelee Park - Delray Beach
*http://www.co.palm-beach.fl.us/parks/specfac/dog_park/index.htm*
7715 Forest Hill Blvd. (off I-95 exit Forest Hill Boulevard, west to the main Okeeheelee Park entrance on the north side of the road; follow the park road to the Pooch Pines sign, turn right and continue to the top of the hill)
Daily dawn-dusk; closed Wed. noon-3 for maintenance
Fenced, 5 acres, paved pathways, shaded sitting areas, disposal bag dispensers and receptacles, trash cans, restrooms and parking nearby, separate areas for large and small dogs, canine drinking stations, dog washing area.

## Bark Park at Snyder Park - Fort Lauderdale
*ci.fort-lauderdale.fl.us/cityparks/snyder/barkpark*
3299 S.W. 4th Ave.
Daily 7 a.m.-7:30 p.m., Apr.-Sept.; 7-6:30, rest of year. Closed Jan. 1 and Dec. 25.
Fee Mon.-Fri. $2; senior citizens and ages 6-12, $1.50.
Fee Sat.-Sun. and holidays $2.50; senior citizens and ages 6-12, $1.50.
Fenced, two open-air pavilions, benches, disposal bags, trash cans, parking, restrooms, water, separate area for small dogs, two hose stations, drinking fountains, agility equipment, small nature area with more than 20 labeled native trees. Freshwater dog swim Sat.-Sun. and holidays 10-5, first weekend in Mar.-first Sun. in Dec.; fee $1. Dogs must remain in the car until arrival at Bark Park and are not permitted in the remainder of Snyder Park. Access for the disabled.

## Dog Wood Off-Leash Park - Gainesville
*dogwoodpark.com*
5505 S.W. Archer Rd. (1 mile west of I-75)
Sat.-Sun. noon-5; once in the park, visitors may stay until dusk
Fee $9 plus tax for the first dog, $1 plus tax for each additional dog per family (otherwise $2.50 plus tax for each additional dog in the group)
Six-foot fence, 15 acres, double-gated entry and exit, jogging trail, hammocks, gazebo, picnic tables, lounge chairs, swinging and regular benches, multiple clean-up stations with disposal bags, indoor restrooms, free bottled water, soft drinks for sale, two large swimming ponds for dogs, wading pools, dog shower, agility course, sunny and shady areas for small dogs, park-provided tennis balls. Park also offers a do-it-yourself dog wash, a doggie boutique, dog day care, a dog photography studio and agility and obedience training. Some breeds must be neutered in order to enter the park; phone (352) 335-1919 for details.

## Paw Park of Historic Sanford - Sanford
*pawparksanford.org*
427 French Ave. (US 17/92) in Sanford's Historic District, 20 minutes north of downtown Orlando. From I-4, take the SR 46 exit (exit 101C, Sanford/Mount Dora), proceed east on SR 46 approximately 4 miles to French Avenue, turn right (southbound) and get into the left thru-lane; the Paw Park is on the left just past the Burger King
Daily 7:30 a.m.-8 p.m.
Fenced, double-gated entry, shaded with mature oak trees, historic lighting, paved walkway, benches, tables, disposal bag dispensers, parking, self-watering bowls, water misting station, dog showers, separate area for small dogs, community bulletin board. Access for the disabled.

## 17th Street Park & Paw Park - Sarasota
*scgov.net*
4570 17th St.
Daily dawn-dusk
Six-foot fence, 6 acres, lighted, double-gated entry, trees, benches, tables, disposal bags, trash cans, parking, restrooms, water, dog shower, separate area for small dogs, community bulletin board.

## Lakeview Park - Sarasota
*scgov.net*
7150 Lago St.
Daily dawn-midnight
Six-foot fence, double-gated entry, many trees, benches, tables, disposal bags, trash cans, parking, restrooms, water, dog shower, separate area for small dogs, community bulletin board. Access for the disabled.

## Brohard Beach & Paw Park - Venice
*scgov.net*
1600 Harbor Dr. South
Paw Park daily dawn-midnight. Dog Beach daily 7:30 a.m.-dusk
Six-foot fence, trees, benches, tables, shelter, disposal bags, trash cans, parking, water, dog shower, separate area for small dogs, community bulletin board. Dog Beach is accessed by boardwalk from Paw Park. Dogs are permitted in a restricted area along Brohard Beach as indicated by beach signs. Access for the disabled.

## Woodmere Park & Woodmere Paw Park - Venice
*scgov.net*
3951 Woodmere Park Blvd. (two blocks north of U.S. 41 on Jacaranda Boulevard)
Daily dawn-dusk
Fenced, double-gated entry, trees, benches, tables, disposal bags, trash cans, parking, restrooms, water, double-gated section for small dogs near the front gate, dog shower, community bulletin board.

# MICHIGAN

### Orion Oaks Bark Park - Lake Orion
*co.oakland.mi.us/parksrec/ppark/lyon.html*
Joslyn Road, south of Clarkston Road (park at the north Joslyn Road entrance and follow the signs)
Daily half-hour before dawn to half-hour after dusk
Park pass required; a daily pass is available at the Lake Orion Township office (open Mon.-Fri.) on Joslyn Road south of the park; or at Independence Oaks County Park (open daily) on Sashabaw Road 2.5 miles north of I-75. Resident fee $5 per day, $28 for an annual pass. Non-resident fee $10 per vehicle for daily entry, $49 for an annual pass; over 62, $3 per vehicle for daily entry, $23 for an annual pass.
Fenced, 7 acres, trees, benches, tables, disposal bags, trash cans, parking, portable toilet, water. A portion of Lake Sixteen is reserved for canine swimmers. Access for the disabled.

### Lyon Oaks Bark Park - Lyon Township
*co.oakland.mi.us/parksrec/ppark/orion.html*
Pontiac Trail between Wixom and Old Plank roads
Daily half-hour before dawn to half-hour after dusk
Park pass required; daily and annual passes are available at the park. Resident fee $5 per day, $28 for an annual pass. Non-resident fee $10 per vehicle for daily entry, $49 for an annual pass; over 62, $3 per vehicle for daily entry, $23 for an annual pass.
Fenced, 13 acres of open fields, benches, tables, disposal bags, trash cans, parking, restrooms, water pump.

# MINNESOTA

**Note:** In the greater Minneapolis area there are nine off-leash sites within a 15-minute drive of downtown Minneapolis/St. Paul. There are an additional eight sites in rural/suburban areas of the seven-county metropolitan area. All Minneapolis city parks require a permit for use, and the Minnehaha site also requires a permit for parking; phone (612) 348-4250 for information. Nearby dog parks in Maplewood, Roseville, St. Paul and Shoreview do not require a permit for use. Please read descriptions carefully.

### Alimagnet Dog Park - Burnsville (south metro suburb)
*alimagnetdogpark.org*
1200 Alimagnet Pkwy. (from central St. Paul, go south on I-35E to the CR 42 exit, east to CR 11, then north on CR 11 to Alimagnet Parkway and turn right; the dog park is on the right)
Daily 5 a.m.-10 p.m. Permit required; phone the Recreation Department at (952) 895-4500.
Fenced, 7 acres, double-gated entry, wooded areas, open fields, mowed prairie-grass trail, benches, tables, disposal bags, trash cans, parking, phones, restrooms, water, pond.

### Coates/Dakota County (south metro rural)
*Blaine Avenue south of CR 46 (160th Street E.) in the center of Dakota County near Coates*
Daily 5 a.m.-10 p.m. Permit required.
Fenced, 16 acres of wooded and open spaces with a walking trail loop, tables, disposal bag dispensers and receptacles, parking, portable toilets, no surface water; bring drinking water for your dog.

### Elm Creek Park Reserve - Dayton (northwest metro rural)
*threeriversparkdistrict.org/trails/trails_pet.cfm*
13080 Territorial Rd.
Daily 5 a.m.-dusk. Permit required; day permits are available at the site. Annual special-use permits may be obtained by phoning Park Guest Services at (763) 559-9000.
Fenced, 30 acres with a mowed trail, trees, tables, trash cans, parking, restrooms.

### Battle Creek Off-Leash Site - Maplewood (east central metro)
*co.ramsey.mn.us/parks/parks/offleash.asp*
Lower Afton and McKnight
Daily dawn-dusk. No permit required.
Partially fenced, 12 acres, tables, trash cans, parking.

### Columbia Park - Minneapolis
*dogromp.org*
St. Anthony Parkway off Central Avenue
Daily 6 a.m.-10 p.m. Permit required.
Fully fenced, 2 acres, double-gated entry at the east and west ends of the park, bench, disposal bag dispensers, parking.

### Franklin Terrace - Minneapolis
*dogromp.org*
Franklin Terrace and 30th Avenue S.
Daily 6 a.m.-10 p.m. Permit required.
Fully fenced, 2.6 acres, double-gated entry at the east and west ends of the site, bench, disposal bag dispensers, on-street parking.

### Lake of the Isles Park - Minneapolis
*dogromp.org*
Lake of the Isles Parkway and W. 28th Street
Daily 6 a.m.-10 p.m. Permit required.
Fully fenced, 2.6 acres, double-gated entry at the northern end of the site, lighted at the southern end, benches, disposal bag dispensers.

### Minnehaha Park - Minneapolis
*dogromp.org*
Minnehaha Avenue and E. 54th Street
Daily 6 a.m.-10 p.m. Permit required.
Partially fenced, 4.2 acres along the Mississippi River (where dogs can swim), disposal bag dispensers, lighted parking area (parking permit required), portable toilet in parking area.

### Egan Park's Off-Leash Area - Plymouth
*http://www2.ci.plymouth.mn.us, Parks & Recreation Dept. phone (763) 509-5200*
CR 47 in northwest Plymouth, about two blocks west of Dunkirk Lane on the south side of CR 47
Daily dawn-dusk. No permit required.
Unfenced, 10 acres, trash cans; bring your own drinking water.

# MINNESOTA (CONT'D)

## Cleary Lake Regional Park - Prior Lake (south metro rural)
*threeriversparkdistrict.org/trails/trails_pet.cfm*
18106 Texas Ave.
Daily 5 a.m.-dusk. Permit required; day permits are available at the site. Annual special-use permits may be obtained by phoning Park Guest Services at (763) 559-9000.
Fenced, 35 acres, tables, trash cans, parking, restrooms, pond. Trails are mowed in summer, packed in winter.

## Lake Sarah Regional Park - Rockford (west metro rural)
*threeriversparkdistrict.org/trails/trails_pet.cfm*
Lake Sarah Drive, 30 miles west of Minneapolis and east of CR 92 (take US 55 west to CR 92, proceed south to Lake Sarah Drive, turn left and then left again onto the first gravel road; the parking lot for the off-leash area is on the left side)
Daily 5 a.m.-dusk. Permit required; day permits are available at the site. Annual special-use permits may be obtained by phoning Park Guest Services at (763) 559-9000.
Unfenced, 30 acres, trees, mowed parking area, trash cans, restrooms.

## Crow-Hassan Park Reserve - Rogers (northwest metro rural)
*threeriversparkdistrict.org/trails/trails_pet.fmc*
Sylvan Lake Road west of Rogers (from I-94, take the Rogers exit and go south through town to the T intersection, turn right on CR 116 and proceed to CR 203, turn left and follow CR 203 to the park entrance)
Daily 5 a.m.-dusk. Permit required; day permits are available at the site. Annual special-use permits may be obtained by phoning Park Guest Services at (763) 559-9000.
Fenced, 30 acres with a mowed trail, trees, tables, trash cans, parking, restrooms.

## Woodview Dog Park - Roseville (central)
*co.ramsey.mn.us/parks/parks/offleash.asp*
Larpenteur Avenue, just east of Dale Street (access gate to main off-leash area is about 100 yards down the bike trail)
Daily dawn-dusk. No permit required.
Partially fenced (along bike trail only), 3 acres, trees, tables, disposal bags, trash cans, parking, water, separate fenced area for small dogs. Access for the disabled.

## Rice Creek Off-Leash Site - Shoreview (northeast metro)
*co.ramsey.mn.us/parks/parks/offleash.asp*
Lexington Avenue, just south of CR J
Daily dawn-dusk. No permit required.
Unfenced, 12 acres of flat prairie vegetation, tables, trash cans, parking, small pond.

## Bass Lake/Belt Line - St. Louis Park (west central)
*stlouispark.org/PermitsForms/2005Off-LeashApp.pdf*
West 36th Street and Belt Line Boulevard at Bass Lake Preserve, east of the tennis courts
Daily dawn-dusk. Permit required (see link above)
Fenced, 1.5 acres; bring drinking water for your dog.

## Arlington-Arkwright (ArlArk) Dog Park - St. Paul
*dogromp.org*
Arkwright Street at Arlington Avenue (from I-35E, take the Maryland Avenue exit east to Arkwright Street, then go north; the park is on the right-hand side)
Daily dawn-9 p.m. No permit required.
Fenced, 4.5 acres with trails and woods, tables, disposal bags, trash cans, parking. Park users sometimes leave gates open; keep your dog under voice control to prevent escapes.

## Otter Lake Dog Park - White Bear Township (northeast suburban)
*dogromp.org*
Otter Lake Road (take I-35E to the CR J exit, then CR J east to Otter Lake Road, following it south to the dog park; the entrance is next to the boat launch)
Daily dawn-dusk. No permit required.
Partially fenced, 10 acres of rolling hills with wooded and open prairie vegetation, separate 1-acre fenced area for small dogs. The park is fenced adjacent to Otter Lake Road and along most of the south boundary, bounded on the east by a large wetland and on the north by Otter Lake.

# NEVADA

All Clark County/Las Vegas dog park areas include water, seating and waste receptacles.

## Desert Breeze Park Dog Park - Clark County/Las Vegas (NW)
*accessclarkcounty.com/parks, (702) 455-8200*
8425 W. Spring Mountain Rd. at Durango
Daily 6 a.m.-11 p.m.

## Desert Inn Dog Park - Clark County/Las Vegas (SE)
*accessclarkcounty.com/parks, (702) 455-8200*
3570 Vista del Monte, near Lamb and Boulder Highway
Daily 6 a.m.-11 p.m.

## Dog Fancier's Park - Clark County/Las Vegas (SE)
*accessclarkcounty.com/parks, (702) 455-8200*
5800 E. Flamingo Rd., off E. Flamingo and Jimmy Durante
Daily 6 a.m.-11 p.m.
This 12-acre park is also used for dog shows and training.

## Molasky Park Dog Park - Clark County/Las Vegas (SE)
*accessclarkcounty.com/parks, (702) 455-8200*
1065 E. Twain, west of Maryland Parkway; dog run is south of Twain
Daily 6 a.m.-11 p.m.

## Shadow Rock Dog Park - Clark County/Las Vegas (NE)
*accessclarkcounty.com/parks, (702) 455-8200*
2650 Los Feliz (cross streets Lake Mead past Hollywood); dog run is east of the park area
Daily 6 a.m.-11 p.m.

## NEVADA (cont'd)

**Sunset Park - Clark County/Las Vegas (SE)**
accessclarkcounty.com/parks, (702) 455-8200
2601 E. Sunset Rd.; closest parking is off Eastern
between Sunset and Warm Springs roads
Daily 6 a.m.-11 p.m.

## NEW YORK

**New York City (Manhattan and boroughs)**
urbanhound.com
nycgovparks.org/sub_things_to_do/facilities/
af_dog_runs.html

**Canine Court, Van Cortlandt Park - Bronx**
West 252nd Street and Broadway (enter on the path on
252nd and follow it about 100 feet to the left)
Daily dawn-dusk
Fenced with two large runs: a basic dog run and a canine
agility playground with teeter-totter, hurdles, ladder, three
chutes and a hanging tire.

**Ewen Park ("John's Run") - Bronx (Riverdale)**
Riverdale to Johnson avenues, south of West 232nd
Street and down the steps in the clearing on the right
Daily dawn-dusk
Unfenced, plastic lawn furniture, scenic views.

**Seton Park - Bronx (Riverdale)**
West 235th Street and Independence Avenue (west of
Independence on 235th Street, near the Spuyten Duyvil
Library)
Daily dawn-dusk

**Prospect Park - Brooklyn**
fidobrooklyn.org, (888) 604-3422
Grand Army Plaza and Flatbush; off-leash areas may be
accessed from all park entrances
Daily 9 p.m.-9 a.m., Apr.-Oct.; 5 p.m.-9 a.m., rest of year
(in the 80-acre Long Meadow and 6-acre Peninsula
Meadow). Dogs may be off-leash in the 15-acre
Nethermead Mon.-Fri. 5 p.m-9 a.m. year-round (closed
holidays). On holidays and weekends, the hours above
apply to Nethermead as well. At all other times, dogs must
be on a leash, minimum fine for non-compliance $100.
Trees, restrooms (at Long Meadow only; may not be
available early in the morning), water (some fountains
equipped with troughs for dogs). No separate area for
small dogs. Small swimming area in the Long Meadow
near the 9th Street entrance. Note: Use of the park is at
the owner's risk. Dogs may be off-leash with appropriate
supervision in three large meadows at the hours specified
above; please observe all off-leash rules. Rules are posted
online and at park entrances. Dogs must be on a leash at
all other places and times.

**Owl's Head Park - Brooklyn (Bay Ridge)**
68th Street and Shore Road
Tree, grass surface, disposal bags.

**Hillside Park - Brooklyn Heights**
Columbia Heights and Middagh Street
Daily 24 hours
Fenced.

**Palmetto Playground - Brooklyn Heights**
Columbia Place and State Street (in the corner by the
Brooklyn-Queens Expressway)
Daily 24 hours
Benches, one park light, water.

**Tompkins Square Park - Manhattan (East Village)**
East 9th Street at Avenue B
Daily 6 a.m.-midnight
Benches, picnic tables, water, a canine memorial.

**Madison Square Park - Manhattan (Gramercy/Flatiron/
Union Square)**
East 24th Street at Fifth Avenue
Daily 6 a.m.-midnight
Trees, benches, disposal bags, water.

**Thomas Jefferson Park - Manhattan (Harlem)**
East 112th Street at First Avenue
Daily 24 hours
Benches, wood chips surface.

**J. Hood Wright Park - Manhattan (Inwood/Ft. George/
Washington Heights)**
West 173rd Street between Fort Washington Avenue and
Haven Avenue

**Fishbridge Park - Manhattan (Lower East Side)**
Dover Street at Pearl Street, just south of the Brooklyn
Bridge
Daily dawn-dusk
Benches, water hose, summer wading pool, lockbox for
toys, lockbox with newspapers for picking up after your
dog.

**Peter Detmold Park — Manhattan (Midtown East)**
East 49th Street at FDR Drive (behind Beeckman Place)
Daily dawn-9 p.m., June-Sept.; dawn-8 p.m., Mar.-May
and Oct.-Nov.; dawn-7 p.m., rest of year
Trees, benches, historical lamps, disposal bags.

**Carl Shurz Park - Manhattan (Upper East Side)**
East 86th Street at East End Avenue
Daily dawn-1 a.m.
Benches, scoops, pea gravel surface. A second run for
small dogs (past the main run, toward the East River) has
a scenic view of the river and the 59th Street Bridge.

**Riverside Park at 72nd Street - Manhattan (Upper West
Side/Morningside Heights)**
West 72nd Street
Daily 6 a.m.-1 a.m.
Bench, hanging flowerpots, disposal bags, scoopers.

**Riverside Park at 87th Street - Manhattan (Upper West
Side/Morningside Heights)**
West 87th Street
Daily dawn-dusk
Separate areas for large and small dogs, fountain and
hose.

**Riverside Park at 105th Street - Manhattan (Upper
West Side/Morningside Heights)**
riversidedog.org
West 105th Street, Riverside Park Central Promenade
Daily dawn-dusk
Trees, crushed granite surface, benches, disposal bag
dispensers, drinking fountain, dog water faucet, separate
area for small dogs.

# NEW YORK (CONT'D)

### Theodore Roosevelt Park - Manhattan (Upper West Side/Morningside Heights)
West 81st Street at Columbus Avenue
Daily 8 a.m.-10 p.m.
Shade trees, benches, dog water faucet, separate run for small dogs.

### Washington Square Park - Manhattan (West Village)
West 4th Street at Thompson Street
Daily 6 a.m.-midnight
Trees, pea gravel surface, benches, scoopers, water hose, water bowls.

### Doughboy Plaza - Queens (Woodside)
Woodside Avenue from 54th to 56th streets (also south of Woodside at 56th Street) at Windmuller Park
Daily dawn-dusk
Fenced, trash can.

# OHIO

### Mt. Airy Dog Park - Cincinnati
cincinnati-oh.gov/cityparks/pages/-4327-/
Westwood Northern Boulevard within Mt. Airy Forest's Highpoint Picnic Area, between Montana Avenue and North Bend Road
Daily dawn-dusk
Fenced, trees, benches, tables, shelter, trash cans, parking, restrooms, water. Access for the disabled.

# OREGON

### Alton Baker Park - Eugene
www.eugene-or.gov
South of Leo Harris Parkway; park in the lot south of Autzen Stadium and cross the pedestrian bridge to the dog park
Daily 6 a.m.-11 p.m.
Fenced, benches, tables, simple shelters for protection from sun and rain, disposal bag receptacles, water.

### Amazon Park - Eugene
www.eugene-or.gov
East of 29th Street and Amazon Parkway
Daily 6 a.m.-11 p.m.
Fenced, benches, tables, simple shelters for protection from sun and rain, disposal bag receptacles, water, parking nearby.

### Morse Ranch - Eugene
www.eugene-or.gov
Crest Drive and Lincoln Street (park in the main parking area at 595 Crest Dr. and take the trail east)
Daily 6 a.m.-11 p.m.
Fenced, benches, tables, simple shelters for protection from sun and rain, disposal bag receptacles, water.

### Brentwood Park - Portland
http://www.portlandonline.com/parks/index.cfm?c=39523
SE 60th Avenue and Duke Street
Daily 5 a.m.-midnight
Fenced.

### Chimney Park - Portland
http://www.portlandonline.com/parks/index.cfm?c=39523
9360 N. Columbia Blvd.
Daily 5 a.m.-midnight
Unfenced, 6 acres of off-leash meadow and trails. Dogs should be under excellent voice command.

### East Delta Park - Portland
http://www.portlandonline.com/parks/index.cfm?c=39523
N. Denver and Martin Luther King Jr. Boulevard (off I-5 exit 307 across from the East Delta Sports Complex)
Daily 5 a.m.-midnight, May-Oct. (open during dry season only)
Fenced, 5 acres of off-leash field, trees, benches; bring drinking water for your dog. Dogs are not allowed on the sports fields.

### Gabriel Park - Portland
http://www.portlandonline.com/parks/index.cfm?c=39523
S.W. 45th Street and Vermont
Daily 5 a.m.-midnight, May-Oct. (open during dry season only)
Fenced, 1 5 acres of off-leash area, trees, picnic tables, water. Dogs must remain leashed when not in the off-leash area.

### Normandale Park - Portland
http://www.portlandonline.com/parks/index.cfm?c=39523
NE 57th Avenue and Halsey Street
Daily 5 a.m.-midnight
Fenced.

# TEXAS

### White Rock Lake Dog Park - Dallas
dallasdogparks.org
Mockingbird Point within White Rock Lake Park
Tues.-Sun. 5 a.m.-midnight
Fenced, 2.5 acres, trees, benches, disposal bags, trash cans, parking, restrooms, water fountains, separate fenced areas for large and small dogs, fenced swimming area for dogs in White Rock Lake.

# VIRGINIA

**Note:** Disposal bag receptacles are provided at Alexandria parks; patrons must provide their own bags.

### Ben Brenman Park - Alexandria
ci.alexandria.va.us/recreation/parks/dogpark.html#fenced
Cameron Station along Backlick Creek
Daily 6 a.m.-10 p.m.
Fenced, disposal bag receptacles, trash cans, parking.

### Dog Park - Alexandria
ci.alexandria.va.us/recreation/parks/dogpark.html#fenced
5000 block of Duke Street east of the Charles E. Beatley Jr. Library
Daily 6 a.m.-10 p.m.
Fenced, disposal bag receptacles, trash cans, parking.

### Montgomery Park - Alexandria
ci.alexandria.va.us/recreation/parks/dogpark.html#fenced
Fairfax and 1st streets
Daily 6 a.m.-10 p.m.
Fenced, disposal bag receptacles, trash cans, parking.

# VIRGINIA (CONT'D)

### Simpson Stadium Park - Alexandria
ci.alexandria.va.us/recreation/parks/dogpark.html#fenced
Monroe Avenue
Daily 6 a.m.-10 p.m.
Fenced, disposal bag receptacles, trash cans, parking, dog water fountains.

### Off-leash, unfenced, under voice control areas:

### Beauregard Street - Alexandria
ci.alexandria.va.us/recreation/parks/dogpark.html#unfenced
Southeast corner of Armistead and Beauregard streets
Daily 6 a.m.-10 p.m.
Unfenced.

### Braddock Road - Alexandria
ci.alexandria.va.us/recreation/parks/dogpark.html#unfenced
Southeast corner of Braddock Road and Commonwealth Avenue
Daily 6 a.m.-10 p.m.
Unfenced.

### Chambliss Street - Alexandria
ci.alexandria.va.us/recreation/parks/dogpark.html#unfenced
Chambliss Street at Grigsby Avenue, south of the tennis courts
Daily 6 a.m.-10 p.m.
Unfenced; area is marked by traffic barriers.

### Chinquapin Park - Alexandria
ci.alexandria.va.us/recreation/parks/dogpark.html#unfenced
King Street at the east end of the loop road
Daily 6 a.m.-10 p.m.
Unfenced; area is marked by traffic barriers.

### Edison Street - Alexandria
ci.alexandria.va.us/recreation/parks/dogpark.html#unfenced
Edison Street, west of the cul-de-sac between the bike trail and Berkey Photo Processing
Daily 6 a.m.-10 p.m.
Unfenced; area is marked by traffic barriers.

### Ft. Williams - Alexandria
ci.alexandria.va.us/recreation/parks/dogpark.html#unfenced
Ft. Williams and New Ft. Williams Parkway
Daily 6 a.m.-10 p.m.
Unfenced; area is marked by traffic barriers.

### Founders Park - Alexandria
ci.alexandria.va.us/recreation/parks/dogpark.html#unfenced
Oronoco Street and Union Street, northeast corner
Daily 6 a.m.-10 p.m.
Unfenced; 100-by-100-foot area is marked by traffic barriers.

### Hooff's Run - Alexandria
ci.alexandria.va.us/recreation/parks/dogpark.html#unfenced
East of Commonwealth Avenue between Oak and Chapman streets
Daily 6 a.m.-10 p.m.
Unfenced; area is marked by traffic barriers.

### Monticello Park - Alexandria
ci.alexandria.va.us/recreation/parks/dogpark.html#unfenced
Beverly Drive, east of the entrance
Daily 6 a.m.-10 p.m.
Unfenced; 50-by-200-foot area is marked by traffic barriers.

### North Fort Ward Park - Alexandria
ci.alexandria.va.us/recreation/parks/dogpark.html#unfenced
Braddock Road, east side of entrance
Daily 6 a.m.-10 p.m.
Unfenced; 100-by-100-foot area is marked by traffic barriers.

### Tarleton Park - Alexandria
ci.alexandria.va.us/recreation/parks/dogpark.html#unfenced
Old Mill Run west of Gordon Street
Daily 6 a.m.-10 p.m.
Unfenced.

### Timberbranch Parkway - Alexandria
ci.alexandria.va.us/recreation/parks/dogpark.html#unfenced
Median to Timberbranch Parkway between Braddock Road and Oakley Place
Daily 6 a.m.-10 p.m.
Unfenced; area is marked by traffic barriers.

### Windmill Hill Park - Alexandria
ci.alexandria.va.us/recreation/parks/dogpark.html#unfenced
Gibbon and Union streets
Daily 6 a.m.-10 p.m.
Unfenced.

### W&OD Railroad - Alexandria
ci.alexandria.va.us/recreation/parks/dogpark.html#unfenced
Raymond Avenue (200 feet of the W&OD Railroad right-of-way south of Raymond)
Daily 6 a.m.-10 p.m.
Unfenced; area is marked by traffic barriers.

### Benjamin Banneker Park - Arlington County
arlingtondogs.org
1600 block of North Sycamore Street (take I-66 west to Sycamore Street/exit 69, turn left on Sycamore and proceed past the East Falls Church Metro Station, turn right onto North 16th Street and take the first right, which dead-ends at the dog exercise area)
Daily dawn to half-hour after dusk
Fully fenced, picnic table and benches, water.

### Fort Barnard Park - Arlington County
arlingtondogs.org
South Pollard Street and South Walter Reed Drive (from Rte. 50, take Glebe Road south, turn right on South Walter Reed Drive and proceed to Pollard Street; the park is on the right side)
Daily dawn to half-hour after dusk
Fully fenced, picnic table and benches, water.

### Glencarlyn Park - Arlington County
arlingtondogs.org
301 South Harrison St. (from Rte. 50, head west to Carlin Springs Road, exit right and then turn left at the stop sign, pass under Rte. 50 and follow Carlin Springs to 4th Street, turn left on 4th Street and proceed five blocks until the road ends at the Glencarlyn Park sign, following the park road until it ends; park and walk over a small bridge and stream to the exercise area)
Daily dawn to half-hour after dusk
Unfenced area near a creek and woods, picnic table, benches.

# VIRGINIA (CONT'D)

### Shirlington Park - Arlington County
arlingtondogs.org
2601 S. Arlington Mill Dr., bordering South Four Mile Run between Shirlington Road and South Walter Reed Drive along the bicycle path between a storage facility and the water, near but not in Jennie Dean Park (from South Four Mile Run, turn south onto Nelson and park behind the storage facility; there are no signs indicating the dog park)
Daily dawn to half-hour after dusk
Partially fenced, picnic table, benches, water.

### Utah Park - Arlington County
arlingtondogs.org
3308 S. Stafford St. (from I-395, take the Shirlington exit to Quaker Lane, turn right onto 32nd Road S., turn right onto S. Stafford Street and follow the curve to the yield sign, turn left onto 32nd Street and park at the bottom of the hill or along the street; the dog exercise area is on the far side of the softball diamond from the parking lot)
Daily dawn to half-hour after dusk
Fully fenced, picnic table, benches, water.

### Red Wing Park - Virginia Beach
vbgov.com/e-gov/vbcsg/faqinfo/0,1172,5353,00.html
1398 General Booth Blvd.
Daily 7:30 a.m.-dusk; closed Jan. 1, Martin Luther King Day, Veterans Day, Thanksgiving and Dec. 25
Annual fee for first-time visitors $5; owners must register at the park office, show proof of pet's rabies shot and vaccines, and obtain a city dog license.
Fenced, benches, disposal bags, parking, restrooms, water. Access for the disabled.

### Woodstock Community Park - Virginia Beach
vbgov.com/e-gov/vbcsg/faqinfo/0,1172,5353,00.html
5709 Providence Rd.
Daily 7:30 a.m.-dusk; closed Jan. 1, Martin Luther King Day, Veterans Day, Thanksgiving and Dec. 25
Annual fee for first-time visitors $5; owners must register at the park office, show proof of pet's rabies shot and vaccines, and obtain a city dog license.
Fenced, benches, disposal bags, restrooms, parking. Access for the disabled.

# WASHINGTON

### I-5 Colonnade Park - Seattle
coladog.org
Lakeview Boulevard and Franklin Avenue East in the Eastlake neighborhood beneath I-5, south of East Howe Street
Daily 6 a.m.-11 p.m.
Fenced, 1.2 acres, double-gated entry, dog water fountain; the I-5 freeway deck provides shelter from the elements.

### I-90 "Blue Dog Pond" - Seattle
coladog.org
Martin Luther King Jr. Way and South Massachusetts Street, on the northwest corner
Daily 6 a.m.-11 p.m.
Fenced, 1 acre, parking, dog water fountain, Blue Dog sculpture. No off-leash areas in I-90 Lid Park, just east of Blue Dog Pond.

### Dr. Jose Rizal Park - Seattle
coladog.org
1008 12th Ave. S. on North Beacon Hill; off-leash area is in the lower portion of the park
Daily 6 a.m.-11 p.m.
Fenced, 4 acres, double-gated entry, parking, dog water fountain, scenic view of downtown.

### Genesee Park - Seattle
coladog.org
46th Avenue South and South Genesee Street
Daily 6 a.m.-11 p.m.
Fenced, 3 acres, double-gated entry, parking, dog water fountain.

### Golden Gardens Park - Seattle
coladog.org
8498 Seaview Pl. N.W. in Ballard
Daily 6 a.m.-11 p.m.
Fenced, lighted, 1 acre, parking, dog water fountain. The off-leash area is in the upper (eastern) portion of the park; dogs are not allowed on the lower beach area.

### Magnuson Park - Seattle
coladog.org
6500 Sandpoint Way N.E. (enter the park at 74th Street and drive to the end of the road)
Daily 6 a.m.-11 p.m.
Fenced, 9 acres, double-gated entry, shelter, parking, separate area for small/shy dogs, dog water fountain, beach access.

### Northacres Park - Seattle
coladog.org
N. 130th Street, west of I-5; off-leash area is in the northeast corner of the park at 12530 Third Ave. N.E., north of the ball field. Parking is available on the west side of the park along 1st Street N.E. and on the south side along North 125th Street
Daily 6 a.m.-11 p.m.
Fenced, double-gated entry, parking, dog water fountain.

### Plymouth Pillars Park - Seattle
coladog.org
Boren Avenue and Pike Street on Capitol Hill above I-5
Daily 6 a.m.-11 p.m.
Fenced, 9,800 square feet, double-gated entry, dog water fountain, scenic view of downtown Seattle.

### Regrade Park - Seattle
coladog.org
3rd Avenue and Bell Street, downtown
Fenced, 13,000 square feet, double-gated entry, dog water fountain.

### Westcrest Park - Seattle
coladog.org
8806 8th Ave. S.W. in West Seattle
Daily 6 a.m.-11 p.m.
Fenced, 5 acres, parking, dog water fountain. The off-leash area is along the east side of the reservoir.

### Woodland Park - Seattle
coladog.org
West Green Lake Way North, west of the tennis courts
Daily 6 a.m.-11 p.m.
Fenced, 1 acre, double-gated entry, parking, dog water fountain.

# Canada

## ALBERTA

### 91 Street Right of Way - Edmonton
*gov.edmonton.ab.ca, (780) 496-1475*
Berm east of 91 Street from 10 Avenue north to
Whitemud Freeway and east to 76 Street
Unfenced.

### Buena Vista Great Meadow - Edmonton
*gov.edmonton.ab.ca, (780) 496-1475*
North of Laurier Park and Buena Vista Drive and south of
Melton Ravine in the vicinity of 88 Avenue
Unfenced; area does not include the pedestrian bridge
access trail, Yorath property or the trail north to McKenzie
Ravine. This is a hot-air balloon site, so please leash your
dog during balloon launches.

### Hermitage Park North - Edmonton
*gov.edmonton.ab.ca, (780) 496-1475*
129 Avenue to 137 Avenue; also 22 Street along the
riverbank where signs designate an off-leash area.
Unfenced. This is a multi-use area in the valley north of
the park's fishing pond and picnic area.

### Jackie Parker Park - Edmonton
*gov.edmonton.ab.ca, (780) 496-1475*
Whitemud Freeway and 50th Street
Unfenced. Includes the area south of the 44 Avenue
entrance; dogs are not allowed on the golf course.

### Keehewin Blackmud - Edmonton
*gov.edmonton.ab.ca, (780) 496-1475*
Pipeline corridor, 104 Street and 20 Avenue to the south
end of 109 Street (excludes Bearspaw Drive West and
Blackmud Creek and Ravine)
Unfenced.

### Kennedale - Edmonton
*gov.edmonton.ab.ca, (780) 496-1475*
Ravine west of the 40 Street loop, west to 47 Street and
the top of the bank
Unfenced.

### Lauderdale - Edmonton
*gov.edmonton.ab.ca, (780) 496-1475*
South end of Grand Trunk Park, from 127 to 129 Avenue
and 113A to 109 Street
Unfenced.

### Mill Creek Ravine - Edmonton
*gov.edmonton.ab.ca, (780) 496-1475*
68 Avenue and 93 Street; access is from the west or
north sides of Argyll Park
Unfenced. A granular trail along the bottom of the ravine
leads to the Whyte (82) Avenue overpass.

### Terwillegar Park - Edmonton
gov.edmonton.ab.ca, (780) 496-1475
Rabbit Hill Road
Unfenced. This is a multi-use area.

## MANITOBA

### Bourkevale Park - Winnipeg
winnipeg.ca/publicworks/parks/fieldsforfido.asp
100 Ferry Rd., south of the dike along the riverbank
Daily 6 a.m.-10 p.m.
Unfenced, trash cans, parking; bring your own disposal
bags.

### Juba Park & Pioneer Avenue - Winnipeg
winnipeg.ca/publicworks/parks/fieldsforfido.asp
Pioneer Avenue, all vacant land west of the walkway to
Juba Park
Daily 6 a.m.-10 p.m.
Unfenced, trash cans, parking; bring your own disposal
bags.

### Kil-Cona Park - Winnipeg
winnipeg.ca/publicworks/parks/fieldsforfido.asp
Lagimodiere Boulevard in the area north of the west
parking lot
Daily 6 a.m.-10 p.m.
Unfenced, trash cans, parking; bring your own disposal
bags.

### King's Park - Winnipeg
winnipeg.ca/publicworks/parks/fieldsforfido.asp
King's Drive, south end of park, south of the lake
Daily 6 a.m.-10 p.m.
Unfenced, trash cans, parking; bring your own disposal
bags.

### Maple Grove Park - Winnipeg
winnipeg.ca/publicworks/parks/fieldsforfido.asp
Frobisher Road, north area of park
Daily 6 a.m.-10 p.m.
Unfenced, trash cans, parking; bring your own disposal
bags.

### Westview Park - Winnipeg
winnipeg.ca/publicworks/parks/fieldsforfido.asp
Midland Street; entire park is an off-leash area
Daily 6 a.m.-10 p.m.
Unfenced, trash cans, parking; bring your own disposal
bags.

# United States

## CALIFORNIA

 **Disneyland® Resort**

(714) 781-4565, 1313 S. Harbor Blvd. via I-5 Disneyland Drive and Disney Way exits, Anaheim
Disneyland® Resort consists of two family-oriented theme parks — Disneyland Park and Disney's California Adventure Park — and the shops, restaurants and entertainment of Downtown Disney®. Indoor kennel facilities $15. Mon.-Fri. 10-8, Sat. 9 a.m.-midnight, Sun. 9 a.m.-10 p.m. Extended hours in summer; phone ahead to confirm. Admission to either park $59; over 60, $57; ages 3-9, $49. Parking fee. disneyland.disney.go.com

 **SeaWorld Adventure Park**

(619) 226-3901 or (800) 257-4268, 500 SeaWorld Dr., San Diego
SeaWorld offers four major animal shows, rides and playgrounds, a marina and exhibits featuring marine creatures from around the world. Pet facility provided for a nominal charge on a first-come, first-serve basis. Opens daily at 9, mid-June through Labor Day; at 10, rest of year. Closing times vary. Admission $56; ages 3-9, $46. Parking fee.
www.seaworld.com/ca

 **Universal Studios Hollywood**

(800) 864-8377, 100 Universal City Plaza, Universal City
In addition to thrill rides and arcade games, Universal Studios gives visitors a behind-the-scenes look at the workings of a major film and TV studio. Complimentary kennel service. Daily 9-8 in summer, 10-6 rest of year. Box office closes at 5 in summer, at 4 rest of year. Hours may vary; phone ahead to confirm. Closed Thanksgiving and Dec. 25. Admission $55; over 59, $51; under 48 inches tall $45. Parking fee.
themeparks.universalstudios.com

## DISTRICT OF COLUMBIA

 **Washington Monument**

(202) 426-6841, 15th Street and Constitution Avenue N.W., Washington, D.C.
This instantly recognizable 555-foot marble obelisk commemorates our nation's first president and is surrounded by expansive grounds. Pets on leash. Daily 9-5; closed Dec. 25. Free. www.nps.gov/wamo

## FLORIDA

**Busch Gardens Tampa Bay**

(866) 353-8622 or (888) 800-5447, 3000 E. Busch Blvd., Tampa
This African-themed family entertainment park and outstanding zoological facility features all kinds of thrill rides and numerous opportunities for animal observation. Outdoor kennel facilities. Generally open daily at 9 a.m.; closing times vary. Phone ahead to confirm hours. Admission $57.95; ages 3-9, $47.95. Parking fee.
www.buschgardens.com

 **SeaWorld Orlando**

(407) 351-3600 or (800) 327-2424, 7007 SeaWorld Dr. at I-4 and SR 528 (Beachline Expressway), Orlando
A research facility as well as a theme park, SeaWorld Orlando presents crowd-pleasing animal shows starring a family of performing killer whales. Air-conditioned kennels. Generally opens daily at 9; closing times vary. Phone ahead to confirm hours. Admission $61.95; ages 3-9, $49.95.
Parking fee. www.seaworld.com

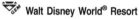 **Universal Orlando Resort**

(407) 363-8000, off I-4 exit 75A (eastbound) or 74B (westbound) following signs, Orlando
At Universal Orlando you can "ride the movies" at the Universal Studios theme park, cavort with superheroes and cartoon characters at the Islands of Adventure theme park, or visit the specialty shops, celebrity-themed restaurants and entertainment venues at CityWalk. Air-conditioned and outdoor kennels. Theme parks open daily at 9 a.m.; closing times vary by season. Phone ahead to confirm hours. CityWalk open daily 11 a.m.-2 a.m. Admission to Universal Orlando Resort $63; ages 3-9, $52. Individual CityWalk venue charges vary. Parking fee.
themeparks.universalstudios.com

 **Walt Disney World® Resort**

(407) 824-4321, theme parks accessible from US 192, Osceola Parkway and several I-4 exits, Lake Buena Vista
Walt Disney World has — count 'em — four theme parks: Magic Kingdom® Park, Epcot®, Disney's Animal Kingdom® Theme Park and Disney-MGM Studios, plus shopping, dining and entertainment at the Downtown Disney® Area. Air-conditioned and outdoor kennels. Theme parks generally open daily at 9 a.m., closing times vary. One-day, one-park admission $63; ages 3-9, $52. Parking fee. disneyworld.disney.go.com

## GEORGIA

 **Six Flags Over Georgia**

(770) 948-9290, 275 Riverside Pkwy. (off I-20), Austell
Six Flags offers more than 100 rides, attractions and shows, a 12,000-seat concert amphitheater, Broadway-style musical shows and a July 4 fireworks display. Air-conditioned kennels (water provided, but not food). Open daily at 10 a.m., late May to mid-Aug.; Sat.-Sun. at 10, mid-Mar. to late May and mid-Aug. to late Oct. Closing times vary. Admission $45.99, over 54 and under 49 inches tall $29.99, under 2 free. Parking fee.
www.sixflags.com

# ILLINOIS

 **Six Flags Great America**

(847) 249-4636 or (847) 249-1776, 542 N. Route 21, Gurnee
Batman the Ride, Iron Wolf and Raging Bull are among the thrill rides at this family theme park, which also has a section of rides and attractions for children under 54 inches tall. Kennel facilities. Open daily at 10 a.m., late Apr. to mid-Sept.; Sat.-Sun. at 10, mid-Sept. to late Oct. Closing times vary; phone ahead to confirm hours. Admission $44.99, over 60 and under 55 inches tall $29.99, under 3 free. Parking fee. www.sixflags.com

# IOWA

 **Pella Historical Village**

(641) 628-2409 or 628-4311, 507 Franklin St., Pella
A country store, log cabin, grist mill, windmill, smithy and other buildings (including Wyatt Earp's boyhood home) are reminders of this town's Dutch Heritage. Pets on leash (grounds only). Mon.-Sat. 9-5, Mar.-Dec. Admission $8; ages 5-18, $2.

# MASSACHUSETTS

 **Bunker Hill Monument**

(617) 242-5641, in Monument Square on Breed's Hill, Charlestown
Part of Boston National Historical Park, this 221-foot-tall granite obelisk commemorates the site of the Battle of Bunker Hill on June 17, 1775. Pets on leash (grounds only); must pick up after pet. Visitor lodge and exhibits daily 9-5. Free. www.nps.gov/bost/Bunker_Hill/htm

# MISSISSIPPI

 **Vicksburg National Military Park**

(601) 636-0583, 3201 Clay St. (entered on the eastern edge off US 80)
More than 1,260 memorials, monuments, statues and markers honor the Union and Confederate troops who engaged in the siege of Vicksburg in 1863. Pets on leash. Grounds open daily dawn-dusk; visitor center daily 8-5. Admission $8 per private vehicle. www.nps.gov/vick

# MISSOURI

 **The Gateway Arch**

(877) 982-1410, Memorial Drive and Market Street, St. Louis
This curved, stainless steel monument soars 630 feet high and symbolizes the gateway to the West. A tram ride takes visitors to an observation deck. Pets on leash (grounds only). Tram ticket center open daily 8 a.m.-10 p.m., Memorial Day-Labor Day; 9-6, rest of year. Closed Jan. 1, Thanksgiving and Dec. 25. Tram ride $10; ages 13-16, $7; ages 3-12, $3. www.gatewayarch.com

# NORTH CAROLINA

 **Paramount's Carowinds Theme Park**

(704) 588-2600 in N.C., (803) 548-5300 or (800) 888-4386, 10 miles south on I-77 to exit 90, Charlotte
Themed areas at this park depict the past and present of the Carolinas, and offer roller coasters and water rides, children's play areas and other family entertainment. Air-conditioned kennels. Open daily, Jun.-Jul.; various times from late Mar. through May 31 and Aug. 1 to early Nov. Hours vary seasonally; phone ahead. Admission $46.99; over 55 and ages 3-6 or under 48 inches tall, $29.99. Parking fee. www.carowinds.com

# OHIO

 **Paramount's Kings Island**

(513) 754-5700 or (800) 288-0808, Kings Island Drive (off I-71 exits 24 and 25), Kings Mills
Kings Island is a family entertainment park featuring 12 hair-raising roller coasters; WaterWorks, a water recreation playground; costumed cartoon characters; and a variety of live shows. Outdoor kennel facilities (fee). Open daily at 9 a.m., late May-Labor Day weekend; Sat.-Sun. at 9 a.m., early Apr. to mid-May. Phone ahead to confirm hours. Admission $44.99; over 59, ages 3-6 or under 48 inches tall, $26.99. Parking fee. www.pki.com

# PENNSYLVANIA

 **Hersheypark**

(800) 437-7439, 100 W. Hersheypark Dr. (just off SR 743 and US 422), Hershey
The emphasis is on thrill rides at Hersheypark, plus live entertainment that includes a marine mammal show, song and dance reviews and big-name performers. Kennel facilities. Open daily at 10 a.m., mid-May to late Sept.; Fri.-Sun. at 10, selected weekends in May. Closing times vary; phone ahead to confirm hours. Admission $41.95; over 54 and ages 3-8, $24.95; 70 and over $17.95. Parking fee. www.hersheypark.com

# TEXAS

### SeaWorld San Antonio

(800) 700-7786, 2595 N. Ellison Dr. (off SR 151 at the junction of Westover Hills Boulevard), San Antonio
Killer and beluga whales, sea lions, otters, walruses and dolphins perform at this marine life park, which also has shark exhibits, a penguin habitat and a children's playground. Outdoor kennel facilities (owner must provide food and water containers). Open daily at 10 a.m., early Mar.-late Nov.; closing times vary. Admission $46.99; ages 3-9, $36.99 (phone to confirm times and admission). Parking fee. www.seaworld.com

### Six Flags Over Texas

(817) 530-6000, 2201 Road to Six Flags (at the junction of I-30 and SR 360 exit 30), Arlington
Themed areas, each featuring thrill rides, food and entertainment, depict Texas under six different flags: Spain, France, Mexico, the Republic of Texas, the Confederate States of America and the United States. Air-conditioned kennels. Open daily, June 1 to mid-Aug.; Sat.-Sun (also Labor Day), late Mar. through May 31, mid-Aug. through Oct. 31 and early to mid-Dec. Hours vary; phone ahead to confirm schedule. Admission $42.99; over 54, the physically impaired and under 48 inches tall, $22.99; under 3 free. Parking fee. www.sixflags.com

# VIRGINIA

### Busch Gardens Williamsburg

(800) 343-7946, 3 miles east on US 60 or off I-64 exit 242A, Williamsburg
This European-themed adventure park offers something for the entire family, from thrill rides to dance and music shows to villages representing England, Germany, France and other nations. Outdoor kennel facilities (England parking lot); fee $6 per pet per day. Open daily at 10 a.m., early May-Labor Day; closing times vary. Open at 10, late Mar.-early May and day after Labor Day-late Oct.; days and closing times vary. Admission $51.95; ages 3-6, $44.95. Parking fee. www.buschgardens.com

### Paramount's Kings Dominion

(804) 876-5000, 16000 Theme Park Dr. (on SR 30 1/2 mile east off I-95 exit 98), Doswell
Eight themed areas make up Kings Dominion, a full-scale theme park with thrill rides, kiddie play areas, costumed characters, live shows and specialty shopping. Kennel facilities (fee); water provided, but not food. Park open daily, Memorial Day-Labor Day; Sat.-Sun., mid-Mar. to day before Memorial Day and first Sat. after Labor Day to mid-Oct. Hours vary seasonally; phone ahead. Admission $45.99; over 54, $39.99; ages 3-6, $31.99. Parking fee. www.kingsdominion.com

# WASHINGTON

### Hovander Homestead Park

(360) 384-3444, 1 mile south via Hovander Road, Ferndale
This restored house, dating from 1903 and furnished with antiques, is within a large park encompassing gardens, picnic sites and a children's farm zoo. Pets on leash (grounds only). Grounds open daily 8 a.m.-dusk; house open Thurs.-Sun. noon-4:30, June 1-Labor Day. Grounds $4 per private vehicle. House $1; ages 5-12, 50 cents. www.co.whatcom.wa.us/parks/hovander/hovander.jsp

# Canada

# ONTARIO

### Upper Canada Village

(613) 543-4328 or (800) 437-2233, 7 miles (11 kilometers) east on CR 2 off Hwy. 401, Morrisburg
Upper Canada Village re-creates life during the 1860s through a working community of artisans and costumed interpreters who perform chores typical of the era. Pets on leash (grounds only). Daily 9:30-5, May 20-Oct. 8. Village admission $16.95; over 65, $15.95; students with ID $10.50; ages 5-12, $7.50. www.uppercanadavillage.com

### Paramount Canada's Wonderland

(905) 832-7000 or 832-8131, off Hwy. 400 (Rutherford Road exit northbound or Major MacKenzie Drive E. exit southbound) at 9580 Jane St., Vaughan
Thrill rides at this theme park include the Top Gun coaster and Drop Zone, a free-fall plunge, while Scooby Doo's Haunted Mansion and Hanna-Barbera Land will entertain little ones. Air-conditioned kennels (fee). Open daily at 10 a.m., late May-Labour Day; some weekends early to late May and day after Labour Day-second Sun. in Oct. Closing times vary. Grounds admission $25.99. Grounds and rides passport $49.99; over 59 and ages 3-6, $24.99. Parking fee. www.canadas-wonderland.com

# NATIONAL PUBLIC LANDS

The National Public Lands listed below permit pets on a leash. Keep in mind that animals may be prohibited from entering public buildings and even some areas outdoors, particularly those that are ecologically sensitive. Specific pet policies vary from park to park and are subject to change. Always check in advance regarding any applicable regulations and to confirm that pets are still permitted where you are going.

Never leave your pet unattended. Keep him leashed or crated at all times. Follow park guidelines faithfully, and monitor your pet's behavior; the National Park Service may confiscate pets that harm wildlife or other visitors. *For additional information on outdoor vacations, see The Great Outdoors, p. 16.*

## United States

### ALABAMA

**Conecuh National Forest**
On the Alabama-Florida border.
(334) 222-2555
[Bicycling] [Camping] [Hiking] [Picnicking] [Swimming]

**Eufaula National Wildlife Refuge**
On the Chattahoochee River.
(334) 687-4065
[Bicycling] [Hiking] [Picnicking] [Visitor center]

**Horseshoe Bend National Military Park**
12 mi. north of Dadeville on SR 49.
(256) 234-7111
[Bicycling] [Hiking] [Picnicking] [Swimming] [Visitor center]

**Talladega National Forest**
In central Alabama.
(256) 362-2909
[Camping] [Hiking] [Picnicking] [Swimming] [Visitor center] [Food service]

**Tuskegee National Forest**
Northeast of Tuskegee.
(334) 727-2652
[Camping] [Hiking] [Picnicking] [Visitor center]

**William B. Bankhead National Forest**
In northwestern Alabama.
(205) 489-5111
[Bicycling] [Camping] [Hiking] [Picnicking] [Swimming] [Visitor center]

**Wheeler National Wildlife Refuge**
Between Decatur and Huntsville.
(256) 353-7243
[Bicycling] [Hiking] [Picnicking] [Visitor center]

### ALASKA

**Chugach National Forest**
Along the Gulf of Alaska from Cape Suckling to Seward.
(907) 743-9500
[Bicycling] [Camping] [Hiking] [Picnicking] [Visitor center]

**Denali National Park and Preserve**
In south-central Alaska.
(907) 683-2294
[Bicycling] [Camping] [Hiking] [Picnicking] [Visitor center] [Food service]

**Glacier Bay National Park and Preserve**
North of Cross Sound to the Canadian border.
(907) 697-2230
[Bicycling] [Camping] [Hiking] [Visitor center]

**Kenai Fjords National Park**
Southeastern side of the Kenai Peninsula.
(907) 224-7500 or 224-2132
[Camping] [Hiking] [Picnicking] [Visitor center]

**Lake Clark National Park and Preserve**
In southern Alaska.
(907) 271-3751
[Camping] [Hiking] [Visitor center]

**Tongass National Forest**
In southeastern Alaska.
(907) 586-8751 or 228-6220
[Bicycling] [Camping] [Hiking] [Picnicking] [Visitor center]

**Wrangell-St. Elias National Park and Preserve**
In southeastern Alaska, northwest of Tongass National Forest.
(907) 822-5234
[Bicycling] [Camping] [Hiking] [Picnicking] [Visitor center] [Food service]

### ARIZONA

**Apache-Sitgreaves National Forests**
In east-central Arizona.
(928) 333-4301
[Bicycling] [Camping] [Hiking] [Picnicking] [Visitor center] [Food service]

**Bill Williams River National Wildlife Refuge**
Off SR 95 near Parker.
(928) 667-4144
[Bicycling] [Hiking] [Picnicking] [Swimming] [Visitor center]

**Buenos Aires National Wildlife Refuge**
North of Sasabe on SR 286.
(520) 823-4251
[Bicycling] [Camping] [Hiking] [Picnicking] [Visitor center]

**Coconino National Forest**
In north-central Arizona.
(928) 527-3600
[Bicycling] [Camping] [Hiking] [Picnicking] [Swimming] [Visitor center] [Food service]

---

[Bicycling] Bicycling  [Camping] Camping  [Hiking] Hiking  [Picnicking] Picnicking
[Swimming] Swimming  [Visitor center] Visitor center  [Food service] Food service

**Coronado National Forest**
In southeastern Arizona and southwestern New Mexico.
(520) 388-8300
🚴 🔼 🥾 🏕 👫

**Glen Canyon National Recreation Area**
In north-central Arizona.
(928) 608-6200
🔼 🥾 🏕 🛥 👫 🍴

**Grand Canyon National Park**
In northwestern Arizona.
(928) 638-7888
🔼 🥾 🏕 👫 🍴

**Kaibab National Forest**
In north-central Arizona.
(928) 635-4061 or (800) 863-0546
🚴 🔼 🥾 🏕 👫 🍴

**Lake Mead National Recreation Area**
In northwestern Arizona and southeastern Nevada.
(702) 293-8990
🚴 🔼 🥾 🏕 🛥 👫 🍴

**Petrified Forest National Park**
In east-central Arizona, east of Holbrook.
(928) 524-6228
🥾 🏕 👫 🍴

**Prescott National Forest**
In central Arizona.
(928) 443-8000 or TDD (928) 443-8001
🚴 🔼 🥾 🏕 🍴

**Saguaro National Park**
Two districts, 15 mi. east and west of Tucson.
(520) 733-5153
🚴 🥾 🏕 👫

**Tonto National Forest**
In central Arizona.
(602) 225-5200
🚴 🔼 🥾 🏕 🛥 🍴

# ARKANSAS

**Buffalo National River**
In northwestern Arkansas.
(870) 741-5443
🔼 🥾 🏕 🛥 👫 🍴

**Felsenthal National Wildlife Refuge**
7 mi. west of Crossett on US 82.
(870) 364-3167
🔼 🥾 🏕 👫

**Hot Springs National Park**
In western Arkansas.
(501) 624-2701 or TDD (501) 624-2308
🔼 🥾 🏕 👫

**Ouachita National Forest**
In west-central Arkansas and southeastern Oklahoma.
(501) 321-5202
🚴 🔼 🥾 🏕 🛥 👫 🍴

**Ozark-St. Francis National Forest**
In northwestern and east-central Arkansas.
(479) 964-7200
🚴 🔼 🥾 🏕 🛥 👫 🍴

**Pea Ridge National Military Park**
East of Rogers in northwest Arkansas.
(479) 451-8122
🚴 🥾 🏕 👫

# CALIFORNIA

**Angeles National Forest**
In southern California.
(626) 574-5200
🚴 🔼 🥾 🏕 🛥 👫 🍴

**Cleveland National Forest**
In southwestern California.
(858) 673-6180
🚴 🔼 🥾 🏕 👫 🍴

**Death Valley National Park**
Along the Nevada border in east-central California.
(760) 786-2331
🚴 🔼 🥾 🏕 👫 🍴

**Eldorado National Forest**
In central California.
(530) 644-6048
🚴 🔼 🥾 🏕 🛥 👫 🍴

**Golden Gate National Recreation Area**
North of the Golden Gate Bridge and in northern and western San Francisco.
(415) 561-4700
🚴 🔼 🥾 🏕 🛥 👫 🍴

**Inyo National Forest**
In central California.
(760) 873-2400
🚴 🔼 🥾 🏕 🛥 👫 🍴

**Joshua Tree National Park**
East of Desert Hot Springs.
(760) 367-5500
🚴 🔼 🥾 🏕 👫

**Klamath National Forest**
In northern California.
(530) 842-6131
🚴 🔼 🥾 🏕 🛥 👫 🍴

**Lassen National Forest**
In northeastern California.
(530) 257-2151
🚴 🔼 🥾 🏕 🛥 👫 🍴

**Lassen Volcanic National Park**
In northeastern California.
(530) 595-4444
🚴 🔼 🥾 🏕 🛥 👫 🍴

**Los Padres National Forest**
In southern California.
(805) 968-6640 or TDD (805) 968-6790
🚴 🔼 🥾 🏕 🛥 👫 🍴

**Mendocino National Forest**
In northwestern California.
(530) 934-2350 or 934-3316, or TDD (530) 934-7724
🚲 🏕 🥾 ⛱ 🏊 👥

**Modoc National Forest**
In northeastern California.
(530) 233-5811
🚲 🏕 🥾 ⛱ 🏊 👥

**Mojave National Preserve**
Between I-15 and I-40 in southeastern California.
(760) 252-6100
🚲 🏕 🥾 ⛱ 👥

**Plumas National Forest**
In northern California.
(530) 283-2050
🚲 🏕 🥾 ⛱ 🏊 🍽

**Point Reyes National Seashore**
Along the California coast just north of San Francisco.
(415) 464-5100
🚲 🏕 🥾 ⛱ 👥

**Redwood National Park**
On the northern California coast.
(707) 464-6101, ext. 5064 or 5265
🚲 🏕 🥾 ⛱ 👥

**San Bernardino National Forest**
In southern California.
(909) 382-2600
🚲 🏕 🥾 ⛱ 🏊 👥 🍽

**Santa Monica Mountains National Recreation Area**
West from Griffith Park in Los Angeles to the Ventura
County line.
(805) 370-2301
🚲 🏕 🥾 ⛱ 👥 🍽

**Sequoia and Kings Canyon National Parks**
In east-central California.
(559) 565-3341
🏕 🥾 ⛱ 👥 🍽

**Sequoia National Forest**
In south-central California.
(559) 784-1500
🚲 🏕 🥾 ⛱ 🏊 👥 🍽

**Shasta-Trinity National Forests**
In northern California.
(530) 226-2500
🚲 🏕 🥾 ⛱ 🏊 👥 🍽

**Sierra National Forest**
In central California.
(559) 297-0706
🚲 🏕 🥾 ⛱ 🏊 👥 🍽

**Six Rivers National Forest**
In northwestern California.
(707) 441-3523 or (707) 442-1721
🚲 🏕 🥾 ⛱ 🏊 👥 🍽

**Smith River National Recreation Area**
Within Six Rivers National Forest in northwestern
California.
(707) 457-3131
🚲 🏕 🥾 ⛱ 🏊

**Stanislaus National Forest**
In central California.
(209) 532-3671
🚲 🏕 🥾 ⛱ 🏊 🍽

**Tahoe National Forest**
In north-central California.
(530) 265-4531
🚲 🏕 🥾 ⛱ 🏊 👥 🍽

**Whiskeytown-Shasta-Trinity National Recreation Area**
North and west of Redding.
(530) 242-3400, (530) 275-1589 in Shasta
or (530) 623-2121 in Trinity
🚲 🏕 🥾 ⛱ 🏊 👥

**Yosemite National Park**
In central California.
(209) 372-0200
🚲 🏕 🥾 ⛱ 🏊 👥 🍽

## COLORADO

**Arapaho and Roosevelt National Forests**
In north-central Colorado.
(970) 295-6700
🚲 🏕 🥾 ⛱ 🏊 👥 🍽

**Arapaho National Recreation Area**
In north-central Colorado.
(970) 887-4100
🚲 🏕 🥾 ⛱ 👥

**Black Canyon of the Gunnison National Park**
In western Colorado.
(970) 641-2337
🚲 🏕 🥾 ⛱ 👥

**Curecanti National Recreation Area**
In south-central Colorado between Gunnison and
Montrose, paralleling US 50.
(970) 641-2337
🚲 🏕 🥾 ⛱ 🏊 👥 🍽

**Grand Mesa-Uncompahgre-Gunnison National Forests**
In west-central Colorado.
(970) 874-6600
🚲 🏕 🥾 ⛱ 👥 🍽

---

🚲 Bicycling   🏕 Camping   🥾 Hiking   ⛱ Picnicking
🏊 Swimming   👥 Visitor center   🍽 Food service

**Mesa Verde National Park**
In southwestern Colorado.
(970) 529-4465 or 4461
▲ 𝔥 ☷ ⭑ ⬤

**Pike National Forest**
In central Colorado.
(719) 553-1400
⚲ ▲ 𝔥 ☷ ⭑

**Rio Grande National Forest**
In south-central Colorado.
(719) 852-5941
⚲ ▲ 𝔥 ☷ ⭑

**Rocky Mountain National Park**
In north-central Colorado.
(970) 586-1206 or 586-1333
▲ 𝔥 ☷ ⭑

**Routt National Forest**
In northwestern Colorado.
(970) 879-1870
⚲ ▲ 𝔥 ☷ ⬗ ⭑

**San Isabel National Forest**
In south-central Colorado.
(719) 553-1400
⚲ ▲ 𝔥 ☷ ⭑

**San Juan National Forest**
In southwestern Colorado.
(970) 247-4874
⚲ ▲ 𝔥 ☷ ⬗ ⭑ ⬤

**White River National Forest**
In west-central Colorado.
(970) 945-2521
⚲ ▲ 𝔥 ☷ ⬗ ⭑

# DELAWARE
**Bombay Hook National Wildlife Refuge**
South of Smyrna.
(302) 653-9345
⚲ 𝔥 ☷ ⭑

**Prime Hook National Wildlife Refuge**
North of Milton via SR 1.
(302) 684-8419
⚲ 𝔥 ☷ ⭑

# FLORIDA
**Apalachicola National Forest**
In northwestern Florida.
(850) 926-3561
⚲ ▲ 𝔥 ☷ ⬗ ⭑

**Biscayne National Park**
In southeast Florida.
(305) 230-7275
▲ ☷ ⬗ ⭑

**Canaveral National Seashore**
North of the Kennedy Space Center.
(321) 267-11105
⚲ ▲ 𝔥 ☷ ⬗ ⭑

**Hobe Sound National Wildlife Refuge**
13640 S.E. US 1.
(772) 546-6141
⚲ ⬗

**J.N. "Ding" Darling National Wildlife Refuge**
1 Wildlife Dr. in Sanibel.
(239) 472-1100
⚲ 𝔥

**Ocala National Forest**
In north-central Florida.
(352) 236-0288
⚲ ▲ 𝔥 ☷ ⬗ ⭑ ⬤

**Osceola National Forest**
Near the Georgia border.
(386) 752-2577
⚲ ▲ 𝔥 ☷ ⬗ ⭑

# GEORGIA
**Chattahoochee and Oconee National Forests**
In central and northern Georgia.
(770) 297-3000
⚲ ▲ 𝔥 ☷ ⬗ ⭑ ⬤

**Chattahoochee River National Recreation Area**
North of Atlanta.
(678) 538-1200
⚲ 𝔥 ☷ ⭑

**Chickamauga and Chattanooga National Military Park**
On the Georgia-Tennessee border.
(706) 866-9241
⚲ 𝔥 ☷ ⭑

**Kennesaw Mountain National Battlefield Park**
Northwest of Marietta.
(770) 427-4686
𝔥 ☷ ⭑

# IDAHO
**Boise National Forest**
In southwestern Idaho.
(208) 373-4007
⚲ ▲ 𝔥 ☷ ⬗ ⭑ ⬤

**Caribou-Targhee National Forest**
In southeastern Idaho.
(208) 524-7500 or 624-3151
⚲ ▲ 𝔥 ☷ ⬗ ⭑ ⬤

**Clearwater National Forest**
In northeastern Idaho.
(208) 476-4541
⚲ ▲ 𝔥 ☷ ⬗ ⭑ ⬤

**Hells Canyon National Recreation Area**
In western Idaho and northeastern Oregon.
(509) 758-0616
🚲 🏕 🥾 ⛱ 🏊 🛈

**Idaho Panhandle National Forests**
In northern and northwestern Idaho.
(208) 765-7223
🚲 🏕 🥾 ⛱ 🏊 🛈

**Nez Perce National Forest**
In northwestern Idaho.
(208) 983-1950
🚲 🏕 🥾 ⛱ 🏊 🛈 🍽

**Payette National Forest**
In west-central Idaho.
(208) 634-0700
🚲 🏕 🥾 ⛱ 🏊 🛈

**Salmon-Challis National Forest**
In east-central Idaho.
(208) 756-5100
🚲 🏕 🥾 ⛱ 🏊 🛈 🍽

**Sawtooth National Forest**
In south-central Idaho.
(208) 737-3200 or 800-260-5970 or TDD (208) 737-3235
🚲 🏕 🥾 ⛱ 🏊 🛈 🍽

**Sawtooth National Recreation Area**
In south-central Idaho.
(208) 727-5013 or (800) 260-5970
🚲 🏕 🥾 ⛱ 🏊 🛈 🍽

# ILLINOIS

**Chautauqua National Wildlife Refuge**
Near Havana.
(309) 535-2290
🚲 🥾 ⛱

**Shawnee National Forest**
In southern Illinois.
(618) 253-7114 or (800) 699-6637
🏕 🥾 ⛱ 🏊 🛈

# INDIANA

**George Rogers Clark National Historical Park**
Off US 50 and US 41 near Vincennes.
(812) 882-1776, ext. 110
🥾 ⛱ 🛈

**Hoosier National Forest**
In southern Indiana.
(812) 275-5987
🚲 🏕 🥾 ⛱ 🏊

**Indiana Dunes National Lakeshore**
On the southern shore of Lake Michigan.
(219) 926-7561, ext. 225
🚲 🏕 🥾 ⛱ 🏊 🛈

**Muscatatuck National Wildlife Refuge**
East of jct. I-65 and US 50 near Seymour.
(812)522-4352
🚲 🥾 ⛱ 🛈

# KANSAS

**Kirwin National Wildlife Refuge**
702 E. Xavier Rd.
(785) 543-6673
🚲 🥾 🛈

# KENTUCKY

**Big South Fork National River and Recreation Area**
In southeastern Kentucky and northeastern Tennessee.
(423) 286-7275 or (606) 376-5073
🚲 🏕 🥾 ⛱ 🏊 🛈

**Cumberland Gap National Historical Park**
At the borders of Kentucky, Tennessee and Virginia.
(606) 248-2817
🚲 🏕 🥾 ⛱ 🛈 🍽

**Daniel Boone National Forest**
Six districts in eastern and southeastern Kentucky.
(859) 745-3100
🚲 🏕 🥾 ⛱ 🏊 🛈

**Land Between the Lakes National Recreation Area**
In western Kentucky and Tennessee.
(270) 924-2000 or (800) 525-7077
🚲 🏕 🥾 ⛱ 🏊 🛈

**Mammoth Cave National Park**
In south-central Kentucky 10 mi. west of Cave City.
(270) 758-2180
🚲 🏕 🥾 ⛱ 🛈 🍽

# LOUISIANA

**Bayou Sauvage National Wildlife Refuge**
Within the New Orleans city limits.
(985) 882-2000
🚲 🥾 ⛱ 🛈

**Kisatchie National Forest**
In central and northern Louisiana.
(318) 473-7160
🚲 🏕 🥾 ⛱ 🏊 🛈

**Sabine National Wildlife Refuge**
8 mi. south of Hackberry on SR 27.
(337) 762-3816
🥾 🛈

# MAINE

**Acadia National Park**
Along the Atlantic coast southeast of Bangor.
(207) 288-3338
🚲 🏕 🥾 ⛱ 🏊 🛈 🍽

---

🚲 Bicycling    🏕 Camping    🥾 Hiking    ⛱ Picnicking
🏊 Swimming    🛈 Visitor center    🍽 Food service

**Moosehorn National Wildlife Refuge**
Near Baring and Dennysville.
(207) 454-7167
🔥 🏇

## MARYLAND
**Assateague Island National Seashore**
In southeastern Maryland south of Ocean City.
(410) 641-1441 or 641-3030
🔥 ▲ 🏇 ⛱ ⚐ ⚑

**Chesapeake and Ohio Canal National Historical Park**
From Georgetown to Cumberland.
(301) 739-4200
🔥 ▲ 🏇 ⛱ ⚑

## MASSACHUSETTS
**Cape Cod National Seashore**
Occupies 40 miles along the shoreline.
(508)349-3785, ext. 200
🔥 🏇 ⛱ ⚐ ⚑

## MICHIGAN
**Hiawatha National Forest**
In Michigan's Upper Peninsula.
(906) 786-4062
🔥 ▲ 🏇 ⛱ ⚐ ⚑ 📷

**Huron-Manistee National Forests**
In the northern part of the Lower Peninsula.
(231) 775-2421 or (800) 821-6263
🔥 ▲ 🏇 ⛱ ⚐ ⚑ 📷

**Ottawa National Forest**
In Michigan's Upper Peninsula.
(906) 932-1330 or (800) 562-1201
🔥 ▲ 🏇 ⛱ ⚐ ⚑ 📷

**Pictured Rocks National Lakeshore**
Along Lake Superior in Michigan's Upper Peninsula.
(906) 387-2607
▲ 🏇 ⛱ ⚐ ⚑

**Sleeping Bear Dunes National Lakeshore**
Along Lake Michigan in the northwestern part of the Lower
Peninsula.
(231) 326-5134
▲ 🏇 ⛱ ⚐ ⚑ 📷

## MINNESOTA
**Chippewa National Forest**
In north-central Minnesota.
(218) 335-8600 or TDD (218) 335-8632
🔥 ▲ 🏇 ⛱ ⚐ ⚑ 📷

**Minnesota Valley National Wildlife Refuge**
3815 E. 80th St.
(952) 854-5900
🔥 🏇 ⚑

**Superior National Forest**
In northeastern Minnesota.
(218) 626-4300
🔥 ▲ 🏇 ⛱ ⚐ ⚑ 📷

## MISSISSIPPI
**Bienville National Forest**
In central Mississippi.
(601) 469-3811
▲ 🏇 ⛱ ⚐ ⚑ 📷

**Gulf Islands National Seashore**
Along the Gulf of Mexico in southern Mississippi.
(228) 875-9057
🔥 ⛱ ⚐ ⚑

## MISSOURI
**Mark Twain National Forest (Big Bay)**
1 mi. southeast of Shell Knob on SR 39, then 3 mi.
southeast on CR YY.
(573) 364-4621
🔥 ⛱ ⚐

**Mark Twain National Forest (Council Bluff)**
13 mi. s. of Potosi on CR P, 4 mi. w. on CR C , then 8
mi. s. on CR DD.
(573) 364-4621
🔥 ▲ 🏇 ⛱ ⚐

**Mark Twain National Forest (Crane Lake)**
12 mi. south of Ironton off SR 49 and CR E.
(573) 364-4621
🔥 🏇 ⛱ ⚐

**Mark Twain National Forest (Fourche Lake)**
18 mi. west of Doniphan on SR 160.
(573) 364-4621
🏇 ⛱ ⚐

**Mark Twain National Forest (Noblett Lake)**
8 mi. west of Willow Springs on SR 76, then 1.5 mi. south
on SR 181, 3 mi. southeast on CR AP and 1 mi.
southwest on FR 857.
(573) 364-4621
🔥 🏇 ⛱

**Mark Twain National Forest (Pinewoods Lake)**
2 mi. west of Ellsinore on SR 60.
(573) 364-4621
🔥 🏇 ⛱ ⚐

**Mark Twain National Forest (Red Bluff)**
1 mi. east of Davisville on CR V, then 1 mi. north on FR
2011.
(573) 364-4621
▲ 🏇 ⛱ ⚐

**Ozark National Scenic Riverways**
In southeastern Missouri.
(573) 323-4236
▲ 🏇 ⛱ ⚐ ⚑ 📷

## MONTANA
**Beaverhead-Deerlodge National Forest**
In southwestern Montana.
(406) 683-3900
🔥 ▲ 🏇 ⛱

**Bighorn Canyon National Recreation Area**
In southern Montana and northern Wyoming.
(406) 666-2412
Ⓐ 🐾 🏕️ 🏊 👥 🍴

**Bitterroot National Forest**
In western Montana.
(406) 363-7100
Ⓐ 🐾 🏕️ 🏊 👥 🍴

**Custer National Forest**
In southeastern Montana.
(406) 657-6200
🚲 Ⓐ 🐾 🏕️ 🏊 🍴

**Flathead National Forest**
In northwestern Montana.
(406) 758-5204
🚲 Ⓐ 🐾 🏕️ 🏊 👥

**Gallatin National Forest**
In south-central Montana.
(406) 522-2520
🚲 Ⓐ 🐾 🏕️ 🏊 👥

**Glacier National Park**
In northwestern Montana.
(406) 888-7800
Ⓐ 🐾 🏕️ 🏊 👥 🍴

**Helena National Forest**
In west-central Montana.
(406) 449-5201
🚲 Ⓐ 🐾 🏕️ 🏊 👥

**Kootenai National Forest**
In northwestern Montana.
(406) 293-6211
🚲 Ⓐ 🐾 🏕️ 🏊 👥 🍴

**Lewis and Clark National Forest**
In central Montana.
(406) 791-7700
🚲 Ⓐ 🐾 🏕️ 👥

# NEBRASKA

**Fort Niobrara National Wildlife Refuge**
East of Valentine on SR 12.
(402) 376-3789
🐾 🏕️

**Nebraska National Forest**
In central and northwestern Nebraska.
(308) 432-0300 or TDD (308) 432-0304
🚲 Ⓐ 🐾 🏕️ 🏊

**Oglala National Grassland**
In northwestern Nebraska, 6 mi. north of Crawford via SR 2.
(308) 432-4475 or 665-3900
Ⓐ 🐾 🏕️ 👥

# NEVADA

**Great Basin National Park**
In central Nevada, 5 mi. west of Baker near the Nevada-Utah border.
(775) 234-7331
Ⓐ 🐾 🏕️ 👥 🍴

**Humboldt-Toiyabe National Forest**
In central, western, northern and southern Nevada and eastern California.
(775) 331-6444
🚲 Ⓐ 🐾 🏕️ 🍴

**Lake Mead National Recreation Area**
In southeastern Nevada and northwestern Arizona.
(702) 293-8906
🚲 Ⓐ 🐾 🏕️ 🏊 👥 🍴

# NEW HAMPSHIRE

**White Mountain National Forest**
In northern New Hampshire.
(603) 528-8721 or TDD (603) 528-8722
🚲 Ⓐ 🐾 🏕️ 🏊 👥 🍴

# NEW JERSEY

**Edwin B. Forsythe National Wildlife Refuge**
US 9 and Great Creek Road near Oceanville
(609) 652-1665
🚲 🐾 🏕️ 👥

**Gateway National Recreation Area**
In northeastern New Jersey (Sandy Hook Unit).
(732) 872-5970
🚲 🐾 🏕️ 🏊 👥 🍴

**Morristown National Historical Park**
Four units in Morristown and southwest.
(973) 539-2085
🚲 🐾 👥

# NEW MEXICO

**Carson National Forest**
In north-central New Mexico.
(505) 758-6200
🚲 Ⓐ 🐾 🏕️ 👥 🍴

**Chaco Culture National Historical Park**
In northwestern New Mexico.
(505) 786-7014
🚲 Ⓐ 🐾 🏕️ 👥

**Cibola National Forest**
In central New Mexico.
(505) 346-3900
🚲 Ⓐ 🐾 🏕️ 🏊 👥 🍴

**Gila National Forest**
In southwestern New Mexico.
(505) 388-8201
🚲 Ⓐ 🐾 🏕️ 👥 🍴

---

🚲 Bicycling   Ⓐ Camping   🐾 Hiking   🏕️ Picnicking
🏊 Swimming   👥 Visitor center   🍴 Food service

**Lincoln National Forest**
In south-central New Mexico.
(505) 434-7200 or TTY (505) 434-7296
⟦♿⟧ ⟦▲⟧ ⟦🚶⟧ ⟦🏕⟧ ⟦🍴⟧

**Santa Fe National Forest**
In north-central New Mexico between the San Pedro Mountains and the Sangre de Cristo Mountains.
(505) 438-7840
⟦♿⟧ ⟦▲⟧ ⟦🚶⟧ ⟦🏕⟧ ⟦🚻⟧

# NEW YORK

**Finger Lakes National Forest**
In south-central New York on a ridge between Seneca and Cayuga lakes, via I-90, I-81 and SR 17.
(607) 546-4470
⟦♿⟧ ⟦▲⟧ ⟦🚶⟧ ⟦🏕⟧

**Fire Island National Seashore**
In southeastern New York on Fire Island, off the south shore of Long Island.
(631) 289-4810
⟦▲⟧ ⟦🚶⟧ ⟦🏕⟧ ⟦⚓⟧ ⟦🚻⟧ ⟦🍴⟧

**Gateway National Recreation Area (Jamaica Bay Unit)**
In Brooklyn and Queens boroughs in New York City.
(718) 354-4606
⟦♿⟧ ⟦🚶⟧ ⟦🏕⟧ ⟦⚓⟧ ⟦🚻⟧ ⟦🍴⟧

**Gateway National Recreation Area (Staten Island Unit)**
On Staten Island borough in New York City.
(718) 354-4606
⟦♿⟧ ⟦🚶⟧ ⟦🏕⟧ ⟦⚓⟧ ⟦🚻⟧ ⟦🍴⟧

**Saratoga National Historical Park**
8 miles south of Schuylerville on US 4.
(518) 664-9821, ext. 224
⟦♿⟧ ⟦🚶⟧ ⟦🏕⟧ ⟦🚻⟧

# NORTH CAROLINA

**Cape Hatteras National Seashore**
In eastern North Carolina along the Outer Banks.
(252) 473-2111 or 441-5711
⟦♿⟧ ⟦▲⟧ ⟦🚶⟧ ⟦🏕⟧ ⟦⚓⟧ ⟦🚻⟧ ⟦🍴⟧

**Croatan National Forest**
In southeastern North Carolina.
(252) 638-5628
⟦♿⟧ ⟦▲⟧ ⟦🚶⟧ ⟦🏕⟧ ⟦⚓⟧

**Great Smoky Mountains National Park**
In western North Carolina and eastern Tennessee.
(865) 436-1200
⟦♿⟧ ⟦▲⟧ ⟦🚶⟧ ⟦🏕⟧ ⟦⚓⟧ ⟦🚻⟧

**Nantahala National Forest**
At North Carolina's southwestern tip.
(828) 257-4200 or 526-3765
⟦♿⟧ ⟦▲⟧ ⟦🚶⟧ ⟦🏕⟧ ⟦⚓⟧

**Nantahala National Forest (Hanging Dog)**
5 mi. northwest of Murphy on SR 1326.
(828) 257-4200 or 526-3765
⟦▲⟧ ⟦🚶⟧

**Nantahala National Forest (Jackrabbit Mountain)**
10 mi. northeast of Hayesville via US 64, SR 175 and SR 1155.
(828) 257-4200 or 526-3765
⟦▲⟧ ⟦🚶⟧ ⟦🏕⟧ ⟦⚓⟧

**Nantahala National Forest (Standing Indian Mountain)**
9 mi. west of Franklin on US 64, then 2 mi. east on old US 64 and 2 mi. south on FR 67.
(828) 257-4200 or 526-3765
⟦▲⟧ ⟦🚶⟧ ⟦🏕⟧

**Pisgah National Forest**
In western North Carolina.
(828) 257-4200
⟦♿⟧ ⟦▲⟧ ⟦🚶⟧ ⟦🏕⟧ ⟦⚓⟧ ⟦🚻⟧ ⟦🍴⟧

**Pisgah National Forest (Lake Powhatan)**
7 mi. southwest of Asheville on SR 191 and FR 3807.
(828) 257-4200
⟦♿⟧ ⟦▲⟧ ⟦🚶⟧ ⟦🏕⟧ ⟦⚓⟧

**Pisgah National Forest (Rocky Bluff)**
3 mi. south of Hot Springs on SR 209.
(828) 257-4200
⟦▲⟧ ⟦🚶⟧ ⟦🏕⟧

**Uwharrie National Forest**
In central North Carolina.
(910) 576-6391
⟦♿⟧ ⟦▲⟧ ⟦🚶⟧ ⟦🏕⟧ ⟦⚓⟧ ⟦🚻⟧

# NORTH DAKOTA

**Little Missouri National Grassland**
Between the Missouri River and South Dakota.
(701) 225-5151
⟦♿⟧ ⟦▲⟧ ⟦🚶⟧ ⟦🏕⟧ ⟦🚻⟧

**Sheyenne National Grassland**
Along the Sheyenne River south of Fargo.
(701) 683-4342
⟦▲⟧ ⟦🚶⟧

**Theodore Roosevelt National Park (North Unit)**
In western North Dakota.
(701) 842-2333
⟦▲⟧ ⟦🚶⟧ ⟦🏕⟧ ⟦🚻⟧

**Theodore Roosevelt National Park (South Unit)**
In western North Dakota.
(701) 623-4466
⟦▲⟧ ⟦🚶⟧ ⟦🏕⟧ ⟦🚻⟧ ⟦🍴⟧

# OHIO

**Cuyahoga Valley National Park**
In northeastern Ohio.
(216) 524-1497
⟦♿⟧ ⟦🚶⟧ ⟦🏕⟧ ⟦🚻⟧ ⟦🍴⟧

**Hopewell Culture National Historical Park**
About 3 mi. north of Chillicothe on SR 104.
(740) 774-1125
⟦🏕⟧ ⟦🚻⟧

**Wayne National Forest**
In southeast Ohio.
(740) 753-0101
🚲 ⛺ 🥾 ⛱ 🏊 👥

## OKLAHOMA

**Chickasaw National Recreation Area**
In south-central Oklahoma.
(580) 622-3165 or 3161
🚲 ⛺ 🥾 ⛱ 🏊 👥

**Ouachita National Forest**
In southeastern Oklahoma and west-central Arkansas.
(501) 321-5202
🚲 ⛺ 🥾 ⛱ 🏊 👥 🍴

**Salt Plains National Wildlife Refuge**
Off SR 38, 2 mi. south of jct. SRs 11 and 38 at Cherokee.
(580) 626-4794
🥾 👥

## OREGON

**Crater Lake National Park**
On the crest of the Cascade Range off SR 62.
(541) 594-3100
🚲 ⛺ 🥾 ⛱ 👥 🍴

**Deschutes National Forest**
In central Oregon 6 mi. south of Bend via US 97.
(541) 383-5300
🚲 ⛺ 🥾 ⛱ 🏊 👥 🍴

**Fremont-Winema National Forests**
In south-central Oregon.
(541) 947-2151
🚲 ⛺ 🥾 ⛱ 🏊 👥

**Hells Canyon National Recreation Area**
In northeastern Oregon and western Idaho.
(541) 523-3356 or (800) 523-1235
🚲 ⛺ 🥾 ⛱ 👥

**Malheur National Forest**
In eastern Oregon.
(541) 575-3000
🚲 ⛺ 🥾 ⛱ 🏊 🍴

**Mount Hood National Forest**
In northwestern Oregon.
(888) 622-4822
🚲 ⛺ 🥾 ⛱ 🏊 👥 🍴

**Ochoco National Forest**
In central Oregon off US 26.
(541) 416-6500
🚲 ⛺ 🥾 ⛱ 🏊

**Oregon Dunes National Recreation Area**
Between North Bend and Florence.
(541) 271-3611
🚲 ⛺ 🥾 ⛱ 🏊 👥 🍴

**Rogue River-Siskiyou National Forest**
In southwestern Oregon off I-5 from Medford.
(541) 858-2200
🚲 ⛺ 🥾 ⛱ 🏊 👥 🍴

**Siuslaw National Forest**
In western Oregon.
(541) 750-7000
🚲 ⛺ 🥾 ⛱ 🏊 👥 🍴

**Umatilla National Forest**
In northeastern Oregon.
(541) 278-3716
🚲 ⛺ 🥾 ⛱ 🏊 👥

**Umpqua National Forest**
In southwestern Oregon 33 mi. east of Roseburg on SR 138.
(541) 672-6601
🚲 ⛺ 🥾 ⛱ 🏊 👥 🍴

**Wallowa-Whitman National Forest**
In northeastern Oregon.
(541) 523-6391
🚲 ⛺ 🥾 ⛱ 🏊 👥 🍴

**Willamette National Forest**
In western Oregon.
(541) 225-6300
🚲 ⛺ 🥾 ⛱ 🏊 🍴

## PENNSYLVANIA

**Allegheny National Forest**
In northwestern Pennsylvania.
(814) 723-5150 or TDD (814) 726-2710
🚲 ⛺ 🥾 ⛱ 🏊 👥

**Delaware Water Gap National Recreation Area**
In eastern Pennsylvania and northwestern New Jersey.
(570) 588-2457 or (570) 588-7044
🚲 ⛺ 🥾 ⛱ 🏊 👥

**Gettysburg National Military Park**
Surrounding the town of Gettysburg at SR 134.
(717) 334-1124
🚲 🥾 ⛱ 👥

**John Heinz National Wildlife Refuge at Tinicum**
I-95S exit 14 near Philadelphia
(215) 365-3118
🚲 🥾 👥

**Valley Forge National Historical Park**
Extending east of Valley Forge along SR 23.
(610) 783-1077
🚲 🥾 ⛱ 👥

---

| 🚲 Bicycling | ⛺ Camping | 🥾 Hiking | ⛱ Picnicking |
| 🏊 Swimming | 👥 Visitor center | 🍴 Food service | |

# SOUTH CAROLINA

**Francis Marion National Forest**
On the Coastal Plain north of Charleston.
(803) 561-4000
🚶 ⛺ 🏍 🏕 🚤 🏠 🍴

**Kings Mountain National Military Park**
South of Kings Mountain, N.C., off I-85.
(864) 936-7921
⛺ 🏍

**Sumter National Forest**
In western South Carolina.
(803) 561-4000
🚶 ⛺ 🏍 🏕 🚤 🍴

# SOUTH DAKOTA

**Badlands National Park**
In southwestern South Dakota.
(605) 433-5361, ext. 100
⛺ 🏍 🏕 🏠

**Black Hills National Forest**
In southwestern South Dakota.
(605) 673-9200 or TDD (605) 673-4954
🚶 ⛺ 🏍 🏕 🚤 🏠 🍴

**Custer National Forest**
In northwestern South Dakota and southeastern Montana.
(605) 797-4432
🚶 ⛺ 🏍 🏕

**Wind Cave National Park**
In southwestern South Dakota.
(605) 745-4600
⛺ 🏍 🏕 🏠

# TENNESSEE

**Big South Fork National River and Recreation Area**
In northeastern Tennessee and southeastern Kentucky.
(423) 286-7275 or (606) 376-5073
🚶 ⛺ 🏍 🏕 🚤 🏠

**Cherokee National Forest**
In eastern Tennessee.
(423) 476-9700
🚶 ⛺ 🏍 🏕 🚤 🏠

**Chickamauga and Chattanooga National Military Park**
On the Georgia-Tennessee border.
(706) 866-9241
🚶 🏍 🏕 🏠

**Great Smoky Mountains National Park**
In eastern Tennessee and western North Carolina.
(865) 436-1200
🚶 ⛺ 🏍 🏕 🏠

**Land Between the Lakes National Recreation Area**
In western Kentucky and Tennessee.
(270) 924-2000 or (800) 525-7077
🚶 ⛺ 🏍 🏕 🚤 🏠

# TEXAS

**Amistad National Recreation Area**
Northwest of Del Rio via US 90.
(830) 775-7491
⛺ 🏍 🏕 🚤 🏠

**Big Bend National Park**
Southeast of Alpine on SR 118 and US 385.
(432) 477-2251 or 1158
🚶 ⛺ 🏍 🏕 🏠 🍴

**Davy Crockett National Forest**
In east Texas.
(936) 655-2299
⛺ 🏍 🏕 🚤 🍴

**Guadalupe Mountains National Park**
110 mi. east of El Paso on US 62/180.
(915) 828-3251
⛺ 🏍 🏕 🏠

**Lake Meredith National Recreation Area**
45 mi. northeast of Amarillo and 9 mi. west of Borger via SR 136.
(806) 857-3151
⛺ 🏍 🏕 🚤 🍴

**Padre Island National Seashore**
On Padre Island near Corpus Christi.
(361) 949-8068
🚶 ⛺ 🏍 🏕 🚤 🏠 🍴

**Sabine National Forest**
In east Texas.
(409) 787-3870
⛺ 🏍 🏕 🚤

**Sam Houston National Forest**
40 mi. north of Houston in east Texas.
(936) 344-6205 or (888) 361-6908
🚶 ⛺ 🏍 🏕 🚤 🍴

# UTAH

**Arches National Park**
5 mi. northwest of Moab on US 191.
(435) 719-2100 or TTY (435) 259-5279
⛺ 🏍 🏕 🏠

**Ashley National Forest**
In northeastern Utah.
(435) 789-1181
🚶 ⛺ 🏍 🏕 🚤 🏠

**Bryce Canyon National Park**
26 mi. southeast of Panguitch via US 89 and SRs 12 and 63.
(435) 834-5322
⛺ 🏍 🏕 🏠 🍴

**Canyonlands National Park**
In southeastern Utah.
(435) 719-2100 or TTY (435) 259-5279
⛺ 🏍 🏕 🏠

**Capitol Reef National Park**
10 mi. east of Torrey on SR 24.
(435) 425-3791, ext. 111
🚲 ⛺ 🥾 ⛱ 🏛

**Dixie National Forest**
In southwestern Utah.
(435) 865-3700
🚲 ⛺ 🥾 ⛱ 🏊 🏛 🍽

**Fishlake National Forest**
In south-central Utah.
(435) 896-9233
🚲 ⛺ 🥾 ⛱ 🏊 🏛 🍽

**Flaming Gorge National Recreation Area**
In northeastern Utah.
(435) 784-3445
🚲 ⛺ 🥾 ⛱ 🏊 🏛 🍽

**Glen Canyon National Recreation Area**
In south-central Utah.
(928) 608-6200
⛺ 🥾 ⛱ 🏊 🏛 🍽

**Manti-La Sal National Forest**
In southeastern Utah.
(435) 637-2817
🚲 ⛺ 🥾 ⛱

**Uinta National Forest**
In central Utah.
(801) 377-5780
🚲 ⛺ 🥾 ⛱ 🏛

**Wasatch-Cache National Forest**
In north-central and northeastern Utah.
(801) 236-3400
🚲 ⛺ 🥾 ⛱ 🏊 🏛 🍽

**Zion National Park**
In southwestern Utah.
(435) 772-3256
🚲 ⛺ 🥾 ⛱ 🏛 🍽

# VERMONT

**Green Mountain National Forest**
In south-central Vermont.
(802) 747-6700
🚲 ⛺ 🥾 ⛱ 🏊 🍽

**Marsh-Billings-Rockefeller National Historical Park**
Off SR 12 near Woodstock.
(802) 457-3368, ext. 22
🥾 ⛱

# VIRGINIA

**George Washington and Jefferson National Forests**
In western Virginia and the eastern edge of West Virginia.
(540) 265-5100 or (888) 265-0019
🚲 ⛺ 🥾 ⛱ 🏊 🏛 🍽

**Mount Rogers National Recreation Area**
In southwestern Virginia.
(276) 783-5196 or (800) 628-7202
🚲 ⛺ 🥾 ⛱ 🏊 🏛 🍽

**Shenandoah National Park**
In northwestern Virginia.
(540) 999-3500
🚲 ⛺ 🥾 ⛱ 🏛 🍽

# WASHINGTON

**Gifford Pinchot National Forest**
In southwestern Washington.
(360) 891-5000
🚲 ⛺ 🥾 ⛱ 🏊 🏛

**Lake Roosevelt National Recreation Area**
In northeastern Washington.
(509) 633-9441
🚲 ⛺ 🥾 ⛱ 🏊 🏛

**Mount Baker-Snoqualmie National Forest (Douglas Fir)**
2 mi. east of Glacier on SR 542.
(425) 775-9702 or (800) 627-0062, ext. 0
⛺ 🥾 ⛱

**Mount Baker-Snoqualmie National Forest (Horseshoe Cove)**
14 mi. north of Concrete on Baker Lake.
(425) 775-9702 or (800) 627-0062, ext. 0
⛺ 🥾 🏊

**Mount Baker-Snoqualmie National Forest (Shannon Creek)**
24 mi. north of Concrete on Baker Lake.
(425) 775-9702 or (800) 627-0062, ext. 0
⛺ 🥾 ⛱ 🏊

**Olympic National Forest**
In northwestern Washington.
(360) 956-2400
🚲 ⛺ 🥾 ⛱ 🏊 🏛 🍽

# WEST VIRGINIA

**Monongahela National Forest**
In eastern West Virginia.
(304) 636-1800
🚲 ⛺ 🥾 ⛱ 🏊 🏛 🍽

**New River Gorge National River**
Between Fayetteville and Hinton.
(304) 465-0508
🚲 ⛺ 🥾 ⛱ 🏊 🏛 🍽

**Spruce Knob-Seneca Rocks National Recreation Area**
In east-central West Virginia.
(304) 257-4488
🚲 ⛺ 🥾 ⛱ 🏛

---

🚲 Bicycling   ⛺ Camping   🥾 Hiking   ⛱ Picnicking
🏊 Swimming   🏛 Visitor center   🍽 Food service

# WISCONSIN

## Apostle Islands National Lakeshore
Off northern Wisconsin's Bayfield Peninsula in Lake Superior.
(715) 779-3397

## Chequamegon-Nicolet National Forest
In north-central and northeastern Wisconsin.
(715) 762-2461 or TTY (715) 762-5701 (Chequamegon),
(715) 362-1300 or TTY (715) 362-1383 (Nicolet)

## St. Croix National Scenic Riverway
Running 252 mi. from Cable to Prescott.
(715) 483-3284

# WYOMING

## Bighorn Canyon National Recreation Area
In Montana and northern Wyoming.
(307) 548-2251

## Bighorn National Forest
In north-central Wyoming.
(307) 674-2600

## Devils Tower National Monument
Between Sundance and Hulett.
(307) 467-5283

## Flaming Gorge National Recreation Area
On the Wyoming-Utah border.
(435) 784-3445

## Fossil Butte National Monument
14 mi. west of Kemmerer on US 30.
(307) 877-4455

## Grand Teton National Park
In northwestern Wyoming.
(307) 739-3300

## Medicine Bow National Forest
In southeastern Wyoming.
(307) 745-2300

## Shoshone National Forest
In northwestern Wyoming.
(307) 527-6241

## Yellowstone National Park
In northwestern Wyoming.
(307) 344-7311

# Canada

# ALBERTA

## Banff National Park of Canada
In southwestern Alberta, west of Calgary.
(403) 762-1550

## Elk Island National Park of Canada
In central Alberta, east of Edmonton.
(780) 992-2950

## Jasper National Park of Canada
In west-central Alberta along the British Columbia border.
(780) 852-6176

## Waterton Lakes National Park of Canada
In Alberta's southwestern corner.
(403) 859-5133, or 859-2224 during the winter

# BRITISH COLUMBIA

## Glacier National Park of Canada
In southeastern British Columbia.
(250) 837-7500

## Kootenay National Park of Canada
In southeastern British Columbia.
(250) 347-9615 or (800) 748-7275

## Mount Revelstoke National Park of Canada
In southeastern British Columbia.
(250) 837-7500

## Pacific Rim National Park Reserve of Canada
On the southwestern coast of Vancouver Island.
(250) 726-7721 or 726-4212, Jun. 1 to mid-Sept.

## Yoho National Park of Canada
On the British Columbia-Alberta border.
(250) 343-6783

## MANITOBA
**Riding Mountain National Park of Canada**
In southwestern Manitoba.
(204) 848-7275
🚴 🅰 🚶 🌳 🏊 👥 🍽

## NEW BRUNSWICK
**Fundy National Park of Canada**
On Hwy. 114, 130 km. southwest of Moncton.
(506) 887-6000
🚴 🅰 🚶 🌳 🏊 👥 🍽

**Kouchibouguac National Park of Canada**
On Hwy. 134, north of Moncton.
(506) 876-2443 or TDD (506) 876-4205
🚴 🅰 🚶 🌳 🏊 👥 🍽

## NEWFOUNDLAND
**Gros Morne National Park of Canada**
On Newfoundland's western coast.
(709) 458-2417, 458-2066 or TDD (709) 772-4564
🅰 🚶 🌳 🏊 👥

**Terra Nova National Park of Canada**
In eastern Newfoundland.
(709) 533-2801 or 2942
🚴 🅰 🚶 🌳 🏊 👥 🍽

## NORTHWEST TERRITORIES
**Nahanni National Park Reserve of Canada**
145 km. west of Fort Simpson in southwestern Northwest Territories.
(867) 695-3151
🅰 🚶 👥

**Wood Buffalo National Park of Canada**
On the Northwest Territories-Alberta border.
(867) 872-7960
🚴 🅰 🚶 🌳 🏊 👥

## NOVA SCOTIA
**Cape Breton Highlands National Park of Canada**
5 km. northeast of Chéticamp on Cabot Tr.
(902) 224-2306 or (888) 773-8888
🚴 🅰 🚶 🌳 🏊 👥 🍽

**Kejimkujik National Park and National Historic Site of Canada**
In southwestern Nova Scotia off Hwy. 8 at Maitland Bridge.
(902) 682-2772
🚴 🅰 🚶 🌳 🏊 👥 🍽

## ONTARIO
**Bruce Peninsula National Park of Canada**
In southwestern Ontario.
(519) 596-2233
🅰 🚶 🌳 🏊 👥

**Point Pelee National Park of Canada**
South of Leamington.
(519) 322-2365 or (888) 773-8888
🚴 🚶 🌳 🏊 👥 🍽

## PRINCE EDWARD ISLAND
**Port La Joye-Fort Amherst National Historic Site of Canada**
West of Charlottetown on Hwy. 1.
(902) 566-7626
🚶 🌳 👥 🍽

**Prince Edward Island National Park of Canada**
Along the island's northern shore.
(902) 566-7050
🚴 🅰 🚶 🌳 🏊 👥 🍽

## QUEBEC
**Forillon National Park of Canada**
20 km. northeast of Gaspé via Hwy. 132.
(418) 368-5505 or (888) 773-8888
🚴 🅰 🚶 🌳 🏊 👥 🍽

**La Mauricie National Park of Canada**
North of Trois-Rivières via Hwy. 55.
(819) 538-3232 or (888) 773-8888
🚴 🅰 🚶 🌳 🏊 👥 🍽

## SASKATCHEWAN
**Grasslands National Park of Canada**
Between Val Marie and Killdeer in southern Saskatchewan.
(306) 298-2257
🅰 🚶 🌳 👥

**Prince Albert National Park of Canada**
In central Saskatchewan.
(306) 663-4522
🚴 🅰 🚶 🌳 🏊 👥

## YUKON TERRITORY
**Kluane National Park of Canada**
West of Haines Junction.
(867) 634-7250
🚴 🅰 🚶 🌳 🏊 👥 🍽

---

🚴 Bicycling   🅰 Camping   🚶 Hiking   🌳 Picnicking
🏊 Swimming   👥 Visitor center   🍽 Food service

# ANIMAL CLINICS

This list of animal clinics in the United States and Canada is provided by the Veterinary Emergency & Critical Care Society as a service to the community for information purposes only. This is not to be construed as a certification or an endorsement of any clinic listed. For further information, contact the society at (210) 698-5575 or online at www.veccs.org. Note: Hours frequently change, and not all clinics are open 24 hours or in the evening. In addition, not all facilities listed here are emergency clinics. In non-emergency situations, it's best to call first.

If you are traveling to an area not covered in this list, be prepared for an emergency by asking your regular veterinarian to recommend a clinic or veterinarian at your destination. The American Animal Hospital Association also provides a veterinary locator service to clinics that meet the association's high standards for veterinary care. Contact the association at (303) 986-2800 or online at www.healthypet.com.

# United States

## ALABAMA

**Village Veterinary Clinic**
403 Opelika Rd., Auburn
(334) 821-7730

**Emergency and Specialty Animal Medical Center**
2864 Acton Rd., Birmingham
(205) 967-7389

**Lakeview Pet Wellness Center**
3222 6th Ave. S., Birmingham
(205) 323-1536

**Animal Emergency Clinic of North Alabama**
2112 S. Memorial Pkwy., Huntsville
(256) 533-7600

**Rehm Animal Clinic**
951 Hillcrest Rd., Mobile
(251) 639-9120

**Carriage Hills Animal Clinic**
3200 E. Bypass, Montgomery
(334) 277-2867

## ALASKA

**Pet Emergency Treatment**
2320 E. Dowling Rd., Anchorage
(907) 274-5636

## ARIZONA

**Emergency Animal Clinic**
86 W. Juniper Ave., Gilbert
(480) 497-0222

**Franklin Veterinary Hospital**
1721 E. University Dr., Mesa
(480) 890-8283

**Mesa Veterinary Hospital**
858 N. Country Club Dr., Mesa
(480) 833-7330

**Emergency Animal Clinic**
9875 W. Peoria Ave., Peoria
(623) 974-1520

**Emergency Animal Clinic**
2260 West Glendale Ave., Phoenix
(602) 995-3757

**Palo Verde Animal Hospital**
1215 E. Northern Ave., Phoenix
(602) 944-9661

**Emergency Animal Clinic**
14202 N. Scottsdale Rd., Suite 163, Scottsdale
(480) 949-8001

**VCA Paradise Valley Emergency Animal Hospital**
6969 E. Shea Blvd., #225, Scottsdale
(480) 991-1845

**Animal Emergency Service**
4832 E. Speedway St., Tucson
(520) 327-5624

**Grant Road Small Animal Hospital**
1675 West Grant Rd., Tucson
(520) 792-1858

## ARKANSAS

**Animal Emergency & Specialty Clinic**
8735 Sheltie Dr., Suite G, Maumelle
(501) 224-3784

## CALIFORNIA

**Animal Hospital of Antioch**
2204 A St., Antioch
(925) 754-6700

**Antioch Veterinary Hospital**
1432 West 10th St., Antioch
(925) 757-2233

**Central Coast Pet Emergency Clinic**
1558 W. Branch St., Arroyo Grande
(805) 489-6573

**Animal Emergency and Urgent Care**
4300 Easton Dr., #1, Bakersfield
(661) 322-6019

**Pet Emergency Treatment Service Inc.**
1048 University Ave., Berkeley
(510) 548-6684

**United Emergency Animal Clinic**
1657 S. Bascom Ave., Campbell
(408) 371-6252

**Acacia Veterinary Hospital**
479 East Ave., Chico
(530) 345-1338

**Contra Costa Veterinary Emergency Center**
1410 Monument Blvd., Concord
(925) 798-2900

**Solano Pet Emergency Clinic**
4437 Central Pl., Cordelia
(707) 864-1444

**East Valley Emergency Pet Clinic**
938 N. Diamond Bar Blvd., Diamond Bar
(909) 861-5737

**Dublin Veterinary Hospital**
7410 Amador Valley Blvd., #D, Dublin
(925) 828-5520

**Emergency Pet Clinic of San Gabriel Valley**
3254 Santa Anita Ave., El Monte
(626) 579-4550

**Greenback Veterinary Hospital**
8311 Greenback Ln., Fair Oaks
(916) 725-1541

**VCA All Care Animal Referral Center**
18440 E. Amistad St., Fountain Valley
(714) 963-0909

**Central Veterinary Hospital & Emergency Service**
5245 Central Ave., Fremont
(510) 797-7387

**Veterinary Emergency Services**
1639 N. Fresno St., Fresno
(559) 486-0520

**Orange County Emergency Pet Clinic**
12750 Garden Grove Blvd., Garden Grove
(714) 537-3032

**Pet Medical Center Chatoak**
17659 Chatsworth St., Granada Hills
(818) 363-7444

**Animal Emergency Clinic**
12022 La Crosse Ave., Grand Terrace
(909) 825-9350

**North Orange County Emergency Pet Clinic**
1474 S. Harbor Blvd., La Habra
(714) 441-2925

**Pet Emergency & Specialty Center**
5232 Jackson Dr., #105, La Mesa
(619) 462-4800

**Loomis Basin Veterinary Clinic**
3901 Sierra College Blvd., Loomis
(916) 652-5816

**Adobe Animal Hospital**
396 First St., Los Altos
(650) 948-9661

**Animal Surgical Emergency Center**
1535 South Sepulveda Blvd., Los Angeles
(310) 473-1561

**Eagle Rock Emergency Pet Clinic**
4254 Eagle Rock Blvd., Los Angeles
(323) 254-7382

**VCA/West Los Angeles Animal Hospital**
1818 South Sepulveda Blvd., Los Angeles
(310) 473-2951

**Animal Urgent Care**
28085 Hillcrest, Mission Viejo
(949) 364-6228

**Monterey Animal Hospital**
725 Foam St., Monterey
(831) 373-0711

**Crossroads Animal Emergency & Referral Center**
11057 E. Rosecrans Ave., Norwalk
(562) 863-2522

**Emergency Veterinary Clinic - South Peninsula**
3045 Middlefield Rd., Palo Alto
(650) 494-1461

**Animal Emergency Clinic of Pasadena**
2121 E. Foothill Blvd., Pasadena
(626) 564-0704

**McClave Veterinary Hospital**
6950 Reseda Blvd., Reseda
(818) 881-5102

**Rimforest Animal Hospital**
1299 Bear Springs Rd., Rimforest
(909) 337-8589

**Animal Care Center of Sonoma County**
6470 Redwood Dr., Rohnert Park
(707) 584-4343

**Sacramento Emergency Veterinary Clinic**
2201 El Camino Ave., Sacramento
(916) 922-3425

**VCA Sacramento Veterinary Surgical Services**
9700 Business Park Dr., #404, Sacramento
(916) 362-3111

**San Clemente Veterinary Hospital**
1833 South El Camino Real, San Clemente
(949) 492-5777

**VCA Hillcrest Animal Center**
246 W. Washington St., San Diego
(619) 299-7387

**Emergency Animal Hospital & Referral Center**
2317 Hotel Cir. South, San Diego
(619) 299-2400

**All Animals Emergency Hospital**
1333 9th Ave., San Francisco
(415) 566-0531

**Mission Pet Hospital**
720 Valencia St., San Francisco
(415) 552-1969

**Pets Unlimited**
2343 Fillmore St., San Francisco
(415) 563-6700

**South Bay Veterinary Specialists**
5440 Thornwood Dr., #H, San Jose
(408) 363-8066

**Bay Area Veterinary Specialists**
14790 Washington Ave., San Leandro
(510) 352-6080

**California Veterinary Specialist**
100 N. Rancho Santa Fe Rd., Ste. #133, San Marcos
(760) 734-4433

**North Peninsula Veterinary Emergency Clinic**
227 N. Amphlett Blvd., San Mateo
(650) 348-2575

**Santa Cruz Veterinary Hospital**
2585 Soquel Dr., Santa Cruz
(831) 475-5400

**Pet Care Veterinary Hospital**
1370 Fulton Rd., Santa Rosa
(707) 579-5900

**Beverly Oaks Animal Hospital**
14302 Ventura Blvd., Sherman Oaks
(818) 788-2022

**American Veterinary Hospital**
2109 Tapo St., #3, Simi Valley
(805) 581-9111

**Rancho Sequoia Veterinary Hospital**
3380 Los Angeles Ave., Simi Valley
(805) 522-7476

**Animal Emergency Center**
11730 Ventura Blvd., Studio City
(818) 760-3882

**Emergency Pet Clinic of Temecula**
27443 Jefferson Ave., Temecula
(951) 695-5044

**Pet Emergency Clinic of Thousand Oaks**
2967 North Moorpark Rd., Thousand Oaks
(805) 492-2436

**Animal Emergency Clinic of the Desert**
72374 Ramon Rd., Thousand Palms
(760) 343-3438

**Emergency Pet Clinic of South Bay**
2325 Torrance Blvd., Torrance
(310) 320-8300

**Central Animal Hospital**
281 North Central Ave., Upland
(909) 981-2855

**Pet Emergency Clinic of Ventura**
2301 S. Victoria Ave., Ventura
(805) 642-8562

**Washington Boulevard Animal Hospital**
12116 East Washington Blvd., Whittier
(562) 693-8233

## COLORADO

**All Pets Veterinary Clinic**
5290 Manhattan Cir., Boulder
(303) 499-5335

**Boulder Emergency Pet Clinic**
1658 30th St., Boulder
(303) 440-7722

**Animal Emergency Care Center**
5752 North Academy Blvd., Colorado Springs
(719) 260-7141

**Animal Emergency Care Center**
3775 Airport Rd., Colorado Springs
(719) 578-9300

**Alameda East Veterinary Hospital**
9770 E. Alameda Ave., Denver
(303) 366-2639

**Colorado State University Veterinary Teaching Hospital**
300 W. Drake Rd., Fort Collins
(970) 221-4535

**Centennial Veterinary Clinic**
5151 S. Federal Blvd., Ste. #H-6, Littleton
(303) 795-0130

**Wheat Ridge Animal Hospital**
3695 Kipling St., Wheat Ridge
(303) 424-3325

## CONNECTICUT

**East of the River Veterinary Emergency Clinic**
222 Boston Tpk., Bolton
(860) 646-6134

**Shoreline Animal Emergency Clinic**
7365 Main St., Suite 5, Stratford
(203) 375-6500

**Connecticut Veterinary Center**
470 Oakwood Ave., West Hartford
(860) 233-8564

## FLORIDA

**Veterinary Emergency Clinic of Central Florida**
195 Concord Dr., Casselberry
(407) 644-4449

**Volusia Animal Emergency Clinic**
US 92, Daytona Beach
(386) 252-4300

**American Animal Emergency of Deerfield Beach**
103 N. Powerline Rd., Deerfield Beach
(954) 428-9888

**Animal Emergency and Referral Center**
3984 S. US 1, Fort Pierce
(772) 466-3441

**Affiliated Pet Emergency Services**
7520 W. University Ave., Gainesville
(352) 373-4444

**Chasewood Animal Hospital**
6390 W. Indiantown Rd., #16, Jupiter
(561) 745-4944

**Veterinary Emergency Care**
3609 Hwy. 98 S., Lakeland
(863) 665-3199

**Lantana-Atlantis Animal Clinic**
3530 Lantana Rd., Lantana
(561) 439-0694

**VCA Promenade Animal Hospital**
4424 N. University Dr., Lauderhill
(954) 748-9600

**Veterinary Emergency Clinic of Lake County**
33040 Professional Dr., Leesburg
(352) 728-4440

**Animal Emergency Clinic South**
8429 S.W. 132nd St., Miami
(305) 251-2096

**Knowles Emergency Clinic**
1000 N.W. 27th Ave., Miami
(305) 649-1234

**Knowles Snapper Creek Animal Clinic**
9933 Sunset Dr., Miami
(305) 279-2323

**Emergency Veterinary Clinic Okaloosa/Walton**
210 A Government Ave., Niceville
(850) 729-3335

**Veterinary Emergency Clinic of Central Florida**
2080 Principal Row, Orlando
(407) 438-4449

**Pet Emergency of Palm Beach County**
3816 Northlake Blvd., Palm Beach Gardens
(561) 691-9999

**Emergency Animal Clinic**
6602 Pines Blvd., Pembroke Pines
(954) 962-0300

**Animal Hospital**
8560 N. Davis Hwy., Pensacola
(850) 479-9484

**Animal Emergency of Pasco**
8740 US Hwy. 19 N., Port Richey
(727) 841-6575

**Emergency Veterinary Clinic of Sarasota**
7517 S. Tamiami Tr., #107, Sarasota
(941) 923-7260

**Animal Emergency of Hernando**
3496 Deltona Blvd., Spring Hill
(352) 666-0904

**Animal Emergency Clinic of St. Petersburg**
3165 22nd Ave. N., St. Petersburg
(727) 323-1311

**Allied Veterinary Emergency Hospital**
401 East 9th Ave., Tallahassee
(850) 222-0123

**Northwood Animal Hospital**
1881-B North Martin Luther King Jr. Blvd., Tallahassee
(850) 385-8181

**Murphy Animal Hospital**
6845 N. Dale Mabry, Tampa
(813) 879-6090

**American Animal Emergency Clinic**
3425 Forest Hill Blvd., West Palm Beach
(561) 433-2244

**Summit Boulevard Animal Hospital**
1000 S. Military Tr., #B and C, West Palm Beach
(561) 439-7900

# GEORGIA

**Animal Emergency Clinic of Sandy Springs**
228 Sandy Springs Pl. N.E., Atlanta
(404) 252-7881

**Augusta Animal Emergency**
208 Hudson Trace, Augusta
(706) 733-7458

**Animal Emergency Care**
2009 Mercer University Dr., Macon
(478) 750-0911

**Cobb Emergency Veterinary Clinic**
630 Cobb Pkwy. N., Ste. C, Marietta
(770) 424-9157

**Peachtree Corners Animal Clinic**
4020 Holcomb Bridge Rd., Norcross
(770) 448-0700

**Animal Emergency Center of North Fulton**
900 Mansell Rd., #19, Roswell
(770) 594-2266

**Chattahoochee Animal Clinic**
1176 Alpharetta St., Roswell
(770) 993-6329

**Savannah Veterinary Emergency and Specialty Referral Center**
317 Eisenhower Dr., Savannah
(912) 355-6113

# ILLINOIS

**Animal Emergency Center**
2005 Mall St., Collinsville
(618) 346-1843

**Emergency Veterinary Care South**
13715 S. Cicero Ave., Crestwood
(708) 388-3771

**Animal Emergency and Treatment Center**
1810 Belvidere Rd., Grayslake
(847) 548-5300

**Emergency Veterinary Services**
820 Ogden Ave., Lisle
(630) 960-2900

**Animal Emergency and Critical Care Center**
1810 Frontage Rd., Northbrook
(847) 564-5775

**Emergency Veterinary Services of St. Charles**
530 Dunham Rd., St. Charles
(630) 584-7447

# INDIANA

**All Pet Emergency Clinic**
104B South Heidelbach, Evansville
(812) 422-3300

**Northeast Indiana Veterinary Emergency & Specialty Hospital**
5818 Maplecrest Rd., Fort Wayne
(260) 426-1062

**Indianapolis Veterinary Emergency and Medical Center**
5245 Victory Dr., Indianapolis
(317) 782-4418

**Veterinary Centers of America**
4030 W. 86th St., Indianapolis
(317) 872-0200

**New Carlisle Animal Clinic**
8935 East US 20, New Carlisle
(574) 654-3129

Calumet Emergency Veterinary Clinic
216 W. Lincoln Hwy., Schererville
(219) 865-0970

Arbor View Animal Hospital
244 W. US Hwy. 6, Valparaiso
(219) 762-6586

# IOWA

Animal Emergency Clinic & Referral Center of Central Iowa
6110 Crescent Ave., Des Moines
(515) 280-3051

# KANSAS

Mission Medvet
5914 Johnson Dr., Mission
(913) 722-5566

Veterinary Specialty & Emergency Center
11950 W. 110th St., Overland Park
(913) 642-9563

Wichita Emergency Veterinary Clinic
727 S. Washington St., Wichita
(316) 262-5321

# KENTUCKY

Colonial Animal Clinic
1601 Argillite Rd., Flatwoods
(606) 836-8112

Hagyard Davidson McGee Veterinarians
4250 Ironworks Pike, Lexington
(859) 255-8741

Jefferson Animal Hospital & Emergency Center
4504 Outer Loop, Louisville
(502) 966-4104

# LOUISIANA

Westbank Pet Emergency Clinic, Inc.
1152 Terry Pkwy., Terrytown
(504) 392-1932

Animal Emergency Clinic
1955 Veterans Memorial Blvd., Metairie
(504) 835-8508

# MAINE

Animal Emergency Clinic of Mid Maine
37 Strawberry Ave., Lewiston
(207) 777-1110

Norway Veterinary Hospital
Route 26, 10 Main St., Norway
(207) 743-6384

Animal Emergency Clinic
352 Warren Ave., Portland
(207) 878-3121

# MARYLAND

Anne Arundel Veterinary Emergency Clinic, Inc.
808 Bestgate Rd., Annapolis
(410) 224-0331

Emergency Veterinary Clinic
32 Mellor Ave., Catonsville
(410) 788-7040

Veterinary Referral Associates, Inc.
15021 Dufief Mill Rd., Gaithersburg
(301) 340-3224

Beltway Emergency Animal Hospital
11660 Annapolis Rd., Glenn Dale
(301) 464-3737

Emergency Animal Center
3051 Thurston Rd., Urbana
(301) 831-1088

Metropolitan Emergency Animal Clinic
12106 Nebel St., Rockville
(301) 770-5225

Animal Emergency Center and Chesapeake Veterinary Referral
1209 Cromwell Bridge Rd., Towson
(410) 252-8387

Southern Maryland Veterinary Referral Center and Emergency
3485 Rockefeller Ct., Waldorf
(301) 638-0988

Westminster Veterinary Hospital-Emergency Trauma Center
269 W. Main St., Westminster
(410) 848-3363

# MASSACHUSETTS

Angell Animal Center
350 S. Huntington Ave., Boston
(617) 522-7282

Roberts Animal Hospital
516 Washington St., Hanover
(781) 826-2306

Holyoke Animal Hospital
320 Easthampton Rd., Holyoke
(413) 538-8700

Animal Health Care Associates
Martha's Vineyard Airport, Martha's Vineyard
(508) 693-6515

Highland Animal Hospital
31 Wellesley Ave., Needham
(781) 433-0467

Tufts University School Of Veterinary Medicine
200 Westboro Rd., North Grafton
(508) 839-5395

South Deerfield Veterinary Clinic
Elm Street and Route 5 & 10, South Deerfield
(413) 665-3626

Veterinary Associates of Cape Cod
16 Commonwealth Ave., South Yarmouth
(508) 394-3566

Angell Animal Medical Center
171 Union St., Springfield
(413) 785-1221

**VCA/Wakefield Animal Hospital**
19 Main St., Wakefield
(781) 245-0045

## MICHIGAN
**Michigan Veterinary Specialists**
3412 E. Walton Blvd., Auburn Hills
(248) 371-3713

**Lansing Veterinary Urgent Care**
5133 S. Martin Luther King Jr. Blvd., Lansing
(517) 393-9200

**Veterinary Medical Center**
243 N. Jebavy Dr., Ludington
(231) 845-0585

**Veterinary Emergency Service & Critical Care**
28223 John R Rd., Madison Heights
(248) 547-4677

**Veterinary Emergency Service West**
40850 Ann Arbor Rd., Plymouth
(734) 207-8500

**Michigan Veterinary Specialists**
29080 Inkster Rd., Southfield
(248) 354-6660

**Affiliated Veterinary Emergency Services**
14085 Northline Rd., Southgate
(734) 284-1700

**Union Lake Veterinary Hospital**
6545 Cooley Lake Rd., Waterford
(248) 363-1508

## MINNESOTA
**South Metro Animal Emergency Care Clinic**
14690 Pennock Ave., Apple Valley
(952) 953-3737

**Affiliated Emergency Veterinary Service**
1615 Coon Rapids Blvd., Coon Rapids
(763) 754-9434

**Affiliated Emergency Veterinary Service**
4708 Olson Memorial Hwy., Golden Valley
(763) 529-6560

**Animal Emergency Clinic**
301 University Ave., St. Paul
(651) 293-1800

## MISSISSIPPI
**Bienville Animal Medical Center**
1524 Bienville Blvd., Ocean Springs
(228) 872-1231

## MISSOURI
**Animal Emergency Clinic**
12501 Natural Bridge Rd., Bridgeton
(314) 739-1500

**Animal Emergency Clinic**
9937 Big Bend Blvd., St. Louis
(314) 822-7600

## MONTANA
**Animal Medical Clinic**
5100 9th Ave. South, Great Falls
(406) 761-8183

## NEBRASKA
**VCA-Rohrig Animal Hospital**
8022 W. Dodge Rd., Omaha
(402) 399-8100

## NEVADA
**Carson Tahoe Veterinary Hospital**
3389 S. Carson St., Carson City
(775) 883-8238

**Animal Emergency Center**
3340 E. Patrick Ln., Las Vegas
(702) 457-8050

**VCA Painted Desert Animal Hospital**
4601 N. Rancho Dr., Las Vegas
(702) 645-2543

**Animal Emergency Center**
6425 S. Virginia St., Reno
(775) 851-3600

## NEW HAMPSHIRE
**Animal Emergency Clinic of Southern New Hampshire**
2626 Brown Ave., Pine Island Plaza, Manchester
(603) 666-6677

**State Line Veterinary Hospital**
325 S. Daniel Webster Hwy., Nashua
(603) 888-2751

**Animal Medical Center**
1550 Woodbury Ave., Portsmouth
(603) 436-4922

## NEW JERSEY
**Ocean County Veterinary Hospital**
838 River Ave., Lakewood
(732) 363-7202

**Oradell Animal Hospital**
580 Winters Ave., Paramus
(201) 262-0010

**Alliance Emergency Veterinary Clinic**
540 Route 10 West, Randolph
(973) 328-2844

## NEW MEXICO
**Albuquerque Animal Emergency Clinic**
4000 Montgomery N.E., Albuquerque
(505) 884-3433

**Great Plains Veterinary Clinic**
2720 Lovington Hwy., Hobbs
(505) 392-5513

**Ruidoso Animal Clinic**
160 Sudderth, Ruidoso
(505) 257-4027

**Emergency Veterinary Clinic of Santa Fe**
1311 Calle Nava, Santa Fe
(505) 984-0625

# NEW YORK

**Central Veterinary Hospital**
388 Central Ave., Albany
(518) 434-2115

**Greater Buffalo Veterinary Services**
4949 Main St., Amherst
(716) 839-4043

**Bayside Animal Clinic**
36-43 Bell Blvd., Bayside
(718) 224-4451

**Bellerose Animal Hospital**
242-01 Jamaica Ave., Bellerose
(718) 347-1057

**Brooklyn Veterinary Emergency Service**
453 Bay Ridge Ave., Brooklyn
(718) 748-5180

**Far Rockaway Animal Hospital**
1833 Cornaga Ave., Far Rockaway
(718) 327-0256

**Boulevard Animal Clinic**
112-49 Queens Blvd., Forest Hills
(718) 261-1231

**Terrace Animal Clinic**
501 Great Neck Rd., Great Neck
(516) 466-9191

**Homer Animal Clinic**
66 S. West St., Homer
(607) 749-7223

**Animal Emergency Center of Queens P.C.**
187-11 Hillside Ave., Jamaica
(718) 454-4141

**Animal Emergency Clinic**
1112 Morton Blvd., Kingston
(845) 336-0713

**Hilton Hospital for Animals**
120 Merrick Rd., Lynbrook
(516) 887-2914

**Animal Medical Center/Bobst Hospital**
510 East 62nd St., New York
(212) 838-8100

**VCA/Manhattan Veterinary Group**
240 East 80th St., New York
(212) 988-1000

**Riverside Animal Hospital**
250 West 108th St., New York
(212) 865-2224

**Orchard Park Veterinary Medical Center**
3507 Orchard Park Rd., Orchard Park
(716) 662-6660

**Animal Emergency Clinic of Hudson Valley**
84 Patrick Ln., Poughkeepsie
(845) 471-8242

**Animal Hospital**
640 Willowbrook Rd., Staten Island
(718) 494-0050

**Veterinary Emergency Center**
1293 Clove Rd., Staten Island
(718) 720-4211

**The Veterinary Medical Center**
2612 Erie Blvd. East, Syracuse
(315) 446-7933

**Valley Cottage Animal Hospital**
202 Route 303, Valley Cottage
(845) 268-9263

**Central Veterinary Associates**
73 W. Merrick Rd., Valley Stream
(516) 825-3066

**Animal Care Hospital**
4535 Old Vestal Rd., Vestal
(607) 770-9999

**Schroon River Animal Hospital**
150 Schroon River Rd., Warrensburg
(518) 623-3181

**Nassau Animal Emergency Clinic**
740 Old Country Rd., Westbury
(516) 333-6262

# NORTH CAROLINA

**Freedom Animal Hospital**
3055 Freedom Dr., Charlotte
(704) 399-6534

**Triangle Pet Emergency Treatment Service**
3319 Chapel Hill Blvd., Durham
(919) 489-0615

**Veterinary Emergency Clinic of Gaston County**
728 E. Franklin Blvd., Gastonia
(704) 866-7918

**Cabarrus Emergency Veterinary Clinic**
1317 S. Cannon Blvd., Kannapolis
(704) 932-1182

**Emergency Veterinary Clinic**
2440 Plantation Center Dr., Matthews
(704) 844-6440

**After Hours Small Animal Emergency Clinic**
409 Vick Ave., Raleigh
(919) 781-5145

**Ansede Animal Hospital**
3535 South Wilmington St., Raleigh
(919) 661-1515

**Wilmington Animal Emergency Clinic**
5333 Oleander Dr., Wilmington
(910) 791-7387

**Forsyth After Hours Veterinary Emergency Clinic**
7781 Northpoint Blvd., Winston-Salem
(336) 896-0902

# OHIO

**Animal Emergency Clinic**
5320 West 140th St., Brook Park
(216) 362-6000

**Animal Medical & Emergency Hospital**
2527 West Dublin-Granville Rd., Columbus
(614) 889-2556

**Dayton Emergency Veterinary Clinic**
2714 Springboro West, Dayton
(937) 293-2714

**Lorain Animal Emergency Center**
1909 North Ridge Rd., Lorain
(440) 240-1400

**County Animal Hospital**
1185 Reading Rd., Mason
(513) 398-8000

**Aaron Animal Clinic and Emergency Hospital**
7640 Broadview Rd., Parma
(216) 901-9980

**Columbus Veterinary Emergency Service & MedVet**
300 E. Wilson Bridge Rd., Worthington
(614) 846-5800

# OKLAHOMA
**Midtown Animal Hospital**
1101 S.W. Park Ave., Lawton
(580) 353-3438

**Veterinary Emergency and Critical Care Hospital**
1800 W. Memorial Rd., Oklahoma City
(405) 749-6989

**Animal Emergency Center**
7220 E. 41st St., Tulsa
(918) 665-0508

# OREGON
**Willamette Veterinary Clinic**
650 S.W. Third St., Corvallis
(541) 753-5750

**Dove Lewis Emergency Animal Hospital**
1984 N.W. Pettygrove St., Portland
(503) 228-7281

**Salem Veterinary Emergency Clinic**
3215 Market St. N.E., Salem
(503) 588-8082

**Emergency Veterinary Clinic of Tualatin**
19314 S.W. Mohave Ct., Tualatin
(503) 691-7922

# PENNSYLVANIA
**Providence Veterinary Hospital**
24th and Providence Ave., Chester
(610) 872-4000

**Center for Animal Referral & Emergency Services**
2010 Cabot Blvd., Langhorne
(215) 750-2774

**Allegheny Veterinary Trauma & Specialty**
4224 Northern Pike, Monroeville
(412) 373-4200

**Metropolitan Veterinary Center**
560 McNeilly Rd., Pittsburgh
(412) 344-6888

**VCA Castle Shannon Animal Hospital**
3610 Library Rd., Pittsburgh
(412) 885-2500

**Tri-County Veterinary Emergency Service**
2250 N. Old Bethlehem Pike, Quakertown
(215) 536-6245

**Valley Central Emergency Veterinary Hospital**
210 Fullerton Ave., Whitehall
(610) 435-5588

**Animal Emergency Clinic of York**
3256 N. Susquehanna Tr., York
(717) 767-5355

# RHODE ISLAND
**North Kingstown Animal Hospital**
3736 Quaker Ln., North Kingstown
(401) 295-9777

**Warwick Animal Hospital**
1950 Elmwood Ave., Warwick
(401) 785-2222

# SOUTH CAROLINA
**South Carolina Veterinary Emergency Care Center**
132 Stonemark Ln., Columbia
(803) 798-3837

**Animal Hospital of North Myrtle Beach**
2501 Hwy. 17 S., North Myrtle Beach
(843) 272-8121

**Veterinary Emergency Clinic**
1291 Ashville Hwy., Spartanburg
(864) 591-1923

# TENNESSEE
**Keith Street Animal Clinic**
1990 Keith St., Cleveland
(423) 476-1804

**After Hours Pet Emergency Clinic**
215 Center Park Dr., Knoxville
(865) 966-3888

# TEXAS
**I-20 Animal Medical Center**
5820 I-20 West, Arlington
(817) 478-9238

**Animal Emergency Hospital of Austin**
4106 N. Lamar Blvd., Austin
(512) 459-4336

**Emergency Animal Hospital of Northwest Austin**
4434 Frontier Tr., Austin
(512) 899-0955

**Emergency Animal Hospital of Northwest Austin**
12034 Research Blvd., #8, Austin
(512) 331-6121

**North Texas Emergency Pet Clinic**
1712 W. Frankford Rd., Carrollton
(972) 323-1310

**Emergency Animal Clinic**
12101 Greenville Ave., #118, Dallas
(972) 994-9110

**Whiterock Animal Hospital**
11414 East Northwest Hwy., Dallas
(214) 328-3255

**El Paso Animal Emergency Center**
2101 Texas Ave., El Paso
(915) 545-1148

**Airport Freeway Animal Emergency Clinic**
411 N. Main St., Euless
(817) 571-2088

**VCA Fort Worth Animal Medical Center**
8331 W. Freeway, Fort Worth
(817) 560-8387

**Animal Emergency Clinic**
8921 Katy Frwy., Houston
(713) 932-9589

**Animal Emergency Clinic Caldera Road**
1100 Gulf Frwy. S., #104, League City
(281) 332-1678

**Permian Basin Emergency Veterinary Clinic**
13528 W. US Hwy. 80, Midland
(432) 561-8301

**Lake Olympia Animal Hospital**
3603 Glenn Lakes, Missouri City
(281) 499-7242

**Emergency Pet Clinic**
8503 Broadway, #105, San Antonio
(210) 822-2873

**Emergency Pet Center**
503 E. Sonterra Blvd., San Antonio
(210) 404-2873

**VCA Southwest Freeway Animal Hospital**
15575 Southwest Frwy., Sugar Land
(281) 491-8387

## UTAH

**Animal Medical Services**
469 W. Center St., Orem
(801) 225-3346

**Central Emergency Animal Clinic**
55 E. Miller Ave., Salt Lake City
(801) 487-1325

## VERMONT

**Lamoille Valley Veterinary Services**
278 Vermont Route #15 East, Hyde Park
(802) 888-7911

## VIRGINIA

**Alexandria Animal Hospital**
2660 Duke St., Alexandria
(703) 823-3601

**Albemarle Veterinary Hospital**
445 Westfield Rd., Charlottesville
(434) 973-6146

**Animal Emergency Clinic of Fredericksburg**
1210 Snowden St., Fredericksburg
(540) 371-0554

**Animal Emergency Hospital & Referral Center**
2 Cardinal Park Dr., #101B, Leesburg
(703) 777-5755

**Animal Emergency & Critical Care of Lynchburg**
3432 Odd Fellows Rd., Lynchburg
(434) 846-1504

**Veterinary Internal Medicine Practice**
8614 Centreville Rd., Manassas
(703) 330-8809

**Veterinary Emergency Center**
3312 W. Cary St., Richmond
(804) 353-9000

**Springfield Emergency Veterinary Hospital**
6651-F Backlick Rd., Springfield
(703) 451-8900

**Silver Spring Veterinary Hospital**
241 Garber Ln., Winchester
(540) 662-2301

## WASHINGTON

**After Hours Animal Emergency Clinic**
718 Auburn Way N., Auburn
(253) 939-6272

**Aerowood Animal Hospital**
2975 156th Ave. S.E., Bellevue
(425) 746-6557

**Snoqualmie Valley Animal Hospital**
32020 S.E. 40th St., Fall City
(425) 222-7220

**Vista Veterinary Hospital**
5603 W. Canal Dr., Kennewick
(509) 783-2131

**Veterinary Specialty Center**
20115 44th Ave. W., Lynnwood
(425) 697-6106

**Animal Emergency and Trauma Center**
320 Lindvig Way, Poulsbo
(360) 697-7771

**Emerald City Emergency Clinic**
4102 Stone Way N., Seattle
(206) 634-9000

**VCA Five Corners Animal Hospital**
15707 1st Ave. S., Seattle
(206) 243-2982

**Pet Emergency Clinic**
21 E. Mission Ave., Spokane
(509) 326-6670

**Animal Emergency Clinic**
5608 South Durango, Tacoma
(253) 474-0791

**Emergency Veterinary Service**
6818 E. 4th Plain Blvd., Suite C, Vancouver
(360) 694-3007

## WEST VIRGINIA

**Middletown Animal Clinic**
1615 Bobbeck Ln., Fairmont
(304) 366-6130

**Kanawha Valley Animal Emergency Clinic**
5304 MacCorkle Ave. S.W., South Charleston
(304) 768-2911

## WISCONSIN

**Fox Valley Animal Referral Center**
4706 New Horizons Blvd., Appleton
(920) 993-9193

**Animal Emergency Center**
2100 W. Silver Spring Dr., Glendale
(414) 540-6710

**Emergency Clinic for Animals**
229 W. Beltline Hwy., Madison
(608) 274-7772

**Animal Clinic**
2734 Calumet Dr., Sheboygan
(920) 458-3636

**Emergency Veterinary Service**
360 Bluemound Rd., Waukesha
(262) 542-3241

# Canada

## BRITISH COLUMBIA

**Animal Emergency Clinic**
#103-6337 198th St., Langley
(604) 514-1711

**Vancouver Animal Emergency Clinic, Ltd.**
1590 West 4th Ave., Vancouver
(604) 734-5104

## ONTARIO

**Park Animal Hospital**
1958 Burnham Thorpe Rd. E., Mississauga
(905) 625-5222

**Niagara Veterinary Emergency Clinic**
2F Tremont Dr., #1, St. Catharines
(905) 641-3185

# PET-FRIENDLY LODGINGS

How to Use the Listings
U.S. Lodgings
Canadian Lodgings
Campground Listings

# How to Use the Listings

Some 13,000 AAA-RATED® properties across North America accept traveling pets. This guide provides listings for those lodgings in the United States and Canada that roll out the welcome mat for pets as well as the people who love them.

For the purpose of this book, "pets" are domestic cats or dogs. If you are planning to travel with any other kind of animal — particularly such exotic pets as birds or reptiles — check with the property before making definite plans. Expect to keep nontraditional pets crated at all times.

**Note:** Always inform the management that you are traveling with an animal; you may be fined if you do not declare your pet. Many properties require guests with pets to sign a waiver or release form and to pay for the room with a credit card. Of course, whether you pay in cash or by credit card, you will be held liable for any damages caused by your pet, even if the property does not charge a deposit or pet fee. It is not a good idea to leave your pet unattended in the room, but if you must, crate him and notify the management. When in public areas, keep your pet leashed and do not allow him to disturb other guests.

## About the Listings

Geographic listings are used for accuracy and consistency; lodgings are listed under the city or town in which they physically are located — or in some cases under the nearest recognized city or town. For a complete list of all cities within a state or province, see the comprehensive City Index at the beginning of the corresponding section.

U.S. properties are shown first, followed by Canadian properties. Most listings are alphabetically organized by state or province, city and establishment name. Reflecting contemporary travel patterns, properties in some cities or towns may instead be listed within destination cities or areas. Such "vicinity cities" and their listings will be shown alphabetically in the destination city or area, and the vicinity city also will appear in alphabetical order in the City Index, along with the page number on which the listings begin.

Each listing provides the following information (see sample listing, next page):

❶ Symbol denoting Official Appointment (OA) properties. The OA program permits properties to display and advertise the AAA or CAA logo. OAs have a special interest in serving AAA/CAA members. Ask if they offer special member amenities such as free breakfast, early check-in/late check-out, free room upgrade, free local phone calls, etc.

❷ Diamond rating. See next page.

❸ Property name.

❹ Lodging classification. See p. 61.

❺ Special amenities offered. These properties provide an additional benefit to pets, such as treats, toys or gifts, pet sitting and/or walking, a pet menu, food/water dishes, pet sheets or pillows, pet beds or other extras.

❻ Telephone number.

❼ Two-person (2P) rate year-round, and cancellation notice validity period (if more than 48 hours). Rates listed are usually daily, but weekly rates also may be listed. **Note:** Most properties accept any or all of the major credit cards, including American Express, MasterCard and VISA. If a property accepts only cash, the phrase "(no credit cards)" follows the rates.

❽ Physical address and highway location, if available.

❾ Exterior or interior corridors.

❿ Pet policies. If the phrase "pets accepted" appears, the property does accept pets but specific information was unavailable at press time. Otherwise, pet-specific policies are denoted as follows:

**Size.** "Very small" denotes pets weighing up to 10 pounds; "small," up to 25 pounds; "medium," up to 50 pounds; and "large," up to 100 pounds. If no size is specified, the property accepts pets of all sizes.

**Species.** "Other" indicates the property accepts animals other than dogs and cats. Always call ahead and specify the type of pet you plan to bring.

**Deposits and fees.** Includes the dollar amount, the type of charge (refundable deposit or nonrefundable fee), the frequency of the charge and whether the charge is per pet or per room.

**Designated rooms.** Guests with pets are placed in certain rooms, often smoking rooms or those on the ground floor.

**Housekeeping service.** The phrase "service with restrictions" denotes properties that require the pet to be crated, removed or attended by the owner during housekeeping service.

**Supervision.** The pet is required to be supervised at all times.

**Crate.** The pet must be crated when the owner is not present.

⓫ Property discounts and amenities:

- 🆂🆅 Minimum 10% discount.
- 🅰🆂🅺 May offer discount.
- 🆂🅳 Senior discount.
- ⊠ Non-smoking rooms.
- 🅺🅼 Semi-accessible or 🅺🅼 fully accessible.
- ⑦ Hearing impaired.
- 🅺 Roll-in showers.
- 🅱 Refrigerator.
- ▣ Coffee maker.

⟨Ⅱ⟩ Restaurant on premises.

⟨≈⟩ Pool.

⟨⊠⟩ Recreational activities.

⟨Ⅺ⟩ No air conditioning.

⟨Ⅶ⟩ No TV.

⟨☎⟩ No telephones.

Please note: Some in-room amenities represented by the icons in the listings may be available only in selected rooms, and may incur an extra fee. Please inquire when making your reservations.

It is important to remember that animal policies do change; always confirm policies, restrictions and fees with the lodging when making reservations and again 1-2 days before departure.

Listing information is subject to change. All listing information was accurate at press time. However, lodging rates and policies change and the publisher cannot be held liable for changes occurring after publication. AAA cannot guarantee the safety of guests or their pets at any facility.

# AAA Diamond Ratings

Before a property is listed by AAA, it must satisfy a set of minimum standards regarding basic lodging needs as identified by AAA members. If a property meets those requirements, it is assigned a diamond rating reflecting the overall quality of the establishment.

AAA ratings range from one to five diamonds and indicate the property's physical and service standards as measured against the standards of each diamond level. The rating process takes into account the property's classification; i.e., its physical structure and style of operation.

◆ These establishments typically appeal to the budget-minded traveler. They provide essential, no-frills accommodations. They meet the basic requirements pertaining to comfort, cleanliness, and hospitality.

◆◆ These establishments appeal to the traveler seeking more than the basic accommodations. There are modest enhancements to the overall physical attributes, design elements, and amenities of the facility typically at a modest price.

◆◆◆ These establishments appeal to the traveler with comprehensive needs. Properties are multifaceted with a distinguished style, including marked upgrades in the quality of physical attributes, amenities and level of comfort provided.

◆◆◆◆ These establishments are upscale in all areas. Accommodations are progressively more refined and stylish. The physical attributes reflect an obvious enhanced level of quality throughout. The fundamental hallmarks at this level include an extensive array of amenities combined with a high degree of hospitality, service, and attention to detail.

◆◆◆◆◆ These establishments reflect the characteristics of the ultimate in luxury and sophistication. Accommodations are first-class. The physical attributes are extraordinary in every manner. The fundamental hallmarks at this level are to meticulously serve and exceed all guest expectations while maintaining an impeccable standard of excellence. Many personalized services and amenities enhance an unmatched level of comfort.

# Lodging Classifications

**BB Bed & Breakfast:** Usually smaller establishments emphasizing a more personal relationship between operators and guests, leading to an "at home" feeling. Guest units tend to be individually decorated. Rooms may not include some modern amenities such as televisions and telephones, and may have a shared bathroom. Usually owner-operated, with a common room or parlor separate from the innkeeper's living quarters, where guests and operators can interact during evening and breakfast hours. Evening office closures are normal. A continental or full, hot breakfast is served and is included in the room rate.

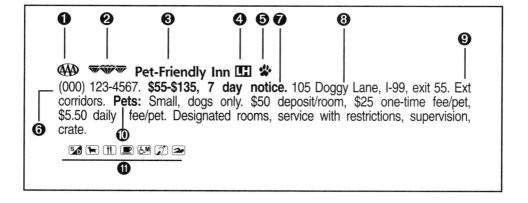

**CA Cabin/Cottage:** Vacation-oriented, small-scale, free-standing houses or cabins. Units vary in design and decor and often contain one or more bedrooms, living room, kitchen, dining area and bathroom. Studio-type models combine the sleeping and living areas into one room. Typically, basic cleaning supplies, kitchen utensils, and complete bed and bath linens are supplied. The guest registration area may be located off-site.

**CI Country Inn:** Although similar in definition to a bed and breakfast, country inns are usually larger in size, provide more spacious public areas and offer a dining facility that serves at least breakfast and dinner. May be located in a rural setting or downtown area.

**CO Condominium:** Establishments that primarily offer guest accommodations that are privately owned by individuals and available for rent. These can include apartment-style units or homes. A variety of room styles and decor treatments are offered, and limited housekeeping service is typical. May have off-site registration.

**LH Large-scale Hotel:** A multistory establishment with interior room entrances. A variety of guest unit styles are offered. Public areas are spacious and include a variety of facilities such as a restaurant, shops, fitness center, spa, business center or meeting rooms.

**M Motel:** Low-rise or multistory establishment offering limited public and recreational facilities.

**RA Ranch:** Often offers rustic decor treatments and food and beverage facilities. Entertainment and recreational activities are geared to a Western-style adventure vacation. May provide some meeting facilities.

**SH Small-scale Hotel:** A multistory establishment typically with interior room entrances. A variety of guest unit styles are offered. Public areas are limited in size and/or the variety of facilities available.

**VH Vacation Home:** Vacation-oriented or extended-stay, large-scale, freestanding houses that are routinely available for rent through a management company. Houses vary in design and décor and often contain two or more bedrooms, living room, full kitchen, dining room and multiple bathrooms. Typically, basic cleaning supplies, kitchen utensils, and complete bed and bath linens are supplied. The guest registration area may be located off-site.

# Campground Listings

Geographic listings are used for accuracy and consistency. Campgrounds are listed under the city or town in which they physically are located — or in some cases under the nearest recognized city or town. Not all listings include physical addresses. U.S. campgrounds are given first, followed by Canadian campgrounds. Listings are alphabetically organized by state or province, city and campground name.

**Note:** Call first before taking your pet on a camping trip, as campground policies regarding pets may change.

Each listing provides the following information (see sample listing):

❶ Location.

❷ Campground name.

❸ Symbol denoting Official Appointment (OA) campgrounds. The OA program permits privately operated campgrounds to display and advertise the AAA or CAA logo. OAs have a special interest in serving AAA/CAA members.

❹ Telephone number.

❺ Fee range for a specified number of persons, including the fee for an extra person (XP) staying at the campground.

❻ Most campgrounds accept any or all of the major credit cards, including American Express, MasterCard and Visa. If a campground accepts only cash, the sentence "(no credit cards)." appears.

❼ Physical address (if available), highway location and mailing address (if available).

❽ Pet policies (as applicable). When pets up to 25 pounds are permitted, the phrase "small pets allowed" will appear. If no size is specified, the campground accepts pets of all sizes.

❾ Campground discounts and amenities:

    🆂 10% senior discount for members over 59

    🆇 No Tents.

    🆇 Pool.

    🆇 Recreational activities.

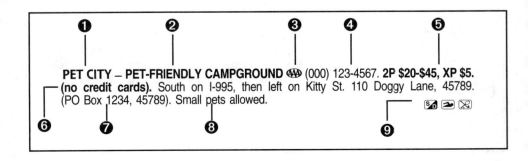

PET CITY – PET-FRIENDLY CAMPGROUND 🆎 (000) 123-4567. **2P $20-$45, XP $5. (no credit cards).** South on I-995, then left on Kitty St. 110 Doggy Lane, 45789. (PO Box 1234, 45789). Small pets allowed.

# United States

# ALABAMA

## CITY INDEX

## ABBEVILLE

### ▼▼ Best Western-Abbeville Inn M
(334) 585-5060. **$59-$75.** 1237 US Hwy 431. Jct SR 27. Ext corridors. **Pets:** $8 daily fee/pet. Service with restrictions, supervision.

(ASK) (S6) (X) 🔒 💻 ➿

## ALBERTVILLE

### ▼▼ Jameson Inn SH
(256) 891-2600. **$54-$104.** 315 Martling Rd. On US 431, just e of SR 75. Ext corridors. **Pets:** Very small, other species. $10 daily fee/room. Service with restrictions, supervision.

(ASK) (X) (&) 🔒 💻 ➿

## ALEXANDER CITY

### ▼▼ Jameson Inn SH
(256) 234-7099. **$54-$104.** 4335 US Hwy 280. US 280, just s of jct SR 22; just w of jct SR 63. Ext corridors. **Pets:** Very small, other species. $10 daily fee/room. Service with restrictions, supervision.

(ASK) (X) (&) 🔒 💻 ➿

## ANDALUSIA

### ▼▼ Days Inn M
(334) 427-0050. **$59.** 1604 Dr. MLK Jr Expwy. On US 84 Bypass. Ext corridors. **Pets:** Medium. $10 daily fee/room. Designated rooms, service with restrictions, supervision.

(ASK) (S6) (X) 🔒 💻 ➿

### ▼▼ Scottish Inn M ❖
(334) 222-7511. **$39-$64.** 1421 Dr. MLK Jr Expwy. On US 84 Bypass. Ext corridors. **Pets:** $10 daily fee/pet. Service with restrictions, supervision.

(SAVE) (S6) (X) 🔒 ➿

## ANNISTON

### ▼▼ Long Leaf Lodge at McClellan M
(256) 820-9494. **$60-$75.** 74 Exchange Ave. I-20, exit 185, 1 mi n on SR 21, then 1.5 mi e to McClellan-Baltzgate. Ext corridors. **Pets:** Accepted.

(ASK) (S6) (X) (&M) 🔒 💻

## ARAB

### ▼▼ Jameson Inn SH
(256) 586-5777. **$54-$104.** 706 N Brindlee Mountain Pkwy. On US 231, 0.5 mi n of jct SR 69. Ext corridors. **Pets:** Very small, other species. $10 daily fee/room. Service with restrictions, supervision.

(ASK) (X) (&) 🔒 💻 ➿

## ARDMORE

### ▼▼ Budget Inn M
(256) 423-6699. **$39-$69.** I-65 & Hwy 53. I-65, exit 365, just se. Ext corridors. **Pets:** Accepted.

(SAVE) (S6) (X) 🔒

## ATHENS

### ▼▼ Best Western Athens Inn SH
(256) 233-4030. **$49-$99.** 1329 Hwy 72. I-65, exit 351, just w. Ext corridors. **Pets:** Medium. $10 daily fee/pet. Service with restrictions, supervision.

(SAVE) (S6) (X) 🔒 💻 ➿

### ▼▼ Country Hearth Inn SH
(256) 232-1520. **$39-$79, 7 day notice.** 1500 Hwy 72 E. I-65, exit 351, just e on US 72. Ext corridors. **Pets:** Medium. $5 daily fee/pet. Service with restrictions, supervision.

(ASK) (S6) (X) 🔒 💻 ➿

### ▼▼▼ Hampton Inn Athens SH ❖
(256) 232-0030. **$85-$95.** 1488 Thrasher Blvd. I-65, exit 351, just ne. Ext corridors. **Pets:** $25 one-time fee/room. Service with restrictions.

(ASK) (X) 🔒 💻 ➿

## ATTALLA

### ▼▼ Americas Best Value Inn & Suites SH
(256) 570-0117. **$55-$130.** 915 E 5th Ave. I-59, exit 183 southbound, just e; exit northbound, through first set of lights, then just e. Ext corridors. **Pets:** Accepted.

(SAVE) (S6) (X) 🔒

### ▼▼ Days Inn Gadsden/Attalla SH
(256) 538-7861. **$63.** 801 Cleveland Ave. I-59, exit 183 northbound, just e; exit southbound, through first set of lights, then just e. Ext corridors. **Pets:** Accepted.

(ASK) (S6) (X) (&) 🔒 💻 ➿

### ▼▼ Econo Lodge SH
(256) 538-9925. **$49-$64.** 507 Cherry St. I-59, exit 183, just w. Int corridors. **Pets:** Small, dogs only. $25 deposit/pet. Service with restrictions, supervision.

(SAVE) (S6) (X) 🔒 💻 (♆) ➿

## AUBURN

### ▼▼ Best Western University Convention Center SH
(334) 821-7001. **$75.** 1577 S College St. I-85, exit 51, 1.4 mi n on US 29/SR 147. Ext corridors. **Pets:** Accepted.

(SAVE) (S6) (X) 🔒 💻 ➿

### ▼▼▼ The Hotel at Auburn University Hotel & Dixon Conference Center LH
(334) 821-8200. **$109-$245.** 241 S College St. I-85, exit 51, 3.5 mi n on US 29/SR 147. Int corridors. **Pets:** Accepted.

(SAVE) (X) (&M) (♦) 🔒 💻 (♆) ➿

### ▼▼ Jameson Inn M
(334) 502-5020. **$54-$104.** 1212 Mall Pkwy. I-85, exit 58, 1.5 mi w on US 280, then 2.1 mi s on US 29/SR 14. Ext corridors. **Pets:** Very small, other species. $10 daily fee/room. Service with restrictions, supervision.

(ASK) (X) 🔒 💻 ➿

# BIRMINGHAM METROPOLITAN AREA

## BESSEMER

**Best Western Hotel & Suites** SH
(205) 481-1950. **$89-$250.** 5041 Academy Ln. I-20/59, exit 108, just sw. Int corridors. **Pets:** Accepted.

**Comfort Inn** SH
(205) 428-3999. **$80-$140.** 5051 Academy Ln. I-20/59, exit 108, just sw. Int corridors. **Pets:** Accepted.

**Jameson Inn** SH
(205) 428-3194. **$54-$104.** 5021 Academy Ln. I-20/59, exit 108, just sw. Ext corridors. **Pets:** Very small, other species. $10 daily fee/room. Service with restrictions, supervision.

**Motel 6 #426** M
(205) 426-9646. **$39-$55.** 1000 Shiloh Ln. I-20/59, exit 108, 1 mi ne on US 11. Ext corridors. **Pets:** Accepted.

**Sleep Inn** SH 🐾
(205) 424-0000. **$59-$169.** 1259 Greenmor Dr. I-459, exit 6, just e, then just s. Int corridors. **Pets:** Medium. $15 daily fee/pet. Designated rooms, service with restrictions, supervision.

## BIRMINGHAM

**AmeriSuites (Birmingham/Inverness)** SH
(205) 995-9242. **$100-$150, 14 day notice.** 4686 Hwy 280 E. I-459, exit 19 (US 280), 1.7 mi e. Int corridors. **Pets:** Small, other species. $10 daily fee/pet. Designated rooms, service with restrictions, crate.

**Baymont Inn & Suites Birmingham** SH
(205) 995-9990. **$69-$83.** 513 Cahaba Park Cir. I-459, exit 19 (US 280), 1.2 mi e. Int corridors. **Pets:** Medium. Service with restrictions.

**Best Western Carlton Suites** SH
(205) 940-9990. **$98-$140.** 140 State Farm Pkwy. I-65, exit 255 (Lakeshore Pkwy), just w to Wildwood Pkwy, then just n. Int corridors. **Pets:** Very small, dogs only. $10 daily fee/pet. Designated rooms, service with restrictions, supervision.

**Best Western Mountain Brook** SH
(205) 991-9977. **$70-$200.** 4627 Hwy 280 E. I-459, exit 19 (US 280), 1.4 mi e. Ext corridors. **Pets:** Accepted.

**Days Inn-Birmingham** SH
(205) 324-4510. **$55-$180.** 905 11th Ct W. I-20/59, exit 123, just sw. Ext/int corridors. **Pets:** Accepted.

**Drury Inn & Suites-Birmingham Southwest** SH
(205) 940-9500. **$90-$140.** 160 State Farm Pkwy. I-65, exit 255, 0.5 mi on northwest frontage road. Int corridors. **Pets:** Accepted.

**Embassy Suites Birmingham** LH
(205) 879-7400. **$139-$219.** 2300 Woodcrest Pl. Just n of jct US 31 and 280, exit 21st Ave southbound, then 0.3 mi s. Int corridors. **Pets:** Accepted.

**Holiday Inn-Airport** SH
(205) 591-6900. **$80-$89.** 5000 Richard Arrington Blvd. I-20/59, exit 129, just s. Int corridors. **Pets:** Accepted.

**Homestead Studio Suites Hotel-Birmingham/Perimeter Park South** SH
(205) 967-3800. **$44-$64.** 12 Perimeter Park S. I-459, exit 19 (US 280), 0.5 mi e, then just s. Ext corridors. **Pets:** $25 daily fee/pet. Service with restrictions, supervision.

**Homewood Suites by Hilton** SH
(205) 995-9823. **$129-$169.** 215 Inverness Center Dr. I-459, exit 19 (US 280), 1.8 mi e, then just s. Int corridors. **Pets:** Accepted.

**Pickwick Hotel & Conference Center** SH
(205) 933-9555. **$88.** 1023 20th St S. 1.5 mi s of downtown (Five Points area). Int corridors. **Pets:** Other species. $75 one-time fee/room. Service with restrictions, supervision.

**Residence Inn By Marriott** SH
(205) 991-8686. **$134.** 3 Green Hill Pkwy. I-459, exit 19 (US 280), 2 mi e. Ext corridors. **Pets:** Accepted.

**Sheraton Birmingham Hotel** LH
(205) 324-5000. **$99-$209.** 2101 Richard Arrington Blvd N. I-20/59, exit 22nd St. Int corridors. **Pets:** Accepted.

**The Tutwiler-A Wyndham Historic Hotel** LH
(205) 322-2100. **$119-$185.** 2021 Park Pl N. Downtown. Int corridors. **Pets:** Accepted.

## CALERA

**Holiday Inn Express** SH
(205) 668-3641. **$65-$95.** 357 Hwy 304. I-65, exit 231, just se. Ext corridors. **Pets:** Accepted.

## HOMEWOOD

**La Quinta Inn & Suites Birmingham (Homewood)** SH
(205) 290-0150. **$86-$117.** 60 State Farm Pkwy. I-65, exit 255, 0.9 mi on northwest frontage road. Int corridors. **Pets:** Medium. Service with restrictions.

**Microtel** SH
(205) 945-5550. **$35-$65.** 251 Summit Pkwy. I-65, exit 256 northbound; exit 256A southbound, just w. Int corridors. **Pets:** Other species. $15 one-time fee/room. Service with restrictions, supervision.

**Ramada Inn** SH
(205) 916-0464. **$49-$199, 30 day notice.** 226 Summit Pkwy. I-65, exit 256 northbound; exit 256A southbound, just w. Int corridors. **Pets:** Very small. $25 one-time fee/pet. Service with restrictions, supervision.

**Red Roof Inn** M
(205) 942-9414. **$43-$58.** 151 Vulcan Rd. I-65, exit 256 northbound; exit 256A southbound, just nw. Ext corridors. **Pets:** Accepted.

**▲▲▲ ▼▼▼▼ Residence Inn by Marriott 🆂🅷**
(205) 943-0044. **$95-$165.** 50 State Farm Pkwy. I-65, exit 255, 1 mi on northwest frontage road. Int corridors. **Pets:** Accepted.
🆂🅰🆅🅴 ⑤ ✕ ⑤ 🅱 🖃 ⌇ ✕

**▼▼ ▼▼ Super 8 Motel 🆂🅷**
(205) 945-9888. **$47-$53.** 140 Vulcan Rd. I-65, exit 256 northbound; exit 256A southbound, just nw. Int corridors. **Pets:** Medium, other species. $5 daily fee/pet. Service with restrictions.
🅰🆂🅺 ⑤ ✕ 🅱 🖃

**▼▼▼▼ TownePlace Suites by Marriott 🆂🅷**
(205) 943-0114. **$75-$119.** 500 Wildwood Cir. I-65, exit 255, 0.6 mi w, then just n. Int corridors. **Pets:** Accepted.
🅰🆂🅺 ⑤ ✕ 🅼 🖃 🅱 🖃 ⌇

# HOOVER

**▼▼▼▼ AmeriSuites (Birmingham/Riverchase) 🆂🅷**
(205) 988-8444. **$119-$129.** 2980 John Hawkins Pkwy. I-459, exit 13, 0.5 mi s on US 31, then 0.8 mi w on SR 150. Int corridors. **Pets:** Small. $10 daily fee/room. Designated rooms, service with restrictions, supervision.
🅰🆂🅺 ⑤ ✕ 🖃 🅱 🖃 ⌇

**▲▲▲ ▼▼▼▼ La Quinta Inn & Suites Birmingham (Hoover/Riverchase) 🆂🅷**
(205) 403-0096. **$81-$110.** 120 Riverchase Pkwy E. I-65, exit 247 (Valleydale Rd), just w. Int corridors. **Pets:** Medium. No service.
🆂🅰🆅🅴 ✕ 🖃 🅱 🖃 ⌇

**▲▲▲ ▼▼▼ ▼▼▼ The Wynfrey Hotel 🅻🅷 🐾**
(205) 987-1600. **$169-$255.** 1000 Riverchase Galleria. I-459, exit 13 (US 31), adjacent to the Riverchase Galleria. Int corridors. **Pets:** $150 deposit/pet. Service with restrictions.
🆂🅰🆅🅴 ⑤ ✕ 🖃 🅱 🖃 🅸🅸 ⌇ ✕

# IRONDALE

**▼▼▼▼ Best Western Rime Garden Inn & Suites 🆂🅷**
(205) 951-1200. **$99-$129, 7 day notice.** 5320 Beacon Dr. I-20, exit 133 westbound, just sw. Ext corridors. **Pets:** Accepted.
🅰🆂🅺 ⑤ ✕ 🅱 🖃 🅸🅸 ⌇

# LEEDS

**▲▲▲ ▼▼▼ Days Inn of Leeds 🅼**
(205) 699-9833. **$54-$60.** 1838 Ashville Rd. I-20, exit 144A eastbound; exit 144B westbound, just s. Ext corridors. **Pets:** Medium. $7 daily fee/pet. Service with restrictions.
🆂🅰🆅🅴 ⑤ ✕ 🅱 ⌇

# MOODY

**▼▼ ▼▼ Super 8 Motel 🅼**
(205) 640-7091. **$67-$78.** 2451 Moody Pkwy. I-20, exit 144, 1 mi n on US 411. Ext corridors. **Pets:** Accepted.
🅰🆂🅺 ⑤ ✕ 🅱

# ONEONTA

**▲▲▲ ▼▼▼ Best Western Colonial Inn 🆂🅷**
(205) 274-2200. **$60-$70, 14 day notice.** 293 Valley Rd. On SR 75, 0.5 mi n of jct US 231. Ext corridors. **Pets:** Accepted.
🆂🅰🆅🅴 ⑤ ✕ 🖃 🅱 🖃 ⌇

# PELHAM

**▲▲▲ ▼▼▼ Comfort Inn 🆂🅷**
(205) 444-9200. **$79-$160, 7 day notice.** 110 Cahaba Valley Pkwy. I-65, exit 246, just nw. Ext corridors. **Pets:** Small. $75 one-time fee/room. Designated rooms, no service, supervision.
🆂🅰🆅🅴 ⑤ ✕ 🅱 🖃 ⌇

# TRUSSVILLE

**▼▼ ▼▼ Jameson Inn 🆂🅷**
(205) 661-9323. **$54-$104.** 4730 Norrell Dr. I-59, exit 141, just e on Chalkville Rd, then just n. Ext corridors. **Pets:** Very small, other species. $10 daily fee/room. Service with restrictions, supervision.
🅰🆂🅺 ✕ 🖃 🅱 🖃 ⌇

---

# END METROPOLITAN AREA

# BOAZ

**▼▼ ▼▼ Days Inn 🆂🅷**
(256) 593-0000. **$49-$75.** 12960 US Hwy 431 S. On US 431, 1 mi s of jct SR 168. Ext corridors. **Pets:** Accepted.
🅰🆂🅺 ✕ 🅱 🖃

**▼▼ ▼▼ Key West Inn 🆂🅷**
(256) 593-0800. **$50-$125.** 10535 SR 168. 0.5 mi w of jct US 431. Ext corridors. **Pets:** Medium. $5 daily fee/pet. Service with restrictions, crate.
🅰🆂🅺 ⑤ ✕ 🅱 🖃

# CHICKASAW

**▼▼ ▼▼ America's Best Inn 🅼**
(251) 457-4006. **$59-$99.** 370 W Lee St. I-65, exit 10, just e. Ext corridors. **Pets:** Accepted.
✕ 🅱 🖃 ⌇

# CHILDERSBURG

**▲▲▲ ▼▼▼ Days Inn 🆂🅷**
(256) 378-6007. **$60-$250.** 33669 US Hwy 280. 0.8 mi s of jct SR 76. Ext corridors. **Pets:** Accepted.
🆂🅰🆅🅴 ⑤ ✕ 🅱 🖃 ⌇

# CLANTON

**▲▲▲ ▼▼▼▼ Best Western Inn 🆂🅷**
(205) 280-1006. **$75-$85, 5 day notice.** 801 Bradberry Ln. I-65, exit 205, 0.5 mi e. Ext corridors. **Pets:** Accepted.
🆂🅰🆅🅴 ✕ 🖃 🅱 🖃 ⌇

**▲▲▲ ▼▼▼ GuestHouse International Inn 🆂🅷**
(205) 280-0306. **$54-$66.** 946 Lake Mitchell Rd. I-65, exit 208, just w. Ext corridors. **Pets:** Medium, other species. $20 deposit/pet. Service with restrictions, supervision.
🆂🅰🆅🅴 ⑤ ✕ 🅱 🖃 ⌇

# CULLMAN

**▲▲▲ ▼▼▼▼ Best Western Fairwinds Inn 🆂🅷**
(256) 737-5009. **$53-$98.** 1917 Commerce Ave NW. I-65, exit 310, just e. Ext corridors. **Pets:** Small. $9 daily fee/room. Designated rooms, service with restrictions, supervision.
🆂🅰🆅🅴 ⑤ ✕ 🅱 🖃 ⌇

**▼▼ ▼▼ Comfort Inn 🆂🅷**
(256) 734-1240. **$80-$120.** 5917 Alabama Hwy 157 NW. I-65, exit 310, just e. Ext corridors. **Pets:** Small. Service with restrictions, supervision.
🅰🆂🅺 ⑤ ✕ 🅱 🖃 ⌇

**Days Inn** SH
(256) 739-3800. **$60-$80.** 1841 4th St SW. I-65, exit 308, just e. Ext corridors. **Pets:** Other species. $5 daily fee/room. Service with restrictions.

## DECATUR

**Comfort Inn & Suites** SH
(256) 355-1999. **$70-$90.** 2212 Danville Rd SW. SR 67, jct Beltline Rd SW. Int corridors. **Pets:** Accepted.

**Holiday Inn Hotel & Suites** SH
(256) 355-3150. **$51-$175.** 1101 6th Ave NE. Just w of jct US 31, 72A and SR 20. Ext/int corridors. **Pets:** Medium. $25 one-time fee/room. Designated rooms, service with restrictions, supervision.

**Jameson Inn** SH
(256) 355-2229. **$54-$104.** 2120 Jameson Pl SW. SR 67, 1.6 mi s of jct US 72A, 3.9 mi n of jct US 31. Ext corridors. **Pets:** Very small, other species. $10 daily fee/room. Service with restrictions, supervision.

**Microtel Inn & Suites** SH
(256) 301-9995. **$49-$75.** 2226 Beltline Rd SW. On SR 67, 4 mi w of jct US 31. Int corridors. **Pets:** Small. $15 one-time fee/pet. Service with restrictions, supervision.

## DEMOPOLIS

**Riverview Inn** M
(334) 289-0690. **$50.** 110 Yacht Basin Dr. 1.8 mi n on S Walnut from jct US 80. Ext corridors. **Pets:** Accepted.

## DOTHAN

**Americas Best Value Inn & Suites** M
(334) 793-5200. **$40-$65.** 2901 Ross Clark Cir. 0.8 mi s of jct US 84; west end of town. Ext corridors. **Pets:** Accepted.

**Comfort Inn** SH
(334) 793-9090. **$86-$107.** 3593 Ross Clark Cir. Just w of jct US 231; northwest part of town. Int corridors. **Pets:** Medium. $10 daily fee/pet. Service with restrictions, supervision.

**Days Inn** M
(334) 793-2550. **$46-$51.** 2841 Ross Clark Cir. 0.9 mi s of jct US 84; west end of town. Ext corridors. **Pets:** $5 daily fee/pet. Service with restrictions, supervision.

**Holiday Inn Express** M
(334) 671-3700. **$63-$75.** 3071 Ross Clark Cir. Just s of jct US 84; west end of town. Ext corridors. **Pets:** Large, other species. $15 one-time fee/room. Service with restrictions.

**Holiday Inn-South** SH
(334) 794-8711. **$75-$105, 10 day notice.** 2195 Ross Clark Cir. Just e of US 231; in south part of town. Ext corridors. **Pets:** Accepted.

**Howard Johnson Express Inn** SH
(334) 792-3339. **$55-$69.** 2244 Ross Clark Cir. 1.4 mi s of jct SR 52; west end of town. Ext corridors. **Pets:** Medium, dogs only. $10 daily fee/pet. Service with restrictions, supervision.

**Motel 6 #1233** M
(334) 793-6013. **$37-$49.** 2907 Ross Clark Cir. 0.8 mi s of jct US 84; west end of town. Ext corridors. **Pets:** Accepted.

**Quality Inn** M
(334) 794-6601. **$65-$75.** 3053 Ross Clark Cir. Just s of jct US 84, west end of town. Ext corridors. **Pets:** Accepted.

## ENTERPRISE

**Comfort Inn** SH
(334) 393-2304. **$70.** 615 Boll Weevil Cir. On US 84 Bypass. Ext corridors. **Pets:** Other species. $25 one-time fee/pet. Designated rooms, service with restrictions, supervision.

## EUFAULA

**Eufaula Comfort Suites** SH
(334) 616-0114. **$72-$90, 14 day notice.** 12 Paul Lee Pkwy. 1.7 mi s on US 431 from jct US 82 E, then just e. Int corridors. **Pets:** Other species. $25 one-time fee/room. Service with restrictions, supervision.

**Jameson Inn** M
(334) 687-7747. **$54-$104.** 136 Towne Center Blvd. On US 431, 1 mi s of US 82 E. Ext corridors. **Pets:** Very small, other species. $10 daily fee/room. Service with restrictions, supervision.

## EVERGREEN

**Comfort Inn** M
(251) 578-4701. **$59-$108.** 1671 Ted Bates Rd. I-65, exit 96, just w. Ext corridors. **Pets:** Medium. $10 daily fee/pet. Designated rooms, service with restrictions, supervision.

**Days Inn of Evergreen** M
(251) 578-2100. **$55-$70.** Rt 2. I-65, exit 96, just w. Ext corridors. **Pets:** Accepted.

## FAIRHOPE

**Key West Inn** M
(251) 990-7373. **$69-$99.** 231 S Greeno Rd. On US 98, 1.9 mi s of jct SR 104. Ext corridors. **Pets:** Accepted.

## FLORENCE

**Jameson Inn** SH
(256) 764-5326. **$54-$104.** 115 Ana Dr. On US 43/72, just nw of jct SR 133 (Cox Creek Pkwy). Ext corridors. **Pets:** Very small, other species. $10 daily fee/room. Service with restrictions, supervision.

**Knights Inn Florence** M
(256) 766-2620. **$50-$90.** 1915 Florence Blvd. On US 72. Ext corridors. **Pets:** Very small. $10 one-time fee/room. No service, supervision.

**Super 8 Motel** M
(256) 757-2167. **$47-$59.** 101 Hwy 72 & 43 E. 3.8 mi e on US 43/72 from jct SR 133 (Cox Creek Pkwy). Ext corridors. **Pets:** Medium. $10 deposit/pet. Service with restrictions, crate.

# FOLEY

**Holiday Inn Express** SH
(251) 943-9100. **$63-$168.** 2682 S McKenzie St. On SR 59, 1.9 mi s of jct US 98. Ext corridors. **Pets:** Small, other species. $20 one-time fee/room. Service with restrictions, crate.

**Key West Inn** M
(251) 943-1241. **$49-$129.** 2520 S McKenzie St. On SR 59, 1.8 mi s of jct US 98. Ext corridors. **Pets:** Medium. $10 daily fee/pet. Designated rooms, service with restrictions, supervision.

# FORT PAYNE

**Econo Lodge** M ☃
(256) 845-4013. **$55-$65.** 1412 Glenn Blvd SW. I-59, exit 218, just w. Ext corridors. **Pets:** Medium, other species. $10 daily fee/room. Designated rooms, service with restrictions, supervision.

# GADSDEN

**Motel 6 #1495** SH
(256) 543-1105. **$40-$52.** 1600 Rainbow Dr. I-759, exit 4A, 0.8 mi s on US 411. Ext corridors. **Pets:** Accepted.

# GREENVILLE

**Days Inn** M
(334) 382-3118. **$55-$80.** 946 Fort Dale Rd. I-65, exit 130, just s on SR 185. Ext corridors. **Pets:** Other species. $10 daily fee/pet. Service with restrictions, supervision.

**Jameson Inn** M
(334) 382-6300. **$54-$104.** 71 Jameson Ln. I-65, exit 130, just n on SR 185, then just w on Cahaba Rd. Ext corridors. **Pets:** Very small, other species. $10 daily fee/room. Service with restrictions, supervision.

# GULF SHORES

**La Quinta Inn** SH
(251) 967-3500. **$60-$309.** 213 W Fort Morgan Rd. On SR 180, just w of jct SR 59. Int corridors. **Pets:** Accepted.

# GUNTERSVILLE

**Super 8 Motel-Guntersville** M
(256) 582-8444. **$44-$49.** 14341 Hwy 431 S. On US 431, 2 mi s of jct SR 69. Ext corridors. **Pets:** Accepted.

# HAMILTON

**Days Inn** SH
(205) 921-1790. **$50-$63.** 1849 Military St S. US 78, exit 14, 1 mi n, then 1 mi w on US 43. Ext corridors. **Pets:** Other species. $10 daily fee/pet. Service with restrictions, supervision.

**Econo Lodge Inn & Suites** SH
(205) 921-7831. **$59-$64.** 2031 Military St S. US 78, exit 14, 1 mi n, then 1 mi n on US 43. Ext corridors. **Pets:** Accepted.

# HUNTSVILLE

**Americas Best Inn** M
(256) 539-9671. **$59-$79.** 1304 N Memorial Pkwy. I-565, exit 19B, 0.5 mi n on US 231/431, Cook Ave exit. Ext corridors. **Pets:** Very small. Designated rooms, service with restrictions, supervision.

**Baymont Inn & Suites Huntsville** SH
(256) 830-8999. **$78-$94.** 4890 University Dr SE. I-565, exit 14B, 2.6 mi n on Research Park Blvd, then 1 mi e on US 72. Int corridors. **Pets:** Medium. Service with restrictions.

**Holiday Inn Express Hotel & Suites** SH
(256) 721-1000. **$69-$79.** 3808 University Dr. I-565, exit 17A, just e. Int corridors. **Pets:** Small. $25 one-time fee/room. Service with restrictions, supervision.

**La Quinta Inn Huntsville (Research Park)** SH
(256) 830-2070. **$76-$90.** 4870 University Dr NW. I-565, exit 14B, 2.6 mi n on Research Park Blvd, then 1 mi e on US 72. Ext corridors. **Pets:** Medium. Service with restrictions.

**La Quinta Inn Huntsville (Space Center)** SH
(256) 533-0756. **$74-$86.** 3141 University Dr (Hwy 72). I-565, exit 17A, 1.1 mi n on SR 53 (Jordan Ln), then 0.6 mi e on US 72. Ext corridors. **Pets:** Medium. Service with restrictions.

**Select Hotel by Holiday Inn** LH
(256) 533-1400. **$100-$219.** 401 Williams Ave SW. Just w of Church St; downtown. Int corridors. **Pets:** Large. $25 one-time fee/room. Designated rooms, no service, crate.

# JASPER

**Jameson Inn** SH
(205) 387-7710. **$54-$104.** 1100 Hwy 118. SR 118, 1.8 mi w of jct SR 69. Ext corridors. **Pets:** Very small, other species. $10 daily fee/room. Service with restrictions, supervision.

# MADISON

**Motel 6–1087** M
(256) 772-7479. **$39-$51.** 8995 Madison Blvd. I-565, exit 8, just n on Wall Triana Hwy, then just w. Ext corridors. **Pets:** Accepted.

# MOBILE

**Americas Best Value Inn & Suites** M
(251) 344-2121. **$40-$75.** 162 W I-65 Service Rd. I-65, exit 4, just w on Dauphin St, then 0.5 mi s. Ext corridors. **Pets:** Accepted.

**Drury Inn-Mobile** SH
(251) 344-7700. **$70-$113.** 824 W I-65 Service Rd S. I-65, exit 3 (Airport Blvd), just w, then just s on service road. Int corridors. **Pets:** Accepted.

**Econo Lodge Mobile** SH
(251) 343-4911. **$52-$62.** 156 Beltline Hwy S. I-65, exit 4, just w on Dauphin St, then 0.5 mi s. Int corridors. **Pets:** Accepted.

**Family Inns of America** M
(251) 344-5500. **$37-$75.** 900 W I-65 Service Rd S. I-65, exit 3 (Airport Blvd), just w, then just s. Ext corridors. **Pets:** Accepted.

**Holiday Inn-Bellingrath Gardens** SH
(251) 666-5600. **$84-$111.** 5465 Hwy 90 W. I-10, exit 15B, just e on US 90, then just s on Coca Cola Rd. Int corridors. **Pets:** Accepted.

**◆◆◆ ▼▼ La Quinta Inn Mobile Ⓜ**
(251) 343-4051. **$74-$90.** 816 W I-65 Service Rd S. I-65, exit 3 (Airport Blvd), just w, then just s. Ext/int corridors. **Pets:** Medium. Service with restrictions.
ⓈⒶⓋⒺ ⓧ 🛏 💻 ⌖

**▼ Motel 6 #608 Ⓜ**
(251) 660-1483. **$42-$55.** 5488 Inn Rd. I-10, exit 15B, just e on US 90, then just n. Ext corridors. **Pets:** Accepted.
Ⓢ🄳 ⓧ Ⓖ 🛏 ⌖

**◆◆◆ ▼ Olsson Motel Ⓜ**
(251) 661-5331. **$65, 15 day notice.** 4137 Government Blvd. I-65, exit 1, 2 mi w on US 90. Ext corridors. **Pets:** Accepted.
ⓈⒶⓋⒺ Ⓢ🄳 ⓧ 🛏

**▼▼▼ Quality Inn 🆂🅷**
(251) 343-4949. **$52-$149.** 150 S Beltline Hwy. I-65, exit 4, just w on Dauphin St, then 0.4 mi s on West I65 Service Rd. Int corridors. **Pets:** Accepted.
Ⓐ🆂🅺 Ⓢ🄳 ⓧ 🛏 💻 ⌖

**▼▼▼ Ramada Civic Center 🆂🅷**
(251) 433-6923. **$79-$109, 3 day notice.** 255 Church St. I-10, exit 26B eastbound, just w on Church St; westbound, just w on Government St to Joachim St, then just s, downtown. Ext/int corridors. **Pets:** Accepted.
Ⓐ🆂🅺 Ⓢ🄳 ⓧ 🛏 💻 🍴 ⌖ ⓧ

**▼▼▼ Ramada Inn I-65 Ⓜ**
(251) 342-3220. **$65-$85.** 850 W I-65 Service Rd S. I-65, exit 3, just w on Airport Rd, then just s on service road. Ext corridors. **Pets:** Accepted.
Ⓐ🆂🅺 Ⓢ🄳 ⓧ 🛏 💻 🍴 ⌖ ⓧ

**▼▼ Red Roof Inn North Ⓜ**
(251) 476-2004. **$46-$59.** 33 I-65 Service Rd E. I-65, exit 4, just e on Dauphin St, just s on Springdale Blvd, then just w. Ext corridors. **Pets:** Accepted.
ⓧ

**▼▼ Red Roof Inn-South Ⓜ**
(251) 666-1044. **$46-$65.** 5450 Coca Cola Rd. I-10, exit 15B, just e on US 90. Ext corridors. **Pets:** Accepted.
ⓧ Ⓐ Ⓖ

**▼▼▼ Residence Inn by Marriott Mobile 🆂🅷**
(251) 304-0570. **$119-$159.** 950 W I-65 Service Rd S. I-65, exit 3 (Airport Blvd), just w, then 0.4 mi s. Int corridors. **Pets:** Accepted.
Ⓐ🆂🅺 ⓧ Ⓖ🅼 Ⓖ 🛏 💻 ⌖ ⓧ

**▼▼▼ SuiteOne of Mobile Ⓜ**
(251) 662-8080. **$49-$59.** 5498 Inn Rd. I-10, exit 15B, just e on US 90, then just n. Ext corridors. **Pets:** Other species. $50 one-time fee/pet. Service with restrictions.
Ⓐ🆂🅺 Ⓢ🄳 ⓧ Ⓖ 🛏 💻

**▼▼▼ TownePlace Suites by Marriott 🆂🅷**
(251) 345-9588. **$59-$149.** 1075 Montlimar Dr. I-65, exit 3 (Airport Blvd), 0.5 mi w, then 0.5 mi s. Int corridors. **Pets:** Other species. $75 one-time fee/room. Service with restrictions.
Ⓐ🆂🅺 Ⓢ🄳 ⓧ 🛏 💻 ⌖

## MONROEVILLE

**◆◆◆ ▼▼ America's Best Value Inn Ⓜ**
(251) 743-3154. **$50-$150.** 50 Hwy 21 S. On SR 21, just s of jct US 84. Ext corridors. **Pets:** Accepted.
ⓈⒶⓋⒺ Ⓢ🄳 ⓧ 🛏

**◆◆◆ ▼▼▼ Holiday Inn Express 🆂🅷**
(251) 743-3333. **$80-$250.** 120 Hwy 21 S. On SR 21, just s of jct US 84. Int corridors. **Pets:** Accepted.
ⓈⒶⓋⒺ Ⓢ🄳 ⓧ Ⓖ🅼 Ⓖ 🛏 💻 ⌖

## MONTGOMERY

**▼▼ America's Best Inns 🆂🅷**
(334) 270-9199. **$66-$99, 3 day notice.** 5135 Carmichael Rd. I-85, exit 6, just s on Eastern Blvd, then just w. Int corridors. **Pets:** Other species. Service with restrictions, supervision.
Ⓐ🆂🅺 ⓧ Ⓐ Ⓖ 🛏 💻 ⌖

**◆◆◆ ▼▼▼ Baymont Inn & Suites Montgomery 🆂🅷**
(334) 277-6000. **$76-$89.** 5225 Carmichael Rd. I-85, exit 6, just s on Eastern Blvd, then just w. Int corridors. **Pets:** Medium. Service with restrictions.
ⓈⒶⓋⒺ ⓧ Ⓖ🅼 Ⓐ 🛏 💻 ⌖

**◆◆◆ ▼▼▼ Best Western Monticello Inn Ⓜ**
(334) 277-4442. **$59.** 5837 Monticello Dr. I-85, exit 6, just n on Eastern Blvd, then just e. Ext corridors. **Pets:** Accepted.
ⓈⒶⓋⒺ Ⓢ🄳 ⓧ 🛏 💻 ⌖

**◆◆◆ ▼▼▼ Days Inn Midtown Ⓜ**
(334) 269-9611. **$54-$74, 5 day notice.** 2625 Zelda Rd. I-85, exit 3, just s on Ann St. Ext corridors. **Pets:** $5 daily fee/pet. Service with restrictions, supervision.
ⓈⒶⓋⒺ Ⓢ🄳 ⓧ 🛏 💻 ⌖

**▼▼▼▼ Drury Inn & Suites-Montgomery 🆂🅷**
(334) 273-1101. **$80-$130.** 1124 Eastern Blvd. I-85, exit 6, just n. Int corridors. **Pets:** Accepted.
Ⓐ🆂🅺 ⓧ 🛏 💻 ⌖

**▼▼▼ Econo Lodge Ⓜ**
(334) 284-3400. **$55-$60.** 4135 Troy Hwy. On US 82/231, 0.7 mi e of jct South and East blvds. Ext corridors. **Pets:** Accepted.
Ⓐ🆂🅺 ⓧ 🛏 💻 ⌖

**◆◆◆ ▼▼▼ Embassy Suites Montgomery Conference Center 🅻🅷**
(334) 269-5055. **$99-$219.** 300 Tallapoosa St. Between Motton and Commerce sts; in historic downtown. Int corridors. **Pets:** $25 one-time fee/room. Service with restrictions, crate.
ⓈⒶⓋⒺ ⓧ Ⓖ🅼 Ⓐ Ⓖ 🛏 💻 🍴 ⌖ ⓧ

**▼▼▼ GuestHouse International Hotel & Suites 🆂🅷**
(334) 264-2231. **$79.** 120 Madison Ave. Corner of N Lawrence St; in historic downtown. Int corridors. **Pets:** Accepted.
Ⓐ🆂🅺 Ⓢ🄳 ⓧ Ⓖ 🛏 💻 🍴 ⌖

**▼▼▼ Holiday Inn-East 🆂🅷**
(334) 272-0370. **$65-$79.** 1185 Eastern Bypass. I-85, exit 6, just n. Ext/int corridors. **Pets:** Accepted.
Ⓐ🆂🅺 Ⓢ🄳 ⓧ Ⓖ🅼 Ⓐ Ⓖ 🛏 💻 🍴 ⌖ ⓧ

**◆◆◆ ▼▼▼▼ La Quinta Inn Montgomery Ⓜ**
(334) 271-1620. **$76-$86.** 1280 East Blvd. I-85, exit 6, just s. Ext corridors. **Pets:** Medium. Service with restrictions.
ⓈⒶⓋⒺ ⓧ 🛏 💻 ⌖

**▼ Motel 6 #149 Ⓜ**
(334) 277-6748. **$45-$57.** 1051 Eastern Blvd. I-85, exit 6, just n. Ext corridors. **Pets:** Accepted.
Ⓢ🄳 ⓧ ⌖

**▼▼ Quality Inn & Suites–Governors House & Covention Center 🆂🅷**
(334) 288-2800. **Call for rates.** 2705 E South Blvd. I-85, exit 6, 3.7 mi s on East Blvd. Ext corridors. **Pets:** Medium. $35 one-time fee/pet. Service with restrictions, supervision.
ⓧ 🛏 💻 🍴 ⌖

**◆◆◆ ▼▼▼▼ Residence Inn by Marriott 🆂🅷**
(334) 270-3300. **$144-$164.** 1200 Hilmar Ct. I-85, exit 6, just s on Eastern Blvd, then just e. Ext/int corridors. **Pets:** Accepted.
ⓈⒶⓋⒺ Ⓢ🄳 ⓧ Ⓐ Ⓖ 🛏 💻 ⌖ ⓧ

▼▼▼ **TownePlace Suites by Marriott** SH
(334) 396-5505. **$94-$119.** 5047 Townplace Dr. I-85, exit 6, just s on Eastern Blvd, then just w on Carmichael Rd. Int corridors. **Pets:** Accepted.

⊠ 👍M 🖊 👍 🖥 💻 🏊

## OPELIKA

▼▼ **Days Inn Opelika** M
(334) 749-5080. **$54-$64, 14 day notice.** 1014 Anand Ave. I-85, exit 62, just e on US 280. Ext corridors. **Pets:** Accepted.

ASK 🛏 ⊠ 🖊 💻 🏊

## OXFORD

🔶 ▼▼▼ **Best Western-Anniston/Oxford** SH
(256) 831-3410. **$49-$89.** US 78 & SR 21. I-20, exit 185, just n. Ext corridors. **Pets:** Accepted.

SAVE 🛏 ⊠ 🖊 💻 🍴 🏊

▼▼ **Jameson Inn Oxford** M
(256) 825-2170. **$54-$104.** 161 Colonial Dr. I-20, exit 188, just n, then w. Ext corridors. **Pets:** Very small, other species. $10 daily fee/room. Service with restrictions, supervision.

ASK ⊠ 🖊 💻 🏊

▼ **Motel 6 #542** M
(256) 831-5463. **$39-$49.** 202 Grace St. I-20, exit 185, just s. Ext corridors. **Pets:** Accepted.

🛏 ⊠ 🖊 🏊

## OZARK

🔶 ▼▼▼ **All American Ozark Inn** M 🐾
(334) 774-5166. **$53-$58.** 2064 Hwy 231 S. 1 mi s of jct SR 249. Ext corridors. **Pets:** Medium, other species. Service with restrictions, crate.

SAVE 🛏 ⊠ 🖊 💻 🏊

▼▼ **Jameson Inn** M
(334) 774-0233. **$54-$104.** 1360 S US Hwy 231. 0.3 mi s of jct SR 249. Ext corridors. **Pets:** Very small, other species. $10 daily fee/room. Service with restrictions, supervision.

ASK ⊠ 👍M 🖊 💻 🏊

▼▼▼ **Quality Inn & Suites-Ozark/Ft Rucker** SH
(334) 774-7300. **$70.** 858 US 231 S. Just n of jct SR 249. Ext corridors. **Pets:** Other species. $25 one-time fee/pet. Service with restrictions.

ASK 🛏 ⊠ 🖊 💻 🍴 🏊

## PRATTVILLE

▼▼ **Jameson Inn** SH
(334) 361-6463. **$54-$104.** 104 Jameson Ct. I-65, exit 179, 1 mi w. Ext corridors. **Pets:** Very small, other species. $10 daily fee/room. Service with restrictions, supervision.

ASK ⊠ 🖊 💻 🏊

## PRICEVILLE

🔶 ▼▼▼ **Comfort Inn** SH
(256) 355-1037. **$90.** 3239 Point Mallard Pkwy. I-65, exit 334, just w. Int corridors. **Pets:** Small. $10 daily fee/room. Service with restrictions, supervision.

SAVE 🛏 ⊠ 🖊 💻 🏊

▼▼ **Days Inn** SH 🐾
(256) 355-3297. **$69-$89.** 63 Marco Dr. I-65, exit 334, just e. Ext corridors. **Pets:** Dogs only. $10 daily fee/room. Service with restrictions, crate.

ASK 🛏 ⊠ 🖊 💻 🏊

## SCOTTSBORO

▼▼ **Americas Best Value Inn & Suites** SH
(256) 259-4300. **$50-$59.** 46 Micah Way. On US 72, just s of jct SR 35. Ext corridors. **Pets:** Accepted.

ASK ⊠ 🖊 💻 🏊

▼▼ **Jameson Inn** SH
(256) 574-6666. **$54-$104.** 208 Micah Way. On US 72, just s of jct SR 35. Ext corridors. **Pets:** Very small, other species. $10 daily fee/room. Service with restrictions, supervision.

ASK ⊠ 🖊 💻 🏊

## SELMA

▼▼ **Comfort Inn** SH
(334) 875-5700. **$60-$70.** 1812 Hwy 14 E. Jct SR 14 and US 80 Bypass. Int corridors. **Pets:** Accepted.

ASK 🛏 ⊠ 🖊 💻 🏊

▼▼ **Jameson Inn** M
(334) 874-8600. **$54-$104.** 2420 Broad St. On SR 22, just n of jct US 80. Ext corridors. **Pets:** Very small, other species. $10 daily fee/pet. Service with restrictions, supervision.

ASK ⊠ 🖊 💻 🏊

▼▼ **Ramada Inn** SH
(334) 872-0461. **$60-$65.** 1710 W Highland Ave. On US 80. Ext corridors. **Pets:** Other species. $20 daily fee/pet. Service with restrictions, supervision.

ASK 🛏 ⊠ 🖊 🖊 💻 🍴 🏊

## STEVENSON

🔶 ▼ **Budget Host Inn** M
(256) 437-2215. **$45-$50, 3 day notice.** 42973 US Hwy 72. On US 72, just s of CR 85. Ext corridors. **Pets:** Very small. $5 daily fee/pet. Designated rooms, service with restrictions, supervision.

SAVE 🛏 ⊠ 🖊 💻

## SYLACAUGA

▼▼ **Jameson Inn** SH
(256) 245-4141. **$54-$104.** 89 Gene Stewart Blvd. Off US 280, just s. Ext corridors. **Pets:** Very small, other species. $10 daily fee/room. Service with restrictions, supervision.

ASK ⊠ 🖊 💻 🏊

## TROY

▼▼ **Holiday Inn Express** M
(334) 670-0012. **$76.** Hwy 231 at US 29. On US 231, just n of jct US 29. Ext corridors. **Pets:** Accepted.

ASK 🛏 ⊠ 🖊 💻

🔶 ▼▼▼ **Holiday Inn of Troy** SH
(334) 566-1150. **$75-$89.** Hwy 231 at US 29. On US 231, just n of jct US 29. Ext corridors. **Pets:** Accepted.

SAVE 🛏 ⊠ 🖊 💻 🍴 🏊

## TUSCALOOSA

▼▼ **Americas Best Value Inn** SH
(205) 556-7950. **$45-$145.** 3501 McFarland Blvd. I-59/20, exit 73, just ne on US 82. Ext corridors. **Pets:** Very small. Designated rooms, service with restrictions, supervision.

ASK 🛏 ⊠ 🖊 💻 🏊

▼▼ **Jameson Inn** SH
(205) 345-5018. **$54-$104.** 5021 Oscar Baxter Rd. I-59/20, exit 71A, just s. Ext corridors. **Pets:** Very small, other species. $10 daily fee/room. Service with restrictions, supervision.

ASK ⊠ 🖊 💻 🏊

▼▼▼ **La Quinta Inn Tuscaloosa** 🆂🅷
(205) 349-3270. **$67-$83.** 4122 McFarland Blvd E. I-59/20, exit 73, just
sw on US 82. Ext corridors. **Pets:** Medium. Service with restrictions.

ⒶⓈ🄺 ⊠ 🛈 🖥 🏊

🔺🔺🔺 ▼ **Masters Inn** Ⓜ
(205) 556-2010. **$32-$36.** 3600 McFarland Blvd. I-59/20, exit 73, just
nw on US 82. Ext corridors. **Pets:** Accepted.

🆂🅰🆅🅴 ⊠ 🛈 🏊

▼ **Motel 6 #432** Ⓜ
(205) 759-4942. **$39-$53.** 4700 McFarland Blvd E. I-59/20, exit 73, just
se on US 82. Ext corridors. **Pets:** Accepted.

🆂🅾 ⊠ ♿ 🛈 🏊

# VANCE

▼▼▼ **Wellesley Inn & Suites** 🆂🅷
(205) 556-3606. **$72-$140.** 11170 Will Walker Rd/Daimler Benz Blvd.
I-59/20, exit 89 southbound, just s; exit northbound, 0.8 mi n on
Mercedes Dr, 0.3 mi w, then just s. Int corridors. **Pets:** Accepted.

ⒶⓈ🄺 🆂🅾 ⊠ ♿🄼 ♿ 🛈 🖥

# ALASKA

## ANCHORAGE

**Best Western Barratt Inn** SH ❖
(907) 243-3131. **$79-$189.** 4616 Spenard Rd. International Airport Rd, just ne of jct Jewel Lake and Spenard rds. Ext/int corridors. **Pets:** Other species. $50 deposit/room, $10 daily fee/room. Designated rooms, service with restrictions, crate.

**Comfort Inn Ship Creek** SH
(907) 277-6887. **$79-$249.** 111 W Ship Creek Ave. At 3rd and E sts, 0.3 mi n on E St, across the railway, just e on Ship Creek Ave; downtown. Int corridors. **Pets:** Medium. $10 daily fee/pet. Designated rooms, service with restrictions, supervision.

**Days Inn Downtown** SH
(907) 276-7226. **$69-$250.** 321 E 5th Ave. At Cordova and E 5th Ave; downtown. Ext/int corridors. **Pets:** Other species. $10 daily fee/pet. Designated rooms, service with restrictions, crate.

**Hilton Anchorage** LH
(907) 272-7411. **$99-$329, 3 day notice.** 500 W 3rd Ave. At E St; downtown. Int corridors. **Pets:** Dogs only. $25 daily fee/pet. Service with restrictions, supervision.

**Long House Alaskan Hotel** SH
(907) 243-2133. **$69-$219.** 4335 Wisconsin St. International Airport Rd, 1.5 mi ne on Spenard Rd, nw on Wisconsin St at 43rd Ave, then just e. Int corridors. **Pets:** Large, other species. $50 deposit/room, $10 daily fee/pet. Designated rooms, service with restrictions, supervision.

**Merrill Field Inn** M ❖
(907) 276-4547. **$70-$156.** 420 Sitka St. 1 mi e via US 1 (Glenn Hwy). Ext corridors. **Pets:** Medium. $7 daily fee/pet. Service with restrictions, supervision.

**Microtel Inn & Suites** SH
(907) 245-5002. **$63-$135.** 5205 Northwood Dr. 1.7 mi e of airport. Int corridors. **Pets:** Accepted.

**Millennium Alaskan Hotel Anchorage** LH
(907) 243-2300. **$170-$310.** 4800 Spenard Rd. International Airport Rd, just ne from jct Jewel Lake and Spenard rds. Int corridors. **Pets:** Accepted.

**Motel 6–4216** M
(907) 677-8000. **$58-$135.** 5000 A St. Jct C St and International Airport Rd. Int corridors. **Pets:** Accepted.

**Ramada Anchorage Downtown** SH
(907) 272-7561. **$79-$239.** 115 E 3rd Ave. Jct Barrow St; downtown. Ext/int corridors. **Pets:** Accepted.

**Red Roof Inn** M ❖
(907) 274-1650. **$59-$139.** 1104 E 5th Ave. At Karluk St. Ext/int corridors. **Pets:** Medium, other species. Service with restrictions, supervision.

**Residence Inn by Marriott** SH
(907) 563-9844. **$129-$344.** 1025 E 35th Ave. Corner of US 1 (New Seward Hwy) and 36th Ave. Int corridors. **Pets:** Other species. $10 daily fee/room, $75 one-time fee/room. Service with restrictions.

**Sheraton Anchorage Hotel** LH ❖
(907) 276-8700. **$99-$279.** 401 E 6th Ave. 6th Ave and Denali St. Int corridors. **Pets:** Small, dogs only. Designated rooms, service with restrictions, supervision.

**Super 8 Motel-Anchorage** SH
(907) 276-8884. **$70-$150.** 3501 Minnesota Dr. At 36th Ave, just n of Spenard Rd. Int corridors. **Pets:** Other species. $25 deposit/room. Service with restrictions, supervision.

**Westmark Anchorage** LH
(907) 276-7676. **$109-$219.** 720 W 5th Ave. At G St and W 5th Ave; downtown. Int corridors. **Pets:** Accepted.

## CANTWELL

**Backwoods Lodge** M ❖
(907) 768-2232. **$90-$130, 10 day notice.** Denali Hwy MM 133.8. Parks Hwy, (Milepost 210), just e on Denali Hwy. Ext corridors. **Pets:** Medium. Service with restrictions, supervision.

## DENALI NATIONAL PARK AND PRESERVE

**McKinley Chalet Resort** LH ❖
(907) 683-8200. **$3-$249, 7 day notice.** Milepost 238 (Parks Hwy). Milepost 238.5 on SR 3 (Parks Hwy) Ext corridors. **Pets:** Service with restrictions, supervision.

## EAGLE RIVER

**Eagle River Microtel Inn & Suites** SH
(907) 622-3232. **$60-$140.** 13049 Old Glenn Hwy. Jct Glenn Hwy (SR 1), Eagle River exit, just e, just s. Int corridors. **Pets:** Other species. $10 daily fee/room. Designated rooms, service with restrictions, crate.

**Eagle River Motel** M
(907) 694-5000. **$59-$109, 3 day notice.** 11111 Old Eagle River Rd. Glenn Hwy, exit Eagle River, just e; center. Ext corridors. **Pets:** Dogs only. $7 daily fee/pet. Designated rooms, service with restrictions, crate.

# FAIRBANKS

**▼▼ ▼▼ Best Western Fairbanks Inn SH**
(907) 456-6602. **$72-$160.** 1521 S Cushman St. Just s of Airport Way. Int corridors. **Pets:** Large, other species. $10 daily fee/pet. Designated rooms, service with restrictions, supervision.

ASK S☉ ✕ ⤒M 🛏 🖳 ❙❙

**▲▲▲ ▼▼ ▼▼ Comfort Inn-Chena River SH**
(907) 479-8080. **$79-$179.** 1908 Chena Landings Loop. Airport Way, just n on Peger Rd, then just e on Phillips Field Rd, follow signs in wooded area south of road. Int corridors. **Pets:** Other species. $10 daily fee/pet. Designated rooms, service with restrictions, supervision.

SAVE ✕ ⤒M ⤓ 🛏 🖳 ⤮

**▲▲▲ ▼▼▼▼ Pike's Waterfront Lodge SH**
(907) 456-4500. **$99-$279.** 1850 Hoselton Rd. Jct Airport and Hoselton rds. Ext/int corridors. **Pets:** Accepted.

SAVE ✕ 🛏 🖳 ❙❙ ✕

**▼▼ Regency Fairbanks Hotel SH**
(907) 452-3200. **$99-$250.** 95 10th Ave. Just w of SR 2 (Steese Expwy). Int corridors. **Pets:** Accepted.

✕ 🛏 🖳 ❙❙

**▼▼ Super 8 Motel M**
(907) 451-8888. **$71-$154.** 1909 Airport Way. Airport Way at Wilbur St. Int corridors. **Pets:** Accepted.

ASK S☉ ✕ 🛏

# HAINES

**▲▲▲ ▼▼ Captain's Choice Inc Motel M**
(907) 766-3111. **$86-$172.** 108 2nd Ave N. Jct 2nd Ave and Dalton St. Ext corridors. **Pets:** Other species. $10 one-time fee/room. Service with restrictions, supervision.

SAVE ✕ 🛏 🖳 ℀

# HOMER

**▲▲▲ ▼▼ ▼▼ Best Western Bidarka Inn M**
(907) 235-8148. **$65-$179.** 575 Sterling Hwy. 0.3 mi n on Sterling Hwy (SR 1). Ext/int corridors. **Pets:** Large, other species. $10 daily fee/pet. Designated rooms, service with restrictions, supervision.

SAVE S☉ ✕ 🛏 🖳 ❙❙ ℀

# JUNEAU

**▼▼ Best Western Country Lane Inn M**
(907) 789-5005. **$100-$130.** 9300 Glacier Hwy. Just e off Egan Dr. Ext corridors. **Pets:** Accepted.

ASK S☉ ✕ 🛏 🖳

**▲▲▲ ▼▼ ▼▼ Frontier Suites Airport Hotel SH**
(907) 790-6600. **$89-$159.** 9400 Glacier Hwy. At Juneau International Airport. Ext/int corridors. **Pets:** Medium, dogs only. $50 one-time fee/room. Service with restrictions, crate.

SAVE ✕ ⤒M 🛏 🖳 ❙❙ ✕ ℀

**▼▼ Juneau Super 8 SH**
(907) 789-4858. **$80-$114.** 2295 Trout St. At Juneau International Airport, just nw to Glacier Hwy, then just e. Int corridors. **Pets:** Accepted.

S☉ ✕ ℀

**▲▲▲ ▼▼ Westmark Baranof SH**
(907) 586-2660. **$125-$143.** 127 N Franklin St. At 2nd and Franklin sts; downtown. Int corridors. **Pets:** Accepted.

SAVE ✕ ⤓ 🛏 🖳 ❙❙ ℀

# KETCHIKAN

**▲▲▲ ▼▼▼▼ Best Western Landing SH**
(907) 225-5166. **$145-$207.** 3434 Tongass Ave. Across from the Alaska Marine Hwy ferry terminal. Ext/int corridors. **Pets:** Large, other species. $10 daily fee/pet. Designated rooms, service with restrictions, crate.

SAVE S☉ ✕ 🛏 🖳 ❙❙

**▼▼ Ketchikan Super 8 Motel SH**
(907) 225-9088. **$97-$125.** 2151 Sea Level Dr. From Alaska Marine Hwy ferry terminal, 0.9 mi se to Washington St, then just s; from airport ferry terminal, 1.3 mi se. Int corridors. **Pets:** Accepted.

ASK S☉ ✕ 🛏 ℀

# KODIAK

**▲▲▲ ▼▼ ▼▼ Best Western Kodiak Inn SH**
(907) 486-5712. **$99-$169.** 236 W Rezanof Dr. 0.3 mi w of ferry terminal; center. Ext/int corridors. **Pets:** Accepted.

SAVE S☉ ✕ ⤓ 🛏 🖳 ❙❙ ℀

# MOOSE PASS

**▲▲▲ ▼▼ Trail Lake Lodge M**
(907) 288-3101. **$79-$105.** MM 29.5 Seward Hwy. US 9 (Seward Hwy) at MM 29.5. Ext corridors. **Pets:** Very small, cats only. Designated rooms, no service, supervision.

SAVE S☉ ✕ ❙❙ ℀

# PALMER

**▼▼ Peak Inn Motel M**
(907) 746-5757. **$50-$95, 3 day notice.** 775 W Evergreen Ave. Just w of Glenn Hwy (SR 1). Ext corridors. **Pets:** Medium. $50 deposit/room, $10 daily fee/room. Designated rooms, service with restrictions, supervision.

ASK S☉ 🛏 🖳 ❙❙ ℀

# SITKA

**▼▼ ▼▼ Super 8 Motel-Sitka SH**
(907) 747-8804. **$100-$129.** 404 Sawmill Creek Rd. Just e from corner of Lake St and Halibut Point/Sawmill Creek rds; center. Int corridors. **Pets:** Accepted.

ASK S☉ ✕ ⤓ 🛏

# SKAGWAY

**▲▲▲ ▼▼ Westmark Inn Skagway SH**
(907) 983-6000. **$119.** 3rd & Spring St. Downtown. Ext/int corridors. **Pets:** Accepted.

SAVE S☉ ✕ ⤒M 🛏 🖳 ❙❙ ℀

# SOLDOTNA

**▲▲▲ ▼▼ ▼▼ Alaskan Serenity Bed and Breakfast BB**
(907) 262-6648. **$60-$160, 30 day notice.** 41598 Aksala Ln. Sterling Hwy (SR 1), 1.5 mi e, 1.6 mi n on Mackey Lake Rd, then 0.5 mi e on Denise Lake Rd. Ext/int corridors. **Pets:** $10 daily fee/room. Designated rooms, service with restrictions, supervision.

SAVE ✕ 🛏 🖳 ℀

# TOK

**▲▲▲ ▼▼ ▼▼ Cleft of the Rock Bed & Breakfast CA** 🐾
(907) 883-4219. **$65-$135, 3 day notice.** MM 0.5 Sundog Tr. Jct SR 1 and 2 (Alaskan Hwy), 3 mi w on SR 2 (Alaskan Hwy) to Sundog Tr, then 0.5 mi n. Ext/int corridors. **Pets:** $5 one-time fee/pet. Supervision.

SAVE ✕ 🛏 🖳 ✕ ℀

**▲▲▲ ▼▼ ▼▼ Westmark Inn Tok M**
(907) 883-5174. **$129.** Jct Alaska Hwy & Glenn Hwy. On SR 1; jct SR 2 (Alaskan Hwy). Ext corridors. **Pets:** Accepted.

SAVE S☉ ✕ 🖳 ❙❙

# TRAPPER CREEK

**▼▼ ▼▼ Gate Creek Cabins CA**
(907) 733-1393. **$90-$130, 10 day notice.** Mile 10.5 Petersville Rd. From MM 114 (Parks Hwy), 10.5 mi w at Petersville Rd. Ext corridors. **Pets:** Accepted.

ASK ✕ 🛏 🖳 ✕ ℀ ⊠

## VALDEZ

**AAA ◆◆ Best Western Valdez Harbor Inn SH**
(907) 835-3434. **$82-$140.** 100 N Harbor Dr. Just s at Meals Dr. Int corridors. **Pets:** Medium. $25 one-time fee/pet. Designated rooms, service with restrictions, supervision.

SAVE S🐾 ✕ 🐾 🛢 🖵 ⑪ 🅰

## WASILLA

**AAA ◆◆ Best Western Lake Lucille Inn SH**
(907) 373-1776. **$89-$169.** 1300 W Lake Lucille Dr. George Parks Hwy (SR 3), just w on Hallea Ln; center. Int corridors. **Pets:** Medium. $10 daily fee/pet. Service with restrictions, supervision.

SAVE S🐾 ✕ 🐾 🛢 🖵 ⑪ ✕ 🅰

**AAA ◆◆ Grandview Inn & Suites SH**
(907) 357-7666. **$80-$170.** 2900 E Parks Hwy. 1 mi n of jct Parks Hwy and Fairview Loop exit. Int corridors. **Pets:** Medium. $10 daily fee/room. Designated rooms, service with restrictions, crate.

SAVE S🐾 ✕ 🛢 🖵 ⑪ 🏊

## WILLOW

**◆◆ Alaskan Host Bed & Breakfast BB**
(907) 495-6800. **$90-$115, 14 day notice.** Milepost 66.5 Old Parks Hwy. Parks Hwy, Milepost 66, 1 mi e at Old Parks Hwy. Ext/int corridors. **Pets:** Small, dogs only. $10 daily fee/pet. Service with restrictions, supervision.

✕ 🛢 ✕ 🅰 ☎

# ARIZONA

## AJO

**La Siesta Motel** M
(520) 387-6569. **$53.** 2561 N Ajo-Gila Bend Hwy. On SR 85, 1.8 mi n of town plaza. Ext corridors. **Pets:** Accepted.

## BELLEMONT

**Bellemont Microtel Inn** SH
(928) 556-9599. **$33-$54.** 12380 W Interstate Hwy 40. I-40, exit 185, just n. Int corridors. **Pets:** Small, dogs only. $15 one-time fee/pet. Designated rooms, service with restrictions, supervision.

## BENSON

**Quail Hollow Inn** M
(520) 586-3646. **$65-$90.** 699 N Ocotillo Ave. I-10, exit 304, just s. Ext corridors. **Pets:** $20 deposit/room. Designated rooms, service with restrictions, supervision.

**Super 8 Motel** M
(520) 586-1530. **$50-$109, 3 day notice.** 855 N Ocotillo Ave. I-10, exit 304, just n. Ext corridors. **Pets:** Medium. $40 deposit/pet. Designated rooms, service with restrictions, supervision.

## BISBEE

**Audrey's Inn** CO
(520) 227-6120. **$95-$110.** 20 Brewery Ave. Just ne of Main St; in historic district. Int corridors. **Pets:** Accepted.

**San Jose Lodge** M
(520) 432-5761. **$75-$125, 3 day notice.** 1002 Naco Hwy. 1.5 mi s from jct SR 92. Ext corridors. **Pets:** $10 daily fee/pet. Designated rooms, service with restrictions, supervision.

## BULLHEAD CITY

**Best Western Bullhead City Inn** SH
(928) 754-3000. **$74-$99.** 1126 Hwy 95. 1.8 mi s of Laughlin Bridge. Ext corridors. **Pets:** Medium. $20 one-time fee/room. Service with restrictions, supervision.

**Budget Host Inn** M
(928) 763-1002. **$65-$75.** 1616 Hwy 95. Jct SR 68, 3.2 mi s on SR 95. Int corridors. **Pets:** Small, dogs only. $10 one-time fee/pet. Designated rooms, service with restrictions, supervision.

**Lake Mohave Resort Motel** M
(928) 754-3245. **$85-$115, 3 day notice.** 2690 E Katherine Spur Rd. Jct SR 95, 1.5 mi e on SR 68, 1 mi n, then 5.4 mi e; at Katherine Landing; in Lake Mead National Recreation area. Ext corridors. **Pets:** Large, other species. $10 daily fee/pet. Service with restrictions, supervision.

## CAMP VERDE

**Comfort Inn-Camp Verde** SH
(928) 567-9000. **$59-$139.** 340 N Goswick Way. I-17, exit 287, just e, then just s. Int corridors. **Pets:** Accepted.

**Days Inn & Suites of Camp Verde** SH
(928) 567-3700. **$45-$95.** 1640 W Hwy 260. I-17, exit 287, just e, then just n. Int corridors. **Pets:** Other species. $10 one-time fee/pet. Designated rooms, service with restrictions, supervision.

**Super 8 Motel-Camp Verde** M
(928) 567-2622. **$54-$129.** 1550 W Hwy 260. I-17, exit 287, just e. Int corridors. **Pets:** Accepted.

## CASA GRANDE

**Best Western Casa Grande** SH
(520) 836-1600. **$80-$150.** 665 Via Del Cielo. I-10, exit 194 (SR 287), 1 mi w. Ext corridors. **Pets:** Accepted.

**Holiday Inn Casa Grande** SH
(520) 426-3500. **$69-$99.** 777 N Pinal Ave. I-10, exit 194 (SR 287), 3.9 mi w. Int corridors. **Pets:** Medium. Service with restrictions, supervision.

**Motel 6-1263** M
(520) 836-3323. **$41-$63.** 4965 N Sunland Gin Rd. I-10, exit 200. Ext corridors. **Pets:** Accepted.

**Super 8 Motel** SH
(520) 836-8800. **$55-$150.** 2066 E Florence Blvd. I-10, exit 194 (SR 287), 0.6 mi w. Int corridors. **Pets:** Other species. $10 daily fee/pet. Service with restrictions, supervision.

## CHAMBERS

**Chieftain Inn** M
(928) 688-2754. **$75-$150.** I-40 & 191 Interchange. I-40, exit 333, just s at jct US 191 N. Ext corridors. **Pets:** Accepted.

# CHINLE

**Best Western Canyon de Chelly Inn** M
(928) 674-5875. **$79-$119.** 100 Main St, Rt 7. US 191, just e. Ext corridors. **Pets:** Accepted.
[SAVE] [S⌀] [✕] [⊟] [⊑] [¶] [≋]

# COTTONWOOD

**Best Western Cottonwood Inn** M
(928) 634-5575. **$69-$109.** 993 S Main St. On SR 89A, at SR 260. Ext corridors. **Pets:** Accepted.
[SAVE] [S⌀] [✕] [⌂] [⊟] [⊑] [≋]

**Budget Inn & Suites** M
(928) 634-3678. **$54-$99.** 1089 Hwy 260. On SR 260, just e of jct SR 89A. Ext corridors. **Pets:** Small. $15 daily fee/pet. Designated rooms, service with restrictions, supervision.
[SAVE] [S⌀] [✕] [⊟] [⊑]

**Little Daisy Motel** M
(928) 634-7865. **$50-$55.** 34 S Main St. On SR 89A, just n. Ext corridors. **Pets:** Other species. $20 deposit/room, $5 daily fee/pet. Service with restrictions, crate.
[SAVE] [S⌀] [✕] [⊟]

**Pines Motel** M
(928) 634-9975. **$54-$79.** 920 S Camino Real. Jct SR 260, just nw on SR 89A, then just s. Ext corridors. **Pets:** $10 one-time fee/room. Service with restrictions, supervision.
[SAVE] [S⌀] [✕] [⊟] [⊑] [≋]

**Quality Inn** M
(928) 634-4207. **$65-$99.** 301 W Hwy 89A. On SR 89A, 1.8 mi s of jct SR 260. Ext corridors. **Pets:** Small. $20 one-time fee/room. Designated rooms, service with restrictions, supervision.
[SAVE] [S⌀] [✕] [⊟] [⊑] [¶] [≋]

**The View Motel** M
(928) 634-7581. **$48-$58.** 818 S Main St. On SR 89A, 0.4 mi nw of jct SR 260. Ext corridors. **Pets:** Accepted.
[SAVE] [S⌀] [✕] [⊟] [≋]

# DOUGLAS

**Motel 6 #305** M
(520) 364-2457. **$36-$46.** 111 16th St (SR 80). 1.2 mi e of jct SR 191. Ext corridors. **Pets:** Large, other species. Service with restrictions, supervision.
[ASK] [S⌀] [✕] [⊟] [≋]

# EAGAR

**Best Western Sunrise Inn** M
(928) 333-2540. **$75, 14 day notice.** 128 N Main St. From jct SR 260, just n; from jct US 60, 1.5 mi s. Ext corridors. **Pets:** Small. $10 one-time fee/pet. Service with restrictions, supervision.
[ASK] [S⌀] [✕] [⊘] [⊟] [⊑]

# EHRENBERG

**Best Western Flying J Motel** SH
(928) 923-9711. **$79-$199.** S Frontage Rd. I-10, exit 1, just s; 0.5 mi e of the Colorado River. Int corridors. **Pets:** Accepted.
[SAVE] [S⌀] [✕] [⊟] [⊑] [≋]

# ELOY

**Super 8 Motel** M
(520) 466-7804. **$49-$99, 7 day notice.** 3945 W Houser Rd. I-10, exit 203 (Toltec Rd), just e, then just s. Ext corridors. **Pets:** Accepted.
[ASK] [S⌀] [✕] [⊟] [≋]

# FLAGSTAFF

**AmeriSuites (Flagstaff/Interstate Crossroads)** SH
(928) 774-8042. **$59-$129.** 2455 S Beulah Blvd. I-40, exit 195, just n to Forest Meadows St, just w, then just s. Int corridors. **Pets:** Accepted.
[SAVE] [S⌀] [✕] [⊘] [⌂] [⊟] [⊑] [≋]

**Best Western Kings House** M
(928) 774-7186. **$45-$125.** 1560 E Route 66. I-40, exit 198 (Butler Ave), just w, just n on Enterprise, then just w. Ext corridors. **Pets:** Medium. $15 daily fee/pet. Service with restrictions, supervision.
[SAVE] [S⌀] [✕] [⊟] [⊑] [≋]

**Best Western Pony Soldier Inn and Suites** SH
(928) 526-2388. **$59-$119.** 3030 E Route 66. I-40, exit 201, just n, then 1 mi w. Int corridors. **Pets:** Small. $15 one-time fee/room. Designated rooms, service with restrictions, supervision.
[SAVE] [S⌀] [✕] [⊘] [⊟] [⊑] [≋]

**Comfort Inn I-17/I-40** SH
(928) 774-2225. **$59-$139.** 2355 S Beulah Blvd. I-40, exit 195, just n to Forest Meadows St, then 1 blk w. Int corridors. **Pets:** Small. $5 daily fee/pet. Service with restrictions, supervision.
[SAVE] [S⌀] [✕] [⊘] [⊟] [⊑] [≋]

**Days Inn East** SH
(928) 527-1477. **$39-$169.** 3601 E Lockett Rd. I-40, exit 201, just n, 0.5 mi w on I-40 business loop, then just n. Int corridors. **Pets:** Other species. $10 one-time fee/room. Designated rooms, crate.
[SAVE] [S⌀] [✕] [⊟] [⊑] [≋]

**Days Inn Route 66** M
(928) 774-5221. **$40-$129.** 1000 W Route 66. I-40, exit 195, 1.5 mi n on Milton Rd, then just w. Ext corridors. **Pets:** Accepted.
[SAVE] [S⌀] [✕] [⊘] [⊟] [⊑] [≋]

**Econo Lodge** SH
(928) 774-7701. **$60-$119, 7 day notice.** 2480 E Lucky Ln. I-40, exit 198 (Butler Ave), just n, then just e. Int corridors. **Pets:** Accepted.
[ASK] [S⌀] [✕] [⊟] [⊑] [≋]

**Econo Lodge-University** M
(928) 774-7326. **$45-$109.** 914 S Milton Rd. I-40, exit 195, 1.2 mi n. Ext corridors. **Pets:** Large, other species. $5 daily fee/pet. Supervision.
[SAVE] [S⌀] [✕] [⊟] [⊑] [≋]

**Holiday Inn Express** SH
(928) 714-1000. **$59-$139.** 2320 E Lucky Ln. I-40, exit 198 (Butler Ave), just n, then just e. Int corridors. **Pets:** Other species. $25 one-time fee/room. Service with restrictions, crate.
[SAVE] [S⌀] [✕] [⊘] [⌂] [⊟] [⊑] [¶] [≋] [✕]

**Howard Johnson Inn-Lucky Lane** M
(928) 779-5121. **$49-$109.** 2520 E Lucky Ln. I-40, exit 198 (Butler Ave), just n, then just e. Ext corridors. **Pets:** Accepted.
[SAVE] [S⌀] [✕] [⊘] [⊟] [⊑] [≋]

**Motel 6 Flagstaff-Butler Ave #301** M
(928) 774-1801. **$42-$55.** 2010 E Butler Ave. I-40, exit 198 (Butler Ave), just n. Ext corridors. **Pets:** Accepted.
[S⌀] [✕] [≋]

**Motel 6-Flagstaff West #1000** M
(928) 779-3757. **$42-$55.** 2745 S Woodlands Village. I-40, exit 195, just n to Forest Meadows St, w to Beulah Blvd, just s, then just w. Ext corridors. **Pets:** Accepted.
[S⌀] [✕] [⌂M] [⌂] [⊟] [≋]

**Parkside Family Inn & Suites** M
(928) 774-8820. **$25-$149.** 121 S Milton Rd. I-40, exit 195, 2.5 mi n. Ext corridors. **Pets:** Accepted.
[SAVE] [S⌀] [✕] [⊟]

**Quality Inn I-40/I-17** SH
(928) 774-8771. **$39-$99.** 2000 S Milton Rd. I-40, exit 195, just n to Forest Meadows, then right. Int corridors. **Pets:** Other species. $10 daily fee/pet. Service with restrictions, supervision.

**Quality Inn-Lucky Lane** M
(928) 226-7111. **$49-$109.** 2500 E Lucky Ln. I-40, exit 198 (Butler Ave), just n, then just e. Ext corridors. **Pets:** Other species. $10 daily fee/room. Service with restrictions, supervision.

**Ramada Limited-Lucky Lane** M
(928) 779-3614. **$49-$109.** 2350 E Lucky Ln. I-40, exit 198 (Butler Ave), just n, then just e. Ext corridors. **Pets:** Medium, other species. $10 daily fee/room. Service with restrictions, supervision.

**Ramada Limited West** SH
(928) 773-1111. **$49-$144.** 2755 S Woodlands Village Blvd. I-40, exit 195, just n to Fores: Meadows St, w to Beulah Blvd, just s, then w. Ext corridors. **Pets:** Large. $10 daily fee/room. Designated rooms, service with restrictions, supervision.

**Residence Inn by Marriott Flagstaff** M
(928) 526-5555. **$60-$199.** 3440 N Country Club Dr. I-40, exit 201, 0.5 mi s. Ext/int corridors. **Pets:** Accepted.

**Rodeway Inn East** SH
(928) 526-2200. **$35-$89.** 2650 E Route 66. I-40, exit 201, 0.5 mi n, then 1.6 mi w. Ext corridors. **Pets:** Very small, other species. $10 one-time fee/pet. Service with restrictions, supervision.

**Sleep Inn** M
(928) 556-3000. **$55-$130.** 2765 S Woodlands Village Blvd. I-40, exit 195, just n to Forest Meadows St, w to Beaulah Rd, just s, then just w. Int corridors. **Pets:** Other species. $20 daily fee/room. Service with restrictions, supervision.

**Super 8-Lucky Lane** M
(928) 773-4888. **$49-$109.** 2540 E Lucky Ln. I-40, exit 198 (Butler Ave), just n, then just e. Ext corridors. **Pets:** $10 one-time fee/room. Designated rooms, service with restrictions.

**Super 8 Motel** M
(928) 774-4581. **$39-$125.** 602 W Route 66. I-40, exit 195, 1.5 mi n on SR 89A (Milton Rd), just w. Ext corridors. **Pets:** Accepted.

**Super 8 Motel East Flagstaff** M
(928) 526-0818. **$39-$149.** 3725 Kasper Ave. I-40, exit 201, just n, 0.5 mi w on I-40 business loop, then just n. Int corridors. **Pets:** Small, other species. $20 daily fee/pet. Designated rooms, service with restrictions, supervision.

**Travel Inn** M
(928) 774-3381. **$36-$39.** 801 W Route 66. I-40, exit 195, 1.2 mi n on Milton Rd, then just w. Ext corridors. **Pets:** Other species. $10 one-time fee/room. Service with restrictions, supervision.

**Travelodge-Grand Canyon/Flagstaff** M
(928) 526-1399. **$29-$130.** 2610 E Route 66. I-40, exit 201, just n, then 1.7 mi w on I-40 business loop. Ext corridors. **Pets:** $10 daily fee/pet. No service, supervision.

**Travelodge Hotel** SH
(928) 779-6944. **$34-$179.** 2200 E Butler Ave. I-40, exit 198 (Butler Ave), just n. Int corridors. **Pets:** Other species. $10 daily fee/pet. No service, supervision.

# FLORENCE

**Rancho Sonora Inn** M
(520) 868-8000. **$79-$89, 3 day notice.** 9198 N Hwy 79. On SR 79, 5 mi s of SR 287. Ext corridors. **Pets:** $10 one-time fee/pet. Designated rooms, crate.

# FOREST LAKES

**Forest Lakes Lodge** M
(928) 535-4727. **$55-$74.** 876 AZ Hwy 260. On SR 260. Ext corridors. **Pets:** Small, dogs only. $10 one-time fee/pet. Service with restrictions, supervision.

# GILA BEND

**America's Choice Inn & Suites** M
(928) 683-6311. **$59-$75.** 2888 Butterfield Tr. I-8, exit 119, just nw. Int corridors. **Pets:** Medium. $10 one-time fee/room. Designated rooms, service with restrictions, supervision.

**Best Western Space Age Lodge** M
(928) 683-2273. **$69-$119.** 401 E Pima St. Business Loop I-8; center. Ext corridors. **Pets:** Medium, other species. Service with restrictions.

# GLOBE

**Comfort Inn at Round Mountain Park** SH
(928) 425-7575. **$69-$209.** 1515 South St. On US 60, 1 mi e of town. Ext corridors. **Pets:** Accepted.

**Motel 6 #4223** SH
(928) 425-5741. **$43-$50.** 1699 E Ash St. On US 60, 1.3 mi e of town. Ext/int corridors. **Pets:** Accepted.

# GOLD CANYON

**Gold Canyon Golf Resort** LH
(480) 982-9090. **$135-$310, 3 day notice.** 6100 S Kings Ranch Rd. US 60, exit Kings Ranch Rd, 1 mi n. Ext corridors. **Pets:** Dogs only. $75 one-time fee/pet. Service with restrictions, supervision.

# GRAND CANYON NATIONAL PARK

## GRAND CANYON NATIONAL PARK SOUTH RIM

▼▼▼▼ **The Grand Hotel** SH
(928) 638-3333. **$99-$189, 3 day notice.** Hwy 64. On SR 64; 2 mi s of South Rim entrance. Int corridors. **Pets:** Accepted.
(ASK) (S⌀) (✕) (⌂) (🔥) (🔌) (🍴) (≋)

🔶🔶 ◈ ▼▼ **Red Feather Lodge** SH
(928) 638-2414. **$75-$145.** Hwy 64. On SR 64; 2 mi s of South Rim entrance. Ext/int corridors. **Pets:** Other species. $50 deposit/room. Designated rooms, service with restrictions, supervision.
(SAVE) (S⌀) (✕) (⌂) (🔥) (🔌) (🍴) (≋)

# END AREA

## HEBER

🔶🔶 ▼▼▼ **Best Western Sawmill Inn** SH
(928) 535-5053. **$59-$99.** 1877 Hwy 260. 0.5 mi e of center. Ext corridors. **Pets:** Other species. $10 daily fee/pet. Service with restrictions, supervision.
(SAVE) (S⌀) (✕) (⌂) (🔥) (🔌)

## HOLBROOK

🔶🔶 ▼▼ **American Best Inn** M
(928) 524-2654. **$37-$57.** 2211 E Navajo Blvd. I-40, exit 289, 1 mi w. Ext corridors. **Pets:** Other species. $5 deposit/pet. No service, crate.
(SAVE) (S⌀) (✕) (🔥) (🔌)

🔶🔶 ▼▼ **Best Western Adobe Inn** M
(928) 524-3948. **$49-$79.** 615 W Hopi Dr. I-40, exit 285, 1 mi e on US 180 (Hopi Dr). Ext corridors. **Pets:** Other species. $10 daily fee/pet. Service with restrictions, supervision.
(SAVE) (S⌀) (✕) (🔥) (🔌) (≋)

🔶🔶 ▼▼▼ **Best Western Arizonian Inn** SH
(928) 524-2611. **$77-$91.** 2508 Navajo Blvd. I-40, exit 289, 0.5 mi w. Ext corridors. **Pets:** Accepted.
(SAVE) (S⌀) (✕) (🔥) (🔌) (≋)

🔶🔶 ▼▼▼ **Comfort Inn** SH
(928) 524-6131. **$59-$75.** 2602 E Navajo Blvd. I-40, exit 289, just w. Ext corridors. **Pets:** Accepted.
(SAVE) (S⌀) (✕) (🔥) (🔌) (≋)

🔶🔶 ▼▼▼ **Econo Lodge** SH
(928) 524-1448. **$40-$55.** 2596 E Navajo Blvd. I-40, exit 289, just w. Ext corridors. **Pets:** Accepted.
(SAVE) (S⌀) (✕) (🔥) (🔌) (≋)

▼▼◈▼▼ **Holbrook Holiday Inn Express** M ❀
(928) 524-1466. **$74-$89.** 1308 E Navajo Blvd. I-40, exit 286, just e. Int corridors. **Pets:** Very small, dogs only. $25 one-time fee/pet. Designated rooms, supervision.
(ASK) (S⌀) (✕) (🔥) (🔌) (≋)

## JEROME

🔶🔶 ▼▼◈▼▼ **Connor Hotel of Jerome** SH ❀
(928) 634-5006. **$85-$145, 3 day notice.** 164 Main St. Center. Int corridors. **Pets:** Other species. Service with restrictions, supervision.
(SAVE) (S⌀) (✕) (🔥) (🔌)

## KAYENTA

▼▼◈▼▼ **Hampton Inn of Kayenta** SH
(928) 697-3170. **$59-$139, 3 day notice.** Hwy 160. On US 160, just w. Int corridors. **Pets:** Accepted.
(ASK) (✕) (S⌀M) (⌂) (🔥) (🔌) (🍴) (≋)

## KINGMAN

🔶🔶 ▼▼◈▼▼ **Best Western A Wayfarer's Inn** SH
(928) 753-6271. **$78-$97.** 2815 E Andy Devine Ave. I-40, exit 53, 0.5 mi w on Route 66. Ext corridors. **Pets:** Medium. $8 one-time fee/room. Designated rooms, service with restrictions, supervision.
(SAVE) (S⌀) (✕) (⌂) (🔥) (🔌) (≋)

🔶🔶 ▼▼◈▼▼ **Best Western King's Inn & Suites** SH
(928) 753-6101. **$78-$97.** 2930 E Route 66. I-40, exit 53, just w on Route 66. Ext corridors. **Pets:** Accepted.
(SAVE) (S⌀) (✕) (⌂) (🔥) (🔌) (≋)

🔶🔶 ▼▼▼ **Brunswick Hotel** SH
(928) 718-1800. **$55-$66.** 315 E Andy Devine Ave. On Route 66; downtown. Int corridors. **Pets:** Medium, dogs only. $10 one-time fee/room. No service, supervision.
(SAVE) (S⌀) (✕) (⌂) (🔥) (🍴)

🔶🔶 ▼▼▼ **Days Inn West** M
(928) 753-7500. **$39-$89.** 3023 E Andy Devine Ave. I-40, exit 53, just w on Route 66. Ext corridors. **Pets:** Accepted.
(SAVE) (S⌀) (✕) (🔥) (≋)

🔶🔶 ▼▼ **Hill Top Motel** M
(928) 753-2198. **$38-$75, 3 day notice.** 1901 E Andy Devine Ave. I-40, exit 53, 2 mi w on Route 66. Ext corridors. **Pets:** Dogs only. $5 daily fee/pet. Service with restrictions, supervision.
(SAVE) (S⌀) (✕) (🔥) (🔌)

▼▼ **Motel 6–1114** M
(928) 753-9222. **$47-$61.** 424 W Beale St. I-40, exit 48, just se on Business Loop I-40/US 93. Ext corridors. **Pets:** Accepted.
(S⌀) (✕) (⌂) (🔥) (≋)

▼▼ **Motel 6–1366** M
(928) 757-7151. **$43-$53.** 3351 E Andy Devine Ave. I-40, exit 53, just e on Route 66. Ext corridors. **Pets:** Accepted.
(S⌀) (✕) (🔥) (≋)

▼▼▼ **Quality Inn** M
(928) 753-4747. **$56-$150.** 1400 E Andy Devine Ave. I-40, exit 48, 2 mi e on Route 66. Ext corridors. **Pets:** Medium. $10 one-time fee/pet. Designated rooms, service with restrictions.
(ASK) (S⌀) (✕) (⌂) (🔥) (🔌) (≋) (✕)

🔶🔶 ▼▼▼ **Super 8 Motel** SH ❀
(928) 757-4808. **$44-$159.** 3401 E Andy Devine Ave. I-40, exit 53, just e on Route 66. Int corridors. **Pets:** $10 daily fee/pet. Designated rooms, service with restrictions, supervision.
(SAVE) (S⌀) (✕) (🔥)

## KOHLS RANCH

▼▼▼ **Kohl's Ranch Lodge** CO ❀
(928) 478-4211. **Call for rates.** 202 S Kohl's Ranch Lodge Rd. Jct SR 87 and 260E, 16.6 mi e, just s. Ext/int corridors. **Pets:** Other species. Service with restrictions.
(✕) (⌂) (🔥) (🔌) (🍴) (≋) (✕)

# LAKE HAVASU CITY

**Best Western Lake Place Inn** 🆂🅷
(928) 855-2146. **$69-$300.** 31 Wing's Loop. 1 mi e of SR 95 via Swanson Ave; downtown. Ext corridors. **Pets:** $10 daily fee/room. Service with restrictions, supervision.

**Hampton Inn Lake Havasu** 🆂🅷
(928) 855-4071. **$89-$129.** 245 London Bridge Rd. 0.5 mi n of London Bridge. Int corridors. **Pets:** Other species. $10 daily fee/pet. Designated rooms, service with restrictions, supervision.

**The Havasu Inn** 🅼
(928) 855-7841. **$59-$159.** 1700 N McCulloch. At Riviera Blvd. Ext corridors. **Pets:** Accepted.

**Island Inn Hotel** 🆂🅷
(928) 680-0606. **$69-$300.** 1300 W McCulloch Blvd. 0.7 mi w of London Bridge/SR 95. Int corridors. **Pets:** Accepted.

**Island Suites** 🆂🅷
(928) 855-7333. **$82-$300.** 236 S Lake Havasu Ave. Just s of jct McCulloch Blvd. Int corridors. **Pets:** Accepted.

**Lake Havasu City Super 8** 🅼
(928) 855-8844. **$55-$169.** 305 London Bridge Rd. Just w of SR 95, exit Palo Verde; 0.5 mi n of London Bridge. Int corridors. **Pets:** Small. $10 one-time fee/pet. Designated rooms, service with restrictions, supervision.

**Motel 6 Lake Havasu** 🅼
(928) 855-3200. **$47-$131.** 111 London Bridge Rd. 0.3 mi n of London Bridge. Int corridors. **Pets:** $10 daily fee/room. Service with restrictions, supervision.

**Ramada Inn Havasu** 🅼
(928) 855-1111. **$69-$299.** 271 S Lake Havasu Ave. SR 95, just e on Swanson Ave, just s. Ext corridors. **Pets:** Accepted.

**Travelodge-Lake Havasu City** 🆂🅷
(928) 680-9202. **$50-$160, 3 day notice.** 480 London Bridge Rd. 1 mi n of London Bridge. Int corridors. **Pets:** Accepted.

# NOGALES

**Best Western Siesta Motel** 🅼
(520) 287-4671. **$70-$75.** 673 N Grand Ave. On Business Loop I-19, 1 mi n of International border. Ext corridors. **Pets:** Small. Service with restrictions, supervision.

**Motel 6 Nogales #71** 🅼
(520) 281-2951. **$47-$61.** 141 W Mariposa Rd. I-19, exit 4, 0.9 mi e. Ext corridors. **Pets:** Accepted.

# PAGE

**Best Western Arizona Inn** 🆂🅷
(928) 645-2466. **$44-$109.** 716 Rimview Dr. 0.7 mi e of US 89 via SR 89L. Int corridors. **Pets:** Accepted.

**Lake Powell Days Inn & Suites** 🆂🅷
(928) 645-2800. **$49-$119.** 961 N Hwy 89. On US 89, just s. Int corridors. **Pets:** Other species. $10 daily fee/pet. Service with restrictions, supervision.

**Linda's Lake Powell Condos** 🅲🅾
(928) 353-4591. **$88-$114, 3 day notice.** 1019 Tower Butte. 6 mi n on US 89. Ext corridors. **Pets:** Accepted.

**Motel 6-Page/Lake Powell #4013** 🆂🅷
(928) 645-5888. **$39-$69, 3 day notice.** 637 S Lake Powell Blvd. On Business Loop SR 89L, just e of US 89. Int corridors. **Pets:** Accepted.

**Quality Inn, At Lake Powell** 🆂🅷
(928) 645-8851. **$40-$150.** 287 N Lake Powell Blvd. 0.8 mi e of US 89/SR 89L. Int corridors. **Pets:** Other species. Designated rooms, service with restrictions.

**Super 8 Gateway to Lake Powell** 🆂🅷
(928) 645-5858. **$44-$84, 3 day notice.** 649 S Lake Powell Blvd. On SR 89L, just e of US 89. Int corridors. **Pets:** Small, other species. $10 one-time fee/pet. Designated rooms, service with restrictions, supervision.

# PARKER

**Best Western Parker Inn** 🆂🅷
(928) 669-6060. **$69-$129.** 1012 Geronimo Ave. SR 95, just e. Int corridors. **Pets:** Small. Designated rooms, service with restrictions, supervision.

# PAYSON

**Americas Best Value Inn** 🅼
(928) 474-2283. **$45-$99.** 811 S Beeline Hwy. On SR 87, 0.7 mi s of SR 260. Ext/int corridors. **Pets:** Medium. $10 daily fee/pet. Service with restrictions, supervision.

**Best Western Payson Inn** 🆂🅷
(928) 474-3241. **$69-$149.** 801 N Beeline Hwy. On SR 87, 0.6 mi n of SR 260. Ext corridors. **Pets:** Dogs only. $10 daily fee/room. Service with restrictions, supervision.

**Comfort Inn** 🅼
(928) 474-5241. **$52-$189.** 809 E Hwy 260. On SR 260, 0.8 mi e of SR 87. Ext corridors. **Pets:** Accepted.

**Days Inn & Suites** 🆂🅷
(928) 474-9800. **$59-$149.** 301-A S Beeline Hwy. On SR 87, just s of SR 260. Int corridors. **Pets:** Small. $10 daily fee/pet. Designated rooms, service with restrictions, supervision.

**Majestic Mountain Inn** 🆂🅷 ❀
(928) 474-0185. **$65-$150.** 602 E Hwy 260. On SR 260, 0.5 mi e of SR 87. Ext corridors. **Pets:** Small. $20 one-time fee/pet. Designated rooms, service with restrictions, supervision.

▼▼▼ Motel 6 #4201 Ⓜ
(928) 474-4526. **$45-$85.** 101 W Phoenix St. On SR 87, 1.1 mi s of SR 260. Int corridors. **Pets:** Accepted.
[S🐾] [✕] [🛏]

Ⓐ ▼▼▼ Paysonglo Lodge 🆂🅷
(928) 474-2382. **$55-$92.** 1005 S Beeline Hwy. On SR 87, 0.9 mi s of SR 260. Ext corridors. **Pets:** Small. Designated rooms, service with restrictions, supervision.
[SAVE] [S🐾] [✕] [🛏] [💻] [🌊]

# PHOENIX METROPOLITAN AREA

## APACHE JUNCTION

Ⓐ ▼▼ Apache Junction Motel Ⓜ ❀
(480) 982-7702. **$43-$69, 3 day notice.** 1680 W Apache Tr. US 60, exit 195, 2 mi n, then just w. Ext corridors. **Pets:** Very small, dogs only. $20 one-time fee/pet. Service with restrictions, supervision.
[SAVE] [S🐾] [✕] [🛏]

Ⓐ ▼▼▼ Apache Junction Super 8 🆂🅷
(480) 288-8888. **$59-$114.** 251 E 29th Ave. US 60, exit 196 (Idaho Rd/SR 88 E), just n. Ext/int corridors. **Pets:** Small, dogs only. $50 deposit/pet. Designated rooms, service with restrictions, supervision.
[SAVE] [S🐾] [✕] [🎦] [💺] [🛏] [🌊]

## BUCKEYE

▼▼▼ Days Inn-Buckeye 🆂🅷
(623) 386-5400. **$70-$200.** 25205 W Yuma Rd. I-10, exit 114 (Miller Rd), just sw. Ext corridors. **Pets:** Accepted.
[ASK] [S🐾] [✕] [🎦] [🛏] [💻] [🌊]

## CAREFREE

Ⓐ ▼▼▼▼ The Boulders Resort & Golden Door
Spa 🅻🅷
(480) 488-9009. **$199-$575, 21 day notice.** 34631 N Tom Darlington Dr. Scottsdale Rd, 11 mi n of Bell Rd. Ext corridors. **Pets:** Accepted.
[SAVE] [✕] [🎦] [🛏] [💻] [🍴] [🌊] [✕]

Ⓐ ▼▼▼▼ Carefree Resort & Villas 🅻🅷 ❀
(480) 488-5300. **$79-$239.** 37220 Mule Train Rd. SR 101, exit 36 (Pima Rd), 12.2 mi n to Cave Creek Rd, 1 mi w, then 0.4 mi n. Ext/int corridors. **Pets:** $50 one-time fee/room. Service with restrictions, crate.
[SAVE] [S🐾] [✕] [💺] [🛏] [💻] [🍴] [🌊] [✕]

## CAVE CREEK

Ⓐ ▼▼ Cave Creek Tumbleweed Hotel Ⓜ
(480) 488-3668. **$89-$199, 14 day notice.** 6333 E Cave Creek Rd. Jct Scottsdale Rd/Tom Darlington Rd, 1.3 mi w. Ext corridors. **Pets:** Accepted.
[SAVE] [✕] [🛏] [💻] [🌊]

## CHANDLER

▼▼ Chandler Super 8 🆂🅷
(480) 961-3888. **$59-$75.** 7171 W Chandler Blvd. I-10, exit 160 (Chandler Blvd), just e. Int corridors. **Pets:** Accepted.
[ASK] [S🐾] [✕] [🛏] [🌊]

Ⓐ ▼▼ Comfort Inn 🆂🅷
(480) 705-8882. **$69-$119.** 255 N Kyrene Rd. I-10, exit 160 (Chandler Blvd), 1.5 mi e, then just n. Int corridors. **Pets:** Accepted.
[SAVE] [S🐾] [✕] [♿M] [💺] [🛏] [💻] [🌊]

▼▼▼▼ Hawthorn Suites Chandler 🆂🅷
(480) 705-8881. **$89-$169.** 5858 W Chandler Blvd. I-10, exit 160 (Chandler Blvd), 1.5 mi e. Int corridors. **Pets:** Accepted.
[ASK] [S🐾] [✕] [💺] [🛏] [💻] [🌊] [✕]

▼▼▼▼ Homewood Suites by Hilton 🆂🅷
(480) 753-6200. **$79-$239.** 7373 W Detroit St. I-10, exit 160 (Chandler Blvd), 0.4 mi e, n on 54th St, then just w. Int corridors. **Pets:** Accepted.
[ASK] [✕] [♿M] [💺] [🛏] [💻] [🌊]

▼▼▼▼ Park Plaza Phoenix/Chandler 🆂🅷
(480) 961-4444. **$72-$128.** 7475 W Chandler Blvd. I-10, exit 160 (Chandler Blvd), just e, then just s on Southgate Dr. Int corridors. **Pets:** Accepted.
[ASK] [S🐾] [✕] [💻] [🍴] [🌊] [✕]

▼▼▼ Red Roof Inn-Chandler 🆂🅷
(480) 857-4969. **$46-$74.** 7400 W Boston St. I-10, exit 160 (Chandler Blvd), just e, then s on Southgate Dr. Int corridors. **Pets:** Accepted.
[✕] [♿M] [🎦] [💺] [🛏] [💻] [🌊]

▼▼▼▼ Residence Inn-Chandler Fashion Center 🆂🅷
(480) 782-1551. **$99-$199, 14 day notice.** 200 N Federal St. I-10, exit 160 (Chandler Blvd), 4.2 mi e, just n on N Metro Blvd, then just e. Int corridors. **Pets:** Accepted.
[ASK] [S🐾] [✕] [♿M] [💺] [🛏] [💻] [🌊] [✕]

Ⓐ ▼▼▼▼ San Marcos Resort and Conference
Center 🅻🅷
(480) 812-0900. **$79-$219, 3 day notice.** 1 San Marcos Pl. Just s on Arizona Ave from jct Chandler Blvd, just w on Buffalo St; in historic downtown. Ext corridors. **Pets:** Accepted.
[SAVE] [S🐾] [✕] [🛏] [💻] [🍴] [🌊] [✕]

▼▼▼ Southgate Motel Ⓜ
(480) 940-0308. **$45-$80.** 7445 W Chandler Blvd. I-10, exit 160 (Chandler Blvd), just e, then just s on Southgate Dr. Ext corridors. **Pets:** Accepted.
[ASK] [S🐾] [✕] [💺] [🛏] [💻] [🌊]

Ⓐ ▼▼▼▼ Windmill Suites of Chandler 🆂🅷
(480) 812-9600. **$84-$149.** 3535 W Chandler Blvd. I-10, exit 160 (Chandler Blvd), 4 mi e. Int corridors. **Pets:** Accepted.
[SAVE] [S🐾] [✕] [💺] [🛏] [🌊] [✕]

## GLENDALE

Ⓐ ▼▼▼ Best Western Phoenix-Glendale 🆂🅷
(623) 939-9431. **$59-$119.** 7116 N 59th Ave. I-17, exit 205 (Glendale Ave), 4.3 mi w, then just n. Ext corridors. **Pets:** $10 daily fee/pet. Service with restrictions.
[SAVE] [S🐾] [✕] [🛏] [💻] [🌊]

▼▼▼ Ramada Limited 🆂🅷
(623) 412-2000. **$53-$149.** 7885 W Arrowhead Towne Ctr Dr. Loop 101, exit 14 (Bell Rd), 0.3 mi e, then just n on 79th Ave. Ext corridors. **Pets:** Accepted.
[ASK] [S🐾] [✕] [🎦] [💺] [🛏] [💻] [🌊]

## GOODYEAR

▼▼▼ Best Western Phoenix Goodyear Inn Ⓜ ❀
(623) 932-3210. **$69-$149.** 55 N Litchfield Rd. I-10, exit 128, 0.8 mi s. Ext/int corridors. **Pets:** Small, other species. $10 daily fee/room. Service with restrictions, crate.
[ASK] [S🐾] [✕] [🛏] [💻] [🍴] [🌊]

▼▼▼▼ Hampton Inn & Suites 🆂🅷
(623) 536-1313. **$99-$179.** 2000 N Litchfield Rd. I-10, exit 128, 0.5 mi n. Int corridors. **Pets:** Accepted.
[ASK] [✕] [♿M] [💺] [🛏] [💻] [🌊] [✕]

▼▼▼ **Holiday Inn Express** SH
(623) 535-1313. **$99-$199.** 1313 N Litchfield Rd. I-10, exit 128, just n. Int corridors. **Pets:** Accepted.

ASK S X         ☒

▼▼▼ **Residence Inn by Marriott** SH
(623) 866-1313. **$139-$299.** 2020 N Litchfield Rd. I-10, exit 128, 0.6 mi n. Int corridors. **Pets:** Other species. $75 one-time fee/room.

ASK S X         ☒

▼▼▼ **Wingate Inn & Suites** SH
(623) 547-1313. **$99-$169.** 1188 N Dysart Rd. I-10, exit 129 (Dysart Rd), just n. Int corridors. **Pets:** Other species. $35 one-time fee/pet. Service with restrictions, crate.

ASK S X      

# LITCHFIELD PARK

AAA ▼▼▼▼ **The Wigwam Resort** LH ❀
(623) 935-3811. **$229-$669, 7 day notice.** 300 Wigwam Blvd. I-10, exit 128 (Litchfield Rd), 2.4 mi n, then 0.4 mi e. Ext corridors. **Pets:** Small, dogs only. Service with restrictions, crate.

SAVE S X       ⑪   ☒

# MESA

AAA ▼▼▼ **Arizona Golf Resort & Conference Center** LH ❀
(480) 832-3202. **$129-$199.** 425 S Power Rd. 1.3 mi n of US 60 (Superstition Frwy), exit 188 (Power Rd); southeast corner of Broadway and Power rds; entrance on Broadway Rd. Ext corridors. **Pets:** Other species. Service with restrictions.

SAVE X       ⑪   ☒

AAA ▼▼▼ **Best Western Dobson Ranch Inn** SH ❀
(480) 831-7000. **$62-$170.** 1666 S Dobson Rd. Just s of US 60 (Superstition Frwy), exit 177 (Dobson Rd). Ext/int corridors. **Pets:** Medium, dogs only. Service with restrictions, crate.

SAVE X       ⑪

AAA ▼▼▼ **Best Western Mesa Inn** SH ❀
(480) 964-8000. **$60-$100.** 1625 E Main St. 2 mi n of US 60 (Superstition Frwy), exit Stapley Dr, 0.5 mi e. Ext corridors. **Pets:** Other species. $20 one-time fee/pet. Service with restrictions, supervision.

SAVE S X    

AAA ▼▼▼ **Best Western Mezona Inn** SH
(480) 834-9233. **$59-$149.** 250 W Main St. Just e of Country Club Dr; downtown. Ext corridors. **Pets:** Other species. Supervision.

SAVE S X    

AAA ▼▼▼ **Best Western Superstition Springs Inn** SH
(480) 641-1164. **$59-$129.** 1342 S Power Rd. Just n of US 60 (Superstition Frwy), exit 188 (Power Rd); northwest corner of Power Rd and Hampton Ave. Ext corridors. **Pets:** Small. $10 daily fee/pet. Designated rooms, service with restrictions, supervision.

SAVE S X    

AAA ▼▼▼ **Days Inn** SH
(480) 844-8900. **$49-$129.** 333 W Juanita. US 60 (Superstition Frwy), exit 179 (Country Club Dr), just s, then just e. Int corridors. **Pets:** Accepted.

SAVE S X       ☒

▼▼ **Days Inn-East Mesa** M
(480) 981-8111. **$59-$109.** 5531 E Main St. 0.5 mi e of Higley Rd. Ext corridors. **Pets:** Accepted.

ASK S X      

AAA ▼▼▼ **Holiday Inn Hotel & Suites** LH
(480) 964-7000. **$65-$139.** 1600 S Country Club Dr. US 60 (Superstition Frwy), exit 179, just s. Ext/int corridors. **Pets:** Accepted.

SAVE S X       ⑪  

▼▼▼ **Homestead Studio Suites Hotel Phoenix-Mesa** SH
(480) 752-2266. **$55-$85.** 1920 W Isabella. Just s of US 60 (Superstition Frwy), exit 177 (Dobson Rd). Ext corridors. **Pets:** $25 daily fee/pet. Service with restrictions, supervision.

ASK S X    

▼▼▼ **La Quinta Inn & Suites Phoenix (Mesa East)** SH
(480) 654-1970. **$99-$144.** 6530 E Superstition Springs Blvd. US 60 (Superstition Frwy), exit 187 (Superstition Springs Blvd) eastbound, just se; exit 188 (Power Rd) westbound, just sw. Int corridors. **Pets:** Medium. Service with restrictions.

ASK X           ☒

▼▼▼ **La Quinta Inn & Suites Phoenix (Mesa West)** SH
(480) 844-8747. **$76-$136.** 902 W Grove Ave. US 60 (Superstition Frwy), exit 178 (Alma School Rd), just n, then just e. Int corridors. **Pets:** Medium. Service with restrictions.

ASK X      

▼▼ **Motel 6-Mesa South #1030** M
(480) 834-0066. **$39-$61.** 1511 S Country Club Dr. US 60 (Superstition Frwy), exit 179 (Country Club Dr), northeast corner. Ext corridors. **Pets:** Accepted.

S X    

▼▼▼ **Residence Inn by Marriott Mesa** SH
(480) 610-0100. **$89-$214.** 941 W Grove Ave. US 60 (Superstition Frwy), exit 178 (Alma School Rd), just n, then just e. Ext corridors. **Pets:** Medium. $75 one-time fee/room. Service with restrictions, supervision.

ASK S X           ☒

▼▼ **Sleep Inn of Mesa** SH
(480) 807-7760. **$59-$109.** 6347 E Southern Ave. US 60 (Superstition Frwy), exit 188 (Power Rd), 0.8 mi n, then 0.4 mi w to mall entrance. Int corridors. **Pets:** Accepted.

ASK S X         ☒

▼▼ **Super 8 Motel-Mesa/Gilbert Rd** SH
(480) 545-0888. **$56-$81.** 1550 S Gilbert Rd. US 60 (Superstition Frwy), exit 182 (Gilbert Rd), 1 blk n. Int corridors. **Pets:** Other species. $5 daily fee/pet. Service with restrictions, supervision.

ASK S X    

▼▼ **Travelodge Suites Mesa** SH
(480) 832-5961. **$39-$109.** 4244 E Main St. US 60 (Superstition Frwy), exit 185 (Greenfield Rd), 2 mi n, then just w. Ext corridors. **Pets:** Small. $30 deposit/pet. $10 daily fee/pet. Service with restrictions, supervision.

ASK S X    

AAA ▼▼▼ **Windemere Hotel and Conference Center** SH
(480) 985-3600. **$69-$139.** 5750 E Main St. 0.7 mi e of Higley Rd. Ext corridors. **Pets:** Accepted.

SAVE S X     ⑪  

# PARADISE VALLEY

▼▼▼ **Hermosa Inn** SH
(602) 955-8614. **$115-$690, 7 day notice.** 5532 N Palo Cristi Rd. 1 mi s of Lincoln Dr; corner of Stanford Dr. Ext corridors. **Pets:** Accepted.

ASK S X     ⑪   ☒

AAA ▼▼▼▼ **Sanctuary on Camelback Mountain** LH ❀
(480) 948-2100. **$165-$645, 7 day notice.** 5700 E McDonald Dr. US 101, exit McDonald Dr, 3.9 mi w. Ext corridors. **Pets:** Crate.

SAVE X     ⑪   ☒

# PEORIA

### ◆◆ Comfort Suites by Choice Hotels/Sports Complex SH
(623) 334-3993. **$55-$169.** 8473 W Paradise Ln. Loop 101, exit 14 (Bell Rd), just e to 83rd Ave, just s, then just w. Int corridors. **Pets:** Accepted.

(ASK) SD ⊠ ⌂ ⌂ ⊟ ⏧ ➾

### ◆◆◆ Holiday Inn Express Hotel & Suites SH
(623) 853-1313. **$89-$179.** 16771 N 84th Ave. Loop 101, exit 14 (Bell Rd), just w, then just s. Int corridors. **Pets:** Accepted.

(ASK) SD ⊠ ⌂M ⌂ ⊟ ⏧ ➾

### ◆◆◆ La Quinta Inn & Suites Phoenix (West/Peoria) SH
(623) 487-1900. **$96-$180.** 16321 N 83 Ave. Loop 101, exit 14 (Bell Rd), just e, then just s. Int corridors. **Pets:** Medium. Service with restrictions.

(ASK) ⊠ ⌂ ⌂ ⊟ ⏧ ➾

### ◆◆◆ Residence Inn by Marriott SH
(623) 979-2074. **$90-$210, 14 day notice.** 8435 W Paradise Ln. Loop 101, exit 14 (Bell Rd), just e, just s on 83rd Ave, then just w. Int corridors. **Pets:** Accepted.

(ASK) SD ⊠ ⌂ ⊟ ⏧ ➾ ⊠

# PHOENIX

### ◉◉◉ ◆◆◆ AmeriSuites (Phoenix/Metro Center) SH
(602) 997-8800. **$89-$179.** 10838 N 25th Ave. I-17, exit 208 (Peoria Ave), just e, then 0.3 mi n. Int corridors. **Pets:** Accepted.

(SAVE) SD ⊠ ⌂ ⊟ ⏧ ➾

### ◉◉◉ ◆◆◆◆ Arizona Biltmore Resort & Spa LH ❀
(602) 955-6600. **$195-$1845, 7 day notice.** 2400 E Missouri. Jct Camelback Rd, 0.5 mi n on 24th St, then 0.4 mi w. Ext/int corridors. **Pets:** Medium. $50 deposit/pet, $50 one-time fee/pet. Designated rooms, supervision.

(SAVE) ⊠ ⌂ ⏧ ⏧ ➾ ⊠

### ◉◉◉ ◆◆◆ Best Western Airport Inn SH
(602) 273-7251. **$69-$149.** 2425 S 24th St. I-10, exit 150B westbound, just s; exit 151 (University Dr) eastbound, just n to I-10 westbound, 1 mi w to exit 150B (24th St), then just s. Ext/int corridors. **Pets:** Accepted.

(SAVE) SD ⊠ ⌂ ⊟ ⏧ ⏧ ➾

### ◉◉◉ ◆◆◆ Best Western Bell Hotel SH
(602) 993-8300. **$54-$139.** 17211 N Black Canyon Hwy. I-17, exit 212, just e, then just n. Ext corridors. **Pets:** Accepted.

(SAVE) SD ⊠ ⌂ ⊟ ⏧ ➾

### ◉◉◉ ◆◆◆ Best Western InnSuites Hotel Phoenix Northern/Airport SH
(602) 997-6285. **$69-$139.** 1615 E Northern Ave. Loop 51, 0.3 mi w. Ext corridors. **Pets:** Accepted.

(SAVE) SD ⊠ ⌂ ⌂ ⊟ ⏧ ➾

### ◉◉◉ ◆◆ Best Western Phoenix I-17 MetroCenter Inn SH
(602) 864-6233. **$69-$99.** 8101 N Black Canyon Hwy. I-17, exit 206 (Northern Ave), just e, then just n; on east side of freeway. Ext corridors. **Pets:** Accepted.

(SAVE) SD ⊠ ⌂ ⊟ ⏧ ➾

### ◆◆ Candlewood Suites SH ❀
(602) 861-4900. **$40-$199.** 11411 N Black Canyon Hwy. I-17, exit 208 (Peoria Ave), just e, then 0.4 mi n. Int corridors. **Pets:** Other species. $75 one-time fee/room. Supervision.

(ASK) SD ⊠ ⌂ ⊟ ⏧ ➾

### ◉◉◉ ◆◆◆ Clarion Hotel @ Phoenix Tech Center SH ❀
(480) 893-3900. **$69-$159.** 5121 E La Puenta Ave. I-10, exit 157 (Elliot Rd), just w, just n on 51st St, then just e. Ext corridors. **Pets:** Medium, other species. $25 one-time fee/room. Service with restrictions, supervision.

(SAVE) SD ⊠ ⌂ ⊟ ⏧ ➾

### ◆◆◆ Comfort Inn Black Canyon SH
(602) 242-8011. **$59-$129.** 5050 N Black Canyon Hwy. I-17, exit 203 (Camelback Rd), just w, then just n on west side of freeway. Ext corridors. **Pets:** Accepted.

(ASK) SD ⊠ ⌂ ⊟ ⏧ ➾

### ◆◆◆ Comfort Suites by Choice Hotels SH
(602) 861-3900. **$49-$149.** 10210 N 26th Dr. I-17, exit 208 (Peoria Ave), just e, just s on 25th Ave, then 0.3 mi w on W Beryl Ave. Int corridors. **Pets:** Accepted.

(ASK) SD ⊠ ⌂M ⌂ ⊟ ⏧ ➾

### ◆◆ Comfort Suites Conference Center SH
(602) 279-3211. **$62-$143.** 3210 NW Grand Ave. I-17, exit 201 (Thomas Rd), just w to 27th Ave, just n, then 0.7 mi nw. Ext corridors. **Pets:** Accepted.

(ASK) SD ⊠ ⌂ ⊟ ⏧ ➾

### ◉◉◉ ◆◆◆ Crowne Plaza Phoenix SH
(602) 943-2341. **$59-$169.** 2532 W Peoria Ave. I-17, exit 208 (Peoria Ave), just e, then just n on 25th Ave. Int corridors. **Pets:** $25 one-time fee/room. Service with restrictions, supervision.

(SAVE) SD ⊠ ⌂M ⌂ ⌂ ⊟ ⏧ ⏧ ➾

### ◉◉◉ ◆◆◆ Crowne Plaza Phoenix Airport SH
(602) 273-7778. **$69-$159.** 4300 E Washington St. Loop 202, exit 2 (44th St), 0.7 mi s. Int corridors. **Pets:** $50 one-time fee/room. Service with restrictions, supervision.

(SAVE) SD ⊠ ⌂ ⌂ ⊟ ⏧ ⏧ ➾

### ◉◉◉ ◆◆ Days Inn-Airport M
(602) 244-8244. **$65-$99.** 3333 E Van Buren St. Loop 202, exit 1C (32nd St), 0.6 mi s, then just e. Ext/int corridors. **Pets:** Other species. $20 one-time fee/pet. Service with restrictions, supervision.

(SAVE) SD ⊠ ⌂ ⊟ ⏧ ⏧ ➾

### ◆◆ Econo Lodge Inn & Suites-Downtown SH
(602) 528-9100. **$59-$159.** 202 E McDowell Rd. Just e of Central Ave. Int corridors. **Pets:** Accepted.

(ASK) SD ⊠ ⊟ ⏧ ➾

### ◆◆◆ Embassy Suites Phoenix Airport at 24th St SH
(602) 957-1910. **$99-$199.** 2333 E Thomas Rd. SR 51, exit 2, just e. Ext corridors. **Pets:** Accepted.

SD ⊠ ⌂ ⊟ ⏧ ⏧ ➾ ⊠

### ◆◆◆ Embassy Suites Phoenix-Biltmore SH
(602) 955-3992. **$129-$309.** 2630 E Camelback Rd. Just n of Camelback Rd, on 26th St. Int corridors. **Pets:** Accepted.

SD ⊠ ⌂ ⊟ ⏧ ➾

### ◉◉◉ ◆◆◆ Embassy Suites Phoenix North LH
(602) 375-1777. **$129-$232.** 2577 W Greenway Rd. I-17, exit 211, just e. Ext corridors. **Pets:** Other species. $10 daily fee/room, $50 one-time fee/room. Service with restrictions, supervision.

(SAVE) SD ⊠ ⌂ ⌂ ⊟ ⏧ ⏧ ➾ ⊠

### ◆◆ Extended StayAmerica Phoenix-Chandler-E Chandler Blvd SH
(480) 753-6700. **$60-$90.** 5035 E Chandler Blvd. I-10, exit 160 (Chandler Blvd), just w. Ext corridors. **Pets:** $25 daily fee/pet. Service with restrictions, supervision.

(ASK) SD ⊠ ⌂ ⊟ ⏧ ➾

**Extended StayAmerica Phoenix/Airport/E Oak St** SH
(602) 225-2998. **$50-$95.** 4357 E Oak St. Loop 202, exit 2 (44th St), 1 mi n. Ext corridors. **Pets:** $25 daily fee/pet. Service with restrictions, supervision.
ASK SÒ ✕ &M 🔲 💻 🗪

**Extended StayAmerica Phoenix-Metro Center** SH
(602) 870-2999. **$50-$80.** 11211 N Black Canyon Hwy. I-17, exit 208 (Peoria Ave), just e, then 0.3 mi n; on east side of freeway. Ext corridors. **Pets:** $25 daily fee/pet. Service with restrictions, supervision.
ASK SÒ ✕ &M 🔲 💻 🗪

**Extended Stay Deluxe Phoenix-Biltmore** SH
(602) 265-6800. **$75-$125.** 5235 N 16th St. Jct SR 51, just w on Camelback Rd, then just n. Int corridors. **Pets:** $25 daily fee/pet. Service with restrictions, supervision.
ASK SÒ ✕ 🔲 💻 🗪

**Extended Stay Deluxe (Phoenix/Midtown)** SH
(602) 279-9000. **$65-$100.** 217 W Osborn Rd. Just w of Central Ave; between Indian School and Thomas rds. Int corridors. **Pets:** $25 daily fee/pet. Service with restrictions, supervision.
ASK SÒ ✕ &M 🖉 🖪 🔲 💻 🗪

**Hilton Suites-Phoenix** LH
(602) 222-1111. **$89-$249.** 10 E Thomas Rd. Just e of Central Ave; in Phoenix Plaza. Int corridors. **Pets:** Large. $50 deposit/pet. Service with restrictions, crate.
SAVE SÒ ✕ &M 🖉 🖪 💻 🍴 🗪 🗙

**Holiday Inn Express Hotel & Suites** SH
(602) 453-9900. **$69-$119.** 3401 E University Dr. I-10, exit 151 (University Dr), just n. Int corridors. **Pets:** Accepted.
ASK SÒ ✕ 🖪 🔲 💻 🗪

**Holiday Inn Express Hotel & Suites** SH
(480) 785-8500. **$79-$119.** 15221 S 50th St. I-10, exit 160 (Chandler Blvd), just w. Int corridors. **Pets:** Medium. Designated rooms, service with restrictions.
SAVE SÒ ✕ 🖪 🔲 💻 🗪

**Holiday Inn West** SH
(602) 484-9009. **$99-$129.** 1500 N 51st Ave. I-10, exit 139 (51st Ave), just n. Int corridors. **Pets:** Accepted.
SAVE SÒ ✕ &M 🖉 🖪 🔲 💻 🍴 🗪

**Homestead Studio Suites Hotel-Phoenix North/Metro Center** M
(602) 944-7828. **$45-$75.** 2102 W Dunlap Ave. I-17, exit 207, 0.7 mi e. Ext corridors. **Pets:** $25 daily fee/pet. Service with restrictions, supervision.
ASK SÒ ✕ 🖪 🔲 💻

**Homewood Suites by Hilton** SH
(602) 508-0937. **$89-$219.** 2001 E Highland Ave. Just e of 20th St. Int corridors. **Pets:** Accepted.
ASK ✕ 🖪 🔲 💻 🗪 🗙

**Homewood Suites Hotel** SH 🐾
(602) 674-8900. **$79-$159.** 2536 W Beryl Ave. I-17, exit 208 (Peoria Ave), just e, just s on 25th Ave, then just w. Int corridors. **Pets:** Other species. $200 deposit/room, $50 one-time fee/room. Service with restrictions, crate.
SAVE ✕ &M 🖪 🔲 💻 🗪

**La Quinta Inn & Suites Phoenix (Chandler)** SH
(480) 961-7700. **$96-$136.** 15241 S 50th St. I-10, exit 160 (Chandler Blvd), just w, then just n. Int corridors. **Pets:** Medium. Service with restrictions.
ASK ✕ &M 🖉 🖪 🔲 💻 🗪

**La Quinta Inn Phoenix Airport North** SH
(602) 956-6500. **$60-$120.** 4727 E Thomas Rd. Just w of 48th St. Ext/int corridors. **Pets:** Medium. $50 deposit/room. Service with restrictions, supervision.
SAVE SÒ ✕ 🖪 🔲 💻 🗪

**La Quinta Inn Phoenix (North)** SH
(602) 993-0800. **$86-$116.** 2510 W Greenway Rd. I-17, exit 211, just e. Ext corridors. **Pets:** Medium. Service with restrictions.
ASK ✕ 🖉 &M 🖪 🔲 💻 🗪 🗙

**La Quinta Inn Phoenix (Thomas Road)** M
(602) 258-6271. **$69-$108.** 2725 N Black Canyon Hwy. I-17, exit 201 (Thomas Rd), just e, then just s on east side of freeway. Ext corridors. **Pets:** Medium. Service with restrictions.
ASK ✕ &M 🖪 🔲 💻 🗪

**MainStay Suites** SH
(602) 395-0900. **$59-$139.** 9455 N Black Canyon Hwy. I-17, exit 207, just e, then 0.4 mi n. Int corridors. **Pets:** Small. $100 one-time fee/pet. Service with restrictions, supervision.
ASK SÒ ✕ &M 🖪 🔲 💻 🗪

**Motel 6 Phoenix-Black Canyon #1304** M
(602) 277-5501. **$41-$57.** 4130 N Black Canyon Hwy. I-17, exit 202 (Indian School Rd), just w. Ext corridors. **Pets:** Accepted.
SÒ ✕ 🗪

**Motel 6 Phoenix East #18** M
(602) 267-8555. **$45-$61.** 5315 E Van Buren St. Loop 202 eastbound, exit 4 (52nd/Van Buren sts) just s, then just e. Ext corridors. **Pets:** Accepted.
SÒ ✕ &M 🖪 🗪

**Motel 6 Phoenix-North #344** M
(602) 993-2353. **$42-$63.** 2330 W Bell Rd. I-17, exit 212A, just e. Ext corridors. **Pets:** Accepted.
SÒ &M 🗪

**Motel 6 Phoenix-Northern Ave #1185** M
(602) 995-7592. **$41-$57.** 8152 N Black Canyon Hwy. I-17, exit 206, just w, then just s. Ext corridors. **Pets:** Accepted.
SÒ ✕ &M 🗪

**Motel 6 Phoenix West #696** M
(602) 272-0220. **$45-$67.** 1530 N 52nd Dr. I-10, exit 139, just n to McDowell, just w, then just s. Ext corridors. **Pets:** Accepted.
SÒ ✕ &M 🗪

**The Phoenix Place Hotel & Suites** SH
(602) 604-4900. **$59-$89.** 3600 N 2nd Ave. Just n of Osborn Rd, 0.5 mi s of Indian School; downtown. Ext/int corridors. **Pets:** Accepted.
ASK SÒ ✕ &M 🖪 🔲 💻 🗪 🗙

**Pointe Hilton Squaw Peak Resort** LH 🐾
(602) 997-2626. **$79-$299, 3 day notice.** 7677 N 16th St. Loop 51, exit Glendale Ave, 0.4 mi w, then 0.6 mi n. Ext corridors. **Pets:** $75 deposit/pet. Supervision.
SAVE ✕ 🖉 &M 🖪 🔲 💻 🍴 🗪 🗙

**Pointe Hilton Tapatio Cliffs Resort** LH 🐾
(602) 866-7500. **$79-$299, 3 day notice.** 11111 N 7th St. I-17, exit 207 (Dunlap Ave), 3 mi e, then 2 mi n. Ext corridors. **Pets:** $75 deposit/room. Designated rooms, service with restrictions, crate.
SAVE ✕ &M 🖉 &M 🖪 💻 🍴 🗪 🗙

**Premier Inns** M
(602) 943-2371. **$39-$109.** 10402 Black Canyon Fwy. I-17, exit 208 (Peoria Ave), 0.3 mi w to 28th Dr, just s, just e on Metro Pkwy E, then just n on 27th Ave. Ext corridors. **Pets:** Accepted.
SAVE SÒ ✕ &M 🗪

**Prime Hotel Phoenix North** SH
(602) 978-2222. **$75-$123.** 2641 W Union Hills Dr. I-17, exit 214A (Union Hills Dr), just w. Int corridors. **Pets:** Accepted.
ASK ✕ 🖉 🖪 🔲 💻 🍴 🗪

**Radisson Hotel Phoenix Airport North** SH
(602) 220-4400. **$109-$239.** 427 N 44th St. Loop 202, exit 2 (44th St), 0.5 mi s. Int corridors. **Pets:** Accepted.
ASK SÒ ✕ &M 🖉 🖪 🔲 💻 🍴 🗪

**Ramada Plaza Hotel and Suites** SH
(602) 866-7000. **$69-$130.** 12027 N 28th Dr. I-17, exit 209 (Cactus Rd), just w, then just s. Int corridors. **Pets:** Medium. $25 daily fee/pet. Designated rooms, service with restrictions, crate.

**Red Roof Inn** SH
(602) 233-8004. **$57-$75.** 5215 W Willetta. I-10, exit 139 (51st Ave), just n, just e on McDowell Rd, then just s. Int corridors. **Pets:** Accepted.

**Red Roof Inn-Camelback** SH
(602) 264-9290. **$45-$51.** 502 W Camelback Rd. I-17, exit 203 (Camelback Rd), 1.8 mi e. Int corridors. **Pets:** Accepted.

**Residence Inn by Marriott** SH
(602) 864-1900. **$79-$122.** 8242 N Black Canyon Hwy. I-17, exit 207 (Dunlap Ave), just w, then 0.8 mi s. Ext/int corridors. **Pets:** Medium, dogs only. $75 deposit/pet. Service with restrictions, supervision.

**Residence Inn by Marriott Phoenix Airport** SH
(602) 273-9220. **$69-$250.** 801 N 44th St. Loop 202, exit 152 (40th and 44th sts) eastbound; exit 152 (44th St) westbound, just s. Int corridors. **Pets:** Small. $75 one-time fee/room. Service with restrictions.

**The Ritz-Carlton, Phoenix** LH
(602) 468-0700. **$159-$519.** 2401 E Camelback Rd. Southeast corner of Camelback Rd and 24th St. Int corridors. **Pets:** Accepted.

**Royal Palms Resort and Spa** LH
(602) 840-3610. **$135-$325, 7 day notice.** 5200 E Camelback Rd. Just e of 52nd St. Ext/int corridors. **Pets:** Accepted.

**Sheraton Crescent Hotel** LH
(602) 943-8200. **$75-$259.** 2620 W Dunlap Ave. I-17, exit 207 (Dunlap Ave), just e. Int corridors. **Pets:** Accepted.

**Sheraton Wild Horse Pass Resort & Spa** LH
(602) 225-0100. **$125-$300, 7 day notice.** 5594 W Wild Horse Pass Blvd. I-10, exit 162, 2.4 mi w. Int corridors. **Pets:** Accepted.

**Sleep Inn Phoenix North** SH
(602) 504-1200. **$49-$143.** 18235 N 27th Ave. I-17, exit 214A, just w, then just s. Int corridors. **Pets:** Small, other species. $50 deposit/pet, $15 daily fee/pet. Designated rooms, service with restrictions, crate.

**Sleep Inn Sky Harbor Airport** SH
(480) 967-7100. **$65-$169.** 2621 S 47th Pl. I-10, exit 151 (University Dr), 2 mi n, then just w. Int corridors. **Pets:** Accepted.

**Studio 6 Phoenix-Deer Valley #6030** SH
(602) 843-1151. **$49-$77.** 18405 N 27th Ave. I-17, exit 214A (Union Hills Dr), just w, then just s. Ext corridors. **Pets:** Accepted.

**Super 8 Motel-Phoenix** SH
(602) 415-0888. **$69-$199.** 1242 N 53rd Ave. I-10, exit 139 (51st Ave), just s to Latham Rd, then just w. Int corridors. **Pets:** Other species. $25 daily fee/room. Designated rooms, service with restrictions, supervision.

**TownePlace Suites by Marriott** SH
(602) 943-9510. **$80-$150.** 9425 N Black Canyon Hwy. I-17, exit 207, just e, then 0.3 mi n. Int corridors. **Pets:** Accepted.

**Travelers Inn** SH
(602) 233-1988. **$49.** 5102 W Latham St. I-10, exit 139 (51st Ave), just sw. Ext corridors. **Pets:** $15 one-time fee/pet. Supervision.

**Wingate Inn Phoenix** SH
(602) 716-9900. **$69-$129.** 2520 N Central Ave. I-10, exit 145 (7th St), just n to McDowell Rd, 0.4 mi w, then 0.7 mi n. Int corridors. **Pets:** Small, other species. $75 deposit/room. Service with restrictions, supervision.

# SCOTTSDALE

**AmeriSuites (Scottsdale/Old Town)** SH
(480) 423-9944. **$59-$199.** 7300 E 3rd Ave. Just e of Scottsdale Rd. Int corridors. **Pets:** Small, other species. Service with restrictions, supervision.

**Best Western Papago Inn & Resort** SH
(480) 947-7335. **$59-$159, 3 day notice.** 7017 E McDowell Rd. From Scottsdale Rd, just w. Ext corridors. **Pets:** Accepted.

**Best Western Scottsdale Airpark Suites** SH
(480) 951-4000. **$79-$179.** 7515 E Butherus Dr. 0.8 mi n of Thunderbird Rd; 0.5 mi e of Scottsdale Rd. Ext corridors. **Pets:** Accepted.

**Camelback Inn, A JW Marriott Resort & Spa** LH
(480) 948-1700. **$149-$499, 7 day notice.** 5402 E Lincoln Dr. 0.5 mi e of Tatum Blvd; north side of Lincoln Dr. Ext corridors. **Pets:** Service with restrictions, crate.

**Chaparral Suites Resort** SH
(480) 949-1414. **$159-$219.** 5001 N Scottsdale Rd. At Chaparral Rd. Ext corridors. **Pets:** Medium, dogs only. $25 one-time fee/pet. Service with restrictions, supervision.

**Comfort Suites by Choice Hotels-Old Town** SH
(480) 946-1111. **$50-$170.** 3275 N Drinkwater Blvd. N of Thomas Rd; just e of Scottsdale Rd. Int corridors. **Pets:** Accepted.

**Country Inn & Suites By Carlson** SH
(480) 314-1200. **$65-$155.** 10801 N 89th Pl. Loop 101, exit 41, just e on Shea Blvd, then just n. Int corridors. **Pets:** Medium. $50 one-time fee/room. Service with restrictions, supervision.

**DoubleTree Paradise Valley Resort-Scottsdale** LH
(480) 947-5400. **$75-$289.** 5401 N Scottsdale Rd. Just n of Chaparral Rd; on east side of Scottsdale Rd. Ext corridors. **Pets:** Small. $50 one-time fee/room. Service with restrictions, crate.

**Extended Stay Deluxe Phoenix-Scottsdale** SH
(480) 483-1333. **$75-$115.** 10660 N 69th St. From jct Scottsdale Rd, just w on Shea Blvd, then just n. Int corridors. **Pets:** $25 daily fee/pet. Service with restrictions, supervision.

**The Fairmont Scottsdale Princess** 🏨 🐾
(480) 585-4848. **$139-$499, 14 day notice.** 7575 E Princess Dr. 0.6 mi n of Bell Rd, 0.5 mi e of Scottsdale Rd; on south side of Princess Dr. Ext/int corridors. **Pets:** Small. $30 daily fee/room. Supervision.

**Four Seasons Resort Scottsdale at Troon North** 🏨 🐾
(480) 515-5700. **$185-$4500, 7 day notice.** 10600 E Crescent Moon Dr. SR 101, exit 36 (Pima Rd), 4.7 mi n, 2 mi e on Happy Valley, then 1.5 mi n on Alma School Rd. Ext corridors. **Pets:** Small. Service with restrictions, supervision.

**Hampton Inn-Oldtown/Fashion Square Scottsdale** 🏨 🐾
(480) 941-9400. **$69-$179.** 4415 N Civic Center Plaza. Scottsdale Rd, just e on Camelback Rd, just s on 75th St. Ext/int corridors. **Pets:** Other species. $50 one-time fee/room. Service with restrictions.

**Hilton Scottsdale Resort & Villas** 🏨 🐾
(480) 948-7750. **$89-$359, 3 day notice.** 6333 N Scottsdale Rd. Loop 101, exit 45, 2.1 mi w on McDonald Dr, then 0.3 mi n. Int corridors. **Pets:** Small, dogs only. $75 deposit/room, $25 one-time fee/room. Service with restrictions, crate.

**Holiday Inn Express Hotel & Suites-Scottsdale** 🏨
(480) 675-7665. **$69-$189.** 3131 N Scottsdale Rd. Northeast corner of Scottsdale Rd and Earll Dr. Int corridors. **Pets:** Small, other species. $75 deposit/room. Service with restrictions, supervision.

**Homestead Studio Suites Hotel-Phoenix-Scottsdale** 🏨
(480) 994-0297. **$55-$95.** 3560 N Marshall Way. Just w of Scottsdale Rd on Goldwater, just s. Ext corridors. **Pets:** $25 daily fee/pet. Service with restrictions, supervision.

**The Inn at Pima, A Condominium Suite Hotel** 🏨 🐾
(480) 948-3800. **$59-$189.** 7330 N Pima Rd. 0.4 mi n of Indian Bend Rd; on west side of Pima Rd. Ext/int corridors. **Pets:** Other species. $10 daily fee/room. Designated rooms, service with restrictions, supervision.

**La Quinta Inn & Suites Phoenix (Scottsdale)** 🏨
(480) 614-5300. **$96-$158.** 8888 E Shea Blvd. Loop 101, exit Shea Blvd, northeast corner. Int corridors. **Pets:** Medium. Service with restrictions.

**Millennium Resort Scottsdale, McCormick Ranch** 🏨
(480) 948-5050. **$69-$279.** 7401 N Scottsdale Rd. 0.8 mi n of Indian Bend Rd. Int corridors. **Pets:** Accepted.

**Motel 6 Scottsdale #29** 🅼
(480) 946-2280. **$55-$78.** 6848 E Camelback Rd. Just w of Scottsdale Rd. Ext corridors. **Pets:** Accepted.

**The Phoenician** 🏨
(480) 941-8200. **$375-$775, 7 day notice.** 6000 E Camelback Rd. 0.5 mi w of 64th St. Ext/int corridors. **Pets:** Accepted.

**Ramada Limited Scottsdale** 🅼
(480) 994-9461. **$50-$150.** 6935 5th Ave. Just w of Scottsdale Rd; just n of Indian School Rd; on south side of 5th Ave. Ext corridors. **Pets:** Small. $15 daily fee/pet. Service with restrictions, supervision.

**Renaissance Scottsdale Resort** 🏨
(480) 991-1414. **$129-$369.** 6160 N Scottsdale Rd. Just n of McDonald Dr; on west side of Scottsdale Rd. Ext corridors. **Pets:** Accepted.

**Residence Inn by Marriott, Scottsdale/Paradise Valley** 🏨
(480) 948-8666. **$79-$309.** 6040 N Scottsdale Rd. Just n of McDonald Dr. Ext/int corridors. **Pets:** Other species. $75 one-time fee/room. Service with restrictions.

**Residence Inn Scottsdale North** 🏨 🐾
(480) 563-4120. **$89-$239.** 17011 N Scottsdale Rd. SR 101, exit 34 (Scottsdale Rd), 1.1 mi s, then just e on 17050 N. Int corridors. **Pets:** Small. $75 one-time fee/room. Designated rooms, service with restrictions, crate.

**Rodeway Inn of Scottsdale** 🅼
(480) 946-3456. **$54-$109.** 7110 E Indian School Rd. Just w of Scottsdale Rd, on north side of Indian School Rd. Ext corridors. **Pets:** Accepted.

**Scottsdale Marriott at McDowell Mountains** 🏨
(480) 502-3836. **$119-$329.** 16770 N Perimeter Dr. Loop 101, exit 36 (Princess Dr), just w to N Perimeter Dr, then 0.6 mi s. Int corridors. **Pets:** Small. $50 daily fee/pet. Designated rooms, service with restrictions, supervision.

**Sleep Inn** 🏨 🐾
(480) 998-9211. **$54-$139.** 16630 N Scottsdale Rd. Just s of Bell Rd. Int corridors. **Pets:** Large, other species. $10 daily fee/room. Service with restrictions, supervision.

**Summerfield Suites by Wyndham-Scottsdale** 🏨
(480) 946-7700. **$89-$329.** 4245 N Drinkwater Blvd. 0.3 mi e of Scottsdale Rd. Ext corridors. **Pets:** Accepted.

**TownePlace Suites by Marriott** 🏨
(480) 551-1100. **$59-$139.** 10740 N 90th St. Loop 101, exit Shea Blvd, just e to 90th St, then just n. Int corridors. **Pets:** Other species. $75 one-time fee/room. Service with restrictions.

**The Westin Kierland Resort & Spa** 🏨 🐾
(480) 624-1000. **$169-$569, 7 day notice.** 6902 E Greenway Pkwy. 0.5 mi w of Scottsdale Rd. Int corridors. **Pets:** Other species. Designated rooms.

## SURPRISE

**Days Inn & Suites** 🏨
(623) 933-4000. **$60-$175.** 12477 W Bell Rd. US 60 (Grand Ave), 1.1 mi e, then just s on Greasewood St. Int corridors. **Pets:** Accepted.

**Windmill Suites at Sun City West** 🏨
(623) 583-0133. **$76-$157.** 12545 W Bell Rd. US 60 (Grand Ave), 1 mi e. Int corridors. **Pets:** Accepted.

# TEMPE

**AAA** ▼▼▼▼ **AmeriSuites (Tempe/Arizona Mills)** SH
(480) 831-9800. **$69-$179.** 1520 W Baseline Rd. I-10, exit 155 (Baseline Rd), 0.4 mi e. Int corridors. **Pets:** Medium. $10 daily fee/pet. Service with restrictions, supervision.
SAVE ⬛ ✕ ⬛ ⬛ ⬛ ≋

**AAA** ▼▼▼▼ **AmeriSuites (Tempe/Phoenix Airport)** SH
(480) 804-9544. **$79-$189.** 1413 W Rio Salado Pkwy. Just w of Priest Dr. Int corridors. **Pets:** Accepted.
SAVE ⬛ ✕ ⬛ ⬛ ⬛ ≋

**AAA** ▼▼▼ **Best Western Inn of Tempe** SH
(480) 784-2233. **$69-$129, 15 day notice.** 670 N Scottsdale Rd. SR 202 Loop (Red Mountain Frwy), exit 7, just s. Int corridors. **Pets:** Accepted.
SAVE ⬛ ✕ ⬛ ⬛ ⬛ ≋

▼▼▼▼ **Candlewood Suites** SH
(480) 777-0440. **$46-$120.** 1335 W Baseline Rd. I-10, exit 155 (Baseline Rd), 0.5 mi e; just e of Priest Dr. Int corridors. **Pets:** Medium. $150 one-time fee/pet. Service with restrictions, supervision.
ASK ⬛ ✕ ⬛ ⬛ ⬛ ≋

**AAA** ▼▼▼▼ **Comfort Inn & Suites Tempe/ASU** SH
(480) 966-7202. **$49-$129.** 1031 E Apache Blvd. SR 202 Loop (Red Mountain Frwy), exit 7 (Rural Rd S), 1.5 mi s, then just e. Int corridors. **Pets:** Other species. $50 deposit/room. Service with restrictions, supervision.
SAVE ⬛ ✕ ⬭ ⬛ ⬛ ⬛ ≋ ✕

**AAA** ▼▼▼▼ **Country Inn & Suites By Carlson** SH
(480) 345-8585. **$72-$110.** 1660 W Elliot Rd. I-10, exit 157, just e. Ext corridors. **Pets:** Large, other species. $50 deposit/room. Service with restrictions.
ASK ⬛ ✕ ⬭ ⬛ ⬛ ≋

**AAA** ▼▼ **Econo Lodge/Tempe ASU** M
(480) 966-5832. **$42-$72.** 2101 E Apache Blvd. Loop 101, exit Broadway southbound, just e to Price Rd, then just s; exit Rio Salado Pkwy northbound, just s. Ext corridors. **Pets:** Accepted.
SAVE ✕ ⬛ ⬛ ≋

**AAA** ▼▼ **Fiesta Inn Resort** LH
(480) 967-1441. **$85-$165.** 2100 S Priest Dr. I-10, exit 153 (Broadway Rd), 0.5 mi e. Ext corridors. **Pets:** Small. $50 deposit/room. Designated rooms, service with restrictions, supervision.
SAVE ⬛ ✕ ⬭ ⬛ ⬛ ⬛ ⬛ ⧍ ≋ ✕

**AAA** ▼▼▼▼ **Hampton Inn & Suites** SH
(480) 675-9799. **$89-$159.** 1429 N Scottsdale Rd. SR 202 Loop (Red Mountain Frwy), exit 7, 0.5 mi n. Ext corridors. **Pets:** Other species. $50 one-time fee/room. Service with restrictions, supervision.
SAVE ⬛ ✕ ⬭ ⬛ ⬛ ⬛ ≋ ✕ ✿

▼▼▼▼ **Hawthorn Suites–Tempe** SH ✿
(480) 633-2744. **$69-$159.** 2301 E Southern Ave. Loop 101, exit Southern Ave/Baseline Rd; at southeast corner. Int corridors. **Pets:** Other species. $75 one-time fee/room. Service with restrictions, supervision.
ASK ⬛ ✕ ⬙ ⬭ ⬛ ⬛ ⬛ ≋

**AAA** ▼▼ **Holiday Inn** SH
(480) 968-3451. **$59-$116.** 915 E Apache Blvd. US 60 (Superstition Frwy), exit 174 (Rural Rd), 2 mi n. Int corridors. **Pets:** Large. $50 deposit/room. Service with restrictions, supervision.
SAVE ⬛ ✕ ⬭ ⬛ ⬛ ⬛ ⧍ ≋ ✕

▼▼▼ **Holiday Inn Express/Tempe** SH
(480) 820-7500. **$59-$99.** 5300 S Priest Dr. I-10, exit 155 (Baseline Rd), 0.4 mi e, then just s. Int corridors. **Pets:** Small. $25 one-time fee/pet. Service with restrictions, supervision.
ASK ⬛ ✕ ⬛ ⬛ ≋

▼▼▼▼ **Homestead Studio Suites**
**Hotel-Phoenix/Airport/Tempe** SH
(480) 557-8880. **$65-$95.** 2165 W 15th St. I-10, exit 153 (Broadway Rd), 0.3 mi ne, just nw on S 52nd St, then just w. Int corridors. **Pets:** $25 daily fee/pet. Service with restrictions, supervision.
ASK ⬛ ✕ ⬭ ⬛ ⬛ ≋

**AAA** ▼▼▼▼ **InnSuites Hotels & Suites Tempe/Phoenix**
**Airport** SH
(480) 897-7900. **$69-$119.** 1651 W Baseline Rd. I-10, exit 155 (Baseline Rd), just e. Ext corridors. **Pets:** Accepted.
SAVE ⬛ ✕ ⬛ ⬛ ⧍ ≋ ✕

▼▼▼ **La Quinta Inn Phoenix (Sky Harbor South)** SH
(480) 967-4465. **$70-$142.** 911 S 48th St. I-10, exit 153 (Broadway Rd) eastbound; exit 153A (University Dr) westbound, 0.8 mi n; on south side of University Dr; east side of SR 143 (Hohokam Expwy). Ext corridors. **Pets:** Medium. Service with restrictions.
ASK ✕ ⬙ ⬭ ⬛ ⬛ ≋

▼ **Motel 6 #1315** M
(480) 945-9506. **$45-$65.** 1612 N Scottsdale Rd. Loop 202(Red Mountain Frwy), exit 7, 0.6 mi n. Ext corridors. **Pets:** Accepted.
⬛ ✕ ≋

**AAA** ▼▼▼ **Quality Inn Tempe/Airport** M
(480) 967-3000. **$59-$139.** 1550 S 52nd St. I-10, exit 153 (Broadway Rd), 0.3 mi ne. Ext corridors. **Pets:** Accepted.
SAVE ⬛ ✕ ⬙ ⬛ ⬛ ≋

**AAA** ▼▼▼ **Ramada Limited** SH ✿
(480) 413-1188. **$59-$69.** 1701 W Baseline Rd. I-10, exit 155 (Baseline Rd), just e. Ext corridors. **Pets:** $15 daily fee/pet. Supervision.
SAVE ⬛ ✕ ⬙ ⬭ ⬛ ⬛ ≋

**AAA** ▼▼ **Ramada Limited Tempe-University** M
(480) 736-1700. **$49-$99.** 1915 E Apache Blvd. US 60 (Superstition Frwy), exit 175, 1.9 mi n on McClintock Dr, then 0.3 mi e. Ext corridors. **Pets:** Small, dogs only. $50 deposit/room. Service with restrictions, supervision.
SAVE ⬛ ✕ ⬙ ⬭ ⬛ ⬛ ≋

▼▼▼ **Red Roof Inn Phoenix Airport** SH
(480) 449-3205. **$54-$75.** 2135 W 15th St. I-10, exit 153 (Broadway Rd), just nw on S 52nd St, then just w. Int corridors. **Pets:** Accepted.
✕ ⬭ ⬛ ≋

▼▼▼▼ **Residence Inn by Marriott** SH
(480) 756-2122. **$79-$229.** 5075 S Priest Dr. I-10, exit 155 (Baseline Rd), 0.4 mi e, then just n. Ext/int corridors. **Pets:** Other species. $75 one-time fee/room. Service with restrictions, supervision.
✕ ⬙ ⬭ ⬛ ⬛ ≋ ✕

**AAA** ▼▼▼▼ **Sheraton Phoenix Airport Hotel** LH
(480) 967-6600. **$119-$239.** 1600 S 52nd St. I-10, exit 153B Broadway Rd westbound; exit 153A 48th St eastbound, 0.3 mi ne. Int corridors. **Pets:** Accepted.
SAVE ⬛ ✕ ⬙ ⬭ ⬛ ⬛ ⧍ ≋ ✕

▼▼ **Studio 6 Extended Stay #6031** SH
(602) 414-4470. **$49-$77.** 4909 S Wendler Dr. I-10, exit 155 (Baseline Rd), just w, then 0.4 mi n. Ext corridors. **Pets:** Accepted.
⬛ ✕ ⬭ ⬛ ≋

**AAA** ▼▼▼▼ **Tempe Mission Palms Hotel** SH
(480) 894-1400. **$109-$219, 3 day notice.** 60 E 5th St. Just e of Mill Ave, 0.3 mi n of University Dr; downtown. Int corridors. **Pets:** Accepted.
SAVE ⬛ ✕ ⬙ ⬭ ⬛ ⬛ ⧍ ≋ ✕

▼▼ **Tempe Super 8** M
(480) 967-8891. **$39-$99.** 1020 E Apache Blvd. Just e of Rural Rd. Ext corridors. **Pets:** Other species. $15 one-time fee/room. Designated rooms, service with restrictions, supervision.
ASK ⬛ ✕ ⬛ ≋

**Wyndham Buttes Resort** SH
(602) 225-9000. **$119-$239.** 2000 Westcourt Way. I-10, exit 153 (Broadway Rd) westbound, 0.8 mi w to 48th St, then 0.3 mi s; exit 48th St eastbound, 0.5 mi s. Int corridors. **Pets:** Accepted.

SAVE ☒ 🖉 🖵 🍴 🔄 ☒

# YOUNGTOWN

**Best Western Inn & Suites of Sun City** SH ❀
(623) 933-8211. **$65-$130.** 11201 Grand Ave. On US 60, just se of 113th Ave. Ext/int corridors. **Pets:** Medium, other species. Designated rooms, service with restrictions, supervision.

SAVE S❍ ☒ 🖉 🖳 🖬 🖵 🔄

## END METROPOLITAN AREA

# PINETOP-LAKESIDE

**Bear Mountain Inn & Suites** SH
(928) 368-6600. **$49-$109.** 1637 White Mountain Blvd. On SR 260. Int corridors. **Pets:** Accepted.

SAVE S❍ ☒ 🖬

**Best Western Inn of Pinetop** M
(928) 367-6667. **$95.** 404 E White Mountain Blvd. On SR 260. Ext corridors. **Pets:** Large. $10 daily fee/pet. Service with restrictions, supervision.

SAVE S❍ ☒ 🖬 🖵

**Holiday Inn Express** SH
(928) 367-6077. **$79-$169.** 431 E White Mountain Blvd. On SR 260. Int corridors. **Pets:** Accepted.

SAVE S❍ ☒ 🖬 🖵 ☒

**Lazy Oaks Resort** CA
(928) 368-6203. **$69-$126 (no credit cards), 21 day notice.** 1075 Larson Rd. Jct SR 260, 0.8 mi s on Rainbow Lake Dr, then 0.6 mi w. Ext corridors. **Pets:** Medium. No service, supervision.

🖬 🖵 ☒ 🐾 🌀

**Northwoods Resort** CA
(928) 367-2966. **$79-$149, 14 day notice.** 165 E White Mountain Blvd. On SR 260. Ext corridors. **Pets:** Other species. $12 daily fee/pet. No service, supervision.

☒ 🖬 🖵 ☒ 🐾 🌀

**Super 8 Motel** SH
(928) 367-3161. **$125-$150.** 1202 E White Mountain Blvd. On SR 260, east end of town. Int corridors. **Pets:** Accepted.

SAVE S❍ ☒ 🖬 🔄

**Timber Lodge** M
(928) 367-4463. **$59-$69.** 1078 E White Mountain Blvd. On SR 260. Ext corridors. **Pets:** Other species. $10 daily fee/pet. Service with restrictions, supervision.

ASK S❍ ☒ 🖬 🖵 🐾

**Woodland Inn & Suites** M
(928) 367-3636. **$69-$149, 3 day notice.** 458 E White Mountain Blvd. On SR 260. Ext corridors. **Pets:** Medium, other species. $50 deposit/pet, $10 daily fee/pet. Service with restrictions, supervision.

SAVE S❍ ☒ 🖬 🖵

# PRESCOTT

**Best Western Prescottonian Motel** M
(928) 445-3096. **$79-$139.** 1317 E Gurley St. On SR 89, just s of jct SR 69. Ext corridors. **Pets:** Accepted.

ASK S❍ ☒ 🖉 🖬 🖵 🍴 🔄

**Comfort Inn of Prescott** M
(928) 778-5770. **$59-$139.** 1290 White Spar Rd. On SR 89, 1.5 mi s of town center. Ext corridors. **Pets:** Medium, dogs only. $10 daily fee/pet. Designated rooms, service with restrictions, supervision.

SAVE S❍ ☒ 🖳 🖬 🖵

**Motel 6 #0166** M
(928) 776-0160. **$45-$61.** 1111 E Sheldon St. 0.4 mi e of jct SR 89; center. Ext corridors. **Pets:** Accepted.

S❍ ☒ 🖳 🖬 🔄

**Prescott Cabin Rentals** M
(928) 778-9573. **$106-$249.** 5555 Onyx Dr. Jct SR 89, 5 mi e on SR 69, 0.4 mi s on dirt/gravel road. Ext corridors. **Pets:** Accepted.

☒ 🖬 🖵 ☒

**Prescott Super 8 Motel** M
(928) 776-1282. **$51-$66.** 1105 E Sheldon St. 0.4 mi e of jct SR 89. Int corridors. **Pets:** Accepted.

SAVE S❍ ☒ 🖉 🖬 🖵 🔄

**Quality Inn & Suites and Conference Center** SH
(928) 777-0770. **$89-$209.** 4499 Hwy 69. On SR 69, 3.6 mi e of jct SR 89. Int corridors. **Pets:** Accepted.

SAVE S❍ ☒ 🖳 🖬 🖵 🍴 🔄 ☒

# PRESCOTT VALLEY

**Days Inn/Prescott Valley** M
(928) 772-8600. **$79-$120.** 7875 E Hwy 69. On SR 69; corner of Windsong Rd. Ext corridors. **Pets:** Other species. $50 deposit/room. Service with restrictions.

SAVE S❍ ☒ 🖳 🖬 🔄

# QUARTZSITE

**Super 8 Motel-Quartzsite** M
(928) 927-8080. **$75-$135.** 2050 W Dome Rock Rd. I-10, exit 17, just s to Frontage Rd, then 0.6 mi w. Int corridors. **Pets:** Other species. $5 daily fee/pet. Supervision.

ASK ☒ 🖳 🖬

# RIO RICO

**Esplendor Resort at Rio Rico** LH
(520) 281-1901. **$99-$250.** 1069 Camino Caralampi. I-19, exit 17 (Rio Rico Dr), 0.5 mi w. Ext corridors. **Pets:** $25 deposit/pet. Service with restrictions.

ASK S❍ ☒ 🖳M 🖳 🖬 🖵 🍴 🔄 ☒

# SAFFORD

**Best Western Desert Inn** M
(928) 428-0521. **$65-$75.** 1391 W Thatcher Blvd. US 191, 1 mi w on US 70. Ext corridors. **Pets:** Accepted.

SAVE S❍ ☒ 🖬 🖵 🔄

**Comfort Inn** M
(928) 428-5851. **$67-$74.** 1578 W Thatcher Blvd. US 191, 1.3 mi w on US 70. Ext corridors. **Pets:** Accepted.

ASK S❍ ☒ 🖬 🖵 🔄

**Days Inn** M
(928) 428-5000. **$80-$150, 30 day notice.** 520 E Hwy 70. US 191, 0.5 mi e. Ext corridors. **Pets:** Medium, other species. $10 daily fee/room. Service with restrictions, crate.

SAVE S❍ ☒ 🖳M 🖉 🖳 🖬 🖵 🔄

◆ **Econo Lodge** **M**
(928) 348-0011. **$51.** 225 E Hwy 70. Just e of jct US 191 and 70. Ext corridors. **Pets:** Accepted.

**◆◆◆◆ Quality Inn & Suites** **SH**
(928) 428-3200. **$85-$215.** 420 E Hwy 70. US 191, 0.5 mi e. Ext/int corridors. **Pets:** Accepted.

## ST. JOHNS

◆ **Days Inn** **M**
(928) 337-4422. **$75-$85.** 125 E Commercial St. Center. Ext corridors. **Pets:** Accepted.

## ST. MICHAELS

**◆◆◆ ◆◆◆◆ Navajoland Days Inn** **SH**
(928) 871-5690. **$70-$95.** 392 W Hwy 264. From jct SR 12, 1.5 mi w. Ext corridors. **Pets:** Small. $20 daily fee/pet. Service with restrictions, supervision.

## SEDONA

**◆◆◆ ◆◆◆◆ Best Western Inn of Sedona** **SH**
(928) 282-3072. **$134-$209.** 1200 W Hwy 89A. Jct SR 179, 1.2 mi w. Ext corridors. **Pets:** Large, other species. $20 daily fee/room. Designated rooms, service with restrictions, supervision.

**◆◆◆ ◆◆◆ Desert Quail Inn** **M**
(928) 284-1433. **$69-$139.** 6626 Hwy 179. Jct Bell Rock Blvd, 0.9 mi s. Ext corridors. **Pets:** Small, dogs only. $10 daily fee/pet. Designated rooms, service with restrictions, supervision.

**◆◆◆ ◆◆◆◆ El Portal Sedona** **BB**
(928) 203-9405. **$225-$495, 15 day notice.** 95 Portal Ln. Jct SR 89A, just s on SR 179, then just w. Ext/int corridors. **Pets:** Other species. Designated rooms, service with restrictions, supervision.

**◆◆◆ ◆◆◆◆ Hilton Sedona Resort & Spa** **LH**
(928) 284-4040. **$139-$299, 3 day notice.** 90 Ridge Trail Dr. Jct SR 89A, 7.3 mi s on SR 179. Int corridors. **Pets:** Accepted.

**◆◆◆ ◆◆◆◆ La Quinta Inn Sedona** **SH**
(928) 284-0711. **$105-$125.** 6176 Hwy 179. Jct Bell Rock Blvd, just s. Int corridors. **Pets:** Medium. Service with restrictions, crate.

**◆◆◆ ◆◆◆◆ ◆◆◆◆ L'Auberge de Sedona Resort** **SH**
(928) 282-1661. **$189-$319, 14 day notice.** 301 L Ln. Jct SR 179, just ne on SR 89A to L'Auberge Ln; east side of SR 89A, just n down the hill. Ext/int corridors. **Pets:** Medium, dogs only. $100 deposit/pet, $50 one-time fee/pet. Service with restrictions.

**◆◆◆◆ ◆◆◆◆ The Lodge at Sedona** **BB** ❖
(928) 204-1942. **$165-$325, 14 day notice.** 125 Kallof Pl. Jct SR 179, 1.8 mi w on SR 89A, then just s. Ext/int corridors. **Pets:** Dogs only. $200 deposit/room, $35 daily fee/pet. Designated rooms, service with restrictions, supervision.

**◆◆◆ ◆◆◆◆ Matterhorn Inn** **M** ❖
(928) 282-7176. **$69-$159.** 230 Apple Ave. Jct SR 179, just ne on SR 89A; uptown. Ext corridors. **Pets:** Large, other species. $10 daily fee/room. Designated rooms, service with restrictions, crate.

**◆◆◆ ◆◆◆◆ Quality Inn-King's Ransom** **SH** ❖
(928) 282-7151. **$69-$189.** 771 Hwy 179. 0.7 mi s of jct SR 89A. Ext/int corridors. **Pets:** Small. $15 one-time fee/room. Designated rooms, service with restrictions, supervision.

**◆◆◆◆ ◆◆◆◆ Radisson Poco Diablo Resort** **LH**
(928) 282-7333. **$99-$139.** 1752 S Hwy 179. Jct SR 179, 2 mi s of SR 89A. Ext corridors. **Pets:** Accepted.

**◆◆◆ ◆◆◆◆ Sedona Real Inn & Suites** **SH**
(928) 282-1414. **$99-$319.** 95 Arroyo Pinon. Jct SR 179, 3.4 mi w on SR 89A, just sw. Ext corridors. **Pets:** Medium, other species. $20 one-time fee/pet. Designated rooms, service with restrictions, crate.

**◆◆◆◆ ◆◆◆◆ Sedona Rouge Hotel & Spa** **SH** ❖
(928) 203-4111. **$279-$309, 3 day notice.** 2250 W Hwy 89A. Jct SR 179, 2 mi w. Ext/int corridors. **Pets:** Medium. $100 deposit/room, $25 one-time fee/room. Designated rooms, service with restrictions, supervision.

**◆◆◆◆ ◆◆◆◆ Sedona Super 8** **SH** ❖
(928) 282-1533. **$69-$109.** 2545 W Hwy 89A. Jct SR 179, 2.4 mi w. Int corridors. **Pets:** Medium. $25 one-time fee/pet. Service with restrictions, supervision.

**◆◆◆ ◆◆◆◆ Sky Ranch Lodge** **M**
(928) 282-6400. **$75-$250.** Airport Rd. Jct SR 179, 1 mi w on SR 89A, then 1 mi s on west side. Ext corridors. **Pets:** Accepted.

**◆◆◆ ◆◆◆◆ The Views Inn Sedona** **M**
(928) 284-2487. **$65-$150.** 65 E Cortez Dr. Jct Bell Rock Blvd, 0.9 mi s on SR 179, just e. Ext corridors. **Pets:** Other species. $50 deposit/pet, $15 daily fee/pet. Designated rooms, no service, supervision.

**◆◆◆ ◆◆◆ Village Lodge** **M**
(928) 284-3626. **$49-$59.** 78 Bell Rock Blvd. Jct SR 179, just w. Ext/int corridors. **Pets:** Medium, other species. Service with restrictions, supervision.

## SELIGMAN

**◆◆◆ ◆◆◆ Canyon Lodge** **M**
(928) 422-3255. **$47-$50.** 114 E Chino Ave. I-40, exit 121, 1 mi n, then 0.7 mi e on Route 66. Ext corridors. **Pets:** Small. $10 one-time fee/pet. Designated rooms, service with restrictions, supervision.

## SHOW LOW

**◆◆◆ ◆◆◆ Best Western Paint Pony Lodge** **M**
(928) 537-5773. **$84-$204.** 581 W Deuce of Clubs Ave. On US 60 and SR 260. Ext corridors. **Pets:** Other species. $10 daily fee/pet. Designated rooms, service with restrictions, supervision.

**◆◆◆ ◆◆◆ Days Inn** **M**
(928) 537-4356. **$65-$85.** 480 W Deuce of Clubs Ave. On US 60 and SR 260. Ext/int corridors. **Pets:** Small. $10 daily fee/room. Service with restrictions, crate.

**◆◆◆ ◆◆◆ Kiva Motel** **M**
(928) 537-4542. **$48-$58, 3 day notice.** 261 E Deuce of Clubs Ave. On US 60 and SR 260. Ext corridors. **Pets:** Medium, dogs only. $5 daily fee/pet. Service with restrictions, supervision.

▼▼ Motel 6 #4102 **M**
(928) 537-7694. **$50-$74.** 1941 E Deuce of Clubs Ave. Just e of jct SR 260. Ext corridors. **Pets:** Medium. Designated rooms, service with restrictions, supervision.

[ASK] [S🐾] [✕] [🍴]

**AAA** ▼▼▼ Sleep Inn **SH**
(928) 532-7323. **$74-$115.** 1751 W Deuce of Clubs Ave. On SR 260, 0.5 mi w of US 60. Int corridors. **Pets:** Other species. $10 daily fee/pet. Service with restrictions, supervision.

[SAVE] [S🐾] [✕] [&M] [🐾] [🛁] [🍴] [💻] [🏊]

## SIERRA VISTA

**AAA** ▼▼▼ Best Western Mission Inn **M**
(520) 458-8500. **$69-$80.** 3460 E Fry Blvd. Just w of jct SR 90 and 92. Ext corridors. **Pets:** Medium, other species. Service with restrictions, supervision.

[SAVE] [S🐾] [✕] [&M] [🍴] [💻] [🏊]

**AAA** ▼▼▼ Quality Inn **SH**
(520) 458-7900. **$79-$99, 14 day notice.** 1631 S Hwy 92. On SR 92, 1 mi s of jct SR 90. Int corridors. **Pets:** Large. $10 daily fee/pet. Designated rooms, service with restrictions, crate.

[SAVE] [S🐾] [✕] [🍴] [💻] [🏊]

**AAA** ▼▼ Super 8 Motel **M**
(520) 459-5380. **$49-$59.** 100 Fab Ave. Jct Business SR 90 and Fry Blvd, then just e of main gate to Fort Huachuca. Ext corridors. **Pets:** Accepted.

[SAVE] [S🐾] [✕] [🐾] [🍴] [💻] [🏊]

▼▼▼ Windemere Hotel & Conference Center **SH**
(520) 459-5900. **$139.** 2047 S Hwy 92. 1.5 mi s of jct SR 90. Int corridors. **Pets:** $50 deposit/pet. Service with restrictions, crate.

[ASK] [S🐾] [✕] [🍴] [💻] [🍴] [🏊]

## TAYLOR

**AAA** ▼▼▼ Silver Creek Inn **M**
(928) 536-2600. **$53-$69.** 825 N Main St. On SR 77. Ext corridors. **Pets:** Other species. $10 daily fee/room. Service with restrictions, crate.

[SAVE] [S🐾] [✕] [🍴] [💻]

# TOMBSTONE

**AAA** ▼▼▼ Best Western Lookout Lodge **SH**
(520) 457-2223. **$75-$95.** 801 US Hwy 80 W. On SR 80, 1 mi n. Ext corridors. **Pets:** Accepted.

[SAVE] [S🐾] [✕] [🍴] [💻] [🏊]

**AAA** ▼▼▼ Tombstone Motel **M**
(520) 457-3478. **$59-$79.** 502 E Fremont St. On SR 80; between 5th and 6th sts. Ext corridors. **Pets:** Small. $25 deposit/pet. Designated rooms, service with restrictions, supervision.

[SAVE] [✕] [🍴] [💻]

**AAA** ▼▼ Trail Riders Inn **M**
(520) 457-3573. **$55.** 13 N 7th St. Just e; center. Ext corridors. **Pets:** Medium, dogs only. $6 daily fee/pet. Service with restrictions, supervision.

[SAVE] [S🐾] [✕] [🏊]

## TUBAC

▼▼▼▼ Tubac Golf Resort **SH**
(520) 398-2211. **$99-$345, 7 day notice.** 1 Otero Rd. I-19, exit 40, on east side, then 2 mi s. Ext corridors. **Pets:** Accepted.

[ASK] [✕] [🐾] [🍴] [💻] [🍴] [🏊] [🐾]

## TUBA CITY

**AAA** ▼▼▼ Quality Inn **SH**
(928) 283-4545. **$85-$110.** Main St & Moenave Rd. 1 mi n of US 160. Int corridors. **Pets:** Medium. $10 one-time fee/pet. Service with restrictions, supervision.

[SAVE] [S🐾] [✕] [🍴] [💻] [🍴]

# TUCSON METROPOLITAN AREA

## CATALINA

▼▼▼ Super 8 Motel-Tucson/Catalina **M**
(520) 818-9500. **$51-$75.** 15691 N Oracle Rd. 4.6 mi n of Tangerine Rd. Ext/int corridors. **Pets:** Dogs only. $100 deposit/pet, $5 daily fee/pet. Service with restrictions, supervision.

[ASK] [S🐾] [✕] [🐾] [🍴] [💻] [🏊]

## GREEN VALLEY

**AAA** ▼▼▼▼ Baymont Inn & Suites **SH**
(520) 399-3736. **$74-$144.** 90 W Esperanza Blvd. I-19, exit 65, just w. Int corridors. **Pets:** Medium. $50 deposit/pet. Designated rooms, service with restrictions, supervision.

[SAVE] [S🐾] [✕] [🐾] [🐾] [🍴] [💻] [🏊]

**AAA** ▼▼▼▼ Best Western Green Valley **SH**
(520) 625-2250. **$59-$124.** 111 S La Canada Dr. I-19, exit 65, just w, then just s. Int corridors. **Pets:** Small, dogs only. $25 one-time fee/pet. Designated rooms, service with restrictions, supervision.

[SAVE] [S🐾] [✕] [🍴] [💻] [🍴] [🏊]

▼▼ Holiday Inn Express **SH**
(520) 625-0900. **$70-$135.** 19200 S I-19 Frontage Rd. I-19, exit 69 (Duval Mine Rd), west side of interstate, then just s. Int corridors. **Pets:** Accepted.

[ASK] [S🐾] [✕] [🐾] [🐾] [🍴] [💻] [🏊]

## MARANA

**AAA** ▼▼▼ La Quinta Inn & Suites **SH**
(520) 572-4235. **$59-$199.** 6020 W Hospitality Rd. I-10, exit 246 (Cortaro Rd), just w, then just n. Int corridors. **Pets:** Service with restrictions, supervision.

[SAVE] [S🐾] [✕] [&M] [🐾] [🍴] [💻] [🏊]

▼▼ Red Roof Inn Tucson North **SH**
(520) 744-8199. **$47-$73.** 4940 W Ina Rd. I-10, exit 248 (Ina Rd), just w. Int corridors. **Pets:** Accepted.

[✕] [🐾] [🍴] [🏊]

▼▼ Super 8 Motel **SH**
(520) 572-0300. **$79-$109.** 8351 N Cracker Barrel Rd. I-10, exit 246 (Cortaro Rd), just w. Int corridors. **Pets:** $10 daily fee/room. Service with restrictions, supervision.

[ASK] [✕] [🐾] [🍴] [🏊]

▼▼ Travelodge **SH**
(520) 744-3382. **$50-$150.** 4910 W Ina Rd. I-10, exit 248 (Ina Rd), just w. Ext corridors. **Pets:** Accepted.

[ASK] [S🐾] [✕] [🐾] [🍴] [💻] [🏊]

# ORO VALLEY

**△△△ ▼▼▼ ▼▼▼ Hilton Tucson El Conquistador Golf & Tennis Resort** 🄻🄷
(520) 544-5000. **$79-$299.** 10000 N Oracle Rd. I-10, exit 248 (Ina Rd), 5.4 mi e, then 4.4 mi n. Ext/int corridors. **Pets:** Medium. $50 one-time fee/room. Designated rooms, service with restrictions, crate.
SAVE ⊠ &M 🄴 🄱 🄻🄿 🄸🄸 ⊷ ⊠

# TUCSON

**△△△ ▼▼ Americas Best Value Inn-Tucson** 🄼
(520) 884-5800. **$50-$139.** 810 E Benson Hwy. I-10, exit 262, just s. Ext corridors. **Pets:** Other species. $25 deposit/room. Service with restrictions, supervision.
SAVE 🄢🄳 ⊠ 🄱 ⊷

**△△△ ▼▼▼ AmeriSuites (Tucson/Airport)** 🄢🄷
(520) 295-0405. **$79-$189.** 6885 S Tucson Blvd. Just n of Tucson International Airport. Int corridors. **Pets:** Service with restrictions, supervision.
SAVE 🄢🄳 ⊠ &M 🄢 🄴 🄱 🄻🄿 ⊷

**△△△ ▼▼▼ Best Western Executive Inn** 🄢🄷
(520) 791-7551. **$65-$89.** 333 W Drachman St. I-10, exit 257 (Speedway Blvd), 0.4 mi e to Main St, then 0.3 mi n. Int corridors. **Pets:** Medium, other species. $25 one-time fee/pet. Designated rooms, service with restrictions, supervision.
SAVE 🄢🄳 ⊠ 🄢 🄱 🄻🄿 ⊷

**△△△ ▼▼▼ Best Western InnSuites Hotel & Suites Tucson-Catalina Foothills** 🄢🄷
(520) 297-8111. **$69-$149.** 6201 N Oracle Rd. I-10, exit 250 (Orange Grove Rd), 4 mi e, then just s. Ext corridors. **Pets:** Accepted.
SAVE 🄢🄳 🄴 🄱 🄻🄿 ⊷ ⊠

**▼▼▼ Clarion Hotel-Randolph Park** 🄢🄷
(520) 795-0330. **$74-$164, 3 day notice.** 102 N Alvernon. Jct Campbell Ave, 2.2 mi e on Broadway, then just n. Ext/int corridors. **Pets:** $25 one-time fee/pet. Service with restrictions, crate.
ASK 🄢🄳 ⊠ 🄱 🄻🄿 🄸🄸 ⊷ ⊠

**△△△ ▼▼▼ Comfort Suites** 🄢🄷
(520) 295-4400. **$59-$159.** 6935 S Tucson Blvd. Just n of Tucson International Airport. Int corridors. **Pets:** Medium, other species. $25 one-time fee/room. Service with restrictions.
SAVE 🄢🄳 ⊠ 🄴 🄱 🄻🄿 ⊷

**▼▼▼ Comfort Suites at Tucson Mall** 🄢🄷
(520) 888-6676. **$69-$150.** 515 W Auto Mall Dr. I-10, exit 254 (Prince Rd), 1.9 mi then 1.2 mi n. Int corridors. **Pets:** Other species. $10 one-time fee/pet. Service with restrictions, crate.
ASK 🄢🄳 ⊠ 🄴 🄱 🄻🄿 ⊷ ⊠

**△△△ ▼▼▼ Comfort Suites Tanque Verde/Sabino Canyon** 🄢🄷 🐾
(520) 298-2300. **$79-$179.** 7007 E Tanque Verde Rd. Jct Grand Rd, 0.4 mi ne. Ext corridors. **Pets:** Medium. $25 one-time fee/room. Service with restrictions, supervision.
SAVE 🄢🄳 ⊠ 🄱 🄻🄿 ⊷

**▼▼▼ Country Inn & Suites By Carlson** 🄢🄷
(520) 575-9255. **$79-$139.** 7411 N Oracle Rd. SR 77 (Oracle Rd), just n of Ina Rd. Ext corridors. **Pets:** Medium. $25 one-time fee/room. Service with restrictions.
ASK 🄢🄳 ⊠ &M 🄢 🄴 🄱 🄻🄿 ⊷ ⊠

**△△△ ▼▼▼ ▼▼▼ DoubleTree Hotel at Reid Park** 🄻🄷
(520) 881-4200. **$74-$289.** 445 S Alvernon Way. I-10, exit 259 (22nd St), 4 mi e, then just n. Ext/int corridors. **Pets:** Accepted.
SAVE 🄢🄳 ⊠ 🄢 🄴 🄱 🄻🄿 🄸🄸 ⊷ ⊠

**△△△ ▼▼ Econo Lodge** 🄼
(520) 622-6714. **$38-$199.** 1136 N Stone Ave. I-10, exit 257 (St Mary Blvd) eastbound, just e, then just n. Ext corridors. **Pets:** Dogs only. $10 deposit/pet. Designated rooms, service with restrictions, supervision.
SAVE 🄢🄳 ⊠ 🄱 ⊷

**△△△ ▼▼▼▼ Hampton Inn North** 🄢🄷
(520) 206-0602. **$79-$149.** 1375 W Grant Rd. I-10, exit 256 (Grant Rd), just w. Int corridors. **Pets:** Medium. Designated rooms, service with restrictions, supervision.
SAVE 🄢🄳 ⊠ &M 🄴 🄱 🄻🄿 ⊷

**△△△ ▼▼▼▼ Holiday Inn Express Hotel & Suites Tucson Airport** 🄢🄷
(520) 889-6600. **$79-$159.** 2548 E Medina Rd. 0.5 mi n of entrance to Tucson International Airport. Int corridors. **Pets:** Accepted.
SAVE 🄢🄳 ⊠ &M 🄴 🄱 🄻🄿 ⊷

**▼▼▼▼ The Hotel Arizona** 🄻🄷
(520) 624-8711. **$98-$189.** 181 W Broadway. I-10, exit 258 (Broadway Blvd/Congress St), just e. Int corridors. **Pets:** Accepted.
ASK 🄢🄳 ⊠ 🄴 🄱 🄻🄿 🄸🄸 ⊷

**△△△ ▼▼▼ InnSuites Hotels & Suites Tucson City Center** 🄢🄷
(520) 622-3000. **$79-$155.** 475 N Granada Ave. I-10, exit 258 (Broadway Blvd/Congress St), just e, then 0.4 mi n. Ext/int corridors. **Pets:** Accepted.
SAVE 🄢🄳 ⊠ 🄱 🄻🄿 🄸🄸 ⊷ ⊠

**△△△ ▼▼▼▼ La Quinta Inn & Suites Tucson Airport** 🄢🄷
(520) 573-3333. **$96-$123.** 7001 S Tucson Blvd. Just n of Tucson International Airport. Int corridors. **Pets:** Medium. Service with restrictions.
SAVE ⊠ &M 🄢 🄴 🄱 🄻🄿 ⊷

**▼▼▼▼ La Quinta Inn Downtown** 🄢🄷 🐾
(520) 624-4455. **$59-$119.** 750 Starr Pass Blvd. I-10, exit 259 (Starr Pass Blvd), just w. Int corridors. **Pets:** Other species. $10 one-time fee/room.
ASK 🄢🄳 ⊠ 🄴 🄱 🄻🄿 ⊷

**▼▼▼▼ La Quinta Inn Tucson (East)** 🄢🄷
(520) 747-1414. **$74-$116.** 6404 E Broadway. Just e of Wilmot Rd. Ext corridors. **Pets:** Medium. Service with restrictions.
ASK ⊠ 🄱 🄻🄿 ⊷

**△△△ ▼▼▼ ▼▼▼ The Lodge At Ventana Canyon** 🄻🄷
(520) 577-4000. **$79-$549, 21 day notice.** 6200 N Clubhouse Ln. I-10, exit 256 (Grant Rd), 8.6 mi e to Tanque Verde Rd, 0.6 mi e to Sabino Canyon Rd, 2 mi n, then 3.2 mi n on Kolb Rd. Ext/int corridors. **Pets:** Accepted.
SAVE ⊠ 🄴 🄱 🄻🄿 🄸🄸 ⊷ ⊠

**△△△ ▼▼▼▼ Lodge on the Desert** 🄢🄷 🐾
(520) 325-3366. **$89-$289.** 306 N Alvernon Way. I-10, exit 258 (Broadway Blvd/Congress St), 4 mi e, then just n. Ext corridors. **Pets:** $50 deposit/room, $15 daily fee/pet. Service with restrictions, supervision.
SAVE ⊠ 🄱 🄻🄿 🄸🄸 ⊷

**△△△ ▼▼▼ ▼▼▼ Loews Ventana Canyon Resort** 🄻🄷 🐾
(520) 299-2020. **$99-$379, 7 day notice.** 7000 N Resort Dr. I-10, exit 256 (Grant Rd), 8.6 mi e, 0.6 mi ne on Tanque Verde Rd, 2 mi n on Sabino Canyon Rd, then 3.5 mi n on Kolb Rd. Ext/int corridors. **Pets:** Large, other species. Designated rooms.
SAVE 🄢🄳 ⊠ &M 🄢 🄴 🄱 🄻🄿 🄸🄸 ⊷ ⊠

**▼▼ Motel 6 Tucson-22nd Street #1196** 🄼
(520) 624-2516. **$41-$85.** 1222 S Freeway Rd. I-10, exit 259 (Starr Pass Blvd), just w, then just s on frontage road. Ext corridors. **Pets:** Accepted.
🄢🄳 ⊠ ⊷

◆ Motel 6 Tucson-Benson Hwy South #271 **M**
(520) 628-1264. **$41-$85.** 1031 E Benson Hwy. I-10, exit 262, 0.3 mi se. Ext corridors. **Pets:** Accepted.
⬛ ✕ ⬛

◆ Motel 6 Tucson-Congress Street #50 **M**
(520) 628-1339. **$44-$85.** 960 S Freeway. I-10, exit 258 (Broadway Blvd/Congress St), 0.7 mi s on west side of interstate. Ext corridors. **Pets:** Accepted.
⬛ ✕ ⬛ ⬛

◆ Motel 6 Tucson North #1127 **M**
(520) 744-9300. **$40-$85.** 4630 W Ina Rd. I-10, exit 248 (Ina Rd), just e to Camino de Oeste, then just n. Int corridors. **Pets:** Accepted.
⬛ ✕ ⬛ ⬛

◆◆ ◆◆ ◆◆ Omni Tucson National Golf Resort & Spa **LH**
(520) 297-2271. **$109-$439, 7 day notice.** 2727 W Club Dr. I-10, exit 246 (Cortaro Rd), 3.5 mi e, then n on Shannon Rd. Ext corridors. **Pets:** Accepted.
⬛ ⬛ ✕ ⬛ ⬛ ⬛ ⬛ ⬛ ⬛ ⬛

◆ ◆ Quality Inn at Tucson Airport **SH**
(520) 294-2500. **$59-$180.** 2803 E Valencia Rd. 1 mi ne of Tucson International Airport; just e of Tucson Blvd. Ext/int corridors. **Pets:** Large. $10 daily fee/pet. Service with restrictions, supervision.
⬛ ⬛ ✕

◆◆ ◆◆◆◆ Radisson Suites Tucson **LH**
(520) 721-7100. **$69-$199.** 6555 E Speedway Blvd. Just e of Wilmot Rd. Ext corridors. **Pets:** Medium. $50 one-time fee/room. Designated rooms, service with restrictions, supervision.
⬛ ⬛ ✕ ⬛ ⬛ ⬛ ⬛ ⬛

◆◆ ◆◆◆ Ramada Inn & Suites Foothills Resort **SH** ☘
(520) 886-9595. **$49-$199.** 6944 E Tanque Verde Rd. Jct Campbell Ave, 5.5 mi e on Grant Rd, then just ne. Ext corridors. **Pets:** Very small, dogs only. $30 one-time fee/pet.
⬛ ⬛ ✕ ⬛ ⬛ ⬛ ⬛

◆◆ ◆◆◆ Ramada Limited Tucson West **M**
(520) 628-6491. **$59-$94.** 665 N Freeway. I-10, exit 257 (St. Mary's Rd/Speedway Blvd), just s. Ext corridors. **Pets:** Other species. Service with restrictions, supervision.
⬛ ⬛ ✕ ⬛ ⬛ ⬛

◆ Red Roof Inn-Tucson South **M**
(520) 571-1400. **$50-$74.** 3704 E Irvington Rd. I-10, exit 264 westbound; exit 264B eastbound. Ext corridors. **Pets:** Accepted.
✕ ⬛ ⬛

◆ ◆◆ Residence Inn by Marriott **SH** ☘
(520) 721-0991. **$99-$189, 10 day notice.** 6477 E Speedway Blvd. Just e of Wilmot Rd. Ext corridors. **Pets:** Other species. $75 one-time fee/room. Service with restrictions.
⬛ ✕ ⬛ ⬛ ⬛ ⬛ ⬛ ⬛

◆◆◆◆ Residence Inn by Marriott Williams Centre **SH**
(520) 790-6100. **$69-$249.** 5400 E Williams Cir. Jct Campbell Ave, 3.8 mi e on Broadway Blvd, then just s and just e on Williams Centre. Int corridors. **Pets:** Other species. $75 one-time fee/room.
⬛ ⬛ ✕ ⬛ ⬛ ⬛ ⬛ ✕

◆◆ ◆◆ Riverpark Inn **SH**
(520) 622-6611. **$69-$169.** 350 S Freeway. I-10, exit 158 (Broadway Blvd/Congress St), just w, then 0.4 mi s. Ext/int corridors. **Pets:** Accepted.
⬛ ⬛ ✕ ⬛ ⬛ ⬛ ⬛ ✕

◆◆ ◆◆◆ Rodeway Inn I-10 & Grant Rd **M**
(520) 622-7791. **$69-$139, 15 day notice.** 1365 W Grant Rd. I-10, exit 256 (Grant Rd), just w. Ext corridors. **Pets:** Other species. $20 one-time fee/room. Service with restrictions, crate.
⬛ ⬛ ✕ ⬛ ⬛ ⬛ ⬛ ⬛

◆◆◆ Sheraton Tucson Hotel & Suites **SH**
(520) 323-6262. **$164-$289.** 5151 E Grant Rd. Jct Campbell Ave, 3.6 mi e. Ext/int corridors. **Pets:** Accepted.
⬛ ⬛ ✕ ⬛ ⬛ ⬛ ⬛ ⬛ ⬛ ⬛ ✕

◆◆ ◆◆ Studio 6 Extended Stay #6002 **M**
(520) 746-0030. **$48-$77.** 4950 S Outlet Center Dr. I-10, exit 264A eastbound; exit 264B westbound, just s, then just nw on Julian Dr. Ext corridors. **Pets:** Accepted.
⬛ ✕ ⬛ ⬛ ⬛

◆◆◆ ◆◆◆ TownePlace Suites by Marriott **SH**
(520) 292-9697. **$89-$179.** 405 W Rudasill Rd. Jct Orange Grove Rd, 0.5 mi s on Oracle Rd, then just e. Int corridors. **Pets:** $85 one-time fee/pet. Designated rooms, service with restrictions.
⬛ ⬛ ✕ ⬛ ⬛ ⬛ ⬛

◆◆◆ ◆ Travelodge **M**
(520) 622-8089. **$49-$110.** 1000 S Freeway. I-10, exit 259 (22nd St), just w, then just n. Int corridors. **Pets:** Accepted.
⬛ ✕ ⬛

◆◆◆ ◆◆ ◆◆ The Westin La Paloma Resort & Spa **LH** ☘
(520) 742-6000. **$109-$489, 7 day notice.** 3800 E Sunrise Dr. From SR 77 (Oracle Rd), 4.6 mi e on Ina Rd via Skyline and Sunrise drs, just s on Via Palomita. Ext corridors. **Pets:** Medium. Designated rooms, service with restrictions, supervision.
⬛ ⬛ ✕ ⬛ ⬛ ⬛ ⬛ ⬛ ✕

◆◆◆ ◆◆◆◆ Windmill Suites at St. Philip's Plaza **SH**
(520) 577-0007. **$69-$165.** 4250 N Campbell Ave. I-10, exit 254 (Prince Rd), 4 mi e, then 1 mi n. Int corridors. **Pets:** Accepted.
⬛ ⬛ ✕ ⬛ ⬛ ⬛ ✕

---

## END METROPOLITAN AREA

## WICKENBURG

◆◆ ◆◆ AmericInn **SH**
(928) 684-5461. **$65-$86, 5 day notice.** 850 E Wickenburg Way. 1.3 mi se on US 60. Int corridors. **Pets:** Small. $7 daily fee/pet. Service with restrictions, supervision.
⬛ ⬛ ✕ ⬛ ⬛ ⬛ ⬛ ⬛

◆◆ ◆◆ Best Western Rancho Grande **SH**
(928) 684-5445. **$64-$111.** 293 E Wickenburg Way. On US 60; center. Ext corridors. **Pets:** Accepted.
⬛ ⬛ ✕ ⬛ ⬛ ⬛ ⬛ ✕

◆◆ ◆◆ Super 8 Motel **M**
(928) 684-0808. **$70-$80.** 975 N Tegner St. 1 mi n of US 60 and 93. Ext/int corridors. **Pets:** Other species. $10 daily fee/pet. Designated rooms, service with restrictions, supervision.
⬛ ⬛ ✕ ⬛ ⬛ ⬛

## WILLCOX

◆◆◆ ◆◆ ◆◆ Best Western Plaza Inn **SH**
(520) 384-3556. **$63-$89.** 1100 W Rex Allen Dr. I-10, exit 340, just s. Ext corridors. **Pets:** Medium. $15 daily fee/pet. Service with restrictions, supervision.
⬛ ⬛ ✕ ⬛ ⬛ ⬛ ⬛ ⬛

**AAA ▼▼ Days Inn M**
(520) 384-4222. **$52-$65.** 724 N Bisbee Ave. I-10, exit 340, just s. Ext corridors. **Pets:** Medium. $6 daily fee/pet. Service with restrictions, supervision.
[SAVE] [S☉] [✕] [⊟] [⊇]

**▼ Motel 6 Willcox #410 M**
(520) 384-2201. **$39-$51.** 921 N Bisbee Ave. I-10, exit 340, just s. Ext corridors. **Pets:** Accepted.
[S☉] [✕] [⊟] [⊇]

# WILLIAMS

**AAA ▼▼ The Canyon Motel M ☙**
(928) 635-9371. **$39-$74.** 1900 E Rodeo Rd/Route 66. I-40, exit 165 (Grand Canyon), 1 mi s on Business Loop 40, then just w. Ext corridors. **Pets:** Other species. $7 daily fee/pet. Designated rooms, no service, crate.
[SAVE] [✕] [⊟] [⊟] [⊇] [⊠]

**AAA ▼▼ Days Inn M**
(928) 635-4051. **$52-$128.** 2488 W Route 66. I-40, exit 161, just e. Int corridors. **Pets:** Accepted.
[SAVE] [S☉] [✕] [⊘] [⊟] [⊇]

**AAA ▼▼ El Rancho Motel M ☙**
(928) 635-2552. **$33-$73.** 617 E Route 66. I-40, exit 163, 0.6 mi s, then just e. Ext corridors. **Pets:** $5 daily fee/pet. Designated rooms, service with restrictions, supervision.
[SAVE] [S☉] [✕] [⊟] [⊟] [⊇]

**AAA ▼ Highlander Motel M**
(928) 635-2541. **$40-$85.** 533 W Route 66. I-40, exit 161, 1.3 mi e. Ext corridors. **Pets:** Accepted.
[SAVE] [S☉] [✕]

**AAA ▼▼▼ Holiday Inn Williams SH**
(928) 635-4114. **$69-$159.** 950 N Grand Canyon Blvd. I-40, exit 163, just s. Int corridors. **Pets:** Other species. Service with restrictions.
[SAVE] [✕] [⟨.M⟩] [⊘] [⟨.⟩] [⊟] [⊟] [⊟] [⊇]

**AAA ▼▼ Motel 6–4010 M**
(928) 635-9000. **$35-$99.** 831 W Route 66. I-40, exit 161, 1 mi e. Int corridors. **Pets:** Accepted.
[SAVE] [S☉] [✕] [⊟] [⊇]

**AAA ▼▼▼ Mountainside Inn SH**
(928) 635-4431. **$59-$109.** 642 E Route 66. I-40, exit 163, 0.6 mi s, then just e. Ext corridors. **Pets:** Accepted.
[SAVE] [S☉] [✕] [⊘] [⊟] [⊟] [⊟] [⊇]

**AAA ▼▼▼▼ Quality Inn Mountain Ranch Resort SH**
(928) 635-2693. **$59-$109.** 6701 E Mountain Ranch Rd. I-40, exit 171 (Deer Farm Rd), just s. Ext corridors. **Pets:** $25 one-time fee/room. Service with restrictions, supervision.
[SAVE] [S☉] [✕] [⊟] [⊟] [⊟] [⊇] [⊠]

**AAA ▼ Rodeway Inn M ☙**
(928) 635-2619. **$29-$75, 7 day notice.** 334 E Route 66. I-40, exit 163, 0.5 mi s, then just e. Ext corridors. **Pets:** Small, other species. $50 deposit/pet, $10 daily fee/pet, $10 one-time fee/pet. Designated rooms, service with restrictions, crate.
[SAVE] [S☉] [✕] [⊟] [⊟]

**AAA ▼ Travelodge Williams M**
(928) 635-2651. **$39-$99.** 430 E Route 66. I-40, exit 163, 0.5 mi s, then just e. Ext corridors. **Pets:** Dogs only. $8 one-time fee/pet. Designated rooms, service with restrictions, supervision.
[SAVE] [S☉] [✕] [⊟] [⊟] [⊇]

# WINDOW ROCK

**AAA ▼▼ Quality Inn Navajo Nation Capital SH**
(928) 871-4108. **$75-$80.** 48 W Hwy 264. Center. Ext corridors. **Pets:** Medium, other species. $50 deposit/room. Service with restrictions, supervision.
[SAVE] [S☉] [✕] [⊟] [⊟] [⊓]

# WINSLOW

**AAA ▼▼▼ Best Western Adobe Inn SH ☙**
(928) 289-4638. **$80-$130, 30 day notice.** 1701 N Park Dr. I-40, exit 253. Int corridors. **Pets:** Small, other species. $10 daily fee/pet. Service with restrictions, supervision.
[SAVE] [S☉] [✕] [⟨.⟩] [⊟] [⊟] [⊓] [⊇]

**AAA ▼▼▼ Days Inn SH**
(928) 289-1010. **$55-$60.** 2035 W Hwy 66. I-40, exit 252, just s. Int corridors. **Pets:** Other species. $10 daily fee/pet. Designated rooms, no service, supervision.
[SAVE] [S☉] [✕] [⟨.⟩] [⊇]

**AAA ▼▼▼ Econo Lodge SH**
(928) 289-4687. **$59-$119.** 1706 N Park Dr. I-40, exit 253. Ext corridors. **Pets:** Small. $5 one-time fee/room. Service with restrictions, supervision.
[SAVE] [S☉] [✕] [⊘] [⊟] [⊟] [⊇]

**▼▼▼▼ Holiday Inn Express-Winslow SH**
(928) 289-2960. **$99-$109.** 816 Transcon Ln. I-40, exit 255, just n. Int corridors. **Pets:** Accepted.
[ASK] [S☉] [✕] [⟨.⟩] [⊟] [⊟] [⊇]

**▼▼▼▼ La Posada Hotel SH**
(928) 289-4366. **$89-$129, 3 day notice.** 303 E 2nd St. I-40, exit 253, 1 mi s to Route 66 (2nd St), then just e; in historic downtown. Int corridors. **Pets:** Other species. $10 one-time fee/room. Designated rooms, service with restrictions.
[✕] [⟨.M⟩] [⟨.⟩] [⊟] [⊓] [⊠]

**AAA ▼▼▼ Motel 6 Winslow #4012 M**
(928) 289-9581. **$39-$57.** 520 W Desmond St. I-40, exit 253, just s on N Park Dr, then just w. Int corridors. **Pets:** Accepted.
[SAVE] [S☉] [✕] [⟨.⟩] [⊇]

**AAA ▼▼ Super 8 Motel M**
(928) 289-4606. **$51-$79.** 1916 W Third St. I-40, exit 252, just e on Route 66. Int corridors. **Pets:** Medium, other species. $10 one-time fee/pet. Designated rooms, service with restrictions, supervision.
[SAVE] [S☉] [✕] [⊟]

# YUMA

**AAA ▼▼▼ Best Western Coronado Motor Hotel M**
(928) 783-4453. **$69-$150.** 233 4th Ave. I-8, exit 4th Ave eastbound, 0.5 mi s; exit 1 (Giss Pkwy) westbound, 1 mi w. Ext corridors. **Pets:** Accepted.
[SAVE] [S☉] [✕] [⊟] [⊟] [⊓] [⊇]

**AAA ▼▼▼ Best Western InnSuites Hotel & Suites Yuma SH**
(928) 783-8341. **$69-$169.** 1450 Castle Dome Ave. I-8, exit 2 (16th St/US 95), just ne. Ext corridors. **Pets:** Accepted.
[SAVE] [S☉] [✕] [⊘] [⊟] [⊟] [⊓] [⊇] [⊠]

**▼▼▼▼ Clarion Suites SH**
(928) 726-4830. **$137-$284.** 2600 S 4th Ave. I-8, exit 2 (16 St/US 95) eastbound, 1 mi w, then 1.3 mi s; exit 3 (SR 280) westbound, 0.5 mi s, then 2 mi w. Ext corridors. **Pets:** Accepted.
[ASK] [S☉] [✕] [⊟] [⊟] [⊇]

**▼▼▼ Comfort Inn SH**
(928) 782-1200. **$99-$179, 7 day notice.** 1691 S Riley Ave. I-8, exit 2 (16th St/US 95), just w. Int corridors. **Pets:** Medium. $10 daily fee/room. Service with restrictions, supervision.
[ASK] [S☉] [✕] [⟨.M⟩] [⟨.⟩] [⊟] [⊟] [⊇]

▼▼▼ Holiday Inn 🆂🅷
(928) 782-9300. **Call for rates (no credit cards).** 1901 E 18th St. I-8, exit 2, 0.4 mi e on 16th St, just s on Pacific Ave, then just w. Int corridors. **Pets:** Medium, dogs only. $10 daily fee/pet. Service with restrictions, crate.
☒ 🚹ᴹ 🛇 🔋 🖥 🍴 ⇌

🔷🔷 ▼▼▼ Howard Johnson Inn 🆂🅷
(928) 344-1420. **$70-$120.** 3181 S 4th Ave. I-8, exit 3E (SR 280 S), 1 mi s to 32nd St, then 2 mi w. Ext corridors. **Pets:** Other species. $10 daily fee/room. Service with restrictions, crate.
SAVE ☒ 🛇 🔋 🖥 ⇌

▼▼ Microtel Inn & Suites 🆂🅷
(928) 345-1777. **$54-$140.** 11274 S Fortuna Rd, Suite H. I-8, exit 12 (Fortuna Rd), just s, then w on Frontage Rd. Int corridors. **Pets:** Small, other species. Supervision.
ASK ☒ 🛇 🔋 🖥 ⇌

▼▼ Motel 6 Yuma East #1031 🅼
(928) 782-9521. **$43-$63.** 1445 E 16th St. I-8, exit 2 (16th St/US 95), just e. Ext corridors. **Pets:** Accepted.
🆂 ☒ 🛇 ⇌

▼▼ Oak Tree Inn 🆂🅷
(928) 539-9000. **$85-$109, 7 day notice.** 1730 Sunridge Dr. I-8, exit 2 (16th St/US 95), just e, then just s. Int corridors. **Pets:** Medium. $10 daily fee/pet. No service, supervision.
ASK 🆂 ☒ 🔋 🖥 ⇌

🔷🔷🔷 ▼▼▼ Quality Inn Airport 🆂🅷
(928) 726-4721. **$79-$149.** 711 E 32nd St. I-8, exit 3E (SR 280), 1.2 mi s, then 1.9 mi w. Ext corridors. **Pets:** Accepted.
SAVE 🆂 ☒ 🛇 🔋 🖥 🍴 ⇌

🔷🔷🔷 ▼▼ Ramada Inn Chilton Conference Center 🆂🅷
(928) 344-1050. **$94-$119.** 300 E 32nd St. I-8 business loop, 2.3 mi s of jct US 95. Ext corridors. **Pets:** Accepted.
SAVE 🆂 ☒ 🔋 🖥 🍴 ⇌

🔷🔷🔷 ▼▼▼ Shilo Inn Hotel-Yuma 🆂🅷 🐾
(928) 782-9511. **$113-$190.** 1550 S Castle Dome Rd. I-8, exit 2 (16th St/US 95), just ne. Int corridors. **Pets:** $10 daily fee/pet. Service with restrictions, supervision.
SAVE 🆂 ☒ 🛇 🔋 🖥 🍴 ⇌ ☒

🔷🔷🔷 ▼▼▼ Yuma Cabana Motel 🅼
(928) 783-8311. **$47-$80.** 2151 S 4th Ave. I-8, exit 2 (16th St/US 95), 1 mi w, then 0.5 mi s. Int corridors. **Pets:** Accepted.
SAVE 🆂 ☒ 🔋 ⇌

▼▼ Yuma Super 8 Motel 🆂🅷
(928) 782-2000. **$89-$169, 7 day notice.** 1688 S Riley Ave. I-8, exit 2 (16th St/US 95), just w. Int corridors. **Pets:** Medium. $10 daily fee/room. Service with restrictions, supervision.
ASK 🆂 ☒ 🚹ᴹ 🛇 🔋 🖥 ⇌

# ARKANSAS

## ARKADELPHIA

**Best Western-Continental Inn** SH
(870) 246-5592. **$60-$99.** 136 Valley St. I-30, exit 78, just e. Ext corridors. **Pets:** Medium, other species. $5 daily fee/room. Designated rooms, service with restrictions, supervision.

**Comfort Inn** SH
(870) 246-3800. **$63-$80.** 100 Crystal Palace Dr. I-30, exit 78, just sw. Int corridors. **Pets:** Other species. $25 daily fee/pet. Designated rooms, service with restrictions, supervision.

**Super 8 Motel** SH
(870) 246-8585. **$48-$62.** 118 Valley St. I-30, exit 78, just e. Ext corridors. **Pets:** Accepted.

## BATESVILLE

**Ramada Inn of Batesville** SH
(870) 698-1800. **$72-$76.** 1325 N St Louis St. 1 mi n on US 167. Ext corridors. **Pets:** Medium. Service with restrictions, supervision.

**Super 8 Motel-Batesville** M
(870) 793-5888. **$47-$72.** 1287 N St. Louis St. 1 mi n on US 167. Int corridors. **Pets:** Accepted.

## BEEBE

**Days Inn** SH
(501) 882-2008. **$69-$125.** 100 Tammy Ln. US 67/167, exit 28, just e. Ext corridors. **Pets:** Small, dogs only. $10 daily fee/pet. Service with restrictions, supervision.

## BENTON

**Americas Best Inn** SH
(501) 776-1515. **$42-$55.** 1221 Hot Springs Rd. I-30, exit 117. Int corridors. **Pets:** $5 daily fee/pet. Designated rooms, service with restrictions, supervision.

**Days Inn** SH
(501) 776-3200. **$41-$55, 10 day notice.** 17701 I-30. I-30, exit 118, on eastbound service road. Ext corridors. **Pets:** Accepted.

## BENTONVILLE

**TownePlace Suites by Marriott Bentonville/Rogers** SH
(479) 621-0202. **$124-$179.** 3100 SE 14th St. I-540, exit 86, just e. Int corridors. **Pets:** Other species. $75 one-time fee/room.

## BLYTHEVILLE

**Comfort Inn of Blytheville** SH
(870) 762-5721. **$60, 7 day notice.** 1520 E Main. I-55, exit 67, just w. Ext corridors. **Pets:** Accepted.

**Hampton Inn** SH
(870) 763-5220. **$76-$86.** 301 N Access Rd. I-55, exit 67, just nw. Ext corridors. **Pets:** Accepted.

**Holiday Inn** SH
(870) 763-5800. **$99-$135.** 1121 E Main. I-55, exit 67, just w. Ext/int corridors. **Pets:** Accepted.

**Super 8 Motel** SH
(870) 763-2300. **$50-$74.** 239 N Service Rd. I-55, exit 67, just nw. Int corridors. **Pets:** Accepted.

## BRYANT

**Americas Best Value Inn & Suites** M
(501) 653-7800. **$49-$69.** 407 W Commerce St. I-30, exit 123, just sw. Ext corridors. **Pets:** Medium. $8 daily fee/pet. Designated rooms, service with restrictions, supervision.

**Super 8 Motel** M
(501) 847-7888. **$52-$56.** 201 Dell Dr. I-30, exit 123, just e. Ext corridors. **Pets:** Dogs only. $20 deposit/room $5 one-time fee/pet. Service with restrictions, supervision.

## CABOT

**Super 8 of Cabot** M
(501) 941-3748. **$62.** 15 Ryeland Dr. US 67/167, exit 19 (SR 89), just e. Ext corridors. **Pets:** Accepted.

## CAMDEN

**Holiday Inn Express** SH
(870) 836-8100. **$80-$100, 7 day notice.** 1450 Hwy 278 W. 1 mi w of jct US 79 and 278. Int corridors. **Pets:** Small. Service with restrictions, supervision.

## CLARKSVILLE

**Best Western Sherwood Inn** SH
(479) 754-7900. **$42-$74, 10 day notice.** 1203 S Rogers Ave. I-40, exit 58, just n. Ext corridors. **Pets:** Other species. Service with restrictions, supervision.

**AAA ▼▼▼ Comfort Inn SH**
(479) 754-3000. **$65-$130, 3 day notice.** 1167 S Rogers Ave. I-40, exit 58, just n. Ext ccrridors. **Pets:** Medium. $25 daily fee/room. Designated rooms, service with restrictions, supervision.
[SAVE] [S♦] [✕] [📶] [💻] [≈]

# CONWAY

**AAA ▼▼▼ Days Inn SH**
(501) 450-7575. **$60-$75.** 1002 E Oak St. I-40, exit 127, just n. Ext corridors. **Pets:** Accepted.
[SAVE] [S♦] [✕] [📶] [💻] [≈]

**▼ Motel 6 #260 M**
(501) 327-6623. **$40-$51.** 1105 Hwy 65 N. I-40, exit 125, just se. Ext corridors. **Pets:** Accepted.
[S♦] [✕] [🔧] [&] [≈]

**AAA ▼▼▼ Quality Inn SH**
(501) 329-0300. **$61-$159.** 150 Hwy 65 N. I-40, exit 125, just n. Ext corridors. **Pets:** Medium. $20 one-time fee/room. Service with restrictions.
[SAVE] [S♦] [✕] [🔧] [📶] [💻] [≈]

# EL DORADO

**▼▼▼▼ La Quinta Inn El Dorado SH**
(870) 863-6677. **$55-$65.** 2303 Junction City Rd. Just e of jct US 167 and 82B. Ext/int corridors. **Pets:** Accepted.
[ASK] [S♦] [✕] [🔧] [📶] [💻] [≈]

# EUREKA SPRINGS

**AAA ▼▼▼▼ 1886 Crescent Hotel & Spa SH**
(479) 253-9766. **$84-$164, 3 day notice.** 75 Prospect Ave. 1.3 mi n of jct SR 23 on US 62B Historic Loop. Int corridors. **Pets:** Small. $10 daily fee/pet. Designated rooms, service with restrictions.
[SAVE] [S♦] [✕] [🔧] [📶] [💻] [🍴] [≈] [✕]

**▼▼▼▼ Arsenic & Old Lace B&B BB** 🐾
(479) 253-5454. **$139-$229, 15 day notice.** 60 Hillside Ave. 1.2 mi n on SR 23, just sw: downtown. Ext/int corridors. **Pets:** Medium, dogs only. $30 one-time fee/room. Designated rooms, service with restrictions, crate.
[ASK] [S♦] [✕]

**▼▼ Basin Park Hotel SH**
(479) 253-7837. **$74-$137, 3 day notice.** 12 Spring St. 0.7 mi n of jct US 62 via SR 23 N; downtown. Int corridors. **Pets:** Service with restrictions.
[ASK] [S♦] [✕] [🔧] [💻] [🍴] [≈]

**▼▼ Bavarian Inn SH**
(479) 253-8128. **$68-$128, 3 day notice.** 325 W Van Buren St. 1 mi w of jct US 62 and SR 23. Ext corridors. **Pets:** Accepted.
[✕] [🔧] [💻] [≈]

**AAA ▼▼◆ Best Western Inn of the Ozarks SH** 🐾
(479) 253-9768. **$49-$119.** 207 W Van Buren St. On US 62, 0.5 mi w of jct SR 23. Ext corridors. **Pets:** Dogs only. $5 one-time fee/pet. Service with restrictions, supervision.
[SAVE] [S♦] [✕] [🔧] [&] [🔧] [💻] [🍴] [≈] [✕]

**▼▼ Brackenridge Lodge M**
(479) 253-6803. **$49-$149, 7 day notice.** 352 W Van Buren St. 1 mi w of jct US 62 and SR 23. Ext corridors. **Pets:** Accepted.
[ASK] [✕] [🔧] [💻] [≈] [✅]

**AAA ▼▼▼ Colonial Mansion Inn SH** 🐾
(479) 253-7300. **$38-$95, 3 day notice.** 154 Huntsville Rd. Just s of jct US 62 and SR 23. Ext/int corridors. **Pets:** Small. Designated rooms, service with restrictions, crate.
[SAVE] [S♦] [✕] [🔧] [💻] [≈]

**▼▼ Comfort Inn SH**
(479) 253-5241. **$49-$179.** 196 E Van Buren St. Just w of jct US 62 and SR 23 S. Ext/int corridors. **Pets:** Accepted.
[ASK] [S♦] [✕] [🔧] [🔧] [💻] [≈]

**▼▼ Days Inn M**
(479) 253-8863. **$49-$149, 3 day notice.** 120 W Van Buren St. On US 62, just w of jct SR 23 N. Ext corridors. **Pets:** Medium, dogs only. $15 daily fee/pet. Service with restrictions, supervision.
[ASK] [S♦] [✕] [🔧] [💻] [≈]

**AAA ▼▼▼ Howard Johnson Express SH**
(479) 253-6665. **$42-$120.** 4042 E Van Buren St. 1.8 mi e of jct US 62 and SR 23. Ext corridors. **Pets:** Accepted.
[SAVE] [S♦] [✕] [💻] [≈]

**▼ The Joy Motel M**
(479) 253-9568. **$39-$93, 3 day notice.** 216 W Van Buren St. 0.5 mi w of jct US 62 and SR 23. Ext corridors. **Pets:** Accepted.
[ASK] [S♦] [✕] [🔧] [💻] [≈]

**▼ Road Runner Inn M**
(479) 253-8166. **$69-$79, 7 day notice.** 3034 Mundell Rd. On US 62, 4.3 mi w, 3.9 mi s on SR 187, then 3 mi se. Ext corridors. **Pets:** Large, other species. $10 one-time fee/pet. Service with restrictions, supervision.
[ASK] [✕] [🔧] [💻] [✅]

**▼ Travelers Inn M**
(479) 253-8386. **$38-$58, 3 day notice.** 2044 E Van Buren St. On US 62, just e of jct US 62 and SR 23. Ext corridors. **Pets:** Accepted.
[ASK] [S♦] [✕] [🔧] [≈]

**AAA ▼▼▼ Travelodge SH**
(479) 253-8992. **$42-$120.** 110 Huntsville Dr. Jct US 62 and SR 23. Ext corridors. **Pets:** Accepted.
[SAVE] [S♦] [✕] [🔧] [💻] [≈]

# FAYETTEVILLE

**AAA ▼▼▼ Best Western Windsor Suites SH**
(479) 587-1400. **$59-$199.** 1122 S Futrall Dr. I-540, exit 62, just se. Ext corridors. **Pets:** Small, other species. $20 one-time fee/pet. Designated rooms, service with restrictions.
[SAVE] [S♦] [✕] [🔧] [💻] [≈]

**▼▼ Quality Inn SH**
(479) 444-9800. **$68-$100, 3 day notice.** 523 S Shiloh Dr. I-540, exit 62, just w. Ext corridors. **Pets:** Accepted.
[ASK] [S♦] [✕] [🔧] [💻] [≈]

**AAA ▼▼▼▼ Radisson Hotel Fayetteville LH**
(479) 442-5555. **$119-$155, 30 day notice.** 70 N East Ave. Just w of US 71B and SR 471; downtown. Int corridors. **Pets:** Accepted.
[SAVE] [S♦] [✕] [&] [🔧] [💻] [🍴] [≈]

**▼▼ Sleep Inn by Choice Hotels SH**
(479) 587-8700. **$74-$144.** 728 Millsap Rd. I-540, exit 67, 1.6 mi e, then just s on US 71B. Int corridors. **Pets:** Accepted.
[ASK] [S♦] [✕] [&] [🔧] [💻]

# FORDYCE

**▼▼ Days Inn SH**
(870) 352-2400. **$72-$90.** 2500 W 4th St. On US 79/167; 1 mi w of center. Ext/int corridors. **Pets:** Small. $50 deposit/room, $10 daily fee/pet. Service with restrictions, supervision.
[ASK] [S♦] [✕] [🔧] [💻] [≈]

# FORREST CITY

**▼▼▼▼ Holiday Inn SH**
(870) 633-6300. **$72-$89.** 200 Holiday Dr. I-40, exit 241B, just n. Ext corridors. **Pets:** Small, other species. Service with restrictions, supervision.
[ASK] [S♦] [✕] [🔧] [💻] [🍴] [≈]

# FORT SMITH

**▼▼ ▼▼ Americas Best Value Kings Row Inn & Suites** 🆂🅷
(479) 452-4200. **$55-$70.** 5801 Rogers Ave. I-540, exit 8A (Rogers Ave), just w. Ext corridors. **Pets:** Small, other species. $30 deposit/pet. Service with restrictions, supervision.
🅰🆂🅺 🆂🔟 ⊠ 🕹 🛢 🖥 🏊

**▼▼▼▼ Aspen Hotel & Suites** 🆂🅷
(479) 452-9000. **$94-$120.** 2900 S 68th St. I-540, exit 8B (Rogers Ave), just e. Int corridors. **Pets:** Other species. Service with restrictions, supervision.
🅰🆂🅺 🆂🔟 ⊠ 🛢 🖥 🏊

**▼▼ ▼▼ Baymont Inn & Suites Fort Smith** 🆂🅷
(479) 484-5770. **$76-$86.** 2123 Burnham Rd. I-540, exit 8A (Rogers Ave), just w. Int corridors. **Pets:** Medium. Service with restrictions.
🅰🆂🅺 ⊠ 🕹 🛢 🖥 🏊

**▼▼ ▼▼ Comfort Inn** 🆂🅷
(479) 484-0227. **$99.** 2120 Burnham Rd. I-540, exit 8A (Rogers Ave), just w. Int corridors. **Pets:** Other species. Service with restrictions, crate.
🅰🆂🅺 ⊠ 🕹 🛢 🖥 🏊 🚫

**▼▼ ▼▼ Holiday Inn Express** 🆂🅷
(479) 452-7500. **Call for rates (no credit cards).** 6813 Phoenix Ave. I-540, exit 8A (Rogers Ave), 0.6 mi e, then 0.5 mi s. Int corridors. **Pets:** Accepted.
⊠ 🔅 🛢 🖥 🏊

**▼▼▼▼ Holiday Inn Fort Smith City Center** 🅻🅷
(479) 783-1000. **$109.** 700 Rogers Ave. Just s of US 64 (Garrison Ave); downtown. Int corridors. **Pets:** Accepted.
🅰🆂🅺 🆂🔟 ⊠ 🅻🅼 🕹 🔅 🛢 🖥 🍽 🏊 🚫

**▼▼ Motel 6 Fort Smith #0133** 🅼
(479) 484-0576. **$40-$54.** 6001 Rogers Ave. I-540, exit 8B (Rogers Ave), just w. Ext corridors. **Pets:** Accepted.
🆂🔟 ⊠ 🔅 🏊

**▼▼▼▼ Residence Inn by Marriott** 🆂🅷
(479) 478-8300. **$79-$139.** 3005 S 74th. I-540, exit 8A (Rogers Ave), 0.8 mi e. Int corridors. **Pets:** Large, other species. $75 one-time fee/room. Service with restrictions, supervision.
🅰🆂🅺 🆂🔟 ⊠ 🕹 🔅 🛢 🖥 🏊 🚫

**▼▼ Super 8 Motel** 🅼
(479) 646-3411. **$55-$60, 7 day notice.** 3810 Towson Ave. 2 mi s of SR 22. Ext corridors. **Pets:** Accepted.
🅰🆂🅺 🆂🔟 ⊠ 🕹 🛢 🏊

# GENTRY

**▼▼▼▼ Apple Crest Inn Bed & Breakfast** 🅱🅱
(479) 736-8201. **$100-$180, 14 day notice.** 12758 S Hwy 59. On SR 59, 1 mi s. Int corridors. **Pets:** Medium, other species. $25 one-time fee/room. Designated rooms, service with restrictions, crate.
🅰🆂🅺 🆂🔟 ⊠

# HARRISON

**▼▼ ▼▼ Comfort Inn** 🆂🅷
(870) 741-7676. **$65-$95.** 1210 Hwy 62/65 N. 1 mi n on US 62/65/412. Ext/int corridors. **Pets:** Small. $25 daily fee/room. Service with restrictions, supervision.
🅰🆂🅺 🆂🔟 ⊠ 🕹 🛢 🖥 🏊

**🅰🅰🅰 ▼▼ Family Budget Inn** 🅼 🐾
(870) 743-1000. **$37-$40.** 401 S Main (Hwy 65B S). 0.7 mi s of jct SR 7. Ext corridors. **Pets:** Medium, other species. $5 daily fee/room. Designated rooms, no service, supervision.
🆂🅰🆅🅴 🆂🔟 ⊠ 🛢 🖥 🏊

**▼▼ ▼▼ Holiday Inn Express Hotel & Suites** 🆂🅷
(870) 741-3636. **$65-$105.** 117 Hwy 43 E. Just e from jct US 62/65/412 and SR 43. Int corridors. **Pets:** Small. $25 one-time fee/pet. Service with restrictions, supervision.
🅰🆂🅺 🆂🔟 ⊠ 🔅 🛢 🖥 🏊 🚫

# HAZEN

**▼▼▼▼ Super 8 Motel** 🆂🅷 🐾
(870) 255-2888. **$55-$75.** 2809 Hwy 63. I-40, exit 193, just s. Ext corridors. **Pets:** Other species. $5 daily fee/pet. Service with restrictions, crate.
🅰🆂🅺 🆂🔟 ⊠ 🛢 🖥 🏊

# HOPE

**🅰🅰🅰 ▼▼▼▼ Best Western of Hope** 🆂🅷 🐾
(870) 777-9222. **$60-$65.** 1800 Holiday Dr. I-30, exit 30, just nw. Ext corridors. **Pets:** Other species. Service with restrictions, crate.
🆂🅰🆅🅴 🆂🔟 ⊠ 🛢 🖥 🏊

# HOT SPRINGS

**🅰🅰🅰 ▼▼▼▼ Clarion Resort** 🆂🅷
(501) 525-1391. **$69-$159.** 4813 Central Ave. 5.5 mi s of jct US 270 and SR 7. Int corridors. **Pets:** Medium. $10 daily fee/room, $25 one-time fee/room. Designated rooms, service with restrictions, supervision.
🆂🅰🆅🅴 🆂🔟 ⊠ 🔅 🛢 🖥 🍽 🏊 🚫

**🅰🅰🅰 ▼▼▼▼ Embassy Suites Hot Springs** 🅻🅷 🐾
(501) 624-9200. **$129-$169.** 400 Convention Blvd. Just w of jct US 70. Int corridors. **Pets:** Medium, other species. $25 daily fee/room. Service with restrictions, crate.
🆂🅰🆅🅴 ⊠ 🅻🅼 🕹 🔅 🛢 🖥 🍽 🏊 🚫

**▼▼▼▼ Lake Hamilton Resort** 🆂🅷
(501) 767-8606. **$84-$160.** 2803 Albert Pike Rd. 5 mi w on US 270. Int corridors. **Pets:** Accepted.
🅰🆂🅺 🆂🔟 ⊠ 🛢 🖥 🍽 🏊 🚫

**🅰🅰🅰 ▼▼ Travelier Inn** 🅼
(501) 624-4681. **$48-$62.** 1045 E Grand Ave. 1 mi e of jct US 270B and 70. Ext corridors. **Pets:** Other species. Service with restrictions, crate.
🆂🅰🆅🅴 🆂🔟 ⊠ 🛢 🏊

**🅰🅰🅰 ▼▼▼▼ Velda Rose Resort Hotel & Spa** 🅻🅷 🐾
(501) 623-3311. **$64-$84.** 217 Park Ave. On US 70B and SR 7; center. Int corridors. **Pets:** Medium, other species. Designated rooms, service with restrictions, supervision.
🆂🅰🆅🅴 🆂🔟 ⊠ 🛢 🖥 🍽 🏊

# JACKSONVILLE

**▼▼ ▼▼ Days Inn** 🅼
(501) 982-1543. **$50-$60.** 1414 John Harden Dr. US 67/167, exit 10B southbound; exit 11 northbound. Ext corridors. **Pets:** Large. $5 daily fee/pet. Designated rooms, service with restrictions, supervision.
🅰🆂🅺 🆂🔟 ⊠ 🛢 🏊

# JONESBORO

**▼▼ ▼▼ Baymont Inn-Jonesboro** 🆂🅷
(870) 802-2200. **$65-$80.** 2910 Kazi St. US 63, exit Stadium Blvd/Caraway Rd, just n. Int corridors. **Pets:** Medium. Service with restrictions.
🅰🆂🅺 🆂🔟 ⊠ 🔅 🛢 🖥 🏊

**🅰🅰🅰 ▼▼▼▼ Comfort Inn & Suites** 🆂🅷
(870) 972-9000. **$65-$99.** 2911 Gilmore Dr. US 63, exit Stadium Blvd/Caraway Rd, just n. Int corridors. **Pets:** $10 one-time fee/room. Service with restrictions, supervision.
🆂🅰🆅🅴 ⊠ 🕹 🛢 🖥 🏊

**▼▼▼▼ Holiday Inn Express** 🆂🅷
(870) 932-5554. **$85-$100.** 2407 Phillips Dr. US 63, exit Stadium Blvd/Caraway Rd, just n. Int corridors. **Pets:** Accepted.
🅰🆂🅺 🆂🔟 ⊠ 🛢 🖥 🏊

◆◆ Motel 6–0187
(870) 932-1050. **$37-$50.** 2300 S Caraway Rd. US 63, exit Stadium Blvd/Caraway Rd, 0.6 mi n. Ext corridors. **Pets:** Accepted.

❎ ➥

## LITTLE ROCK

◆◆ Airport Travelodge 🆂🅷
(501) 490-2200. **$58-$64.** 7615 Fluid Dr. I-440, exit 5, just n. Ext corridors. **Pets:** Accepted.

A$K 🆂 ❎ 🅗 🖿

◆◆ Baymont Inn & Suites Little Rock West 🆂🅷
(501) 225-7007. **$70-$80.** 1010 Breckenridge Rd. I-430, exit 8, just e to Breckenridge Rd, then just s. Int corridors. **Pets:** Medium. Service with restrictions.

A$K ❎ 🔀 🅗 🖿

◈ ◆◆◆ Comfort Inn & Suites, Downtown Little Rock @ The Clinton Library 🆂🅷
(501) 687-7700. **$72-$99.** 707 I-30. I-30, exit 140A, just e. Int corridors. **Pets:** Medium. $25 one-time fee/room. Service with restrictions, supervision.

SAVE 🆂 ❎ 🅖M 🅗 🖿 ➥

◈ ◆◆◆ Embassy Suites Hotel Little Rock 🅻🅷
(501) 312-9000. **$109-$500.** 11301 Financial Center Pkwy. Jct I-430 and 630, just w. Int corridors. **Pets:** Medium. $50 one-time fee/room. Service with restrictions, crate.

SAVE ❎ 🅖M 🔀 🅖 🅗 🖿 🍴 ➥ ❎

◈ ◆◆◆ Hampton Inn Little Rock I-30 🆂🅷
(501) 562-6667. **$74.** 6100 Mitchell Dr. I-30, exit 133. Int corridors. **Pets:** Accepted.

SAVE 🆂 ❎ 🖿 ➥

◆◆◆ Holiday Inn Select 🆂🅷
(501) 223-3000. **$80-$108.** 201 S Shackleford Rd. Jct I-430 and 630. Ext/int corridors. **Pets:** Small. $25 daily fee/pet. Service with restrictions, crate.

A$K ❎ 🔀 🅗 🖿 🍴 ➥

◈ ◆◆◆ La Quinta Inn Litle Rock (West) 🆂🅷
(501) 224-0900. **$69-$79.** 200 S Shackleford Rd. I-430, exit 6; I-630, exit Shackleford Rd N; jct I-430 and 630. Ext corridors. **Pets:** Medium. Service with restrictions.

SAVE ❎ 🖿 ➥

◆◆◆ La Quinta Inn Little Rock (Medical Center Area) 🆂🅷
(501) 664-7000. **$69-$79.** 901 Fair Park Blvd. I-630, exit 4, just s. Ext corridors. **Pets:** Medium. Service with restrictions.

A$K ❎ 🅖M 🔀 🅗 🖿 ➥

◈ ◆◆◆ La Quinta Inn Little Rock (Otter Creek Area) 🆂🅷
(501) 455-2300. **$73-$33.** 11701 I-30. I-30, exit 128, just e. Ext corridors. **Pets:** Medium. Service with restrictions.

SAVE ❎ 🖿 ➥

## LONOKE

◈ ◆◆ Days Inn 🆂🅷
(501) 676-5138. **$65-$80.** 105 Dee Dee Ln. I-40, exit 175, just n. Ext corridors. **Pets:** Small, other species. $10 one-time fee/pet. Service with restrictions, supervision.

SAVE 🆂 ❎ 🅙 🅗 🖿 ➥

## MARION

◆◆ Best Western-Regency Motor Inn 🆂🅷
(870) 739-3278. **$65-$75.** 3635 I-55. I-55, exit 10, just nw. Ext corridors. **Pets:** Medium. Service with restrictions, crate.

A$K 🆂 ❎ 🔀 🅗 🖿 ➥

## MAUMELLE

◆◆◆ Comfort Suites 🆂🅷
(501) 851-8444. **$74-$139.** 14322 Frontier Dr. I-40, exit 142, just sw. Int corridors. **Pets:** Accepted.

A$K 🆂 ❎ 🔀 🅗 🖿 ➥

◆◆ Quality Inn-Maumelle 🆂🅷
(501) 851-3500. **$75.** 14325 Frontier Dr. I-40, exit 142, just sw. Ext corridors. **Pets:** Medium. $10 one-time fee/room. Designated rooms, service with restrictions, supervision.

A$K 🆂 ❎ 🅗 🖿 ➥

## MOUNTAIN HOME

◆◆ Best Western Carriage Inn 🆂🅷
(870) 425-6001. **$45-$75.** 963 Hwy 62 E. 1.3 mi e on US 62B. Ext corridors. **Pets:** Small, other species. $10 one-time fee/room. Designated rooms, service with restrictions, supervision.

A$K 🆂 ❎ 🖿 ➥

◆◆ Holiday Inn Express 🆂🅷
(870) 425-6200. **Call for rates.** 1005 Coley Dr. 1.4 mi e on US 62B. Int corridors. **Pets:** Accepted.

❎ 🅖M 🅙 🅗 🖿 ➥

◈ ◆◆◆ Teal Point Resort 🅒🅐
(870) 492-5145. **$69-$341, 45 day notice.** 715 Teal Point Rd. 7 mi e on US 62, 0.6 mi n on CR 406, follow signs. Ext corridors. **Pets:** Other species. $7 daily fee/pet. Designated rooms, supervision.

SAVE 🅗 ➥ ❎ 🅩

## MOUNTAIN VIEW

◆◆ Best Western Fiddlers Inn 🅼
(870) 269-2828. **$54-$95.** 601 Sylomore. 1 mi n on SR 5, 9 and 14. Ext corridors. **Pets:** Small, dogs only. $5 daily fee/pet.

A$K 🆂 ❎ 🅗 🖿 ➥

## NEWPORT

◈ ◆◆ Fortune Inn and Suites 🅼
(870) 523-5851. **$65-$70.** 901 Hwy 367 N. US 67, exit 83, 1 mi w, then 0.3 mi n. Ext corridors. **Pets:** Other species. Service with restrictions, supervision.

SAVE 🆂 ❎ 🅗 🖿 ➥

## NORTH LITTLE ROCK

◈ ◆◆ Baymont Inn 🆂🅷
(501) 758-8888. **$75-$90.** 4100 E McCain Blvd. Jct US 67/167, exit 1A northbound; exit 1 southbound. Ext corridors. **Pets:** Medium. Service with restrictions.

SAVE ❎ 🔀 🖿 ➥

◆◆ Days Inn 🆂🅷
(501) 851-3297. **$64-$85.** 7200 Bicentennial Rd. I-40, exit 142. Ext corridors. **Pets:** Accepted.

A$K 🆂 ❎ 🔀 🅗

◆◆ Hampton Inn 🆂🅷
(501) 771-2090. **$74-$79.** 500 W 29th St. I-40, exit 152. Int corridors. **Pets:** Accepted.

A$K 🆂 ❎ 🔀 🖿 ➥

◈ ◆◆◆ Holiday Inn-North 🆂🅷
(501) 758-1851. **$62-$82.** 120 W Pershing Blvd. I-40, exit 152 westbound; exit 153A eastbound. Int corridors. **Pets:** Other species. $20 one-time fee/room.

SAVE 🆂 ❎ 🖿 🍴 ➥

◆◆ La Quinta Inn 🆂🅷
(501) 945-0808. **$81-$91.** 4311 Warden Rd. US 67/167, exit 1B northbound; exit 1 southbound. Int corridors. **Pets:** Medium. Service with restrictions.

A$K ❎ 🔀 🅙 🅗 🖿 ➥

**AAA** ▼▼▼ **Red Roof Inn** SH
(501) 945-0080. **$60-$65.** 5711 Pritchard Dr. I-40, exit 157, just s. Int corridors. **Pets:** Small. Service with restrictions, supervision.
SAVE S☐ ✕ 🖥 ➾

▼▼▼▼ **Residence Inn by Marriott-North** SH
(501) 945-7777. **$90-$160, 14 day notice.** 4110 Healthcare Dr. I-40, exit 156. Int corridors. **Pets:** Accepted.
ASK S☐ ✕ ✎ 🖥 ➾ ✕

## OZARK

▼ **Oxford Inn** M
(479) 667-1131. **$45.** 305 N 18th St. I-40, exit 35, 3 mi s on SR 23. Ext corridors. **Pets:** Medium. $10 daily fee/pet. No service, supervision.
ASK S☐ ✕ 🖥 ➾

## PINE BLUFF

▼▼▼ **Hampton Inn Pine Bluff** SH
(870) 850-0444. **$76-$80.** 3103 E Market St. I-530, exit 46, just n. Int corridors. **Pets:** Small. Service with restrictions, supervision.
S☐ ✕ ✎ ✎ 🖥 ➾

▼▼▼ **Holiday Inn Express Hotel & Suites** SH
(870) 879-3800. **$72-$150.** 3620 Camden Rd. I-530, exit 39, just sw. Int corridors. **Pets:** Small, other species. $25 one-time fee/pet. Service with restrictions, supervision.
ASK S☐ ✕ ✎M ✎ 🖥 ➾

## POCAHONTAS

▼▼ **Days Inn & Suites** SH
(870) 892-9500. **$75.** 2805 Hwy 67 S. 1.7 mi s. Int corridors. **Pets:** Medium. $25 deposit/pet, $10 daily fee/pet. Designated rooms, service with restrictions, supervision.
ASK S☐ ✕ 🖥 ➾

## ROGERS

▼▼▼▼ **AmeriSuites (Rogers/Bentonville)** SH
(479) 633-8555. **$59-$139.** 4610 W Walnut. I-540, exit 85, just e. Int corridors. **Pets:** Other species. Service with restrictions, crate.
ASK S☐ ✕ ✎M ✎ ✎ 🖥 ➾

**AAA** ▼▼▼ **Embassy Suites Northwest Arkansas** LH
(479) 254-8400. **$99-$239.** 3303 Pinnacle Hills Pkwy. I-540, exit 83, just w, then 0.6 mi s. Int corridors. **Pets:** Medium. Service with restrictions, crate.
SAVE ✕ ✎M ✎ ✎ 🖥 🍴 ➾ ✕

▼▼▼ **Residence Inn by Marriott** SH
(479) 636-5900. **$109-$169.** 4611 W Locust St.. I-540, exit 85, 0.4 mi n on 46th St. Int corridors. **Pets:** Small, other species. $75 one-time fee/pet. Crate.
ASK S☐ ✕ ✎M ✎ 🖥 ➾ ✕

## RUSSELLVILLE

▼▼ **Comfort Inn** M
(479) 967-7500. **$59-$69.** 3019 E Parkway Dr. I-40, exit 84, just s. Ext corridors. **Pets:** Medium. $10 daily fee/pet. Service with restrictions, supervision.
ASK S☐ ✕ 🖥 ➾

**AAA** ▼▼ **Holiday Inn** SH
(479) 968-4300. **$75.** 2407 N Arkansas Ave. I-40, exit 81, just s. Ext corridors. **Pets:** Other species. $10 one-time fee/pet.
SAVE S☐ ✕ 🖥 🍴 ➾

▼ **Motel 6 Russellville #265** M
(479) 968-3666. **$37-$48.** 215 W Birch St. I-40, exit 81, just n. Ext corridors. **Pets:** Accepted.
S☐ ✕ ✎ 🖥 ➾

▼ **Super 8 Motel-Russellville** SH
(479) 968-8898. **$60-$70.** 2404 N Arkansas Ave. I-40, exit 81, just s. Int corridors. **Pets:** Small. $10 daily fee/pet. Service with restrictions, supervision.
ASK S☐ ✕ ✎ 🖥 ➾

## SEARCY

▼▼▼▼ **Hampton Inn** SH
(501) 268-0654. **$77-$87.** 3204 E Race Ave. US 67, exit 46, just w. Ext/int corridors. **Pets:** Accepted.
ASK ✕ ✎ 🖥 🖥 ➾ ✕

**AAA** ▼ **Royal Inn** M
(501) 268-3511. **$45-$50.** 2203 E Race Ave. US 67, exit 46, 1.1 mi w. Ext corridors. **Pets:** Small, dogs only. $5 daily fee/pet. Designated rooms, service with restrictions, supervision.
SAVE S☐ ✕ 🖥 🖥

## SILOAM SPRINGS

▼▼ **Super 8 Motel** M
(479) 524-8898. **$55-$59.** 1800 Hwy 412 W. Center. Ext corridors. **Pets:** Very small, dogs only. Service with restrictions, supervision.
ASK S☐ ✕ ✎ 🖥 🖥 ➾

## SPRINGDALE

▼▼ **Baymont Inn & Suites Springdale** SH
(479) 751-2626. **$80-$90.** 1300 S 48th St. I-540, exit 72, just e on US 412. Int corridors. **Pets:** Medium. Service with restrictions.
ASK ✕ ✎M ✎ ✎ 🖥 🖥 ➾ ✕

**AAA** ▼▼▼▼ **Comfort Suites** SH
(479) 725-1777. **$82, 30 day notice.** 1099 Rieff St. I-540, exit 72, just w. Int corridors. **Pets:** Accepted.
SAVE S☐ ✕ ✎ 🖥 🖥 ➾ ✕

**AAA** ▼▼▼ **Hampton Inn & Suites** SH
(479) 756-3500. **$139-$169.** 1700 S 48th St. I-540, exit 72, just e. Int corridors. **Pets:** $50 deposit/room, $50 one-time fee/room. Service with restrictions, crate.
SAVE S☐ ✕ ✎M ✎ ✎ 🖥 🖥 ➾

**AAA** ▼▼▼ **Holiday Inn Northwest AR Hotel & Convention Center** LH
(479) 751-8300. **$69-$300.** 1500 S 48th St. I-540, exit 72, just e on US 412. Int corridors. **Pets:** Other species. $20 deposit/room. Service with restrictions, crate.
SAVE S☐ ✕ ✎ ✎ 🖥 🖥 🍴 ➾ ✕

▼▼▼ **Residence Inn by Marriott** SH
(479) 872-9100. **$119-$149.** 1740 S 48th St. I-540, exit 72, just e to 48th St, then just s. Int corridors. **Pets:** Accepted.
ASK S☐ ✕ ✎ 🖥 🖥 ➾ ✕

## STAR CITY

▼▼ **Super 8 Motel-Star City** SH
(870) 628-6883. **$69.** 1308 N Lincoln St. Just n on US 425. Int corridors. **Pets:** Accepted.
ASK ✕ 🖥 🖥 ➾

## STUTTGART

**AAA** ▼▼ **Holiday Inn Express** SH
(870) 673-3616. **$65-$112.** 708 W Michigan. Just w on US 63/79. Ext corridors. **Pets:** Medium. $5 daily fee/room. Designated rooms, service with restrictions, supervision.
SAVE S☐ ✕ 🖥 🖥 ➾

# TEXARKANA

**Best Value Inn Kings Row Suites** M
(870) 774-3851. **$62-$72.** 4200 N State Line Ave. I-30, exit 223A, just s. Ext/int corridors. **Pets:** Accepted.
ASK SO X ☐ ☐ ☐ ☐

**Holiday Inn Texarkana** SH
(870) 774-3521. **$65.** 5100 N State Line Ave. I-30, exit 223B, just n. Int corridors. **Pets:** Accepted.
SAVE SO X ☐ ☐ ☐ ☐ ☐ ☐

**La Quinta Inn** SH
(870) 773-1000. **$73-$83.** 5102 N State Line Ave. I-30, exit 223B, just n. Int corridors. **Pets:** Medium. Service with restrictions.
ASK X ☐ ☐ ☐ ☐

**Quality Inn** SH
(870) 772-0070. **$63-$90.** 5210 N State Line Ave. I-30, exit 223B, just n. Ext corridors. **Pets:** Other species. $25 one-time fee/room. Service with restrictions.
SAVE SO X ☐ ☐ ☐

# TRUMANN

**Days Inn & Suites** SH
(870) 483-8383. **$65-$75.** 400 Commerce Dr. US 63, exit 29, just e. Ext/int corridors. **Pets:** Other species. $10 daily fee/pet. Service with restrictions, supervision.
SAVE SO X ☐ ☐ ☐ ☐ ☐

# VAN BUREN

**Comfort Inn** SH
(479) 474-2223. **$65-$109.** 3131 Cloverleaf. I-540, exit 2A, just s. Int corridors. **Pets:** Small, dogs only. $25 one-time fee/pet. Service with restrictions, supervision.
ASK SO X ☐ ☐ ☐

**Holiday Inn Express** SH
(479) 474-8100. **$68.** 1903 N 6th St. I-40, exit 5, just n. Ext corridors. **Pets:** Accepted.
X ☐ ☐

**Motel 6 Van Buren #1264** M
(479) 474-8001. **$40-$52.** 1716 Fayetteville Rd. I-40, exit 5, just s. Ext corridors. **Pets:** Accepted.
SO X ☐ ☐

# CALIFORNIA

## CITY INDEX

## ADELANTO

 Days Inn **M**
(760) 246-8777. **Call for rates.** 11628 Bartlett Ave. US 395, just e. Ext corridors. **Pets:** Accepted.

## ALTURAS

 Best Western Trailside Inn **M**
(530) 233-4111. **$80-$90.** 343 N Main St. On US 395. Ext corridors. **Pets:** Accepted.

# ANAHEIM

**ΑΑΑ ▼▼▼ Anabella Hotel** 🆂🅷
(714) 905-1050. **$119-$149, 3 day notice.** 1030 W Katella Ave. I-5, exit Katella Ave, 1 mi w. Ext corridors. **Pets:** Medium. $100 one-time fee/room. Designated rooms, service with restrictions, supervision.
🆂🅰🆅🅴 🆂�幅 🗙 🅷 💷 🍽 🏊

**▼▼▼ Anaheim Marriott Hotel** 🅻🅷
(714) 750-8000. **$129-$249.** 700 W Convention Way. I-5, exit Katella Ave, 0.6 mi w to Harbor Blvd, 0.3 mi s, then just w. Int corridors. **Pets:** Accepted.
🅰🆂🅺 🗙 🅼 🅿 🅷 💷 🍽 🏊 🗙

**ΑΑΑ ▼▼▼ Anaheim Plaza Hotel & Suites** 🆂🅷
(714) 772-5900. **$99-$119.** 1700 S Harbor Blvd. I-5, exit Katella Ave, 0.5 mi w, then just n. Ext corridors. **Pets:** Medium. $10 daily fee/room. Designated rooms, supervision.
🆂🅰🆅🅴 🆂 🗙 🅷 💷 🍽 🏊

**ΑΑΑ ▼▼▼ Anaheim Quality Inn Maingate** 🅼
(714) 750-5211. **$59-$129.** 2200 S Harbor Blvd. I-5, exit Chapman Ave, 1.5 mi w, then just n. Ext corridors. **Pets:** Accepted.
🆂🅰🆅🅴 🆂 🗙 🅷 💷

**ΑΑΑ ▼▼▼ Anaheim Stardust** 🅼
(714) 774-7600. **$69-$129.** 1057 W Ball Rd. I-5, exit Ball Rd, just w. Ext corridors. **Pets:** Accepted.
🆂🅰🆅🅴 🆂 🗙 🅷 💷

**ΑΑΑ ▼▼▼ Anaheim TownePlace Suites By Marriott** 🅼
(714) 939-9700. **$139-$159.** 1730 S State College Blvd. I-5, exit Katella Ave, 1.0 mi e, then just n. Int corridors. **Pets:** Small, other species. $75 one-time fee/room. Service with restrictions, supervision.
🆂🅰🆅🅴 🆂 🗙 🅷 💷 🏊 🗙

**ΑΑΑ ▼▼▼ Clarion Hotel Anaheim Resort** 🅻🅷
(714) 750-3131. **$69-$199, 3 day notice.** 616 Convention Way. I-5, exit Katella Ave, 0.6 mi w to Harbor Blvd, then 0.3 mi s. Int corridors. **Pets:** Small. $10 daily fee/room, $25 one-time fee/room. Service with restrictions, crate.
🆂🅰🆅🅴 🆂 🗙 🅷 💷 🍽 🏊

**ΑΑΑ ▼▼▼ Embassy Suites Hotel Anaheim-North Near Disneyland Resort** 🅻🅷
(714) 632-1221. **$134-$234.** 3100 E Frontera St. SR 91, exit Glassell St, just se. Int corridors. **Pets:** Accepted.
🆂🅰🆅🅴 🗙 🅷 💷 🍽 🏊 🗙

**▼▼▼ Hilton Anaheim** 🅻🅷
(714) 750-4321. **$89-$299.** 777 Convention Way. I-5, exit Katella Ave, just w to Harbor Blvd, just s, then just w. Int corridors. **Pets:** Small. $150 deposit/room. Designated rooms, service with restrictions, supervision.
🗙 🅼 🅷 💷 🍽 🏊 🗙

**▼▼▼ La Quinta Inn and Suites** 🆂🅷
(714) 635-5000. **$79-$159.** 1752 S Clementine St. I-5, exit Katella Ave, just n. Int corridors. **Pets:** Accepted.
🗙 🅷 💷 🏊

**ΑΑΑ ▼▼▼ Lemon Tree Hotel** 🅼
(714) 772-0200. **$79-$129, 3 day notice.** 1600 E Lincoln Ave. I-5, exit Lincoln Ave, 2 mi e. Ext/int corridors. **Pets:** Accepted.
🆂🅰🆅🅴 🆂 🗙 🅷 💷

**▼▼▼ Red Roof Inn Anaheim-Maingate** 🅼
(714) 520-9696. **$55-$76.** 100 Disney Way. I-5, exit Disney Way. Ext corridors. **Pets:** Accepted.
🗙 🅷 🏊

**ΑΑΑ ▼▼▼ Residence Inn by Marriott Anaheim Maingate** 🆂🅷
(714) 533-3555. **$149-$329, 3 day notice.** 1700 S Clementine St. I-5, exit Katella Ave, just w, then just n. Ext corridors. **Pets:** Medium. $75 one-time fee/room. Service with restrictions, crate.
🆂🅰🆅🅴 🗙 🅼 🅿 🅷 💷 🏊 🗙

**▼▼▼ Sheraton Anaheim Hotel** 🅻🅷 🐾
(714) 778-1700. **$119-$239.** 900 S Disneyland Dr. I-5, exit Ball Rd. Int corridors. **Pets:** Small, dogs only. $25 daily fee/room. Designated rooms, service with restrictions, supervision.
🅰🆂🅺 🆂 🗙 🅿 🅷 💷 🍽 🏊 🗙

**ΑΑΑ ▼▼▼ Staybridge Suites by Holiday Inn-Anaheim Resort** 🆂🅷
(714) 748-7700. **$84-$269.** 1855 S Manchester Ave. I-5, exit Katella Ave, just s; adjacent to west side of freeway. Int corridors. **Pets:** Accepted.
🆂🅰🆅🅴 🆂 🗙 🅷 💷 🏊 🗙

# ANAHEIM HILLS

**▼▼▼ Best Western Anaheim Hills** 🅼
(714) 779-0252. **$69-$79.** 5710 E La Palma Ave. SR 91, exit Imperial Hwy, 0.3 mi n. Ext/int corridors. **Pets:** Small. $15 daily fee/pet. Designated rooms, service with restrictions, supervision.
🅰🆂🅺 🆂 🗙 🅷 💷 🏊 🗙

# ANDERSON

**▼▼▼ AmeriHost Inn-Anderson** 🅼
(530) 365-6100. **$69.** 2040 Factory Outlet Dr. I-5, exit Factory Outlet Dr, just w. Int corridors. **Pets:** Accepted.
🅰🆂🅺 🆂 🗙 🅼 🅿 🅷 💷 🏊 🗙

**ΑΑΑ ▼▼▼ Best Western Knights Inn** 🅼
(530) 365-2753. **$60-$80.** 2688 Gateway Dr. I-5, exit Central Anderson eastbound; exit Lassen Park westbound, just e. Ext corridors. **Pets:** Accepted.
🆂🅰🆅🅴 🆂 🗙 🅷 💷 🏊

# ANGELS CAMP

**ΑΑΑ ▼▼▼ Angels Inn Motel** 🅼
(209) 736-4242. **$75-$95.** 600 N Main St. SR 49, north end of town. Ext corridors. **Pets:** Dogs only. $50 deposit/room, $10 daily fee/room. Service with restrictions, supervision.
🆂🅰🆅🅴 🆂 🗙 🅷 🏊

**ΑΑΑ ▼▼▼ Best Western Cedar Inn & Suites** 🅼
(209) 736-4000. **$69-$169.** 444 S Main St. On SR 49; center. Ext/int corridors. **Pets:** Accepted.
🆂🅰🆅🅴 🆂 🗙 🅼 🅷 💷 🏊

**ΑΑΑ ▼▼▼ Gold Country Inn** 🅼
(209) 736-4611. **$50-$145.** 720 S Main St. 1 mi s of jct SR 49 and 4. Ext corridors. **Pets:** Medium. $10 daily fee/pet. Service with restrictions, supervision.
🆂🅰🆅🅴 🆂 🗙 🅷 💷

**ΑΑΑ ▼▼▼ Jumping Frog Motel** 🅼
(209) 736-2191. **$55-$150.** 330 Murphys Grade Rd. SR 49, n of Angels Camp Center, just left. Ext corridors. **Pets:** Small, dogs only. $50 deposit/pet, $15 daily fee/pet. Designated rooms, service with restrictions, supervision.
🆂🅰🆅🅴 🗙 🅷 💷

# APTOS

**▼▼▼ Bayview Hotel** 🅲🅸
(831) 688-8654. **$149-$269, 10 day notice.** 8041 Soquel Dr. SR 1, exit State Park Dr E, 0.8 mi s. Int corridors. **Pets:** Accepted.
🅰🆂🅺 🆂 🗙 🍽 🅰🅲

# ARCATA

**AAA** **WWW** **Arcata Super 8** SH
(707) 822-8888. **$53-$99.** 4887 Valley West Blvd. US 101, exit Giuntoli Ln/Janes Rd, just e, then just s. Int corridors. **Pets:** Other species. $5 daily fee/pet. Service with restrictions, supervision.
SAVE SD X ⬛

**AAA** **WWWW** **Best Western Arcata Inn** M
(707) 826-0313. **$89-$175.** 4827 Valley West Blvd. US 101, exit Giuntoli Ln/Janes Rd, just e, then just s. Ext corridors. **Pets:** Large, dogs only. $20 one-time fee/room. Designated rooms, service with restrictions, supervision.
SAVE SD X ⬛ ⬛ ⬛ ⬛

**AAA** **WWWW** **Comfort Inn** M
(707) 826-2827. **$65-$150.** 4701 Valley West Blvd. US 101, exit Giuntoli Ln/Janes Rd, just e, then 0.3 mi s. Ext corridors. **Pets:** Large, dogs only. $10 daily fee/pet. Designated rooms, service with restrictions, supervision.
SAVE SD X ⬛ ⬛ ⬛ ⬛ ⬛

**AAA** **WW WWW** **Hotel Arcata** SH
(707) 826-0217. **$79-$200.** 708 9th St. Corner of G St; downtown. Int corridors. **Pets:** Accepted.
SAVE SD X ⬛ ⬛ ⬛

**AAA** **WWWW** **Quality Inn Arcata** SH
(707) 822-0409. **$70-$130.** 3535 Janes Rd. US 101, exit Giuntoli Ln/Janes Rd, just w. Int corridors. **Pets:** Other species. $10 daily fee/pet. Designated rooms, service with restrictions, supervision.
SAVE SD X ⬛ ⬛ ⬛ ⬛

# ARROYO GRANDE

**AAA** **WWW** **Premier Inns** M
(805) 481-4774. **$44-$119.** 555 Camino Mercado. US 101, exit Oak Park Rd, just e, then 0.3 mi s. Ext corridors. **Pets:** Accepted.
SAVE SD X ⬛ ⬛

# AUBURN

**AAA** **WWWW** **Best Western Golden Key** M ❀
(530) 885-8611. **$78-$130.** 13450 Lincoln Way. I-80, exit Foresthill Rd. Ext corridors. **Pets:** $15 one-time fee/pet. Designated rooms, service with restrictions, supervision.
SAVE SD X ⬛ ⬛ ⬛ ⬛ ⬛

**AAA** **WWW** **Foothills Motel** M
(530) 885-8444. **$60-$70.** 13431 Bowman Rd. I-80, exit Foresthill Rd. Ext corridors. **Pets:** Dogs only. $50 deposit/room, $10 daily fee/pet. Designated rooms, service with restrictions, supervision.
SAVE SD X ⬛ ⬛ ⬛

**WWW** **Holiday Inn-Auburn** SH
(530) 887-8787. **$109-$149.** 120 Grassy Valley Hwy. I-80, exit SR 49. Int corridors. **Pets:** Accepted.
ASK X ⬛ ⬛ ⬛ ⬛

**AAA** **WWW** **Motel 6 #4152** M
(530) 888-7829. **$65-$89.** 1819 Auburn Ravine Rd. I-80, exit Foresthill and Auburn Ravine rds. Int corridors. **Pets:** Accepted.
SAVE X ⬛ ⬛ ⬛

**AAA** **WWW** **Travelodge** M
(530) 885-7025. **$75-$125, 15 day notice.** 13490 Lincoln Way. I-80, exit Foresthill Rd. Ext/int corridors. **Pets:** Small. $15 daily fee/pet. Designated rooms, service with restrictions, supervision.
SAVE SD X ⬛ ⬛ ⬛ ⬛

# BAKERSFIELD

**AAA** **WW WW** **Americas Best Inn** M
(661) 764-5221. **$54-$64.** 200 Trask St. I-5, exit Stockdale Hwy, just e. Ext corridors. **Pets:** Medium. $5 daily fee/pet. Designated rooms, service with restrictions, supervision.
SAVE SD X ⬛ ⬛ ⬛

**WWW** **Bakersfield Red Lion Hotel** SH
(661) 327-0681. **$69-$169.** 2400 Camino Del Rio Ct. SR 99, exit SR 58 (Rosedale Hwy), just w, then just s. Ext/int corridors. **Pets:** Medium. $25 daily fee/pet. Service with restrictions, supervision.
ASK SD X ⬛ ⬛ ⬛ ⬛ ⬛ ⬛

**AAA** **WW WW** **Best Western Crystal Palace Inn & Suites** SH
(661) 327-9651. **$69-$139.** 2620 Buck Owens Blvd. SR 99, exit Buck Owens Blvd northbound; exit SR 58 (Rosedale Hwy) southbound. Int corridors. **Pets:** Accepted.
SAVE SD X ⬛ ⬛ ⬛ ⬛ ⬛ ⬛

**AAA** **WW WW** **Best Western Heritage Inn** M
(661) 764-6268. **$75-$90.** 253 Trask St. I-5, exit Stockdale Hwy, just e. Ext corridors. **Pets:** Accepted.
SAVE SD X ⬛ ⬛ ⬛ ⬛

**AAA** **WWWW** **Best Western Hill House** SH ❀
(661) 327-4064. **$59-$119.** 700 Truxtun Ave. SR 99, exit California Ave, 1.2 mi e, 0.4 mi n on Chester Ave, then 0.4 mi e. Int corridors. **Pets:** Medium. $10 daily fee/pet. Service with restrictions, supervision.
SAVE SD X ⬛ ⬛ ⬛ ⬛ ⬛

**WW WW** **Candlewood Suites** SH
(661) 328-8181. **Call for rates.** 3600 Chester Ln. SR 99, exit California Ave, just w to Real Rd, just s, then just w. Int corridors. **Pets:** Accepted.
X ⬛ ⬛ ⬛ ⬛ ⬛

**WW WW** **Days Inn** M
(661) 324-5555. **$69.** 4500 Buck Owens Blvd. SR 99, exit SR 58 (Rosedale Hwy) southbound, just e to Pierce Rd, then 0.7 mi n; exit Airport Dr northbound to Buck Owens Blvd, then just s. Ext corridors. **Pets:** Accepted.
ASK SD X ⬛ ⬛ ⬛ ⬛

**WW WW WW** **DoubleTree Hotel Bakersfield** LH
(661) 323-7111. **$109-$169.** 3100 Camino Del Rio Ct. SR 99, exit SR 58 (Rosedale Hwy), just w. Int corridors. **Pets:** Accepted.
ASK SD X ⬛ ⬛ ⬛ ⬛ ⬛ ⬛ ⬛ ⬛

**AAA** **WW WWW** **Holiday Inn Select Convention Center** LH
(661) 323-1900. **$99-$129.** 801 Truxtun Ave. SR 99, exit California Ave, 1.2 mi e, 0.4 mi n on Chester Ave, then 0.3 mi e. Int corridors. **Pets:** Accepted.
SAVE X ⬛ ⬛ ⬛ ⬛ ⬛ ⬛ ⬛ ⬛

**WW WW** **Howard Johnson Express Inn** M
(661) 396-1425. **$55-$85, 3 day notice.** 2700 White Ln. SR 99, exit White Ln, just e. Ext corridors. **Pets:** $10 daily fee/pet. Service with restrictions, supervision.
ASK SD X ⬛ ⬛ ⬛

**AAA** **WW WW WW** **La Quinta Inn Bakersfield** M
(661) 325-7400. **$79-$119.** 3232 Riverside Dr. SR 99, exit SR 58 (Rosedale Hwy) southbound; exit Buck Owens Blvd northbound, just n of SR 58 (Rosedale Hwy). Ext corridors. **Pets:** Medium. Service with restrictions.
SAVE X ⬛ ⬛ ⬛ ⬛ ⬛

**AAA** **WW** **Liberty Inn Motel** M ❀
(661) 366-1630. **$45-$65.** 8230 E Brundage Ln. SR 99, 7 mi e on SR 58 (Rosedale Hwy), exit SR 284 (Weed Patch Hwy), just n, then just e. Ext/int corridors. **Pets:** Small, other species. $5 one-time fee/pet. Service with restrictions, supervision.
SAVE SD X ⬛ ⬛

**AAA ▼▼▼ Quality Inn M**
(661) 325-0772. **$72-$140.** 1011 Oak St. SR 99, exit California Ave, just e, then just s. Ext/int corridors. **Pets:** Accepted.
[SAVE] [S☉] [X] [📶] [💻] [🏊]

**AAA ▼▼▼ Ramada Limited-Central M** ❀
(661) 831-1922. **$70-$100.** 830 Wible Rd. SR 99, exit Ming Ave, 0.8 mi ne. Ext corridors. **Pets:** Medium. $10 daily fee/pet. Service with restrictions, supervision.
[SAVE] [S☉] [X] [⚖] [📶] [💻] [🏊]

**▼▼▼ Residence Inn by Marriott SH** ❀
(661) 321-9800. **$179-$249.** 4241 Chester Ln. SR 99, exit California Ave, 0.5 mi w, then just n. Ext corridors. **Pets:** Other species. $75 one-time fee/room. Service with restrictions, supervision.
[ASK] [X] [🔔M] [✎] [⚖] [📶] [💻] [🏊] [⊠]

**AAA ▼▼ Super 8 Motel Bakersfield M**
(661) 322-1012. **$65-$75.** 901 Real Rd. SR 99, exit California Ave, just w, then just s. Ext corridors. **Pets:** Small. $10 daily fee/pet. Service with restrictions, supervision.
[SAVE] [S☉] [X] [📶] [🏊]

**AAA ▼▼▼ Vagabond Inn North M**
(661) 392-1800. **$45-$55.** 6100 Knudsen Dr. SR 99, exit Olive Dr; west side. Ext corridors. **Pets:** Accepted.
[SAVE] [S☉] [X] [📶] [💻] [🏊]

**AAA ▼▼▼ Vagabond Inn South M**
(661) 831-9200. **$49-$55.** 6501 Colony St. SR 99, exit Panama Ln, just e, then just s. Ext corridors. **Pets:** Dogs only. $20 deposit/pet, $5 daily fee/pet. Service with restrictions, supervision.
[SAVE] [S☉] [X] [📶] [💻] [🏊]

# BANNING

**AAA ▼▼▼ Banning Travelodge M**
(951) 849-1000. **$57-$199, 3 day notice.** 1700 W Ramsey St. I-10, exit 22nd St, 0.5 mi e, then just n. Ext corridors. **Pets:** Accepted.
[SAVE] [S☉] [X] [📶] [💻] [🏊]

**▼▼ Days Inn M**
(951) 849-0092. **$58-$185.** 2320 W Ramsey St. I-10, exit 22nd St, just n, then just w. Ext corridors. **Pets:** Accepted.
[X] [📶] [💻] [🏊]

**AAA ▼▼ Super 8 Motel M**
(951) 849-8888. **$57-$199, 3 day notice.** 1690 W Ramsey St. I-10, exit 22nd St, just n, then 0.4 mi e. Int corridors. **Pets:** Accepted.
[SAVE] [S☉] [X] [📶] [💻] [🏊]

# BARSTOW

**AAA ▼▼▼ Barstow-Super 8 Motel M**
(760) 256-8443. **$59-$79.** 170 Coolwater Ln. I-15/40, exit E Main St, 0.3 mi w, then just s. Ext corridors. **Pets:** $5 one-time fee/pet. Service with restrictions, supervision.
[SAVE] [S☉] [X] [📶] [💻] [🏊]

**AAA ▼▼▼▼ Best Western Desert Villa Inn M**
(760) 256-1781. **$69-$139.** 1984 E Main St. I-15/40, exit Main St westbound; exit Montara eastbound; 0.5 mi e of I-15. Ext corridors. **Pets:** $15 one-time fee/pet. Service with restrictions, supervision.
[SAVE] [S☉] [X] [🔔M] [✎] [⚖] [📶] [💻] [🍽] [🏊]

**AAA ▼▼▼ Days Inn M**
(760) 256-1737. **$54-$59.** 1590 Coolwater Ln. I-15/40, exit E Main St, just w, then just s on Roberta St. Ext corridors. **Pets:** Small. $10 daily fee/pet. Service with restrictions, supervision.
[SAVE] [S☉] [X] [📶]

**AAA ▼▼ Executive Inn M**
(760) 256-7581. **$45-$70.** 1261 E Main St. I-15/40, exit E Main St, 0.8 mi w. Ext corridors. **Pets:** Dogs only. $3 daily fee/pet, $15 one-time fee/pet. Service with restrictions, supervision.
[SAVE] [S☉] [X] [📶] [🏊]

**AAA ▼▼ Gateway Motel M**
(760) 256-8931. **$45-$95.** 1630 E Main St. I-15/40, exit E Main St, just e. Ext corridors. **Pets:** Accepted.
[SAVE] [S☉] [X] [📶] [🏊]

**▼▼▼ Holiday Inn Express, Barstow-Historic Route 66 SH**
(760) 256-1300. **$89-$109.** 1861 W Main St. I-15/40, exit W Main St, 0.8 mi ne. Int corridors. **Pets:** Other species. $20 deposit/room. Service with restrictions, supervision.
[ASK] [S☉] [X] [📶] [💻] [🏊]

**▼▼▼ Holiday Inn Express Hotel & Suites SH**
(760) 253-9200. **$108-$258.** 2700 Lenwood Rd. I-15/40, exit Lenwood Rd, just e, then 0.5 mi s. Int corridors. **Pets:** Other species. $25 deposit/room. Service with restrictions, crate.
[ASK] [S☉] [X] [🔔M] [✎] [⚖] [📶] [💻] [🏊] [⊠]

**▼▼ Motel 6 Barstow #1355 M**
(760) 256-1752. **$41-$51.** 150 N Yucca Ave. I-15/40, exit E Main St, 0.5 mi w, then just n. Ext corridors. **Pets:** Accepted.
[S☉] [X] [🏊]

**▼▼▼ Ramada Inn SH**
(760) 256-5673. **$85-$109.** 1511 E Main St. I-15/40, exit E Main St, 0.3 mi w. Int corridors. **Pets:** Medium. $20 one-time fee/room. Service with restrictions, supervision.
[ASK] [S☉] [X] [🔔M] [📶] [💻] [🍽] [🏊]

**AAA ▼▼ Stardust Inn M**
(760) 256-7116. **$35-$60.** 901 E Main St. I-15/40, exit Barstow Rd, 0.8 mi n, then 0.4 mi e. Ext corridors. **Pets:** Small. $5 daily fee/pet. Designated rooms, service with restrictions, supervision.
[SAVE] [S☉] [X] [📶] [🏊]

# BEAUMONT

**AAA ▼▼ Americas Best Value Inn M**
(951) 845-2185. **$70-$170.** 625 E 5th St. I-10, exit SR 79 (Beaumont Ave), just n. Ext corridors. **Pets:** Medium. $5 daily fee/pet. Service with restrictions, supervision.
[SAVE] [S☉] [X] [📶] [🏊]

**AAA ▼▼▼ Best Western El Rancho Motor Inn M**
(951) 845-2176. **$85-$180.** 480 E 5th St. I-10, exit SR 79 (Beaumont Ave), just n, then just e. Ext corridors. **Pets:** Very small, other species. $10 daily fee/pet. Designated rooms, service with restrictions, supervision.
[SAVE] [S☉] [X] [📶] [💻] [🍽] [🏊]

# BENICIA

**AAA ▼▼▼▼ Best Western Heritage Inn SH**
(707) 746-0401. **$99-$109.** 1955 E 2nd St. I-780, exit Central Benicia/E 2nd St, just e. Int corridors. **Pets:** Small. $25 one-time fee/pet. Service with restrictions, supervision.
[SAVE] [S☉] [X] [📶] [💻] [🏊]

# BEN LOMOND

**AAA ▼▼ Econo Lodge M**
(831) 336-2292. **$69-$189, 7 day notice.** 9733 Hwy 9. SR 9, 0.3 mi n; on San Lorenzo River. Ext corridors. **Pets:** Accepted.
[SAVE] [S☉] [X] [📶] [💻] [🏊]

# BERKELEY

**♦♦♦ ▼▼ Best Value Golden Bear Inn M**
(510) 525-6770. **$65-$109.** 1620 San Pablo Ave. I-80, exit Gilman E, just 2 mi s. Ext corridors. **Pets:** $10 daily fee/room. Supervision.
SAVE ⬛ ✕ ⬛ ⬛

**▼▼▼▼ The Claremont Resort and Spa LH**
(510) 843-3000. **$205-$735.** 41 Tunnel Rd. SR 13 and 24, 1 mi n; in Berkeley Hills. Int corridors. **Pets:** Accepted.
⬛ ✕ ⬛ 🍴 ⬛ ✕

**♦♦♦ ▼▼▼▼ DoubleTree Hotel and Executive Meeting Center Berkeley Marina SH**
(510) 548-7920. **$94-$270.** 200 Marina Blvd. I-80, exit University Ave, 0.5 mi w; on Berkeley Marina. Int corridors. **Pets:** Medium. $75 one-time fee/room. Designated rooms, service with restrictions, crate.
SAVE ⬛ ✕ ⬛ ⬛ ⬛ 🍴 ⬛ ✕

# BERRY CREEK

**▼▼▼▼ Lake Oroville Bed & Breakfast BB**
(530) 589-0700. **$125-$175.** 240 Sunday Dr. SR 162, 15 mi e to Bell Ranch Rd, 0.5 mi w. Int corridors. **Pets:** Accepted.
ASK ✕ ⬛ ⬛ ⬛

# BIG BEAR LAKE

**◆◆ ▼▼ Alpine Village Suites Lodge M 🐾**
(909) 866-5460. **$89-$209, 3 day notice.** 546 Pine Knot Ave. SR 18 business route; in the village. Ext/int corridors. **Pets:** Large, other species. $100 deposit/room. Service with restrictions.
ASK ⬛ ✕ ⬛ ⬛ ⬛

**▼▼▼▼ Bear Manor Cabins CA**
(909) 866-6800. **$119-$299, 15 day notice.** 40393 Big Bear Blvd. SR 18, 0.8 mi w of village. Ext corridors. **Pets:** Very small, dogs only. $100 deposit/room. Designated rooms, service with restrictions, supervision.
ASK ⬛ ✕ ⬛ ⬛ ⬛

**▼▼▼▼ Best Western Big Bear Chateau SH 🐾**
(909) 866-6666. **$79-$299, 3 day notice.** 42200 Moonridge Rd. SR 18, 1.5 mi e of Pine Knot Ave, then 0.5 mi s. Int corridors. **Pets:** Dogs only. $15 daily fee/pet. Service with restrictions, supervision.
ASK ✕ ⬛ ⬛ 🍴 ⬛ ✕

**◆◆◆ ▼▼ Big Bear Lakefront Lodge M**
(909) 866-8271. **$49-$209, 3 day notice.** 40360 Lakeview Dr. SR 18, 0.5 mi w of Pine Knot Ave, 0.5 mi nw. Ext/int corridors. **Pets:** Accepted.
SAVE ⬛ ✕ ⬛ ⬛ ✕ ⬛

**◆◆◆ ▼▼▼ Cozy Hollow Lodge CA**
(909) 866-9694. **$49-$279, 15 day notice.** 40409 Big Bear Blvd. SR 18, 0.8 mi w. Ext corridors. **Pets:** Medium, dogs only. $100 deposit/room, $10 daily fee/pet, $25 one-time fee/room. Designated rooms, service with restrictions, crate.
SAVE ⬛ ✕ ⬛ ⬛ ⬛

**▼▼ Eagle's Nest Bed & Breakfast BB 🐾**
(909) 866-6465. **$85-$165, 5 day notice.** 41675 Big Bear Blvd. SR 18, 1 mi e of Pine Knot Ave. Ext/int corridors. **Pets:** Other species. $10 daily fee/pet. Designated rooms, service with restrictions, crate.
ASK ⬛ ✕ ⬛ ⬛

**◆◆◆ ▼▼ Golden Bear Cottages CA**
(909) 866-2010. **$79-$179, 30 day notice.** 39367 Big Bear Blvd. SR 18, 2 mi w of village. Ext corridors. **Pets:** Accepted.
SAVE ⬛ ✕ ⬛ ⬛ ⬛ ✕ ⬛

**◆◆◆ ▼▼▼ Grey Squirrel Resort CA**
(909) 866-4335. **$85-$145, 14 day notice.** 39372 Big Bear Blvd. SR 18, 2.5 mi w of village. Ext corridors. **Pets:** Other species. $10 daily fee/pet. Service with restrictions, crate.
SAVE ⬛ ✕ ⬛ ⬛ ⬛ ✕ ⬛

**▼▼ Majestic Moose Lodge CA**
(909) 866-2435. **$69-$229, 7 day notice.** 39328 Big Bear Blvd. SR 18, 2.5 mi w of village. Ext/int corridors. **Pets:** Accepted.
ASK ✕ ⬛ ⬛ ⬛ ✕ ⬛

**▼▼▼ Pine Knot Guest Ranch CA 🐾**
(909) 866-6500. **$89-$189.** 908 Pine Knot Ave. Just s of SR 18 business route and downtown area. Ext corridors. **Pets:** Other species. $10 one-time fee/pet. Designated rooms.
ASK ⬛ ✕ ⬛ ⬛

**◆◆◆ ▼▼▼ Sleepy Forest Cottages CA**
(909) 866-7444. **$65-$199, 15 day notice.** 426 Eureka Dr. SR 18, 0.7 mi e of Pine Knot Ave, then just n. Ext corridors. **Pets:** Accepted.
SAVE ⬛ ✕ ⬛ ⬛

**◆◆◆ ▼▼▼ Stage Coach Lodge CA**
(909) 878-3008. **$60-$165, 14 day notice.** 652 Jeffries Rd. SR 18, 0.5 mi e of Pine Knot Ave, then 0.3 mi s. Ext corridors. **Pets:** Other species. $75 deposit/room, $10 daily fee/pet. Designated rooms, service with restrictions, supervision.
SAVE ⬛ ⬛ ⬛ ✕ ⬛

**◆◆◆ ▼▼▼ Timber Haven Lodge CA 🐾**
(909) 866-7207. **$96-$265, 14 day notice.** 877 Tulip Ln. SR 18, 1.8 mi w of Pine Knot Ave, 0.4 mi s. Ext corridors. **Pets:** Dogs only. $10 daily fee/pet. Designated rooms, service with restrictions, supervision.
SAVE ⬛ ✕ ⬛ ⬛ ✕ ⬛

**◆◆◆ ◆ ▼▼▼ The Timberline Lodge CA 🐾**
(909) 866-4141. **$79-$220, 10 day notice.** 39921 Big Bear Blvd. SR 18, 1.5 mi w of Pine Knot Ave. Ext corridors. **Pets:** Large, other species. $10 daily fee/pet. No service, supervision.
SAVE ⬛ ✕ ⬛ ⬛ ⬛ ✕ ⬛

# BIG PINE

**▼▼ Big Pine Motel M**
(760) 938-2282. **$45.** 370 S Main St. On US 395. Ext corridors. **Pets:** Accepted.
ASK ✕ ⬛ ⬛

**◆◆◆ ▼▼ Bristlecone Motel M**
(760) 938-2067. **$48-$68.** 101 N Main St. On US 395. Ext corridors. **Pets:** $4 daily fee/room. Service with restrictions, supervision.
SAVE ⬛ ✕ ⬛ ⬛

# BISHOP

**◆◆◆ ▼▼▼▼ Best Western Bishop Holiday Spa Lodge M**
(760) 873-3543. **$89-$135.** 1025 N Main St. On US 395. Ext corridors. **Pets:** Accepted.
SAVE ⬛ ✕ ⬛ ⬛ ⬛

**◆◆◆ ▼▼▼▼ Comfort Inn M**
(760) 873-4284. **$84-$113.** 805 N Main St. On US 395. Ext corridors. **Pets:** Accepted.
SAVE ⬛ ✕ ⬛ ⬛ ⬛

**◆◆◆ ▼▼▼▼ Holiday Inn Express Hotel & Suites SH**
(760) 872-2423. **$99-$199.** 636 N Main St. On US 395. Int corridors. **Pets:** Medium, dogs only. $20 daily fee/pet. Designated rooms, service with restrictions, supervision.
SAVE ⬛ ✕ ⬛ ⬛ ⬛ ⬛ ⬛ ⬛ ✕

**▼▼▼ Motel 6–4094 M**
(760) 873-8426. **$49-$89.** 1005 N Main St. On US 395. Ext corridors. **Pets:** Large, other species. Service with restrictions, supervision.
✕ ⬛ ⬛

**▼▼▼ Ramada Limited M**
(760) 872-1771. **$99-$169.** 155 E Elm St. On US 395, just e. Ext corridors. **Pets:** Accepted.
ASK ⬛ ✕ ⬛ ⬛ ⬛ ⬛

**Rodeway Inn** M
(760) 873-3564. **$70-$150.** 150 E Elm St. From US 395, just e. Ext/int corridors. **Pets:** Medium. $5 daily fee/pet. Service with restrictions, supervision.
[ASK] [S⬦] [✕] [🛏] [💻] [⇌]

**Thunderbird Motel** M
(760) 873-4215. **$55-$150.** 190 W Pine St. Just w of US 395. Ext corridors. **Pets:** Accepted.
[ASK] [S⬦] [✕] [🛏] [💻]

**Vagabond Inn** M
(760) 873-6351. **$74-$185.** 1030 N Main St. On US 395. Ext corridors. **Pets:** Accepted.
[SAVE] [S⬦] [✕] [🛏] [💻] [⇌] [✕]

## BLYTHE

**Best Western Sahara Motel** M
(760) 922-7105. **$69-$149.** 825 W Hobsonway. I-10, exit Lovekin Blvd, just n, then just w. Ext corridors. **Pets:** Small. Service with restrictions, supervision.
[SAVE] [S⬦] [✕] [🛏] [💻] [⇌]

**Comfort Suites** M
(760) 922-9209. **$60-$145.** 545 E Hobsonway. I-10, exit 7th St, just n, then just w. Ext corridors. **Pets:** Accepted.
[SAVE] [S⬦] [✕] [🛏] [💻]

**Super 8 Motel** M
(760) 922-8881. **$60-$150, 3 day notice.** 550 W Donlon St. I-10, exit Lovekin Blvd, just s. Int corridors. **Pets:** Small. $10 daily fee/pet. Service with restrictions, supervision.
[SAVE] [S⬦] [✕] [⇌]

**Travelers Inn Express** M
(760) 922-3334. **$69-$139, 3 day notice.** 1781 E Hobsonway. I-10, exit Intake Blvd, just n, then just w. Ext corridors. **Pets:** Medium, other species. Designated rooms, service with restrictions, supervision.
[SAVE] [S⬦] [✕] [🛏] [💻] [🍴] [⇌]

## BORREGO SPRINGS

**Borrego Springs Resort Hotel** SH
(760) 767-5700. **$75-$115.** 1112 Tilting T Dr. SR 22, 1.5 mi s on Borrego Valley Rd, just w. Int corridors. **Pets:** Very small. $50 deposit/pet. Designated rooms, service with restrictions, supervision.
[SAVE] [S⬦] [✕] [⬚] [🛏] [💻] [🍴] [⇌] [✕]

## BRAWLEY

**Brawley Inn** M
(760) 344-1199. **$79-$150.** 575 W Main St. On SR 86 and 78. Ext/int corridors. **Pets:** $50 one-time fee/pet. Service with restrictions, crate.
[SAVE] [✕] [🛏] [💻] [🍴] [⇌]

## BREA

**Homestead Studio Suites Hotel-Orange County-Brea** M
(714) 528-2500. **$65-$80.** 3050 E Imperial Hwy. SR 57, exit Imperial Hwy, 1.4 mi e. Ext corridors. **Pets:** $25 daily fee/pet. Service with restrictions, supervision.
[ASK] [S⬦] [✕] [🛏] [💻]

**Woodfin Suite Hotel** M
(714) 579-3200. **$114-$164.** 3100 E Imperial Hwy. SR 57, exit Imperial Hwy, 1.5 mi e. Ext corridors. **Pets:** Other species. $150 deposit/room, $5 daily fee/pet. Service with restrictions, crate.
[SAVE] [S⬦] [✕] [🛏] [💻] [⇌]

## BRIDGEPORT

**Best Western Ruby Inn** M
(760) 932-7241. **$100-$170.** 333 Main St. On US 395; center. Ext corridors. **Pets:** Accepted.
[SAVE] [S⬦] [✕] [🛏] [💻]

**Redwood Motel** M 🐾
(760) 932-7060. **$55-$159, 5 day notice.** 425 Main St. On US 395; on north side of town. Ext corridors. **Pets:** Large. $10 daily fee/pet. Designated rooms, service with restrictions, supervision.
[SAVE] [S⬦] [✕] [⬚] [🛏] [💻]

**Silver Maple Inn** M 🐾
(760) 932-7383. **$60-$120.** 310 Main St. On US 395; center. Ext corridors. **Pets:** Other species. Supervision.
[SAVE] [S⬦] [✕] [🛏] [💻] [⬚]

**Walker River Lodge** M
(760) 932-7021. **$55-$200.** 100 Main St. On US 395; at south end of town. Ext corridors. **Pets:** Medium. Service with restrictions, supervision.
[SAVE] [S⬦] [✕] [⬚] [🛏] [💻] [⇌]

## BUELLTON

**Quality Inn Solvang/Buellton** M
(805) 688-0022. **$59-$179.** 630 Ave of the Flags. US 101, exit Ave of the Flags/McMurray Rd southbound, just s; exit northbound, just w. Ext/int corridors. **Pets:** Medium. $25 one-time fee/room. Designated rooms, service with restrictions, supervision.
[SAVE] [S⬦] [✕] [🛏] [💻]

**Santa Ynez Valley Marriott** SH 🐾
(805) 688-1000. **$149-$329.** 555 McMurray Rd. US 101, exit SR 246, just e, then just n. Int corridors. **Pets:** $50 one-time fee/room. Designated rooms, service with restrictions.
[ASK] [S⬦] [✕] [⬚M] [⬚] [🛏] [💻] [🍴] [⇌] [✕]

## BURNEY

**Burney Motel** M
(530) 335-4500. **$45-$69, 3 day notice.** 37448 Main St. 0.8 mi e on SR 299. Ext corridors. **Pets:** Accepted.
[✕] [🛏] [💻]

**Charm Motel** M 🐾
(530) 335-2254. **$55-$95, 3 day notice.** 37363 Main St. 0.8 mi e on SR 299. Ext corridors. **Pets:** Other species. $5 daily fee/pet. Service with restrictions, supervision.
[SAVE] [S⬦] [✕] [🛏] [💻]

**Green Gables Motel** M 🐾
(530) 335-2264. **$55-$95, 3 day notice.** 37385 Main St. 0.8 mi e on SR 299. Ext corridors. **Pets:** Other species. $5 daily fee/pet. Service with restrictions, supervision.
[SAVE] [S⬦] [✕] [🛏] [💻] [⇌]

**Shasta Pines Motel** M
(530) 335-2201. **$49-$116, 5 day notice.** 37386 Main St. 0.8 mi e on SR 299. Ext corridors. **Pets:** Small. $7 daily fee/pet. Designated rooms, service with restrictions, supervision.
[SAVE] [S⬦] [✕] [⬚M] [🛏] [💻] [⇌]

## BUTTONWILLOW

**Super 8 Motel** M
(661) 764-5117. **$57-$68.** 20681 Tracy Ave. I-5, exit SR 58, just e. Ext corridors. **Pets:** Accepted.
[SAVE] [S⬦] [✕] [⬚] [⇌]

**Willow Inn & Suites** M
(661) 764-5121. **$55-$69.** 20645 Tracy Road. I-5, exit SR 58, just e, then just n. Ext corridors. **Pets:** Accepted.
[SAVE] [S⬦] [✕] [🛏] [💻] [⇌]

## CALIMESA

**AAA ▽▽▽ Calimesa Inn Motel M**
(909) 795-2536. **$70-$130.** 1205 Calimesa Blvd. I-10, exit Calimesa Blvd, just ne. Ext corridors. **Pets:** Small. $10 daily fee/pet. Service with restrictions, supervision.

[SAVE] [S🐾] [✕] [🛏] [≈]

## CALIPATRIA

**AAA ▽▽▽ Calipatria Inn & Suites M 🐾**
(760) 348-7348. **$80-$205.** 700 N Sorenson Ave. On SR 111. Ext corridors. **Pets:** $20 deposit/pet. Service with restrictions, supervision.

[SAVE] [S🐾] [✕] [🛏] [💻] [🍽] [≈]

## CAMBRIA

**▽▽ Cambria Shores Inn M 🐾**
(805) 927-8644. **$105-$200, 7 day notice.** 6276 Moonstone Beach Dr. SR 1, exit Moonstone Beach Dr, just w, then 0.8 mi s. Ext corridors. **Pets:** Dogs only. $25 daily fee/pet. Service with restrictions, supervision.

[✕] [🛏] [💻] [⚿]

**▽▽▽ Fog Catcher Inn M**
(805) 927-1400. **$89-$279.** 6400 Moonstone Beach Dr. SR 1, exit Moonstone Beach Dr, just w, then 0.7 mi s. Ext corridors. **Pets:** Accepted.

[ASK] [S🐾] [✕] [🛏] [💻] [≈] [⚿]

**AAA ▽▽ Mariners Inn by the Sea M**
(805) 927-4624. **$79-$189, 5 day notice.** 6180 Moonstone Beach Dr. SR 1, exit Moonstone Beach Dr, just w, then 1 mi s. Ext corridors. **Pets:** Accepted.

[SAVE] [✕] [🛏] [⚿]

**▽▽▽ Sea Otter Inn M**
(805) 927-5888. **$89-$329, 3 day notice.** 6656 Moonstone Beach Dr. SR 1, exit Moonstone Beach Dr, just w, then 0.5 mi s. Ext corridors. **Pets:** Accepted.

[ASK] [S🐾] [✕] [🛏] [💻] [≈] [⚿]

## CAMERON PARK

**▽▽▽ Cameron Park Inn & Suites SH**
(530) 677-2203. **$89-$179.** 3361 Coach Ln. 12 mi w of Placerville on US 50, exit Cameron Park Dr. Ext corridors. **Pets:** Accepted.

[ASK] [S🐾] [✕] [♿M] [🛏] [💻] [≈]

## CAMINO

**▽▽ Camino Hotel-Seven Mile House BB**
(530) 644-7740. **$86-$119, 7 day notice.** 4103 Carson Rd. US 50, exit Camino, just n. Int corridors. **Pets:** Accepted.

[ASK] [S🐾] [✕] [♿M] [⚿] [📶] [🗨]

## CAMPBELL

**AAA ▽▽▽ Campbell Inn M**
(408) 374-4300. **$89-$99.** 675 E Campbell Ave. SR 17, exit Hamilton Ave E, 0.3 mi to Bascom Ave, 0.3 mi s, then 0.3 mi w. Ext corridors. **Pets:** Medium, other species. $50 one-time fee/room. Service with restrictions, supervision.

[SAVE] [S🐾] [✕] [🛏] [💻] [≈] [🗨]

**▽▽▽ Residence Inn by Marriott-San Jose M 🐾**
(408) 559-1551. **$135-$179.** 2761 S Bascom Ave. SR 17, exit Camden Ave E, just n. Ext corridors. **Pets:** Other species. $75 one-time fee/room. Service with restrictions, crate.

[ASK] [S🐾] [✕] [💻] [≈]

## CAPAY

**AAA ▽▽▽ Capay Valley Bed & Breakfast BB 🐾**
(530) 796-3738. **$89-$390.** 15875 State Hwy 16. I-505, exit SR 16, 10 mi w. Ext/int corridors. **Pets:** Designated rooms.

[SAVE] [S🐾] [✕] [♿M] [⚿] [≈] [🗨]

## CAPITOLA

**AAA ▽▽▽ Best Western Capitola By-the-Sea Inn & Suites SH 🐾**
(831) 477-0607. **$79-$219.** 1435 41st Ave. SR 1, exit 41st Ave, 0.8 mi w. Int corridors. **Pets:** Dogs only. $10 daily fee/pet. Service with restrictions.

[SAVE] [S🐾] [✕] [♿M] [⚿] [🛏] [💻] [≈]

**AAA ▽▽▽ Capitola Inn M**
(831) 462-3004. **$50-$158.** 822 Bay Ave. SR 1, exit Bay Ave, just w. Ext/int corridors. **Pets:** Medium. $20 one-time fee/pet. Designated rooms, service with restrictions, supervision.

[SAVE] [S🐾] [✕] [🛏] [≈]

## CARLSBAD

**AAA ▽▽▽▽ Four Seasons Resort Aviara LH 🐾**
(760) 603-6800. **$420-$570, 3 day notice.** 7100 Four Seasons Point. I-5, exit Poinsettia Ln/Aviara Pkwy, 1 mi e on Poinsettia Ln, then 1 mi s on Aviara Pkwy. Int corridors. **Pets:** Small. Designated rooms.

[SAVE] [✕] [💻] [🍽] [≈] [🗨]

**AAA ▽▽▽ Quality Inn & Suites M**
(760) 931-1185. **$100-$190.** 751 Raintree Dr. I-5, exit Poinsetta Ln, just w to Ave Encinas, then just n. Ext corridors. **Pets:** Large. $10 daily fee/pet. Designated rooms, service with restrictions, supervision.

[SAVE] [S🐾] [✕] [🛏] [💻] [🍽] [≈]

## CARPINTERIA

**AAA ▽▽▽ Holiday Inn Express Hotel & Suites SH**
(805) 566-9499. **$99-$229.** 5606 Carpinteria Ave. US 101, exit Casitas Pass Rd, just s, then just e. Int corridors. **Pets:** Accepted.

[SAVE] [S🐾] [✕] [♿M] [🗨] [⚿] [🛏] [💻] [≈]

## CASSEL

**▽▽▽ Burney Mountain Guest Ranch RA**
(530) 335-4087. **$175-$300, 61 day notice.** 22800 Hat Creek Powerhouse #2. I-5, exit 299E, 2.7 mi; from jct SR 89/299. Ext corridors. **Pets:** Accepted.

[ASK] [S🐾] [✕] [🛏] [💻] [≈] [🗨]

## CASTAIC

**AAA ▽▽▽ Comfort Inn M**
(661) 295-1100. **$59-$99.** 31558 Castaic Rd. I-5, exit Parker Rd northbound, 0.3 mi ne; exit Lake Hughes Rd southbound, 0.5 mi se. Ext corridors. **Pets:** Other species. $10 one-time fee/pet. Designated rooms, service with restrictions, supervision.

[SAVE] [S🐾] [✕] [🗨] [🛏] [💻] [≈]

## CASTRO VALLEY

**▽▽▽ Holiday Inn Express SH**
(510) 538-9501. **$87-$119.** 2532 Castro Valley Blvd. I-580, exit Castro Valley Blvd, 0.3 mi n. Int corridors. **Pets:** Accepted.

[ASK] [S🐾] [✕] [🛏] [💻] [≈]

## CATHEDRAL CITY

**▽▽ Comfort Suites M**
(760) 324-5939. **$49-$169.** 69-151 E Palm Canyon Dr. I-10, exit Date Palm Dr, 5 mi s, then just e. Ext corridors. **Pets:** Small. $10 daily fee/pet. Service with restrictions, supervision.

[ASK] [S🐾] [✕] [🛏] [💻] [≈]

**AAA ▽▽▽▽ Doral Desert Princess Resort, Palm Springs LH**
(760) 322-7000. **$159-$299, 3 day notice.** 67-967 Vista Chino. I-10, exit Date Palm Dr, 0.5 mi s, then 1 mi w. Int corridors. **Pets:** Medium. $150 deposit/room, $75 one-time fee/room. Designated rooms, service with restrictions, crate.

[SAVE] [✕] [🛏] [💻] [🍽] [≈] [🗨]

# CAYUCOS

**▼▼ ◆◆ Beachwalker Inn** Ⓜ
(805) 995-2133. **$65-$199, 3 day notice.** 501 S Ocean Ave. On SR 1 business route. Ext corridors. **Pets:** Small. $10 daily fee/room. Service with restrictions, supervision.
Ⓐ$Ⓚ Ⓢ🔒 ☒ 🔋 💻 🎾

**▼▼▼ Cayucos Beach Inn** Ⓜ 🐾
(805) 995-2828. **$85-$185, 3 day notice.** 333 S Ocean Ave. On SR 1 business route. Ext corridors. **Pets:** Other species. $5 daily fee/pet, $10 one-time fee/pet. Service with restrictions, crate.
☒ 🔋 💻

**ⒶⒶⒶ ◆ Cypress Tree Motel** Ⓜ 🐾
(805) 995-3917. **$45-$107.** 125 S Ocean Ave. On SR 1 business route. Ext corridors. **Pets:** Large, other species. $10 one-time fee/room. Service with restrictions.
ⓈⒶⓋⒺ Ⓢ🔒 ☒ 🔋 💻 🎾

**ⒶⒶⒶ ◆ Dolphin Inn** Ⓜ
(805) 995-3810. **$49-$199, 3 day notice.** 399 S Ocean Ave. On SR 1 business route. Ext corridors. **Pets:** Medium. $10 daily fee/pet. Designated rooms, service with restrictions, supervision.
ⓈⒶⓋⒺ Ⓢ🔒 ☒ 🔋 💻 🎾

**ⒶⒶⒶ ◆ Estero Bay Motel** Ⓜ
(805) 995-3614. **$49-$169, 7 day notice.** 25 S Ocean Ave. On SR 1 business route. Ext corridors. **Pets:** Small, dogs only. $10 one-time fee/pet. Designated rooms, service with restrictions, supervision.
ⓈⒶⓋⒺ ☒ 🔋 💻 🎾

**ⒶⒶⒶ ◆ Shoreline Inn** Ⓜ
(805) 995-3681. **$95-$195.** 1 N Ocean Ave. On SR 1 business route. Ext corridors. **Pets:** Accepted.
ⓈⒶⓋⒺ Ⓢ🔒 ☒ 🔋 💻 🎾

# CEDARVILLE

**ⒶⒶⒶ ▼▼ Sunrise Motel** Ⓜ
(530) 279-2161. **$60-$65, 4 day notice.** 54889 Hwy 299. On SR 299, 0.5 mi w. Ext corridors. **Pets:** Medium. $5 daily fee/pet. Designated rooms, service with restrictions, supervision.
ⓈⒶⓋⒺ Ⓢ🔒 ☒ 🔋 💻

# CHESTER

**ⒶⒶⒶ ▼▼ Chester Manor Motel** Ⓜ 🐾
(530) 258-2441. **$77-$90.** 306 Main St. On SR 36. Ext corridors. **Pets:** Large. $18 daily fee/pet. Service with restrictions, supervision.
ⓈⒶⓋⒺ Ⓢ🔒 ☒ 🔋 💻 🎾

# CHICO

**ⒶⒶⒶ ◆ Budget Inn of Chico** 🆂🅷
(530) 342-9472. **$45-$150.** 1717 Park Ave. SR 99, exit 20th St E, then right. Ext corridors. **Pets:** Small, dogs only. $10 daily fee/pet. Designated rooms, service with restrictions, supervision.
ⓈⒶⓋⒺ Ⓢ🔒 ☒ 🔋 ☒

**ⒶⒶⒶ ▼▼ Deluxe Inn** Ⓜ
(530) 342-8386. **$45-$39.** 2507 Esplanade. 2 mi n on SR 99 business route. Ext corridors. **Pets:** Small, dogs only. $10 daily fee/pet. Designated rooms, service with restrictions, supervision.
ⓈⒶⓋⒺ Ⓢ🔒 ☒ 🔋 🎾

**ⒶⒶⒶ ▼▼ Heritage Inn Express** Ⓜ
(530) 343-4527. **$85-$110.** 725 Broadway. SR 32, exit SR 99, 1 mi w. Ext corridors. **Pets:** Medium. $20 one-time fee/room. Designated rooms, service with restrictions, supervision.
ⓈⒶⓋⒺ Ⓢ🔒 ☒ 🔋 💻 🎾

**ⒶⒶⒶ ▼▼ ◆ Holiday Inn of Chico** 🆂🅷
(530) 345-2491. **$109-$139.** 685 Manzanita Ct. Just w of SR 99, via Cohasset Rd. Int corridors. **Pets:** Medium, other species. $50 one-time fee/room. Designated rooms, service with restrictions, supervision.
ⓈⒶⓋⒺ Ⓢ🔒 ☒ 🔼🅼 ♿ 🔋 💻 🍴 🏊

**▼▼▼ Music Express Inn** 🅱🅱
(530) 345-8376. **$76-$125.** 1145 El Monte Ave. SR 99, exit SR 32, 1 mi e to El Monte Ave, then just n. Ext/int corridors. **Pets:** $15 daily fee/pet. Service with restrictions, crate.
Ⓐ$Ⓚ Ⓢ🔒 ☒ 🔼🅼 ♿ 🔋

**▼▼▼ Oxford Suites** 🆂🅷 🐾
(530) 899-9090. **$95.** 2035 Business Ln. SR 99, exit 20th St E. Int corridors. **Pets:** Medium. $25 one-time fee/pet. Designated rooms, service with restrictions, supervision.
Ⓐ$Ⓚ Ⓢ🔒 ☒ 🔼🅼 ♿ 🔋 💻 🎾 ☒

**▼▼▼ Residence Inn** 🆂🅷
(530) 894-5500. **Call for rates.** 2485 Carmichael Dr. SR 99, exit Park Ave, 0.5 mi nw. Int corridors. **Pets:** Accepted.
☒ 🔋 💻 🎾 ☒

**ⒶⒶⒶ ◆ Safari Garden Motel** Ⓜ
(530) 343-3201. **$45-$55.** 2352 Esplanade. 2 mi n on SR 99 business route. Ext corridors. **Pets:** Small, dogs only. Designated rooms, service with restrictions, supervision.
ⓈⒶⓋⒺ Ⓢ🔒 ☒ 🔋 💻 🎾

**ⒶⒶⒶ ▼▼▼ Super 8 Motel** Ⓜ
(530) 345-2533. **$60-$80.** 655 Manzanita Ct. Just w of SR 99, via Cohasset Rd. Int corridors. **Pets:** Medium. $6 daily fee/pet. Service with restrictions, supervision.
ⓈⒶⓋⒺ Ⓢ🔒 ☒ 🔋 💻 🎾

# CHOWCHILLA

**ⒶⒶⒶ ▼▼ Days Inn** Ⓜ
(559) 665-1994. **$65-$75.** 220 E Robertson Blvd. SR 99, exit Robertson Blvd W. Ext corridors. **Pets:** Other species. $10 daily fee/pet. Service with restrictions.
ⓈⒶⓋⒺ Ⓢ🔒 ☒ 🔋 💻 🎾

# CLIO

**▼▼▼ Molly's Bed & Breakfast** 🅱🅱 🐾
(530) 836-4436. **$90-$110, 7 day notice.** 276 Lower Main St. Just e of SR 89. Int corridors. **Pets:** $10 daily fee/pet. Designated rooms, service with restrictions, supervision.
Ⓐ$Ⓚ ☒ Ⓦ ☒

# COALINGA

**ⒶⒶⒶ ▼▼▼ Best Western Big Country Inn** Ⓜ
(559) 935-0866. **$79-$129.** 25020 W Dorris Ave. I-5, exit SR 198/ Hanford-Lemoore, just w. Ext corridors. **Pets:** Medium. $10 daily fee/pet. Service with restrictions, supervision.
ⓈⒶⓋⒺ Ⓢ🔒 ☒ 🔋 💻 🎾

**ⒶⒶⒶ ▼▼▼ The Inn at Harris Ranch** 🆂🅷
(559) 935-0717. **$123-$139.** 24505 W Dorris Ave. I-5, exit SR 198/ Hanford-Lemoore, just e. Ext/int corridors. **Pets:** Accepted.
ⓈⒶⓋⒺ Ⓢ🔒 ☒ 🔼🅼 💻 🍴 🎾

# COLUMBIA

**▼▼ Columbia Gem Motel** Ⓜ
(209) 532-4508. **$69-$129.** 22131 Parrotts Ferry Rd. 3 mi n of Sonora; 1 mi from Columbia State Historic Park. Ext corridors. **Pets:** Dogs only. Service with restrictions, supervision.
☒ 🔋 💻 ☒

# CONCORD

**Best Western Heritage Inn** M
(925) 686-4466. **$69-$109.** 4600 Clayton Rd. 3 mi e at Wharton Way. Ext corridors. **Pets:** Accepted.

**Holiday Inn Concord** LH
(925) 687-5500. **$70-$144.** 1050 Burnett Ave. I-680, exit E Concord Ave, just e. Ext/int corridors. **Pets:** Medium, other species. $25 one-time fee/pet. Crate.

**Premier Inns** M
(925) 674-0888. **$54-$74.** 1581 Concord Ave. SR 242, exit Clayton Rd northbound; exit Concord Ave southbound, just e. Ext corridors. **Pets:** Small. Service with restrictions, supervision.

# CORNING

**Best Western Inn Corning** M
(530) 824-2468. **$75-$109.** 2165 Solano St. I-5, exit 631 (Central Corning), 1 blk e. Ext corridors. **Pets:** Medium. $10 one-time fee/pet. Designated rooms, service with restrictions, supervision.

**Comfort Inn** M
(530) 824-5200. **$64-$117.** 910 Hwy 99 W. I-5, exit 631 (Central Corning), just e. Int corridors. **Pets:** Accepted.

**Days Inn** M
(530) 824-2000. **$50-$199.** 3475 Hwy 99 W. I-5, exit 630 (South Ave), 0.3 mi s. Int corridors. **Pets:** Other species. $5 daily fee/pet. Designated rooms, service with restrictions, supervision.

**Holiday Inn Express Hotel & Suites** SH
(530) 824-6400. **$74-$129.** 3350 Sunrise Way. I-5, exit 630 (South Ave), just s. Int corridors. **Pets:** Other species. $10 one-time fee/pet. Designated rooms, service with restrictions, supervision.

# CORONA

**Hotel Paseo "Dynasty Suites"** M
(951) 371-7185. **$99.** 1805 W 6th St. SR 91, exit 6th St eastbound; exit Maple St westbound, just s. Ext corridors. **Pets:** Small. $20 daily fee/pet. Service with restrictions, supervision.

**Residence Inn by Marriott Corona** SH
(951) 371-0107. **$115-$280.** 1015 Montecito Dr. I-15, exit Magnolia, just e, just n on El Camino, just w on Carly Way, then just n. Int corridors. **Pets:** Medium, other species. $75 one-time fee/room. Service with restrictions, supervision.

# COSTA MESA

**Hilton Costa Mesa** LH
(714) 540-7000. **$99-$269, 3 day notice.** 3050 Bristol St. I-405, exit Bristol St, just s. Int corridors. **Pets:** Very small. $25 one-time fee/pet. Service with restrictions, supervision.

**Holiday Inn-Costa Mesa/Orange County Airport** LH
(714) 557-3000. **$89-$149.** 3131 Bristol St. I-405, exit Bristol St, just s. Int corridors. **Pets:** Medium, other species. $50 one-time fee/room. Designated rooms, service with restrictions.

**La Quinta Inn Costa Mesa (John Wayne/Orange Co. Airport)** M
(714) 957-5841. **$75-$115.** 1515 S Coast Dr. I-405, exit Harbor Blvd, just n, then just w. Ext corridors. **Pets:** Medium. Service with restrictions.

**Ramada Limited & Suites** SH
(949) 645-2221. **$79-$143.** 1680 Superior Ave. Just w of SR 55 (Newport Blvd) at 17th St. Ext corridors. **Pets:** Small. $10 daily fee/room. Designated rooms, service with restrictions, supervision.

**Residence Inn by Marriott** SH
(714) 241-8800. **$109-$189.** 881 W Baker St. SR 73, exit Bear St; SR 55, exit Baker St. Ext corridors. **Pets:** Medium, other species. $75 one-time fee/room. Service with restrictions, supervision.

**Vagabond Inn** M
(714) 557-8360. **$59-$99, 3 day notice.** 3205 Harbor Blvd. I-405, exit Harbor Blvd, just s; entrance from Gisler Ave, just w of Harbor. Ext corridors. **Pets:** Small. $10 daily fee/pet. Designated rooms, service with restrictions, supervision.

**The Westin South Coast Plaza Hotel** LH
(714) 540-2500. **$109-$185.** 686 Anton Blvd. I-405, exit Bristol St, just n, then just e. Int corridors. **Pets:** Accepted.

**Wyndham Orange County Airport** LH
(714) 751-5100. **$119-$189.** 3350 Ave of the Arts. I-405, exit Bristol St, n to Anton Blvd, just e, then just n. Int corridors. **Pets:** Accepted.

# CRESCENT CITY

**Americas Best Value Inn** M
(707) 464-4141. **$45-$95.** 440 Hwy 101 N. On US 101; center. Ext corridors. **Pets:** Medium, dogs only. $7 daily fee/pet. Designated rooms, service with restrictions.

**Hiouchi Motel** M
(707) 458-3041. **$60-$65.** 2097 Hwy 199. On US 199, 5.5 mi e of jct US 101. Ext corridors. **Pets:** Dogs only. Service with restrictions, supervision.

**Super 8** M
(707) 464-4111. **$50-$110, 7 day notice.** 685 Hwy 101 S. On US 101. Ext corridors. **Pets:** Small, dogs only. $10 daily fee/pet. Designated rooms, service with restrictions, supervision.

# CROMBERG

**Long Valley Resort** CA
(530) 836-0754. **$75-$85, 14 day notice.** 59532 Hwy 70. On SR 70. Ext corridors. **Pets:** Other species. $8 daily fee/pet. Designated rooms, no service, supervision.

# CUPERTINO

**Cypress Hotel** LH
(408) 253-8900. **$99-$279.** 10050 S De Anza Blvd. I-280, exit De Anza Blvd, just s. Int corridors. **Pets:** Other species. Designated rooms, service with restrictions, supervision.

# CYPRESS

**▼▼◈◈ Homestead Studio Suites Hotel-Orange County-Cypress** 🆂🅷
(714) 761-2766. **$90.** 5990 Corporate Ave. I-605, exit Katella Ave, 3 mi e, 0.4 mi n on Valley View Ave, then just w. Int corridors. **Pets:** $25 daily fee/pet. Service with restrictions, supervision.
[A$K] [S🔒] [✕] [🛏] [💻] [🌊]

**◈◈◈ ▼▼▼ Woodfin Suite Hotel-Cypress** 🆂🅷 ❀
(714) 828-4000. **$130.** 5905 Corporate Ave. I-605, exit Katella Ave, 3 mi e, 0.4 mi n on Valley View Ave, then just w. Int corridors. **Pets:** Other species. $5 daily fee/pet, $150 one-time fee/room. Designated rooms, service with restrictions, supervision.
[SAVE] [S🔒] [✕] [🛏] [💻] [🌊]

# DANA POINT

**◈◈◈ ▼▼◈◈ Laguna Cliffs Marriott Resort & Spa** 🅻🅷
(949) 661-5000. **$199-$209, 3 day notice.** 25135 Park Lantern. I-5, exit Pacific Coast Hwy, just w on Harbor Dr. Int corridors. **Pets:** Accepted.
[SAVE] [S🔒] [✕] [🛏] [💻] [🍽] [🌊] [✕]

**◈◈◈ ▼▼◈◈ The St. Regis Monarch Beach Resort & Spa** 🅻🅷 ❀
(949) 234-3200. **$345-$1295, 7 day notice.** One Monarch Beach Resort. I-5, exit Pacific Coast Hwy northbound, 3 mi n; exit Crown Valley Pkwy southbound, 3 mi w, 1 mi s on Pacific Coast Hwy, then 0.5 mi e on Niguel Rd. Int corridors. **Pets:** Small. $100 one-time fee/pet. Designated rooms, service with restrictions, supervision.
[SAVE] [✕] [⚥M] [🔲] [🎾] [🍽] [🌊] [✕]

# DAVIS

**◈◈◈ ▼▼◈◈ Best Western University Lodge** 🆂🅷
(530) 756-7890. **$79-$99.** 123 B St. Just e of University of California Davis campus. Ext corridors. **Pets:** Medium. $10 daily fee/pet. Service with restrictions, supervision.
[SAVE] [S🔒] [✕] [🛏] [💻] [✕]

**◈◈◈ ▼▼◈◈ Howard Johnson Hotel** 🅼
(530) 792-0800. **$69-$99.** 4100 Chiles Rd. I-80, exit Mace Blvd, just s, then 0.3 mi w. Int corridors. **Pets:** Accepted.
[SAVE] [S🔒] [✕] [⚥M] [🎾] [🛏] [💻] [🍽] [🌊]

**◈◈◈ ▼▼◈◈ University Park Inn & Suites** 🆂🅷
(530) 756-0910. **$75-$134.** 1111 Richards Blvd. I-80, exit Richards Blvd, just n. Ext corridors. **Pets:** Accepted.
[SAVE] [S🔒] [✕] [⚥M] [🛏] [💻] [🌊]

# DEATH VALLEY NATIONAL PARK

**▼▼ Stovepipe Wells Village** 🅼
(303) 297-2757. **$67-$112.** SR 190. On SR 190; 24 mi nw of visitor center. Ext corridors. **Pets:** $20 deposit/room. Service with restrictions, supervision.
[✕] [⚥M] [🎾] [🛏] [🍽] [🌊] [🐕]

# DELANO

**◈◈◈ ▼▼◈◈ Comfort Inn** 🅼
(661) 725-1022. **$65-$85.** 2211 Girard St. SR 99, exit County Line Rd, just e. Ext corridors. **Pets:** Small. $10 daily fee/pet. Service with restrictions, supervision.
[SAVE] [S🔒] [✕] [🛏] [💻] [🌊]

# DINUBA

**▼▼◈◈ Reedley Country Inn** 🅱🅱
(559) 638-2585. **$85-$95.** SR 99, exit Manning Ave, 10 mi e, then 1 mi s on Rd 52 (Reed Ave). Ext/int corridors. **Pets:** Accepted.
[✕]

# DIXON

**◈◈◈ ▼▼◈◈ Best Western Inn Dixon** 🆂🅷
(707) 678-1400. **$95-$135, 3 day notice.** 1345 Commercial Way. I-80, exit Pitt School Rd; 8 mi w of University of California Davis campus. Ext/int corridors. **Pets:** Other species. $10 one-time fee/room. Designated rooms, service with restrictions, supervision.
[SAVE] [S🔒] [✕] [⚥M] [🎾] [🛏] [💻] [🌊]

**▼▼◈◈ Super 8** 🆂🅷 ❀
(707) 678-3399. **$65-$105.** 2500 Plaza Ct. I-80, exit W A St, just s. Int corridors. **Pets:** Other species. $10 daily fee/pet. Supervision.
[A$K] [S🔒] [✕] [🛏] [🌊]

# DOWNIEVILLE

**▼▼◈◈ Riverside Inn** 🅼
(530) 289-1000. **$75-$100, 3 day notice.** 206 Commercial St. SR 49; center. Ext corridors. **Pets:** Accepted.
[✕] [🛏] [🎾] [✕] [🅰]

# DUBLIN

**▼▼◈◈ AmeriSuites (San Francisco/Dublin)** 🆂🅷
(925) 828-9006. **$99.** 4950 Hacienda Dr. I-580, exit Hacienda Dr, then n. Int corridors. **Pets:** Other species. $10 one-time fee/room. Service with restrictions, supervision.
[A$K] [S🔒] [✕] [⚥M] [🎾] [🛏] [💻] [🌊]

# DUNNIGAN

**▼▼◈◈ Americas Best Value Inn** 🆂🅷 ❀
(530) 724-3333. **$61-$119.** 3930 Rd 89. I-5, exit Dunnigan. Int corridors. **Pets:** Medium, other species. $10 daily fee/pet. Service with restrictions.
[A$K] [S🔒] [✕] [🛏] [💻] [🌊]

**◈◈◈ ▼▼◈◈ Best Western Country** 🅼 ❀
(530) 724-3471. **$65-$139.** 3930 Rd 89. I-5, exit Dunnigan. Ext corridors. **Pets:** Medium, other species. $10 daily fee/pet. Service with restrictions.
[SAVE] [S🔒] [✕] [⚥M] [🛏] [💻] [🌊]

# DUNSMUIR

**◈◈◈ ▼▼◈◈ Caboose Motel-Railroad Park Resort** 🅼 ❀
(530) 235-4440. **$90-$100, 3 day notice.** 100 Railroad Park Rd. I-5, exit 728 (Railroad Park Rd), 1 mi s. **Pets:** Large, dogs only. $10 daily fee/pet. Service with restrictions, supervision.
[SAVE] [✕] [🛏] [💻] [🍽] [🌊]

**◈◈◈ ▼▼◈◈ Cedar Lodge Motel** 🅼
(530) 235-4331. **$59-$125, 3 day notice.** 4201 Dunsmuir Ave. I-5, exit 732, 0.5 mi w. Ext corridors. **Pets:** Medium, dogs only. $7 daily fee/pet. Designated rooms, service with restrictions, supervision.
[SAVE] [✕] [🛏] [💻]

# EL CENTRO

**▼▼◈◈ Barbara Worth Golf Resort and Convention Center** 🆂🅷
(760) 356-2806. **$93-$99.** 2050 Country Club Dr. I-8, exit Bowker Rd, 2 mi n, then 3 mi e on CR S-80; 9 mi e of SR 86. Ext/int corridors. **Pets:** Accepted.
[A$K] [S🔒] [✕] [🛏] [💻] [🍽] [🌊] [✕]

**◈◈◈ ▼▼ Days Inn** 🅼
(760) 352-5511. **$49-$69.** 1425 Adams Ave. I-8, exit Imperial Ave, 1.4 mi n, then just w on SR 86 and I-8 business loop. Ext corridors. **Pets:** Small. $10 one-time fee/pet. Designated rooms, service with restrictions, supervision.
[A$K] [S🔒] [✕] [🛏] [🌊]

**◈◈◈ ▼▼◈◈ Ramada Inn El Centro** 🅼
(760) 352-5152. **$69-$79.** 1455 Ocotillo Dr. I-8, exit Imperial Ave, just n, then just e. Ext corridors. **Pets:** Accepted.
[SAVE] [S🔒] [✕] [🛏] [💻] [🍽] [🌊]

**▼▼ Super Star Inn-El Centro M**
(760) 352-0715. **$49-$69.** 611 N Imperial Ave. I-8, exit Imperial Ave, 1.4 mi n. Ext corridors. **Pets:** Small. $10 one-time fee/pet. Designated rooms, service with restrictions, supervision.

ASK SZ X B ~

**▼▼ Vacation Inn M**
(760) 352-9700. **$75-$95.** 2015 Cottonwood Cir. I-8, exit Imperial Ave, just n, then just w. Ext corridors. **Pets:** Accepted.

ASK SZ X B ~ TT ~

## EL PORTAL

**AAA ▼▼▼ Yosemite View Lodge M**
(209) 379-2681. **$85-$699, 7 day notice.** 11136 Hwy 140. Just w of Yosemite National Park West Gate. Ext corridors. **Pets:** Other species. $10 daily fee/pet. Supervision.

SAVE X SM ~ ~ B ~ ~ X

## EMERYVILLE

**AAA ▼▼▼ Woodfin Suite Hotel San Francisco Bay Bridge LH**
(510) 601-5880. **$179-$229.** 5800 Shellmound St. I-80, exit Powell St. Int corridors. **Pets:** Other species. $150 deposit/room, $5 daily fee/pet. Designated rooms, service with restrictions.

SAVE X B ~ ~ X

## ENCINITAS

**AAA ▼▼▼ Best Western Encinitas Inn & Suites at Moonlight Beach M**
(760) 942-7455. **$100-$150, 3 day notice.** 85 Encinitas Blvd. I-5, exit Encinitas Blvd, just w. Ext corridors. **Pets:** Small. $50 one-time fee/room. Designated rooms, service with restrictions, supervision.

SAVE X ~ TT ~

**▼▼▼ La Quinta Encinitas/San Diego M**
(760) 944-3800. **$79-$159.** 607 Leucadia Blvd. I-5, exit Leucadia Blvd, east side. Ext corridors. **Pets:** Accepted.

ASK SZ B ~ ~

## ESCONDIDO

**AAA ▼▼▼ Best Western Escondido SH**
(760) 740-1700. **$79-$129, 7 day notice.** 1700 Seven Oaks Rd. I-15, exit El Norte Pkwy, just e. Int corridors. **Pets:** Small, other species. $25 one-time fee/pet. Service with restrictions, supervision.

SAVE SZ X B ~

**AAA ▼ Rodeway Inn M**
(760) 746-0441. **$54-$149.** 250 W El Norte Pkwy. I-15, exit El Norte Pkwy, 1 mi e. Ext corridors. **Pets:** Accepted.

SAVE SZ X B ~

## ETNA

**▼ Motel Etna M**
(530) 467-5330. **$45.** 317 Collier Way. Just w of SR 3. Ext corridors. **Pets:** Accepted.

X B

## EUREKA

**▼▼▼ Bayview Motel M**
(707) 442-1673. **$80-$150.** 2844 Fairfield St. E of US 101, at Henderson St, top of hill. Ext corridors. **Pets:** Small. $5 daily fee/room. Designated rooms, service with restrictions, supervision.

ASK SZ X ~ B ~ X

**AAA ▼▼▼ Best Western Bayshore Inn M**
(707) 268-8005. **$89-$159.** 3500 Broadway. US 101; south end of town. Ext corridors. **Pets:** Dogs only. $40 one-time fee/pet. Designated rooms, service with restrictions, supervision.

SAVE SZ X ~ B ~ TT ~ X

**AAA ▼▼▼ Carter House Inns CI**
(707) 444-8062. **$155-$595, 3 day notice.** 301 L St. Just w of US 101 S. Int corridors. **Pets:** Medium. $50 daily fee/room. Designated rooms, service with restrictions, supervision.

SAVE SZ X B TT X

**AAA ▼▼ Eureka Town House Motel M**
(707) 443-4536. **$50-$125.** 933 4th St. On US 101 southbound; corner of K St. Ext corridors. **Pets:** Small, dogs only. $10 daily fee/pet. Designated rooms, service with restrictions, supervision.

SAVE SZ X B ~ X

**▼ Eureka Travelodge M**
(707) 443-6345. **$54-$150.** 4 4th St. On US 101; corner of 4th and B sts. Ext corridors. **Pets:** Accepted.

ASK SZ X B ~ ~ X

**▼▼▼ Quality Inn Eureka M**
(707) 443-1601. **$78-$200.** 1209 4th St. On US 101 southbound; between M and N sts. Ext corridors. **Pets:** Accepted.

ASK SZ X B ~ ~ X

**AAA ▼▼ Ramada Eurekan SH**
(707) 443-2206. **$72-$125.** 270 5th St. On US 101 northbound; corner of D St. Int corridors. **Pets:** Medium, other species. $30 deposit/pet, $12 daily fee/pet. Designated rooms, service with restrictions, supervision.

SAVE SZ X B ~ X X

**AAA ▼▼▼ Red Lion Hotel Eureka SH ☙**
(707) 445-0844. **$79-$150.** 1929 4th St. On US 101 southbound; between T and V sts. Int corridors. **Pets:** Medium. $15 one-time fee/room. Service with restrictions, supervision.

SAVE SZ X ~ B ~ TT ~

**AAA ▼▼▼ Sunrise Inn & Suites M**
(707) 443-9751. **$49-$99.** 129 4th St. On US 101 southbound; corner of C St. Ext corridors. **Pets:** Small. $8 daily fee/pet. Service with restrictions, supervision.

SAVE SZ X B X

## FAIRFIELD

**AAA ▼ Econo Lodge Inn & Suites M**
(707) 864-2426. **$59-$109.** 4625 Central Way. I-80, exit Suisun Valley Rd, just e. Ext corridors. **Pets:** Accepted.

SAVE SZ X SM B ~

## FALLBROOK

**AAA ▼▼▼ Best Western Franciscan Inn M**
(760) 728-6174. **$65-$119.** 1635 S Mission Rd. I-15, exit CR S-13, 6.5 mi sw. Ext corridors. **Pets:** Accepted.

SAVE SZ X B ~

## FALL RIVER MILLS

**AAA ▼▼▼ Hi-Mont Motel M ☙**
(530) 336-5541. **$86-$94, 3 day notice.** 43021 Bridge St. 1 mi w on SR 299. Ext corridors. **Pets:** Other species. $5 daily fee/pet. Service with restrictions, supervision.

SAVE SZ X ~ B ~

## FERNDALE

**▼▼▼ Collingwood Inn Bed & Breakfast BB ☙**
(707) 786-9219. **$99-$300, 14 day notice.** 831 Main St. Center. Int corridors. **Pets:** Other species. $25 daily fee/pet.

ASK SZ X X W ~

**AAA ▼▼▼ Shaw House Inn Bed & Breakfast BB**
(707) 786-9958. **$100-$285, 14 day notice.** 703 Main St. Center. Ext/int corridors. **Pets:** Accepted.

SAVE X X W ~

# FIREBAUGH

**AAA** ▼▼▼▼ **Best Western Apricot Inn** 🅼
(559) 659-1444. **$70-$125.** 46290 W Panoche Rd. I-5, exit W Panoche Rd, just w. Ext corridors. **Pets:** Medium. $5 daily fee/pet. Service with restrictions, supervision.
SAVE ⬛ ✖ ⬛ ⬛ ⬛ ⬌

# FISH CAMP

**AAA** ▼▼▼▼ **Apple Tree Inn** 🅲🅰
(559) 683-5111. **$99-$209, 12 day notice.** 1110 Hwy 41. 2 mi from South Gate to Yosemite National Park. Ext corridors. **Pets:** Other species. $50 one-time fee/pet. Designated rooms, service with restrictions, supervision.
SAVE ⬛ ✖ ⬛ ⬛ ⬛ ⬛ ⬌ ✖ 🅚

**▼▼** **The Narrow Gauge Inn** 🅼 ❀
(559) 683-7720. **$79-$225, 4 day notice.** 48571 Hwy 41. 4 mi from South Gate to Yosemite National Park. Ext corridors. **Pets:** Medium. $25 one-time fee/pet. Designated rooms, service with restrictions, supervision.
✖ ⬛ ⬛ ⬛ ⬌

# FOLSOM

**▼▼▼** **Residence Inn by Marriott** 🆂🅷
(916) 983-7289. **$170-$185, 14 day notice.** 2555 Iron Point Rd. US 50, exit Bidwell St, just n. Int corridors. **Pets:** Accepted.
A$K ⬛ ✖ ⬛ ⬛ ⬛ ⬌ ✖

# FORTUNA

**AAA** ▼▼▼▼ **Best Western Country Inn** 🅼
(707) 725-6822. **$89-$145.** 2025 Riverwalk Dr. US 101, exit 687 (Kenmar Rd), just w. Ext corridors. **Pets:** Medium, dogs only. $10 one-time fee/pet. Service with restrictions, supervision.
SAVE ⬛ ✖ ⬛ ⬛ ⬛ ⬛ ⬛ ⬌

**AAA** ▼▼▼ **Fortuna Super 8** 🅼
(707) 725-2888. **$60-$105.** 1805 Alamar Way. US 101, exit 687 (Kenmar Rd), 0.3 mi w on Riverwalk Dr to Alamar Way. Ext corridors. **Pets:** Small, dogs only. $10 daily fee/pet. Designated rooms, service with restrictions, supervision.
SAVE ⬛ ✖ ⬛ ⬛ ⬛

**▼▼▼** **Holiday Inn Express** 🅼
(707) 725-5500. **$99-$199.** 1859 Alamar Way. US 101, exit 687 (Kenmar Rd), 0.3 mi w on Riverwalk Dr to Alamar Way. Ext corridors. **Pets:** Accepted.
A$K ⬛ ✖ ⬛ ⬛ ⬌

**AAA** ▼ ▼ **Travel Inn** 🅼
(707) 725-6993. **$59-$89, 3 day notice.** 275 12th St. US 101, exit 12th St, 0.5 mi w. Ext corridors. **Pets:** Very small. $10 daily fee/pet. Service with restrictions, supervision.
SAVE ⬛ ✖ ⬛ ⬛ 🅚

# FOUNTAIN VALLEY

**▼▼▼** **Residence Inn by Marriott** 🆂🅷
(714) 965-8000. **$119-$189.** 9930 Slater Ave. I-405, exit Brookhurst St, just n, then just w. Ext corridors. **Pets:** Large, other species. $75 one-time fee/room. Service with restrictions, supervision.
✖ ⬛ ⬛ ⬛ ⬌ ✖

# FREMONT

**AAA** ▼▼▼▼ **AmeriSuites (Silicon Valley/Fremont)** 🆂🅷 ❀
(510) 623-6000. **$64-$107.** 3101 W Warren Ave. I-880, exit Warren Ave/Mission Blvd, just w. Int corridors. **Pets:** Medium. $10 daily fee/pet. Designated rooms, service with restrictions, supervision.
SAVE ⬛ ✖ ⬛ ⬛ ⬛ ⬛ ⬌

**AAA** ▼▼▼▼ **Best Western Garden Court Inn** 🆂🅷 ❀
(510) 792-4300. **$59-$89.** 5400 Mowry Ave. I-880, exit Mowry Ave, just e. Int corridors. **Pets:** Medium. $15 daily fee/room. Designated rooms, service with restrictions, supervision.
SAVE ⬛ ✖ ⬛ ⬛ ⬛ ⬌

**▼▼▼▼** **Fremont Marriott** 🅻🅷
(510) 413-3700. **$149-$199.** 46100 Landing Pkwy. I-880, exit Fremont Blvd/Cushing Pkwy, then w. Int corridors. **Pets:** Small. Service with restrictions, supervision.
⬛ ✖ ⬛ ⬛ ⬛ ⬛ ⬌

**▼▼** **Homestead Studio Suites Hotel-Fremont Blvd. South** 🆂🅷
(510) 353-1664. **$77.** 46080 Fremont Blvd. I-880, exit Fremont Blvd/Cushing Pkwy, just w. Int corridors. **Pets:** $20 daily fee/pet. Service with restrictions, supervision.
A$K ⬛ ✖ ⬛ ⬛

**▼▼▼▼** **La Quinta Inn & Suites Fremont** 🆂🅷
(510) 445-0808. **$79-$109.** 46200 Landing Pkwy. I-880, exit Fremont Blvd/Cushing Pkwy, just w. Int corridors. **Pets:** Medium. Service with restrictions.
A$K ✖ ⬛ ⬛ ⬛ ⬌

# FRESNO

**AAA** ▼▼▼ **Comfort Inn** 🅼
(559) 275-2374. **$95-$145.** 5455 W Shaw Ave. SR 99, exit Shaw Ave. Int corridors. **Pets:** Small. $25 one-time fee/pet. Designated rooms, service with restrictions, supervision.
SAVE ⬛ ✖ ⬛ ⬛ ⬛ ⬛ ⬌

**AAA** ▼▼▼ **Days Inn-Parkway** 🅼 🐾
(559) 268-6211. **$54-$99, 15 day notice.** 1101 N Parkway Dr. SR 99, exit Olive Ave, just w. Ext corridors. **Pets:** Medium. $5 daily fee/pet. Service with restrictions, supervision.
SAVE ⬛ ✖ ⬛ ⬌

**▼▼▼** **Holiday Inn Express Hotel & Suites-Barcus** 🅼
(559) 277-5700. **$100-$160.** 5046 N Barcus. SR 99, exit Shaw Ave, just e. Int corridors. **Pets:** Medium, other species. $20 one-time fee/room. Service with restrictions, supervision.
SAVE ⬛ ✖ ⬛ ⬛ ⬛ ⬛ ⬌

**▼▼▼▼** **La Quinta Inn Fresno/Yosemite** 🅼
(559) 442-1110. **$74-$112.** 2926 Tulare St. SR 99, exit Fresno St, 2 mi e to R St, then s. Ext corridors. **Pets:** Medium. Service with restrictions.
A$K ✖ ⬛ ⬛ ⬛ ⬌

**▼▼** **Quality Inn** 🅼
(559) 275-2727. **$97.** 4278 W Ashlan Ave. SR 99, exit Ashlan Ave, just w. Ext corridors. **Pets:** Accepted.
A$K ⬛ ✖ ⬛ ⬛ ⬌

**▼▼** **Red Roof Inn** 🅼
(559) 276-1910. **$48-$71.** 5021 N Barcus Ave. SR 99, exit Shaw Ave. Ext corridors. **Pets:** Small. No service, supervision.
✖ ⬛ ⬌

**AAA** ▼▼▼ **Red Roof Inn** 🅼
(559) 431-3557. **$57-$77.** 6730 N Blackstone Ave. SR 41, exit Herndon Ave, then w. Ext corridors. **Pets:** Small, other species. $75 deposit/room. Service with restrictions, supervision.
SAVE ⬛ ✖ ⬛ ⬌

**▼▼▼▼** **Residence Inn by Marriott** 🅼
(559) 222-8900. **$139-$189.** 5322 N Diana Ave. SR 41, exit Shaw Ave, 0.3 mi w, n on Blackstone Ave, then e on Barstow Ave. Int corridors. **Pets:** Accepted.
✖ ⬛ ⬛ ⬛ ⬛ ⬛ ⬌ ✖

**AAA ♦♦ Super 8-Downtown M**
(559) 268-0621. **$85-$95, 4 day notice.** 2127 Inyo St. SR 99, exit Ventura St, 0.5 mi e. Ext corridors. **Pets:** Small. $15 one-time fee/pet. Designated rooms, service with restrictions, supervision.
[SAVE] [S&] [✕] [🐾] [▯] [🖵] [🏊]

**AAA ♦♦♦ Super 8-Parkway M**
(559) 268-0741. **$59-$89.** 1087 N Parkway Dr. SR 99, exit Olive Ave, just w. Ext corridors. **Pets:** Medium. $10 daily fee/pet. Service with restrictions, supervision.
[SAVE] [S&] [✕] [▯] [🖵] [🏊]

**AAA ♦♦♦♦ TownePlace Suites by Marriott M**
(559) 435-4600. **$85-$150.** 7127 N Fresno St. SR 41, exit Herndon Ave E. Int corridors. **Pets:** Small, other species. $75 one-time fee/room. Service with restrictions, supervision.
[SAVE] [S&] [✕] [&M] [&°] [▯] [🖵] [🏊]

**AAA ♦♦♦ Travelodge Blackstone M**
(559) 229-9840. **$45-$99.** 3876 N Blackstone Ave. SR 41, exit Shields Ave, 0.3 mi w. Ext corridors. **Pets:** Medium. $5 daily fee/pet. Service with restrictions, supervision.
[SAVE] [S&] [✕] [▯] [🖵] [🏊]

**♦ University Inn M**
(559) 294-0224. **$49-$65.** 2655 E Shaw Ave. SR 41, exit Shaw Ave, 1.5 mi e. Ext corridors. **Pets:** Small, other species. $75 deposit/room. Service with restrictions, supervision.
[ASK] [S&] [✕] [▯] [🏊]

**AAA ♦♦ Valley Inn M**
(559) 233-3913. **$38-$45.** 933 N Parkway Dr. SR 99, exit Olive Ave, then w. Ext corridors. **Pets:** Small, dogs only. $5 daily fee/room. Service with restrictions, supervision.
[SAVE] [S&] [✕] [▯]

## FULLERTON

**AAA ♦♦♦ Fullerton Inn M**
(714) 773-4900. **$65-$75.** 2601 W Orangethorpe Ave. SR 91, exit Magnolia Ave, just n, then just e. Ext corridors. **Pets:** Small. $10 daily fee/pet. Designated rooms, service with restrictions, supervision.
[SAVE] [S&] [✕] [▯] [🏊]

**♦♦♦♦ Fullerton Marriott Hotel at California State Univ SH**
(714) 738-7800. **$89-$169.** 2701 E Nutwood Ave. SR 57, exit Nutwood Ave, just w. Int corridors. **Pets:** Accepted.
[ASK] [✕] [&M] [🐾] [▯] [🖵] [🍴] [🏊] [✕°]

## GALT

**AAA ♦ Royal Delta Inn M**
(209) 745-9181. **$49.** 1040 N Lincoln Way. SR 99, exit Pringle Ave. Ext corridors. **Pets:** Small. $100 deposit/pet. Service with restrictions, supervision.
[SAVE] [✕] [&M] [🏊]

## GARBERVILLE

**AAA ♦♦♦♦ Best Western Humboldt House Inn M**
(707) 923-2771. **$96-$129.** 701 Redwood Dr. US 101, exit Garberville, just e. Ext corridors. **Pets:** Medium, dogs only. $10 one-time fee/room. Designated rooms, service with restrictions, supervision.
[SAVE] [S&] [✕] [&°] [▯] [🖵] [🏊]

**AAA ♦♦ Motel Garberville M**
(707) 923-2422. **$49-$89.** 948 Redwood Dr. On US 101 business route. Ext corridors. **Pets:** Very small, dogs only. $10 daily fee/pet. Designated rooms, service with restrictions, supervision.
[SAVE] [S&] [✕] [▯] [🖵]

**♦♦ Sherwood Forest Motel M**
(707) 923-2721. **$86-$96.** 814 Redwood Dr. US 101, exit Garberville, just e. Ext corridors. **Pets:** Accepted.
[ASK] [S&] [✕] [▯] [🖵]

## GARDEN GROVE

**♦♦♦ Anaheim Marriott Suites SH ❀**
(714) 750-1000. **$119-$199.** 12015 Harbor Blvd. I-5, exit Chapman Ave, 1.5 mi w, then just s. Int corridors. **Pets:** Other species. $15 daily fee/pet. Designated rooms, service with restrictions, supervision.
[ASK] [S&] [✕] [▯] [🖵] [🍴] [🏊] [✕°]

**♦♦♦ Candlewood Suites Anaheim-South SI**
(714) 539-4200. **$89-$129.** 12901 Garden Grove Blvd. SR 22, exit Haster St westbound, just w; exit Fairview St eastbound, just nw. Int corridors. **Pets:** Accepted.
[ASK] [S&] [✕] [▯] [🖵]

**♦♦♦ Homewood Suites by Hilton-Anaheim/Maingate SH**
(714) 740-1800. **$139-$179, 14 day notice.** 12005 Harbor Blvd. I-5, exit Chapman Ave, 1.4 mi w, then just n. Int corridors. **Pets:** Very small, dogs only. $200 one-time fee/pet. Service with restrictions, supervision.
[ASK] [S&] [✕] [▯] [🖵]

**AAA ♦♦♦ Residence Inn Anaheim Resort Area SH**
(714) 591-4000. **$139-$369, 3 day notice.** 11931 Harbor Blvd. I-5, exit Chapman Ave, 1 mi w, then just n. Int corridors. **Pets:** Medium. $75 one-time fee/pet. Service with restrictions, supervision.
[SAVE] [S&] [✕] [&M] [🐾] [&°] [▯] [🖵] [🏊] [✕°]

## GILROY

**AAA ♦♦♦ Leavesley Inn M**
(408) 847-5500. **$68-$75.** 8430 Murray Ave. US 101, exit Leavesley Rd, just w. Ext corridors. **Pets:** Medium. $20 one-time fee/pet. Service with restrictions, supervision.
[SAVE] [S&] [✕] [▯] [🏊]

## GRAEAGLE

**♦♦♦♦ Chalet View Lodge SH**
(530) 832-5528. **$80-$181.** 72056 Hwy 70. 5 mi e on SR 70 (Feather River Hwy) from jct SR 89. Ext corridors. **Pets:** $15 daily fee/pet. Service with restrictions, supervision.
[ASK] [S&] [✕] [▯] [🖵] [🍴] [🏊] [✕°]

## GRASS VALLEY

**AAA ♦♦♦ Alta Sierra Village Inn M ♣**
(530) 273-9102. **$59-$175, 7 day notice.** 11858 Tammy Way. 6 mi s, 1.1 mi e on Alta Sierra Dr, 0.8 mi w on Norlene, then 0.5 mi e; follow signs to Alta Sierra Country Club. Ext corridors. **Pets:** Other species. $10 one-time fee/room. Service with restrictions, supervision.
[SAVE] [✕] [&M] [▯] [🖵] [🌊]

**AAA ♦♦♦ Best Western Gold Country Inn M**
(530) 273-1393. **$75-$125.** 11972 Sutton Way. SR 20 and 49, exit Brunswick Rd, just e; midway between Grass Valley and Nevada City. Ext corridors. **Pets:** $15 one-time fee/pet. Service with restrictions, supervision.
[SAVE] [S&] [✕] [&M] [▯] [🖵] [🏊]

**AAA ♦ Coach N' Four Motel M**
(530) 273-8009. **$62-$124, 3 day notice.** 628 S Auburn St. SR 49, exit E Empire St, 0.3 mi e, then just s. Ext corridors. **Pets:** Other species. $50 deposit/pet, $10 daily fee/pet. Designated rooms, service with restrictions, supervision.
[SAVE] [S&] [✕] [&M] [▯]

**AAA ♦♦♦ Golden Chain Resort Motel M**
(530) 273-7279. **$62-$102.** 13413 SR 49. On SR 49, 2.5 mi s. Ext corridors. **Pets:** Medium. $10 one-time fee/pet. Service with restrictions, supervision.
[SAVE] [S&] [✕] [&M] [▯] [🖵]

**♦♦♦ Grass Valley Courtyard Suites SI ❀**
(530) 272-7696. **$140-$265, 3 day notice.** 210 ■ Auburn St. SR 49, exit Central Grass Valley. Ext corridors. **Pets:** Dogs only. $25 one-time fee/pet. Supervision.
[ASK] [S&] [✕] [&M] [&°] [▯] [🖵] [🏊] [✕°]

**AAA** **WW** Stagecoach Motel **M**
(530) 272-3701. **$65-$135, 3 day notice.** 405 S Auburn St. SR 49, exit Colfax Ave, 0.4 mi s. Ext corridors. **Pets:** Other species. $15 one-time fee/room. Designated rooms, service with restrictions, supervision.
[SAVE] [SÓ] [X] [&M] [📶] [💻]

# GRIDLEY

**AAA** **WWW** Gridley Inn **M** ❀
(530) 846-4520. **$60-$80.** 1490 Hwy 99, Suite A. On SR 99, 1 mi s. Ext corridors. **Pets:** $10 one-time fee/pet. Service with restrictions, supervision.
[SAVE] [X] [📶] [💻]

**AAA** **WWW** Pacific Motel **M**
(530) 846-4580. **$58-$68, 3 day notice.** 1308 Hwy 99. On SR 99, 1 mi s. Ext corridors. **Pets:** Accepted.
[SAVE] [SÓ] [X] [📶] [💻] [🐾]

# GROVELAND

**AAA** **WWW** Americas Best Value Inn -Yosemite Westgate Lodge **M**
(209) 962-5281. **$69-$179, 3 day notice.** 7633/7647 Hwy 120. On SR 120, 12 mi e. Ext corridors. **Pets:** $15 daily fee/pet. Designated rooms, service with restrictions, supervision.
[SAVE] [SÓ] [X] [📶] [💻] [🐾]

**AAA** **WWWW** Groveland Hotel at Yosemite National Park **CI**
(209) 962-4000. **$145-$185.** 18767 Main St. Center. Int corridors. **Pets:** Accepted.
[SAVE] [X] [💻] [🍴]

# HANFORD

**AAA** **WWWW** Sequoia Inn **SH**
(559) 582-0338. **$65-$105.** 1655 Mall Dr. SR 198, exit 12th Ave, then n. Int corridors. **Pets:** Accepted.
[SAVE] [SÓ] [X] [📶] [💻] [🐾]

# HAYWARD

**AAA** **WWWW** Comfort Inn **M**
(510) 538-4466. **$79-$160.** 24997 Mission Blvd. 1.8 mi e of I-880, exit SR 92 (Jackson St), 0.5 mi s on SR 238 (Mission Blvd). Ext corridors. **Pets:** Small, other species. $100 deposit/room, $15 daily fee/pet. Designated rooms, service with restrictions, supervision.
[SAVE] [SÓ] [X] [📶] [💻]

**WWWW** La Quinta Inn & Suites Hayward/Oakland Airport **SH**
(510) 732-6300. **$89-$108.** 20777 Hesperian Blvd. I-880, exit A St, 0.5 mi w. Int corridors. **Pets:** Accepted.
[ASK] [SÓ] [X] [&] [📶] [💻] [🐾]

**AAA** **WWWW** MainStay Suites **SH**
(510) 731-3571. **$75-$129.** 835 West A St. I-880, exit A St, just w. Int corridors. **Pets:** Small. $15 daily fee/pet. Service with restrictions, supervision.
[SAVE] [SÓ] [X] [&] [💻] [🐾]

# HEMET

**AAA** **WW** Best Western Inn of Hemet **M**
(951) 925-6605. **$79-$126.** 2625 W Florida Ave. 2.4 mi w of SR 79 N (San Jacinto St) on SR 74/79. Ext corridors. **Pets:** Very small. $10 one-time fee/pet. Service with restrictions, supervision.
[SAVE] [SÓ] [X] [📶] [💻] [🐾]

**AAA** **WW** Coach Light Motel **M**
(951) 658-3237. **$60-$75.** 1640 W Florida Ave. 1.7 mi w of SR 74 N (San Jacinto St) on SR 74/79. Ext corridors. **Pets:** Dogs only. $10 daily fee/pet. Designated rooms, no service, supervision.
[SAVE] [SÓ] [X] [📶] [🐾]

**AAA** **WW** Country Inn of Hemet **M**
(951) 766-1902. **$80-$90.** 1201 W Florida Ave. 1.5 mi w of SR 79 N (San Jacino St), on SR 74/79. Ext corridors. **Pets:** Accepted.
[SAVE] [SÓ] [X] [📶] [💻] [🐾]

# HESPERIA

**AAA** **WWW** Days Inn Suites-Hesperia/Victorville **M**
(760) 948-0600. **$69-$179.** 14865 Bear Valley Rd. I-15, exit Bear Valley Rd, 0.5 mi e of Victor Valley Mall. Ext corridors. **Pets:** Accepted.
[SAVE] [SÓ] [X] [📶] [💻]

**AAA** **WWWW** Holiday Inn Express Hotel & Suites **SH**
(760) 244-7674. **$69-$189.** 9750 Key Pointe Dr. I-15, exit Main St, just w, then just n. Int corridors. **Pets:** Small, dogs only. $10 daily fee/pet. Designated rooms, service with restrictions, supervision.
[SAVE] [SÓ] [X] [&M] [📶] [♿] [📶] [💻] [🐾]

**WWWW** La Quinta Inn & Suites Victorville **SH**
(760) 949-9900. **$90-$100.** 12000 Mariposa Rd. I-15, exit Bear Valley Rd, just e, then just s. Int corridors. **Pets:** Accepted.
[ASK] [SÓ] [X] [📶] [💻] [🐾] [X]

# HUNTINGTON BEACH

**AAA** **WWWW** Hilton Waterfront Beach Resort **LH**
(714) 845-8000. **$189-$384, 3 day notice.** 21100 Pacific Coast Hwy. I-405, exit Beach Blvd, 6 mi s, then just w. Int corridors. **Pets:** Accepted.
[SAVE] [X] [📶] [💻] [🍴] [🐾] [X]

# IDYLLWILD

**WW** Cedar Street Inn **CA**
(951) 659-4789. **$80-$170, 10 day notice.** 25880 Cedar St. From SR 243 and town center, 0.3 mi ne on N Circle Dr. Ext corridors. **Pets:** Accepted.
[ASK] [SÓ] [X] [📶] [💻] [K] [Z]

**WW** Woodland Park Manor **M**
(951) 659-2657. **$89-$182, 10 day notice.** 55350 S Circle Dr. From SR 243 and town center, 1 mi ne. Ext corridors. **Pets:** Designated rooms, supervision.
[X] [📶] [💻] [🐾] [K] [Z]

# IMPERIAL

**WW** Imperial Valley Inn **M**
(760) 355-4500. **$59-$89.** 1093 Airport Blvd. On SR 86. Ext corridors. **Pets:** Accepted.
[X] [📶] [💻] [🍴] [🐾]

# INDEPENDENCE

**AAA** **WW** Independence Courthouse Motel **M** ❀
(760) 878-2732. **$45-$75.** 157 N Edwards. On US 395. Ext corridors. **Pets:** Other species. $5 daily fee/pet. Service with restrictions, crate.
[SAVE] [SÓ] [X] [📶]

**AAA** **WWW** Ray's Den Motel **M**
(760) 878-2122. **$55-$75.** 405 N Edwards. On US 395. Ext corridors. **Pets:** Dogs only. $6 one-time fee/pet. Service with restrictions, supervision.
[SAVE] [SÓ] [X] [📶] [💻]

# INDIAN WELLS

**AAA** **WWWW** Hyatt Grand Champions Resort **LH**
(760) 341-1000. **$99-$319.** 44-600 Indian Wells Ln. I-10, exit Cook St, 4.4 mi s, 1.5 mi e on SR 111, then just n. Ext/int corridors. **Pets:** Accepted.
[SAVE] [X] [&M] [&] [📶] [💻] [🍴] [🐾] [X]

# INDIO

**Best Western Date Tree Hotel** M
(760) 347-3421. **$59-$249, 3 day notice.** 81-909 Indio Blvd. I-10, exit Monroe St westbound, 0.5 mi s; exit Indio Blvd eastbound, 2.4 mi s. Int corridors. **Pets:** Accepted.

**Indian Palms Country Club & Resort** SH
(760) 775-4444. **$84-$209.** 48-630 Monroe St. I-10, exit Monroe St, 2 mi s. Ext corridors. **Pets:** Medium, dogs only. $30 daily fee/pet. Designated rooms, service with restrictions, crate.

**Palm Shadow Inn** M
(760) 347-3476. **$59-$144.** 80-761 Hwy 111. I-10, exit Jefferson Ave, 2.5 mi s, then 0.7 mi e. Ext corridors. **Pets:** Accepted.

**Quality Inn** M
(760) 347-4044. **$60-$170.** 43505 Monroe St. I-10, exit Monroe St, 0.5 mi s. Int corridors. **Pets:** Accepted.

**Super 8 Motel** M
(760) 342-0264. **$45-$189.** 81753 Hwy 111. I-10, exit 142S (Monroe St), 1.5 mi s, then 0.5 mi w. Ext corridors. **Pets:** $100 deposit/room, $15 daily fee/pet. Service with restrictions, supervision.

# IRVINE

**Candlewood Suites-Irvine Spectrum** SH
(949) 788-0500. **$109-$139.** 16150 Sand Canyon Ave. I-5, exit Sand Canyon Ave, 1.4 mi w to Hospital Rd, then 0.3 mi s. Int corridors. **Pets:** Accepted.

**Hilton Irvine/Orange County Airport** LH ❖
(949) 833-9999. **$109-$299.** 18800 MacArthur Blvd. I-405, exit MacArthur Blvd, 0.5 mi s. Int corridors. **Pets:** Large. $50 one-time fee/room. Designated rooms, service with restrictions.

**La Quinta Inn Irvine Spectrum (Old Historic Site)** M
(949) 551-0909. **$89-$129.** 14972 Sand Canyon Ave. I-5, exit Sand Canyon Ave, just w. Ext/int corridors. **Pets:** Medium. Service with restrictions.

**Residence Inn by Marriott Irvine John Wayne Airport** SH
(949) 261-2020. **$119-$209.** 2855 Main St. I-405, exit Jamboree Rd, just n, then just e. Int corridors. **Pets:** Other species. $75 one-time fee/room. Service with restrictions, supervision.

**Residence Inn by Marriott-Irvine Spectrum** SH ❖
(949) 380-3000. **$109-$189.** 10 Morgan. I-5, exit Alton Pkwy, 2 mi e. Ext corridors. **Pets:** Medium, other species. $50 one-time fee/room. Service with restrictions, supervision.

# JACKSON

**Amador Motel** M
(209) 223-0970. **$54-$66, 5 day notice.** 12408 Kennedy Flat Rd. 1.5 mi n at jct SR 49 and 88 on Frontage Rd. Ext corridors. **Pets:** Large, dogs only. $20 daily fee/pet. Designated rooms, service with restrictions, supervision.

**Best Western Amador Inn** SH
(209) 223-0211. **$79-$95.** 200 S Hwy 49. On SR 49. Int corridors. **Pets:** Accepted.

**El Campo Casa Resort Motel** M
(209) 223-0100. **$57-$108.** 12548 Kennedy Flat Rd. 1.5 mi w in Martell; jct SR 49 and 88 on Frontage Rd; approach off SR 88. Ext corridors. **Pets:** Accepted.

**The Jackson Lodge** M
(209) 223-0486. **$55-$120.** 850 N Hwy 49/88. On SR 88/49, 0.5 mi w. Ext corridors. **Pets:** Accepted.

# JAMESTOWN

**1859 Historic National Hotel, A Country Inn** CI ❖
(209) 984-3446. **$150, 3 day notice.** 18183 Main St. Downtown. Int corridors. **Pets:** Medium, other species. $10 daily fee/pet. Service with restrictions, supervision.

**Country Inn Sonora** M
(209) 984-0315. **$69-$209.** 18730 Hwy 108. On SR 108 and 49, 1 mi e of town. Ext corridors. **Pets:** Accepted.

**Jamestown Hotel** BB ❖
(209) 984-3902. **$90-$175, 7 day notice.** 18153 Main St. 0.5 mi n of jct SR 49 and 108; downtown. Int corridors. **Pets:** Small, dogs only. $25 daily fee/pet. Designated rooms, service with restrictions, crate.

# JUNE LAKE

**Double Eagle Resort/Spa** CA
(760) 648-7004. **$189-$229, 30 day notice.** 5587 Hwy 158. On SR 158; 3 mi w of village. Ext corridors. **Pets:** $15 daily fee/pet. Designated rooms, service with restrictions.

**Gull Lake Lodge** M
(760) 648-7516. **$75-$185, 7 day notice.** 132 Leonard Ave. Just n of SR 158; via Knoll and Bruce sts; in village. Ext corridors. **Pets:** Other species. Service with restrictions, supervision.

**June Lake Villager** M ❖
(760) 648-7712. **$85, 30 day notice.** 85 Boulder Dr. On SR 158; center of village. Ext corridors. **Pets:** Other species. Service with restrictions, supervision.

# KERNVILLE

**River View Lodge** M
(760) 376-6019. **$79-$129, 3 day notice.** 2 Sirretta St. On Kernville Rd; at the bridge; center. Ext corridors. **Pets:** Medium. $20 daily fee/pet. Service with restrictions, supervision.

# KETTLEMAN CITY

**Best Western Kettleman Inn and Suites** M
(559) 386-0804. **$79-$169.** 33410 Powers Dr. E of and adjacent to I-5, exit SR 41 N, 0.3 mi to Bernard, then 0.3 mi n. Ext corridors. **Pets:** Other species. $5 daily fee/pet. Designated rooms, service with restrictions, supervision.

(AAA) ◆◆◆ Super 8 M
(559) 386-9530. **$49-$79.** 33415 Powers Dr. E of and adjacent to I-5, exit SR 41 N, 0.3 mi to Bernard, then 0.3 mi n. Ext corridors. **Pets:** Small. $40 deposit/room, $10 one-time fee/pet. Designated rooms, service with restrictions, supervision.

(SAVE) (Sᴰ) (✕) (⌂) (⇌)

## KING CITY

◆◆ ◆◆ Courtesy Inn M
(831) 385-4646. **$49-$89, 7 day notice.** 4 Broadway Cir. US 101, exit Broadway St, just w. Ext corridors. **Pets:** Small, dogs only. $45 deposit/pet. No service, supervision.

(A$K) (Sᴰ) (✕) (&M) (📷) (⌂) (🛏) (💻) (⇌)

## KINGSBURG

(AAA) ◆◆◆ Swedish Inn M
(559) 897-1022. **$63-$68.** 401 Conejo St. SR 99, exit Conejo St, just w. Ext corridors. **Pets:** Accepted.

(SAVE) (Sᴰ) (✕) (🛏) (💻) (⇌)

## KLAMATH

(AAA) ◆◆◆ Motel Trees M
(707) 482-3152. **$60-$70.** 15495 Hwy 101 N. On US 101, 4.5 mi n. Ext corridors. **Pets:** $25 daily fee/pet. Service with restrictions, crate.

(SAVE) (Sᴰ) (✕) (🛏) (💻) (🍴) (🐾)

## KYBURZ

(AAA) ◆◆ ◆◆ Kyburz Resort Motel M
(530) 293-3382. **$59-$99.** 13668 Hwy 50. On US 50; halfway between Placerville and South Lake Tahoe. Ext corridors. **Pets:** Accepted.

(SAVE) (Sᴰ) (✕) (&M) (🛏) (💻) (🐾)

## LAGUNA BEACH

(AAA) ◆◆◆◆ Best Western Laguna Brisas Spa Hotel M
(949) 497-7272. **$129-$399.** 1600 S Coast Hwy. SR 133, 1 mi s on SR 1. Ext/int corridors. **Pets:** Medium, other species. $50 daily fee/pet, $50 one-time fee/pet. No service, supervision.

(SAVE) (Sᴰ) (✕) (🛏) (💻) (⇌)

◆◆◆◆ The Carriage House-Bed & Breakfast BB
(949) 494-8945. **$140-$175, 3 day notice.** 1322 Catalina St. SR 133, 1 mi s on S Coast Hwy to Cress St, then just e. Ext corridors. **Pets:** Other species. $10 daily fee/pet. Service with restrictions, supervision.

(✕) (🛏) (💻) (🍴) (⇌)

(AAA) ◆◆◆◆ Casa Laguna Inn BB 🐾
(949) 494-2996. **$150-$225, 5 day notice.** 2510 S Coast Hwy. SR 133, 1.3 mi s on SR 1. Ext corridors. **Pets:** Other species. $25 daily fee/pet. Supervision.

(SAVE) (Sᴰ) (✕) (🛏) (💻) (⇌)

(AAA) ◆◆ ◆◆ The Tides Inn M
(949) 494-2494. **$99-$250.** 460 N Coast Hwy. SR 133, 0.5 mi n on SR 1. Ext corridors. **Pets:** Medium. $25 daily fee/pet. Designated rooms, service with restrictions, supervision.

(SAVE) (Sᴰ) (✕) (🛏) (💻)

## LAKE ARROWHEAD

(AAA) ◆◆◆◆ Arrowhead Saddleback Inn CI
(909) 336-3571. **$98-$350, 7 day notice.** On SR 173, jct SR 189; across from entrance to Lake Arrowhead Village. Ext/int corridors. **Pets:** Other species. $8 daily fee/pet. Designated rooms, service with restrictions, supervision.

(SAVE) (✕) (🛏) (💻) (🍴)

◆◆◆◆ Storybook Inn BB 🐾
(909) 337-0011. **$99-$119, 7 day notice.** 28717 SR 18. SR 18, 1.1 mi e of jct SR 173. Ext/int corridors. **Pets:** Other species. Designated rooms, service with restrictions.

(A$K) (Sᴰ) (✕) (🛏) (💻) (🍴)

## LAKE FOREST

◆◆ ◆◆ Candlewood Suites-Irvine East SH
(949) 598-9105. **$89-$119.** 3 S Pointe Dr. I-5, exit Bake Pkwy, 2.6 mi e, then just s. Int corridors. **Pets:** Accepted.

(A$K) (✕) (🛏) (💻)

# LAKE TAHOE AREA

## SOUTH LAKE TAHOE

◆◆ ◆◆ Alder Inn M
(530) 544-4485. **$48-$180, 14 day notice.** 1072 Ski Run Blvd. 2.5 blks s off US 50 on Ski Run Blvd; 0.8 mi below Heavenly Valley Ski Lift Terminal. Ext corridors. **Pets:** Accepted.

(A$K) (Sᴰ) (✕) (🛏) (💻) (⇌) (🐾)

(AAA) ◆◆ ◆◆ Alpenrose Inn M
(530) 544-2985. **$50-$150, 7 day notice.** 4074 Pine Blvd. 0.3 mi n of US 50 via Park Ave. Ext corridors. **Pets:** Accepted.

(SAVE) (Sᴰ) (✕) (🛏) (💻)

(AAA) ◆◆ ◆◆ Ambassador Motor Lodge M
(530) 544-6461. **$55-$110.** 4130 Manzanita Ave. Just s of US 50 on Stateline Ave. Ext corridors. **Pets:** Accepted.

(SAVE) (Sᴰ) (✕) (🛏) (💻) (⇌) (🐾)

(AAA) ◆◆ ◆◆ Americas Best Value Inn & Suites–Blue Jay Lodge M
(530) 544-5232. **$49-$129.** 4133 Cedar Ave. 2 blks from casino center. Ext corridors. **Pets:** Accepted.

(SAVE) (Sᴰ) (✕) (&M) (⌂) (🛏) (💻) (⇌)

(AAA) ◆◆ ◆◆ Best Western Timber Cove Lodge M
(530) 541-6722. **$89-$209.** 3411 Lake Tahoe Blvd. 1.5 mi w of casino center; 0.5 mi w of Ski Run Blvd. Ext corridors. **Pets:** Medium, other species. $100 deposit/room, $25 daily fee/pet. Designated rooms, service with restrictions, supervision.

(SAVE) (Sᴰ) (✕) (⌂) (💻) (🍴) (⇌) (🐾)

(AAA) ◆◆ Budget Inn M
(530) 544-2834. **$32-$150, 3 day notice.** 3496 Lake Tahoe Blvd. On US 50, 1.5 mi w of casino center. Ext corridors. **Pets:** Dogs only. $5 daily fee/pet. Service with restrictions, supervision.

(SAVE) (✕) (🛏) (⇌) (🐾)

(AAA) ◆◆ Cal Va Rado Motel M
(530) 541-3900. **$39-$79.** 988 Stateline Ave. Just n of US 50; near casino center. Ext corridors. **Pets:** Medium, other species. $25 deposit/pet. Designated rooms, service with restrictions.

(SAVE) (Sᴰ) (✕) (🛏) (🐾)

(AAA) ◆◆ Capri Motel M
(530) 544-3665. **$55-$110.** 932 Stateline Ave. Just s of US 50. Ext corridors. **Pets:** Accepted.

(SAVE) (Sᴰ) (✕) (🛏) (💻) (⇌) (🐾)

**▲▲▲ ▽▽ Cedar Inn & Suites M**
(530) 543-0159. **$39-$69.** 890 Stateline Ave. US 50, 2 blks n; at Stateline and Manzanita aves. Ext corridors. **Pets:** Medium. $10 daily fee/pet. Supervision.
SAVE ⬛⬛⬛⬛⬛⬛

**▽▽ Cedar Lodge M**
(530) 544-6453. **$40-$60, 3 day notice.** 4069 Cedar Ave. N off US 50, toward the lake; at Cedar and Friday aves; 3 blks from the casino center. Ext corridors. **Pets:** Accepted.
ASK ⬛⬛⬛⬛⬛

**▲▲▲ ▽▽▽ Days Inn-Casino Area/South Lake Tahoe M**
(530) 541-4800. **$49-$279, 5 day notice.** 968 Park Ave. 1 blk n off US 50, toward the lake; at Park and Cedar aves; 3 blks w of casino center. Int corridors. **Pets:** $10 daily fee/pet. Designated rooms, service with restrictions, supervision.
SAVE ⬛⬛⬛⬛

**▲▲▲ ▽▽▽ Fireside Lodge B & B BB ❀**
(530) 544-5515. **$89-$145, 30 day notice.** 515 Emerald Bay Rd. SR 89, 1 mi n of US 50. Ext corridors. **Pets:** Dogs only. $100 deposit/room, $20 daily fee/pet. Service with restrictions, supervision.
SAVE ⬛⬛⬛⬛⬛

**▲▲▲ ▽▽▽ High Country Lodge M**
(530) 541-0508. **$40-$150.** 1227 Emerald Bay Rd. US 50, 0.5 mi n of airport. Ext corridors. **Pets:** Very small, dogs only. $10 one-time fee/pet. Designated rooms, service with restrictions, supervision.
SAVE ⬛⬛⬛⬛⬛

**▲▲▲ ▽▽ Pistantes Coyote Den M ❀**
(530) 541-2282. **$35-$175, 4 day notice.** 1211 Emerald Bay Rd. US 50, 0.5 mi n of airport. Ext corridors. **Pets:** Dogs only. Designated rooms, supervision.
SAVE ⬛⬛⬛⬛⬛

**▲▲▲ ▽▽ Rodeway Inn M**
(530) 541-7150. **$39-$299, 3 day notice.** 4127 Pine Blvd. N off US 50; between Stateline and Park aves. Ext/int corridors. **Pets:** Very small. $15 one-time fee/room. Designated rooms, service with restrictions, supervision.
SAVE ⬛⬛⬛⬛⬛

**▲▲▲ ▽▽ South Lake Tahoe Lodge M**
(530) 541-8589. **$59-$99.** 1341 Emerald Bay Rd. US 50, 0.5 mi n of airport. Ext corridors. **Pets:** Accepted.
SAVE ⬛⬛⬛⬛⬛

**▲▲▲ ▽▽ Super 8 M**
(530) 544-3476. **$36-$205.** 3600 Lake Tahoe Blvd. US 50, just w of Ski Run Blvd. Ext corridors. **Pets:** Accepted.
SAVE ⬛⬛⬛⬛⬛⬛⬛⬛

**▽▽▽ Tahoe Hacienda Inn M**
(530) 541-3805. **$48-$198, 3 day notice.** 3820 Lake Tahoe Blvd. US 50, 0.7 mi w of casino center. Ext corridors. **Pets:** Small. $50 deposit/pet, $10 daily fee/pet. Designated rooms, service with restrictions, supervision.
ASK ⬛⬛⬛⬛⬛⬛⬛

**▲▲▲ ▽▽▽▽ Tahoe Keys Resort CO ❀**
(530) 544-5397. **$100-$1300.** 599 Tahoe Keys Blvd. US 50, exit Tahoe Keys Blvd, 1 mi w. Ext corridors. **Pets:** Dogs only. $100 deposit/pet, $25 one-time fee/pet. Designated rooms, service with restrictions, supervision.
SAVE ⬛⬛⬛⬛⬛⬛⬛⬛

**▲▲▲ ▽▽ Tahoe Valley Lodge M**
(530) 541-0353. **$95-$495, 7 day notice.** 2241 Lake Tahoe Blvd. 0.5 mi e of jct US 50 and SR 89. Ext corridors. **Pets:** Small, dogs only. $10 daily fee/pet. Designated rooms, service with restrictions, supervision.
SAVE ⬛⬛⬛⬛⬛⬛

## TAHOE CITY

**▽▽ Mother Nature's Inn M**
(530) 581-4278. **$55-$115, 3 day notice.** 551 N Lake Blvd. SR 28, 0.5 mi e of jct SR 89; behind Mother Nature's Store. Int corridors. **Pets:** Accepted.
ASK ⬛⬛⬛⬛

## TAHOE VISTA

**▽▽ Holiday House M ❀**
(530) 546-2369. **$125-$225, 14 day notice.** 7276 N Lake Blvd. SR 28, 1 mi w of SR 267. Ext corridors. **Pets:** Other species. $30 one-time fee/pet. Service with restrictions, supervision.
⬛⬛⬛⬛⬛⬛

## TRUCKEE

**▽▽ The Inn at Truckee M**
(530) 587-8888. **$90-$140, 3 day notice.** 11506 Deerfield Dr. I-80, exit SR 89, just s. Int corridors. **Pets:** Accepted.
ASK ⬛⬛⬛⬛⬛⬛

---

## END AREA

## LANCASTER

**▲▲▲ ▽▽▽ Best Western Antelope Valley Inn M**
(661) 948-4651. **$125.** 44055 N Sierra Hwy. SR 14, exit Ave K, 2.3 mi e. Ext/int corridors. **Pets:** Accepted.
SAVE ⬛⬛⬛⬛⬛⬛⬛

**▽▽▽ Oxford Inn & Suites M ❀**
(661) 949-3423. **$105-$115.** 1651 W Ave K. SR 14, exit Ave K, just w. Int corridors. **Pets:** $50 one-time fee/pet. Service with restrictions, supervision.
ASK ⬛⬛⬛⬛⬛⬛⬛⬛

## LA PALMA

**▽▽▽▽ La Quinta Inn & Suites Orange County (Buena Park) SH**
(714) 670-1400. **$85-$135.** 3 Center Pointe Dr. SR 91, exit Orangethorpe Ave/Valley View St, just n. Int corridors. **Pets:** Medium. Service with restrictions.
ASK ⬛⬛⬛⬛⬛

## LATHROP

**▽▽ Days Inn M**
(209) 982-1959. **$80-$86.** 14750 S Harlan Rd. I-5, exit Lathrop Rd. Int corridors. **Pets:** Small. $10 daily fee/pet. Service with restrictions, supervision.
ASK ⬛⬛⬛⬛⬛

## LEBEC

**▽▽ Best Rest Inn M**
(661) 248-2700. **$49-$79.** 51541 N Peace Valley Rd. I-5, exit Frazier Park, just w. Int corridors. **Pets:** Other species. $10 daily fee/pet. Designated rooms, service with restrictions, supervision.
ASK ⬛⬛⬛⬛⬛⬛

**▲▲▲ ▽▽▽▽ Ramada Limited Grapevine M**
(661) 248-1530. **$69-$99.** 9000 Country Side Ct. I-5, exit Grapevine, just w. Ext corridors. **Pets:** Medium, other species. $10 daily fee/pet. Designated rooms, service with restrictions.
SAVE ⬛⬛⬛⬛⬛⬛⬛

## LEE VINING

**AAA** ♦♦♦ **Murphey's Motel** **M**
(760) 647-6316. **$53-$113.** 51493 Hwy 395. On US 395; in town. Ext corridors. **Pets:** Medium. $5 one-time fee/pet. Service with restrictions, supervision.
SAVE ⊠ 🛢 🖵

## LEMOORE

♦♦ **Days Inn- Lemoore** **M** ❀
(559) 924-1261. **$85.** 877 E "D" St. SR 198, exit Houston St, 0.8 ni nw. Ext corridors. **Pets:** Other species. $50 deposit/room. Service with restrictions, supervision.
ASK S🔒 ⊠ &M 🛢 🖵 ⩘

## LINDSAY

**AAA** ♦♦♦ **Super 8 Motel** **M** ❀
(559) 562-5188. **$69-$99.** 390 N Hwy 65. On SR 65. Ext corridors. **Pets:** Small. $10 one-time fee/room. Designated rooms, no service, supervision.
SAVE S🔒 ⊠ 🛢 ⩘

## LIVERMORE

♦♦ **AmeriHost Inn & Suites** **SH**
(925) 373-9600. **$69-$149.** 7700 Southfront Rd. I-580, exit Greenville Rd, just s. Int corridors. **Pets:** Small. $50 one-time fee/pet. Designated rooms, service with restrictions, crate.
ASK S🔒 ⊠ 🛢 🖵 ⩘ ⊠

♦♦♦ **Residence Inn by Marriott** **M**
(925) 373-1800. **$149-$174.** 1000 Airway Blvd. I-580, exit Airway Blvd/Collier Canyon Rd, just n. Ext corridors. **Pets:** Accepted.
ASK S🔒 ⊠ 🖵 ⩘ ⊠

## LODI

**AAA** ♦♦ **El Rancho Motel** **M** ❀
(209) 368-0651. **$55-$65.** 603 N Cherokee Ln. SR 99, exit Turner Rd, just s. Ext corridors. **Pets:** Very small. $10 one-time fee/pet. Service with restrictions, supervision.
SAVE S🔒 ⊠ &M 🖵 ⩘

♦♦♦ **Wine & Roses Hotel and Restaurant** **CI**
(209) 334-6988. **$159-$239, 7 day notice.** 2505 W Turner Rd. I-5, exit Turner Rd, 5 mi e; SR 99, exit Turner Rd, 2 mi w. Int corridors. **Pets:** Medium, other species. $25 daily fee/room. Designated rooms, service with restrictions, crate.
ASK S🔒 ⊠ &M 🛢 🖵 🍴

## LOMPOC

**AAA** ♦♦♦ **Americas Best Value Inn** **M**
(805) 735-3737. **$69-$169.** 1200 N H St. SR 1, 1.3 mi n. Ext corridors. **Pets:** Small. $25 daily fee/pet. Service with restrictions, supervision.
SAVE S🔒 ⊠ 🛢 🏊

**AAA** ♦♦♦ **Quality Inn & Executive Suites** **SH**
(805) 735-8555. **$89-$179, 7 day notice.** 1621 N H St. On SR 1, 1.8 mi n. Int corridors. **Pets:** Accepted.
SAVE S🔒 ⊠ 🛢 🖵 ⩘ ⊠

## VAGABOND INN

**AAA** ♦♦♦ **Vagabond Inn** **M**
(805) 735-7744. **$89-$179.** 1122 N H St. SR 1, 1.2 mi n. Ext/int corridors. **Pets:** Medium. $25 one-time fee/room. Service with restrictions, crate.
SAVE ⊠ 🛢 🖵 ⩘

**AAA** ♦♦♦ **White Oaks Hotel** **M** ❀
(805) 733-5000. **$69-$139.** 3955 Apollo Way. SR 1, exit Constellation Blvd, just e; 3.5 mi n of Ocean Ave. Ext/int corridors. **Pets:** Dogs only. $50 deposit/pet, $10 daily fee/pet. Designated rooms, service with restrictions, supervision.
SAVE S🔒 ⊠ 🛢 🖵 ⩘ ⊠

## LONE PINE

**AAA** ♦♦♦ **Best Western Frontier Motel** **M**
(760) 876-5571. **$59-$109.** 1008 S Main St. On US 395; at south end of town. Ext corridors. **Pets:** Accepted.
SAVE S🔒 ⊠ &M 🏊 🖵 🛢 🖵 ⩘

**AAA** ♦♦♦ **Dow Villa Motel** **M**
(760) 876-5521. **$66-$135.** 310 S Main St. On US 395. Ext corridors. **Pets:** Medium. $50 deposit/room. Designated rooms, service with restrictions, supervision.
SAVE S🔒 ⊠ &M 🏊 🖵 🛢 🖵 ⩘

**AAA** ♦♦ **Lone Pine Budget Inn Motel** **M**
(760) 876-5655. **$45-$99, 3 day notice.** 138 W Willow St. US 395, just w. Ext corridors. **Pets:** Accepted.
SAVE ⊠ 🛢 🖵

**AAA** ♦♦♦ **National 9 Trails Motel** **M**
(760) 876-5555. **$45-$99, 3 day notice.** 633 S Main St. On US 395. Ext corridors. **Pets:** Accepted.
SAVE 🛢 🖵 ⩘

## LOS ALAMITOS

♦♦♦ **Residence Inn by Marriott-Cypress/Orange County** **SH** ❀
(714) 484-5700. **$159-$229.** 4931 Katella Ave. I-605, exit Katella Ave, 1.5 mi e. Int corridors. **Pets:** Small. $75 one-time fee/pet. Service with restrictions, supervision.
ASK ⊠ 🛢 🖵 ⩘ ⊠

## LOS ALTOS

♦♦♦ **Marriott Residence Inn-Palo Alto/Los Altos** **M** ❀
(650) 559-7890. **$109-$289.** 4460 El Camino Real. US 101, exit San Antonio Rd, 2 mi w to SR 82, then just n. Int corridors. **Pets:** $75 one-time fee/pet. Service with restrictions, crate.
ASK ⊠ &M 🖵 ⩘ ⊠

## LOS ANGELES METROPOLITAN AREA

### ARCADIA

▼▼▼▼ Residence Inn by Marriott SH ❖
(626) 446-6500. **$209.** 321 E Huntington Dr. I-210, exit Huntington Dr,
0.5 mi w, then just n on Gateway Dr. Ext corridors. **Pets:** Other species.
$75 one-time fee/room. Service with restrictions.

ASK ☒ ⓜ ⌑ ⌂ 🛏 ▦ ☎ ⌦

### BEVERLY HILLS

▼▼▼▼ Avalon Hotel SH
(310) 277-5221. **$289-$359.** 9400 W Olympic Blvd. I-10, exit Robertson
Blvd, 1.7 mi n, then 0.8 mi w. Ext/int corridors. **Pets:** Accepted.

☒ ▦ ❙❙ ☎

🔷 ▼▼▼▼ The Beverly Hills Hotel and
Bungalows ☖ ❖
(310) 276-2251. **$470-$535.** 9641 Sunset Blvd. I-405, exit Sunset Blvd,
3.7 mi e. Int corridors. **Pets:** Small, dogs only. $200 one-time fee/pet.
Designated rooms.

SAVE ☒ ⓜ ⌑ ⌂ ❙❙ ☎ ⌦

🔷 ▼▼▼▼ Luxe Hotel Rodeo Drive SH
(310) 273-0300. **$380.** 360 N Rodeo Dr. I-405, exit Wilshire Blvd, 4.4 mi
e, then just n. Int corridors. **Pets:** Accepted.

SAVE ⑤ ☒ 🛏 ▦ ❙❙

▼▼▼▼ The Mosaic Hotel SH
(310) 278-0303. **$320-$420.** 125 S Spalding Dr. I-405, exit Wilshire
Blvd, 2.2 mi e, then just s. Ext/int corridors. **Pets:** Accepted.

ASK ☒ 🛏 ▦ ❙❙ ☎

🔷 ▼▼▼▼ The Peninsula Beverly Hills SH ❖
(310) 551-2888. **$425-$3500.** 9882 S Santa Monica Blvd. I-405, exit
Santa Monica Blvd, 2.2 mi e at Wilshire Blvd. Int corridors. **Pets:** Other
species. $35 daily fee/pet.

SAVE ☒ ⓜ ⌑ ▦ ❙❙ ☎ ⌦

🔷 ▼▼▼▼ Raffles L'Ermitage Beverly Hills SH ❖
(310) 278-3344. **$438-$895, 7 day notice.** 9291 Burton Way. I-10, exit
Robertson Blvd, 3.1 mi n, then just w. Int corridors. **Pets:** Medium. $150
one-time fee/room. Designated rooms, service with restrictions, supervision.

SAVE ⑤ ☒ ⓜ ⌑ ⌂ ▦ ❙❙ ☎ ⌦

▼▼▼▼ Regent Beverly Wilshire ☖ ❖
(310) 275-5200. **$400-$515.** 9500 Wilshire Blvd. I-405, exit Wilshire
Blvd, 4.5 mi e. Int corridors. **Pets:** Very small. Service with restrictions,
supervision.

☒ ⓜ ⌑ ⌂ ❙❙ ☎ ⌦

### BURBANK

▼▼▼▼ Burbank Airport Hilton & Convention Center ☖
(818) 843-6000. **$109-$219.** 2500 Hollywood Way. I-5, exit Hollywood
Way, 1 mi s. Int corridors. **Pets:** Accepted.

⑤ ☒ 🛏 ▦ ❙❙ ☎

▼▼▼ The Graciela Burbank SH ❖
(818) 842-8887. **$240-$325.** 322 N Pass Ave. SR 134, exit Hollywood
Way westbound, just w on Alameda Ave, then 0.5 mi n on Pass Ave;
exit Pass Ave eastbound, 0.5 mi n. Ext corridors. **Pets:** Medium. $75
one-time fee/pet. Designated rooms, service with restrictions.

ASK ⑤ ☒ 🛏 ▦ ❙❙ ⌦

🔷 ▼▼▼▼ Safari Inn, A Coast Hotel M ❖
(818) 845-8586. **$103-$199.** 1911 W Olive Ave. I-5, exit Olive Ave, 1.3
mi sw. Ext corridors. **Pets:** Other species. $200 deposit/room, $25 one-
time fee/room. Supervision.

SAVE ⑤ ☒ ⌑ ⌂ ▦ ❙❙ ☎

### CERRITOS

▼▼▼▼ Sheraton Cerritos Hotel at Towne Center SH
(562) 809-1500. **$239-$249.** 12725 Center Court Dr. SR 91, exit
Artesia/Bloomfield Dr, just s. Int corridors. **Pets:** Accepted.

ASK ⑤ ☒ ⓜ ▦ ❙❙ ☎

### CHATSWORTH

▼▼▼ Ramada Inn SH
(818) 998-5289. **$75-$95.** 21340 Devonshire St. SR 118, exit De Soto
Ave, 1.5 mi s, then 0.5 mi w. Int corridors. **Pets:** Small. $50 deposit/pet,
$10 daily fee/pet. Designated rooms, service with restrictions, supervision.

ASK ⑤ ☒ ⓜ ⌑ 🛏 ▦ ❙❙ ☎

### CLAREMONT

▼▼▼ Hotel Claremont & Tennis Club M
(909) 621-4831. **$99-$129.** 840 S Indian Hill Blvd. I-10, exit Indian Hill,
just s; enter on Auto Center Dr. Ext corridors. **Pets:** Accepted.

ASK ⑤ 🛏 ▦ ☎ ⌦

### CULVER CITY

🔷 ▼▼▼▼ Radisson Hotel-LA Westside ☖
(310) 649-1776. **$99-$159.** 6161 W Centinela Ave. I-405, exit Jefferson
Blvd, just s, then just nw. Int corridors. **Pets:** Accepted.

SAVE ⑤ ☒ 🛏 ▦ ❙❙ ☎

### DOWNEY

🔷 ▼▼▼▼ Embassy Suites Hotel ☖
(562) 861-1900. **$119-$299.** 8425 Firestone Blvd. I-605, exit Firestone
Blvd, 2 mi w. Int corridors. **Pets:** Accepted.

SAVE ☒ 🛏 ▦ ❙❙ ☎ ⌦

### EL SEGUNDO

▼▼▼▼ Embassy Suites-LAX South ☖
(310) 640-3600. **$149-$189.** 1440 E Imperial Ave. I-405, exit Imperial
Hwy, 1.6 mi w. Int corridors. **Pets:** Accepted.

☒ 🛏 ▦ ❙❙ ☎

▼▼▼▼ Homestead Studio Suites Hotel-Los Angeles-LAX
Airport-El Segundo M
(310) 607-4000. **$105.** 1910 E Mariposa Ave. I-105, exit Sepulveda
Blvd, 1 mi s. Ext corridors. **Pets:** $25 daily fee/pet. Service with restric-
tions, supervision.

ASK ⑤ ☒ ⓜ ⌑ ⌂ 🛏 ▦

▼▼▼▼ Summerfield Suites by Wyndham-El Segundo M
(310) 725-0100. **$89-$149.** 810 S Douglas St. I-405, exit Rosecrans
Ave, 0.5 mi e, then just n. Ext/int corridors. **Pets:** Accepted.

ASK ☒ ⓜ ⌑ ⌂ 🛏 ▦ ☎ ⌦

### GLENDALE

▼▼▼ Homestead Studio Suites Hotel-Los
Angeles-Glendale SH
(818) 956-6665. **$104.** 91 W Glenoaks Blvd. I-5, exit Western Ave,
0.4 mi e, then 0.6 mi s. Int corridors **Pets:** $25 daily fee/pet. Service with
restrictions, supervision.

ASK ⑤ ☒ ⓜ ⌑ ⌂ 🛏 ▦

▼▼▼ Los Angeles Days Inn-Glendale SH
(818) 956-0202. **$120-$144, 7 day notice.** 450 W Pioneer Dr. SR 134,
exit Pacific Ave, just s, then just e. Int corridors. **Pets:** Small, other
species. $50 deposit/room. Designated rooms, service with restrictions,
supervision.

ASK ⑤ ☒ 🛏 ▦ ❙❙ ☎

△△△ ▼◇▼ Vagabond Inn Glendale **M**
(818) 240-1700. **$89-$109.** 120 W Colorado St. SR 134, exit Brand Blvd, 1 mi s, then just w. Ext corridors. **Pets:** Small. $10 daily fee/pet. Designated rooms, service with restrictions, crate.
⟨SAVE⟩ ⟨S🔖⟩ ⟨⊠⟩ ⟨🔖M⟩ ⟨🌀⟩ ⟨🖧⟩ ⟨🛢⟩ ⟨💻⟩ ⟨🌊⟩

# HAWTHORNE

▼◇ ▼ TownePlace Suites by Marriott **M**
(310) 725-9696. **$94-$210.** 14400 Aviation Blvd. I-405, exit Rosecrans Ave, 0.4 mi w. Int corridors. **Pets:** Medium. $75 one-time fee/room. Service with restrictions, supervision.
⟨A$K⟩ ⟨S🔖⟩ ⟨⊠⟩ ⟨🛢⟩ ⟨💻⟩ ⟨🌊⟩

# HOLLYWOOD

△△△ ▼◇▼◇ Best Western Hollywood Hills Hotel **M**
(323) 464-5181. **$99-$199.** 6141 Franklin Ave. US 101, exit Gower St, just n, then just e. Ext/int corridors. **Pets:** Small. $25 daily fee/room. Designated rooms.
⟨SAVE⟩ ⟨S🔖⟩ ⟨⊠⟩ ⟨🛢⟩ ⟨💻⟩ ⟨🍴⟩ ⟨🌊⟩

△△△ ▼◇▼◇ Ramada Inn and Conference Center-Hollywood Near Universal Studios **SH**
(323) 315-1800. **$80-$120.** 1160 N Vermont Ave. US 101, exit Vermont Ave, 0.5 mi n. Int corridors. **Pets:** Medium. $35 daily fee/pet. Designated rooms, service with restrictions, supervision.
⟨SAVE⟩ ⟨S🔖⟩ ⟨⊠⟩ ⟨🛢⟩ ⟨💻⟩ ⟨🍴⟩ ⟨🌊⟩ ⟨⊠⟩

# INDUSTRY

▼◇▼◇ Pacific Palms Conference Resort **LH**
(626) 810-4455. **$149-$209.** One Industry Hills Pkwy. SR 60, exit Azusa Ave, 1.3 mi n, 0.5 mi w. Int corridors. **Pets:** Accepted.
⟨A$K⟩ ⟨S🔖⟩ ⟨⊠⟩ ⟨🖧⟩ ⟨💻⟩ ⟨🍴⟩ ⟨🌊⟩ ⟨⊠⟩

# LA MIRADA

▼◇▼◇ Residence Inn by Marriott **SH**
(714) 523-2800. **$149-$199.** 14419 Firestone Blvd. I-5, exit Valley View, just n, then 0.5 mi e. Ext corridors. **Pets:** Small, other species. $75 one-time fee/room. Service with restrictions, supervision.
⟨A$K⟩ ⟨S🔖⟩ ⟨⊠⟩ ⟨🛢⟩ ⟨💻⟩ ⟨🌊⟩ ⟨⊠⟩

# LONG BEACH

△△△ ▼◇▼◇ The Coast Long Beach Hotel **SH**
(562) 435-7676. **$120-$175.** 700 Queensway Dr. I-710, exit Harbor Scenic Dr (Queen Mary), 1 mi s. Ext corridors. **Pets:** $100 deposit/room. Service with restrictions, crate.
⟨SAVE⟩ ⟨⊠⟩ ⟨🛢⟩ ⟨💻⟩ ⟨🍴⟩ ⟨🌊⟩ ⟨⊠⟩

△△△ ▼◇▼ Days Inn-City Center **M**
(562) 591-0088. **$70-$75.** 1500 E Pacific Coast Hwy. I-710, exit SR 1 (Pacific Coast Hwy), 2 mi e. Ext corridors. **Pets:** Accepted.
⟨SAVE⟩ ⟨S🔖⟩ ⟨⊠⟩ ⟨🔖M⟩ ⟨🖧⟩ ⟨🛢⟩ ⟨💻⟩

△△△ ▼◇▼◇ GuestHouse Hotel Long Beach **M**
(562) 597-1341. **$89-$109.** 5325 E Pacific Coast Hwy. I-405, exit SR 22 (Long Beach) northbound, 2 mi nw; exit Lakewood Blvd southbound, 2 mi se on SR 1. Ext corridors. **Pets:** Medium. $10 daily fee/room. Service with restrictions, crate.
⟨SAVE⟩ ⟨S🔖⟩ ⟨⊠⟩ ⟨🌀⟩ ⟨🖧⟩ ⟨🛢⟩ ⟨💻⟩ ⟨🍴⟩ ⟨🌊⟩

▼◇▼◇ Hilton Long Beach **LH**
(562) 983-3400. **$124-$334.** Two World Trade Center. I-710, exit Broadway/Downtown, just e to Daisy Ave, just s to Ocean Blvd, then just w. Int corridors. **Pets:** Accepted.
⟨A$K⟩ ⟨S🔖⟩ ⟨⊠⟩ ⟨💻⟩ ⟨⊠⟩

△△△ ▼◇▼◇ Holiday Inn-Long Beach Airport **LH**
(562) 597-4401. **$99-$179.** 2640 Lakewood Blvd. I-405, exit Lakewood Blvd, just s. Ext/int corridors. **Pets:** Small, other species. $100 deposit/pet, $25 one-time fee/pet. Designated rooms, service with restrictions, supervision.
⟨SAVE⟩ ⟨⊠⟩ ⟨🛢⟩ ⟨💻⟩ ⟨🍴⟩ ⟨🌊⟩

▼◇▼◇ Renaissance Long Beach Hotel **LH**
(562) 437-5900. **$132-$259.** 111 E Ocean Blvd. I-710, exit Broadway/Downtown, 0.8 mi e to Long Beach Blvd, just s, then just w. Int corridors. **Pets:** Accepted.
⟨A$K⟩ ⟨⊠⟩ ⟨💻⟩ ⟨🍴⟩ ⟨🌊⟩ ⟨⊠⟩

▼◇▼◇ The Westin Long Beach **LH** ❖
(562) 436-3000. **$319-$490.** 333 E Ocean Blvd. I-710, exit Broadway/Downtown, 0.8 mi e to Long Beach Blvd, then just s. **Pets:** Medium, other species. $75 one-time fee/room. Service with restrictions, supervision.
⟨A$K⟩ ⟨S🔖⟩ ⟨⊠⟩ ⟨💻⟩ ⟨🍴⟩ ⟨🌊⟩ ⟨⊠⟩

# LOS ANGELES

△△△ ▼◇▼◇ Best Western Dragon Gate Inn **SH**
(213) 617-3077. **$109-$159.** 818 N Hill St. US 101, exit Broadway, 0.6 mi n to Alpine St, just e, then just n. Ext corridors. **Pets:** Accepted.
⟨SAVE⟩ ⟨S🔖⟩ ⟨⊠⟩ ⟨🔖M⟩ ⟨🌀⟩ ⟨🖧⟩ ⟨🛢⟩ ⟨💻⟩

△△△ ▼◇▼ Beverly Laurel Motor Hotel **M**
(323) 651-2441. **$98-$113.** 8018 Beverly Blvd. I-10, exit Fairfax Ave, 2.8 mi n, then just w. Ext corridors. **Pets:** Medium. $25 daily fee/pet. Service with restrictions, supervision.
⟨SAVE⟩ ⟨S🔖⟩ ⟨⊠⟩ ⟨🛢⟩ ⟨🍴⟩ ⟨🌊⟩

▼◇▼◇ Crowne Plaza Hotel and Resort LA Airport **LH**
(310) 642-7500. **$99-$199.** 5985 W Century Blvd. I-405, exit Century Blvd, 1.2 mi w. Int corridors. **Pets:** Accepted.
⟨A$K⟩ ⟨S🔖⟩ ⟨⊠⟩ ⟨💻⟩ ⟨🍴⟩ ⟨🌊⟩ ⟨⊠⟩

△△△ ▼◇▼◇ Four Points by Sheraton LAX **LH** ❖
(310) 645-4600. **$109-$119.** 9750 Airport Blvd. I-405, exit Century Blvd, 1.5 mi w, then just n. Ext/int corridors. **Pets:** Medium. $25 one-time fee/room. Designated rooms, service with restrictions, supervision.
⟨SAVE⟩ ⟨S🔖⟩ ⟨⊠⟩ ⟨🛢⟩ ⟨💻⟩ ⟨🍴⟩ ⟨🌊⟩

△△△ ▼◇▼◇ Four Seasons Hotel Los Angeles at Beverly Hills **LH** ❖
(310) 273-2222. **$385-$5000.** 300 S Doheny Dr. I-10, exit Robertson Blvd, 3 mi n to Burton Way, then just w. Int corridors. **Pets:** Very small. Service with restrictions, supervision.
⟨⊠⟩ ⟨🔖M⟩ ⟨🌀⟩ ⟨💻⟩ ⟨🍴⟩ ⟨🌊⟩ ⟨⊠⟩

△△△ ▼◇▼◇ Hotel Angeleno **LH**
(310) 476-6411. **$129-$229.** 170 N Church Ln. I-405, exit Sunset Blvd, just w, then just n. Int corridors. **Pets:** Accepted.
⟨SAVE⟩ ⟨S🔖⟩ ⟨⊠⟩ ⟨🛢⟩ ⟨💻⟩ ⟨🍴⟩ ⟨🌊⟩

▼◇▼◇ Hotel Bel-Air **SH**
(310) 472-1211. **$395-$600, 3 day notice.** 701 Stone Canyon Rd. I-405, exit Sunset Blvd, 2 mi e, then 0.8 mi n. Ext corridors. **Pets:** Accepted.
⟨⊠⟩ ⟨🛢⟩ ⟨🍴⟩ ⟨🌊⟩

△△△ ▼◇▼◇ Hyatt Regency Century Plaza **LH** ❖
(310) 277-2000. **$460.** 2025 Avenue of the Stars. I-10, exit Robertson Blvd, 2.7 mi n to Olympic Blvd, 1.9 mi w, then just n. Int corridors. **Pets:** $30 daily fee/pet. Service with restrictions, supervision.
⟨SAVE⟩ ⟨⊠⟩ ⟨🔖M⟩ ⟨🌀⟩ ⟨🖧⟩ ⟨💻⟩ ⟨🍴⟩ ⟨🌊⟩ ⟨⊠⟩

▼◇▼◇ Le Meridien at Beverly Hills **LH**
(310) 247-0400. **$299-$350.** 465 S La Cienega Blvd. I-10, exit La Cienega Blvd, 2.5 mi n. Ext corridors. **Pets:** Accepted.
⟨⊠⟩ ⟨🔖M⟩ ⟨🌀⟩ ⟨🖧⟩ ⟨💻⟩ ⟨🍴⟩ ⟨🌊⟩ ⟨⊠⟩

**🔺🔺 ▽▽▽▽ Loews Beverly Hills Hotel LH** ❀
(310) 277-2800. **$179-$279.** 1224 S Beverwil Dr. I-10, exit Robertson Blvd, 1.8 mi n, then 0.7 mi e. Int corridors. **Pets:** Other species. Designated rooms.
⬛ ⬛ ⬛ ⬛ ⬛ ⬛

**▽▽▽▽ Los Angeles Airport Hilton & Towers LH**
(310) 410-4000. **$119-$319.** 5711 W Century Blvd. I-405, exit Century Blvd, 0.8 mi w. Int corridors. **Pets:** Medium. $25 daily fee/room. Designated rooms, service with restrictions, supervision.
⬛ ⬛ ⬛ ⬛ ⬛ ⬛ ⬛ ⬛

**▽▽▽▽ Los Angeles Airport Marriott Hotel LH**
(310) 641-5700. **$129-$229.** 5855 W Century Blvd. I-405, exit Century Blvd, 1 mi w. Int corridors. **Pets:** Accepted.
⬛ ⬛ ⬛ ⬛ ⬛ ⬛ ⬛ ⬛ ⬛

**🔺🔺 ▽▽▽▽ Luxe Hotel Sunset Boulevard SH**
(310) 476-6571. **$250, 3 day notice.** 11461 Sunset Blvd. I-405, exit Sunset Blvd, just w. Int corridors. **Pets:** Large. $100 one-time fee/pet. Designated rooms, service with restrictions, supervision.
⬛ ⬛ ⬛ ⬛ ⬛ ⬛ ⬛ ⬛

**🔺🔺 ▽▽▽ ▽▽▽ Omni Los Angeles Hotel LH**
(213) 617-3300. **$139-$275.** 251 S Olive St. SR 110, exit 4th St southbound; exit 6th St northbound, just e, then just n. Int corridors. **Pets:** Small. $50 one-time fee/pet. Service with restrictions, crate.
⬛ ⬛ ⬛ ⬛ ⬛ ⬛ ⬛ ⬛

**▽▽▽ Radisson Hotel at Los Angeles Airport LH**
(310) 670-9000. **$99-$189, 3 day notice.** 6225 W Century Blvd at Sepulveda Blvd. I-405, exit Century Blvd, 1.6 mi w. Int corridors. **Pets:** Accepted.
⬛ ⬛ ⬛ ⬛ ⬛

**▽▽▽ Residence Inn by Marriott-Beverly Hills SH**
(310) 277-4427. **$189-$289.** 1177 S Beverly Dr. I-10, exit Robertson Blvd, 1.6 mi n to Pico Blvd, then 0.6 mi w. Int corridors. **Pets:** Accepted.
⬛ ⬛ ⬛ ⬛ ⬛

**▽▽▽ Sheraton Gateway Hotel, Los Angeles Airport LH** 🐾
(310) 642-1111. **$99-$129, 3 day notice.** 6101 W Century Blvd. I-405, exit Century Blvd, 1.3 mi w. Int corridors. **Pets:** Large, dogs only. Service with restrictions, supervision.
⬛ ⬛ ⬛ ⬛ ⬛ ⬛

**🔺🔺 ▽▽▽ ▽▽▽ Sheraton Los Angeles Downtown LH**
(213) 488-3500. **$129-$329.** 711 S Hope St. SR 110, exit 6th St southbound, just e, then just s. Int corridors. **Pets:** Accepted.
⬛ ⬛ ⬛ ⬛ ⬛ ⬛ ⬛ ⬛ ⬛

**🔺🔺 ▽▽▽ Travelodge Hotel at Lax SH**
(310) 649-4000. **$62-$99.** 5547 W Century Blvd. I-405, exit Century Blvd, 0.5 mi w. Ext/int corridors. **Pets:** Small. $10 daily fee/pet. Designated rooms, service with restrictions, crate.
⬛ ⬛ ⬛ ⬛ ⬛ ⬛

**🔺🔺 ▽▽▽ Vagabond Inn Los Angeles-USC M**
(213) 746-1531. **$89-$109.** 3101 S Figueroa St. SR 110, exit Adams Blvd, 0.5 mi s. Ext corridors. **Pets:** Medium. $10 daily fee/pet. Designated rooms, service with restrictions, supervision.
⬛ ⬛ ⬛ ⬛ ⬛

**▽▽▽ The Westin Hotel-Los Angeles Airport LH**
(310) 216-5858. **$109-$259.** 5400 W Century Blvd. I-405, exit Century Blvd, just w. Int corridors. **Pets:** Accepted.
⬛ ⬛ ⬛ ⬛ ⬛ ⬛ ⬛

# MANHATTAN BEACH

**▽▽▽▽ Residence Inn by Marriott SH**
(310) 421-3100. **$119-$239, 3 day notice.** 1700 N Sepulveda Blvd. I-405, exit Rosecrans Ave, 1.5 mi w, then 1 mi s on SR 1. Ext corridors. **Pets:** Small. $75 one-time fee/pet. Designated rooms, service with restrictions, crate.
⬛ ⬛ ⬛ ⬛ ⬛ ⬛ ⬛ ⬛ ⬛ ⬛

# MISSION HILLS

**🔺🔺 ▽▽▽▽ GuestHouse International Inn M**
(818) 891-1771. **$83.** 10621 Sepulveda Blvd. I-405, exit Devonshire St, just e, then just n; SR 118 (Simi Valley Frwy), just s. Ext/int corridors. **Pets:** Small, other species. $20 daily fee/pet. Designated rooms, service with restrictions, supervision.
⬛ ⬛ ⬛ ⬛ ⬛ ⬛ ⬛ ⬛ ⬛

# MONROVIA

**▽▽▽ Homestead Studio Suites Hotel-Los Angeles-Monrovia SH**
(626) 256-6999. **$95.** 930 S Fifth Ave. I-210, exit Huntington Dr, just w, then just n. Int corridors. **Pets:** $25 daily fee/pet. Service with restrictions, supervision.
⬛ ⬛ ⬛ ⬛ ⬛ ⬛ ⬛

# PASADENA

**🔺🔺 ▽▽▽▽ Quality Inn Pasadena M**
(626) 796-9291. **$81-$99, 5 day notice.** 3321 E Colorado Blvd. I-210, exit Madre St, just s, then 0.3 mi e. **Pets:** Accepted.
⬛ ⬛ ⬛ ⬛ ⬛

**🔺🔺 ▽▽▽ ▽▽▽ The Ritz-Carlton, Huntington Hotel & Spa LH** ❀
(626) 568-3900. **$310-$320.** 1401 S Oak Knoll Ave. I-210, exit Lake Ave, 2 mi s. Ext/int corridors. **Pets:** Medium. $125 one-time fee/room.
⬛ ⬛ ⬛ ⬛ ⬛ ⬛ ⬛ ⬛ ⬛ ⬛

**▽▽▽▽ Sheraton Pasadena Hotel LH** 🐾
(626) 449-4000. **$139-$245.** 303 E Cordova St. I-210, exit Los Robles Ave, 0.7 mi s, then just w. Int corridors. **Pets:** Medium, dogs only. Designated rooms.
⬛ ⬛ ⬛ ⬛ ⬛ ⬛ ⬛ ⬛ ⬛

**🔺🔺 ▽▽ Super 8 M**
(626) 449-3020. **$63-$99.** 2863 E Colorado Blvd. I-210, exit San Gabriel Blvd, 0.3 mi s, then just e. Ext corridors. **Pets:** Very small. $10 daily fee/pet. Designated rooms, service with restrictions, supervision.
⬛ ⬛ ⬛ ⬛ ⬛

**🔺🔺 ▽▽ Vagabond Inn M**
(626) 449-3170. **$65-$105.** 1203 E Colorado Blvd. I-210, exit Hill Ave, just s, then just w. Ext/int corridors. **Pets:** Accepted.
⬛ ⬛ ⬛ ⬛ ⬛

**▽▽▽▽ The Westin-Pasadena LH**
(626) 792-2727. **$145-$239.** 191 N Los Robles Ave. I-210, exit Los Robles Ave, just s; in Plaza Las Fuentes. Int corridors. **Pets:** Accepted.
⬛ ⬛ ⬛ ⬛ ⬛ ⬛ ⬛ ⬛ ⬛

**🔺🔺 ▽▽▽ Westway Inn M**
(626) 304-9678. **$75-$350, 30 day notice.** 1599 E Colorado Blvd. I-210, exit Allen Ave westbound; exit Hill Ave eastbound, 0.8 mi s. Ext corridors. **Pets:** Medium. $10 daily fee/pet. Designated rooms, service with restrictions, supervision.
⬛ ⬛ ⬛ ⬛ ⬛

# POMONA

**▼▼▼ Sheraton Suites Fairplex 🏠**
(909) 622-2220. **$215.** 601 W McKinley Ave. I-10, exit White Ave eastbound, 0.5 mi n, then just w; exit Fairplex Dr westbound, 1 mi n, then 0.7 mi e. Int corridors. **Pets:** Medium, other species. $150 deposit/room. Service with restrictions, supervision.
🅰️ ⊠ 🛢 💻 🍴 🛬 ⊠

**▼▼ Shilo Inn Pomona Hotel 🆂🅷 ❀**
(909) 598-0073. **$81-$142.** 3200 Temple Ave. SR 57, exit Temple Ave, just w. Int corridors **Pets:** $10 daily fee/pet. Service with restrictions, supervision.
🅰️ 🆂 ⊠ 🛢 💻 🍴 🛬 ⊠

# SAN DIMAS

**▼▼ Red Roof Inn 🅼**
(909) 599-2362. **$66-$85.** 204 N Village Ct. SR 57, exit Arrow Hwy, just e, then just n. Ext corridors. **Pets:** Accepted.
🅰️ 🆂 ⊠ 🆅 ⬚ 🛢 🛬

# SAN PEDRO

**▼▼▼ Marina Hotel San Pedro 🏠**
(310) 514-3344. **$109-$239.** 2800 Via Cabrillo Marina. I-110, exit Gaffey St, 1.5 mi s, then 0.5 mi e on 22nd St. Int corridors. **Pets:** $50 deposit/room. Service with restrictions, crate.
🅰️ 🆂 ⊠ 🛢 💻 🍴 🛬 ⊠

**▼ Vagabond Inn 🅼**
(310) 831-8911. **$65-$75.** 215 S Gaffey St. I-110, exit Gaffey St, just s of terminus. Ext corridors. **Pets:** Accepted.
🆂🅰️🆅 ⊠ 🛢 💻 🛬

# SANTA CLARITA

**▼▼▼ Best Western Valencia Inn 🅼**
(661) 255-0555. **$99-$149.** I-5, exit Magic Mountain Pkwy, just e. Ext corridors. **Pets:** Accepted.
🆂🅰️🆅 🆂 ⊠ 🛢 💻 🛬

**▼▼▼ Residence Inn by Marriott 🆂🅷 ❀**
(661) 290-2800. **$129-$159.** 25320 The Old Rd. I-5, exit Lyons Ave, just w. Int corridors. **Pets:** Large, other species. $10 daily fee/pet, $75 one-time fee/room. Service with restrictions, crate.
🅰️ ⊠ 🆅 ⬚ ⬚ 🛢 💻 🛬 ⊠

# SANTA MONICA

**▼▼▼▼ The Fairmont Miramar Hotel Santa Monica 🏠 ❀**
(310) 576-7777. **$269-$1599.** 101 Wilshire Blvd. I-10, exit Lincoln Blvd, 0.6 mi n, then 0.6 mi w. Ext/int corridors. **Pets:** Small. $25 deposit/pet. Service with restrictions, supervision.
🆂🅰️🆅 ⊠ 💻 🍴 🛬 ⊠

**▼▼▼ The Georgian 🆂🅷 ❀**
(310) 395-9945. **$235-$276.** 1415 Ocean Ave. I-10, exit Lincoln Blvd, just n, then 0.5 mi w on Broadway. Int corridors. **Pets:** Medium. $200 one-time fee/room. Service with restrictions, supervision.
🅰️ 🆂 ⊠ 🛢 💻 🍴

**▼▼▼▼ Le Merigot–A JW Marriott Hotel & Spa 🏠**
(310) 395-9700. **$339-$599.** 1740 Ocean Ave. I-10, exit Lincoln Blvd, 0.3 mi s, 0.6 mi w on Pico Blvd, then just n. Int corridors. **Pets:** Accepted.
🆂🅰️🆅 🆂 ⊠ 🍴 🛬 ⊠

**▼▼▼ Loews Santa Monica Beach Hotel 🏠 ❀**
(310) 458-6700. **$289-$540.** 1700 Ocean Ave. I-10, exit Lincoln Blvd, 0.3 mi s, 0.6 mi w on Pico Blvd, then just n. Int corridors. **Pets:** Service with restrictions, supervision.
🆂🅰️🆅 ⊠ 🆅 ⬚ ⬚ 🍴 🛬 ⊠

**▼▼▼ Sheraton Delfina Santa Monica 🏠**
(310) 399-9344. **$279-$439.** 530 Pico Blvd. I-10, exit Lincoln Blvd, just s. Int corridors. **Pets:** Accepted.
🅰️ 🆂 ⊠ 🛢 💻 🍴 🛬

**▼▼▼ Travelodge-Santa Monica/Pico Blvd 🅼**
(310) 450-5766. **$89-$159.** 3102 W Pico Blvd. I-10, exit Centinela Ave, just n, then just w. Ext corridors. **Pets:** Small. $100 deposit/pet. Designated rooms, service with restrictions, supervision.
🆂🅰️🆅 🆂 ⊠ 🛢 💻

# SHERMAN OAKS

**▼▼▼ Best Western Carriage Inn 🅼**
(818) 787-2300. **$99-$169.** 5525 Sepulveda Blvd. I-405, exit Burbank Blvd, just e, then just s. Ext/int corridors. **Pets:** Accepted.
🆂🅰️🆅 🆂 ⊠ ⬚ 🛢 💻 🍴 🛬

# TARZANA

**▼▼▼ St. George Motor Inn 🅼**
(818) 345-6911. **$67-$92.** 19454 Ventura Blvd. US 101, exit Tampa Ave, just s, then just w. Ext corridors. **Pets:** Accepted.
🆂🅰️🆅 🆂 ⊠ 🛢 💻 🛬

# TORRANCE

**▼▼ Homestead Studio Suites Hotel-Los Angeles-Torrance 🆂🅷**
(310) 543-0048. **$95.** 3995 Carson St. I-405, exit Hawthorne Blvd, 3.6 mi s; I-110, exit Carson St, 4.5 mi w. Int corridors. **Pets:** $25 daily fee/pet. Service with restrictions, supervision.
🅰️ 🆂 ⊠ 🆅 ⬚ ⬚ 🛢 💻

**▼▼▼ Residence Inn by Marriott 🆂🅷**
(310) 543-4566. **$99-$179.** 3701 Torrance Blvd. I-405, exit Hawthorne Blvd, 3.2 mi s, then just e. Ext corridors. **Pets:** Accepted.
🅰️ 🆂 ⊠ 🛢 💻 🛬 ⊠

**▼▼▼ Staybridge Suites 🅼 ❀**
(310) 371-8525. **$109-$290.** 19901 Prairie Ave. I-405, exit Crenshaw Blvd, just s to 190th St, 1 mi w, then just s. Ext/int corridors. **Pets:** Small. $10 daily fee/pet, $250 one-time fee/room. Service with restrictions, supervision.
🅰️ 🆂 ⊠ 🛢 💻 🛬 ⊠

# WEST HOLLYWOOD

**▼▼▼ Bel Age 🏠**
(310) 854-1111. **$199-$229.** 1020 N San Vicente Blvd. I-10, exit La Cienega Blvd, 2.6 mi n, then 1.5 mi nw. Int corridors. **Pets:** Accepted.
🆂🅰️🆅 ⊠ 💻 🍴 🛬

**▼▼▼ The Grafton on Sunset 🆂🅷**
(323) 654-4600. **$165-$335.** 8462 Sunset Blvd. I-10, exit La Cienega Blvd, 4.4 mi n, then just e. Int corridors. **Pets:** Accepted.
🅰️ ⊠ 🆅 ⬚ ⬚ 🛢 🍴 🛬

**▼▼▼ Le Montrose Suite Hotel 🆂🅷**
(310) 855-1115. **$210-$290.** 900 Hammond St at Cynthia St. I-10, exit La Cienega Blvd, 2.6 mi n to San Vicente Blvd, 1.3 mi nw, then just w on Cynthia St. Int corridors. **Pets:** Accepted.
🅰️ 🆂 ⊠ 🛢 💻 🍴 🛬 ⊠

▼▼▼▼ Le Parc Suite Hotel **LH**
(310) 855-8888. **$200-$400.** 733 N West Knoll Dr. I-10, exit La Cienega Blvd, 3.5 mi n, just w on Melrose Ave, then just n. Int corridors. **Pets:** Large, other species. $75 one-time fee/pet. Designated rooms, service with restrictions, supervision.

(A$K) (S⌀) (✕) (▮) (⬛) (Ⴌ) (⤇) (☒)

▲▲▲ ▼▼▼ Ramada Plaza Hotel **LH**
(310) 652-6400. **$109-$199.** 8585 Santa Monica Blvd. I-10, exit La Cienega Blvd, 4 mi n, then just w. Int corridors. **Pets:** Small. $150 one-time fee/pet. Designated rooms, service with restrictions, supervision.

(SAVE) (S⌀) (✕) (▮) (⬛) (Ⴌ) (⤇)

## WHITTIER

▲▲▲ ▼▼▼▼ Radisson Hotel Whittier **LH**
(562) 945-8511. **$69-$129.** 7320 Greenleaf Ave. I-605, exit Whittier Blvd, 2.5 mi e, then 0.6 mi n. Int corridors. **Pets:** Accepted.

(SAVE) (S⌀) (✕) (Ⴆᴹ) (▮) (⬛) (Ⴌ) (⤇)

▲▲ ▼▼ Vagabond Inn **M**
(562) 698-9701. **$60-$85.** 14125 E Whittier Blvd. I-605, exit Whittier Blvd, 3.5 mi e. Ext corridors. **Pets:** Accepted.

(SAVE) (S⌀) (✕) (▮) (⬛) (⤇)

## WOODLAND HILLS

▲▲▲ ▼▼▼▼ Warner Center Marriott Hotel **LH** ❧
(818) 887-4800. **$119-$229.** 21850 Oxnard St. US 101, exit Topanga Canyon Blvd, 0.6 mi n, then just e. Int corridors. **Pets:** Other species. $50 one-time fee/room. Service with restrictions, crate.

(SAVE) (S⌀) (✕) (▮) (⬛) (Ⴌ) (⤇) (☒)

---

# END METROPOLITAN AREA

---

## LOS BANOS

▲▲▲ ▼▼▼ Best Western Executive Inn **SH**
(209) 827-0954. **$66-$88.** 301 W Pacheco Blvd. On SR 152. Int corridors. **Pets:** Accepted.

(SAVE) (S⌀) (✕) (Ⴆᴹ) (Ⴆ) (▮) (⬛) (⤇) (☒)

▲▲▲ ▼▼ Regency Inn **M** ❧
(209) 826-3871. **$45-$55.** 349 W Pacheco Blvd. On SR 152; center. Ext corridors. **Pets:** Other species. $5 daily fee/pet. Supervision.

(SAVE) (S⌀) (✕) (▮) (⬛) (⤇)

## LOS GATOS

▲▲▲ ▼▼▼▼ Los Gatos Lodge **M**
(408) 354-3300. **$145-$165.** 50 Los Gatos Saratoga Rd. SR 17, exit E Los Gatos, just e. Ext/int corridors. **Pets:** Service with restrictions, supervision.

(SAVE) (S⌀) (✕) (Ⴆᴹ) (Ⴆ) (▮) (⬛) (Ⴌ) (⤇) (☒)

▲▲▲ ▼▼▼ Toll House Hotel **SH**
(408) 395-7070. **$179-$219.** 140 S Santa Cruz Ave. I-880/SR 17, exit SR 9, 0.3 mi w. Int corridors. **Pets:** Accepted.

(SAVE) (S⌀) (✕) (⟲) (▮) (⬛) (Ⴌ) (☒)

## LOS OLIVOS

▲▲▲ ▼▼▼ ▼▼ Fess Parker's Wine Country Inn & Spa **CI**
(805) 688-7788. **$265-$450, 7 day notice.** 2860 Grand Ave. SR 154, 0.5 mi s. Ext/int corridors. **Pets:** Accepted.

(SAVE) (S⌀) (✕) (▮) (Ⴌ) (⤇) (☒)

## LOS OSOS

▲▲▲ ▼▼▼▼ Sea Pines Golf Resort **M**
(805) 528-5252. **$99-$149.** 1945 Solano St. SR 1, exit Los Osos/Baywood Park, 4 mi s on S Bay Blvd, 1.6 mi w on Los Osos Valley Rd, 0.3 mi n on Pecho Rd, then just w on Skyline Dr. Ext corridors. **Pets:** Medium. $15 daily fee/pet. Designated rooms, service with restrictions, supervision.

(SAVE) (S⌀) (✕) (Ⴆᴹ) (Ⴆ) (▮) (⬛) (Ⴌ) (☒)

## MADERA

▲▲▲ ▼▼▼▼ Madera Valley Inn **M**
(559) 664-0100. **$89-$119.** 317 North G St. SR 99, exit Central Madera, just e. Int corridors. **Pets:** Accepted.

(SAVE) (S⌀) (✕) (▮) (⬛) (Ⴌ) (⤇)

▼▼ Motel 6 #4247 **M**
(559) 675-8697. **$54-$85, 3 day notice.** 22683 Ave 18 1/2. SR 99, exit Ave 18 1/2, just w. Int corridors. **Pets:** Accepted.

(A$K) (S⌀) (✕) (Ⴆ) (▮) (⤇)

▼▼ Super 8 **M**
(559) 661-1131. **$60-$70.** 1855 W Cleveland Ave. SR 99, exit Cleveland Ave, just w. Ext corridors. **Pets:** $5 daily fee/pet. Service with restrictions, supervision.

(A$K) (S⌀) (✕) (▮) (⬛) (⤇)

## MAMMOTH LAKES

▲▲▲ ▼▼▼ Econo Lodge Wildwood Inn **M**
(760) 934-6855. **$79-$199, 7 day notice.** 3626 Main St. On SR 203, 0.7 mi w of Old Mammoth Rd. Ext corridors. **Pets:** Medium. $10 daily fee/pet. Designated rooms, service with restrictions, supervision.

(SAVE) (S⌀) (✕) (▮) (⬛) (⤇) (Ⴗ)

▼▼▼ Mammoth Ski & Racquet Club **CO**
(760) 934-7368. **$150-$450, 30 day notice.** 248 Mammoth Slopes Dr. From Old Mammoth Rd, 1 mi w on SR 203; SR 203, just n: Canyon Blvd, 0.8 mi w, then just s. Int corridors. **Pets:** Dogs only. $25 daily fee/room. Designated rooms, no service, supervision.

(A$K) (✕) (▮) (⬛) (⤇) (☒) (Ⴗ)

▼▼▼ Shilo Inn **SH** ❧
(760) 934-4500. **$100-$200.** 2963 Main St. On SR 203, just e of Old Mammoth Rd. Int corridors. **Pets:** $10 daily fee/pet. Service with restrictions, supervision.

(A$K) (S⌀) (✕) (Ⴆᴹ) (⟲) (▮) (⬛) (⤇) (☒)

▲▲▲ ▼▼▼ Sierra Lodge **SH**
(760) 934-8881. **$59-$189.** 3540 Main St. On SR 203, 0.6 mi w of Old Mammoth Rd. Int corridors. **Pets:** Other species. $10 daily fee/pet. Service with restrictions, supervision.

(SAVE) (S⌀) (✕) (▮) (Ⴗ)

▲▲▲ ▼▼▼ Sierra Nevada Rodeway Inn **SH**
(760) 934-2515. **$99-$449, 7 day notice.** 164 Old Mammoth Rd. Just s of SR 203. Ext/int corridors. **Pets:** Accepted.

(SAVE) (✕) (▮) (⬛) (⤇) (Ⴗ)

▼▼ Summit Condominiums **CO** ❧
(760) 934-5771. **$142-$733, 30 day notice.** 3253 Meridian Blvd. 1 mi w of Old Mammoth Rd. Int corridors. **Pets:** $500 deposit/pet. Crate.

(✕) (▮) (⬛) (⤇) (☒) (Ⴗ)

**▼▼ ▼▼ Swiss Chalet Motel** Ⓜ
(760) 934-2403. **$70-$120, 7 day notice.** 3776 Viewpoint Rd. 0.7 mi w of Old Mammoth Rd; adjacent to SR 203. Ext corridors. **Pets:** Dogs only. $10 one-time fee/pet. Designated rooms, service with restrictions, supervision.
(A$K) (S⌀) (✕) (🛏) (🐾)

# MANTECA

**▲▲▲ ▼▼▼▼ Best Western Executive Inn & Suites** Ⓜ
(209) 825-1415. **$75-$80.** 1415 E Yosemite Ave. Jct SR 99 and 120, exit Yosemite Ave. Ext corridors. **Pets:** $25 one-time fee/pet. Service with restrictions, supervision.
(SAVE) (S⌀) (✕) (&M) (🛏) (💻) (🐾)

# MARIPOSA

**▲▲▲ ▼▼▼▼ Americas Best Value Inn–Mariposa Lodge** Ⓜ
(209) 966-3607. **$49-$129, 3 day notice.** 5052 Hwy 140. Center. Ext corridors. **Pets:** Medium. $10 daily fee/pet. Service with restrictions, supervision.
(SAVE) (S⌀) (✕) (🛏) (💻) (🐾)

**▲▲▲ ▼▼▼▼ Best Western Yosemite Way Station Motel** Ⓜ
(209) 966-7545. **$44-$96.** 4999 Hwy 140. SR 140 at SR 49 S. Ext corridors. **Pets:** Small, dogs only. $10 daily fee/pet. Designated rooms, service with restrictions, supervision.
(SAVE) (S⌀) (✕) (&M) (💻) (🐾)

**▼▼ ▼▼ Miners Inn** Ⓜ
(209) 742-7777. **$64-$149.** 5181 Hwy 49 N. On SR 49, n at SR 140. Ext/int corridors. **Pets:** Other species. $10 daily fee/pet. Designated rooms, service with restrictions, supervision.
(A$K) (S⌀) (✕) (🛏) (💻) (🍽) (🐾)

# MARYSVILLE

**▲▲▲ ▼▼▼▼ Americas Best Value Inn** Ⓜ
(530) 743-1531. **$50-$85.** 904 E St. Jct SR 70 and 20. Ext corridors. **Pets:** Accepted.
(SAVE) (✕) (&M) (🗶) (🛏)

# MERCED

**▲▲▲ ▼▼▼▼ Merced-Yosemite Travelodge** Ⓜ
(209) 722-6224. **$55-$75.** 1260 Yosemite Pkwy. SR 99, exit SR 140, just e. Ext corridors. **Pets:** Medium, dogs only. $25 deposit/pet, $10 daily fee/pet. Service with restrictions, supervision.
(SAVE) (S⌀) (✕) (&M) (🛏) (💻) (🐾)

# MILPITAS

**▲▲▲ ▼▼▼▼ Best Western Brookside Inn** Ⓜ
(408) 263-5566. **$69-$109.** 400 Valley Way. I-880, exit Calaveras Blvd (SR 237), just e. Ext/int corridors. **Pets:** Accepted.
(SAVE) (S⌀) (✕) (🗶) (🛏) (💻) (🐾) (🗙)

**▲▲▲ ▼▼▼▼ Beverly Heritage Hotel** LH
(408) 943-9080. **$69-$229.** 1820 Barber Ln. Northwest quadrant of I-880 and Montague Expwy. Int corridors. **Pets:** Accepted.
(SAVE) (S⌀) (✕) (🗶) (🛏) (💻) (🍽) (🐾) (🗙)

**▼▼▼▼ Embassy Suites Milpitas/Silicon Valley** LH
(408) 942-0400. **$159-$179.** 901 E Calaveras Blvd. I-680, exit Calaveras Blvd (SR 237), just w. Int corridors. **Pets:** Medium. $50 one-time fee/pet. Service with restrictions, supervision.
(A$K) (S⌀) (✕) (🛏) (💻) (🍽) (🐾) (🗙)

**▼▼ ▼▼ Homestead Studio Suites Hotel-San Jose-Milpitas** Ⓜ
(408) 433-9700. **$100.** 330 Cypress Dr. SR 237, exit McCarthy S. Ext/int corridors. **Pets:** $25 daily fee/pet. Service with restrictions, supervision.
(A$K) (S⌀) (✕) (🗶) (💻)

**▲▲▲ ▼▼▼ Inns of America** Ⓜ
(408) 946-8889. **$69-$109.** 270 S Abbott Ave. I-880, exit Calaveras Blvd (SR 237), just e. Ext corridors. **Pets:** Medium. $10 one-time fee/pet. Service with restrictions.
(SAVE) (S⌀) (✕) (🛏) (💻) (🐾)

**▼▼▼▼ Residence Inn by Marriott** SH
(408) 941-9222. **$89-$159.** 1501 California Cir. I-880, exit Dixon Landing Rd E, just s. Int corridors. **Pets:** Accepted.
(A$K) (S⌀) (✕) (🗶) (💻) (🐾) (🗙)

**▲▲▲ ▼▼▼▼ ▼▼▼▼ Sheraton San Jose at Silicon Valley** LH
(408) 943-0600. **$79-$259.** 1801 Barber Ln. 4 mi n of San Jose International Airport; 0.3 mi nw of I-880 and Montague Expwy. Ext/int corridors. **Pets:** Large. Service with restrictions, supervision.
(SAVE) (S⌀) (✕) (🛏) (💻) (🍽) (🐾) (🗙)

**▼▼▼▼ TownePlace Suites by Marriott** SH
(408) 719-1959. **$69-$199.** 1428 Falcon Dr. I-680, exit Montague Expwy, just w, then just n. Int corridors. **Pets:** Medium. $75 one-time fee/pet. Service with restrictions, supervision.
(A$K) (S⌀) (✕) (💻) (🐾)

# MIRANDA

**▲▲▲ ▼▼▼▼ Miranda Gardens Resort** CA
(707) 943-3011. **$105-$245, 7 day notice.** 6766 Ave of the Giants. US 101, exit 650 (Miranda), just e on French Rd, 0.3 mi s on Maple Hills Rd, then 1.5 mi e. Ext corridors. **Pets:** Accepted.
(SAVE) (S⌀) (✕) (🛏) (💻) (🐾) (🍽) (🗙)

# MODESTO

**▲▲▲ ▼▼▼ Best Western Town House Lodge** Ⓜ
(209) 524-7261. **$75-$80.** 909 16th St. SR 99, exit Central Modesto, 1 mi e, at I St. Ext corridors. **Pets:** $20 one-time fee/room. Service with restrictions, supervision.
(SAVE) (S⌀) (✕) (&M) (🛏) (💻) (🐾)

**▲▲▲ ▼▼▼▼ Days Inn** Ⓜ
(209) 527-1010. **$59-$99.** 1312 McHenry Ave. SR 99, exit Briggsmore Ave, 2.3 mi e, then 0.5 mi s. Ext/int corridors. **Pets:** Accepted.
(SAVE) (S⌀) (✕) (🗶) (🛏) (💻) (🐾)

**▲▲▲ ▼▼▼ Howard Johnson Express Inn** Ⓜ
(209) 537-4821. **$79-$99.** 1672 Herndon Rd. SR 99, exit Hatch Rd E, then s. Ext corridors. **Pets:** Small, other species. $100 deposit/pet. Designated rooms, service with restrictions, supervision.
(SAVE) (S⌀) (✕) (🛏) (💻) (🐾)

**▲▲▲ ▼▼▼ Microtel Inn & Suites** SH
(209) 538-6466. **$79-$99.** 1760 Herndon Rd. SR 99, exit Hatch Rd E, just s. Int corridors. **Pets:** Small, other species. $100 deposit/pet. Designated rooms, service with restrictions, supervision.
(SAVE) (S⌀) (✕) (&M) (🗶) (🛏) (💻) (🐾)

**▼▼▼▼ Red Lion Hotel Modesto** SH
(209) 521-1612. **$109-$169.** 1612 Sisk Rd. SR 99, exit Briggsmore Ave, just e. Int corridors. **Pets:** Medium, other species. $50 one-time fee/room. Service with restrictions, supervision.
(A$K) (S⌀) (✕) (&M) (🛏) (💻) (🍽) (🐾) (🗙)

**▲▲▲ ▼▼ Travelodge** Ⓜ
(209) 524-3251. **$47-$60.** 722 Kansas Ave. SR 99, exit Kansas Ave, then w. Ext corridors. **Pets:** $10 one-time fee/pet. Crate.
(SAVE) (✕) (&M) (🛏) (💻)

# MOJAVE

**▲▲▲ ▼▼▼ Americas Best Value Inn** Ⓜ
(661) 824-9317. **$60-$80.** 16352 Sierra Hwy. On SR 14 and 58. Ext corridors. **Pets:** Medium, other species. $5 daily fee/room. Service with restrictions, supervision.
(SAVE) (S⌀) (✕) (🛏) (💻) (🐾)

**(AAA) ▼▼▼▼ Best Western Desert Winds M**
(661) 824-3601. **$79.** 16200 Sierra Hwy. On SR 14 and 58. Ext corridors. **Pets:** Very small. $10 daily fee/pet. Service with restrictions, supervision.
[SAVE] [S♦] [X] [🛏] [📶] [🐾]

**(AAA) ▼▼▼ Desert Inn M**
(661) 824-2518. **$49-$59.** 1954 Hwy 58. Just e of SR 14. Ext corridors. **Pets:** Medium. Service with restrictions, crate.
[SAVE] [S♦] [X] [🛏] [📶]

**(AAA) ▼▼▼ Econo Lodge M**
(661) 824-2463. **$48-$69.** 2145 Hwy 58. Just e of SR 14. Ext corridors. **Pets:** $7 daily fee/pet. Service with restrictions, supervision.
[SAVE] [S♦] [X] [🛏] [📶] [🐾]

**(AAA) ▼▼▼▼ Mariah Country Inn & Suites SH**
(661) 824-4980. **$95.** 1385 Hwy 58. 1.5 mi e of SR 14. Int corridors. **Pets:** Very small. $10 daily fee/pet. Service with restrictions, supervision.
[SAVE] [S♦] [X] [&M] [📶] [🐾] [🛏] [📶] [🍴] [🐾]

# MONTEREY PENINSULA AREA

## CARMEL-BY-THE-SEA

**(AAA) ▼▼▼▼ Best Western Carmel Mission Inn SH**
(831) 624-1841. **$89-$389.** 3665 Rio Rd. 1 mi s on SR 1. Ext/int corridors. **Pets:** Medium. $35 one-time fee/room. Designated rooms, service with restrictions, supervision.
[SAVE] [S♦] [X] [🛏] [📶] [🍴] [🐾]

**(AAA) ▼▼▼▼ Briarwood Inn BB**
(831) 626-9056. **$110-$275, 7 day notice.** 3 blks n off Ocean Ave; at San Carlos St and 4th Ave. Ext corridors. **Pets:** Medium, dogs only. $25 daily fee/pet. Service with restrictions, supervision.
[SAVE] [S♦] [X] [🛏] [📶] [🔑]

**▼▼▼▼ Carmel Country Inn BB**
(831) 625-3263. **$150-$325, 7 day notice.** 4 blks n of Ocean Ave; at Dolores St and 3rd Ave. Ext corridors. **Pets:** Accepted.
[X] [🛏] [📶] [🔑]

**(AAA) ▼▼▼▼ Carmel Fireplace Inn Bed & Breakfast BB**
(831) 624-4862. **$105-$285, 7 day notice.** 3 blks n off Ocean Ave; at San Carlos St and 4th Ave. Ext corridors. **Pets:** Medium, dogs only. $25 daily fee/pet. Designated rooms, service with restrictions, supervision.
[SAVE] [S♦] [X] [🛏] [📶] [🔑]

**(AAA) ▼▼▼▼ Carmel Garden Court BB**
(831) 624-6926. **$150-$245, 7 day notice.** 3 blks n off Ocean Ave; at 4th Ave and Torres St. Ext corridors. **Pets:** Medium. $50 one-time fee/pet. Service with restrictions, supervision.
[SAVE] [X] [🛏] [📶] [🔑]

**▼▼▼ Carmel River Inn M ❀**
(831) 624-1575. **$80-$469, 3 day notice.** 1 mi s on SR 1; n of Carmel River Bridge at Oliver Rd. Ext corridors. **Pets:** Other species. $13 daily fee/room. Service with restrictions, supervision.
[ASK] [S♦] [X] [🛏] [📶] [🐾] [🔑]

**▼▼▼▼ Carmel Tradewinds Inn SH**
(831) 624-2776. **$195-$575, 3 day notice.** 4 blks n off Ocean Ave; at Mission St and 3rd Ave. Ext corridors. **Pets:** Medium. $25 daily fee/pet. Designated rooms, supervision.
[ASK] [S♦] [X] [🛏] [📶] [🔑]

**(AAA) ▼▼▼▼ Coachman's Inn M**
(831) 624-6421. **$135-$425, 3 day notice.** Just s of Ocean Ave on San Carlos St; between 7th and 8th aves. Ext corridors. **Pets:** Dogs only. $20 daily fee/pet. Designated rooms, service with restrictions, supervision.
[SAVE] [S♦] [X] [&M] [🛏] [📶] [🔑]

**▼▼▼▼ Cypress Inn SH**
(831) 624-3871. **$125-$550, 3 day notice.** Just s off Ocean Ave; at Lincoln St and 7th Ave. Ext/int corridors. **Pets:** Accepted.
[X] [🍴] [🔑]

**(AAA) ▼▼▼ Hofsas House M ❀**
(831) 624-2745. **$85-$275, 3 day notice.** 3 blks n off Ocean Ave; between 3rd and 4th aves on San Carlos St. Ext corridors. **Pets:** Medium, dogs only. $20 daily fee/pet. Designated rooms, supervision.
[SAVE] [S♦] [X] [🛏] [📶] [🐾] [🔑]

**(AAA) ▼▼▼▼ Wayside Inn M ❀**
(831) 624-5336. **$99-$414, 7 day notice.** 1 blk s off Ocean Ave; at Mission St and 7th Ave. Ext corridors. **Pets:** Medium, other species. Designated rooms, service with restrictions, supervision.
[SAVE] [S♦] [X] [🛏] [📶] [🔑]

## CARMEL VALLEY

**▼▼▼ Carmel Valley Lodge M ❀**
(831) 659-2261. **$159-$219, 7 day notice.** 8 Ford Rd. 11.5 mi e of SR 1; at Carmel Valley and Ford rds. Ext corridors. **Pets:** Dogs only. $10 daily fee/pet. Service with restrictions, supervision.
[S♦] [X] [🌀] [🛏] [📶] [🐾] [🔑]

**▼▼▼ Los Laureles Lodge M ❀**
(831) 659-2233. **$99-$595, 3 day notice.** 313 W Carmel Valley Rd. 10.5 mi e of SR 1. Ext corridors. **Pets:** Medium, dogs only. $20 daily fee/pet. Service with restrictions, supervision.
[ASK] [S♦] [X] [🛏] [📶] [🍴] [🐾] [🔑]

## MONTEREY

**(AAA) ▼▼▼▼ Bay Park Hotel SH ❀**
(831) 649-1020. **$79-$269.** 1425 Munras Ave. SR 1, exit Soledad Dr/Munras Ave, just w. Int corridors. **Pets:** Medium, other species. $20 daily fee/pet. Designated rooms, service with restrictions, supervision.
[SAVE] [S♦] [X] [&M] [🌀] [🔑] [🛏] [📶] [🍴] [🏊]

**(AAA) ▼▼▼▼ Best Western The Beach Resort SH ❀**
(831) 394-3321. **$99-$429.** 2600 Sand Dunes Dr. SR 1, exit Del Rey Oaks, just w. Ext corridors. **Pets:** Other species. $25 daily fee/room. Designated rooms, service with restrictions, supervision.
[SAVE] [S♦] [X] [🛏] [📶] [🍴] [🐾]

**(AAA) ▼▼▼▼ Best Western Victorian Inn M ❀**
(831) 373-8000. **$129-$279, 3 day notice.** 487 Foam St. SR 1, exit Monterey, 3.4 mi w. Ext/int corridors. **Pets:** Other species. $100 deposit/room, $35 one-time fee/room. Designated rooms, service with restrictions.
[SAVE] [S♦] [X] [&M] [🌀] [🔑] [🛏] [📶] [🔑]

**(AAA) ▼▼▼ El Adobe Inn M ❀**
(831) 372-5409. **$45-$195, 3 day notice.** 936 Munras Ave. SR 1, exit Soledad Dr/Munras Ave, 0.6 mi w. Ext corridors. **Pets:** Medium, dogs only. $15 daily fee/pet. Designated rooms, service with restrictions, supervision.
[SAVE] [X] [🌀] [🛏] [📶] [🔑]

**(AAA) ▼▼▼▼ Hyatt Regency-Monterey Resort & Conference Center LH**
(831) 372-1234. **$99-$255.** 1 Old Golf Course Rd. SR 1, exit Aguajito Rd northbound; exit Monterey southbound, just e. Int corridors. **Pets:** Accepted.
[SAVE] [X] [&M] [🌀] [🔑] [🛏] [📶] [🍴] [🏊] [🐾] [🔑]

**Monterey Bay Lodge** M
(831) 372-8057. **$89-$319.** 55 Camino Aguajito. SR 1, exit Aguajito Rd, just w. Ext corridors. **Pets:** Accepted.

**Monterey Fireside Lodge** M
(831) 373-4172. **$79-$499, 3 day notice.** 1131 10th St. SR 1, exit Aguajito Rd or Monterey, just w. Ext corridors. **Pets:** Other species. $20 daily fee/pet. Designated rooms, no service, supervision.

## PACIFIC GROVE

**Bide-A-Wee Inn & Cottages** M
(831) 372-2330. **$69-$169, 3 day notice.** 221 Asilomar Blvd. 1 mi n of SR 68. Ext corridors. **Pets:** $10 daily fee/pet. Service with restrictions, supervision.

**Olympia Lodge** M
(831) 373-2777. **$110-$180, 3 day notice.** 1140 Lighthouse Ave. 1 mi w. Ext corridors. **Pets:** Accepted.

**Sea Breeze Inn and Cottages** M
(831) 372-7771. **$79-$289.** 1100 Lighthouse Ave. Just w of Seventeen Mile Dr; jct Lighthouse Ave and Grove Acre. Ext/int corridors. **Pets:** $25 one-time fee/pet. Designated rooms, service with restrictions, crate.

**Sea Breeze Lodge** M
(831) 372-3431. **$69-$259.** 1101 Lighthouse Ave. Just w of Seventeen Mile Dr. Ext corridors. **Pets:** $25 one-time fee/pet. Designated rooms, service with restrictions, crate.

## PEBBLE BEACH

**The Lodge at Pebble Beach** LH
(831) 624-3811. **$580-$1072, 3 day notice.** 1700 Seventeen Mile Dr. Off SR 1. Ext/int corridors. **Pets:** Medium, dogs only.

## SEASIDE

**Econo Lodge Bay Breeze** M
(831) 899-7111. **$49-$199.** 2049 Fremont Blvd. SR 1, exit Sand City/Seaside, just e. Ext/int corridors. **Pets:** Small. Service with restrictions, supervision.

# END AREA

## MORENO VALLEY

**Comfort Inn** M
(951) 242-0699. **$64-$149.** 23330 Sunnymead Blvd. SR 60, exit Pigeon Pass Rd, just s, then 0.5 mi e. Ext/int corridors. **Pets:** Medium, other species. $50 deposit/pet, $10 daily fee/pet. Service with restrictions, crate.

## MORGAN HILL

**Quality Inn** SH
(408) 779-0447. **$69-$199.** 16525 Condit Rd. US 101, exit Tennant Ave or E Dunne Ave, just e. Int corridors. **Pets:** Accepted.

**Residence Inn by Marriott** SH
(408) 782-8311. **$108-$127, 14 day notice.** 18620 Madrone Pkwy. US 101, exit Cochrane W, just n. Int corridors. **Pets:** Accepted.

## MORRO BAY

**Best Western El Rancho** M
(805) 772-2212. **$85-$185.** 2460 Main St. SR 1, exit SR 41, 0.5 mi n. Ext corridors. **Pets:** Accepted.

**Days Inn** M
(805) 772-2711. **$59-$149, 3 day notice.** 1095 Main St. SR 1, exit Morro Bay Blvd, 0.7 mi w, then just n. Ext corridors. **Pets:** Accepted.

**Morro Bay Sandpiper/Keystone Inn** M
(805) 772-7503. **$49-$185, 3 day notice.** 540 Main St. SR 1, exit Morro Bay Blvd, 0.7 mi w, then 0.4 mi s. Ext corridors. **Pets:** Accepted.

**Sundown Inn** M
(805) 772-7381. **$38-$149.** 640 Main St. SR 1, exit Morro Bay Blvd, 0.7 mi w, then just s. Ext corridors. **Pets:** Small, dogs only. $8 daily fee/pet. Designated rooms, service with restrictions, supervision.

## MOUNTAIN VIEW

**Homestead Studio Suites Hotel-Mountain View/Silicon Valley** M
(650) 962-1500. **$95.** 190 E El Camino Real. On SR 82, just w of SR 85. Ext corridors. **Pets:** $25 daily fee/pet. Service with restrictions, supervision.

**Tropicana Lodge** M
(650) 961-0220. **$75-$100.** 1720 El Camino Real W. US 101, exit Shoreline Blvd, 2 mi to SR 82, then just n. Ext/int corridors. **Pets:** Other species. Designated rooms, service with restrictions, crate.

## MOUNT SHASTA

**A-1 Choice Inn** M
(530) 926-4811. **$69-$109, 3 day notice.** 1340 S Mount Shasta Blvd. I-5, exit McCloud/SR 89, just n at 1st left, then 1 mi. Ext corridors. **Pets:** Very small, dogs only. $10 daily fee/pet. Designated rooms, service with restrictions, supervision.

**Best Western Tree House Motor Inn** M
(530) 926-3101. **$91-$162.** 111 Morgan Way. I-5, exit Central Mount Shasta, just e. Ext/int corridors. **Pets:** Medium. $10 daily fee/pet. Service with restrictions, supervision.

**Mt Shasta Ranch Bed & Breakfast** BB
(530) 926-3870. **$70-$125, 3 day notice.** 1008 W A Barr Rd. I-5, exit Central Mount Shasta, 1.5 mi w. Ext/int corridors. **Pets:** Other species. $10 one-time fee/pet. Supervision.

**AAA ▼▼▼ Swiss Holiday Lodge M ❖**
(530) 926-3446. **$59-$80.** 2400 S Mount Shasta Blvd. I-5, exit McCloud/SR 89, just n at 1st left. Ext corridors. **Pets:** Medium. $8 daily fee/pet. Designated rooms, service with restrictions, supervision.
[SAVE] [S⚡] [X] [🖥] [�]

## NEEDLES

**▼▼ Americas Best Value Inn M**
(760) 326-4501. **$55-$69.** 1102 E Broadway. I-40, exit US 95 (E Broadway), just sw. Ext corridors. **Pets:** Medium. $10 daily fee/room. Designated rooms, service with restrictions, supervision.
[ASK] [S⚡] [X] [🖥] [🌐]

**AAA ▼▼ Best Western Colorado River Inn M**
(760) 326-4552. **$60-$80.** 2371 W Broadway. I-40, exit W Broadway/River Rd, 0.3 mi e; on Business Loop I-40. Ext corridors. **Pets:** Medium. $25 deposit/pet. Designated rooms, service with restrictions, supervision.
[SAVE] [S⚡] [X] [🖥] [🖥] [🌐]

**AAA ▼▼ Best Western Royal Inn M**
(760) 326-5660. **$60-$80.** 1111 Pashard St. I-40, exit W Broadway. Ext corridors. **Pets:** Medium. $25 deposit/pet. Designated rooms, service with restrictions, supervision.
[SAVE] [S⚡] [X] [🖥] [🖥] [🌐]

**AAA ▼▼ Days Inn & Suites M**
(760) 326-5836. **$50-$250.** 1215 Hospitality Ln. I-40, exit J St, just se. Ext corridors. **Pets:** Other species. $10 one-time fee/pet. Service with restrictions, supervision.
[SAVE] [S⚡] [X] [🌐] [🖥] [🌐]

**AAA ▼▼ Travelers Inn M**
(760) 326-4900. **$40-$65.** 1195 3rd St Hill. I-40, exit J St, just e, then just s. Ext corridors. **Pets:** Medium, other species. $50 deposit/room. Designated rooms, service with restrictions, supervision.
[SAVE] [S⚡] [X] [🌀] [🖥] [🌐]

## NEVADA CITY

**AAA ▼▼ Nevada City Inn M ❖**
(530) 265-2253. **$79-$155.** 760 Zion St. SR 20 and 49, exit Gold Flat/Ridge Rd, 0.3 mi w, then 0.3 mi n. Ext corridors. **Pets:** Other species. $10 daily fee/pet. Designated rooms, supervision.
[SAVE] [S⚡] [X] [&M] [🖥]

## NEWARK

**▼▼▼ Homewood Suites by Hilton SH**
(510) 791-7700. **$119-$159, 3 day notice.** 39270 Cedar Blvd. I-880, exit Mowry Ave, w to Cedar Blvd, then 0.3 mi s. Int corridors. **Pets:** Accepted.
[ASK] [S⚡] [X] [&] [🖥] [🖥] [🌐] [X]

**▼▼▼ Residence Inn by Marriott Newark/Silicon Valley SH**
(510) 739-6000. **$65-$139.** 34566 Dumbarton Ct. SR 84, exit Newark Blvd, just s. Int corridors. **Pets:** Accepted.
[ASK] [X] [&M] [&] [🖥] [🌐] [X]

**AAA ▼▼▼ Woodfin Suites M**
(510) 795-1200. **$99.** 39150 Cedar Blvd. I-880, exit Mowry Ave, just w, then 0.3 mi s. Ext corridors. **Pets:** Accepted.
[SAVE] [S⚡] [X] [&] [🖥] [🌐]

## NEWPORT BEACH

**▼▼▼▼ The Island Hotel Newport Beach LH**
(949) 759-0808. **$360-$3950.** 690 Newport Center Dr. SR 73, exit MacArthur Blvd northbound, 3 mi s to San Joaquin Hills Rd, then 0.5 mi w; exit Jamboree Rd southbound, 2.5 mi s to San Joaquin Hills Rd, then 0.5 mi e. Int corridors. **Pets:** Accepted.
[X] [&M] [🌀] [&] [🖥] [🍽] [🌐] [X]

## NIPOMO

**▼▼ Kaleidoscope Inn & Gardens B&B BB ❖**
(805) 929-5444. **$125, 7 day notice.** 130 E Dana St. US 101, exit Tefft St, 0.7 mi e, just s on Thompson Rd, then just e. Ext/int corridors. **Pets:** Other species. Designated rooms, service with restrictions, crate.
[X] [&] [🌐] [🌀]

## NOVATO

**AAA ▼▼▼ Inn Marin SH**
(415) 883-5952. **$99-$149.** 250 Entrada Dr. US 101, exit Ignacio Blvd, just w, then just n on Enfrente Rd. Ext corridors. **Pets:** Accepted.
[SAVE] [S⚡] [X] [&M] [&] [🖥] [🖥] [🍽] [🌐]

**AAA ▼▼ Novato Days Inn SH**
(415) 897-7111. **$69-$109.** 8141 Redwood Blvd. US 101, exit San Marin Dr, 1 mi n. Ext corridors. **Pets:** Small, dogs only. $10 daily fee/pet. Service with restrictions, supervision.
[SAVE] [S⚡] [X] [&M] [🖥] [🖥] [🍽] [🌐]

**AAA ▼▼ Novato Travelodge M**
(415) 892-7500. **$69-$94.** 7600 Redwood Blvd. US 101, exit San Marin Dr, just w. Ext corridors. **Pets:** Small. $10 daily fee/pet. Service with restrictions, supervision.
[SAVE] [S⚡] [X] [&M] [🖥] [🖥] [🌐]

## OAKHURST

**AAA ▼▼▼ Best Western Yosemite Gateway Inn M**
(559) 683-2378. **$59-$112.** 40530 Hwy 41. SR 49, 0.8 mi n. Ext corridors. **Pets:** Accepted.
[SAVE] [S⚡] [X] [&M] [🌀] [&] [🖥] [🖥] [🌐] [X]

**AAA ▼▼▼ Comfort Inn-Oakhurst M**
(559) 683-8282. **$49-$99.** 40489 Hwy 41. SR 49, 0.5 mi n. Ext corridors. **Pets:** Other species. $10 daily fee/room. Service with restrictions, supervision.
[SAVE] [S⚡] [X] [🌀] [🖥] [🖥] [🌐]

**AAA ▼▼▼ Days Inn M**
(559) 642-2525. **$49-$119.** 40662 Hwy 41. SR 49, 0.8 mi n. Ext corridors. **Pets:** Accepted.
[SAVE] [S⚡] [X] [🖥] [🖥] [🌐]

## OAKLAND

**AAA ▼▼▼ Best Western Inn at the Square SH**
(510) 452-4565. **$99-$159.** 233 Broadway. I-880, exit Broadway, 0.3 mi w. Int corridors. **Pets:** Small. $150 deposit/room. Designated rooms, service with restrictions, supervision.
[SAVE] [S⚡] [X] [🖥] [🖥] [🌐]

**▼▼▼ Hilton Oakland Airport LH**
(510) 635-5000. **$99-$499.** 1 Hegenberger Rd. I-880, exit Hegenberger Rd, 1 mi w; 1.3 mi e of Metropolitan Oakland International Airport. Int corridors. **Pets:** Accepted.
[S⚡] [X] [&M] [&] [🖥] [🖥] [🍽] [🌐]

**▼▼▼ Homewood Suites SH**
(510) 663-2700. **$169.** 1103 Embarcadero. I-880, exit 16th Ave/Embarcadero southbound; exit 5th Ave/Embarcadero northbound, just w. Int corridors. **Pets:** Medium, other species. $300 deposit/room, $50 one-time fee/room. Service with restrictions, crate.
[ASK] [S⚡] [X] [🖥] [🖥] [🌐]

**▼▼ Quality Inn M**
(510) 562-4888. **$79-$89.** 8471 Enterprise Way. I-880, exit Hegenberger Rd, just e. Ext corridors. **Pets:** Medium, dogs only. $10 daily fee/pet. Service with restrictions.
[ASK] [S⚡] [X] [🖥] [🖥]

# OCEANO

**Oceano Inn** M
(805) 473-0032. **$69-$219.** 1252 Pacific Blvd. On SR 1. Ext corridors. **Pets:** Very small. $15 daily fee/pet. Service with restrictions, supervision.

# OCEANSIDE

**La Quinta Inn** SH ❀
(760) 450-0730. **$99-$129.** 937 N Coast Hwy. I-5, exit Coast Hwy, just w. Int corridors. **Pets:** Other species. $100 deposit/room. Service with restrictions, supervision.

**Motel 6 #4208** M
(760) 721-1543. **$60-$80.** 909 N Coast Hwy. I-5, exit Coast Hwy, just w. Int corridors. **Pets:** Accepted.

# OJAI

**Best Western Casa Ojai** M
(805) 646-8175. **$95-$135.** 1302 E Ojai Ave. 0.8 mi e on SR 150. Ext corridors. **Pets:** Accepted.

**Blue Iguana Inn** M ❀
(805) 646-5277. **$95-$269, 7 day notice.** 11794 N Ventura Ave. 2.5 mi w of town on SR 33. Ext corridors. **Pets:** Medium, dogs only. $20 daily fee/pet. Service with restrictions, supervision.

**Oakridge Inn** M
(805) 649-4018. **$85-$140.** 780 N Ventura Ave. In Oak View; 4 mi s on SR 33; 2 mi e of Lake Casitas. Ext corridors. **Pets:** Medium. $15 daily fee/pet. Designated rooms, service with restrictions, supervision.

**Ojai Valley Inn & Spa** LH
(805) 646-1111. **$400-$5400, 3 day notice.** 905 Country Club Rd. 1 mi w on SR 150, 0.3 mi s. Ext/int corridors. **Pets:** Accepted.

# ONTARIO

**AmeriSuites (Los Angeles/Ontario Mills)** SH
(909) 980-2200. **$145-$209.** 4760 E Mills Cir. I-10, exit Milliken Ave, just n, then 0.5 mi e on Ontario Mills Pkwy. Int corridors. **Pets:** Small, other species. $10 daily fee/pet. Service with restrictions, crate.

**Best Western InnSuites Ontario** SH
(909) 466-9600. **$79-$129.** 3400 Shelby St. I-10, exit Haven Ave, just n to Inland Empire Blvd, w to Lotus Ave, then just s. Ext corridors. **Pets:** Accepted.

**Best Western Ontario Airport** M ❀
(909) 937-6800. **$89-$139, 3 day notice.** 209 N Vineyard Ave. I-10, exit Vineyard Ave, 0.3 mi s. Ext corridors. **Pets:** Small, other species. $10 daily fee/pet. Designated rooms, service with restrictions, supervision.

**DoubleTree Hotel Ontario** LH
(909) 937-0900. **$105-$219.** 222 N Vineyard Ave. I-10, exit Vineyard Ave, 0.4 mi s. Int corridors. **Pets:** Accepted.

**Hilton Ontario Airport** LH
(909) 980-0400. **$89-$239, 3 day notice.** 700 N Haven Ave. I-10, exit Haven Ave, just n. Int corridors. **Pets:** Accepted.

**La Quinta Inn & Suites Ontario (Airport)** SH
(909) 476-1112. **$109-$139.** 3555 Inland Empire Blvd. I-10, exit Haven Ave, just n, then just e. Int corridors. **Pets:** Medium. Service with restrictions.

**Nites Inn** SH
(909) 983-3600. **$68-$100.** 1801 E G St. I-10, exit Vineyard Ave, just s, then just w. Ext corridors. **Pets:** Small. $10 daily fee/pet. Designated rooms, service with restrictions, supervision.

**Residence Inn by Marriott** SH ❀
(909) 937-6788. **$129-$189.** 2025 Convention Center Way. I-10, exit Vineyard Ave, just s, then 1 blk e. Ext corridors. **Pets:** Large, other species. $100 one-time fee/room. Service with restrictions, crate.

# ORLAND

**Amber Light Inn Motel** M ❀
(530) 865-7655. **$52-$59.** 828 Newville Rd. I-5, exit Chico (SR 32), 0.3 mi e. Ext corridors. **Pets:** Small, other species. $8 one-time fee/pet. Service with restrictions, supervision.

**Orland Inn** M
(530) 865-7632. **$57-$63.** 1052 South St. I-5, exit South St northbound; exit CR 16 southbound, just e; in Stony Creek Shopping Center. Ext corridors. **Pets:** Other species. $5 one-time fee/pet. Service with restrictions, crate.

# OROVILLE

**Americas Best Value Inn** M ❀
(530) 533-7070. **$65-$110.** 580 Oro Dam Blvd. SR 70, exit Oroville Dam Blvd, 0.3 mi e. Ext corridors. **Pets:** Other species. $20 deposit/room, $6 daily fee/pet. Designated rooms, service with restrictions, supervision.

**Comfort Inn** M
(530) 533-9673. **$79-$109.** 1470 Feather River Blvd. SR 70, exit E Montgomery St. Int corridors. **Pets:** Accepted.

**Days Inn-Oroville** M
(530) 533-3297. **$65-$129.** 1745 Feather River Blvd. SR 70, exit E Montgomery St, just e to Feather River Blvd, then 0.5 mi s. Ext corridors. **Pets:** Medium. $10 daily fee/pet. Service with restrictions, supervision.

**Sunset Inn** M
(530) 533-8201. **$49-$149.** 1835 Feather River Blvd. SR 70, exit E Montgomery St, 0.5 mi s. Ext corridors. **Pets:** Accepted.

# OXNARD

**Best Western Oxnard Inn** M
(805) 483-9581. **$89-$139.** 1156 S Oxnard Blvd. US 101, exit Rose Ave northbound, 3 mi s, then 1 mi w; exit Oxnard Blvd southbound, 3.5 mi s. Ext corridors. **Pets:** Medium. $20 one-time fee/pet. Designated rooms, service with restrictions, supervision.

**Residence Inn At River Ridge** SH
(805) 278-2200. **$149-$189.** 2101 W Vineyard Ave. US 101, exit Vineyard Ave, 1.8 mi w. Ext corridors. **Pets:** Accepted.

### Vagabond Inn Oxnard M
(805) 983-0251. **$69-$99.** 1245 N Oxnard Blvd. US 101, exit Vineyard Ave northbound; exit Oxnard Blvd southbound, 1.5 mi s. Ext corridors. **Pets:** Other species. $5 daily fee/room. Service with restrictions, supervision.

## PALMDALE

### Residence Inn by Marriott SH
(661) 947-4204. **$135-$220, 14 day notice.** 514 W Ave P. SR 14, exit Ave P, just w. Int corridors. **Pets:** Accepted.

## PALM DESERT

### Best Western Palm Desert Resort M ❀
(760) 340-4441. **$69-$229.** 74-695 Hwy 111. I-10, exit Cook St, 4.4 mi s, then 0.3 mi w. Ext corridors. **Pets:** Medium, other species. $50 deposit/room. Designated rooms, service with restrictions, supervision.

### Casa Larrea Inn M
(760) 568-0311. **Call for rates.** 73-771 Larrea St. I-10, exit Cook St, 4.4 mi s to SR 111, 1.2 mi w to San Luis Rey Ave, just s, then just e. Ext corridors. **Pets:** Other species. $10 daily fee/pet. Service with restrictions, supervision.

### Comfort Suites M
(760) 360-3337. **$79-$249.** 39-585 Washington St. I-10, exit Washington St, just n. Int corridors. **Pets:** Medium, other species. $15 one-time fee/room. Service with restrictions, supervision.

### Fairfield Inn M
(760) 341-9100. **$79-$164.** 72-322 Hwy 111. I-10, exit Monterey Ave, 5.7 mi s, then 0.6 mi w. Int corridors. **Pets:** Small, other species. $75 one-time fee/room. Service with restrictions, supervision.

### The Inn at Deep Canyon M
(760) 346-8061. **$47-$127, 3 day notice.** 74470 Abronia Tr. I-10, exit Cook St, 4.4 mi s to SR 111, 0.5 mi w, then just s on Deep Canyon Rd. Ext corridors. **Pets:** Large, other species. $10 daily fee/pet. Designated rooms, service with restrictions.

### International Lodge CO
(760) 346-6161. **$93-$159, 3 day notice.** 74-380 El Camino. I-10, exit Cook St, 4.4 mi s to SR 111, 0.6 mi w to Panorama Dr, just s, then just e. Ext corridors. **Pets:** Small, other species. $10 daily fee/pet. Designated rooms, service with restrictions.

### Residence Inn by Marriott SH
(760) 776-0050. **$99-$369.** 38-305 Cook St. I-10, exit Cook St, 0.8 mi s. Ext corridors. **Pets:** Medium, other species. $75 one-time fee/pet. Service with restrictions, supervision.

## PALM SPRINGS

### A Place In The Sun M ❀
(760) 325-0254. **$99-$259, 7 day notice.** 754 San Lorenzo Rd. Just e of Palm Canyon Dr via Mesquite Ave and Random Rd. Ext corridors. **Pets:** Other species. $15 daily fee/pet. Service with restrictions, supervision.

### Casa Cody Country Inn M
(760) 320-9346. **$69-$359, 3 day notice.** 175 S Cahuilla Rd. SR 111, just w on Tahquitz Canyon Way, then just s. Ext corridors. **Pets:** Accepted.

### Hilton Palm Springs Resort LH
(760) 320-6868. **$118-$178, 3 day notice.** 400 E Tahquitz Canyon Way. Just e of Indian Canyon Dr. Int corridors. **Pets:** Accepted.

### Hotel California M ❀
(760) 322-8855. **$79-$250, 3 day notice.** 424 E Palm Canyon Dr. 1.5 mi s of Tahquitz Canyon Way. Ext corridors. **Pets:** Small, dogs only. $100 deposit/room, $15 daily fee/pet. Designated rooms, service with restrictions, supervision.

### Howard Johnson Express Inn M
(760) 320-0555. **$69-$129.** 2000 N Palm Canyon Dr. 1.5 mi n of Tahquitz Canyon Way. Ext corridors. **Pets:** Accepted.

### Palm Springs Riviera Resort LH
(760) 327-8311. **$69-$219.** 1600 N Indian Canyon Dr. 1.5 mi n of Tahquitz Canyon Way. Int corridors. **Pets:** Accepted.

### Quality Inn Resort M
(760) 323-2775. **$49-$149.** 1269 E Palm Canyon Dr. 2.3 mi se of Tahquitz Canyon Way. Ext corridors. **Pets:** Medium. Designated rooms, service with restrictions, supervision.

### Ramada Resort Inn & Conference Center SH
(760) 323-1711. **$59-$179.** 1800 E Palm Canyon Dr. 2.7 mi se of Tahquitz Canyon Way. Ext/int corridors. **Pets:** Accepted.

### Shilo Inn Suites M ❀
(760) 320-7676. **$88-$163.** 1875 N Palm Canyon Dr. 1.5 mi n of Tahquitz Canyon Way. Ext corridors. **Pets:** Small. $25 daily fee/pet. Designated rooms, service with restrictions, supervision.

### Super 8 Lodge M
(760) 322-3757. **$58-$75.** 1900 N Palm Canyon Dr. 1.4 mi n of Tahquitz Canyon Way. Ext corridors. **Pets:** Accepted.

### Vagabond Inn Palm Springs M ❀
(760) 325-7211. **$59-$129.** 1699 S Palm Canyon Dr. 1.5 mi s of Tahquitz Canyon Way. Ext corridors. **Pets:** Small, other species. $10 daily fee/pet. Service with restrictions, supervision.

### Wyndham Palm Springs LH
(760) 322-6000. **$99-$119.** 888 Tahquitz Canyon Way. 0.4 mi e of Indian Canyon Dr. Int corridors. **Pets:** Accepted.

## PALO ALTO

### Crowne Plaza Cabana Hotel SH
(650) 857-0787. **$189-$224.** 4290 El Camino Real. US 101, exit San Antonio Rd, 0.4 mi n. Ext/int corridors. **Pets:** Accepted.

## PARADISE

### Comfort Inn M
(530) 876-0191. **$69-$99.** 5475 Clark Rd. SR 191, 0.5 mi s of Pearson Rd. Int corridors. **Pets:** Accepted.

### Lantern Inn M
(530) 877-5553. **$65-$98.** 5799 Wildwood Ln. 1 blk w off Skyway. Ext corridors. **Pets:** Dogs only. $10 daily fee/pet. Service with restrictions, supervision.

**⚠️ ▼▼▼▼ Paradise Inn 🅜**
(530) 877-2127. **$59-$99.** 5423 Skyway. 1.5 mi w. Ext corridors. **Pets:** Small, dogs only. $10 daily fee/pet. Service with restrictions, supervision.
SAVE 🅢🅓 ✕ 🅱 🖥 🏊

**⚠️ ▼▼▼▼ Ponderosa Gardens Motel 🅜**
(530) 872-9094. **$75-$95.** 7010 Skyway. 2 blks e; center. Ext corridors. **Pets:** $6 daily fee/pet. Designated rooms, service with restrictions, supervision.
SAVE ✕ 🅶🅜 ♿ 🅱 🖥 🏊

## PASO ROBLES

**⚠️ ▼▼▼▼ Hampton Inn & Suites 🆂🅷**
(805) 226-9988. **$106-$199.** 212 Alexa Ct. US 101, exit SR 46 (Fresno/Bakersfield) W, just sw. Int corridors. **Pets:** Small. $50 deposit/room. Service with restrictions, supervision.
SAVE 🅢🅓 ✕ 🅶🅜 ♿ 🅱 🖥 🏊

## PHELAN

**⚠️ ▼▼▼ Best Western Cajon Pass 🅜**
(760) 249-6777. **$69-$149.** 8317 Hwy 138. I-15, exit Silver Lake/US 138, just w. Ext corridors. **Pets:** Accepted.
SAVE 🅢🅓 ✕ 🅱 🖥 🏊

## PIRU

**▼▼▼▼ Heritage Valley Inn 🅲🅘**
(805) 521-0700. **$135-$195, 3 day notice.** 691 N Main St. SR 126, 0.7 mi n. Int corridors. **Pets:** Other species. $100 deposit/room. Service with restrictions, crate.
ASK 🅢🅓 ✕ 🍴

## PISMO BEACH

**▼▼▼▼ Cliffs Resort 🆂🅷 ✿**
(805) 773-5000. **$139-$399, 3 day notice.** 2757 Shell Beach Rd. US 101, exit Spyglass Dr northbound; exit Shell Beach Rd southbound, just w, then just n. Int corridors. **Pets:** Dogs only. $10 daily fee/room. Designated rooms, service with restrictions.
ASK 🅢🅓 ✕ 🅶🅜 🅰 ♿ 🅱 🖥 🍴 🏊 🐾

**▼▼▼▼ Cottage Inn by the Sea 🅜**
(805) 773-4617. **$89-$279.** 2351 Price St. US 101, exit Shell Beach Rd northbound, just w, 0.5 mi s; exit Price St southbound, just w, then just s. Ext corridors. **Pets:** Accepted.
ASK 🅢🅓 ✕ 🅶🅜 🅰 ♿ 🅱 🖥 🏊 🐾

**⚠️ ▼▼▼▼ Oxford Suites 🆂🅷 ✿**
(805) 773-3773. **$99-$199.** 651 Five Cities Dr. US 101, exit 4th St, just w, then just n. Ext corridors. **Pets:** Medium, other species. $10 daily fee/pet. Designated rooms, service with restrictions, supervision.
SAVE 🅢🅓 ✕ 🅶🅜 🅰 🅱 🖥

**▼▼▼ Sandcastle Inn 🅜**
(805) 773-2422. **$109-$339.** 100 Stimson Ave. US 101, exit Price St northbound, 0.3 mi s, then just w; exit Hinds Ave southbound, just w, then just s. Ext/int corridors. **Pets:** Other species. $10 daily fee/pet. Designated rooms, service with restrictions, supervision.
ASK 🅢🅓 ✕ 🅶🅜 🅰 ♿ 🅱 🖥

**▼▼▼ Sea Gypsy Motel 🅒🅞**
(805) 773-1801. **$55-$170.** 1020 Cypress St. US 101, exit Wadsworth Ave northbound, 0.3 mi w to Cypress St, then just s; exit SR 1 southbound, just w on Wadsworth Ave, then just s. Ext/int corridors. **Pets:** Other species. $15 daily fee/pet. Service with restrictions, supervision.
✕ 🅱 🖥 🏊 🐾

**⚠️ ▼▼▼ Shell Beach Inn 🅜**
(805) 773-4373. **$69-$159.** 653 Shell Beach Rd. US 101, exit Shell Beach Rd northbound, just w, then 1.2 mi s; exit Price St southbound, just w, then 1 mi n. Ext corridors. **Pets:** $15 daily fee/pet. Service with restrictions, supervision.
SAVE 🅢🅓 ✕ 🅱 🖥 🏊 🐾

**▼▼▼▼ Spyglass Inn 🆂🅷**
(805) 773-4855. **$89-$279.** 2705 Spyglass Dr. US 101, exit Spyglass Dr northbound; exit Shell Beach Rd southbound, just w, then just n. Ext corridors. **Pets:** Accepted.
ASK 🅢🅓 ✕ 🅶🅜 🅰 ♿ 🅱 🖥 🍴 🏊 🐾

## PLACENTIA

**▼▼▼▼ Residence Inn by Marriott 🆂🅷**
(714) 996-0555. **$89-$149.** 700 W Kimberly Ave. SR 57, exit Orangethorpe Ave, just w, just n on Placentia Ave, then just e. Ext corridors. **Pets:** Large, other species. $75 one-time fee/room. Service with restrictions.
ASK ✕ 🅱 🖥 🏊 🐾

## PLACERVILLE

**⚠️ ▼▼▼▼ Best Western Placerville Inn 🆂🅷**
(530) 622-9100. **$89-$299.** 6850 Green Leaf Dr. US 50, exit Missouri Flat Rd S, 0.5 mi w. Int corridors. **Pets:** Other species. $20 daily fee/room. Service with restrictions.
SAVE 🅢🅓 ✕ 🅶🅜 🅱 🖥 🏊

**⚠️ ▼▼▼ Mother Lode Motel 🅜**
(530) 622-0895. **$60-$78, 7 day notice.** 1940 Broadway. 2 mi e; adjacent to US 50, exit Point View Dr. Ext corridors. **Pets:** Accepted.
SAVE 🅢🅓 ✕ 🅶🅜 ♿ 🅱 🖥 🏊

## PLEASANT HILL

**▼▼▼▼ Residence Inn by Marriott-Pleasant Hill 🅜**
(925) 689-1010. **$179-$259.** 700 Ellinwood Way. I-680, exit Willow Pass Rd W to S Contra Costa Blvd, e on Ellinwood Dr, then n. Ext/int corridors. **Pets:** Accepted.
ASK 🅢🅓 ✕ 🖥 🏊 🐾

**▼▼▼▼ Summerfield Suites by Wyndham-Pleasant Hill 🆂🅷**
(925) 934-3343. **$99-$279.** 2611 Contra Costa Blvd. I-680, exit Contra Costa Blvd, then w. Int corridors. **Pets:** Accepted.
ASK ✕ 🅶🅜 ♿ 🖥 🏊 🐾

## PLEASANTON

**⚠️ ▼▼▼▼ Crowne Plaza Hotel Pleasanton 🅛🅗 ✿**
(925) 847-6000. **$69-$139.** 11950 Dublin Canyon Rd. I-580, exit Foothill Rd, 0.3 mi s. Int corridors. **Pets:** $25 one-time fee/room. Designated rooms, service with restrictions, crate.
SAVE 🅢🅓 ✕ 🅶🅜 ♿ 🅱 🖥 🍴 🏊

**▼▼▼▼ Extended Stay Deluxe 🆂🅷**
(925) 730-0000. **$69-$149.** 4555 Chabot Dr. I-580, exit Hopyard Rd, 1 mi s, e on Stoneridge Dr, then s. Int corridors. **Pets:** $25 daily fee/pet. Service with restrictions, supervision.
ASK 🅢🅓 ✕ 🖥 🏊

**⚠️ ▼▼▼▼ Larkspur Landing Home Suite Hotel Pleasanton 🆂🅷**
(925) 463-1212. **$125-$145.** 5535 Johnson Dr. I-580, exit Hopyard Rd S, w on Owen. Int corridors. **Pets:** Accepted.
SAVE 🅢🅓 ✕ 🖥

**▼▼▼ Ramada Inn 🅜**
(925) 463-1300. **$79-$109.** 5375 Owens Ct. I-580, exit Hopyard Rd, just s. Ext corridors. **Pets:** Accepted.
ASK 🅢🅓 ✕ 🅱 🖥 🏊

**⚠️ ▼▼▼▼ Residence Inn by Marriott 🆂🅷**
(925) 227-0500. **$83-$149.** 11920 Dublin Canyon Rd. I-580, exit Foothill Blvd S, then w. Int corridors. **Pets:** Accepted.
SAVE 🅢🅓 ✕ 🅶🅜 ♿ 🖥 🏊 🐾

**▼▼▼▼ Summerfield Suites by Wyndham-Pleasanton 🅜**
(925) 730-0070. **$84-$259.** 4545 Chabot Dr. I-580, exit Hopyard Rd, 1 mi s, e on Stoneridge Dr, then s. Ext corridors. **Pets:** Accepted.
ASK ✕ 🅶🅜 ♿ 🖥 🏊 🐾

**♦♦♦ ▼▼▼▼ Wyndham Garden Hotel-Pleasanton** 🆂🅷
(925) 463-3330. **$79-$149.** 5990 Stoneridge Mall Rd. Jct I-580 and 680, 0.5 mi sw; I-580, exit Foothill Rd, 0.3 mi s, then 0.3 mi e on Canyon Way. Int corridors. **Pets:** Accepted.
🆂🅰🆅🅴 ✕ 🔌 💻 🏊 ✕

## POLLOCK PINES

**♦♦♦ ▼▼▼▼ Best Western Stagecoach Inn** Ⓜ
(530) 644-2029. **$99-$149.** 5940 Pony Express Tr. US 50, exit Pollock Pines eastbound, 1 mi e; exit Sly Park westbound. Ext corridors. **Pets:** Accepted.
🆂🅰🆅🅴 🆂🔟 ✕ 🅑M 💻 🏊

**♦♦♦ ▼▼▼▼ Westhaven Inn** Ⓜ 🐾
(530) 644-7800. **$79-$89.** 5658 Pony Express Tr. US 50, exit Pollock Pines, just n. Ext corridors. **Pets:** Small. $10 daily fee/pet. Designated rooms, no service, supervision.
🆂🅰🆅🅴 🆂🔟 ✕ 🅑M 🔌 💻

## PORTERVILLE

**♦♦♦ ▼▼▼▼ Best Western Porterville Inn** 🆂🅷
(559) 781-7411. **$89-$96.** 350 W Montgomery Ave. SR 65, 0.8 mi e, just s on Jaye St, then just e; adjacent to SR 190. Int corridors. **Pets:** Accepted.
🆂🅰🆅🅴 🆂🔟 ✕ 🅑M 🖈 🔌 🔌 💻 🏊 ✕

## PORTOLA

**▼ Sleepy Pines Motel** Ⓜ
(530) 832-4291. **$61-$96.** 74631 Hwy 70. On SR 70. Ext corridors. **Pets:** Dogs only. Service with restrictions, supervision.
✕ 🔌 💻 🅺

## QUINCY

**♦♦♦ ▼ Pine Hill Motel** Ⓜ 🐾
(530) 283-1670. **$75-$85.** 42075 Hwy 70. 1 mi n. Ext corridors. **Pets:** Medium. $5 daily fee/pet. Service with restrictions, supervision.
🆂🅰🆅🅴 ✕ 🔌 💻 ✕

## RANCHO CORDOVA

**♦♦♦ ▼▼▼▼ AmeriSuites (Sacramento/Rancho Cordova)** 🆂🅷 🐾
(916) 635-4799. **$79-$129.** 10744 Gold Center Dr. US 50, exit Zinfandel Dr, just s. Int corridors. **Pets:** $25 deposit/room. Service with restrictions, supervision.
🆂🅰🆅🅴 🆂🔟 ✕ 🅑M 🖈 🔌 💻 🏊

**♦♦♦ ▼▼▼▼ Best Western, The Venetian Court** Ⓜ
(916) 635-4040. **$99-$109.** 11269 Point East Dr. US 50, exit Sunrise Blvd S; 12 mi e of Sacramento. Int corridors. **Pets:** Large, other species. $25 one-time fee/pet. Service with restrictions, supervision.
🆂🅰🆅🅴 🆂🔟 ✕ 🅑M 🔌 💻 🍽 🏊

**♦♦♦ ▼▼ Days Inn** Ⓜ
(916) 351-1213. **$64-$99.** 12249 Folsom Blvd. US 50, exit Hazel Ave, just s. Ext corridors. **Pets:** Accepted.
🆂🅰🆅🅴 🆂🔟 ✕ 🅑M 🖈 🔌 💻 🏊

**▼▼▼▼ Residence Inn by Marriott** Ⓜ
(916) 851-1550. **$99-$199, 14 day notice.** 2779 Prospect Park Dr. US 50, exit Zinfandel Dr. Int corridors. **Pets:** Accepted.
🅰🆂🅺 ✕ 🅑M 🖈 💻 🏊 ✕

**♦♦♦ ▼▼▼▼ Wingate Inn** 🆂🅷
(916) 858-8680. **$70-$100.** 10745 Gold Center Dr. US 50, exit Zinfandel Dr, just s. Int corridors. **Pets:** Small, other species. $75 deposit/room. Service with restrictions, supervision.
🆂🅰🆅🅴 🆂🔟 ✕ 🅑M 🖈 🔌 💻 🏊

## RANCHO MIRAGE

**♦♦♦ ▼▼▼▼ ▼▼▼▼ The Westin Mission Hills Resort** 🅻🅷
(760) 328-5955. **$129-$450, 7 day notice.** 71-333 Dinah Shore Dr. I-10, exit Bob Hope Dr/Ramon Rd, 0.3 mi w on Ramon Rd, 1 mi s on Bob Hope Dr, then 0.6 mi w. Ext corridors. **Pets:** Accepted.
🆂🅰🆅🅴 🆂🔟 ✕ 💻 🍽 🏊 ✕

## RED BLUFF

**♦♦♦ ▼▼▼ Americas Best Value Inn & Suites** Ⓜ
(530) 529-2028. **$60-$120, 7 day notice.** 30 Gilmore Rd. I-5, exit SR 36 W (Central District), just s. Ext corridors. **Pets:** Medium. $6 daily fee/pet. Designated rooms, service with restrictions, supervision.
🆂🅰🆅🅴 🆂🔟 ✕ 🅑M 🖈 🔌 💻 🏊

**▼▼▼ Days Inn & Suites** Ⓜ
(530) 527-6130. **$60-$66.** 5 John Sutter St. I-5, exit 647 northbound, just e; exit 647A southbound, 0.4 mi e. Ext corridors. **Pets:** Accepted.
🅰🆂🅺 🆂🔟 ✕ 🏊

**▼▼ Econo Lodge** Ⓜ
(530) 528-8890. **$50-$100.** 1142 N Main St. I-5, exit 351 northbound, just s; exit Antelope Blvd southbound, 0.5 mi w, then just n. Ext corridors. **Pets:** Accepted.
🅰🆂🅺 🆂🔟 ✕ 🔌 💻 🏊

**♦♦♦ ▼▼▼ Lamplighter Lodge** Ⓜ
(530) 527-1150. **$85-$95.** 210 S Main St. I-5, exit business loop. Ext corridors. **Pets:** Medium, dogs only. $10 daily fee/pet. Designated rooms, service with restrictions, supervision.
🆂🅰🆅🅴 🆂🔟 ✕ 🔌 🏊

**♦♦♦ ▼ Sportsman Lodge** Ⓜ
(530) 527-2888. **$60-$120.** 768 Antelope Blvd. I-5, exit SR 36 W (Central District), 1.5 mi e. Ext corridors. **Pets:** $7 daily fee/pet. Service with restrictions, supervision.
🆂🅰🆅🅴 🆂🔟 ✕ 🔌 💻 🏊

**♦♦♦ ▼▼▼▼ Super 8 Motel** Ⓜ
(530) 527-8882. **$60-$110.** 203 Antelope Blvd. I-5, exit SR 36 W (Central District). Int corridors. **Pets:** Large, other species. $7 daily fee/pet. Service with restrictions, supervision.
🆂🅰🆅🅴 🆂🔟 ✕ 🔌 🏊

**♦♦♦ ▼▼▼ Travelodge Red Bluff** Ⓜ
(530) 527-6020. **$60-$120.** 38 Antelope Blvd. I-5, exit SR 36 W (Central District), just w. Ext corridors. **Pets:** Medium. $7 daily fee/pet. Service with restrictions, supervision.
🆂🅰🆅🅴 🆂🔟 ✕ 🅑M 🖈 🔌 💻 🏊

## REDCREST

**♦♦♦ ▼▼▼ Redcrest Resort** 🅲🅰 🐾
(707) 722-4208. **$50-$140, 14 day notice.** 26459 Ave of the Giants. US 101, exit Redcrest southbound; exit Redcrest/Holmes northbound, just e, then just n. Ext corridors. **Pets:** $7 daily fee/pet. Designated rooms, no service, supervision.
🆂🅰🆅🅴 ✕ 🔌 💻 ✕ 🅺 🅩

## REDDING

**♦♦♦ ▼▼▼ Americas Best Value Ponderosa Inn** 🆂🅷
(530) 241-6300. **$50-$99.** 2220 Pine St. I-5, exit Cypress Ave, 1.5 mi w. Ext corridors. **Pets:** Accepted.
🆂🅰🆅🅴 🆂🔟 ✕ 🔌 💻 🏊

**♦♦♦ ▼▼▼▼ AmeriHost Inn & Suites-Redding** 🆂🅷
(530) 722-9100. **$94-$150.** 2600 Larkspur Ln. I-5, exit Cypress Ave, just e, then right at Larkspur Ln. Int corridors. **Pets:** Accepted.
🆂🅰🆅🅴 🆂🔟 ✕ 🔌 💻 🏊

**(AAA) ▼▼▼ Best Western Hospitality House** SH
(530) 241-6464. **$65-$99.** 532 N Market St. I-5, exit Lake Blvd northbound, just w, 0.5 mi to Market St, then 0.5 mi s; exit Market St southbound, 2 mi s. Ext corridors. **Pets:** Small, dogs only. $20 daily fee/pet. Designated rooms, service with restrictions, supervision.
SAVE ⊠ 🔋 🎫 ▦ 🍴 ➥

**(AAA) ▼▼▼ Grand Manor Inn & Suites** SH
(530) 221-4472. **$88-$200.** 850 Mistletoe Ln. I-5, exit Cypress Ave E, 0.8 mi n on Hilltop Dr. Int corridors. **Pets:** Accepted.
SAVE 🔸 ⊠ 🎫 🔋 ▦ ➥

**(AAA) ▼▼▼ Holiday Inn Express** SH
(530) 241-5500. **$89-$139.** 1080 Twin View Blvd. I-5, exit Twin View Blvd, just w. Int corridors. **Pets:** Large, other species. $30 daily fee/room. Designated rooms, service with restrictions, supervision.
SAVE 🔸 ⊠ 🎫 🎫 🔋 ▦ ➥

**(AAA) ▼▼▼ La Quinta Inn Redding** SH
(530) 221-8200. **$82-$125.** 2180 Hilltop Dr. I-5, exit Cypress Ave E, 0.5 mi n. Int corridors. **Pets:** Medium. Service with restrictions.
SAVE ⊠ 🔋 🎫 ▦ ➥

**(AAA) ▼▼▼ Oxford Suites** SH 🐾
(530) 221-0100. **$85-$125.** 1967 Hilltop Dr. I-5, exit Cypress Ave E, 0.5 mi n. Ext/int corridors. **Pets:** Medium. $25 one-time fee/room. Service with restrictions, supervision.
SAVE 🔸 ⊠ 🎫 🔋 ▦ ➥

**(AAA) ▼▼▼ Quality Inn** M
(530) 221-6530. **$85-$169.** 2059 Hilltop Dr. I-5, exit Cypress Ave E, 0.3 mi n. Ext corridors. **Pets:** Small. $15 one-time fee/pet. Service with restrictions, supervision.
SAVE 🔸 ⊠ 🔋 ▦ ➥

**(AAA) ▼▼▼ Ramada Limited** SH
(530) 246-2222. **$90-$120.** 1286 Twin View Blvd. I-5, exit Twin View Blvd E, just n. Int corridors. **Pets:** Medium, other species. $15 one-time fee/room. Designated rooms, service with restrictions, crate.
SAVE 🔸 ⊠ 🎫 🎫 🔋 ▦ ➥

**(AAA) ▼▼▼ Redding Travelodge** SH
(530) 243-5291. **$65-$107.** 540 N Market St. I-5, exit Lake Blvd northbound, just w, 0.5 mi to Market St, then 0.5 mi s; exit Market St southbound, 2 mi s. Ext corridors. **Pets:** Accepted.
SAVE 🔸 ⊠ 🎫 🔋 ▦ ➥

**(AAA) ▼▼▼ Red Lion Hotel Redding** SH
(530) 221-8700. **$77-$135.** 1830 Hilltop Dr. I-5, exit SR 44 and Hilltop Dr. Int corridors. **Pets:** Accepted.
SAVE 🔸 ⊠ 🎫 🎫 🔋 ▦ 🍴 ➥ 🗙

# REDLANDS

**(AAA) ▼▼ Best Western Sandman Motel** M
(909) 793-2001. **$72-$84.** 1120 W Colton Ave. I-10, exit Tennessee St, just s, then just e. Ext corridors. **Pets:** Accepted.
SAVE 🔸 ⊠ 🔋 ▦ ➥

**(AAA) ▼▼▼ Dynasty Suites-Redlands** M
(909) 793-6648. **$80-$100.** 1235 W Colton Ave. I-10, exit Tennessee St, just s, then just w. Ext corridors. **Pets:** Small. $15 daily fee/pet. Service with restrictions, supervision.
SAVE ⊠ 🔋 ▦ ➥ 🗙

# REDWAY

**(AAA) ▼▼▼ Dean Creek Resort** M
(707) 923-2555. **$58-$145, 3 day notice.** 4112 Redwood Dr. US 101, exit Redwood Dr northbound; exit Redway/Shelter Cove southbound, just w. Ext corridors. **Pets:** $100 deposit/pet. Service with restrictions, supervision.
SAVE 🔸 ⊠ 🔋 ▦ ➥ 🗙

# REDWOOD CITY

**▼▼▼ ▼▼▼ Sofitel San Francisco Bay** LH 🐾
(650) 598-9000. **$249.** 223 Twin Dolphin Dr. US 101, exit Marine World Pkwy E, 0.5 mi s. Int corridors. **Pets:** Designated rooms, service with restrictions, supervision.
ASK ⊠ 🎫 🎫 🍴 ➥

# REEDLEY

**(AAA) ▼▼▼ Edgewater Inn** M
(559) 637-7777. **$76-$88.** 1977 W Manning Ave. 12 mi e of SR 99 via Manning Ave. Ext corridors. **Pets:** Medium, dogs only. $8 daily fee/pet. Designated rooms, service with restrictions, supervision.
SAVE 🔸 ⊠ 🔋 ▦ ➥

# RIALTO

**(AAA) ▼▼▼ Best Western Empire Inn** M
(909) 877-0690. **$80-$150, 3 day notice.** 475 W Valley Blvd. I-10, exit Riverside Ave, just n, then 0.5 mi w. Ext corridors. **Pets:** Medium. $50 deposit/room, $10 daily fee/pet. Designated rooms, no service, supervision.
SAVE 🔸 ⊠ 🔋 ▦ 🍴 ➥

# RIDGECREST

**(AAA) ▼▼▼ Best Western China Lake Inn** M
(760) 371-2300. **$90-$110.** 400 S China Lake Blvd. On US 395 business route. Ext corridors. **Pets:** Large, other species. $10 one-time fee/pet. Designated rooms, service with restrictions, crate.
SAVE 🔸 ⊠ 🎫 🎫 🔋 ▦ ➥

**(AAA) ▼▼ Carriage Inn** M
(760) 446-7910. **$89.** 901 N China Lake Blvd. On SR 178 and US 395 business route. Ext corridors. **Pets:** Small. $25 one-time fee/room. Designated rooms, service with restrictions, supervision.
SAVE 🔸 ⊠ 🎫 🎫 🎫 🔋 ▦ 🍴 ➥ 🗙

**(AAA) ▼▼▼ Comfort Inn** M
(760) 375-9731. **$85-$130.** 507 S China Lake Blvd. On US 395 business route. Ext corridors. **Pets:** Small. $10 one-time fee/pet. Service with restrictions, supervision.
SAVE 🔸 ⊠ 🎫 🎫 🔋 ▦ ➥

**(AAA) ▼▼ Econo Lodge** M
(760) 446-2551. **$67-$78.** 201 Inyokern Rd. On SR 178 and US 395 business route, just w of China Lake Blvd. Ext corridors. **Pets:** Small, dogs only. Service with restrictions, supervision.
SAVE ⊠ 🔋 ▦ ➥

**(AAA) ▼▼▼ Heritage Inn & Suites** SH
(760) 446-7951. **$75-$88.** 1050 N Norma. On US 395 business route, just w. Int corridors. **Pets:** $100 deposit/room. Service with restrictions, crate.
SAVE 🔸 ⊠ 🎫 🎫 🔋 ▦ 🍴 ➥

**▼▼ Rodeway Inn** M
(760) 384-3575. **$50-$80.** 131 W Upjohn Ave. Business Rt US 395, just w. Ext corridors. **Pets:** Medium, other species. $5 one-time fee/pet. Service with restrictions, supervision.
ASK 🔸 ⊠ 🔋 ▦

**(AAA) ▼▼▼ Vagabond Inn** M
(760) 375-2220. **$65-$86.** 426 China Lake Blvd. On US 395 business route. Ext corridors. **Pets:** Small. $10 one-time fee/pet. Service with restrictions, supervision.
SAVE 🔸 ⊠ 🎫 🎫 🎫 🔋 ▦

# RIO DELL

**(AAA) ▼▼ Humboldt Gables Motel** M
(707) 764-5609. **$50-$75.** 40 W Davis St. US 101, exit Wildwood Ave, 0.5 mi w. Ext corridors. **Pets:** Accepted.
SAVE 🔸 ⊠ 🎫 🔋 ▦ 🗙

# RIVERSIDE

**(AAA) ▼▼ Best Western of Riverside M**
(951) 359-0770. **$109-$229.** 10518 Magnolia Ave. SR 91, exit Tyler St, 0.5 mi nw, then 0.3 mi sw. Ext corridors. **Pets:** Medium. $100 deposit/room, $20 daily fee/room. Designated rooms, service with restrictions, supervision.
(SAVE) (S) (X) (H) (P) (≈)

**(AAA) ▼▼▼ Dynasty Suites Hotel M**
(951) 369-8200. **$89-$129, 3 day notice.** 3735 Iowa Ave. I-215 and SR 60, exit University Ave, just w, then just n. Ext corridors. **Pets:** Small. $10 daily fee/pet. Designated rooms, service with restrictions, supervision.
(SAVE) (S) (X) (H) (P) (≈)

# ROCKLIN

**(AAA) ▼▼▼▼ Howard Johnson Hotel SH**
(916) 624-4500. **$99-$159.** 4420 Rocklin Rd. I-80 E, exit Rocklin Rd. Int corridors. **Pets:** Small, other species. $100 deposit/room, $20 one-time fee/room. Designated rooms, service with restrictions, supervision.
(SAVE) (S) (X) (&M) (🐾) (&) (H) (P) (≈)

**(AAA) ▼▼▼▼ Rocklin Park Hotel SH**
(916) 630-9400. **$119-$169.** 5450 China Garden Rd. I-80, exit Rocklin Rd, just e, s on Aguilar Rd, then e. Int corridors. **Pets:** Other species. $75 one-time fee/room. Designated rooms, service with restrictions.
(SAVE) (S) (X) (&M) (&) (H) (P) (▼) (≈) (X)

# ROSEVILLE

**(AAA) ▼▼▼ Best Western Roseville Inn M**
(916) 782-4434. **$70-$90.** 220 Harding Blvd. I-80, exit Douglas Blvd, just w, then just n. Ext corridors. **Pets:** Medium, other species. $10 daily fee/pet. Designated rooms, service with restrictions, supervision.
(SAVE) (S) (X) (&M) (H) (P) (≈)

**(AAA) ▼▼▼▼ Oxford Suites M**
(916) 784-2222. **$89-$159.** 130 N Sunrise Ave. I-80, exit Douglas Blvd, just e, then 0.3 mi n. Ext/int corridors. **Pets:** Small. $50 one-time fee/room. Service with restrictions, supervision.
(SAVE) (X) (&M) (&) (P) (≈)

**▼▼▼▼ Residence Inn by Marriott SH**
(916) 772-5500. **$124-$147, 14 day notice.** 1930 Taylor Rd. I-80, exit Eureka-Taylor Rd, just s. Int corridors. **Pets:** Accepted.
(ASK) (S) (X) (&M) (&) (P) (≈) (X)

# SACRAMENTO

**(AAA) ▼▼▼ Best Western Expo Inn M**
(916) 922-9833. **$95-$150.** 1413 Howe Ave. Jct SR 16 and US 50, exit Howe Ave, 2.5 mi n. Int corridors. **Pets:** Other species. $25 one-time fee/room. Designated rooms, service with restrictions, crate.
(SAVE) (S) (X) (H) (P) (≈)

**(AAA) ▼▼▼▼ Best Western Harbor Inn & Suites SH**
(916) 371-2100. **$114.** 1250 Halyard Dr. 4 mi w; exit Business Rt I-80 via Harbor Blvd. Ext/int corridors. **Pets:** Other species. $25 daily fee/pet. Designated rooms, service with restrictions, supervision.
(SAVE) (S) (X) (&M) (&) (H) (P) (≈)

**▼▼▼ Canterbury Inn M**
(916) 927-0927. **$59-$89.** 1900 Canterbury Rd. Business Rt I-80, exit Exposition Blvd, 0.4 mi w to Leisure Ln; just n of SR 160. Ext corridors. **Pets:** Accepted.
(ASK) (S) (X) (&M) (H) (P) (≈)

**▼▼ Clarion Hotel Mansion Inn SH**
(916) 444-8000. **$89-$139, 3 day notice.** 700 16th St. On SR 160, 1.3 mi n of Business Rt I-80, exit 16th St. Int corridors. **Pets:** Accepted.
(ASK) (S) (X) (&M) (🐾) (&) (H) (P) (▼) (≈)

**(AAA) ▼▼ Clarion Hotel Near Calexpo SH**
(916) 487-7600. **$99-$169.** 2600 Auburn Blvd. Business Rt I-80, exit Fulton Ave. Int corridors. **Pets:** Accepted.
(SAVE) (S) (X) (&M) (H) (P) (▼) (≈)

**▼▼▼ DoubleTree Hotel LH**
(916) 929-8855. **$95-$235.** 2001 Point West Way. 1 blk off Business Rt I-80, exit via Arden Way. Int corridors. **Pets:** Accepted.
(ASK) (S) (X) (&M) (&) (H) (P) (▼) (≈)

**(AAA) ▼▼▼ Econo Lodge M**
(916) 443-6631. **$49-$129.** 711 16th St. Business Rt I-80, exit 15th St eastbound; exit 16th St westbound; I-5, exit J St (Old Sacramento). Ext corridors. **Pets:** Accepted.
(SAVE) (S) (X) (&M) (H)

**(AAA) ▼▼▼▼ Holiday Inn Express Sacramento SH**
(916) 444-4436. **$89-$139, 3 day notice.** 728 16th St. On SR 160. Int corridors. **Pets:** Accepted.
(SAVE) (S) (X) (&M) (&) (H) (P) (≈)

**▼▼ Homestead Studio Suites Hotel-Sacramento-S. Natomas M**
(916) 564-7500. **$82.** 2810 Gateway Oaks Dr. I-5, exit W El Camino Ave, just w, then 0.4 mi n. Ext corridors. **Pets:** $25 daily fee/pet. Service with restrictions, supervision.
(ASK) (S) (X) (&M) (&) (P)

**▼▼ Host Airport Hotel SH**
(916) 922-8071. **$100-$175.** 6945 Airport Blvd. 11 mi nw of state capitol; 6 mi nw of I-80; off I-5. Ext corridors. **Pets:** Medium. $50 one-time fee/room. Designated rooms, service with restrictions, supervision.
(ASK) (S) (X) (&M) (P)

**▼▼▼ La Quinta Inn Sacramento (Downtown) M**
(916) 448-8100. **$89-$134.** 200 Jibboom St. I-5, exit Richards Blvd W, 2.3 mi nw of Business Loop I-80. Ext corridors. **Pets:** Medium. Service with restrictions.
(ASK) (X) (&M) (H) (P) (≈)

**▼▼▼ La Quinta Inn Sacramento (North) M**
(916) 348-0900. **$84-$129.** 4604 Madison Ave. I-80, exit Madison Ave, 0.3 mi e. Ext corridors. **Pets:** Medium. Service with restrictions.
(ASK) (X) (&M) (P) (≈)

**(AAA) ▼▼▼▼ Larkspur Landing Home Suite Hotel Sacramento SH**
(916) 646-1212. **$139-$149.** 555 Howe Ave. US 50, exit Howe Ave, 1.5 mi n. Int corridors. **Pets:** Small. $10 daily fee/pet, $75 one-time fee/pet. Designated rooms, service with restrictions, crate.
(SAVE) (S) (X) (&M) (&) (H) (P)

**▼▼▼▼ Marriott Residence Inn M**
(916) 920-9111. **$159.** 1530 Howe Ave. 2.5 mi n of jct SR 16 and US 50, exit Howe Ave. Ext corridors. **Pets:** Accepted.
(ASK) (S) (X) (&M) (🐾) (H) (P) (≈)

**▼▼ Quality Inn M**
(916) 927-7117. **$57-$77.** 3796 Northgate Blvd. I-80, exit Northgate Blvd, just s. Ext corridors. **Pets:** Accepted.
(ASK) (S) (X) (≈)

**(AAA) ▼▼▼▼ Radisson Hotel SH**
(916) 922-2020. **$109-$229.** 500 Leisure Ln. Business Rt I-80, exit Exposition Blvd, 0.4 mi w. Ext corridors. **Pets:** Accepted.
(SAVE) (S) (X) (&M) (🐾) (&) (P) (▼) (≈) (X)

**▼▼▼▼ Red Lion Hotel Sacramento M**
(916) 922-8041. **$95-$140.** 1401 Arden Way. I-80, exit Arden Way; in Arden Fair Shopping Plaza. Ext/int corridors. **Pets:** Accepted.
(ASK) (S) (X) (&M) (H) (P) (▼) (≈)

**▼▼▼ Residence Inn by Marriott M** ❖
(916) 649-1300. **$89-$154.** 2410 W El Camino Ave. I-5, exit W El Camino Ave. Ext corridors. **Pets:** $75 one-time fee/room. Service with restrictions.

ASK S✗ ✗ ᴹ 🖥 💻 ⛵ ✗

**▲▲▲ ▼▼▼ Vagabond Executive Inn Old Town SH**
(916) 446-1481. **$79-$119.** 909 3rd St. I-5, exit J St (Old Sacramento); 8 blks w of state capitol. Ext corridors. **Pets:** Small. $10 daily fee/pet. Service with restrictions, supervision.

SAVE S✗ ✗ ᴹ ✍ 🖥 💻 ⛵

# SALINAS

**▲▲▲ ▼▼▼ Ramada Limited M**
(831) 424-4801. **$59-$199.** 109 John St. US 101, exit John St, 0.7 mi w. Ext corridors. **Pets:** Small, dogs only. $10 daily fee/pet. Designated rooms, service with restrictions, supervision.

SAVE S✗ ✗ ✗ 🖥 💻

**▼▼▼ Residence Inn by Marriott-Salinas SH**
(831) 775-0410. **$109-$200, 14 day notice.** 17215 El Rancho Way. US 101, exit Laurel Dr, just w. Int corridors. **Pets:** Accepted.

ASK S✗ ✗ ᴹ ✗ 💻 ⛵ ✗

**▲▲▲ ▼▼▼ Vagabond Inn M**
(831) 758-4693. **$50-$300.** 131 Kern St. US 101, exit Market St, just e. Ext corridors. **Pets:** Medium. $10 daily fee/pet. Service with restrictions, supervision.

SAVE S✗ ✗ ᴹ 🖥 💻 ⛵

# SAN ANDREAS

**▼▼▼ The Robins Nest BB** ❖
(209) 754-1076. **$95-$175, 7 day notice.** 247 W St. Charles St. SR 49; north end of town. Int corridors. **Pets:** Other species. Designated rooms, service with restrictions, supervision.

ASK S✗ ✗ 🖥 💻

# SAN BERNARDINO

**▲▲▲ ▼▼ Econo Lodge M**
(909) 383-1188. **$75-$80.** 606 N "H" St. I-215, exit 5th St, just e, then just n. Ext corridors. **Pets:** Accepted.

SAVE S✗ ✗ 🖥 💻 ⛵

**▼▼▼▼ Hilton-San Bernardino LH**
(909) 889-0133. **$129-$470.** 285 E Hospitality Ln. I-10, exit Waterman Ave, just n, then just w. Int corridors. **Pets:** Accepted.

✗ 🖥 💻 🍴 ⛵ ✗

**▼▼▼▼ La Quinta Inn San Bernardino M**
(909) 888-7571. **$95-$125.** 205 E Hospitality Ln. I-10, exit Waterman Ave, just n, then 0.3 mi w. Ext corridors. **Pets:** Medium. Service with restrictions.

ASK ✗ ᴹ ✍ 🖥 💻 ⛵

# SAN CLEMENTE

**▲▲▲ ▼▼▼▼ Country Plaza Inn SH**
(949) 498-8800. **$79-$139.** 35 Via Pico Plaza. I-5, exit Avenida Pico, just w, then just s. Int corridors. **Pets:** Small, dogs only. $100 deposit/room, $30 daily fee/pet. Designated rooms, service with restrictions, supervision.

SAVE S✗ ✗ ᴹ ✍ ✗ 🖥 💻 ⛵

**▼▼▼▼ Holiday Inn-San Clemente Resort SH**
(949) 361-3000. **$119-$159.** 111 S Avenida de la Estrella. I-5, exit Avenida Palizada southbound; exit Avenida Presidio northbound, just s, then just w. Int corridors. **Pets:** Large, other species. $10 daily fee/pet. Service with restrictions, supervision.

S✗ ✗ 🖥 💻 🍴 ⛵

# SAN DIEGO METROPOLITAN AREA

# CHULA VISTA

**▼▼▼▼ La Quinta Inn San Diego (Chula Vista) M**
(619) 691-1211. **$102-$145.** 150 Bonita Rd. I-805, exit E St/Bonita Rd, just w. Ext corridors. **Pets:** Medium. Service with restrictions.

ASK ✗ 💻 ⛵

# CORONADO

**▼▼▼▼ Coronado Island Marriott Resort LH**
(619) 435-3000. **$250-$345, 3 day notice.** 2000 2nd St. I-5, exit Coronado Bridge, 1.5 mi w to Glorietta Blvd, then just ne. Ext corridors. **Pets:** Other species. $75 one-time fee/room. Service with restrictions.

ASK S✗ ✗ ✗ 🖥 💻 🍴 ⛵ ✗

**▼▼▼ Crown City Inn M** ❖
(619) 435-3116. **$99-$209.** 520 Orange Ave. I-5, exit Coronado Bridge, 1.5 mi w, then just s. Ext corridors. **Pets:** Other species. $8 daily fee/pet. Designated rooms, service with restrictions, supervision.

✗ ᴹ ✗ 🖥 💻 🍴 ⛵

**▲▲▲ ▼▼▼ ▼▼▼ Loews Coronado Bay Resort LH** ❖
(619) 424-4000. **$279-$349.** 4000 Coronado Bay Rd. I-5, exit Coronado Bridge, 1.7 mi w to Orange Ave, 1 mi sw to Silver Strand Blvd, then 4.5 mi s to Coronado Cays. Ext/int corridors. **Pets:** $25 one-time fee/room. Service with restrictions, supervision.

SAVE S✗ ✗ 🖥 💻 🍴 ⛵ ✗

# DEL MAR

**▲▲▲ ▼▼▼▼ Del Mar Inn, A Clarion Carriage House SH**
(858) 755-9765. **$99-$199, 3 day notice.** 720 Camino Del Mar. I-5, exit Del Mar Heights Rd, 1 mi w, then 0.3 mi n. Int corridors. **Pets:** Accepted.

SAVE S✗ ✗ 🖥 💻 ⛵

**▼▼▼▼ Hilton San Diego Del Mar LH**
(858) 792-5200. **$159-$599.** 15575 Jimmy Durante Blvd. I-5, exit Via de la Valle, just w. Int corridors. **Pets:** Large. $150 deposit/pet, $50 one-time fee/pet. Service with restrictions, supervision.

ASK S✗ ✗ 🖥 💻 🍴 ⛵

# EL CAJON

**▲▲▲ ▼▼▼ Quality Inn & Suites Grossmont SH**
(619) 588-8808. **$75-$125.** 1250 El Cajon Blvd. I-8, exit Severin Dr westbound, 1 mi e on Murray Rd; exit El Cajon Blvd eastbound, 0.5 mi w. Ext corridors. **Pets:** Accepted.

SAVE S✗ ✗ 🖥 💻 ⛵

# LA JOLLA

**▲▲▲ ▼▼▼ La Jolla Cove Suites SH** ❖
(858) 459-2621. **$199-$549.** 1155 Coast Blvd. I-5, exit La Jolla Village Dr, 1 mi w to Torrey Pines Rd, 2.5 mi to Prospect St, 0.5 mi s to Girard Ave, then just w. Ext corridors. **Pets:** Medium. $25 daily fee/room. Designated rooms, service with restrictions, supervision.

SAVE S✗ ✗ 🖥 💻 ✗

**La Jolla Village Lodge** M ❀
(858) 551-2001. **$70-$220.** 1141 Silverado St. I-5, exit La Jolla Pkwy northbound, 1.5 mi w to Torrey Pines Rd, 1 mi w, then 0.8 mi sw; exit La Jolla Village Dr southbound, 1 mi w to Torrey Pines Rd, then 3.6 mi sw. Ext corridors. **Pets:** Other species. $20 one-time fee/pet. Supervision.

**La Valencia Hotel** LH
(858) 454-0771. **$275-$3500.** 1132 Prospect St. I-5, exit La Jolla Pkwy northbound, 1.5 mi w to Torrey Pines Rd, 1 mi w, then 0.6 mi sw; exit La Jolla Village Dr southbound, 1 mi w to Torrey Pines Rd, 2.7 mi sw, then 0.6 mi sw. Ext/int corridors. **Pets:** Medium. $75 one-time fee/room. Service with restrictions, supervision.

**Residence Inn by Marriott La Jolla** SH
(858) 587-1770. **$149-$359.** 8901 Gilman Dr. I-5, exit Gilman Dr, 1.5 mi nw. Ext corridors. **Pets:** Accepted.

**San Diego Marriott La Jolla** LH
(858) 587-1414. **$149-$229.** 4240 La Jolla Village Dr. I-5, exit La Jolla Village Dr, 0.5 mi e. Int corridors. **Pets:** $75 one-time fee/pet. Designated rooms, service with restrictions.

## LA MESA

**Motel 6 San Diego-La Mesa #1319** M
(619) 464-7151. **$51-$69.** 7621 Alvarado Rd. I-8, exit Fletcher Pkwy, just s, then just w. Ext corridors. **Pets:** Accepted.

## NATIONAL CITY

**Howard Johnson Express Inn-San Diego South** M
(619) 474-6517. **$45-$129.** 521 Roosevelt Ave. I-5, exit 8th St southbound; exit Plaza Blvd northbound, just e, then just n. Ext corridors. **Pets:** Accepted.

## POWAY

**Best Western Country Inn** M
(858) 748-6320. **$69-$109.** 13845 Poway Rd. I-15, exit Poway Rd, 4 mi e. Ext corridors. **Pets:** Accepted.

**Ramada Limited** M
(858) 748-7311. **$69-$119.** 12448 Poway Rd. I-15, exit Poway Rd, 3 mi e. Ext corridors. **Pets:** Accepted.

## RANCHO BERNARDO

**Courtyard by Marriott San Diego/Rancho Bernardo** SH
(858) 613-2000. **$113-$149.** 11611 Bernardo Plaza Ct. I-15, exit Rancho Bernardo Rd, just e to Bernardo Center Dr, then just s. Int corridors. **Pets:** Accepted.

**La Quinta Inn San Diego (Rancho Penasquitos)** SH
(858) 484-8800. **$89-$125.** 10185 Paseo Montril. I-15, exit Rancho Penasquitos Blvd, just w. Ext corridors. **Pets:** Medium. Service with restrictions.

**Rancho Bernardo Inn** SH
(858) 487-1611. **$179-$219, 3 day notice.** 17550 Bernardo Oaks Dr. I-15, exit Rancho Bernardo Rd, 1 mi e, then 1 mi n. Ext/int corridors. **Pets:** Dogs only. $100 one-time fee/room. Service with restrictions, supervision.

**Rancho Bernardo Travelodge** M
(858) 487-0445. **$60-$450.** 16929 W Bernardo Dr. I-15, exit Rancho Bernardo Rd, just w, then just s. Ext corridors. **Pets:** Accepted.

**Residence Inn San Diego Rancho Bernardo/Carmel Mountain Ranch** SH
(858) 673-1900. **$139-$219.** 11002 Rancho Carmel Dr. I-15, exit Carmel Mountain Rd, just e. Ext/int corridors. **Pets:** Accepted.

**Staybridge Suites Carmel Mountain** SH
(858) 487-0900. **$159-$699.** 11855 Ave of Industry. I-15, exit Carmel Mountain Rd, 1 mi ne to second Rancho Carmel Dr, just w to Innovation Dr, just n, then just e. Int corridors. **Pets:** Medium, other species. $75 one-time fee/pet. Service with restrictions.

## RANCHO SANTA FE

**The Inn at Rancho Santa Fe** SH
(858) 756-1131. **$230-$950, 3 day notice.** 5951 Linea del Cielo. I-5, exit Lomas Sante Fe Dr, 4 mi e on CR S-8. Ext/int corridors. **Pets:** Medium. $125 one-time fee/room. Designated rooms, service with restrictions, supervision.

**Morgan Run Resort & Club** SH
(858) 756-2471. **$149-$259.** 5690 Cancha de Golf. I-5, exit Via De La Valle, 3 mi e. Ext/int corridors. **Pets:** Accepted.

## SAN DIEGO

**Best Western Lamplighter Inn & Suites** M
(619) 582-3088. **$75-$130.** 6474 El Cajon Blvd. I-8, exit 70th St, 0.5 mi s, then 1 mi w. Ext corridors. **Pets:** $10 daily fee/pet. Service with restrictions, supervision.

**The Bristol** LH
(619) 232-6141. **$119-$159.** 1055 First Ave. I-5, exit Front St, 0.5 mi s at C St; downtown. Int corridors. **Pets:** Large, dogs only. $45 deposit/pet. Designated rooms, service with restrictions, supervision.

**Doubletree Club Hotel San Diego Zoo/SeaWorld Area** LH
(619) 881-6900. **$119-$199, 3 day notice.** 1515 Hotel Cir S. I-8, exit Hotel Cir, south side. Int corridors. **Pets:** Accepted.

**DoubleTree Hotel San Diego-Mission Valley** LH ❀
(619) 297-5466. **$129-$259.** 7450 Hazard Center Dr. SR 163, exit Friars Rd, 0.3 mi e to Frazee Rd, then just s. Int corridors. **Pets:** Medium. $50 one-time fee/room. Designated rooms, service with restrictions, crate.

**Four Points by Sheraton San Diego** SH
(858) 277-8888. **$115-$225.** 8110 Aero Dr. SR 163, southbound exit Balboa Ave E, 1 mi se via Kearny Villa Rd; exit Kearny Villa Rd northbound, 0.8 mi ne. Int corridors. **Pets:** Accepted.

**Hampton Inn SeaWorld/Airport** SH
(619) 299-6633. **$129-$179.** 3888 Greenwood St. I-8, exit Sports Arena Blvd, 0.5 mi s, 0.3 mi e on Hancock St, then 0.4 mi s on Kurtz St. Int corridors. **Pets:** Medium. $75 one-time fee/pet. Service with restrictions, supervision.

**Holiday Inn on the Bay** LH
(619) 232-3861. **$129-$189.** 1355 N Harbor Dr at Ash St. I-5, exit Hawthorn St northbound, 0.4 mi w, then 0.4 mi s; exit Front Ave southbound, 0.5 mi s to Ash St, then just w. Int corridors. **Pets:** Accepted.

**Homestead Studio Suites Hotel-San Diego/Mission Valley** M
(619) 299-2292. **$85-$105.** 7444 Mission Valley Rd. SR 163, exit Friars Rd, 1 mi ne via Mission Center Dr. Ext corridors. **Pets:** $25 daily fee/pet. Service with restrictions, supervision.

**Homestead Studio Suites Hotel-San Diego/Sorrento Mesa** M
(858) 623-0100. **$105-$115.** 9880 Pacific Heights Blvd. I-805, exit Mira Mesa Blvd, 1 mi e. Ext corridors. **Pets:** $25 daily fee/pet. Service with restrictions, supervision.

**Horton Grand Hotel** SH
(619) 544-1886. **$189-$289, 3 day notice.** 311 Island Ave. I-5, exit Front St southbound, 1.2 mi s, then just e; exit J St northbound, 1 mi w, just n on 3rd Ave, then just e. Int corridors. **Pets:** Small, dogs only. $100 one-time fee/room. Designated rooms, service with restrictions, supervision.

**Motel 6 San Diego-Downtown #1419** M
(619) 236-9292. **$55-$75.** 1546 2nd Ave. I-5, exit 6th Ave northbound, 0.3 mi w, then just s; exit 2nd Ave southbound, just s. Int corridors. **Pets:** Accepted.

**Motel 6 San Diego North #1020** M
(858) 268-9758. **$57-$83.** 5592 Clairemont Mesa Blvd. I-805, exit Clairemont Mesa Blvd, just w. Ext corridors. **Pets:** Accepted.

**Ocean Villa Inn** M ❖
(619) 224-3481. **$89-$299.** 5142 W Point Loma Blvd. I-8, exit Sunset Cliff Blvd, 1.5 mi sw. Ext corridors. **Pets:** $25 one-time fee/room. Designated rooms, service with restrictions, supervision.

**Old Town Inn** M
(619) 260-8024. **$65-$145.** 4444 Pacific Hwy. I-5, exit SeaWorld Dr, just w, then 1 mi s. Ext corridors. **Pets:** $10 daily fee/pet. Service with restrictions, supervision.

**Pacific Inn Hotel & Suites** M
(619) 232-6391. **$59-$269.** 1655 Pacific Hwy. I-5, exit Front St southbound, just s to Cedar St, 0.3 mi w, then just n; exit Hawthorn St northbound, 0.4 mi w, then just s. **Pets:** Accepted.

**Pacific Shores Inn** M
(858) 483-6300. **$69-$159.** 4802 Mission Blvd. I-5, exit Garnet Ave, 2.5 mi w, then 0.3 mi n. Ext corridors. **Pets:** Accepted.

**Premier Inns Mission Valley/Hotel Circle** M
(619) 291-8252. **$49-$129.** 2484 Hotel Circle Pl. I-8, exit Taylor St, just n. Ext corridors. **Pets:** Medium. Service with restrictions, supervision.

**Premier Inn-Sports Arena/Mission Bay** M
(619) 223-9500. **$44-$139.** 3333 Channel Way. I-5/8, exit Rosecrans St, 0.5 mi s, 1 mi nw on Sports Arena Blvd, then just e. Ext corridors. **Pets:** Accepted.

**Red Lion Hanalei Hotel** LH ❖
(619) 297-1101. **$98-$144.** 2270 Hotel Cir S. I-8, exit Tayor St, just n, then just e. Ext corridors. **Pets:** Medium, dogs only. $75 deposit/pet. Designated rooms, service with restrictions, supervision.

**Residence Inn by Marriott-San Diego Central** SH
(858) 278-2100. **$129-$209.** 5400 Kearny Mesa Rd. SR 163, exit Clairemont Mesa Blvd. Ext corridors. **Pets:** Medium, other species. $75 one-time fee/room. Service with restrictions, supervision.

**Residence Inn by Marriott San Diego Downtown** SH
(619) 338-8200. **$159-$199.** 1747 Pacific Hwy. I-5, exit Front St southbound, just s to Grape St, 0.3 mi w, then just n; exit Hawthorn St northbound, 0.4 mi w, then just s. Int corridors. **Pets:** Other species. $75 one-time fee/room.

**Residence Inn San Diego/Mission Valley/ SeaWorld Area** SH ❖
(619) 881-3600. **$159-$359, 3 day notice.** 1865 Hotel Cir S. I-8, exit Hotel Cir, south side. Int corridors. **Pets:** Large. $75 one-time fee/pet. Service with restrictions, supervision.

**Residence Inn San Diego Ranch Bernardo/Scripps Poway** SH
(858) 635-5724. **$159-$219.** 12011 Scripps Highland Dr. I-805, exit Mercy Rd/Scripps Poway Pkwy, just e, then just n. Int corridors. **Pets:** Large, other species. $75 one-time fee/pet. Supervision.

**Residence Inn San Diego-Sorrento Mesa** SH
(858) 552-9100. **$116-$189.** 5995 Pacific Mesa Ct. I-805, exit Mira Mesa Blvd, 1.5 mi e. Int corridors. **Pets:** Other species. $75 one-time fee/room.

**San Diego Marriott Hotel & Marina** LH ❖
(619) 234-1500. **$400-$3500.** 333 W Harbor Dr. I-5, exit Front St, 1.3 mi s, then just w. Int corridors. **Pets:** Other species. $75 deposit/pet. Service with restrictions.

**Shelter Pointe Hotel** SH
(619) 221-8000. **$139-$249.** 1551 Shelter Island Dr. I-5, exit Rosecrans St southbound, 3 mi sw; exit Hawthorn St northbound, 3 mi nw on Harbor Dr to Scott Rd, then 0.5 mi w. Ext/int corridors. **Pets:** Accepted.

**Sheraton San Diego Hotel and Marina** LH
(619) 291-2900. **$189-$389.** 1380 Harbor Island Dr. I-5, exit Hawthorn St northbound, just e to Harbor Dr, 1.5 mi w, then just s; exit Kettern/Hancock southbound, just s to Laurel St, just w to Harbor Dr, 1.5 mi w, then just s. Ext/int corridors. **Pets:** Accepted.

**Sheraton San Diego Hotel, Mission Valley** LH ❖
(619) 260-0111. **$259-$299.** 1433 Camino del Rio S. I-8, exit Mission Center Rd, south side. Int corridors. **Pets:** Dogs only. $75 one-time fee/room. Service with restrictions, supervision.

**Sheraton Suites San Diego** LH
(619) 696-9800. **$189-$249.** 701 A St/7th Ave. I-5, exit Front St, 0.5 mi s. Int corridors. **Pets:** Accepted.

**▼▼▼▼ Sommerset Suites Hotel SH**
(619) 692-5200. **$89-$279.** 606 Washington St. SR 163, just w. Ext/int corridors. **Pets:** Accepted.
ⒶⓈⓀ 🆂🔟 ⓧ 🏊

**▼▼▼▼ Staybridge Suites by Holiday Inn-Sorrento Mesa SH**
(858) 453-5343. **$169-$269.** 6639 Mira Mesa Blvd. I-805, exit Mira Mesa Blvd, 2.3 mi e. Int corridors. **Pets:** Other species. $75 one-time fee/room.
ⒶⓈⓀ 🆂🔟 ⓧ ⓜ 🗐 🔳 🍴 🔲 🏊

**▼▼▼▼ Staybridge Suites Riviera-San Diego Downtown SH**
(619) 795-4000. **$155-$315.** 1110 A St. SR 163, exit Ash St, just e. Int corridors. **Pets:** Large. $75 one-time fee/room. Service with restrictions, supervision.
ⒶⓈⓀ 🆂🔟 ⓧ ⓜ 🗐 🔳 🍴 🔲

**♦♦♦ ▼▼ Vagabond Inn-Point Loma M ✷**
(619) 224-3371. **$64-$164.** 1325 Scott St. I-8, exit Nimintz Blvd, 2 mi s to Rosecrans St, just w to Jarvis St, then just s; in Point Loma area. Ext corridors. **Pets:** Medium. $10 daily fee/pet. Designated rooms, service with restrictions, supervision.
SAVE 🆂🔟 ⓧ 🍴 🔲 🏊

**▼▼▼▼ The Westin Horton Plaza LH**
(619) 239-2200. **$189-$369.** 910 Broadway Cir. I-5, exit Front St southbound, 0.9 mi s to Broadway, just e, then just s; exit 6th Ave northbound, 0.6 mi s, just w, then just s. Int corridors. **Pets:** Accepted.
ⒶⓈⓀ ⓧ ⓜ 🗐 🔳 🍴 🔲 🍴 🏊 🔲

**♦♦♦ ▼▼▼▼ Woodfin Suite Hotel SH**
(858) 597-0500. **$299-$399.** 10044 Pacific Mesa Blvd. I-805, exit Mira Mesa Blvd, 1.1 mi e, then just n. Int corridors. **Pets:** Accepted.
SAVE 🆂🔟 ⓧ ⓜ 🗐 🔳 🔲 🍴 🏊

# SAN FRANCISCO METROPOLITAN AREA

## BELMONT

**▼▼▼▼ Summerfield Suites by Wyndham-Belmont/Redwood Shores SH**
(650) 591-8600. **$109-$209.** 400 Concourse Dr. US 101, exit Marine World Pkwy, just e, then just n on Oracle Pkwy. Ext corridors. **Pets:** Accepted.
ⒶⓈⓀ ⓧ ⓜ 🔳 🔲 🏊

## BRISBANE

**▼▼▼ Homewood Suites By Hilton SH ✷**
(650) 589-1600. **$149-$229.** 2000 Shoreline Ct. US 101, exit Sierra Point Pkwy, just e. Int corridors. **Pets:** $75 one-time fee/room. Designated rooms, service with restrictions, supervision.
ⒶⓈⓀ 🆂🔟 ⓧ ⓜ 🗐 🔳 🍴 🔲 🏊

## BURLINGAME

**▼▼▼▼ Crowne Plaza LH ✷**
(650) 342-9200. **$89-$149.** 1177 Airport Blvd. US 101, exit Broadway-Burlingame or Old Bayshore, just e. Int corridors. **Pets:** Large, other species. $100 deposit/room. Designated rooms, service with restrictions, supervision.
ⒶⓈⓀ 🆂🔟 ⓧ ⓜ 🗐 🔳 🍴 🔲 🍴 🏊

**♦♦♦ ▼▼▼▼ DoubleTree Hotel-San Francisco Airport LH ✷**
(650) 344-5500. **$89-$189.** 835 Airport Blvd. US 101, exit Broadway-Burlingame or Anza Blvd, just e. Int corridors. **Pets:** Medium, other species. $20 one-time fee/room. Designated rooms, service with restrictions.
SAVE 🆂🔟 ⓧ ⓜ 🗐 🔳 🍴 🔲 🍴

**▼▼ Red Roof Inn M**
(650) 342-7772. **$65-$100.** 777 Airport Blvd. US 101, exit Broadway-Burlingame or E Anza Blvd; just s of airport. Ext corridors. **Pets:** Accepted.
ⓧ ⓜ 🗐 🔳 🏊

**▼▼▼ ♦♦♦♦ San Francisco Airport Marriott LH**
(650) 692-9100. **$104-$179.** 1800 Old Bayshore Hwy. US 101, exit Millbrae Ave, just e. Int corridors. **Pets:** Accepted.
ⒶⓈⓀ 🆂🔟 ⓧ ⓜ 🗐 🔳 🍴 🔲 🍴 🏊 🔲

**♦♦♦ ▼▼▼▼ Sheraton Gateway Hotel-San Francisco International Airport LH ✷**
(650) 340-8500. **$159-$209.** 600 Airport Blvd. US 101, exit Broadway-Burlingame or Anza Blvd, 0.3 mi e. Int corridors. **Pets:** Dogs only. Supervision.
SAVE 🆂🔟 ⓧ ⓜ 🗐 🔳 🔲 🍴 🏊

**♦♦♦ ▼▼ Vagabond Inn-SFO M**
(650) 692-4040. **$59-$99.** 1640 Bayshore Hwy. US 101, exit Millbrae Ave, just e. Ext corridors. **Pets:** Small. $10 daily fee/pet. Designated rooms, service with restrictions, supervision.
SAVE 🆂🔟 ⓧ ⓜ 🔳 🔲

## CORTE MADERA

**♦♦♦ ▼▼ Marin Suites Hotel SH**
(415) 924-3608. **$154-$204.** 45 Tamal Vista Blvd. US 101, exit Tamalpais Rd/Paradise Dr. Ext corridors. **Pets:** Other species. $10 daily fee/pet. Service with restrictions, supervision.
SAVE 🆂🔟 ⓧ ⓜ 🔳 🔲 🏊 🕱

## HALF MOON BAY

**♦♦♦ ▼▼▼▼ Comfort Inn Half Moon Bay SH ✷**
(650) 712-1999. **$79-$159.** 2930 N Cabrillo Hwy. On SR 1. Ext corridors. **Pets:** Large, other species. $20 daily fee/room. Service with restrictions, supervision.
SAVE 🆂🔟 ⓧ ⓜ 🔳 🍴 🔲

**♦♦♦ ▼▼ Harbor View Inn M**
(650) 726-2329. **$86-$186.** 51 Ave Alhambra. 4 mi n of jct SR 92 and 1; e of SR 1. Ext corridors. **Pets:** Accepted.
SAVE 🆂🔟 ⓧ ⓜ 🍴 🕱

**♦♦♦ ▼▼▼▼ Holiday Inn Express M ✷**
(650) 726-3400. **$89-$149.** 230 S Cabrillo Hwy. On SR 1, just s of SR 92. Ext corridors. **Pets:** Large. $10 daily fee/pet. Designated rooms, service with restrictions, supervision.
SAVE 🆂🔟 ⓧ ⓜ 🍴 🔲

**▼▼▼ Ramada Limited M**
(650) 726-9700. **$69-$275.** 3020 N Cabrillo Hwy. 2 mi n of jct SR 92 and 1; w of SR 1. Ext corridors. **Pets:** Accepted.
ⒶⓈⓀ 🆂🔟 ⓧ ⓜ 🔲

**▼▼▼▼ ▼▼ The Ritz-Carlton, Half Moon Bay LH ✷**
(650) 712-7000. **$295-$395, 7 day notice.** 1 Miramontes Point Rd. 3 mi s of jct SR 92 and 1; w of SR 1 at Miramontes Point Rd. Ext/int corridors. **Pets:** Small. $100 one-time fee/room. Designated rooms, service with restrictions, supervision.
ⒶⓈⓀ ⓧ 🔳 🍴 🏊 🕱

## MILLBRAE

**♦♦♦ ▼▼▼▼ Clarion Hotel-San Francisco Airport LH**
(650) 692-6363. **$148.** 401 E Millbrae Ave. US 101, exit Millbrae Ave, just e. Int corridors. **Pets:** Medium, other species. Designated rooms, service with restrictions, supervision.
SAVE 🆂🔟 ⓧ ⓜ 🔳 🔲 🍴 🏊

▼▼▼ The Westin Hotel-San Francisco Airport 🏨 ❖
(650) 692-3500. **$329.** 1 Old Bayshore Hwy. Just e of US 101, exit Millbrae Ave. Int corridors. **Pets:** Medium, dogs only. Supervision.
[A$K] [✕] [&M] [🐾] [🛋] [💻] [🍴] [🏊] [✕]

## SAN BRUNO

🔷🔷🔷 ▼▼▼ Regency Inn Ⓜ
(650) 589-7535. **$69-$99.** 411 E San Bruno Ave. US 101, exit San Bruno Ave, 0.4 mi w. Ext corridors. **Pets:** Other species. $15 daily fee/pet. Service with restrictions, supervision.
[SAVE] [S🐾] [✕] [&M] [🛋] [💻]

🔷🔷🔷 ▼▼▼▼ Staybridge Suites Ⓜ
(650) 588-0770. **$149-$199.** 1350 Huntington Ave. I-380, exit El Camino Real N, e on Sneath Ln. Ext corridors. **Pets:** Large, other species. $150 one-time fee/room.
[SAVE] [S🐾] [✕] [&M] [🛋] [💻] [🏊] [✕]

## SAN CARLOS

▼▼ ▼▼ Homestead Studio Suites Hotel-San
    Carlos-Downtown Ⓜ
(650) 368-2600. **$86.** 3 Circle Star Way. US 101, exit Whipple Ave, w to Industrial, then just n. Int corridors. **Pets:** $25 daily fee/pet. Service with restrictions, supervision.
[A$K] [S🐾] [✕] [&M] [🛋] [💻]

## SAN FRANCISCO

🔷🔷🔷 ▼▼▼ ▼▼▼ Argonaut Hotel 🏨 ❖
(415) 563-0800. **$139-$269.** 495 Jefferson St. Fisherman's Wharf; adjacent to The Cannery. Int corridors. **Pets:** Small. $50 deposit/pet. Designated rooms, service with restrictions, supervision.
[SAVE] [S🐾] [✕] [&M] [🛋] [💻] [🍴]

▼▼▼ Beresford Arms 🆂🅷 ❖
(415) 673-2600. **$99-$119.** 701 Post St. 3 blks w of Union Square. Int corridors. **Pets:** Other species. Designated rooms, service with restrictions, supervision.
[A$K] [S🐾] [✕] [&M] [🛋] [💻] [🐾]

🔷🔷🔷 ▼▼▼◆ Best Western Tuscan Inn at Fisherman's
    Wharf 🆂🅷 ❖
(415) 561-1100. **$139-$239.** 425 Northpoint St. Just s of Fisherman's Wharf at Mason St. Int corridors. **Pets:** Medium, other species. Designated rooms, service with restrictions, supervision.
[SAVE] [S🐾] [✕] [🐾] [💻] [🍴]

🔷🔷🔷 ▼▼ ▼▼ Campton Place Hotel 🆂🅷
(415) 781-5555. **$345-$480.** 340 Stockton St. Just n of Union Square. Int corridors. **Pets:** Accepted.
[A$K] [S🐾] [✕] [🛋] [🍴]

🔷🔷🔷 ▼▼ ▼▼ Cartwright Hotel 🆂🅷 ❖
(415) 421-2865. **$125-$269.** 524 Sutter St. Union Square at Powell St. Int corridors. **Pets:** Large, other species. Service with restrictions.
[SAVE] [S🐾] [✕] [🛋] [💻]

🔷🔷🔷 ▼▼◆▼ Comfort Inn by the Bay 🆂🅷
(415) 928-5000. **$79-$225.** 2775 Van Ness Ave. On US 101 (Van Ness Ave) at Lombard St. Int corridors. **Pets:** Accepted.
[SAVE] [S🐾] [✕] [♿] [🛋] [🛋] [💻]

🔷🔷🔷 ▼▼◆▼ Crowne Plaza Union Square 🏨
(415) 398-8900. **$129-$269.** 480 Sutter St. Just n off Union Square; corner of Powell St. Int corridors. **Pets:** Accepted.
[SAVE] [✕] [&M] [🐾] [🛋] [🛋] [💻] [🍴]

▼▼◆▼ Diva Hotel 🆂🅷
(415) 885-0200. **$129-$199.** 440 Geary St. Just w of Union Square. Int corridors. **Pets:** Accepted.
[A$K] [S🐾] [✕] [🍴]

🔷🔷🔷 ▼▼▼ Executive Hotel Vintage Court 🆂🅷
(415) 392-4666. **$199-$329.** 650 Bush St. 2 blks n of Union Square. Int corridors. **Pets:** Accepted.
[SAVE] [S🐾] [✕] [&M]

▼▼▼▼ The Fairmont San Francisco 🏨 ❖
(415) 772-5000. **$199-$389.** 950 Mason St. Atop Nob Hill at California St. Int corridors. **Pets:** Small, other species. $25 daily fee/room. Service with restrictions.
[A$K] [✕] [&M] [🐾] [🛋] [🍴]

▼▼▼▼ Four Seasons Hotel San Francisco 🏨
(415) 633-3000. **$435-$480.** 757 Market St. Between 3rd and 4th sts. Int corridors. **Pets:** Accepted.
[A$K] [✕] [&M] [🛋] [🍴] [🏊] [✕]

🔷🔷🔷 ▼▼▼▼ Harbor Court Hotel 🆂🅷
(415) 882-1300. **$159-$309.** 165 Steuart St. On Embarcadero; between Howard and Mission sts. Int corridors. **Pets:** Accepted.
[SAVE] [S🐾] [✕] [&M] [🍴] [🐾]

🔷🔷🔷 ▼▼▼▼ Holiday Inn Civic Center 🏨
(415) 626-6103. **$85-$169.** 50 8th St. 2 blks from civic auditorium; just s of Market St and BART Station. Int corridors. **Pets:** Accepted.
[SAVE] [✕] [&M] [🐾] [🛋] [🛋] [🍴] [🐾]

🔷🔷🔷 ▼▼▼▼ Holiday Inn Fisherman's Wharf 🏨
(415) 771-9000. **$109-$229.** 1300 Columbus Ave. Jct North Point St. Int corridors. **Pets:** Designated rooms, service with restrictions, crate.
[SAVE] [✕] [&M] [🐾] [🛋] [🛋] [💻] [🍴] [🐾]

▼▼▼ Hotel Beresford 🆂🅷 ❖
(415) 673-9900. **$89-$119.** 635 Sutter St. 1 blk nw of Union Square at Mason St. Int corridors. **Pets:** Other species. Designated rooms, service with restrictions, supervision.
[A$K] [S🐾] [✕] [&M] [🍴] [🐾]

▼▼▼ Hotel Metropolis 🆂🅷 ❖
(415) 775-4600. **$85-$159.** 25 Mason St. US 101 (Van Ness Ave), exit Market St, just w. Int corridors. **Pets:** Medium, other species. $50 one-time fee/room. Service with restrictions, supervision.
[A$K] [S🐾] [✕] [🛋] [🛋] [🐾]

🔷🔷🔷 ▼▼▼ ▼▼▼ Hotel Monaco 🏨 ❖
(415) 292-0100. **$209-$299.** 501 Geary St. Just w of Union Square at Taylor St. Int corridors. **Pets:** Other species. Designated rooms, service with restrictions, crate.
[SAVE] [S🐾] [✕] [&M] [🛋] [💻] [🍴] [✕]

🔷🔷🔷 ▼▼▼ ▼▼▼ Hotel Nikko San Francisco 🏨
(415) 394-1111. **$185-$380.** 222 Mason St. Just w of Union Square. Int corridors. **Pets:** Accepted.
[SAVE] [✕] [&M] [🐾] [💻] [🍴] [🏊] [✕]

🔷🔷🔷 ▼▼▼ ▼▼▼ Hotel Palomar 🆂🅷 ❖
(415) 348-1111. **$149-$449.** 12 4th St. At Market St; downtown. Int corridors. **Pets:** Designated rooms, service with restrictions, supervision.
[SAVE] [✕] [&M] [🛋] [🛋] [🍴]

🔷🔷🔷 ▼▼▼ ▼▼▼ Hotel Triton 🆂🅷
(415) 394-0500. **$149-$259.** 342 Grant Ave. Near Union Square at Bush St. Int corridors. **Pets:** Accepted.
[SAVE] [S🐾] [✕] [&M]

▼▼◆▼ Hotel Union Square 🆂🅷
(415) 397-3000. **$89-$209.** 114 Powell St. US 101 (Van Ness Ave), exit Market St E to Powell St; just n of cable car turnaround. Int corridors. **Pets:** Accepted.
[A$K] [S🐾] [✕] [🍴]

▼▼▼ Kensington Park Hotel 🆂🅷
(415) 788-6400. **$125-$205.** 450 Post St. US 101 (Van Ness Ave), exit 5th St, right to Ellis St, right on Taylor St. Int corridors. **Pets:** Accepted.
[A$K] [S🐾] [✕] [🛋] [🍴] [🍴]

▼▼▼ **La Quinta Inn & Suites** 🆂🅷
(415) 673-4711. **$79-$159.** 1050 Van Ness Ave. On US 101 (Van Ness Ave). Int corridors. **Pets:** Accepted.
[A$K] [✕] [💻]

🆂 ▼▼▼▼ **The Laurel Inn** 🆂🅷 ❖
(415) 567-8467. **$165-$190.** 444 Presidio Ave. 1 mi w of US 101 (Van Ness Ave); 1 mi e of Park Presidio Blvd (SR 1) at California St. Int corridors. **Pets:** Service with restrictions, supervision.
[SAVE] [✕] [👪] [🖉] [🛏] [💻] [🐾]

▼▼▼ ▼▼▼ **Mandarin Oriental, San Francisco** 🅻🅷 ❖
(415) 276-9888. **$505-$775.** 222 Sansome St. US 101, 1.2 mi e on Bush St, then just n. Int corridors. **Pets:** Small, dogs only. $25 one-time fee/pet. Service with restrictions, supervision.
[A$K] [✕] [🖉] [📶] [🛏] [💻] [🍽]

🆂 ▼▼▼▼ **Monticello Inn** 🆂🅷
(415) 392-8800. **$199-$249.** 127 Ellis St. Just w of Union Square. Int corridors. **Pets:** Accepted.
[SAVE] [🆂] [✕] [💻] [🍽]

▼▼▼ ▼▼▼ **Omni San Francisco Hotel** 🅻🅷 ❖
(415) 677-9494. **$189-$599.** 500 California St. At Montgomery St; in financial district. Int corridors. **Pets:** Small. $50 one-time fee/room. Service with restrictions, crate.
[A$K] [🆂] [✕] [👪] [📶] [💻] [🍽]

▼▼ ▼▼ **Pacific Heights Inn** 🅼
(415) 776-3310. **$69-$150.** 1555 Union St. Just w of US 101 (Van Ness Ave). Ext corridors. **Pets:** Medium. $10 daily fee/room. Service with restrictions, supervision.
[A$K] [✕] [👪] [📶] [🛏] [💻] [🐾]

▼▼▼ ▼▼▼ **Palace Hotel** 🅻🅷
(415) 512-1111. **$219-$539.** 2 New Montgomery St. Just e of Union Square at Market St. Int corridors. **Pets:** Accepted.
[A$K] [✕] [🖉] [📶] [🍽] [🏊] [🚫]

▼▼▼ ▼▼▼ **Pan Pacific Hotel San Francisco** 🅻🅷
(415) 771-8600. **$159-$400.** 500 Post St. Just w of Union Square at Mason St. Int corridors. **Pets:** Small. $75 one-time fee/pet. Designated rooms, service with restrictions, supervision.
[A$K] [🆂] [✕] [👪] [📶] [💻] [🍽]

🆂 ▼▼▼▼ **The Prescott Hotel** 🆂🅷 ❖
(415) 563-0303. **$169-$360.** 545 Post St. Just w of Union Square. Int corridors. **Pets:** Medium. Service with restrictions, supervision.
[SAVE] [✕] [🍽]

▼▼▼ ▼▼▼ **San Francisco Marriott Fisherman's Wharf** 🅻🅷
(415) 775-7555. **$149-$229.** 1250 Columbus Ave. Just s of Fisherman's Wharf at Bay St. Int corridors. **Pets:** Accepted.
[SAVE] [🆂] [✕] [👪] [🖉] [📶] [🛏] [💻] [🍽]

▼▼▼ ▼▼▼ **Serrano Hotel** 🆂🅷
(415) 885-2500. **$149-$259.** 405 Taylor St. Just w of Union Square at O'Farrell St. Int corridors. **Pets:** Accepted.
[SAVE] [🆂] [✕] [👪] [📶] [🍽] [🚫]

▼▼▼ ▼▼▼▼ **Sheraton Fisherman's Wharf** 🅻🅷 ❖
(415) 362-5500. **$119-$299.** 2500 Mason St. Just se of Fisherman's Wharf at Beach St. Int corridors. **Pets:** Large, dogs only. Service with restrictions, supervision.
[SAVE] [🆂] [✕] [👪] [🖉] [📶] [🛏] [💻] [🍽] [🏊]

🆂 ▼▼▼ **Sir Francis Drake Hotel** 🅻🅷
(415) 392-7755. **$139-$239.** 450 Powell St. Just off Union Square at Sutter St. Int corridors. **Pets:** Accepted.
[SAVE] [🆂] [✕] [🍽]

🆂 ▼▼▼▼ **The Stanford Court, A Renaissance Hotel** 🅻🅷
(415) 989-3500. **$169-$259.** 905 California St. Atop Nob Hill; corner of California and Powell sts. Int corridors. **Pets:** Accepted.
[SAVE] [🆂] [✕] [👪] [🖉] [📶] [🛏] [🍽]

▼▼ ▼▼ **Travelodge By The Bay** 🅼
(415) 673-0691. **$69-$139.** 1450 Lombard St. On US 101. Ext corridors. **Pets:** Dogs only. $20 daily fee/pet. Designated rooms, service with restrictions, supervision.
[SAVE] [✕] [👪] [📶] [🛏] [💻]

🆂 ▼▼▼ **Villa Florence Hotel** 🆂🅷
(415) 397-7000. **$229-$259.** 225 Powell St. Just s of Union Square; between O'Farrell and Geary sts. Int corridors. **Pets:** Accepted.
[SAVE] [🆂] [✕] [🖉] [💻] [🍽]

🆂 ▼▼▼ ▼▼▼ **The Westin St. Francis** 🅻🅷 ❖
(415) 397-7000. **$149-$489.** 335 Powell St. On Union Square. **Pets:** Medium, dogs only. $75 one-time fee/room. Supervision.
[SAVE] [🆂] [✕] [📶] [🛏] [💻] [🍽] [🚫]

## SAN MATEO

▼▼ ▼▼ **Homestead Studio Suites Hotel-San Francisco-San Mateo-SFO** 🅼
(650) 574-1744. **$86.** 1830 Gateway Dr. SR 92, exit Edgewater Blvd; se of jct US 101 and SR 92. Ext corridors. **Pets:** $25 daily fee/pet. Service with restrictions, supervision.
[A$K] [🆂] [✕] [👪] [📶] [🛏] [💻]

▼▼▼ ▼▼▼ **Radisson Villa Hotel** 🆂🅷
(650) 341-0966. **$79-$179.** 4000 S El Camino Real. US 101, exit W Hillsdale Blvd, 0.5 mi s on SR 82; 8 mi s of San Francisco International Airport. Ext/int corridors. **Pets:** Accepted.
[SAVE] [🆂] [✕] [👪] [📶] [🛏] [💻] [🍽] [🏊]

▼▼ ▼▼ **Residence Inn by Marriott** 🅼 ❖
(650) 574-4700. **$159-$189.** 2000 Winward Way. 0.8 mi se from jct US 101 and SR 92; exit SR 92 via Edgewater Blvd. Ext corridors. **Pets:** Medium. $75 one-time fee/pet. Service with restrictions, supervision.
[A$K] [🆂] [✕] [👪] [📶] [🛏] [💻] [🏊] [🚫]

## SAN RAFAEL

▼▼ ▼▼ **Villa Inn** 🅼
(415) 456-4975. **$69-$79.** 1600 Lincoln Ave. Off US 101 at Lincoln Ave off-ramp; exit Central San Rafael northbound, 0.3 mi w on 4th St, then 0.5 mi n. Ext corridors. **Pets:** Medium, dogs only. $20 deposit/room. Designated rooms, service with restrictions, supervision.
[A$K] [🆂] [✕] [👪] [📶] [🛏] [💻] [🏊]

## SOUTH SAN FRANCISCO

▼▼▼ ▼▼ **Howard Johnson Express Inn** 🅼
(650) 589-9055. **$49-$109.** 222 S Airport Blvd. US 101, exit S Airport Blvd, just e. Ext corridors. **Pets:** Accepted.
[SAVE] [🆂] [✕] [📶] [🛏] [💻]

▼▼▼ ▼▼▼ **La Quinta Inn San Francisco (Airport)** 🅼
(650) 583-2223. **$92-$132.** 20 S Airport Blvd. US 101, exit S Airport Blvd, just w. Int corridors. **Pets:** Medium. Service with restrictions.
[SAVE] [✕] [👪] [📶] [🛏] [💻] [🏊]

## END METROPOLITAN AREA

# SAN JOSE

**(AAA)** ▼▼▼ **Best Western Gateway Inn** 🆂🅷
(408) 435-8800. **$89-$99.** 2585 Seaboard Ave. US 101, exit Trimble Rd E; 1 mi ne of San Jose International Airport. Int corridors. **Pets:** Small. $100 deposit/room. Designated rooms, service with restrictions, supervision.
🆂🅰🆅🅴 🆂🔟 ☒ 🅼 ⬛ ⬜ 🍴 ➰

**(AAA)** ▼▼▼ **Crowne Plaza Hotel and Resort San Jose** 🅻🅷
(408) 998-0400. **$79-$189.** 282 Almaden Blvd. 6 blks n off I-280, exit Almaden-Vine. Int corridors. **Pets:** Accepted.
🆂🅰🆅🅴 🆂🔟 ☒ 🅼 🅼 ⬛ ⬜ 🍴

**(AAA)** ▼▼▼▼ **DoubleTree Hotel San Jose** 🅻🅷
(408) 453-4000. **$89-$289.** 2050 Gateway Pl. 0.3 mi e of San Jose International Airport via Airport Blvd; w of US 101, exit N 1st St; US 101 northbound, exit Brokaw Rd. Int corridors. **Pets:** Large. $50 deposit/room. Service with restrictions, supervision.
🆂🅰🆅🅴 🆂🔟 ☒ ⬛ ⬜ 🍴 ➰

**▼▼▼▼ Extended Stay Deluxe** 🆂🅷
(408) 453-3000. **$79-$199.** 55 E Brokaw Rd. US 101, exit 1st St/Brokaw Rd, just e. Int corridors. **Pets:** $25 daily fee/pet. Service with restrictions, supervision.
🅰🆂🅺 🆂🔟 ☒ 🅼 ⬜ ➰

**▼▼▼▼ The Fairmont San Jose** 🅻🅷
(408) 998-1900. **$136-$289.** 170 S Market St. At Fairmont Plaza. Int corridors. **Pets:** Accepted.
🅰🆂🅺 🆂🔟 ☒ 🍴 ➰ ⊠

**(AAA)** ▼▼▼▼ **Hilton San Jose** 🅻🅷
(408) 287-2100. **$89-$299.** 300 Almaden Blvd. Downtown. Int corridors. **Pets:** Medium, other species. $100 deposit/pet. Service with restrictions, supervision.
🆂🅰🆅🅴 🆂🔟 ☒ 🅼 ⬛ ⬜ 🍴 ➰

**▼▼ Homestead Studio Suites Hotel-San Jose-Downtown** 🆂🅷
(408) 573-0648. **$100.** 1560 N 1st St. 1 mi e of San Jose International Airport; US 101, exit N 1st St, then s. Int corridors. **Pets:** $25 daily fee/pet. Service with restrictions, supervision.
🅰🆂🅺 🆂🔟 ☒ ⬜

**▼▼▼▼ Homewood Suites by Hilton** 🆂🅷
(408) 428-9900. **$149-$225.** 10 W Trimble Rd. 2 mi n of San Jose International Airport; US 101, exit Trimble Rd, 1.3 mi e. Ext/int corridors. **Pets:** Small, dogs only. $50 one-time fee/room. Service with restrictions.
🅰🆂🅺 ☒ 🅼 🅼 ⬜ ➰ ⊠

**(AAA)** ▼▼▼▼ **Hotel De Anza** 🅻🅷
(408) 286-1000. **$99-$399.** 233 W Santa Clara St. Downtown. Int corridors. **Pets:** Small. $30 one-time fee/room. Service with restrictions.
🆂🅰🆅🅴 🆂🔟 ☒ ⬜ 🍴

**(AAA)** ▼▼▼ **Howard Johnson Express Inn** Ⓜ
(408) 280-5300. **$69-$159.** 1215 S 1st St. Jct I-280 and SR 82, 0.8 mi s. Ext corridors. **Pets:** Accepted.
🆂🅰🆅🅴 🆂🔟 ☒ ⬛ ⬜

**▼▼▼▼ Residence Inn by Marriott** 🆂🅷
(408) 226-7676. **$163-$189.** 6111 San Ignacio Ave. US 101, exit Bernal Rd, then e. Int corridors. **Pets:** Medium, other species. $75 one-time fee/room. Service with restrictions, crate.
🅰🆂🅺 🆂🔟 ☒ 🅼 🅼 ⬛ ⬜ ➰ ⊠

**(AAA)** ▼▼▼▼ **Staybridge Suites San Jose** Ⓜ
(408) 436-1600. **$99-$169.** 1602 Crane Ct. US 101, exit 1st St/Brokaw Rd, 0.4 mi e to Bering S, then 0.5 mi. Ext corridors. **Pets:** Accepted.
🆂🅰🆅🅴 🆂🔟 ☒ ⬛ ⬜ ➰

**▼▼▼▼ TownePlace Suites by Marriott San Jose/Cupertino** 🆂🅷
(408) 984-5903. **$89-$149.** 440 Saratoga Ave. I-280, exit Saratoga Ave, just n. Int corridors. **Pets:** Accepted.
🅰🆂🅺 🆂🔟 ☒ ⬜ ➰

**(AAA)** ▼▼▼ **Vagabond Inn San Jose** Ⓜ
(408) 453-8822. **$69-$99.** 1488 N 1st St. I-880, exit N 1st St, then w. Ext corridors. **Pets:** Accepted.
🆂🅰🆅🅴 🆂🔟 ☒ ⬛ ⬜ ➰

# SAN JUAN BAUTISTA

**(AAA)** ▼▼▼ **San Juan Inn** Ⓜ
(831) 623-4380. **$69-$99.** 410 The Alameda. Jct SR 156. Ext corridors. **Pets:** Other species. $15 daily fee/pet. Designated rooms.
🆂🅰🆅🅴 🆂🔟 ☒ ⬛ ⬜ ➰

# SAN JUAN CAPISTRANO

**(AAA)** ▼▼▼ **Best Western Capistrano Inn** Ⓜ
(949) 493-5661. **$80-$180.** 27174 Ortega Hwy. I-5, exit SR 74 (Ortega Hwy), just e. Ext corridors. **Pets:** Other species. $25 one-time fee/room.
🆂🅰🆅🅴 🆂🔟 ☒ ⬛ ⬜ ➰

# SAN LUIS OBISPO

**(AAA)** ▼▼▼ **Best Western Royal Oak Hotel** Ⓜ 🐾
(805) 544-4410. **$79-$169.** 214 Madonna Rd. US 101, exit Madonna Rd, just s. Ext/int corridors. **Pets:** Large. $10 one-time fee/pet. Service with restrictions, supervision.
🆂🅰🆅🅴 🆂🔟 ☒ 🅼 🎵 🦽 ⬛ ⬜ ➰

**(AAA)** ▼▼▼ **Days Inn** Ⓜ 🐾
(805) 549-9911. **$59-$199.** 2050 Garfield St. US 101, exit Monterey St, just sw. Ext corridors. **Pets:** Medium, dogs only. $10 daily fee/pet. Designated rooms, service with restrictions, supervision.
🆂🅰🆅🅴 🆂🔟 ☒ 🅼 🎵 🦽 ⬛ ⬜ ➰ ⊠

**▼▼▼ Heritage Inn Bed & Breakfast** 🅱🅱
(805) 544-7440. **$85-$150, 7 day notice.** 978 Olive St. US 101, exit SR 1/Morro Bay northbound, just w on Santa Rosa St, then just s; exit Santa Rosa St southbound, just ne. Int corridors. **Pets:** Small, other species. $25 one-time fee/pet. Designated rooms, service with restrictions, supervision.
☒ 🧥 🕎 �️

**▼▼▼ Holiday Inn Express** 🆂🅷
(805) 544-8600. **$89-$149.** 1800 Monterey St. US 101, exit Monterey St, just w. Int corridors. **Pets:** Accepted.
🅰🆂🅺 🆂🔟 ☒ 🅼 🎵 🦽 ⬛ ⬜ ➰

**(AAA)** ▼▼▼ **Ramada Inn Olive Tree** Ⓜ
(805) 544-2800. **$59-$199.** 1000 Olive St. US 101, exit SR 1/Morro Bay northbound, just w on Santa Rosa St, then just s; exit Santa Rosa St southbound, just ne. Ext corridors. **Pets:** Small, dogs only. $50 deposit/pet, $10 daily fee/pet. Designated rooms, service with restrictions, supervision.
🆂🅰🆅🅴 🆂🔟 ☒ 🅼 🎵 🦽 ⬛ ⬜ ➰

**(AAA)** ▼▼▼ **Sands Suites & Motel** Ⓜ
(805) 544-0500. **$59-$219.** 1930 Monterey St. US 101, exit Monterey St, just sw. Ext corridors. **Pets:** Other species. $10 one-time fee/pet. Designated rooms, service with restrictions, supervision.
🆂🅰🆅🅴 🆂🔟 ☒ 🅼 ⬛ ⬜ ➰

**▼▼▼ San Luis Creek Lodge** 🆂🅷 🐾
(805) 541-1122. **$119-$299, 3 day notice.** 1941 Monterey St. US 101, exit Monterey St, just e. Ext/int corridors. **Pets:** Small, dogs only. $25 one-time fee/pet. Designated rooms, service with restrictions, supervision.
🅰🆂🅺 🆂🔟 ☒ 🅼 🦽 ⬛ ⬜

# SAN MARCOS

**▼▼▼▼ Lake San Marcos Resort** SH ❀
(760) 744-0120. **$129-$169.** 1025 La Bonita Dr. SR 78, exit Rancho Santa Fe Rd, 2 mi s, then 0.5 mi e via Lake San Marcos Dr and San Marino Dr; at Lake San Marcos. Ext/int corridors. **Pets:** Other species. $50 one-time fee/room. Designated rooms.

(ASK) (S🐾) ⊠ 🛏 🖵 🍴 🏊 ⊠

# SAN RAMON

**◆◆ Homestead Studio Suites Hotel-San Ramon-Bishop Ranch** M
(925) 277-0833. **$100.** 18000 San Ramon Valley Blvd. I-680, exit Bollinger Canyon Rd E, just n. Ext corridors. **Pets:** Service with restrictions, supervision.

(ASK) (S🐾) ⊠ 🛋 🛏 🖵

**▼▼▼ Residence Inn by Marriott** M
(925) 277-9292. **$89-$234.** 1071 Market Pl. I-680, exit Bollinger Canyon Rd E, 0.5 mi e. Ext corridors. **Pets:** Large, other species. $75 one-time fee/room. Service with restrictions.

(ASK) (S🐾) ⊠ 🛋 🛏 🖵 🏊 ⊠

**▼▼▼ San Ramon Marriott at Bishop Ranch** LH
(925) 867-9200. **$79-$229.** 2600 Bishop Dr. I-680, exit Bollinger Canyon Rd E, n on Sunset, then just w. Int corridors. **Pets:** Accepted.

(ASK) ⊠ 🛏 🖵 🍴 🏊 ⊠

**▼▼▼▼ Sierra Suites Hotel San Ramon** SH
(925) 743-1882. **$89-$199.** 2323 San Ramon Valley Blvd. I-680, exit Crow Canyon Rd W, just n. Int corridors. **Pets:** Accepted.

(ASK) (S🐾) ⊠ (&M) 🛋 🛏 🖵

# SAN SIMEON

**▼▼▼ California Seacoast Lodge** SH
(805) 927-3878. **$79-$229, 3 day notice.** 9215 Hearst Dr. Just w of SR 1. Int corridors. **Pets:** Accepted.

⊠ 🛏 🖵 🏊 🐾

**◆◆◆ ▼▼▼ Courtesy Inn** M
(805) 927-4691. **$50-$110.** 9450 Castillo Dr. East side of SR 1. Ext corridors. **Pets:** Dogs only. $10 one-time fee/pet. Service with restrictions, supervision.

(SAVE) (S🐾) ⊠ 🛏 🖵 🏊

**▼▼ Motel 6 Premiere–1212** SH
(805) 927-8691. **$45-$78.** 9070 Castillo Dr. Just e of SR 1. Int corridors. **Pets:** Accepted.

(S🐾) ⊠ (&M) 🚭 🛋 🛏 🍴 🏊

**▼▼ San Simeon Lodge** SH
(805) 927-4601. **$55-$210.** 9520 Castillo Dr. On SR 1. Ext corridors. **Pets:** Medium. $10 daily fee/pet. Designated rooms, supervision.

(ASK) (S🐾) ⊠ 🛏 🖵 🍴 🏊 🐾

**◆◆◆ ▼▼▼ Silver Surf Motel** M
(805) 927-4661. **$39-$186.** 9390 Castillo Dr. Just e of SR 1. Ext corridors. **Pets:** Other species. $10 daily fee/pet. Designated rooms, service with restrictions, supervision.

(SAVE) (S🐾) ⊠ 🛏 🖵 🏊 🐾

# SANTA ANA

**▼▼ Motel 6 #738** M
(714) 558-0500. **$44-$59.** 1623 E 1st St. I-5, exit 4th St, just s on Mabury St, then just w. Ext corridors. **Pets:** Accepted.

(S🐾) ⊠

**▼▼▼ Red Roof Inn** M
(714) 542-0311. **$54-$84.** 2600 N Main St. I-5, exit Main St, 0.3 mi n. Ext/int corridors. **Pets:** Accepted.

(ASK) (S🐾) ⊠ 🛏 🏊

# SANTA BARBARA

**◆◆◆ ▼▼▼ Best Western Beachside Inn** M
(805) 965-6556. **$145-$299.** 336 W Cabrillo Blvd. US 101, exit Bath St northbound, just w on Haley St to Castillo St, then 0.4 mi s; exit Castillo St southbound, 0.3 mi s. Ext corridors. **Pets:** Other species. $20 daily fee/pet. Service with restrictions, supervision.

(SAVE) ⊠ 🛏 🖵 🏊

**◆◆◆ ▼▼ Blue Sands Motel** M
(805) 965-1624. **$85-$239, 3 day notice.** 421 S Milpas St. US 101, exit Milpas St, 0.3 mi s. Ext corridors. **Pets:** Accepted.

(SAVE) (S🐾) ⊠ 🛏 🖵 🏊 🐾

**▼▼▼▼▼ Four Seasons Biltmore Santa Barbara** LH
(805) 969-2261. **$650-$700, 3 day notice.** 1260 Channel Dr. US 101, exit Olive Mill Rd, 0.3 mi s. Ext/int corridors. **Pets:** Accepted.

(ASK) ⊠ 🛏 🖵 🍴 🏊 ⊠

**◆◆◆ ▼▼▼ Harbor House Inn** M ❀
(805) 962-9745. **$109-$275.** 104 Bath St. US 101, exit Cabrillo Blvd (left hand exit), 3 mi n, then just e; exit Castillo St southbound, 0.4 mi w, just s on Cabrillo Blvd, then just e. Ext corridors. **Pets:** $15 daily fee/pet. Designated rooms, service with restrictions, supervision.

(SAVE) (S🐾) ⊠ 🛏 🖵 🐾

**◆◆◆ ▼▼▼▼ Hotel MarMonte** LH
(805) 963-0744. **$169-$359, 3 day notice.** 1111 E Cabrillo Blvd. US 101, exit Milpas St, 0.3 mi s, then just e. Int corridors. **Pets:** Dogs only. $75 one-time fee/room. Designated rooms, service with restrictions, crate.

(SAVE) ⊠ (&M) 🚭 🛋 🛏 🖵 🍴 🏊 ⊠

**▼▼▼▼ Marina Beach Motel** M
(805) 963-9311. **$89-$269.** 21 Bath St. US 101, exit Garden St, 0.3 mi w to Cabrillo Blvd, 0.4 mi n to Bath St, then just e. Ext corridors. **Pets:** Small. $15 daily fee/pet. Designated rooms, supervision.

(ASK) (S🐾) ⊠ 🛏 🖵

**▼▼◆◆ Pacifica Suites** SH
(805) 683-6722. **$129-$279.** 5490 Hollister Ave. US 101, exit Patterson Ave, 0.5 mi s, then 0.5 mi w. Ext/int corridors. **Pets:** Accepted.

(ASK) (S🐾) ⊠ (&M) 🚭 🛋 🛏 🖵

**▼▼◆◆ The Parkside Inn** M
(805) 963-0744. **$99-$179, 3 day notice.** 424 Por La Mar. US 101, exit Milpas St, 0.3 mi s, just e on Cabrillo Blvd, then just n. Int corridors. **Pets:** Accepted.

(ASK) ⊠ 🛏 🖵 🏊 ⊠

# SANTA CATALINA ISLAND

**◆◆◆ ▼▼▼▼ Best Western Catalina Canyon Hotel & Spa** M
(310) 510-0325. **$79-$299, 3 day notice.** 888 Country Club Dr. 0.5 mi from the harbor via Sumner Ave. Ext corridors. **Pets:** Accepted.

(SAVE) (S🐾) ⊠ 🖵 🍴 🏊 ⊠

# SANTA CLARA

**▼▼▼▼ GuestHouse Inn & Suites** M
(408) 241-3010. **$69-$109, 3 day notice.** 2930 El Camino Real. SR 82, 0.5 mi w of San Tomas Expwy; US 101, exit S Bowers Ave. Ext corridors. **Pets:** Other species. $10 daily fee/pet.

(ASK) (S🐾) ⊠ (&M) 🛏 🖵 🏊

**▼▼ Ramada Limited** M
(408) 244-8313. **$65-$95.** 1655 El Camino Real. I-880, exit The Alameda, 2 mi w. Ext corridors. **Pets:** Accepted.

(ASK) (S🐾) ⊠ 🛏 🖵 🏊

**▼▼▼▼ Santa Clara Marriott Hotel** LH
(408) 988-1500. **$199-$249.** 2700 Mission College Blvd. 0.5 mi e off US 101, exit Great America Pkwy; 0.8 mi s of Great America Theme Park. Int corridors. **Pets:** Designated rooms, service with restrictions, crate.

(ASK) ⊠ (&M) 🚭 🛋 🛏 🖵 🍴 🏊 ⊠

▼▼▼▼ **Sierra Suites Hotel-Santa Clara** ⚏
(408) 486-0800. **$99-$209.** 3915 Rivermark Plaza. US 101, exit Montague Expwy E. Int corridors. **Pets:** Accepted.

🅰🆂🅺 ⑤ ⊠ 🅱 💻 ➿

**AAA** ▼▼▼ **The Vagabond Inn** Ⓜ
(408) 241-0771. **$39-$109.** 3580 El Camino Real. On SR 82, southeast corner of Lawrence Expwy cloverleaf. Ext corridors. **Pets:** Medium, other species. $10 daily fee/pet. Designated rooms, service with restrictions, supervision.

🆂🅰🆅🅴 ⑤ ⊠ 🅱 💻 ➿

▼▼ ▼▼ **Wellesley Inn (Santa Clara)** ⚏
(408) 257-8600. **$79-$99.** 5405 Stevens Creek Blvd. I-280 and Lawrence Expwy, exit Stevens Creek Blvd, just w. Int corridors. **Pets:** Small. $10 one-time fee/room. Service with restrictions, supervision.

🅰🆂🅺 ⑤ ⊠ 🅱 💻 ➿

▼▼▼ ▼▼▼ **The Westin Hotel-Santa Clara** Ⓛ
(408) 986-0700. **$109-$349.** 5101 Great America Pkwy. 0.8 mi e off US 101, exit Great America Pkwy. Int corridors. **Pets:** Accepted.

🅰🆂🅺 ⑤ ⊠ 🅼 ⊘ 🅱 💻 ⑪ ➿ ⊠

## SANTA CRUZ

**AAA** ▼▼▼ **Bay Front Inn** Ⓜ
(831) 423-8564. **$48-$250.** 325 Pacific Ave. 6 blks se of SR 1. Ext corridors. **Pets:** Other species. $10 daily fee/pet. Service with restrictions, supervision.

🆂🅰🆅🅴 ⑤ ⊠ 🅱 ➿

**AAA** ▼▼▼ **Continental Inn** Ⓜ
(831) 429-1221. **$75-$260.** 414 Ocean St. 5 blks from beach; between Broadway and Soquel aves. Ext corridors. **Pets:** Accepted.

🆂🅰🆅🅴 ⑤ ⊠ 🅱 💻 ➿

**AAA** ▼▼▼ **GuestHouse International Pacific Inn** Ⓜ
(831) 425-3722. **$60-$200 (no credit cards).** 330 Ocean St. 1 mi from jct SR 1 and 17. Int corridors. **Pets:** Medium, dogs only. $10 daily fee/pet. Designated rooms, service with restrictions, supervision.

🆂🅰🆅🅴 ⑤ ⊠ 🅱 💻 ➿

**AAA** ▼▼▼▼ **Hilton Santa Cruz/Scotts Valley** ⚏ ❀
(831) 440-1000. **$169-$329.** 6001 La Madrona Dr. SR 17, exit Mt. Hermon Rd. Int corridors. **Pets:** Dogs only. $25 daily fee/pet. Designated rooms, service with restrictions, supervision.

🆂🅰🆅🅴 ⊠ 🅼 ⑤ 🅱 💻 ⑪ ➿

**AAA** ▼▼▼ **The Inn at Pasatiempo** Ⓜ
(831) 423-5000. **$150-$220.** 555 Hwy 17. 0.8 mi n of jct SR 1 and 17; exit SR 17, exit Pasatiempo Dr. Ext corridors. **Pets:** Accepted.

🆂🅰🆅🅴 ⑤ ⊠ 🅱 💻 ⑪ ➿ 🏧

**AAA** ▼▼▼ **Ocean Pacific Lodge** Ⓜ
(831) 457-1234. **$70-$250.** 301 Pacific Ave. SR 1 and 17, exit Ocean St, 1 mi w to Broadway, turn right, left on Front St to Pacific Ave, then just right. Ext corridors. **Pets:** Accepted.

🆂🅰🆅🅴 ⑤ ⊠ 🅱 ➿

## SANTA MARIA

**AAA** ▼▼▼▼ **Best Western Big America** Ⓜ
(805) 922-5200. **$89-$149.** 1725 N Broadway. US 101, exit Broadway, 0.5 mi w. Ext corridors. **Pets:** Medium. Service with restrictions, supervision.

🆂🅰🆅🅴 ⑤ ⊠ 🅱 💻 ➿

▼▼▼▼ **Historic Santa Maria Inn** Ⓛ
(805) 928-7777. **$129-$169.** 801 S Broadway. US 101, exit Main St, 1 mi w, then 0.5 mi s. Int corridors. **Pets:** Medium. $50 one-time fee/pet. Service with restrictions, supervision.

🅰🆂🅺 ⑤ ⊠ 🅼 ⊘ 🅱 💻 ⑪ ➿ ⊠

**AAA** ▼▼▼▼ **Holiday Inn Hotel & Suites** Ⓛ
(805) 928-6000. **$120-$150.** 2100 N Broadway. US 101, exit Broadway, just w. Int corridors. **Pets:** Accepted.

🆂🅰🆅🅴 ⑤ ⊠ 🅼 ⊘ 🅱 💻 ⑪ ➿ ⊠

## SANTA NELLA

**AAA** ▼▼▼ **Comfort Inn** Ⓜ
(209) 827-8700. **$69-$85.** 28821 W Gonzaga Rd. 3 mi w of I-5; SR 152, exit Gonzaga Rd, just s. Ext corridors. **Pets:** Small, dogs only. $10 daily fee/pet. Designated rooms, service with restrictions, crate.

🆂🅰🆅🅴 ⑤ ⊠ 🅱 💻 ➿

**AAA** ▼▼▼▼ **Holiday Inn Express** Ⓜ
(209) 826-8282. **$75-$95.** 28976 W Plaza Dr. I-5, exit SR 33, just e. Ext corridors. **Pets:** Medium. $8 daily fee/room. Designated rooms, service with restrictions, supervision.

🆂🅰🆅🅴 ⑤ ⊠ 🅱 💻 ➿

**AAA** ▼▼▼ **Ramada Inn Mission de Oro** ⚏
(209) 826-4444. **$70-$95, 3 day notice.** 13070 Hwy 33 S. I-5, exit SR 33, just w. Ext/int corridors. **Pets:** Other species. $10 daily fee/room.

🆂🅰🆅🅴 ⑤ ⊠ 🅱 💻 ⑪ ➿

## SCOTTS VALLEY

▼▼▼▼ **Best Western Inn Scotts Valley** ⚏ ❀
(831) 438-6666. **$109-$145.** 6020 Scotts Valley Dr. SR 17, exit Granite Creek, just w. Ext corridors. **Pets:** Medium, dogs only. $100 deposit/pet. Designated rooms, service with restrictions, supervision.

⊠ 🅼 ⊘ 🅱 💻 ➿

## SELMA

**AAA** ▼▼ **Super 8 Motel** ⚏
(559) 896-2800. **$75-$110.** 3142 S Highland Ave. SR 99, exit Floral Ave. Int corridors. **Pets:** Accepted.

🆂🅰🆅🅴 ⑤ ⊠ 🅱 ➿

## SHASTA LAKE

**AAA** ▼▼▼ **Bridge Bay Resort** Ⓜ ❀
(530) 275-3021. **$78-$103, 3 day notice.** I-5, exit 690, e of I-5, exit Bridge Bay Rd; 12 mi n of Redding. Ext corridors. **Pets:** Medium. $50 deposit/pet, $10 daily fee/pet. Designated rooms, service with restrictions, supervision.

🆂🅰🆅🅴 ⑤ ⊠ 🅱 💻 ⑪ ➿ ⊠

**AAA** ▼▼▼ **Fawndale Lodge & RV Resort** Ⓜ ❀
(530) 275-8000. **$59-$83, 5 day notice.** I-5, exit 689, 1 mi s of Shasta Lake; e of I-5, exit Fawndale Rd; 10 mi n of Redding. Ext corridors. **Pets:** Supervision.

🆂🅰🆅🅴 ⑤ ⊠ 🅱 💻 ➿

## SHELTER COVE

**AAA** ▼▼▼▼ **Inn of the Lost Coast** Ⓜ
(707) 986-7524. **$135-$250.** 205 Wave Dr. US 101, exit Shelter Cove, 1.7 mi s on Redwood Dr, 21.1 mi w on Briceland Rd/Shelter Cove Rd, 0.4 mi n on Upper Pacific Rd, then just w on Lower Pacific Rd. Ext corridors. **Pets:** $10 daily fee/pet. Designated rooms, service with restrictions, supervision.

🆂🅰🆅🅴 ⑤ ⊠ 🅱 💻 ⑪ 🏧 🄴

## SIERRA CITY

**AAA** ▼▼▼ **Herrington's Sierra Pines** Ⓜ
(530) 862-1151. **$74-$105, 7 day notice.** 104 Main St. 0.5 mi w on SR 49; 12 mi n of Downieville Center. Ext corridors. **Pets:** Other species. Supervision.

🆂🅰🆅🅴 ⑤ ⊠ 🅱 💻 ⑪ ⊠ 🏧 🄴

# SMITH RIVER

**▼▼▼ Ship Ashore Motel M**
(707) 487-3141. **$69-$90.** 12370 Hwy 101. On US 101; 3.7 mi s of Oregon Stateline. Ext corridors. **Pets:** Accepted.
(SAVE) (S♠) (✕) (🛏) (💻) (🍴) (AC)

# SOLEDAD

**♦♦♦ ▼▼▼ Best Western Valley Harvest Inn M**
(831) 678-3833. **$89-$180.** 1155 Front St. US 101, exit Soledad, just e. Ext/int corridors. **Pets:** Small, dogs only. $10 daily fee/pet. Designated rooms, service with restrictions, supervision.
(SAVE) (S♠) (✕) (🛏) (💻) (🍴) (2~)

# SOLVANG

**▼▼▼ Meadowlark Inn M**
(805) 688-4631. **$125-$275, 7 day notice.** 2644 Mission Dr. On SR 246, 1.6 mi e. Ext corridors. **Pets:** Accepted.
(ASK) (✕) (🛏) (💻) (2~)

**♦♦♦ ▼▼▼ Royal Copenhagen Inn M ❀**
(805) 688-5561. **$65-$179, 3 day notice.** 1579 Mission Dr. On SR 246. Ext/int corridors. **Pets:** Other species. Designated rooms, service with restrictions, supervision.
(SAVE) (S♠) (✕) (🛏) (💻) (2~)

# SONORA

**♦♦♦ ▼▼▼ Aladdin Motor Inn SH**
(209) 533-4971. **$76-$79.** 14260 Mono Way (Hwy 108). On SR 108, 3.5 mi e. Ext/int corridors. **Pets:** Accepted.
(SAVE) (✕) (🛏) (💻) (2~)

**♦♦♦ ▼▼▼▼ Best Western Sonora Oaks M**
(209) 533-4400. **$99-$121.** 19551 Hess Ave. 3.5 mi e on SR 108. Ext/int corridors. **Pets:** $20 daily fee/pet. Designated rooms, service with restrictions, supervision.
(SAVE) (S♠) (✕) (🎜) (🛏) (💻) (2~)

**♦♦♦ ▼ Miners Motel M**
(209) 532-7850. **$59-$75, 3 day notice.** 18740 SR 108. On SR 108 and 49, 1 mi e of Jamestown. Ext corridors. **Pets:** Small, dogs only. $10 daily fee/pet. No service.
(SAVE) (S♠) (✕) (🛏) (💻) (2~)

**♦♦♦ ▼▼▼ Sonora Days Inn M**
(209) 532-2400. **$69-$109.** 160 S Washington St. Downtown. Ext/int corridors. **Pets:** Dogs only. $10 one-time fee/pet. Designated rooms, no service, supervision.
(SAVE) (S♠) (✕) (🛏) (💻) (🍴) (2~)

**♦♦♦ ▼ Sonora Gold Lodge M**
(209) 532-3952. **$49-$125.** 480 Stockton St. 0.5 mi sw on SR 108 business route and 49. Ext corridors. **Pets:** Other species. $25 one-time fee/room. Designated rooms, service with restrictions, supervision.
(SAVE) (✕) (💻) (2~)

**▼▼▼▼ Union Hill Inn BB**
(209) 533-1494. **$150-$195, 5 day notice.** 21645 Parrotts Ferry Rd. Jct SR 49 and Parrotts Ferry Rd; 3 mi n of downtown. Ext corridors. **Pets:** Accepted.
(ASK) (S♠) (✕) (🛏) (💻) (2✓)

# STOCKTON

**♦♦♦ ▼▼ Americas Best Value Inn M**
(209) 466-7777. **$58.** 1707 W Fremont St. I-5, exit Fremont St southbound; exit Pershing Ave northbound, just w. Ext corridors. **Pets:** Small. $25 deposit/room. Designated rooms, service with restrictions, supervision.
(SAVE) (S♠) (✕) (🎜M) (🛏) (💻) (2~)

**♦♦♦ ▼▼▼ Comfort Inn M**
(209) 478-4300. **$55-$105.** 2654 W March Ln. I-5, exit March Ln, just e. Ext corridors. **Pets:** Small, other species. $75 deposit/room. Service with restrictions, supervision.
(SAVE) (S♠) (✕) (🎜M) (🛏) (💻) (2~)

**♦♦♦ ▼ Econo Lodge of Stockton M**
(209) 466-5741. **$50-$60.** 2210 S Manthey Rd. I-5, exit 8th St W, 0.3 mi s of jct SR 4. Int corridors. **Pets:** Very small. $25 deposit/room. Designated rooms, service with restrictions, supervision.
(SAVE) (S♠) (✕) (🎜M) (🛏) (💻)

**▼▼▼ Holiday Inn SH**
(209) 474-3301. **$89-$139.** 111 E March Ln. I-5, exit March Ln, 2 mi e; corner of El Dorado St. Int corridors. **Pets:** Accepted.
(ASK) (S♠) (✕) (🎜M) (🎜') (🛏) (💻) (🍴)

**▼▼▼ Howard Johnson Express Inn-Marina M**
(209) 948-6151. **$65-$129.** 33 N Center St. 1 blk n; w off El Dorado St via Weber; SR 99, exit Wilson Way southbound; exit northbound, w via Mariposa Rd to Charter Way; I-5, exit downtown. Ext corridors. **Pets:** Small. $10 daily fee/pet. Designated rooms, service with restrictions, supervision.
(ASK) (S♠) (✕) (🛏) (💻) (2~)

**♦♦♦ ▼▼▼ La Quinta Inn Stockton M**
(209) 952-7800. **$85-$115.** 2710 W March Ln. I-5, exit March Ln, just w. Ext corridors. **Pets:** Medium. Service with restrictions.
(SAVE) (✕) (🎜M) (💻) (2~)

**♦♦♦ ▼▼▼ Residence Inn by Marriott SH**
(209) 472-9800. **$139-$250.** 3240 W March Ln. I-5, exit March Ln, 0.5 mi w. Int corridors. **Pets:** Other species. $75 one-time fee/room. No service, supervision.
(SAVE) (S♠) (✕) (🎜M) (🎜') (💻) (2~) (✕2)

# SUNNYVALE

**♦♦♦ ▼▼▼ Four Points by Sheraton Sunnyvale SH**
(408) 738-4888. **$229-$259.** 1250 Lakeside Dr. US 101, exit Lawrence Expwy S, e on Oakmead. Int corridors. **Pets:** Accepted.
(SAVE) (S♠) (✕) (🎜M) (🛏) (💻) (🍴) (2~) (✕2)

**▼▼▼ Homestead Studio Suites Hotel-San Jose-Sunnyvale M**
(408) 734-3431. **$92.** 1255 Orleans Dr. N of SR 237, exit Mathilda Ave, e on Moffett Park Dr. Ext corridors. **Pets:** $25 daily fee/pet. Service with restrictions, supervision.
(ASK) (S♠) (✕) (💻)

**♦♦♦ ▼▼▼ Maple Tree Inn SH ❀**
(408) 720-9700. **$99.** 711 E El Camino Real. On SR 82; between Fair Oaks and Wolfe Rd; 2.5 mi w of US 101. Int corridors. **Pets:** Medium, other species. $10 daily fee/pet. Designated rooms, service with restrictions, crate.
(SAVE) (S♠) (✕) (🎜') (🛏) (2~)

**▼▼▼ Quality Inn-Sunnyvale SH**
(408) 744-1100. **$69-$189.** 1280 Persian Dr. US 101, exit Lawrence Expwy N, 1 mi n to Persian Dr, then 0.3 mi w. Int corridors. **Pets:** Accepted.
(ASK) (S♠) (✕) (🛏) (💻) (2~)

**▼▼▼ Residence Inn by Marriott SH**
(408) 720-8893. **$164-$189.** 1080 Stewart Dr. US 101, exit Lawrence Expwy S, w on Duane Ave W. Ext corridors. **Pets:** Accepted.
(✕) (🎜M) (🎜') (🛏) (💻) (2~) (✕2)

**▼▼▼ Staybridge Suites M ❀**
(408) 745-1515. **$100-$164.** 900 Hamlin Ct. SR 237, exit Mathilda Ave S, w on Ross Dr. Ext corridors. **Pets:** Medium, other species. $150 one-time fee/room. Service with restrictions.
(ASK) (S♠) (✕) (🛏) (💻) (2~) (✕2)

**▼▼▼ TownePlace Suites by Marriott Sunnyvale/Mountain View** SH
(408) 733-4200. **$79-$159.** 606 S Bernardo Ave. SR 85, exit SR 82, 0.5 mi s. Int corridors. **Pets:** Accepted.
[ASK] [S&] [X] [▦]

**◆◆◆ ▼▼ Vagabond Inn** M
(408) 734-4607. **$54-$269.** 816 Ahwanee Ave. US 101, exit Matilda Ave S, then s. Ext corridors. **Pets:** Accepted.
[SAVE] [S&] [X] [▯] [▦] [≈]

**▼▼▼ Wild Palms Hotel** M
(408) 738-0500. **$59-$129.** 910 E Fremont Ave. I-280, exit Wolfe Rd, just e. Ext/int corridors. **Pets:** Accepted.
[ASK] [S&] [X] [▯] [≈]

## SUSANVILLE

**▼▼ Americas Best Inns** M
(530) 257-4522. **Call for rates.** 2705 Main St. 1.5 mi e on SR 36. Ext corridors. **Pets:** Other species. $10 daily fee/pet. Service with restrictions, supervision.
[ASK] [S&] [X] [▯]

**◆◆◆ ▼▼▼ River Inn** M
(530) 257-6051. **$50-$60.** 1710 Main St. 0.8 mi e on SR 36. Ext corridors. **Pets:** Medium, dogs only. $10 daily fee/pet. Designated rooms, service with restrictions, supervision.
[SAVE] [S&] [X] [▯] [≈]

**◆◆◆ ▼▼ Super 8 Motel** M
(530) 257-2782. **$60-$70.** 2975 Johnstonville Rd. SR 36, 1.8 mi e. Ext corridors. **Pets:** Accepted.
[SAVE] [S&] [X] [▯] [▦] [≈]

## TEHACHAPI

**◆◆◆ ▼▼ Best Western Mountain Inn** M
(661) 822-5591. **$85-$89.** 418 W Tehachapi Blvd. SR 58, exit SR 202, 1 mi e. Ext corridors. **Pets:** Other species. Designated rooms, service with restrictions.
[SAVE] [S&] [X] [▯] [▦] [≈]

**◆◆◆ ▼▼ Tehachapi Summit Travelodge** M
(661) 823-8000. **$72-$85.** 500 Steuber Rd. SR 58, exit Monolith eastbound; exit Tehachapi Blvd westbound. Int corridors. **Pets:** Other species. $7 daily fee/pet. Service with restrictions, supervision.
[SAVE] [S&] [X] [▯] [▦] [≈]

## THOUSAND OAKS

**▼▼▼ Best Western Thousand Oaks Inn** SH ❀
(805) 497-3701. **$100-$118.** 75 W Thousand Oaks Blvd. US 101, exit Moorpark Rd, just n, then just w. Ext corridors. **Pets:** Small, other species. $75 one-time fee/room. Service with restrictions, supervision.
[ASK] [S&] [X] [&M] [⌂] [▯] [▦] [≈]

**▼ Motel 6 #1360 Thousand Oaks** M
(805) 499-0711. **$47-$61.** 1516 Newbury Rd. US 101, exit Ventu Park Rd, just w, then just n. Ext corridors. **Pets:** Accepted.
[S&] [X] [≈]

**◆◆◆ ▼▼ Premier Inns** M
(805) 499-0755. **$49-$69.** 2434 W Hillcrest Dr. US 101, exit Borchard Rd, just e, then just n. Ext corridors. **Pets:** Designated rooms, service with restrictions, supervision.
[SAVE] [S&] [X] [&M] [▯] [≈]

## THOUSAND PALMS

**◆◆◆ ▼▼ Red Roof Inn** M
(760) 343-1381. **$58-$89.** 72-215 Varner Rd. I-10, exit Ramon Rd, just n, then just w. Ext corridors. **Pets:** Small, other species. $75 deposit/room. Service with restrictions, supervision.
[SAVE] [S&] [X] [▯] [▦] [≈]

## THREE RIVERS

**◆◆◆ ▼▼ Americas Best Value Inn–Lazy J Ranch** M ❀
(559) 561-4449. **$90-$115, 3 day notice.** 39625 Sierra Dr. SR 198, 2.5 mi sw of town center. Ext corridors. **Pets:** Other species. $5 one-time fee/pet. Service with restrictions, supervision.
[SAVE] [S&] [X] [▯] [▦] [≈] [X]

**◆◆◆ ▼▼▼ Buckeye Tree Lodge** M ❀
(559) 561-5900. **$68-$134, 3 day notice.** 46000 Sierra Dr. SR 198, 6 mi ne of town center; 0.5 mi sw of entrance to Sequoia National Park. Ext corridors. **Pets:** Other species. $5 daily fee/pet. Service with restrictions, supervision.
[SAVE] [S&] [X] [▯] [▦] [≈]

**◆◆◆ ▼▼▼ Gateway Lodge** M
(559) 561-4133. **$79-$129, 7 day notice.** 45978 Sierra Dr. SR 198, 6 mi ne of town center; 0.5 mi sw of entrance to Sequoia National Park. Ext corridors. **Pets:** Other species. $10 daily fee/pet. Service with restrictions.
[SAVE] [S&] [X] [▯] [▦] [▥] [Z]

**◆◆◆ ▼▼▼ Sequoia Village Inn** CA
(559) 561-3652. **$69-$259, 14 day notice.** 45971 Sierra Dr. SR 198, 6 mi ne of town center; 0.5 mi sw of entrance to Sequoia National Park. Ext corridors. **Pets:** $5 daily fee/pet. Service with restrictions, supervision.
[SAVE] [S&] [X] [▯] [▦] [≈] [Z]

**▼▼ Sierra Lodge** M
(559) 561-3681. **$50-$112, 7 day notice.** 43175 Sierra Dr. SR 198, 1 mi se of town center; 3 mi sw of entrance to Sequoia National Park. Ext corridors. **Pets:** Medium. $20 deposit/room, $5 daily fee/pet. Designated rooms, service with restrictions, supervision.
[ASK] [S&] [X] [▯] [▦] [≈]

## TRINIDAD

**◆◆◆ ▼▼ Bishop Pine Lodge** CA
(707) 677-3314. **$90-$110, 14 day notice.** 1481 Patricks Point Dr. US 101, exit Seawood Dr, just w, then 0.8 mi s. Ext corridors. **Pets:** $15 daily fee/pet. No service, supervision.
[SAVE] [S&] [X] [▯] [▦] [⌂]

**▼▼▼ Lost Whale Bed & Breakfast Inn** BB
(707) 677-3425. **$140-$275, 7 day notice.** 3452 Patricks Point Dr. US 101, exit Patricks Point Dr, 1.1 mi w. Int corridors. **Pets:** Accepted.
[ASK] [X] [⌂]

**▼▼▼ Trinidad Inn** SH
(707) 677-3349. **$90-$150.** 1170 Patricks Point Dr. US 101, exit Trinidad, just w on Main St, then 1.3 mi n. Ext corridors. **Pets:** Accepted.
[SAVE] [X] [▯] [▦] [⌂]

## TULARE

**◆◆◆ ▼▼▼ Best Western Town & Country Lodge** M
(559) 688-7537. **$79-$150.** 1051 N Blackstone St. SR 99, exit Prosperity Ave/Blackstone St, just w. Int corridors. **Pets:** Accepted.
[SAVE] [S&] [X] [&] [▯] [▦] [≈]

**◆◆◆ ▼▼▼ Charter Inn** SH
(559) 685-9500. **$78-$91.** 1016 E Prosperity Ave. SR 99, exit Prosperity Ave/Blackstone St, just e. Int corridors. **Pets:** $10 daily fee/pet. Service with restrictions, supervision.
[SAVE] [S&] [X] [&M] [⌂] [&] [▯] [▦] [≈]

**◆◆◆ ▼▼▼ Days Inn** M
(559) 686-0985. **$55-$65.** 1183 N Blackstone St. SR 99, exit Prosperity Ave/Blackstone St, just w. Ext corridors. **Pets:** Other species. $10 daily fee/pet. Service with restrictions, supervision.
[SAVE] [S&] [X] [▯] [≈]

**Quality Inn M**
(559) 686-3432. **$75-$80.** 1010 E Prosperity Ave. SR 99, exit Prosperity Ave/Blackstone St, just e. Int corridors. **Pets:** Small, dogs only. $10 daily fee/pet. Service with restrictions, supervision.

## TURLOCK

**Best Western Orchard Inn M**
(209) 667-2827. **$80-$86.** 5025 N Golden State Blvd. SR 99, exit Taylor Rd, just e. Ext corridors. **Pets:** Other species. $25 one-time fee/pet.

**Travelodge M**
(209) 668-3400. **$62-$78.** 201 W Glenwood Ave. SR 99, exit Lander W. Ext corridors. **Pets:** Medium, dogs only. $25 deposit/room. Designated rooms, service with restrictions, supervision.

## TWAIN HARTE

**McCaffrey House B & B Inn BB**
(209) 586-0757. **$125-$160, 8 day notice.** 23251 Hwy 108. 0.5 mi on SR 108; just beyond 4000' elevation marker. Int corridors. **Pets:** Dogs only. $25 daily fee/pet. Designated rooms, service with restrictions, supervision.

## TWENTYNINE PALMS

**Best Western Gardens Inn & Suites M**
(760) 367-9141. **$85-$129.** 71487 Twentynine Palms Hwy. On SR 62; 1.8 mi w of town center. Ext/int corridors. **Pets:** Small, dogs only. $20 one-time fee/room. Designated rooms, service with restrictions, supervision.

**Circle C Lodge M**
(760) 367-7615. **$94-$135.** 6340 El Rey Ave. On SR 62, just n; 1.5 mi w of town center. Ext corridors. **Pets:** Medium. $10 daily fee/pet. Designated rooms, service with restrictions, crate.

**Roughley Manor BB**
(760) 367-3238. **$135-$160, 5 day notice.** 74744 Joe Davis Rd. SR 62, 0.5 mi n on Utal Trail, 0.5 mi e on Joe Davis Rd, then just n. Ext/int corridors. **Pets:** Medium, dogs only. Designated rooms, service with restrictions, supervision.

**Sunnyvale Garden Suites Hotel CO**
(760) 361-3939. **$89-$99.** 73843 Sunnyvale Dr. SR 62, 0.7 mi n on Adobe Rd, just e on S Slope, just n on Ocotillo, then just e. Ext corridors. **Pets:** Accepted.

## VACAVILLE

**Best Western Heritage Inn M**
(707) 448-8453. **$85-$100.** 1420 E Monte Vista Ave. I-80, exit Monte Vista Ave, just n. Ext corridors. **Pets:** Medium, other species. Designated rooms, service with restrictions, supervision.

**Residence Inn by Marriott SH**
(707) 469-0300. **$110-$270.** 360 Orange Dr. I-80, exit Orange Dr eastbound, 0.5 mi; exit Monte Vista westbound, freeway overpass to E Nut Tree Pkwy. Int corridors. **Pets:** Accepted.

**Vacaville Super 8 M**
(707) 449-8884. **$64-$84.** 101 Allison Ct. I-80, exit Monte Vista Ave, just n. Int corridors. **Pets:** Accepted.

## VALLEJO

**Holiday Inn at Napa Gateway SH**
(707) 644-1200. **$89-$209.** 1000 Fairgrounds Dr. I-80, exit Marine World Pkwy (SR 37), 0.3 mi n. Int corridors. **Pets:** Medium, dogs only. $50 one-time fee/room. Designated rooms, service with restrictions, crate.

**Ramada Inn M**
(707) 643-2700. **$99-$160.** 1000 Admiral Callaghan Ln. I-80 S, exit Columbus Pkwy, 0.5 mi w. Ext corridors. **Pets:** $25 one-time fee/room. Service with restrictions, supervision.

## VENTURA

**La Quinta Inn Ventura M**
(805) 658-6200. **$79-$119.** 5818 Valentine Rd. US 101, exit Victoria Ave, just s, then just n. Ext/int corridors. **Pets:** Medium. Service with restrictions.

**Marriott Ventura Beach Hotel LH**
(805) 643-6000. **$149-$379.** 2055 Harbor Blvd. US 101, exit Seaward Ave, just w, then 0.5 mi n. Int corridors. **Pets:** Accepted.

**Vagabond Inn Ventura M**
(805) 648-5371. **$69-$179.** 756 E Thompson Blvd. US 101, exit California St northbound, just n, then just s; exit Ventura Ave southbound, 0.6 mi e. Ext corridors. **Pets:** Other species. $10 daily fee/room. Service with restrictions, supervision.

## VICTORVILLE

**Comfort Suites Hotel SH**
(760) 245-6777. **$109-$129, 3 day notice.** 12281 Mariposa Rd. I-15, exit Bear Valley Rd, just e, then just n. Int corridors. **Pets:** Accepted.

**Red Roof Inn M**
(760) 241-1577. **$67-$71.** 13409 Mariposa Rd. I-15, exit Bear Valley Rd northbound, just e, then 1.5 mi n; exit Green Tree Blvd southbound, just e, then 1.5 mi s. Ext corridors. **Pets:** Medium. $50 deposit/room. Service with restrictions, crate.

**Travelodge Victorville M**
(760) 241-7200. **$65-$105.** 12175 Mariposa Rd. I-15, exit Bear Valley Rd, just e, then just n. Ext corridors. **Pets:** Small, dogs only. $7 one-time fee/pet. Service with restrictions, supervision.

## VISALIA

**Best Western Visalia Inn M**
(559) 732-4561. **$69-$85.** 623 W Main St. SR 198, exit SR 63 S (Mooney Blvd), just n, then 0.9 mi e. Ext corridors. **Pets:** Small, dogs only. $10 daily fee/pet. Service with restrictions, supervision.

**Lamp Liter Inn M**
(559) 732-4511. **$79-$119.** 3300 W Mineral King Ave. SR 198, exit SR 63 S (Mooney Blvd), 0.5 mi w. Ext corridors. **Pets:** Accepted.

**Super 8 M**
(559) 627-2885. **$49-$105.** 4801 W Noble Ave. SR 198, exit Akers St, just s, then 0.5 mi e on frontage road. Ext corridors. **Pets:** Other species. $10 daily fee/pet. Service with restrictions.

**AAA ◆◆◆◆ Visalia Holiday Inn Hotel & Conference Center** LH
(559) 651-5000. **$109-$159.** 9000 W Airport Dr. SR 99, exit SR 198, just e to Plaza Dr, then just s. Int corridors. **Pets:** Medium. $25 one-time fee/pet. Designated rooms, service with restrictions, supervision.
SAVE SÒ ✕ 🖥 💻 ❚❙ 🏊 ✕

## VISTA

**◆◆◆◆ La Quinta Inn San Diego (Vista)** M
(760) 727-8180. **$89-$129.** 630 Sycamore Ave. SR 78, exit Sycamore Ave, just sw. Ext/int corridors. **Pets:** Medium. Service with restrictions.
ASK ✕ 🖥 🏊

## WALNUT CREEK

**◆◆◆◆ Embassy Suites Hotel** LH
(925) 934-2500. **$129-$229.** 1345 Treat Blvd. I-680, exit Geary Rd/Treat Blvd northbound; exit Oak Park Blvd southbound, then e; at Pleasant Hill BART Station. Int corridors. **Pets:** Accepted.
ASK SÒ ✕ 🏖 🖥 💻 ❚❙ 🏊 ✕

**AAA ◆◆◆◆ Holiday Inn Walnut Creek** SH
(925) 932-3332. **$71-$159.** 2730 N Main St. I-680, exit N Main St, just n. Int corridors. **Pets:** Accepted.
SAVE SÒ ✕ 🖥 💻 ❚❙ 🏊

## WATSONVILLE

**AAA ◆◆◆ Best Western Rose Garden Inn** M 🐾
(831) 724-3367. **$59-$159.** 740 Freedom Blvd. On SR 152. Ext corridors. **Pets:** Dogs only. $10 daily fee/pet. Service with restrictions.
SAVE SÒ ✕ 🖥 💻 🏊

**◆◆ Red Roof Inn** SH
(831) 740-4520. **Call for rates.** 1620 W Beach St. SR 1, exit Riverside Dr (SR 129), just w. Int corridors. **Pets:** Accepted.
✕ 🖥 💻 🏊

## WEAVERVILLE

**AAA ◆◆◆ 49er Gold Country Inn** M
(530) 623-4937. **$45-$120, 3 day notice.** 718 Main St. On SR 299. Ext corridors. **Pets:** Medium. Service with restrictions, supervision.
SAVE SÒ ✕ 🖥 💻 🏊

**AAA ◆◆◆◆ Best Western Weaverville Victorian Inn** SH
(530) 623-4432. **$85-$169.** 1709 Main St. On SR 299. Ext corridors. **Pets:** Medium. $25 one-time fee/room. Designated rooms, service with restrictions, supervision.
SAVE SÒ ✕ 🖉 🖥 💻 ❚❙ 🏊

**AAA ◆◆ Motel Trinity** M
(530) 623-2129. **$45-$85, 3 day notice.** 1112 Main St. Just s on SR 3. Ext corridors. **Pets:** Medium, other species. $5 daily fee/pet. Service with restrictions, supervision.
SAVE SÒ ✕ 🖥 💻 🏊

**◆◆ Red Hill Motel** CA
(530) 623-4331. **$37-$84.** Red Hill Rd. SR 299, just w of SR 3. Ext corridors. **Pets:** Other species. $5 one-time fee/pet. Service with restrictions, supervision.
🖥 💻

## WEED

**AAA ◆◆◆◆ Comfort Inn** M
(530) 938-1982. **$69-$99.** 1844 Shastina Dr. I-5, exit S Weed, just e. Int corridors. **Pets:** Accepted.
SAVE SÒ ✕ 🖉 🖥 💻 🏊

**AAA ◆◆◆◆ Holiday Inn Express** M
(530) 938-1308. **$69-$89.** 1830 Black Butte Dr. Just e of I-5; in town. Int corridors. **Pets:** Accepted.
SAVE SÒ ✕ 🖥 💻

**AAA ◆◆ Sis-Q-Inn Motel** M
(530) 938-4194. **$85-$95.** 1825 Shastina Dr. I-5, exit S Weed. Int corridors. **Pets:** Accepted.
SAVE SÒ ✕ 🖥

## WESTLEY

**AAA ◆◆◆ Econo Lodge** M
(209) 894-3900. **$65-$90, 3 day notice.** 7100 McCracken Rd. I-5, exit Westley, then e. Ext corridors. **Pets:** $10 daily fee/pet. No service, supervision.
SAVE SÒ ✕ 🖥 💻 🏊

**AAA ◆◆◆◆ Holiday Inn Express** SH 🐾
(209) 894-8940. **$79-$109.** 4525 Howard Rd. I-5, exit Westley, then e. Int corridors. **Pets:** Small. $25 one-time fee/pet. Service with restrictions, supervision.
SAVE SÒ ✕ 🖥 💻 🏊

## WESTMORLAND

**AAA ◆◆◆ Super 8 Motel** M
(760) 351-7100. **$65-$85.** 351 W Main St. On SR 86. Int corridors. **Pets:** Medium. $10 daily fee/pet. Designated rooms, service with restrictions, supervision.
SAVE SÒ ✕ 🖥 🏊

## WILLIAMS

**AAA ◆◆◆ Comfort Inn** M
(530) 473-2381. **$65-$85.** 400 C St. I-5, exit Williams, just w on E St, then just n on 4th St. Ext corridors. **Pets:** Accepted.
SAVE SÒ ✕ 🖥M 🖥 💻 🏊

**AAA ◆◆◆◆ Granzella's Inn** M
(530) 473-3310. **$72-$100.** 391 6th St. I-5, exit Williams, 0.5 mi w. Int corridors. **Pets:** Other species. $10 one-time fee/room. Service with restrictions, supervision.
SAVE SÒ ✕ 🖥M 🖉 🖥 💻 ❚❙ 🏊

**AAA ◆◆ Holiday Inn Express Hotel & Suites** M
(530) 473-5120. **$85-$105.** 374 Ruggieri Way. I-5, exit Williams, just e. Int corridors. **Pets:** Accepted.
SAVE SÒ ✕ 🖥M 🖉 🖥 💻

**AAA ◆ Stage Stop Inn** M
(530) 473-2281. **$43-$50.** 300 N 7th St. I-5, exit SR 20 business route, 3 blks w. Ext corridors. **Pets:** Accepted.
SAVE SÒ ✕ 🖥 🏊

## WILLOW CREEK

**AAA ◆ Bigfoot Motel** M
(530) 629-2142. **$55-$99.** 39039 Hwy 299. On SR 299; just e of SR 96; center. Ext corridors. **Pets:** Accepted.
SAVE ✕ 🖥 🏊

## WILLOWS

**AAA ◆◆◆◆ Best Western Golden Pheasant Inn** M 🐾
(530) 934-4603. **$75-$80.** 249 N Humboldt Ave. I-5, exit 162 (Willows-Elk Creek-Glenn Rd), just e. Ext corridors. **Pets:** Large, other species. $10 one-time fee/room. Service with restrictions.
SAVE SÒ ✕ 🖥M 🖥 💻 ❚❙ 🏊

**AAA ◆◆ Days Inn** M
(530) 934-4444. **$49-$79.** 475 N Humboldt Ave. I-5, exit 162 (Willows-Elk Creek-Glenn Rd), just e. Ext corridors. **Pets:** Accepted.
SAVE SÒ ✕ 🖥M 🖥 💻 🏊

**AAA ◆ Economy Inn** M
(530) 934-4224. **$50-$70.** 435 N Tehama St. I-5, exit SR 162 (Willows-Elk Creek-Glenn Rd), 1 mi e. Ext corridors. **Pets:** Small. $5 one-time fee/pet. Designated rooms, service with restrictions, supervision.
SAVE SÒ ✕ 🖥

**AAA ▼▼▼ Motel 6 #4273 M ❖**
(530) 934-7026. **$62-$96.** 452 N Humboldt Ave. I-5, exit 162 (Willows-Elk Creek-Glenn Rd), just e. Ext corridors. **Pets:** Medium. $7 daily fee/pet, $7 one-time fee/pet. Service with restrictions, supervision.
SAVE ⑤ ⊠ 🖥 💻 ➥

**▼▼ Super 8 Motel of Willows M**
(530) 934-2871. **$55-$150.** 457 Humboldt Ave. I-5, exit 162 (Willows-Elk Creek-Glenn Rd). Int corridors. **Pets:** Accepted.
ASK ⑤ ⊠ 🖥 ➥

## WINE COUNTRY AREA

# ALBION

**▼▼▼▼ Fensalden Inn BB**
(707) 937-4042. **$119-$239, 7 day notice.** 33810 Navarro Ridge Rd. 0.5 mi e of jct SR 1. Ext/int corridors. **Pets:** Accepted.
ASK ⑤ ⊠ 🖥 💻 ⫽ 𝒲 ☑

# ANCHOR BAY

**▼▼▼ North Coast Country Inn BB ❖**
(707) 884-4537. **$156-$225, 5 day notice.** 34591 S Hwy 1. On SR 1, 4.5 mi n. Ext corridors. **Pets:** Other species. $25 one-time fee/pet. Service with restrictions, supervision.
ASK ⑤ ⊠ 🖥 💻 ⫽ 𝒲 ☑

# BODEGA BAY

**▼▼▼ Bodega Coast Inn M ❖**
(707) 875-2217. **$129-$299.** 521 SR 1 N. 2 blks s. Ext corridors. **Pets:** Medium, other species. $30 daily fee/pet. Designated rooms, service with restrictions, supervision.
ASK ⑤ ⊠ ৬M 🖥 💻 ⫽

# CALISTOGA

**▼▼ Brannan Cottage Inn BB**
(707) 942-4200. **$135-$200, 7 day notice.** 109 Wapoo Ave. At Lincoln Ave. Ext corridors. **Pets:** Medium, other species. $100 deposit/room, $25 daily fee/pet. Service with restrictions, crate.
ASK ⊠

**▼▼ Washington Street Lodging CA**
(707) 942-6968. **$95-$140 (no credit cards), 3 day notice.** 1605 Washington St. On SR 29. Ext corridors. **Pets:** Other species. $15 one-time fee/pet. Service with restrictions.
⊠ ৬M 🖥 💻 ☑

# CLOVERDALE

**AAA ▼▼ Cloverdale Oaks Inn M**
(707) 894-2404. **$59-$109, 3 day notice.** 123 S Cloverdale Blvd. US 101, exit Citrus Fair Dr, 0.4 mi w to S Cloverdale Blvd, then just n. Ext corridors. **Pets:** Very small, dogs only. $15 daily fee/pet. Designated rooms, service with restrictions, supervision.
SAVE ⑤ ⊠ ৬M 🖥 💻

# FORT BRAGG

**AAA ▼▼▼ Americas Best Value Inn Seabird Lodge M**
(707) 964-4731. **$76-$130, 3 day notice.** 191 South St. 0.8 mi n of Noyo River Bridge; 1 blk e off SR 1. Ext corridors. **Pets:** Medium. $8 daily fee/room. Designated rooms, service with restrictions, supervision.
SAVE ⑤ ⊠ 🖥 💻 ➥ ⫽

**AAA ▼▼▼▼ Beachcomber Motel M ❖**
(707) 964-2402. **$69-$260.** 1111 N Main St. 1 mi n on SR 1. Ext corridors. **Pets:** Other species. $10 daily fee/pet. Designated rooms, service with restrictions, supervision.
SAVE ⊠ 🖥 💻 ⫽

**AAA ▼▼▼▼ Beach House Inn M ❖**
(707) 961-1700. **$59-$175.** 100 Pudding Creek Rd. 0.7 mi n on SR 1. Int corridors. **Pets:** Medium, other species. $10 one-time fee/pet. Service with restrictions, supervision.
SAVE ⑤ ⊠ 🖥 💻 ⫽

**AAA ▼▼▼ Chelsea Inn & Suites M**
(707) 964-4787. **$49-$159.** 763 N Main St. SR 1, 0.5 mi n. Ext corridors. **Pets:** Accepted.
SAVE ⑤ ⊠ 🖥 💻 ⫽

**▼▼ Cleone Gardens Inn M**
(707) 964-2788. **$86-$140, 3 day notice.** 24600 N Hwy 1. On SR 1, 0.4 mi n of MacKerricher State Park entrance. Ext corridors. **Pets:** Accepted.
⊠ 🖥 💻 ⫽

**▼▼▼ The Emerald Dolphin Inn M ❖**
(707) 964-6699. **$55-$180, 7 day notice.** 1211 S Main St. On SR 1. Ext corridors. **Pets:** Dogs only. $10 daily fee/pet. Designated rooms, service with restrictions, supervision.
ASK ⑤ ⊠ 🖥 💻 ⫽

**AAA ▼▼▼▼ Quality Inn M**
(707) 964-4761. **$59-$150.** 400 S Main St. 6 blks s on SR 1. Ext corridors. **Pets:** Accepted.
SAVE ⑤ ⊠ 🖥 💻 ¶ ➥ ⊠ ⫽

**▼▼ Super 8 Motel-Fort Bragg M**
(707) 964-4003. **$46-$123.** 888 S Main St. On SR 1, 0.6 mi n of jct SR 20. Ext corridors. **Pets:** Medium, dogs only. $10 one-time fee/pet. Designated rooms, service with restrictions, supervision.
ASK ⑤ ⊠ 🖥 💻

**AAA ▼▼▼ Surf Motel M**
(707) 964-5361. **$51-$110.** 1220 S Main St. 1 mi s on SR 1; s of Noyo River Bridge; 0.3 mi n of jct SR 20. Ext corridors. **Pets:** Accepted.
SAVE ⑤ ⊠ 🖥 💻 ⫽

# GUALALA

**▼▼◆ Gualala Country Inn M**
(707) 884-4343. **$95-$165.** 47955 Center St. On SR 1; south end of town. Ext/int corridors. **Pets:** Other species. $10 one-time fee/pet. Service with restrictions, supervision.
⊠ 🖥 💻 ⫽

**▼▼ Surf Motel M**
(707) 884-3571. **$95-$179, 3 day notice.** 39170 S Hwy 1. Center. Ext/int corridors. **Pets:** Other species. $10 one-time fee/pet. Service with restrictions, supervision.
⊠ 🖥 💻 ⫽

# GUERNEVILLE

**AAA ▼▼▼ Ferngrove Cottages CA ❖**
(707) 869-8105. **$89-$239, 3 day notice.** 16650 Hwy 116. On SR 116, just sw. Ext corridors. **Pets:** Large, other species. $15 daily fee/pet. Designated rooms, service with restrictions, supervision.
SAVE ⑤ ⊠ ৬M 🖥 💻 ➥ ⊠ ⫽ ☑

# HEALDSBURG

**AAA ▼▼◆ Americas Best Value Inn & Suites M**
(707) 433-5548. **$69-$149.** 74 Healdsburg Ave. US 101, exit Central Healdsburg, just e. Ext corridors. **Pets:** $10 daily fee/pet. Service with restrictions, supervision.
SAVE ⑤ ⊠ ৬M 🖥 💻 ➥

**Best Western Dry Creek Inn** M ❖
(707) 433-0300. **$79-$265.** 198 Dry Creek Rd. US 101, exit Dry Creek Rd, just e. Ext corridors. **Pets:** $25 daily fee/pet. Service with restrictions, crate.
SAVE (S) ✕ (M) ▢ ▢ ▢ ≋

**Duchamp** CA ❖
(707) 431-1300. **$275-$450, 14 day notice.** 421 Foss St. US 101, exit Central Healdsburg. Ext corridors. **Pets:** Medium, dogs only. $50 daily fee/pet. Service with restrictions, supervision.
ASK ✕ (M) ▢ ≋

# JENNER

**Jenner Inn & Cottages** CI ❖
(707) 865-2377. **$98-$178, 10 day notice.** 10400 Hwy 1. On SR 1 at SR 116. Ext corridors. **Pets:** Medium, dogs only. $35 one-time fee/pet. Designated rooms, service with restrictions, supervision.
(S) ✕ (M) ▢ ▢ ▢ ▢ ▢

# LEGGETT

**Redwoods River Resort** CA ❖
(707) 925-6249. **$55-$145, 7 day notice.** 75000 Hwy 101. 6.5 mi n of jct SR 1. Ext corridors. **Pets:** Dogs only. $10 daily fee/pet. Designated rooms, no service, supervision.
SAVE ✕ ▢ ▢ ≋ ▢ ▢ ▢

# LITTLE RIVER

**Auberge Mendocino-Rachel's Inn** BB ❖
(707) 937-0088. **$169-$375, 14 day notice.** 8200 N Hwy 1. On SR 1, 2 mi s of Mendocino. Ext/int corridors. **Pets:** Medium, dogs only. $100 deposit/room, $35 one-time fee/room. Designated rooms, service with restrictions, supervision.
SAVE (S) ✕ ▢ ▢ ▢ ▢ ▢

**The Inn at Schoolhouse Creek** BB ❖
(707) 937-5525. **$110-$350, 14 day notice.** 7001 N Hwy 1. On SR 1, 0.8 mi s of Van Damme State Park entrance. Ext corridors. **Pets:** Other species. $50 one-time fee/room. Service with restrictions.
ASK (S) ✕ ▢ ▢ ▢ ▢

**Stevenswood Spa Resort** CI ❖
(707) 937-2810. **$139-$365, 14 day notice.** 8211 SR 1. 2 mi s of Mendocino. Int corridors. **Pets:** $50 one-time fee/room. Supervision.
SAVE (S) ✕ ▢ ▢ ▢ ▢ ▢ ▢

# MENDOCINO

**Abigail's Bed & Breakfast** BB ❖
(707) 937-0934. **$99-$299, 14 day notice.** 951 Ukiah St. Just e of Lansing St; center. Ext/int corridors. **Pets:** Medium, dogs only. $25 one-time fee/pet. Service with restrictions, supervision.
ASK (S) ✕ ▢ ▢ ▢ ▢

**Blackberry Inn** M ❖
(707) 937-5281. **$95-$215, 5 day notice.** 44951 Larkin Rd. Just e of jct SR 1. Ext corridors. **Pets:** Medium, other species. $10 daily fee/pet. Designated rooms, supervision.
SAVE ✕ ▢ ▢ ▢

**Hill House Inn** CI ❖
(707) 937-0554. **$108-$225, 5 day notice.** 10701 Pallette Dr. Just w on Little Lake St from jct SR 1, just n on Lansing St. Ext corridors. **Pets:** Medium. $15 one-time fee/room. Designated rooms, service with restrictions, supervision.
ASK (S) ✕ ▢ ▢ ▢ ▢

**MacCallum House Inn** CI ❖
(707) 937-0289. **$135-$375, 7 day notice.** 45020 Albion St. Just w of Lansing St; center. Ext/int corridors. **Pets:** Other species. $25 daily fee/pet. Designated rooms, crate.
SAVE ✕ ▢ ▢ ▢ ▢ ▢ ▢

**Mendocino Seaside Cottage** BB ❖
(707) 485-0239. **$187-$301, 14 day notice.** 10940 Lansing St. Just w on Little Lake Rd from jct SR 1, 0.3 mi n. Ext/int corridors. **Pets:** Other species. $25 one-time fee/pet. No service, supervision.
SAVE (S) ✕ ▢ ▢ ▢ ▢

**Stanford Inn by the Sea & Spa** CI ❖
(707) 937-5615. **$235-$475, 7 day notice.** 44850 Comptche-Ukiah Rd. SR 1, exit Comptche-Ukiah Rd, 0.5 mi s of town, then 0.5 mi e. Ext corridors. **Pets:** Other species. $25 one-time fee/pet.
SAVE (S) ✕ (M) ▢ ▢ ▢ ▢ ≋ ▢ ▢

# NAPA

**The Napa Inn** BB
(707) 257-1444. **$145-$295, 10 day notice.** 1137 Warren St. SR 29, exit 1st St, 0.5 mi e, then 0.3 mi n. Int corridors. **Pets:** Accepted.
SAVE (S) ✕ (M) ▢ ▢

**Napa River Inn** SH ❖
(707) 251-8500. **$199-$599.** 500 Main St. Downtown. Int corridors. **Pets:** Medium. $50 daily fee/pet. Designated rooms, supervision.
ASK (S) ✕ (M) ▢ ▢ ▢

**Napa Valley Redwood Inn** M ❖
(707) 257-6111. **$67-$152.** 3380 Solano Ave. Just w off SR 29 via Redwood Rd, just s. Ext corridors. **Pets:** Other species. $10 one-time fee/pet. No service.
SAVE (S) ✕ (M) ▢ ▢ ≋

# OCCIDENTAL

**Occidental Lodge** M
(707) 874-3623. **$69-$149, 3 day notice.** 3610 Bohemian Hwy. In the village. Ext corridors. **Pets:** Medium, dogs only. $8 daily fee/pet. Service with restrictions, supervision.
SAVE (S) ✕ (M) ▢ ▢ ≋

# PETALUMA

**Quality Inn-Petaluma** SH
(707) 664-1155. **$95-$185.** 5100 Montero Way. US 101, exit Old Redwood Hwy-Penngrove; exit Petaluma Blvd N-Penngrove southbound (east side). Ext/int corridors. **Pets:** Large, other species. $15 daily fee/room. Service with restrictions, supervision.
SAVE (S) ✕ (M) ▢ ▢ ▢ ≋ ▢

**Sheraton Sonoma County-Petaluma** SH ❖
(707) 283-2888. **$129-$269.** 745 Baywood Dr. US 101, exit SR 116 (Lakeville Hwy), just se. Int corridors. **Pets:** Medium, dogs only. $100 deposit/pet. Designated rooms, service with restrictions, crate.
SAVE (S) ✕ (M) ▢ ▢ ▢ ▢ ≋

# POINT ARENA

**Wharf Master's Inn** M
(707) 882-3171. **$79-$195, 3 day notice.** 785 Port Rd. 1 mi w on Iversen Ave from jct SR 1; at wharf. Ext corridors. **Pets:** Accepted.
SAVE ✕ (M) ▢ ▢ ▢

# ROHNERT PARK

**Best Western Inn** SH
(707) 584-7435. **$89-$130, 3 day notice.** 6500 Redwood Dr. US 101, exit Rohnert Park Expwy, just w. Ext corridors. **Pets:** $10 one-time fee/room. Designated rooms, service with restrictions, crate.
SAVE (S) ✕ (M) ▢ ≋

# ST. HELENA

**El Bonita Motel** M
(707) 963-3216. **$89-$299, 3 day notice.** 195 Main St. 0.8 mi s on SR 29. Ext corridors. **Pets:** Other species. $5 daily fee/pet. Service with restrictions, supervision.
SAVE ✕ (M) ▢ ▢ ▢ ≋

(AAA) ▽▽▽ ▽▽▽ Harvest Inn SH
(707) 963-9463. $239-$579, 7 day notice. One Main St. 1.5 mi s on
SR 29. Ext corridors. Pets: Accepted.
SAVE ✕ &M ☾ 🖪 📇 ➾ ✕

## SANTA ROSA

(AAA) ▽▽▽ Americas Best Value Inn M
(707) 523-3480. $59-$109. 1800 Santa Rosa Ave. US 101, exit Baker
Ave northbound; exit Corby Ave southbound. Ext corridors.
Pets: Large, other species. $15 one-time fee/room. Service with restrictions,
crate.
SAVE S❺ ✕ &M 🖪

(AAA) ▽▽▽▽ Best Western Garden Inn M ❀
(707) 546-4031. $75-$129. 1500 Santa Rosa Ave. US 101, exit Baker
Ave northbound; exit Corby Ave southbound. Ext corridors.
Pets: Medium, dogs only. $15 daily fee/room. Service with restrictions,
supervision.
SAVE S❺ ✕ &M ☾ 🖪 📇 ¶↑ ➾

(AAA) ▽▽ ▽▽ Fountaingrove Inn, Hotel & Conference
Center SH ❀
(707) 578-6101. $119-$169. 101 Fountaingrove Pkwy. 2.5 mi n on US
101, exit Mendocino Ave/Old Redwood Hwy, just e. Int corridors.
Pets: Other species. $50 daily fee/room. Service with restrictions, crate.
SAVE S❺ ✕ &M ⌖ 🖪 📇 ¶↑ ➾

(AAA) ▽▽▽▽ Hillside Inn Motel M
(707) 546-9353. $82-$98, 3 day notice. 2901 4th St. US 101, 2.5 mi s
on SR 12; at Farmers Ln and 4th St. Ext corridors. Pets: Accepted.
SAVE ✕ &M 📇 ¶↑ ➾

(AAA) ▽▽▽▽ Holiday Inn Express M
(707) 545-9000. $89-$159. 870 Hopper Ave. US 101, exit Mendocino
Ave/Old Redwood Hwy northbound, just w; exit Hopper Ave southbound. Ext corridors. Pets: Medium, other species. $20 one-time fee/
room. Designated rooms, service with restrictions, supervision.
SAVE S❺ ✕ &M 🖪 📇 ➾

(AAA) ▽▽▽ Travelodge M
(707) 542-3472. $50-$119. 1815 Santa Rosa Ave. 1.5 mi s on US 101
business route; US 101, exit Baker Ave northbound; exit Corby Ave
southbound. Ext corridors. Pets: $15 daily fee/pet. Service with restric-
tions, supervision.
SAVE ✕ &M 🖪 📇 ➾

## THE SEA RANCH

(AAA) ▽▽▽ Sea Ranch Lodge SH ❀
(707) 785-2371. $225-$495, 7 day notice. 60 Sea Walk Dr. Just w of
SR 1. Ext corridors. Pets: Large, dogs only. $50 one-time fee/pet. Service
with restrictions, supervision.
SAVE S❺ ✕ &M 📇 ¶↑ ✕ AC

## SONOMA

(AAA) ▽▽▽▽ Best Western Sonoma Valley Inn M
(707) 938-9200. $108-$360, 3 day notice. 550 2nd St W. 1 blk w of
town plaza. Ext corridors. Pets: Accepted.
SAVE S❺ ✕ &M ☾ 🖪 📇 ➾

## UKIAH

(AAA) ▽▽▽▽ Days Inn M
(707) 462-7584. $60-$129, 7 day notice. 950 N State St. US 101, exit
N State St, 0.5 mi s. Ext corridors. Pets: Other species. $10 daily fee/pet.
Service with restrictions, supervision.
SAVE S❺ ✕ 🖪 📇 ➾

(AAA) ▽▽▽▽ Discovery Inn M
(707) 462-8873. $69-$129, 3 day notice. 1340 N State St. 1.5 mi n on
US 101 business route; US 101, exit N State St. Ext corridors.
Pets: Accepted.
SAVE S❺ ✕ ☾ 🖪 📇 ➾

▽▽▽ Regency Inn M
(707) 462-6657. $49-$99, 7 day notice. 1070 S State St. US 101, exit
Talmage Rd, 1 mi w. Ext corridors. Pets: Other species. $10 daily
fee/pet. Service with restrictions, crate.
ASK S❺ ✕ 🖪 ➾

(AAA) ▽▽▽ Rodeway Inn M ❀
(707) 462-2906. $69-$99. 1050 S State St. US 101, exit Talmage Rd,
0.5 mi w. Ext corridors. Pets: Dogs only. $10 daily fee/pet. Service with
restrictions, supervision.
SAVE S❺ ✕ 🖪 📇 ➾

(AAA) ▽▽ Super 8 Motel M
(707) 468-8181. $59-$79. 693 S Orchard Ave. US 101, exit Gobbi St
W. Ext corridors. Pets: $5 daily fee/pet. Service with restrictions, supervi-
sion.
SAVE S❺ ✕ 🖪 📇 ➾

## WESTPORT

▽▽▽ DeHaven Valley Farm BB
(707) 961-1660. $94-$151, 3 day notice. 39247 N Hwy 1. On SR 1,
just n of Branscomb Rd. Ext/int corridors. Pets: Accepted.
ASK S❺ ✕ 🖪 📇 ¶↑ AC 🐾

## WILLITS

▽▽▽ Baechtel Creek Inn & Spa M
(707) 459-9063. $69-$185. 101 Gregory Ln. US 101, just w. Ext corridors. Pets: Accepted.
ASK S❺ ✕ 🖪 📇 ➾

## YOUNTVILLE

(AAA) ▽▽▽ ▽▽▽ Vintage Inn SH
(707) 944-1112. $230-$610, 7 day notice. 6541 Washington St. SR 29,
exit Yountville; center. Ext corridors. Pets: Accepted.
SAVE S❺ ✕ &M ☾ 🖪 📇 ➾ ✕

---

## END AREA

---

## WOODLAND

(AAA) ▽▽▽ Days Inn SH
(530) 666-3800. $65-$95. 1524 E Main St. I-5, exit Main St (Woodland)
northbound; exit SR 113 (Davis) southbound. Int corridors. Pets: $10
daily fee/pet. Service with restrictions.
SAVE S❺ ✕ &M 🖪 ➾

## YERMO

(AAA) ▽▽▽ Oak Tree Inn SH
(760) 254-1148. $65-$75. 35450 Yermo Rd. I-15/40, exit Ghost Town
Rd, just e, then just s. Int corridors. Pets: Accepted.
SAVE S❺ ✕ 🖪 📇 ¶↑ ➾

# YOSEMITE NATIONAL PARK

▼▼ The Redwoods In Yosemite VH
(209) 375-6666. **$119-$682, 10 day notice.** 8038 Chilnualna Falls Rd. 6 mi inside the southern entrance via SR 41 and Chilnualna Falls Rd. Ext corridors. **Pets:** Other species. $10 daily fee/pet. Designated rooms, service with restrictions, supervision.

ASK S△ ✕ ⊟ ▣

# YREKA

▲▲▲ ▼▼▼ AmeriHost Inn-Yreka M
(530) 841-1300. **$70-$95.** 148 Moonlit Oaks Ave. I-5, exit SR 3 (Fort Jones Rd). Int corridors. **Pets:** Accepted.

SAVE S△ ✕ 🛔 ⊟ ▣ ⤷ ✕

▲▲▲ ▼▼▼ Best Western Miner's Inn M ❀
(530) 842-4355. **$78-$113.** 122 E Miner St. I-5, exit Central Yreka, just w. Ext corridors. **Pets:** Medium. $10 daily fee/pet. Designated rooms, service with restrictions, supervision.

SAVE S△ ✕ 🛔 ⊟ ▣ ⤷

▲▲▲ ▼▼▼ Comfort Inn M
(530) 842-1612. **$59-$95.** 1804-B Fort Jones Rd. I-5, exit SR 3 (Fort Jones Rd). Int corridors. **Pets:** Medium. $20 deposit/room, $6 daily fee/pet. Service with restrictions, supervision.

SAVE S△ ✕ 🛔M 🛔 ⊟ ⤷

▲▲▲ ▼▼▼ Econo Lodge Inn & Suites M
(530) 842-4404. **$49-$95.** 526 S Main St. I-5, exit Central Yreka, 0.3 mi s. Ext corridors. **Pets:** Medium, other species. $20 deposit/room, $7 daily fee/pet. Designated rooms, service with restrictions, supervision.

SAVE S△ ✕ 🛔M 🛔 ⊟ ⤷

▲▲▲ ▼▼▼ Mountain View Inn/Motel M
(530) 842-1940. **$43-$89.** 801 N Main St. I-5, exit Montague Rd, 0.5 mi w. Ext corridors. **Pets:** Small. $5 daily fee/pet. Designated rooms, no service, supervision.

SAVE S△ ✕ ⊟ ▣

▲▲▲ ▼▼▼ Super 8-Yreka M
(530) 842-5781. **$59-$79.** 136 Montague Rd. I-5, exit Montague Rd, just w. Ext corridors. **Pets:** Accepted.

SAVE S△ ✕ 🛔 ▣ ⤷

# YUBA CITY

▲▲▲ ▼▼▼ Comfort Inn M
(530) 674-1592. **$50-$99.** 730 Palora Ave. SR 99, exit Bridge St, 0.5 mi s of jct SR 20. Int corridors. **Pets:** Accepted.

SAVE S△ ✕ 🛔M 🛔 ⊟ ▣ ⤷

▼▼ Days Inn & Suites SH
(530) 674-0201. **$50-$80.** 4228 S Hwy 99. On SR 99, 4.5 mi s of SR 20. Ext corridors. **Pets:** $10 daily fee/pet. Designated rooms, service with restrictions, supervision.

ASK S△ ✕ 🛔M 🛔 ⊟ ▣ ⟦⟧ ⤷

▲▲▲ ▼▼ Days Inn-Downtown-Yuba City M
(530) 674-1711. **$45-$80.** 700 N Palora Ave. SR 99, exit Bridge St, 0.5 mi s of SR 20. Ext corridors. **Pets:** Accepted.

SAVE S△ ✕ 🛔M 🛔 ⊟ ▣ ⤷

# YUCCA VALLEY

▲▲▲ ▼▼ Americas Best Value Inn & Suites-Oasis of Eden M
(760) 365-6321. **$49-$139.** 56377 Twentynine Palms Hwy. 1 mi w of jct SR 62 and 247. Ext corridors. **Pets:** Small. $10 daily fee/pet. Designated rooms, supervision.

SAVE S△ ✕ 🛔 ▣ ⤷

▼▼ Super 8 Motel M
(760) 228-1773. **$64-$119.** 57096 Twentynine Palms Hwy. On SR 62, 0.3 mi w of jct SR 247. Int corridors. **Pets:** Accepted.

ASK S△ ✕ 🛔 ▣ ⤷

# COLORADO

## CITY INDEX

## ALAMOSA

**Best Western Alamosa Inn** SH ❄
(719) 589-2567. **$59-$81.** 2005 Main St. 1 mi w on US 160 and 285. Ext corridors. **Pets:** Medium. $15 daily fee/room. Service with restrictions, supervision.
SAVE | SD | X | 🛏 | 💻 | 🏊

**Inn of the Rio Grande** SH
(719) 589-5833. **$79-$89.** 333 Sante Fe Ave. Just e of jct SR 17 on US 160. Int corridors. **Pets:** Other species. $25 deposit/pet. Supervision.
SAVE | SD | X | &M | 🗟 | 🛏 | 💻 | 🍴 | 🏊 | X

## ASPEN

**Aspen Meadows Resort A Dolce Conference Destination** LH
(970) 925-4240. **$136-$610, 14 day notice.** 845 Meadows Rd. 3 blks e of SR 82 via 7th Ave. Ext/int corridors. **Pets:** Accepted.
ASK | X | 🗟 | 🛏 | 💻 | 🍴 | 🏊 | X | 🎾

**Aspen Mountain Lodge** SH
(970) 925-7650. **$89-$359.** 311 W Main St. Just w on SR 82; between 2nd and 3rd sts. Int corridors. **Pets:** Accepted.
ASK | X | 🛏 | 💻 | 🏊

**Hotel Aspen** SH ❄
(970) 925-3441. **$119-$405, 30 day notice.** 110 W Main St. On SR 82, just w. Ext/int corridors. **Pets:** Dogs only. $20 daily fee/room. Designated rooms.
ASK | SD | X | 🛏 | 💻 | 🏊

**Hotel Jerome** SH
(970) 920-1000. **$460-$1475, 30 day notice.** 330 E Main St. On SR 82; downtown. Int corridors. **Pets:** Accepted.
SAVE | X | X | 🍴 | 🏊 | X

**Hotel Lenado** BB
(970) 925-6246. **$115-$525, 30 day notice.** 200 S Aspen St. Just s of SR 82 via Aspen St at jct Hopkins St. Ext/int corridors. **Pets:** Accepted.
ASK | X | 🛏 | 💻

**Limelite Lodge** M
(970) 925-3025. **$69-$350, 7 day notice.** 228 E Cooper St. Just s of SR 82, at Monarch and Cooper sts. Ext corridors. **Pets:** Large. $10 daily fee/pet. Service with restrictions, supervision.
SAVE | X | 🗟 | 🗟 | 🛏 | 💻 | 🏊

**The Little Nell** LH ❄
(970) 920-4600. **$430-$6000, 30 day notice.** 675 E Durant Ave. Beside the gondola at base of Aspen Mountain. Int corridors. **Pets:** Other species. Service with restrictions, supervision.
ASK | SD | 🛏 | 🍴 | 🏊 | X

**St. Regis Aspen** LH
(970) 920-3300. **$145-$2400, 30 day notice.** 315 E Dean St. SR 82, s on Monarch St, then just e. Int corridors. **Pets:** Accepted.
ASK | X | 🗟 | 🍴 | 🏊 | X

**Sky Hotel** LH
(970) 925-6760. **$145-$1165, 14 day notice.** 709 E Durant Ave. At base of Aspen Mountain. Ext/int corridors. **Pets:** Accepted.
SAVE | SD | X | 💻 | 🍴 | 🏊 | X

## BEAVER CREEK

**Comfort Inn-Vail/Beaver Creek** SH
(970) 949-5511. **$59-$189.** 161 W Beaver Creek Blvd. I-70, exit 167, just s on Avon Rd, then just w. Int corridors. **Pets:** Medium, other species. $25 one-time fee/room. Designated rooms, service with restrictions, supervision.
ASK | SD | X | 🗟 | 🛏 | 💻 | 🏊

**The Ritz-Carlton, Bachelor Gulch** LH ❄
(970) 748-6200. **$195-$1150.** 0130 Daybreak Ridge. I-70, exit 167, s on Avon and Village rds (beyond gatehouse), w on Prater Rd, follow signs to Bachelor Gulch. Int corridors. **Pets:** Dogs only. $125 one-time fee/room. Service with restrictions, supervision.
SAVE | X | &M | 🗟 | 🗟 | 💻 | 🍴 | 🏊 | X

## BOULDER

**Best Western Boulder Inn** SH
(303) 449-3800. **$89-$114.** 770 28th St. US 36 at Baseline Rd. Int corridors. **Pets:** Other species. $100 deposit/room. Designated rooms, supervision.
SAVE | SD | X | 🛏 | 💻 | 🍴 | 🏊 | X

**Boulder Broker Inn** SH
(303) 444-3330. **$109-$149.** 555 30th St. US 36 (28th St), exit Baseline Rd, 0.3 mi e to 30th St, then just s. Int corridors. **Pets:** Medium. $10 one-time fee/room. Designated rooms, service with restrictions, supervision.
ASK | SD | X | 🛏 | 💻 | 🍴 | 🏊 | X

**Boulder Outlook Hotel & Suites** SH ❄
(303) 443-3322. **$69-$129.** 800 28th St. US 36 (28th St), exit Baseline Rd via Frontage Rd. Ext/int corridors. **Pets:** Other species. $10 daily fee/room. Designated rooms, service with restrictions, crate.
SAVE | SD | X | 🗟 | 🗟 | 🛏 | 💻 | 🍴 | 🏊 | X

**▲▲▲ ▼▼ ▼▼ Boulder University Inn M ❖**
(303) 417-1700. **$60-$119.** 1632 Broadway. From US 36, exit Baseline (CO 93), 0.3 mi s, then 3 mi nw. Ext corridors. **Pets:** Medium, other species. $100 deposit/room. Designated rooms, service with restrictions, supervision.

SAVE S❻ ✕ 🖥 💻 🏊

**▲▲▲ ▼▼ ▼▼ Foot of The Mountain Motel M**
(303) 442-5688. **$70-$85.** 200 Arapahoe Ave. 1.8 mi w of US 36 (28th St). Ext corridors. **Pets:** $50 deposit/room, $5 daily fee/pet. Designated rooms, service with restrictions, supervision.

SAVE ✕ 🖥 🏧

**▼▼ ▼▼ Homewood Suites by Hilton SH**
(303) 499-9922. **$139-$169.** 4950 Baseline Rd. 0.3 mi e of US 36; SR 157 (Foothills Pkwy), exit Baseline Rd, just w; entry off Baseline Rd. Ext/int corridors. **Pets:** Other species. $50 one-time fee/room. Service with restrictions, crate.

ASK S❻ ✕ 🗐 🐾 🖥 💻 🏊 ✕

**▲▲▲ ▼▼▼▼ Millennium Harvest House Boulder LH**
(303) 443-3850. **$99-$215.** 1345 28th St. Just s of jct Arapahoe Rd and 28th St (US 36). Int corridors. **Pets:** Accepted.

SAVE S❻ ✕ 🗐 🖥 🍴 🏊 ✕

**▲▲▲ ▼▼▼▼ Quality Inn & Suites Boulder Creek SH ❖**
(303) 449-7550. **$79-$149.** 2020 Arapahoe Ave. US 36 (28th St), 0.5 mi w. Ext/int corridors. **Pets:** Medium, other species. $100 deposit/room, $15 daily fee/pet. Designated rooms, supervision.

SAVE S❻ ✕ 🖥 💻 🏊 ✕

**▼▼ ▼▼ Residence Inn by Marriott SH**
(303) 449-5545. **$99-$179.** 3030 Center Green Dr. 0.5 mi e of US 36 (28th St); e on Valmont Rd; corner of Foothills Pkwy. Ext corridors. **Pets:** Accepted.

ASK ✕ 🗐 🐾 🖥 💻 🏊 ✕

# BRECKENRIDGE

**▼▼▼▼ Great Divide Lodge LH**
(970) 547-5550. **$89-$249, 21 day notice.** 550 Village Rd. I-70, exit 203, 10.7 mi s on SR 9, just w on S Park Ave, then just s on Village Rd. **Pets:** Accepted.

ASK S❻ ✕ 🐾 🖥 💻 🍴 🏊 ✕ 🐕

**▼▼▼▼ The Hunt Placer Inn BB ❖**
(970) 453-7573. **$149-$218, 14 day notice.** 275 Ski Hill Rd. SR 9 (Main St), just w toward Peak 8. Int corridors. **Pets:** Medium, dogs only. $25 daily fee/room. Designated rooms, service with restrictions, supervision.

ASK S❻ ✕ 🐾 🐕

**▼▼▼▼ Liftside Suites in Breckenridge SH**
(970) 453-2000. **$109-$215, 21 day notice.** 535 S Park Ave. 0.3 mi w of SR 9. Int corridors. **Pets:** Accepted.

ASK S❻ ✕ 🐾 🖥 💻 🍴 🏊 ✕

**▼▼▼▼ The Village at Breckenridge Hotel SH**
(970) 453-2000. **$89-$199, 21 day notice.** 535 S Park Ave. 0.3 mi w of SR 9. Int corridors. **Pets:** $30 daily fee/room. Designated rooms, service with restrictions.

ASK S❻ ✕ 🐾 🖥 💻 🏊 ✕

**▼▼ ▼▼ Wildwood Suites CO**
(970) 453-0232. **$75-$425, 30 day notice.** 120 Sawmill Rd. From SR 9, just w on Ski Hill Rd, then just s. Int corridors. **Pets:** Large, dogs only. $75 one-time fee/room. Designated rooms, service with restrictions.

ASK S❻ ✕ 🖥 💻 ✕ 🐕

# BROOMFIELD

**▲▲▲ ▼▼▼▼ ▼▼▼▼ Omni Interlocken Resort LH ❖**
(303) 438-6600. **$189-$259.** 500 Interlocken Blvd. US 36 (Boulder Tpke), exit Interlocken Loop, then w, just s via signs. Int corridors. **Pets:** Small. $50 one-time fee/pet. Service with restrictions, crate.

SAVE S❻ ✕ 🐾 🗐 🐕 🖥 💻 🍴 🏊 ✕

**▼▼ ▼▼ TownePlace Suites by Marriott
Boulder/Broomfield SH ❖**
(303) 466-2200. **$109-$139.** 480 Flatiron Blvd. US 36 W (Boulder Tpke), exit Interlocken Loop, to first traffic light, w on Interlocken Blvd, then s. Int corridors. **Pets:** Medium. $25 one-time fee/pet. Service with restrictions.

ASK ✕ 🐾 🗐 🐕 🖥 💻 🏊

# BRUSH

**▲▲▲ ▼▼ ▼▼ Americas Best Value Inn Brush SH**
(970) 842-5146. **$50-$70.** 1208 N Colorado Ave. I-76, exit 90B, just n. Ext/int corridors. **Pets:** Accepted.

SAVE S❻ ✕ 🖥 💻 🏊

**▼▼ ▼▼ Microtel Inn SH**
(970) 842-4241. **$54-$68.** 975 N Colorado Ave. I-76, exit 90A, just s. Int corridors. **Pets:** Dogs only. $20 deposit/room, $15 daily fee/pet. Designated rooms, service with restrictions, supervision.

ASK S❻ ✕ 🐕 🖥 🏊

# BUENA VISTA

**▲▲▲ ▼▼ Alpine Lodge M**
(719) 395-2415. **$55-$75, 15 day notice.** 12845 Hwy 24 & 285. 2 mi s on US 24, 0.5 mi e on US 24 and 285. Ext corridors. **Pets:** Accepted.

SAVE S❻ ✕ 🖥

**▲▲▲ ▼▼▼▼ Best Western Vista Inn M**
(719) 395-8009. **$72-$149.** 733 US Hwy 24 N. 0.5 mi n. Int corridors. **Pets:** Medium, dogs only. $50 deposit/room, $10 daily fee/pet. Designated rooms, service with restrictions, supervision.

SAVE S❻ ✕ 🗐 🖥 💻 🏊

# BURLINGTON

**▼▼ ▼▼ Burlington Comfort Inn SH**
(719) 346-7676. **$69-$109, 14 day notice.** 282 S Lincoln St. I-70, exit 437, just n on US 385. Int corridors. **Pets:** Medium, other species. $50 deposit/room, $10 daily fee/room. Designated rooms, service with restrictions, supervision.

ASK S❻ ✕ 🐕 🖥 💻 🏊

**▲▲▲ ▼▼▼▼ Chaparral Motor Inn M**
(719) 346-5361. **$45-$59.** 405 S Lincoln St. I-70, exit 437, just n on jct US 385. Ext corridors. **Pets:** Small. $7 daily fee/pet. Service with restrictions, supervision.

SAVE S❻ ✕ 🖥 💻 🏊

# CANON CITY

**▼▼ ▼▼ Best Western Royal Gorge Motel M**
(719) 275-3377. **$50-$100, 7 day notice.** 1925 Fremont Dr. 0.8 mi e on US 50. Ext/int corridors. **Pets:** Accepted.

ASK S❻ ✕ 🖥 💻 🍴 🏊 ✕

**▲▲▲ ▼▼ ▼▼ Budget Host Royal Gorge Inn M**
(719) 269-1100. **$60-$99.** 217 N Raynolds Ave. 1 mi e on US 50, just n. Int corridors. **Pets:** Accepted.

SAVE ✕ 🖥 🏊

**▼▼ ▼▼ Comfort Inn SH**
(719) 276-6900. **$59-$99.** 311 Royal Gorge Blvd. On US 50, just w of downtown. Int corridors. **Pets:** Accepted.

ASK S❻ ✕ 🐾 🐕 🖥 💻 🏊

**▼▼▼▼ Holiday Inn Express SH**
(719) 275-2400. **$69-$125.** 110 Latigo Ln. 2.5 mi e of SR 115 on US 50. Int corridors. **Pets:** Small, dogs only. $15 one-time fee/pet. Designated rooms, service with restrictions, supervision.

ASK S❻ ✕ 🐾 🐕 🖥 💻 🏊

**▼▼ Quality Inn & Suites M**
(719) 275-8676. **$79-$189.** 3075 E Hwy 50. 2 mi e of jct SR 115 and US 50; center. Int corridors. **Pets:** Accepted.

(ASK) (S♂) (✕) (⌂) (▣) (🍴) (⇌)

## CARBONDALE

**♨♨ ▼▼▼ Comfort Inn & Suites SH ✿**
(970) 963-8880. **$79-$169.** 920 Cowen Dr. Jct of SR 82 and 133, just s via signs. Int corridors. **Pets:** Large, other species. $10 daily fee/pet. Designated rooms, service with restrictions, supervision.

(SAVE) (S♂) (✕) (⌂) (▣) (⇌) (✕)

**♨♨ ▼▼ Days Inn-Carbondale SH**
(970) 963-9111. **$59-$139, 3 day notice.** 950 Cowen Dr. Jct SR 82 and 133. Int corridors. **Pets:** Accepted.

(SAVE) (S♂) (✕) (⌂) (▣) (⇌) (✕)

**♨♨ ▼▼ Thunder River Lodge M ✿**
(970) 963-2543. **$46-$85.** 179 Hwy 133. Just s on SR 133, from jct SR 82. Ext corridors. **Pets:** $20 deposit/room, $5 daily fee/pet. Designated rooms, service with restrictions, supervision.

(SAVE) (✕)

## CASTLE ROCK

**♨♨ ▼▼▼ Best Western Inn & Suites of Castle Rock SH**
(303) 814-8800. **$79-$129.** 595 Genoa Way. I-25, exit 184 (Meadows Pkwy), just w to Castleton Way, just s, then e on Genoa Way. Int corridors. **Pets:** Medium. $15 daily fee/pet. Designated rooms, service with restrictions, supervision.

(SAVE) (S♂) (✕) (🐾) (⌂) (▣) (⇌)

**▼▼▼ Comfort Suites SH ✿**
(303) 814-9999. **$55-$99.** 4755 Castleton Way. I-25, exit 184 (Meadows Pkwy), w to Castleton Way; entry on east side. Int corridors. **Pets:** Other species. $10 daily fee/room.

(ASK) (S♂) (✕) (⅙M) (🐾) (⌂) (▣) (⇌) (✕)

**▼▼▼ Hampton Inn SH ✿**
(303) 660-9800. **$89-$159.** 4830 Castleton Way. I-25, exit 184 (Meadows Pkwy), sw to N Castleton Rd, just s, then e. Int corridors. **Pets:** Large, other species. $25 one-time fee/room. Service with restrictions, supervision.

(ASK) (S♂) (✕) (⅙M) (🐾) (⌂) (▣) (⇌)

**▼▼▼ Holiday Inn Express SH**
(303) 660-9733. **$59-$109.** 884 Park St. I-25, exit 182, just w. Int corridors. **Pets:** Medium, other species. $10 daily fee/pet. Service with restrictions, supervision.

(ASK) (S♂) (✕) (⌂) (▣) (⇌)

## CEDAREDGE

**♨♨ ▼▼▼ Howard Johnson Express Inn M**
(970) 856-7824. **$69-$99.** 530 S Grand Mesa Dr. Just s on SR 65. Int corridors. **Pets:** Accepted.

(SAVE) (✕) (⌂) (▣) (⇌)

---

# COLORADO SPRINGS METROPOLITAN AREA

## COLORADO SPRINGS

**♨♨ ▼▼▼ The Academy Hotel LH**
(719) 598-5770. **$79-$119, 3 day notice.** 8110 N Academy Blvd. I-25, exit 150, just s. Int corridors. **Pets:** Medium, other species. $60 deposit/pet. Service with restrictions, crate.

(SAVE) (S♂) (✕) (⅙M) (🐾) (⌂) (▣) (🍴) (⇌) (✕)

**▼▼ Airport Value Inn & Suites SH**
(719) 596-5588. **$59-$99.** 6875 Space Village Ave. I-25, exit 141, 1 mi e on Cimarron Ave, 0.7 mi n on Wahsatch Ave, 6.3 mi e on Platte Ave, then exit Space Village Ave. Ext/int corridors. **Pets:** Medium. $5 daily fee/pet, $35 one-time fee/room. Designated rooms, service with restrictions, supervision.

(ASK) (S♂) (✕) (⅙M) (⌂) (▣)

**♨♨ ▼▼▼▼ AmeriSuites (Colorado Springs/Garden of the Gods) SH**
(719) 265-9385. **$89-$149.** 503 W Garden of the Gods Rd. I-25, exit 146, just w. Int corridors. **Pets:** Large. $10 daily fee/pet. Service with restrictions, crate.

(SAVE) (✕) (🐾) (⌂) (▣) (⇌)

**♨♨ ▼▼ Apollo Park Executive Suites CO ✿**
(719) 634-0286. **$55-$105, 3 day notice.** 805 S Circle Dr, 2-B. I-25, exit 138, 2.5 mi e. Int corridors. **Pets:** Other species. $5 daily fee/room. Designated rooms, service with restrictions, supervision.

(SAVE) (S♂) (✕) (⌂) (▣) (⇌)

**♨♨ ▼▼ Best Western Airport Inn SH**
(719) 574-7707. **$69-$99.** 1780 Aeroplaza Dr. I-25, exit 139, 4 mi e on US 24 Bypass. Int corridors. **Pets:** Accepted.

(SAVE) (✕) (⅙M) (⌂) (▣) (⇌)

**♨♨ ▼▼▼ Best Western Executive Inn & Suites SH ✿**
(719) 576-2371. **$70-$140.** 1440 Harrison Rd. I-25, exit 138, just w; on northwest corner of interchange; entry through restaurant. Int corridors. **Pets:** Medium, dogs only. $10 daily fee/pet. Designated rooms, service with restrictions, supervision.

(SAVE) (S♂) (✕) (⅙M) (🐾) (⌂) (▣) (⇌)

**♨♨ ▼▼▼▼ The Broadmoor LH ✿**
(719) 634-7711. **$230-$530, 7 day notice.** 1 Lake Ave. I-25, exit 138, 3 mi w on Circle Dr (which becomes Lake Ave). Int corridors. **Pets:** Other species. $35 daily fee/pet. Service with restrictions, supervision.

(SAVE) (✕) (⅙M) (🐾) (⌂) (▣) (🍴) (⇌) (✕)

**♨♨ ▼▼ Chief Motel M**
(719) 473-5228. **$35-$65.** 1624 S Nevada Ave. I-25, exit 140. Ext corridors. **Pets:** Accepted.

(SAVE) (S♂) (✕) (⌂)

**♨♨ ▼▼▼ Comfort Inn North SH**
(719) 262-9000. **$49-$129.** 6450 Corporate Dr. I-25, exit 149 (Woodmen Rd), just w to 2nd light, then 0.3 mi s. Int corridors. **Pets:** Medium. $10 daily fee/pet. Supervision.

(SAVE) (S♂) (✕) (⅙M) (🐾) (⌂) (▣) (⇌)

**♨♨ ▼▼▼ Comfort Inn South SH**
(719) 579-6900. **$59-$109.** 1410 Harrison Rd. I-25, exit 138 (Circle Dr), just w to Rand Rd, then ne. Int corridors. **Pets:** $25 deposit/pet. Designated rooms, service with restrictions, supervision.

(SAVE) (S♂) (✕) (🐾) (⌂) (▣) (⇌)

**▼▼▼ Comfort Suites SH**
(719) 536-0731. **$99-$139.** 1055 Kelly Johnson Blvd. I-25, exit 150, just s on Academy Blvd to Kelly Johnson Blvd, then w. Int corridors. **Pets:** Other species. $20 one-time fee/room. Designated rooms, crate.

(ASK) (S♂) (✕) (⅙M) (🐾) (⌂) (▣) (⇌) (✕)

▼▼ **Days Inn-Air Force Academy** SH
(719) 266-1317. **$49-$94.** 8350 Razorback Rd. I-25, exit 150, just s, then e. Int corridors. **Pets:** Accepted.
ASK S🔥 ✕ 🐾M 🛏 💻 🏊

▼▼ **Doubletree Hotel Colorado Springs, World Arena** SH 🐾
(719) 576-8900. **$109-$199.** 1775 E Cheyenne Mountain Blvd. I-25, exit 138, just w. Int corridors. **Pets:** Medium, other species. $10 daily fee/pet. Service with restrictions, supervision.
ASK ✕ 🐾M 🗞 🖋 💻 🍽 🏊 ✕

▼▼▼ **Drury Inn-Pikes Peak** SH
(719) 598-2500. **$65-$135.** 8155 N Academy Blvd. I-25, exit 150, just s, then e. Int corridors. **Pets:** Accepted.
ASK ✕ 🗞 🛏 💻 🏊 ✕

AAA ▼▼▼ **Econo Lodge Inn & Suites** SH 🐾
(719) 632-6651. **$45-$85.** 1623 S Nevada Ave. I-25, exit 140, just s. Ext corridors. **Pets:** Other species. $10 deposit/pet, $10 one-time fee/pet. Service with restrictions, supervision.
SAVE S🔥 🖋 🛏 💻 🏊

▼▼▼ **Fairfield Inn by Marriott-South** SH
(719) 576-1717. **$69-$139.** 2725 Geyser Dr. I-25, exit 138, just w to E Cheyenne Mountain Blvd, then just s. Int corridors. **Pets:** Accepted.
ASK S🔥 ✕ 🐾M 🗞 🖋 🛏 💻 🏊

AAA ▼▼▼ **Holiday Inn Express Air Force Academy** SH 🐾
(719) 592-9800. **$59-$179.** 7110 Commerce Center Dr. I-25, exit 149, just w on Woodmen Rd, then just n. Int corridors. **Pets:** Medium, dogs only. $25 daily fee/pet. Designated rooms, service with restrictions, supervision.
SAVE S🔥 ✕ 🐾M 🖋 🛏 💻 🏊 ✕

▼▼ **Homewood Suites by Hilton** SH
(719) 265-6600. **$129-$219.** 9130 Explorer Dr. I-25, exit 151, 0.8 mi e; across from Focus on the Family. Int corridors. **Pets:** Medium, other species. $25 one-time fee/pet. Service with restrictions, crate.
ASK S🔥 ✕ 🗞 🖋 🛏 💻 🏊

▼▼▼ **Homewood Suites by Hilton Colorado Springs Airport** SH
(719) 574-2701. **$102-$123.** 2875 Zeppelin Rd. I-25, exit 139, 4 mi e on US 24 Bypass, 1.1 mi s on Powers Blvd, then just e. Int corridors. **Pets:** Small. $50 one-time fee/pet. Service with restrictions, crate.
ASK S🔥 ✕ 🗞 🛏 💻 🏊

AAA ▼▼▼ **La Quinta Inn & Suites Colorado Springs (South/Airport)** SH
(719) 527-4788. **$89-$149.** 2750 Geyser Dr. I-25, exit 138 (Circle Dr), just w to Cheyenne Mountain Blvd, then just s. Int corridors. **Pets:** Medium. Service with restrictions.
SAVE ✕ 🐾M 🗞 🖋 🛏 💻 🏊

AAA ▼▼▼ **La Quinta Inn Colorado Springs (Garden of the Gods)** SH
(719) 528-5060. **$62-$135.** 4385 Sinton Rd. I-25, exit 146, just e. Ext/int corridors. **Pets:** Medium. Service with restrictions.
SAVE ✕ 🗞 🛏 💻 🏊

▼▼▼ **Park Plaza Colorado Springs** LH
(719) 598-7656. **$69-$119.** 505 Popes Bluff Tr. I-25, exit 146, just w, then n on Hilton Pkwy. Int corridors. **Pets:** Medium. $50 deposit/room. Supervision.
ASK S🔥 ✕ 🐾M 🛏 💻 🍽 🏊 ✕

AAA ▼▼▼ **Radisson Inn & Suites** LH
(719) 597-7000. **$109-$119.** 1645 N Newport Rd. I-25, exit 139, 4 mi e on US 24 Bypass (Fountain Blvd). Int corridors. **Pets:** Medium, dogs only. $100 deposit/pet, $25 daily fee/room. Service with restrictions, crate.
SAVE S🔥 ✕ 🐾M 🗞 🖋 🛏 💻 🍽 🏊 ✕

AAA ▼▼▼ **Rainbow Lodge and Inn** M
(719) 632-4551. **$55-$95, 7 day notice.** 3709 W Colorado Ave. I-25, exit 141, 2.5 mi w on US 24, just n on 31st, then 0.7 mi w. Ext corridors. **Pets:** Accepted.
SAVE S🔥 ✕ 🛏 💻 🏊

▼▼ **Ramada Inn** SH
(719) 632-7077. **$59-$99.** 1703 S Nevada Ave. I-25, exit 140, 0.4 mi sw. Ext corridors. **Pets:** Accepted.
ASK S🔥 ✕ 🛏 💻 🏊

▼▼ **Ramada Limited East-Airport** SH
(719) 596-7660. **$59-$89.** 520 N Murray Blvd. I-25, exit 141, 1 mi e on Cimarron Ave, 0.7 mi n on Wahsatch Ave, 3.7 mi e on Platte Ave, the just n. Ext/int corridors. **Pets:** Other species. $25 deposit/pet. Designated rooms, service with restrictions, supervision.
ASK S🔥 ✕ 🖋 🛏 💻 🏊

▼▼▼▼ **Residence Inn by Marriott-Central** SH 🐾
(719) 574-0370. **$69-$139.** 3880 N Academy Blvd. I-25, exit 146, 6 mi e on Austin Bluffs Pkwy to Academy Blvd (SR 83), 0.3 mi s. Ext corridors. **Pets:** Other species. $75 one-time fee/room.
ASK S🔥 ✕ 🗞 🛏 💻 🏊 ✕

▼▼▼ **Residence Inn by Marriott Colorado Springs North at Interguest Pkwy** SH
(719) 388-9300. **$89-$299.** 9805 Federal Dr. I-25, exit 153, just e, then s. Int corridors. **Pets:** Small. $75 one-time fee/pet. Service with restrictions, supervision.
ASK S🔥 ✕ 🐾M 🛏 💻 🏊 ✕

▼▼▼ **Residence Inn by Marriott-Colorado Springs South** SH 🐾
(719) 576-0101. **$119-$189.** 2765 Geyser Dr. I-25, exit 138, just w to E Cheyenne Mountain Blvd, then just s. Int corridors. **Pets:** Other species. $75 one-time fee/room. Service with restrictions.
ASK S🔥 ✕ 🐾M 🛏 💻 🏊 ✕

▼▼ **Rodeway Inn** SH
(719) 471-0990. **$50-$60.** 2409 E Pikes Peak Ave. I-25, exit 143, e on Uintah to Union, s to Pikes Peak, then e; exit 138, ne on Circle Dr to Pikes Peak Ave, then w. Ext corridors. **Pets:** Accepted.
S🔥 ✕ 🛏 💻 🏊

▼▼▼ **Sheraton Colorado Springs Hotel** LH
(719) 576-5900. **$159-$199.** 2886 S Circle Dr. I-25, exit 138, just e. Int corridors. **Pets:** Accepted.
ASK S🔥 ✕ 🗞 🛏 💻 🍽 🏊 ✕

▼▼ **Sleep Inn** SH
(719) 260-6969. **$69-$99.** 1075 Kelly Johnson Blvd. I-25, exit 150, just s on Academy Blvd to Kelly Johnson Blvd, then w. Int corridors. **Pets:** Other species. $20 one-time fee/room. Designated rooms, crate.
ASK S🔥 ✕ 🐾M 🖋 🛏 💻 🏊

AAA ▼ **Stagecoach Motel** M 🐾
(719) 633-3894. **$39-$69.** 1647 S Nevada Ave. I-25, exit 140, just s. Ext corridors. **Pets:** Very small, other species. $5 daily fee/pet. Designated rooms, service with restrictions, crate.
SAVE S🔥 ✕ 🛏

AAA ▼▼▼▼ **Staybridge Suites-Air Force Academy** SH
(719) 590-7829. **$99-$199.** 7130 Commerce Center Dr. I-25, exit 149, just w, then n. Int corridors. **Pets:** Other species. $150 one-time fee/room. Designated rooms, service with restrictions, supervision.
SAVE S🔥 ✕ 🐾M 🗞 🖋 🛏 💻 🏊 ✕

▼▼▼ **TownePlace Suites by Marriott-Colorado Springs** SH
(719) 594-4447. **$79-$109.** 4760 Centennial Blvd. I-25, exit 146, 1 mi w on Garden of the Gods Rd, just n on Centennial Blvd, then first left. Int corridors. **Pets:** Accepted.
ASK S🔥 ✕ 🐾M 🖋 🛏 💻 🏊

**Travel Inn M**
(719) 636-3986. **$29-$89.** 512 S Nevada Ave. I-25, exit 141, just e to Nevada Ave, then just s. Ext/int corridors. **Pets:** Other species. $20 deposit/pet, $5 one-time fee/pet. Service with restrictions, supervision.

**Travelodge SH**
(719) 632-4600. **$40-$75.** 2625 Ore Mill Rd. I-25, exit 141, 2.3 mi nw on US 24; entry via 26th St. Int corridors. **Pets:** Medium. $20 one-time fee/pet. Service with restrictions, supervision.

**Wyndham Colorado Springs LH**
(719) 260-1800. **$79-$189.** 5580 Tech Center Dr. I-25, exit 147 (Rockrimmon Blvd), 0.5 mi w. Int corridors. **Pets:** Accepted.

## MANITOU SPRINGS

**Best Western Skyway Inn & Suites SH**
(719) 685-5991. **$79-$129, 3 day notice.** 311 Manitou Ave. I-25, exit 141, 4 mi w on US 24, then just sw on US 24 business route. Ext corridors. **Pets:** Accepted.

**Park Row Lodge M ❀**
(719) 685-5216. **$40-$70.** 54 Manitou Ave. I-25, exit 141, 4 mi w on US 24, then just ne on US 24 business route. Ext corridors. **Pets:** Small. $10 one-time fee/room. Service with restrictions, supervision.

**Red Wing Motel M**
(719) 685-5656. **$38-$120.** 56 El Paso Blvd. I-25, exit 141, 4 mi w on US 24, just ne on US 24 business route/Manitour Ave, then just w on Beckers Ln. Ext corridors. **Pets:** Medium. $7 daily fee/room. Service with restrictions, supervision.

**Silver Saddle Motel M ❀**
(719) 685-5611. **$65-$95, 30 day notice.** 215 Manitou Ave. I-25, exit 141, 4 mi w on US 24, then just sw on US 24 business route. Ext corridors. **Pets:** Other species. Service with restrictions, supervision.

## END METROPOLITAN AREA

## COPPER MOUNTAIN

**Copper Mountain Resort CO**
(970) 968-2882. **$134-$269.** 0509 Copper Rd. I-70, exit 195. Int corridors. **Pets:** Accepted.

## CORTEZ

**Anasazi Motor Inn M**
(970) 565-3773. **$55-$75.** 640 S Broadway. 0.5 mi sw on US 160 and 491. Ext corridors. **Pets:** Medium, other species. $50 deposit/pet. Designated rooms, service with restrictions, supervision.

**Best Western Turquoise Inn & Suites SH ❀**
(970) 565-3778. **$69-$159.** 535 E Main St. On US 160. Ext corridors. **Pets:** $15 one-time fee/room. Service with restrictions, supervision.

**Budget Host Inn M**
(970) 565-3738. **$44-$92.** 2040 E Main St. 1.3 mi e on US 160, w of jct SR 145. Ext corridors. **Pets:** $5 daily fee/pet. Designated rooms, service with restrictions, supervision.

**CareFree Inn Sands M**
(970) 565-3761. **$50-$89.** 1120 E Main St. 0.3 mi e on US 160. Ext/int corridors. **Pets:** Other species. $10 daily fee/pet. Designated rooms, service with restrictions, supervision.

**Comfort Inn SH**
(970) 565-3400. **$69-$149.** 2321 E Main St. 1.3 mi e on US 160. Ext/int corridors. **Pets:** Other species. $10 one-time fee/pet. Service with restrictions, supervision.

**Days Inn SH**
(970) 565-8577. **$49-$119.** US Hwy 160 at State 145. 1.5 mi e on US 160, at jct SR 145. Ext/int corridors. **Pets:** Large, other species. $10 one-time fee/room. Service with restrictions.

**Econo Lodge M**
(970) 565-3474. **$42-$89.** 2020 E Main St. 1.3 mi e on US 160. Ext corridors. **Pets:** Accepted.

**Holiday Inn Express SH**
(970) 565-6000. **$89-$159.** 2121 E Main St. 1.3 mi e on US 160. Int corridors. **Pets:** Other species. Designated rooms, service with restrictions, supervision.

**Tomahawk Lodge M**
(970) 565-8521. **$45-$79.** 728 S Broadway. 1 mi sw on US 160 and 491. Ext corridors. **Pets:** Dogs only. $25 deposit/pet. Designated rooms, service with restrictions, supervision.

**Travelodge M**
(970) 565-7778. **$40-$79.** 440 S Broadway. 0.8 mi sw on US 160 and 491. Ext corridors. **Pets:** Accepted.

## CRAIG

**Best Western Deer Park Inn and Suites SH**
(970) 824-9282. **$69-$129.** 262 Commerce St (Hwy 13). Jct US 40, just 0.3 mi s on SR 13. Int corridors. **Pets:** Medium. $50 deposit/room, $10 daily fee/room. No service, supervision.

**Black Nugget Motel M**
(970) 824-8161. **$40-$65.** 2855 W Victory Way. 1.5 mi w on US 40, 0.3 mi w of jct SR 13. Ext corridors. **Pets:** Large, other species. $5 daily fee/pet. Service with restrictions, supervision.

**Craig Holiday Inn SH**
(970) 824-4000. **$79-$159.** 300 S Hwy 13. 0.3 mi s on SR 13, from jct US 40. Int corridors. **Pets:** Accepted.

# CRESTED BUTTE

**▼▼▼▼ Grand Lodge Crested Butte** 🔲
(970) 349-8000. **$69-$229, 3 day notice.** 6 Emmons Loop. 2.5 mi n on SR 135. Int corridors. **Pets:** Dogs only. $30 one-time fee/room. Designated rooms, service with restrictions, supervision.

(A$K) (S🔲) (✕) (🔲) (🔲) (🔲) (🍴) (🏊) (✕)

**▼▼▼ Old Town Inn** 🔲
(970) 349-6184. **$59-$98, 14 day notice.** 708 6th St. Se on SR 135. Int corridors. **Pets:** $10 daily fee/room. Designated rooms, supervision.

(A$K) (S🔲) (✕) (🔲)

# DELTA

**▼▼▼ Best Western Sundance** 🔲
(970) 874-9781. **$95-$105, 7 day notice.** 903 Main St. 0.5 mi s on US 50. Ext corridors. **Pets:** Other species. $10 daily fee/pet. Service with restrictions, crate.

(SAVE) (S🔲) (✕) (🔲) (🔲) (🍴) (🏊) (✕)

**▼▼▼ Comfort Inn** 🔲
(970) 874-1000. **$60-$72.** 180 Gunnison River Dr. Just n, w of jct US 50 and 92. Int corridors. **Pets:** Accepted.

(A$K) (S🔲) (✕) (🔲) (🔲)

**▼▼▼ Southgate Inns** 🔲
(970) 874-9726. **$45-$80.** 2124 S Main St. 1.5 mi s on US 50. Ext corridors. **Pets:** Medium, dogs only. $10 one-time fee/room. Designated rooms, service with restrictions, supervision.

(SAVE) (S🔲) (✕) (🔲) (🔲) (🏊)

# DENVER METROPOLITAN AREA

# AURORA

**▼▼▼▼ AmeriSuites (Denver/Airport)** 🔲
(303) 371-0700. **$99-$169, 10 day notice.** 16250 E 40th Ave. I-70, exit 283 (Chambers Rd), just n, then 0.5 mi e. Int corridors. **Pets:** $30 one-time fee/room. Service with restrictions, supervision.

(SAVE) (S🔲) (✕) (🔲) (🔲) (🔲) (🔲) (🔲) (🏊)

**▼▼▼▼ Best Western Gateway Inn & Suites** 🔲
(720) 748-4800. **$69-$129.** 800 S Abilene St. I-225, exit 7 (Mississippi Ave), e to Abilene St, then 3 blks n. Int corridors. **Pets:** Accepted.

(SAVE) (S🔲) (✕) (🔲) (🔲) (🔲) (🏊) (✕)

**▼▼ Comfort Inn Denver Southeast** 🔲
(303) 755-8000. **$49-$89.** 14071 E Iliff Ave. I-225, exit 5, just e. Int corridors. **Pets:** Accepted.

(A$K) (S🔲) (✕) (🔲) (🔲) (🔲) (🔲)

**▼▼▼ Crestwood Suites** 🔲
(303) 481-0379. **$59-$99.** 14090 E Evans. I-225, exit 5 (E Iliff Ave), e to Blackhawk St, then 0.4 mi nw. Int corridors. **Pets:** Accepted.

(A$K) (S🔲) (✕) (🔲) (🔲)

**▼▼▼ Extended Stay Deluxe** 🔲
(303) 337-7000. **$69-$89.** 14095 E Evans Ave. I-225, exit 5 (E Iliff Ave), just e to Blackhawk St, then just n. Int corridors. **Pets:** $25 daily fee/pet. Service with restrictions, supervision.

(A$K) (S🔲) (✕) (🔲) (🔲) (🔲) (🔲) (🔲) (🏊)

**▼▼▼ Homestead Studio Suites Hotel-Denver/Aurora** 🔲
(303) 750-9116. **$52-$62.** 13941 E Harvard Ave. I-225, exit 5, just e on E Iliff Ave to Blackhawk St, then just s. Ext corridors. **Pets:** $25 daily fee/pet. Service with restrictions, supervision.

(A$K) (S🔲) (✕) (🔲) (🔲) (🔲) (🔲) (🔲)

**▼▼▼▼ La Quinta Inn Denver (Aurora)** 🔲
(303) 337-0206. **$65-$109.** 1011 S Abilene St. I-225, exit 7, just e, then n. Ext corridors. **Pets:** Medium. Service with restrictions.

(A$K) (✕) (🔲) (🔲) (🔲) (🏊)

**▼▼▼▼ Sleep Inn Denver International Airport** 🔲
(303) 373-1616. **$54-$139.** 15900 E 40th Ave. I-70, exit 283; from airport, Pena Blvd S to 40th Ave W. Int corridors. **Pets:** Accepted.

(SAVE) (S🔲) (✕) (🔲) (🔲) (🔲) (🔲) (🏊)

# CENTENNIAL

**▼▼▼ Days Inn Denver Tech Center** 🔲
(303) 768-9400. **$50-$100.** 9719 E Geddes Ave. I-25, exit 196 (Dry Creek Rd), just e to S Clinton St, just n, then just e. Int corridors. **Pets:** Accepted.

(A$K) (S🔲) (✕) (🔲) (🔲) (🔲)

**▼▼▼▼ Embassy Suites Denver Tech Center** 🔲
(303) 792-0433. **$79-$229.** 10250 E Costilla Ave. I-25, exit 197, 1 mi e on Arapahoe Rd, 0.3 mi s on Havana St, then w. Int corridors. **Pets:** Medium, other species. $75 one-time fee/room. Service with restrictions, supervision.

(SAVE) (✕) (🔲) (🔲) (🔲) (🔲) (🔲) (🍴) (🏊)

# DENVER

**▼▼▼ Best Western Central Denver** 🔲
(303) 296-4000. **$65-$79.** 200 W 48th Ave. I-25, exit 215 northbound; exit 214B southbound. Int corridors. **Pets:** Medium, dogs only. $10 daily fee/pet. Designated rooms, service with restrictions, crate.

(SAVE) (S🔲) (✕) (🔲) (🔲) (🍴) (🏊)

**▼▼▼ ▼▼▼ Brown Palace Hotel & Spa** 🔲
(303) 297-3111. **$149-$199.** 321 17th St, Tremont & Broadway. I-25, exit 210 (E Colfax Ave) to Lincoln St, n to Tremont, then just w. Int corridors. **Pets:** Accepted.

(SAVE) (S🔲) (✕) (🔲) (🔲) (🔲) (🔲) (🍴) (✕)

**▼▼▼ Cameron Motel** 🔲 🐾
(303) 757-2100. **$52-$65.** 4500 E Evans Ave. I-25, exit 203, then w. Ext corridors. **Pets:** Medium, other species. $5 daily fee/pet. Designated rooms, service with restrictions, supervision.

(SAVE) (✕) (🔲)

**▼▼▼ Comfort Inn Central** 🔲 🐾
(303) 297-1717. **$84-$114.** 401 E 58th Ave. I-25, exit 215, just e, then left on Logan St. Int corridors. **Pets:** Medium, dogs only. $10 daily fee/room. Designated rooms, service with restrictions, crate.

(SAVE) (S🔲) (✕) (🔲) (🔲) (🔲) (🍴) (🏊)

**▼▼▼▼ Comfort Inn Downtown Denver** 🔲
(303) 296-0400. **$89-$149.** 401 17th St. I-25, exit 210 (E Colfax Ave) to Lincoln St, n to Tremont, then just w; opposite Brown Palace Hotel. Int corridors. **Pets:** Accepted.

(SAVE) (S🔲) (✕) (🔲) (🔲) (🍴)

**▼▼▼▼ Denver Marriott Tech Center** 🔲
(303) 779-1100. **$89-$199.** 4900 S Syracuse St. I-25, exit 199, exit Bellview e to Syracuse St, then just n. Int corridors. **Pets:** Accepted.

(A$K) (S🔲) (✕) (🔲) (🔲) (🔲) (🔲) (🍴) (🏊)

**▼▼▼ DoubleTree Hotel Denver** LH
(303) 321-3333. **$74-$189.** 3203 Quebec St. I-70, exit 278, 0.5 mi s; I-270, exit 4. Int corridors. **Pets:** Accepted.

ASK SD ✕ 🐾 🛏 🖥 🍴 ≈ ✕

**▼▼▼▼ Drury Inn-Denver East** SH
(303) 373-1983. **$70-$120.** 4380 E Peoria St. I-70, exit 281, just n. Int corridors. **Pets:** Accepted.

ASK ✕ 🐾 🛏 🖥 ≈

**▼▼▼▼ Embassy Suites Denver-Aurora** LH
(303) 375-0400. **$89-$199.** 4444 N Havana St. I-70, exit 280, just n. Int corridors. **Pets:** Accepted.

ASK ✕ 🚹M 🐾 🛏 🖥 🍴 ≈ ✕

**▼▼▼▼ The Four Points by Sheraton Denver Southeast** LH
(303) 758-7000. **$199.** 6363 E Hampden Ave. I-25, exit 201, just e. Ext/int corridors. **Pets:** Accepted.

ASK SD ✕ 🚹M 🐾 🛏 🖥 🍴 ≈ ✕

**🅰🅰🅰 ▼▼▼ Guesthouse Hotel Denver Stapleton** SH
(303) 388-6161. **$69-$155.** 3737 Quebec St. I-70, exit 278, just s. Int corridors. **Pets:** Other species. $25 one-time fee/room. Designated rooms, service with restrictions, supervision.

SAVE SD ✕ 🛏 🖥 🍴 ≈

**▼▼▼▼ Hampton Inn & Suites Denver Tech Center** SH 🐾
(303) 804-9900. **$59-$149.** 5001 S Ulster St. I-25, exit 199, e to Ulster St, then just n. Int corridors. **Pets:** Medium. $100 deposit/room. Service with restrictions, supervision.

ASK SD ✕ 🚹M 🐾 🛏 🖥 ≈

**🅰🅰🅰 ▼▼▼▼ Hampton Inn DIA** SH
(303) 371-0200. **$86-$100.** 6290 Tower Rd. I-70, exit 186 (Tower Rd), 3.5 mi n. Int corridors. **Pets:** Accepted.

SAVE SD ✕ 🚹M 🐾 🛏 ≈

**🅰🅰🅰 ▼▼▼▼ Holiday Chalet A Victorian Bed & Breakfast** BB 🐾
(303) 437-8245. **$94-$160.** 1820 E Colfax Ave. I-25, exit 210, 2.3 mi e on US 40. Int corridors. **Pets:** Other species. $5 daily fee/room. No service, supervision.

SAVE ✕ 🛏 🖥

**▼▼▼ Holiday Inn-Denver Central** LH
(303) 292-9500. **$89-$129.** 4849 Bannock St. I-25, 215 northbound; exit 214B southbound, 1 mi s. Ext/int corridors. **Pets:** Accepted.

ASK SD ✕ 🚹M 🐾 🛒 🛏 🖥 🍴 ≈

**🅰🅰🅰 ▼▼▼▼ Holiday Inn DIA** LH 🐾
(303) 371-9494. **$87, 3 day notice.** 15500 E 40th Ave. I-70, exit 283 (Chambers Rd), just n, then just e. Int corridors. **Pets:** Other species. $25 one-time fee/room. Designated rooms, service with restrictions, crate.

SAVE SD ✕ 🚹M 🐾 🛒 🛏 🖥 🍴 ≈ ✕

**▼▼ Homestead Studio Suites Hotel-Denver/Tech Center-North** SH
(303) 689-9443. **$64-$74.** 4885 S Quebec St. I-25, exit 199, just w to Quebec St, then just n; next to Mountain View Golf Course. Ext corridors. **Pets:** $25 daily fee/pet. Service with restrictions, supervision.

ASK SD ✕ 🚹M 🐾 🛒 🛏 🖥

**🅰🅰🅰 ▼▼▼▼ Hotel Monaco Denver** SH 🐾
(303) 296-1717. **$169-$289.** 1717 Champa St. I-25, exit 212A (Speer Blvd S), s to Curtis St, w to 19th St, 1 blk s to Champa St, then 2 blks w. Int corridors. **Pets:** Other species. Service with restrictions, supervision.

SAVE SD ✕ 🚹M 🐾 🛒 🛏 🖥 🍴 ✕

**🅰🅰🅰 ▼▼▼ ▼▼ Hotel Teatro** SH 🐾
(303) 228-1100. **$185-$1400.** 1100 14th St. I-25, exit 212 (Speer Blvd), just ne on Lawrence St, then e to 14th St; exit Auraria Pkwy northbound. Int corridors. **Pets:** Dogs only.

SAVE ✕ 🐾 🚹M 🐾 🛏 🖥 🍴 ✕

**▼▼▼▼ The Inn at Cherry Creek** SH
(303) 377-8577. **$169-$229.** 234 Columbine St. Entrance on Clayton St; between 2nd and 3rd aves; in Cherry Creek Village. Int corridors. **Pets:** Dogs only. Designated rooms, service with restrictions, supervision.

ASK SD ✕ 🖥 🍴

**🅰🅰🅰 ▼▼▼ ▼▼▼ JW Marriott Denver At Cherry Creek** SH 🐾
(303) 316-2700. **$189-$289.** 150 Clayton Ln. I-25, exit 5 (University Blvd), 2.4 mi n to 1st Ave, just e, then just n. Int corridors. **Pets:** Other species. Service with restrictions, supervision.

SAVE SD ✕ 🚹M 🐾 🖥 🍴 ✕

**▼▼▼▼ La Quinta Inn & Suites Denver (Airport/DIA)** SH
(303) 371-0888. **$82-$119.** 6801 Tower Rd. I-70, exit 286, 4.2 mi n; 0.8 mi s of Pena Blvd. Int corridors. **Pets:** Medium. Service with restrictions.

ASK ✕ 🚹M 🐾 🛒 🛏 🖥 ≈

**▼▼▼▼ La Quinta Inn Denver (Central)** SH
(303) 458-1222. **$77-$127.** 3500 Park Ave W. I-25, exit 213, take 38th Ave, just s, left at Fox St, left on Park Ave to 2nd light, then U-turn. Ext/int corridors. **Pets:** Medium. Service with restrictions.

ASK ✕ 🚹M 🐾 🛒 🖥 ≈

**🅰🅰🅰 ▼▼▼▼ La Quinta Inn Denver (Cherry Creek)** SH
(303) 758-8886. **$72-$119.** 1975 S Colorado Blvd. I-25, exit 204, just s. Ext corridors. **Pets:** Medium. Service with restrictions.

SAVE ✕ 🐾 🛏 🖥 ≈

**▼▼▼▼ Magnolia Hotel-Downtown** SH 🐾
(303) 607-9000. **$99-$249.** 818 17th St. I-25, exit 212A (Speer Blvd S) to Market St, e to 17th St, then s to jct 17th and Stout sts. Int corridors. **Pets:** Medium. $20 daily fee/pet. Designated rooms, service with restrictions, crate.

ASK ✕ 🐾 🐾 🛒 🛏 🖥

**▼▼▼▼ Marriott Courtyard Denver Cherry Creek** SH
(303) 757-8797. **$89-$179.** 1475 S Colorado Blvd. I-25, exit 204, 0.5 mi n; entry on Arkansas St. Int corridors. **Pets:** Accepted.

ASK SD ✕ 🚹M 🐾 🛒 🛏 🖥 ≈

**🅰🅰🅰 ▼▼▼ Quality Inn Denver East** SH
(303) 371-5640. **$80-$100.** 3975 Peoria Way. I-70, exit 281, exit 281 eastbound; exit 282 westbound, just s. Ext corridors. **Pets:** Medium, other species. $15 daily fee/room. Designated rooms, service with restrictions, supervision.

SAVE SD ✕ 🛏 🖥 ≈

**🅰🅰🅰 ▼▼▼▼ Radisson Hotel Denver Stapleton Plaza** LH
(303) 321-3500. **$79-$109.** 3333 Quebec St. I-70, exit 278, 0.3 mi s; I-270, exit 4. Int corridors. **Pets:** Accepted.

SAVE SD ✕ 🚹M 🐾 🛒 🖥 🍴 ≈ ✕

**▼▼▼▼ Ramada Continental Hotel** SH
(303) 433-6677. **$60-$80.** 2601 Zuni St. I-25, exit 212B, just w on Speer Blvd, then just e. **Pets:** Other species. $25 one-time fee/room. Designated rooms, service with restrictions, crate.

ASK 🐾 🛒 🛏 🖥 🍴 ≈

**▼▼▼▼ Ramada Inn Denver Downtown** LH
(303) 831-7700. **$79-$129.** 1150 E Colfax Ave. I-25, exit 210 (E Colfax Ave), 1 mi e on US 40; 0.5 mi e of State Capitol. Int corridors. **Pets:** Other species. $100 deposit/room. Service with restrictions.

ASK SD ✕ 🐾 🛏 🖥 🍴 ≈

**Ramada Suites at Denver International Airport** SH
(303) 373-1600. **$90-$100.** 7020 Tower Rd. I-70, exit 186 (Tower Rd), 4.5 mi n. Int corridors. **Pets:** Medium. $35 deposit/room. Service with restrictions, supervision.

SAVE Sₒ X ᕘM ᐧᕍ 🛢 🖵 🌊

**Red Lion Denver Central** SH
(303) 321-6666. **$49-$129.** 4040 Quebec St. I-70, exit 278, just s. Ext/int corridors. **Pets:** Accepted.

ASK Sₒ X ᐧᕍ 🛢 🖵 ¶ 🌊

**Red Lion Hotel Denver Downtown at Invesco Field** SH
(303) 433-8331. **$109-$139.** 1975 Bryant St. I-25, exit 210B, just w. Int corridors. **Pets:** Accepted.

SAVE Sₒ X 🛢 🖵 ¶ 🌊

**Red Roof Inn & Suites** SH
(303) 371-5300. **$63-$93.** 6890 Tower Rd. I-70, exit 286, 4.2 mi n; 0.8 mi s of Pena Blvd. Int corridors. **Pets:** Small, other species. $75 deposit/room. Service with restrictions, supervision.

SAVE Sₒ X ᕘ ᐧᕍ 🛢 🖵 🌊

**Residence Inn by Marriott Denver Downtown** SH ❀
(303) 458-5318. **$119-$199.** 2777 Zuni St. I-25, exit 212B, just w. Ext corridors. **Pets:** Large. $75 one-time fee/pet. Service with restrictions.

ASK Sₒ X ᕘ 🛢 🖵 🌊 ⊠

**TownePlace Suites by Marriott-Denver Southeast** SH ❀
(303) 759-9393. **$49-$99.** 3699 S Monaco Pkwy. I-25, exit 201, just e to Monaco Pkwy, then s. Int corridors. **Pets:** Large. $75 one-time fee/pet. Service with restrictions, supervision.

X ᐧᕍ 🛢 🖵 🌊

**TownePlace Suites by Marriott Downtown Denver** SH
(303) 722-2322. **$129-$159.** 685 Speer Blvd. I-25, exit Speer Blvd S, 1.5 mi s, stay in right lane, just past second Bannock St, exit towards Broadway, then right on Acoma St. Int corridors. **Pets:** Accepted.

ASK Sₒ X ᕘ ᐧᕍ 🖵 🌊

**The Warwick Hotel-Denver** SH ❀
(303) 861-2000. **$260.** 1776 Grant St at 18th Ave. I-25, exit 210 (E Colfax Ave) to Logan St, n to 18th St, then just w. Int corridors. **Pets:** Dogs only. $200 deposit/room. Designated rooms, service with restrictions.

SAVE Sₒ X ᕘ ᐧᕍ 🛢 🖵 ¶ 🌊

**The Westin Tabor Center Denver** LH
(303) 572-9100. **$225.** 1672 Lawrence St. I-25, exit 212A, 1 mi s to Lawrence St, then e. Int corridors. **Pets:** Accepted.

SAVE Sₒ X ᕘM ᕘ ᐧᕍ 🖵 ¶ 🌊 ⊠

# ENGLEWOOD

**AmeriSuites (Denver/Tech Center)** SH
(303) 804-0700. **$99-$159, 30 day notice.** 8300 E Crescent Pkwy. I-25, exit 199 (Bellview Ave), 0.4 mi e to Crescent Pkwy, then s. Int corridors. **Pets:** Accepted.

SAVE Sₒ X ᕘ ᐧᕍ 🛢 🖵 🌊

**Drury Inn & Suites-Denver Near the Tech Center** SH
(303) 694-3400. **$70-$110.** 9445 E Dry Creek Rd. I-25, exit 196 (Dry Creek Rd), just w, on northwest corner. Int corridors. **Pets:** Accepted.

ASK X ᐧᕍ 🛢 🖵 🌊

**Holiday Inn Express Hotel & Suites** SH
(303) 662-0777. **$81-$100.** 7380 S Clinton St. I-25, exit 196 (Dry Creek Rd), e to S Clinton St, then just n. Int corridors. **Pets:** Medium, other species. $35 one-time fee/room. Service with restrictions.

ASK Sₒ X ᕘ ᐧᕍ 🛢 🖵 🌊

**Homestead Studio Suites Hotel-Denver/Tech South/Inverness** M
(303) 708-8888. **$52-$76.** 9650 E Geddes Ave. I-25, exit 196 (Dry Creek Rd), just e, then n on S Clinton St. Ext corridors. **Pets:** $25 daily fee/pet. Service with restrictions, supervision.

ASK Sₒ X ᕘ ᐧᕍ 🛢 🖵

**Quality Suites Denver Tech** SH
(303) 858-0700. **$80-$85.** 7374 S Clinton St. I-25, exit 196 (Dry Creek Rd), just e, then n. Int corridors. **Pets:** Accepted.

ASK Sₒ X ᕘM ᕘ ᐧᕍ 🛢 🖵 🌊

**Residence Inn by Marriott-Denver Tech Center** SH
(303) 740-7177. **$89-$179.** 6565 S Yosemite St. I-25, exit 197, just w on Arapahoe Rd, then n. Ext corridors. **Pets:** Accepted.

ASK Sₒ X ᕘM 🛢 🖵 🌊 ⊠

**Residence Inn Park Meadows** SH
(720) 895-0200. **$74-$199.** 8322 S Valley Hwy. I-25, exit 195 (County Line Rd), just e to S Valley Hwy, then just s. Int corridors. **Pets:** Other species. $75 one-time fee/room. Service with restrictions.

ASK Sₒ X ᕘM 🛢 🖵 🌊 ⊠

**TownePlace Suites Denver Tech Center** SH
(720) 875-1113. **$66-$94.** 7877 S Chester St. I-25, exit 196 (Dry Creek Rd), just w to Chester St, then 0.3 mi s. Int corridors. **Pets:** Accepted.

ASK Sₒ X ᕘM ᐧᕍ 🛢 🖵 🌊

# GLENDALE

**Four Points Cherry Creek Denver** SH ❀
(303) 757-3341. **$199.** 600 S Colorado Blvd. I-25, exit 204, 1.4 mi n. Int corridors. **Pets:** $25 one-time fee/pet. Service with restrictions, supervision.

SAVE X 🖵 ¶ 🌊

**Homestead Studio Suites Hotel-Denver/Cherry Creek** SH
(303) 388-3880. **$64-$74.** 4444 Leetsdale Dr. I-25, exit 204, 1.5 mi n to E Virginia Ave, just e to S Birch St, then just n. Ext corridors. **Pets:** $25 daily fee/pet. Service with restrictions, supervision.

ASK Sₒ X ᕘM ᐧᕍ 🖵

**Loews Denver Hotel** LH ❀
(303) 782-9300. **$129-$229.** 4150 E Mississippi Ave. I-25, exit 204, 1 mi n on Colorado Blvd, then just e. Int corridors. **Pets:** Large, other species. Service with restrictions.

SAVE X ᕘM ᕘ ᐧᕍ 🛢 🖵 ¶

**Staybridge Suites Denver/Cherry Creek** SH
(303) 321-5757. **$109-$169.** 4220 E Virginia Ave. I-25, exit 204, 1.5 mi n on Colorado Blvd to Virginia Ave, then just e. Int corridors. **Pets:** Accepted.

ASK Sₒ X ᕘM ᕘ ᐧᕍ 🛢 🖵 ⊠

# GOLDEN

**Clarion Collection The Golden Hotel** SH ❀
(303) 279-0100. **$99-$269.** 800 11th St. At 11th St and Washington Ave; downtown. Int corridors. **Pets:** Medium, other species. $100 deposit/pet, $15 daily fee/pet. Service with restrictions, supervision.

ASK Sₒ X ᕘ 🛢 🖵 ¶

**Days Inn Denver West** SH
(303) 277-0200. **$79-$139.** 15059 W Colfax Ave. I-70, exit 262 (Colfax Ave), just e. Int corridors. **Pets:** Other species. $7 daily fee/pet. Service with restrictions, crate.

ASK Sₒ X ᕘ ᐧᕍ 🛢 🖵 ¶ 🌊 ⊠

▼▼▼ Denver Marriott West **LH**
(303) 279-9100. **$159.** 1717 Denver W Blvd. I-70, exit 263, just n, then w. Int corridors. **Pets:** $50 one-time fee/room. Designated rooms, service with restrictions, supervision.

(ASK) (S⚡) (✕) (&M) (🐾) (📠) (📶) (🛏) (🍴) (🏊) (🚫)

▼▼▼ Holiday Inn Denver West **LH**
(303) 279-7611. **$74-$94, 3 day notice.** 14707 W Colfax Ave. I-70, exit 262 (Colfax Ave), just e. Ext/int corridors. **Pets:** Accepted.

(ASK) (S⚡) (✕) (&M) (🐾) (📶) (📶) (🛏) (🍴) (🏊) (🚫)

◆◆◆ ▼▼▼ La Quinta Inn Denver (Golden) **SH**
(303) 279-5565. **$78-$124.** 3301 Youngfield Service Rd. I-70, exit 264 (32nd Ave), just w, then n. Ext corridors. **Pets:** Medium. Service with restrictions.

(SAVE) (✕) (🐾) (📶) (🏊)

▼▼▼ Residence Inn by Marriott Denver West/Golden **SH**
(303) 271-0909. **$89-$129.** 14600 W 6th Ave Frontage Rd. US 6, exit Indiana Ave to frontage road, just e. Int corridors. **Pets:** Other species. $75 one-time fee/pet.

(ASK) (✕) (&M) (🐾) (📶) (📶) (🏊) (🚫)

◆◆◆ ▼▼▼ Table Mountain Inn **SH**
(303) 277-9898. **$113-$187.** 1310 Washington Ave. US 6, exit 19th St, 0.5 mi n to Washington Ave, 0.5 mi w; downtown, just s of arch. Int corridors. **Pets:** Accepted.

(SAVE) (S⚡) (✕) (&M) (🐾) (📶) (📶) (🍴)

# GREENWOOD VILLAGE

▼▼▼ Hampton Inn Denver Southeast **SH** 🐾
(303) 792-9999. **$109-$155.** 9231 E Arapahoe Rd. I-25, exit 197, just e. Int corridors. **Pets:** Medium, other species. $25 daily fee/pet. Designated rooms, service with restrictions, crate.

(ASK) (✕) (&M) (🐾) (📶) (📶) (🏊)

▼▼▼ Homestead Studio Suites Hotel-Denver/Tech South/
Greenwood Village **SH**
(303) 858-1669. **$59-$74.** 9253 E Costilla Ave. I-25, exit 197, just e on Arapahoe Rd, se on Clinton St to Costilla St, then w. Int corridors. **Pets:** $25 daily fee/pet. Service with restrictions, supervision.

(ASK) (S⚡) (✕) (&M) (🐾) (📶) (📶)

▼▼▼ La Quinta Inn & Suites Denver (Tech Center) **SH**
(303) 649-9969. **$95-$135.** 7077 S Clinton St. I-25, exit 197, e to Clinton St, then s. Int corridors. **Pets:** Medium. Service with restrictions.

(ASK) (✕) (&M) (🐾) (📶) (📶) (🏊)

▼▼▼ Sheraton Denver Tech Center Hotel **SH** 🐾
(303) 799-6200. **$229.** 7007 S Clinton St. I-25, exit 197, e on Arapahoe Rd, then s. Int corridors. **Pets:** Medium, dogs only. Designated rooms, service with restrictions, supervision.

(ASK) (S⚡) (✕) (&M) (🐾) (📶) (📶) (🍴) (🏊)

▼▼▼ Sleep Inn Denver Tech Center **SH**
(303) 662-9950. **$54-$63.** 9257 Costilla Ave. I-25, exit 197, just e to Clinton St, s to Costilla Ave, then w. Int corridors. **Pets:** Accepted.

(ASK) (S⚡) (✕) (&M) (🐾) (📶) (📶) (🏊)

◆◆◆ ▼▼▼ Summerfield Suites by Wyndham-Denver Tech
Center **SH**
(303) 706-1945. **$79-$189.** I-25, exit 197, e to Clinton St, then just s. Int corridors. **Pets:** Accepted.

(SAVE) (✕) (&M) (🐾) (📶) (📶) (📶) (🏊) (🚫)

◆◆◆ ▼▼▼ Woodfield Suites Denver-Tech Center **SH**
(303) 799-4555. **$90-$110.** 9009 E Arapahoe Rd. I-25, exit 197, just e. Int corridors. **Pets:** Medium. Service with restrictions.

(SAVE) (✕) (&M) (🐾) (📶) (📶) (📶) (🏊) (🚫)

# HIGHLANDS RANCH

▼▼▼ Residence Inn Denver South Highlands Ranch **SH**
(303) 683-5500. **$142.** 93 Centennial Blvd. SR 470, exit Broadway, just s, then w. Int corridors. **Pets:** Large, other species. $75 one-time fee/pet. Service with restrictions.

(ASK) (✕) (&M) (🐾) (📶) (📶) (📶) (🏊) (🚫)

# LAKEWOOD

◆◆◆ ▼▼▼ Best Western-Denver Southwest **SH**
(303) 989-5500. **$49-$75.** 3440 S Vance St. Just ne of jct US 285 (Hampden Ave) and S Wadsworth Blvd, e on Girton Dr, then just s. Int corridors. **Pets:** $75 deposit/room. Designated rooms, service with restrictions, supervision.

(SAVE) (S⚡) (✕) (🐾) (📶) (📶) (🏊)

▼▼▼ Comfort Suites **SH**
(303) 231-9929. **$89-$109.** 11909 W 6th. US 6, exit Simms/Union, westbound travelers must turn right at stop light, but do not use right turn lane, follow signs to frontage road. Int corridors. **Pets:** Medium. $10 daily fee/pet. Service with restrictions, supervision.

(ASK) (S⚡) (✕) (🐾) (📶) (📶) (🏊) (🚫)

◆◆◆ ▼▼▼ La Quinta Inn & Suites Denver
(Southwest/Lakewood) **M**
(303) 969-9700. **$75-$129.** 7190 W Hampden Ave. Just se of jct US 285 (W Hampden Ave) and Wadsworth Blvd, e on Jefferson Ave, just n, then e on frontage road. Int corridors. **Pets:** Medium. Service with restrictions.

(SAVE) (✕) (&M) (🐾) (📶) (📶) (🏊)

▼▼▼ Quality Suites Lakewood **SH**
(303) 988-8600. **$79-$129.** 7260 W Jefferson Ave. Just se of US 285 (W Hampden Ave) and Wadsworth Blvd, then e. Int corridors. **Pets:** Medium, dogs only. $10 daily fee/pet. Designated rooms, service with restrictions, crate.

(ASK) (S⚡) (✕) (🐾) (📶) (📶) (🏊)

▼▼▼ Residence Inn by Marriott Denver
SW/Lakewood **SH**
(303) 985-7676. **$107-$116.** 7050 W Hampden Ave. Just se of jct US 285 (W Hampden Ave) and Wadsworth Blvd, e on Jefferson Ave, then n on frontage road. Int corridors. **Pets:** Medium, other species. $75 one-time fee/room.

(ASK) (S⚡) (✕) (&M) (🐾) (📶) (📶) (📶) (🏊) (🚫)

◆◆◆ ▼▼▼ Sheraton-Denver West Hotel **LH**
(303) 987-2000. **$69-$119.** 360 Union Blvd. US 6, exit Simms/Union, s on Union Blvd; 3 mi e of jct I-70, exit 261. Int corridors. **Pets:** Accepted.

(SAVE) (✕) (📶) (📶) (🍴) (🏊) (🚫)

▼▼▼ Super 8 Motel-SW Denver **M**
(303) 989-4600. **$49-$89.** 7240 W Jefferson Ave. Just se of US 285 (W Hampden Ave) and Wadsworth Blvd, then e. Int corridors. **Pets:** Medium, dogs only. $10 daily fee/pet. Designated rooms, service with restrictions, crate.

(ASK) (S⚡) (✕) (📶) (📶)

▼▼▼ TownePlace Suites by Marriott-Lakewood **SH** 🐾
(303) 232-7790. **$89-$99.** 800 Tabor St. US 6, exit Simms/Union, just n to 8th, then w. Int corridors. **Pets:** Other species. $20 daily fee/room.

(ASK) (S⚡) (✕) (&M) (🐾) (📶) (📶) (🏊)

# LONE TREE

▼▼▼ Staybridge Suites Denver South-Lone Tree **SH**
(303) 649-1010. **$99-$162.** 7820 Park Meadows Dr. I-25, exit 195 (County Line Rd), w on County Line Rd to Acres Green, s to E Park Meadows Dr, then just w; SR-470, exit Quebec St, just se. Int corridors. **Pets:** Accepted.

(ASK) (S⚡) (✕) (&M) (🐾) (📶) (📶) (📶) (🏊) (🚫)

# NORTHGLENN

**(AAA) ▼▼▼** Ramada Plaza and Convention Center Denver/Northglenn SH
(303) 452-4100. **$79-$159.** 10 E 120th Ave. I-25, exit 223, just e. Int corridors. **Pets:** Accepted.
SAVE S🐾 ✕ &M 🐾 🐾 🍴 🖵 🍴 ⚓ 🐾

# THORNTON

**(AAA) ▼▼** Sleep Inn North Denver SH 🐾
(303) 280-9818. **$64-$104.** 12101 Grant St. I-25, exit 223, e to Grant St, then n. Int corridors. **Pets:** Medium, other species. $5 daily fee/pet. Service with restrictions.
SAVE S🐾 ✕ &M 🐾 🐾 🍴 🖵 ⚓

# WESTMINSTER

**▼▼** Comfort Inn-Northwest SH
(303) 428-3333. **$59-$89, 30 day notice.** 8500 Turnpike Dr. US 36 (Boulder Tpke), exit Sheridan Ave, just s, left on Turnpike Dr at 87th Ave, then 0.4 mi. Int corridors. **Pets:** $10 daily fee/pet. Designated rooms, service with restrictions.
ASK S🐾 ✕ &M 🐾 🐾 🍴 🖵 ⚓

**(AAA) ▼▼▼** DoubleTree Hotel Denver North SH
(303) 427-4000. **$79-$149.** 8773 Yates Dr. US 36 (Boulder Tpke), exit Sheridan Ave, n to 92nd Ave, e to Yates Dr, then 0.5 mi s. Int corridors. **Pets:** Other species. Service with restrictions, supervision.
SAVE ✕ 🐾 🖵 🍴 ⚓ 🐾

**▼▼▼** Hampton Inn by Hilton SH
(303) 427-0700. **$84.** 5030 W 88th Pl. US 36 (Boulder Tpke), exit Sheridan Ave, 0.3 mi n to 92nd Ave, e to Yates Dr, then 0.4 mi s. Int corridors. **Pets:** Accepted.
ASK S🐾 ✕ &M 🐾 🐾 🍴 🖵 ⚓

**(AAA) ▼▼▼** La Quinta Inn & Suites Westminster (Promenade) SH
(303) 438-5800. **$67-$129.** 10179 Church Ranch Way. US 36 (Boulder Tpke), exit Church Ranch Blvd, just s to 103rd Pl, then e. Int corridors. **Pets:** Medium, other species. Service with restrictions, crate.
SAVE S🐾 ✕ &M 🐾 🍴 🖵 ⚓

**▼▼▼** La Quinta Inn Denver (Northglenn) SH
(303) 252-9800. **$72-$112.** 345 W 120th Ave. I-25, exit 223, just w. Ext/int corridors. **Pets:** Medium. Service with restrictions.
ASK ✕ 🐾 🍴 🖵 ⚓

**(AAA) ▼▼▼** La Quinta Inn Denver (Westminster Mall) SH
(303) 425-9099. **$75-$120.** 8701 Turnpike Dr. US 36 (Boulder Tpke), exit Sheridan Ave, just s, then left on Turnpike Dr at 87th Ave. Ext/int corridors. **Pets:** Medium. Service with restrictions.
SAVE ✕ &M 🐾 🍴 🖵 ⚓

**▼▼▼** Residence Inn by Marriott SH
(303) 427-9500. **$119-$129, 14 day notice.** 5010 W 88th Pl. US 36 (Boulder Tpke), exit Sheridan Ave, n to 92nd Ave, e to Yates Dr, then s. Int corridors. **Pets:** Accepted.
ASK S🐾 ✕ &M 🐾 🐾 🍴 🖵 ⚓ 🐾

**▼▼▼** The Westin Westminster LH
(303) 410-5000. **$109-$279.** 10600 Westminster Blvd. US 36 (Boulder Tpke), exit 104th Ave, just n. Int corridors. **Pets:** Accepted.
ASK S🐾 ✕ &M 🐾 🐾 🍴 🖵 🍴 ⚓ 🐾

**▼▼** Westminster-Super 8 SH
(303) 451-7200. **$69-$79.** 12055 Melody Dr. I-25, exit 223, just w. Int corridors. **Pets:** $5 daily fee/pet. Service with restrictions, supervision.
ASK S🐾 ✕ 🐾 🐾 🍴 🖵 🐾

---

## END METROPOLITAN AREA

---

# DILLON

**(AAA) ▼▼▼** Best Western Ptarmigan Lodge SH
(970) 468-2341. **$60-$149, 7 day notice.** 652 Lake Dillon Dr. I-70, exit 205, 1.3 mi se on US 6, then 0.3 mi s. Ext/int corridors. **Pets:** Other species. $15 one-time fee/pet. Designated rooms, service with restrictions, crate.
SAVE ✕ 🍴 🖵 🐾 🐾

**(AAA) ▼▼** Dillon Super 8 Motel SH
(970) 468-8888. **$60-$126.** 808 Little Beaver Tr. I-70, exit 205, just s, then e. Int corridors. **Pets:** Medium. $15 one-time fee/pet. Service with restrictions, supervision.
SAVE S🐾 ✕ 🍴 🖵

# DURANGO

**(AAA) ▼▼** Adobe Inn M
(970) 247-2743. **$33-$89.** 2178 Main Ave. On US 550, 1.4 mi n of jct US 160. Ext corridors. **Pets:** Small. $5 one-time fee/room. Service with restrictions, supervision.
SAVE S🐾 ✕ 🍴 🖵 ⚓

**(AAA) ▼▼** Alpine Inn M
(970) 247-4042. **$48-$94.** 3515 N Main Ave. 2.7 mi n of jct US 160 W and 550, on US 550. Ext corridors. **Pets:** Other species. $5 daily fee/room. Service with restrictions, supervision.
SAVE S🐾 ✕ 🍴

**(AAA) ▼** Caboose Motel M
(970) 247-1191. **$38-$125.** 3363 Main Ave. 2.5 mi n of jct US 550 and 160. Ext corridors. **Pets:** Medium, dogs only. $10 daily fee/pet. Designated rooms, service with restrictions, supervision.
SAVE S🐾 ✕ 🍴 🖵

**▼▼** Comfort Inn SH
(970) 259-5373. **$50-$139.** 2930 N Main Ave. 2.1 mi n of jct US 160 and 550, on US 550. Ext corridors. **Pets:** Medium, other species. $10 one-time fee/pet. Designated rooms, service with restrictions, supervision.
ASK S🐾 ✕ 🖵 ⚓

**▼▼** Days Inn Durango M
(970) 259-1430. **$69-$136.** 1700 CR 203. 4.5 mi n on US 550; entry just s of establishment, then w. Int corridors. **Pets:** Other species. Service with restrictions, supervision.
ASK S🐾 ✕ 🖵 ⚓ 🐾

**▼▼▼** DoubleTree Hotel Durango SH
(970) 259-6580. **$69-$229.** 501 Camino Del Rio. Jct US 160 and 550. Int corridors. **Pets:** Accepted.
✕ &M 🐾 🐾 🍴 🖵 🍴 ⚓ 🐾

**(AAA) ▼▼▼** Holiday Inn SH
(970) 247-5393. **$71-$160.** 800 Camino Del Rio. On US 550, just n of jct US 160. Ext corridors. **Pets:** Accepted.
SAVE S🐾 ✕ 🐾 🐾 🍴 🖵 ⚓ 🐾

**▼▼** Iron Horse Inn M
(970) 259-1010. **$59-$189.** 5800 N Main Ave. 4.5 mi n on US 550. Ext corridors. **Pets:** Designated rooms, service with restrictions, supervision.
ASK ✕ 🍴 ⚓ 🐾

**(AAA) ▼▼▼** Quality Inn & Suites SH
(970) 259-7900. **$79-$300.** 455 S Camino Del Rio. On US 160 (Frontage Rd), 1.5 mi e of jct US 550. Int corridors. **Pets:** $10 daily fee/pet. Service with restrictions, supervision.
SAVE S🐾 ✕ &M 🐾 🍴 🖵 ⚓ 🐾

**▼▼▼▼ Residence Inn by Marriott** 🆂🅷
(970) 259-6200. **$109-$234, 3 day notice.** 21691 Hwy 160 W. On US 160, just w. Int corridors. **Pets:** Medium, other species. $75 one-time fee/room. Service with restrictions, supervision.

🅰🆂🅺 🆂🔟 ☒ 🖎 🛢 💻 ⇆ ☒

**▼▼▼ The Rochester Hotel** 🅱🅱 🐾
(970) 385-1920. **$109-$229, 14 day notice.** 726 E 2nd Ave. Just e of Main Ave via 7th St, then just n. Int corridors. **Pets:** Other species. $20 daily fee/pet. Designated rooms, service with restrictions, supervision.

🅰🆂🅺 🆂🔟 ☒ 🛢 💻

**⚑⚑⚑ ▼ Siesta Motel** 🅼
(970) 247-0741. **$34-$98.** 3475 N Main Ave. 2.6 mi n of jct US 160 W and 550, on US 550. Ext corridors. **Pets:** Dogs only. $10 daily fee/pet. Designated rooms, service with restrictions, supervision.

🆂🅰🆅🅴 ☒ 🛢 💻

**⚑⚑⚑ ▼▼▼ Travelodge** 🅼
(970) 247-1741. **$59-$119.** 2970 Main Ave. 2.2 mi n of jct US 160 and 550, on US 550. Ext corridors. **Pets:** Other species. $8 daily fee/pet. Designated rooms, service with restrictions, crate.

🆂🅰🆅🅴 🆂🔟 ☒ 🛢 💻

# EAGLE

**⚑⚑⚑ ▼▼▼ AmericInn Lodge & Suites** 🆂🅷
(970) 328-5155. **$119-$159.** 0085 Pond Rd. I-70, exit 147, just n, then w. Int corridors. **Pets:** Medium, other species. $35 one-time fee/room. Service with restrictions, supervision.

🆂🅰🆅🅴 🆂🔟 ☒ 🖎🅼 🍳 🖎 🛢 💻 ⇆ ☒

**⚑⚑⚑ ▼▼▼ Best Western Eagle Lodge & Suites** 🆂🅷
(970) 328-6316. **$80-$99.** 200 Loren Ln. I-70, exit 147, just s. Int corridors. **Pets:** Accepted.

🆂🅰🆅🅴 🆂🔟 ☒ 🖎 🛢 💻 ⇆ ☒

**▼▼ Holiday Inn Express** 🆂🅷
(970) 328-8088. **$60-$140.** 0075 Pond Rd. I-70, exit 147, just n, then w. Int corridors. **Pets:** Accepted.

🅰🆂🅺 🆂🔟 ☒ 🖎🅼 🍳 🖎 🛢 💻 ⇆

# EDWARDS

**⚑⚑⚑ ▼▼▼▼ Inn and Suites at Riverwalk** 🆂🅷
(970) 926-0606. **$90-$1200, 14 day notice.** 27 Main St. I-70, exit 163, 0.3 mi s. Int corridors. **Pets:** Large, other species. $5 daily fee/pet, $25 one-time fee/pet. No service, crate.

🆂🅰🆅🅴 🆂🔟 ☒ 🍳 🛢 💻 🍴 ⇆

# ESTES PARK

**⚑⚑⚑ ▼▼▼ Budget Host Four Winds Motor Lodge** 🅼
(970) 586-3313. **$45-$99, 5 day notice.** 1120 Big Thompson Ave. 1 mi e on US 34. Ext corridors. **Pets:** Medium. $15 daily fee/pet. Designated rooms, service with restrictions, supervision.

🆂🅰🆅🅴 ☒ 🛢 💻 ⇆ ☒

**⚑⚑⚑ ▼▼▼ Castle Mountain Lodge** 🅲🅰
(970) 586-3664. **$85-$235, 30 day notice.** 1520 Fall River Rd. 1 mi w on US 34. Ext corridors. **Pets:** Accepted.

🆂🅰🆅🅴 🆂🔟 🛢 ☒ 🎿 🧖

**⚑⚑⚑ ▼▼▼▼ Holiday Inn** 🆂🅷
(970) 586-2332. **$64-$159, 3 day notice.** 101 S St Vrain Ave. 0.5 mi se; on SR 7 at jct US 36. Int corridors. **Pets:** Medium. $10 deposit/pet. Designated rooms, service with restrictions, supervision.

🆂🅰🆅🅴 🆂🔟 ☒ 🖎🅼 🍳 🖎 🛢 💻 🍴 ⇆ ☒

**⚑⚑⚑ ▼▼▼ Lake Estes Inn & Suites** 🅼
(970) 586-3386. **$69-$259, 7 day notice.** 1650 Big Thompson Ave. 1.7 mi e on US 34. Ext corridors. **Pets:** Medium. $25 deposit/room. Designated rooms, service with restrictions, supervision.

🆂🅰🆅🅴 ☒ 🛢 💻 ⇆ ☒ 🧖

**⚑⚑⚑ ▼▼▼▼ Silver Moon Inn** 🅼
(970) 586-6006. **$68-$150.** 175 Spruce Dr. Just w on US 34, then just ne. Ext corridors. **Pets:** Large, dogs only. Designated rooms, service with restrictions, supervision.

🆂🅰🆅🅴 ☒ 🛢 💻 ⇆

**▼▼ Timber Creek Chalets** 🅲🅰
(970) 586-8803. **$60-$270, 30 day notice.** 2115 Fall River Rd. Jct US 34 and 36, 2.9 mi w. Ext corridors. **Pets:** Accepted.

☒ 🛢 💻 ⇆ 🧖

# EVANS

**⚑⚑⚑ ▼▼▼ Sleep Inn Greeley/Evans** 🆂🅷 🐾
(970) 356-2180. **$59-$99.** 3025 8th Ave. Just sw of jct US 34 and 85 Bypass. Int corridors. **Pets:** Other species. $15 one-time fee/pet. Service with restrictions, crate.

🆂🅰🆅🅴 🆂🔟 ☒ 🖎🅼 🍳 🖎 🛢 💻 ⇆

# EVERGREEN

**▼▼▼▼ Quality Suites Evergreen** 🆂🅷 🐾
(303) 526-2000. **$90-$130.** I-70, exit 252 (Evergreen Pkwy), on west side of El Rancho Restaurant; exit 251 eastbound. Int corridors. **Pets:** Other species. $50 deposit/room. Designated rooms, service with restrictions, crate.

🅰🆂🅺 🆂🔟 ☒ 🖎🅼 🖎 🛢 💻 ⇆ ☒

# FAIRPLAY

**⚑⚑⚑ ▼▼▼ The Western Inn** 🅼
(719) 836-2026. **$53-$75.** 490 Hwy 285. US 285, 0.8 mi n of jct SR 9. Ext corridors. **Pets:** Accepted.

🆂🅰🆅🅴 🆂🔟 ☒ 🛢 💻 🧖

# FORT COLLINS

**⚑⚑⚑ ▼▼▼ AmericInn Lodge & Suites** 🆂🅷
(970) 226-1232. **$89-$159.** 7645 Westgate Dr. I-25, exit 262, just se off SR 392. Int corridors. **Pets:** Medium. $10 daily fee/room. Designated rooms, service with restrictions.

🆂🅰🆅🅴 ☒ 🖎🅼 🍳 🖎 🛢 💻 ⇆ ☒

**⚑⚑⚑ ▼▼▼ Best Western University Inn** 🅼 🐾
(970) 484-1984. **$69-$99.** 914 S College Ave. I-25, exit 268, 4 mi w to College Ave, then just n on US 267. Ext/int corridors. **Pets:** Other species. $10 daily fee/pet. Designated rooms, service with restrictions, supervision.

🆂🅰🆅🅴 🆂🔟 ☒ 🛢 💻 ⇆

**▼▼▼▼ Comfort Suites by Choice Hotels** 🆂🅷
(970) 206-4597. **$85-$105.** 1415 Oakridge Dr. I-25, exit 265, 3.3 mi w to McMurray Ave, just s, then w. Int corridors. **Pets:** Medium. $15 daily fee/pet. Service with restrictions, supervision.

🅰🆂🅺 🆂🔟 ☒ 🍳 🖎 🛢 💻 ⇆

**▼▼▼▼ Courtyard by Marriott** 🆂🅷
(970) 282-1700. **$85-$119.** 1200 Oakridge Dr. I-25, exit 265, 3.3 mi w; entry via Lemay Ave. Int corridors. **Pets:** $25 daily fee/room. Designated rooms, service with restrictions, supervision.

🅰🆂🅺 ☒ 🖎🅼 🍳 🖎 🛢 💻 🍴 ⇆

**▼▼▼▼ Fort Collins Marriott** 🅻🅷
(970) 226-5200. **$89-$145.** 350 E Horsetooth Rd. I-25, exit 265, 4 mi w to John F Kennedy, then n; just beyond Horsetooth Rd. Int corridors. **Pets:** Medium. $10 daily fee/pet. Designated rooms, supervision.

🅰🆂🅺 🆂🔟 ☒ 🖎🅼 🍳 🖎 🛢 💻 🍴 ⇆

**▼▼▼▼ Hampton Inn** 🆂🅷
(970) 229-5927. **$79-$149.** 1620 Oakridge Dr. I-25, exit 265, 3.3 mi w, s on McMurray Ave to Oakridge Dr, then just e. Int corridors. **Pets:** Large. $25 one-time fee/pet. Service with restrictions, supervision.

🅰🆂🅺 🆂🔟 ☒ 🖎🅼 🖎 🛢 💻 ⇆

**Hilton Ft Collins** 🆂🅗 ❀
(970) 482-2626. **$89-$229.** 425 W Prospect Rd. I-25, exit 268, 4.3 mi w. Int corridors. **Pets:** $25 one-time fee/room. Service with restrictions, crate.

🆂🅰🆅🅴 🆂🅾 ⊠ 🎲 🖫 🖬 🖳 🍴 ⇶ ⊠

**Quality Inn & Suites** 🆂🅗
(970) 282-9047. **$94-$189.** 4001 S Mason St. I-25, exit 265, 4.6 mi w to Mason St, then 0.5 mi n. Int corridors. **Pets:** Dogs only. $50 deposit/pet. Designated rooms, service with restrictions, supervision.

🆂🅰🆅🅴 🆂🅾 ⊠ 🖫ᴹ 🎲 🖫 🖬 🖳 ⇶

**Residence Inn Fort Collins** 🆂🅗 ❀
(970) 223-5700. **$89-$169.** 1127 Oakridge Dr. I-25, exit 265, 3.3 mi w on Harmony Rd to Lemay Ave, then s to Oakridge Dr. Int corridors. **Pets:** Other species. $75 one-time fee/room. Crate.

🅰🆂🅺 ⊠ 🖫 🖬 🖳 ⇶ ⊠

**Sleep Inn** 🆂🅗
(970) 484-5515. **$70-$100.** 3808 E Mulberry St. I-25, exit 269B, just nw. Int corridors. **Pets:** Medium. $10 daily fee/pet. Service with restrictions, supervision.

🅰🆂🅺 🆂🅾 ⊠ 🖫 🖬 🖳

**Super 8 Motel** 🆂🅗
(970) 493-7701. **$50-$80.** 409 Centro Way. I-25, exit 269B, just w. Int corridors. **Pets:** Other species. $5 daily fee/pet. Service with restrictions, supervision.

🅰🆂🅺 🆂🅾 ⊠ 🖬 ⊠

# FORT MORGAN

**Best Western Park Terrace Inn** 🆂🅗 ❀
(970) 867-8256. **$52-$85.** 725 Main St. I-76, exit 80, 0.5 mi s. Ext corridors. **Pets:** Other species. $10 one-time fee/pet. Designated rooms, service with restrictions, supervision.

🅰🆂🅺 🆂🅾 ⊠ 🖬 🖳 🍴 ⇶

**Central Motel** 🅼
(970) 867-2401. **$44-$61.** 201 W Platte Ave. I-76, exit 80, 0.6 mi s, then w on US 34. Ext corridors. **Pets:** Other species. $5 one-time fee/room. Service with restrictions, supervision.

🆂🅰🆅🅴 🆂🅾 ⊠ 🖬 🖳

**Roadway Inn** 🅼 ❀
(970) 867-9481. **$55-$75.** 1409 Barlow Rd. I-76, exit 82, just n. Ext/int corridors. **Pets:** Large. $15 daily fee/room. Designated rooms, service with restrictions, supervision.

🅰🆂🅺 🆂🅾 ⊠ 🖬 🍴 ⇶

# FRISCO

**Best Western Lake Dillon Lodge** 🆂🅗
(970) 668-5094. **$79-$209, 7 day notice.** 1202 Summit Blvd. I-70, exit 203, just s. Int corridors. **Pets:** Dogs only. $15 one-time fee/room. Designated rooms, service with restrictions, supervision.

🆂🅰🆅🅴 🆂🅾 ⊠ 🖬 🖳 🍴 ⇶ ⊠

**Holiday Inn-Frisco** 🆂🅗
(970) 668-5000. **$69-$169, 21 day notice.** 1129 N Summit Blvd. I-70, exit 203, just s. Ext/int corridors. **Pets:** Accepted.

🆂🅰🆅🅴 🆂🅾 ⊠ 🖫ᴹ 🎲 🖫 🖬 🖳 🍴 ⇶ ⊠

**Hotel Frisco** 🆂🅗
(970) 668-5009. **$69-$159, 14 day notice.** 308 Main St.. I-70, exit 201, 0.7 mi s; center. Ext/int corridors. **Pets:** Accepted.

🅰🆂🅺 ⊠ 🖬 🖳 🦮

**New Summit Inn** 🆂🅗
(970) 668-3220. **$49-$140, 3 day notice.** 1205 N Summit Blvd. I-70, exit 203, just s, then just e. Int corridors. **Pets:** Dogs only. $10 daily fee/pet. Designated rooms, no service, supervision.

🆂🅰🆅🅴 🆂🅾 ⊠ 🖬 🖳

**Ramada Limited Frisco** 🆂🅗
(970) 668-8783. **$59-$149.** 990 Lakepoint Dr. I-70, exit 203, just s. Int corridors. **Pets:** Other species. $10 daily fee/room. Designated rooms, service with restrictions, supervision.

🆂🅰🆅🅴 🆂🅾 ⊠ 🖫ᴹ 🎲 🖬 🖳

**Snowshoe Motel** 🅼
(970) 668-3444. **$48-$130.** 521 Main St. I-70, exit 203 westbound, 1 mi s to Main St, then just w; exit 201 eastbound. Ext corridors. **Pets:** Medium. $10 deposit/pet, $10 one-time fee/pet. Designated rooms, service with restrictions, supervision.

🆂🅰🆅🅴 ⊠ 🖬 🖳 🦮

# FRUITA

**Balanced Rock Motel** 🅼
(970) 858-7333. **$45-$50, 3 day notice.** 126 S Coulson. I-70, exit 19, just n to Aspen Ave, then just w. Ext corridors. **Pets:** Dogs only. $5 daily fee/pet. Designated rooms, service with restrictions, supervision.

🆂🅰🆅🅴 ⊠ 🖬

**Comfort Inn** 🆂🅗 ❀
(970) 858-1333. **$69-$135.** 400 Jurassic Ave. I-70, exit 19, 0.3 mi s; just e of Dinosaur Discovery Museum. Int corridors. **Pets:** Other species. Designated rooms, service with restrictions, supervision.

🆂🅰🆅🅴 🆂🅾 ⊠ 🖫ᴹ 🎲 🖫 🖬 🖳 ⇶

**H-Motel** 🅼
(970) 858-7198. **$35-$55, 3 day notice.** 333 Hwy 6 & 50. I-70, exit 19, just n, follow signs to US 6 E, then just e. Ext corridors. **Pets:** Large, dogs only. $5 daily fee/pet. Designated rooms, service with restrictions, supervision.

🆂🅰🆅🅴 ⊠ 🖬

**La Quinta Inn & Suites** 🆂🅗
(970) 858-8850. **$89-$139.** 570 Raptor Rd. I-70, exit 19, 0.3 mi s. Int corridors. **Pets:** Service with restrictions, supervision.

🅰🆂🅺 🆂🅾 ⊠ 🖫 🖬 🖳 ⇶

**Super 8** 🆂🅗
(970) 858-0808. **$49-$86.** 399 Jurassic Ave. I-70, exit 19, 0.3 mi s; just e of Dinosaur Discovery Museum. Int corridors. **Pets:** Other species. $5 daily fee/pet. Designated rooms, service with restrictions, supervision.

🆂🅰🆅🅴 🆂🅾 ⊠ 🖫ᴹ 🎲 🖫 🖬 ⇶

# GEORGETOWN

**Georgetown Mountain Inn** 🅼
(303) 569-3201. **$59-$87.** 1100 Rose St. I-70, exit 228, just s, then 0.3 mi w. Ext corridors. **Pets:** Other species. $10 one-time fee/room. Designated rooms, service with restrictions, supervision.

🆂🅰🆅🅴 🆂🅾 ⊠ 🖬 ⇶ 🦮

# GLENWOOD SPRINGS

**Caravan Inn** 🅼
(970) 945-7451. **$59-$109.** 1826 Grand Ave. I-70, exit 116, 1.3 mi s on SR 82. Ext corridors. **Pets:** $8 daily fee/pet. Designated rooms, service with restrictions, crate.

🆂🅰🆅🅴 🆂🅾 ⊠ 🖬 ⇶

**Hotel Colorado** 🆂🅗 ❀
(970) 945-6511. **$149-$169.** 526 Pine St. I-70, exit 116, just ne. Int corridors. **Pets:** Dogs only. $15 daily fee/pet. Service with restrictions.

🆂🅰🆅🅴 🆂🅾 ⊠ 🖫 🖬 🖳 🍴 ⊠ 🦮

**Quality Inn & Suites** 🆂🅗
(970) 945-5995. **$89-$189.** 2650 Gilstrap. I-70, exit 114, just s, then w. Int corridors. **Pets:** Accepted.

🅰🆂🅺 🆂🅾 ⊠ 🖫ᴹ 🎲 🖫 🖬 🖳 ⇶

▼▼▼▼ **Ramada Inn & Suites** SH ❀
(970) 945-2500. **$65-$149.** 124 W 6th St. I-70, exit 116, just w. Ext/int corridors. **Pets:** Other species. $10 daily fee/room. Designated rooms, service with restrictions, crate.

ASK S♂ ✕ ⊟ 🖵 ⊞ ⇌

▲▲▲ ▼▼▼ **Silver Spruce Motel** M ❀
(970) 945-5458. **$45-$100.** 162 W 6th St. I-70, exit 116, just w on frontage road. Ext corridors. **Pets:** Other species. $7 daily fee/pet. Service with restrictions, supervision.

SAVE S♂ ✕ ⊟

# GRANBY

▲▲▲ ▼▼▼▼ **The Inn at Silver Creek** LH ❀
(970) 887-2131. **$59-$338, 16 day notice.** 62927 Hwy 40. 2 mi se on US 40. Int corridors. **Pets:** $25 one-time fee/pet. Designated rooms, service with restrictions, supervision.

SAVE S♂ ✕ ⊟ 🖵 ⇌ ✕ 🐾

# GRAND JUNCTION

▲▲▲ ▼▼▼ **Americas Best Value Inn** SH ❀
(970) 245-1410. **$55-$84.** 754 Horizon Dr. I-70, exit 31, 0.3 mi n. Ext corridors. **Pets:** Other species. Service with restrictions, supervision.

SAVE S♂ ✕ ⚊M ⚙ ⊟ 🖵 ⇌

▲▲▲ ▼▼▼ **Best Western Sandman Motel** SH ❀
(970) 243-4150. **$45-$105.** 708 Horizon Dr. I-70, exit 31, 0.3 mi s. Ext/int corridors. **Pets:** Dogs only. Designated rooms, service with restrictions, supervision.

SAVE S♂ ✕ ⊟ 🖵 ⇌

▲▲▲ ▼▼▼ **Budget Host Inn** M ❀
(970) 243-6050. **$50-$95.** 721 Horizon Dr. I-70, exit 31, 0.3 mi s. Ext corridors. **Pets:** Other species. $50 deposit/room. Service with restrictions, supervision.

SAVE S♂ ✕ ⊟ 🖵 ⇌

▲▲▲ ▼▼▼▼ **DoubleTree Hotel Grand Junction** LH
(970) 245-8198. **$74-$174.** 743 Horizon Dr. I-70, exit 31, just s. Int corridors. **Pets:** Accepted.

SAVE S♂ ✕ 🐾 ⊟ 🖵 ⊞ ⇌ ✕

▲▲▲ ▼▼▼ **Grand Junction Super 8** SH
(970) 248-8080. **$49-$86.** 728 Horizon Dr. I-70, exit 31, just s. Int corridors. **Pets:** Accepted.

SAVE S♂ ✕ ⊟ ⇌

▲▲▲ ▼▼▼▼ **Grand Vista Hotel** SH
(970) 241-8411. **$65-$79.** 2790 Crossroads Blvd. I-70, exit 31, 0.3 mi n. Int corridors. **Pets:** Accepted.

SAVE S♂ ✕ ⊟ 🖵 ⊞ ⇌

▼▼▼▼ **Hampton Inn** SH
(970) 243-3222. **$100-$124.** 205 Main St. At 2nd and Main sts; downtown. Int corridors. **Pets:** Accepted.

ASK S♂ ✕ ⚊M 🐾 ⚙ ⊟ 🖵 ⇌ ✕

▼▼▼▼ **Hawthorn Suites** SH
(970) 242-2525. **$99-$209.** 225 Main St. At 2nd and Main sts; downtown. Int corridors. **Pets:** Other species. $25 daily fee/pet. Service with restrictions, crate.

ASK S♂ ✕ ⚊M ⚙ ⊟ 🖵 ⇌ ✕

▲▲▲ ▼▼▼▼ **Holiday Inn** SH ❀
(970) 243-6790. **$79-$99.** 755 Horizon Dr. I-70, exit 31, northwest corner. Ext/int corridors. **Pets:** Other species. Service with restrictions, supervision.

SAVE S♂ ✕ 🐾 ⚙ ⊟ 🖵 ⊞ ⇌ ✕

▲▲▲ ▼▼▼▼ **La Quinta Inn & Suites Grand Junction** SH
(970) 241-2929. **$92-$132.** 2761 Crossroads Blvd. I-70, exit 31, n to Crossroads Blvd, then just w. Int corridors. **Pets:** Medium. Service with restrictions.

SAVE ✕ ⚊M 🐾 ⚙ ⊟ 🖵 ⇌

▲▲▲ ▼▼▼ **Mesa Inn** M
(970) 245-3080. **$45-$80.** 704 Horizon Dr. I-70, exit 31, 0.5 mi s. Ext corridors. **Pets:** $50 deposit/room. Designated rooms, service with restrictions, supervision.

SAVE S♂ ✕ ⊟ 🖵 ⇌

▲▲▲ ▼▼▼ **Quality Inn of Grand Junction** SH
(970) 245-7200. **$65-$99.** 733 Horizon Dr. I-70, exit 31, just s. Int corridors. **Pets:** $50 deposit/room. Designated rooms, service with restrictions, supervision.

SAVE S♂ ✕ ⊟ 🖵 ⊞ ⇌

▲▲▲ ▼▼▼ **Ramada Inn** SH ❀
(970) 243-5150. **$49-$109.** 752 Horizon Dr. I-70, exit 31, just n. Int corridors. **Pets:** Other species. Service with restrictions, supervision.

SAVE S♂ ✕ 🖵 ⊞ ⇌

▲▲▲ ▼▼▼ **West Gate Inn** M
(970) 241-3020. **$60-$75.** 2210 Hwy 6 & 50. I-70, exit 26, just se. Ext corridors. **Pets:** Other species. $50 deposit/room. Designated rooms, service with restrictions, crate.

SAVE S♂ ✕ 🖵 ⊞ ⇌

# GRAND LAKE

▲▲▲ ▼▼▼ **Spirit Lake Lodge** M
(970) 627-3344. **$55-$160, 7 day notice.** 829 Grand Ave. Just e of US 34; downtown. Ext corridors. **Pets:** Medium, other species. $10 daily fee/pet. No service, supervision.

SAVE S♂ ✕ ⊟ ⇌ 🐾

# GREAT SAND DUNES NATIONAL PARK AND PRESERVE

▼▼ **Great Sand Dunes Lodge** M
(719) 378-2900. **$89-$95.** 7900 Hwy 150 N. From Alamosa, 16 mi e on US 160, 16 mi n on SR 150; at entrance to Great Sand Dunes National Monument. Ext corridors. **Pets:** Accepted.

✕ ⇌

# GREELEY

▲▲▲ ▼▼▼▼ **Best Western Regency Hotel** SH
(970) 353-8444. **$65-$225.** 701 8th St. On US 85 business route; downtown. Int corridors. **Pets:** Accepted.

SAVE S♂ ✕ ⚊M 🐾 ⚙ ⊟ 🖵 ⊞ ⇌

▼▼▼▼ **Country Inn & Suites By Carlson** SH
(970) 330-3404. **$85-$110.** 2501 W 29th St. US 34 Bypass, exit 23rd Ave, just s, then w. Int corridors. **Pets:** Accepted.

ASK S♂ ✕ ⚊M 🐾 ⊟ 🖵 ⇌

▼▼▼▼ **Holiday Inn Express** SH
(970) 330-7495. **$70-$90.** 2563 W 29th St. US 34 Bypass, exit 23rd Ave, just s, then w. Int corridors. **Pets:** Accepted.

ASK S♂ ✕ ⚊M 🐾 ⚙ ⊟ 🖵 ⇌ ✕

▼▼▼▼ **Super 8 Motel** SH
(970) 330-8880. **$58-$133.** 2423 W 29th St. US 34 Bypass, exit 23rd Ave, just s, then just w. Int corridors. **Pets:** Other species. $15 daily fee/room. Service with restrictions, crate.

ASK ✕ ⊟ 🖵

# GUNNISON

**AAA VVV ABC Motel M**
(970) 641-2400. **$42-$79.** 212 E Tomichi Ave. On US 50; near Western State College. Ext corridors. **Pets:** Medium, other species. $5 daily fee/ pet. Designated rooms, service with restrictions, supervision.
SAVE Sb X B P

**VVV Alpine Inn M**
(970) 641-2804. **$59-$125, 15 day notice.** 1011 W Rio Grande. Jct US 50 and SR 135, 1.1 mi w. Int corridors. **Pets:** Accepted.
ASK Sb X B P

**AAA VVV Gunnison Inn M**
(970) 641-0700. **$50-$75.** 412 E Tomichi Ave. On US 50; near Western State College. Ext corridors. **Pets:** Other species. $5 daily fee/pet. Designated rooms, service with restrictions, supervision.
SAVE Sb X B

**AAA VVV Water Wheel Inn SH**
(970) 641-1650. **$49-$99.** 37478 W Hwy 50. Jct SR 135, 2.5 mi w. Ext/int corridors. **Pets:** Medium. Designated rooms, service with restrictions, supervision.
SAVE Sb X B P

# HERMOSA

**VV The Inn at Durango Mountain & Silverpick Condos & Townhomes M**
(970) 247-9669. **$69-$179.** 49617 US 550 N. 26.4 mi n, then just w. Int corridors. **Pets:** Accepted.
ASK Sb X B P

# HOT SULPHUR SPRINGS

**AAA VV Canyon Motel M**
(970) 725-3395. **$54-$99.** 221 Byers Ave. On US 40. Ext corridors. **Pets:** Other species. $10 daily fee/room. Designated rooms, service with restrictions, supervision.
SAVE Sb X B P

# JULESBURG

**AAA VV Budget Host Platte Valley Inn SH**
(970) 474-3336. **$44-$65.** 15225 Hwy 385 & I-76. I-76, exit 180, just n. Ext corridors. **Pets:** Dogs only. $7 daily fee/pet. Designated rooms, service with restrictions, supervision.
SAVE Sb X P

# KEYSTONE

**AAA VVV The Inn at Keystone SH**
(970) 496-4825. **$79-$310, 21 day notice.** 23044 Hwy 6. I-70, exit 205, 6.5 mi e on US 6; at Keystone Ski area. Int corridors. **Pets:** Other species. $25 daily fee/room. Designated rooms, service with restrictions.
SAVE Sb X B P

# LA JUNTA

**VVV Holiday Inn Express M**
(719) 384-2900. **$79-$99.** 27994 US Hwy 50 Frontage Rd. On US 50, 0.8 mi w. Int corridors. **Pets:** Other species. $10 daily fee/room. Service with restrictions, supervision.
ASK Sb X B P

**VV Travel Inn M**
(719) 384-2504. **$38-$45.** 110 E 1st St. On US 50. Ext corridors. **Pets:** Accepted.
ASK Sb X B

# LAKE CITY

**AAA VV Matterhorn Mountain Motel M**
(970) 944-2210. **$80-$95, 30 day notice.** 409 Bluff St. SR 149, just w via 4th St. Ext corridors. **Pets:** Other species. $10 one-time fee/pet. No service, supervision.
SAVE X B P

# LAMAR

**AAA VVV Best Western Cow Palace Inn M**
(719) 336-7753. **$80-$105.** 1301 N Main St. 0.8 mi n on US 50 and 287. Ext/int corridors. **Pets:** Accepted.
SAVE Sb X B P

**AAA VVV Blue Spruce Motel M**
(719) 336-7454. **$45-$65.** 1801 S Main St. 1.3 mi s on US 287 and 385. Ext corridors. **Pets:** Other species. $5 daily fee/pet. Designated rooms, service with restrictions, supervision.
SAVE Sb X B P

**AAA VVV El Mar Budget Host Motel M**
(719) 336-4331. **$42-$60.** 1210 S Main St. 1 mi s on US 287 and 385. Ext corridors. **Pets:** Other species. $5 daily fee/pet. Service with restrictions, supervision.
SAVE Sb X B P

# LAS ANIMAS

**AAA VVVV Best Western Bent's Fort Inn M**
(719) 456-0011. **$63-$73.** 10950 E US 50. On US 50, 1.5 mi e on frontage road. Int corridors. **Pets:** Other species. Service with restrictions, supervision.
SAVE Sb X B P

# LEADVILLE

**AAA VVV Alps Motel M**
(719) 486-1223. **$59-$115, 5 day notice.** S Hwy 24. Just s on US 24. Int corridors. **Pets:** Large. $15 daily fee/pet. Designated rooms, service with restrictions, supervision.
SAVE X B P

# LIMON

**VV Best Western Limon Inn SH**
(719) 775-0277. **$60-$105.** 925 T Ave. I-70, exit 359. Int corridors. **Pets:** Large. $10 one-time fee/pet. Designated rooms, no service, supervision.
ASK Sb X B P

**VV Midwest Country Inn M**
(719) 775-2273. **$55-$65.** 795 Main St. I-70, exit 361, 1 mi w. Ext/int corridors. **Pets:** Accepted.
ASK Sb X

**AAA VVV Safari Motel M**
(719) 775-2363. **$42-$92.** 637 Main St. I-70, exit 361, 0.8 mi w. Ext corridors. **Pets:** Other species. $5 one-time fee/pet. Service with restrictions, supervision.
SAVE Sb X

**AAA VVV Super 8 Motel SH**
(719) 775-2889. **$65-$102.** 937 Hwy 24. I-70, exit 359, just s. Int corridors. **Pets:** Other species. $10 one-time fee/room. Service with restrictions, supervision.
SAVE Sb X B P

**AAA VVV Tyme Square Inn SH**
(719) 775-0700. **$61-$105.** 2505 6th St. I-70, exit 359, then s. Int corridors. **Pets:** Other species. $10 daily fee/pet. Designated rooms, no service, supervision.
SAVE X SM B P

# LONGMONT

**AAA** ▼▼▼▼ **Hawthorn Suites** SH
(303) 774-7100. **$89-$116.** 2000 Sunset Way. 1 mi s on US 287, 1.3 mi sw on SR 119, just n on Sunset St, then just w on Korte Pkwy. Int corridors. **Pets:** Other species. $100 one-time fee/room. Service with restrictions, supervision.
(SAVE) (S/D) (X) (&M) (&) 🐾 🛏 🍴 ➿ (X)

**AAA** ▼▼▼▼ **Radisson Hotel & Conference Center Longmont-Boulder** SH
(303) 776-2000. **$80-$151.** 1900 Ken Pratt Blvd. 1 mi s on US 287, 1.3 mi sw on SR 119. Int corridors. **Pets:** Other species. $50 deposit/room. Designated rooms, service with restrictions, crate.
(SAVE) (S/D) (X) 🐾 (&) 🛏 🍴 🍽 ➿ (X)

▼▼▼▼ **Residence Inn by Marriott Boulder/Longmont** SH
(303) 702-9933. **$99-$199.** 1450 Dry Creek Dr. I-25, exit 235, jct Hover Rd and SR 119. Int corridors. **Pets:** Other species. $50 one-time fee/room. Service with restrictions, supervision.
(ASK) (S/D) (X) (&M) 🐾 (&) 🛏 🍴 ➿

▼▼ **Super 8 Motel** M
(303) 772-0888. **$50-$86.** 10805 Turner Blvd. I-25, exit 240, jct SR 119; 7 mi e of town. Int corridors. **Pets:** Accepted.
(ASK) (S/D) (X)

# LOUISVILLE

**AAA** ▼▼▼▼ **Comfort Inn of Boulder County** SH
(303) 604-0181. **$59-$129.** 1196 Dillon Rd. US 36 (Boulder Tpke), exit Superior (SR 170), just n on McCaslin Blvd, then just w. Int corridors. **Pets:** $100 deposit/room, $10 one-time fee/pet. Designated rooms, service with restrictions, supervision.
(SAVE) (S/D) (X) (&M) (&) 🛏 🍴

**AAA** ▼▼▼▼ **La Quinta Inn & Suites Denver (Louisville/Boulder)** SH
(303) 664-0100. **$89-$150.** 902 Dillon Rd. US 36 (Boulder Tpke), exit Superior (SR 170), just n on McCaslin Blvd, then e. Int corridors. **Pets:** Medium. Service with restrictions.
(SAVE) (X) (&M) 🐾 (&) 🛏 🍴 ➿

▼▼▼▼ **Quality Inn and Suites** SH
(303) 327-1215. **$59-$149.** 960 W Dillon Rd. US 36 (Boulder Tpke), exit Superior (SR 170), n on McCaslin Blvd to Dillon Rd, then e. Int corridors. **Pets:** $15 daily fee/pet. Service with restrictions, supervision.
(ASK) (S/D) (X) (&) 🛏 🍴 ➿

▼▼▼▼ **Residence Inn by Marriott-Boulder/Louisville** SH
(303) 665-2661. **$139-$149.** 845 Coal Creek Cir. US 36 (Boulder Tpke), exit Superior (SR 170), n on McCaslin Blvd to Dillon Rd, then 0.6 mi e. Int corridors. **Pets:** Other species. $75 one-time fee/room. Service with restrictions.
(ASK) (S/D) (X) (&M) 🐾 (&) 🛏 🍴 ➿ (X)

# LOVELAND

**AAA** ▼▼▼▼ **Best Western Coach House** SH
(970) 667-7810. **$69-$129.** 5542 E US Hwy 34. I-25, exit 257B, just w. Ext/int corridors. **Pets:** Other species. $15 daily fee/pet. Designated rooms, service with restrictions, supervision.
(SAVE) (S/D) (X) 🛏 🍴 ➿

**AAA** ▼▼ **Budget Host Exit 254 Inn** M 🐾
(970) 667-5202. **$54-$76.** 2716 SE Frontage Rd. I-25, exit 254, just e. Ext corridors. **Pets:** Small, dogs only. $7 daily fee/pet. Service with restrictions, supervision.
(SAVE) (S/D) (X) 🛏 ➿

# MARBLE

▼▼▼▼ **Ute Meadows Inn Bed & Breakfast** BB 🐾
(970) 963-7088. **$119-$159, 14 day notice.** 2880 CR 3. From jct SR 133, 3 mi e. Int corridors. **Pets:** Dogs only. $15 daily fee/pet. Service with restrictions, supervision.
(ASK) (S/D) (X) 🍴 🐾 (X) (X) 🐾

# MESA VERDE NATIONAL PARK

**AAA** ▼▼▼ **Far View Lodge in Mesa Verde** M
(970) 529-4421. **$119-$145, 3 day notice.** 1 Navajo Hill, MM 15. 15 mi from park gate; near park visitors center. Ext corridors. **Pets:** Accepted.
(SAVE) (S/D) (X) (&) 🛏 🍴 🍴 (X) 🍽

# MONTE VISTA

**AAA** ▼▼▼▼ **Best Western Movie Manor Motel** SH
(719) 852-5921. **$60-$115, 7 day notice.** 2830 W Hwy 160. On US 160, 2 mi w. Ext corridors. **Pets:** Accepted.
(SAVE) (X) 🛏 🍴

**AAA** ▼▼▼ **Comfort Inn** M 🐾
(719) 852-0612. **$80-$110.** 1519 Grande Ave. 0.3 mi e on US 160. Int corridors. **Pets:** Other species. Service with restrictions, supervision.
(SAVE) (S/D) (X) 🛏 ➿

# MONTROSE

▼▼▼ **Affordable Inns** M
(970) 249-6644. **$58.** 1480 S Townsend Ave. 1 mi s on US 550. Ext corridors. **Pets:** Medium, dogs only. $8 one-time fee/pet. Service with restrictions, supervision.
(ASK) (S/D) (X) 🛏 ➿

▼▼▼ **Best Western Red Arrow** SH 🐾
(970) 249-9641. **$69-$109.** 1702 E Main St. 1 mi e on US 50. Ext/int corridors. **Pets:** Other species. $8 daily fee/room. Service with restrictions, crate.
(ASK) (S/D) (X) 🛏 🍴 ➿ (X)

**AAA** ▼▼▼ **Black Canyon Motel** M 🐾
(970) 249-3495. **$45-$95.** 1605 E Main St. 1 mi e on US 50. Ext corridors. **Pets:** Medium. $5 daily fee/room. Designated rooms, service with restrictions, supervision.
(SAVE) (S/D) (X) (&) 🛏 🍴 ➿

**AAA** ▼▼▼ **Canyon Trails Inn** M
(970) 249-3426. **$38-$69.** 1225 E Main St. 0.8 mi e on US 50. Ext corridors. **Pets:** Other species. $20 deposit/room. Designated rooms, service with restrictions, supervision.
(SAVE) (S/D) (X) 🛏 ➿

**AAA** ▼▼ **Days Inn** SH
(970) 249-3411. **$39-$69.** 1655 E Main St. 1 mi e on US 50. Int corridors. **Pets:** Accepted.
(ASK) (S/D) (X) 🛏 🍴 ➿

**AAA** ▼▼▼▼ **Holiday Inn Express Hotel & Suites** SH
(970) 240-1800. **$89-$159.** 1391 S Townsend Ave. 1 mi s on US 550, e on Niagara Ave. Int corridors. **Pets:** Accepted.
(SAVE) (S/D) (X) (&M) 🐾 (&) 🛏 🍴 ➿

▼▼▼ **Quality Inn & Suites-Montrose** SH
(970) 249-1011. **$59-$109.** 2751 Commercial Way. 2 mi s on US 550, w on O'Delle. Int corridors. **Pets:** Dogs only. $5 one-time fee/pet. Designated rooms, service with restrictions, supervision.
(ASK) (S/D) (X) 🐾 (&) 🛏 🍴 ➿

▼▼ **Uncompahgre Bed & Breakfast** BB 🐾
(970) 240-4000. **$70-$115.** 21049 Uncompahgre Rd. 8 mi s on US 550. Int corridors. **Pets:** Dogs only. Service with restrictions, supervision.
(ASK) (S/D) (X) 🛏

**△△△ ▽▽▽ Western Motel Ⓜ**
(970) 249-3481. **$45-$105.** 1200 E Main St. 0.8 mi e on US 50. Ext corridors. **Pets:** Small, dogs only. $25 deposit/room, $5 daily fee/pet. Designated rooms, service with restrictions, supervision.

(SAVE) (S🐾) (✕) (🏠) (🖥) (🌊)

## NEDERLAND

**△△△ ▽▽▽▽ Best Western Lodge at Nederland SH**
(303) 258-9463. **$110-$125, 3 day notice.** 55 Lakeview Dr. SR 119; across street from Visitor's Center. Int corridors. **Pets:** Accepted.

(SAVE) (S🐾) (✕) (🏠) (🖥) (✕)

## NEW CASTLE

**▽▽ New Castle Rodeway Inn SH**
(970) 984-2363. **$70-$110.** 781 Burning Mountain Ave. I-70, exit 105, just n, then w. Int corridors. **Pets:** Other species. $10 one-time fee/pet. Service with restrictions, crate.

(ASK) (S🐾) (✕) (♿) (🏠) (🖥) (🌊)

## OURAY

**▽▽ Comfort Inn Ⓜ**
(970) 325-7203. **$59-$135.** 191 5th Ave. Just w of US 550. Ext corridors. **Pets:** Dogs only. $10 daily fee/pet. Designated rooms, service with restrictions.

(✕) (♿) (🏠) (🖥)

**△△△ ▽▽▽ Ouray Riverside Inn & Cabins Ⓜ 🐾**
(970) 325-4061. **$35-$160, 3 day notice.** 1805 N Main St. Just n on US 550. Ext corridors. **Pets:** Designated rooms, service with restrictions, supervision.

(SAVE) (✕) (🏠) (🖥)

**△△△ ▽▽▽ Ouray Victorian Inn & Resort Accommodations Ⓜ**
(970) 325-7222. **$65-$100.** 50 3rd Ave. Just w of US 550. Ext corridors. **Pets:** Other species. Designated rooms, service with restrictions, supervision.

(SAVE) (S🐾) (✕) (🏠) (🖥) (🎿)

**△△△ ▽▽▽ Rivers Edge Motel Ⓜ**
(970) 325-4621. **$50-$100.** 110 7th Ave. Just w of US 550 via 7th Ave. Ext corridors. **Pets:** Dogs only. $10 daily fee/pet. Service with restrictions, supervision.

(SAVE) (S🐾) (✕) (🏠) (🖥) (🎿)

## PAGOSA SPRINGS

**△△△ ▽▽▽ Americas Best Value High Country Lodge Ⓜ 🐾**
(970) 264-4181. **$65-$96.** 3821 E Hwy 160. On US 160, 3 mi e. Ext corridors. **Pets:** Other species. $15 one-time fee/room. Service with restrictions, supervision.

(SAVE) (S🐾) (✕) (🏠) (🖥) (✕)

**△△△ ▽▽▽ Best Western Oak Ridge Lodge Ⓜ**
(970) 264-4173. **$59-$149, 3 day notice.** 158 Hot Springs Blvd. Just s of US 160. Int corridors. **Pets:** Accepted.

(SAVE) (S🐾) (✕) (🏠) (🖥) (🍴) (🌊) (✕)

**▽▽ Econo Lodge Ⓜ**
(970) 731-2701. **$59-$109.** 315 Navajo Trail Dr. 4 mi w on US 160. Int corridors. **Pets:** Medium. $10 daily fee/room. Service with restrictions, supervision.

(ASK) (S🐾) (✕) (♿) (🏠) (🌊)

**▽▽ Fireside Inn Cabins ⒸⒶ 🐾**
(970) 264-9204. **$95-$164.** 1600 E Hwy 160. 1.3 mi e on US 160. Ext corridors. **Pets:** Other species. $8 daily fee/pet. No service, supervision.

(ASK) (S🐾) (✕) (🏠) (🖥) (✕) (🎿)

**△△△ ▽▽▽▽ Pagosa Lodge SH**
(970) 731-4141. **$90-$125.** 3505 W Hwy 160. 3.5 mi w on US 160. Int corridors. **Pets:** Small, dogs only. $45 one-time fee/pet. Service with restrictions, supervision.

(SAVE) (S🐾) (✕) (♿) (🏠) (🖥) (🍴) (🌊) (✕)

**▽▽ The Pagosa Springs Inn & Suites SH**
(970) 731-3400. **$60-$119.** 519 Village Dr. 3.8 mi w on US 160. Int corridors. **Pets:** Medium. $10 daily fee/pet. Designated rooms, service with restrictions, supervision.

(ASK) (S🐾) (✕) (🏠) (🖥) (🌊)

**△△△ ▽▽ Super 8 Motel Ⓜ**
(970) 731-4005. **$40-$100.** 8 Solomon Dr. 2.5 mi w on US 160. Ext/int corridors. **Pets:** Other species. No service, supervision.

(SAVE) (S🐾) (✕) (🏠)

## PUEBLO

**▽▽▽▽ Best Western Eagle Ridge Inn & Suites SH**
(719) 543-4644. **$55-$120.** 4727 N Elizabeth St. I-25, exit 102, just w, then just n. Int corridors. **Pets:** Large. $15 daily fee/pet. Service with restrictions, supervision.

(ASK) (S🐾) (✕) (🏠) (🖥) (🌊) (✕)

**△△△ ▽▽▽ Best Western Town House Motel Ⓜ**
(719) 543-6530. **$44-$80.** 730 N Santa Fe Ave. I-25, exit 99B, just w, then just s. Ext corridors. **Pets:** Medium, other species. $10 one-time fee/room. Service with restrictions.

(SAVE) (S🐾) (✕) (♿) (🏠) (🖥) (🍴) (🌊)

**▽▽▽▽ Hampton Inn SH 🐾**
(719) 544-4700. **$69-$109.** 4703 N Freeway. I-25, exit 102, just w. Ext corridors. **Pets:** Small, other species. $10 one-time fee/room. Designated rooms, service with restrictions, crate.

(ASK) (S🐾) (✕) (🏠) (🖥) (🌊)

**▽▽▽▽ La Quinta Inn & Suites Pueblo SH**
(719) 542-3500. **$76-$129.** 4801 N Elizabeth St. I-25, exit 102, just nw. Int corridors. **Pets:** Medium. Service with restrictions.

(ASK) (✕) (📷) (♿) (🏠) (🌊)

**▽▽▽ Microtel Inn & Suites SH**
(719) 242-2020. **$60-$95.** 3343 Gateway Dr. I-25, exit 94. Int corridors. **Pets:** Accepted.

(ASK) (✕) (♿) (🏠) (🖥)

**▽▽ Motel 6–1186 Ⓜ**
(719) 543-8900. **$39-$55.** 960 Hwy 50 W. I-25, exit 101, 0.3 mi w. Ext corridors. **Pets:** Accepted.

(S🐾) (✕) (♿) (🏠)

**▽▽▽ Quality Inn & Suites SH**
(719) 544-5500. **$69-$175.** 3910 Outlook Blvd. I-25, exit 101 (US 50), 0.9 mi w, just s on Fortino Blvd, e on frontage road, then just s. Int corridors. **Pets:** Small. $20 daily fee/pet. Designated rooms, no service, crate.

(ASK) (S🐾) (✕) (♿) (🏠) (🖥) (🌊)

**▽▽▽ Ramada Inn Pueblo SH**
(719) 543-8050. **$49-$109.** 4001 N Elizabeth St. I-25, exit 101 (US 50 W), 0.3 mi n on service road. Ext/int corridors. **Pets:** Accepted.

(ASK) (S🐾) (✕) (🏠) (🖥) (🍴) (🌊) (✕)

**▽▽ Sleep Inn SH**
(719) 583-4000. **$55-$105.** 3626 N Freeway. I-25, exit 101, just ne on frontage road. Int corridors. **Pets:** Accepted.

(ASK) (S🐾) (✕) (♿) (🏠) (🖥) (🌊)

# PUEBLO WEST

**▼▼▼ Inn at Pueblo West** M
(719) 547-2111. **$79-$199.** 201 S McCulloch Blvd. I-25, exit 101, 7.5 mi w on US 50, then 0.5 mi s. Ext/int corridors. **Pets:** Other species. $50 deposit/room. Designated rooms, no service, supervision.

⑤🅢⑥ ✕ ⑥🅜 ⑥ 🚪 🖵 🍴 🏊

# RIDGWAY

**◈◈ ▼▼▼ Chipeta Sun Lodge and Spa** BB
(970) 626-3737. **$75-$250.** 304 S Lena St. Jct US 550, just w on SR 62, then just s. Ext/int corridors. **Pets:** Accepted.

SAVE 🅢⑥ ✕ 🚪 🖵 🏊 ✕ 🅐𝒦

**◈◈ ▼▼▼ Ridgway-Ouray Lodge & Suites** M
(970) 626-5444. **$60-$98.** 373 Palomino Tr. From US 550, just ne on SR 62, then just e. Int corridors. **Pets:** Large. $10 daily fee/pet. Designated rooms, service with restrictions, supervision.

SAVE 🅢⑥ ✕ 🚪 🖵 🏊 ✕

# RIFLE

**◈◈ ▼▼▼ Rusty Cannon Motel** M
(970) 625-4404. **$74-$82, 14 day notice.** 701 Taughenbaugh Blvd. I-70, exit 90, just s. Ext corridors. **Pets:** Dogs only. $25 deposit/pet, $25 one-time fee/pet. Designated rooms, service with restrictions, supervision.

SAVE 🅢⑥ ✕ 🚪 🖵 🏊

# SALIDA

**◈◈ ▼▼▼ Aspen Leaf Lodge** M ❀
(719) 539-6733. **$50-$99.** 7350 W Hwy 50. Just w of Hot Springs Pool. Ext corridors. **Pets:** Medium, other species. $5 daily fee/room. Service with restrictions, supervision.

SAVE 🅢⑥ ✕ 🚪

**◈◈ ▼▼ Circle R Motel** M
(719) 539-6296. **$44-$89.** 304 E US Hwy 50.. Ext corridors. **Pets:** $5 one-time fee/pet. Service with restrictions, crate.

SAVE ✕ 🚪 🖵

**◈◈ ▼▼ Days Inn** SH
(719) 539-6651. **$50-$110.** 407 E Hwy 50. US 50. Int corridors. **Pets:** Accepted.

SAVE 🅢⑥ ✕ 🚪 🖵

**◈◈ ▼▼ Econo Lodge** SH
(719) 539-2895. **$49-$199.** 1310 E Hwy 50. Just e on US 50; between Blake and Palmer sts. Ext corridors. **Pets:** Medium. $10 daily fee/pet. Designated rooms, supervision.

SAVE 🅢⑥ ✕ 🚪 🖵

**◈◈ ▼▼▼ Great Western Colorado Lodge** M
(719) 539-2514. **$69-$100.** 352 W Rainbow Blvd. On US 50. Ext corridors. **Pets:** Other species. $10 daily fee/pet. Designated rooms, service with restrictions, supervision.

SAVE 🅢⑥ ✕ 🚪 🖵 🏊

**◈◈ ▼▼▼ Silver Ridge Lodge** M
(719) 539-2553. **$45-$100, 3 day notice.** 545 W Rainbow Blvd. US 50, just w of Chamber of Commerce. Ext corridors. **Pets:** Small. $10 daily fee/pet. Designated rooms, service with restrictions, supervision.

SAVE 🅢⑥ ✕ 🚪 🖵

**▼▼ Super 8 Motel** M
(719) 539-6689. **$59-$129.** 525 W Rainbow Blvd. On US 50. Ext corridors. **Pets:** Medium. Service with restrictions, crate.

ASK 🅢⑥ ✕ 🚪 🖵 🏊

**◈◈ ▼▼ Travelodge** M
(719) 539-2528. **$59-$109.** 7310 Hwy 50. On US 50 W. Ext corridors. **Pets:** Other species. $5 daily fee/pet. Designated rooms, service with restrictions.

SAVE 🅢⑥ ✕ 🚪 🖵 🏊

**▼▼▼ The Tudor Rose Bed & Breakfast** BB
(719) 539-2002. **$72-$175, 7 day notice.** 6720 CR 104. Just e on US 50, s on CR 104, 0.5 mi up the hill, follow signs. Int corridors. **Pets:** Accepted.

✕ 🚪 ✕ 🅐𝒦

**◈◈ ▼▼▼ Woodland Motel** M ❀
(719) 539-4980. **$44-$102.** 903 W 1st St. From center of historic downtown, 0.5 mi w on 1st St (SR 291). Ext corridors. **Pets:** Other species.

SAVE ✕ 🚪 🖵

# SILVERTHORNE

**◈◈ ▼▼▼ Days Inn Summit County** SH
(970) 468-8661. **$59-$139.** 580 Silverthorne Ln. I-70, exit 205, just n on SR 9, just e on Rainbow Dr, then just e on Tanglewood Ln. Int corridors. **Pets:** Medium, other species. $10 daily fee/pet. Service with restrictions, supervision.

SAVE 🅢⑥ ✕ 🅜 ⑥ 🅐 🚪

**▼▼▼ La Quinta Inn & Suites** SH
(970) 468-6200. **$69-$179, 3 day notice.** 560 Silverthorne Ln. I-70, exit 205, just n on SR 9, just e on Rainbow Rd, then just e on Tanglewood Ln. Int corridors. **Pets:** Small, other species. Designated rooms, service with restrictions, supervision.

ASK 🅢⑥ ✕ 🅜 ⑥ 🅐 🚪 🖵 🍴 🏊

**▼▼▼ Quality Inn & Suites** SH
(970) 513-1222. **$79-$219.** 530 Silverthorne Ln. I-70, exit 205, just n on SR 9, just e on Rainbow Rd, then just e on Tanglewood Ln. Int corridors. **Pets:** Accepted.

ASK 🅢⑥ ✕ 🅜 ⑥ 🅐 🚪 🖵 🏊

# SILVERTON

**◈◈ ▼▼▼ Silverton's Inn of the Rockies at the Historic Alma House** BB
(970) 387-5336. **$85-$120, 7 day notice.** 220 E 10th St. From SR 110 (Greene St), just se. Int corridors. **Pets:** Accepted.

SAVE 🅢⑥ ✕ 🅐𝒦 ✉

**▼▼ Villa Dallavalle B & B** BB
(970) 387-5555. **$79-$125.** 1257 Blair St. SR 110, off US 550, se on 12th to Blair St, then just n. Int corridors. **Pets:** Medium, dogs only. $5 daily fee/room. Service with restrictions, supervision.

ASK 🅢⑥ ✕ 🅐𝒦

**◈◈ ▼▼▼ The Wyman Hotel & Inn** BB ❀
(970) 387-5372. **$145-$165, 14 day notice.** 1371 Greene St. Northeast corner of Greene (Main) and 14th sts. Int corridors. **Pets:** Other species. $25 one-time fee/pet. Designated rooms, supervision.

SAVE ✕ 🚪 🍴 🅐𝒦

# SNOWMASS VILLAGE

**▼▼▼ Silvertree Hotel** LH
(970) 923-3520. **$79-$659.** 100 Elbert Ln. 4 mi sw of SR 82 via Brush Creek and Snowmelt rds, Lot 8. Int corridors. **Pets:** Accepted.

ASK 🅢⑥ ✕ ⑥ 🚪 🖵 🍴 🏊 ✕ 🅐𝒦

**◈◈ ▼▼▼ Snowmass Mountain Chalet** SH
(970) 923-3900. **$89-$325, 45 day notice.** 115 Daly Ln. 4 mi sw of SR 82 via Brush Creek and Lower Village rds, Lot 5. Ext/int corridors. **Pets:** Accepted.

SAVE 🅢⑥ ✕ 🚪 🖵 🏊 ✕ 🅐𝒦

# SOUTH FORK

**▼▼ Comfort Inn** M
(719) 873-5600. **$100-$110.** 0182 E Frontage Rd. On US 160. Int corridors. **Pets:** Accepted.

ASK 🅢⑥ ✕ 🚪 🖵 🏊

**Ute Bluff Lodge and RV Park** M
(719) 873-5595. **$59-$64, 30 day notice.** 27680 W Hwy 160. 2.5 mi e of jct US 160 and SR 149. Ext corridors. **Pets:** Medium. $5 daily fee/pet. Designated rooms, service with restrictions, supervision.

ASK SD X 🗑 💻 🐾

**Wolf Creek Ski Lodge** M
(719) 873-5547. **$59-$109, 15 day notice.** 31042 Hwy 160 W. On US 160. Ext corridors. **Pets:** Dogs only. $10 daily fee/pet. Designated rooms, service with restrictions, supervision.

SAVE SD X 🗑 💻 🍽 🐾

# STEAMBOAT SPRINGS

**The Alpiner Lodge** M
(970) 879-1430. **$59-$99, 3 day notice.** 424 Lincoln Ave. US 40, just w of Hot Springs Pool. Ext/int corridors. **Pets:** Accepted.

SAVE SD X 🗑 💻

**Best Western Ptarmigan Inn** SH ❀
(970) 879-1730. **$79-$234.** 2304 Apres Ski Way. 2.3 mi e on US 40, 0.8 mi n on Mt Werner Rd, then take Apres Ski Way. Int corridors. **Pets:** Other species. $25 one-time fee/room. Supervision.

SAVE SD X 🗑 💻 🐾 🐾

**Comfort Inn** SH
(970) 879-6669. **$75-$279.** 1055 Walton Creek Rd. 2.8 mi e on US 40. Int corridors. **Pets:** Accepted.

ASK SD X 🐾 🐾 🗑 💻 🐾

**Fairfield Inn & Suites by Marriott** SH
(970) 870-9000. **$69-$139, 4 day notice.** 3200 S Lincoln Ave. 3 mi e on US 40. Int corridors. **Pets:** Accepted.

SAVE SD X 🐾 🐾 🐾 🗑 💻

**Hampton Inn & Suites** SH ❀
(970) 871-8900. **$119-$309, 3 day notice.** 725 S Lincoln Ave. 1.1 mi e on US 40. Int corridors. **Pets:** Medium. $25 one-time fee/pet. Designated rooms, service with restrictions, supervision.

ASK SD X 🐾 🐾 🐾 🗑 💻 🐾 🐾

**Holiday Inn Steamboat** SH ❀
(970) 879-2250. **$109-$159, 3 day notice.** 3190 S Lincoln Ave. 3 mi e on US 40. Int corridors. **Pets:** Other species. $25 deposit/room, $10 daily fee/room. Designated rooms, service with restrictions, supervision.

SAVE SD X 🐾 🐾 🐾 🗑 💻 🍽 🐾

**Iron Horse Inn-Steamboat Springs** SH
(970) 879-6505. **$59-$125.** 333 S Lincoln Ave. 1 mi e on US 40. Ext/int corridors. **Pets:** Accepted.

SAVE SD X 🗑 💻 🐾

**La Quinta Inn** SH
(970) 871-1219. **Call for rates.** 3155 Ingels Ln. On US 40, just e on Ingles Ln. Int corridors. **Pets:** Other species. $10 one-time fee/room. Designated rooms, service with restrictions, crate.

ASK SD X 🗑 💻 🐾

**Nordic Lodge** M
(970) 879-0531. **$59-$199, 14 day notice.** 1036 Lincoln Ave. Between 10th and 11th sts; downtown. Ext corridors. **Pets:** $10 daily fee/pet. Service with restrictions

SAVE SD X 🗑 🐾

**Rabbit Ears Motel** M ❀
(970) 879-1150. **$99-$129, 3 day notice.** 201 Lincoln Ave. Just e on US 40. Ext corridors. **Pets:** $12 one-time fee/room. Service with restrictions, supervision.

SAVE SD X 🗑 💻

**Sheraton Steamboat Resort** LH
(970) 879-2220. **$129-$379, 30 day notice.** 2200 Village Inn Ct. 2.3 mi e on US 40, 1 mi n on Mt Werner Rd; at ski area. Int corridors. **Pets:** Large, dogs only. $25 one-time fee/room. Service with restrictions, supervision.

ASK SD X 🐾 🐾 🗑 💻 🍽 🐾 🐾

**Super 8 Motel** SH
(970) 879-5230. **$59-$108.** 3195 S Lincoln Ave. 3 mi e on US 40. Int corridors. **Pets:** Medium, dogs only. Designated rooms, supervision.

ASK SD X 🗑 💻 🐾

# STERLING

**Best Western Sundowner** M ❀
(970) 522-6265. **$77-$119.** 125 Overland Trail St. I-76, exit 125, just w. Ext/int corridors. **Pets:** Other species. $10 daily fee/pet. Designated rooms, service with restrictions, supervision.

SAVE SD X 🗑 💻 🐾

**Colonial Motel** M
(970) 522-3382. **$45-$64.** 915 S Division. I-76, exit 125, 1.8 mi w on US 6 to 3rd traffic light (4th St), then 1.7 mi s. Ext corridors. **Pets:** Accepted.

SAVE SD X 🗑

**Ramada Inn** SH
(970) 522-2625. **$80-$100.** 22140 E Hwy 6. I-76, exit 125, 0.5 mi e on US 6. Ext/int corridors. **Pets:** Other species. $25 deposit/room. Service with restrictions, supervision.

SAVE SD X 🐾 🗑 💻 🍽 🐾 🐾

# STRATTON

**Best Western Golden Prairie Inn** SH
(719) 348-5311. **$65-$99.** 700 Colorado Ave. I-70, exit 419, just n. Ext corridors. **Pets:** Accepted.

SAVE SD X 🗑 💻 🍽 🐾

# TELLURIDE

**Hotel Columbia** SH ❀
(970) 728-0660. **$150-$460, 30 day notice.** 300 W San Juan Ave. Just s of SR 145 Spur, at Aspen St and San Juan Ave; opposite gondola. Int corridors. **Pets:** Dogs only. $20 daily fee/room. Service with restrictions, supervision.

SAVE SD X 🗑 💻 🍽 🐾

**The Hotel Telluride** SH ❀
(970) 369-1188. **$129-$269.** 199 N Cornet St. Just n of jct SR 145 (Colorado Ave). Ext/int corridors. **Pets:** Medium, other species. $100 one-time fee/room. Designated rooms, service with restrictions.

ASK SD X 🐾 🐾 🐾 🗑 💻 🐾

**Peaks Resort & Golden Door Spa** LH
(970) 728-6800. **$99-$950, 30 day notice.** 136 Country Club Dr. 1.8 mi s of jct SR 145 (Colorado Ave) and 145 Spur, 2.5 mi e on Mountain Village Blvd, follow ski area signs; in Telluride Mountain Village. Ext/int corridors. **Pets:** Accepted.

ASK X 🐾 🗑 💻 🍽 🐾 🐾 🐾

# TRINIDAD

**Best Western Trinidad Inn** M
(719) 846-2215. **$99-$119.** 900 W Adams St. I-25, exit 13A northbound, just ne; exit Cross Bridge southbound, then just ne. Ext corridors. **Pets:** Accepted.

SAVE SD X 🗑 💻 🍽 🐾

**Budget Host Derrick Motel** M ❀
(719) 846-3307. **$59-$69.** 10301 Santa Fe Trail Dr. I-25, exit 11, 0.5 mi ne. Ext corridors. **Pets:** Medium. $10 daily fee/pet. Service with restrictions, supervision.

SAVE SD X 🗑 💻

**▼▼ Budget Summit Inn M**
(719) 846-2251. **$50-$65.** 9800 Santa Fe Trail Dr. I-25, exit 11, just se. Ext/int corridors. **Pets:** Accepted.

[ASK] [SÒ] [✕] [🐾] [🖑] [🖪]

**(AAA) ▼▼▼▼ Quality Inn Trinidad SH**
(719) 846-4491. **$85-$129.** 3125 Toupal Dr. I-25, exit 11, just w. Int corridors. **Pets:** Medium, dogs only. $50 deposit/pet, $15 one-time fee/pet. Designated rooms, no service, supervision.

[SAVE] [SÒ] [✕] [🖪] [🖳] [🍴] [🛋] [✕]

**▼▼ Super 8 Motel M**
(719) 846-8280. **$55-$90.** 1924 Freedom Rd. I-25, exit 15, just ne. Int corridors. **Pets:** Medium. $10 one-time fee/pet. Service with restrictions, supervision.

[ASK] [SÒ] [✕] [🖪] [🖳]

# VAIL

**(AAA) ▼▼▼▼ Antlers at Vail CO**
(970) 476-2471. **$128-$1500, 60 day notice.** 680 W Lionshead Pl. I-70, exit 176, 0.5 mi w, then just s on Lionshead Cir. Ext corridors. **Pets:** Accepted.

[SAVE] [✕] [🐾] [🖑] [🖪] [🖳] [🛋] [✕] [🏋]

**▼▼▼▼ Holiday Inn Apex Vail SH**
(970) 476-2739. **Call for rates.** 2211 N Frontage Rd. I-70, exit 173, just w. Int corridors. **Pets:** Medium, dogs only. $25 one-time fee/pet. Designated rooms, supervision.

[✕] [🛆M] [🖑] [🖪] [🖳] [🍴] [🛋] [✕]

**▼▼ ▼▼ Sonnenalp Resort of Vail SH**
(970) 476-5656. **$240-$2055.** 20 Vail Rd. I-70, exit 176, just s. Int corridors. **Pets:** Accepted.

[ASK] [SÒ] [✕] [🐾] [🍴] [🛋] [✕]

**(AAA) ▼▼▼ ▼▼▼ Vail Cascade Resort & Spa LH**
(970) 476-7111. **$249-$479, 14 day notice.** 1300 Westhaven Dr. I-70, exit 176, 2 mi w; 1 mi e of exit 173 on south frontage road. Int corridors. **Pets:** Accepted.

[SAVE] [✕] [🛆M] [🐾] [🖑] [🖪] [🖳] [🍴] [🛋] [✕] [🏋]

# WALSENBURG

**(AAA) ▼▼ Anchor Motel M**
(719) 738-2800. **$35-$65.** 1001 Main St. I-25, exit 49, 0.5 mi nw. Ext corridors. **Pets:** Small, other species. Designated rooms, service with restrictions, supervision.

[SAVE] [✕] [🖪] [🖳]

**(AAA) ▼▼ ▼▼ Best Western Rambler SH**
(719) 738-1121. **$63-$120.** 457 US Hwy 85-87. I-25, exit 52, just w. Ext corridors. **Pets:** $25 deposit/room. Designated rooms, service with restrictions, supervision.

[SAVE] [SÒ] [✕] [🖳] [🍴] [🛋]

**(AAA) ▼▼ Country Budget Host Motel M**
(719) 738-3800. **$42-$64.** 553 US Hwy 85 & 87. I-25, exit 52, 0.3 mi w. Ext corridors. **Pets:** Accepted.

[SAVE] [SÒ] [✕]

# WINDSOR

**(AAA) ▼▼ Super 8 Motel SH 🐾**
(970) 686-5996. **$64-$84.** 1265 Main St. I-25, exit 262, 3.8 mi e; in shopping/restaurant complex. Int corridors. **Pets:** Other species. $15 daily fee/pet. Service with restrictions, crate.

[SAVE] [SÒ] [✕] [🛆M] [🖪] [🖳]

# WINTER PARK

**▼▼▼▼ The Vintage Resort and Conference Center at Winter Park SH**
(970) 726-8801. **Call for rates.** 100 Winter Park Dr. In ski resort area. Int corridors. **Pets:** Accepted.

[ASK] [SÒ] [🖪] [🖳] [🍴] [🛋] [✕] [🏋]

**(AAA) ▼▼▼▼ Winter Park Mountain Lodge SH**
(970) 726-4211. **$69-$299.** 81699 US Hwy 40. 2.3 mi se on US 40; near Winter Park ski area. Int corridors. **Pets:** Accepted.

[SAVE] [✕] [🛆M] [🐾] [🖳] [🍴] [🛋] [✕]

# YAMPA

**(AAA) ▼▼ ▼▼ Oak Tree Inn SH**
(970) 638-1000. **$75.** 98 Moffat Ave. Just off SR 131. Int corridors. **Pets:** Other species. $10 one-time fee/room. Service with restrictions, supervision.

[SAVE] [SÒ] [✕] [🖪] [🖳] [🍴]

# CONNECTICUT

## CITY INDEX

## BETHEL

### ⬥⬥ Microtel Inn & Suites 🆂🅷
(203) 748-8318. **$79-$92.** 80 Benedict Rd. I-84, exit 8, 1 mi e on US 6. Int corridors. **Pets:** $100 deposit/room, $10 daily fee/pet. Service with restrictions, crate.

(ASK) 🆂 ⊠ ⬚ ⬚ 🛏 🖥

## BRIDGEPORT

### ⬥⬥⬥ Bridgeport Holiday Inn & Convention Center 🆂🅷
(203) 334-1234. **$107-$149.** 1070 Main St. SR 8, exit 2 northbound, 0.7 mi se; exit southbound, just s, then just e. Int corridors. **Pets:** Medium, other species. $50 deposit/room. Service with restrictions, supervision.

(ASK) 🆂 ⊠ 🛏 🖥 ⊞ 🛥

## BROOKFIELD

### ⬥⬥ Twin Tree Inn Ⓜ
(203) 775-0220. **$85-$95.** 1030 Federal Rd (Rt 7 & 202). Jct SR 25 and US 202, 1 mi n. Ext/int corridors. **Pets:** Dogs only. $10 one-time fee/pet. Designated rooms, service with restrictions, crate.

(ASK) 🆂 ⊠ ⬚ 🛏

## DANBURY

### ⬥⬥⬥ Ethan Allen Hotel 🆂🅷
(203) 744-1776. **$119.** 21 Lake Ave Extension. I-84, exit 4, 0.3 mi w on US 6 and 202. Int corridors. **Pets:** Large, other species. $15 daily fee/pet. Designated rooms, service with restrictions, supervision.

(ASK) 🆂 ⊠ ⬚ 🛏 🖥 ⊞ 🛥

### ⬥⬥⬥ Holiday Inn 🆂🅷
(203) 792-4000. **$114-$144.** 80 Newtown Rd. I-84, exit 8 (Newtown Rd), 0.5 mi s on US 6 W. Int corridors. **Pets:** Large, other species. $15 daily fee/pet. Designated rooms, service with restrictions.

(SAVE) 🆂 ⊠ ⬚ 🛏 🖥 ⊞ 🛥

### ⬥⬥⬥ Maron Hotel & Suites 🆂🅷
(203) 791-2200. **$119-$179.** 42 Lake Ave Extension. I-84, exit 4, 0.5 mi w on US 6 and 202. Int corridors. **Pets:** Medium, other species. $10 daily fee/room. Designated rooms, service with restrictions.

(SAVE) ⊠ ⊠M ⬚ ⬚ 🛏 🖥 ⊞

### ⬥⬥⬥ Residence Inn by Marriott 🆂🅷 🐾
(203) 797-1256. **$114-$229.** 22 Segar St. I-84, exit 4 eastbound, just n; exit westbound, just e on Lake Ave Extension, then just s. Int corridors. **Pets:** Other species. $75 one-time fee/room. Service with restrictions.

(SAVE) ⊠ ⬚ ⬚ 🛏 🖥 🛥

### ⬥⬥⬥ Sheraton Danbury 🅻🅷
(203) 794-0600. **$79-$169.** 18 Old Ridgebury Rd. I-84, exit 2 eastbound; exit 2A westbound. Int corridors. **Pets:** Accepted.

(ASK) 🆂 ⊠ ⬚ ⬚ 🛏 🖥 ⊞ 🛥 ⊠

### ⬥⬥ Super 8 Motel 🆂🅷
(203) 743-0064. **$63-$69.** 3 Lake Ave Extension. I-84, exit 4, just w on US 6 and 202. Int corridors. **Pets:** Accepted.

(SAVE) 🆂 ⊠ 🛏

## DAYVILLE

### ⬥⬥⬥ Holiday Inn Express 🆂🅷
(860) 779-3200. **$114-$134.** 16 Tracy Rd. I-395, exit 94, just w. Int corridors. **Pets:** Small. $10 daily fee/pet. Designated rooms, service with restrictions, crate.

(ASK) 🆂 ⊠ ⊠M ⬚ 🛏 🖥 🛥

## GRISWOLD

### ⬥⬥⬥ AmericInn Lodge & Suites 🆂🅷
(860) 376-3200. **$69-$179.** 375 Voluntown Rd. I-395, exit 85, w on SR 138. Int corridors. **Pets:** Accepted.

(SAVE) 🆂 ⊠ ⊠M ⬚ 🛏 🖥 🛥

# HARTFORD METROPOLITAN AREA

## AVON

### ⬥⬥⬥ Residence Inn by Marriott Hartford-Avon 🆂🅷
(860) 678-1666. **$159.** 55 Simsbury Rd (SR 202). Jct US 44, just n. Int corridors. **Pets:** Accepted.

(ASK) 🆂 ⊠ ⊠M ⬚ ⬚ 🛏 🖥 🛥 ⊠

## BERLIN

### ⬥⬥⬥ Hawthorne Inn 🆂🅷 🐾
(860) 828-4181. **$110-$150.** 2387 Berlin Tpke. I-91, exit 17 northbound, 4.7 mi n on SR 15 (Berlin Tpke); exit 22N southbound, 2.5 mi n on SR 9 to exit 22, follow signs onto US 5 and SR 15 S (Berlin Tpke) for 3 mi. Int corridors. **Pets:** Other species. Service with restrictions.

(SAVE) 🆂 ⊠ ⬚ 🛏 ⊞ 🛥 ⊠

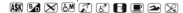

# CROMWELL

▼▼ Comfort Inn SH ❀
(860) 635-4100. **$67-$150.** 111 Berlin Rd. I-91, exit 21, just e on SR 372. Int corridors. **Pets:** Other species. $15 daily fee/room. Designated rooms, service with restrictions, supervision.

(ASK) (S6) (X) (🔓) (💻)

AAA ▼▼▼ Crowne Plaza Hartford-Cromwell LH
(860) 635-2000. **$109-$169.** 100 Berlin Rd. I-91, exit 21, just e on SR 372. Int corridors. **Pets:** Accepted.

(SAVE) (S6) (X) (&M) (🔓) (🔓) (💻) (¶) (≈) (✕)

# EAST HARTFORD

AAA ▼▼▼ Holiday Inn SH
(860) 528-9611. **$79-$129.** 363 Roberts St. I-84, exit 58, just w. Int corridors. **Pets:** Medium, dogs only. $25 deposit/pet, $25 daily fee/pet. Designated rooms, service with restrictions, supervision.

(SAVE) (S6) (X) (🔓) (🔓) (🔓) (💻) (¶) (≈)

▼▼▼ Sheraton Hartford Hotel SH ❀
(860) 528-9703. **$89-$159.** 100 E River Dr. I-84, exit 53 eastbound, just s; exit 54 westbound to exit 3 (Darlin St), just n. Int corridors. **Pets:** Large. Service with restrictions, supervision.

(ASK) (S6) (X) (&M) (🔓) (🔓) (🔓) (💻) (¶) (≈)

# EAST WINDSOR

▼▼▼ Holiday Inn Express Hartford Airport Area M
(860) 627-6585. **$79-$104.** 260 Main St (US 5). I-91, exit 44, just s. Int corridors. **Pets:** Accepted.

(ASK) (X) (&M) (🔓) (🔓) (🔓) (💻)

# ENFIELD

▼ Motel 6-Enfield #1042 M
(860) 741-3685. **$48-$65.** 11 Hazard Ave. I-91, exit 47E, just e. Ext corridors. **Pets:** Accepted.

(S6) (X) (🔓)

▼▼ Red Roof Inn # 7105 M
(860) 741-2571. **$55-$81.** 5 Hazard Ave. I-91, exit 47E. Ext corridors. **Pets:** Accepted.

(X) (&M) (🔓) (🔓) (🔓)

# FARMINGTON

AAA ▼▼▼ Centennial Inn Suites CO
(860) 677-4647. **$99-$239.** 5 Spring Ln. US 6, 0.3 mi e of jct SR 177. Ext/int corridors. **Pets:** Large, other species. $15 daily fee/pet. Designated rooms, service with restrictions.

(SAVE) (S6) (X) (&M) (🔓) (🔓) (💻) (≈)

▼▼▼ Homewood Suites by Hilton SH
(860) 321-0000. **$159-$169.** 2 Farm Glen Blvd. I-84, exit 39, 0.6 mi e on SR 4. Int corridors. **Pets:** Accepted.

(X) (&M) (🔓) (🔓) (💻) (≈)

# HARTFORD

▼▼▼ Crowne Plaza Hartford Downtown LH
(860) 549-2400. **$129-$199.** 50 Morgan St. I-91, exit 32B; I-84, exit 50 eastbound; exit 52 westbound. Int corridors. **Pets:** Very small. $50 one-time fee/room. Designated rooms, service with restrictions, supervision.

(ASK) (S6) (X) (&M) (🔓) (🔓) (🔓) (💻) (¶) (≈)

▼▼▼ Goodwin Hotel SH
(860) 246-7500. **$99-$1050.** 1 Haynes St. Downtown; entrance on Asylum St. Int corridors. **Pets:** Accepted.

(ASK) (S6) (X) (&M) (🔓) (🔓) (💻) (¶)

▼▼ Residence Inn by Marriott Downtown Hartford SH
(860) 524-5550. **$139-$249.** 942 Main St. I-91, exit 29A northbound; exit 31 southbound. Int corridors. **Pets:** Other species. $75 one-time fee/pet. Service with restrictions, crate.

(ASK) (S6) (X) (🔓) (🔓) (💻)

# MANCHESTER

▼▼▼ Extended StayAmerica SH
(860) 643-5140. **$91.** 340 Tolland Tpke. I-84, exit 63, 0.3 mi se on SR 30, then just sw. Int corridors. **Pets:** Accepted.

(ASK) (S6) (X) (&M) (🔓) (🔓) (💻)

▼▼▼ Residence Inn Manchester SH
(860) 432-4242. **$159-$199.** 201 Hale Rd. I-84, exit 63, 0.5 mi nw, then 0.6 mi sw. Int corridors. **Pets:** Other species. $75 one-time fee/room. Service with restrictions.

(ASK) (S6) (X) (&M) (🔓) (🔓) (🔓) (💻) (≈) (✕)

# MIDDLETOWN

▼▼▼ Inn at Middletown SH
(860) 854-6300. **$129-$169.** 70 Main St. SR 9, exit 15, just sw on Dr. Martin Luther King Jr Way, then 0.4 mi se. Int corridors. **Pets:** Medium. $75 one-time fee/pet. Designated rooms, service with restrictions, crate.

(ASK) (S6) (X) (&M) (🔓) (🔓) (🔓) (💻) (¶) (≈)

# PLAINVILLE

▼▼ Ramada Inn SH
(860) 747-6876. **$80-$110.** 400 New Britain Ave. I-84, exit 34 eastbound, 0.6 mi n on Crooked St; exit 34 westbound, 0.6 mi n on Crooked St. Int corridors. **Pets:** Accepted.

(ASK) (S6) (X) (🔓) (💻) (¶) (≈)

# SIMSBURY

▼▼ The Ironhorse Inn M
(860) 658-2216. **$86-$96.** 969 Hopmeadow St. On US 202/SR 10, 0.4 mi n. Int corridors. **Pets:** Accepted.

(ASK) (S6) (X) (🔓) (≈)

# SOUTHINGTON

▼ Motel 6-1018 M
(860) 621-7351. **$48-$61.** 625 Queen St. I-84, exit 32, just ne. Ext corridors. **Pets:** Accepted.

(S6) (X) (🔓)

AAA ▼▼▼ Residence Inn by Marriott SH
(860) 621-4440. **$119-$189.** 778 West St. I-84, exit 31, just s. Int corridors. **Pets:** Accepted.

(SAVE) (S6) (X) (&M) (🔓) (🔓) (💻) (≈) (✕)

# WETHERSFIELD

AAA ▼▼ Best Western Camelot Inn SH
(860) 563-2311. **$79-$109.** 1330 Silas Deane Hwy. I-91, exit 24, 0.4 mi n. Int corridors. **Pets:** Small, dogs only. $10 daily fee/pet. Designated rooms, service with restrictions, supervision.

(SAVE) (X) (&M) (🔓) (💻) (≈) (✕)

▼ Motel 6-1028 M
(860) 563-5900. **$48-$62.** 1341 Silas Deane Hwy. I-91, exit 24, just n on SR 99. Ext corridors. **Pets:** Accepted.

(S6) (X) (🔓)

# WINDSOR

▼▼▼ The Residence Inn by Marriott Hartford-Windsor SH
(860) 688-7474. **$129-$169.** 100 Dunfey Ln. I-91, exit 37, just w on SR 305 to Dunfey Ln, then 0.3 mi n. Ext corridors. **Pets:** Other species. $75 one-time fee/room. Service with restrictions.

(ASK) (S6) (X) (&M) (🔓) (🔓) (💻) (≈) (✕)

# WINDSOR LOCKS

**AAA** **WWW** Baymont Inn & Suites Hartford-Airport **SH**
(860) 623-3336. **$80-$115.** 64 Ella T Grasso Tpke. I-91, exit 40, 2.5 mi
w on SR 20, then just n on SR 75. Int corridors. **Pets:** Medium. Service
with restrictions.
[SAVE] [X] [&M] [⚙] [📦] [💻]

**WWW** Homewood Suites by Hilton **SH**
(860) 627-8463. **$79-$289.** 65 Ella T Grasso Tpke. I-91, exit 40, 2.5 mi
w on SR 20, then just n on SR 75. Ext/int corridors. **Pets:** Accepted.
[ASK] [Sб] [X] [&M] [⚙] [📦] [💻] [🏊] [🍽]

**WW** Motel 6–763 **M**
(860) 292-6200. **$49-$62.** 3 National Dr. Jct SR 20, 0.7 mi n on SR 75,
then just e. Ext corridors. **Pets:** Accepted.
[Sб] [X] [🏊]

**WWW** Ramada Inn Bradley International Airport **SH** ❀
(860) 623-9494. **$109-$159.** 5 Ella T Grasso Tpke. I-91, exit 40, 2.5 mi
w on SR 20, then just n on SR 75. Int corridors. **Pets:** Other species.
$20 one-time fee/room. Service with restrictions.
[ASK] [X] [📦] [💻] [🍽] [🏊]

**WWW** Sheraton Hotel At Bradley International
Airport **LH** ❀
(860) 627-5311. **$99-$169.** 1 Bradley International Airport. At Bradley
International Airport terminal. Int corridors. **Pets:** Large. $50 deposit/pet.
Service with restrictions, supervision.
[ASK] [Sб] [X] [&M] [⚙] [📦] [💻] [🍽] [🏊]

---

## END METROPOLITAN AREA

---

# LAKEVILLE

**AAA** **WWW** Inn at Iron Masters **M** ❀
(860) 435-9844. **$95-$195.** 229 Main St (Rt 44 & 41). 0.5 mi ne. Ext
corridors. **Pets:** Dogs only. Supervision.
[SAVE] [X] [📦] [💻] [🏊]

**AAA** **WWW** Interlaken Inn Resort and Conference
Center **SH** ❀
(860) 435-9878. **$139-$349, 7 day notice.** 74 Interlaken Rd. On SR
112, 0.5 mi w of jct SR 41. Ext/int corridors. **Pets:** $10 daily fee/room.
Designated rooms, service with restrictions, supervision.
[SAVE] [X] [⚙] [📦] [💻] [🍽] [🏊] [🏊]

# LEDYARD

**WW** Almost In Mystic/Mares Inn **BB**
(860) 572-7556. **$100-$200, 14 day notice.** 333 Colonel Ledyard Hwy.
I-95, exit 89, 1 mi ne to Gold Star Hwy, 0.6 mi w, then 0.7 mi n. Int
corridors. **Pets:** Designated rooms, no service, supervision.
[X] [📦] [💻] [🐾]

# LITCHFIELD

**AAA** **WWW** Litchfield Inn **CI** ❀
(860) 567-4503. **$150-$250, 3 day notice.** 432 Bantam Rd. 1.5 mi w
on US 202. Int corridors. **Pets:** Medium, dogs only. $25 daily fee/pet.
Designated rooms, service with restrictions, supervision.
[SAVE] [Sб] [X] [📦] [💻] [🍽]

# MERIDEN

**WWW** Four Points by Sheraton Meriden **SH**
(203) 238-2380. **$109-$189.** 275 Research Pkwy. I-91, exit 17 southbound; exit 16 northbound, 0.5 mi e, then 0.5 mi s. Int corridors.
**Pets:** Dogs only. $25 one-time fee/room. Supervision.
[ASK] [Sб] [X] [&M] [⚙] [&✶] [📦] [💻] [🍽] [🏊]

**WWW** Residence Inn by Marriott **SH**
(203) 634-7770. **$89-$139.** 390 Bee St. I-91, exit 16 northbound, just e
on E Main St, then 0.7 mi n; exit 19 southbound, 0.5 mi w on Baldwin
Ave, then 0.5 mi s. Ext/int corridors. **Pets:** Accepted.
[ASK] [X] [&M] [&✶] [📦] [💻] [🏊] [🏊]

# MILFORD

**WWW** Residence Inn by Marriott **SH**
(203) 283-2100. **$85-$179.** 62 Rowe Ave. I-95, exit 35, just nw. Int
corridors. **Pets:** Medium. $75 one-time fee/room. Service with restrictions,
crate.
[ASK] [Sб] [X] [&✶] [📦] [💻] [🏊]

# MYSTIC

**AAA** **WWW** AmeriSuites (Mystic/I-95 & Seaport) **SH**
(860) 536-9997. **$89-$229.** 224 Greenmanville Ave. I-95, exit 90, just
se. Int corridors. **Pets:** Small. $25 daily fee/pet. Service with restrictions,
crate.
[SAVE] [Sб] [X] [&M] [⚙] [&✶] [📦] [💻] [🏊]

**AAA** **WWW** Best Western Mystic **SH**
(860) 536-4281. **$149-$249.** 9 Whitehall Ave. I-95, exit 90, just n. Int
corridors. **Pets:** Medium. $20 daily fee/room. No service, supervision.
[SAVE] [Sб] [X] [📦] [💻] [🍽] [🏊] [🏊]

**AAA** **WWW** The Inn at Mystic **M**
(860) 536-9604. **$95-$315.** 3 Williams Ave. On US 1 at SR 27. Ext/int
corridors. **Pets:** $15 deposit/pet. Designated rooms, service with restric-
tions, supervision.
[SAVE] [X] [⚙] [📦] [💻] [🍽] [🏊] [🏊]

**AAA** **WWW** Residence Inn by Marriott **SH**
(860) 536-5150. **$149-$399.** 40 Whitehall Ave. I-95, exit 90, just n on
SR 27. Int corridors. **Pets:** Other species. $75 one-time fee/room. Service
with restrictions.
[SAVE] [X] [⚙] [&✶] [📦] [💻] [🏊] [🏊]

# NEW HAVEN

**AAA** **WWWW** Omni New Haven Hotel at Yale **LH**
(203) 772-6664. **$209-$419.** 155 Temple St. Center of downtown. Int
corridors. **Pets:** Small. $50 one-time fee/room. Designated rooms, service
with restrictions, supervision.
[SAVE] [Sб] [X] [&M] [⚙] [&✶] [📦] [💻] [🍽]

**WWW** Residence Inn by Marriott **SH**
(203) 777-5337. **$134-$161.** 3 Long Wharf Dr. I-95, exit 46, 0.6 mi nw.
Ext corridors. **Pets:** Accepted.
[ASK] [X] [⚙] [📦] [💻] [🏊] [🏊]

# NEW LONDON

**WW** Red Roof Inn #7145 **M**
(860) 444-0001. **$59-$106.** 707 Colman St. I-95, exit 82A northbound,
0.8 mi n, just w, then 0.6 mi on Bayonet St; exit 83 southbound, 0.6 mi
s. Ext corridors. **Pets:** Accepted.
[X] [⚙] [&✶]

# NEW MILFORD

**WW** The Homestead Inn **BB**
(860) 354-4080. **$105-$160.** 5 Elm St. Just e of village green off Main
St; center. Ext/int corridors. **Pets:** Large, other species. $10 daily fee/pet.
Designated rooms, service with restrictions, supervision.
[ASK] [Sб] [X] [📦]

# NIANTIC

**▼ Motel 6–1063** Ⓜ
(860) 739-6991. **$47-$65.** 269 Flanders Rd. I-95, exit 74, just s. Ext corridors. **Pets:** Accepted.

# NORTH STONINGTON

**▼▼▼ Antiques and Accommodations** BB
(860) 535-1736. **$99-$189, 14 day notice.** 32 Main St. I-95, exit 92, 2.5 mi nw on SR 2, then 0.3 mi n. Ext/int corridors. **Pets:** Accepted.

**ⒶⒶⒶ ▼▼▼▼ Cedar Park Inn & Whirlpool Suites** Ⓜ
(860) 535-7829. **$69-$249.** 85 Norwich Westerly Rd. I-95, exit 92, 1 mi w on SR 2. Ext corridors. **Pets:** Accepted.

**▼▼▼ The Inn at Lower Farm** BB
(860) 535-9075. **$95-$160, 7 day notice.** 119 Mystic Rd. I-95, exit 90, 1.5 mi n on SR 27, 1.4 mi e on SR 184, then 3.4 mi n on SR 201. Int corridors. **Pets:** Accepted.

# NORWALK

**▼▼ Homestead Studio Suites Hotel-Norwalk** SH
(203) 847-6888. **$125.** 400 Main Ave. I-95, exit 15, 3.5 mi n via US 7, just e, then 1 mi s. Int corridors. **Pets:** $25 daily fee/pet. Service with restrictions, supervision.

**ⒶⒶⒶ ▼▼ ▼ The Silvermine Tavern** CI
(203) 847-4558. **$120-$180, 3 day notice.** 194 Perry Ave. Merritt Pkwy, exit 40A, 0.5 mi s on Main Ave, then 1.7 mi ne. Int corridors. **Pets:** Accepted.

# OLD LYME

**ⒶⒶⒶ ▼▼▼▼ Old Lyme Inn** CI ❖
(860) 434-2600. **$135-$185, 10 day notice.** 85 Lyme St. I-95, exit 70 northbound, just n on SR 156, then 0.5 mi e on US 1; exit southbound, just n. Int corridors. **Pets:** Other species. $50 deposit/room. Designated rooms, service with restrictions, crate.

# OLD SAYBROOK

**ⒶⒶⒶ ▼▼ ▼▼ Saybrook Point Inn & Spa** SH
(860) 395-2000. **$229-$699, 3 day notice.** 2 Bridge St. On SR 154, 2.2 mi s of jct US 1; at Saybrook Point. Int corridors. **Pets:** Accepted.

# PUTNAM

**ⒶⒶⒶ ▼▼ ▼ King's Inn** SH
(860) 928-7961. **$68-$98.** 5 Heritage Rd. I-395, exit 96, just sw. Int corridors. **Pets:** Accepted.

# RIVERTON

**▼▼ Old Riverton Inn** CI
(860) 379-8678. **$95-$200, 10 day notice.** 436 E River Rd (SR 20). Center. Int corridors. **Pets:** Accepted.

# SHELTON

**▼▼ Homestead Studio Suites Hotel-Shelton** SH
(203) 926-6868. **$110.** 945 Bridgeport Ave. SR 8, exit 11, 0.5 mi w. Int corridors. **Pets:** $25 daily fee/pet. Service with restrictions, supervision.

**▼▼▼▼ Residence Inn by Marriott** SH
(203) 926-9000. **$107-$152.** 1001 Bridgeport Ave. SR 8, exit 11, 0.3 mi w. Ext corridors. **Pets:** Other species. $75 one-time fee/room. Service with restrictions, crate.

# SOUTHBURY

**▼▼▼▼ Crowne Plaza–Southbury** SH
(203) 598-7600. **$139-$159.** 1284 Strongtown Rd. I-84, exit 16, just n on SR 188. Int corridors. **Pets:** Medium. $50 deposit/room. Designated rooms, service with restrictions, supervision.

# STAMFORD

**ⒶⒶⒶ ▼ Amsterdam Hotel–Greenwich/Stamford** SH
(203) 327-4300. **$70-$90.** 19 Clark's Hill Ave. I-95, exit 8 northbound, just n on Atlantic St, 0.6 mi ne on Tresser Blvd, then just s; exit southbound, just nw on Elm St, ne on Main St, then just s. Int corridors. **Pets:** $20 daily fee/pet. Designated rooms, service with restrictions, crate.

**▼▼▼▼ Sheraton Stamford Hotel** LH
(203) 359-1300. **$309.** 2701 Summer St. I-95, exit 8 northbound, 1.7 mi w on Atlantic and Bedford sts; exit 7 southbound, n on Atlantic and Bedford sts. Int corridors. **Pets:** Accepted.

**▼▼▼▼ Stamford Marriott Hotel & Spa** LH 🐾
(203) 357-9555. **$249-$310.** Two Stamford Forum. I-95, exit 8, just n under viaduct, then n on Tresser Blvd. Int corridors. **Pets:** Other species. $20 one-time fee/pet. Designated rooms, service with restrictions, crate.

**ⒶⒶⒶ ▼▼ ▼ Super 8 Motel** SH
(203) 324-8887. **$80-$120.** 32 Grenhart Rd. I-95, exit 6, just n. Int corridors. **Pets:** $20 daily fee/room. Designated rooms, service with restrictions, supervision.

**▼▼▼ The Westin Stamford** LH
(203) 967-2222. **$89-$199.** 1 First Stamford Pl. I-95, exit 7 northbound, just s on Greenwich Ave, then just w; exit 6 southbound, just s on West Ave, 0.3 mi w on Baxter Ave, just n on Fairfield Ave, then just e. Int corridors. **Pets:** Accepted.

# STONINGTON

**ⒶⒶⒶ ▼▼ ▼ Another Second Penny Inn** BB 🐾
(860) 535-1710. **$99-$189, 8 day notice.** 870 Pequot Tr. I-95, exit 91, 0.8 mi s on SR 234. Int corridors. **Pets:** Medium, other species. $25 one-time fee/pet. Designated rooms, service with restrictions, supervision.

# STRATFORD

**▼▼▼▼ Homewood Suites by Hilton** SH
(203) 377-3322. **$143-$179.** 6905 Main St. SR 15, exit 53, just n. Int corridors. **Pets:** Accepted.

# TORRINGTON

**ⒶⒶⒶ ▼▼ ▼ Quality Inn & Suites** Ⓜ
(860) 496-8808. **$79-$139.** 395 Winsted Rd. SR 8 northbound, exit 45, just n, then 0.7 mi sw; exit southbound, just sw. Ext/int corridors. **Pets:** Accepted.

## WATERBURY

◈◈◈ House on the Hill Bed & Breakfast 🅱🅱
(203) 757-9901. **$150-$250, 7 day notice.** 92 Woodlawn Terr. I-84, exit 21, 0.6 mi n on Meadow St, then 0.4 mi ne on Pine St. Int corridors. **Pets:** Service with restrictions, supervision.
Ⓐ$Ⓚ S🅳 ⊠ 🗑 🖵

## WATERFORD

🔺 ◈ Oakdell Motel Ⓜ
(860) 442-9446. **$60-$145.** 983 Hartford Tpke. I-95, exit 82, 2 mi n on SR 85. Ext/int corridors. **Pets:** Dogs only. $25 deposit/room. Supervision.
SAVE 🗑 🌊

## WESTPORT

◈◈◈ The Westport Inn Ⓜ 🐾
(203) 259-5236. **$129-$199.** 1595 Post Rd E. I-95, exit 18 northbound, n to US 1, then 1.5 mi e; exit 19 southbound, 1 mi w. Ext/int corridors. **Pets:** Small, other species. Designated rooms, service with restrictions, supervision.
Ⓐ$Ⓚ S🅳 ⊠ 🌀 🗑 🖵 🌊

## WILLINGTON

🔺 ◈◈ Econo Lodge 🆂🅷
(860) 684-1400. **$85-$95.** 327 Ruby Rd. I-84, exit 71, just s. Int corridors. **Pets:** Accepted.
SAVE S🅳 ⊠ 🅼 🌀 🦽 🌊

# DELAWARE

## CLAYMONT

**Holiday Inn Select Wilmington**
(302) 792-2700. **$130-$155.** 630 Naamans Rd. I-95, exit 11, just w on SR 92; I-495, exit 6 (Naamans Rd). Int corridors. **Pets:** Accepted.

## DEWEY BEACH

**Atlantic Oceanside Motel**
(302) 227-8811. **$35-$209, 7 day notice.** 1700 Hwy 1. Jct SR 1 and McKinley St. Ext corridors. **Pets:** Dogs only. $5 daily fee/pet. Service with restrictions.

**Bellbuoy Motel**
(302) 227-6000. **$75-$250, 3 day notice.** 21 Van Dyke St. SR 1, on oceanside block of Van Dyke St. Ext corridors. **Pets:** Dogs only. $15 daily fee/pet. Service with restrictions.

**Best Western Gold Leaf**
(302) 226-1100. **$59-$289, 3 day notice.** 1400 Hwy 1. On SR 1; center. Int corridors. **Pets:** Accepted.

**Sea-Esta Motel I**
(302) 227-7666. **$44-$179.** 2306 Hwy 1. SR 1 at Houston St. Ext corridors. **Pets:** Large, other species. $8 daily fee/pet. Service with restrictions, crate.

**Sea-Esta Motel III**
(302) 227-4343. **$44-$199.** 1409 Hwy 1. Jct SR 1 and Rodney St. Ext corridors. **Pets:** Large, other species. $8 daily fee/pet. Service with restrictions, crate.

## DOVER

**Comfort Suites-Dover**
(302) 736-1204. **$89-$199.** 1654 N DuPont Hwy. SR 1, exit 104, 0.3 mi s on US 13. Int corridors. **Pets:** Small. $20 daily fee/pet. Designated rooms, no service, crate.

**Little Creek Inn**
(302) 730-1300. **$150-$195.** 2623 N Little Creek Rd. SR 1, exit 98, 1 mi e on SR 8; 2.2 mi e of jct US 13. Int corridors. **Pets:** Accepted.

**Sheraton Dover Hotel**
(302) 678-8500. **$129.** 1570 N DuPont Hwy. SR 1, exit 104, 1 mi s on US 13. Int corridors. **Pets:** Accepted.

## FENWICK ISLAND

**Atlantic Coast Inn**
(302) 539-7673. **$49-$169, 7 day notice.** Lighthouse Rd & Coastal Hwy. Jct SR 1 and 54. Ext corridors. **Pets:** Accepted.

## GEORGETOWN

**Comfort Inn & Suites-Georgetown**
(302) 854-9400. **$60-$240, 3 day notice.** 507 N DuPont Hwy. On US 113, 0.5 mi n of jct SR 404. Int corridors. **Pets:** Accepted.

## HARRINGTON

**AmericInn Lodge & Suites of Harrington**
(302) 398-3900. **$90-$110.** 1259 Corn Crib Rd. On US 13, 0.6 mi s of jct SR 14. Int corridors. **Pets:** Dogs only. $20 daily fee/pet. Service with restrictions, crate.

## LEWES

**The Inn at Canal Square**
(302) 644-3377. **$105-$290, 7 day notice.** 122 Market St. On the canal. Int corridors. **Pets:** Accepted.

**Sleep Inn & Suites**
(302) 645-6464. **$59-$249.** 1595 Hwy 1. On SR 1, 1.5 mi s. Int corridors. **Pets:** Other species. $20 daily fee/pet. Designated rooms, service with restrictions, crate.

## LONG NECK

**Sea Esta II**
(302) 945-5900. **$44-$139.** A19 Long Neck Rd. On SR 23, 1.1 mi s of jct SR 24, 5 and 23. Ext corridors. **Pets:** Accepted.

## MILLSBORO

**Atlantic Inn-Millsboro**
(302) 934-6711. **$69-$169.** 210 E DuPont Hwy. US 113, just s of SR 24. Ext corridors. **Pets:** Accepted.

## NEWARK

**Best Western Delaware Inn and Conference Center-Wilmington/Newark**
(302) 738-3400. **$89-$169.** 260 Chapman Rd. I-95, exit 3 southbound; exit 3A northbound, 0.3 mi e on SR 273 E, then just n. Int corridors. **Pets:** Accepted.

**Days Inn Wilmington/Newark**
(302) 368-2400. **$59.** 900 Churchmans Rd. I-95, exit 4B, 0.3 mi n on SR 7, exit 166, then 0.3 mi w on SR 58 (Churchmans Rd). Ext corridors. **Pets:** $10 daily fee/pet. Service with restrictions, crate.

**Hilton Wilmington/Christiana**
(302) 454-1500. **$109-$249.** 100 Continental Dr. I-95, exit 4B, 0.3 mi n on SR 7, exit 166, then 0.4 mi w on SR 58 (Churchmans Rd). Int corridors. **Pets:** Small. Designated rooms, service with restrictions, crate.

▼▼ Homestead Studio Suites
Hotel-Newark/Christiana 🆂🅷
(302) 283-0800. **$84-$104.** 333 Continental Dr. I-95, exit 4B, 0.3 mi n on SR 7, exit 166, then 0.4 mi w on SR 58 (Churchmans Rd). Int corridors. **Pets:** $25 daily fee/pet. Service with restrictions, supervision.

(A$K) 🆂 ✕ 🕭ᴍ 🕭 🕭 🖬 🖵 🌫

▼▼▼ Homewood Suites by Hilton Newark/Wilmington
South 🆂🅷 🐾
(302) 453-9700. **$109-$219.** 640 S College Ave. I-95, exit 1B southbound; exit 1 northbound, 0.8 mi n on SR 896. Int corridors. **Pets:** Small, other species. $15 one-time fee/room. Service with restrictions, crate.

✕ 🕭ᴍ 🕭 🕭 🖬 🖵 🌫

🔺 ▼▼ Howard Johnson Inn &
Suites-Wilmington/Newark 🆂🅷 🐾
(302) 368-8521. **$55-$99.** 1119 S College Ave. I-95, exit 1B southbound; exit 1 northbound, 0.3 mi n on SR 896. Int corridors. **Pets:** $15 one-time fee/pet. Service with restrictions, supervision.

(SAVE) 🆂 ✕ 🕭 🖬 🖵 🌫

🔺 ▼▼ Quality Inn University 🅼
(302) 368-8715. **$60-$125.** 1120 S College Ave. I-95, exit 1B southbound; exit 1 northbound, 0.3 mi n on SR 896. Ext corridors. **Pets:** Accepted.

(SAVE) 🆂 ✕ 🕭 🖬 🖵 🌫

▼▼ Red Roof Inn-Wilmington 🅼
(302) 292-2870. **$61-$76.** 415 Stanton Christiana Rd. I-95, exit 4B, 0.5 mi n on SR 7. Ext corridors. **Pets:** Accepted.

✕ 🕭ᴍ 🕭 🕭 🖬

▼▼▼ Residence Inn by Marriott 🆂🅷
(302) 453-9200. **$99-$169.** 240 Chapman Rd. I-95, exit 3 southbound; exit 3A northbound, 0.3 mi e on SR 273 E, then 0.5 mi s. Ext corridors. **Pets:** Accepted.

✕ 🕭 🕭 🖬 🖵 🌫 ✕

## NEW CASTLE

▼ Dutch Inn 🅼
(302) 328-6246. **$55.** 111 S DuPont Hwy. I-295, exit Dover/Shore Points, 2.5 mi s on US 13, 40 and 301. Ext corridors. **Pets:** Accepted.

(A$K) 🆂 ✕ 🖬

🔺 ▼▼▼ Quality Inn Skyways 🅼 🐾
(302) 328-6666. **$94-$104.** 147 N DuPont Hwy. I-95, exit 5A, 0.8 mi s on SR 141, exit 1B, 0.5 mi s on US 13, 40 and 301; I-295, exit New Castle Airport/US 13 S, 1.8 mi s on US 13, 40 and 301. Ext/int corridors. **Pets:** Large, other species. $10 daily fee/room. Designated rooms, service with restrictions, supervision.

(SAVE) 🆂 ✕ 🕭ᴍ 🕭 🕭 🖬 🖵 🌫

# REHOBOTH BEACH

▼▼ AmericInn Lodge & Suites of Rehoboth Beach 🆂🅷
(302) 226-0700. **$59-$249.** 329Z Airport Rd. Just w of SR 1; 1.3 mi n of jct SR 1A. Int corridors. **Pets:** Large, dogs only. $20 daily fee/pet. Designated rooms, service with restrictions, supervision.

(A$K) ✕ 🕭ᴍ 🕭 🕭 🖬 🖵 🌫

▼▼ The Atlantis Inn 🅼
(302) 227-9446. **$79-$275, 7 day notice.** 154 Rehoboth Ave. At Rehoboth Ave and 2nd St; downtown. Ext corridors. **Pets:** Accepted.

(A$K) 🆂 ✕ 🖬 🖵 🌫

▼▼ The Breakers Hotel & Suites 🅼
(302) 227-6688. **$55-$299, 3 day notice.** 105 2nd St. Just n of Rehoboth Ave. Ext corridors. **Pets:** Accepted.

(A$K) 🆂 ✕ 🖬 🖵 🌫

🔺 ▼▼ Sea-Esta IV 🅼
(302) 227-5882. **$44-$179.** 3101 Hwy 1. 1 mi s. Ext corridors. **Pets:** Large, other species. $8 daily fee/pet. Service with restrictions, crate.

(SAVE) ✕ 🖬 🌫

# WILMINGTON

🔺 ▼▼▼ Best Western Brandywine Valley Inn 🅼
(302) 656-9436. **$99-$165.** 1807 Concord Pike. I-95, exit 8, 1 mi n on US 202. Ext corridors. **Pets:** Other species. $25 one-time fee/room. Designated rooms, supervision.

(SAVE) 🆂 ✕ 🕭 🖬 🖵 🌫

🔺 ▼▼▼ Days Inn Wilmington 🅼
(302) 478-0300. **$69-$99.** 5209 Concord Pike. I-95, exit 8, 4 mi n on US 202; jct SR 92 (Naamans Rd). Ext corridors. **Pets:** Large. $10 daily fee/pet. Service with restrictions, crate.

(SAVE) 🆂 ✕ 🕭 🖬 🖵 🌫

🔺 ▼▼▼ Sheraton Suites Wilmington 🅻🅷
(302) 654-8300. **$99-$225.** 422 Delaware Ave. I-95, exit 7, 0.3 mi e; downtown. Int corridors. **Pets:** Accepted.

(SAVE) 🆂 ✕ 🕭ᴍ 🕭 🖬 🖵 🕇 🌫

▼▼▼ The Spencer Hotel 🅻🅷
(302) 655-0400. **$169-$199.** 700 N King St. King and 7th sts; downtown. Int corridors. **Pets:** Accepted.

(A$K) ✕ 🕭ᴍ 🕭 🕭 🖬 🖵 🕇 🌫

# DISTRICT OF COLUMBIA

## WASHINGTON

**▼▼▼ Doubletree Guest Suites, Washington DC** SH
(202) 785-2000. **$159-$600.** 801 New Hampshire Ave NW. Just sw at Washington Circle. Int corridors. **Pets:** $20 deposit/pet. Crate.
⊠ ⅏ ⚑ ✦ ▤ ▥ ≈

**AAA ▼▼▼▼ The Fairmont Washington, D.C.** LH ❀
(202) 429-2400. **$169-$549.** 2401 M St NW. 24th and M sts NW. Int corridors. **Pets:** Other species. Service with restrictions, supervision.
SAVE ⅏ ⊠ ⅏ ⚑ ✦ ▥ ┤┤ ≈ ⊠

**AAA ▼▼▼▼ Four Seasons Hotel Washington**
(202) 342-0444. **$375-$795.** 2800 Pennsylvania Ave NW. Located in Georgetown. Int corridors. **Pets:** Very small. Service with restrictions, supervision.
SAVE ⅏ ⊠ ⚑ ✦ ▤ ▥ ┤┤ ≈ ⊠

**AAA ▼▼▼ Grand Hyatt Washington at Washington Center** LH
(202) 582-1234. **$149-$369.** 1000 H St NW. Jct 11th and H St NW. Int corridors. **Pets:** Accepted.
SAVE ⊠ ⚑ ✦ ▤ ▥ ┤┤ ≈ ⊠

**▼▼▼ Hamilton Crowne Plaza Hotel Washington DC** LH
(202) 682-0111. **$109-$439.** 1001 14th St NW. 14th and K sts NW. Int corridors. **Pets:** Accepted.
ASK ⅏ ⊠ ⅏ ⚑ ✦ ▤ ▥ ┤┤

**▼▼▼ The Hay-Adams** SH
(202) 638-6600. **$239-$975.** 16th & H Sts NW. 16th and H sts NW, just n of the White House. Int corridors. **Pets:** Accepted.
⊠ ⚑ ✦ ▤ ┤┤

**AAA ▼▼▼ Holiday Inn-Central** SH
(202) 483-2000. **$119-$249.** 1501 Rhode Island Ave NW. Just e of Scott Circle. Int corridors. **Pets:** Accepted.
SAVE ⅏ ⊠ ⚑ ✦ ▤ ▥ ┤┤ ≈

**AAA ▼▼▼ Holiday Inn Downtown** SH
(202) 737-1200. **$169-$249, 7 day notice.** 1155 14th St NW. Massachusetts Ave, at Thomas Circle NW. Int corridors. **Pets:** Accepted.
SAVE ⅏ ⊠ ⚑ ✦ ▤ ▥ ┤┤ ≈

**AAA ▼▼▼ The Hotel George** SH ❀
(202) 347-4200. **$174-$434.** 15 E St NW. On Capitol Hill, just n of Capitol grounds. Int corridors. **Pets:** Other species. Service with restrictions, crate.
SAVE ⅏ ⊠ ⅏ ⚑ ✦ ▤ ▥ ┤┤

**AAA ▼▼▼ Hotel Helix** SH ❀
(202) 462-9001. **$129-$329.** 1430 Rhode Island Ave NW. Just e of Scott Circle. Int corridors. **Pets:** Other species. Designated rooms, service with restrictions, supervision.
SAVE ⅏ ⊠ ⚑ ✦ ▤ ▥ ┤┤

**AAA ▼▼▼ Hotel Madera** SH ❀
(202) 296-7600. **$149-$359.** 1310 New Hampshire Ave NW. Between 20th and N sts NW. Int corridors. **Pets:** Other species. Service with restrictions, crate.
SAVE ⅏ ⊠ ⚑ ✦ ▤ ▥ ┤┤

**AAA ▼▼▼ Hotel Monaco Washington DC** SH ❀
(202) 628-7177. **$170-$386.** 700 F St NW. Between 7th and 8th sts NW. Int corridors. **Pets:** Large, other species. Designated rooms, service with restrictions, crate.
SAVE ⅏ ⊠ ⚑ ✦ ▥ ┤┤

**AAA ▼▼▼ Hotel Rouge** SH ❀
(202) 232-8000. **$129-$339.** 1315 16th St NW. Just n of Scott Circle. Int corridors. **Pets:** Other species. Designated rooms, service with restrictions, supervision.
SAVE ⅏ ⊠ ⚑ ✦ ▤ ▥ ┤┤

**AAA ▼▼▼ Hotel Washington** LH
(202) 638-5900. **$250-$350.** 515 15th St NW. 1 blk e of the White House at Pennsylvania Ave and 15th St NW; 2 blks from Metro Center. Int corridors. **Pets:** Accepted.
SAVE ⅏ ⊠ ⚑ ✦ ▤ ▥ ┤┤

**AAA ▼▼▼ The Jefferson, A Loews Hotel** SH
(202) 347-2200. **$289-$637.** 1200 16th St NW. 16th and M sts NW. Int corridors. **Pets:** Accepted.
SAVE ⅏ ⊠ ⅏ ✦ ▤ ▥ ┤┤

**▼▼▼ L'Enfant Plaza Hotel** LH
(202) 484-1000. **$290-$880.** 480 L SW. I-395, exit L'Enfant Plaza/12th St. Int corridors. **Pets:** Accepted.
ASK ⅏ ⊠ ⚑ ▤ ▥ ┤┤ ≈ ⊠

**AAA ▼▼▼ Lincoln Suites Downtown** SH
(202) 223-4320. **$119-$209.** 1823 L St NW. Between 18th and 19th sts NW. Int corridors. **Pets:** Accepted.
SAVE ⅏ ⊠ ⚑ ✦ ▤ ▥

**AAA ▼▼▼ The Madison** LH
(202) 862-1600. **$229-$559.** 1177 15th St NW. 15th and M sts NW. Int corridors. **Pets:** Accepted.
SAVE ⅏ ⊠ ⚑ ✦ ▤ ┤┤ ⊠

**▼▼▼ ▼▼▼ Mandarin Oriental, Washington D.C.** LH ❀
(202) 554-8588. **$405-$8000.** 1330 Maryland Ave SW. Jct Independence Ave SW, just s on 12th St SW. Int corridors. **Pets:** Medium. $100 one-time fee/room. Service with restrictions.
⊠ ⅏ ⚑ ✦ ┤┤ ≈

**▼▼▼ Marriott Wardman Park Hotel** LH
(202) 328-2000. **$299-$409.** 2660 Woodley Rd NW. Just w of Connecticut Ave; at Woodley Park/Zoo Metro Station. Int corridors. **Pets:** Small. $50 one-time fee/room. Service with restrictions, supervision.
ASK ⊠ ⅏ ⚑ ✦ ▤ ▥ ┤┤ ≈ ⊠

**AAA ▼▼▼ The Melrose Hotel, Washington DC** LH
(202) 955-6400. **$199-$339.** 2430 Pennsylvania Ave NW. Between 24th and 25th sts NW. Int corridors. **Pets:** Accepted.
⊠ ⚑ ▥ ┤┤

**AAA ▼▼▼ Omni Shoreham Hotel** LH
(202) 234-0700. **$229-$429.** 2500 Calvert St NW. Just w of Connecticut Ave. Int corridors. **Pets:** Accepted.
SAVE ⅏ ⊠ ⚑ ✦ ▤ ▥ ┤┤ ≈ ⊠

**AAA ▼▼▼ Park Hyatt Washington, D.C.** LH
(202) 789-1234. **$188-$517.** 1201 24th St NW. 24th and M sts NW. Int corridors. **Pets:** Accepted.
SAVE ⊠ ⅏ ⚑ ✦ ┤┤ ≈ ⊠

**▼▼▼ Red Roof Inn Downtown Washington, D.C.** SH
(202) 289-5959. **$110-$170.** 500 H St NW. At 5th and H sts NW; in Chinatown. Int corridors. **Pets:** Accepted.
⊠ ⚑ ✦ ▤ ▥

**AAA ▼▼▼ Renaissance Mayflower Hotel** LH
(202) 347-3000. **$180-$369.** 1127 Connecticut Ave NW. Just n of K St NW; in business district. Int corridors. **Pets:** Accepted.
SAVE ⊠ ⅏ ⚑ ✦ ┤┤

**▼▼▼▼ Residence Inn by Marriott Capitol** SH
(202) 484-8280. **$229.** 333 E St SW. Between 3rd and 4th sts SW. Int corridors. **Pets:** Medium, other species. $10 daily fee/room, $200 one-time fee/room. Designated rooms, service with restrictions, crate.
ASK SD ☒ ⅏M ⟨⟩ 🛏 ▣ ☄

**▼▼▼ Residence Inn by Marriott-Dupont Circle** SH
(202) 466-6800. **$109-$349.** 2120 P St NW. Between 21st and 22nd sts NW; just w of Dupont Circle. Int corridors. **Pets:** Accepted.
ASK SD ☒ ⅏M ⟨⟩ 🛏 ▣

**▼▼▼ Residence Inn by Marriott-Washington DC-Vermont Ave** SH
(202) 898-1100. **$259.** 1199 Vermont Ave NW. Jct 14th St and Vermont Ave NW, at Thomas Circle. Int corridors. **Pets:** Medium. $8 daily fee/pet, $150 one-time fee/pet. Service with restrictions.
ASK SD ☒ ⅏M ⟨⟩ 🛏 ▣

**▼▼▼▼ The Ritz-Carlton, Georgetown** SH ✿
(202) 912-4100. **$260-$550.** 3100 South St NW. Just s of jct M St and Wisconsin Ave, off Wisconsin Ave, just e. Int corridors. **Pets:** Small. $50 one-time fee/pet. Service with restrictions, supervision.
☒ ⟨⟩ ⟨⟩ 🛏 ▣ ⟨⟩ ✕

**▼▼▼▼ The Ritz-Carlton, Washington, DC** LH
(202) 835-0500. **$259-$645.** 1150 22nd St NW. At 22nd and M sts NW. Int corridors. **Pets:** Accepted.
☒ ⟨⟩ ⟨⟩ ▣ ⟨⟩ ☄ ✕

**▼▼▼ The River Inn** SH
(202) 337-7600. **$119-$269.** 924 25th St NW. Between K and I sts NW. Int corridors. **Pets:** Accepted.
ASK SD ☒ ⟨⟩ 🛏 ▣ ⟨⟩

**AAA ▼▼▼ ▼▼▼ The St. Regis, Washington, D.C.** LH
(202) 638-2626. **$259-$415.** 923 16th St NW. Just n of the White House, 16th and K sts. Int corridors. **Pets:** Accepted.
SAVE SD ☒ ⟨⟩ ⟨⟩

**AAA ▼▼▼ ▼▼▼ Sofitel Lafayette Square Washington DC** SH ✿
(202) 730-8800. **$500-$800.** 806 15th St NW. Jct 15th and H sts NW. Int corridors. **Pets:** Other species. Designated rooms.
SAVE ☒ ⅏M ⟨⟩ ⟨⟩ ⟨⟩

**AAA ▼▼▼ Topaz Hotel** SH
(202) 393-3000. **$139-$339.** 1733 N St NW. Just e of Connecticut Ave. Int corridors. **Pets:** Accepted.
SAVE SD ☒ ⟨⟩ ⟨⟩ ⟨⟩

**▼▼▼ Travelodge Gateway** SH
(202) 832-8600. **$69-$139.** 1917 Bladensburg Rd NE. US 50 (New York Ave) and Alternate Rt 1; just w of entrance to Baltimore-Washington Pkwy. Ext/int corridors. **Pets:** Small. $25 one-time fee/pet. Designated rooms, service with restrictions, crate.
ASK SD ☒ ⟨⟩ ⟨⟩ 🛏 ▣ ⟨⟩ ☄

**AAA ▼▼▼ Washington Suites Georgetown** SH
(202) 333-8060. **$209-$329.** 2500 Pennsylvania Ave NW. Jct 25th St NW and Pennsylvania Ave; 2 blks from Foggy Bottom metro station. Int corridors. **Pets:** Accepted.
SAVE SD ☒ ⅏M ⟨⟩ ⟨⟩ 🛏 ▣

**▼▼▼▼ The Westin Embassy Row** SH
(202) 293-2100. **$349.** 2100 Massachusetts Ave NW. Just w of Dupont Circle; at 21st St. Int corridors. **Pets:** Accepted.
ASK ☒ ⟨⟩ ⟨⟩ 🛏 ▣ ⟨⟩ ✕

**▼▼▼▼ The Westin Grand** LH ✿
(202) 429-0100. **$209-$289.** 2350 M St NW. 24th and M sts NW. Int corridors. **Pets:** Medium, dogs only. Service with restrictions, supervision.
ASK SD ☒ ⟨⟩ ⟨⟩ ▣ ⟨⟩ ☄

**▼▼▼▼ The Willard InterContinental** LH ✿
(202) 628-9100. **$269-$650.** 1401 Pennsylvania Ave NW. Just e of the White House. Int corridors. **Pets:** Medium. Service with restrictions, crate.
ASK SD ☒ ⅏M ⟨⟩ ⟨⟩ ▣ ⟨⟩ ✕

# FLORIDA

## CITY INDEX

## ALACHUA

### (AAA) ▽▽▽ Comfort Inn/FL-339 [SH] ✿

(386) 462-2414. **$85, 7 day notice.** 15920 NW Hwy 441. I-75, exit 399, just e. Ext corridors. **Pets:** Dogs only. $10 daily fee/pet. Designated rooms, service with restrictions, supervision.

[SAVE] [S⊘] [✕] [🔒] [💻] [⇔]

## APALACHICOLA

### (AAA) ▽▽▽ Coombs House Inn [BB]

(850) 653-9199. **$89-$169, 5 day notice.** 80 6th St. Corner of US 98 and 6th St; center. Int corridors. **Pets:** Accepted.

[SAVE] [S⊘] [✕] [🔒] [💻]

### (AAA) ▽▽▽ Gibson Inn [CI] ✿

(850) 653-2191. **$85-$185, 14 day notice.** Market St & Ave C. On US 98 at west end of bridge. Int corridors. **Pets:** $15 daily fee/pet. Designated rooms, service with restrictions, supervision.

[SAVE] [S⊘] [✕]

## ARCADIA

### (AAA) ▽▽◇ Best Western Arcadia Inn [M]

(863) 494-4884. **$69-$149.** 504 S Brevard Ave. 0.6 mi s of SR 70 on US 17. Ext corridors. **Pets:** Accepted.

[SAVE] [S⊘] [✕] [🔒] [💻] [⇔]

## AVON PARK

### (AAA) ▽▽◇ Econo Lodge [M]

(863) 453-2000. **$60-$90.** 2511 US Hwy 27 S. On US 27; 2.5 mi s of jct SR 17 and 64. Ext corridors. **Pets:** Other species. $10 daily fee/room. Service with restrictions.

[SAVE] [S⊘] [✕] [🌀] [💻] [⇔]

## BOCA RATON

### (AAA) ▽▽▽▽ Hilton Suites Boca Raton [SH]

(561) 483-3600. **$169-$289.** 7920 Glades Rd. Florida Tpke, exit 75 (SR 808/Glades Rd); in Arvida Parkway Center. Int corridors. **Pets:** Accepted.

[SAVE] [S⊘] [✕] [🌀] [♿] [🔒] [💻] [⇔] [✕]

### ▽▽ Homestead Studio Suites Hotel-Boca Raton/Commerce [M]

(561) 994-2599. **$64-$114.** 501 NW 77th St. I-95, exit 50, just s on Congress Ave to NW 6th Ave. Ext corridors. **Pets:** $25 daily fee/pet. Service with restrictions, supervision.

[A$K] [S⊘] [✕] [♿] [🔒] [💻]

### (AAA) ▽▽▽ Residence Inn-By Marriott-Boca Raton [SH] ✿

(561) 994-3222. **$99-$229.** 525 NW 77th St. I-95, exit 50, just w of Congress Ave. Ext corridors. **Pets:** $75 one-time fee/room. Service with restrictions, supervision.

[SAVE] [S⊘] [✕] [🌀] [♿] [🔒] [💻] [⇔] [✕]

### ▽▽▽ TownePlace Suites by Marriott [SH] ✿

(561) 994-7232. **$99-$239, 3 day notice.** 5110 NW 8th Ave. I-95, exit 48B (Yamato Rd), just w; in Arvida Corporate Park. Int corridors. **Pets:** Medium. $75 one-time fee/room. Service with restrictions, crate.

[A$K] [S⊘] [✕] [♿M] [🌀] [♿] [🔒] [💻] [⇔]

## BONITA SPRINGS

### ▽▽▽ AmericInn Hotel & Suites [SH]

(239) 495-9255. **$79-$200.** 28600 Trails Edge Blvd. I-75, exit 116, 0.7 mi s of Bonita Beach Rd on US 41. Int corridors. **Pets:** Accepted.

[A$K] [S⊘] [✕] [♿M] [🌀] [♿] [🔒] [💻] [⇔]

### ▽▽▽ Baymont Inn-Bonita Springs [SH]

(239) 949-9400. **$60-$130.** 27991 Oakland Dr. I-75, exit 116, just w. Int corridors. **Pets:** Accepted.

[A$K] [S⊘] [✕] [🔒] [💻] [⇔]

**♦♦♦ ▼▼▼ Comfort Inn Hotel SH**
(239) 992-5001. **$49-$159.** 9800 Bonita Beach Rd. I-75, exit 116, 2.5 mi w on CR 865. Int corridors. **Pets:** Accepted.
SAVE S⭕ ✕ ⌂ 🔲 🔲 ⚬

**▼▼▼▼ Staybridge Suites by Holiday Inn SH**
(239) 949-5913. **$149-$249.** 8900 Brighton Ln. I-75, exit 116, 3.5 mi w on CR 865, 1.4 mi n on US 41 (Tamiami Tr), then e on Highland Woods Blvd. Int corridors. **Pets:** Accepted.
ASK S⭕ ✕ ⚬M ⌂ ⚬ 🔲 🔲 ⚬

## BOYNTON BEACH

**▼▼▼▼ Holiday Inn-Boynton Beach SH**
(561) 737-4600. **$99-$149.** 1601 N Congress Ave. I-95, exit 59 (Gateway Blvd), 1.2 mi w to SR 807 (Congress Ave); 0.3 mi s of jct SR 806 (Gateway Blvd); adjacent to Catalina Shopping Center. Ext/int corridors. **Pets:** Small. $50 one-time fee/room. Designated rooms, service with restrictions, supervision.
ASK S⭕ ✕ ⌂ ⚬ 🔲 🔲 ⚬ ⚬

## BRADENTON

**▼▼ ▼ Econo Lodge Airport M**
(941) 758-7199. **$59-$99.** 6727 14th St W. On US 41, 2 mi s of jct SR 70. Ext corridors. **Pets:** Dogs only. $10 daily fee/pet. Designated rooms, service with restrictions, supervision.
ASK S⭕ ✕ ⚬ 🔲 ⚬

**♦♦♦ ▼▼▼ Howard Johnson Express Inn M**
(941) 756-8399. **$60-$124.** 6511 14th St W. On US 41, 1.5 mi s of jct SR 70. Ext corridors. **Pets:** Small, dogs only. $10 daily fee/pet. Service with restrictions, supervision.
SAVE S⭕ ✕ ⚬ 🔲 ⚬

**▼▼ ▼ Motel 6 #678 M**
(941) 747-6005. **$45-$70.** 660 67th St Cir E. I-75, exit 220 southbound; exit 220B northbound, just w on SR 64. Ext corridors. **Pets:** Accepted.
S⭕ ✕ ⚬

## BRADENTON BEACH

**♦♦♦ ▼▼▼▼ Tortuga Inn Beach Resort M**
(941) 778-6611. **$115-$270, 14 day notice.** 1325 Gulf Dr N. On SR 789, 0.3 mi n of jct SR 684. Ext corridors. **Pets:** Accepted.
SAVE ✕ ⚬ 🔲 ⚬

**♦♦♦ ▼▼▼▼ Tradewinds Resort CA**
(941) 779-0010. **$145-$325, 14 day notice.** 1603 Gulf Dr N. On SR 789, 0.5 mi n of jct SR 684. Ext corridors. **Pets:** Small. $25 one-time fee/pet. Designated rooms, service with restrictions, supervision.
SAVE ✕ ⚬ 🔲 ⚬

## BROOKSVILLE

**▼▼ ▼ Best Western Brooksville I-75 M**
(352) 796-9481. **$69-$99.** 30307 Cortez Blvd. I-75, exit 301, just w on US 98/SR 50. Ext corridors. **Pets:** Other species. $25 one-time fee/room. Designated rooms, service with restrictions, supervision.
ASK S⭕ ✕ ⚬M ⌂ 🔲 ⚬

**♦♦♦ ▼▼▼ Days Inn Heritage Inn M**
(352) 796-9486. **$64-$109.** 6320 Windmere Rd. I-75, exit 301, just e on US 98/SR 50. Ext corridors. **Pets:** Other species. $15 one-time fee/pet. Service with restrictions.
SAVE S⭕ ✕ ⚬M ⌂ ⚬ 🔲 🔲 ⚬

## BUSHNELL

**♦♦♦ ▼▼▼ Best Western Guest House Inn M**
(352) 793-5010. **$49-$99.** 2224 W Hwy 48. I-75, exit 314, just e. Ext corridors. **Pets:** Accepted.
SAVE S⭕ ✕ ⚬ 🔲 ⚬

## CAPE CORAL

**♦♦♦ ▼▼▼ Dockside Inn M**
(239) 542-0061. **$85-$155, 7 day notice.** 3817 Del Prado Blvd. 1.2 mi n of jct Cape Coral Pkwy. Ext corridors. **Pets:** Other species. $20 one-time fee/room. Service with restrictions, crate.
SAVE S⭕ ✕ ⚬ ⚬ ✕

**▼▼▼▼ Quality Hotel SH**
(239) 542-2121. **$80-$135.** 1538 Cape Coral Pkwy. Jct Del Prado Blvd. Int corridors. **Pets:** Accepted.
ASK S⭕ ✕ ⚬ ⌂ ⚬ 🔲 ⚬

## CARRABELLE

**▼▼ ▼ The Moorings At Carrabelle SH**
(850) 697-2800. **$100-$175.** 1000 US 98. On US 98, just e of bridge. Ext corridors. **Pets:** Accepted.
ASK S⭕ ⚬ 🔲 ⚬ ✕

## CEDAR KEY

**♦♦♦ ▼▼ ▼ Park Place Motel & Condominiums M**
(352) 543-5737. **$65-$100.** 211 2nd St. At A St. Ext corridors. **Pets:** Small, other species. $7 daily fee/pet. Designated rooms, service with restrictions, supervision.
SAVE ✕ ⚬ 🔲

**♦♦♦ ▼▼▼▼ Seahorse Landing Condominiums CO**
(352) 543-5860. **$150-$165.** 4050 G St. Just w on 6th St. Ext corridors. **Pets:** Very small, other species. $20 daily fee/room. Designated rooms, no service.
SAVE ✕ ⚬ 🔲 ⚬ ✕

## CHARLOTTE HARBOR

**▼ Banana Bay Waterfront Motel M**
(941) 743-4441. **$450-$850 (weekly).** 23285 Bayshore Rd. Jct US 41. Ext corridors. **Pets:** Accepted.
✕ ⚬ 🔲 ✕

## CHIEFLAND

**▼▼▼▼ Holiday Inn Express SH**
(352) 493-9400. **$65-$91.** 809 NW 21st Ave. US 19/98, 1.5 mi n of jct US 129. Ext corridors. **Pets:** Accepted.
ASK S⭕ ✕ ⚬M ⌂ ⚬ ⚬ ⚬

## CHIPLEY

**▼▼ ▼ Super 8 Motel M**
(850) 638-8530. **$59-$74.** 1150 Motel Dr. I-10, exit 120, just n. Ext corridors. **Pets:** Other species. $5 daily fee/pet. Service with restrictions.
ASK S⭕ ✕ ⚬

## COCOA

**▼▼ ▼ Best Western Cocoa Inn SH**
(321) 632-1065. **$65-$139.** 4225 W King St. I-95, exit 201 (SR 520), 0.3 mi e. Ext corridors. **Pets:** Medium. $10 one-time fee/pet. Service with restrictions, crate.
ASK S⭕ ✕ ⚬ ⚬ 🔲 🔲 ⚬

**♦♦♦ ▼▼▼ Econo Lodge-Space Center SH**
(321) 632-4561. **$55-$175.** 3220 N Cocoa Blvd. US 1, just n of jct SR 528. Ext corridors. **Pets:** Accepted.
SAVE S⭕ ✕ ⚬ ⚬ 🔲 🔲 ⚬

## COCOA BEACH

**♦♦♦ ▼▼▼▼ Holiday Inn Cocoa Beach Oceanfront Resort SH**
(321) 783-2271. **$120-$350.** 1300 N Atlantic Ave. SR A1A, 1.8 mi s of jct SR 520. Ext corridors. **Pets:** Accepted.
SAVE S⭕ ✕ ⚬M ⚬ ⚬ 🔲 🔲 ⚬ ⚬ ✕

**△△△ ▽▽▽ La Quinta Inn Cocoa Beach SH**
(321) 783-2252. **$59-$279.** 1275 N Atlantic Ave. On SR A1A, 1.7 mi s.
Ext corridors. **Pets:** Other species. Service with restrictions, supervision.
[SAVE] [S♦] [✕] [🐾] [🔔] [▣] [❒] [⊪] [≈]

**▽▽▽▽ Quality Suites Cocoa Beach SH**
(321) 783-6868. **$99-$299.** 3655 N Atlantic Ave. SR A1A, 0.3 mi s of jct
SR 520. Int corridors. **Pets:** Accepted.
[ASK] [S♦] [✕] [♿M] [🐾] [🔔] [▣]

**▽▽▽ Surf Studio Beach Resort M**
(321) 783-7100. **$85-$195, 7 day notice.** 1801 S Atlantic Ave. SR A1A
northbound, 5 mi s of jct SR 520 at Francis St; 1.3 mi n of Partrick
AFB. Ext corridors. **Pets:** Medium. $20 daily fee/pet. Service with restric-
tions, supervision.
[🐾] [🔔] [❒] [≈]

## CRESCENT BEACH

**△△△ ▽▽▽▽ Beacher's Lodge SH**
(904) 471-8849. **$79-$225.** 6970 A1A S. Just s of jct SR 206. Ext
corridors. **Pets:** Small, other species. $50 one-time fee/pet. Designated
rooms, service with restrictions, supervision.
[SAVE] [S♦] [✕] [🔔] [❒] [≈]

**△△△ ▽▽▽▽ Channel Marker 71 Barrier Island Inn and
Restaurant SH 🐾**
(904) 461-4288. **$118-$298, 14 day notice.** 7601 A1A S. 1.4 mi s of
SR 206. Int corridors. **Pets:** Medium, dogs only. $75 deposit/pet. No
service, supervision.
[SAVE] [S♦] [✕] [🔔] [⊪] [✕]

## CRESCENT CITY

**▽▽▽ Lake View Motel M**
(386) 698-1090. **$55-$85.** 1004 N Summit St. 1 mi n on US 17. Ext
corridors. **Pets:** Medium. $5 daily fee/pet. Designated rooms, service with
restrictions, supervision.
[ASK] [✕] [🔔] [❒] [≈]

## CRESTVIEW

**△△△ ▽▽▽ Holiday Inn SH**
(850) 682-6111. **$90.** 4050 S Ferdon Blvd. I-10, exit 56, 0.5 mi s. Ext
corridors. **Pets:** Small. $25 one-time fee/room. Service with restrictions.
[SAVE] [S♦] [✕] [🐾] [🔔] [❒] [⊪] [≈]

**▽▽▽▽ Jameson Inn SH**
(850) 683-1778. **$54-$104.** 151 Cracker Barrel Dr. I-10, exit 56, just s.
Int corridors. **Pets:** Very small, other species. $10 daily fee/room. Service
with restrictions, supervision.
[ASK] [✕] [🔔] [❒] [≈]

**△△△ ▽▽▽ Super 8 Motel M**
(850) 682-9649. **$49-$69.** 3925 S Ferdon Blvd. I-10, exit 56, 0.3 mi s.
Ext corridors. **Pets:** Other species. $5 daily fee/pet. Designated rooms,
service with restrictions.
[SAVE] [S♦] [✕] [🔔]

## CRYSTAL RIVER

**△△△ ▽▽▽▽ Best Western Crystal River Resort SH**
(352) 795-3171. **$92-$140.** 614 NW Hwy 19. On US 19/98, 0.8 mi n of
jct SR 44. Ext corridors. **Pets:** Medium, other species. $3 daily fee/pet.
Service with restrictions, supervision.
[SAVE] [S♦] [✕] [🐾] [🐾] [🔔] [❒] [≈] [✕]

**△△△ ▽▽▽ Days Inn SH**
(352) 795-2111. **$60-$130.** 2380 NW US 19. US 19, 2.2 mi n of jct SR
44. Ext corridors. **Pets:** $10 daily fee/pet. Designated rooms, service with
restrictions, supervision.
[SAVE] [S♦] [✕] [🐾] [🔔] [⊪]

## DAYTONA BEACH

**△△△ ▽▽▽ Bermuda House SH**
(386) 672-1440. **$59-$350, 7 day notice.** 2560 N Atlantic Ave. On SR
A1A, 4 mi n of jct US 92. Ext/int corridors. **Pets:** Accepted.
[SAVE] [S♦] [✕] [🔔] [❒] [≈]

**△△△ ▽▽▽▽ Best Western LaPlaya Resort SH**
(386) 672-0990. **$69-$479, 7 day notice.** 2500 N Atlantic Ave. On SR
A1A, 3.3 mi n of jct US 92. Ext corridors. **Pets:** Accepted.
[SAVE] [S♦] [✕] [🐾] [🔔] [❒] [⊪] [≈] [✕]

**△△△ ▽▽▽ Days Inn Speedway M**
(386) 255-0541. **$59-$249, 30 day notice.** 2900 W International
Speedway Blvd. I-95, exit 261B southbound; exit 261 northbound, just
w on US 92. Ext corridors. **Pets:** Accepted.
[SAVE] [S♦] [✕] [🔔] [⊪] [≈]

**△△△ ▽▽▽▽ La Quinta Inn & Suites SH**
(386) 944-0060. **$69-$299, 3 day notice.** 816 N Atlantic Ave. On SR
A1A, 1.4 mi n of jct US 92. Ext corridors. **Pets:** Accepted.
[SAVE] [S♦] [✕] [🐾] [🔔] [❒] [≈]

**△△△ ▽▽▽ La Quinta Inn Daytona Beach M**
(386) 255-7412. **$75-$95.** 2725 International Speedway Blvd. I-95, exit
261 northbound; exit 261B southbound, just e. Int corridors.
**Pets:** Medium. Service with restrictions.
[SAVE] [✕] [♿M] [🐾] [🐾] [❒] [≈]

**△△△ ▽▽▽▽ Plaza Ocean Club SH**
(386) 239-9800. **$89-$429.** 640 N Atlantic Ave. On SR A1A, 1 mi n of
jct SR 90. Int corridors. **Pets:** Medium, dogs only. $15 daily fee/pet.
Designated rooms, service with restrictions.
[SAVE] [S♦] [✕] [♿M] [🐾] [🐾] [🔔] [❒] [⊪] [≈]

**△△△ ▽▽▽ Ramada Inn Speedway SH 🐾**
(386) 255-2422. **$89-$399, 7 day notice.** 1798 W International Speedway Blvd. I-95, exit 261A southbound; exit 261 northbound, 2 mi e on
US 92. Ext corridors. **Pets:** Medium, other species. $25 one-time fee/
room. Designated rooms, service with restrictions.
[ASK] [S♦] [✕] [🐾] [🔔] [❒] [⊪] [≈]

**▽▽ Scottish Inns M**
(386) 258-5742. **$49-$245, 30 day notice.** 1515 S Ridgewood Ave.
I-95, exit 260A, 2.5 mi e on SR 400, then just n on US 1. Ext
corridors. **Pets:** Accepted.
[ASK] [S♦] [✕] [🔔] [≈]

## DAYTONA BEACH SHORES

**△△△ ▽▽▽ Atlantic Ocean Palm Inn M**
(386) 761-8450. **$59-$189, 30 day notice.** 3247 S Atlantic Ave. On SR
A1A, 5 mi s of jct US 92. Ext corridors. **Pets:** Small, dogs only. $15 daily
fee/pet. Designated rooms, service with restrictions, supervision.
[SAVE] [S♦] [✕] [🔔] [≈]

## DE FUNIAK SPRINGS

**▽▽▽ Best Western Crossroads Inn SH**
(850) 892-5111. **$69-$99.** 2343 Freeport Rd. I-10, exit 85, just s. Ext/int
corridors. **Pets:** Small. $10 one-time fee/room. Designated rooms, service
with restrictions, supervision.
[ASK] [S♦] [✕] [🔔] [❒] [⊪] [≈]

**▽▽▽ Days Inn SH**
(850) 892-6115. **$55-$90, 3 day notice.** 472 Hugh Adams Rd. I-10, exit
85, just n. Ext corridors. **Pets:** Accepted.
[ASK] [S♦] [✕] [🔔] [≈]

# DELAND

**AAA** ▼▼▼▼ **Holiday Inn** SH
(386) 738-5200. **$59-$229.** 350 E International Speedway Blvd. 0.3 mi ne on US 92 from jct US 17. Int corridors. **Pets:** Small, dogs only. $25 one-time fee/pet. Designated rooms, service with restrictions, crate.

SAVE S⌀ ✕ ⌐ ⌐ ■ ⌐ ♚ ≈

**AAA** ▼▼ ▼▼ **University Inn** M
(386) 734-5711. **$69-$179.** 644 N Woodland Blvd. US 17, 0.9 mi n of jct SR 44. Ext corridors. **Pets:** Medium. $10 daily fee/pet. Service with restrictions, supervision.

SAVE S⌀ ✕ ⌐ ■ ⌐ ≈

# DELRAY BEACH

**AAA** ▼▼▼▼ **The Colony Hotel & Cabana Club** SH
(561) 276-4123. **$125-$310, 3 day notice.** 525 E Atlantic Ave. On SR 806 (Atlantic Ave) at US 1 northbound; center. Int corridors. **Pets:** Accepted.

SAVE ✕ ⌐ ⌐ ≈

▼▼▼▼ **Residence Inn Delray Beach** SH
(561) 276-7441. **$199-$659.** 1111 E Atlantic Ave. I-95, exit 52, 1.7 mi e. Int corridors. **Pets:** Accepted.

ASK S⌀ ✕ ⌐M ⌐ ⌐ ■ ⌐ ≈

# DELTONA

**AAA** ▼▼▼▼ **Best Western Deltona Inn** SH
(386) 860-3000. **$79-$249.** 481 Deltona Blvd. I-4, exit 108, just ne. Ext corridors. **Pets:** Small, other species. $10 daily fee/pet. Designated rooms, service with restrictions, crate.

SAVE S⌀ ✕ ⌐ ■ ⌐ ♚ ≈

# ELKTON

**AAA** ▼▼ ▼▼ **Comfort Inn St. Augustine** SH
(904) 829-3435. **$69-$109.** 2625 SR 207. I-95, exit 311, just w. Ext corridors. **Pets:** $15 daily fee/room. Service with restrictions, crate.

SAVE S⌀ ✕ ■ ⌐ ≈

# ELLENTON

▼▼ ▼▼ **GuestHouse International Inn** M
(941) 729-0600. **$60-$110.** 4915 17th St E. I-75, exit 224, 0.3 mi s on US 301, just w on 51st Ave E, then just n. Ext corridors. **Pets:** Small. Designated rooms, no service, crate.

ASK S⌀ ✕ ⌐M ⌐ ⌐ ■ ⌐ ≈

▼▼ ▼▼ **Sleep Inn & Suites Riverfront** M
(941) 721-4933. **$69-$199.** 5605 18th St E. I-75, exit 224, just n on US 301, just e on 19th St E, then 0.3 mi sw. Int corridors. **Pets:** Accepted.

✕ ⌐M ⌐ ■ ⌐ ≈

# FLAGLER BEACH

▼▼ ▼▼ **Beach Front Motel** M
(386) 439-0089. **$54-$69, 3 day notice.** 1544 S A1A. On SR A1A, 1 mi s of SR 100. Ext corridors. **Pets:** Medium. $15 one-time fee/room. Service with restrictions, supervision.

ASK S⌀ ✕ ■ ≈

**AAA** ▼▼ ▼▼ **Topaz Motel** SH
(386) 439-3301. **$65-$180.** 1224 S Oceanshore Blvd. On SR A1A, 0.5 mi s of SR 100. Ext/int corridors. **Pets:** Accepted.

SAVE ✕ ⌐ ■ ⌐ ♚ ≈

# FLORAL CITY

▼▼ ▼▼ **Moonrise Resort** CA
(352) 726-2553. **$70-$110 (no credit cards), 21 day notice.** 8801 E Moonrise Ln, Lot 18. Just e on CR 48, then 1.5 mi n on Old Floral City Rd. Ext corridors. **Pets:** $20 daily fee/pet. No service.

■ ⌐ ✕ ⌐

---

# THE FLORIDA KEYS AREA

## ISLAMORADA

**AAA** ▼▼ ▼▼ **Sands of Islamorada** M
(305) 664-2791. **$99-$285, 3 day notice.** 80051 Overseas Hwy. US 1 at MM 80. Ext corridors. **Pets:** Other species. $20 daily fee/pet. Service with restrictions.

SAVE ⌐ ■ ⌐ ≈ ✕

## KEY LARGO

**AAA** ▼▼ ▼▼ **Howard Johnson Resort Key Largo** SH
(305) 451-1400. **$99-$199.** 102400 Overseas Hwy. US 1 at MM 102 (Bayside). Int corridors. **Pets:** Accepted.

SAVE S⌀ ✕ ⌐M ⌐ ⌐ ■ ⌐ ♚ ≈ ✕

▼▼▼▼ **Marina Del Mar Resort & Marina** SH
(305) 451-4107. **$99-$199, 3 day notice.** 527 Caribbean Dr. US 1 at MM 100. Ext corridors. **Pets:** Accepted.

ASK S⌀ ✕ ⌐ ■ ⌐ ♚ ≈ ✕

**AAA** ▼▼▼▼ **Sheraton Beach Resort, Key Largo** LH
(305) 852-5553. **$109-$409.** 97000 S Overseas Hwy. US 1 at MM 97. Ext corridors. **Pets:** Accepted.

SAVE S⌀ ✕ ⌐ ⌐ ■ ⌐ ♚ ✕

## KEY WEST

▼▼▼▼ **Ambrosia Too At Fleming St** BB
(305) 296-9838. **$125-$445, 30 day notice.** 622 Fleming St. Just n of Simonton St; in Old Town. Ext corridors. **Pets:** Accepted.

✕ ■ ⌐ ≈

▼▼▼▼ **Center Court Historic Inn & Cottages** BB ❧
(305) 296-9292. **$98-$708, 30 day notice.** 915 Center St. 0.5 mi n of jct US 1; between Duval and Simonton sts; in Old Town. Ext/int corridors. **Pets:** Other species. $10 daily fee/pet. Service with restrictions.

✕ ■ ≈ ✕

**AAA** ▼▼▼▼ **Chelsea House** BB
(305) 296-2211. **$89-$275, 10 day notice.** 707 Truman Ave. Corner of Elizabeth St and Truman Ave. Ext/int corridors. **Pets:** Accepted.

SAVE ✕ ■ ⌐ ≈

**AAA** ▼▼ ▼▼ **Courtney's Place Historic Cottages & Inn** CA ❧
(305) 294-3480. **$79-$259, 21 day notice.** 720 Whitmarsh Ln. Just e of jct Petronia and Simonton sts; in Old Town. Ext corridors. **Pets:** Other species. $25 one-time fee/room. Designated rooms.

SAVE ⌐ ■ ⌐ ≈

▼▼▼▼ **The Cuban Club Suites** M
(305) 294-5269. **$129-$599, 14 day notice.** 1108 Duval St. Corner of Duval and Amelia sts; in Old Town. Int corridors. **Pets:** Accepted.

ASK S⌀ ✕ ■ ≈

**(AAA) ▼▼▼ Curry Mansion Inn** BB
(305) 294-5349. **$175-$325, 14 day notice.** 511 Caroline St. Just n of jct Duval St; in Old Town. Ext/int corridors. **Pets:** Small, other species. Service with restrictions, supervision.
(SAVE) ☒ 🛏 ➴

**(AAA) ▼▼▼ Frances Street Bottle Inn** BB
(305) 294-8530. **$89-$209, 14 day notice.** 535 Frances St. US 1/Roosevelt Blvd, w on White St, then just s on Southard St; corner of Frances and Southard sts; in Old Town. Int corridors. **Pets:** Other species. $35 one-time fee/pet. Designated rooms.
(SAVE) ☒ 🛏 ☑

**(AAA) ▼▼▼ The Palms Hotel** BB
(305) 294-3146. **$120-$205, 7 day notice.** 820 White St. Just w of Truman Ave. Ext corridors. **Pets:** Accepted.
(SAVE) ➴

**(AAA) ▼▼▼▼ Pier House Resort & Caribbean Spa** LH
(305) 296-4600. **$200-$2000, 7 day notice.** One Duval St. At the foot of Duval St; in Old Town. Ext/int corridors. **Pets:** Accepted.
(SAVE) ☒ 🗂 🖙 🛏 🖵 🍴 ➴ 🗶

**(AAA) ▼▼▼▼ Sheraton Suites-Key West** LH ❀
(305) 292-9800. **$149-$425, 3 day notice.** 2001 S Roosevelt Blvd. Jct US 1 and SR A1A, 3 mi s. Ext/int corridors. **Pets:** Medium, dogs only. Service with restrictions, supervision.
(SAVE) (S̄D) ☒ (&M) 🗂 🖙 🖵 🍴 ➴ 🗶

## MARATHON

**▼▼ Ramada Marathon Oceanview Florida Keys** SH
(305) 743-8550. **$69-$399.** 13351 Overseas Hwy. US 1 at MM 54. Int corridors. **Pets:** Accepted.
(ASK) (S̄D) ☒ 🛏 🖵 ➴

---

# FORT LAUDERDALE METROPOLITAN AREA

## CORAL SPRINGS

**(AAA) ▼▼▼▼ La Quinta Inn Ft. Lauderdale (Coral Springs)** SH
(954) 753-9000. **$89-$135.** 3701 University Dr. SR 817, just n of jct SR 834 (Sample Rd). Int corridors. **Pets:** Medium. Service with restrictions.
(SAVE) ☒ (&M) 🗂 🖙 🛏 🖵 ➴

**▼▼ Studio 6 #6027** M
(954) 796-0011. **$58-$79.** 5645 University Dr. SR 869 (Sawgrass Expwy), exit 12 (University Dr), just s. Ext corridors. **Pets:** Accepted.
(S̄D) ☒ 🖙 🛏 🖵

**(AAA) ▼▼▼ Wellesley Inn (Coral Springs)** SH
(954) 344-2200. **$99-$119.** 3100 N University Dr. SR 817, just s of jct Sample Rd (SR 834). Int corridors. **Pets:** Small, dogs only. $10 daily fee/pet. Designated rooms, service with restrictions, supervision.
(SAVE) (S̄D) ☒ 🗂 🛏 🖵 ➴

## DANIA BEACH

**▼▼ Motel 6–Dania Beach #376** M
(954) 921-5505. **$45-$70.** 825 E Dania Beach Blvd. I-95, exit 22, 1.1 mi e on Stirling Rd, just n on US 1 (Federal Hwy), then 0.8 mi e. Ext corridors. **Pets:** Accepted.
(S̄D) ☒ 🖙 ➴

**(AAA) ▼▼▼▼ Sheraton Fort Lauderdale Airport Hotel** LH
(954) 920-3500. **$110-$309.** 1825 Griffin Rd. I-95, exit 23. Int corridors. **Pets:** Accepted.
(SAVE) (S̄D) ☒ (&M) 🗂 🖙 🛏 🖵 🍴 ➴ 🗶

## DAVIE

**▼▼ Homestead Studio Suites Hotel-Plantation/Davie** M
(954) 476-1211. **$64-$104.** 7550 SR 84 E. I-595, exit University Dr/SR 817, 0.3 mi. Ext corridors. **Pets:** $25 daily fee/pet. Service with restrictions, supervision.
(ASK) (S̄D) ☒ (&M) 🗂 🖙 🛏 🖵

## DEERFIELD BEACH

**(AAA) ▼▼▼ Comfort Suites** SH
(954) 570-8887. **$79-$169.** 1040 E Newport Center Dr. I-95, exit 41, jct SW 10th St to SW 12th Ave, then s; in Newport Center Complex. Ext corridors. **Pets:** Accepted.
(SAVE) (S̄D) ☒ 🗂 🖙 🛏 🖵 ➴

**▼▼▼ Embassy Suites-Deerfield Beach Resort** LH
(954) 426-0478. **$119-$450.** 950 Ocean Dr (SR A1A). SR A1A, 0.5 mi s of jct SR 810 (Hillsboro Blvd). Int corridors. **Pets:** Accepted.
(ASK) ☒ 🗂 🖙 🛏 🖵 🍴 ➴ 🗶

**▼▼ Holiday Park Hotels & Suites** M
(954) 427-2200. **$59-$110.** 1250 W Hillsboro Blvd. I-95, exit 42B, just w on SR 810 (Hillsboro Blvd), then just s on 12th Ave SW. Ext corridors. **Pets:** Accepted.
(ASK) (S̄D) ☒ 🗂 🖙 🛏 🖵 🍴 ➴

**(AAA) ▼▼▼ La Quinta Inn Ft. Lauderdale (Deerfield Beach)** M
(954) 421-1004. **$72-$129.** 351 W Hillsboro Blvd. I-95, exit 42A, 0.3 mi e on SR 810. Ext corridors. **Pets:** Medium. Service with restrictions.
(SAVE) ☒ (&M) 🗂 🛏 🖵 ➴

**(AAA) ▼▼▼ Travelers Inn** M
(954) 421-5000. **$59-$169.** 1401 S Federal Hwy. On US 1, 1.3 mi s of jct SR 810 (Hillsboro Blvd). Ext/int corridors. **Pets:** Accepted.
(SAVE) (S̄D) ☒ 🛏 🖵 🍴 ➴

**▼▼▼ Wellesley Inn (Deerfield Beach)** SH
(954) 428-0661. **$65-$159.** 100 12th Ave SW. I-95, exit 42B, just w on SR 810 (Hillsboro Blvd), then just s. Int corridors. **Pets:** Accepted.
(ASK) (S̄D) ☒ 🗂 🖙 🛏 🖵

## FORT LAUDERDALE

**(AAA) ▼▼▼▼ AmeriSuites (Fort Lauderdale/17th Street)** SH
(954) 763-7670. **$119-$169.** 1851 SE Tenth Ave. SR A1A/17th St Cswy, just s. Int corridors. **Pets:** Medium, other species. $10 daily fee/pet. Designated rooms, service with restrictions, supervision.
(SAVE) ☒ (&M) 🗂 🖙 🛏 🖵 ➴

**▼▼ Birch Patio Motel** M
(954) 563-9540. **$50-$140, 28 day notice.** 617 N Birch Rd. 0.4 mi s on SR A1A from jct SR 838 (Sunrise Blvd), w on Aurumar St. Ext corridors. **Pets:** Accepted.
(ASK) ☒ 🛏 🖵 ➴

**▼▼▼ Embassy Suites-Fort Lauderdale** LH
(954) 527-2700. **$139-$299.** 1100 SE 17th St Cswy. On SR A1A, just e of jct US 1 (Federal Hwy). Int corridors. **Pets:** Accepted.
(ASK) ☒ 🗂 🖙 🛏 🖵 ➴ 🗶

**▼▼ Flying Cloud Motel** M
(954) 563-7062. **$49-$135, 14 day notice.** 533 Orton Ave. Just w of SR A1A; between Terramar and Rio Mar sts, 0.5 mi s of SR 838 (Sunrise Blvd). Ext corridors. **Pets:** Accepted.
(ASK) 🛏 ➴

**▼▼▼ Hampton Inn Fort Lauderdale Airport North** SH
(954) 524-9900. **$99-$143.** 2301 SW 12th Ave. I-95, exit 25 (SR 84), 0.7 mi e to SW 12th Ave, then just n. Int corridors. **Pets:** Accepted.
(ASK) (S̄D) ☒ (&M) 🗂 🖙 🛏 🖵 ➴

**La Quinta Inn Ft. Lauderdale (Cypress Creek/I-95) SH**
(954) 491-7666. **$69-$130.** 999 W Cypress Creek Rd. I-95, exit 33 southbound, 0.8 mi; exit 33B northbound, at Powerline Rd. Int corridors. **Pets:** Medium. Service with restrictions.

**Motel 6–Ft. Lauderdale #55 SH**
(954) 760-7999. **$55-$75.** 1801 SR 84. I-95, exit 25 (SR 84 E), just e, then U-turn at light. Int corridors. **Pets:** Accepted.

**Ramada Inn-Fort Lauderdale Airport/Cruise Port M**
(954) 584-4000. **$69-$124.** 2275 SR 84/Marina Mile Rd. I-95, exit 25 (SR 84), just w. Ext corridors. **Pets:** Accepted.

**Red Roof Inn SH**
(954) 776-6333. **$55-$85.** 4800 Powerline Rd. I-95, exit 32, just w of jct Commercial Blvd, then n. Int corridors. **Pets:** Accepted.

**Royal Saxon Apartments M ❖**
(954) 566-7424. **$65-$175, 14 day notice.** 551 Breakers Ave. Just w of SR A1A, 0.5 mi s of SR 838 (Sunrise Blvd); corner of Breakers Ave and Terramar St. Ext corridors. **Pets:** Other species. $100 deposit/pet. Designated rooms, service with restrictions, supervision.

**Sea Chateau Resort Motel M**
(954) 566-8331. **$65-$100 (no credit cards), 10 day notice.** 555 N Birch Rd & Terramar St. 2 blks w of SR A1A; 0.5 mi s of SR 838 (Sunrise Blvd). Ext corridors. **Pets:** Accepted.

**Sheraton Suites Cypress Creek LH ❖**
(954) 772-5400. **$99-$169.** 555 NW 62nd St. I-95, exit 33B northbound, then w; exit 33 southbound, then w (Cypress Creek Rd). Int corridors. **Pets:** Medium. Designated rooms, service with restrictions, supervision.

**TownePlace Suites by Marriott SH ❖**
(954) 484-2214. **$99-$199, 3 day notice.** 3100 Prospect Rd. I-95, exit 33, 2.7 mi w, then 0.5 mi s on NW 31st St. Int corridors. **Pets:** $75 one-time fee/room. Service with restrictions.

**The Westin, Fort Lauderdale LH ❖**
(954) 772-1331. **$109-$209.** 400 Corporate Dr. I-95, exit 33 southbound, then e; exit 33A northbound, then e; in Radice Corporate Park. Int corridors. **Pets:** Medium. $50 one-time fee/room. Service with restrictions.

# HOLLYWOOD

**Days Inn Fort Lauderdale/Hollywood Airport South SH**
(954) 923-7300. **$79-$249.** 2601 N 29th Ave. I-95, exit 21, just nw on SR 822 (Sheridan St). Int corridors. **Pets:** Accepted.

**Econo Lodge Inn & Suites Hollywood Blvd M ❖**
(954) 981-1800. **$59-$199.** 4900 Hollywood Blvd. I-95, exit 20, 1.6 mi w; Florida Tpke, exit 49, 1.3 mi e. Ext corridors. **Pets:** Medium, other species. $15 daily fee/pet. Designated rooms, service with restrictions, supervision.

**La Quinta Inn & Suites Ft. Lauderdale (Airport)**
(954) 922-2295. **$99-$169.** 2620 N 26th Ave. I-95, exit 21, just e to Oakwood, then just left. Int corridors. **Pets:** Medium. Service with restrictions.

**Sandy Shores Motel & Family Lodging M**
(954) 923-3750. **$55-$95, 7 day notice.** 342 Van Buren St. From SR 820 (Hollywood Blvd), just s on SR A1A (S Ocean Dr), then e. Ext corridors. **Pets:** Accepted.

**Seminole Hard Rock Hotel & Casino Hollywood LH**
(954) 327-7625. **$189-$349, 7 day notice.** 1 Seminole Way. I-95, exit 22, 2.9 mi w, then just n on SR 7/US 441; Florida Tpke, exit 53, 0.5 mi e, then 0.8 mi s. Int corridors. **Pets:** Accepted.

# PLANTATION

**Holiday Inn Plantation/Sawgrass SH**
(954) 472-5600. **$79-$149.** 1701 N University Dr. SR 817, just s of jct SR 838 (Sunrise Blvd). Ext/int corridors. **Pets:** Accepted.

**La Quinta Inn & Suites Ft. Lauderdale (Plantation) SH**
(954) 476-6047. **$95-$149.** 8101 Peters Rd. I-595, exit 5 (SR 817 N/University Dr), just n, then just w; in Crossroad Office Park. Int corridors. **Pets:** Medium. Service with restrictions.

**Residence Inn by Marriott-Ft. Lauderdale/Plantation SH**
(954) 723-0300. **$109-$189.** 130 N University Dr. I-595, exit 5 (SR 817/University Dr), 0.7 mi n; just n of jct SR 842 (Broward Blvd). Int corridors. **Pets:** Other species. $75 one-time fee/room. Service with restrictions, crate.

**Sheraton Suites-Plantation LH ❖**
(954) 424-3300. **$279-$700.** 311 N University Dr. I-595, exit 5 (SR 817/University Dr), 0.7 mi n; 0.3 mi n of jct Broward Blvd (SR 842); at Fashion Mall. Int corridors. **Pets:** Medium. $25 daily fee/pet. Service with restrictions, supervision.

**Staybridge Suites Ft Lauderdale-Plantation SH**
(954) 577-9696. **$124-$219.** 410 N Pine Island Rd. I-595, exit 4, 1.7 mi n. Int corridors. **Pets:** Medium. $70 deposit/room, $30 one-time fee/room. Service with restrictions.

**Wellesley Inn (Plantation) SH**
(954) 473-8257. **$89-$169.** 7901 SW 6th St. 0.3 mi w of SR 817 (University Dr); 0.5 mi sw of jct SR 842 (Broward Blvd). Int corridors. **Pets:** Accepted.

# POMPANO BEACH

**Extended Stay Deluxe SH**
(954) 783-1050. **$67-$118.** 1401 SW 15th St. I-95, exit 33B (Cypress Creek Rd) to Andrews Ave, just s, then left on McNab St. Int corridors. **Pets:** $25 daily fee/pet. Service with restrictions, supervision.

**Motel 6–Pompano Beach #371 M**
(954) 977-8011. **$50-$65.** 1201 NW 31st Ave. Florida Tpke, exit 67 (Coconut Creek Pkwy/Martin Luther King Blvd), just s. **Pets:** Accepted.

## SUNRISE

**ⒶⒶⒶ ▼▼▼▼ Baymont Inn & Suites Sunrise at Sawgrass** 𝗦𝗛
(954) 846-1200. **$95-$129.** 13651 NW 2nd St. SW 136th Ave, 0.3 mi n of jct I-595, exit 1A and SR 84; 0.5 mi e of jct I-75 and Sawgrass Expwy. Int corridors. **Pets:** Medium. Service with restrictions.
[SAVE] ⊠ 🔌 🛏 🖥 ⤳

**ⒶⒶⒶ ▼▼▼ Wellesley Inn & Suites (Sunrise)** 𝗦𝗛
(954) 845-9929. **$79-$159.** 13600 NW 2nd St. SW 136th Ave, 0.3 mi n of jct I-595, exit 1A and SR 84; 0.5 mi e of jct I-75 and Sawgrass Expwy. Int corridors. **Pets:** Small, other species. $10 daily fee/pet. Designated rooms, service with restrictions, supervision.
[SAVE] ⊠ 🔌 🛏 🖥 ⤳

## TAMARAC

**ⒶⒶⒶ ▼▼▼ Baymont Inn & Suites Ft. Lauderdale** 𝗦𝗛
(954) 485-7900. **$69-$109.** 3800 W Commercial Blvd. On SR 870 (Commercial Blvd), 0.8 mi e of Florida Tpke, exit 62; just e of jct SR 7 and US 441. Int corridors. **Pets:** Medium. Service with restrictions.
[SAVE] ⊠ 🔌 🛏 🖥 ⤳

**▼▼ Homestead Studio Suites Hotel-Ft Lauderdale/Tamarac** 𝗠
(954) 733-6644. **$44-$84.** 3873 W Commercial Blvd. SR 870 (Commercial Blvd), 0.7 mi e of Florida Tpke, exit 62; just e of jct US 441 and SR 7. Ext corridors. **Pets:** $25 daily fee/pet. Service with restrictions, supervision.
[ASK] [SD] ⊠ 🔌 🛏 🖥

## WESTON

**ⒶⒶⒶ ▼▼▼▼ AmeriSuites (Ft. Lauderdale/Weston)** 𝗦𝗛
(954) 659-1555. **$109-$199.** 2201 N Commerce Pkwy. I-75, exit 15, 0.5 mi w on Arvida Pkwy to Weston Rd, n to N Commerce Pkwy, then just e. Int corridors. **Pets:** Small. $10 daily fee/room. Service with restrictions, crate.
[SAVE] ⊠ 🔌 🛏 🖥 ⤳

**▼▼▼ Residence Inn by Marriott Weston** 𝗦𝗛
(954) 659-8585. **$119-$249.** 2605 Weston Rd. I-75, exit 15 to Weston Rd, just s. Int corridors. **Pets:** Other species. $79 one-time fee/room. Service with restrictions, supervision.
[ASK] [SD] ⊠ 🔌 🛏 🖥 ⤳ ⊠

**▼▼▼ TownePlace Suites by Marriott Weston** 𝗦𝗛
(954) 659-2234. **$69-$209.** 1545 Three Village Rd. I-75, exit 15, 1 mi e on Arvida Pkwy to Bonaventure Blvd, n to Three Village Rd, then w. Int corridors. **Pets:** Accepted.
[ASK] [SD] ⊠ 🛏 🖥 ⤳

---

## END METROPOLITAN AREA

---

## FORT MYERS

**▼▼ Best Western Airport Inn** 𝗦𝗛 ✿
(239) 561-7000. **$90-$189.** 8955 Daniels Pkwy. I-75, exit 131, 0.6 mi w. Int corridors. **Pets:** Medium. $10 daily fee/pet. Designated rooms, service with restrictions, supervision.
[ASK] [SD] ⊠ 🛏 🖥 ⤳ ⊠

**▼▼▼ Best Western Coral Bridge Inn & Suites** 𝗦𝗛
(239) 454-6363. **$60-$159.** 9200 College Pkwy. 1.3 mi w of US 41 at McGregor Blvd; in Southpointe Commons. **Pets:** Medium, other species. $10 daily fee/room. Service with restrictions, supervision.
[ASK] [SD] ⊠ [M] 🔌 🛏 🖥 ⤳ ⊠

**ⒶⒶⒶ ▼▼▼ Best Western Fort Myers Island Gateway** 𝗦𝗛
(239) 466-1200. **$69-$229.** 20091 Summerlin Rd SW. Jct John Morris Rd. Ext corridors. **Pets:** Other species. $25 one-time fee/room. Service with restrictions, supervision.
[SAVE] [SD] ⊠ 🔌 🛏 🖥 ⏸ ⤳

**ⒶⒶⒶ ▼▼▼ Best Western Springs Resort** 𝗠
(239) 267-7900. **$79-$144.** 18051 S Tamiami Tr. On US 41 at Constitution Blvd. Ext corridors. **Pets:** Medium. $20 daily fee/pet. Service with restrictions, crate.
[SAVE] [SD] ⊠ 🛏 🖥 ⏸ ⤳

**▼▼▼ Comfort Inn-Ft. Myers** 𝗦𝗛
(239) 694-9200. **$79-$129.** 4171 Boatways Rd. I-75, exit 141, just e on SR 80, then just s on Orange River Blvd. Int corridors. **Pets:** Accepted.
[ASK] [SD] ⊠ [M] 🔌 🛏 🖥 ⤳

**ⒶⒶⒶ ▼▼▼ Comfort Suites Airport/University** 𝗠
(239) 768-0005. **$109-$169.** 13651 Indian Paint Ln. I-75, exit 131, just w. Int corridors. **Pets:** Accepted.
[SAVE] [SD] ⊠ 🔌 🛏 🖥 ⤳

**ⒶⒶⒶ ▼▼▼ Country Inn & Suites By Carlson Sanibel-Gateway** 𝗦𝗛
(239) 454-9292. **$109-$289.** 13901 Shell Point Plaza. Jct McGregor Blvd; in Shell Point. Int corridors. **Pets:** Medium. $10 daily fee/room. Service with restrictions, crate.
[SAVE] [SD] ⊠ [M] 🔌 🛏 🖥 ⤳

**▼▼▼ Holiday Inn Select Ft. Myers Airport Area** 𝗟𝗛
(239) 482-2900. **$139-$309, 3 day notice.** 13051 Bell Tower Dr. Jct Daniels Pkwy; in Bell Tower Shops. Int corridors. **Pets:** Medium, other species. $50 one-time fee/room. Designated rooms, service with restrictions, supervision.
[ASK] ⊠ [M] 🔌 🛏 🖥 ⏸ ⤳ ⊠

**▼▼▼ Homewood Suites by Hilton-Ft. Myers** 𝗦𝗛
(239) 275-6000. **$99-$289, 3 day notice.** 5255 Big Pine Way. Just e of jct US 41; in Bell Tower Shops. Int corridors. **Pets:** Medium. $75 one-time fee/room. Service with restrictions, crate.
[ASK] [SD] ⊠ [M] 🔌 🛏 🖥 ⤳

**▼▼▼ Howard Johnson-Fort Myers** 𝗠
(239) 936-3229. **$89-$125.** 4811 S Cleveland Ave. On US 41, just s of jct N Airport Rd. Ext corridors. **Pets:** Accepted.
[ASK] ⊠ 🔌 🛏 🖥 ⏸ ⤳

**ⒶⒶⒶ ▼▼▼ La Quinta Inn Fort Myers** 𝗠
(239) 275-3300. **$79-$149.** 4850 S Cleveland Ave. On US 41, just s of jct N Airport Rd. Ext corridors. **Pets:** Medium. Service with restrictions.
[SAVE] ⊠ [M] 🔌 🛏 🖥 ⤳

**ⒶⒶⒶ ▼▼▼ Quality Hotel Historic District** 𝗦𝗛
(239) 332-3232. **$69-$179.** 2431 Cleveland Ave. On US 41, just n. Int corridors. **Pets:** Accepted.
[SAVE] [SD] ⊠ 🔌 🛏 🖥 ⏸ ⤳

**▼▼▼ Residence Inn by Marriott** 𝗦𝗛
(239) 936-0110. **$124-$329.** 2960 Colonial Blvd. I-75, exit 136, 3.5 mi w on SR 884 (Colonial Blvd). Int corridors. **Pets:** Accepted.
[ASK] [SD] ⊠ [M] 🔌 🛏 🖥 ⤳ ⊠

◆◆◆ **Suburban Extended Stay Hotel** SH
(239) 938-0100. **$54-$140.** 10150 Metro Pkwy. I-75, exit 136, 3.5 mi w on SR 884 (Colonial Blvd). Int corridors. **Pets:** $25 one-time fee/pet. Designated rooms, service with restrictions, supervision.

ASK SD ✕ ⓜ ⊟ ▣ ≈

◆◆◆ **Wynstar Inn & Suites** SH
(239) 791-5000. **$59-$259.** 10150 Daniels Pkwy. I-75, exit 131, just e. Int corridors. **Pets:** Small. $100 deposit/room, $25 daily fee/pet. Designated rooms, service with restrictions, supervision.

ASK SD ✕ ⓜ ⟲ ⓖ ⊟ ▣ ≈

# FORT MYERS BEACH

⬥⬥⬥ ◆◆◆ **Best Western Beach Resort** SH
(239) 463-6000. **$109-$269, 7 day notice.** 684 Estero Blvd. 0.4 mi n of Matanzas Pass Bridge. Ext corridors. **Pets:** Small, other species. $10 daily fee/pet. Designated rooms, service with restrictions, supervision.

SAVE SD ✕ ⟲ ⓖ ⊟ ▣ ≈ ✕

⬥⬥⬥ ◆◆◆ **Lighthouse Resort Inn & Suites** SH
(239) 463-9392. **$79-$295, 3 day notice.** 1051 5th St. Jct Matanzas Pass Bridge (SR 865). Ext corridors. **Pets:** Accepted.

SAVE SD ✕ ⊟ ▣ ⓣ ≈

◆◆◆ **Silver Sands Villas** M
(239) 463-6554. **$79-$219, 21 day notice.** 1207 Estero Blvd. Just s of Matanzas Pass Bridge (SR 865). Ext corridors. **Pets:** Accepted.

ASK ✕ ⊟ ▣ ≈

◆ **Sun Deck Resort** M
(239) 463-1842. **$49-$235, 30 day notice.** 1051 Third St. Just s of Matanzas Pass Bridge (SR 865). Ext corridors. **Pets:** Accepted.

ASK SD ✕ ⊟ ▣ ⓩ

# FORT PIERCE

◆◆ **Days Inn Hutchinson Island** M
(772) 461-8737. **$69-$105.** 1920 Seaway Dr. SR A1A southbound, Hutchinson Island, 2.5 mi e of jct US 1. Ext/int corridors. **Pets:** Other species. $10 daily fee/pet. Designated rooms, service with restrictions, supervision.

ASK SD ✕ ⟲ ⊟ ▣ ≈

◆◆◆ **Holiday Inn Express** SH
(772) 464-5000. **$79-$165.** 7151 Okeechobee Rd. I-95, exit 129, 0.7 mi w on SR 70; Florida Tpke, exit 152. Ext corridors. **Pets:** Small, other species. $25 one-time fee/room. Designated rooms, service with restrictions, supervision.

ASK SD ✕ ⓜ ⟲ ⓖ ▣ ≈

◆◆ **Motel 6-Fort Pierce #1207** M
(772) 461-9937. **$47-$69.** 2500 Peters Rd. I-95, exit 129, just w, then n. Ext corridors. **Pets:** Accepted.

SD ✕ ≈

# GAINESVILLE

⬥⬥⬥ ◆◆◆ **Best Western Gateway Grand** SH
(352) 331-3336. **$89-$129.** 4200 NW 97th Blvd. I-75, exit 390, just n of SR 222, then just w. Int corridors. **Pets:** Accepted.

SAVE SD ✕ ⓜ ⓖ ⊟ ▣ ⓣ ≈ ✕

⬥⬥⬥ ◆ **Comfort Inn West** SH ✿
(352) 264-1771. **$79-$169.** 3440 SW 40th Blvd. I-75, exit 384, just e, then just n. Int corridors. **Pets:** $10 daily fee/pet. Designated rooms, service with restrictions.

SAVE SD ✕ ⓜ ⓖ ⊟ ▣ ≈

⬥⬥⬥ ◆ **Econo Lodge University** M
(352) 373-7816. **$43-$119, 3 day notice.** 2649 SW 13th St. I-75, exit 382, 2 mi e on SR 331, then 0.5 mi n on US 441. Ext corridors. **Pets:** Small. $10 daily fee/pet. Designated rooms, service with restrictions, supervision.

SAVE SD ✕ ⊟ ▣ ≈

◆◆ **Extended StayAmerica** SH
(352) 375-0073. **$61-$86.** 3600 SW 42nd St. I-75, exit 384. Ext corridors. **Pets:** Accepted.

ASK SD ✕ ⓖ ⊟ ▣

⬥⬥⬥ ◆◆ **Holiday Inn Express** SH
(352) 376-0004. **$87-$189.** 3905 SW 43rd St. I-75, exit 384, just w; behind Cracker Barrel Restaurant. Int corridors. **Pets:** Medium, other species. $10 daily fee/room. Designated rooms, service with restrictions, supervision.

SAVE SD ✕ ⓜ ⓖ ⊟ ▣ ≈

⬥⬥⬥ ◆◆◆ **Holiday Inn-West** SH
(352) 332-7500. **$79-$129.** 7417 Newberry Rd. I-75, exit 387, just w. Ext corridors. **Pets:** Accepted.

SAVE ✕ ⊟ ▣ ⓣ ≈

◆◆◆ **La Quinta Inn Gainesville** SH
(352) 332-6466. **$80-$106.** 920 NW 69th Terrace. I-75, exit 387, just e, then just n. Ext corridors. **Pets:** Medium. Service with restrictions.

ASK ✕ ⟲ ⊟ ▣ ≈

◆ **Motel 6 #414** SH
(352) 373-1604. **$41-$53.** 4000 SW 40th Blvd. I-75, exit 384, just e. Ext corridors. **Pets:** Accepted.

SD ✕ ⊟ ≈

◆◆ **Quality Inn** SH
(352) 378-2405. **$54-$131.** 3455 SW Williston Rd. I-75, exit 382, just w. Ext/int corridors. **Pets:** Accepted.

ASK SD ✕ ⊟ ▣ ≈

⬥⬥⬥ ◆◆ **Ramada Limited** SH
(352) 332-8001. **$69-$109.** 7413 W Newberry Rd. I-75, exit 387, just w. Ext corridors. **Pets:** Accepted.

SAVE SD ✕ ⊟ ▣ ⓣ ≈

◆◆ **Red Roof Inn-Gainesville** SH
(352) 336-3311. **$49-$65.** 3500 SW 42nd St. I-75, exit 384, just e. Int corridors. **Pets:** Accepted.

✕ ⓜ ⟲ ⓖ ⊟ ≈

# HAINES CITY

⬥⬥⬥ ◆◆◆ **Best Western Lake Hamilton** M
(863) 421-6929. **$59-$87.** 605 B Moore Rd. On US 27, just s of jct SR 544; 2 mi s of jct US 17-92. Ext corridors. **Pets:** Accepted.

SAVE SD ✕ ⓜ ⊟ ▣ ≈ ✕

⬥⬥⬥ ◆◆◆ **Howard Johnson Inn** M
(863) 422-8621. **$59-$99.** 33224 Hwy 27 S. On US 27, 1.8 mi s of jct US 17-92. Ext corridors. **Pets:** Accepted.

SAVE ✕ ⟲ ⊟ ▣ ⓣ ≈

# HERNANDO

◆◆◆ **Best Western Citrus Hills Lodge** SH
(352) 527-0015. **$78-$103.** 350 E Norvell Bryant Hwy. CR 486 at Citrus Hills Blvd, 3.3 mi w of US 41. Ext corridors. **Pets:** Accepted.

ASK SD ✕ ⓜ ⟲ ⊟ ▣ ⓣ ≈

# HOLMES BEACH

⬥⬥⬥ ◆ **Haley's Motel** M ✿
(941) 778-5405. **$79-$259, 30 day notice.** 8102 Gulf Dr N. On CR 789, 1.2 mi n of jct SR 64, jct Palm Dr; on Anna Maria Island. Ext corridors. **Pets:** Other species. $30 one-time fee/pet.

SAVE ✕ ⊟ ≈

# HOMOSASSA SPRINGS

◆◆ **Park Inn** SH
(352) 628-4311. **$69-$89.** 4076 S Suncoast Blvd. Just s of jct CR 490 and US 19. Ext corridors. **Pets:** Accepted.

ASK SD ✕ ⊟ ▣ ≈ ✕

## INDIALANTIC

▼▼▼ Oceanfront Cottages CA
(321) 725-8474. $790-$1190 (weekly), 60 day notice. 612 Wavecrest Ave. Just s of east end of US 192. Ext corridors. Pets: Accepted.
🗶 🛢 💷 🏊

## INDIAN HARBOUR BEACH

AAA ▼▼▼ Wellesley Inn-Melbourne/Indian Harbour
Beach SH
(321) 773-0325. $79-$139. 1894 S Patrick Dr. I-95, exit 183, 8 mi e, then 1 mi n on SR 513. Ext/int corridors. Pets: Accepted.
SAVE 🔊 🗶 🎢 🐾 🛢 💷 🏊

## INVERNESS

▼▼▼ Van der Valk Inverness VH
(352) 637-1140. $125-$275, 28 day notice. 4555 E Windmill Dr. 2.7 mi n on US 41. Pets: Accepted.
ASK 🔊 🗶 🛢 💷 🏊

# JACKSONVILLE METROPOLITAN AREA

## BALDWIN

AAA ▼▼▼ Best Western Baldwin Inn M
(904) 266-9759. $65-$155. 1088 US 301 S. I-10, exit 343, just s. Ext corridors. Pets: Medium, other species. $8 daily fee/pet. Designated rooms, service with restrictions, supervision.
SAVE 🔊 🗶 💷 🏊

## FERNANDINA BEACH

AAA ▼▼▼ ▼▼▼ Amelia Island Plantation LH
(904) 261-6161. $206-$769, 14 day notice. 6800 First Coast Hwy. In Fernandina Beach; SR A1A, 6.5 mi s of the bridge. Ext/int corridors. Pets: Accepted.
SAVE 🗶 🎢 🐾 🛢 💷 🍽 🏊 🗶

▼▼▼ Hoyt House BB
(904) 277-4300. $119-$219, 7 day notice. 804 Atlantic Ave. In Fernandina Beach; on Atlantic Ave/SR 200 at Centre and S 8th sts; in the historic district. Int corridors. Pets: Accepted.
ASK 🗶

## JACKSONVILLE

▼▼ AmeriSuites (Jacksonville/Baymeadows) SH
(904) 737-4477. $79. 8277 Western Way Cir. I-95, exit 341, just e. Int corridors. Pets: Accepted.
ASK 🔊 🗶 🎢 🐾 🛢 💷 🏊

AAA ▼▼▼ Baymont Inn & Suites Jacksonville SH
(904) 268-9999. $67-$109. 3199 Hartley Rd. I-295, exit 5A northbound; exit 5 southbound at SR 13. Int corridors. Pets: Medium. Service with restrictions.
SAVE 🗶 🎢 🛢 💷 🏊

AAA ▼▼▼ Best Western Hotel JTB/Southpoint LH 🐾
(904) 281-0900. $80-$189, 14 day notice. 4660 Salisbury Rd. I-95, exit 344 (SR 202), just ne, then just s. Int corridors. Pets: Medium. $10 daily fee/pet. Designated rooms, service with restrictions, supervision.
SAVE 🔊 🗶 🎢 🛢 💷 🏊 🗶

▼▼▼ Candlewood Suites SH
(904) 296-7785. $79-$89. 4990 Belfort Rd. I-95, exit 344 (SR 202), ne to Belfort Rd, then just s. Int corridors. Pets: Accepted.
ASK 🔊 🗶 🐾 🎢 🐾 🛢 💷

AAA ▼▼▼ Hampton Inn Jacksonville Airport SH
(904) 741-4980. $69-$119. 1170 Airport Entrance Rd. I-95, exit 363B, just w, then just s on Duval Rd. Ext corridors. Pets: Accepted.
SAVE 🔊 🗶 🐾 🎢 🐾 🛢 💷 🏊

▼▼▼ Holiday Inn Express & Suites Jacksonville SH
(904) 696-3333. $82-$139. 10148 New Berlin Rd. I-95, exit 362A southbound, 4.9 mi s on SR 9A to Heckscher Dr, then just w; exit 358A northbound, 5.8 mi ne on Hecksher Dr. Int corridors. Pets: Medium, other species. $50 deposit/room. Designated rooms, service with restrictions, supervision.
ASK 🔊 🗶 🐾 🛢 💷 🏊 🗶

▼▼▼ Homestead Studio Suites
Hotel-Jacksonville/Baymeadows SH
(904) 739-1881. $60-$115. 8300 Western Way. I-95, exit 341, just e to Western Way, then just s. Int corridors. Pets: $25 daily fee/pet. Service with restrictions, supervision.
ASK 🔊 🗶 🎢 🐾 🛢 💷

▼▼▼ Homestead Studio Suites
Hotel-Jacksonville/Southeast SH
(904) 296-0661. $70-$115. 4693 Jacksonville-Salisbury Rd S. I-95, exit 344, e on J Turner Butler Blvd, then just s. Int corridors. Pets: $25 daily fee/pet. Service with restrictions, supervision.
ASK 🔊 🗶 🍖 🎢 🐾 🛢 💷 🏊

▼▼ Homestead Studio Suites
Hotel-Jacksonville/Southside M
(904) 642-9911. $60-$105. 10020 Skinner Lake Rd. I-95, exit 344, 3.5 mi e on J Turner Butler Blvd to Gate Pkwy, just n, then just w. Ext corridors. Pets: $25 daily fee/pet. Service with restrictions, supervision.
ASK 🔊 🗶 🍖 🐾 🛢 💷

▼▼▼ Homewood Suites by Hilton SH
(904) 733-9299. $99-$199. 8737 Baymeadows Rd. I-95, exit 341, 0.3 mi w. Ext/int corridors. Pets: Small. $125 one-time fee/pet. Service with restrictions, crate.
ASK 🔊 🗶 🛢 💷 🏊 🗶

▼▼▼ Jameson Inn SH
(904) 296-0968. $54-$104. 7030 Bonneval Rd. I-95, exit 344, just w. Int corridors. Pets: Very small, other species. $10 daily fee/room. Service with restrictions, supervision.
ASK 🗶 🛢 💷 🏊

▼▼▼ La Quinta Inn & Suites Jacksonville (Butler Blvd) SH
(904) 296-0703. $99-$115. 4686 Lenoir Ave S. I-95, exit 344 (SR 202), just sw, then just nw. Int corridors. Pets: Medium. Service with restrictions.
ASK 🗶 🍖 🎢 🐾 🛢 💷 🏊

AAA ▼▼▼ La Quinta Inn Jacksonville (Airport/North) SH
(904) 751-6960. $80-$106. 812 Dunn Ave. I-95, exit 360, southwest corner. Ext corridors. Pets: Medium. Service with restrictions.
SAVE 🗶 🎢 🛢 💷 🏊

▼▼▼ La Quinta Inn Jacksonville (Baymeadows) M
(904) 731-9940. $86-$105. 8255 Dix Ellis Tr. I-95, exit 341, southwest corner. Ext corridors. Pets: Medium. Service with restrictions.
ASK 🗶 🛢 💷 🏊

**La Quinta Inn Jacksonville (Orange Park)** SH
(904) 778-9539. **$81-$96.** 8555 Blanding Blvd. I-295, exit 12, just s on SR 21. Ext corridors. **Pets:** Medium. Service with restrictions.

**Masters Inn Butler Blvd/Southpoint** SH
(904) 281-2244. **$49-$59.** 4940 Mustang Rd. I-95, exit 344 (SR 202), just sw, then just nw. Int corridors. **Pets:** Medium. $15 daily fee/pet. Designated rooms, service with restrictions, supervision.

**Motel 6 Jacksonville SW (Orange Park) #415** M
(904) 777-6100. **$43-$55.** 6107 Youngerman Cir. I-295, exit 12, just sw. Ext corridors. **Pets:** Accepted.

**Omni Jacksonville Hotel** LH
(904) 355-6664. **$105-$399.** 245 Water St. Corner of Pearl and Water sts; on northside of St. Johns River; downtown; adjacent to The Landing. Int corridors. **Pets:** Small. $50 one-time fee/pet. Service with restrictions, supervision.

**Radisson Hotel Jacksonville Butler Boulevard** SH
(904) 281-9700. **$71-$139.** 4700 Salisbury Rd. I-95, exit 344, just e on Butler Blvd, then just s. Int corridors. **Pets:** Accepted.

**Ramada Inn Conference Center** SH
(904) 268-8080. **$89-$99.** 3130 Hartley Rd. I-295, exit 5A northbound; exit 5 southbound; jus: n on SR 13. Ext corridors. **Pets:** Accepted.

**Red Roof Inn-Airport** M
(904) 741-4488. **$50-$61.** 14701 Airport Entrance Rd. I-95, exit 363, just w. Ext corridors. **Pets:** Accepted.

**Residence Inn by Marriott** SH
(904) 733-8088. **$119-$299.** 8365 Dix Ellis Tr. I-95, exit 341 (SR 152), just w to Freedom Commerce Pkwy, then just s to Dix Ellis Tr. Ext corridors. **Pets:** Other species. $75 one-time fee/room. Service with restrictions.

**Residence Inn by Marriott** SH
(904) 996-8900. **$99-$179.** 10551 Deerwood Park Blvd. I-95, exit 344, 3.5 mi e on J Turner Butler Blvd to Gate Blvd, just s, then just w. Int corridors. **Pets:** Other species. $75 one-time fee/room. Service with restrictions, crate.

## JACKSONVILLE BEACH

**Quality Suites Oceanfront** SH
(904) 435-3535. **$159-$299.** 11 1st St N. Just n of Beach Blvd (US 90). Int corridors. **Pets:** Medium. $35 daily fee/pet. Service with restrictions, supervision.

## ORANGE PARK

**Comfort Inn** SH
(904) 644-4444. **$65-$95.** 341 Park Ave. I-295, exit 10 (US 17), just s. Ext corridors. **Pets:** Other species. $30 one-time fee/pet. Service with restrictions, supervision.

## PONTE VEDRA BEACH

**The Sawgrass Marriott Resort & Beach Club** LH
(904) 285-7777. **$175-$284.** 1000 PGA Tour Blvd. 2.5 mi s of J Turner Butler Blvd. Int corridors. **Pets:** Accepted.

# END METROPOLITAN AREA

## JENSEN BEACH

**River Palm Cottages** CA
(772) 334-0401. **$149-$199, 14 day notice.** 2325 NE Indian River Dr. On SR 707 (NE Indian River Dr); 1.4 mi s of jct SR 732. Ext corridors. **Pets:** Other species. $20 daily fee/pet. Designated rooms, supervision.

## JUNO BEACH

**Holiday Inn Express-North Palm Beach** SH
(561) 622-4366. **$99-$169.** 13950 US Hwy 1. Jct Donald Ross Rd. Ext/int corridors. **Pets:** Accepted.

## JUPITER

**Wellesley Inn (Jupiter)** SH
(561) 575-7201. **$79-$149.** 34 Fishermans Wharf. SR 706 (Indiantown Rd); 0.3 mi w of jct US 1; in Fisherman's Wharf Plaza. Int corridors. **Pets:** Medium, other species. $20 daily fee/pet. Designated rooms, service with restrictions, crate.

## LAKE CITY

**Best Western Inn** SH
(386) 752-3801. **$60-$110.** 3598 W US Hwy 90. I-75, exit 427, just w. Ext corridors. **Pets:** Small. $10 daily fee/pet. Designated rooms, service with restrictions, supervision.

**Days Inn I-10** SH
(386) 758-4224. **$75-$200.** 3430 N US 441. I-10, exit 303, just s. Ext corridors. **Pets:** $10 daily fee/pet. Designated rooms, service with restrictions, crate.

**Driftwood Inn** M
(386) 755-3545. **$38-$60.** 2764 W US Hwy 90. I-75, exit 427, 0.7 mi e. Ext corridors. **Pets:** Small, dogs only. $10 daily fee/pet. Designated rooms, service with restrictions, supervision.

**Econo Lodge South** M
(386) 755-9311. **$60-$70, 7 day notice.** 14113 S US Hwy 441. I-75, exit 414, at US 441. Ext corridors. **Pets:** Very small. $10 daily fee/pet. Designated rooms, service with restrictions, supervision.

**Jameson Inn** SH
(386) 758-8440. **$54-$104.** 285 SW Commerce Blvd. I-75, exit 427, just e, then just s. Int corridors. **Pets:** Very small, other species. $10 daily fee/room. Service with restrictions, supervision.

**Rodeway Inn** M
(386) 755-5203. **$45-$75.** 205 SW Commerce Dr. I-75, exit 427, just e. Ext corridors. **Pets:** Other species. $5 daily fee/pet. Designated rooms, service with restrictions, crate.

**Scottish Inns** M
(386) 755-0230. **$46.** 2916 W US Hwy 90. I-75, exit 427, 0.6 mi e. Ext corridors. Pets: Accepted.
[SAVE] [X] [bullet]

## LAKELAND

**AmeriSuites Lakeland Center** SH
(863) 413-1122. **$79-$159.** 525 W Orange St. I-4, exit 32, 3.2 mi s on US 98, then just w. Int corridors. Pets: Small. $10 daily fee/pet. Designated rooms, service with restrictions, supervision.
[SAVE] [S] [X] [&M] [icons]

**Baymont Inn & Suites Lakeland** SH
(863) 815-0606. **$85-$129.** 4315 Lakeland Park Dr. I-4, exit 33; jct SR 33, just nw. Int corridors. Pets: Medium. Service with restrictions.
[SAVE] [X] [&M] [icons]

**Comfort Inn & Suites** SH
(863) 859-0100. **$99-$149.** 3520 Hwy US 98 N. I-4, exit 32, just nw; at Lakeland Square Mall. Int corridors. Pets: Accepted.
[SAVE] [S] [X] [&M] [icons]

**Holiday Inn Lakeland Hotel & Conference Center** SH
(863) 688-8080. **$71-$99.** 3260 US Hwy 98 N. I-4, exit 32, just e. Int corridors. Pets: Accepted.
[ASK] [S] [X] [icons]

**Imperial Swan Hotel & Suites** SH
(863) 647-3000. **$99-$239, 30 day notice.** 4141 S Florida Ave. SR 37, 3.5 mi s of US 98 business route. Int corridors. Pets: Accepted.
[SAVE] [X] [&M] [icons]

**Jameson Inn** SH
(863) 858-9070. **$54-$104.** 4375 Lakeland Park Dr. I-4, exit 33, just nw. Int corridors. Pets: Very small, other species. $10 daily fee/room. Service with restrictions, supervision.
[ASK] [X] [&M] [icons]

**Lakeland Residence Inn by Marriott** SH
(863) 680-2323. **$129-$200.** 3701 Harden Blvd. I-4, exit 27 (Polk Pkwy), se on SR 570 (toll) to exit 5, then just n. Int corridors. Pets: Other species. $75 one-time fee/room. Service with restrictions, crate.
[ASK] [X] [icons]

**La Quinta Inn & Suites Lakeland** SH
(863) 859-2866. **$79-$129.** 1024 Crevasse St. I-4, exit 32, just n on US 98. Int corridors. Pets: Medium. No service.
[SAVE] [X] [&M] [icons]

## LAKE WORTH

**Lago Motor Inn** M
(561) 585-5246. **$95-$115, 14 day notice.** 714 S Dixie Hwy. I-95, exit 63, 0.7 mi e, then just s on US 1; US 1, just s of jct 6th Ave S. Ext corridors. Pets: Accepted.
[SAVE] [X] [bullet] [icons]

## LANTANA

**Motel 6 Lantana #688** M
(561) 585-5833. **$45-$72.** 1310 W Lantana Rd. I-95, exit 61 (SR 812), just e, then s. Ext corridors. Pets: Accepted.
[S] [X] [icons]

## LIVE OAK

**Econo Lodge** SH
(386) 362-7459. **$60-$69.** 6811 N US 129 & I-10. I-10, exit 283, just s. Ext corridors. Pets: Large, other species. $10 one-time fee/pet. Service with restrictions, supervision.
[SAVE] [S] [X] [icons]

**Suwannee River Best Western Inn** SH
(386) 362-6000. **$50-$175, 7 day notice.** 6819 US 129 N. I-10, exit 283, 0.3 mi s. Ext corridors. Pets: Accepted.
[SAVE] [S] [X] [icons]

## LONGBOAT KEY

**Riviera Beach Resort** M
(941) 383-2552. **$798-$1258 (weekly), 30 day notice.** 5451 Gulf of Mexico Dr. On SR 789, 5 mi s of jct SR 684 (Cortez Rd). Ext corridors. Pets: Small, dogs only. $100 deposit/pet. No service, supervision.
[SAVE] [X] [icons]

## MACCLENNY

**Econo Lodge** M [paw]
(904) 259-3000. **$49-$85.** 151 Woodlawn Rd. I-10, exit 335, just s of jct SR 121. Ext corridors. Pets: Large, other species. $10 one-time fee/pet. Service with restrictions.
[SAVE] [S] [X] [icons]

## MARIANNA

**Best Western Marianna Inn** SH
(850) 526-5666. **$59-$79.** 2086 Hwy 71 S. I-10, exit 142, 0.3 mi s. Ext corridors. Pets: $10 daily fee/pet. Service with restrictions.
[SAVE] [S] [X] [icons]

**Quality Inn** SH
(850) 526-5600. **$69-$99.** 2175 Hwy 71 S. I-10, exit 142, just n. Ext corridors. Pets: Medium. $12 daily fee/pet. Service with restrictions, supervision.
[ASK] [S] [X] [icons]

## MELBOURNE

**Crane Creek Inn Waterfront Bed & Breakfast** BB [paw]
(321) 768-6416. **$100-$199, 14 day notice.** 907 E Melbourne Ave. Jct US 192, just s on Babcock, then 0.9 mi e. Ext/int corridors. Pets: Dogs only. $10 daily fee/pet. Service with restrictions, supervision.
[X] [icons]

**Hilton Melbourne Rialto Place** SH
(321) 768-0200. **$129-$269.** 200 Rialto Pl. 1 mi w of US 1, 0.8 mi n of US 192 via Airport Blvd. Int corridors. Pets: Medium, other species. $50 deposit/room. Service with restrictions, supervision.
[X] [&M] [icons]

**La Quinta Inn & Suites Melbourne** SH
(321) 242-9400. **$105-$159.** 7200 George T Edwards Dr. I-95, exit 191 (CR 509), just w. Int corridors. Pets: Medium. Service with restrictions.
[SAVE] [X] [icons]

**Super 8** M
(321) 723-4430. **$69-$89.** 1515 S Harbor City Blvd. I-95, exit 180, 7 mi e to US 1 on US 192, then 0.5 mi n. Int corridors. Pets: Accepted.
[SAVE] [S] [X] [&M] [icons]

**Wisteria Inn Bed & Breakfast** BB
(321) 727-0717. **$95-$145, 14 day notice.** 1924 Catterton Dr. I-95, exit 180, 4.5 mi e on US 192, then just n. Int corridors. Pets: Accepted.
[X] [icons]

# MIAMI-MIAMI BEACH METROPOLITAN AREA

## AVENTURA

**WWW WWW The Fairmont Turnberry Isle Resort & Club** 🔲 ❀
(305) 932-6200. **$143-$4200, 3 day notice.** 19999 W Country Club Dr. 0.5 mi w of SR A1A via SR 856; from US 1 at NE 199th St and Biscayne Blvd. Ext/int corridors. **Pets:** Small. $25 daily fee/pet. Service with restrictions, supervision.

🅂🄰🆅 🆂🄾 ⊠ 🔏 🖋 🔲 💻 🍴 🏊 🗙

**WWWW Residence Inn by Marriott-Aventura Mall** 🔲
(786) 528-1001. **$89-$409.** 19900 W Country Club Dr. 0.5 mi w of SR A1A via SR 856; from US 1 at NE 199th St and Biscayne Blvd. Int corridors. **Pets:** Accepted.

🄰🅂🄺 🆂🄾 ⊠ 🆕 🔏 🖋 🔏 🔲 💻 🏊

## BAL HARBOUR

**WWW WWW Sheraton Bal Harbour Beach Resort** 🔲 ❀
(305) 865-7511. **$309-$499, 3 day notice.** 9701 Collins Ave. On SR A1A, just n on SR 922. Int corridors. **Pets:** Medium, dogs only. Service with restrictions, supervision.

🅂🄰🆅 🆂🄾 ⊠ 🔏 🖋 🔏 🔲 💻 🍴 🏊 🗙

## COCONUT GROVE

**WWW WWW Mayfair Hotel & Spa** 🔲
(305) 441-0000. **$99-$389.** 3000 Florida Ave. At Florida Ave and Virginia St; center. Ext/int corridors. **Pets:** Accepted.

🅂🄰🆅 ⊠ 🔏 🖋 💻 🍴 🏊 🗙

**WWWW Residence Inn by Marriott** 🔲 ❀
(305) 285-9303. **$123-$229.** 2835 Tigertail Ave. S Bayshore Dr, w on SW 27th Ave/Cornelia Dr, then s; in CocoWalk and May Fair Shops. Ext corridors. **Pets:** Other species. $75 one-time fee/room. Service with restrictions.

🄰🅂🄺 🆂🄾 ⊠ 🔏 💻 🏊

## CUTLER RIDGE

**WWWW Baymont Inn & Suites Miami-Cutler Ridge** 🔲
(305) 278-0001. **$79-$109.** 10821 Caribbean Blvd. Florida Tpke, exit 12 (US 1), northwest corner. Int corridors. **Pets:** Medium. Service with restrictions.

🅂🄰🆅 ⊠ 🆕 🔏 🖋 🔏 🔲 💻 🏊

**WWWW Best Western Floridian Hotel** 🔲
(305) 253-9960. **$79-$129.** 10775 Caribbean Blvd. Florida Tpke, exit 12 (US 1), then w. Ext corridors. **Pets:** Accepted.

🅂🄰🆅 🆂🄾 ⊠ 🔏 🔲 💻 🍴 🏊

## FLORIDA CITY

**WWW WW Coral Roc Motel** 🄼
(305) 246-2888. **$32-$129, 3 day notice.** 1100 N Krome Ave. On SR 997; just w of US 1; 0.5 mi s of Homestead. Ext corridors. **Pets:** Small, dogs only. $50 deposit/pet. Service with restrictions, supervision.

🅂🄰🆅 🆂🄾 ⊠ 🔏 🏊

**WWWW Hampton Inn** 🄼
(305) 247-8833. **$84-$124.** 124 E Palm Dr. On US 1, 0.3 mi s of Florida Tpke terminus. Ext corridors. **Pets:** Accepted.

🄰🅂🄺 🆂🄾 ⊠ 🔏 🔏 🔲 💻 🏊

## HIALEAH

**WWW WW Days Inn Miami Lakes/Westland Mall** 🔲
(305) 823-2121. **$75-$94.** 1950 W 49th St. SR 826 (Palmetto Expwy), exit NW 103rd St, just e. Int corridors. **Pets:** Accepted.

🅂🄰🆅 🆂🄾 ⊠ 🔏 💻

**WWW WW Ramada Inn-Miami Airport North** 🔲
(305) 823-2000. **$65-$119.** 1950 W 49th St. SR 826 (Palmetto Expwy), exit NW 103rd St, just e. Int corridors. **Pets:** Accepted.

🅂🄰🆅 🆂🄾 ⊠ 🆕 🔏 🔏 🔲 💻 🍴 🏊

## HIALEAH GARDENS

**WWW WW Howard Johnson Plaza Hotel & Conference Center-Miami Airport** 🔲
(305) 825-1000. **$109-$199.** 7707 NW 103rd St. SR 826 (Palmetto Expwy), exit NW 103rd St, just w. Int corridors. **Pets:** Large, other species. $100 one-time fee/room. Service with restrictions, supervision.

🅂🄰🆅 🆂🄾 ⊠ 🔏 🔲 💻 🏊 🗙

## HOMESTEAD

**WW WW Days Inn Homestead** 🄼
(305) 245-1260. **$75-$139, 3 day notice.** 51 S Homestead Blvd. US 1, 1.2 mi n of Florida Tpke, jct 320 St SW and US 1. Ext corridors. **Pets:** Accepted.

🄰🅂🄺 🆂🄾 ⊠ 🔏 🔏 🍴 🏊

**WWW WW Everglades Motel** 🄼
(305) 247-4117. **$32-$109.** 605 S Krome Ave. Just w of US 1; between Lucy and 6th sts; on SR 997, 0.5 mi s of center of town. Ext corridors. **Pets:** Accepted.

🅂🄰🆅 🆂🄾 ⊠ 🔏 🏊

## KENDALL

**WWW WWW AmeriSuites (Miami/Kendall)** 🔲
(305) 279-8688. **$119-$189.** 11520 SW 88th St. Florida Tpke, exit 20 (SW 88th/Kendall Dr), just e on SR 94, then 0.3 mi s. Int corridors. **Pets:** Small. $10 daily fee/room. Service with restrictions, crate.

🅂🄰🆅 🆂🄾 ⊠ 🆕 🔏 🔏 🔏 🔲 🏊

**WWW WWW Wellesley Inn (Miami/Kendall)** 🔲
(305) 270-0359. **$96-$146.** 11750 Mills Dr. Florida Tpke, exit 20, SW 88th (Kendall Dr), 0.3 mi e on SR 94, then 0.3 mi n on SW 117th Ave. Int corridors. **Pets:** Other species. $20 daily fee/room. Designated rooms, service with restrictions, crate.

🅂🄰🆅 🆂🄾 ⊠ 🆕 🔏 🔏 🔏 🔲 🏊

## KEY BISCAYNE

**WWW WWWW The Ritz-Carlton, Key Biscayne** 🔲
(305) 365-4500. **$199-$1599, 7 day notice.** 455 Grand Bay Dr. Crandon Blvd, just e. Int corridors. **Pets:** Accepted.

⊠ 🔏 🍴 🏊 🗙

## MIAMI

**WW WW America's Best Inn-Miami Airport** 🄼
(305) 592-5440. **$69-$99.** 7330 NW 36th St. Just e of jct SR 826 (Palmetto Expwy). Int corridors. **Pets:** Accepted.

🄰🅂🄺 🆂🄾 ⊠ 💻 🏊

**WWW WWW AmeriSuites (Miami/Airport West)** 🔲
(305) 718-8292. **$89-$139.** 3655 NW 82nd Ave. 0.4 mi w on NW 36th St from jct SR 826 (Palmetto Expwy). Int corridors. **Pets:** Small. $10 daily fee/room. Service with restrictions, crate.

🅂🄰🆅 🆂🄾 ⊠ 🆕 🔏 🔏 🔏 🔲 💻 🏊

**▼▼▼ Candlewood Suites Miami Airport West SH**
(305) 591-9099. **$79-$129.** 8855 NW 27th St. SR 826 (Palmetto Expwy), 0.8 mi w on nw 36th St, 0.4 mi s. Int corridors. **Pets:** Large. $150 one-time fee/pet. Service with restrictions, crate.

ASK S X 5M / 5 8 ● ⚊

**▲▲▲ ▼▼▼ ▼▼▼ Four Seasons Hotel Miami LH**
(305) 358-3535. **$275-$1950.** 1435 Brickell Ave. On US 1 (Brickell Ave) and 14th St. Int corridors. **Pets:** Accepted.

SAVE X 5M / 5 8 ● ⚊ ¶¶ ⚊ ⊠

**▲▲▲ ▼▼▼ ▼▼▼ Hampton Inn-Miami Airport West SH**
(305) 513-0777. **$79-$169.** 3620 NW 79th Ave. SR 826 (Palmetto Expwy), exit NW 36th St, just s of jct NW 58th St, just s; in Boykin Center. Int corridors. **Pets:** Accepted.

SAVE S X 5M / 5 8 ● ⚊

**▼▼ ▼ Homestead Studio Suites Hotel-Miami/Airport/Blue Lagoon M**
(305) 260-0085. **$54-$94.** 6605 NW 7th St. SR 836 (Dolphin Expwy), exit Milam Dairy Rd S, 0.3 mi e; in Blue Lagoon Office Park. Ext corridors. **Pets:** $25 daily fee/pet. Service with restrictions, supervision.

ASK S X 5M / 5 8 ●

**▼▼ ▼ Homestead Studio Suites Hotel-Miami/Airport/Doral M**
(305) 436-1811. **$54-$99.** 8720 NW 33rd St. SR 826 (Palmetto Expwy), 0.8 mi w on NW 36th St, just s. Ext corridors. **Pets:** $25 daily fee/pet. Service with restrictions, supervision.

ASK S X / 5 8 ● ⚊

**▼▼▼ Homewood Suites by Hilton-Miami Airport/Blue Lagoon SH**
(305) 261-3335. **$119-$199.** 5500 Blue Lagoon Dr. Se of jct SR 836 (Dolphin Expwy), exit Red Rd. Int corridors. **Pets:** Accepted.

ASK S X 5M / 5 8 ● ⚊ ⊠

**▲▲▲ ▼▼▼ La Quinta Inn & Suites Miami (Airport West) SH**
(305) 436-0830. **$89-$129.** 8730 NW 27th St. SR 836 (Dolphin Expwy), just n on 87th NW Ave. Int corridors. **Pets:** Medium. Service with restrictions.

SAVE X 5M / 5 8 ● ⚊

**▲▲▲ ▼▼▼ La Quinta Inn Miami (Airport North) M**
(305) 599-9902. **$75-$99.** 7401 NW 36th St. Just e of jct SR 826 (Palmetto Expwy). Ext corridors. **Pets:** Medium. Service with restrictions.

SAVE X / 8 ● ⚊

**▲▲▲ ▼▼▼ Mandarin Oriental, Miami LH 🐾**
(305) 913-8288. **$415-$860.** 500 Brickell Key Dr. US 1 (Brickell Ave), just e on SE 8th St (Brickell Key Dr). Int corridors. **Pets:** Small. $100 deposit/room, $100 one-time fee/room. Supervision.

SAVE X 5M / 5 8 ● ¶¶ ⚊ ⊠

**▼▼ ▼ Miami River Inn BB**
(305) 325-0045. **$69-$199, 3 day notice.** 118 SW South River Dr. I-95, exit 1B (SW 7th St), just w to SW 5th Ave, just n to SW 2nd St, then e. Ext/int corridors. **Pets:** $25 one-time fee/room.

ASK S X ⚊

**▲▲▲ ▼▼▼ Quality Inn-South at The Falls M**
(305) 251-2000. **$79-$119.** 14501 S Dixie Hwy (US 1). US 1 at SW 145th St. Ext corridors. **Pets:** Medium, other species. $10 daily fee/room. Service with restrictions.

SAVE S X / 8 ● ¶¶ ⚊

**▼▼▼ Residence Inn by Marriott SH**
(305) 591-2211. **$99-$189.** 1212 NW 82nd Ave. SR 836 (Dolphin Expwy), exit 87th Ave NW, just n to NW 82nd Ave, then e. Ext corridors. **Pets:** Accepted.

ASK S X / 8 ● ⚊ ⊠

**▼▼▼ ▼▼▼ Sofitel Miami LH**
(305) 264-4888. **$279.** 5800 Blue Lagoon Dr. Just sw of jct SR 836 (Dolphin Expwy), exit Red Rd. Int corridors. **Pets:** Service with restrictions.

ASK S X 8 ¶¶ ⚊ ⊠

**▼▼▼ ▼▼▼ Staybridge Suites Miami-Airport West-Doral SH**
(305) 500-9100. **$102-$159, 3 day notice.** 3265 NW 87th Ave. 0.4 mi s of jct NW 36th St. Int corridors. **Pets:** $125 one-time fee/pet. Service with restrictions, supervision.

ASK S X / 5 8 ● ⚊

**▼▼▼ Summerfield Suites by Wyndham-Miami Airport SH**
(305) 269-1922. **$109-$284.** 5710 Blue Lagoon Dr. Se of jct SR 836 (Dolphin Expwy), exit Red Rd, just w. Int corridors. **Pets:** Accepted.

ASK X 5M / 5 8 ● ⚊

**▼▼▼ TownePlace Suites by Marriott SH**
(305) 718-4144. **$49-$179, 14 day notice.** 10505 NW 36th St. Florida Tpke, exit 29, 1.2 mi e to 107th Ave, then just s. Int corridors. **Pets:** Accepted.

ASK S X 8 ● ⚊

**▼▼ ▼ Wellesley Inn (Miami Airport) SH**
(305) 592-4799. **$58-$72.** 8436 NW 36th St. 0.8 mi w of jct SR 826 (Palmetto Expwy). Int corridors. **Pets:** Accepted.

ASK S X / 8 ● ⚊

## MIAMI BEACH

**▼▼▼ Cadet Hotel SH**
(305) 672-6688. **$99-$225, 3 day notice.** 1701 James Ave. Just w of SR A1A (Collins Ave) on 17th St; corner of James Ave and 17th St. Int corridors. **Pets:** Accepted.

ASK X

**▲▲▲ ▼▼▼ Casa Grande Suite Hotel SH**
(305) 672-7003. **$215-$1500, 3 day notice.** 834 Ocean Dr. E of SR A1A (Collins Ave) and 8th St. Int corridors. **Pets:** Accepted.

SAVE S X / 5 8 ●

**▼▼▼ Century Hotel SH**
(305) 674-8855. **$80-$215, 7 day notice.** 140 Ocean Dr. Just e of SR A1A (Collins Ave), just s of 2nd St. Int corridors. **Pets:** Accepted.

ASK S

**▼▼▼ Crowne Plaza Royal Palm on South Beach LH**
(305) 604-5700. **$264-$454, 3 day notice.** 1545 Collins Ave. On SR A1A (Collins Ave), just s of 16th Ave. Ext/int corridors. **Pets:** Accepted.

ASK S X 5 8 ● ¶¶ ⚊ ⊠

**▲▲▲ ▼▼▼ Eden Roc, A Renaissance Resort & Spa LH**
(305) 531-0000. **$159-$424, 3 day notice.** 4525 Collins Ave. SR A1A (Collins Ave), just n of 41st St. Int corridors. **Pets:** Small, dogs only. $75 one-time fee/room. Service with restrictions.

SAVE S X / 5 8 ● ¶¶ ⚊ ⊠

**▲▲▲ ▼▼▼ Fontainebleau Resort LH**
(305) 538-2000. **$199-$1200.** 4441 Collins Ave. On SR A1A. Int corridors. **Pets:** Accepted.

SAVE S X / 5 8 ● ¶¶ ⚊ ⊠

**▼▼▼ Hotel Ocean SH 🐾**
(305) 672-2579. **$190-$675, 3 day notice.** 1230 Ocean Dr. E of jct SR A1A (Collins Ave) and 12th St. Int corridors. **Pets:** Other species. $15 daily fee/pet. Crate.

X 8 ¶¶

**▼▼▼ The Kent Hotel SH 🐾**
(305) 604-5068. **$140-$175, 3 day notice.** 1131 Collins Ave. On SR A1A, at Collins Ave and 11th St. Int corridors. **Pets:** Other species. $50 one-time fee/room. Supervision.

ASK S X / 8

### Loews Miami Beach Hotel LH ❀
(305) 604-1601. **$219-$4000, 3 day notice.** 1601 Collins Ave. On SR A1A, at Collins and 16th aves. Int corridors. **Pets:** Other species. Service with restrictions, supervision.

### The Marlin SH
(305) 604-3595. **$135-$895, 14 day notice.** 1200 Collins Ave. On SR A1A, at Collins Ave and 12th St. Int corridors. **Pets:** Accepted.

### Marriott South Beach LH ❀
(305) 536-7700. **$199-$389, 3 day notice.** 161 Ocean Dr. Just e of SR A1A (Collins Ave); just s of 2nd St. Int corridors. **Pets:** Large. $150 one-time fee/room. Designated rooms, service with restrictions, crate.

### The Ritz-Carlton, South Beach LH ❀
(786) 276-4000. **$599-$5500, 3 day notice.** 1 Lincoln Rd. Jct SR A1A (Collins Ave) and Lincoln Rd. Int corridors. **Pets:** Small, dogs only. $250 one-time fee/room. Supervision.

### Rodeway Inn South Beach M
(305) 673-1199. **$89-$129.** 1506 Collins Ave. On SR A1A (Collins Ave), just s of 15th St. Ext corridors. **Pets:** Small, other species. $100 deposit/room. Designated rooms, service with restrictions, supervision.

### The Tides Hotel SH
(305) 604-5070. **$420-$650, 3 day notice.** 1220 Ocean Dr. E of jct SR A1A (Collins Ave) and 12th St. Int corridors. **Pets:** Accepted.

### Villa Capri All Suites Hotel SH
(305) 531-7742. **$170-$415, 3 day notice.** 3010 Collins Ave. On SR A1A; at 30th St. Int corridors. **Pets:** Accepted.

### The Waldorf Towers Hotel SH
(305) 531-7684. **$109-$219.** 860 Ocean Dr. Corner of 8th St and Ocean Dr; just e of Collins Ave (SR A1A). Int corridors. **Pets:** Accepted.

## MIAMI LAKES

### TownePlace Suites by Marriott SH
(305) 512-9191. **$104-$144.** 8079 NW 154th St. SR 826 (Palmetto Expwy), exit 154th St, 0.4 mi w. Int corridors. **Pets:** Accepted.

### Wellesley Inn (Miami Lakes) SH
(305) 821-8274. **$89-$169.** 7925 NW 154th St. Jct SR 826 (Palmetto Expwy), just w. Int corridors. **Pets:** Very small, other species. $10 daily fee/pet. Designated rooms, service with restrictions, supervision.

## MIAMI SPRINGS

### Baymont Inn & Suites Miami-Airport SH
(305) 871-1777. **$75-$149.** 3501 NW Le Jeune Rd. SR 953 (Le Jeune Rd) at jct SR 112. Int corridors. **Pets:** Medium. Service with restrictions.

### Holiday Inn Express Miami International Airport SH
(305) 887-2153. **$169-$199.** 5125 NW 36th St. Between Le Jeune Rd and SR 826 (Palmetto Expwy). Int corridors. **Pets:** Other species. $50 one-time fee/pet. Designated rooms, service with restrictions, crate.

### Homestead Studio Suites Hotel-Miami/Airport/Miami Springs SH
(305) 870-0448. **$74-$109.** 101 Fairway Dr. I-95 to SR 112 W, exit NW 36th St, then w, right on Palmetto Dr, then w; between Le Jeune Rd and SR 826 (Palmetto Expwy); behind Clarion Hotel. Int corridors. **Pets:** $25 daily fee/pet. Service with restrictions, supervision.

### Red Roof Inn Miami Airport SH
(305) 871-4221. **$63-$100.** 3401 NW Le Jeune Rd. On SR 953 at SR 112; 0.5 mi n of airport entrance. Int corridors. **Pets:** Accepted.

### Sleep Inn-Miami Airport SH
(305) 871-7553. **$89-$169.** 105 Fairway Dr. I-95 to SR 112 W, exit NW 36th St, then w, right on Palmetto Dr, then w; between Le Jeune Rd and SR 826 (Palmetto Expwy). Int corridors. **Pets:** Medium. $25 one-time fee/pet. Designated rooms, service with restrictions.

## SUNNY ISLES BEACH

### Newport Beachside Hotel & Resort LH
(305) 949-1300. **$99-$325.** 16701 Collins Ave. SR A1A, jct SR 826 and Sunny Isles Blvd. Int corridors. **Pets:** Small, other species. $50 one-time fee/pet. Service with restrictions.

### Trump International Sonesta Beach Resort LH
(305) 692-5600. **$199-$850, 3 day notice.** 18001 Collins Ave. On SR A1A, just s of The William Lehman Cswy. Int corridors. **Pets:** Small, dogs only. $100 one-time fee/pet. Service with restrictions, supervision.

---

# END METROPOLITAN AREA

## MILTON

### Comfort Inn SH
(850) 623-1511. **$59-$149.** 4962 S Hwy 87. I-10, exit 31, just s. Int corridors. **Pets:** Accepted.

### Red Roof Inn & Suites SH ❀
(850) 995-6100. **$89-$110, 3 day notice.** 2672 Avalon Blvd. I-10, exit 22, just s. Int corridors. **Pets:** Medium, other species. Service with restrictions, supervision.

## MOSSY HEAD

### Ramada Limited SH
(850) 951-9780. **$54-$59.** 326 Green Acres Dr. I-10, exit 70, just s. Ext corridors. **Pets:** Large. $25 daily fee/pet. Service with restrictions, supervision.

## NAPLES

### Baymont Inn & Suites Naples SH
(239) 352-8400. **$69-$169.** 185 Bedzel Cir. I-75, exit 101, just w. Int corridors. **Pets:** Medium. Service with restrictions.

**△△△ ▽▽▽ The Fairways Resort M**
(239) 597-8181. **$65-$240, 3 day notice.** 103 Palm River Blvd. I-75, exit 111, 2.2 mi w on CR 846. Ext corridors. **Pets:** Accepted.
⟦SAVE⟧ ⟦S⟧ ⟦✕⟧ ⟦🛏⟧ ⟦💻⟧ ⟦🏊⟧

**△△△ ▽▽▽▽ The Hawthorn Suites of Naples SH**
(239) 593-1300. **$89-$269.** 3557 Pine Ridge Rd. I-75, exit 107, 0.7 mi w. Int corridors. **Pets:** Medium. $125 one-time fee/room. Designated rooms, service with restrictions, crate.
⟦SAVE⟧ ⟦S⟧ ⟦✕⟧ ⟦&M⟧ ⟦🖉⟧ ⟦🛏⟧ ⟦💻⟧ ⟦🏊⟧ ⟦✕⟧

**△△△ ▽▽▽▽ Holiday Inn M**
(239) 263-3434. **$74-$189.** 1100 Tamiami Tr N. I-75, exit 107, 3.8 mi w on CR 896, then 3.8 mi s on US 41 (Tamiami Tr). Ext corridors. **Pets:** Accepted.
⟦SAVE⟧ ⟦S⟧ ⟦✕⟧ ⟦🛏⟧ ⟦💻⟧ ⟦🍴⟧ ⟦🏊⟧

**▽▽▽▽ LaPlaya Beach & Golf Resort LH**
(239) 597-3123. **$269-$799, 14 day notice.** 9891 Gulf Shore Dr. North end of town; US 41 (Tamiami Tr), 1.3 mi w on Vanderbilt Beach Rd (SR 862), then 0.5 mi n. Ext/int corridors. **Pets:** Accepted.
⟦ASK⟧ ⟦✕⟧ ⟦&⟧ ⟦💻⟧ ⟦🍴⟧ ⟦🏊⟧ ⟦✕⟧

**△△△ ▽▽▽▽ Quality Inn & Suites SH**
(239) 649-5500. **$89-$299.** 4055 Tamiami Tr N. I-75, exit 107, 3.5 mi n on US 41, then just n of Park Shore Dr. Int corridors. **Pets:** Accepted.
⟦SAVE⟧ ⟦S⟧ ⟦✕⟧ ⟦&M⟧ ⟦🛏⟧ ⟦💻⟧ ⟦🏊⟧

**▽▽ Red Roof Inn M**
(239) 774-3117. **$50-$90.** 1925 Davis Blvd. I-75, exit 101, 6.5 mi w on SR 84; just e of jct US 41 (Tamiami Tr). Ext corridors. **Pets:** Accepted.
⟦✕⟧ ⟦&⟧ ⟦🛏⟧ ⟦💻⟧ ⟦🏊⟧

**▽▽▽▽ Residence Inn by Marriott, Naples SH** 🐾
(239) 659-1300. **$89-$329.** 4075 Tamiami Tr N. I-75, exit 107, 3.8 mi w on CR 896 (Pine Ridge Rd), then 1 mi s on US 41 (Tamiami Tr). Int corridors. **Pets:** Other species. $75 one-time fee/room. Service with restrictions.
⟦ASK⟧ ⟦S⟧ ⟦✕⟧ ⟦&M⟧ ⟦🖉⟧ ⟦&⟧ ⟦🛏⟧ ⟦💻⟧ ⟦🏊⟧ ⟦✕⟧

**△△△ ▽▽ Spinnaker Inn of Naples M** 🐾
(239) 434-0444. **$46-$86.** 6600 Dudley Dr. I-75, exit 107, just w. Ext corridors. **Pets:** Other species. $10 daily fee/room. Service with restrictions, supervision.
⟦SAVE⟧ ⟦S⟧ ⟦✕⟧ ⟦🛏⟧ ⟦💻⟧ ⟦🏊⟧

**▽▽▽▽ Staybridge Suites by Holiday Inn SH**
(239) 643-8002. **$130-$280, 3 day notice.** 4805 Tamiami Tr N. I-75, exit 107, 3.8 mi w on Pine Ridge Rd to US 41 (Tamiami Tr), then just s. Int corridors. **Pets:** Other species. $100 deposit/room, $150 one-time fee/room. Service with restrictions.
⟦ASK⟧ ⟦S⟧ ⟦✕⟧ ⟦&M⟧ ⟦🖉⟧ ⟦&⟧ ⟦🛏⟧ ⟦💻⟧ ⟦🏊⟧

**△△△ ▽▽▽ Wellesley Inn (Naples) SH**
(239) 793-4646. **$139-$199.** 1555 5th Ave S. I-75, exit 101, 6.5 mi w on SR 84. Int corridors. **Pets:** Accepted.
⟦SAVE⟧ ⟦✕⟧ ⟦🖉⟧ ⟦&⟧ ⟦🛏⟧ ⟦💻⟧ ⟦🏊⟧

## NEW SMYRNA BEACH

**▽▽ Buena Vista Inn M** 🐾
(386) 428-5565. **$65-$95, 14 day notice.** 500 N Causeway. 2 mi e on SR Business Rt 44, at west end of North Causeway Bridge. Ext corridors. **Pets:** Other species. $5 daily fee/pet. No service.
⟦ASK⟧ ⟦S⟧ ⟦✕⟧ ⟦🛏⟧ ⟦💻⟧ ⟦✕⟧

**△△△ ▽▽▽▽ Night Swan Intracoastal Bed & Breakfast BB**
(386) 423-4940. **$100-$200, 3 day notice.** 512 S Riverside Dr. Just s of SR 44 Intracoastal Waterway bridge; west side of Intracoastal Waterway. Ext/int corridors. **Pets:** Medium, other species. Designated rooms.
⟦SAVE⟧ ⟦S⟧ ⟦✕⟧ ⟦&⟧ ⟦🛏⟧ ⟦💻⟧ ⟦✕⟧

## NORTH FORT MYERS

**△△△ ▽▽▽ Econo Lodge M**
(239) 995-0571. **$49-$145.** 13301 N Cleveland Ave. On US 41, 1.1 mi n of Caloosahatchee Bridge. Ext corridors. **Pets:** Accepted.
⟦SAVE⟧ ⟦S⟧ ⟦✕⟧ ⟦🛏⟧ ⟦💻⟧ ⟦🏊⟧

**▽▽▽ Howard Johnson Express Inn M**
(239) 656-4000. **$49-$209, 3 day notice.** 13000 N Cleveland Ave. On US 41, 1 mi n of Caloosahatchee Bridge; jct North Key Dr. Ext corridors. **Pets:** Accepted.
⟦ASK⟧ ⟦S⟧ ⟦✕⟧ ⟦🖉⟧ ⟦🛏⟧ ⟦💻⟧ ⟦🏊⟧

## OCALA

**△△△ ▽▽▽ Budget Host Inn M**
(352) 732-6940. **$45-$92.** 4013 NW Bonnie Heath Blvd. I-75, exit 354, 0.3 mi n on US 27. Ext corridors. **Pets:** Medium, other species. $10 daily fee/pet. Service with restrictions, supervision.
⟦SAVE⟧ ⟦S⟧ ⟦✕⟧ ⟦🛏⟧

**△△△ ▽▽▽ Comfort Inn SH**
(352) 629-8850. **$65-$130.** 4040 W Silver Springs Blvd. I-75, exit 352, just w on SR 40. Ext corridors. **Pets:** Medium, other species. $5 daily fee/pet. Designated rooms, service with restrictions, crate.
⟦SAVE⟧ ⟦S⟧ ⟦✕⟧ ⟦🛏⟧ ⟦💻⟧ ⟦🍴⟧ ⟦🏊⟧

**△△△ ▽▽ Days Inn SH**
(352) 629-7041. **$65-$150.** 3811 NW Bonnie Heath Blvd. I-75, exit 354, just n on US 27. Ext/int corridors. **Pets:** $5 daily fee/pet. Service with restrictions, supervision.
⟦SAVE⟧ ⟦S⟧ ⟦✕⟧ ⟦🛏⟧ ⟦💻⟧ ⟦🏊⟧

**▽▽▽ Days Inn SH**
(352) 629-0091. **$49-$95.** 3620 W Silver Springs Blvd. I-75, exit 352, just e. Ext/int corridors. **Pets:** Accepted.
⟦ASK⟧ ⟦S⟧ ⟦✕⟧ ⟦🛏⟧ ⟦🏊⟧

**▽▽▽ Hilton Ocala LH**
(352) 854-1400. **$109-$229.** 3600 SW 36th Ave. I-75, exit 350, 0.3 mi e on SR 200. Int corridors. **Pets:** Accepted.
⟦ASK⟧ ⟦S⟧ ⟦✕⟧ ⟦🖉⟧ ⟦🛏⟧ ⟦💻⟧ ⟦🍴⟧ ⟦🏊⟧ ⟦✕⟧

**△△△ ▽▽▽▽ Howard Johnson Inn M**
(352) 629-7021. **$50-$200.** 3951 NW Bonnie Heath Blvd. I-75, exit 354, just w. Ext corridors. **Pets:** Accepted.
⟦SAVE⟧ ⟦S⟧ ⟦✕⟧ ⟦🛏⟧ ⟦💻⟧ ⟦🍴⟧ ⟦🏊⟧ ⟦✕⟧

**△△△ ▽▽▽▽ La Quinta Inn & Suites Ocala SH**
(352) 861-1137. **$92-$155.** 3530 SW 36th Ave. I-75, exit 350, just e on SR 200. Int corridors. **Pets:** Medium. Service with restrictions.
⟦SAVE⟧ ⟦✕⟧ ⟦&M⟧ ⟦🖉⟧ ⟦&⟧ ⟦🛏⟧ ⟦💻⟧ ⟦🏊⟧

**△△△ ▽▽▽ Quality Inn Ocala Hotel and Conference Center SH**
(352) 629-0381. **$49-$129.** 3621 W Silver Springs Blvd. I-75, exit 352, just e on SR 40. Ext corridors. **Pets:** Large. $20 one-time fee/room. Service with restrictions.
⟦SAVE⟧ ⟦S⟧ ⟦✕⟧ ⟦🛏⟧ ⟦💻⟧ ⟦🍴⟧ ⟦🏊⟧

**△△△ ▽▽▽▽ Red Roof Inn & Suites SH**
(352) 732-4590. **$60-$90.** 120 NW 40th Ave. I-75, exit 352, just w. Int corridors. **Pets:** Accepted.
⟦SAVE⟧ ⟦✕⟧ ⟦🛏⟧ ⟦💻⟧ ⟦🏊⟧

**▽▽▽ Seven Sisters Inn BB**
(352) 867-1170. **$119-$279, 7 day notice.** 820 SE Fort King St. Just s of jct SR 40 on SE Winona Ave; in downtown historic district. Int corridors. **Pets:** Accepted.
⟦ASK⟧ ⟦✕⟧ ⟦&⟧ ⟦💻⟧

**AAA** ▼▼▼ **Steinbrenner's Ramada Inn & Conference Center** SH
(352) 732-3131. **$79-$139.** 3810 NW Bonnie Heath Blvd. I-75, exit 354, just w. Ext corridors. **Pets:** Medium. $25 one-time fee/pet. Designated rooms, service with restrictions, supervision.
SAVE S X & 🖶 🖵 ❚❙ 🛁 ⊠

## OKEECHOBEE

**AAA** ▼ **Budget Inn** M
(863) 763-3185. **$69-$145.** 201 S Parrott Ave (US 441). US 98 and 441, just s of jct SR 70. Ext corridors. **Pets:** Accepted.
SAVE S X 🖶 🛁

**AAA** ▼ **Economy Inn** M
(863) 763-1148. **$89-$169, 3 day notice.** 507 N Parrott Ave. US 441, 0.3 mi n of jct SR 70. Ext corridors. **Pets:** Small. $10 daily fee/pet. Service with restrictions, supervision.
SAVE S X 🖶

## OLD TOWN

**AAA** ▼▼▼ **Suwanee Gables Motel** M
(352) 542-7752. **$79-$99, 7 day notice.** 27659 SE Hwy 19, Alt 27. US 19, 98 and 27A; 2 mi s of jct SR 349. Ext corridors. **Pets:** Accepted.
SAVE S X 🖶 🛁

## ORANGE CITY

**AAA** ▼▼▼ **Comfort Inn** M
(386) 775-7444. **$75-$225, 30 day notice.** 445 S Volusia Ave. I-4, exit 114, 2.8 mi w on SR 472, then 2 mi s on US 17-92. Ext corridors. **Pets:** Medium. $25 deposit/room, $15 daily fee/pet. Service with restrictions, crate.
SAVE S X 🖶 🖵 🛁

---

# ORLANDO METROPOLITAN AREA

## ALTAMONTE SPRINGS

▼▼▼▼ **Candlewood Suites** SH
(407) 767-5757. **$79-$99.** 644 Raymond Ave. I-4, exit 92, just w to Douglas Ave, 0.8 mi n to Central Pkwy, then just e. Int corridors. **Pets:** Accepted.
ASK S X &M 🗐 🖵 🖶 🖵 🛁

**AAA** ▼▼▼ **Days Inn Altamonte Springs** M
(407) 788-1411. **$50-$150, 3 day notice.** 150 S Westmonte Dr. I-4, exit 92, 0.3 mi w on SR 436, then just s. Ext corridors. **Pets:** Other species. $10 daily fee/pet. Designated rooms, no service, crate.
SAVE S X 🗐 🖵 🖶 🖵 🛁

**AAA** ▼▼▼▼ **Embassy Suites Orlando North** SH
(407) 834-2400. **$120-$220.** 225 E Altamonte Dr. I-4, exit 92, 0.3 mi e on SR 436, then just n on North Lake Blvd. Int corridors. **Pets:** Medium. $20 daily fee/pet. Designated rooms, service with restrictions.
SAVE X &M 🗐 🖵 🖶 🖵 ❚❙ 🛁 ⊠

**AAA** ▼▼▼▼ **Holiday Inn Orlando North/Altamonte Springs** SH ❀
(407) 862-4455. **$72-$109, 7 day notice.** 230 W SR 436. I-4, exit 92, just sw. Ext/int corridors. **Pets:** Medium. $40 one-time fee/room. Designated rooms, service with restrictions, supervision.
SAVE S X &M 🗐 🖵 🖶 🖵 ❚❙ 🛁

▼▼▼▼ **Homestead Studio Suites Hotel-Orlando/Altamonte Springs** SH
(407) 332-9300. **$49-$69.** 302 S North Lake Blvd. I-4, exit 92, just e, then 0.3 mi s. Int corridors. **Pets:** $25 daily fee/pet. Service with restrictions, supervision.
ASK S X &M 🗐 🖵 🖶 🖵

▼▼▼▼ **Residence Inn by Marriott** SH
(407) 788-7991. **$89-$289.** 270 Douglas Ave. I-4, exit 92, just w on SR 436, then just n. Ext corridors. **Pets:** Small. $75 one-time fee/pet. Service with restrictions, supervision.
ASK S X &M 🗐 🖵 🖶 🖵 🛁 ⊠

## DAVENPORT

**AAA** ▼▼▼ **Best Western Maingate South** SH
(863) 424-2596. **$69-$89.** 2425 Frontage Rd. I-4, exit 55, just s on US 27. Ext corridors. **Pets:** Small. $10 daily fee/room. Service with restrictions, supervision.
SAVE S X &M 🗐 🖶 🖵 🛁

▼▼▼▼ **Calabay Parc-The Florida Store** VH
(407) 846-1722. **$110-$215, 30 day notice.** 3479 W Vine St. I-4, exit 68, 3.5 mi s on SR 535, then 3.8 mi e on US 192. Ext corridors. **Pets:** Accepted.
ASK S X 🖶 🖵 🛁

▼▼▼▼ **Hampton Inn Orlando-S of Walt Disney Resort** SH
(863) 420-9898. **$79-$120.** 44117 Hwy 27. I-4, exit 55, just nw. Int corridors. **Pets:** Medium, other species. $25 daily fee/room. Designated rooms, service with restrictions.
ASK S X &M 🗐 🖵 🖶 🖵 🛁

**AAA** ▼▼▼ ▼▼▼ **Omni Orlando Resort at ChampionsGate** LH
(407) 390-6664. **$189-$269, 3 day notice.** 1500 Masters Blvd. I-4, exit 58, 0.3 mi w. Int corridors. **Pets:** Accepted.
SAVE X &M 🗐 🖵 🖶 🖵 ❚❙ ⊠

**AAA** ▼▼▼▼ **Regal Palms Resort at Highlands Reserve** CO
(863) 424-8411. **$119-$199, 3 day notice.** 2700 Sand Mine Rd. Jct US 192 and 27, 1 mi s. Ext corridors. **Pets:** Small. $300 deposit/room, $200 one-time fee/room. Designated rooms, no service, supervision.
SAVE S X 🖶 🖵 ❚❙ 🛁 ⊠

▼▼▼▼ **Regal Palms Resort at Highlands Reserve** VH
(863) 424-8411. **$149-$239, 3 day notice.** 2700 Sand Mine Rd. On US 192, 1 mi e of US 27. Ext corridors. **Pets:** Accepted.
ASK S 🖶 🖵 🛁 ⊠

▼▼▼▼ **Southern Dunes-The Florida Store** VH
(407) 846-1722. **$115-$215, 30 day notice.** 3479 W Vine St. I-4, exit 68, 3.5 mi s on SR 535, then 3.8 mi e on US 192. Ext corridors. **Pets:** Accepted.
ASK S X 🖶 🖵 ❚❙ 🛁 ⊠

▼▼ **Super 8 Motel Maingate South** SH
(863) 420-8888. **$39-$120.** 44199 Hwy 27. I-4, exit 55, 0.5 mi n. Ext corridors. **Pets:** Medium, other species. $10 daily fee/room. Designated rooms, service with restrictions, crate.
ASK S X 🗐 🖵 🖶 🖵 🛁

## KISSIMMEE

**AAA** ▼▼▼▼ **AmeriSuites (Orlando/Lake Buena Vista South)** SH
(407) 997-1300. **$99-$184.** 4991 Calypso Cay Way. I-4, exit 68, 3 mi s on SR 535. Int corridors. **Pets:** Medium. $10 daily fee/pet. Service with restrictions, supervision.
SAVE S X &M 🗐 🖵 🖶 🖵 🛁 ⊠

**Best Western Maingate East Hotel & Suites** SH
(407) 870-2000. **$89-$169.** 4018 W Vine St. I-4, exit 64A, 7 mi e on US 192. Ext corridors. **Pets:** Small. $50 one-time fee/room. Service with restrictions, supervision.

**Clear Creek-The Florida Store** VH
(407) 846-1722. **$110-$215, 30 day notice.** 3479 W Vine St. I-4, exit 68, 3.5 mi s on SR 535, then 3.8 mi e on US 192. Ext corridors. **Pets:** Accepted.

**Country Inn & Suites at Calypso Cay** SH
(407) 997-1400. **$99-$179.** 5001 Calypso Cay Way. I-4, exit 68, 3 mi s on SR 535; just s of Osceola Pkwy; just n of US 192. Int corridors. **Pets:** Medium. $10 daily fee/pet. Service with restrictions, supervision.

**County Hearth Inn & Suites** SH
(407) 396-6100. **$39-$79.** 6075 W Irlo Bronson Memorial Hwy. I-4, exit 64A, 1 mi e on US 192; between MM 8 and 9. Ext corridors. **Pets:** Accepted.

**Days Inn-Kissimmee** SH
(407) 846-7136. **$40-$100, 3 day notice.** 2095 E Irlo Bronson Memorial Hwy. Florida Tpke, exit 244, 0.3 mi w on US 192. Ext corridors. **Pets:** Accepted.

**Days Inn Maingate East** SH
(407) 396-7969. **$59-$129, 3 day notice.** 5840 W Irlo Bronson Memorial Hwy. I-4, exit 64A, 1 mi e on US 192. Ext corridors. **Pets:** Accepted.

**Fantasy World Club Villas** CO
(407) 396-1808. **$99-$195.** 5005 Kyngs Heath Rd. I-4, exit 64A, 3.5 mi e on US 192 and just n; at MM 11. Ext corridors. **Pets:** Accepted.

**Flamingo Inn** M
(407) 846-1935. **$29-$39, 3 day notice.** 801 E Vine St. 0.3 mi e of jct US 441 and 192 on US 192. Ext corridors. **Pets:** Small, dogs only. $8 daily fee/pet.

**Florida Pines-The Florida Store** VH
(407) 846-1722. **$115-$215, 30 day notice.** 3479 W Vine St. I-4, exit 68, 3.5 mi s on SR 535, then 3.8 mi e on US 192. Ext corridors. **Pets:** Accepted.

**Hampton Lakes-The Florida Store** VH
(407) 846-1722. **$90-$270, 30 day notice.** 3479 W Vine St. I-4, exit 68, 3.5 mi s on SR 535, then 3.8 mi e on US 192. Ext corridors. **Pets:** Accepted.

**Howard Johnson Enchantedland Hotel** SH
(407) 396-4343. **$49-$125.** 4985 W Irlo Bronson Memorial Hwy. I-4, exit 64A, 3.2 mi e on US 192. Ext corridors. **Pets:** Small. $10 daily fee/pet. Designated rooms, service with restrictions, crate.

**Howard Johnson Express Inn Parkside** SH
(407) 396-7100. **$39-$59, 7 day notice.** 4311 W Vine St/W Hwy 192. I-4, exit 64A, 3.5 mi w of jct US 17-92 and 441. Ext corridors. **Pets:** $10 daily fee/room. Designated rooms, service with restrictions, supervision.

**Howard Johnson Maingate Resort West** SH
(407) 396-4500. **$39-$129.** 8660 W Irlo Bronson Memorial Hwy. I-4, exit 64B, 5.6 mi w on SR 192. Ext corridors. **Pets:** Small, other species. $35 one-time fee/room. Designated rooms, service with restrictions, supervision.

**Indian Creek-The Florida Store** VH
(407) 846-1722. **$110-$215, 30 day notice.** 3479 W Vine St. I-4, exit 68, 3.5 mi s on SR 535, then 3.8 mi e on US 192. Ext corridors. **Pets:** Accepted.

**Lake Marion Resort Community** CO
(863) 427-3911. **$70-$158, 3 day notice.** 687 Lake Marion Golf Dr.. Ext corridors. **Pets:** Medium. $50 deposit/pet. Service with restrictions, supervision.

**La Quinta Inn & Suites Kissimmee (Orlando Maingate)** SH
(407) 997-1700. **$99-$179.** 3484 Polynesian Isle Blvd. I-4, exit 68, s on SR 535, then just e. Int corridors. **Pets:** Medium, other species. $25 deposit/room. Service with restrictions.

**MainStay Suites Maingate** SH
(407) 396-2056. **$79-$129.** 4786 W Irlo Bronson Memorial Hwy. I-4, exit 64A, 4 mi e on US 192; 4.8 mi w of jct US 17-92 and 441. Ext corridors. **Pets:** Medium, other species. $10 daily fee/room. Service with restrictions.

**Masters Inn-Kissimmee** SH
(407) 396-4020. **$39-$59, 3 day notice.** 5367 W Irlo Bronson Memorial Hwy. I-4, exit 25, 2.5 mi e on US 192. Ext corridors. **Pets:** Accepted.

**Masters Inn-Main Gate** SH
(407) 396-7743. **$39-$150, 3 day notice.** 2945 Entry Point Blvd. I-4, exit 25, 2.5 mi w on US 192; 1 mi w of Disney World main gate. Ext corridors. **Pets:** Accepted.

**Motel 6-#0436** SH
(407) 396-6422. **$39-$49.** 7455 W Irlo Bronson Memorial Hwy. I-4, exit 64B, 1.3 mi w on US 192. Ext corridors. **Pets:** Accepted.

**Motel 6-#0464** M
(407) 396-6333. **$39-$49.** 5731 W Hwy 192. I-4, exit 64A, 2 mi e. Ext corridors. **Pets:** Accepted.

**The Palms Hotel and Villas** SH
(407) 396-2229. **$87-$140, 3 day notice.** 3100 Parkway Blvd. I-4, exit 64A, 0.3 mi e on US 192, then 0.5 mi n. Ext/int corridors. **Pets:** Accepted.

**Quality Suites Maingate East** SH
(407) 396-8040. **$89-$299, 3 day notice.** 5876 W Irlo Bronson Memorial Hwy. I-4, exit 64A, 1 mi e on US 192. Ext corridors. **Pets:** Small, dogs only. $10 daily fee/pet. Designated rooms, service with restrictions, crate.

**Radisson Resort WorldGate** LH
(407) 396-1400. **$89-$159, 3 day notice.** 3011 Maingate Ln. US 192, 2.8 mi w of I-4, 1 mi w of Disney World main gate access road. Int corridors. **Pets:** Medium, other species. $75 one-time fee/room. Designated rooms, service with restrictions crate.

**AAA** ▼▼▼ **Ramada Inn Resort Eastgate** SH ❀
(407) 396-1111. **$49-$129.** 5150 W Irlo Bronson Memorial Hwy. I-4, exit 64A, 2.8 mi e on US 192. Int corridors. **Pets:** Medium, other species. $10 daily fee/pet. Designated rooms, no service, supervision.
SAVE SD X 🐾 🔧 🔲 🍴 ⬌ ✕

**AAA** ▼▼▼◆ **Ramada Plaza Hotel and Inn Gateway** LH
(407) 396-4400. **$69-$119.** 7470 W Irlo Bronson Memorial Hwy. I-4, exit 64B, 2.3 mi w on US 192; 1 mi w of Disney World main gate. Ext/int corridors. **Pets:** Small. $25 one-time fee/room. Designated rooms, service with restrictions, crate.
SAVE SD X 🐾 🔧 🔲 🍴 ⬌ ✕

**AAA** ▼▼▼ **Red Roof Inn** SH
(407) 396-0065. **$40-$85.** 4970 Kyngs Heath Rd. I-4, exit 64A, 3.6 mi e on US 192; jct SR 535. Ext corridors. **Pets:** Accepted.
SAVE X 🔧 ⬌

**AAA** ▼▼▼ **Rodeway Inn Maingate** SH
(407) 396-4300. **$35-$90, 7 day notice.** 5995 W Irlo Bronson Memorial Hwy. I-4, exit 64A, 1 mi e. Ext corridors. **Pets:** Accepted.
ASK SD X 🐾 🔧 🔲 ⬌

**AAA** ▼▼▼◆ **Seralago Hotel & Suites Main Gate East** SH ❀
(407) 396-4488. **$59-$99.** 5678 W Irlo Bronson Memorial Hwy. I-4, exit 64A; between MM 9 and 10. Ext corridors. **Pets:** Small, dogs only. $25 one-time fee/room. Designated rooms.
SAVE SD X 🐾M 🔧 🔲 🍴 ⬌ ✕

**AAA** ▼▼▼ **Travelodge Hotel Maingate East** SH
(407) 396-4222. **$49-$129.** 5711 W Irlo Bronson Memorial Hwy. I-4, exit 64A, 2 mi e on US 192. Int corridors. **Pets:** Accepted.
SAVE SD X 🐾 🔧 🔲 🍴 ⬌ ✕

**AAA** ▼▼▼ **Travelodge Kissimmee Heritage Park** SH
(407) 846-2221. **$59-$129.** 2261 E Irlo Bronson Memorial Hwy. US 192 and 441 at Florida Tpke, exit 244. Ext corridors. **Pets:** Accepted.
SAVE SD X 🐾 🔧 🔲 ⬌ ✕

▼▼▼ **Ventura Resort Rentals-Kissimmee** VH
(407) 273-8770. **$83-$196, 91 day notice.** 5946 Curry Ford Rd. 0.6 mi e of SR 436. Ext corridors. **Pets:** Accepted.
ASK SD 🐾 🔧 🔲 ⬌

**AAA** ▼▼▼ **Westgate Inn** SH
(863) 424-2621. **$39-$65.** 9200 W US Hwy 192. I-4, exit 64B, 6 mi w. Ext corridors. **Pets:** Accepted.
SAVE SD X 🔧 🔲 ⬌

## LADY LAKE

**AAA** ▼▼▼◆ **Comfort Suites** SH
(352) 259-6578. **$99-$150.** 1202 Avenida Central N. Just n on US 441. Int corridors. **Pets:** Medium, other species. $35 one-time fee/pet. Designated rooms, service with restrictions, supervision.
SAVE SD X 🔧 🔲 ⬌

**AAA** ▼▼▼◆ **Holiday Inn Express Hotel & Suites** SH
(352) 750-3888. **$94-$98.** 1205 Avenida Central N. Just n on US 441. Int corridors. **Pets:** Accepted.
SAVE SD X 🔧 🔲 ⬌

## LAKE BUENA VISTA

**AAA** ▼▼▼◆ **Buena Vista Suites** SH
(407) 239-8588. **$109-$159.** 8203 World Center Dr. I-4, exit 67, 1.3 mi e; jct SR 535 and 536. Int corridors. **Pets:** Accepted.
SAVE SD X 🐾 🛠 🔧 🔲 🍴 ⬌ ✕

**AAA** ▼▼▼◆ **Comfort Inn Lake Buena Vista** SH ❀
(407) 996-7300. **$59-$89.** 8442 Palm Pkwy. I-4, exit 68, 0.6 mi n on SR 535, then 0.5 mi e. Ext corridors. **Pets:** Medium, other species. $10 daily fee/pet. Service with restrictions.
SAVE SD X 🐾M 🔧 🔧 🔧 🔲 🍴 ⬌

**AAA** ▼▼▼ **Days Inn Lake Buena Vista Hotel** SH
(407) 239-4441. **$69-$129.** 12799 Apopka-Vineland Rd. I-4, exit 68, just n. Int corridors. **Pets:** Accepted.
SAVE SD X 🐾 🔧 🔲 ⬌

▼▼▼ **Embassy Suites Hotel-Lake Buena Vista Resort** SH
(407) 239-1144. **$109-$229, 3 day notice.** 8100 Lake Ave. I-4, exit 68, 0.6 mi n on SR 535, 1 mi e on Palm Pkwy, then just se. Ext/int corridors. **Pets:** Accepted.
ASK X 🐾M 🔧 🛠 🔧 🔲 🍴 ⬌ ✕

**AAA** ▼▼▼ **Holiday Inn-SunSpree Resort-Lake Buena Vista** LH
(407) 239-4500. **$79-$129.** 13351 SR 535. I-4, exit 68, 0.3 mi se. Ext corridors. **Pets:** Accepted.
SAVE SD X 🐾M 🔧 🛠 🔧 🔲 🍴 ⬌ ✕

**AAA** ▼▼▼◆ **Sheraton Safari Hotel** SH
(407) 239-0444. **$109-$249, 3 day notice.** 12205 Apopka-Vineland Rd. I-4, exit 68, 0.5 mi n on SR 535. Ext/int corridors. **Pets:** Accepted.
SAVE SD X 🐾M 🔧 🛠 🔧 🔲 🍴 ⬌ ✕

**AAA** ▼▼▼◆ **Westgate Blue Tree at Lake Buena Vista** SH
(407) 597-2200. **$89-$189, 7 day notice.** 12007 Cypress Run Rd. I-4, exit 68, 0.5 mi n on SR 535, just n on Apopka-Vineland Rd, then just e on Vining's Way Blvd. Ext corridors. **Pets:** Accepted.
SAVE 🐾 🛠 🔧 🔲 ⬌ ✕

## LAKE MARY

▼▼▼ **Candlewood Suites Lake Mary-Heathrow** SH
(407) 585-3000. **$69-$139.** 1130 Greenwood Blvd. I-4, exit 98, just e to Lake Emma Rd, 0.5 mi s to Greenwood Blvd, then 0.6 mi w. Int corridors. **Pets:** Large, other species. $150 one-time fee/room. Service with restrictions.
ASK SD X 🐾 🛠 🔧 🔲 ⬌

▼▼▼ **Homestead Studio Suites-Orlando/Lake Mary** SH
(407) 829-2332. **$49-$79.** 1040 Greenwood Blvd. I-4, exit 98, 0.5 mi s on Lake Emma Rd; in Commerce Park. Int corridors. **Pets:** $25 daily fee/pet. Service with restrictions, supervision.
ASK SD X 🐾M 🐾 🛠 🔧 🔲 ⬌

**AAA** ▼▼▼◆ **Homewood Suites by Hilton** SH
(407) 805-9111. **$99-$149.** 755 Currency Cir. I-4, exit 98, just ne via Lake Mary Blvd and Primera. Int corridors. **Pets:** Accepted.
SAVE X 🐾M 🐾 🛠 🔧 🔲 ⬌

**AAA** ▼▼▼◆ **La Quinta Inn & Suites Orlando (Lake Mary)** SH
(407) 805-9901. **$89-$109.** 1060 Greenwood Blvd. I-4, exit 98, just se via Lake Mary Blvd. Int corridors. **Pets:** Medium. Service with restrictions.
SAVE X 🐾M 🐾 🛠 🔧 🔲 ⬌

## LEESBURG

**AAA** ▼▼▼◆ **GuestHouse International Inn & Suites** SH
(352) 787-1210. **$49-$99.** 1308 N 14th St. Jct US 27 and 441. Ext corridors. **Pets:** Other species. $15 one-time fee/room. Service with restrictions.
SAVE SD X 🐾 🔧 🔲 ⬌

**AAA** ▼▼▼ **Super 8 Motel** SH
(352) 787-6363. **$36-$106.** 1392 North Blvd W. Jct US 27 and 441. Int corridors. **Pets:** Medium, other species. $10 daily fee/pet. Service with restrictions, supervision.
SAVE SD X 🐾M 🐾 🔧 ⬌

# LONGWOOD

▼▼▼ **Comfort Inn & Conference Center** SH
(407) 862-4000. **$79-$149.** 2025 W SR 434. I-4, exit 94, just nw. Ext corridors. **Pets:** Accepted.

[ASK] [S▾] [✕] [◇] [🛏] [▣] [🍴] [≈]

# MAITLAND

AAA ▼▼▼ **Homewood Suites by Hilton Orlando North** SH
(407) 875-8777. **$99-$339.** 290 Southhall Ln. I-4, exit 90, just w, then just s on Lake Destiny. Int corridors. **Pets:** $75 one-time fee/room. Service with restrictions, crate.

[SAVE] [S▾] [✕] [&M] [◇] [☼] [🛏] [▣] [≈]

# OCOEE

▼▼▼ **Best Western Turnpike West-Orlando** SH
(407) 656-5050. **$69-$94.** 10945 W Colonial Dr. I-4, exit 84, 10 mi w on SR 50; 0.5 mi e of Florida Tpke, exit 267B. Ext corridors. **Pets:** Accepted.

[ASK] [S▾] [✕] [◇] [☼] [🛏] [▣] [🍴] [≈]

▼◆▼ **Red Roof Inn Orlando West** SH
(407) 347-0140. **$59-$84.** 11241 W Colonial Dr. I-4, exit 84, 10 mi w on SR 50; 0.6 mi e of Florida Tpke, exit 267. Int corridors. **Pets:** Accepted.

[ASK] [S▾] [✕] [◇] [🛏] [▣] [≈]

# ORLANDO

▼▼▼ **Americas Best Value Inn & Suites** SH
(407) 351-4410. **$59-$99.** 5858 International Dr. I-4, exit 75A, just s on (SR 435 (Kirkman Rd), then just w. Ext corridors. **Pets:** Accepted.

[ASK] [S▾] [✕] [◇] [☼] [🛏] [▣] [≈]

AAA ▼▼▼ **AmeriSuites (Orlando Airport/Northeast)** SH
(407) 240-3939. **$90-$200.** 7500 Augusta National Dr. SR 528 (Bee Line Expwy), exit 11, 0.5 mi n on SR 436, just e on TG Lee Blvd, then just s. Int corridors. **Pets:** Small. $10 daily fee/pet. Service with restrictions, supervision.

[SAVE] [S▾] [✕] [◇] [☼] [🛏] [▣] [≈]

AAA ▼◆▼ **AmeriSuites (Orlando Airport/Northwest)** SH
(407) 816-7800. **$89-$199.** 5435 Forbes Pl. SR 528 (Bee Line Expwy), exit 11, 0.5 mi n on SR 436, then just w. Int corridors. **Pets:** Small, other species. $10 daily fee/pet. Designated rooms, service with restrictions, supervision.

[SAVE] [S▾] [✕] [&M] [◇] [☼] [🛏] [▣] [≈]

AAA ▼▼▼ **AmeriSuites (Orlando/Universal)** SH
(407) 351-0627. **$139-$179.** 5895 Caravan Ct. I-4, exit 75B, 0.6 mi ne. Int corridors. **Pets:** Accepted.

[SAVE] [S▾] [✕] [&M] [◇] [☼] [🛏] [▣] [≈]

AAA ▼▼▼ **Baymont Inn & Suites Orlando South** SH
(407) 240-0500. **$85-$105.** 2051 Consulate Dr. US 17-92 and 441, just s of SR 528 (Bee Line Expwy); off Florida Tpke, exit 254. Int corridors. **Pets:** Medium. Service with restrictions.

[SAVE] [✕] [◇] [☼] [🛏] [▣] [≈]

AAA ▼▼▼ **Best Western Orlando West** SH
(407) 841-8600. **$59-$125, 14 day notice.** 2014 W Colonial Dr. I-4, exit 84, 1.5 mi w on SR 50; 0.4 mi e of SR 423. Int corridors. **Pets:** Accepted.

[SAVE] [S▾] [✕] [◇] [☼] [🛏] [▣] [🍴] [≈]

AAA ▼▼▼ **Comfort Inn-North** SH
(407) 629-4000. **$63-$69.** 830 Lee Rd. I-4, exit 88, 0.4 mi w on SR 423. Int corridors. **Pets:** Accepted.

[SAVE] [S▾] [✕] [◇] [🛏] [▣] [≈] [✕]

▼▼▼ **Comfort Inn Universal Studios** SH
(407) 363-7886. **$69-$89.** 6101 Sand Lake Rd. I-4, exit 74A, 0.3 mi e on SR 482 (Sand Lake Rd), at Universal Blvd. Ext corridors. **Pets:** Accepted.

[ASK] [S▾] [✕] [&M] [◇] [☼] [🛏] [▣] [≈]

AAA ▼▼▼ **Comfort Suites Orlando** SH 🐾
(407) 351-5050. **$69-$129.** 9350 Turkey Lake Rd. I-4, exit 74A, just w on SR 482 (Sand Lake Rd), then 1.5 mi s. Ext corridors. **Pets:** Large, other species. $10 daily fee/pet. Service with restrictions, crate.

[SAVE] [S▾] [✕] [&M] [◇] [☼] [🛏] [▣] [≈]

AAA ▼▼▼ **Days Inn North of Universal** SH
(407) 841-3731. **$40-$150.** 2500 W 33rd St. I-4, exit 79, just e. Ext corridors. **Pets:** Accepted.

[SAVE] [S▾] [✕] [◇] [☼] [🛏] [🍴] [≈]

▼▼ **Extended StayAmerica-Orlando Convention Center/Sea World/Disney Area** SH
(407) 352-3454. **Call for rates.** 6451 Westwood Blvd. I-4, exit 72, just e on SR 528 (Bee Line Expwy) to exit 1 (International Dr), just s, then just w. Int corridors. **Pets:** Accepted.

[✕] [🛏] [▣]

▼▼▼ **Extended Stay Deluxe (Orlando/Southpark)** SH
(407) 248-8010. **$85-$119.** 8687 Commodity Cir. Just sw of jct SR 423 (John Young Pkwy) and 482 (Sand Lake Rd). Int corridors. **Pets:** $25 daily fee/pet. Service with restrictions, supervision.

[ASK] [S▾] [✕] [◇] [☼] [🛏] [▣] [≈]

AAA ▼▼▼ **Hawthorn Suites Orlando Airport** SH 🐾
(407) 438-2121. **$89-$149.** 7450 Augusta National Dr. SR 528 (Bee Line Expwy), exit 11, 0.5 mi n on SR 436, just e, then just s. Int corridors. **Pets:** Medium, dogs only. $20 daily fee/room. Designated rooms, service with restrictions, supervision.

[SAVE] [S▾] [✕] [&M] [◇] [☼] [🛏] [▣] [≈] [✕]

AAA ▼▼▼ **Holiday Inn & Suites At Universal Orlando** SH
(407) 351-3333. **$89-$169, 3 day notice.** 5905 S Kirkman Rd. I-4, exit 75B, 0.5 mi n on SR 435 (Kirkman Rd). Int corridors. **Pets:** Accepted.

[SAVE] [S▾] [✕] [&M] [◇] [☼] [🛏] [▣] [🍴] [≈]

▼◆▼ **Holiday Inn-International Drive Resort** SH
(407) 351-3500. **$89-$159.** 6515 International Dr. I-4, exit 74A, just e on SR 482 (Sand Lake Rd), then 0.5 mi n. Ext/int corridors. **Pets:** $35 daily fee/room. Service with restrictions, crate.

[ASK] [✕] [&M] [◇] [☼] [🛏] [▣] [≈] [✕]

▼▼▼ **Homestead Studio Suites Hotel-Orlando/South** SH
(407) 352-5577. **$49-$74.** 4101 Equity Row. Just sw of jct SR 423 (John Young Pkwy) and 482 (Sand Lake Rd). Int corridors. **Pets:** $25 daily fee/pet. Service with restrictions, supervision.

[ASK] [S▾] [✕] [&M] [◇] [☼] [🛏] [▣]

▼▼ **Howard Johnson Inn-International Drive** SH
(407) 351-2900. **$89-$125.** 6603 International Dr. I-4, exit 74A, just e on SR 482 (Sand Lake Rd), then 0.4 m n. Ext corridors. **Pets:** Small. $25 daily fee/room. Designated rooms, no service, supervision.

[ASK] [✕] [◇] [🛏] [▣] [≈]

▼▼ **I-Drive Inn** SH
(407) 351-4430. **$69-$109.** 6323 International Dr. I-4, exit 74A, just e on SR 482 (Sand Lake Rd), then 0.7 mi n. Int corridors. **Pets:** Accepted.

[ASK] [S▾] [✕] [&M] [◇] [☼] [🛏] [▣] [≈]

AAA ▼▼▼ **La Quinta Inn & Suites Orlando (Airport North)** SH
(407) 240-5000. **$79-$95.** 7160 N Frontage Rd. SR 528 (Bee Line Expwy), exit 11, 0.5 mi n on SR 436, then just w. Int corridors. **Pets:** Medium. Service with restrictions.

[SAVE] [✕] [&M] [◇] [☼] [🛏] [▣] [≈]

◬ ▽◆▽◆▽ **La Quinta Inn & Suites Orlando (Convention Center)** SH
(407) 345-1365. **$89-$109.** 8504 Universal Blvd. I-4, exit 74A, 0.5 mi e on SR 482 (Sand Lake Rd), then 0.5 mi s. Int corridors. **Pets:** Medium. Service with restrictions.
[SAVE] [✕] [&M] [🐾] [🎛] [🖥] [💻] [➰]

◬ ▽◆▽◆▽ **La Quinta Inn & Suites Orlando (U.C.F.)** SH
(407) 737-6075. **$79-$95.** 11805 Research Pkwy. Just se of jct University Blvd and SR 434 (Alafaya Tr). Int corridors. **Pets:** Medium. Service with restrictions.
[SAVE] [✕] [&M] [🐾] [🎛] [🖥] [💻] [➰]

◬ ▽◆▽◆▽ **La Quinta Inn Orlando (Airport West)** SH
(407) 857-9215. **$69-$89.** 7931 Daetwyler Dr. SR 528 (Bee Line Expwy), exit 9 (Tradeport), via McCoy Rd. Ext corridors. **Pets:** Medium. Service with restrictions.
[SAVE] [🐾] [💻] [➰]

◬ ▽◆▽◆▽ **La Quinta Inn Orlando (International Drive)** SH
(407) 351-1660. **$75-$125.** 8300 Jamaican Ct. I-4, exit 74A, just e on SR 482 (Sand Lake Rd), then just s on International Dr. Ext corridors. **Pets:** Medium. Service with restrictions.
[SAVE] [✕] [&M] [🐾] [🎛] [🖥] [💻] [➰] [✕]

◬ ▽◆▽◆▽ **La Quinta Inn Orlando-Winter Park** SH
(407) 645-5600. **$69-$249.** 626 Lee Rd. I-4, exit 88 (Lee Rd), just w on SR 438. Int corridors. **Pets:** Small. Designated rooms, service with restrictions, supervision.
[SAVE] [S&] [✕] [🐾] [🎛] [🖥] [💻] [🍴] [➰]

▽◆▽◆▽ **Masters Inn International Drive** SH
(407) 345-1172. **$49-$120, 3 day notice.** 8222 Jamaican Ct. I-4, exit 74A, e on SR 482 (Sand Lake Rd), then just s on International Dr. Ext corridors. **Pets:** Accepted.
[SAVE] [S&] [✕] [🐾] [🖥] [➰]

▽◆▽ **Motel 6 Orlando-International Drive #1079** SH
(407) 351-6500. **$45-$61.** 5909 American Way. I-4, exit 75A, just w of SR 435, then just n. Int corridors. **Pets:** Accepted.
[S&] [✕] [🐾] [➰]

▽◆▽ **Motel 6 Orlando-Winter Park #791** M
(407) 647-1444. **$45-$57.** 5300 Adanson Rd. I-4, exit 88, 0.5 mi w on SR 423 (Lee Rd). Ext corridors. **Pets:** Accepted.
[S&] [➰]

▽◆▽ **Quality Inn International** SH 🐾
(407) 996-1600. **$59-$99.** 7600 International Dr. I-4, exit 74A, just e on SR 482 (Sand Lake Rd), then just n. Ext corridors. **Pets:** Medium. $10 daily fee/pet. Service with restrictions, crate.
[ASK] [S&] [✕] [&M] [🐾] [🎛] [🖥] [💻] [🍴] [➰]

▽◆▽ **Quality Inn Plaza** SH
(407) 996-8585. **$59-$99.** 9000 International Dr. I-4, exit 74A, just e on SR 482 (Sand Lake Rd), then 1 mi s. Ext corridors. **Pets:** Medium, other species. $10 daily fee/pet. Designated rooms, service with restrictions.
[ASK] [S&] [✕] [&M] [🐾] [🎛] [🖥] [💻] [🍴] [➰] [✕]

◬ ▽◆▽ **Red Horse Inn** SH
(407) 351-4100. **$59-$119, 3 day notice.** 5825 International Dr. I-4, exit 75A, just w. Ext corridors. **Pets:** Accepted.
[SAVE] [S&] [✕] [🐾] [🖥] [💻] [➰]

▽◆▽ **Red Roof Inn Convention Center** SH
(407) 352-1507. **$46-$100.** 9922 Hawaiian Ct. I-4, exit 72, 0.9 mi e on SR 528 (Bee Line Expwy) to exit 1, then just n. Ext corridors. **Pets:** Accepted.
[✕] [&M] [🐾] [🎛] [🖥] [➰]

▽◆▽◆▽ **Residence Inn by Marriott Orlando Convention Center** SH
(407) 226-0288. **$89-$189.** 8800 Universal Blvd. I-4, exit 74A, 0.5 mi e on SR 482 (Sand Lake Rd), then 0.8 mi s. Int corridors. **Pets:** Accepted.
[ASK] [S&] [✕] [&M] [🐾] [🎛] [🖥] [💻] [➰] [✕]

▽◆▽◆▽ **Residence Inn by Marriott/Orlando East** SH 🐾
(407) 513-9000. **$159-$209.** 11651 University Blvd. 2.2 mi e of SR 417 on University Blvd; just w of SR 434 (Alafaya Tr). Int corridors. **Pets:** Medium. $150 one-time fee/room. Service with restrictions, crate.
[ASK] [S&] [✕] [🐾] [🎛] [🖥] [💻] [➰] [✕]

◬ ▽◆▽◆▽ **Residence Inn by Marriott-Orlando International Dr** SH
(407) 345-0117. **$119-$229.** 7975 Canada Ave. I-4, exit 74A, just e on SR 482 (Sand Lake Rd). Ext corridors. **Pets:** Accepted.
[SAVE] [S&] [✕] [&M] [🐾] [🎛] [🖥] [💻] [➰] [✕]

◬ ▽◆▽◆▽ **Residence Inn by Marriott SeaWorld International Center** SH
(407) 313-3600. **$79-$145.** 11000 Westwood Blvd. I-4, exit 72. Int corridors. **Pets:** Medium, other species. $75 one-time fee/room. Service with restrictions.
[SAVE] [S&] [✕] [&M] [🐾] [🎛] [🖥] [💻] [🍴] [➰] [✕]

▽◆▽ **Rodeway Inn International** SH
(407) 996-4444. **$49-$95.** 6327 International Dr. I-4, exit 74A, just e on SR 482 (Sand Lake Rd), then 0.7 mi n. Ext/int corridors. **Pets:** Accepted.
[ASK] [S&] [✕] [&M] [🐾] [🎛] [🖥] [💻] [🍴] [➰]

◬ ▽◆▽◆▽ **Sheraton Studio City Hotel** SH
(407) 351-2100. **$79-$299, 3 day notice.** 5905 International Dr. I-4, exit 75A, just w of SR 435 (Kirkman Rd). Int corridors. **Pets:** Large. $50 one-time fee/room. Designated rooms, service with restrictions, supervision.
[SAVE] [S&] [✕] [🐾] [🖥] [💻] [🍴] [➰] [✕]

◬ ▽◆▽◆▽ **Sheraton Suites Orlando Airport** SH
(407) 240-5555. **$99-$179.** 7550 Augusta National Dr. 2 mi n of airport terminal via SR 436 and TG Lee Blvd. Int corridors. **Pets:** Accepted.
[SAVE] [S&] [✕] [&M] [🐾] [🎛] [🖥] [💻] [🍴] [➰]

▽◆▽ **Sheraton World Resort** LH
(407) 352-1100. **$259-$310, 3 day notice.** 10100 International Dr. I-4, exit 72, just s on International Dr; SR 528 (Bee Line Expwy), exit 1, just e. Ext/int corridors. **Pets:** Accepted.
[ASK] [S&] [✕] [&M] [🐾] [🎛] [🖥] [💻] [🍴] [➰] [✕]

▽◆▽ **StudioPlus-Orlando Convention Center/Sea World/ Disney Area** SH
(407) 351-1982. **Call for rates.** 6443 Westwood Blvd. I-4, exit 72, just e on SR 528 (Bee Line Expwy) to exit 1 (International Dr), just s, then just w. Int corridors. **Pets:** Accepted.
[✕] [🐾] [🖥] [💻] [➰]

▽◆▽◆▽ **TownePlace Suites by Marriott Orlando East/UCF** SH
(407) 243-6100. **$109-$139.** 11801 High Tech Ave. 2.2 mi e of SR 417 on University Blvd. Int corridors. **Pets:** Accepted.
[ASK] [S&] [✕] [🐾] [🎛] [🖥] [💻]

◬ ▽◆▽◆▽ **Universal's Hard Rock Hotel, A Loews Hotel** LH
(407) 503-2000. **$229-$466, 5 day notice.** 5800 Universal Blvd. I-4, exit 75A, 1 mi n, follow signs. Int corridors. **Pets:** Accepted.
[SAVE] [✕] [&M] [🐾] [🎛] [🖥] [💻] [🍴] [➰] [✕]

**Universal's Portofino Bay Hotel, A Loews Hotel** LH
(407) 503-1000. **$264-$488, 5 day notice.** 5601 Universal Blvd. I-4, exit 74B westbound; exit 75A eastbound, 1 mi n, follow signs. Int corridors. **Pets:** Accepted.

[SAVE] [X] [&M] [⌀] [ɛˣ] [⬛] [⬜] [¶¶] [⇌] [X]

**Universal's Royal Pacific Resort, A Loews Hotel** LH
(407) 503-3000. **$199-$428, 5 day notice.** 6300 Hollywood Way. I-4, exit 74B, just n. Int corridors. **Pets:** Accepted.

[SAVE] [X] [⌀] [⬛] [⬜] [¶¶] [⇌] [X]

**Ventura Resort Rentals Orlando** CO
(407) 273-8770. **$64-$152, 91 day notice.** 5946 Curry Ford Rd. 0.6 mi e of SR 436. Ext corridors. **Pets:** Accepted.

[ASK] [Sʒ] [⌀] [⬛] [⬜] [⇌] [X]

**Westin Grand Bohemian** LH
(407) 313-9000. **$239-$439.** 325 S Orange Ave. Downtown. Int corridors. **Pets:** Accepted.

[SAVE] [X] [&M] [⌀] [ɛˣ] [⬜] [¶¶] [⇌] [X]

**Wyndham Orlando Resort** LH
(407) 351-2420. **$129-$195, 3 day notice.** 8001 International Dr. I-4, exit 74A, just e at SR 482 (Sand Lake Rd). Ext/int corridors. **Pets:** Accepted.

[SAVE] [X] [&M] [⌀] [ɛˣ] [⬛] [⬜] [¶¶] [⇌] [X]

## ST. CLOUD

**Budget Inn of St Cloud** M
(407) 892-2858. **$45-$90, 3 day notice.** 602 13th St. On US 192, 0.5 mi e of The Water Tower, 2 mi w of jct CR 15. Ext corridors. **Pets:** Small, dogs only. $10 daily fee/pet. Service with restrictions, supervision.

[SAVE] [Sʒ] [X] [⌀] [⬛]

## TAVARES

**Budget Inn** M
(352) 343-4666. **$49-$59, 7 day notice.** 101 W Burleigh Blvd. On US 441, 0.3 mi e of jct SR 19 S. Ext corridors. **Pets:** Accepted.

[ASK] [Sʒ] [X] [⬛] [⇌]

---

# END METROPOLITAN AREA

---

# ORMOND BEACH

**Comfort Inn Interstate** SH
(386) 672-8621. **$250, 7 day notice.** 1567 N US 1. I-95, exit 273, just e. Ext corridors. **Pets:** Small. $10 daily fee/pet. Designated rooms, no service, supervision.

[SAVE] [Sʒ] [X] [⌀] [⬛] [⬜] [⇌]

**Comfort Inn On The Beach** M
(386) 677-8550. **$85-$225, 10 day notice.** 507 S Atlantic Ave. On SR A1A, 1 mi s of jct SR 40. Ext corridors. **Pets:** Very small. $15 daily fee/pet. Service with restrictions, supervision.

[SAVE] [Sʒ] [X] [⬛] [⬜] [⇌]

**Jameson Inn** SH
(386) 672-3675. **$54-$104.** 175 Interchange Blvd. I-95, exit 268, just w, then just s. Int corridors. **Pets:** Very small, other species. $10 daily fee/room. Service with restrictions, supervision.

[ASK] [X] [&M] [⌀] [ɛˣ] [⬛] [⬜] [⇌]

# OSPREY

**Ramada Inn-Sarasota South** M
(941) 966-2121. **$129-$139.** 1660 S Tamiami Tr. On US 41, 1.8 mi n of jct SR 681. Ext/int corridors. **Pets:** Accepted.

[ASK] [Sʒ] [X] [⬛] [⬜] [¶¶] [⇌]

# PALM BAY

**Jameson Inn** SH
(321) 725-2952. **$54-$104.** 890 Palm Bay Rd. I-95, exit 176. Int corridors. **Pets:** Very small, other species. $10 daily fee/room. Service with restrictions, supervision.

[ASK] [X] [&M] [⌀] [ɛˣ] [⬛] [⬜] [⇌]

# PALM BEACH

**Brazilian Court Hotel** SH
(561) 655-7740. **$250-$3000, 3 day notice.** 301 Australian Ave. From Royal Palm Way (SR 204), s on Cocoanut Row, 2 blks to Australian Ave, then just e; corner of Hibiscus and Australian aves. Int corridors. **Pets:** Accepted.

[ASK] [Sʒ] [X] [ɛˣ] [⬛] [¶¶] [⇌] [X]

**The Chesterfield Hotel** SH
(561) 659-5800. **$140-$1600, 3 day notice.** 363 Cocoanut Row. Just w of SR A1A; at Australian Ave and Cocoanut Row. Int corridors. **Pets:** Accepted.

[SAVE] [Sʒ] [X] [⌀] [⬛] [¶¶] [⇌] [X]

**The Four Seasons Resort, Palm Beach** LH
(561) 582-2800. **$295-$785, 7 day notice.** 2800 S Ocean Blvd. SR A1A, 0.3 mi n of jct SR 802. Int corridors. **Pets:** Accepted.

[SAVE] [X] [&M] [⌀] [ɛˣ] [⬛] [⬜] [¶¶] [⇌] [X]

**Heart of Palm Beach Hotel** SH
(561) 655-5600. **$99-$1000, 3 day notice.** 160 Royal Palm Way. Just e of SR A1A; center. Int corridors. **Pets:** Accepted.

[ASK] [X] [⌀] [⬛] [⬜] [⇌]

# PALM BEACH SHORES

**Best Western Seaspray Inn** SH
(561) 844-0233. **$100-$230, 14 day notice.** 123 S Ocean Ave. On Singer Island; 0.5 mi s of SR A1A. Int corridors. **Pets:** Accepted.

[SAVE] [X] [⬛] [⬜] [¶¶] [⇌]

# PALM COAST

**Microtel Inn & Suites** SH
(386) 445-8976. **$57-$159, 30 day notice.** 16 Kingswood Dr. I-95, exit 289, 0.5 mi se via Old Kings Rd. Int corridors. **Pets:** Very small, dogs only. $25 one-time fee/pet. Designated rooms, service with restrictions, supervision.

[ASK] [X] [&M] [ɛˣ] [⬛] [⬜] [⇌]

**Palm Coast Villas** M ✿
(386) 445-3525. **$54-$79.** 5454 N Oceanshore Blvd. I-95, exit 289, 2.8 mi e to SR A1A, then 1.8 mi n. Ext corridors. **Pets:** Other species. $5 daily fee/pet. Designated rooms, no service, supervision.

[SAVE] [Sʒ] [X] [⬛] [⬜] [⇌]

# PANAMA CITY

**Days Inn Bayside** SH
(850) 763-4622. **$72-$125.** 711 W Beach Dr. Business Rt US 98, 0.5 mi w of jct US 231. Ext corridors. **Pets:** Medium. $10 daily fee/room. Designated rooms, service with restrictions, supervision.

[SAVE] [Sʒ] [X] [⬛] [⬜] [¶¶] [⇌]

▼▼ ▼▼ **Howard Johnson Inn** SH
(850) 785-0222. **$54-$129, 3 day notice.** 4601 W Hwy 98. US 98, 0.8
mi e of Hathaway Bridge. Ext/int corridors. **Pets:** Small. $25 one-time
fee/room. Designated rooms, no service, crate.

[ASK] [S🐾] [✕] [🖥] [💷] [🍴] [≈]

▲▲▲ ▼▼▼▼ **La Quinta Inn & Suites Panama City** SH
(850) 914-0022. **$102-$135.** 1030 E 23rd St. Jct US 231 and CR 390A.
Int corridors. **Pets:** Medium. Service with restrictions.

[SAVE] [✕] [&M] [✍] [🖥] [💷] [≈]

▼▼ **Super 8 Motel** M
(850) 784-1988. **$50-$109.** 207 Hwy 231 N. Just n of jct US 98. Ext/int
corridors. **Pets:** Small, dogs only. $15 daily fee/pet. Designated rooms,
service with restrictions.

[ASK] [S🐾] [✕] [🖥] [≈]

# PENSACOLA

▲▲▲ ▼▼ ▼▼ **Americas Best Value Inn & Suites** SH
(850) 479-1099. **$59-$89.** 8240 N Davis Hwy. I-10, exit 13, 0.8 mi n.
Ext/int corridors. **Pets:** Medium. $10 one-time fee/pet. Service with restrictions, supervision.

[SAVE] [S🐾] [✕] [✍] [🖥] [💷] [≈]

▼▼▼ ▼▼▼ **Ashton Inn & Suites** SH
(850) 454-0280. **$75-$99.** 4 New Warrington Rd. Just n of jct US 98
and SR 295. Int corridors. **Pets:** Other species. $50 one-time fee/room.
Service with restrictions, supervision.

[ASK] [S🐾] [✕] [🖥] [💷] [≈]

▼▼▼ ▼▼▼ **Comfort Inn-NAS Corry** SH
(850) 455-3233. **$77, 3 day notice.** 3 New Warrington Rd. Just n of jct
US 98 and SR 295. Ext corridors. **Pets:** Large, other species. $30
one-time fee/room. Designated rooms, service with restrictions.

[ASK] [✕] [🖥] [💷] [≈]

▲▲▲ ▼▼▼▼ **Holiday Inn Pensacola-University Mall** SH
(850) 474-0100. **$70-$80.** 7200 Plantation Rd. I-10, exit 13, just s; use
University Mall entrance. Ext corridors. **Pets:** Accepted.

[SAVE] [✕] [✍] [✍] [🖥] [💷] [🍴] [≈]

▼▼▼ ▼▼▼ **La Quinta Inn Pensacola** SH
(850) 474-0411. **$76-$100.** 7750 N Davis Hwy. I-10, exit 13, just n. Ext
corridors. **Pets:** Medium. No service.

[ASK] [✕] [✍] [🖥] [💷] [≈]

▼▼ **Motel 6 #1105** M
(850) 474-1060. **$40-$53.** 7226 Plantation Rd. I-10, exit 13, sw on Mall
Rd. Ext corridors. **Pets:** Accepted.

[S🐾] [✕] [✍] [≈]

▼▼ **Motel 6 #1183** M
(850) 476-5386. **$39-$51.** 7827 N Davis Hwy. I-10, exit 13, 0.3 mi n.
Ext corridors. **Pets:** Accepted.

[S🐾] [✕] [✍] [≈]

▲▲▲ ▼▼▼ **Quality Inn** SH
(850) 477-0711. **$59-$79.** 6550 N Pensacola Blvd. I-10, exit 10A, 1.2 mi
s on US 29. Ext/int corridors. **Pets:** Accepted.

[SAVE] [S🐾] [✕] [✍] [🖥] [💷] [≈]

▲▲▲ ▼▼▼ **Ramada Limited** SH
(850) 944-0333. **$59-$89.** 8060 Lavalle Way. I-10, exit 7, just s. Ext
corridors. **Pets:** Accepted.

[SAVE] [S🐾] [✕] [🖥] [💷] [≈]

▼▼ ▼▼ **Red Roof Inn** M
(850) 476-7960. **$43-$58.** 7340 Plantation Rd. I-10, exit 13, just s. Ext
corridors. **Pets:** Accepted.

[✕] [🖥]

▲▲▲ ▼▼▼▼ **Residence Inn By Marriott** SH
(850) 479-1000. **$144-$195.** 7230 Plantation Rd. I-10, exit 13, just s.
Ext corridors. **Pets:** Accepted.

[SAVE] [✕] [&M] [✍] [🖥] [💷] [≈] [✕]

# PENSACOLA BEACH

▼▼ ▼▼ **Comfort Inn Pensacola Beach** SH
(850) 934-5400. **$85-$250.** 40 Ft Pickens Rd. Just off SR 399. Ext
corridors. **Pets:** Accepted.

[ASK] [S🐾] [✕] [&M] [✍] [🖥] [💷] [≈]

# PERRY

▲▲▲ ▼▼ **Best Budget Inn** M
(850) 584-6231. **$43-$46.** 2220 US 19 S. US 19 and 98, 0.4 mi s of jct
US 221. Ext corridors. **Pets:** Other species. $10 daily fee/pet. Service with
restrictions, supervision.

[SAVE] [S🐾] [✕] [🖥] [≈]

# PORT ST. LUCIE

▼▼▼ ▼▼▼ **Holiday Inn-Port St Lucie** SH
(772) 337-2200. **$19-$229.** 10120 S Federal Hwy, Rt 1. US 1, 0.5 mi n
of jct SR 716, Port St Lucie Blvd. Int corridors. **Pets:** Accepted.

[ASK] [S🐾] [✕] [✍] [🖥] [💷] [🍴] [≈]

# PUNTA GORDA

▼▼ **Motel 6 #1231** M
(941) 639-9585. **$45-$82.** 9300 Knights Dr. I-75, exit 161, just w on CR
768. Ext corridors. **Pets:** Accepted.

[S🐾] [✕] [&M] [✍] [🖥] [≈]

# QUINCY

▼▼▼ ▼▼▼ **Allison House Inn** BB 🌢
(850) 875-2511. **$85-$140, 14 day notice.** 215 N Madison St. Just e of
town center; in historic district. Int corridors. **Pets:** Small, dogs only.
Designated rooms, service with restrictions, supervision.

[ASK] [S🐾] [✕]

# ST. AUGUSTINE

▲▲▲ ▼▼ ▼▼ **Avenida Inn Saint Augustine** SH
(904) 829-6581. **$56-$199.** 2800 N Ponce de Leon Blvd. US 1 at SR
16; in historic district. Ext corridors. **Pets:** Medium, dogs only. $10 daily
fee/pet. Designated rooms, service with restrictions, supervision.

[SAVE] [S🐾] [✕] [✍] [🖥] [🍴] [≈]

▼▼▼ ▼▼▼ **Bayfront Westcott House** BB
(904) 824-4301. **$119-$279, 7 day notice.** 146 Avenida Menendez. 1
blk s of the Bridge of Lions. Ext/int corridors. **Pets:** Small, other species.
$15 daily fee/pet. Designated rooms, no service, supervision.

[ASK] [S🐾] [✕]

▲▲▲ ▼▼ ▼▼ **Best Western St. Augustine I-95** M
(904) 829-1999. **$59-$150.** 2445 SR 16. I-95, exit 318, just w. Ext
corridors. **Pets:** Accepted.

[SAVE] [S🐾] [✕] [💷] [≈]

▲▲▲ ▼▼ ▼▼ **The Cozy Inn** M
(904) 824-2449. **$49-$99.** 202 San Marco Ave. 0.3 mi s of jct SR 16.
Ext corridors. **Pets:** Accepted.

[SAVE] [S🐾] [✕] [🖥] [💷]

▲▲▲ ▼▼ ▼▼ **Days Inn-West** SH
(904) 824-4341. **$59-$199, 14 day notice.** 2560 SR 16. I-95, exit 318,
just w. Ext corridors. **Pets:** Small, dogs only. $10 daily fee/pet. Designated
rooms, service with restrictions, supervision.

[SAVE] [S🐾] [✕] [🖥] [💷] [≈]

▼▼ **The Inn At Camachee Harbor** SH ❀
(904) 825-0003. **$99-$159, 3 day notice.** 201 Yacht Club Dr. On Intra-coastal Waterway at west side of Usine Bridge; 1 mi e of jct N SR A1A and San Marco Blvd. Ext/int corridors. **Pets:** Other species. $15 daily fee/pet. Service with restrictions, crate.

▲▲▲ ▼▼▼ **La Quinta Inn St. Augustine** SH
(904) 824-3383. **$59-$150.** 1300 Ponce de Leon Blvd. US 1, 1 mi n. Ext corridors. **Pets:** Accepted.

▲▲▲ ▼▼▼ **Ramada Limited** M
(904) 829-5643. **$69-$109.** 2535 SR 16. I-95, exit 318, just w. Ext corridors. **Pets:** Other species. $10 daily fee/room. Service with restrictions, supervision.

▲▲▲ ▼▼▼▼ **St. Francis Inn** BB
(904) 824-6068. **$119-$239, 7 day notice.** 279 St George St. Just s; in the historic district. Ext/int corridors. **Pets:** Medium, other species. $15 daily fee/pet. Designated rooms, service with restrictions.

▲▲▲ ▼▼▼ **Scottish Inns** M
(904) 824-2871. **$50-$110.** 110 San Marco Ave. Old Mission and San Marco aves; center. Ext corridors. **Pets:** Small, dogs only. $10 daily fee/pet. Service with restrictions, supervision.

▲▲▲ ▼▼▼▼ **World Golf Village Renaissance Resort** LH
(904) 940-8000. **$109-$499, 3 day notice.** 500 S Legacy Tr. I-95, exit 323, just w, then 2 mi follow signs. Int corridors. **Pets:** Accepted.

## ST. AUGUSTINE BEACH

▲▲▲ ▼▼▼ **Comfort Inn at St. Augustine Beach** SH
(904) 471-1474. **$69-$107.** 901 A1A Beach Blvd. On Business Rt SR A1A, 1.6 mi s of jct SR 312 and A1A. Ext corridors. **Pets:** Accepted.

▲▲▲ ▼▼▼ **Holiday Inn-St Augustine Beach** SH
(904) 471-2555. **$114-$169.** 860 A1A Beach Blvd. On Business Rt SR A1A, 1.8 mi s of jct SR 312 and A1A. Ext/int corridors. **Pets:** Small, other species. $20 daily fee/pet. Designated rooms, service with restrictions, supervision.

▲▲▲ ▼▼▼ **Super 8 By The Beach** SH
(904) 471-2330. **$49-$229.** 311 A1A Beach Blvd. On Business Rt SR A1A, 1 mi s of jct SR 312 and A1A. Ext corridors. **Pets:** Small. $15 one-time fee/pet. Designated rooms, service with restrictions, supervision.

## SARASOTA

▲▲▲ ▼▼▼▼ **Comfort Inn Sarasota Airport** SH
(941) 351-7734. **$70-$150.** 5000 N Tamiami Tr. On US 41, just s of jct University Pkwy. Ext corridors. **Pets:** Small, other species. $10 daily fee/pet. Service with restrictions, supervision.

▲▲▲ ▼▼▼ **Coquina on the Beach Resort** M
(941) 388-2141. **$89-$259.** 1008 Benjamin Franklin Dr. On St. Armands Key of Lido Beach, 0.9 mi s of St. Armands Circle. Ext corridors. **Pets:** Accepted.

▲▲▲ ▼▼▼▼ **Hibiscus Suites Inn** M
(941) 921-5797. **$129-$429, 3 day notice.** 1735 Stickney Point Rd. On SR 72, 0.3 mi sw of jct US 41. Ext corridors. **Pets:** Medium, dogs only. $25 daily fee/room. Service with restrictions, crate.

▲▲▲ ▼▼▼▼ **Hyatt Sarasota** LH
(941) 953-1234. **$135-$265.** 1000 Blvd of the Arts. Just w of jct US 41. Int corridors. **Pets:** Accepted.

▼▼▼▼▼ **The Ritz-Carlton, Sarasota** LH ❀
(941) 309-2000. **$349-$539.** 1111 Ritz-Carlton Dr. On US 41, jct John Ringling Blvd. Int corridors. **Pets:** Small. $125 one-time fee/room. Desig-nated rooms, service with restrictions, crate.

▼▼▼ **The Sunset Lodge Motel** M
(941) 925-1151. **$65-$105, 21 day notice.** 1765 Dawn St. 0.3 mi sw of jct US 41 on SR 72, just s on Ave C, then just w. Ext corridors. **Pets:** Accepted.

▼▼▼ **The Tides Inn** M
(941) 924-7541. **$60-$120, 21 day notice.** 1800 Stickney Point Rd. On SR 72, 0.3 mi sw of jct US 41. Ext corridors. **Pets:** Accepted.

## SATELLITE BEACH

▲▲▲ ▼▼▼ **Days Inn** M
(321) 777-3552. **$70-$200.** 180 SR A1A. 0.3 mi s of jct SR 404. Ext corridors. **Pets:** Small, other species. $10 daily fee/pet. Service with restric-tions, crate.

## SEBRING

▼▼▼▼▼ **The Chateau Elan Hotel & Spa** SH
(863) 655-6252. **$99, 3 day notice.** 150 Midway Dr. From US 27, 2.2 mi e on SR 98; at entrance to Sebring International Raceway. Int corridors. **Pets:** Accepted.

▲▲▲ ▼▼▼▼ **Inn On The Lakes** SH
(863) 471-9400. **$79-$109.** 3100 Golfview Rd. On US 27, 1.5 mi n of jct SR 17. Ext/int corridors. **Pets:** Medium, other species. $40 one-time fee/room. Designated rooms, service with restrictions.

▲▲▲ ▼▼▼ **Kenilworth Lodge** SH
(863) 385-0111. **$60-$160, 3 day notice.** 1610 Lakeview Dr. US 27, 1 mi e on SR 17. Ext/int corridors. **Pets:** Accepted.

▲▲▲ ▼▼▼▼ **Quality Inn & Suites Conference Center** SH
(863) 385-4500. **$70-$100.** 6525 US 27 N. On US 27, 7 mi n of jct SR 17. Ext corridors. **Pets:** Medium, other species. $10 daily fee/pet. Desig-nated rooms, service with restrictions, crate.

## SIESTA KEY

▲▲▲ ▼▼▼ **Tropical Breeze Resort & Spa of Siesta Key** M ❀
(941) 349-1125. **$103-$398, 14 day notice.** 5150 Ocean Blvd. Jct Avenida Messina; in Siesta Village. Ext corridors. **Pets:** Other species. $75 one-time fee/room. Designated rooms, service with restrictions.

▼▼▼▼ **Turtle Beach Resort** M
(941) 349-4554. **$295-$435, 60 day notice.** 9049 Midnight Pass Rd. 2.8 mi s of jct SR 72. Ext corridors. **Pets:** Other species. $44 one-time fee/pet.

# SILVER SPRINGS

**Days Inn** M
(352) 236-2891. **$65-$85.** 5001 E Silver Springs Blvd. SR 40, 0.5 mi w of jct CR 35. Ext corridors. **Pets:** Other species. $10 daily fee/pet. Service with restrictions.

**Sun Plaza Motel** M
(352) 236-2343. **$50-$70.** 5461 E Silver Springs Blvd. SR 40, jct CR 35. Ext corridors. **Pets:** Dogs only. $10 one-time fee/pet. Service with restrictions, supervision.

# STARKE

**Best Western Motor Inn** SH
(904) 964-6744. **$69-$125, 14 day notice.** 1290 N Temple Ave. 1 mi n on US 301 from jct SR 100. Ext corridors. **Pets:** Medium. $10 daily fee/pet. Service with restrictions, supervision.

**Days Inn** SH
(904) 964-7600. **$62-$149, 7 day notice.** 1101 N Temple Ave. 10 mi s of jct SR 16. Ext corridors. **Pets:** Other species. $10 daily fee/pet. Designated rooms, service with restrictions.

# STEINHATCHEE

**Steinhatchee Landing Resort** CO
(352) 498-3513. **$132-$425, 14 day notice.** SR 51 N. SR 51, 8 mi w of jct US 19/98. Ext corridors. **Pets:** Accepted.

**Steinhatchee River Inn** M
(352) 498-4049. **$60-$89, 14 day notice.** 1111 Riverside Dr. Center. Ext corridors. **Pets:** Accepted.

# STUART

**Hutchinson Island Marriott Beach Resort & Marina** LH
(772) 225-3700. **$139-$379, 3 day notice.** 555 NE Ocean Blvd. 4 mi ne on SR A1A; south end of Hutchinson Island at east end of causeway. Ext/int corridors. **Pets:** Accepted.

**Pirates Cove Resort & Marina** SH
(772) 287-2500. **$145-$220.** 4307 SE Bayview St. 0.3 mi e of SR A1A. Ext corridors. **Pets:** Large, other species. $20 one-time fee/pet. Designated rooms, service with restrictions, supervision.

# TALLAHASSEE

**Best Western Seminole Inn** M
(850) 656-2938. **$70-$150, 7 day notice.** 6737 Mahan Dr. I-10, exit 209A, just w on US 90. Ext corridors. **Pets:** Small. $5 daily fee/pet. Supervision.

**Days Inn** SH
(850) 222-3219. **$70-$199.** 1350 W Tennessee St. 1.6 mi w of US 27. Int corridors. **Pets:** Accepted.

**Econo Lodge** M
(850) 385-6155. **$52-$109.** 2681 N Monroe St. I-10, exit 199, 0.5 mi s. Ext corridors. **Pets:** Other species. $10 daily fee/pet. Service with restrictions, supervision.

**Homewood Suites by Hilton** SH
(850) 402-9400. **$89-$299.** 2987 Apalachee Pkwy. US 27, 3.5 mi s. Int corridors. **Pets:** Accepted.

**La Quinta Inn Tallahassee (North)** SH
(850) 385-7172. **$84-$121.** 2905 N Monroe St. I-10, exit 199, just s on US 27. Ext corridors. **Pets:** Medium. Service with restrictions.

**La Quinta Inn Tallahassee (South)** SH
(850) 878-5099. **$79-$125.** 2850 Apalachee Pkwy. 3 mi se on US 27. Ext corridors. **Pets:** Medium. Service with restrictions.

**Motel 6 #1073** SH
(850) 877-6171. **$45-$55.** 1027 Apalachee Pkwy. 1 mi se on US 27. Ext corridors. **Pets:** Accepted.

**Motel 6 #1191** SH
(850) 386-7878. **$39-$51.** 2738 N Monroe St. I-10, exit 199, just s on US 27. Ext corridors. **Pets:** Accepted.

**Motel 6–420** M
(850) 668-2600. **$43-$57.** 1481 Timberlane Rd. I-10, exit 203, just n, then w. Ext corridors. **Pets:** Accepted.

**Ramada Conference Center** LH
(850) 386-1027. **Call for rates.** 2900 N Monroe St. I-10, exit 199, just s. Ext/int corridors. **Pets:** Medium, other species. $10 daily fee/room. Service with restrictions, crate.

# TAMPA BAY METROPOLITAN AREA

## APOLLO BEACH

**▼▼ Ramada Inn on Tampa Bay** **M**
(813) 641-2700. **$65-$150.** 6414 Surfside Blvd. I-75, exit 246, 1.8 mi w on CR 672, 1.8 mi s on US 41, then 2.4 mi w on Apollo Beach Blvd. Ext corridors. **Pets:** Accepted.
[ASK] [S] [X] [⌀] [E] [●] [H] [≋] [X]

## BRANDON

**▼▼ Homestead Studio Suites Hotel-Tampa/Brandon** **M**
(813) 643-5900. **$59-$74.** 330 Grand Regency Blvd. I-75, exit 257, just e on SR 60, then 0.4 mi n; in Regency Office Park. Ext corridors. **Pets:** $25 daily fee/pet. Service with restrictions, supervision.
[ASK] [S] [X] [&M] [⌀] [E] [●] [■]

**⧫⧫ ▼▼▼ La Quinta Inn & Suites Tampa Bay**
**(Brandon)** **SH**
(813) 643-0574. **$89-$149.** 310 Grand Regency Blvd. I-75, exit 257, just e on SR 60, then 0.5 mi n; in Regency Office Park. Int corridors. **Pets:** Medium. Service with restrictions.
[SAVE] [X] [&M] [⌀] [&] [E] [●] [≋]

## CLEARWATER

**⧫⧫ ▼▼▼▼ Belleview Biltmore Resort & Spa** **SH**
(727) 373-3000. **$149-$179.** 25 Belleview Blvd. 2 mi s on US Alternate 19 (Ft Harrison Ave); from jct SR 60; 0.5 mi w. Int corridors. **Pets:** Small. $25 daily fee/room. Designated rooms, service with restrictions, supervision.
[SAVE] [S] [X] [⌀] [&] [E] [●] [H] [≋] [X]

**⧫⧫ ▼▼ Days Inn-St. Pete/Clearwater Airport** **SH**
(727) 573-3334. **$84-$114.** 3910 Ulmerton Rd. I-275, exit 31 southbound; exit 30 northbound, 2 mi w on SR 688. Int corridors. **Pets:** Small, other species. $20 one-time fee/room. Designated rooms, service with restrictions.
[SAVE] [S] [X] [&M] [⌀] [&] [E] [●] [≋]

**▼▼▼▼ Hampton Inn-Clearwater/St. Petersburg Airport** **M**
(727) 577-9200. **$79-$109.** 3655 Hospitality at Ulmerton Rd. I-275, exit 31 southbound; exit 30 northbound, 1.8 mi w on SR 688. Ext corridors. **Pets:** Accepted.
[ASK] [S] [X] [&] [●] [≋] [X]

**▼▼ Homestead Studio Suites**
**Hotel-Tampa/Clearwater** **M**
(727) 572-4800. **$49-$69.** 2311 Ulmerton Rd. I-275, exit 31 southbound; exit 30 northbound, 1.3 mi w on SR 688. Ext corridors. **Pets:** $25 daily fee/pet. Service with restrictions, supervision.
[ASK] [S] [X] [⌀] [&] [E] [●] [≋]

**▼▼▼▼ Homewood Suites by Hilton** **SH**
(727) 573-1500. **$99-$169.** 2233 Ulmerton Rd. I-275, exit 31 southbound; exit 30 northbound, 1.3 mi w on SR 688. Int corridors. **Pets:** Small. $150 one-time fee/pet. Designated rooms, service with restrictions.
[ASK] [S] [X] [&M] [⌀] [&] [E] [●] [≋]

**▼▼ Howard Johnson Inn & Suites** **M**
(727) 796-0135. **$60-$96.** 27988 US Hwy 19 N. On US 19, 0.6 mi n of jct SR 580. Ext corridors. **Pets:** Accepted.
[ASK] [S] [X] [&] [E] [●] [≋] [X]

**⧫⧫ ▼▼▼▼ La Quinta Inn Tampa Bay**
**(Clearwater-Airport)** **SH**
(727) 572-7222. **$85-$105.** 3301 Ulmerton Rd. I-275, exit 31 southbound; exit 30 northbound, 1.7 mi w on SR 688; in The Centres Office Park. Int corridors. **Pets:** Medium. Service with restrictions.
[SAVE] [X] [⌀] [&] [E] [●] [≋] [X]

**▼▼▼ Radisson Hotel Clearwater Central** **SH**
(727) 799-1181. **$75-$89.** 20967 US 19 N. On US 19, just n of jct SR 60. Ext/int corridors. **Pets:** Accepted.
[ASK] [S] [X] [&M] [⌀] [&] [E] [●] [H] [≋] [X]

**⧫⧫⧫ ▼▼▼ Residence Inn by Marriott** **SH** ✿
(727) 573-4444. **$159-$229.** 5050 Ulmerton Rd. On SR 688, 1 mi e of jct US 19. Ext corridors. **Pets:** Medium, other species. $75 one-time fee/room. Service with restrictions, supervision.
[SAVE] [X] [⌀] [&] [E] [●] [≋] [X]

**⧫⧫⧫ ▼▼▼ Super 8 Clearwater/St. Petersburg Airport** **SH**
(727) 572-8881. **$69-$129.** 13260 34th St N. I-275, exit 31 southbound; exit 30 northbound, 1.8 mi w on SR 688 (Ulmerton Rd), then just s. Int corridors. **Pets:** Medium. $10 daily fee/pet. Designated rooms, no service, supervision.
[SAVE] [S] [X] [E] [≋]

**▼▼▼ TownePlace Suites by Marriott St.**
**Petersburg/Clearwater** **SH**
(727) 299-9229. **$149-$199.** 13200 49th St N. I-275, exit 31 southbound; exit 30 northbound, 3 mi w on SR 688, then just s; in Turtle Creek. Int corridors. **Pets:** Accepted.
[ASK] [S] [X] [&M] [⌀] [&] [E] [●] [≋]

## CLEARWATER BEACH

**⧫⧫⧫ ▼▼▼ ▼▼▼ Sheraton Sand Key Resort** **LH**
(727) 595-1611. **$219-$299.** 1160 Gulf Blvd. 2 mi s on SR 699; at south end of Clearwater Pass Bridge. Int corridors. **Pets:** Accepted.
[SAVE] [S] [X] [&M] [⌀] [&] [E] [●] [H] [≋] [X]

## INDIAN ROCKS BEACH

**▼▼ Sea Star Motel & Apartments** **M** ✿
(727) 596-2525. **$60-$110, 30 day notice.** 1805 Gulf Blvd. On SR 699, 1.2 mi n of jct SR 688 (Walsingham Rd). Ext corridors. **Pets:** Other species. $10 daily fee/pet. No service, crate.
[ASK] [X] [E] [●] [X] [Z]

## MADEIRA BEACH

**⧫⧫⧫ ▼▼▼ Snug Harbor Inn Waterfront Bed &**
**Breakfast** **M**
(727) 395-9256. **$65-$116, 28 day notice.** 13655 Gulf Blvd. On SR 699, 0.9 mi s of jct Tom Stuart Cswy. Ext corridors. **Pets:** Accepted.
[SAVE] [X] [E] [●] [≋] [X]

## NEW PORT RICHEY

**⧫⧫⧫ ▼▼▼ Econo Lodge** **M**
(727) 845-4990. **$60-$120, 7 day notice.** 7631 US 19. On US 19, 0.8 mi n of jct Main St. Ext corridors. **Pets:** Small. $6 daily fee/room. Designated rooms, service with restrictions, supervision.
[SAVE] [S] [X] [E] [●]

## PALM HARBOR

**⧫⧫⧫ ▼▼▼ Best Western Palm Harbor Hotel** **SH**
(727) 942-0358. **$89-$185.** 37611 US 19 N. On US 19, 3 mi s of jct SR 582. Ext corridors. **Pets:** Accepted.
[SAVE] [S] [X] [&] [E] [●] [H] [≋] [X]

**▼▼ Knights Inn-Clearwater/Palm Harbor** **M**
(727) 789-2002. **$45-$119.** 34106 US 19 N. On US 19, 1.8 mi n of CR 752 (Tampa Rd). Ext corridors. **Pets:** Medium, other species. $10 daily fee/room. Service with restrictions, supervision.
[ASK] [S] [X] [E] [●] [≋]

**(AAA) ▼▼▼ Red Roof Inn M**
(727) 786-2529. **$45-$99.** 32000 US 19 N. On US 19, 0.4 mi s of jct CR 752 (Tampa Rd). Ext corridors. **Pets:** Accepted.
[SAVE] [S] [X] [⌂] [⌨] [🖥] [🖨] [≈]

**(AAA) ▼▼▼▼ The Westin Innisbrook Golf Resort CO**
(727) 942-2000. **$109-$239, 3 day notice.** 36750 US Hwy 19 N. On US 19, 2.8 mi s of jct SR 582. Int corridors. **Pets:** Accepted.
[SAVE] [S] [X] [🖥] [🖨] [🍴] [≈] [⊗]

## PINELLAS PARK

**(AAA) ▼▼▼ La Quinta Inn Tampa (Pinellas Park/Clearwater) SH**
(727) 545-5611. **$75-$105.** 7500 US Hwy 19 N. I-275, exit 28, 1.4 mi s on Gandy Blvd (SR 694), then just n. Ext/int corridors. **Pets:** Medium. No service.
[SAVE] [X] [&M] [⌂] [🖥] [🖨] [≈]

## PLANT CITY

**(AAA) ▼▼▼ Ramada Inn Plantation House M**
(813) 752-3141. **$69-$189.** 2011 N Wheeler St. I-4, exit 21, just se on SR 39. Ext corridors. **Pets:** Accepted.
[SAVE] [S] [X] [&M] [⌂] [⌨] [🖥] [🖨] [🍴] [≈]

## PORT RICHEY

**▼▼ Comfort Inn M**
(727) 863-3336. **$70-$90.** 11810 US 19. On US 19, just s of jct SR 52. Ext corridors. **Pets:** Medium, other species. $10 daily fee/pet. Service with restrictions.
[ASK] [S] [X] [⌂] [🖥] [🖨] [≈]

## SAFETY HARBOR

**(AAA) ▼▼▼▼ Safety Harbor Resort and Spa on Tampa Bay SH**
(727) 726-1161. **$209-$284, 3 day notice.** 105 N Bayshore Dr. Jct SR 590 (Main St); downtown. Int corridors. **Pets:** Medium. $75 one-time fee/pet. Designated rooms, service with restrictions, supervision.
[SAVE] [S] [X] [&M] [⌂] [⌨] [🖥] [🖨] [🍴] [≈] [⊗]

## ST. PETE BEACH

**▼▼ Bay Palm Resort M**
(727) 360-7642. **$59-$109, 14 day notice.** 4237 Gulf Blvd. On SR 699, 0.5 mi n of Pinellas Bayway. Ext corridors. **Pets:** Accepted.
[X] [🖥] [🖨] [≈]

**(AAA) ▼▼▼ Bayview Plaza Waterfront Resort M ❀**
(727) 367-1387. **$45-$159, 14 day notice.** 4321 Gulf Blvd. On SR 699; 0.8 mi n of Pinellas Bayway. Ext corridors. **Pets:** Medium. $10 daily fee/pet. Crate.
[SAVE] [S] [X] [🖥]

**(AAA) ▼▼▼▼ Beach House Suites By The Don Cesar SH ❀**
(727) 363-0001. **$169-$454, 5 day notice.** 3860 Gulf Blvd. On SR 699, 0.4 mi n of jct Pinellas Bayway. Ext corridors. **Pets:** Other species. $25 one-time fee/pet. Designated rooms, service with restrictions.
[SAVE] [S] [X] [⌂] [🖥] [🖨] [≈] [⊗]

**(AAA) ▼▼▼▼ Don CeSar Beach Resort, A Loews Hotel LH ❀**
(727) 360-1881. **$164-$524, 5 day notice.** 3400 Gulf Blvd. On SR 699, jct Pinellas Bayway. Int corridors. **Pets:** Other species. $25 one-time fee/pet. Service with restrictions, supervision.
[SAVE] [S] [X] [&M] [⌂] [⌨] [🖥] [🖨] [🍴] [≈] [⊗]

**(AAA) ▼▼ Lamara Motel Apartments M**
(727) 360-7521. **$55-$100, 7 day notice.** 520 73rd Ave. Just w of Gulf Blvd (SR 699). Ext corridors. **Pets:** Accepted.
[SAVE] [S] [X] [🖥] [≈]

## ST. PETERSBURG

**▼▼ Days Inn Tropicana Field North M**
(727) 522-3191. **$54-$79.** 2595 54th Ave N. I-275, exit 26; exit 26B northbound, 0.3 mi w. Ext corridors. **Pets:** Accepted.
[ASK] [S] [X] [⌂] [🖥] [🖨] [≈]

**(AAA) ▼▼▼▼ La Quinta Inn Tampa Bay Area (St. Petersburg) M**
(727) 527-8421. **$79-$99.** 4999 34th St N. I-275, exit 26; exit 26B northbound, just w on 54th Ave N, then just s on US 19. Ext corridors. **Pets:** Medium. Service with restrictions.
[SAVE] [X] [&M] [⌂] [🖪] [🖥] [🖨] [≈]

**(AAA) ▼▼▼ Mansion House B & B BB**
(727) 821-9391. **$119-$220, 14 day notice.** 105 5th Ave NE. 0.5 mi n at 1st St N; downtown. Ext/int corridors. **Pets:** Small, dogs only. $25 daily fee/room. Designated rooms, service with restrictions, supervision.
[SAVE] [X] [🖥] [≈]

**(AAA) ▼▼▼ Ramada Inn Mirage M**
(727) 525-1181. **$65-$130.** 5005 34th St N. I-275, exit 26; exit 26B northbound, just w on 54th Ave N, then just s on US 19. Ext corridors. **Pets:** Small. $25 one-time fee/pet. Service with restrictions, supervision.
[SAVE] [S] [X] [🖥] [🖨] [≈]

## TAMPA

**(AAA) ▼▼▼ AmeriSuites (Tampa Airport/Westshore) SH**
(813) 282-1037. **$99-$200.** 4811 W Main St. I-275, exit 40A, 0.5 mi n on Westshore Blvd; exit 39A northbound, 1 mi e on Kennedy Blvd, 1 mi s on Westshore Blvd, then just w. Int corridors. **Pets:** Accepted.
[SAVE] [S] [X] [&M] [⌂] [⌨] [🖥] [🖨] [≈]

**(AAA) ▼▼▼ AmeriSuites (Tampa near Busch Gardens) SH**
(813) 979-1922. **$99-$149.** 11408 N 30th St. I-275, exit 51, 1.8 mi e on SR 582, then just s. Int corridors. **Pets:** Accepted.
[SAVE] [S] [X] [&M] [⌂] [⌨] [🖥] [🖨] [≈]

**(AAA) ▼▼▼ AmeriSuites (Tampa/Sabal Corporate Park) M**
(813) 622-8557. **$79-$189.** 10007 Princess Palm Ave. I-75, exit 260 southbound; exit 260B northbound, 0.5 mi w on SR 574 (Dr. Martin Luther King Jr Blvd), just s on Falkenburg Rd, then just w; in Sabal Corporate Park. Int corridors. **Pets:** Accepted.
[SAVE] [S] [X] [🖥] [🖨] [≈]

**(AAA) ▼▼▼ Baymont Inn & Suites Tampa-Brandon SH**
(813) 684-4007. **$89-$109.** 602 S Falkenburg Rd. I-75, exit 257, just w on SR 60, then just n. Int corridors. **Pets:** Medium. Service with restrictions.
[SAVE] [X] [⌂] [🖥] [🖨] [≈]

**(AAA) ▼▼▼ Baymont Inn & Suites Tampa/near Busch Gardens SH**
(813) 930-6900. **$69-$109.** 9202 N 30th St. I-275, exit 50, 2 mi e on SR 580, then just n. Ext corridors. **Pets:** Medium. Service with restrictions.
[SAVE] [X] [⌂] [⌨] [🖥] [🖨] [≈]

**(AAA) ▼▼▼ Baymont Inn Tampa-Fairgrounds M**
(813) 626-0885. **$59-$79.** 4811 US 301 N. I-4, exit 6 westbound; exit 6A eastbound, just se. Int corridors. **Pets:** Medium. Service with restrictions.
[SAVE] [X] [⌂] [🖥] [🖨] [≈]

**(AAA) ▼▼▼▼ Best Western All Suites Hotel Near USF Behind Busch Gardens SH**
(813) 971-8930. **$89-$129.** 3001 University Center Dr. I-275, exit 51, 1.8 mi e on SR 582 (Fowler Ave), then 0.5 mi s on N 30th St. Ext corridors. **Pets:** Large, other species. $25 one-time fee/pet. Service with restrictions, supervision.
[SAVE] [S] [X] [🖥] [🖨] [🍴] [≈]

**Best Western Brandon Hotel & Conference Center M**
(813) 621-5555. **$79-$109.** 9331 Adamo Dr. I-75, exit 257, 1.2 mi w on SR 60. Ext corridors. **Pets:** Accepted.

**Best Western-The Westshore Hotel LH**
(813) 282-3636. **$89-$139.** 1200 N Westshore Blvd. I-275, exit 40A, 0.4 mi n; exit 39A northbound, 0.5 mi e on Kennedy Blvd, then 1.2 mi n. Ext corridors. **Pets:** Accepted.

**Chase Suite Hotel by Woodfin M**
(813) 281-5677. **$99-$229.** 3075 N Rocky Point Dr. I-275, exit 39 southbound; exit 39B northbound, 3 mi w on SR 60, then just n; in Rocky Point Harbor. Ext corridors. **Pets:** Small. $100 one-time fee/pet. Designated rooms, service with restrictions, supervision.

**Comfort Inn and Conference Center Near Busch Gardens SH**
(813) 933-4011. **$79-$109.** 820 E Busch Blvd. I-275, exit 50, just e on SR 580. Ext/int corridors. **Pets:** Small, other species. $25 one-time fee/room. Designated rooms, service with restrictions, crate.

**Comfort Inn Hotel & Suites Tampa Stadium/Airport M**
(813) 877-6061. **$70-$269.** 4732 N Dale Mabry Hwy. I-275, exit 41B, 2 mi n. Ext corridors. **Pets:** Accepted.

**Extended Stay Deluxe SH**
(813) 637-8990. **$69-$159, 30 day notice.** 1805 N Westshore Blvd. I-275, exit 40A southbound, 0.5 mi n; exit 39A northbound, 0.5 mi e on Kennedy Blvd, then 1.3 mi n. Int corridors. **Pets:** $25 daily fee/pet. Service with restrictions, supervision.

**Hampton Inn Veterans Expressway SH**
(813) 901-5900. **$109-$149.** 5628 W Waters Ave. SR 589 (Veteran's Expwy), exit 6A, just e on CR 584. Int corridors. **Pets:** Medium. $10 daily fee/room. Service with restrictions, supervision.

**Hard Rock Seminole Casino & Hotel LH**
(813) 627-7625. **$134-$305, 3 day notice.** 5223 N Orient Rd. I-4, exit 6, just w. Int corridors. **Pets:** Medium, other species. $50 one-time fee/pet. Designated rooms, service with restrictions, supervision.

**Holiday Inn Express & Suites SH**
(813) 910-7171. **$89-$169.** 8310 Galbraith Rd. I-75, exit 270, 0.3 mi n on CR 581 (Bruce B Downs Blvd), just w on Highwoods Preserve Pkwy, then just n; in Highwoods Preserve. Int corridors. **Pets:** Small, other species. $50 one-time fee/pet. Designated rooms, service with restrictions, supervision.

**Holiday Inn Tampa Near Busch Gardens SH**
(813) 971-4710. **$69-$179.** 2701 E Fowler Ave. I-275, exit 51, 1.5 mi e on SR 582. Ext/int corridors. **Pets:** Accepted.

**Homestead Studio Suites Hotel-Tampa/North Airport M**
(813) 243-1913. **$49-$69.** 5401 Beaumont Ctr Blvd. SR 589 (Veterans Expwy), exit 4, just w on SR 580. Ext/int corridors. **Pets:** $25 daily fee/pet. Service with restrictions, supervision.

**La Quinta Inn & Suites Tampa Bay (U.S.F./Near Busch Gardens) SH**
(813) 910-7500. **$89-$119.** 3701 E Fowler. I-275, exit 51, 2.2 mi e on SR 582. Int corridors. **Pets:** Medium. Service with restrictions.

**La Quinta Inn Tampa Bay (Airport) M**
(813) 287-0440. **$79-$135.** 4730 Spruce St. I-275, exit 40A, 0.7 mi w on Westshore Blvd; exit 39A, 1 mi n on Kennedy Blvd, 1.2 mi w on Westshore Blvd, then just s. Ext corridors. **Pets:** Medium. Service with restrictions.

**La Quinta Inn Tampa South SH**
(813) 835-6262. **$120-$150.** 4620 W Gandy Blvd. Just e of jct S West Shore Blvd. Int corridors. **Pets:** Small. Designated rooms, service with restrictions, supervision.

**Motel 6 #1192 M**
(813) 628-0888. **$42-$55.** 6510 US 301 N. I-4, exit 6 westbound; exit 6B eastbound, 0.7 mi n. Ext corridors. **Pets:** Accepted.

**Red Roof Inn M**
(813) 932-0073. **$44-$75.** 2307 E Busch Blvd. I-275, exit 50, 1.4 mi e on SR 580. Ext corridors. **Pets:** Accepted.

**Red Roof Inn-Fairgrounds M**
(813) 623-5245. **$48-$79.** 5001 N US 301. I-4, exit 7 westbound; exit 7A eastbound, just se. Ext corridors. **Pets:** Accepted.

**Residence Inn by Marriott Sabal Park SH**
(813) 627-8855. **$114-$149.** 9719 Princess Palm Ave. I-75, exit 260 southbound; exit 260B northbound, just w on SR 574 (Dr. Martin Luther King Jr Blvd), just s on Falkenburg Rd, then 0.4 mi w; in Sabal Corporate Center. Int corridors. **Pets:** Accepted.

**Sheraton Suites Tampa Airport LH**
(813) 873-8675. **$285.** 4400 W Cypress St. I-275, exit 40B, n to Cypress St, then 0.3 mi w. Int corridors. **Pets:** Large. Service with restrictions, supervision.

**Tahitian Inn M**
(813) 877-6721. **$109-$219.** 601 S Dale Mabry Hwy. I-275, exit 41A, 1.1 mi s. Ext/int corridors. **Pets:** Other species. $25 one-time fee/room. Designated rooms, service with restrictions.

**Wingate Inn-USF Near Busch Gardens SH**
(813) 979-2828. **$116-$125.** 3751 E Fowler Ave. I-275, exit 51, 2.2 mi e on SR 582. Int corridors. **Pets:** Accepted.

**Wyndham Westshore-Tampa LH**
(813) 286-4400. **$145-$309.** 4860 W Kennedy Blvd. I-275, exit 40A, 0.5 mi s; jct SR 60 and Westshore Blvd. Int corridors. **Pets:** Accepted.

# TEMPLE TERRACE

**Extended StayAmerica SH**
(813) 989-2264. **$65-$115.** 12242 Morris Bridge Rd. I-75, exit 266, just w on Fletcher Ave (CR 582A). Int corridors. **Pets:** Accepted.

**Residence Inn by Marriott Tampa North SH**
(813) 972-4400. **Call for rates.** 13420 N Telecom Pkwy. I-75, exit 266, 1.1 mi w on Fletcher Ave (CR 582A); in Telecom Tampa Park. Int corridors. **Pets:** Accepted.

# TREASURE ISLAND

**⬧⬧⬧** ◈◈ **Best Western Sea Castle Suites** Ⓜ
(727) 367-2704. **$79-$195.** 10750 Gulf Blvd. On SR 699, jct Treasure Island Cswy. Ext corridors. **Pets:** Accepted.
[SAVE] 🛏 ✕ 🔒 💻 ⌫ ✕

# WESLEY CHAPEL

**⬧⬧⬧** ◈◈◈ **Masters Inn Tampa North** Ⓜ
(813) 973-0155. **$49-$63.** 27807 SR 54 W. I-75, exit 279, just w. Ext corridors. **Pets:** Accepted.
[SAVE] 🛏 ✕ 🗑 🔒 🍴 ⌫

## END METROPOLITAN AREA

# TITUSVILLE

**⬧⬧⬧** ◈◈◈ **Best Western Space Shuttle Inn Kennedy Space Center** 🆂🅷
(321) 269-9100. **$69-$169.** 3455 Cheney Hwy. I-95, exit 215, just e on SR 50. Ext corridors **Pets:** Accepted.
[SAVE] 🛏 ✕ 🗑 🔒 💻 🍴 ⌫ ✕

**⬧⬧⬧** ◈◈◈ **Days Inn-Kennedy Space Center** 🆂🅷
(321) 269-4480. **$59-$125.** 3755 Cheney Hwy. I-95, exit 215 (SR 50). Ext corridors. **Pets:** Accepted.
[SAVE] 🛏 ✕ 🗑 🔒 💻 ⌫

**⬧⬧⬧** ◈◈◈ **Hampton Inn Titusville/Kennedy Space Center** 🆂🅷
(321) 383-9191. **$89-$189.** 4760 Helen Hauser Blvd. I-95, exit 215, just w. Int corridors. **Pets:** Medium. $25 one-time fee/pet. Designated rooms, service with restrictions, supervision.
[SAVE] 🛏 ✕ 🔒 💻 ⌫

**⬧⬧⬧** ◈◈◈ **Ramada Inn & Suites-Kennedy Space Center** 🆂🅷
(321) 269-5510. **$59-$109.** 3500 Cheney Hwy. I-95, exit 215, just e on SR 50. Int corridors. **Pets:** Medium. $25 daily fee/room. Service with restrictions, supervision.
[SAVE] 🛏 ✕ 🗑 🔒 💻 🍴 ⌫ ✕

# VENICE

**⬧⬧⬧** ◈◈◈ **Holiday Inn Venice** Ⓜ ❄
(941) 485-5411. **$69-$169.** 455 US 41 Bypass N. 0.5 mi s of jct US 41. Ext/int corridors. **Pets:** Medium, other species. $30 one-time fee/pet. Service with restrictions, crate.
[SAVE] 🛏 ✕ 🛗 🗑 🔒 💻 🍴 ⌫ ✕

**⬧⬧⬧** ◈◈◈ **Horse and Chaise Inn A Bed & Breakfast** 🅱🅱
(941) 488-2702. **$125-$169, 3 day notice.** 317 Ponce de Leon. Just s of jct Venice Ave on Nassau St, just sw; downtown. Ext/int corridors. **Pets:** Accepted.
[SAVE] ✕ 🔒 ✉

◈ **Motel 6–364** Ⓜ
(941) 485-8255. **$45-$75.** 281 US 41 Bypass N. Just n of jct Venice Ave. Ext corridors. **Pets:** Accepted.
🛏 ✕ 🗑 🛗 ⌫

# WEEKI WACHEE

**⬧⬧⬧** ◈ ◈ **Best Western Weeki Wachee Resort** Ⓜ
(352) 596-2007. **$65-$109.** 6172 Commercial Way. On US 19, jct SR 50 (Cortez Blvd). Ext corridors. **Pets:** Other species. No service, supervision.
[SAVE] 🛏 ✕ 🗑 💻 ⌫

# WEST MELBOURNE

◈ ◈ **Howard Johnson** 🆂🅷
(321) 768-8439. **$70-$110.** 4431 W New Haven Ave. I-95, exit 180, just e on US 192. Ext corridors. **Pets:** Accepted.
🛏 ✕ 🗑 🔒 💻 ⌫

# WEST PALM BEACH

**⬧⬧⬧** ◈◈◈ **Comfort Inn-Palm Beach Lakes** Ⓜ
(561) 689-6100. **$109-$159.** 1901 Palm Beach Lakes Blvd. I-95, exit 71, just w. Int corridors. **Pets:** Accepted.
[SAVE] 🛏 ✕ 🔒 💻

◈◈◈ **Hibiscus House Bed & Breakfast** 🅱🅱
(561) 863-5633. **$95-$210, 14 day notice.** 501 30th St. 1.2 mi n on Flagler Dr from jct Palm Beach Lakes Blvd, 0.3 mi w. Int corridors. **Pets:** Other species.
[ASK] 🛏 ✕ 🔒 ⌫

◈◈◈ **La Quinta Inn** Ⓜ
(561) 697-3388. **$89-$129.** 5981 Okeechobee Blvd. SR 704, at east side of Florida Tpke, exit 99. Ext corridors. **Pets:** Accepted.
[ASK] 🛏 ✕ 🗑 🛗 🔒 💻 ⌫

◈◈ **Red Roof Inn-West Palm Beach** Ⓜ
(561) 697-7710. **$66-$100.** 2421 Metrocenter Blvd E. I-95, exit 74 (45th St), just w on CR 702; in Metrocenter Corporate Park. Ext/int corridors. **Pets:** Accepted.
✕ 🛗 🗑 🛗 🔒 ⌫

◈◈◈ **Residence Inn by Marriott West Palm Beach** 🆂🅷
(561) 687-4747. **$119-$359.** 2461 Metrocenter Blvd. I-95, exit 74, just w on 45th St; in Metrocenter Corporate Park. Int corridors. **Pets:** Other species. $75 one-time fee/room. Service with restrictions, crate.
[ASK] ✕ 🛗 🗑 🛗 🔒 💻 ⌫ ✕

◈◈ **Studio 6 Extended Stay #6026** Ⓜ
(561) 640-3335. **$63-$93.** 1535 Centrepark Dr N. I-95, exit 69 (Belvedere Rd), w to Australian Ave, n to Centrepark Dr, then e straight ahead. Ext corridors. **Pets:** Accepted.
🛏 ✕ 🛗 🛗 🔒

**⬧⬧⬧** ◈◈ **Wellesley Inn (West Palm Beach)** 🆂🅷
(561) 689-8540. **$79-$159.** 1910 Palm Beach Lakes Blvd. I-95, exit 71, just w. Int corridors. **Pets:** Small. Designated rooms, service with restrictions, crate.
[SAVE] 🛏 ✕ 🛗 🔒 💻 ⌫

# WILLISTON

◈ **Williston Motor Inn** Ⓜ
(352) 528-4801. **$38.** 606 W Noble Ave. 0.5 mi n on US 27 alternate route. Ext corridors. **Pets:** Accepted.
✕ 🔒 💻 🍴 ⌫

# WINTER HAVEN

**⬧⬧⬧** ◈◈◈ **Best Western Admiral's Inn** 🆂🅷
(863) 324-5950. **$98-$249.** 5665 Cypress Gardens Blvd. SR 540, 3 mi e of jct US 17; 3.9 mi w of jct US 27. Ext/int corridors. **Pets:** Accepted.
[SAVE] 🛏 ✕ 🔒 💻 🍴 ⌫ ✕

## CITY INDEX

## ADAIRSVILLE

### 🔺🔺 ▽▽▽ Comfort Inn SH
(770) 773-2886. **$50-$85.** 107 Princeton Blvd. I-75, exit 306, just w. Ext corridors. **Pets:** Small. $10 daily fee/pet. Service with restrictions, supervision.
SAVE S🔒 ✖ 🔒M 🔒 🔒 💻 ➰

### ▽▽▽▽ Ramada Limited SH
(770) 769-9726. **$50-$110.** 500 Georgia North Cir. I-75, exit 306, 0.3 mi w. Ext corridors. **Pets:** Medium. $8 daily fee/pet. Designated rooms, service with restrictions, supervision.
ASK S🔒 ✖ 🔒M 🔒 🔒 💻 ➰

## ADEL

### ▽▽▽▽ Hampton Inn SH
(229) 896-3099. **$70-$72.** 1500 W 4th St. I-75, exit 39, just w. Int corridors. **Pets:** Other species. $10 daily fee/pet. Designated rooms, service with restrictions, supervision.
ASK S🔒 ✖ 🔒M 🔒 🔒 💻 ➰

### ▽▽ Super 8 Motel I-75 SH
(229) 896-2244. **$44-$49.** 1103 W 4th St. I-75, exit 39, just e. Ext corridors. **Pets:** Accepted.
ASK S🔒 ✖ ➰

## ALBANY

### ▽▽ Jameson Inn SH
(229) 435-3737. **$54-$104.** 2720 Dawson Rd. 0.5 mi s of jct US 82 and SR 520. Ext corridors. **Pets:** Very small, other species. $10 daily fee/room. Service with restrictions, supervision.
ASK ✖ 🔒 💻 ➰

### ▽ Motel 6 #172 SH
(229) 439-0078. **$35-$47.** 201 S Thornton Dr. Just e of US 19/82. Ext corridors. **Pets:** Accepted.
S🔒 ✖ ➰

### ▽▽ Quality Inn-Merry Acres SH
(229) 435-7721. **$65-$179.** 1500 Dawson Rd. 3.3 mi w. Ext corridors. **Pets:** Small, dogs only. $10 daily fee/pet. Designated rooms, service with restrictions, crate.
ASK S🔒 ✖ 🔒 💻 🍽 ➰

### ▽▽▽ Wingate Inn SH
(229) 883-9800. **$105.** 2735 Dawson Rd. Jct US 82 and SR 520, 0.4 mi s. Int corridors. **Pets:** Accepted.
ASK S🔒 ✖ 🔒 💻 ➰

## AMERICUS

### 🔺🔺 ▽▽▽▽ 1906 Pathway Inn Bed & Breakfast BB 🐾
(229) 928-2078. **$89-$145.** 501 S Lee St. 0.5 mi s of US 280 on SR 377. Int corridors. **Pets:** Small, other species. $50 deposit/room, $20 daily fee/pet. Designated rooms, service with restrictions, supervision.
SAVE ✖

### ▽▽▽ Holiday Inn Express SH
(229) 928-5400. **$80-$110.** 1611 E Lomar St. On US 280, just w of jct US 27. Ext corridors. **Pets:** Accepted.
ASK S🔒 ✖ 🔒 💻 ➰

### ▽▽ Jameson Inn Americus SH
(229) 924-2726. **$54-$104.** 1605 E Lamar St. On US 280, just w of jct US 27. Ext corridors. **Pets:** Very small, other species. $10 daily fee/room. Service with restrictions, supervision.
ASK ✖ 🔒 🔒 💻 ➰

### ▽▽ Ramada Inn SH
(229) 924-4431. **$51-$70.** 1205 Martin Luther King Jr Blvd. On US 19 S, 1 mi w of downtown. Ext corridors. **Pets:** Small, other species. $10 daily fee/pet. Designated rooms, service with restrictions.
ASK S🔒 ✖ 🔒 💻 🍽 ➰

## ASHBURN

### 🔺🔺 ▽▽▽ Best Western Ashburn Inn SH
(229) 567-0080. **$50-$69.** 820 Shoney's Dr. I-75, exit 82, just w. Ext corridors. **Pets:** Small, dogs only. $10 daily fee/pet. Designated rooms, service with restrictions, supervision.
SAVE ✖ 🔒 💻 ➰

### 🔺🔺 ▽▽▽ Days Inn SH
(229) 567-3346. **$48-$58.** 823 E Washington Ave. I-75, exit 82, just w on SR 112. Ext corridors. **Pets:** Small. $10 daily fee/pet. Designated rooms, service with restrictions, supervision.
SAVE ✖ 🔒 ➰

### 🔺🔺 ▽▽▽ Ramada Limited SH
(229) 567-3295. **$52.** 156 Whittle Cir. I-75, exit 82, just w. Ext corridors. **Pets:** Accepted.
SAVE S🔒 🔒 💻 ➰

▼▼/▼▼ Super 8 Motel **SH**
(229) 567-4688. **$59.** 749 E Washington Ave. I-75, exit 82, just w. Ext corridors. **Pets:** Other species. $5 daily fee/pet. Designated rooms, service with restrictions, supervision.

A$K ⓢ ☒ 🖶

## ATHENS

▲▲▲ ▼▼/▼▼ Best Western-Colonial Inn **SH**
(706) 546-7311. **$59-$119.** 170 N Milledge Ave. Jct US 78 business route (Broad St), 0.5 mi w on SR 15. Ext corridors. **Pets:** Accepted.

SAVE ☒ 🖶 🖵 ⌇

▼▼/▼▼ Holiday Inn **LH**
(706) 549-4433. **$74-$99.** 197 E Broad St. On US 78 business route (Broad St); center. Ext/int corridors. **Pets:** Accepted.

A$K ⓢ ☒ 🔲 🖶 🖵 ⍟

▼▼/▼▼ Holiday Inn Express **SH**
(706) 546-8122. **$69-$84.** 513 W Broad St. On US 78 business route (Broad St); center. Int corridors. **Pets:** Accepted.

A$K ⓢ ☒ 🔲 🖶 🖵 ⌇

▼▼ Microtel Inn **SH**
(706) 548-5676. **$54-$130.** 1050 Ultimate Dr. Jct US 78 business route (Broad St) and SR 10 Loop, 1.4 mi e. Int corridors. **Pets:** Small, dogs only. $25 one-time fee/room. Designated rooms, service with restrictions, crate.

A$K ⓢ ☒ 🔲 🖶

# ATLANTA METROPOLITAN AREA

## ACWORTH

▼▼/▼▼ Acworth Comfort Suites **SH**
(678) 574-4222. **$74-$84.** 200 N Point Way. I-75, exit 277, just e. Int corridors. **Pets:** Small, dogs only. $10 one-time fee/pet. Service with restrictions, supervision.

A$K ⓢ ☒ 🔲 🖶 🖵 ⌇

▲▲▲ ▼▼/▼▼ America's Best Inn **M**
(770) 974-5400. **$45-$50, 7 day notice.** 5320 Cherokee St. I-75, exit 278, just w. Ext corridors. **Pets:** $5 daily fee/pet. Service with restrictions, supervision.

SAVE ⓢ ☒ 🔲 🖶 ⌇

▲▲▲ ▼▼/▼▼ Best Western Acworth Inn **SH**
(770) 974-0116. **$60-$85.** 5155 Cowan Rd. I-75, exit 277, just w. Ext corridors. **Pets:** Accepted.

SAVE ⓢ ☒ 🖶 🖵 ⌇

▲▲▲ ▼▼/▼▼ Days Inn **M**
(770) 974-1700. **$50-$80.** 5035 Cowan Rd. I-75, exit 277, just w. Ext corridors. **Pets:** Accepted.

SAVE ⓢ ☒ ⌇

▲▲▲ ▼▼/▼▼ Econo Lodge **SH**
(770) 974-1922. **$50-$80.** 4980 Cowan Rd. I-75, exit 277, just w. Ext corridors. **Pets:** Accepted.

SAVE ⓢ ☒ 🖶 🖵 ⌇

▲▲▲ ▼▼/▼▼ Super 8 Motel **SH**
(770) 966-9700. **$45-$79.** 4970 Cowan Rd. I-75, exit 277, just w. Ext corridors. **Pets:** Accepted.

SAVE ⓢ ☒ 🔲 🖶 ⌇

## ALPHARETTA

▲▲▲ ▼▼/▼▼ AmeriSuites (Atlanta Alpharetta/North Point Mall) **SH**
(770) 594-8788. **$89-$129, 30 day notice.** 7500 North Point Pkwy. SR 400, exit 8, just e to North Point Pkwy, then just n. Int corridors. **Pets:** Small, dogs only $10 daily fee/pet. Service with restrictions, supervision.

SAVE ⓢ ☒ 🅼 🔲 🖶 🖵 ⌇

▲▲▲ ▼▼/▼▼ AmeriSuites (Atlanta Alpharetta/Windward Parkway) **SH**
(770) 343-9566. **$109-$159.** 5595 Windward Pkwy. SR 400, exit 11, just w. Int corridors. **Pets:** Accepted.

SAVE ⓢ ☒ 🅼 🔲 🖶 🖵 ⌇

▼▼/▼▼ DoubleTree Hotel Alpharetta **SH**
(678) 347-0022. **$79-$159.** 2925 Jordan Ct. SR 400, exit 11, 0.7 mi w. Int corridors. **Pets:** Accepted.

A$K ⓢ ☒ 🅼 🔲 🖶 🖵 ⌇

▼▼/▼▼ Extended StayAmerica **SH**
(770) 475-2676. **$54-$64.** 1950 Rock Mill Rd. SR 400, exit 9, just e. Int corridors. **Pets:** Accepted.

A$K ⓢ 🅼 🔲 🖶 🖵

▼▼/▼▼ Extended Stay Deluxe **SH**
(770) 569-1730. **$50-$65.** 3329 Old Milton Pkwy. SR 400, exit 10, just e. Int corridors. **Pets:** $25 daily fee/pet. Service with restrictions, supervision.

A$K ⓢ ☒ 🅼 🔲 🖶 🖵 ⌇

▲▲▲ ▼▼/▼▼ Homewood Suites **SH**
(770) 998-1622. **$144-$189.** 10775 Davis Dr. SR 400, exit 8, northwest corner. Int corridors. **Pets:** Other species. $100 one-time fee/room.

SAVE ⓢ ☒ 🅼 🔲 🖶 🖵 ⌇

▼▼/▼▼ La Quinta Inn & Suites Atlanta (Alpharetta) **SH**
(770) 754-7800. **$98-$118.** 1350 North Point Dr. SR 400, exit 9, 0.5 mi e. Int corridors. **Pets:** Medium. No service.

A$K ☒ 🅼 🔲 🖶 🖵 ⌇

▲▲▲ ▼▼/▼▼ Residence Inn by Marriott **SH**
(770) 664-0664. **$124-$169.** 5465 Windward Pkwy W. SR 400, exit 11, 0.4 mi w. Ext/int corridors. **Pets:** Accepted.

SAVE ☒ 🅼 🔲 🖶 🖵 ⌇ ☒

▼▼/▼▼ Sierra Suites Alpharetta **SH**
(678) 339-0505. **$75-$129.** 12505 Cingular Way. SR 400, exit 11, 0.5 mi w. Int corridors. **Pets:** Accepted.

A$K ⓢ ☒ 🅼 🔲 🖶 🖵 ⌇

▼▼/▼▼ Staybridge Suites **SH**
(770) 569-7200. **$69-$209.** 3980 North Point Pkwy. SR 400, exit 10, 0.5 mi e. Int corridors. **Pets:** Medium. $150 one-time fee/room. Service with restrictions.

A$K ⓢ ☒ 🅼 🔲 🖶 🖵 ⌇

▼▼ StudioPlus **SH**
(770) 475-7871. **Call for rates.** 3331 Old Milton Pkwy. SR 400, exit 10, just e. Int corridors. **Pets:** Accepted.

☒ 🅼 🔲 🖶 🖵 ⌇

▼▼/▼▼ TownePlace Suites by Marriott **SH**
(770) 664-1300. **$49-$129.** 7925 S Westside Pkwy. SR 400, exit 9, 0.3 mi w. Int corridors. **Pets:** Medium. $75 one-time fee/room. Service with restrictions.

A$K ⓢ ☒ 🅼 🔲 🖶 🖵 ⌇

▼▼/▼▼ Wingate Inn **SH**
(770) 649-0955. **$80-$115.** 1005 Kingswood Pl. SR 400, exit 8, 0.7 mi w. Int corridors. **Pets:** Service with restrictions, crate.

A$K ⓢ ☒ 🅼 🔲 🖶 🖵

# ATLANTA

**AAA ▼▼▼▼ AmeriSuites (Atlanta/Buckhead) SH**
(404) 869-6161. **$89-$199.** 3242 Peachtree Rd NE. Jct Peachtree and Piedmont rds NE, just s. Int corridors. **Pets:** Accepted.

**AAA ▼▼▼▼ AmeriSuites (Atlanta/Perimeter Center) SH**
(770) 730-9300. **$79-$149.** 1005 Crestline Pkwy. SR 400, exit 5A (Dunwoody), 0.3 mi e. Int corridors. **Pets:** Accepted.

**AAA ▼▼▼ Baymont Inn & Suites**
**Atlanta-Buckhead/Lenox SH**
(404) 321-0999. **$69-$89.** 2535 Chantilly Dr NE. I-85, exit 88 southbound; exit 86 northbound, 2 mi on Buford Hwy to Lenox Rd, then just e under highway. Int corridors. **Pets:** Medium. Service with restrictions.

**AAA ▼▼▼▼ Best Western Granada Suite Hotel SH**
(404) 876-6100. **$95-$279.** 1302 W Peachtree St. I-75/85, exit 250 (14th St), just e, then just n on W Peachtree St to 16th St. Int corridors. **Pets:** Small. $50 one-time fee/pet. Designated rooms, service with restrictions, supervision.

**AAA ▼▼▼▼ Best Western Inn at the Peachtrees SH**
(404) 577-6970. **$95-$229.** 330 W Peachtree St. I-75/85, exit 248C northbound, 0.4 mi w to Peachtree St, then 0.3 mi n; exit 249C southbound, just s to Peachtree Pl, then just e. Ext/int corridors. **Pets:** Medium. $50 one-time fee/room. Service with restrictions, crate.

**▼▼ Beverly Hills Inn BB**
(404) 233-8520. **$99-$199, 3 day notice.** 65 Sheridan Dr NE. Jct Piedmont and Peachtree rds, 1.1 mi s on Peachtree Rd to Sheridan Dr, then just e. Int corridors. **Pets:** $50 one-time fee/room. Service with restrictions, supervision.

**▼▼▼ Crowne Plaza Atlanta Perimeter NW LH**
(770) 955-1700. **$69-$169.** 6345 Powers Ferry Rd NW. I-285, exit 22, southeast corner. Int corridors. **Pets:** Small. $75 one-time fee/room. Service with restrictions, supervision.

**▼▼▼ Extended StayAmerica SH**
(404) 679-4333. **Call for rates.** 3115 Clairmont Rd. I-85, exit 91, 0.6 mi w. Int corridors. **Pets:** Accepted.

**▼▼▼ Extended StayAmerica SH**
(770) 396-5600. **Call for rates.** 905 S Crestline Pkwy. I-285, exit 28 westbound, 0.7 mi n; exit 26 eastbound, 0.5 mi n to Hammond Dr, 0.5 mi e, then 0.3 mi n. Int corridors. **Pets:** Accepted.

**▼▼▼ Extended Stay Deluxe SH**
(770) 933-8010. **$75-$109.** 2010 Powers Ferry Rd. I-75, exit 260 (Windy Hill Rd). Int corridors. **Pets:** $25 daily fee/pet. Service with restrictions, supervision.

**▼▼▼ Extended Stay Deluxe SH**
(404) 237-9100. **$89-$129.** 3967 Peachtree Rd. I-85, exit 89, 2.8 mi w. Int corridors. **Pets:** $25 daily fee/pet. Service with restrictions, supervision.

**▼▼▼ Extended Stay Deluxe (Atlanta/Windy Hill) SH**
(770) 226-0242. **$55-$80.** 2225 Interstate North Pkwy. I-75, exit 260 (Windy Hill Rd), just e to Interstate North Pkwy, then just s. Int corridors. **Pets:** $25 daily fee/pet. Service with restrictions, supervision.

**▼▼▼ Extended Stay Deluxe SH**
(770) 379-0111. **$75-$109.** 6330 Peachtree-Dunwoody Rd NE. I-285, exit 28 westbound, 0.7 mi n; exit 26 eastbound, 0.5 mi n to Hammond Dr, 0.5 mi e, then 0.3 mi n. Int corridors. **Pets:** $25 daily fee/pet. Service with restrictions, supervision.

**▼▼▼▼ Fairfield Inn-Atlanta/Buckhead SH**
(404) 846-0900. **$89-$129.** 3092 Piedmont Rd NE. Jct Piedmont and Peachtree rds NE, just s. Int corridors. **Pets:** Accepted.

**AAA ▼▼▼▼▼ Four Seasons Hotel Atlanta SH 🐾**
(404) 881-9898. **$365-$1650.** 75 14th St. I-75/85, exit 250 (14th St), 0.3 mi e. Int corridors. **Pets:** Very small. Designated rooms, service with restrictions, supervision.

**AAA ▼▼▼ ▼▼▼ Grand Hyatt Atlanta LH**
(404) 365-8100. **$165-$305.** 3300 Peachtree Rd. Corner of Peachtree and Piedmont rds. Int corridors. **Pets:** Accepted.

**AAA ▼▼▼▼ Hampton Inn-Perimeter Center SH**
(404) 303-0014. **$59-$109.** 769 Hammond Dr. I-285, exit 26 eastbound, 0.5 mi n to Hammond Dr, then 0.5 mi e; exit 28 westbound, 0.5 mi n to Hammond Dr, then 0.5 mi w. Int corridors. **Pets:** Accepted.

**AAA ▼▼▼▼ Hawthorn Suites-Atlanta NW SH**
(770) 952-9595. **$99-$109.** 1500 Parkwood Cir. I-75, exit 260 (Windy Hill Rd), 0.5 mi e, then 0.3 mi s on Powers Ferry Rd. Ext corridors. **Pets:** Accepted.

**▼▼▼▼ Holiday Inn Express Hotel & Suites-Atlanta Buckhead SH**
(404) 262-7880. **$95-$229.** 505 Pharr Rd. Jct Pharr Rd and Maple Dr; just w of Piedmont Rd. Ext/int corridors. **Pets:** Accepted.

**▼▼▼▼ Holiday Inn Select Atlanta Perimeter SH**
(770) 457-6363. **$84-$124.** 4386 Chamblee-Dunwoody Rd. I-285, exit 30 eastbound, southwest corner; westbound, follow access road 1.3 mi to Chamblee-Dunwoody Rd, then just s. Int corridors. **Pets:** Accepted.

**▼▼ Homestead Studio Suites Hotel-Atlanta/North Druid Hills SH**
(404) 325-1223. **$44-$74.** 1339 Executive Park Dr NE. I-85, exit 89, just e to Executive Park Dr, then just s. Ext corridors. **Pets:** $25 daily fee/pet. Service with restrictions, supervision.

**▼▼ Homestead Studio Suites Hotel-Atlanta/Perimeter SH**
(770) 522-0025. **$54-$74.** 1050 Hammond Dr. I-285, exit 26 eastbound, 0.5 mi n to Hammond Dr, then 0.5 mi e; exit 28 westbound, just n to Hammond Dr, then just w. Ext corridors. **Pets:** $25 daily fee/pet. Service with restrictions, supervision.

**▼▼▼ Homewood Suites-Cumberland SH**
(770) 988-9449. **$99-$189.** 3200 Cobb Pkwy SW. I-285, exit 19 eastbound; exit 20 westbound, 0.7 mi se on US 41 (Cobb Pkwy). Ext/int corridors. **Pets:** Accepted.

**▼▼▼ Hotel Indigo SH 🐾**
(404) 874-9200. **$89-$209.** 683 Peachtree St NE. I-75/85, exit 249D, 0.5 mi e to Peachtree St, then just n. Int corridors. **Pets:** Other species. Designated rooms.

▼▼▼▼ **La Quinta Inn & Suites Atlanta (Paces Ferry/Vinings)** SH
(770) 801-9002. **$86-$106.** 2415 Paces Ferry Rd SE. I-285, exit 18, just w. Int corridors. **Pets:** Medium. Service with restrictions.
ASK ⊠ ᎧM ⬚ ⬚ ⬚ ⬚ ⬚ ⊸

▲▲▲ ▼▼▼▼ **La Quinta Inn & Suites Atlanta (Perimeter/ Medical Center)** SH
(770) 350-6177. **$77-$125.** 6260 Peachtree-Dunwoody. I-285, exit 28 westbound, 0.7 mi n; exit 26 eastbound, 0.5 mi n to Hammond Dr, 0.7 mi e, then 0.5 mi n. Int corridors. **Pets:** Medium. No service.
SAVE ⊠ ᎧM ⬚ ⬚ ⬚ ⬚ ⊸

▲▲▲ ▼▼▼ ▼▼▼ **Omni Hotel at CNN Center** LH
(404) 659-0000. **$389, 3 day notice.** 100 CNN Center. I-75/85, exit 248C northbound, 0 8 mi w; exit 249C southbound to International Blvd, then 0.5 mi w. Int corridors. **Pets:** Small, other species. $50 one-time fee/pet. Designated rooms, service with restrictions, crate.
SAVE SᏰ ⊠ ⬚ ⬚ ⬚ ⬚ ⬚ ⊸ ⊠

▼▼ **Red Roof Inn-Druid Hills** M
(404) 321-1653. **$55-$71.** 1960 N Druid Hills Rd. I-85, exit 89, just w. Ext corridors. **Pets:** Accepted.
⊠ ⬚

▼▼▼▼ **Residence Inn Atlanta Midtown at 17th Street** SH
(404) 745-1000. **$79-$302.** 1365 Peachtree St. I-75/85, exit 250 (14th St), 0.5 mi e to Peachtree St, then 0.3 mi n. Int corridors. **Pets:** Medium. $75 one-time fee/room. Service with restrictions, crate.
ASK SᏰ ⊠ ᎧM ⬚ ⬚ ⬚ ⬚ ⊸ ⊠

▼▼▼▼ **Residence Inn-Buckhead/Lenox** SH
(404) 467-1660. **$174-$194.** 2220 Lake Blvd. I-85, exit 89, 1.6 mi w on N Druid Hills (becomes E Roxboro), just n on Lenox Park Blvd. Int corridors. **Pets:** Medium. $75 one-time fee/room. Service with restrictions, supervision.
ASK SᏰ ⊠ ᎧM ⬚ ⬚ ⬚ ⬚ ⊸ ⊠

▲▲▲ ▼▼▼▼ **Residence Inn by Marriott-Atlanta/Buckhead** SH
(404) 239-0677. **$169.** 2960 Piedmont Rd NE. Jct Piedmont and Pharr rds, just s. Ext corridors. **Pets:** Medium, other species. $75 one-time fee/room.
SAVE SᏰ ⊠ ⬚ ⬚ ⬚ ⬚ ⊸ ⊠

▼▼▼▼ **Residence Inn by Marriott-Atlanta Downtown** SH
(404) 522-0950. **$85-$169.** 134 Peachtree St NW. I-75/85, exit 248C northbound, 0.4 mi w, then just s; exit 249A southbound to International Blvd, just w, then just s. Int corridors. **Pets:** Accepted.
ASK SᏰ ⊠ ⬚ ⬚ ⬚ ⬚

▲▲▲ ▼▼▼▼ **Residence Inn by Marriott Atlanta Dunwoody** SH
(770) 455-4446. **$75-$169.** 1901 Savoy Dr. I-285, exit 30, just e. Ext corridors. **Pets:** Accepted.
SAVE ⊠ ⬚ ⬚ ⬚ ⊸ ⊠

▼▼▼▼ **Residence Inn by Marriott Midtown** SH
(404) 872-8885. **$74-$234.** 1041 W Peachtree St. I-75/85, exit 250 (10th St), just e to W Peachtree St, then just n; corner of 11th St. Int corridors. **Pets:** Accepted.
ASK SᏰ ⊠ ⬚ ⬚ ⬚ ⬚

▲▲▲ ▼▼▼▼ **Residence Inn by Marriott-Perimeter Center** SH ☙
(404) 252-5066. **$99-$189.** 6096 Barfield Rd. I-285, exit 26 eastbound, 0.5 mi n on Glenridge to Hammond Dr, then 0.3 mi e to Barfield Rd; exit 28 westbound (Peachtree-Dunwoody Rd), 0.5 mi n to Hammond Dr, then just w. Ext corridors. **Pets:** Other species. $75 one-time fee/room. Service with restrictions.
SAVE ⊠ ⬚ ⬚ ⬚ ⊸ ⊠

▲▲▲ ▼▼▼ ▼▼▼ **The Ritz-Carlton, Atlanta** LH ☙
(404) 659-0400. **$285-$2000.** 181 Peachtree St NE. I-75/85, exit 248C northbound, 0.4 mi w, then just s; exit 249A southbound, just s to International Blvd, just w, then just s. Int corridors. **Pets:** Small, other species. $150 one-time fee/pet. Service with restrictions, supervision.
SAVE ⊠ ᎧM ⬚ ⬚ ⬚ ⊠

▲▲▲ ▼▼▼ ▼▼▼ **The Ritz-Carlton, Buckhead** LH
(404) 237-2700. **$335-$2500.** 3434 Peachtree Rd NE. I-85, exit 86, 1.8 mi n on Cheshire Bridge-Lenox Rd. Int corridors. **Pets:** Accepted.
SAVE ⊠ ⬚ ⬚ ⬚ ⬚ ⬚ ⊸ ⊠

▼▼▼▼ **Sheraton Atlanta Hotel** LH
(404) 659-6500. **$89-$142.** 165 Courtland St. I-75/85, exit 249A southbound; exit 248C northbound, just w. Int corridors. **Pets:** Accepted.
ASK SᏰ ⊠ ⬚ ⬚ ⬚ ⬚ ⬚ ⊸ ⊠

▲▲▲ ▼▼▼ ▼▼▼ **Sheraton Buckhead Hotel Atlanta** LH ☙
(404) 261-9250. **$109-$289.** 3405 Lenox Rd NE. I-85, exit 88 southbound; exit 86 northbound, 1.8 mi n. Int corridors. **Pets:** Service with restrictions.
SAVE SᏰ ⊠ ⬚ ⬚ ⬚ ⬚ ⊸

▲▲▲ ▼▼▼▼ **Sheraton Midtown Atlanta Hotel at Colony Square** LH ☙
(404) 892-6000. **$89-$289.** 188 14th St NE. I-75/85, exit 250 (14th St), 0.5 mi e. Int corridors. **Pets:** Medium. $25 daily fee/pet. Designated rooms, service with restrictions, crate.
SAVE SᏰ ⊠ ᎧM ⬚ ⬚ ⬚ ⬚ ⬚ ⊸

▼▼▼▼ **Sheraton Suites Galleria** LH
(770) 955-3900. **$89-$189.** 2844 Cobb Pkwy SE. I-285, exit 20 westbound; exit 19 eastbound, just s on US 41 (Cobb Pkwy). Int corridors. **Pets:** Accepted.
ASK SᏰ ⊠ ⬚ ⬚ ⬚ ⬚ ⬚ ⊸

▼▼▼▼ **Staybridge Suites** SH
(404) 842-0800. **$99-$249.** 540 Pharr Rd. Jct Pharr and Piedmont rds, just w. Int corridors. **Pets:** Accepted.
ASK SᏰ ⊠ ⬚ ⬚ ⬚ ⬚ ⊸

▼▼▼▼ **Staybridge Suites-Atlanta-Mt. Vernon** SH
(404) 250-0110. **$160.** 760 Mt Vernon Hwy NE. I-285, exit 25, 0.8 mi n on Roswell Rd, then 1 mi e. Ext/int corridors. **Pets:** Accepted.
ASK SᏰ ⊠ ⬚ ⬚ ⬚ ⊸ ⊠

▼▼▼▼ **Staybridge Suites Atlanta Perimeter** SH
(678) 320-0111. **$144.** 4601 Ridgeview Rd. I-285, exit 29 (Ashford-Dunwoody Rd), 0.5 mi n, 0.5 mi w on Perimeter Center W to Crowne Pointe Dr, then just n. Int corridors. **Pets:** Accepted.
ASK SᏰ ⊠ ᎧM ⬚ ⬚ ⬚ ⊸

▲▲▲ ▼▼▼ **University Inn at Emory** SH ☙
(404) 634-7327. **$79-$159.** 1767 N Decatur Rd. I-85, exit 91, 3.8 mi s on Clairmont Rd to N Decatur Rd, then 0.8 mi w. Ext corridors. **Pets:** Large, other species. $15 daily fee/pet. Service with restrictions.
SAVE SᏰ ⊠ ⬚ ⬚ ⬚ ⊸

▲▲▲ ▼▼▼ ▼▼▼ **W Atlanta** LH ☙
(770) 396-6800. **$329-$399.** 111 Perimeter Center W. I-285, exit 29 (Ashford-Dunwoody Rd), 0.5 mi n. Int corridors. **Pets:** Medium, other species. $25 daily fee/pet, $100 one-time fee/room. Designated rooms, service with restrictions, supervision.
SAVE ⊠ ᎧM ⬚ ⬚ ⬚ ⬚ ⊸ ⊠

▼▼▼▼ **The Westin Atlanta North** LH
(770) 395-3900. **$169-$300.** 7 Concourse Pkwy. I-285, exit 28 westbound; exit 26 eastbound, 0.5 mi n to Hammond Dr, then 0.4 mi e. Int corridors. **Pets:** Accepted.
ASK SᏰ ⊠ ⬚ ⬚ ⬚ ⬚ ⬚ ⊸ ⊠

**△△△ ▽▽▽▽▽▽▽▽ The Westin Buckhead Atlanta** 🏠
(404) 365-0065. **$159-$389.** 3391 Peachtree Rd NE. Adjacent to Lenox Mall. Int corridors. **Pets:** Accepted.
[SAVE] [S△] [✕] [🐾] 🅵 🖥 [🍴] [≈] [✕]

**▽▽▽▽ The Westin Peachtree Plaza** 🏠
(404) 659-1400. **$109-$385, 3 day notice.** 210 Peachtree St. I-75/85, exit 248C northbound, 0.4 mi w; exit 249C southbound, 0.5 mi s. Int corridors. **Pets:** Accepted.
[ASK] [S△] [✕] [🐾] [♿] 🅵 🖥 [🍴] [≈]

# AUSTELL

**▽▽▽▽ La Quinta Inn Atlanta (West/Near Six Flags)** 🆂🅷
(770) 944-2110. **$69-$105.** 7377 Six Flags Dr. I-20, exit 46 eastbound; exit 46B westbound, just n. Ext/int corridors. **Pets:** Medium. Service with restrictions.
[ASK] [✕] [🐾] 🅵 🖥 [≈]

# COLLEGE PARK

**△△△ ▽▽▽▽ AmeriSuites (Atlanta/Airport)** 🆂🅷
(770) 994-2997. **$99-$149.** 1899 Sullivan Rd. I-85, exit 71, just e to Sullivan Rd, then just s; I-285, exit 60 (Riverdale Rd N), 1 mi to Sullivan Rd, then just s. Int corridors. **Pets:** Small. $15 daily fee/pet. Service with restrictions, supervision.
[SAVE] [S△] [✕] [♿] [🐾] 🅵 🖥 [≈]

**▽▽ Howard Johnson Express Inn** 🆂🅷
(404) 766-0000. **$55-$75, 3 day notice.** 2480 Old National Pkwy. I-285, exit 62, just s. Int corridors. **Pets:** Small. $15 daily fee/pet. Designated rooms, service with restrictions, crate.
[ASK] [S△] [✕] 🅵 🖥

**▽ Motel 6-1487 Atlanta Airport** 🅼
(404) 761-9701. **$41-$51.** 2471 Old National Pkwy. I-85, exit 69; I-285, exit 62, just s. Ext corridors. **Pets:** Accepted.
[S△] [✕] 🖥

**▽▽ Ramada Hotel Atlanta Airport South** 🆂🅷
(770) 996-4321. **$59-$99.** 1551 Phoenix Blvd. I-285, exit 60 (Riverdale Rd N), just sw. Ext/int corridors. **Pets:** Designated rooms, service with restrictions, supervision.
[ASK] [S△] [✕] [🐾] [♿] 🅵 🖥 [🍴] [≈]

**▽▽ Super 8 Motel-Atlanta Airport** 🆂🅷
(770) 991-8985. **Call for rates.** 2010 Sullivan Rd. I-85, exit 71. Int corridors. **Pets:** Accepted.
[✕] 🅵 🖥

# DECATUR

**▽▽ Best Inn & Suites** 🆂🅷
(404) 286-2500. **$58-$65.** 4095 Covington Hwy. I-285, exit 43, just w. Ext corridors. **Pets:** $10 daily fee/pet. No service, supervision.
[ASK] [S△] [✕] [♿] [🐾] 🅵 [≈]

# DORAVILLE

**△△△ ▽ Masters Inn** 🅼
(770) 454-8373. **$43-$52.** 3092 Presidential Pkwy. I-85, exit 94, just e, then n. Ext corridors. **Pets:** Accepted.
[SAVE] [S△] [✕] [🐾] 🅵 [≈]

# DOUGLASVILLE

**▽▽ Days Inn** 🅼
(770) 949-1499. **$49-$85, 15 day notice.** 5489 Westmoreland Plaza. I-20, exit 37, just n. Ext corridors. **Pets:** Small. $20 daily fee/pet. Designated rooms, service with restrictions, supervision.
[ASK] [S△] [✕] 🅵 [≈]

# DULUTH

**▽▽▽▽ AmeriSuites (Atlanta/Duluth-John's Creek)** 🆂🅷
(770) 622-5858. **$59-$99.** 11505 Medlock Bridge Rd. Jct SR 141 and 120, 0.7 mi n. Int corridors. **Pets:** Accepted.
[ASK] [S△] [✕] [♿] [🐾] [♿] 🅵 🖥 [≈]

**△△△ ▽▽▽▽ AmeriSuites (Atlanta/Gwinnett Mall)** 🆂🅷
(770) 623-9699. **$85-$149.** 3530 Venture Pkwy. I-85, exit 104, just w to Venture Pkwy, then just n. Int corridors. **Pets:** Accepted.
[SAVE] [S△] [✕] [♿] [🐾] 🅵 🖥 [≈]

**▽▽▽▽ Candlewood Suites-Atlanta** 🆂🅷
(678) 380-0414. **$69-$79.** 3665 Shackleford Rd. I-85, exit 104, just e, then just s. Int corridors. **Pets:** Large, other species. $150 one-time fee/room. Service with restrictions, crate.
[ASK] [S△] [✕] [♿] [🐾] [♿] 🅵 🖥

**△△△ ▽▽ Days Inn Gwinnett Place** 🆂🅷
(770) 476-8700. **$70-$100.** 1920 Pleasant Hill Rd. I-85, exit 104; northwest corner. Int corridors. **Pets:** Accepted.
[SAVE] [S△] 🖥

**▽▽ Extended StayAmerica** 🆂🅷
(770) 622-0270. **Call for rates.** 3430 Venture Pkwy. I-85, exit 104, just w to Venture Pkwy, then just n. Int corridors. **Pets:** Accepted.
[✕] [♿] [🐾] [♿] 🅵 🖥

**△△△ ▽▽▽▽ Hampton Inn & Suites-Gwinnett** 🆂🅷
(770) 931-9800. **$109-$129.** 1725 Pineland Rd. I-85, exit 104, 0.3 mi e to Crestwood, then just s. Int corridors. **Pets:** Small. $75 one-time fee/room. Designated rooms, no service, supervision.
[SAVE] [S△] [✕] [♿] [🐾] [♿] 🅵 🖥 [≈]

**△△△ ▽▽▽▽ Holiday Inn-Gwinnett Center** 🆂🅷
(770) 476-2022. **$74-$139.** 6310 Sugarloaf Pkwy. I-85, exit 108, just w. Int corridors. **Pets:** Other species. $75 one-time fee/room. Service with restrictions, crate.
[SAVE] [S△] [✕] [♿] [🐾] [♿] 🅵 🖥 [🍴] [≈]

**▽▽▽▽ La Quinta Inn Duluth** 🆂🅷
(678) 957-0500. **$79-$89.** 2370 Stephen Center Dr. I-85, exit 107, just w. Int corridors. **Pets:** Other species. Service with restrictions, supervision.
[ASK] [S△] [✕] [♿] [🐾] 🅵 🖥 [≈]

**△△△ ▽▽ Quality Inn–Gwinnett Mall** 🆂🅷
(770) 623-9300. **$50-$90.** 3500 Venture Pkwy. I-85, exit 104, just w to Venture Pkwy, then just n. Ext/int corridors. **Pets:** Other species. $10 daily fee/pet. Service with restrictions, supervision.
[SAVE] [S△] [✕] [🐾] 🅵 🖥 [≈]

**▽▽▽▽ Residence Inn-Atlanta Gwinnett** 🆂🅷 🐾
(770) 921-2202. **$144-$189.** 1760 Pineland Rd. I-85, exit 104, just e to Shackleford Rd, just s to Pineland Rd, then just e. Int corridors. **Pets:** Small, other species. $75 one-time fee/room. Service with restrictions, crate.
[ASK] [S△] [✕] [♿] [🐾] [♿] 🅵 🖥 [≈] [✕]

**▽▽ Studio 6 #6023** 🆂🅷
(770) 931-3113. **$47-$61.** 3525 Breckinridge Blvd. I-85, exit 104, just e to Breckinridge Blvd, then just n. Ext corridors. **Pets:** Accepted.
[S△] [✕] [♿] 🅵 🖥

**△△△ ▽▽▽▽ Wellesley Inn & Suites (Atlanta/Gwinnett Mall)** 🆂🅷
(770) 623-6800. **$89-$99, 3 day notice.** 3390 Venture Pkwy NW. I-85, exit 104, just w to Venture Pkwy, then just n. Int corridors. **Pets:** Medium, other species. $10 daily fee/pet. Service with restrictions, supervision.
[SAVE] [S△] [✕] [♿] [🐾] 🅵 🖥 [≈]

# EAST POINT

▼▼▼▼ AmeriSuites (Atlanta Airport/North) SH
(404) 768-8484. **$99-$199, 14 day notice.** 3415 Norman Berry Dr. I-85, exit 73 southbound, just e to Bobby Brown Pkwy, then just n; exit 73B northbound. Int corridors. **Pets:** Accepted.

ASK Sb X M 🖊 🖉 🖥 🖵 ⤬

⊕ ▼▼▼▼ Comfort Inn & Suites Atlanta Airport Camp
Creek SH
(404) 762-5566. **$79-$109.** 3601 N Desert Dr. I-285, exit 2, just e. Int corridors. **Pets:** Accepted.

SAVE Sb X M 🖊 🖥 🖵 ⤬

▼▼▼ Crowne Plaza Hotel and Resort Atlanta Airport LH
(404) 768-6660. **$79-$179.** 1325 Virginia Ave. I-85, exit 73 southbound; exit 73B northbound, just w. Int corridors. **Pets:** Accepted.

ASK Sb X M 🖊 🖉 🖥 🖵 ⤬

▼▼▼ Drury Inn & Suites-Atlanta Airport SH
(404) 761-4900. **$90-$130.** 1270 Virginia Ave. I-85, exit 73 southbound; exit 73A northbound, just e. Int corridors. **Pets:** Accepted.

ASK X M 🖊 🖉 🖥 🖵 ⤬

⊕ ▼▼▼ Holiday Inn Atlanta Airport North LH
(404) 762-8411. **$79-$139.** 1380 Virginia Ave. I-85, exit 73 southbound; exit 73B northbound, just w. Ext/int corridors. **Pets:** Accepted.

SAVE Sb X M 🖊 🖉 🖥 🖵 ⤬

▼▼ Red Roof Inn-Atlanta Airport North SH
(404) 209-1800. **$71-$76.** 1200 Virginia Ave. I-85, exit 73 southbound; exit 73A northbound, just e. Int corridors. **Pets:** Accepted.

ASK X M 🖊 🖉 🖥 🖵 ⤬

⊕ ▼▼▼ Wellesley Inn (Atlanta/Hartsfield Int'l
Airport) SH
(404) 762-5111. **$69-$89.** 1377 Virginia Ave. I-85, exit 73 southbound; exit 73B northbound, just w. Int corridors. **Pets:** Small, other species. $10 daily fee/pet. Designated rooms, service with restrictions, supervision.

SAVE Sb X 🖊 🖉 🖥 🖵 🍴 ⤬

# FOREST PARK

▼▼ Days Inn-Airport East SH
(404) 768-6400. **$60-$150.** 5116 Hwy 85. I-75, exit 237A southbound; exit 237 northbound, 0.5 mi w. **Pets:** Other species. $25 daily fee/room. No service, supervision.

ASK Sb X 🖥 🖵 ⤬

⊕ ▼▼▼ Super 8 Motel SH
(404) 363-8811. **$59-$99.** 410 Old Dixie Way. I-75, exit 235, just e. Ext corridors. **Pets:** Small, dogs only. $7 daily fee/pet. Service with restrictions, supervision.

SAVE Sb X 🖉 🖥 ⤬

# HAPEVILLE

⊕ ▼▼▼▼ Hilton Atlanta Airport LH
(404) 767-9000. **$89-$239.** 1031 Virginia Ave. I-85, exit 73 southbound; exit 73A northbound, just e. Int corridors. **Pets:** Large. $100 deposit/room. Designated rooms, service with restrictions, supervision.

SAVE X M 🖊 🖥 🖵 🍴 ⤬ 🖾

⊕ ▼▼▼ Residence Inn Atlanta Airport SH
(404) 761-0511. **$119-$189.** 3401 International Blvd. I-85, exit 73 southbound; exit 73A northbound, 0.5 mi e to International Blvd, then just n. Ext/int corridors. **Pets:** Accepted.

SAVE Sb X 🖊 🖉 🖥 🖵 ⤬ 🖾

# JONESBORO

⊕ ▼▼▼ Americas Best Value Inn & Suites SH
(770) 968-5018. **$39-$110.** 6358 Old Dixie Rd. I-75, exit 235, just w. Ext corridors. **Pets:** Accepted.

SAVE Sb X 🖥 🖵 ⤬

⊕ ▼▼▼ Holiday Inn Atlanta South Jonesboro SH
(770) 968-4300. **$90-$160.** 6288 Old Dixie Hwy. I-75, exit 235, just w. Int corridors. **Pets:** Medium. $15 one-time fee/room. Supervision.

SAVE Sb X M 🖊 🖉 🖥 🖵 🍴 ⤬

# KENNESAW

⊕ ▼▼▼ Best Western Kennesaw Inn SH
(770) 424-7666. **$54-$125.** 3375 Busbee Dr. I-75, exit 271, just e. Ext corridors. **Pets:** Small, other species. $10 daily fee/pet. Designated rooms, service with restrictions, supervision.

SAVE X 🖥 🖵 ⤬

▼▼ Extended StayAmerica SH
(770) 422-1403. **Call for rates.** 3000 George Busbee Pkwy. I-75, exit 269, just e to George Busbee Pkwy, then 0.8 mi n. Int corridors. **Pets:** Accepted.

X M 🖊 🖉 🖥 🖵

▼▼ Red Roof Inn-Town Center Mall M
(770) 429-0323. **$45-$52.** 520 Roberts Ct NW. I-75, exit 269, southeast corner. Ext corridors. **Pets:** Accepted.

X M 🖊 🖉 🖥

⊕ ▼▼▼ Residence Inn by Marriott Town
Center SH 🐾
(770) 218-1018. **$80-$200.** 3443 Busbee Dr. I-75, exit 271, just e. Int corridors. **Pets:** Other species. $75 one-time fee/room. Service with restrictions.

SAVE Sb X M 🖊 🖉 🖥 🖵 ⤬ 🖾

▼▼ Rodeway Inn M
(770) 590-0519. **$45-$70.** 1460 George Busbee Pkwy. I-75, exit 273, just e. Ext corridors. **Pets:** Accepted.

ASK Sb X 🖥 🖵 ⤬

▼▼ StudioPlus SH
(770) 425-6101. **Call for rates.** 3316 Busbee Dr. I-75, exit 271, just e to Busbee Dr, then just s. Int corridors. **Pets:** Accepted.

X M 🖊 🖥 🖵 ⤬

▼▼▼ TownePlace Suites by Marriott SH
(770) 794-8282. **$75-$169.** 1074 Cobb Place Blvd NW. I-75, exit 269, 1.1 mi w to Second Cobb Place Blvd entrance. Int corridors. **Pets:** Accepted.

ASK Sb X M 🖊 🖉 🖥 🖵 ⤬

# LAWRENCEVILLE

⊕ ▼▼▼ Days Inn M
(770) 995-7782. **$49-$60.** 731 Duluth Hwy. Jct SR 316, just e on SR 120. Ext corridors. **Pets:** $20 one-time fee/pet. Supervision.

SAVE Sb X 🖥

▼▼▼ Hampton Inn SH
(770) 338-9600. **$84-$114.** 1135 Lakes Pkwy. I-85, exit 106 northbound, 4 mi e to Riverside Pkwy, then just n; exit 115 southbound, 4.4 mi s on SR 20 to SR 316, then 1.1 mi w. Int corridors. **Pets:** Small. $50 one-time fee/pet. Service with restrictions, supervision.

ASK Sb X M 🖊 🖉 🖥 🖵 ⤬

# LITHIA SPRINGS

▼▼ SuiteOne Hotel of Douglas County SH
(770) 948-8331. **$69-$99.** 637 W Market Cir. I-20, exit 44, 1 mi n. Ext corridors. **Pets:** Accepted.

ASK Sb X 🖉 🖥 🖵 ⤬

# LITHONIA

▼▼▼▼ AmeriSuites (Lithonia/Stonecrest Mall) SH
(770) 484-4384. **$109-$199.** 7900 Mall Ring Rd. I-20, exit 75, just s on Turner Hill Rd, then 0.7 mi w; at rear of Stonecrest Mall. Int corridors. **Pets:** Accepted.

ASK Sb X 🖉 🖥 🖵 ⤬

# MARIETTA

**▼▼▼▼ Comfort Inn-Marietta** SH
(770) 952-3000. **$79-$109.** 2100 Northwest Pkwy. I-75, exit 261, 0.3 mi w to Franklin Rd, then just s. Ext corridors. **Pets:** Small. $25 one-time fee/pet. Designated rooms, service with restrictions, supervision.

[ASK] [S$] [✕] [⚏] [🛏] [📺] [≈]

**▼▼▼▼ Drury Inn & Suites-Atlanta Northwest** SH
(770) 612-0900. **$75-$125.** 1170 Powers Ferry Pl. I-75, exit 261, just e. Int corridors. **Pets:** Accepted.

[ASK] [✕] [⚏M] [⚏] [⚏] [🛏] [📺] [≈]

**▼▼▼ Extended StayAmerica** SH
(770) 690-9477. **Call for rates.** 1967 Leland Dr. I-75, exit 260, just e to Leland Dr, then just n. Int corridors. **Pets:** Accepted.

[✕] [⚏M] [⚏] [🛏] [📺]

**ⒶⒶⒶ ▼▼▼▼ Holiday Inn Hotel & Suites**
**Atlanta-Marietta** SH
(770) 952-7581. **$80-$125.** 2265 Kingston Ct. I-75, exit 261, 0.3 mi w to Franklin Rd, just n to Kingston Ct, then just e. Int corridors. **Pets:** Accepted.

[SAVE] [S$] [✕] [⚏M] [⚏] [⚏] [🛏] [📺] [🍴] [≈]

**▼▼▼▼ Homestead Studio Suites Hotel-Atlanta/Powers**
**Ferry/Galleria Area** SH
(770) 303-0043. **$49-$69.** 2239 Powers Ferry Rd. I-285, exit 22, just n. Int corridors. **Pets:** $25 daily fee/pet. Service with restrictions, supervision.

[ASK] [S$] [✕] [⚏M] [⚏] [⚏] [🛏] [📺]

**ⒶⒶⒶ ▼▼▼▼ Hyatt Regency Suites Perimeter**
**Northwest** LH
(770) 956-1234. **$89-$185.** 2999 Windy Hill Rd. I-75, exit 260, 0.5 mi e at Powers Ferry Rd. Int corridors. **Pets:** Accepted.

[SAVE] [⚏M] [⚏] [⚏] [🛏] [📺] [🍴] [≈] [✕]

**ⒶⒶⒶ ▼▼▼▼ La Quinta Inn Atlanta (Marietta)** SH
(770) 951-0026. **$68-$95.** 2170 Delk Rd. I-75, exit 261, 0.3 mi w. Ext/int corridors. **Pets:** Medium. Service with restrictions.

[SAVE] [✕] [⚏] [🛏] [📺] [≈]

**▼▼▼▼ Marietta Garden Hotel** SH
(770) 428-4400. **$69-$109.** 1775 Parkway Pl NW. I-75, exit 263, southwest corner. Int corridors. **Pets:** Accepted.

[ASK] [✕] [⚏M] [⚏] [🛏] [📺] [🍴] [≈]

**ⒶⒶⒶ ▼ Masters Inn Marietta** M
(770) 951-2005. **$41-$48.** 2682 Windy Hill Rd. I-75, exit 260, just w to Circle 75 Pkwy, then just s. Ext corridors. **Pets:** Accepted.

[SAVE] [S$] [✕] [🛏]

**▼▼▼ Quality Inn Atlanta/Marietta** SH
(770) 955-0004. **$59-$99.** 1255 Franklin Rd. I-75, exit 261, 0.3 mi w to Franklin Rd, then just s. Int corridors. **Pets:** Accepted.

[ASK] [S$] [✕] [⚏] [🛏] [📺] [≈]

**ⒶⒶⒶ ▼▼▼ Ramada Limited Suites** SH
(770) 919-7878. **$49-$59.** 630 Franklin Rd. I-75, exit 263, 0.3 mi w to Franklin Rd, then 0.3 mi s. Ext corridors. **Pets:** Accepted.

[SAVE] [S$] [✕] [⚏] [⚏] [🛏] [📺] [≈]

**ⒶⒶⒶ ▼▼▼ Super 8 Motel** SH
(770) 919-2340. **$49-$59.** 610 Franklin Rd. I-75, exit 263, 0.3 mi w to Franklin Rd, then 0.3 mi s. Ext corridors. **Pets:** Medium. $7 daily fee/pet. Service with restrictions, supervision.

[SAVE] [S$] [✕] [⚏] [🛏] [≈]

# MORROW

**▼▼ Best Western Southlake Inn** SH
(770) 961-6300. **$44-$69, 3 day notice.** 6437 Jonesboro Rd. I-75, exit 233, just e. Ext corridors. **Pets:** Accepted.

[ASK] [S$] [✕] [🛏] [📺] [≈]

**ⒶⒶⒶ ▼▼ Days Inn** SH
(770) 961-6044. **$58-$73.** 1599 Adamson Pkwy. I-75, exit 233, just e. Ext/int corridors. **Pets:** Small. $25 deposit/room, $10 daily fee/room. Designated rooms, service with restrictions, supervision.

[SAVE] [S$] [✕] [⚏M] [⚏] [🛏] [≈]

**▼▼▼ Drury Inn & Suites-Atlanta South** SH
(770) 960-0500. **$75-$126.** 6520 S Lee St. I-75, exit 233, just e. Int corridors. **Pets:** Accepted.

[ASK] [✕] [⚏M] [⚏] [⚏] [🛏] [📺] [≈]

**ⒶⒶⒶ ▼▼▼▼ Hampton Inn Southlake** SH 🐾
(770) 968-8990. **$79-$99.** 1533 Southlake Pkwy. I-75, exit 233, just w, then just s on Mt Zion Rd. Int corridors. **Pets:** Medium. $50 one-time fee/pet. Service with restrictions, crate.

[SAVE] [S$] [✕] [⚏] [🛏] [📺] [≈]

**ⒶⒶⒶ ▼▼▼▼ Quality Inn & Suites** SH
(770) 960-1957. **$49-$69.** 6597 Hwy 54. I-75, exit 233, just w. Ext corridors. **Pets:** Accepted.

[SAVE] [S$] [✕] [🛏] [📺] [≈]

**▼▼▼ Red Roof Inn-South** M
(770) 968-1483. **$45-$60.** 1348 Southlake Plaza Dr. I-75, exit 233, just e to Southlake Plaza Dr, then just n. Ext corridors. **Pets:** Accepted.

[✕] [⚏] [🛏]

**ⒶⒶⒶ ▼▼▼ Sleep Inn** SH
(770) 472-9800. **$54-$169.** 2185 Mt Zion Pkwy. I-75, exit 231, just w to Mt Zion Pkwy, then just s. Int corridors. **Pets:** Other species. $50 deposit/pet, $10 daily fee/pet. Designated rooms, service with restrictions, supervision.

[SAVE] [S$] [✕] [⚏M] [🛏] [📺] [≈]

# NORCROSS

**ⒶⒶⒶ ▼▼▼▼ Amberley Suite Hotel** SH
(770) 263-0515. **$69-$79.** 5885 Oakbrook Pkwy. I-85, exit 99, 0.5 mi e to Live Oak Pkwy, 0.8 mi n, then w. Int corridors. **Pets:** Accepted.

[SAVE] [S$] [✕] [⚏M] [⚏] [🛏] [📺] [🍴] [≈] [✕]

**ⒶⒶⒶ ▼▼▼▼ AmeriSuites (Atlanta/Peachtree Corners)** SH
(770) 416-7655. **$84.** 5600 Peachtree Pkwy. I-285, exit 31B, 4 mi n on SR 141, then 1 mi n. Int corridors. **Pets:** Medium. $10 daily fee/pet. Designated rooms, service with restrictions.

[SAVE] [✕] [⚏M] [⚏] [⚏] [🛏] [📺] [≈]

**ⒶⒶⒶ ▼▼▼▼ Best Western/Diplomat Inn** SH
(770) 448-8686. **$80-$90, 7 day notice.** 6187 Dawson Blvd. I-85, exit 99, just e to McDonough Dr, then just s. Ext corridors. **Pets:** Accepted.

[SAVE] [S$] [✕] [🛏] [📺] [≈]

**ⒶⒶⒶ ▼▼▼ Days Inn Atlanta NE** SH
(770) 368-0218. **$44-$94.** 5990 Western Hills Dr. I-85, exit 99, 0.8 mi w to Norcross Tucker Rd to Western Hills Dr, then just n. Ext corridors. **Pets:** Very small. $10 daily fee/pet. Designated rooms, no service, supervision.

[SAVE] [S$] [✕] [🛏] [≈]

**▼▼▼▼ Drury Inn & Suites-Atlanta Northeast** SH
(770) 729-0060. **$70-$120.** 5655 Jimmy Carter Blvd. I-85, exit 99, just w. Int corridors. **Pets:** Accepted.

[ASK] [✕] [⚏M] [⚏] [⚏] [🛏] [📺] [≈]

**ⒶⒶⒶ ▼▼▼ GuestHouse Inn** SH
(770) 564-0492. **$49-$74, 7 day notice.** 2050 Willowtrail Pkwy. I-85, exit 101, just e. Ext corridors. **Pets:** Small, other species. $15 one-time fee/pet. Designated rooms, service with restrictions, supervision.

[SAVE] [S$] [✕] [🛏] [📺] [≈]

▼▼▼ **Hilton Atlanta Northeast** LH
(770) 447-4747. **$69-$169.** 5993 Peachtree Industrial Blvd. I-285, exit 31B, 4.5 mi ne. Int corridors. **Pets:** Medium, other species. Service with restrictions.

ASK S✕ ⌖M ⊘ 🖥 💻 ⏹ 🍴 ⊛ ✕

▼▼ **Homestead Studio Suites Hotel-Atlanta/Norcross** SH
(770) 449-9966. **$65-$75.** 7049 Jimmy Carter Blvd. I-85, exit 99, 4 mi n; I-285, exit 31B, 4 mi n. Ext corridors. **Pets:** $25 daily fee/pet. Service with restrictions, supervision.

ASK S✕ ⌖M ⊘ 🖥 💻

▼▼▼ **Homewood Suites by Hilton** SH
(770) 448-4663. **$114.** 450 Technology Pkwy. I-85, exit 99, 4 mi w to Peachtree Industrial Blvd, 0.4 mi n, w on Holcomb Bridge Rd, then 2 blks n on Peachtree Pkwy; I-285, exit 31B, 5 mi n on SR 141. Ext/int corridors. **Pets:** Accepted.

ASK S✕ ⌖M ⊘ 🖥 💻 ⊛ ✕

▲ ▼▼▼ **La Quinta Inn** SH
(770) 368-9400. **$59-$79.** 5945 Oakbrook Pkwy. I-85, exit 99, 0.5 mi e to Live Oak Pkwy, then 0.8 mi w. Int corridors. **Pets:** Medium. Service with restrictions.

SAVE S✕ ⌖M 🖥 💻 ⊛

▼▼▼ **La Quinta Inn Atlanta (Peachtree Industrial)** SH
(770) 449-5144. **$63-$74.** 5375 Peachtree Industrial Blvd. I-285, exit 31B, 5.5 mi n; I-85, exit 99, 4 mi w to Peachtree Industrial Blvd, then 1.5 mi n. Ext/int corridors. **Pets:** Medium. Service with restrictions.

ASK ✕ ⊘ 🖥 💻 ⊛

▼▼ **Ramada Limited** SH
(770) 449-7322. **$79-$99.** 6045 Oakbrook Pkwy. I-85, exit 99, just e to Live Oak Pkwy, 1 mi n, then w. Ext/int corridors. **Pets:** Accepted.

ASK S✕ ✕ 💻 ⊛

▼▼ **Red Roof Inn & Suites** SH
(770) 446-2882. **$50-$94.** 5395 Peachtree Industrial Blvd. I-285, exit 31B, 5.5 mi n; I-85, exit 99, 4 mi w to Peachtree Industrial Blvd, then 1.5 mi n. Int corridors. **Pets:** Small, other species. Service with restrictions, supervision.

ASK S✕ ⊘ 🖥 💻 ⊛

▼▼ **Red Roof Inn-Indian Trail** M
(770) 448-8944. **$41-$57.** 5171 Brook Hollow Pkwy. I-85, exit 101, just w to Brook Hollow Pkwy, then just s. Ext corridors. **Pets:** Accepted.

✕ ⊘ ⌖

▼▼ **StudioPlus** SH
(770) 582-9984. **$64.** 7065 Jimmy Carter Blvd. I-85, exit 99, 4 mi n; I-285, exit 31B, 4 mi n. Int corridors. **Pets:** Other species. $75 one-time fee/pet. Service with restrictions, crate.

ASK S✕ ⌖M ⊘ ⌖ 🖥 💻

## ROSWELL

▲ ▼▼▼ **Baymont Inn & Suites Atlanta-Roswell** SH
(770) 552-0200. **$59-$75.** 575 Old Holcomb Bridge Rd. SR 400, exit 7B, just w. Int corridors. **Pets:** Medium. Service with restrictions.

SAVE ✕ ⌖M ⊘ 🖥 💻 ⊛

▼▼▼ **Brookwood Inn** SH
(770) 587-5161. **$55-$60.** 9995 Old Dogwood Rd. SR 400, exit 7B, just w to Old Dogwood Rd, then just n. Ext corridors. **Pets:** Accepted.

ASK ✕ ⊘ 🖥 💻 ⊛

▼▼ **Studio 6 #6025** SH
(770) 992-9449. **$47-$59.** 9955 Old Dogwood Rd. SR 400, exit 7B, just w. Ext corridors. **Pets:** Accepted.

S✕ ⌖M ⊘ ⌖ 🖥 💻

## SMYRNA

▼▼ **AmeriHost Inn** SH
(404) 794-1600. **$69-$89.** 5130 S Cobb Dr. I-285, exit 15, 0.3 mi w. Int corridors. **Pets:** Accepted.

ASK S✕ ⌖M ⊘ ⌖ 🖥 💻 ⊛ ✕

▲ ▼▼▼ **AmeriSuites (Atlanta/Galleria)** SH
(770) 384-0060. **$98, 3 day notice.** 2876 Springhill Pkwy. I-285, exit 20 westbound; exit 19 eastbound, just n to Spring Rd, then just w. Int corridors. **Pets:** Small, other species. $10 daily fee/pet. Designated rooms, service with restrictions, supervision.

SAVE S✕ ✕ ⌖M ⊘ 🖥 💻 ⊛

▼▼▼ **Best Western, Atlanta Galleria Inn and Suites** SH
(770) 541-1499. **$45-$70.** 2221 Corporate Plaza. I-75, exit 260, just w. Int corridors. **Pets:** Accepted.

ASK S✕ ✕ ⊘ ⌖ 🖥 💻 ⊛ ✕

▼▼▼ **Comfort Inn & Suites** SH
(678) 309-1200. **$68-$128, 14 day notice.** 2800 Highlands Pkwy. I-285, exit 15, just w to Highlands Pkwy, then just s. Int corridors. **Pets:** Accepted.

ASK S✕ ✕ ⌖M ⊘ ⌖ 🖥 💻 ⊛

▼▼ **Homestead Studio Suites Hotel-Atlanta/Cumberland** SH
(770) 432-4000. **$49-$69.** 3103 Sports Ave. I-285, exit 20 westbound; exit 19 eastbound, just n to Spring Rd, then 0.3 mi w. Ext corridors. **Pets:** $25 daily fee/pet. Service with restrictions, supervision.

ASK S✕ ⌖M ⊘ ⌖ 🖥 💻

▼▼ **Red Roof Inn-North** M
(770) 952-6966. **$43-$51.** 2200 Corporate Plaza. I-75, exit 260, just w to Corporate Plaza, then just s. Ext corridors. **Pets:** Accepted.

✕ ⌖M ⊘ ⌖

▲ ▼▼▼ **Residence Inn-Atlanta Cumberland** SH
(770) 433-8877. **$99.** 2771 Cumberland Blvd. I-285, exit 20 westbound; exit 19 eastbound, just n to Spring Rd, 0.3 mi w to Cumberland Blvd, then just n. Ext corridors. **Pets:** Accepted.

SAVE S✕ ✕ ⊘ ⌖ 🖥 💻 ⊛ ✕

## STONE MOUNTAIN

▲ ▼▼▼ **Best Western Stone Mountain** SH
(770) 465-1022. **$79-$99.** 1595 E Park Place Blvd. US 78, exit E Park Place Blvd, just n. Ext corridors. **Pets:** Small. $25 daily fee/pet. Designated rooms, service with restrictions, supervision.

SAVE S✕ ✕ ⌖ 🖥 💻 ⊛

## SUWANEE

▲ ▼▼▼ **Comfort Inn** SH
(770) 945-1608. **$69-$105.** 2945 Hwy 317. I-85, exit 111, just e. Ext corridors. **Pets:** Medium, other species. $25 one-time fee/room. Service with restrictions.

SAVE S✕ ✕ 🖥 💻 ⊛

## TUCKER

▲ ▼▼▼ **Atlanta Northlake TownePlace Suites** SH
(770) 938-0408. **$64-$94.** 3300 Northlake Pkwy. I-285, exit 36 southbound, just w; exit 37 northbound, just w to Parklake Dr, 0.5 mi n, then just w. Int corridors. **Pets:** $75 one-time fee/room. Service with restrictions.

SAVE ✕ ⌖M ⊘ ⌖ 🖥 💻 ⊛

▲ ▼▼▼ **Econo Lodge** M
(770) 939-8440. **$48-$59.** 1820 Mountain Industrial Blvd. US 78, exit 4, just n. Int corridors. **Pets:** $5 daily fee/pet. Designated rooms, no service, supervision.

SAVE S✕ ✕ 🖥

**ⒶⒶⒶ ▼▼ Masters Inn Tucker Ⓜ**
(770) 938-3552. **$43-$52.** 1435 Montreal Rd. I-285, exit 38, just w. Ext corridors. **Pets:** Accepted.
[SAVE] [Ⓢ] [✕] [⬛] [↝]

**▼▼ ▼▼ Quality Inn Atlanta/Northlake ⓈⒽ**
(770) 491-7444. **$55-$90.** 2155 Ranchwood Dr. I-285, exit 37, 0.4 mi w, then just n. Ext/int corridors. **Pets:** Medium. $50 deposit/pet, $10 daily fee/pet. Designated rooms, service with restrictions, supervision.
[ASK] [Ⓢ] [✕] [ⓜ] [🔊] [🖉] [⬛] [↝]

**▼▼ ▼▼ Red Roof Inn-Atlanta Tucker NE Ⓜ**
(770) 496-1311. **$43-$53.** 2810 Lawrenceville Hwy. I-285, exit 38, just w. Ext corridors. **Pets:** Accepted.
[✕] [🔊]

## UNION CITY

**▼▼▼▼ Holiday Inn Express Hotel & Suites ⓈⒽ**
(770) 969-4567. **$59-$129.** 6743 Shannon Pkwy. I-85, exit 64, 0.3 mi w, then just n. Int corridors. **Pets:** Accepted.
[ASK] [Ⓢ] [✕] [ⓜ] [🔊] [🖉] [⬛] [⬛] [↝]

**▼▼ ▼▼ Microtel Inn & Suites ⓈⒽ**
(770) 306-3800. **$45-$69.** 6690 Shannon Pkwy. I-85, exit 64, 0.3 mi w to Shannon Pkwy, then just n. Int corridors. **Pets:** Small, other species. $10 daily fee/pet. Designated rooms, service with restrictions, supervision.
[ASK] [Ⓢ] [✕] [ⓜ] [🔊] [🖉] [⬛] [⬛]

**▼▼ ▼▼ Ramada Limited ⓈⒽ**
(770) 964-5100. **$62-$78.** 7420 Oakley Rd. I-85, exit 64, just e. Ext corridors. **Pets:** Small. $25 one-time fee/room. Designated rooms, service with restrictions, crate.
[ASK] [Ⓢ] [✕] [⬛] [⬛]

---

# END METROPOLITAN AREA

---

## AUGUSTA

**ⒶⒶⒶ ▼▼▼▼ AmeriSuites (Augusta/River Watch Pkwy) ⓈⒽ**
(706) 733-4656. **$59-$129.** 1062 Claussen Rd. I-20, exit 200 westbound, 0.4 mi sw on service road; exit 199 eastbound, 0.3 mi w, then 0.6 mi nw on service road. Int corridors. **Pets:** Accepted.
[SAVE] [✕] [ⓜ] [🔊] [🖉] [⬛] [⬛] [↝] [✕]

**▼▼▼▼ Augusta Suites Inn ⓈⒽ**
(706) 868-1800. **$99.** 3038 Washington Rd. I-20, exit 199 (Washington Rd), just w. Ext corridors. **Pets:** Accepted.
[ASK] [Ⓢ] [✕] [⬛] [⬛] [🍴] [↝]

**▼▼▼▼ Augusta Towers Hotel & Convention Center ⓈⒽ**
(706) 855-8100. **$79-$119.** 2651 Perimeter Pkwy. I-520, exit 1C (Wheeler Rd), just w to Perimeter Pkwy, then just n. Int corridors. **Pets:** Large. $25 one-time fee/room. Designated rooms, service with restrictions, crate.
[ASK] [Ⓢ] [✕] [ⓜ] [⬛] [⬛] [🍴] [↝] [✕]

**ⒶⒶⒶ ▼▼▼▼ Comfort Inn ⓈⒽ**
(706) 855-6060. **$63-$99.** 629 Frontage Rd NW. I-20, exit 196B, 0.3 mi n to Scott Nixon Memorial, just w, then 0.3 mi s. Int corridors. **Pets:** Large, other species. $25 one-time fee/room. Service with restrictions, crate.
[SAVE] [Ⓢ] [✕] [⬛] [⬛] [↝]

**ⒶⒶⒶ ▼▼▼▼ Comfort Inn Medical Center ⓈⒽ**
(706) 722-2224. **$65, 10 day notice.** 1455 Walton Way. I-20, exit 199 (Washington Rd), 4.5 mi e on SR 28, then just sw on 15th St. Ext corridors. **Pets:** Medium, other species. $50 deposit/room. Service with restrictions, crate.
[SAVE] [Ⓢ] [✕] [🖉] [⬛] [⬛] [↝]

**▼▼▼▼ Country Suites Augusta Riverwalk ⓈⒽ**
(706) 774-1400. **$129-$139.** 3 9th St. I-20, exit 200 (River Watch Pkwy), 5.4 mi se, then just n. Int corridors. **Pets:** Accepted.
[ASK] [Ⓢ] [✕] [ⓜ] [🔊] [🖉] [⬛] [⬛] [↝] [✕]

**▼▼▼▼ Holiday Inn Gordon Highway at Bobby Jones ⓈⒽ**
(706) 737-2300. **$82-$92.** 2155 Gordon Hwy. I-520, exit 3A (US 78), just w. Ext corridors. **Pets:** Medium. $35 one-time fee/room. Service with restrictions, crate.
[ASK] [Ⓢ] [✕] [⬛] [⬛] [🍴] [↝]

**ⒶⒶⒶ ▼▼▼▼ Howard Johnson Inn Ⓜ**
(706) 863-2882. **$49-$54.** 601 Frontage Rd NW. I-20, exit 196B (Bobby Jones Expwy), just nw. Ext corridors. **Pets:** Other species. $10 daily fee/pet. Designated rooms, service with restrictions, crate.
[ASK] [Ⓢ] [✕] [⬛] [⬛] [↝]

**ⒶⒶⒶ ▼▼▼▼ La Quinta Inn Augusta ⓈⒽ**
(706) 733-2660. **$66-$85.** 3020 Washington Rd. I-20, exit 199 (Washington Rd), just w. Ext/int corridors. **Pets:** Medium. Service with restrictions.
[SAVE] [✕] [ⓜ] [🖉] [⬛] [⬛] [↝]

**ⒶⒶⒶ ▼▼▼▼ The Partridge Inn ⓈⒽ**
(706) 737-8888. **$109-$189.** 2110 Walton Way. 1.3 mi w off 15th St. Int corridors. **Pets:** Accepted.
[SAVE] [Ⓢ] [✕] [⬛] [⬛] [🍴] [↝]

**▼▼▼▼ Radisson Riverfront Hotel ⓁⒽ**
(706) 722-8900. **$129-$139.** 2 10th St. I-20, exit 200 (River Watch Pkwy), 5.4 mi se, then just n; downtown. Int corridors. **Pets:** Accepted.
[ASK] [Ⓢ] [✕] [ⓜ] [🔊] [🖉] [⬛] [⬛] [🍴] [↝] [✕]

## BAINBRIDGE

**▼▼ ▼▼ Jameson Inn ⓈⒽ**
(229) 243-7000. **$54-$104.** 1403 Tallahassee Hwy. Just s of US 84 Bypass on US 27. Ext corridors. **Pets:** Very small, other species. $10 daily fee/room. Service with restrictions, supervision.
[ASK] [✕] [🖉] [⬛] [⬛] [↝]

## BAXLEY

**▼▼ Scottish Inn Ⓜ**
(912) 367-3652. **$40-$50.** 1179 Hatch Pkwy S. Jct US 1 and SR 15, just s. Ext corridors. **Pets:** Accepted.
[ASK] [Ⓢ] [✕] [⬛]

## BLUE RIDGE

**▼▼ ▼▼ Douglas Inn & Suites Ⓜ**
(706) 258-3600. **$59-$89.** 1192 Windy Ridge Rd. Just off SR 515 and US 76. Ext corridors. **Pets:** Medium. $10 daily fee/pet. Service with restrictions, supervision.
[ASK] [Ⓢ] [✕] [⬛] [⬛] [↝]

# BRASELTON

🔺🔺 ▼▼▼ **Chateau Elan Lodge by Holiday Inn Express** SH
(770) 867-8100. **$69-$119.** 2069 Hwy 211 NW. I-85, exit 126, just w. Int corridors. **Pets:** Other species. $30 one-time fee/room. Service with restrictions, crate.
SAVE S🔴 ▣ ⌦

# BREMEN

🔺🔺 ▼▼▼ **Days Inn** SH ❀
(770) 537-4646. **$45-$165.** 35 Price Creek Rd. I-75, exit 11, just n. Ext corridors. **Pets:** Medium. $10 daily fee/pet. Service with restrictions, supervision.
SAVE S🔴 ✕ ▤ ▣ ⌦

# BRUNSWICK

🔺🔺 ▼▼▼▼ **Best Western Brunswick Inn** SH
(912) 264-0144. **$68-$108.** 5323 New Jesup Hwy. I-95, exit 36B (New Jesup Hwy/US 25), just nw. Ext corridors. **Pets:** Accepted.
SAVE S🔴 ✕ ▤ ▣ 🍴 ⌦

▼▼▼▼ **Embassy Suites Hotel** SH
(912) 264-6100. **$109-$179.** 500 Mall Blvd. I-95, exit 38 (Golden Isles Pkwy), 2 mi se, then just e. Int corridors. **Pets:** Accepted.
✕ 🔂 ▤ ▣ ⌦

🔺🔺 ▼▼▼▼ **Hampton Inn** SH
(912) 261-0002. **$99-$109.** 230 Warren Mason Blvd. I-95, exit 36A (New Jesup Hwy/US 25), just se, then just sw on Tourist Dr. Ext/int corridors. **Pets:** Large, other species. $10 one-time fee/pet. Service with restrictions.
SAVE S🔴 ✕ 🔂 ▤ ▣ ⌦

▼▼ **Jameson Inn Brunswick** SH
(912) 267-0800. **$54-$104.** 661 Scranton Rd. I-95, exit 38 (Golden Isles Pkwy), 1.6 mi se, then just sw. Ext corridors. **Pets:** Very small, other species. $10 daily fee/room. Service with restrictions, supervision.
A$K ✕ ▤ ▣ ⌦

🔺🔺 ▼▼▼ **La Quinta Inn & Suites Brunswick** SH
(912) 265-7725. **$72-$82.** 165 Warren Mason Blvd. I-95, exit 36A (New Jesup Hwy/US 25), just se, then sw on Tourist Dr. Int corridors. **Pets:** Medium. Service with restrictions.
SAVE ✕ 🔂 ▤ ▣ ⌦

▼▼ **Motel 6 #790** M
(912) 264-8582. **$38-$53.** 403 Butler Dr. I-95, exit 36B (New Jesup Hwy/US 25), just nw, then sw on I-95 south entrance service road. Ext corridors. **Pets:** Accepted.
S🔴 ✕ 🔳 ⌦

🔺🔺 ▼▼▼ **The Park Inn** SH
(912) 264-4033. **$79-$129.** 5252 New Jesup Hwy. I-95, exit 36B (New Jesup Hwy/US 25), just nw. Ext corridors. **Pets:** Other species. $25 one-time fee/room. Service with restrictions, supervision.
SAVE S🔴 ✕ 🔳 ▤ ▣ 🍴 ⌦

▼▼ **Red Roof Inn & Suites I-95** SH
(912) 264-4720. **$59-$104.** 25 Tourist Dr. I-95, exit 36A (New Jesup Hwy/US 25), just se. Int corridors. **Pets:** Accepted.
A$K S🔴 ✕ 🔂 ▤ ▣ ⌦

🔺🔺 ▼▼ **Super 8 Motel** M
(912) 264-8800. **$50-$56, 7 day notice.** 5280 New Jesup Hwy. I-95, exit 36B (New Jesup Hwy/US 25), just nw. Int corridors. **Pets:** Medium. $10 daily fee/pet. Service with restrictions, supervision.
SAVE S🔴 ✕ ▤

# BYRON

🔺🔺 ▼▼▼▼ **Best Western Inn and Suites** SH ❀
(478) 956-3056. **$59.** 101 Dunbar Rd. I-75, exit 149 (SR 49), just ne. Ext corridors. **Pets:** Medium. $10 daily fee/pet. Service with restrictions, crate.
SAVE S🔴 ✕ 🔳 ▤ ▣ ⌦

🔺🔺 ▼▼▼▼ **Comfort Inn** SH
(478) 956-1600. **$69-$89.** 115 Chapman Rd. I-75, exit 149 (SR 49), just sw, then n. Ext corridors. **Pets:** Small. $10 daily fee/pet. No service, supervision.
SAVE S🔴 ✕ 🔳 ▤ ▣ ⌦

# CALHOUN

🔺🔺 ▼▼▼ **Americas Best Inn** M
(706) 625-1511. **$40-$65.** 1438 US Hwy 41 N. I-75, exit 318, just w. Ext corridors. **Pets:** Accepted.
SAVE S🔴 ✕ ▤ ▣ ⌦

🔺🔺 ▼▼▼ **Budget Host Shepherd Motel** M
(706) 629-8644. **$40-$48.** 1007 Fairmount Hwy 53. I-75, exit 312, just e. Ext corridors. **Pets:** Accepted.
SAVE S🔴 ✕ 🔳 ▤ ⌦

▼▼▼ **Comfort Inn** SH
(706) 629-8271. **$60-$65.** 742 Hwy 53 SE. I-75, exit 312, just w. Ext corridors. **Pets:** Other species. $5 daily fee/pet. Service with restrictions.
A$K S🔴 ✕ ▤ ▣ 🍴 ⌦

▼▼▼ **Jameson Inn** SH
(706) 629-8133. **$54-$104.** 189 Jameson St. I-75, exit 312, just w. Ext corridors. **Pets:** Very small, other species. Service with restrictions, supervision.
A$K ✕ 🔂 🔳 ▤ ▣ ⌦

▼▼▼ **Knights Inn of Calhoun** M
(706) 629-4521. **$35-$40.** 2261 US 41 NE. I-75, exit 318, just e. Ext corridors. **Pets:** Accepted.
A$K S🔴 ✕ ▤

🔺🔺 ▼▼▼ **Quality Inn Calhoun** SH ❀
(706) 629-9501. **$65-$75.** 915 Hwy 53 E SE. I-75, exit 312, just e. Ext corridors. **Pets:** Small. $6 daily fee/pet. Service with restrictions.
SAVE S🔴 ✕ ▤ ▣ 🍴 ⌦

▼▼ **Ramada Limited** SH
(706) 629-9207. **$45-$65.** 1204 Red Bud Rd NE. I-75, exit 315, just w. Ext corridors. **Pets:** Accepted.
A$K S🔴 ✕ 🔂 ▤ ▣ ⌦

# CARROLLTON

▼▼ **Jameson Inn** SH
(770) 834-2600. **$54-$104.** 700 S Park St. On US 27, just s of downtown. Ext corridors. **Pets:** Very small, other species. $10 daily fee/room. Service with restrictions, supervision.
A$K 🔳 🔳 ▤ ▣ ⌦

# CARTERSVILLE

▼▼ **Budget Host Inn** M
(770) 386-0350. **$38-$51.** 851 Cass-White Rd. I-75, exit 296, just w. Ext corridors. **Pets:** Small. $5 daily fee/pet. Service with restrictions, supervision.
A$K S🔴 ✕ ▤ ⌦

🔺🔺 ▼▼▼ **Comfort Inn** SH
(770) 387-1800. **$45-$62.** 28 SR 20 Spur. I-75, exit 290, 0.3 mi se. Ext corridors. **Pets:** $5 daily fee/pet. Service with restrictions, supervision.
SAVE S🔴 ✕ ▤ ▣ ⌦

**▼▼▼▼ Country Inn & Suites by Carlson** SH
(770) 386-5888. **$71-$80.** 43 SR 20 Spur. I-75, exit 290, 0.3 mi se. Int corridors. **Pets:** Accepted.
ASK S6 ✕ &M ♿ 🛅 💻 ➳

**△△△ ▼▼▼ Days Inn** SH 🐾
(770) 382-1824. **$44-$88, 7 day notice.** 5618 Hwy 20 SE. I-75, exit 290, just w. Ext corridors. **Pets:** Other species. $7 daily fee/pet.
SAVE S6 ✕ 🛅 ➳

**▼▼▼▼ Holiday Inn** SH
(770) 386-0830. **$70.** 2336 Hwy 411 NE. I-75, exit 293, southwest corner. Int corridors. **Pets:** Accepted.
✕ &M 🖉 🛅 💻 🍴 ➳

**△△△ ▼▼▼ Howard Johnson Express** M
(770) 386-0700. **$45-$75.** 25 Carson Loop NW. I-75, exit 296, just w. Ext corridors. **Pets:** Accepted.
SAVE S6 ✕ 🛅 💻 🍴 ➳

**△△△ ▼▼▼ Knights Inn** M
(770) 386-7263. **$55-$70, 14 day notice.** 420 E Church St. I-75, exit 288, 1.5 mi w. Ext corridors. **Pets:** Medium. $10 one-time fee/pet. Designated rooms, service with restrictions, crate.
SAVE S6 ✕ 🛅 ➳

**▼▼▼ Motel 6–4046** M
(770) 386-1449. **$42-$46.** 5657 Hwy 20 NE. I-75, exit 290, 0.3 mi e. Ext corridors. **Pets:** Accepted.
S6 ✕ 🖉 ➳

**△△△ ▼▼▼▼ Quality Inn** SH
(770) 386-0510. **$59-$85.** 235 Dixie Ave. I-75, exit 288, 2.5 mi w. Ext corridors. **Pets:** Small. $5 daily fee/pet. Designated rooms, service with restrictions, supervision.
SAVE S6 ✕ 🛅 💻 🍴 ➳

**△△△ ▼▼▼ Super 8 Motel** M
(770) 382-8881. **$40-$70.** 41 SR 20 Spur SE. I-75, exit 290, 0.3 mi e. Int corridors. **Pets:** $5 daily fee/pet. Service with restrictions, supervision.
SAVE S6 ✕ 🖉 🛅

# CEDARTOWN

**▼▼▼ Country Hearth Inn** SH
(770) 749-9951. **$45-$85.** 925 N Main St. 1.5 mi n on US 27. Int corridors. **Pets:** Accepted.
ASK S6 ✕ &M 🖉 ♿ 🛅 💻

# CHATSWORTH

**▼▼▼ Key West Inn** M
(706) 517-1155. **$49-$55.** 501 GI Maddox Pkwy. Jct SR 76 and US 411. Ext corridors. **Pets:** Medium, other species. $5 daily fee/pet. Service with restrictions, supervision.
ASK S6 ✕ 🛅

# CLAYTON

**▼▼▼ Quality Inn & Suites** SH
(706) 782-2214. **$59-$99.** 834 Hwy 441 S. 0.8 mi s. Ext corridors. **Pets:** Accepted.
ASK S6 ✕ 🛅 💻 ➳

**△△△ ▼▼ Regal Inn** M
(706) 782-4269. **$37-$95, 3 day notice.** 707 Hwy 441 S. 0.8 mi s. Ext corridors. **Pets:** Small, dogs only. $5 daily fee/pet. Designated rooms, service with restrictions, supervision.
SAVE S6 ✕ 🛅

**△△△ ▼▼▼ Stonebrook Inn** SH
(706) 782-4702. **$39-$99.** 698 Hwy 441 S. 0.8 mi s. Int corridors. **Pets:** Small. $50 deposit/pet, $5 daily fee/pet. Service with restrictions, crate.
SAVE S6 ✕ 🛅 💻

# COLUMBUS

**△△△ ▼▼▼▼ Baymont Inn & Suites Columbus** SH
(706) 323-4344. **$75-$89.** 2919 Warm Springs Rd. I-185, exit 7 southbound; exit 7A northbound, just e. Int corridors. **Pets:** Medium. Service with restrictions.
SAVE ✕ 🖉 🛅 💻 ➳

**▼▼▼ Howard Johnson Inn & Suites** SH
(706) 322-6641. **$77-$87.** 1011 Veterans Pkwy. I-185, exit 7 southbound; exit 7A northbound, 1.2 mi w tc Veterans Pkwy, then 3.2 mi s. Ext corridors. **Pets:** Large. $25 one-time fee/room. Service with restrictions, supervision.
ASK S6 ✕ ♿ 🛅 💻 🍴 ➳

**△△△ ▼▼▼ La Quinta Inn Columbus** SH
(706) 568-1740. **$80-$104.** 3201 Macon Rd. I-185, exit 6, just w. Ext corridors. **Pets:** Medium. Service with restrictions.
ASK ✕ 🖉 🛅 💻 ➳

**▼▼ Motel 6 #58** M
(706) 687-7214. **$44-$57.** 3050 Victory Dr. I-185, exit 1B, 3 mi w. Ext corridors. **Pets:** Accepted.
S6 ✕ ♿ 🛅

**▼▼▼ Super 8 Motel of Columbus** M
(706) 322-6580. **$52-$68.** 2935 Warm Springs Rd. I-185, exit 7 southbound; exit 7A northbound, just e. Int corridors. **Pets:** Accepted.
ASK S6 ✕ ♿ 🛅

# COMMERCE

**▼▼▼ Comfort Inn** SH
(706) 335-9001. **$75-$85.** 165 Eisenhower Dr. I-85, exit 149, just nw. Ext corridors. **Pets:** Medium. $20 daily fee/pet. Service with restrictions.
ASK ✕ 🖉 🛅 💻 ➳

**▼▼▼ Howard Johnson Inn & Suites** SH
(706) 335-5581. **$50-$85.** 148 Eisenhower Dr. I-85, exit 149, just w. Ext corridors. **Pets:** Medium. $10 one-time fee/pet. Service with restrictions, supervision.
ASK S6 ✕ 🛅 💻 ➳

**△△△ ▼▼ Scottish Inn** M 🐾
(706) 335-5147. **$34-$120.** 30934 US 441 S. I-85, exit 149, 0.3 mi e. Ext corridors. **Pets:** Other species. $10 daily fee/pet. Service with restrictions, supervision.
SAVE S6 ✕ 🛅 ➳

**▼▼▼ Super 8 Motel** SH
(706) 336-8008. **$53-$88.** 152 Eisenhower Dr. I-85, exit 149, just w. Ext corridors. **Pets:** Medium. $10 one-time fee/pet. Service with restrictions, supervision.
ASK S6 ✕

# CONYERS

**△△△ ▼▼▼ Comfort Inn** SH
(770) 760-0300. **$69-$99, 7 day notice.** 1363 Klondike Rd. I-20, exit 80. Int corridors. **Pets:** Accepted.
SAVE S6 ✕ &M 🛅 💻 ➳

**▼▼▼ Hampton Inn** SH
(770) 483-8838. **$89-$99.** 1340 Dogwood Dr. I-20, exit 82, just n, then just e. Int corridors. **Pets:** Other species. $25 one-time fee/room.
ASK S6 ✕ &M 🖉 ♿ 🛅 💻 ➳

**▼▼▼▼ Holiday Inn** SH
(770) 483-3220. **$68-$75.** 1351 Dogwood Dr. I-20, exit 80, just n to Dogwood Dr, then 0.4 mi w. Ext corridors. **Pets:** Very small, dogs only. $25 one-time fee/room. Service with restrictions, supervision.
ASK S6 ✕ &M 🖉 🛅 💻 🍴 ➳

**▼▼ Jameson Inn** 🆂🅷
(770) 760-1230. **$54-$104.** 1164 Dogwood Dr. I-20, exit 82, just n to Dogwood Dr, then just w. Ext corridors. **Pets:** Very small, other species. $10 daily fee/room. Service with restrictions, supervision.

🄰🅂🄺 ⊠ 🖥 💻 🏊

**▼▼▼ La Quinta Inn & Suites Atlanta (Conyers)** 🆂🅷
(770) 918-0092. **$85-$124.** 1184 Dogwood Dr. I-20, exit 82, just n to Dogwood Dr, then just w. Int corridors. **Pets:** Small. Service with restrictions, crate.

🄰🅂🄺 ⊠ 🄼 🕖 🄺 🖥 💻 🏊

# CORDELE

**🄰🄰🄰 ▼▼▼ Best Western Colonial Inn** 🆂🅷
(229) 273-5420. **$64-$69.** 1706 E 16th Ave (US 280). I-75, exit 101 (US 280), just w. Ext/int corridors. **Pets:** Accepted.

🆂🄰🅅🄴 🆂🄳 ⊠ 🖥 💻 🏊

**🄰🄰🄰 ▼▼▼ Ramada Inn** 🆂🅷 🐾
(229) 273-5000. **$75.** 2016 E 16th Ave (US 280). I-75, exit 101 (US 280), just e. Ext corridors. **Pets:** Medium. $10 daily fee/room. Service with restrictions, supervision.

🆂🄰🅅🄴 🆂🄳 ⊠ 🖥 💻 🏊

# CORNELIA

**▼▼ Comfort Inn** 🆂🅷
(706) 778-9573. **$49-$98.** 2965 J Warren Rd. Jct SR 365 and US 441 business route, just w. Int corridors. **Pets:** Medium. $25 daily fee/room. Designated rooms, service with restrictions, supervision.

🄰🅂🄺 🆂🄳 ⊠ 🄼 🖥 💻 🏊

**▼▼ Holiday Inn Express** 🆂🅷
(706) 778-3600. **$70-$130.** 1105 Business 441. Jct SR 365 and US 441, just e. Int corridors. **Pets:** $25 one-time fee/pet. Designated rooms, service with restrictions, crate.

🄰🅂🄺 🆂🄳 ⊠ 🄼 🕖 🄺 🖥 💻 🏊

# COVINGTON

**▼▼▼ Best Western Executive Inn** 🆂🅷
(770) 787-4900. **$68-$82.** 10111 Alcovy Rd. I-20, exit 92, just n. Ext corridors. **Pets:** Accepted.

🄰🅂🄺 🆂🄳 ⊠ 🄼 🄺 🖥 💻 🏊

**🄰🄰🄰 ▼▼▼ Super 8 Motel-Covington** 🆂🅷
(770) 786-5800. **$50-$81.** 10130 Alcovy Rd. I-20, exit 92, just n. Ext corridors. **Pets:** $10 daily fee/pet, $20 one-time fee/pet. Service with restrictions, supervision.

🆂🄰🅅🄴 🆂🄳 ⊠ 🖥 💻 🏊

# CUMMING

**▼▼▼ Hampton Inn** 🆂🅷
(770) 889-0877. **$89-$104, 3 day notice.** 915 Northside Forsyth Dr. SR 400, exit 14, just e. Int corridors. **Pets:** Small. $20 daily fee. Designated rooms, service with restrictions, supervision.

🄰🅂🄺 🆂🄳 ⊠ 🄼 🕖 🄺 🖥 💻 🏊

# DAHLONEGA

**🄰🄰🄰 ▼▼▼ Super 8 Motel** 🅼
(706) 864-4343. **$45-$99, 7 day notice.** 20 Mountain Dr. 0.5 mi s on US 19 and SR 60. Ext corridors. **Pets:** Accepted.

🆂🄰🅅🄴 🆂🄳 ⊠ 🕖 🖥 🏊

# DALTON

**🄰🄰🄰 ▼▼▼ Americas Best Inns** 🆂🅷
(706) 226-1100. **$42-$59.** 1529 W Walnut Ave. I-75, exit 333, just e. Ext corridors. **Pets:** Medium, other species. $5 daily fee/pet. Service with restrictions, supervision.

🆂🄰🅅🄴 🆂🄳 ⊠ 🕖 🖥 💻 🏊

**🄰🄰🄰 ▼▼▼ Best Western Inn of Dalton** 🆂🅷
(706) 226-5022. **$54.** 2106 Chattanooga Rd. I-75, exit 336, just w. Ext corridors. **Pets:** Very small, dogs only. $5 daily fee/pet. Designated rooms, service with restrictions, supervision.

🆂🄰🅅🄴 🆂🄳 ⊠ 🖥 💻 🍽 🏊

**🄰🄰🄰 ▼▼▼▼ Comfort Inn & Suites** 🆂🅷
(706) 259-2583. **$64-$99.** 905 Westbridge Rd. I-75, exit 333, just w to Westbridge Rd, then just s. Int corridors. **Pets:** Medium, other species. $15 daily fee/pet. Designated rooms, service with restrictions, supervision.

🆂🄰🅅🄴 🆂🄳 ⊠ 🄼 🕖 🄺 🖥 💻 🏊

**▼▼ Econo Lodge** 🅼
(706) 278-4300. **$65.** 2007 Tampico Way. I-75, exit 336, just e. Int corridors. **Pets:** Accepted.

🄰🅂🄺 🆂🄳 ⊠ 🖥 💻 🏊

**▼▼ Jameson Inn** 🆂🅷
(706) 281-1880. **$54-$104.** 422 Holiday Dr. I-75, exit 333, just w, then 0.3 mi n. Ext corridors. **Pets:** Very small, other species. $10 daily fee/room. Service with restrictions, supervision.

🄰🅂🄺 ⊠ 🕖 🄺 🖥 💻 🏊

**▼ Motel 6 #761** 🅼
(706) 278-5522. **$35-$47.** 2200 Chattanooga Rd. I-75, exit 336, 0.3 mi w. Ext corridors. **Pets:** Accepted.

🆂🄳 ⊠ 🄼 🕖 🄺

**▼▼▼ Quality Inn & Suites** 🆂🅷
(706) 278-0500. **$59-$79, 7 day notice.** 515 Holiday Dr. I-75, exit 333, northwest corner. Ext corridors. **Pets:** Accepted.

🄰🅂🄺 🆂🄳 ⊠ 🕖 🖥 💻 🏊

**▼▼▼ Wingate Inn** 🆂🅷
(706) 272-9099. **$81-$90.** 309 Holiday Dr. I-75, exit 333, just w to Holiday Dr, then 0.5 mi n. Int corridors. **Pets:** Small, other species. $10 daily fee/pet. Designated rooms, service with restrictions, supervision.

🄰🅂🄺 🆂🄳 ⊠ 🄼 🄺 🖥 💻 🏊

# DARIEN

**🄰🄰🄰 ▼▼▼ Comfort Inn** 🆂🅷
(912) 437-4200. **$89-$129.** 703 Frontage Rd. I-95, exit 49 (SR 251), just nw. Int corridors. **Pets:** Small. $10 daily fee/pet. Service with restrictions, supervision.

🆂🄰🅅🄴 🆂🄳 ⊠ 🄺 🖥 💻 🏊

# DAWSONVILLE

**🄰🄰🄰 ▼▼▼▼ Best Western (Dawson Village Inn)** 🆂🅷
(706) 216-4410. **$60-$159.** 76 N Georgia Ave. Jct SR 400/53, 0.5 mi s. Int corridors. **Pets:** Small. $20 deposit/pet, $5 daily fee/pet. Designated rooms, service with restrictions, supervision.

🆂🄰🅅🄴 🆂🄳 ⊠ 🄼 🄺 🖥 💻 🏊

**▼▼▼ Comfort Inn** 🆂🅷
(706) 216-1900. **$64-$94.** 127 Beartooth Pkwy. Jct SR 400/53, 0.5 mi s. Int corridors. **Pets:** Accepted.

🄰🅂🄺 🆂🄳 ⊠ 🄼 🖥 💻 🏊

# DILLARD

**🄰🄰🄰 ▼▼▼▼ Dillard House** 🆂🅷
(706) 746-5348. **$49-$159.** 768 Franklin St. US 441, just e via Old Dillard Rd. Ext corridors. **Pets:** Small. $5 daily fee/pet. Designated rooms.

🆂🄰🅅🄴 ⊠ 🄺 🖥 💻 🍽 🗙

**▼▼ Ramada Limited** 🅼
(706) 746-5321. **$49-$119.** 3 Best Inn Way. Center. Ext corridors. **Pets:** Accepted.

🄰🅂🄺 🆂🄳 ⊠ 🖥 💻 🏊

# DOUGLAS

### ▼▼ Jameson Inn M
(912) 384-9432. **$54-$104.** 1628 S Peterson Ave. Jct US 221/441/SR 31 and SR 206/353, just s. Ext corridors. **Pets:** Accepted.

ASK ✕ 🛑 💷 ⋙

# DUBLIN

### ◆◆◆ ▼▼▼ Best Western Executive Inn & Suites SH
(478) 275-2650. **$60-$85.** 2121 Hwy 441 S. I-16, exit 51 (US 441), 0.5 mi n. Ext corridors. **Pets:** Accepted.

SAVE S⊙ ✕ 🛑 💷 ⋙

### ▼▼ Comfort Inn SH
(478) 274-8000. **$50-$70.** 2110 Hwy 441 S. I-16, exit 51 (US 441), 0.6 mi n. Ext corridors. **Pets:** Accepted.

ASK S⊙ ✕ &M 🛑 💷 ⋙

### ▼ Econo Lodge M
(478) 296-1223. **$49-$120 (no credit cards).** 2184 Hwy 441 S. I-16, exit 51 (US 441), just n. Ext corridors. **Pets:** Accepted.

ASK S⊙ ✕ 🛑

### ▼▼ Jameson Inn M
(478) 275-3008. **$54-$104.** 100 PM Watson Dr. I-16, exit 51 (US 441), just n. Ext corridors. **Pets:** Very small, other species. $10 daily fee/room. Service with restrictions, supervision.

ASK ✕ 🛑 💷 ⋙

# FITZGERALD

### ▼▼ Country Hearth Inn SH
(229) 409-9911. **$50-$95.** 125 Stuart Way. Just n of US 319/107, just e. Int corridors. **Pets:** Accepted.

ASK S⊙ ✕ 🛑 💷

### ▼▼ Western Motel SH
(229) 424-9500. **$54-$104.** 111 Bull Run Rd. Just n of US 319/107, on US 129. Ext corridors. **Pets:** Accepted.

ASK ✕ 🛑 💷 ⋙

# FORSYTH

### ◆◆◆ ▼▼ Econo Lodge SH ❀
(478) 994-5603. **$48-$64.** 320 Cabiness Rd. I-75, exit 187 (SR 83), just ne. Int corridors. **Pets:** Medium. $6 daily fee/pet. Service with restrictions, supervision.

SAVE S⊙ 💷 ⋙

### ▼▼▼ Holiday Inn Forsyth SH ❀
(478) 994-5691. **$94-$109.** 480 Holiday Cir. I-75, exit 186 (Juliette Rd), just w, then just s on Aaron St. Ext corridors. **Pets:** Large, other species. $25 one-time fee/room. Service with restrictions, supervision.

ASK S⊙ ✕ 🞩 ⟨ 🛑 💷 ⊓ ⋙

### ▼▼ Super 8 Motel SH
(478) 994-5101. **$45-$135.** 436 Tift College Dr. I-75, exit 186 (Juliette Rd), just w. Ext/int corridors. **Pets:** Small. $10 one-time fee/pet. Designated rooms, service with restrictions, supervision.

ASK S⊙ ✕ 🛑 ⋙

# GAINESVILLE

### ▼▼ Days Inn-Gainesville SH
(770) 535-8100. **$55-$70.** 520 Queen City Pkwy SW. I-985, exit 20, 1.8 mi nw on SR 60. Ext corridors. **Pets:** Accepted.

ASK S⊙ ✕ 🛑 💷 ⋙

### ▼▼ Ramada Limited M
(770) 287-3205. **$45-$89.** 766 Jesse Jewell Pkwy. I-985, exit 20, 1.9 mi w to Jesse Jewell Pkwy, then just w. Ext corridors. **Pets:** Small. $10 daily fee/pet. Service with restrictions, supervision.

ASK S⊙ ✕ 🛑 💷

# GARDEN CITY

### ◆◆◆ ▼▼ Masters Inn Garden City SH
(912) 964-4344. **$47-$52.** 4200 Hwy 21 N (Augusta Rd). I-95, exit 109 (SR 21), 6.7 mi s. Ext/int corridors. **Pets:** Accepted.

SAVE S⊙ ✕ 🞩 🛑 ⋙

# GLENNVILLE

### ◆◆◆ ▼ Cheeri-O Inn M
(912) 654-2176. **$40-$42.** 820 Musgrove St. 0.8 mi s on US 25 and 301. Ext corridors. **Pets:** Medium. $5 daily fee/pet. Designated rooms, service with restrictions, supervision.

SAVE S⊙ ✕ 🛑 💷

---

## GOLDEN ISLES AREA

---

# JEKYLL ISLAND

### ◆◆◆ ▼▼ Quality Inn & Suites SH
(912) 635-2202. **$72-$182.** 700 N Beachview Dr. Jct Ben Fortson Pkwy (SR 520)/Beachview Dr, 1.5 mi n. Ext corridors. **Pets:** Small, other species. $10 daily fee/pet. Service with restrictions, supervision.

SAVE S⊙ ✕ ⟨ 🛑 💷 ⋙ ✕

### ◆◆◆ ▼▼▼ Villas by the Sea CO ❀
(912) 635-2521. **$114-$304, 7 day notice.** 1175 N Beachview Dr. Jct Ben Fortson Pkwy (SR 520)/Beachview Dr, 4 mi n. Ext corridors. **Pets:** Medium. $125 one-time fee/room. Designated rooms, service with restrictions, supervision.

SAVE S⊙ ✕ &M 🞩 ⟨ 🛑 💷 ⊓ ⋙ ✕

---

## END AREA

---

# GRAY

### ▼▼ Days Inn M
(478) 986-4200. **$58.** 288 W Clinton St. Jct SR 44/US 129, 0.9 mi w on US 129. Ext/int corridors. **Pets:** Accepted.

ASK S⊙ ✕ ⟨ 🛑 ⋙

# GREENSBORO

### ▼ Microtel Inn M
(706) 453-7300. **$55-$90.** 2470 Old Eatonton Rd. I-20, exit 130, just n on SR 44. Int corridors. **Pets:** Accepted.

ASK S⊙ ✕ &M 🞩 ⟨ 🛑

▼▼ ▼▼ **The Ritz-Carlton Lodge, Reynolds Plantation** 🄻🄷 ❀
(706) 467-0600. **$225-$5000.** 1 Lk Oconee Tr. I-20, exit 130, 1.3 mi sw on SR 44 (Old Eatonton Rd), 1.5 mi e on Linger Longer Rd, then 2 mi ne. Ext/int corridors. **Pets:** Small. $125 one-time fee/room. Designated rooms, service with restrictions.

(ASK) (S🄳) (✕) (&M) (⌀) 🖬 🖵 (¶¶) (⇌) (⌧)

# GRIFFIN

▼▼ ▼▼ **Howard Johnson Inn & Suites** 🅂🄷
(770) 227-1516. **$39-$199, 5 day notice.** 1690 N Expressway. 1.5 mi n on US 41 and 19. Ext corridors. **Pets:** Large. $25 one-time fee/room. Designated rooms, service with restrictions, supervision.

(ASK) (S🄳) (✕) (&·) 🖬 🖵 (⇌)

# GROVETOWN

▼▼ ▼▼ **Motel 6 of Augusta** 🅂🄷
(706) 651-8300. **$37-$69.** 459 Parkwest Dr. I-20, exit 194 (SR 383), just s, then w. Int corridors. **Pets:** Accepted.

(ASK) (S🄳) (✕) (&·) 🖬 (⇌)

# HAHIRA

▼▼ ▼▼ **Super 8 Motel I-75** 🅂🄷
(229) 794-8000. **$39-$49.** 1300 Georgia Hwy 122 W. I-75, exit 29, just w. Ext corridors. **Pets:** Accepted.

(ASK) (S🄳) (✕)

# HAMPTON

▼▼ ▼▼ **Country Hearth Inn** 🅂🄷
(770) 707-1477. **$60-$67.** 1078 Bear Creek Blvd. 1 mi w of center of town; at US 41 and 19. Int corridors. **Pets:** Other species. $25 one-time fee/room. Service with restrictions, supervision.

(ASK) (S🄳) (✕) (&M) (⌀) (&·) 🖬 🖵

# HELEN

▼▼ ▼▼ **Blue Ridge Cabin Rentals** 🄲🄰
(706) 878-1773. **$99-$399, 8 day notice.** 2990 Hwy 356. 1 mi n on SR 75, 2.9 mi e. Ext corridors. **Pets:** Accepted.

(ASK) 🖬 🖵

▼▼ ▼▼ **The Helendorf River Inn & Conference Center** 🅂🄷
(706) 878-2271. **$54-$104, 10 day notice.** 33 Munichstrasse. SR 17 and 75; center. Ext corridors. **Pets:** Other species. $10 daily fee/pet. Designated rooms, service with restrictions, supervision.

(✕) 🖬 🖵 (⇌)

▼▼ ▼▼ **Kountry Peddler Tanglewood Resort Cabins** 🄲🄰
(706) 878-3286. **$87-$535, 14 day notice.** 3387 Hwy 356. 1 mi n on SR 75, then 3 mi ne. Ext corridors. **Pets:** Accepted.

(ASK) (S🄳) (✕) 🖬 🖵 (⌧)

▲▲▲ ▼▼▼▼ **Premier Vacation Rentals Inc** 🅅🄷
(706) 348-8323. **$90-$475, 14 day notice.** 5156 Helen Hwy. 3.5 mi s on SR 75. Ext corridors. **Pets:** Very small, dogs only. $15 daily fee/pet. Designated rooms, no service, supervision.

(SAVE) (S🄳) 🖬 🖵

# HIAWASSEE

▼▼ ▼▼ **Enota B & B, Cabins & Conference Lodge** 🄲🄰 ❀
(706) 896-9966. **$100-$165, 10 day notice.** 1000 Hwy 180. E on US 76 to SR 75/17, 6 mi s to SR 180, then 3 mi w. Ext corridors. **Pets:** Other species. $15 daily fee/pet.

(✕) 🖬 🖵 (⌧) (☤)

# HINESVILLE

▼▼▼▼ ▼▼ **Quality Inn at Fort Stewart** 🅂🄷
(912) 876-4466. **$55-$75.** 706 E Oglethrope Hwy. Just sw of jct US 84 and SR 38C. Ext corridors. **Pets:** Other species. $10 daily fee/room. Service with restrictions, crate.

(ASK) (S🄳) (✕) (⌀) (&·) 🖬 🖵 (⇌)

# HIRAM

▼▼▼▼ ▼▼ **Country Inn & Suites by Carlson** 🅂🄷
(770) 222-0456. **$69-$110, 3 day notice.** 70 Enterprise Path. Jct SR 92/6 and US 278, 0.3 mi w. Int corridors. **Pets:** Accepted.

(ASK) (S🄳) (✕) (&·) 🖬 🖵 (⇌)

# HOGANSVILLE

▲▲▲ ▼▼ ▼▼ **Econo Lodge** 🅂🄷
(706) 637-9395. **$55-$105.** 1888 E Main St. I-85, exit 28, just w. Ext corridors. **Pets:** Small, dogs only. $10 daily fee/pet. Designated rooms, service with restrictions, supervision.

(SAVE) (S🄳) (✕) 🖬 🖵 (⇌)

▼▼ ▼▼ **Garden Inn & Suites** 🅂🄷
(706) 637-5400. **$50-$55.** 1630 Bass Cross Rd. I-85, exit 28, just w. Ext corridors. **Pets:** Accepted.

(ASK) (S🄳) (✕) 🖬 (⇌)

# JASPER

▲▲▲ ▼▼ ▼▼ **Super 8 Motel** 🅂🄷
(706) 253-3297. **$75-$85.** 100 Whitfield Dr. Jct SR 515/53; in Lawsons Crossing. Ext corridors. **Pets:** Accepted.

(SAVE) (S🄳) (✕) (&M) (&·) 🖬 🖵 (⇌)

# JESUP

▼▼ ▼▼ **Jameson Inn of Jesup** 🄼
(912) 427-6800. **$54-$104.** 205 N Hwy 301. Jct US 341, just n. Ext corridors. **Pets:** Very small, other species. $10 daily fee/room. Service with restrictions, supervision.

(ASK) (✕) (⌀) 🖬 🖵 (⇌)

# KINGSLAND

▲▲▲ ▼▼▼▼ **Best Western/Kings Bay Inn** 🅂🄷
(912) 729-7666. **$75-$139, 3 day notice.** 1353 Hwy 40 E. I-95, exit 3 (SR 40), just se. Ext corridors. **Pets:** Small, other species. $7 one-time fee/pet. Service with restrictions, crate.

(SAVE) (S🄳) (✕) (⌀) 🖬 🖵 (⇌)

▼▼ ▼▼ **Econo Lodge** 🄼
(912) 673-7336. **$52-$60.** 1135 E King Ave. I-95, exit 3 (SR 40), just nw. Ext corridors. **Pets:** Medium. $5 daily fee/pet. Service with restrictions, supervision.

(ASK) (S🄳) (✕) (&M) (⌀) (&·) 🖬 🖵 (⇌)

▼▼ ▼▼ **Jameson Inn** 🄼
(912) 729-9600. **$54-$104.** 105 May Creek Blvd. I-95, exit 3 (SR 40), just w, then s at Boone Ave. Ext corridors. **Pets:** Very small, other species. $10 daily fee/room. Service with restrictions, supervision.

(ASK) (✕) (&M) 🖬 🖵 (⇌)

▲▲▲ ▼▼▼▼ **Ramada Inn & Suites** 🅂🄷 ❀
(912) 729-3000. **$65-$109.** 1215 E King Ave. I-95, exit 3 (SR 40), just nw. Ext corridors. **Pets:** Medium, other species. $10 daily fee/pet.

(SAVE) (S🄳) (✕) (&·) 🖬 🖵 (¶¶) (⇌)

▲▲▲ ▼▼ **Super 8 Motel** 🅂🄷
(912) 729-6888. **$42-$150.** 120 Edenfield Dr. I-95, exit 3 (SR 40), just se. Int corridors. **Pets:** Medium. $5 daily fee/pet. Service with restrictions, supervision.

(SAVE) (S🄳) (✕) 🖬

# LA FAYETTE

▲▲▲ ▼▼ ▼▼ **Days Inn** 🅂🄷
(706) 639-9362. **$55-$100.** 2209 N Main St. 2.5 mi n on US 27. Ext corridors. **Pets:** Other species. $10 daily fee/pet. Service with restrictions, crate.

(SAVE) (S🄳) (✕) 🖬 (⇌)

▼▼ Key West Inn **M**
(706) 638-8200. **$60-$75, 14 day notice.** 2221 N Main St. 2.5 mi n on US 27. Ext corridors. **Pets:** Medium. $10 daily fee/pet. Service with restrictions.
(ASK) (S☼) (✕) (♿M) (🔌) (≈)

# LAGRANGE

(AAA) ▼▼ AmeriHost Inn-LaGrange **SH**
(706) 885-9002. **$59.** 107 Hoffman Dr. I-85, exit 18 (Lafayette Pkwy), just w. Int corridors. **Pets:** Small. $10 daily fee/pet. Service with restrictions, crate.
(SAVE) (S☼) (✕) (🔌) (🔌) (≈)

(AAA) ▼▼▼ Best Western Lafayette Garden Inn **SH**
(706) 884-6175. **$60-$91.** 1513 Lafayette Pkwy. I-85, exit 18 (Lafayette Pkwy), just w. Ext corridors. **Pets:** Accepted.
(SAVE) (S☼) (✕) (🔌) (🔌) (🍴) (≈)

(AAA) ▼▼ Days Inn-LaGrange/Callaway Gardens **SH**
(706) 882-8881. **$67.** 2606 Whitesville Rd. I-85, exit 13, just e. Ext corridors. **Pets:** $10 daily fee/pet. No service, supervision.
(SAVE) (S☼) (✕) (🔌) (🔌) (🔌) (≈)

▼▼ Econo Lodge **SH**
(706) 882-9540. **$65-$130.** 1601 Lafayette Pkwy. I-85, exit 18 (Lafayette Pkwy), just e. Ext corridors. **Pets:** Accepted.
(✕) (🔌) (🔌) (≈)

▼▼ Jameson Inn **SH**
(706) 882-8700. **$54-$104.** 110 Jameson Dr. I-85, exit 18 (Lafayette Pkwy), 0.3 mi w. Ext corridors. **Pets:** Very small, other species. $10 daily fee/room. Service with restrictions, supervision.
(ASK) (✕) (♿M) (🔌) (🔌) (🔌) (≈)

# LAKE PARK

▼▼ Days Inn **SH**
(229) 559-0229. **$59-$69.** 4913 Timber Dr. I-75, exit 5, just w, then n. Ext corridors. **Pets:** Accepted.
(ASK) (S☼) (✕) (🔌) (≈)

▼▼ Holiday Inn Express **SH**
(229) 559-5181. **$75.** 1198 Lakes Blvd. I-75, exit 5, just e. Ext corridors. **Pets:** Accepted.
(✕) (🔌) (🔌) (≈)

(AAA) ▼▼ Super 8 Motel **SH**
(229) 559-8111. **$50-$70.** 4907 Timber Dr. I-75, exit 5, just w, then n. Ext corridors. **Pets:** Accepted.
(SAVE) (✕) (🔌)

(AAA) ▼▼ Travelodge **SH**
(229) 559-0110. **$40-$65.** 4912 Timber Dr. I-75, exit 5, just w, then just n. Int corridors. **Pets:** Accepted.
(SAVE) (S☼) (✕) (♿M) (🔌) (🔌) (≈)

# LAVONIA

(AAA) ▼▼ Super 8 Motel-Lavonia **SH**
(706) 356-8848. **$49-$99.** 14227 Jones St. I-85, exit 173, just w. Ext corridors. **Pets:** Other species. $10 daily fee/room. Designated rooms, service with restrictions, supervision.
(ASK) (S☼) (✕) (♿M) (🔌) (🔌) (🔌) (🔌) (≈)

# LOCUST GROVE

(AAA) ▼▼▼ Econo Lodge **M**
(770) 957-2601. **$45-$100, 3 day notice.** 4829 Bill Gardner Pkwy. I-75, exit 212, just e. Ext corridors. **Pets:** Small. $7 daily fee/pet. Designated rooms, service with restrictions, supervision.
(SAVE) (S☼) (✕) (🔌) (🔌)

(AAA) ▼▼▼ Red Roof Inn & Suites **SH**
(678) 583-0004. **$53-$94.** 4832 Bill Gardner Pkwy. I-75, exit 212, just e. Int corridors. **Pets:** Accepted.
(SAVE) (S☼) (✕) (♿M) (🔌) (🔌) (🔌) (🔌) (≈)

# LOUISVILLE

(AAA) ▼▼ Louisville Motor Lodge **M**
(478) 625-7168. **$43-$48.** 308 Hwy 1 Bypass. Jct SR 24/US 1 Bypass, 0.6 mi n. Ext corridors. **Pets:** Small. $6 daily fee/pet. Service with restrictions, supervision.
(SAVE) (✕) (🔌)

# MACON

▼▼ Best Inns & Suites **M**
(478) 405-0106. **$-$.** 130 Holiday North Dr. I-75, exit 169 (Arkwright Rd), just sw to US 23 (Riverside Dr), just se to Holiday North Dr, then just sw. Ext corridors. **Pets:** Accepted.
(ASK) (S☼) (✕) (🔌) (🔌)

(AAA) ▼▼▼ Best Western Inn & Suites of Macon **M**
(478) 781-5300. **$59.** 4681 Chambers Rd. I-475, exit 3 (Eisenhower Pkwy/US 80), just ne, then just se. Ext corridors. **Pets:** Medium. $10 daily fee/pet. Designated rooms, service with restrictions, crate.
(SAVE) (S☼) (✕) (🔌) (🔌) (🔌) (≈)

(AAA) ▼▼▼ Best Western Riverside Inn **SH** 🐾
(478) 743-6311. **$59-$69.** 2400 Riverside Dr. I-75, exit 167 (Riverside Dr), just w, then 0.4 mi se. Int corridors. **Pets:** Medium. $10 daily fee/pet. Designated rooms, service with restrictions, supervision.
(SAVE) (S☼) (✕) (🔌) (🔌) (≈)

(AAA) ▼▼▼ Crowne Plaza Hotel **LH**
(478) 746-1461. **$62-$119, 3 day notice.** 108 First St. Between Walnut St and Riverside Dr; downtown. Int corridors. **Pets:** $50 one-time fee/room. Designated rooms, service with restrictions, supervision.
(SAVE) (S☼) (✕) (🔌) (🔌) (🍴) (≈) (✕)

▼▼ Days Inn-Macon West **M**
(478) 784-1000. **$60-$80, 7 day notice.** 6000 Harrison Rd. I-475, exit 3 (Eisenhower Pkwy/US 80), just w. Ext corridors. **Pets:** Accepted.
(ASK) (S☼) (✕) (🔌) (🔌) (≈)

(AAA) ▼▼▼ Econo Lodge **M** 🐾
(478) 474-1661. **$40-$60.** 4951 Romeiser Dr. I-475, exit 3 (Eisenhower Pkwy/US 80), just sw, then s. Ext corridors. **Pets:** Other species. $11 daily fee/pet. No service, supervision.
(SAVE) (S☼) (✕) (🔌) (≈)

▼▼▼ Hawthorn Inn & Suites **SH**
(478) 471-2121. **$81, 11 day notice.** 107 Holiday North Dr. I-75, exit 169 (Arkwright Rd), just sw to Riverside Dr, then just se. Ext corridors. **Pets:** Accepted.
(ASK) (S☼) (✕) (🔌) (🔌) (🔌) (≈)

▼▼▼ Holiday Inn Macon Conference Center **SH**
(478) 474-2610. **$64-$65.** 3590 Riverside Dr. I-75, exit 169 (Arkwright Rd), just sw, then just se. Ext corridors. **Pets:** Small. $25 one-time fee/pet. Service with restrictions, supervision.
(ASK) (✕) (🔌) (🔌) (🍴) (≈)

(AAA) ▼▼▼ Holiday Inn West **SH**
(478) 788-0120. **$69.** 4755 Chambers Rd. I-475, exit 3 (Eisenhower Pkwy/US 80), just nw, then se. Ext corridors. **Pets:** Accepted.
(SAVE) (S☼) (✕) (🔌) (🔌) (🍴) (≈)

▼▼▼ Jameson Inn **M**
(478) 474-8004. **$54-$104.** 150 Plantation Inn Dr. I-475, exit 9 (Zebulon Rd), just e to Peake Rd, then just s. Ext corridors. **Pets:** Accepted.
(ASK) (✕) (🔌) (🔌) (≈)

◆◆◆ ♦♦♦ La Quinta Inn & Suites Macon 🆂🅷
(478) 475-0206. **$93-$128.** 3944 River Place Dr. I-75, exit 169 (Arkwright Rd), just n, then e. Int corridors. **Pets:** Medium. Service with restrictions.
[SAVE] [✕] [⅍M] [📶] [🛏] [💻] [🏊]

♦♦ Motel 6 #4246 Ⓜ
(478) 474-2870. **$40-$46.** 4991 Harrison Rd. I-475, exit 3 (Eisenhower Pkwy/US 80), just ne, then n. Ext corridors. **Pets:** Accepted.
[✕] [🛏] [🏊]

♦♦ Red Roof Inn 🆂🅷
(478) 477-7477. **$41-$50.** 3950 River Place Dr. I-75, exit 169 (Arkwright Rd), just n, then e. Int corridors. **Pets:** Accepted.
[✕] [📶] [🛏] [🏊]

◆◆◆ ♦♦ Rodeway Inn Ⓜ 🐾
(478) 476-3471. **$49.** 4999 Eisenhower Pkwy. I-475, exit 3 (Eisenhower Pkwy/US 80), just ne. Ext corridors. **Pets:** Medium. $5 daily fee/pet. Service with restrictions, crate.
[SAVE] [S⃝] [✕] [🛏] [💻] [🏊]

◆◆◆ ♦♦♦ Sleep Inn I-475 🆂🅷
(478) 476-8111. **$63.** 140 Plantation Inn Dr. I-475, exit 9 (Zebulon Rd), just e to Peake Rd, then just s. Int corridors. **Pets:** Accepted.
[SAVE] [S⃝] [✕] [⅍M] [📶] [📶] [🛏] [💻] [🏊]

## MADISON

◆◆◆ ♦♦♦ Days Inn 🆂🅷
(706) 342-1839. **$49.** 2001 Eatonton Hwy. I-20, exit 114, just n. Ext corridors. **Pets:** Accepted.
[SAVE] [S⃝] [✕] [🛏] [💻] [🏊]

## MCDONOUGH

◆◆◆ ♦♦♦♦ Comfort Inn 🆂🅷
(770) 954-9110. **$70-$185.** 80 Hwy 81 W. I-75, exit 218, just nw. Ext corridors. **Pets:** Medium. $7 daily fee/pet. Service with restrictions, crate.
[SAVE] [S⃝] [✕] [📶] [🛏] [💻] [🏊]

◆◆◆ ♦♦♦ Country Hearth Inn & Suites Ⓜ
(770) 957-2458. **$50.** 1170 Hampton Rd. I-75, exit 218, just e. Ext/int corridors. **Pets:** Other species. $10 daily fee/room. Designated rooms, service with restrictions, supervision.
[SAVE] [S⃝] [✕] [🛏]

◆◆◆ ♦♦ Days Inn 🆂🅷
(770) 957-5261. **$56-$80.** 744 SR 155 S & I-75. I-75, exit 216, just e. Ext corridors. **Pets:** Accepted.
[SAVE] [S⃝] [✕] [📶] [🛏] [💻] [🏊]

◆◆◆ ♦♦ Econo Lodge Ⓜ
(770) 957-2651. **$45-$140.** 1279 Hampton Rd. I-75, exit 218, just w. Ext corridors. **Pets:** Accepted.
[SAVE] [S⃝] [✕] [🛏] [💻] [🏊]

◆◆◆ ♦♦ Masters Inn Ⓜ
(770) 957-5818. **$45-$139.** 1311 Hampton Rd. I-75, exit 218, just w. Ext corridors. **Pets:** Accepted.
[SAVE] [S⃝] [✕] [🛏] [💻]

◆◆◆ ♦♦♦♦ Quality Inn & Suites Conference Center 🆂🅷
(770) 957-5291. **$69-$150.** 930 Hwy 155 S. I-75, exit 216, just w. Ext corridors. **Pets:** Other species. $5 daily fee/room. Service with restrictions, crate.
[SAVE] [S⃝] [✕] [⅍M] [📶] [🛏] [💻] [🍴] [🏊]

## MILLEDGEVILLE

♦♦♦ Holiday Inn Express 🆂🅷
(478) 454-9000. **$77-$99, 3 day notice.** 1839 N Columbia St. US 441, 2 mi n of downtown. Int corridors. **Pets:** Accepted.
[ASK] [S⃝] [✕] [⅍M] [📶] [📶] [🛏] [💻]

## MONROE

♦♦♦ Country Hearth Inn 🆂🅷
(770) 207-1977. **$65-$70.** 1222 W Spring St. 1 mi w of downtown on Business Rt SR 10. Int corridors. **Pets:** Accepted.
[✕] [⅍M] [📶] [🛏] [💻]

## NEWNAN

◆◆◆ ♦♦ Best Western-Shenandoah Inn 🆂🅷
(770) 304-9700. **$60-$80.** 620 Hwy 34 E. I-85, exit 47, just w. Ext corridors. **Pets:** Medium, other species. $10 daily fee/pet. Designated rooms, service with restrictions, supervision.
[SAVE] [S⃝] [✕] [⅍M] [📶] [🛏] [💻] [🏊]

♦♦♦ Jameson Inn 🆂🅷
(770) 252-1236. **$54-$104.** 40 Lakeside Way. I-85, exit 47, 0.6 mi e. Int corridors. **Pets:** Very small, other species. $10 daily fee/room. Service with restrictions, supervision.
[ASK] [✕] [⅍M] [📶] [📶] [🛏] [💻] [🏊]

♦♦♦ Ramada Limited 🆂🅷
(770) 683-1499. **$52-$80.** 1310 Hwy 29 S. I-85, exit 41, just w. Ext corridors. **Pets:** Small. $15 daily fee/pet. Service with restrictions, supervision.
[ASK] [S⃝] [✕] [📶] [🛏] [💻] [🏊]

## OAKWOOD

♦♦♦♦ Country Inn & Suites by Carlson 🆂🅷
(770) 535-8080. **$85-$185.** 4535 Oakwood Rd. I-985, exit 16, just sw. Int corridors. **Pets:** Accepted.
[ASK] [S⃝] [✕] [📶] [📶] [🛏] [💻] [🏊]

♦♦ Jameson Inn of Oakwood/Gainesville 🆂🅷
(770) 533-9400. **$54-$104.** 3780 Merchants Way. I-985, exit 16, 0.4 mi nw. Ext corridors. **Pets:** Accepted.
[ASK] [✕] [⅍M] [🛏] [💻]

## PEACHTREE CITY

♦♦ Sleep Inn 🆂🅷
(770) 486-0044. **$99-$129.** 109 City Cir. Jct SR 74 and 54; in Avenues Shopping Center. Int corridors. **Pets:** Small. $45 one-time fee/pet. Service with restrictions, supervision.
[S⃝] [✕] [⅍M] [📶] [🛏] [💻]

## PERRY

♦♦ Best Inns 🆂🅷
(478) 987-4454. **$39-$69.** 110 Perimeter Rd. I-75, exit 136 (Sam Nunn Blvd), just se. Ext corridors. **Pets:** Other species. $10 daily fee/room. Service with restrictions, crate.
[ASK] [S⃝] [✕] [🛏] [🏊]

◆◆◆ ♦♦♦♦ Best Western Bradbury Inn & Suites 🆂🅷
(478) 218-5200. **$69-$89.** 205 Lect Dr. I-75, exit 135 (US 41), just e, then just n. Int corridors. **Pets:** Accepted.
[SAVE] [S⃝] [✕] [📶] [🛏] [💻] [🏊]

◆◆◆ ♦♦♦♦ Comfort Inn Perry 🆂🅷
(478) 987-7710. **$53-$119.** 1602 Sam Nunn Blvd. I-75, exit 136 (Sam Nunn Blvd), just w. Ext corridors. **Pets:** Medium. $15 daily fee/room. Service with restrictions, supervision.
[SAVE] [S⃝] [✕] [📶] [🛏] [💻] [🏊]

◆◆◆ ♦♦♦♦ Days Inn & Suites of Perry 🆂🅷
(478) 987-8777. **$59-$89.** 201 Lect Dr. I-75, exit 135 (US 41), just e, then just n. Ext/int corridors. **Pets:** Accepted.
[SAVE] [S⃝] [✕] [⅍M] [📶] [📶] [🛏] [💻] [🏊] [✕]

◆◆◆ ♦♦♦♦ Henderson Village 🅲🅸
(478) 988-8696. **$175-$350, 3 day notice.** 125 S Langston Cir. I-75, exit 127 (SR 26), 1.3 mi w. Ext/int corridors. **Pets:** Accepted.
[SAVE] [S⃝] [✕] [🛏] [💻] [🍴] [🏊] [✕]

◆◆ **Jameson Inn-Perry** Ⓜ
(478) 987-5060. **$54-$104.** 200 Market Place Dr. I-75, exit 136 (Sam Nunn Blvd), just se, then sw. Ext corridors. **Pets:** Accepted.
[ASK] ✕ 🖥 🖵 🏊

◆◆◆ ◆◆ **New Perry Hotel** 🆂🅷
(478) 987-1000. **$59-$125.** 800 Main St. I-75, exit 136 (Sam Nunn Blvd) southbound, 1.2 mi se on US 341, then just w; exit 135 (US 41) northbound, 1.5 mi ne, then just s. Ext/int corridors. **Pets:** Accepted.
[SAVE] [S🅳] ✕ 🅖 🖥 🖵 🍽 🏊

◆◆◆ ◆◆ **Quality Inn** Ⓜ
(478) 987-1345. **$59-$95.** 1504 Sam Nunn Blvd. I-75, exit 136 (Sam Nunn Blvd), just nw. Ext corridors. **Pets:** $10 daily fee/room. Designated rooms, service with restrictions, supervision.
[SAVE] [S🅳] ✕ 🖥 🖵 🍽 🏊

◆◆◆ ◆◆ ◆◆ **Super 8 Motel** 🆂🅷
(478) 987-0999. **$50-$70, 3 day notice.** 102 Plaza Dr. I-75, exit 136 (Sam Nunn Blvd), just se. Ext corridors. **Pets:** Accepted.
[SAVE] [S🅳] ✕ 🅖 🖥 🏊

# PINE MOUNTAIN

◆◆◆◆ **Callaway Gardens' Mountain Creek Inn** 🅻🅷
(706) 663-2281. **$114-$144, 7 day notice.** Hwy 27. On US 27, 2.8 mi s. Ext corridors. **Pets:** Accepted.
[ASK] ✕ 🅖🅜 🖇 🅖 🖵 🍽 🏊 ✕

◆◆◆ ◆◆ **Days Inn** 🆂🅷
(706) 663-2121. **$60-$89.** 368 S Main Ave. Just s on US 27 and SR 18. Ext corridors. **Pets:** $10 daily fee/pet. Designated rooms, service with restrictions, supervision.
[SAVE] [S🅳] ✕ 🖇 🅖 🖥 🏊

◆◆ **White Columns Motel** Ⓜ
(706) 663-8008. **$50-$65.** 524 S Main St. 1 mi s on US 27. Ext corridors. **Pets:** Accepted.
[ASK] [S🅳] ✕ 🖥

# POOLER

◆◆◆ ◆◆◆◆ **Best Western Bradbury Suites** 🆂🅷 🐾
(912) 330-0330. **$79-$159.** 155 Bourne Ave. I-95, exit 102 (US 80), just e. Int corridors. **Pets:** Medium, other species. Service with restrictions, crate.
[SAVE] [S🅳] ✕ 🅖🅜 🖇 🅖 🖥 🖵 🏊 ✕

◆◆◆◆ **Comfort Inn & Suites Conference Center** 🆂🅷
(912) 748-6464. **$70-$100.** 301 Governor Treutlen Dr. I-95, exit 102 (US 80), just nw, then just se. Int corridors. **Pets:** Accepted.
[ASK] [S🅳] ✕ 🖥 🖵 🏊

◆◆◆ ◆◆ **Econo Lodge–Savannah Pooler** Ⓜ
(912) 748-4124. **$55-$99.** 500 E Hwy 80. I-95, exit 102 (US 80), just nw. Ext corridors. **Pets:** Other species. $10 daily fee/room. Designated rooms, service with restrictions.
[SAVE] [S🅳] ✕ 🖇 🅖 🖥 🖵 🏊

◆◆◆ **Jameson Inn** 🆂🅷
(912) 748-0017. **$54-$104.** 125 Bourne Ave. I-95, exit 102 (US 80), just e. Int corridors. **Pets:** Very small, other species. $10 daily fee/room. Service with restrictions, supervision.
[ASK] ✕ 🖇 🅖 🖥 🖵 🏊

◆◆ **Red Roof Inn & Suites** 🆂🅷
(912) 748-4050. **$74-$89.** 20 Mill Creek Cir. I-95, exit 104 (Pooler Pkwy), just w. Int corridors. **Pets:** Accepted.
[ASK] [S🅳] ✕ 🖇 🅖 🖥 🖵 🏊

# RINGGOLD

◆◆◆ ◆◆◆◆ **Comfort Inn** 🆂🅷
(706) 935-4000. **$69-$109.** 177 Industrial Blvd. I-75, exit 348, just w. Int corridors. **Pets:** Small. $10 daily fee/pet. Designated rooms, service with restrictions, supervision.
[SAVE] [S🅳] ✕ 🅖 🖥 🖵 🏊

◆◆ ◆◆ **Super 8 Motel** Ⓜ
(706) 965-7080. **$47-$100.** 5400 Alabama Hwy. I-75, exit 348, just e. Ext corridors. **Pets:** Accepted.
[ASK] [S🅳] ✕ 🅖🅜 🖥 🏊

# ROCKMART

◆◆ ◆◆ **Days Inn** Ⓜ
(770) 684-9955. **$50-$60.** 105 GTM Pkwy. Jct US 278 and SR 101, just n. Ext corridors. **Pets:** Small. $5 daily fee/pet. Designated rooms, service with restrictions, supervision.
[ASK] [S🅳] ✕ 🅖🅜 🖇 🖥

# ROME

◆◆◆◆ **Holiday Inn-Sky Top Center** 🆂🅷
(706) 295-1100. **$80.** 20 US 411 E. 2 mi e. Ext corridors. **Pets:** Accepted.
[ASK] ✕ 🅖🅜 🖇 🅖 🖥 🍽 🏊

◆◆ ◆◆ **Howard Johnson Express Inn of Rome** 🆂🅷
(706) 291-1994. **$52-$60.** 1610 Martha Berry Blvd. 2 mi n on US 27. Ext corridors. **Pets:** Accepted.
[ASK] [S🅳] ✕ 🖇 🅖 🖥 🖵

◆◆ ◆◆ **Jameson Inn** 🆂🅷
(706) 291-7797. **$54-$104.** 40 Grace Dr. On US 411, 2.2 mi e. Int corridors. **Pets:** Very small, other species. $10 daily fee/room. Service with restrictions, supervision.
[ASK] ✕ 🅖🅜 🖇 🅖 🖥 🖵 🏊

# SANDERSVILLE

◆◆◆ ◆◆ **Villa South Inn** Ⓜ
(478) 552-1234. **$61-$80, 11 day notice.** 725 S Harris St (SR 15). Jct SR 15/242, just s on SR 15. Ext corridors. **Pets:** Accepted.
[SAVE] ✕ 🖥 🖵 🍽 🏊

# SAVANNAH

◆◆◆ ◆◆ **Americas Best Value Inn** Ⓜ
(912) 927-2999. **$45-$65, 5 day notice.** 390 Canebrake Rd. I-95, exit 94 (SR 204), just e, then just s. Ext corridors. **Pets:** Small, other species. $5 daily fee/pet. Designated rooms, service with restrictions, supervision.
[SAVE] [S🅳] ✕ 🖇 🖥 🖵 🏊

◆◆◆ ◆◆◆ ◆◆◆ **Ballastone Inn** 🅱🅱
(912) 236-1484. **$215-$395, 15 day notice.** 14 E Oglethorpe Ave. Between Bull and Drayton sts. Int corridors. **Pets:** Small, dogs only. $50 deposit/pet, $50 one-time fee/pet. Designated rooms, service with restrictions, crate.
[SAVE] ✕

◆◆◆ ◆◆ ◆◆ **Baymont Inn & Suites Savannah** 🆂🅷
(912) 927-7660. **$59-$99.** 8484 Abercorn St. 2.4 mi s of jct SR 21/204 (Abercorn St). Int corridors. **Pets:** Medium. Service with restrictions.
[SAVE] ✕ 🖇 🖥 🖵

◆◆◆ ◆◆ ◆◆ **Best Western Central** 🆂🅷
(912) 355-1000. **$60-$100.** 45 Eisenhower Dr. 1.3 mi s of jct SR 21/204 (Abercorn St), then just w. Ext corridors. **Pets:** Accepted.
[SAVE] ✕ 🖇 🖥 🖵 🏊

◆◆ ◆◆ ◆◆ **Catherine Ward House Inn** 🅱🅱
(912) 234-8564. **$159-$375, 14 day notice.** 118 E Walburg St. Between Drayton and Abercorn sts. Ext/int corridors. **Pets:** Accepted.
[ASK] ✕ 🖥 🖵

**Clarion Inn & Suites** SH
(912) 920-3200. **$70-$139.** 16 Gateway Blvd E. I-95, exit 94 (SR 204), just e. Int corridors. **Pets:** Medium, other species. $20 daily fee/pet. Designated rooms, service with restrictions, supervision.

**ClubHouse Inn & Suites** SH
(912) 356-1234. **$109-$129.** 6800 Abercorn St. 1 mi s of jct SR 21/204 (Abercorn St). Int corridors. **Pets:** Accepted.

**Days Inn-Airport** SH
(912) 966-5000. **$69-$100.** 2500 Dean Forest Rd. I-95, exit 102 (US 80), 2.7 mi e to SR 307, then 1.9 mi n. Ext corridors. **Pets:** Accepted.

**East Bay Inn** CI
(912) 238-1225. **$159-$199, 7 day notice.** 225 E Bay St. I-16, exit 167 (Montgomery St), 0.8 mi ne, then 0.4 mi se; in historic district. Int corridors. **Pets:** Accepted.

**The Forsyth Park Inn** BB
(912) 233-6800. **$150-$230, 7 day notice.** 102 W Hall St. Between Whitaker and Howard sts; on Forsyth Park. Int corridors. **Pets:** Small. $40 one-time fee/pet. Designated rooms, service with restrictions.

**Hawthorn Suites** SH
(912) 966-0020. **$109-$119.** 4 Stephen S Green Ave. I-95, exit 104, 0.4 mi e. Int corridors. **Pets:** Small. $100 one-time fee/room. Designated rooms, service with restrictions, supervision.

**Holiday Inn-Midtown** SH
(912) 352-7100. **$90.** 7100 Abercorn St. 1.2 mi s of jct SR 21/204 (Abercorn St). Ext corridors. **Pets:** Accepted.

**Homewood Suites by Hilton** SH
(912) 353-8500. **$129-$229.** 5820 White Bluff Rd. Jct SR 21/204, 0.5 mi s. Ext/int corridors. **Pets:** Accepted.

**Joan's on Jones B & B** BB 🐾
(912) 234-3863. **$165-$185 (no credit cards), 7 day notice.** 17 W Jones St. Between Whitaker and Bull sts. Ext corridors. **Pets:** Dogs only. $50 one-time fee/room. Crate.

**La Quinta Inn Savannah (I-95)** M
(912) 925-9505. **$69-$84.** 6 Gateway Blvd S. I-95, exit 94 (SR 204), just e, then s. Ext corridors. **Pets:** Medium. Service with restrictions.

**La Quinta Inn Savannah (Midtown)** SH
(912) 355-3004. **$68-$105.** 6805 Abercorn St. 1 mi s of jct SR 21/204 (Abercorn St). Ext/int corridors. **Pets:** Medium. Service with restrictions.

**The Olde Georgian Inn** BB
(912) 236-2911. **$105-$250, 7 day notice.** 212 W Hall St. Between Jefferson and Barnard sts; just w of Forsyth Park. Int corridors. **Pets:** Accepted.

**Olde Harbour Inn** BB
(912) 234-4100. **$149-$350, 7 day notice.** 508 E Factors Walk. Lincoln St ramp off E Bay St; in historic riverfront district. Ext corridors. **Pets:** Accepted.

**Quality Inn Savannah South** M
(912) 925-2770. **$47-$94.** 3 Gateway Blvd S. I-95, exit 94 (SR 204), just e, then just s. Ext corridors. **Pets:** Small. $10 daily fee/pet. Designated rooms, service with restrictions, supervision.

**Red Roof Inn** SH
(912) 920-3535. **$50-$90.** 405 Al Henderson Blvd. I-95, exit 94 (SR 204), just e. Int corridors. **Pets:** Accepted.

**Savannah Residence Inn by Marriott** SH
(912) 356-3266. **$119-$179.** 5710 White Bluff Rd. Jct SR 21, 0.5 mi s. Int corridors. **Pets:** Accepted.

**Suites on Lafayette** CO
(912) 233-7815. **$149-$209, 14 day notice.** 201-205 E Charlton St. Off Abercorn St at Lafayette Square. Int corridors. **Pets:** Accepted.

**Travelodge** M
(912) 925-2640. **$40-$199.** 1 Ft Argyle Rd. I-95, exit 94 (SR 204), just w. Ext corridors. **Pets:** $10 daily fee/pet. Designated rooms, supervision.

**Westin Savannah Harbor Resort and Spa** LH
(912) 201-2000. **$149-$299, 3 day notice.** 1 Resort Dr. On Hutchinson Island; 1 mi se of first exit after Eugene Talmadge Memorial Bridge and US 17. Int corridors. **Pets:** Accepted.

# STATESBORO

**Best Western University Inn** M
(912) 681-7900. **$62-$68.** 1 Jameson Ave. Jct US 25/301 and SR 67, 0.9 mi s on US 25/301. Ext corridors. **Pets:** Accepted.

**Hometown Inn** M
(912) 681-4663. **Call for rates.** 126 Rushing Ln. Jct US 301 Bypass and SR 67, just n, then w. Ext corridors. **Pets:** Accepted.

**La Quinta Inn Statesboro** SH
(912) 871-2525. **$70-$100.** 1 Lanier Dr. Jct US 301 Bypass and SR 67, 1.2 mi w on US 301, just n of Georgia Southern University. Int corridors. **Pets:** $50 deposit/pet. No service, supervision.

**Statesboro Inn & Restaurant** CI
(912) 489-8628. **$95-$115.** 106 S Main St (US 301/25). US 301/25, just s of town center; downtown. Int corridors. **Pets:** Accepted.

# STOCKBRIDGE

**Best Western Atlanta South** SH
(770) 474-8771. **$60-$100.** 619 Hwy 138. I-75, exit 228, just e; I-675, exit 1, 0.5 mi w. Ext corridors. **Pets:** Accepted.

**Motel 6–1117** M
(770) 389-1142. **$43-$55.** 7233 Davidson Pkwy N. I-675, exit 1, just e, then just n; I-75, exit 228, 1 mi e. Ext corridors. **Pets:** Accepted.

**Super 8 Motel Atlanta South** SH
(770) 474-5758. **$55-$75.** 1451 Hudson Bridge Rd. I-75, exit 224, just w. Ext corridors. **Pets:** Accepted.

# SWAINSBORO

**ααα ▼▼▼ Bradford Inn** Ⓜ
(478) 237-2400. **$50-$65.** 688 S Main St. I-16, exit 90 (US 1), 12.4 mi n. Ext corridors. **Pets:** Small. $10 daily fee/pet. Service with restrictions, supervision.

🅂🄰🅅🄴 S🄰 ⊠ 🄸 🄻🄳

# TALLAPOOSA

**▼▼ Comfort Inn** SH 🐾
(770) 574-5575. **$90-$300.** 788 Hwy 100. I-20, exit 5, just s. Int corridors. **Pets:** Very small, other species. $10 daily fee/pet. Designated rooms, service with restrictions, supervision.

🄰🅂🄺 S🄰 ⊠ 🄻🄼 🄻🄳 🄸 🄻🄳 🄿🄰

# THOMASTON

**▼▼ Best Western Thomaston Inn** SH
(706) 648-2900. **$52-$75, 7 day notice.** 1207 Hwy 19 N. 2.8 mi n; center of town. Ext corridors. **Pets:** Accepted.

🄰🅂🄺 S🄰 ⊠ 🄸 🄻🄳 🄿🄰

**▼▼ Jameson Inn** SH
(706) 648-2232. **$54-$104.** 1010 Hwy 19 N. Jct SR 74, 2.3 mi n. Ext corridors. **Pets:** Very small, other species. $10 daily fee/room. Service with restrictions, supervision.

🄰🅂🄺 ⊠ 🄸 🄻🄳 🄿🄰

# THOMASVILLE

**▼▼ Comfort Inn** SH
(229) 228-5555. **$65-$76.** 14866 US 19 S. Jct SR 300/I-19 and I-84 and SR 122; southeast corner. Ext corridors. **Pets:** Medium, other species. $30 deposit/room. Service with restrictions, crate.

🄰🅂🄺 S🄰 🄸 🄻🄳 🄿🄰

**▼▼ Jameson Inn** SH
(229) 227-9500. **$54-$104.** 1670 Remington Ave. US 19, just w on CR 122. Ext corridors. **Pets:** Very small, other species. $10 daily fee/room. Service with restrictions, supervision.

🄰🅂🄺 ⊠ 🄻🄼 🄻🄳 🄻🄳 🄸 🄻🄳 🄿🄰

**▼▼▼ Quality Inn & Suites Conference Center** SH
(229) 225-2134. **$72.** 15138 Hwy 19 S. 0.3 mi s of US 319. Ext corridors. **Pets:** Accepted.

🄰🅂🄺 S🄰 ⊠ 🄻🄼 🄻🄳 🄸 🄻🄳 🄸🄸 🄿🄰

# THOMSON

**ααα ▼▼▼ Best Western White Columns Inn** SH 🐾
(706) 595-8000. **$59-$89, 14 day notice.** 1890 Washington Rd. I-20, exit 172 (US 78), just s. Ext corridors. **Pets:** $10 daily fee/room. Service with restrictions, crate.

🅂🄰🅅🄴 S🄰 ⊠ 🄸 🄻🄳 🄸🄸 🄿🄰 🆇

**ααα ▼ Days Inn** Ⓜ
(706) 595-2262. **$59-$69.** 2658 Cobbham Rd. I-20, exit 175 (SR 150), just n. Ext corridors. **Pets:** Medium, other species. $15 daily fee/pet. No service, supervision.

🅂🄰🅅🄴 S🄰 ⊠ 🄸

# TIFTON

**▼▼ Days Inn & Suites** SH
(229) 382-8505. **$54-$75.** 1199 Hwy 82 W. I-75, exit 62, just w. Int corridors. **Pets:** Accepted.

🄰🅂🄺 S🄰 ⊠ 🄸 🄻🄳 🄿🄰

**ααα ▼▼▼ Hampton Inn** SH
(229) 382-8800. **$90-$99.** 720 Hwy 319 S. I-75, exit 62, just e. Ext corridors. **Pets:** Accepted.

🅂🄰🅅🄴 ⊠ 🄸 🄻🄳 🄿🄰

**ααα ▼▼ Holiday Inn** SH
(229) 382-6687. **$65-$75.** 1208 Hwy 82 W. I-75, exit 62, at jct US 82 and 319. Ext corridors. **Pets:** Other species. Designated rooms, service with restrictions, supervision.

🅂🄰🅅🄴 S🄰 ⊠ 🄻🄳 🄸 🄻🄳 🄸🄸 🄿🄰

**▼▼ Microtel Inns & Suites** SH
(229) 387-0112. **$49-$75.** 196 S Virginia Ave. I-75, exit 62, just n. Int corridors. **Pets:** Other species. $10 one-time fee/pet. Designated rooms, service with restrictions, crate.

🄰🅂🄺 S🄰 ⊠ 🄻🄼 🄻🄳 🄸 🄻🄳 🄿🄰

**▼ Motel 6 #4074** SH
(229) 388-8777. **$38, 7 day notice.** 579 Old Omega Rd. I-75, exit 61, just w. Int corridors. **Pets:** Accepted.

🄰🅂🄺 S🄰 ⊠ 🄿🄰

**▼ Ramada Limited and Conference Center** SH
(229) 382-8500. **$53-$64.** 1211 Hwy 82 W. I-75, exit 62, just w. Ext corridors. **Pets:** Accepted.

🄰🅂🄺 S🄰 ⊠ 🄸 🄻🄳 🄿🄰

# TOWNSEND

**▼ Days Inn** Ⓜ
(912) 832-4411. **$60-$65.** Hwy 57. I-95, exit 58 (SR 57), just nw. Ext corridors. **Pets:** Medium, other species. $10 daily fee/pet. Service with restrictions, supervision.

🄰🅂🄺 S🄰 ⊠ 🄸 🄿🄰

# TRENTON

**▼▼ Days Inn** SH
(706) 657-2550. **$53-$55.** 95 Killian Ave. I-59, exit 11, just e. Ext corridors. **Pets:** Other species. $10 daily fee/pet.

🄰🅂🄺 S🄰 ⊠ 🄻🄼 🄸 🄻🄳

# UNADILLA

**▼ Scottish Inn** Ⓜ
(478) 627-3228. **$36-$40.** 1062 Pine St (US 41). I-75, exit 121 (US 41), just ne. Ext corridors. **Pets:** Accepted.

🄰🅂🄺 S🄰 ⊠ 🄸 🄿🄰

# VALDOSTA

**▼▼ Best Western King of the Road** SH
(229) 244-7600. **$69-$79.** 1403 N St Augustine Rd. I-75, exit 18, just w off of SR 94. Ext corridors. **Pets:** Accepted.

🄰🅂🄺 S🄰 ⊠ 🄻🄳 🄸 🄻🄳 🄸🄸 🄿🄰

**ααα ▼▼▼ Comfort Inn Conference Center** SH
(229) 242-1212. **$73-$149.** 2101 W Hill Ave. I-75, exit 16, just w. Ext/int corridors. **Pets:** Small, other species. Designated rooms, service with restrictions, supervision.

🅂🄰🅅🄴 S🄰 ⊠ 🄸 🄻🄳 🄸🄸 🄿🄰 🆇

**▼▼ Days Inn Conference Center** SH
(229) 249-8800. **$49-$62.** 1827 W Hill Ave. I-75, exit 16, just e. Ext corridors. **Pets:** Accepted.

🄰🅂🄺 S🄰 ⊠ 🄻🄼 🄻🄳 🄸 🄻🄳 🄿🄰

**▼▼ Days Inn I-75 North** SH
(229) 244-4460. **$49-$59.** 4598 N Valdosta Rd. I-75, exit 22, just w. Ext corridors. **Pets:** Accepted.

🄰🅂🄺 S🄰 ⊠ 🄸 🄿🄰

**ααα ▼▼▼ Econo Lodge** SH
(229) 671-1511. **$60-$100.** 3022 James Rd. I-75, exit 18, southwest corner. **Pets:** Medium. $25 one-time fee/pet. Designated rooms, service with restrictions, supervision.

🅂🄰🅅🄴 S🄰 🄸 🄻🄳 🄿🄰

**AAA ▼▼▼ Holiday Inn** SH
(229) 242-3881. **$69.** 1309 St Augustine Rd. I-75, exit 18, just e on SR 94. Ext corridors. **Pets:** Small, other species. $10 one-time fee/pet. Designated rooms, service with restrictions, crate.

SAVE 🔲 ✖ 🔲 🔲 🍽 🏊

**▼▼ Howard Johnson Express Inn & Suites** SH
(229) 249-8900. **$49-$62.** 1330 St Augustine Rd. I-75, exit 18, just e. Ext corridors. **Pets:** Accepted.

ASK 🔲 ✖ 🔲 🔲 🏊

**▼▼ Jameson Inn** SH
(229) 253-0009. **$54-$104.** 1725 Gornto Rd. I-75, exit 18, 0.3 mi e on north side of SR 94. Ext corridors. **Pets:** Very small, other species. $10 daily fee/room. Service with restrictions, supervision.

ASK ✖ 🔲 🔲 🔲 🏊

**▼▼▼ La Quinta Inn & Suites Valdosta** SH
(229) 247-7755. **$76-$119.** 1800 Clubhouse Dr. I-75, exit 18, 0.3 mi e, then just s off SR 94. Int corridors. **Pets:** Accepted.

ASK 🔲 ✖ 🔲 🔲 🔲 🏊

**AAA ▼▼▼ Quality Inn North** SH
(229) 248-8510. **$69-$74.** 1209 St Augustine Rd. I-75, exit 18, 0.3 mi e on SR 94. Ext corridors. **Pets:** Small, dogs only. $5 daily fee/pet. Designated rooms, service with restrictions.

SAVE ✖ 🔲 🔲 🔲 🏊 ✖

**▼▼ Quality Inn South** SH
(229) 244-4520. **$49-$99.** 1902 W Hill Ave. I-75, exit 16, just e on US 84. Ext corridors. **Pets:** Medium. Service with restrictions.

ASK 🔲 ✖ 🔲 🔲 🏊

**▼▼▼ Ramada Limited** SH
(229) 242-1225. **$79.** 2008 W Hill Ave. I-75, exit 16, just e on US 84. Ext corridors. **Pets:** Other species. $10 daily fee/pet. Service with restrictions, crate.

ASK 🔲 ✖ 🔲 🔲 🏊

**▼▼ Super 8 Motel I-75** SH
(229) 249-8000. **$49-$59.** 1825 W Hill Ave. I-75, exit 16, just e. Int corridors. **Pets:** Accepted.

ASK 🔲 ✖ 🔲 🔲 🔲 🏊

# VIDALIA

**AAA ▼▼▼ Days Inn** SH
(912) 537-9251. **$50-$65, 7 day notice.** 1503 Lyons E. 1 mi e on US 280. Ext corridors. **Pets:** Medium. $5 daily fee/pet. Service with restrictions, supervision.

SAVE 🔲 ✖ 🔲 🔲 🔲 🏊

**▼▼▼ Holiday Inn Express** SH
(912) 537-9000. **$67-$90.** 2619 E First St. 2.5 mi e on US 280. Ext corridors. **Pets:** Service with restrictions, supervision.

ASK 🔲 ✖ 🔲 🔲 🔲 🏊

# VILLA RICA

**▼▼ Days Inn** SH
(770) 459-8888. **$50-$80.** 195 Hwy 61 Connector. I-20, exit 24, just n. Int corridors. **Pets:** Very small, dogs only. $7 one-time fee/pet. Designated rooms, service with restrictions, supervision.

ASK 🔲 ✖ 🔲 🔲 🏊

# WARM SPRINGS

**▼▼▼▼ Best Western White House Inn** SH
(706) 655-2750. **$65-$119.** 2526 White House Pkwy. Jct US 41/27, 1.4 mi s. Ext/int corridors. **Pets:** Accepted.

ASK 🔲 ✖ 🔲 🔲 🔲 🔲 🏊

# WARNER ROBINS

**AAA ▼▼▼ Best Western Peach Inn** SH
(478) 953-3800. **$48-$65.** 2739 Watson Blvd. I-75, exit 146 (SR 247C), 4.1 mi e. Ext corridors. **Pets:** Small. $10 daily fee/pet. Designated rooms, no service, supervision.

SAVE 🔲 ✖ 🔲 🔲 🔲 🏊

**AAA ▼▼▼▼ Comfort Inn & Suites** SH
(478) 922-7555. **$65-$149.** 95 S Hwy 247. Jct SR 247C and US 129/SR 247, 1.6 mi s on US 129/SR 247. Ext/int corridors. **Pets:** Small, other species. $25 one-time fee/room. Service with restrictions, supervision.

SAVE 🔲 ✖ 🔲 🔲 🔲 🏊

**▼▼ Jameson Inn-Warner Robins** SH
(478) 953-5522. **$54-$104.** 2731 Watson Blvd. I-75, exit 146 (SR 247C), 4.1 mi e. Ext corridors. **Pets:** Very small, other species. $10 daily fee/room. Service with restrictions, supervision.

ASK ✖ 🔲 🔲 🔲 🏊

# WAYCROSS

**▼▼ Comfort Inn Waycross** SH
(912) 283-3300. **$89-$95.** 1903 Memorial Dr. Between US 1 and 82, at S City Blvd. Ext corridors. **Pets:** Accepted.

ASK 🔲 ✖ 🔲 🔲 🔲 🏊

**▼▼▼▼ Holiday Inn Waycross** SH
(912) 283-4490. **$70-$90.** 1725 Memorial Dr. Jct US 1 and 82. Ext corridors. **Pets:** Medium. $15 one-time fee/room. Service with restrictions, crate.

ASK 🔲 ✖ 🔲 🔲 🔲 🔲 🍽 🏊 ✖

**▼▼ Jameson Inn** SH
(912) 283-3800. **$54-$104.** 950 City Blvd. Between US 1 and 82, east of city. Ext corridors. **Pets:** Very small, other species. $10 daily fee/room. Service with restrictions, supervision.

ASK ✖ 🔲 🔲 🔲 🔲 🏊

# WAYNESBORO

**▼▼ Jameson Inn** M
(706) 437-0500. **$54-$104.** 1436 N Liberty St. 0.9 mi n of downtown center on US 25. Ext corridors. **Pets:** Very small, other species. $10 daily fee/room. Service with restrictions, supervision.

ASK ✖ 🔲 🔲 🔲 🏊

# WEST POINT

**▼▼ Travelodge** M
(706) 643-9922. **$51.** 1870 SR 18. I-85, exit 2, just e. Int corridors. **Pets:** Accepted.

ASK 🔲 ✖ 🔲 🔲 🏊

# WINDER

**▼▼ Jameson Inn** M
(770) 867-1880. **$54-$104.** 9 Stafford St. Jct SR 81, 11, 53 and 8; center. Ext corridors. **Pets:** Accepted.

ASK ✖ 🔲 🔲 🔲 🏊

# WOODSTOCK

**▼▼ SuiteOne of Woodstock** SH
(770) 592-7848. **$54-$79.** 470 Parkway 575. I-575, exit 7, just e to Parkway 575, then just n. Ext corridors. **Pets:** Accepted.

ASK 🔲 ✖ 🔲 🔲 🔲 🔲

# YOUNG HARRIS

**AAA ▼▼▼▼ Brasstown Valley Resort** LH
(706) 379-9900. **$119-$219, 3 day notice.** 6321 US Hwy 76. US 76 and US 76/SR 515. Int corridors. **Pets:** Small, dogs only. $75 one-time fee/pet. Designated rooms, service with restrictions, crate.

SAVE ✖ 🔲 🔲 🔲 🔲 🍽 🏊 ✖

# HAWAII

## HONOLULU

**AAA** ▼▼▼▼ Kahala Mandarin Oriental Hawaii **LH** ❀
(808) 739-8888. **$395-$795, 3 day notice.** 5000 Kahala Ave. E of
Diamond Head at end of Kahala Ave. Int corridors. **Pets:** Very small.
Service with restrictions, supervision.
[SAVE] [✕] [&M] [⟋] [☞] [🍴] [⇌] [✕]

## END METROPOLITAN AREA

## KAANAPALI

▼▼▼▼ The Westin Maui Resort & Spa **LH**
(808) 667-2525. **$400-$715, 3 day notice.** 2365 Kaanapali Pkwy. Off
SR 30, via Kaanapali Pkwy; in Kaanapali Beach resort area. Int corridors. **Pets:** Accepted.
[ASK] [SD] [✕] [&M] [☞] [🖥] [💻] [🍴] [⇌] [✕]

## KAUPULEHU

**AAA** ▼▼▼▼ Four Seasons Resort Hualalai at Historic
Ka'upulehu **LH**
(808) 325-8000. **$560-$8350, 21 day notice.** 100 Ka'upulehu Dr. Off
SR 19, 6 mi n of Kona International Airport. Ext corridors.
**Pets:** Accepted.
[SAVE] [✕] [&M] [⟋] [☞] [💻] [🍴] [⇌] [✕]

## WAILEA

**AAA** ▼▼▼▼ Four Seasons Resort, Maui at
Wailea **LH** ❀
(808) 874-8000. **$385-$1250, 14 day notice.** 3900 Wailea Alanui Dr.
From end of SR 31, 0.5 mi s. Int corridors. **Pets:** Very small, other
species. Service with restrictions.
[SAVE] [✕] [&M] [⟋] [☞] [🖥] [💻] [🍴] [⇌] [✕]

# IDAHO

## CITY INDEX

## AMERICAN FALLS

**Hillview Motel M**
(208) 226-5151. **$42-$56.** 2799 Lakeview Rd. I-86, exit 40, just s, then just w. Ext corridors. **Pets:** Medium. $5 daily fee/pet. Service with restrictions, supervision.

## BLACKFOOT

**Best Western Blackfoot Inn SH**
(208) 785-4144. **$59-$99.** 750 Jensen Grove Dr. I-15, exit 93, just e on Bergener, then 0.4 mi n on Parkway. Int corridors. **Pets:** Other species. Service with restrictions, supervision.

**Super 8 SH**
(208) 785-9333. **$55-$80.** 1279 Parkway Dr. I-15, exit 93, just e; shared driveway with McDonald's Restaurant. Int corridors. **Pets:** Other species. $10 one-time fee/room. Service with restrictions, crate.

## BLISS

**Amber Inn Motel SH**
(208) 352-4441. **$42.** 17286 US Hwy 30. I-84, exit 141, just s. Int corridors. **Pets:** Other species. $10 daily fee/pet. Service with restrictions, supervision.

## BOISE

**AmeriSuites (Boise/Towne Square Mall) SH**
(208) 375-1200. **$99-$119.** 925 N Milwaukee St. I-84, exit 49 (Franklin St), just w, then 0.5 mi n. Int corridors. **Pets:** Accepted.

**Boise Super 8 Motel SH**
(208) 344-8871. **$53-$69.** 2773 Elder St. I-84, exit 53 (Vista Ave), just n. Int corridors. **Pets:** Other species. $25 deposit/room. Designated rooms, service with restrictions, supervision.

**Budget Host Inn M**
(208) 322-4404. **$55-$75.** 8002 Overland Rd. I-84, exit 50A westbound, just s, just w, then just n; exit 50B eastbound, just w, then just n. Ext corridors. **Pets:** Other species. $10 one-time fee/room. Service with restrictions, crate.

**Doubletree Club Hotel SH**
(208) 345-2002. **$69-$169.** 475 W Parkcenter Blvd. I-84, exit 54 (Broadway Ave), 2 mi n, then 0.3 mi e on Beacon and Parkcenter Blvd. Int corridors. **Pets:** Accepted.

**DoubleTree Hotel Riverside SH**
(208) 343-1871. **$76-$300.** 2900 Chinden Blvd. I-184, exit Fairview Ave, just n, then just w on Garden. Int corridors. **Pets:** Accepted.

**Extended StayAmerica SH**
(208) 363-9040. **$60-$70.** 2500 S Vista Ave. I-84, exit 53 (Vista Ave), 0.7 mi n. Int corridors. **Pets:** Medium, other species. $25 daily fee/pet. Service with restrictions.

**Fairfield Inn by Marriott SH**
(208) 331-5656. **$66-$94.** 3300 S Shoshone St. I-84, exit 53 (Vista Ave), just n to Elder St, then just w. Int corridors. **Pets:** Accepted.

**Hampton Inn SH**
(208) 331-5600. **$139.** 3270 S Shoshone St. I-84, exit 53 (Vista Ave), just n to Elder St, then just w. Int corridors. **Pets:** Small. $20 daily fee/pet. Service with restrictions, supervision.

**Holiday Inn Boise Airport SH**
(208) 343-4900. **$89-$119.** 3300 Vista Ave. I-84, exit 53 (Vista Ave), just n. Int corridors. **Pets:** Accepted.

**Owyhee Plaza Hotel SH**
(208) 343-4611. **$95-$145.** 1109 Main St. At 11th and Main sts; center. Ext/int corridors. **Pets:** Accepted.

**Oxford Suites SH**
(208) 322-8000. **$69-$159.** 1426 S Entertainment Ave. I-84, exit 50A westbound; exit 50B eastbound, just s to Spectrum St, just w, then just n. **Pets:** Medium, other species. $50 one-time fee/room. Designated rooms, service with restrictions, supervision.

**Red Lion Hotel Boise Downtowner LH**
(208) 344-7691. **$69-$195.** 1800 Fairview Ave. I-84, exit Fairview Ave, 1 mi n. Int corridors. **Pets:** Accepted.

**Red Lion ParkCenter Suites–Boise SH**
(208) 342-1044. **$59-$119.** 424 E Parkcenter Blvd. I-84, exit 54 (Broadway Ave), 2.3 mi n, then just e on Beacon and Parkcenter Blvd. Int corridors. **Pets:** Accepted.

**Residence Inn by Marriott-Boise Central SH**
(208) 344-1200. **$134-$175.** 1401 Lusk Ave. I-84, exit 53 (Vista Ave), 2.4 mi n. Ext corridors. **Pets:** Other species. $75 one-time fee/room. Service with restrictions.

**Residence Inn by Marriott-Boise West SH**
(208) 385-9000. **Call for rates.** 7303 W Denton. I-84, exit 50A westbound; exit 50B eastbound, 2 mi n on Cole Rd, just w, then just n. Int corridors. **Pets:** Other species. $75 one-time fee/room. Designated rooms, service with restrictions, crate.

**Rodeway Inn of Boise SH**
(208) 376-2700. **$65-$110.** 1115 N Curtis Rd. I-84, exit 2, just se. Ext/int corridors. **Pets:** Accepted.

**Safari Inn Downtown** SH
(208) 344-6556. **$75-$85.** 1070 Grove St. At 11th and Grove sts; center. Int corridors. **Pets:** Accepted.

**Shilo Inn Suites-Boise Airport** SH
(208) 343-7662. **$57-$110.** 4111 Broadway Ave. I-84, exit 54 (Broadway Ave), just sw. Int corridors. **Pets:** $10 daily fee/pet. Service with restrictions, supervision.

**SpringHill Suites Boise** SH
(208) 939-8266. **$85-$133.** 6325 N Cloverdale Rd. I-84, exit 46 (Eagle Rd), 4.3 mi n to Chinden, 0.9 mi e, then just s. Int corridors. **Pets:** Other species. $15 daily fee/room. Designated rooms, service with restrictions, crate.

**University Inn** M
(208) 345-7170. **$65-$83.** 2360 University Dr. I-84, exit 53 (Vista Ave), 2.5 mi n. Ext corridors. **Pets:** Medium. $10 one-time fee/room. Designated rooms, service with restrictions, supervision.

## BONNERS FERRY

**Best Western Kootenai River Inn Casino & Spa**
(208) 267-8511. **$85-$129.** 7169 Plaza St. On US 95; city center. Int corridors. **Pets:** Small. $15 one-time fee/pet. Service with restrictions, supervision.

## BURLEY

**Best Western Burley Inn & Convention Center** SH
(208) 678-3501. **$60-$73.** 800 N Overland Ave. I-84, exit 208, just s. Ext/int corridors. **Pets:** Medium. Service with restrictions, supervision.

**Budget Motel** M
(208) 678-2200. **$50-$68.** 900 N Overland Ave. I-84, exit 208, just s. Ext corridors. **Pets:** Accepted.

## CALDWELL

**Best Western Caldwell Inn & Suites** M
(208) 454-7225. **$81-$93.** 908 Specht Ave. I-84, exit 29, just s. Int corridors. **Pets:** Large. $5 daily fee/pet. Service with restrictions, supervision.

**La Quinta Inn Caldwell** SH
(208) 454-2222. **$59-$99.** 901 Specht Ave. I-84, exit 29, just s. Int corridors. **Pets:** Other species. Service with restrictions, supervision.

## COEUR D'ALENE

**Best Western Coeur d'Alene Inn & Conference Center** SH
(208) 765-3200. **$95-$179.** W 414 Appleway Ave. I-90, exit 12, just nw. Int corridors. **Pets:** Large, dogs only. $25 daily fee/pet. Service with restrictions, supervision.

**The Coeur d'Alene Resort** LH
(208) 765-4000. **$125-$389, 7 day notice.** 115 S 2nd St. I-90, exit 11, 2 mi s. Ext/int corridors. **Pets:** Accepted.

**Days Inn-Coeur d'Alene** SH
(208) 667-8668. **$45-$135.** 2200 Northwest Blvd. I-90, exit 11, just se. Int corridors. **Pets:** Accepted.

**Guest House Inn & Suites** SH
(208) 765-3011. **$39-$99.** 330 W Appleway. I-90, exit 12, just n, then just e. Int corridors. **Pets:** Dogs only. $10 one-time fee/room. Service with restrictions, supervision.

**La Quinta Inn & Suites Coeur D'Alene (East)** SH
(208) 667-6777. **$44-$199.** 2209 E Sherman Ave. I-90, exit 15 (Sherman Ave), just s. Int corridors. **Pets:** Other species. Service with restrictions.

**La Quinta Inn Coeur D'Alene (Appleway)** SH
(208) 765-5500. **$59-$169.** 280 W Appleway Ave. I-90, exit 12, just ne. Int corridors. **Pets:** Medium, other species. Service with restrictions, crate.

**The Roosevelt, A Bed & Breakfast Inn** BB
(208) 765-5200. **$89-$329, 14 day notice.** 105 Wallace Ave. I-90, exit 13, 2 mi s, then just w; downtown. Int corridors. **Pets:** Other species. $25 one-time fee/room. Designated rooms, service with restrictions, crate.

**Shilo Inn Suites Coeur d'Alene** SH
(208) 664-2300. **$78-$133.** 702 W Appleway Ave. I-90, exit 12, just n, then just w. Int corridors. **Pets:** $10 daily fee/pet. Service with restrictions, supervision.

## DRIGGS

**Best Western Teton West Motel** SH
(208) 354-2363. **$65-$105.** 476 N Main St. 0.7 mi n on SR 33. Int corridors. **Pets:** Accepted.

**Intermountain Lodge** CA
(208) 354-8153. **$49-$74, 7 day notice.** 34 Ski Hill Rd. 0.8 mi e on Little Ave from SR 33 E. Ext corridors. **Pets:** Dogs only. $10 daily fee/pet. Designated rooms, service with restrictions, supervision.

## HAGERMAN

**Hagerman Valley Inn** M
(208) 837-6196. **$54-$79.** 661 Frog's Landing. South end of town on US 30. Ext/int corridors. **Pets:** $5 daily fee/pet. Designated rooms, service with restrictions, supervision.

## HAILEY

**Airport Inn** M
(208) 788-2477. **$78-$95.** 820 4th Ave S. Just n of SR 75 at 4th Ave; near airport. Ext corridors. **Pets:** $10 daily fee/pet. Designated rooms, service with restrictions, supervision.

**Wood River Inn** SH
(208) 578-0600. **$89-$147.** 603 N Main. Just n of downtown on SR 75. Int corridors. **Pets:** Medium, other species. $25 one-time fee/room. Service with restrictions, supervision.

# HEYBURN

**Super 8–Burley** 🆂🅷
(208) 678-7000. **$61-$78.** 336 S 600 W. I-84, exit 208, just n. Int corridors. **Pets:** Small, dogs only. $7 one-time fee/pet. Designated rooms, service with restrictions, supervision.

# IDAHO FALLS

**Best Western Driftwood Inn** 🆂🅷
(208) 523-2242. **$59-$129.** 575 River Pkwy. I-15, exit 118 (Broadway), 0.5 mi n, then 0.3 mi n. Ext corridors. **Pets:** Accepted.

**Comfort Inn** 🆂🅷
(208) 528-2804. **$73-$100.** 195 S Colorado Ave. I-15, exit 118 (Broadway), just w to Colorado Ave, then just s. Int corridors. **Pets:** Accepted.

**GuestHouse Inn & Suites** 🆂🅷
(208) 523-6260. **$56-$109.** 850 Lindsay Blvd. I-15, exit 119, just e. Ext/int corridors. **Pets:** Large, other species. $10 one-time fee/room. Designated rooms, service with restrictions, crate.

**Le Ritz Hotel & Suites** 🆂🅷
(208) 528-0880. **$79-$89.** 720 Lindsay Blvd. I-15, exit 118 (Broadway), 0.5 mi e, then just n. Int corridors. **Pets:** $15 one-time fee/room. Designated rooms, service with restrictions, supervision.

**Red Lion Hotel on the Falls** 🆂🅷
(208) 523-8000. **$64-$104.** 475 River Pkwy. I-15, exit 118 (Broadway), 0.5 mi e, then just n. Ext/int corridors. **Pets:** $25 one-time fee/room. Designated rooms, service with restrictions, crate.

**Shilo Inn Suites Conference Hotel** 🆂🅷
(208) 523-0088. **$75-$125.** 780 Lindsay Blvd. I-15, exit 119, just se. Int corridors. **Pets:** $10 daily fee/pet. Designated rooms, service with restrictions, supervision.

# JEROME

**Best Western Sawtooth Inn and Suites** 🆂🅷
(208) 324-9200. **$79-$109.** 2653 S Lincoln. I-84, exit 168, just n on SR 79. Int corridors. **Pets:** Other species. $50 deposit/room. Designated rooms, service with restrictions, supervision.

# KELLOGG

**Silverhorn Motor Inn** 🆂🅷
(208) 783-1151. **$75.** 699 W Cameron Ave. I-90, exit 49, just ne. Int corridors. **Pets:** Other species. Supervision.

**Super 8 Motel-Kellogg** 🆂🅷
(208) 783-1234. **$53-$59.** 601 Bunker Ave. I-90, exit 49, 0.5 mi s. Int corridors. **Pets:** Service with restrictions, supervision.

# KETCHUM

**Best Western Tyrolean Lodge** 🆂🅷
(208) 726-5336. **$85-$144, 3 day notice.** 260 Cottonwood. South end of town; just w of SR 75 (Main St) on Rivers St, just s on 3rd Ave. Int corridors. **Pets:** Accepted.

**Tamarack Lodge** 🅼
(208) 726-3344. **$99-$174, 14 day notice.** 291 Walnut Ave N. Just ne on Sun Valley Rd from jct SR 75 (Main St); downtown. Ext/int corridors. **Pets:** Small, dogs only. $10 daily fee/pet. Service with restrictions, supervision.

# KOOSKIA

**Reflections Inn** 🅱🅱
(208) 926-0855. **$69-$94, 3 day notice.** HCR 75, Box 32, US Hwy 12. 11 mi e on US 12, between MM 84 and 85. Ext corridors. **Pets:** Accepted.

# LEWISTON

**Comfort Inn** 🆂🅷
(208) 798-8090. **$60-$156.** 2128 8th Ave. 1.2 mi s on US 12 from jct US 95, just s on 21st St. Int corridors. **Pets:** Other species. $10 one-time fee/room. Supervision.

**GuestHouse Inn & Suites** 🆂🅷
(208) 746-3311. **$49-$89.** 1325 Main St. Downtown. Int corridors. **Pets:** $10 one-time fee/pet. Designated rooms, service with restrictions, supervision.

**Holiday Inn Express** 🆂🅷
(208) 750-1600. **$69-$99.** 2425 Nez Perce Dr. 1.2 mi s on US 12 from jct US 95, 1.2 mi s on 21st St, then just e. Int corridors. **Pets:** Other species. $20 one-time fee/room. Service with restrictions, supervision.

**Super 8 Motel** 🆂🅷
(208) 743-8808. **$50.** 3120 North & South Hwy. Just e on US 12 from jct US 95. Int corridors. **Pets:** Accepted.

# MCCALL

**Best Western McCall** 🆂🅷
(208) 634-6300. **$63-$115.** 415 3rd St. SR 55, just s of jct with Lake St. Ext/int corridors. **Pets:** Accepted.

**McCall Super 8 Lodge** 🅼
(208) 634-4637. **$68-$149.** 303 S 3rd St. South end of town on SR 55. Int corridors. **Pets:** Accepted.

# MONTPELIER

**Best Western Clover Creek Inn** 🆂🅷
(208) 847-1782. **$70-$100.** 243 N 4th St. Just n on US 30 from jct US 89 S. Ext corridors. **Pets:** Dogs only. $10 daily fee/pet. Service with restrictions, supervision.

# MOSCOW

**Best Western University Inn** 🆂🅷
(208) 882-0550. **$94-$135, 3 day notice.** 1516 Pullman Rd. Jct US 95, 1 mi w on SR 8. Int corridors. **Pets:** Small, other species. $25 daily fee/room. Designated rooms, service with restrictions, crate.

**La Quinta Inn** 🆂🅷
(208) 882-5365. **$79-$99.** 185 Warbonnet Dr. 1.6 mi w on SR 8 from jct US 93, just n. Int corridors. **Pets:** Other species. Service with restrictions, supervision.

▼▼ **Super 8 Motel** 🆂🅷
(208) 883-1503. **$49-$99.** 175 Peterson Dr. Jct US 95, 0.8 mi w on SR 8, just n. Int corridors. **Pets:** Medium. $10 daily fee/pet. Service with restrictions, supervision.
🅰🆂🅺 🆂🔟 ✕ 🛢

# MOUNTAIN HOME

▼▼▼ **Best Western Foothills Motor Inn** 🆂🅷
(208) 587-8477. **$89-$119.** 1080 Hwy 20. I-84, exit 95, just n. Ext corridors. **Pets:** Accepted.
🅰🆂🅺 🆂🔟 ✕ 🔁🅼 🖉 🖎 🛢 🖵 🌊

▼▼ **Sleep Inn** 🆂🅷
(208) 587-9743. **$77-$97.** 1180 Hwy 20. I-84, exit 95, just n. Int corridors. **Pets:** Accepted.
🅰🆂🅺 🆂🔟 ✕ 🛢 🖵

# NAMPA

▼▼▼ **Hampton Inn & Suites at the Idaho Center** 🆂🅷 🐾
(208) 442-0036. **$89-$109.** 5750 E Franklin Rd. I-84, exit 38, 0.4 mi n on Garrity Blvd just e; in front of Idaho Center. Int corridors. **Pets:** Large, other species. $20 one-time fee/room. Service with restrictions, supervision.
🅰🆂🅺 🆂🔟 ✕ 🔁🅼 🖎 🛢 🖵 🌊

▼▼ **Shilo Inn-Nampa Boulevard** 🆂🅷 🐾
(208) 466-8993. **$49-$80.** 617 Nampa Blvd. I-84, exit 35, just sw. Int corridors. **Pets:** $10 daily fee/pet. Service with restrictions, supervision.
🅰🆂🅺 🆂🔟 ✕ 🖉 🛢 🖵 🌊 ✕

▼▼ **Shilo Inn Nampa Suites** 🆂🅷 🐾
(208) 465-3250. **$64-$103.** 1401 Shilo Dr. I-84, exit 36, just nw. Int corridors. **Pets:** $10 daily fee/pet. Service with restrictions, supervision.
🅰🆂🅺 🆂🔟 ✕ 🖉 🛢 🖵 🍽 🌊 ✕

# OROFINO

▼▼▼ **Best Western Lodge at River's Edge** 🆂🅷
(208) 476-9999. **$76-$99.** 615 Main St. Downtown. Int corridors. **Pets:** Very small. $20 daily fee/pet. Designated rooms, service with restrictions, supervision.
🅰🆂🅺 🆂🔟 ✕ 🛢 🖵 🍽 🌊

🔺 ▼▼ **Konkolville Motel** 🅼
(208) 476-5584. **$52-$56.** 2000 Konkolville Rd. 2.7 mi e on Michigan Ave. Ext corridors. **Pets:** Other species. $10 daily fee/pet. Designated rooms, service with restrictions, supervision.
🆂🅰🆅🅴 🆂🔟 ✕ 🛢 🖵 🌊

# POCATELLO

🔺 ▼▼ **Best Western CottonTree Inn** 🆂🅷
(208) 237-7650. **$78.** 1415 Bench Rd. I-15, exit 71, just e. Int corridors. **Pets:** Other species. $25 deposit/room. Service with restrictions.
🆂🅰🆅🅴 🆂🔟 ✕ 🛢 🖵 🌊

▼▼ **Comfort Inn** 🆂🅷 🐾
(208) 237-8155. **$70-$100.** 1333 Bench Rd. I-15, exit 71, just e. Int corridors. **Pets:** Dogs only. $10 daily fee/pet. Designated rooms, service with restrictions, supervision.
🅰🆂🅺 🆂🔟 ✕ 🖉 🛢 🖵 🌊

▼▼▼ **Holiday Inn-Pocatello** 🆂🅷
(208) 237-1400. **$66-$89.** 1399 Bench Rd. I-15, exit 71, just e. Ext/int corridors. **Pets:** Medium, other species. $10 daily fee/room. Designated rooms, service with restrictions, supervision.
🅰🆂🅺 🆂🔟 ✕ 🖉 🖎 🛢 🖵 🍽 🌊 ✕

🔺 ▼▼ **Pocatello Super 8 Motel** 🆂🅷
(208) 234-0888. **$53-$99.** 1330 Bench Rd. I-15, exit 71, just e. Int corridors. **Pets:** Accepted.
🆂🅰🆅🅴 🆂🔟 ✕ 🖎 🛢

▼▼ **Ramada Inn & Convention Center** 🆂🅷
(208) 237-0020. **$60-$96.** 133 W Burnside. I-86, exit 61, just n. Int corridors. **Pets:** Accepted.
🅰🆂🅺 🆂🔟 ✕ 🛢 🖵 🍽 🌊 ✕

▼▼ **Red Lion Hotel Pocatello** 🆂🅷
(208) 233-2200. **$68-$85.** 1555 Pocatello Creek Rd. I-15, exit 71, just e. Int corridors. **Pets:** Accepted.
🅰🆂🅺 🆂🔟 ✕ 🛢 🖵 🍽 🌊 ✕

▼ **Thunderbird Motel** 🅼
(208) 232-6330. **$46-$55.** 1415 S 5th Ave. I-15, exit 67, 1.3 mi n; just s of Idaho State University. Ext corridors. **Pets:** Other species. $5 daily fee/pet. Service with restrictions, supervision.
🅰🆂🅺 🆂🔟 ✕ 🛢 🌊

# PONDERAY

🔺 ▼▼ **Monarch Mountain Lodge** 🆂🅷
(208) 263-1222. **$60-$105.** 363 Bonner Mall Way. 0.5 mi n on US 95 N from jct SR 200. Int corridors. **Pets:** Accepted.
🆂🅰🆅🅴 ✕ 🛢

▼ **Sandpoint Motel 6–4163** 🆂🅷
(208) 263-5383. **$55.** 477255 Hwy 95 N. 1.2 mi n on US 95 from jct SR 200. Int corridors. **Pets:** Accepted.
✕ 🔁🅼 🖎 🛢

▼▼ **Super 8 Motel** 🆂🅷
(208) 263-2210. **$40-$69.** 476841 Hwy 95 N. 0.7 mi n on US 95 from jct SR 200. Int corridors. **Pets:** Other species. $5 daily fee/room, $25 one-time fee/pet. Service with restrictions, supervision.
🅰🆂🅺 🆂🔟 ✕ 🔁🅼 🛢

# POST FALLS

🔺 ▼▼▼ **Comfort Inn** 🆂🅷
(208) 773-8900. **$69-$159.** 3175 E Seltice Way. I-90, exit 7, just sw. Int corridors. **Pets:** Accepted.
🆂🅰🆅🅴 ✕ 🔁🅼 🖉 🛢 🖵

🔺 ▼▼ **Howard Johnson Express** 🆂🅷 🐾
(208) 773-4541. **$54-$145.** 3647 W 5th Ave. I-90, exit 2, just ne. Int corridors. **Pets:** Medium. $10 daily fee/pet. Designated rooms, service with restrictions, crate.
🆂🅰🆅🅴 🆂🔟 ✕ 🔁🅼 🖉 🖎 🛢 🖵 🌊

🔺 ▼▼▼ **Red Lion Templin's Hotel on the River–Post Falls** 🆂🅷
(208) 773-1611. **$79-$159.** 414 E First Ave. I-90, exit 5 eastbound, just s to First Ave; exit 6 westbound, 0.7 mi w on Seltice Way to Spokane St, 0.5 mi s, then just e. Int corridors. **Pets:** Other species. $20 daily fee/pet. Designated rooms, service with restrictions, supervision.
🆂🅰🆅🅴 🆂🔟 ✕ 🔁🅼 🖉 🖎 🛢 🖵 🍽 🌊 ✕

🔺 ▼▼ **Sleep Inn** 🆂🅷
(208) 777-9394. **$59-$179.** 157 S Pleasant View Rd. I-90, exit 2, just s. Int corridors. **Pets:** Accepted.
🆂🅰🆅🅴 🆂🔟 ✕ 🖉 🖎 🖵 🌊

# PRIEST RIVER

▼▼ **Eagle's Nest Motel** 🅼
(208) 448-2000. **$45-$89.** 1007 Albeni Hwy (US 2). US 2, 0.5 mi w. Ext corridors. **Pets:** $100 deposit/room. Designated rooms, supervision.
🅰🆂🅺 ✕ 🔁🅼 🖎 🛢 🖵

# REXBURG

▼▼▼ **AmericInn Lodge & Suites** 🆂🅷
(208) 356-5333. **$69-$209.** 1098 Golden Beauty Dr. US 20, exit 332. Int corridors. **Pets:** Other species. $100 deposit/room, $20 daily fee/room. Designated rooms, service with restrictions, crate.
🅰🆂🅺 🆂🔟 ✕ 🛢 🖵 🌊 ✕

**△△△ ▽▽ ▽▽ Best Western CottonTree Inn SH**
(208) 356-4646. **$71-$96.** 450 W 4th St S. US 20, exit 332 (S Rexburg), 1 mi e. Int corridors. **Pets:** Very small. Designated rooms, service with restrictions, supervision.
SAVE S⚬ ✕ 🛏 💻 🍽 ≋

**△△△ ▽▽ ▽▽ Comfort Inn SH**
(208) 359-1311. **$55-$109.** 885 W Main St. US 20, exit 333 (Salmon), just e. Int corridors. **Pets:** Other species. Service with restrictions, supervision.
SAVE S⚬ ✕ 🛏 💻 ≋

**△△△ ▽▽▽ Days Inn M**
(208) 356-9222. **$58-$73.** 271 S 2nd W. US 20, exit 332 (S Rexburg), 1.8 mi e, then just n. Ext corridors. **Pets:** Small. Designated rooms, service with restrictions, supervision.
SAVE S⚬ ✕ 🛏 💻

# RIGGINS

**△△△ ▽▽▽▽ Best Western Salmon Rapids Lodge SH**
(208) 628-2743. **$79-$120.** 1010 S Main St. Just e of US 95; downtown. Int corridors. **Pets:** Accepted.
SAVE S⚬ ✕ 🛏 🛏 💻 ≋

**▽▽ Pinehurst Resort Cottages CA**
(208) 628-3323. **$45-$70, 7 day notice.** MM 182 on US 95. On US 95, 13 mi s. Ext corridors. **Pets:** Accepted.
✕ 🛏 💻 🅦 🖉

# SAGLE

**▽▽ ▽▽ Bottle Bay Resort & Marina CA**
(208) 263-5916. **$85-$105, 90 day notice.** 115 Resort Rd. 8.3 mi e on Bottle Bay Rd from US 95. Ext corridors. **Pets:** Accepted.
🛏 💻 🍽 ✕ 🅚 🖉

# ST. ANTHONY

**▽▽ ▽▽ GuestHouse Int'l Inn Henry's Fork SH**
(208) 624-3711. **$46-$89.** 115 S Bridge St. US 20, exit St. Anthony, just w. Ext corridors. **Pets:** Other species. $10 one-time fee/room. Service with restrictions, crate.
ASK S⚬ ✕ 💻 🍽

# SALMON

**▽▽ Motel DeLuxe M**
(208) 756-2231. **$40-$88.** 112 S Church St. Just s of Main St; downtown. Ext corridors. **Pets:** Other species. $5 one-time fee/room. Supervision.
ASK S⚬ ✕ 🛏 💻

# SANDPOINT

**▽▽ Best Western Edgewater Resort SH**
(208) 263-3194. **$89-$209.** 56 Bridge St. Just e of US 95 N; downtown. Int corridors. **Pets:** Other species. $10 daily fee/pet. Service with restrictions, supervision.
ASK S⚬ ✕ 🛏 💻 🍽 ≋ ✕

**▽▽▽▽ Coit House Bed & Breakfast BB**
(208) 265-4035. **$69-$140, 3 day notice.** 502 N Fourth Ave. Just ne of US 95 at Fourth Ave and Alder St. Int corridors. **Pets:** Accepted.
ASK S⚬ ✕

**▽▽ The K2 Inn M**
(208) 263-3441. **$39-$139, 3 day notice.** 501 N Fourth Ave. US 95, just e. Ext corridors. **Pets:** Accepted.
ASK S⚬ ✕ 🛏 💻

**△△△ ▽▽▽▽ La Quinta Inn Sandpoint SH 🐾**
(208) 263-9581. **$89-$149.** 415 Cedar St. Jct US 95 and 2; downtown. Ext/int corridors. **Pets:** Dogs only. Service with restrictions, supervision.
SAVE S⚬ ✕ 🅜 🍳 🛏 💻 🍽 ≋

**▽▽ ▽▽ Quality Inn Sandpoint SH**
(208) 263-2111. **$59-$179.** 807 N 5th. US 2 and 95, just s of jct SR 200. Int corridors. **Pets:** Other species. $10 daily fee/pet. Service with restrictions, supervision.
ASK ✕ 🛏 💻 🍽 ≋

# STANLEY

**▽▽ ▽▽ Mountain Village Lodge SH**
(208) 774-3661. **$54-$74.** Corner US 75 & SR 21. Jct US 75 and SR 21. Ext corridors. **Pets:** Accepted.
ASK ✕ 🛏 💻 🍽 🅚

**△△△ ▽▽ Salmon River Cabins & Motel CA**
(208) 774-3566. **$68-$125 (no credit cards), 30 day notice.** 55 Lower Stanley. 1 mi n on US 75 from jct SR 21. Ext corridors. **Pets:** Small. $10 daily fee/pet. Service with restrictions, supervision.
SAVE ✕ 🛏 💻 🅚

# TWIN FALLS

**△△△ ▽▽ ▽▽ Best Western Apollo Motor Inn M**
(208) 733-2010. **$59-$85.** 296 Addison Ave W. I-84, exit 173, 5.7 mi s on US 93, then 1.2 mi w. Ext corridors. **Pets:** Small. $8 daily fee/pet. Designated rooms, service with restrictions, supervision.
SAVE S⚬ ✕ 🛏 💻 ≋

**▽▽ ▽▽ Comfort Inn M**
(208) 734-7494. **$79-$149.** 1893 Canyon Springs Rd. I-84, exit 173, 3.5 mi s on US 93. Int corridors. **Pets:** Accepted.
ASK ✕ 🛏 💻 ≋

**△△△ ▽▽ ▽▽ Days Inn M**
(208) 324-6400. **$55-$95.** 1200 Centennial Spur. I-84, exit 173, just n on US 93. Int corridors. **Pets:** Medium, other species. $50 deposit/pet, $10 one-time fee/pet. Designated rooms, service with restrictions, supervision.
SAVE S⚬ ✕ 🅜 🛏 💻

**△△△ ▽▽▽▽ Red Lion Hotel Canyon Springs SH**
(208) 734-5000. **$82-$120.** 1357 Blue Lakes Blvd N. I-84, exit 173, 4 mi s on US 93. Int corridors. **Pets:** Medium. $50 deposit/room. Service with restrictions, supervision.
SAVE S⚬ ✕ 🅜 🍳 🅜 🛏 💻 🍽 ≋ ✕

**▽▽▽▽ Shilo Inn, Twin Falls, LLC SH ✿**
(208) 733-7545. **$89-$130.** 1586 Blue Lakes Blvd N. I-84, exit 173, 3.7 mi s on US 93. Int corridors. **Pets:** $10 daily fee/pet. Service with restrictions, supervision.
ASK S⚬ ✕ 🅜 🍳 🅜 🛏 💻 ≋ ✕

**▽▽▽▽ Twin Falls Super 8 Motel M**
(208) 734-5801. **$85, 5 day notice.** 1260 Blue Lakes Blvd N. I-84, exit 173, 4.1 mi s on US 93. Int corridors. **Pets:** Accepted.
ASK S⚬ ✕ 🛏 💻

# WALLACE

**▽▽ ▽▽ Stardust Motel M**
(208) 752-1213. **$54-$68.** 410 Pine St. I-90, exit 61 (Business Rt 90), 0.7 mi e; downtown. Ext corridors. **Pets:** Other species. $15 daily fee/pet. Service with restrictions, supervision.
ASK S⚬ ✕ 🛏 💻

**△△△ ▽▽▽▽ The Wallace Inn SH**
(208) 752-1252. **$73-$98.** 100 Front St. I-90, exit 61 (Business Rt 90), just se. Int corridors. **Pets:** Other species. $15 daily fee/pet. Service with restrictions, supervision.
SAVE S⚬ ✕ 🅜 🛏 🛏 💻 🍽 ≋ ✕

# WORLEY

**△△△ ▽▽▽▽ Coeur d'Alene Casino Resort Hotel SH**
(208) 686-0248. **$60-$400.** 27068 S Hwy 95. On US 95, 3 mi n. Int corridors. **Pets:** Accepted.
SAVE ✕ 🛏 🛏 💻 🍽 ≋ ✕

# ILLINOIS

## ALTON

#### ▼▼▼▼ Comfort Inn SH
(618) 465-9999. **$82-$97.** 11 Crossroads Ct. Off SR 3, jct SR 140. Int corridors. **Pets:** Other species. Service with restrictions, supervision.

(ASK) (S∂) (X) (&M) (🌣) (&) (🖬) (💻) (🏊)

#### ▼▼ Super 8 Motel SH
(618) 465-8885. **$52-$75.** 1800 Homer Adams Pkwy. On SR 111, 1.8 mi e of jct US 67. Int corridors. **Pets:** Small. $50 deposit/room. Service with restrictions, supervision.

(ASK) (S∂) (X) (&M) (🖬) (💻)

## ARCOLA

#### ▼▼ Comfort Inn SH
(217) 268-4000. **$47-$120.** 610 E Springfield Rd. I-57, exit 203 (SR 133), just w. Int corridors. **Pets:** Small, other species. $7 daily fee/pet. Service with restrictions, supervision.

(ASK) (X) (🌣) (🖬) (💻) (🏊)

## BELLEVILLE

#### ⬭⬭⬭ ▼▼▼ The Shrine Hotel SH
(618) 397-1162. **$95-$115.** 451 S Demazenod Dr. I-255, exit 17A, 1 mi e on SR 15; in Shrine of Our Lady of the Snows Complex. Int corridors. **Pets:** Other species. Service with restrictions, crate.

(SAVE) (S∂) (X) (🖬) (💻) (🍴) (🚫)

## BLOOMINGTON

#### ▼▼▼ The Chateau of Bloomington LH
(309) 662-2020. **$109-$179.** 1601 Jumer Dr. I-55, exit 167, follow I-55 business route (Veterans Pkwy); 1.3 mi n of jct SR 9; 1 mi s of jct I-55. Int corridors. **Pets:** Accepted.

(ASK) (S∂) (X) (🌣) (🖬) (💻) (🍴) (🏊) (🚫)

#### ▼▼▼ Country Inn & Suites By Carlson
#### Bloomington/Normal-Airport SH 🐾
(309) 662-3100. **$76-$106.** 2403 E Empire St. Jct I-55 business route (Veterans Pkwy) and SR 9, 0.8 mi e. Int corridors. **Pets:** $5 daily fee/room. Designated rooms, service with restrictions, supervision.

(ASK) (S∂) (X) (🌣) (&) (🖬) (💻) (🏊) (🚫)

#### ▼▼▼▼ Country Inn & Suites By Carlson
#### Bloomington/Normal-West SH 🐾
(309) 828-7177. **$90-$96.** 923 Maple Hill Rd. I-55/74, exit 160B (SR 9), 0.3 mi w to Wylie Dr, just n, then just e. Int corridors. **Pets:** $10 daily fee/pet. No service.

(ASK) (S∂) (X) (&M) (&) (🖬) (💻) (🏊)

#### ▼▼ Days Inn-Bloomington SH
(309) 829-6292. **$70-$80.** 1707 W Market St. I-55/74, exit 160A (SR 9), 0.5 mi e. Int corridors. **Pets:** Accepted.

(ASK) (S∂) (X) (&M) (🖬) (🏊)

#### ▼▼▼ DoubleTree Hotel LH
(309) 664-6446. **$135.** 10 Brickyard Dr. I-55 business route (Veterans Pkwy), just n of US 150. Int corridors. **Pets:** Accepted.

(ASK) (S∂) (X) (🌣) (&) (🖬) (💻) (🍴) (🏊) (🚫)

#### ▼▼ Eastland Suites Hotel & Conference Center SH
(309) 662-0000. **$69-$159.** 1801 Eastland Dr. Jct I-55 business route (Veterans Pkwy) and SR 9, just s to Eastland Dr, then just e. Ext/int corridors. **Pets:** Accepted.

(ASK) (X) (🖬) (💻) (🏊) (🚫)

#### ▼▼ Econo Lodge M 🐾
(309) 829-3100. **$45-$100.** 403 Brock Dr. I-55/74, exit 160A (SR 9), just e. Ext corridors. **Pets:** Medium. $10 daily fee/pet. Service with restrictions, supervision.

(ASK) (S∂) (X) (🖬) (💻)

#### ▼▼ Ramada Limited & Suites
#### Bloomington/Normal-West SH
(309) 828-0900. **$77-$105.** 919 Maple Hill Rd. I-55/74, exit 160B (SR 9), 0.3 mi w to Wylie Rd, just n, then just e. Int corridors. **Pets:** Other species. $10 daily fee/room. Service with restrictions, supervision.

(ASK) (S∂) (X) (🖬) (💻) (🏊)

#### ▼▼▼ Wingate Inn SH
(309) 820-9990. **$79.** 1031 Wylie Dr. I-55/74, exit 160B (SR 9), just w, then just n. Int corridors. **Pets:** Other species. $10 daily fee/pet. Designated rooms, service with restrictions, crate.

(ASK) (S∂) (X) (🌣) (&) (🖬) (💻) (🏊)

## BOURBONNAIS

**▼▼ ▼▼ Hampton Inn Bradley/Kankakee** SH
(815) 932-8369. **$88-$127.** 60 Ken Hayes Dr. I-57, exit 315 (SR 50). Int corridors. **Pets:** Medium, dogs only. $50 deposit/room. Service with restrictions, supervision.
ASK SO X LM BI ID ~

## CARBONDALE

**▼▼▼▼ Hampton Inn** SH
(618) 549-6900. **$86-$119.** 2175 Reed Station Pkwy. I-57, exit 54B, 12 mi w on SR 13. Int corridors. **Pets:** Accepted.
ASK SO X LM J LM BI ID ~

**▼▼ ▼▼ Super 8 Motel** SH
(618) 457-8822. **$56-$85.** 1180 E Main St. 1 mi e on SR 13. Int corridors. **Pets:** Service with restrictions, supervision.
ASK SO X J BI ID

## CASEY

**AAA ▼▼▼▼ Comfort Inn** SH
(217) 932-2212. **$75-$115, 7 day notice.** 933 SR 49. I-70, exit 129, 0.3 mi se. Int corridors. **Pets:** Large, other species. $5 daily fee/pet. Service with restrictions, supervision.
SAVE SO X BI ID ~

## CHAMPAIGN

**▼▼ ▼▼ Baymont Inn & Suites** SH
(217) 356-8900. **$70-$125.** 302 W Anthony Dr. I-74, exit 182 (Neil St), just nw. Int corridors. **Pets:** Large. Designated rooms, service with restrictions, supervision.
ASK SO X J LM BI ID

**AAA ▼▼▼▼ Country Inn & Suites By Carlson** SH
(217) 355-6666. **$89.** 602 W Marketview Dr. I-74, exit 181 (Prospect Rd), just n, then just e. Int corridors. **Pets:** Small. Designated rooms, service with restrictions, crate.
SAVE SO X LM J LM BI ID ~

**▼▼▼▼ Drury Inn & Suites-Champaign** SH
(217) 398-0030. **$105-$140.** 905 W Anthony Dr. I-74, exit 181 (Prospect Blvd), just n. Int corridors. **Pets:** Accepted.
ASK X LM J LM BI ID ~

**AAA ▼▼▼▼ La Quinta Inn Champaign** SH
(217) 356-4000. **$69-$126.** 1900 Center Dr. I-74, exit 182B (Neil St), just n. Int corridors. **Pets:** Medium. Service with restrictions.
SAVE X LM J BI ID ~

**AAA ▼▼ ▼▼ Microtel Inn** SH
(217) 398-4136. **$55-$89.** 1615 Rion Dr. I-57, exit 238, just w. Int corridors. **Pets:** Small. $10 one-time fee/room. Designated rooms, service with restrictions, supervision.
SAVE SO X BI

**▼▼ ▼▼ Red Roof Inn #170** SH
(217) 352-0101. **$45-$68.** 212 W Anthony Dr. I-74, exit 182B (Neil St), just n to Anthony Dr, then just w. Ext corridors. **Pets:** Accepted.
X J BI

## CHARLESTON

**▼▼ ▼▼ Days Inn Charleston** SH
(217) 345-7689. **Call for rates.** 810 W Lincoln Hwy. SR 130, 1.8 mi w on SR 16 (Lincoln Hwy). Ext/int corridors. **Pets:** Accepted.
ASK X BI ID

## CHESTER

**AAA ▼▼▼▼ Best Western Reids' Inn** SH
(618) 826-3034. **$64.** 2150 State St. SR 150, 1 mi e of SR 3. Int corridors. **Pets:** Accepted.
SAVE SO X LM BI ID ~

# CHICAGO METROPOLITAN AREA

## ALGONQUIN

**AAA ▼▼▼▼ Holiday Inn Express Hotel & Suites** SH
(847) 458-6000. **$89-$104, 5 day notice.** 2595 Bunker Hill Rd. I-90, exit Randall Rd N, 6.1 mi n to Bunker Hill Rd, then just w. Int corridors. **Pets:** Small. $50 one-time fee/room. Designated rooms, service with restrictions, supervision.
SAVE SO X LM BI ID ~ X

## ALSIP

**▼▼ ▼▼ Baymont Inn-Midway South** SH
(708) 597-3900. **$59-$75.** 12801 S Cicero Ave. I-294, exit Cicero Ave S. Int corridors. **Pets:** Medium, other species. Designated rooms, service with restrictions, crate.
ASK SO X J LM BI ID

**AAA ▼▼▼▼ DoubleTree Hotel Chicago/Alsip** LH
(708) 371-7300. **$79-$159.** 5000 W 127th St. I-294, exit Cicero Ave S, just w. Int corridors. **Pets:** Medium, other species. $50 deposit/pet. Designated rooms, service with restrictions, crate.
SAVE SO X LM J BI ID TI ~

## ANTIOCH

**AAA ▼▼ ▼▼ Best Western Regency Inn** SH
(847) 395-3606. **$83-$155, 3 day notice.** 350 Rt 173. SR 173, 0.5 mi w of jct SR 83. Int corridors. **Pets:** Medium. $25 deposit/pet. Designated rooms, service with restrictions, supervision.
SAVE SO X BI ID ~

## ARLINGTON HEIGHTS

**AAA ▼▼▼▼ AmeriSuites (Chicago/Arlington Heights)** SH
(847) 956-1400. **$99-$129.** 2111 S Arlington Heights Rd. I-90, exit Arlington Heights Rd, 0.6 mi n. Int corridors. **Pets:** Small. $10 daily fee/pet. Designated rooms, service with restrictions, supervision.
SAVE SO X J LM BI ID X

**▼▼▼▼ La Quinta Inn Chicago (Arlington Heights)** SH
(847) 253-8777. **$77-$134.** 1415 W Dundee Rd. SR 53, exit Dundee Rd, just e. Int corridors. **Pets:** Medium. Service with restrictions.
ASK X J BI ID ~

**▼▼ Motel 6-1048** SH
(847) 806-1230. **$47-$59.** 441 W Algonquin Rd. I-90, exit Arlington Heights Rd, 0.5 mi n, then 0.5 mi w. Int corridors. **Pets:** Accepted.
SO X LM

**▼▼ Red Roof Inn #7102** M
(847) 228-6650. **$52-$77.** 22 W Algonquin Rd. I-90, exit Arlington Heights Rd, 0.5 mi n, then just w. Ext corridors. **Pets:** Accepted.
X LM

**▼▼▼▼ Sheraton Chicago Northwest** LH
(847) 394-2000. **$99-$269.** 3400 W Euclid Ave. SR 53, exit Euclid Ave, just e. Int corridors. **Pets:** Accepted.
ASK SO X J BI ID TI ~ X

# AURORA

**▼▼▼▼ Staybridge Suites by Holiday Inn Aurora/Naperville** ⑤⧉ ❀
(630) 978-2222. **$139-$164.** 4320 Meridian Pkwy. I-88, exit SR 59, 2 mi s to Meridian Pkwy, then just w. Int corridors. **Pets:** Other species. $75 one-time fee/pet. Designated rooms, service with restrictions, supervision.

[ASK] [SO] [X] [&M] [&] [⊟] [⊡] [↝] [X]

# BANNOCKBURN

**⬥⬥⬥ ▼▼▼▼ Woodfield Suites Chicago-Bannockburn/Deerfield** ⑤⧉
(847) 317-7300. **$119-$124.** 2000 S Lakeside Dr. I-94, exit Half Day Rd (SR 22), just e to Lakeside Dr, then just s. Int corridors. **Pets:** Medium. Service with restrictions.

[SAVE] [X] [&M] [⌂] [&] [⊟] [⊡] [↝] [X]

# BLOOMINGDALE

**▼▼▼▼ Residence Inn by Marriott** ⑤⧉
(630) 893-9200. **$99-$179, 14 day notice.** 295 Knollwood Dr. I-355, exit Army Trail Rd, 4 mi w, then just n. Int corridors. **Pets:** Accepted.

[ASK] [SO] [X] [&M] [⌂] [&] [⊟] [⊡] [↝] [X]

# BOLINGBROOK

**▼▼▼▼ Holiday Inn Hotel & Suites** ⑭
(630) 679-1600. **$129.** 205 Remington Blvd. I-55, exit 267, just n, then 0.4 mi sw. Int corridors. **Pets:** Accepted.

[ASK] [SO] [X] [&M] [⌂] [&] [⊟] [⊡] [¶] [↝] [X]

**▼▼▼▼ La Quinta Inn Bolingbrook** ⑤⧉ ❀
(630) 226-0000. **$79-$109.** 225 W South Frontage Rd. I-55, exit 267, 0.5 mi sw. Int corridors. **Pets:** Other species. $25 one-time fee/room. Designated rooms, no service, supervision.

[ASK] [SO] [X] [⌂] [⊟] [⊡] [↝]

# BRIDGEVIEW

**⬥⬥⬥ ▼ Exel Inn of Bridgeview** ⑤⧉
(708) 430-1818. **$65-$95.** 9625 S 76th Ave. I-294, exit 95th St, just s. Int corridors. **Pets:** Small, other species. Designated rooms, service with restrictions, supervision.

[SAVE] [SO] [X] [⊟] [⊡]

# BURR RIDGE

**⬥⬥⬥ ▼▼ Ramada/Burr Ridge/Chicago Southwest** ⑤⧉ ❀
(630) 325-2900. **$69-$129.** 300 S Frontage Rd. I-55, exit 276A (County Line Rd), just sw. Int corridors. **Pets:** Medium. $50 one-time fee/room. Designated rooms, service with restrictions, supervision.

[SAVE] [SO] [X] [⊟] [⊡] [¶] [↝] [X]

# CALUMET CITY

**▼▼ ▼▼ Baymont Inn & Suites-South Chicago** ⑤⧉
(708) 891-2900. **$89-$99.** 510 E End Ave. I-94, exit 71B (Sibley Blvd), just e. Int corridors. **Pets:** Very small, dogs only. $50 one-time fee/pet. Service with restrictions, crate.

[ASK] [SO] [X] [&M] [⌂] [&] [⊟] [⊡] [↝]

# CHICAGO

**⬥⬥⬥ ▼▼▼▼ Allegro Chicago, A Kimpton Hotel** ⑤⧉
(312) 236-0123. **$109-$289.** 171 W Randolph St. Jct La Salle St; in theater district. Int corridors. **Pets:** Accepted.

[SAVE] [SO] [X] [⊟] [⊡] [¶]

**⬥⬥⬥ ▼▼▼▼ The Allerton Crowne Plaza** ⑭
(312) 440-1500. **$149-$439.** 701 N Michigan Ave. Jct Huron St. Int corridors. **Pets:** Small, dogs only. $75 deposit/room, $25 one-time fee/ room. Service with restrictions, crate.

[SAVE] [SO] [X] [⌂] [&] [⊟] [⊡] [¶] [X]

**⬥⬥⬥ ▼▼▼▼ Amalfi Hotel Chicago** ⑤⧉ ❀
(312) 395-9000. **$179-$369.** 20 W Kinzie St. Between State and Dearborn sts. Int corridors. **Pets:** Small. Service with restrictions.

[SAVE] [SO] [X] [&M] [⌂] [&] [⊟] [⊡] [X]

**⬥⬥⬥ ▼▼▼ Carlton Inn Midway** Ⓜ ❀
(773) 582-0900. **$99-$139.** 4944 S Archer Ave. I-55, exit 287 (Pulaski), 1.8 mi s to Archer Ave, then just e. Ext corridors. **Pets:** Medium. $50 deposit/pet. Designated rooms, service with restrictions, supervision.

[SAVE] [X] [&] [⊟] [⊡]

**▼▼▼ ▼▼▼ Conrad Chicago** ⑭ ❀
(312) 645-1500. **$359-$434.** 521 N Rush St at Michigan Ave. Jct Grand Ave. Int corridors. **Pets:** Medium, dogs only.

[X] [&M] [⌂] [&] [⊟] [⊡] [¶] [X]

**▼▼▼ ▼▼▼ The Drake Hotel, Chicago** ⑭
(312) 787-2200. **$289-$369.** 140 E Walton Pl. N Michigan Ave at Lake Shore Dr and Walton Pl. Int corridors. **Pets:** Accepted.

[X] [⌂] [&] [⊟] [⊡] [¶]

**▼▼▼ ▼▼▼ The Fairmont Chicago** ⑭ ❀
(312) 565-8000. **$169-$469.** 200 N Columbus Dr. Jct Michigan Ave and Wacker Dr, just e. Int corridors. **Pets:** Small. $25 daily fee/room. Service with restrictions, supervision.

[ASK] [X] [⌂] [¶]

**⬥⬥⬥ ▼▼▼▼ Four Seasons Hotel Chicago** ⑭ ❀
(312) 280-8800. **$450-$675.** 120 E Delaware Pl. Jct Michigan Ave, just nw of John Hancock building. Int corridors. **Pets:** Medium. Designated rooms, service with restrictions.

[SAVE] [X] [&M] [⌂] [&] [⊟] [⊡] [¶] [↝] [X]

**⬥⬥⬥ ▼▼▼▼ Hard Rock Hotel Chicago** ⑭ ❀
(312) 345-1000. **$159-$399.** 230 N Michigan Ave. Between Lake St and Wacker Dr. Int corridors. **Pets:** Other species. $25 daily fee/pet.

[SAVE] [SO] [X] [&M] [⌂] [&] [⊟] [⊡] [¶] [X]

**⬥⬥⬥ ▼▼▼▼ Hilton Chicago** ⑭
(312) 922-4400. **$154-$384.** 720 S Michigan Ave. I-290 (Congress Pkwy), just s. Int corridors. **Pets:** Accepted.

[SAVE] [X] [⌂] [&] [⊟] [¶] [↝] [X]

**⬥⬥⬥ ▼▼▼▼ Hilton Chicago O'Hare Airport** ⑭
(773) 686-8000. **$329.** Opposite and connected to terminal buildings at O'Hare International Airport, accessed via I-190. Int corridors. **Pets:** Accepted.

[SAVE] [X] [⌂] [⊡] [¶] [↝] [X]

**⬥⬥⬥ ▼▼▼▼ Holiday Inn Chicago Mart Plaza** ⑭
(312) 836-5000. **$379.** 350 N Orleans. Atop the Mart Center along the Chicago River. Int corridors. **Pets:** Accepted.

[SAVE] [SO] [X] [⌂] [&] [⊟] [⊡] [¶] [↝] [X]

**⬥⬥⬥ ▼▼▼▼ Holiday Inn Chicago-O'Hare** ⑤⧉
(773) 693-2323. **$80-$160.** 8201 W Higgins Rd. I-90, exit 79B (Cumberland Ave N), just n to Higgins Rd (SR 72), then just e. Int corridors. **Pets:** Other species. $50 one-time fee/room. Service with restrictions, supervision.

[SAVE] [SO] [X] [⌂] [⊟] [⊡] [¶] [↝]

**⬥⬥⬥ ▼▼▼▼ Hotel Burnham Chicago** ⑤⧉ ❀
(312) 782-1111. **$179-$449.** One W Washington St. Jct State St. Int corridors. **Pets:** Other species. Designated rooms, service with restrictions, supervision.

[SAVE] [SO] [X] [⌂] [&] [⊡] [¶] [X]

**⬥⬥⬥ ▼▼▼▼ Hotel Monaco Chicago** ⑤⧉ ❀
(312) 960-8500. **$169-$359.** 225 N Wabash Ave. Jct Wacker Dr. Int corridors. **Pets:** Other species. Crate.

[SAVE] [SO] [X] [⌂] [&] [⊡] [¶] [X]

**House of Blues Hotel, A Loews Hotel** LH
(312) 245-0333. **$125-$365.** 333 N Dearborn St. Between Dearborn and State sts. Int corridors. **Pets:** Accepted.
SAVE ⑤ ✕ ⑦ 🐾 🏢 ⑪

**Omni Ambassador East** LH 🐾
(312) 787-7200. **$169-$269.** 1301 N State Pkwy. Jct Goethe St and N State Pkwy. Int corridors. **Pets:** Small, other species. $50 daily fee/pet. No service, supervision.
SAVE ⑤ ✕ ⑦ 🐾 🏢 ⑪ ✕

**Omni Chicago Hotel** LH
(312) 944-6664. **$329-$899.** 676 N Michigan Ave. Jct Huron St. Int corridors. **Pets:** Accepted.
SAVE ⑤ ✕ 🐾M ⑦ 🏢 🏢 ⑪ 🏊 ✕

**The Palmer House Hilton** LH
(312) 726-7500. **$109-$359.** 17 E Monroe St. Between State St and Wabash Ave. Int corridors. **Pets:** Accepted.
SAVE ✕ ⑦ 🏢 ⑪ 🏊 ✕

**Park Hyatt Chicago** LH
(312) 335-1234. **$239-$459.** 800 N Michigan Ave. Jct Chicago and Michigan aves at Water Tower Square. Int corridors. **Pets:** Accepted.
SAVE ✕ ⑦ 🏢 ⑪ 🏊 ✕

**The Peninsula Chicago** LH 🐾
(312) 337-2888. **$490-$1100.** 108 E Superior St. Jct Michigan Ave. Int corridors. **Pets:** Small. Service with restrictions, supervision.
SAVE ⑤ ✕ ⑦ 🐾 🏢 ⑪ 🏊 ✕

**Radisson Hotel & Suites Chicago** LH
(312) 787-2900. **$319.** 160 E Huron St. Just e of N Michigan Ave. Int corridors. **Pets:** Small, other species. $100 deposit/pet. Service with restrictions, supervision.
SAVE ⑤ ✕ ⑦ 🐾 🏢 🏢 ⑪ 🏊

**Red Roof Inn Chicago Downtown #7281** SH
(312) 787-3580. **$87-$139.** 162 E Ontario St. Just e of Michigan Ave. Int corridors. **Pets:** Accepted.
✕ ⑦

**Renaissance Chicago Hotel** LH
(312) 372-7200. **$179-$419.** One W Wacker Dr. Jct State St. Int corridors. **Pets:** Small. $45 one-time fee/room. Service with restrictions, supervision.
SAVE ⑤ ✕ 🐾M ⑦ 🐾 🏢 ⑪ 🏊 ✕

**Residence Inn by Marriott Chicago Downtown** SH 🐾
(312) 943-9800. **$129-$579.** 201 E Walton St. Just e of Michigan Ave at Mies van der Rohe. Int corridors. **Pets:** $75 daily fee/room. Service with restrictions.
✕ ⑦ 🐾 🏢 🏢

**The Ritz-Carlton, Chicago (A Four Seasons Hotel)** LH
(312) 266-1000. **$450-$625.** 160 E Pearson St. Jct N Michigan Ave. Int corridors. **Pets:** Accepted.
SAVE ⑤ ✕ ⑦ 🐾 🏢 🏢 ⑪ 🏊 ✕

**Sheraton Chicago Hotel & Towers** LH 🐾
(312) 464-1000. **$129-$399.** 301 E North Water St. Columbus Dr at Chicago River; just e of Michigan Ave. Int corridors. **Pets:** Small. $100 deposit/room. Service with restrictions, supervision.
SAVE ⑤ ✕ ⑦ 🏢 🏢 ⑪ 🏊 ✕

**Sofitel Chicago Water Tower** LH 🐾
(312) 324-4000. **$335-$475.** 20 E Chestnut St. Jct Wabash Ave and Chestnut St, 0.5 blk w of Rush St. Int corridors. **Pets:** Small. Service with restrictions, supervision.
SAVE ⑤ ✕ 🐾M ⑦ 🐾 ⑪ ✕

**The Sutton Place Hotel** LH 🐾
(312) 266-2100. **$179-$299.** 21 E Bellevue Pl. Jct Rush St. Int corridors. **Pets:** Small, dogs only. $200 deposit/pet, $50 one-time fee/pet. Service with restrictions, crate.
SAVE ⑤ ✕ ⑦ 🏢 ⑪

**W Chicago-City Center** LH
(312) 332-1200. **$179-$499.** 172 W Adams St. Between La Salle and Wells sts. Int corridors. **Pets:** Accepted.
ASK ⑤ ✕ ⑦ 🐾 🏢 🏢 ⑪ ✕

**W Chicago Lakeshore** LH 🐾
(312) 943-9200. **$250-$275.** 644 N Lake Shore Dr. Jct Ontario St. Int corridors. **Pets:** Medium. $100 one-time fee/room. Designated rooms, service with restrictions, crate.
ASK ✕ ⑦ 🐾 🏢 🏊

**The Westin Chicago River North** LH
(312) 744-1900. **$179-$459.** 320 N Dearborn St. Just n of Chicago River; between Dearborn and Clark sts; in River North area. Int corridors. **Pets:** Accepted.
SAVE ⑤ ✕ ⑦ 🏢 🏢 ⑪ ✕

**The Westin Michigan Avenue Chicago** LH
(312) 943-7200. **$369-$479.** 909 N Michigan Ave. Across from John Hancock Center. Int corridors. **Pets:** Accepted.
SAVE ⑤ ✕ 🐾M ⑦ 🐾 🏢 ⑪ ✕

**The Whitehall Hotel** SH
(312) 944-6300. **$179-$389.** 105 E Delaware Pl. Just w of Michigan Ave. Int corridors. **Pets:** Accepted.
ASK ⑤ ✕ ⑪

# CRYSTAL LAKE

**Comfort Inn by Choice Hotels** SH
(815) 444-0040. **$89-$199.** 595 E Tracy Tr. Jct US 14 and SR 31, 0.4 mi w, then just s on Pingree St. Int corridors. **Pets:** Accepted.
ASK ⑤ ✕ ⑦ 🏢 🏢 🏊

**Super 8 Motel** SH
(815) 788-8888. **$48-$92, 7 day notice.** 577 Crystal Point Dr. On US 14, 1 mi w of jct SR 31. Int corridors. **Pets:** Medium. $10 daily fee/pet. Service with restrictions, supervision.
ASK ⑤ ✕ 🏢 🏢

# DOWNERS GROVE

**Red Roof Inn #7087** M
(630) 963-4205. **$55-$81.** 1113 Butterfield Rd. I-355, exit Butterfield Rd (SR 56), on frontage road; I-88, exit Highland Ave N, just w. Ext corridors. **Pets:** Accepted.
✕ ⑦ 🏢

# ELGIN

**Quality Inn-Elgin** SH
(847) 608-7300. **$55-$75.** 500 Tollgate Rd. I-90, exit SR 31 N, just n. Int corridors. **Pets:** Other species. $10 daily fee/room. Service with restrictions, crate.
SAVE ✕ 🐾M ⑦ 🐾 🏢 🏢

# ELK GROVE VILLAGE

**Best Western Chicago West** SH
(847) 981-0010. **$84-$179.** 1600 Oakton St. Jct SR 72 (Higgins Rd) and 83 (Busse Rd). Int corridors. **Pets:** Accepted.
SAVE ⑤ ✕ 🏢 🏢 ⑪ 🏊 ✕

**♦♦♦ ▽ Exel Inn of Elk Grove Village SH**
(847) 895-2085. **$56-$86.** 1000 W Devon Ave. I-290, exit Thorndale Ave, 0.5 mi w to Rohlwing Rd, 0.3 mi n to Devon Ave, then 0.3 mi e. Int corridors. **Pets:** Small, other species. Designated rooms, service with restrictions, supervision.

SAVE SO X 🐾 🖥 🛏 🖵

**♦♦♦ ▽ Exel Inn of O'Hare SH**
(847) 803-9400. **$65-$95.** 2881 Touhy Ave. Jct SR 72 (Higgins Rd) and 83 (Busse Rd), 1.5 mi e on SR 72 (Higgins Rd). Int corridors. **Pets:** Small, other species. Designated rooms, service with restrictions, supervision.

SAVE SO X 🐾 🖥 🛏 🖵

**▽▽▽ Holiday Inn Elk Grove Village LH**
(847) 437-6010. **$72-$118.** 1000 Busse Rd. 0.3 mi s of jct SR 72 (Higgins Rd). Int corridors. **Pets:** Accepted.

ASK SO X 🐾 🖥 🛏 🖵 🍴 🏊 ⊠

**▽▽▽ La Quinta Inn Chicago (O'Hare Airport) SH**
(847) 439-6767. **$89-$139.** 1900 E Oakton St. Jct SR 72 (Higgins Rd) and 83 (Busse Rd). Int corridors. **Pets:** Medium. Service with restrictions.

ASK X 🐾 🛏 🖵 🏊

**▽▽▽ Sheraton Suites Elk Grove Village LH 🐾**
(847) 290-1600. **$109-$209.** 121 Northwest Point Blvd. I-90, exit Arlington Heights Blvd, just s; in Northwest Point Corporate Park. Int corridors. **Pets:** Medium, dogs only. $50 deposit/room. Service with restrictions, supervision.

ASK SO X 🖥 🖵 🍴 🏊 ⊠

**♦♦♦ ▽▽ Super 8 Motel O'Hare SH**
(847) 827-3133. **$57-$85.** 2951 Touhy Ave. Jct SR 72 (Higgins Rd) and 83 (Busse Rd), 1.5 mi e on SR 72 (Higgins Rd). Int corridors. **Pets:** Accepted.

SAVE SO X 🖥 🖵 🏊

## ELMHURST

**♦♦♦ ▽▽▽ Holiday Inn Chicago-Elmhurst SH**
(630) 279-1100. **$95-$350.** 624 N York St. I-290, exit 12 (York Rd), just n. Int corridors. **Pets:** Small. $20 daily fee/pet. Designated rooms, service with restrictions, supervision.

SAVE SO X 🐾 🛏 🖵 🍴 🏊 ⊠

## EVANSTON

**♦♦♦ ▽▽▽▽ Hotel Orrington LH 🐾**
(847) 866-8700. **$108-$252.** 1710 Orrington Ave. Jct Church St. Int corridors. **Pets:** Other species. $50 one-time fee/room. Designated rooms, service with restrictions, crate.

SAVE SO X 🖥 🛏 🖵 🍴

## FRANKLIN PARK

**♦♦♦ ▽▽ Comfort Inn by Choice Hotels SH**
(847) 233-9292. **$79-$89.** 3001 N Mannheim Rd. Jct US 12/45 (Mannheim Rd) and Grand Ave, just n. Int corridors. **Pets:** Medium, other species. $50 deposit/pet, $10 daily fee/pet. Service with restrictions, supervision.

SAVE SO X 🖵 🛏 🖵 🏊

**♦♦♦ ▽▽ Super 8 O'Hare South SH**
(847) 288-0600. **$54-$149.** 3010 N Mannheim Rd. Jct US 12/45 (Mannheim Rd) and Grand Ave, just n. Int corridors. **Pets:** Small. $20 one-time fee/pet. Designated rooms, service with restrictions, supervision.

SAVE SO X 🛏

## GLEN ELLYN

**▽▽ Holiday Inn-Glen Ellyn SH**
(630) 629-6000. **$71-$120.** 1250 Roosevelt Rd. I-355, exit Roosevelt Rd, 0.8 mi e on SR 38. Int corridors. **Pets:** Accepted.

ASK SO X 🖵 🐾 🖵 🛏 🖵 🍴 🏊

## GLENVIEW

**▽▽ Baymont Inn & Suites Chicago-Glenview SH**
(847) 635-8300. **$49-$149.** 1625 Milwaukee Ave. I-294, exit Willow Rd, 0.4 mi e to Landwehr Rd, 1.3 mi s to Lake Ave, then 0.5 mi w. Int corridors. **Pets:** Medium. Service with restrictions.

ASK SO X 🐾 🛏 🖵

**♦♦♦ ▽▽▽ Staybridge Suites SH**
(847) 657-0002. **$99-$155.** 2600 Lehigh Ave. I-294, exit Willow Rd, 2.4 mi e. Int corridors. **Pets:** Accepted.

SAVE SO X 🖵M 🐾 🖵 🛏 🖵 🏊

## GURNEE

**♦♦♦ ▽▽▽ Baymont Inn & Suites Chicago-Gurnee SH**
(847) 662-7600. **$76-$131.** 5688 N Ridge Rd. I-94, exit Grand Ave (SR 132), just e via service road. Int corridors. **Pets:** Medium. Service with restrictions.

SAVE X 🖵M 🐾 🖵 🛏 🖵 🏊

**▽▽▽ Comfort Suites by Choice Hotels SH**
(847) 782-0890. **Call for rates.** 5430 Grand Ave. I-94, exit Grand Ave (SR 132 E), 0.5 mi e. Int corridors. **Pets:** Medium, dogs only. $50 one-time fee/room. Service with restrictions, supervision.

ASK SO X 🖵M 🐾 🖵 🛏 🖵 🏊 ⊠

**▽▽▽ Country Inn & Suites By Carlson SH**
(847) 625-9700. **$59-$299, 3 day notice.** 5420 Grand Ave. I-94, exit Grand Ave (SR 132), 0.5 mi e. Int corridors. **Pets:** Medium, dogs only. $50 one-time fee/room. Service with restrictions, supervision.

ASK SO X 🖵M 🐾 🖵 🛏 🖵 🏊 ⊠

## HOFFMAN ESTATES

**♦♦♦ ▽▽▽▽ AmeriSuites (Chicago/Hoffman Estates) SH**
(847) 839-1800. **$89-$167.** 2750 Greenspoint Pkwy. I-90, exit Barrington Rd westbound, 0.3 mi s; exit SR 59 eastbound, 0.5 mi n to SR 72 (Higgins Rd), 2 mi e to Barrington Rd, then just n. Int corridors. **Pets:** Small. $10 daily fee/pet. Service with restrictions, supervision.

SAVE SO X 🐾 🖵 🛏 🖵 🏊

**▽▽ Baymont Inn & Suites Chicago-Hoffman Estates SH**
(847) 882-8848. **$65-$105.** 2075 Barrington Rd. I-90, exit Barrington Rd westbound, 0.3 mi s; exit SR 59 eastbound, 0.5 mi n to SR 72 (Higgins Rd), 2 mi e to Barrington Rd, then just n. Int corridors. **Pets:** Medium. $50 deposit/room. Designated rooms, service with restrictions, supervision.

ASK SO X 🐾 🛏 🖵

**▽▽▽ La Quinta Inn Chicago (Hoffman Estates) SH**
(847) 882-3312. **$78-$124.** 2280 Barrington Rd. I-90, exit Barrington Rd westbound, 0.3 mi s; exit SR 59 eastbound, 0.5 mi n to SR 72 (Higgins Rd), 2 mi e to Barrington Rd, then just n. Int corridors. **Pets:** Medium. Service with restrictions.

ASK X 🐾 🖵 🛏 🖵 🏊

**▽ Red Roof Inn #7199 M**
(847) 885-7877. **$54-$88.** 2500 Hassell Rd. I-90, exit Barrington Rd westbound, 0.3 mi s; exit SR 59 eastbound, 0.5 mi n to SR 72 (Higgins Rd), 2 mi e to Barrington Rd, then just n. Ext corridors. **Pets:** Accepted.

X 🐾 🛏

## ITASCA

**♦♦♦ ▽▽▽▽ AmeriSuites (Chicago/Itasca) SH**
(630) 875-1400. **$89-$159.** 1150 Arlington Heights Rd. I-290, exit Thorndale Ave, 0.6 mi e on Thorndale Heights Rd, then 0.5 mi n. Int corridors. **Pets:** Accepted.

SAVE SO X 🖵M 🐾 🖵 🛏 🖵 🏊

# JOLIET

**▼▼▼ Comfort Inn by Choice Hotels North** 🆂🄷
(815) 436-5141. **$80-$100.** 3235 Norman Ave. I-55, exit 257, just e. Int corridors. **Pets:** Accepted.
🄰🅂🄺 🆂ⅾ ☒ 🕖 🃏 🛇 💻 🌊

**▼▼▼ Comfort Inn by Choice Hotels-South** 🆂🄷
(815) 744-1770. **$80-$100.** 135 S Larkin Ave. I-80, exit 130B, 0.5 mi n. Int corridors. **Pets:** Accepted.
🄰🅂🄺 🆂ⅾ ☒ 🕖 🃏 🛇 💻 🌊

**▼▼▼▼ Holiday Inn Express-Joliet** 🆂🄷
(815) 729-2000. **$69-$139.** 411 S Larkin Ave. I-80, exit 130B, just nw. Int corridors. **Pets:** Small, dogs only. Designated rooms, no service, supervision.
🄰🅂🄺 🆂ⅾ ☒ 🄼 🕖 🃏 🛇 💻 🌊

**▼ Red Roof Inn #7071** 🄼
(815) 741-2304. **$48-$80.** 1750 McDonough St. I-80, exit 130B, just off Larkin Ave. Ext corridors. **Pets:** Accepted.
☒ 🕖 🛇

**▲▲▲ ▼▼▼ Super 8 Motel I-55 North** 🆂🄷
(815) 439-3838. **$54-$60.** 3401 Mall Loop Dr. I-55, exit 257, 0.4 mi e on US 30, then just s. Int corridors. **Pets:** Accepted.
🅂🄰🅅🄴 🆂ⅾ ☒ 🕖 🃏 🛇 💻

# LANSING

**▼ Red Roof Inn #7078** 🄼
(708) 895-9570. **$55-$88.** 2450 E 173rd St. I-80/94, exit 161 (Torrence Ave), just n. Ext corridors. **Pets:** Accepted.
☒ 🕖 🛇

# LIBERTYVILLE

**▼▼ Candlewood Suites Chicago-Libertyville** 🆂🄷
(847) 247-9900. **$97-$127.** 1100 N US 45. I-94, exit 137 (Buckley Rd), 5.6 mi w to US 45, then 1.4 mi s. Int corridors. **Pets:** Accepted.
🄰🅂🄺 🆂ⅾ ☒ 🄼 🕖 🃏 🛇 💻

**▼ Days Inn** 🆂🄷
(847) 816-8006. **$75-$115, 7 day notice.** 1809 N Milwaukee Ave. Jct SR 21 (Milwaukee Ave) and 137 (Buckley Rd). Int corridors. **Pets:** Other species. $5 daily fee/pet. Service with restrictions, supervision.
🄰🅂🄺 🆂ⅾ ☒ 🕖 🛇 💻 🌊

**▼▼▼ Holiday Inn Express Hotel & Suites** 🆂🄷
(847) 549-7878. **$89-$129.** 77 Buckley Rd. I-94, exit SR 137 (Buckley Rd), 2.3 mi w. Int corridors. **Pets:** Medium, dogs only. $50 one-time fee/pet. Service with restrictions, supervision.
🄰🅂🄺 🆂ⅾ ☒ 🃏 🛇 💻

# LINCOLNSHIRE

**▼▼▼▼ Homewood Suites by Hilton Chicago-Lincolnshire** 🆂🄷
(847) 945-9300. **$129-$199.** 10 Westminister Way. I-94, exit Half Day Rd, just w. Int corridors. **Pets:** Accepted.
🄰🅂🄺 🆂ⅾ ☒ 🕖 🛇 💻 🌊 ☒

**▲▲▲ ▼▼▼ ▼▼▼ Lincolnshire Marriott Resort** 🄻🄷
(847) 634-0100. **$189-$259.** 10 Marriott Dr. I-94, exit Half Day Rd, 2 mi w to jct US 45, SR 21 and 22, then just s. Int corridors. **Pets:** Accepted.
🅂🄰🅅🄴 ☒ 🄼 🕖 🃏 🛇 💻 🍴 🌊 ☒

**▼▼▼ Staybridge Suites** 🆂🄷
(847) 821-0002. **$129-$299.** 100 Barclay Blvd. I-94, exit Half Day Rd, 2.2 mi w to Barclay Blvd, then just s; just w of jct US 45 and SR 21; in Lincolnshire Corporate Center. Int corridors. **Pets:** Accepted.
🄰🅂🄺 🆂ⅾ ☒ 🄼 🕖 🃏 🛇 💻 🌊

# LOMBARD

**▲▲▲ ▼▼▼▼ AmeriSuites (Chicago/Lombard/Oak Brook)** 🆂🄷
(630) 932-6501. **$99-$169.** 2340 S Fountain Square Dr. I-88, exit Highland Ave, just n to Butterfield Rd (SR 56), 0.9 mi e, then just n. Int corridors. **Pets:** Small. $10 daily fee/room. Service with restrictions, supervision.
🅂🄰🅅🄴 🆂ⅾ ☒ 🄼 🕖 🃏 🛇 💻 🌊

**▼▼ Homestead Studio Suites Hotel-Chicago/Lombard/Oak Brook** 🆂🄷
(630) 928-0202. **$74-$89.** 2701 Technology Dr. I-88, exit Highland Ave, just n, 0.6 mi e on Butterfield Rd (SR 56), then just s. Int corridors. **Pets:** $25 daily fee/pet. Service with restrictions, supervision.
🄰🅂🄺 🆂ⅾ ☒ 🕖 🃏 🛇 💻

# MATTESON

**▲▲▲ ▼▼▼ Baymont Inn & Suites Chicago-Matteson** 🆂🄷
(708) 503-0999. **$69-$145.** 5210 W Southwick Dr. I-57, exit 340A, 0.3 mi e on US 30, then 0.3 mi s on Cicero Ave. Int corridors. **Pets:** Medium. Service with restrictions.
🅂🄰🅅🄴 ☒ 🕖 🃏 🛇 💻

**▼▼▼ Country Inn & Suites by Carlson** 🆂🄷
(708) 748-4740. **$89-$139.** 950 Lake Superior Dr. I-57, exit 340A, 0.3 mi e, then 0.3 mi n. Int corridors. **Pets:** Small. $10 daily fee/pet. Designated rooms, service with restrictions, supervision.
🄰🅂🄺 🆂ⅾ ☒ 🄼 🕖 🃏 🛇 💻 🌊 ☒

# MUNDELEIN

**▼▼▼▼ Crowne Plaza Chicago North Shore** 🆂🄷 ❀
(847) 949-5100. **$209-$249.** 510 SR 83 E. Jct US 45 and SR 83. Int corridors. **Pets:** Designated rooms, service with restrictions, supervision.
🄰🅂🄺 🆂ⅾ ☒ 🕖 🛇 💻 🍴 🌊

**▼ Super 8 Motel** 🆂🄷
(847) 949-8842. **Call for rates.** 1950 S Lake St. Jct US 45, SR 60 and 83. Int corridors. **Pets:** Accepted.
🄰🅂🄺 ☒ 🛇

# NAPERVILLE

**▲▲▲ ▼▼ Exel Inn of Naperville** 🆂🄷
(630) 357-0022. **$56-$86.** 1585 N Naperville/Wheaton Rd. I-88, exit Naperville Rd, 0.5 mi s. Int corridors. **Pets:** Small, other species. Designated rooms, service with restrictions, supervision.
🅂🄰🅅🄴 🆂ⅾ ☒ 🛇 💻

**▼▼▼ Fairfield Inn & Suites by Marriott Naperville/Aurora** 🆂🄷
(630) 548-0966. **$99-$130.** 1847 W Diehl Rd. I-88, exit SR 59, just s. Int corridors. **Pets:** Accepted.
🄰🅂🄺 ☒ 🄼 🕖 🃏 🛇 💻 🌊

**▲▲▲ ▼▼▼▼ Holiday Inn Select Hotel & Conference Center** 🄻🄷
(630) 505-4900. **$119-$169.** 1801 N Naper Blvd. I-88, exit Naperville Rd, just s. Int corridors. **Pets:** Accepted.
🅂🄰🅅🄴 ☒ 🕖 🛇 💻 🍴 🌊

**▼▼ Homestead Studio Suites Hotel-Chicago/Naperville** 🆂🄷
(630) 577-0200. **$70-$85.** 1827 Centre Point Cir. I-88, exit Naperville Rd, just s to Diehl Rd, 0.8 mi w, then just n. Int corridors. **Pets:** $25 daily fee/pet. Service with restrictions, supervision.
🄰🅂🄺 🆂ⅾ ☒ 🕖 🃏 🛇 💻

**▼▼▼ Naperville TownePlace Suites** 🆂🄷
(630) 548-0881. **$113-$141.** 1843 W Diehl Rd. I-88, exit SR 59, just s to Diehl Rd, then just w. Int corridors. **Pets:** Accepted.
🄰🅂🄺 ☒ 🕖 🃏 🛇 💻 🌊 ☒

▼ Red Roof Inn #7195 **M**
(630) 369-2500. **$58-$80.** 1698 W Diehl Rd. I-88, exit SR 59, just s. Ext corridors. **Pets:** Accepted.

⊠ 🖉 🛏

## NORTH AURORA

🔺 ▼▼ Baymont Inn & Suites North Aurora **SH**
(630) 897-7695. **$84-$139.** 308 S Lincoln Way. I-88, exit SR 31. Int corridors. **Pets:** Service with restrictions, supervision.

SAVE S⊠ ⊠ 🖉 🛏 🖃 ≈

## NORTHBROOK

🔺 ▼▼▼ Radisson Hotel Northbrook **LH**
(847) 298-2525. **$79-$209.** 2875 N Milwaukee Ave. I-294, exit Willow Rd, 1 mi w to SR 21 and US 45, then 0.6 mi s. Int corridors. **Pets:** Medium. $25 one-time fee/pet. Service with restrictions, supervision.

SAVE S⊠ ⊠ 🖉 🖉 🛏 ⏏ ≈

▼ Red Roof Inn #7188 **M**
(847) 205-1755. **$55-$77.** 340 Waukegan Rd. I-94, exit SR 43 (Waukegan Rd). Ext corridors. **Pets:** Accepted.

⊠

## OAK BROOK

▼▼▼ Residence Inn by Marriott Chicago/Oak Brook **SH**
(630) 571-1200. **$89-$229.** 790 Jorie Blvd. I-88, exit Midwest Rd eastbound, just n to 22nd St (Cermak Rd), 1.7 mi e to Jorie Blvd, then just sw; exit 22nd St (Cermak Rd) westbound, 0.4 mi e to Jorie Blvd. Int corridors. **Pets:** Medium, other species. $75 one-time fee/pet. Service with restrictions, crate.

⊠ 🖉M 🖉 🖉 🛏 🖃 ≈ 🐾

## OAKBROOK TERRACE

🔺 ▼▼ Comfort Suites-Oakbrook Terrace/O'Hare Chicago **SH**
(630) 916-1000. **$64-$198.** 17 W 445 Roosevelt Rd. SR 38, just w of jct SR 83. Int corridors. **Pets:** Small, dogs only. $10 daily fee/pet. Designated rooms, supervision.

SAVE S⊠ ⊠ 🛏 🖃 ≈ 🐾

🔺 ▼▼◆ Holiday Inn-Chicago/Oak Brook **SH**
(630) 833-3600. **$89-$109, 7 day notice.** 17 W 350 22nd St. I-88, exit Midwest Rd eastbound, just n, then 0.3 mi e; 0.5 mi w of jct SR 83. Int corridors. **Pets:** Accepted.

SAVE S⊠ ⊠ 🖉 🛏 🖃 ⏏ ≈ 🐾

🔺 ▼▼◆ La Quinta Inn Chicago (Oak Brook) **SH**
(630) 495-4600. **$85-$139.** 1 S 666 Midwest Rd. I-88, exit Midwest Rd eastbound, 0.4 mi n, then just n of 22nd St (Cermak Rd); exit 22nd St (Cermak Rd) westbound, 1.1 mi w to Midwest Rd, then just n. Int corridors. **Pets:** Medium. Service with restrictions.

SAVE ⊠ 🖉 🛏 🖃 ≈

▼▼▼ Staybridge Suites Chicago-Oakbrook Terrace **SH**
(630) 953-9393. **$81-$198.** 200 Royce Blvd. I-88, exit Midwest Rd eastbound to 22nd St, 0.4 mi w to SR 56, just n, then just n on Renaissance Blvd; exit Cermak Rd/22nd St westbound, 2.5 mi w on 22nd St to SR 56, just n, then just n on Renaissance Blvd. Int corridors. **Pets:** Medium, other species. $75 one-time fee/room. Service with restrictions.

ASK S⊠ ⊠ 🖉M 🖉 🖉 🛏 🖃 🐾

## PALATINE

▼▼▼ Holiday Inn Express Palatine/Arlington Heights **SH** 🐾
(847) 934-4900. **$79-$199.** 1550 E Dundee Rd. SR 53, exit Dundee Rd (SR 68), just w. Int corridors. **Pets:** Medium, other species. Designated rooms, service with restrictions, crate.

ASK S⊠ ⊠ 🖉M 🖉 🖉 🛏 🖃 ≈ 🐾

## PROSPECT HEIGHTS

🔺 ▼ Exel Inn of Prospect Heights **SH**
(847) 459-0545. **$51-$81.** 540 Milwaukee Ave. Jct SR 21 and US 45. Int corridors. **Pets:** Small, other species. Designated rooms, service with restrictions, supervision.

SAVE S⊠ ⊠ 🖉 🛏 🖃

## RICHMOND

▼▼ Save Inn Richmond/Geneva Lakes **SH**
(815) 678-4711. **$75-$105.** 11200 N Rt 12. 0.5 mi n of jct SR 173. Int corridors. **Pets:** Other species. $10 daily fee/pet. Designated rooms, service with restrictions, supervision.

ASK S⊠ ⊠ 🖃 ≈

## ROSEMONT

🔺 ▼▼▼ Crowne Plaza Chicago O'Hare **LH**
(847) 671-6350. **$109-$219.** 5440 N River Rd. I-190, exit 1B, just s. Int corridors. **Pets:** Accepted.

SAVE S⊠ ⊠ 🖉M 🖉 🖉 🛏 🖃 ⏏ ≈ 🐾

▼▼▼ Doubletree Hotel Chicago O'Hare Airport-Rosemont **LH**
(847) 292-9100. **$79-$269.** 5460 N River Rd. I-190, exit 1B, just s. Int corridors. **Pets:** Accepted.

ASK ⊠ 🖉M 🖉 🖉 🖃 ⏏ ≈ 🐾

🔺 ▼▼▼ Embassy Suites Hotel O'Hare Rosemont **LH**
(847) 678-4000. **$109-$349.** 5500 N River Rd. I-190, exit 1B, just s. Int corridors. **Pets:** Medium. Service with restrictions, supervision.

SAVE ⊠ 🖉 🖉 🛏 🖃 ⏏ ≈ 🐾

▼▼▼ Residence Inn by Marriott Chicago-O'Hare **SH**
(847) 375-9000. **$139-$189.** 7101 Chestnut St. Jct US 12 and 45 and Touhy Ave. Int corridors. **Pets:** Accepted.

ASK ⊠ 🖉 🖉 🛏 🖃 ≈ 🐾

▼▼▼ Sheraton Gateway Suites O'Hare **LH** 🐾
(847) 699-6300. **$99-$289.** 6501 N Mannheim Rd. On US 12 and 45, at SR 72 (Higgins Rd). Int corridors. **Pets:** Medium, dogs only. Service with restrictions, supervision.

ASK ⊠ 🖉 🖉 🛏 🖃 ⏏ ≈ 🐾

🔺 ▼▼▼▼ The Westin O'Hare **LH** 🐾
(847) 698-6000. **$99-$289.** 6100 N River Rd. I-190, exit 1B, just n. Int corridors. **Pets:** Medium. Service with restrictions, supervision.

SAVE S⊠ ⊠ 🖉M 🖉 🖉 🖃 ⏏ ≈ 🐾

▼▼▼ Wyndham O'Hare **LH**
(847) 297-1234. **$109-$135.** 6810 N Mannheim Rd. On US 12 and 45, 0.3 mi n of SR 72 (Higgins Rd). Int corridors. **Pets:** Accepted.

ASK S⊠ ⊠ 🖉 🖉 🛏 🖃 ⏏ ≈ 🐾

## ST. CHARLES

🔺 ▼▼ Best Western Inn of St. Charles **SH**
(630) 584-4550. **$79-$99.** 1635 E Main St. On SR 64, 0.5 mi e of SR 25. Ext/int corridors. **Pets:** Dogs only. $10 daily fee/pet. Service with restrictions, crate.

SAVE S⊠ ⊠ 🛏 🖃 ≈

🔺 ▼▼ Holiday Inn Express **SH**
(630) 584-5300. **$69-$129.** 1600 E Main St. On SR 64, 0.5 mi e of SR 25. Int corridors. **Pets:** Accepted.

SAVE S⊠ ⊠ 🛏 🖃

▼▼ Quality Inn by Choice Hotels **SH**
(630) 513-6500. **Call for rates.** 100 S Tyler Rd. Jct SR 25, 0.5 mi e on SR 64, then just s. Int corridors. **Pets:** Medium, dogs only. $25 one-time fee/pet. Service with restrictions, supervision.

⊠ 🖉 🛏 🖃 ≈

**AAA ◈ Super 8 Motel-St. Charles** SH
(630) 377-8388. **$70-$90.** 1520 E Main St. On SR 64, 1 mi e. Int corridors. **Pets:** Accepted.
SAVE Sō ✕ ⊞

## SCHAUMBURG

**AAA ◈◈◈ AmeriSuites (Chicago/Schaumburg)** SH
(847) 330-1060. **$79-$140.** 1851 McConnor Pkwy. I-290, exit 1A (Woodfield/Golf rds) northbound, just n to Golf Rd, just w to McConnor Pkwy, then just n; exit 1B (Woodfield/Golf rds) southbound. Int corridors. **Pets:** Small. $10 daily fee/pet. Designated rooms, supervision.
SAVE Sō ✕ ⓈM ⓕ ⓙ ⊞ ⊡ ⋈ ✕

**◈◈ Drury Inn-Schaumburg** SH
(847) 517-7737. **$80-$130.** 600 N Martingale Rd. I-290, exit SR 72 (Higgins Rd), just w, then just n. Int corridors. **Pets:** Accepted.
ASK ✕ ⓙ ⓕ ⊞ ⊡ ⋈

**◈◈ Holiday Inn Schaumburg** SH
(847) 310-0500. **$89-$115.** 1550 N Roselle Rd. I-90, exit Roselle Rd, 0.8 mi s. Int corridors. **Pets:** Accepted.
ASK Sō ✕ ⓙ ⓕ ⊞ ⊡ Ⓨ ⋈

**◈ Homestead Studio Suites Hotel-Chicago/Schaumburg** SH
(847) 882-6900. **$74-$89.** 51 E State Pkwy. I-90, exit Roselle Rd, 0.8 mi s, then just e. Int corridors. **Pets:** $25 daily fee/pet. Service with restrictions, supervision.
ASK Sō ✕ ⓈM ⓙ ⓕ ⓕ ⊡

**◈◈◈ Homewood Suites by Hilton-Schaumburg** SH
(847) 605-0400. **$79-$139.** 815 E American Ln. I-290, exit SR 72 (Higgins Rd), 0.5 mi w, 0.8 mi n on Meacham Rd, then 0.8 mi w. Ext/int corridors. **Pets:** Accepted.
ASK Sō ✕ ⓈM ⓙ ⓕ ⊞ ⊡ ⋈ ✕

**AAA ◈◈◈ La Quinta Inn (Schaumburg)** SH
(847) 517-8484. **$80-$144.** 1730 E Higgins Rd. I-290, exit Higgins Rd (SR 72), just w. Int corridors. **Pets:** Medium. Service with restrictions.
SAVE ✕ ⓙ ⓕ ⊞ ⊡ ⋈

**◈◈ Residence Inn by Marriott-Chicago/Schaumburg** SH ✿
(847) 517-9200. **$89-$219, 7 day notice.** 1610 McConnor Pkwy. I-290, exit 1A (Woodfield/Golf rds) northbound, follow signs just n to Golf Rd, just w to McConnor Pkwy, then just n; exit 1B (Woodfield/Golf rds) southbound. Int corridors. **Pets:** Large, other species. $75 one-time fee/room. Service with restrictions, crate.
ASK Sō ✕ ⓈM ⓙ ⓕ ⊞ ⊡ ⋈ ✕

**◈◈◈ Staybridge Suites Chicago/Schaumburg** SH
(847) 619-6677. **$134-$154.** 901 E Woodfield Office Ct. I-290, exit SR 72 (Higgins Rd), 1.5 mi w, then 0.3 mi n on Plum Grove Rd. Ext/int corridors. **Pets:** Medium, other species. $200 one-time fee/pet. Designated rooms, service with restrictions, crate.
ASK Sō ✕ ⓙ ⓕ ⊞ ⊡ ⋈ ✕

## SCHILLER PARK

**AAA ◈◈◈ Comfort Suites O'Hare** SH
(847) 233-9000. **$79-$149.** 4200 N River Rd. Jct SR 19 (Irving Park Rd) and Des Plaines St/River Rd, just n. Int corridors. **Pets:** Medium, other species. $25 one-time fee/room. Service with restrictions, crate.
SAVE Sō ✕ ⓈM ⓙ ⓕ ⓕ ⊞ ⊡ Ⓨ

**AAA ◈◈◈◈ Four Points by Sheraton Chicago O'Hare Airport** LH
(847) 671-6000. **$189-$210.** 10249 W Irving Park Rd. Jct US 12 and 45 and SR 19 (Irving Park Rd). Int corridors. **Pets:** Small. $50 deposit/pet. Service with restrictions, supervision.
SAVE Sō ✕ ⓈM ⓙ ⓕ ⊞ ⊡ Ⓨ ⋈ ✕

## SKOKIE

**AAA ◈◈◈ Comfort Inn Northshore-Skokie** SH
(847) 679-4200. **$119-$149.** 9333 Skokie Blvd. I-94, exit Old Orchard Rd, 0.4 mi e to Skokie Blvd (US 41), then 0.3 mi s. Int corridors. **Pets:** Medium, other species. Service with restrictions, supervision.
SAVE Sō ✕ ⓈM ⓕ ⊞ ⊡ Ⓨ ⋈ ✕

**◈◈◈ Holiday Inn Chicago-Skokie & Conference Center** SH
(847) 679-8900. **$102-$179.** 5300 W Touhy Ave. I-94, exit 39A, 0.5 mi w. Ext/int corridors. **Pets:** Small. $25 one-time fee/pet. Designated rooms, service with restrictions, supervision.
ASK Sō ✕ ⓙ ⓕ ⊞ ⊡ Ⓨ ⋈ ✕

## TINLEY PARK

**AAA ◈◈◈ La Quinta Inn & Suites Chicago-Tinley Park** SH
(708) 633-1200. **$75-$155.** 7255 W 183rd St. I-80, exit 148B, 0.5 mi n to 183rd St, then just w to North Creek Business Center. Int corridors. **Pets:** Medium. Service with restrictions.
SAVE ✕ ⓈM ⓙ ⓕ ⊞ ⊡ ⋈

## VERNON HILLS

**◈◈ Homestead Studio Suites Hotel-Chicago/Vernon Hills/Lincolnshire** SH
(847) 955-1111. **$74-$89.** 675 Woodlands Pkwy. I-94, exit SR 60 (Town Line Rd), 2.1 mi w to SR 21 (Milwaukee Ave), 1.9 mi s to Woodlands Pkwy, then just w. Int corridors. **Pets:** $25 daily fee/pet. Service with restrictions, supervision.
✕ ⓙ ⓕ ⊞ ⊡

## WARRENVILLE

**◈◈◈ Residence Inn by Marriott Chicago Naperville/Warrenville** SH
(630) 393-3444. **$149-$249.** 28500 Bella Vista Pkwy. I-88, exit Winfield Rd, just n to Ferry Rd, then just e. Int corridors. **Pets:** Other species. $75 one-time fee/room. Service with restrictions, crate.
ASK Sō ✕ ⓈM ⓙ ⓕ ⊞ ⊡ ⋈ ✕

## WAUKEGAN

**AAA ◈◈ Best Western of Waukegan** SH
(847) 244-6100. **$80-$100.** 411 S Green Bay Rd. I-94, exit SR 120 (Belvidere Rd) eastbound, 2.3 mi e to Green Bay Rd, then just n. Ext/int corridors. **Pets:** Accepted.
SAVE Sō ✕ ⓕ ⊞ ⊡ ⋈

**◈◈ Candlewood Suites Chicago/Waukegan** SH
(847) 578-5250. **$79-$119.** 1151 S Waukegan Rd. I-94, exit SR 137 (Buckley Rd), 0.5 mi e to SR 43 (Waukegan Rd), then 1.9 mi n. Int corridors. **Pets:** Accepted.
ASK Sō ✕ ⓙ ⓕ ⊞ ⊡

**◈◈◈ Residence Inn by Marriott-Waukegan/Gurnee** SH
(847) 689-9240. **$99-$169.** 1440 S White Oak Dr. I-94, exit SR 137 (Buckley Rd), 0.5 mi e to SR 43 (Waukegan Rd), 1.5 mi n to Lakeside Dr, then just e. Int corridors. **Pets:** Other species. $75 one-time fee/room.
ASK ✕ ⓈM ⓙ ⓕ ⊞ ⊡ ⋈ ✕

## WEST DUNDEE

**◈◈ TownePlace Suites by Marriott** SH 🐾
(847) 608-6320. **$54-$89.** 2185 Marriott Dr. I-90, exit SR 31, 0.4 mi n to Marriott Dr, then just e. Int corridors. **Pets:** Large, other species. $75 one-time fee/room. Service with restrictions.
ASK ✕ ⓙ ⓕ ⊞ ⊡ ⋈

## WESTMONT

◈◈ **Homestead Studio Suites Hotel-Chicago/Westmont/Oak Brook** SH
(630) 323-9292. **$65-$80.** 855 Pasquinelli Dr. SR 83, exit US 34 (Ogden Ave), just w to Pasquinelli Dr, then 0.5 mi n. Int corridors. **Pets:** $25 daily fee/pet. Service with restrictions, supervision.
(A$K) (S₀) (X) (&M) (∅) (⅗) (🛏) (💻)

## WILLOWBROOK

◬ ◈ **Baymont Inn & Suites Chicago-Willowbrook** SH
(630) 654-0077. **$88-$145.** 855 79th St. I-55, exit 274, just n. Int corridors. **Pets:** Medium. Service with restrictions.
(SAVE) (X) (∅) (🛏) (💻)

◈ **Red Roof Inn #7167** M
(630) 323-8811. **$55-$95.** 7535 Kingery Hwy. I-55, exit 274, 0.5 mi n on SR 83. Ext corridors. **Pets:** Accepted.
(X) (∅) (🛏)

◈◈ **Super 8 Motel-Willowbrook** SH
(630) 789-6300. **$73-$92.** 820 W 79th St. I-55, exit 274, 0.3 mi n to Midway Dr, then e on frontage road. Ext/int corridors. **Pets:** Other species. $10 one-time fee/room. Service with restrictions, supervision.
(A$K) (S₀) (X) (∅) (🛏) (💻) (🏊)

## WOODSTOCK

◈ **Super 8 Motel** SH
(815) 337-8808. **$55-$106, 3 day notice.** 1220 Davis Rd. On SR 47, s of jct US 14. Int corridors. **Pets:** Accepted.
(A$K) (S₀) (X) (🛏)

---

## END METROPOLITAN AREA

---

## CHILLICOTHE

◈◈ **Super 8 Motel** SH
(309) 274-2568. **$65-$85, 3 day notice.** 615 S Fourth St. 1.1 mi s on SR 29. Int corridors. **Pets:** Large. Service with restrictions, supervision.
(A$K) (S₀) (X) (🛏)

## COLLINSVILLE

◈◈◈ **Drury Inn-St. Louis/Collinsville** SH
(618) 345-7700. **$74-$146.** 602 N Bluff Rd. I-55/70, exit 11 (SR 157), just n. Int corridors. **Pets:** Accepted.
(A$K) (X) (&M) (∅) (🛏) (💻) (🏊)

◈◈◈ **Holiday Inn Collinsville/St. Louis** SH
(618) 345-2800. **$110.** 1000 Eastport Plaza Dr. I-55/70, exit 11 (SR 157), just nw. Int corridors. **Pets:** Accepted.
(A$K) (X) (🛏) (💻) (⑪) (🏊) (X)

## DANVILLE

◬ ◈◈ **Best Western Regency Inn** SH
(217) 446-2111. **$70-$100.** 360 Eastgate Dr. I-74, exit 220 (Lynch Dr), just n. Ext/int corridors. **Pets:** Small, dogs only. $10 daily fee/pet. Designated rooms, service with restrictions, supervision.
(SAVE) (S₀) (X) (🛏) (💻) (🏊)

◬ ◈◈ **Best Western Riverside Inn** SH
(217) 431-0020. **$70-$110.** 57 S Gilbert St. I-74, exit 215B, 0.8 mi n on US 150 and SR 1. Ext/int corridors. **Pets:** Very small, dogs only. $10 daily fee/pet. Designated rooms, service with restrictions, supervision.
(SAVE) (S₀) (X) (🛏) (💻) (🏊)

◈◈ **Comfort Inn by Choice Hotels** SH
(217) 443-8004. **$64-$95.** 383 Lynch Dr. I-74, exit 220 (Lynch Dr), just n. Int corridors. **Pets:** Service with restrictions, supervision.
(A$K) (S₀) (X) (∅) (🛏) (💻) (🏊)

◈◈ **Sleep Inn & Suites** SH
(217) 442-6600. **$59-$99.** 361 Lynch Dr. I-74, exit 220 (Lynch Dr), just n. Int corridors. **Pets:** Small, dogs only. $10 daily fee/pet. Designated rooms, service with restrictions, supervision.
(A$K) (S₀) (X) (🛏) (💻) (🏊)

◈◈ **Super 8** SH
(217) 443-4499. **$51-$58.** 377 Lynch Dr. I-74, exit 220 (Lynch Dr), just n. Int corridors. **Pets:** Accepted.
(A$K) (S₀) (X) (🛏) (💻)

## DECATUR

◈◈◈ **Country Inn & Suites By Carlson** SH
(217) 872-2402. **$79.** 5150 Hickory Point Frontage Rd. I-72, exit 141B (US 51 N), s on frontage road. Int corridors. **Pets:** Accepted.
(A$K) (S₀) (X) (&M) (∅) (⅗) (🛏) (💻) (🏊) (X)

◈◈ **Ramada Limited Decatur** SH
(217) 876-8011. **$73-$79.** 355 E Hickory Point Rd. I-72, exit 141B (US 51 N), just n, then s via frontage road. Int corridors. **Pets:** Accepted.
(A$K) (S₀) (X) (∅) (⅗) (🛏) (💻) (🏊)

◬ ◈◈ **Sleep Inn of Decatur** SH
(217) 872-7700. **$68-$85.** 3920 E Hospitality Ln. I-72, exit 144 (SR 48), just s to Brush College Rd, then just e. Int corridors. **Pets:** Small, dogs only. $10 one-time fee/room. Service with restrictions, supervision.
(SAVE) (S₀) (X) (∅) (⅗) (🛏) (💻) (🏊) (X)

◈◈ **Wingate Inn** SH
(217) 875-5500. **$69, 10 day notice.** 5170 Wingate Dr. I-72, exit 141, 0.5 mi n on US 51, then just e. Int corridors. **Pets:** Medium, other species. $10 one-time fee/room. Service with restrictions, supervision.
(A$K) (S₀) (X) (&M) (∅) (⅗) (🛏) (💻) (🏊) (X)

## DEKALB

◈◈ **Baymont Inn & Suites Dekalb/Sycamore** SH 🐾
(815) 748-4800. **$69-$99, 5 day notice.** 1314 W Lincoln Hwy. I-88, exit Annie Glidden Rd, 2 mi n to W Lincoln Hwy (SR 38), then 0.4 mi w. Int corridors. **Pets:** Medium. $50 deposit/room. Designated rooms, service with restrictions, supervision.
(A$K) (S₀) (X) (&M) (∅) (⅗) (🛏) (💻) (🏊)

◬ ◈◈◈ **Best Western DeKalb Inn & Suites** SH
(815) 758-8661. **$79-$149.** 1212 W Lincoln Hwy. I-88, exit Annie Glidden Rd, 2 mi n to W Lincoln Hwy (SR 38), then just w. Ext/int corridors. **Pets:** Accepted.
(SAVE) (S₀) (X) (∅) (🛏) (💻) (🏊)

## DIXON

◬ ◈◈ **Comfort Inn by Choice Hotels** SH
(815) 284-0500. **$69-$84.** 136 Plaza Dr. I-88, exit SR 26, just n, then just e. Int corridors. **Pets:** Medium, other species. $100 deposit/pet. Service with restrictions, supervision.
(SAVE) (S₀) (X) (🛏) (💻) (🏊)

**◆◆◆ ▼◆▼ Quality Inn & Suites by Choice Hotels** 🆂🅷
(815) 288-2001. **$79-$105.** 154 Plaza Dr. I-88, exit SR 26, just n, then just e. Int corridors. **Pets:** Medium, other species. $15 daily fee/room. Service with restrictions, supervision.
[SAVE] 🆂 ✕ 🔲 🖵 ➳ ✕

# EAST MOLINE

**▼◆▼◆ Ramada-East Moline** 🆂🅷
(309) 792-4660. **$75-$119.** 2209 John Deere Expwy. I-74, exit 5B, 5 mi e; I-80, exit 4A, 6 mi w. Int corridors. **Pets:** Accepted.
[ASK] 🆂 ✕ 🅜 🖵 🔲 🖵 ➳

**▼◆ Super 8 Motel-East Moline** 🆂🅷
(309) 796-1999. **$60-$90.** 2201 John Deere Rd. I-74, exit 4B (John Deere Rd), 5.5 mi e on SR 5. Int corridors. **Pets:** Accepted.
[ASK] 🆂 ✕ 🔲

# EAST PEORIA

**▼◆ ▼◆ Super 8 Motel** 🆂🅷
(309) 698-8889. **$56-$95.** 725 Taylor St. I-74, exit 96, just e. Int corridors. **Pets:** Small. $50 deposit/room. Designated rooms, service with restrictions, supervision.
[ASK] 🆂 ✕ 🔲 🖵

# EFFINGHAM

**◆◆◆ ▼◆▼ Best Western Raintree Inn** 🆂🅷
(217) 342-4121. **$45-$65.** 1811 W Fayette Ave. I-57/70, exit 159, just n. Ext/int corridors. **Pets:** Small. Designated rooms, service with restrictions, supervision.
[SAVE] 🆂 ✕ 🔲 🖵 ➳

**▼◆▼ Comfort Inn** 🆂🅷
(217) 347-5050. **$59-$75.** 1304 W Evergreen Dr. I-57/70, exit 160 (SR 32/33), just e, then just n. Int corridors. **Pets:** Accepted.
[ASK] 🆂 ✕ 🅜 🔲 🖵 🖵 ➳ ✕

**▼◆▼◆ Comfort Suites** 🆂🅷
(217) 342-3151. **$59-$89.** 1310 W Fayette Ave. I-57/70, exit 159, 0.4 mi e. Int corridors. **Pets:** Accepted.
[ASK] 🆂 ✕ 🅜 🖵 🔲 🖵 ➳

**◆◆◆ ▼◆▼ Days Inn** Ⓜ
(217) 342-9271. **$39-$64.** 1412 W Fayette Ave. I-57/70, exit 159, just e. Ext corridors. **Pets:** $5 daily fee/pet. Service with restrictions, crate.
[SAVE] 🆂 ✕ 🔲 🖵 ➳

**▼◆▼◆ Holiday Inn Express** 🆂🅷
(217) 540-1111. **Call for rates.** 1103 Ave of Mid-America. I-57/70, exit 160 (SR 32/33), just n. Int corridors. **Pets:** Accepted.
[ASK] ✕ 🅜 🖵 🔲 🖵 ➳

**◆◆◆ ▼◆ Paradise Inn** Ⓜ
(217) 342-2165. **$40-$46.** 1000 W Fayette Ave. I-57/70, exit 159, 1 mi e. Ext corridors. **Pets:** Small. $10 daily fee/pet. Designated rooms, service with restrictions, supervision.
[SAVE] ✕ 🔲

**▼◆ ▼◆ Super 8 Motel-Effingham** Ⓜ
(217) 342-6888. **$59-$88.** 1400 Thelma Keller Ave. I-57/70, exit 160 (SR 32/33), 0.5 mi n. Int corridors. **Pets:** Other species. Service with restrictions, supervision.
[ASK] 🆂 ✕ 🖵 🔲 🖵

# FAIRVIEW HEIGHTS

**▼◆▼◆ Drury Inn & Suites-Fairview Heights** 🆂🅷
(618) 398-8530. **$86-$130.** 12 Ludwig Dr. I-64, exit 12 (SR 159). Int corridors. **Pets:** Accepted.
[ASK] ✕ 🔲 🖵 ➳

**◆◆◆ ▼◆▼ Ramada Inn Fairview Heights** 🅻🅷
(618) 632-4747. **$69-$89.** 6900 N Illinois Ave. I-64, exit 12 (SR 159), just n. Int corridors. **Pets:** Medium. $15 one-time fee/room. Service with restrictions, crate.
[SAVE] 🆂 ✕ 🔲 🖵 🖵 ▥ ➳

**▼◆ ▼◆ Super 8 Motel** 🆂🅷
(618) 398-8338. **$68-$90.** 45 Ludwig Dr. I-64, exit 12 (SR 159). Int corridors. **Pets:** Other species. Service with restrictions, crate.
[ASK] 🆂 ✕ 🖵 🔲

# FLORA

**▼◆▼◆ Best Western Lorson Inn** 🆂🅷
(618) 662-3054. **$66-$92.** 201 Gary Hagen Dr. Jct US 45 and 50. Int corridors. **Pets:** Other species. $25 deposit/room. Service with restrictions, supervision.
[ASK] 🆂 ✕ 🅜 🔲 🖵 ✕

# FORSYTH

**▼◆▼ Comfort Inn by Choice Hotels** 🆂🅷
(217) 875-1166. **$59-$89.** 134 Barnett Ave. I-72, exit 141B (US 51), 0.5 mi n. Int corridors. **Pets:** Accepted.
[ASK] 🆂 ✕ 🖵 🔲 🖵 ➳

# FREEPORT

**◆◆◆ ▼◆▼◆ AmeriHost Inn & Suites-Freeport** 🆂🅷
(815) 599-8510. **$65-$85.** 1060 Riverside Dr. Jct US 20 Bypass and SR 26, just s. Int corridors. **Pets:** Other species. $25 one-time fee/room. Service with restrictions, supervision.
[SAVE] 🆂 ✕ 🔲 🖵 ➳

# GALENA

**◆◆◆ ▼◆▼ Best Western Quiet House & Suites** 🆂🅷 🐾
(815) 777-2577. **$70-$205.** 9915 US Route 20 W. 1 mi e. Ext/int corridors. **Pets:** $15 one-time fee/pet. Designated rooms, service with restrictions, supervision.
[SAVE] ✕ 🔲 🖵 ➳

**◆◆◆ ▼◆▼◆ Eagle Ridge Resort & Spa** 🅻🅷
(815) 777-2444. **$149-$309, 7 day notice.** 444 Eagle Ridge Dr. 6 mi e on US 20, then 4.5 mi n. Ext/int corridors. **Pets:** Small, dogs only. $75 one-time fee/room. Service with restrictions, crate.
[SAVE] ✕ 🖵 🔲 🖵 ▥ ➳ ✕

# GALESBURG

**◆◆◆ ▼◆▼◆ Best Western Prairie Inn** 🆂🅷
(309) 343-7151. **$92.** 300 S Soangetaha Rd. I-74, exit 48 (Main St), just e, then just s. Int corridors. **Pets:** Large, other species. Designated rooms, service with restrictions.
[SAVE] 🆂 ✕ 🖵 🖵 🔲 🖵 ▥ ➳ ✕

**▼◆ ▼◆ Comfort Inn by Choice Hotels** 🆂🅷
(309) 344-5445. **$64-$104.** 907 W Carl Sandburg Dr. US 34, exit US 150 E. Int corridors. **Pets:** $15 one-time fee/room. Service with restrictions, supervision.
[ASK] 🆂 ✕ 🅜 🖵 🔲 🖵

# GALVA

**▼◆ ▼◆ Super 8 Motel** 🆂🅷
(309) 932-2841. **$60-$80.** 100 Commercial St. On SR 34; downtown. Int corridors. **Pets:** Accepted.
[ASK] 🆂 ✕ 🖵 🔲 🖵

# GILMAN

**◆◆◆ ▼◆▼ Super 8 Motel** 🆂🅷 🐾
(815) 265-7000. **$67-$79.** 1301 S Crescent St. I-57, exit 283, 0.3 mi e. Int corridors. **Pets:** Small. $25 deposit/pet, $5 daily fee/pet. Service with restrictions, supervision.
[SAVE] 🆂 ✕ 🖵 🔲

▼▼ Travel Inn **M**
(815) 265-7283. **$65-$75.** 834 US 24 W. I-57, exit 283, just e. Ext/int corridors. **Pets:** Large. $5 one-time fee/pet. Designated rooms, service with restrictions, supervision.

ASK ⊠ ⤜

## GRAYVILLE

▼▼ Best Western Windsor Oaks Inn **SH**
(618) 375-7930. **$73-$88.** 2200 S Court St. I-64, exit 130 (SR 1), just n. Int corridors. **Pets:** Other species. $5 daily fee/room. Service with restrictions, crate.

ASK SM ⊠ ⚗ 🛗 🖵 ⊺¶ ⤜

▼▼ Super 8 Motel **SH**
(618) 375-7288. **$59-$90, 14 day notice.** 2060 Co Rd. I-64, exit 130 (SR 1), just n. Int corridors. **Pets:** Other species. $10 one-time fee/room. Service with restrictions, supervision.

ASK SM ⊠ ⚹M ⚗ 🛗 🖵

## GREENVILLE

◈◈◈ ▼▼ Best Western Country View Inn **SH**
(618) 664-3030. **$45-$75.** 1731 S SR 127. I-70, exit 45; from jct SR 127 and I-70, just n. Ext/int corridors. **Pets:** Accepted.

SAVE SM ⊠ ⚗ 🛗 🖵 ⤜

## HIGHLAND

▼▼▼ Holiday Inn Express **SH**
(618) 651-1100. **$81-$142, 3 day notice.** 20 Central Blvd. I-70, exit 24 (SR 143), 4 mi s. Int corridors. **Pets:** Accepted.

ASK SM ⊠ 🛗 🖵 ⤜

## JACKSONVILLE

◈◈◈ ▼ Starlite Motel **M** ❦
(217) 245-7184. **$45-$52, 5 day notice.** 1910 W Morton Ave. I-72, exit 64, 2.3 mi n on SR 267 (Main St) to SR 104 (Morton Ave), then 1.8 mi w. Ext corridors. **Pets:** Small. $5 daily fee/pet. Service with restrictions, crate.

SAVE SM ⊠ 🛗

▼ Super 8 Motel **SH**
(217) 479-0303. **$40-$75.** 1003 W Morton Ave. I-72, exit 64, 2.3 mi n on SR 267 (Main St) to SR 104 (Morton Ave), then 0.8 mi w. Int corridors. **Pets:** Medium, other species. $10 daily fee/pet. Crate.

ASK SM ⊠ 🛗

## LINCOLN

▼▼ Holiday Inn Express **SH**
(217) 735-5800. **$79-$125.** 130 Olson Dr. I-55, exit 126 (US 121), just e to Heitman Dr, just w to Olson Dr, then just n. Int corridors. **Pets:** Medium, other species. Designated rooms, service with restrictions, supervision.

SM ⊠ ⚗ ⚹ 🛗 🖵 ⤜

## LITCHFIELD

▼▼▼ Holiday Inn Express **SH**
(217) 324-4556. **$72-$87.** 1405 W Hudson Dr. I-55, exit 52 (SR 16), just e to Ohren Ln, just s to W Hudson Dr, then just w. Int corridors. **Pets:** Small. Designated rooms, service with restrictions, supervision.

ASK SM ⊠ 🛗 🖵 ⤜

## MACOMB

▼ Super 8 Motel **SH**
(309) 836-8888. **$45-$125.** 313 University Dr. 1.1 mi n on US 67 to University Dr, 0.5 mi w. Int corridors. **Pets:** Accepted.

ASK SM ⊠ ⚗ 🛗

## MANTENO

◈◈◈ ▼▼▼ Country Inn & Suites by Carlson **SH**
(815) 468-2600. **$79-$149.** 380 S Cypress St. I-57, exit 322, just se via frontage road. Int corridors. **Pets:** Accepted.

SAVE SM ⊠ ⚹M ⚗ ⚹ 🛗 🖵 ⤜

## MARION

▼▼ Comfort Inn **SH** ❦
(618) 993-6221. **$63-$80.** 2600 W Main St. I-57, exit 53 (Main St), just w. Int corridors. **Pets:** Medium. Designated rooms, service with restrictions, crate.

ASK SM ⊠ ⚗ 🛗 🖵 ⤜

▼▼▼ Drury Inn-Marion **SH**
(618) 997-9600. **$80-$130.** 2706 W DeYoung St. I-57, exit 54B (SR 13), 0.5 mi w. Int corridors. **Pets:** Accepted.

ASK ⊠ ⚹M ⚗ ⚹ 🛗 🖵 ⤜

▼▼ Super 8 Motel **SH** ❦
(618) 993-5577. **$50-$80.** 2601 W DeYoung St. I-57, exit 54B (SR 13), just w. Int corridors. **Pets:** Other species. Service with restrictions, crate.

ASK SM ⊠ ⚗ 🛗 🖵

## MATTOON

▼▼ Super 8 Motel **M**
(217) 235-8888. **$51-$100.** 205 McFall Rd. I-57, exit 190B, just w. Int corridors. **Pets:** Small, other species. $10 daily fee/pet. Designated rooms, supervision.

ASK SM ⊠ 🛗 🖵

## METROPOLIS

▼▼▼ Isle of View Bed & Breakfast **BB**
(618) 524-5838. **$95-$145, 7 day notice.** 205 Metropolis St. I-24, exit 37, 3 mi w, then 0.3 mi s of US 45. Int corridors. **Pets:** Other species. Supervision.

## MONTICELLO

◈◈◈ ▼▼▼ Best Western Monticello Gateway Inn **SH**
(217) 762-9436. **$50-$85, 3 day notice.** 805 Iron Horse Pl. I-72, exit 166, just s. Ext/int corridors. **Pets:** Small. $10 daily fee/pet. Designated rooms.

SAVE SM ⊠ 🛗 🖵 ⤜

## MORRIS

▼▼ Days Inn & Suites **SH**
(815) 942-9000. **$70-$75.** 80 Hampton Rd. I-80, exit 112, just n. Int corridors. **Pets:** Other species. Service with restrictions.

ASK SM ⊠ ⚹ 🛗 🖵 ⤜

▼▼ Holiday Inn **SH**
(815) 942-6600. **$90-$100.** 200 Gore Rd. I-80, exit 112, 0.3 mi nw. Int corridors. **Pets:** Accepted.

ASK SM ⊠ ⚹ 🛗 🖵 ⊺¶ ⤜ ⊠

## MORTON

◈◈◈ ▼▼▼ Best Western Ashland House Inn & Conference Center **SH**
(309) 263-5116. **$69-$99.** 201 E Ashland St. I-74, exit 102, 0.3 mi ne. Int corridors. **Pets:** Accepted.

SAVE SM ⊠ 🛗 🖵 ⊺¶ ⤜ ⊠

▼▼ Quality Inn **SH**
(309) 266-8310. **$59-$69.** 115 E Ashland St. I-74, exit 102B, just w. Ext/int corridors. **Pets:** Accepted.

ASK SM ⊠ 🛗 🖵

# MOUNT VERNON

**▼▼▼▼ Drury Inn-Mount Vernon** 🆂🅷
(618) 244-4550. **$76-$128.** 145 N 44th St. I-57/64, exit 95 (SR 15), just
e, then just n; entry through restaurant parking lot. Int corridors.
**Pets:** Accepted.
Ⓐ🆂🅺 ⊠ 🗐 🛢 🖵 🛥

**Ⓐ ▼▼▼▼ Holiday Inn** 🅻🅷
(618) 244-7100. **$91-$120.** 222 Potomac Blvd. I-57/64, exit 95 (SR 15),
just w to Potomac Blvd, then just n. Int corridors. **Pets:** Medium. $10
one-time fee/pet. Designated rooms, supervision.
🆂🅰🆅🅴 🆂🅳 ⊠ 🗐 🛢 🖵 🍴 🛥 ⊠

**▼▼ Super 8 Motel** 🆂🅷 🐾
(618) 242-8800. **$59-$85.** 401 S 44th St. I-57/64, exit 95 (SR 15), just
e, then just s. Int corridors. **Pets:** Other species. Service with restrictions,
supervision.
Ⓐ🆂🅺 🆂🅳 ⊠ 🗐 🛢 🖵

# NASHVILLE

**Ⓐ ▼▼▼▼ Best Western U.S. Inn** 🆂🅷
(618) 478-5341. **$65-$79.** 11640 SR 127. I-64, exit 50 (SR 127), 0.3 mi
s. Int corridors. **Pets:** Medium. $10 daily fee/pet. Designated rooms, serv-
ice with restrictions, supervision.
🆂🅰🆅🅴 🆂🅳 ⊠ 🗐 🛢 🖵 🏊

# NORMAL

**Ⓐ ▼▼▼▼ Best Western University Inn** 🆂🅷
(309) 454-4070. **$77-$37.** 6 Traders Cir. I-55, exit 165A (US 51), just s,
then return on frontage road. Int corridors. **Pets:** $10 one-time fee/room.
Service with restrictions, supervision.
🆂🅰🆅🅴 🆂🅳 ⊠ 🗐 🛢 🖵

**▼▼ Comfort Suites by Choice Hotels
Bloomington/Normal** 🆂🅷
(309) 452-8588. **$80-$110.** 310 B Greenbriar Dr. I-55, exit 167, follow
I-55 business route (Veterans Pkwy), 1.3 mi s; jct Fort Jesse Rd. Int
corridors. **Pets:** Accepted.
Ⓐ🆂🅺 🆂🅳 ⊠ 🗐 🛢 🖵 🛥

**▼▼ Holiday Inn Bloomington-Normal** 🆂🅷
(309) 452-8300. **$89-$99.** 8 Traders Cir. I-55, exit 165A, 0.5 mi e, return
on service road. Int corridors. **Pets:** Accepted.
Ⓐ🆂🅺 🆂🅳 ⊠ 🗐 🛢 🖵 🍴 🛥 ⊠

**▼▼ Signature Inn-Bloomington/Normal** 🆂🅷
(309) 454-4044. **$74-$99.** 101 S Veterans Pkwy. I-55, exit 167, follow
I-55 business route (Veterans Pkwy), 1.5 mi s. Int corridors. **Pets:** Very
small, other species. $10 daily fee/room. Service with restrictions, supervi-
sion.
Ⓐ🆂🅺 ⊠ 🗐 🛢 🖵

# O'FALLON

**Ⓐ ▼▼▼▼ Comfort Inn** 🆂🅷
(618) 624-6060. **$69-$129.** 1100 Eastgate Dr. I-64, exit 19B (SR 158),
0.5 mi n, then just sw. Int corridors. **Pets:** Other species. $50 deposit/pet.
🆂🅰🆅🅴 🆂🅳 ⊠ 🗐 🛢 🖵

**▼▼ Quality Inn** 🆂🅷
(618) 628-8895. **$55-$99.** 1409 W Hwy 50. I-64, exit 14 (US 50), 0.4 mi
w. Int corridors. **Pets:** Other species. $10 daily fee/room. Designated
rooms, service with restrictions, supervision.
Ⓐ🆂🅺 🆂🅳 ⊠ 🗐 🛢 🖵

# OGLESBY

**▼▼ Holiday Inn Express** 🆂🅷
(815) 883-3535. **$79-$159.** 900 Holiday St. I-39, exit 54, just e. Int
corridors. **Pets:** Other species. Designated rooms, service with restrictions,
supervision.
Ⓐ🆂🅺 🆂🅳 ⊠ 🗐 🖵 🛥

# OTTAWA

**▼▼▼▼ Hampton Inn** 🆂🅷
(815) 434-6040. **$93-$213.** 4115 Holiday Ln. I-80, exit 90 (SR 23), just
n. Int corridors. **Pets:** Accepted.
Ⓐ🆂🅺 🆂🅳 ⊠ 🅼 🗐 🛢 🖵 🛥 ⊠

**▼▼ Holiday Inn Express** 🆂🅷
(815) 433-0029. **$85-$115.** 120 W Stevenson Rd. I-80, exit 90 (SR 23),
just n. Int corridors. **Pets:** Medium, other species. Designated rooms,
service with restrictions, supervision.
Ⓐ🆂🅺 🆂🅳 ⊠ 🗐 🛢 🖵 🛥

# PEKIN

**Ⓐ ▼▼▼▼ Econo Lodge Inn & Suites** 🆂🅷
(309) 353-4047. **$65-$90.** 3240 Vandever Ave. Just n of SR 9; 3 mi e of
jct SR 29. Int corridors. **Pets:** Accepted.
🆂🅰🆅🅴 🆂🅳 ⊠ 🗐 🛢 🖵 🛥

# PEORIA

**▼▼ AmericInn Lodge & Suites** 🆂🅷
(309) 692-9200. **$95-$175.** 9106 N Lindbergh Dr. SR 6, exit 6, 0.5 mi s.
Int corridors. **Pets:** Small. $15 daily fee/room. Service with restrictions,
supervision.
Ⓐ🆂🅺 🆂🅳 ⊠ 🗐 🛢 🖵 🛥 ⊠

**▼▼ Best Western Signature Inn** 🆂🅷
(309) 685-2556. **$74-$99.** 4112 N Brandywine Dr. I-74, exit 89 (US
150/War Memorial Dr), just e, then just n. Int corridors. **Pets:** Very
small, other species. $10 daily fee/room. Service with restrictions, supervi-
sion.
Ⓐ🆂🅺 ⊠ 🗐 🛢 🖵

**▼▼ Comfort Suites by Choice Hotels** 🆂🅷
(309) 688-3800. **$90-$95.** 1812 W War Memorial Dr. I-74, exit 89 (US
150/War Memorial Dr), just e, then just s. Int corridors. **Pets:** Accepted.
Ⓐ🆂🅺 🆂🅳 ⊠ 🗐 🛢 🖵 🛥

**▼ Red Roof Inn #7057** 🅼
(309) 685-3911. **$45-$67.** 1822 W War Memorial Dr. I-74, exit 89 (US
150/War Memorial Dr), just e. Ext corridors. **Pets:** Accepted.
⊠ 🗐 🛢 🖵

**▼▼▼ Residence Inn by Marriott** 🆂🅷
(309) 681-9000. **$130-$170, 14 day notice.** 2000 W War Memorial Dr.
I-74, exit 89 (US 150/War Memorial Dr), just w; entrance through
Northwoods Mall. Int corridors. **Pets:** Accepted.
Ⓐ🆂🅺 🆂🅳 ⊠ 🗐 🛢 🖵 ⊠

**▼▼▼▼ Staybridge Suites Peoria-Downtown** 🆂🅷
(309) 673-7829. **$99-$199.** 300 W Romeo B Garrett Ave. I-74, exit 92
(Glendale Ave), 0.5 mi w (Glendale Ave becomes William Kumpf St),
then just w on Fourth Ave. Int corridors. **Pets:** Small, dogs only. $75
one-time fee/pet. Designated rooms, service with restrictions, crate.
Ⓐ🆂🅺 🆂🅳 ⊠ 🗐 🛢 🖵 ⊠

**▼ Super 8 Motel** 🆂🅷
(309) 688-8074. **$61-$81.** 1816 W War Memorial Dr. I-74, exit 89 (US
150/War Memorial Dr), just e. Int corridors. **Pets:** Other species. $50
deposit/pet. Service with restrictions, supervision.
Ⓐ🆂🅺 🆂🅳 ⊠ 🗐 🛢 🖵

# PERU

**▼▼ La Quinta Inn Peru** 🆂🅷
(815) 224-9000. **$72-$76.** 4389 Venture Dr. I-80, exit 75 (SR 251), 0.4
mi s to 38th St, just w to Venture Dr, then 0.4 mi nw. Int corridors.
**Pets:** Small. Service with restrictions, supervision.
Ⓐ🆂🅺 🆂🅳 ⊠ 🗐 🛢 🖵 🛥 ⊠

## PONTIAC

### ▼▼ Comfort Inn by Choice Hotels SH
(815) 842-2777. **$69-$125, 14 day notice.** 1821 W Reynolds St. I-55, exit 197 (SR 116), just e. Int corridors. **Pets:** Accepted.
(ASK) (S&) (X) (🛏) (💻) (🏊)

## PONTOON BEACH

### ◆◆◆ ▼▼▼ Best Western Camelot Inn SH
(618) 931-2262. **$53-$83, 7 day notice.** 1240 E Old Chain of Rocks Rd. I-270, exit 6B (SR 111), just n. Int corridors. **Pets:** Accepted.
(SAVE) (S&) (X) (🛏) (💻) (🏊)

---

## QUAD CITIES AREA

## MOLINE

### ▼▼ Comfort Inn by Choice Hotels SH
(309) 762-7000. **$60-$90.** 2600 52nd Ave. I-280/74, exit 18A eastbound; exit 5B westbound, just s to traffic light, then 0.5 mi w on 27th St. Int corridors. **Pets:** Accepted.
(ASK) (S&) (X) (🛏) (💻) (🏊)

### ▼▼ Econo Lodge SH
(309) 762-1548. **$59-$89.** 6920 27th St. I-280/74, exit 18A eastbound; exit 5B westbound, just s on US 6 and 150, then just nw. Int corridors. **Pets:** Medium. $10 daily fee/pet. Designated rooms, service with restrictions, supervision.
(ASK) (S&) (X) (🛏) (💻) (🏊)

### ◆◆◆ ▼ Exel Inn of Moline SH
(309) 797-5580. **$44-$64.** 2501 52nd Ave. I-280/74, exit 18A eastbound; exit 5B westbound, just s on US 6 and 150, then 1 mi nw on 27th St. Int corridors. **Pets:** Small, other species. Designated rooms, service with restrictions, supervision.
(SAVE) (S&) (X) (🚭) (🛏) (💻)

### ◆◆◆ ▼▼ Holiday Inn Express-Moline Airport SH
(309) 762-8300. **$89-$159.** 6910 27th St. I-280/74, exit 18A eastbound; exit 5B westbound, just s on US 6 and 150, then just nw. Int corridors. **Pets:** Accepted.
(SAVE) (S&) (X) (🚭) (🛏) (💻)

### ◆◆◆ ▼▼▼ La Quinta Inn Moline SH
(309) 762-9008. **$65-$105.** 5450 27th St. I-280/74, exit 18A eastbound; exit 5B westbound, just s on US 6 and 150 to traffic light, then just nw. Int corridors. **Pets:** Medium. Service with restrictions.
(SAVE) (X) (🚭) (🛏) (💻) (🏊)

### ▼▼ Quality Inn & Suites by Choice Hotels SH
(309) 762-1711. **$69-$109.** 6920 27th St. I-280/74, exit 18A eastbound; exit 5B westbound, just s on US 6 and 150, then just nw. Int corridors. **Pets:** Medium. $10 daily fee/pet. Designated rooms, service with restrictions, supervision.
(ASK) (S&) (X) (🛏) (💻) (🏊)

## ROCK ISLAND

### ◆◆◆ ▼▼▼ Four Points by Sheraton LH
(309) 794-1212. **$90-$160.** 226 17th St. Just e of Centennial Bridge; at 3rd Ave and 17th St; downtown. Int corridors. **Pets:** Accepted.
(SAVE) (S&) (X) (🚭) (🛏) (💻) (🍽) (🏊) (⊠)

---

## END AREA

## QUINCY

### ▼▼ Comfort Inn by Choice Hotels SH
(217) 228-2700. **$59-$89.** 4122 Broadway. I-172, exit 14 (SR 104), 1.3 mi w. Int corridors. **Pets:** Accepted.
(ASK) (S&) (X) (🛏) (💻) (🏊)

### ◆◆◆ ▼ Super 8 Motel SH
(217) 228-8808. **$60-$103, 14 day notice.** 224 N 36th St. I-172, exit 14 (SR 104), 1.8 mi w, then just s. Int corridors. **Pets:** Other species. Service with restrictions, crate.
(SAVE) (S&) (X) (&M) (🛏)

## RANTOUL

### ◆◆◆ ▼▼▼ Best Western Heritage Inn SH
(217) 892-9292. **$59-$110.** 420 S Murray Rd. I-57, exit 250 (US 136), 0.5 mi e, then just s. Ext corridors. **Pets:** Small, other species. $5 daily fee/pet. Service with restrictions, crate.
(SAVE) (S&) (X) (🛏) (💻) (🏊)

### ▼▼ Super 8 Motel SH
(217) 893-8888. **$56-$63, 4 day notice.** 207 S Murray Rd. I-57, exit 250 (US 136), just e. Int corridors. **Pets:** Accepted.
(ASK) (S&) (X) (🛏) (💻)

## ROBINSON

### ▼▼ Best Western Robinson Inn SH
(618) 544-8448. **$71-$110.** 1500 W Main St. 1 mi w on SR 33. Int corridors. **Pets:** Other species. $5 daily fee/room. Service with restrictions, supervision.
(ASK) (S&) (X) (🚭) (🛏) (💻)

## ROCHELLE

### ◆◆◆ ▼▼ AmeriHost Inn-Rochelle SH 🐾
(815) 562-9530. **$69-$169.** 567 E Hwy 38. I-39, exit 99 (SR 38), 1 mi w. Int corridors. **Pets:** Other species. $25 deposit/room. Designated rooms, service with restrictions, supervision.
(SAVE) (S&) (X) (🛏) (💻) (🏊)

### ◆◆◆ ▼▼▼ Comfort Inn & Suites SH 🐾
(815) 562-5551. **$74-$189.** 1131 N 7th St. I-39, exit 99 (SR 38), 2.5 mi w; jct SR 38 and 251; downtown. Int corridors. **Pets:** Other species. $25 one-time fee/room. Designated rooms, service with restrictions, supervision.
(SAVE) (S&) (X) (🛏) (💻) (🍽) (🏊) (⊠)

### ▼▼▼ Holiday Inn Express SH 🐾
(815) 562-9994. **$99.** 1240 Dement Rd. I-39, exit 99, just nw. Int corridors. **Pets:** Other species. $25 one-time fee/room. Designated rooms, service with restrictions, supervision.
(ASK) (S&) (X) (&M) (🚭) (🛏) (💻) (🏊)

## ROCK FALLS

### ▼ Rock Falls Super 8 SH
(815) 626-8800. **$60-$80.** 2100 First Ave. I-88, exit 41 (SR 40), 0.3 mi n, then just w on W 21st St. Int corridors. **Pets:** Other species. $20 one-time fee/room. No service, supervision.
(ASK) (S&) (X) (🛏)

# ROCKFORD

**Baymont Inn & Suites Rockford** SH
(815) 229-8200. **$59-$180.** 662 N Lyford Rd. I-90, exit US 20 business route, just e, then just n. Int corridors. **Pets:** Small. Service with restrictions, supervision.

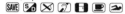

**Comfort Inn by Choice Hotels** SH
(815) 398-7061. **$69-$94.** 7392 Argus Dr. I-90, exit US 20 business route, just w to Bell School Rd, then just n. Int corridors. **Pets:** Accepted.

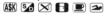

**Exel Inn of Rockford** SH
(815) 332-4915. **$46-$76.** 220 S Lyford Rd. I-90, exit US 20 business route, just e, then just s. Int corridors. **Pets:** Small, other species. Designated rooms, service with restrictions, supervision.

**Quality Suites** SH
(815) 227-1300. **$89-$209.** 7401 Walton St. I-90, exit US 20 business route, just w to Bell School Rd, then just s. Int corridors. **Pets:** Medium, other species. Service with restrictions, crate.

**Red Roof Inn #7035** M
(815) 398-9750. **$49-$70.** 7434 E State St. I-90, exit US 20 business route, just w. Ext corridors. **Pets:** Accepted.

**Residence Inn by Marriott** SH
(815) 227-0013. **$89-$199, 14 day notice.** 7542 Colosseum Dr. I-90, exit US 20 business route, just w. Int corridors. **Pets:** Accepted.

**Sleep Inn-Rockford** SH
(815) 398-8900. **$55-$100.** 725 Clark Dr. I-90, exit US 20 business route, just w to Bell School Rd, just n to Clark Dr, then 0.4 mi ne. Int corridors. **Pets:** Accepted.

**Sweden House Lodge** SH
(815) 398-4130. **$50-$75, 7 day notice.** 4605 E State St. I-90, exit US 20 business route, 4 mi w. Ext/int corridors. **Pets:** Accepted.

# SALEM

**Super 8 Motel of Salem** SH
(618) 548-5882. **$60-$87.** 118 Woods Ln. I-57, exit 116 (US 50), just w. Ext/int corridors. **Pets:** Designated rooms, service with restrictions, supervision.

# SAVOY

**Best Western Paradise Inn** SH
(217) 356-1824. **$72-$95, 7 day notice.** 709 N Dunlap. I-57, exit 229, 1 mi e to US 45, then 2.5 mi n. Ext corridors. **Pets:** Small. $25 deposit/room, $5 daily fee/pet. Service with restrictions, supervision.

# SOUTH JACKSONVILLE

**Comfort Inn-South Jacksonville** SH
(217) 245-8372. **$61-$109.** 200 Comfort Dr. I-72, exit 64, just n. Int corridors. **Pets:** Accepted.

**Econo Lodge Inn & Suites by Choice Hotels** SH
(217) 245-9575. **$70-$95.** 1914 Southbrooke Rd. I-72, exit 64, just n. Int corridors. **Pets:** Other species. $20 one-time fee/room. Designated rooms, service with restrictions, supervision.

# SPRINGFIELD

**Baymont Inn Springfield** SH
(217) 529-6655. **$75, 3 day notice.** 5871 S 6th St. I-55, exit 90 (Toronto Rd), just e to 6th St, then just n. Int corridors. **Pets:** Accepted.

**Comfort Inn by Choice Hotels** SH
(217) 787-2250. **$69-$99.** 3442 Freedom Dr. I-72, exit 93 (Veterans Pkwy), 0.7 mi n to Lindbergh Blvd, just w to Freedom Dr, then just s. Int corridors. **Pets:** Accepted.

**Days Inn** M
(217) 529-0171. **$70-$90, 3 day notice.** 3000 Stevenson Dr. I-55, exit 94 (Stevenson Dr), just w. Ext corridors. **Pets:** Accepted.

**Drury Inn & Suites-Springfield** SH
(217) 529-3900. **$95-$125.** 3180 S Dirksen Pkwy. I-55, exit 94 (Stevenson Dr), just w to Dirksen Pkwy, then just n. Int corridors. **Pets:** Accepted.

**Microtel Inn & Suites** SH
(217) 753-2636. **$65-$99.** 2636 Sunrise Dr. I-55, exit 94 (Stevenson Dr), just w to Dirksen Pkwy, then 0.4 mi n. Int corridors. **Pets:** Small. $5 daily fee/pet. Service with restrictions, crate.

**Pear Tree Inn by Drury-Springfield** SH
(217) 529-9100. **$75-$108.** 3190 S Dirksen Pkwy. I-55, exit 94 (Stevenson Dr), just w. Int corridors. **Pets:** Accepted.

**Ramada Limited (South)** SH
(217) 529-1410. **$49-$119.** 5970 S 6th St. I-55, exit 90 (Toronto Rd), 0.3 mi e. Int corridors. **Pets:** Accepted.

**Red Roof Inn #7040** M
(217) 753-4302. **$45-$65.** 3200 Singer Ave. I-55, exit 96B, just w. Ext corridors. **Pets:** Accepted.

**Sleep Inn by Choice Hotels** SH
(217) 787-6200. **$70-$110.** 3470 Freedom Dr. I-72, exit 93 (Veterans Pkwy), 0.7 mi n to Lindbergh Blvd, just w to Freedom Dr, then just s. Int corridors. **Pets:** Accepted.

**The State House Inn, A Clarion Collection Hotel** SH
(217) 528-5100. **$89-$130.** 101 E Adams St. Jct 1st and Adams sts; just n of the State House. Int corridors. **Pets:** Accepted.

**Staybridge Suites Springfield South** SH
(217) 793-6700. **$99-$159.** 4231 Schooner Dr. I-72, exit 93, 0.4 mi se. Int corridors. **Pets:** Medium. $75 deposit/room, $75 one-time fee/room. Service with restrictions, supervision.

# STAUNTON

**Staunton Super 8** SH
(618) 635-5353. **$39-$70.** 1527 Herman Rd. I-55, exit 41, 0.3 mi w. Int corridors. **Pets:** Medium. $10 one-time fee/pet. Service with restrictions, supervision.

# STOCKTON

**▼▼▼▼ Country Inn & Suites By Carlson** SH
(815) 947-6060. **$79-$121.** 200 Dillon Ave. On US 20, just e of SR 78. Int corridors. **Pets:** Medium. $20 daily fee/room. Designated rooms, service with restrictions, supervision.
ASK SD X GM S H ED

# SYCAMORE

**▼▼▼ Americas Best Value Inn & Suites** SH
(815) 899-6500. **$59-$99.** 1860 Dekalb Ave. On SR 23, 0.9 mi s of Peace Rd. Int corridors. **Pets:** Accepted.
ASK SD X GM S H ED

**♦♦♦ ▼▼▼ AmeriHost Inn-Sycamore** SH
(815) 895-4979. **$99-$109.** 1475 S Peace Rd. I-88, exit Peace Rd, 5.5 mi n to jct SR 23. Int corridors. **Pets:** Accepted.
SAVE X GM S H ED

# TUSCOLA

**▼▼▼ AmeriHost Inn-Tuscola** SH
(217) 253-3500. **$56-$100.** 1006 Southline Rd. I-57, exit 212 (US 36), 0.3 mi w. Int corridors. **Pets:** Accepted.
ASK SD X GM S H ED

**▼▼▼ Holiday Inn Express** SH
(217) 253-6363. **$66-$89.** 1201 Tuscola Blvd. I-57, exit 212 (US 36), 0.3 mi w to Progress Blvd, just s to Tuscola Blvd, then 0.4 mi se. Int corridors. **Pets:** Medium. Designated rooms, service with restrictions, supervision.
ASK SD X GM S H ED

**▼▼▼ Super 8 Motel-Tuscola** SH
(217) 253-5488. **$69, 10 day notice.** 1007 E Southline Dr. I-57, exit 212 (US 36), 0.4 mi w. Int corridors. **Pets:** Other species. $10 daily fee/pet. Designated rooms, no service, supervision.
ASK SD X H ED

# URBANA

**♦♦♦ ▼▼▼ Ramada Limited-Urbana/Champaign** SH ❀
(217) 328-4400. **$79-$102.** 902 W Killarney St. I-74, exit 183 (Lincoln Ave), just s to Killarney St, then just w. Int corridors. **Pets:** $50 deposit/room. Service with restrictions, crate.
SAVE SD X H ED

**▼▼ Sleep Inn** SH ❀
(217) 367-6000. **$76-$105, 7 day notice.** 1908 N Lincoln Ave. I-74, exit 183 (Lincoln Ave), 0.5 mi s. Int corridors. **Pets:** Other species. $7 one-time fee/room. Service with restrictions, supervision.
ASK SD X S H ED

# VANDALIA

**♦♦♦ ▼▼ Days Inn** M
(618) 283-4400. **$61-$81.** 1920 Kennedy Blvd. I-70, exit 63 (US 51), 0.6 mi n. Ext corridors. **Pets:** Other species. $10 deposit/room. Service with restrictions, crate.
SAVE SD X H ED

**♦♦♦ ▼▼ Jay's Inn** M
(618) 283-1200. **$49-$61.** 720 Gochenour St. I-70, exit 63 (US 51), just s. Ext corridors. **Pets:** Other species. Service with restrictions.
SAVE SD X H ED

**♦♦♦ ▼▼ Ramada Limited Vandalia** SH
(618) 283-1400. **$57-$70.** 2707 Veterans Ave. I-70, exit 61, just s. Int corridors. **Pets:** Other species. $10 one-time fee/pet. Designated rooms, no service, crate.
SAVE X H ED

# WASHINGTON

**▼ Super 8 Motel-Peouia Area** SH
(309) 444-8881. **$60-$80.** 1884 Washington Rd. On Business Rt SR 24, 1.5 mi w. Int corridors. **Pets:** Accepted.
ASK SD X H

# WATSEKA

**♦♦♦ ▼▼▼ Super 8 Motel** SH ❀
(815) 432-6000. **$68-$82.** 710 W Walnut. On US 24; center of downtown. Int corridors. **Pets:** Small. $25 deposit/pet, $5 daily fee/pet. Service with restrictions, supervision.
SAVE SD X H

# WEST CITY

**▼▼ Super 8 Motel of Benton/West City** SH
(618) 438-8205. **$65-$89.** 711 1/2 W Main St. I-57, exit 71 (SR 14), just e. Int corridors. **Pets:** Accepted.
ASK SD X S

# INDIANA

## ANGOLA

**WWW Ramada Inn** SH
(260) 665-9471. **$72-$200.** 3855 N SR 127. I-69, exit 154, just e, then 0.4 mi s. Int corridors **Pets:** $25 daily fee/pet. Service with restrictions, supervision.

## AUBURN

**WWW Holiday Inn Express** SH
(260) 925-1900. **$95.** 404 Touring Dr. I-69, exit 129, just e off SR 8. Int corridors. **Pets:** Other species. Designated rooms, service with restrictions, supervision.

**WWW La Quinta Inn Auburn** SH
(260) 920-1900. **$81-$83.** 306 Touring Dr. I-69, exit 129, 0.5 mi e on SR 8. Int corridors. **Pets:** Accepted.

**WW Super 8 Motel-Auburn** SH
(260) 927-8800. **$68-$78.** 503 Ley Dr. I-69, exit 129, just e. Int corridors. **Pets:** Other species. $50 deposit/room, $15 one-time fee/room. Designated rooms, service with restrictions, supervision.

## BEDFORD

**WW Bedford Super 8** SH
(812) 275-8881. **$65-$125.** 501 Bell Back Rd. Jct SR 37 and 58, just e on SR 58. Int corridors. **Pets:** $10 daily fee/pet. Supervision.

## BERNE

**AAA WWW Black Bear Inn & Suites** SH ❖
(260) 589-8955. **$69.** 1335 US 27 N. On US 27, 1 mi n. Int corridors. **Pets:** Medium. Designated rooms, service with restrictions, supervision.

## BLOOMINGTON

**WWW Fairfield Inn by Marriott** SH
(812) 331-1122. **$79-$219.** 120 Fairfield Dr. Just e from SR 37 at 3rd St. Int corridors. **Pets:** Small. $25 one-time fee/pet. Service with restrictions, supervision.

**WWW Hampton Inn** SH
(812) 334-2100. **$94-$249, 30 day notice.** 2100 N Walnut St. 1 mi e of jct SR 37 on SR 45/46 Bypass, then just s on College Ave/Walnut St. Int corridors. **Pets:** Small. Designated rooms, service with restrictions, supervision.

**WWW TownePlace Suites By Marriott** SH
(812) 334-1234. **$89-$169.** 105 S Franklin Rd. Just e from SR 37 at 3rd St, then 0.3 mi n. Int corridors. **Pets:** Other species. $75 one-time fee/room. No service.

## BLUFFTON

**W Budget Inn** M
(260) 824-0820. **$40-$55.** 1090 N Main St. Jct SR 1 and 116; north side of town. Ext corridors. **Pets:** Dogs only. $5 daily fee/pet. Service with restrictions, supervision.

## CHESTERTON

**WWW Gray Goose Inn** BB ❖
(219) 926-5781. **$95-$125, 10 day notice.** 350 Indian Boundary Rd. I-94, exit 26A, 0.6 mi s to Indian Boundary Rd, then 0.3 mi w. Int corridors. **Pets:** Service with restrictions, crate.

# NEARBY OHIO
# CINCINNATI METROPOLITAN AREA

## LAWRENCEBURG

**▼▼▼ Quality Inn & Suites** 🅂🄷
(812) 539-4770. **$89-$129.** 1000 E Eads Pkwy. I-275, exit 16, 0.5 mi w on US 50. Int corridors. **Pets:** Medium, other species. $20 daily fee/pet. Service with restrictions, crate.
(ASK) 🅂🄾 ⊠ 🄴 🄱 🄳 ⇌

# END METROPOLITAN AREA

## CLARKSVILLE

**🅐🅐🅐 ▼▼▼ Best Western Green Tree Inn** 🅼
(812) 288-9281. **$75.** 1425 Broadway St. I-65, exit 4, just w. Ext corridors. **Pets:** Medium, dogs only. $20 deposit/room. Service with restrictions, crate.
(SAVE) 🅂🄾 ⊠ 🄱 🄳 ⇌

## CLOVERDALE

**▼▼ Super 8 Motel Cloverdale/Greencastle** 🅂🄷
(765) 795-7373. **$55-$80.** 1020 N Main St. I-70, exit 41, just s. Int corridors. **Pets:** Small, dogs only. Service with restrictions, supervision.
(ASK) 🅂🄾 ⊠ 🄴 🄱 🄳 ⇌

## COLUMBIA CITY

**🅐🅐🅐 ▼▼▼ AmeriHost Inn & Suites** 🅂🄷
(260) 248-4551. **$69-$89.** 701 W Connexion Way. 1 mi w, just off US 30. Int corridors. **Pets:** $10 daily fee/pet. Service with restrictions, supervision.
(SAVE) 🅂🄾 ⊠ 🄻🄼 🄴 🄱 🄳 ⇌

## COLUMBUS

**🅐🅐🅐 ▼▼▼ Columbus Holiday Inn and Conference Center** 🅂🄷
(812) 372-1541. **$96-$140.** 2480 Jonathan Moore Pike. I-65, exit 68, just e on SR 46. Ext/int corridors. **Pets:** $25 one-time fee/room. Designated rooms, service with restrictions, supervision.
(SAVE) 🅂🄾 ⊠ 🄻🄼 🄽 🄴 🄱 🄳 🍴 ⇌ ⊠

**🅐🅐🅐 ▼▼▼ Days Inn Columbus** 🅂🄷
(812) 376-9951. **$54-$89.** 3445 Jonathan Moore Pike. I-65, exit 68, just w. Int corridors. **Pets:** Accepted.
(SAVE) 🅂🄾 ⊠ 🄱 🄳 ⇌

## CRAWFORDSVILLE

**🅐🅐🅐 ▼▼▼ Comfort Inn** 🅂🄷
(765) 361-0665. **$79-$179.** 2991 N Gandhi Dr. I-74, exit 34, just s on US 231. Int corridors. **Pets:** $15 daily fee/room. Designated rooms, service with restrictions, supervision.
(SAVE) 🅂🄾 ⊠ 🄱 🄳 ⇌

**▼▼▼▼ Holiday Inn-Crawfordsville** 🅂🄷
(765) 362-8700. **$76-$90.** 2500 N Lafayette Rd. I-74, exit 34, 0.3 mi s on US 231. Ext corridors. **Pets:** Small. $15 daily fee/room. Designated rooms, service with restrictions, supervision.
(ASK) 🅂🄾 ⊠ 🄻🄼 🄽 🄴 🄱 🄳 🍴 ⇌

## DALE

**▼▼▼▼ Baymont Inn & Suites Dale** 🅂🄷
(812) 937-7000. **$60-$235.** 1339 N Washington St. I-64, exit 57 (US 231), just s. Int corridors. **Pets:** Medium, other species. $25 deposit/room. Designated rooms, service with restrictions, supervision.
(ASK) 🅂🄾 ⊠ 🄻🄼 🄴 🄱 🄳 ⇌

**▼▼ Motel 6 #4068** 🅂🄷
(812) 937-2294. **$43-$96.** 1334 N Washington St. I-64, exit 57 (US 231), just s. Int corridors. **Pets:** Accepted.
(ASK) 🅂🄾 ⊠ 🄴 🄱 🄳 ⇌

## DECATUR

**🅐🅐🅐 ▼▼▼ AmeriHost Inn Decatur** 🅂🄷
(260) 728-4600. **$84.** 1201 S 13th St. On US 27 and 33, 1 mi s of jct US 224. Int corridors. **Pets:** $25 deposit/room. Service with restrictions, supervision.
(SAVE) 🅂🄾 ⊠ 🄻🄼 🄽 🄴 🄱 🄳 ⇌

**▼▼▼ Comfort Inn of Decatur** 🅂🄷
(260) 724-8888. **$75-$89.** 1302 S 13th St. 1 mi s on US 27 and 33. Int corridors. **Pets:** Small, dogs only. $5 daily fee/pet. Designated rooms, service with restrictions, crate.
(ASK) 🅂🄾 ⊠ 🄻🄼 🄽 🄴 🄱 🄳 ⇌

**▼▼▼ Days Inn** 🅂🄷
(260) 728-2196. **$53-$79.** 1033 N 13th St. On US 27 and 33, 0.5 mi n of jct US 224. Ext/int corridors. **Pets:** Small, dogs only. $5 daily fee/pet. Service with restrictions, supervision.
(ASK) 🅂🄾 ⊠ 🄱 🄳 ⇌

## ELKHART

**🅐🅐🅐 ▼▼▼ Econo Lodge** 🅼
(574) 262-0540. **$49-$65.** 3440 Cassopolis St. I-80/90, exit 92, 0.3 mi n. Ext corridors. **Pets:** Small. $5 daily fee/pet. Designated rooms, service with restrictions, supervision.
(SAVE) 🅂🄾 ⊠ 🄱 🄳

**▼▼▼ Jameson Inn** 🅂🄷
(574) 264-7222. **$74-$99.** 3010 Brittany Ct. I-80/90, exit 92, 0.3 mi s on SR 19. Int corridors. **Pets:** Very small, other species. $10 daily fee/room. Service with restrictions, supervision.
(ASK) ⊠ 🄽 🄱 🄳 ⇌

**▼▼▼ Ramada** 🅂🄷
(574) 262-1581. **$79-$240, 30 day notice.** 3011 Belvedere Rd. I-80/90, exit 92, 0.3 mi s on SR 19. Int corridors. **Pets:** Small. $10 daily fee/pet. Designated rooms, service with restrictions, supervision.
(ASK) 🅂🄾 ⊠ 🄻🄼 🄴 🄱 🄳 🍴 ⇌

**▼▼▼ Red Roof Inn-Elkhart #7018** 🅼
(574) 262-3691. **$49-$77.** 2902 Cassopolis St. I-80/90, exit 92, 0.5 mi s. Ext corridors. **Pets:** Accepted.
⊠ 🄽 🄴 🄱

## EVANSVILLE

**▼▼▼▼ Baymont Inn & Suites Evansville East** 🅂🄷
(812) 477-2677. **$79-$135.** 8005 E Division St. I-164, exit 7B (SR 66/Lloyd Expwy), 0.5 mi w to Cross Pointe Blvd, just n to Division St, then 0.5 mi e. Int corridors. **Pets:** Small. Designated rooms, service with restrictions, supervision.
(ASK) 🅂🄾 ⊠ 🄻🄼 🄴 🄱 🄳 ⇌

▼▼▼ Baymont Inn & Suites Evansville West SH
(812) 421-9773. **$74-$184.** 5737 Pearl Dr. Jct US 41 and SR 62, 5.7 mi w on SR 62, then just s on Boehne Camp Rd. Int corridors. **Pets:** Small. $15 one-time fee/room. No service, supervision.

[ASK] [S❄] [✕] [⅙M] [♿] [🍴] [💻] [➰] [✕]

♦♦♦ ▼▼▼ Best Western Gateway Inn & Suites SH ❀
(812) 868-8000. **$64-$99.** 324 Rusher Creek Rd. I-64, exit 25A (US 41), 0.5 mi s, then just w. Int corridors. **Pets:** Other species. $15 one-time fee/pet. Service with restrictions, supervision.

[SAVE] [S❄] [✕] [⅙M] [♿] [🍴] [💻] [➰]

♦♦♦ ▼▼▼ Casino Aztar Hotel LH
(812) 433-4000. **$79-$375.** 421 NW Riverside Dr. SR 62 (Lloyd Expwy), just s on Fulton. Int corridors. **Pets:** Small. $100 deposit/room. Service with restrictions.

[SAVE] [S❄] [✕] [⅙M] [♿] [🍴] [💻] [🍴]

▼▼▼ Comfort Inn East SH
(812) 476-3600. **$69-$190.** 8331 E Walnut St. I-164, exit 7B (SR 66/Lloyd Expwy), 0.5 mi w to Eagle Crest Blvd, 0.3 mi se to Fuquay St, just s to Walnut St, then 0.4 mi e. Int corridors. **Pets:** Medium. $10 daily fee/room. Service with restrictions.

[ASK] [S❄] [✕] [⅙M] [🔲] [♿] [🍴] [💻] [➰]

▼▼▼ Drury Inn & Suites-Evansville East SH
(812) 471-3400. **$90-$125.** 100 Cross Pointe Blvd. I-164, exit 7B (SR 66/Lloyd Expwy), 0.5 mi w. Int corridors. **Pets:** Accepted.

[ASK] [✕] [⅙M] [🔲] [♿] [🍴] [💻] [➰] [✕]

▼▼▼ Drury Inn & Suites-Evansville North SH
(812) 423-5818. **$90-$125.** 3901 US 41 N. On US 41, 2.5 mi n of jct SR 62 and 66 (Lloyd Expwy), 3.3 mi sw of Regional Airport entrance. Int corridors. **Pets:** Accepted.

[ASK] [✕] [🍴] [💻] [➰] [✕]

▼ ▼ Econo Lodge SH
(812) 477-2211. **$55-$79.** 5006 Morgan Ave. I-164, exit 9, 1.5 mi w on SR 62. Int corridors. **Pets:** Accepted.

[ASK] [✕] [🔲] [♿] [🍴] [💻]

▼ ▼ Evansville Microtel Inn & Suites SH
(812) 471-9340. **$49-$109.** 1930 Cross Pointe Blvd. I-164, exit 9, just w. Int corridors. **Pets:** Accepted.

[ASK] [S❄] [✕] [🍴] [💻]

▼ ▼ Holiday Inn Express SH
(812) 867-1100. **$56-$78.** 19600 Elpers Rd. I-64, exit 25A (US 41), 0.6 mi s. Int corridors. **Pets:** Accepted.

[ASK] [✕] [⅙M] [♿] [🍴] [💻]

▼ ▼ HomeLife Studios & Suites M
(812) 475-1700. **$35-$99.** 100 S Green River Rd. I-164, exit 7B (SR 66/Lloyd Expwy), 2 mi w to Green River Rd, then just s. Ext corridors. **Pets:** Large. $75 deposit/room, $25 one-time fee/room. Service with restrictions.

[ASK] [S❄] [✕] [🔲] [♿] [🍴] [💻] [➰]

♦♦♦ ▼▼▼ Quality Inn & Suites East SH
(812) 471-3414. **$70-$150, 4 day notice.** 8015 E Division St. I-164, exit 7B (SR 66/Lloyd Expwy), 0.5 mi w to Cross Pointe Blvd, just n, then 0.5 mi e. Int corridors. **Pets:** Very small. $10 daily fee/room. Designated rooms, service with restrictions, supervision.

[SAVE] [S❄] [✕] [⅙M] [♿] [🍴] [💻] [➰]

▼▼▼ Residence Inn Hotel SH
(812) 471-7191. **$109-$159.** 8283 E Walnut St. I-164, exit 7B (SR 66/Lloyd Expwy), 0.5 mi w to Eagle Crest Blvd, 0.3 mi se to Fuquay St, then 0.3 mi e. Int corridors. **Pets:** Accepted.

[✕] [⅙M] [🔲] [♿] [🍴] [💻] [➰] [✕]

▼ ▼ Signature Inn Evansville SH
(812) 476-9626. **$74-$99.** 1101 N Green River Rd. I-164, exit 9 (SR 62 E/Morgan Ave), 1.5 mi w on SR 62, then just s. Int corridors. **Pets:** Very small, other species. $10 daily fee/room. Service with restrictions, supervision.

[ASK] [✕] [🔲] [🍴] [💻] [➰]

# FORT WAYNE

▼ ▼ Baymont Inn Fort Wayne SH
(260) 489-2220. **$52-$91.** 1005 W Washington Center Rd. I-69, exit 111B, just w on SR 3, then just n. Int corridors. **Pets:** Small. $50 deposit/room. Designated rooms, service with restrictions, crate.

[ASK] [S❄] [✕] [⅙M] [🔲] [🍴] [💻]

♦♦♦ ▼ ▼ Best Western Luxury Inn Fort Wayne SH
(260) 436-0242. **$76-$83.** 5501 Coventry Ln. I-69, exit 102. Int corridors. **Pets:** Medium, other species. $10 one-time fee/pet. Crate.

[SAVE] [S❄] [✕] [🍴] [💻] [➰]

♦♦♦ ▼▼▼ Don Hall's Guesthouse SH
(260) 489-2524. **$89-$109.** 1313 W Washington Center Rd. I-69, exit 111B, just n on SR 3, then 0.3 mi e. Ext/int corridors. **Pets:** Small, dogs only. Service with restrictions, supervision.

[SAVE] [S❄] [✕] [🍴] [💻] [🍴] [➰] [✕]

▼ ▼ Fort Wayne Marriott LH
(260) 484-0411. **$189.** 305 E Washington Center Rd. I-69, exit 112A. Int corridors. **Pets:** Accepted.

[ASK] [✕] [🔲] [🍴] [💻] [🍴] [➰] [✕]

▼▼▼ Residence Inn by Marriott Fort Wayne SH
(260) 484-4700. **$89-$149.** 4919 Lima Rd. I-69, exit 111A, just s on US 27. Ext corridors. **Pets:** Accepted.

[ASK] [S❄] [✕] [🔲] [🍴] [💻] [➰] [✕]

▼▼▼ Residence Inn Southwest SH
(260) 432-8000. **$99-$119.** 7811 W Jefferson Blvd. I-69, exit 102, 0.5 mi e. Int corridors. **Pets:** Accepted.

[ASK] [S❄] [✕] [🔲] [🍴] [💻] [➰] [✕]

# FRANKFORT

▼▼▼ Holiday Inn Express SH
(765) 659-4400. **$64.** 592 S CR 200 W. I-65, exit 158, 6.1 mi e; jct US 421/SR 38/39, 1.8 mi w. Int corridors. **Pets:** Accepted.

[ASK] [S❄] [✕] [🔲] [♿] [🍴] [💻] [➰]

▼ ▼ Super 8 Motel SH
(765) 654-0088. **$51-$66.** 1875 W SR 28. I-65, exit 158, 6.4 mi e; jct US 421/SR 38/39, 1.6 mi w. Int corridors. **Pets:** Accepted.

[ASK] [S❄] [✕] [🍴] [➰]

# GEORGETOWN

▼ Motel 6–4097 SH
(812) 923-0441. **$49-$56.** 1079 N Luther Rd. I-64, exit 118, just w on SR 64. Int corridors. **Pets:** Accepted.

[ASK] [S❄] [✕] [♿] [🍴] [➰]

# GOSHEN

♦♦♦ ▼▼ ▼ Best Western Inn M
(574) 533-0408. **$79.** 900 Lincolnway E. 1 mi se on US 33. Ext corridors. **Pets:** Service with restrictions, crate.

[SAVE] [S❄] [✕] [🍴] [💻]

# GREENCASTLE

♦♦♦ ▼ College Inn M
(765) 653-4167. **$45-$65.** 315 Bloomington St. I-70, exit 41, 8 mi n on US 231. Ext corridors. **Pets:** Accepted.

[SAVE] [S❄] [✕] [🍴]

## GREENSBURG

**▼▼▼▼ Holiday Inn Express** SH
(812) 663-5500. **$75-$129.** 915 Ann Blvd. I-74, exit 134A, 1.4 mi s on SR 3. Int corridors. **Pets:** Other species. Designated rooms, service with restrictions, supervision.

[ASK] [S⊘] [✕] [⌘M] [⌖] [⛱] [⊟] [⊡] [≋]

## HAMMOND

**▼▼ Best Western Northwest Indiana Inn** SH
(219) 844-2140. **$94-$104.** 3830 179th St. I-80/94, exit 5 (Cline Ave), 0.6 mi s to frontage road, then 0.6 mi n. Int corridors. **Pets:** Medium, other species. $30 deposit/pet, $5 daily fee/pet. Designated rooms, service with restrictions, supervision.

[ASK] [S⊘] [✕] [⌖] [⊟] [⊡] [¶] [≋]

**▼▼▼▼ Residence Inn by Marriott Chicago Southeast** SH
(219) 844-8440. **$199-$229.** 7740 Corinne Dr. I-80/94, exit 3 (Kennedy Ave S), just s. Int corridors. **Pets:** Small, other species. $75 one-time fee/room. Service with restrictions, crate.

[ASK] [S⊘] [✕] [⌘M] [⌖] [⛱] [⊟] [⊡] [≋] [✕]

## HAUBSTADT

**⒜⒜⒜ ▼▼▼▼ Quality Inn Evansville North** SH
(812) 768-5878. **$64-$74.** RR 1, Box 252 (Hwy 41 & I-64). I-64, exit 25B, 0.4 mi n on US 41 to Warrenton Rd, just w to frontage road, then 0.3 mi s. Int corridors. **Pets:** Large, other species. $15 one-time fee/room. Service with restrictions, crate.

[SAVE] [S⊘] [✕] [⛱] [⊟] [⊡] [≋]

## HOWE

**⒜⒜⒜ ▼▼▼ Super 8 Motel** SH
(260) 562-2828. **$64-$99.** 7333 N SR 9. I-80/90, exit 121 (US 66), 0.5 mi s. Int corridors. **Pets:** Other species. Service with restrictions, supervision.

[SAVE] [S⊘] [✕] [⌘M] [⌖] [⛱] [⊟]

## HUNTINGBURG

**⒜⒜⒜ ▼▼▼ Quality Inn** SH
(812) 683-2334. **$59-$129.** 406 E 22nd St. I-64, exit 57, 9 mi n on US 231, then just w. Ext corridors. **Pets:** Small. $10 daily fee/pet. Service with restrictions, crate.

[SAVE] [S⊘] [✕] [⊟] [⊡] [¶] [≋]

## HUNTINGTON

**▼▼ ▼▼ AmeriHost Inn & Suites Huntington** SH
(260) 359-9000. **$69-$148.** 2820 Hotel Ave. 0.6 mi nw of jct US 24/224 and SR 5. Int corridors. **Pets:** Accepted.

[ASK] [✕] [⛱] [⌖] [⊟] [⊡] [≋]

---

# INDIANAPOLIS METROPOLITAN AREA

## ANDERSON

**▼▼ ▼▼ Super 8 Motel** SH 🐾
(765) 642-2222. **$55-$64.** 2215 E 59th St. I-69, exit 26, just w. Int corridors. **Pets:** Medium. $10 one-time fee/pet. No service.

[ASK] [S⊘] [✕] [⊟] [⊡] [≋]

## CARMEL

**▼▼▼▼ Residence Inn by Marriott Indianapolis/Carmel** SH
(317) 846-2000. **$149-$359.** 11895 N Meridian St. I-465, exit 31, 2 mi n on US 31, just e on 116th St, then just n on Pennsylvania Rd. Int corridors. **Pets:** Small, other species. $75 one-time fee/room. Service with restrictions, supervision.

[ASK] [✕] [⌘M] [⛱] [⌖] [⊟] [⊡] [≋] [✕]

**▼▼ ▼▼ Signature Inn Carmel** SH
(317) 816-1616. **$74-$99.** 10201 N Meridian St. I-465, exit 31, 0.3 mi n on US 31. Int corridors. **Pets:** Very small, other species. $10 daily fee/room. Service with restrictions, supervision.

[ASK] [✕] [⛱] [⊟] [⊡] [≋] [✕]

## CHESTERFIELD

**▼▼ Super 8 Motel** SH
(765) 378-0888. **$49-$57.** 15701 W Commerce Rd. I-69, exit 34, just w. Ext/int corridors. **Pets:** $25 deposit/room, $5 one-time fee/room. Service with restrictions, supervision.

[ASK] [S⊘] [✕] [⊟]

## EDINBURGH

**⒜⒜⒜ ▼▼▼ Best Western Horizon Inn** SH 🐾
(812) 526-9883. **$65-$139.** 11780 N US 31. I-65, exit 76B, just n. Int corridors. **Pets:** Dogs only. $10 daily fee/room. Service with restrictions, supervision.

[SAVE] [S⊘] [✕] [⊟] [⊡] [≋]

## FISHERS

**⒜⒜⒜ ▼▼▼▼ Comfort Suites** SH 🐾
(317) 578-1200. **$79-$225.** 9760 Crosspoint Blvd. I-69, exit 3, just w on 96th St, then just n. Int corridors. **Pets:** Medium, other species. $10 daily fee/pet. Service with restrictions, crate.

[SAVE] [S⊘] [✕] [⌖] [⊟] [⊡] [≋]

**▼▼▼▼ Frederick-Talbott Inn** BB
(317) 578-3600. **$99-$179, 7 day notice.** 13805 Allisonville Rd. I-465, exit 35 (Allisonville Rd), 6.2 mi n; I-69, exit 5, 1.8 mi w on 116th St to Allisonville Rd, then 2.2 mi n. Int corridors. **Pets:** Accepted.

[ASK] [S⊘] [✕]

**▼▼▼▼ Ramada Inn Indianapolis Northeast** SH
(317) 558-4100. **$99-$185.** 9791 North by Northeast Blvd. I-69, exit 3, just ne. Int corridors. **Pets:** Medium.

[ASK] [S⊘] [✕] [⌖] [⊟] [⊡] [≋]

**▼▼▼▼ Residence Inn by Marriott Indianapolis/Fishers** SH 🐾
(317) 842-1111. **$89-$189.** 9765 Crosspoint Blvd. I-69, exit 3, just nw. Int corridors. **Pets:** Other species. $75 one-time fee/room. Service with restrictions.

[ASK] [S⊘] [✕] [⌘M] [⛱] [⌖] [⊟] [⊡] [≋] [✕]

**▼▼▼▼ Staybridge Suites Indianapolis-Fishers** SH 🐾
(317) 577-9500. **$109-$169.** 9780 Crosspoint Blvd. I-69, exit 3, just nw. Int corridors. **Pets:** Medium, other species. $75 one-time fee/room. Service with restrictions, supervision.

[ASK] [S⊘] [✕] [⌘M] [⛱] [⌖] [⊟] [⊡] [≋] [✕]

## GREENWOOD

**▼▼▼ Red Roof Inn** M
(317) 887-1515. **$39-$65.** 110 Sheek Rd. I-65, exit 99, just w. Ext corridors. **Pets:** Accepted.

[ASK] [S⊘] [✕] [⊟] [⊡] [≋]

# INDIANAPOLIS

**AAA** ▼▼▼ **AmeriSuites**
**(Indianapolis/Airport-Speedway)** SH
(317) 227-0950. **$129-$169.** 5500 Bradbury Ave. I-465, exit 11A, 0.3 mi e on Airport Expwy to Executive Dr exit. Int corridors. **Pets:** Medium. $10 daily fee/pet. Designated rooms, supervision.
[SAVE] [S] [X] [M] [] [] [] [↝]

**AAA** ▼▼▼ **AmeriSuites (Indianapolis/Keystone)** SH
(317) 843-0064. **$79-$225.** 9104 Keystone Crossing. I-465, exit 33, 0.5 mi s on SR 431, just e on 86th St, then 0.5 mi n. Int corridors. **Pets:** Accepted.
[SAVE] [S] [X] [] [] [] [] [↝]

**AAA** ▼▼▼ **Baymont Inn & Suites Indianapolis-Airport** SH
(317) 244-8100. **$85-$125.** 2650 Executive Dr. I-465, exit 11, 0.3 mi e. Int corridors. **Pets:** Medium. No service.
[SAVE] [X] [] [] []

**AAA** ▼▼▼ **Baymont Inn & Suites Indianapolis East** SH
(317) 897-2300. **$71-$145.** 2349 Post Dr. I-70, exit 91 (Post Rd), just n. Int corridors. **Pets:** Medium. Service with restrictions.
[SAVE] [X] [M] [] [] [] []

**AAA** ▼▼▼ **Best Western Airport Suites** SH
(317) 246-1505. **$89-$180.** 55 S High School Rd. I-465, exit 13B, just w. Int corridors. **Pets:** Accepted.
[SAVE] [S] [X] [] []

▼▼▼ **Comfort Inn & Suites City Centre** SH
(317) 631-9000. **$129-$250.** 530 S Capitol Ave. Just s of South St. Int corridors. **Pets:** Accepted.
[ASK] [S] [X] [M] [] [] [] [] [↝]

▼▼▼ **Drury Inn-Indianapolis** SH
(317) 876-9777. **$90-$125.** 9320 N Michigan Rd. I-465, exit 27, just s. Int corridors. **Pets:** Accepted.
[ASK] [X] [] [] [] [↝]

▼▼ **Extended Stay Deluxe** SH
(317) 241-0700. **$79-$99.** 5350 W Southern Ave. I-465, exit 11A, just e to Lynhurst Dr, just s, then just w. Int corridors. **Pets:** $25 daily fee/pet. Service with restrictions, supervision.
[ASK] [X] [] [] [] [] [↝]

▼▼▼ **Hawthorn Suites East** SH
(317) 322-0011. **$89-$129.** 7035 Western Select Dr. I-70, exit 89, 0.5 mi w of jct I-465. Int corridors. **Pets:** Accepted.
[ASK] [S] [X] [M] [] [] [] [↝]

**AAA** ▼▼▼ **Hilton Indianapolis North Hotel** LH
(317) 849-6668. **$109-$249.** 8181 N Shadeland Ave. I-69, exit 1, just e. Int corridors. **Pets:** Accepted.
[SAVE] [S] [X] [] [] [] [] [] [↝] [⊠]

▼▼▼ **Holiday Inn East** SH
(317) 359-5341. **$99-$139.** 6990 E 21st St. I-70, exit 89, 0.5 mi w of jct I-465. Int corridors. **Pets:** Medium. $25 one-time fee/room. Service with restrictions, supervision.
[ASK] [S] [X] [] [] [] [] [↝] [⊠]

▼▼ **Homestead Studio Suites**
**Hotel-Indianapolis/Northwest** SH
(317) 334-7829. **$81-$96.** 8520 Northwest Blvd. I-465, exit 23, just e. Int corridors. **Pets:** $25 daily fee/pet. Service with restrictions, supervision.
[ASK] [S] [X] [M] [] [] [] [↝]

▼▼▼ **Indianapolis Marriott East** LH
(317) 352-1231. **$89-$149.** 7202 E 21st St. I-70, exit 89, 0.3 mi se; 0.5 mi w of jct I-465. Int corridors. **Pets:** Accepted.
[ASK] [S] [X] [] [] [] [] [] [↝] [⊠]

▼▼ **Jameson Inn** SH
(317) 849-8555. **$74-$99.** 8380 Kelly Ln. I-465, exit 35 (Allisonville Rd), just s. Int corridors. **Pets:** Very small, other species. $10 daily fee/room. Service with restrictions, supervision.
[ASK] [X] [] [] [] [↝]

**AAA** ▼▼▼ **La Quinta Inn Indianapolis Airport** SH
(317) 247-4281. **$94-$134.** 5316 W Southern Ave. I-465, exit 11A, 0.5 mi e on Airport Expwy to Lynhurst Dr. Int corridors. **Pets:** Medium. Service with restrictions.
[SAVE] [X] [] [] [] [↝]

▼▼▼ **La Quinta Inn Indianapolis (East)** SH
(317) 359-1021. **$59-$129.** 7304 E 21st St. I-70, exit 89, just s, then just e; 0.5 mi w of jct I-465. Int corridors. **Pets:** Accepted.
[ASK] [S] [X] [] [] [] [↝]

▼▼ **Microtel Inn & Suites** SH
(317) 870-7765. **$45-$170.** 9140 N Michigan Rd. I-465, exit 27, just s. Int corridors. **Pets:** Accepted.
[ASK] [S] [X] [] []

**AAA** ▼▼▼▼ **Omni Severin Hotel** LH
(317) 634-6664. **$99-$259.** 40 W Jackson Pl. Opposite Union Station. Int corridors. **Pets:** Small, dogs only. $50 one-time fee/room. Service with restrictions, crate.
[SAVE] [S] [X] [] [] [] [] [] [↝]

▼▼▼ **Quality Inn & Suites Airport** SH
(317) 381-1000. **$69-$199.** 2631 S Lynhurst Dr. I-465, exit 11A, 0.5 mi e on Airport Expwy to Lynhurst Dr. Int corridors. **Pets:** Other species. $10 one-time fee/pet. Service with restrictions, supervision.
[ASK] [S] [X] [] [] [] [↝]

▼▼ **Quality Inn South** SH
(317) 788-0811. **$59-$119, 14 day notice.** 450 Bixler Rd. I-465, exit 2B, just s. Int corridors. **Pets:** Accepted.
[ASK] [S] [X] [] [] [↝]

**AAA** ▼▼▼▼ **Ramada-Indianapolis** SH
(317) 897-4000. **$75-$125.** 7701 E 42nd St. I-465, exit 42 (Pendleton Pike), just e. Int corridors. **Pets:** Small. $20 one-time fee/pet. Designated rooms, service with restrictions, crate.
[SAVE] [S] [X] [] [] [] [] [↝]

▼▼▼ **Red Roof Inn-South #7013** M
(317) 788-9551. **$48-$63.** 5221 Victory Dr. I-465/74, exit 52 (Emerson Ave), just s. Ext corridors. **Pets:** Accepted.
[X] [] [] []

▼▼▼ **Red Roof Inn-Speedway #7074** M
(317) 293-6881. **$46-$61.** 6415 Debonair Ln. I-465, exit 16A, just se. Ext corridors. **Pets:** Accepted.
[X] [] []

▼▼▼ **Renaissance Tower Historic Inn** SH
(317) 261-1652. **$105, 3 day notice.** 230 E 9th St. Between Alabama and Delaware sts. Int corridors. **Pets:** Accepted.
[ASK] [X] [] []

▼▼▼ **Residence Inn by Marriott Indianapolis**
**Airport** SH 🐾
(317) 244-1500. **$99-$299.** 5224 W Southern Ave. I-465, exit 11A, 0.5 mi e on Airport Expwy to Lynhurst Dr. Int corridors. **Pets:** Small, other species. $75 one-time fee/room. Service with restrictions, crate.
[ASK] [S] [X] [] [] [] [] [↝] [⊠]

▼▼▼ **Residence Inn by Marriott Indianapolis Downtown on**
**the Canal** SH
(317) 822-0840. **$169-$209.** 350 W New York St. At New York St and Senate Ave. Int corridors. **Pets:** Other species. $75 one-time fee/room. Service with restrictions, crate.
[ASK] [X] [M] [] [] [] [↝]

▼▼▼ **Residence Inn by Marriott Northwest-Indianapolis** SH
(317) 275-6000. **$129-$134.** 6220 Digital Way. I-465, exit 21, just w. Int corridors. **Pets:** Medium. $75 one-time fee/room. Designated rooms, service with restrictions, crate.

ASK S🐾 ✕ ᴹ ☐ ☐ 🚱 ✕

▼▼▼ **Sheraton Indianapolis Hotel & Suites** LH
(317) 846-2700. **$209-$249.** 8787 Keystone Crossing. I-465, exit 33, 0.5 mi s on SR 431, just e on 86th St, then just n. Int corridors. **Pets:** Accepted.

ASK S🐾 ✕ ᴹ ⬡ ☐ ☐ ⧄ 🚱 ✕

▼▼▼ **Signature Inn-Indianapolis East** SH
(317) 353-6966. **$49-$104.** 7610 Old Trails Rd. I-465, exit 46, just sw. Int corridors. **Pets:** Accepted.

ASK ✕ ⬡ ☐ ☐ 🚱

▼▼▼ **Signature Inn-South** SH
(317) 784-7006. **$74-$99.** 4402 E Creekview Dr. I-65, exit 103, just w. Int corridors. **Pets:** Very small, other species. $10 daily fee/room. Service with restrictions, supervision.

ASK ✕ ⬡ ☐ ☐ 🚱

▼▼▼ **Super 8 Indianapolis-Northeast** SH
(317) 841-8585. **$55-$59.** 7202 E 82nd St. I-69, exit 1, 0.3 mi e to Clear Vista, just n, then just w on Clear Vista Ln. Ext corridors. **Pets:** Accepted.

ASK S🐾 ✕ ☐ ☐ ☐ 🚱

▼▼▼ **TownePlace Suites by Marriott Keystone** SH
(317) 255-3700. **Call for rates.** 8468 Union Chapel Rd. I-465, exit 31, 1.2 mi s on Meridian St, 2.8 mi e on 86th St, then just s. Int corridors. **Pets:** Accepted.

✕ ☐ ☐ 🚱

▼▼▼ **TownePlace Suites by Marriott Park 100** SH
(317) 290-8900. **Call for rates.** 5802 W 71st St. I-465, exit 21, 0.3 mi e. Int corridors. **Pets:** Accepted.

✕ ☐ ☐ ☐ 🚱

ⒶⒶⒶ ▼▼▼ **The Westin Indianapolis** LH 🐾
(317) 262-8100. **$169-$349.** 50 S Capitol Ave. At Washington and Maryland sts and Capitol Ave. Int corridors. **Pets:** Small, dogs only. Service with restrictions.

SAVE S🐾 ✕ ⬡ ☐ ☐ ☐ ⧄ 🚱

# END METROPOLITAN AREA

# JASPER

▼▼▼ **Days Inn Jasper** SH 🐾
(812) 482-6000. **$60-$114.** 272 Brucke Strasse. Jct SR 164, just w. Ext/int corridors. **Pets:** Other species. $10 daily fee/pet. Service with restrictions, supervision.

ASK S🐾 ✕ ⬡ ☐ ☐ ☐ ⧄ 🚱 ✕

# JEFFERSONVILLE

▼▼▼ **TownePlace Suites by Marriott** SH
(812) 280-8200. **$75-$95.** 703 N Shore Dr. I-65, exit 0, just w. Int corridors. **Pets:** Accepted.

ASK S🐾 ✕ ☐ ☐ ☐ 🚱

# KENDALLVILLE

ⒶⒶⒶ ▼▼▼ **Best Western Kendallville Inn** SH
(260) 347-5263. **$74-$129.** 621 Professional Way. 1 mi e on US 6. Int corridors. **Pets:** Large, dogs only. $25 one-time fee/room. Designated rooms, service with restrictions, supervision.

SAVE S🐾 ✕ ☐ ☐ 🚱 ✕

# LEBANON

ⒶⒶⒶ ▼▼▼ **Comfort Inn** SH
(765) 482-4800. **$79-$179.** 210 N Sam Ralston Rd. I-65, exit 140. Int corridors. **Pets:** $10 daily fee/room. Supervision.

SAVE S🐾 ✕ ☐ ☐ 🚱

▼▼▼ **Super 8 Motel** SH
(765) 482-9999. **$56-$149.** 405 N Mount Zion Rd. I-65, exit 140, just w. Int corridors. **Pets:** Accepted.

ASK S🐾 ✕ ☐ ☐ 🚱

# NOBLESVILLE

▼▼▼ **Quality Inn & Suites** SH
(317) 770-6772. **$59-$159.** 16025 Prosperity Dr. 1.7 mi s of jct SR 32, 37 and 38. Int corridors. **Pets:** Medium, other species. $30 daily fee/room. Service with restrictions, crate.

✕ ☐ ☐ ☐ 🚱

# PLAINFIELD

ⒶⒶⒶ ▼▼▼ **AmeriHost Inn-Plainfield/Indianapolis** SH
(317) 838-9300. **$79-$215.** 6105 Cambridge Way. I-70, exit 66, just n. Int corridors. **Pets:** Other species. $25 deposit/pet. Service with restrictions, supervision.

SAVE S🐾 ✕ ⬡ ☐ ☐ ☐ 🚱

# SHELBYVILLE

▼▼▼ **Best Western Shelbyville Inn** SH
(317) 398-0472. **$65-$100.** 68 E Rampart St. I-74, exit 113, just w. Int corridors. **Pets:** Accepted.

ASK S🐾 ✕ ᴹ ☐ ☐ 🚱

# KOKOMO

ⒶⒶⒶ ▼▼▼ **Best Western/Signature Inn Kokomo** SH
(765) 455-1000. **$74-$99.** 4021 S LaFountain St. US 31, 2.8 mi s of jct US 35. Int corridors. **Pets:** Very small, other species. $10 daily fee/room. Service with restrictions, supervision.

SAVE ✕ ⬡ ☐ ☐ 🚱

▼▼▼ **Comfort Inn by Choice Hotels** SH
(765) 452-5050. **$65-$85.** 522 Essex Dr. Jct US 35, 0.3 mi n on US 31. Int corridors. **Pets:** Accepted.

ASK S🐾 ✕ ⬡ ☐ ☐ 🚱

▼▼▼ **Days Inn & Suites** M
(765) 453-7100. **$56-$85.** 264 S 00 EW. US 31, 2.8 mi s of jct US 35. Ext corridors. **Pets:** $10 one-time fee/room. Service with restrictions, supervision.

ASK S🐾 ✕ ☐ ☐ ⧄ 🚱

▼▼▼ **Hampton Inn & Suites** SH
(765) 455-2900. **$109-$159.** 2920 S Reed Rd (US Hwy 31). US 31, 2 mi s of jct US 35. Int corridors. **Pets:** Service with restrictions, crate.

ASK S🐾 ✕ ᴹ ⬡ ☐ ☐ ☐ 🚱 ✕

▼▼ Super 8 Motel SH
(765) 455-3288. **$54-$81.** 5110 Clinton Dr. US 31, 2.8 mi s of jct US 35. Int corridors. **Pets:** Accepted.
ASK 🔊 ✕ 🛋 📶 💻 ⊇

## LAFAYETTE

AAA ▼▼▼ Best Western Lafayette Executive Plaza & Conference Center SH
(765) 447-0575. **$84-$199, 30 day notice.** 4343 SR 26 E. I-65, exit 172, just w. Int corridors. **Pets:** Accepted.
SAVE 🔊 ✕ 🛋 ♿ 📶 💻 🍴 ⊇ ✕

AAA ▼▼▼ Comfort Suites-Lafayette SH
(765) 447-0016. **$80-$200.** 31 Frontage Rd. I-65, exit 172, just e. Int corridors. **Pets:** Small. $20 daily fee/pet. Designated rooms, no service, crate.
SAVE 🔊 ✕ ♿M 🛋 📶 💻 ⊇ ✕

▼▼ Days Inn & Suites SH
(765) 446-8558. **$60-$100, 30 day notice.** 151 Frontage Rd. I-65, exit 172, just e. Int corridors. **Pets:** Accepted.
ASK 🔊 ✕ 📶 💻

AAA ▼▼▼ Holiday Inn Express SH
(765) 449-4808. **$89-$200.** 201 Frontage Rd. I-65, exit 172, just e on SR 26, then just n. Int corridors. **Pets:** Other species. Service with restrictions, crate.
SAVE 🔊 ✕ 🛋 📶 💻

▼▼▼ Homewood Suites by Hilton SH
(765) 448-9700. **$119-$189.** 3939 SR 26 E. I-65, exit 172, 0.8 mi w. Ext/int corridors. **Pets:** Accepted.
ASK ✕ 🛋 📶 💻 ⊇ ✕

▼▼▼ Loeb House Inn BB
(765) 420-7737. **$95-$175, 14 day notice.** 708 Cincinnati St. SR 38, 0.4 mi n on 9th St, then just w. Int corridors. **Pets:** Accepted.
ASK 🔊 ✕

▼▼ Red Roof Inn-Lafayette #7062 M
(765) 448-4671. **$47-$62.** 4201 SR 26 E. I-65, exit 172, 0.3 mi w. Ext corridors. **Pets:** Accepted.
✕ 🛋 📶

▼▼ Signature Inn Lafayette SH
(765) 447-4142. **$74-$99.** 4320 SR 26 E. I-65, exit 172, just w. Int corridors. **Pets:** Very small, other species. $10 daily fee/room. Service with restrictions, supervision.
ASK ✕ 🛋 📶 💻 ⊇

▼▼▼ TownePlace Suites by Marriott SH
(765) 446-8668. **$119-$159, 30 day notice.** 163 Frontage Rd. I-65, exit 172, just e. Int corridors. **Pets:** Accepted.
ASK 🔊 ✕ 📶 💻 ⊇

## LOGANSPORT

▼▼ Holiday Inn SH
(574) 753-6351. **$92-$150.** 3550 E Market St. 2.5 mi e on Business Rt US 24. Int corridors. **Pets:** Accepted.
ASK 🔊 ✕ ♿M 🛋 📶 💻 🍴 ⊇

## MADISON

▼▼ Country Hearth Inn SH
(812) 273-0757. **$53-$129.** 308 Demaree Dr. Jct SR 7 and 62, 2 mi e on SR 62. Int corridors. **Pets:** Other species. $10 daily fee/pet. Service with restrictions, crate.
ASK 🔊 ✕ 📶 💻

AAA ▼▼ Super 8 Motel SH
(812) 273-4443. **$55-$70.** 3767 Clifty Dr. Jct SR 56/62/256. Int corridors. **Pets:** Dogs only. $10 daily fee/pet.
SAVE 🔊 ✕ 🛋 📶 💻 ⊇

## MARION

AAA ▼▼▼ Comfort Suites-Marion SH
(765) 651-1006. **$79-$125.** 1345 N Baldwin Ave. 1.5 mi n of jct SR 9 and 18. Int corridors. **Pets:** Small. $20 daily fee/pet. Designated rooms, no service, crate.
SAVE 🔊 ✕ 🛋 💻 ⊇ ✕

## MARKLE

▼▼ Super 8 Motel Fort Wayne South/Markle SH 🐾
(260) 758-8888. **$56.** 610 Annette Dr. I-69, exit 86, just e. Int corridors. **Pets:** Medium. $7 daily fee/pet. Service with restrictions, supervision.
ASK 🔊 ✕ 📶 💻

## MERRILLVILLE

▼▼▼ Residence Inn by Marriott Merrillville SH
(219) 791-9000. **$139-$159.** 8018 Delaware Pl. I-65, exit 253B (US 30), 0.3 mi nw. Int corridors. **Pets:** Accepted.
ASK ✕ ♿M 🛋 📶 💻 ⊇ ✕

AAA ▼▼ Super 8 Motel SH
(219) 736-8383. **$47-$65, 7 day notice.** 8300 Louisiana St. I-65, exit 253A (US 30), 0.5 mi se. Int corridors. **Pets:** Medium, other species. Designated rooms, service with restrictions, supervision.
SAVE 🔊 ✕ ♿M 🛋 📶

## MICHIGAN CITY

▼▼ Red Roof Inn-Michigan City #7007 M
(219) 874-5251. **$50-$80.** 110 W Kieffer Rd. I-94, exit 34B, 0.3 mi n on US 421. Ext corridors. **Pets:** Accepted.
✕ 🛋 📶

## MONTGOMERY

▼▼ Gasthof Amish Village Inn SH
(812) 486-2600. **$60-$100.** CR 650 E. US 50, 0.8 mi n on First St. Int corridors. **Pets:** Accepted.
ASK 🔊 ✕ 🛋 📶 💻 🍴 ⊇

## MONTICELLO

AAA ▼▼▼ Best Western Brandywine Inn & Suites SH
(574) 583-6333. **$79-$189.** 728 S 6th St. SR 24, just s. Int corridors. **Pets:** Accepted.
SAVE 🔊 ✕ ♿M 🛋 📶 💻 ⊇ ✕

## MOUNT VERNON

▼▼ Four Seasons Motel M
(812) 838-4821. **$57-$89.** 70 Hwy 62 W. 1.8 mi w. Ext corridors. **Pets:** Accepted.
ASK 🔊 ✕ 📶 💻 ⊇

▼▼ Mt. Vernon Inn SH
(812) 838-8888. **$65-$75.** 6225 Hwy 69 S. On SR 69 Bypass, just n of SR 62. Int corridors. **Pets:** Accepted.
ASK ✕ 📶 ⊇

## MUNCIE

▼▼ Muncie Days Inn SH
(765) 288-2311. **$48-$64.** 3509 N Everbrook Ln. I-69, exit 41, 6.3 mi e on SR 332, then just n. Int corridors. **Pets:** Dogs only. $10 one-time fee/room. Service with restrictions, supervision.
ASK 🔊 ✕ 📶 💻

▼▼▼ The Roberts Hotel LH
(765) 741-7777. **$89-$250.** 420 S High St. Opposite Horizon Convention Center. Int corridors. **Pets:** $10 daily fee/pet. Service with restrictions, crate.
ASK 🔊 ✕ 📶 🍴 ⊇

▼▼▼ **Signature Inn-Muncie** 🆂🅷
(765) 284-4200. **$74-$99.** 3400 N Chadam Ln. I-69, exit 41, 6.3 mi e on SR 332. Int corridors. **Pets:** Very small, other species. $10 daily fee/room. Service with restrictions, supervision.

🄰🅂🄺 ⊠ 🕭 🛏 💻 ➳

▼▼ **Super 8 Motel** 🆂🅷
(765) 286-4333. **$45-$72.** 3601 W Fox Ridge Ln. I-69, exit 41, 6.3 mi e on SR 332. Int corridors. **Pets:** Accepted.

🄰🅂🄺 🆂🄳 ⊠ 🛏

## NEW ALBANY

🄰🄰🄰 ▼▼▼ **Holiday Inn Express** 🆂🅷
(812) 945-2771. **$79-$199.** 411 W Spring St. I-64, exit 123. Int corridors. **Pets:** Other species. $15 one-time fee/room. Designated rooms, service with restrictions, crate.

🆂🄰🆅🄴 🆂🄳 ⊠ 🖐 🛏 💻 ➳

## NEW CASTLE

🄰🄰🄰 ▼▼▼ **Best Western Raintree Inn** 🆂🅷
(765) 521-0100. **$63-$80.** 2836 S SR 3. I-70, exit 123, 2.5 mi n. Ext/int corridors. **Pets:** Small, other species. $20 one-time fee/pet. Service with restrictions, supervision.

🆂🄰🆅🄴 🆂🄳 ⊠ 🖐 🛏 💻 🍴 ➳ ⊠

## NORTH VERNON

▼▼ **Comfort Inn** 🆂🅷
(812) 352-9999. **$79-$119.** 150 FDR Dr. Jct US 50, 0.6 mi n on SR 7. Int corridors. **Pets:** Accepted.

🄰🅂🄺 🆂🄳 ⊠ 🖐 🛏 💻

## PERU

▼▼▼ **Best Western Circus City Inn** 🆂🅷
(765) 473-8800. **$79-$160.** 2642 Business 31 S. Just e of jct US 31. Int corridors. **Pets:** Accepted.

🄰🅂🄺 🆂🄳 ⊠ 🕭 🖐 🛏 💻 ➳

## PLYMOUTH

▼▼ **Super 8 Motel** 🆂🅷
(574) 936-8856. **$55-$130.** 2160 N Oak Rd. US 30, just s. Int corridors. **Pets:** Accepted.

🄰🅂🄺 🆂🄳 ⊠ 🛏 💻 ➳

▼▼▼ **Swan Lake Resort** 🆂🅷
(574) 935-5680. **$98-$258, 3 day notice.** 5203 Plymouth-LaPorte Tr. 2.5 mi w on US 30, 4 mi nw on Queen Rd/Plymouth-LaPorte Tr. Int corridors. **Pets:** Accepted.

🄰🅂🄺 🆂🄳 ⊠ 🛏 💻 🍴 ➳ ⊠

## PORTAGE

▼▼ **Super 8 Motel Portage** 🆂🅷
(219) 762-8857. **$45-$80.** 6118 Melton Rd. I-94, exit 19, just s on SR 249, then just w on US 20. Int corridors. **Pets:** Small. $25 one-time fee/room. Designated rooms, service with restrictions, supervision.

🄰🅂🄺 🆂🄳 ⊠ 🛏 💻

## PORTLAND

▼▼ **Hoosier Inn** 🅼
(260) 726-7113. **$48-$55.** 1620 Meridian St. 1.4 mi n on US 27. Ext corridors. **Pets:** Dogs only. $5 one-time fee/pet. Service with restrictions, supervision.

🄰🅂🄺 🆂🄳 ⊠ 🛏 💻

## PRINCETON

▼▼ **Fairfield Inn by Marriott** 🆂🅷
(812) 385-4300. **$64-$85.** 2828 Dixon St. Jct US 41 and SR 64, 0.3 mi w. Int corridors. **Pets:** $50 one-time fee/room. Designated rooms, service with restrictions, supervision.

🄰🅂🄺 🆂🄳 ⊠ 🖐 🕭 🛏 💻 ➳

## REMINGTON

▼▼ ▼▼ **Super 8 Motel-Remington** 🆂🅷
(219) 261-2883. **$65-$100.** 4278 W US 24. I-65, exit 201, 0.5 mi w. Int corridors. **Pets:** Small, dogs only. $10 daily fee/pet. Designated rooms, service with restrictions, supervision.

🄰🅂🄺 🆂🄳 ⊠ 🖐 🛏 ➳

## RENSSELAER

🄰🄰🄰 ▼▼▼▼ **Holiday Inn Express** 🆂🅷
(219) 866-7111. **$82-$102, 10 day notice.** 4788 Nesbitt Dr. I-65, exit 215, just e. Int corridors. **Pets:** Other species. $10 one-time fee/pet. Designated rooms, supervision.

🆂🄰🆅🄴 🆂🄳 ⊠ 🖐🄼 🖐 🛏 💻

## RICHMOND

▼▼ **Days Inn** 🅼
(765) 966-4900. **$55-$75.** 5775 National Rd E. I-70, exit 156A, just s. Ext corridors. **Pets:** Accepted.

🄰🅂🄺 🆂🄳 ⊠

▼▼◆ **Holiday Inn-Richmond** 🆂🅷 🐾
(765) 966-7511. **$85-$325.** 5501 National Rd E. I-70, exit 156A, 0.3 mi w. Int corridors. **Pets:** Large. $15 daily fee/pet. Designated rooms, service with restrictions, supervision.

🄰🅂🄺 🆂🄳 ⊠ 🖐🄼 🕭 🖐 🛏 💻 🍴 ➳ ⊠

🄰🄰🄰 ▼▼▼ **Knights Inn** 🆂🅷
(765) 966-1505. **$49-$79.** 3020 E Main St. I-70, exit 156A, 2 mi w. Ext corridors. **Pets:** $5 daily fee/pet. Service with restrictions, supervision.

🆂🄰🆅🄴 🆂🄳 ⊠ 🛏 💻

▼▼◆ **Lees Inn & Suites** 🆂🅷
(765) 966-6559. **$89-$109.** 6030 National Rd E. I-70, exit 156A, jct US 40. Int corridors. **Pets:** Accepted.

🄰🅂🄺 🆂🄳 ⊠ 🛏 💻 ➳

▼▼ **Motel 6 Richmond #4170** 🅼
(765) 966-6682. **$39-$89.** 419 Commerce Dr. I-70, exit 156A, just s on US 40. Ext corridors. **Pets:** Accepted.

🄰🅂🄺 🆂🄳 ⊠ ➳

## ROCKVILLE

▼▼ **Billie Creek Village & Inn** 🆂🅷
(765) 569-3430. **$49-$129, 3 day notice.** 1659 E US Hwy 36. On US 36, 1.4 mi e. Int corridors. **Pets:** Accepted.

🄰🅂🄺 ⊠ 🖐🄼 💻 ➳

## ROSELAND

🄰🄰🄰 ▼▼▼ **Comfort Suites South Bend** 🆂🅷
(574) 272-1500. **$89-$325, 30 day notice.** 52939 SR 933 N. I-80/90, exit 77, just e to Business Rt US 31/33, then 1 mi n. Int corridors. **Pets:** Small. $20 daily fee/pet. Designated rooms, no service, crate.

🆂🄰🆅🄴 🆂🄳 ⊠ 🖐 🛏 💻 ➳ ⊠

▼▼ **Quality Inn-University Area** 🆂🅷
(574) 272-6600. **$70-$100.** 515 Dixie Way N. I-80/90, exit 77, on US 31 and SR 933, 0.8 mi n. Ext/int corridors. **Pets:** Accepted.

🄰🅂🄺 🆂🄳 ⊠ 🖐 🛏 💻 🍴 ➳

▼▼ **Ramada South Bend** 🅻🅷
(574) 272-5220. **$59-$219.** 52890 SR 933 N. I-80/90, exit 77, 1 mi n. Ext/int corridors. **Pets:** Accepted.

🄰🅂🄺 🆂🄳 ⊠ 🛏 💻 🍴 ➳

## SCOTTSBURG

🄰🄰🄰 ▼▼▼ **Mariann Travel Inn** 🅼
(812) 752-3396. **$58-$61.** I-65 and SR 56. I-65, exit 29A, just e. Ext corridors. **Pets:** Dogs only. Designated rooms, service with restrictions, crate.

🆂🄰🆅🄴 🆂🄳 ⊠ 🛏 🍴 ➳ ⊠

# SELLERSBURG

◆◆ **Home Lodge** SH
(812) 246-6332. **$319-$369 (weekly), 14 day notice.** 363 Triangle Dr.
I-65, exit 9, just e. Int corridors. **Pets:** Accepted.

⊠ 🗇 🖪 💻

◆◆◆ **Ramada Limited & Suites** SH
(812) 246-3131. **$109-$129.** 360 Triangle Dr. I-65, exit 9, just e. Int
corridors. **Pets:** Accepted.

A$K S�🔒 ⊠ 🖪 💻 ⊸

# SEYMOUR

◆◆ **Holiday Inn** SH
(812) 522-6767. **$79-$107.** 2025 E Tipton St. I-65, exit 50B, 0.5 mi w
on US 50. Ext corridors. **Pets:** Other species.

A$K S�🔒 ⊠ 🖪 💻 ❫❪ ⊸

◆ **Motel 6 Seymour #4153** SH
(812) 524-7443. **$36-$99.** 365 Tanger Blvd. I-65, exit 50A. Int corridors.
**Pets:** Accepted.

A$K S�🔒 ⊠ 🕭M 🗇 🖪 💻 ⊸

# SHIPSHEWANA

AAA ◆◆ **Super 8 Motel** SH
(260) 768-4004. **$55-$110.** 740 S Van Buren St. US 20, 0.8 mi n on SR
5. Int corridors. **Pets:** Accepted.

SAVE S�🔒 ⊠ 🗇 🕭 🖪 💻

# SOUTH BEND

◆◆◆ **Oliver Inn Bed & Breakfast** BB
(574) 232-4545. **$140-$299, 14 day notice.** 630 W Washington St. 0.3
mi w of jct US 933 and 31 S. Int corridors. **Pets:** Accepted.

A$K S�🔒 ⊠

◆◆◆ **Quality Inn & Suites** SH
(574) 288-3800. **$79-$149.** 4124 Lincolnway W. I-80/90, exit 72 (US 31)
south, 1.5 mi s to South Bend Airport exit, then 2 mi e. Int corridors.
**Pets:** Medium. $10 daily fee/pet. Service with restrictions, supervision.

A$K S�🔒 ⊠ 🕭M 🕭 🖪 💻 ⊠

◆◆ **Super 8 Motel** SH
(574) 243-0200. **$64-$89.** 4124 Ameritech Dr. I-80/90, exit 72 (US 31),
0.7 mi n, just e on Cleveland Rd, then just s. Int corridors.
**Pets:** Medium, other species. $10 daily fee/pet. Designated rooms, service
with restrictions, supervision.

A$K S�🔒 ⊠ 🗇 🖪 💻 ⊸

# TAYLORSVILLE

◆◆ **Red Roof Inn** M
(812) 526-9747. **$49-$150.** 10330 US 31. I-65, exit 76A, just s. Ext
corridors. **Pets:** Accepted.

A$K S�🔒 ⊠ 🗇 🖪 💻 ⊸

# TELL CITY

◆◆ **Ramada Limited** SH
(812) 547-3234. **$63.** 235 Orchard Hill Dr. Just off SR 66, 1.7 mi se of
jct SR 37. Int corridors. **Pets:** Other species. $50 deposit/room. Service
with restrictions, supervision.

A$K S�🔒 ⊠ 🕭 🗇 🖪 💻 ⊸

# TERRE HAUTE

◆◆ **Comfort Suites by Choice Hotels** SH
(812) 235-1770. **$79-$120.** 501 E Margaret Ave. I-70, exit 7 (US
41/150), just ne. Int corridors. **Pets:** Accepted.

A$K S�🔒 ⊠ 🕭M 🕭 🖪 💻 ⊸

◆◆◆ **Drury Inn-Terre Haute** SH
(812) 238-1206. **$95-$140.** 3040 Hwy 41 S. I-70, exit 7 (US 41/150),
just n. Int corridors. **Pets:** Accepted.

A$K ⊠ 🕭M 🕭 🖪 💻 ⊸ ⊠

◆ **Econo Lodge** M
(812) 234-9931. **$54-$69.** 401 E Margaret Ave. I-70, exit 7 (US 41/150),
just n, then e. Ext corridors. **Pets:** Large, other species. $10 one-time
fee/room. Service with restrictions.

A$K S�🔒 ⊠ 🖪 💻 ⊸

◆◆◆ **Holiday Inn** LH 🐾
(812) 232-6081. **$109-$159.** 3300 US 41 S. I-70, exit 7 (US 41/150),
just s. Int corridors. **Pets:** Small, other species. Service with restrictions,
supervision.

A$K ⊠ 🗇 🖪 💻 ❫❪ ⊸ ⊠

◆◆ **Pear Tree Inn by Drury-Terre Haute** SH
(812) 234-4268. **$75-$105.** 3050 US 41 S. I-70, exit 7 (US 41/150), just
n. Int corridors. **Pets:** Accepted.

A$K ⊠ 🕭 💻

◆ **Super 8 Motel-Terre Haute** SH
(812) 232-4890. **$47-$90.** 3089 S 1st St. I-70, exit 7 (US 41/150), just
nw. Int corridors. **Pets:** Service with restrictions, supervision.

A$K S☈ ⊠ 🖪

# VALPARAISO

◆◆◆ **Courtyard by Marriott Valparaiso** SH
(219) 465-1700. **$89-$129.** 2301 E Morthland Dr. US 30, w of jct SR 49
Bypass. Int corridors. **Pets:** Accepted.

⊠ 🗇 🖪 💻 ❫❪ ⊸

# WARREN

◆◆◆ **Comfort Inn Warren** SH
(260) 375-4800. **$65.** 7275 S 75 E. I-69, exit 78, just n on SR 5. Int
corridors. **Pets:** Medium. Service with restrictions, supervision.

A$K S☈ ⊠ 🕭M 🕭 🖪 💻 ⊸

◆◆ **Super 8 Motel** SH
(260) 375-4688. **$45.** 7281 S 75 E. I-69, exit 78. Int corridors.
**Pets:** Accepted.

A$K S☈ ⊠

# WARSAW

AAA ◆◆◆ **Comfort Inn & Suites-Warsaw** SH
(574) 269-6655. **$92-$150.** 3328 E Center St. 3.2 mi e of SR 15 on US
30. Int corridors. **Pets:** Medium, other species. $10 daily fee/pet. Service
with restrictions, crate.

SAVE S☈ ⊠ 🗇 🕭 🖪 💻 ⊸ ⊠

◆◆◆ **Ramada Plaza Hotel of Warsaw** SH 🐾
(574) 269-2323. **$94-$109.** 2519 E Center St. 2.8 mi e of SR 15 on US
30, just s. Int corridors. **Pets:** Other species. Service with restrictions.

A$K S☈ ⊠ 🖪 💻 ❫❪ ⊸ ⊠

# WASHINGTON

◆◆◆ **Baymont Inn & Suites Washington** SH
(812) 254-7000. **$67-$117.** 7 Cumberland Dr. Just ne of jct US 50 and
SR 257. Int corridors. **Pets:** Medium, dogs only. $50 deposit/room. Serv-
ice with restrictions, supervision.

A$K S☈ ⊠ 🗇 🖪 💻 ⊸ ⊠

# WEST LAFAYETTE

◆◆ **Super 8 Motel-West Lafayette** SH
(765) 567-7100. **$60-$70.** 2030 Northgate Dr. I-65, exit 178, just n on
SR 43. Int corridors. **Pets:** Small. $25 daily fee/pet. Designated rooms,
service with restrictions, supervision.

A$K S☈ ⊠ 🕭M 🕭 🖪

# IOWA

## ADAIR

**Adair Budget Inn** M
(641) 742-5553. **$39-$49.** 100 S 5th St. I-80, exit 76. Ext corridors. **Pets:** $20 deposit/room. Designated rooms, service with restrictions, supervision.

**Adair Super 8** SH
(641) 742-5251. **$54-$79.** 111 S 5th St. I-80, exit 76. Int corridors. **Pets:** Very small. $20 deposit/room. Service with restrictions, supervision.

## ALBIA

**Indian Hills Inn** SH
(641) 932-7181. **$66-$104, 3 day notice.** 100 Hwy 34 E. Just e of jct US 34 and SR 5. Ext/int corridors. **Pets:** $6 daily fee/pet. Designated rooms, service with restrictions, supervision.

## ALGONA

**AmericInn Motel** SH
(515) 295-3333. **$76-$124.** 600 Hwy 18 W. Just w of jct US 169/18. Int corridors. **Pets:** Other species. Supervision.

## ALTOONA

**Heartland Inn-Altoona** SH
(515) 967-2400. **$76-$105.** 300 34th Ave NW. I-80, exit 142, 0.5 mi s. Int corridors. **Pets:** Small. $10 daily fee/room. Designated rooms, service with restrictions, supervision.

**Motel 6 Des Moines East #1420** SH
(515) 967-5252. **$41-$55.** 3225 Adventureland Dr. I-80, exit 142A. Int corridors. **Pets:** Accepted.

**Settle Inn & Suites-Altoona** SH
(515) 967-7888. **$69-$89.** 2101 Adventureland Dr. I-80, exit 142A, just se. Int corridors. **Pets:** Accepted.

# AMANA COLONIES AREA

## HOMESTEAD

**Die Heimat Country Inn & Bed & Breakfast** BB
(319) 622-3937. **$70-$90, 14 day notice.** 4430 V St. Just s of US 6, e on Main St, then just e of jct US 151. Int corridors. **Pets:** Medium, dogs only. $10 daily fee/room. Designated rooms, supervision.

# END AREA

## AMES

**AmericInn & Suites** SH
(515) 233-1005. **$59-$159.** 2507 SE 16th St. I-35, exit 111B, just w on US 30, then exit 150. Int corridors. **Pets:** Accepted.

**Baymont Inn & Suites** SH
(515) 296-2500. **$79-$159.** 2500 Elwood Dr. I-35, exit 111B, 3.5 mi w on US 30, exit 146 (Elwood Dr), then just s. Int corridors. **Pets:** Service with restrictions, supervision.

**Comfort Inn-Ames** SH
(515) 232-0689. **$55-$100.** 1605 S Dayton Ave. I-35, exit 111B, just w on US 30, then exit 150. Int corridors. **Pets:** Accepted.

**♦♦♦ ▼▼▼▼ Comfort Suites** 🆂🅷
(515) 268-8808. **$89-$134.** 2609 Elwood Dr. I-35, exit 111B, 3.5 mi w on US 30, exit 146 (Elwood Dr), then just s. Int corridors. **Pets:** Small. $10 daily fee/pet. Designated rooms, service with restrictions, supervision.
[SAVE] [S☉] [✕] [ᕕM] [⌐] [⌂] [🛏] [💻] [🛆] [✕]

**▼▼▼▼ GrandStay Residential Suites** 🆂🅷
(515) 232-8363. **Call for rates.** 1606 S Kellogg Ave. I-35, exit 111, 1 mi w, then just nw on Duff Ave to Kellogg Ave. Int corridors. **Pets:** Accepted.
[✕] [ᕕM] [⌂] [🛏] [💻] [🛆]

**▼▼▼ Heartland Inn-Ames** 🆂🅷
(515) 233-6060. **$78-$88.** 2600 SE 16th St. I-35, exit 111B, just w on US 30, then exit 150. Int corridors. **Pets:** Small. $10 daily fee/room. Designated rooms, service with restrictions, supervision.
[ASK] [S☉] [✕] [🛏] [💻] [🛆]

**▼▼▼▼ The Hotel at Gateway Center** 🅻🅷
(515) 292-8600. **$139.** US 30 & Elwood Dr. I-35, exit 111B, 3.5 mi w on US 30, exit 146 (Elwood Dr). Int corridors. **Pets:** Medium. $150 deposit/room. Designated rooms, service with restrictions, crate.
[ASK] [S☉] [✕] [ᕕM] [⌐] [⌂] [🛏] [💻] [🍴] [🛆] [✕]

**♦♦♦ ▼▼▼ Quality Inn & Suites Starlite Village Conference Center** 🆂🅷
(515) 232-9260. **$100-$130.** 2601 E 13th St. I-35, exit 113 (13th St), 0.5 mi w. Int corridors. **Pets:** Accepted.
[SAVE] [S☉] [✕] [⌐] [⌂] [🛏] [💻] [🍴] [🛆] [✕]

## ANAMOSA

**▼▼▼ Super 8 Motel-Anamosa** 🆂🅷
(319) 462-3888. **$54-$58.** 100 Grant Wood Dr. Just e on US 64 from US 151. Int corridors. **Pets:** Small. $20 daily fee/pet. Designated rooms, no service, crate.
[ASK] [S☉] [✕] [⌐]

## ANKENY

**♦♦♦ ▼▼▼ Best Western Metro North** 🆂🅷
(515) 964-1717. **$69-$89, 30 day notice.** 133 SE Delaware Ave. I-35, exit 92, just w. Int corridors. **Pets:** Accepted.
[SAVE] [S☉] [✕] [🛏] [💻] [🍴] [🛆] [✕]

**▼▼▼ Heartland Inn** 🆂🅷
(515) 964-8202. **$80-$95.** 201 SE Delaware Ave. I-35, exit 92, just w. Int corridors. **Pets:** Small. $10 daily fee/room. Designated rooms, service with restrictions, supervision.
[ASK] [S☉] [✕] [🛏] [💻] [🛆]

## ARNOLDS PARK

**▼▼▼ Fillenwarth Beach** 🆂🅷
(712) 332-5646. **$64-$820 (no credit cards), 21 day notice.** 87 Lake Shore Dr. Just w of US 71; on West Lake Okoboji. Ext corridors. **Pets:** Other species.
[✕] [🛏] [💻] [🛆] [✕]

## ATLANTIC

**♦♦♦ ▼▼▼ Days Inn** 🆂🅷
(712) 243-4067. **$65-$70.** 64968 Boston Rd. I-80, exit 60 (US 71), 0.5 mi s. Int corridors. **Pets:** Medium, other species. $5 one-time fee/room. Designated rooms, service with restrictions, supervision.
[SAVE] [S☉] [✕] [🛏] [💻] [🛆]

**▼▼▼ Super 8 Motel** 🆂🅷
(712) 243-4723. **$65-$70.** 1902 E 7th St. I-80, exit 60 (US 71), 6 mi s, then 2 mi w; east side of town. Int corridors. **Pets:** Medium, other species. $25 deposit/room. Designated rooms, service with restrictions, crate.
[ASK] [S☉] [✕] [⌂] [🛏] [💻] [🛆]

## BURLINGTON

**♦♦♦ ▼▼▼▼ Best Western Pzazz Fun City** 🆂🅷
(319) 753-2223. **$109-$199, 30 day notice.** 3001 Winegard Dr. Jct US 61 and 34, just n. Int corridors. **Pets:** Other species. Designated rooms, service with restrictions.
[SAVE] [S☉] [✕] [ᕕM] [⌐] [⌂] [🛏] [💻] [🍴] [🛆] [✕]

**▼▼▼▼ Comfort Suites Hotel & Conference Center** 🆂🅷
(319) 753-1300. **Call for rates.** 1780 Stonegate Center Dr. On US 61, 2 mi s of US 34. Int corridors. **Pets:** Accepted.
[✕] [ᕕM] [⌂] [🛏] [💻] [🍴] [🛆] [✕]

**♦♦♦ ▼▼▼ Quality Inn** 🆂🅷
(319) 753-0000. **$75-$85, 10 day notice.** 3051 Kirkwood Ave. Jct US 61 and 34, just n. Int corridors. **Pets:** $10 daily fee/pet. Service with restrictions, supervision.
[SAVE] [S☉] [✕] [🛏] [💻] [🛆]

**▼▼▼ Super 8 Motel-Burlington** 🆂🅷
(319) 752-9806. **$45-$79.** 3001 Kirkwood Ave. Jct US 61 and 34, just n. Int corridors. **Pets:** Small. $10 daily fee/pet. Designated rooms, no service, crate.
[ASK] [S☉] [✕] [🛏]

## CARROLL

**▼▼▼ Super 8 Motel** 🆂🅷
(712) 792-4753. **$53-$63.** 1757 US 71 N. Just n of jct US 30 and 71. Int corridors. **Pets:** Accepted.
[ASK] [S☉] [✕]

## CARTER LAKE

**♦♦♦ ▼▼▼▼ Holiday Inn Express Hotel & Suites** 🆂🅷
(402) 505-4900. **$84-$129.** 2510 Abbott Plaza. I-480 W, exit 4 to 10th St, 2 mi n, follow Eppley Airfield signs. Int corridors. **Pets:** Medium. $100 deposit/room, $10 daily fee/room. Designated rooms, service with restrictions, supervision.
[SAVE] [S☉] [✕] [ᕕM] [⌐] [⌂] [🛏] [💻] [🛆]

**♦♦♦ ▼▼▼ Super 8 Motel** 🆂🅷 🐾
(712) 347-5588. **$58-$68.** 3000 Airport Dr. I-480 W, exit 4 to 10th St 2.3 mi n, follow Eppley Airfield signs. Int corridors. **Pets:** Other species. $10 one-time fee/room. Service with restrictions, crate.
[SAVE] [✕] [ᕕM] [⌂] [🛏] [🛆]

## CEDAR FALLS

**♦♦♦ ▼▼▼ Days Inn** 🅼
(319) 266-1222. **$69-$89.** 5826 University Ave, Suite 2. 0.7 mi e of jct SR 58. Int corridors. **Pets:** Accepted.
[SAVE] [S☉] [✕] [🛏] [💻]

**♦♦♦ ▼▼▼ University Inn** 🅼 🐾
(319) 277-1412. **$45-$69.** 4711 University Ave. 1.6 mi e of jct SR 58. Ext/int corridors. **Pets:** Large. $30 deposit/pet. Designated rooms, service with restrictions, crate.
[SAVE] [S☉] [✕] [🛏] [💻] [✕]

## CEDAR RAPIDS

**▼▼▼ Best Western Cooper's Mill Hotel & Restaurant** 🆂🅷
(319) 366-5323. **$69-$89.** 100 F Ave NW. I-380, exit 19C northbound, take a right at end of the exit, make an immediate U-turn and go under I-380; exit 20A southbound, cross river, right on 1st St NW. Int corridors. **Pets:** Medium. $5 daily fee/pet. Designated rooms, service with restrictions, crate.
[ASK] [S☉] [✕] [🛏] [💻] [🍴] [🛆] [✕]

**(AAA) ▽▽▽ Best Western Longbranch Hotel & Convention Center** SH
(319) 377-6386. **$89-$99.** 90 Twixt Town Rd NE. I-380, exit 24A (SR 100/Collins Rd), 2.5 mi e, then just n. Int corridors. **Pets:** Medium, other species. $5 daily fee/pet. Designated rooms, service with restrictions, supervision.
SAVE S⬚ ✕ 🖥 💻 🍴 ≈ ✕

**(AAA) ▽▽▽ Clarion Hotel & Convention Center** LH ✿
(319) 366-8671. **$82-$90.** 525 33rd Ave SW. I-380, exit 17 (33rd Ave SW), just w. Int corridors. **Pets:** Medium. $15 one-time fee/room. Designated rooms, service with restrictions.
SAVE S⬚ ✕ 🖥 💻 🍴 ≈ ✕

**▽▽ Comfort Inn by Choice Hotels North** SH
(319) 393-8247. **$64-$99.** 5055 Rockwell Dr NE. I-380, exit 24A (SR 100/Collins Rd), 1.3 mi e. Int corridors. **Pets:** Accepted.
ASK S⬚ ✕ 🖥 💻

**▽▽ Comfort Inn by Choice Hotels-South** SH
(319) 363-7934. **$64-$99.** 390 33rd Ave SW. I-380, exit 17 (33rd Ave SW), just w. Int corridors. **Pets:** Accepted.
ASK S⬚ ✕ 🖥 💻

**(AAA) ▽▽ Country Inn & Suites Cedar Rapids Airport** SH
(319) 363-3789. **$89-$139.** 9100 Atlantic Dr SW. I-380, exit 13, just w. Int corridors. **Pets:** Large, other species. $10 daily fee/room. Service with restrictions, supervision.
SAVE S⬚ ✕ &M 🖥 💻 ≈

**(AAA) ▽▽▽ Crowne Plaza Five Seasons** LH
(319) 363-8161. **$82-$299.** 350 1st Ave NE. I-380, exit 20B, just e; downtown. Int corridors. **Pets:** Accepted.
SAVE ✕ 🖥 💻 🍴 ≈ ✕

**▽▽ Economy Inn & Suites of Cedar Rapids** SH
(319) 365-4339. **$49-$79.** 3245 Southgate Pl SW. I-380, exit 17 (33rd Ave SW), just w. Int corridors. **Pets:** Accepted.
ASK S⬚ ✕ 🖥 💻 ≈

**(AAA) ▽▽▽ Exel Inn of Cedar Rapids** SH
(319) 366-2475. **$46-$76.** 616 33rd Ave SW. I-380, exit 17 (33rd Ave SW), 0.3 mi w. Int corridors. **Pets:** Small, other species. Designated rooms, service with restrictions, supervision.
SAVE S⬚ ✕ 🖥 💻

**▽▽▽ Hawthorn Suites Ltd** SH
(319) 294-8700. **$122-$133.** 4444 Czech Ln NE. I-380, exit 24A (SR 100/Collins Rd), just s. Int corridors. **Pets:** Other species. Service with restrictions, crate.
ASK S⬚ ✕ &M 🖥 💻 ≈

**▽▽ Heartland Inn** SH
(319) 362-9012. **$78-$93.** 3315 Southgate Ct SW. I-380, exit 17 (33rd Ave SW), just sw. Int corridors. **Pets:** Small. $10 daily fee/room. Designated rooms, service with restrictions, supervision.
ASK S⬚ ✕ 🖥 💻 ≈ ✕

**▽▽▽ Mainstay Suites** SH
(319) 363-7829. **$75-$120.** 5145 Rockwell Dr NE. I-380, exit 24A (SR 100/Collins Rd), 1 mi e, then just n. Int corridors. **Pets:** Medium, other species. $10 daily fee/pet. Service with restrictions, crate.
ASK S⬚ ✕ &M 🖥 💻 ≈ ✕

**(AAA) ▽▽▽ Marriott Cedar Rapids** LH
(319) 393-6600. **$129-$189.** 1200 Collins Rd NE. I-380, exit 24A (SR 100/Collins Rd), 1 mi e. Int corridors. **Pets:** Accepted.
SAVE S⬚ ✕ &M 🖥 💻 🍴 ≈

**▽▽ Motel 6 #1485** M
(319) 366-7523. **$35-$47.** 3325 Southgate Ct SW. I-380, exit 17 (33rd Ave SW), just sw. Ext corridors. **Pets:** Accepted.
S⬚ ✕ &M

**▽▽ Ramada Limited** SH
(319) 396-5000. **$65-$110.** 4011 16th Ave SW. I-380, exit 16 (US 30), 2.4 mi w, 1.4 mi n (exit 250) on Edgewood Rd to 16th Ave, then just w. Int corridors. **Pets:** Small. Service with restrictions, crate.
ASK S⬚ ✕ &M 🖥 💻 ≈

**▽▽ Ramada Limited Suites** SH
(319) 378-8888. **$69-$135.** 2025 Werner Ave NE. I-380, exit 24A (SR 100/Collins Rd), just se. Int corridors. **Pets:** Small. Service with restrictions, supervision.
ASK S⬚ ✕ 🖥 💻 ≈

**▽▽▽ Residence Inn by Marriott** SH
(319) 395-0111. **$79-$149.** 1900 Dodge Rd NE. I-380, exit 24A (SR 100/Collins Rd), just e. Int corridors. **Pets:** Accepted.
ASK S⬚ ✕ &M 🖥 💻 ≈ ✕

**▽▽ Super 8 Motel** SH
(319) 363-1755. **$55.** 400 33rd Ave SW. I-380, exit 17 (33rd Ave SW), just w. Int corridors. **Pets:** $10 one-time fee/pet. Service with restrictions, supervision.
ASK S⬚ ✕ 🖥

**▽▽ Super 8 Motel** SH
(319) 362-6002. **$56-$61.** 720 33rd Ave SW. I-380, exit 17 (33rd Ave SW), 0.4 mi w. Int corridors. **Pets:** Accepted.
ASK S⬚ ✕ &M 🖥

**▽▽ Travel Inn & Suites** SH
(319) 378-3948. **$45-$51.** 2215 Blairs Ferry Rd NE. I-380, exit 24B, just e. Int corridors. **Pets:** Accepted.
✕ &M 🖥 💻 ≈

# CHARLES CITY

**(AAA) ▽▽ Hartwood Inn** M
(641) 228-4352. **$40.** 1312 Gilbert St. Jct US 18 and CR B35, exit 212, 2.2 mi e. Ext corridors. **Pets:** Other species. $5 daily fee/pet. Service with restrictions.
SAVE S⬚ ✕ &M 🖥 💻 ≈

**▽▽ Super 8 Motel-Charles City** SH
(641) 228-2888. **$49-$69.** 1411 S Grand Ave. Jct US 18 and 218 (exit 229), 0.8 mi n on US 218 business route; south side of town. Int corridors. **Pets:** Small. Designated rooms, no service, crate.
ASK S⬚ ✕ &M 🖥

# CHEROKEE

**(AAA) ▽▽ Best Western La Grande Hacienda** SH
(712) 225-5701. **$65-$85, 3 day notice.** 1401 N 2nd St. Jct US 59 and SR 2, 0.4 mi s. Int corridors. **Pets:** Other species. $50 deposit/room, $10 one-time fee/room. Service with restrictions, supervision.
SAVE S⬚ ✕ &M 🖥 💻 🍴 ≈

# CLARINDA

**▽▽ Clarinda Super 8 Motel** SH
(712) 542-6333. **$59-$68.** 1203 S 12th St. Jct US 71 and SR 2, just e. Int corridors. **Pets:** Small. Service with restrictions, supervision.
ASK S⬚ ✕ &M 🖥 💻

# CLEAR LAKE

**▽▽ AmericInn Lodge & Suites of Clear Lake** SH
(641) 357-8954. **$70-$120.** 1406 25th St. I-35, exit 194 (SR 122). Int corridors. **Pets:** Service with restrictions, supervision.
ASK ✕ 🖥 💻 ≈ ✕

**(AAA) ▽▽ Best Western Holiday Lodge** SH
(641) 357-5253. **$66-$78.** 2023 7th Ave N. I-35, exit 194 (SR 122), 0.3 mi w. Ext/int corridors. **Pets:** Other species. $10 daily fee/room. Designated rooms, service with restrictions, supervision.
SAVE S⬚ ✕ &M 🖥 💻 🍴 ≈

**AAA ▼▼ Budget Inn SH**
(641) 357-8700. **$45-$75.** 1306 N 25th St. I-35, exit 194 (US 18), just nw. Int corridors. **Pets:** Service with restrictions, supervision.
[SAVE] [S◇] [✕] [🛏] [⊶]

**▼▼ Heartland Inn SH**
(641) 357-5123. **$77-$130.** 1603 S Shore Dr. I-35, exit 193, 1.3 mi w to S Shore Dr, then 1 mi s. Int corridors. **Pets:** Small. $10 daily fee/room. Designated rooms, service with restrictions, supervision.
[ASK] [S◇] [✕] [🛏] [▣] [⊶] [✕]

**▼ Lake Country Inn M ❀**
(641) 357-2184. **$35-$70.** 518 Hwy 18. I-35, exit 194 (US 18), 2 mi w. Ext corridors. **Pets:** Dogs only. $5 daily fee/pet. Designated rooms, service with restrictions, supervision.
[ASK] [S◇] [✕] [🛏] [▣]

**▼▼ Microtel Inn SH**
(641) 357-0966. **$57-$77.** 1305 N 25th St. I-35, exit 194 (SR 122), just nw. Int corridors. **Pets:** Other species. Service with restrictions, crate.
[ASK] [S◇] [✕] [⅏M] [▣]

**▼▼ Super 8 Motel SH**
(641) 357-7521. **$46-$65.** 2809 4th Ave S. I-35, exit 193, just e. Int corridors. **Pets:** $5 one-time fee/pet. Service with restrictions, supervision.
[ASK] [S◇] [✕]

# CLINTON

**AAA ▼▼ Best Western-Frontier Motor Inn SH**
(563) 242-7112. **$69-$39.** 2300 Lincoln Way. On US 30, just e of jct US 30 and 67. Ext/int corridors. **Pets:** Medium. Service with restrictions, crate.
[SAVE] [S◇] [✕] [⌖] [⅏] [🛏] [▣] [🍴] [⊶] [✕]

**AAA ▼▼▼ Country Inn & Suites By Carlson SH**
(563) 244-9922. **$69-$99.** 2224 Lincoln Way. On US 30, just e of jct US 30 and 67. Int corridors. **Pets:** Medium. $10 daily fee/pet. Service with restrictions, crate.
[SAVE] [S◇] [✕] [⅏M] [⌖] [⅏] [🛏] [▣] [⊶]

**▼▼ Super 8 Motel-Clinton SH**
(563) 242-8870. **$46-$80.** 1711 Lincoln Way. On US 30, 0.7 mi e of jct US 67. Int corridors. **Pets:** Small. Designated rooms, no service, crate.
[ASK] [S◇] [✕] [⅏M] [⌖] [🛏]

# CLIVE

**AAA ▼▼▼ Baymont Inn & Suites West Des Moines-Clive SH**
(515) 221-9200. **$59-$109.** 1390 NW 118th St. I-80/35, exit 124 (University Ave). Int corridors. **Pets:** Medium. Service with restrictions.
[SAVE] [✕] [⅏M] [⌖] [⅏] [🛏] [▣] [⊶]

**AAA ▼▼▼ Chase Suite Hotel by Woodfin SH**
(515) 223-7700. **$99-$139.** 11428 Forest Ave. I-80/35, exit 124 (University Ave), just ne. Ext corridors. **Pets:** Other species. $150 deposit/pet, $5 daily fee/pet. Service with restrictions, crate.
[SAVE] [S◇] [✕] [⅏M] [⌖] [⅏] [🛏] [▣] [⊶] [✕]

**▼▼ Heartland Inn-West Des Moines SH**
(515) 226-0414. **$77-$87.** 11414 Forest Ave. I-80/35, exit 124 (University Ave), just e. Int corridors. **Pets:** Small. $10 daily fee/room. Designated rooms, service with restrictions, supervision.
[ASK] [S◇] [✕] [🛏] [▣] [✕]

# COLFAX

**▼▼ Comfort Inn SH**
(515) 674-4455. **$65-$179.** 1402 N Walnut. I-80, exit 155, just ne. Int corridors. **Pets:** Large, other species. $13 daily fee/room. Service with restrictions, supervision.
[ASK] [S◇] [✕] [⅏M] [⌖] [🛏] [▣] [⊶] [✕]

# COLUMBUS JUNCTION

**▼▼ Columbus Motel M**
(319) 728-8080. **$51-$58.** 265 Colonels Dr. Just e of jct US 92 and SR 70 on US 92. Int corridors. **Pets:** Accepted.
[ASK] [✕] [🛏] [▣]

# CORALVILLE

**▼▼ Days Inn M**
(319) 354-4400. **$55-$129.** 205 2nd St. I-80, exit 242, 1 mi s to 2nd St, then just w. Ext corridors. **Pets:** Medium. $20 daily fee/pet. Designated rooms, service with restrictions, supervision.
[ASK] [S◇] [✕] [🛏]

**▼▼ Heartland Inn SH**
(319) 351-8132. **$85-$95.** 87 2nd St. I-80, exit 242, 1 mi s on US 6, then just e. Int corridors. **Pets:** Small. $10 daily fee/room. Designated rooms, service with restrictions, supervision.
[ASK] [S◇] [✕] [🛏] [▣] [⊶]

**▼▼ Super 8 Motel-Iowa City SH**
(319) 337-8388. **$54-$69.** 611 1st Ave. I-80, exit 242, 0.4 mi s. Int corridors. **Pets:** Small. $20 daily fee/pet. No service, crate.
[ASK] [S◇] [✕] [⅏M] [⌖] [🛏]

# COUNCIL BLUFFS

**AAA ▼▼ Best Western Crossroads of the Bluffs SH**
(712) 322-3150. **$69-$129.** 2216 27th Ave. I-29/80, exit 1B (24th St), just ne. Int corridors. **Pets:** Accepted.
[SAVE] [S◇] [✕] [⌖] [⅏] [🛏] [▣] [⊶]

**AAA ▼▼ Days Inn SH**
(712) 323-2200. **$55-$100.** 3619 9th Ave. I-29, exit 53A (9th Ave). Int corridors. **Pets:** $10 daily fee/pet. Designated rooms, service with restrictions, supervision.
[SAVE] [S◇] [✕] [⌖] [🛏] [▣]

**▼▼ Days Inn SH**
(712) 366-9699. **$45-$70, 14 day notice.** 3208 S 7th St. I-29/80, exit 3 (US 92), just sw. Int corridors. **Pets:** Accepted.
[ASK] [S◇] [✕] [⌖] [⅏] [🛏] [▣]

**▼▼ Heartland Inn SH**
(712) 322-8400. **$78-$93.** 1000 Woodbury Ave. I-80, exit 5 (Madison Ave). Int corridors. **Pets:** Small. $10 daily fee/room. Designated rooms, service with restrictions, supervision.
[ASK] [S◇] [✕] [🛏] [▣] [⊶]

**▼▼ Motel 6 Council Bluffs, IA #1153 SH**
(712) 366-2405. **$45-$65.** 3032 S Expressway St. I-29/80, exit 3 (US 92). Int corridors. **Pets:** Accepted.
[S◇] [✕] [⌖] [⅏] [🛏] [▣] [⊶]

**AAA ▼▼ Quality Inn & Suites SH ❀**
(712) 328-3171. **$59-$129.** 3537 W Broadway. I-29, exit 53A (9th Ave), just e, 0.5 mi n on S 35th St, then just w. Ext/int corridors. **Pets:** Other species. $10 daily fee/room. Service with restrictions.
[SAVE] [S◇] [✕] [⌖] [⅏] [🛏] [▣] [⊶]

**▼ Super 8 Motel SH**
(712) 322-2888. **$58-$64.** 2712 S 24th St. I-80, exit 1B (24th St). Int corridors. **Pets:** Service with restrictions, supervision.
[ASK] [S◇] [✕] [⌖]

**AAA ▼▼ Western Inn SH**
(712) 322-4499. **$65-$86.** 1842 Madison Ave. I-80, exit 5 (Madison Ave). Int corridors. **Pets:** Medium. $10 one-time fee/room. Designated rooms, service with restrictions, crate.
[SAVE] [✕] [⌖] [⊶]

# CRESCO

**AAA** ▼▼ Cresco Motel **M** ❀
(563) 547-2240. **$48-$74.** 620 2nd Ave SE. On SR 9; on east side of town. Ext corridors. **Pets:** Other species. $7 daily fee/room. Service with restrictions, supervision.
SAVE Sₒ ✕ ᴹ ✆ 🖪

# CRESTON

▼▼ Super 8 Motel-Creston **SH**
(641) 782-6541. **$60-$73.** 804 W Taylor. Jct US 34 and SR 25, on US 34. Int corridors. **Pets:** Small. Designated rooms, no service, crate.
ASK Sₒ ✕ ᴹ ✆ 🖪

# DECORAH

▼▼ Heartland Inn **SH**
(563) 382-2269. **$75-$97.** 705 Commerce Dr. Jct US 52, 1.8 mi e on SR 9. Int corridors. **Pets:** Small. $10 daily fee/room. Designated rooms, service with restrictions, supervision.
ASK Sₒ ✕ 🖪 🖳 ⇌

# DENISON

▼▼ Denison Super 8 **SH**
(712) 263-5081. **Call for rates.** 502 Boyer Valley Rd. Jct US 30/59 and SR 141, 0.3 mi sw. Int corridors. **Pets:** Small. $5 daily fee/pet. Service with restrictions, crate.
ASK ✕ 🖪

# DES MOINES

**AAA** ▼▼ American Inn & Suites **M**
(515) 265-7511. **$46-$50, 7 day notice.** 5020 NE 14th St. I-80/35, exit 136 (US 69), just n. Ext/int corridors. **Pets:** Other species. Service with restrictions, supervision.
SAVE Sₒ ✕ ✆ 🖳

▼▼ Bavarian Inn **SH**
(515) 265-5611. **$49-$59.** 5220 NE 14th St. I-80/35, exit 136 (US 69), 0.3 mi n. Int corridors. **Pets:** Small. $10 one-time fee/room. Service with restrictions, supervision.
ASK Sₒ ✕ 🖪 🖳 ❤️ ⇌

▼▼ Comfort Inn by Choice Hotels **SH**
(515) 287-3434. **$64-$134.** 5231 Fleur Dr. Opposite the airport. Int corridors. **Pets:** Accepted.
ASK Sₒ ✕ ᴹ 🖉 🖪 🖳 ⇌

**AAA** ▼▼▼ Four Points Sheraton Des Moines Airport **SH**
(515) 287-6464. **$89-$149.** 1810 Army Post Rd. Across from airport. Int corridors. **Pets:** Accepted.
SAVE Sₒ ✕ ᴹ ✆ 🖪 🖳 ❤️ ⇌

▼▼ Heartland Inn-Airport **SH**
(515) 256-0603. **$88-$103.** 1901 Hackley Ave. Opposite the airport. Int corridors. **Pets:** Small. $10 daily fee/room. Designated rooms, service with restrictions, supervision.
ASK Sₒ ✕ 🖉 ✆ 🖪 🖳 ⇌

▼ Hickman Motor Lodge **M**
(515) 276-8591. **$49-$56.** 6500 Hickman Rd. I-80/35, exit 125, 2.5 mi e. Ext corridors. **Pets:** Accepted.
ASK Sₒ 🖪

▼▼▼ Hotel Fort Des Moines **LH**
(515) 243-1161. **$69-$179.** 1000 Walnut St. Downtown. Int corridors. **Pets:** Other species. Service with restrictions, crate.
ASK ✕ 🖪 🖳 ❤️ ⇌ ⨯

▼▼ Motel 6-30 **M**
(515) 287-6364. **$43-$55.** 4817 Fleur Dr. Opposite the airport. Ext corridors. **Pets:** Accepted.
Sₒ ✕ ✆

▼▼ Quality Inn & Suites **SH**
(515) 278-2381. **$59-$109.** 4995 Merle Hay Rd. I-80/35, exit 131 (Merle Hay Rd), just s. Int corridors. **Pets:** Large. $25 one-time fee/room. Designated rooms, service with restrictions.
ASK Sₒ ✕ ᴹ 🖉 ✆ 🖪 🖳 ⇌ ⨯

**AAA** ▼▼▼ Quality Inn & Suites Event Center **LH**
(515) 282-5251. **$69-$108, 14 day notice.** 929 3rd St. I-235, exit 3rd St; downtown. Int corridors. **Pets:** Medium. Designated rooms, service with restrictions, supervision.
SAVE Sₒ ✕ 🖉 🖪 🖳 ❤️ ⇌

**AAA** ▼▼ Ramada **SH**
(515) 265-4777. **$74-$84.** 4685 NE 14th St. I-80, exit 137 (US 69), just s. Int corridors. **Pets:** $10 daily fee/pet. Designated rooms, service with restrictions, supervision.
SAVE Sₒ ✕ 🖪 🖳 ❤️ ⇌ ⨯

**AAA** ▼▼ Red Roof Inn & Suites **SH**
(515) 266-6800. **$68-$94.** 4950 NE 14th St. I-80, exit 137 (US 69). Int corridors. **Pets:** Medium. Service with restrictions, crate.
SAVE Sₒ ✕ ᴹ ✆ 🖪 🖳

▼▼ Super 8 Lodge **SH**
(515) 278-8858. **$45-$80.** 4755 Merle Hay Rd. I-80/35, exit 131 (Merle Hay Rd), just s. Int corridors. **Pets:** Small, other species. $10 daily fee/pet. Service with restrictions, supervision.
ASK Sₒ ✕ 🖪

# DE SOTO

▼ Edgetowner Motel **M**
(515) 834-2641. **$55.** 804 Guthrie. I-80, exit 110, just s. Ext corridors. **Pets:** Dogs only. Service with restrictions, supervision.
✕

# DUBUQUE

**AAA** ▼▼▼ Best Western Midway Hotel **LH**
(563) 557-8000. **$89-$125.** 3100 Dodge St. US 20, 2.3 mi w of jct US 52/61/151 and Mississippi Bridge. Int corridors. **Pets:** Medium. $10 one-time fee/room. Designated rooms, service with restrictions, supervision.
SAVE Sₒ ✕ 🖉 🖪 🖳 ⇌ ⨯

▼▼ Comfort Inn by Choice Hotels **SH**
(563) 556-3006. **$64-$114.** 4055 McDonald Dr. US 20, 3.8 mi w of jct US 52/61/151 and Mississippi Bridge. Int corridors. **Pets:** Accepted.
ASK Sₒ ✕ 🖉 🖪 🖳 ⇌

▼▼ Days Inn-Dubuque **SH**
(563) 583-3297. **$55-$105.** 1111 Dodge St. US 20, 0.8 mi w of jct US 52/61/151 and Mississippi Bridge, exit Hill/Bryant. Ext corridors. **Pets:** Other species. $5 daily fee/pet. Service with restrictions, supervision.
ASK Sₒ ✕ 🖪 🖳 ❤️ ⇌

▼▼ Heartland Inn-South **SH**
(563) 556-6555. **$80-$90.** 2090 Southpark Ct. US 151 and 61 at jct US 52; 2.5 mi s of jct US 20 and Mississippi Bridge. Int corridors. **Pets:** Small. $10 daily fee/room. Designated rooms, service with restrictions, supervision.
ASK Sₒ ✕ 🖪 🖳 ⨯

▼▼ Heartland Inn-West **SH**
(563) 582-3752. **$80-$90.** 4025 McDonald Dr. US 20, 3.8 mi w of jct US 52/61/151 and Mississippi Bridge. Int corridors. **Pets:** Small. $10 daily fee/room. Designated rooms, service with restrictions, supervision.
ASK Sₒ ✕ 🖪 🖳 ⇌ ⨯

**AAA** ▼▼▼ Holiday Inn Dubuque/Galena **LH**
(563) 556-2000. **$89-$119.** 450 Main St. At Main and 4th sts; downtown. Int corridors. **Pets:** Large. $25 one-time fee/room. Designated rooms, service with restrictions, crate.
SAVE Sₒ ✕ ᴹ ✆ 🖪 🖳 ❤️ ⇌ ⨯

▼▼▼ MainStay Suites **SH**
(563) 557-7829. **$69-$119.** 1275 Associates Dr. Just n of jct US 20 and NW Arterial Rd; west side of town. Int corridors. **Pets:** Very small, other species. $20 one-time fee/pet. Service with restrictions, supervision.
[ASK] [S✿] [✕] [&M] [✎] [🛏] [💻]

## DYERSVILLE

▼▼ ▼▼ Comfort Inn-Dyersville **SH**
(563) 875-7700. **$75-$160.** 527 16th Ave SE. US 20, exit 294 (SR 136), just nw. Int corridors. **Pets:** Medium. $13 daily fee/pet. Designated rooms, service with restrictions, supervision.
[ASK] [S✿] [✕] [&M] [✎] [🛏] [💻] [≈] [✕]

▼▼ ▼▼ Super 8 Motel-Dyersville **SH**
(563) 875-8885. **$49-$79.** 925 15th Ave SE. US 20, exit 294 (SR 136), just n. Int corridors. **Pets:** Accepted.
[ASK] [S✿] [✕] [&M] [🛏]

## ELDRIDGE

▼▼▼ Quality Inn & Suites **SH**
(563) 285-4600. **$65-$135.** 1000 E Iowa St. Just w of jct US 61 and CR F45 (exit 127). Int corridors. **Pets:** Medium, other species. $50 deposit/room. Service with restrictions, crate.
[ASK] [S✿] [✕] [✎] [🛏] [💻] [≈] [✕]

## ELK HORN

▼▼ AmericInn Motel & Suites **SH**
(712) 764-4000. **$75-$118.** 4037 Main St. I-80, exit 54 (SR 173), 6.4 mi n. Int corridors. **Pets:** Other species. $50 deposit/room. Designated rooms, service with restrictions, crate.
[ASK] [✕] [&M] [✎] [🛏] [💻] [≈]

## ESTHERVILLE

▼▼▼▼ Sleep Inn & Suites **SH**
(712) 362-5522. **$84-$94.** 2008 Central Ave. Jct SR 4 and 9, 1 mi e. Int corridors. **Pets:** $13 daily fee/room. Service with restrictions, supervision.
[ASK] [S✿] [✕] [✎] [🛏] [💻]

## EVANSDALE

▼▼ ▼▼ Days Inn **SH**
(319) 235-1111. **$89.** 450 Evansdale Dr. I-380, exit 68, just n. Int corridors. **Pets:** Small, other species. $50 deposit/pet, $10 daily fee/pet. Service with restrictions, supervision.
[ASK] [S✿] [✕] [&M] [🛏] [💻] [≈]

## FAIRFIELD

(AAA) ▼▼ ▼▼ Best Western Fairfield Inn **SH**
(641) 472-2200. **$75-$82.** 2200 W Burlington Ave. On US 34, 1 mi w of jct SR 1. Int corridors. **Pets:** Accepted.
[SAVE] [S✿] [✕] [✎] [🛏] [💻] [🍴] [≈]

## FORT DODGE

(AAA) ▼▼ ▼▼ Comfort Inn **SH**
(515) 573-5000. **$80-$160, 30 day notice.** 2938 5th Ave S. US 20, exit 124 (Coalville), 6 mi n on CR P59, then 2 mi w on 5th Ave and Business Rt US 20. Int corridors. **Pets:** Medium. $10 daily fee/pet. Designated rooms, service with restrictions, supervision.
[SAVE] [S✿] [✕] [&M] [🐾] [🛏] [💻] [≈]

▼▼ ▼▼ Days Inn **SH**
(515) 576-8000. **$49-$64.** 3040 5th Ave S. US 20, exit 124 (Coalville), 3.7 mi n on CR P59, then 1.2 mi w on Business Rt US 20. Int corridors. **Pets:** Accepted.
[ASK] [S✿] [✕] [✎] [💻]

▼▼▼▼ Quality Inn **SH**
(515) 955-3621. **$63.** 2001 US 169. US 20, 2 mi n. Ext/int corridors. **Pets:** Accepted.
[ASK] [S✿] [✕] [&M] [🛏] [💻] [🍴] [≈] [✕]

▼▼▼ Super 8 Motel-Fort Dodge Iowa **SH**
(515) 576-8788. **$62-$100.** 3638 Maple Dr. US 20, exit 124 (Coalville), 6 mi n, then just w. Int corridors. **Pets:** Accepted.
[ASK] [S✿] [✕] [&M] [🛏]

## FORT MADISON

(AAA) ▼▼▼▼ Comfort Inn & Suites **SH**
(319) 372-6800. **$88-$189.** 6169 Reve Ct S 61. Just e of jct US 61 and SR 2, on US 61. Int corridors. **Pets:** Accepted.
[SAVE] [S✿] [✕] [✎] [🛏] [💻] [≈] [✕]

(AAA) ▼▼▼▼ The Madison Inn Motel **M**
(319) 372-7740. **$45-$100, 7 day notice.** 3440 Ave L. US 2 and 61, 2 mi w. Ext corridors. **Pets:** Medium. $10 daily fee/pet. Designated rooms, service with restrictions, supervision.
[SAVE] [S✿] [✕] [🛏] [💻]

▼▼▼ Super 8 Motel-Ft Madison **SH**
(319) 372-8500. **$52-$65.** US 61 W, 5107 Ave O. US 61, 1 mi e of jct US 61 and SR 2. Ext/int corridors. **Pets:** Small. Designated rooms, no service, crate.
[ASK] [S✿] [✕] [✏] [🛏]

## GLENWOOD

▼▼ Lincoln Bluff View Motel **SH**
(712) 622-8191. **$48-$53.** 57902 190 St. I-29, exit 35 (US 34). Int corridors. **Pets:** Accepted.
[✕] [🛏] [🍴]

## GRIMES

▼▼▼▼ AmericInn Lodge & Suites **SH** 🐾
(515) 986-9900. **$70-$180.** 251 Gateway. Just sw of jct US 44 and SR 141. Int corridors. **Pets:** Dogs only. $50 deposit/room, $10 daily fee/room. Designated rooms, service with restrictions, supervision.
[ASK] [✕] [&M] [✎] [🛏] [💻] [≈] [✕]

## HAMPTON

▼▼ ▼▼ AmericInn Lodge & Suites **SH**
(641) 456-5559. **$76-$130.** 702 Central Ave W. On SR 3 (Central Ave W), 0.7 mi w of jct US 65 and SR 3. Int corridors. **Pets:** Medium, other species. $100 deposit/pet. Designated rooms, service with restrictions, supervision.
[ASK] [✕] [🐾] [✎] [🛏] [💻] [≈] [✕]

▼▼ ▼▼ Country Heritage Bed & Breakfast **BB**
(641) 456-4036. **$65-$95.** 1034 Hwy 3. I-35, exit 165, 4 mi e. Int corridors. **Pets:** Accepted.
[✕] [💻] [🔧]

## IDA GROVE

▼▼ Delux Motel **M**
(712) 364-3317. **$45-$60.** 5981 US Hwy 175. Jct US 59 S and 175. Ext corridors. **Pets:** Accepted.
[✕] [🛏]

## INDEPENDENCE

▼▼ ▼▼ Super 8 Motel **SH**
(319) 334-7041. **$66-$125.** 2000 1st St W. US 20, exit 252, 1.4 mi n. Int corridors. **Pets:** Small. $10 daily fee/pet. Designated rooms, service with restrictions, crate.
[ASK] [S✿] [✕] [&M] [🛏]

## IOWA CITY

(AAA) ▼▼▼▼ Quality Inn & Suites **LH**
(319) 354-2000. **$69-$139.** 2525 N Dodge. I-80, exit 246, just ne. Int corridors. **Pets:** Accepted.
[SAVE] [S✿] [✕] [✎] [🛏] [💻] [🍴] [≈] [✕]

**🛆🛆🛆** 🛇🛇🛇🛇 **Sheraton Iowa City Hotel** �LⱧ
(319) 337-4058. **$239.** 210 S Dubuque St. Dubuque and Burlington sts (SR 1); downtown. Int corridors. **Pets:** Accepted.
🆂🅰🆅🅴 🆂🅳 ⊠ ⓜ ⊘ 💺 📳 📠 💻 🍴 🏊 ⊠

**🛆🛆🛆** 🛇🛇🛇 **Travelodge** 🆂🅷 🐾
(319) 351-1010. **$61-$76.** 2216 N Dodge St. I-80, exit 246, just sw on SR 1. Ext/int corridors. **Pets:** Medium. $6 daily fee/pet. Designated rooms, service with restrictions, supervision.
🆂🅰🆅🅴 🆂🅳 ⊠ ⓜ ⊘ 💺 📳 📠 💻 🏊

## JEFFERSON

🛇🛇🛇 **The Redwood Motel** 🅼
(515) 386-3116. **$40-$45, 3 day notice.** 209 E Gallup Rd. Just e of jct US 30 and SR 4. Ext corridors. **Pets:** Accepted.
🅰🆂🅺 🆂🅳 ⊠

## JOHNSTON

**🛆🛆🛆** 🛇🛇🛇 **Americas Best Inn** 🆂🅷
(515) 270-1111. **$49-$90.** 5050 Merle Hay Rd. I-80/35, exit 131 (Merle Hay Rd), just n. Int corridors. **Pets:** Other species. $10 one-time fee/room. Service with restrictions, supervision.
🆂🅰🆅🅴 🆂🅳 ⊠ ⓜ ⊘ 📳 📠 💻 🏊

**🛆🛆🛆** 🛇🛇🛇 **Best Western-Des Moines North** 🆂🅷
(515) 276-5411. **$67-$82, 30 day notice.** 5055 Merle Hay Rd. I-80/35, exit 131 (Merle Hay Rd), just n. Int corridors. **Pets:** Accepted.
🆂🅰🆅🅴 🆂🅳 ⊠ ⊘ 📳 📠 💻 🍴 🏊

## KEOKUK

🛇🛇 **Super 8 Motel-Keokuk** 🆂🅷
(319) 524-3888. **$52-$65.** 3511 Main St. On Business US 61/US 218, 2 mi n of jct US 136. Int corridors. **Pets:** Small. Designated rooms, no service, crate.
🅰🆂🅺 🆂🅳 ⊠ ⓜ 📳 💻

## LE CLAIRE

**🛆🛆🛆** 🛇🛇🛇 **Comfort Inn & Suites-Riverview** 🆂🅷
(563) 289-4747. **$70-$150.** 902 Mississippi View Ct. I-80, exit 306 (US 67), 0.5 mi n to Eagle Ridge Rd, then just sw. Int corridors. **Pets:** Medium. $25 deposit/room. Service with restrictions, crate.
🆂🅰🆅🅴 🆂🅳 ⊠ ⓜ 💺 📳 📠 🏊

**🛆🛆🛆** 🛇🛇🛇🛇 **Holiday Inn Express** 🆂🅷
(563) 289-9978. **$60-$105, 30 day notice.** 1201 Canal Shore Dr. I-80, exit 306, just n. Int corridors. **Pets:** Other species. $15 daily fee/room. Service with restrictions, supervision.
🆂🅰🆅🅴 🆂🅳 ⊠ 💺 📳 📠 🏊

**🛆🛆🛆** 🛇🛇🛇 **Super 8 of LeClaire** 🆂🅷
(563) 289-5888. **$62-$105.** 1552 Welcome Center Dr. I-80, exit 306 (US 67), 0.5 mi n to Eagle Ridge Rd, then just sw to Mississippi View Ct. Int corridors. **Pets:** Medium. $25 deposit/pet. Service with restrictions, crate.
🆂🅰🆅🅴 🆂🅳 ⊠ ⓜ 💺 📳 💻

## LE MARS

🛇🛇🛇 **Super 8 Motel** 🆂🅷
(712) 546-8800. **$50-$80, 30 day notice.** 1201 Hawkeye Ave SW. 1.2 mi s of jct US 75/SR 3, on US 75; south end of town. Int corridors. **Pets:** Dogs only. $10 daily fee/pet. Designated rooms, service with restrictions, supervision.
🅰🆂🅺 🆂🅳 ⊠ ⓜ 📳 💻 🏊

## MANCHESTER

🛇🛇 **Super 8 of Manchester** 🆂🅷
(563) 927-2533. **$61-$98.** 1020 W Main. Jct US 20 and SR 13, exit 275, 1.3 mi n, then 0.3 mi e. Int corridors. **Pets:** Medium. $10 daily fee/pet. Designated rooms, service with restrictions, supervision.
🅰🆂🅺 🆂🅳 ⊠ ⓜ 📳 💻

## MARION

🛇🛇 **Microtel Inn & Suites** 🆂🅷
(319) 373-7400. **$55-$85.** 5500 Dyer Ave. Jct US 151 and SR 13. Int corridors. **Pets:** Accepted.
⊠ ⓜ 💺 📳 💻

## MARQUETTE

🛇 **The Frontier Motel** 🅼
(563) 873-3497. **$55-$100.** 101 S 1st St. Just s of jct US 18 and SR 76; between Mississippi River Bridge and casino. Ext corridors. **Pets:** Accepted.
⊠ 📳 💻 🏊

## MARSHALLTOWN

🛇🛇🛇 **Best Western Regency Inn** 🆂🅷 🐾
(641) 752-6321. **$77-$92.** 3303 S Center St. Jct US 30 and SR 14. Int corridors. **Pets:** Other species. $10 one-time fee/room. Service with restrictions, supervision.
🅰🆂🅺 🆂🅳 ⊠ ⓜ ⊘ 💺 📳 📠 💻 🍴 🏊

🛇🛇 **Comfort Inn** 🆂🅷
(641) 752-6000. **$70-$85.** 2613 S Center St. 0.5 mi n of jct US 30 and SR 14. Int corridors. **Pets:** Other species. $10 one-time fee/room. Service with restrictions, supervision.
🅰🆂🅺 🆂🅳 ⊠ ⓜ ⊘ 💺 📳 📠 💻

🛇🛇 **Super 8 Motel** 🆂🅷 🐾
(641) 753-3333. **$57-$70.** 3315 S Center St. Just n of jct US 30 and SR 14. Int corridors. **Pets:** Other species. $10 one-time fee/room. Service with restrictions, supervision.
🅰🆂🅺 🆂🅳 ⊠ ⊘ 📳 💻

## MASON CITY

**🛆🛆🛆** 🛇🛇🛇 **Americas Best Value Inn** 🅼
(641) 424-2910. **$40-$69.** 24 5th St SW. Just w of jct US 65 and SR 122; just s of downtown. Ext/int corridors. **Pets:** Medium, other species. Service with restrictions, crate.
🆂🅰🆅🅴 🆂🅳 ⊠ 📳 🏊

🛇🛇 **Days Inn Mason City** 🆂🅷
(641) 424-0210. **$54-$66.** 2301 4th St SW. I-35, exit 194 (SR 122), 6 mi e. Int corridors. **Pets:** Accepted.
🅰🆂🅺 🆂🅳 ⊠ 💺 📳 💻

**🛆🛆🛆** 🛇🛇🛇🛇 **Holiday Inn** 🆂🅷
(641) 423-1640. **$84-$99.** 2101 4th St SW (Hwy 122). I-35, exit 194 (SR 122), 6 mi e. Ext/int corridors. **Pets:** Medium. $10 one-time fee/pet. Service with restrictions, crate.
🆂🅰🆅🅴 🆂🅳 ⊠ ⓜ 💺 📳 💻 🍴 🏊 ⊠

## MONTICELLO

🛇🛇 **The Blue Inn** 🆂🅷
(319) 465-6116. **$62-$100.** 250 N Main St. North end of town on US 151. Int corridors. **Pets:** Other species. $6 daily fee/pet. Designated rooms, service with restrictions, supervision.
🅰🆂🅺 🆂🅳 ⊠ 💻 🍴 🏊

## MOUNT PLEASANT

🛇🛇 **Brazelton Hotel** 🆂🅷
(319) 385-0571. **$71-$79.** 1200 E Baker. US 218/27, exit 45, 0.6 mi s on Grand Ave. Int corridors. **Pets:** Accepted.
🅰🆂🅺 🆂🅳 ⊠ ⊘ 💺 📳 📠 💻 🏊 ⊠

🛇🛇 **Heartland Inn** 🆂🅷
(319) 385-2102. **$74-$84.** 810 N Grand Ave. US 218/27, exit 45, 0.6 mi s. Int corridors. **Pets:** Small. $10 daily fee/room. Designated rooms, service with restrictions, supervision.
🅰🆂🅺 🆂🅳 ⊠ 📳 💻 🏊 ⊠

▼▼ **Super 8 Motel-Mt Pleasant** 🆂🅷
(319) 385-8888. **$59-$64.** 1000 N Grand Ave. US 218/27, exit 45, 0.6 mi s. Int corridors. **Pets:** Small. Designated rooms, no service, crate.
A$K 🔊 ✕ 🔋 🖵

## MOUNT VERNON

🛆🛆 ▼▼▼ **Sleep Inn & Suites** 🆂🅷 🐾
(319) 895-0055. **$69-$149.** 310 Virgil Ave. Jct US 30 and SR 1, just se. Int corridors. **Pets:** Medium. $12.50 one-time fee/room. Service with restrictions, supervision.
SAVE 🔊 ✕ 🔊ᴹ 🔦 🔋 🖵 ⇌

## MUSCATINE

▼▼▼ **Holiday Inn Muscatine** 🆂🅷
(563) 264-5550. **$80-$96.** 2915 N Hwy 61. Jct US 61 and SR 38, just n. Int corridors. **Pets:** Small, other species. $50 deposit/room, $10 daily fee/pet. Designated rooms, service with restrictions, crate.
A$K 🔊 ✕ 🔋 🖵 🍴 ⇌ ✕

▼▼ **Super 8 Motel-Muscatine** 🆂🅷
(563) 263-9100. **$44-$72.** 2900 N Hwy 61. Jct US 61 and SR 38. Int corridors. **Pets:** Small. Designated rooms, no service, crate.
A$K 🔊 ✕ ⌀ 🔋

## NEWTON

▼▼▼ **Days Inn of Newton** 🆂🅷
(641) 792-2330. **$65-$95.** 1605 W 19th St S. I-80, exit 164 (SR 14), just n. Int corridors. **Pets:** Other species. $10 daily fee/pet, $10 one-time fee/pet. Service with restrictions, supervision.
A$K 🔊 ✕ 🔦 🔋 🖵

🛆🛆 ▼▼▼ **Holiday Inn Express** 🆂🅷
(641) 792-7722. **$80-$120.** 1700 W 19th St S. I-80, exit 164 (SR 14), just nw. Int corridors. **Pets:** Small. $10 daily fee/room. Service with restrictions, supervision.
SAVE 🔊 ✕ 🔦 🔋 🖵 ⇌

🛆🛆 ▼▼▼ **HomeRidge Inn & Suites** 🆂🅷
(641) 792-3333. **$105-$115.** 208 W 4th St N. Downtown. Int corridors. **Pets:** Accepted.
SAVE 🔊 ✕ 🔊ᴹ 🔦 🔋 🖵 ⇌

🛆🛆 ▼▼▼ **Ramada Limited** 🆂🅷
(641) 792-8100. **$60-$85.** 1405 W 19th St S. I-80, exit 164 (SR 14), just n. Int corridors. **Pets:** Medium. $10 daily fee/pet. Designated rooms, service with restrictions, supervision.
SAVE 🔊 ✕ 🔋 🖵

## OELWEIN

▼▼ **Super 8 Motel-Oelwein** 🅼
(319) 283-2888. **Call for rates.** 210 10th St SE. Jct SR 3 and 150, 1 mi s. Int corridors. **Pets:** Medium. $10 daily fee/pet. Service with restrictions.
A$K ✕ 🔋 🖵

## OKOBOJI

▼▼ **AmericInn Lodge & Suites** 🆂🅷
(712) 332-9000. **$75-$195, 7 day notice.** 1005 Brooks Park Dr. Jct US 71 and SR 9, 2.5 mi s on US 71. Int corridors. **Pets:** Large, dogs only. $50 deposit/pet, $10 one-time fee/pet. Service with restrictions, supervision.
✕ 🔊ᴹ 🔦 🔋 🖵 🏊

▼▼▼ **Arrowwood Resort & Conference Center** 🆂🅷
(712) 332-2161. **$89-$329, 7 day notice.** 1405 US 71 S. Jct US 71 and SR 9, 3 mi s. Ext/int corridors. **Pets:** Accepted.
A$K 🔊 ✕ 🔊ᴹ ⌀ 🔦 🔋 🖵 🍴 ⇌ ✕

## OSCEOLA

▼▼▼ **AmericInn Lodge & Suites** 🆂🅷
(641) 342-9400. **$69-$149.** 111 Ariel Cir. I-35, exit 33. Int corridors. **Pets:** Medium. $50 deposit/room, $10 one-time fee/pet. Designated rooms, service with restrictions, supervision.
A$K 🔊 ✕ 🔊ᴹ 🔦 🔋 🖵 🏊

## OSKALOOSA

🛆🛆 ▼▼▼ **Americas Best Value Inn** 🅼
(641) 673-8351. **$62-$73.** 1315 A Ave E. On SR 92, just w of jct SR 23. Ext/int corridors. **Pets:** Medium, dogs only. $5 daily fee/pet. Designated rooms, service with restrictions, crate.
SAVE 🔊 ✕ 🔋 🖵

▼▼▼ **Comfort Inn** 🆂🅷
(641) 672-0375. **$85-$119.** 2401 A Ave W. Just e of jct SR 163, exit 57 (SR 92). Int corridors. **Pets:** Accepted.
A$K 🔊 ✕ 🔦 🔋 🖵 ⇌ ✕

## OTTUMWA

▼▼ **Colonial Motor Inn** 🅼
(641) 683-1661. **$41-$52.** 1534 Albia Rd. W on US 34, s at Quincy St, 0.5 mi to Albia Rd, then just w. Ext/int corridors. **Pets:** Accepted.
A$K 🔊 ✕ 🔋

▼▼▼ **Heartland Inn** 🆂🅷
(641) 682-8526. **$73-$83.** 125 W Joseph Ave. Jct US 63 and 34, 2 mi n. Int corridors. **Pets:** Small. $10 daily fee/room. Service with restrictions, supervision.
A$K 🔊 ✕ ⌀ 🔋 🖵 ⇌

▼▼▼ **Super 8 Motel** 🆂🅷
(641) 684-5055. **$59-$90.** 2823 N Court Rd. Jct US 63 and 34, 1.8 mi n. Int corridors. **Pets:** Accepted.
A$K 🔊 ✕ 🔋 🖵 ⇌ ✕

## PELLA

🛆🛆 ▼▼▼ **AmeriHost Inn & Suites-Pella** 🆂🅷
(641) 628-0085. **$59-$89.** 2104 Washington St. SR 163 Bypass at CR G28, exit 40. Int corridors. **Pets:** Medium. $10 daily fee/room. Designated rooms, service with restrictions, crate.
SAVE 🔊 ✕ 🔊ᴹ 🔦 🔋 🖵 ⇌ ✕

▼▼▼ **Super 8 Motel-Pella** 🆂🅷
(641) 628-8181. **$54-$89.** 105 E Oskaloosa St. SR 163, exit 42, 1 mi n, then 0.5 mi e. Int corridors. **Pets:** Small. Designated rooms, no service, crate.
A$K 🔊 ✕ 🔊ᴹ ⌀ 🔋 🖵

## PERCIVAL

🛆🛆 ▼▼▼ **Nebraska City Super 8 Motel** 🆂🅷
(712) 382-2828. **$50-$83.** 2103 249th St. I-29, exit 10, just w. Int corridors. **Pets:** Dogs only. $10 one-time fee/room. Designated rooms, supervision.
SAVE ✕ 🔊ᴹ 🔦 🔋 🖵

## PLEASANT HILL

🛆🛆 ▼▼▼ **Sleep Inn & Suites** 🆂🅷
(515) 299-9922. **$79-$169, 7 day notice.** 5850 Morning Star Ct. US 65, exit 79 (SR 163/E University Ave), just e. Int corridors. **Pets:** Medium. $13 daily fee/room. Service with restrictions, supervision.
SAVE 🔊 ✕ 🔦 🔋 🖵 🏊 ✕

# QUAD CITIES AREA

## BETTENDORF

**Heartland Inn-Bettendorf** SH
(563) 355-6336. **$78-$88.** 815 Golden Valley Dr. I-74, exit 2, just e, just n on Utica Ridge Rd, then just w. Int corridors. **Pets:** Small. $10 daily fee/room. Designated rooms, service with restrictions, supervision.

**The Lodge-Hotel & Conference Center** LH
(563) 359-7141. **$86-$176.** 900 Spruce Hills Dr. I-74, exit 2, just e. Int corridors. **Pets:** Small, other species. $50 deposit/room. Designated rooms, service with restrictions, crate.

**Signature Inn Bettendorf** SH
(563) 355-7575. **$49-$104.** 3020 Utica Ridge Rd. I-74, exit 2, just e. Int corridors. **Pets:** Accepted.

## DAVENPORT

**Baymont Inn & Suites Davenport** SH
(563) 386-1600. **$61-$98.** 400 Jason Way Ct. I-80, exit 295A (US 61), just s to 65th St, then 0.5 mi ne on frontage road. Int corridors. **Pets:** Medium. Service with restrictions.

**Best Western SteepleGate Inn** SH
(563) 386-6900. **$89-$119.** 100 W 76th St. I-80, exit 295A (US 61), 0.5 mi s to 65th St and frontage road entrance, then just nw. Int corridors. **Pets:** Medium. $10 daily fee/room. Service with restrictions, crate.

**Comfort Inn Davenport** SH
(563) 391-8222. **$54-$140, 30 day notice.** 7222 Northwest Blvd. I-80, exit 292 (Northwest Blvd), 0.3 mi s. Ext corridors. **Pets:** Accepted.

**Country Inn & Suites by Carlson** SH
(563) 388-6444. **$69-$99.** 140 E 55th St. I-80, exit 295A (US 61), 1.4 mi s. Int corridors. **Pets:** Accepted.

**Davenport Holiday Inn** SH
(563) 391-1230. **$74-$189.** 5202 Brady St. I-80, exit 295A (US 61), 1.6 mi s. Int corridors. **Pets:** Medium. $25 daily fee/pet. Service with restrictions, supervision.

**Davenport Super 8 Motel** SH
(563) 388-9810. **$57-$70, 7 day notice.** 410 E 65th St. I-80, exit 295A (US 61), 0.5 mi s, then just e. Int corridors. **Pets:** Accepted.

**Exel Inn of Davenport** SH
(563) 386-6350. **$43-$73.** 6310 N Brady St. I-80, exit 295A (US 61), 0.5 mi s. Int corridors. **Pets:** Small, other species. Designated rooms, service with restrictions, supervision.

**Heartland Inn** SH
(563) 386-8336. **$78-$88.** 6605 Brady St. I-80, exit 295A (US 61), just se. Int corridors. **Pets:** Small. $10 daily fee/room. Designated rooms, service with restrictions, supervision.

**Howard Johnson Plaza Hotel** LH ❀
(563) 326-1786. **Call for rates.** 227 LeClare St. Downtown. Int corridors. **Pets:** Medium, dogs only. $20 one-time fee/room. Designated rooms, service with restrictions, supervision.

**Residence Inn by Marriott** SH
(563) 391-8877. **$94-$140, 14 day notice.** 120 E 55th St. I-80, exit 295 (US 61), 1.4 mi s. Int corridors. **Pets:** Accepted.

**Rhythm City Casino Blackhawk Hotel** LH
(563) 328-6000. **$59-$195.** 200 E 3rd St. Between Brady St (US 61 N) and Pershing Ave; downtown. Int corridors. **Pets:** Other species. $50 deposit/room. Service with restrictions, supervision.

# END AREA

## RED OAK

**Super 8-Red Oak** SH
(712) 623-6919. **$62-$72.** 800 Senate Ave. Just e of jct US 34 and SR 48 on US 34. Int corridors. **Pets:** Other species. $5 daily fee/pet. Service with restrictions, supervision.

## SIBLEY

**Super 8 Motel** SH
(712) 754-3603. **$60-$70.** 1108 2nd Ave. On SR 60. Int corridors. **Pets:** Accepted.

## SIOUX CITY

**AmericInn Lodge & Suites** SH
(712) 255-1800. **$79-$129, 7 day notice.** 4230 S Lewis Blvd. I-29, exit 143, just e. Int corridors. **Pets:** Other species. $50 deposit/room, $10 daily fee/room. Designated rooms, service with restrictions, supervision.

**Clarion Hotel and Conference Center** LH
(712) 277-4101. **$82-$92.** 707 4th St. Downtown. Int corridors. **Pets:** Accepted.

**Comfort Inn by Choice Hotels** SH
(712) 274-1300. **$74-$104.** 4202 S Lakeport St. I-29, exit 144A, 1 mi e on US 20, then just s; do not use Business Rt US 20. Int corridors. **Pets:** Accepted.

**Motel 6-45** M
(712) 277-3131. **$40-$53.** 6166 Harbor Dr. I-29, exit 141, just w. Int corridors. **Pets:** Accepted.

**Quality Inn Hotel & Conference Center** M
(712) 277-3211. **$49-$79.** 1401 Zenith Dr. I-29, exit 149 (Hamilton Blvd). Int corridors. **Pets:** Other species. Service with restrictions, crate.

**♦♦ Super 8 Motel SH**
(712) 274-1520. **$53-$80.** 4307 Stone Ave. I-29, exit 144A, US 75 to exit 4B, 1 mi n on Gordon Dr; exit 147B southbound to Gordon Dr, 3 mi s. Int corridors. **Pets:** Dogs only. $10 daily fee/pet. Designated rooms, service with restrictions, supervision.

(ASK) (S6) (X) (&M) (☎) (➥)

## SLOAN

**♦ Winna Vegas Inn SH**
(712) 428-4280. **$58-$68.** 1862 Hwy 141. I-29, exit 127, just e. Int corridors. **Pets:** Accepted.

(ASK) (S6) (X) (&M) (⚡) (☎) (➥)

## SPIRIT LAKE

**♦ Oaks Motel M**
(712) 336-2940. **$56-$100, 10 day notice.** 1701 Chicago. Jct US 71 and SR 9, just e. Ext corridors. **Pets:** Accepted.

(X) (☎)

**♦ Shamrock Inn SH**
(712) 336-2668. **$49-$119, 3 day notice.** 1905 18th St. 0.6 mi e on SR 9 from jct US 71. Ext/int corridors. **Pets:** Accepted.

(ASK) (S6) (X) (☎) (➥) (➤)

**♦♦ Spirit Lake Super 8 SH**
(712) 336-4901. **$55-$99, 3 day notice.** 2203 Circle Dr W. Jct US 71 and SR 9. Int corridors. **Pets:** $10 one-time fee/room. Service with restrictions, supervision.

(ASK) (X) (&M) (☎) (➤)

## SPRINGDALE

**♦ Econo Lodge M ❧**
(319) 627-2171. **$49-$70.** 1943 Garfield Ave. I-80, exit 259, just sw. Ext corridors. **Pets:** Medium. $5 daily fee/pet. Service with restrictions, supervision.

(ASK) (S6) (X) (➤)

## STORM LAKE

**♦ Super 8 Motel-Storm Lake SH**
(712) 732-3063. **$49-$59.** 101 W Milwaukee. Jct Business Rt US 71 and SR 7. Int corridors. **Pets:** Small. $20 daily fee/pet. Designated rooms, no service, crate.

(ASK) (S6) (X) (🕗) (☎) (➤)

## STORY CITY

**♦♦♦ Comfort Inn SH**
(515) 733-6363. **$62-$89.** 425 Timberland Dr. I-35, exit 124, just sw. Int corridors. **Pets:** Accepted.

(ASK) (S6) (X) (⚡) (☎) (➤) (➥) (➤)

**♦♦ Super 8 Motel SH**
(515) 733-5281. **$53-$70.** 515 Factory Outlet Dr. I-35, exit 124, just sw. Int corridors. **Pets:** Medium. $5 daily fee/pet. Service with restrictions, supervision.

(ASK) (S6) (X) (&M) (☎)

**♦♦ Viking Hotel M ❧**
(515) 733-4306. **$48-$68.** 1520 Broad St. I-35, exit 124, just w. Int corridors. **Pets:** Other species. $5 daily fee/room. Service with restrictions, supervision.

(ASK) (S6) (X) (☎) (➥)

## STUART

**♦♦ AmericInn Motel & Suites SH**
(515) 523-9000. **$65-$110.** 420 SW 8th St. I-80, exit 93, just w. Int corridors. **Pets:** Other species. $50 deposit/room, $10 daily fee/pet. Designated rooms, service with restrictions, supervision.

(ASK) (S6) (X) (&M) (🕗) (⚡) (☎) (➤) (➥) (➤)

**♦♦ Super 8 Motel SH**
(515) 523-2888. **Call for rates.** 203 SE 7th St. I-80, exit 93. Int corridors. **Pets:** Accepted.

(ASK) (X) (&M) (☎) (➤) (➥)

## TOLEDO

**AAA ♦♦ Designer Inn & Suites SH**
(641) 484-5678. **$50-$60.** 403 US 30 W. On US 30, just w of jct US 63 and 30. Int corridors. **Pets:** Accepted.

(SAVE) (S6) (X) (☎) (➥)

**AAA ♦♦ Super 8 Motel-Toledo SH ❧**
(641) 484-5888. **$54-$63.** 207 Hwy 30 W. On US 30, just w of jct US 63 and 30. Ext/int corridors. **Pets:** Other species. $5 daily fee/room. Service with restrictions, crate.

(SAVE) (S6) (X) (&M) (☎) (➥)

## URBANA

**♦♦ Super 8 Urbana Iowa SH**
(319) 443-8888. **$60-$96.** 5369 Hutton Dr. I-380, exit 43, just s on east access road. Int corridors. **Pets:** Accepted.

(ASK) (S6) (X) (☎) (➥) (➤) (➤)

## URBANDALE

**AAA ♦♦ Comfort Inn-Merle Hay SH**
(515) 270-1037. **$69-$89.** 5900 Sutton Dr. I-80, exit 131 (Merle Hay Rd), just s, then w. Int corridors. **Pets:** Other species. $5 daily fee/pet. Service with restrictions, supervision.

(SAVE) (S6) (X) (🕗) (☎) (➤) (➥) (➤)

**♦♦♦ Holiday Inn Northwest SH**
(515) 278-0271. **$76-$84.** 5000 Merle Hay Rd. I-35/80, exit 131 (Merle Hay Rd), just s. Ext/int corridors. **Pets:** Accepted.

(ASK) (S6) (X) (&M) (☎) (➤) (➥) (🍴) (➥) (➤)

**♦♦ Microtel Inn and Suites SH ❧**
(515) 727-5424. **$55-$105.** 8711 Plum Dr. I-35/80, exit 129. Int corridors. **Pets:** Other species. $25 deposit/room. Service with restrictions, supervision.

(ASK) (S6) (X) (&M) (⚡) (☎) (➥)

**♦♦ Sleep Inn SH**
(515) 270-2424. **$69-$169.** 11211 Hickman Rd. I-35/80, exit 125 (Hickman Rd), just ne. Int corridors. **Pets:** Accepted.

(ASK) (S6) (X) (&M) (🕗) (⚡) (☎) (➥) (➤) (➤)

## WALNUT

**♦♦ Super 8 Motel SH**
(712) 784-2221. **$55-$89.** 2109 Antique City Dr. I-80, exit 46, just n. Int corridors. **Pets:** Medium, other species. $5 daily fee/pet. Designated rooms, service with restrictions, supervision.

(ASK) (S6) (X) (&M) (⚡) (☎) (➥) (➥)

## WASHINGTON

**♦♦ Super 8 Motel-Washington M**
(319) 653-6621. **$56-$62.** 119 Westview Dr. 1.5 mi w on SR 1 and 92. Int corridors. **Pets:** $25 deposit/pet. Designated rooms, service with restrictions, supervision.

(ASK) (S6) (X) (☎) (➥)

## WATERLOO

**♦♦ Comfort Inn by Choice Hotels SH**
(319) 234-7411. **$69-$104.** 1945 La Porte Rd. I-380, exit 72 (E San Marnan). Int corridors. **Pets:** Accepted.

(ASK) (S6) (X) (🕗) (☎) (➥) (➥)

▼▼ **Heartland Inn-Crossroads** 🆂🅷
(319) 235-4461. **$80-$90.** 1809 La Porte Rd. I-380, exit 72 (E San Marnan), just nw. Int corridors. **Pets:** Small. $10 daily fee/room. Designated rooms, service with restrictions, supervision.
(ASK) 🆂 ✕ 🅑 🔌 🌊

▼▼ **Heartland Inn-Greyhound Park** 🆂🅷
(319) 232-7467. **$80-$90.** 3052 Marnie Ave. 1 mi n of jct US 20 and 63, exit 227. Int corridors. **Pets:** Small. $10 daily fee/room. Designated rooms, service with restrictions, supervision.
(ASK) 🆂 ✕ 🅑 🔌 🌊 ✕

▼▼ **Holiday Inn Express** 🆂🅷
(319) 233-9191. **$81.** 2141 La Porte Rd. I-380, exit 72 (E San Marnan). Int corridors. **Pets:** Large, other species. $10 one-time fee/room. Service with restrictions, supervision.
(ASK) 🆂 ✕ 🅜 🔌 🅑 🔌 🌊 ✕

▼▼ **Quality Inn & Suites** 🆂🅷
(319) 235-0301. **$79-$119, 7 day notice.** 226 W 5th St. Downtown. Int corridors. **Pets:** Medium. $50 deposit/pet, $10 daily fee/pet. Designated rooms, service with restrictions, supervision.
(ASK) 🆂 ✕ 🅜 🔌 🅑 🔌

▼▼ **Ramada Hotel & Convention Center** 🅻🅷
(319) 233-7560. **$59-$99.** 205 W 4th St. 4th and Commercial sts; downtown. Int corridors. **Pets:** Other species. Designated rooms, service with restrictions.
(ASK) 🆂 ✕ 🅜 🔌 🅑 🔌 🍴 🌊 ✕

# WAVERLY

▼▼ **AmeriHost Inn-Waverly** 🆂🅷
(319) 352-0399. **$73-$149.** 404 29th Ave SW. Business Rt US 218, exit 198, 0.5 mi n. Int corridors. **Pets:** Small. $10 daily fee/pet. Designated rooms, service with restrictions, supervision.
(ASK) 🆂 ✕ 🅜 🔌 🅑 🔌 🌊 ✕

▼▼ **Red Fox Inn** 🆂🅷
(319) 352-5330. **$65-$150.** 1900 Heritage Way. On SR 3, 2 mi e of jct US 218 and SR 3 (exit 203). Ext/int corridors. **Pets:** Accepted.
(ASK) ✕ 🔌 🅑 🔌 🍴 🌊 ✕

◆▼ **Super 8 Waverly** 🆂🅷
(319) 352-0888. **$52-$129.** 301 13th Ave SW. Business Rt US 218 S, exit 198, 1.2 mi n. Int corridors. **Pets:** Medium. $10 daily fee/pet. Designated rooms, service with restrictions, supervision.
(ASK) 🆂 ✕ 🅜 🅑

# WEBSTER CITY

▼▼ **AmericInn Motel & Suites of Webster City** 🆂🅷 🐾
(515) 832-3999. **$85-$125.** 411 Closz Dr. Just s of jct US 20 and SR 17. Int corridors. **Pets:** Other species. $50 deposit/room. Designated rooms, service with restrictions, supervision.
(ASK) ✕ 🅜 🔌 🅑 🔌 🌊

▼▼ **The Executive Inn** 🆂🅷
(515) 832-3631. **$45-$75.** 1700 Superior St. Jct US 20 and SR 17, exit 140, 0.5 mi n. Int corridors. **Pets:** Accepted.
✕ 🅑 🔌 🔌

# WEST BURLINGTON

▼▼ **AmericInn** 🆂🅷
(319) 758-9000. **$59-$125.** 628 S Gear Ave. US 34, exit 260 (Gear Ave), just ne. Int corridors. **Pets:** Accepted.
(ASK) ✕ 🅜 🔌 🔌 🅑 🔌 🌊 ✕

# WEST DES MOINES

◆▼◆ **Candlewood Suites-West Des Moines** 🆂🅷
(515) 221-0001. **$85-$129.** 7625 Office Plaza Dr N. I-80, exit 121 (Jordan Creek Pkwy), just sw. Int corridors. **Pets:** Medium, other species. $75 one-time fee/pet. Service with restrictions, crate.
(ASK) 🆂 ✕ 🅜 🔌 🅑 🔌

◆▼◆ **Hawthorn Suites Ltd** 🆂🅷
(515) 223-0000. **$102-$103.** 6905 Lake Dr. I-80, exit 121 (Jordan Creek Pkwy), just ne. Int corridors. **Pets:** Service with restrictions, crate.
(ASK) 🆂 ✕ 🅜 🔌 🅑 🔌 🌊 ✕

◆▼ **Motel 6–1408** 🆂🅷
(515) 267-8885. **$42-$55.** 7655 Office Plaza Dr N. I-80, exit 121 (Jordan Creek Pkwy), just sw. Int corridors. **Pets:** Accepted.
🆂 ✕ 🅜 🔌 🌊

◆▼◆ **Residence Inn-Des Moines West** 🆂🅷
(515) 267-0338. **Call for rates.** 160 S Jordan Creek Pkwy. I-35, exit 70 (Mills Civic Pkwy), 1.2 mi w to 68th, then just nw. Int corridors. **Pets:** Accepted.
✕ 🔌 🅑 🔌 🌊

🅰🅰🅰 ◆▼◆◆ **Sheraton West Des Moines** 🅻🅷 🐾
(515) 223-1800. **$89-$189.** 1800 50th St. I-80/35, exit 124 (University Ave), just e. Int corridors. **Pets:** Medium. $25 one-time fee/room. Designated rooms, service with restrictions, supervision.
(SAVE) 🆂 ✕ 🔌 🔌 🅑 🔌 🍴 🌊 ✕

◆▼◆ **Valley West Inn** 🆂🅷
(515) 225-2524. **$79-$109.** 3535 Westown Pkwy. I-235, exit 1 (Valley W Dr), just nw. Int corridors. **Pets:** $10 daily fee/room. Crate.
(ASK) 🆂 ✕ 🔌 🅑 🔌 🍴 🌊 ✕

◆▼◆ **West Des Moines Marriott** 🅻🅷
(515) 267-1500. **$89-$129.** 1250 Jordan Creek Pkwy. I-80, exit 121 (Jordan Creek Pkwy). Int corridors. **Pets:** Medium. $50 one-time fee/room. Service with restrictions, supervision.
(ASK) 🆂 ✕ 🅜 🔌 🅑 🔌 🍴 🌊 ✕

# WILLIAMS

▼▼ **Best Western Norseman Inn** 🅼
(515) 854-2281. **$61-$66.** 3086 220th St. I-35, exit 144, just e. Int corridors. **Pets:** Medium, dogs only. Service with restrictions, supervision.
(ASK) 🆂 ✕ 🅑 🔌

# WILLIAMSBURG

◆▼◆ **Amana Holiday Inn** 🆂🅷
(319) 668-1175. **$119-$159.** 2211 U Ave. I-80, exit 225 (US 151). Int corridors. **Pets:** Other species. No service, crate.
(ASK) 🆂 ✕ 🔌 🔌 🅑 🔌 🍴 🌊 ✕

🅰🅰🅰 ◆▼◆ **Best Western Quiet House Suites** 🆂🅷
(319) 668-9777. **$85-$140.** 1708 N Highland St. I-80, exit 220, 0.8 mi n. Int corridors. **Pets:** Accepted.
(SAVE) 🆂 ✕ 🔌 🔌 🅑 🔌 🌊

◆▼◆ **Comfort Inn Amana Colonies** 🆂🅷
(319) 668-2700. **$68-$125.** 2185 U Ave. I-80, exit 225 (US 151), just n. Int corridors. **Pets:** Accepted.
(ASK) 🆂 ✕ 🔌 🔌 🅑 🔌 🔌

🅰🅰🅰 ◆▼◆ **Crest Country Inn** 🅼
(319) 668-1522. **$57-$65.** 340 W Evans St. I-80, exit 220, just nw. Ext corridors. **Pets:** Accepted.
(SAVE) ✕ 🔌

🅰🅰🅰 ◆▼◆ **Super 8 Motel** 🆂🅷
(319) 668-9718. **$70-$100.** 1708 N Highland St. I-80, exit 220, 0.8 mi n. Ext/int corridors. **Pets:** Accepted.
(SAVE) 🆂 ✕ 🔌

# KANSAS

## ABILENE

**AAA** **WWW** Best Western President's Inn **SH**
(785) 263-2050. **$44-$56.** 2210 N Buckeye. I-70, exit 275. Ext corridors.
**Pets:** Service with restrictions, supervision.
[SAVE] [S] [X] [&M] [icons] [icons] [icons]

**WW** Days Inn-Abilene Pride **SH**
(785) 263-2800. **$39-$68.** 1709 N Buckeye Ave. I-70, exit 275, 0.5 mi s.
Ext/int corridors. **Pets:** Accepted.
[ASK] [S] [X] [icons] [icons]

**AAA** **WWW** Diamond Motel **M**
(785) 263-2360. **$34-$49, 3 day notice.** 1407 NW 3rd St. I-70, exit
275, 1.3 mi s, then 1 mi w. Ext corridors. **Pets:** Small. $5 daily fee/pet.
Designated rooms, service with restrictions, supervision.
[SAVE] [X] [icon]

**WWWW** Holiday Inn Express Hotel & Suites **SH**
(785) 263-4049. **$76.** 110 E Lafayette Ave. I-70, exit 275, just n. Int
corridors. **Pets:** Accepted.
[ASK] [S] [X] [&M] [icons]

**WW** Super 8 Motel **SH**
(785) 263-4545. **$55-$65.** 2207 N Buckeye. I-70, exit 275, just s. Int
corridors. **Pets:** Other species. $50 deposit/room, $10 daily fee/pet. Service
with restrictions, supervision.
[ASK] [S] [X] [&M] [icons]

## ATCHISON

**WW** AmericInn Lodge & Suites **SH**
(913) 367-4000. **$75-$175, 30 day notice.** 500 US 73. Just s at jct US
59 and 73. Int corridors. **Pets:** $50 deposit/room, $10 daily fee/pet. Service with restrictions, supervision.
[ASK] [X] [&M] [icons]

## BAXTER SPRINGS

**WW** Baxter Inn-4-Less **SH**
(620) 856-2106. **$40-$50.** 2451 Military Ave. On US 69 alternate route,
1 mi s of jct US 166. Int corridors. **Pets:** Service with restrictions,
supervision.
[ASK] [S] [X] [icon]

## BELLEVILLE

**WW** Super 8 Motel **SH**
(785) 527-2112. **$52-$100.** 1410 28th St. On US 36, 0.5 mi e of jct US
81. Int corridors. **Pets:** Small, dogs only. $5 daily fee/pet. Designated
rooms, service with restrictions, supervision.
[ASK] [S] [X] [icon]

## BELOIT

**WW** Super 8 Motel-Beloit **SH**
(785) 738-4300. **$59, 3 day notice.** 205 W Hwy 24. Just e of jct SR 14.
Ext/int corridors. **Pets:** Medium. Designated rooms, service with restrictions, supervision.
[ASK] [X] [&M] [icons]

## BURLINGTON

**WW** Country Haven Inn **SH**
(620) 364-8260. **$57-$65.** 207 Cross St. Just e of US 75; 1 mi n of
center. Int corridors. **Pets:** Accepted.
[ASK] [S] [X] [icons]

## CHANUTE

**AAA** **WW** Guest House Motor Inn **M**
(620) 431-0600. **$33-$38.** 1814 S Santa Fe. US 169, exit 35th St, 2.5
mi ne. Ext corridors. **Pets:** Small. $5 daily fee/pet. Service with restric-
tions.
[SAVE] [X] [icon]

## CLAY CENTER

**WW** Cedar Court Motel **SH**
(785) 632-2148. **$50-$66.** 905 Crawford. On US 24, just e of jct SR 15.
Ext corridors. **Pets:** Accepted.
[ASK] [X] [&M] [icons]

## COFFEYVILLE

**AAA** **WWW** Appletree Inn **M**
(620) 251-0002. **$67-$91.** 820 E 11th St. 0.8 mi e of center. Int corridors. **Pets:** Very small. $3 daily fee/pet. Service with restrictions, supervi-
sion.
[SAVE] [S] [X] [icons]

**AAA** **WWW** Super 8 Motel **M**
(620) 251-2250. **$64-$74.** 104 W 11th St. On US 169 and 166; center.
Ext corridors. **Pets:** Medium, dogs only. $10 one-time fee/pet. Designated
rooms, service with restrictions, supervision.
[SAVE] [S] [X] [icons]

## COLBY

**AAA** **WWWW** Best Western Crown Motel **M** 🐾
(785) 462-3943. **$65-$95.** 2320 S Range. I-70, exit 53 (SR 25), just s.
Ext corridors. **Pets:** Other species.
[SAVE] [S] [X] [icons]

**AAA** **WWWW** Comfort Inn **SH** 🐾
(785) 462-3833. **$79-$119.** 2225 S Range. I-70, exit 53 (SR 25), just s.
Int corridors. **Pets:** Other species. $5 daily fee/pet. Designated rooms,
supervision.
[SAVE] [S] [X] [icons]

**♦♦♦ ▼▼▼ Days Inn** SH
(785) 462-8691. **$56-$80.** 1925 S Range. I-70, exit 53 (SR 25), 0.3 mi n. Int corridors. **Pets:** $5 daily fee/pet. Designated rooms, service with restrictions, supervision.
SAVE S X 🛏 💻 ≈

**♦♦♦ ▼▼▼▼ Holiday Inn Express Hotel & Suites** SH
(785) 462-8787. **$85-$110, 7 day notice.** 645 W Willow. I-70, exit 53 (SR 25), just ne. Int corridors. **Pets:** Other species. $10 daily fee/room. Service with restrictions, crate.
SAVE S X 🛏 💻 ≈ ⊠

**▼ Motel 6 #4245** SH
(785) 462-8201. **$41-$51.** 1985 S Range. I-70, exit 53 (SR 25), just n. Ext/int corridors. **Pets:** Accepted.
ASK S X

**♦♦♦ ▼▼▼ Quality Inn** SH
(785) 462-3933. **$55-$85, 7 day notice.** 1950 S Range. I-70, exit 53 (SR 25), just n. Ext/int corridors. **Pets:** Other species. $20 deposit/room. Designated rooms, service with restrictions, supervision.
SAVE S X 🛏 💻 ⊤ ≈

**▼▼ Super 8 Motel** SH
(785) 462-8248. **$47-$74.** 1040 Zelfer Ave. I-70, exit 53 (SR 25), 0.3 mi n, then just w. Int corridors. **Pets:** Accepted.
ASK S X

## CONCORDIA

**▼▼ Super 8 Motel-Concordia** SH
(785) 243-4200. **$54-$69.** 1320 Lincoln. On US 81, 1 mi s of center. Ext/int corridors. **Pets:** Other species. $10 one-time fee/room. Service with restrictions, crate.
ASK S X 🛏 💻

## COTTONWOOD FALLS

**♦♦♦ ▼▼▼ ▼▼▼ Grand Central Hotel** CI
(620) 273-6763. **$150-$180.** 215 Broadway. Just w of US 177; center of downtown. Int corridors. **Pets:** Dogs only. Service with restrictions, supervision.
SAVE S X 🛏 💻 ⊤

## COUNCIL GROVE

**♦♦♦ ▼▼▼ The Cottage House Hotel & Motel** SH
(620) 767-6828. **$65-$180, 7 day notice.** 25 N Neosho. Just n of Main St; downtown. Ext/int corridors. **Pets:** Other species. $10 daily fee/pet. Designated rooms, service with restrictions, supervision.
SAVE S X 🛏 💻

## DODGE CITY

**♦♦♦ ▼▼▼ Comfort Inn** SH
(620) 338-8700. **$90-$105.** 2000 W Wyatt Earp Blvd. 1.3 mi w on US 50 business route. Int corridors. **Pets:** Other species. $50 deposit/room.
SAVE S X 🛏 💻 ≈

**▼▼ Econo Lodge of Dodge City** SH
(620) 225-0231. **$47-$60.** 1610 W Wyatt Earp Blvd. 1 mi w on US 50 business route. Int corridors. **Pets:** Accepted.
ASK S X ⌂ 🛏 💻 ⊤ ≈

**▼▼▼▼ Holiday Inn Express** SH
(620) 227-5000. **$90-$100.** 2320 W Wyatt Earp Blvd. 1.4 mi w on US 50 business route. Int corridors. **Pets:** Other species. Service with restrictions, crate.
ASK S X ⌂ 🛏 💻 ≈

**▼▼ Super 8 Motel** SH
(620) 225-3924. **$90-$100.** 1708 W Wyatt Earp Blvd. 1.2 mi w on US 50 business route. Int corridors. **Pets:** Other species. Service with restrictions, crate.
ASK S X ⌂ 🛏 💻 ≈

## EL DORADO

**♦♦♦ ▼▼▼ Best Western Red Coach Inn** SH
(316) 321-6900. **$60-$115, 3 day notice.** 2525 W Central Ave. I-35, exit 71, 0.5 mi e. Ext corridors. **Pets:** Small, dogs only. $15 one-time fee/pet. Designated rooms, service with restrictions, supervision.
SAVE S X ⌂ 🛏 💻 ⊤ ≈ ⊠

**▼ Super 8 Motel-El Dorado** M
(316) 321-4888. **$52-$74.** 2530 W Central Ave. I-35, exit 71, 0.5 mi e. Int corridors. **Pets:** Small. $20 daily fee/pet. Designated rooms, no service, crate.
ASK S X 🛏 💻

## ELLSWORTH

**♦♦♦ ▼▼▼ Best Western Garden Prairie Inn** SH
(785) 472-3116. **$69-$89, 14 day notice.** Jct SR 140 & 156. Jct SR 140 and 156. Ext/int corridors. **Pets:** Medium. No service, supervision.
SAVE S X M ⌂ 🛏 💻 ≈

## EMPORIA

**♦♦♦ ▼ Americas Best Value Inn** M
(620) 342-7567. **$50-$64.** 2913 W Hwy 50. I-35, exit 127, 0.8 mi e. Int corridors. **Pets:** Accepted.
SAVE S X 💻

**▼▼ Candlewood Suites** SH
(620) 343-7756. **$79-$99.** 2602 Candlewood Dr. I-35, exit 128 (Industrial St), just n, then e. Int corridors. **Pets:** Accepted.
ASK S X ⌂ 🛏 💻

**▼ Motel 6 #4148** SH
(620) 343-1240. **$42-$61, 15 day notice.** 2630 W 18th Ave. I-35, exit 128 (Industrial St), just s, then e. Int corridors. **Pets:** Accepted.
ASK S X 🛏

## FORT SCOTT

**▼ 1st Interstate Inn** M
(620) 223-5330. **$44-$59, 15 day notice.** 2222 1/2 S Main. On US 69 Bypass, 2.5 mi s of US 54. Int corridors. **Pets:** Small, dogs only. $5 daily fee/room. Service with restrictions, supervision.
ASK S X ⌂

**▼▼ Best Western Fort Scott Inn** SH
(620) 223-0100. **$78.** 101 State St. On US 69 Bypass, exit US 54 southbound; exit 3rd St northbound. Ext/int corridors. **Pets:** Small. $10 daily fee/pet. Designated rooms, service with restrictions, supervision.
ASK S X 🛏 💻 ⊤ ≈ ⊠

## GARDEN CITY

**▼▼ Americas Best Value Inn** SH
(620) 275-5095. **$62-$72.** 1818 Commanche Dr. W of US 50 and 83 Bypass, on SR 156. Ext corridors. **Pets:** Accepted.
ASK S X 🛏 ≈

**▼▼ AmericInn Lodge & Suites** SH 🐾
(620) 272-9860. **$85-$160.** 3020 E Kansas Ave. Jct US 50, 83 and SR 156. Int corridors. **Pets:** $50 deposit/room, $10 daily fee/pet. Service with restrictions, supervision.
ASK S X ⌂ ⌂ 🛏 💻 ≈ ⊠

**▼▼ Best Western Red Baron Hotel** SH
(620) 275-4164. **$67-$73.** 2205 E Hwy 50. 2.3 mi e on US 50 business route, at US 83 Bypass. Ext corridors. **Pets:** Accepted.
ASK S X 🛏 💻 ⊤ ≈

**♦♦♦ ▼▼▼ Best Western Wheat Lands Hotel & Conference Center** SH
(620) 276-2387. **$64-$89.** 1311 E Fulton. 1 mi e on US 50 business route. Ext corridors. **Pets:** Other species. Service with restrictions, crate.
SAVE S X ⌂ 🛏 💻 ⊤ ≈

**AAA ◈◈◈ Comfort Inn** SH
(620) 275-5800. **$60-$150.** 2608 E Kansas Ave. Jct US 50, 83 and SR 156. Int corridors. **Pets:** Medium, other species. $10 daily fee/pet. Designated rooms, service with restrictions, supervision.

SAVE ✕ ⬡ 🛏 💻 🏊 ✕

**◈◈◈◈ Holiday Inn Express Hotel & Suites** SH
(620) 275-5900. **$92-$102.** 2502 E Kansas Ave. Jct US 50, 83 and SR 156. Int corridors. **Pets:** Other species. Service with restrictions, crate.

ASK S⬡ ✕ ⬡ ⬡ 🛏 💻 🏊

**◈ National 9 Inn** M
(620) 275-0677. **$51-$56.** 123 Honey Bee Ct. 2.3 mi e on US 50 business route, at US 83 Bypass. Ext corridors. **Pets:** Accepted.

ASK S⬡ ✕ ⬡

**AAA ◈◈ Plaza Hotel** SH
(620) 275-7471. **$82-$38.** 1911 E Kansas Ave. 0.5 mi w of US 50 and 83 Bypass, on SR 156. Int corridors. **Pets:** Other species. Supervision.

SAVE S⬡ ✕ ⬡ 🛏 💻 🍴 🏊 ✕

# GODDARD

**AAA ◈◈ Express Inn** M
(316) 794-3366. **$44-$50.** 19941 W Kellogg Dr. Just se of jct US 54/400 and 199th St. Ext corridors. **Pets:** Medium, other species. $5 one-time fee/room. Service with restrictions, supervision.

SAVE ✕ 🛏

# GOODLAND

**AAA ◈◈◈ Best Western Buffalo Inn** SH 🐾
(785) 899-3621. **$59-$70.** 830 W Hwy 24. I-70, exit 17 or 19, n to jct US 24 and SR 27. Ext corridors. **Pets:** Other species. $25 deposit/room. Designated rooms, service with restrictions, supervision.

SAVE S⬡ ✕ 🛏 💻 🍴 🏊

**AAA ◈◈◈ Comfort Inn** SH
(785) 899-7181. **$79.** 2519 Enterprise Rd. I-70, exit 17, just n. Int corridors. **Pets:** Medium. $15 one-time fee/pet. Designated rooms, service with restrictions, supervision.

SAVE S⬡ ✕ ⬡M ⬡ 🛏 💻 🏊

# GREAT BEND

**AAA ◈◈◈ Best Western Angus Inn** SH
(620) 792-3541. **$75.** 2920 10th St. 0.8 mi w on US 56 and SR 96/156. Ext/int corridors. **Pets:** Small, dogs only. Service with restrictions, supervision.

SAVE S⬡ ✕ ⬡ 🛏 💻 🍴 🏊 ✕

**AAA ◈◈◈ Highland Hotel & Convention Center** SH
(620) 792-2431. **$49-$71.** 3017 10th St. 1 mi w on US 56 and SR 96/156. Ext/int corridors. **Pets:** Other species. $10 daily fee/pet. Designated rooms, service with restrictions, crate.

SAVE S⬡ ✕ ⬡ 🛏 💻 🍴 🏊 ✕

# GREENSBURG

**◈◈ Best Western J-Hawk Motel** SH
(620) 723-2121. **$74.** 515 W Kansas Ave. Just w on US 54. Ext corridors. **Pets:** Other species. Supervision.

ASK S⬡ ✕ 🛏 💻 🏊

# HAYS

**◈◈ Best Western Vagabond Motel** M
(785) 625-2511. **$57-$75.** 2524 Vine St. I-70, exit 159 (US 183), 1 mi s. Ext corridors. **Pets:** Designated rooms, service with restrictions, supervision.

ASK S⬡ ✕ ⬡ 🛏 💻 🍴 🏊

**AAA ◈◈◈ Hampton Inn-Hays** SH 🐾
(785) 625-8103. **$64-$89.** 3801 Vine St. I-70, exit 159 (US 183), just sw. Ext/int corridors. **Pets:** Service with restrictions, supervision.

SAVE S⬡ ✕ ⬡ ⬡ 💻

**◈◈◈ Holiday Inn-Hays** SH
(785) 625-7371. **$59-$99.** 3603 Vine St. I-70, exit 159 (US 183), just s. Ext/int corridors. **Pets:** Accepted.

ASK ✕ ⬡M ⬡ ⬡ 🛏 💻 🍴 🏊 ✕

**◈ Motel 6-167** M
(785) 625-4282. **$41-$61.** 3404 Vine St. I-70, exit 159 (US 183), 0.3 mi s. Ext corridors. **Pets:** Accepted.

S⬡ ✕ 🏊

**◈◈◈ Super 8 Motel-Hays** SH
(785) 625-8048. **$54-$79.** 3730 Vine St. I-70, exit 159 (US 183), just s. Int corridors. **Pets:** Small. $20 daily fee/pet. Designated rooms, no service, crate.

ASK S⬡ ✕ ⬡ 🛏

# HAYSVILLE

**AAA ◈◈ Haysville Inn** M
(316) 522-1000. **$42-$48.** 301 E 71st St. I-35, exit 39, just w. Ext corridors. **Pets:** Medium. $5 one-time fee/pet. Service with restrictions, supervision.

SAVE S⬡ ✕ ⬡ 🛏

# HESSTON

**◈◈◈ AmericInn Lodge & Suites-Hesston** SH
(620) 327-2053. **$67-$90.** 2 Leonard Ct. I-135, exit 40, just e. Int corridors. **Pets:** Small. $50 deposit/room. Designated rooms, service with restrictions, supervision.

ASK S⬡ ✕ 🛏 💻 🏊

# HILLSBORO

**◈◈◈ Country Haven Inn** SH
(620) 947-2929. **$59.** 804 Western Heights. On US 56; center. Int corridors. **Pets:** Small. $40 deposit/room, $10 one-time fee/room. Designated rooms, service with restrictions, supervision.

ASK S⬡ ✕ 🛏

# HUTCHINSON

**AAA ◈◈ Americas Best Value Inn** M
(620) 662-6394. **$47-$62.** 1315 E 11th Ave. Just se of jct SR 61. Int corridors. **Pets:** Accepted.

SAVE S⬡ ✕ ⬡ 💻

**AAA ◈ Astro Motel** M
(620) 663-1151. **$36-$69, 20 day notice.** 15 E 4th Ave. Just e of Main St. Ext corridors. **Pets:** Accepted.

SAVE ✕ 🛏 🏊

**◈◈ Comfort Inn** SH
(620) 663-7822. **$55-$129.** 1621 Super Plaza. Just w of jct SR 61 and N 17th Ave. Int corridors. **Pets:** Accepted.

ASK S⬡ ✕ ⬡ ⬡ 🛏 💻 🏊

**AAA ◈◈◈ Grand Prairie Hotel & Convention Center** LH
(620) 669-9311. **$69-$129.** 1400 N Lorraine St. Just nw of jct SR 61 and N 11th Ave. Ext/int corridors. **Pets:** Accepted.

SAVE S⬡ ✕ ⬡ 🛏 💻 🍴 🏊 ✕

**◈◈◈ Holiday Inn Express Hotel & Suites** SH
(620) 669-5200. **$90-$100.** 1601 Super Plaza. Just w of jct SR 61 and N 17th Ave. Int corridors. **Pets:** Other species. Service with restrictions, crate.

ASK S⬡ ✕ ⬡M ⬡ ⬡ 🛏 💻 🏊 ✕

**▼▼ Microtel Inn & Suites** 🆂🅷
(620) 665-3700. **$54-$145.** 1420 N Lorraine. Just nw of jct SR 61 and N 11th Ave. Int corridors. **Pets:** Medium. $6 one-time fee/pet. Designated rooms, service with restrictions, supervision.

A$K 🆂🛑 ⊠ 🕭 🛢 🖵

# INDEPENDENCE

**▼▼ Appletree Inn** 🆂🅷
(620) 331-5500. **$78-$82.** 201 N 8th St. At 8th and Laurel sts. Ext/int corridors. **Pets:** Other species. Service with restrictions, supervision.

⊠ 🛢 🌊

**⨁⨁⨁ ▼▼▼ Knights Inn** 🆂🅷
(620) 331-7300. **$49-$59.** 3222 W Main St. 1.4 mi e of jct US 75 and 160. Ext corridors. **Pets:** Small. $10 one-time fee/pet. Designated rooms, service with restrictions, supervision.

SAVE 🆂🛑 ⊠ 🛢 🖵 🌊

**▼▼ Microtel Inn & Suites** 🆂🅷
(620) 331-0088. **$66-$83.** 2917 W Main St. 1.2 mi e of jct US 75 and 160. Int corridors. **Pets:** Other species. $3 one-time fee/pet. Service with restrictions, crate.

A$K 🆂🛑 ⊠ 🛢🅼 🗐 🕭 🛢 🖵

# IOLA

**⨁⨁⨁ ▼▼▼ Best Western Inn** 🅼
(620) 365-5161. **$54-$58.** 1315 N State St. Jct US 54 and 169, 1.5 mi w on US 54, then 0.8 mi n. Ext corridors. **Pets:** Accepted.

SAVE 🆂🛑 ⊠ 🗐 🕭 🛢 🖵 🍽 🌊

**▼▼ Super 8 Iola** 🆂🅷
(620) 365-3030. **$69-$79.** 200 Bills Way. Jct US 54 and 169. Int corridors. **Pets:** Medium. Service with restrictions, supervision.

A$K 🆂🛑 ⊠ 🛢 🖵 🌊

# JUNCTION CITY

**▼▼▼▼ Courtyard by Marriott Junction City** 🆂🅷
(785) 210-1500. **$79-$149.** 310 Hammons Dr. I-70, exit 298. Int corridors. **Pets:** $75 one-time fee/room. Service with restrictions, supervision.

A$K 🆂🛑 ⊠ 🛢🅼 🕭 🛢 🖵 🌊

**▼▼ Days Inn** 🆂🅷
(785) 762-2727. **$58-$75.** 1024 S Washington St. I-70, exit 296, just n. Ext/int corridors. **Pets:** Other species. Designated rooms, service with restrictions.

A$K 🆂🛑 ⊠ 🗐 🛢 🖵 🌊 ⊠

**▼▼ Econo Lodge** 🅼
(785) 238-8181. **$40-$80.** 211 Flint Hills Blvd. I-70, exit 299 (Grandview Plaza). Int corridors. **Pets:** Accepted.

A$K 🆂🛑 ⊠ 🛢 🖵

**⨁⨁⨁ ▼▼ Golden Wheat Budget Host** 🅼
(785) 238-5106. **$30-$75, 3 day notice.** 820 S Washington St. I-70, exit 296, 0.5 mi n. Ext corridors. **Pets:** Very small, dogs only. $5 daily fee/pet. Designated rooms, service with restrictions, supervision.

SAVE 🆂🛑 ⊠ 🛢

**▼▼▼ Holiday Inn Express** 🆂🅷
(785) 762-4200. **$84-$124, 15 day notice.** 120 N East St. I-70, exit 298, just nw. Int corridors. **Pets:** Accepted.

A$K 🆂🛑 ⊠ 🛢🅼 🗐 🛢 🖵 🌊 ⊠

---

# KANSAS CITY METROPOLITAN AREA

# GARDNER

**▼▼ Super 8** 🆂🅷
(913) 856-8887. **$60-$180, 30 day notice.** 2001 E Santa Fe. I-35, exit 210. Int corridors. **Pets:** Large. $10 daily fee/pet. Service with restrictions, crate.

A$K 🆂🛑 ⊠ 🛢🅼 🛢

# KANSAS CITY

**▼▼ Best Western Inn and Conference Center** 🆂🅷
(913) 677-3060. **$89-$99.** 501 Southwest Blvd. I-35, exit 234 (7th St), just s. Int corridors. **Pets:** Other species. Service with restrictions, supervision.

A$K 🆂🛑 ⊠ 🛢 🖵 🌊

**▼▼ Microtel Inn & Suites at the Speedway** 🆂🅷
(913) 334-3028. **$59-$69.** 7721 Elizabeth St. I-70, exit 414 (78th St N), just ne. Int corridors. **Pets:** Accepted.

A$K 🆂🛑 ⊠ 🛢🅼 🕭 🛢 🖵 🌊

# LENEXA

**▼▼ Days Inn Lenexa** 🅼
(913) 492-7200. **$57-$75, 7 day notice.** 9630 Rosehill Rd. I-35, exit 224 (95th St), just e. Ext corridors. **Pets:** Small. Designated rooms, service with restrictions, supervision.

A$K 🆂🛑 ⊠ 🛢🅼 🕭 🛢 🌊

**▼▼▼▼ Extended StayAmerica of Lenexa** 🆂🅷
(913) 894-5550. **$68-$77.** 8015 Lenexa Dr. I-35, exit 227 (75th St), 1 mi s on east frontage road. Ext corridors. **Pets:** $25 daily fee/pet. Service with restrictions, supervision.

A$K 🆂🛑 ⊠ 🛢🅼 🗐 🕭 🛢 🖵 🌊

**▼▼▼▼ La Quinta Inn Kansas City (Lenexa)** 🆂🅷
(913) 492-5500. **$79-$119.** 9461 Lenexa Dr. I-35, exit 224 (95th St), just ne; entrance left on Monrovia Rd, off 95th St. Int corridors. **Pets:** Medium. Service with restrictions.

A$K ⊠ 🕭 🛢 🖵 🌊

**▼▼ Super 8 Motel-Lenexa** 🆂🅷
(913) 888-8899. **$52-$72.** 9601 Westgate Dr. I-35, exit 224 (95th St), just se. Int corridors. **Pets:** Small. $20 daily fee/pet. Designated rooms, no service, crate.

A$K 🆂🛑 ⊠ 🛢🅼 🗐 🛢 🖵

# MERRIAM

**▼▼ Comfort Inn-Merriam** 🆂🅷
(913) 262-2622. **$44-$100.** 6401 E Frontage Rd. I-35, exit 228B (Shawnee Mission Pkwy), just se. Int corridors. **Pets:** Small. $10 daily fee/pet. Designated rooms, service with restrictions, supervision.

A$K 🆂🛑 ⊠ 🗐 🛢 🖵 🌊

**▼▼▼ Drury Inn-Merriam/Shawnee Mission Parkway** 🆂🅷
(913) 236-9200. **$80-$130.** 9009 W Shawnee Mission Pkwy. I-35, exit 228B (Shawnee Mission Pkwy). Int corridors. **Pets:** Accepted.

A$K ⊠ 🛢🅼 🗐 🛢 🖵 🌊

**▼▼ Hampton Inn & Suites** 🆂🅷
(913) 722-0800. **$100-$110.** 7400 W Frontage Rd. I-35, exit 227, just nw. Int corridors. **Pets:** Small, other species. Service with restrictions, crate.

A$K 🆂🛑 ⊠ 🛢🅼 🕭 🛢 🖵 🌊

**▼▼ Homestead Studio Suites Hotel-Kansas City/Shawnee Mission** 🅼
(913) 236-6006. **$64-$73.** 6451 E Frontage Rd. I-35, exit 228B (Shawnee Mission Pkwy), just se. Ext corridors. **Pets:** $25 daily fee/pet. Service with restrictions, supervision.

A$K 🆂🛑 ⊠ 🛢🅼 🗐 🕭 🛢 🖵

**ΔΔΔ** ▼▼▼ **Quality Inn** 🆂🅷
(913) 262-4448. **$42-$100.** 6601 E Frontage Rd. I-35, exit 228A, just ne. Ext/int corridors. **Pets:** Very small. $10 daily fee/pet. Designated rooms, service with restrictions, supervision.
〔SAVE〕 🔟 ⊠ 🚻 📷 📖 🅱 📺 ➿

## OLATHE

▼▼▼▼ **Holiday Inn** 🆂🅷
(913) 829-4000. **$81-$102.** 101 W 151st St. I-35, exit 215 (151st St). Int corridors. **Pets:** Other species. Service with restrictions, crate.
〔ASK〕 🔟 ⊠ 📷 🅱 📺 🍴 ➿

**ΔΔΔ** ▼▼▼ **Sleep Inn** 🆂🅷
(913) 390-9500. **$69-$79.** 20662 W 151st St. I-35, exit 215 (151st St), 0.4 mi sw. Int corridors. **Pets:** Small. $10 one-time fee/pet. Service with restrictions, crate.
〔SAVE〕 🔟 ⊠ 🚻 📷 📖 🅱 📺 ➿

## OVERLAND PARK

**ΔΔΔ** ▼▼▼▼ **AmeriSuites (Overland Park/Convention Center)** 🆂🅷
(913) 491-9002. **$119-$179.** 5001 W 110th St. I-435, exit 77B (Nall Ave), just se. Int corridors. **Pets:** Small, dogs only. $10 one-time fee/pet. Service with restrictions, supervision.
〔SAVE〕 🔟 ⊠ 🚻 📖 🅱 📺 ➿

**ΔΔΔ** ▼▼▼▼ **AmeriSuites (Overland Park/Metcalf)** 🆂🅷
(913) 451-2553. **$119-$179.** 6801 W 112th St. I-435, exit 79 (Metcalf Ave/US 169), 0.6 mi s. Int corridors. **Pets:** Small. $25 one-time fee/room. Designated rooms, service with restrictions, supervision.
〔SAVE〕 🔟 ⊠ 🚻 📖 🅱 📺 ➿

▼▼▼▼ **Candlewood Suites** 🆂🅷
(913) 469-5557. **$75-$92.** 11001 Oakmont. I-435, exit 82 (Quivira Rd), 0.5 mi s, 0.3 mi w on College Ave, then just n. Int corridors. **Pets:** Small, other species. $25 one-time fee/pet. Service with restrictions.
〔ASK〕 🔟 ⊠ 🚻 📖 🅱 📺

**ΔΔΔ** ▼▼▼▼ **Chase Suites by Woodfin** 🆂🅷 🐾
(913) 491-3333. **$119-$219.** 6300 W 110th. I-435, exit 79 (Metcalf Ave/US 169), 0.3 mi s on US 169, 0.5 mi e on College Blvd to Lamar Ave, then just n. Ext corridors. **Pets:** $50 deposit/pet, $5 daily fee/pet. Designated rooms, service with restrictions, crate.
〔SAVE〕 🔟 ⊠ 🚻 📷 📖 🅱 📺 ➿ ⊠

▼▼▼▼ **ClubHouse Inn & Suites** 🆂🅷
(913) 648-5555. **$67-$76.** 10610 Marty Ave. I-435, exit 79 (Metcalf Ave/US 169). Int corridors. **Pets:** Accepted.
〔ASK〕 🔟 ⊠ 📖 🅱 📺 ➿ ⊠

▼▼▼▼ **Comfort Inn & Suites** 🆂🅷 🐾
(913) 648-7858. **Call for rates.** 7200 W 107th St. I-435, exit 79 (Metcalf Ave), just nw. Int corridors. **Pets:** Other species. $10 daily fee/room. Service with restrictions.
⊠ 📖 🅱 📺 ➿

▼▼▼▼ **Drury Inn & Suites-Overland Park** 🆂🅷
(913) 345-1500. **$75-$125.** 10963 Metcalf Ave. I-435, exit 79 (Metcalf Ave/US 169), just se. Int corridors. **Pets:** Accepted.
〔ASK〕 ⊠ 🚻 📖 🅱 📺 ➿ ⊠

▼▼▼▼ **Extended Stay Deluxe Kansas City-Overland Park-Metcalf** 🆂🅷
(913) 642-2299. **$68-$86.** 7201 W 106th St. I-435, exit 79 (Metcalf Ave/US 169), just nw. Int corridors. **Pets:** $25 daily fee/pet. Service with restrictions, supervision.
〔ASK〕 🔟 ⊠ 🚻 📖 🅱 📺

▼▼▼▼ **Holiday Inn of Mission-Overland Park** 🅻🅷
(913) 262-3010. **$59-$179.** 7240 Shawnee Mission Pkwy. I-35, exit 228B (Shawnee Mission Pkwy), 1 mi e. Ext/int corridors. **Pets:** Accepted.
〔ASK〕 🔟 ⊠ 🚻 📷 📖 🅱 📺 🍴 ➿ ⊠

▼▼▼▼ **Holtze Executive Village** 🆂🅷
(913) 344-8100. **$179-$199.** 11400 College Blvd. I-435, exit 82 (Quivira Rd), 0.5 mi s, then just e. Ext/int corridors. **Pets:** Accepted.
〔ASK〕 🔟 ⊠ 🚻 📷 📖 🅱 📺 ➿

▼▼▼▼ **Homestead Studio Suites Hotel-Kansas City/Overland Park** 🆂🅷
(913) 661-7111. **$68-$86.** 5401 W 110th St. I-435, exit 77B (Nall Ave), just s. Int corridors. **Pets:** $25 daily fee/pet. Service with restrictions, supervision.
〔ASK〕 🔟 ⊠ 🚻 📷 🅱 📺

▼▼ **Microtel Inn and Suites of Overland Park/Lenexa** 🆂🅷
(913) 541-2664. **Call for rates.** 8750 Ballentine St. I-35, exit 225A, just se. Int corridors. **Pets:** Accepted.
〔ASK〕 ⊠ 🚻 📷 🅱 📺 ➿

▼▼▼▼ **Pear Tree Inn by Drury-Overland Park** 🆂🅷
(913) 451-0200. **$60-$110.** 10951 Metcalf Ave. I-435, exit 79 (Metcalf Ave/US 169), just se. Int corridors. **Pets:** Accepted.
〔ASK〕 ⊠ 🚻 📷 🅱 📺 ➿

▼▼▼▼ **Red Roof Inn-Overland Park** 🅼
(913) 341-0100. **$49-$86.** 6800 W 108th St. I-435, exit 79 (Metcalf Ave/US 169), just ne. Ext corridors. **Pets:** Accepted.
⊠ 🚻 📷

▼▼▼▼ **Residence Inn by Marriott** 🆂🅷
(913) 491-4444. **$69-$259.** 12010 Blue Valley Pkwy. I-435, exit 79 (Metcalf Ave/US 169), 1.3 mi s. Int corridors. **Pets:** Accepted.
〔ASK〕 🔟 ⊠ 🚻 📷 🅱 📺 ➿ ⊠

**ΔΔΔ** ▼▼▼ **Settle Inn & Suites** 🆂🅷 🐾
(913) 381-5700. **$49-$89.** 4401 W 107th St. I-435, exit 77A (Roe Ave), just ne. Ext/int corridors. **Pets:** Small, dogs only. $15 daily fee/pet. Service with restrictions, supervision.
〔SAVE〕 🔟 ⊠ 🚻 📷 📖 🅱 📺 ➿

▼▼▼▼ **Sheraton Overland Park Hotel at the Convention Center** 🅻🅷 🐾
(913) 234-2100. **$165-$185.** 6100 College Blvd. I-435, exit 79 (Metcalf Ave/US 169), just s to College Blvd, then 0.6 mi e. Int corridors. **Pets:** Medium. Service with restrictions, supervision.
⊠ 🚻 📖 📺 🍴 ➿

▼▼ **Super 8 Motel** 🆂🅷
(913) 341-4440. **$49-$129.** 10750 Barkley St. I-435, exit 79 (Metcalf Ave/US 169), just n to 107th St, then just e. Int corridors. **Pets:** Small, other species. $25 one-time fee/room. Service with restrictions, supervision.
〔ASK〕 🔟 ⊠ 🚻 🅱

▼▼ **White Haven Motor Lodge** 🅼
(913) 649-8200. **$55-$60.** 8039 Metcalf Ave. I-435, exit 79 (Metcalf Ave/US 169), 3.5 mi n. Ext corridors. **Pets:** Medium, other species. Service with restrictions, supervision.
⊠ 📷 🅱 ➿

▼▼▼▼ **Wyndham Garden Hotel-Overland Park** 🆂🅷
(913) 383-2550. **$64-$124.** 7000 W 108th St. I-435, exit 79 (Metcalf Ave/US 169), just ne. Int corridors. **Pets:** Accepted.
〔ASK〕 ⊠ 🚻 📷 📖 🅱 📺 🍴 ➿

## END METROPOLITAN AREA

# LANSING

**▽▽ Econo Lodge** SH
(913) 727-2777. **$55-$59.** 504 N Main. I-70, exit 224 (Leavenworth), 10 mi n on US 73 and SR 7. Int corridors. **Pets:** Accepted.
ASK ⑤ ✕ 🛏 🖥

**▽▽▽ Holiday Inn Express Hotel & Suites** SH
(913) 250-1000. **$82-$91.** 120 Express Dr. I-70, exit 224 (Leavenworth), 10 mi n on US 73 and SR 7. Int corridors. **Pets:** Medium, other species. $20 one-time fee/room. Service with restrictions, crate.
ASK ⑤ ✕ ⑥M ⑤ 🛏 🖥 🌊 ✕

# LARNED

**⊕ ▽▽ Best Western Townsman Inn** SH
(620) 285-3114. **$54-$66.** 123 E 14th St. Jct US 56 and SR 156. Ext corridors. **Pets:** Small, dogs only. Service with restrictions, supervision.
SAVE ⑤ ✕ ⑦ 🛏 🖥 🌊

# LAWRENCE

**▽▽ Americas Best Value Hallmark Inn** M
(785) 841-6500. **$59-$99, 5 day notice.** 730 Iowa St. I-70, exit 202, 1 mi s on US 59. Ext corridors. **Pets:** Accepted.
ASK ⑤ ✕ 🖥

**⊕ ▽▽▽ Best Western Lawrence** SH
(785) 843-9100. **$69-$99.** 2309 Iowa St. On US 59; jct SR 10. Ext/int corridors. **Pets:** Other species. Designated rooms, service with restrictions, supervision.
SAVE ⑤ ✕ ⑥M ⑤ 🛏 🖥 🌊

**⊕ ▽▽ Golden Rule Motel** SH
(785) 842-5721. **$50-$65.** 515 McDonald Dr. I-70, exit 202, 0.8 mi s, then just w. Int corridors. **Pets:** Accepted.
SAVE ⑤ ✕ 🛏 🖥

**▽▽ Quality Inn** SH 🐾
(785) 842-5100. **$65-$125.** 801 N Iowa St. I-70, exit 202, 1 mi s on US 59. Ext/int corridors. **Pets:** Medium, other species. $10 one-time fee/pet. Service with restrictions, crate.
ASK ⑤ ✕ 🛏 🖥 🌊

# LEAVENWORTH

**▽▽ Days Inn** M
(913) 651-6000. **$50-$129.** 3211 S 4th St. I-70, exit 224 (Leavenworth), 12 mi n on US 73 and SR 7. Ext corridors. **Pets:** Accepted.
ASK ✕ 🛏 🖥 🌊

# LIBERAL

**▽▽ Best Western LaFonda Motel** SH
(620) 624-5601. **$46-$94.** 229 W Pancake Blvd. Just w of jct US 54 and 83B (Kansas Ave). Ext corridors. **Pets:** Accepted.
ASK ⑤ ✕ ⑦ 🛏 🖥 🍴 🌊

**⊕ ▽ Cimarron Inn** M
(620) 624-6203. **$45.** 564 E Pancake Blvd. 0.8 w of jct US 54 and 83. Ext corridors. **Pets:** $5 daily fee/pet. Designated rooms, service with restrictions, supervision.
SAVE ⑤ ✕ 🛏 🖥 🌊

**⊕ ▽▽▽ Liberal Inn** SH
(620) 624-7254. **$60-$75.** 603 E Pancake Blvd. 0.5 mi w of jct US 54 and 83. Int corridors. **Pets:** Medium. Designated rooms, service with restrictions, crate.
SAVE ⑤ ✕ 🛏 🖥 🍴 🌊

**▽▽ Liberal Super 8 Motel** SH
(620) 624-8880. **$52-$68, 7 day notice.** 747 E Pancake Blvd. Just w of jct US 54 and 83. Int corridors. **Pets:** Accepted.
ASK ⑤ ✕ 🛏 🖥 🌊

# LINDSBORG

**▽▽ Viking Motel** M
(785) 227-3336. **$49-$66.** 446 Harrison. I-135, exit 78, 4 mi sw. Ext corridors. **Pets:** Accepted.
✕ 🌊

# MANHATTAN

**▽▽ Hampton Inn** SH
(785) 539-5000. **$88-$95.** 501 E Poyntz Ave. SR 177, 0.3 mi e on US 24 (Frontage Rd). Int corridors. **Pets:** Accepted.
ASK ⑤ ✕ ⑥M ⑤ 🛏 🖥 🌊

**⊕ ▽▽▽ Holiday Inn/Holidome** LH
(785) 539-5311. **$79-$199.** 530 Richards Dr. On SR 18 (Ft Riley Blvd), 0.3 mi e of jct SR 113. Ext/int corridors. **Pets:** Accepted.
SAVE ⑤ ✕ ⑤ 🛏 🖥 🍴 🌊 ✕

**▽▽ Motel 6-152** M
(785) 537-1022. **$45-$58.** 510 Tuttle Creek Blvd. 0.3 mi ne on US 24 (Frontage Rd) and SR 177. Ext corridors. **Pets:** Accepted.
⑤ ✕ ⑥M ⑦ ⑤ 🌊

**▽▽▽ Ramada Plaza Hotel** SH 🐾
(785) 539-7531. **$89-$149.** 1641 Anderson. 1 mi n of SR 18 (Ft Riley Blvd). Int corridors. **Pets:** Other species. $10 daily fee/room. Service with restrictions, supervision.
ASK ⑤ ✕ 🛏 🖥 🍴 🌊 ✕

**▽▽ Super 8 Motel-Manhattan** SH
(785) 537-8468. **$53-$75.** 200 Tuttle Creek Blvd. Jct US 24 (Frontage Rd) and SR 177. Int corridors. **Pets:** Small. $20 daily fee/pet. Designated rooms, no service, crate.
ASK ⑤ ✕ ⑦ 🛏 🖥

# MARYSVILLE

**▽▽ Best Western Surf Motel** SH
(785) 562-2354. **$45-$65.** 2105 Center St. 1 mi e on US 36 (Pony Express Hwy). Ext/int corridors. **Pets:** Accepted.
ASK ⑤ ✕ ⑤ 🛏 🖥 ✕

**⊕ ▽▽ Oak Tree Inn-Marysville** SH
(785) 562-1234. **$65.** 1127 Pony Express Hwy. 1.6 mi e on US 36 (Pony Express Hwy). Int corridors. **Pets:** Accepted.
SAVE ⑤ ✕ ⑥M ⑤ 🛏 🖥 🍴

**▽▽ Super 8 Motel** SH
(785) 562-5588. **$62-$69.** 1155 Pony Express Hwy. 2 mi e on US 36 (Pony Express Hwy). Int corridors. **Pets:** Other species. $10 one-time fee/room. Designated rooms, service with restrictions, supervision.
ASK ⑤ ✕ ⑥M 🛏

# MCPHERSON

**⊕ ▽▽▽ Americas Best Value Inn** M
(620) 241-8881. **$48-$62.** 2110 E Kansas Ave. I-135, exit 60, just w. Int corridors. **Pets:** Accepted.
SAVE ⑤ ✕ ⑥M ⑤ 🖥

**▽▽ Best Western Holiday Manor Motel** SH
(620) 241-5343. **$66-$120.** 2211 E Kansas Ave. I-135, exit 60, just w. Ext/int corridors. **Pets:** Medium. $10 daily fee/pet. Designated rooms, service with restrictions, crate.
ASK ⑤ ✕ ⑦ 🛏 🖥 🍴 🌊

ⓐ ▼ Red Coach Inn 🆂🅷
(620) 241-6960. **$59-$111.** 2111 E Kansas Ave. I-135, exit 60, just w. Ext/int corridors. **Pets:** Accepted.
[SAVE] 🆂 ⊠ 🍴 ⊅ ⊠

## MEADE

ⓐ ▼ Dalton's Bedpost Motel Ⓜ
(620) 873-2131. **$44-$49.** 519 Carthage. On US 54. Ext corridors. **Pets:** Accepted.
[SAVE] ⊠

## NEWTON

ⓐ ▼ Americas Best Value Inn Ⓜ
(316) 283-7611. **$45-$57.** 1620 E 2nd St. I-135, exit 31, just e. Int corridors. **Pets:** Accepted.
[SAVE] 🆂 ⊠ 🖬 🖵

▼▼ Best Western Red Coach Inn 🆂🅷
(316) 283-9120. **$61-$119, 14 day notice.** 1301 E 1st St. I-135, exit 31, just w. Ext/int corridors. **Pets:** Other species. Supervision.
[ASK] 🆂 ⊠ 🖉 🖬 🖵 🍴 ⊅ ⊠

▼▼ Days Inn Newton 🆂🅷
(316) 283-3330. **$66-$68.** 105 Manchester St. I-135, exit 31, just e. Int corridors. **Pets:** Accepted.
[ASK] 🆂 ⊠ 🖬 🖵 ⊅

## OAKLEY

▼▼ Golden Plains Motel Ⓜ
(785) 672-3254. **$58-$65.** 3506 US 40. I-70, exit 76, 1.7 mi w. Ext corridors. **Pets:** Small. Service with restrictions, supervision.
[ASK] 🆂 ⊠ 🖵 ⊅

## OBERLIN

ⓐ ▼ Frontier Motel Ⓜ
(785) 475-2203. **$49-$79.** 207 E Frontier Pkwy. On US 36, 0.5 mi e of jct US 83. Ext corridors. **Pets:** Medium. $25 daily fee/pet. Service with restrictions, supervision.
[SAVE] ⊠ 🖬 🍴 ⊅

## OTTAWA

▼▼ Best Western Ottawa Inn 🆂🅷
(785) 242-2224. **$65-$99.** 606 E 23rd St. I-35, exit 183 (US 59). Ext/int corridors. **Pets:** Small. $5 one-time fee/pet. Designated rooms, service with restrictions, supervision.
[ASK] 🆂 ⊠ ♿ 🖬 ⊅

▼▼ Days Inn Ⓜ
(785) 242-4842. **$50-$85, 7 day notice.** 1641 S Main. I-35, exit 183 (US 59), 1 mi n. Ext corridors. **Pets:** Accepted.
[ASK] 🆂 ⊠ ♿ 🖬 🖵 ⊅

ⓐ ▼▼ Econo Lodge 🆂🅷
(785) 242-3400. **$49-$125.** 2331 S Cedar Rd. I-35, exit 183 (US 59). Int corridors. **Pets:** Accepted.
[SAVE] 🆂 ⊠ 🖬 ⊅

## PARK CITY

▼ Super 8 Motel-Wichita North/Park City 🆂🅷
(316) 744-2071. **$51-$73.** 6075 Air Cap Dr. I-135, exit 14, just sw. Int corridors. **Pets:** Small. $10 daily fee/pet. Designated rooms, service with restrictions, supervision.
[ASK] 🆂 ⊠ ♿ 🖬

## PARSONS

▼ Super 8 Motel-Parsons 🆂🅷
(620) 421-8000. **$55-$80.** 229 E Main. 1.3 mi e of jct US 400 and 59. Int corridors. **Pets:** Small. $50 deposit/room. Designated rooms, no service, crate.
[ASK] 🆂 ⊠ 🖬 🖵 ⊅

## PHILLIPSBURG

ⓐ ▼▼ Cottonwood Inn Ⓜ
(785) 543-2125. **$70-$100, 7 day notice.** 1200 State St. 2 mi e on US 36 and 183. Ext corridors. **Pets:** Accepted.
[SAVE] 🆂 ⊠ 🖬 ⊅

## PITTSBURG

▼▼ Econo Lodge 🆂🅷 🐾
(620) 231-8300. **$69-$74.** 2408 S Broadway. Jct US 69 and Broadway; south side of town. Ext corridors. **Pets:** Small. $10 daily fee/pet. Designated rooms, service with restrictions, supervision.
[ASK] 🆂 ⊠ 🖬 ⊅

## PRATT

▼▼ Days Inn 🆂🅷
(620) 672-9465. **$53-$85.** 1901 E 1st St. 1.7 mi e on US 54. Ext corridors. **Pets:** Accepted.
[ASK] 🆂 ⊠ 🖬 🖵 ⊅

▼▼ Econo Lodge 🆂🅷
(620) 672-6407. **$47-$65.** 1336 E 1st St. 1 mi e on US 54. Ext corridors. **Pets:** Accepted.
[ASK] 🆂 ⊠ 🖬 🖵 ⊅

ⓐ ▼ Economy Inn Ⓜ
(620) 672-5588. **$38-$50, 4 day notice.** 1401 E 1st St. 1 mi e on US 54. Ext corridors. **Pets:** Medium. $5 one-time fee/pet. Designated rooms, service with restrictions, supervision.
[SAVE] 🆂 ⊠ 🖬 ⊅

▼ Evergreen Inn Ⓜ
(620) 672-6431. **$40-$50.** 20001 W US Hwy 54. On US 54, 3 mi w. Ext corridors. **Pets:** Dogs only. $5 one-time fee/pet. Designated rooms, service with restrictions, supervision.
[ASK] 🆂 ⊠ 🖬 ⊅

▼▼▼ Leisure Hotel 🆂🅷
(620) 672-9433. **$78-$89.** 1401 W Hwy 54. On US 54, 2 mi w. Int corridors. **Pets:** Other species. Service with restrictions, supervision.
[ASK] 🆂 ⊠ 🖉 🖬 🖵 ⊅

## RUSSELL

▼▼▼ AmericInn Lodge & Suites 🆂🅷 🐾
(785) 483-4200. **$74.** 1430 S Fossil St. I-70, exit 184 (US 281), just n. Int corridors. **Pets:** Other species. $50 deposit/room, $10 daily fee/pet. Designated rooms, service with restrictions, supervision.
[ASK] ⊠ ♿ ♿ 🖬 🖵 ⊅ ⊠

▼ Days Inn Ⓜ
(785) 483-6660. **$55-$74.** 1225 S Fossil St. I-70, exit 184 (US 281), just n. Ext corridors. **Pets:** Other species. $5 daily fee/pet. Service with restrictions, supervision.
[ASK] 🆂 ⊠ 🖬 ⊅

## SABETHA

▼▼ Sabetha Country Inn 🆂🅷
(785) 284-2300. **$51-$56.** 1423 S 75 Hwy. US 75, 1 mi s of jct SR 246 and US 75. Int corridors. **Pets:** Accepted.
⊠ ♿ 🖬

# SALINA

**▼ 1st Inn Gold** ⑤Ⅱ
(785) 827-5511. **$49-$64.** 2403 S 9th St. I-135, exit 90 (Magnolia), just e. Ext corridors. **Pets:** Accepted.
ASK Ⓢ ✕ ▤ ▣ ⊸

**▼▼ Americas Best Inn** ⑤Ⅱ
(785) 825-2500. **$48-$61.** 429 W Diamond Dr. I-70, exit 252, just n. Int corridors. **Pets:** Medium, dogs only. $5 daily fee/pet. Designated rooms, service with restrictions, supervision.
ASK Ⓢ ✕ ⓜ ▤

**▼▼ Baymont Inn & Suites** ⑤Ⅱ
(785) 493-9800. **$70-$90.** 745 W Schilling Rd. I-135, exit 89 (Schilling Rd), just w. Int corridors. **Pets:** Small. $10 one-time fee/pet. Designated rooms, service with restrictions, supervision.
ASK Ⓢ ✕ ⓜ ⓔ ▤ ▣ ⊸ ✕

**◈◈ ▼▼ Best Western Mid-America Inn** ⑤Ⅱ
(785) 827-0356. **$64-$85.** 1846 N 9th St. I-70, exit 252, just s. Ext corridors. **Pets:** $50 deposit/pet. Service with restrictions, supervision.
SAVE Ⓢ ✕ ⓜ ⓔ ▣ ⑪ ⊸

**▼▼▼ Candlewood Suites** ⑤Ⅱ
(785) 826-6939. **$49-$92.** 2650 Planet Ave. I-135, exit 89 (Schilling Rd), just e to S 9th St, 0.5 mi n to Belmont, then just w. Int corridors. **Pets:** Medium. $20 one-time fee/pet. Service with restrictions, crate.
ASK ✕ ⓜ ⓓ ⓔ ▤ ▣

**▼▼ Comfort Inn** ⑤Ⅱ
(785) 826-1711. **$90.** 1820 W Crawford St. I-135, exit 92, just e. Int corridors. **Pets:** Accepted.
ASK Ⓢ ✕ ⓓ ▤ ▣ ⊸

**▼▼▼ Holiday Inn Express Hotel & Suites-Salina** ⑤Ⅱ
(785) 827-9000. **$79-$109.** 201 E Diamond Dr. I-70, exit 252, just ne. Int corridors. **Pets:** Other species. $11 one-time fee/pet. Service with restrictions.
ASK ✕ ⓜ ⓓ ⓔ ▤ ▣ ⊸

**▼▼ Holiday Inn of Salina** ⑤Ⅱ ✿
(785) 823-1739. **$75-$95.** 1616 W Crawford St. I-135, exit 92, 0.5 mi e. Int corridors. **Pets:** Medium. $25 one-time fee/room. Designated rooms, service with restrictions, supervision.
ASK Ⓢ ✕ ⓜ ⓓ ⓔ ▤ ▣ ⑪ ⊸ ✕

**◈◈ ▼▼ Red Coach Inn** ⑤Ⅱ
(785) 825-2111. **$62.** 2110 W Crawford St. I-135, exit 92, just w. Int corridors. **Pets:** Small, dogs only. $15 one-time fee/pet. Designated rooms, service with restrictions, supervision.
SAVE Ⓢ ✕ ⓜ ⓓ ⓔ ▤ ▣ ⑪ ⊸ ✕

**◈◈ ▼▼ Super 8 I-70** ⑤Ⅱ
(785) 823-8808. **$59-$81.** 120 E Diamond Dr. I-70, exit 252, just ne. Int corridors. **Pets:** Accepted.
SAVE Ⓢ ✕ ⓜ ⓓ ▤ ▣ ⊸

**◈◈ ▼▼ TraveLodge** ⑤Ⅱ
(785) 825-8211. **$45-$50.** 1949 N 9th St. I-70, exit 252, just s. Ext corridors. **Pets:** Accepted.
SAVE ✕ ▤ ▣ ⊸

# SHARON SPRINGS

**▼ ▼ Oak Tree Inn** ⑤Ⅱ
(785) 852-4664. **$68-$78.** 801 N Hwy 27. Jct US 40 and SR 27. Ext/int corridors. **Pets:** Other species. $10 deposit/room. Service with restrictions, crate.
ASK Ⓢ ✕ ⓓ ⓔ ▤ ▣ ⑪

# TOPEKA

**◈◈◈ ▼▼▼ AmeriSuites (Topeka/Northwest)** ⑤Ⅱ
(785) 273-0066. **$79-$129.** 6021 SW Sixth Ave. I-70, exit 356 (Wanamaker Rd), just n. Int corridors. **Pets:** $10 daily fee/pet. Service with restrictions, crate.
SAVE ✕ ⓜ ⓔ ▤ ▣ ⊸

**▼▼ Best Western Candlelight Inn** Ⓜ
(785) 272-9550. **$44-$139.** 2831 SW Fairlawn Rd. I-470, exit 3. Ext corridors. **Pets:** Small. $8 daily fee/pet. Service with restrictions, supervision.
ASK Ⓢ ✕ ⓓ ▤ ▣ ⊸ ✕

**◈◈◈ ▼▼ Best Western Meadow Acres Motel** Ⓜ
(785) 267-1681. **$55-$120.** 2950 S Topeka Blvd. I-470, exit 6, 1.5 mi n. Ext corridors. **Pets:** Accepted.
SAVE Ⓢ ▤ ▣ ⊸

**◈◈◈ ▼▼▼ Capitol Plaza Hotel** ⒧Ⓗ
(785) 431-7200. **$119-$129.** 1717 SW Topeka Blvd. I-70, exit SE 8th Ave, 1.6 mi s; I-470, exit Topeka Blvd, 2.9 mi n. Int corridors. **Pets:** Accepted.
SAVE ✕ ⓜ ⓓ ⓔ ▤ ▣ ⑪ ⊸ ✕

**▼▼▼ ClubHouse Inn & Suites** ⑤Ⅱ
(785) 273-8888. **$119-$149.** 924 SW Henderson. I-70, exit 356 (Wanamaker Rd). Int corridors. **Pets:** Accepted.
ASK Ⓢ ✕ ⓓ ⓔ ▤ ▣ ⊸

**▼▼ Comfort Inn by Choice Hotels** ⑤Ⅱ
(785) 273-5365. **$64-$119.** 1518 SW Wanamaker Rd. I-470, exit 1 (Wanamaker Rd). Int corridors. **Pets:** Accepted.
ASK Ⓢ ✕ ▤ ▣ ⊸

**▼▼▼ Country Inn & Suites By Carlson-Topeka-West** ⑤Ⅱ
(785) 478-9800. **$79-$99.** 6020 SW 10th St. I-70, exit 356 (Wanamaker Rd). Int corridors. **Pets:** Other species. $10 one-time fee/room. Service with restrictions, supervision.
ASK Ⓢ ✕ ⓓ ⓔ ▤ ▣ ⊸

**▼▼ Quality Inn** ⑤Ⅱ
(785) 273-6969. **$59-$129.** 1240 SW Wanamaker Rd. I-470, exit 1 (Wanamaker Rd), just ne; I-70, exit 356A (Wanamaker Rd), 1 mi s. Int corridors. **Pets:** Accepted.
ASK Ⓢ ✕ ⓓ ▤ ▣ ⊸

**▼▼ Ramada Inn Downtown** ⒧Ⓗ
(785) 234-5400. **$64.** 420 SE Sixth St. I-70, exit 362B, just e. Int corridors. **Pets:** Accepted.
✕ ⓜ ⓔ ▤ ▣ ⑪ ⊸ ✕

**▼▼▼ Residence Inn by Marriott** ⑤Ⅱ
(785) 271-8903. **$89-$159, 14 day notice.** 1620 SW Westport Dr. I-470, exit 1 (Wanamaker Rd), just se. Int corridors. **Pets:** Accepted.
ASK Ⓢ ✕ ⓜ ⓓ ⓔ ▤ ▣ ⊸ ✕

**▼▼▼ The Senate Luxury Suites** ⑤Ⅱ
(785) 233-5050. **$80-$95, 3 day notice.** 900 SW Tyler. Just w of state capitol; downtown. Int corridors. **Pets:** Accepted.
ASK Ⓢ ✕ ▤ ▣

# ULYSSES

**▼▼ Single Tree Inn** ⑤Ⅱ
(620) 356-1500. **$71-$81.** 2033 W Oklahoma St. 1.5 mi w on US 160. Int corridors. **Pets:** Other species. $25 deposit/room. Service with restrictions, crate.
ASK Ⓢ ✕ ⓓ ▤ ▣

# WAMEGO

**◈◈◈ ▼ Simmer Motel** Ⓜ
(785) 456-2304. **$50-$55.** 1215 Hwy 24 W. Jct SR 99, 0.5 mi w. Ext corridors. **Pets:** Accepted.
SAVE ✕ ▤ ▣ ⊸

# WICHITA

**AAA ▼▼ Best Western Airport Inn & Conference Center** SH
(316) 942-5600. **$89.** 6815 W Kellogg. I-235, exit 7, 0.6 mi w on US 54 (S Frontage Rd). Int corridors. **Pets:** Accepted.

SAVE S X ✎ 🖥 💻 ▯▯ ⇨ ⊠

**AAA ▼▼ Best Western Governors Inn & Suites** SH
(316) 522-0775. **$69-$109.** 4742 S Emporia. I-135, exit 1B, just sw. Int corridors. **Pets:** Accepted.

SAVE S X 🖥 💻 ⇨

**AAA ▼▼ Best Western Wichita North/Park City** SH
(316) 832-9387. **$74-$94.** 915 E 53rd St N. I-135, exit 13, just w. Ext/int corridors. **Pets:** Medium, dogs only. $25 one-time fee/room. Service with restrictions, supervision.

SAVE S X ✎ 🖥 💻 ▯▯ ⇨ ⊠

**▼▼ Candlewood Suites** SH
(316) 942-0400. **$87-$129.** 570 S Julia. I-235, exit 7, 0.4 mi nw on Dugan Rd. Int corridors. **Pets:** Accepted.

ASK S X ✎ ✎ 🖥 💻

**▼▼ Candlewood Suites-Wichita Northeast** SH
(316) 634-6070. **$77.** 3141 N Webb Rd. SR 96, exit Webb Rd, just nw. Int corridors. **Pets:** Accepted.

ASK S X ⚹M ✎ ✎ 🖥 💻

**▼▼ ClubHouse Inn & Suites** SH
(316) 684-1111. **$69-$109.** 515 S Webb Rd. I-35, exit 50, just e. Int corridors. **Pets:** Accepted.

ASK S X ✎ 🖥 💻 ⇨

**AAA ▼▼ Comfort Inn** SH
(316) 522-1800. **$71-$81.** 4849 S Laura. I-135, exit 1A/B (47th St S), just e. Int corridors. **Pets:** Medium, other species. $10 daily fee/room. Service with restrictions, supervision.

SAVE S X ✎ ✎ 🖥 💻 ⇨

**▼▼ Comfort Inn by Choice Hotels** SH
(316) 686-2844. **$74-$104.** 9525 E Corporate Hills Dr. I-35, exit 50, just ne. Int corridors. **Pets:** Accepted.

ASK S X ✎ ✎ 🖥 💻 ⇨

**AAA ▼▼ Comfort Suites Airport** SH
(316) 945-2600. **$77-$95.** 658 Westdale. Jct I-235 and US 54. Int corridors. **Pets:** Very small. $10 daily fee/pet. Service with restrictions, supervision.

SAVE S X ✎ ✎ 🖥 💻 ⇨

**▼▼ Cresthill Suites Hotel** SH
(316) 689-8000. **Call for rates.** 12111 E Central Ave. 1.7 mi e of jct Rock Rd. Int corridors. **Pets:** Other species. $50 one-time fee/room. Service with restrictions

X 🖥 💻

**▼▼ Days Inn Wichita North** M
(316) 832-1131. **$52-$63, 3 day notice.** 901 E 53rd St N. I-135, exit 13, just w. Int corridors. **Pets:** Accepted.

ASK S X ✎ 🖥 💻

**▼▼▼ The Four Points by Sheraton Wichita Airport** SH
(316) 942-7911. **$69-$129.** 5805 W Kellogg. I-235, exit 7A, just w. Int corridors. **Pets:** Accepted.

ASK S X ✎ 🖥 💻 ▯▯ ⇨

**▼▼ Hampton Inn by Hilton** SH
(316) 686-3576. **$89-$129.** 9449 E Corporate Hills Dr. I-35, exit 50, just ne. Int corridors. **Pets:** Accepted.

ASK S X ⚹M ✎ ✎ 🖥 💻 ⇨

**▼▼▼ Hawthorn Suites at Reflection Ridge** SH
(316) 729-5700. **$101-$118.** 2405 N Ridge Rd. I-235, exit 10, 1.7 mi w on Zoo Blvd/21st St N, then just n. Int corridors. **Pets:** $20 one-time fee/room. Service with restrictions, crate.

ASK S X ✎ 🖥 💻 ⊠

**▼▼ Holiday Inn Express** SH
(316) 529-4848. **$83-$97.** 4848 S Laura. I-35, exit 1B, just ne. Int corridors. **Pets:** Other species. $25 one-time fee/room. Service with restrictions, crate.

ASK X ✎ ✎ 💻 ⇨

**▼▼ Holiday Inn Express-North** SH
(316) 634-3900. **$84-$119.** 7824 E 32nd St N. SR 96 E, exit Rock Rd, just sw. Int corridors. **Pets:** Accepted.

ASK S X ✎ ✎ 🖥 💻 ⇨

**AAA ▼▼ Holiday Inn Select** SH
(316) 686-7131. **$74-$104.** 549 S Rock Rd. I-35, exit 50, 0.5 mi w. Ext/int corridors. **Pets:** Small. $25 one-time fee/pet. Designated rooms, service with restrictions, crate.

SAVE S X ✎ ✎ 🖥 💻 ▯▯ ⇨ ⊠

**AAA ▼▼ Holiday Inn Wichita/Airport** SH
(316) 943-2181. **$79-$89.** 5500 W Kellogg. I-235, exit 7, just w. Int corridors. **Pets:** Small. $15 daily fee/pet. Service with restrictions, supervision.

SAVE X ✎ ✎ 🖥 💻 ▯▯ ⇨ ⊠

**AAA ▼▼ Inn at the Park** BB
(316) 652-0500. **$99-$160.** 3751 E Douglas St. US 54, exit Hillside Ave, 0.4 mi n, then just e. Int corridors. **Pets:** $150 deposit/pet. Designated rooms, service with restrictions.

SAVE X 🖥

**▼▼ The Kansas Inn** SH
(316) 269-9999. **$55-$57.** 1011 N Topeka Ave. I-135, exit 8 (13th St), 0.7 mi w, then 0.3 mi s. Int corridors. **Pets:** Accepted.

ASK S X ✎ ✎ 🖥 💻

**▼▼▼ La Quinta Inn & Suites Wichita Downtown** SH
(316) 269-2090. **$69-$159.** 221 E Kellogg. Just sw of jct US 54/400 and Broadway. Int corridors. **Pets:** Accepted.

ASK S X ⚹M ✎ ✎ 🖥 💻 ▯▯ ⇨ ⊠

**▼▼ La Quinta Inn Wichita (Towne East Mall)** SH
(316) 681-2881. **$75-$111.** 7700 E Kellogg. I-35, exit 50, 0.5 mi w. Int corridors. **Pets:** Medium. Service with restrictions.

ASK X ✎ ✎ 🖥 💻 ⇨

**AAA ▼▼ Quality Inn-Airport** SH
(316) 722-8730. **$59-$69.** 600 S Holland. I-235, exit 7, 1.1 mi w on US 54. Int corridors. **Pets:** Other species. $10 one-time fee/room. Designated rooms, service with restrictions, supervision.

SAVE S X ✎ 🖥 💻 ⇨

**▼▼▼ Residence Inn by Marriott** SH
(316) 686-7331. **$154.** 411 S Webb Rd. I-35, exit 50, just ne. Ext corridors. **Pets:** Accepted.

ASK S X 🖥 💻 ⇨ ⊠

**▼▼ Super 8 Motel-Wichita/East** M
(316) 686-3888. **$51-$73.** 527 S Webb Rd. I-35, exit 50, just e. Int corridors. **Pets:** Medium. $25 daily fee/pet. Designated rooms, no service, supervision.

ASK S X ✎ 🖥 💻

**▼▼ TownePlace Suites by Marriott** SH
(316) 631-3773. **$64-$119.** 9444 E 29th St N. SR 96, exit Webb Rd, just sw. Int corridors. **Pets:** Accepted.

ASK X ⚹M ✎ ✎ 🖥 💻 ⊠

▼▼ **Wesley Inn** 🆂🅷
(316) 858-3343. **$49-$59.** 3343 E Central Ave. Just e of jct Hillside. Int corridors. **Pets:** Accepted.
(ASK) ⊠ 🐾 🔋 💻

# WINFIELD

▼▼ **Comfort Inn** 🆂🅷
(620) 221-7529. **$76-$175.** 3800 S Pike Rd. On US 77, 1 mi s. Ext/int corridors. **Pets:** $10 daily fee/pet. Designated rooms, service with restrictions, crate.
(ASK) 🆂🅾 ⊠ 🐾 🔋 💻 🏊

▼▼ **Econo Lodge** 🅼
(620) 221-9050. **$56-$71.** 1710 Main St. 0.5 mi s of jct US 77 and 160. Ext corridors. **Pets:** Small. $10 daily fee/pet. Designated rooms, service with restrictions, supervision.
(ASK) 🆂🅾 ⊠ 🔋 💻

# YATES CENTER

▼ **Star Motel** 🅼
(620) 625-2175. **$33-$39.** 206 S Fry. On US 54, at US 75. Ext corridors. **Pets:** Accepted.
⊠

# KENTUCKY

## CITY INDEX

## ASHLAND

### ◆◆◆ ▼▼ Knights Inn Ⓜ
(606) 928-9501. **$46-$60.** 7216 US Rt 60. I-64, exit 185, 5 mi sw on US 60, then 4.3 mi n. Ext corridors. **Pets:** Accepted.

🅢🅐🅥🅔 Ⓢ ⊠ 🔋 💻 ⇌

## BARDSTOWN

### ◆◆◆ ▼▼ Bardstown-Parkview Motel Ⓜ
(502) 348-5983. **$60-$85.** 418 E Stephen Foster Ave. 0.5 mi e on US 150; e of jct US 62. Ext corridors. **Pets:** Accepted.

🅢🅐🅥🅔 Ⓢ ⊠ 🔋 🍴 ⇌

### ▼▼ Best Western General Nelson Motel ⑤ℍ
(502) 348-3977. **$59-$79, 7 day notice.** 411 W Stephen Foster Ave. 0.5 mi w on US 62. Ext corridors. **Pets:** Small. $10 one-time fee/pet. Service with restrictions, crate.

🅐🅢🅚 Ⓢ ⊠ 🔋 💻 ⇌

### ◆◆◆ ▼▼ Days Inn-Bardstown ⑤ℍ
(502) 348-9253. **$69.** 1875 New Haven Rd. Bluegrass Pkwy, exit 21. Ext corridors. **Pets:** Accepted.

🅢🅐🅥🅔 Ⓢ ⊠ 🔋 💻 🍴 ⇌ ⊠

### ◆◆◆ ▼▼▼ Hampton Inn ⑤ℍ
(502) 349-0100. **$72-$97.** 985 Chambers Blvd. Just s of US 245. Int corridors. **Pets:** Medium, other species. $50 one-time fee/room. Service with restrictions, crate.

🅢🅐🅥🅔 Ⓢ ⊠ 🔥ᴹ 🕗 🐾 🔋 💻 ⇌

### ▼▼▼ Old Bardstown Inn ⑤ℍ
(502) 349-0776. **$49-$59, 3 day notice.** 510 E Stephen Foster Ave. 0.5 mi e on US 150, e of jct US 62. Ext corridors. **Pets:** $10 daily fee/pet. Designated rooms, service with restrictions, crate.

🅐🅢🅚 Ⓢ ⊠ 🔋 💻 ⇌

### ◆◆◆ ▼ Old Kentucky Home Motel Ⓜ
(502) 348-5979. **$35-$35.** 414 W Stephen Foster Ave. 0.5 mi w on US 62. Ext corridors. **Pets:** $5 daily fee/room. Service with restrictions, supervision.

🅢🅐🅥🅔 Ⓢ ⊠ 🔋 💻 ⇌

### ▼▼ Ramada Inn ⑤ℍ
(502) 349-0363. **$50-$85.** 523 N 3rd St. 0.5 mi n on US 150. Ext corridors. **Pets:** $10 daily fee/pet. Service with restrictions, supervision.

🅐🅢🅚 Ⓢ ⊠ 🔋 💻 ⇌

## BEAVER DAM

### ▼▼ Days Inn Beaver Dam ⑤ℍ
(270) 274-0851. **$64-$69.** 1750 US Hwy 231. Kentucky Pkwy, exit 75, just n. Int corridors. **Pets:** Accepted.

🅐🅢🅚 ⊠ 🔋 💻 ⇌

## BENTON

### ▼▼▼ Holiday Inn Express Hotel & Suites ⑤ℍ
(270) 527-5300. **$80-$140.** 173 Carroll Rd. Purchase Pkwy, exit 47. Int corridors. **Pets:** Accepted.

⊠ 🔥ᴹ 🕗 🐾 🔋 💻 ⇌

## BEREA

### ◆◆◆ ▼▼▼ Boone Tavern Hotel-Berea College ⑤ℍ
(859) 985-3700. **$83-$100.** 100 Main St. I-75, exit 76, 1.5 mi ne on SR 21. Int corridors. **Pets:** Other species. $100 deposit/room. Service with restrictions, supervision.

🅢🅐🅥🅔 Ⓢ ⊠ 🐾 💻 🍴

### ▼▼▼ Comfort Inn & Suites ⑤ℍ
(859) 985-5500. **$55-$99.** 1003 Paint Lick Rd. I-75, exit 76, just w. Int corridors. **Pets:** $10 daily fee/pet. Service with restrictions, supervision.

🅐🅢🅚 Ⓢ ⊠ 🔥ᴹ 🐾 🔋 💻 ⇌

### ◆◆◆ ▼▼ Knights Inn Berea Ⓜ
(859) 986-2384. **$40-$60.** 715 Chestnut St. I-75, exit 76, 0.3 mi e. Ext corridors. **Pets:** Other species. $5 daily fee/pet. Service with restrictions, supervision.

🅢🅐🅥🅔 Ⓢ ⊠ 🔋

## BOWLING GREEN

### ◆◆◆ ▼▼ Continental Inn ⑤ℍ
(270) 781-5200. **$58-$65.** 700 Interstate Dr. I-65, exit 28, 0.3 mi w. Ext corridors. **Pets:** Small. $10 daily fee/pet. Designated rooms, service with restrictions, supervision.

🅢🅐🅥🅔 Ⓢ ⊠ 💻 ⇌

### ◆◆◆ ▼▼ Country Hearth Inn ⑤ℍ
(270) 783-4443. **$40-$54.** 395 Corvette Dr. I-65, exit 28, just w. Int corridors. **Pets:** Medium. $10 daily fee/pet. Service with restrictions, crate.

🅢🅐🅥🅔 Ⓢ ⊠ 🔥ᴹ 🔋 💻

### ◆◆◆ ▼▼▼ Days Inn ⑤ℍ
(270) 781-6470. **$60-$130.** 4617 Scottsville Rd. I-65, exit 22 (Scottsville Rd), 0.3 mi n. Int corridors. **Pets:** Accepted.

🅢🅐🅥🅔 ⊠ 🕗 🔋 💻 ⇌

### ▼▼▼ Drury Inn-Bowling Green ⑤ℍ
(270) 842-7100. **$90-$130.** 3250 Scottsville Rd. I-65, exit 22 (Scottsville Rd), just w. Int corridors. **Pets:** Accepted.

🅐🅢🅚 ⊠ 🔥ᴹ 🐾 🔋 💻 ⇌

### ◆◆◆ ▼▼▼ Holiday Inn University Plaza 🅛🅗 🐾
(270) 745-0088. **$99-$149.** 1021 Wilkinson Trace. I-65, exit 22 (Scottsville Rd), 2.5 mi w, then just n. Int corridors. **Pets:** Large. $25 one-time fee/room. Service with restrictions, crate.

🅢🅐🅥🅔 Ⓢ ⊠ 🐾 🔋 💻 🍴 ⇌ ⊠

**(AAA) ▼▼▼ News Inn of Bowling Green M**
(270) 781-3460. **$49-$79.** 3160 Scottsville Rd. I-65, exit 22 (Scottsville Rd). Ext corridors. **Pets:** Medium. $5 daily fee/pet. Service with restrictions, supervision.
[SAVE] [S�référ] [X] [▤] [≈]

**(AAA) ▼▼▼ Red Roof Inn SH**
(270) 781-6550. **$59-$89.** 3140 Scottsville Rd. I-65, exit 22 (Scottsville Rd), 0.3 mi w. Ext corridors. **Pets:** Medium. Designated rooms, service with restrictions, supervision.
[SAVE] [S�).] [X] [▤]

# CADIZ

**▼▼▼ Holiday Inn Express SH**
(270) 522-3700. **$72-$80.** 153 Broad Bent Blvd. I-24, exit 65, just s. Int corridors. **Pets:** Accepted.
[ASK] [S�) ] [X] [▤] [▣] [≈]

**▼▼ Super 8 Motel SH**
(270) 522-7007. **$54-$64, 14 day notice.** 154 Hospitality Ln. I-24, exit 65. Ext corridors. **Pets:** Accepted.
[ASK] [S�) ] [X] [▤] [≈]

# CAMPBELLSVILLE

**(AAA) ▼▼▼▼ Best Western Campbellsville Lodge SH**
(270) 465-7001. **$54-$60.** 1400 E Broadway. 2 mi e on US 68 and SR 55. Int corridors. **Pets:** Very small. $10 daily fee/pet. Service with restrictions, supervision.
[SAVE] [S�) ] [X] [▤] [▣] [≈]

**▼▼▼▼ Holiday Inn Express SH**
(270) 465-2727. **$69.** 102 Plantation Dr. Jct US 68 and SR 55, 0.5 mi n. Int corridors. **Pets:** Other species. $10 daily fee/room. Service with restrictions.
[ASK] [S�) ] [X] [&M] [♿] [▤] [▣]

**▼▼ Lakeview Motel SH 🐾**
(270) 465-8139. **$45-$48.** 1291 Old Lebanon Rd. 1 mi n on SR 289. Ext corridors. **Pets:** Medium, dogs only. $50 deposit/room, $10 daily fee/pet. Service with restrictions, supervision.
[ASK] [S�) ] [X] [▤] [▣]

# CARROLLTON

**(AAA) ▼▼▼▼ Best Western Executive Inn SH**
(502) 732-8444. **$65-$119.** 10 Slumber Ln. I-71, exit 44, just nw. Int corridors. **Pets:** Large, other species. $10 daily fee/pet. Service with restrictions, supervision.
[SAVE] [X] [&M] [♨] [♿] [▤] [▣] [≈]

**(AAA) ▼▼▼ Days Inn Carrollton SH**
(502) 732-9301. **$49-$99.** 61 Inn Rd. I-71, exit 44, just nw. Int corridors. **Pets:** Accepted.
[SAVE] [S�) ] [X] [▤] [▣] [≈]

**▼▼▼ Super 8 Carrollton SH**
(502) 732-0252. **$55-$99.** 130 Slumber Ln. I-71, exit 44, just nw. Int corridors. **Pets:** Accepted.
[ASK] [S�) ] [X] [▤]

# CAVE CITY

**(AAA) ▼▼▼ Comfort Inn SH**
(270) 773-2030. **$35-$125.** 801 Mammoth Cave St. I-65, exit 53, just ne. Ext corridors. **Pets:** Very small. $10 daily fee/pet. Service with restrictions, supervision.
[SAVE] [S�) ] [X] [♿] [▤] [▣] [≈]

**(AAA) ▼▼▼ Super 8 Motel SH**
(270) 773-2500. **$39-$89.** 799 Mammoth Cave St. I-65, exit 53, just ne. Ext corridors. **Pets:** Accepted.
[SAVE] [S�) ] [X] [&M] [♿] [▤] [▣] [≈]

# CORBIN

**▼▼▼▼ Baymont Inn & Suites-Corbin SH**
(606) 523-9040. **$65-$95.** 174 Adams Rd. I-75, exit 29. Int corridors. **Pets:** Medium. $8 daily fee/pet. Designated rooms, service with restrictions, supervision.
[ASK] [S�) ] [X] [&M] [♨] [♿] [▤] [▣] [🔊] [≈]

**(AAA) ▼▼▼ Best Western-Corbin Inn SH**
(606) 528-2100. **$54-$89.** 2630 Cumberland Falls Hwy. I-75, exit 25. Ext corridors. **Pets:** Small. $10 daily fee/pet. Designated rooms, service with restrictions, supervision.
[SAVE] [S�) ] [X] [▤] [▣] [≈]

# COVINGTON

**▼▼▼ Embassy Suites Cincinnati RiverCenter LH 🐾**
(859) 261-8400. **$209-$325.** 10 E RiverCenter Blvd. I-71/75, exit 192, 0.8 mi e on 5th St, then 0.3 mi n on Madison Ave. Int corridors. **Pets:** Medium. Service with restrictions, supervision.
[ASK] [S�) ] [X] [&M] [♨] [▤] [▣] [🔊] [≈]

# DANVILLE

**▼▼▼ Holiday Inn Express-Danville SH**
(859) 236-8600. **$59-$79.** 96 Daniel Dr. Just e of US 127 on US 150 Bypass. Int corridors. **Pets:** Small. Designated rooms, no service, crate.
[ASK] [S�) ] [X] [&M] [♿] [▤] [▣]

# DRY RIDGE

**▼▼▼ Holiday Inn Express SH**
(859) 824-7121. **$64-$79.** 1050 Fashion Ridge Rd. I-75, exit 159, just nw. Int corridors. **Pets:** Accepted.
[ASK] [S�) ] [X] [♿] [▤] [▣]

**▼▼▼ Microtel Inn and Suites SH 🐾**
(859) 824-2000. **$46-$50.** 79 Blackburn Ln. I-75, exit 159, just ne. Int corridors. **Pets:** Other species. $5 daily fee/pet. Service with restrictions.
[ASK] [S�) ] [X] [♿] [▤] [▣]

# EDDYVILLE

**▼▼▼ Eddy Creek Resort & Marina CA**
(270) 388-2271. **$74, 45 day notice.** 7312 SR 93 S. I-24, exit 45, 4 mi s. Ext corridors. **Pets:** Medium. $100 deposit/room. Designated rooms, service with restrictions, supervision.
[X] [▤] [▣] [🔊] [≈] [⊠] [⊡]

# ELIZABETHTOWN

**(AAA) ▼▼▼▼ Best Western Atrium Gardens SH**
(270) 769-3030. **$74-$84, 7 day notice.** 1043 Executive Dr. I-65, exit 94, just nw. Int corridors. **Pets:** Accepted.
[SAVE] [S�) ] [X] [▤] [▣] [≈]

**▼▼▼ Country Hearth Inn & Suites SH**
(270) 769-2344. **$72-$90.** 1058 N Mulberry St. I-65, exit 94, just nw. Ext corridors. **Pets:** Accepted.
[ASK] [S�) ] [X] [♨] [▤] [▣] [🔊] [≈]

**▼▼▼ Holiday Inn Express SH**
(270) 769-1334. **$81-$90.** 107 Buffalo Creek Dr. I-65, exit 94, just w. Int corridors. **Pets:** Small, other species. $25 daily fee/pet. Designated rooms, service with restrictions, crate.
[ASK] [S�) ] [X] [&M] [♨] [♿] [▤] [▣] [≈]

**(AAA) ▼▼▼ Kentucky Cardinal Inn SH**
(270) 765-6139. **$74-$84, 7 day notice.** 642 E Dixie Ave. I-65, exit 91 (US 31 W), 0.3 mi nw. Ext/int corridors. **Pets:** Accepted.
[SAVE] [S�) ] [X] [▣] [≈]

**Quality Inn & Suites** SH
(270) 765-4166. **$59-$99.** 2009 N Mulberry St. I-65, exit 94, just sw. Int corridors. **Pets:** Medium. $10 daily fee/pet. Service with restrictions, supervision.
[SAVE] [S] [X] [M] [&] [] [] []

## ERLANGER

**Baymont Inn & Suites Cincinnati-Airport (Erlanger, KY)** SH
(859) 746-0300. **$89-$99.** 1805 Airport Exchange Blvd. I-275, exit 2. Int corridors. **Pets:** Large, other species. Service with restrictions.
[ASK] [S] [X] [M] [] [&] [] [] []

**Residence Inn by Marriott, Cincinnati Airport** SH
(859) 282-7400. **$139-$189.** 2811 Circleport Dr. I-275, exit 2. Int corridors. **Pets:** Accepted.
[ASK] [X] [M] [] [] [] [X]

## FLORENCE

**AmeriSuites (Cincinnati/Airport)** SH
(859) 647-1170. **$89-$149.** 300 Meijer Dr. I-71/75, exit 182, 0.4 mi sw. Int corridors. **Pets:** Accepted.
[SAVE] [S] [X] [M] [] [&] [] [] []

**Ashley Quarters** SH
(859) 525-9997. **$92-$110.** 4880 Houston Rd. I-71/75, exit 182, 0.6 mi w on Turfway and Houston rds. Int corridors. **Pets:** Small. $50 one-time fee/room. Designated rooms, service with restrictions, supervision.
[SAVE] [S] [X] [&] [] [] []

**Best Western Inn Florence** SH
(859) 525-0090. **$55-$100.** 7821 Commerce Dr. I-71/75, exit 181, just ne. Int corridors. **Pets:** Small. $10 daily fee/pet. Designated rooms, service with restrictions, supervision.
[SAVE] [S] [X] [M] [&] [] [] []

**Florence Super 8** SH 🐾
(859) 283-1221. **$54-$65, 10 day notice.** 7928 Dream St. I-71/75, exit 180, just e on US 42, then just n. Int corridors. **Pets:** Medium. $5 daily fee/pet. Service with restrictions, supervision.
[SAVE] [S] [X] []

**Knights Inn Florence** M
(859) 371-9711. **$39-$79.** 8049 Dream St. I-71/75, exit 180, just e on US 42, then just n. Ext corridors. **Pets:** Accepted.
[ASK] [S] [X] [] [] []

**Motel 6-Florence #496** SH
(859) 283-0909. **$35-$55.** 7937 Dream St. I-75/71, exit 180, just e on US 42, then just n. Ext corridors. **Pets:** Accepted.
[S] [X] [M] [&] []

**Red Roof Inn** M
(859) 647-2700. **$53-$70.** 7454 Turfway Rd. I-71/75, exit 182, 0.8 mi sw. Int corridors. **Pets:** Medium. Service with restrictions, supervision.
[ASK] [S] [X] [] []

## FORT MITCHELL

**Best Western Fort Mitchell** SH
(859) 331-1500. **$89-$130.** 2100 Dixie Hwy. I-71/75, exit 188, just w. Ext/int corridors. **Pets:** Accepted.
[SAVE] [S] [X] [&] [] [] [] [X]

## FRANKFORT

**Americas Best Value Inn** SH
(502) 875-3220. **$52-$72.** 1225 US Hwy 127 S. I-64, exit 53B, 1.2 mi n. Int corridors. **Pets:** Accepted.
[SAVE] [S] [X] []

**Bluegrass Inn** M
(502) 695-1800. **$48-$64.** 635 Versailles Rd. I-64, exit 58, 1 mi n on US 60. Ext corridors. **Pets:** Medium, dogs only. $10 daily fee/pet. Designated rooms, service with restrictions, supervision.
[SAVE] [S] [X] [] []

**Holiday Inn Capital Plaza** LH
(502) 227-5100. **$82.** 405 Wilkinson Blvd. Adjacent to Frankfort Civic Center. Int corridors. **Pets:** Accepted.
[ASK] [S] [X] [M] [] [&] [] [] [] [] []

## FRANKLIN

**Best Western Franklin Inn** SH
(270) 598-0070. **$37-$75.** 162 Anand Dr. I-65, exit 2, just w. Ext corridors. **Pets:** Small, dogs only. $12 daily fee/pet. Designated rooms, service with restrictions, supervision.
[SAVE] [S] [X] [M] [&] [] [] []

**Comfort Inn** SH
(270) 586-6100. **$55-$99.** 3794 Nashville Rd. I-65, exit 2. Ext corridors. **Pets:** $7 daily fee/pet. Service with restrictions, supervision.
[SAVE] [S] [X] [M] [] [] []

**Days Inn** SH
(270) 598-0163. **$50-$99.** 103 Trotter Ln. I-65, exit 6, just w. Ext corridors. **Pets:** Small. $5 daily fee/pet. Service with restrictions, supervision.
[SAVE] [S] [X] [M] [] [] []

**Super 8 Motel** SH
(270) 586-5090. **$45-$65.** 3811 Nashville Rd. I-65, exit 2, just w. Ext corridors. **Pets:** Small. $5 daily fee/pet. Designated rooms, service with restrictions, supervision.
[ASK] [S] [X] [M] [] [] []

## GEORGETOWN

**Days Inn of Georgetown** M
(502) 863-5000. **$33-$75.** 385 Cherry Blossom Way. I-75, exit 129, just se. Ext corridors. **Pets:** $5 daily fee/pet. Service with restrictions, supervision.
[ASK] [S] [X] [&] [] [] []

## GLASGOW

**Comfort Inn** SH
(270) 651-9099. **$70-$90.** 210 Calvary Dr. Cumberland Pkwy, exit 11, just n. Ext corridors. **Pets:** Small. $10 daily fee/room. Service with restrictions.
[ASK] [S] [X] [&] [] [] []

## GRAND RIVERS

**Best Western Kentucky-Barkley Lakes Inn** SH
(270) 928-2700. **$56-$73.** 720 Complex Dr. I-24, exit 31 (SR 453), just s. Ext/int corridors. **Pets:** Accepted.
[SAVE] [S] [X] [] [] []

**Microtel Inn & Suites** SH
(270) 928-2740. **$51-$74.** 1017 Dover Rd. I-24, exit 31 (SR 453), just n. Int corridors. **Pets:** Accepted.
[X] [M] [] [&] [] []

## GRAYSON

**Super 8 Motel** SH
(606) 474-8811. **$39-$89.** 125 Super 8 Ln. I-64, exit 172, just s. Int corridors. **Pets:** Small, other species. $10 daily fee/pet. Designated rooms, service with restrictions, supervision.
[ASK] [S] [X] [M] [] [&] [] []

# HARLAN

**Holiday Inn Express Harlan** SH
(606) 573-3385. **$69-$79.** 2608 S Hwy 421. On US 421, 2.8 mi s. Int corridors. **Pets:** Small. Designated rooms, no service, crate.

# HARRODSBURG

**Best Western Danville and Harrodsburg** SH
(859) 734-9431. **$60-$65.** 1680 Danville Rd. 3 mi s on US 127. Ext/int corridors. **Pets:** Accepted.

**Country Hearth Inn** SH
(859) 734-2400. **$54-$70.** 105 Commercial Dr. 0.6 mi n on College St. Int corridors. **Pets:** Small. $20 one-time fee/pet. Service with restrictions, supervision.

# HEBRON

**Radisson Hotel Cincinnati Airport** LH
(859) 371-6166. **$89-$119.** Cincinnati N KY Airport. I-71/75 via I-275, 4 mi w, exit 4B from I-275 (SR 212), then 1.3 mi w on SR 212. Int corridors. **Pets:** Accepted.

# HENDERSON

**Ramada Inn** SH
(270) 826-6600. **$75-$80.** 2044 US 41 N. 1 mi n on US 41. Int corridors. **Pets:** Accepted.

# HOPKINSVILLE

**Holiday Inn** SH
(270) 886-4413. **$85.** 2910 Ft Campbell Blvd. Pennyrile Pkwy, exit 7A, 0.6 mi n on US 41A. Int corridors. **Pets:** Small, other species. Service with restrictions, supervision.

**Hopkinsville Best Western** SH
(270) 886-9000. **$65-$79.** 4101 Ft Campbell Blvd. Pennyrile Pkwy, exit 7A, just s on US 41A. Int corridors. **Pets:** Accepted.

# HORSE CAVE

**Country Hearth Inn & Suites** SH
(270) 786-2165. **$33-$77.** I-65 & Hwy 218. I-65, exit 58, just ne. Ext corridors. **Pets:** Small. $5 daily fee/pet. Designated rooms, no service, supervision.

**Hampton Inn** SH
(270) 786-5000. **$59-$79.** 750 Flint Ridge Rd. I-65, exit 58, just nw. Int corridors. **Pets:** Accepted.

# KUTTAWA

**Days Inn** SH
(270) 388-4060. **$64-$104.** 139 Days Inn Dr. I-24, exit 40 (US 62), just s. Ext corridors. **Pets:** Large, other species. $10 one-time fee/room. Crate.

# LEBANON

**Country Hearth Inn** SH
(270) 692-4445. **$58-$66.** 720 W Main St. 1.4 mi s on SR 55 and US 68. Int corridors. **Pets:** Accepted.

# LEITCHFIELD

**Hatfield Inn** SH
(270) 259-0464. **$63-$80.** 769 White St. Western Kentucky Pkwy, exit 107, just nw. Int corridors. **Pets:** Other species. $10 daily fee/pet. Service with restrictions, supervision.

# LEWISPORT

**Best Western Hancock Inn** M
(270) 295-3234. **$59.** 9040 US Hwy 60 W. On US 60. Int corridors. **Pets:** Other species. $50 deposit/pet. Service with restrictions, supervision.

# LEXINGTON

**Days Inn-South** SH
(859) 263-3100. **$53-$62.** 5575 Athens-Boonesboro Rd. I-75, exit 104, just e. Ext corridors. **Pets:** Small. $10 daily fee/pet. Service with restrictions, supervision.

**Griffin Gate Marriott Resort** LH ❀
(859) 231-5100. **$124-$189.** 1800 Newtown Pike. I-75, exit 115, 0.5 mi sw. Int corridors. **Pets:** Medium. $50 one-time fee/room. Designated rooms, service with restrictions, supervision.

**Hampton Inn I-75** SH
(859) 299-2613. **$79-$119.** 2251 Elkhorn Rd. I-75, exit 110, 0.4 mi nw. Int corridors. **Pets:** Service with restrictions, crate.

**Holiday Inn Express Hotel & Suites-Lexington** SH
(859) 389-6800. **$79-$139.** 1000 Export St. I-75, exit 113, 4.5 mi s, then just e. Int corridors. **Pets:** $25 one-time fee/room. Designated rooms, service with restrictions, supervision.

**Holiday Inn-Lexington North** SH ❀
(859) 233-0512. **$89-$179.** 1950 Newtown Pike. I-75/64, exit 115, just s. Ext/int corridors. **Pets:** Medium. $25 one-time fee/room. Designated rooms, service with restrictions, supervision.

**Holiday Inn Lexington South** SH
(859) 263-5241. **$75-$89.** 5532 Athens-Boonesboro Rd. I-75, exit 104, just e. Int corridors. **Pets:** Small, other species. $15 daily fee/room. Service with restrictions.

**La Quinta Inn Lexington** SH
(859) 231-7551. **$75-$103.** 1919 Stanton Way. I-75/64, exit 115, just se off SR 922. Int corridors. **Pets:** Medium. Service with restrictions.

**Microtel Inn** SH
(859) 299-9600. **$45-$125, 14 day notice.** 2240 Buena Vista Rd. I-75, exit 110, just w. Int corridors. **Pets:** Small, other species. $20 one-time fee/room. Service with restrictions, supervision.

**Radisson Plaza Hotel Lexington** LH
(859) 231-9000. **$99, 7 day notice.** 369 W Vine St. Corner of Vine St and Broadway. Int corridors. **Pets:** Accepted.

**Ramada Inn & Conference Center** SH
(859) 299-1261. **$89-$109.** 2143 N Broadway. I-75/64, exit 113, just e. Int corridors. **Pets:** $10 daily fee/pet. Service with restrictions, supervision.

**▼ Red Roof Inn-North** 🆂🅷
(859) 293-2626. **$45-$67.** 1980 Haggard Ct. I-75/64, exit 113, 0.3 mi nw. Ext corridors. **Pets:** Accepted.

⊠

**▼ Red Roof Inn South** 🆂🅷
(859) 277-9400. **$55-$73.** 2651 Wilhite Dr. Jct US 27 and SR 4. Ext corridors. **Pets:** Accepted.

⊠ 🅼 🔋

**▼▼ Red Roof Inn Southeast** 🆂🅷
(859) 543-1877. **$45-$64, 7 day notice.** 100 Canebrake Dr. I-75, exit 104, just e. Int corridors. **Pets:** Accepted.

🅰🆂🅺 🆂 ⊠ 🔋 💻 ➤

**▼▼▼▼ Residence Inn by Marriott** 🆂🅷 🐾
(859) 231-6191. **$89-$169.** 1080 Newtown Pike. I-75/64, exit 115, 1 mi s on SR 922. Ext corridors. **Pets:** Other species. $75 one-time fee/room.

🅰🆂🅺 🆂 ⊠ 🅴 🔋 💻 ➤ ⊠

**▼▼▼▼ Residence Inn South @ Hamburg** 🆂🅷
(859) 263-9979. **$99-$179.** 2688 Pink Pigeon Pkwy. I-75, exit 108, just se. Int corridors. **Pets:** Large, other species. $75 one-time fee/room. Service with restrictions, crate.

🅰🆂🅺 ⊠ 🅼 📶 🅴 🔋 💻 🍽 ➤ ⊠

**▼▼ Sleep Inn Lexington** 🆂🅷
(859) 543-8400. **$69-$129.** 1920 Plaudit Pl. I-75, exit 108, just sw. Int corridors. **Pets:** Accepted.

🅰🆂🅺 🆂 ⊠ 🅴 🔋 💻 ➤

# LIBERTY

**🅐🅐🅐 ▼ Royal Inn Express** 🆂🅷
(606) 787-6224. **$42-$44.** 579 N Wallace Wilkinson Blvd. 1 mi n on US 127; 0.5 mi n of jct SR 70. Ext corridors. **Pets:** Medium. $5 daily fee/pet. Service with restrictions, supervision.

🆂🅰🆅🅴 ⊠ 🔋

# LONDON

**▼ Budget Host Westgate Inn** 🆂🅷 🐾
(606) 878-7330. **$45-$54, 3 day notice.** 254 W Daniel Boone Pkwy. I-75, exit 41, just w on SR 80. Ext/int corridors. **Pets:** Small. Designated rooms, service with restrictions, supervision.

🆂 ⊠ 🅼 🅴 🔋 ➤

**▼▼ Red Roof Inn** 🆂🅷
(606) 862-8844. **$49-$69.** 110 Melcon Ln. I-75, exit 41, southwest corner. Int corridors. **Pets:** Accepted.

🅰🆂🅺 🆂 ⊠ 🅼 🔋 💻 ➤

---

# LOUISVILLE METROPOLITAN AREA

# BROOKS

**▼▼ Comfort Inn** 🆂🅷 🐾
(502) 957-6900. **$62-$250.** 149 Willabrook Dr. I-65, exit 121, just nw. Int corridors. **Pets:** Other species. $15 daily fee/room. Service with restrictions.

🅰🆂🅺 🆂 ⊠ 🔋 ➤ ⊠

# HURSTBOURNE

**▼▼▼ Drury Inn & Suites-Louisville** 🆂🅷
(502) 326-4170. **$90-$140.** 9501 Blairwood Rd. I-64, exit 15. Int corridors. **Pets:** Accepted.

🅰🆂🅺 ⊠ 🅼 📶 🅴 🔋 💻 ➤

**▼ Red Roof Inn Louisville–East #034** 🆂🅷
(502) 426-7621. **$52-$65.** 9330 Blairwood Rd. I-64, exit 15, 0.3 mi nw of Hurstbourne Pkwy. Ext corridors. **Pets:** Accepted.

⊠ 🅼

# JEFFERSONTOWN

**🅐🅐🅐 ▼▼▼ AmeriSuites (Louisville/East)** 🆂🅷
(502) 426-0119. **$109-$149.** 701 S Hurstbourne Pkwy. I-64, exit 15, 1 mi n. Int corridors. **Pets:** Accepted.

🆂🅰🆅🅴 🆂 ⊠ 📶 🔋 💻 ➤

**🅐🅐🅐 ▼▼▼ Clarion Hotel and Conference Center** 🅻🅷
(502) 491-4830. **$59-$299.** 9700 Bluegrass Pkwy. I-64, exit 15, 0.5 mi se of Hurstbourne Pkwy. Int corridors. **Pets:** Small. $25 one-time fee/room. Service with restrictions, supervision.

🆂🅰🆅🅴 🆂 ⊠ 📶 🔋 💻 🍽 ➤ ⊠

**▼▼▼ Comfort Suites** 🆂🅷
(502) 266-6509. **$79-$119.** 1850 Resource Way. I-64, exit 17, 0.5 mi s of Blankenbaker Rd. Int corridors. **Pets:** Very small. $20 daily fee/room. Service with restrictions, supervision.

🅰🆂🅺 🆂 ⊠ 🅼 🔋 💻 ➤

**▼▼▼ Holiday Inn-Hurstbourne** 🅻🅷
(502) 426-2600. **$69-$99.** 1325 S Hurstbourne Pkwy. I-64, exit 15. Ext/int corridors. **Pets:** Small. $35 one-time fee/pet. Service with restrictions, supervision.

🅰🆂🅺 🆂 ⊠ 📶 🔋 💻 🍽 ➤ ⊠

**▼▼▼ Homestead Studio Suites Hotel-Louisville/East** 🆂🅷
(502) 267-4454. **$63-$109.** 1650 Alliant Ave. I-64, exit 17, just s. Int corridors. **Pets:** $25 daily fee/pet. Service with restrictions, supervision.

🅰🆂🅺 🆂 ⊠ 🅼 🅴 🔋 💻 ➤

**▼▼▼ Jameson Inn** 🆂🅷
(502) 267-8100. **$54-$104.** 1301 Kentucky Mills Dr. I-64, exit 17. Ext/int corridors. **Pets:** Very small, other species. $10 daily fee/room. Service with restrictions, supervision.

🅰🆂🅺 ⊠ 🅼 🅴 🔋 💻 ➤ ⊠

**▼▼ Microtel Inn** 🆂🅷
(502) 266-6590. **$50-$65.** 1221 Kentucky Mills Dr. I-64, exit 17. Int corridors. **Pets:** Small. $20 one-time fee/pet. Designated rooms, service with restrictions, supervision.

🅰🆂🅺 🆂 ⊠ 🅼 📶 🅴

**▼▼ Sleep Inn** 🆂🅷
(502) 266-6776. **$59-$250.** 1850 Priority Way. I-64, exit 17, 0.5 mi s of Blankenbaker Rd. Int corridors. **Pets:** Accepted.

🅰🆂🅺 🆂 ⊠ 🔋 💻

**▼▼ Super 8 Motel & Suites** 🆂🅷
(502) 267-8889. **$50-$350.** 1501 Alliant Ave. I-64, exit 17, just e. Int corridors. **Pets:** Small, other species. $20 daily fee/pet. No service, supervision.

🅰🆂🅺 🆂 ⊠ 🅼 🅴 🔋 ➤

# LA GRANGE

**▼▼▼ Comfort Suites** 🆂🅷
(502) 225-4125. **$72-$180.** 1500 Crystal Dr. I-71, exit 22, just e. Int corridors. **Pets:** Accepted.

🅰🆂🅺 🆂 ⊠ 🅼 🅴 🔋 💻 ➤ ⊠

# LOUISVILLE

**▼▼▼ Aleksander House Bed and Breakfast** 🅱🅱 🐾
(502) 637-4985. **$95-$169, 3 day notice.** 1213 S 1st St. I-65, exit 135 (St Catherine St), just s. Int corridors. **Pets:** $20 one-time fee/pet. Designated rooms, service with restrictions, crate.

🅰🆂🅺 ⊠ 🔋 💻

▼▼▼▼ **Breckinridge Inn** LH
(502) 456-5050. **$69-$99.** 2800 Breckinridge Ln. I-264, exit 18A, just s. Int corridors. **Pets:** $25 one-time fee/pet. Service with restrictions, supervision.

ASK SD X 🕮 🖃 ❘❘ ⌁ X

▼▼▼▼ **Executive West** LH
(502) 367-2251. **$129, 7 day notice.** 830 Phillips Ln. I-264, exit 11 (Fairgrounds/Expo Center Main Gate). Int corridors. **Pets:** Other species. $50 daily fee/pet. Service with restrictions, crate.

ASK SD X ⌀ 🕮 🕮 🖃 ❘❘ ⌁ X

AAA ▼▼▼▼ **Holiday Inn Airport East** SH
(502) 452-6361. **$85-$159.** 4004 Gardiner Point Dr. I-264, exit 15B westbound; exit 15 eastbound. Int corridors. **Pets:** Small. $35 one-time fee/room. Designated rooms, service with restrictions, supervision.

SAVE X 🕮 🕮 🖃 ❘❘ ⌁

▼▼▼▼ **Holiday Inn South-Airport** LH
(502) 964-3311. **$89-$145.** 3317 Fern Valley Rd. I-65, exit 128 (Fern Valley Rd), northeast corner. Int corridors. **Pets:** Accepted.

ASK SD X ⌀M 🕮 🖃 ❘❘ ⌁

▼▼▼ **Jameson Inn Airport South** SH
(502) 968-4100. **$54-$104.** 6515 Signature Dr. I-65, exit 128 (Fern Valley Rd), southeast corner. Int corridors. **Pets:** Very small, other species. $10 daily fee/room. Service with restrictions, supervision.

ASK X 🕮 🖃 ⌁

AAA ▼▼▼ **La Quinta Inn & Suites Airport & Expo-Louisville** SH 🐾
(502) 368-0007. **$79-$125.** 4125 Preston Hwy. I-65, exit 130, 1 mi w. Int corridors. **Pets:** Medium. $50 deposit/room. Service with restrictions, supervision.

SAVE SD X ⌀M ⌀ 🕮 🖃

▼▼ **Red Roof Inn-Airport-Fairgrounds** SH
(502) 968-0151. **$50-$65.** 4704 Preston Hwy. I-65, exit 130, northeast corner. Ext corridors. **Pets:** Accepted.

X

▼▼ ▼▼ **Red Roof Inn-Southeast-Fairgrounds** SH
(502) 456-2993. **$49-$67.** 3322 Red Roof Inn Pl. I-264, 15B westbound, 0.3 mi s; exit 15 eastbound. Ext corridors. **Pets:** Accepted.

X 🕮

▼▼▼ **Residence Inn by Marriott-Louisville Airport** SH
(502) 363-8800. **$119-$229.** 700 Phillips Ln. I-264, exit 11 (Fairgrounds/ Expo Center Main Gate), 0.4 mi w. Int corridors. **Pets:** Accepted.

ASK SD X ⌀M ⌀ 🕮 🖃 ⌁ X

▼▼▼▼ **Residence Inn by Marriott-Louisville NE** SH
(502) 412-1311. **$139-$189.** 3500 Springhurst Commons Dr. I-265, exit 32, 0.5 mi w on Westport Rd, then just n. Int corridors. **Pets:** Medium, other species. $75 one-time fee/room. Service with restrictions.

ASK SD X ⌀M 🕮 🖃 ⌁ X

▼▼▼▼ **Residence Inn Louisville East** SH
(502) 425-1821. **$79-$99.** 120 N Hurstbourne Pkwy. I-64, exit 15, 1.8 mi n. Ext corridors. **Pets:** Accepted.

X 🕮 🖃 ⌁ X

AAA ▼▼▼▼ **The Seelbach Hilton Louisville** LH
(502) 585-3200. **$119-$219.** 500 4th St. I-65, exit 136C (Muhammad Ali), 0.3 mi w, then just s. Int corridors. **Pets:** Large. $50 deposit/room. Service with restrictions.

SAVE X ⌀M ⌀ 🕮 🖃 ❘❘ X

▼▼▼ **Sleep Inn Fairgrounds** SH
(502) 368-9597. **$49-$275.** 3330 Preston Hwy. I-264, exit 11 (Fairgrounds/Expo Center Main Gate), 0.5 mi e on Phillips Ln, then just n. Int corridors. **Pets:** Small. $10 daily fee/pet. Designated rooms, service with restrictions, crate.

X ⌀ 🕮 🖃

▼▼▼ **Staybridge Suites by Holiday Inn** SH
(502) 244-9511. **$110-$149.** 11711 Gateworth Way. I-64, exit 17, just n. Int corridors. **Pets:** Accepted.

ASK X ⌀M ⌀ 🕮 🖃 ⌁

## SHEPHERDSVILLE

AAA ▼▼▼ **Best Western South** SH
(502) 543-7097. **$69-$79, 30 day notice.** 211 S Lakeview Dr. I-65, exit 117 (SR 44 W), just se. Int corridors. **Pets:** Small. Service with restrictions, crate.

SAVE SD X 🕮 🖃 ⌁

## SHIVELY

▼▼▼▼ **Holiday Inn-Southwest** LH
(502) 448-2020. **$89-$159.** 4110 Dixie Hwy. I-264, exit 8B, just n on US 31 W and 60. Int corridors. **Pets:** Small. $25 one-time fee/room. Service with restrictions, supervision.

ASK SD X ⌀ 🕮 🖃 ❘❘ ⌁

---

## END METROPOLITAN AREA

---

## MADISONVILLE

▼▼ ▼▼ **Days Inn Madisonville** SH
(270) 821-8620. **$62-$67.** 1900 Lantaff Blvd. Pennyrile Pkwy, exit 44. Int corridors. **Pets:** Other species. $10 daily fee/room. Service with restrictions.

ASK SD X ⌀ 🕮 🖃 ❘❘

## MAYFIELD

▼▼ **Super 8 Motel** SH
(270) 247-8899. **$53-$73.** 1100 Links Ln. Purchase Pkwy, exit 24, just s on SR 121. Int corridors. **Pets:** Small, dogs only. $10 daily fee/pet. Designated rooms, service with restrictions, crate.

ASK SD X 🕮 🖃

## MAYSVILLE

▼▼ ▼▼ **Super 8 Motel, Maysville KY** SH
(606) 759-8888. **$57-$63.** 550 Tucker Dr. Just e of US 68. Int corridors. **Pets:** Accepted.

ASK SD X 🕮

## MOREHEAD

AAA ▼▼▼▼ **Comfort Inn & Suites** SH 🐾
(606) 780-7378. **$52-$92.** 2650 Kentucky 801 N. I-64, exit 133, just s. Int corridors. **Pets:** Other species. $10 daily fee/room. Service with restrictions, crate.

SAVE SD X ⌀M ⌀ 🕮 🖃 ⌁

AAA ▼▼▼▼ **Holiday Inn Express of Morehead** SH
(606) 784-5796. **$60-$89.** 110 Toms Dr. I-64, exit 137 (SR 32), just sw. Int corridors. **Pets:** Small, other species. $10 daily fee/pet. Service with restrictions, supervision.

SAVE SD X ⌀M ⌀ 🕮 🖃 ⌁

# MORGANTOWN

▼▼◆◆ **Motel 6 #4120** 🆂🅷
(270) 526-9481. **$-$.** 1460 S Main St. William H Natcher Pkwy, exit 26, just w. Int corridors. **Pets:** Accepted.

Ⓐ🆂🅺 🆂💰 ⊠ 👩🏻‍🦽 📄 👨‍🦽 🍽 🛏 🏊

# MORTONS GAP

🅰🅰🅰 ▼▼◆◆ **Best Western Pennyrile Inn** 🆂🅷 🐾
(270) 258-5201. **$54-$62, 14 day notice.** White City Rd. Pennyrile Pkwy, exit 37 (US 41). Ext corridors. **Pets:** Medium. $7 daily fee/pet. Service with restrictions, crate.

🆂🅰🆅🅴 🆂💰 ⊠ 🛏 🏊 🏊

# MOUNT STERLING

▼▼▼◆ **Ramada Limited** 🆂🅷
(859) 497-9400. **$70.** 115 Stone Trace Dr. I-64, exit 110. Int corridors. **Pets:** Accepted.

Ⓐ🆂🅺 🆂💰 ⊠ 👩🏻‍🦽 👨‍🦽 🛏 🏊 🏊

# MOUNT VERNON

🅰🅰🅰 ▼◆ **Kastle Inn Motel** Ⓜ
(606) 256-5156. **$52-$70.** Hwy 25 S. I-75, exit 59. Ext corridors. **Pets:** Medium, other species. Service with restrictions, supervision.

🆂🅰🆅🅴 🆂💰 ⊠ 🍴 🏊

# MURRAY

▼▼ ◆◆ **Days Inn-Murray, KY** 🆂🅷
(270) 753-6706. **$44-$79.** 517 S 12th St. 1 mi s on US 641. Ext corridors. **Pets:** Accepted.

Ⓐ🆂🅺 🆂💰 ⊠ 🛏 🏊 🏊

# NEWPORT

▼▼▼◆ **Comfort Suites Riverfront** 🆂🅷
(859) 291-6700. **$99-$135.** 420 Riverboat Row. I-471, exit 5, just e on SR 8. Int corridors. **Pets:** Accepted.

Ⓐ🆂🅺 🆂💰 ⊠ 👩🏻‍🦽 🛏 🏊

# OAK GROVE

🅰🅰🅰 ▼▼▼◆ **Comfort Inn-Oak Grove** 🆂🅷
(270) 439-3311. **$74-$89.** 201 Auburn St. I-24, exit 86, just s. Ext corridors. **Pets:** Small. $20 daily fee/pet. Designated rooms, no service, supervision.

🆂🅰🆅🅴 🆂💰 ⊠ 👩🏻‍🦽 📄 👨‍🦽 🛏 🏊 🏊

▼▼▼◆ **Holiday Inn Express** 🆂🅷
(270) 439-0022. **$89-$149.** 12759 Ft Campbell Blvd. I-24, exit 86. Int corridors. **Pets:** $10 daily fee/pet. Designated rooms, service with restrictions, crate.

Ⓐ🆂🅺 🆂💰 ⊠ 👩🏻‍🦽 📄 🛏 🏊 🏊

# OWENSBORO

▼◆ **Motel 6 #205** 🆂🅷
(270) 686-8606. **$41-$53.** 4585 Frederica St. US 60 Bypass, exit 4 at jct US 431, just n. Ext corridors. **Pets:** Accepted.

🆂💰 ⊠ 👩🏻‍🦽 📄 👨‍🦽 🛏 🏊

▼▼ ◆◆ **Super 8 Motel-Owensboro** 🆂🅷
(270) 685-3388. **$60-$70.** 1027 Goetz Dr. US 60 Bypass, exit 4 at jct US 431. Int corridors. **Pets:** Small. $5 one-time fee/pet. Designated rooms, service with restrictions, supervision.

Ⓐ🆂🅺 🆂💰 ⊠ 👨‍🦽 🛏 🏊

# OWINGSVILLE

▼▼ ◆ **Super 8 Owingsville** 🆂🅷
(606) 674-2200. **$54-$60.** 201 Williams Ave. I-64, exit 121, just n. Int corridors. **Pets:** Large. Service with restrictions.

Ⓐ🆂🅺 🆂💰 ⊠ 👨‍🦽 🛏

# PADUCAH

▼▼ ◆◆ **Baymont Inn-Paducah** 🆂🅷
(270) 443-4343. **$55-$65.** 5300 Old Cairo Rd. I-24, exit 3 (SR 305), just w. Int corridors. **Pets:** Small. Designated rooms, service with restrictions, supervision.

Ⓐ🆂🅺 🆂💰 ⊠ 📄 👨‍🦽 🛏 🏊

▼▼ ◆◆ **Days Inn** 🆂🅷
(270) 442-7500. **$55-$80.** 3901 Hinkleville Rd. I-24, exit 4 (US 60), just e. Ext corridors. **Pets:** Accepted.

Ⓐ🆂🅺 🆂💰 ⊠ 🛏 🏊 🏊

▼▼▼◆▼ **Drury Inn-Paducah** 🆂🅷
(270) 443-3313. **$90-$133.** 3975 Hinkleville Rd. I-24, exit 4 (US 60), just e. Int corridors. **Pets:** Accepted.

Ⓐ🆂🅺 ⊠ 👨‍🦽 🛏 🏊 🏊

▼▼▼◆▼ **Drury Suites-Paducah** 🆂🅷
(270) 441-0024. **$96-$135.** 2930 James-Sanders Blvd. I-24, exit 4 (US 60), just w. Int corridors. **Pets:** Accepted.

Ⓐ🆂🅺 ⊠ 👨‍🦽 🛏 🏊 🏊 ⊠

▼▼▼◆▼ **Hampton Inn-Paducah** 🆂🅷
(270) 442-4500. **$91-$131.** 5006 Hinkleville Rd. I-24, exit 4 (US 60), just w. Int corridors. **Pets:** Accepted.

Ⓐ🆂🅺 ⊠ 👩🏻‍🦽 📄 🛏 🏊

▼▼▼◆▼ **Holiday Inn Express** 🆂🅷
(270) 442-8874. **$85-$117.** 3994 Hinkleville Rd. I-24, exit 4 (US 60), just e. Int corridors. **Pets:** Accepted.

Ⓐ🆂🅺 🆂💰 ⊠ 🛏 🏊 🏊

▼▼ ◆◆ **Pear Tree Inn by Drury-Paducah** 🆂🅷
(270) 444-7200. **$70-$105.** 5002 Hinkleville Rd. I-24, exit 4 (US 60), just w. Ext corridors. **Pets:** Accepted.

Ⓐ🆂🅺 ⊠ 🛏 🏊 🏊

# PRESTONSBURG

▼▼ ◆◆ **Super 8 Prestonsburg** Ⓜ
(606) 886-3355. **$54-$59, 7 day notice.** 550 US 23 S. Jct US 114 and 23. Int corridors. **Pets:** Accepted.

Ⓐ🆂🅺 🆂💰 ⊠ 🏊

# RICHMOND

▼▼▼◆▼ **Holiday Inn Express Hotel & Suites** 🆂🅷
(859) 624-4005. **$84-$159.** 1990 Colby Taylor Dr. I-75, exit 87, just w. Int corridors. **Pets:** Other species. $15 daily fee/pet. Service with restrictions.

Ⓐ🆂🅺 🆂💰 ⊠ 👩🏻‍🦽 📄 👨‍🦽 🛏 🏊 🏊

▼▼▼◆▼ **Jameson Inn** 🆂🅷
(859) 623-0063. **$54-$104.** 1007 Colby Taylor Dr. I-75, exit 87, just w. Int corridors. **Pets:** Very small, other species. $10 daily fee/room. Service with restrictions, supervision.

Ⓐ🆂🅺 ⊠ 👩🏻‍🦽 📄 👨‍🦽 🛏 🏊

🅰🅰🅰 ▼▼▼◆ **La Quinta Inn Richmond** 🆂🅷
(859) 623-9121. **$55-$65.** 1751 Lexington Rd. I-75, exit 90 northbound; exit 90A southbound. Int corridors. **Pets:** Medium. Service with restrictions, crate.

🆂🅰🆅🅴 🆂💰 ⊠ 📄 🛏 🏊 🏊

▼▼ ◆◆ **Red Roof Inn** Ⓜ
(859) 625-0084. **$49-$69.** 111 Bahama Ct. I-75, exit 90 northbound; exit 90A southbound. Int corridors. **Pets:** Medium. Service with restrictions.

Ⓐ🆂🅺 ⊠ 👨‍🦽 🛏 🏊

🅰🅰🅰 ▼▼▼◆ **Super 8 Motel** 🆂🅷
(859) 624-1550. **$45-$50, 7 day notice.** 107 N Keeneland Dr. I-75, exit 90. Int corridors. **Pets:** Very small. $6 daily fee/pet. Designated rooms, service with restrictions, supervision.

🆂🅰🆅🅴 🆂💰 ⊠ 👩🏻‍🦽 🛏 🏊

# SCOTTSVILLE

**AAA** ▼▼ **Executive Inn** SH
(270) 622-7770. **$55-$61.** 57 Burnley Rd. US 31 E, jct SR 231. Ext corridors. **Pets:** Large. $10 one-time fee/pet. Designated rooms, service with restrictions, crate.

SAVE ⑤ ✕ 🖥 ≋

# SHELBYVILLE

**AAA** ▼▼ **Best Western Shelbyville Lodge** SH
(502) 633-4400. **$69-$109.** 115 Isaac Shelby Dr. I-64, exit 32, 0.5 mi n on SR 55. Int corridors. **Pets:** Accepted.

SAVE ⑤ ✕ 🖥 🖵 ≋

▼▼ **Holiday Inn Express** SH
(502) 647-0109. **$87-$97.** 110 Club House Dr. I-64, exit 35, just s. Int corridors. **Pets:** Accepted.

ASK ⑤ ✕ ☳ⁿ ⨀ 🔦 🖥 🖵 ≋

# SMITHS GROVE

**AAA** ▼▼ **Bryce Inn** SH
(270) 563-5141. **$45-$59.** 592 S Main St. I-65, exit 38, 0.3 mi w. Ext corridors. **Pets:** Small, dogs only. $5 daily fee/pet. Service with restrictions, supervision.

SAVE ⑤ ✕ 🖥 🖵 ≋

# SOMERSET

▼▼▼ **Comfort Inn** SH
(606) 677-1500. **$69-$89, 3 day notice.** 82 Jolin Dr. Cumberland Pkwy, 4.3 mi s on US 27. Int corridors. **Pets:** $10 daily fee/pet. Service with restrictions, supervision.

ASK ⑤ ✕ ☳ⁿ 🔦 🖥 🖵 ≋

# SPARTA

▼▼▼ **Ramada Limited & Suites** SH
(859) 567-7223. **$69-$99, 3 day notice.** 525 Dale Dr. I-71, exit 57, just w. Int corridors. **Pets:** Medium, other species. $25 one-time fee/room. Designated rooms, service with restrictions.

ASK ⑤ ✕ ☳ⁿ 🔦 🖥 🖵 ≋

# VERSAILLES

▼▼▼▼ **1823 Historic Rose Hill Inn** BB 🐾
(859) 873-5957. **$109-$179, 7 day notice.** 233 Rose Hill. Just s on SR 33 (S Main St), then just w. Ext/int corridors. **Pets:** Dogs only. $15 one-time fee/room. Designated rooms.

✕ 🖥 🖵

# WEST LIBERTY

▼▼ **Days Inn** SH
(606) 743-4206. **$58-$84.** 1613 W Main St. Jct SR 519 and 460, just w. Int corridors. **Pets:** Accepted.

ASK ⑤ ✕ ☳ⁿ 🔦

# WILLIAMSBURG

▼▼▼ **Cumberland Inn** SH 🐾
(606) 539-4100. **$74-$79.** 649 S 10th St. I-75, exit 11. Int corridors. **Pets:** Small. $15 one-time fee/room. Designated rooms, service with restrictions, supervision.

ASK ⑤ ✕ ☳ⁿ 🖥 🖵 🍴 ≋

# WILLIAMSTOWN

▼▼ **Americas Best Value Inn & Suites** SH
(859) 824-7177. **$32-$48.** 10 Skyway Dr. I-75, exit 154, just w. Ext corridors. **Pets:** Accepted.

ASK ⑤ ✕ 🖥 ≋

**AAA** ▼▼ **Days Inn** SH
(859) 824-5025. **$49-$66.** 211 SR 36 W. I-75, exit 154, just n. Ext corridors. **Pets:** Accepted.

SAVE ⑤ ✕ 🖥 🖵 ≋

# WINCHESTER

**AAA** ▼▼ **Best Western-Country Squire** SH
(859) 744-7210. **$59-$119.** 1307 W Lexington Rd. I-64, exit 94 (US 60), 0.9 mi se. Ext corridors. **Pets:** Small. $5 daily fee/pet. Designated rooms, service with restrictions, supervision.

SAVE ⑤ ✕ 🖥 🖵 ≋

# LOUISIANA

## CITY INDEX

## ALEXANDRIA

### ◬◬ ▽▽▽ Best Western of Alexandria Inn & Suites & Conference Center SH
(318) 445-5530. $78. 2720 W MacArthur Dr. I-49, exit 86 (MacArthur Dr), 1.3 mi sw. Ext/int corridors. Pets: Small. $25 one-time fee/room. Designated rooms, service with restrictions, crate.

SAVE S🐾 ☒ 🛏 💻 ⊶

### ◬◬ ▽▽▽ Clarion Hotel Alexandria SH
(318) 487-4261. $96-$189. 2716 N MacArthur Dr. I-49, exit 86 (MacArthur Dr), 1.2 mi sw. Ext/int corridors. Pets: Medium. $15 one-time fee/pet. Service with restrictions, supervision.

SAVE S🐾 ☒ ✧ 🛏 💻 🍴 ⊶

### ▽▽▽ La Quinta Inn & Suites Alexandria SH
(318) 442-3700. $115-$127. 6116 W Calhoun Dr. I-49, exit 90 (Air Base Rd), just w. Int corridors. Pets: Medium. Service with restrictions.

ASK ☒ �ṀM 📁 ✧ 🛏 💻 ⊶

### ◬◬ ▽▽▽ Ramada Limited SH ❀
(318) 448-1611. $60-$70. 742 MacArthur Dr. 0.4 mi s of jct SR 28 and US 71/165 (MacArthur Dr). Ext corridors. Pets: Other species. $25 deposit/room. Crate.

SAVE S🐾 ☒ 🛏 💻 ⊶

### ◬◬ ▽▽▽ Super 8 Motel M
(318) 445-6541. $49-$70. 700 MacArthur Dr. I-49, exit 86 (MacArthur Dr), 2.4 mi sw. Ext/int corridors. Pets: Other species. $25 one-time fee/room. Designated rooms, service with restrictions, supervision.

SAVE S🐾 ☒ 💻 ⊶

## BATON ROUGE

### ▽▽▽ AmeriSuites (Baton Rouge/East) SH
(225) 769-4400. $99-$135. 6080 Bluebonnet Blvd. I-10, exit 162. Int corridors. Pets: Medium. $10 daily fee/pet. Service with restrictions, crate.

ASK S🐾 ☒ 📁 ✧ 🛏 💻 ⊶

### ◬◬ ▽▽▽ Baymont Inn & Suites Baton Rouge SH
(225) 291-6600. $78-$88. 10555 Rieger Rd. I-10, exit 163 (Siegen Ln), just n, then just e. Int corridors. Pets: Medium. Service with restrictions.

SAVE ☒ 📁 🛏 💻 ⊶

### ◬◬ ▽▽▽ Chase Suites by Woodfin SH ❀
(225) 927-5630. $99-$179. 5522 Corporate Blvd. I-10, exit 158, just n on College Dr, then just e. Ext corridors. Pets: Medium, other species. $150 deposit/pet. Service with restrictions, crate.

SAVE S🐾 ☒ ✧ 🛏 💻 ⊶ ☒

### ▽▽▽ Comfort Inn SH
(225) 236-4000. $69-$100. 2445 S Acadian Thruway. I-10, exit 157B, just n. Int corridors. Pets: Accepted.

ASK S🐾 ☒ 📁 ✧ 🛏 💻 ⊶

### ▽▽▽ Crestwood Suites Hotel SH
(225) 291-5200. $50-$100. 5222 S Sherwood Forest Blvd. I-12, exit 4, 1.7 mi s. Int corridors. Pets: Small. $50 daily fee/pet. Designated rooms, service with restrictions, supervision.

☒ 🛏 💻

### ◬◬ ▽▽▽ Holiday Inn Select & Executive Center Baton Rouge LH
(225) 925-2244. $89-$109. 4728 Constitution Ave. I-10, exit 158, just se on frontage road. Int corridors. Pets: Accepted.

SAVE ☒ ⓑM 📁 🛏 💻 🍴 ⊶

### ◬◬ ▽▽▽ La Quinta Inn Baton Rouge SH
(225) 924-9600. $93-$103. 2333 S Acadian Thruway. I-10, exit 157B. Ext corridors. Pets: Medium. Service with restrictions.

SAVE ☒ 📁 🛏 💻 ⊶

### ▽▽▽ Microtel Inn & Suites SH
(225) 927-9997. $40-$50. 10311 Plaza Americana Dr. I-12, exit 2B, just n, then e. Int corridors. Pets: Accepted.

ASK S🐾 ☒ ✧ 🛏 💻 ⊶

### ▽▽ Motel 6 Baton Rouge Southeast #1124 M
(225) 291-4912. $43-$55. 10445 Rieger Rd. I-10, exit 163, just n. Ext corridors. Pets: Accepted.

S🐾 ☒ ✧ ⊶

### ▽▽▽ Ramada I-12/Airline Highway SH
(225) 706-5500. $68. 10045 Gwenadele Ave. I-12, exit 2B, just n on US 61. Ext corridors. Pets: $25 daily fee/pet. Designated rooms, no service, crate.

S🐾 ☒ ⓑM 📁 🛏 💻 ⊶

### ▽▽▽ Residence Inn by Marriott-Baton Rouge SH
(225) 293-8700. $75-$149. 10333 N Mall Dr. I-10, exit 163 westbound, just s on Siegen Ln, then just e; exit eastbound, 0.5 mi to S Mall Dr, just e to Andrea (at Lowe's), then just n. Int corridors. Pets: Small. $75 one-time fee/room. Service with restrictions, supervision.

ASK ☒ ⓑM 📁 ✧ 🛏 💻 ⊶ ☒

### ◬◬ ▽▽▽ Sheraton Baton Rouge Convention Center Hotel LH ❀
(225) 242-2600. $220. 102 France St. I-110, exit 1A (Government St), 0.8 mi w to St. James, then just s. Int corridors. Pets: Dogs only. Service with restrictions, supervision.

SAVE S🐾 ☒ ✧ 🛏 💻 🍴 ⊶

### ▽▽▽ TownePlace Suites by Marriott SH
(225) 819-2112. $85-$95. 8735 Summa Ave. I-10, exit 162 (Bluebonnet Blvd), just s to Picardy, just w to Summa Ave, then 0.5 mi nw. Int corridors. Pets: Accepted.

ASK S🐾 ☒ ⓑM 📁 ✧ 🛏 💻 ⊶

## BOSSIER CITY

### ▽▽ Best Western-Airline Motor Inn SH
(318) 742-6000. $95-$125, 7 day notice. 1984 Airline Dr. I-20, exit 22 (Airline Dr), just n. Ext corridors. Pets: Accepted.

ASK S🐾 ☒ 🛏 💻 🍴 ⊶

### ▽▽ Econo Lodge Inn & Suites SH
(318) 746-5050. $49-$79. 4300 Industrial Dr. I-20, exit 23 (Industrial Dr). Ext corridors. Pets: Accepted.

ASK S🐾 ☒ 🛏 💻 ⊶

▼▼▼ **Hampton Inn** 〈SH〉
(318) 752-1112. **$84-$144.** 1005 Gould Dr. I-20, exit 21, 0.5 mi ne on service road. Int corridors. **Pets:** Accepted.

ⒶⓈⓀ ☒ Ⓛⓜ 🐾 Ⓘ 🛏 🖥 ⌁

ⒶⒶⒶ ▼▼▼▼ **La Quinta Inn Bossier City** 〈SH〉
(318) 747-4400. **$90-$110.** 309 Preston Blvd. I-20, exit 21, just n. Ext corridors. **Pets:** Medium. Service with restrictions.

〔SAVE〕 ☒ 🐾 🖥 ⌁

▼▼ **Microtel Inn & Suites** 〈SH〉
(318) 742-7882. **$70.** 2713 Village Ln. I-20, exit 22 (Airline Dr), just s, then just w. Int corridors. **Pets:** Medium, other species. $25 one-time fee/room. Service with restrictions, supervision.

ⒶⓈⓀ 〔Sⓓ〕 ☒ Ⓛⓜ 🐾 Ⓖ 🛏 🖥

▼▼▼▼ **Quality Inn & Suites** 〈SH〉
(318) 742-7890. **$76-$86.** 2717 Village Ln. I-20, exit 22 (Airline Dr), just s, then just w. Int corridors. **Pets:** Accepted.

ⒶⓈⓀ 〔Sⓓ〕 ☒ Ⓛⓜ 🐾 Ⓖ 🛏 🖥 ⌁

▼▼▼ **Residence Inn by Marriott-Shreveport/Bossier City** 〈SH〉
(318) 747-6220. **$109-$209.** 1001 Gould Dr. I-20, exit 21, just ne. Ext corridors. **Pets:** Other species. $75 one-time fee/room. Service with restrictions.

ⒶⓈⓀ 〔Sⓓ〕 ☒ Ⓖ 🛏 🖥 ⌁ ☒

# BREAUX BRIDGE

ⒶⒶⒶ ▼▼▼ **Best Western of Breaux Bridge** 〈M〉
(337) 332-1114. **$74-$169.** 2088-B Rees St. I-10, exit 109 (Breaux Bridge). Ext corridors. **Pets:** Small. $10 daily fee/pet. Service with restrictions, supervision.

〔SAVE〕 〔Sⓓ〕 ☒ 🛏 🖥 ⌁

▼▼▼▼ **Holiday Inn Express of Breaux Bridge** 〈SH〉
(337) 667-8913. **$73-$89.** 2942 H Grand Point Hwy. I-10, exit 115, just n. Int corridors. **Pets:** Accepted.

☒ Ⓛⓜ Ⓖ 🛏 🖥 ⌁

# CONVENT

▼▼▼▼ **Poche Plantation Bed & Breakfast and RV Resort** 〈BB〉
(225) 562-7728. **$119, 10 day notice.** 6554 Louisiana Hwy 44. Jct SR 44 and 641; 10.1 mi s of Sunshine Bridge (SR 70), then 10.2 mi n. Ext/int corridors. **Pets:** Other species. $15 daily fee/room. Service with restrictions, supervision.

ⒶⓈⓀ 〔Sⓓ〕 ☒ 🛏 🖥 ⌁

# CROWLEY

▼▼ **Days Inn of Crowley** 〈SH〉
(337) 783-2378. **$46-$79.** 9571 Egan Hwy. I-10, exit 80. Ext corridors. **Pets:** Accepted.

ⒶⓈⓀ 〔Sⓓ〕 ☒ 🛏 🖥 ⌁

# DERIDDER

ⒶⒶⒶ ▼▼◈ **Stagecoach Inn** 〈SH〉
(337) 462-0022. **$75.** 505 E 1st St. 2 mi on east side; between US 171 NS. Ext corridors. **Pets:** Accepted.

〔SAVE〕 ☒ Ⓛⓜ 🛏 🖥 ⌁

# HAMMOND

ⒶⒶⒶ ▼▼◈ **Best Western Hammond Inn & Suites** 〈SH〉
(985) 419-2001. **$55-$75.** 107 Duo Dr. I-12, exit 40 (US 51), just ne. Ext corridors. **Pets:** Small, other species. $10 daily fee/pet. Service with restrictions, supervision.

〔SAVE〕 〔Sⓓ〕 ☒ Ⓖ 🛏 🖥 ⌁

ⒶⒶⒶ ▼▼▼▼ **Michabelle-A Little Inn** 〈CI〉
(985) 419-0550. **$75-$100, 5 day notice.** 1106 S Holly St. I-12, exit 40 (US 51), 0.8 mi n, just e on Old Covington Hwy, then n, follow signs. Ext/int corridors. **Pets:** Accepted.

〔SAVE〕 〔Sⓓ〕 ☒ 🖥 🍴 🎞

# IOWA

▼▼▼ **Howard Johnson Express Inn** 〈SH〉
(337) 582-2440. **$55-$64.** 107 E Frontage Rd. I-10, exit 43, just n, then just e. Int corridors. **Pets:** Accepted.

ⒶⓈⓀ 〔Sⓓ〕 ☒ 🛏 🖥

# KINDER

ⒶⒶⒶ ▼▼▼ **Best Western Inn At Coushatta** 〈SH〉
(337) 738-4800. **$69-$119.** 12102 US Hwy 165 N. 5 mi n of jct US 190/165. Int corridors. **Pets:** Small. $15 deposit/pet, $10 one-time fee/pet. Designated rooms, service with restrictions, supervision.

〔SAVE〕 〔Sⓓ〕 ☒ 🛏 🖥 ⌁

▼▼▼ **Holiday Inn Express Hotel & Suites** 〈SH〉
(337) 738-3381. **$79-$150.** 11750 US Hwy 165. 5.2 mi n of jct US 190/165, 5.1 mi on US 165. Ext/int corridors. **Pets:** Accepted.

ⒶⓈⓀ 〔Sⓓ〕 ☒ Ⓛⓜ Ⓖ 🛏 🖥 ⌁

# LAFAYETTE

▼▼▼ **America's Best Suites of Lafayette** 〈SH〉
(337) 235-1367. **$89-$139.** 125 E Kaliste Saloom Rd. I-10, exit 103A, 1 mi w of jct E Kaliste Saloom Rd and US 90 (SW Evangeline Thruway). Int corridors. **Pets:** Small, other species. Service with restrictions, supervision.

ⒶⓈⓀ 〔Sⓓ〕 ☒ Ⓖ 🛏 🖥 ⌁

ⒶⒶⒶ ▼▼▼▼ **Best Western Hotel Acadiana** 〈SH〉
(337) 233-8120. **$89-$99, 3 day notice.** 1801 W Pinhook Rd. SR 182, 1.5 mi s of US 90 (Evangeline Thruway). Int corridors. **Pets:** Accepted.

〔SAVE〕 〔Sⓓ〕 ☒ 🐾 Ⓖ 🛏 🖥 🍴 ⌁

▼▼ **Comfort Inn Lafayette** 〈SH〉
(337) 232-9000. **$81.** 1421 SE Evangeline Thruway. 3 mi s of I-10 at jct US 90 (Evangeline Thruway). Int corridors. **Pets:** Service with restrictions, crate.

ⒶⓈⓀ 〔Sⓓ〕 ☒ 🐾 🛏 🖥 🍴 ⌁

▼▼ **Days Inn-Lafayette** 〈M〉
(337) 237-8880. **$48-$65.** 1620 N University. I-10, exit 101. Ext corridors. **Pets:** Other species. $10 one-time fee/pet. No service, crate.

ⒶⓈⓀ 〔Sⓓ〕 ☒ 🛏 🖥 ⌁

▼▼▼▼ **Drury Inn & Suites-Lafayette** 〈SH〉
(337) 262-0202. **$77-$118.** 120 Alcide Dominique. I-10, exit 101 (SR 182), just s on University Ave, then just w. Int corridors. **Pets:** Accepted.

ⒶⓈⓀ ☒ Ⓛⓜ 🛏 🖥 ⌁

▼▼ **Hilton Lafayette & Towers** 〈LH〉
(337) 235-6111. **$69-$189.** 1521 W Pinhook Rd. SR 182, 1.3 mi sw of US 90 (Evangeline Thruway). Int corridors. **Pets:** Small, other species. $25 one-time fee/room. Designated rooms, service with restrictions, crate.

ⒶⓈⓀ ☒ Ⓖ 🛏 🖥 🍴 ⌁

▼▼ **Jameson Inn of Lafayette** 〈SH〉
(337) 291-2916. **$54-$104.** 2200 NE Evangeline Thruway. I-10, exit 103A, just s. Int corridors. **Pets:** Very small, other species. $10 daily fee/room. Service with restrictions, supervision.

ⒶⓈⓀ ☒ Ⓖ 🛏 🖥 ⌁

▼▼▼▼ **La Quinta Inn & Suites Lafayette Oil Center** 〈SH〉
(337) 291-1088. **$87-$109.** 1015 W Pinhook Rd. I-10, exit 101 (University Ave), 3.5 mi to SR 182 (Pinhook Rd), then 0.5 mi w. Int corridors. **Pets:** Small, other species. $100 one-time fee/room. Designated rooms, service with restrictions, supervision.

ⒶⓈⓀ 〔Sⓓ〕 ☒ Ⓖ 🛏 🖥 ⌁

**AAA** ♦♦♦ **La Quinta Inn Lafayette (North)** SH
(337) 233-5610. **$75-$95.** 2100 NE Evangeline Thruway. I-10, exit 103A, 0.3 mi s on US 167. Ext corridors. **Pets:** Medium. Service with restrictions.
SAVE ⊠ 🐾 🛁 💻 🏊

♦♦ **Motel 6 #461** M
(337) 233-2055. **$39-$49.** 2724 NE Evangeline Thruway. I-49, exit 1B (Pont des Mouton Rd), just e, then just s on frontage road. Ext corridors. **Pets:** Accepted.
🐾 ⊠ 🏊

♦♦ ♦ **Ramada Inn** SH
(337) 235-0858. **$57-$71.** 120 E Kaliste Saloom Rd. I-10, exit 103A, 4.4 mi e on US 90 (Evangeline Thruway), then 1 mi s. Ext corridors. **Pets:** Accepted.
ASK 🐾 ⊠ 🛁 💻 🏊

## LAKE CHARLES

♦♦♦ **Best Suites of America** SH
(337) 439-2444. **$94-$150.** 401 Lakeshore Dr. I-10, exit 29 (business district/tourist bureau) eastbound; exit 30B (Ryan St business district) westbound, just s to Pine, then just w. Int corridors. **Pets:** Accepted.
ASK 🐾 ⊠ 🐾 🛁 💻 🏊

**AAA** ♦♦♦ **La Quinta Inn Lake Charles** SH
(337) 436-5998. **$60-$150.** 1320 MLK Hwy 171 N. I-10, exit 33, 0.8 mi n. Int corridors. **Pets:** Medium. $50 deposit/room. Service with restrictions, supervision.
SAVE 🐾 ⊠ 🐾 🛁 💻 🏊

## LIVONIA

♦♦ ♦ **Oak Tree Inn** SH
(225) 637-2590. **$53.** 7875 Airline Hwy. Jct SR 77 and US 190, 0.3 mi w. Ext corridors. **Pets:** Accepted.
ASK 🐾 ⊠ 🐾 🛁 💻

## MINDEN

**AAA** ♦♦♦♦ **Best Western Minden Inn** SH
(318) 377-1001. **$60-$70.** I-20, exit 47, just n. Ext corridors. **Pets:** $10 daily fee/pet. Service with restrictions, supervision.
SAVE 🐾 ⊠ 🐾 🛁 💻 🏊

## MONROE

♦♦♦♦ **Holiday Inn Hotel & Suites Conference Center** SH
(318) 387-5100. **$69-$150.** 1051 Hwy 165 Bypass. I-20, exit 118B, just ne on US 165 service road. Ext/int corridors. **Pets:** Other species. $20 one-time fee/pet. No service, supervision.
🐾 ⊠ 🐾 🐾 🛁 💻 🍴 🏊 🚭

**AAA** ♦♦♦♦ **La Quinta Inn Monroe** SH
(318) 322-3900. **$85-$102.** 1035 Hwy 165 Bypass. I-20, exit 118B, just ne on US 165 service road. Ext corridors. **Pets:** Medium. Service with restrictions.
SAVE ⊠ 🐾 💻 🏊

## MORGAN CITY

♦♦♦♦ **Holiday Inn-Morgan City** SH
(985) 385-2200. **$78-$179.** 520 Roderick St. 1.5 mi s of jct US 90 and SR 70. Ext corridors. **Pets:** Accepted.
ASK 🐾 ⊠ 🐾 🐾 🐾 🛁 💻 🍴 🏊

## NEW IBERIA

**AAA** ♦♦♦ **Best Western Inn & Suites** SH
(337) 364-3030. **$70-$80.** 2714 Hwy 14. 0.3 mi e of jct US 90. Ext/int corridors. **Pets:** Accepted.
SAVE 🐾 ⊠ 🛁 💻 🍴 🏊

♦♦ ♦ **Holiday Inn New Iberia-Avery Island** SH
(337) 367-1201. **$57-$105.** 2915 Hwy 14. SR 14, just e of jct US 90. Ext corridors. **Pets:** Medium. $75 deposit/room, $25 one-time fee/room. Service with restrictions, supervision.
ASK 🐾 ⊠ 🛁 💻 🍴 🏊

---

# NEW ORLEANS METROPOLITAN AREA

## COVINGTON

♦♦♦♦ **Holiday Inn & Suites Covington Northshore** SH
(985) 893-3580. **$79-$99.** 501 N Hwy 190. I-12, exit 63B, just n. Ext/int corridors. **Pets:** Medium, other species. $45 one-time fee/pet. Service with restrictions, supervision.
ASK 🐾 ⊠ 🐾 🛁 💻 🍴 🏊 🚭

## GRETNA

**AAA** ♦♦ ♦ **La Quinta Inn New Orleans (West Bank)** SH
(504) 368-5600. **$90-$105.** 50 Terry Pkwy. S US 90 business route, exit 9A (Terry Pkwy); N US 90 (Westbank Expwy), exit 9 (Terry Pkwy/General DeGaulle). Ext corridors. **Pets:** Medium. Service with restrictions.
SAVE ⊠ 🐾 🛁 💻 🏊

## KENNER

**AAA** ♦♦♦♦ **Hilton New Orleans Airport** LH
(504) 469-5000. **$109-$219.** 901 Airline Dr. I-10, exit 223A (Williams Blvd), just n then 0.8 mi w. Int corridors. **Pets:** Small. $50 one-time fee/pet. Designated rooms, service with restrictions, crate.
SAVE ⊠ 🐾 🐾 🛁 💻 🍴 🏊

♦♦♦♦ **La Quinta Inn New Orleans (Airport)** SH
(504) 466-1401. **$106-$116.** 2610 Williams Blvd. I-10, exit 223A (Williams Blvd), 0.3 mi s. Int corridors. **Pets:** Medium. Service with restrictions.
⊠ 🛁 💻 🏊

## LA PLACE

**AAA** ♦♦ ♦ **Best Western La Place Inn** SH
(985) 651-4000. **$79-$139.** 4289 Main St. I-10, exit 209, just s. Ext corridors. **Pets:** Small. $25 one-time fee/pet. Service with restrictions, supervision.
SAVE 🐾 ⊠ 🐾 🛁 🏊

♦♦♦♦ **Quality Inn-La Place** SH
(985) 652-5544. **$79-$109.** 3900 Hwy 51. I-10, exit 209, 0.5 mi s. Ext corridors. **Pets:** Accepted.
ASK 🐾 ⊠ 🐾 🛁 💻 🍴 🏊

## METAIRIE

**AAA** ♦♦ ♦ **La Quinta Inn New Orleans (Causeway)** SH
(504) 835-8511. **$85-$105.** 3100 I-10 Service Rd. I-10, exit 228 (Causeway Blvd), just s. Ext corridors. **Pets:** Medium. Service with restrictions.
SAVE ⊠ 🐾 🐾 🛁 💻 🏊

**AAA** ♦♦ ♦ **La Quinta Inn New Orleans (Veterans)** SH
(504) 456-0003. **$93-$103.** 5900 Veterans Memorial Blvd. I-10, exit 225, just n. Ext corridors. **Pets:** Medium. Service with restrictions.
SAVE ⊠ 🐾 🐾 🛁 💻 🏊

♦♦♦♦ **Residence Inn by Marriott-Metairie** SH
(504) 832-0888. **$104, 3 day notice.** 3 Galleria Blvd. I-10, exit 228 (Causeway Blvd), just se to 36th St, then just e. Int corridors. **Pets:** Accepted.
ASK 🐾 ⊠ 🐾 🛁 💻 🏊 🚭

# NEW ORLEANS

**AAA** ▼▼▼ **Ambassador Hotel** SH
(504) 527-5271. **$69-$229, 3 day notice.** 535 Tchoupitoulas St. Between Poydras and Lafayette; downtown. Int corridors. **Pets:** Accepted.
SAVE S❍ ☒ ⚙ 🛏 ▣ ⊞ ❢

**AAA** ▼▼▼ **Best Western St. Christopher Hotel** SH
(504) 648-0444. **$99-$149.** 114 Magazine St. Between Canal and Common sts. Int corridors. **Pets:** Accepted.
SAVE S❍ ☒ ⚙ ▣

**AAA** ▼▼▼ **Chateau Sonesta Hotel** LH
(504) 586-0800. **$109-$259.** 800 Iberville St. Between Dauphine and Bourbon sts. Int corridors. **Pets:** Accepted.
SAVE S❍ ☒ ⟋ ⚙ ▣ ⊞ ❢

▼▼▼ **Drury Inn & Suites-New Orleans** SH
(504) 529-7800. **$95-$180.** 820 Poydras St. Between Baronne and Carondelet sts. Int corridors. **Pets:** Accepted.
ASK ☒ ⚙ 🛏 ▣ ❢

**AAA** ▼▼▼ **Elysian Fields Inn** BB
(504) 948-9420. **$99-$250, 14 day notice.** 930 Elysian Fields Ave. I-610, exit 3 (Elysian Fields), 1.2 mi s. Int corridors. **Pets:** Accepted.
SAVE ☒

**AAA** ▼▼▼ **The Fairmont New Orleans** LH
(504) 529-7111. **$89-$305, 3 day notice.** 123 Baronne St. Between Canal and University sts; entrance on University St; downtown. Int corridors. **Pets:** Accepted.
SAVE S❍ ☒ ⟋ ⚙ 🛏 ⊞ ❢ ⊠

**AAA** ▼▼ **French Quarter Suites Hotel** SH ❀
(504) 524-7725. **$59-$299, 7 day notice.** 1119 N Rampart St. Between Ursuline and Governor Nicholls. Ext corridors. **Pets:** Other species. $15 daily fee/pet. Service with restrictions.
SAVE ☒ 🛏 ▣ ❢

**AAA** ▼▼▼ **Garden District Hotel Clarion Collection** SH
(504) 566-1200. **$69-$209.** 2203 St. Charles Ave. 1 mi w of US 90; at corner of Jackson Ave. Int corridors. **Pets:** Accepted.
SAVE S❍ ☒ ⟋ ⚙ 🛏 ⊞

**AAA** ▼◆▼ **Holiday Inn French Quarter** SH
(504) 529-7211. **$109-$329.** 124 Royal St. Between Iberville and Canal sts. Int corridors. **Pets:** Accepted.
SAVE ☒ ⚙M ⟋ ⚙ 🛏 ▣ ⊞ ❢

**AAA** ▼▼▼ **Hotel Monaco New Orleans** SH
(504) 561-0010. **$99-$499.** 333 St. Charles Ave. Jct Perdido St. Int corridors. **Pets:** Accepted.
SAVE S❍ ☒ ⚙ ▣ ⊞

**AAA** ▼▼▼ **The Iberville Suites** SH
(504) 523-2400. **$93-$268, 3 day notice.** 910 Iberville St. Between Burgundy and Dauphine sts. Int corridors. **Pets:** Accepted.
SAVE S❍ ☒ ⚙ 🛏 ▣

**AAA** ▼▼▼ **JW Marriott New Orleans** LH
(504) 525-6500. **$139-$419, 3 day notice.** 614 Canal St. Registration and parking on Common St. Int corridors. **Pets:** Accepted.
SAVE ☒ ⟋ ⚙ 🛏 ▣ ⊞ ❢

**AAA** ▼◆▼ **La Quinta Inn & Suites New Orleans (Downtown)** SH
(504) 598-9977. **$125-$179.** 301 Camp St. Corner of Gravier and Camp sts; downtown. Int corridors. **Pets:** Medium. Service with restrictions.
SAVE ☒ ⚙M ⟋ ⚙ 🛏 ▣ ❢

▼▼ **La Quinta Inn New Orleans (Bullard)** SH
(504) 246-3003. **$79-$93.** 12001 I-10 Service Rd. I-10, exit 245 (Bullard Rd). Ext corridors. **Pets:** Medium. No service.
ASK ☒ ⚙ 🛏 ▣ ❢

**AAA** ▼▼▼ **Loews New Orleans Hotel** LH ❀
(504) 595-3300. **$149-$319, 3 day notice.** 300 Poydras St. Corner of S Peters St; downtown. Int corridors. **Pets:** Other species. No service.
SAVE S❍ ☒ ⚙ 🛏 ▣ ⊞ ❢ ⊠

**AAA** ▼▼▼ **The Maison Orleans-Ritz Carlton** SH
(504) 670-2900. **$422.** 904 Iberville St. Between Burgundy and Dauphine sts. Int corridors. **Pets:** Accepted.
SAVE ☒ ⚙M ⚙ ⊞ ❢ ⊠

**AAA** ▼▼▼ **Maison St. Charles Quality Inn & Suites** SH
(504) 522-0187. **$87-$223.** 1319 St. Charles Ave. I-90 business, exit St. Charles Ave, just w; between Thalia and Erato sts. Ext corridors. **Pets:** Accepted.
SAVE S❍ ☒ ⟋ ⚙ 🛏 ▣ ⊞ ❢

▼ **Motel 6- Six Flags Area** M
(504) 240-2862. **$42-$60.** 12330 I-10 Service Rd. I-10, exit 245 (Bullard Rd), just s, then 0.4 mi e on eastbound access road. Int corridors. **Pets:** Accepted.
☒ ⚙M ⚙ ❢

▼▼▼ **Omni Royal Crescent Hotel** SH
(504) 527-0006. **$89-$169.** 535 Gravier St. 0.3 mi w of Canal St; downtown. Int corridors. **Pets:** Accepted.
ASK S❍ ☒ ⟋ ⚙ 🛏 ▣ ⊞ ⊠

▼▼▼ **Omni Royal Orleans Hotel** LH
(504) 529-5333. **$95-$379, 3 day notice.** 621 St. Louis St. At Royal and St. Louis sts. Int corridors. **Pets:** Small. $50 one-time fee/room. Service with restrictions, supervision.
ASK S❍ ☒ ⚙ 🛏 ▣ ⊞

**AAA** ▼▼▼ **The Pontchartrain Hotel** SH
(504) 524-0581. **$109-$259.** 2031 St. Charles Ave. 1 mi w of US 90. Int corridors. **Pets:** Medium. $50 one-time fee/room. Service with restrictions, crate.
SAVE S❍ ☒ ⟋ 🛏 ▣ ⊞

▼▼▼ **Residence Inn by Marriott** SH
(504) 522-1300. **$99-$289, 3 day notice.** 345 St. Joseph's St. Jct Tchoupitoulas St. Int corridors. **Pets:** Large. $75 one-time fee/pet. Service with restrictions, crate.
ASK S❍ ☒ ⚙M ⚙ 🛏 ▣ ⊞ ⊠

**AAA** ▼▼▼ **The Ritz-Carlton New Orleans** LH
(504) 524-1331. **$419-$459.** 921 Canal St. Between Dauphine and Burgundy sts. Int corridors. **Pets:** Accepted.
SAVE ☒ ⚙M ⟋ ⚙ ⊞ ❢

**AAA** ▼▼▼ **Royal Sonesta Hotel New Orleans** LH
(504) 586-0300. **$109-$329, 3 day notice.** 300 Bourbon St. Garage entrance on Conti or Bienville sts. Int corridors. **Pets:** Small. $50 one-time fee/room. Designated rooms, service with restrictions, supervision.
SAVE S❍ ☒ ⚙M ⟋ ⚙ 🛏 ❢ ⊞

▼▼▼ **St. James Hotel** SH
(504) 304-4000. **$99-$249, 3 day notice.** 330 Magazine St. Jct Magazine and Natchez sts; downtown. Int corridors. **Pets:** Accepted.
ASK S❍ ☒ ⚙ ▣ ⊞

**AAA** ▼▼▼ **The Sheraton New Orleans Hotel** LH ❀
(504) 525-2500. **$109-$249, 3 day notice.** 500 Canal St. Between Camp and Magazine sts. Int corridors. **Pets:** Large, dogs only. Service with restrictions, supervision.
SAVE S❍ ☒ ⟋ ⚙ ▣ ⊞ ❢ ⊠

**◈◈ Studio 6 New Orleans #6000** 🆂🅷
(504) 240-9778. **$49-$61.** 12330 I-10 Service Rd. I-10, exit 245 (Bullard Rd), 0.4 mi e on eastbound access road. Int corridors. **Pets:** Accepted.
🆂⬛ ❌ 🚪 💻 ⌁

**◈◈◈ W French Quarter** 🆂🅷 🐾
(504) 581-1200. **$479-$519, 3 day notice.** 316 rue Chartres St. Between Conti and Eienville sts. Int corridors. **Pets:** Medium. $25 daily fee/pet, $100 one-time fee/pet. Service with restrictions, supervision.
A$K 🆂⬛ ❌ 🗝 💻 🍽 ⌁

**◈◈◈ Windsor Court Hotel** 🅻🅷 🐾
(504) 523-6000. **$200-$455.** 300 Gravier St. Between Magazine and Tchoupitoulas sts. Int corridors. **Pets:** Other species. $150 one-time fee/room. Service with restrictions.
SAVE ❌ 🎵 🚪 🍽 ⌁ 🏊

**◈◈◈ W New Orleans** 🅻🅷
(504) 525-9444. **$129-$469, 3 day notice.** 333 Poydras St. Close to Riverfront area/convention center; jct Poydras and S Peters sts; downtown. Int corridors. **Pets:** Accepted.
SAVE 🆂⬛ ❌ 🅶🅼 🎵 🗝 💻 🍽 ⌁

# SLIDELL

**◈◈ ◈◈◈◈ La Quinta Inn New Orleans/Slidell** 🆂🅷
(985) 643-9770. **$79-$89.** 794 E I-10 Service Rd. I-10, exit 266 (Gause Blvd), just se. Ext corridors. **Pets:** Medium. Service with restrictions.
SAVE ❌ 🗝 🚪 💻 ⌁

**◈◈◈ Sleep Inn** 🆂🅷
(985) 641-2143. **$47-$89.** 142 Oak Ct. I-10, exit 261, just n. Int corridors. **Pets:** Accepted.
A$K 🆂⬛ ❌ 🅶🅼 ♿ 🚪 💻 ⌁

---

## END METROPOLITAN AREA

---

# OPELOUSAS

**◈◈ ◈◈ Days Inn & Suites** 🆂🅷
(337) 407-0004. **$70-$150.** 5761 I-49 S Service Rd. I-49, exit 18 (Creswell Ln). Ext corridors. **Pets:** Accepted.
SAVE 🆂⬛ ❌ ♿ 🚪 💻 ⌁

# PORT ALLEN

**◈◈ ◈◈ Best Western Magnolia Manor** 🆂🅷
(225) 344-3638. **$60-$75.** 234 Lobdell Hwy. I-10, exit 151, just n. Int corridors. **Pets:** Accepted.
SAVE 🆂⬛ ❌ 🚪 💻 ⌁

**◈ Motel 6 Baton Rouge-Port Allen #406** 🅼
(225) 343-5945. **$41-$51.** 2800 I-10 Frontage Rd. I-10, exit 151, just s. Ext corridors. **Pets:** Accepted.
🆂⬛ ❌ 🚪 💻 ⌁

# RAYVILLE

**◈◈◈ Days Inn** 🅼
(318) 728-4500. **$50-$55.** 125 Maxwell St. I-20, exit 138, just n. Ext corridors. **Pets:** Accepted.
A$K 🆂⬛ ❌ 🚪 💻 ⌁

# RUSTON

**◈◈ Budget Lodge** 🆂🅷
(318) 255-0354. **$59.** 1301 Goodwin Rd. I-20, exit 85, just n on US 167, then just e on N Service Rd. Ext corridors. **Pets:** Accepted.
A$K 🆂⬛ ❌ 🗝 🚪 💻 ⌁

**◈◈ ◈◈ Days Inn** 🆂🅷
(318) 251-2360. **$64-$89.** 1801 N Service Rd E. I-20, exit 86, just ne. Ext corridors. **Pets:** Very small. $50 deposit/pet. Designated rooms, service with restrictions, supervision.
SAVE 🆂⬛ ❌ 🗝 🚪 💻 ⌁

**◈◈ Ramada Inn** 🆂🅷
(318) 255-5901. **$76-$85.** 401 N Service Rd. I-20, exit 85, just ne. Ext corridors. **Pets:** Accepted.
❌ 🚪 💻 🍽 ⌁

# ST. FRANCISVILLE

**◈◈ Lake Rosemound Inn Bed & Breakfast** 🅱🅱
(225) 635-3176. **$70-$125, 3 day notice.** 10473 Lindsey Ln. 13 mi n on SR 61, then 3 mi w using Rosemound Loop, Sligo Rd, Lake Rosemound Rd and Lindsey Ln, follow signs. Ext/int corridors. **Pets:** Other species. Service with restrictions.
❌ 🏊

# SCOTT

**◈◈ Howard Johnson** 🆂🅷
(337) 593-0849. **$60-$70.** 103 Harold Gauthe Dr. I-10, exit 97. Int corridors. **Pets:** Accepted.
A$K 🆂⬛ ❌ 🚪 💻 ⌁

# SHREVEPORT

**◈◈◈ Clarion Hotel Shreveport** 🅻🅷
(318) 797-9900. **$89-$129.** 1419 E 70th St. I-20, exit 19A (SR 1 S), 6 mi s to E 70th St, then 0.4 mi w. Int corridors. **Pets:** Accepted.
❌ 🎵 🚪 💻 🍽 ⌁

**◈◈◈ Holiday Inn Downtown** 🅻🅷
(318) 222-7717. **$77-$89.** 102 Lake St. I-20, exit 19A (Spring St), just n. Int corridors. **Pets:** Accepted.
🆂⬛ ❌ 🅶🅼 🎵 🚪 💻 🍽 ⌁

**◈◈ ◈◈◈◈ La Quinta Inn & Suites Shreveport** 🆂🅷
(318) 671-1100. **$99-$116.** 6700 Financial Cir. I-20, exit 10 (Pines Rd), 0.5 mi e on frontage road. Int corridors. **Pets:** Medium. Service with restrictions.
SAVE ❌ 🅶🅼 🗝 🚪 💻 ⌁

**◈◈◈ Residence Inn by Marriott** 🆂🅷
(318) 635-8000. **Call for rates.** 4910 W Monkhouse. I-20, exit 13, just nw. Int corridors. **Pets:** Small, other species. $75 one-time fee/room. Service with restrictions.
❌ 🅶🅼 🎵 🗝 🚪 💻 ⌁ 🏊

# SULPHUR

**◈◈◈ Wingate Inn** 🆂🅷
(337) 527-5151. **$69-$79.** 300 Texaco Rd. I-10, exit 20 (SR 27), just s, then just w. Int corridors. **Pets:** Accepted.
A$K 🆂⬛ ❌ 🗝 🚪 💻 ⌁

# WEST MONROE

▼▼▼ **Holiday Inn Express** 🆂🅷
(318) 807-6000. **$81-$90.** 603 Constitution Dr. I-20, exit 114 (Thomas Rd), just s to Constitution Dr, then 1.1 mi w. Int corridors. **Pets:** Small. $25 one-time fee/pet. Service with restrictions, supervision.

🅰🆂🅺 🆂🅾 ✖ 🆕 📷 🐾 🔲 💻 🏊

▼▼ **Jameson Inn** 🆂🅷
(318) 361-0750. **$54-$104.** 213 Constitution Dr. I-20, exit 114 (Thomas Rd), just s to Constitution Dr, then just w. Int corridors. **Pets:** Very small, other species. $10 daily fee/room. Service with restrictions, supervision.

🅰🆂🅺 ✖ 🔲 💻 🏊

▼▼▼ **Quality Inn & Suites-West Monroe** 🆂🅷
(318) 387-2711. **$65-$75.** 503 Constitution Dr. I-20, exit 114 (Thomas Rd), just s to Constitution Dr, then 0.6 mi w. Int corridors. **Pets:** Accepted.

🅰🆂🅺 🆂🅾 ✖ 🆕 📷 🐾 🔲 💻 🏊

▼▼ **Red Roof Inn** Ⓜ
(318) 388-2420. **$41-$60.** 102 Constitution Dr. I-20, exit 114 (Thomas Rd), just s. Ext corridors. **Pets:** Accepted.

✖ 🐾

# MAINE

## AUBURN

### ▼▼▼ A Fireside Inn & Suites SH
(207) 777-1777. **$70-$180.** 1777 Washington St. I-95 (Maine Tpke), exit 75, 5 mi s on US 202, SR 4 and 100. Ext/int corridors. **Pets:** Accepted.
ASK S☐ ☒ ☐ ☐ ☐ ⏻ ☞

### ▲▲▲ ▼▼ Econo Lodge SH
(207) 784-1331. **$89-$180.** 170 Center St. North side on SR 4. Ext/int corridors. **Pets:** $10 daily fee/pet. Designated rooms, service with restrictions, supervision.
SAVE S☐ ☒ ☐

### ▲▲▲ ▼ Sleepy Time Motel M ☙
(207) 783-1435. **$62-$85.** 46 Danville Corner Rd. I-95 (Maine Tpke), exit 75, 0.5 mi ne on US 202, just e. Ext corridors. **Pets:** Medium, other species. $10 one-time fee/pet. Service with restrictions, supervision.
SAVE S☐ ☒ ☐

## AUGUSTA

### ▲▲▲ ▼▼▼▼ Best Western Senator Inn & Spa SH
(207) 622-5804. **$99-$259.** 284 Western Ave. I-95, exit 109 (Augusta-Winthrop) northbound; exit 109A southbound, on US 202, SR 11 and 100. Ext/int corridors. **Pets:** Accepted.
SAVE S☐ ☒ ☐ ☐ ☐ ⏻ ☞ ☒

### ▼▼▼ Comfort Inn SH
(207) 623-1000. **$94-$199, 3 day notice.** 281 Civic Center Dr. I-95, exit 112B northbound; exit 112 southbound. Int corridors. **Pets:** Large. Service with restrictions, supervision.
ASK ☒ ☐ ☐ ☐ ⏻ ☞

### ▲▲▲ ▼▼▼ Econo Lodge Inn & Suites SH
(207) 622-6371. **$59-$249.** 390 Western Ave. I-95, exit 109 (Augusta-Winthrop) northbound; exit 109B southbound on US 202, SR 11 and 100. Ext corridors. **Pets:** Service with restrictions, supervision.
SAVE S☐ ☒ ☐ ☐ ⏻ ☞

### ▼▼▼▼ Holiday Inn SH
(207) 622-4751. **$94-$179, 3 day notice.** 110 Community Dr. I-95, exit 112A northbound; exit 112 southbound, just s on SR 8, 11 and 27. Int corridors. **Pets:** Large. Service with restrictions, supervision.
ASK ☒ ☐ ☐ ☐ ☐ ☐ ⏻ ☞

## BANGOR

### ▼▼▼ America's Best Inn SH
(207) 942-1234. **$85-$120, 7 day notice.** 570 Main St. I-395, exit 3B. Int corridors. **Pets:** Accepted.
ASK S☐ ☒ ☐ ☐ ⏻

### ▼▼▼▼ Best Western White House SH ☙
(207) 862-3737. **$70-$130.** 155 Littlefield Ave. I-95, exit 180 (Coldbrook Rd), 5.5 mi s of downtown. Ext/int corridors. **Pets:** Other species. $100 deposit/room. Designated rooms, service with restrictions, supervision.
ASK S☐ ☒ ☐ ☐ ☞

### ▼▼▼ Comfort Inn SH
(207) 942-7899. **$79-$129.** 750 Hogan Rd. I-95, exit 187 (Hogan Rd), 0.5 mi w. Int corridors. **Pets:** Other species. $6 one-time fee/room. Service with restrictions, supervision.
ASK S☐ ☒ ☐ ☞

### ▼▼ Days Inn SH
(207) 942-8272. **$59-$109.** 250 Odlin Rd. I-95, exit 182B, 0.3 mi e on US 2 and SR 100. Int corridors. **Pets:** Dogs only. $10 one-time fee/pet. Service with restrictions, supervision.
ASK S☐ ☒ ☐M ☐ ☞

### ▼▼ Econo Lodge M
(207) 945-0111. **$49-$120.** 327 Odlin Rd. I-95, exit 182B, just e on US 2 and SR 100. Int corridors. **Pets:** Accepted.
ASK S☐ ☒ ☐ ☐

### ▼▼▼▼ Four Points by Sheraton Bangor SH
(207) 947-6721. **$130-$160.** 308 Godfrey Blvd. At Bangor International Airport. Int corridors. **Pets:** Medium. $20 one-time fee/room. Service with restrictions, supervision.
ASK S☐ ☒ ☐M ☐ ☐ ⏻ ☞

### ▼▼▼▼ Holiday Inn-Bangor SH
(207) 947-0101. **$139-$149.** 404 Odlin Rd. I-95, exit 182B at jct Odlin Rd and I-395. Int corridors. **Pets:** Accepted.
ASK S☐ ☒ ☐M ☐ ☐ ⏻ ☞

### ▼▼▼ Holiday Inn Bangor-Civic Center SH
(207) 947-8651. **$81-$99.** 500 Main St. I-395, exit 3B, just n. Int corridors. **Pets:** Other species. Designated rooms, service with restrictions, supervision.
ASK S☐ ☒ ☐ ☐ ⏻ ☞

### ▼▼▼ Ramada Inn SH
(207) 947-6961. **$89-$119.** 357 Odlin Rd. I-95, exit 182B, at jct Odlin Rd and I-395. Int corridors. **Pets:** Small. Service with restrictions, crate.
ASK S☐ ☒ ☐ ☐ ⏻ ☞

### ▼▼▼ Riverside Inn SH
(207) 973-4100. **$69-$129, 7 day notice.** 495 State St. Adjacent to Eastern Maine Medical Center. Int corridors. **Pets:** Accepted.
☒ ☐ ☐

### ▼▼ Travelodge M ☙
(207) 942-6301. **$50-$100.** 482 Odlin Rd. I-95, exit 182B, just left. Ext corridors. **Pets:** Medium, dogs only. $10 daily fee/pet. Designated rooms, service with restrictions, supervision.
ASK S☐ ☒ ☐ ☐

## BAR HARBOR

### ▲▲▲ ▼▼▼ Anchorage Motel M
(207) 288-3959. **$54-$129, 3 day notice.** 51 Mt Desert St. In town on SR 3. Ext corridors. **Pets:** $15 daily fee/room. Service with restrictions, supervision.
SAVE ☒ ☐

**◆◆ A Wonder View Inn & Suites** 🆂🅷 ❖
(207) 288-3358. **$50-$230, 3 day notice.** 50 Eden St. 0.5 mi w on SR 3. Ext corridors. **Pets:** Medium. $10 daily fee/pet. Service with restrictions, supervision.
❎ 🛎 🖥 🍽 ≈

**◆◆◆ ◆◆◆◆ Balance Rock Inn 1903** 🅱🅱
(207) 288-2610. **$115-$525, 14 day notice.** 21 Albert Meadow. S on Main St, just e; center. Ext/int corridors. **Pets:** Accepted.
🆂🅰🆅🅴 ❎ 🍽 ≈

**◆◆◆ ◆◆◆ Best Western Inn** 🆂🅷
(207) 288-5823. **$75-$150.** 452 State Hwy 3. 4.8 mi w. Ext corridors. **Pets:** Small, dogs only. Designated rooms, service with restrictions, supervision.
🆂🅰🆅🅴 🆂🔒 ❎ 🛎 🖥 ≈

**◆◆◆ ◆◆ Days Inn** 🅼
(207) 288-3321. **$89-$229.** 120 Eden St. 1 mi w on SR 3. Ext corridors. **Pets:** $10 one-time fee/pet. Service with restrictions, crate.
🆂🅰🆅🅴 🆂🔒 ❎ 🛎

**◆ Hutchins Mountain View Cottages** 🅲🅰 ❖
(207) 288-4833. **$58-$98, 14 day notice.** 286 State Rt 3. 4 mi w. Ext corridors. **Pets:** Other species. Service with restrictions, crate.
🛎 🖥 ≈ 🅇 🆉

**◆◆◆ ◆◆◆◆ The Ledgelawn Inn** 🅱🅱
(207) 288-4596. **$80-$325, 14 day notice.** 66 Mt Desert St. Center. Ext/int corridors. **Pets:** Large. $25 daily fee/pet. Designated rooms, service with restrictions, supervision.
🆂🅰🆅🅴 ❎ ≈

**◆◆◆◆ Primrose Inn Bed and Breakfast** 🅱🅱
(207) 288-4031. **$85-$210, 14 day notice.** 73 Mt Desert St. Center. Int corridors. **Pets:** Dogs only. $75 one-time fee/room. Designated rooms, service with restrictions, crate.
❎ 🛎

# BATH

**◆◆◆ ◆◆◆◆ Holiday Inn Bath/Brunswick** 🆂🅷
(207) 443-9741. **$79-$299.** 139 Richardson St. 0.3 mi s on US 1. Int corridors. **Pets:** $75 deposit/pet. Service with restrictions, crate.
🆂🅰🆅🅴 🆂🔒 ❎ 🅻🅼 🅰 🅴 🛎 🖥 🍽 ≈ 🅇

# BELFAST

**◆◆ ◆◆ Belfast Harbor Inn** 🆂🅷
(207) 338-2740. **$54-$139.** 91 Searsport Ave (Rt 1). On US 1, 1.2 mi n from jct SR 3. Ext/int corridors. **Pets:** Dogs only. $10 daily fee/pet. Designated rooms, service with restrictions, supervision.
🅰🆂🅺 🆂🔒 ❎ ≈

**◆◆◆◆◆ Comfort Inn Ocean's Edge** 🆂🅷 ❖
(207) 338-2090. **$79-$189.** 159 Searsport Ave. On US 1, 2 mi n from jct SR 3. Int corridors. **Pets:** Other species. $10 daily fee/pet. Designated rooms, service with restrictions, supervision.
🅰🆂🅺 🆂🔒 ❎ 🅻🅼 🅰 🅴 🛎 🖥 🍽 ≈ 🅇

**◆ Gull Motel** 🅼
(207) 338-4030. **$39-$89, 3 day notice.** US Rt 1. On US 1, 3 mi n from jct SR 3. Ext corridors. **Pets:** $10 daily fee/pet. Designated rooms, service with restrictions, supervision.
🅰🆂🅺 ❎ 🛎

**◆◆◆ ◆◆◆◆ Penobscot Bay Inn** 🅲🅸
(207) 338-5715. **$50-$145.** 192 Northport Ave (US 1). US 1, 2 mi s from jct SR 3. Ext/int corridors. **Pets:** Medium, dogs only. $100 deposit/room, $15 daily fee/pet. Designated rooms, service with restrictions, supervision.
🆂🅰🆅🅴 🆂🔒 ❎ 🛎 🍽

**◆◆ ◆◆ Seascape Motel & Cottages** 🅼
(207) 338-2130. **$59-$129, 3 day notice.** 202 Searsport Ave. On US 1, 3 mi n from jct SR 3. Ext corridors. **Pets:** Small. $10 one-time fee/pet. Designated rooms, service with restrictions, supervision.
🅰🆂🅺 🆂🔒 ❎ 🛎 ≈

# BETHEL

**◆◆ ◆◆ Briar Lea Inn & Restaurant** 🅲🅸 ❖
(207) 824-4717. **$79-$139, 14 day notice.** 150 Mayville Rd (US 2). 1 mi n of jct US 2, SR 5 and 26. Int corridors. **Pets:** Dogs only. $10 daily fee/pet. Service with restrictions, crate.
🅰🆂🅺 ❎ 🍽

**◆◆ ◆◆ The Inn At the Rostay** 🅼
(207) 824-3111. **$55-$130, 14 day notice.** 186 Mayville Rd (US 2). On US 2, 2 mi e. Ext corridors. **Pets:** Accepted.
🅰🆂🅺 🆂🔒 ❎ 🛎 🍽 ≈

**◆◆◆ ◆◆◆◆ L'Auberge Country Inn & Bistro** 🅲🅸
(207) 824-2774. **$79-$279, 14 day notice.** 15 L'Auberge Ln. Center. Int corridors. **Pets:** Accepted.
🆂🅰🆅🅴 🆂🔒 ❎ 🍽 🅿 🆉

# BOOTHBAY

**◆◆ ◆◆ Hillside Acres Cabins & Motel** 🅼
(207) 633-3411. **$50-$85.** 301 Adams Pond Rd. US 1, 9 mi s on SR 27, then just w. Ext/int corridors. **Pets:** Designated rooms, service with restrictions, supervision.
❎ 🛎 🖥 ≈ 🅇 🆉

**◆◆◆◆ Kenniston Hill Inn** 🅱🅱
(207) 633-2159. **$80-$140, 14 day notice.** 988 Wiscasset Rd. US 1 to SR 27, 10 mi s. Ext/int corridors. **Pets:** Accepted.
🅰🆂🅺 🆂🔒 ❎ 🆉

**◆◆◆ ◆◆ White Anchor Inn** 🅼
(207) 633-3788. **$50-$84.** 609 Wiscasset Rd. US 1 to SR 27, 7.5 mi s. Ext/int corridors. **Pets:** Large, other species. $10 one-time fee/room. Designated rooms, service with restrictions, supervision.
🆂🅰🆅🅴 ❎ 🛎

# BOOTHBAY HARBOR

**◆◆◆ ◆◆◆◆ Welch House Inn** 🅱🅱
(207) 633-3431. **$85-$195, 14 day notice.** 56 McKown St. Center. Ext/int corridors. **Pets:** Accepted.
🆂🅰🆅🅴 ❎

# BREWER

**◆ Brewer Motor Inn** 🆂🅷
(207) 989-4476. **$49-$62.** 359 Wilson St. I-395, exit 4, n on SR 15 to US 1A, then 0.7 mi e. Ext/int corridors. **Pets:** Accepted.
❎ 🍽

# BRIDGTON

**◆◆ ◆◆ Pleasant Mountain Inn** 🅼
(207) 647-4505. **$60-$125, 7 day notice.** 656 N High St. On US 302, 3 mi w of center. Ext corridors. **Pets:** Accepted.
🅰🆂🅺 ❎ 🛎 🖥

# BRUNSWICK

**◆◆◆ ◆◆◆ Viking Motor Inn** 🅼
(207) 729-6661. **$59-$139.** 287 Bath Rd. US 1, exit Cooks Corner, left on Bath Rd, then 1 mi w. Ext/int corridors. **Pets:** Medium. $10 daily fee/pet. Service with restrictions, supervision.
🆂🅰🆅🅴 ❎ 🛎

# BRYANT POND

◆ **Mollyockett Motel & Swim Spa** Ⓜ
(207) 674-2345. **$70-$95.** 1132 S Main St. 1.3 mi n on SR 26 from jct SR 219. Ext/int corridors. **Pets:** Dogs only. Service with restrictions, supervision.
(ASK) (S♦) (✕) (🏠) (💳) (🏊) (✕)

# CALAIS

◆◆◆ ◆◆◆ **Calais Motor Inn** 🆂🅷
(207) 454-7111. **$44-$99.** 633 Main St. 0.5 mi s on US 1. Ext/int corridors. **Pets:** $10 daily fee/pet. Service with restrictions, supervision.
(SAVE) (S♦) (✕) (🏠) (💳) (🍽) (🏊)

◆◆◆ ◆◆◆ **International Motel** Ⓜ
(207) 454-7515. **$55-$95.** 626 Main St. 0.5 mi s on US 1. Ext corridors. **Pets:** Dogs only. Designated rooms, service with restrictions, supervision.
(SAVE) (S♦) (✕) (🏠) (💳)

# CAMDEN

◆◆◆ ◆◆◆◆ **Blue Harbor House, A Village Inn** 🅱🅱 ❖
(207) 236-3196. **$95-$195, 14 day notice.** 67 Elm St. On US 1; center. Ext/int corridors. **Pets:** Medium, dogs only. $25 one-time fee/room. Designated rooms, service with restrictions, supervision.
(SAVE) (✕) (🍽)

◆◆◆◆ **Camden Harbour Inn** 🅱🅱
(207) 236-4200. **$155-$275, 7 day notice.** 83 Bayview St. Off US 1, 0.3 mi e; center. Int corridors. **Pets:** Accepted.
(✕) (🐾)

◆◆◆◆ **The Camden Riverhouse Hotel & Inns** 🆂🅷
(207) 236-0500. **$99-$250, 14 day notice.** 11 Tannery Ln. Center. Int corridors. **Pets:** Accepted.
(ASK) (S♦) (✕) (🏠) (💳) (🏊)

◆◆◆ ◆◆◆◆ **Lord Camden Inn** 🅱🅱 ❖
(207) 236-4325. **$89-$299.** 24 Main St. Center. Int corridors. **Pets:** Other species. $20 daily fee/room. Service with restrictions, supervision.
(SAVE) (S♦) (✕) (🏠) (💳)

# CAPE ELIZABETH

◆◆◆ ◆◆◆◆ **Inn By The Sea** 🆂🅷 ❖
(207) 799-3134. **$299-$709, 14 day notice.** 40 Bowery Beach Rd (SR 77). On SR 77, 7 mi s. Ext/int corridors. **Pets:** Other species. Designated rooms, service with restrictions, supervision.
(SAVE) (S♦) (✕) (🈹M) (🏠) (💳) (🍽) (🏊) (✕) (🐾)

# CARIBOU

◆◆◆ ◆◆◆◆ **Caribou Inn & Convention Center** 🆂🅷 ❖
(207) 498-3733. **$88-$124.** 19 Main St. 3 mi s on US 1. Int corridors. **Pets:** Other species. $25 deposit/room. Service with restrictions, crate.
(SAVE) (S♦) (✕) (🏠) (💳) (🍽) (🏊) (✕)

# CASTINE

◆◆◆◆ **Pentagoet Inn** 🅲🅸
(207) 326-8616. **$95-$205, 14 day notice.** 26 Main St. Center. Int corridors. **Pets:** Accepted.
(✕) (🍽) (🐾) (🍷) (🚭)

# CORNISH

◆◆ **Midway Motel** Ⓜ
(207) 625-8835. **$49-$99, 7 day notice.** 712 S Hiram Rd. 0.7 mi w on SR 25, just past jct SR 25. Ext/int corridors. **Pets:** Accepted.
(✕) (🏠) (💳) (🏊)

# EAGLE LAKE

◆◆ **Overlook Motel & Lakeside Cabins** Ⓜ
(207) 444-4535. **$53-$124.** 3232 Aroostook Rd. On SR 11; center. Ext/int corridors. **Pets:** Other species. $4 daily fee/pet. Service with restrictions, supervision.
(🏠) (💳) (✕)

# EAST BOOTHBAY

◆◆◆ ◆◆◆ **Smuggler's Cove Inn** 🆂🅷
(207) 633-2800. **$49-$199.** 727 Ocean Point Rd. Jct SR 27, 4.5 mi e on SR 96. Ext corridors. **Pets:** $50 deposit/room, $25 daily fee/room. Designated rooms, service with restrictions, supervision.
(SAVE) (S♦) (✕) (🏠) (💳) (🍽) (🏊)

# EDGECOMB

◆◆◆ **Sheepscot River Inn** 🆂🅷 ❖
(207) 882-6343. **$79-$199, 7 day notice.** 306 Eddy Rd. 1 mi w on US 1; on east side of Davies Bridge, 1 mi e of Wiscasset. Ext/int corridors. **Pets:** Dogs only. $10 daily fee/pet. Designated rooms, service with restrictions, crate.
(ASK) (S♦) (✕) (🏠) (💳) (✕)

# ELLSWORTH

◆◆◆ **The Colonial Inn** 🆂🅷
(207) 667-5548. **$54-$130.** 321 High St. 1.3 mi e on SR 3. Ext/int corridors. **Pets:** Accepted.
(ASK) (✕) (🈹) (💳) (🍽) (🏊)

◆◆◆ **Holiday Inn** 🆂🅷
(207) 667-9341. **$90-$160.** 215 High St. Jct US 1, 1A and SR 3. Int corridors. **Pets:** $10 daily fee/pet. Service with restrictions, supervision.
(ASK) (✕) (🈹M) (🏠) (💳) (🍽) (🏊) (✕)

◆◆◆ ◆◆◆ **Jasper's Motel** 🆂🅷
(207) 667-5318. **$48-$87, 3 day notice.** 200 High St. 1 mi e on US 1 and SR 3. Ext corridors. **Pets:** Accepted.
(SAVE) (S♦) (✕) (🏠) (🍽)

◆◆◆ ◆◆◆ **Twilite Motel** Ⓜ
(207) 667-8165. **$66-$119, 3 day notice.** 147 Bucksport Rd. Jct US 1A, 1.5 mi w on US 1/SR 3. Ext corridors. **Pets:** Small, dogs only. $10 daily fee/pet. Designated rooms, service with restrictions, supervision.
(SAVE) (✕) (🏠) (💳)

# FARMINGTON

◆◆◆ ◆◆ **Mount Blue Motel** Ⓜ
(207) 778-6004. **$60.** 454 Wilton Rd. 2 mi w on US 2 and SR 4. Ext corridors. **Pets:** Accepted.
(SAVE) (S♦) (✕) (🏠)

# FREEPORT

◆◆◆ ◆◆◆ **Best Western Freeport Inn** 🆂🅷
(207) 865-3106. **$85-$170.** 31 US 1 S. I-295, exit 17, 1 mi n. Ext/int corridors. **Pets:** Accepted.
(SAVE) (S♦) (✕) (🏠) (💳) (🍽) (🏊)

◆◆ **Econo Lodge** Ⓜ
(207) 865-3777. **$59-$159.** 537 US Rt 1. I-295, exit 20, 0.3 mi s. Ext corridors. **Pets:** Accepted.
(ASK) (S♦) (✕) (🏠) (💳)

◆◆◆ ◆◆◆◆ **Harraseeket Inn** 🅲🅸 ❖
(207) 865-9377. **$119-$295, 3 day notice.** 162 Main St. I-295, exit 22, 0.5 mi e. Int corridors. **Pets:** Dogs only. $25 daily fee/pet. Designated rooms, service with restrictions, supervision.
(SAVE) (S♦) (✕) (🈹M) (🌀) (🈹) (🏠) (💳) (🍽) (🏊)

# GREENVILLE

**◆◆◆ Chalet Moosehead Lakefront Motel Ⓜ**
(207) 695-2950. **$69-$135, 3 day notice.** 12 N Birch St. 1.5 mi w on SR 15. Ext corridors. **Pets:** Dogs only. $10 daily fee/pet. Designated rooms, service with restrictions, supervision.

⊠ 🖬 🖃 ⊠

**AAA ◆◆◆ Kineo View Motor Lodge Ⓜ**
(207) 695-4470. **$69-$99.** Overlook Dr. 2.5 mi s on SR 15. Ext corridors. **Pets:** $10 daily fee/room. Designated rooms, service with restrictions, supervision.

SAVE S🖬 ⊠ 🖬 🖃

# HANCOCK

**◆◆◆ The White Birches 🄢🄷**
(207) 667-3621. **$50-$110.** 19 Thorsen Rd. US 1, 1.5 mi n of jct SR 3. Ext corridors. **Pets:** Accepted.

A$K S🖬 ⊠ 🖬 🖃 ⑪

# KENNEBUNKPORT

**AAA ◆◆◆◆ The Captain Jefferds Inn 🄱🄱**
(207) 967-2311. **$130-$350, 14 day notice.** 5 Pearl St. From Dock Square, 0.3 mi e on Maine St, just s; corner of Pearl and Pleasant sts. Ext/int corridors. **Pets:** Accepted.

SAVE ⊠ 🖬

**AAA ◆◆◆◆ The Colony Hotel 🄢🄷 ❖**
(207) 967-3331. **$225-$550, 3 day notice.** 140 Ocean Ave. From Dock Square, 1 mi s. Int corridors. **Pets:** Other species. $25 daily fee/pet.

SAVE S🖬 ⊠ 🖉 🖬 ⑪ 🖃 ⊠

**AAA ◆◆◆◆ Lodge At Turbat's Creek Ⓜ ❖**
(207) 967-8700. **$79-$169, 14 day notice.** 7 Turbat's Creek Rd. From Dock Square, 0.5 mi e on Maine St, 0.6 mi ne on Wildes, then just se. Ext corridors. **Pets:** Other species. $25 one-time fee/room. Designated rooms, service with restrictions, supervision.

SAVE S🖬 ⊠ 🖙 🖬 ⊠

**AAA ◆◆◆ ◆◆◆ The Yachtsman Lodge & Marina Ⓜ**
(207) 967-2511. **$169-$369, 30 day notice.** 57 Ocean Ave. From Dock Square, 0.3 mi e. Ext corridors. **Pets:** Accepted.

SAVE ⊠ 🖬 🖃 ⊠

# KITTERY

**◆◆◆ Enchanted Nights Bed & Breakfast 🄱🄱 ❖**
(207) 439-1489. **$55-$350, 15 day notice.** 29 Wentworth St. I-95, exit 2 (Kittery), 1 mi s on SR 236, then just right on SR 103. Ext/int corridors. **Pets:** Other species. $10 one-time fee/room. Supervision.

A$K S🖬 ⊠ 🖬 🖃

# LEWISTON

**AAA ◆◆◆ Chalet Motel 🄢🄷**
(207) 784-0600. **$60-$70.** 1243 Lisbon St. I-95 (Maine Tpke), exit 80. Ext/int corridors. **Pets:** Accepted.

SAVE S🖬 ⊠ 🖬 ⑪ 🖃 ⊠

# LINCOLNVILLE

**◆◆◆ Abbingtons Seaview Motel & Cottages Ⓜ ❖**
(207) 236-3471. **$50-$135, 3 day notice.** 6 Seaview Dr. On US 1, 1.2 mi s of jct SR 173. Ext corridors. **Pets:** Other species. $10 daily fee/pet. Designated rooms, supervision.

A$K S🖬 ⊠ 🖬 🖃 🖙

**◆◆◆ Pine Grove Cottages 🄲🄰**
(207) 236-2929. **$75-$160, 7 day notice.** 2076 Atlantic Hwy. On US 1, 2 mi s of jct SR 173. Ext corridors. **Pets:** Accepted.

⊠ 🖬 🖃

# LUBEC

**◆◆◆ ◆◆◆ The Eastland Motel Ⓜ**
(207) 733-5501. **$58-$74.** 395 County Rd. Jct US 1 and SR 189, 8.4 mi e on SR 189. Ext/int corridors. **Pets:** Medium, dogs only. $10 daily fee/pet. Designated rooms, service with restrictions, supervision.

SAVE ⊠ 🖬

# MACHIAS

**◆◆◆ ◆◆◆ The Bluebird Motel Ⓜ**
(207) 255-3332. **$60-$70, 3 day notice.** Dublin St. On US 1, 1 mi s. Ext corridors. **Pets:** Accepted.

SAVE S🖬 ⊠ 🄴🄼 🖬

**◆◆◆ ◆◆◆ Machias Motor Inn Ⓜ**
(207) 255-4861. **$65-$110.** 26 E Main St. 0.5 mi e on US 1. Ext corridors. **Pets:** Medium, dogs only. $5 daily fee/pet. Service with restrictions, supervision.

SAVE S🖬 ⊠ 🖬 🖃

# MEDWAY

**◆◆◆ Katahdin Shadows Motel Ⓜ**
(207) 746-5162. **$54, 10 day notice.** I-95, exit 244, 1.5 mi w on SR 157. Ext corridors. **Pets:** Service with restrictions, supervision.

⊠ 🖬 🖙 ⊠

# MILFORD

**◆◆◆ ◆◆◆ Milford Motel On The River Ⓜ**
(207) 827-3200. **$57-$95.** 174 Main Rd. 0.5 mi n on US 2. Ext/int corridors. **Pets:** Accepted.

⊠ 🖬

# MILLINOCKET

**◆◆◆ ◆◆◆ Americas Best Value Heritage Inn 🄢🄷**
(207) 723-9777. **$79-$89.** 935 Central St. 0.8 mi e on SR 11 and 157. Int corridors. **Pets:** Service with restrictions, supervision.

A$K S🖬 ⊠ 🖃 ⑪ 🖙

**◆◆◆ ◆◆◆ Econo Lodge-Inn & Suites 🄢🄷**
(207) 723-4555. **$59-$125, 3 day notice.** 740 Central St. On SR 157; center. Int corridors. **Pets:** $10 daily fee/pet. Service with restrictions, supervision.

SAVE ⊠ 🖬 🖙 ⊠

# OGUNQUIT

**◆◆◆ ◆◆◆ Studio East Motor Inn Ⓜ**
(207) 646-7297. **$49-$169, 7 day notice.** 267 Main St. On US 1; center. Ext corridors. **Pets:** Accepted.

A$K S🖬 ⊠ 🖬

# OLD ORCHARD BEACH

**◆◆◆ ◆◆◆ Alouette Beach Resort Ⓜ**
(207) 934-4151. **$49-$265, 14 day notice.** 91 E Grand Ave. 0.9 mi e on SR 9 (E Grand Ave). Ext/int corridors. **Pets:** Accepted.

SAVE ⊠ 🖬 🖃 ⑪ 🖙

**◆◆◆ ◆◆◆ Old Colonial Motel Ⓜ ❖**
(207) 934-9862. **$65-$230, 14 day notice.** 61 W Grand Ave. On SR 9 (W Grand Ave), 0.5 mi w. Ext corridors. **Pets:** Small, other species. $8 daily fee/pet. Designated rooms, service with restrictions, crate.

SAVE S🖬 ⊠ 🖬 🖙 ⊠

**◆◆◆ ◆◆◆ Sea View Motel 🄢🄷**
(207) 934-4180. **$50-$260, 14 day notice.** 65 W Grand Ave. 0.5 mi w on SR 9 (W Grand Ave). Ext corridors. **Pets:** Medium, dogs only. $100 deposit/pet, $10 daily fee/pet. Designated rooms, no service, supervision.

SAVE S🖬 ⊠ 🖬 🖙

# ORONO

▼▼▼ **Best Western Black Bear Inn & Conference Center** SH
(207) 866-7120. **$89-$119.** 4 Godfrey Dr. I-95, exit 193 (Stillwater Ave). Int corridors. **Pets:** $3 daily fee/pet. Service with restrictions, supervision.
(ASK) S✿ ✕ ⟨&M⟩ 🛏 💻

▼▼ **University Inn Academic Suites** SH ❖
(207) 866-4921. **$69-$82.** 5 College Ave. I-95, exit 191, 1.6 mi n on US 2; 8 mi n of Bangor. Int corridors. **Pets:** Other species. Designated rooms, service with restrictions, supervision.
(ASK) ✕ 🛏 💻 ⤴

# PORTLAND

▼▼▼▼ **Doubletree Hotel** LH
(207) 774-5611. **$89-$269.** 1230 Congress St. I-295, exit 5 southbound, w on SR 22; exit 5B northbound. Int corridors. **Pets:** Medium, other species. $50 one-time fee/room. Designated rooms, service with restrictions, supervision.
(ASK) ✕ ⟨&M⟩ ⟨&⟩ 🛏 💻 🍴 ⤴

🅰🅰🅰 ▼▼▼▼ **Eastland Park Hotel** LH
(207) 775-5411. **$99-$209.** 157 High St. At Congress Square; center. Int corridors. **Pets:** Accepted.
(SAVE) S✿ ✕ 🛏 💻 🍴 ✕

🅰🅰🅰 ▼▼▼ **Embassy Suites Hotel** LH
(207) 775-2200. **$99-$299.** 1050 Westbrook St. At Portland International Jetport. Int corridors. **Pets:** Other species.
(SAVE) ✕ ⟨&M⟩ 🌀 🛏 💻 🍴 ⤴ ✕

🅰🅰🅰 ▼▼▼▼ **Holiday Inn-West** SH
(207) 774-5601. **$110-$210.** 81 Riverside St. I-95 (Maine Tpke), exit 48. Int corridors. **Pets:** Designated rooms, service with restrictions, supervision.
(SAVE) S✿ ✕ ⟨&M⟩ 🌀 ⟨&⟩ 🛏 💻 🍴 ⤴ ✕

🅰🅰🅰 ▼▼▼▼ **Howard Johnson Plaza Hotel** SH
(207) 774-5861. **$85-$195.** 155 Riverside St. I-95 (Maine Tpke), exit 48, jct SR 25. Int corridors. **Pets:** $50 deposit/room. Service with restrictions, supervision.
(SAVE) S✿ ✕ 🛏 💻 🍴 ⤴

🅰🅰🅰 ▼▼▼ ▼▼▼ **Portland Harbor Hotel** SH
(207) 775-9090. **$179-$299.** 468 Fore St. In the Old Port. Int corridors. **Pets:** Accepted.
(SAVE) S✿ ✕ ⟨&M⟩ 🛏 🍴

# PRESQUE ISLE

🅰🅰🅰 ▼▼ **Northern Lights Motel** M ❖
(207) 764-4441. **$57-S90.** 72 Houlton Rd. 2 mi s on US 1. Ext corridors. **Pets:** Medium. Designated rooms, service with restrictions, supervision.
(SAVE) ✕ 🛏

🅰🅰🅰 ▼▼▼ **Presque Isle Inn & Convention Center** SH ❖
(207) 764-3321. **$78-$124.** 116 Main St. 1 mi s on US 1. Int corridors. **Pets:** Other species. $25 deposit/room. Service with restrictions, crate.
(SAVE) S✿ ✕ 🛏 💻 🍴 ⤴

# RANGELEY

▼▼ ▼▼ **Country Club Inn** CI
(207) 864-3831. **$92-$120, 7 day notice.** 56 Country Club Rd. 2.5 mi w on SR 4 and 16, 0.8 mi s, follow signs. Ext/int corridors. **Pets:** Large. $10 daily fee/pet. Service with restrictions, supervision.
(ASK) ✕ 🍴 ⤴ 🐾 🐾 🐾

🅰🅰🅰 ▼▼▼▼ **Rangeley Inn & Motor Lodge** SH
(207) 864-3341. **$84-$129, 15 day notice.** 2443 Main St. Center. Ext/int corridors. **Pets:** Medium, other species. $20 daily fee/pet. Designated rooms, service with restrictions, supervision.
(SAVE) ✕ 🛏 💻 🍴

# ROCKLAND

🅰🅰🅰 ▼▼▼ **Navigator Motor Inn** SH
(207) 594-2131. **$59-$139.** 520 Main St. On US 1. Ext/int corridors. **Pets:** Dogs only. Designated rooms, service with restrictions, supervision.
(SAVE) S✿ ✕ 🛏 🍴

🅰🅰🅰 ▼▼▼ **Trade Winds Motor Inn** SH
(207) 596-6661. **$59-$155.** 2 Park Dr. On US 1; center. Ext/int corridors. **Pets:** Other species. Designated rooms, supervision.
(SAVE) S✿ ✕ 🛏 🍴 ⤴ ✕

# ROCKPORT

🅰🅰🅰 ▼▼▼▼ **The Country Inn At Camden-Rockport** SH ❖
(207) 236-2725. **$94-$209, 3 day notice.** 8 Country Inn Way. Jct SR 90, 0.9 mi n on US 1. Ext/int corridors. **Pets:** $10 daily fee/room. Designated rooms, service with restrictions, supervision.
(SAVE) S✿ ✕ 🛏 💻 ⤴ ✕

# RUMFORD

🅰🅰🅰 ▼▼▼ **Linnell Motel & RestInn Conference Center** SH
(207) 364-4511. **$60-$75.** 986 Prospect Ave. 2 mi w, just off US 2. Ext/int corridors. **Pets:** Accepted.
(SAVE) S✿ ✕ 🛏

# SACO

🅰🅰🅰 ▼▼▼▼ **Hampton Inn** SH ❖
(207) 282-7222. **$79-$149.** 48 Industrial Park Rd. I-95 (Maine Tpke), exit 36; I-195, exit 1. Int corridors. **Pets:** Other species. Designated rooms, service with restrictions, supervision.
(SAVE) S✿ ✕ ⟨&M⟩ ⟨&⟩ 🛏 💻 ⤴

🅰🅰🅰 ▼▼ **Saco Motel** M
(207) 284-6952. **$50-$85, 3 day notice.** 473 Main St. I-95 (Maine Tpke), exit 36, 0.5 mi s on US 1. Ext corridors. **Pets:** Accepted.
(SAVE) S✿ ✕ 🛏 ⤴

▼▼ **Wagon Wheel Motel** M ❖
(207) 284-6387. **$55-$125, 3 day notice.** 726 Portland Rd. 1.8 mi n on US 1; 0.8 mi n of jct I-95 (Maine Tpke), exit 36. Ext corridors. **Pets:** Dogs only. Designated rooms, service with restrictions, supervision.
✕ 🛏 💻 ⤴

# SANFORD

▼▼ **Super 8 Motel** SH
(207) 324-8823. **$60-$100.** 1892 Main St (Rt 109). I-95 (Maine Tpke), exit 19, 7 mi w. Int corridors. **Pets:** Accepted.
(ASK) S✿ ✕ 🌀 🛏

# SCARBOROUGH

▼▼ **Pride Motel & Cottages** CA
(207) 883-4816. **$45-$155.** 677 US 1. I-95 (Maine Tpke), exit 36, 0.5 mi e to US 1, then 4.5 mi n. Ext corridors. **Pets:** Other species. $5 daily fee/pet. Service with restrictions, supervision.
✕ 🛏 ⤴ ✕

▼▼▼▼ **Residence Inn by Marriott** SH
(207) 883-0400. **$125-$216.** 800 Roundwood Dr. I-95 (Maine Tpke), exit 42, 1.5 mi n on Payne Rd. Int corridors. **Pets:** Large, other species. $75 one-time fee/pet. Service with restrictions, supervision.
(ASK) S✿ ✕ ⟨&M⟩ 🌀 ⟨&⟩ 🛏 💻 ⤴ ✕

▼▼▼ **TownePlace Suites by Marriott** SH ❖
(207) 883-6800. **$99-$189.** 700 Roundwood Dr. I-95 (Maine Tpke), exit 42, 1.5 mi n on Payne Rd. Int corridors. **Pets:** Other species. $75 one-time fee/room. Service with restrictions, crate.
(ASK) S✿ ✕ ⟨&M⟩ ⟨&⟩ 🛏 💻 ⤴

# SEARSPORT

### 🆔 ▼▼▼ The Yardarm Motel Ⓜ
(207) 548-2404. **$58-$115, 3 day notice.** 172 E Main St. 0.5 mi n on US 1. Ext corridors. **Pets:** Medium. Designated rooms, service with restrictions, supervision.

🆂🅰🆅🅴 ⊠ 📠

# SKOWHEGAN

### 🆔 ▼▼ Breezy Acres Motel Ⓜ
(207) 474-2703. **$58-$68.** 315 Waterville Rd. 1.5 mi s on US 201. Ext corridors. **Pets:** Accepted.

🆂🅰🆅🅴 🆂 ⊠ 📠 💻 ⤳ ⊠

# SOUTHPORT

### 🆔 ▼▼▼ The Lawnmere Inn 🆑
(207) 633-2544. **$89-$250.** 65 Hendricks Hill Rd. 2 mi s of Boothbay Harbor on SR 27, just s of bridge to Southport Island. Ext/int corridors. **Pets:** Accepted.

🆂🅰🆅🅴 ⊠ 📠 🍴

### 🆔 ▼▼▼▼ Ocean Gate Inn 🆂🅷
(207) 633-3321. **$69-$189, 3 day notice.** 70 Ocean Gate Rd. SR 27, 2.5 mi s of Boothbay Harbor, 0.5 mi s of bridge to Southport Island. Ext corridors. **Pets:** Accepted.

🆂🅰🆅🅴 🆂 ⊠ 📠 💻 ⤳ ⊠

# SOUTH PORTLAND

### ▼▼▼▼ Best Western Merry Manor Inn 🆂🅷
(207) 774-6151. **$99-$159.** 700 Main St. I-95 (Maine Tpke), exit 45, 1.3 mi e to US 1. Ext/int corridors. **Pets:** Medium, other species. Service with restrictions, crate.

🅰🆂🅺 🆂 ⊠ 🅼 🅺 📠 💻 🍴 ⤳ ⊠

### ▼▼▼ Hampton Inn Hotel 🆂🅷
(207) 773-4400. **$119-$209.** 171 Philbrook Ave. I-95 (Maine Tpke), exit 45. Int corridors. **Pets:** Accepted.

🅰🆂🅺 🆂 ⊠ 🅼 📀 📠 💻

### 🆔 ▼▼▼ Howard Johnson Hotel 🆂🅷
(207) 775-5343. **$89-$199.** 675 Main St. I-95 (Maine Tpke), exit 45, 1.3 mi e to US 1. Int corridors. **Pets:** Designated rooms, service with restrictions, supervision.

🆂🅰🆅🅴 🆂 ⊠ 📠 💻 ⤳

### ▼▼▼▼ Portland Marriott Hotel & Golf Resort 🅻🅷
(207) 871-8000. **$159-$299.** 200 Sable Oaks Dr. I-95 (Maine Tpke), exit 45, just n on Maine Mall Rd, then just w on Running Hill Rd. Int corridors. **Pets:** Accepted.

🅰🆂🅺 🆂 ⊠ 🅼 📀 📠 💻 🍴 ⤳ ⊠

### 🆔 ▼▼▼ Sable Oaks Suites 🆂🅷
(207) 775-3900. **$99-$199.** 303 Sable Oaks Dr. I-95 (Maine Tpke), exit 45, just n on Maine Mall Rd, then just w on Running Hill Rd. Int corridors. **Pets:** Other species. $20 one-time fee/room. Service with restrictions, supervision.

🆂🅰🆅🅴 🆂 ⊠ 🅼 🅺 📠 💻 ⤳

# SPRUCE HEAD

### 🆔 ▼▼▼▼ Craignair Inn 🆑 🐾
(207) 594-7644. **$70-$159, 14 day notice.** 5 Third St. 2.5 mi w on SR 73, 1.5 mi s on Clark Island Rd; 10 mi s of Rockland. Ext/int corridors. **Pets:** Medium. $10 daily fee/room. Designated rooms, service with restrictions, supervision.

🆂🅰🆅🅴 ⊠ 🍴

# WATERVILLE

### 🆔 ▼▼▼ Budget Host Airport Inn 🆂🅷 🐾
(207) 873-3366. **$40-$110.** 400 Kennedy Memorial Dr. I-95, exit 127, 0.3 mi e on SR 11 (Kennedy Memorial Dr). Ext/int corridors. **Pets:** $10 daily fee/pet. Designated rooms, service with restrictions, supervision.

🆂🅰🆅🅴 🆂 ⊠ 🅺 📠 🍴

### 🆔 ▼▼▼ Econo Lodge 🆂🅷
(207) 872-5577. **$39-$109.** 455 Kennedy Memorial Dr. I-95, exit 127 on SR 11 (Kennedy Memorial Dr) at Waterville-Oakland. Ext/int corridors. **Pets:** Dogs only. $10 daily fee/pet. Supervision.

🆂🅰🆅🅴 🆂 ⊠ 💻 ⤳

### ▼▼▼▼ Holiday Inn 🆂🅷
(207) 873-0111. **$105-$185.** 375 Main St. I-95, exit 130 (Main St) on SR 104. Int corridors. **Pets:** Other species. Service with restrictions, supervision.

🅰🆂🅺 🆂 ⊠ 📠 💻 🍴 ⤳ ⊠

# WELLS

### 🆔 ▼▼▼ Ne'r Beach Motel Ⓜ 🐾
(207) 646-2636. **$44-$119 (no credit cards).** 395 Post Rd (Rt 1). US 1, 0.8 mi s of jct SR 9B. Ext corridors. **Pets:** Medium, other species. $75 deposit/pet, $10 daily fee/pet. Designated rooms, service with restrictions, supervision.

🆂🅰🆅🅴 🆂 ⊠ 📠 ⤳

# WEST FORKS

### ▼▼ Inn by the River 🆑 🐾
(207) 663-2181. **$75-$150, 30 day notice.** US Rt 201. Center. Int corridors. **Pets:** Other species. $25 deposit/room. Designated rooms, service with restrictions.

🅰🆂🅺 🆂 ⊠ 💻 🍴 ⊠ 🆆 🆉

# WESTPORT

### ▼▼▼ The Squire Tarbox Inn 🆑
(207) 882-7693. **$130-$195, 14 day notice.** 1181 Main Rd. Jct US 1 and SR 144; in Wiscasset; 8.5 mi s on SR 144, follow signs. Ext/int corridors. **Pets:** Accepted.

⊠ 🍴 ⊠ 🆆 🆉

# WILTON

### 🆔 ▼▼▼ Whispering Pines Motel Ⓜ
(207) 645-3721. **$60-$90, 3 day notice.** 183 Lake Rd. SR 2, 1 mi w of jct SR 4. Ext corridors. **Pets:** Accepted.

🆂🅰🆅🅴 🆂 ⊠ 📠 💻 ⊠

# YARMOUTH

### 🆔 ▼▼▼ Down-East Village Motel Ⓜ
(207) 846-5161. **$65-$117.** 705 US Rt 1. I-295, exit 15 northbound; exit 17 southbound. Ext corridors. **Pets:** Accepted.

🆂🅰🆅🅴 🆂 ⊠ 💻 🍴 ⤳

# MARYLAND

## CITY INDEX

## BALTIMORE METROPOLITAN AREA

### ABERDEEN

**Clarion Aberdeen** SH
(410) 273-6300. **$79-$109.** 980 Hospitality Way. I-95, exit 85, just e on SR 22. Int corridors. **Pets:** Other species. Service with restrictions, crate.

**Holiday Inn Chesapeake House** SH
(410) 272-8100. **$120-$130.** 1007 Beards Hill Rd. I-95, exit 85, just e on SR 22. Int corridors. **Pets:** Medium. Service with restrictions, crate.

**Red Roof Inn** SH
(410) 273-7800. **$61-$72.** 988 Hospitality Way. I-95, exit 85, just e on SR 22. Ext corridors. **Pets:** Accepted.

### ANNAPOLIS

**Homestead Studio Suites Hotel-Annapolis** SH
(410) 571-6600. **$84-$154.** 120 Admiral Cochrane Dr. 2.3 mi sw on US 50 and 301, exit 22, just s, then just e. Int corridors. **Pets:** $25 daily fee/pet. Service with restrictions, supervision.

**Loews Annapolis Hotel** LH ❖
(410) 263-7777. **$119-$289.** 126 West St. US 50 and 301, exit 24 eastbound; exit 24A westbound, 1.4 mi s on SR 70, just sw on Calvert St, then just w. Int corridors. **Pets:** Other species. Designated rooms.

**Radisson Hotel Annapolis** SH
(410) 224-3150. **$89-$169.** 210 Holiday Ct. 2.3 mi sw on US 50 and 301, exit 22 to Riva Rd, 0.3 mi n. Int corridors. **Pets:** Accepted.

**Residence Inn by Marriott-Annapolis** SH
(410) 573-0300. **$179-$289.** 170 Admiral Cochrane Dr. 2.3 mi sw on US 50 and 301, exit 22 to Riva Rd, just s on Riva Rd, then just e. Ext corridors. **Pets:** Accepted.

**Sheraton Annapolis Hotel** LH
(410) 266-3131. **$279-$309.** 173 Jennifer Rd. North side of US 50 and 301, exit 23B westbound; exit 23 eastbound. Int corridors. **Pets:** Accepted.

### ANNAPOLIS JUNCTION

**TownePlace Suites by Marriott-Baltimore/Ft. Meade** SH
(301) 498-7477. **$59-$139.** 120 National Business Pkwy. I-95, exit 38A, 2.5 mi e on SR 32 to exit 11 (Dorsey Run Rd), then 1.3 e. Int corridors. **Pets:** Accepted.

### BALTIMORE

**Admiral Fell Inn** SH ❖
(410) 522-7377. **$199-$239.** 888 S Broadway St. Corner of Broadway and Thames sts; facing the waterfront. Int corridors. **Pets:** Other species. Designated rooms, service with restrictions.

**Baltimore's Tremont Park Hotel** SH
(410) 576-1200. **$79-$199.** 8 E Pleasant St. Just s of US 40 E, off Charles St. Int corridors. **Pets:** Large. $10 daily fee/room. Designated rooms, service with restrictions, crate.

**Brookshire Suites** SH ❖
(410) 625-1300. **$89-$206.** 120 E Lombard St. Corner of Calvert and Lombard sts. Int corridors. **Pets:** Other species. $25 ceposit/room. Designated rooms, service with restrictions, supervision.

**Hampton Inn & Suites-Inner Harbor** SH ❖
(410) 539-7888. **$166-$224.** 131 E Redwood St. Between Lombard and Baltimore sts; corner of Calvert and E Redwood sts. Int corridors. **Pets:** Small. $50 one-time fee/pet. Service with restrictions, crate.

**Peabody Court-A Clarion Hotel** SH
(410) 727-7101. **$135-$2000.** 612 Cathedral St. Cathedral St and Mt Vernon Square. Int corridors. **Pets:** Accepted.

**Pier 5 Hotel** SH
(410) 539-2000. **$239-$349.** 711 Eastern Ave. On the Inner Harbor, at Pier 5. Int corridors. **Pets:** Accepted.

**Sheraton Inner Harbor Hotel** LH
(410) 962-8300. **$169-$339.** 300 S Charles St. On S Charles St at Conway St. Int corridors. **Pets:** Accepted.

### COLUMBIA

**Extended Stay Deluxe Columbia Corporate Park** SH
(410) 872-2994. **$119-$149.** 8890 Stanford Blvd. I-95, exit 41B, 1.3 mi w on SR 175 (Little Patuxent Pkwy), 0.5 mi s on Snowden River Pkwy, just w on McGaw Rd, then 0.3 mi nw. Int corridors. **Pets:** $25 daily fee/pet. Service with restrictions, supervision.

**Homewood Suites by Hilton** SH ❀
(410) 872-9200. **$79-$239.** 8320 Benson Dr. I-95, exit 41B, 0.5 mi w on SR 175 (Little Patuxent Pkwy), just nw on SR 108, then just w on Lark Brown Rd. Int corridors. **Pets:** Other species. $75 one-time fee/room. Service with restrictions.

**Sheraton Columbia Hotel** LH ❀
(410) 730-3900. **$149-$269.** 10207 Wincopin Cir. 1.2 mi w on SR 175 (Little Patuxent Pkwy) from jct US 29, then just s; center. Int corridors. **Pets:** Small, dogs only. $50 one-time fee/room. Supervision.

**Staybridge Suites Baltimore-Columbia** SH
(410) 964-9494. **$99-$239.** 8844 Columbia 100 Pkwy. I-95, exit 43B, 4 mi w on SR 100, exit 1B, then just e. Int corridors. **Pets:** Accepted.

# EDGEWOOD

**Best Western Invitation Inn** SH
(410) 679-9700. **$62-$99.** 1709 Edgewood Rd. I-95, exit 77A, just e on SR 24. Ext corridors. **Pets:** Accepted.

# ELLICOTT CITY

**Residence Inn by Marriott Columbia** SH
(410) 997-7200. **$79-$159.** 4950 Beaver Run Way. I-95, exit 43B, 4 mi w on SR 100, exit 1B (Executive Park Dr). Int corridors. **Pets:** Accepted.

# GLEN BURNIE

**Days Inn-Glen Burnie** SH
(410) 761-8300. **$72-$139.** 6600 Ritchie Hwy. I-695, exit 3B eastbound; exit 2 westbound, 0.5 mi s on SR 2. Ext corridors. **Pets:** Large. $20 daily fee/pet. Service with restrictions, crate.

# HANOVER

**Red Roof Inn-BWI Parkway** M
(410) 712-4070. **$59-$71.** 7306 Parkway Dr S. I-95, exit 43A, 2 mi e on SR 100 to exit 8, 0.5 mi se. Ext corridors. **Pets:** Accepted.

**Residence Inn by Marriott-Arundel Mills/BWI** SH ❀
(410) 799-7332. **$114-$239.** 7035 Arundel Mills Cir. I-95, exit 43A, 3.6 mi e on SR 100 to exit 10A (Arundel Mills Blvd). Int corridors. **Pets:** Medium, other species. $75 one-time fee/room.

# JESSUP

**Red Roof Inn-Columbia/Jessup** M
(410) 796-0380. **$70-$96.** 8000 Washington Blvd. I-95, exit 41A; 0.3 mi s of jct US 1 and SR 175. Ext corridors. **Pets:** Accepted.

# LINTHICUM HEIGHTS

**AmeriSuites (Baltimore/BWI Airport)** SH
(410) 859-3366. **$149-$209.** 940 International Dr. I-695, exit 7A, 1 mi s on SR 295, then just e on W Nursery Rd. Int corridors. **Pets:** Accepted.

**Candlewood Suites-BWI** SH
(410) 850-9214. **$117-$129.** 1247 Winterson Rd. I-695, exit 7A, 1 mi s on SR 295, 1.3 mi e on W Nursery Rd, then 0.3 mi w. Int corridors. **Pets:** Medium, other species. $75 one-time fee/room. Service with restrictions.

**Comfort Inn Airport** SH ❀
(410) 789-9100. **$89-$149.** 6921 Baltimore Annapolis Blvd. I-695, exit 6A eastbound; exit 5 westbound, at jct SR 170 and 648. Int corridors. **Pets:** Other species. Service with restrictions.

**Comfort Suites-BWI Airport** SH ❀
(410) 691-1000. **$89-$249.** 815 Elkridge Landing Rd. I-695, exit 7A, 1 mi s on SR 295, then 1.3 mi e on W Nursery Rd. Int corridors. **Pets:** Other species. $25 one-time fee/pet. Service with restrictions, crate.

**Extended StayAmerica BWI Airport** SH
(410) 850-0400. **$94-$109.** 1500 Aero Dr. I-695, exit 7A, 1 mi s on SR 295, 0.6 mi e on W Nursery Rd, then just n. Int corridors. **Pets:** $25 daily fee/pet. Service with restrictions, supervision.

**Four Points by Sheraton BWI Airport** SH
(410) 859-3300. **$93-$239.** 7032 Elm Rd. I-195, exit 1A, 0.5 mi n on SR 170, then just e. Int corridors. **Pets:** Medium. $25 daily fee/pet. Service with restrictions, crate.

**Hampton Inn BWI Airport** SH
(410) 850-0600. **$89-$179.** 829 Elkridge Landing Rd. I-695, exit 7A, 1 mi s on SR 295, 1.3 mi e on W Nursery Rd, then just w. Int corridors. **Pets:** Accepted.

**Holiday Inn-BWI Airport Conference Center** LH
(410) 859-8400. **$99-$162.** 890 Elkridge Landing Rd. I-695, exit 7A, 1 mi s on SR 295, 1.3 mi e on W Nursery Rd, then 0.5 mi w. Int corridors. **Pets:** Medium. $20 one-time fee/pet. Designated rooms, service with restrictions, supervision.

**Homestead Studio Suites Hotel-Baltimore Washington Int'l Airport** M
(410) 691-2500. **$94-$109.** 939 International Dr. I-695, exit 7A, 1 mi s on SR 295, then just e on W Nursery Rd. Ext corridors. **Pets:** $25 daily fee/pet. Service with restrictions, supervision.

**Homewood Suites by Hilton-BWI Airport** SH
(410) 684-6100. **$129-$189.** 1181 Winterson Rd. I-695, exit 7A, 1 mi s on SR 295, 0.7 mi e on W Nursery Rd, then just n. Int corridors. **Pets:** Accepted.

**Microtel Inn & Suites-BWI Airport** SH ❀
(410) 865-7500. **$115-$125.** 1170 Winterson Rd. I-695, exit 7A, 1 mi s on SR 295, 0.7 mi e on W Nursery Rd, then just n. Int corridors. **Pets:** Other species. $75 one-time fee/room. Service with restrictions, crate.

**Motel 6 Baltimore-Linthicum Heights #1201** M
(410) 636-9070. **$55-$75.** 5179 Raynor Ave. I-695, exit 8, just e on SR 168. Ext corridors. **Pets:** Accepted.

**Red Roof Inn-BWI Airport** SH
(410) 850-7600. **$76-$105.** 827 Elkridge Landing Rd. I-695, exit 7A, 1 mi s on SR 295, 1.3 mi e on W Nursery Rd, then just w. Ext corridors. **Pets:** Accepted.

**Residence Inn by Marriott-BWI Airport** SH
(410) 691-0255. **$119-$199.** 1160 Winterson Rd. I-695, exit 7A, 1 mi s on SR 295, 0.7 mi e on W Nursery Rd, then just n. Int corridors. **Pets:** Accepted.

[AAA] ▼▼▼ Sleep Inn & Suites Airport SH ✿
(410) 789-7223. **$89-$139.** 6055 Belle Grove Rd. I-695, exit 6A eastbound; exit 5 westbound, 0.3 mi n to jct SR 170/648. Int corridors. **Pets:** Other species. Service with restrictions.
[SAVE] [S🐾] [✕] [&M] [🖉] [&] [🖥] [🖵]

## OWINGS MILLS

[AAA] ▼▼▼▼ AmeriSuites (Baltimore/Owings Mills) SH
(410) 998-3630. **$144-$154.** 4730 Painters Mill Rd. I-795, exit 4 (Owings Mills Blvd), 0.5 mi s, then 0.7 mi e on Red Run Blvd. Int corridors. **Pets:** Small. $50 one-time fee/room. Service with restrictions, supervision.
[SAVE] [S🐾] [✕] [&M] [🖉] [&] [&] [🖥] [🖵] [≈]

## SYKESVILLE

▼▼▼▼ Inn at Norwood BB
(410) 549-7868. **$120-$190, 7 day notice.** 7514 Norwood Ave. I-70, exit 80 (SR 32), 8 mi n, just w on Main St, then just w on Church St. Int corridors. **Pets:** Medium, dogs only. $20 daily fee/pet. Designated rooms, supervision.
[ASK] [✕] [&] [🖥] [🖵] [🖉]

## TIMONIUM

▼▼ ▼▼ Red Roof Inn-Timonium M
(410) 666-0380. **$63-$98.** 111 W Timonium Rd. I-83, exit 16A northbound; exit 16 southbound, just e. Ext corridors. **Pets:** Accepted.
[✕] [&]

## TOWSON

[AAA] ▼▼▼▼ Holiday Inn Baltimore-Townson SH
(410) 823-4410. **$109-$149.** 1100 Cromwell Bridge Rd. I-695, exit 29A, just s. Int corridors. **Pets:** Medium. $25 one-time fee/room. Service with restrictions, supervision.
[SAVE] [S🐾] [✕] [🖉] [&] [🖥] [🖵] [¶] [≈]

▼▼▼ Sheraton Baltimore North LH
(410) 321-7400. **$89-$229.** 903 Dulaney Valley Rd. I-695, exit 27A, 0.3 mi s. Int corridors. **Pets:** Accepted.
[ASK] [S🐾] [✕] [🖉] [&] [🖥] [🖵] [¶] [≈] [✕]

## WESTMINSTER

▼▼ The Boston Inn M
(410) 848-9095. **$50-$66.** 533 Baltimore Blvd. 0.9 mi se on SR 97/140 from jct SR 27. Ext corridors. **Pets:** Dogs only. $50 deposit/pet. Service with restrictions, crate.
[ASK] [✕] [&] [🖥]

▼▼ ▼▼ Days Inn-Westminster SH
(410) 857-0500. **$74-$89.** 25 S Cranberry Rd. 0.4 mi se on SR 97/140 from jct SR 27, just n. Int corridors. **Pets:** Accepted.
[ASK] [S🐾] [✕] [🖉] [&] [🖥] [🖵] [≈]

## WHITE MARSH

▼▼▼ Residence Inn by Marriott Baltimore/White Marsh SH
(410) 933-9554. **$119-$249.** 4980 Mercantile Rd. I-95, exit 67B, just w. Int corridors. **Pets:** Medium, other species. $75 one-time fee/room. Service with restrictions, supervision.
[ASK] [✕] [&] [&] [🖥] [🖵] [≈] [✕]

# END METROPOLITAN AREA

## CAMBRIDGE

[AAA] ▼▼▼ ▼▼▼ Hyatt Regency Chesapeake Bay Golf Resort, Spa and Marina LH
(410) 901-1234. **$139-$335, 3 day notice.** 100 Heron Blvd. US 50 E, 1.2 mi e of Frederick C Malkus Jr Bridge. Int corridors. **Pets:** Accepted.
[SAVE] [✕] [&M] [🖉] [&] [&] [🖥] [🖵] [¶] [≈] [✕]

## CHESTERTOWN

▼▼▼ Brampton Bed & Breakfast Inn BB
(410) 778-1860. **$155-$265, 10 day notice.** 25227 Chestertown Rd. SR 213 to 291, 0.5 mi w to SR 20, 1 mi s. Ext/int corridors. **Pets:** Accepted.
[✕] [🖥] [🖉]

## CRISFIELD

[AAA] ▼▼ Pines Motel M
(410) 968-0900. **$45-$109.** 127A N Somerset Ave. 0.4 mi e of SR 413. Ext corridors. **Pets:** Other species. $5 daily fee/pet. Designated rooms, service with restrictions, supervision.
[SAVE] [S🐾] [✕] [&] [🖥] [≈]

## CUMBERLAND

▼▼▼ Holiday Inn SH
(301) 724-8800. **$80-$109, 3 day notice.** 100 S George St. I-68, exit 43C, just n; downtown. Int corridors. **Pets:** $10 one-time fee/room. Service with restrictions, crate.
[ASK] [✕] [&] [&] [🖥] [¶] [≈]

[AAA] ▼▼▼ ▼▼▼ Rocky Gap Lodge & Golf Resort LH ✿
(301) 784-8400. **$79-$190, 3 day notice.** 16701 Lakeview Rd NE. I-68, exit 50, just n. Int corridors. **Pets:** Dogs only. $75 one-time fee/room. Service with restrictions, crate.
[SAVE] [S🐾] [✕] [&M] [&] [&] [🖥] [🖵] [¶] [≈] [✕]

## DISTRICT OF COLUMBIA METROPOLITAN AREA

## BELTSVILLE

**▼▼▼ Sheraton-College Park Hotel** 🅢🅗 ☙
(301) 937-4422. **$89-$149.** 4095 Powder Mill Rd. I-95, exit 29B, just w on SR 212; 2 mi n of I-495 (Capital Beltway). Int corridors. **Pets:** Medium, dogs only. Service with restrictions, supervision.
🆎🅂 ✕ 🐾M 🖉 ᕤ 🆓 🔲 🍽 ⊯

## BETHESDA

**▼▼ Residence Inn by Marriott-Bethesda-Downtown** 🅢🅗
(301) 718-0200. **$239-$279.** 7335 Wisconsin Ave. I-495, exit 34, 2.5 mi s on SR 355; entrance on Waverly St. Int corridors. **Pets:** Medium. $10 daily fee/room, $200 one-time fee/room. Service with restrictions, supervision.
✕ 🖉 🐾 ᕤ 🔲 ⊯ ✕

## BOWIE

**▼▼▼ Comfort Inn Hotel & Conference Center-Bowie** 🅢🅗
(301) 464-0089. **$109-$150.** 4500 NW Crain Hwy. US 50, exit 13A, jct US 50/301 and SR 3. Int corridors. **Pets:** Small, other species. $15 daily fee/pet. Designated rooms, service with restrictions, supervision.
🆎🅂 🅂 ✕ 🐾M 🖉 🐾 ᕤ 🆓 🔲 🍽 ⊯

**▼▼▼ Hampton Inn-Bowie** 🅢🅗
(301) 809-1800. **$109-$159.** 15202 Major Lansdale Blvd. US 50, exit 11, 0.4 mi s on SR 197. Int corridors. **Pets:** Small, other species. $25 daily fee/pet. Service with restrictions, crate.
🆎🅂 🅂 ✕ 🐾M 🐾 ᕤ 🆓 ⊯

## CAMP SPRINGS

**⚞⚟ ▼▼ Days Inn-Camp Springs/Andrews AFB** 🅢🅗
(301) 423-2323. **$74-$89.** 5001 Mercedes Blvd. I-95/495, exit 7B, 0.3 mi n on Auth Rd. Int corridors. **Pets:** Other species. $10 daily fee/pet. Service with restrictions, supervision.
🆂🅰🆅🅴 🅂 ✕ ᕤ 🆓 ⊯

## GAITHERSBURG

**⚞⚟ ▼▼▼ Comfort Inn Shady Grove** 🅢🅗
(301) 330-0023. **$79-$139.** 16216 Frederick Rd. I-270, exit 8, 1 mi e on Shady Grove Rd at jct SR 355. Int corridors. **Pets:** Other species. $15 daily fee/pet. Service with restrictions, crate.
🆂🅰🆅🅴 🅂 ✕ 🖉 ᕤ 🔲 ⊯

**⚞⚟ ▼▼▼ Holiday Inn-Gaithersburg** 🅛🅗
(301) 948-8900. **$109-$149.** 2 Montgomery Village Ave. I-270, exit 11, 0.3 mi e. Int corridors. **Pets:** Small. Service with restrictions, crate.
🆂🅰🆅🅴 🅂 ✕ 🐾M 🖉 🐾 ᕤ 🔲 🍽 ⊯ ✕

**▼▼ Homestead Studio Suites Hotel-Gaithersburg/Rockville** 🅢🅗
(301) 987-9100. **$110-$130.** 2621 Research Blvd. I-270, exit 8, just w, then just n. Int corridors. **Pets:** $25 daily fee/pet. Service with restrictions, supervision.
🆎🅂 🅂 ✕ 🐾M 🖉 🐾 ᕤ 🔲

**▼▼▼ Residence Inn by Marriott-Gaithersburg** 🅢🅗
(301) 590-3003. **$99-$179.** 9721 Washingtonian Blvd. I-270, exit 9B (I-370/Sam Eig Hwy), just w to Fields Rd, 0.8 mi se, then just ne. Int corridors. **Pets:** Accepted.
🆎🅂 🅂 ✕ 🐾M 🖉 🐾 ᕤ 🔲 ⊯ ✕

**▼▼▼ Summerfield Suites by Wyndham-Gaithersburg** 🅢🅗
(301) 527-6000. **$109-$157.** 200 Skidmore Blvd. I-370, exit SR 355, just n to Westland Rd. Ext corridors. **Pets:** Accepted.
🆎🅂 ✕ 🐾M 🖉 🐾 ᕤ 🔲 ⊯ ✕

**▼▼▼ TownePlace Suites by Marriott-Gaithersburg** 🅢🅗 ☙
(301) 590-2300. **$79-$189.** 212 Perry Pkwy. I-270, exit 10 northbound, just e; exit 11 southbound, just e on SR 124 to SR 355, 0.3 mi s, then 0.5 mi sw. Int corridors. **Pets:** Medium. $75 one-time fee/room.
🆎🅂 🅂 ✕ 🐾M 🖉 🐾 ᕤ 🔲 ⊯

## GERMANTOWN

**▼▼ Homestead Studio Suites Hotel-Germantown** 🅜
(301) 515-4500. **$95-$100.** 20141 Century Blvd. I-270, exit 15B, just w to Aircraft Dr, then just n. Ext corridors. **Pets:** $25 daily fee/pet. Service with restrictions, supervision.
🆎🅂 🅂 ✕ 🐾M 🖉 🐾 ᕤ 🔲

## GREENBELT

**▼▼▼ Residence Inn by Marriott-Greenbelt** 🅢🅗
(301) 982-1600. **$129-$249.** 6320 Golden Triangle Dr. I-95/495, exit 23, 0.5 mi sw of jct SR 201; off SR 193, just n on Walker Dr. Int corridors. **Pets:** Accepted.
🆎🅂 🅂 ✕ 🐾M 🖉 🐾 ᕤ 🔲 ⊯ ✕

## LANHAM

**▼▼ Red Roof Inn-Lanham** 🅜
(301) 731-8830. **$62-$86.** 9050 Lanham Severn Rd. I-95/495, exit 20A, 0.3 mi e on SR 450. Ext corridors. **Pets:** Accepted.
✕ ᕤ

## LARGO

**▼▼ Radisson Hotel Largo/Washington, D.C.** 🅢🅗
(301) 773-0700. **$89-$149.** 9100 Basil Ct. I-95/495, exit 17A (SR 202); off Capital Beltway. Int corridors. **Pets:** Accepted.
🆎🅂 🅂 ✕ 🐾M 🖉 🐾 ᕤ 🔲 🍽 ⊯

## LAUREL

**▼▼ Comfort Suites Laurel Lakes** 🅢🅗
(301) 206-2600. **$99-$134.** 14402 Laurel Pl. On US 1, 0.9 mi s of jct SR 198. Int corridors. **Pets:** Medium. $75 one-time fee/pet. Designated rooms, service with restrictions.
✕ 🖉 ᕤ 🔲 ⊯

**⚞⚟ ▼▼▼ Quality Inn & Suites Laurel** 🅢🅗
(301) 725-8800. **$85-$209.** One Second St. On US 1, 0.5 mi n of jct SR 198. Ext/int corridors. **Pets:** Small. $15 daily fee/room. Designated rooms, service with restrictions, crate.
🆂🅰🆅🅴 🅂 ✕ 🐾 ᕤ 🔲 ⊯

**▼▼ Ramada Inn-Laurel** 🅢🅗
(301) 498-0900. **$89-$99.** 3400 Fort Meade Rd. SR 198, 0.5 mi w of jct Baltimore-Washington Pkwy. Ext/int corridors. **Pets:** Accepted.
🆎🅂 🅂 ✕ 🖉 ᕤ 🔲 🍽 ⊯

**▼▼ Red Roof Inn-Laurel** 🅜
(301) 498-8811. **$65-$90.** 12525 Laurel Bowie Rd. On SR 197, 0.3 mi w of Baltimore-Washington Pkwy. Ext corridors. **Pets:** Accepted.
✕ 🖉 🐾 ᕤ

## ROCKVILLE

**⚞⚟ ▼▼▼ The Atrium Court Hotel, a Clarion Collection** 🅢🅗
(301) 840-0200. **$119-$199.** 3 Research Ct. I-270, exit 8 (Shady Grove Rd), just sw. Int corridors. **Pets:** Accepted.
🆂🅰🆅🅴 🅂 ✕ 🖉 🐾 ᕤ 🔲 ⊯

🔺 ▼▼💎 **Best Western Washington Gateway Hotel** 🔲
(301) 424-4940. **$79-$189.** 1251 W Montgomery Ave. I-270, exit 6B, just w on SR 28. Int corridors. **Pets:** Accepted.
[SAVE] [S🔒] [✕] [🌙] [🛏] [🔌] [💻] [🍴] [🏊]

▼▼ **Red Roof Inn-Rockville** 🔲
(301) 987-0965. **$76-$110.** 16001 Shady Grove Rd. I-270, exit 8 (Shady Grove Rd), 0.5 mi e. Ext corridors. **Pets:** Accepted.
[✕] [&M] [🌙] [🛏] [🔌]

🔺 ▼▼💎 **Woodfin Suites Hotel** 🔲
(301) 590-9880. **$204-$274.** 1380 Piccard Dr. I-270, exit 8 (Shady Grove Rd), 0.3 mi s; 1 mi w of SR 355 via Redland Rd. Ext corridors. **Pets:** Accepted.
[SAVE] [S🔒] [✕] [🌙] [🛏] [🔌] [💻] [🏊] [✕]

# END METROPOLITAN AREA

## EMMITSBURG

🔺 ▼▼💎 **Sleep Inn & Suites in Emmitsburg** 🔲
(301) 447-0044. **$77-$129.** 501 Silo Hill Pkwy. US 15. Int corridors. **Pets:** Large. $25 daily fee/pet. Designated rooms, service with restrictions, supervision.
[SAVE] [S🔒] [✕] [🛏] [🔌] [💻] [🏊]

## FREDERICK

▼▼💎▼ **Frederick Residence Inn by Marriott** 🔲
(301) 360-0010. **$99-$134.** 5230 Westview Dr. I-270, exit 31B, 0.5 mi sw on SR 85, 0.3 mi n on Crestwood Blvd. Int corridors. **Pets:** Accepted.
[ASK] [✕] [🛏] [🔌] [💻] [🏊] [✕]

🔺 ▼▼💎▼ **Hampton Inn** 🔲
(301) 698-2500. **$89-$129.** 5311 Buckeystown Pike (SR 85). I-270, exit 31B, 0.6 mi w. Int corridors. **Pets:** Accepted.
[SAVE] [S🔒] [✕] [🌙] [🛏] [🔌] [💻] [🍴] [🏊]

▼▼💎▼ **Holiday Inn Express-FSK Mall** 🔲
(301) 695-2881. **$84-$104.** 5579 Spectrum Dr. I-270, exit 31A, just e on SR 85. Int corridors. **Pets:** Other species. $25 deposit/room. Service with restrictions, supervision.
[ASK] [S🔒] [✕] [🌙] [🛏] [🔌] [💻]

▼▼💎▼ **Holiday Inn-Francis Scott Key Mall** 🔲 🐾
(301) 694-7500. **$99-$129.** 5400 Holiday Dr. I-270, exit 31A, just se of SR 85. Int corridors. **Pets:** Medium. $25 one-time fee/room. Service with restrictions, supervision.
[ASK] [S🔒] [✕] [🌙] [🛏] [🔌] [💻] [🍴] [🏊] [✕]

🔺 ▼▼💎▼ **Holiday Inn-Frederick/Ft Detrick** 🔲
(301) 662-5141. **$84-$114.** 999 W Patrick St. Just w on US 40 from jct US 15. Ext corridors. **Pets:** Accepted.
[SAVE] [S🔒] [✕] [🌙] [🛏] [🔌] [💻] [🍴] [🏊] [✕]

▼▼💎▼ **MainStay Suites** 🔲
(301) 668-4600. **$109-$149.** 7310 Executive Way. I-270, exit 31B. Int corridors. **Pets:** Small. $10 daily fee/pet, $100 one-time fee/room. Service with restrictions, supervision.
[ASK] [S🔒] [✕] [🛏] [🔌] [💻] [🏊]

▼▼ **Quality Inn Historic Frederick** 🔲
(301) 695-6200. **$69-$125.** 420 Prospect Blvd. US 15, exit Jefferson St, just se. Int corridors. **Pets:** Accepted.
[ASK] [S🔒] [✕] [🌙] [🛏] [🔌] [💻] [🏊] [✕]

## FROSTBURG

🔺 ▼▼💎 **Days Inn & Suites** 🔲
(301) 689-2050. **$69-$99.** 11100 New Georges Creek Rd. I-68, exit 34, 1 mi n on SR 36. Int corridors. **Pets:** Accepted.
[SAVE] [S🔒] [✕] [🌙] [🛏] [💻] [✕]

## GRANTSVILLE

▼▼💎▼ **Comfort Inn** 🔲
(301) 895-5993. **$69-$79.** 2541 Chestnut Ridge Rd. I-68, exit 22, just s on US 219. Int corridors. **Pets:** Accepted.
[S🔒] [✕] [🛏] [💻] [🏊]

## GRASONVILLE

🔺 ▼▼💎 **Best Western Kent Narrows Inn** Ⓜ ❀
(410) 827-6767. **$79-$199.** 3101 Main St. US 50 and 301, exit 42; at Kent Narrows Bridge. Ext corridors. **Pets:** Large, other species. $10 daily fee/room. Designated rooms, service with restrictions, supervision.
[SAVE] [S🔒] [✕] [🌙] [🛏] [🔌] [💻] [🏊] [✕]

## HAGERSTOWN

🔺 ▼▼ **Clarion Hotel & Conference Center Antietam Creek** 🔲
(301) 733-5100. **$69-$119.** 901 Dual Hwy. I-70, exit 32B, 2.3 mi w on US 40. Int corridors. **Pets:** Accepted.
[SAVE] [S🔒] [✕] [🌙] [🛏] [🔌] [💻] [🍴] [🏊]

▼▼ **Halfway Hagerstown Super 8** 🔲 🐾
(301) 582-1992. **$53-$69.** 16805 Blake Rd. I-81, exit 5B, just w. Int corridors. **Pets:** Medium. $15 deposit/pet, $11 one-time fee/pet. Service with restrictions, supervision.
[ASK] [S🔒] [✕] [🌙] [🛏] [🔌]

▼▼ **Motel 6-1259** Ⓜ
(301) 582-4445. **$45-$59.** 11321 Massey Blvd. I-81, exit 5, 0.5 mi e, 0.5 mi n of jct I-81 and 70. Ext corridors. **Pets:** Accepted.
[S🔒] [✕] [🌙] [🏊]

🔺 ▼▼💎 **Quality Inn Antietam Creek** 🔲
(301) 733-2700. **$59.** 1101 Dual Hwy. I-70, exit 32B, 2.2 mi w on US 40. Int corridors. **Pets:** Small, dogs only. $10 daily fee/pet. Service with restrictions, supervision.
[SAVE] [S🔒] [✕] [🛏] [💻]

🔺 ▼▼💎 **Sleep Inn & Suites** 🔲
(301) 766-9449. **$79-$149.** 18216 Col Henry K Douglas Dr. I-70, exit 29, just s. Int corridors. **Pets:** Other species. $10 one-time fee/pet. Service with restrictions, supervision.
[SAVE] [S🔒] [✕] [🌙] [🛏] [🔌] [💻]

## INDIAN HEAD

🔺 ▼▼💎 **Super 8 Motel** 🔲
(301) 753-8100. **$60-$80.** 4694 Indian Head Hwy. SR 210, 0.6 mi s of jct SR 225. Int corridors. **Pets:** Small, dogs only. $10 daily fee/pet. Designated rooms, service with restrictions, supervision.
[SAVE] [S🔒] [✕] [&M] [🛏]

## LA PLATA

🔺 ▼▼💎 **Best Western La Plata Inn** 🔲
(301) 934-4900. **$69-$109.** 6900 Crain Hwy. Jct SR 6, 0.4 mi s on US 301. Int corridors. **Pets:** Medium. $25 one-time fee/room. Designated rooms, service with restrictions, supervision.
[SAVE] [✕] [&M] [🌙] [🛏] [💻] [🏊]

## LA VALE

🔷🔷 Red Roof Inn **SH**
(301) 729-6700. **$70-$90.** 12310 Winchester Rd SW. I-68, exit 40, 0.6 mi s. Ext/int corridors. **Pets:** Accepted.
[SAVE] [S🔟] [✕] [🔟] [🔟] [🔟] [🔟]

🔷🔷 Super 8 Motel **M**
(301) 729-6265. **$54.** 1301 National Hwy. I-68, exit 40, 0.4 mi n. Int corridors. **Pets:** Accepted.
[ASK] [S🔟] [✕] [🔟]

## LEXINGTON PARK

🔺🔷🔷 Best Western Lexington Park **SH**
(301) 862-4100. **$69.** Rt 235. 3.2 mi n. Int corridors. **Pets:** Small, other species. $25 one-time fee/room. Service with restrictions, crate.
[SAVE] [S🔟] [✕] [🔟] [🔟] [🔟] [🔟]

## MCHENRY

🔷🔷 Comfort Inn at Deep Creek **SH**
(301) 387-4200. **$59-$169.** 2704 Deep Creek Dr. 1 mi s on US 219 from jct SR 42. Int corridors. **Pets:** Accepted.
[ASK] [S🔟] [✕] [🔟] [🔟] [🔟]

🔷🔷🔷 Wisp Mountain Resort/Hotel & Conference Center **SH** 🐾
(301) 387-5581. **$79-$259, 14 day notice.** 290 Marsh Hill Rd. 1 mi s on US 219 from jct SR 42, just w on Sang Run Rd, 0.3 mi s. Int corridors. **Pets:** Medium, dogs only. $50 one-time fee/pet. Designated rooms, service with restrictions, supervision.
[ASK] [S🔟] [✕] [🔟] [🔟] [🔟] [🔟] [🔟] [🔟] [🔟]

## NORTH EAST

🔷🔷🔷 Crystal Inn **SH**
(410) 287-7100. **$69-$119.** 1 Center Dr. I-95, exit 100, 0.3 mi se on SR 272. Int corridors. **Pets:** Accepted.
[ASK] [S🔟] [✕] [🔟] [🔟] [🔟] [🔟] [🔟]

## OCEAN CITY

🔺🔷🔷 Best Western Sea Bay Inn **SH**
(410) 524-6100. **$39-$289, 3 day notice.** 6007 Coastal Hwy. Jct 60th St and Coastal Hwy. Int corridors. **Pets:** Accepted.
[SAVE] [S🔟] [✕] [🔟] [🔟] [🔟] [🔟]

🔺🔷🔷🔷 Clarion Resort Fontainebleau Hotel **LH** 🐾
(410) 524-3535. **$99-$369, 3 day notice.** 10100 Coastal Hwy. 101st St and the ocean. Int corridors. **Pets:** Large. $30 daily fee/pet. Designated rooms, service with restrictions, supervision.
[SAVE] [S🔟] [✕] [🔟] [🔟] [🔟] [🔟] [🔟] [🔟]

🔺🔷🔷 Fenwick Inn **SH**
(410) 250-1100. **$39-$269, 3 day notice.** 13801 Coastal Hwy. 138th St and Coastal Hwy. Int corridors. **Pets:** Small, other species. $10 daily fee/pet. Designated rooms, service with restrictions.
[SAVE] [✕] [🔟] [🔟] [🔟] [🔟]

## PERRYVILLE

🔺🔷🔷 Ramada Perryville **SH**
(410) 642-2866. **$69-$109.** 61 Heather Ln. I-95, exit 93, just e. Ext corridors. **Pets:** Accepted.
[SAVE] [S🔟] [✕] [🔟] [🔟] [🔟]

## PRINCESS ANNE

🔷🔷🔷 Waterloo Country Inn **CI**
(410) 651-0883. **$125-$255, 7 day notice.** 28822 Mt. Vernon Rd. 3.3 mi w on SR 362 from jct US 13. Int corridors. **Pets:** Accepted.
[✕] [🔟] [🔟] [🔟] [🔟] [🔟]

## ROCK HALL

🔷🔷🔷 Inn at Huntingfield Creek **BB** 🐾
(410) 639-7779. **$125-$200, 10 day notice.** 4928 Eastern Neck Rd. 1.8 mi s on SR 445 from jct SR 20. Ext/int corridors. **Pets:** Large. Designated rooms, service with restrictions, crate.
[ASK] [S🔟] [✕] [🔟] [🔟] [🔟] [🔟] [🔟]

🔷 Mariners Motel **M** 🐾
(410) 639-2291. **$75-$85.** 5681 S Hawthorne Ave. 0.3 mi e of SR 20. Ext corridors. **Pets:** Crate.
[✕] [🔟] [🔟] [🔟]

## ST. MICHAELS

🔺🔷🔷 The Parsonage Inn **BB**
(410) 745-5519. **$125-$195, 10 day notice.** 210 N Talbot St. 0.3 mi w on SR 33. Ext/int corridors. **Pets:** Small, dogs only. $25 one-time fee/pet. Designated rooms, service with restrictions, supervision.
[SAVE] [S🔟] [✕] [🔟]

## SALISBURY

🔺🔷🔷 Americas Best Value Inn Salisbury **SH** 🐾
(410) 742-7194. **$49-$149, 3 day notice.** 2625 N Salisbury Blvd. US 13, 1 mi n of jct US 50 Bypass. Ext corridors. **Pets:** Other species. $10 daily fee/pet. Service with restrictions, crate.
[SAVE] [S🔟] [✕] [🔟] [🔟] [🔟] [🔟]

🔺🔷🔷 Best Western Salisbury Plaza **M**
(410) 546-1300. **$59-$145.** 1735 N Salisbury Blvd. US 13 business route, 0.5 mi s of US 50 Bypass. Ext corridors. **Pets:** Other species. $10 daily fee/pet. Service with restrictions, crate.
[SAVE] [S🔟] [✕] [🔟] [🔟] [🔟]

🔺🔷🔷 Comfort Inn Salisbury **SH**
(410) 543-4666. **$64-$134.** 2701 N Salisbury Blvd. US 13, 0.5 mi n of jct US 13 business route and Bypass. Int corridors. **Pets:** Accepted.
[SAVE] [S🔟] [✕] [🔟] [🔟] [🔟]

🔷🔷🔷 Ramada Inn and Conference Center **LH**
(410) 546-4400. **$70-$149.** 300 S Salisbury Blvd. US 13 business route, 0.4 mi s of jct Business US 50; downtown. Int corridors. **Pets:** Medium, dogs only. $25 one-time fee/pet. Service with restrictions, supervision.
[ASK] [S🔟] [✕] [🔟] [🔟] [🔟] [🔟]

## SNOW HILL

🔷🔷🔷 River House Inn **BB**
(410) 632-2722. **$125-$300, 7 day notice.** 201 E Market St. 1 mi w on SR 394 from jct SR 113. Ext/int corridors. **Pets:** Accepted.
[ASK] [S🔟] [✕] [🔟] [🔟] [🔟] [🔟]

## SOLOMONS

🔷🔷 Comfort Inn Beacon Marina **SH**
(410) 326-6303. **$89-$199.** 255 Lore Rd. Off SR 2/4. Int corridors. **Pets:** Small. $20 daily fee/pet. Designated rooms, no service, crate.
[ASK] [S🔟] [✕] [🔟] [🔟] [🔟] [🔟]

## THURMONT

🔺🔷🔷 Rambler Inn **M**
(301) 271-2424. **$42-$108, 3 day notice.** US 15 at SR 550. Ext/int corridors. **Pets:** Medium, other species. $7 daily fee/pet. Designated rooms, service with restrictions, supervision.
[SAVE] [S🔟] [✕] [🔟]

# WHITEHAVEN

◆◆ **Whitehaven Bed & Breakfast** BB
(410) 873-3294. **$95-$105, 3 day notice.** 23844 River St. SR 352 to
Whitehaven Rd, then w. Int corridors. **Pets:** Accepted.
⊠ 🖵 📶 ☎

# WILLIAMSPORT

◆◆◆ ◆◆ **Red Roof Inn** SH
(301) 582-3500. **$54-$79, 11 day notice.** 310 E Potomac St. I-81, exit
2, 0.3 mi sw on US 11. Ext corridors. **Pets:** Small. $5 daily fee/pet.
Service with restrictions, supervision.
SAVE S📶 ⊠ 📶 🖫

# MASSACHUSETTS

## AMHERST

**WWWW The Lord Jeffery Inn** SH
(413) 253-2576. **$89-$239.** 30 Boltwood Ave. I-91, exit 19, 6 mi e on SR 9 to Commons. Int corridors. **Pets:** $15 daily fee/pet. Designated rooms, service with restrictions, supervision.
[ASK] [X] [D] [II]

**WW University Lodge** M
(413) 256-8111. **$50-$170.** 345 N Pleasant St. 0.6 mi n. Ext corridors. **Pets:** Medium, dogs only. $20 daily fee/pet. Designated rooms, service with restrictions, supervision.
[ASK] [SD] [X] [D] [D]

## AUBURN

**WWW WWW Baymont Inn & Suites Worcester-Auburn** SH
(508) 832-7000. **$85-$125.** 446 Southbridge St. I-90, exit 10, 1.2 mi n on SR 12. Int corridors. **Pets:** Medium. Service with restrictions.
[SAVE] [X] [D] [D]

## BARRE

**WWW WWW Jenkins Inn** CI ✿
(978) 355-6444. **$165-$190, 7 day notice.** 7 West St. On SR 122 and 32. Int corridors. **Pets:** Dogs only. $5 daily fee/pet. Service with restrictions, supervision.
[SAVE] [SD] [X] [D] [II]

---

# BOSTON METROPOLITAN AREA

## ANDOVER

**WWW WWWW Comfort Suites** SH
(978) 475-6000. **$89-$109.** 4 Riverside Dr. I-93, exit 45, 0.5 mi e. Int corridors. **Pets:** Medium. $10 daily fee/room, $50 one-time fee/pet. Designated rooms, service with restrictions, crate.
[SAVE] [SD] [X] [LM] [D] [D] [D] [D] [D] [X]

**WWWWW La Quinta Inn** SH
(978) 685-6200. **$89-$140.** 131 River Rd. I-93, exit 45, 2 mi n of I-495, exit 40B. Int corridors. **Pets:** Medium. Service with restrictions.
[ASK] [X] [D] [D] [D]

**WWWW Residence Inn by Marriott Boston-Andover** SH
(978) 683-0382. **$144-$179.** 500 Minuteman Rd. I-93, exit 45, 0.3 mi w, then 0.5 mi n. Int corridors. **Pets:** Medium, other species. $75 one-time fee/room. Designated rooms, service with restrictions, crate.
[ASK] [SD] [X] [LM] [D] [D] [D] [D] [D] [X]

**WWW WWW Staybridge Suites Boston/Andover** SH
(978) 686-2000. **$129-$159.** 4 Tech Dr. I-93, exit 45, just sw via Shattuck Rd. Int corridors. **Pets:** Accepted.
[SAVE] [SD] [X] [LM] [D] [D] [D] [D]

**WWW WWWW Wyndham Andover Hotel** LH
(978) 975-3600. **$89-$179.** 123 Old River Rd. I-93, exit 45, just e on River Rd. Int corridors. **Pets:** Accepted.
[SAVE] [X] [D] [D] [D] [D] [II] [D] [X]

## ARLINGTON

**WWWW Hawthorn Suites Ltd** SH
(781) 643-7258. **$139-$229.** 1 Massachusetts Ave. On SR 2A, just n of SR 16. Int corridors. **Pets:** Accepted.
[ASK] [SD] [X] [LM] [D] [D] [D]

## BILLERICA

**WWWWW Homewood Suites by Hilton** SH
(978) 670-7111. **$159-$189.** 35 Middlesex Tpke. I-95, exit 32B, 2.5 mi n. Int corridors. **Pets:** Accepted.
[ASK] [SD] [X] [D] [D] [D] [D] [D] [D]

## BOSTON

**WWWW Boston Harbor Hotel** LH ✿
(617) 439-7000. **$245-$635.** 70 Rowes Wharf. At Rowes Wharf. Int corridors. **Pets:** Large, other species. Designated rooms, service with restrictions, crate.
[X] [D] [II] [D] [X]

**WWW WWWW Boston Omni Parker House Hotel** LH
(617) 227-8600. **$199-$409.** 60 School St. Corner of Tremont and School sts; northeast corner of Boston Common. Int corridors. **Pets:** Accepted.
[SAVE] [SD] [X] [D] [II]

**WWW WWW The Boston Park Plaza Hotel & Towers** LH
(617) 426-2000. **$139-$429.** 64 Arlington St. Just s of Boston Common and Public Gardens. Int corridors. **Pets:** Accepted.
[SAVE] [SD] [X] [D] [D] [D] [D] [II]

**WWW WWW Comfort Inn Boston** SH
(617) 287-9200. **$89-$179.** 900 William T Morrissey Blvd. I-93, exit 13 northbound, 0.5 mi sw; exit 12 southbound, follow signs. Int corridors. **Pets:** Other species. Service with restrictions, supervision.
[SAVE] [SD] [X] [D] [D] [D] [D]

**WWWW Courtyard by Marriott Boston, Copley Square** SH
(617) 437-9300. **$149-$349.** 88 Exeter St. I-90, exit 22, just n; between Huntington Ave and Boylston St. Int corridors. **Pets:** Accepted.
[ASK] [SD] [X] [LM] [D] [D] [D] [D]

▼▼▼ DoubleTree Guest Suites-Boston/Cambridge SH
(617) 783-0090. **$109-$309.** 400 Soldiers Field Rd. I-90, exit 20 westbound; exit 18 eastbound. Int corridors. **Pets:** $250 deposit/room. Designated rooms, service with restrictions, crate.

⬡⬡ ▼▼▼ ▼▼▼ The Eliot Hotel SH ❀
(617) 267-1607. **$285-$465.** 370 Commonwealth Ave. Corner of Commonwealth and Massachusetts aves. Int corridors. **Pets:** Other species. Service with restrictions, crate.

⬡⬡ ▼▼▼ Embassy Suites Boston at Logan Airport SH
(617) 567-5000. **$109-$309.** 207 Porter St. I-90, exit 20, at Logan Airport; rental car returns. Int corridors. **Pets:** Accepted.

⬡⬡ ▼▼▼ ▼▼▼ The Fairmont Copley Plaza
Boston LH ❀
(617) 267-5300. **$159-$479.** 138 St. James Ave. At Copley Square. Int corridors. **Pets:** $25 daily fee/pet. Service with restrictions, supervision.

⬡⬡ ▼▼▼ ▼▼▼ Fifteen Beacon SH
(617) 670-1500. **$350-$1900.** 15 Beacon St. Just e of State House; just ne of Boston Common; center. Int corridors. **Pets:** Accepted.

⬡⬡ ▼▼▼ ▼▼▼ Four Seasons Hotel Boston LH
(617) 338-4400. **$425-$825.** 200 Boylston St. Between Arlington and Charles sts. Int corridors. **Pets:** Accepted.

⬡⬡ ▼▼▼ ▼▼▼ Hilton Boston Logan Airport LH
(617) 568-6700. **$119-$475.** 85 Terminal Rd. At General Edward Lawrence Logan International Airport. Int corridors. **Pets:** Medium. Service with restrictions, crate.

⬡⬡ ▼▼▼ ▼▼▼ Hotel Commonwealth LH ❀
(617) 933-5000. **$159-$449.** 500 Commonwealth Ave. On SR 2 at Beacon St and Brookine Ave. Int corridors. **Pets:** Small. $25 one-time fee/pet. Service with restrictions, supervision.

▼ Howard Johnson Hotel Fenway SH
(617) 267-8300. **$109-$279.** 1271 Boylston St. I-90, exit Brookline Ave S, backing onto Fenway Park. Int corridors. **Pets:** Accepted.

⬡⬡ ▼▼▼ ▼▼▼ Hyatt Regency Boston LH
(617) 912-1234. **$139-$315.** One Ave de Lafayette. Just e of Boston Common at Lafayette Pl. Int corridors. **Pets:** Accepted.

⬡⬡ ▼▼▼ ▼▼▼ Langham Hotel Boston LH
(617) 451-1900. **$330-$445.** 250 Franklin St. Center; on Post Office Square. Int corridors. **Pets:** Accepted.

⬡⬡ ▼▼▼ ▼▼▼ Nine Zero Hotel SH
(617) 772-5800. **$249-$5000.** 90 Tremont St. Just ne of Boston Common; motor entrance on Bosworth, just s of property; center. Int corridors. **Pets:** Accepted.

⬡⬡ ▼▼▼ ▼▼▼ Onyx Hotel SH
(617) 557-9955. **$159-$369.** 155 Portland St. Just n corner of Merrimac and Traverse sts; 3 blks s of Fleet Center. Int corridors. **Pets:** Accepted.

⬡⬡ ▼▼▼ Ramada Boston SH
(617) 287-9100. **$89-$179.** 800 William T Morrissey Blvd. I-93, exit 13 northbound, 0.5 mi sw; exit 12 southbound, follow signs. Int corridors. **Pets:** Other species. Service with restrictions, supervision.

⬡⬡ ▼▼▼ Residence Inn by Marriott Boston Harbor on
Tudor Wharf SH
(617) 242-9000. **$169-$399.** 34-44 Charles River Ave. Just se of SR 99 at Charlestown Bridge. Int corridors. **Pets:** Other species. $75 one-time fee/room. Service with restrictions.

⬡⬡ ▼▼▼ ▼▼▼ The Ritz-Carlton, Boston LH
(617) 536-5700. **$335-$575.** 15 Arlington St. At Arlington and Newbury sts; overlooks the Public Gardens. Int corridors. **Pets:** Accepted.

⬡⬡ ▼▼▼ ▼▼▼ The Ritz-Carlton Boston Common SH
(617) 574-7100. **$295-$725.** 10 Avery St. At Washington and Avery sts; 1 blk e of Boston Common. Int corridors. **Pets:** Accepted.

⬡⬡ ▼▼▼ ▼▼▼ Seaport Hotel LH
(617) 385-4000. **$179-$299.** 1 Seaport Ln. At World Trade Center/Commonwealth Pier. Int corridors. **Pets:** Accepted.

⬡⬡ ▼▼▼ Sheraton Boston LH ❀
(617) 236-2000. **$99-$1500.** 39 Dalton St. I-90, exit 22. Int corridors. **Pets:** Medium. Service with restrictions, supervision.

⬡⬡ ▼▼▼ ▼▼▼ The Westin Copley Place Boston LH
(617) 262-9600. **$199-$479, 3 day notice.** 10 Huntington Ave. I-90, exit 22, at Copley Square. Int corridors. **Pets:** Accepted.

## BOXBOROUGH

▼▼▼ Holiday Inn Boxborough Woods SH
(978) 263-8701. **$117-$159 (no credit cards).** 242 Adams Pl. I-495, exit 28, just e on SR 111. Int corridors. **Pets:** Accepted.

## BRAINTREE

⬡⬡ ▼▼▼ Holiday Inn Express-Braintree SH ❀
(781) 848-1260. **$69-$139.** 190 Wood Rd. I-93, exit 6, just n on SR 37, then 0.4 mi w. Int corridors. **Pets:** Other species. $10 daily fee/pet. Designated rooms, no service, supervision.

▼▼▼ Sheraton Braintree Hotel LH ❀
(781) 848-0600. **$149-$189.** 37 Forbes Rd. I-93, exit 6, just s on SR 37, then just w. Int corridors. **Pets:** Medium, dogs only. Service with restrictions, crate.

## BROOKLINE

▼▼▼ Holiday Inn Brookline SH
(617) 277-1200. **$109-$259.** 1200 Beacon St. 1 mi sw of Kenmore Square; at Beacon and St. Paul sts. Int corridors. **Pets:** Accepted.

## BURLINGTON

▼▼ Homestead Studio Suites
Hotel-Boston/Burlington SH
(781) 359-9099. **$105.** 40 South Ave. I-95, exit 32B, just n. Int corridors. **Pets:** $25 daily fee/pet. Service with restrictions, supervision.

▼▼▼ **Staybridge Suites Boston-Burlington** SH ❀
(781) 221-2233. **$134-$169.** 11 Old Concord Rd. I-95, exit 32B, just s on Middlesex Tpke. Int corridors. **Pets:** Medium, other species. $12 daily fee/pet. Service with restrictions.
ASK S⊘ ⊠ &M ⊘ ⊡ ❚ ▣ ⇌

▼▼▼ **Summerfield Suites by Wyndham-Boston/Burlington** SH
(781) 270-0800. **$129-$199.** 2 Van de Graaff Dr. I-95/SR 128, exit 33A, just s on US 3, then 0.5 mi w on Wayside Rd. Int corridors. **Pets:** Accepted.
ASK ⊠ &M ⊘ ⊡ ❚ ▣ ⇌ ⊠

# CAMBRIDGE

▼▼▼ **Best Western Hotel Tria** SH ❀
(617) 491-8000. **$149-$299.** 220 Alewife Brook Pkwy. Jct SR 2, 16 and US 3; in N Cambridge; I-90 (Massachusetts Tpke), exit Cambridge/Allston to SR 2 W (Fresh Pond Pkwy). Int corridors. **Pets:** $25 daily fee/room.
ASK S⊘ ⊠ ⊘ ⊡ ❚ ▣ ⑪ ⇌

🆀 ▼▼▼ ▼▼▼ **The Charles Hotel, Harvard Square** LH
(617) 864-1200. **$399-$599.** One Bennett St. Corner of Eliot and Bennett sts; just s of Harvard Square. Int corridors. **Pets:** Accepted.
SAVE S⊘ ⊠ &M ⊘ ⊡ ❚ ▣ ⑪ ⇌ ⊠

🆀 ▼▼▼ ▼▼▼ **Hotel @ MIT** SH
(617) 577-0200. **$119-$459.** 20 Sidney St. On SR 2A, 1 mi n of the river. Int corridors. **Pets:** Accepted.
SAVE ⊠ &M ⊘ ⊡ ❚ ▣ ⑪

🆀 ▼▼▼ ▼▼▼ **Hotel Marlowe** SH
(617) 868-8000. **$139-$299.** 25 Edwin H Land Blvd. Just sw of jct SR 28. Int corridors. **Pets:** Accepted.
SAVE S⊘ ⊠ &M ⊘ ⊡ ❚ ▣ ⑪ ⊠

🆀 ▼▼▼ ▼▼▼ **Hyatt Regency Cambridge** LH
(617) 492-1234. **$139-$295.** 575 Memorial Dr. On US 3 and SR 2. Int corridors. **Pets:** Accepted.
SAVE ⊠ &M ⊘ ⊡ ❚ ▣ ⑪ ⇌ ⊠

▼▼▼ **Residence Inn by Marriott Cambridge** LH
(617) 349-0700. **$329-$529.** 6 Cambridge Center. Corner of Ames St and Broadway. Int corridors. **Pets:** Large, other species. $150 one-time fee/room. Designated rooms, service with restrictions.
ASK S⊘ ⊠ &M ⊘ ⊡ ❚ ▣ ⇌

▼▼▼ **Sheraton Commander Hotel** SH ❀
(617) 547-4800. **$99-$320.** 16 Garden St. Just n of Harvard Square. Int corridors. **Pets:** Medium, dogs only. Service with restrictions, supervision.
ASK S⊘ ⊠ &M ⊘ ⊡ ❚ ▣ ⑪

# CONCORD

▼▼ **Best Western at Historic Concord** SH
(978) 369-6100. **$109-$159.** 740 Elm St. 1.8 mi w, just off SR 2 and 2A. Int corridors. **Pets:** Other species. $10 daily fee/room. Designated rooms, service with restrictions, supervision.
ASK S⊘ ⊠ ❚ ▣ ⇌

# DANVERS

▼ **Motel 6 Boston-Danvers #1078** M
(978) 774-8045. **$60-$81.** 65 Newbury St. On US 1 northbound, just n of SR 114. Int corridors. **Pets:** Accepted.
S⊘ ⊠ ⇌

▼▼▼ **Residence Inn by Marriott** SH ❀
(978) 777-7171. **$139-$199.** 51 Newbury St (Rt 1). US 1 N, just s of jct SR 114. Ext corridors. **Pets:** $75 one-time fee/room. Service with restrictions, supervision.
ASK S⊘ ⊠ ♿ ❚ ▣ ⇌ ⊠

🆀 ▼▼▼ **Sheraton Ferncroft Resort** LH ❀
(978) 777-2500. **$79-$199.** 50 Ferncroft Rd. I-95, exit 50, follow signs for US 1 S to Ferncroft Village. Int corridors. **Pets:** Medium, dogs only. Service with restrictions, supervision.
SAVE ⊠ &M ⊘ ⊡ ❚ ▣ ⑪ ⇌ ⊠

🆀 ▼▼▼ **TownePlace Suites by Marriott** SH
(978) 777-6222. **$109-$159.** 238 Andover St. Southwest corner of jct US 1 and SR 114; SR 114 eastbound, enter just w of US 1 (no westbound entrance); US 1 southbound, enter through shopping center. Int corridors. **Pets:** Accepted.
⊠ &M ⊘ ⊡ ❚ ▣

# DEDHAM

🆀 ▼▼▼ **Holiday Inn Boston/Dedham Hotel & Conference Center** SH
(781) 329-1000. **$104-$139.** 55 Ariadne Rd. I-95, exit 15A, on US 1. Int corridors. **Pets:** $25 one-time fee/room. Designated rooms, service with restrictions, supervision.
SAVE S⊘ ⊠ &M ❚ ▣ ⑪ ⇌

🆀 ▼▼▼ **Residence Inn by Marriott** SH
(781) 407-0999. **$109-$219.** 259 Elm St. I-95, exit 15A, just n, then 0.4 mi e. Int corridors. **Pets:** Accepted.
SAVE S⊘ ⊠ ⊘ ⊡ ❚ ▣ ⇌ ⊠

# FOXBORO

▼▼▼ **Foxborough Residence Inn by Marriott** SH
(508) 698-2800. **$109-$179.** 250 Foxborough Blvd. I-95, exit 7A, 0.6 mi s on SR 140, 0.7 mi e, then just r. Int corridors. **Pets:** Medium. $75 one-time fee/room. Service with restrictions, crate.
ASK ⊠ &M ⊘ ⊡ ❚ ▣ ⇌ ⊠

# FRAMINGHAM

▼▼ **Best Western Framingham** SH
(508) 872-8811. **$99-$129.** 130 Worcester Rd. I-90, exit 13, 0.5 mi s to SR 9; 1 mi w of Speen St; just w of Shopper's World Mall. Int corridors. **Pets:** Designated rooms, service with restrictions, supervision.
ASK S⊘ ⊠ ❚ ▣ ⑪ ⇌

▼▼ **Red Roof Inn #7068** M
(508) 872-4499. **$72-$96.** 650 Cochituate Rd. I-90, exit 13, follow SR 30 E. Ext corridors. **Pets:** Accepted.
⊠ ❚ ▣

🆀 ▼▼▼ **Residence Inn by Marriott** SH
(508) 370-0001. **$174-$209.** 400 Staples Dr. SR 9 W to Crossing Blvd, then s. Int corridors. **Pets:** Large, other species. $75 one-time fee/room.
SAVE S⊘ ⊠ &M ⊘ ⊡ ❚ ▣ ⇌

▼▼▼ **Sheraton-Framingham** LH
(508) 879-7200. **$259.** 1657 Worcester Rd. I-90, exit 12, follow signs to SR 9 W. Int corridors. **Pets:** Accepted.
ASK ⊠ ⊘ ⊡ ❚ ▣ ⑪ ⇌ ⊠

# FRANKLIN

▼▼▼ **Franklin Residence Inn by Marriott** SH ❀
(508) 541-8188. **$89-$189.** 4 Forge Pkwy. I-495, exit 17, 0.7 mi nw off SR 140 N. Int corridors. **Pets:** $75 one-time fee/room. Service with restrictions, supervision.
ASK S⊘ ⊠ &M ⊘ ⊡ ❚ ▣ ⇌

▼▼▼ **Hawthorn Suites Ltd** SH
(508) 553-3500. **$99-$220.** 835 Upper Union St. I-495, exit 16, just s, then 0.3 mi e. Int corridors. **Pets:** Accepted.
ASK S⊘ ⊠ &M ⊘ ⊡ ❚ ▣ ⇌

# GLOUCESTER

▼▼/▼▼ Cape Ann Motor Inn **M**
(978) 281-2900. **$75-$160, 7 day notice.** 33 Rockport Rd. 2 mi n of terminus of SR 128 via SR 127A. Ext corridors. **Pets:** Service with restrictions, supervision

⊗ 🖬 ⚠

# HAVERHILL

⚠ ▼▼/▼▼ Best Western Merrimack Valley **SH**
(978) 373-1511. **$69-$179, 3 day notice.** 401 Lowell Ave. I-495, exit 49 (SR 110). Int corridors. **Pets:** Medium. $20 daily fee/pet. Service with restrictions, supervision.

SAVE 🖬 ⊗ 🖬 ⚌ ➦

# LAWRENCE

▼▼/▼▼ Hampton Inn Boston/North Andover **SH**
(978) 975-4050. **$79-$129.** 224 Winthrop Ave. I-495, exit 42A, just s on SR 114. Int corridors. **Pets:** Accepted.

ASK 🖬 ⊗ ⚊M ⚑ 🖬 ⚌

# LEXINGTON

⚠ ▼▼/▼▼ Sheraton Lexington Hotel **SH** ⚘
(781) 862-8700. **$99-$139.** 727 Marrett Rd. Jct I-95 and SR 128, exit 30B (SR 2A). Int corridors. **Pets:** Medium, dogs only. $25 one-time fee/room. Service with restrictions, supervision.

SAVE 🖬 ⊗ 🖬 ⚌ 🍴

# MARLBOROUGH

▼▼/▼▼ Embassy Suites Hotel-Boston Marlborough **LH**
(508) 485-5900. **$129-$189.** 123 Boston Post Rd W. I-495, exit 24B, 0.5 mi w; just off US 20. Int corridors. **Pets:** Accepted.

ASK ⊗ ⚊M ⚑ 🖬 ⚌ 🍴 ➦ ⊗

▼▼ Homestead Studio Suites
Hotel-Boston/Marlborough **SH**
(508) 490-9911. **$105.** 19 Northborough Rd E. I-495, exit 24B, just w on US 20. Int corridors. **Pets:** $25 daily fee/pet. Service with restrictions, supervision.

ASK 🖬 ⊗ ⚑ 🖬 ⚌

# NATICK

⚠ ▼▼ Boston/Natick Travelodge **M**
(508) 655-2222. **$59-$129.** 1350 Worcester St. I-90 (Massachusetts Tpke), exit 13, SR 9W; eastbound side. Ext corridors. **Pets:** Accepted.

SAVE ⊗ 🖬 ⚌

# NEEDHAM

▼▼/▼▼ Sheraton Needham Hotel **LH** ⚘
(781) 444-1110. **$159-$209.** 100 Cabot St. I-95, exit 19A, just e. Int corridors. **Pets:** Small. Service with restrictions, supervision.

ASK 🖬 ⊗ 🖬 ⚌ 🍴 ➦ ⊗

# NEWTON

⚠ ▼▼/▼▼ Holiday Inn Newton **SH**
(617) 969-5300. **$149-$189.** 399 Grove St. I-95, exit 22, just e; 0.3 mi s of I-90. Int corridors. **Pets:** Accepted.

SAVE 🖬 ⊗ ⚑ 🖬 ⚌ 🍴 ➦

⚠ ▼▼/▼▼ Sheraton Newton Hotel **LH**
(617) 969-3010. **$105-$129.** 320 Washington St. I-90 (Massachusetts Tpke), exit 17 (SR 16). Int corridors. **Pets:** Accepted.

SAVE ⊗ ⚑ 🖬 ⚌ 🍴 ➦

# NORTH CHELMSFORD

▼▼/▼▼ Hawthorn Suites, LTD **SH** ⚘
(978) 256-5151. **$69-$124.** 25 Research Pl. US 3, exit 32, 0.3 mi ne on SR 4. Int corridors. **Pets:** Medium, other species. $10 daily fee/room, $50 one-time fee/room. Designated rooms, service with restrictions, crate.

ASK 🖬 ⊗ ⚊M ⚑ 🖬 ⚌ ➦

# PEABODY

▼▼/▼▼ Homestead Studio Suites
Hotel-Boston/Peabody **SH**
(978) 531-6632. **$85.** 200 Jubilee Dr. SR 128, exit 28, just s to Centennial Dr, w to the end, n to Jubilee Dr, then 1.1 mi e. Int corridors. **Pets:** $25 daily fee/pet. Service with restrictions.

ASK 🖬 ⊗ ⚑ ⚑ 🖬 ⚌ ➦

▼▼/▼▼ Homewood Suites by Hilton **SH**
(978) 536-5050. **$99-$199.** 57 Newbury St. On US 1, northbound; I-95 and SR 128, exit 44B, just n, then left on Dearborn Rd. Int corridors. **Pets:** Accepted.

ASK 🖬 ⊗ ⚊M ⚑ ⚑ 🖬 ⚌ ➦

# REVERE

▼▼/▼▼ Comfort Inn & Suites Boston Airport **SH**
(781) 485-3600. **$79-$149.** 85 American Legion Hwy. Jct SR 1A and 60, 3 mi n of General Edward Lawrence Logan International Airport. Int corridors. **Pets:** Medium, other species. $10 daily fee/room. Service with restrictions, supervision.

ASK 🖬 ⊗ ⚑ 🖬 ⚌ 🍴 ➦

▼▼/▼▼ Hampton Inn Boston Logan Airport **SH**
(781) 286-5665. **$99-$179.** 230 Lee Burbank Hwy. On SR 1A, 1.9 mi n of General Edward Lawrence Logan International Airport; 0.6 mi s of terminus SR 60. Int corridors. **Pets:** Medium. $25 one-time fee/pet. Service with restrictions, supervision.

ASK 🖬 ⊗ ⚊M ⚑ ⚑ 🖬 🖬 ⚌ ➦

# SALEM

▼▼/▼▼ Hawthorne Hotel **SH** ⚘
(978) 744-4080. **$104-$209, 3 day notice.** 18 Washington Square W. On SR 1A. Int corridors. **Pets:** Other species. $10 daily fee/pet. Designated rooms, service with restrictions, supervision.

ASK 🖬 ⊗ 🖬 🍴

▼▼/▼▼ The Salem Inn **BB**
(978) 741-0680. **$119-$250, 7 day notice.** 7 Summer St. On SR 114 at Essex St; SR 128, exit 25A, 3 mi e. Int corridors. **Pets:** Other species. $15 daily fee/pet. Designated rooms, service with restrictions, supervision.

⊗ 🖬 ⚌

# SAUGUS

▼▼ Red Roof Inn #7305 **SH**
(781) 941-1400. **$84-$116.** 920 Broadway (US 1). I-95, exit 44 northbound, 3.2 mi s on US 1; exit Main St/Saugus southbound to U-turn. Int corridors. **Pets:** Accepted.

⊗ ⚊M ⚑ 🖬

# SUDBURY

▼▼/▼▼ Clarion Carriage House Inn **SH**
(978) 443-2223. **$129-$219.** 738 Boston Post Rd. I-495, exit 24A, 7.5 mi e on US 20; 4.7 mi w of jct SR 27 on US 20. Int corridors. **Pets:** Other species. $10 daily fee/pet. Service with restrictions, supervision.

ASK 🖬 ⊗ 🖬 ⚌

# TEWKSBURY

⚠ ▼▼/▼▼ Holiday Inn Tewksbury/Andover **SH**
(978) 640-9000. **$75-$129.** 4 Highwood Dr. I-495, exit 39, just w on SR 133. Int corridors. **Pets:** $50 one-time fee/room. Designated rooms, service with restrictions, supervision.

SAVE 🖬 ⊗ ⚑ 🖬 ⚌ 🍴 ➦ ⊗

**▼ Motel 6 Boston-Tewksbury #1403 M**
(978) 851-8677. **$63-$81.** 95 Main St. I-495, exit 38, just s on SR 38.
Ext corridors. **Pets:** Accepted.

**▼▼▼ Residence Inn by Marriott-Boston/Tewksbury SH**
(978) 640-1003. **$79-$169.** 1775 Andover St. I-495, exit 39, 0.3 mi w on
SR 133. Ext corridors. **Pets:** Large, other species. $75 one-time fee/room.
Service with restrictions.

**▼▼▼ TownePlace Suites by Marriott SH**
(978) 863-9800. **$54-$124.** 20 International Pl. I-495, exit 39, 0.3 mi nw.
Int corridors. **Pets:** Accepted.

## WAKEFIELD

**▼▼▼ Sheraton Colonial Hotel & Golf Club Boston
North LH**
(781) 245-9300. **$79-$229.** 1 Audubon Rd. I-95, exit 42, just n. Int
corridors. **Pets:** Accepted.

## WALTHAM

**▼▼▼ Courtyard by Marriott Boston-Waltham SH**
(781) 419-0900. **$151-$180.** 387 Winter St. I-95, exit 27A, on northeast
corner. Int corridors. **Pets:** $50 one-time fee/room. Supervision.

**▼▼▼ Extended Stay Deluxe Boston-Waltham SH**
(781) 622-1900. **$95.** 32 Fourth Ave. I-95, exit 27A, just se. Int corri-
dors. **Pets:** $25 daily fee/pet. Service with restrictions, supervision.

**▼▼▼ Holiday Inn Express Boston/Waltham SH**
(781) 890-2800. **$98-$125.** 385 Winter St. I-95, exit 27A, just ne. Ext/int
corridors. **Pets:** $50 one-time fee/room. Supervision.

**▼▼ Homestead Studio Suites Hotel-Boston/Waltham SH**
(781) 890-1333. **$90.** 52 Fourth Ave. I-95, exit 27A, just se; behind The
Westin, Waltham-Boston. Int corridors. **Pets:** $25 daily fee/pet. Service
with restrictions, supervision.

**▼▼▼ Home Suites Inn of Boston-Waltham SH**
(781) 890-3000. **$112-$140.** 455 Totten Pond Rd. I-95, exit 27A, just s.
Int corridors. **Pets:** Other species. $50 one-time fee/room. Supervision.

**AAA ▼▼▼ Hyatt House SH**
(781) 290-0026. **$149-$189.** 54 Fourth Ave. I-95, exit 27A, just e;
behind The Westin, Waltham-Boston. Int corridors. **Pets:** Accepted.

**▼▼▼ The Westin, Waltham-Boston LH 🐾**
(781) 290-5600. **$109-$309.** 70 Third Ave. I-95, exit 27A, just se. Int
corridors. **Pets:** Large. Service with restrictions, supervision.

## WESTFORD

**▼▼▼ Residence Inn by Marriott SH**
(978) 392-1407. **$149-$199.** 7 Lan Dr. I-495, exit 32, just s, then 0.5 w
on SR 110. Int corridors. **Pets:** Accepted.

## WOBURN

**▼▼▼ Crowne Plaza Hotel and Resort
Boston/Woburn LH**
(781) 932-0999. **$169-$209.** 2 Forbes Rd. I-95, exit 36, 0.5 mi s via
Washington St, then just e at Getty Station; jct Cedar St. Int corridors.
**Pets:** Accepted.

**▼▼▼ Extended Stay Deluxe Boston-Woburn SH**
(781) 938-3737. **$100.** 831 Main St. I-95, exit 35, just n on SR 38. Int
corridors. **Pets:** $25 daily fee/pet. Service with restrictions, supervision.

**▼▼▼ Holiday Inn Select SH**
(781) 935-8760. **$81-$119.** 15 Middlesex Canal Park Rd. I-95, exit 35, s
via SR 38. Int corridors. **Pets:** Accepted.

**▼▼ Red Roof Inn Woburn #7238 SH**
(781) 935-7110. **$79-$116.** 19 Commerce Way. I-95, exit 36, just n,
then just w on Mishawum Rd. Int corridors. **Pets:** Accepted.

**▼▼▼ Residence Inn by Marriott-Boston/Woburn SH**
(781) 376-4000. **$79-$239.** 300 Presidential Way. I-93, exit 37C, just
nw. Int corridors. **Pets:** Other species. $75 one-time fee/room. Service with
restrictions, supervision.

---

# END METROPOLITAN AREA

---

# BROCKTON

**▼▼▼ Residence Inn by Marriott SH**
(508) 583-3600. **$109-$179, 5 day notice.** 124 Liberty St. SR 24, exit
17B, just w, just s on Pearl St, then 0.3 mi se via Mill St connector. Int
corridors. **Pets:** Medium, other species. $75 one-time fee/room. Service
with restrictions.

# CAPE COD AREA

## BUZZARDS BAY

**△△△ ▽▽▽ Bay Motor Inn** CA
(508) 759-3989. **$51-$129, 10 day notice.** 223 Main St. SR 25, 0.5 mi w of Bourne rotary, exit 2. Ext corridors. **Pets:** Dogs only. $10 daily fee/room. Service with restrictions, supervision.
[SAVE] [S○] [✕] [🛏] [≈]

## CENTERVILLE

**△△△ ▽▽▽ Centerville Corners Inn** M
(508) 775-7223. **$50-$160, 14 day notice.** 369 S Main St. 1 mi s of SR 28, jct Craigville Beach Rd. Ext corridors. **Pets:** Medium, dogs only. $10 daily fee/pet. Service with restrictions, supervision.
[SAVE] [✕] [🛏] [≈]

## FALMOUTH

**▽▽ Capeside Cottage Bed & Breakfast** BB
(508) 548-6218. **$100-$160, 14 day notice.** 320 Woods Hole Rd. 2.2 mi s on SR 28. Int corridors. **Pets:** Accepted.
[✕] [🛏] [≈] [▽] [✓]

**△△△ ▽▽▽ Mariner Motel** M
(508) 548-1331. **$59-$169, 14 day notice.** 555 Main St. 0.5 mi e on SR 28. Ext corridors. **Pets:** Accepted.
[SAVE] [✕] [🛏] [≈]

**△△△ ▽▽▽▽ Village Green Inn** BB
(508) 548-5621. **$90-$275, 15 day notice.** 40 W Main St. On the Village Green. Int corridors. **Pets:** Accepted.
[SAVE] [S○] [✕] [🛏] [✓]

## HYANNIS

**▽▽▽▽ Comfort Inn** SH ❖
(508) 771-4804. **$95-$190.** 1470 Iyanough Rd. On SR 132; US 6, exit 6, 1.3 mi se. Ext/int corridors. **Pets:** Large, other species. $50 deposit/room. Designated rooms, service with restrictions, supervision.
[ASK] [S○] [✕] [⊘] [🛏] [▣] [≈] [✕]

## ORLEANS

**△△△ ▽▽▽▽ Skaket Beach Motel** M ❖
(508) 255-1020. **$58-$169, 10 day notice.** 203 Cranberry Hwy (Rt 6A). US 6, exit 12, just e. Ext corridors. **Pets:** $9 daily fee/pet. Designated rooms, service with restrictions, supervision.
[SAVE] [✕] [🛏] [▣] [≈]

## PROVINCETOWN

**▽▽▽▽ Anchor Inn Beach House** SH
(508) 487-0432. **$125-$385, 21 day notice.** 175 Commercial St. 2 blks se of SR 6A, just sw of the post office; center. Ext/int corridors. **Pets:** Accepted.
[ASK] [✕] [👁] [🛏]

**▽▽▽▽ Bayshore & Chandler** CO
(508) 487-9133. **$100-$250, 14 day notice.** 493 Commercial St. 0.8 mi n of Town Hall. Ext corridors. **Pets:** $15 daily fee/pet. Service with restrictions.
[✕] [🛏] [▣]

**△△△ ▽▽▽▽ Cape Inn** SH
(508) 487-1711. **$99-$189, 3 day notice.** 698 Commercial St. 1.5 mi se on SR 6A. Ext corridors. **Pets:** $10 daily fee/pet. Designated rooms, service with restrictions, supervision.
[SAVE] [S○] [✕] [⊘] [🛏] [▣] [🍴] [≈]

**△△△ ▽▽▽▽ Surfside Hotel & Suites** SH ❖
(508) 487-1726. **$89-$319.** 542-543 Commercial St. 1 mi e of Town Hall. Ext/int corridors. **Pets:** Dogs only. $20 daily fee/pet. Designated rooms, service with restrictions.
[SAVE] [S○] [✕] [🛏] [▣] [≈]

**▽▽▽▽ White Wind Inn** BB
(508) 487-1526. **$90-$270, 14 day notice.** 174 Commercial St. Just w of Town Hall. Int corridors. **Pets:** Medium, dogs only. $20 daily fee/pet. Designated rooms, crate.
[✕] [🛏]

## SANDWICH

**▽▽▽▽ The Earl of Sandwich Motel** M
(508) 888-1415. **$55-$109, 7 day notice.** 378 SR 6A. At MM 5.1. Ext corridors. **Pets:** Accepted.
[✕] [🛏] [≈]

**△△△ ▽▽▽▽ Sandwich Lodge & Resort** M
(508) 888-2275. **$62-$199, 7 day notice.** 54 SR 6A. On SR 6A, 1 mi w. Ext/int corridors. **Pets:** Other species. $10 daily fee/pet. Designated rooms, service with restrictions, supervision.
[SAVE] [S○] [✕] [🛏] [≈] [✕]

# END AREA

## CHICOPEE

**▽▽ Motel 6-1059** M
(413) 592-5141. **$45-$65.** 36 Johnny Cake Hollow Rd. I-90 (Massachusetts Tpke), exit 6, just n. Ext corridors. **Pets:** Accepted.
[S○] [✕] [≈]

**△△△ ▽▽▽ Quality Inn-Chicopee** SH ❖
(413) 592-6171. **$59-$109.** 463 Memorial Dr. I-90 (Massachusetts Tpke), exit 5, just ne; upon exiting, use jug handle overpass to SR 33 N. Int corridors. **Pets:** $25 one-time fee/room. Service with restrictions, supervision.
[SAVE] [S○] [✕] [🛏] [▣] [≈]

## DARTMOUTH

**▽▽▽ Comfort Inn** SH
(508) 996-0800. **$79-$129.** 171 Faunce Corner Rd. I-195, exit 12A westbound; exit 12 eastbound, then s. Int corridors. **Pets:** Other species. $50 one-time fee/room. Service with restrictions, crate.
[ASK] [S○] [✕] [🛏] [▣] [≈]

**▽▽▽ Residence Inn by Marriott** SH
(508) 984-5858. **$109-$259.** 181 Faunce Corner Rd. I-195, exit 12 westbound; exit 12 eastbound, just s. Int corridors. **Pets:** $75 one-time fee/room. Service with restrictions.
[ASK] [✕] [👁M] [⊘] [👁] [🛏] [▣] [≈] [✕]

# DEERFIELD

◆◆◆ Deerfield Inn 🄲 ❀
(413) 774-5587. **$159-$250, 7 day notice.** 81 Old Main St. Center. Int corridors. **Pets:** Small, dogs only. $15 daily fee/room. Designated rooms, service with restrictions, crate.

ASK S🔒 X 🍴

# EAST WAREHAM

◆◆◆ ◆◆◆ Atlantic Motel 🄼
(508) 295-0210. **$69-$189, 10 day notice.** 7 Depot St. Between east-bound and westbound lanes of US 6/SR 28; jct SR 25, exit 1. Ext corridors. **Pets:** Medium, dogs only. $15 daily fee/pet. Designated rooms, service with restrictions, supervision.

SAVE S🔒 X 🗄 ≈

# FAIRHAVEN

◆◆◆ ◆◆◆ Holiday Inn Express Harborfront 🅂🅷 ❀
(508) 997-1281. **$89-$149.** 110 Middle St. I-195, exit 15, 1 mi s, then just off US 6. Int corridors. **Pets:** Other species. $10 one-time fee/room. Service with restrictions, crate.

SAVE S🔒 X 🗄 💻

# FITCHBURG

◆◆◆ ◆◆◆ Best Western Royal Plaza Hotel & Trade Center 🅻🅷
(978) 342-7100. **$89-$159.** 150 Royal Plaza Dr. Just s on SR 31; SR 2, exit 28. Int corridors. **Pets:** Service with restrictions, supervision.

SAVE S🔒 X 🗄 🗄 💻 🍴 ≈ 🗄

# GARDNER

◆◆◆ ◆◆ Super 8 Motel 🄼
(978) 630-2888. **$78-$93, 14 day notice.** 22 Pearson Blvd. SR 2, exit 23, just n. Int corridors. **Pets:** Medium. $10 daily fee/pet. Service with restrictions, supervision.

ASK S🔒 X 🗄

# GREAT BARRINGTON

◆◆◆ ◆◆ Monument Mountain Motel 🄼
(413) 528-3272. **$55-$199, 14 day notice.** 247 Stockbridge Rd. On US 7, 1.2 mi s of jct SR 183. Ext corridors. **Pets:** Medium, dogs only. $15 daily fee/pet. Designated rooms, service with restrictions, supervision.

SAVE S🔒 X 🗄 ≈

◆◆◆ ◆◆◆ Travelodge 🄼
(413) 528-2340. **$65-$259, 14 day notice.** 400 Stockbridge Rd. On US 7, 1.2 mi s of jct SR 183. Ext corridors. **Pets:** $15 daily fee/pet. Designated rooms, service with restrictions, supervision.

SAVE S🔒 X 🗄 💻 ≈

# GREENFIELD

◆◆◆ ◆◆◆ The Brandt House B&B 🅱🅱 ❀
(413) 774-3329. **$85-$295, 30 day notice.** 29 Highland Ave. I-91, exit 26, 1.8 mi e on SR 2A, then se via Cresent St. Int corridors. **Pets:** Dogs only. $25 one-time fee/pet. Service with restrictions, supervision.

SAVE X 🗄

# HADLEY

◆◆◆ ◆◆◆ Howard Johnson 🅂🅷
(413) 586-0114. **$60-$193.** 401 Russell St. I-91, exit 19 northbound, 4.3 mi e on SR 9; exit 24 southbound, 10 mi s on SR 116, then just w on SR 9. Int corridors. **Pets:** Medium, dogs only. $20 daily fee/pet. Designated rooms, service with restrictions, supervision.

SAVE S🔒 X 🗄🄼 🗄 🗄 💻 ≈

◆◆◆ ◆◆◆ Quality Inn 🅂🅷
(413) 584-9816. **$75-$145, 3 day notice.** 237 Russell St. I-91, exit 19 northbound; exit 20 southbound, 3 mi e on SR 9. Int corridors. **Pets:** Medium, dogs only. $25 one-time fee/pet. Service with restrictions, supervision.

SAVE S🔒 X 🗄 🗄 💻 ≈

# HOLLAND

◆◆◆ Restful Paws Bed & Breakfast 🅱🅱 ❀
(413) 245-7792. **$140, 7 day notice.** 70 Allen Hill Rd. SR 20. 2.1 mi s on E. Brimfield Rd, 0.4 mi on Alexander Rd, then 0.7 mi n. Int corridors. **Pets:** Service with restrictions, supervision.

ASK S🔒 X 💻 🗄 🗄

# LANESBORO

◆◆ Mt View Motel 🄼
(413) 442-1009. **$48-$145, 7 day notice.** 499 S Main St. 1 mi s on US 7. Ext corridors. **Pets:** Accepted.

ASK S🔒 X 🗄 💻

◆◆◆ ◆◆ The Weathervane Motel 🄼
(413) 443-3230. **$35-$110, 15 day notice.** 475 S Main St. 1.3 mi s on US 7. Ext corridors. **Pets:** Very small. $10 daily fee/pet. Designated rooms, no service, supervision.

SAVE X 🗄 💻

# LEE

◆◆◆ ◆◆ Rodeway Inn 🄼
(413) 243-0813. **$69-$169, 14 day notice.** 200 Laurel St. On US 20, 1.8 mi w of I-90 exit 2. Ext corridors **Pets:** Accepted.

SAVE S🔒 X 🗄 💻 ≈

# LENOX

◆◆ ◆◆ Seven Hills Country Inn & Restaurant 🅂🅷
(413) 637-0060. **$85-$340, 15 day notice.** 40 Plunkett St. Jct US 7/20, 0.6 mi se on US 20, 0.8 mi w. Ext/int corridors. **Pets:** Accepted.

ASK X 🗄 🗄 💻 🍴 ≈ 🗄

# MANSFIELD

◆◆◆ ◆◆◆ Holiday Inn Mansfield 🅂🅷
(508) 339-2200. **$111-$159.** 31 Hampshire St. I-95, exit 7A, 0.5 mi s on SR 140, then 1 mi w on Forbes Rd; -495, exit 12, 2 mi n on SR 140, then w on Forbes Rd. Int corridors. **Pets:** $10 daily fee/pet. Designated rooms, service with restrictions, crate.

SAVE S🔒 X 🗄 🗄 💻 🍴 ≈ 🗄

# MARTHA'S VINEYARD AREA

## VINEYARD HAVEN

 The Doctor's House **BB**
(508) 696-0859. **$125-$325, 21 day notice.** 60 Mt. Aldworth Rd. 0.4 mi sw to road to Edgartown, 1 blk e. Int corridors. **Pets:** Accepted.
[SAVE] [X] [Z]

# END AREA

## MIDDLEBORO

Days Inn-Plymouth/Middleboro **SH** ❖
(508) 946-4400. **$74-$119.** 30 E Clark St. I-495, exit 4, at SR 105. Int corridors. **Pets:** Large, other species. $10 daily fee/pet. Designated rooms, service with restrictions, supervision.
[SAVE] [S] [X] [&] [H] [P] [≈]

## MILFORD

Days Inn **SH**
(508) 634-2499. **$65-$90.** 3 Fortune Blvd. I-495, exit 20, 0.3 mi s on SR 85, then just e. Int corridors. **Pets:** Accepted.
[SAVE] [S] [X] [&] [H] [P]

Holiday Inn Express **SH**
(508) 634-1054. **$79-$129.** 50 Fortune Blvd. I-495, exit 20, just sw on SR 85, then just se. Int corridors. **Pets:** $25 one-time fee/room. Designated rooms, service with restrictions.
[SAVE] [X] [&M] [⌂] [&] [H] [P] [≈]

La Quinta **SH**
(508) 478-8243. **$70-$114.** 24 Beaver St. I-495, exit 19, just w on SR 109. Int corridors. **Pets:** Medium. Service with restrictions.
[ASK] [X] [H] [P]

## NORTH ADAMS

Jae's Inn **CI**
(413) 664-0100. **$75-$150, 3 day notice.** 1111 S State St. Center; 2 mi s on SR 8. Int corridors. **Pets:** Other species. $20 daily fee/pet. Designated rooms, service with restrictions.
[SAVE] [X] [H] [¶] [≈] [X]

## NORTHAMPTON

Clarion Hotel & Conference Center **SH**
(413) 586-1211. **$99-$179.** One Atwood Dr. I-91, exit 18, just s on US 5. Int corridors. **Pets:** $20 daily fee/room. Designated rooms, service with restrictions, crate.
[ASK] [S] [X] [&M] [⌂] [&] [H] [P] [¶] [≈] [X]

## NORTHBOROUGH

Econolodge Inn & Suites **SH**
(508) 842-8941. **Call for rates.** 380 SW Cutoff. Jct of US 20 and SR 9. Ext corridors. **Pets:** Other species. $10 daily fee/room. Service with restrictions, supervision.
[ASK] [X] [H] [P]

## ORANGE

Executive Inn **M**
(978) 544-8864. **$55-$85, 7 day notice.** 110 Daniel Shay Hwy. US 202, exit 16, just n of jct SR 2. Ext/int corridors. **Pets:** $7 daily fee/pet. Service with restrictions, crate.
[SAVE] [X] [H]

## PITTSFIELD

Crowne Plaza Hotel and Resort Pittsfield Berkshires **LH**
(413) 499-2000. **$119-$275.** 1 West St, Berkshire Common. Center. Int corridors. **Pets:** $25 one-time fee/pet. Service with restrictions, supervision.
[ASK] [S] [X] [&M] [⌂] [&] [H] [P] [¶] [≈] [X]

## RAYNHAM

Days Inn Taunton **M**
(508) 824-8647. **$70-$119.** 164 New State Hwy. SR 24, exit 13B, 0.8 mi w on US 44. Ext/int corridors. **Pets:** $10 daily fee/pet. Designated rooms, service with restrictions, crate.
[SAVE] [S] [X] [&] [≈]

## REHOBOTH

Five Bridge Inn Bed & Breakfast **BB** ❖
(508) 252-3190. **$98-$125, 7 day notice.** 154 Pine St. 1.6 mi n of US 44; 3.3 mi w of jct SR 118; US 44, n on Blanding, e on Broad, n on Salisbury, then w. Int corridors. **Pets:** Medium, other species. $15 one-time fee/room. Designated rooms, service with restrictions, crate.
[ASK] [S] [X] [H] [P] [≈] [X]

## ROCKLAND

Best Western Rockland **SH** ❖
(781) 871-5660. **$109-$150.** 909 Hingham St. SR 3, exit 14, 0.3 mi sw on SR 228. Int corridors. **Pets:** $20 daily fee/pet. Designated rooms, service with restrictions.
[SAVE] [X] [H] [P]

## SCITUATE

The Inn at Scituate Harbor **M**
(781) 545-5550. **$99-$239, 7 day notice.** 7 Beaver Dam Rd. Jct Front St; at Scituate Harbor. Int corridors. **Pets:** Accepted.
[ASK] [S] [X] [H] [¶] [≈]

## SEEKONK

Motel 6-1289 **M**
(508) 336-7800. **$57-$70.** 821 Fall River Ave. I-195, exit 1, just n on SR 114A. Int corridors. **Pets:** Accepted.
[S] [X] [⌂] [&]

Ramada Inn-Providence **SH**
(508) 336-7300. **$104-$149, 7 day notice.** 940 Fall River Ave. I-195, exit 1, just s. Int corridors. **Pets:** Accepted.
[ASK] [S] [X] [H] [P] [¶] [≈] [X]

## SOMERSET

Quality Inn-Fall River/Somerset **SH**
(508) 678-4545. **$79-$165.** 1878 Wilbur Ave. Jct SR 103 and I-195, exit 4 eastbound; exit 4A westbound. Int corridors. **Pets:** Accepted.
[SAVE] [S] [X] [H] [P] [≈] [X]

# SOUTHBOROUGH

### ▼▼ Red Roof Inn **M**
(508) 481-3904. **$64-$94.** 367 Turnpike Rd. I-495, exit 23A, just e on SR 9. Ext corridors. **Pets:** Accepted.
⊠ 🖥

# SPRINGFIELD

### ▲▲▲ ▼▼▼ Holiday Inn **LH**
(413) 781-0900. **$114-$149.** 711 Dwight St. I-291, exit 2A, just e. Int corridors. **Pets:** Other species. $35 one-time fee/room. Service with restrictions.
SAVE ⊠ 👨 🐾 🖥 💻 🍽 🏊 ⊠

### ▲▲▲ ▼ Howard Johnson Express Inn **M**
(413) 783-2111. **$54-$95.** 1356 Boston Rd. I-90, exit 7, 2.2 mi s on SR 21, then just w on US 20. Ext/int corridors. **Pets:** Accepted.
SAVE 👨 ⊠ 🖥 💻 🏊

### ▼▼▼▼ Sheraton Springfield Monarch Place **LH**
(413) 781-1010. **$109-$239.** 1 Monarch Pl. I-91, exit 6 northbound; exit 7 southbound, just n; downtown. Int corridors. **Pets:** Accepted.
ASK 👨 ⊠ 👨 🐾 🖥 💻 🍽 🏊 ⊠

# STURBRIDGE

### ▲▲▲ ▼▼▼ Best Western-American Motor Lodge **M**
(508) 347-9121. **$69-$109.** 350 US 20 St. Jct US 20 and SR 131. Int corridors. **Pets:** Medium. $5 daily fee/pet. Designated rooms, service with restrictions, supervision.
SAVE 👨 ⊠ 🍽 🏊

### ▲▲▲ ▼▼▼ Comfort Inn & Suites Colonial **SH**
(508) 347-3306. **$89-$259.** 215 Charlton Rd. I-90 (Massachusetts Tpke), exit 9, 0.5 mi e; I-84, exit 3A. Ext/int corridors. **Pets:** $15 daily fee/room. Designated rooms, service with restrictions.
SAVE 👨 ⊠ 👨 🐾 🖥 💻 🏊

### ▼▼ Days Inn **M** 🐾
(508) 347-3391. **$49-$149, 15 day notice.** 66-68 Haynes St (SR 15). I-84, exit 2, 0.5 mi n, follow signs to SR 131, on I-84 service road. Ext/int corridors. **Pets:** $7 daily fee/room. Service with restrictions, supervision.
ASK 👨 ⊠ 💻 🏊

### ▲▲▲ ▼▼ Publick House Historic Inn & Country Lodge **SH** 🐾
(508) 347-3313. **$69-$165.** 295 Main St. I-90, I-90 (Massachusetts Tpke), exit 9; I-84, exit 3B, 0.5 mi s of jct US 20. Ext/int corridors. **Pets:** Large, other species. $10 daily fee/pet. Designated rooms, service with restrictions, supervision.
SAVE 👨 ⊠ 🖥 💻 🍽 🏊

### ▼▼ Quality Inn & Conference Center **SH**
(508) 347-1978. **$59-$149.** 400 Haynes Rd (SR 15). I-84, exit 1, 0.5 mi w. Int corridors. **Pets:** Accepted.
ASK 👨 ⊠ 🐾 🐾 🖥 💻 🍽 🏊

### ▼▼ Sturbridge Coach Motor Lodge **M**
(508) 347-7327. **$39-$149, 15 day notice.** 408 Main St. I-90 (Massachusetts Tpke), exit 9, 0.8 mi w on US 20; I-84, exit 3B. Ext corridors. **Pets:** Accepted.
ASK 👨 ⊠ 💻 🏊

### ▲▲▲ ▼ Sturbridge Heritage Motel **M**
(508) 347-3943. **$45-$65.** 499 Main St. I-84, exit 3B, 1.5 mi w on US 20. Ext corridors. **Pets:** Accepted.
SAVE 👨 ⊠ 🖥

### ▲▲▲ ▼▼▼▼ Sturbridge Host Hotel and Conference Center on Cedar Lake **LH**
(508) 347-7393. **$99-$149.** 366 Main St. I-90 (Massachusetts Tpke), exit 9, just w on US 20; I-84, exit 3B. Int corridors. **Pets:** Accepted.
SAVE ⊠ 🐾 🖥 💻 🍽 🏊 ⊠

### ▲▲▲ ▼▼▼ Super 8 **M**
(508) 347-9000. **$49-$149.** 358 Main St. I-90 (Massachusetts Tpke), exit 9; I-84, exit 3B on US 20. Ext corridors. **Pets:** Other species. $10 daily fee/pet. Designated rooms, service with restrictions, supervision.
SAVE 👨 ⊠ 🖥 💻 🏊

# UXBRIDGE

### ▲▲▲ ▼▼ Quaker Inn & Conference Center **M**
(508) 278-2445. **$62-$85.** 442 Quaker Hwy. 0.6 mi e of SR 146 on 146A. Ext/int corridors. **Pets:** Accepted.
SAVE 👨 ⊠ 🖥 🏊

# WESTBOROUGH

### ▼▼▼▼ Extended Stay Deluxe Boston-Westborough-Computer Dr **SH**
(508) 366-6100. **$105.** 1800 Computer Dr. I-495, exit 23B, just w; north side of SR 9. Int corridors. **Pets:** $25 daily fee/pet. Service with restrictions, supervision.
ASK 👨 ⊠ 👨 🐾 🐾 🖥 💻 🏊

### ▲▲▲ ▼▼▼▼ Residence Inn by Marriott Boston/Westborough **SH** 🐾
(508) 366-7700. **$99-$249.** 25 Connector Rd. I-495, exit 23B, just w on SR 9, exit Computer/Research Dr, then 0.3 mi s. Ext/int corridors. **Pets:** Large, other species. $75 one-time fee/room. Designated rooms, crate.
SAVE 👨 ⊠ 👨 🐾 🐾 🖥 💻 🏊 ⊠

### ▲▲▲ ▼▼▼▼ Wyndham Westborough **LH**
(508) 366-5511. **$99-$219.** 5400 Computer Dr. I-495, exit 23B, just w on SR 9, exit Computer/Research Dr. Int corridors. **Pets:** Accepted.
SAVE ⊠ 👨 🐾 🐾 🖥 💻 🍽 🏊 ⊠

# WESTFIELD

### ▲▲▲ ▼▼▼ Econo Lodge & Suites **SH**
(413) 568-2821. **$55-$120.** 2 Southampton Rd. I-90, exit 3, at jct SR 202 and 10. Int corridors. **Pets:** Medium. $25 daily fee/pet. Service with restrictions, supervision.
SAVE 👨 ⊠ 🖥 💻 🏊

# WEST SPRINGFIELD

### ▲▲▲ ▼▼▼▼ Hampton Inn **SH** 🐾
(413) 732-1300. **$89-$99.** 1011 Riverdale St (US 5). I-91, exit 13B, 0.3 mi s. Int corridors. **Pets:** Large. $75 one-time fee/room. Service with restrictions, supervision.
SAVE 👨 ⊠ 👨 🐾 🐾 🖥 💻 🏊

### ▲▲▲ ▼▼▼ Quality Inn **SH**
(413) 739-7261. **$55-$145.** 1150 Riverdale St. I-91, exit 13B, jct US 5. Int corridors. **Pets:** $35 one-time fee/pet. Service with restrictions, crate.
SAVE 👨 ⊠ 🖥 💻 🍽 🏊

### ▼▼▼ Red Roof Inn #7193 **M**
(413) 731-1010. **$59-$94.** 1254 Riverdale St. I-91, exit 13A. Ext corridors. **Pets:** Accepted.
⊠ 👨 🐾

### ▼▼▼▼ Residence Inn by Marriott **SH**
(413) 732-9543. **$110-$200, 14 day notice.** 64 Border Way. I-91, exit 13A, on US 5. Int corridors. **Pets:** Accepted.
ASK 👨 ⊠ 👨 🐾 🐾 🖥 💻 🏊 ⊠

# WEST STOCKBRIDGE

### ▲▲▲ ▼ Pleasant Valley Motel **M** 🐾
(413) 232-8511. **$45-$195, 15 day notice.** 42 Stockbridge Rd. I-90 (Massachusetts Tpke), exit B3 eastbound, 0.5 mi s on SR 22, then 3.5 mi e on SR 102; exit 1 westbound, 0.4 mi e. Ext corridors. **Pets:** Medium. $15 daily fee/pet. Designated rooms, service with restrictions.
SAVE ⊠ 🖥 🏊

# WILLIAMSTOWN

### ▼▼ ◆ Cozy Corner Motel [M]
(413) 458-8006. **$55-$125, 10 day notice.** 284 Sand Springs Rd (US 7). On US 7, 1.5 mi n of jct SR 2. Ext corridors. **Pets:** Other species. $10 daily fee/pet. Service with restrictions, crate.

[X] [▣]

### ◆◆◆ ▼ The Villager Motel [M]
(413) 458-4046. **$55-$125, 14 day notice.** 953 Simonds Rd. On US 7, 1.7 n of jct SR 2. Ext corridors. **Pets:** Accepted.

[SAVE] [S◊] [X] [▣]

# WORCESTER

### ◆◆◆ ▼▼▼ Crowne Plaza Hotel [LH]
(508) 791-1600. **$99-$199.** 10 Lincoln Square. I-290, exit 17 eastbound; exit 18 westbound, 0.3 mi s. Int corridors. **Pets:** Medium. $25 daily fee/pet. Service with restrictions, supervision.

[SAVE] [S◊] [X] [&M] [≈] [≈] [▣] [▣] [¶] [≈] [X]

### ◆◆◆ ▼▼▼ Holiday Inn [SH]
(508) 852-4000. **$84-$169.** 500 Lincoln St. I-290, exit 20, 0.5 mi n on SR 70. Int corridors. **Pets:** Other species. $25 daily fee/room. Service with restrictions, crate.

[SAVE] [S◊] [X] [&M] [≈] [≈] [▣] [▣] [¶] [≈]

# MICHIGAN

## ALGONAC

▼▼ Linda's Lighthouse Inn BB ❄️
(810) 794-2992. $95-$135, 7 day notice. 5965 Pointe Tremble Rd (SR 29). I-94, exit 243 (23 Mile Rd), 14.3 mi e. Int corridors. Pets: Other species. $15 deposit/pet. Crate.
ASK ✕ ✕ 🐾 ✍

## ALLEGAN

▼▼▼ Castle In The Country B & B Inn BB
(269) 673-8054. $125-$225, 7 day notice. 340 SR 40 S. SR 40 S, 6 mi s. Int corridors. Pets: Accepted.
✕ ✕ ✍

## ALLENDALE

▼▼ Sleep Inn & Suites SH
(616) 892-8000. $59-$150. 4869 Becker Dr. I-96, exit 16, 6 mi s, then 2.5 mi e on SR 45. Int corridors. Pets: Medium. $10 one-time fee/pet. Designated rooms, service with restrictions, crate.
ASK S✕ ✕ &M ✒ 🛏 ⬛ ➰

## ALPENA

▼▼ Holiday Inn SH
(989) 356-2151. $80-$110. 1000 Hwy 23 N. On US 23, 1 mi n. Int corridors. Pets: Accepted.
ASK S✕ ✕ ✒ 🛏 ⬛ 🍴 ➰ ✕

## ANN ARBOR

▼▼ Best Value Inn & Suites M
(734) 665-3500. $59-$99, 3 day notice. 3505 S State St. I-94, exit 177 (State St), just ne. Ext corridors. Pets: Large. $25 one-time fee/room. Designated rooms, service with restrictions, supervision.
ASK S✕ ✕ 🛏 ⬛

Ⓐ ▼▼▼ Best Western Executive Plaza SH
(734) 665-4444. $69-$159. 2900 Jackson Rd. I-94, exit 172 (Jackson Rd), just e. Ext/int corridors. Pets: Accepted.
SAVE S✕ ✕ 🛏 ⬛ 🍴 ➰ ✕

▼▼ Candlewood Suites SH
(734) 663-2818. $74-$169. 701 Waymarket Way. I-94, exit 175 (Ann Arbor/Saline Rd), just e on Eisenhower Rd. Int corridors. Pets: Large, other species. $150 one-time fee/room. Service with restrictions, crate.
ASK ✕ &M ✒ ✒ 🛏 ⬛

▼▼◆ Extended StayAmerica SH
(734) 332-1980. $69. 1501 Briarwood Circle Dr. I-94, exit 177 (State St), just ne. Int corridors. Pets: Accepted.
ASK S✕ ✕ &M ✒ ✒ 🛏 ⬛

▼▼◆ Hampton Inn-North SH ❄️
(734) 996-4444. $84-$164. 2300 Green Rd. US 23, exit 41 (Plymouth Rd), just nw. Int corridors. Pets: Large, other species. $25 one-time fee/room. No service, crate.
ASK S✕ ✕ &M ✒ 🛏 ⬛ 🍴 ➰

▼▼◆ Hawthorn Suites SH
(734) 327-0011. $113-$149. 3535 Green Rd. US 23, exit 41 (Plymouth Rd), just sw. Int corridors. Pets: Other species. $100 one-time fee/room. Service with restrictions.
ASK S✕ &M ✒ ✒ 🛏 ⬛ ➰ ✕

▼▼ Red Roof Inn #7045 M
(734) 996-5800. $59-$83. 3621 Plymouth Rd. US 23, exit 41 (Plymouth Rd), just nw. Ext corridors. Pets: Accepted.
✕ ✒ ✒ 🛏

▼▼ Residence Inn by Marriott SH 🐾
(734) 996-5666. $89-$229. 800 Victor's Way. I-94, exit 177 (State St), just ne. Ext/int corridors. Pets: Other species. $15 daily fee/pet. Service with restrictions.
ASK ✕ ✒ ✒ 🛏 ⬛ ➰ ✕

## AU GRES

▼▼ Best Western Pinewood Lodge SH
(989) 876-4060. $56-$89. 510 W US 23. On US 23, just w. Int corridors. Pets: $10 one-time fee/pet. Designated rooms, service with restrictions, supervision.
S✕ ✕ 🛏 ⬛ ➰

## BAD AXE

Ⓐ ▼▼▼ Econo Lodge Inns & Suites SH
(989) 269-3200. $39-$80. 898 N Van Dyke Rd. Just s of jct SR 142 and 53 (Van Dyke Rd). Int corridors. Pets: Medium. $10 one-time fee/pet. Service with restrictions, supervision.
SAVE S✕ ✕ ➰

# BARAGA

**▼▼ Super 8 Motel** 🆂🅷
(906) 353-6680. **$54-$59.** 790 Michigan Ave. 1 mi w on SR 38. Int corridors. **Pets:** Accepted.

⟨ASK⟩ 🆂🗙 ▦ ▣

# BATTLE CREEK

**▼▼ Baymont Inn & Suites-Battle Creek** 🆂🅷
(269) 979-5400. **$129.** 4725 Beckley Rd. I-94, exit 97 (Capital Ave), just sw. Int corridors. **Pets:** Medium, other species. $10 daily fee/room. Service with restrictions, supervision.

⟨ASK⟩ 🆂🗙 ⟨⟩ ⟨⟩ ▦ ▣ ≋

**▼▼ Days Inn** 🅼
(269) 979-3561. **$42-$57.** 4786 Beckley Rd. I-94, exit 97 (Capital Ave), just s. Ext corridors. **Pets:** Accepted.

⟨ASK⟩ 🆂🗙 ▦

**▼ Motel 6-4250** 🅼
(269) 979-1141. **$42-$50.** 4775 Beckley Rd. I-94, exit 97 (Capital Ave), just sw. Ext corridors. **Pets:** Accepted.

🆂🗙 ⟨M⟩ ⟨⟩ ≋

**▼▼ Ramada Inn & Suites** 🅼
(269) 979-1100. **$69-$109, 14 day notice.** 5050 Beckley Rd. I-94, exit 97 (Capital Ave), just s. Ext corridors. **Pets:** Service with restrictions, supervision.

⟨ASK⟩ 🆂🗙 ▦ ▣ 🍴 ≋

# BAY VIEW

**▲ ▼▼ Comfort Inn** 🆂🅷 🐾
(231) 347-3220. **$60-$200.** 1314 US 31 N. Jct US 31 and SR 119. Int corridors. **Pets:** Other species. Service with restrictions, supervision.

⟨SAVE⟩ 🆂🗙 ▦ ▣

# BEAR LAKE

**▲ ▼ Bella Vista Inn** 🅼
(231) 864-3000. **$57-$59, 7 day notice.** 12273 US 31. On US 31; center. Ext corridors. **Pets:** Dogs only. $10 daily fee/pet. Service with restrictions, supervision.

⟨SAVE⟩ 🗙 ▦ ▣ ≋

# BENTON HARBOR

**▲ ▼▼ Best Western T.C. Inn & Suites** 🆂🅷
(269) 925-1880. **$59-$99.** 1598 Mall Dr. I-94, exit 29 (Pipestone Rd), just n to Mall Dr, then just w. Int corridors. **Pets:** Accepted.

⟨SAVE⟩ 🗙 ▦ ▣ ≋

**◆▼ Red Roof Inn #7043** 🅼
(269) 927-2484. **$45-$75.** 1630 Mall Dr. I-94, exit 29 (Pipestone Rd), just n, then just w. Ext corridors. **Pets:** Accepted.

🗙 ⟨M⟩ ⟨⟩ ▦

# BIG RAPIDS

**◆▼▼ Holiday Inn Hotel & Conference Center** 🆂🅷
(231) 796-4400. **$94-$139.** 1005 Perry St. US 131, exit 139, 1.3 mi e on SR 20. Int corridors. **Pets:** Accepted.

⟨ASK⟩ 🆂🗙 ⟨M⟩ ⟨⟩ ▦ ▣ 🍴 ≋ 🗙

**▲ ▼▼ Quality Inn & Suites** 🅼
(231) 592-5150. **$69-$119.** 1705 S State St. US 131, exit 139, 2.1 mi e on SR 20, then 1 mi s. Ext/int corridors. **Pets:** Medium. $10 daily fee/pet. Designated rooms, no service, supervision.

⟨SAVE⟩ 🆂🗙 ▦ ▣ ≋

# BIRCH RUN

**▲ ▼▼ Super 8 Motel** 🆂🅷
(989) 624-4440. **$47-$83.** 9235 E Birch Run Rd. I-75, exit 136 (Birch Run Rd), just e. Int corridors. **Pets:** Medium. Designated rooms, service with restrictions, supervision.

⟨SAVE⟩ 🆂🗙 ▦ 🗙

# BRIDGEPORT

**▼▼ Baymont Inn & Suites-Frankenmuth/Bridgeport** 🆂🅷
(989) 777-3000. **$49-$129.** 6460 Dixie Hwy. I-75, exit 144A. Int corridors. **Pets:** Accepted.

⟨ASK⟩ 🆂🗙 ⟨⟩ ▦ ▣ ≋

# BROOKLYN

**▼▼ Super 8 Motel** 🆂🅷
(517) 592-0888. **$58-$130.** 155 Wamplers Rd. Jct Main St (SR 50) and SR 124; downtown. Int corridors. **Pets:** Other species. $5 daily fee/pet. Service with restrictions, supervision.

⟨ASK⟩ 🆂🗙 ⟨M⟩ ⟨⟩ ▦

# BYRON CENTER

**▲ ▼▼ AmeriHost Inn-Grand Rapids South** 🆂🅷
(616) 827-9900. **$69-$169.** 7625 Caterpillar Ct SW. US 131, exit 75. Int corridors. **Pets:** Accepted.

⟨SAVE⟩ 🆂🗙 ⟨⟩ ▦ ▣ ≋

**▼▼▼ Baymont Inn & Suites Grand Rapids Southwest/ Byron Center** 🆂🅷
(616) 583-9535. **$79-$99.** 8282 Pfeiffer Farms Dr SW. US 131, exit 74, just w. Int corridors. **Pets:** Large. Service with restrictions, supervision.

⟨ASK⟩ 🆂🗙 ⟨M⟩ ⟨⟩ ⟨⟩ ▦ ▣ 🍴 ≋ 🗙

# CADILLAC

**▲ ▼ Econo Lodge** 🆂🅷
(231) 775-6700. **$44-$85.** 2501 Sunnyside Dr. Jct SR 55 and 115. Ext/int corridors. **Pets:** $10 daily fee/room. Service with restrictions, crate.

⟨SAVE⟩ 🆂🗙 ▦ ▣

**▲ ▼▼▼ McGuires Resort** 🆂🅷 🐾
(231) 775-9947. **$79-$129, 7 day notice.** 7880 Mackinaw Tr. US 131, exit 177, 0.7 mi n, then 0.5 mi w. Int corridors. **Pets:** $15 daily fee/room. Designated rooms, service with restrictions, crate.

⟨SAVE⟩ 🗙 ▦ ▣ 🍴 ≋ 🗙

# CALUMET

**▼▼ AmericInn of Calumet** 🆂🅷
(906) 337-6463. **$89-$139.** 56925 S 6th St. On US 41, just w of Visitors Center. Int corridors. **Pets:** Accepted.

⟨ASK⟩ 🗙 ⟨⟩ ▦ ▣ ≋ 🗙

# CASCADE

**▼▼ AmeriSuites Grand Rapids/Airport** 🆂🅷
(616) 940-8100. **$69-$129.** 5401 28th St Ct SE. I-96, exit 43B, just e on SR 11. Int corridors. **Pets:** Accepted.

⟨ASK⟩ 🆂🗙 ▦ ▣ 🗙

**▼▼ Baymont Inn-Grand Rapids Airport** 🆂🅷
(616) 956-3300. **$69-$89.** 2873 Kraft Ave SE. I-96, exit 43B, just e. Int corridors. **Pets:** Medium. Service with restrictions, supervision.

⟨ASK⟩ 🆂🗙 ▦ ▣

**▼▼ Country Inn & Suites by Carlson of Grand Rapids** 🆂🅷 🐾
(616) 977-0909. **$71-$79.** 5399 28th St. I-96, exit 43B, just e on SR 11. Int corridors. **Pets:** Large, other species. Service with restrictions, supervision.

⟨ASK⟩ 🆂🗙 ⟨M⟩ ⟨⟩ ⟨⟩ ▦ ▣ ≋

▼▼▼ **Crowne Plaza Grand Rapids** LH ❀
(616) 957-1770. **$119-$145.** 5700 28th St SE. I-96, exit 43B, 0.3 mi e on SR 11. Int corridors. **Pets:** Small. $50 deposit/room, $10 daily fee/room. Designated rooms, service with restrictions, supervision.

A$K S⬧ ✕ ⬧ ⬧ ⬧ ⬧ ⬧ ⬧ ⬧

▲▲ ▼ **Exel Inn of Grand Rapids** SH
(616) 957-3000. **$50-$80.** 4855 28th St SE. I-96, exit 43A, 0.5 mi w on SR 11. Int corridors. **Pets:** Small, other species. Designated rooms, service with restrictions, supervision.

SAVE S⬧ ✕ ⬧ ⬧

▼▼ **Hampton Inn** SH ❀
(616) 956-9304. **$82-$92.** 4981 28th St SE. I-96, exit 43A, 0.5 mi w on SR 11. Int corridors. **Pets:** Other species. Service with restrictions, crate.

A$K S⬧ ✕ ⬧ ⬧ ⬧ ⬧

▼▼ **Howard Johnson Express Inn & Suites** SH
(616) 940-1777. **$69-$109.** 2985 Kraft Ave SE. I-96, exit 43B, 0.5 mi se. Int corridors. **Pets:** Accepted.

A$K S⬧ ⬧ ⬧

▼▼ **La Quinta Inn & Suites** SH
(616) 949-8400. **$64-$74.** 5500 28th St SE. I-96, exit 43B, just e on SR 11. Int corridors. **Pets:** Accepted.

A$K S⬧ ✕ ⬧ ⬧ ⬧ ⬧

## CEDARVILLE

▲▲ ▼▼ **Cedarville Inn** SH
(906) 484-2266. **$69-$109.** 106 W M-134. On SR 134; just w of SR 129. Int corridors. **Pets:** Accepted.

SAVE ✕ ⬧ ⬧ ⬧ ⬧

## CHARLEVOIX

▼▼▼ **AmericInn Lodge & Suites** SH ❀
(231) 237-0988. **$89-$199.** 11800 US 31 N. On US 31, 2.4 mi n. Int corridors. **Pets:** Dogs only. $50 deposit/room, $25 daily fee/pet. Service with restrictions, supervision.

A$K S⬧ ✕ ⬧ ⬧ ⬧ ⬧ ⬧

## CHARLOTTE

▲▲▲ ▼▼▼ **Super 8 Motel** SH
(517) 543-8288. **$72-$90.** 828 E Shepherd St. I-69, exit 60 (SR 50), just w. Int corridors. **Pets:** Other species. Service with restrictions, supervision.

SAVE S⬧ ✕ ⬧

## CHEBOYGAN

▲▲▲ ▼ **Birch Haus Motel** M
(231) 627-5862. **$40-$70.** 1301 Mackinaw Ave. On US 23, 0.8 mi nw. Ext corridors. **Pets:** Small. $5 daily fee/pet. Service with restrictions, supervision.

SAVE ✕ ⬧

▼ **Continental Inn** M
(231) 627-7164. **$49-$120.** 613 N Main St. Jct US 23 and SR 27. Ext corridors. **Pets:** Other species. $6 daily fee/room. Designated rooms, service with restrictions, supervision.

A$K S⬧ ✕ ⬧ ⬧ ⬧

▲▲▲ ▼ **Pine River Motel** M ❀
(231) 627-5119. **$30-$70, 3 day notice.** 102 Lafayette. 0.5 mi e on US 23. Ext corridors. **Pets:** $10 one-time fee/pet. Service with restrictions, supervision.

SAVE S⬧ ✕ ⬧

## CHELSEA

▼▼▼ **Chelsea Comfort Inn & Conference Center** SH
(734) 433-8000. **$94-$199.** 1645 Commerce Park Dr. I-94, exit 159 (SR 52/Main St), just n. Int corridors. **Pets:** Other species. Service with restrictions, supervision.

A$K S⬧ ✕ ⬧M ⬧ ⬧ ⬧ ⬧

## CHRISTMAS

▲▲▲ ▼▼▼ **Pair-A-Dice Inn** SH
(906) 387-3500. **$49-$109, 3 day notice.** E7889 W Hwy M-28. On SR 28; center. Int corridors. **Pets:** Dogs only. $10 one-time fee/room. Service with restrictions, supervision.

SAVE S⬧ ✕ ⬧

## COLDWATER

▲▲▲ ▼▼▼ **Red Roof Inn** SH
(517) 279-1199. **$59-$169.** 348 S Willowbrook Rd. I-69, exit 13 (US 12), just e. Int corridors. **Pets:** Small. Service with restrictions, supervision.

SAVE S⬧ ✕ ⬧M ⬧ ⬧ ⬧

▲▲▲ ▼▼▼ **Super 8 Motel** SH
(517) 278-8833. **$61-$75.** 600 Orleans Blvd. I-69, exit 13 (US 12), 0.3 mi w on E Chicago St, just n on N Michigan Ave, then just e. Int corridors. **Pets:** Accepted.

SAVE S⬧ ✕ ⬧M ⬧ ⬧

## COMSTOCK PARK

▼ **Swan Inn** M
(616) 784-1224. **$48-$80.** 5182 Alpine Ave. Jct I-96 and Alpine Ave, 3 mi n on SR 37. Ext corridors. **Pets:** Other species. Crate.

✕ ⬧ ⬧ ⬧ ⬧

## COOPERSVILLE

▲▲▲ ▼▼▼ **AmeriHost Inn-Coopersville** SH
(616) 837-8100. **$69-$99.** 1040 O'Malley Dr. I-96, exit 16, just n. Int corridors. **Pets:** Small. $25 one-time fee/pet. No service, supervision.

SAVE S⬧ ✕ ⬧M ⬧ ⬧ ⬧ ⬧

## COPPER HARBOR

▼ **Lake Fanny Hooe Resort** M
(906) 289-4451. **$69-$99, 7 day notice.** 505 2nd St. Just s on Manganese Rd. Ext corridors. **Pets:** Other species. $7 daily fee/pet. Service with restrictions, supervision.

✕ ⬧ ⬧ ✕ ⬧ ⬧

# DETROIT METROPOLITAN AREA

## ALLEN PARK

**Best Western Greenfield Inn** SH
(313) 271-1600. **$100-$150.** 3000 Enterprise Dr. I-94, exit 206 (Oakwood Blvd), just s, then just w. Int corridors. **Pets:** Medium, dogs only. $100 deposit/room. Designated rooms, service with restrictions, supervision.

**Holiday Inn Express & Suites** SH
(313) 323-3500. **$99-$149.** 3600 Enterprise Dr. I-94, exit 206 (Oakwood Blvd), just s, then just w. Int corridors. **Pets:** Accepted.

## AUBURN HILLS

**AmeriSuites (Detroit/Auburn Hills)** SH
(248) 475-9393. **$59-$149.** 1545 Opdyke Rd. I-75, exit 79 (University Dr), just w to Opdyke Rd, then just n. Int corridors. **Pets:** Small, other species. $10 daily fee/pet. Designated rooms, service with restrictions, supervision.

**Candlewood Suites** SH
(248) 373-3342. **$89-$109.** 1650 N Opdyke Rd. I-75, exit 79 (University Dr), just w, then 0.4 mi n. Int corridors. **Pets:** Accepted.

**Homestead Studio Suites Hotel-Detroit/Auburn Hills** SH
(248) 340-8888. **$80-$95.** 3315 University Dr. I-75, exit 79 (University Dr), 0.9 mi e. Int corridors. **Pets:** $25 daily fee/pet. Service with restrictions, supervision.

**Staybridge Suites** SH
(248) 322-4600. **$144-$159.** 2050 Featherstone Rd. I-75, exit 79 (University Dr), just w, 0.5 mi s on Opdyke Rd, then just e. Int corridors. **Pets:** Large, other species. $75 one-time fee/room. Service with restrictions, crate.

## BELLEVILLE

**Red Roof Inn Metro Airport #7183** M
(734) 697-2244. **$60-$77.** 45501 N I-94 Service Dr. I-94, exit 190 (Belleville Rd), just n. Ext corridors. **Pets:** Accepted.

**Super 8 Motel** SH
(734) 699-1888. **$55-$95.** 45707 S I-94 Service Dr. I-94, exit 190 (Belleville Rd), just s. Int corridors. **Pets:** Accepted.

## BIRMINGHAM

**Barclay Inn Birmingham** SH
(248) 646-7300. **$79-$250.** 34952 Woodward Ave. On SR 1, jct Woodward Ave and Maple Rd; center. Ext/int corridors. **Pets:** Medium. $25 one-time fee/room. Designated rooms, service with restrictions, crate.

**Holiday Inn Express–Birmingham** SH
(248) 642-6200. **$119-$129.** 35270 Woodward Ave. Jct Woodward Ave and Maple Rd; center. Int corridors. **Pets:** Small. $25 daily fee/room. Designated rooms, service with restrictions, supervision.

## CANTON

**Baymont Inn & Suites Detroit-Canton** SH
(734) 981-1808. **$74-$114.** 41211 Ford Rd. I-275, exit 25 (Ford Rd), just w to jct Haggerty Rd. Int corridors. **Pets:** Medium. Service with restrictions.

**Super 8 Motel-Canton** SH
(734) 722-8880. **$64-$89.** 3933 Lotz Rd. I-275, exit 22 (Michigan Ave), just e on US 12, then just s. Int corridors. **Pets:** Accepted.

## DEARBORN

**Red Roof Inn-Dearborn #7182** M
(313) 278-9732. **$64-$91.** 24130 Michigan Ave. Jct US 24 (Telegraph Rd) and 12 (Michigan Ave). Ext corridors. **Pets:** Accepted.

**The Ritz-Carlton, Dearborn** LH
(313) 441-2000. **$249-$324.** 300 Town Center Dr. SR 39 (Southfield Frwy); between Ford Rd and Michigan Ave exits, on Service Dr. Int corridors. **Pets:** Medium. $125 one-time fee/room. Designated rooms, service with restrictions, crate.

**TownePlace Suites** SH
(313) 271-0200. **$100-$130.** 6141 Mercury Dr. SR 39 (Southfield Frwy), exit 7 (Ford Rd), just e, then 0.8 mi n. Int corridors. **Pets:** Accepted.

## DETROIT

**Holiday Inn Express** LH
(313) 887-7000. **$90-$180.** 1020 Washington Blvd. Corner of Washington Blvd and Michigan Ave. Int corridors. **Pets:** Medium. $25 one-time fee/room. Service with restrictions, supervision.

**Residence Inn By Marriott-Dearborn** SH
(313) 441-1700. **$59-$199.** 5777 Southfield Service Dr. SR 39 (Southfield Frwy), exit Ford Rd, just w. Ext corridors. **Pets:** Accepted.

## FARMINGTON HILLS

**Candlewood Suites** SH
(248) 324-0540. **$49-$249.** 37555 Hills Tech Dr. I-696, exit I-96 E/I-275 S/SR 5, just s to SR 5 N, 2 mi n to 12 Mile Rd, 1.3 mi e, then 0.3 mi s on Halsted Rd. Int corridors. **Pets:** Large, other species. $150 one-time fee/room. Service with restrictions.

**Red Roof Inn-Farmington Hills #7038** M
(248) 478-8640. **$57-$74.** 24300 Sinacola Ct. I-96/275 and SR 5, exit 165 (Grand River Ave), just w. Ext corridors. **Pets:** Accepted.

## LAKE ORION

**Best Western Palace Inn** SH
(248) 391-2755. **$80-$90.** 2755 N Lapeer Rd. I-75, exit 81 (Lapeer Rd), 3.3 mi n. Ext/int corridors. **Pets:** Accepted.

## LIVONIA

**AmeriSuites (Detroit/Livonia)** SH
(734) 953-9224. **$129-$209.** 19300 Haggerty Rd. I-275, exit 169 (7 Mile Rd), just w. Int corridors. **Pets:** Accepted.

▼▼▼ Residence Inn Detroit-Livonia SH
(734) 462-4201. $129-$139. 17250 Fox Dr. I-275, exit 170 (6 Mile Rd), just w. Int corridors. Pets: Accepted.

ASK S▲ ✕ ◆M ⬡ ⬢ ◨ ◻ ⤳ ⊠

## MADISON HEIGHTS

▼ Motel 6 Madison Heights #1109 M
(248) 583-0500. $45-$58. 32700 Barrington Rd. I-75, exit 65A (14 Mile Rd), just e. Ext corridors. Pets: Accepted.

S▲ ✕ ◆M ⬡ ⬢

▼ ▼ Red Roof Inn #7084 M
(248) 583-4700. $57-$77. 32511 Concord Dr. I-75, exit 65A (14 Mile Rd), just e, then just s. Ext corridors. Pets: Accepted.

✕ ⬡ ◨

▼ ▼ Residence Inn by Marriott-Detroit Troy/Madison
    Heights SH
(248) 583-4322. $159. 32650 Stephenson Hwy. I-75, exit 65B (14 Mile Rd), just w, then just s. Ext corridors. Pets: Accepted.

✕ ⬡ ◨ ◻ ⤳ ⊠

## NOVI

▼▼▼ Residence Inn by Marriott-Detroit/Novi SH
(248) 735-7400. $159-$199. 27477 Caberet Dr. I-96, exit 162 (Novi Rd), just n to 12 Mile Rd, then just w. Int corridors. Pets: Large, other species. $75 one-time fee/room. Service with restrictions, crate.

ASK S▲ ✕ ◆M ⬡ ⬢ ◨ ◻ ⤳

▼▼▼ Sheraton-Detroit-Novi LH
(248) 349-4000. $89-$219. 21111 Haggerty Rd. I-275, exit 167 (8 Mile Rd), just w to Haggerty Rd, then just n. Int corridors. Pets: Accepted.

ASK S▲ ✕ ◆M ⬡ ⬢ ◨ ◻ ¶ ⤳ ⊠

▼ ▼ StudioPlus Deluxe Studios SH
(248) 344-4555. $48-$70. 39640 Orchard Hill Pl. I-275, exit 167 (8 Mile Rd), 0.4 mi w, then just n. Int corridors. Pets: Accepted.

ASK S▲ ✕ ⬢ ◨ ◻

▼ ▼ TownePlace Suites SH
(248) 305-5533. $129-$169. 42600 11 Mile Rd. I-96, exit 162 (Novi Rd), just s, 0.5 mi e on Crescent Dr, then just s on Town Center Dr. Int corridors. Pets: Medium. $75 one-time fee/room. Service with restrictions, supervision.

ASK S▲ ✕ ⬢ ◨ ◻ ⤳

## PLYMOUTH

▼ ▼ Red Roof Inn-Plymouth #7016 M
(734) 459-3300. $62-$83. 39700 Ann Arbor Rd. I-275, exit 28 (Ann Arbor Rd), just e. Ext corridors. Pets: Accepted.

✕ ⬡ ⬢ ◨

## PONTIAC

▼▼▼ Residence Inn by Marriott Detroit Pontiac/Auburn
    Hills SH
(248) 858-8664. $99-$199. 3333 Centerpoint Pkwy. I-75, exit 75 (Square Lake Rd), w via Opdyke Rd. Int corridors. Pets: Accepted.

ASK S▲ ✕ ⬡ ⬢ ◨ ◻ ⤳ ⊠

## ROCHESTER HILLS

▼ ▼ Red Roof Inn #7191 M
(248) 853-6400. $60-$86. 2580 Crooks Rd. Jct Hall (SR 59) and Crooks rds. Ext corridors. Pets: Accepted.

✕ ⬡ ⬢ ◨

## ROMULUS

▼ ▼ Baymont Inn & Suites Detroit-Airport SH
(734) 722-6000. $70-$124. 9000 Wickham Rd. I-94, exit 198 (Merriman Rd), just n, then just w. Int corridors. Pets: Medium. Service with restrictions.

ASK ✕ ⬡ ◨ ◻

▼▼▼ Detroit Metro Airport Marriott SH
(734) 729-7555. $79-$179, 14 day notice. 30559 Flynn Dr. I-94, exit 198 (Merriman Rd), just n, then 0.3 mi e. Int corridors. Pets: Accepted.

ASK S▲ ✕ ◆M ⬡ ◨ ◻ ¶ ⤳

▼ ▼ Extended StayAmerica SH
(734) 722-7780. $65. 30325 Flynn Dr. I-94, exit 198 (Merriman Rd), just n, then 0.4 mi e. Int corridors. Pets: Accepted.

✕ ◨ ◻

▼ ▼ Four Points by Sheraton Detroit Metro Airport SH
(734) 729-9000. $170. 8800 Wickham Rd. I-94, exit 198 (Merriman Rd), just n, then just e. Int corridors. Pets: Medium, dogs only. Service with restrictions, supervision.

ASK S▲ ✕ ⬡ ◨ ◻ ¶ ⤳

▼ Northwest Inn SH
(734) 595-7400. $52-$69. 9095 Wickham Rd. I-94, exit 198 (Merriman Rd), just n, then just w. Int corridors. Pets: Accepted.

ASK S▲ ✕ ⬢ ◨ ◻

⬢⬢⬢ ▼ ▼ Ramada Detroit Airport SH
(734) 728-2322. $54. 31119 Flynn Dr. I-94, exit 198 (Merriman Rd). Ext/int corridors. Pets: Other species. $20 daily fee/pet. Service with restrictions, supervision.

SAVE S▲ ✕ ◆M ⬡ ⬢ ◻ ⤳

▼ ▼ Super 8 Motel-Romulus SH
(734) 946-8808. $54-$60. 9863 Middlebelt Rd. I-94, exit 199 (Middlebelt Rd), 0.8 mi s. Int corridors. Pets: $25 one-time fee/room. Service with restrictions, crate.

ASK S▲ ✕ ◆M ◨

⬢⬢⬢ ▼ ▼ ▼ The Westin Detroit Metropolitan
    Airport LH ❀
(734) 942-6500. $99-$279. 2501 Worldgateway Pl. I-94, exit 198 (Merriman Rd); at McNamara Terminal. Int corridors. Pets: Medium, dogs only. Service with restrictions, supervision.

SAVE S▲ ✕ ◆M ⬢ ◨ ◻ ¶ ⤳

## ROSEVILLE

▼▼▼ Baymont Inn & Suites Detroit-Roseville SH
(586) 296-6910. $59-$84. 20675 13 Mile Rd. I-94, exit 232 (Little Mack Ave), just s. Int corridors. Pets: Large. $50 deposit/room. Designated rooms, service with restrictions, supervision.

ASK S▲ ✕ ⬡ ◨ ◻

▼▼▼ Best Western Georgian Inn M
(586) 294-0400. $69-$189. 31327 Gratiot Ave. I-94, exit 232 (Little Mack Ave), just s, 0.5 mi n on 13 Mile Rd, then just n. Ext corridors. Pets: Dogs only. $8 daily fee/pet. Service with restrictions.

ASK S▲ ✕ ◨ ◻ ¶ ⤳

▼ ▼ Red Roof Inn #7012 M
(586) 296-0310. $51-$77. 31800 Little Mack Ave. I-94, exit 232 (Little Mack Ave), just n. Ext corridors. Pets: Accepted.

✕ ⬢

## SOUTHFIELD

▼ ▼ Candlewood Suites SH
(248) 945-0010. $59-$189. 1 Corporate Dr. SR 10 (Northwestern Hwy), exit Lasher Rd, just e. Int corridors. Pets: Medium. $75 one-time fee/pet. Service with restrictions, crate.

ASK S▲ ✕ ◆M ⬢ ◨ ◻

▼▼▼▼ **Hawthorn Suites Ltd** SH
(248) 350-2400. **$89-$149.** 25100 Northwestern Hwy. SR 10 (Northwestern Hwy), exit 10 Mile Rd. Int corridors. **Pets:** Accepted.

ASK ✕ &M ⟨⟩ ⊟ ▣ ⨦

▼▼ **Holiday Inn-Southfield** LH
(248) 353-7700. **$99.** 26555 Telegraph Rd. I-696, exit 9 (Telegraph Rd), just s on US 24 (Telegraph Rd). Int corridors. **Pets:** Accepted.

ASK S⊙ ✕ ⟨⟩ ⟨⟩ ⊟ ▣ ⫟ ⨦ ⊠

▼▼ **Homestead Studio Suites**
  **Hotel-Detroit/Southfield** SH
(248) 213-4500. **$74-$89.** 28500 Northwestern Hwy. I-696, exit 9, just nw of jct US 24 (Telegraph Rd). Int corridors. **Pets:** $25 daily fee/pet. Service with restrictions, supervision.

ASK S⊙ ✕ &M ⟨⟩ ⟨⟩ ⊟ ▣

⟨AAA⟩ ▼▼▼ **Marvin's Garden Inn** M
(248) 353-6777. **$109-$259.** 27650 Northwestern Hwy. I-696, exit 9 (Telegraph Rd), just nw of Telegraph Rd. Ext/int corridors. **Pets:** $100 deposit/room. Designated rooms, service with restrictions, supervision.

SAVE S⊙ ✕ ⟨⟩ ⊟ ▣ ⨦

▼▼ **Red Roof Inn-Southfield #7133** M
(248) 353-7200. **$68-$84.** 27660 Northwestern Hwy. I-696, exit 9 (Telegraph Rd), just nw. Ext corridors. **Pets:** Accepted.

✕ &M ⟨⟩ ⊟

▼▼ **Residence Inn by Marriott** SH
(248) 352-8900. **$119-$169.** 26700 Central Park Blvd. I-696, exit 11 (Evergreen Rd), just sw of jct 11 Mile and Evergreen rds. Ext corridors. **Pets:** Accepted.

ASK ✕ &M ⟨⟩ ⊟ ▣ ⨦

⟨AAA⟩ ▼▼▼ ▼▼▼ **Westin Hotel Southfield-Detroit** LH
(248) 827-4000. **$89-$239.** 1500 Town Center. SR 10 (Northwestern Hwy), exit 10 Mile/Evergreen rds, 0.3 mi n. Int corridors. **Pets:** Accepted.

SAVE S⊙ ✕ &M ⟨⟩ ⟨⟩ ⊟ ▣ ⫟ ⨦

## SOUTHGATE

⟨AAA⟩ ▼▼▼ **Americas Best Value Inn & Suites** M
(734) 287-8340. **$54-$70.** 18777 Northline Rd. I-75, exit 37 (Northline Rd), just w. Ext corridors. **Pets:** Small, other species. $5 daily fee/pet. Designated rooms, no service.

SAVE S⊙ ✕ ⟨⟩ ⊟ ▣ ⨦

⟨AAA⟩ ▼▼▼ **Baymont Inn & Suites Detroit-Southgate** SH
(734) 374-3000. **$67-$124.** 12888 Reeck Rd. I-75, exit 37 (Northline Rd), just w. Int corridors. **Pets:** Medium. Service with restrictions.

SAVE ✕ ⟨⟩ ⊟ ▣

## STERLING HEIGHTS

▼▼ **TownePlace Suites** SH
(586) 566-0900. **$89-$119.** 14800 Lakeside Cir. 1 mi e of jct SR 53 (Van Dyke Ave) and 59 (Hall Rd). Int corridors. **Pets:** Accepted.

ASK S⊙ ✕ &M ⟨⟩ ⊟ ▣ ⨦

## TAYLOR

▼▼ **Red Roof Inn-Taylor #7189** M
(734) 374-1150. **$61-$82.** 21230 Eureka Rd. I-75, exit 36 (Eureka Rd), just w. Ext corridors. **Pets:** Accepted.

✕ ⊟

## TROY

▼▼▼▼ **Drury Inn & Suites-Troy** SH
(248) 528-3330. **$85-$125.** 575 W Big Beaver Rd. I-75, exit 69 (Big Beaver Rd), just e. Int corridors. **Pets:** Accepted.

ASK ✕ ⟨⟩ ⟨⟩ ⊟ ▣ ⫟ ⨦

▼▼ **Holiday Inn-Troy** SH
(248) 689-7500. **$72-$129.** 2537 Rochester Ct. I-75, exit 67 (Rochester Rd), 0.3 mi sw, then just w. Int corridors. **Pets:** Dogs only. $30 one-time fee/room. Service with restrictions, crate.

ASK S⊙ ✕ ⊟ ▣ ⫟ ⨦

▼▼ **Red Roof Inn-Troy #7021** M
(248) 689-4391. **$61-$86.** 2350 Rochester Ct. I-75, exit 67 (Rochester Rd), 0.3 mi sw. Ext corridors. **Pets:** Accepted.

✕ ⟨⟩

▼▼▼ **Residence Inn by Marriott** SH
(248) 689-6856. **$89-$169.** 2600 Livernois Rd. I-75, exit 69 (Big Beaver Rd), 0.5 mi e to Livernois Rd, then 0.5 mi s. Ext corridors. **Pets:** Accepted.

ASK S⊙ ✕ ⟨⟩ ⊟ ▣ ⨦ ⊠

## UTICA

⟨AAA⟩ ▼▼▼▼ **AmeriSuites (Detroit/Utica)** SH
(586) 803-0100. **$49-$129.** 45400 Park Ave. Jct Van Dyke Ave (SR 53) and Hall Rd (SR 59). Int corridors. **Pets:** Small. $10 one-time fee/pet. Service with restrictions, crate.

SAVE S⊙ ✕ &M ⟨⟩ ⊟ ▣ ⨦

⟨AAA⟩ ▼▼▼ **Baymont Inn & Suites Detroit-Utica** SH
(586) 731-4700. **$89-$159.** 45311 Park Ave. Jct Van Dyke Ave (SR 53) and Hall Rd (SR 59), just n. Int corridors. **Pets:** Medium. Service with restrictions.

SAVE ✕ ⟨⟩ ⟨⟩ ⊟ ▣ ⨦

⟨AAA⟩ ▼▼▼ **Staybridge Suites-Utica** SH
(586) 323-0101. **$129-$199.** 46155 Utica Park Blvd. Jct Van Dyke Ave (SR 53) and Hall Rd (SR 59), just n. Int corridors. **Pets:** Large, other species. $75 one-time fee/room. Service with restrictions, supervision.

SAVE S⊙ ✕ ⊟ ▣ ⨦

## WARREN

⟨AAA⟩ ▼▼▼ **Baymont Inn & Suites Detroit-Warren Tech**
  **Center** SH
(586) 574-0550. **$69-$104.** 30900 Van Dyke Ave. I-696, exit 23 (Van Dyke Ave), 2 mi n on SR 53. Int corridors. **Pets:** Medium. Service with restrictions.

SAVE ✕ ⟨⟩ ⊟ ▣

⟨AAA⟩ ▼▼▼▼ **Hawthorn Suites Ltd** SH
(586) 264-8800. **$89-$94.** 7601 Chicago Rd. I-696, exit 23 (Van Dyke Ave), 1.8 mi n. Int corridors. **Pets:** $75 one-time fee/pet. Service with restrictions.

SAVE S⊙ ✕ ⊟ ▣ ⨦

▼▼▼▼ **Homewood Suites by Hilton** SH ❀
(586) 558-7870. **$79-$159, 3 day notice.** 30180 N Civic Center Blvd. I-696, exit 23 (Van Dyke Rd), 2 mi n. Ext/int corridors. **Pets:** $100 one-time fee/room. Service with restrictions, crate.

ASK S⊙ ✕ &M ⟨⟩ ⊟ ▣ ⨦

▼▼ **Quality Inn** SH ❀
(586) 264-0100. **$53-$72.** 32035 Van Dyke Ave. I-696, exit 23 (Van Dyke Ave), 2.7 mi n. Int corridors. **Pets:** Medium, other species. $10 daily fee/pet. Designated rooms, service with restrictions, crate.

ASK S⊙ ✕ ⟨⟩ ⊟ ▣ ⫟ ⨦ ⊠

▼▼ **Red Roof Inn-Warren #7070** M
(586) 573-4300. **$57-$81.** 26300 Dequindre Rd. I-696, exit 20 (Dequindre Rd), just ne. Ext corridors. **Pets:** Accepted.

✕ ⟨⟩ ⊟

# DE WITT

**AAA ▼▼▼ Sleep Inn** SH
(517) 669-8823. **$93-$103.** 1101 Commerce Park Dr. I-69, exit 87 (Business US 127), 0.8 mi n. Int corridors. **Pets:** Medium, dogs only. $10 daily fee/pet. Designated rooms, service with restrictions, supervision.
SAVE S♦ ✕ 🔌 🛏 🖥 🏊

# DOUGLAS

**▼▼ AmericInn of Saugatuck/Douglas** SH 🐾
(269) 857-8581. **$63-$254, 7 day notice.** 2905 Blue Star Hwy. I-196, exit 36, 0.3 mi n. Int corridors. **Pets:** Dogs only. $30 daily fee/pet. Designated rooms, service with restrictions, supervision.
ASK ✕ &M 🔌 🛏 🖥 🏊

# DOWAGIAC

**AAA ▼▼▼ AmeriHost Inn & Suites-Dowagiac** SH
(269) 782-4270. **$84-$99.** 29291 Amerihost Dr. 0.4 mi s of jct SR 51 and 62. Int corridors. **Pets:** Medium. $20 deposit/room. Designated rooms, service with restrictions, supervision.
SAVE S♦ ✕ 🔌 🛏 🖥 🏊

# EAGLE HARBOR

**▼ Shoreline Resort** M
(906) 289-4441. **$70-$77.** 201 Front St, F #2015. On SR 26. Ext corridors. **Pets:** Accepted.
ASK S♦ 🖥 🍴 🎿 🏷

# EAST LANSING

**▼▼▼ Candlewood Suites** SH
(517) 351-8181. **$59-$179.** 3545 Forest Rd. 1 mi e of I-496 and US 127, exit 11 (Jolly Rd). Int corridors. **Pets:** $75 one-time fee/room. Service with restrictions, crate.
ASK S♦ ✕ &M 🔌 🛏 🖥 🍴

**▼▼▼ Residence Inn by Marriott** SH 🐾
(517) 332-7711. **$89-$159.** 1600 E Grand River Ave. US 127, exit Grand River Ave, 2.6 mi se on SR 43. Ext corridors. **Pets:** Other species. $75 one-time fee/room. Service with restrictions.
ASK S♦ ✕ 🔌 🛏 🖥 🏊 🏷

**▼▼ TownePlace Suites** SH
(517) 203-1000. **$84-$99.** 2855 Hannah Blvd. I-96, exit 110 (Okemos Rd), just n, 0.5 mi w on Jolly Rd, then 0.4 mi n on Hagedorn Rd. Int corridors. **Pets:** Accepted.
ASK S♦ ✕ 🔌 🛏 🖥 🏊

# EAST TAWAS

**▼▼▼ Holiday Inn-Tawas Bay Resort** SH
(989) 362-8601. **$77-$185, 3 day notice.** 300 E Bay St. On US 23 N. Int corridors. **Pets:** Other species. $30 daily fee/room. Service with restrictions, supervision.
ASK S♦ ✕ 🛏 🖥 🍴 🏊 🏷

# ESCANABA

**AAA ▼ Hiawatha Motel** M
(906) 786-1341. **$50-$60.** 2400 Ludington St. 0.5 mi w on US 2/41. Ext corridors. **Pets:** $5 one-time fee/pet. No service, crate.
SAVE S♦ ✕ 🛏

# FENTON

**▼▼▼ Holiday Inn Express Hotel & Suites** SH
(810) 714-7171. **$79-$159.** 17800 Silver Pkwy. US 23, exit 78 (Owen Rd), just w, then 0.4 mi n. Int corridors. **Pets:** Medium. Service with restrictions, supervision.
ASK S♦ ✕ &M 🔌 🛏 🖥 🏊

# FLINT

**AAA ▼▼▼ Baymont Inn & Suites-Flint** SH
(810) 732-2300. **$60-$99.** 4160 Pier North Blvd. I-75, exit 122 (Pierson Rd), just w. Int corridors. **Pets:** Accepted.
SAVE S♦ ✕ 🔌 🛏 🖥 🏊

**▼▼▼ Holiday Inn Express** SH
(810) 238-7744. **$80-$169.** 1150 Robert T Longway Blvd. I-475, exit 8A (Robert T Longway Blvd), just w. Int corridors. **Pets:** Small. $50 deposit/pet. Designated rooms, service with restrictions, supervision.
ASK S♦ ✕ 🔌 🛏 🖥

**▼ Howard Johnson Express Inn** M
(810) 733-5910. **$45-$70.** G-3277 Miller Rd. I-75, exit 117B (Miller Rd) northbound; exit 117 (Miller Rd) southbound, just w. Ext corridors. **Pets:** Other species. $10 daily fee/pet. Designated rooms, service with restrictions, supervision.
✕ 🛏 🖥 🏊

**▼▼ Red Roof Inn-Flint #7004** M
(810) 733-1660. **$48-$68.** G-3219 Miller Rd. I-75, exit 117B (Miller Rd), just w. Ext corridors. **Pets:** Accepted.
🔌 🛏 🖥

**▼▼▼ Residence Inn by Marriott** SH
(810) 424-7000. **$110-$250, 14 day notice.** 2202 W Hill Rd. US 23, exit 90 (Hill Rd), just e. Int corridors. **Pets:** Accepted.
ASK S♦ ✕ &M 🔌 🛏 🖥 🏊 🏷

# FRANKENMUTH

**▼▼ Drury Inn & Suites-Frankenmuth** SH
(989) 652-2800. **$95-$157.** 260 S Main St. On SR 83; downtown. Int corridors. **Pets:** Accepted.
ASK ✕ &M 🔌 🛏 🖥 🏊

# GAYLORD

**AAA ▼▼▼ Americas Best Value Royal Crest Inn** SH
(989) 732-6451. **$49-$99.** 803 S Otsego Ave. I-75, exit 279, 2.3 mi ne on I-75 business loop. Int corridors. **Pets:** Accepted.
SAVE S♦ ✕ 🛏 🖥 🏊 🏷

**AAA ▼▼▼ Best Western Alpine Lodge** SH 🐾
(989) 732-2431. **$69-$109.** 833 W Main St. I-75, exit 282, 0.3 mi e on SR 32. Ext/int corridors. **Pets:** Medium, dogs only. Service with restrictions, supervision.
SAVE S♦ ✕ 🛏 🖥 🍴 🏊 🏷

**AAA ▼ Downtown Motel** M
(989) 732-5010. **$46-$66.** 208 S Otsego Ave. I-75, exit 282, 0.5 mi e and 0.3 mi s on I-75 business loop. Ext/int corridors. **Pets:** Dogs only. $5 daily fee/pet. Service with restrictions, supervision.
SAVE S♦ ✕ 🛏

**AAA ▼▼ Quality Inn** SH 🐾
(989) 732-7541. **$59-$109.** 137 West St. I-75, exit 282, 0.3 mi e on SR 32. Int corridors. **Pets:** Other species. $10 daily fee/room. Designated rooms, service with restrictions, supervision.
SAVE S♦ ✕ 🛏 🖥 🍴 🏊 🏷

**▼▼ Red Roof Inn** SH
(989) 731-6331. **$46-$99.** 510 S Wisconsin Ave. I-75, exit 282, just e on SR 32, then 0.4 mi s. Int corridors. **Pets:** Medium, other species. No service, supervision.
ASK S♦ ✕ &M 🔌 🛏 🖥 🏊

**Timberly Motel M**
(989) 732-5166. **$48-$84, 10 day notice.** 881 S Otsego Ave. I-75, exit 279, 2.5 mi n on I-75 business loop (Old US 27). Ext corridors. **Pets:** Other species. $5 daily fee/pet. Designated rooms, service with restrictions, supervision.
SAVE 🔊 ❌

# GRAND MARAIS

**ArborGate Inn M**
(906) 494-2681. **$55-$65.** 21795 Randolph Rd. Just e of SR 77. Ext corridors. **Pets:** Accepted.
SAVE 🔊 ❌ 🔲 🅺 📶

**Voyageur's Motel M**
(906) 494-2389. **$68-$88.** 21914 E Wilson St. 0.5 mi e of SR 77. Ext corridors. **Pets:** Dogs only. $10 daily fee/pet. Designated rooms, service with restrictions, supervision.
ASK 🔊 ❌ 🔲 📶 🅺

# GRAND RAPIDS

**Homewood Suites by Hilton SH**
(616) 285-7100. **$99-$149, 14 day notice.** 3920 Stahl Dr SE. I-96, exit 43A (28th St SW), 1.5 mi w to E Paris Ave, then just n. Int corridors. **Pets:** Accepted.
ASK 🔊 ❌ 🔲 📶

**Radisson Hotel Grand Rapids Riverfront LH**
(616) 363-9001. **$89-$119.** 270 Ann St NW. US 131, exit 88, 1.8 mi n. Int corridors. **Pets:** Medium. $20 one-time fee/room. Designated rooms, service with restrictions, supervision.
SAVE 🔊 ❌ 🔲 📶 🏊 ❌

# GRANDVILLE

**Comfort Suites SH**
(616) 667-0733. **$74-$109, 7 day notice.** 4520 Kenowa Ave SW. I-196, exit 67, just sw. Int corridors. **Pets:** Accepted.
SAVE 🔊 ❌ 🔲 📶 🏊

**Residence Inn by Marriott Grand Rapids West SH**
(616) 538-1100. **$85-$199.** 3451 Rivertown Point Ct SW. I-196, exit 67, 1.7 mi e. Int corridors. **Pets:** Accepted.
ASK ❌ 🔲 📶 🏊 ❌

# GRAYLING

**Holiday Inn SH** 🐾
(989) 348-7611. **$79-$185.** 2650 S Business Loop. I-75 business loop, 0.8 mi s. Ext/int corridors. **Pets:** Other species. Service with restrictions.
ASK 🔊 ❌ 📶 🔲 🏊 ❌

**North Country Lodge M**
(989) 348-8471. **$56-$175.** 617 N I-75 Business Loop. 1 mi n. Ext corridors. **Pets:** Accepted.
SAVE ❌ 🔲

**Super 8 Motel SH**
(989) 348-8888. **$57-$74.** 5828 Nelson A Miles Pkwy. I-75, exit 251, just w. Int corridors. **Pets:** Accepted.
ASK ❌ 🔲 📶 🏊 ❌

# HANCOCK

**Best Western Copper Crown Motel SH**
(906) 482-6111. **$65.** 235 Hancock Ave. On US 41 S; downtown. Ext/int corridors. **Pets:** $10 daily fee/room. Designated rooms, service with restrictions, supervision.
ASK 🔊 ❌ 📶 🏊 ❌

# HARRISON

**Lakeside Motel & Cottages M** ❀
(989) 539-3796. **$55-$89.** 515 Park St. US 127, exit US 127 business route/SR 61, 2.2 mi w. Ext corridors. **Pets:** Other species. Service with restrictions, supervision.
SAVE 🔊 ❌ 🔲 📶 ❌

# HART

**Budget Host Motel SH**
(231) 873-1855. **$59-$119, 14 day notice.** 4143 Polk Rd. US 31, exit Mears/Hart, just e on US 31 business route. Int corridors. **Pets:** Very small. $25 deposit/room. Designated rooms, service with restrictions, supervision.
❌ 📶

**Comfort Inn SH**
(231) 873-3456. **$70-$180.** 2248 N Comfort Dr. US 31, exit Mears/Hart, just e on US 31 business route. Int corridors. **Pets:** Other species. $10 daily fee/pet. Service with restrictions, supervision.
SAVE 🔊 ❌ ♿ 🔲 📶 🏊 ❌

# HOLLAND

**Best Western Kelly Inn & Suites SH**
(616) 994-0400. **$69-$109.** 2888 W Shore Dr. US 31, exit Felch St E, just n. Ext/int corridors. **Pets:** Accepted.
SAVE 🔊 ❌ ♿ 📶 ♿ 🔲 📶 🏊 ❌

**Comfort Inn SH**
(616) 392-1000. **$69-$139.** 422 E 32nd St. Just w of US 31. Int corridors. **Pets:** Accepted.
ASK 🔊 ❌ 🔲 📶

**Residence Inn by Marriott SH**
(616) 393-6900. **$113-$149.** 631 Southpoint Ridge Rd. I-196, exit 49, 0.7 mi n on SR 40. Int corridors. **Pets:** Accepted.
ASK ❌ ♿ 🔲 📶 🏊 ❌

# HOUGHTON

**Best Value King's Inn SH**
(906) 482-5000. **$69-$110.** 215 Shelden Ave. On US 41; downtown. Int corridors. **Pets:** Accepted.
ASK 🔊 ❌ 🔲 📶 🏊 ❌

**Best Western-Franklin Square Inn SH**
(906) 487-1700. **$91-$111.** 820 Shelden Ave. On US 41; downtown. Int corridors. **Pets:** Accepted.
SAVE 🔊 ❌ 🔲 📶 🍴 🏊 ❌

# HOUGHTON LAKE

**Hillside Motel M**
(989) 366-5711. **$64-$74, 3 day notice.** 3419 W Houghton Lake Dr. On SR 55, 6 mi e of US 27; 10 mi w of I-75. Ext corridors. **Pets:** Supervision.
ASK 🔊 ❌ 🔲

**Holiday Inn Express SH** 🐾
(989) 422-7829. **$49-$149.** 200 Cloverleaf Ln. Jct US 127 and SR 55, just e. Int corridors. **Pets:** Other species. $25 one-time fee/room. Service with restrictions.
ASK 🔊 ❌ ♿ 🔲 🏊

**Super 8 Motel SH**
(989) 422-3119. **$65-$139.** 9580 W Lake City Rd. Jct US 127 and SR 55. Int corridors. **Pets:** $5 daily fee/pet. Service with restrictions, supervision.
ASK 🔊 ❌ 🔲 🏊 ❌

# HOWELL

### ▼▼ ▼▼ Best Western Howell Ⓜ
(517) 548-2900. **$89-$145.** 1500 Pinckney Rd. I-96, exit 137 (Pickney Rd), just s on CR D19. Ext corridors. **Pets:** Small, dogs only. $15 daily fee/pet. Designated rooms, service with restrictions, supervision.

⟨ASK⟩ ⟨S⟩ ⟨✕⟩ ⟨🖥⟩ ⟨💻⟩ ⟨🏊⟩

# HUDSONVILLE

### ◆▼ AmeriHost Inn-Hudsonville ⓈⒽ
(616) 662-4000. **$69-$150.** 3301 Highland Dr. I-196, exit 62 (32nd Ave), just nw. Int corridors. **Pets:** Small, other species. $25 one-time fee/room. Service with restrictions, supervision.

⟨ASK⟩ ⟨✕⟩ ⟨&M⟩ ⟨♿⟩ ⟨🖥⟩ ⟨💻⟩ ⟨🏊⟩

# IMLAY CITY

### ▲▲ ▼▼ Days Inn ⓈⒽ
(810) 724-8005. **$59-$82.** 6692 Newark Rd. I-69, exit 168 (SR 53/Van Dyke Rd), 0.3 mi n, then w. Int corridors. **Pets:** Medium. $50 deposit/room, $10 one-time fee/pet. Service with restrictions, supervision.

⟨SAVE⟩ ⟨S⟩ ⟨✕⟩ ⟨♪⟩ ⟨🖥⟩ ⟨💻⟩ ⟨🏊⟩

### ▼▼ ◆ Super 8 Motel-Imlay City ⓈⒽ
(810) 724-8700. **$52-$99.** 6951 Newark Rd. I-69, exit 168 (SR 53/Van Dyke Rd), just n to Newark Rd, then just e. Int corridors. **Pets:** $10 one-time fee/room. Service with restrictions, supervision.

⟨ASK⟩ ⟨S⟩ ⟨✕⟩ ⟨🖥⟩

# INDIAN RIVER

### ▲▲ ▼▼ Nor Gate Motel Ⓜ
(231) 238-7788. **$44-$50, 3 day notice.** 4846 S Straits Hwy. I-75, exit 310, 0.3 mi w, then 2 mi s on Old US 27. Ext corridors. **Pets:** Accepted.

⟨SAVE⟩ ⟨S⟩ ⟨✕⟩ ⟨🖥⟩ ⟨💻⟩ ⟨✕⟩

# IONIA

### ▲▲ ▼▼ Super 8 Motel ⓈⒽ
(616) 527-2828. **$62-$110.** 7245 S State Rd. I-96, exit 67 (SR 66). Int corridors. **Pets:** Accepted.

⟨SAVE⟩ ⟨S⟩ ⟨✕⟩ ⟨&M⟩ ⟨♪⟩ ⟨♿⟩ ⟨🖥⟩ ⟨💻⟩

# IRON MOUNTAIN

### ◆ Americans Best Inn ⓈⒽ
(906) 776-8000. **$40-$60.** 1609 S Stephenson Ave. 1 mi e on US 2. Ext/int corridors. **Pets:** Other species. Designated rooms, supervision.

⟨ASK⟩ ⟨✕⟩ ⟨🖥⟩ ⟨🏊⟩ ⟨✕⟩

### ▲▲ ▼▼ Budget Host Inn Ⓜ ❀
(906) 774-6797. **$52-$57.** 1663 N Stephenson Ave. 1.5 mi nw on US 2 and 141. Ext corridors. **Pets:** Medium. $5 daily fee/room. Designated rooms, service with restrictions, supervision.

⟨SAVE⟩ ⟨S⟩ ⟨✕⟩ ⟨🖥⟩

### ▼▼ ▼▼ Days Inn ⓈⒽ
(906) 774-2181. **$50-$110.** W8176 S US 2. On US 2, 1.8 mi e. Ext/int corridors. **Pets:** Dogs only. $10 one-time fee/room. Designated rooms, service with restrictions, supervision.

⟨ASK⟩ ⟨S⟩ ⟨✕⟩ ⟨🖥⟩ ⟨🏊⟩ ⟨✕⟩

# IRONWOOD

### ▲▲ ▼▼ AmericInn of Ironwood ⓈⒽ
(906) 932-7200. **$74-$179.** 1117 E Cloverland Dr. 0.8 mi e on US 2. Int corridors. **Pets:** Other species. $25 one-time fee/room. Designated rooms, service with restrictions, supervision.

⟨SAVE⟩ ⟨S⟩ ⟨✕⟩ ⟨&M⟩ ⟨♿⟩ ⟨🖥⟩ ⟨💻⟩ ⟨🏊⟩ ⟨✕⟩

### ▲▲ ▼▼ Crestview Motel Ⓜ ❀
(906) 932-4845. **$45-$80.** 424 W Cloverland Dr. 0.4 mi w on US 2. Ext corridors. **Pets:** $8 one-time fee/room. No service, supervision.

⟨SAVE⟩ ⟨✕⟩ ⟨🖥⟩ ⟨💻⟩

### ▲▲ ▼▼ Royal Motel Ⓜ
(906) 932-4230. **$41-$46, 7 day notice.** 715 W Cloverland Dr. 0.7 mi w on US 2. Ext corridors. **Pets:** Very small, dogs only. Designated rooms, service with restrictions, supervision.

⟨SAVE⟩ ⟨✕⟩

### ▼▼ Super 8 Motel ⓈⒽ
(906) 932-3395. **$65-$95, 30 day notice.** 160 E Cloverland Dr. Jct US 2 and 2 business route. Int corridors. **Pets:** Other species. $10 daily fee/room. Service with restrictions, supervision.

⟨ASK⟩ ⟨S⟩ ⟨✕⟩ ⟨🖥⟩ ⟨💻⟩ ⟨✕⟩

# ISHPEMING

### ▲▲ ▼▼ ▼▼ Best Western Country Inn ⓈⒽ
(906) 485-6345. **$80-$119.** 850 US 41 W. On US 41, just n of town. Int corridors. **Pets:** Designated rooms, service with restrictions, supervision.

⟨SAVE⟩ ⟨S⟩ ⟨✕⟩ ⟨🖥⟩ ⟨🍴⟩ ⟨🏊⟩ ⟨✕⟩

# JACKSON

### ▲▲ ▼▼ ▼▼ Baymont Inn-Jackson ⓈⒽ
(517) 789-6000. **$75-$85.** 2035 Service Dr. I-94, exit 138 (US 127), just nw. Int corridors. **Pets:** Accepted.

⟨SAVE⟩ ⟨S⟩ ⟨✕⟩ ⟨&M⟩ ⟨♪⟩ ⟨🖥⟩ ⟨💻⟩

### ▼▼▼▼ Holiday Inn ⓈⒽ
(517) 783-2681. **$79-$300.** 2000 Holiday Inn Dr. I-94, exit 138 (US 127), just n to Springport Rd, then just w. Ext/int corridors. **Pets:** Accepted.

⟨ASK⟩ ⟨S⟩ ⟨✕⟩ ⟨♪⟩ ⟨♿⟩ ⟨🖥⟩ ⟨💻⟩ ⟨🍴⟩ ⟨🏊⟩ ⟨✕⟩

### ▼▼ Motel 6-1088 Ⓜ
(517) 789-7186. **$42-$52.** 830 Royal Dr. I-94, exit 138 (US 127), just se. Ext corridors. **Pets:** Accepted.

⟨S⟩ ⟨✕⟩ ⟨♪⟩ ⟨♿⟩ ⟨🏊⟩

### ▼▼ Super 8 Motel-Jackson ⓈⒽ
(517) 788-8780. **$45-$64.** 2001 Shirley Dr. I-94, exit 138 (US 127), just ne. Int corridors. **Pets:** Accepted.

⟨ASK⟩ ⟨S⟩ ⟨✕⟩ ⟨♪⟩ ⟨🖥⟩

# KALAMAZOO

### ▲▲ ▼▼▼▼ Best Western Hospitality Inn ⓈⒽ
(269) 381-1900. **$60-$130.** 3640 E Cork St. I-94, exit 80 (Sprinkle Rd), just nw. Int corridors. **Pets:** Large, other species. $15 daily fee/pet. Service with restrictions, supervision.

⟨SAVE⟩ ⟨S⟩ ⟨✕⟩ ⟨🖥⟩ ⟨💻⟩ ⟨🏊⟩ ⟨✕⟩

### ▲▲ ▼▼▼▼ Clarion Hotel ⓈⒽ
(269) 385-3922. **$74-$179.** 3600 E Cork St. I-94, exit 80 (Sprinkle Rd), just n, then just w. Int corridors. **Pets:** Accepted.

⟨SAVE⟩ ⟨S⟩ ⟨✕⟩ ⟨🖥⟩ ⟨💻⟩ ⟨🍴⟩ ⟨🏊⟩ ⟨✕⟩

### ▲▲ ▼▼ ▼▼ Comfort Inn ⓈⒽ
(269) 381-7000. **$72-$100.** 3820 Sprinkle Rd. I-94, exit 80 (Sprinkle Rd), 0.3 mi s. Int corridors. **Pets:** Other species. $50 one-time fee/pet. Service with restrictions, supervision.

⟨SAVE⟩ ⟨S⟩ ⟨✕⟩ ⟨♿⟩ ⟨🖥⟩ ⟨💻⟩ ⟨🏊⟩

### ▲▲ ▼▼ ▼▼ Econo Lodge ⓈⒽ
(269) 388-3551. **$45-$69.** 3750 Easy St. I-94, exit 80 (Sprinkle Rd), just w. Int corridors. **Pets:** $10 daily fee/pet. Service with restrictions, crate.

⟨SAVE⟩ ⟨S⟩ ⟨✕⟩ ⟨🖥⟩ ⟨💻⟩ ⟨🏊⟩

### ▲▲ ▼▼ Knights Inn Ⓜ ❀
(269) 381-5000. **$50-$70.** 1211 S Westnedge Ave. I-94, exit 76B, 3 mi n, w on Park Pl, then just s. Ext/int corridors. **Pets:** $25 one-time fee/pet. Designated rooms, no service, supervision.

⟨SAVE⟩ ⟨S⟩ ⟨✕⟩ ⟨🖥⟩

▼▼ **Red Roof Inn-East #7003** **M**
(269) 382-6350. **$52-$80.** 3701 E Cork St. I-94, exit 80 (Sprinkle Rd), just n, then just w. Ext corridors. **Pets:** Accepted.
✕ &M ☞

▼▼ **Red Roof Inn-West #7025** **SH**
(269) 375-7400. **$45-$69.** 5425 W Michigan Ave. US 131, exit 36B, just nw. Ext corridors. **Pets:** Accepted.
✕ ☞

# KENTWOOD

▼▼ **Best Western Midway Hotel** **SH**
(616) 942-2550. **$74-$99.** 4101 28th St SE. I-96, exit 43A, 1.5 mi w on SR 11. Int corridors. **Pets:** Accepted.
A$K S☐ ✕ ☐ ☐ ⊞ ☞ ☒

▼▼ **Comfort Inn** **SH** ❖
(616) 957-2080. **$59-$109.** 4155 28th St SE. I-96, exit 43A, 1.5 mi w on SR 11. Int corridors. **Pets:** Medium, other species. Service with restrictions, crate.
A$K S☐ ✕ ☞ ☐ ☐

▼▼▼ **Residence Inn by Marriott East** **SH**
(616) 957-8111. **$69-$169.** 2701 E Beltline Ave. Jct SR 11 and E Beltline Ave (SR 37). Ext corridors. **Pets:** Other species. $75 one-time fee/room. Service with restrictions.
A$K ✕ ☞ ☐ ☐ ☞ ☒

▼▼▼ **Staybridge Suites by Holiday Inn** **SH** ❖
(616) 464-3200. **$95-$159.** 3000 Lake Eastbrook Blvd SE. I-96, exit 43A, 2 mi w on SR 11, then just s. Int corridors. **Pets:** Other species. $75 one-time fee/room. Designated rooms.
A$K S☐ ✕ &M ☞ ☐ ☐ ☞

# LAKE CITY

AAA ▼ **Northcrest Motel** **M**
(231) 839-2075. **$59-$79.** 1341 S Lakeshore. 1 mi s on SR 55 and 66. Ext corridors. **Pets:** Accepted.
SAVE S☐ ☐ ☐ ☞

# LAKESIDE

▼▼▼ **White Rabbit Inn** **BB**
(269) 469-4620. **$95-$200, 7 day notice.** 14634 Red Arrow Hwy. I-94, exit 6 (Union Pier Rd), 1 mi w, then 2 mi n. Ext corridors. **Pets:** Accepted.
✕ ☐ ☐ ☑

# LANSING

AAA ▼▼ **Best Western Midway Hotel** **SH**
(517) 627-8471. **$79-$99.** 7711 W Saginaw Hwy. I-96, exit 93B (SR 43/Saginaw Hwy), just e. Int corridors. **Pets:** Accepted.
SAVE S☐ ✕ ☐ ☐ ⊞ ☞ ☒

AAA ▼▼▼ **Hampton Inn of Lansing** **SH** ❖
(517) 627-8381. **$84-$99.** 525 N Canal Rd. I-96, exit 93B (SR 43/Saginaw Hwy), just e. Int corridors. **Pets:** Medium. $100 deposit/room. Service with restrictions, crate.
SAVE ✕ ☞ ☐ ☐

▼▼ **Motel 6 Lansing West #1089** **M**
(517) 321-1444. **$45-$58.** 7326 W Saginaw Hwy. I-96, exit 93B (SR 43/Saginaw Hwy), just e. Ext corridors. **Pets:** Accepted.
S☐ ✕ ☞ ☞

▼▼ **Red Roof Inn-East #7029** **M**
(517) 332-2575. **$56-$74.** 3615 Dunckel Rd. Just e of I-496 and US 127, exit 11 (Jolly Rd). Ext corridors. **Pets:** Accepted.
✕ ☞ ☐

▼▼ **Red Roof Inn-West #7020** **SH**
(517) 321-7246. **$51-$73.** 7412 W Saginaw Hwy. I-96, exit 93B (SR 43/Saginaw Hwy), just e. Ext corridors. **Pets:** Accepted.
✕

▼▼▼ **Residence Inn by Marriott West** **SH**
(517) 886-5030. **$100-$160, 14 day notice.** 922 Delta Commerce Dr. I-96, exit 93B (SR 43/Saginaw Hwy), 0.4 mi e; behind Bennigans. Int corridors. **Pets:** Accepted.
A$K S☐ ✕ &M ☞ ☐ ☐ ☞ ☒

▼▼▼ **Sheraton Lansing Hotel** **SH** ❖
(517) 323-7100. **$91-$250.** 925 S Creyts Rd. I-496, exit 1 (Creyts Rd), just n. Int corridors. **Pets:** Medium. $30 one-time fee/room. Service with restrictions, supervision.
A$K S☐ ✕ ☞ ☐ ☐ ⊞ ☞

# LUDINGTON

AAA ▼▼ **Holiday Inn Express** **SH** ❖
(231) 845-7004. **$71-$206.** 5323 W US 10. Jct US 31, 1.3 mi w on US 10. Int corridors. **Pets:** Other species. $10 one-time fee/pet. Designated rooms, service with restrictions, supervision.
SAVE S☐ ✕ ☞ ☐ ☐ ☞ ☒

▼▼ **Super 8 Motel** **SH**
(231) 843-2140. **$54-$279.** 5005 W US 10. Jct US 31, 1 mi w. Int corridors. **Pets:** Medium. $5 daily fee/pet. Designated rooms, service with restrictions, supervision.
A$K S☐ ✕ ☞ ☐ ☞ ☒

# MACKINAW CITY

AAA ▼▼▼ **Baymont Inn & Suites-Mackinaw City** **SH**
(231) 436-7737. **$69-$149.** 109 S Nicolet St. I-75, exit 338, just n. Int corridors. **Pets:** Small. $50 deposit/room. Designated rooms, service with restrictions, supervision.
SAVE S☐ ✕ ☞ ☐ ☐ ☞

AAA ▼ **Beachcomber Motel on the Water** **M** ❖
(231) 436-8451. **$39-$125, 3 day notice.** 1011 S Huron Ave. 1 mi s on US 23. Ext corridors. **Pets:** Small, dogs only. $5 daily fee/pet. Designated rooms, service with restrictions, supervision.
SAVE S☐ ✕ ☐

AAA ▼ **The Beach House** **CA**
(231) 436-5353. **$44-$170, 14 day notice.** 11490 W US 23. 1.3 mi s. Ext corridors. **Pets:** Medium, dogs only. $15 one-time fee/pet. Service with restrictions.
SAVE ☐ ☞ ☒ ☑

▼ **Budget Inns-Starlite** **M** ❖
(231) 436-5959. **$26-$129.** 116 Old US 31. I-75, exit 338 southbound, 0.3 mi e; exit 337 northbound, just ne. Ext corridors. **Pets:** Small, dogs only. $15 daily fee/pet. Designated rooms, service with restrictions, supervision.
A$K S☐ ✕ ☐ ☞ ☒

AAA ▼ **Capri Motel** **M**
(231) 436-5498. **$38-$188, 3 day notice.** 801 S Nicolet St. I-75, exit 338 southbound, just s. Ext corridors. **Pets:** Small, dogs only. $10 daily fee/pet. Service with restrictions, supervision.
SAVE S☐ ✕ ☐ ☐ ☞ ☒

AAA ▼▼▼ **Days Inn & Suites "Bridgeview Lodge"** **M**
(231) 436-8961. **$39-$259.** 206 N Nicolet St. I-75, exit 339; at bridge. Ext/int corridors. **Pets:** Medium, dogs only. $50 deposit/room. Designated rooms, service with restrictions, supervision.
SAVE S☐ ✕ ☐ ☐ ☞

**AAA ▼▼ Days Inn Lakeview M**
(231) 436-5557. **$59-$209.** 825 S Huron Ave. I-75, exit 337 northbound, 0.5 mi n to US 23, 0.3 mi e; exit 338 southbound, 0.8 mi se on US 23. Ext corridors. **Pets:** Medium, dogs only. $50 deposit/pet. Designated rooms, service with restrictions, supervision.

SAVE 🛏️ ✕ 🛢️ 💻 🍽️ 🏊

**AAA ▼▼ Holiday Inn Express at the Bridge SH**
(231) 436-7100. **$39-$269.** 364 Louvingny. I-75, exit 339. Int corridors. **Pets:** Medium, dogs only. $50 deposit/room. Designated rooms, service with restrictions, supervision.

SAVE 🛏️ ✕ &M 🛢️ 💻 🏊 ✕

**AAA ▼ Kings Inn M**
(231) 436-5322. **$29-$89, 3 day notice.** 1020 S Nicolet St. I-75, exit 337 northbound, 0.5 mi n; exit 338 southbound, 0.5 mi s. Ext corridors. **Pets:** Accepted.

SAVE 🛏️ ✕ 🛢️ 🏊

**AAA ▼▼ Super 8 Motel Bridgeview SH**
(231) 436-5252. **$38-$198, 3 day notice.** 601 N Huron Ave. I-75, exit 339 northbound, just n, then just e. Ext/int corridors. **Pets:** Large, other species. $50 deposit/room. Service with restrictions, supervision.

SAVE 🛏️ ✕ 🖴 🛢️ 💻 🏊 ✕

## MANISTIQUE

**AAA ▼ Beachcomber Motel M ❀**
(906) 341-2567. **$48-$78.** 751 E Lakeshore Dr. 1 mi e on US 2. Ext corridors. **Pets:** Supervision.

SAVE 🛏️ ✕ 🛢️

**▼▼ Comfort Inn SH**
(906) 341-6981. **$69-$169.** 617 E Lakeshore Dr. 0.5 mi e on US 2. Int corridors. **Pets:** Other species. $10 daily fee/pet. Service with restrictions, supervision.

ASK 🛏️ ✕ 🛢️ 💻 ✕

**▼▼ Econo Lodge Lakeshore M**
(906) 341-6014. **$60-$120.** 1101 E Lakeshore Dr. 1.5 mi e on US 2. Ext/int corridors. **Pets:** Medium. $10 daily fee/room. Designated rooms, service with restrictions, supervision.

ASK 🛏️ ✕ 🖴 🛢️ 💻 ✕

## MARQUETTE

**AAA ▼ Birchmont Motel M**
(906) 228-7538. **$45-$75, 10 day notice.** 2090 US 41 S. On US 41 and SR 28, 4.3 mi s. Ext corridors. **Pets:** Other species. $6 daily fee/pet. Designated rooms, service with restrictions, supervision.

SAVE ✕ 🛢️ 🏊

**▼▼ Holiday Inn SH**
(906) 225-1351. **$98-$125.** 1951 US 41 W. On US 41 and SR 28, 1.8 mi w. Int corridors. **Pets:** Medium, dogs only. $25 daily fee/pet. Designated rooms, service with restrictions, crate.

ASK 🛏️ ✕ &M 🖴 🛢️ 💻 🍽️ 🏊 ✕

**AAA ▼▼ Nordic Bay Lodge M**
(906) 226-7516. **$55-$104.** 1880 US 41 S. On US 41 and SR 28, 1.8 mi se. Ext corridors. **Pets:** Dogs only. Designated rooms, service with restrictions, supervision.

SAVE 🛏️ ✕ 🛢️ 💻 🍽️ ✕

**▼▼ Ramada Inn SH**
(906) 228-6000. **$119-$124.** 412 W Washington St. 0.5 w on US 41 business route. Int corridors. **Pets:** $10 one-time fee/pet. Designated rooms, service with restrictions, supervision.

ASK 🛏️ ✕ 🛢️ 💻 🍽️ 🏊 ✕

## MARSHALL

**AAA ▼ Arbor Inn of Historic Marshall M**
(269) 781-7772. **$50-$69.** 15435 W Michigan Ave. I-69, exit 36 (Michigan Ave), just w. Ext corridors. **Pets:** Other species. $5 daily fee/pet. Designated rooms, service with restrictions, crate.

SAVE 🛏️ ✕ 🛢️ 🏊

## MENOMINEE

**AAA ▼▼ Econo Lodge On The Bay SH**
(906) 863-4431. **$100-$158.** 2516 10th St. 1 mi n on US 41. Int corridors. **Pets:** Very small. $25 daily fee/pet. Designated rooms, service with restrictions, supervision.

SAVE 🛏️ ✕ 🛢️ 💻

## MIDLAND

**AAA ▼▼ Best Western Valley Plaza Resort SH**
(989) 496-2700. **$89-$99.** 5221 Bay City Rd. US 10, exit Midland/Bay City Rd. Int corridors. **Pets:** Small, dogs only. Designated rooms, service with restrictions, supervision.

SAVE ✕ 🛢️ 💻 🍽️ 🏊 ✕

**▼▼ Fairview Inn & Suites SH**
(989) 631-0070. **$79-$99.** 2200 W Wackerly St. Jct US 10 and Eastman Rd. Int corridors. **Pets:** Accepted.

ASK 🛏️ ✕ 🛢️ 💻 🏊

**▼▼ Holiday Inn SH**
(989) 631-4220. **$86-$123.** 1500 W Wackerly St. Jct US 10 and Eastman Rd. Ext/int corridors. **Pets:** Accepted.

ASK ✕ 🛢️ 💻 🍽️ 🏊 ✕

**AAA ▼▼ Plaza Suites Hotel SH**
(989) 496-0100. **$99-$109.** 5221 Bay City Rd. US 10, exit Midland/Bay City Rd. Int corridors. **Pets:** Accepted.

SAVE ✕ 🛢️ 💻

## MIO

**▼ Mio Motel M**
(989) 826-3248. **$50-$70, 3 day notice.** 415 N Morenci St. Just n on SR 33 and 72. Ext corridors. **Pets:** Dogs only. Service with restrictions, supervision.

✕ 🛢️

## MONROE

**▼▼ Comfort Inn SH**
(734) 384-1500. **$60-$200.** 6500 Albain Rd. I-75, exit 11 (Laplaisance Rd), just w. Int corridors. **Pets:** Accepted.

ASK 🛏️ ✕ 🖴 🛢️ 💻 🏊

## MOUNT PLEASANT

**▼▼▼ Holiday Inn SH**
(989) 772-2905. **$89-$159.** 5665 E Pickard Ave. Jct US 127 and SR 20 E. Ext/int corridors. **Pets:** Medium, dogs only. Designated rooms, service with restrictions, supervision.

ASK 🛏️ ✕ &M 🖴 🛢️ 💻 🍽️ 🏊 ✕

## MUNISING

**AAA ▼ Alger Falls Motel M**
(906) 387-3536. **$40-$65.** E9427 E Hwy M-28. 2 mi e on SR 28 and 94. Ext corridors. **Pets:** Small, dogs only. $5 one-time fee/pet. Designated rooms, service with restrictions, supervision.

SAVE ✕ 🛢️

**▼▼ AmericInn of Munising SH**
(906) 387-2000. **$70-$210.** E 9926 Hwy M-28 E. On SR 28, 2.7 mi e. Int corridors. **Pets:** Accepted.

ASK 🛏️ ✕ &M 🖴 🛢️ 💻 🏊 ✕

**Best Western** M
(906) 387-4864. **$69-$129, 3 day notice.** E 10160 E Hwy M-28. On SR 28, 3 mi e. Ext/int corridors. **Pets:** Accepted.

**Comfort Inn** SH
(906) 387-5292. **$65-$110.** E9589 E Hwy M-28. On SR 28, 1.5 mi e. Int corridors. **Pets:** Accepted.

**Days Inn** SH
(906) 387-2493. **$55-$110.** 420 E Hwy M-28. On SR 28, 0.5 mi e. Int corridors. **Pets:** Accepted.

**Sunset Motel on the Bay** M
(906) 387-4574. **$50-$82.** 1315 Bay St. 1 mi e on E Munising Ave (CR H58). Ext corridors. **Pets:** Dogs only. $10 one-time fee/pet. Designated rooms, service with restrictions, supervision.

**Terrace Motel** M ✿
(906) 387-2735. **$40-$55.** 420 Prospect. 0.5 mi e, just off SR 28. Ext corridors. **Pets:** Medium. $3 daily fee/pet. Designated rooms, service with restrictions, crate.

# NEW BUFFALO

**Best Western Plaza Hotel** SH ✿
(269) 469-4193. **$90-$190.** 18800 La Porte Rd. I-94, exit 1 (La Porte Rd), just w. Int corridors. **Pets:** Very small. $25 one-time fee/pet. Designated rooms, service with restrictions, supervision.

# NORWAY

**AmericInn of Norway** SH
(906) 563-7500. **$80-$82.** W 6002 US Hwy 2. 0.7 mi w. Int corridors. **Pets:** Accepted.

# PAW PAW

**Comfort Inn & Suites** SH ✿
(269) 655-0303. **$59-$119.** 153 Ampey Rd. I-94, exit 60 (SR 40), just nw. Int corridors. **Pets:** Medium, other species. $50 deposit/room. Service with restrictions, crate.

# PELLSTON

**Holiday Inn Express Pellston** SH ✿
(231) 539-7000. **$59-$179.** 1600 US 31 N. 1.2 mi n. Int corridors. **Pets:** Other species. $20 one-time fee/room. No service, supervision.

# PETOSKEY

**Days Inn Petoskey** M
(231) 348-3900. **$60-$140.** 1420 US 131 S. 1.3 mi s. Ext corridors. **Pets:** Other species. $10 daily fee/pet. Service with restrictions, supervision.

# PLAINWELL

**Comfort Inn** SH
(269) 685-9891. **$73-$200.** 622 Allegan St. US 131, exit 49A, just e. Int corridors. **Pets:** Medium. $10 daily fee/pet. Designated rooms, service with restrictions, supervision.

# PORT HURON

**AmeriHost Inn-Port Huron** SH
(810) 364-8000. **$59-$159.** 1611 Range Rd. I-94, exit 269 (Range Rd), just w. Int corridors. **Pets:** Medium. $8 daily fee/pet. No service, supervision.

**Hampton Inn** SH ✿
(810) 966-9000. **$89-$159.** 1655 Yeager St. I-94, exit 274 (Water St), just s, then just w. Int corridors. **Pets:** Other species. Designated rooms, service with restrictions, supervision.

# PORTLAND

**Best Western American Heritage Inn** SH
(517) 647-2200. **$74-$84.** 1681 Grand River Ave. I-96, exit 77, just n. Int corridors. **Pets:** Accepted.

# SAGINAW

**Best Western–Saginaw** SH
(989) 755-0461. **$59-$99.** 1408 S Outer Dr. I-75, exit 149B (SR 46). Int corridors. **Pets:** Other species. $25 one-time fee/room. Service with restrictions, supervision.

**Four Points by Sheraton Saginaw** SH
(989) 790-5050. **$79.** 4960 Towne Centre Rd. I-675, exit 6, just w on Tittabawassee Rd. Int corridors. **Pets:** Accepted.

**Howard Johnson Plaza Hotel** SH
(989) 753-6608. **$79-$189.** 400 Johnson St. I-675, exit 2, just s. Int corridors. **Pets:** Accepted.

**Motel 6 Saginaw #1496** M
(989) 754-8414. **$42-$55.** 966 S Outer Dr. I-75, exit 149B (SR 46). Ext corridors. **Pets:** Accepted.

**Ramada Inn & Suites** SH
(989) 793-7900. **$50-$99.** 3325 Davenport Ave. I-675, exit 3, 2 mi w on SR 58. Int corridors. **Pets:** Medium, other species. Designated rooms, service with restrictions.

**Super 8 Motel** SH
(989) 791-3003. **$58-$75.** 4848 Towne Centre Rd. I-675, exit 6, 0.3 mi w, then just s. Int corridors. **Pets:** $10 daily fee/room. Service with restrictions, supervision.

# ST. IGNACE

**Bay View Motel** M ✿
(906) 643-9444. **$36-$72.** 1133 N State St. 3 mi n of bridge tollgate on I-75 business route. Ext corridors. **Pets:** Other species. $5 one-time fee/pet. Service with restrictions, crate.

**Budget Host Inn** SH
(906) 643-9666. **$58-$146.** 700 N State St. 1.8 mi n of bridge tollgate on I-75 business route. Ext/int corridors. **Pets:** Other species. $40 deposit/room. Service with restrictions, supervision.

**Quality Inn St. Ignace** SH
(906) 643-9700. **$59-$139.** 913 Boulevard Dr. Jct I-75 and US 2 W. Int corridors. **Pets:** $10 daily fee/pet. Service with restrictions, supervision.

**ⒶⒶⒶ ▼ Wayside Motel Ⓜ**
(906) 643-8944. **$40-$65, 3 day notice.** 751 N State St. 2 mi n of bridge tollgate on I-75 business route. Ext corridors. **Pets:** Small, dogs only. $5 daily fee/pet. Designated rooms, service with restrictions, supervision.
Ⓢ𝔸𝕍𝔼 Ⓢ Ⓧ 🔲

## ST. JOSEPH

**ⒶⒶⒶ ▼ Econo Lodge St. Joseph Ⓜ**
(269) 982-3333. **$49-$89.** 2723 Niles Ave. I-94, exit 27 (Niles Ave), 2 mi w. Ext corridors. **Pets:** Accepted.
Ⓢ𝔸𝕍𝔼 Ⓧ 🔲 🏊

## SAULT STE. MARIE

**ⒶⒶⒶ ▼▼ Best Western Sault Ste Marie 🆂🅷 🐾**
(906) 632-2170. **$59-$109.** 4335 I-75 business loop. I-75, exit 392, 0.3 mi ne. Int corridors. **Pets:** $15 one-time fee/room. Service with restrictions, supervision.
Ⓢ𝔸𝕍𝔼 Ⓢ Ⓧ ⓔ 🔲 🔲 🏊 Ⓧ

**ⒶⒶⒶ ▼ Budget Host Crestview Inn Ⓜ**
(906) 635-5213. **$59-$79.** 1200 Ashmun St. I-75, exit 392, 2.8 mi ne on I-75 business loop. Ext corridors. **Pets:** Other species. Designated rooms, service with restrictions, supervision.
Ⓢ𝔸𝕍𝔼 Ⓢ Ⓧ 🔲

**ⒶⒶⒶ ▼▼ Colonial Inn & Suites Ⓜ 🐾**
(906) 632-4366. **$49-$99.** 4281 I-75 Business Loop. I-75, exit 392, 0.3 mi ne. Ext corridors. **Pets:** Other species. $15 one-time fee/room. Designated rooms, service with restrictions, supervision.
Ⓢ𝔸𝕍𝔼 Ⓢ Ⓧ 🔲 🔲

**ⒶⒶⒶ ▼▼ Days Inn 🆂🅷**
(906) 632-6000. **$49-$199.** 3651 I-75 Business Spur. I-75, exit 392, 0.8 mi ne on I-75 business loop. Int corridors. **Pets:** Accepted.
Ⓢ𝔸𝕍𝔼 Ⓢ Ⓧ 🔲 🔲 🏊 Ⓧ

**▼ Econo Lodge 🆂🅷**
(906) 632-6000. **$49-$99.** 3525 I-75 business spur. I-75, exit 392, 0.7 mi ne. Int corridors. **Pets:** Small. $10 one-time fee/room. Designated rooms, service with restrictions, supervision.
Ⓐ𝕊𝕂 Ⓢ Ⓧ ⓔⓂ ⓔ 🔲 🔲

**ⒶⒶⒶ ▼ La France Terrace Motel Ⓜ**
(906) 632-7823. **$42-$75.** 1608 Ashmun St. I-75, exit 392, 2.3 mi ne on I-75 business loop. Ext corridors. **Pets:** Dogs only. Designated rooms, service with restrictions, crate.
Ⓢ𝔸𝕍𝔼 Ⓢ Ⓧ 🔲 🏊

**ⒶⒶⒶ ▼ Mid-City Motel Ⓜ**
(906) 632-6832. **$46-$58.** 304 E Portage Ave. Just e of town, on I-75 business loop. Ext corridors. **Pets:** Medium, dogs only. $5 daily fee/pet. Service with restrictions, supervision.
Ⓢ𝔸𝕍𝔼 Ⓢ Ⓧ

**▼ Royal Motel Ⓜ**
(906) 632-6323. **$46-$54.** 1707 Ashmun St. I-75, exit 392, 2 mi ne on I-75 business loop. **Pets:** Small, dogs only. Service with restrictions, supervision.
Ⓐ𝕊𝕂 Ⓢ Ⓧ 🔲 🔲

**▼ Super 8 Motel 🆂🅷 🐾**
(906) 632-8882. **$49-$79.** 3826 I-75 Business Loop. I-75, exit 392, 0.5 mi ne. Int corridors. **Pets:** $50 deposit/room. Designated rooms, service with restrictions, supervision.
Ⓐ𝕊𝕂 Ⓢ Ⓧ ⓔ 🔲

## SILVER CITY

**ⒶⒶⒶ ▼ America's Choice Rainbow Lodging Ⓜ**
(906) 885-5348. **$59-$85, 7 day notice.** 32739 W State Hwy M 64. SR 64, just e of jct SR 107. Ext corridors. **Pets:** Medium, dogs only. $25 one-time fee/pet. Designated rooms, service with restrictions, supervision.
Ⓢ𝔸𝕍𝔼 Ⓢ Ⓧ 🔲 🔲 🍴 Ⓧ

**▼▼ AmericInn Lodge & Suites 🆂🅷**
(906) 885-5311. **$100-$160, 4 day notice.** 120 Lincoln Ave. On SR 107, 0.3 mi w of SR 64. Int corridors. **Pets:** Dogs only. $10 daily fee/room. Designated rooms, service with restrictions, supervision.
Ⓐ𝕊𝕂 Ⓢ Ⓧ ⓔ 🔲 🔲 🍴 🏊 Ⓧ

**▼ Mountain View Lodges 🅲🅰**
(906) 885-5256. **$125-$190, 30 day notice.** 237 Lincoln Ave. Jct SR 107 and 64, 0.8 mi w. Ext corridors. **Pets:** Dogs only. $40 one-time fee/pet. Designated rooms, no service, supervision.
Ⓧ 🔲 🔲 Ⓚ

## SPRING LAKE

**▼▼ Grand Haven Waterfront Holiday Inn 🆂🅷 🐾**
(616) 846-1000. **$89-$185.** 940 W Savidge St. On SR 104, just e of US 131. Int corridors. **Pets:** Dogs only. $25 daily fee/pet. Designated rooms, service with restrictions, supervision.
Ⓐ𝕊𝕂 Ⓢ Ⓧ ⓔ 🔲 🔲 🍴 🏊 Ⓧ

## STEVENSVILLE

**▼▼ Baymont Inn & Suites-St. Joseph (Stevensville) 🆂🅷**
(269) 428-9111. **$49-$99.** 2601 W Marquette Woods Rd. I-94, exit 23 (Red Arrow Hwy), just w. Int corridors. **Pets:** Accepted.
Ⓐ𝕊𝕂 Ⓢ Ⓧ ⓔⓂ 🔲 ⓔ 🔲 🔲

**ⒶⒶⒶ ▼▼ Candlewood Suites 🆂🅷**
(269) 428-4400. **$79-$117.** 2567 W Marquette Woods Rd. I-94, exit 23 (Red Arrow Hwy), just w. Int corridors. **Pets:** Medium. $55 one-time fee/pet. Designated rooms, service with restrictions.
Ⓢ𝔸𝕍𝔼 Ⓧ ⓔⓂ ⓔ 🔲 🔲

**▼▼ Hampton Inn 🆂🅷**
(269) 429-2700. **$74-$149.** 5050 Red Arrow Hwy. I-94, exit 23 (Red Arrow Hwy), just se. Int corridors. **Pets:** Accepted.
Ⓐ𝕊𝕂 Ⓢ Ⓧ ⓔⓂ ⓔ 🔲 🔲 🏊

**ⒶⒶⒶ ▼▼ Park Inn International 🆂🅷**
(269) 429-3218. **$70-$150.** 4290 Red Arrow Hwy. I-94, exit 23 (Red Arrow Hwy), 0.5 mi n. Ext/int corridors. **Pets:** Other species. Service with restrictions, supervision.
Ⓢ𝔸𝕍𝔼 Ⓢ Ⓧ ⓔ 🔲 🔲 🍴 🏊 Ⓧ

## STURGIS

**ⒶⒶⒶ ▼ Americas Best Value Inn Ⓜ**
(269) 651-2361. **$35-$59.** 71381 S Centerville Rd. I-80/90, exit 121 (SR 66), 0.4 mi n. Ext corridors. **Pets:** Very small, dogs only. $5 daily fee/pet. Service with restrictions, supervision.
Ⓢ𝔸𝕍𝔼 Ⓢ Ⓧ 🏊

## SUTTONS BAY

**▼ Red Lion Motor Lodge Ⓜ**
(231) 271-6694. **$59-$165.** 4290 S West Bay Shore Rd. 5 mi s on SR 22. Ext corridors. **Pets:** Medium. $10 one-time fee/pet. Service with restrictions, supervision.
Ⓧ 🔲 🔲 Ⓩ

## TAWAS CITY

**ⒶⒶⒶ ▼ Tawas Motel-Resort Ⓜ**
(989) 362-3822. **$45-$80.** 1124 US 23 S. On US 23, 1.8 mi s. Ext corridors. **Pets:** Medium. $5 one-time fee/pet. Service with restrictions, crate.
Ⓢ𝔸𝕍𝔼 Ⓢ Ⓧ 🔲 🔲 🏊 Ⓧ

# TECUMSEH

**◊ Tecumseh Inn Motel M**
(517) 423-7401. **$135.** 1445 W Chicago Blvd. On SR 50, 1.5 mi w of city center. Ext corridors. **Pets:** Other species.

(ASK) (S⌀) (✕) (🛏) (💻) (🍽)

# THREE RIVERS

**◊◊ Super 8 Motel SH**
(269) 279-8888. **$59-$89.** 711 US 131. Jct US 131 and SR 60 (W Broadway St). Int corridors. **Pets:** Accepted.

(✕) (⌀M) (💺) (🛏) (≈)

# TRAVERSE CITY

**◊◊◊ ◊◊ Best Western Four Seasons M**
(231) 946-8424. **$49-$229, 7 day notice.** 305 Munson Ave. 2 mi e on US 31. Ext/int corridors. **Pets:** Large. $10 daily fee/room. Service with restrictions, supervision.

(SAVE) (S⌀) (✕) (🛏) (💻) (≈)

**◊◊◊ ◊◊ Days Inn & Suites SH**
(231) 941-0208. **$45-$199.** 420 Munson Ave. 2 mi e on US 31. Int corridors. **Pets:** Medium, other species. $10 daily fee/pet. Service with restrictions, supervision.

(SAVE) (S⌀) (✕) (🛏) (💻) (≈) (✕)

**◊◊◊ ◊◊◊ Holiday Inn SH** 🐾
(231) 947-3700. **$79-$229.** 615 E Front St. 0.5 mi e on US 31. Int corridors. **Pets:** Other species. $10 daily fee/room. Supervision.

(SAVE) (S⌀) (✕) (⌀M) (📶) (💺) (🛏) (💻) (🍽) (≈) (✕)

**◊◊ Park Place Hotel SH**
(231) 946-5000. **$189-$269.** 300 E State St. Corner of E State and Park sts; downtown. Int corridors. **Pets:** Accepted.

(ASK) (S⌀) (✕) (📶) (🛏) (💻) (🍽) (≈) (✕)

**◊◊◊ ◊◊ Quality Inn SH** 🐾
(231) 929-4423. **$39-$169.** 1492 US 31 N. On US 31, 3.3 mi e. Ext/int corridors. **Pets:** Other species. $10 daily fee/room. Designated rooms, service with restrictions, supervision.

(SAVE) (S⌀) (✕) (💺) (🛏) (💻) (≈)

**◊◊ Traverse Victorian Inn SH**
(231) 947-5525. **$60-$150.** 461 Munson Ave. 2.4 mi e on US 31. Int corridors. **Pets:** Accepted.

(ASK) (S⌀) (✕) (🛏) (💻) (≈)

# WALKER

**◊◊◊ ◊◊ AmeriHost Inn-Grand Rapids North SH**
(616) 791-8500. **$94-$189.** 2171 Holton Ct. I-96, exit 28 (Walker Ave), just s. Int corridors. **Pets:** Small. $25 one-time fee/pet. No service, supervision.

(SAVE) (S⌀) (✕) (💺) (🛏) (💻) (≈)

**◊◊ Baymont Inn & Suites-Grand Rapids North SH**
(616) 735-9595. **$79-$99.** 2151 Holton Ct NW. I-96, exit 28 (Walker Ave), just s. Int corridors. **Pets:** Medium. Service with restrictions, supervision.

(ASK) (S⌀) (✕) (💺) (🛏) (💻) (≈)

# WATERSMEET

**◊◊ Dancing Eagles Resort Lac Vieux Desert Casino SH**
(906) 358-4949. **$60-$150.** N5384 US Hwy 45. 1.8 mi n of US 2. Int corridors. **Pets:** Large. $100 deposit/room, $10 daily fee/room. Designated rooms, service with restrictions, supervision.

(ASK) (S⌀) (✕) (💺) (🛏) (💻) (≈) (✕)

# WEST BRANCH

**◊◊ Super 8 Motel SH**
(989) 345-8488. **$71-$89.** 2596 Austin's Way. I-75, exit 212 (Cook Rd). Int corridors. **Pets:** Medium. No service, supervision.

(✕) (💺) (🛏) (💻) (≈)

# WHITEHALL

**◊◊◊ ◊ Lake Land Motel M**
(231) 894-5644. **$40-$75.** 1002 E Colby St. On US 31 business route, 0.8 mi w of US 31. Ext corridors. **Pets:** Large. $5 one-time fee/pet. Service with restrictions, crate.

(SAVE) (✕) (💻)

# WHITMORE LAKE

**◊◊◊ ◊◊ Best Western Whitmore Lake M**
(734) 449-2058. **$75-$115.** 9897 Main St. US 23, exit 53, just e. Ext corridors. **Pets:** Medium. $25 daily fee/pet. Service with restrictions, crate.

(SAVE) (S⌀) (✕) (🛏) (💻) (≈)

# WYOMING

**◊ Super 8 Motel SH**
(616) 530-8588. **$80.** 727 44th St SW. US 131, exit 79. Int corridors. **Pets:** Accepted.

(ASK) (S⌀) (✕) (🛏)

# MINNESOTA

## CITY INDEX

## AITKIN

### ▼▼ 40 Club Inn SH
(218) 927-2903. **$59-$89.** 950 2nd St NW. SR 210, 1 mi w of jct US 169. Int corridors. **Pets:** Accepted.

ASK ⊠ & ▤ ▦ ⇌

### ▼ Ripple River Motel & RV Park M
(218) 927-3734. **$58-$105.** 701 Minnesota Ave S. US 169, 0.8 mi s of jct SR 210. Ext corridors. **Pets:** $10 daily fee/pet. Designated rooms, service with restrictions, crate.

ASK ⊠ ▤

## ALBERT LEA

### ▲ ▼▼ Albert Lea Countryside Inn Motel M ❖
(507) 373-2446. **$49-$79, 3 day notice.** 2102 E Main St. I-35, exit 11, 1.3 mi w on CR 46. Ext/int corridors. **Pets:** $7 daily fee/pet. Designated rooms, service with restrictions, supervision.

SAVE S⊘ ⊠ ▤

### ▲ ▼▼▼ Comfort Inn SH
(507) 377-1100. **$69-$129.** 810 Happy Trails Ln. I-35, exit 11, just se. Int corridors. **Pets:** Other species. $10 one-time fee/pet. Designated rooms, service with restrictions, supervision.

SAVE S⊘ ⊠ &M ▧ & ▤ ▦ ⇌ ⊠

### ▲ ▼▼▼ Country Inn & Suites By Carlson SH
(507) 373-5513. **$84-$104.** 2214 E Main St. I-35, exit 12 southbound; exit 11 northbound, 1 mi w. Int corridors. **Pets:** Small. $20 one-time fee/pet. Designated rooms, service with restrictions, supervision.

SAVE S⊘ ⊠ &M & ▤ ▦ ⇌

### ▲ ▼▼▼ Days Inn SH
(507) 373-8291. **$65-$90.** 2301 E Main St. I-35, exit 11, 1 mi w on CR 46. Int corridors. **Pets:** Medium, other species. $8 daily fee/pet. Designated rooms, service with restrictions, supervision.

SAVE S⊘ ⊠ & ▤ ▦ ⇌ ⊠

## ALEXANDRIA

### ▲ ▼▼▼ Country Inn & Suites By Carlson SH
(320) 763-9900. **$80-$115.** 5304 Hwy 29 S. I-94, exit 103, just sw. Int corridors. **Pets:** Other species. $10 one-time fee/room. Designated rooms, service with restrictions, supervision.

SAVE S⊘ ⊠ &M ▧ & ▤ ▦ ⇌

### ▼▼▼ Holiday Inn Alexandria SH ❖
(320) 763-6577. **$80-$150.** 5637 State Hwy 29 S. I-94, exit 103, just s. Int corridors. **Pets:** Other species. Designated rooms, service with restrictions, crate.

ASK ⊠ ▤ ▦ ▥ ⇌ ⊠

### ▲ ▼▼▼ Ramada Limited SH
(320) 762-5161. **$52-$119.** 507 50th Ave W. I-94, exit 103, just ne. Int corridors. **Pets:** Accepted.

SAVE S⊘ ⊠ ▧ ▤ ▦ ⇌

### ▲ ▼▼▼ Super 8 Motel SH
(320) 763-6552. **$61-$83, 14 day notice.** 4620 SR 29 S. I-94, exit 103, 0.3 mi n. Int corridors. **Pets:** Accepted.

SAVE S⊘ ⊠ ▤

## AUSTIN

### ▲ ▼▼▼ Country Side Inn SH
(507) 437-7774. **$45-$90.** 3303 Oakland Ave W. I-90, exit 175 (Oakland Ave), just nw. Int corridors. **Pets:** Other species. $5 one-time fee/room. Service with restrictions, crate.

SAVE S⊘ ⊠ ▤ ▦

### ▼▼ Days Inn SH
(507) 433-8600. **$50-$80.** 700 16th Ave NW. I-90, exit 178A (4th St NW), just nw. Int corridors. **Pets:** Small. $15 one-time fee/pet. Designated rooms, service with restrictions, supervision.

ASK S⊘ ⊠ ▧ ▤ ▦

### ▼▼▼ Holiday Inn & Austin Conference Center SH
(507) 433-1000. **$89-$159.** 1701 4th St NW. I-90, exit 178A (4th St NW), just nw. Int corridors. **Pets:** Small. $25 one-time fee/pet. Designated rooms, service with restrictions, supervision.

ASK S⊘ ⊠ &M ▧ & ▤ ▦ ▥ ⇌ ⊠

## BABBITT

### ▼▼▼ Timber Bay Lodge & Houseboats CA ❖
(218) 827-3682. **$730-$3500 (weekly), 60 day notice.** 8347 Timber Bay Rd. 2.8 mi e of jct CR 21 via CR 70 and 623. Ext corridors. **Pets:** $14 daily fee/pet. No service, crate

▤ ▦ ⊠ ▨

## BAUDETTE

### ▼▼▼ AmericInn Lodge & Suites Lake of the Woods SH
(218) 634-3200. **$74-$140.** 1179 Main St W. 0.5 mi w on SR 11. Int corridors. **Pets:** Accepted.

ASK S⊘ ⊠ &M ▧ & ▤ ▦ ⇌ ⊠

# BAXTER

**▼◆▼** **Country Inn & Suites by Carlson** 🆂🅷
(218) 828-2161. **$94-$149.** 15058 Dellwood Dr N. Jct SR 371 and 210, 1 mi n on SR 371. Int corridors. **Pets:** Medium, dogs only. Service with restrictions, supervision.

🅰🆂🅺 🆂� ⊠ 🔬 🕭 🛏 💻 ⇌

**▼◆▼** **Hawthorn Inn & Suites** 🆂🅷
(218) 822-1133. **$80-$200.** 2300 Fairview Rd N. Just nw of jct SR 371 on SR 210. Int corridors. **Pets:** Medium, other species. $50 deposit/pet, $10 one-time fee/pet. Designated rooms, service with restrictions, supervision.

🅰🆂🅺 🆂� ⊠ 🔬 🕭 🛏 💻 ⇌ ⊠

# BEMIDJI

**△△△** **▼◆▼** **AmericInn Lodge & Suites** 🆂🅷
(218) 751-3000. **$65-$128.** 1200 Paul Bunyan Dr NW. 0.5 mi e of the northwest jct US 2, 71 and SR 197. Int corridors. **Pets:** Medium. $30 one-time fee/pet. Service with restrictions, supervision.

🆂🅰🆅🅴 🆂� ⊠ 🕭 🛏 💻 ⇌ ⊠

**△△△** **▼◆▼** **Best Western Bemidji** 🆂🅷 🐾
(218) 751-0390. **$45-$99.** 2420 Paul Bunyan Dr. Jct US 71 N and SR 197. Int corridors. **Pets:** Other species. $10 one-time fee/room. Designated rooms, service with restrictions, supervision.

🆂🅰🆅🅴 🆂� ⊠ 🕭 🛏 💻 ⇌ ⊠

**△△△** **▼◆▼** **Ruttger's Birchmont Lodge** 🅲🅰
(218) 444-3463. **$52-$374, 30 day notice.** 7598 Bemidji Rd NE. Jct SR 197, 3.6 mi n on CR 21 (Bemidji Ave N). Ext/int corridors. **Pets:** Large, other species. $10 daily fee/pet. Designated rooms, service with restrictions, supervision.

🆂🅰🆅🅴 🆂🔄 ⊠ 🛏 💻 🍴 ⇌ ⊠

# BLUE EARTH

**▼◆▼** **Super 8 Motel** 🆂🅷
(507) 526-7376. **$60-$70.** 1420 Giant Dr. I-90, exit 119 (US 169), just s. Int corridors. **Pets:** Other species. $5 one-time fee/pet. Service with restrictions, supervision.

🅰🆂🅺 🆂🔄 ⊠ 🛏 💻

# BRAINERD

**△△△** **▼◆▼** **Ramada Inn Brainerd** 🆂🅷
(218) 829-1441. **$69-$135, 4 day notice.** 2115 S 6th St. On SR 371 business route, 1.8 mi s of jct SR 210. Ext/int corridors. **Pets:** Other species. $10 daily fee/pet. Service with restrictions, supervision.

🆂🅰🆅🅴 🆂🔄 ⊠ 🔬 🛏 💻 🍴 ⊠

# BRECKENRIDGE

**△△△** **▼◆▼** **Select Inn of Breckenridge/Wahpeton** 🆂🅷
(218) 643-9201. **$55-$74.** 821 Hwy 75 N. Just sw of jct US 75 N and 210. Int corridors. **Pets:** Other species. $50 deposit/pet, $10 one-time fee/pet.

🆂🅰🆅🅴 🆂🔄 ⊠ 🔬 🛏 💻 ⇌

# CALEDONIA

**▼◆▼** **AmericInn Lodge & Suites** 🆂🅷
(507) 725-8000. **$72-$120.** 508 N Kruckow Ave. Just n of Main St on SR 44, just w on Esch Dr. Int corridors. **Pets:** Medium. $50 deposit/pet. Service with restrictions, supervision.

🅰🆂🅺 ⊠ 🔬 🛏 💻 ⇌ ⊠

**▼◆▼** **Crest Red Carpet Inn** 🅼 🐾
(507) 724-3311. **$65.** 15944 State 76. Jct SR 44 and 76; on north end of town, 1.9 mi s. Ext/int corridors. **Pets:** $10 one-time fee/room. Designated rooms, crate.

🅰🆂🅺 ⊠ 🛏

# CANNON FALLS

**△△△** **▼◆▼** **Best Western Saratoga Inn** 🆂🅷
(507) 263-7272. **$69-$145.** 31591 64th Ave. 1 mi s on US 52. Int corridors. **Pets:** Accepted.

🆂🅰🆅🅴 🆂🔄 ⊠ 🛏 💻 ⇌

# CLOQUET

**▼◆▼** **Super 8 Motel** 🆂🅷
(218) 879-1250. **$62-$158.** 121 Big Lake Rd. I-35, exit 237 (SR 33), 2 mi nw. Int corridors. **Pets:** Medium, dogs only. $50 deposit/pet. Designated rooms, service with restrictions, supervision.

🅰🆂🅺 🆂🔄 ⊠ 🔬 🛏

# CROOKSTON

**▼◆▼** **Northland Inn of Crookston** 🆂🅷
(218) 281-5210. **$69-$89.** 2200 University Ave. On US 2 W and 75 N, 1.5 mi n. Int corridors. **Pets:** Other species. $10 one-time fee/room. Service with restrictions, supervision.

🅰🆂🅺 🆂🔄 ⊠ 🔬 🍴 ⇌

# DETROIT LAKES

**△△△** **▼◆▼** **AmericInn Lodge & Suites** 🆂🅷
(218) 847-8795. **$74-$145.** 777 Hwy 10 E. 1.4 mi se. Int corridors. **Pets:** Other species. $10 daily fee/room. Service with restrictions, supervision.

🆂🅰🆅🅴 🆂🔄 ⊠ 🔬 🕭 🛏 💻 ⇌ ⊠

**△△△** **▼◆▼** **Best Western Holland House & Suites** 🆂🅷 🐾
(218) 847-4483. **$79-$209, 3 day notice.** 615 Hwy 10 E. 1.3 mi se. Ext/int corridors. **Pets:** Medium. $10 daily fee/pet. Designated rooms, service with restrictions, supervision.

🆂🅰🆅🅴 ⊠ 🔬 🛏 💻 ⇌ ⊠

**△△△** **▼◆▼** **Budget Host Inn** 🅼 🐾
(218) 847-4454. **$49-$112.** 895 Hwy 10 E. 1.5 mi se. Ext corridors. **Pets:** Medium. $10 daily fee/pet. Service with restrictions, supervision.

🆂🅰🆅🅴 🆂🔄 ⊠ 🛏 💻

**△△△** **▼◆▼** **Country Inn & Suites By Carlson** 🆂🅷
(218) 847-2000. **$69-$112.** 1330 Hwy 10 E. Just e of jct US 10 and CR 54 E. Int corridors. **Pets:** $20 one-time fee/room. Service with restrictions, supervision.

🆂🅰🆅🅴 🆂🔄 ⊠ 🔬 🛏 💻 ⇌

# DULUTH

**△△△** **▼◆▼** **AmericInn Hotel & Suites of Duluth/Proctor** 🆂🅷
(218) 624-1026. **$90-$200.** 185 US 2. Jct I-35 and US 2, 0.8 mi n. Int corridors. **Pets:** $10 daily fee/pet. Service with restrictions, supervision.

🆂🅰🆅🅴 🆂🔄 ⊠ 🔬 🕭 🛏 💻 🍴 ⇌

**△△△** **▼◆▼** **Best Western Downtown Motel** 🅼
(218) 727-6851. **$44-$129.** 131 W 2nd St. 2nd St at 2nd Ave W; center. Ext/int corridors. **Pets:** Other species. Service with restrictions, supervision.

🆂🅰🆅🅴 🆂🔄 ⊠ 🛏 💻

**△△△** **▼◆▼** **Best Western Edgewater Resort & Waterpark** 🅼 🐾
(218) 728-3601. **$79-$309.** 2400 London Rd. I-35, exit 258 (21st Ave E), just nw. Ext/int corridors. **Pets:** $25 daily fee/pet. Designated rooms, service with restrictions, supervision.

🆂🅰🆅🅴 🆂🔄 ⊠ 🔬 🕭 🛏 💻 ⇌ ⊠

**△△△** **▼◆▼** **Country Inn & Suites By Carlson** 🆂🅷
(218) 628-0668. **$89-$175.** 9330 W Skyline Pkwy. I-35, exit 249 (Boundary Ave), just se. Int corridors. **Pets:** Accepted.

🆂🅰🆅🅴 🆂🔄 ⊠ 🔬 🛏 💻 ⇌ ⊠

▼▼▼▼ **Country Inn & Suites-Duluth North** 🆂🅷
(218) 740-4500. **$99-$199.** 4257 Haines Rd. Just n of US 53 at jct Haines Rd. **Pets:** Other species. $10 daily fee/room. Designated rooms, service with restrictions, supervision.
ASK SD ✕ 🛢 💻 ⊇ ✕

▼▼ **Days Inn-Duluth** 🆂🅷
(218) 727-3110. **$55-$159.** 909 Cottonwood Ave. SR 194, just n of jct US 53. Int corridors. **Pets:** Other species. Service with restrictions, supervision.
ASK SD ✕ 🖋 🛢

🅐🅐🅐 ▼▼ **Econo Lodge Airport** 🆂🅷 🐾
(218) 722-5522. **$49-$159.** 4197 Haines Rd. West side on US 53 and SR 194. Int corridors. **Pets:** $50 deposit/room, $10 one-time fee/room. Designated rooms, service with restrictions, supervision.
SAVE ✕ 💻 ⊇ ✕

🅐🅐🅐 ▼▼▼ **Hawthorn Suites at Waterfront Plaza** 🆂🅷 🐾
(218) 727-4663. **$89-$299.** 325 Lake Ave S. In Canal Park area. Int corridors. **Pets:** $75 deposit/room. Designated rooms, service with restrictions, supervision.
SAVE SD ✕ 🛢M 🖉 🖋 🛢 💻 🍽 ⊇ ✕

🅐🅐🅐 ▼▼▼ **The Inn on Lake Superior** 🆂🅷 🐾
(218) 726-1111. **$119-$299.** 350 Canal Park Dr. In Canal Park area. Int corridors. **Pets:** Medium, other species. $25 daily fee/room. Designated rooms, service with restrictions, supervision.
SAVE SD ✕ 🛢M 🖉 🖋 🛢 💻 ⊇ ✕

▼▼▼ **Radisson Hotel Duluth-Harborview** 🅻🅷
(218) 727-8981. **$89-$199.** 505 W Superior St. At 5th Ave W; center. Int corridors. **Pets:** $10 daily fee/room. Designated rooms, service with restrictions, supervision.
ASK SD ✕ 🛢 💻 🍽 ⊇ ✕

▼▼ **Voyageur Lakewalk Inn** 🅼 🐾
(218) 722-3911. **$40-$71.** 333 E Superior St. I-35, exit 256 (Superior St), just n at jct 4th Ave E and Superior St. Ext corridors. **Pets:** $10 one-time fee/room. Service with restrictions, supervision.
✕ 🛢 💻

## ELY

🅐🅐🅐 ▼▼▼ **Grand Ely Lodge Resort and Conference Center** 🆂🅷 🐾
(218) 365-6565. **$90-$175.** 400 N Pioneer Rd. SR 169 to Central Ave, just n to Pioneer Rd, then 1 mi n. Ext/int corridors. **Pets:** Large, other species. $15 daily fee/pet. Designated rooms, service with restrictions, crate.
SAVE SD ✕ 🖉 🖋 🛢 💻 🍽 ⊇ ✕

▼ **Motel Ely-Budget Host** 🅼
(218) 365-3237. **$69-$89.** 1047 E Sheridan St. SR 1 and 169. Ext corridors. **Pets:** Dogs only. $10 one-time fee/room. Designated rooms, service with restrictions, supervision.
ASK SD ✕ 💻

## EVELETH

▼▼ **Super 8 Motel** 🆂🅷
(218) 744-1661. **$57-$95.** 1080 Industrial Park Dr. On US 53, 0.5 mi n of jct SR 37. Int corridors. **Pets:** Accepted.
ASK SD ✕ 🛢M 🖋 🛢 💻 ⊇ ✕

## FAIRMONT

▼▼ **Comfort Inn** 🆂🅷
(507) 238-5444. **$75-$95.** 2225 N State St. I-90, exit 102 (SR 15), just sw. Int corridors. **Pets:** Accepted.
ASK SD ✕ 🛢M 🛢 💻 ⊇

▼▼▼ **Holiday Inn** 🆂🅷
(507) 238-4771. **$89-$109.** 1201 Torgerson Dr. I-90, exit 102 (SR 15), just se. Int corridors. **Pets:** Accepted.
ASK SD ✕ 🛢 🛢 💻 🍽 ⊇ ✕

▼▼ **Super 8 Motel** 🆂🅷
(507) 238-9444. **$47-$65.** 1200 Torgerson Dr. I-90, exit 102 (SR 15), just se. Int corridors. **Pets:** Accepted.
ASK SD ✕ 🛢

## FARIBAULT

🅐🅐🅐 ▼▼ **AmericInn Motel** 🆂🅷
(507) 334-9464. **$80-$160.** 1801 Lavender Dr. I-35, exit 59 (SR 21), 0.3 mi e. Int corridors. **Pets:** Large. $15 one-time fee/pet. Designated rooms, service with restrictions, supervision.
SAVE ✕ 🖉 🖋 🛢 💻 ⊇ ✕

▼▼ **Days Inn & Suites** 🆂🅷
(507) 334-6835. **$60-$85.** 1920 Cardinal Ln. I-35, exit 59 (SR 21), just ne. Int corridors. **Pets:** $10 daily fee/pet. Service with restrictions, supervision.
ASK ✕ 🛢M 🖉 🖋 🛢 💻 ⊇

🅐🅐🅐 ▼▼ **Select Inn** 🅼
(507) 334-2051. **$48-$70.** 4040 SR 60 W. I-35, exit 56, just w. Int corridors. **Pets:** Accepted.
SAVE ✕ 🖋 🛢 💻 ⊇

## FERGUS FALLS

🅐🅐🅐 ▼▼ **AmericInn Lodge & Suites** 🆂🅷
(218) 739-3900. **$76-$99.** 526 Western Ave N. I-94, exit 54 (SR 210), just se. Int corridors. **Pets:** Other species. $50 deposit/room, $10 one-time fee/room. Designated rooms, service with restrictions, crate.
SAVE ✕ 🛢M 🖉 🖋 🛢 💻 ⊇ ✕

▼ **Motel 7** 🅼
(218) 736-2554. **$42-$65.** 616 Frontier Dr. I-94, exit 54 (SR 210), just ne. Int corridors. **Pets:** Dogs only. $10 daily fee/pet. Designated rooms, service with restrictions, supervision.
✕ 🛢

## FINLAYSON

▼▼ **Banning Junction-North Country Inn** 🆂🅷
(320) 245-5284. **$59-$99.** 60671 State Hwy 23. I-35, exit 195 (SR 23), just ne. Int corridors. **Pets:** Accepted.
ASK SD ✕ 🛢

## FOSSTON

▼▼ **Super 8 Motel** 🆂🅷
(218) 435-1088. **$56-$70.** 108 S Amber. US 2, 0.5 mi e. Int corridors. **Pets:** Dogs only. $5 one-time fee/room. Service with restrictions, supervision.
ASK SD ✕ 🛢

## GARRISON

▼▼▼ **Garrison Inn & Suites by Ruttger's** 🆂🅷
(320) 692-4050. **$59-$129.** 9243 Hwy 169. SR 169, just s of jct SR 18. Int corridors. **Pets:** $50 deposit/room, $10 daily fee/pet. Designated rooms, service with restrictions, supervision.
ASK SD ✕ 🛢 💻 ⊇

## GAYLORD

▼▼ **Gold Leaf Inn & Suites** 🅼
(507) 237-5860. **$56-$129.** 330 Main Ave E. 1.5 mi e. Int corridors. **Pets:** Medium. Designated rooms, service with restrictions, supervision.
✕ 🖋 🛢

# GRAND MARAIS

**▲▲▲ ▼▼▼▼ Best Western Superior Inn & Suites** 🆂🅷 ❀
(218) 387-2240. **$79-$259, 3 day notice.** 104 1st Ave E. SR 61, just ne of center. Int corridors. **Pets:** Medium. $10 daily fee/room. Designated rooms, service with restrictions, supervision.
[SAVE] [✕] [🐾] [▦]

**▼▼▼▼ Gunflint Lodge** 🆅🅷
(218) 388-2294. **$150-$400, 60 day notice.** 143 S Gunflint Lake. 43 mi n of town; 0.8 mi e of jct CR 12 (Gunflint Tr) and 50. Ext corridors. **Pets:** Accepted.
[ᏜM] [🔒] [▦] [🍴] [✕] [🐾] [🐕]

**▼▼ Nor'Wester Lodge and Outfitter** 🅲🅰
(218) 388-2252. **$99-$239, 60 day notice.** 7778 Gunflint Tr. 30 mi nw on CR 12 (Gunflint Tr) from jct SR 61. Ext corridors. **Pets:** Accepted.
[🔒] [▦] [✕] [🐾] [📶] [🐕]

**▼▼ Outpost Motel** 🅼
(218) 387-1833. **$45-$59.** 2935 SR 61 E. 9 mi ne. Ext corridors. **Pets:** Other species. $10 daily fee/pet. Supervision.
[✕] [🔒] [▦] [✕] [🐾]

**▲▲▲ ▼▼ Wedgewood Motel** 🅼
(218) 387-2944. **$49-$69, 3 day notice.** 1663 E Hwy 61. On SR 61, 2.5 mi ne. Ext corridors. **Pets:** Dogs only. $5 daily fee/pet. Designated rooms, service with restrictions, supervision.
[SAVE] [ᏕØ] [✕] [🔒] [🐾] [🐕]

# GRAND RAPIDS

**▲▲▲ ▼▼ Budget Host Inn** 🅼
(218) 326-3457. **$50-$78, 7 day notice.** 311 E Hwy 2. Jct US 2 E and 169 N. Ext/int corridors. **Pets:** Accepted.
[SAVE] [ᏕØ] [✕]

**▲▲▲ ▼▼▼▼ Country Inn By Carlson** 🆂🅷
(218) 327-4960. **$89-$130.** 2601 S Hwy 169. US 2, 2 mi s. Int corridors. **Pets:** Accepted.
[SAVE] [ᏕØ] [✕] [ᏜM] [Ø] [Ꮬⁿ] [🔒] [▦] [🐾]

**▲▲▲ ▼▼▼▼ Sawmill Inn** 🆂🅷
(218) 326-8501. **$79-$99.** 2301 S Hwy 169. US 2, 2 mi s on US 169. Ext/int corridors. **Pets:** Service with restrictions, supervision.
[SAVE] [ᏕØ] [✕] [Ø] [🔒] [▦] [🍴] [🐾] [✕]

# GRANITE FALLS

**▼▼ Super 8 Motel** 🆂🅷
(320) 564-4075. **$50-$92.** 845 W SR 212. Jct SR 23 and 212, 0.5 mi w. Int corridors. **Pets:** Accepted.
[ASK] [ᏕØ] [✕] [ᏜM] [Ꮬⁿ] [🔒] [🐾]

# HIBBING

**▼▼▼ Super 8 Motel** 🆂🅷
(218) 263-8982. **Call for rates.** 1411 E 40th St. Just e of US 169 and SR 37. Int corridors. **Pets:** Accepted.
[✕]

# HINCKLEY

**▼▼▼ Days Inn** 🆂🅷
(320) 384-7751. **$59-$129.** 104 Grindstone Ct. I-35, exit 183 (SR 48), just e. Int corridors. **Pets:** Small, other species. $10 daily fee/pet. Service with restrictions, supervision.
[ASK] [ᏕØ] [✕] [Ꮬⁿ] [🔒] [▦] [🐾]

**▼▼▼ Travelodge** 🅼
(320) 384-6112. **$45-$109.** 325 Fire Monument Rd. I-35, exit 183 (SR 48), just w. Ext/int corridors. **Pets:** Small, other species. $10 daily fee/room. Service with restrictions, supervision.
[ASK] [ᏕØ] [✕] [Ø] [🔒] [▦]

# HUTCHINSON

**▼▼▼ AmericInn Motel** 🆂🅷
(320) 587-5515. **$78-$139.** 1115 Hwy 7 E. On SR 7, just e. Int corridors. **Pets:** Accepted.
[ASK] [ᏕØ] [✕] [ᏜM] [Ø] [Ꮬⁿ] [🔒] [▦] [🐾] [✕]

# INTERNATIONAL FALLS

**▼▼ Hilltop Motel** 🅼
(218) 283-2505. **$49-$89.** 2002 2nd Ave W. US 53, 1 mi s of jct US 53 and SR 11. Ext corridors. **Pets:** Small, other species. $10 daily fee/pet. Service with restrictions, supervision.
[ASK] [ᏕØ] [✕]

**▼▼▼▼ Holiday Inn** 🆂🅷
(218) 283-8000. **$95-$175.** 1500 US 71 W. 1.5 mi w on US 71 and SR 11 W. Int corridors. **Pets:** Designated rooms, service with restrictions, supervision.
[ASK] [✕] [Ꮬⁿ] [🔒] [▦] [🍴] [🐾] [✕]

# JACKSON

**▼▼▼▼ AmericInn Lodge & Suites** 🆂🅷
(507) 847-2444. **$85-$140.** 110 Belmont Ln. I-90, exit 73, just sw. Int corridors. **Pets:** Dogs only. $50 deposit/room, $10 daily fee/pet. Designated rooms, service with restrictions, supervision.
[✕] [ᏜM] [🔒] [▦] [🐾]

**▼▼ Budget Host Inn Praire Winds** 🅼
(507) 847-2020. **$40-$56.** 950 US 71. I-90, exit 73 (US 71), 0.4 mi s. Ext corridors. **Pets:** Accepted.
[ASK] [✕] [ᏜM] [🔒]

**▼▼▼ Econo Lodge** 🆂🅷
(507) 847-3110. **$60-$70.** 2007 Hwy 71 N. I-90, exit 73 (US 71), just n. Ext/int corridors. **Pets:** Accepted.
[ASK] [ᏕØ] [✕] [▦] [🍴] [🐾]

**▼▼▼ Super 8 Motel** 🆂🅷
(507) 847-3498. **$65-$70.** 2025 Hwy 71 N. I-90, exit 73 (US 71), just n. Int corridors. **Pets:** Accepted.
[ASK] [ᏕØ] [✕] [ᏜM] [Ꮬⁿ] [🔒]

# LAMBERTON

**▼▼ Lamberton Motel** 🅼
(507) 752-7242. **$35-$55.** 601 1st Ave W. Just s of jct US 14 and Ilex St. Ext corridors. **Pets:** Other species. $5 one-time fee/pet. Designated rooms, service with restrictions, supervision.
[ASK] [ᏕØ] [✕] [🔒] [▦]

# LITCHFIELD

**▼▼ ScotWood Motel** 🅼
(320) 693-2496. **$50-$80.** 1017 E Frontage Rd. On US 12. Int corridors. **Pets:** Accepted.
[ASK] [ᏕØ] [✕] [🔒] [🐾]

# LITTLE FALLS

**▼▼▼▼ Country Inn & Suites By Carlson** 🆂🅷
(320) 632-1000. **$94-$139.** 209 16th St NE. Just ne of jct SR 10 and 27. Int corridors. **Pets:** Accepted.
[ᏕØ] [✕] [ᏜM] [Ꮬⁿ] [🔒] [▦] [🐾]

# LONG PRAIRIE

**▲▲▲ ▼▼▼ Budget Host Inn** 🅼
(320) 732-6118. **$55-$72.** 417 Lake St. On US 71 and SR 27, just s of jct SR 287. Ext corridors. **Pets:** Medium. $5 daily fee/room. Designated rooms, service with restrictions, supervision.
[SAVE] [ᏕØ] [✕] [🔒] [▦]

# LUTSEN

### ❖❖❖ Cascade Lodge [CI]
(218) 387-1112. **$45-$99, 14 day notice.** 3719 W SR 61. On SR 61, 7 mi ne of jct CR 4 (Caribou Tr). Ext/int corridors. **Pets:** Medium, dogs only. $10 daily fee/pet. Designated rooms, service with restrictions, supervision.
[SAVE] [S₀] [X] [T] [P] [Y] [X]

### ❖❖❖ Solbakken Resort [M]
(218) 663-7566. **$51-$91, 14 day notice.** 4874 W SR 61. On SR 61, 1.3 mi n of jct CR 4 (Caribou Tr). Ext corridors. **Pets:** Medium. $10 daily fee/pet. Designated rooms, service with restrictions, supervision.
[SAVE] [S₀] [X] [☞] [T] [P] [X] [K]

# MANKATO

### ❖❖❖ AmericInn of Mankato at MSU [SH]
(507) 345-8011. **$50-$200.** 240 Stadium Rd. From jct US 14, 1.6 mi s on SR 22, 0.4 mi w on SR 83, just s on Victory Dr, then 1.5 mi w. Int corridors. **Pets:** Accepted.
[ASK] [X] [S.M] [☞] [T] [P] [⇒] [X]

### ❖❖❖❖ Best Western Hotel, Restaurant & Conference Center [SH]
(507) 625-9333. **$72-$114.** 1111 Range St. 1.3 mi n on US 169. Int corridors. **Pets:** Designated rooms, service with restrictions, supervision.
[SAVE] [S₀] [X] [T] [P] [Y] [⇒] [X]

### ❖❖ Comfort Inn by Choice Hotels [SH]
(507) 388-5107. **$64-$109.** 131 Apache Pl. Just s of jct US 14 and SR 22 S. Int corridors. **Pets:** $10 daily fee/room. Service with restrictions, supervision.
[ASK] [S₀] [X] [☞] [T] [P] [⇒]

### ❖❖❖ Days Inn [SH] ❖
(507) 387-3332. **$45-$95.** 1285 Range St. US 169, 0.3 mi s of jct US 14. Int corridors. **Pets:** $5 daily fee/pet. Designated rooms, service with restrictions, supervision.
[SAVE] [S₀] [X] [T] [P] [⇒]

### ❖❖❖ Grandstay Residential Suites [SH]
(507) 388-8688. **$90-$110.** 1000 Raintree Rd. 1.3 mi s of jct US 14 and SR 22 on CR 3. Int corridors. **Pets:** Accepted.
[ASK] [X] [☞] [☞] [T] [P] [⇒]

### ❖❖❖ Holiday Inn [SH]
(507) 345-1234. **$70-$139.** 101 E Main St. Main St at Riverfront Dr; downtown. Int corridors. **Pets:** Accepted.
[ASK] [X] [S.M] [☞] [☞] [T] [P] [Y] [⇒] [X]

### ❖❖ Super 8 Motel [SH]
(507) 387-4041. **$60-$95.** 51578 US Hwy 169. Jct US 169 N and 14, just n. Int corridors. **Pets:** Dogs only. $100 deposit/room. Designated rooms, service with restrictions, supervision.
[ASK] [S₀] [X] [T] [P]

# MARSHALL

### ❖❖❖ Best Western Marshall Inn [SH]
(507) 532-3221. **$79-$139.** 1500 E College Dr. SR 19, just w of jct SR 23. Int corridors. **Pets:** $10 daily fee/room. Service with restrictions, supervision.
[SAVE] [X] [T] [P] [Y] [⇒] [X]

### ❖❖❖ Comfort Inn [SH]
(507) 532-3070. **$70-$105.** 1511 E College Dr. SR 19, w of jct SR 23. Int corridors. **Pets:** $10 daily fee/pet. Service with restrictions, crate.
[ASK] [S₀] [X] [S.M] [☞] [☞] [T] [P] [⇒]

### ❖❖ Super 8 Motel [SH]
(507) 537-1461. **$60-$75.** 1106 E Main St. 0.3 mi se on US 59 from jct SR 23. Int corridors. **Pets:** Other species. $10 daily fee/room. Service with restrictions, supervision.
[ASK] [S₀] [X] [☞] [T]

# MCGREGOR

### ❖❖ Country Meadows Inn [SH]
(218) 768-7378. **$60-$119.** 403 Meadows Dr. Jct SR 65 and 210. Int corridors. **Pets:** Other species. $6 daily fee/pet. Designated rooms, service with restrictions, supervision.
[ASK] [S₀] [X] [☞] [T] [P] [⇒]

---

## MINNEAPOLIS-ST. PAUL METROPOLITAN AREA

# ANNANDALE

### ❖❖ AmericInn Lodge & Suites [SH]
(320) 274-3006. **$69-$129.** 620 Elm St E. On SR 55. Int corridors. **Pets:** Medium, other species. $50 deposit/room. Designated rooms, service with restrictions, crate.
[ASK] [S₀] [X] [S.M] [☞] [☞] [T] [P] [⇒]

# ARDEN HILLS

### ❖❖ Super 8 Arden Hills/Minneapolis/St. Paul [SH] ❖
(651) 484-6557. **$59-$90.** 1125 Red Fox Rd. I-694, exit 43A (Lexington Ave), just sw. Int corridors. **Pets:** Medium. $50 deposit/room, $8 daily fee/pet. Service with restrictions, supervision.
[ASK] [S₀] [X] [T] [P]

# BECKER

### ❖❖❖ Sleep Inn & Suites [SH]
(763) 262-7700. **$69-$109.** 14435 Bank St. Just e on US 10. Int corridors. **Pets:** $100 deposit/room, $10 daily fee/pet. Service with restrictions, supervision.
[SAVE] [S₀] [X] [T] [P] [⇒] [X]

# BLOOMINGTON

### ❖❖❖ AmeriSuites (Minneapolis/Mall of America) [SH] ❖
(952) 854-0700. **$89-$189.** 7800 International Dr. I-494, exit 1B (34th Ave), just sw. Int corridors. **Pets:** Very small. Designated rooms, service with restrictions, supervision.
[SAVE] [S₀] [X] [S.M] [☞] [T] [P] [⇒]

### ❖❖❖ Baymont Inn Minneapolis-Airport (Bloomington) [SH]
(952) 881-7311. **$85-$121.** 7815 Nicollet Ave S. I-494, exit 4A (Nicollet Ave), just s. Int corridors. **Pets:** Medium. Service with restrictions.
[SAVE] [X] [☞] [T] [P]

### ❖❖❖ Hilton Minneapolis/St. Paul Airport Mall of America [LH]
(952) 854-2100. **$89-$209.** 3800 American Blvd E. I-494, exit 1B (34th Ave), just se. Int corridors. **Pets:** Medium. Service with restrictions, crate.
[SAVE] [S₀] [X] [S.M] [☞] [☞] [T] [P] [Y] [⇒] [X]

**(AAA) ▼▼▼▼ Homewood Suites by Hilton** 🆂🅷
(952) 854-0900. **$119-$199.** 2261 Killebrew Dr. I-494, exit 2A (24th Ave), 1 mi s, then just w. Int corridors. **Pets:** Medium. $100 one-time fee/room. Service with restrictions.
〔SAVE〕 ⛄ ⊠ ⅆ ▯ 🖭 ⇝

**(AAA) ▼▼▼ Le Bourget Aero Suites** 🆂🅷
(952) 893-9999. **$79-$189.** 7770 Johnson Ave. I-494, exit 6B (France Ave), 0.5 mi nw on frontage road (78th St). Int corridors. **Pets:** Small. $100 deposit/pet. Service with restrictions, supervision.
〔SAVE〕 ⛄ ⊠ ⅋ ☒ ▯ 🖭 ⇝ ⊠

**▼▼▼ Ramada Inn Mall of America** 🆂🅷
(952) 854-3411. **$79-$199.** 2201 E 78th St. I-494, exit 2A (24th Ave), just s. Int corridors. **Pets:** Accepted.
〔ASK〕 ⛄ ⊠ ⅋ ☒ ▯ 🖭 🍴 ⇝ ⊠

**▼▼▼ Residence Inn by Marriott** 🆂🅷
(952) 876-0900. **$159-$220.** 7850 Bloomington Ave S. I-494, exit 3, on south frontage road. Int corridors. **Pets:** Accepted.
〔ASK〕 ⊠ ☒ ▯ 🖭 ⇝

**▼▼▼ Sheraton Bloomington Hotel Minneapolis**
   **South** 🆻🅷 🐾
(952) 835-7800. **$239-$349.** 7800 Normandale Blvd. I-494, exit 7 (SR 100). Int corridors. **Pets:** Medium. $50 deposit/room. Service with restrictions, supervision.
〔ASK〕 ⛄ ⊠ ☒ ▯ 🖭 🍴 ⇝ ⊠

**(AAA) ▼▼▼▼ Sofitel Minneapolis** 🆻🅷 🐾
(952) 835-1900. **$159-$259.** 5601 W 78th St. Just nw of jct I-494 and SR 100, access via SR 100 and Industrial Blvd. Int corridors. **Pets:** Medium, dogs only. Designated rooms, service with restrictions.
〔SAVE〕 ⊠ ⅋ ☒ ☒ ▯ 🍴 ⇝ ⊠

**▼▼▼▼ Staybridge Suites** 🆂🅷
(952) 831-7900. **$109-$149.** 5150 American Blvd. I-494, exit 6B (France Ave), just se of SR 100, then 1 mi w on frontage road. Int corridors. **Pets:** Medium, other species. $150 one-time fee/room. Service with restrictions, supervision.
〔ASK〕 ⛄ ⊠ ☒ ⅋ ☒ ▯ 🖭 ⇝ ⊠

## BROOKLYN CENTER

**(AAA) ▼▼▼ Baymont Inn & Suites Minneapolis-Brooklyn**
   **Center** 🆂🅷
(763) 561-8400. **$66-$116.** 6415 James Cir N. I-94/694, exit 34 (Shingle Creek Pkwy), just ne. Int corridors. **Pets:** Medium. Service with restrictions.
〔SAVE〕 ⊠ ☒ ▯ 🖭

**▼▼ Comfort Inn by Choice Hotels** 🆂🅷
(763) 560-7464. **$69-$99.** 1600 James Cir N. I-694, exit 34 (Shingle Creek Pkwy), just ne. Int corridors. **Pets:** Accepted.
〔ASK〕 ⛄ ⊠ ⅋ ☒ ☒ ▯ 🖭

**(AAA) ▼▼▼▼ Crowne Plaza Minneapolis North** 🆂🅷 🐾
(763) 566-8000. **$89-$109.** 2200 Freeway Blvd. I-94/694, exit 34 (Shingle Creek Pkwy). Int corridors. **Pets:** Medium, dogs only. $100 deposit/room, $25 daily fee/pet. Designated rooms, service with restrictions, supervision.
〔SAVE〕 ⛄ ⊠ ☒ ▯ 🖭 🍴 ⇝ ⊠

## BROOKLYN PARK

**▼▼ Sleep Inn** 🆂🅷
(763) 971-8000. **$74-$99.** 7011 Northland Cir. I-94/694, exit 30 (Boone Ave), just ne. Int corridors. **Pets:** Accepted.
〔ASK〕 ⛄ ⊠ ⅋ ☒ ▯ 🖭

## BURNSVILLE

**▼▼ Red Roof Inn** Ⓜ
(952) 890-1420. **$42-$79.** 12920 Aldrich Ave S. I-35W, exit 2 (Burnsville Pkwy), just sw. Ext corridors. **Pets:** Accepted.
⊠ ☒

**(AAA) ▼▼▼ Super 8 Motel** Ⓜ
(952) 894-3400. **$52-$72.** 1101 Burnsville Pkwy. I-35W, exit 2 (Burnsville Pkwy), just sw. Int corridors. **Pets:** Accepted.
〔SAVE〕 ⛄ ⊠ ▯

## CHANHASSEN

**(AAA) ▼▼▼▼ AmericInn Hotel & Suites** 🆂🅷
(952) 934-3888. **$81-$165.** 570 Pond Promenade. Just se of jct SR 5 and 101 S. Int corridors. **Pets:** $100 deposit/room, $30 daily fee/room. Designated rooms, service with restrictions, crate.
〔SAVE〕 ⛄ ⊠ ⅋ ☒ ▯ 🖭 ⇝ ⊠

## CHASKA

**(AAA) ▼▼▼▼ Best Western Chaska River Inn &**
   **Suites** 🆂🅷 🐾
(952) 448-7877. **$60-$100.** One Riverbend. Jct US 212, 0.3 mi s on SR 41. Int corridors. **Pets:** Other species. $30 deposit/room. Service with restrictions.
〔SAVE〕 ⊠ ⅋ ☒ ▯ 🖭 🍴 ⇝ ⊠

## COON RAPIDS

**(AAA) ▼▼▼ Comfort Inn-Northtown** 🆂🅷
(763) 785-4746. **$79-$109.** 9052 University Ave NE. Just ne of jct US 10, exit University Ave. Int corridors. **Pets:** Other species. $10 daily fee/pet. Designated rooms, service with restrictions, supervision.
〔SAVE〕 ⛄ ⊠ ▯ 🖭 ⇝

**(AAA) ▼▼▼▼ Country Suites By Carlson** 🆂🅷 🐾
(763) 780-3797. **$89-$149.** 155 Coon Rapids Blvd. 0.5 mi e of SR 610. Int corridors. **Pets:** Medium. $10 daily fee/pet. Designated rooms, service with restrictions, crate.
〔SAVE〕 ⛄ ⊠ ☒ ☒ ▯ 🖭 ⇝

## EAGAN

**▼▼ Days Inn** 🆂🅷
(651) 681-1770. **$79-$109.** 4510 Erin Dr. Just ne of jct SR 77 and Cliff Rd. Int corridors. **Pets:** Designated rooms, service with restrictions, supervision.
〔ASK〕 ⛄ ⊠ ⅋ ☒ ▯ 🖭 ⇝ ⊠

**▼▼ Homestead Studio Suites Hotel-Airport/Eagan** 🆂🅷
(651) 905-1778. **$75.** 3015 Denmark Ave. I-35E, exit 98 (Lone Oak Rd), just se. Int corridors. **Pets:** $25 daily fee/pet. Service with restrictions, supervision.
〔ASK〕 ⛄ ⊠ ☒ ☒ ▯ 🖭

**▼▼ Microtel Inn & Suites** 🆂🅷
(651) 405-0988. **$59-$89.** 3000 Denmark Ave. I-35E, exit 98 (Lone Oak Rd), just se. Int corridors. **Pets:** $10 one-time fee/room. Designated rooms, service with restrictions, supervision.
〔ASK〕 ⛄ ⊠ ☒ ▯ 🖭

**▼▼▼▼ Residence Inn by Marriott-Mpls/St. Paul**
   **Airport** 🆂🅷 🐾
(651) 688-0363. **$89-$139.** 3040 Eagandale Pl. I-35E, exit 98 (Lone Oak Rd), just sw. Ext corridors. **Pets:** Other species. $75 deposit/room. Crate.
⊠ ☒ 🖭 ⇝ ⊠

**▼▼▼▼ Staybridge Suites** 🆂🅷 🐾
(651) 994-7810. **$129-$149.** 4675 Rahncliff Rd. I-35E, exit 93 (Cliff Rd), just w, then just s. Int corridors. **Pets:** $150 one-time fee/room. Service with restrictions.
〔ASK〕 ⛄ ⊠ ☒ ☒ ▯ 🖭 ⇝

▼▼▼ TownePlace Suites SH
(651) 994-4600. **$79-$149.** 3615 Crestridge Dr. I-35E, exit 71 (Pilot Knob Rd), just se. Int corridors. **Pets:** Small. $75 one-time fee/room. Service with restrictions, crate.

(A$K) (S6) (×) (8) (•) (🛏)

# EDEN PRAIRIE

♦♦♦ ▼▼▼▼ AmeriSuites (Minneapolis/Eden Prairie) SH
(952) 944-9700. **$142-$191.** 11369 Viking Dr. I-494, exit 11A, just w. Int corridors. **Pets:** Accepted.

(SAVE) (S6) (×) (&M) (☞) (8) (•) (🛏)

▼▼▼ Best Western Eden Prairie Inn SH
(952) 829-0888. **$89-$165.** 11500 W 78th St. I-494, exit 11A, just sw. Int corridors. **Pets:** Small, dogs only. $10 one-time fee/pet. Designated rooms, service with restrictions, supervision.

(A$K) (S6) (×) (8) (•)

▼▼ Homestead Studio Suites Hotel-Minneapolis/Eden Prairie SH
(952) 942-6818. **$69-$84.** 11905 Technology Dr. Just sw of jct I-494 and US 212 (Flying Cloud Dr). Int corridors. **Pets:** $25 daily fee/pet. Service with restrictions, supervision.

(A$K) (S6) (×) (&M) (☞) (8) (•)

▼▼▼▼ The Residence Inn by Marriott-Minneapolis SW SH
(952) 829-0033. **$89-$159.** 7780 Flying Cloud Dr. I-494, exit 11A, on US 169 S and 212 (Flying Cloud Dr). Int corridors. **Pets:** Accepted.

(A$K) (×) (☞) (8) (•) (🛏)

▼▼▼▼ TownePlace Suites By Marriott SH
(952) 942-6001. **$51-$129.** 11588 Leona Rd. I-494, se of jct US 212 (Flying Cloud Dr). Int corridors. **Pets:** Accepted.

(×) (8) (•) (🛏)

# EDINA

▼▼▼▼ Residence Inn Minneapolis-Edina SH
(952) 893-9300. **$119-$289.** 3400 Edinborough Way. I-494, exit 6B (France Ave), 0.3 mi n to Minnesota Dr, then just e. Int corridors. **Pets:** Small, dogs only. $75 one-time fee/pet. Designated rooms, service with restrictions, supervision.

(A$K) (S6) (×) (🐾) (8) (•)

# ELK RIVER

▼▼▼ AmericInn Lodge & Suites of Elk River M
(763) 441-8554. **$79-$199.** 17432 Hwy 10. 1.5 mi se on US 10/169. Int corridors. **Pets:** Accepted.

(A$K) (S6) (×) (☞) (•)

# FOREST LAKE

▼▼▼ AmericInn Motel SH
(651) 464-1930. **$69-$95.** 1291 W Broadway. I-35, exit 131 (CR 2), just ne. Int corridors. **Pets:** Medium. $10 daily fee/room. Designated rooms, service with restrictions, supervision.

(A$K) (S6) (×) (☞) (8) (•) (🛏)

# HASTINGS

▼▼▼▼ Country Inn & Suites By Carlson SH
(651) 437-8870. **$79-$149.** 300 33rd St. Just e of US 61. Int corridors. **Pets:** Large. $75 deposit/room, $10 daily fee/room. Designated rooms, service with restrictions, supervision.

(A$K) (S6) (×) (☞) (8) (•) (🛏)

# LAKE ELMO

♦♦♦ ▼▼▼▼ A Wildwood Lodge SH
(651) 714-8068. **$162.** 8511 Hudson Blvd. I-94, exit 250 (Inwood/Radio), just ne. Int corridors. **Pets:** Small, other species. $150 one-time fee/room. Designated rooms, no service, supervision.

(SAVE) (S6) (×) (&M) (🐾) (8) (•) (🍴) (🛏) (×)

# MAPLE GROVE

▼▼▼▼ Staybridge Suites Minneapolis-Maple Grove SH
(763) 494-8856. **$119-$339.** 7821 Elm Creek Blvd. Just ne of jct I-94/494/694. Int corridors. **Pets:** Medium. $150 one-time fee/pet. Service with restrictions, crate.

(A$K) (S6) (×) (&M) (🐾) (☞) (8) (•) (🛏) (×)

# MINNEAPOLIS

♦♦♦ ▼▼▼ ▼▼▼ Graves 601 Hotel LH
(612) 677-1100. **$184-$284.** 601 1st Ave N. Between 6th and 7th sts. Int corridors. **Pets:** Accepted.

(SAVE) (S6) (×) (🐾) (☞) (8) (🍴)

▼▼▼ Hilton Minneapolis LH
(612) 376-1000. **$119-$359.** 1001 Marquette Ave. Between S 10th and S 11th sts. Int corridors. **Pets:** Small. $150 deposit/room. Service with restrictions, crate.

(A$K) (S6) (🐾) (☞) (8) (•) (🍴) (🛏) (×)

▼▼▼ Holiday Inn Minneapolis Metrodome LH
(612) 333-4646. **$159-$172.** 1500 Washington Ave S. Jct Washington and S 15th aves. Int corridors. **Pets:** Accepted.

(A$K) (×) (🐾) (☞) (8) (•) (🍴) (🛏) (×)

♦♦♦ ▼▼▼ ▼▼▼ The Marquette Hotel LH
(612) 333-4545. **$109-$469.** 7th St & Marquette Ave. Jct Marquette Ave and S 7th St. Int corridors. **Pets:** Accepted.

(SAVE) (S6) (×) (🐾) (☞) (8) (•) (🍴)

♦♦♦ ▼▼▼ Millenium Hotel Minneapolis LH 🐾
(612) 332-6000. **$99.** 1313 Nicollet Mall. Jct Nicollet Ave and Grant St. Int corridors. **Pets:** $10 daily fee/pet. Service with restrictions.

(SAVE) (×) (&M) (🐾) (8) (•) (🍴) (🛏) (×)

♦♦♦ ▼▼▼ Minneapolis Marriott City Center LH
(612) 349-4000. **$189-$259.** 30 S 7th St. Between Hennepin and Nicollet aves; in City Center Shopping Complex. Int corridors. **Pets:** Accepted.

(SAVE) (S6) (×) (&M) (🐾) (8) (•) (🍴) (×)

♦♦♦ ▼▼▼ ▼▼▼ Radisson Plaza Hotel Minneapolis LH
(612) 339-4900. **$159-$299.** 35 S 7th St. Between Nicollet and Hennepin aves. Int corridors. **Pets:** Small. $50 one-time fee/room. Service with restrictions, supervision.

(SAVE) (S6) (×) (&M) (🐾) (☞) (8) (•) (🍴) (×)

▼▼▼ Residence Inn Milwaukee Road Depot SH
(612) 340-1300. **$119-$229.** 425 S 2nd St. Jct S 2nd St and 5th Ave S. Int corridors. **Pets:** Large, other species. $75 one-time fee/pet. Designated rooms, service with restrictions, crate.

(A$K) (S6) (×) (🐾) (☞) (8) (•)

# MINNETONKA

▼▼▼ Minneapolis Marriott-Southwest LH 🐾
(952) 935-5500. **$169-$219.** 5801 Opus Pkwy. Just nw of jct US 169 and Cross Town SR 62, exit Bren Rd off US 169. Int corridors. **Pets:** Medium, dogs only. $250 deposit/room. Service with restrictions, crate.

(A$K) (×) (🐾) (8) (•) (🍴) (🛏) (×)

♦♦♦ ▼▼▼ ▼▼▼ Sheraton Minneapolis West Hotel SH
(952) 593-0000. **$99-$189.** 12201 Ridgedale Dr. I-394, exit 1C (Plymouth Rd), 0.3 mi s. Int corridors. **Pets:** Accepted.

(SAVE) (S6) (×) (8) (•) (🍴) (🛏) (×)

# MONTICELLO

♦♦♦ ▼▼▼ ▼▼▼ Best Western Chelsea Inn & Suites SH
(763) 271-8880. **$79-$139.** 89 Chelsea Rd. I-94, exit 193, just se. Int corridors. **Pets:** Accepted.

(SAVE) (S6) (×) (☞) (8) (•) (🛏)

**Days Inn** SH
(763) 295-1111. **$59-$79.** 200 E Oakwood Dr. I-94, exit 193, 0.3 mi se. Int corridors. **Pets:** Large, other species. $12 one-time fee/pet. Designated rooms, service with restrictions, supervision.

**Silver Fox Inn** SH
(763) 295-4000. **$72-$86.** 1114 Cedar St. I-94, exit 193, 0.3 mi se. Int corridors. **Pets:** Accepted.

## OAKDALE

**Wingate Inn** SH ❀
(651) 578-8466. **$105-$155.** 970 Helena Ave N. I-694, exit 57, just e, then just s. Int corridors. **Pets:** Medium. $50 deposit/room. Designated rooms, service with restrictions, supervision.

## PLYMOUTH

**Best Western Kelly Inn** SH
(763) 553-1600. **$89-$124.** 2705 N Annapolis Ln. I-494, exit 22 (SR 55), just e. Int corridors. **Pets:** Service with restrictions, supervision.

**Radisson Hotel & Conference Center Minneapolis** LH
(763) 559-6600. **$99-$169.** 3131 Campus Dr. I-494, exit 22 (SR 55), just e to CR 61 (Northwest Blvd), then 0.8 mi nw. Int corridors. **Pets:** Accepted.

**Red Roof Inn** M
(763) 553-1751. **$63-$96.** 2600 Annapolis Ln N. I-494, exit 22 (SR 55), just se. Ext corridors. **Pets:** Accepted.

## RICHFIELD

**Candlewood Suites** SH
(612) 869-7704. **$95-$115.** 351 W 77th St. I-494, exit 4B (Lyndale Ave), just ne. Int corridors. **Pets:** Medium. $75 one-time fee/pet. Service with restrictions, crate.

## ROGERS

**AmericInn Lodge & Suites** SH
(763) 428-4346. **$75-$105.** 21800 Industrial Blvd. I-94, exit 207 (SR 101), just sw. Int corridors. **Pets:** Dogs only. $100 deposit/room, $10 daily fee/pet. Designated rooms, supervision.

## ROSEVILLE

**Residence Inn** SH ❀
(651) 636-0680. **$89-$159.** 2985 Centre Pointe Dr. I-35W, exit 25A (CR D), just se. Int corridors. **Pets:** Other species. $75 one-time fee/room. Service with restrictions, crate.

## ST. LOUIS PARK

**Lakeland Inn** SH
(952) 926-6575. **$60-$75.** 4025 Hwy 7. SR 7, 0.5 mi e of SR 100. Int corridors. **Pets:** Large. $5 daily fee/pet. Designated rooms, service with restrictions, supervision.

**TownePlace Suites-Minneapolis West** SH
(952) 847-6900. **$69-$159.** 1400 Zarthan Ave S. I-394, exit 5 (Park Place Blvd), 0.3 mi w on 16th, then just n. Int corridors. **Pets:** Accepted.

## ST. PAUL

**Best Western Kelly Inn** SH
(651) 227-8711. **$89-$119.** 161 St. Anthony Ave. Jct I-35E and 94. Int corridors. **Pets:** Service with restrictions, supervision.

**Exel Inn of St. Paul** SH
(651) 771-5566. **$58-$88.** 1739 Old Hudson Rd. I-94, exit 245 (White Bear Ave), just nw. Int corridors. **Pets:** Small, other species. Designated rooms, service with restrictions, supervision.

**Holiday Inn Express Bandana Square** SH
(651) 647-1637. **$79-$149.** 1010 Bandana Blvd W. I-94, exit 239B (Lexington Pkwy), 1.3 mi n, then 0.3 mi w on Energy Park Dr. Int corridors. **Pets:** $20 one-time fee/room. Designated rooms, service with restrictions, crate.

## SHAKOPEE

**Canterbury Inn** SH
(952) 445-3644. **$69-$119.** 1244 Canterbury Rd. Just nw of US 169. Int corridors. **Pets:** Accepted.

**Sandalwood Studios & Suites** SH
(952) 277-0100. **$54-$129.** 3910 12th Ave E. Just nw of US 169. Int corridors. **Pets:** Small. $10 daily fee/room. Designated rooms, service with restrictions, supervision.

## STILLWATER

**Days Inn-Stillwater** SH
(651) 430-1300. **$59-$99.** 1750 W Frontage Rd. SR 36 at Washington Ave, just ne. Int corridors. **Pets:** $10 daily fee/pet. Service with restrictions, supervision.

**Super 8 Motel** M
(651) 430-3990. **$55-$89.** 2190 W Frontage Rd. SR 36 at Washington Ave, 3.3 mi sw. Int corridors. **Pets:** Other species. $10 one-time fee/room. Service with restrictions, supervision.

## TAYLORS FALLS

**The Springs Country Inn** M
(651) 465-6565. **$59-$159.** 361 Government St. US 8 and SR 95, just w. Ext corridors. **Pets:** Accepted.

## WHITE BEAR LAKE

**Best Western White Bear Country Inn** SH
(651) 429-5393. **$90-$180.** 4940 N Hwy 61. Jct SR 96, 1 mi n. Int corridors. **Pets:** $10 daily fee/pet. Service with restrictions, supervision.

## WOODBURY

**AAA** **♦♦♦♦** **Holiday Inn Express Hotels & Suites** SH
(651) 702-0200. **$109, 7 day notice.** 9840 Norma Ln. I-94, exit 251, just sw. Int corridors. **Pets:** Accepted.
[SAVE] [S🐾] [✕] [🏃] [📶] [🖥] [🌊] [✕]

**♦♦♦** **Red Roof Inn #7063** M
(651) 738-7160. **$50-$80.** 1806 Wooddale Dr. I-494, exit 59 (Valley Creek Rd), just se. Ext corridors. **Pets:** Accepted.
[✕] [🐾]

---

## END METROPOLITAN AREA

---

## MONTEVIDEO

**♦♦♦♦♦** **Country Inn & Suites By Carlson** SH
(320) 269-8000. **$80-$145.** 1805 E Hwy 7. On SR 7. Int corridors. **Pets:** $200 deposit/room. Designated rooms, supervision.
[ASK] [S🐾] [✕] [🏃] [🖥] [🌊]

## MOORHEAD

**AAA** **♦♦♦** **Days Inn and Conference Center of Moorhead** SH
(218) 287-7100. **$69-$139.** 600 30th Ave SW. I-94, exit 1A (US 75), just sw. Int corridors. **Pets:** $11 daily fee/room. Designated rooms, service with restrictions, supervision.
[SAVE] [S🐾] [✕] [🏃] [🖥] [🍴] [🌊] [✕]

**AAA** **♦** **Grand Inn Of Moorhead** SH
(218) 233-7501. **$45-$57.** 810 Belsly Blvd. I-94, exit 1A (US 75), 0.5 mi s. Int corridors. **Pets:** $25 deposit/room. Designated rooms, service with restrictions, supervision.
[SAVE] [S🐾] [✕]

**AAA** **♦♦♦♦** **Travelodge & Suites** SH
(218) 233-5333. **$60-$90.** 3027 S Frontage Rd. Just s of US 10 E; east of downtown. Int corridors. **Pets:** Medium. Designated rooms, service with restrictions, supervision.
[SAVE] [S🐾] [✕] [🅼] [🏃] [📶] [🖥] [🌊]

## MOOSE LAKE

**♦♦♦♦♦** **AmericInn Lodge & Suites** SH
(218) 485-8885. **$70-$180.** 400 Park Place Dr. I-35, exit 214 (SR 73), just sw. Int corridors. **Pets:** Other species. $50 deposit/room, $10 daily fee/room. Designated rooms, service with restrictions.
[ASK] [✕] [🏃] [🖥] [🌊]

## MORRIS

**AAA** **♦♦♦** **Best Western Prairie Inn** SH
(320) 589-3030. **$60-$92.** 200 SR 28 E. Jct US 59 and SR 28, just sw. Int corridors. **Pets:** Accepted.
[SAVE] [S🐾] [✕] [🏃] [🖥] [🍴] [🌊]

## NEW ULM

**♦♦♦** **Holiday Inn** SH
(507) 359-2941. **$69-$139, 7 day notice.** 2101 S Broadway. SR 15/68, 1.8 mi se. Int corridors. **Pets:** Accepted.
[ASK] [✕] [🏃] [🖥] [🍴] [🌊] [✕]

**AAA** **♦♦♦** **Microtel Inn & Suites** SH
(507) 354-9800. **$58-$105.** 424 20th St S. Just e of jct SR 15/68 and CR 37. Int corridors. **Pets:** Medium, other species. $5 daily fee/room, $10 one-time fee/room. Designated rooms, service with restrictions, supervision.
[SAVE] [S🐾] [✕] [🅼] [🏃] [🖥] [🌊]

## NISSWA

**AAA** **♦♦♦** **Nisswa Motel** M
(218) 963-7611. **$59-$82.** 5370 Merrill Ave. Just sw of Main St; center. Ext corridors. **Pets:** Medium, dogs only. $5 daily fee/pet. Designated rooms, service with restrictions, crate.
[SAVE] [✕] [🏃] [🖥]

## OLIVIA

**♦♦♦** **The Sheep Shedde Inn** SH
(320) 523-5000. **$55.** 2425 W Lincoln Ave. Just e of jct US 71 and 212. Int corridors. **Pets:** $5 daily fee/room. Service with restrictions, supervision.
[✕] [🏃] [🖥] [🍴]

## ONAMIA

**♦♦♦** **Econo Lodge** SH 🐾
(320) 532-3838. **$70-$100.** 40847 US 169. On US 169; 6 mi n. Int corridors. **Pets:** Medium, dogs only. $10 one-time fee/pet. Designated rooms, service with restrictions, supervision.
[ASK] [S🐾] [✕] [🏃] [🖥]

## ORR

**♦♦♦♦** **AmericInn Lodge & Suites** SH
(218) 757-3613. **$80-$210.** 4675 Hwy 53. Just n on US 53. Int corridors. **Pets:** Other species. $20 one-time fee/room. Designated rooms, supervision.
[ASK] [S🐾] [✕] [🐾] [🏃] [🖥] [🍴] [🌊] [✕]

**♦♦♦** **North Country Inn** SH
(218) 757-3778. **$60-$90.** 4483 Hwy 53. 0.3 mi s. Int corridors. **Pets:** $10 one-time fee/pet. Service with restrictions, supervision.
[✕] [🅼] [🏃]

## OWATONNA

**AAA** **♦♦♦** **Microtel Inn & Suites** SH
(507) 446-0228. **$49-$54.** 150 St. John Dr NW. I-35, exit 41 (Bridge St), just nw. Int corridors. **Pets:** Accepted.
[SAVE] [S🐾] [✕] [🅼] [🐾] [🏃] [🖥]

**♦♦♦** **Owatonna Grand Hotel** SH
(507) 455-0606. **$69-$109.** 1212 N I-35. I-35, exit 42B, 0.3 mi nw. Int corridors. **Pets:** Accepted.
[ASK] [S🐾] [✕] [🐾] [🏃] [🖥] [🌊] [✕]

## PEQUOT LAKES

**AAA** **♦♦♦♦** **AmericInn Lodge & Suites** SH 🐾
(218) 568-8400. **$69-$229.** 32912 Paul Bunyan Trail Dr (SR 371/CR 16). SR 371, n of downtown. Int corridors. **Pets:** Very small, dogs only. $10 deposit/pet. Designated rooms, service with restrictions, supervision.
[SAVE] [S🐾] [✕] [🏃] [🖥] [🌊] [✕]

## PERHAM

**♦♦** **Super 8 Motel** SH
(218) 346-7888. **$66-$73.** 106 Jake St SE. SR 78, just nw of jct US 10. Int corridors. **Pets:** Large. $5 daily fee/pet. Service with restrictions, supervision.
[ASK] [S🐾] [✕] [🏃]

## PINE RIVER

**♦♦♦** **Econo Lodge** M
(218) 587-4499. **$50-$100.** 2684 SR 371 SW. 1 mi s. Ext corridors. **Pets:** Large, dogs only. $10 daily fee/pet. Service with restrictions, supervision.
[ASK] [S🐾] [✕] [🏃] [🖥] [✕]

# RED WING

**Best Western Quiet House & Suites** SH
(651) 388-1577. **$60-$180.** 752 Withers Harbor Dr. 1.5 mi n on US 61, at Withers Harbor Dr. opposite side of US 61 from Pottery Mall. Ext/int corridors. **Pets:** Large. $15 daily fee/pet. Designated rooms, service with restrictions, supervision.

**Days Inn** M
(651) 388-3568. **$62-$95.** 955 E 7th St. US 61/63, 1.7 mi se. Ext corridors. **Pets:** $7 daily fee/pet. Designated rooms, service with restrictions, supervision.

# ROCHESTER

**Days Inn-South** M
(507) 286-1001. **$55-$90.** 111 28th St SE. Jct US 52 and 63 (Broadway), 0.5 mi n. Int corridors. **Pets:** Accepted.

**Econo Lodge-South** SH
(507) 282-9905. **$50-$70.** 1850 S Broadway. Jct US 52 and 63 (Broadway), 1 mi s. Int corridors. **Pets:** Dogs only. $8 daily fee/pet. Designated rooms, service with restrictions, supervision.

**Hilton Garden Inn Rochester Downtown** SH
(507) 285-1234. **$113-$139.** 225 S Broadway. US 63 (Broadway); downtown. Int corridors. **Pets:** Accepted.

**Holiday Inn South** SH
(507) 288-1844. **$77-$87.** 1630 S Broadway. On US 63 (Broadway), 0.5 mi s of jct US 14. Ext/int corridors. **Pets:** $15 daily fee/pet. Designated rooms, service with restrictions, supervision.

**The Kahler Grand Hotel** LH
(507) 282-2581. **$159.** 20 2nd Ave SW. Opposite Mayo Clinic and Methodist Hospital. Int corridors. **Pets:** Accepted.

**Kahler Inn & Suites** SH
(507) 289-8646. **$85-$110, 7 day notice.** 9 NW 3rd Ave. Just n of Mayo Clinic. Int corridors. **Pets:** Accepted.

**Marriott Hotel** LH
(507) 280-6000. **$209-$249.** 101 1st Ave SW. Just e of Mayo Clinic. Int corridors. **Pets:** Accepted.

**Microtel Inn & Suites** SH
(507) 286-8780. **$54-$80.** 4210 Hwy 52 N. US 52, exit 41st St NW, just w. Int corridors. **Pets:** Other species. $5 daily fee/room. Service with restrictions.

**Quality Inn & Suites** SH
(507) 282-8091. **$90.** 1620 1st Ave SE. On US 63 (Broadway) from jct US 14, 0.5 mi s, just e on 16th St, then just s. Ext/int corridors. **Pets:** Other species. $5 daily fee/pet.

**Radisson Plaza Hotel** LH
(507) 281-8000. **$169-$209, 7 day notice.** 150 S Broadway. On US 63 (Broadway); downtown. Int corridors. **Pets:** Large. Designated rooms, service with restrictions, crate.

**Staybridge Suites** SH
(507) 289-6600. **$129-$229.** 1211 2nd St SW. SR 52, exit 2nd St SW, just e. Int corridors. **Pets:** Accepted.

# ROSEAU

**AmericInn Lodge & Suites** SH
(218) 463-1045. **$70-$160.** 1090 3rd St NW. 1 mi w on SR 11. Int corridors. **Pets:** $25 one-time fee/room. Designated rooms, supervision.

**North Country Inn** SH
(218) 463-9444. **$70-$130.** 902 3rd St NW. 0.8 mi w on SR 11. Int corridors. **Pets:** Accepted.

# ST. CLOUD

**AmericInn Lodge & Suites** SH
(320) 253-6337. **$65-$125.** 4385 Clearwater Rd. I-94, exit 171 (CR 75), just ne. Int corridors. **Pets:** Other species. $10 daily fee/pet. Service with restrictions, supervision.

**Best Western Americanna Inn & Conference Center** SH
(320) 252-8700. **$62-$128.** 520 S US Hwy 10. Jct SR 23, 0.3 mi s. Ext/int corridors. **Pets:** Accepted.

**Best Western Kelly Inn** SH
(320) 253-0606. **$85-$139.** 100 4th Ave S. SR 23 at 4th Ave S; center. Int corridors. **Pets:** Service with restrictions, supervision.

**Comfort Inn** SH
(320) 251-1500. **$59-$149.** 4040 2nd St S. Jct SR 15 and 23 W, just w. Int corridors. **Pets:** Small, other species. $10 one-time fee/pet. Designated rooms, supervision.

**Country Inn & Suites By Carlson** SH
(320) 259-8999. **$77-$95.** 235 S Park Ave. Jct SR 15 and 23 W, just w. Int corridors. **Pets:** Accepted.

**Days Inn Hotel and Waterslide** SH
(320) 253-4444. **$44-$129.** 70 37th Ave S. Jct SR 15 and 23, just e. Int corridors. **Pets:** Small. $10 daily fee/pet. Service with restrictions, supervision.

**Holiday Inn Express** SH
(320) 240-8000. **$69-$200.** 4322 Clearwater Rd. I-94, exit 171 (CR 75), just ne. Int corridors. **Pets:** Designated rooms, service with restrictions, supervision.

**Holiday Inn Hotel & Suites** SH
(320) 253-9000. **$79-$104.** 75 S 37th Ave. Jct SR 15 and 23. Int corridors. **Pets:** Large, other species. Service with restrictions, supervision.

**Ramada Limited & Suites** SH
(320) 253-3200. **$55-$118.** 121 Park Ave S. Jct SR 15 and 23, just w. Int corridors. **Pets:** $5 daily fee/pet. Service with restrictions, supervision.

**Thrifty Motel** M
(320) 253-6320. **$36-$78.** 130 14th Ave NE. Jct US 10 and SR 23, 0.3 mi e. Int corridors. **Pets:** Accepted.

## SAUK CENTRE

**AAA ▼▼ AmericInn Lodge & Suites SH ☙**
(320) 352-2800. **$73-$129.** 1230 Timberlane Dr. I-94, exit 127, just ne. Int corridors. **Pets:** Medium, dogs only. $10 one-time fee/pet. Designated rooms, service with restrictions, crate.

SAVE ⊠ 🖩 🖥 💻 🏊 ⊠

## SILVER BAY

**AAA ▼▼▼ AmericInn Lodge & Suites SH ☙**
(218) 226-4300. **$100-$259.** 150 Mensing Dr. On SR 61, 0.5 mi ne of jct SR 61 and Outer Dr. Int corridors. **Pets:** $20 daily fee/pet. Designated rooms, service with restrictions, supervision.

SAVE S☉ ⊠ 🖥 🔲 🖩 🖥 💻 🏊 ⊠

**AAA ▼▼▼ Mariner Motel M ☙**
(218) 226-4488. **$50-$70, 3 day notice.** 46 Outer Dr. Just w off SR 61; at traffic signal. Ext corridors. **Pets:** Dogs only. $5 daily fee/pet. Service with restrictions, supervision.

SAVE ⊠ 🖩 💻 🖾

## SLEEPY EYE

**AAA ▼▼▼ Inn of Seven Gables SH**
(507) 794-5390. **$69-$89.** 1100 E Main St. US 14, 0.8 mi e of jct CR 4 and US 14. Int corridors. **Pets:** $8 daily fee/room. Designated rooms, service with restrictions, crate.

SAVE S☉ ⊠ 🖩 💻 🏊

## SPICER

**▼▼ Northern Inn Hotel & Suites SH**
(320) 796-2091. **$59-$139.** 154 Lake Ave S. On SR 23; center. Int corridors. **Pets:** $10 daily fee/pet. Designated rooms, service with restrictions, supervision.

ASK ⊠ 🖩 💻 🏊

## SPRING VALLEY

**AAA ▼▼▼ Spring Valley Inn & Suites SH**
(507) 346-7788. **$62-$80.** 745 N Broadway. Just w on US 63. Int corridors. **Pets:** Accepted.

SAVE S☉ ⊠ 🖥 🖩 💻

## STEWARTVILLE

**AAA ▼▼▼ AmericInn Motel M**
(507) 533-4747. **$65-$80.** 1700 NW 2nd Ave. I-90, exit 209A, 1 mi s on US 63. Int corridors. **Pets:** Accepted.

SAVE S☉ ⊠ 🖥 🖩 🖾 🖩 🖥 💻

## TOFTE

**AAA ▼▼▼ AmericInn Lodge & Suites SH ☙**
(218) 663-7899. **$59-$229.** 7261 W SR 61. On SR 61. Int corridors. **Pets:** $10 daily fee/room. Designated rooms, service with restrictions, supervision.

SAVE ⊠ 🖥 🖩 💻 🏊 ⊠

**▼▼▼ Bluefin Bay on Lake Superior CO**
(218) 663-7296. **$59-$550, 5 day notice.** 7198 W SR 61. On SR 61. Ext corridors. **Pets:** Other species. $20 daily fee/pet. Designated rooms, service with restrictions, crate.

⊠ 🖩 💻 🍴 🏊 ⊠ 🖾

## TWO HARBORS

**AAA ▼▼▼ AmericInn Lodge & Suites SH ☙**
(218) 834-3000. **$66-$219.** 1088 SR 61. On SR 61, 0.7 mi s. Int corridors. **Pets:** Dogs only. $20 one-time fee/room. Designated rooms, service with restrictions, supervision.

SAVE S☉ ⊠ 🖥 🖩 🖩 💻 🏊 ⊠

**AAA ▼▼▼▼ Superior Shores Resort CO ☙**
(218) 834-5671. **$49-$479, 14 day notice.** 1521 Superior Shores Dr. On SR 61, 1.5 mi n of center. Ext/int corridors. **Pets:** $20 one-time fee/room. Designated rooms, service with restrictions, supervision.

SAVE ⊠ 🖩 💻 🍴 🏊 ⊠

## VERGAS

**▼▼▼ The Log House & Homestead on Spirit Lake BB**
(218) 342-2318. **$115-$215.** 44854 Fredholm Rd. 5 mi sw on CR 4. Ext/int corridors. **Pets:** Dogs only.

⊠ 🖩 💻 ⊠ 🖾 🖾

## VIRGINIA

**▼▼▼ AmericInn Lodge & Suites SH ☙**
(218) 741-7839. **$79-$159.** 5480 Mountain Iron Dr. US 53, just s of jct US 169. Int corridors. **Pets:** $10 one-time fee/pet. Designated rooms, supervision.

S☉ ⊠ 🖾 🖩 🖩 💻 🏊 ⊠

**▼▼ Lakeshor Motor Inn Downtown M**
(218) 741-3360. **$49-$99.** 404 6th Ave N. Just n of Chestnut St; center. Ext corridors. **Pets:** Accepted.

ASK S☉ ⊠ 🖩 💻

**▼▼ Ski-View Motel M**
(218) 741-8918. **$44-$75.** 903 N 17th St. Jct US 53 and 169, 0.5 mi n on US 53, 0.7 mi e on 9th St N, then 0.5 mi n on 9th Ave W. Ext/int corridors. **Pets:** Dogs only. $5 daily fee/room. Service with restrictions, supervision.

⊠ 💻

## WABASHA

**▼▼▼ AmericInn Lodge & Suites SH**
(651) 565-5366. **$69-$99.** 150 Commerce Dr. Just ne of jct US 61 and SR 60. Int corridors. **Pets:** Accepted.

ASK ⊠ 🖾 🖩 🖩 💻 ⊠

## WALKER

**▼▼▼▼ Country Inn & Suites By Carlson SH**
(218) 547-1400. **$58-$98.** 442 Walker Bay Blvd. 1 mi s on SR 371. Int corridors. **Pets:** Medium, other species. $5 one-time fee/pet. Designated rooms, service with restrictions, crate.

ASK S☉ ⊠ 🖾 🖩 💻 🏊

## WARROAD

**▼▼ Can-Am Motel SH**
(218) 386-3807. **$53-$64.** 406 Main Ave NE. 0.5 mi w on SR 11. Int corridors. **Pets:** Medium. Designated rooms, no service, supervision.

ASK S☉ ⊠ 🖾 🖩

**▼▼ The Patch Motel SH**
(218) 386-2723. **$52-$60.** 801 N State Ave W. 0.6 mi w on SR 11. Int corridors. **Pets:** Accepted.

ASK S☉ ⊠ 🖾 🖩 🖩 🍴

## WILLMAR

**▼▼▼ Comfort Inn SH**
(320) 231-2601. **$90-$130.** 2200 E US 12. 1.8 mi e. Int corridors. **Pets:** Small. $50 deposit/room. Designated rooms, service with restrictions, crate.

ASK S☉ ⊠ 🖾 🖩 🖩 💻 🏊 ⊠

**▼▼ Days Inn-Willmar SH**
(320) 231-1275. **$66-$73.** 225 28th St SE. 2.3 mi e on US 12. Int corridors. **Pets:** Small. $50 deposit/room. Designated rooms, service with restrictions, crate.

ASK S☉ ⊠ 🖾 🖩 💻

▼▼▼ Holiday Inn & Willmar Conference Center SH
(320) 235-6060. **$100-$110.** 2100 US 12 E. 1.8 mi e. Int corridors.
**Pets:** Small. $50 deposit/room. Designated rooms, service with restrictions,
crate.

# WINDOM

▲▲▲ ▼▼ Guardian Inn Motel M
(507) 831-1809. **$58-$65.** 1955 1st Ave. Just ne on SR 60 from jct US
71. Int corridors. **Pets:** $6 one-time fee/pet. Designated rooms, service
with restrictions, supervision.

▼▼ Super 8 of Windom M
(507) 831-1120. **$48-$59.** 222 3rd Ave S. South end of town, just n of
jct US 71 and SR 60. Int corridors. **Pets:** Accepted.

# WINONA

▲▲▲ ▼▼▼▼ Best Western Riverport Inn & Suites SH ☙
(507) 452-0606. **$79-$119.** 900 Bruski Dr. Jct US 14/61 and SR 43. Int
corridors. **Pets:** Other species. $15 one-time fee/room. Designated rooms,
service with restrictions, supervision.

▼▼▼ Holiday Inn Hotel and Suites SH
(507) 453-0303. **$99-$179.** 1025 Hwy 61 E. Jct SR 43, just sw. Int
corridors. **Pets:** Other species. $25 daily fee/room. Designated rooms,
service with restrictions, supervision.

▼▼ Quality Inn SH
(507) 454-4390. **$70-$150.** 956 Mankato Ave. Jct US 14/61 and SR 43.
Ext/int corridors. **Pets:** Accepted.

# WORTHINGTON

▲▲▲ ▼▼▼▼ AmericInn Motel SH
(507) 376-4500. **$69-$120, 7 day notice.** 1475 Darling Dr. I-90, exit 43
(US 59), just se. Int corridors. **Pets:** Other species. $10 one-time fee/
room. Service with restrictions, supervision.

▼▼ Days Inn SH
(507) 376-6155. **$65-$79.** 207 Oxford St. I-90, exit 42, 0.7 mi s on SR
266, then just e. Ext/int corridors. **Pets:** Other species. $20 deposit/pet,
$6 one-time fee/pet. Service with restrictions, supervision.

▼▼ Super 8 Motel SH
(507) 372-7755. **$64-$150.** 850 Lucy Dr. I-90, exit 42, just sw. Int
corridors. **Pets:** Other species. $10 one-time fee/room. Service with restric-
tions, supervision.

## ABERDEEN

🛇🛇 ▽▽▽ **Best Western Aberdeen Inn** SH
(662) 369-4343. **$66-$72.** 801 E Commerce St. On US 45, just n of jct SR 25 and Tenn-Tom Bridge. Ext corridors. **Pets:** Accepted.
SAVE S🛇 ✕ 🖥 🔲 🍽 ⌦

## BATESVILLE

▽▽ **Comfort Inn** SH
(662) 563-1188. **$70-$95.** 290 Power Dr. I-55, exit 243B, just ne on frontage road. Ext corridors. **Pets:** Accepted.
ASK S🛇 ✕ 🖥 🔲 ⌦

## BAY ST. LOUIS

▽▽ **Casino Magic Inn** LH
(228) 467-9257. **$59-$129.** 711 Casino Magic Dr. US 90, 0.6 mi n on Meadow Rd, then e, follow signs. Int corridors. **Pets:** Accepted.
ASK ✕ 🖥 🔲 🍽 ⌦ ✕

▽▽ **Key West Inn** SH
(228) 466-0444. **$50-$135, 3 day notice.** 1000 Hwy 90. 2.5 mi e of jct SR 603. Ext corridors. **Pets:** Accepted.
ASK S🛇 ✕ 🖥 🔲

## BILOXI

▽▽▽ **Father Ryan House Bed & Breakfast Inn** BB
(228) 435-1189. **$100-$175, 7 day notice.** 1196 Beach Blvd. I-110, exit 1B, 0.8 mi w on US 90. Ext/int corridors. **Pets:** Accepted.
ASK ✕ 🖥 🔲 ⌦

▽▽ **Gulf Beach Resort Hotel** SH
(228) 385-5555. **$45-$75.** 2428 Beach Blvd. I-110, exit 1B, 5.5 mi w on US 90. Int corridors. **Pets:** Accepted.
ASK S🛇 ✕ 🖥 🔲 ⌦

▽▽▽ **Holiday Inn Express** SH
(228) 388-1000. **$80-$180.** 2416 Beach Blvd. I-110, exit 1B, 5.5 mi w on US 90. Ext corridors. **Pets:** Accepted.
ASK S🛇 ✕ 🖥 🔲 ⌦

## BOONEVILLE

▽▽ **Super 8 Motel** SH
(662) 720-1688. **$55-$65.** 110 Hospitality Ave. Jct US 45 and SR 4/30, 1.7 mi e to SR 145, then 0.5 mi s. Int corridors. **Pets:** Accepted.
ASK S🛇 ✕ 🖥 ⌦

## CANTON

🛇🛇 ▽▽▽ **Best Western-Canton Inn** SH
(601) 859-8600. **$60-$65.** 137 Soldier Colony Rd. I-55, exit 119, just se. Int corridors. **Pets:** Accepted.
SAVE S🛇 ✕ 🖥 🔲 ⌦

🛇🛇 ▽▽▽ **Comfort Inn** SH
(601) 859-7575. **$61-$74.** 145 Soldier Colony Rd. I-55, exit 119, just se. Int corridors. **Pets:** $50 deposit/pet. Service with restrictions, supervision.
SAVE S🛇 ✕ 🖥 🔲 ⌦

## CLARKSDALE

▽▽▽ **Best Western Executive Inn** SH
(662) 627-9292. **$65-$74.** 710 S State St. 1 mi s of jct US 49 and SR 161. Ext/int corridors. **Pets:** Accepted.
ASK S🛇 ✕ 🖥 🔲 ⌦

🛇🛇 ▽▽▽ **Econo Lodge** M
(662) 621-1110. **$59-$69, 3 day notice.** 350 S State St. 0.5 mi s of jct US 49 amd SR 161. Ext corridors. **Pets:** Medium, other species. $10 daily fee/pet. Service with restrictions, supervision.
SAVE S🛇 ✕ 🖥

## CLEVELAND

▽▽ **Comfort Inn of Cleveland** SH
(662) 843-4060. **$59-$79.** 721 N Davs Ave. On US 61, 1 mi n of jct US 61 and SR 8. Ext corridors. **Pets:** Accepted.
ASK S🛇 ✕ 🔑 🖥 🔲 ⌦

## COLUMBIA

▽▽▽ **Comfort Inn** SH
(601) 731-9955. **$74-$114.** 820 Hwy 98 Bypass. Just e of jct US 98 Bypass and SR 13. Int corridors. **Pets:** Accepted.
ASK S🛇 ✕ 🔑 🖥 🔲 ⌦

## COLUMBUS

▽▽ **Master Hosts Inns & Suites** SH
(662) 328-5202. **$47-$67.** 506 Hwy 45 N. US 82, exit US 45 N, just s. Ext corridors. **Pets:** Medium. $5 daily fee/room. Service with restrictions, supervision.
ASK S🛇 ✕ 🖥 🔲 🍽 ⌦

## CORINTH

▽▽ **Comfort Inn** SH
(662) 287-4421. **$41-$50.** 2101 Hwy 72 W. Jct US 72 and 45, just e. Ext corridors. **Pets:** Other species. $25 deposit/room. Service with restrictions.
ASK S🛇 ✕ 🖥 🔲 ⌦

## D'IBERVILLE

▽▽▽ **Wingate Inn D'Iberville Biloxi** SH
(228) 396-0036. **$59-$119.** 12009 Incan River Rd. I-10, exit 46B, just ne. Int corridors. **Pets:** Medium, other species. $10 daily fee/pet. Service with restrictions, supervision.
ASK S🛇 ✕ 🔑 🖥 🔲 ⌦

## DURANT

▽▽ **Super 8 Motel of Duran** M
(662) 653-3881. **Call for rates.** 312 Hwy 12. I-55, exit 156, just e. Ext corridors. **Pets:** Accepted.
✕ 🖥 ⌦

# FOREST

**⬨⬨ ▽▽▽ Apple Tree Inn** SH ❀
(601) 469-2640. **$61-$67, 3 day notice.** 1846 Hwy 35 S. I-20, exit 88, just n. Ext corridors. **Pets:** Large, other species. Service with restrictions, supervision.
SAVE ⬩ ✕ 📖 💻 ❢ ⌒

**⬨⬨ ▽▽ Comfort Inn** SH
(601) 469-2100. **$55-$65.** 1250 Hwy 35 S. I-20, exit 88, just n. Ext corridors. **Pets:** Small. $12 daily fee/pet. Service with restrictions, supervision.
SAVE ⬩ ✕ 📖 💻 ⌒

# GREENVILLE

**▽▽ Comfort Inn of Greenville** SH
(662) 378-4976. **$59-$129.** 3080 US 82 E. 3 mi e of center. Ext corridors. **Pets:** Accepted.
ASK ⬩ ✕ ⬩ 📖 💻 ⌒

# GREENWOOD

**▽▽ Comfort Inn** SH
(662) 453-5974. **$64-$79.** 401 Hwy 82 W. 0.4 mi w of Main St. Ext corridors. **Pets:** Accepted.
ASK ⬩ ✕ 📖 💻 ⌒

# GRENADA

**▽▽ Americas Best Value Inn** SH
(662) 226-7816. **$42-$59.** 1750 Sunset Dr. I-55, exit 206, just ne on frontage road. Ext corridors. **Pets:** Large. $5 daily fee/pet. Service with restrictions, supervision.
ASK ⬩ ✕ 📖 💻 ⌒

**▽▽▽ Country Inn & Suites by Carlson** SH
(662) 227-8444. **$68-$93.** 255 SW Frontage Rd. I-55, exit 206, just sw. Int corridors. **Pets:** Small. $25 one-time fee/pet. Service with restrictions, supervision.
ASK ⬩ ✕ 📖 💻 ⌒

# GULFPORT

**▽▽▽ Americas Best Value Inn** SH
(228) 868-8500. **$69-$135.** 9375 Hwy 49. I-10, exit 34A, just sw. Ext corridors. **Pets:** Accepted.
ASK ⬩ ✕ 📖 💻 ⌒

**⬨⬨ ▽▽▽ Best Western Seaway Inn** SH
(228) 864-0050. **$50-$210.** 9475 Hwy 49. I-10, exit 34A, just sw. Ext corridors. **Pets:** Accepted.
SAVE ⬩ ✕ ⬩ ⬩ 📖 💻 ⌒

**▽▽▽ Comfort Inn-Beachview** SH
(228) 896-7436. **$59-$149.** 1034 Beach Blvd. I-10, exit 38 (Lorranine-Cowan), 4.5 mi s to US 90, then just w. Int corridors. **Pets:** Accepted.
ASK ⬩ ✕ ⬩M ⬩ 📖 💻 ⌒

**⬨⬨ ▽▽▽ Crystal Inn** SH
(228) 822-9600. **$69-$135, 3 day notice.** 9379 Canal Rd. I-10, exit 31, just s. Int corridors. **Pets:** Medium. $25 deposit/pet. Service with restrictions, supervision.
SAVE ⬩ ✕ ⬩ 📖 💻 ⌒

**▽▽▽ Holiday Inn Airport** SH
(228) 868-8200. **$62-$82.** 9415 Hwy 49. I-10, exit 34A, 0.6 mi s. Ext corridors. **Pets:** Accepted.
ASK ✕ ⬩ 📖 💻 ❢ ⌒

**⬨⬨ ▽▽▽ Holiday Inn Express** SH
(228) 864-7222. **$69-$129, 3 day notice.** 9435 Hwy 49. I-10, exit 34A, 0.6 mi s. Ext corridors. **Pets:** Small. $35 one-time fee/room. Service with restrictions, supervision.
SAVE ⬩ ✕ ⬩ ⬩ 📖 💻

**▽▽ Motel 6 #416** M
(228) 863-1890. **$36-$71.** 9355 US Hwy 49. I-10, exit 34A, just s. Ext corridors. **Pets:** Accepted.
⬩ ✕ ⬩ ⌒

# HATTIESBURG

**▽▽▽ Comfort Inn University-The Lodge** SH
(601) 264-1881. **$85-$105.** 6541 US Hwy 49. I-59, exit 67A, just s. Ext/int corridors. **Pets:** Accepted.
ASK ⬩ ✕ 📖 💻 ⌒

**⬨⬨ ▽▽▽ Hampton Inn of Hattiesburg** SH
(601) 264-8080. **$81-$139.** 4301 Hardy St. I-59, exit 65, just nw. Ext/int corridors. **Pets:** Small, dogs only. Service with restrictions, supervision.
SAVE ⬩ ✕ ⬩ 📖 💻 ⌒

**⬨⬨ ▽▽▽ Inn on the Hill** SH ❀
(601) 599-2001. **$71.** 6595 Hwy 49 N. I-59, exit 67A, just se. Ext corridors. **Pets:** Medium. $25 one-time fee/room. Service with restrictions, supervision.
SAVE ⬩ ✕ 📖 💻 ❢ ⌒

**▽▽ Motel 6 #0235** M
(601) 544-6096. **$45-$55.** 6508 US Hwy 49 N. I-59, exit 67A, 0.5 mi e. Ext corridors. **Pets:** Accepted.
⬩ ✕ ⬩ ⌒

**▽▽ University Inn** SH
(601) 268-2850. **$74.** 6563 Hwy 49 N. I-59, exit 67A, just se. Int corridors. **Pets:** Accepted.
ASK ⬩ ✕ 💻 ❢ ⌒

# HOLLY SPRINGS

**▽▽▽ Hampton Inn** SH
(662) 252-5444. **$79-$129.** 100 Brooks Rd. US 78, exit 30, just sw. Int corridors. **Pets:** Accepted.
ASK ⬩ ✕ ⬩ ⬩ 📖 💻 ⌒

# HORN LAKE

**⬨⬨ ▽▽▽ Days Inn** SH
(662) 349-3493. **$64-$89.** 801 Desoto Cove. I-55, exit 289, just nw. Int corridors. **Pets:** Small, dogs only. $10 daily fee/pet. Service with restrictions, supervision.
SAVE ⬩ ✕ ⬩M ⬩ 📖 💻 ⌒

**▽▽▽ Drury Inn & Suites-Memphis South** SH
(662) 349-6622. **$85-$125.** 735 Goodman Rd W. I-55, exit 289, just sw. Int corridors. **Pets:** Accepted.
ASK ✕ ⬩M ⬩ ⬩ 📖 💻 ⌒

**▽▽ Motel 6** SH
(662) 349-4439. **$54-$66.** 701 Southwest Dr. I-55, exit 289, just se. Int corridors. **Pets:** Accepted.
⬩ ✕ ⬩ ⌒

# JACKSON

**▽▽▽ Cabot Lodge Millsaps** SH
(601) 948-8650. **$85-$105.** 2375 N State St. I-55, exit 98A northbound, 1 mi w on Woodrow Wilson Blvd, then just s. Int corridors. **Pets:** Accepted.
ASK ✕ ⬩ 💻 ⌒

**▽▽▽ The Edison Walthall Hotel** LH
(601) 948-6161. **$89-$99.** 225 E Capitol St. I-55, exit 96A (Pearl St), 0.8 mi w; between West and Lamar sts; downtown. Ext/int corridors. **Pets:** Accepted.
ASK ⬩ ✕ 📖 💻 ❢ ⌒

**⬨⬨ ▽▽▽ Holiday Inn Hotel & Suites** LH
(601) 366-9411. **$84-$99, 14 day notice.** 5075 I-55 N. I-55, exit 102A, s on west frontage road. Ext/int corridors. **Pets:** Accepted.
SAVE ✕ ⬩ 📖 💻 ❢ ⌒

**(AAA) ▼▼▼ Jackson Inn & Suites SH**
(601) 899-9000. **$84-$130.** 5411 I-55 N. I-55, exit 102A northbound; exit 102 southbound, s on west service road. Int corridors. **Pets:** Small, other species. $35 daily fee/room, $70 one-time fee/room. Service with restrictions, supervision.
(SAVE) (X) (Ø) (Ø) (Ø) (Ø) (≈)

**▼▼▼ Jameson Inn SH**
(601) 206-8923. **$54-$104.** 585 Beasley Rd. I-55, exit 102, just w. Int corridors. **Pets:** Very small, other species. $10 daily fee/room. Service with restrictions, supervision.
(ASK) (X) (&M) (Ø) (Ø) (Ø) (Ø) (≈)

**▼▼▼ La Quinta Inn Jackson (North) SH**
(601) 957-1741. **$59-$75.** 616 Briarwood Dr. I-55, exit 102A northbound, just ne on Frontage Rd. Ext corridors. **Pets:** Medium. Service with restrictions.
(ASK) (X) (&M) (Ø) (Ø) (≈)

**▼ Motel 6-1167 M**
(601) 956-8848. **$36-$46.** 6145 I-55 N/Frontage Rd. I-55, exit 103, 0.5 mi sw on Frontage Rd. Ext corridors. **Pets:** Accepted.
(Sб) (X) (≈)

**(AAA) ▼▼▼ Quality Inn & Suites SH**
(601) 969-2230. **$70-$90.** 400 Greymont Ave. I-55, exit 96B (High St), just w, then just s. Ext corridors. **Pets:** Accepted.
(SAVE) (X) (Ø) (Ø) (Ø)

**▼▼ Red Roof Inn Fairgrounds M**
(601) 969-5006. **$42-$61.** 700 Larson St. I-55, exit 96B (High St), e to Greymont, then just ne. Ext corridors. **Pets:** Accepted.
(X) (Ø) (Ø) (Ø)

**(AAA) ▼▼▼ Regency Hotel & Conference Center SH**
(601) 969-2141. **$100-$109.** 400 Greymont Ave. I-55, exit 96B, just w, then just s. Ext/int corridors. **Pets:** Medium. $25 daily fee/pet. Service with restrictions, crate.
(SAVE) (X) (&M) (Ø) (Ø) (Ø) (Ø) (≈)

**▼▼▼ Residence Inn by Marriott SH ❦**
(601) 355-3599. **$109-$160, 7 day notice.** 881 E River Pl. I-55, exit 96C, just e. Ext corridors. **Pets:** Other species. $75 one-time fee/room. Service with restrictions.
(ASK) (X) (Ø) (Ø) (Ø) (Ø) (≈) (X)

## KOSCIUSKO

**(AAA) ▼▼▼ Americas Best Value Inn SH**
(662) 289-6252. **$53-$67.** 1052 Veterans Memorial Dr/Hwy 35 Bypass. Just sw of jct SR 35 and Natchez Trace Pkwy. Ext corridors. **Pets:** Medium, other species. $5 daily fee/pet. Service with restrictions, supervision.
(SAVE) (Sб) (X) (Ø) (Ø) (≈)

**▼▼ Super 8 Motel Kosciusko M**
(662) 289-7880. **Call for rates.** 718 Veterans Memorial Dr. Just sw of jct SR 35 and Natchez Trace Pkwy. Ext corridors. **Pets:** Accepted.
(X) (Ø) (Ø) (≈)

## LAUREL

**▼▼▼ Comfort Suites SH**
(601) 649-2620. **$85-$150.** 1820 Jefferson St. I-59, exit 95B, just se. Int corridors. **Pets:** Accepted.
(ASK) (Sб) (X) (Ø) (Ø) (Ø) (≈)

## MCCOMB

**(AAA) ▼▼▼ Hawthorn Inn & Suites SH**
(601) 684-8655. **$80-$110.** 2001 Veteran's Blvd. I-55, exit 18, just off interstate. Int corridors. **Pets:** Accepted.
(SAVE) (Sб) (X) (&M) (Ø) (Ø) (Ø) (≈)

# MERIDIAN

**▼▼▼ Baymont Inn & Suites Meridian SH**
(601) 693-2300. **$73-$89.** 1400 Roebuck Dr. I-20/59, exit 153, just s. Int corridors. **Pets:** Medium. Service with restrictions.
(ASK) (X) (Ø) (Ø) (≈)

**▼ Days Inn M**
(601) 483-3812. **$59-$69.** 145 Hwy 11 & 80 E. I-20/59, exit 154 westbound; exit 154B eastbound, just n to Frontage Rd, then just e. Ext corridors. **Pets:** Large, other species. $6 daily fee/pet. Service with restrictions, crate.
(ASK) (Sб) (X) (Ø) (Ø) (≈)

**▼▼ Econo Lodge M**
(601) 693-9393. **$45-$60.** 2405 S Frontage Rd. I-20/59, exit 153, 0.5 mi sw. Ext corridors. **Pets:** Accepted.
(ASK) (Sб) (X) (Ø)

**▼▼ Holiday Inn Northeast SH**
(601) 485-5101. **$85-$130.** 111 US 11 & 80. I-20/59, exit 154 westbound, just n to frontage road, then just e; exit 154B eastbound. Ext corridors. **Pets:** Accepted.
(ASK) (Sб) (X) (&M) (Ø) (Ø) (Ø) (Ø) (Ø) (≈)

**▼▼ Jameson Inn SH**
(601) 483-3315. **$54-$104.** 524 Bonita Lakes Dr. I-20/59, exit 154 southbound; exit 154A northbound, just s. Ext corridors. **Pets:** Very small, other species. $10 daily fee/room. Service with restrictions, supervision.
(ASK) (X) (&M) (Ø) (Ø) (Ø) (Ø) (≈)

**▼ Motel 6 M**
(601) 482-1182. **$35-$38.** 2309 S Frontage Rd. I-20/59, exit 153, 0.5 mi sw. Ext corridors. **Pets:** Other species. Service with restrictions, supervision.
(X) (Ø) (≈)

**▼▼▼ Quality Inn M**
(601) 693-4521. **$60-$70.** 1401 Roebuck Dr. I-20/59, exit 153, just s. Ext corridors. **Pets:** Medium. Service with restrictions, supervision.
(ASK) (Sб) (X) (Ø) (Ø) (Ø) (≈)

# MOSS POINT

**(AAA) ▼▼▼ Best Western Flagship Inn SH**
(228) 475-5000. **$59-$79.** 4830 Amoco Dr. I-10, exit 69, just s. Ext corridors. **Pets:** Accepted.
(SAVE) (Sб) (X) (Ø) (Ø) (Ø) (≈)

**(AAA) ▼▼▼ Holiday Inn Express SH**
(228) 474-2100. **$69-$89.** 4800 Amoco Dr. I-10, exit 69, just s. Int corridors. **Pets:** Accepted.
(SAVE) (Sб) (X) (&M) (Ø) (Ø) (Ø) (≈)

# NATCHEZ

**(AAA) ▼▼▼ Cedar Grove Plantation CI**
(601) 445-0585. **$120-$240, 10 day notice.** 617 Kingston Rd. Jct US 84 and 98, 3.4 mi s on US 61, then 6.3 mi se. Ext/int corridors. **Pets:** Accepted.
(SAVE) (X) (Ø) (≈) (X) (Ø)

**(AAA) ▼▼ Days Inn of Natchez SH**
(601) 445-8291. **$64-$90.** 109 US Hwy 61 S. Just se of jct US 61, 84 and 98. Ext corridors. **Pets:** Medium. $5 daily fee/pet. Service with restrictions, crate.
(SAVE) (Sб) (X) (Ø) (Ø) (≈)

# NEWTON

**▼▼ Days Inn M**
(601) 683-3361. **$50-$75.** 261 Eastside Dr. I-20, exit 109, just s on SR 15. Ext corridors. **Pets:** Accepted.
(X) (Ø) (Ø) (≈)

# OCEAN SPRINGS

**🏶 ▼▼▼ Comfort Inn Biloxi/Ocean Springs** 🖼️
(228) 818-0300. **$69-$149.** 7827 Lamar Poole Rd. I-10, exit 50, just nw on service road. Int corridors. **Pets:** Small. $25 one-time fee/pet. Service with restrictions, crate.

**▼▼▼▼ Holiday Inn Express** 🖼️
(228) 875-7555. **$60-$130.** 7304 Washington Ave. I-10, exit 50, 0.4 mi s on SR 609. Ext corridors. **Pets:** Accepted.

**▼▼ Ramada Limited** 🖼️
(228) 872-2323. **$64-$169.** 8011 Tucker Rd. I-10, exit 50, just n. Ext corridors. **Pets:** Medium, other species. $10 daily fee/pet. Designated rooms, service with restrictions, crate.

# OLIVE BRANCH

**▼▼▼ Comfort Inn** 🖼️
(662) 895-0456. **$79.** 7049 Enterprise. US 78, exit 2, SR 302, just w. Int corridors. **Pets:** Small. $12 daily fee/pet. Designated rooms, service with restrictions, supervision.

**🏶 ▼▼▼ Holiday Inn Express Hotel & Suites** 🖼️
(662) 893-8700. **$89-$109.** 8900 Expressway Dr. US 78, exit 4, just e. Int corridors. **Pets:** $10 daily fee/room. Designated rooms, service with restrictions, crate.

**▼▼▼ Whispering Woods Hotel and Conference Center** 🖼️
(662) 895-2941. **$130, 3 day notice.** 11200 E Goodman Rd. US 78, exit SR 302, 3.6 mi e. Int corridors. **Pets:** Medium, other species. $100 deposit/room, $25 one-time fee/room. Service with restrictions.

# PASCAGOULA

**🏶 ▼▼ LaFont Inn** 🖼️
(228) 762-7111. **$55-$85.** 2703 Denny Ave. I-10, exit 69, 3.5 mi s on SR 63, then 2 mi w on US 90. Ext corridors. **Pets:** Accepted.

**▼▼ Super 8 Motel** 🅼
(228) 762-9414. **$109-$180.** 4919 Denny Ave. I-10, exit 69, 3.5 mi s on SR 63, then just w on US 90. Int corridors. **Pets:** Accepted.

# PASS CHRISTIAN

**▼▼▼▼ Harbour Oaks Inn** 🅱🅱
(228) 452-9399. **$83-$138, 14 day notice.** 126 W Scenic Dr. Just off US 90. Int corridors. **Pets:** Accepted.

# PEARL

**▼▼▼▼ Jameson Inn of Pearl** 🖼️
(601) 932-6030. **$54-$104.** 434 Riverwind Dr. I-20, exit 48, just nw. Int corridors. **Pets:** Very small, other species. $10 daily fee/room. Service with restrictions, supervision.

**🏶 ▼▼▼▼ La Quinta Inn & Suites Jackson Airport (Pearl)** 🖼️
(601) 664-0065. **$65-$85.** 501 S Pearson Rd. I-20, exit 48, just s. Int corridors. **Pets:** Accepted.

# PHILADELPHIA

**▼▼ Deluxe Inn & Suites** 🖼️
(601) 656-0052. **$40-$200.** 1004 Central Dr. Jct SR 15 and 16. Ext corridors. **Pets:** Small. $10 daily fee/room. Service with restrictions, supervision.

# PICAYUNE

**▼▼ Days Inn** 🖼️
(601) 799-1339. **$59-$149.** 450 S Lofton Ave. I-59, exit 4, just nw. Ext corridors. **Pets:** Medium, other species. $10 daily fee/pet. Designated rooms, service with restrictions, supervision.

# PONTOTOC

**▼▼ Days Inn** 🅼
(662) 489-5200. **$52-$90.** 217 Hwy 15 N. Just n of jct SR 6 and 15. Ext corridors. **Pets:** Accepted.

# RICHLAND

**▼▼ Days Inn** 🖼️
(601) 932-5553. **$55-$75.** 1035 US Hwy 49 S. I-20, exit 47, 4 mi s. Ext corridors. **Pets:** $6 daily fee/pet. No service, supervision.

**▼▼ Executive Inn & Suites** 🖼️
(601) 664-3456. **$49-$59.** 390 Hwy 49 S. I-20, exit 47, just s. Ext corridors. **Pets:** Medium, dogs only. $5 one-time fee/pet. Designated rooms, service with restrictions, crate.

# RIDGELAND

**▼▼▼ Drury Inn & Suites-Jackson, MS** 🖼️
(601) 956-6100. **$80-$135.** 610 E County Line Rd. I-55, exit 103 (County Line Rd), just w. Int corridors. **Pets:** Accepted.

**▼▼ Econo Lodge** 🅼
(601) 956-7740. **$55-$60.** 839 Ridgewood Rd. I-55, exit 103 (County Line Rd), just e, then just n. Ext corridors. **Pets:** Accepted.

**▼▼▼ Homewood Suites by Hilton** 🖼️
(601) 899-8611. **$94-$139.** 853 Centre St. I-55, exit 103 (County Line Rd), just e to Ridgewood Rd, 0.4 mi ne, then just e. Int corridors. **Pets:** Other species. $100 one-time fee/room. Designated rooms, service with restrictions, supervision.

**▼▼ Quality Inn North** 🖼️
(601) 956-6203. **$54-$79, 7 day notice.** 839 Ridgewood Rd. I-55, exit 103 (County Line Rd), just ne. Ext corridors. **Pets:** Accepted.

**▼▼ Red Roof Inn Ridgeland** 🅼
(601) 956-7707. **$43-$55.** 810 Adcock St. I-55, exit 103 (County Line Rd), just ne on Frontage Rd. Ext corridors. **Pets:** Accepted.

# SOUTHAVEN

**▼▼ Southern Inn & Suites** 🖼️
(662) 393-4174. **$55-$95.** 8945 Hamilton Rd. I-55, exit 291, just se. Ext corridors. **Pets:** Accepted.

# STARKVILLE

**(AAA) ▼▼▼▼ Best Western Starkville Inn** [M]
(662) 324-5555. **$65-$149.** 119 Hwy 12 W. SR 12, 1.5 mi w of jct US 82. Ext corridors. **Pets:** Accepted.
[SAVE] [S&] [X] [H] [P] [≈]

# TUNICA

**▼▼▼▼ Best Western Tunica North** [SH]
(662) 363-6711. **$59-$149.** 7500 Casino Strip Resort Blvd. Jct US 61 and SR 304. Int corridors. **Pets:** Accepted.
[ASK] [S&] [X] [&M] [⊘] [☞] [H] [P] [≈]

**(AAA) ▼▼▼ Cottage Inn** [CA] ❀
(662) 363-2900. **$50-$150.** 4325 Casino Center Dr. On US 61. Ext corridors. **Pets:** Medium, other species. Crate.
[SAVE] [S&] [X] [H] [P]

# TUPELO

**(AAA) ▼▼▼▼ AmeriHost Inn-Tupelo** [SH]
(662) 844-7660. **$79-$129.** 625 Spicer Dr. On SR 145, 0.4 mi n of McCullough Blvd. Int corridors. **Pets:** Small. $25 one-time fee/room. Designated rooms, service with restrictions, supervision.
[SAVE] [S&] [X] [&M] [☞] [H] [P] [≈] [X]

**▼▼▼ Comfort Inn** [SH]
(662) 842-5100. **$74-$94.** 1190 N Gloster St. Jct McCullough Blvd and SR 145, 1.3 mi s to McCullough Blvd, w to N Gloster St, then 0.3 mi n. Ext corridors. **Pets:** Small, other species. $25 deposit/room. Service with restrictions, supervision.
[ASK] [S&] [X] [H] [P]

**▼▼ Jameson Inn** [SH]
(662) 840-2380. **$54-$104.** 879 Mississippi Dr. US 45, exit Barnes Crossing, 1 mi sw. Ext corridors. **Pets:** Very small, other species. $10 daily fee/room. Service with restrictions, supervision.
[ASK] [X] [☞] [H] [P] [≈]

**▼▼ Red Roof Inn Tupelo** [M]
(662) 844-1904. **$43-$56.** 1500 McCullough Blvd. Just w of jct SR 145. Ext corridors. **Pets:** Accepted.
[X] [☞] [H] [≈]

**(AAA) ▼▼▼ Super 8 Motel** [M]
(662) 842-0448. **$46-$58.** 3898 McCullough Blvd. Exit 81, just sw US 78. Ext corridors. **Pets:** Very small. $10 daily fee/pet. Designated rooms, service with restrictions, supervision.
[SAVE] [S&] [X] [H] [≈]

# VICKSBURG

**(AAA) ▼▼▼▼ Annabelle Bed & Breakfast** [BB]
(601) 638-2000. **$99, 7 day notice.** 501 Speed St. I-20, exit 1A, 2.3 mi n on Washington St, then just w. Ext/int corridors. **Pets:** Small. $35 daily fee/pet. Service with restrictions, supervision.
[SAVE] [X] [H] [P] [≈]

**(AAA) ▼▼▼ Battlefield Inn** [SH]
(601) 638-5811. **$50-$75.** 4137 I-20 N Frontage Rd. I-20, exit 4B, 1 mi ne. Ext/int corridors. **Pets:** Other species. $10 daily fee/pet. Service with restrictions.
[SAVE] [S&] [X] [H] [▮▮] [≈] [X]

**(AAA) ▼▼▼▼ Cedar Grove Mansion Inn** [CI]
(601) 636-1000. **$100-$260, 3 day notice.** 2200 Oak St. I-20, exit 1A, 2.3 mi n on Washington St, then w on Klein St to gated entrance. Ext/int corridors. **Pets:** Small, other species. $50 one-time fee/room. Designated rooms.
[SAVE] [S&] [X] [H] [P] [▮▮] [≈] [X]

**▼▼▼ The Corners Bed & Breakfast Inn** [BB]
(601) 636-7421. **$90-$130, 3 day notice.** 601 Klein St. I-20, exit 1A, 2.3 mi n on Washington St, then just w. Ext/int corridors. **Pets:** Other species. Service with restrictions.
[ASK] [X] [H] [P]

**▼ Econo Lodge of Vicksburg** [M]
(601) 634-8766. **$50-$70.** 3330-A Clay St. I-20, exit 4B (Clay St), just n. Ext corridors. **Pets:** Other species. $10 one-time fee/room. Service with restrictions, supervision.
[ASK] [S&] [X] [H] [P]

**▼▼▼▼ Hampton Inn of Vicksburg** [SH]
(601) 636-6100. **$87-$97, 3 day notice.** 3332 Clay St. I-20, exit 4B (Clay St), just n. Ext corridors. **Pets:** Accepted.
[ASK] [S&] [X] [H] [P] [≈]

**▼▼ Jameson Inn** [SH]
(601) 619-7799. **$54-$104.** 3975 S Frontage Rd. I-20, exit 4A, on southeast frontage road. Ext corridors. **Pets:** Very small, other species. $10 daily fee/pet. Service with restrictions, supervision.
[ASK] [X] [&M] [⊘] [☞] [H] [P] [≈]

**▼▼ Motel 6 #4189** [SH]
(601) 638-5077. **$55-$115, 7 day notice.** 4127 N Frontage Rd. I-20, exit 4B (Clay St), just ne on Frontage Rd. Int corridors. **Pets:** Accepted.
[X] [≈]

# WAVELAND

**▼▼▼ Coast Inn & Suites** [SH]
(228) 467-9261. **$59-$89, 3 day notice.** 404 Hwy 90. Just w of jct SR 603/43. Ext corridors. **Pets:** Accepted.
[ASK] [S&] [X] [☞] [H] [P] [▮▮] [≈]

# YAZOO CITY

**(AAA) ▼▼▼ Comfort Inn** [SH]
(662) 746-6444. **$62-$69.** 1600 Jerry Clower Blvd. US 49 E, 1.8 mi n of jct US 49 W. Int corridors. **Pets:** Accepted.
[SAVE] [S&] [X] [H] [P] [≈]

# MISSOURI

## ARNOLD

 **Drury Inn-Arnold** SH
(636) 296-9600. **$75-$120.** 1201 Drury Ln. I-55, exit 191 (SR 141), 0.3 mi e. Int corridors. **Pets:** Accepted.

ASK ✕ ♿ 🖥 ≈

## AVA

**Ava Super 8** SH
(417) 683-1343. **$55-$75.** 1711 S Jefferson St. Jct SR 5 S and 76. Int corridors. **Pets:** Other species. $10 one-time fee/room. Designated rooms, service with restrictions, supervision.

ASK SD ✕ ♿M 🖥 🖥

## BETHANY

**Best Western Bethany Inn** SH
(660) 425-8006. **$58-$125.** 496 S 39th St. I-35, exit 92, just nw. Int corridors. **Pets:** Accepted.

ASK SD ✕ ♿ 🖥 🖥 ≈

**Family Budget Inn** M
(660) 425-7915. **$49-$54.** 4014 Miller St. I-35, exit 92. Int corridors. **Pets:** Accepted.

SAVE SD ✕ ♿ 🖥 ≈

## BOONVILLE

**Boonville Comfort Inn** SH 🌸
(660) 882-5317. **$59-$109.** 2427 Mid America Industrial Dr. I-70, exit 101, just sw. Int corridors. **Pets:** Small, dogs only. $10 daily fee/pet. Designated rooms, service with restrictions, supervision.

SAVE SD ✕ 🖥 🖥 ≈

**Boonville Days Inn** SH
(660) 882-8624. **$60-$82.** 2401 Pioneer St. I-70, exit 103, just n. Int corridors. **Pets:** Medium, other species. $15 one-time fee/pet. Service with restrictions, supervision.

✕ ♿M 🖥 🖥

## BRANSON

**Best Western Landing View Inn & Suites** SH
(417) 334-6464. **$54-$94.** 403 W Main (Hwy 76). 0.3 mi e from SR 76 and US 65. Ext corridors. **Pets:** Medium. $10 daily fee/room. Service with restrictions, crate.

SAVE SD ✕ 🖥 🖥 🖥 ≈ ✕

**Chateau on the Lake Resort Spa & Convention Center** LH
(417) 334-1161. **$89-$249, 3 day notice.** 415 N State Hwy 265. Just n of jct SR 165 and 265. Int corridors. **Pets:** Small, dogs only. $25 one-time fee/pet. Designated rooms, service with restrictions, supervision.

SAVE SD ✕ ♿M 🖥 🖥 🖥 ⑪ ≈ ✕

**Eagles Inn a Rodeway Inn** SH
(417) 336-2666. **$45-$85.** 3221 Shepherd of the Hills Expwy. 0.3 mi e of jct SR 76. Ext corridors. **Pets:** Accepted.

ASK SD ✕ 🖥 ≈

**Foxborough Inn** SH
(417) 335-4369. **Call for rates.** 235 Expressway Ln. US 65, exit Shepherd of The Hills Expwy, 2.3 mi w, just sw. Ext corridors. **Pets:** Small, other species. $25 one-time fee/room. Designated rooms, service with restrictions, crate.

✕ 🖥 ≈

**Holiday Inn Express Hotel & Suites** SH
(417) 336-1100. **$82-$93.** 1970 W Hwy 76 (Country Music Blvd). 1.8 mi w of jct SR 76 (Country Music Blvd) and US 65. Int corridors. **Pets:** Other species. $25 one-time fee/room. Designated rooms, service with restrictions, supervision.

ASK SD ✕ ♿M 🖥 🖥 🖥 ≈

**Howard Johnson** SH
(417) 336-5151. **$49-$79.** 3027-A W Hwy 76. On SR 76 (Country Music Blvd), 3.5 mi w of jct US 65. Ext corridors. **Pets:** Medium. $10 daily fee/pet. Designated rooms, service with restrictions, supervision.

ASK SD ✕ 🖥 🖥 ⑪ ≈

**La Quinta Inn Branson (Music City Centre)** SH
(417) 336-1600. **$65-$85.** 1835 W Hwy 76. 1.6 mi w of jct US 65. Ext/int corridors. **Pets:** Other species. Service with restrictions, crate.

ASK SD ✕ 🖥 🖥 ≈ ✕

**Ozark Valley Inn** M
(417) 336-4666. **$34-$75.** 2693 Shephard of the Hills Expwy. Jct SR 76 (Country Music Blvd), 0.9 mi e. Ext corridors. **Pets:** $10 one-time fee/room. Designated rooms, service with restrictions.

SAVE ✕ 🖥 🖥 ≈

**Quality Inn** SH
(417) 335-6776. **$45-$90.** 3269 Shepherd of the Hills Expwy. 0.3 mi e of jct SR 76 (Country Music Blvd). Ext/int corridors. **Pets:** Small, dogs only. $10 daily fee/pet. Designated rooms, service with restrictions, crate.

ASK SD ✕ 🖥 🖥 🖥 ⑪ ≈ ✕

**▼▼ Ramada Inn & Conference Center** 🆂🅷
(417) 334-1000. **$39-$89.** 1700 Hwy 76 W. Jct SR 76 (Country Music Blvd) and US 65, 1.5 mi w. Ext corridors. **Pets:** Medium. $20 one-time fee/room. Designated rooms, no service, crate.

ASK 🆂 ⊠ 🖼 🖥 💻 🍴 ⊇ ⊠

**▼▼ Ramada Limited** 🆂🅷
(417) 337-5207. **$45-$125.** 2316 Shepherd of the Hills Expwy. Jct SR 76 (Country Music Blvd), 1.3 mi e. Ext corridors. **Pets:** Large, other species. $10 daily fee/room. Service with restrictions.

ASK 🆂 ⊠ 🖼 💻 ⊇

**▼▼ Residence Inn by Marriott** 🆂🅷
(417) 336-4077. **$69-$199.** 280 Wildwood Dr S. 2 mi w on SR 76 (Country Music Blvd), just s. Int corridors. **Pets:** Other species. $75 one-time fee/room. Service with restrictions.

ASK 🆂 ⊠ 🖼 🖼 🖼 🖥 💻 ⊇ ⊠

**▼ Rock View Resort** Ⓜ
(417) 334-4678. **$53-$87, 21 day notice.** 1049 Park View Dr. Jct US 65, 4.4 mi w on SR 165, 0.3 mi s via Dale Dr, then 0.7 mi w. Ext corridors. **Pets:** $7 daily fee/pet. Service with restrictions, supervision.

⊠ 🖥 💻 ⊇ ⊠ 🖼

**AAA ▼▼ Scenic Hills Inn** 🆂🅷
(417) 336-8855. **$58.** 2422 Shepherd of the Hills Expwy. Jct SR 76 (Country Music Blvd), 1.1 mi e. Int corridors. **Pets:** Small, other species. $7 daily fee/pet. Designated rooms, service with restrictions.

SAVE 🆂 ⊠ 🖥 💻 ⊇

**AAA ▼▼ Settle Inn Resort & Conference Center** 🆂🅷
(417) 335-4700. **$59-$99.** 3050 Green Mountain Dr. Jct SR 76 (Country Music Blvd) and US 65, 3 mi w on SR 76, 0.8 mi s. Int corridors. **Pets:** Other species. $10 daily fee/pet. Designated rooms, service with restrictions, supervision.

SAVE 🆂 ⊠ 🖼 🖼 🖥 💻 🍴 ⊇ ⊠

# BRANSON WEST

**▼▼ Shady Acre Motel** Ⓜ
(417) 338-2316. **$36-$42.** 8722 Hwy 76. Jct SR 265, 1.1 mi w. Ext corridors. **Pets:** Small, dogs only. $10 one-time fee/room. Service with restrictions, crate.

⊠ 🖥 💻 ⊇

# BUTLER

**▼▼ Days Inn** 🆂🅷
(660) 679-4544. **$45-$90.** 100 S Fran Ave. Just e of jct US 71 and SR 52. Int corridors. **Pets:** Accepted.

ASK 🆂 ⊠ 🖥 ⊇

**▼ Super 8 Motel–Butler** Ⓜ
(660) 679-6183. **$39-$65.** 1114 W Fort Scott St. Just e of jct US 71 and SR 52. Ext corridors. **Pets:** Medium, other species. $5 daily fee/pet. Service with restrictions, supervision.

ASK 🆂 ⊠ 🖥

# CAMERON

**AAA ▼▼ Best Western Acorn Inn** Ⓜ
(816) 632-2187. **$69-$79.** 2210 E US 36. I-35, exit 54, 0.3 mi e. Ext corridors. **Pets:** Medium, other species. Service with restrictions, supervision.

SAVE 🆂 ⊠ 🖼 🖼 🖥 💻 ⊇

**AAA ▼▼ Comfort Inn** 🆂🅷 🐾
(816) 632-5655. **$65-$90.** 1803 Comfort Ln. I-35, exit 54, just e. Int corridors. **Pets:** Designated rooms, service with restrictions, supervision.

SAVE 🆂 ⊠ 🖼 🖥 💻 ⊇

**AAA ▼▼ Econo Lodge** Ⓜ 🐾
(816) 632-6571. **$49-$69.** 220 E Grand. I-35, exit 54, 0.5 mi w on US 36, then just s on US 69. Ext corridors. **Pets:** Other species. $5 daily fee/pet. Service with restrictions, supervision.

SAVE 🆂 ⊠ 🖥 ⊇

**▼▼ Super 8 Motel** 🆂🅷
(816) 632-8888. **$62.** 1710 N Walnut St. I-35, exit 54, 0.5 mi w on US 36. Int corridors. **Pets:** Small. $10 one-time fee/room. Designated rooms, service with restrictions, supervision.

ASK 🆂 ⊠ 🖥 ⊇

# CANTON

**▼▼ Comfort Inn Canton** 🆂🅷
(573) 288-8800. **$65-$105.** 1701 Oak St. US 61, exit CR P, just e. Int corridors. **Pets:** Medium. $13 daily fee/pet. Service with restrictions, supervision.

ASK 🆂 ⊠ 🖥 💻 ⊇ ⊠

# CAPE GIRARDEAU

**▼▼ Drury Lodge-Cape Girardeau** 🆂🅷
(573) 334-7151. **$100-$140.** 104 S Vantage Dr. I-55, exit 96 (William St), just e. Ext/int corridors. **Pets:** Accepted.

ASK ⊠ 🖼 🖥 💻 🍴 ⊇

**▼▼▼ Drury Suites-Cape Girardeau** 🆂🅷
(573) 339-9500. **$98-$133.** 3303 Campster Dr. I-55, exit 96 (William St), just w. Int corridors. **Pets:** Accepted.

ASK ⊠ 🖼 🖼 🖼 🖥 💻 ⊇

**▼▼▼ Hampton Inn-Cape Girardeau** 🆂🅷
(573) 651-3000. **$102-$150.** 103 Cape W Pkwy. I-55, exit 96 (William St), 0.3 mi sw. Int corridors. **Pets:** Accepted.

ASK ⊠ 🖼 🖼 🖼 🖥 💻

**▼▼▼ Pear Tree Inn by Drury-Cape Girardeau** 🆂🅷
(573) 334-3000. **$70-$110.** 3248 William St. I-55, exit 96 (William St), just e. Int corridors. **Pets:** Accepted.

ASK ⊠ ⊇

**▼▼▼ Victorian Inn & Suites** 🆂🅷
(573) 651-4486. **$74-$130.** 3265 William St. I-55, exit 96 (William St), just e. Ext/int corridors. **Pets:** Accepted.

ASK 🆂 ⊠ 🖼 🖼 🖼 🖥 💻 ⊇ ⊠

# CARTHAGE

**AAA ▼▼ Best Western Precious Moments Hotel** 🆂🅷
(417) 359-5900. **$65-$135.** 2701 Hazel St. Just e of jct US 71 and SR HH. Int corridors. **Pets:** Accepted.

SAVE 🆂 ⊠ 🖼 🖼 🖥 💻 ⊇

**AAA ▼▼ Econo Lodge** 🆂🅷
(417) 358-3900. **$54-$79.** 1441 W Central. On SR 96; jct US 71. Ext/int corridors. **Pets:** Accepted.

SAVE 🆂 ⊠ 🖼 🖥 ⊇

**▼▼ Super 8 Motel** 🆂🅷
(417) 359-9000. **$64-$125.** 416 W Fir Rd. Just e of jct US 71 and SR HH. Int corridors. **Pets:** Small. $5 daily fee/pet. Designated rooms, service with restrictions.

ASK 🆂 ⊠ 🖥

# CASSVILLE

**▼ Budget Inn** Ⓜ 🐾
(417) 847-4196. **$42-$62.** Hwy 112/248. On SR 76, 86 and 112, just e of jct SR 248. Ext corridors. **Pets:** Small, dogs only. $20 deposit/pet. Service with restrictions, supervision.

ASK 🆂 ⊠ 🖥 💻 ⊇

**▼ Super 8 Motel** 🆂🅷
(417) 847-4888. **$58-$65.** 101 S Hwy 37. Just s of jct SR 76, 86 and 37 business route. Int corridors. **Pets:** Small, dogs only. $20 deposit/room, $5 daily fee/pet. Designated rooms, service with restrictions, supervision.

ASK 🆂 ⊠ 🖼 🖥 ⊇

# CHARLESTON

**◆◆◆ ▼▼▼ Comfort Inn** Ⓜ
(573) 683-4200. **$60-$99.** 102 Drake St. I-57, exit 10, just nw. Ext corridors. **Pets:** Small. $15 daily fee/pet. Designated rooms, service with restrictions, supervision.
ⓈAVE Ⓢ Ⓧ Ⓗ Ⓛ ⌐

# CHILLICOTHE

**▼▼ Best Western Inn** ⓈⒽ
(660) 646-0572. **$64-$110.** 1020 S Washington St. Jct US 36 and 65 (Washington St). Ext/int corridors. **Pets:** Accepted.
ⒶⓈK Ⓢ Ⓧ Ⓛᴹ Ⓗ Ⓛ ⌐

**▼ Chillicothe Super 8 Motel** ⓈⒽ
(660) 646-7888. **$70-$77.** 580 Old Hwy 36 E. Jct US 36 and 65 (Washington St), 0.8 mi e. Int corridors. **Pets:** Small, other species. $10 one-time fee/room. Service with restrictions, supervision.
ⒶⓈK Ⓢ Ⓧ Ⓗ

# CLINTON

**◆◆◆ ▼ Motel USA Inn** Ⓜ
(660) 885-2267. **$35-$55.** 1508 N 2nd St. Jct SR 7 and 13. Ext corridors. **Pets:** Small, dogs only. $10 daily fee/pet. Designated rooms, no service, supervision.
ⓈAVE Ⓢ Ⓧ Ⓗ

# COLUMBIA

**▼▼▼ Drury Inn-Columbia** ⓈⒽ
(573) 445-1800. **$80-$175.** 1000 Knipp St. I-70, exit 124 (Stadium Blvd), just s. Int corridors. **Pets:** Accepted.
ⒶⓈK Ⓧ ⓩ Ⓗ Ⓛ ⌐

**▼▼▼ Holiday Inn Select Executive Center** ⒽⒾ
(573) 445-8531. **$84.** 2200 I-70 Dr SW. I-70, exit 124 (Stadium Blvd), just w. Int corridors. **Pets:** Accepted.
ⒶⓈK Ⓢ Ⓧ Ⓛᴹ ⓩ Ⓗ Ⓛ Ⓣ ⌐ Ⓧ

**▼▼ La Quinta Inn Columbia** ⓈⒽ
(573) 443-4141. **$69-$109, 3 day notice.** 901 Conley Rd. I-70, exit 128A (US 63). Int corridors. **Pets:** Small. $10 daily fee/pet. Designated rooms, service with restrictions, supervision.
ⒶⓈK Ⓢ Ⓧ Ⓛᴹ Ⓗ Ⓛ ⌐

**◆◆◆ ▼▼ Quality Inn Columbia** ⓈⒽ
(573) 449-2491. **$69-$99.** 1612 N Providence Rd. I-70, exit 126 (Providence Rd). Ext/int corridors. **Pets:** $10 daily fee/pet. Designated rooms, service with restrictions, supervision.
ⓈAVE Ⓢ Ⓧ Ⓛᴹ Ⓗ Ⓛ ⌐ Ⓧ

**▼▼ Red Roof Inn-Columbia** Ⓜ
(573) 442-0145. **$49-$72.** 201 E Texas Ave. I-70, exit 126 (Providence Rd), just n. Ext corridors. **Pets:** Accepted.
Ⓧ Ⓛ

**▼▼ Super 8 Columbia/Lake of the Woods** ⓈⒽ
(573) 474-8307. **$61-$100.** 5700 Freedom Dr. I-70, exit 131, just ne. Int corridors. **Pets:** Other species. $15 one-time fee/pet. Supervision.
Ⓧ Ⓗ Ⓛ ⌐

**▼▼ Super 8 Motel-Columbia** Ⓜ
(573) 474-8488. **$62-$90.** 3216 Clark Ln. I-70, exit 128A, northeast corner. Int corridors. **Pets:** Other species. $15 daily fee/pet. Designated rooms, service with restrictions, supervision.
Ⓧ Ⓗ Ⓛ

# CUBA

**◆◆◆ ▼ Super 8 Motel** Ⓜ
(573) 885-2087. **$45-$100.** 28 Hwy P. I-44, exit 208 (SR 19), just nw. Ext/int corridors. **Pets:** $10 one-time fee/room. Designated rooms, service with restrictions, supervision.
ⓈAVE Ⓢ Ⓧ ⓩ Ⓗ Ⓛ

# FESTUS

**◆◆◆ ▼▼▼ Baymont Inn & Suites** ⓈⒽ
(636) 937-2888. **$69-$79.** 1303 Veterans Blvd. I-55, exit 175, just w. Int corridors. **Pets:** Accepted.
ⓈAVE Ⓢ Ⓧ Ⓗ Ⓛ

**▼▼ Drury Inn-Festus** ⓈⒽ
(636) 933-2400. **$70-$106.** 1001 Veterans Blvd. I-55, exit 175, just e. Int corridors. **Pets:** Accepted.
ⒶⓈK Ⓧ Ⓗ Ⓛ ⌐

# FULTON

**▼▼ Holiday Inn Express Fulton** ⓈⒽ
(573) 642-2600. **$67-$75.** 2205 Cardinal Dr. US 54, exit CR HH, just s. Int corridors. **Pets:** Other species. $10 daily fee/pet. Designated rooms, service with restrictions, supervision.
ⒶⓈK Ⓢ Ⓧ Ⓗ Ⓛ ⌐ Ⓧ

**▼▼▼ Loganberry Inn Bed & Breakfast Inc** ⒷⒷ ❧
(573) 642-9229. **$99-$189, 14 day notice.** 310 W 7th St. 1 mi e of jct US 54 and CR F, n on Westminster, then just e. Int corridors. **Pets:** Dogs only. $10 one-time fee/pet. Designated rooms, service with restrictions, crate.
ⒶⓈK Ⓢ Ⓧ Ⓗ Ⓛ

# HANNIBAL

**◆◆◆ ▼▼▼ Quality Inn & Suites** ⓈⒽ
(573) 221-4001. **$79-$119.** 120 Lindsey Dr. 2 mi w on US 36, exit Shinn Ln to south service road. Int corridors. **Pets:** Medium. $10 daily fee/pet. Designated rooms, service with restrictions, supervision.
ⓈAVE Ⓢ Ⓧ Ⓗ Ⓛ ⌐ Ⓧ

# HARRISONVILLE

**◆◆◆ ▼▼ Best Western Harrisonville** Ⓜ
(816) 884-3200. **$55-$95, 30 day notice.** 2201 Rockhaven Rd. Just n of jct US 71 and SR 291. Ext corridors. **Pets:** Small. $10 daily fee/pet. Designated rooms, service with restrictions, supervision.
ⓈAVE Ⓢ Ⓧ Ⓗ Ⓛ ⌐

**▼ Budget Host Caravan Motel** Ⓜ
(816) 884-4100. **$39-$60.** 1705 Hwy 291 N. Just n of jct US 71. Ext corridors. **Pets:** Medium. $5 deposit/room. Service with restrictions, supervision.
ⒶⓈK Ⓢ Ⓧ Ⓗ

**◆◆◆ ▼ Slumber Inn Motel** Ⓜ
(816) 884-3100. **$37-$48, 7 day notice.** 21400 E 275th St. Jct US 71 and SR 7 S (Clinton exit), just w. Ext corridors. **Pets:** Medium. $10 daily fee/pet. Service with restrictions, supervision.
ⓈAVE Ⓢ Ⓧ Ⓗ ⌐

# HAYTI

**▼▼ Drury Inn & Suites-Caruthersville** ⓈⒽ
(573) 359-2702. **$78-$140.** 1317 Hwy 84. I-55, exit 19 (US 412/SR 84), just w. Int corridors. **Pets:** Accepted.
ⒶⓈK Ⓧ ⓩ Ⓗ Ⓛ ⌐

# HIGGINSVILLE

**▼▼ Super 8 Motel-Higginsville** ⓈⒽ
(660) 584-7781. **$60-$76.** 6471 Oakview Ln. I-70, exit 49 (SR 13), just se. Int corridors. **Pets:** Other species. $10 deposit/room, $5 daily fee/pet. No service, supervision.
ⒶⓈK Ⓢ Ⓧ Ⓔ

# HOUSTON

**▼ Southern Inn Motel** ⓈⒽ
(417) 967-4591. **$50-$55.** 1493 S Hwy 63. 1.3 mi s on US 63. Ext corridors. **Pets:** Accepted.
ⒶⓈK Ⓢ Ⓧ

# JACKSON

**▼▼▼ Drury Inn & Suites-Jackson,MO** 🆂🅷
(573) 243-9200. **$85-$125.** 225 Drury Ln. I-55, exit 105 (SR 61), 0.3 mi
w. Int corridors. **Pets:** Accepted.

🅰🆂🅺 ⊗ ♿ 🗳 💻 ⇌

# JEFFERSON CITY

**▼▼ Ramada Inn-Jefferson City** 🆂🅷
(573) 635-7171. **$69-$77, 14 day notice.** 1510 Jefferson St. US 54,
exit Ellis Blvd, 0.5 mi nw. Ext/int corridors. **Pets:** Other species. $10 daily
fee/pet. Service with restrictions, crate.

🅰🆂🅺 🆂🅓 ⊗ 🖉 🗳 💻 🍽 ⇌

# JOPLIN

**▼▼ Baymont Inn & Suites** 🆂🅷
(417) 623-0000. **$66-$86.** 3510 S Range Line Rd. I-44, exit 8B, just n.
Ext/int corridors. **Pets:** Accepted.

🅰🆂🅺 🆂🅓 ⊗ 🖉 🗳 💻 ⇌

**▼▼▼ Best Western Oasis Inn & Suites** 🆂🅷
(417) 781-6776. **$55-$62.** 3508 S Range Line Rd. I-44, exit 8B, just nw.
Ext corridors. **Pets:** Small, dogs only. $10 daily fee/pet. No service, super-
vision.

🆂🅐🆅🅴 🆂🅓 ⊗ 🗳 💻 ⇌

**▼▼ Drury Inn & Suites-Joplin** 🆂🅷
(417) 781-8000. **$80-$130.** 3601 Range Line Rd. I-44, exit 8B, just ne.
Int corridors. **Pets:** Accepted.

🅰🆂🅺 ⊗ 🖉 🗳 💻 ⇌ ⊗

**Ⓐ ▼▼▼ Holiday Inn** 🆂🅷
(417) 782-1000. **$99-$139.** 3615 Range Line Rd. I-44, exit 8B, just ne.
Int corridors. **Pets:** Accepted.

🆂🅐🆅🅴 🆂🅓 ⊗ 🖉 🗳 💻 🍽 ⇌ ⊗

**▼ Microtel Inn & Suites Joplin** 🆂🅷
(417) 626-8282. **$47-$52.** 4101 Richard Joseph Blvd. I-44, exit 8A, just
s. Int corridors. **Pets:** Small, other species. Service with restrictions, supervision.

🅰🆂🅺 🆂🅓 ⊗ 🖉 🗳 💻 ⇌

**Ⓐ ▼▼▼ Sleep Inn** 🆂🅷
(417) 782-1212. **$69-$89.** I-44 & State Hwy 43 S. I-44, exit 4, just s. Int
corridors. **Pets:** Accepted.

🆂🅐🆅🅴 🆂🅓 ⊗ 🖉 💻

**▼ Super 8 Motel-Joplin** 🅼
(417) 782-8765. **$50-$95.** 2830 E 36th St. I-44, exit 8B, just n. Int
corridors. **Pets:** Accepted.

🅰🆂🅺 🆂🅓 ⊗ 🗳

# KANSAS CITY METROPOLITAN AREA

## BLUE SPRINGS

**▼ Econo Lodge of Blue Springs** 🅼
(816) 229-6363. **$55-$75.** 1110 N 7 Hwy. I-70, exit 20, just n. Ext
corridors. **Pets:** Medium, dogs only. $10 one-time fee/room. Designated
rooms, service with restrictions, supervision.

🅰🆂🅺 🆂🅓 ⇌

**Ⓐ ▼▼ Sleep Inn** 🆂🅷
(816) 224-1199. **$55-$65.** 451 NW Jefferson St. I-70, exit 20, just n on
SR 7 to NW Jefferson St, then just e. Int corridors. **Pets:** Other species.
$5 one-time fee/pet.

🆂🅐🆅🅴 🆂🅓 ⊗ 🕭🅼 🖉 🗳 💻 ⇌

## INDEPENDENCE

**ⒶⒶ ▼▼▼ Best Western Truman Inn** 🅼
(816) 254-0100. **$49-$64.** 4048 S Lynn Court Dr. I-70, exit 12, just n on
Noland Rd, then just w. Ext corridors. **Pets:** Medium, other species. $30
deposit/room, $8 daily fee/pet. Service with restrictions, crate.

🆂🅐🆅🅴 🆂🅓 ⊗ 🗳 💻 ⇌

**▼▼ Red Roof Inn** 🅼
(816) 373-2800. **$50-$80.** 13712 E 42nd Terrace. I-70, exit 12, just sw.
Ext corridors. **Pets:** Accepted.

⊗ 🕭🅼 🖉

**ⒶⒶ ▼▼▼ Super 8 Motel** 🆂🅷
(816) 833-1888. **$44-$59.** 4032 S Lynn Court Dr. I-70, exit 12, just nw.
Int corridors. **Pets:** Medium. $30 deposit/room, $8 daily fee/pet. Service
with restrictions, crate.

🆂🅐🆅🅴 🆂🅓 ⊗ 🗳 ⇌

## KANSAS CITY

**ⒶⒶ ▼▼▼▼ AmeriSuites KCI Airport** 🆂🅷
(816) 891-0871. **$89-$116.** 7600 NW 97th Terr. I-29, exit 10, just sw. Int
corridors. **Pets:** Small. $10 daily fee/pet. Service with restrictions, supervi-
sion.

🆂🅐🆅🅴 🆂🅓 ⊗ 🖉 🗳 💻 ⇌

**ⒶⒶ ▼▼▼ Baymont Inn & Suites Kansas City South** 🆂🅷
(816) 822-7000. **$71-$105.** 8601 Hillcrest Rd. I-435, exit 69 (87th St).
Int corridors. **Pets:** Medium. Service with restrictions.

🆂🅐🆅🅴 ⊗ 🕭🅼 🖉 🖉 🗳 💻

**ⒶⒶ ▼▼▼ Best Western Country Inn-North** 🅼
(816) 459-7222. **$45-$139.** 2633 NE 43rd St. I-35, exit 8C (Antioch Rd),
just s on SR 1, then just e. Ext corridors. **Pets:** Accepted.

🆂🅐🆅🅴 🆂🅓 ⊗ 🖉 🗳 💻 ⇌

**ⒶⒶ ▼▼▼ Best Western Seville Plaza Hotel** 🆂🅷
(816) 561-9600. **$97-$179.** 4309 Main St. 43rd and Main sts, just se. Int
corridors. **Pets:** Medium, dogs only. $20 one-time fee/pet. Designated
rooms, service with restrictions, supervision.

🆂🅐🆅🅴 🆂🅓 ⊗ 🕭🅼 🗳 💻

**ⒶⒶ ▼▼▼▼ Chase Suites by Woodfin** 🆂🅷
(816) 891-9009. **$149-$189.** 9900 NW Prairie View Rd. I-29, exit 10.
Ext corridors. **Pets:** Accepted.

🆂🅐🆅🅴 🆂🅓 ⊗ 🖉 🖉 🗳 💻 ⇌ ⊗

**▼▼▼ Clarion Hotel KCI** 🆂🅷
(816) 464-2345. **$69-$99.** 11832 Plaza Cir. I-29, exit 13, just e. Int
corridors. **Pets:** Accepted.

🅰🆂🅺 🆂🅓 ⊗ 🗳 💻 🍽 ⇌ ⊗

**▼▼ Days Inn** 🅼
(816) 746-1666. **$70-$190.** 11120 NW Ambassador Dr. I-29, exit 12,
just e, then s. Int corridors. **Pets:** Medium. $15 daily fee/pet. Designated
rooms, service with restrictions, supervision.

🅰🆂🅺 ⊗ 🕭🅼 🖉 🗳 ⇌

**▼▼▼▼ Drury Inn & Suites-Kansas City Airport** 🆂🅷
(816) 880-9700. **$80-$130.** 7900 NW Tiffany Springs Pkwy. I-29, exit
10, just w. Int corridors. **Pets:** Accepted.

🅰🆂🅺 ⊗ 🕭🅼 🖉 🖉 🗳 💻 ⇌ ⊗

**▼▼▼ Drury Inn & Suites-Kansas City Stadium** 🆂🅷
(816) 923-3000. **$80-$130.** 3830 Blue Ridge Cutoff. I-70, exit 9 (Blue
Ridge Cutoff), just nw. Int corridors. **Pets:** Accepted.

🅰🆂🅺 ⊗ 🕭🅼 🖉 🗳 💻 ⇌

**♦♦♦ ▼▼▼▼ Embassy Suites Hotel KCI Airport** SH
(816) 891-7788. **$99-$209.** 7640 NW Tiffany Springs Pkwy. I-29, exit 10, just e. Int corridors. **Pets:** Small. $10 daily fee/room. Service with restrictions, supervision
SAVE ✕ ⛬M ⟲ ⛭ ⬛ ⬛ ⏐⏐ ⇝ ✕

**♦♦♦ ▼▼▼ Fairfield Inn Kansas City-Liberty** SH
(816) 792-4000. **$74-$99.** 8101 N Church Rd. I-35, exit 16 (SR 152), just w, then s. Int corridors. **Pets:** Large, other species. $75 one-time fee/room. Designated rooms, service with restrictions, supervision.
SAVE S⛬ ✕ ⛬M ⟲ ⬛ ⬛ ⇝

**▼▼▼▼ Holiday Inn At The Plaza, Kansas City** SH 🐾
(816) 753-7400. **$139-$189.** One E 45th St. In Country Club Plaza. Int corridors. **Pets:** Medium. $25 one-time fee/room. Service with restrictions, crate.
A$K S⛬ ✕ ⛬M ⟲ ⛭ ⬛ ⬛ ⏐⏐ ⇝

**▼▼▼ Holiday Inn Express Westport Plaza** SH
(816) 931-1000. **$79-$129.** 801 Westport Rd. In Westport Plaza area. Int corridors. **Pets:** Accepted.
A$K S⛬ ✕ ⛬M ⟲ ⬛ ⬛

**▼▼▼▼ Holiday Inn-Sports Complex** SH
(816) 353-5300. **$79, 14 day notice.** 4011 Blue Ridge Cutoff. I-70, exit 9 (Blue Ridge Cutoff), just se. Int corridors. **Pets:** $50 deposit/room. Service with restrictions, crate.
A$K S⛬ ✕ ⛬M ⟲ ⛭ ⬛ ⬛ ⏐⏐ ⇝ ✕

**▼▼ Homestead Studio Suites Hotel-Kansas City/Country Club Plaza** SH
(816) 531-2212. **$86-$104.** 4535 Main St. Just ne of Country Club Plaza. Int corridors. **Pets:** $25 daily fee/pet. Service with restrictions, supervision.
A$K S⛬ ✕ ⛬M ⛭ ⬛ ⬛

**♦♦♦ ▼▼▼ Homewood Suites by Hilton** SH
(816) 880-9880. **$89-$189.** 7312 NW Polo Dr. I-29, exit 10, just e. Int corridors. **Pets:** Accepted.
SAVE ✕ ⟲ ⛭ ⬛ ⬛ ⇝ ✕

**♦♦♦ ▼▼▼ The InterContinental Kansas City** LH
(816) 756-1500. **$189-$339.** 401 Ward Pkwy. Corner of Wornall and Ward Pkwy; in Country Club Plaza. Int corridors. **Pets:** Accepted.
SAVE S⛬ ✕ ⟲ ⏐⏐ ⇝ ✕

**▼▼▼▼ Kansas City Marriott Downtown** LH
(816) 421-6800. **$142-$200.** 200 W 12th St. Just s of I-70, US 24 and 40. Int corridors. **Pets:** $25 one-time fee/room. Crate.
A$K S⛬ ✕ ⟲ ⛭ ⬛ ⬛ ⏐⏐ ⇝ ✕

**▼▼▼ La Quinta Inn** SH
(816) 483-7900. **$69-$84.** 1051 N Cambridge Ave. I-435, exit 57, just w to Cambridge Ave, then just s. Int corridors. **Pets:** Other species. Service with restrictions, crate.
A$K S⛬ ✕ ⟲ ⛭ ⬛ ⬛ ⇝ ✕

**♦♦♦ ▼▼ ▼▼ Quality Inn & Suites Airport** SH
(816) 587-6262. **$70-$80.** 6901 NW 83rd St. I-29, exit 8. Int corridors. **Pets:** Accepted.
SAVE S⛬ ✕ ⛭ ⬛ ⬛ ⇝

**▼▼▼▼ Radisson Hotel & Suites Kansas City, City Center** SH
(816) 474-6664. **$109.** 1301 Wyandotte St. Just s of I-70, US 24 and 40. Int corridors. **Pets:** Accepted.
✕ ⟲ ⛭ ⬛ ⬛ ⏐⏐ ⇝

**▼▼▼▼ Radisson Hotel Kansas City Airport** SH
(816) 464-2423. **$89-$119.** 11828 NW Plaza Cir. I-29, exit 13, just se. Int corridors. **Pets:** Accepted.
A$K S⛬ ✕ ⛬M ⟲ ⛭ ⬛ ⬛ ⏐⏐ ⇝ ✕

**▼▼ Red Roof Inn-North** M
(816) 452-8585. **$48-$86.** 3636 NE Randolph Rd. I-435, exit 55B northbound; exit 55 southbound, just e on SR 210, then just n. Ext corridors. **Pets:** Accepted.
✕ ⛬M ⛭

**▼▼▼ Residence Inn by Marriott Downtown/Union Hill** SH
(816) 561-3000. **$89-$189.** 2975 Main St. Just n of 31st St. Ext corridors. **Pets:** Accepted.
A$K S⛬ ✕ ⟲ ⛭ ⬛ ⬛ ⇝ ✕

**▼▼▼ Residence Inn Kansas City Country Club Plaza** SH
(816) 753-0033. **Call for rates (no credit cards).** 4601 Broadway Blvd. In Country Club Plaza. Int corridors. **Pets:** Small. $75 one-time fee/room.
✕ ⛭ ⬛ ⬛ ⇝

**▼▼▼ Sheraton Suites Country Club Plaza** LH 🐾
(816) 931-4400. **$165-$190.** 770 W 47th St. Corner of Summit and 47th St; in Country Club Plaza. Int corridors. **Pets:** Medium, dogs only. Service with restrictions, supervision.
A$K ✕ ⛬M ⟲ ⛭ ⬛ ⬛ ⏐⏐ ⇝

**♦♦♦ ▼▼▼ ▼▼▼ The Westin Crown Center** LH
(816) 474-4400. **$129-$299.** 1 E Pershing Rd. 0.5 mi s. Int corridors. **Pets:** Accepted.
SAVE S⛬ ✕ ⛬M ⟲ ⛭ ⬛ ⏐⏐ ⇝ ✕

# KEARNEY

**▼▼ Kearney Super 8 Motel** SH
(816) 628-6800. **$61-$100.** 210 Platte Clay Way. I-35, exit 26, just e on SR 92, then just n. Int corridors. **Pets:** Medium, dogs only. $10 one-time fee/room. Designated rooms, service with restrictions.
A$K S⛬ ✕

# LEE'S SUMMIT

**▼▼ Comfort Inn & Suites** SH
(816) 554-6688. **$80-$160.** 3701 NE Ralph Powell Rd. I-470, exit 12 (Woods Chappel Rd), 0.3 mi sw. Int corridors. **Pets:** Medium, dogs only. $25 one-time fee/room. Service with restrictions, supervision.
A$K S⛬ ✕ ⛭ ⬛ ⬛ ⇝

**▼▼ Comfort Inn by Choice Hotels** SH
(816) 524-8181. **$69-$119.** 607 SE Oldham Pkwy. Jct US 50 and SR 291 N. Int corridors. **Pets:** Accepted.
A$K S⛬ ✕ ⛬M ⬛ ⬛ ⇝

**▼▼▼ Lee's Summit Holiday Inn Express** SH
(816) 795-6400. **$84-$109.** 4825 NE Lakewood Way. I-470, exit 14, just e on Bowlin Rd, then 0.4 mi s. Int corridors. **Pets:** Accepted.
A$K S⛬ ✕ ⛬M ⛭ ⬛ ⬛ ⇝

# NORTH KANSAS CITY

**▼▼▼ Baymont Inn & Suites Kansas City North** SH
(816) 221-1200. **$75-$125.** 2214 Taney Rd. I-29/35, exit 6A, just e on SR 210, then just n. Int corridors. **Pets:** Medium. Service with restrictions.
A$K S⛬ ✕ ⟲ ⬛ ⬛

**♦♦♦ ▼▼ North Kansas City Days Inn** SH
(816) 421-6000. **$52-$67.** 2232 Taney St. I-29/35, exit 6A, just e on SR 210, then just n. Int corridors. **Pets:** Accepted.
SAVE S⛬ ✕ ⛬M ⟲ ⛭ ⬛

# OAK GROVE (JACKSON COUNTY)

**♦♦♦ ▼▼▼ Econo Lodge** M
(816) 690-3681. **$60.** 410 SE 1st St. I-70, exit 28, just s on Broadway St, just e on SE 4th St, then just n. Ext corridors. **Pets:** Small. $5 daily fee/pet. Service with restrictions, supervision.
SAVE S⛬ ✕ ⬛

# KINGDOM CITY

▼▼ Super 8 Motel-Kingdom City **M**
(573) 642-2888. **$42-$74.** 3370 Gold Ave. I-70, exit 148 (US 54), 0.3 mi s. Int corridors. **Pets:** Small. $5 daily fee/pet. Designated rooms, no service, crate.

ASK S✗ ✕ &M ⟲ 🖶

# KIRKSVILLE

▼▼ Comfort Inn by Choice Hotels **M**
(660) 665-2205. **$75-$105.** 2209 N Baltimore. US 63 N. Int corridors. **Pets:** Very small, dogs only. $15 one-time fee/pet. Service with restrictions, supervision.

✕ &M ⟲ 🖶 ▱

▼▼ Super 8 Motel-Kirksville **M**
(660) 665-8826. **$52-$75.** 1101 Country Club Dr. On US 63 and SR 6. Int corridors. **Pets:** Other species. $10 daily fee/pet. Designated rooms, service with restrictions, supervision.

ASK S✗ ✕ 🖶

# LAKE OZARK

▼▼▼ The Resort at Port Arrowhead **LH** 🐾
(573) 365-2334. **$99-$179, 3 day notice.** 3080 Bagnell Dam Blvd. 2.6 mi s of Bagnell Dam, on US 54 business route. Ext/int corridors. **Pets:** Dogs only. $50 deposit/pet, $12 daily fee/pet. Service with restrictions, supervision.

ASK S✗ ✕ &M ⟲ ⟨🌊⟩ 🖶 ▱ 🍴 ⇌ ✕

# LEBANON

AAA ▼▼ Best Western Wyota Inn **SH**
(417) 532-6171. **$60.** 1225 Mill Creek Rd. I-44, exit 130, just nw. Ext corridors. **Pets:** Accepted.

SAVE S✗ ✕ 🖶 ▱ 🍴 ⇌

▼▼ Holiday Inn Express **SH**
(417) 532-1111. **$87-$147.** 1955 W Elm St. I-44, exit 127, just n. Int corridors. **Pets:** Very small. $25 one-time fee/pet. Designated rooms, service with restrictions.

ASK S✗ ✕ 🖶 ▱ ⇌

# LICKING

▼▼ Scenic Rivers Inn **M**
(573) 674-4809. **$50-$52.** 209 S Hwy 63. On US 63. Ext corridors. **Pets:** Small. $5 daily fee/pet. Designated rooms, service with restrictions, supervision.

ASK S✗ ✕ ⟨🌊⟩ 🖶 ▱

# LOUISIANA

AAA ▼ River's Edge Motel **M**
(573) 754-4522. **$50-$65.** 201 Mansion St. On US 54; at Champ Clark Bridge. Ext corridors. **Pets:** Large, dogs only. $5 one-time fee/pet. Service with restrictions, supervision.

SAVE S✗ ✕ 🖶 ▱

# MACON

▼▼ Best Western Inn **M**
(660) 385-2125. **$51-$59.** 28933 Sunset Dr. On Outer Rd S; at US 36 and Long Branch Lake exit. Ext corridors. **Pets:** Accepted.

ASK S✗ ✕ 🖶 ▱ ⇌

▼▼ Super 8 Motel **SH**
(660) 385-5788. **$55-$80.** 203 E Briggs Dr. Jct US 36 and 63. Int corridors. **Pets:** Other species. $10 daily fee/pet. Service with restrictions, supervision.

ASK S✗ ✕ 🖶

# MARSHFIELD

▼▼ ▼▼ Holiday Inn Express **SH**
(417) 859-6000. **$66-$89.** 1301 Banning St. I-44, exit 100 (SR 38), on southeast corner. Int corridors. **Pets:** Medium. $20 deposit/room. Designated rooms, service with restrictions, supervision.

ASK S✗ ✕ &M 🖶 ▱ ⇌

# MARYVILLE

▼▼ Super 8 Motel-Maryville **SH**
(660) 582-8088. **$55.** 222 Summit Dr. On Business Rt US 71; just n of US 71 Bypass. Int corridors. **Pets:** Other species. $20 deposit/room. Service with restrictions, supervision.

ASK S✗ ✕ 🖶 ▱

# MINER

AAA ▼▼ Best Western Coach House Inn **SH**
(573) 471-9700. **$65-$130.** 220 S Interstate Dr. I-55, exit 67, just e, then 0.5 mi s on Interstate Dr (frontage road). Int corridors. **Pets:** Small. $25 one-time fee/room. Designated rooms, service with restrictions, supervision.

SAVE S✗ ✕ ⟲ 🖶 ▱ ⇌

▼▼ Drury Inn-Sikeston **SH**
(573) 471-4100. **$89-$128.** 2602 E Malone. I-55, exit 67, just sw. Int corridors. **Pets:** Accepted.

✕ &M ⟲ ⟨🌊⟩ 🖶 ▱ ⇌

▼▼ Pear Tree Inn by Drury-Sikeston **SH**
(573) 471-8660. **$60-$100.** 2602 E Malone Rear. I-55, exit 67, just sw. Ext corridors. **Pets:** Accepted.

ASK ✕ &M ⟲ ▱ ⇌

# MOBERLY

▼▼ Best Western Moberly Inn **SH**
(660) 263-6540. **$70-$105, 10 day notice.** 1200 Hwy 24 E. Jct US 24 and 63 business route. Int corridors. **Pets:** Small, dogs only. $30 one-time fee/room. Service with restrictions, supervision.

ASK S✗ ✕ &M 🖶 ▱ 🍴 ⇌

# MOUNTAIN GROVE

▼ Days Inn of Mountain Grove **SH**
(417) 926-5555. **$48-$64.** 300 E 19th St. Jct US 60 and 95, just se. Ext corridors. **Pets:** Accepted.

ASK S✗ ✕ ⇌

▼▼ TraveLodge **M**
(417) 926-3152. **$60-$70.** 111 E 17th St. Jct US 60 and 95, just s. Ext corridors. **Pets:** Accepted.

ASK S✗ ✕ ▱ ⇌

# MOUNT VERNON

▼▼ Super 8 **SH**
(417) 461-0230. **$63-$95.** 1200 E Industrial Blvd. I-44, exit 46, just n, then just se. Int corridors. **Pets:** Small. $10 one-time fee/pet. Service with restrictions, supervision.

ASK S✗ ✕ ⟨🌊⟩ 🖶 ⇌

# NEOSHO

▼▼ Super 8 Motel-Neosho **SH**
(417) 455-1888. **$52-$69.** 3085 Gardner/Edgewood Dr. Just s of jct US 60B and 71B. Int corridors. **Pets:** Small. $10 daily fee/pet. Designated rooms, no service, crate.

ASK S✗ ✕ ⟲ 🖶

# NEVADA

▼▼ Days Inn of Nevada **SH** 🐾
(417) 667-6777. **$49-$69.** 2345 Marvel Rd. US 71, exit Camp Clark, just w. Ext/int corridors. **Pets:** Small. $5 daily fee/pet. Designated rooms, service with restrictions, supervision.

ASK S✗ ✕ 🖶 ▱

◆ **Super 8 Motel** SH
(417) 667-8888. **$54-$57.** 2301 E Austin Blvd. US 71, exit Camp Clark, just w. Int corridors. **Pets:** Accepted.

ASK S$ ✕ 🖥 ⌇

## NEW FLORENCE

◆◆ **Days Inn Booneslick Lodge** SH
(573) 835-7777. **Call for rates.** 403 Booneslick Rd. I-70, exit 175, just w. Int corridors. **Pets:** Accepted.

ASK ✕ 🖥 ⌇

## OSAGE BEACH

▲▲▲ ◆◆ **Best Western Dogwood Hills Resort Inn** SH
(573) 348-1735. **$50-$110, 14 day notice.** 1252 State Hwy KK. 0.5 mi n, off US 54. Ext corridors. **Pets:** Accepted.

SAVE S$ ✕ 🖥 🖥 🍴 ⌇

◆◆ **Econo Lodge Lake of the Ozarks** M
(573) 348-1781. **$39-$129, 7 day notice.** 5760 Hwy 54. On US 54, 0.4 mi e of SR KK. Ext/int corridors. **Pets:** Medium, other species. $10 daily fee/pet, $20 one-time fee/pet. Designated rooms, service with restrictions, crate.

ASK S$ ✕ 🖥 🖥 ⌇

▲▲▲ ◆◆ **Lake Chateau Resort** M
(573) 348-2791. **$49-$139.** 5066 Hwy 54. Just s of Grand Glaize Bridge. Ext corridors. **Pets:** Accepted.

SAVE S$ ✕ 🖥 🖥 🍴 ⌇ ✕

▲▲▲ ◆ **Scottish Inns** M
(573) 348-3123. **$40-$95, 3 day notice.** 5404 Hwy 54. 1 mi w of Grand Glaize Bridge. Ext/int corridors. **Pets:** Small. $5 daily fee/pet. Designated rooms, service with restrictions, crate.

SAVE S$ ✕ ⌇

## PACIFIC

▲▲▲ ◆◆ **Quality Inn Near Six Flags** M
(636) 257-8400. **$70-$90.** 1400 W Osage St. I-44, exit 257, just se. Ext/int corridors. **Pets:** Medium. $15 daily fee/pet. Designated rooms, service with restrictions, crate.

SAVE S$ ✕ ⌧ 🖥 🖥 ⌇

## POPLAR BLUFF

◆◆ **Comfort Inn** SH
(573) 686-5200. **$75-$110.** 2582 N Westwood Blvd. 1.3 mi s from jct US 60 E. Int corridors. **Pets:** Medium, dogs only. $50 one-time fee/room. Designated rooms, service with restrictions, supervision.

ASK S$ ✕ ⌖M ⌖ 🖥 🖥 ⌇

◆◆ **Drury Inn-Poplar Bluff** SH
(573) 686-2451. **$90-$130.** 2220 N Westwood Blvd. On US 67, 1.4 mi s from jct US 60 E. Int corridors. **Pets:** Accepted.

ASK ✕ ⌧ 🖥 🖥 ⌇

◆ **Pear Tree Inn by Drury-Poplar Bluff** M
(573) 785-7100. **$65-$100.** 2218 N Westwood Blvd. On US 67, 1.4 mi s from jct US 60 E. Ext corridors. **Pets:** Accepted.

ASK ✕ ⌧ 🖥 ⌇

◆ **Super 8** SH
(573) 785-0176. **$52-$72.** 2831 N Westwood Blvd. On US 67, 0.8 mi s from jct US 60 E. Int corridors. **Pets:** Medium, dogs only. $25 one-time fee/room. Service with restrictions, supervision.

ASK S$ ✕ ⌧ 🖥

## POTOSI

◆ **Potosi Super 8** SH
(573) 438-8888. **$50-$59.** 820 E High St. Jct SR 8 and 21. Ext/int corridors. **Pets:** Other species. $10 daily fee/pet. Service with restrictions.

S$ ✕ 🖥

## REPUBLIC

◆◆ **AmericInn Lodge & Suites of Republic** SH ❀
(417) 732-5335. **Call for rates.** 950 Austin Ln. I-44, exit 67, 4.4 mi s to SR 174 (flashing red light/4-way stop), 0.7 mi e to Highland Park Town Center. Int corridors. **Pets:** Small. $50 deposit/room, $10 daily fee/pet. Designated rooms, service with restrictions, crate.

✕ 🖥 🖥 ⌇

## RICH HILL

▲▲▲ ◆ **Apache Motel** M
(417) 395-2161. **$38-$40.** Hwy 71 and B. Just e of jct US 71 and CR B. Ext corridors. **Pets:** Accepted.

SAVE S$ ✕

## ROLLA

▲▲▲ ◆◆ **AmeriHost Inn & Suites** SH
(573) 364-7000. **$95.** 1801 Martin Springs Dr. I-44, exit 184, just sw. Int corridors. **Pets:** Medium, dogs only. Service with restrictions.

SAVE S$ ✕ 🖥 🖥 ⌇

▲▲▲ ◆◆ **Best Western Coachlight** M
(573) 341-2511. **$64-$159.** 1403 Martin Springs Dr. Jct I-44 and Business Rt 44 S, exit 184. Ext corridors. **Pets:** Accepted.

SAVE S$ ✕ 🖥 🖥 ⌇

◆◆ **Drury Inn-Rolla** SH
(573) 364-4000. **$62-$110.** 2006 N Bishop. I-44, exit 186 (US 63), just ne. Ext/int corridors. **Pets:** Accepted.

ASK ✕ 🖥 🖥 ⌇

## ST. CLAIR

▲▲▲ ◆◆ **Budget Lodging** M
(636) 629-1000. **$69-$79.** 866 S Outer Rd W. I-44, exit 240, just w. Ext/int corridors. **Pets:** Other species. $10 daily fee/pet. Designated rooms, service with restrictions, supervision.

SAVE S$ ✕ 🖥 🖥 ⌇

## ST. JOSEPH

◆◆◆ **Drury Inn & Suites-St. Joseph** SH
(816) 364-4700. **$75-$115.** 4213 Frederick Blvd. I-29, exit 47. Int corridors. **Pets:** Accepted.

ASK ✕ ⌖M ⌧ 🖥 🖥 ⌇ ✕

▲▲▲ ◆◆ **Ramada Inn** LH ❀
(816) 233-6192. **$57-$81.** 4016 Frederick Blvd. I-29, exit 47. Int corridors. **Pets:** Other species. $25 one-time fee/room. Designated rooms, service with restrictions, supervision.

SAVE S$ ✕ 🖥 🖥 🍴 ⌇ ✕

◆◆◆ **St. Joseph Holiday Inn-Riverfront** LH
(816) 279-8000. **$84-$139, 3 day notice.** 102 S Third St. I-229, exit Edmond St northbound; exit Felix St southbound; downtown. Int corridors. **Pets:** Large. $10 daily fee/pet. Service with restrictions, supervision.

ASK S$ ✕ ⌖M ⌧ 🖥 🖥 🍴 ⌇ ✕

# ST. LOUIS METROPOLITAN AREA

## CHESTERFIELD

**◆◆◆ Homewood Suites by Hilton** SH
(636) 530-0305. **$79-$129.** 840 Chesterfield Pkwy W. I-64, exit 20, 1 mi n. Int corridors. **Pets:** Accepted.
ASK S⊘ ⊠ ⛊ 🔋 💻 ⇌

## CLAYTON

**◆◆◆ ◆◆◆◆ Crowne Plaza St Louis-Clayton** SH
(314) 726-5400. **$169-$189.** 7750 Carondelet Ave. I-64/US 40, exit 31 (Brentwood Blvd), 1.3 mi n, then 0.7 mi e. Int corridors. **Pets:** Designated rooms, service with restrictions, crate.
SAVE ⊠ ⛊ 🔋 💻 ⍾ ⇌ ⊠

**◆◆◆ ◆◆◆◆ The Ritz-Carlton, St. Louis** LH ❖
(314) 863-6300. **$224-$299.** 100 Carondelet Plaza. I-64, exit 32B, 1.2 mi n on Hanley Rd, then just e. Int corridors. **Pets:** Small. $125 one-time fee/room. Service with restrictions, supervision.
SAVE ⊠ ⛊ 🔋 ⍾ ⇌ ⊠

**◆◆◆ ◆◆◆◆ Sheraton Clayton Plaza Hotel** SH
(314) 863-0400. **$229, 3 day notice.** 7730 Bonhomme Ave. I-64/US 40, exit 31 (Brentwood Blvd), 1.3 mi n, then 0.7 mi e. Int corridors. **Pets:** Small. Service with restrictions, supervision.
SAVE S⊘ ⊠ ⛊ 🔋 💻 ⍾ ⇌

## CREVE COEUR

**◆◆◆◆ Drury Inn & Suites-Creve Coeur** SH
(314) 989-1100. **$95-$146.** 11980 Olive Blvd. I-270, exit 14 (Olive Blvd). Int corridors. **Pets:** Accepted.
ASK ⊠ ⟪M ⛊ 🔋 💻 ⇌

## EARTH CITY

**◆◆◆ Residence Inn St. Louis Airport/Earth City** SH
(314) 209-0995. **$134-$169.** 3290 Rider Tr S. I-70, exit 231B (Earth City Expwy N), exit 231B (Earth City Expwy N), just e. Int corridors. **Pets:** Accepted.
ASK ⊠ ⟪M ⛊ 🔋 💻 ⇌ ⊠

## EDMUNDSON

**◆◆◆ Drury Inn-St. Louis Airport** SH
(314) 423-7700. **$85-$145.** 10490 Natural Bridge Rd. I-70, exit 236 (Lambert Airport), just se. Int corridors. **Pets:** Accepted.
ASK ⊠ ⟪M ⛊ 🔋 💻 ⇌

## EUREKA

**◆◆◆ ◆◆◆◆ Holiday Inn at Six Flags** SH
(636) 938-6661. **$89-$229 (no credit cards), 3 day notice.** 4901 Six Flags Rd. I-44, exit 261 (Allenton Rd). Ext/int corridors. **Pets:** Accepted.
SAVE ⊠ 💻 ⍾ ⇌ ⊠

## FENTON

**◆◆◆◆ Drury Inn & Suites-Fenton** SH
(636) 343-7822. **$85-$120.** 1088 S Highway Dr. I-44, exit 274 (Bowles Ave), just se. Int corridors. **Pets:** Accepted.
ASK ⊠ ⛊ 🔋 💻 ⇌

**◆◆◆ Pear Tree Inn by Drury-Fenton** SH
(636) 343-8820. **$73-$103.** 1100 S Highway Dr. I-44, exit 274 (Bowles Ave), just s. Int corridors. **Pets:** Accepted.
ASK ⊠ ⛊ 🔋 💻 ⇌

**◆◆◆ TownePlace Suites by Marriott** SH
(636) 305-7000. **$83-$135.** 1662 Fenton Business Park Ct. I-44, exit 275 westbound; exit 274 eastbound to S Highway Dr, just s. Int corridors. **Pets:** Accepted.
ASK S⊘ ⊠ ⟪M ⛊ 🔋 💻 ⇌

## FORISTELL

**◆◆◆ ◆◆◆◆ Best Western West 70 Inn** SH
(636) 673-2900. **$73-$95, 10 day notice.** 12 Hwy W. I-70, exit 203 (CR W), just n. Int corridors. **Pets:** Large. $10 one-time fee/pet. Service with restrictions, supervision.
SAVE S⊘ ⊠ 🔋 💻 ⇌

## HAZELWOOD

**◆◆◆◆ La Quinta Inn St. Louis (Airport)** SH
(314) 731-3881. **$78-$115.** 5781 Campus Ct. I-270, exit 23 (McDonnell Blvd), just s. Int corridors. **Pets:** Medium. Service with restrictions.
⊠ ⛊ 🔋 💻 ⇌

## KIRKWOOD

**◆◆◆◆ Best Western Kirkwood Inn** SH ❖
(314) 821-3950. **$79-$129, 7 day notice.** 1200 S Kirkwood Rd. I-44, exit 277B (Lindbergh Blvd), just n. Int corridors. **Pets:** Medium, other species. $10 daily fee/pet. Designated rooms, service with restrictions, crate.
ASK S⊘ ⊠ ⛊ 🔋 💻 ⍾ ⇌

## MARYLAND HEIGHTS

**◆◆◆◆ Drury Inn & Suites-St. Louis-Westport** SH
(314) 576-9966. **$77-$118.** 12220 Dorsett Rd. I-270, exit 17 (Dorsett Rd), just se. Int corridors. **Pets:** Accepted.
ASK ⊠ ⛊ 🔋 💻 ⇌

**◆◆◆ ◆◆◆◆ Sheraton (West Port) Hotel-Lakeside Chalet** LH
(314) 878-1500. **$139-$159.** 191 Westport Plaza Dr. I-270, exit 16A (Page Ave), 0.8 mi e to Lackland Rd exit, just w to Craig Rd, then 0.4 mi n. Int corridors. **Pets:** Other species. Service with restrictions, crate.
SAVE S⊘ ⊠ ⟪M ⛊ 🔋 💻 ⍾ ⇌

**◆◆◆ ◆◆◆◆ The Sheraton (West Port) Plaza Tower** LH
(314) 878-1500. **$95-$125.** 900 Westport Plaza Dr. I-270, exit 16A (Page Ave), 0.8 mi e, exit Lackland Rd, just w to Craig Rd, then 0.4 mi n. Int corridors. **Pets:** Other species. Service with restrictions, crate.
SAVE S⊘ ⊠ ⟪M ⛊ 🔋 💻 ⍾ ⇌ ⊠

**◆◆◆◆ Staybridge Suites** SH
(314) 878-1555. **$142-$163.** 1855 Craigshire Rd. I-270, exit 16A (Page Ave), 0.8 mi e, exit Lackland Rd, 1 mi w, then s via Lackland and Craigshire rds. Ext/int corridors. **Pets:** Large. $100 one-time fee/pet. Service with restrictions, supervision.
⊠ ⛊ 🔋 💻 ⇌ ⊠

## MEHLVILLE

**◆◆◆◆ Holiday Inn St. Louis-South I-55** SH
(314) 894-0700. **$89-$175.** 4234 Butler Hill Rd. I-55, exit 195 (Butler Hill Rd), just se. Ext/int corridors. **Pets:** $50 deposit/room. Service with restrictions, supervision.
ASK S⊘ ⊠ ⛊ 🔋 💻 ⍾ ⇌ ⊠

## O'FALLON

**◆◆◆ ◆◆◆◆ Comfort Inn & Suites** SH
(636) 696-8000. **$89-$199.** 100 Comfort Inn Ct. I-70, exit 219, just sw. Int corridors. **Pets:** Medium, other species. $10 daily fee/pet. Designated rooms, service with restrictions, supervision.
SAVE S⊘ ⊠ ⛊ 🔋 💻 ⇌ ⊠

# A FAMILY VACATION SHOULD INCLUDE THE WHOLE FAMILY.

**Best Western Advantages:**

*Exclusive AAA Preferred Gold Crown Club® International frequent-guest program*

*Swimming pools at most locations*

*Continental or hot breakfast\**

*Fresh in-room coffee*

*Free high-speed internet access*

*Free local calls*

*Go to bestwestern.com for the complete list*

**AT OVER 1,900 BEST WESTERNS PETS ARE NOT ONLY ALLOWED, THEY'RE WELCOMED.**

Best Western® invites you to bring your pet on your next family trip. Your best friend will love being part of the fun, while the rest of you enjoy the 17 services and amenities that have made Best Western the choice for vacation travel.

Visit our website and click on "Trip Planner" to find one of our pet-friendly hotels. And plan your getaway today.

bestwestern.com | 1.800.WESTERN

**Best Western**

The World's Largest Hotel Chain®

# MAKE YOUR STAY MORE REWARDING.

**Best Western Advantages:**

**2,000+ AAA approved hotels in US, Canada & Caribbean**

**Continental or hot breakfast**

**Free high-speed internet access**

**Free local calls**

## MORE POINTS. LOW RATES.

Now your AAA membership is even more valuable at Best Western® when you join the new AAA Preferred Gold Crown Club® International frequent-guest program. Membership is free and offers exclusive benefits when you stay at Best Western, including 10% bonus points with every qualified stay. Points can be used toward free room nights, merchandise, airline miles, dining, shopping and entertainment gift cards, and much more. Best of all you always get the lowest rate available.

**bestwestern.com/aaa | 1.866.430.9022**
**Program Code: AAA/CAA  Over 1,100 AAA Offices**

The World's Largest Hotel Chain®

# RICHMOND HEIGHTS

▼▼▼▼ **Residence Inn By Marriott-St. Louis Galleria** 🆂🅷
(314) 862-1900. **$89-$179.** 1100 McMorrow Ave. I-170, exit 1C (Brentwood Ave) northbound; exit Brentwood Ave southbound, 0.5 mi e of Galleria via Galleria Pkwy. Ext corridors. **Pets:** Accepted.
[A$K] [✕] [🛏M] [🗩] [♿] [🛢] [🖵] [🐾] [🐾]

# ST. ANN

▼▼▼▼ **Hampton Inn-St. Louis Airport** 🆂🅷
(314) 429-2000. **$90-$140.** 10820 Pear Tree Ln. I-70, exit 236 (Airport Dr), just sw. Int corridors. **Pets:** Accepted.
[A$K] [✕] [🛢] [🖵] [🐾]

▼▼▼ **Pear Tree Inn-St. Louis Airport** 🆂🅷
(314) 427-3400. **$75-$130.** 10810 Pear Tree Ln. I-70, exit 236 (Airport Dr), just sw. Int corridors. **Pets:** Accepted.
[A$K] [✕] [🛢] [🖵] [🐾]

# ST. CHARLES

🅰🅰🅰 ▼▼▼▼ **Comfort Suites-St. Charles** 🆂🅷 ❄
(636) 949-0694. **$90-$120.** 1400 S 5th St. I-70, exit 229 (5th St), just ne. Int corridors. **Pets:** Service with restrictions, crate.
[SAVE] [🛏] [✕] [🗝] [🛢] [🖵] [🐾]

🅰🅰🅰 ▼▼▼ **Travelodge** 🆂🅷
(636) 949-8700. **$59-$69.** 2781 Veteran's Memorial Pkwy. I-70, exit 228 (First Capitol), 0.8 mi w on service road (Bogey Rd). Int corridors. **Pets:** Accepted.
[SAVE] [✕] [🛢] [🖵] [🐾]

# ST. LOUIS

▼▼▼▼ **Drury Inn & Suites-St. Louis-Convention Center** 🅻🅷
(314) 231-8100. **$96-$156.** 711 N Broadway. I-70, exit 250B, at convention center. Int corridors. **Pets:** Accepted.
[A$K] [✕] [🛢] [🖵] [🍴] [🐾] [🐾]

▼▼▼▼ **Drury Inn-St. Louis/Union Station** 🆂🅷
(314) 231-3900. **$100-$172.** 201 S 20th St. Just e of Jefferson Ave; between Market St and Clark Ave. Int corridors. **Pets:** Accepted.
[A$K] [✕] [🛏M] [🗝] [🛢] [🖵] [🍴] [🐾]

🅰🅰🅰 ▼▼▼▼ **Drury Plaza Hotel-St. Louis At the Arch** 🆂🅷
(314) 231-3003. **$105-$177.** 4th & Market St. I-70, 250B (Stadium/Memorial Dr), just w on Pine St to Broadway, just s to Walnut St, just e to Fourth St, then just n. Int corridors. **Pets:** Accepted.
[SAVE] [✕] [🛏M] [🗝] [🛢] [🖵] [🍴] [🐾]

▼▼▼▼ **Hampton Inn-St. Louis/Union Station** 🆂🅷
(314) 241-3200. **$100-$174.** 2211 Market St. I-64/US 40, exit 39, just n on Jefferson Ave, then just e. Int corridors. **Pets:** Accepted.
[A$K] [✕] [🛢] [🖵] [🍴] [🐾] [🐾]

🅰🅰🅰 ▼▼▼▼ **Hyatt Regency St. Louis At Union Station** 🅻🅷
(314) 231-1234. **$105-$219.** 1 St. Louis Union Station. Just e on Jefferson Ave, off US 40 at 18th and Market sts. Int corridors. **Pets:** Accepted.
[SAVE] [✕] [🗩] [🛢] [🖵] [🍴] [🐾]

▼▼▼▼ **Omni Majestic Hotel** 🆂🅷
(314) 436-2355. **$174-$204, 12 day notice.** 1019 Pine St. Between 10th and 11th sts. Int corridors. **Pets:** Medium. $50 one-time fee/room. Service with restrictions, crate.
[A$K] [🛏] [✕] [🗩] [🖵] [🍴]

▼▼▼ ▼▼▼ **Renaissance Grand Hotel St. Louis** 🅻🅷
(314) 621-9600. **$169-$219.** 800 Washington Ave. Across from Convention Center. Int corridors. **Pets:** Accepted.
[A$K] [✕] [🛏M] [🗩] [♿] [🛢] [🖵] [🍴] [🐾]

▼▼▼ ▼▼▼ **The Renaissance St. Louis Suites Hotel** 🆂🅷
(314) 621-9700. **$189-$229.** 827 Washington Ave. Next to America's Center (Convention Center). Int corridors. **Pets:** Accepted.
[A$K] [✕] [🛏M] [🗩] [♿] [🛢] [🖵] [🍴] [🐾]

🅰🅰🅰 ▼▼▼ **Sheraton St. Louis City Center Hotel & Suites** 🅻🅷 ❄
(314) 231-5007. **$299-$599.** 400 S 14th St. I-40, exit 39B (14th St), just ne. Int corridors. **Pets:** Medium, dogs only. Service with restrictions, supervision.
[SAVE] [🛏] [✕] [🗩] [♿] [🛢] [🖵] [🍴] [🐾] [🐾]

🅰🅰🅰 ▼▼▼ ▼▼▼ **The Westin St. Louis** 🅻🅷 ❄
(314) 621-2000. **$174-$379.** 811 Spruce St. Just w of Busch Stadium. Int corridors. **Pets:** Medium, other species. Service with restrictions.
[SAVE] [✕] [🛏M] [🗩] [♿] [🛢] [🖵] [🍴]

# ST. PETERS

▼▼▼▼ **Drury Inn-St. Charles/St. Peters** 🆂🅷
(636) 397-9700. **$86-$140.** 170 Westfield Dr. I-70, exit 222 (Mid Rivers Mall Dr), just se. Int corridors. **Pets:** Accepted.
[A$K] [✕] [🛏M] [🗩] [🛢] [🖵] [🐾]

# SUNSET HILLS

🅰🅰🅰 ▼▼▼▼ **Holiday Inn-Southwest & Viking Conference Center** 🆂🅷 ❄
(314) 821-6600. **$99-$200.** 10709 Watson Rd. I-44, exit 277B, just s. Int corridors. **Pets:** Small. $25 one-time fee/pet. Designated rooms, service with restrictions, supervision.
[SAVE] [🛏] [✕] [🗩] [♿] [🛢] [🖵] [🍴] [🐾] [🐾]

# VALLEY PARK

▼▼▼▼ **Drury Inn & Suites-St. Louis Southwest** 🆂🅷
(636) 861-8300. **$80-$140.** 5 Lambert Drury Pl. I-44, exit 272 (SR 141), just sw. Int corridors. **Pets:** Accepted.
[A$K] [✕] [🛢] [🖵] [🐾]

▼▼▼▼ **Hampton Inn-St. Louis Southwest** 🆂🅷
(636) 529-9020. **$96-$130.** 9 Lambert Drury Pl. I-44, exit 272 (SR 141), just sw. Int corridors. **Pets:** Accepted.
[A$K] [✕] [🛢] [🖵] [🐾]

---

# END METROPOLITAN AREA

---

# ST. ROBERT

🅰🅰🅰 ▼▼▼ **Best Western Montis Inn** 🅼
(573) 336-4299. **$55-$80.** 14086 Hwy Z. I-44, exit 163, just se. Ext corridors. **Pets:** Medium. Service with restrictions, crate.
[SAVE] [🛏] [✕] [🛢] [🖵] [🐾]

▼▼ **Motel 6 #4211** 🆂🅷
(573) 336-3610. **$43-$60.** 545 Hwy Z. I-44, exit 161, just s, then 0.3 mi e on frontage road. Int corridors. **Pets:** Other species. $100 deposit/room. Service with restrictions, crate.
[A$K] [🛏] [✕] [🛏M] [🛢] [🖵]

# SEDALIA

**Hotel Bothwell, A Clarion Collection** SH
(660) 826-5588. **$60-$185.** 103 E 4th St. Corner of 4th and S Ohio sts; downtown. Int corridors. **Pets:** Medium. $25 one-time fee/pet.

# SHELBINA

**Americas Best Value Inn** M
(573) 588-0020. **Call for rates.** 711 N Highway 15. US 36, exit SR 15, 0.3 mi n. Int corridors. **Pets:** Accepted.

# SPRINGFIELD

**Baymont Inn & Suites** SH
(417) 889-8188. **$78-$125.** 3776 S Glenstone Ave. On US 60. Int corridors. **Pets:** Medium. $25 one-time fee/room. Service with restrictions, supervision.

**Best Western Coach House Inn** SH
(417) 862-0701. **$59-$79.** 2535 N Glenstone Ave. I-44, exit 80A, just s. Ext corridors. **Pets:** Small, other species. Service with restrictions, supervision.

**Best Western Route 66 Rail Haven** M
(417) 866-1963. **$54-$74.** 203 S Glenstone Ave. I-44, exit 80A, 3 mi s. Ext corridors. **Pets:** Small, other species. $10 daily fee/room. Service with restrictions, crate.

**Clarion Hotel** SH
(417) 883-6550. **$60-$79.** 3333 S Glenstone Ave. On US 60 (James River Expwy), 0.5 mi n. Int corridors. **Pets:** Small, other species. $10 daily fee/pet. Service with restrictions, supervision.

**Crystal Suites** SH
(417) 886-5090. **$89-$109.** 1260 E Independence St. US 60 (James River Expwy), exit National Ave. Ext corridors. **Pets:** Small. $10 one-time fee/pet. Designated rooms, service with restrictions.

**Drury Inn & Suites-Springfield** SH
(417) 863-8400. **$88-$148.** 2715 N Glenstone Ave. I-44, exit 80A (Glenstone Ave), just s. Int corridors. **Pets:** Accepted.

**Holiday Inn Express Hotel & Suites** SH
(417) 862-0070. **$98-$169.** 1117 E St. Louis St. Just w of National Ave. Int corridors. **Pets:** Small. $20 one-time fee/room. Service with restrictions, supervision.

**Holiday Inn North** SH ♣
(417) 865-8600. **$99-$249.** 2720 N Glenstone Ave. I-44, exit 80A, just se. Int corridors. **Pets:** Medium, other species. $25 one-time fee/room.

**Krystal Aire-A Non-Smoking Hotel** SH
(417) 869-0001. **$61-$87.** 2745 N Glenstone Ave. I-44, exit 80A, just sw. Ext/int corridors. **Pets:** Accepted.

**La Quinta Inn Springfield** SH
(417) 520-8800. **$69-$99.** 1610 E Evergreen. I-44, exit 80A. Int corridors. **Pets:** Small, other species. Designated rooms, service with restrictions, supervision.

**Quality Inn & Suites** SH
(417) 888-0898. **$62-$72.** 3930 S Overland Ave. US 60 (James River Expwy), exit Kansas Expwy, just n to Chesterfield Blvd, then just w. Int corridors. **Pets:** Small. $25 deposit/pet, $10 daily fee/pet. Designated rooms, service with restrictions, supervision.

**Residence Inn-Springfield** SH
(417) 890-0020. **$99-$179.** 1303 E Kingsley St. James River Expwy, exit National St, just s, then just e. Int corridors. **Pets:** Other species. $75 one-time fee/room. Service with restrictions, supervision.

**Sleep Inn of Springfield** SH
(417) 886-2464. **$50-$85.** 233 E Camino Alto. US 60 (James River Expwy), exit Campbell Ave, just se. Int corridors. **Pets:** Other species. $10 daily fee/pet. Designated rooms, service with restrictions, supervision.

**University Plaza Hotel and Convention Center** LH
(417) 864-7333. **$89-$149, 7 day notice.** 333 John Q Hammons Pkwy. 0.5 mi e on St. Louis St. Int corridors. **Pets:** Small, other species. $10 daily fee/pet. Designated rooms, service with restrictions, crate.

# SWEET SPRINGS

**People's Choice Motel** M
(660) 335-6315. **$34-$37.** 1001 N Locust St. I-70, exit 66, just se. Ext corridors. **Pets:** $20 deposit/room. Service with restrictions, supervision.

**Super 8 Motel** SH
(660) 335-4888. **$54.** 208 W 40 Hwy. I-70, exit 66, just se. Int corridors. **Pets:** Accepted.

# TRENTON

**Super 8 Motel** SH
(660) 359-2988. **$49-$75.** 1845A E 28th St. US 65, 1 mi n of jct SR 6 and US 65. Int corridors. **Pets:** Accepted.

# UNION

**Super 8 Motel** SH
(636) 583-8808. **$73-$109.** 1015 E Main St. I-44, exit 247 (US 50), 4.7 mi w; just w of jct SR 47. Int corridors. **Pets:** Dogs only. $8 daily fee/pet. Service with restrictions, supervision.

# WARSAW

**Super 8 Motel-Warsaw** SH
(660) 438-2882. **$60-$93.** 1603 Commercial St. US 65 and SR 7, exit Clinton. Ext corridors. **Pets:** Medium, dogs only. $40 deposit/pet, $5 one-time fee/pet. Service with restrictions, supervision.

# WASHINGTON

**Sleep Inn & Suites** SH
(636) 390-8877. **$80-$150.** 4104 S Point Rd. I-44, exit 251, 8.5 mi w on SR 100 to S Point Rd. Int corridors. **Pets:** Medium. $25 daily fee/pet. Designated rooms, service with restrictions, supervision.

**Super 8 Washington** SH
(636) 390-0088. **$70-$130.** 2081 Eckelkamp Ct. I-44, exit 251, 10 mi, w on SR 100; just s of SR 100 and 47. Int corridors. **Pets:** Small, dogs only. $35 deposit/room, $10 daily fee/pet. Service with restrictions, supervision.

# WEST PLAINS

▼▼ **Ramada Inn** 🆂🅷
(417) 256-8191. **$59-$77.** 1301 Preacher Roe Blvd. US 63, exit US 160 Gainsville, just s. Ext/int corridors. **Pets:** Other species. $10 daily fee/pet. Service with restrictions, supervision.
🅰🅢🅚 🆂🔟 ❌ 🔲 🔳 🍽 〰

▼▼ **Super 8 Motel-West Plains** 🆂🅷
(417) 256-8088. **$42-$75.** 1210 Porter Wagoner Blvd. On US 63B, 0.8 mi s of jct US 63. Int corridors. **Pets:** Small, other species. $25 one-time fee/room. Service with restrictions, supervision.
🅰🅢🅚 🆂🔟 ❌

# MONTANA

## ALBERTON

**▲▲▲ ▼▼ The Ghost Rails Inn** BB
(406) 722-4990. **$59-$69.** 702 Railroad Ave. Downtown. Int corridors. **Pets:** Accepted.
[SAVE] [S▲] [✕] [K] [✆]

## BELGRADE

**▼▼▼▼ Gallatin River Lodge** CI
(406) 388-0148. **$170-$270, 7 day notice.** 9105 Thorpe Rd. I-90, exit 298, 2.7 mi s on SR 85, 1 mi w on Valley Center Rd (gravel), then 0.5 mi s, follow sign. Int corridors. **Pets:** Other species. $25 daily fee/pet. Designated rooms, crate.
[ASK] [✕] [¶] [✕] [K]

**▲▲▲ ▼▼▼▼ Holiday Inn Express** SH
(406) 388-0800. **$69-$149.** 6261 Jackrabbit Ln. I-90, exit 298, just s on SR 85. Int corridors. **Pets:** Accepted.
[SAVE] [S▲] [✕] [&M] [&] [🛏] [▭] [¶]

**▲▲▲ ▼▼▼▼ La Quinta Inn & Suites Belgrade (Bozeman/Belgrade)** SH
(406) 388-2222. **$59-$139.** 6445 Jackrabbit Ln. I-90, exit 298, just s on SR 85. Int corridors. **Pets:** Service with restrictions, supervision.
[SAVE] [S▲] [✕] [&] [🛏] [▭] [🏊] [✕]

**▲▲▲ ▼▼▼▼ Super 8 Motel-Belgrade/Bozeman Airport** SH
(406) 388-1493. **$59-$79.** 6450 Jackrabbit Ln. I-90, exit 298, just s. Int corridors. **Pets:** Accepted.
[SAVE] [S▲] [✕] [🛏] [🏊]

## BIGFORK

**▲▲▲ ▼▼▼▼ Mountain Lake Lodge** SH
(406) 837-3800. **$89-$265, 7 day notice.** 1950 Sylvan Dr. On US 35, 5 mi s. Ext corridors. **Pets:** Medium. $15 daily fee/pet. Designated rooms, service with restrictions.
[SAVE] [S▲] [✕] [&M] [🛏] [▭] [¶] [🏊] [✕]

**▲▲▲ ▼▼ Timbers Motel** M
(406) 837-6200. **$52-$118, 7 day notice.** 8540 Hwy 35. Just n on US 35 from jct SR 209. Ext corridors. **Pets:** $10 one-time fee/room. Supervision.
[SAVE] [✕] [&] [▭] [🏊]

## BIG SKY

**▲▲▲ ▼▼▼▼ 320 Guest Ranch** RA
(406) 995-4283. **$100-$338, 30 day notice.** 205 Buffalo Horn Creek Rd. 11.8 mi s on US 191; in Gallatin National Forest. Ext corridors. **Pets:** Other species. $10 daily fee/pet. Service with restrictions, supervision.
[SAVE] [S▲] [✕] [🛏] [▭] [¶] [✕] [K]

**▲▲▲ ▼▼▼▼ Best Western Buck's T-4 Lodge** SH
(406) 995-4111. **$80-$149, 7 day notice.** 46625 Gallatin Rd. US 191, 1 mi s of Big Sky entrance. Ext/int corridors. **Pets:** Large, other species. $10 daily fee/pet. Service with restrictions, supervision.
[SAVE] [S▲] [✕] [&] [🛏] [▭] [¶] [✕]

**▲▲▲ ▼▼▼▼ Rainbow Ranch Lodge** M 🐾
(406) 995-4132. **$185-$295.** 42950 Gallatin Rd. 5 mi s on US 191. Ext corridors. **Pets:** Other species. $40 daily fee/room. Service with restrictions, supervision.
[SAVE] [S▲] [✕] [¶] [✕] [K]

## BIG TIMBER

**▼▼ Big Timber Super 8 Motel** SH
(406) 932-8888. **$54-$94.** 20A Big Timber Loop Rd. I-90, exit 367. Int corridors. **Pets:** Dogs only. $5 daily fee/pet. Designated rooms, service with restrictions, supervision.
[ASK] [S▲] [✕] [&M] [🖨] [🛏]

**▼▼ River Valley Inn** M
(406) 932-4943. **$64-$84.** 600 W 2nd St. I-90, exit 367, just n, then 0.6 mi e. Int corridors. **Pets:** Small. $10 one-time fee/room. Service with restrictions, supervision.
[✕] [🛏]

## BILLINGS

**▼▼▼ Best Western Billings** SH
(406) 248-9800. **$85-$125.** 5610 S Frontage Rd. I-90, exit 446, just s. Ext/int corridors. **Pets:** Service with restrictions, supervision.
[ASK] [S▲] [✕] [&M] [&] [🛏] [▭] [🏊]

**▲▲▲ ▼▼▼ Best Western Clocktower Inn** SH 🐾
(406) 259-5511. **$84-$110.** 2511 1st Ave N. On I-90 business loop; downtown. Ext/int corridors. **Pets:** Large. $10 daily fee/room. Service with restrictions, supervision.
[SAVE] [S▲] [✕] [🖨] [🛏] [▭] [¶] [🏊]

**▼▼▼ Billings Hotel and Convention Center** SH
(406) 248-7151. **$109-$119.** 1223 Mullowney Ln. I-90, exit 446, just s. Int corridors. **Pets:** Medium. $10 one-time fee/pet. Designated rooms, service with restrictions, crate.
[ASK] [S▲] [✕] [🛏] [▭] [¶] [🏊] [✕]

**▼▼▼ Billings Super 8 Motel** SH
(406) 248-8842. **$57-$87.** 5400 Southgate Dr. I-90, exit 447, just n on S Billings Blvd, 0.8 mi w on King Ave, then just s on Parkway Ln. Int corridors. **Pets:** Accepted.
[ASK] [S▲] [✕] [&M] [🖨] [🛏] [▭]

**▲▲▲ ▼▼▼ Cherry Tree Inn** M
(406) 252-5603. **$55-$65.** 823 N Broadway. I-90, exit 450, 2 mi n on 27th St, then just w on 9th Ave. Int corridors. **Pets:** Other species. Service with restrictions, supervision.
[SAVE] [S▲] [✕] [🛏] [▭]

**▼▼▼ Comfort Inn by Choice Hotels** SH
(406) 652-5200. **$85-$105.** 2030 Overland Ave. I-90, exit 446, 0.5 mi n, then just s. Int corridors. **Pets:** Other species. $15 one-time fee/room. Service with restrictions, supervision.
[ASK] [S▲] [✕] [&M] [🖨] [🛏] [▭] [🏊]

▽▽ **Days Inn** 🆂🅷
(406) 252-4007. **$63-$129.** 843 Parkway Ln. I-90, exit 447, just n on S Billings Blvd, 0.8 mi w on King Ave, then just s. Int corridors. **Pets:** Accepted.
🅰️$🅺 🆂🔟 ☒ 🔧 🎗 🔋 ▣

▽ **Dude Rancher Lodge** Ⓜ
(406) 259-5561. **$55-$90.** 415 N 29th St. Just w of the 400 block of N 27th st; downtown. Ext/int corridors. **Pets:** Large, other species. $5 daily fee/room. Designated rooms, service with restrictions, supervision.
🅰️$🅺 🆂🔟 ☒ 🔋 ▣ 🍴

▲▲▲ ▽ **Hilltop Inn** 🆂🅷 ❀
(406) 245-5000. **$62-$72.** 1116 N 28th St. I-90, exit 450, 2 mi n, just w on 11th Ave, then just n. Int corridors. **Pets:** Other species. $5 daily fee/pet. Designated rooms, service with restrictions, supervision.
🆂🅰🆅🅴 🆂🔟 ☒ 🔧🅼 🔋 ▣

▲▲▲ ▽▽▽▽ **Holiday Inn Grand Montana Billings** 🅻🅷
(406) 248-7701. **$76-$109.** 5500 Midland Rd. I-90, exit 446. Int corridors. **Pets:** Accepted.
🆂🅰🆅🅴 ☒ 🔧🅼 ☁ 🎗 🔋 ▣ 🍴 ⤳ ☒

▽▽ **Howard Johnson Express Inn** 🆂🅷 ❀
(406) 248-4656. **$50-$89.** 1001 S 27th St. I-90, exit 450, just n on SR 3 (S 27th St). Int corridors. **Pets:** Other species. $50 deposit/room. Designated rooms, service with restrictions, supervision.
🅰️$🅺 🆂🔟 ☒ 🔧🅼 ☁ 🎗 🔋 ▣

▽ **Kelly Inn** 🆂🅷
(406) 252-2700. **$62-$99.** 5425 Midland Rd. I-90, exit 446, just se. Ext/int corridors. **Pets:** Service with restrictions, supervision.
🅰️$🅺 🆂🔟 ☒ 🎗 🔋 ▣ ⤳

▽ **Motel 6 #178** Ⓜ
(406) 252-0093. **$39-$57.** 5400 Midland Rd. I-90, exit 446, just se. Ext corridors. **Pets:** Accepted.
🆂🔟 ☒ 🔧🅼 ☁ 🎗

▽▽▽ **Quality Inn Homestead** 🆂🅷
(406) 652-1320. **$61-$97.** 2036 Overland Ave. I-90, exit 446, n on King Ave W, then just s, first stoplight. Int corridors. **Pets:** Large. $50 deposit/room. Service with restrictions, supervision.
🅰️$🅺 🆂🔟 ☒ 🔋 ▣ ⤳ ☒

▽▽ **Red Roof Inn #269** 🆂🅷
(406) 248-7551. **$42-$68.** 5353 Midland Rd. I-90, exit 446, just se. Int corridors. **Pets:** Accepted.
☒ 🔧🅼 ☁ 🎗 🔋 ▣

▲▲▲ ▽▽ **Rimview Inn** Ⓜ
(406) 248-2622. **$62-$75.** 1025 N 27th St. I-90, exit 450, 2 mi n. Ext/int corridors. **Pets:** Dogs only. $10 daily fee/pet. Service with restrictions, supervision.
🆂🅰🆅🅴 ☒ 🔋

▲▲▲ ▽▽▽ **Riverstone Billings Inn** 🆂🅷 ❀
(406) 252-6800. **$62-$72.** 880 N 29th St. I-90, exit 27th St, 2 mi n, then just w on 9th Ave. Int corridors. **Pets:** Other species. $5 daily fee/pet. Service with restrictions, supervision.
🆂🅰🆅🅴 🆂🔟 ☒ 🔋 ▣

▽▽▽▽ **Sheraton Downtown Billings Hotel** 🅻🅷
(406) 252-7400. **$89-$99.** 27 N 27th St. I-90 business loop and SR 3. Int corridors. **Pets:** Accepted.
🅰️$🅺 🆂🔟 ☒ 🎗 🔧 🔋 ▣ 🍴 ⤳ ☒

▲▲▲ ▽▽▽ **Western Executive Inn** 🆂🅷
(406) 294-8888. **$57-$100.** 3121 King Ave W. I-90, exit 446, 2.5 mi w. Int corridors. **Pets:** Service with restrictions, supervision.
🆂🅰🆅🅴 🆂🔟 ☒ 🔧🅼 🎗 🔋 ▣

# BOZEMAN

▽▽ **Americas Best Value Inn** 🆂🅷
(406) 585-7888. **$51-$85.** 817 Wheat Dr. I-90, exit 306, just n. Int corridors. **Pets:** Accepted.
🅰️$🅺 ☒ 🔧🅼 🎗 🔋 ⤳

▽▽▽ **AmericInn Lodge & Suites** 🆂🅷
(406) 522-8686. **$89-$169.** 1121 Reeves Rd W. I-90, exit 305, just n. Int corridors. **Pets:** Accepted.
🅰️$🅺 ☒ 🔧🅼 🎗 🔋 ▣ ⤳ ☒

▲▲▲ ▽▽▽▽ **Best Western GranTree Inn** 🆂🅷
(406) 587-5261. **$89-$149.** 1325 N 7th Ave. I-90, exit 306, just s. Int corridors. **Pets:** Designated rooms, service with restrictions, supervision.
🆂🅰🆅🅴 🆂🔟 ☒ 🎗 🔋 ▣ 🍴 ⤳

▽▽ **Bozeman Days Inn** 🆂🅷 ❀
(406) 587-5251. **$59-$179.** 1321 N 7th Ave. I-90, exit 306, just s. Int corridors. **Pets:** Other species. $10 daily fee/pet. Service with restrictions, crate.
🅰️$🅺 🆂🔟 ☒ 🔧🅼 🎗 🔋 ▣ ⤳ ☒

▲▲▲ ▽▽▽ **Bozeman Inn** Ⓜ
(406) 587-3176. **$40-$80.** 1235 N 7th Ave. I-90, exit 306, just s. Ext corridors. **Pets:** $5 one-time fee/room. Service with restrictions, crate.
🆂🅰🆅🅴 🆂🔟 ☒ 🔋 ▣

▽▽ **Bozeman Super 8** 🆂🅷
(406) 586-1521. **$59-$89.** 800 Wheat Dr. I-90, exit 306, just n, then just w. Int corridors. **Pets:** $5 one-time fee/room. Supervision.
🅰️$🅺 🆂🔟 ☒

▲▲▲ ▽▽▽ **Bozeman's Western Heritage Inn** 🆂🅷 ❀
(406) 586-8534. **$58-$103, 7 day notice.** 1200 E Main St. I-90 business loop, exit 309, 0.5 mi w. Int corridors. **Pets:** Dogs only. $5 daily fee/pet. Service with restrictions, supervision.
🆂🅰🆅🅴 🆂🔟 ☒ 🔋 ▣ ☒

▲▲▲ ▽▽▽▽ **Holiday Inn Bozeman** 🆂🅷 ❀
(406) 587-4561. **$89-$129.** 5 Baxter Ln. I-90, exit 306, just s of ject I-90. Int corridors. **Pets:** Medium. $50 deposit/pet. Designated rooms, service with restrictions, crate.
🆂🅰🆅🅴 ☒ 🎗 🔋 ▣ ▣ 🍴 ⤳ ☒

▽▽ **Microtel Inn & Suites** 🆂🅷
(406) 586-3797. **$59-$79, 14 day notice.** 612 Nikles Dr. I-90, exit 306, just ne. Int corridors. **Pets:** $10 one-time fee/room. Supervision.
🅰️$🅺 🆂🔟 ☒ 🎗 🔋 ▣

▲▲▲ ▽▽ **Rainbow Motel** Ⓜ
(406) 587-4201. **$48-$70.** 510 N 7th Ave. I-90, exit 306, 0.8 mi s. Ext corridors. **Pets:** Accepted.
🆂🅰🆅🅴 ☒ 🔋 ▣ ⤳

▽▽ **Ramada Limited** Ⓜ
(406) 585-2626. **$75-$100.** 2020 Wheat Dr. I-90, exit 306, just n, then just w. Int corridors. **Pets:** Small, dogs only. $10 one-time fee/pet. Service with restrictions, supervision.
🅰️$🅺 🆂🔟 ☒ 🔋 ▣ ⤳

▲▲▲ ▽▽▽ **Royal "7" Budget Inn** Ⓜ
(406) 587-3103. **$45-$67.** 310 N 7th Ave. I-90, exit 306, 0.8 mi s. Ext corridors. **Pets:** $2 daily fee/pet. Designated rooms, service with restrictions, supervision.
🆂🅰🆅🅴 🆂🔟 ☒ 🔋 ▣ ⤳

# BROWNING

▲▲▲ ▽▽ **Western Motel LLC** Ⓜ
(406) 338-7572. **$45-$98.** 121 Central Ave E. On US 2; center. Ext corridors. **Pets:** Accepted.
🆂🅰🆅🅴 🆂🔟 ☒ 🔋

# BUTTE

**(AAA) ▼▼▼ Best Western Butte Plaza Inn** SH
(406) 494-3500. **$80-$115.** 2900 Harrison Ave. I-90/15, exit 127 (Harrison Ave). Int corridors. **Pets:** Other species. $50 deposit/pet. Designated rooms, service with restrictions, supervision.
SAVE S6 ✕ 🛏 🖵 ⍾ 🏊 ✕

**▼ ▼ Comfort Inn of Butte** SH
(406) 494-8850. **$99.** 2777 Harrison Ave. I-90/15, exit 127 (Harrison Ave), just s. Int corridors. **Pets:** Accepted.
ASK S6 ✕ ⍾ ⌨ 🛏 🖵 🏊 ✕

**(AAA) ▼▼ Copper King Lodge & Convention Center** SH
(406) 494-6666. **$80-$95.** 4655 Harrison Ave S. I-90/15, exit 127A (Harrison Ave), 2 mi s on SR 2. Int corridors. **Pets:** Accepted.
SAVE S6 ✕ &M 🛏 🖵 ⍾ 🏊 ✕

**▼ ▼ Days Inn** SH
(406) 494-7000. **$80-$100, 7 day notice.** 2700 Harrison Ave. I-90/15, exit 127 (Harrison Ave), just n. Int corridors. **Pets:** Accepted.
ASK S6 ✕ &M ⍾ ⌨ 🛏 🖵 🏊

**(AAA) ▼▼ Red Lion Hotel** SH 🐾
(406) 494-7800. **$72-$109.** 2100 Cornell Ave. I-90/15, exit 127B (Harrison Ave), just n, then just e. Int corridors. **Pets:** Large, other species. $10 deposit/room. Service with restrictions.
SAVE S6 ✕ ⍾ ⌨ 🛏 🖵 ⍾ 🏊 ✕

**(AAA) ▼▼ Rocker Inn** M
(406) 723-5464. **$46-$57.** 122001 W Brown's Gulch Rd. I-90/15, exit 122 (Rocker). Int corridors. **Pets:** Medium. $5 daily fee/room. Designated rooms, service with restrictions, supervision.
SAVE ✕ 🛏

**(AAA) ▼▼ Super 8 Motel of Butte** SH
(406) 494-6000. **$62-$84, 5 day notice.** 2929 Harrison Ave. I-90/15, exit 127 (Harrison Ave), just s. Int corridors. **Pets:** Large. $50 deposit/pet, $5 daily fee/pet. Designated rooms, service with restrictions, supervision.
SAVE S6 ✕

# CHINOOK

**(AAA) ▼▼ Chinook Motor Inn** SH
(406) 357-2248. **$65-$69.** 100 Indiana St. On US 2. Int corridors. **Pets:** Accepted.
SAVE S6 ✕ 🖵 ⍾

# CHOTEAU

**(AAA) ▼ Big Sky Motel** M
(406) 466-5318. **$55.** 209 S Main Ave. Just s of town center on US 89. Ext corridors. **Pets:** Other species. Service with restrictions, supervision.
SAVE S6 ✕ 🛏

**(AAA) ▼▼ Stage Stop Inn** SH 🐾
(406) 466-5900. **$73-$120.** 1005 Main Ave N. N of town center on US 89. Int corridors. **Pets:** $25 daily fee/room.
SAVE S6 ✕ ⌨ 🛏 🏊

# COLSTRIP

**▼ ▼ Super 8 Motel of Colstrip LLC** M
(406) 748-3400. **$56-$70.** 6227 Main St. SR 39. Int corridors. **Pets:** $5 daily fee/room. Designated rooms, service with restrictions, supervision.
ASK S6 ✕ 🛏 🖵

# COLUMBIA FALLS

**(AAA) ▼▼▼ Meadow Lake Resort** CO
(406) 892-8700. **$95-$165, 30 day notice.** 100 St Andrews Dr. Jct US 2 and SR 40, 1.4 mi e on US 2, 1.1 mi n on Meadow Lake Blvd. Ext/int corridors. **Pets:** Accepted.
SAVE S6 ✕ 🛏 🖵 ⍾ 🏊 ✕

# COLUMBUS

**▼ ▼ Super 8 of Columbus** SH
(406) 322-4101. **$55-$75.** 602 8th Ave N. I-90, exit 408, just s on SR 78. Int corridors. **Pets:** Medium, other species. $5 daily fee/pet. Service with restrictions, supervision.
ASK S6 ✕ &M ⍾ ⌨ 🛏 🖵

# CONRAD

**▼ Super 8 Motel** SH
(406) 278-7676. **$55-$75.** 215 N Main. I-15, exit 339, just w. Int corridors. **Pets:** Accepted.
ASK S6 ✕ ⍾ 🛏 🖵

# CUT BANK

**(AAA) ▼▼ Glacier Gateway Inn** SH
(406) 873-5544. **$55-$85.** 1121 E Railroad St. US 2, just e from town center. Int corridors. **Pets:** Dogs only. $5 one-time fee/pet. Service with restrictions, supervision.
SAVE S6 ✕ 🛏

# DEER LODGE

**(AAA) ▼ Scharf's Motor Inn** M
(406) 846-2810. **$70-$80.** 819 Main St. I-90, exit 187, on I-90 business loop; downtown. Ext corridors. **Pets:** Accepted.
SAVE S6 ✕ 🛏

**(AAA) ▼▼ Super 8 Motel** M
(406) 846-2370. **$60-$85.** 1150 N Main St. I-90, exit 184, 0.3 mi s. Int corridors. **Pets:** Accepted.
SAVE S6 ✕ 🛏 🖵

**▼ Western Big Sky Inn** M
(406) 846-2590. **$44-$60.** 210 N Main St. I-90, exit 184, 1 mi w. Ext corridors. **Pets:** Designated rooms, service with restrictions, supervision.
ASK ✕ 🛏 🖵

# DILLON

**(AAA) ▼▼ Best Western Paradise Inn** M
(406) 683-4214. **$51-$79.** 650 N Montana St. I-15, exit 63, 0.3 mi s on SR 41. Ext corridors. **Pets:** Accepted.
SAVE S6 ✕ 🖵 ⍾ 🏊

**▼ ▼ Comfort Inn of Dillon** M
(406) 683-6831. **$65-$99.** 450 N Interchange. I-15, exit 63. Int corridors. **Pets:** Accepted.
ASK S6 ✕ ⍾ 🛏 🖵 🏊

**(AAA) ▼ Dillon Beaverhead Inn** M 🐾
(406) 683-6600. **$52-$82.** 20 Swenson Way. I-15, exit 63, just e, then just s. Ext corridors. **Pets:** Small, dogs only. $5 one-time fee/pet. Designated rooms, service with restrictions, supervision.
SAVE S6 ✕ &M ⌨ 🛏 🖵

**▼▼▼ GuestHouse International Inns & Suites** SH
(406) 683-3636. **$69-$119.** 580 Sinclair St. I-15, exit 63. Int corridors. **Pets:** Accepted.
ASK S6 ✕ &M ⌨ 🛏 🖵 🏊

**(AAA) ▼ Sundowner Motel** M
(406) 683-2375. **$38-$43.** 500 N Montana St. I-15, exit 63, just s. Ext corridors. **Pets:** Accepted.
SAVE ✕ 🛏

**▼▼ Super 8 Motel** M
(406) 683-4288. **$57-$77, 10 day notice.** 550 N Montana St. I-15, exit 63, just n on US 91. Int corridors. **Pets:** Dogs only. $50 deposit/pet, $10 daily fee/pet. Designated rooms, service with restrictions, supervision.
ASK S6 ✕ 🛏

# EAST GLACIER PARK

**Dancing Bears Inn LLC** M
(406) 226-4402. **$55-$146.** 40 Montana Ave. Just off US 2, follow signs; center. Ext/int corridors. **Pets:** Other species. $10 daily fee/pet. Supervision.

# ENNIS

**Fan Mountain Inn** M
(406) 682-5200. **$46-$75, 7 day notice.** 204 N Main. US 287, just nw of city center. Ext corridors. **Pets:** Accepted.

**Sportsman's** CA
(406) 682-4242. **$60-$100, 10 day notice.** 310 US Hwy 287 N. US 287, just nw of city center. Ext corridors. **Pets:** Accepted.

# FORSYTH

**Best Western Sundowner Inn** M
(406) 346-2115. **$69-$85.** 1018 Front St. I-94, exit 95, 0.5 mi nw on north frontage road. Ext corridors. **Pets:** $10 daily fee/room. Service with restrictions, supervision.

**Rails Inn Motel** SH
(406) 346-2242. **$64-$69, 3 day notice.** 3rd & Front sts. I-94, exit 93, just n, then 0.5 mi e on frontage road. Int corridors. **Pets:** $50 deposit/room, $5 daily fee/pet. Service with restrictions, supervision.

**Restwel Motel** M
(406) 346-2771. **$50-$62.** 810 Front St. I-94, exit 95, 0.8 mi nw on north frontage road Ext corridors. **Pets:** Medium. $5 daily fee/pet. Designated rooms, service with restrictions, supervision.

**Westwind Motor Inn** M
(406) 346-2038. **$54-$60, 3 day notice.** 225 Westwind Ln. I-94, exit 93, 0.3 mi n. Int corridors. **Pets:** $50 deposit/room, $5 daily fee/pet. Service with restrictions, supervision.

# GARDINER

**Best Western by Mammoth Hot Springs** SH
(406) 848-7311. **$69-$149, 3 day notice.** S Hwy 89. 0.5 mi n. Ext/int corridors. **Pets:** Accepted.

**Travelodge Yellowstone Park North** M
(406) 848-7520. **$40-$95, 3 day notice.** 109 Hellroaring St. North entrance, just s on US 89, 0.5 mi n of Yellowstone north gate. Ext corridors. **Pets:** Small, dogs only. $10 one-time fee/pet. Service with restrictions, supervision.

**Yellowstone River Motel** M
(406) 848-7303. **$48-$88.** 14 E Park St. Just e of US 89. Ext corridors. **Pets:** Other species. $5 one-time fee/room. Service with restrictions, supervision.

**Yellowstone Super 8-Gardiner** SH
(406) 848-7401. **$49-$109.** Hwy 89 S. On US 89. Int corridors. **Pets:** Other species. $5 daily fee/pet. Designated rooms, service with restrictions, supervision.

# GLASGOW

**Cottonwood Inn** SH
(406) 228-8213. **$60-$80.** 45 1st Ave NE. 0.5 mi e on US 2. Int corridors. **Pets:** Other species. Designated rooms, service with restrictions, supervision.

# GLENDIVE

**Best Western Glendive Inn** SH
(406) 377-5555. **$75-$105, 10 day notice.** 223 N Merrill Ave. I-94, exit 215, on I-94 business loop; downtown. Ext/int corridors. **Pets:** Accepted.

**Super 8 Glendive** M
(406) 365-5671. **$51-$81.** 1904 Merrill Ave. I-94, exit 215, just n. Int corridors. **Pets:** Other species. $5 one-time fee/room. Service with restrictions, supervision.

# GREAT FALLS

**Best Western Heritage Inn** SH
(406) 761-1900. **$89-$109.** 1700 Fox Farm Rd. I-15, exit 278, 0.8 mi e on 10th Ave S and US 87/89 and SR 3/200. Int corridors. **Pets:** Medium. Designated rooms, service with restrictions, supervision.

**Comfort Inn by Choice Hotels** SH
(406) 454-2727. **$95-$115.** 1120 9th St S. I-15, exit 278, 3 mi e on 10th Ave S and US 87/89 and SR 3/200, then just s. Int corridors. **Pets:** Accepted.

**Crystal Inn** SH
(406) 727-7788. **$59-$109.** 3701 31st St SW. I-15, exit 277, just e. Int corridors. **Pets:** Other species. $10 daily fee/pet. Designated rooms, service with restrictions, supervision.

**Days Inn of Great Falls** M
(406) 727-6565. **$64-$89.** 101 14th Ave NW. I-15, exit 280 (Central Ave), 1.3 mi e on Central Ave/Business Rt I-15, 0.8 mi n on 3rd St NW, then just w. Int corridors. **Pets:** Dogs only. $5 daily fee/room. Designated rooms, service with restrictions, supervision.

**The Great Falls Inn** SH ❀
(406) 453-6000. **$68-$74.** 1400 28th St S. I-15, exit 278, 5.3 mi e on 10th Ave S, 0.3 mi s on 26th St S, then just e on 15th Ave S. Int corridors. **Pets:** $5 daily fee/pet. Designated rooms, supervision.

**Great Falls Super 8 Motel** SH
(406) 727-7600. **$45-$90.** 1214 13th St S. I-15, exit 278, 2.7 mi e on 10th Ave S and US 87/89 and SR 3/200, then just s. Int corridors. **Pets:** Large, other species. $10 one-time fee/room. Service with restrictions, supervision.

**Hampton Inn** SH
(406) 453-2675. **$79-$119.** 2301 14th St SW. I-15, exit 278, just sw. Int corridors. **Pets:** Medium, dogs only. $20 one-time fee/pet. Designated rooms, service with restrictions, supervision.

**La Quinta Inn & Suites Great Falls** SH 🐾
(406) 761-2600. **$79-$209.** 600 River Dr S. I-15, exit 278, 1.7 mi e on 10th Ave S, then 0.8 mi n. Int corridors. **Pets:** Service with restrictions, supervision.

**(AAA) ▽▽▽ Motel 6 #4238 M**
(406) 453-1602. **$52-$75.** 2 Treasure State Dr. I-15, exit 278, 0.8 mi e on 10th Ave S and US 87/89 and SR 3/200; next to Best Western. Int corridors. **Pets:** Accepted.
[SAVE] [🛏] [✕] [🏊]

**(AAA) ▽▽▽ Ponderosa Inn SH**
(406) 761-3410. **$64-$99.** 220 Central Ave. Downtown. Ext/int corridors. **Pets:** Small. Service with restrictions, supervision.
[SAVE] [🛏] [✕] [▣] [▦] [🍴] [🏊]

# HAMILTON

**▽▽▽ Town House Inn SH**
(406) 363-6600. **$65-$99.** 1113 N 1st St. North of city center on US 93. Int corridors. **Pets:** Large, other species. $5 daily fee/pet. Service with restrictions, supervision.
[ASK] [🛏] [✕] [♿] [🏊] [▣] [▦]

# HARDIN

**(AAA) ▽▽▽ American Inn of Hardin SH**
(406) 665-1870. **$55-$85.** 1324 N Crawford Ave. I-90, exit 495, just s on SR 47. Ext corridors. **Pets:** Accepted.
[SAVE] [🛏] [✕] [🏊] [▣] [▦] [🍴] [🏊]

**▽ Western Motel M**
(406) 665-2296. **$35-$75.** 830 W 3rd St. I-90, exit 495 eastbound, 1.3 mi s on SR 47 and CR 313, just e; exit 497 westbound, 0.3 mi w on I-90 business loop, continue straight on 3rd St for 0.7 mi. Ext corridors. **Pets:** Accepted.
[✕] [▣]

# HARLOWTON

**▽ Corral Motel M**
(406) 632-4331. **$50-$55, 3 day notice.** 0.5 mi e at jct US 12 and 191. Ext corridors. **Pets:** Dogs only. $5 one-time fee/pet. Service with restrictions, supervision.
[ASK] [🛏] [✕] [▣]

**▽ Countryside Inn M**
(406) 632-4119. **$56-$60.** 309 3rd St NE. US 12 E. Ext corridors. **Pets:** Small, dogs only. $5 daily fee/pet. Designated rooms, service with restrictions, supervision.
[✕] [▣] [✕]

# HELENA

**▽▽▽▽ Barrister Bed & Breakfast BB**
(406) 443-7330. **$95-$110, 4 day notice.** 416 N Ewing St. I-15, exit 192 (Prospect Ave), 1.5 mi sw via Prospect and Montana aves to 9th Ave, 0.8 mi w, then just s. Int corridors. **Pets:** Accepted.
[ASK] [🛏] [✕] [✎]

**▽▽▽▽ Best Western Helena Great Northern Hotel SH**
(406) 457-5500. **$98-$150.** 835 Great Northern Blvd. I-15, exit 193 (Cedar St), just e of jct Lyndale and Benton aves; downtown. Int corridors. **Pets:** Accepted.
[ASK] [🛏] [✕] [♿] [🏊] [♿] [▣] [▦] [🏊] [✕]

**▽▽▽ Days Inn Helena SH ❀**
(406) 442-3280. **$69-$129.** 2001 Prospect Ave. I-15, exit 192 (Prospect Ave), just w. Int corridors. **Pets:** Other species. $10 daily fee/pet. Designated rooms, service with restrictions, supervision.
[ASK] [🛏] [✕] [♿] [🏊] [♿] [▣] [▦] [✕]

**(AAA) ▽▽▽ Elkhorn Mountain Inn SH ❀**
(406) 442-6625. **$71-$73.** 1 Jackson Creek Rd. I-15, exit 187 (Montana City), just w. Int corridors. **Pets:** Other species. $5 daily fee/pet. Supervision.
[SAVE] [🛏] [✕] [♿] [♿] [▣] [▦]

**(AAA) ▽▽▽ Red Lion Colonial Hotel SH**
(406) 443-2100. **$72-$119.** 2301 Colonial Dr. I-15, exit 192 southbound; exit 192B northbound. Int corridors. **Pets:** $20 one-time fee/pet. Service with restrictions, supervision.
[SAVE] [🛏] [✕] [▣] [▦] [🍴] [🏊]

**▽▽ Super 8 Motel SH ❀**
(406) 443-2450. **$45-$65.** 2200 11th Ave. I-15, exit 192B (capitol area) southbound; exit west business district northbound on US 12. Int corridors. **Pets:** $10 one-time fee/room. Designated rooms, service with restrictions, supervision.
[ASK] [🛏] [✕] [🏊] [♿] [▣] [▦]

**▽▽▽ Wingate Inn SH**
(406) 449-3000. **$105-$130.** 2007 Oakes. I-15, exit 193, just sw. Int corridors. **Pets:** Accepted.
[ASK] [🛏] [✕] [♿] [🏊] [♿] [▣] [▦] [🏊]

# HUNGRY HORSE

**(AAA) ▽▽▽ Mini Golden Inns Motel M**
(406) 387-4313. **$85-$150, 30 day notice.** 8955 US 2 E. East end of town. Ext corridors. **Pets:** Accepted.
[SAVE] [🛏] [✕] [♿] [♿] [▣] [▦]

# KALISPELL

**(AAA) ▽▽ Aero Inn SH**
(406) 755-3798. **$44-$89.** 1830 US 93 S. 1.3 mi s on US 93 from jct US 2. Int corridors. **Pets:** $20 deposit/room. Designated rooms, service with restrictions, supervision.
[SAVE] [🛏] [✕] [🏊] [♿] [▣] [▦] [🏊]

**▽▽ Days Inn Kalispell SH**
(406) 756-3222. **$65-$140.** 1550 Hwy 93 N. 1.3 mi n on US 93 from jct US 2. Int corridors. **Pets:** Small. $10 daily fee/pet. Designated rooms, service with restrictions, supervision.
[✕] [▣]

**(AAA) ▽▽▽ Four Seasons Motor Inn SH**
(406) 755-6123. **$53-$113.** 350 N Main St. US 93, just n of jct US 2. Ext/int corridors. **Pets:** Medium. $10 daily fee/room. Designated rooms, service with restrictions, supervision.
[SAVE] [🛏] [✕] [▣] [▦] [🍴]

**▽▽ Kalispell/Glacier Int'l Airport area Super 8 Motel SH**
(406) 755-1888. **$87-$143.** 1341 1st Ave E. 1.2 mi s on US 93 from jct US 2. Int corridors. **Pets:** Other species. $10 one-time fee/room. Designated rooms, supervision.
[ASK] [🛏] [✕] [♿] [🏊] [▣] [▦]

**▽▽ Kalispell Grand Hotel SH**
(406) 755-8100. **$75-$129.** 100 Main St. On US 93; downtown. Int corridors. **Pets:** Accepted.
[ASK] [🛏] [✕] [🍴]

**(AAA) ▽▽▽▽ La Quinta Inn & Suites Kalispell SH**
(406) 257-5255. **$59-$169.** 255 Montclair Dr. Jct US 93 and 2, 1 mi e. Int corridors. **Pets:** Accepted.
[SAVE] [🛏] [✕] [♿] [🏊] [♿] [▣] [▦] [🏊] [✕]

**(AAA) ▽▽▽ Red Lion Inn Kalispell SH**
(406) 755-6700. **$69-$149.** 1330 Hwy 2 W. 1 mi w on US 2 from jct US 93. Int corridors. **Pets:** Accepted.
[SAVE] [🛏] [✕] [▣] [▦] [🍴] [🏊]

**(AAA) ▽▽▽▽ WestCoast Kalispell Center Hotel SH**
(406) 751-5050. **$109-$159.** 20 N Main St. Just s on US 93 from jct of US 2; connected to Kalispell Center Mall. Int corridors. **Pets:** $20 one-time fee/pet. Designated rooms, service with restrictions, supervision.
[SAVE] [🛏] [✕] [♿] [▣] [▦] [🍴] [🏊] [✕]

▼◆ **WestCoast Outlaw Hotel-Kalispell** 🆂🅷
(406) 755-6100. **$69-$199.** 1701 Hwy 93 S. 1.4 mi s on US 93 from jct US 2. Int corridors. **Pets:** Medium. $15 one-time fee/pet. Service with restrictions, supervision.
🅰🆂🅺 🆂🛅 ⊠ 🛅 🖵 🍴 ⇆ ⊠

# LAKESIDE

▼▼ **Bayshore Resort Motel Inc** Ⓜ
(406) 844-3131. **$60-$170.** 616 Lakeside Blvd. On US 93; center. Ext corridors. **Pets:** $7 daily fee/pet. Designated rooms, service with restrictions, supervision.
🅰🆂🅺 ⊠ 🛅 🖵 ⊠ 🅺

# LAUREL

▼▼ **Best Western Yellowstone Crossing** 🆂🅷
(406) 628-6888. **$74-$89, 14 day notice.** 205 SE 4th St. I-90, exit 434, just n, then just e. Int corridors. **Pets:** $10 daily fee/pet. Designated rooms, service with restrictions, supervision.
🅰🆂🅺 🆂🛅 ⊠ Ⓜᴹ 🎬 🛋 🛅 🖵 ⇆

# LEWISTOWN

🅰🅰🅰 ▼ **B & B Motel** Ⓜ
(406) 538-5496. **$48-$65.** 520 E Main St. Downtown. Ext corridors. **Pets:** Accepted.
🆂🅰🆅🅴 ⊠ 🛅

# LIBBY

▼▼ **Sandman Motel** Ⓜ 🐾
(406) 293-8831. **$39-$69.** 688 US Hwy 2 W. Just w on US 2 from jct SR 37. Ext corridors. **Pets:** Medium, dogs only. $20 deposit/room. Designated rooms, service with restrictions, supervision.
🅰🆂🅺 🆂🛅 ⊠ 🛅

🅰🅰🅰 ▼▼ **Super 8 Motel** 🆂🅷
(406) 293-2771. **$53-$99.** 448 US 2 W. Just w on US 2 from jct SR 37. Int corridors. **Pets:** Other species. $10 one-time fee/room. Service with restrictions, supervision.
🆂🅰🆅🅴 🆂🛅 ⊠ 🎬 🛅 ⇆

# LINCOLN

🅰🅰🅰 ▼ **Leeper's Ponderosa Motel** Ⓜ 🐾
(406) 362-4333. **$55-$70.** Hwy 200 & 1st Ave. On SR 200, just w. Ext corridors. **Pets:** $5 daily fee/pet. Service with restrictions, supervision.
🆂🅰🆅🅴 🆂🛅 ⊠ 🛅 🖵 🅺

# LIVINGSTON

🅰🅰🅰 ▼▼ **Best Western Yellowstone Inn & Conference Center** 🆂🅷
(406) 222-6110. **$65-$115.** 1515 W Park St. I-90, exit 333, just n. Int corridors. **Pets:** Medium. $10 daily fee/pet. Service with restrictions, supervision.
🆂🅰🆅🅴 ⊠ 🛅 🖵 ⇆

🅰🅰🅰 ▼ **Del Mar Motel Inc** Ⓜ
(406) 222-3120. **$44-$76, 3 day notice.** 1201 Hwy 10 W. I-90, exit 330, 1.9 mi e on I-90 business loop. Ext corridors. **Pets:** Other species. $5 daily fee/pet. Service with restrictions, supervision.
🆂🅰🆅🅴 🆂🛅 ⊠ 🛅 🖵 ⇆

▼▼ **Econo Lodge** 🆂🅷
(406) 222-0555. **$45-$115.** 111 Rogers Ln. I-90, exit 333, just n on US 89, then just w. Int corridors. **Pets:** Other species. $20 deposit/room, $5 daily fee/room. Designated rooms, service with restrictions, supervision.
🅰🆂🅺 🆂🛅 ⊠ Ⓜᴹ 🎬 🛋 🛅 🖵 ⇆

🅰🅰🅰 ▼▼ **Travelodge Livingston** Ⓜ
(406) 222-6320. **$62-$102.** 102 Rogers Ln. I-90, exit 333, just n on US 89, then just w. Ext/int corridors. **Pets:** Small. $10 one-time fee/pet. Designated rooms, service with restrictions, supervision.
🆂🅰🆅🅴 🆂🛅 ⊠ 🛅 🖵 🍴 ⇆

# LOLO

▼▼ **Days Inn** 🆂🅷
(406) 273-2121. **$59-$99.** 11225 US 93 S. North edge of town. Ext/int corridors. **Pets:** Accepted.
🅰🆂🅺 🆂🛅 ⊠ Ⓜᴹ 🛅 🖵

# MILES CITY

🅰🅰🅰 ▼▼ **Best Western War Bonnet Inn** Ⓜ
(406) 234-4560. **$85-$93.** 1015 S Haynes Ave. I-94, exit 138 (Broadus), 0.3 mi n. Ext corridors. **Pets:** Other species. $5 daily fee/pet. Service with restrictions, supervision.
🆂🅰🆅🅴 ⊠ 🛅 🖵 ⇆ ⊠

▼▼▼ **GuestHouse International Inn & Suites** 🆂🅷
(406) 232-3661. **$65-$150.** 3111 Steel St. I-94, exit 138 (Broadus), just s. Int corridors. **Pets:** $10 daily fee/room. Service with restrictions, supervision.
🅰🆂🅺 🆂🛅 ⊠ Ⓜᴹ 🛋 🛅 🖵 ⇆

# MISSOULA

▼▼ **Americas Best Inn** 🆂🅷
(406) 542-7550. **$65-$99.** 4953 N Reserve St. I-90 W, exit 101 (Reserve St), just s. Int corridors. **Pets:** Medium. $10 daily fee/pet. Designated rooms.
🅰🆂🅺 🆂🛅 ⊠ 🎬 🛋 🛅 🖵

🅰🅰🅰 ▼▼▼ **Best Western Grant Creek Inn** 🆂🅷
(406) 543-0700. **$89-$139.** 5280 Grant Creek Rd. I-90, exit 101 (Reserve St), just n. Int corridors. **Pets:** Small. $10 daily fee/room. Service with restrictions, supervision.
🆂🅰🆅🅴 🆂🛅 ⊠ Ⓜᴹ 🎬 🛋 🛅 🖵 ⇆ ⊠

▼▼ **Campus Inn** Ⓜ
(406) 549-5134. **$45-$99.** 744 E Broadway. I-90, exit 105 (Van Buren St), just s to Broadway, then just w. Ext/int corridors. **Pets:** Large, other species. $6 daily fee/room. Service with restrictions, supervision.
🅰🆂🅺 ⊠ 🎬 🛋 🛅 ⇆

▼▼▼ **Comfort Inn** 🆂🅷
(406) 542-0888. **$72-$139.** 4545 N Reserve St. I-90, exit 101 (Reserve St), 0.5 mi s. Int corridors. **Pets:** Other species. $10 one-time fee/pet. Service with restrictions, supervision.
🅰🆂🅺 🆂🛅 ⊠ Ⓜᴹ 🎬 🛋 🛅 🖵 ⇆

🅰🅰🅰 ▼▼▼ **Days Inn/Missoula Airport** 🆂🅷
(406) 721-9776. **$66-$99.** 8600 Truck Stop Rd. I-90, exit 96, just n. Int corridors. **Pets:** $5 daily fee/pet. Designated rooms, no service, supervision.
🆂🅰🆅🅴 ⊠ 🛅

🅰🅰🅰 ▼▼ **Days Inn University** 🆂🅷
(406) 543-7221. **$64-$84.** 201 E Main St. I-90, exit 104 (Orange St), 0.5 mi s to Broadway, 0.5 mi e to Washington, just s to Main St, then just w. Ext corridors. **Pets:** Medium, dogs only. $25 one-time fee/pet. Designated rooms, service with restrictions, supervision.
🆂🅰🆅🅴 🆂🛅 ⊠ 🛅 🖵 ⇆

🅰🅰🅰 ▼▼▼ **Doubletree Hotel Missoula/Edgewater** 🆂🅷
(406) 728-3100. **$114-$189.** 100 Madison. I-90, exit 105 (Van Buren St), just s, then w on Front St. Int corridors. **Pets:** Accepted.
🆂🅰🆅🅴 ⊠ Ⓜᴹ 🎬 🛋 🛅 🖵 🍴 ⇆

🅰🅰🅰 ▼ **Downtown Motel** Ⓜ
(406) 549-5191. **$41-$52.** 502 E Broadway. I-90, exit 105 (Van Buren St), just w. Ext corridors. **Pets:** Accepted.
🆂🅰🆅🅴 ⊠ 🛅 🖵

🅰🅰🅰 ▼ **Family Inn** Ⓜ
(406) 543-7371. **$75-$80.** 1031 E Broadway. I-90, exit 105 (Van Buren St), just s, then just e. Ext corridors. **Pets:** Medium. $10 daily fee/pet. Service with restrictions, supervision.
🆂🅰🆅🅴 🆂🛅 ⊠ 🛅 ⇆

◆◆◆ **Hampton Inn** SH
(406) 549-1800. **$70-$119, 7 day notice.** 4805 N Reserve St. I-90, exit 101 (Reserve St), just s. Int corridors. **Pets:** Accepted.

◆◆◆◆ **Holiday Inn Missoula-Parkside** SH
(406) 721-8550. **$89-$149, 7 day notice.** 200 S Pattee St. I-90, exit 104 (Orange St), 0.5 mi s to Broadway, just e to Pattee St, then just s. Int corridors. **Pets:** Other species. $20 one-time fee/room. Service with restrictions, supervision.

◆◆ **Microtel Inn & Suites** SH
(406) 543-0959. **$55-$80.** 5059 N Reserve St. I-90, exit 101 (Reserve St), just s. Int corridors. **Pets:** Accepted.

◆◆◆ **Ponderosa Lodge** M
(406) 543-3102. **$50-$65.** 800 E Broadway. I-90, exit 105 (Van Buren St), just s to Broadway, then w. Ext/int corridors. **Pets:** Medium, dogs only. $10 daily fee/pet. Designated rooms, service with restrictions, supervision.

◆◆◆ **Quality Inn & Conference Center** SH
(406) 251-2665. **$85-$135.** 3803 Brooks St. I-90, exit 101 (Reserve St), 5 mi s to Brooks St (US 93), then just w. Int corridors. **Pets:** Medium. $10 daily fee/pet. Designated rooms.

◆◆◆ **Red Lion Inn** SH
(406) 728-3300. **$75-$130.** 700 W Broadway. I-90, exit 104 (Orange St), just s, then just w. Ext corridors. **Pets:** Accepted.

◆◆◆ **Redwood Lodge** M
(406) 721-2110. **$65.** 8060 Hwy 93 N. I-90, exit 96, just s. Ext corridors. **Pets:** No service, supervision.

◆◆◆ **Ruby's Inn & Convention Center** SH
(406) 721-0990. **$89-$109.** 4825 N Reserve St. I-90, exit 101 (Reserve St), just s. Ext/int corridors. **Pets:** Accepted.

◆◆ **Sleep Inn by Choice Hotels** SH
(406) 543-5883. **$85-$105, 18 day notice.** 3425 Dore Ln. I-90, exit 101 (Reserve St), 5 mi s, then just e on Brooks St. Int corridors. **Pets:** Accepted.

◆◆◆ **Southgate Inn** SH
(406) 251-2250. **$45-$80.** 3530 Brooks St. I-90, exit 101 (Reserve St), 5 mi s to Brooks St, then just e. Ext corridors. **Pets:** Accepted.

◆◆ **Super 8-Brooks St** SH
(406) 251-2255. **$54-$76.** 3901 Brooks St. I-90, exit 101 (Reserve St), 5 mi s, then just w. Int corridors. **Pets:** Medium, dogs only. $5 daily fee/pet. Designated rooms, service with restrictions, supervision.

◆◆◆ **Travelers Inn Motel** M
(406) 728-8330. **$52-$75.** 4850 N Reserve St. I-90, exit 101 (Reserve St), just s. Ext corridors. **Pets:** Small, dogs only. $5 daily fee/pet. Designated rooms, service with restrictions, supervision.

## OVANDO

◆◆◆◆ **Lake Upsata Guest Ranch** RA
(406) 793-5890. **$90-$440, 30 day notice.** 201 Lower Lakeside Ln. 7.5 mi w on SR 200 to MM 38, 3.4 mi n on Woodworth Rd, then 1 mi e. Ext corridors. **Pets:** Other species. Crate.

## POLSON

◆◆◆ **Bayview Inn** M
(406) 883-3120. **$48-$83.** 914 Hwy 93. Just s; downtown. Ext corridors. **Pets:** $5 daily fee/pet. Service with restrictions, supervision.

◆◆◆ **Best Western KwaTaqNuk Resort** SH
(406) 883-3636. **$79-$135, 3 day notice.** 303 US Hwy 93 E. Just s of downtown. Int corridors. **Pets:** $10 daily fee/room. Designated rooms, service with restrictions, supervision.

## RED LODGE

◆◆ **Best Western Lu Pine Inr** SH
(406) 446-1321. **$79-$119.** 702 S Hauser. 0.4 mi s, just w of US 212. Int corridors. **Pets:** Accepted.

◆◆ **Comfort Inn of Red Lodge** SH
(406) 446-4469. **$60-$150.** 612 N Broadway. Jct US 212 and SR 78, north entrance. Int corridors. **Pets:** Accepted.

◆◆◆ **Super 8 of Red Lodge** M
(406) 446-2288. **$100-$120, 14 day notice.** 1223 S Broadway Ave. Just s on US 212. Ext/int corridors. **Pets:** Other species. $5 daily fee/pet. Service with restrictions, crate.

◆◆◆ **Yodeler Motel** M
(406) 446-1435. **$50-$99.** 601 S Broadway. Just s on US 212. Ext corridors. **Pets:** Dogs only. $5 one-time fee/pet. Designated rooms, service with restrictions, supervision.

## RONAN

◆◆ **Starlite Motel** M
(406) 676-7000. **$44-$69.** 18 Main St SW. Just w of jct US 93 and Main St. Ext corridors. **Pets:** Large, dogs only. $10 daily fee/pet. Designated rooms, service with restrictions, supervision.

## ST. IGNATIUS

◆◆ **Sunset Motel** M
(406) 745-3900. **$39-$59.** 333 Mountain View. Just s of downtown, exit on US 93. Ext corridors. **Pets:** Dogs only. $5 one-time fee/room. Service with restrictions, supervision.

## ST. REGIS

◆◆◆ **Little River Motel** M
(406) 649-2713. **$40-$70.** 50 Old US Hwy 10 W. I-90, exit 33, just n to flashing light, just w, then just sw. Ext corridors. **Pets:** Small. $5 daily fee/pet. Service with restrictions, supervision.

## SEELEY LAKE

◆◆◆ **Wilderness Gateway Inn** M
(406) 677-2095. **$46-$63.** 2996 Hwy 83 N. South end of town on SR 83. Ext corridors. **Pets:** Accepted.

## SHELBY

◆◆ **Comfort Inn of Shelby** SH
(406) 434-2212. **$55-$75.** 455 McKinley Ave. I-15, exit 363, just e, then just s. Int corridors. **Pets:** Medium, other species. $5 daily fee/pet. Service with restrictions, supervision.

**Crossroads Inn M**
(406) 434-5134. **$56-$70.** 1200 Roosevelt Hwy. Just w of town center on US 2. Int corridors. **Pets:** Other species. $10 daily fee/pet. Designated rooms, supervision.

**O'Haire Manor Motel M**
(406) 434-5555. **$50-$70.** 204 2nd St S. Just s of Main St via Maple St. Ext/int corridors. **Pets:** Large. $5 one-time fee/room. Service with restrictions, supervision.

## SIDNEY

**Richland Motor Inn M**
(406) 433-6400. **$80-$90.** 1200 S Central Ave. 1.5 mi n of jct SR 200 and 16. Int corridors. **Pets:** $5 one-time fee/pet. Service with restrictions.

## SUPERIOR

**Budget Host Big Sky Motel M** ☙
(406) 822-4831. **$56-$65.** 103 4th Ave E. I-90, exit 47, just n. Ext corridors. **Pets:** Medium. $10 one-time fee/pet. Designated rooms, service with restrictions, supervision.

## THOMPSON FALLS

**The Riverfront M**
(406) 827-3460. **$45-$139.** 4907 Hwy 200 W. 1 mi w of city center. Ext corridors. **Pets:** Small, other species. $7 daily fee/pet. Service with restrictions, supervision.

## THREE FORKS

**Broken Spur Motel M**
(406) 285-3237. **$55-$70.** 124 W Elm (Hwy 2). I-90, exit 278 westbound, 1.3 mi sw; exit 274 eastbound, 1 mi s on SR 287 to jct SR 2, then 3 mi se. Ext corridors. **Pets:** $5 daily fee/pet. Service with restrictions, supervision.

**Fort Three Forks Motel & RV Park M** ☙
(406) 285-3233. **$46-$99.** 10776 Hwy 287. I-90, exit 274. Ext corridors. **Pets:** Large, other species. $10 one-time fee/room. Designated rooms, service with restrictions, supervision.

## VICTOR

**Wildlife Adventures Guest Ranch RA**
(406) 642-3262. **$105-$170.** 1765 Pleasant View Dr. Jct US 93 and Fifth St, 0.9 mi w, 3.2 mi s. Int corridors. **Pets:** Other species. $5 daily fee/pet. Service with restrictions, supervision.

## WEST YELLOWSTONE

**Best Western Cross Winds Motor Inn SH**
(406) 646-9557. **$49-$139, 5 day notice.** 201 Firehole Ave. Just w of US 191 and 287, or US 20 at Dunraven St and Firehole Ave. Ext corridors. **Pets:** Large. dogs only. Designated rooms, service with restrictions, supervision.

**Best Western Desert Inn SH**
(406) 646-7376. **$55-$175, 3 day notice.** 133 Canyon Ave. US 191 at US 20; corner of Canyon and Firehole aves. Int corridors. **Pets:** Large, dogs only. Designated rooms, service with restrictions, supervision.

**Brandin' Iron Inn SH**
(406) 646-9411. **$44-$114, 3 day notice.** 201 Canyon Ave. Just w and n of park entrance. Ext corridors. **Pets:** Accepted.

**City Center Motel M**
(406) 646-7337. **$39-$89, 3 day notice.** 214 Madison Ave. W off US 191 at Madison Ave and Dunraven St; just nw of park entrance. Ext corridors. **Pets:** Small. $15 one-time fee/pet. Designated rooms, service with restrictions, supervision.

**ClubHouse Inn SH**
(406) 646-4892. **$59-$159.** 105 S Electric St. Just sw of jct US 191, 187 and 20, just w of park entrance. Int corridors. **Pets:** Service with restrictions, supervision.

**Days Inn West Yellowstone SH**
(406) 646-7656. **$59-$130.** 301 Madison Ave. W off US 191; just nw of park entrance. Ext/int corridors. **Pets:** Small, dogs only. $9 daily fee/pet. Designated rooms, service with restrictions, supervision.

**Gray Wolf Inn & Suites M**
(406) 646-0000. **$69-$139.** 250 S Canyon Ave. Just w of Yellowstone National Park entrance. Int corridors. **Pets:** Other species. $50 deposit/room. Designated rooms, service with restrictions, supervision.

**Kelly Inn SH**
(406) 646-4544. **$69-$189.** 104 S Canyon Ave. S of jct US 191, 287 and 20; just w of park entrance. Ext/int corridors. **Pets:** Service with restrictions, supervision.

**Roundup Motel & Dude Motor Inn M**
(406) 646-7301. **$90-$110.** 3 Madison Ave. Just n of park entrance. Ext corridors. **Pets:** Accepted.

**Stage Coach Inn SH**
(406) 646-7381. **$49-$139, 14 day notice.** 209 Madison Ave. Corner of Dunraven St and Madison Ave, just w of park entrance. Ext/int corridors. **Pets:** Other species. $50 deposit/room. Designated rooms, service with restrictions, supervision.

**The Three Bear Lodge M**
(406) 646-7353. **$59-$105, 14 day notice.** 217 Yellowstone Ave. Just w of park entrance. Ext/int corridors. **Pets:** Other species. $5 one-time fee/pet. Service with restrictions, supervision.

**Travelers Lodge M**
(406) 646-9561. **$79-$109.** 225 Yellowstone Ave. Just w of park entrance. Ext corridors. **Pets:** Accepted.

**Yellowstone Lodge SH** ☙
(406) 646-0020. **$59-$149.** 251 S Electric St. Just w of park entrance. Int corridors. **Pets:** Other species. $10 daily fee/room. Service with restrictions, crate.

## WHITEFISH

**Bay Point on the Lake CO**
(406) 862-2331. **$89-$189, 30 day notice.** 300 Bay Point Dr. Jct US 93 and SR 487, 0.6 mi n on SR 487 to Skyles Pl, 0.3 mi w to Dakota Ave, 0.3 mi n, then just w. Ext corridors. **Pets:** Accepted.

**(AAA) ◊◊◊ Best Western Rocky Mountain Lodge SH ❖**
(406) 862-2569. **$81-$189.** 6510 Hwy 93 S. 1.3 mi s on US 93 from jct SR 487. Ext/int corridors. **Pets:** $15 daily fee/pet. Designated rooms, service with restrictions, crate.
SAVE Sᴅ ✕ ᕼM �᱘ 🐾 🖥 🖵 ≋

**◊ Cheap Sleep Motel SH**
(406) 862-5515. **$50-$70.** 6400 Hwy 93 S. US 93, 1 mi s. Int corridors. **Pets:** Accepted.
✕ ≋

**(AAA) ◊◊◊ Kristianna Mountain Homes CO**
(406) 862-2860. **$135-$1100, 30 day notice.** 3842 Winter Ln. Jct US 93 and SR 487, 2.4 mi n on SR 487, at flashing light go 5.2 mi on Big Mountain Rd, just n on Gelande, then just w on Kristanna Close. Ext/int corridors. **Pets:** Accepted.
SAVE ✕ 🖥 🖵 ✕ ᴀ̸ᴄ

**◊◊◊ North Forty Resort CA**
(406) 862-7740. **$79-$229, 14 day notice.** 3765 Hwy 40 W. 2.5 mi e on SR 40 from jct of US 93. Ext corridors. **Pets:** Other species. $10 daily fee/pet. Designated rooms, service with restrictions, supervision.
✕ 🖥 🖵 ✕ ᴀ̸ᴄ

**(AAA) ◊◊◊ Pine Lodge SH**
(406) 862-7600. **$80-$145.** 920 Spokane Ave. 1 mi s on US 93. Int corridors. **Pets:** Medium. Service with restrictions, supervision.
SAVE Sᴅ ✕ ᕼM �᱘ 🐾 🖥 🖵 ≋

**◊ Super 8 Motel SH**
(406) 862-8255. **$50-$92.** 800 Spokane Ave. 1 mi s on US 93 from jct SR 487. Int corridors. **Pets:** Dogs only. $5 daily fee/pet. Service with restrictions, supervision.
ASK Sᴅ ✕

# WHITE SULPHUR SPRINGS

**(AAA) ◊◊◊ All Seasons Inn & Suites M**
(406) 547-8888. **$59-$87.** 808 3rd Ave SW. On US 89, south end of town. Int corridors. **Pets:** $20 deposit/pet, $6 daily fee/pet. Service with restrictions, supervision.
SAVE Sᴅ ✕ ᕼM �᱘ 🖥

# NEBRASKA

## AINSWORTH

### Comfort Inn 🆂🅷
(402) 387-1050. **$100-$105.** 1124 E 4th St. 0.5 mi e on US 20. Int corridors. **Pets:** Medium, dogs only. $10 daily fee/pet. Designated rooms, service with restrictions, crate.

### Super 8 Motel 🆂🅷
(402) 387-0700. **$50.** 1025 E 4th St. 0.5 mi e on US 20. Int corridors. **Pets:** Accepted.

## ALLIANCE

### Alliance Days Inn 🆂🅷
(308) 762-8000. **$59-$96.** 117 Cody Ave. Jct US 385 and SR 2, 0.4 mi e, just s. Int corridors. **Pets:** Other species. $10 daily fee/pet. Designated rooms, service with restrictions, supervision.

### Sunset Motel & RV Park 🅼
(308) 762-8660. **$40-$80.** 1210 E Hwy 2. Jct US 87, 1 mi e. Ext/int corridors. **Pets:** Dogs only. $5 daily fee/pet. Service with restrictions, supervision.

## BEATRICE

### Beatrice Super 8 Motel 🆂🅷
(402) 228-8808. **$65-$105, 3 day notice.** 3721 N 6th St. 1 mi n on US 77. Int corridors. **Pets:** Accepted.

### Holiday Inn Express Hotel & Suites 🆂🅷
(402) 228-7000. **$68-$117.** 4005 N 6th St. 1 mi n on US 77. Int corridors. **Pets:** Accepted.

## BELLEVUE

### Settle Inn and Suites 🆂🅷
(402) 292-1155. **$60-$140.** 2105 Pratt Ave. US 75, exit Cornhusker, just w. Int corridors. **Pets:** Small, dogs only. $15 daily fee/room. Designated rooms, service with restrictions, supervision.

## CENTRAL CITY

### Super 8 Motel 🆂🅷
(308) 946-5055. **$47-$56.** 1701 31st St. SR 14, 1 mi s of jct US 30. Ext/int corridors. **Pets:** Accepted.

## CHADRON

### Best Western West Hills Inn 🆂🅷
(308) 432-3305. **$60-$126, 14 day notice.** 1100 W 10th St. Jct US 385 and 20. Ext/int corridors. **Pets:** Medium. $10 one-time fee/room. Service with restrictions, supervision.

### Chadron Super 8 Motel 🆂🅷
(308) 432-4471. **$45-$103.** 840 W Hwy 20. 0.8 mi w on US 20; just e of jct US 385. Int corridors. **Pets:** Accepted.

### Grand Westerner Motel 🅼 🐾
(308) 432-5595. **$44-$57.** 1050 W Hwy 20. 0.8 mi w on US 20; just e of jct US 385. Ext corridors. **Pets:** Dogs only. No service, supervision.

### Westerner Motel 🅼
(308) 432-5577. **$44-$57.** 300 Oak St. On US 20, 0.5 mi e of jct US 385 and SR 87. Ext corridors. **Pets:** Dogs only. Designated rooms, service with restrictions, supervision.

## COLUMBUS

### Sleep Inn & Suites Hotel 🆂🅷
(402) 562-5200. **$73-$125.** 303 23rd St. On US 30, 2 mi e of jct US 30 and 81; east side of town. Int corridors. **Pets:** Medium. $10 daily fee/pet. Designated rooms, service with restrictions, crate.

### Super 8 Motel-Columbus 🆂🅷
(402) 563-3456. **$49-$55.** 3324 20th St. On US 30 and 81, just s. Int corridors. **Pets:** Small. Designated rooms, no service, crate.

## COZAD

### Motel 6-Cozad–4091 🆂🅷
(308) 784-4900. **$50-$56.** 809 S Meridian. I-80, exit 222, just n. Int corridors. **Pets:** Accepted.

## CRETE

### Super 8 Motel 🆂🅷
(402) 826-3600. **$61-$88.** 1880 W 12th St. 1.3 mi sw at jct SR 33/103; west end of town. Int corridors. **Pets:** Accepted.

## FREMONT

### Comfort Inn by Choice Hotels 🆂🅷
(402) 721-1109. **$49-$149.** 1649 E 23rd Ave. 2 mi e cn US 30, just e of Business Rt US 275. Int corridors. **Pets:** Large, other species. $5 one-time fee/room. Supervision.

### Holiday Lodge & Conference Center 🆂🅷
(402) 727-1110. **$57-$85.** 1220 E 23rd St. US 30, jct Business Rt US 275 and 30. Ext/int corridors. **Pets:** Small. $25 deposit/pet. Designated rooms, supervision.

# FULLERTON

**▼▼ Fullerton Inn M** 🐾
(308) 536-2699. **$63.** S Hwy 14. Just s of center. Int corridors.
**Pets:** Service with restrictions, supervision.
[S🄌] [✕] [♿M]

# GERING

**▼▼ Monument Inn & Suites SH**
(308) 436-1950. **$65.** 1130 M St. On SR 92, 1 mi e of SR 71. Int
corridors. **Pets:** Accepted.
[ASK] [S🄌] [✕] [♿M] [🄫] [🛢] [🖵]

# GOTHENBURG

**AAA ▼▼ Gothenburg Super 8 SH**
(308) 537-2684. **$58-$84.** 401 Platte River Dr. I-80, exit 211 (SR 47),
just n. Int corridors. **Pets:** Accepted.
[SAVE] [S🄌] [✕] [🛢] [🖵] [🏊]

# GRAND ISLAND

**▼▼▼ Holiday Inn-Interstate 80 SH** 🐾
(308) 384-7770. **$69-$109.** 7838 S US Hwy 281. I-80, exit 312 (US
281), just s. Int corridors. **Pets:** $15 daily fee/room. Service with restric-
tions, supervision.
[ASK] [S🄌] [✕] [♿M] [🄫] [♿] [🛢] [🖵] [🍴] [🏊] [✕]

**▼▼ Howard Johnson Riverside Inn & Conference
Center SH** 🐾
(308) 384-5150. **$54-$81.** 3333 Ramada Rd. I-80, exit 314, 4.2 mi n.
Ext/int corridors. **Pets:** Other species. $10 daily fee/pet. Service with
restrictions, supervision.
[ASK] [S🄌] [✕] [🛢] [🖵] [🍴] [🏊] [✕]

**▼▼ Super 8 Motel SH**
(308) 384-4380. **$58-$63.** 2603 S Locust St. I-80, exit 314, 4.7 mi n. Int
corridors. **Pets:** Medium. $10 one-time fee/pet. Service with restrictions,
supervision.
[ASK] [✕] [🛢] [🖵] [🏊]

**▼▼ Travelodge SH**
(308) 382-5003. **$51-$57.** 1311 S Locust St. I-80, exit 314 (US 281),
5.2 mi n. Int corridors. **Pets:** Other species. $6 one-time fee/room. Service
with restrictions.
[✕] [🄫] [🛢] [🖵]

**▼▼ USA Inns of America M**
(308) 381-0111. **$50-$65.** 7000 S Nine Bridge Rd. I-80, exit 312 (US
281), just n. Ext/int corridors. **Pets:** Medium. $5 daily fee/pet. Designated
rooms, service with restrictions, supervision.
[ASK] [S🄌] [✕] [🛢] [🖵]

# HASTINGS

**AAA ▼▼▼ Holiday Inn-Hastings SH** 🐾
(402) 463-6721. **$63-$129.** 2205 Osborne Dr E. Jct US 34 and 281, 2
mi n. Ext/int corridors. **Pets:** Other species. $30 deposit/room. Designated
rooms, service with restrictions, crate.
[SAVE] [✕] [♿M] [🄫] [🄫] [🛢] [🖵] [🍴] [🏊] [✕]

**AAA ▼ Midlands Lodge M**
(402) 463-2428. **$43-$55, 7 day notice.** 910 W J St. Jct US 6, 34 and
281. Ext corridors. **Pets:** Small, dogs only. $15 daily fee/pet. Designated
rooms, no service, supervision.
[SAVE] [S🄌] [✕] [🛢] [🏊]

**▼▼ Super 8 SH**
(402) 463-8888. **$54-$79.** 2200 N Kansas Ave. Jct US 34 and 281, 2
mi n. Int corridors. **Pets:** Accepted.
[ASK] [S🄌] [✕] [🄫] [🄫] [🛢] [🖵]

# HOLDREGE

**▼▼ Super 8 SH**
(308) 995-2793. **$50-$90.** 420 Broadway. US 183, 0.5 mi w on US
6/34. Int corridors. **Pets:** Small. $10 daily fee/pet. Service with restrictions,
supervision.
[ASK] [S🄌] [✕] [🛢] [🏊]

# KEARNEY

**AAA ▼▼ AmericInn Lodge & Suites of Kearney SH**
(308) 234-7800. **$79-$99.** 215 W Talmadge Rd. I-80, exit 272 (SR 44),
just n. Int corridors. **Pets:** Accepted.
[SAVE] [✕] [♿M] [🄫] [🛢] [🖵] [🏊] [✕]

**AAA ▼▼ Best Western Inn of Kearney SH** 🐾
(308) 237-5185. **$69-$89.** 1010 3rd Ave. I-80, exit 272 (SR 44), 1 mi n,
then just w. Ext/int corridors. **Pets:** Other species. $10 one-time fee/room.
[SAVE] [S🄌] [✕] [🄫] [🛢] [🖵] [🍴] [🏊] [✕]

**AAA ▼▼ Days Inn of Kearney SH**
(308) 234-5699. **$45-$75.** 619 2nd Ave. I-80, exit 272 (SR 44), 0.8 mi n.
Int corridors. **Pets:** Other species. $10 daily fee/pet. Service with restric-
tions, supervision.
[SAVE] [S🄌] [✕] [🛢] [🏊]

**AAA ▼▼ Ramada Inn-Kearney SH**
(308) 237-3141. **$60-$90.** 301 2nd Ave. I-80, exit 272 (SR 44), 0.7 mi n.
Int corridors. **Pets:** Other species. $10 one-time fee/room. Service with
restrictions.
[SAVE] [S🄌] [✕] [🛢] [🖵] [🍴] [🏊] [✕]

**▼ Super 8 Motel M**
(308) 234-5513. **$47-$62.** 15 W 8th St. I-80, exit 272 (SR44), 1 mi n,
then just e. Int corridors. **Pets:** Accepted.
[ASK] [S🄌] [✕] [🖵]

# KIMBALL

**▼▼ Days Inn-Kimball M**
(308) 235-4671. **$62-$105.** 611 E 3rd St. I-80, exit 20, 1.5 ne on SR 71,
then 0.5 mi e on US 30. Ext corridors. **Pets:** Other species. $10 daily
fee/pet. Service with restrictions, supervision.
[ASK] [S🄌] [✕] [🛢] [🏊]

# LEXINGTON

**▼▼▼ Days Inn SH** 🐾
(308) 324-6440. **$50-$85.** 2506 Plum Creek Pkwy. I-80, exit 237 (US
283), 0.6 mi n. Int corridors. **Pets:** Dogs only. $6 daily fee/pet, $6 one-
time fee/pet. Designated rooms, service with restrictions, supervision.
[ASK] [S🄌] [✕] [🛢]

**AAA ▼▼▼▼ Holiday Inn Express Hotel & Suites SH**
(308) 324-9900. **$69-$115.** 2605 Plum Creek Pkwy. I-80, exit 237 (US
283), 0.5 mi n. Int corridors. **Pets:** Large, other species. $10 one-time
fee/room. Designated rooms, service with restrictions, supervision.
[SAVE] [✕] [♿M] [🄫] [🛢] [🖵] [🏊] [✕]

**▼▼ Lexington Comfort Inn SH**
(308) 324-3747. **$62-$85.** 2810 Plum Creek Pkwy. I-80, exit 237 (US
283), 0.3 mi n. Ext/int corridors. **Pets:** Accepted.
[ASK] [S🄌] [✕] [🛢] [🖵] [🏊]

# LINCOLN

**▼▼ Baymont Inn & Suites SH**
(402) 477-1100. **$69-$99.** 3939 N 26th St. I-80, exit 403 (27th St), 2 mi
s. Int corridors. **Pets:** Small. Service with restrictions, supervision.
[ASK] [S🄌] [✕] [♿M] [🄫] [🄫] [🛢] [🖵] [✕]

**▼▼▼ Chase Suites Hotel SH** 🐾
(402) 483-4900. **$88-$159.** 200 S 68th St Pl. On US 34, 4.3 mi e, just
s of jct 68th St. Ext corridors. **Pets:** Other species. $150 deposit/room, $5
daily fee/pet. Designated rooms, service with restrictions, crate.
[ASK] [S🄌] [✕] [♿M] [🄫] [🄫] [🛢] [🖵] [🏊] [✕]

▼▼▼ Country Inns & Suites By Carlson SH ❀
(402) 476-5353. **$95-$115, 3 day notice.** 5353 N 27th St. I-80, exit 403 (27th St), 1.5 mi s. Int corridors. **Pets:** Medium. $75 deposit/room. Designated rooms, service with restrictions, supervision.
A$K S🐾 ✕ &M 🖐️ 🛏️ 🖥️ ｜¶ ⊷

◆◆◆ ▼▼ Days Inn South SH
(402) 423-7111. **$45-$69.** 1140 Calvert St. 2.5 mi s on SR 2. Ext/int corridors. **Pets:** Medium, dogs only. $5 daily fee/pet. Service with restrictions, supervision.
SAVE S🐾 ✕ 🛏️ 🖥️

◆◆◆ ▼▼ Econo Lodge M ❀
(402) 475-4511. **$44-$69.** 1140 W Cornhusker Hwy. I-80, exit 399 (Airport), just w. Ext/int corridors. **Pets:** Small, dogs only. $10 one-time fee/pet. Service with restrictions, supervision.
SAVE S🐾 ✕ &M 🛏️ 🖥️

▼▼▼ Holiday Inn Express SH
(402) 435-0200. **$85-$135.** 1133 Belmont Ave. I-80, exit 401A; 2 mi s on I-180, exit 2 (Cornhusker Hwy), then just e. Int corridors. **Pets:** Other species. Crate.
A$K S🐾 ✕ &M 🖐️ & 🛏️ 🖥️ ⊷ ⊠

▼▼▼ Quality Inn & Suites SH
(402) 464-4400. **$65-$109.** 216 N 48th St. 2.5 mi e on US 6 and 34; just ne of jct O St; entrance off of 48th St. Int corridors. **Pets:** Medium, other species. $10 daily fee/room. Designated rooms, service with restrictions, supervision.
A$K S🐾 ✕ &M 🖐️ & 🛏️ 🖥️

▼▼ Settle Inn & Suites SH
(402) 435-8100. **$69-$109.** 2800 Husker Cir. I-80, exit 403 (27th St), just s to Wildcat Dr, just e, then just n. Int corridors. **Pets:** Accepted.
A$K S🐾 ✕ &M & 🛏️ 🖥️ ⊷

▼▼▼ Staybridge Suites Lincoln-I-80 SH
(402) 438-7829. **$89-$209.** 2701 Fletcher Ave. I-80, exit 403 (27th St), 0.4 mi s. Int corridors. **Pets:** Other species. $25 one-time fee/room. Service with restrictions, crate.
A$K ✕ &M & 🛏️ 🖥️ ⊷ ⊠

▼▼ Super 8 Motel-Lincoln/Cornhusker SH
(402) 467-4488. **$54-$73.** 2545 Cornhusker Hwy. I-80, exit 403 (27th St), 2.5 mi s. Int corridors. **Pets:** Small. Designated rooms, no service, crate.
A$K S🐾 ✕ &M 🖐️ & 🛏️ 🖥️

▼▼ Super 8 Motel-Lincoln/West "O" Street SH
(402) 476-8887. **$54-$73.** 2635 W est O St St. I-80, exit 395, 2 mi e. Int corridors. **Pets:** Small. Designated rooms, no service, crate.
A$K S🐾 ✕ &M 🖐️ 🛏️ 🖥️

◆◆◆ ▼▼▼ Town House Motel SH
(402) 475-3000. **$55-$100.** 1744 M St. Jct 18th and M St; downtown. Int corridors. **Pets:** Other species. Service with restrictions, supervision.
SAVE S🐾 ✕ 🖐️ 🛏️ 🖥️

◆◆◆ ▼▼▼ Villager Courtyard & Gardens Hotel SH
(402) 464-9111. **$63-$88.** 5200 O St. 3 mi e on US 6 city route and 34. Ext corridors. **Pets:** Accepted.
SAVE S🐾 ✕ &M 🖐️ & 🛏️ 🖥️ ｜¶ ⊷ ⊠

# MCCOOK

◆◆◆ ▼▼ Economy 8 Motel M
(308) 345-1141. **$50-$60.** 1103 E B St. Jct US 6 and 34, 0.5 mi e; east side of town. Ext corridors. **Pets:** Medium. Service with restrictions, supervision.
SAVE S🐾 ✕

▼▼▼ Holiday Inn Express SH
(308) 345-4505. **$70-$88.** 1 Holiday Bison Dr. On US 83, just n of jct US 6 and 34. Int corridors. **Pets:** Accepted.
A$K S🐾 ✕ &M 🖐️ 🛏️

# MORRILL

▼▼ Oak Tree Inn SH ❀
(308) 247-2111. **$55-$69.** 707 E Webster. 0.5 mi e on US 26. Ext/int corridors. **Pets:** $5 one-time fee/room. Service with restrictions.
A$K S🐾 ✕ &M & 🛏️ ｜¶ ⊠

# NEBRASKA CITY

◆◆◆ ▼▼ Apple Inn SH
(402) 873-5959. **$57-$65.** 502 S 11th St. Jct 11th St and 4th Corso; center. Ext/int corridors. **Pets:** Small, dogs only. $8 daily fee/room. Designated rooms, service with restrictions, supervision.
SAVE S🐾 ✕ 🖐️ 🛏️ 🖥️ ⊷

# NORFOLK

◆◆◆ ▼▼▼ Norfolk Country Inn SH ❀
(402) 371-4430. **$65.** 1201 S 13th St. Jct US 275 Bypass and US 81. Ext corridors. **Pets:** Service with restrictions, supervision.
SAVE S🐾 ✕ & 🛏️ 🖥️ ｜¶

◆◆◆ ▼▼▼ Norfolk Lodge & Suites- A Clarion Collection Hotel SH
(402) 379-3833. **$89-$159.** 4200 W Norfolk Ave. On US 275 Bypass, 3 mi w of jct US 81. Ext/int corridors. **Pets:** Small. $20 one-time fee/pet. Designated rooms, service with restrictions, crate.
SAVE S🐾 ✕ &M 🖐️ & 🛏️ 🖥️ ｜¶ ⊠

▼▼ Super 8 Motel-Norfolk SH
(402) 379-2220. **$49-$58.** 1223 Omaha Ave. Jct US 275 Bypass and 81. Int corridors. **Pets:** Small. Designated rooms, no service, crate.
A$K S🐾 ✕ 🖐️ 🛏️ 🖥️

▼▼ White House Inn SH
(402) 371-3133. **$55-$60.** 2206 Market Ln. On US 275 Bypass, 1 mi w of jct US 81. Int corridors. **Pets:** Other species. $20 deposit/room, $5 daily fee/room. Designated rooms, service with restrictions, supervision.
A$K S🐾 ✕ 🖐️ 🛏️ 🖥️

# NORTH PLATTE

◆◆◆ ▼▼ Americas Best Value Travelers Inn M
(308) 534-4020. **$40-$60.** 602 E 4th St. I-80, exit 177 (US 83), 1.5 mi n, then 0.3 mi e. Ext corridors. **Pets:** Medium, other species. Service with restrictions, supervision.
SAVE S🐾 ✕ 🛏️ ⊷

◆◆◆ ▼▼▼ Best Western Chalet Lodge M
(308) 532-2313. **$52-$89.** 920 N Jeffers St. I-80, exit 177 (US 83), 2 mi n on US 30 and 83. Ext corridors. **Pets:** Other species. $7 daily fee/pet. Service with restrictions, supervision.
SAVE S🐾 ✕ 🛏️ ⊷

◆◆◆ ▼▼▼ Holiday Inn Express Hotel & Suites SH
(308) 532-9500. **$85-$95.** 300 Holiday Frontage Rd. I-80, exit 177 (US 83), just s. Int corridors. **Pets:** Accepted.
SAVE ✕ &M 🖐️ & 🛏️ 🖥️ ⊷ ⊠

▼▼ Howard Johnson Inn SH
(308) 532-0130. **$50-$90.** 1209 S Dewey. I-80, exit 177 (US 83), 0.5 mi n. Ext corridors. **Pets:** Medium. $10 daily fee/pet. Service with restrictions, supervision.
A$K S🐾 ✕ 🛏️ 🖥️ ｜¶ ⊷

▼▼▼ La Quinta Inn & Suites SH
(308) 534-0700. **$79-$154.** 2600 Eagles Wings Pl. I-80, exit 179, just n, then just w. Int corridors. **Pets:** Other species. Service with restrictions, supervision.
A$K S🐾 ✕ &M 🖐️ & 🛏️ 🖥️ ⊷

**(AAA) ▼▼▼ Quality Inn & Suites SH**
(308) 532-9090. **$73-$169.** 2102 S Jeffers St. I-80, exit 177 (US 83), just n. Ext/int corridors. **Pets:** Other species. $10 daily fee/pet. Designated rooms.
[SAVE] [S$] [X] [&M] [🖉] [&] [🛏] [💻] [🍴] [🏊] [X]

**(AAA) ▼▼▼ Ramada Inn SH**
(308) 534-3120. **$58-$72.** 3201 S Jeffers St. I-80, exit 177 (US 83), 0.3 mi s. Int corridors. **Pets:** Accepted.
[SAVE] [X] [&] [💻] [🍴] [🏊]

# OGALLALA

**(AAA) ▼▼▼ Best Western Stagecoach Inn SH**
(308) 284-3656. **$59-$105.** 201 Stagecoach Tr. I-80, exit 126 (US 26/SR 61), just n, then e on Frontage Rd. Ext corridors. **Pets:** Accepted.
[SAVE] [S$] [X] [&] [💻] [🍴] [🏊] [X]

**(AAA) ▼▼▼ Days Inn M ❖**
(308) 284-6365. **$55-$79.** 601 Stagecoach Tr. I-80, exit 126 (US 26/SR 61), just n, then e on Frontage Rd. Int corridors. **Pets:** Dogs only. $6 daily fee/room. Service with restrictions, supervision.
[SAVE] [S$] [X] [&]

**▼▼ Holiday Inn Express SH**
(308) 284-2266. **$65-$99, 10 day notice.** 501 Stagecoach Tr. I-80, exit 126 (US 26/SR 61), just n, then e on Frontage Rd. Ext/int corridors. **Pets:** Accepted.
[ASK] [S$] [X] [🖉] [&] [&] [💻]

**▼▼ Ogallala Comfort Inn SH**
(308) 284-4028. **$65-$110.** 110 Pony Express Rd. I-80, exit 126 (US 26/SR 61), just s. Ext/int corridors. **Pets:** Medium, other species. $10 daily fee/pet. Designated rooms, supervision.
[ASK] [S$] [X] [🖉] [&] [💻] [🏊]

# OMAHA

**(AAA) ▼▼▼ Baymont Inn Omaha SH**
(402) 592-5200. **$65-$102.** 10760 M St. I-80, exit 445 (L St E), 0.3 mi e, s on 108th St, then just e. Int corridors. **Pets:** Medium. Service with restrictions.
[SAVE] [X] [🖉] [&] [💻]

**(AAA) ▼▼▼ Best Western Kelly Inn Omaha SH ❖**
(402) 339-7400. **$85-$110.** 4706 S 108th St. I-80, exit 445 (L St E), 0.3 mi e, then just s. Int corridors. **Pets:** Other species. Service with restrictions, supervision.
[SAVE] [S$] [X] [🖉] [&] [💻] [🍴] [🏊] [X]

**▼▼ Best Western Settle Inn SH**
(402) 431-1246. **$69-$109.** 650 N 109th Ct. I-680, exit 3 (Dodge St W), 0.8 mi w to 108th St and N Old Mill Rd, then just w on Mill Valley Rd. Int corridors. **Pets:** Small, dogs only. $15 daily fee/room. Designated rooms, service with restrictions, supervision.
[ASK] [S$] [X] [🖉] [&] [&] [💻] [🏊]

**▼▼ Candlewood Suites SH**
(402) 758-2848. **$69-$119, 3 day notice.** 360 S 108th Ave. I-680, exit 3 (Dodge St W), 0.7 mi to 108th St, then 0.8 mi s. Int corridors. **Pets:** Accepted.
[ASK] [S$] [X] [&M] [🖉] [&] [&] [💻]

**▼▼ Clarion Hotel-West SH**
(402) 895-1000. **$49-$249.** 4888 S 118th St. I-80, exit 445 (L St W), 0.3 mi w on US 275/SR 92, then just s on 120th St. Int corridors. **Pets:** Medium. $10 daily fee/room. Designated rooms, service with restrictions, supervision.
[ASK] [S$] [X] [&M] [🖉] [&] [&] [💻] [🍴] [🏊]

**(AAA) ▼▼▼ Comfort Inn SH**
(402) 896-6300. **$60-$180.** 9595 S 145th St. I-80, exit 440, just n, then w. Int corridors. **Pets:** $10 daily fee/pet. Designated rooms, service with restrictions, supervision.
[SAVE] [S$] [X] [&] [&] [💻] [🏊]

**(AAA) ▼▼▼ Comfort Inn-Southwest SH ❖**
(402) 593-2380. **$79-$159, 7 day notice.** 10728 L St. I-80, exit 445 (L St E), just n on 108th St, then e. Int corridors. **Pets:** Medium. $10 daily fee/pet. Service with restrictions, supervision.
[SAVE] [S$] [X] [&] [💻] [🏊]

**(AAA) ▼▼▼ Countryside Suites M**
(402) 884-2644. **$60-$80.** 9477 S 142nd St. I-80, exit 440, just ne. Ext corridors. **Pets:** Very small. $20 deposit/pet, $7 daily fee/pet. Service with restrictions, supervision.
[SAVE] [S$] [X] [&M] [&] [💻]

**▼▼▼ Crowne Plaza Hotel LH ❖**
(402) 496-0850. **$79-$149.** 655 N 108th Ave. I-680, exit 3 (Dodge St W), 0.7 mi to 108th St to 108th Ave and N Old Mill Rd exits, then just n. Int corridors. **Pets:** Medium. $25 one-time fee/pet. Service with restrictions, crate.
[ASK] [X] [🖉] [&] [&] [💻] [🍴] [🏊] [X]

**▼▼▼ DoubleTree Guest Suites Omaha LH**
(402) 397-5141. **$69-$189.** 7270 Cedar St. I-80, exit 449 (72nd St), 1.3 mi n. Int corridors. **Pets:** Accepted.
[X] [🖉] [&] [&] [💻] [🍴] [🏊] [X]

**(AAA) ▼▼▼ Hawthorn Suites SH**
(402) 331-0101. **$99.** 11025 M St. I-80, exit 445 (L St E), 0.3 mi e, just s on 108th St, then just w. Ext corridors. **Pets:** Medium, other species. $6 daily fee/pet. Service with restrictions, crate.
[SAVE] [S$] [X] [🖉] [&] [💻] [🏊] [X]

**▼▼▼ Holiday Inn Express Hotel & Suites-West SH**
(402) 333-5566. **Call for rates.** 17677 Wright St. I-80, exit 445 (L St W), 5.5 mi w, then just s. Int corridors. **Pets:** Accepted.
[X] [&M] [🖉] [&] [&] [💻] [🏊]

**▼▼▼ Homewood Suites SH**
(402) 397-7500. **$122-$132.** 7010 Hascall St. I-80, exit 449 (72nd St), just n, then just e. Ext/int corridors. **Pets:** Accepted.
[ASK] [X] [🖉] [&] [&] [🏊]

**(AAA) ▼▼▼ La Quinta Inn Omaha SH**
(402) 493-1900. **$71-$111.** 3330 N 104th Ave. I-680, exit 4 (Maple St), just w to 108th St, just n to Bedford, then just e. Int corridors. **Pets:** Medium. Service with restrictions.
[SAVE] [S$] [X] [🖉] [&] [💻] [🏊]

**(AAA) ▼▼▼ Park Inn Omaha-Downtown SH**
(402) 345-2222. **$79-$100.** 3001 Chicago. I-480, exit 2B westbound; exit 2A northbound, just w on Dodge St, then just n on 30th St. Int corridors. **Pets:** Accepted.
[SAVE] [S$] [X] [&M] [🖉] [&] [&] [💻]

**▼▼ Ramada Limited SH**
(402) 896-9500. **$62-$68.** 9505 S 142nd St. I-80, exit 440, just ne. Int corridors. **Pets:** Medium, dogs only. $10 daily fee/pet. No service, supervision.
[ASK] [S$] [X] [&] [&] [💻] [🏊]

**(AAA) ▼▼▼ Relax Inn Motel & Suites M**
(402) 731-7300. **$50-$65.** 4578 S 60th St. I-80, exit 450 (60th St), 0.8 mi s. Ext corridors. **Pets:** Very small. $20 deposit/pet, $7 daily fee/pet. Service with restrictions, supervision.
[SAVE] [X] [&] [💻]

**(AAA) ▼▼▼ Residence Inn by Marriott SH**
(402) 553-8898. **$99-$199.** 6990 Dodge St. I-680, exit 3 (Dodge St E), 3 mi e. Ext corridors. **Pets:** Accepted.
[SAVE] [S$] [X] [&] [💻] [🏊] [X]

**(AAA) ⟡⟡ Satellite Motel M**
(402) 733-7373. **$45-$60.** 6006 L St. I-80, exit 450 (60th St), 0.8 mi s; just n of US 275 and SR 92. Ext/int corridors. **Pets:** Very small. $20 deposit/pet, $7 daily fee/pet. Service with restrictions, supervision.
[SAVE] [✕] [🛏] [▣]

**⟡⟡⟡ Sheraton Omaha Hotel LH**
(402) 342-2222. **$219-$229.** 1615 Howard St. Downtown. Int corridors. **Pets:** Accepted.
[ASK] [S♦] [✕] [✎] [&] [🛏] [▣] [¶] [✕]

**(AAA) ⟡⟡ Sleep Inn & Suites SH**
(402) 342-2525. **$60-$70.** 2525 Abbott Dr. I-480 E, exit 14st St (downtown), 2 mi n, follow signs. Int corridors. **Pets:** Small. $20 daily fee/pet. Designated rooms, no service, crate.
[SAVE] [S♦] [✕] [✎] [&] [🛏] [▣]

**⟡⟡ Super 8 Motel-Omaha/Aksarben SH**
(402) 390-0700. **$49-$85.** 7111 Spring St. I-80, exit 449 (72nd St), 0.3 mi n. Int corridors. **Pets:** Small. Designated rooms, no service, crate.
[ASK] [S♦] [✕] [✎] [🛏]

**⟡⟡ Super 8 Motel-Omaha/West L SH**
(402) 339-2250. **$49-$91.** 10829 M St. I-80, exit 445 (L St E), 0.3 mi e, just s on 108th St, then just w. Int corridors. **Pets:** Small. Designated rooms, no service, crate.
[ASK] [S♦] [✕] [✎] [🛏]

## O'NEILL

**(AAA) ⟡ Elms Motel M**
(402) 336-3800. **$46-$56.** 414 E Hwy 20. 1 mi se on US 20/275. Ext corridors. **Pets:** $7 one-time fee/room. Service with restrictions, supervision.
[SAVE] [S♦] [✕] [🛏] [▣]

**⟡⟡⟡ Holiday Inn Express Hotel & Suites SH**
(402) 336-4500. **$70-$80.** 1020 E Douglas St. 0.4 mi e on US 20/275. Int corridors. **Pets:** Small, dogs only. $10 daily fee/pet. Service with restrictions, supervision.
[ASK] [✕] [&M] [&] [🛏] [▣] [≈]

**⟡⟡ Super 8 Motel-O'Neill SH**
(402) 336-3100. **$49-$99.** 106 E Hwy 20. 0.5 mi e on US 20/275. Int corridors. **Pets:** Small Designated rooms, no service, crate.
[ASK] [S♦] [✕] [&M] [✎] [&] [🛏]

## PAXTON

**(AAA) ⟡⟡⟡ Paxton Days Inn M**
(308) 239-4510. **$54-$89.** 851 Paxton Rd. I-80, exit 145, just n. Ext corridors. **Pets:** Other species. $10 one-time fee/room. Service with restrictions, supervision.
[SAVE] [S♦] [✕] [✎] [🛏] [▣] [¶] [✕]

## ST. PAUL

**(AAA) ⟡ Bel-Air Motel & RV Park M**
(308) 754-4466. **$45-$49.** 1158 Highway 281. On US 281, 1 mi s. Ext corridors. **Pets:** Medium. $10 daily fee/pet. Supervision.
[SAVE] [✕] [🛏] [▣]

**⟡⟡ Super 8 Motel SH**
(308) 754-4554. **$58-$70.** 116 Howard Ave. Just e of downtown, jct US 281. Ext/int corridors. **Pets:** $5 daily fee/room. Service with restrictions, supervision.
[ASK] [S♦] [✕] [&] [🛏]

## SCOTTSBLUFF

**(AAA) ⟡ Capri Motel M 🐾**
(308) 635-2057. **$35-$45, 5 day notice.** 2424 Ave I. 1.5 mi nw, just s of 27th St. Ext corridors. **Pets:** Other species. $5 daily fee/pet. Service with restrictions, crate.
[SAVE] [S♦] [✕] [🛏] [▣]

**⟡⟡ Comfort Inn SH**
(308) 632-7510. **$65-$75.** 1902 21st Ave. 1.8 mi e on US 26, just n. Ext/int corridors. **Pets:** Other species. Service with restrictions, supervision.
[ASK] [S♦] [✕] [✎] [&] [🛏] [▣] [≈]

**⟡⟡ Lamplighter American Inn SH**
(308) 632-7108. **$48-$56.** 606 E 27th St. US 26 business route, 0.5 mi e of jct SR 71, just s. Int corridors. **Pets:** Dogs only. $6 daily fee/pet. Service with restrictions, supervision.
[ASK] [S♦] [✕] [🛏] [¶] [≈]

## SEWARD

**⟡⟡ Seward Super 8 M**
(402) 643-3388. **$51-$61.** 1329 Progressive Rd. I-80, exit 379, 3 mi n on SR 15. Ext/int corridors. **Pets:** Small, dogs only. $15 daily fee/pet. Designated rooms, service with restrictions, supervision.
[ASK] [S♦] [✕] [&] [🛏]

## SIDNEY

**(AAA) ⟡⟡⟡ AmericInn Motel & Suites of Sidney SH 🐾**
(308) 254-0100. **$84-$159.** 645 Cabela Dr. I-80, exit 59, just nw. Int corridors. **Pets:** Large, other species. Service with restrictions, supervision.
[SAVE] [S♦] [✕] [&M] [✎] [&] [🛏] [▣] [≈]

**(AAA) ⟡⟡⟡ Days Inn SH**
(308) 254-2121. **$59-$125.** 3042 Silverberg Dr. I-80, exit 59, just n. Int corridors. **Pets:** Medium. $10 daily fee/pet. Designated rooms, service with restrictions, supervision.
[SAVE] [S♦] [✕] [🛏] [▣] [≈]

**⟡⟡⟡ Holiday Inn & Conference Center SH**
(308) 254-2000. **$66-$90.** 664 Chase Blvd. I-80, exit 59, just s. Int corridors. **Pets:** Medium, dogs only. $10 daily fee/room. Designated rooms, service with restrictions, supervision.
[ASK] [✕] [&M] [✎] [&] [🛏] [▣] [¶] [≈]

## SOUTH SIOUX CITY

**⟡⟡⟡ Marina Inn Conference Center SH**
(402) 494-4000. **$99-$149.** 4th & B sts. I-29, exit 148, on banks of Missouri River; e at stop light by Nebraska side of bridge. Int corridors. **Pets:** Accepted.
[ASK] [✕] [&M] [✎] [&] [🛏] [▣] [¶] [≈]

## SYRACUSE

**(AAA) ⟡⟡⟡ Sleep Inn & Suites SH 🐾**
(402) 269-2700. **$70.** 130 N 30th Rd. Jct SR 2, 1 mi n on SR 50. Int corridors. **Pets:** Other species. $10 daily fee/pet.
[SAVE] [✕] [&M] [✎] [&] [🛏] [▣] [≈]

## THEDFORD

**(AAA) ⟡⟡⟡ Roadside Inn SH**
(308) 645-2284. **$51-$76.** HC 58 Box 1D. 1 mi e on SR 2, just w of US 83. Int corridors. **Pets:** Other species. $50 deposit/room, $5 daily fee/pet. Designated rooms, service with restrictions, supervision.
[SAVE] [S♦] [✕] [&M] [✎] [🛏] [▣]

## VALENTINE

**⟡ Dunes Lodge & Suites M**
(402) 376-3131. **$44-$89.** 340 E Hwy 20. Jct US 20/83, 0.3 mi e. Ext corridors. **Pets:** Medium. $10 one-time fee/pet. Designated rooms, service with restrictions, supervision.
[ASK] [S♦] [✕] [🛏]

**⟡ Motel Raine M**
(402) 376-2030. **$40-$60.** 618 W Hwy 20 W. Jct US 20/83, 0.5 mi sw. Ext corridors. **Pets:** Accepted.
[ASK] [✕] [▣]

**(AAA) ▼▼▼ Trade Winds Motel M**
(402) 376-1600. **$40-$74.** E Hwy 20 & 83. Jct US 20/83, 1 mi se. Ext corridors. **Pets:** $5 daily fee/pet. Service with restrictions, supervision.
[SAVE] [Sↄ] [X] [▤] [▣] [≈]

## WAHOO

**▼▼ Wahoo Heritage Inn SH**
(402) 443-1288. **$57-$74.** 950 N Chestnut. On US 77 and SR 92, just nw of downtown. Ext/int corridors. **Pets:** $10 daily fee/pet. Service with restrictions, supervision.
[ASK] [Sↄ] [X] [&M] [▤] [▣]

## WAYNE

**▼▼ Super 8 Motel-Wayne SH**
(402) 375-4898. **$49-$61.** 610 Tomar Dr. SR 35, 0.6 mi e of jct SR 15. Int corridors. **Pets:** Small. $20 daily fee/pet. Designated rooms, no service, crate.
[ASK] [Sↄ] [X] [&M] [∅]

## YORK

**(AAA) ▼▼▼ Best Western Palmer Inn M 🐾**
(402) 362-5585. **$50-$69.** 2426 S Lincoln Ave. I-80, exit 353 (US 81), 1 mi n. Ext corridors. **Pets:** Other species. $10 one-time fee/room. Service with restrictions, supervision.
[SAVE] [Sↄ] [X] [▤] [▣] [≈]

**(AAA) ▼▼▼ Holiday Inn SH**
(402) 362-6661. **$72-$79.** 4619 S Lincoln Ave. I-80, exit 353 (US 81), just s. Int corridors. **Pets:** Small. $25 daily fee/pet. Service with restrictions, supervision.
[SAVE] [Sↄ] [X] [&M] [∅] [&'] [▤] [▣] [¶] [≈]

**▼▼ Yorkshire Inn Motel M**
(402) 362-6633. **$42-$59.** 3402 S Lincoln Ave. I-80, exit 353 (US 81), 0.5 mi n. Ext/int corridors. **Pets:** Accepted.
[ASK] [Sↄ] [X] [▤]

# NEVADA

## AMARGOSA VALLEY

 Longstreet Inn, Casino & RV Park SH
(775) 372-1777. $69-$99. 373 Stateline. 7 mi n of jct SR 127 and 190 (Death Valley Jct) on SR 373; 15 mi s of jct SR 95 and 373 on SR 373. Int corridors. Pets: Accepted.

## BATTLE MOUNTAIN

Comfort Inn SH
(775) 635-5880. $56-$78. 521 E Front St. I-80, exit 229 or 233, just n. Int corridors. Pets: Accepted.

## BEATTY

Burro Inn M
(775) 553-2225. $44. Third St & Hwy 95. 4 blks s on SR 95. Ext corridors. Pets: Accepted.

Exchange Club Motel & Casino M
(775) 553-2333. $45. 119 Main St. SR 95 at SR 374; downtown. Ext corridors. Pets: Other species. $25 deposit/pet, $5 daily fee/pet. Service with restrictions, supervision.

Stagecoach Hotel Casino M
(775) 553-2419. $43-$53. Hwy 95 N. North end of town; west side of US 95. Ext/int corridors. Pets: Other species. $10 deposit/pet, $5 one-time fee/pet. Designated rooms, service with restrictions, supervision.

## CARLIN

Comfort Inn SH
(775) 754-6110. $59-$89. 1018 Fir St. I-80, exit 280, just s. Int corridors. Pets: Accepted.

## CARSON CITY

Americas Best Value Inn M
(775) 882-2007. $33-$199. 2731 S Carson St. 1.3 mi s on US 50 and 395. Ext corridors. Pets: $5 one-time fee/room. Service with restrictions, supervision.

Best Western Trailside Inn M
(775) 883-7300. $45-$209. 1300 N Carson St. 0.5 mi n on US 395. Ext corridors. Pets: Other species. $10 daily fee/pet. Service with restrictions, supervision.

Carson City Super 8 M
(775) 883-7800. $38-$199. 2829 S Carson St. South end of town. Int corridors. Pets: Small, other species. $10 daily fee/pet. No service, supervision.

Days Inn M
(775) 883-3343. $45-$190, 7 day notice. 3103 N Carson St. US 395 N, north end of town. Ext corridors. Pets: $10 daily fee/pet. Service with restrictions, supervision.

Holiday Inn Express & Suites M
(775) 283-4055. $84-$149. 4055 N Carson St. US 395; north end of town. Int corridors. Pets: Accepted.

The Plaza Hotel M
(775) 883-9500. $39-$89, 3 day notice. 801 S Carson St. South end of town. Ext/int corridors. Pets: Dogs only. $100 one-time fee/pet. Designated rooms, supervision.

## ELKO

Best Western Gold Country Motor Inn SH
(775) 738-8421. $99-$139. 2050 Idaho St. I-80, exit 303, just s. Ext corridors. Pets: Accepted.

Comfort Inn SH
(775) 777-8762. $73-$133, 7 day notice. 2970 Idaho St. I-80, exit 303, just s, then just e. Int corridors. Pets: Very small. $10 daily fee/pet. Designated rooms, service with restrictions, supervision.

High Desert Inn SH
(775) 738-8425. $89. 3015 Idaho St. I-80, exit 303, just s. Ext/int corridors. Pets: Medium, other species. $15 one-time fee/room. Designated rooms, service with restrictions, crate.

Oak Tree Inn SH
(775) 777-2222. $59-$99. 95 Spruce Rd. I-80, exit 301, just n. Int corridors. Pets: Accepted.

Red Lion Inn & Casino Elko SH
(775) 738-2111. $89-$159. 2065 Idaho St. I-80, exit 303, just s. Int corridors. Pets: Other species. $15 one-time fee/room. Designated rooms, service with restrictions.

Shilo Inn SH
(775) 738-5522. $69-$123. 2401 Mountain City Hwy. I-80, exit 301, just n. Int corridors. Pets: $10 daily fee/pet. Service with restrictions, supervision.

Thunderbird Motel M
(775) 738-7115. $59-$69. 345 Idaho St. I-80, exit 301 or 303, 1 mi s. Ext corridors. Pets: Accepted.

# ELY

**4 Sevens Motel** M
(775) 289-4747. **$30-$45.** 500 High St. Just n of 5th St; downtown. Ext corridors. **Pets:** Accepted.
SAVE S⊘ ✕ ⊟ ⊑

**Fireside Inn** M
(775) 289-3765. **$40-$50.** McGill Hwy. 2 mi n on US 93. Ext corridors. **Pets:** Accepted.
SAVE S⊘ ✕ ⊟ ⊑

**Historic Hotel Nevada & Gambling Hall** SH
(775) 289-6665. **$30-$50.** 501 Aultman St. Downtown. Int corridors. **Pets:** Accepted.
SAVE S⊘ ✕ ⊟ ⊑ ⊤⊥

**Ramada Inn-Copper Queen Casino** SH
(775) 289-4884. **$74-$134.** 805 Great Basin Blvd. 0.3 mi s of jct US 6, 50 and 93. Ext/int corridors. **Pets:** Accepted.
SAVE S⊘ ✕ &M ⊟ ⊑ ⊤⊥ ≈

# EUREKA

**Best Western Eureka Inn** SH
(775) 237-5247. **$79.** 251 N Main St. On east side of Main St; center. Int corridors. **Pets:** $25 deposit/room, $10 one-time fee/room. Designated rooms, service with restrictions, supervision.
ASK ✕ &M ⊘ & ⊟ ⊑

# FALLON

**Comfort Inn** M
(775) 423-5554. **$60-$100.** 1830 W Williams Ave. US 50, 1 mi w of US 95. Int corridors. **Pets:** Medium. $10 daily fee/pet. Designated rooms, service with restrictions, supervision.
SAVE S⊘ ✕ &M & ⊟ ⊑ ≈

**Motel 6 #4140** M
(775) 423-2277. **$46-$70.** 1705 S Taylor St. 0.5 mi s of US 50. Ext corridors. **Pets:** Accepted.
SAVE S⊘ ✕ ≈

**Super 8 Motel** M
(775) 423-6031. **$55-$60.** 855 W Williams Ave. US 50, 0.5 mi w of US 95. Ext/int corridors. **Pets:** Other species. $5 daily fee/pet. Designated rooms, service with restrictions.
SAVE ✕ ⊤⊥

# FERNLEY

**Best Western Fernley Inn** M
(775) 575-6776. **$75-$125, 7 day notice.** 1405 E Newlands Dr. I-80, exit 48, just s. Ext corridors. **Pets:** Medium, other species. $7 daily fee/pet. Designated rooms, service with restrictions.
SAVE S⊘ ✕ &M ⊘ ⊟ ⊑ ≈

# GARDNERVILLE

**Best Western Topaz Lake Inn** M
(775) 266-4661. **$55-$139.** 3410 Sandy Bowers Ave. US 395 at Topaz Lake, 22 mi s. Ext/int corridors. **Pets:** Medium, dogs only. $10 daily fee/pet. Designated rooms, service with restrictions, supervision.
SAVE S⊘ ✕ &M & ⊟ ⊑ ≈

**Topaz Lodge** M
(775) 266-3338. **$29-$105.** 1979 US 395 S. US 395 S at Topaz Lake, 22 mi s. Ext corridors. **Pets:** Medium, dogs only. $10 daily fee/pet. Designated rooms, service with restrictions, supervision.
SAVE ✕ ⊤⊥ ≈

**Westerner Motel** M
(775) 782-3602. **$45-$85.** 1353 US 395 N. On US 395, south end of town. Ext corridors. **Pets:** Accepted.
SAVE S⊘ ✕ ⊟ ⊑ ≈

# HAWTHORNE

**El Capitan Resort Casino** M
(775) 945-3321. **$55-$60.** 540 F St. Just n of US 95. Ext corridors. **Pets:** Other species. $10 daily fee/room. Designated rooms, service with restrictions.
SAVE ✕ ⊟ ⊑ ⊤⊥ ≈

# JACKPOT

**Horseshu Hotel & Casino** SH
(775) 755-7777. **$29-$65.** 1385 Hwy 93. On US 93. Int corridors. **Pets:** Other species. Designated rooms, service with restrictions.
SAVE ✕ ⊑ ⊤⊥ ≈ ✕

**West Star Resort** M
(775) 755-2600. **$32-$125.** Hwy 93 & Foker St. Just w of US 93. Int corridors. **Pets:** Accepted.
ASK S⊘ ✕ &M & ⊑

---

# NEARBY CALIFORNIA
# LAKE TAHOE AREA

## STATELINE

**Harrah's Hotel, Casino & Resort** LH
(775) 588-6611. **$89-$699, 3 day notice.** US 50. In casino area. Int corridors. **Pets:** Accepted.
SAVE ✕ &M & ⊤⊥ ≈ ✕

**Harveys Hotel, Casino & Resort** LH
(775) 588-2411. **$59-$699, 3 day notice.** US 50. On US 50, in casino center. Int corridors. **Pets:** Accepted.
SAVE ✕ &M & ⊤⊥ ≈ ✕

**Lake Village Resort** CO
(775) 589-6065. **$150-$475, 30 day notice.** 301 Hwy 50. 1 mi e of casino center. Ext corridors. **Pets:** Large, dogs only. $20 daily fee/pet. Service with restrictions.
SAVE S⊘ ✕ ⊟ ⊑ ≈ ✕ ⊼

---

# END AREA

# LAS VEGAS METROPOLITAN AREA

## BOULDER CITY

**Boulder Inn & Suites** M
(702) 369-1000. **$69-$129.** 704 Nevada Way. On US 93. Ext corridors.
**Pets:** Accepted.

**El Rancho Boulder Motel** M
(702) 293-1085. **$70-$120, 7 day notice.** 725 Nevada Way. On US 93.
Ext corridors. **Pets:** Dogs only. $10 daily fee/pet. Service with restrictions,
supervision.

## ECHO BAY

**Echo Bay Resort** M
(702) 394-4000. **$60-$115, 3 day notice.** North Shore Rd. 4 mi e of SR
167; on Lake Mead. Int corridors. **Pets:** Accepted.

## HENDERSON

**Green Valley Ranch** LH
(702) 617-7777. **$300-$500.** 2300 S Paseo Verde Dr. I-215, exit Green
Valley Pkwy, just s. **Pets:** Small, dogs only. $300 deposit/room, $100 daily
fee/pet. Designated rooms, service with restrictions, supervision.

**Hawthorn Inn & Suites** M
(702) 568-7800. **$79-$299, 3 day notice.** 910 S Boulder Hwy. S of
Lake Mead Pkwy. Int corridors. **Pets:** Other species. $15 daily fee/pet.
Service with restrictions, crate.

**Residence Inn-Green Valley** M
(702) 434-2700. **$139.** 2190 Olympic Ave. I-215, exit Green Valley
Pkwy N, 3 mi n at Sunset Rd. Int corridors. **Pets:** Accepted.

**The Ritz-Carlton, Lake Las Vegas** LH
(702) 567-4700. **$179-$5000.** 1610 Lake Las Vegas Pkwy. I-215, e to
end, n on Lake Las Vegas Pkwy, then 0.5 mi. Int corridors.
**Pets:** Accepted.

## INDIAN SPRINGS

**Indian Springs Motor Hotel** M
(702) 879-3700. **$44-$54.** 300 Tonopah Hwy. On US 95. Int corridors.
**Pets:** Accepted.

## LAS VEGAS

**Amerirest Las Vegas Travelodge** M
(702) 733-0001. **$39-$99.** 2601 Westwood Dr. I-15, exit Sahara Ave E,
just se. Int corridors. **Pets:** Accepted.

**Best Western Main Street Inn** M
(702) 382-3455. **$45-$199.** 1000 N Main St. I-15, exit 43E northbound;
exit 44E southbound. Ext corridors. **Pets:** Other species. $15 daily fee/
pet. Service with restrictions.

**Best Western Nellis Motor Inn** M
(702) 643-6111. **$55-$200.** 5330 E Craig Rd. I-15, exit 48, 2.8 mi e; 0.3
mi from Nellis AFB. Ext corridors. **Pets:** Other species. $50 deposit/room,
$10 daily fee/pet. Designated rooms, service with restrictions, supervision.

**Best Western Parkview Inn** M
(702) 385-1213. **$55-$199, 14 day notice.** 921 Las Vegas Blvd N. I-15,
exit US 93-95, 0.3 mi n at Washington. Ext corridors. **Pets:** Other
species. $8 daily fee/pet. Service with restrictions, crate.

**Candlewood Suites** SH
(702) 836-3660. **$109-$249.** 4034 S Paradise Rd. I-15, exit E Flamingo
Rd to Paradise Rd, just ne. Int corridors. **Pets:** Accepted.

**Comfort Inn** M
(702) 399-1500. **$89-$299.** 910 E Cheyenne Ave. I-15, exit Cheyenne
Ave W. Int corridors. **Pets:** $10 daily fee/pet. Service with restrictions,
supervision.

**Extended Stay Deluxe-Las Vegas-East
Flamingo** M
(702) 731-3111. **$82.** 1550 E Flamingo Rd. I-15, exit E Flamingo Rd, 2
mi. Int corridors. **Pets:** $25 daily fee/pet. Service with restrictions, supervi-
sion.

**Four Seasons Hotel Las Vegas** LH
(702) 632-5000. **$275-$580.** 3960 Las Vegas Blvd S. I-15, exit E Tropicana Ave, just s on the Strip. Int corridors. **Pets:** Accepted.

**Hawthorn Suites-Las Vegas** M
(702) 739-7000. **$79-$169, 3 day notice.** 5051 Duke Ellington Way.
I-15, exit E Tropicana Ave, 0.8 mi e to Duke Ellington Way, then just s.
Ext corridors. **Pets:** Accepted.

**Highland Inn Motel** M
(702) 896-4333. **$45-$200, 3 day notice.** 8025 S Industrial Rd. I-15,
exit W Blue Diamond Rd, just nw. Ext corridors. **Pets:** Very small. $10
daily fee/pet. Service with restrictions, supervision.

**Holiday Inn Express Hotel & Suites N Las
Vegas** M
(702) 649-3000. **$99-$229.** 4540 Donovan Way. I-15, exit W Craig Rd.
Int corridors. **Pets:** Accepted.

**Homestead Studio Suites Hotel-Las
Vegas/Midtown** M
(702) 369-1414. **$82.** 3045 S Maryland Pkwy. I-15, exit Sahara Ave E,
just s. Int corridors. **Pets:** $25 daily fee/pet. Service with restrictions,
supervision.

**Howard Johnson Airport Inn** Ⓜ
(702) 798-2777. **$30-$100.** 5100 Paradise Rd. I-15, exit E Tropicana Ave, 1.8 mi to Paradise Rd, then 0.3 mi s. Ext corridors. **Pets:** Small. $50 one-time fee/pet. Designated rooms, service with restrictions, supervision.

**Howard Johnson Las Vegas Strip** Ⓜ
(702) 388-0301. **$40-$300.** 1401 Las Vegas Blvd S. I-15, exit Las Vegas Blvd, just n. Ext/int corridors. **Pets:** Small. $10 daily fee/pet. Designated rooms, service with restrictions, supervision.

**La Quinta Inn & Suites Las Vegas (Summerlin Tech Center)** Ⓜ
(702) 360-1200. **$85-$115.** 7101 Cascade Valley Ct. US 95, exit W Cheyenne Ave. Int corridors. **Pets:** Medium. Service with restrictions.

**La Quinta Inn & Suites Las Vegas (West/Lakes)** Ⓜ
(702) 243-0356. **$99-$199.** 9570 W Sahara Ave. Just w of Fort Apache Rd. Int corridors. **Pets:** Other species. Designated rooms, service with restrictions, supervision.

**La Quinta Inn Las Vegas (Convention Center)** Ⓜ
(702) 796-9000. **$89-$129.** 3970 Paradise Rd. I-15, exit E Flamingo Rd, 0.8 mi s of convention center; 0.5 mi e of the Strip. Int corridors. **Pets:** Medium. Service with restrictions.

**La Quinta Inn Las Vegas (Nellis)** Ⓜ
(702) 632-0229. **$69-$169.** 4288 N Nellis Blvd. I-15, exit Craig Rd, e to N Las Vegas Blvd. Int corridors. **Pets:** Other species. Service with restrictions, crate.

**La Quinta Inn Las Vegas (Tropicana)** Ⓜ
(702) 798-7736. **$69-$139.** 4975 S Valley View Blvd. I-15, exit Tropicana Ave W. Int corridors. **Pets:** Accepted.

**Motel 6 Boulder Highway #1337** Ⓜ
(702) 457-8051. **$47-$57.** 4125 Boulder Hwy. Just s of Sahara Ave. Ext corridors. **Pets:** Accepted.

**Ramada Inn-Speedway Casino** Ⓜ
(702) 399-3297. **$59-$149.** 3227 Civic Center Dr. I-15, exit Cheyenne Ave E. Int corridors. **Pets:** Medium. $10 daily fee/pet. Service with restrictions.

**Residence Inn by Marriott Las Vegas South** Ⓜ
(702) 795-7378. **$119-$329, 14 day notice.** 5875 Industrial Rd. I-15, exit Russell Rd, just sw. Int corridors. **Pets:** Accepted.

**Residence Inn-Hughes Center** Ⓜ
(702) 650-0040. **$159-$399.** 370 Hughes Center Dr. I-15, exit Paradise Rd. Int corridors. **Pets:** Large, other species. $75 one-time fee/room. Service with restrictions.

**Residence Inn Las Vegas Convention Center** Ⓜ ✿
(702) 796-9300. **$169-$399.** 3225 Paradise Rd. Opposite the convention center. Ext corridors. **Pets:** Large, other species. $75 one-time fee/room. Designated rooms, service with restrictions.

**St. Tropez All Suite Hotel** 🆂🅷
(702) 369-5400. **$99-$129.** 455 E Harmon Ave. 2 mi s of convention center at Paradise Rd. Ext/int corridors. **Pets:** Accepted.

**Super 8 Motel Las Vegas Strip** Ⓜ
(702) 794-0888. **$59-$250.** 4250 S Koval Ln. I-15, exit S Koval Ln. Int corridors. **Pets:** Other species. $15 daily fee/pet. Designated rooms, service with restrictions, supervision.

**The Westin Casuarina Las Vegas Hotel & Spa** 🅻🅷
(702) 836-9775. **$329-$699.** 160 E Flamingo Rd. I-15, exit Flamingo Rd E. Int corridors. **Pets:** Accepted.

## LAUGHLIN

**Don Laughlin's Riverside Resort Hotel & Casino** 🅻🅷
(702) 298-2535. **$39-$699.** 1650 S Casino Dr. 2 mi s of Davis Dam. Int corridors. **Pets:** Accepted.

## MESQUITE

**Best Western Mesquite Inn** Ⓜ
(702) 346-7444. **$69-$99.** 390 N Sandhill Blvd. I-15, exit 122. Ext corridors. **Pets:** Medium. $10 daily fee/room. Designated rooms, service with restrictions, supervision.

**Falcon Ridge Hotel** 🆂🅷
(702) 346-2200. **$59-$229.** 1030 W Pioneer Blvd. I-15, exit 120, just w. Int corridors. **Pets:** Accepted.

**Virgin River Hotel Casino Bingo** Ⓜ
(702) 346-7777. **$30-$90.** 100 Pioneer Blvd. I-15, exit 122, just w. Ext corridors. **Pets:** Accepted.

## OVERTON

**Best Western North Shore Inn at Lake Mead** Ⓜ
(702) 397-6000. **$57-$79.** 520 N Moapa Valley Blvd. I-15, exit 93, 10 mi ne on SR 169. Int corridors. **Pets:** Small, dogs only. $10 daily fee/room. Designated rooms, service with restrictions, supervision.

## PAHRUMP

**Best Western Pahrump Station** Ⓜ
(775) 727-5100. **$69-$129.** 1101 S Hwy 160. Downtown. Ext corridors. **Pets:** Medium, dogs only. $6 daily fee/pet Designated rooms, service with restrictions, supervision.

**Saddle West Hotel & Casino** Ⓜ
(775) 727-1111. **$46-$175.** 1220 S Hwy 160. Downtown. Ext corridors. **Pets:** Medium. $100 deposit/room. Designated rooms, service with restrictions, supervision.

---

**END METROPOLITAN AREA**

# LOVELOCK

**◈◈◈ ♛♛♛ Sturgeon's Inn & Casino** 🅂🄷
(775) 273-2971. **$59-$85.** 1420 Cornell Ave. I-80, exit 105 or 107, just n. Ext corridors. **Pets:** Accepted.
[A$K] [S🄳] [✕] [&M] [⌀] [🔋] [▥] [🍽] [⇌]

# MINDEN

**◈◈◈ ♛♛♛♛ Best Western Minden Inn** 🅼
(775) 782-7766. **$65-$109.** 1795 Ironwood Dr. US 395, exit Ironwood Dr W, 0.5 mi n of jct US 395 and SR 88. Ext corridors. **Pets:** Small, dogs only. $15 daily fee/pet. Service with restrictions, supervision.
[SAVE] [S🄳] [✕] [&M] [&] [🔋] [▥] [⇌]

**♛♛ Holiday Lodge** 🅼
(775) 782-2288. **$43-$56.** 1591 US 395 N. Center. Ext corridors. **Pets:** Small, dogs only. $30 deposit/pet. Designated rooms, service with restrictions, supervision.
[A$K] [✕] [🔋] [⇌]

# RENO

**◈◈◈ ♛♛♛ A&A's Rodeway Inn & Spa** 🅼
(775) 786-2500. **$30-$170, 3 day notice.** 2050 Market St. I-395, exit W Mill St. Int corridors. **Pets:** Other species. $10 daily fee/pet. Service with restrictions.
[SAVE] [S🄳] [✕] [🔋] [▥] [⇌]

**◈◈◈ ♛♛♛ Airport Travelodge** 🅼
(775) 786-2506. **$40-$190.** 2050-B Market St. I-395, exit W Mill St, just w. Int corridors. **Pets:** Other species. $10 daily fee/pet. Service with restrictions.
[SAVE] [S🄳] [✕] [🔋] [▥] [⇌]

**◈◈◈ ♛♛♛♛ Atlantis Casino Resort-Reno** 🄻🄷
(775) 825-4700. **$49-$189.** 3800 S Virginia St. 3 mi s on US 395. Ext/int corridors. **Pets:** Accepted.
[SAVE] [S🄳] [✕] [&M] [⌀] [&] [▥] [🍽] [⇌] [✕]

**◈◈◈ ♛♛♛♛ Best Western Airport Plaza Hotel** 🅂🄷
(775) 348-6370. **$59-$249.** 1981 Terminal Way. US 395, exit E Plumb Villanova. Int corridors. **Pets:** Accepted.
[SAVE] [S🄳] [✕] [&M] [&] [🔋] [▥] [🍽] [⇌] [✕]

**◈◈◈ ♛♛ Days Inn** 🅼
(775) 786-4070. **$29-$179.** 701 E 7th St. I-80, exit Wells Ave, just s. Ext corridors. **Pets:** Accepted.
[SAVE] [S🄳] [✕] [🔋] [▥]

**♛♛♛♛ Holiday Inn-Downtown** 🅂🄷
(775) 786-5151. **$59-$199.** 1000 E 6th St. I-80, exit Wells Ave, 2 blks e. Int corridors. **Pets:** Accepted.
[SAVE] [✕] [&M] [⌀] [&] [🔋] [▥] [🍽] [⇌]

**♛♛♛♛ La Quinta Inn Reno (Airport)** 🅼
(775) 348-6100. **$69-$129.** 4001 Market St. US 395, exit airport northbound; exit Villanova Dr southbound. Ext corridors. **Pets:** Medium. Service with restrictions.
[A$K] [✕] [&M] [⌀] [🔋] [▥] [⇌]

**◈◈◈ ♛♛♛ Reno Downtown Travelodge** 🅼
(775) 329-3451. **$29-$199.** 655 W 4th St. I-80, exit Keystone, just e. Ext corridors. **Pets:** Accepted.
[SAVE] [S🄳] [✕] [🔋] [▥] [⇌]

**◈◈◈ ♛♛♛ Residence Inn by Marriott** 🅼
(775) 853-8800. **$84-$164.** 9845 Gateway Dr. US 395, exit S Meadows Pkwy, then e. Int corridors. **Pets:** Accepted.
[SAVE] [✕] [&M] [&] [🔋] [▥] [⇌] [✕]

**◈◈◈ ♛♛♛ Super 8 Motel at Meadow Wood Courtyard** 🅼
(775) 829-4600. **$49-$139.** 5851 S Virginia St. US 395 at S McCarran Blvd. Ext corridors. **Pets:** Accepted.
[SAVE] [S🄳] [✕] [&M] [⌀] [🔋] [▥] [🍽] [⇌]

**◈◈◈ ♛♛♛ Super 8 Motel-University** 🅼
(775) 329-3464. **$39-$140.** 1651 N Virginia St. Opposite University of Nevada. Ext corridors. **Pets:** Accepted.
[SAVE] [S🄳] [✕] [🔋] [▥] [⇌]

# SPARKS

**◈◈◈ ♛♛♛ Quality Inn** 🅼
(775) 358-6900. **$80-$169.** 55 E Nugget Ave. I-80, exit E McCarran Blvd, just s. Int corridors. **Pets:** Accepted.
[SAVE] [S🄳] [✕] [&] [🔋] [▥] [🍽] [⇌]

# TONOPAH

**◈◈◈ ♛♛♛♛ Best Western Hi-Desert Inn** 🅼
(775) 482-3511. **$75-$99.** 320 Main St. On US 6 and 95. Int corridors. **Pets:** Dogs only. Designated rooms, service with restrictions, supervision.
[SAVE] [S🄳] [✕] [&M] [⌀] [&] [🔋] [▥] [⇌]

**◈◈◈ ♛♛♛ Ramada Inn-Tonopah Station** 🅼
(775) 482-9777. **$63-$75.** 1100 Main St. On US 6 and 95. Int corridors. **Pets:** Accepted.
[SAVE] [S🄳] [✕] [&M] [&] [▥] [🍽]

# UNIONVILLE

**◈◈◈ ♛♛♛ Old Pioneer Garden** 🄱🄱
(775) 538-7585. **$95 (no credit cards), 7 day notice.** 2805 Unionville Rd. I-80, exit 149, 16 mi s, then 2.5 mi w. Int corridors. **Pets:** Service with restrictions, supervision.
[SAVE] [✕] [♨] [⌀]

# VIRGINIA CITY

**♛♛ Gold Hill Hotel** 🄱🄱
(775) 847-0111. **$45-$235.** 1540 Main St. 1 mi s on SR 342. Ext/int corridors. **Pets:** Small. $15 one-time fee/pet. Designated rooms, service with restrictions, supervision.
[A$K] [🔋] [▥] [🍽]

# WELLS

**◈◈◈ ♛♛♛ Super 8 Motel** 🅼 🐾
(775) 752-3384. **$48-$64.** 930 6th St. I-80, exit 351 eastbound, 1 mi n, then 0.8 mi e; exit 352A westbound, 0.3 mi n, then 0.5 mi w. Ext corridors. **Pets:** Other species. $5 daily fee/pet. Designated rooms, service with restrictions, supervision.
[SAVE] [S🄳] [✕] [🔋] [⇌]

**◈◈◈ ♛♛♛ The Sage Inn** 🅼
(775) 752-3353. **$44-$62.** 576 6th St. I-80, exit 351 eastbound, 1 mi n, then 0.5 mi e; exit 352A westbound, 0.3 mi n, then 0.7 mi w. Ext corridors. **Pets:** Accepted.
[SAVE] [S🄳] [✕] [🔋] [▥] [⇌]

# WEST WENDOVER

**♛♛ Wendover Super 8** 🅼
(775) 664-2888. **$29-$129, 3 day notice.** 1325 Wendover Blvd. I-80, exit 410, 0.5 mi w. Int corridors. **Pets:** Other species. $8 one-time fee/room. Service with restrictions, supervision.
[A$K] [S🄳] [✕] [🔋]

# WINNEMUCCA

**◈◈◈ ♛♛♛♛ Best Western Gold Country Inn** 🅂🄷 🐾
(775) 623-6999. **$89-$119.** 921 W Winnemucca Blvd. I-80, exit 176 or 178, just s. Int corridors. **Pets:** Other species. $10 one-time fee/pet. Supervision.
[SAVE] [S🄳] [✕] [🔋] [▥] [⇌]

**◈◈◈ ♛♛♛♛ Best Western Holiday Motel** 🅼
(775) 623-3684. **$59-$89.** 670 W Winnemucca Blvd. I-80, exit 176 or 178, just s. Ext corridors. **Pets:** Other species. $20 deposit/room. Service with restrictions, supervision.
[SAVE] [S🄳] [✕] [🔋] [▥] [⇌]

**AAA ◆◆◆◆ Days Inn M**
(775) 623-3661. **$69-$99.** 511 W Winnemucca Blvd. I-80, exit 176 or 178, just s. Ext corridors. **Pets:** $10 one-time fee/room. Service with restrictions, supervision.
[SAVE] [S🐾] [✕] [🔒] [💻] [⌐]

**◆◆◆ Holiday Inn Express SH**
(775) 625-3100. **$72-$119.** 1987 W Winnemucca Blvd. I-80, exit 176, just s. Int corridors. **Pets:** Large. $20 daily fee/pet. Designated rooms, service with restrictions, supervision.
[ASK] [S🐾] [✕] [⛟M] [🗐] [⛭] [🔒] [💻] [⌐]

**AAA ◆◆◆◆ Red Lion Hotel & Casino SH**
(775) 623-2565. **$89-$119.** 741 W Winnemucca Blvd. I-80, exit 176 or 178, just s. Int corridors. **Pets:** Accepted.
[SAVE] [S🐾] [✕] [🗐] [🔒] [💻] [⑪] [⌐]

**AAA ◆◆ Scott Shady Court Motel M**
(775) 623-3646. **$38-$55.** 400 1st St. I-80, exit 176 or 178, 0.3 mi n on Pavilion. Ext corridors. **Pets:** Accepted.
[SAVE] [💻] [⌐]

**◆◆ Super 8 Motel M**
(775) 625-1818. **$59-$108.** 1157 W Winnemucca Blvd. I-80, exit 176, 0.5 mi e. Int corridors. **Pets:** Other species. $50 deposit/room, $10 daily fee/pet. Service with restrictions, supervision.
[ASK] [S🐾] [✕] [🔒]

**AAA ◆◆◆◆ Town House Motel M**
(775) 623-3620. **$44-$63.** 375 Monroe St. I-80, exit 176 or 178, just s. Ext corridors. **Pets:** Medium. Service with restrictions, supervision.
[SAVE] [S🐾] [✕] [🔒] [💻] [⌐]

# NEW HAMPSHIRE

## CITY INDEX

## BARTLETT

(The) Bartlett Inn **BB**
(603) 374-2353. **$79-$215, 14 day notice.** White Mountain Hwy (US 302). On US 302, 2.4 mi w of jct SR 16. Ext/int corridors. **Pets:** Dogs only. Designated rooms, supervision.

The Villager Motel **M**
(603) 374-2742. **$49-$109, 10 day notice.** US 302. 1 mi e on US 302; 1.3 mi w of Attitash Mountain. Ext corridors. **Pets:** Dogs only. $10 daily fee/pet. Designated rooms, service with restrictions, supervision.

## BETHLEHEM

 The Mulburn Inn at Bethlehem **BB**
(603) 869-3389. **$90-$175, 14 day notice.** 2370 Main St. I-93, exit 40, 3.5 mi e on US 302. Int corridors. **Pets:** $25 one-time fee/pet. Designated rooms, service with restrictions, supervision.

## BRETTON WOODS

 The Bretton Arms Country Inn **CI**
(603) 278-1000. **$159-$299, 15 day notice.** US 302. Center. Int corridors. **Pets:** Dogs only. $30 daily fee/pet. Designated rooms.

The Townhomes at Bretton Woods **CO**
(603) 278-2000. **$199-$1200, 15 day notice.** Rt 302. Center. Ext corridors. **Pets:** Accepted.

## CHESTERFIELD

Chesterfield Inn **CI**
(603) 256-3211. **$295, 5 day notice.** 399 Cross Rd. I-91, exit 3, 2 mi e on SR 9. Ext/int corridors. **Pets:** Large, other species. Supervision.

## CHOCORUA

The Lazy Dog Inn **BB**
(603) 323-8350. **$85-$205, 14 day notice.** 201 White Mountain Hwy. On SR 16, 2.8 mi n of jct SR 25. Int corridors. **Pets:** Dogs only. Supervision.

## CLAREMONT

Best Budget Inn **M**
(603) 542-9567. **$54-$74, 3 day notice.** 24 Sullivan St. Just n of jct SR 11/12/103/120; center. Ext corridors. **Pets:** Medium, dogs only. $20 deposit/pet, $15 daily fee/pet. Designated rooms, service with restrictions, supervision.

## COLEBROOK

Northern Comfort Motel **M**
(603) 237-4440. **$64-$78, 3 day notice.** 1 Trooper Scott Phillips Hwy. 1.5 mi s on US 3. Ext corridors. **Pets:** Accepted.

## CONCORD

Best Western Concord Inn & Suites **SH**
(603) 228-4300. **$59-$299.** 97 Hall St. I-93, exit 13, just n on Main St, then 0.5 mi w. Int corridors. **Pets:** Medium, other species. $15 one-time fee/pet. Service with restrictions, supervision.

Concord Comfort Inn **SH**
(603) 226-4100. **$59-$189.** 71 Hall St. I-93, exit 13, just n on Main St, then 0.3 mi w. Int corridors. **Pets:** Dogs only. $15 daily fee/pet. Designated rooms, service with restrictions, supervision.

## CONWAY

White Deer Motel **M**
(603) 447-5366. **$49-$159, 14 day notice.** 379 White Mountain Hwy. 2.1 mi s of jct US 302; 0.5 mi n of village center on SR 16. Ext/int corridors. **Pets:** Accepted.

## DOVER

Days Inn **M**
(603) 742-0400. **$89-$259.** 481 Central Ave. Spaulding Tpke, exit 7, 2 mi n on SR 108; downtown. Ext/int corridors. **Pets:** Other species. $50 deposit/room. Supervision.

## DURHAM

Hickory Pond Inn **CI**
(603) 659-2227. **$89-$146, 3 day notice.** 1 Stagecoach Rd. 2.8 mi s on SR 108. Int corridors. **Pets:** Accepted.

## EATON CENTER

Inn at Crystal Lake & Restaurant **CI**
(603) 447-2120. **$89-$239, 14 day notice.** 2356 Eaton Rd. On SR 153; center. Ext/int corridors. **Pets:** Dogs only. Designated rooms, service with restrictions, supervision.

## FRANCONIA

Franconia Hotel **SH**
(603) 823-7422. **$79-$139, 3 day notice.** 87 Wallace Hill Rd. I-93, exit 38, just e. Int corridors. **Pets:** Accepted.

**AAA ▼▼ ◇ Gale River Motel M** ❀
(603) 823-5655. **$60-$120, 7 day notice.** 1 Main St. I-93, exit 38, 0.8 mi n on SR 18. Ext corridors. **Pets:** $10 daily fee/pet. Service with restrictions, supervision.
[SAVE] [S🐾] [✕] [🛏] [💻] [🏊] [✕]

**▼▼◇▼ Lovetts Inn by Lafayette Brook CI**
(603) 823-7761. **$125-$335, 7 day notice.** 1474 Profile Rd. I-93, exit 38, just w on Wallace Hill Rd, then 2.1 mi s on SR 18. Ext/int corridors. **Pets:** Accepted.
[ASK] [✕] [🛏] [💻] [🍴] [🏊] [✕] [☎]

# GORHAM

**◇ Moose Brook Motel M**
(603) 466-5400. **$39-$89, 7 day notice.** 65 Lancaster Rd. Jct SR 16, 0.5 mi w on US 2. Ext corridors. **Pets:** $5 one-time fee/pet. Designated rooms, service with restrictions, crate.
[✕] [🛏] [🏊]

**▼▼ ▼▼ Royalty Inn SH**
(603) 466-3312. **$50-$110.** 130 Main St. On US 2 and SR 16; center. Ext/int corridors. **Pets:** Other species. $5 daily fee/pet. Designated rooms, service with restrictions.
[✕] [🐾M] [🛏] [💻] [🍴] [🏊] [✕]

**AAA ▼▼ ▼▼ Top Notch Inn M** ❀
(603) 466-5496. **$39-$142.** 265 Main St. On US 2 and SR 16; center. Ext/int corridors. **Pets:** Medium, dogs only. Designated rooms, service with restrictions, supervision.
[SAVE] [S🐾] [✕] [🔑] [🛏] [💻] [🏊]

**▼▼ ▼▼ Town & Country Motor Inn SH**
(603) 466-3315. **$70-$125.** US Rt 2. 0.5 mi e of jct SR 16. Ext/int corridors. **Pets:** $6 daily fee/pet. Designated rooms, service with restrictions, supervision.
[✕] [🛏] [🍴] [🏊] [✕]

# HAMPTON

**AAA ▼▼▼▼ The Inn of Hampton and Conference Center SH**
(603) 926-6771. **$109-$189.** 815 Lafayette Rd. 0.5 mi n on US 1. Int corridors. **Pets:** Medium. Designated rooms, service with restrictions, supervision.
[SAVE] [S🐾] [✕] [🐾M] [✏] [🔑] [🛏] [💻] [🍴] [🏊] [✕]

**AAA ▼▼▼▼ Lamie's Inn and The Old Salt CI** ❀
(603) 926-0330. **$105-$145, 3 day notice.** 490 Lafayette Rd. Jct SR 27 on US 1. Int corridors. **Pets:** Medium. $50 deposit/pet. Service with restrictions, supervision.
[SAVE] [S🐾] [✕] [🔑] [🛏] [🍴]

# HAMPTON FALLS

**AAA ▼▼▼▼ Hampton Falls Inn M**
(603) 926-9545. **$79-$179.** 11 Lafayette Rd. I-95, exit 1, 0.5 mi e on SR 107, then 1 mi n on US 1. Int corridors. **Pets:** Medium, dogs only. $50 deposit/pet. Designated rooms, service with restrictions, supervision.
[SAVE] [S🐾] [✕] [🛏] [🍴] [🏊] [✕]

# HANCOCK

**▼▼◇▼ The Hancock Inn CI**
(603) 525-3318. **$120-$260, 15 day notice.** 33 Main St. Jct of SR 123 and 137; center. Int corridors. **Pets:** Accepted.
[✕] [🍴]

# HARTS LOCATION

**▼▼◇▼ Notchland Inn CI**
(603) 374-6131. **$195-$340, 14 day notice.** US 302. On US 302, 6.4 mi w of Bartlett. Ext/int corridors. **Pets:** $10 daily fee/pet. Designated rooms, service with restrictions, crate.
[✕] [🛏] [💻] [🍴] [✕]

# KEENE

**▼▼ ▼▼ Best Western Sovereign Hotel SH**
(603) 357-3038. **$79-$195.** 401 Winchester St. SR 10, just s of jct SR 12 and 101. Int corridors. **Pets:** Accepted.
[ASK] [S🐾] [✕] [✏] [🛏] [💻] [🍴] [🏊]

**▼▼ ▼▼ Holiday Inn Express SH** ❀
(603) 352-7616. **$125-$189.** 175 Key Rd. SR 101, just n, via Winchester St, 0.3 mi w. Int corridors. **Pets:** Medium, dogs only. $25 daily fee/pet. Designated rooms, service with restrictions, supervision.
[ASK] [S🐾] [✕] [🐾M] [✏] [🔑] [🛏] [💻] [🏊]

**AAA ▼▼ ▼▼ Super 8 Keene SH**
(603) 352-9780. **$72-$200.** 3 Ashbrook Rd. Jct SR 9 and 12, just w. Int corridors. **Pets:** Accepted.
[SAVE] [S🐾] [✕] [🐾M] [🛏]

# LANCASTER

**AAA ▼▼ ▼▼ The Cabot Motor Inn & Restaurant SH**
(603) 788-3346. **$50-$150.** 200 Portland St. On US 2, 1.5 mi e of jct US 3. Ext/int corridors. **Pets:** Other species. $15 daily fee/pet. Designated rooms, service with restrictions.
[SAVE] [✕] [🔑] [🛏] [💻] [🍴] [🏊] [✕]

**AAA ▼▼ ▼▼ Coos Motor Inn SH**
(603) 788-3079. **$39-$90.** 209 Main St. On US 2 and 3; center. Int corridors. **Pets:** Medium. $10 daily fee/pet. Designated rooms, service with restrictions, crate.
[SAVE] [S🐾] [✕] [🔑] [🛏] [💻]

**AAA ▼▼ ▼▼ Lancaster Motor Inn SH** ❀
(603) 788-4921. **$49-$79.** 112 Main St. 0.5 mi w of jct US 2 and 3. Ext corridors. **Pets:** Other species. $4 one-time fee/room. Crate.
[SAVE] [S🐾] [✕] [🛏] [🍴]

# LEBANON

**AAA ▼▼ ◇ Days Inn M**
(603) 448-5070. **$89-$129.** 135 SR 120. I-89, exit 18, 0.8 mi n. Ext/int corridors. **Pets:** Accepted.
[SAVE] [S🐾] [✕] [🛏]

**▼▼◇▼ Residence Inn by Marriott-Lebanon SH**
(603) 643-4511. **$149-$229.** 32 Centerra Pkwy. I-89, exit 18, 2.5 mi n on SR 120. Int corridors. **Pets:** Other species. $75 one-time fee/room. Service with restrictions, crate.
[ASK] [✕] [🐾M] [✏] [🔑] [🛏] [💻] [🏊] [✕]

# LINCOLN

**AAA ▼▼▼▼ Comfort Inn & Suites SH** ❀
(603) 745-6700. **$99-$299, 7 day notice.** 21 Railroad St. I-93, exit 32, just e on SR 112; at Hobo Railroad. Int corridors. **Pets:** Other species. $10 daily fee/pet. Designated rooms, service with restrictions, supervision.
[SAVE] [✕] [🐾M] [🔑] [🛏] [💻] [🏊] [✕]

**AAA ▼▼ Parker's Motel M**
(603) 745-8341. **$39-$109, 3 day notice.** 750 US Rt 3. I-93, exit 33 (US 3), 2 mi ne. Ext corridors. **Pets:** Small. $5 daily fee/pet. Service with restrictions, supervision.
[SAVE] [S🐾] [✕] [🛏] [💻] [🏊] [✕]

# LITTLETON

**▼▼◇▼ Beal House Inn and Restaurant CI** ❀
(603) 444-2661. **$120-$245, 30 day notice.** 2 W Main St. I-93, exit 42, 0.8 mi e on US 302 and SR 10. Int corridors. **Pets:** Dogs only. $150 deposit/room, $25 daily fee/pet. Designated rooms, service with restrictions, supervision.
[ASK] [✕] [🛏] [💻] [🍴]

**Eastgate Motor Inn** M
(603) 444-3971. **$59-$109.** 335 Cottage St. I-93, exit 41, just e. Ext/int corridors. **Pets:** Accepted.

**Thayers Inn** SH
(603) 444-6469. **$49-$109.** 111 Main St. I-93, exit 42, 1.3 mi e on US 302 and SR 10; center. Int corridors. **Pets:** Medium, dogs only. $8 daily fee/room. Designated rooms, service with restrictions, supervision.

# LOUDON

**Red Roof Inn** SH
(603) 225-8399. **$50-$120.** 2 Staniels Rd. I-393, exit 3, 1.5 mi n. Int corridors. **Pets:** Large, other species. Service with restrictions, supervision.

# MANCHESTER

**Comfort Inn** SH
(603) 668-2600. **$99-$299.** 298 Queen City Ave. I-293, exit 4, just w. Int corridors. **Pets:** Accepted.

**Holiday Inn Express Hotel & Suites–Manchester Airport** SH
(603) 669-6800. **$103-$309.** 1298 S Porter St. I-293, exit 1. Int corridors. **Pets:** Large. $50 deposit/room. Service with restrictions, crate.

**Homewood Suites by Hilton** SH
(603) 668-2200. **$79-$249.** 1000 N Perimeter Rd. I-293, exit 2, follow signs to Manchester Airport. Int corridors. **Pets:** Medium. $100 one-time fee/room. Service with restrictions, supervision.

**Radisson Hotel Manchester** LH
(603) 625-1000. **$149-$219.** 700 Elm St. Jct Granite St; downtown. Int corridors. **Pets:** Large, other species. $25 one-time fee/room. Designated rooms, service with restrictions, crate.

**TownePlace Suites by Marriott** SH
(603) 641-2288. **$69-$189.** 686 Huse Rd. I-293, exit 1, 0.5 mi se on SR 28. Int corridors. **Pets:** Other species. $75 one-time fee/room. Supervision.

# MERRIMACK

**Days Inn Merrimack** M
(603) 429-4600. **$55-$65.** 242 Daniel Webster Hwy. Everett Tpke, exit 11, just e, then 0.7 mi s on US 3. Int corridors. **Pets:** Accepted.

**Residence Inn by Marriott** SH
(603) 424-8100. **$129-$229.** 246 Daniel Webster Hwy. Everett Tpke, exit 11, just e, then 0.6 mi s on US 3. Ext/int corridors. **Pets:** Other species. $75 one-time fee/pet. Designated rooms.

# NASHUA

**Holiday Inn Nashua** SH
(603) 888-1551. **$89-$139.** 9 Northeastern Blvd. US 3 (Everett Tpke), exit 4, just w, then 0.3 mi n. Int corridors. **Pets:** $25 one-time fee/room. Service with restrictions, crate.

**Red Roof Inn #7122** M
(603) 888-1893. **$59-$84.** 77 Spitbrook Rd. US 3 (Everett Tpke), exit 1, just e. Ext corridors. **Pets:** Accepted.

**Sheraton Nashua Hotel** LH
(603) 888-9970. **$99-$239.** 11 Tara Blvd. US 3 (Everett Tpke), exit 1, just w. Int corridors. **Pets:** Large, dogs only. Supervision.

# NEWBURY

**Best Western Sunapee Lake Lodge** SH
(603) 763-2010. **$89-$329, 14 day notice.** 1403 SR 103. Jct SR 103B, just e. Int corridors. **Pets:** $10 daily fee/pet. Designated rooms, service with restrictions, supervision.

**Lakeview Motor Lodge at Mt. Sunapee** M
(603) 763-2701. **$79-$119, 7 day notice.** 1349 SR 103. Jct SR 103B, 0.3 mi s on SR 103; near Mount Sunapee. Ext corridors. **Pets:** Other species. $15 daily fee/pet. Designated rooms, service with restrictions, supervision.

# NEW CASTLE

**Wentworth By The Sea Marriott Hotel & Spa** LH
(603) 422-7322. **$199-$429, 3 day notice.** 588 Wentworth Rd. On SR 1B, 2 mi e of SR 1A. Ext/int corridors. **Pets:** Small, dogs only. $50 deposit/pet. Service with restrictions, supervision.

# NEW LONDON

**New London Inn** CI
(603) 526-2791. **$125-$205, 7 day notice.** 353 Main St. Center. Int corridors. **Pets:** Accepted.

# NORTH CONWAY

**Mt Washington Valley Inn** SH
(603) 356-5486. **$49-$189, 3 day notice.** 1567 White Mountain Hwy. 2.5 mi s on US 302/SR 16; village center. Int corridors. **Pets:** Medium, dogs only. $50 deposit/pet. Designated rooms, service with restrictions, supervision.

**North Conway Mountain Inn** M
(603) 356-2803. **$59-$169, 3 day notice.** 2114 White Mountain Hwy. 1 mi s on US 302/SR 16. Ext corridors. **Pets:** Supervision.

**Spruce Moose Lodge and Cottages** BB
(603) 356-6239. **$59-$119, 14 day notice.** 207 Seavey St. US 302/SR 16, 0.5 mi e; village center. Ext/int corridors. **Pets:** Accepted.

# PITTSBURG

**The Glen** CA
(603) 538-6500. **$196-$260 (no credit cards), 7 day notice.** 118 Glen Rd. 9 mi n on US 3, from jct SR 145 to Varney Rd, then 0.3 mi s to Glen Rd, follow signs. Ext/int corridors. **Pets:** Other species. Designated rooms, service with restrictions, crate.

# PLYMOUTH

**The Common Man Inn & Spa** SH
(603) 536-2200. **$89-$199.** 231 Main St. I-93, exit 26, on US 3. Int corridors. **Pets:** Large. Designated rooms, service with restrictions.

# PORTSMOUTH

◆◆ Meadowbrook Inn Ⓜ ❀
(603) 436-2700. **$69-$139.** 549 US Hwy 1 Bypass. I-95, exit 5; jct US 1 Bypass and Portsmouth Traffic Circle. Ext/int corridors. **Pets:** Other species. $10 daily fee/pet. Service with restrictions, supervision.

◆ Motel 6 Portsmouth #1424 Ⓜ
(603) 334-6606. **$55-$85.** 3 Gosling Rd. I-95, exit 4 to Spaulding Tpke (US 4 and SR 16), exit 1, just e. Int corridors. **Pets:** Accepted.

◆◆◆ Residence Inn by Marriott SH
(603) 436-8880. **$89-$259.** 1 International Dr. SR 4/16, exit 1, just s. Int corridors. **Pets:** Accepted.

◆◆◆ Sheraton Harborside Portsmouth Hotel & Conference Center LH ❀
(603) 431-2300. **$189-$209.** 250 Market St. Downtown. Int corridors. **Pets:** Large, dogs only. Service with restrictions, supervision.

# ROCHESTER

◆◆ ◆◆ Anchorage Inn Ⓜ ❀
(603) 332-3350. **$59-$129.** 13 Wadleigh Rd. Jct Spaulding Tpke and SR 125, exit 12. Ext corridors. **Pets:** $15 daily fee/pet. Designated rooms, service with restrictions, supervision.

◆◆◆ The Governor's Inn CI
(603) 332-0107. **$88-$158.** 78 Wakefield St. On SR 125 and 108, just n of monument; center. Int corridors. **Pets:** Accepted.

# SALEM

◆◆ ◆◆◆ Holiday Inn-Salem New Hampshire SH
(603) 893-5511. **$89-$179.** 1 Keewaydin Dr. I-93, exit 2, just sw. Int corridors. **Pets:** Accepted.

◆ Red Roof Inn #7151 Ⓜ
(603) 898-6422. **$59-$100.** 15 Red Roof Ln. I-93, exit 2, just se. Ext corridors. **Pets:** Accepted.

# SUGAR HILL

◆◆◆ The Hilltop Inn BB ❀
(603) 823-5695. **$100-$130, 8 day notice.** 9 Norton Ln. I-93, exit 38, 0.5 mi n on SR 18, then 2.8 mi w on SR 117. Int corridors. **Pets:** Dogs only. $10 daily fee/room. Service with restrictions, supervision.

# SUNAPEE

◆◆ Dexter's Inn BB ❀
(603) 763-5571. **$110-$185, 7 day notice.** 258 Stagecoach Rd. Jct SR 103B and 11, 0.4 mi w on SR 11, 1.75 mi s (Winn Hill Rd). Ext/int corridors. **Pets:** Other species. $10 daily fee/pet. Designated rooms.

# TAMWORTH

◆◆◆ Tamworth Inn CI
(603) 323-7721. **$120-$330.** 15 Cleveland Hill Rd. Jct SR 16 and 113, 3 mi w on SR 113; center. Int corridors. **Pets:** Accepted.

# THORNTON

◆ Shamrock Motel Ⓜ
(603) 726-3534. **$50-$65, 7 day notice.** 2913 US 3. I-93, exit 29, 2.3 mi n. Ext corridors. **Pets:** Accepted.

# WATERVILLE VALLEY

◆◆ Snowy Owl Inn SH ❀
(603) 236-8383. **$102-$430, 15 day notice.** 4 Village Rd. I-93, exit 28, 11 mi e on SR 49. Int corridors. **Pets:** Medium. Service with restrictions, supervision.

# WEST LEBANON

◆◆◆ ◆◆ Airport Economy Inn Ⓜ
(603) 298-8888. **$70-$120.** 45 Airport Rd. I-89, exit 20 (SR 12A), just s, then just e. Int corridors. **Pets:** Accepted.

◆◆◆ Fireside Inn and Suites SH
(603) 298-5900. **$100-$200.** 25 Airport Rd. I-89, exit 20 (SR 12A), just s. Int corridors. **Pets:** Dogs only. $10 daily fee/pet. Designated rooms, service with restrictions, supervision.

# WOLFEBORO

◆◆ The Lake Motel Ⓜ
(603) 569-1100. **$79-$139, 14 day notice.** 280 S Main St. 0.5 mi se on SR 28. Ext/int corridors. **Pets:** Accepted.

# WOODSVILLE

◆◆◆ ◆ All Seasons Motel Ⓜ
(603) 747-2157. **$60-$90.** 36 Smith St. I-91, exit 17, 4.1 mi e on US 302, then just s. Ext corridors. **Pets:** Accepted.

◆◆◆ ◆◆ Nootka Lodge Ⓜ
(603) 747-2418. **$65-$160.** Jct 10 & 302. I-91, exit 17, 4.5 mi e on US 302. Ext corridors. **Pets:** Accepted.

# NEW JERSEY

## CITY INDEX

## ATLANTIC CITY METROPOLITAN AREA

### ATLANTIC CITY

**AAA** ▼▼▼▼ Sheraton Atlantic City Convention Center Hotel **LH**
(609) 344-3535. **$89-$429.** 2 Miss America Way. Garden State Expwy, exit 38 to Atlantic City Expwy to Artic, just e to Michigan, then just n. Int corridors. **Pets:** Accepted.

SAVE 🔒 ✕ 🄰 (✦ 🛄 💻 ¶ ≈

### SOMERS POINT

▼▼▼▼ Residence Inn by Marriott **SH**
(609) 927-6400. **$169-$299.** 900 Mays Landing Rd. Garden State Pkwy, exit 30 southbound; exit 29 northbound, 1 mi e. Ext corridors. **Pets:** Accepted.

ASK 🔒 ✕ 🄰 (✦ 🛄 💻 ≈ ✕

## END METROPOLITAN AREA

### BASKING RIDGE

▼▼▼ The Inn at Somerset Hills **SH**
(908) 580-1300. **$129-$225.** 80 Allen Rd. I-78, exit 33, 0.3 mi n on CR 525, then 0.3 mi w Int corridors. **Pets:** Medium. $25 daily fee/room. Designated rooms, service with restrictions, crate.

ASK 🔒 ✕ 🄰 (✦ 🛄 💻 ¶

▼▼▼ Olde Mill Inn **SH**
(908) 221-1100. **$159-$179.** 225 US 202 & N Maple Ave. I-287, exit 30B (2nd ramp). Ext/int corridors. **Pets:** Accepted.

SAVE 🔒 ✕ 🄰 (✦ 🛄 💻 ¶

### BEACH HAVEN

**AAA** ▼▼▼ Engleside Inn **SH**
(609) 492-1251. **$92-$424, 30 day notice.** 30 Engleside Ave. 6.9 mi s of SR 72 Cswy to Engleside Ave, then just e. Ext corridors. **Pets:** Other species. $10 daily fee/pet. Designated rooms, service with restrictions, crate.

SAVE ✕ (✦ 🛄 💻 ¶ ≈

### BRIDGEWATER

▼▼▼▼ Marriott Bridgewater Hotel **LH**
(908) 927-9300. **$89-$299.** 700 Commons Way. I-287, exit 17 to US 202/206 S, 0.5 mi to Commons Way, then 0.4 mi e. Int corridors. **Pets:** Accepted.

ASK 🔒 ✕ 🄼 🄰 (✦ 🛄 💻 ¶ ≈

▼▼▼▼ Summerfield Suites by Wyndham-Bridgewater **SH**
(908) 725-0800. **$119-$224.** 530 Rt 22 E. I-287, exit 14B northbound; exit 17 southbound to US 22 W, then 0.8 mi. Ext corridors. **Pets:** Accepted.

ASK ✕ 🄼 🄰 (✦ 🛄 💻 ≈ ✕

### CAPE MAY COURT HOUSE

**AAA** ▼▼▼ The Doctors Inn **BB**
(609) 463-9330. **$100-$275, 14 day notice.** 2 N Main St. At Main (US 9) and Mechanic sts; just s of Garden State Pkwy. Int corridors. **Pets:** Small, dogs only. $25 daily fee/pet. Designated rooms, supervision.

SAVE ✕ 🛄

### CLIFTON

**AAA** ▼▼▼ Wellesley Inn & Suites **SH**
(973) 778-6500. **$119-$139.** 265 Rt 3 E. Garden State Pkwy, exit 153, 2.5 mi e; New Jersey Tpke, exit 16W, 4.5 mi w on SR 3, U-turn on Main Ave. Int corridors. **Pets:** Accepted.

SAVE 🔒 ✕ 🄼 🄰 (✦ 🛄 💻 ¶ ≈

### CRANBURY

▼▼▼ Residence Inn by Marriott/Cranbury **SH**
(609) 395-9447. **$169-$199.** 2662 Rt 130. New Jersey Tpke, exit 8A to SR 32 W toward town, 2 mi w on S River Rd. Int corridors. **Pets:** Other species. $75 one-time fee/room. Service with restrictions, supervision.

ASK 🔒 ✕ 🄼 🄰 (✦ 🛄 💻 ≈ ✕

▼▼▼ Staybridge Suites/Cranbury **SH**
(609) 409-7181. **$139-$149.** 1272 S River Rd. New Jersey Tpke, exit 8A to SR 32 toward Cranbury, 2 mi w. Int corridors. **Pets:** Other species. $40 one-time fee/room. Service with restrictions, supervision.

✕ 🛄 💻 ≈

### DENVILLE

▼▼▼ Hampton Inn-The Inn At Denville **SH**
(973) 664-1050. **$175.** 350 Morris Ave. I-80, exit 37 westbound, just s on Green Pond Rd, then just e; eastbound, just n on Hibernia Ave, then just e. Int corridors. **Pets:** Accepted.

ASK 🔒 ✕ 🄼 🄰 (✦ 🛄 💻 ≈ ✕

# EAST BRUNSWICK

▼ **Motel 6, East Brunswick #1083** SH
(732) 390-4545. **$61-$75.** 244 Rt 18 N. New Jersey Tpke, exit 9 (SR 18) to SR 18 S, 1 mi, exit at Edgeboro Rd, w at U-turn, then just e. Ext/int corridors. **Pets:** Accepted.

ⓈⒹ ☒ ⓁM ⌦ ⒧

▼▼ **Studio 6 East Brunswick #6020** SH
(732) 238-3330. **$73-$83.** 246 Rt 18 @ Edgeboro Rd. New Jersey Tpke, exit 9 (SR 18) to SR 18 S, 1 mi, exit at Edgeboro Rd, w at U-turn, then just e. Int corridors. **Pets:** Accepted.

ⓈⒹ ☒ ⓁM ⌦ ⒧ 🖥 ▭

# EAST HANOVER

▼▼▼ **Ramada Inn & Conference Center** SH
(973) 386-5622. **$89-$179.** 130 Rt 10 W. I-287, exit 39, 3 mi e. Int corridors. **Pets:** Accepted.

ⒶⓈⓀ ⓈⒹ ☒ ⓁM ⌦ ⒧ 🖥 ▭ ⑪

# EAST RUTHERFORD

▼▼ **Homestead Studio Suites Hotel-Meadowlands/East Rutherford** SH
(201) 939-8866. **$100.** 300 SR 3 E. New Jersey Tpke, exit 16W (from western spur), sports complex right after toll. Int corridors. **Pets:** $25 daily fee/pet. Service with restrictions, supervision.

ⒶⓈⓀ ⓈⒹ ☒ ⓁM ⌦ ⒧ 🖥 ▭

▼▼▼ **Sheraton Meadowlands** LH 🐾
(201) 896-0500. **$119-$169.** 2 Meadowlands Plaza. New Jersey Tpke, exit 16W (from western spur), sports complex right after toll to Sheraton Plaza Dr. Int corridors. **Pets:** Medium. Service with restrictions, crate.

ⒶⓈⓀ ⓈⒹ ☒ ⓁM ⌦ ⒧ 🖥 ▭ ⑪ 🏊 ☒

# EATONTOWN

ⒶⒶⒶ ▼▼▼ **Crystal Inn** M 🐾
(732) 542-4900. **$60-$109.** 170 Main St. SR 35, just n of Ft Monmouth. Ext/int corridors. **Pets:** Medium. $10 daily fee/pet. Service with restrictions, supervision.

ⓈⒶⓋⒺ ⓈⒹ ☒ ⌦ 🖥 🏊

▼▼◆ **Staybridge Suites Hotel Eatontown-Tinton Falls** SH
(732) 380-9300. **$144-$198.** 4 Industrial Way E. Garden State Pkwy, exit 105, 0.7 mi e on SR 36, then 0.7 mi s on SR 35. Int corridors. **Pets:** Medium. $275 one-time fee/room. Designated rooms, service with restrictions, crate.

ⒶⓈⓀ ⓈⒹ ☒ ⓁM ⌦ ⒧ 🖥 ▭ 🏊

# EDISON

▼▼ **Courtyard by Marriott Edison/Woodbridge** SH
(732) 738-1991. **$79-$154.** 3105 Woodbridge Ave. New Jersey Tpke, exit 10, 0.5 mi se on CR 514, then just e. Int corridors. **Pets:** Large, other species. $75 one-time fee/pet. Service with restrictions.

ⒶⓈⓀ ⓈⒹ ⓁM ⌦ ⒧ 🖥 ▭ 🏊

▼ **Red Roof Inn #7194** M
(732) 248-9300. **$74-$91.** 860 New Durham Rd. I-287, exit 2A northbound, 0.3 mi w via Bridge St, then left; exit 3 southbound, just w. Ext corridors. **Pets:** Accepted.

☒ ⓁM ⌦ ⒧ 🖥

▼▼▼ **Sheraton Edison** LH 🐾
(732) 225-8300. **$249-$289.** 125 Raritan Center Pkwy. New Jersey Tpke, exit 10, 0.5 mi se on CR 514, keep right after tolls. Int corridors. **Pets:** Medium, other species. $50 deposit/room. Service with restrictions, crate.

ⒶⓈⓀ ⓈⒹ ☒ ⓁM ⌦ ⒧ 🖥 ▭ ⑪ 🏊 ☒

▼▼ **Wellesley Inn (Edison)** SH
(732) 287-0171. **$65-$110.** 831 US 1 S. 1.3 mi s of I-287. Int corridors. **Pets:** Accepted.

ⒶⓈⓀ ⓈⒹ ☒ ⒧ 🖥 ▭

# ELIZABETH

ⒶⒶⒶ ▼▼▼▼ **Hilton Newark Airport** LH
(908) 351-3900. **$109-$269.** 1170 Sprng St. New Jersey Tpke, exit 13A, on US 1 and 9 N, U-turn on McClellan St. Int corridors. **Pets:** Accepted.

ⓈⒶⓋⒺ ☒ ⓁM ⌦ ⒧ 🖥 ▭ ⑪ 🏊 ☒

▼▼▼▼ **Residence Inn by Marriott** SH
(908) 352-4300. **$167-$172.** 83 Glimcher Realty Way. New Jersey Tpke, exit 13A, after toll follow signs to Jersey Garden Blvd, 1 mi, left on Kapkowski Rd, then just e. Int corridors. **Pets:** Accepted.

ⒶⓈⓀ ☒ ⓁM ⌦ ⒧ 🖥 ▭ 🏊

# FAIRFIELD

ⒶⒶⒶ ▼▼▼ **Fairfield Wellesley Inns** SH
(973) 575-1742. **$89-$149.** 38 Two Bridges Rd. I-80, exit 52 westbound; exit 47B (Caldwells) eastbound, 7 mi e on US 46, exit Passaic Ave. Int corridors. **Pets:** Accepted.

ⓈⒶⓋⒺ ⓈⒹ ☒ ⓁM ⌦ ⒧ 🖥 ▭ ⑪ 🏊

# FAIR LAWN

ⒶⒶⒶ ▼▼▼ **AmeriSuites (Fair Lawn/Paramus)** SH
(201) 475-3888. **$99-$219.** 41-01 Broadway (Rt 4 W). Garden State Pkwy, exit 161 northbound, 0.7 mi w; exit 163 southbound. Int corridors. **Pets:** $10 daily fee/pet. Designated rooms, service with restrictions, supervision.

ⓈⒶⓋⒺ ☒ ⓁM ⌦ ⒧ 🖥 ▭ 🏊

# FLEMINGTON

ⒶⒶⒶ ▼▼ **The Ramada Inn** M
(908) 782-7472. **$82-$120.** 250 Hwy 202 & SR 31. 0.5 mi s of the circle. Ext corridors. **Pets:** Accepted.

ⓈⒶⓋⒺ ⓈⒹ ☒ ⌦ 🖥 ▭ ⑪ 🏊

# HAZLET

▼▼◆ **Wellesley Inn (Hazlet)** SH
(732) 888-2800. **$89-$159.** 3215 SR 35 N. Garden State Pkwy, exit 117, 1.5 mi s on SR 35, then U-turn on Hazlet Ave. Int corridors. **Pets:** Accepted.

ⒶⓈⓀ ⓈⒹ ☒ ⓁM ⌦ ⒧ 🖥 ▭

# HILLSBOROUGH

▼▼ **Days Inn Hillsborough Executive Inn** SH
(908) 685-9000. **$99.** 118 Rt 206 S. 2.6 mi s of jct SR 28, US 202 and 206, at circle. Int corridors. **Pets:** $20 daily fee/pet. Designated rooms, no service, crate.

ⒶⓈⓀ ⓈⒹ ☒ ⌦ 🖥 ▭ 🏊

# ISELIN

▼▼▼▼ **Sheraton at Woodbridge Place** LH
(732) 634-3600. **$95-$169.** 515 Rt 1 S. Garden State Pkwy, exit 131A northbound, 0.7 mi e, s on Middlesex Essex Tpke, 0.4 mi to Gill Ln, then 1.5 mi w; exit 130 southbound, 0.7 mi on US 1 N to Gill Ln, then U-turn; diagonal to Woodbridge Center. Int corridors. **Pets:** Accepted.

ⒶⓈⓀ ⓈⒹ ☒ ⌦ 🖥 ▭ ⑪ 🏊

# LAWRENCEVILLE

ⒶⒶⒶ ▼▼◆ **Howard Johnson Inn** M
(609) 896-1100. **$75-$150.** 2995 Rt 1 S. On US 1 southbound, 0.5 mi s of I-295. Ext/int corridors. **Pets:** $10 one-time fee/room. Service with restrictions, crate.

ⓈⒶⓋⒺ ⓈⒹ ☒ ⌦ 🖥 ▭ 🏊

▼ **Red Roof Inn-Princeton #7111** M
(609) 896-3388. **$62-$86.** 3203 Brunswick Pike (US 1). I-295, exit 67A, just n. Ext corridors. **Pets:** Accepted.

☒ ⌦ ⒧ 🖥

# LEDGEWOOD

**AAA** **WWW** Days Inn **SH** ❖
(973) 347-5100. **$84-$105.** 1691 US 46 W. I-80, exit 27, 2 mi e (thru US 206 N and 183 N). Int corridors. **Pets:** Other species. $50 deposit/room. Service with restrictions.

⟨SAVE⟩ ⟨S☉⟩ ⟨✕⟩ ⟨◢⟩ ⟨⬚⟩ ⟨⬛⟩ ⟨❢⟩ ⟨≋⟩

# LONG BRANCH

**WWWW** Ocean Place Resort & Spa **LH** ❖
(732) 571-4000. **$125-$314, 7 day notice.** 1 Ocean Blvd. 2.5 mi e from jct SR 71, 0.5 mi s. Int corridors. **Pets:** Large, other species. $50 one-time fee/pet. Service with restrictions.

⟨ASK⟩ ⟨S☉⟩ ⟨✕⟩ ⟨⬛⟩ ⟨⬚⟩ ⟨❢⟩ ⟨≋⟩ ⟨✕⟩

# MAHWAH

**AAA** **WWWW** Sheraton Crossroads Hotel **LH**
(201) 529-1660. **$259-$269.** 1 International Blvd (Rt 17). I-287, exit 66, at SR 17 N. Int corridors. **Pets:** Accepted.

⟨SAVE⟩ ⟨S☉⟩ ⟨✕⟩ ⟨◢⟩ ⟨⬛⟩ ⟨⬚⟩ ⟨❢⟩ ⟨≋⟩ ⟨✕⟩

# MIDDLETOWN

**AAA** **WWW** Comfort Inn **M** ❖
(732) 671-3400. **$99-$169.** 750 Hwy 35 S. Garden State Pkwy, exit 114, 2 mi on Red Hill Rd, 1 mi s on King's Hwy to SR 35, then 0.3 mi s. Int corridors. **Pets:** Other species. $25 daily fee/room. Service with restrictions, supervision.

⟨SAVE⟩ ⟨S☉⟩ ⟨✕⟩ ⟨◢⟩ ⟨⬛⟩ ⟨⬚⟩ ⟨≋⟩

# MONMOUTH JUNCTION

**W** Red Roof Inn/North Princeton #7198 **M**
(732) 821-8800. **$55-$80.** 208 New Rd. On US 1 S. Ext corridors. **Pets:** Accepted.

⟨✕⟩ ⟨◢⟩ ⟨⬛⟩

**WWWW** Residence Inn by Marriott **SH**
(732) 329-9600. **$119-$179.** 4225 Rt 1 S. 0.5 mi s of Raymond Rd. Int corridors. **Pets:** Other species. $75 one-time fee/room.

⟨ASK⟩ ⟨S☉⟩ ⟨✕⟩ ⟨&M⟩ ⟨◢⟩ ⟨⬚⟩ ⟨⬛⟩ ⟨⬚⟩ ⟨≋⟩ ⟨✕⟩

# MORRISTOWN

**AAA** **WWWW** Summerfield Suites by
Wyndham-Morristown **SH**
(973) 971-0008. **$189-$209.** 194 Park Ave. SR 24, exit 2A (Morristown), stay in far left lane. Int corridors. **Pets:** Accepted.

⟨SAVE⟩ ⟨✕⟩ ⟨&M⟩ ⟨◢⟩ ⟨⬚⟩ ⟨⬛⟩ ⟨⬚⟩ ⟨≋⟩ ⟨✕⟩

**AAA** **WWWW** The Westin Governor Morris **LH** ❖
(973) 539-7300. **$229-$309.** 2 Whippany Rd. I-287, exit 36 southbound, left lane to light, left to stop, then left 1 mi; exit 36A northbound thru Morris Ave, 0.8 mi, follow signs. Int corridors. **Pets:** Large, dogs only. Service with restrictions, supervision.

⟨SAVE⟩ ⟨S☉⟩ ⟨✕⟩ ⟨◢⟩ ⟨⬚⟩ ⟨⬛⟩ ⟨❢⟩ ⟨≋⟩

# NEWARK

**WWWW** Sheraton Newark Airport Hotel **LH**
(973) 690-5500. **$109-$269, 4 day notice.** 128 Frontage Rd. New Jersey Tpke, exit 14 via Frontage Rd, 2nd right after toll booth. Int corridors. **Pets:** Accepted.

⟨ASK⟩ ⟨S☉⟩ ⟨✕⟩ ⟨&M⟩ ⟨◢⟩ ⟨⬚⟩ ⟨⬛⟩ ⟨⬚⟩ ⟨❢⟩ ⟨≋⟩ ⟨✕⟩

# NORTH BERGEN

**WWW** Days Inn **SH**
(201) 348-3600. **$140-$165.** 2750 Tonnelle Ave (US 1 & 9). Jct SR 3, 0.4 mi s. Int corridors. **Pets:** Small. $100 deposit/pet. Designated rooms, service with restrictions, supervision.

⟨ASK⟩ ⟨S☉⟩ ⟨✕⟩ ⟨◢⟩ ⟨⬛⟩ ⟨⬚⟩ ⟨❢⟩

# PARAMUS

**WWW** La Quinta Inn **SH**
(201) 265-4200. **$99-$130.** 393 Rt 17 S. Garden State Pkwy, exit 163 northbound to SR 17 N, 0.6 mi to Midland Ave, then U-turn to SR 17 S; exit 165 southbound to Richwood Ave, 1 mi. Int corridors. **Pets:** Small. Service with restrictions, supervision.

⟨ASK⟩ ⟨S☉⟩ ⟨✕⟩ ⟨⬛⟩ ⟨⬚⟩

# PARSIPPANY

**WWW** Embassy Suites **LH**
(973) 334-1440. **$109-$299.** 909 Parsippany Blvd. I-80, exit 42 to US 202 N; just ne of jct US 202 and 46 W. Int corridors. **Pets:** $20 daily fee/room. Designated rooms, service with restrictions.

⟨✕⟩ ⟨◢⟩ ⟨⬛⟩ ⟨⬚⟩ ⟨❢⟩ ⟨≋⟩ ⟨✕⟩

**WWW** Red Roof Inn #7072 **M**
(973) 334-3737. **$73-$78.** 855 US 46 E. I-80, exit 47 westbound; exit 45 eastbound, 0.5 mi e. Ext corridors. **Pets:** Accepted.

⟨✕⟩ ⟨◢⟩ ⟨⬛⟩

**AAA** **WWWW** Sheraton Parsippany Hotel **LH**
(973) 515-2000. **$289-$355.** 199 Smith Rd. I-287, exit 41A northbound; exit 42 to US 46 E, 0.4 mi s. Int corridors. **Pets:** Accepted.

⟨SAVE⟩ ⟨S☉⟩ ⟨✕⟩ ⟨◢⟩ ⟨⬚⟩ ⟨⬛⟩ ⟨⬚⟩ ⟨❢⟩ ⟨≋⟩ ⟨✕⟩

**WWWW** Sierra Suites Hotel-Parsippany **SH**
(973) 428-8875. **$89-$219.** 299 Smith Rd. I-287, exit 41A northbound; exit 42 southbound to US 46 E, 0.5 mi s. Int corridors. **Pets:** Accepted.

⟨ASK⟩ ⟨S☉⟩ ⟨✕⟩ ⟨◢⟩ ⟨⬚⟩ ⟨⬛⟩ ⟨⬚⟩ ⟨≋⟩ ⟨✕⟩

# NEARBY PENNSYLVANIA
# PHILADELPHIA METROPOLITAN AREA

# BORDENTOWN

**AAA** **WWW** Imperial Inn **M**
(609) 298-3355. **$55-$85.** 3312 Rt 206 S. New Jersey Tpke, exit 7, 0.8 mi s. Ext corridors. **Pets:** Accepted.

⟨SAVE⟩ ⟨S☉⟩ ⟨✕⟩ ⟨⬛⟩

# CARNEYS POINT

**AAA** **WWWW** Holiday Inn Express Hotel & Suites **SH**
(856) 351-9222. **$90-$150.** 506 Pennsville-Auburn Rd. I-295, exit 2B, just e. Int corridors. **Pets:** Other species. Supervision.

⟨SAVE⟩ ⟨S☉⟩ ⟨✕⟩ ⟨◢⟩ ⟨⬛⟩ ⟨⬚⟩

# CHERRY HILL

**WWW** Clarion Hotel & Conference Center **LH**
(856) 428-2300. **$119-$169.** 1450 Rt 70 E. I-295, exit 34B, just w. Int corridors. **Pets:** Accepted.

⟨ASK⟩ ⟨S☉⟩ ⟨✕⟩ ⟨&M⟩ ⟨◢⟩ ⟨⬚⟩ ⟨⬛⟩ ⟨⬚⟩ ⟨❢⟩ ⟨≋⟩ ⟨✕⟩

**AAA** **WWWW** Holiday Inn Philadelphia-Cherry Hill **SH** ❖
(856) 663-5300. **$99-$159.** Rt 70 & Sayer Ave. I-295, exit 34B, 2.5 mi w. Int corridors. **Pets:** Other species. $75 deposit/room. Designated rooms, service with restrictions.

⟨SAVE⟩ ⟨S☉⟩ ⟨✕⟩ ⟨◢⟩ ⟨⬚⟩ ⟨⬛⟩ ⟨⬚⟩ ⟨❢⟩ ⟨≋⟩

**▼▼▼▼ Residence Inn by Marriott** 🆂🄷
(856) 429-6111. **$159-$239.** 1821 Old Cuthbert Rd. I-295, exit 34A, just e to Marlkress Rd jughandle, back to Old Cuthbert Rd, then just n. Ext corridors. **Pets:** Accepted.

(A$K) 🆂🄾 ⊠ 🗗 🄴 🗗 🖃 ➾ 🖾

## DEPTFORD

**▼▼▼▼ Residence Inn by Marriott** 🆂🄷
(856) 686-9188. **$162, 14 day notice.** 1154 Hurffville Rd. SR 42, exit Deptford, Woodbury, Runnemede to CR 544, just e to CR 415. Int corridors. **Pets:** Accepted.

(A$K) 🆂🄾 ⊠ 🗗 🄴 🗗 🖃 ➾ 🖾

## HADDONFIELD

**▼▼▼▼ Haddonfield Inn** 🄱🄱
(856) 428-2195. **$139-$299, 7 day notice.** 44 W End Ave. I-295, exit 28, 0.7 mi n on SR 168, 2.6 mi e on Kings Hwy, then just n. Int corridors. **Pets:** Accepted.

(A$K) ⊠ 🄴 🗗

## MOUNT HOLLY

**🄰🄰🄰 ▼▼▼ Best Western Burlington Inn** 🆂🄷
(609) 261-3800. **$84-$129, 3 day notice.** 2020 Rt 541, Rd 1. New Jersey Tpke, exit 5, just n. Int corridors. **Pets:** Other species. $5 daily fee/pet. Service with restrictions, supervision.

(SAVE) 🆂🄾 ⊠ 🗗 🄴 🗗 🖃 ➾

## MOUNT LAUREL

**🄰🄰🄰 ▼▼▼▼ AmeriSuites (Mt. Laurel/Philadelphia)** 🆂🄷
(856) 840-0770. **$69-$159.** 8000 Crawford Pl. New Jersey Tpke, exit 4, 1 mi se on SR 73; I-295, exit 36A, 1.7 mi se on SR 73. Int corridors. **Pets:** Accepted.

(SAVE) 🆂🄾 ⊠ 🄼 ⊠ 🄴 🗗 🄴 🗗 ➾

**▼▼ Candlewood Suites** 🆂🄷
(856) 642-7567. **$109.** 4000 Crawford Pl. New Jersey Tpke, exit 4, 1 mi s on SR 73 S. Int corridors. **Pets:** Accepted.

(A$K) 🆂🄾 ⊠ 🄴 🗗 🖃

**▼▼▼▼ Doubletree Guest Suites Hotel** 🄻🄷
(856) 778-8999. **$124-$214.** 515 Fellowship Rd N. New Jersey Tpke, exit 4, just nw to Fellowship Rd, then just n; I-295, exit 36A, just se on SR 73 to Fellowship Rd, then just n. Int corridors. **Pets:** Accepted.

(A$K) 🆂🄾 ⊠ 🄼 ⊠ 🗗 🖃 🍴 ➾

**▼▼▼▼ Marriott Mt Laurel** 🄻🄷
(856) 234-7300. **$119-$189.** 915 Rt 73 N. New Jersey Tpke, exit 4, northeast corner; I-295, exit 36A, just se. Int corridors. **Pets:** Accepted.

(A$K) 🆂🄾 ⊠ 🗗 ⊠ 🗗 🖃 🍴 ➾ 🖾

**▼▼ Red Roof Inn #7066** 🄼
(856) 234-5589. **$54-$77.** 603 Fellowship Rd. New Jersey Tpke, exit 4, just nw on SR 73 to Fellowship Rd, then just s; I-295, exit 36A, just se on SR 73 to Fellowship Rd, then just s. Ext corridors. **Pets:** Accepted.

⊠ 🗗 🄴

**▼▼▼▼ Staybridge Suites** 🆂🄷
(856) 722-1900. **$126-$177.** 4115 Church Rd. New Jersey Tpke, exit 4, 0.5 mi s on SR 73, then 0.5 mi w. Int corridors. **Pets:** Accepted.

(A$K) 🆂🄾 ⊠ 🗗 🖃 ➾ 🖾

**▼▼▼▼ Summerfield Suites by Wyndham-Mount Laurel** 🆂🄷
(856) 222-1313. **$139-$169.** 3000 Crawford Pl. New Jersey Tpke, exit 4, 1 mi s on SR 73; I-295, exit 36A, 1.5 mi s on SR 73. Ext corridors. **Pets:** Accepted.

(A$K) ⊠ 🄼 ⊠ 🗗 🄴 🗗 🖃 ➾ 🖾

**▼▼▼▼ Wyndham Mount Laurel** 🄻🄷
(856) 234-7000. **$89-$129.** 1111 Rt 73 N. New Jersey Tpke, exit 4; I-295, exit 36A, 0.5 mi se. Int corridors. **Pets:** Accepted.

(A$K) ⊠ ⊠ 🄴 🗗 🄴 🗗 🖃 🍴 ➾ 🖾

---

## END METROPOLITAN AREA

---

## PISCATAWAY

**▼▼▼▼ Embassy Suites Hotel** 🄻🄷 ❁
(732) 980-0500. **$149-$229.** 121 Centennial Ave. I-287, exit 9 (Highland Park), just s to Centennial Ave. Int corridors. **Pets:** Large. $200 deposit/ room, $20 daily fee/room. Designated rooms.

⊠ 🗗 🄴 🗗 🖃 🍴 ➾

**▼▼ Motel 6 Piscataway** 🆂🄷
(732) 981-9200. **$62-$96.** 1012 Stelton Rd. I-287, exit 5, just e. Ext/int corridors. **Pets:** Accepted.

🄴

## PLAINSBORO

**▼▼▼▼ Courtyard by Marriott Princeton** 🆂🄷
(609) 716-9100. **$119-$189.** 3815 US Rt 1. 0.4 mi s of Scudders Mill Rd at Mapleton Rd. Int corridors. **Pets:** Accepted.

(A$K) 🆂🄾 ⊠ 🄼 ⊠ 🗗 🖃 ➾

## PRINCETON

**🄰🄰🄰 ▼▼▼▼ AmeriSuites (Princeton/Carnegie Center West)** 🆂🄷
(609) 720-0200. **$149-$259.** 3565 US 1 S. 1.5 mi s of jct CR 526 and 571. Int corridors. **Pets:** Accepted.

(SAVE) 🆂🄾 ⊠ 🄼 ⊠ 🗗 🖃 ➾

**🄰🄰🄰 ▼▼▼▼ Holiday Inn Princeton** 🆂🄷
(609) 520-1200. **$139.** 100 Independence Way. I-295, exit 67A (SR 1) northbound; exit 67 (SR 1) southbound, 7 mi n. Int corridors. **Pets:** Accepted.

(SAVE) 🆂🄾 ⊠ 🗗 🗗 🖃 🍴 ➾ 🖾

**🄰🄰🄰 ▼▼▼▼ Nassau Inn** 🆂🄷 ❁
(609) 921-7500. **$203-$214.** 10 Palmer Square. Center. Int corridors. **Pets:** Small. $75 one-time fee/room. Designated rooms, service with restrictions, crate.

(SAVE) 🆂🄾 ⊠ 🗗 ⊠ 🗗 🍴

**▼▼▼▼ Residence Inn by Princeton at Carnegie Center** 🆂🄷
(609) 799-0550. **$199-$299.** 3563 US 1 S. 1.5 mi s of jct CR 527 and 571. Int corridors. **Pets:** Accepted.

⊠ 🄼 🗗 ⊠ 🗗 🖃 ➾ 🖾

**▼▼▼▼ Staybridge Suites** 🆂🄷
(609) 951-0009. **$199-$229.** 4375 US 1 S. Just past Ridge Rd. Ext corridors. **Pets:** Accepted.

(A$K) 🆂🄾 ⊠ 🗗 🗗 🖃 ➾ 🖾

**🄰🄰🄰 ▼▼▼▼ Westin Princeton at Forrestal Village** 🄻🄷 ❁
(609) 452-7900. **$319-$359.** 201 Village Blvd. On US 1 southbound, 1.5 mi n of CR 571. Int corridors. **Pets:** Medium, other species. Service with restrictions.

(SAVE) 🆂🄾 ⊠ 🄼 🗗 🗗 🖃 🍴 ➾ 🖾

# RAMSEY

 Best Western SH
(201) 327-6700. **$89-$175.** 1315 Rt 17 S. Jct I-287 and SR 17 S, 3 mi s. Int corridors. **Pets:** Medium. $25 deposit/room. Service with restrictions, supervision.

# RED BANK

Extended StayAmerica Red Bank-Middletown SH
(732) 450-8688. **Call for rates.** 329 Newman Springs Rd. Garden State Pkwy, exit 109, just e. Int corridors. **Pets:** Accepted.

# ROCKAWAY

Best Western-The Inn at Rockaway SH
(973) 625-1200. **$59-$139.** 14 Green Pond Rd. I-80, exit 37, just n. Int corridors. **Pets:** Accepted.

# SECAUCUS

AmeriSuites (Secaucus/Meadowlands) SH
(201) 422-9480. **$199.** 575 Park Plaza Dr. New Jersey Tpke, exits 16E, 17 or 16W via SR 3 to Harmon Meadow Blvd, then just w. Int corridors. **Pets:** Medium. $10 daily fee/pet. Designated rooms, service with restrictions, supervision.

The Holiday Inn Harmon Meadow LH
(201) 348-2000. **$140-$190.** 300 Plaza Dr. New Jersey Tpke, exits 16E, 17, or 16W via SR 3 to Harmon Meadow Blvd. Int corridors. **Pets:** Small. $100 one-time fee/pet. Service with restrictions, supervision.

Homestead Studio Suites
Hotel-Secaucus/Meadowlands SH
(201) 553-9700. **$125.** 1 Plaza Dr. New Jersey Tpke, exit 16E northbound; exit 17E southbound, 0.3 mi e. Int corridors. **Pets:** $25 daily fee/pet. Service with restrictions, supervision.

Red Roof Inn-Meadowlands #7150 M
(201) 319-1000. **$80-$110.** 15 Meadowlands Pkwy. Between eastern and western spurs of New Jersey Tpke, exits 16E, 17 or 16W to SR 3, exit Meadowlands Pkwy. Ext corridors. **Pets:** Accepted.

Wyndham Meadowlands Suites LH
(201) 863-8700. **$109-$289.** 350 Rt 3 W, at Mill Creek Dr. Between eastern and western spurs of New Jersey Tpke, exits 16E, 17 or 16W via SR 3 W and Harmon Meadow Blvd; in Mill Creek Mall. Int corridors. **Pets:** Accepted.

# SHORT HILLS

Hilton Short Hills Hotel and Spa LH ✿
(973) 379-0100. **$389-$829.** 41 John F Kennedy Pkwy. I-78, exit 48 (SR 24), 2.5 mi to Kennedy Pkwy. Int corridors. **Pets:** Medium. $25 daily fee/room. Designated rooms, service with restrictions, supervision.

# SOMERSET

Doubletree Hotel & Executive Meeting Center LH
(732) 469-2600. **$99-$189.** 200 Atrium Dr. I-287, exit 10 (CR 527), just n (direction Bound Brook) to Davidson Ave, 0.5 mi sw; in Atrium Corp Park. Int corridors. **Pets:** Accepted.

Holiday Inn-Somerset SH
(732) 356-1700. **$75-$159.** 195 Davidson Ave. I-287, exit 10 (CR 527), just n (direction Bound Brook), then 0.5 mi sw. Int corridors. **Pets:** Other species. Service with restrictions, supervision.

Residence Inn by Marriott-Somerset SH
(732) 627-0881. **$90-$153.** 37 World Fair Dr. I-287, exit 10 (CR 527), left on ramp (CR 527 S/Easton Ave) 0.3 mi, then 0.5 mi w. Int corridors. **Pets:** Accepted.

Somerset Marriott Hotel LH
(732) 560-0500. **$79-$159, 3 day notice.** 110 Davidson Ave. I-287, exit 10 (CR 527), just n (direction Bound Brook) to Davidson Ave, then just sw. Int corridors. **Pets:** Accepted.

Staybridge Suites SH
(732) 356-8000. **$135-$171.** 260 Davidson Ave. I-287, exit 10 (CR 527), just n (direction Bound Brook) to Davidson Ave, then 0.8 mi sw. Ext corridors. **Pets:** Accepted.

# SOUTH PLAINFIELD

Holiday Inn SH
(908) 753-5500. **$139.** 4701 Stelton Rd. I-287, exit 5, just s. Int corridors. **Pets:** Accepted.

# SPRINGFIELD

Holiday Inn Springfield SH
(973) 376-9400. **$136.** 304 Rt 22 W. Garden State Pkwy, exit 140 northbound, 4 mi w; exit 140A southbound. Int corridors. **Pets:** Service with restrictions, crate.

# TINTON FALLS

Holiday Inn at Tinton Falls SH ✿
(732) 544-9300. **$79-$129.** 700 Hope Rd. Garden State Pkwy, exit 105. Int corridors. **Pets:** Medium. $50 one-time fee/room. Designated rooms, service with restrictions, crate.

Red Roof Inn #7211 M
(732) 389-4646. **$68-$108.** 11 Centre Plaza. Garden State Pkwy, exit 105, just right at 1st light after toll. Ext corridors. **Pets:** Accepted.

Residence Inn by Marriott SH
(732) 389-8100. **$119-$199. 30 day notice.** 90 Park Rd. Garden State Pkwy, exit 105, 1st jughandle after toll, immediate left before Courtyard by Marriott, just n, then e. Ext corridors. **Pets:** Large. $75 one-time fee/pet. Designated rooms, service with restrictions, supervision.

Sunrise Suites Hotel SH
(732) 389-4800. **$89-$159.** 3 Centre Plaza. Garden State Pkwy, exit 105, 1st right at Hope Rd after toll. Ext/int corridors. **Pets:** Accepted.

# TOMS RIVER

Howard Johnson Hotel-Toms River SH ✿
(732) 244-1000. **$85-$199.** 955 Hooper Ave. Garden State Pkwy, exit 82, 1 mi e on SR 37. Int corridors. **Pets:** Medium. $50 daily fee/pet. Designated rooms, service with restrictions, crate.

# VINELAND

**▼▼▼ Ramada Inn Vineland** SH
(856) 696-3800. **$77.** 2216 W Landis Ave. SR 55, exit 32A, just e. Int corridors. **Pets:** Accepted.
ASK S⬛ ✕ 🛏 🖵 ❔ ⇌

# WANTAGE

**▼ High Point Country Inn** M
(973) 702-1860. **$80-$90.** 1328 SR 23 N. 1 mi n of Colesville Village Center. Ext corridors. **Pets:** Accepted.
✕ 🛏 ⇌ 🖉

# WARREN

**▼▼▼ Somerset Hills Hotel** SH
(908) 647-6700. **$135-$325.** 200 Liberty Corner Rd. I-78, exit 33, just n on CR 525. Int corridors. **Pets:** Medium. $25 daily fee/room. Designated rooms, service with restrictions, crate.
ASK S⬛ ✕ 🖉 🛏 🖵 ❔ ⇌

# WAYNE

**▼▼ Ramada Wayne/Fairfield** SH
(973) 256-7000. **$79-$149.** 334 Rt 46 E/Service Rd. I-80, exit 53 westbound (Butler-Verona) thru SR 23 S, service road off US 46 eastbound Caldwells; exit 47B eastbound, 7 mi e on US 46 to service road. Ext corridors. **Pets:** Accepted.
ASK S⬛ ✕ 🖉 🛏 🖵 ❔ ⇌

**◈◈◈ ▼▼▼ Wellesley Inn (Wayne)** SH
(973) 696-8050. **$104-$114.** 1850 Rt 23 & Ratzer Rd. I-80, exit 53 (Butler-Verona) westbound to SR 23 N, 3 mi to Ratzer Rd (service road); exit 54 eastbound to Minisink Rd to U-turn for I-80 W to exit 53. Int corridors. **Pets:** Accepted.
SAVE S⬛ ✕ ♿ 🖉 ♿ 🛏 🖵 ⇌

# WEEHAWKEN

**◈◈◈ ▼▼▼ Sheraton Suites On The Hudson** LH
(201) 617-5600. **$149-$449.** 500 Harbor Blvd. I-495 E toward Lincoln Tunnel, exit Weehawken/Hoboken, bear right at bottom of hill, then 0.4 mi e to Lincoln Harbor Complex. Int corridors. **Pets:** Accepted.
SAVE ✕ 🖉 ♿ 🛏 🖵 ❔ ⇌

# WEST ORANGE

**▼▼▼ Residence Inn by Marriott-West Orange** SH ❧
(973) 669-4700. **$199-$299.** 107 Prospect Ave. I-280, exit 8B, 1 mi n on CR 527 (Prospect Ave). Int corridors. **Pets:** Large. $15 daily fee/pet, $75 one-time fee/pet. Service with restrictions, crate.
ASK ✕ ♿ 🛏 🖵 ⇌

# WHIPPANY

**▼▼ Homestead Studio Suites Hotel-Hanover/Parsippany** SH
(973) 463-1999. **$110.** 125 Rt 10 E. I-287, exit 39, 3.6 mi e. Int corridors. **Pets:** $25 daily fee/pet. Service with restrictions, supervision.
ASK S⬛ ✕ ♿ᴹ 🖉 ♿ 🛏 🖵

**◈◈◈ ▼▼▼ Summerfield Suites by Wyndham-Parsippany/Whippany** SH
(973) 605-1001. **$179-$199.** 1 Ridgedale Ave. I-287, exit 39, just nw. Int corridors. **Pets:** Accepted.
SAVE ✕ ♿ᴹ 🖉 ♿ 🛏 🖵 ⇌

**◈◈◈ ▼▼ Wellesley Inn (Whippany)** SH
(973) 539-8350. **$69-$89.** 1255 Rt 10 E. I-287, exit 39B southbound; exit 39 northbound, just w. Int corridors. **Pets:** Accepted.
SAVE ✕ 🖉 ♿ 🛏 🖵 ⇌

# WOODBRIDGE

**▼▼ Homestead Studio Suites Hotel-Woodbridge** SH
(732) 442-8333. **$95.** 1 Hoover Way. New Jersey Tpke, exit 11, 1.4 mi to US 9 N, then just w on King George Post Rd. Int corridors. **Pets:** $25 daily fee/pet. Service with restrictions, supervision.
ASK S⬛ ✕ ♿ᴹ 🖉 ♿ 🛏 🖵

# NEW MEXICO

## CITY INDEX

## ALAMOGORDO

### ▲▲▲ ▼▼▼▼ Best Western Desert Aire Inn SH
(505) 437-2110. $60-$110. 1021 S White Sands Blvd. 1.5 mi s of jct US 54/70 and 82. Ext corridors. **Pets:** Accepted.

### ▼▼ Super 8 Motel-Alamogordo SH
(505) 439-2741. $55-$79. 3204 N White Sands Blvd. Just s of jct US 54/70 and 82. Int corridors. **Pets:** Medium, other species. Service with restrictions, supervision.

## ALBUQUERQUE

### ▲▲▲ ▼▼▼▼ Airport University Inn SH ☙
(505) 247-0512. $59-$105. 1901 University Blvd SE. I-25, exit 228A southbound; exit 222 northbound, just e. Int corridors. **Pets:** $25 one-time fee/pet. Service with restrictions, crate.

### ▲▲▲ ▼▼▼▼ AmeriSuites (Albuquerque/Airport) SH
(505) 242-9300. $72-$125. 1400 Sunport Place Blvd SE. I-25, exit 221, 0.3 mi s to University Blvd exit, then just n to Woodward Rd. Int corridors. **Pets:** Accepted.

### ▲▲▲ ▼▼▼▼ AmeriSuites (Albuquerque/Midtown) SH
(505) 881-0544. $109-$139. 2500 Menaul Blvd NE. I-40, exit 160, just n to Menaul Blvd, then 0.6 mi w. Int corridors. **Pets:** Small, dogs only. $10 daily fee/pet. Designated rooms, service with restrictions, supervision.

### ▲▲▲ ▼▼▼▼ AmeriSuites (Albuquerque/Uptown) SH
(505) 872-9000. $79-$119. 6901 Arvada Ave NE. I-40, exit 162 westbound; exit 162B eastbound, 0.7 mi n. Int corridors. **Pets:** Small. $10 daily fee/pet. Designated rooms, service with restrictions, supervision.

### ▲▲▲ ▼▼▼▼ Baymont Inn & Suites Albuquerque North SH
(505) 345-7500. $70-$80. 7439 Pan American Frwy NE. I-25, exit 231, just w. Int corridors. **Pets:** Medium. Service with restrictions.

### ▲▲▲ ▼▼▼ Best Western American Motor Inn SH
(505) 298-7426. $69-$169. 12999 Central Ave NE. I-40, exit 167 westbound, 0.3 mi w on Central Ave; exit 166 eastbound, right on Juan Tabo, left on Central Ave, then 0.5 mi e. Ext corridors. **Pets:** Accepted.

### ▲▲▲ ▼▼▼ Best Western InnSuites Hotel & Suites-Airport Albuquerque SH
(505) 242-7022. $69-$159. 2400 Yale Blvd SE. I-25, exit 222 northbound; exit 222A southbound, 1 mi e, then just s. Int corridors. **Pets:** Accepted.

### ▲▲▲ ▼▼▼▼ Brittania & W E Mauger Estate Bed & Breakfast BB ☙
(505) 242-8755. $89-$229, 10 day notice. 701 Roma Ave NW. I-25, exit 225, 1 mi w, then just s on 7th Ave. Int corridors. **Pets:** Dogs only. $30 one-time fee/room. Designated rooms, service with restrictions.

### ▼▼▼▼ Candlewood Suites SH
(505) 888-3424. $59-$109. 3025 Menaul Blvd NE. I-40, exit 160, just n to Menaul Blvd, then 0.5 mi w. Int corridors. **Pets:** Medium. $75 one-time fee/room. Service with restrictions, supervision.

### ▲▲▲ ▼▼▼▼ ClubHouse Inn & Suites SH
(505) 345-0010. $84-$109. 1315 Menaul Blvd NE. I-25, exit 227A, just e to University Blvd, 0.5 mi s to Menaul Blvd, then 0.5 mi w. Int corridors. **Pets:** Accepted.

### ▲▲▲ ▼▼▼ Comfort Inn-Airport SH
(505) 243-2244. $69-$109. 2300 Yale Blvd SE. I-25, exit 222A southbound; exit 222 northbound, 1 mi n, then just s. Ext/int corridors. **Pets:** Medium. $10 one-time fee/pet. Designated rooms, service with restrictions.

### ▼▼▼▼ Comfort Inn & Suites by Choice Hotels SH
(505) 822-1090. $70-$90. 5811 Signal Ave NE. I-25, exit 233, just e via Alameda. Int corridors. **Pets:** Accepted.

### ▲▲▲ ▼▼▼ Comfort Inn East SH
(505) 294-1800. $49-$99. 13031 Central Ave NE. I-40, exit 167, just w. Ext corridors. **Pets:** Accepted.

### ▼▼▼ Comfort Inn-Midtown SH
(505) 881-3210. $54-$110. 2015 Menaul Blvd NE. I-25, exit 225 northbound, 1.6 mi n of Frontage Rd to Menaul Blvd, then just e; exit 227 (Commanche Rd) southbound, s on Frontage Rd, 0.8 mi n to Menaul Blvd, then just e. Ext corridors. **Pets:** Medium. $10 daily fee/pet. Designated rooms, service with restrictions, supervision.

### ▲▲▲ ▼▼▼ Days Inn-Hotel Circle SH
(505) 275-3297. $65. 10321 Hotel Cir NE. I-40, exit 165 (Eubank Blvd), just n. Ext corridors. **Pets:** Accepted.

### ▼▼▼ Days Inn Midtown SH
(505) 884-0250. $45-$109, 15 day notice. 2120 Menaul Blvd NE. I-40, exit 160, just n to Menaul Blvd, then 0.8 mi w. Ext corridors. **Pets:** Small. $10 one-time fee/room. Service with restrictions, supervision.

**▼▼ Days Inn West** Ⓜ
(505) 836-3297. **$53-$85.** 6031 Iliff Rd NW. I-40, exit 155, just s on Coors Rd, then just w. Ext corridors. **Pets:** $5 daily fee/pet. Designated rooms, supervision.
[A$K] [S⬤] [✕] [⅋M] [🐾] [⅋] [⇌]

**▼▼▼◆ Drury Inn & Suites-Albuquerque** SH
(505) 341-3600. **$96-$148.** 4310 The 25 Way NE. I-25, exit Jefferson St NE, northwest quadrant of exchange. Int corridors. **Pets:** Accepted.
[A$K] [✕] [⅋M] [🛏] [⎙] [⇌]

**ⒶⒶⒶ ▼▼▼ Econo Lodge Downtown/University** SH ❖
(505) 243-1321. **$39-$69.** 817 Central Ave NE. I-25, 224A northbound; exit 224B southbound, just e. Ext corridors. **Pets:** Medium. $25 deposit/room, $5 daily fee/pet. Service with restrictions, supervision.
[SAVE] [S⬤] [✕] [🛏] [⎙] [⇌]

**ⒶⒶⒶ ▼▼▼ Econo Lodge Old Town** SH
(505) 243-8475. **$45-$130.** 2321 Central Ave NW. I-40, exit 157A, 0.6 mi s on Rio Grande Blvd, then 0.4 mi w. Ext corridors. **Pets:** Medium, dogs only. $10 daily fee/pet. Designated rooms, service with restrictions, supervision.
[SAVE] [S⬤] [✕] [🛏] [⎙] [⇌]

**ⒶⒶⒶ ▼▼▼ Equus Hotel Suites** Ⓜ ❖
(505) 883-8888. **$69-$109.** 2401 Wellsley Dr NE. I-40, exit 160, just n to Menaul Blvd, just w, then just s. Ext corridors. **Pets:** Large. Designated rooms, service with restrictions, supervision.
[SAVE] [S⬤] [✕] [🛏] [⎙] [⇌]

**ⒶⒶⒶ ▼▼▼▼ Fairfield Inn Airport** SH
(505) 247-1621. **$59-$98.** 2300 Centre Ave SE. I-25, exit 222 northbound; exit 222A southbound, 1 mi e to Yale Blvd; northeast jct of Gibson and Yale blvds. Int corridors. **Pets:** Small, other species. $75 one-time fee/room. Service with restrictions, supervision.
[SAVE] [S⬤] [✕] [⅋M] [🐾] [⅋] [🛏] [⎙] [⇌]

**▼▼ GuestHouse Inn & Suites** SH
(505) 271-8500. **$35-$95, 7 day notice.** 10331 Hotel Ave NE. I-40, exit 165, 2 blks n. Int corridors. **Pets:** Accepted.
[A$K] [S⬤] [✕] [⎙] [⇌]

**ⒶⒶⒶ ▼▼▼▼ Hacienda Antigua Inn** BB ❖
(505) 345-5399. **$134-$189, 10 day notice.** 6708 Tierra Dr NW. I-25, exit 230 (Osuna Dr), 2 mi w, then just n. Ext/int corridors. **Pets:** Other species. $35 one-time fee/pet. Designated rooms, supervision.
[SAVE] [S⬤] [✕] [🛏] [⎙] [⇌]

**ⒶⒶⒶ ▼▼▼ Hampton Inn-North** SH
(505) 344-1555. **$84-$94.** 5101 Ellison NE. I-25, exit 231, just w. Ext corridors. **Pets:** Service with restrictions, supervision.
[SAVE] [S⬤] [✕] [⅋M] [🐾] [🛏] [⎙] [⇌]

**▼▼▼◆ Hawthorn Inn & Suites** SH ❖
(505) 242-1555. **$69-$149.** 1511 Gibson Blvd SE. I-25, exit 222 northbound; exit 222A southbound, just e. Int corridors. **Pets:** Medium. $5 daily fee/pet. Designated rooms, service with restrictions, supervision.
[A$K] [S⬤] [✕] [⅋M] [🐾] [⅋] [🛏] [🍴] [⇌]

**ⒶⒶⒶ ▼▼▼ Holiday Inn Express** SH
(505) 275-8900. **$69.** 10330 Hotel Ave NE. I-40, exit 165 (Eubank Blvd), 2 blks n. Ext corridors. **Pets:** Accepted.
[SAVE] [S⬤] [✕] [🐾] [⅋] [🛏] [⎙] [⇌] [✕]

**▼▼▼◆ Holiday Inn Express-West** SH
(505) 836-8600. **$69-$129.** 6100 Iliff Rd NW. I-40, exit 155, just sw. Ext/int corridors. **Pets:** Other species. $10 one-time fee/pet. Service with restrictions, supervision.
[A$K] [S⬤] [✕] [⅋M] [🐾] [⅋] [🛏] [⎙] [⇌] [✕]

**▼▼▼ Hotel Albuquerque at Old Town** LH
(505) 843-6300. **$89-$254.** 800 Rio Grande Blvd NW. I-40, exit 157A, 0.4 mi s. Int corridors. **Pets:** Accepted.
[A$K] [S⬤] [✕] [🐾] [⅋] [🍴] [⇌] [✕]

**▼▼▼ The Hotel Blue** SH
(505) 924-2400. **$79-$109.** 717 Central Ave NW. 8th and Central Ave; downtown. Ext corridors. **Pets:** Medium. $25 one-time fee/room. Service with restrictions.
[A$K] [S⬤] [✕] [🐾] [⅋] [🛏] [⎙] [⇌]

**▼▼▼ Howard Johnson Express nn** SH
(505) 828-1600. **$60-$75.** 7630 Pan American NE. I-25, exit 231, 0.8 mi n on frontage road. Int corridors. **Pets:** Medium, other species. $10 daily fee/pet. Designated rooms, service with restrictions, crate.
[A$K] [✕] [🐾] [⅋] [🛏] [⎙] [⇌]

**▼▼▼▼ La Quinta Inn Albuquerque (Airport)** SH
(505) 243-5500. **$78-$112.** 2116 Yale Blvd SE. I-25, exit 222 northbound; exit 222A southbound, 1 mi e. Ext/int corridors. **Pets:** Medium. Service with restrictions.
[A$K] [✕] [⅋M] [🐾] [⅋] [🛏] [⎙] [⇌]

**▼▼▼▼ La Quinta Inn Albuquerque (I-40 East)** SH
(505) 884-3591. **$64-$100.** 2424 San Mateo Blvd NE. I-40, exit 161 westbound; exit 161B eastbound, just n. Ext corridors. **Pets:** Medium. Service with restrictions.
[A$K] [✕] [🐾] [⅋] [🛏] [⎙] [⇌]

**ⒶⒶⒶ ▼▼▼▼ La Quinta Inn Albuquerque (North)** SH
(505) 821-9000. **$72-$109.** 5241 San Antonio Dr NE. I-25, exit 231, just e. Ext corridors. **Pets:** Medium. Service with restrictions.
[SAVE] [✕] [⅋M] [🐾] [⅋] [🛏] [⎙] [⇌]

**▼▼▼ La Quinta Inn & Suites Albuquerque (West)** SH
(505) 839-1744. **$99-$129.** 6101 Iliff Rd NW. I-40, exit 155, just sw. Int corridors. **Pets:** Medium. Service with restrictions.
[A$K] [✕] [⅋M] [🐾] [⅋] [🛏] [⎙] [⇌]

**▼▼ Microtel Inn & Suites** SH
(505) 836-1686. **$65.** 9910 Avalon NW. I-40, exit 153, just s; on western edge of city. Int corridors. **Pets:** Accepted.
[A$K] [S⬤] [✕] [⎙]

**▼ Motel 6 #1349** Ⓜ
(505) 243-8017. **$44-$57.** 1000 Avenida Cesar Chavez. I-25, exit 223, just w. Ext corridors. **Pets:** Accepted.
[S⬤] [✕] [🐾] [⅋] [🛏] [⇌]

**▼ Motel 6 Albuquerque East #49** Ⓜ
(505) 294-4600. **$38-$51.** 13141 Central Ave NE. I-40, exit 167 (Tramway Blvd), just s, then just w. Ext corridors. **Pets:** Accepted.
[S⬤] [✕] [⇌]

**▼ Motel 6 Albuquerque North #1290** SH
(505) 821-1472. **$43-$55.** 8510 Pan American Frwy NE. I-25, exit 232 (Paseo del Norte), just n on Frontage Rd. Int corridors. **Pets:** Accepted.
[S⬤] [✕] [⅋M] [⇌]

**ⒶⒶⒶ ▼▼▼ Motel 76** SH
(505) 836-3881. **$38-$52.** 1521 Coors Blvd NW. I-40, exit 155 (Coors Blvd), just s. Ext corridors. **Pets:** Small. $25 deposit/room. Service with restrictions, supervision.
[SAVE] [✕]

**▼▼▼▼ Nativo Lodge** SH ❖
(505) 798-4300. **$89-$179.** 6000 Pan American Frwy NE. I-25, exit 230, just e. Int corridors. **Pets:** Dogs only. $50 one-time fee/room. Service with restrictions.
[A$K] [S⬤] [✕] [🐾] [⅋] [🛏] [⎙] [🍴] [✕]

**ⒶⒶⒶ ▼▼▼ Plaza Inn Albuquerque** SH ❖
(505) 243-5693. **$79-$129.** 900 Medical Arts NE. I-25, exit 225, just e. Int corridors. **Pets:** Large. $25 one-time fee/pet. Service with restrictions, crate.
[SAVE] [S⬤] [✕] [⅋M] [🛏] [⎙] [🍴] [⇌]

**⚑ ▼▼ Quality Inn & Suites Albuquerque**
**Downtown** 🆂🅷
(505) 242-5228. **$53-$95.** 411 McKnight Ave NW. I-40, exit 159A, just s via 4th St N. Int corridors. **Pets:** Accepted.
⬛ 🆂 ⊠ ▭ ⊇

**⚑ ▼▼▼ Quality Suites** 🆂🅷
(505) 797-0850. **$79-$99.** 5251 San Antonio Dr NE. I-25, exit 231, just e. Int corridors. **Pets:** Medium. $6 daily fee/pet. Service with restrictions, supervision.
⬛ 🆂 ⊠ 🚹 ▭ ⊇

**▼▼▼ Radisson Hotel & Conference Center** 🅻🅷
(505) 888-3311. **$89-$179.** 2500 Carlisle Blvd NE. I-40, exit 160, just n. Ext/int corridors. **Pets:** Accepted.
A$K 🆂 ⊠ ♿ ⊘ ⊡ 🚹 ▭ 🍴 ⊇ ⊠

**▼▼▼ Ramada Limited** 🆂🅷
(505) 858-3297. **$69-$79.** 5601 Alameda Blvd NE. I-25, exit 233, just w. Int corridors. **Pets:** Accepted.
A$K 🆂 ⊠ ♿ ⊘ ⊡ 🚹 ▭ ⊇

**⚑ ▼▼ Ramada Limited (Airport)** 🆂🅷
(505) 242-0036. **$45-$70.** 1801 Yale Blvd SE. I-25, exit 222 northbound; exit 222A southbound, 1 mi e, then just n. Int corridors. **Pets:** Accepted.
⬛ 🆂 ⊠ ♿ ⊡ 🚹 ▭ ⊠

**▼▼ Red Roof Inn** 🆂🅷
(505) 831-3400. **$42-$59.** 6015 Iliff Rd NW. I-40, exit 155 (Coors Blvd), just s, then just w. Ext corridors. **Pets:** Accepted.
⊠ ♿ ⊘ ⊡ ⊇

**▼▼▼ Residence Inn North by Marriott** 🆂🅷
(505) 761-0200. **$109-$149.** 4331 The Lane at 25 NE. I-25, exit 229 (Jefferson St), just w, just n to The Lane at 25 NE, then just e. Int corridors. **Pets:** Accepted.
A$K ⊠ ♿ ⊡ 🚹 ▭ ⊇ ⊠

**⚑ ▼▼ Sandia Peak Inn** 🆂🅷
(505) 831-5036. **$49-$99.** 4614 Central Ave SW. I-40, exit 159A (Rio Grande Blvd), just s, then 2 mi w. Ext corridors. **Pets:** Accepted.
⬛ 🆂 ⊠ 🚹 ⊇

**⚑ ▼▼▼ Sheraton Albuquerque Uptown** 🅻🅷
(505) 881-0000. **$89-$199.** 2600 Louisiana Blvd NE. I-40, exit 162, 0.8 mi n. Int corridors. **Pets:** Accepted.
⬛ 🆂 ⊠ ♿ ⊘ ⊡ 🚹 ▭ 🍴 ⊇ ⊠

**⚑ ▼▼▼ Sleep Inn Airport** 🆂🅷
(505) 244-3325. **$70.** 2300 International Ave SE. I-25, exit 222 northbound; exit 222A southbound, 1 mi e to Yale Blvd, then just n. Int corridors. **Pets:** Accepted.
⬛ 🆂 ⊠ ⊘ ⊡ ▭ ⊇

**⚑ ▼ Stardust Inn** 🅼
(505) 243-2891. **$36-$79.** 801 Central Ave NE. I-25, 224A northbound; exit 224B southbound, just e. Ext corridors. **Pets:** Medium. $25 deposit/pet, $5 daily fee/pet. Designated rooms, service with restrictions, crate.
⬛ 🆂 ⊠ 🚹 ⊇

**▼▼▼ Sun Village Corporate Suites** 🅲🅾
(505) 842-6640. **$60-$90, 7 day notice.** 801 Locust NE. From University Blvd, just w on Indian School Rd, then just n. Ext corridors. **Pets:** Accepted.
⊠ 🚹 ▭ ⊇ ⊠

**▼▼ Super 8 Motel East** 🆂🅷
(505) 271-4807. **$50-$125, 5 day notice.** 450 Paisano NE. I-40, exit 166 (Juan Tabo Blvd), just n to Copper, then just s. Int corridors. **Pets:** Accepted.
A$K 🆂 ⊠ ⊡

**▼▼ Super 8 Motel of Albuquerque** 🆂🅷
(505) 888-4884. **$50-$125, 5 day notice.** 2500 University Blvd NE. I-25, exit 225 northbound, 1.9 mi n on frontage road to Menaul Blvd, then just e; exit 227 (Comanche Rd) southbound, 0.9 mi s to Menaul Blvd, then just e. Int corridors. **Pets:** Accepted.
A$K 🆂 ⊠ ⊘ ⊡ 🚹 ▭

**▼▼ Super 8 Motel West (Albuquerque)** 🆂🅷
(505) 836-5560. **$50-$125, 5 day notice.** 6030 Iliff Rd NW. I-40, exit 155, 0.5 mi s. Int corridors. **Pets:** Accepted.
A$K 🆂 ⊠ ⊡

**⚑ ▼▼▼ TownePlace Suites** 🆂🅷
(505) 232-5800. **$59-$109.** 2400 Centre Ave SE. I-25, exit 222 northbound; exit 222A southbound, 1 mi e to Yale Blvd, at northeast jct of Gibson and Yale blvds, then just e. Int corridors. **Pets:** Small, other species. $75 one-time fee/room. Service with restrictions, supervision.
⬛ 🆂 ⊠ ♿ ⊡ 🚹 ⊇

**▼▼▼ Wyndham Albuquerque at International**
**Sunport** 🅻🅷
(505) 843-7000. **$89-$119.** 2910 Yale Blvd SE. I-25, exit 225 northbound; exit 222A southbound, 1 mi e on Gibson Blvd, then 0.5 mi s. Int corridors. **Pets:** Accepted.
A$K ⊠ ♿ ⊘ ⊡ ▭ 🍴 ⊇ ⊠

# ALGODONES

**⚑ ▼▼▼ Hacienda Vargas Bed and Breakfast**
**Inn** 🅱🅱 🐾
(505) 867-9115. **$89-$149, 10 day notice.** 1431 SR 313 (El Camino Real). I-25, exit 248, 0.5 mi w. Int corridors. **Pets:** Large, other species. $10 one-time fee/pet. Service with restrictions, crate.
⬛ 🆂 ⊠ ⊠ 🆆 ⊘

# ARROYO SECO

**▼▼ Adobe and Stars B & B** 🅱🅱
(505) 776-2776. **$110-$185, 32 day notice.** 584 State Hwy 150. 1.1 mi ne on SR 150 at Valdez Rd. Ext/int corridors. **Pets:** Accepted.
A$K ⊠ 🚹 🅰🅲 🆆

# ARTESIA

**⚑ ▼ Artesia Inn** 🅼
(505) 746-9801. **$45-$55.** 1820 S 1st St. 1.5 mi s on US 285. Ext corridors. **Pets:** Accepted.
⬛ 🆂 ⊠ 🚹 ▭ ⊇

# BELEN

**⚑ ▼▼▼ Best Western-Belen** 🆂🅷
(505) 861-3181. **$65-$95.** 2111 Camino del Llano Blvd. I-25, exit 191, just w. Ext/int corridors. **Pets:** Other species. $20 deposit/pet, $5 one-time fee/pet. Designated rooms, supervision.
⬛ 🆂 ⊠ ⊡ 🚹 ▭ ⊇

**▼▼▼ Holiday Inn Express** 🆂🅷
(505) 861-5000. **$89.** 2110 Camino del Llano. I-25, exit 191, just w. Int corridors. **Pets:** Accepted.
A$K 🆂 ⊠ ♿ ⊡ 🚹 ▭ ⊇

# BERNALILLO

**⚑ ▼▼▼ Days Inn-Bernalillo** 🆂🅷
(505) 771-7000. **$40-$80.** 107 N Camino del Pueblo. I-25, exit 242, just w. Int corridors. **Pets:** $30 deposit/pet. Service with restrictions, supervision.
⬛ 🆂 ⊠ 🚹 ⊇

**Hyatt Regency Tamaya Resort and Spa** LH
(505) 867-1234. **$125-$315, 3 day notice.** 1300 Tuyuna Tr. I-25, exit 242, 1 mi w on SR 44 to Tamaya Rd, then 1 mi n, follow signs. Int corridors. **Pets:** Accepted.

**La Hacienda Grande** BB
(505) 867-1887. **$109-$149, 10 day notice.** 21 Barros Rd. I-25, exit 242, 0.3 mi w to Camino del Pueblo, then 0.5 mi n. Ext/int corridors. **Pets:** Large, other species. $10 one-time fee/room. Designated rooms, no service, crate.

## BLOOMFIELD

**Super 8 Motel** M
(505) 632-8886. **$50.** 525 W Broadway Blvd. Jct of US 64 and SR 44. Int corridors. **Pets:** Accepted.

## CARLSBAD

**Best Western Stevens Inn** SH
(505) 887-2851. **$72-$99.** 1829 S Canal St. 1 mi s on US 62, 180 and 285. Ext corridors. **Pets:** $10 daily fee/pet. Service with restrictions, supervision.

**Carlsbad Inn** M
(505) 887-1171. **$36-$49.** 2019 S Canal St. 1.5 mi s on US 62, 180 and 285. Ext corridors. **Pets:** Medium. $5 one-time fee/pet. Designated rooms, service with restrictions, supervision.

**Comfort Inn** SH
(505) 887-1994. **$71-$81.** 2429 W Pierce St. N on US 285. Int corridors. **Pets:** Accepted.

**Days Inn of Carlsbad** SH
(505) 887-7800. **$80-$95, 14 day notice.** 3910 National Parks Hwy. 3.5 mi sw on US 62 and 180. Ext corridors. **Pets:** Very small, dogs only. $10 daily fee/pet. Designated rooms, service with restrictions, supervision.

**Stagecoach Inn** M
(505) 887-1148. **$36-$52.** 1819 S Canal St. 1 mi s on US 62, 180 and 285. Ext corridors. **Pets:** Medium. $10 daily fee/pet. Designated rooms, service with restrictions, supervision.

## CHAMA

**Vista del Rio Lodge** M
(505) 756-2138. **$60-$90.** 2595 US Hwy 84/64. 0.5 mi s of SR 17. Ext corridors. **Pets:** Small, dogs only. Service with restrictions, supervision.

## CHIMAYO

**Casa Escondida Bed & Breakfast** BB
(505) 351-4805. **$89-$149, 14 day notice.** 64 CR 0100. SR 68, 7.1 mi e on SR 76, 0.5 mi nw on CR 100, follow signs. Ext/int corridors. **Pets:** Accepted.

## CIMARRON

**Cimarron Inn & RV Park** M
(505) 376-2268. **$49-$60.** 212 10th St. On US 64. Ext corridors. **Pets:** Other species. Crate.

## CLAYTON

**Best Western Kokopelli Lodge** SH
(505) 374-2589. **$71-$165.** 702 S 1st St. US 87, 0.5 mi se of jct US 56 and 64. Ext corridors. **Pets:** $5 daily fee/pet. Service with restrictions, supervision.

**Days Inn & Suites** SH
(505) 374-0133. **$69-$139.** 1120 S 1st St. US 87, 1 mi s of jct US 56 and 64. Int corridors. **Pets:** $5 daily fee/pet. Service with restrictions, supervision.

**Super 8 Motel** M
(505) 374-8127. **$48-$85.** 1425 S 1st St. US 87, 1 mi se of jct US 56 and 64. Int corridors. **Pets:** Accepted.

## CLOVIS

**Comfort Inn** SH
(505) 762-4591. **$59.** 1616 Mabry Dr. 1 mi e on US 60, 70 and 84. Ext corridors. **Pets:** Accepted.

**Econo Lodge** M
(505) 763-3439. **$59-$129.** 1400 E Mabry Dr. 0.5 mi e on US 60, 70 and 84. Ext corridors. **Pets:** Medium. $10 one-time fee/pet. Designated rooms, service with restrictions, supervision.

**Holiday Inn Clovis** SH
(505) 762-4491. **$59-$109.** 2700 E Mabry Dr. 1.5 mi e on US 60, 70 and 84. Ext corridors. **Pets:** Accepted.

**Howard Johnson Expressway Inn** SH
(505) 769-1953. **$52-$66.** 2920 Mabry Dr. US 60, 70 and 84, just e. Int corridors. **Pets:** Accepted.

**La Quinta Inn & Suites Clovis** SH
(505) 763-8777. **$85-$115.** 4521 N Prince St. Jct US 60/84 and Prince St, 3 mi n. Int corridors. **Pets:** Small, other species. $30 deposit/room. Service with restrictions, supervision.

## DEMING

**Best Western Mimbres Valley Inn** SH
(505) 546-4544. **$47-$85.** 1500 W Pine. I-10, exit 81, just e. Ext corridors. **Pets:** Small. $5 one-time fee/pet. Service with restrictions, supervision.

**Days Inn** M
(505) 546-8813. **$47-$57.** 1601 E Pine St. I-10, exit 85 westbound, 2 mi w on business loop; exit 81 eastbound, 1 mi e on business loop. Ext corridors. **Pets:** Small. $5 daily fee/pet. Service with restrictions, supervision.

**Grand Motor Inn** SI
(505) 546-2632. **$48.** 1721 E Pine St. -10, exit 85 westbound, 2 mi w on business loop; exit 82 eastbound, 1 mi e on business loop. Ext corridors. **Pets:** Medium, other species. $6 daily fee/room. Designated rooms, service with restrictions, supervision.

**Holiday Inn** SH
(505) 546-2661. **$50-$60.** 4600 E Pine St. I-10, exit 85, just w. Ext corridors. **Pets:** Medium, other species. Designated rooms, service with restrictions, supervision.

**La Quinta Inn & Suites** 🆂🅷 ❀
(505) 546-0600. **$69-$99.** 4300 E Pine St. I-10, exit 85, just w. Int corridors. **Pets:** Small. $25 deposit/room. Service with restrictions, supervision.

🅰🆂🅺 🆂🔟 ❌ ⬛ᴹ 🄻 📱 🖵 ⇌

# EDGEWOOD

▽▼▽▼ **Alta Mae's Heritage Inn** 🅱🅱
(505) 281-5000. **$95, 14 day notice.** 1950-C Old Route 66. I-40, exit 187, just s to stop sign, then just e. Ext corridors. **Pets:** Accepted.

🅰🆂🅺 ❌ ❌ 🆉

# ELEPHANT BUTTE

🄰🄰🄰 ▽▼▽▼ **Elephant Butte Inn** 🆂🅷 ❀
(505) 744-5431. **$70-$100, 3 day notice.** 401 Hwy 195. I-25, exit 83, 4 mi e. Ext corridors. **Pets:** Medium. $15 one-time fee/pet. Designated rooms, service with restrictions, supervision.

🆂🅰🆅🅴 🆂🔟 ❌ ⬛ᴹ 🄻 📱 🖵 🍴 ⇌

▽▼ **Marina Suites Motel** 🅼
(505) 744-5269. **$75-$95.** 200 Country Club Dr. I-25, exit 83, 4.7 mi e. Ext corridors. **Pets:** Dogs only. Designated rooms, service with restrictions, supervision.

🅰🆂🅺 🆂🔟 📱 🖵 🆉

# ESPANOLA

🄰🄰🄰 ▽▼▽▼ **Comfort Inn** 🆂🅷
(505) 753-2419. **$55-$125.** 604-B S Riverside Dr. US 84 and 285, just s of jct SR 68. Int corridors. **Pets:** Other species. Service with restrictions, supervision.

🆂🅰🆅🅴 🆂🔟 ❌ 📱 🖵 ⇌

▽▼▽▼ **Espanola Days Inn** 🆂🅷
(505) 747-1242. **$45-$72.** 807 S Riverside Dr. US 84 and 285, 0.7 mi s of jct SR 68. Ext corridors. **Pets:** $6 daily fee/pet. Service with restrictions.

🅰🆂🅺 🆂🔟 ❌ 📱

🄰🄰🄰 ▽▼▽▼ **Super 8 Motel** 🆂🅷
(505) 753-5374. **$40-$105.** 811 S Riverside Dr. US 84 and 285, 0.5 mi s of jct SR 68. Int corridors. **Pets:** Other species. Service with restrictions, supervision.

🆂🅰🆅🅴 🆂🔟 ❌ 📱 🖵

# FARMINGTON

🄰🄰🄰 ▽▼▽▼▽ **Best Western Inn & Suites** 🆂🅷 ❀
(505) 327-5221. **$89-$109.** 700 Scott Ave. 0.8 mi e on US 64 at Bloomfield Blvd and Scott Ave. Int corridors. **Pets:** $10 one-time fee/pet. Designated rooms, service with restrictions, supervision.

🆂🅰🆅🅴 🆂🔟 ❌ 🄬 📱 🖵 🍴 ⇌ ❌

▽▼▽▼ **Brentwood Inn Farmington** 🆂🅷
(505) 325-2288. **$84.** 600 E Broadway. 1 mi e; at Broadway and Scott Ave. Int corridors. **Pets:** Accepted.

🅰🆂🅺 🆂🔟 ❌ 🄬 📱 🖵 🍴 ⇌ ❌

🄰🄰🄰 ▽▼▽▼ **Comfort Inn** 🅼
(505) 325-2626. **$69-$119.** 555 Scott Ave. 0.8 mi e on US 64 (Bloomfield Blvd), just n. Int corridors. **Pets:** Accepted.

🆂🅰🆅🅴 🆂🔟 ❌ 📱 🖵 ⇌

▽▼▽▼ **Days Inn** 🅼
(505) 325-3700. **$60-$80.** 1901 E Broadway. 1.7 mi e on US 64 (Bloomfield Blvd). Int corridors. **Pets:** Accepted.

🅰🆂🅺 🆂🔟 ❌ ⬛ᴹ 🄬 🄻 📱 🖵

🄰🄰🄰 ▽▼▽▼▽ **Holiday Inn Express** 🅼
(505) 325-2545. **$77.** 2110 Bloomfield Blvd. 1.6 mi e on US 64 (Bloomfield Blvd), just past jct Broadway, on frontage road. Int corridors. **Pets:** Medium, dogs only. $25 one-time fee/room. Service with restrictions, supervision.

🆂🅰🆅🅴 🆂🔟 ❌ ⬛ᴹ 🄬 🄻 📱 🖵 ⇌

▽▼▽▼ **La Quinta Inn Farmington** 🅼
(505) 327-4706. **$72-$112.** 675 Scott Ave. 1 mi e on SR 516 (Main St), just s. Ext/int corridors. **Pets:** Medium. Service with restrictions.

🅰🆂🅺 ❌ ⬛ᴹ 🄬 📱 🖵 ⇌

▽▼ **Super 8 Motel** 🅼
(505) 325-1813. **$48-$78.** 1601 E Broadway. Just n of jct SR 64 (Bloomfield Blvd). Int corridors. **Pets:** Other species. $5 daily fee/pet. Service with restrictions, supervision.

🅰🆂🅺 🆂🔟 ❌ 🄻 📱

# GALLUP

▽▼▽▼ **Americas Best Value Inn & Suites** 🆂🅷
(505) 722-0757. **$49-$64, 3 day notice.** 2003 US 66 W. I-40, exit 20, 1 mi w. Ext/int corridors. **Pets:** Accepted.

🅰🆂🅺 🆂🔟 ❌ ⬛ᴹ 📱 🖵 🍴 ⇌

🄰🄰🄰 ▽▼▽▼ **Best Western Inn & Suites** 🆂🅷
(505) 722-2221. **$59-$99.** 3009 US 66 W. I-40, exit 16, 1 mi e. Int corridors. **Pets:** Large, other species. $15 one-time fee/room. Designated rooms, service with restrictions.

🆂🅰🆅🅴 🆂🔟 ❌ 📱 🖵 🍴 ⇌ ❌

🄰🄰🄰 ▽▼▽▼ **Best Western Royal Holiday Motel** 🆂🅷
(505) 722-4900. **$59-$149.** 1903 W Hwy 66. I-40, exit 20, 0.5 mi s to US 66, then 0.8 mi w. Int corridors. **Pets:** Accepted.

🆂🅰🆅🅴 🆂🔟 ❌ 📱 🖵 ⇌

🄰🄰🄰 ▽▼▽▼ **Comfort Inn** 🅼
(505) 722-0982. **$59-$99.** 3208 US 66 W. I-40, exit 16, 0.3 mi e. Int corridors. **Pets:** Small. $10 daily fee/room. Designated rooms, service with restrictions, supervision.

🆂🅰🆅🅴 🆂🔟 ❌ 📱 🖵 ⇌

▽▼▽▼ **Econo Lodge** 🆂🅷
(505) 722-3800. **$35-$85.** 3101 US 66 W. I-40, exit 16, 0.8 mi e. Int corridors. **Pets:** Medium, other species. $5 daily fee/pet. Service with restrictions, supervision.

🅰🆂🅺 🆂🔟 ❌ 📱

🄰🄰🄰 ▽▼ **Economy Inn** 🅼
(505) 863-9301. **$31-$39.** 1709 US 66 W. I-40, exit 20, s to US 66, then 0.5 mi w. Ext corridors. **Pets:** Accepted.

🆂🅰🆅🅴 ❌ 📱

▽▼▽▼ **Gallup Travelodge** 🆂🅷
(505) 722-2100. **$44-$89, 7 day notice.** 3275 US 66 W. I-40, exit 16, just e. Int corridors. **Pets:** Accepted.

🅰🆂🅺 🆂🔟 ❌ ⬛ᴹ 🄻 🖵 ⇌

▽▼▽▼▽ **La Quinta Inn & Suites** 🆂🅷
(505) 722-2233. **$69-$104.** 3880 Hwy 66 E. I-40, exit 26, just e. Int corridors. **Pets:** Accepted.

🅰🆂🅺 ❌ ⬛ᴹ 🄻 📱 🖵 ⇌ ❌

▽▼▽▼ **Ramada Limited** 🆂🅷 ❀
(505) 726-2700. **$69-$99, 7 day notice.** 1440 W Maloney Ave. I-40, exit 20, 1 mi w. Int corridors. **Pets:** Small. $5 daily fee/pet. Designated rooms, service with restrictions, supervision.

🅰🆂🅺 🆂🔟 ❌ ⬛ᴹ 📱 🖵 ⇌

🄰🄰🄰 ▽▼▽▼ **Red Roof Inn** 🅼
(505) 722-7765. **$36-$60.** 3304 W Hwy 66. I-40, exit 16, just se. Ext corridors. **Pets:** Large. $3 daily fee/pet. No service, supervision.

🆂🅰🆅🅴 🆂🔟 ❌ 📱 🖵 ⇌

🄰🄰🄰 ▽▼▽▼ **Sleep Inn** 🆂🅷
(505) 863-3535. **$60-$80.** 3820 E US 66. I-40, exit 26, just e. Int corridors. **Pets:** Other species. $8 daily fee/pet. Service with restrictions, crate.

🆂🅰🆅🅴 🆂🔟 ❌ ⬛ᴹ 🄻 📱 ⇌

**▼▼▼ Super 8 Motel M**
(505) 722-5300. **$55-$62.** 1715 W US 66. I-40, exit 20, s to US 66, then 0.5 mi w. Int corridors. **Pets:** Accepted.
A$K S❺ ⊠ 🗃 💻 ⇌

# GRANTS

**◉◉◉ ▼▼▼ Best Western Inn & Suites SH ❀**
(505) 287-7901. **$69-$89.** 1501 E Santa Fe Ave. I-40, exit 85, just w. Int corridors. **Pets:** Medium. $10 one-time fee/pet. Designated rooms, service with restrictions, supervision.
SAVE S❺ ⊠ 🗃 💻 🍴 ⇌ ⊠

**▼▼ Comfort Inn SH ❀**
(505) 287-8700. **$59-$79, 7 day notice.** 1551 E Santa Fe Ave. I-40, exit 85, 0.3 mi n. Int corridors. **Pets:** Small. $5 daily fee/pet. Designated rooms, service with restrictions, supervision.
A$K S❺ ⊠ 🔊M 🗃 💻 ⇌

**◉◉◉ ▼▼▼ Days Inn SH**
(505) 287-8883. **$50-$90, 3 day notice.** 1504 E Santa Fe Ave. I-40, exit 85, 0.3 mi n. Ext corridors. **Pets:** Small. $5 daily fee/pet. Service with restrictions, supervision.
SAVE S❺ ⊠

**▼▼ Grants Travelodge SH ❀**
(505) 287-7800. **$59-$79, 7 day notice.** 1608 E Santa Fe Ave. I-40, exit 85, 0.3 mi n. Ext corridors. **Pets:** Small. $5 daily fee/pet. Designated rooms, service with restrictions, supervision.
A$K S❺ ⊠ 🔊M 🗃 💻 ⇌

**◉◉◉ ▼▼▼▼ Holiday Inn Express SH**
(505) 285-4676. **$60-$90, 3 day notice.** 1496 E Sante Fe Ave. I-40, exit 85, 0.3 mi n. Int corridors. **Pets:** Small. $10 daily fee/room. Designated rooms, service with restrictions, supervision.
SAVE S❺ ⊠ 🗃 💻 ⇌

**◉◉◉ ▼▼▼ Sands Motel M**
(505) 287-2996. **$40-$43.** 112 McArthur St. I-40, exit 85, 1.5 mi w on Business Loop 40. Ext corridors. **Pets:** $5 daily fee/pet. Service with restrictions, crate.
SAVE S❺ ⊠ 🗃

**▼▼ Super 8 Grants SH**
(505) 287-8811. **$45-$65.** 1604 E Santa Fe Ave. I-40, exit 85, just n. Int corridors. **Pets:** Accepted.
A$K S❺ ⊠ 💻 ⇌

# HOBBS

**▼▼ Best Western Executive Inn SH**
(505) 397-7171. **$70-$100.** 309 N Marland Blvd. US 62/180 and Snyder St. Ext corridors. **Pets:** Other species. $10 daily fee/pet. Service with restrictions, supervision.
⊠ 🗃 💻 ⇌

**◉◉◉ ▼▼▼ Days Inn M**
(505) 397-6541. **$51-$64, 3 day notice.** 211 N Marland Blvd. 2 mi e on US 62 and 180. Ext corridors. **Pets:** Small. $10 one-time fee/pet. Service with restrictions, supervision.
SAVE S❺ ⊠ 🔊 🔊 🗃 💻 ⇌

**◉◉◉ ▼▼▼ Econo Lodge SH**
(505) 397-3591. **$49-$69.** 619 N Marland Blvd. 2.5 mi e on US 62 and 180. Ext corridors. **Pets:** Accepted.
SAVE S❺ ⊠ 🗃 💻 ⇌

**◉◉◉ ▼▼▼ Howard Johnson-Hobbs SH**
(505) 397-3251. **$75.** 501 N Marland Blvd. 2.5 mi e on US 62 and 180. Ext/int corridors. **Pets:** Accepted.
SAVE S❺ ⊠ 🔊 🗃 💻 🍴 ⇌

**◉◉◉ ▼▼▼ Rodeway Inn M**
(505) 393-4101. **$50-$55.** 200 N Marland Blvd. On US 62 and 180, 2 mi e. Ext corridors. **Pets:** Small, dogs only. $25 deposit/pet. Designated rooms, service with restrictions, supervision.
SAVE ⊠ 🗃 💻 ⇌

# LAS CRUCES

**◉◉◉ ▼▼▼▼ Baymont Inn & Suites Las Cruces SH**
(505) 523-0100. **$73-$83.** 1500 Hickory Dr. I-10, exit 140, just se of jct I-25 and Avenida de Mesilla. Int corridors. **Pets:** Medium. Service with restrictions.
SAVE ⊠ 🔊M 🔊 🗃 💻 ⇌

**◉◉◉ ▼▼▼▼ Best Western Mesilla Valley Inn SH ❀**
(505) 524-8603. **$62-$89.** 901 Avenida de Mesilla. I-10, exit 140, just n. Ext/int corridors. **Pets:** Large, other species. Designated rooms, service with restrictions, crate.
SAVE ⊠ 🔊 🗃 💻 🍴 ⇌

**◉◉◉ ▼▼ Best Western Mission Inn SH**
(505) 524-8591. **$59-$79.** 1765 S Main St. I-10, exit 142, 1 mi n. Ext corridors. **Pets:** Designated rooms, service with restrictions, supervision.
SAVE ⊠ 🗃 💻 🍴 ⇌

**▼▼ Comfort Suites by Choice Hotels SH**
(505) 522-1300. **$75-$95.** 2101 S Triviz. I-25, exit 1. Int corridors. **Pets:** Accepted.
A$K S❺ ⊠ 🔊M 🔊 🔊 🗃 💻 ⇌

**◉◉◉ ▼▼ Hampton Inn SH**
(505) 526-8311. **$74-$79, 30 day notice.** 755 Avenida de Mesilla. I-10, exit 140. Ext corridors. **Pets:** Accepted.
SAVE S❺ ⊠ 🗃 💻 ⇌

**▼▼▼ Hilton Las Cruces LH**
(505) 522-4300. **$89-$159.** 705 S Telshore Blvd. I-25, exit 3 (Lohman Ave), just e. Int corridors. **Pets:** Small. $20 daily fee/pet. Designated rooms, service with restrictions, supervision.
A$K S❺ ⊠ 🔊M 🔊 🗃 💻 🍴 ⇌

**▼▼▼ Holiday Inn Express SH ❀**
(505) 527-9947. **$59-$189.** 2200 S Valley Dr. I-10, exit 142, 2 blks w. Ext corridors. **Pets:** Small. Service with restrictions, supervision.
A$K S❺ ⊠ 🔊M 🔊 🗃 💻 ⇌

**▼▼▼ La Quinta Inn Las Cruces SH**
(505) 524-0331. **$80-$90.** 790 Avenida de Mesilla. I-10, exit 140. Int corridors. **Pets:** Medium. Service with restrictions.
A$K ⊠ 🔊M 🔊 🗃 💻 ⇌

**▼▼▼ Lundeen's Inn of the Arts BB ❀**
(505) 526-3326. **$79.** 618 S Alameda Blvd. Center. Int corridors. **Pets:** Medium. $15 one-time fee/pet. Service with restrictions, crate.
A$K ⊠

**▼▼▼ Ramada Palms de Las Cruces SH**
(505) 526-4411. **$65-$195.** 201 E University Ave. I-10, exit 142, just n. Int corridors. **Pets:** Accepted.
A$K S❺ ⊠ 🔊M 🔊 🔊 💻 🍴 ⇌

**▼▼▼ Royal Host Motel M**
(505) 524-8536. **$46-$54.** 2146 W Picacho St. I-10, exit 139, 1 mi n, then 0.5 mi e on I-10 business route (Picacho St). Ext corridors. **Pets:** Medium. $15 one-time fee/pet. No service, supervision.
⊠ 🗃 ⇌

**▼▼▼ Sleep Inn by Choice Hotels SH**
(505) 522-1700. **$70-$90.** 2121 S Triviz. I-25, exit 1. Int corridors. **Pets:** Accepted.
A$K S❺ ⊠ 🔊M 🔊 🔊 🗃 💻 ⇌

# LAS VEGAS

### ◆◆◆ ▼▼▼ Comfort Inn SH
(505) 425-1100. **$60-$125.** 2500 N Grand Ave. I-25, exit 347, just sw, US 85 and I-25 business route. Int corridors. **Pets:** Medium. Designated rooms, service with restrictions, supervision.
SAVE Sₒ ✕ ⓵ 🖥 ⟳

### ◆◆◆ ▼▼ El Camino Motel M
(505) 425-5994. **$50-$65.** 1152 N Grand Ave. I-25, exit 345, 0.3 mi w, US 85 and I-25 business route. Ext corridors. **Pets:** Accepted.
SAVE Sₒ ✕ ⅋

### ◆◆◆ ▼▼▼ Inn on the Santa Fe Trail M ✿
(505) 425-6791. **$64-$84.** 1133 N Grand Ave. I-25, exit 345, 0.5 mi n; I-25 business route and US 84, 0.3 mi w. Ext corridors. **Pets:** $5 daily fee/room. Designated rooms, supervision.
SAVE Sₒ ✕ 🖥 🖥 ⅋ ⟳

### ◆◆◆ ▼▼▼▼ Plaza Hotel SH
(505) 425-3591. **$69-$139.** 230 Plaza. I-25, exit 343W, just w, follow signs to Old Town Plaza. Int corridors. **Pets:** Other species. $10 daily fee/room. Service with restrictions, supervision.
SAVE Sₒ ✕ 🖥 🖥 ⅋

# LORDSBURG

### ◆◆◆ ▼▼▼ Best Western-Western Skies Inn SH
(505) 542-8807. **$69-$109.** 1303 S Main St. I-10, exit 22, just s. Ext corridors. **Pets:** $15 daily fee/pet. Designated rooms, service with restrictions, supervision.
SAVE Sₒ ✕ 🖥 🖥 ⅋ ⟳

### ▼▼▼▼ Holiday Inn Express SH
(505) 542-3666. **$85-$99.** 1408 S Main St. I-10, exit 22, just s. Ext corridors. **Pets:** Accepted.
ASK Sₒ ✕ ⅋M ⓵ 🖥 🖥 ⟳

### ◆◆◆ ▼▼▼ Super 8 Motel SH
(505) 542-8882. **$60-$70.** 110 E Maple. I-10, exit 22, just s. Int corridors. **Pets:** Accepted.
SAVE Sₒ ✕

# LOS LUNAS

### ◆◆◆ ▼▼▼ Days Inn SH
(505) 865-5995. **$50-$80.** 1919 Main St SW. I-25, exit 203, just s to entrance at southeast corner. Int corridors. **Pets:** Medium. $10 one-time fee/room. Service with restrictions, supervision.
SAVE Sₒ ✕ 🖥 🖥 ⟳

### ▼▼▼ Western Skies Inn & Suites SH
(505) 865-0001. **$59-$89.** 2258 Sun Ranch Village Loop. I-25, exit 203, just w. Int corridors. **Pets:** Medium. $10 daily fee/pet. Designated rooms, service with restrictions, supervision.
ASK Sₒ ✕ ⅋M ⓵ ⟳

# LOVINGTON

### ◆◆◆ ▼▼▼ Lovington Inn SH
(505) 396-5346. **$54.** 1600 W Ave D. Jct US 82 and SR 18, 1 mi w. Ext corridors. **Pets:** $10 deposit/room. Service with restrictions.
SAVE Sₒ ✕ ⓵ 🖥 🖥 ⅋

# MESILLA

### ▼▼▼ Meson de Mesilla CI
(505) 525-9212. **$57-$185.** 1803 Avenida de Mesilla. I-10, exit 140, 0.4 mi s. Ext/int corridors. **Pets:** Accepted.
✕ 🖥 ⅋ ⟳

# MORIARTY

### ◆◆◆ ▼▼▼ Days Inn SH
(505) 832-4451. **$55-$79.** 1809 Route 66 W. I-40, exit 194. Int corridors. **Pets:** Small. $10 one-time fee/pet.
SAVE Sₒ ✕ 🖥

### ◆◆◆ ▼▼▼ Econo Lodge SH
(505) 832-4457. **$44-$69.** 1316 Route 66 W. I-40, exit 194, 0.5 mi se on US 66 and I-40 business loop. Int corridors. **Pets:** Other species. $5 daily fee/pet. Service with restrictions, supervision.
SAVE Sₒ ✕ 🖥 🖥

### ◆◆◆ ▼▼▼▼ Holiday Inn Express SH
(505) 832-5000. **$93.** 1507 Route 66. I-40, exit 194, 0.4 mi e. Int corridors. **Pets:** Medium, other species. $10 one-time fee/room. Designated rooms, service with restrictions, supervision.
SAVE Sₒ ✕ ⅋M 🖥 🖥 ⟳

### ◆◆◆ ▼▼ Sunset Motel M
(505) 832-4234. **$47-$54.** 501 E Route 66. I-40, exit 197, 1 mi w, then 0.5 mi e. Ext corridors. **Pets:** Other species. Service with restrictions, supervision.
SAVE Sₒ ✕ 🖥 🖥

### ◆◆◆ ▼▼▼ Super 8 Motel SH
(505) 832-6730. **$60-$70.** 1611 W Old Route 66. I-40, exit 194, 0.5 mi e on Central Ave. Int corridors. **Pets:** Medium, other species. $20 deposit/room. Designated rooms, service with restrictions, supervision.
SAVE Sₒ ✕ ⓵ 🖥

# PINOS ALTOS

### ▼▼▼ Bear Creek Motel & Cabins CA
(505) 388-4501. **$99-$159, 10 day notice.** 88 Main St. 1 mi n on SR 15. Ext corridors. **Pets:** Accepted.
ASK Sₒ 🖥 🖥 ⅋

# POJOAQUE PUEBLO

### ◆◆◆ ▼▼▼ Cities of Gold Hotel SH
(505) 455-0515. **$86-$119.** 10A Cities of Gold Rd. On US 84/265, just n. Int corridors. **Pets:** Other species. Designated rooms, supervision.
SAVE Sₒ ✕ ⅋M ⓵ 🖥 🖥 ⅋

# RANCHOS DE TAOS

### ◆◆◆ ▼▼ Budget Host Inn M
(505) 758-2524. **$48-$70, 3 day notice.** 1798 Paseo Del Pueblo Sur. On SR 68; center. Ext corridors. **Pets:** Other species. $8 one-time fee/pet. Service with restrictions, crate.
SAVE ✕ 🖥 🖥

# RATON

### ◆◆◆ ▼▼ Budget Host Raton M
(505) 445-3655. **$44-$55.** 136 Canyon Dr. I-25, exit 454, 0.8 mi s on I-25 business loop. Ext corridors. **Pets:** Medium. $2 daily fee/pet. Service with restrictions, supervision.
SAVE Sₒ ✕ ⅋M 🖥

### ▼▼ Motel 6 Raton #279 M
(505) 445-2777. **$39-$61.** 1600 Cedar St. I-25, exit 451, just w. Ext corridors. **Pets:** Accepted.
Sₒ ✕ ⟳

### ◆◆◆ ▼▼ The Raton Pass Inn M
(505) 445-3641. **$42-$52.** 308 Canyon Dr. I-25, exit 454, 0.8 mi s. Ext corridors. **Pets:** Medium, dogs only. $2 daily fee/pet. Service with restrictions, supervision.
SAVE Sₒ ✕ 🖥

# RIO RANCHO

**(A)** ▼▼▼ **Best Western Rio Rancho Inn & Conference Center** SH
(505) 892-1700. **$59-$119, 30 day notice.** 1465 Rio Rancho Blvd. I-25, exit 233 (Alameda Blvd), 6.5 mi w; I-40, exit 155, 10 mi n on Coors Rd/Coors Bypass to SR 528, then 1 mi n. Ext corridors. **Pets:** Accepted.
SAVE SD X ⊘ 🛢 🖵 🌊

**(A)** ▼▼▼ **Days Inn** SH
(505) 892-8800. **$45-$105.** 4200 Crestview Dr. I-25, exit 233 (Alameda Blvd), 8 mi w on SR 528; I-40, exit 155, 8 mi n on Coors Rd (SR 448). Ext corridors. **Pets:** Small. $10 one-time fee/pet. Service with restrictions, supervision.
SAVE SD X 🛢 🌊

▼▼▼ **Extended StayAmerica Albuquerque-Rio Rancho Blvd** SH
(505) 892-7900. **$55-$115.** 2221 Rio Rancho Blvd. I-25, exit 233 (Alameda Blvd), 6 mi w (becomes SR 528/Rio Rancho Blvd). Int corridors. **Pets:** $25 daily fee/pet. Service with restrictions, supervision.
ASK SD X ⊘ 🖉 🛢 🖵 🌊

**(A)** ▼▼▼ **Ramada Limited Hotel** SH ❀
(505) 892-5998. **$63-$69.** 4081 High Resort Blvd. I-25, exit 233 (Alameda Blvd), 8 mi w; I-40, exit 155, 8 mi n on Coors Rd (SR 448). Int corridors. **Pets:** Other species. $10 daily fee/pet. Designated rooms, service with restrictions, supervision.
SAVE X 🛢 🖵 🌊

▼▼ **Rio Rancho Super 8 Motel** SH ❀
(505) 896-8888. **$45-$95.** 4100 Barbara Loop. I-25, exit 233 (Alameda Blvd), 0.5 mi w, 3.8 mi nw on SR 528, then just e. Int corridors. **Pets:** Other species. $8 daily fee/pet. Service with restrictions, supervision.
ASK SD X

# ROSWELL

**(A)** ▼▼▼ **Best Western El Rancho Palacio** SH
(505) 622-2721. **$65-$85, 7 day notice.** 2205 N Main St. 1.8 mi n on US 70 and 285. Ext corridors. **Pets:** Service with restrictions, supervision.
SAVE SD X 🛢 🖵 🌊

**(A)** ▼▼▼ **Best Western Sally Port Inn & Suites** SH
(505) 622-6430. **$79-$99.** 2000 N Main St. 1.5 mi n on US 70 and 285. Int corridors. **Pets:** Other species. $10 daily fee/room. Designated rooms, service with restrictions, supervision.
SAVE SD X 🛢 🖵 🍴 🌊 X

**(A)** ▼▼ **Budget Inn-North** M ❀
(505) 623-6050. **$35-$50.** 2101 N Main St. 1.8 mi n on US 70 and 285. Ext corridors. **Pets:** Other species. $5 daily fee/room. Service with restrictions.
SAVE X 🛢 🌊

▼▼ **Budget Inn West** SH
(505) 623-3811. **$35-$55.** 2200 W 2nd St. 2 mi w on US 70 and 380. Ext corridors. **Pets:** Small, dogs only. $2 daily fee/pet. Service with restrictions, supervision.
ASK SD X 🛢 🌊

**(A)** ▼▼▼ **Comfort Inn** SH
(505) 623-4567. **$69-$129.** 3595 N Main St. On US 70 and 285, 3 mi n. Int corridors. **Pets:** Small. Designated rooms, service with restrictions, supervision.
SAVE SD X 🖸ᴹ 🖉 🛢 🖵 🌊

**(A)** ▼▼ **Days Inn** SH
(505) 623-4021. **$60-$90, 7 day notice.** 1310 N Main St. 0.8 mi n on US 70 and 285. Ext corridors. **Pets:** Service with restrictions, supervision.
SAVE SD X ⊘ 🛢 🖵 🌊

**(A)** ▼▼ **Frontier Motel** M
(505) 622-1400. **$36-$44, 30 day notice.** 3010 N Main St. 2.5 mi n on US 70 and 285. Ext corridors. **Pets:** Accepted.
SAVE SD X 🛢 🌊

▼▼▼ **Holiday Inn Express** SH
(505) 627-9900. **$85-$130.** 2300 N Main St. US 70. Int corridors. **Pets:** Medium. Service with restrictions, supervision.
ASK X 🖸ᴹ 🖉 🛢 🖵 🌊 X

**(A)** ▼▼ **Leisure Inn** SH
(505) 622-2575. **$42-$48.** 2700 W 2nd St. 2.5 mi w on US 70 and 380. Ext corridors. **Pets:** Small, dogs only. $5 daily fee/pet. Designated rooms, service with restrictions, supervision.
SAVE SD X 🛢 🖵 🌊 X

▼▼ **Ramada Limited** SH
(505) 623-9440. **$68.** 2803 W 2nd St. 2.5 mi w on US 70 and 380. Ext/int corridors. **Pets:** Accepted.
ASK SD X 🛢 🌊

▼▼ **Western Inn** M
(505) 623-9425. **$62-$67.** 2331 N Main St. Jct US 70/285/380, 2.2 mi n. Ext corridors. **Pets:** Accepted.
ASK SD X 🛢 🌊

# RUIDOSO

**(A)** ▼▼ **Dan Dee Cabins** CA
(505) 257-2165. **$84-$179, 14 day notice.** 310 Main Rd. 0.8 mi w on Upper Canyon Rd. Ext corridors. **Pets:** Other species. $10 one-time fee/pet. No service, supervision.
SAVE SD 🛢 🖵 🗷

▼▼▼ **Hawthorn Suites Conference & Golf Resort** SH
(505) 258-5500. **$195-$215.** 107 Sierra Blanca Dr. 2.5 mi n on SR 48. Int corridors. **Pets:** Designated rooms, service with restrictions, supervision.
X 🖉 🖍 🛢 🖵 🌊 X

**(A)** ▼▼▼ **Holiday Inn Express** SH
(505) 257-3736. **$89-$179.** 400 W Hwy 70. US 70, just w of jct Sudderth Dr. Int corridors. **Pets:** Other species. Service with restrictions.
SAVE SD X 🖸ᴹ 🖉 🖍 🛢 🖵 🌊

**(A)** ▼▼▼▼ **Inn of the Mountain Gods Resort & Casino** LH
(505) 464-7777. **$99-$500, 3 day notice.** 287 Carrizo Canyon Rd (Rt 4). 1.5 mi w; on the Mescalero Apache Reservation. Int corridors. **Pets:** Accepted.
SAVE SD X 🖸ᴹ 🖍 🖵 🍴 🌊 X

**(A)** ▼▼ **Quality Inn** SH
(505) 378-4051. **$60-$170.** 307 Hwy 70 W. Jct US 70 and SR 48. Int corridors. **Pets:** Small, dogs only. $10 daily fee/pet. Service with restrictions, supervision.
SAVE SD X 🛢 🖵 🌊

▼▼ **Travelodge** SH
(505) 378-4471. **$45-$150.** 159 W Hwy 70. Jct of US 70 and SR 48. Ext corridors. **Pets:** Small. $10 daily fee/pet. No service, supervision.
ASK SD X 🛢 🖵 🌊

**(A)** ▼▼▼ **The Village Lodge** CO ❀
(505) 258-5442. **$129, 14 day notice.** 1000 Mechem Dr. 2 mi n on SR 48. Ext corridors. **Pets:** Medium. $10 one-time fee/room. Service with restrictions, supervision.
SAVE SD 🛢 🖵

**(A)** ▼▼▼ **Whispering Pine Cabins** CA ❀
(505) 257-4311. **$89-$265, 14 day notice.** 422 Main Rd. 0.9 mi w of jct SR 48 and Suddenth Dr. Ext corridors. **Pets:** Other species. $10 one-time fee/pet. No service.
SAVE X 🛢 🖵

# RUIDOSO DOWNS

**▼▼▼ Best Western Pine Springs Inn** SH
(505) 378-8100. **$59-$139.** 1420 W Hwy 70. Just n; center. Ext corridors. **Pets:** Other species. Service with restrictions.

A$K S⬚ ☒ ◨ ▭ ⇌

# SANTA FE

**▼▼▼ Alexander's Inn** BB ❈
(505) 986-1431. **$170-$220, 14 day notice.** 529 E Palace Ave. Just e of jct Paseo De Peralta; 6 blks e of historic plaza. Ext/int corridors. **Pets:** Other species. $20 one-time fee/pet. Service with restrictions.

A$K ☒ ◨ ▭ ☒

**▲▲▲ ▼▼▼ Best Western Inn of Santa Fe** SH
(505) 438-3822. **$45-$125.** 3650 Cerrillos Rd. I-25, exit 278, 2.8 mi n. Int corridors. **Pets:** Accepted.

SAVE S⬚ ☒ ⌬ ◨ ▭ ⇌

**▼▼▼▼ Bishop's Lodge Resort & Spa** LH
(505) 983-6377. **$159-$499, 3 day notice.** 1297 N Bishop's Lodge Rd. 3.5 mi n of jct Paseo De Peralta. Ext/int corridors. **Pets:** Accepted.

A$K S⬚ ☒ ⌬ ◨ ▭ ⏐⏐ ⇌ ☒

**▲▲▲ ▼▼ Camel Rock Suites** M
(505) 989-3600. **$89-$99, 3 day notice.** 3007 S St. Frances Dr. 0.8 mi n on S St. Francis Dr, just e on Zia via access drive. Ext corridors. **Pets:** Small. $50 deposit/room. Designated rooms, supervision.

SAVE S⬚ ☒ ⌖M ⌬ ▭ ⇌

**▼▼▼▼ Casapueblo Inn** SH
(505) 988-4455. **$109-$239, 3 day notice.** 138 Park Ave. Jct Guadalupe St. Ext corridors. **Pets:** Large. $50 one-time fee/room. Service with restrictions, crate.

A$K S⬚ ☒ ⌖ ▭

**▲▲▲ ▼▼▼▼ Comfort Inn** SH
(505) 474-7330. **$59-$169.** 4312 Cerrillos Rd. I-25, exit 278, 1.6 mi n. Int corridors. **Pets:** Other species. $10 one-time fee/room. Service with restrictions, supervision.

SAVE S⬚ ☒ ⌬ ⌖ ◨ ▭ ⇌

**▲▲▲ ▼▼▼▼ Eldorado Hotel & Spa** LH
(505) 988-4455. **$219-$1500, 3 day notice.** 309 W San Francisco. Just w of The Plaza at Sandoval St. Int corridors. **Pets:** Medium, other species. $50 one-time fee/room. Service with restrictions, supervision.

SAVE S⬚ ☒ ⌖M ⌬ ▭ ⏐⏐ ⇌ ☒

**▲▲▲ ▼▼▼▼ El Paradero Bed & Breakfast** BB
(505) 988-1177. **$80-$170, 14 day notice.** 220 W Manhattan Ave. 0.3 mi s on Cerrillos Rd, 1/2 blk e. Ext/int corridors. **Pets:** Dogs only. $15 daily fee/room. Service with restrictions, crate.

SAVE ☒ ⌖ ◨ ▭

**▲▲▲ ▼▼▼ ▼▼▼ The Hacienda at Hotel Santa Fe** SH ❈
(505) 982-1200. **$219-$318, 3 day notice.** 1501 Paseo de Peralta. At Cerrillos Rd, 0.6 mi s of The Plaza. Int corridors. **Pets:** Other species. $20 daily fee/room. Service with restrictions, supervision.

SAVE S⬚ ☒ ◨ ▭ ⏐⏐ ⇌ ☒

**▲▲▲ ▼▼▼▼ Hacienda Nicholas** BB ❈
(505) 986-1431. **$100-$190, 14 day notice.** 320 E Marcy St. Just e of jct Paseo De Peralta; 4 blks e of historic plaza. Ext/int corridors. **Pets:** Other species. $20 one-time fee/pet. Service with restrictions, crate.

SAVE ☒

**▲▲▲ ▼▼▼▼ Hampton Inn Santa Fe** SH
(505) 474-3900. **$69-$189.** 3625 Cerrillos Rd. I-25, exit 278, 2.5 mi n. Int corridors. **Pets:** Other species. Service with restrictions.

SAVE S⬚ ☒ ⌖M ⌬ ⌖ ◨ ▭ ⇌ ☒

**▼▼▼▼ Hotel Plaza Real** SH ❈
(505) 988-4900. **$89-$199, 3 day notice.** 125 Washington Ave. Just ne of The Plaza; center. Ext/int corridors. **Pets:** Dogs only. $50 one-time fee/room. Service with restrictions.

A$K S⬚ ☒ ⌬ ◨ ▭ ⏐⏐

**▲▲▲ ▼▼▼▼ Hotel Santa Fe** SH ❈
(505) 982-1200. **$120-$376.** 1501 Paseo de Peralta. At Cerrillos Rd, 0.6 mi s of The Plaza. Int corridors. **Pets:** Other species. $20 daily fee/room. Service with restrictions, supervision.

SAVE S⬚ ☒ ⌬ ◨ ⏐⏐ ⇌ ☒

**▲▲▲ ▼▼▼▼ Inn On The Alameda** SH ❈
(505) 984-2121. **$130-$295, 3 day notice.** 303 E Alameda Ave. 4 blks e of The Plaza; at Paseo de Peralta. Ext/int corridors. **Pets:** Small, other species. $20 daily fee/room. Designated rooms.

SAVE S⬚ ☒ ⌬ ⌖ ◨ ▭ ☒

**▲▲▲ ▼▼▼▼ La Quinta Inn Santa Fe** SH
(505) 471-1142. **$67-$147.** 4298 Cerrillos Rd. I-25, exit 278, 1.8 mi n. Ext/int corridors. **Pets:** Medium. Service with restrictions.

SAVE ☒ ⌬ ⇌

**▲▲▲ ▼▼▼▼ Las Palomas** M
(505) 982-5560. **$149-$279, 14 day notice.** 460 W San Francisco St. Just w of jct Guadalupe St. Ext corridors. **Pets:** Accepted.

SAVE S⬚ ☒ ⌖ ◨ ▭ ☒

**▼ Motel 6–150** M
(505) 473-1380. **$45-$65.** 3007 Cerrillos Rd. I-25, exit 278, 3.8 mi n. Ext corridors. **Pets:** Accepted.

S⬚ ☒ ⌖ ◨ ▭

**▼▼▼ Park Inn** SH ❈
(505) 471-3000. **$49-$114.** 2907 Cerrillos Rd. I-25, exit 278, 7 mi n. Ext corridors. **Pets:** $50 deposit/pet, $10 daily fee/room. Service with restrictions, supervision.

A$K S⬚ ☒ ◨ ▭ ⇌

**▲▲▲ ▼▼▼ Quality Inn** SH
(505) 471-1211. **$49-$160.** 3011 Cerrillos Rd. I-25, exit 278B, 3.8 mi n. Int corridors. **Pets:** Medium, dogs only. $10 daily fee/pet. No service, supervision.

SAVE ☒ ◨ ▭ ⏐⏐ ⇌

**▼▼▼ Residence Inn by Marriott** SH
(505) 988-7300. **$129-$269.** 1698 Galisteo St. I-25, exit 282, 1.7 mi n on St Francis Dr to St Michaels Dr, just e, then just n. Ext corridors. **Pets:** Small. $75 one-time fee/room. Service with restrictions, supervision.

A$K S⬚ ☒ ⌬ ◨ ▭ ⇌ ☒

**▲▲▲ ▼▼▼ Sage Inn** M
(505) 982-5952. **$89-$134.** 725 Cerrillos Rd. 0.4 mi ne of St. Francis Dr (US 84). Ext corridors. **Pets:** Accepted.

SAVE S⬚ ☒ ⌬ ◨ ▭ ⇌

**▲▲▲ ▼▼▼ Santa Fe Motel & Inn** M
(505) 982-1039. **$69-$169, 3 day notice.** 510 Cerrillos Rd. 4 blks sw of The Plaza. Ext corridors. **Pets:** Accepted.

SAVE S⬚ ☒ ◨ ▭

**▲▲▲ ▼▼▼ Santa Fe Plaza Travelodge** SH
(505) 982-3551. **$69-$199.** 646 Cerrillos Rd. 0.8 mi sw of The Plaza. Ext/int corridors. **Pets:** Small. $10 deposit/pet. No service, crate.

SAVE S⬚ ☒ ⌬ ◨ ▭ ⇌

**▼▼ ▼▼▼ Sleep Inn** SH ❈
(505) 474-9500. **$59-$189.** 8376 Cerrillos Rd. I-25, exit 278, 0.3 mi n. Int corridors. **Pets:** Large, other species. $10 one-time fee/room. Designated rooms, service with restrictions, supervision.

A$K S⬚ ☒ ⌖M ⌬ ⌖ ◨ ▭ ⇌

# SANTA ROSA

◆◆◆ ▽▽▽ **Best Western Adobe Inn** 🆂🅷
(505) 472-3446. **$65-$79, 3 day notice.** 1501 Historic Route 66. I-40, exit 275. Ext corridors. **Pets:** Medium. Service with restrictions, supervision.
[SAVE] [S🐾] [✕] [🛏] [▭] [≈]

◆◆◆ ▽▽▽ **Best Western Santa Rosa Inn** 🅼
(505) 472-5877. **$67-$82.** 3022 Historic Route 66. I-40, exit 277, 0.5 mi w. Ext corridors. **Pets:** Accepted.
[SAVE] [S🐾] [✕] [🛏] [▭] [≈]

◆◆◆ ▽▽ **Check Inn Express** 🆂🅷
(505) 472-5412. **$67-$80.** 3300 Historic Route 66. I-40, exit 277, 0.3 mi w. Int corridors. **Pets:** Accepted.
[SAVE] [✕] [🛏] [▭] [≈]

▽▽ **Comfort Inn** 🆂🅷
(505) 472-5570. **$64-$94, 15 day notice.** 3343 E Historic Route 66. I-40, exit 277, 0.3 mi w. Ext corridors. **Pets:** Large. $10 one-time fee/pet. Designated rooms, service with restrictions, supervision.
[ASK] [S🐾] [✕] [🛏] [▭] [≈]

◆◆◆ ▽▽▽ **Days Inn of Santa Rosa** 🆂🅷
(505) 472-5985. **$55-$90.** 1830 Historic Route 66. I-40, exit 275. Ext corridors. **Pets:** Small. $5 one-time fee/pet. Designated rooms, service with restrictions, supervision.
[SAVE] [S🐾] [✕] [🛏] [▭]

◆◆◆ ▽▽▽▽ **La Quinta Inn-Santa Rosa** 🆂🅷
(505) 472-4800. **$73-$77.** 1701 Historic Route 66. I-40, exit 275, just e. Int corridors. **Pets:** Dogs only. Service with restrictions, supervision.
[SAVE] [S🐾] [✕] [🐾⁺] [🛏] [▭] [≈]

▽▽ **Motel 6–273** 🅼
(505) 472-3045. **$43-$58.** 3400 Historic Route 66. I-40, exit 277, 0.3 mi w. Ext corridors. **Pets:** Accepted.
[S🐾] [✕] [🚭] [🐾⁺] [🛏] [≈]

▽▽ **Super 8 Motel-Santa Rosa** 🅼
(505) 472-5388. **$55-$65.** 1201 Historic Route 66. I-40, exit 275, just w. Int corridors. **Pets:** Accepted.
[ASK] [S🐾] [✕] [&M] [🐾⁺] [🛏]

▽▽ **Travelodge** 🆂🅷
(505) 472-3494. **$45-$75.** 1819 Will Rogers Dr. I-40, exit 275, just n. Ext corridors. **Pets:** Small. $5 one-time fee/pet. Designated rooms, no service, supervision.
[ASK] [S🐾] [✕] [🛏] [▭] [≈]

# SILVER CITY

▽▽▽ **Comfort Inn** 🆂🅷
(505) 534-1883. **$50-$175.** 1060 E Hwy 180. 1.5 mi e on US 180 and SR 90. Int corridors. **Pets:** Accepted.
[ASK] [S🐾] [✕] [🛏] [▭] [≈]

◆◆◆ ▽▽ **Econo Lodge Silver City** 🆂🅷
(505) 534-1111. **$45-$99.** 1120 Hwy 180 E. 1.5 mi ne on US 180 and SR 90. Int corridors. **Pets:** Other species. $20 deposit/room, $7 daily fee/pet. Designated rooms, service with restrictions, supervision.
[SAVE] [S🐾] [✕] [&M] [🐾⁺] [🛏] [▭] [≈]

◆◆◆ ▽▽▽ **Holiday Inn Express** 🆂🅷
(505) 538-2525. **$89-$119.** 1103 Superior St. 3 mi ne on US 180 and SR 90. Int corridors. **Pets:** Accepted.
[SAVE] [S🐾] [✕] [▭]

▽▽ **Super 8 Motel** 🆂🅷
(505) 388-1983. **$34-$100.** 1040 E Hwy 180. 1.5 mi ne on US 180 and SR 90. Int corridors. **Pets:** Accepted.
[ASK] [S🐾] [✕] [▭]

# SOCORRO

◆◆◆ ▽▽▽ **Econo Lodge** 🆂🅷 ☙
(505) 835-1500. **$35-$60.** 713 California Ave. I-25, exit 150, 1 mi s. Ext corridors. **Pets:** Small, dogs only. $5 one-time fee/pet. Supervision.
[SAVE] [S🐾] [✕] [🛏] [▭] [≈] [✕]

▽▽▽▽ **Holiday Inn Express** 🆂🅷
(505) 838-0556. **$90.** 1100 California Ave NE. Center. Ext/int corridors. **Pets:** Accepted.
[ASK] [S🐾] [✕] [&M] [🚭] [🐾⁺] [🛏] [▭] [≈]

▽▽ **Motel 6 #392** 🆂🅷
(505) 835-4300. **$39-$51.** 807 S US 85. I-25, exit 147. Ext corridors. **Pets:** Accepted.
[S🐾] [✕] [&M] [🚭] [🐾⁺] [🛏] [≈]

# TAOS

◆◆◆ ▽▽▽ **Adobe Sun God Lodge** 🅼
(505) 758-3162. **$60-$110.** 919 Paseo del Pueblo Sur. SR 68, 1.8 mi sw of jct US 64 and Taos Plaza. Ext corridors. **Pets:** Other species. $10 one-time fee/room. Service with restrictions.
[SAVE] [✕] [🛏] [▭]

◆◆◆ ▽▽▽ **American Artists Gallery House Bed & Breakfast** 🅱🅱
(505) 758-4446. **$95-$195, 14 day notice.** 132 Frontier Ln. 1 mi s of jct US 64 and Taos Plaza, 0.3 mi e. Ext/int corridors. **Pets:** Dogs only. $25 daily fee/pet. Designated rooms, service with restrictions, supervision.
[SAVE] [S🐾] [✕] [🛏] [▭] [✕] [🅺]

◆◆◆ ▽▽▽▽ **Brooks Street Inn Bed and Breakfast** 🅱🅱
(505) 758-1489. **$89-$189, 14 day notice.** 119 Brooks St. 0.3 mi n on US 64 from jct SR 68 and Taos Plaza, just e. Ext/int corridors. **Pets:** Small, dogs only. $10 daily fee/pet. Designated rooms, service with restrictions, supervision.
[SAVE] [✕] [🛏] [▭] [🅺] [🐾]

◆◆◆ ▽▽▽ **Burch Street Casitas** 🅼
(505) 737-9038. **$99-$135, 21 day notice.** 310 Burch St. US 64, just e of jct SR 68, just s. Ext corridors. **Pets:** Medium, dogs only. $25 one-time fee/pet. No service, supervision.
[SAVE] [S🐾] [✕] [🛏] [▭] [🅺]

▽▽▽▽ **Casa Europa Inn & Gallery** 🅱🅱
(505) 758-9798. **$105-$195, 14 day notice.** 840 Upper Ranchitos Rd. 1.7 mi s from jct US 64. Ext/int corridors. **Pets:** Accepted.
[ASK] [✕] [▭] [🅺]

◆◆◆ ▽▽▽▽ **Fechin Inn** 🆂🅷 ☙
(505) 751-1000. **$127-$359, 3 day notice.** 227 Paseo del Pueblo Norte. Just n on US 64 of jct SR 68 and Taos Plaza. Int corridors. **Pets:** Small, dogs only. $50 one-time fee/pet. Designated rooms, service with restrictions, supervision.
[SAVE] [S🐾] [✕] [&M] [🐾⁺] [🛏] [▭] [✕]

◆◆◆ ▽▽▽▽ **Inn On The Rio** 🅱🅱
(505) 758-7199. **$99-$129, 15 day notice.** 910 Kit Carson Rd. US 64, 1.5 mi e of jct SR 68 and Taos Plaza. Ext corridors. **Pets:** Accepted.
[SAVE] [S🐾] [✕] [▭] [≈] [🅺]

◆◆◆ ▽▽▽▽ **Orinda Bed & Breakfast** 🅱🅱
(505) 758-8581. **$89-$130, 14 day notice.** 461 Valverde St. Just w from jct Don Fernando and Camino de la Placita, then just s; look for Orinda sign. Ext/int corridors. **Pets:** Accepted.
[SAVE] [✕] [🛏] [▭]

▽▽ **Quality Inn** 🆂🅷
(505) 758-2200. **$59-$109.** 1043 Pasec del Pueblo Sur. SR 68, 2 mi sw of jct US 64 and Taos Plaza. Ext/int corridors. **Pets:** Other species. $7 daily fee/pet. Service with restrictions, supervision.
[ASK] [S🐾] [✕] [🚭] [🛏] [▭] [🍴] [≈]

**◥◣◥◣ Sagebrush Inn** SH
(505) 758-2254. **$59-$110, 3 day notice.** 1508 Paseo del Pueblo Sur. SR 68, 3 mi sw of jct US 64 and Taos Plaza. Ext corridors. **Pets:** Other species. $7 daily fee/pet. Designated rooms, service with restrictions, supervision.
ASK Sd ✕ ⌀ ☐ ☐ ¶ ≈

**AAA ◥◣◥◣ San Geronimo Lodge** BB
(505) 751-3776. **$95-$150, 10 day notice.** 1101 Witt Rd. 1.3 mi e of jct SR 68 and Taos Plaza on US 64 (Kit Carson Rd), 0.6 mi s. Ext/int corridors. **Pets:** $10 one-time fee/room. Designated rooms, service with restrictions, crate.
SAVE Sd ✕ ⌂ ≈ ⋈

# THOREAU

**◥◣◥◣ Zuni Mountain Lodge** BB
(505) 862-7769. **$95 (no credit cards), 14 day notice.** 40 W Perch Dr. I-40, exit 53, 13 mi s on SR 612, then w. Ext/int corridors. **Pets:** Other species. Service with restrictions, supervision.
✕ ⋈ ⋈ ⊠

# TRUTH OR CONSEQUENCES

**AAA ◥◣◥◣ Best Western Hot Springs Motor Inn** M
(505) 894-6665. **$57-$69.** 2270 N Date St. I-25, exit 79. Ext corridors. **Pets:** Other species. Service with restrictions, supervision.
SAVE Sd ✕ ☐ ☐ ¶ ≈

**◥◣◥◣ Comfort Inn & Suites** SH
(505) 894-1660. **$55-$120.** 2250 N Date St. I-25, exit 79, just e. Int corridors. **Pets:** Accepted.
ASK Sd ⌂M ⌀ ⌂ ☐ ☐ ¶ ≈

**AAA ◥◣◥◣ Super 8 Motel** M
(505) 894-7888. **$43-$98.** 2151 N Date St. I-25, exit 79, just s. Int corridors. **Pets:** Accepted.
SAVE Sd ✕

# TUCUMCARI

**AAA ◥◣ Americana Motel** M
(505) 461-0431. **$30-$40.** 406 E Tucumcari Blvd. I-40, exit 332, 1.5 mi n on SR 18, then 0.5 mi e on US 66. Ext corridors. **Pets:** Accepted.
SAVE Sd ✕

**AAA ◥◣◥◣ Americas Best Value Inn** M
(505) 461-4484. **$35-$43.** 1023 E Tucumcari Blvd. I-40, exit 333, n to Tucumcari Blvd, then 0.6 mi w. Ext corridors. **Pets:** Accepted.
SAVE Sd ✕ ☐ ☐ ≈

**AAA ◥◣◥◣ Best Western Discovery Inn** SH
(505) 461-4884. **$63-$95.** 200 E Estrella. I-40, exit 332. Ext corridors. **Pets:** Other species. $5 daily fee/room. Designated rooms, service with restrictions, supervision.
SAVE Sd ✕ ☐ ☐ ¶ ≈

**AAA ◥◣ Budget Inn** M ❀
(505) 461-4139. **$30-$45.** 824 W Tucumcari Blvd. I-40, exit 332, 1 mi n to Tucumari Blvd, then 1 mi w. Ext corridors. **Pets:** Medium. $3 one-time fee/pet. Service with restrictions, supervision.
SAVE Sd ✕ ☐

**◥◣◥◣ Comfort Inn** SH
(505) 461-4094. **$61-$69, 7 day notice.** 2800 E Tucumcari Blvd. I-40, exit 335, 0.5 mi w. Ext corridors. **Pets:** Medium. $6 daily fee/pet. No service, supervision.
ASK Sd ✕ ☐ ☐ ≈

**AAA ◥◣◥◣ Days Inn** SH
(505) 461-3158. **$55-$70.** 2623 S First St. I-40, exit 332, just n. Ext/int corridors. **Pets:** Medium, other species. $5 daily fee/pet. Supervision.
SAVE Sd ✕ ☐ ☐

**AAA ◥◣◥◣ Holiday Inn** SH
(505) 461-3780. **$79-$99.** 3716 E Tucumcari Blvd. I-40, exit 335, 0.3 mi w on US 66. Ext corridors. **Pets:** Accepted.
SAVE Sd ✕ ⌂M ⌀ ☐ ☐ ¶ ≈ ⊠

**AAA ◥◣◥◣ Microtel Inn-Tucumcari** SH
(505) 461-0600. **$66-$90.** 2420 S 1st St. I-40, exit 332, just n. Int corridors. **Pets:** Small. $6 daily fee/pet. Designated rooms, service with restrictions, supervision.
SAVE Sd ✕ ⌂ ☐ ☐ ≈

**AAA ◥◣◥◣ Super 8 Motel** M 🐾
(505) 461-4444. **$50-$75.** 4001 E Tucumcari Blvd. I-40, exit 335, just w. Int corridors. **Pets:** Medium. $5 one-time fee/room. Service with restrictions, supervision.
SAVE Sd ✕ ☐ ≈

**◥◣◥◣ Tucumcari Inn** SH 🐾
(505) 461-7800. **$39-$45.** 1700 E Tucumcari Blvd. I-40, exit 333, 0.5 mi n to Tucumari Blvd, then just w. Ext corridors. **Pets:** Medium, other species. $5 one-time fee/pet. Designated rooms, service with restrictions, supervision.
ASK Sd ✕ ☐ ≈

# VAUGHN

**AAA ◥◣ Bel-Air Motel** M
(505) 584-2241. **$48-$55.** 1004 US 54/60/285. 1 mi e on US 54, 60 and 285. Ext corridors. **Pets:** Accepted.
SAVE ✕ ☐

**AAA ◥◣ Oak Tree Inn** SH
(505) 584-8733. **$65-$95, 7 day notice.** Jct State Hwy 54/60 & 285. 1.5 mi e on US 54, 60 and 285. Ext/int corridors. **Pets:** $5 one-time fee/room. Service with restrictions.
SAVE Sd ✕ ⌂M ⌀ ⌂ ☐ ☐ ¶

# NEW YORK

## CITY INDEX

## ALBANY

**Albany Clarion Hotel** SH
(518) 438-8431. **$169-$179.** 3 Watervliet Ave. I-90, exit 5 (Everett Rd), just s, then e. Int corridors. **Pets:** Small. $25 daily fee/room. Designated rooms, service with restrictions, supervision.

**Albany Mansion Hill Inn & Restaurant** BB
(518) 465-2038. **$175-$205, 5 day notice.** 115 Philip St at Park Ave. I-787, exit 3B (Madison Ave/US 20 W) to Philip St, 0.4 mi s. Ext/int corridors. **Pets:** Other species.

**Cocca's Inn & Suites, Wolf Rd** M
(518) 459-2240. **$79-$119.** 2 Wolf Rd. I-87, exit 2E, just e. Ext corridors. **Pets:** Accepted.

**CrestHill Suites** SH
(518) 454-0007. **$99-$189.** 1415 Washington Ave. I-90, exit 2 westbound, just s on Fuller Rd, then just e; exit eastbound, just e. Int corridors. **Pets:** Accepted.

**Extended StayAmerica** SH
(518) 446-0680. **$65-$85.** 1395 Washington Ave. I-90, exit 2 westbound, just s on Fuller Rd, then 0.5 mi e; exit eastbound, just e. Int corridors. **Pets:** Accepted.

**Regency Inn and Suites** SH
(518) 462-6555. **$69-$199.** 416 Southern Blvd. On US 9W; I-87, exit 23. Ext/int corridors. **Pets:** Large, other species. $20 one-time fee/room. Service with restrictions.

**TownePlace Suites by Marriott** SH
(518) 435-1900. **$99-$180.** 1379 Washington Ave. I-90, exit 2 westbound, just s on Fuller Rd, then 0.6 mi e; exit eastbound, just e. Int corridors. **Pets:** Accepted.

## ALLEGANY

**Microtel Inn & Suites-Olean/Allegany** SH
(716) 373-5333. **$49-$109, 14 day notice.** 3234 SR 417. I-86, exit 24, 2.1 mi e on SR 417 (State St). Int corridors. **Pets:** Accepted.

## ANGELICA

**Angelica Inn B&B** BB
(585) 466-3063. **$79-$119, 14 day notice.** 64 W Main St. I-86, exit 31, 0.5 mi w. Ext/int corridors. **Pets:** Medium, other species. $75 deposit/pet. Designated rooms, service with restrictions.

## APALACHIN

**Quality Inn** SH
(607) 625-4441. **$80-$130.** 7666 SR 434. SR 17, exit 66, just e. Int corridors. **Pets:** Other species. $10 daily fee/pet. Service with restrictions, supervision.

## AUBURN

**Holiday Inn-Auburn/Finger Lakes** SH
(315) 253-4531. **$95-$159.** 75 North St. SR 34, just n of US 20/SR 5. Int corridors. **Pets:** Accepted.

**Inn at the Finger Lakes** SH
(315) 253-5000. **$79-$159.** 12 Seminary Ave. Jct SR 34/38, just e on US 20/SR 5; center. Int corridors. **Pets:** Large. $15 one-time fee/pet. Designated rooms, service with restrictions, supervision.

## AVERILL PARK

**La Perla at the Gregory House Country Inn & Restaurant** CI
(518) 674-3774. **$110-$150, 14 day notice.** 3016 SR 43. Center. Int corridors. **Pets:** Accepted.

# BALDWINSVILLE

**▼▼ Microtel Inn & Suites** 🆂🅷
(315) 635-9556. **$55-$100.** 131 Downer St. SR 690, exit SR 31 W, 0.6 mi e. Int corridors. **Pets:** Other species. $5 daily fee/pet. Service with restrictions, crate.

🅰🆂🅺 🆂👀 ✕ 🕭M 🌣 🖪 🖳

# BATAVIA

**⏺ ▼ Budget Inn** 🅼
(585) 343-7921. **$45-$99.** 301 Oak St. I-90, exit 48, just n. Int corridors. **Pets:** Medium. $6 daily fee/pet. Designated rooms, service with restrictions, supervision.

🆂🅰🆅🅴 🆂👀 ✕ 🖪

**⏺ ▼▼▼ Comfort Inn** 🆂🅷
(585) 344-9999. **$139-$159.** 4371 Federal Dr. I-90, exit 48, just n on SR 98. Int corridors. **Pets:** Large. $10 daily fee/room. Service with restrictions, supervision.

🆂🅰🆅🅴 ✕ 🕭M 🌣 🖪 🖳 ✈

**⏺ ▼▼ Days Inn** 🆂🅷 🐾
(585) 343-6000. **$49-$119.** 200 Oak St. I-90, exit 48, just s. Ext/int corridors. **Pets:** Large, other species. $10 one-time fee/pet. Service with restrictions, supervision.

🆂🅰🆅🅴 🆂👀 ✕ 🖪 🖳 🍴 ✈

**⏺ ▼▼▼ Holiday Inn-Darien Lake** 🆂🅷
(585) 344-2100. **$59-$129.** 8250 Park Rd. I-90, exit 48, just w. Int corridors. **Pets:** Small, dogs only. $15 daily fee/pet. Service with restrictions, supervision.

🆂🅰🆅🅴 ✕ 🖪 🖳 🍴 ✈ ⊠

**▼▼▼ Quality Inn & Suites** 🆂🅷
(585) 344-7000. **$63-$110.** 8200 Park Rd. I-90, exit 48, just w. Int corridors. **Pets:** Accepted.

🅰🆂🅺 🆂👀 ✕ 🕭M 🌣 🖪 🖳 ✈

**⏺ ▼▼▼ Ramada Limited** 🆂🅷
(585) 343-1000. **$59-$99.** 8204 Park Rd. I-90, exit 48, just w. Int corridors. **Pets:** Other species. Service with restrictions.

🆂🅰🆅🅴 🆂👀 ✕ 🖳 ✈

# BATH

**▼▼ Bath Super 8** 🆂🅷
(607) 776-2187. **$56-$96.** 333 W Morris St. I-86, exit 38, just n. Int corridors. **Pets:** Medium. Service with restrictions, supervision.

🅰🆂🅺 🆂👀 ✕ 🖪

**▼▼ Days Inn** 🆂🅷
(607) 776-7644. **$75-$115, 60 day notice.** 330 W Morris St. I-86, exit 38, just n. Int corridors. **Pets:** Other species. Service with restrictions, supervision.

🅰🆂🅺 🆂👀 ✕ 🖪 🖳 🍴 ✈

# BINGHAMTON

**⏺ ▼▼▼ Comfort Inn** 🆂🅷
(607) 724-3297. **$85-$150.** 1000 Front St. I-81, exit 5, 1 mi n on US 11 (Front St). Int corridors. **Pets:** Large, other species. $5 daily fee/room. Designated rooms, service with restrictions, supervision.

🆂🅰🆅🅴 ✕ 🕭M ✈

**▼▼▼ Grand Royale Hotel-A Clarion Collection Hotel** 🅻🅷
(607) 722-0000. **$70-$300.** 80 State St. Just n of jct Hawley St; downtown. Int corridors. **Pets:** Accepted.

🅰🆂🅺 🆂👀 ✕ 🖪 🖳

**▼▼▼▼ Holiday Inn Arena** 🅻🅷
(607) 722-1212. **$119-$300.** 2-8 Hawley St. Downtown. Int corridors. **Pets:** Accepted.

🅰🆂🅺 🆂👀 ✕ 🕭M 🌣 🖪 🖳 🍴 ✈

**▼▼ Motel 6-1222** 🆂🅷
(607) 771-0400. **$45-$59.** 1012 Front St. I-81, exit 6 southbound, 2 mi s on US 11 (Front St); exit 5 northbound, 1 mi n on US 11 (Front St). Int corridors. **Pets:** Accepted.

🆂👀 ✕ 🕭M 🌣

**⏺ ▼▼▼ Quality Inn & Suites** 🆂🅷
(607) 722-5353. **$79-$159.** 1156 Front St. I-81, exit 6; just n of Broome Community College. Int corridors. **Pets:** Other species. $15 one-time fee/room. Designated rooms, service with restrictions, crate.

🆂🅰🆅🅴 🆂👀 ✕ 🖪 🖳

# BOONVILLE

**⏺ ▼ Headwaters Motor Lodge** 🅼
(315) 942-4493. **$59-$85, 3 day notice.** 13524 Rt 12. Jct SR 12 and 120, 0.7 mi n. Int corridors. **Pets:** Medium. Supervision.

🆂🅰🆅🅴 🆂👀 ✕ 🖪

# BRIGHTON

**▼▼▼ Wellesley Inn (Rochester/South)** 🆂🅷
(585) 427-0130. **$49-$109.** 797 E Henrietta Rd. I-390, exit 16 (Henrietta Rd) northbound; exit 16B (Henrietta Rd) southbound, just s. Int corridors. **Pets:** Accepted.

🅰🆂🅺 🆂👀 ✕ 🕢 🌣 🖪 🖳

# BROCKPORT

**▼▼▼ Holiday Inn Express** 🆂🅷
(585) 395-1000. **$83-$103.** 4908 Lake Rd S. Just s of jct SR 31, on SR 195. Int corridors. **Pets:** Other species. $15 one-time fee/room. No service, supervision.

🅰🆂🅺 🆂👀 ✕ 🕭M 🖪 🖳

---

# BUFFALO METROPOLITAN AREA

# AMHERST

**⏺ ▼▼▼ Buffalo Marriott-Niagara** 🅻🅷
(716) 689-6900. **$99-$199.** 1340 Millersport Hwy. I-290, exit 5B, 0.5 mi n on SR 263 (Millersport Hwy). Int corridors. **Pets:** $50 one-time fee/room. Designated rooms, service with restrictions, supervision.

🆂🅰🆅🅴 🆂👀 ✕ 🕭M 🕢 🌣 🖪 🖳 🍴 ✈ ⊠

**⏺ ▼▼▼ Comfort Inn University** 🆂🅷 🐾
(716) 688-0811. **$89-$139.** 1 Flint Rd. I-290, exit 5B, 0.5 mi n on SR 263 (Millersport Hwy), then just w. Int corridors. **Pets:** Medium, other species. $10 daily fee/pet. Service with restrictions, supervision.

🆂🅰🆅🅴 🆂👀 ✕ 🖪 🖳

**▼▼▼ Extended StayAmerica** 🆂🅷
(716) 564-0620. **$54-$154.** 125 Inn Keepers Ln. I-290, exit 3, just n on US 62 (Niagara Falls Blvd) to access road. Int corridors. **Pets:** Accepted.

🅰🆂🅺 ✕ 🕭M 🌣 🖪 🖳

**▼▼▼ Homewood Suites Buffalo/Amherst** 🆂🅷
(716) 833-2277. **$149-$189.** 1138 Millersport Hwy. I-290, exit 5A, just w. Int corridors. **Pets:** Medium. $75 one-time fee/room. Service with restrictions.

🅰🆂🅺 🆂👀 ✕ 🕭M 🖪 🖳 ✈

**AAA** ▼▼▼ **Lord Amherst Hotel** M
(716) 839-2200. **$69-$109.** 5000 Main St. I-290, exit 7A, just w on SR 5. Ext/int corridors. **Pets:** Service with restrictions, supervision.
SAVE S⚬ ✕ ᕱM 🛏 🖵 ⌲

▼▼ **Motel 6 Buffalo-Amherst #1298** M
(716) 834-2231. **$43-$61.** 4400 Maple Rd. I-290, exit 5B, just n to Maple Rd, then 0.7 mi w. Int corridors. **Pets:** Accepted.
S⚬ ✕

▼▼ **Red Roof Inn #7104** M
(716) 689-7474. **$48-$90.** 42 Flint Rd. I-290, exit 5B, 0.5 mi n on SR 263 (Millersport Hwy). Ext corridors. **Pets:** Accepted.
✕ ᕱM 🛏

## BLASDELL

**AAA** ▼▼▼ **Clarion Hotel** SH
(716) 648-5700. **$69-$149.** 3950 McKinley Pkwy. I-90, exit 56, 0.4 mi e on SR 179, then 0.8 mi s. Int corridors. **Pets:** Accepted.
SAVE S⚬ ✕ 🐾 🛏 🖵

**AAA** ▼▼▼ **Econo Lodge South** M
(716) 825-7530. **$47-$99.** 4344 Milestrip Rd. I-90, exit 56, just e on SR 179. Ext corridors. **Pets:** Designated rooms, service with restrictions, supervision.
SAVE S⚬ ✕ 🗐 🛏 🖵

## BOWMANSVILLE

▼▼ **Red Roof Inn-Buffalo Airport #7137** M
(716) 633-1100. **$48-$87.** 146 Maple Dr. Just e of SR 78; just n of entrance to I-90 (New York State Thruway), exit 49. Ext corridors. **Pets:** Accepted.
✕ 🗐 🛏

## BUFFALO

**AAA** ▼▼▼▼ **Best Western Inn-On The Avenue** SH
(716) 886-8333. **$105-$155.** 510 Delaware Ave. Between Virginia and Allen sts; downtown. Int corridors. **Pets:** Medium, dogs only. Designated rooms, service with restrictions.
SAVE S⚬ ✕ 🐾 🛏 🖵

▼▼▼▼ **Holiday Inn-Downtown** SH
(716) 886-2121. **$120-$160.** 620 Delaware Ave. Between Allen and North sts; downtown. Int corridors. **Pets:** Accepted.
ASK S⚬ ✕ 🛏 🖵 🍴 ⌲

## CHEEKTOWAGA

▼▼▼▼ **Holiday Inn Express Hotel & Suites-Buffalo Airport** SH
(716) 631-8700. **$100-$140.** 131 Buell Ave. I-90, exit 51, just e on SR 33. Int corridors. **Pets:** Small, other species. $30 one-time fee/room. Service with restrictions, supervision.
ASK S⚬ ✕ ᕱM 🗐 🐾 🖵 ⌲ ✕

▼▼▼▼ **Homewood Suites by Hilton** SH
(716) 685-0700. **$159-$199.** 760 Dick Rd. SR 33, exit Dick Rd, 0.3 mi sw. Int corridors. **Pets:** $100 one-time fee/room. No service.
✕ 🐾 🛏 🖵 ⌲

**AAA** ▼▼▼▼ **Oak Tree Inn** SH
(716) 681-2600. **$46-$105.** 3475 Union Rd. Just s of Walden Ave. Int corridors. **Pets:** Accepted.
SAVE S⚬ ✕ ᕱM 🗐 🐾 🛏 🖵

▼▼▼▼ **Residence Inn by Marriott** SH
(716) 892-5410. **$109-$199, 14 day notice.** 107 Anderson Rd. I-90, exit 52 westbound, stay to the left off exit ramp. Int corridors. **Pets:** Accepted.
ASK S⚬ ✕ ᕱM 🗐 🐾 🛏 🖵 ⌲ ✕

## CLARENCE

**AAA** ▼▼▼▼ **Asa Ransom House** CI
(716) 759-2315. **$105-$135, 7 day notice.** 10529 Main St. Jct SR 78 (Transit Rd), 5.3 mi e on SR 5 (Main St). Int corridors. **Pets:** Large, dogs only. $100 deposit/room. Designated rooms, service with restrictions.
SAVE S⚬ ✕ ᕱM 🛏 🍴

## GRAND ISLAND

**AAA** ▼▼ **Chateau Motor Lodge** M 🐾
(716) 773-2868. **$39-$99, 3 day notice.** 1810 Grand Island Blvd. I-190, exit 18A northbound, 0.5 mi n on SR 324 W. Ext/int corridors. **Pets:** Medium. $8 daily fee/pet. Designated rooms, service with restrictions, supervision.
SAVE S⚬ ✕ 🛏

## HAMBURG

**AAA** ▼▼▼▼ **Comfort Inn & Suites** SH
(716) 648-2922. **$69-$179.** 3615 Commerce Pl. I-90, exit 57, just w. Int corridors. **Pets:** Other species. $10 daily fee/room. Service with restrictions, crate.
SAVE S⚬ ✕ ᕱM 🐾 🛏 🖵 ⌲

**AAA** ▼▼▼▼ **Holiday Inn Hamburg** SH
(716) 649-0500. **$49-$109.** 5440 Camp Rd. I-90, exit 57, 0.3 mi se on SR 75. Int corridors. **Pets:** Other species. $10 daily fee/pet. Service with restrictions.
SAVE S⚬ ✕ 🐾 🛏 🖵 🍴 ⌲

▼▼ **Red Roof Inn #7055** M
(716) 648-7222. **$46-$82.** 5370 Camp Rd. I-90, exit 57, just se on SR 75. Ext corridors. **Pets:** Accepted.
✕ 🗐 🛏

**AAA** ▼▼▼▼ **Tallyho-tel** M 🐾
(716) 648-2000. **$39-$129.** 5245 Camp Rd. I-90, exit 57, just nw on SR 75. Ext corridors. **Pets:** Other species. $15 one-time fee/pet. Service with restrictions, supervision.
SAVE ✕ 🛏 ⌲

## KENMORE

▼▼▼▼ **Super 8-Buffalo/Niagara Falls** SH
(716) 876-4020. **$49-$76.** 1288 Sheridan Dr. I-190, exit 15, 1.5 mi e on SR 324 (Sheridan Dr). Int corridors. **Pets:** Service with restrictions, supervision.
✕ 🛏

## SPRINGVILLE

▼▼▼ **Microtel Inn & Suites** SH
(716) 592-3141. **$49-$79.** 270 S Cascade Dr. On SR 219 S. Int corridors. **Pets:** Accepted.
ASK S⚬ ✕ 🗐 🐾 🛏 🖵

## TONAWANDA

**AAA** ▼▼▼ **Days Inn** M
(716) 835-5916. **$50-$140.** 1120 Niagara Falls Blvd. I-290, exit 3 (Niagara Falls Blvd), 1.3 mi s on US 62. Ext corridors. **Pets:** Other species. Service with restrictions.
SAVE S⚬ ✕ 🛏

**AAA** ▼▼▼ **Econo Lodge** M
(716) 694-6696. **$40-$190.** 2000 Niagara Falls Blvd. I-290, exit 3 (Niagara Falls Blvd), 0.5 mi n on US 62. Ext corridors. **Pets:** Accepted.
SAVE S⚬ ✕ 🛏 🖵

▼▼▼ **Microtel-Tonawanda** SH
(716) 693-8100. **$46-$100, 3 day notice.** 1 Hospitality Centre Way. I-290, exit 1B westbound; exit 1 eastbound, 0.5 mi e on Crestmount Ave, then just n on SR 384 (Delaware St). Int corridors. **Pets:** Large. $10 daily fee/pet. Service with restrictions, supervision.
ASK S⚬ ✕ ᕱM 🛏

## WILLIAMSVILLE

**🔷 ▽▽▽ Ramada Limited** Ⓜ
(716) 634-2700. **$45-$99.** 48 Freeman Rd. I-90, exit 49 (SR 78), just n, then just e. Int corridors. **Pets:** Medium. $10 daily fee/pet. Service with restrictions, supervision.

🆂🅰🆅🅴 🆂🅾 ⊠ 🄳 💻 🌊

---

**▽▽▽ Residence Inn by Marriott Buffalo/Amherst** 🆂🅷
(716) 632-6622. **$79-$239.** 100 Maple Rd. I-290, exit 5B, just e on Maple Rd from jct SR 263 (Millersport Hwy). Ext corridors. **Pets:** Accepted.

🅰🆂🅺 🆂🅾 ⊠ 🄶🅼 🖉 🄳 💻 🌊 🖾

---

# END METROPOLITAN AREA

## CALCIUM

**▽▽ Microtel Inn Watertown** 🆂🅷
(315) 629-5000. **$54-$70.** 8000 Virginia Smith Dr. 4 mi e on SR 342; jct US 11. Int corridors **Pets:** Accepted.

🅰🆂🅺 ⊠ 🄳

## CANANDAIGUA

**🔷 ▽▽▽▽ Canandaigua Inn on the Lake** 🆂🅷
(585) 394-7800. **$99-$329.** 770 S Main St. I-90, exit 44 (Canandaigua/SR 332), just s across US 20 and SR 5. Int corridors. **Pets:** Medium, dogs only. $10 daily fee/room. Service with restrictions, supervision.

🆂🅰🆅🅴 🆂🅾 ⊠ 🄶🅼 🖉 🄶 🄳 💻 🍽 🌊 🖾

**🔷 ▽▽▽ Econo Lodge Canandaigua** 🆂🅷
(585) 394-9000. **$59-$122.** 170 Eastern Blvd. Jct SR 332, 5 and US 20, 0.5 mi e. Int corridors. **Pets:** Medium. $10 daily fee/room. Service with restrictions, supervision.

🆂🅰🆅🅴 🆂🅾 ⊠ 🄳 💻

## CANASTOTA

**▽▽ Days Inn** 🆂🅷
(315) 697-3309. **$59-$129, 14 day notice.** 377 N Peterboro St. I-90, exit 34 on SR 13. Int corridors. **Pets:** Other species. Service with restrictions, supervision.

🅰🆂🅺 🆂🅾 ⊠ 🄳

## CATSKILL

**🔷 ▽▽▽ Catskill Quality Inn & Conference Center** 🆂🅷
(518) 943-5800. **$59-$269.** 704 Rt 23B. I-87 (New York State Thruway), exit 21, just w. Ext'int corridors. **Pets:** Large. $20 daily fee/pet. Designated rooms, service with restrictions, supervision.

🆂🅰🆅🅴 🆂🅾 ⊠ 🄳 💻 🍽 🌊

## CHESTER

**▽▽▽▽ Holiday Inn Express Hotel & Suites** 🆂🅷
(845) 469-3000. **$100-$310.** 2 Bryle Pl. SR 17, exit 126, just n on SR 94, then just w on SR 17M (Brookside Ave). Int corridors. **Pets:** $30 one-time fee/room. Designated rooms, supervision.

🅰🆂🅺 🆂🅾 ⊠ 🖳 🄳 💻 🌊 🖾

## CICERO

**🔷 ▽ Budget Inn** Ⓜ
(315) 458-3510. **$45-$105.** 901 S Bay Rd. I-481, exit 10, just s. Ext corridors. **Pets:** Small, dogs only. $10 daily fee/pet. Service with restrictions, supervision.

🆂🅰🆅🅴 🆂🅾 ⊠ 🄳

## CLINTON

**▽▽▽▽ Amidst the Hedges** 🅱🅱 ❀
(315) 853-3031. **$110-$150, 7 day notice.** 180 Sanford Ave. College St, 0.3 mi n on Elm St. Int corridors. **Pets:** Dogs only. $100 deposit/pet. Designated rooms, service with restrictions, supervision.

⊠ 🄳 💻 🌊

## COBLESKILL

**🔷 ▽▽▽▽ Best Western Inn of Cobleskill** 🆂🅷
(518) 234-4321. **$80-$175.** 121 Burgin Dr. I-88, exit 21 eastbound on SR 7, 0.8 mi e of jct SR 10; exit 22 westbound, 2.9 mi w on SR 27. Int corridors. **Pets:** Accepted.

🆂🅰🆅🅴 🆂🅾 ⊠ 🄶🅼 🖉 🄳 💻 🍽 🌊

**▽▽ Super 8** 🆂🅷
(518) 234-4888. **$60-$130.** 955 E Main St. I-88, exit 22 westbound, 2.4 mi w on SR 7; exit 21 eastbound, 3.1 mi e on SR 7. Int corridors. **Pets:** Other species. $10 one-time fee/room. Service with restrictions, crate.

🅰🆂🅺 🆂🅾 ⊠ 🄶🅼 🖉 🖾

## COLONIE

**▽▽ Ambassador Motor Inn** Ⓜ
(518) 456-8982. **$59-$109, 3 day notice.** 1600 Central Ave. I-87, exit 2 (SR 5), 0.8 mi w. Ext corridors. **Pets:** Other species. Service with restrictions, supervision.

🅰🆂🅺 🆂🅾 ⊠

**▽▽ Red Roof Inn #7112** Ⓜ
(518) 459-1971. **$69-$110.** 188 Wolf Rd. I-87, exit 4, just se to Wolf Rd, then just sw. Ext corridors. **Pets:** Accepted.

⊠ 🄶🅼 🄳

## CORNING

**▽▽▽▽ Radisson Hotel Corning** 🆂🅷
(607) 962-5000. **$105-$129.** 125 Denison Pkwy E. On I-86/SR 17; center. Int corridors. **Pets:** $35 one-time fee/room. Designated rooms, service with restrictions, supervision.

🅰🆂🅺 🆂🅾 ⊠ 🄳 💻 🍽 🌊

**▽▽▽▽ Staybridge Suites by Holiday Inn** 🆂🅷
(607) 936-7800. **$140-$185.** 201 Townley Ave. I-86/SR 17, exit 46, just s. Int corridors. **Pets:** Accepted.

🅰🆂🅺 🆂🅾 ⊠ 🄶🅼 🖉 🖳 🄳 💻 🌊 🖾

## CORTLAND

**▽▽▽ Comfort Inn** 🆂🅷
(607) 753-7721. **$79-$199.** 2 1/2 Locust Ave. I-81, exit 11, just e. Int corridors. **Pets:** Accepted.

🅰🆂🅺 🆂🅾 ⊠ 🄳 💻 🍽

**🔷 ▽ Econo Lodge** Ⓜ
(607) 756-2856. **$55-$165.** 10 Church St. I-81, exit 11, 0.8 mi s on SR 13/41 and US 11. Ext corridors. **Pets:** Small. $20 daily fee/pet. Designated rooms, service with restrictions.

🆂🅰🆅🅴 🆂🅾 ⊠ 🄳 💻

**🔷 ▽▽▽ Holiday Inn Cortland** 🆂🅷
(607) 756-4431. **$79-$169.** 2 River St. I-81, exit 11, just s on SR 13. Int corridors. **Pets:** Medium, other species. $25 one-time fee/room. Service with restrictions, supervision.

🆂🅰🆅🅴 🆂🅾 ⊠ 🄳 💻 🍽 🌊

**🔷 ▽▽ Quality Inn Cortland** 🆂🅷
(607) 756-5622. **$79-$179, 3 day notice.** 188 Clinton St. I-81, exit 11, just n. Int corridors. **Pets:** $20 one-time fee/room. Service with restrictions, supervision.

🆂🅰🆅🅴 🆂🅾 ⊠ 🄳 💻

# CUBA

**ⓐⓐⓐ ▼▼▼ Cuba Econo Lodge M**
(585) 968-1992. **$49-$69.** 1 N Branch Rd. I-86, exit 28, n to N Branch Rd, then e. Int corridors. **Pets:** Large, other species. $5 daily fee/room. Service with restrictions, crate.

SAVE Sⓓ ✕ ❚

# DELHI

**ⓐⓐⓐ ▼ Buena Vista Motel M**
(607) 746-2135. **$75-$92.** 18718 State Hwy 28. Jct SR 10, 0.8 mi e. Ext corridors. **Pets:** Medium, dogs only. $15 daily fee/pet. Designated rooms, service with restrictions, supervision.

SAVE ✕ ❚

# DE WITT

**ⓐⓐⓐ ▼▼▼ Econo Lodge M**
(315) 446-3300. **$70-$140.** 3400 Erie Blvd E. I-481, exit 3, 1.2 mi w on SR 5; I-690, exit 17 S (Bridge St), just e on Erie Blvd (SR 5). Ext corridors. **Pets:** Medium. $10 daily fee/pet. Service with restrictions, supervision.

SAVE Sⓓ ✕ ❚ 🖵

# DOVER PLAINS

**ⓐⓐⓐ ▼▼▼ Old Drovers Inn ❑ ❀**
(845) 832-9311. **$190-$460, 14 day notice.** 196 E Duncan Hill Rd. 3 mi s of SR 22 on Old Rt 22 (CR 6). Int corridors. **Pets:** Small, dogs only. $25 daily fee/pet.

SAVE Sⓓ ✕ ❚❚ 🅟 🄯

# DUNKIRK

**ⓐⓐⓐ ▼▼▼ Best Western Dunkirk/Fredonia SH**
(716) 366-7100. **$69-$149.** 3912 Vineyard Dr. I-90, exit 59, just w. Int corridors. **Pets:** Large, other species. $10 daily fee/pet. Service with restrictions, supervision.

SAVE Sⓓ ✕ ❚ ❚ 🖵 ⤳

**ⓐⓐⓐ ▼▼▼ Clarion Hotel & Conference Center SH**
(716) 366-8350. **$80-$170.** 30 Lake Shore Dr E. Jct SR 60, 0.3 mi w on SR 5. Int corridors. **Pets:** Accepted.

SAVE Sⓓ ✕ 🄯 ❚ 🖵 ❚❚ ⤳ 🄯

**ⓐⓐⓐ ▼▼▼ Comfort Inn SH**
(716) 672-4450. **$69-$149.** 3925 Vineyard Dr. I-90, exit 59, just w of jct SR 60. Int corridors. **Pets:** Large, other species. $10 daily fee/pet. Service with restrictions, supervision.

SAVE Sⓓ ✕ ❚ ❚ 🖵

# EAST GREENBUSH

**▼▼▼ Residence Inn by Marriott SH ❀**
(518) 720-3600. **$159-$249.** 3 Tech Valley Dr. I-90, exit 9, just e. Int corridors. **Pets:** Other species. $75 one-time fee/room.

ASK Sⓓ ✕ �Ⓜ 🄯 ❚ 🖵 ⤳ 🄯

# EAST HAMPTON

**▼ The East Hampton Inn M**
(631) 324-4550. **$99-$235.** 488 Montauk Hwy. 1.3 mi e on SR 27 (Montauk Hwy). Ext corridors. **Pets:** Small, other species. $15 daily fee/pet. Service with restrictions, crate.

ASK Sⓓ ❚

# EAST SYRACUSE

**▼▼▼ Candlewood Suites Syracuse SH**
(315) 432-1684. **$109-$159.** 6550 Baptist Way. I-90, exit 35 (Carrier Cir) to SR 298 E to Old Collamer Rd, just n. Int corridors. **Pets:** Medium, other species. $25 deposit/pet. Service with restrictions, crate.

ASK Sⓓ ✕ ⓂⓂ 🄯 🄯 ❚ 🖵

**▼▼▼ Comfort Inn-Carrier Circle SH**
(315) 437-0222. **$69-$119.** 6491 Thompson Rd S. I-90, exit 35 (Carrier Cir). Ext/int corridors. **Pets:** Medium. Service with restrictions, supervision.

ASK Sⓓ ✕ ❚ 🖵

**▼▼▼ Hawthorn Suites at CrestHill SH**
(315) 432-5595. **$109-$179.** 6410 New Venture Gear Dr. I-90, exit 35 (Carrier Cir) to SR 298 E, just s. Int corridors. **Pets:** Accepted.

ASK Sⓓ ✕ 🄯 ❚ 🖵 ⤳

**▼▼▼ Holiday Inn East-Carrier Circle SH**
(315) 437-2761. **$90-$159.** 6555 Old Collamer Rd. I-90, exit 35 (Carrier Cir) to SR 298 E, just n. Ext/int corridors. **Pets:** Other species. $25 one-time fee/room. Service with restrictions, supervision.

ASK Sⓓ ✕ 🄯 ❚ 🖵 ❚❚ ⤳ 🄯

**▼▼ Microtel Inn Syracuse SH**
(315) 437-3500. **$46-$72.** 6608 Old Collamer Rd. I-90, exit 35 (Carrier Cir) to SR 298 E. Int corridors. **Pets:** Accepted.

ASK Sⓓ ✕ ⓂⓂ 🄯

**▼▼ Red Roof Inn #7157 M**
(315) 437-3309. **$50-$83.** 6614 N Thompson Rd. I-90, exit 35 (Carrier Cir), just n. Ext corridors. **Pets:** Accepted.

✕ 🄯 🄯 ❚

**▼▼▼ Residence Inn by Marriott SH**
(315) 432-4488. **$159-$249.** 6420 Yorktown Cir. I-90, exit 35 (Carrier Cir) to SR 298, just e to Old Collamer Rd, then 0.5 mi n. Ext corridors. **Pets:** Other species. $75 one-time fee/room. Service with restrictions, supervision.

ASK Sⓓ ✕ ⓂⓂ 🄯 🄯 ❚ 🖵 ⤳ 🄯

# ELLICOTTVILLE

**ⓐⓐⓐ ▼▼▼ The Jefferson Inn of Ellicottville BB**
(716) 699-5869. **$79-$209, 30 day notice.** 3 Jefferson St. Western jct US 219 and SR 242, just n; eastern jct US 219 and 242, 0.8 mi w. Ext/int corridors. **Pets:** Dogs only. $15 daily fee/room. Designated rooms, no service.

SAVE ✕ ❚

# ELMIRA

**ⓐⓐⓐ ▼▼▼ Coachman Motor Lodge M**
(607) 733-5526. **$70-$100.** 908 Pennsylvania Ave. SR 17, exit 56 (Water St), 0.5 mi w on SR 352 (Church St), 0.5 mi s on Madison Ave, then 1.4 mi s. Ext corridors. **Pets:** Medium. Service with restrictions, supervision.

SAVE Sⓓ ❚ 🖵

# FALCONER

**▼▼ Red Roof Inn Jamestown/Falconer #7273 SH**
(716) 665-3670. **$54-$80.** 1980 E Main St. I-86, exit 13, just w. Int corridors. **Pets:** Accepted.

✕

# FARMINGTON

**ⓐⓐⓐ ▼▼▼ Budget Inn M**
(585) 924-5020. **$54-$79, 3 day notice.** 6001 Rt 96. I-90, exit 44, 1 mi s on SR 332, then just e. Ext corridors. **Pets:** Small, dogs only. $10 daily fee/pet. Service with restrictions, supervision.

SAVE Sⓓ ✕ ❚ 🖵

# FISHKILL

**▼▼▼ Homestead Studio Suites Hotel-Fishkill SH**
(845) 897-2800. **$105.** 25 Merritt Blvd. I-34, exit 13, just n. Int corridors. **Pets:** $25 daily fee/pet. Service with restrictions, supervision.

ASK Sⓓ ✕ 🄯 🄯 ❚ 🖵

**Ramada Inn-Fishkill** SH
(845) 896-4995. **$99-$129.** 20 Schuyler Blvd & Rt 9. I-84, exit 13, just n. Int corridors. **Pets:** Accepted.
SAVE Sb X &M Ⓐ &` 🛏 💻

**Residence Inn by Marriott** SH
(845) 896-5210. **$169-$209.** 14 Schuyler Blvd. I-84, exit 13, just n. Ext corridors. **Pets:** Other species. $75 one-time fee/room. Service with restrictions, crate.
ASK Sb X &M Ⓐ &` 🛏 💻 ⇌ ⊠

# FREDONIA

**Days Inn Dunkirk-Fredonia** SH 🐾
(716) 673-1351. **$65-$140.** 10455 Bennett Rd. I-90, exit 59, just s on SR 60. Ext/int corricors. **Pets:** Other species. $10 one-time fee/room. Designated rooms, service with restrictions, supervision.
ASK Sb X 🛏 💻 ⇌ ⊠

# FULTON

**Riverside Inn** SH
(315) 593-2444. **$49-$109, 7 day notice.** 930 S 1st St. On SR 481. Int corridors. **Pets:** Other species. $100 deposit/room. Service with restrictions, crate.
ASK Sb X 🛏 💻 ⇌ ⊠

# GARDEN CITY

**Wingate Inn** SH
(516) 705-9000. **$169-$199.** 821 Stewart Ave. Meadowbrook Pkwy, exit 3, 0.5 mi w. Int corridors. **Pets:** Small, dogs only. $50 deposit/room, $50 one-time fee/room. Service with restrictions, crate.
ASK Sb X &M &` 🛏 💻 ⇌

# GATES

**Holiday Inn-Rochester Airport** SH
(585) 328-6000. **$79-$129.** 911 Brooks Ave. I-390, exit 18A (SR 204), just e. Int corridors. **Pets:** Medium. $50 deposit/room. Designated rooms, service with restrictions, supervision.
ASK Sb X Ⓐ 🛏 💻 ⇌ ⊠

# GENEVA

**Hampton Inn Geneva** SH
(315) 781-2035. **Call for rates.** 43 Lake St. Jct Exchange St. Int corridors. **Pets:** Other species. $10 daily fee/pet. Service with restrictions, supervision.
X &M Ⓐ &` 🛏 💻 ⇌

**Ramada Inn Geneva Lakefront** SH 🐾
(315) 789-0400. **$112-$160.** 41 Lakefront Dr. I-90, exit 42, 8 mi s on SR 14. Int corridors. **Pets:** $10 one-time fee/pet. Service with restrictions, supervision.
SAVE Sb X &` 🛏 💻 ⇌

# GREAT NECK

**The Andrew Hotel** SH 🐾
(516) 482-2900. **$275-$305.** 75 N Station Plaza. Jct SR 25A, 0.8 mi n on Middle Neck Rd, just e. Int corridors. **Pets:** Small. $150 one-time fee/room. Service with restrictions.
ASK Sb X 🛏

**Inn at Great Neck** SH
(516) 773-2000. **$199-$249.** 30 Cutter Mill Rd. Jct SR 25A, 0.8 mi n on Middle Neck Rd, just w. Int corridors. **Pets:** Medium. Designated rooms, service with restrictions, supervision.
ASK Sb X Ⓐ &` 🛏 💻 ⇌

# GREECE

**Hampton Inn-Rochester North** SH
(585) 663-6070. **$109-$129.** 500 Center Place Dr. I-390, exit 24A, just e on SR 104 (Ridge Rd), then just n on Buckman Rd. Int corridors. **Pets:** Accepted.
ASK Sb X &M &` 🛏 💻

**Residence Inn by Marriott-West** SH
(585) 865-2090. **$109-$249.** 500 Paddy Creek Cir. I-390, exit 24A, just e on SR 104 (Ridge Rd), just s on Hoover Dr, then just w. Int corridors. **Pets:** Accepted.
ASK Sb X &` 🛏 💻 ⇌ ⊠

**Wellesley Inn (Rochester/North)** SH
(585) 621-2060. **$49-$109.** 1635 W Ridge Rd. I-390, exit 24A, just e on SR 104 (Ridge Rd). Int corridors. **Pets:** Accepted.
ASK Sb X &M Ⓐ &` 🛏 💻

# GUILDERLAND

**Best Western Sovereign Hotel Albany** SH
(518) 489-2981. **$89-$169.** 1228 Western Ave. I-87/90, exit 24, follow signs to US 20 (Western Ave), then 1 mi e. Int corridors. **Pets:** Small. $10 one-time fee/pet. Service with restrictions, crate.
SAVE Sb X Ⓐ &` 🛏 💻 ⇌ ⊠

# HANCOCK

**Smith's Colonial Motel** M
(607) 637-2989. **$65-$135.** 23085 State Hwy 97. SR 17, exit 87, 2.7 mi s. Ext corridors. **Pets:** $10 daily fee/pet. Service with restrictions, supervision.

# HAUPPAUGE

**Residence Inn by Marriott** SH 🐾
(631) 724-4188. **$159-$219.** 850 Veterans Memorial Hwy. I-495, exit 57, 1.2 mi nw. Int corridors. **Pets:** Other species. $75 one-time fee/room.
ASK X &M Ⓐ &` 🛏 💻 ⇌ ⊠

**Sheraton Long Island Hotel** LH
(631) 231-1100. **$104-$219.** 110 Vanderbilt Motor Pkwy. I-495, exit 53 (Wicks Rd), just n, then 0.3 mi e. Int corridors. **Pets:** Large, dogs only. Service with restrictions, crate.
ASK X &M Ⓐ &` 🛏 💻 ⇌ ⊠

# HENRIETTA

**Comfort Suites by Choice Hotels of Rochester** SH
(585) 334-6620. **$69-$149.** 2085 Hylan Dr. I-390, exit 13, just e. Int corridors. **Pets:** Accepted.
ASK Sb X &M &` 🛏 💻 ⇌

**Homewood Suites by Hilton-Rochester** SH
(585) 334-9150. **$174, 14 day notice.** 2095 Hylan Dr. I-390, exit 13, just e. Int corridors. **Pets:** Accepted.
ASK Sb X &M Ⓐ &` 🛏 💻 ⇌

**Microtel-Rochester** SH
(585) 334-3400. **$50-$99, 3 day notice.** 905 Lehigh Station Rd. I-390, exit 12 northbound; exit 12A southbound, just w on SR 253. Int corridors. **Pets:** $10 daily fee/room. Designated rooms, service with restrictions, supervision.
ASK Sb X 🛏

**Red Roof Inn-Henrietta #7042** M
(585) 359-1100. **$50-$85.** 4820 W Henrietta Rd. I-390, exit 12 northbound; exit 12A southbound, 0.5 mi w on SR 253, then just s on SR 15 (Henrietta Rd). Ext corridors. **Pets:** Accepted.
X 🛏

◆◆◆ **Residence Inn by Marriott** SH
(585) 272-8850. **$149-$205.** 1300 Jefferson Rd. I-390, exit 14A southbound, 0.5 mi e on SR 252 (Jefferson Rd); exit 14 northbound, just n on SR 15A, then 0.5 mi e on SR 252 (Jefferson Rd). Ext corridors. **Pets:** Other species. $75 one-time fee/room. Crate.
(A$K) (S⌀) (✕) (⌀) (🛢) (💻) (✕)

◆◆◆ **R I T Inn & Conference Center** SH
(585) 359-1800. **$89-$125.** 5257 W Henrietta Rd. I-390, exit 12 northbound; exit 12A southbound, 0.5 mi w on SR 253, then 0.7 mi s. Int corridors. **Pets:** Accepted.
(A$K) (S⌀) (✕) (⌀) (🛢) (💻) (††) (≈) (✕)

◆◆ **The Rochester Marketplace Inn** SH
(585) 475-9190. **$69-$119.** 800 Jefferson Rd. I-390, exit 14A southbound; exit 14 northbound, 0.5 mi w on SR 252 (Jefferson Rd). Int corridors. **Pets:** Accepted.
(A$K) (S⌀) (✕) (🛢) (💻) (≈)

# HERKIMER

◆◆◆ ◆◆ **Herkimer Motel** M
(315) 866-0490. **$68-$88.** 100 Marginal Rd. I-90, exit 30, just n on SR 28. Ext/int corridors. **Pets:** Service with restrictions, supervision.
(SAVE) (S⌀) (✕) (⌵) (🛢) (≈)

# HIGHLAND

◆◆ **Super 8 Motel** M
(845) 691-6888. **Call for rates.** 3423 Rt 9W. Just s of jct SR 299 and US 9W. Int corridors. **Pets:** Accepted.
(✕) (⌵M) (⌵) (🛢)

# HORNELL

◆◆◆ ◆◆ **Econo Lodge** M
(607) 324-0800. **$59-$84, 7 day notice.** 7462 Seneca Rd. Jct I-86 and SR 36, exit 34, just s to SR 21, just e to Seneca Rd, then just s. Ext/int corridors. **Pets:** Other species. $10 daily fee/pet. Service with restrictions.
(SAVE) (S⌀) (✕) (🛢) (💻) (††)

# HUNTER

◆◆◆ **Hunter Inn** SH
(518) 263-3777. **$79-$235, 14 day notice.** Rt 23A. Jct SR 296, 1.9 mi e. Int corridors. **Pets:** Accepted.
(A$K) (✕) (🛢) (✕)

# HUNTINGTON STATION

◆◆◆ ◆◆ **Whitman Motor Lodge** M
(631) 271-2800. **$90-$109.** 295 E Jericho Tpke. On SR 25 (Jericho Tpke), 0.6 mi e of SR 110. Ext/int corridors. **Pets:** Accepted.
(SAVE) (S⌀) (✕) (🛢) (💻)

# ITHACA

◆◆◆ ◆◆ **Comfort Inn** SH
(607) 272-0100. **$69-$199.** 356 Elmira Rd. Jct SR 96, 89 and 79, 1.5 mi sw on SR 13. Ext/int corridors. **Pets:** Accepted.
(SAVE) (S⌀) (✕) (⌵M) (🛢) (💻)

◆◆◆ ◆◆ **Hampton Inn** SH ❀
(607) 277-5500. **$99-$285.** 337 Elmira Rd. On SR 13. Int corridors. **Pets:** Medium, dogs only. $100 deposit/room. Designated rooms, service with restrictions, supervision.
(SAVE) (S⌀) (✕) (⌵M) (⌀) (⌵) (🛢) (💻) (≈)

◆◆◆ **Holiday Inn Ithaca Downtown** SH ❀
(607) 272-1000. **$99-$170.** 222 S Cayuga St. Just n of SR 96B. Int corridors. **Pets:** Large, other species. $20 one-time fee/room. Service with restrictions, crate.
(A$K) (S⌀) (✕) (⌀) (🛢) (💻) (††) (≈)

◆◆◆ ◆◆ **La Tourelle Resort and Spa** CI
(607) 273-2734. **$125-$375, 3 day notice.** 1150 Danby Rd. 2.7 mi s on SR 96B. Int corridors. **Pets:** Accepted
(A$K) (✕) (🛢) (💻) (††) (✕)

◆◆◆ ◆◆ **Meadow Court Inn** M
(607) 273-3885. **$65-$275.** 529 S Meadow St. 1.5 mi s on SR 13 and 96. Ext/int corridors. **Pets:** $10 daily fee/pet. Designated rooms, service with restrictions, crate.
(SAVE) (✕) (⌵M) (⌀) (🛢) (💻) (††)

# JAMESTOWN

◆◆◆ **Comfort Inn** SH
(716) 664-5920. **$79-$169.** 2800 N Main St. I-86, exit 12, just s. Int corridors. **Pets:** Small, other species. $10 one-time fee/pet. Service with restrictions, supervision.
(A$K) (S⌀) (✕) (🛢) (💻)

◆◆◆ ◆◆ **Holiday Inn** LH
(716) 664-3400. **$79-$160.** 150 W 4th St. I-86, exit 12, 2 mi s on SR 60 (Washington St); center. Int corridors. **Pets:** Accepted.
(SAVE) (S⌀) (✕) (⌀) (⌵) (🛢) (💻) (††) (≈)

# JOHNSON CITY

◆◆◆ ◆◆ **Best Western of Johnson City** SH
(607) 729-9194. **$65-$120.** 569 Harry _ Dr. SR 17, exit 70, 0.3 mi n. Int corridors. **Pets:** Other species. $10 daily fee/pet. Designated rooms, service with restrictions, supervision.
(SAVE) (S⌀) (✕) (🛢) (💻)

◆◆◆ **La Quinta Inn** SH
(607) 770-9333. **$65-$135.** 581 Harry _ Dr. SR 17, exit 70, 0.3 mi n. Int corridors. **Pets:** Other species. Designated rooms, service with restrictions, supervision.
(A$K) (✕) (🛢) (💻)

◆◆ **Red Roof Inn-Binghamton #7203** M
(607) 729-8940. **$48-$85.** 590 Fairview St. SR 17, exit 70, 0.3 mi n, then just n on Reynolds Rd. Ext corridors. **Pets:** Accepted.
(✕) (🛢)

# JOHNSTOWN

◆◆◆ **Holiday Inn** SH
(518) 762-4686. **$96-$160.** 308 N Comrie Ave. Jct SR 30A and 29 E, 1.3 mi n. Ext/int corridors. **Pets:** Accepted.
(A$K) (S⌀) (✕) (⌵M) (⌵) (🛢) (💻) (††) (≈)

# KINGSTON

◆◆◆ **Holiday Inn** SH
(845) 338-0400. **$139-$179, 3 day notice.** 503 Washington Ave. I-87, exit 19, just e of traffic circle. Int corridors. **Pets:** Other species. $10 daily fee/room. Service with restrictions, supervision.
(SAVE) (S⌀) (✕) (⌵) (🛢) (💻) (††) (≈) (✕)

# LAKE GEORGE

◆◆ **Balmoral Motel** M
(518) 668-2673. **$49-$195, 10 day notice.** 444 Canada St. I-87, exit 22, 0.3 mi s on US 9. Ext corridors. **Pets:** Medium. $15 daily fee/pet. Designated rooms, service with restrictions, crate.
(A$K) (✕) (🛢) (💻) (≈)

◆ **Green Haven** M
(518) 668-2489. **$54-$134, 10 day notice.** 3136 Lake Shore Dr. I-87, exit 22, 0.8 mi n on SR 9N. Ext corridors. **Pets:** Large, dogs only. $10 deposit/pet. Service with restrictions, supervision.
(✕) (🛢) (💻) (≈) (✕)

**♦♦ ♦♦ Lake Haven Motel M**
(518) 668-2260. **$49-$129, 10 day notice.** 442 Canada St. I-87, exit 22, 0.4 mi s on US 9. Ext corridors. **Pets:** Dogs only. $10 daily fee/pet. Designated rooms, service with restrictions, crate.
⊠ 🛡 ➘

**♦♦♦ ♦♦♦ Travelodge of Lake George M**
(518) 668-5421. **$69-$166.** 2011 SR 9. I-87, exit 21, just s. Ext corridors. **Pets:** Medium, dogs only. $20 daily fee/pet. Service with restrictions, supervision.
SAVE 🛡 ⊠ 🛡 ➘ ⑪ ➘

## LAKE LUZERNE

**♦♦♦ ♦♦ Luzerne Court M ❀**
(518) 696-2734. **$75-$180, 14 day notice.** 508 Lake Ave. I-87, exit 21, 8.7 mi s on SR 9N. Ext corridors. **Pets:** Dogs only. Service with restrictions, supervision.
SAVE ⊠ 🛡 ⑪ ➘ ☑

## LAKE PLACID

**♦♦♦ ♦♦♦ Art Devlin's Olympic Motor Inn, Inc. M**
(518) 523-3700. **$62-$154, 14 day notice.** 2764 Main St. 0.5 mi e on SR 86. Ext corridors. **Pets:** Dogs only. Service with restrictions, supervision.
SAVE ⊠ 🛡 ➘

**♦♦♦ ♦♦♦ Best Western Golden Arrow Hotel SH ❀**
(518) 523-3353. **$99-$249, 7 day notice.** 2559 Main St. On SR 86; center. Int corridors. **Pets:** Other species. $100 deposit/pet, $50 one-time fee/pet. Designated rooms, service with restrictions, supervision.
SAVE 🛡 ⊠ ➘ 🛡 ➘ ⑪ ➘ ⊠

**♦♦♦ ♦♦♦ Comfort Inn on Lake Placid SH**
(518) 523-9555. **$70-$220, 3 day notice.** 2125 Saranac Ave. 0.5 mi w on SR 86. Ext/int corridors. **Pets:** Other species. Service with restrictions, supervision.
SAVE 🛡 ⊠ ➘ 🛡 ➘ ⑪ ➘ ⊠

**♦♦♦ ♦♦♦ Crowne Plaza Resort & Golf Club Lake Placid SH**
(518) 523-2556. **$79-$269, 7 day notice.** 1 Olympic Dr. Downtown. Ext/int corridors. **Pets:** Accepted.
⊠ ➘ 🛡 ➘ ⑪ ➘ ⊠

**♦♦♦ ♦♦♦ Hilton Lake Placid Resort SH**
(518) 523-4411. **$79-$499, 7 day notice.** 1 Mirror Lake Dr. 0.3 mi w on SR 86. Int corridors. **Pets:** Accepted.
ASK 🛡 ⊠ ➘M ➘ ➘ 🛡 ➘ ⑪ ➘ ⊠

**♦♦♦ ♦♦♦ Swiss Acres Inn SH**
(518) 523-3040. **$48-$138, 7 day notice.** 1970 Saranac Ave. 1 mi w on SR 86. Ext/int corridors. **Pets:** Other species. $15 daily fee/pet. Service with restrictions, supervision.
SAVE 🛡 ⊠ 🛡 ➘ ⑪ ➘

## LANSING

**♦♦ ♦♦ The Clarion University Hotel & Conference Center SH**
(607) 257-2000. **$89-$299.** One Sheraton Dr. SR 13, exit Triphammer Rd, just e; n of Ithaca. Int corridors. **Pets:** Medium. $25 one-time fee/room. Designated rooms, service with restrictions, supervision.
ASK 🛡 ⊠ 🛡 ➘ ⑪ ➘ ⊠

**♦♦♦ ♦♦♦ Econo Lodge SH**
(607) 257-1400. **$67-$175.** 2303 N Triphammer Rd. SR 13, exit Triphammer Rd. Int corridors. **Pets:** Other species. $15 daily fee/pet. Service with restrictions, supervision.
SAVE 🛡 ⊠ 🛡 ➘

**♦♦ ♦♦ Ramada Inn-Airport SH**
(607) 257-3100. **$99-$359.** 2310 N Triphammer Rd. Jct SR 13 and 34, 3.5 mi n on SR 13, exit Triphammer Rd, just w. Int corridors. **Pets:** Accepted.
ASK 🛡 ⊠ ➘ 🛡 ➘ ⑪ ➘ ⊠

## LATHAM

**♦♦♦ ♦♦♦ Century House Restaurant & Hotel SH**
(518) 785-0931. **$115-$225.** 997 New Loudon Rd. I-87, exit 7 (SR 7), just e, then 0.5 mi n on US 9 (New Loudon Rd). Int corridors. **Pets:** Large. $15 daily fee/pet. Designated rooms, service with restrictions, supervision.
SAVE 🛡 ⊠ 🛡 ➘ ⑪ ➘

**♦♦♦ ♦♦♦ Comfort Inn Albany Airport & Conference Center SH ❀**
(518) 783-1900. **$99-$180.** 20 Airport Park Blvd. I-87, exit 4, 2.2 mi nw on Albany Shaker Rd. Int corridors. **Pets:** Medium. $75 deposit/pet, $10 daily fee/pet. Designated rooms, service with restrictions, crate.
SAVE 🛡 ⊠ 🛡 ➘ ⑪

**♦♦♦ ♦♦♦ Holiday Inn Express-Airport SH**
(518) 783-6161. **$85-$125.** 946 New Loudon Rd. I-87, exit 7 (SR 7), just e, then just n on US 9 (New Loudon Rd). Ext corridors. **Pets:** Other species. $20 daily fee/room. Service with restrictions, supervision.
ASK 🛡 ⊠ ➘ 🛡 ➘ ➘

**♦♦♦ ♦♦ Microtel Inn, Albany Airport SH**
(518) 782-9161. **$45-$139.** 7 Rensselaer Ave. I-87, exit 6, just w. Int corridors. **Pets:** Small, dogs only. $10 daily fee/pet. Service with restrictions, supervision.
SAVE 🛡 ⊠ ➘M ➘ ➘ 🛡 ➘

**♦♦♦ ♦♦ Quality Inn & Suites SH ❀**
(518) 785-5891. **$109-$159.** 611 Troy-Schenectady Rd. I-87, exit 6, just w on SR 7. Ext/int corridors. **Pets:** Medium, dogs only. Designated rooms, service with restrictions, supervision.
SAVE 🛡 ⊠ ➘ 🛡 ➘

**♦♦♦ ♦♦ Residence Inn by Marriott Albany Airport SH**
(518) 783-0600. **$199-$249.** 1 Residence Inn Dr. I-87, exit 6, 2 mi w on SR 7. Ext corridors. **Pets:** Other species. $75 one-time fee/room. Service with restrictions, supervision.
ASK 🛡 ⊠ ➘ 🛡 ➘ ➘ ⊠

## LITTLE FALLS

**♦♦♦ ♦♦ Best Western Little Falls Motor Inn SH**
(315) 823-4954. **$69-$105, 3 day notice.** 20 Albany St. On SR 5 and 167. Int corridors. **Pets:** Other species. $10 deposit/pet. Designated rooms, service with restrictions, crate.
SAVE 🛡 ⊠ ➘ ⑪

## LIVERPOOL

**♦♦♦ ♦♦♦ Best Western Inn & Suites SH**
(315) 701-4400. **$84-$159, 10 day notice.** 136 Transistor Pkwy. I-90, exit 37 (Electronics Pkwy), just n; I-81, exit 25 (7th North St), 1.3 mi w, just n on Electronics Pkwy, then just w. Int corridors. **Pets:** Small. $25 one-time fee/room. Designated rooms, service with restrictions, crate.
SAVE ⊠ 🛡 ➘ ➘

**♦♦ ♦♦ Holiday Inn Syracuse Airport LH**
(315) 457-1122. **$99-$200.** 441 Electronics Pkwy. I-90, exit 37 (Electronics Pkwy); I-81, exit 25 (7th North St), 1.3 mi nw. Int corridors. **Pets:** Other species. $50 deposit/room. Designated rooms, service with restrictions, crate.
ASK 🛡 ⊠ ➘M ➘ ➘ 🛡 ➘ ⑪ ➘ ⊠

**▽▽▽ Homewood Suites** SH
(315) 451-3800. **$159-$300, 10 day notice.** 275 Elwood Davis Rd.
I-81, exit 25 (7th North St), 1 mi w; I-90, exit 36. Int corridors.
**Pets:** Medium. $150 one-time fee/pet. Service with restrictions, supervision.

ASK ⊠ 🔒 🖥 🏊 🐾

**ΑΑΑ ▽▽▽ Knights Inn** M ❀
(315) 453-6330. **$44-$189.** 430 Electronics Pkwy. I-90, exit 37 (Electronics Pkwy), just s; I-81, exit 25 (7th North St), 1.3 mi nw, then just
s. Ext corridors. **Pets:** Large. $12 daily fee/pet. Service with restrictions,
supervision.

SAVE S🐾 ⊠ 🔒

**▽▽ Super 8 Motel Syracuse/Liverpool** SH
(315) 451-8888. **$60-$129.** 421 7th North St. I-81, exit 25 (7th North
St), just nw; I-90, exit 36. Int corridors. **Pets:** Accepted.

ASK S🐾 ⊠ 🔒

## LONG LAKE

**ΑΑΑ ▽▽▽ Journey's End Cottages** CA
(518) 624-5381. **$600-$750 (weekly), 60 day notice.** Deerland Rd (Rt
30). On SR 30/28 N, 1 mi s. Ext corridors. **Pets:** Accepted.

SAVE 🔒 🖥 ⊠ 🐾 🗲

**▽▽ Long View Lodge** CI
(518) 624-2862. **$70-$130, 7 day notice.** Deerland Rd (Rt 30). On SR
30/28 N, 2.2 mi s. Ext/int corridors. **Pets:** $10 daily fee/room. Designated
rooms, service with restrictions, supervision.

⊠ 🔒 🍴 🐾 🐾

## LOWMAN

**▽▽ Red Jacket Motel** M
(607) 734-1616. **$40-$95, 3 day notice.** 1744 Rt 17 W. SR 17, just e of
CR 8; between MM 195 and 196. Ext corridors. **Pets:** Accepted.

ASK S🐾 ⊠ 🐾 🔒 🏊

## MALONE

**ΑΑΑ ▽▽▽ Four Seasons Motel** M
(518) 483-3490. **$48-$79, 3 day notice.** 206 W Main St. 1 mi w on US
11. Ext corridors. **Pets:** Medium, other species. $5 daily fee/pet. Service
with restrictions, supervision.

SAVE S🐾 ⊠ 🔒 🖥 🏊

**ΑΑΑ ▽▽▽ Sunset Inn** M
(518) 483-3367. **$50-$85, 5 day notice.** 3899 US 11. 1.5 mi e. Ext
corridors. **Pets:** Accepted.

SAVE S🐾 ⊠ 🔒 🖥 🏊

**ΑΑΑ ▽▽▽ Super 8 Motel at Jons** SH
(518) 483-8123. **$78-$113.** 42 Finney Blvd. On SR 30, just s of jct US
11. Int corridors. **Pets:** Medium. Designated rooms, service with restrictions, supervision.

SAVE ⊠ 🅼 🔒

## MASSENA

**ΑΑΑ ▽▽▽ Econo Lodge-Meadow View Motel** SH
(315) 764-0246. **$65-$99.** 15054 SR 37. On SR 37, 2.7 mi sw. Ext/int
corridors. **Pets:** Small. $5 daily fee/pet. Designated rooms, service with
restrictions, supervision.

SAVE S🐾 ⊠ 🔒 🖥 🍴

## MCGRAW

**ΑΑΑ ▽▽▽ Cortland Days Inn** SH
(607) 753-7594. **$69-$159, 10 day notice.** 3775 US Rt 11. I-81, exit 10
(McGraw/Cortland), just n. Int corridors. **Pets:** Very small. $10 daily
fee/pet. Service with restrictions, supervision.

SAVE S🐾 ⊠ 🖥

## MIDDLETOWN

**▽▽ Super 8 Motel** SH
(845) 692-5828. **$70-$150, 3 day notice.** 563 Rt 211 E. I-84, exit 4, 0.5
mi w on SR 17 to exit 120, then C3 mi e. Int corridors. **Pets:** $25
deposit/pet. No service, supervision.

⊠ 🔒

## MONTOUR FALLS

**ΑΑΑ ▽▽ Relax Inn** M
(607) 535-7183. **$39-$125, 4 day notice.** 100 Clawson Blvd. Jct SR 14
and 224. Ext corridors. **Pets:** Small. $10 daily fee/pet. Designated rooms,
service with restrictions, supervision.

SAVE S🐾 ⊠ 🔒

## NEWBURGH

**▽▽ Quality Inn and Suites** SH
(845) 564-9020. **$89-$249.** 90 Rt 17K. I-87, exit 17, then w; I-84, exit 6,
2 mi e. Ext/int corridors. **Pets:** Accepted.

ASK S🐾 ⊠ 🔒 🖥 🍴 🏊

**▽▽ Super 8** M
(845) 564-5700. **Call for rates.** 1287 Rt 300. I-87, exit 17, just w; I-84,
exit 6, 2 mi e. Int corridors. **Pets:** Accepted.

⊠ 🅼

## NEW HAMPTON

**ΑΑΑ ▽▽▽ Days Inn** M
(845) 374-2411. **$69-$139.** 4939 Rt 17M. I-84, exit 3, 0.8 mi e on US 6
and SR 17M. Ext/int corridors. **Pets:** Large. Designated rooms, service
with restrictions, supervision.

SAVE S🐾 ⊠ 🔒 🖥 🏊

## NEW HARTFORD

**▽▽▽ Holiday Inn Utica** SH
(315) 797-2131. **$109-$199, 15 day notice.** 1777 Burrstone Rd. I-90
(New York State Thruway), exit 31, 4.5 mi w on SR 5 W and 12 S, exit
Burrstone Rd, then 1 mi nw. Int corridors. **Pets:** Accepted.

ASK S🐾 ⊠ 🅼 🚬 ♿ 🔒 🖥 🍴 🏊 ⊠

# NEW YORK METROPOLITAN AREA

## ARMONK

**AAA** ▼▼▼▼ **Wellesley Inn** SH
(914) 273-9090. **$149-$300.** 94 Business Park Dr. I-684, exit 3S northbound; exit 3 southbound, 0.3 mi s on SR 22 to Business Park Dr. Int corridors. **Pets:** Small. $10 daily fee/pet. Designated rooms, service with restrictions, supervision.
SAVE ⑤ ⊠ ⓜ ⊘ ⓙ ❚ ▣ ⑪ ⟲

## ELMSFORD

**AAA** ▼▼▼▼ **Hampton Inn White Plains/Tarrytown** SH
(914) 592-5680. **$119-$199.** 200 Tarrytown Rd. I-287, exit 1; I-87, exit 8, just w. Int corridors. **Pets:** Large. $100 one-time fee/room. Designated rooms, service with restrictions, supervision.
SAVE ⑤ ⊠ ⓜ ⊘ ⓙ ▣ ⟲

**AAA** ▼▼▼ **Wellesley Inn (Elmsford)** SH
(914) 592-3300. **$119-$159.** 540 Saw Mill River Rd. SR 9A, 1.5 mi n of SR 119; 1 mi n of I-287, exit 2 westbound; exit 1 eastbound, jct SR 100C. Int corridors. **Pets:** Accepted.
SAVE ⑤ ⊠ ⓜ ⊘ ⓙ ❚ ▣ ⑪ ⟲

## FLUSHING

**AAA** ▼▼▼▼ **Sheraton La Guardia East Hotel** LH
(718) 460-6666. **$409.** 135-20 39th Ave. In Flushing; Grand Central Pkwy to Northern Blvd, 1 mi e to Main St, 0.3 mi s to 39th Ave, then just w. Int corridors. **Pets:** Accepted.
SAVE ⊠ ⊘ ❚ ▣ ⑪

## JAMAICA

▼▼ ▼▼ **Ramada Plaza Hotel at JFK** LH
(718) 995-9000. **$109-$149, 3 day notice.** Bldg 144/JFK International Airport. In Jamaica; Van Wyck Expwy at Belt Pkwy; southwest corner. Int corridors. **Pets:** Medium. $100 deposit/pet. Designated rooms, service with restrictions, supervision.
ASK ⑤ ⊠ ⊘ ⓙ ❚ ▣ ⑪

## LONG ISLAND CITY

▼▼ ▼▼ **Holiday Inn Express** SH
(718) 706-6700. **$119-$189.** 3805 Hunters Point Ave. In Long Island City; I-278, exit I-495 (Midtown tunnel) westbound, exit 15 (Van Dam St), just n to Hunters Point Blvd, w on Greenpoint Ave, then n at 39th St; I-278 westbound, exit 35 (Greenpoint Ave), n on Greenpoint Ave, then e on 39th St. Int corridors. **Pets:** Accepted.
ASK ⑤ ⊠ ⊘ ⓙ ❚ ▣

## MOUNT KISCO

**AAA** ▼▼▼▼ **Holiday Inn** SH ❀
(914) 241-2600. **$129-$179.** 1 Holiday Inn Dr. Saw Mill River Pkwy, exit 37, just e. Int corridors. **Pets:** Medium, other species. $10 daily fee/pet. Service with restrictions, crate.
SAVE ⑤ ⊠ ⓜ ⊘ ⓙ ❚ ▣ ⑪ ⟲

## NANUET

▼▼▼▼ **Candlewood Suites** SH
(845) 371-4445. **$80-$126.** 20 Overlook Blvd. I-287/87 (New York State Thruway), exit 14 (SR 59 W) to New Clarkstown Rd. Int corridors. **Pets:** Accepted.
ASK ⑤ ⊠ ⓙ ❚ ▣

**AAA** ▼▼ ▼▼ **Days Inn Nanuet** SH
(845) 623-4567. **$69-$109.** 367 W Rt 59. I-287/87 (New York State Thruway), exit 14 (SR 59) northbound, just e; exit southbound, just w. Ext/int corridors. **Pets:** $8 daily fee/pet. Service with restrictions.
SAVE ⑤ ⊠ ❚ ▣ ⟲

## NEW YORK

**AAA** ▼▼▼▼ **Affinia 50** SH
(212) 751-5710. **$249-$689.** 155 E 50th St. Between 3rd and Lexington aves. Int corridors. **Pets:** Accepted.
SAVE ⊠ ⊘ ❚ ▣

**AAA** ▼▼▼▼ **Affinia Dumont** SH
(212) 481-7600. **$269-$629.** 150 E 34th St. Between Lexington and 3rd aves. Int corridors. **Pets:** Accepted.
SAVE ⊠ ⊘ ⓙ ❚ ▣ ⑪

**AAA** ▼▼▼▼ **Affinia Gardens** SH ❀
(212) 355-1230. **$359-$609.** 215 E 64th St. Between 2nd and 3rd aves. Int corridors. **Pets:** Medium, other species. Service with restrictions, supervision.
SAVE ⊠ ⊘ ⓙ ❚ ▣

**AAA** ▼▼▼▼ **Affinia Manhattan** LH ❀
(212) 563-1800. **$269-$549.** 371 7th Ave. At 31st St. Int corridors. **Pets:** Service with restrictions.
SAVE ⊠ ⊘ ❚ ▣ ⑪

▼▼▼▼ **Beekman Tower Hotel** SH
(212) 355-7300. **$239-$609.** 3 Mitchell Pl. 49th St and 1st Ave. Int corridors. **Pets:** Accepted.
ASK ⊠ ⊘ ⓙ ❚ ▣ ⑪

**AAA** ▼▼▼▼ **The Benjamin Hotel** SH ❀
(212) 715-2500. **$279-$799.** 125 E 50th St. Between Lexington and 3rd aves. Int corridors. **Pets:** Other species. Service with restrictions, crate.
SAVE ⊠ ⊘ ❚ ▣ ⊠

**AAA** ▼▼▼▼ **The Carlyle** SH ❀
(212) 744-1600. **$725-$825.** 35 E 76th St. At Madison Ave. Int corridors. **Pets:** Small. $50 daily fee/pet.
SAVE ⊠ ⊘ ⓙ ❚ ⑪ ⊠

▼▼▼▼ **Crowne Plaza at the United Nations** LH
(212) 986-8800. **$199-$699.** 304 E 42nd St. Between 1st and 2nd aves. Int corridors. **Pets:** Accepted.
ASK ⑤ ⊠ ⊘ ⓙ ▣ ⑪ ⊠

▼▼▼▼ **DoubleTree Metropolitan Hotel New York City** SH
(212) 752-7000. **$159-$499.** 569 Lexington Ave. At E 51st St. Int corridors. **Pets:** Accepted.
⊠ ⓜ ⊘ ⓙ ❚ ⑪

▼▼▼▼ **Eastgate Tower Hotel** SH ❀
(212) 687-8000. **$239-$529.** 222 E 39th St. Between 2nd and 3rd aves. Int corridors. **Pets:** Other species. Service with restrictions.
ASK ⊠ ⓜ ⊘ ⓙ ❚ ▣ ⑪

▼▼▼▼ **Embassy Suites Hotel New York** LH
(212) 945-0100. **$229-$999.** 102 N End Ave. Between Murray and Vesey sts. Int corridors. **Pets:** Accepted.
⊠ ⓙ ▣

▼▼▼▼ **The Essex House-A Westin Hotel** LH
(212) 247-0300. **$469-$649.** 160 Central Park S. Between 6th (Ave of the Americas) and 7th aves. Int corridors. **Pets:** Accepted.
ASK ⑤ ⊠ ⓜ ⊘ ⓙ ❚ ⑪ ⊠

▼▼▼▼ **Four Points by Sheraton Manhattan Chelsea** SH
(212) 627-1888. **$205-$475.** 160 W 25th St. Between 6th (Ave of the Americas) and 7th aves. Int corridors. **Pets:** Accepted.
ASK ⊠ ⊘ ⓙ ❚ ▣

▼▼◆▼▼ **Four Seasons Hotel New York** 🄻🄷
(212) 758-5700. **$825-$1095.** 57 E 57th St. Between Park and Madison aves. Int corridors. **Pets:** Accepted.
✕ 🅑M 🗕 🖉 🗎 🍴 ✕

🄰🄰🄰 ▼▼◆▼▼ **Hampton Inn-Manhattan/Chelsea** 🄢🄷
(212) 414-1000. **$169-$389.** 108 W 24th St. Between 6th (Ave of the Americas) and 7th aves. Int corridors. **Pets:** Medium. $50 deposit/room. Supervision.
🅂🄰🅅🄴 🅂🕭 ✕ 🖉 🗕 🗎 🖃

▼◆▼ **Hilton New York** 🄻🄷
(212) 586-7000. **$199-$729.** 1335 Ave of the Americas. Between 53rd and 54th sts. Int corridors. **Pets:** Accepted.
✕ 🖉 🗕 🗎 🖃 🍴

🄰🄰🄰 ▼▼◆▼▼ **Hilton Times Square** 🄻🄷
(212) 840-8222. **$269-$899.** 234 W 42nd St. Between 7th and 8th aves. Int corridors. **Pets:** Accepted.
🅂🄰🅅🄴 ✕ 🅑M 🖉 🗕 🗎 🖃 🍴

🄰🄰🄰 ▼▼◆▼▼ **The Holiday Inn Martinique on Broadway** 🄢🄷
(212) 736-3800. **$269-$699.** 49 W 32nd St. Corner of Broadway. Int corridors. **Pets:** Small, dogs only. $25 daily fee/pet. Service with restrictions, supervision.
🅂🄰🅅🄴 ✕ 🅑M 🖉 🗎 🖃 🍴

▼◆▼ ▼◆▼ **Hotel Gansevoort** 🄢🄷 🐾
(212) 206-6700. **$325-$545.** 18 9th Ave. At 13th St. Int corridors. **Pets:** Small. $65 one-time fee/room. Service with restrictions, crate.
🄰🅂🄺 ✕ 🅑M 🖉 🗕 🍴 🏊

▼◆▼ ▼◆▼ **Hotel Plaza Athenee** 🄢🄷 🐾
(212) 734-9100. **$555-$770.** 37 E 64th St. Between Madison and Park aves. Int corridors. **Pets:** Small. Designated rooms, service with restrictions.
✕ 🗕 🗎 🍴 ✕

🄰🄰🄰 ▼▼◆▼▼ **Hotel Wales** 🄢🄷
(212) 876-6000. **$209-$399.** 1295 Madison Ave. Between 92nd and 93rd sts E. Int corridors. **Pets:** Accepted.
🅂🄰🅅🄴 ✕ 🖉 🗎 🍴 ✕

🄰🄰🄰 ▼▼◆▼▼ **Jolly Hotel Madison Towers** 🄻🄷
(212) 802-0600. **$245-$575.** 22 E 38th St. Between Park and Madison aves. Int corridors. **Pets:** Small, dogs only. Service with restrictions, supervision.
🅂🄰🅅🄴 ✕ 🗕 🖃 🍴

▼◆▼ ▼◆▼ **Le Parker Meridien New York** 🄻🄷
(212) 245-5000. **$560-$1500.** 118 W 57th St. Between 6th (Ave of the Americas) and 7th aves; vehicle entrance on 56th St. Int corridors. **Pets:** Accepted.
🄰🅂🄺 ✕ 🖉 🗕 🗎 🍴 🏊 ✕

▼▼◆▼▼ ▼◆▼ **The Lowell Hotel** 🄢🄷
(212) 838-1400. **$495-$6000.** 28 E 63rd St. Between Park and Madison aves. Int corridors. **Pets:** Accepted.
✕ 🖉 🗎 🖃 🍴 ✕

▼▼◆▼▼ **Mandarin Oriental, New York** 🄻🄷
(212) 805-8800. **$725-$1185, 3 day notice.** 80 Columbus Circle at 60th St. At 60th St. Int corridors. **Pets:** Accepted.
✕ 🖉 🗕 🍴 🏊

▼◆▼ ▼◆▼ **The Mark, New York** 🄢🄷 🐾
(212) 744-4300. **$570-$960.** 25 E 77th St. Madison Ave at E 77th St. Int corridors. **Pets:** Small, dogs only. Service with restrictions, supervision.
✕ 🖉 🍴 ✕

🄰🄰🄰 ▼▼◆▼▼ **Millennium Broadway** 🄻🄷
(212) 768-4400. **$419-$559.** 145 W 44th St. Between 6th (Ave of the Americas) and 7th aves; in Times Square. Int corridors. **Pets:** Medium. Designated rooms, service with restrictions, supervision.
🅂🄰🅅🄴 🅂🕭 ✕ 🅑M 🖉 🗕 🗎 🖃 🍴

🄰🄰🄰 ▼▼◆▼▼ ▼◆▼ **The Muse Hotel** 🄢🄷 🐾
(212) 485-2400. **$269-$459.** 130 W 46th St. Between 6th (Ave of the Americas) and 7th aves. Int corridors. **Pets:** Other species. Service with restrictions, crate.
🅂🄰🅅🄴 ✕ 🗕 🗎 🖃 🍴

▼▼◆▼▼ **New York Marriott Marquis** 🄻🄷
(212) 398-1900. **$259-$619.** 1535 Broadway. Between 45th and 46th sts; motor entrance on 46th St. Int corridors. **Pets:** Accepted.
🄰🅂🄺 ✕ 🗕 🖃 🍴

🄰🄰🄰 ▼▼◆▼▼ **The New York Palace** 🄻🄷
(212) 888-7000. **$520-$685.** 455 Madison Ave. Between 50th and 51st sts. Int corridors. **Pets:** Accepted.
🅂🄰🅅🄴 🅂🕭 ✕ 🅑M 🖉 🗕 🗎 🖃 🍴 ✕

🄰🄰🄰 ▼▼◆▼▼ **Novotel New York** 🄻🄷 🐾
(212) 315-0100. **$179-$349.** 226 W 52nd St. At Broadway. Int corridors. **Pets:** Medium. Service with restrictions, crate.
🅂🄰🅅🄴 🅂🕭 ✕ 🖉 🍴

▼▼◆▼▼ ▼◆▼ **Omni Berkshire Place** 🄻🄷
(212) 753-5800. **$389-$589.** 21 E 52nd St. Between Madison and 5th aves. Int corridors. **Pets:** Accepted.
🄰🅂🄺 🅂🕭 ✕ 🅑M 🖉 🗕 🗎 🍴

▼▼◆▼▼ ▼◆▼ **On The Ave Hotel** 🄢🄷
(212) 362-1100. **$209-$279.** 2178 Broadway. At 77th St. Int corridors. **Pets:** Accepted.
🄰🅂🄺 ✕ 🗎 🖃

🄰🄰🄰 ▼▼◆▼▼ **The Peninsula New York** 🄻🄷 🐾
(212) 956-2888. **$560-$790.** 700 5th Ave. At 55th St. Int corridors. **Pets:** Very small.
🅂🄰🅅🄴 ✕ 🖉 🗕 🗎 🍴 🏊 ✕

▼▼◆▼▼ ▼◆▼ **The Pierre New York-a Taj Hotel** 🄻🄷
(212) 838-8000. **$600-$1400.** 2 E 61st St. At 5th Ave. Int corridors. **Pets:** Accepted.
✕ 🅑M 🗕 🗎 🍴 ✕

🄰🄰🄰 ▼▼◆▼▼ **The Regency Hotel** 🄻🄷
(212) 759-4100. **$359-$1500.** 540 Park Ave. At 61st St. Int corridors. **Pets:** Accepted.
🅂🄰🅅🄴 🅂🕭 ✕ 🅑M 🖉 🗕 🗎 🍴

🄰🄰🄰 ▼▼◆▼▼ ▼◆▼ **Renaissance New York Hotel Times Square** 🐾
(212) 765-7676. **$279-$619.** 2 Times Square, 7th Ave at W 48th St. Broadway and 7th Ave; auto access from 7th Ave, s of W 48th St. Int corridors. **Pets:** Medium, dogs only. $50 one-time fee/room. Service with restrictions, crate.
🅂🄰🅅🄴 ✕ 🖉 🖃 🍴

🄰🄰🄰 ▼▼◆▼▼ ▼◆▼ **The Ritz-Carlton New York, Battery Park** 🄢🄷
(212) 344-0800. **$550-$850.** Two West St. Jct Battery Pl. Int corridors. **Pets:** Accepted.
🅂🄰🅅🄴 ✕ 🅑M 🖉 🗕 🗎 🍴

🄰🄰🄰 ▼▼◆▼▼ **The Ritz-Carlton New York, Central Park** 🄻🄷 🐾
(212) 308-9100. **$750-$775.** 50 Central Park S. Between 5th and 6th (Ave of the Americas) aves. Int corridors. **Pets:** Medium. $125 one-time fee/pet. Supervision.
🅂🄰🅅🄴 ✕ 🅑M 🖉 🗕 🗎 🍴

ꚖꚖꚖ Royalton 🄻🄷
(212) 869-4400. **$250-$550.** 44 W 44th St. Between 5th and 6th (Ave of the Americas) aves. Int corridors. **Pets:** Accepted.

✕ 🤙 🍴

🅰🅰🅰 ꚖꚖꚖꚖ The St. Regis New York 🄻🄷
(212) 753-4500. **$695-$975.** 2 E 55th St. Between Madison and 5th aves. Int corridors. **Pets:** Accepted.

🆂🅰🆅🅴 ✕ 🤙 🎱 🍴 ✕

ꚖꚖꚖ Shelburne Murray Hill Hotel 🆂🄷
(212) 689-5200. **$249-$549.** 303 Lexington Ave. Between 37th and 38th sts. Int corridors. **Pets:** Accepted.

🅰🆂🅺 ✕ 🤙 🎱 📟 🍴

ꚖꚖꚖ Sheraton Manhattan Hotel 🄻🄷
(212) 581-3300. **$179-$299.** 790 7th Ave. Between 51st and 52nd sts. Int corridors. **Pets:** Accepted.

🅰🆂🅺 🆂 ✕ 🤙 🤙 🎱 📟 🍴 🏊 ✕

ꚖꚖꚖ Sheraton New York Hotel & Towers 🄻🄷
(212) 581-1000. **$179-$299.** 811 7th Ave. At 52nd St. Int corridors. **Pets:** Accepted.

🅰🆂🅺 🆂 ✕ 🤙 🎱 📟 🍴 ✕

🅰🅰🅰 ꚖꚖꚖꚖ Sofitel New York 🄻🄷
(212) 354-8844. **$379-$709.** 45 W 44th St. Between 5th and 6th (Ave of the Americas) aves. Int corridors. **Pets:** Medium. Service with restrictions, crate.

🆂🅰🆅🅴 ✕ 🤙 🎱 📟 🍴

ꚖꚖꚖ The SoHo Grand Hotel 🆂🄷
(212) 965-3000. **$309-$3500.** 310 W Broadway. In SoHo; jct Grand St. Int corridors. **Pets:** Accepted.

✕ 🎱 🍴

🅰🅰🅰 ꚖꚖꚖꚖ Surrey Hotel 🆂🄷
(212) 288-3700. **$299-$649.** 20 E 76th St. E 76th St and Madison Ave. Int corridors. **Pets:** Accepted.

🆂🅰🆅🅴 ✕ 🤙 🎱 📟 🍴

🅰🅰🅰 ꚖꚖꚖꚖ Swissotel The Drake, New York 🆂🄷
(212) 421-0900. **$239-$2000.** 440 Park Ave. At 56th St; between Park and Madison aves. Int corridors. **Pets:** Accepted.

🆂🅰🆅🅴 🆂 ✕ 🤙 🎱 📟 🍴 ✕

ꚖꚖꚖ Tribeca Grand Hotel 🆂🄷
(212) 519-6600. **$309-$2300.** 2 Ave of the Americas. At 6th Ave (Ave of the Americas) and White St. Int corridors. **Pets:** Accepted.

✕ 🎱 🍴

ꚖꚖꚖꚖ Trump International Hotel & Tower 🆂🄷
(212) 299-1000. **$645-$735.** 1 Central Park W. Jct Central Park S; at Columbus Circle. Int corridors. **Pets:** Accepted.

✕ 🤙 🎱 📟 🍴 🏊 ✕

ꚖꚖꚖ The Wall Street District Hotel 🄻🄷
(212) 232-7700. **$199-$469.** 15 Gold St. Corner of Gold and Platt sts. Int corridors. **Pets:** Accepted.

🅰🆂🅺 🆂 ✕ 🤙 🎱 📟 🍴

🅰🅰🅰 ꚖꚖꚖꚖ The Westin New York at Times Square 🄻🄷
(212) 201-2700. **$529-$739.** 270 W 43rd St. Corner of 8th Ave. Int corridors. **Pets:** Accepted.

🆂🅰🆅🅴 🆂 ✕ 🤙 🎱 📟 🍴 ✕

ꚖꚖꚖ W New York 🄻🄷
(212) 755-1200. **$429-$519.** 541 Lexington Ave. At 49th St. Int corridors. **Pets:** Accepted.

🅰🆂🅺 🆂 ✕ 🤙 🤙 🎱 📟 🍴

ꚖꚖꚖ W New York Times Square 🄻🄷
(212) 930-7400. **$429-$519.** 1567 Broadway at 47th St. Corner of 47th St. Int corridors. **Pets:** Accepted.

🅰🆂🅺 🆂 ✕ 🤙 🤙 🎱 📟 🍴

ꚖꚖꚖ W New York-Union Square 🆂🄷
(212) 253-9119. **$549-$649.** 201 Park Ave S. At 17th St. Int corridors. **Pets:** Accepted.

✕ 🤙 🤙 🎱 📟 🍴

## PEEKSKILL

🅰🅰🅰 ꚖꚖ Peekskill Inn 🅼
(914) 739-1500. **$125-$140.** 634 Main St. Jct US 6 and 9, e to top of Main St. Ext corridors. **Pets:** Accepted.

🆂🅰🆅🅴 🆂 ✕ 🎱 🍴 🏊

## RYE BROOK

🅰🅰🅰 ꚖꚖꚖ Hilton Rye Town 🄻🄷
(914) 939-6300. **$119-$369.** 699 Westchester Ave. I-287 (Cross Westchester Expwy), exit 10 eastbound, 0.6 mi ne on SR 120A; exit westbound, 0.3 mi n on Webb Ave, then 0.4 mi ne on SR 120A. Int corridors. **Pets:** Small, other species. $50 one-time fee/room. Designated rooms, service with restrictions, supervision.

🆂🅰🆅🅴 ✕ 🤙 🤙 🎱 📟 🍴 🏊 ✕

## STATEN ISLAND

🅰🅰🅰 ꚖꚖꚖ Hilton Garden Inn Staten Island 🆂🄷 🐾
(718) 477-2400. **$159-$199.** 1100 South Ave. I-278, exit 6 (South Ave) westbound, just s; exit 5 eastbound to SR 440 S, exit South Ave, just s to South Ave, 1 mi n to Lois Ln, then just w. Int corridors. **Pets:** Medium. $35 daily fee/pet. Service with restrictions, supervision.

🆂🅰🆅🅴 ✕ 🤙 🎱 📟 🍴 🏊 ✕

🅰🅰🅰 ꚖꚖꚖ The Staten Island Hotel 🄻🄷
(718) 698-5000. **$154-$159.** 1415 Richmond Ave. I-278, exit Richmond Ave, 0.5 mi se. Int corridors. **Pets:** Other species. Designated rooms, service with restrictions, supervision.

🆂🅰🆅🅴 🆂 ✕ 🎱 📟 🍴

## SUFFERN

🅰🅰🅰 ꚖꚖꚖ Wellesley Inn (Suffern) 🆂🄷
(845) 368-1900. **$99-$109.** 17 N Airmont Rd. I-87 (New York State Thruway), exit 14B, just s. Int corridors. **Pets:** Accepted.

🆂🅰🆅🅴 🆂 ✕ 🤙 🎱 📟

## WHITE PLAINS

🅰🅰🅰 ꚖꚖꚖ Renaissance Westchester Hotel 🄻🄷
(914) 694-5400. **$129-$279.** 80 W Red Oak Ln. I-287 (Cross Westchester Expwy), exit 9N-S eastbound, 0.5 mi e on Westchester Ave, just n on Kenilworth Rd, then 0.7 mi w on Westchester Ave; exit westbound, 0.8 mi w on Westchester Ave. Int corridors. **Pets:** Accepted.

🆂🅰🆅🅴 🆂 ✕ 🤙 🤙 🎱 📟 🍴 🏊 ✕

ꚖꚖꚖ Summerfield Suites By Wyndham-Westchester 🆂🄷
(914) 251-9700. **$149-$239.** 101 Corporate Park Dr. I-287 (Cross Westchester Expwy), exit 9A eastbound, 0.6 mi e on Westchester Ave, then 0.3 mi n; exit 9N-S westbound, 0.9 mi w on Westchester Ave. Int corridors. **Pets:** Accepted.

🅰🆂🅺 ✕ 🤙 🎱 📟 🍴 ✕

## END METROPOLITAN AREA

# NIAGARA FALLS METROPOLITAN AREA

## LOCKPORT

### ▼▼▼▼ Holiday Inn Lockport SH
(716) 434-6151. **$80-$130.** 515 S Transit Rd. 1 mi s on SR 78. Int corridors. **Pets:** $10 daily fee/pet. Service with restrictions.

ASK SO X GM 🔌 📶 🔋 💻 🍴 ➡

## NEWFANE

### ▼ Lake Ontario Motel M
(716) 778-5004. **$55-$84.** 3330 Lockport-Olcott Rd. 2.5 mi n of jct SR 104 on SR 78. Int corridors. **Pets:** Other species. $5 daily fee/room. Service with restrictions, supervision.

ASK X 🔋

## NIAGARA FALLS

### ▼▼▼ Best Western Summit Inn SH
(716) 297-5050. **$79-$139, 7 day notice.** 9500 Niagara Falls Blvd. I-190, exit 22, 2.1 mi e on US 62 S. Int corridors. **Pets:** Accepted.

SAVE SO X 🔋 💻 ➡

### ▼ Budget Host Inn M
(716) 283-3839. **$39-$179.** 6621 Niagara Falls Blvd. I-190, exit 22, just e on US 62 S. Ext corridors. **Pets:** Small. $8 daily fee/room. Service with restrictions, supervision.

SAVE SO X 🔋 ➡

### ▼▼▼ Howard Johnson Hotel-Closest to the Falls and Casino SH ❀
(716) 285-5261. **$49-$255.** 454 Main St. I-190, exit 21 (Robert Moses Pkwy) to City Traffic exit, just n to Niagara St, then just w to SR 104 (Main St). Int corridors. **Pets:** Other species. $10 daily fee/pet. Service with restrictions, supervision.

SAVE SO X GM 🔋 💻 ➡

### ▼▼ Quality Hotel and Suites "At the Falls" SH
(716) 282-1212. **$79-$299.** 240 Rainbow Blvd. I-190, exit 21 (Robert Moses Pkwy), eastbound use City Traffic exit, just w; downtown. Int corridors. **Pets:** Large. $20 daily fee/pet. Designated rooms, service with restrictions, supervision.

ASK SO X 🔌 🔋 💻 🍴 ➡

### ▼ Thriftlodge M
(716) 297-2660. **$39-$110.** 9401 Niagara Falls Blvd. I-190, exit 22, 1.8 mi e. Ext corridors. **Pets:** Very small, dogs only. $20 daily fee/pet. Service with restrictions, supervision.

SAVE SO X 🔋 ➡

# END METROPOLITAN AREA

## NORTH SYRACUSE

### ▼▼▼▼ Candlewood Suites Syracuse Airport SH
(315) 454-8999. **$109-$159, 3 day notice.** 5414 South Bay Rd. I-90, exit 36; I-81, exit 26 (Mattydale Rd), follow South Bay Rd signs, just n. Int corridors. **Pets:** Medium. $100 deposit/room. Service with restrictions, crate.

ASK SO X 🔌 🔋 💻

### ▼▼▼▼ Comfort Inn & Suites/Syracuse Airport SH
(315) 457-4000. **$79-$149.** 6701 Buckley Rd. I-81, exit 25 (7th North St), 0.8 mi w; I-90, exit 36. Int corridors. **Pets:** Medium. $10 daily fee/room. Service with restrictions, supervision.

ASK SO X 🔌 🔋 💻 🍴 ➡ ❌

### ▼▼▼ Quality Inn North M
(315) 451-1212. **$79-$169.** 1308 Buckley Rd. I-81, exit 25 (7th North St), 0.3 mi w, then just n. Ext/int corridors. **Pets:** Accepted.

SAVE SO X 🔋 💻 🍴 ➡

## NORWICH

### ▼▼ Howard Johnson Hotel SH
(607) 334-2200. **$95-$179.** 75 N Broad St. On SR 12; downtown. Int corridors. **Pets:** Accepted.

ASK SO X 🔋 💻 🍴 ➡

### ▼▼ Super 8 Motel of Norwich SH
(607) 336-8880. **$60-$88, 7 day notice.** 6067 State Hwy 12. On SR 12, 0.9 mi n. Int corridors. **Pets:** Medium. $5 daily fee/pet. Service with restrictions, supervision.

ASK SO X 🔋 💻

## OGDENSBURG

### ▼▼▼▼ Quality Inn Gran-View M
(315) 393-4550. **$85-$150.** 6765 State Hwy 37. On SR 37, 3 mi sw. Ext/int corridors. **Pets:** Large, other species. $10 one-time fee/pet. Designated rooms, service with restrictions.

SAVE SO X 🔋 💻 🍴 ➡ ❌

### ▼▼▼ The Stonefence Resort & Motel M
(315) 393-1545. **$69-$179.** 7191 SR 7. Jct SR 68, 0.5 mi w. Ext/int corridors. **Pets:** Medium. $22 one-time fee/pet. Designated rooms, service with restrictions, supervision.

SAVE SO X 🔋 💻 🍴 ➡ 🔳

## OLD FORGE

### ▼▼ Best Western Sunset Inn M
(315) 369-6836. **$69-$209, 7 day notice.** 2752 SR 28. 0.3 mi s. Ext/int corridors. **Pets:** Accepted.

ASK SO X 🔋 ➡ ❌

## ONEONTA

### ▼▼▼▼ Holiday Inn Oneonta/Cooperstown Area SH
(607) 433-2250. **$79-$209.** 5206 State Hwy 23. I-88, exit 15 (SR 23 and 28), 1.5 mi e. Int corridors. **Pets:** Accepted.

SAVE SO X 🔌 🔋 💻 🍴 ➡ ❌

### ▼▼ Super 8 Motel SH
(607) 432-9505. **$56-$149.** 4973 SR 23. I-88, exit 15 (SR 23 and 28), 0.3 mi e. Int corridors. **Pets:** Other species. Service with restrictions, supervision.

ASK SO X GM 🔋

## OWEGO

### ▼▼▼ Sunrise Motel M
(607) 687-5667. **$56-$59.** 3778 Waverly Rd. SR 17, exit 64 (SR 96 N) across river w to SR 17C, 2 mi w. Ext corridors. **Pets:** Very small. $7 daily fee/room. Service with restrictions, crate.

SAVE SO X

## PAINTED POST

### ▼▼▼ Best Western Lodge on the Green M
(607) 962-2456. **$50-$100.** 3171 Canada Rd. SR 17, exit 44, just s on US 15 to SR 417 and Gang Mills exit, then just n. Ext corridors. **Pets:** Other species. Service with restrictions, crate.

SAVE X 🔋 💻 🍴 ➡

▼▼ ▼▼ Econo Lodge 🆂🅷
(607) 962-4444. **$57-$95.** 200 Robert Dann Dr. Jct US 15 and SR 17, exit 44, s to Gang Mills exit. Int corridors. **Pets:** Other species. $10 one-time fee/pet. Service with restrictions, supervision.

A$K 🆂 ✕ ⚕M ⬛ 🖥 🖵

🅰 ▼▼ Erwin Motel Ⓜ
(607) 962-7411. **$42-$79, 4 day notice.** 806 Addison Rd. US 15, exit Erwin Addison, 0.5 mi e. Ext corridors. **Pets:** Dogs only. $10 daily fee/pet. Designated rooms, service with restrictions, supervision.

SAVE ✕ 🖥 🖵

# PEMBROKE

▼▼ ▼▼ Darien Lakes Econo Lodge 🆂🅷 ❀
(585) 599-4681. **$44-$129.** 8493 SR 77. I-90, exit 48A, just s. Int corridors. **Pets:** Other species. Designated rooms, service with restrictions, supervision.

A$K 🆂 ✕ 🖥 🖵

# PENN YAN

▼▼▼ ▼▼ Best Western Vineyard Inn & Suites 🆂🅷
(315) 536-8473. **$89.** 142 Lake St. I-90, exit 43, SR 14 S to SR 54 N; corner of SR 54 and 14A. Int corridors. **Pets:** Accepted.

A$K 🆂 ✕ 🖥 🖵 🖵

# PINE VALLEY

🅰 ▼▼ ▼▼ Best Western Marshall Manor Ⓜ
(607) 739-3891. **$55-$90.** 3527 Watkins Rd. SR 17, exit 52, 5 mi n on SR 14. Ext corridors. **Pets:** Accepted.

SAVE 🆂 ✕ 🖥 🖵 🖵

# PLAINVIEW

▼▼▼ ▼▼ Residence Inn by Marriott 🆂🅷
(516) 433-6200. **$199-$229.** 9 Gerhard Rd. I-495, exit 44, 1.6 mi s on SR 135, exit 10, then just e on Old Country Rd. Int corridors. **Pets:** Accepted.

✕ ⚕M ⬛ 🖥 🖵 🖵 🏊 🖵

# PLATTSBURGH

🅰 ▼▼▼ ▼▼ Baymont Inn & Suites Plattsburgh 🆂🅷
(518) 562-4000. **$73-$115.** 16 Plaza Blvd. I-87, exit 37, just w. Int corridors. **Pets:** Medium. Service with restrictions.

SAVE ✕ ⚕M ⬛ 🖥 🖵

🅰 ▼▼ ▼▼ Best Western The Inn at Smithfield 🆂🅷 ❀
(518) 561-7750. **$69-$129.** 446 Rt 3. I-87, exit 37, just w. Int corridors. **Pets:** Other species. $10 one-time fee/room. Designated rooms, service with restrictions, crate.

SAVE 🆂 ✕ ⬛ 🖥 🖵 🖵 🏊 🖵

▼▼ ▼▼ Microtel Inn and Suites 🆂🅷
(518) 324-3800. **$49-$84, 3 day notice.** 554 SR 3. I-87, exit 37, just w. Int corridors. **Pets:** Accepted.

A$K ✕ ⚕M ⬛ 🖥 🖵

🅰 ▼▼▼ Quality Inn Ⓜ ❀
(518) 563-0222. **$55-$99.** 19 Booth Dr. I-87, exit 37, just w. Ext corridors. **Pets:** Dogs only. $25 deposit/room. Service with restrictions, supervision.

SAVE 🆂 ✕ 🖥 🖵

▼▼ Super 8 Motel Ⓜ
(518) 562-8888. **$49-$75.** 7129 Rt 9 N. I-87, exit 39, just e, then just n. Int corridors. **Pets:** Dogs only. $10 daily fee/pet. Designated rooms, service with restrictions, supervision.

A$K ✕ ⚕M ⬛ 🖥 🖵

# PORT JERVIS

🅰 ▼▼ ▼▼ Comfort Inn 🆂🅷
(845) 856-6611. **$99-$149.** 2247 Greenville Tpke. I-84, exit 1, just se. Int corridors. **Pets:** Accepted.

SAVE 🆂 ✕ ⬛ 🖥 🖵 🖵

# POUGHKEEPSIE

🅰 ▼▼▼ ▼▼ Best Western Inn & Conference Center 🆂🅷
(845) 462-4600. **$90-$170.** 2170 South Rd (US 9). Jct US 44 and SR 55, 4.7 mi s. Int corridors. **Pets:** Other species. $50 deposit/room. Supervision.

SAVE 🆂 ✕ ⬛ 🖥 🖵 🖵

▼▼ ▼▼ Econo Lodge 🆂🅷
(845) 452-6600. **$80-$135.** 2625 US 9. I-84, exit 13N, 1.6 mi s of Mid-Hudson Bridge. Ext corridors. **Pets:** Accepted.

A$K 🆂 ✕ ⚕M ⬛ 🖥 🖵

# PULASKI

🅰 ▼▼ Redwood Motel Ⓜ ❀
(315) 298-4717. **$57-$69.** 3723 SR 13. I-81, exit 36, just e. Ext/int corridors. **Pets:** $20 deposit/room. Designated rooms, service with restrictions, supervision.

SAVE ✕ ⬛ 🖥 🖵 🖵

# RHINEBECK

▼▼▼ ▼▼ Beekman Arms & Delamater Inn and Conference Center 🅲�🅸
(845) 876-7077. **$100-$200, 14 day notice.** 6387 Mill St (Rt 9). Jct US 9 and SR 308; center of village. Ext/int corridors. **Pets:** Accepted.

✕ 🐾 🖥 🖵 🖵

# RICHMONDVILLE

▼▼ ▼▼ Econo Lodge Cobleskill/Richmondville Ⓜ
(518) 294-7739. **$70-$100.** 555 Ploss Rd. I-88, exit 20, just e on SR 7, then just s. Ext corridors. **Pets:** Accepted.

A$K 🆂 ✕ ⬛ 🖥

# RIVERHEAD

▼▼▼ ▼▼ Best Western East End 🆂🅷
(631) 369-2200. **$169-$249, 3 day notice.** 1830 SR 25. I-495, exit 72 (SR 25 E). Int corridors. **Pets:** Medium. $50 daily fee/pet. Designated rooms, service with restrictions, supervision.

A$K 🆂 ✕ 🐾 ⬛ 🖥 🖵 🖵

# ROCK HILL

🅰 ▼▼▼ ▼▼ The Lodge at Rock Hill 🆂🅷 ❀
(845) 796-3100. **$99-$239.** 283 Rock Hill Dr. SR 17, exit 109, just e. Int corridors. **Pets:** Other species. $25 one-time fee/pet. Service with restrictions, supervision.

SAVE 🆂 ✕ 🖊 🐾 ⬛ 🖥 🖵 🖵 🏊 🖵

# ROCKVILLE CENTRE

🅰 ▼▼▼ ▼▼ Best Western Mill River Manor 🆂🅷
(516) 678-1300. **$109-$136.** 173 Sunrise Hwy. On SR 27; between N Village and N Centre aves. Ext corridors. **Pets:** Other species. $15 daily fee/pet.

SAVE 🆂 ✕ ⚕M 🖊 🐾 ⬛ 🖥 🖵 🖵

# ROME

▼▼ Adirondack Thirteen Pines Motel Ⓜ ❀
(315) 337-4930. **$45-$65, 3 day notice.** 7353 River Rd. Jct SR 49, 0.5 mi e on SR 365. Ext corridors. **Pets:** Other species. No service, supervision.

A$K 🆂 ✕ ⬛ 🖵 🖵

**AAA** ◆◆◆◆ **Inn at the Beeches** **M**
(315) 336-1776. **$79-$195.** 7900 Turin Rd. Jct SR 46, 2 mi n on SR 26 (Turin Rd). Ext corridors. **Pets:** Small. $10 daily fee/pet. Designated rooms, service with restrictions, supervision.
[SAVE] [S◆] [✕] [♿] [🛏] [≈]

**AAA** ◆◆◆ **Quality Inn of Rome** **SH**
(315) 336-4300. **$90-$150.** 200 S James St. On SR 49; downtown. Ext/int corridors. **Pets:** Medium. $25 daily fee/pet. Designated rooms, service with restrictions, crate.
[SAVE] [S◆] [✕] [♿] [💻] [🛏] [≈]

# ROSCOE

**AAA** ◆◆ **Roscoe Motel** **M**
(607) 498-5220. **$55-$75, 7 day notice.** 2054 Old Rt 17. SR 17, exit 94, 0.5 mi n on SR 206, then just w. Ext corridors. **Pets:** Accepted.
[SAVE] [♿] [💻]

# ROTTERDAM

◆◆ ◆◆ **Super 8 Schenectady** **SH**
(518) 355-2190. **$55-$85.** 3083 Carman Rd. I-890, exit 9 (Curry Rd), 0.4 mi w; I-90, exit 25. Int corridors. **Pets:** Accepted.
[ASK] [S◆] [✕]

# SACKETS HARBOR

◆◆ ◆◆ **Ontario Place Hotel** **SH**
(315) 646-8000. **$79-$350.** 103 General Smith Dr. Center. Int corridors. **Pets:** Other species. $10 one-time fee/room. Designated rooms, service with restrictions, supervision.
[✕] [♿] [💻]

# SALAMANCA

◆◆◆◆ **Holiday Inn Express Hotel & Suites** **SH** 🐾
(716) 945-7600. **$100-$150.** 779 Broad St. I-86, exit 20, just n. Int corridors. **Pets:** Other species. $25 one-time fee/room. Designated rooms, service with restrictions, supervision.
[ASK] [S◆] [✕] [♿] [📶] [♿] [💻] [🛏]

# SARANAC LAKE

**AAA** ◆◆ **Adirondack Motel** **M**
(518) 891-2116. **$60-$160.** 248 Lake Flower Ave. 0.7 mi e on SR 86. Ext corridors. **Pets:** Dogs only. $10 daily fee/room. Service with restrictions, crate.
[SAVE] [✕] [♿] [💻] [✕]

**AAA** ◆◆◆ **Best Western Mountain Lake Inn** **SH**
(518) 891-1970. **$74-$170.** 487 Lake Flower Ave. 0.8 mi e on SR 86. Int corridors. **Pets:** $20 one-time fee/pet. Designated rooms, service with restrictions, supervision.
[SAVE] [S◆] [✕] [♿] [💻] [🛏] [≈]

**AAA** ◆◆ ◆◆ **The Hotel Saranac of Paul Smith's College** **SH**
(518) 891-2200. **$62-$112, 3 day notice.** 100 Main St. Center. Int corridors. **Pets:** Other species. $15 daily fee/pet. Designated rooms, service with restrictions, supervision.
[SAVE] [S◆] [✕] [📶] [♿] [💻] [🛏]

◆◆ **Lake Flower Inn** **M**
(518) 891-2310. **$48-$128, 14 day notice.** 234 Lake Flower Ave. 0.6 mi e on SR 86. Ext corridors. **Pets:** Dogs only. Designated rooms, supervision.
[✕] [♿] [≈] [✕]

# SARATOGA SPRINGS

**AAA** ◆◆◆◆ **Holiday Inn** **SH**
(518) 584-4550. **$109-$549, 3 day notice.** 232 Broadway. On US 9, jct SR 50. Int corridors. **Pets:** Other species. Service with restrictions, crate.
[SAVE] [S◆] [✕] [📶] [♿] [💻] [🛏] [≈]

◆◆◆◆ **Residence Inn by Marriott-Saratoga Springs** **LH**
(518) 584-9600. **Call for rates.** 295 Excelsior Ave. I-87, exit 15, Just n, just s, then just e. Int corridors. **Pets:** Accepted.
[✕] [♿] [♿] [♿] [💻] [≈] [✕]

◆◆ **Saratoga Motel** **M**
(518) 584-0920. **$69-$189, 14 day notice.** 440 Church St. On SR 9N, 2.3 mi w of jct US 9/SR 50. Ext corridors. **Pets:** Accepted.
[ASK] [S◆] [✕] [♿] [💻]

◆◆ **Super 8 Motel** **SH**
(518) 287-6244. **Call for rates.** 17 Old Gick Rd. I-87, exit 15, just e, then just n. Int corridors. **Pets:** Large, other species. Service with restrictions, crate.
[♿] [♿] [♿]

**AAA** ◆◆◆◆ **Union Gables Bed & Breakfast** **BB**
(518) 584-1558. **$140-$410, 14 day notice.** 55 Union Ave. I-87, exit 14, 1.5 mi w. Int corridors. **Pets:** Large, dogs only. $25 one-time fee/pet. Designated rooms, service with restrictions, supervision.
[SAVE] [✕] [♿]

# SAUGERTIES

**AAA** ◆◆ ◆◆ **Comfort Inn** **SH** 🐾
(845) 246-1565. **$89-$159, 14 day notice.** 2790 SR 32. I-87, exit 20, just n. Int corridors. **Pets:** Other species. $25 one-time fee/room. Service with restrictions, supervision.
[SAVE] [S◆] [✕] [♿] [💻]

# SCHENECTADY

◆◆ ◆◆ **Days Inn** **SH**
(518) 370-3297. **$69-$99.** 167 Nott Terrace. Jct State St (SR 5) and Nott Terrace, 2 blks e; downtown. Int corridors. **Pets:** Accepted.
[ASK] [S◆] [✕] [📶] [♿] [💻]

# SCHROON LAKE

**AAA** ◆◆ **Blue Ridge Motel** **M** 🐾
(518) 532-7521. **$85-$95, 21 day notice.** 2455 US Rt 9. I-87, exit 28, 4 mi n. Ext/int corridors. **Pets:** $10 daily fee/pet. Service with restrictions, supervision.
[SAVE] [S◆] [✕] [♿] [💻] [🛏] [📷]

# SCHUYLERVILLE

◆◆ ◆◆ **Burgoyne Motor Inn** **M**
(518) 695-3282. **$49-$145, 3 day notice.** 220 Broad St. US 4 and SR 32, just n of jct SR 29. Ext/int corridors. **Pets:** Small, dogs only. Service with restrictions, supervision.
[ASK] [✕] [♿] [♿] [💻]

# SKANEATELES

**AAA** ◆◆◆◆ **Skaneateles Suites** **M**
(315) 685-7568. **$75-$299, 10 day notice.** 4114 W Genesee St. On US 20, 2 mi w. Ext corridors. **Pets:** Other species. $35 one-time fee/pet. Designated rooms, service with restrictions.
[SAVE] [S◆] [✕] [♿] [💻]

# SOLVAY

◆◆ ◆◆ **Comfort Inn Fairgrounds** **SH**
(315) 453-0045. **$79-$179.** 7010 Interstate Island Rd. I-90, exit 39 to I-690 E, exit 2 (Jones Rd), just sw. Int corridors. **Pets:** Other species. $15 one-time fee/room. Service with restrictions, supervision.
[ASK] [S◆] [✕] [♿] [💻]

◆◆ ◆◆ **Holiday Inn/Farrell Road** **SH**
(315) 457-8700. **$89-$149.** 100 Farrell Rd. I-90, exit 39 to I-690 E, exit John Glenn Blvd. Int corridors. **Pets:** Dogs only. $25 daily fee/pet. Service with restrictions, supervision.
[ASK] [S◆] [✕] [📶] [♿] [♿] [💻] [🛏] [≈]

## SOUTHAMPTON

**AAA** ▼▼▼▼ **Southampton Inn** SH ❖
(631) 283-6500. **$119-$489, 30 day notice.** 91 Hill St. 0.3 mi n from corner of Main St and Jobs Ln. Ext corridors. **Pets:** Other species. $39 daily fee/pet. Designated rooms, service with restrictions, supervision.
SAVE SÓ ⊠ 👁 🖥 🍽 ⚊ ⊠

## SYLVAN BEACH

▼▼ **Cinderella's Suites** M
(315) 762-4280. **$59-$179, 16 day notice.** 1208 N Main St. On SR 13; center. Ext corridors. **Pets:** Accepted.
ASK ⊠ 🖥 🍽

## SYRACUSE

**AAA** ▼▼▼▼ **Marx Hotel & Conference Centre** LH
(315) 479-7000. **$99-$145.** 701 E Genesee St. Jct Almond St; downtown. Int corridors. **Pets:** Medium. $50 daily fee/room. Designated rooms, service with restrictions, supervision.
SAVE SÓ ⊠ 👁M ⊘ 👁 🖥 🍽

**AAA** ▼▼▼▼ **Sheraton Syracuse University Hotel &**
**Conference Center** LH ❖
(315) 475-3000. **$139-$369.** 801 University Ave. I-81, exit 18. Int corridors. **Pets:** Medium, dogs only. Designated rooms, service with restrictions, supervision.
SAVE SÓ ⊠ 🖥 🍽 ⚊ ⊠

## TICONDEROGA

**AAA** ▼▼ **Circle Court Motel** M
(518) 585-7660. **$60-$79.** 6 Montcalm St. SR 9N; at Liberty Monument traffic circle. Ext corricors. **Pets:** $6 daily fee/pet. Service with restrictions, supervision.
SAVE SÓ ⊠ 🖥 🖥

## TROY

**AAA** ▼▼▼▼ **Best Western-Rensselaer Inn** SH
(518) 274-3210. **$89-$99.** 1800 6th Ave. I-787, exit 9, 0.5 mi e, exit downtown, then 0.5 mi s. Int corridors. **Pets:** Accepted.
SAVE SÓ ⊠ 🖥 🖥 🍽 ⚊

## TUPPER LAKE

**AAA** ▼ **Red Top Inn** M
(518) 359-9209. **$55-$30, 3 day notice.** 1562 SR 30. 3 mi s. Ext/int corridors. **Pets:** Accepted.
SAVE ⊠ 🖥 🖥

## UTICA

**AAA** ▼▼ **A-1 Motel** M
(315) 735-6698. **$45-$75.** 238 N Genesee St. I-90 (New York State Thruway), exit 31, just s. Int corridors. **Pets:** Small, dogs only. $10 deposit/room. Designated rooms, service with restrictions, crate.
SAVE SÓ ⊠ 🖥

▼▼ **Best Western Gateway Adirondack Inn** SH
(315) 732-4121. **$79-$159.** 175 N Genesee St. I-90 (New York State Thruway), exit 31, 0.5 mi s. Int corridors. **Pets:** Large. $10 one-time fee/room. Designated rooms, service with restrictions.
ASK SÓ ⊠ ⊘ 🖥 🖥

▼▼ **Red Roof Inn #7180** M
(315) 724-7128. **$52-$101.** 20 Weaver St. I-90 (New York State Thruway), exit 31. Ext corridors. **Pets:** Accepted.
⊠ 🖥

## VALATIE

**AAA** ▼ **Blue Spruce Inn & Suites** M ❖
(518) 758-9711. **$75-$100.** 3093 Rt 9. I-90 (New York State Thruway), exit 12, 4 mi s on US 9 via New York State Thruway Extension, exit B1. Ext corridors. **Pets:** Service with restrictions, supervision.
SAVE SÓ ⊠ 🖥 🖥 🍽 ⚊

## VESTAL

▼▼▼ **Holiday Inn at the University** SH
(607) 729-6371. **$79-$189.** 4105 Vestal Pkwy E. SR 17, exit 70, 2.5 mi s on US 201 to SR 434 W, then right on Bunn Hill Rd. Int corridors. **Pets:** Accepted.
ASK SÓ ⊠ 👁M 🖥 🖥 🍽 ⚊

## VICTOR

**AAA** ▼▼▼▼ **Hampton Inn and Suites-Rochester/Victor** SH
(585) 924-4400. **$129-$164.** 7637 SR 96. I-90 (New York State Thruway), exit 45, just n. Int corridors. **Pets:** Small. Service with restrictions, supervision.
SAVE SÓ ⊠ 👁 🖥 🖥 ⚊

## WARRENSBURG

▼▼ **Super 8 Warrensburg** M
(518) 623-2811. **$70-$165.** 3619 SR 9. I-87, exit 23, just w. Int corridors. **Pets:** Large, other species. $20 daily fee/pet. Designated rooms, service with restrictions, supervision.
ASK ⊠

## WATERLOO

**AAA** ▼▼▼▼ **Holiday Inn Waterloo-Seneca Falls** SH
(315) 539-5011. **$89-$229.** 2468 SR 414. I-90 (New York State Thruway), exit 41, 4 mi s; just n of jct SR 414/5 and US 20. Int corridors. **Pets:** Accepted.
SAVE ⊠ 🖥 🖥 🍽 ⚊ ⊠

**AAA** ▼▼▼ **Microtel Inn & Suites** SH
(315) 539-8438. **$51-$90.** 1966 Rt 5 & 20. I-90 (New York State Thruway), exit 41, 4 mi s on SR 414, then just e. Int corridors. **Pets:** $15 daily fee/room. Supervision.
SAVE ⊠ 👁M 👁 🖥 🖥

## WATERTOWN

**AAA** ▼▼ **Davidson's Motel** M ❖
(315) 782-3861. **$60.** 26177 NYS Rt 3. From Town Square, 3.5 mi e. Ext corridors. **Pets:** Medium, other species. $5 daily fee/pet. Service with restrictions.
SAVE ⊠ 🖥 ⚊

**AAA** ▼▼▼ **Ramada Inn** SH ❖
(315) 788-0700. **$82-$104.** 6300 Arsenal St. I-81, exit 45, just w. Int corridors. **Pets:** $100 deposit/room. Service with restrictions, supervision.
SAVE SÓ ⊠ 🖥 🖥 🍽 ⚊ ⊠

## WATKINS GLEN

**AAA** ▼▼▼ **Anchor Inn and Marina** M ❖
(607) 535-4159. **$59-$159, 10 day notice.** 3425 Salt Point Rd. just n on SR 14, 0.8 mi n. Ext corridors. **Pets:** Medium. $25 deposit/pet. Service with restrictions, supervision.
SAVE SÓ ⊠ 👁 🖥 ⊠

**AAA** ▼▼▼ **Chieftain Motel** M ❖
(607) 535-4759. **$59-$159, 10 day notice.** 3815 SR 14. Jct SR 14A; 3 mi n of town. Ext corridors. **Pets:** Medium. $25 deposit/pet. Service with restrictions, supervision.
SAVE SÓ ⊠ 👁 🖥 ⚊

# WELLSVILLE

**AAA** ◆ **Long Vue Inn & Suites** M
(585) 593-2450. **$54-$69.** 5081 Rt 417 W. Jct SR 19, 3 mi w. Ext corridors. **Pets:** Other species. Designated rooms, service with restrictions, supervision.
[SAVE] [S0] [X] [B] [≡]

◆◆ **Microtel Inn & Suites** SH
(585) 593-3449. **$49-$89.** 30 W Dyke St. Just n off SR 19 and 417. Int corridors. **Pets:** Other species. $10 daily fee/pet. Service with restrictions, supervision.
[ASK] [S0] [X] [&M] [&'] [B] [≡]

# WEST COXSACKIE

◆◆ **Best Western New Baltimore Inn** SH
(518) 731-8100. **$89-$139.** 12600 Rt 9W. I-87 (New York State Thruway), exit 21B, 0.5 mi s. Int corridors. **Pets:** Accepted.
[ASK] [S0] [X] [&'] [B] [≡] [≈] [X]

# WESTMORELAND

**AAA** ◆ **Carriage Motor Inn** M
(315) 853-3561. **$42-$65, 5 day notice.** 5370 SR 233. I-90 (New York State Thruway), exit 32, just n. Ext corridors. **Pets:** Medium. $5 daily fee/pet. Service with restrictions, supervision.
[SAVE] [S0] [X] [B]

# WILMINGTON

**AAA** ◆ **Grand View Motel** M
(518) 946-2209. **$59-$99.** 5941 NYS Rt 86. On SR 86, 1 mi e. Ext corridors. **Pets:** Accepted.
[SAVE] [S0] [X] [B] [≈] [X]

**AAA** ◆◆ **Hungry Trout Resort** M
(518) 946-2217. **$69-$149, 14 day notice.** 5239 Rt 86. On SR 86, 2 mi w. Ext corridors. **Pets:** Dogs only. $10 daily fee/pet. Service with restrictions, crate.
[SAVE] [X] [B] [≡] [¶] [≈] [X]

**AAA** ◆◆◆ **Ledge Rock at Whiteface Mountain** M
(518) 946-2379. **$79-$149, 10 day notice.** 5078 NYS Rt SR 86. On SR 86, 3 mi w. Ext corridors. **Pets:** $25 daily fee/pet. Service with restrictions, supervision.
[SAVE] [S0] [X] [B] [≡] [≈] [X]

◆◆ **Mountain Brook Lodge** M
(518) 946-2262. **$65-$99, 7 day notice.** 5712 Rt 86. Center. Ext corridors. **Pets:** Accepted.
[X] [B] [≡] [≈]

**AAA** ◆◆ **North Pole Motor Inn** M
(518) 946-7733. **$49-$139, 7 day notice.** 5636 NYS Rt 86. On SR 86, just w of jct CR 431. Ext corridors. **Pets:** Dogs only. $7 daily fee/pet. No service, supervision.
[SAVE] [S0] [X] [B] [≡] [≈] [X]

# WOODBURY

**AAA** ◆◆◆ **Executive Inn at Woodbury** M
(516) 921-8500. **$109-$169.** 8030 Jericho Tpke (SR 25). Jct SR 25 and 135, 1 mi e. Ext corridors. **Pets:** Accepted.
[SAVE] [S0] [X] [&'] [B] [≡] [≈]

# NORTH CAROLINA

## ABERDEEN

 **Best Western Pinehurst Motor Inn** M
(910) 944-2367. **$70-$30.** 1500 Sandhills Blvd. Jct US 15/501 N, just s on US 1. Ext corridors. **Pets:** Dogs only. $10 daily fee/pet. Designated rooms, service with restrictions, crate.

**Innkeeper Southern Pines** M
(910) 944-2324. **$58-$72, 3 day notice.** 1405 N Sandhills Blvd. Jct US 15/501 N, just s on US 1. Ext/int corridors. **Pets:** $10 one-time fee/room. Service with restrictions, supervision.

**Motel 6-1234** M
(910) 944-5633. **$43-$55.** 1408 Sandhills Blvd. Jct US 15/501N, just s on US 1. Ext corridors. **Pets:** Accepted.

## ALBEMARLE

**Best Western Executive Inn** SH
(704) 983-6990. **$65-$85.** 735 SR 24/27 Bypass. Jct US 52 S, 1.4 mi e. Ext corridors. **Pets:** Accepted.

**Sleep Inn & Suites** SH
(704) 983-2770. **$69-$199.** 621 Hwy 24/27 Bypass. Jct US 52 S, 1.1 mi e. Int corridors. **Pets:** Accepted.

## ARCHDALE

**Best Western-High Point** SH
(336) 861-3000. **$55-$199.** 1202 Liberty Rd. I-85, exit 113, just s on SR 62. Int corridors. **Pets:** Accepted.

**Comfort Inn Archdale** SH
(336) 434-4797. **$59-$195.** 10123 N Main St. I-85, exit 111, just n on US 311, then just sw on Balfour Dr. Int corridors. **Pets:** Small, other species. $25 one-time fee/pet. Designated rooms, service with restrictions, crate.

## ARDEN

**Quality Inn & Suites Asheville South** SH
(828) 684-6688. **$79-$189.** 1 Skyland Inn Dr. I-26, exit 37. Int corridors. **Pets:** Medium. $25 one-time fee/room. Designated rooms, service with restrictions, supervision.

## ASHEBORO

 **Comfort Inn** SH
(336) 626-3680. **$69-$130.** 242 Lake Crest Rd. US 64, just w on SR 42. Ext corridors. **Pets:** Small, other species. $15 one-time fee/pet. Service with restrictions, crate.

## ASHEVILLE

**1889 WhiteGate Inn & Cottage** BB
(828) 253-2553. **$160-$340, 14 day notice.** 173 E Chestnut St. I-240, exit 5B (Charlotte St), just n, then just w; in historic district. Ext/int corridors. **Pets:** Small, dogs only. $50 one-time fee/room. Designated rooms, service with restrictions, crate.

**1900 Inn on Montford** BB ❖
(828) 254-9569. **$125-$365, 14 day notice.** 296 Montford Ave. I-240, exit 4C (Montford Ave/Haywood St), 0.7 mi n; in historic district. Ext/int corridors. **Pets:** Medium. $50 deposit/room. Designated rooms, service with restrictions, crate.

**Best Western Asheville Biltmore** SH
(828) 253-1851. **$64-$194.** 22 Woodfin St. I-240, exit 5A (Merrimon Ave). Int corridors. **Pets:** Accepted.

**Best Western of Asheville Biltmore East** M
(828) 298-5562. **$49-$109.** 501 Tunnel Rd. I-240, exit 7, 0.5 mi e on SR 70. Ext corridors. **Pets:** Small, dogs only. $10 daily fee/pet. Service with restrictions, crate.

**Biltmore Village Inn** BB
(828) 274-8707. **$175-$325, 14 day notice.** 119 Dodge St. I-40, exit 50/50B (US 25 N), 0.5 mi n, just e on Lula St, just n on Reed St, just e on Warren Ave, then just s. Ext/int corridors. **Pets:** Accepted.

**Black Walnut B&B Inn** BB ❖
(828) 254-3878. **$125-$265, 15 day notice.** 288 Montford Ave. I-240, exit 4C (Montford Ave/Haywood St), 0.5 mi n; in the historic district. Ext/int corridors. **Pets:** Other species. Designated rooms, service with restrictions, crate.

**▼▼ Carolina Bed & Breakfast** BB
(828) 254-3608. **$120-$200.** 177 Cumberland Ave. I-240, exit 4C (Montford Ave/Haywood St), 0.5 mi n on Montford Ave, just e on Chestnut St, then just n. Ext/int corridors. **Pets:** $10 daily fee/pet. Designated rooms, service with restrictions.
☒ 🏠 💻 ☒

**▼▼ Comfort Inn River Ridge** SH
(828) 298-9141. **$59-$139.** 800 Fairview Rd. I-240, exit 8; jct I-40 and US 74. Ext/int corridors. **Pets:** Large, other species. $25 one-time fee/room. Designated rooms, service with restrictions.
ASK 🏠 ☒ 🍴 🔒 💻 〰 ☒

**▲▲▲ ▼▼▼ Comfort Suites-Biltmore Square Mall** SH ☘
(828) 665-4000. **$70-$149.** 890 Brevard Rd. I-26, exit 33, 0.3 mi w. Int corridors. **Pets:** Small, other species. $20 daily fee/room. Crate.
ASK 🏠 ☒ ⛑ 🍴 🔒 💻 〰

**▼▼▼ Crowne Plaza Resort** SH
(828) 254-3211. **$79-$189.** 1 Holiday Inn Dr. I-240, exit 3B (Holiday Inn Dr), just w. Int corridors. **Pets:** Accepted.
ASK 🏠 ☒ 🍴 ⛑ 🔒 💻 🍴 〰 ☒

**▲▲▲ ▼▼▼ Days Inn-Asheville Mall** M
(828) 252-4000. **$30-$179.** 201 Tunnel Rd. I-240, exit 6, 0.5 mi e, on south side of road. Ext corridors. **Pets:** Accepted.
SAVE ☒ 🍴 🔒 💻 〰

**▲▲▲ ▼▼▼ Days Inn-Biltmore East** SH
(828) 298-4000. **$35-$159.** 1435 Tunnel Rd. I-40, exit 55, just n. Int corridors. **Pets:** Small. $15 daily fee/pet. No service, crate.
SAVE 🏠 ☒ 🔒 💻 〰

**▼▼▼ Holiday Inn-Biltmore East at the Blue Ridge Parkway** SH
(828) 298-5611. **$79-$169.** 1450 Tunnel Rd. I-40, exit 55, just n. Int corridors. **Pets:** Accepted.
ASK 🏠 ☒ 💻 🍴 〰

**▲▲▲ ▼ The Log Cabin Motor Court** CA
(828) 645-6546. **$50-$120, 14 day notice.** 330 Weaverville Hwy. 4 mi n on US 19 and 23, exit New Bridge northbound, then 1 mi n on Weaverville Hwy; exit New Stock Rd southbound, 1 mi s. Ext corridors. **Pets:** Other species. $15 daily fee/pet. Service with restrictions, crate.
SAVE 🔒 💻 ☒

**▼ Motel 6-1134** M
(828) 299-3040. **$39-$57.** 1415 Tunnel Rd. I-40, exit 55. Ext corridors. **Pets:** Accepted.
🏠 ☒ ⛑ 〰

**▲▲▲ ▼▼▼ The Pines Cottages** CA
(828) 645-9661. **$45-$165, 14 day notice.** 346 Weaverville Hwy. 4 mi n on US 19 and 23, exit New Bridge northbound, 1.1 mi n on Weaverville Hwy; exit New Stock Rd southbound, 1 mi s. Ext corridors. **Pets:** $15 one-time fee/pet. Service with restrictions.
SAVE 🔒 💻 ☒

**▲▲▲ ▼▼▼ Quality Inn & Suites** SH
(828) 298-5519. **$45-$140.** 1430 Tunnel Rd. I-40, exit 55, just n. Ext corridors. **Pets:** Medium. $25 daily fee/pet. Designated rooms, service with restrictions, supervision.
SAVE 🏠 ☒ 🍴 ⛑ 🔒 💻 〰

**▼▼ Red Roof Inn-West** M
(828) 667-9803. **$40-$80.** 16 Crowell Rd. I-40, exit 44, just n on US 19 and 23, just w on Old Haywood Rd, then just s. Ext corridors. **Pets:** Accepted.
☒ ⛑ 🔒

**▲▲▲ ▼▼▼ Sleep Inn Biltmore** SH
(828) 277-1800. **$69-$159.** 117 Hendersonville Rd. I-40, exit 50, 0.3 mi n on US 25. Int corridors. **Pets:** Accepted.
SAVE 🏠 ☒ ⛑ ⛑ 💻

**▲▲▲ ▼▼▼ Sleep Inn Biltmore West** SH
(828) 670-7600. **$60-$120.** 1918 Old Haywood Rd. I-40, exit 44, just n on US 19 and 23, then just w. Int corridors. **Pets:** Other species. $8 daily fee/room. Service with restrictions, crate.
SAVE 🏠 ☒ 🍴 🔒 💻

**▼▼ Super 8 Motel at Biltmore Square** SH
(828) 670-8800. **$39-$149.** 9 Wedgefield Dr. I-26, exit 33, just nw. Int corridors. **Pets:** Medium, other species. $15 one-time fee/room. Service with restrictions, supervision.
ASK 🏠 ☒ ⛑ 🔒 🔒 💻

**▼ Super 8 Motel Central** M ☘
(828) 667-8706. **$39-$159.** 8 Crowell Rd. I-40, exit 44, just n on US 19 and 23. Int corridors. **Pets:** Medium. $15 one-time fee/room. Service with restrictions, crate.
ASK 🏠 ☒ ⛑ 🔒 💻

# BANNER ELK

**▼◆▼◆▼ Banner Elk Inn B&B and Cottages** BB
(828) 898-6223. **$100-$225, 30 day notice.** 407 Main St E. Jct SR 184 and 194, 0.3 mi n on SR 194. Int corridors. **Pets:** Dogs only. Designated rooms, service with restrictions, supervision.
☒ 🔒 💻

**▼◆▼◆▼ Best Western Mountain Lodge at Banner Elk** SH ☘
(828) 898-4571. **$79-$209, 3 day notice.** 1615 Tynecastle Hwy. 1 mi se on SR 184. Ext corridors. **Pets:** Other species. $25 deposit/pet. Designated rooms, service with restrictions.
ASK 🏠 ☒ ⛑ 🍴 ⛑ 🔒 💻 🍴 〰

# BOONE

**▲▲▲ ▼▼▼▼ Hampton Inn** SH
(828) 264-0077. **$69-$179.** 1075 Hwy 105. Jct US 321, just sw. Int corridors. **Pets:** Very small, dogs only. $45 one-time fee/pet. Service with restrictions, crate.
SAVE 🏠 ☒ 🍴 🔒 💻 〰

# BREVARD

**▼▼▼ Holiday Inn Express** SH
(828) 862-8900. **$69-$125.** 1570 Asheville Hwy. 3 mi e on US 64. Int corridors. **Pets:** Small. $50 one-time fee/pet. Service with restrictions, supervision.
ASK 🏠 ☒ ⛑ 🍴 ⛑ 🔒 💻 〰

# BURLINGTON

**▼▼▼ La Quinta Inn** SH
(336) 229-5203. **$79.** 2444 Maple Ave. I-40/85, exit 145, just n. Int corridors. **Pets:** Small, other species. $25 one-time fee/pet. Service with restrictions, supervision.
ASK 🏠 ☒ ⛑ 🍴 🔒 💻 🍴 〰

**▼ Motel 6-1257** M
(336) 226-1325. **$37-$51.** 2155 Hanford Rd. I-40/85, exit 145, just s on SR 49, just w. Ext corridors. **Pets:** Accepted.
🏠 ☒ 🍴 ⛑ 〰

**▲▲▲ ▼▼▼ Red Roof Inn** SH
(336) 227-1270. **$53-$70, 3 day notice.** 2133 W Hanford Rd. I-40/85, exit 145, just s on SR 49, then just w. Int corridors. **Pets:** Medium. Service with restrictions.
SAVE 🏠 ☒ 🔒 〰

# CANDLER

**▲▲▲ ▼▼▼ Owl's Nest Inn and Engadine Cabins** BB ☘
(828) 665-8325. **$145-$250.** 2630 Smoky Park Hwy. I-40, exit 37, 0.5 mi w on SR 19/23. Ext/int corridors. **Pets:** Other species. $50 one-time fee/room. Designated rooms.
SAVE 🏠 ☒ 🔒

# CARY

**(AAA) ▼▼▼▼ Best Western Cary Inn & Suites SH**
(919) 481-1200. **$79-$99.** 1722 Walnut St. I-40, exit 293, 0.3 mi sw on US 1/64, exit Walnut St, then just w. Int corridors. **Pets:** Accepted.
SAVE ⬡ ✕ 🄯 🛏 💻 🐾 🚫

**▼▼▼▼ Candlewood Suites SH**
(919) 468-4222. **$119-$139.** 1020 Buck Jones Rd. I-40, exit 293, just sw on US 1/64, exit Walnut St, just w, then 0.5 mi n; in Buck Jones Village. Int corridors. **Pets:** Accepted.
ASK ⬡ ✕ 🄯 🖫 🛏 💻

**▼▼▼▼ Comfort Suites Hotel SH**
(919) 852-4318. **$69-$109.** 350 Ashville Ave. US 1, exit 98A, 0.8 mi e on Tryon Rd, then just n. Int corridors. **Pets:** Accepted.
ASK ⬡ ✕ 🖫 🖫 🛏 💻 🐾 🚫

**(AAA) ▼▼▼▼ Hampton Inn SH**
(919) 859-5559. **$59-$89.** 201 Ashville Ave. US 1, exit 98A, 0.8 mi e on Tryon Rd, then just n. Int corridors. **Pets:** Medium. $50 one-time fee/pet. Designated rooms, service with restrictions, supervision.
SAVE ⬡ ▼▼▼▼ 🖫 🄯 🖫 🛏 💻

**(AAA) ▼▼▼▼ Homewood Suites SH**
(919) 467-4444. **$129-$169.** 100 MacAlyson Ct. US 1, exit 98B, just w on US 64, then just s on Edinburgh Dr; in MacGregor Park. Int corridors. **Pets:** Accepted.
SAVE ⬡ ✕ 🖫 🄯 🖫 🛏 💻 🐾 🚫

**▼▼▼▼ La Quinta Inn & Suites Raleigh (Cary) SH**
(919) 851-2850. **$82-$116.** 191 Crescent Commons Dr. US 1, exit 98A, 0.5 mi e on Tryon Rd, then just n. Int corridors. **Pets:** Medium. Service with restrictions.
ASK ✕ 🖫 🄯 🖫 🛏 💻 🐾

**▼▼ Red Roof Inn SH**
(919) 469-3400. **$45-$57.** 1800 Walnut St. I-40, exit 293, 0.3 mi sw on US 1/64 W; exit Walnut St, just e. Int corridors. **Pets:** Accepted.
✕ 🖫 🄯 🖫 🛏

**▼▼▼▼ Residence Inn SH**
(919) 467-4080. **$59-$189.** 2900 Regency Pkwy. US 1, exit 98A, 0.5 mi e on Tryon Rd, then just s. Int corridors. **Pets:** $75 one-time fee/room. Service with restrictions.
ASK ✕ 🖫 🖫 🛏 💻 🐾 🚫

**▼▼▼▼ TownePlace Suites SH**
(919) 678-0005. **$99.** 120 Sage Commons Way. I-40, exit 287, 0.5 mi s on Harrison Ave, 2.3 w on Weston Pkwy, then just n. Int corridors. **Pets:** Accepted.
ASK ⬡ ✕ 🖫 🖫 🛏 💻 🐾

# CASHIERS

**▼▼▼▼ High Hampton Inn & Country Club SH**
(828) 743-2411. **$176-$260, 10 day notice.** 1525 Hwy 107 S. Jct US 64, 1.5 mi s. Ext/int corridors. **Pets:** Accepted.
🍽 🚫 🄰 🄿 🄯

# CHAPEL HILL

**▼▼▼▼ Holiday Inn SH ❄**
(919) 929-2171. **$89-$109.** 1301 N Fordham Blvd. I-40, exit 270, 2 mi s on US 15/501. Ext corridors. **Pets:** Medium. $35 one-time fee/room. Service with restrictions.
ASK ⬡ ✕ 🄯 🛏 💻 🍽 🐾

**(AAA) ▼▼▼▼ The Siena Hotel SH ❄**
(919) 929-4000. **$119-$245.** 1505 E Franklin St. I-40, exit 270, 2 mi s on US 15/501, then 0.5 mi w. Int corridors. **Pets:** Dogs only. $75 one-time fee/pet. Service with restrictions, supervision.
SAVE ⬡ ✕ 🖫 🄯 🖫 🛏 🍽

---

# CHARLOTTE METROPOLITAN AREA

## CHARLOTTE

**(AAA) ▼ Americas Best Value Inn M**
(704) 398-3144. **$49-$59.** 3200 Queen City Dr. I-85, exit 33, just w, then just n. Ext corridors. **Pets:** Accepted.
SAVE ⬡ ✕ 🛏 🐾

**(AAA) ▼▼▼▼ AmeriSuites (Charlotte/Arrowood) SH**
(704) 522-8400. **$79-$139.** 7900 Forest Point Blvd. I-77, exit 3 southbound; exit 2 northbound, just e. Int corridors. **Pets:** Small. $10 daily fee/room. Service with restrictions, supervision.
SAVE ⬡ ✕ 🖫 🄯 🖫 🛏 💻 🐾

**(AAA) ▼▼▼▼ AmeriSuites (Charlotte/Coliseum) SH**
(704) 357-8555. **$99-$134.** 4119 S Stream Blvd. I-77, exit 6B, 2 mi nw on Billy Graham Pkwy, exit Coliseum/Tyvola Rd, then 0.8 mi se on Tyvola Rd. Int corridors. **Pets:** Accepted.
SAVE ⬡ ✕ 🛏 💻 🏊

**(AAA) ▼▼▼▼ Ballantyne Resort LH**
(704) 248-4000. **$179-$289, 3 day notice.** 10000 Ballantyne Commons Pkwy. I-485, exit 61 or 61B, just s. Int corridors. **Pets:** Accepted.
SAVE ⬡ ✕ 🖫 🖫 🄯 🖫 🍽 🐾 🚫

**▼▼▼▼ Candlewood Suites-Coliseum SH**
(704) 529-7500. **$72.** 5840 Westpark Dr. I-77, exit 5 (Tyvola Rd), just e, then 0.5 mi s. Int corridors. **Pets:** Accepted.
ASK ⬡ ✕ 🖫 🄯 🛏 💻

**▼▼▼ Comfort Inn Carowinds SH ❄**
(704) 339-0574. **$49-$159.** 3725 Avenue of the Carolinas. I-77, exit 90, just nw. Int corridors. **Pets:** Other species. $25 one-time fee/room. Designated rooms, service with restrictions.
ASK ⬡ ✕ 🄯 🛏 💻 🐾

**(AAA) ▼▼▼▼ Comfort Inn-Executive Park SH**
(704) 525-2626. **$49-$129.** 5822 Westpark Dr. I-77, exit 5 (Tyvola Rd), just e, then 0.5 mi s. Int corridors. **Pets:** Medium. $25 one-time fee/pet. Service with restrictions, supervision.
SAVE ✕ 🄯 🖫 🛏 💻 🐾

**▼▼▼ Comfort Suites-University SH**
(704) 547-0049. **$80-$130.** 7735 University City Blvd. I-85, exit 45A, 1 mi e on SR 24, then 0.5 mi s on SR 49. Int corridors. **Pets:** Medium. $25 one-time fee/pet. Service with restrictions, supervision.
ASK ⬡ ✕ 🖫 🄯 🖫 🛏 🐾

**(AAA) ▼▼▼▼ Doubletree Guest Suites-South Park SH**
(704) 364-2400. **$70-$159.** 6300 Morrison Blvd. I-77, exit 5 (Tyvola Rd), 3.3 mi e on Tyvola/Fairview rds, just n on Barclay Downs, then just e. Int corridors. **Pets:** Medium. $75 deposit/pet, $15 daily fee/pet. Service with restrictions, crate.
SAVE ✕ 🄯 🖫 🛏 💻 🍽 🐾 🚫

**▼▼▼▼ Drury Inn & Suites-Charlotte North SH**
(704) 593-0700. **$75-$135.** 415 W WT Harris Blvd. I-85, exit 45A, just e on SR 24. Int corridors. **Pets:** Accepted.
ASK ✕ 🖫 🄯 🛏 💻 🐾

**Hampton Inn University Place** SH
(704) 548-0905. **$75-$105.** 8419 N Tryon St. I-85, exit 45A, 0.5 mi e on SR 24, then just s on US 29 (N Tryon St). Int corridors. **Pets:** Accepted.

**Holiday Inn Airport** SH
(704) 394-4301. **$86-$96.** 2707 Little Rock Rd. I-85, exit 32, just e. Int corridors. **Pets:** Accepted.

**Holiday Inn at University Executive Park** SH
(704) 547-0999. **$99.** 8520 University Executive Park Dr. I-85, exit 45A, just e on SR 24, then just s. Int corridors. **Pets:** Accepted.

**Holiday Inn Center City** SH
(704) 335-5400. **$159.** 230 N College St. I-77, exit 10 or 10B, 1 mi e on Trade St, then just n; jct 6th St. Int corridors. **Pets:** Accepted.

**Homestead Studio Suites Hotel-Charlotte/Coliseum** SH
(704) 676-0083. **$77-$154.** 710 Yorkmont Rd. I-77, exit 6B northbound, just w, just s on S Tryon St, then just w; exit southbound, just s on S Tryon St, then just w. Ext corridors. **Pets:** $25 daily fee/pet. Service with restrictions, supervision.

**Homewood Suites by Hilton Airport/Coliseum** SH
(704) 357-0500. **$109-$209.** 2770 Yorkmont Rd. I-77, exit 6B, 2 mi nw on Billy Graham Pkwy, exit Coliseum/Tyvola Rd, just se on Tyvola Rd, then just w. Int corridors. **Pets:** $75 one-time fee/room. Service with restrictions, crate.

**La Quinta Inn & Suites Charlotte (Coliseum)** SH
(704) 523-5599. **$81-$114.** 4900 S Tryon St. I-77, exit 6B northbound, just w, then just s; exit southbound, just s. Int corridors. **Pets:** Medium. No service.

**MainStay Suites** SH
(704) 521-3232. **$71-$80.** 7926 Forest Pine Dr. I-77, exit 3 southbound; exit 2 northbound, just e, then just s. Int corridors. **Pets:** Accepted.

**Omni Charlotte Hotel** LH
(704) 377-0400. **$179.** 132 E Trade St. I-77, exit 10 or 10B, 0.8 mi e; jct Tryon St. Int corridors. **Pets:** Medium, dogs only. $50 one-time fee/room. Service with restrictions, crate.

**The Plaza Hotel on Carowinds** LH
(803) 548-2400. **$59-$199.** 225 Carowinds Blvd. I-77, exit 90, just nw. Int corridors. **Pets:** Accepted.

**Quality Inn & Suites-Crown Point** SH
(704) 845-2810. **$69-$79.** 2501 Sardis Rd N. I-485, exit 51A, 3.3 mi w on US 74, then just s. Int corridors. **Pets:** Accepted.

**Quality Inn-Executive Park** SH
(704) 525-0747. **$59-$109.** 440 Griffith Rd. I-77, exit 5 (Tyvola Rd), just e, just s on Westpark Dr, then just e. Int corridors. **Pets:** Accepted.

**Ramada Woodlawn Conference Center "Airport South"** SH
(704) 525-8350. **$89-$149.** 212 Woodlawn Rd. I-77, exit 6A, just e. Int corridors. **Pets:** Small. $50 one-time fee/room. Service with restrictions, supervision.

**Red Roof Inn-Airport** M
(704) 392-2316. **$48-$73.** 3300 Queen City Dr. I-85, exit 33, just w, then just s. Ext corridors. **Pets:** Accepted.

**Residence Inn by Marriott** SH
(704) 547-1122. **$74-$119.** 8503 N Tryon St. I-85, exit 45A, 0.5 mi e on SR 24, then just s on US 29. Ext corridors. **Pets:** $75 one-time fee/room. Service with restrictions.

**Residence Inn by Marriott-Charlotte Uptown** SH
(704) 340-4000. **$149-$199.** 404 S Mint St. I-77, exit 10 or 10B, 0.6 mi e, then just s. Int corridors. **Pets:** Accepted.

**Residence Inn by Marriott-Piper Glen** SH
(704) 319-3900. **$89-$159.** 5115 Piper Station Dr. I-485, exit 59, just s on Rea Rd, then just e. Int corridors. **Pets:** Accepted.

**Residence Inn by Marriott-Tyvola Executive Park** SH
(704) 527-8110. **$108-$134.** 5816 Westpark Dr. I-77, exit 5 (Tyvola Rd), just e, then 0.4 mi s. Ext/int corridors. **Pets:** $75 one-time fee/pet. Designated rooms, service with restrictions, crate.

**Sheraton Charlotte Airport Hotel** LH
(704) 392-1200. **$139-$199.** 3315 Scott Futrell Dr. I-85, exit 33, just e, then just s. Int corridors. **Pets:** Medium, dogs only. $50 deposit/pet. Service with restrictions, crate.

**Sleep Inn** SH
(704) 549-4544. **$59-$169.** 8525 N Tryon St. I-85, exit 45A, 0.5 mi e on SR 24, just s on US 29. Int corridors. **Pets:** Large, other species. $25 one-time fee/room. Service with restrictions, supervision.

**Sleep Inn-Charlotte Coliseum** SH
(704) 525-5005. **$68-$99.** 701 Yorkmont Rd. I-77, exit 6B northbound, just w, just s on S Tryon St, then just w; exit southbound, just s on Tryon St, then just w. Int corridors. **Pets:** Accepted.

**Staybridge Suites-Arrowood** SH
(704) 527-6767. **Call for rates.** 7924 Forest Pine Dr. I-77, exit 3 southbound; exit 2 northbound, just e then just s. Int corridors. **Pets:** Accepted.

**Staybridge Suites Charlotte-Ballantyne** SH
(704) 248-5000. **$109-$199.** 15735 John J Delaney Dr. I-485, exit 61 or 61B, just s. Int corridors. **Pets:** Accepted.

**Studio 6 Airport-#6006** SH
(704) 394-4993. **$45-$57.** 3420 Queen City Dr. I-85, exit 33, just w, then just s. Int corridors. **Pets:** Accepted.

**Summerfield Suites by Wyndham-Charlotte** SH
(704) 525-2600. **$99-$119.** 4920 S Tryon St. I-77, exit 6B northbound, just w, then just s; exit southbound, just s. Int corridors. **Pets:** Accepted.

**TownePlace Suites by Marriott** SH
(704) 548-0388. **$59-$179.** 8710 Research Dr. I-85, exit 45B, just w on SR 24, then just n. Int corridors. **Pets:** Accepted.

**▼▼▼ TownePlace Suites by Marriott-Arrowood** SH
(704) 227-2000. **$49-$59, 14 day notice.** 7805 Forest Point Blvd. I-77, exit 3 southbound; exit 2 northbound, just e. Int corridors. **Pets:** Accepted.
(ASK) (Sₒ) (✕) (&M) (🎵) (&) 🔒 🖥 ➔

**▼▼▼ The Westin Charlotte** LH
(704) 375-2600. **$249.** 601 S College St. I-277, exit College St, just n; jct E Stonewall St. Int corridors. **Pets:** Accepted.
(ASK) (Sₒ) (✕) (&M) (🎵) (&) 🔒 🖥 (❬❭) ➔ (✕)

## CORNELIUS

**AAA ▼▼▼ Best Western Lake Norman** SH
(704) 896-0660. **$64-$89, 14 day notice.** 19608 Liverpool Pkwy. I-77, exit 28, just w, then s. Int corridors. **Pets:** Accepted.
(SAVE) (Sₒ) (✕) 🔒 🖥 ➔

**▼▼▼ Holiday Inn Lake Norman** SH
(704) 892-9120. **$65.** 19901 Holiday Ln. I-77, exit 28, just e, then just n. Ext corridors. **Pets:** Other species. $25 one-time fee/room. Service with restrictions, supervision.
(ASK) (Sₒ) (✕) (&M) (🎵) 🔒 🖥 (❬❭) ➔

## HUNTERSVILLE

**▼▼▼ Candlewood Suites** SH
(704) 895-3434. **$65-$180, 3 day notice.** 16530 Northcross Dr. I-77, exit 25, just w on SR 73, then just s. Int corridors. **Pets:** Accepted.
(ASK) (Sₒ) (✕) 🔒 🖥

**▼▼ Quality Inn** SH
(704) 892-6597. **$54-$125.** 16825 Caldwell Creek Dr. I-77, exit 25, just e on SR 73, just n on US 21, then just w. Ext/int corridors. **Pets:** Medium. $25 or e-time fee/room. Service with restrictions, crate.
(ASK) (Sₒ) (✕) (&) 🔒 🖥

**▼▼ Sleep Inn** SH
(704) 766-2500. **$89-$99.** 16508 Northcross Dr. I-77, exit 25, just w on SR 73, then just s. Int corridors. **Pets:** Accepted.
(ASK) (Sₒ) (✕) 🔒 🖥

## MATTHEWS

**AAA ▼▼▼ Country Inn & Suites-Matthews** SH
(704) 846-8000. **$74-$79.** 2001 Mount Harmony Church Rd. I-485, exit 51B, 0.5 mi e on US 74, just n on Independence Commerce Dr, then just w. Int corridors. **Pets:** Medium. $10 daily fee/pet. Designated rooms, service with restrictions, crate.
(SAVE) (Sₒ) (✕) (&M) (&) 🔒 🖥 ➔

## PINEVILLE

**▼▼▼▼ Hampton Inn & Suites** SH
(704) 889-2700. **$92-$112.** 401 Towne Centre Blvd. I-485, exit 64B, 0.3 mi s on SR 51, then just e. Int corridors. **Pets:** Accepted.
(ASK) (Sₒ) (✕) (&M) (🎵) (&) 🔒 🖥 ➔

**AAA ▼▼▼▼ Quality Suites** SH
(704) 889-7095. **$69-$129.** 9840 Pineville Matthews Rd. I-485, exit 64B, 0.3 mi s on SR 51. Int corridors. **Pets:** Accepted.
(SAVE) (Sₒ) (✕) (&M) (🎵) (&) 🔒 🖥 ➔

# END METROPOLITAN AREA

## CHEROKEE

**AAA ▼▼▼ Baymont Inn-Cherokee/Smoky Mountains** SH
(828) 497-2102. **$59-$149.** 1455 Acquoni Rd. 2.5 mi n, just w off US 441 N. Int corridors. **Pets:** Medium. $10 daily fee/pet. Designated rooms, service with restrictions, supervision.
(SAVE) (Sₒ) (✕) (&M) (🎵) (&) 🔒 🖥 ➔

**AAA ▼▼▼ Best Western Great Smokies Inn** M
(828) 497-2020. **$49-$99.** 1636 Acquoni Rd. US 441 N, 2.5 mi n; downtown. Ext corridors. **Pets:** Medium. $10 daily fee/pet. Service with restrictions, crate.
(SAVE) (Sₒ) (✕) (🎵) 🔒 🖥 (❬❭) ➔

**AAA ▼▼▼ Microtel Inn & Suites** SH
(828) 497-7800. **$39-$69.** 674 Casino Tr. Jct US 441 and Business Rt US 441 S. Int corridors. **Pets:** Medium. $25 daily fee/pet. Designated rooms, service with restrictions, supervision.
(SAVE) (Sₒ) (✕) (&M) (&) 🔒 🖥 ➔

**AAA ▼▼ Pioneer Motel** M
(828) 497-2435. **$38-$78, 3 day notice.** 0.8 mi w on US 19 S. Ext corridors. **Pets:** Small, dogs only. $10 one-time fee/pet. Designated rooms, service with restrictions, supervision.
(SAVE) (Sₒ) (✕) 🔒 🖥 ➔ (✕)

## CLAREMONT

**AAA ▼▼▼ Super 8 Motel** M
(828) 459-7777. **$62.** 3054 N Oxford St. I-40, exit 135, just s. Ext/int corridors. **Pets:** Medium. $12 daily fee/pet. Service with restrictions, supervision.
(SAVE) (Sₒ) (✕) (&) 🔒 🖥 ➔

## CLAYTON

**▼▼ Sleep Inn** SH
(919) 772-7771. **$50-$70.** 105 Commerce Pkwy. I-40, exit 312, just w on SR 42, then just s. Int corridors. **Pets:** Accepted.
(ASK) (Sₒ) (✕) (&M) (🎵) (&) 🔒 🖥 ➔

## CLEMMONS

**▼▼ The Village Inn Golf & Conference Center** SH
(336) 766-9121. **$62-$75.** 6205 Ramada Dr. I-40, exit 184, just s, then just e. Int corridors. **Pets:** Accepted.
(ASK) (Sₒ) (✕) (🎵) (&) 🔒 🖥 (❬❭) ➔

## CONOVER

**▼▼ Days Inn** SH 🐾
(828) 465-2378. **$64-$94.** 1710 Fairgrove Church Rd SE. I-40, exit 128, just s. Ext corridors. **Pets:** Medium, other species. $25 one-time fee/pet. Service with restrictions, crate.
(ASK) (Sₒ) (✕) (&M) (🎵) 🔒 🖥 ➔

## DORTCHES

**▼▼ Econo Lodge** M
(252) 937-6300. **$50-$70.** 5350 Dortches Blvd. I-95, exit 141, just w, then just n on service road. Ext corridors. **Pets:** Accepted.
(ASK) (Sₒ) (✕) (🎵) 🔒 🖥 (❬❭) ➔

## DUNN

**▼▼ Jameson Inn** M
(910) 891-5758. **$54-$104.** 901 Jackson Rd. I-95, exit 73, just w, then just s. Ext corridors. **Pets:** Very small, other species. $10 daily fee/room. Service with restrictions, supervision.
(ASK) (✕) (&M) (🎵) 🔒 🖥 ➔

# DURHAM

**Americas Best Value Carolina Duke Inn** M
(919) 286-0771. **$45-$120.** 2517 Guess Rd. I-85, exit 175, just e. Ext corridors. **Pets:** Accepted.

**Best Western Skyland Inn** M
(919) 383-2508. **$69-$89.** 5400 US 70 W. I-85, exit 170, 0.3 mi e on US 70, then just n. Ext corridors. **Pets:** Other species. $10 daily fee/pet. Service with restrictions, supervision.

**Candlewood Suites** SH
(919) 484-9922. **$107.** 1818 E NC Hwy 54. I-40, exit 278, just s, then just w. Int corridors. **Pets:** Accepted.

**Extended Stay Deluxe-RTP** SH
(919) 998-0400. **$94-$129.** 4919 S Miami Blvd. I-40, exit 281, just s. Int corridors. **Pets:** $20 daily fee/pet. Service with restrictions, supervision.

**Hampton Inn** SH
(919) 471-6100. **$79-$99.** 1816 Hillandale Rd. I-85, exit 174A, just w. Int corridors. **Pets:** Medium. $50 one-time fee/pet. Service with restrictions, supervision.

**Hilton-Raleigh-Durham Airport at Research Triangle Park** SH
(919) 941-6000. **$89-$249.** 4810 Old Page Rd. I-40, exit 282, just s, then just w on Creekstone Dr. Int corridors. **Pets:** Medium. $50 one-time fee/pet. Designated rooms, service with restrictions, crate.

**Homestead Studio Suites Hotel-Durham/University** SH
(919) 402-1700. **$71-$134.** 1920 Ivy Creek Blvd. I-40, exit 270, 2 mi n on US 15/501, exit 105B, then just e on Martin Luther King Jr Pkwy; in University Place. Ext corridors. **Pets:** $20 daily fee/pet. Service with restrictions, supervision.

**Homestead Studio Suites Hotel-Raleigh/Durham/ Research Triangle Park** SH
(919) 544-9991. **$61-$134.** 4515 NC Hwy 55. I-40, exit 278, just s. Ext corridors. **Pets:** $25 daily fee/pet. Service with restrictions, supervision.

**La Quinta Inn & Suites Raleigh (Durham-Chapel Hill)** SH
(919) 401-9660. **$96-$129.** 4414 Durham Chapel Hill Blvd. I-40, exit 270, 1.7 mi n on US 15/501. Int corridors. **Pets:** Medium. No service.

**La Quinta Inn & Suites Raleigh (Research Triangle Park)** SH
(919) 484-1422. **$82-$105.** 1910 W Park Dr. I-40, exit 278, just n on SR 55, then just e. Int corridors. **Pets:** Medium. Service with restrictions.

**Quality Inn & Suites** M
(919) 382-3388. **$55-$80.** 3710 Hillsborough Rd. I-85, exit 173, just e, then just s. Ext/int corridors. **Pets:** Medium. $25 daily fee/room. Designated rooms, service with restrictions, supervision.

**Residence Inn by Marriott** SH
(919) 361-1266. **$85-$149, 3 day notice.** 201 Residence Inn Blvd. I-40, exit 278, just s, then just w. Ext/int corridors. **Pets:** Accepted.

**Sleep Inn-RTP** SH
(919) 993-3393. **$69-$99.** 5208 New Page Rd. I-40, exit 282, just s. Int corridors. **Pets:** Designated rooms, service with restrictions, supervision.

**Wyndham Garden Hotel-Durham** SH
(919) 941-6066. **$89-$139.** 4620 S Miami Blvd. I-40, exit 281, just n. Int corridors. **Pets:** Accepted.

# EDEN

**Jameson Inn** SH
(336) 627-0472. **$54-$104.** 716 Linden Dr. Jct SR 700/770, 1.4 mi s on SR 87/14, then just e. Ext corridors. **Pets:** Very small, other species. $10 daily fee/room. Service with restrictions, supervision.

# ELIZABETH CITY

**Quality Inn** SH
(252) 338-3951. **$69-$130.** 522 S Hughes Blvd. Jct US 158, 1.2 mi s on US 17. Ext corridors. **Pets:** $25 daily fee/room. Service with restrictions.

# FAYETTEVILLE

**Comfort Inn Cross Creek** SH
(910) 867-1777. **$66-$134.** 1922 Skibo Rd. All American Frwy, exit US 401 Bypass, 0.8 mi s. Int corridors. **Pets:** Large, other species. $25 daily fee/room. Service with restrictions, supervision.

**Comfort Inn-Fayetteville** M
(910) 323-8333. **$75-$95.** 1957 Cedar Creek Rd. I-95, exit 49, just w. Ext corridors. **Pets:** Other species. $10 one-time fee/room. Designated rooms, service with restrictions, supervision.

**Econo Lodge I-95** M
(910) 433-2100. **$49-$99.** 1952 Cedar Creek Rd. I-95, exit 49, just w. Ext corridors. **Pets:** Other species. $5 one-time fee/room. Crate.

**Holiday Inn Bordeaux** SH
(910) 323-0111. **$89-$129.** 1707 Owen Dr. Jct I-95 business route/US 301 S, 2.3 mi w. Ext/int corridors. **Pets:** Accepted.

**Holiday Inn I-95** SH
(910) 323-1600. **$84-$118.** 1944 Cedar Creek Rd. I-95, exit 49, just w. Ext/int corridors. **Pets:** $20 one-time fee/room. Designated rooms, service with restrictions.

**Motel 6 #1075** M
(910) 485-8122. **$41-$51.** 2076 Cedar Creek Rd. I-95, exit 49, just e. Ext corridors. **Pets:** Accepted.

**Quality Inn-East** SH
(910) 323-9850. **$49-$149.** 2111 Cedar Creek Rd. I-95, exit 49, just e. Int corridors. **Pets:** Accepted.

**Ramada Inn** SH
(910) 484-8101. **$-$.** 511 Eastern Blvd. Jct SR 24, 0.8 mi s on US 301. Int corridors. **Pets:** Accepted.

**Ramada Limited** SH
(910) 485-6866. **$55-$179.** 1725 Jim Johnson Rd. I-95, exit 49, just w, then just s. Int corridors. **Pets:** Accepted.

▼▼▼▼ Red Roof Inn 🆂🅷
(910) 321-1460. **$60-$75.** 1569 Jim Johnson Rd. I-95, exit 49, just w on SR 53, then just n. Int corridors. **Pets:** Accepted.

## FLETCHER

🅰🅰🅰 ▼▼▼▼ Holiday Inn Asheville-Airport 🆂🅷 🐾
(828) 684-1213. **$89-$129.** 550 Airport Rd. I-26, exit 40, just e. Int corridors. **Pets:** $25 one-time fee/room. Service with restrictions, supervision.

## FOREST CITY

▼▼◆ Jameson Inn 🅼
(828) 287-8788. **$54-$104.** 164 Jameson Dr. US 74 Bypass, exit 181, 1.8 mi nw on US 74A. Ext corridors. **Pets:** Very small, other species. $10 daily fee/room. Service with restrictions, supervision.

## FRANKLIN

🅰🅰🅰 ▼ Country Inn Town Motel 🅼
(828) 524-4451. **$35-$99, 3 day notice.** 668 E Main St. 0n US 441 S business route. Ext corridors. **Pets:** Medium. $7 daily fee/pet. Designated rooms, service with restrictions, supervision.

🆂🅰🆅🅴 🆂🅾 ⊠ 🔒 🖵 🏊

▼ Days Inn-Franklin 🅼
(828) 524-6491. **$49-$120.** 1320 E Main St. Jct US 23 and 441 Bypass, just nw on US 441 business route. Ext corridors. **Pets:** Accepted.

🅰🆂🅺 🆂🅾 ⊠ 🔒 🖵 🏊

🅰🅰🅰 ▼ Franklin Motel Inn & Suites 🅼
(828) 524-4431. **$30-$80.** 17 W Palmer St. Jct US 441 Bypass, 1 mi n on US 441 business route; downtown. Ext corridors. **Pets:** Other species. $10 one-time fee/room. Service with restrictions, crate.

🆂🅰🆅🅴 🆂🅾 ⊠ 🔒 🖵 🏊

▼ Microtel Inn & Suites 🆂🅷
(828) 349-9000. **$39-$99.** 81 Allman Dr. Jct US 441 Bypass, 0.4 mi s on US 441 and 23. Int corridors. **Pets:** Accepted.

🅰🆂🅺 🆂🅾 ⊠ 🔒 🖵

▼ Mountainside Vacation Lodging 🅼
(828) 524-6209. **$60-$75, 7 day notice.** 8356 Sylva Rd. 4.8 mi n on US 441 and 23. Ext corridors. **Pets:** Accepted.

⊠ 🔒 🖵 🎬

## GARNER

▼▼ Holiday Inn Express 🆂🅷
(919) 662-4890. **$85-$100.** 1595 Mechanical Blvd. I-40, exit 298A, 1.9 mi e on US 70, then just n. Int corridors. **Pets:** Small. $20 daily fee/pet. Designated rooms, service with restrictions, supervision.

🅰🆂🅺 🆂🅾 ⊠ 🔒

## GASTONIA

▼▼ Best Western Executive Inn Gastonia 🅼
(704) 868-2000. **$59-$69, 5 day notice.** 360 Best Western Ct. I-85, exit 20 (New Hope Rd), just n, then just e. Ext/int corridors. **Pets:** Accepted.

⊠ 🔒 🖵 🏊

▼▼ Ramada Limited 🅼
(704) 864-8744. **$39-$99.** 1400 E Franklin Blvd. I-85, exit 20 (New Hope Rd), 0.5 mi s, then just w on US 29/74. Ext corridors. **Pets:** Small, other species. $100 deposit/room, $10 one-time fee/room. Designated rooms, service with restrictions, supervision.

🅰🆂🅺 ⊠ 🔒 🖵

## GOLDSBORO

🅰🅰🅰 ▼▼◆ Best Western Goldsboro Inn 🅼
(919) 735-7911. **$69, 14 day notice.** 801 US 70 E Bypass. US 70 E Bypass, exit Williams St eastbound, just n, just w on Eleventh St, then 0.4 mi sw on service road; exit westbound, straight on Eleventh St, then 0.4 mi sw on service road. Ext corridors. **Pets:** Accepted.

🆂🅰🆅🅴 🆂🅾 ⊠ 🔒 🖵 🍴 🏊

🅰🅰🅰 ▼▼◆ Holiday Inn Express 🆂🅷 🐾
(919) 751-1999. **$85-$143.** 909 N Spence Ave. US 70 E Bypass, exit Spence Ave, just s. Int corridors. **Pets:** Other species. $20 one-time fee/room. Service with restrictions, supervision.

🆂🅰🆅🅴 🆂🅾 ⊠ 🔒 🖵 🏊

▼▼ Jameson Inn 🆂🅷
(919) 778-9759. **$54-$104.** 1408 Harding Dr. US 70 E Bypass, exit Spence Ave, just n, then just e on North Park Dr. Int corridors. **Pets:** Very small, other species. $10 daily fee/room. Service with restrictions, supervision.

🅰🆂🅺 ⊠ 🔒 🖵 🏊

## GREENSBORO

🅰🅰🅰 ▼▼◆ AmeriSuites (Greensboro/Wendover) 🆂🅷
(336) 852-1443. **$109, 14 day notice.** 1619 Stanley Rd. I-40, exit 214 or 214A, just sw on Wendover Ave, then just e. Int corridors. **Pets:** Small. $75 one-time fee/room. Service with restrictions, supervision.

🆂🅰🆅🅴 🆂🅾 ⊠ 🔒 🖵 🏊

▼▼▼◆ Best Western Wendover Plaza 🆂🅷
(336) 297-1055. **$69-$169.** 1103 Lanada Rd. I-40, exit 214 westbound; exit 214A eastbound, just sw on Wendover Ave, then just e on Stanley Rd. Int corridors. **Pets:** Small, other species. $25 one-time fee/room. Service with restrictions, supervision.

🅰🆂🅺 🆂🅾 ⊠ 🔒 🖵

▼▼▼◆ Best Western Windsor Suites 🆂🅷
(336) 294-9100. **$86-$190.** 2006 Veasley St. I-40, exit 217, just s, then just w. Int corridors. **Pets:** Small, other species. $25 one-time fee/pet. Service with restrictions, supervision.

🅰🆂🅺 🆂🅾 ⊠ 🔒 🖵 🏊

▼▼ Biltmore Greensboro Hotel 🆂🅷
(336) 272-3474. **$78-$199, 3 day notice.** 111 W Washington St. Just s on Elm St, just w; downtown. Int corridors. **Pets:** Accepted.

🅰🆂🅺 🆂🅾 ⊠ 🖵

▼▼ Candlewood Suites 🆂🅷
(336) 454-0078. **Call for rates.** 7623 Thorndike Rd. I-40, exit 210 (SR 68), just s, then just w. Int corridors. **Pets:** Accepted.

⊠ 🔒 🖵

🅰🅰🅰 ▼▼▼ Comfort Inn 🆂🅷
(336) 294-6220. **$80-$130, 3 day notice.** 2001 Veasley St. I-40, exit 217, just s on High Point Rd, then just w. Int corridors. **Pets:** Accepted.

🆂🅰🆅🅴 🆂🅾 🔒 🖵

▼▼▼◆ Drury Inn & Suites-Greensboro 🆂🅷
(336) 856-9696. **$80-$125.** 3220 High Point Rd. I-40, exit 217, just s. Int corridors. **Pets:** Accepted.

🅰🆂🅺 ⊠ 🔒 🖵 🏊

▼▼▼◆ La Quinta Inn & Suites Greensboro 🆂🅷
(336) 316-0100. **$91-$125.** 1201 Lanada Rd. I-40, exit 214 or 214A, just sw on Wendover Ave, then just e on Stanley Rd. Int corridors. **Pets:** Medium. Service with restrictions.

🅰🆂🅺 ⊠ 🔒 🖵 🏊

▼▼◆ Red Roof Inn Airport 🅼
(336) 271-2636. **$44-$62.** 615 Regional Rd S. I-40, exit 210 (SR 68), just s, then just e. Ext corridors. **Pets:** Accepted.

⊠ 🔒 🖵

▼▼▼ **Residence Inn by Marriott** SH
(336) 294-8600. **$59-$194.** 2000 Veasley St. I-40, exit 217, just s on High Point Rd, then 0.4 mi w. Ext corridors. **Pets:** Other species. $75 one-time fee/room. Service with restrictions, crate.

ASK S✈ ✕ ⎙ 🛏 ▣ ➿ ✕

# GREENVILLE

▼▼ **Jameson Inn** M
(252) 752-7382. **$54-$104.** 920 Crosswinds St. Jct US 264 business route, just s on US 13/SR 11, then just w. Ext corridors. **Pets:** Very small, other species. $10 daily fee/room. Service with restrictions, supervision.

ASK ✕ 🛗 ⎙ 🛏 ▣ ➿

# HAYESVILLE

▼ **Chatuge Mountain Inn** M
(828) 389-9340. **$54-$60.** 4238 Hwy 64 E. Jct SR 69, 4.2 mi e. Ext corridors. **Pets:** Accepted.

ASK ✕ 🛏 ▣

▼▼ **Deerfield Inn** M
(828) 389-8272. **$55-$80.** 40 Chatuge Ln. 3 mi e on US 64. Ext corridors. **Pets:** Other species. $10 daily fee/pet. Designated rooms, supervision.

ASK S✈ ✕ 🛏 ▣

# HENDERSON

▼▼ **Jameson Inn** SH
(252) 430-0247. **$54-$104.** 400 N Cooper Dr. I-85, exit 212, just w on Ruin Creek Rd, then just n. Int corridors. **Pets:** Very small, other species. $10 daily fee/room. Service with restrictions, supervision.

ASK ✕ 🛗 ⎙ 🖵 🛏 ▣ ➿

▼▼ **Lamplight Inn B&B** BB
(252) 438-6311. **$80-$120, 5 day notice.** 1680 Flemingtown Rd. I-85, exit 220, 1.5 mi nw. Int corridors. **Pets:** Small. Service with restrictions, crate.

ASK S✈ ✕ ✕ ⛢

# HENDERSONVILLE

AAA ▼▼▼ **Best Western Hendersonville Inn** M
(828) 692-0521. **$69-$139.** 105 Sugarloaf Rd. I-26, exit 49A, just e. Ext corridors. **Pets:** Medium, other species. $10 one-time fee/pet. Service with restrictions, crate.

SAVE S✈ ✕ 🛏 ▣ 🍴 ➿

AAA ▼▼ **Comfort Inn** SH
(828) 693-8800. **$45-$109, 15 day notice.** 206 Mitchell Dr. I-26, exit 49B, just w. Ext corridors. **Pets:** Accepted.

SAVE S✈ ✕ ⎙ 🛏 ▣ ➿

# HICKORY

▼▼ **Jameson Inn** M
(828) 304-0410. **$54-$104.** 1120 13th Ave Dr SE. I-40, exit 125, just s, then 0.4 mi w. Ext corridors. **Pets:** Very small, other species. $10 daily fee/pet. Service with restrictions, supervision.

ASK ✕ 🛗 🖵 🛏 ▣ ➿

▼ **Red Roof Inn Hickory** M
(828) 323-1500. **$47-$56.** 1184 Lenoir Rhyne Blvd. I-40, exit 125, just n. Ext corridors. **Pets:** Accepted.

✕ ⎙ 🖵 🛏

# HIGHLANDS

AAA ▼▼ **Mountain High Lodge** M
(828) 526-2790. **$49-$189, 7 day notice.** 200 Main St. Just w on US 64; downtown. Ext corridors. **Pets:** Accepted.

SAVE S✈ ✕ 🛏 ▣

# HIGH POINT

▼▼▼ **Radisson Hotel High Point** SH
(336) 889-8888. **$149-$169.** 135 S Main St. On US 311 business route; center. Int corridors. **Pets:** Accepted.

ASK S✈ ✕ ⎙ 🛏 ▣ 🍴 ➿

# HILLSBOROUGH

AAA ▼▼▼ **Holiday Inn Express** SH
(919) 644-7997. **$75-$159.** 202 Cardinal Dr. I-85, exit 164, just e, then just s. Int corridors. **Pets:** Medium. $25 daily fee/pet. Designated rooms, no service, supervision.

SAVE S✈ ✕ 🛗 🖵 🛏 ▣ ➿

AAA ▼▼ **Microtel Inn & Suites** SH
(919) 245-3102. **$50-$70.** 120 Old Dogwood St. I-85, exit 164, just w, then s. Int corridors. **Pets:** Accepted.

SAVE S✈ ✕ 🛏 ▣

# JACKSONVILLE

AAA ▼▼▼ **Hampton Inn** SH 🐾
(910) 347-6500. **$94-$104.** 474 Western Blvd. 2.5 mi n on US 17, just e. Ext corridors. **Pets:** Small. $25 one-time fee/room. Service with restrictions, crate.

SAVE S✈ ✕ ⎙ 🛏 ▣ ➿

AAA ▼▼ **Super 8 Motel** SH
(910) 455-6888. **$57-$77.** 2149 N Marine Blvd. 2.8 mi n on US 17. Int corridors. **Pets:** Accepted.

SAVE S✈ ✕ 🛏 ▣

# JONESVILLE

AAA ▼▼▼ **Comfort Inn** SH
(336) 835-9400. **$64-$96.** 1633 Winston Rd. I-77, exit 82, just w. Ext corridors. **Pets:** Medium, other species. $10 daily fee/pet. Designated rooms, service with restrictions, crate.

SAVE ✕ 🛗 ⎙ 🛏 ▣ ➿

▼▼▼ **Holiday Inn Express** SH
(336) 835-6000. **$59-$69.** 1713 NC 67 Hwy. I-77, exit 82, just e. Int corridors. **Pets:** Small. $10 daily fee/pet. Designated rooms, service with restrictions, supervision.

ASK S✈ ✕ 🖵 ⎙ 🖵 🛏 ▣ ➿

# KANNAPOLIS

▼▼ **Mainstay Suites** SH
(704) 788-2140. **$61-$69.** 3200 Cloverleaf Pkwy. I-85, exit 58, just n on US 29, just e on Cloverleaf Plaza, then just s. Ext/int corridors. **Pets:** Accepted.

ASK S✈ ✕ 🛏 ▣

# KENLY

▼▼ **Days Inn** M
(919) 284-3400. **$50-$70.** 1139 Johnston Pkwy. I-95, exit 106, just w, then just n. Ext corridors. **Pets:** Accepted.

ASK S✈ ✕ 🛗 ➿

# KINGS MOUNTAIN

▼▼ **Comfort Inn** M 🐾
(704) 739-7070. **$55-$75.** 720-A York Rd. I-85, exit 8, just nw on SR 161. Ext corridors. **Pets:** Medium, other species. $15 one-time fee/room. Service with restrictions, supervision.

ASK S✈ ✕ 🛏 ▣ ➿

# LAURINBURG

▼▼▼ **Hampton Inn** SH
(910) 277-1516. **$63-$67.** 115 Hampton Cir. Jct US 74/501, just s on US 15/401 Bypass, just e. Int corridors. **Pets:** Accepted.

ASK ✕ ⎙ 🖵 🛏 ▣ ➿

▼▼ Jameson Inn **M**
(910) 277-0080. **$54-$104.** 14 Jameson Inn Ct. Jct US 74/501, just n on US 15/401 Bypass, just e. Ext corridors. **Pets:** Very small, other species. $10 daily fee/room. Service with restrictions, supervision.

(A$K) ⊠ ⊟ ⊑ ⊅

# LENOIR

▼▼ Jameson Inn **M**
(828) 758-1200. **$54-$104.** 350 Wilkesboro Blvd. Jct US 321, 0.4 mi ne on SR 18. Ext corridors. **Pets:** Very small, other species. $10 daily fee/room. Service with restrictions, supervision.

(A$K) ⊠ ⅗M ⊟ ⊑ ⊅

# LEXINGTON

▼▼▼ Comfort Suites of Lexington **SH** ❀
(336) 357-2333. **$90, 3 day notice.** 1620 Cotton Grove Rd. I-85, exit 91, just s on SR 8, then just ne. Ext/int corridors. **Pets:** Small, other species. $25 daily fee/room. No service.

(A$K) (S⅗) ⊠ ⅗M ⊟ ⊑ ⊅

▲▲▲ ▼▼ Quality Inn **M**
(336) 249-0111. **$60-$119.** 418 Piedmont Dr. I-85, exit 96, 3.5 mi w on US 64. Ext corridors. **Pets:** Accepted.

(SAVE) (S⅗) ⊠ ⊟ ⊑ ⊅

# LINCOLNTON

▼▼ Days Inn **M**
(704) 735-8271. **$54-$59.** 614 Clark Dr. US 321, exit 24, 1 mi w on SR 150. Ext corridors. **Pets:** Other species. $10 daily fee/room. Designated rooms, service with restrictions, supervision.

(A$K) (S⅗) ⊠ ⊟ ⊑ ⊅

# LITTLE SWITZERLAND

▲▲▲ ▼▼▼ Switzerland Inn **CI**
(828) 765-2153. **$110-$200, 7 day notice.** Jct SR 226A and Blue Ridge Pkwy, MM 334. Ext/int corridors. **Pets:** Other species. $10 one-time fee/room. Designated rooms, no service.

(SAVE) (S⅗) ⊠ ⊟ ⊑ ⊟ ⊅ ⊠

# LUMBERTON

▲▲▲ ▼▼▼ Best Western Inn **M**
(910) 618-9799. **$79-$129.** 201 Jackson Ct. I-95, exit 22, just e, then just s. Ext corridors. **Pets:** Medium. $10 daily fee/pet. Service with restrictions, supervision.

(SAVE) (S⅗) ⊠ ⅔ ⊟ ⊑ ⊅

▲▲▲ ▼▼▼ Quality Inn and Suites **SH**
(910) 738-8261. **$60-$100.** 3608 Kahn Dr. I-95, exit 20, just e, enter at K-Mart entrance, then just w. Ext/int corridors. **Pets:** Accepted.

(SAVE) (S⅗) ⊠ ⊟ ⊑ ⊟ ⊅

# MAGGIE VALLEY

▼ Applecover Inn Motel **M**
(828) 926-9100. **$35-$100, 3 day notice.** 4077 Soco Rd. US 19, 4.5 mi w of US 276. Ext corridors. **Pets:** Other species. $50 deposit/room, $10 one-time fee/room. Designated rooms, no service, supervision.

⊠ ⊟

# MOCKSVILLE

▼▼ Comfort Inn **SH**
(336) 751-7310. **$65-$125.** 1500 Yadkinville Rd. I-40, exit 170, just s on US 601. Ext corridors. **Pets:** Accepted.

(A$K) (S⅗) ⊠ ⅔ ⊟ ⊑ ⊅

▼▼ Comfort Inn & Suites **SH**
(336) 751-5966. **$65-$95.** 629 Madison Rd. I-40, exit 170, just s on US 601, then just w. Int corridors. **Pets:** $25 one-time fee/pet. Service with restrictions, supervision.

(A$K) (S⅗) ⊠ ⅗M ⅔ ⅔ ⊟ ⊑ ⊅

# MOREHEAD CITY

▼▼▼ Holiday Inn Express Hotel & Suites **SH**
(252) 247-5001. **$75-$185.** 5063 Executive Dr. Jct US 70 and SR 24. Int corridors. **Pets:** Accepted.

(A$K) (S⅗) ⊠ ⅔ ⊟ ⊑ ⊅

# MORGANTON

▲▲▲ ▼▼▼▼ Comfort Inn & Suites **SH**
(828) 430-4000. **$59-$159.** 1273 Burkemont Ave. I-40, exit 103, just s. Int corridors. **Pets:** Accepted.

(SAVE) (S⅗) ⊠ ⅗M ⅔ ⊟ ⊑ ⊅

▼▼▼ Holiday Inn **SH**
(828) 437-0171. **$69-$84.** 2400 S Sterling St. I-40, exit 105 (SR 18), just s. Ext corridors. **Pets:** Other species. $25 one-time fee/room. Crate.

(A$K) (S⅗) ⊠ ⅗M ⅔ ⅔ ⊟ ⊑ ⊟ ⊅

▼▼▼ Sleep Inn **SH**
(828) 433-9000. **$56.** 2400A S Sterling St. I-40, exit 105 (SR 18), just s. Int corridors. **Pets:** Accepted.

(A$K) (S⅗) ⊠ ⅔ ⊟ ⊑

# MORRISVILLE

▼▼▼ La Quinta Inn & Suites Raleigh (Raleigh-Durham Int'l Airport) **SH**
(919) 461-1771. **$87-$147.** 1001 Hospitality Ct. I-40, exit 284 and 284A, just s, just e on Aerial Center Pkwy, then just ne; in Aerial Center Park. Int corridors. **Pets:** Medium. Service with restrictions.

(A$K) ⊠ ⅗M ⅔ ⅔ ⊟ ⊑ ⊅

▼▼▼ Staybridge Suites Raleigh Durham Airport **SH**
(919) 468-0180. **$111-$151, 3 day notice.** 1012 Airport Blvd. I-40, exit 284 and 284A, just s; enter between Hampton Inn and Holiday Inn Express. Int corridors. **Pets:** $150 one-time fee/room. Service with restrictions, crate.

⊠ ⅗M ⅔ ⅔ ⊟ ⊑ ⊠

# MOUNT AIRY

▼▼ Comfort Inn **M**
(336) 789-2000. **$62-$125.** 2136 Rockford St. Jct US 52, 0.6 mi s on US 601. Ext corridors. **Pets:** Accepted.

(A$K) (S⅗) ⊠ ⅔ ⊟ ⊑ ⊅

# MURPHY

▲▲▲ ▼▼▼ Best Western of Murphy **M**
(828) 837-3060. **$59-$119.** 1522 Andrews Rd. US 74, 19 and SR 129, exit Andrews Rd. Ext corridors. **Pets:** Small. $10 daily fee/pet. Designated rooms, service with restrictions, supervision.

(SAVE) (S⅗) ⊠ ⊟ ⊑ ⊅

▲▲▲ ▼▼▼ Days Inn **M**
(828) 837-8030. **$59-$109.** 754 Hwy 64 W. US 64 W/19 S/74 W and 129 S. Ext corridors. **Pets:** Accepted.

(SAVE) (S⅗) ⊠ ⊟ ⊑ ⊅

# OUTER BANKS AREA

## KILL DEVIL HILLS

**ⒶⒶⒶ ▼▼▼ Ramada Plaza Outer Banks Resort & Conference Center** SH
(252) 441-2151. **$79-$285.** 1701 S Virginia Dare Tr. SR 12, at MM 9.5. Int corridors. **Pets:** $20 daily fee/pet. Designated rooms, service with restrictions, supervision.

[SAVE] 🗑 ⊠ 🛢 💻 🍴 🏊 ⊠

**ⒶⒶⒶ ▼▼▼ Travelodge-Nags Head Beach** SH 🐾
(252) 441-0411. **$49-$309, 3 day notice.** 804 N Virginia Dare Tr. SR 12, at MM 8.1. Ext/int corridors. **Pets:** Medium. $20 daily fee/pet. Designated rooms, service with restrictions.

[SAVE] 🗑 ⊠ 🛢 💻 🏊

## NAGS HEAD

**ⒶⒶⒶ ▼▼▼ Comfort Inn Oceanfront South** SH
(252) 441-6315. **$55-$330.** 8031 Old Oregon Inlet Rd. SR 12 (Beach Rd), at MM 17. Int corridors. **Pets:** Other species. $10 daily fee/pet. Designated rooms, service with restrictions, supervision.

[SAVE] 🗑 ⊠ 🗂 🛢 💻 🏊 ⊠

**▼▼ Dolphin Oceanfront Motel** M
(252) 441-7488. **$49-$399, 30 day notice.** 8017 Old Oregon Inlet Rd (SR 1243). Jct SR 12, just s, at MM 16.5. Ext corridors. **Pets:** Other species. $10 daily fee/pet. Service with restrictions.

⊠ 🛢 💻 🏊

## OCRACOKE

**ⒶⒶⒶ ▼▼▼ The Anchorage Inn** 3H
(252) 928-1101. **$89-$199, 3 day notice.** 205 Irvin Garrish Hwy (SR 12). From Cedar Island Ferry, just n. Ext corridors. **Pets:** $20 daily fee/room. Designated rooms, service with restrictions, supervision.

[SAVE] ⊠ 🛢 💻 🏊 ⊠

# END AREA

## PINEHURST

**▼▼▼ Homewood Suites by Hilton** SH 🐾
(910) 255-0300. **$109-$250, 7 day notice.** 250 Central Park Ave. Jct SR 5 and 211; in Olmsted Village. Int corridors. **Pets:** $50 one-time fee/pet. Designated rooms, service with restrictions, supervision.

[ASK] 🗑 ⊠ 🗂ᴹ 🖑 🛢 💻 🏊

**▼▼▼ Springhill Suites by Marriott** SH
(910) 695-0234. **$112-$117.** 10024 US 15/501. Jct US 1, 2.3 mi n. Int corridors. **Pets:** Other species. $50 one-time fee/pet.

[ASK] 🗑 ⊠ 🗂ᴹ 🗂 🖑 🛢 💻 🏊 ⊠

## RALEIGH

**ⒶⒶⒶ ▼▼▼▼ AmeriSuites (Raleigh/Wake Forest Rd)** SH
(919) 877-9997. **$93-$179.** 1105 Navaho Dr. I-440, exit 10 (Wake Forest Rd), just n, then just w. Int corridors. **Pets:** Accepted.

[SAVE] ⊠ 🗂ᴹ 🗂 🖑 🛢 💻 🏊

**ⒶⒶⒶ ▼▼▼▼ Best Western Raleigh North** SH
(919) 872-5000. **$52-$70.** 2715 Capital Blvd. I-440, exit 11 or 11B, just n on US 1. Int corridors. **Pets:** Small. $25 daily fee/pet. Designated rooms, service with restrictions, supervision.

[SAVE] ⊠ 🗂 🛢 💻 🏊

**▼▼▼▼ Candlewood Suites-Crabtree** SH
(919) 789-4840. **$39-$89.** 4433 Lead Mine Rd. I-440, exit 7 or 7B, just w, then just n. Int corridors. **Pets:** Medium, dogs only. $75 one-time fee/room. Designated rooms, service with restrictions.

[ASK] 🗑 ⊠ 🗂ᴹ 🖑 🛢 💻

**ⒶⒶⒶ ▼▼▼ Days Inn** M
(919) 878-9310. **$45-$50.** 3201 Wake Forest Rd. I-440, exit 10 (Wake Forest Rd), just n, then just w. Ext corridors. **Pets:** $10 daily fee/room. Designated rooms, service with restrictions, supervision.

[SAVE] 🗑 ⊠ 🗂 🛢 🏊

**ⒶⒶⒶ ▼▼▼ Econo Lodge of Raleigh/North** M
(919) 856-9800. **$49-$79, 3 day notice.** 2641 Appliance Ct. I-440, exit 11 or 11B, just n, then 0.3 mi e. Ext/int corridors. **Pets:** $20 daily fee/pet, $20 one-time fee/pet. No service, supervision.

[SAVE] 🗑 ⊠ 🗂ᴹ 🗂 🖑 🛢 🏊

**ⒶⒶⒶ ▼▼▼▼ Hampton Inn Crabtree** SH
(919) 782-1112. **$79-$104.** 6209 Glenwood Ave. I-440, exit 7 or 7B, 2.5 mi w on US 70. Int corridors. **Pets:** Accepted.

[SAVE] 🗑 ⊠ 🗂ᴹ 🗂 🖑 🛢 💻 🏊

**▼▼▼▼ Holiday Inn at Crabtree Valley Mall** LH
(919) 782-8600. **$89-$149.** 4100 Glenwood Ave. I-440, exit 7, just w on US 70. Int corridors. **Pets:** Accepted.

[ASK] 🗑 ⊠ 🗂ᴹ 🗂 🖑 🛢 💻 🍴 🏊

**ⒶⒶⒶ ▼▼▼▼ Holiday Inn Raleigh-North** LH 🐾
(919) 872-3500. **$79-$99.** 2805 Highwoods Blvd. I-440, exit 11 or 11B, just n on US 1, then just w. Int corridors. **Pets:** Dogs only. $35 one-time fee/room. Service with restrictions, supervision.

[SAVE] 🗑 ⊠ 🗂ᴹ 🗂 🖑 🛢 💻 🍴 🏊

**▼▼ Homestead Studio Suites Hotel-Raleigh/Crabtree Valley** SH
(919) 510-8551. **$67-$134.** 4810 Bluestone Dr. I-440, exit 7 or 7B, 1.6 mi w on US 70, then just s. Ext corridors. **Pets:** $25 daily fee/pet. Service with restrictions, supervision.

[ASK] 🗑 ⊠ 🖑 🛢 💻

**▼▼ Homestead Studio Suites Hotel-Raleigh/North** SH
(919) 981-7353. **$67-$134.** 3531 Wake Forest Rd. I-440, exit 10 (Wake Forest Rd), 0.5 mi n. Ext corridors. **Pets:** $25 daily fee/pet. Service with restrictions, supervision.

[ASK] 🗑 ⊠ 🗂ᴹ 🗂 🖑 🛢 💻

**▼▼▼ Homestead Studio Suites Hotel-Raleigh/Northeast** SH
(919) 807-9970. **$61-$134.** 2601 Appliance Ct. I-440, exit 11 or 11B, just n on US 1, then just e. Int corridors. **Pets:** $25 daily fee/pet. Service with restrictions, supervision.

[ASK] 🗑 ⊠ 🗂 🖑 🛢 💻 🏊

**▼▼▼ Homewood Suites by Hilton** SH
(919) 785-1131. **$139.** 5400 Homewood Banks Dr. I-440, exit 7 or 7B, just w on US 70, then s on Blue Ridge Rd, just w on Crabtree Valley, then just s. Int corridors. **Pets:** Medium. $75 one-time fee/pet. Designated rooms, service with restrictions, crate.

[ASK] 🗑 ⊠ 🗂ᴹ 🗂 🖑 🛢 💻 🏊

**La Quinta Inn & Suites Raleigh (Crabtree)** SH
(919) 785-0071. **$93-$125.** 2211 Summit Park Ln. I-440, exit 7 or 7B, just w on US 70, just s on Blue Ridge Rd, then just e. Int corridors. **Pets:** Medium. Service with restrictions.

**Quality Suites Hotel** SH
(919) 876-2211. **$79-$119.** 4400 Capital Blvd. I-440, exit 11 and 11B, 2.5 mi n on US 1. Int corridors. **Pets:** Accepted.

**Red Roof Inn-South** SH
(919) 833-6005. **$53-$66.** 1813 S Saunders St. I-40, exit 298B, just n. Int corridors. **Pets:** Accepted.

**Residence Inn by Marriott Crabtree** SH
(919) 279-3000. **$125.** 2200 Summit Park Ln. I-440, exit 7 or 7B, just w on US 70, just s on Blue Ridge Rd, then just e. Int corridors. **Pets:** Accepted.

**Residence Inn by Marriott-North Raleigh** SH
(919) 878-6100. **$69-$169.** 1000 Navaho Dr. I-440, exit 10 (Wake Forest Rd), just n, then w. Ext corridors. **Pets:** Accepted.

**Sheraton Capital Center** LH
(919) 834-9900. **$159-$209.** 421 S Salisbury St. Downtown; just s. Int corridors. **Pets:** Accepted.

# REIDSVILLE

**Americas Best Value Inn & Suites** M
(336) 342-0341. **$60-$70.** 2100 Barnes St. US 29, exit 150 (Barnes St), just e. Ext corridors. **Pets:** Small. $10 daily fee/pet. Designated rooms, service with restrictions, supervision.

**Comfort Inn** M
(336) 634-1275. **$60-$205.** 2203 Barnes St. US 29, exit 150 (Barnes St), just e. Ext corridors. **Pets:** Small. $25 one-time fee/pet. Designated rooms, no service, supervision.

# RESEARCH TRIANGLE PARK

**Radisson Hotel in Research Triangle Park** SH
(919) 549-8631. **$-$.** 150 Park Dr. I-40, exit 280, just s, then just w. Int corridors. **Pets:** Accepted.

# ROANOKE RAPIDS

**Jameson Inn** M
(252) 533-0022. **$54-$104.** 101 S Old Farm Rd. I-95, exit 173, 0.5 mi w on US 158, then just s. Ext corridors. **Pets:** Very small, other species. $10 daily fee/room. Service with restrictions, supervision.

# ROBBINSVILLE

**Microtel Inn & Suites** SH
(828) 479-6772. **$49-$69.** 111 Rodney Orr Bypass (US 129). Center of downtown. Int corridors. **Pets:** Accepted.

# ROCKY MOUNT

**Best Western Inn I-95 Gold Rock** M
(252) 985-1450. **$65-$95.** 7095 NC 4. I-95, exit 145, just e. Ext corridors. **Pets:** Small, other species. $10 daily fee/pet. Supervision.

**Comfort Inn** SH ❖
(252) 937-7765. **$65-$79.** 200 Gateway Blvd. I-95, exit 138, 1 mi e on US 64, exit Winstead Ave, then just s. Int corridors. **Pets:** Other species. $25 one-time fee/room. Designated rooms, service with restrictions, crate.

**GuestHouse International Inn Battleboro/Rocky Mt.** M
(252) 407-8100. **$54-$64.** 7797 NC Hwy 48. I-95, exit 145, just e, then just n. Ext corridors. **Pets:** Other species. $6 one-time fee/pet. Supervision.

**Red Roof Inn** SH
(252) 984-0907. **$41-$61.** 1370 N Weslyan Blvd. Jct US 64 Bypass, 1.5 mi n on US 301. Int corridors. **Pets:** Accepted.

**Residence Inn by Marriott** SH ❖
(252) 451-5600. **$125-$145.** 230 Gateway Blvd. I-95, exit 138, 1 mi e on US 64, exit Winstead Ave, just s, then just e. Int corridors. **Pets:** Other species. $75 one-time fee/room. Service with restrictions, crate.

**Super 8 Motel** M
(252) 442-8075. **Call for rates.** 7522 NC 48. I-95, exit 145, just e, then just s. Ext corridors. **Pets:** Accepted.

# ROWLAND

**Holiday Inn Express** M
(910) 422-3377. **$60-$180.** 14733 US Hwy 301. I-95, exit 1B, just w. Ext corridors. **Pets:** Accepted.

# SALISBURY

**Hampton Inn** SH
(704) 637-8000. **$89-$200, 3 day notice.** 1001 Klumac Rd. I-85, exit 75, just w, then just s. Int corridors. **Pets:** Other species. Designated rooms, service with restrictions, supervision.

# SALUDA

**The Oaks Bed & Breakfast** BB
(828) 749-9613. **$115-$175, 3 day notice.** 339 Greenville St. I-26, exit 59, 1.1 mi sw, 0.3 mi w on US 176, then cross railway tracks. Ext/int corridors. **Pets:** Designated rooms.

# SANFORD

**Jameson Inn** M
(919) 708-7400. **$54-$104.** 2614 S Horner Blvd. Jct US 1, 4.1 mi s on US 421 and SR 87. Ext corridors. **Pets:** Very small, other species. $10 daily fee/room. Service with restrictions, supervision.

# SHELBY

**Hampton Inn** SH
(704) 482-5666. **$59-$72.** 2012 E Marion St. Jct US 74 Bypass E and US 74 business route. Int corridors. **Pets:** Small. Designated rooms, no service, crate.

**Super 8** M
(704) 484-2101. **$45-$53.** 1716 E Dixon Blvd. Jct SR 150, 0.4 mi w on US 74 Bypass. Ext corridors. **Pets:** Small. $25 deposit/pet. Service with restrictions, crate.

# SMITHFIELD

▼▼ **Jameson Inn** Ⓜ
(919) 989-5901. **$54-$104.** 125 S Equity Dr. I-95, exit 95, just w, just n on Industrial Park Blvd, then just w. Ext corridors. **Pets:** Very small, other species. $10 daily fee/room. Service with restrictions, supervision.

Ⓐ🅂🅺 ⊠ 🄼 🄪 🄳 🄫 ⌇

🛆 ▼▼▼ **Log Cabin Motel** Ⓜ
(919) 934-1534. **$45-$47.** 2491 US 70 E (Business Route). I-95, exit 95, 0.5 mi e. Ext corridors. **Pets:** Other species. $5 daily fee/pet. Designated rooms, service with restrictions.

🅂🄰🅅🄴 ⊠ 🄳 🍴 ⌇

🛆 ▼▼▼ **Super 8 Motel** 🆂🅷
(919) 989-8988. **$57-$103.** 735 Industrial Park Dr. I-95, exit 95, just w, then just n. Int corridors. **Pets:** Small. $4 daily fee/room. Designated rooms, service with restrictions, supervision.

🅂🄰🅅🄴 🆂🄳 ⊠ 🄼 🄪 🄶 🄳 ⌇

# SOUTHERN PINES

🛆 ▼▼▼ **Hampton Inn** 🆂🅷
(910) 692-9266. **$99, 7 day notice.** 1675 US 1 S. On US 1, 1 mi s. Ext corridors. **Pets:** Small, dogs only. $10 daily fee/pet. Service with restrictions, supervision.

🅂🄰🅅🄴 🆂🄳 ⊠ 🄳 🄫 ⌇

▼▼▼ **Microtel Inn** 🆂🅷
(910) 693-3737. **$47-$65, 7 day notice.** 205 Windstar Pl. 1 mi s on US 1, just e. Int corridors. **Pets:** Accepted.

Ⓐ🅂🅺 🆂🄳 ⊠ 🄶

▼▼▼ **Residence Inn by Marriott** 🆂🅷
(910) 693-3400. **$99-$119.** 105 Brucewood Rd. Jct US 1, 1.2 mi n on US 15/501, then just e. Int corridors. **Pets:** Accepted.

Ⓐ🅂🅺 🆂🄳 ⊠ 🄶 🄳 🄫 ⌇ ⊠

# SPRING LAKE

🛆 ▼▼▼ **Holiday Inn Express Hotel & Suites** 🆂🅷
(910) 436-1900. **$73-$100.** 103 Brook Ln. Jct SR 210, 0.9 mi nw on SR 24/87. Int corridors. **Pets:** Other species. $65 one-time fee/pet. Service with restrictions, supervision.

🅂🄰🅅🄴 🆂🄳 ⊠ 🄼 🄶 🄳 🄫 ⌇ ⊠

🛆 ▼▼ **Super 8 Motel** 🆂🅷
(910) 436-8588. **$55-$85.** 256 S Main St. Jct SR 210, just se on SR 24/87, just s. Int corridors. **Pets:** Medium. $15 daily fee/pet. Designated rooms, service with restrictions, supervision.

Ⓐ🅂🅺 🆂🄳 ⊠ 🄪 🄳

# SPRUCE PINE

🛆 ▼▼▼ **Richmond Inn** 🅱🅱 ☙
(828) 765-6993. **$75-$80.** 51 Pine Ave. Exit off US 19 E and 226 to Oak Ave, just n on Walnut Ave, follow signs; center. Int corridors. **Pets:** $10 daily fee/room.

🅂🄰🅅🄴 🆂🄳 ⊠ 🄳 🄫 🄩

# STATESVILLE

🛆 ▼▼ **Best Western Statesville Inn** 🆂🅷
(704) 881-0111. **$69-$175.** 1121 Morland Dr. I-77, exit 49A, just e on US 70 E. Ext/int corridors. **Pets:** Medium. $10 daily fee/pet. Designated rooms, service with restrictions, supervision.

🅂🄰🅅🄴 🆂🄳 ⊠ 🄶 🄳 🄫 ⌇

▼▼▼ **Holiday Inn Express Hotel & Suites** Ⓜ
(704) 872-4101. **$59-$99.** 740 Sullivan Rd. I-40, exit 151, just s. Ext corridors. **Pets:** Medium, other species. $25 one-time fee/pet. Service with restrictions, supervision.

Ⓐ🅂🅺 🆂🄳 ⊠ 🄼 🄪 🄳 🄫 ⌇

# SUNSET BEACH

🛆 ▼▼▼ **Sea Trail Golf Resort & Conference Center** 🄲🄾
(910) 287-1100. **$62-$462, 3 day notice.** 211 Clubhouse Rd. US 17, 2.2 mi e on SR 904, then 1.5 mi s on SR 179. Ext corridors. **Pets:** Large. $80 one-time fee/pet. Designated rooms, service with restrictions, supervision.

🅂🄰🅅🄴 🆂🄳 ⊠ 🄳 🄫 🍴 ⌇ ⊠

# THOMASVILLE

🛆 ▼▼ **Days Inn** 🆂🅷
(336) 472-6600. **$55-$60.** 895 Lake Rd. I-85, exit 102, just w, then just s. Int corridors. **Pets:** Medium. $25 daily fee/pet. Designated rooms, service with restrictions, crate.

🅂🄰🅅🄴 🆂🄳 ⊠ 🄳 🍴 ⌇

# TRYON

🛆 ▼▼▼ **Pine Crest Inn & Restaurant** 🄲🄸
(828) 859-9135. **$99-$229, 7 day notice.** 85 Pine Crest Ln. I-26, exit 67, 4 mi s on SR 108 W, follow signs. Ext/int corridors. **Pets:** Accepted.

🅂🄰🅅🄴 🆂🄳 ⊠ 🄳 🄫 🍴

# WAYNESVILLE

▼▼ **The Lodge of Waynesville** Ⓜ
(828) 452-0353. **$39-$125.** 909 Russ Ave. US 23/74, exit 102, just se. Ext corridors. **Pets:** Dogs only. $7 daily fee/pet. Service with restrictions, supervision.

🆂🄳 ⊠ 🄳 🄫 ⌇

# WELDON

🛆 ▼▼ **Days Inn** Ⓜ ☙
(252) 536-4867. **$60-$87.** 1611 Julian R Allsbrook Hwy. I-95, exit 173, just e on US 158. Ext corridors. **Pets:** $6 daily fee/pet. Designated rooms, service with restrictions, supervision.

🅂🄰🅅🄴 🆂🄳 ⊠ 🄪 🄳 ⌇

# WEST JEFFERSON

▼▼ **Nation's Inn** Ⓜ
(336) 246-2080. **$58.** 107 Beaver Creek School Rd. Jct US 221, just n on SR 194, just w. Ext corridors. **Pets:** Accepted.

Ⓐ🅂🅺 ⊠ 🄼 🄳

# WILKESBORO

▼▼ **Addison Inn** Ⓜ
(336) 838-1000. **$69-$135.** Hwy 421 N. 2 mi n on US 421, 0.5 mi w of US 421 business route. Ext corridors. **Pets:** Accepted.

Ⓐ🅂🅺 🆂🄳 ⊠ 🄼 🄪 🄳 🄫 ⌇

# WILLIAMSTON

▼▼▼ **Hampton Inn** 🆂🅷
(252) 809-1100. **$79-$84.** 1099 Hampton Ct. US 64, exit 514, just s on US 17, then just w. Int corridors. **Pets:** Accepted.

Ⓐ🅂🅺 🆂🄳 ⊠ 🄶 🄳 🄫 ⌇

▼▼▼▼ **Holiday Inn** SH
(252) 792-3184. **$69-$79.** 101 East Blvd. US 64, exit 514, 1.5 mi n on US 17 business route. Ext/int corridors. **Pets:** Medium. Service with restrictions, supervision.
A$K S⬤ ✕ ⟶ 🛇 🖥 ⏹ 🍽 ⇝

# WILMINGTON

▼▼ **Baymont Inn** M
(910) 392-6767. **$69-$99.** 306 S College Rd. US 17, 0.3 mi s on SR 132. Ext/int corridors. **Pets:** Accepted.
A$K S⬤ ✕ ⟶ 🛇 🖥 ⏹ ⇝

⬥⬥⬥ ▼▼▼ **Comfort Inn Wilmington** SH
(910) 791-4841. **$65-$135.** 151 S College Rd. US 17, just s on SR 132. Int corridors. **Pets:** Large, other species. $25 daily fee/pet. Designated rooms, service with restrictions, crate.
SAVE S⬤ ✕ ⟶ 🛇 🖥 ⏹ ⇝

▼▼▼ **Days Inn** M ❀
(910) 799-6300. **$45-$99.** 5040 Market St. Jct SR 132, 0.6 mi s on US 17. Ext corridors. **Pets:** Large. $15 daily fee/room. Service with restrictions, crate.
A$K S⬤ ✕ ⟶ 🛇 🖥 ⏹ 🍽 ⇝

▼▼▼▼ **Hilton Wilmington Riverside** LH
(910) 763-5900. **$129-$250.** 301 N Water St. On Cape Fear River waterfront. Int corridors. **Pets:** Accepted.
✕ ⟶ 🛇 ✦ 🖥 ⏹ 🍽 ⇝

▼▼ **Jameson Inn** SH
(910) 452-5660. **$54-$104.** 5102 Dunlea Ct. Jct SR 132, 0.5 mi s on US 17, just w on New Centre Dr. Int corridors. **Pets:** Very small, other species. $10 daily fee/room. Service with restrictions, supervision.
A$K ✕ ✦ 🛇 🖥 ⏹ ⇝

⬥⬥⬥ ▼▼▼▼ **MainStay Suites** SH
(910) 392-1741. **$79-$149.** 5229 Market St. Jct SR 132, just s on US 17. Int corridors. **Pets:** Small. $100 one-time fee/room. Designated rooms, service with restrictions.
SAVE S⬤ ✕ ⟶ ✦ 🛇 🖥 ⏹

⬥⬥⬥ ▼▼▼ **Quality Inn** M
(910) 791-8850. **$60-$130.** 4926 Market St. Jct SR 132, 0.9 mi s on US 17. Ext corridors. **Pets:** Small. $5 daily fee/pet, $25 one-time fee/pet. Service with restrictions, supervision.
SAVE S⬤ ✕ ⟶ 🛇 🖥 ⏹ ⇝

▼▼▼▼ **Residence Inn-Landfall** SH
(910) 256-0098. **$99-$189.** 1200 Culbreth Dr. Jct SR 132, 2.8 mi e on US 74, 0.4 mi n on Military Cutoff Rd, then just e. Int corridors. **Pets:** Other species. $75 one-time fee/pet. Supervision.
A$K ✕ ⟶ ✦ 🛇 🖥 ⏹ ⇝ ✕

▼▼ **Super 8 Motel** SH
(910) 343-9778. **$60-$180.** 3604 Market St. Jct SR 132, 1.8 mi s on US 17. Int corridors. **Pets:** Small, dogs only. $25 daily fee/pet. Designated rooms, service with restrictions, supervision.
A$K S⬤ ✕ ⟶ 🛇

# WILSON

⬥⬥⬥ ▼▼▼ **Best Western-Wilson** M
(252) 237-8700. **$48-$110.** 817-A Ward Blvd. US 264, exit 42, 2.6 mi n on Downing St, then just w. Ext corridors. **Pets:** Large. $10 daily fee/pet. Designated rooms, no service, supervision.
SAVE S⬤ ✕ 🛇 🖥 ⏹ ⇝

▼▼▼▼ **Jameson Inn** M
(252) 234-7172. **Call for rates.** 5016 Hayes Pl. I-95, exit 121, just w, then just n. Ext corridors. **Pets:** Accepted.
✕ ⟶ 🛇 🖥 ⏹ ⇝

# WINSTON-SALEM

⬥⬥⬥ ▼▼▼▼ **Augustus T Zevely Inn** BB
(336) 748-9299. **$90-$140, 14 day notice.** 803 S Main St. In Old Salem Historic District. Ext/int corridors. **Pets:** Medium. $15 daily fee/pet. Designated rooms, service with restrictions, crate.
SAVE ✕ 🛇

⬥⬥⬥ ▼▼▼ **Best Western Salem Inn & Suites** SH
(336) 725-8561. **$75-$110.** 127 S Cherry St. I-40 business route, exit 5C (Cherry St) eastbound, just e on High St, then just s; exit westbound, just w on 1st St, just s on Marshall St, just e on High St, then just s. Ext corridors. **Pets:** Medium. $25 one-time fee/room. Designated rooms, service with restrictions, crate.
SAVE S⬤ ✕ ⟶ 🛇 🖥 ⏹ ⇝

⬥⬥⬥ ▼▼▼ **Days Inn-North** M
(336) 744-5755. **$53-$61.** 5218 Germanton Rd. US 52, exit 114, just n on SR 8. Ext corridors. **Pets:** Accepted.
SAVE S⬤ ✕ 🛇

⬥⬥⬥ ▼▼▼▼ **The Hawthorne Inn & Conference Center** SH
(336) 777-3000. **$59-$99.** 420 High St. I-40 business route, exit 5C (Cherry St) eastbound, just e; exit westbound, just w on 1st St, then just s on Marshall St. Int corridors. **Pets:** Medium. $15 daily fee/pet. Designated rooms, service with restrictions.
SAVE S⬤ ✕ ✦M ⟶ ✦ 🛇 🖥 ⏹ 🍽 ⇝

▼▼▼▼ **Holiday Inn Hanes Mall** SH
(336) 765-6670. **$68.** 2008 S Hawthorne Rd. I-40 business route, exit 2A, 0.5 mi s on Silas Creek Pkwy, then just e. Ext corridors. **Pets:** Accepted.
A$K ✕ ✦M ⟶ ✦ 🖥 ⏹ 🍽 ⇝

▼▼▼▼ **La Quinta Inns & Suites Winston-Salem** SH
(336) 765-8777. **$88-$125.** 2020 Griffith Rd. I-40, exit 189 (Stratford Rd), just s, just e on Hanes Mall Blvd, then just s. Int corridors. **Pets:** Medium. Service with restrictions.
A$K ✕ ✦M ⟶ ✦ 🖥 ⏹ ⇝

⬥⬥⬥ ▼▼▼ **Quality Inn-Coliseum** SH
(336) 767-8240. **$73-$135.** 531 Akron Dr. US 52, exit 112, just e. Int corridors. **Pets:** Small. $15 daily fee/pet. Service with restrictions, supervision.
SAVE S⬤ ✕ ⟶ 🛇 🖥 ⏹ ⇝

▼▼▼ **Quality Inn University** SH
(336) 767-9009. **$66-$76, 30 day notice.** 5719 University Pkwy. US 52, exit 115B, 0.4 mi s. Ext corridors. **Pets:** $25 one-time fee/room. Service with restrictions, crate.
A$K S⬤ ✕ ⟶ 🛇 ⏹ ⇝

▼▼▼ **Residence Inn by Marriott** SH
(336) 759-0777. **$99-$149.** 7835 N Point Blvd. US 52 N, exit 115B, 2 mi s on University Pkwy, then just e. Ext corridors. **Pets:** $75 one-time fee/room. Service with restrictions, crate.
A$K S⬤ ✕ ⟶ 🛇 🖥 ⏹ ⇝ ✕

# YANCEYVILLE

▼▼▼ **Days Inn** M
(336) 694-9494. **$55-$150.** 1858 NC Hwy 86 N. Jct US 158 W, just s. Ext corridors. **Pets:** $10 daily fee/pet. No service, supervision.
A$K S⬤ ✕ ✦ 🛇 ⇝

# NORTH DAKOTA

## CITY INDEX

## BEULAH

**▼▼▼ AmericInn Motel & Suites** 🆂🅷
(701) 873-2220. **$76-$126.** 2100 2nd Ave NW. Jct SR 49/200, 1.2 mi s. Int corridors. **Pets:** Other species. $100 deposit/room. Service with restrictions, supervision.
(ASK) 🆂🅾 ✕ 🅖🅜 🖉 🄵 🍴 📺 ⇌ ✕

## BISMARCK

**▲▲▲ ▼▼▼ Best Western Doublewood Inn** 🆂🅷
(701) 258-7000. **$83-$150.** 1400 E Interchange Ave. I-94, exit 159 (US 83), just s. Int corridors. **Pets:** Small. $10 daily fee/room. Designated rooms, service with restrictions, supervision.
(SAVE) 🆂🅾 ✕ 🅖🅜 🖉 🄵 🍴 📺 🍴 ⇌ ✕

**▲▲▲ ▼▼▼▼ Best Western Ramkota Hotel** 🆂🅷
(701) 258-7700. **$99-$125.** 800 S 3rd St. Just s of jct I-94 business loop (Bismarck Expy) and S 3rd St. Int corridors. **Pets:** Accepted.
(SAVE) 🆂🅾 ✕ 🅖🅜 🖉 🄵 🍴 📺 🍴 ⇌ ✕

**▼▼ Comfort Inn** 🆂🅷
(701) 223-1911. **$64-$90.** 1030 Interstate Ave. I-94, exit 159 (US 83), 0.3 mi nw. Int corridors. **Pets:** Small. Service with restrictions, supervision.
(ASK) 🆂🅾 ✕ 🄵 🍴 📺 ⇌ ✕

**▲▲▲ ▼▼ Days Inn-Bismarck** 🆂🅷
(701) 223-9151. **$55-$84, 7 day notice.** 1300 E Capitol Ave. I-94, exit 159 (US 83), just s. Int corridors. **Pets:** $5 daily fee/pet. Designated rooms, service with restrictions, supervision.
(SAVE) 🆂🅾 ✕ 🍴 🄵 📺 ⇌ ✕

**▼▼ Expressway Inn** 🆂🅷
(701) 222-2900. **$54-$85.** 200 Bismarck Expwy. Jct I-94 business loop (Bismarck Expwy) and S 3rd St. Int corridors. **Pets:** Large, other species. $10 one-time fee/room. Designated rooms, service with restrictions, supervision.
(ASK) 🆂🅾 ✕ 🅖🅜 🖉 🄵 📺 ⇌ ✕

**▼▼ Kelly Inn** 🆂🅷
(701) 223-8001. **$79-$99.** 1800 N 12 St. I-94, exit 159 (US 83), 0.3 mi s. Int corridors. **Pets:** Service with restrictions, supervision.
(ASK) 🆂🅾 ✕ 🅖🅜 🖉 🄵 🍴 📺 🍴 ⇌ ✕

**▲▲▲ ▼▼▼ Radisson Hotel Bismarck** 🅻🅷
(701) 255-6000. **$79-$99.** 605 E Broadway Ave. Jct 6th St; center. Int corridors. **Pets:** Accepted.
(SAVE) 🆂🅾 ✕ 🅖🅜 🖉 🄵 📺 🍴 ⇌ ✕

**▲▲▲ ▼▼▼ Ramada Limited Suites** 🆂🅷
(701) 221-3030. **$65-$99.** 3808 E Divide Ave. I-94, exit 161 (Bismarck Expwy), just s. Int corridors. **Pets:** Other species. $10 daily fee/room. Crate.
(SAVE) 🆂🅾 ✕ 🅖🅜 🖉 🄵 🍴 📺 ⇌

**▲▲▲ ▼▼ Select Inn** 🆂🅷
(701) 223-8060. **$48-$70.** 1505 Interchange Ave. I-94, exit 159 (US 83), just se. Int corridors. **Pets:** $25 deposit/room, $5 daily fee/room. Designated rooms, service with restrictions, supervision.
(SAVE) 🆂🅾 ✕ 🖉 🄵 🍴 📺

## BOWMAN

**▲▲▲ ▼▼▼ North Winds Lodge** 🅼
(701) 523-5641. **$40-$58.** 503 Hwy 85 S. On US 85, just s of US 12. Ext corridors. **Pets:** Accepted.
(SAVE) 🆂🅾 ✕ 🍴 📺 ⇌

## CARRINGTON

**▼▼▼ Chieftain Conference Center** 🆂🅷
(701) 652-3131. **$50-$75.** 60 4th Ave S. Jct US 52 and 281, 0.5 mi e on US 52; just s of jct SR 200. Ext/int corridors. **Pets:** Small. $5 daily fee/room. Designated rooms, service with restrictions, supervision.
(ASK) 🆂🅾 ✕ 🍴 🍴

**▼▼ Super 8 Motel** 🆂🅷
(701) 652-3982. **$57-$74.** 101 4th Ave S. Jct US 52 and 281, 0.5 mi e on US 52; just s of jct SR 200. Int corridors. **Pets:** Medium, other species. $5 daily fee/pet. Designated rooms, service with restrictions, supervision.
(ASK) 🆂🅾 ✕ 🍴

## CASSELTON

**▲▲▲ ▼▼▼ Governors' Inn** 🆂🅷
(701) 347-4524. **$65-$109.** 2050 Governors Dr. I-94, exit 331 (SR 18), just n. Int corridors. **Pets:** Other species. $9 daily fee/pet. Designated rooms, service with restrictions, crate.
(SAVE) 🆂🅾 ✕ 🅖🅜 🍴 📺

## DEVILS LAKE

**▼▼ Comfort Inn** 🆂🅷
(701) 662-6760. **$70-$90.** 215 Hwy 2 E. Jct US 2 and SR 20. Int corridors. **Pets:** Accepted.
(ASK) 🆂🅾 ✕ 🖉 🄵 🍴 📺 ⇌ ✕

**▲▲▲ ▼ Trails West Motel** 🅼
(701) 662-5011. **$47.** 111 1st St W. 0.8 mi sw on US 2. Int corridors. **Pets:** $5 daily fee/pet. Service with restrictions, supervision.
(SAVE) 🆂🅾 ✕

## DICKINSON

**▼▼ AmericInn Motel & Suites of Dickinson** 🆂🅷
(701) 225-1400. **$89-$135.** 229 15th St W. I-94, exit 61 (SR 22), just n, then e. Int corridors. **Pets:** Accepted.
(ASK) 🆂🅾 ✕ 🅖🅜 🖉 🄵 🍴 📺 ⇌

**▼▼ Comfort Inn** 🆂🅷
(701) 264-7300. **$66-$140.** 493 Elks Dr. I-94, exit 61 (SR 22), just n, then w. Int corridors. **Pets:** Other species. Service with restrictions, supervision.
(ASK) 🆂🅾 ✕ 🅖🅜 🖉 🄵 🍴 📺 ⇌ ✕

**▲▲▲ ▼▼▼ Hartfiel Inn** 🅱🅱
(701) 225-6710. **$79.** 509 3rd Ave W. I-94, exit 61 (SR 22), 0.8 mi s. Int corridors. **Pets:** Medium, dogs only. Designated rooms, supervision.
(SAVE) ✕ 🍴 📺

**▼▼▼ Holiday Inn Express Hotel & Suites** 🆂🅷
(701) 456-8000. **$69-$85.** 103 14th St W. I-94, exit 61 (SR 22), just n, then just e. Int corridors. **Pets:** Accepted.
(ASK) 🆂🅾 ✕ 🅖🅜 🖉 🄵 🍴 📺 ⇌ ✕

**⬧ ▽▽ Quality Inn & Suites-Dickinson** SH
(701) 225-9510. **$60-$140.** 71 Museum Dr. I-94, exit 61 (SR 22), just s, then e. Int corridors. **Pets:** Small. $10 daily fee/pet. Designated rooms, no service, supervision.
[SAVE] [S5] [✕] [🔒] [💻] [⇌] [✕]

# EDGELEY

**▽▽ Prairie Rose Inn** SH 🐾
(701) 493-2075. **$54-$67.** 111 Frontage Rd. Jct US 281 and SR 13. Ext/int corridors. **Pets:** Dogs only. $25 deposit/room. Service with restrictions, crate.
[ASK] [S5] [✕] [🔒]

# FARGO

**▽▽ Airport/Dome Days Inn & Suites** SH
(701) 232-0000. **$84-$104.** 1507 19th Ave N. I-29, exit 67, 1.2 mi e. Int corridors. **Pets:** Accepted.
[ASK] [S5] [✕] [🔒] [💻] [⇌]

**⬧ ▽▽ AmericInn Lodge & Suites** SH
(701) 234-9946. **$70-$149.** 1423 35th St SW. I-29, exit 64 (13th Ave S), just se. Int corridors. **Pets:** Other species. $10 one-time fee/room. Designated rooms, service with restrictions, supervision.
[SAVE] [S5] [✕] [🔒] [💻] [⇌] [✕]

**⬧ ▽▽ Best Western Fargo Doublewood Inn** SH 🐾
(701) 235-3333. **$67-$72.** 3333 13th Ave S. I-29, exit 64 (13th Ave S), 0.3 mi e. Int corridors. **Pets:** Small, dogs only. $25 deposit/room. Service with restrictions, supervision.
[SAVE] [S5] [✕] [🔒] [💻] [🍴] [⇌] [✕]

**⬧ ▽▽ Best Western Kelly Inn** SH
(701) 282-2143. **$89-$105.** 3800 Main Ave. I-29, exit 65 (Main Ave), just w. Ext/int corridors. **Pets:** Service with restrictions, supervision.
[SAVE] [S5] [✕] [🔒] [💻] [🍴] [⇌] [✕]

**▽▽ Comfort Inn by Choice Hotels East** SH
(701) 280-9666. **$64-$109.** 1407 35th St S. I-29, exit 64 (13th Ave S), just se. Int corridors. **Pets:** Accepted.
[ASK] [S5] [✕] [🔒] [💻] [⇌]

**▽▽ Comfort Inn by Choice Hotels West** SH
(701) 282-9596. **$64-$109.** 3825 9th Ave SW. I-29, exit 64 (13th Ave S), just nw. Int corridors. **Pets:** Accepted.
[ASK] [S5] [✕] [🔒] [💻] [⇌]

**▽▽ Comfort Suites by Choice Hotels** SH
(701) 237-5911. **$74-$119.** 1415 35th St SW. I-29, exit 64 (13th Ave S), just se. Int corridors. **Pets:** Accepted.
[ASK] [S5] [✕] [💻] [⇌] [✕]

**▽▽ Econo Lodge by Choice Hotels** SH
(701) 232-3412. **$54-$94.** 1401 35th St S. I-29, exit 64 (13th Ave S), just se. Int corridors. **Pets:** Accepted.
[ASK] [S5] [✕] [🔒] [💻]

**▽▽ Expressway Inn** SH
(701) 235-3141. **$80-$83.** 1340 21st Ave S. I-94, exit 351, just sw. Ext/int corridors. **Pets:** Medium. $15 daily fee/room. Designated rooms, service with restrictions, crate.
[ASK] [S5] [✕] [💻] [🍴] [⇌] [✕]

**⬧ ▽▽ Grand Inn of Fargo** SH
(701) 232-1321. **$45-$58.** 3402 14th Ave S. I-29, exit 64 (13th Ave S), just se. Int corridors. **Pets:** Large. Designated rooms, service with restrictions, supervision.
[SAVE] [S5] [✕] [🔒]

**⬧ ▽▽ Holiday Inn** LH
(701) 282-2700. **$80-$99.** 3803 13th Ave S. I-29, exit 64 (13 Ave S), just nw. Int corridors. **Pets:** Other species. Service with restrictions, supervision.
[SAVE] [S5] [✕] [💻] [🔒] [💻] [🍴] [⇌] [✕]

**▽▽▽ Holiday Inn Express Fargo** SH
(701) 282-2000. **$90-$95.** 1040 40th St S. I-29, exit 64 (13th Ave S), just nw. Int corridors. **Pets:** Accepted.
[S5] [✕] [💻] [🔒] [💻] [⇌] [✕]

**▽▽▽ Kelly Inn 13th Avenue** SH
(701) 277-8821. **$74-$114.** 4207 13th Ave SW. I-29, exit 64 (13th Ave S), 0.5 mi w. Ext/int corridors. **Pets:** Service with restrictions, supervision.
[ASK] [S5] [✕] [💻] [🔒] [💻] [⇌]

**▽▽▽ MainStay Suites** SH
(701) 277-4627. **$72-$139.** 1901 44th St SW. I-94, exit 348 (45th St), just n, then just e. Int corridors. **Pets:** Accepted.
[ASK] [S5] [✕] [💻] [🔒] [💻] [⇌] [✕]

**▽ Motel 6 #1158** M
(701) 232-9251. **$41-$55.** 1202 36th S. I-29, exit 64 (13th Ave S), just n on east frontage road. Int corridors. **Pets:** Accepted.
[S5] [✕] [🔒] [💻] [⇌]

**⬧ ▽ Select Inn** SH 🐾
(701) 282-6300. **$46-$59.** 1025 38th St SW. I-29, exit 64 (13th Ave S), just w, then n. Int corridors. **Pets:** Large. $25 deposit/room, $5 daily fee/room. Designated rooms, service with restrictions, supervision.
[SAVE] [S5] [✕] [🔒] [💻] [💻]

**▽▽ Sleep Inn** SH
(701) 281-8240. **$69-$84.** 1921 44 St SW. I-94, exit 348 (45th St), just n, then just e. Int corridors. **Pets:** Accepted.
[ASK] [S5] [✕] [🔒] [💻] [💻] [⇌] [✕]

**▽▽ Super 8 Motel** SH
(701) 232-9202. **$39-$109.** 3518 Interstate Blvd. I-29, exit 64 (13th Ave S), just n on east frontage road. Int corridors. **Pets:** $4 daily fee/room. Designated rooms, service with restrictions, supervision.
[ASK] [S5] [✕] [🔒] [💻] [⇌]

# GRAFTON

**▽▽ AmericInn Motel & Suites** SH
(701) 352-2788. **$65-$185.** 1015 12th St W. SR 17, 1.2 mi w. Int corridors. **Pets:** Accepted.
[ASK] [S5] [✕] [💻] [🔒] [💻] [⇌] [✕]

# GRAND FORKS

**⬧ ▽ Americas Best Value Inn of Grand Forks** M
(701) 775-0555. **$45-$75.** 1000 N 42nd St. I-29, exit 141 (Gateway Dr), jct US 2, then just se. Int corridors. **Pets:** Other species. $6 daily fee/pet. Designated rooms, service with restrictions, supervision.
[SAVE] [✕] [🔒] [💻]

**▽▽ AmericInn Motel & Suites** SH
(701) 780-9925. **$64-$180.** 1820 S Columbia Rd. I-29, exit 138 (32nd Ave), 0.7 mi e, then 0.8 mi n. Int corridors. **Pets:** Accepted.
[ASK] [S5] [✕] [💻] [🔒] [💻] [⇌] [✕]

**⬧ ▽▽ Days Inn** SH
(701) 775-0060. **$55-$79.** 3101 34th St S. I-29, exit 138 (32nd Ave), 0.5 mi e. Int corridors. **Pets:** Small. $5 one-time fee/pet. Designated rooms, service with restrictions, supervision.
[SAVE] [S5] [✕] [🔒] [💻]

**▽▽ Travelodge** SH
(701) 772-8151. **$57-$77.** 2100 S Washington St. I-29, exit 140 (Demers Ave), 2.5 mi e, then 1.5 mi s. Int corridors. **Pets:** Small, dogs only. $5 daily fee/room. Designated rooms, supervision.
[ASK] [S5] [✕] [🔒] [💻] [✕]

# JAMESTOWN

**▽▽ Comfort Inn by Choice Hotels** SH
(701) 252-7125. **$64-$119.** 811 20 St SW. I-94, exit 258 (US 281), just n, then just w. Int corridors. **Pets:** Accepted.
[ASK] [S5] [✕] [🔒] [💻] [⇌]

**Quality Inn & Suites** SH
(701) 252-3611. **$79.** 507 25th St SW. I-94, exit 258 (US 281), just s. Int corridors. **Pets:** Large, other species. $10 one-time fee/room. Designated rooms, service with restrictions, crate.

## KENMARE

**Quilt Inn** SH
(701) 385-4100. **$55.** 1232 Central Ave N. Just n on US 52. Int corridors. **Pets:** Accepted.

## MANDAN

**Best Western Seven Seas Inn & Conference Center** SH
(701) 663-7401. **$85-$87.** 2611 Old Red Tr. I-94, exit 152 (Sunset Dr), just nw. Int corridors. **Pets:** Accepted.

## MEDORA

**AmericInn Motel & Suites** SH
(701) 623-4800. **$69-$220.** 75 E River Rd S. I-94, exit 24, just se of downtown. Int corridors. **Pets:** Other species. $12 one-time fee/room. Designated rooms, service with restrictions, supervision.

## MINOT

**Best Western Kelly Inn** SH
(701) 852-4300. **$69-$159.** 1510 26th Ave SW. US 2 and 52 Bypass, at 16th St SW. Ext/int corridors. **Pets:** Service with restrictions, supervision.

**Comfort Inn** SH
(701) 852-2201. **$70-$150.** 1515 22nd Ave SW. US 2 and 52 Bypass, at 16th St SW. Int corridors. **Pets:** Other species. Service with restrictions, supervision.

**Dakota Inn** SH
(701) 838-2700. **$47-$65.** 2401 US 2 & 52 Bypass. Jct US 83, 1 mi w. Int corridors. **Pets:** Accepted.

**Days Inn** SH
(701) 852-3646. **$52-$95.** 2100 4th St SW. Jct US 2 and 52 Bypass, just n. Int corridors. **Pets:** $5 daily fee/pet. Supervision.

**Holiday Inn Riverside Minot** LH
(701) 852-2504. **$67-$104.** 2200 Burdick Expwy E. 1.3 mi e on US 2 business route (Burdick Expwy E). Int corridors. **Pets:** Small, dogs only. $50 one-time fee/room. Designated rooms, service with restrictions, supervision.

**International Inn** LH
(701) 852-3161. **$62-$72.** 1505 N Broadway. 1.5 mi n on US 83. Int corridors. **Pets:** Accepted.

**Sleep Inn & Suites** LH
(701) 837-3100. **$90-$170.** 2400 10th St SW. US 2 and 52 Bypass at 16th St SW; southeast corner of Dakota Square Mall. Int corridors. **Pets:** Accepted.

## VALLEY CITY

**AmericInn Lodge & Suites** SH ❖
(701) 845-5551. **$65-$170.** 280 Winter Snow Rd SE. I-94, exit 292, just ne. Int corridors. **Pets:** Other species. $10 one-time fee/room. Designated rooms, service with restrictions.

**Super 8 Motel-Valley City** M
(701) 845-1140. **$57-$75.** 860 11th St SW. I-94, exit 292, just nw. Int corridors. **Pets:** Accepted.

**Wagon Wheel Inn & Suites** SH
(701) 845-5333. **$52-$62.** 455 Winter Snow Rd. I-94, exit 292, just ne. Ext/int corridors. **Pets:** Small. Designated rooms, service with restrictions, supervision.

## WAHPETON

**AmericInn Lodge & Suites** SH
(701) 642-8365. **$71-$101, 7 day notice.** 2029 Two-Ten Dr. 1 mi n on SR 210 Bypass. Int corridors. **Pets:** Small. $50 deposit/room. Designated rooms, service with restrictions, supervision.

**Comfort Inn by Choice Hotels** SH
(701) 642-1115. **$54-$79.** 209 13th St S. SR 13, 0.3 mi e of jct SR 210 Bypass. Int corridors. **Pets:** Accepted.

**Hospitality Inn & Suites** SH ❖
(701) 642-5000. **$59-$95, 7 day notice.** 1800 Two-Ten Dr. 1 mi n on SR 210 Bypass. Int corridors. **Pets:** Medium. $10 deposit/room. Designated rooms, service with restrictions, supervision.

**Wahpeton Super 8** SH
(701) 642-8731. **$40-$80.** 995 21st Ave N. 1.5 mi n on SR 210 Bypass. Int corridors. **Pets:** Other species. $5 one-time fee/pet. Designated rooms, service with restrictions, supervision.

## WATFORD CITY

**McKenzie Inn** M
(701) 444-3980. **$47-$52.** 132 SW 3rd St. US 85, just w. Ext corridors. **Pets:** Small, dogs only. $5 daily fee/pet. Designated rooms, service with restrictions, supervision.

**Roosevelt Inn & Suites** SH
(701) 842-3686. **$53-$85.** 600 2nd Ave SW. US 85, 0.3 mi w. Int corridors. **Pets:** $5 daily fee/room. Service with restrictions, supervision.

## WEST FARGO

**West Fargo Days Inn** SD
(701) 281-0000. **$60-$77.** 525 E Main Ave. I-29, exit 65 (Main Ave), 2.3 mi w. Int corridors. **Pets:** Accepted.

## WILLISTON

**El Rancho Motor Hotel** SH
(701) 572-6321. **$52-$60.** 1623 2nd Ave W. 1 mi n on US 2 and 85 N Bypass. Ext/int corridors. **Pets:** Accepted.

**Marquis Plaza & Suites** SH
(701) 774-3250. **$72-$78.** 1525 9th Ave NW. US 2 and 85, 4 mi e of jct US 85. Int corridors. **Pets:** Small. $10 daily fee/room. Designated rooms, service with restrictions, supervision.

## CITY INDEX

## AKRON

**Quality Inn Conference Center** SH
(330) 644-7126. **$69-$129, 3 day notice.** 2940 Chenoweth Rd. I-77, exit 120, just n. Int corridors. **Pets:** $40 one-time fee/room. Service with restrictions, crate.

**Red Roof Inn-Akron South #0207** M
(330) 644-7748. **$62-$80.** 2939 S Arlington Rd. I-77, exit 120, just n. **Pets:** Accepted.

## ALLIANCE

**Holiday Inn Express Hotel & Suites** SH
(330) 821-6700. **$79-$199.** 2341 W State St. 2 mi w on US 62. Int corridors. **Pets:** Small, dogs only. $10 one-time fee/pet. Designated rooms, service with restrictions, crate.

**Super 8 Motel** M
(330) 821-5688. **$49-$76.** 2330 W State St. 2 mi w on US 62. Ext corridors. **Pets:** $5 daily fee/pet. Service with restrictions.

## AMHERST

**Days Inn** M
(440) 985-1428. **$50-$80.** 934 N Leavitt Rd. SR 58, 0.3 mi n of SR 2. Ext/int corridors. **Pets:** Accepted.

## ASHLAND

**Days Inn** M
(419) 289-0101. **$40-$65.** 1423 CR 1575. I-71, exit 186, just w. Ext corridors. **Pets:** Accepted.

**The Surrey Inn** SH
(419) 289-7700. **$59-$120.** 1065 Claremont Ave. 1 mi s. Int corridors. **Pets:** Small, dogs only. $5 one-time fee/room. Designated rooms, service with restrictions, supervision.

## ASHTABULA

**Cedars Motel** M
(440) 992-5406. **$55-$75.** 2015 W Prospect Rd. Jct SR 11, 3 mi w on US 20. Ext corridors. **Pets:** Other species. $5 daily fee/pet. Service with restrictions, supervision.

**Ho Hum Motel** M
(440) 969-1136. **$60-$75.** 3801 N Ridge Rd W. I-90, exit 223, 3 mi n on SR 45, then 1 mi e on SR 20. Ext corridors. **Pets:** Other species. $5 daily fee/pet. Service with restrictions, crate.

## ATHENS

**Budget Host-Coach Inn** M
(740) 594-2294. **$41-$95, 3 day notice.** 100 Albany Rd (Hwy 50 W). US 50, exit westbound, just past Richland Ave exit; exit eastbound, e on Township Rd 60. Ext corridors. **Pets:** Small, dogs only. $10 daily fee/room. Designated rooms, service with restrictions, supervision.

**Super 8 Motel** SH
(740) 594-4900. **$50-$130, 21 day notice.** 2091 E State St. US 33, exit State St, 2.7 mi e. Int corridors. **Pets:** $5 daily fee/pet. Designated rooms, service with restrictions, crate.

## AUSTINBURG

**Comfort Inn-Ashtabula** SH
(440) 275-2711. **$69-$99.** 1860 Austinburg Rd. I-90, exit 223, just n. Int corridors. **Pets:** Large, other species. $10 daily fee/room. Designated rooms, service with restrictions, crate.

## AUSTINTOWN

**Austintown Super 8 Motel** M
(330) 793-7788. **$42-$100.** 5280 76 Dr. I-80, exit 223, just s on SR 46. Int corridors. **Pets:** Medium, other species. $8 daily fee/pet. Service with restrictions, supervision.

**(AAA) ▼▼▼ Best Western Meander Inn** 🆂🅷
(330) 544-2378. **$79-$109.** 870 N Canfield-Niles Rd. I-80, exit 223, 0.3 mi s on SR 46. Int corridors. **Pets:** Accepted.
🆂🅰🆅🅴 🆂🅳 ⊠ 🔊 🅺 🍴 🞐 🍴 ⇒

**(AAA) ▼▼▼ Econo Lodge** Ⓜ
(330) 270-2865. **$55-$60, 5 day notice.** 5431 1/2 76th Dr. I-80, exit 223, just s on SR 46. Ext corridors. **Pets:** Accepted.
🆂🅰🆅🅴 🆂🅳 ⊠

## BEAVERCREEK

**▼▼▼▼ Residence Inn by Marriott** 🆂🅷
(937) 427-3914. **$129-$149, 14 day notice.** 2779 Fairfield Commons. I-675, exit 17, just e, just s on New Germany-Trebein, then just e. Int corridors. **Pets:** Accepted.
🅰🆂🅺 🆂🅳 ⊠ 🅼 🔊 🅺 🞐 🞐 ⇒ ⊠

## BLUFFTON

**(AAA) ▼▼▼▼ Comfort Inn** 🆂🅷
(419) 358-6000. **$75-$110.** 117 Commerce Ln. I-75, exit 142, just w on SR 103. Int corridors. **Pets:** Medium, other species. $15 one-time fee/pet. Service with restrictions.
🆂🅰🆅🅴 🆂🅳 ⊠ 🔊 🅺 🞐 🞐 ⇒ ⊠

## BOARDMAN

**(AAA) ▼ Days Inn** Ⓜ
(330) 758-2371. **$36-$85, 3 day notice.** 8392 Market St. I-76, exit 232, 1.8 mi n on SR 7. Ext corridors. **Pets:** Accepted.
🆂🅰🆅🅴 🆂🅳 ⊠ 🞐 ⇒

**▼▼ Microtel Inn Youngstown** 🆂🅷
(330) 758-1816. **$47-$89.** 7393 South Ave. Jct I-680 and US 224, 0.3 mi w. Int corridors. **Pets:** Other species. $50 one-time fee/room. Service with restrictions, supervision.
🅰🆂🅺 🆂🅳 ⊠ 🔊 🅺 🞐

**(AAA) ▼▼▼ Ramada Limited** 🆂🅷
(330) 549-0157. **$59-$79.** 9988 Market St. 0.5 mi n on SR 7. Int corridors. **Pets:** $10 daily fee/room. Designated rooms, service with restrictions, supervision.
🆂🅰🆅🅴 🆂🅳 ⊠ 🅼 🅺 🞐 🞐

## BOWLING GREEN

**▼ Days Inn** Ⓜ
(419) 352-5211. **$49-$89, 3 day notice.** 1550 E Wooster St. I-75, exit 181, just w. Ext corridors. **Pets:** Other species. $10 one-time fee/room. Service with restrictions, supervision.
🅰🆂🅺 🆂🅳 ⊠ 🔊 🞐 🞐

**(AAA) ▼▼▼ Quality Inn & Suites** 🆂🅷
(419) 352-2521. **$59-$69.** 1630 E Wooster St. I-75, exit 181, just w. Int corridors. **Pets:** Medium, other species. $10 daily fee/room. No service, supervision.
🆂🅰🆅🅴 🆂🅳 ⊠ 🞐 🞐 ⇒

## BROOKVILLE

**(AAA) ▼▼▼ Brookville Days Inn** Ⓜ
(937) 833-4003. **$50-$60.** 100 Parkview Dr. I-70, exit 21, just s. Ext corridors. **Pets:** Other species. $10 one-time fee/pet. Service with restrictions.
🆂🅰🆅🅴 🆂🅳 ⊠ ⇒

## BRUNSWICK

**▼▼ Sleep Inn** 🆂🅷
(330) 273-1112. **$48-$72.** 1435 S Carpenter Rd. I-71, exit 226, just w. Ext corridors. **Pets:** Accepted.
🅰🆂🅺 🆂🅳 ⊠ 🞐 🞐 ⇒

## BRYAN

**(AAA) ▼▼▼ Colonial Manor Motel** Ⓜ
(419) 636-3123. **$68-$125.** 924 E High St. US 127, 0.8 mi e on SR 2/34. Ext corridors. **Pets:** Designated rooms, no service, supervision.
🆂🅰🆅🅴 ⊠ 🅺 🞐 🞐 🍴

## CAMBRIDGE

**(AAA) ▼▼▼ Best Western Cambridge** 🆂🅷 🐾
(740) 439-3581. **$49-$89.** 1945 Southgate Pkwy. I-70, exit 178, 0.3 mi n on SR 209. Ext corridors. **Pets:** Small. Service with restrictions, supervision.
🆂🅰🆅🅴 🆂🅳 ⊠ 🔊 🅺 🞐 🞐 ⇒

**▼ Budget Inn** Ⓜ
(740) 432-2304. **$40-$50.** 6405 Glenn Hwy. I-70, exit 176, just e on US 40. Ext/int corridors. **Pets:** Small. $10 daily fee/pet. Designated rooms, service with restrictions, supervision.
🅰🆂🅺 🆂🅳 ⊠ 🞐 🞐

**(AAA) ▼▼▼ Comfort Inn** 🆂🅷
(740) 435-3200. **$64-$139.** 2327 Southgate Pkwy. I-70, exit 178, just n on SR 209. Int corridors. **Pets:** Accepted.
🆂🅰🆅🅴 🆂🅳 ⊠ 🅺 🞐 🞐 ⇒

**▼▼ Days Inn-Cambridge** 🆂🅷
(740) 432-5691. **$59-$89, 3 day notice.** 2328 Southgate Pkwy. I-70, exit 178, just n on SR 209. Int corridors. **Pets:** Service with restrictions.
🅰🆂🅺 🆂🅳 ⊠ 🔊 🞐 🞐 ⇒

**▼▼ Deer Creek Express** Ⓜ
(740) 432-6391. **$43-$69.** 2321 Southgate Pkwy. I-70, exit 178, just ne on SR 209. Ext corridors. **Pets:** Other species. $5 one-time fee/room. Designated rooms, service with restrictions, supervision.
🅰🆂🅺 🆂🅳 ⊠ 🞐 🞐 ⇒

**▼▼▼ Holiday Inn Cambridge/Salt Fork Area** 🆂🅷
(740) 432-7313. **$54-$99.** 2248 Southgate Pkwy. I-70, exit 178, just n on SR 209. Int corridors. **Pets:** Medium. Service with restrictions, crate.
🅰🆂🅺 🆂🅳 ⊠ 🔊 🞐 🞐 🍴 ⇒ ⊠

**(AAA) ▼▼▼ Super 8 Motel-Cambridge** 🆂🅷
(740) 435-8080. **$40-$60.** 8779 Georgetown Rd. I-70, exit 178, just n. Ext corridors. **Pets:** Other species. $10 daily fee/pet. Supervision.
🆂🅰🆅🅴 🆂🅳 ⊠ 🞐

## CANTON

**▼▼ Red Roof Inn #7019** Ⓜ
(330) 499-1970. **$48-$74.** 5353 Inn Circle Ct NW. I-77, exit 109, just w on Everhard Rd. Ext corridors. **Pets:** Accepted.
⊠ 🔊

**▼▼▼ Residence Inn by Marriott** 🆂🅷
(330) 493-0004. **$90-$150, 14 day notice.** 5280 Broadmoor Cir NW. I-77, exit 109, 0.5 mi e on Everhard Rd. Int corridors. **Pets:** Accepted.
🅰🆂🅺 🆂🅳 ⊠ 🅼 🔊 🞐 🞐 ⇒ ⊠

## CARROLLTON

**▼▼▼ Carrollton Days Inn** 🆂🅷
(330) 627-9314. **$79-$130.** 1111 Canton Rd. On SR 43, 0.5 mi n of SR 39. Int corridors. **Pets:** Medium. $20 one-time fee/pet. Service with restrictions, supervision.
🅰🆂🅺 🆂🅳 ⊠ 🞐 🞐 ⇒

## CEDARVILLE

**▼▼▼ Hearthstone Inn & Suites** 🆂🅷 🐾
(937) 766-3000. **$99-$129.** 10 S Main St. I-70, exit 54, 11 mi s. Int corridors. **Pets:** Small, dogs only. $15 daily fee/pet. Service with restrictions, supervision.
🅰🆂🅺 ⊠ 🞐 🞐

# CELINA

**Comfort Inn Grand Lake** 🆂🅷
(419) 586-4656. **$70-$199, 7 day notice.** 1421 SR 703 E. Jct SR 29. Ext corridors. **Pets:** Accepted.

[SAVE] [S🌀] [✕] [🛗] [💻]

# CHILLICOTHE

**Best Western Adena Inn** 🆂🅷
(740) 775-7000. **$69-$149.** 1250 N Bridge St. US 35, exit Bridge St, 0.8 mi n. Int corridors. **Pets:** $10 daily fee/pet. Service with restrictions, supervision.

[ASK] [S🌀] [✕] [🛗] [💻] [🏊]

---

## CINCINNATI METROPOLITAN AREA

# BATAVIA

**Hampton Inn-Cincinnati Eastgate** 🆂🅷
(513) 752-8584. **$71-$119.** 858 Eastgate North Dr. I-275, exit 63B (SR 32), just e, just n on Gleneste Withamsville Rd, then just w; behind Longhorn Steak House. Int corridors. **Pets:** Accepted.

[ASK] [S🌀] [✕] [🛗] [💻] [🏊]

**Holiday Inn-Cincinnati Eastgate** 🅻🅷
(513) 752-4400. **$80-$120.** 4501 Eastgate Blvd. I-275, exit 63B (SR 32), 0.5 mi e to Eastgate Mall exit, then 0.5 mi n. Int corridors. **Pets:** Other species. Service with restrictions.

[SAVE] [S🌀] [✕] [🌀] [🛗] [💻] [🍴] [🏊] [✕]

# BLUE ASH

**AmeriSuites (Cincinnati/Blue Ash)** 🆂🅷
(513) 489-3666. **$99-$129.** 11435 Reed-Hartman Hwy. I-275, exit 47, 0.8 mi s. Int corridors. **Pets:** Small, other species. $10 daily fee/pet. Service with restrictions, supervision.

[SAVE] [S🌀] [✕] [🅼] [🌀] [🛗] [💻] [🏊]

**Homestead Studio Suites Hotel-Cincinnati/Blue Ash** 🆂🅷
(513) 985-9992. **$70-$85.** 4630 Creek Rd. I-275, exit 47, 2.3 mi s on Reed-Hartman Hwy, then just e. Int corridors. **Pets:** $25 daily fee/pet. Service with restrictions, supervision.

[ASK] [S🌀] [✕] [🌀] [🅰] [🛗] [💻] [🏊]

**Red Roof Inn Northeast (Blue Ash)** Ⓜ
(513) 793-8811. **$51-$78.** 5900 Pfeiffer Rd. I-71, exit 15, just w. Ext corridors. **Pets:** Accepted.

[✕] [🅼] [🅰] [🛗]

**Residence Inn by Marriott-Blue Ash** 🆂🅷 🐾
(513) 530-5060. **$139-$159.** 11401 Reed-Hartman Hwy. I-275, exit 47, 0.8 mi s. Ext corridors. **Pets:** Medium, other species. $75 one-time fee/room. Service with restrictions.

[ASK] [S🌀] [✕] [🅼] [🌀] [🅰] [🛗] [💻] [🏊] [✕]

**TownePlace Suites by Marriott Blue Ash** 🆂🅷 🐾
(513) 469-8222. **$109-$119.** 4650 Cornell Rd. I-275, exit 47, 0.9 mi s on Reed-Hartman Hwy, then just w. Int corridors. **Pets:** Large, other species. $75 one-time fee/room. Service with restrictions, supervision.

[ASK] [S🌀] [✕] [🅰] [🛗] [💻] [🏊]

# CHERRY GROVE

**Best Western Clermont** Ⓜ
(513) 528-7702. **$69-$99.** 4004 Williams Dr. I-275, exit 65, just w, then just s. Ext corridors. **Pets:** Small. $25 one-time fee/room. Designated rooms, service with restrictions.

[✕] [🌀] [🅰] [🛗] [💻] [🏊]

**Red Roof Inn Cincinnati East #7080** Ⓜ
(513) 528-2741. **$45-$65.** 4035 Mt. Carmel-Tobasco Rd. I-275, exit 65, just w on SR 125, then just n. Ext corridors. **Pets:** Accepted.

[✕] [🅰] [🛗]

# CINCINNATI

**Millennium Hotel Cincinnati** 🅻🅷
(513) 352-2100. **$199.** 141 W 6th St. Between Elm and Race sts. Int corridors. **Pets:** Accepted.

[SAVE] [S🌀] [✕] [🅰] [🛗] [💻] [🍴] [🏊]

**The Westin Cincinnati** 🅻🅷
(513) 621-7700. **$139-$329.** 21 E 5th St. Between Vine and Walnut sts. Int corridors. **Pets:** Accepted.

[ASK] [S🌀] [✕] [🅼] [🌀] [🅰] [🛗] [💻] [🍴] [🏊]

# FAIRFIELD

**Holiday Inn Express** 🆂🅷
(513) 860-2900. **$87-$105.** 6755 Fairfield Business Park Dr. I-275, exit 41 (SR 4), 1.5 mi n. Int corridors. **Pets:** Small, other species. Designated rooms, service with restrictions, supervision.

[ASK] [S🌀] [✕] [🅼] [🌀] [🅰] [🛗] [💻] [🏊]

# FOREST PARK

**AmeriSuites (Cincinnati/North)** 🆂🅷
(513) 825-9035. **$89-$159.** 12001 Chase Plaza Dr. I-275, exit 39, just s, then just w. Int corridors. **Pets:** Accepted.

[SAVE] [S🌀] [✕] [🌀] [🛗] [💻] [🏊]

# HAMILTON

**The Hamiltonian Hotel** 🆂🅷
(513) 896-6200. **$72-$82.** 1 Riverfront Plaza. Just off High St, on Front St. Int corridors. **Pets:** Accepted.

[ASK] [S🌀] [✕] [🌀] [🛗] [💻] [🍴] [🏊]

# HARRISON

**Comfort Inn** 🆂🅷
(513) 367-9666. **$45-$110.** 391 Comfort Dr. I-74, exit 1, just n on New Haven Rd, then just e. Int corridors. **Pets:** Accepted.

[ASK] [S🌀] [✕] [🅼] [🅰] [🛗] [💻] [🏊]

# MASON

**AmeriSuites (Cincinnati/Deerfield Crossing)** 🆂🅷
(513) 754-0003. **$99-$159.** 5070 Natorp Blvd. I-71, exit 19, 0.5 mi w. Int corridors. **Pets:** Small. $10 daily fee/pet. Designated rooms, service with restrictions, supervision.

[SAVE] [S🌀] [✕] [🅼] [🅰] [🛗] [💻] [🏊]

**(AAA) ▼▼▼ Baymont Inn & Suites Cincinnati-North** SH
(513) 459-1111. **$85-$159.** 9918 Escort Dr. I-71, exit 19, just w, then just s. Int corridors. **Pets:** Medium. Service with restrictions.
SAVE ⊠ 🐾 🖾 🔒 💻 ➔

**(AAA) ▼▼▼ Microtel Inn & Suites Kings Island** SH
(513) 754-1500. **$50-$169.** 5324 Beach Blvd. I-71, exit 25, just nw. Int corridors. **Pets:** Small, dogs only. $20 daily fee/room. Service with restrictions.
SAVE S🐾 ⊠ 🖾M 🖾 🔒 💻

**▼▼▼ TownePlace Suites by Marriott** SH
(513) 774-0610. **$79-$139.** 9369 Waterstone Blvd. I-71, exit 19, 0.5 mi e on Fields-Ertel Rd, then 0.9 mi n. Int corridors. **Pets:** Other species. $75 one-time fee/room. Service with restrictions.
ASK S🐾 ⊠ 🖾M 🖾 🔒 💻 ➔

## MIDDLETOWN

**(AAA) ▼▼▼▼ Best Western Regency Inn** SH
(513) 424-3551. **$65-$145, 7 day notice.** 6475 Culbertson Rd. I-75, exit 32. Int corridors. **Pets:** Accepted.
SAVE S🐾 ⊠ 🖾 🔒 💻 ➔

**▼▼▼ Fairfield Inn by Marriott** SH
(513) 424-5444. **$83-$103.** 6750 Roosevelt Pkwy. I-75, exit 32, 0.5 mi w on SR 122. Int corridors. **Pets:** Accepted.
ASK S🐾 ⊠ 🖾M 🖾 🔒 💻 ➔

**▼▼▼ The Manchester Inn & Conference Center** SH
(513) 422-5481. **$72-$167.** 1027 Manchester Ave. Just w of SR 4 and 73. Int corridors. **Pets:** Accepted.
ASK S🐾 ⊠ 🔒 💻 ⍟

**▼▼▼ Ramada Inn Middletown** SH
(513) 424-1201. **$55-$75.** 6147 W SR 122. I-75, exit 32, just e. Int corridors. **Pets:** Accepted.
ASK S🐾 ⊠ 🖾 🔒 💻 ⍟ ➔

**▼▼ Super 8 Motel Middletown** SH
(513) 422-4888. **$49-$69.** 3553 Commerce Dr. I-75, exit 32, just e, then just n. Int corridors. **Pets:** Dogs only. $10 daily fee/room. Designated rooms, service with restrictions, supervision.
ASK S🐾 ⊠ 🔒

## MOUNT ORAB

**(AAA) ▼▼▼▼ Best Western Mount Orab Inn** SH
(937) 444-6666. **$59-$99.** 100 Leininger St. Jct US 68 and SR 32, just n on US 68. Int corridors. **Pets:** Accepted.
SAVE S🐾 ⊠ 🖾 🔒 💻 ➔

## NORWOOD

**▼▼ Howard Johnson East** SH
(513) 631-8500. **$66-$86.** 5410 Ridge Rd. I-71, exit 8 southbound; exit 8B northbound, 0.4 mi nw. Int corridors. **Pets:** Accepted.
ASK S🐾 ⊠ 🔒 💻 ⍟ ➔

## SHARONVILLE

**(AAA) ▼▼▼▼ Arcadia Residential Suites** SH
(513) 354-1000. **$82-$149.** 11180 Down Rd. I-75, exit 15, just e on Sharon Rd, then just n. Int corridors. **Pets:** Very small. $100 one-time fee/room. Designated rooms, crate.
SAVE S🐾 ⊠ 🖾 🔒 💻 ➔

**▼▼▼▼ Homewood Suites by Hilton-Cincinnati North** SH
(513) 772-8888. **$109-$139.** 2670 E Kemper Rd. I-275, exit 44, jct Mosteller Rd. Int corridors. **Pets:** Small. $15 daily fee/pet. Service with restrictions, crate.
ASK ⊠ 🔒 💻 ➔ ⊠

**(AAA) ▼▼▼▼ LaQuinta Inn & Suites** SH
(513) 771-0300. **$95-$109.** 11029 Down Dr. I-75, exit 15, just e. Int corridors. **Pets:** Medium. Service with restrictions.
SAVE ⊠ 🖾M 🖾 🔒 💻 ➔ ⊠

**▼▼▼ Ramada Limited Sharonville** SH
(513) 772-4114. **$49-$69.** 11171 Dowlin Dr. I-75, exit 15, just e, then just n. Ext/int corridors. **Pets:** Accepted.
ASK S🐾 ⊠ 🖾 🔒 💻 ➔

**▼▼▼ Residence Inn by Marriott** SH 🐾
(513) 771-2525. **$104-$149.** 11689 Chester Rd. I-75, exit 15, 0.3 mi w on Sharon Rd, then 1 mi n. Ext corridors. **Pets:** Medium. $75 one-time fee/room. Service with restrictions, crate.
ASK S🐾 ⊠ 🖾M 🖾 🔒 💻 ➔ ⊠

## WEST CHESTER

**(AAA) ▼▼▼▼ Staybridge Suites Cincinnati North** SH 🐾
(513) 874-1900. **$119-$229.** 8955 Lakota Dr W. I-75, exit 19, just w on Union Center Blvd, then just n. Int corridors. **Pets:** Other species. No service, supervision.
SAVE S🐾 ⊠ 🖾M 🖾 🖾 🔒 💻 ➔ ⊠

## WILMINGTON

**(AAA) ▼▼▼ AmeriHost Inn & Suites** SH
(937) 383-3950. **$74-$109.** 201 Carrie Dr. Jct US 22 and 68, 1.5 mi e on US 22. Int corridors. **Pets:** $25 one-time fee/room. Designated rooms, service with restrictions, crate.
SAVE S🐾 ⊠ 🔒 💻 ➔ ⊠

**(AAA) ▼▼▼▼ Holiday Inn & Roberts Convention Centre** LH
(937) 283-3200. **$129-$159.** 123 Gano Rd. I-71, exit 50, just w. Int corridors. **Pets:** Accepted.
SAVE S🐾 ⊠ 🖾M 🖾 🔒 💻 ⍟ ➔

**▼▼▼ Holiday Inn Express** SH
(937) 382-5858. **$81-$99.** 155 Holiday Dr. 1.6 mi e on US 22. Int corridors. **Pets:** Accepted.
ASK S🐾 ⊠ 🖾M 🖾 🖾 🔒 💻 ➔ ⊠

## END METROPOLITAN AREA

# CLEVELAND METROPOLITAN AREA

## BEACHWOOD

**Hilton Cleveland East/Beachwood** LH
(216) 464-5950. **$99-$169.** 3663 Park East Dr. I-271, exit Chagrin Blvd, just w. Int corridors. **Pets:** Accepted.

**Holiday Inn-Beachwood** SH
(216) 831-3300. **$99-$129.** 3750 Orange Pl. I-271, exit Chagrin Blvd, just e. Int corridors. **Pets:** Accepted.

**Homestead Studio Suites Hotel-Cleveland/Beachwood** SH
(216) 896-5555. **$70-$85.** 3625 Orange Pl. I-271, exit Chagrin Blvd, just e. Int corridors. **Pets:** $25 daily fee/pet. Service with restrictions, supervision.

**Residence Inn by Marriott Cleveland-Beachwood** SH
(216) 831-3030. **$109-$159.** 3628 Park East Dr. Jct US 422 and I-271, exit Chagrin Blvd, just w. Int corridors. **Pets:** Accepted.

**Super 8 Motel-Beachwood** M
(216) 831-7200. **$49-$94.** 3795 Orange Pl. I-271, exit Chagrin Blvd, just e, then s. Ext/int corridors. **Pets:** Small, dogs only. $25 one-time fee/pet. Service with restrictions, supervision.

## CLEVELAND

**Baymont Inn & Suites Cleveland-Airport** SH
(216) 251-8500. **$85-$125.** 4222 W 150th St. I-71, exit 240, just n. Int corridors. **Pets:** Medium. Service with restrictions.

**Cleveland Airport Marriott** LH
(216) 252-5333. **$109-$189.** 4277 W 150th St. I-71, exit 240, just s. Int corridors. **Pets:** Accepted.

**Crowne Plaza Cleveland City Centre Hotel** LH
(216) 771-7600. **$99-$209.** 777 St. Clair Ave. E 6th St and St. Clair Ave. Int corridors. **Pets:** Large, dogs only. $25 one-time fee/room. Service with restrictions, supervision.

**Residence Inn by Marriott** SH
(216) 443-9043. **$99-$169.** 527 Prospect Ave. Between E 9th St and Ontario. Int corridors. **Pets:** Medium. $75 one-time fee/room.

**The Ritz-Carlton, Cleveland** LH ❖
(216) 623-1300. **$239-$259.** 1515 W 3rd St. In Tower City Center (3rd St side). Int corridors. **Pets:** Medium, dogs only. $100 one-time fee/room. Service with restrictions, supervision.

**Sheraton Cleveland Airport Hotel** SH
(216) 267-1500. **$89-$269.** 5300 Riverside Dr. I-71, exit 237, follow signs; just s of I-480 on SR 237. Int corridors. **Pets:** Accepted.

## INDEPENDENCE

**AmeriSuites (Cleveland/Independence)** SH
(216) 328-1060. **$99-$129.** 6025 Jefferson Dr. I-77, exit Rockside Rd, just w to W Creek Rd, then just n. Int corridors. **Pets:** Small. $10 daily fee/room. Service with restrictions, supervision.

**Baymont Inn & Suites Cleveland-Independence** SH
(216) 447-1133. **$72-$149.** 6161 Quarry Ln. I-77, exit Rockside Rd, just e. Int corridors. **Pets:** Medium. Service with restrictions.

**Clarion Hotel & Conference Center Cleveland South** SH
(216) 524-0700. **$79-$119.** 5300 Rockside Rd. I-77, exit Rockside Rd, just w. Int corridors. **Pets:** Other species. $25 deposit/room, $10 daily fee/pet. Designated rooms, service with restrictions, supervision.

**Red Roof Inn #7028** M
(216) 447-0030. **$62-$78.** 6020 Quarry Ln. I-77, exit Rockside Rd, just e. Ext corridors. **Pets:** Accepted.

**Residence Inn by Marriott** SH
(216) 520-1450. **$89-$139.** 5101 W Creek Rd. I-77, exit Rockside Rd, just w to W Creek Rd, then just n. Ext corridors. **Pets:** Accepted.

## LAKEWOOD

**Days Inn** SH
(216) 226-4800. **$59-$89.** 12019 Lake Ave. I-90, exit 166, 1 mi n on W 117th St, then just w. **Pets:** Other species. $100 deposit/room. Service with restrictions, supervision.

**Travelodge** SH
(216) 221-9000. **$59-$79.** 11837 Edgewater Dr. I-90, exit 166, 1 mi n on W 117th St, then just w. Int corridors. **Pets:** Other species. $100 deposit/room. Service with restrictions, supervision.

## MACEDONIA

**Baymont Inn & Suites Cleveland-Macedonia** SH
(330) 468-5400. **$83-$139.** 268 E Highland Rd. I-271, exit 18, just s; I-80/90 (Ohio Tpke), exit 180, just n. Int corridors. **Pets:** Medium. Service with restrictions.

**Knights Inn-Cleveland/Macedonia** M
(330) 467-1981. **$39-$75.** 240 E Highland Rd. I-271, exit 18, just s; I-80/90 (Ohio Tpke), exit 180, 3 mi n. Ext corridors. **Pets:** Other species. $5 daily fee/pet. Designated rooms, service with restrictions, supervision.

## MAYFIELD HEIGHTS

**Baymont Inn & Suites-Cleveland (Mayfield Heights)** SH
(440) 442-8400. **$69-$89.** 1421 Golden Gate Blvd. I-271, exit 34, 0.3 mi w off US 322. Int corridors. **Pets:** Other species. Service with restrictions, supervision.

# MEDINA

**Americas Best Value Inn** M
(330) 722-4335. **$51-$61.** 5200 Montville Dr. I-71, exit 218, just e. Ext corridors. **Pets:** Accepted.

**Red Roof Inn** M
(330) 725-1395. **$49-$70.** 5021 EastPointe Dr. I-71, exit 218, just w. Ext corridors. **Pets:** Accepted.

**Travelers Choice Hotel** SH
(330) 725-4571. **$45.** 2875 Medina Rd. I-71, exit 218, just e. Int corridors. **Pets:** Accepted.

# MIDDLEBURG HEIGHTS

**Comfort Inn-Cleveland Airport** SH
(440) 234-3131. **$89-$119, 3 day notice.** 17550 Rosbough Dr. I-71, exit 235, 0.3 mi w to Engle Rd, then 0.3 mi n. Int corridors. **Pets:** $35 one-time fee/room. Service with restrictions, supervision.

**Ramada Airport South** M
(440) 243-2277. **$60-$80.** 7233 Engle Rd. I-71, exit 235, just w. Ext corridors. **Pets:** $10 one-time fee/room. Service with restrictions, crate.

**Red Roof Inn-Middleburg Heights #7060** SH
(440) 243-2441. **$54-$78.** 17555 Bagley Rd. I-71, exit 235, just w. Ext/int corridors. **Pets:** Accepted.

**Residence Inn by Marriott** SH
(440) 234-6688. **$89-$179.** 17525 Rosbough Dr. I-71, exit 235, just w on Bagley Rd, then just n on Engle Rd. Ext/int corridors. **Pets:** Other species. $75 one-time fee/room. Designated rooms, service with restrictions, crate.

**TownePlace Suites** SH
(440) 816-9300. **$109-$139.** 7325 S Engle Rd. I-71, exit 235, just w on Bagley Rd. Int corridors. **Pets:** Accepted.

# NORTH OLMSTED

**Candlewood Suites** SH
(440) 716-0584. **$89.** 24741 Country Club Blvd. I-480, exit 6B, just n on SR 252. Int corridors. **Pets:** Large, other species. $150 one-time fee/room.

**Homestead Studio Suites Hotel-Cleveland/Airport/North Olmsted** SH
(440) 777-8585. **$50-$65.** 24851 Country Club Blvd. I-480, exit 6B, just n on SR 252. Ext corridors. **Pets:** $25 daily fee/pet. Service with restrictions, supervision.

**Radisson Hotel Cleveland Airport** SH
(440) 734-5060. **$119-$139.** 25070 Country Club Blvd. I-480, exit 6B, just n on SR 252. Int corridors. **Pets:** $50 one-time fee/pet. Supervision.

# NORTH RIDGEVILLE

**Motel 6, Cleveland, North Ridgeville** M
(440) 327-6311. **$50-$60.** 32751 Lorain Rd. I-80, exit 152, 0.6 mi ne on SR 10. Ext corridors. **Pets:** Dogs only. $10 deposit/room. No service, supervision.

# RICHFIELD

**Quality Inn & Suites** SH
(330) 659-6151. **$69-$129.** 4742 Brecksville Rd. I-80, exit 173, just s. Int corridors. **Pets:** Accepted.

# SOLON

**Hampton Inn** SH
(440) 542-0400. **$109-$129.** 6035 Enterprise Pkwy. US 422, exit Harper Rd, 0.6 mi s, then 0.4 mi e. Int corridors. **Pets:** Other species. Service with restrictions, supervision.

# STRONGSVILLE

**Motel 6-Strongsville #1497** M
(440) 238-0170. **$43-$55.** 15385 Royalton Rd. I-71, exit 231A, just e; I-76 (Ohio Tpke), exit 161, 1 mi s. Ext corridors. **Pets:** Accepted.

# TWINSBURG

**Twinsburg Super 8 Motel** SH
(330) 425-2889. **$50-$99.** 8848 Twins Hills Dr. I-480, exit 36, just w on SR 82. Int corridors. **Pets:** Accepted.

# WESTLAKE

**Red Roof Inn-Westlake #7094** M
(440) 892-7920. **$55-$85.** 29595 Clemens Rd. I-90, exit 156, just n. Ext corridors. **Pets:** Accepted.

**Residence Inn by Marriott** SH
(440) 892-2254. **$89-$139.** 30100 Clemens Rd. I-90, exit 156, just n. Ext corridors. **Pets:** Accepted.

# WICKLIFFE

**Clarion Hotel Cleveland East** SH
(440) 585-2750. **$59-$99.** 28500 Euclid Ave. I-90, exit 186, just n. Int corridors. **Pets:** Accepted.

# WILLOUGHBY

**Red Roof Inn-East #7053** M
(440) 946-9872. **$50-$89.** 4166 SR 306. I-90, exit 193, just s. Ext corridors. **Pets:** Accepted.

# END METROPOLITAN AREA

# CLYDE

**▼▼▼▼ Red Roof Inn** 🆂🅷
(419) 547-6660. **$59-$119.** 1363 W McPherson Hwy. 1 mi w on SR 20. Int corridors. **Pets:** Small, dogs only. $50 deposit/pet. Designated rooms, service with restrictions, supervision.
(ASK) 🅂🔟 ⊠ 🔛 ⌨ 🍴 ⇔

# COLUMBUS METROPOLITAN AREA

## COLUMBUS

**AAA ▼▼▼▼ AmeriSuites (Columbus/Worthington)** 🆂🅷
(614) 846-4355. **$89-$139.** 7490 Vantage Dr. I-270, exit 23, just ne. Int corridors. **Pets:** Accepted.
(SAVE) 🅂🔟 ⊠ 🔛 🎱 ⌨ 🍴 🖥 ⇔

**▼▼▼▼ Baymont Inn & Suites-Polaris** 🆂🅷
(614) 791-9700. **$81-$89, 3 day notice.** 8400 Lyra Dr. I-71, exit 121, just w. Int corridors. **Pets:** Accepted.
(ASK) 🅂🔟 ⊠ ⌨ 🍴 🖥 ⇔

**AAA ▼▼▼▼ Best Western Columbus North** 🆂🅷
(614) 888-8230. **$90.** 888 E Dublin-Granville Rd. I-71, exit 117, 0.5 mi w on SR 161. Int corridors. **Pets:** Medium, other species. $25 deposit/pet. Crate.
(SAVE) ⊠ ⌨ 🍴 🖥 🍴 ⇔ ⊠

**AAA ▼▼▼▼ Columbus Marriott North** 🅻🅷
(614) 885-1885. **$79-$169.** 6500 Doubletree Ave. I-71, exit 117, 0.3 mi w on SR 161, then 0.8 mi on Busch Blvd to Kingsmill Pkwy. Int corridors. **Pets:** Accepted.
(SAVE) 🅂🔟 ⊠ 🔛 🎱 ⌨ 🍴 🖥 🍴 ⇔ ⊠

**▼▼▼ Cross Country Inn Airport** Ⓜ
(614) 237-3403. **$69-$89.** 4240 International Gateway. At Port Columbus International Airport. Ext corridors. **Pets:** Accepted.
(ASK) 🅂🔟 ⊠ ⌨ ⇔

**AAA ▼▼▼ Days Inn Fairgrounds** Ⓜ
(614) 299-4300. **$45-$125.** 1700 Clara St. I-71, exit 111, just w. Ext corridors. **Pets:** Medium. $10 daily fee/room. Service with restrictions, crate.
(SAVE) ⊠ 🍴 🖥 ⇔

**▼▼▼▼ Doubletree Guest Suites** 🅻🅷 ❖
(614) 228-4600. **$109-$249.** 50 S Front St. Corner of Front and State sts, just n. Int corridors. **Pets:** Large, dogs only. $50 one-time fee/room. Service with restrictions, crate.
⊠ 🎱 🍴 🖥 🍴

**▼▼▼▼ Drury Inn & Suites-Columbus Convention Center** 🆂🅷
(614) 221-7008. **$115-$160.** 88 E Nationwide Blvd. 0.3 mi n on US 23. Int corridors. **Pets:** Accepted.
(ASK) ⊠ 🔛 🎱 ⌨ 🍴 🖥 ⇔

**▼▼▼▼ Extended Stay Deluxe Columbus/Polaris** 🆂🅷
(614) 431-5522. **$83-$109.** 8555 Lyra Dr. I-71, exit 121, just w on Polaris Pkwy. Int corridors. **Pets:** $25 daily fee/pet. Service with restrictions, supervision.
(ASK) 🅂🔟 ⊠ 🔛 ⌨ 🍴 🖥 ⇔

**▼▼▼▼ Holiday Inn Columbus East** 🆂🅷
(614) 868-1380. **$99-$209.** 4560 Hilton Corporate Dr. I-70, exit 107, just se. Int corridors. **Pets:** Accepted.
(ASK) 🅂🔟 ⊠ 🔛 ⌨ 🍴 🖥 🍴 ⇔ ⊠

**AAA ▼▼▼▼ Holiday Inn-Columbus/Worthington Area** 🅻🅷
(614) 885-3334. **$109-$159.** 175 Hutchinson Ave. I-270, exit 23, just n of jct US 23 N. Int corridors. **Pets:** Accepted.
(SAVE) ⊠ 🔛 🎱 ⌨ 🍴 🖥 🍴 ⇔ ⊠

**AAA ▼▼▼▼ Holiday Inn on the Lane** 🆂🅷 ❖
(614) 294-4848. **$109-$229, 7 day notice.** 328 W Lane Ave. 0.5 mi e of SR 315, exit Lane Ave. Int corridors. **Pets:** Other species. Service with restrictions.
(SAVE) 🅂🔟 ⊠ 🔛 🎱 🍴 🖥 🍴 ⇔ ⊠

**AAA ▼▼▼ Knights Inn-Columbus East** Ⓜ
(614) 864-0600. **$50-$90.** 4320 Groves Rd. I-70, exit 107, just sw. Ext corridors. **Pets:** $35 deposit/pet. Service with restrictions, crate.
(SAVE) 🅂🔟 ⊠ 🍴

**▼▼▼ Microtel Inn-Columbus/Worthington** 🆂🅷
(614) 436-0556. **$43-$73.** 7500 Vantage Dr. I-270, exit 23, just n of US 23 N. Int corridors. **Pets:** Accepted.
(ASK) 🅂🔟 ⊠ 🔛 🍴

**▼▼▼ Motel 6 #1486** Ⓜ
(614) 431-2525. **$37-$55.** 7474 N High St. I-270, exit 23, just n. Ext corridors. **Pets:** Accepted.
🅂🔟 ⊠

**▼▼▼ Motel 6 OSU #1491** Ⓜ
(614) 846-8520. **$39-$52.** 750 Morse Rd. I-71, exit 116, just w. Ext corridors. **Pets:** Accepted.
🅂🔟 ⊠ 🔛 ⌨

**▼▼▼ Red Roof Inn-Downtown #7262** 🆂🅷
(614) 224-6539. **$90-$119.** 111 E Nationwide Blvd. Nationwide Blvd at Third St. Int corridors. **Pets:** Accepted.
⊠ 🔛 🎱 ⌨ 🍴

**▼▼▼ Red Roof Inn-OSU #7121** 🆂🅷
(614) 267-9941. **$60-$70.** 441 Ackerman Rd. SR 315, exit Ackerman Rd, 0.3 mi e. Ext corridors. **Pets:** Accepted.
⊠ ⌨

**▼▼▼ Red Roof Inn-West #7009** Ⓜ
(614) 878-9245. **$58-$80.** 5001 Renner Rd. I-70, exit 91 eastbound; exit 91B westbound, just nw. Ext corridors. **Pets:** Accepted.
⊠ 🔛 ⌨ 🍴

**▼▼▼ Red Roof Inn-Worthington #7310** 🆂🅷
(614) 846-3001. **$54-$70.** 7480 N High St. I-270, exit 23, jct US 23 N, just n. Ext/int corridors. **Pets:** Accepted.
⊠ ⌨ 🍴

**▼▼▼▼ Residence Inn by Marriott** 🆂🅷 ❖
(614) 885-0799. **$69-$159.** 7300 Huntington Park Dr. I-270, exit 23, just n, just e on E Campus View Blvd, then just s. Int corridors. **Pets:** Other species. $75 one-time fee/room. Service with restrictions.
(ASK) 🅂🔟 ⊠ ⌨ 🍴 🖥 ⇔ ⊠

**▼▼▼▼ The Residence Inn by Marriott-Columbus North** 🆂🅷
(614) 431-1819. **$89-$139.** 6191 W Zumstein Dr. I-71, exit 117, just nw. Ext corridors. **Pets:** Accepted.
(ASK) 🅂🔟 ⊠ ⌨ 🍴 🖥 ⇔ ⊠

**▼▼▼▼ Residence Inn by Marriott-Columbus Southeast** 🆂🅷
(614) 864-8844. **$129-$189.** 2084 S Hamilton Rd. I-70, exit 107, just e. Ext corridors. **Pets:** Accepted.
(ASK) 🅂🔟 ⊠ 🔛 ⌨ 🍴 🖥 ⇔ ⊠

**▼▼▼▼ Residence Inn by Marriott Easton** SH
(614) 414-1000. **Call for rates.** 3999 Easton Loop W. I-270, exit 33, 1 mi w, then just n. Int corridors. **Pets:** Accepted.
ASK ⊠ 🐾 🅱 🖵 ➳ ⊠

**▼▼▼▼ Sheraton Suites Columbus** LH
(614) 436-0004. **$99-$229.** 201 Hutchinson Ave. I-270, exit 23, just ne. Int corridors. **Pets:** Accepted.
⊠ 🐾 🅱 🖵 🍴 ➳

**▼▼▼▼ Signature Inn Columbus North** SH
(614) 890-8111. **$74-$99.** 6767 Schrock Hill Ct. I-270, exit 27, n off Cleveland Ave; enter off Schrock Rd. Int corridors. **Pets:** Very small, other species. $10 daily fee/room. Service with restrictions, supervision.
ASK ⊠ 🅱 🖵 ➳

**▼▼▼▼ TownePlace Suites by Marriott** SH
(614) 885-1557. **$89-$109.** 7272 Huntington Park Dr. I-270, exit 23, just e of Vantage Dr. Int corridors. **Pets:** Accepted.
ASK 🆂 ⊠ 🐾 🅱 🖵 ➳

**AAA ▼▼▼▼ The University Plaza Hotel & Conference Center** SH
(614) 267-7461. **$105-$149.** 3110 Olentangy River Rd. 0.5 mi s of N Broadway, exit off SR 315. Int corridors. **Pets:** Accepted.
SAVE 🆂 ⊠ 🅱 🖵 🍴 ➳

**AAA ▼▼▼▼▼ The Westin Great Southern Columbus** LH 🐾
(614) 228-3800. **$125-$155.** 310 S High St. Corner of Main and High sts. Int corridors. **Pets:** Service with restrictions, supervision.
SAVE 🆂 ⊠ 🐾 🅱 🖵 🍴 ⊠

# DELAWARE

**▼▼ The Delaware Hotel** SH
(740) 363-1262. **$49-$129, 3 day notice.** 351 S Sandusky St. 0.5 mi s. Int corridors. **Pets:** Accepted.
ASK 🆂 ⊠ 🅱 🖵 🍴 ➳ ⊠

**AAA ▼ Travelodge** M
(740) 369-4421. **$58-$145.** 1001 US Rt 23 N. 0.5 mi n of downtown. Ext/int corridors. **Pets:** Medium, other species. $10 daily fee/pet. Service with restrictions, supervision.
SAVE 🆂 ⊠ 🅱 🖵

# DUBLIN

**AAA ▼▼▼▼ AmeriSuites (Columbus/Dublin)** SH
(614) 799-1913. **$79-$149.** 6161 Park Center Cir. I-270, exit 15 (Tuttle Crossing Blvd), just e. Int corridors. **Pets:** Small. $10 one-time fee/room. Service with restrictions, supervision.
SAVE 🆂 ⊠ 🐾 🛇 🅱 🖵 ➳

**AAA ▼▼▼ Baymont Inn & Suites Columbus-Dublin** SH
(614) 792-8300. **$79-$149.** 6145 Parkcenter Cir. I-270, exit 15 (Tuttle Crossing Blvd), just e. Int corridors. **Pets:** Medium. Service with restrictions.
SAVE ⊠ 🐾 🅱 🖵

**AAA ▼▼▼▼ Columbus Marriott Northwest** LH
(614) 791-1000. **$175-$200.** 5605 Paul Blazer Memorial Pkwy. I-270, exit 15 (Tuttle Crossing Blvd), 0.3 mi e. Int corridors. **Pets:** Accepted.
SAVE ⊠ 🐾 🛇 🅱 🖵 🍴 ➳

**▼▼▼▼ Drury Inn & Suites-Columbus Northwest** SH
(614) 798-8802. **$85-$130.** 6170 Parkcenter Cir. I-270, exit 15 (Tuttle Crossing Blvd), just e. Int corridors. **Pets:** Large, other species. Service with restrictions, supervision.
ASK ⊠ 🅱 🖵 ➳

**▼▼▼▼ Dublin Homewood Suites by Hilton** SH
(614) 791-8675. **$99-$139, 14 day notice.** 5300 Parkcenter Ave. I-270, exit 15 (Tuttle Crossing Blvd), just e, just n on Blazer Pkwy, then just e. Int corridors. **Pets:** Accepted.
ASK ⊠ 🐾 🛇 🅱 🖵 ➳ ⊠

**▼▼▼▼ Extended Stay Deluxe (Columbus/Dublin)** SH
(614) 760-0245. **$64-$125.** 5530 Tuttle Crossing Blvd. I-270, exit 15 (Tuttle Crossing Blvd), 0.3 mi w. Int corridors. **Pets:** $25 daily fee/pet. Service with restrictions, supervision.
ASK 🆂 ⊠ 🐾 🅱 🖵

**▼▼ ▼ Red Roof Inn-Dublin #7127** M
(614) 764-3993. **$53-$79.** 5125 Post Rd. I-270, exit 17A, just ne. Ext corridors. **Pets:** Accepted.
⊠ 🐾 🅱

**AAA ▼▼▼▼ Residence Inn Dublin by Marriott** SH 🐾
(614) 791-0403. **$69-$239.** 435 Metro Pl S. I-270, exit 17A, 0.5 mi e to Frantz Rd, then 0.5 mi s. Ext/int corridors. **Pets:** Other species. $75 one-time fee/room.
SAVE 🆂 ⊠ 🐾 🛇 🅱 🖵 ➳ ⊠

**▼▼▼▼ Staybridge Suites** SH
(614) 734-9882. **$99, 21 day notice.** 6095 Emerald Pkwy. I-270, exit 15 (Tuttle Crossing Blvd), just w. Int corridors. **Pets:** Accepted.
ASK 🆂 ⊠ 🐾 🅱 🖵 ➳ ⊠

**▼▼▼▼ Woodfin Suites Hotel** SH 🐾
(614) 766-7762. **$99-$150.** 4130 Tuller Rd. I-270, exit 20, 0.3 mi s on Sawmill Rd via Dublin Center Dr. Ext corridors. **Pets:** Other species. $50 one-time fee/room. Designated rooms, service with restrictions.
ASK 🆂 ⊠ 🛇 🅱 🖵 ➳

# GAHANNA

**▼▼ Candlewood Suites Columbus Airport** SH 🐾
(614) 863-4033. **$100-$160.** 590 Taylor Rd. I-270, exit 37, just e, 0.6 mi s on Morrison Rd, then just e. Int corridors. **Pets:** Medium, other species. Service with restrictions.
ASK 🆂 ⊠ 🐾 🅱 🖵

**▼▼ TownePlace Suites by Marriott Columbus Airport** SH 🐾
(614) 861-1400. **$69-$109.** 695 Taylor Rd. I-270, exit 37, just e, 0.6 mi s on Morrison Rd, then just e. Int corridors. **Pets:** Other species. $75 one-time fee/room. Service with restrictions, supervision.
ASK 🆂 ⊠ 🛇 🐾 🅱 🖵 ➳

# GROVE CITY

**AAA ▼▼▼ Best Western Executive Inn** M
(614) 875-7770. **$69-$83.** 4026 Jackpot Rd. I-71, exit 100, just e. Ext corridors. **Pets:** Medium, dogs only. $10 daily fee/pet. Designated rooms, service with restrictions.
SAVE 🆂 ⊠ 🅱 🖵 ➳

**▼▼ Motel 6-South Columbus #1492** M
(614) 875-8543. **$43-$55.** 1900 Stringtown Rd. I-71, exit 100, just w. Ext corridors. **Pets:** Accepted.
🆂 ⊠ 🐾

**▼▼ Red Roof Inn** M
(614) 871-9617. **$65-$150.** 4055 Jackpot Rd. I-71, exit 100, 1.3 mi s of jct I-270. Ext corridors. **Pets:** Medium. $100 deposit/pet. Service with restrictions, supervision.
ASK 🆂 ⊠ 🐾 🅱 🖵 ➳

# HEATH

**AAA ▼▼▼ Quality Inn** SH
(740) 522-1165. **$55-$99.** 733 Hebron Rd. I-70, exit 129B, 7 mi n on SR 79. Ext corridors. **Pets:** Medium. $5 daily fee/pet. Service with restrictions, crate.
SAVE 🆂 ⊠ 🅱 🖵 🍴 ➳

**▼▼ Super 8 Motel-Heath** 🆂🅷
(740) 788-9144. **Call for rates.** 1177 S Hebron Rd. I-70, exit 129B, 6 mi n. Int corridors. **Pets:** Accepted.
⊠ 🖪

## HEBRON

**▼▼ Red Roof Inn** 🆂🅷
(740) 467-7663. **$60-$70.** 10668 Lancaster Rd SW. I-70, exit 126, just s. Int corridors. **Pets:** Accepted.
A$K 🆂🅾 ⊠ 🕭ᴹ 🕭

## HILLIARD

**▼▼▼ Comfort Suites by Choice Hotels-Columbus** 🆂🅷
(614) 529-8118. **$90-$110.** 3831 Park Mill Run Dr. I-270, exit 13A northbound; exit 13 southbound. Int corridors. **Pets:** Accepted.
A$K 🆂🅾 ⊠ 🕭ᴹ 🕭 🖪 💻 🏊

**▼▼▼ Homewood Suites by Hilton-Columbus** 🆂🅷
(614) 529-4100. **$39-$149, 14 day notice.** 3841 Park Mill Run Dr. I-270, exit 13 southbound; exit 13A northbound. Int corridors. **Pets:** Accepted.
A$K ⊠ 🕭ᴹ 🕮 🕭 🖪 💻 🏊 ⊠

## LANCASTER

**▼▼▼ Holiday Inn Express Hotel & Suites** 🆂🅷
(740) 654-4445. **$69-$79.** 1861 Riverway Dr. 2.5 mi nw on US 33. Int corridors. **Pets:** Small. $10 daily fee/pet. Supervision.
A$K 🆂🅾 ⊠ 🕭 🖪 💻 🏊

**ⒶⒶⒶ ▼▼ Rodeway Inn & Rockmill Conference Center** 🆂🅷
(740) 653-3040. **$60-$75, 3 day notice.** 1858 N Memorial Dr. 2 mi nw on US 33. Ext/int corridors. **Pets:** Medium. Service with restrictions, crate.
SAVE 🆂🅾 ⊠ 🖪 💻 🍴 🏊

## LONDON

**ⒶⒶⒶ ▼▼▼ Alexandra's Bed & Breakfast** 🅱🅱
(740) 852-5993. **$80-$140.** 117 N Main St. I-70, exit 79, 4 mi s on SR 42, then just w. Int corridors. **Pets:** Accepted.
SAVE 🆂🅾 ⊠ 🕮

## MARYSVILLE

**ⒶⒶⒶ ▼▼▼ AmeriHost Inn-Marysville** 🆂🅷
(937) 644-0400. **$119-$219.** 16420 Allenby Dr. Jct US 33 and 36. Int corridors. **Pets:** Medium, other species. $35 one-time fee/room. Service with restrictions, supervision.
SAVE 🆂🅾 ⊠ 🕭 🕭 🖪 💻 🏊 ⊠

**▼▼ Super 8 Marysville** 🆂🅷
(937) 644-8821. **$45-$75.** 16510 Square Dr. Just e of US 36, exit off US 33. Ext corridors. **Pets:** Accepted.
A$K 🆂🅾 ⊠ 🖪 💻

## NEWARK

**ⒶⒶⒶ ▼▼▼▼ Cherry Valley Lodge** 🆂🅷 🐾
(740) 788-1200. **$145-$163.** 2299 Cherry Valley Rd. 3.5 mi w on SR 16, then 0.3 mi s. Int corridors. **Pets:** Other species. $150 deposit/room. Designated rooms, service with restrictions, crate.
SAVE 🆂🅾 ⊠ 🕭ᴹ 🕭 🖪 💻 🍴 🏊 ⊠

## REYNOLDSBURG

**▼▼▼ Columbus East Fairfield Inn & Suites** 🆂🅷
(614) 864-4555. **$74-$159.** 2826 Taylor Rd SW. I-70, exit 112 (SR 256 W), just n on SR 256, then e. Int corridors. **Pets:** Other species. $50 one-time fee/room. Service with restrictions.
A$K 🆂🅾 ⊠ 🕭 🖪 💻 🏊

**ⒶⒶⒶ ▼▼ Days Inn & Suites Columbus East** 🆂🅷
(614) 864-1280. **$70-$79.** 2100 Brice Rd. I-70, exit 110 westbound; exit 110B eastbound, just n. Int corridors. **Pets:** Other species. Service with restrictions, supervision.
SAVE 🆂🅾 ⊠ 🕭 🖪 💻 🍴 🏊

**▼▼ Extended StayAmerica-Columbus-East** 🆂🅷
(614) 759-1451. **Call for rates.** 2200 Lake Club Dr. I-70, exit 110 westbound; exit 110B eastbound, 0.5 mi n on Brice Rd, just w on Channingway, then just s. Int corridors. **Pets:** Accepted.
A$K ⊠ 🖪 💻 🏊

**ⒶⒶⒶ ▼▼▼▼ La Quinta Inn Columbus (Airport)** 🆂🅷
(614) 866-6456. **$75-$115.** 2447 Brice Rd. I-70, exit 110 westbound; exit 110B eastbound, 0.3 mi n. Int corridors. **Pets:** Medium. Service with restrictions.
SAVE ⊠ 🖪 💻 🏊

**▼▼ Red Roof Inn-East #7033** 🅼
(614) 864-3683. **$52-$74.** 2449 Brice Rd. I-70, exit 110 westbound; exit 110B eastbound. Ext corridors. **Pets:** Accepted.
⊠ 🕭 🖪

## SUNBURY

**ⒶⒶⒶ ▼▼ Days Inn of Sunbury** 🆂🅷
(740) 362-6159. **$65-$100.** 7323 SR 37 E. I-71, exit 131, just nw. Int corridors. **Pets:** Medium. $10 daily fee/pet. Service with restrictions, supervision.
SAVE 🆂🅾 ⊠ 🕭 🖪 🏊

---

## END METROPOLITAN AREA

## CONNEAUT

**ⒶⒶⒶ ▼▼ Days Inn of Conneaut** 🆂🅷
(440) 593-6000. **$81-$129.** 600 Days Blvd. I-90, exit 241, 0.3 mi n. Int corridors. **Pets:** Accepted.
SAVE 🆂🅾 ⊠ 💻 🏊

## CUYAHOGA FALLS

**ⒶⒶⒶ ▼▼▼▼ Akron Sheraton Suites Cuyahoga Falls** 🆂🅷
(330) 929-3000. **$119-$219.** 1989 Front St. SR 8, exit Broad Blvd, just w. Int corridors. **Pets:** Accepted.
SAVE 🆂🅾 ⊠ 🕭ᴹ 🕮 🖪 💻 🍴 🏊 ⊠

## DAYTON

**▼▼ Comfort Inn by Choice Hotels-North** 🆂🅷
(937) 890-9995. **$90-$110.** 7125 Miller Ln. I-75, exit 59 (Wyse/ Benchwood rds), just w on Benchwood Rd, then 0.6 mi n. Int corridors. **Pets:** Accepted.
A$K 🆂🅾 ⊠ 🕭ᴹ 🕮 🕭 🖪 💻 🏊

**▼▼▼▼ Dayton Marriott Hotel** 🅻🅷 🐾
(937) 223-1000. **$104-$169.** 1414 S Patterson Blvd. I-75, exit 51 (Edwin C Moses Blvd), 1 mi e. Int corridors. **Pets:** $100 one-time fee/room. Service with restrictions, supervision.
A$K 🆂🅾 ⊠ 🕮 🕭 🖪 💻 🍴 🏊 ⊠

**▼▼▼▼ DoubleTree Hotel Dayton Downtown** 🅻🅷
(937) 461-4700. **$129-$169.** 11 S Ludlow St. At Courthouse Square; downtown. Int corridors. **Pets:** Accepted.
⊠ 🕭 🖪 💻 🍴 🏊 ⊠

**▼▼▼ Extended StayAmerica-Dayton North SH**
(937) 898-9221. **$74-$84.** 6688 Miller Ln. I-75, exit 59 (Wyse/Benchwood rds), just w on Benchwood Rd, then just n. Int corridors. **Pets:** $25 daily fee/pet. Service with restrictions, supervision.
ASK S6 ✕ 🔲 📖 🔳 📖

**🅐🅐🅐 ▼▼▼ Howard Johnson Express Inn SH**
(937) 454-0550. **$54-$63.** 7575 Poe Ave. I-75, exit 59 (Wyse/Benchwood rds), just e on Wyse Rd, just sw on Poe Ave/Wyse Rd connector, then 0.8 mi n. Int corridors. **Pets:** Other species. $10 daily fee/pet. Designated rooms, supervision.
SAVE S6 ✕ 🔲 🔳 📖 📖 🌊

**▼ Motel 6-603 SH**
(937) 898-3606. **$40-$53.** 7130 Miller Ln. I-75, exit 59 (Wyse/Benchwood rds), just w on Benchwood Rd, then 0.6 mi n. Ext corridors. **Pets:** Accepted.
S6 ✕ 🔳 🌊

**▼ Red Roof Inn-North #7023 SH**
(937) 898-1054. **$45-$67.** 7370 Miller Ln. I-75, exit 59 (Wyse/Benchwood rds), just w on Benchwood Rd, then 0.8 mi n. Ext corridors. **Pets:** Accepted.
✕ 🔳 📖 🔲

**▼▼▼ Residence Inn by Marriott-Dayton North SH 🐾**
(937) 898-7764. **$119-$200.** 7070 Poe Ave. I-75, exit 59 (Wyse/Benchwood rds), just e on Wyse Rd, just sw on Poe Ave/Wyse Rd connector, then 0.6 mi n. Ext corridors. **Pets:** Other species. $75 one-time fee/room. Service with restrictions, crate.
ASK S6 ✕ 🔳 🔳 🔲 📖 🌊 ✕

**▼▼ Rodeway Inn SH**
(937) 890-9500. **$49-$104.** 4079 Little York Rd. I-75, exit 59 (Wyse/Benchwood rds), just w on Benchwood Rd, then 1 mi n on Miller Ln. Ext/int corridors. **Pets:** Other species. $10 one-time fee/pet. Service with restrictions.
ASK S6 ✕ 🔳 🔲 📖 🍴 🌊

## DOVER

**▼ Hospitality Inn M 🐾**
(330) 364-7724. **$40-$75.** 889 Commercial Pkwy. I-77, exit 83, just e. Ext corridors. **Pets:** Other species. $10 one-time fee/pet. Service with restrictions, supervision.
ASK S6 ✕ 🔳 🔲 🌊

## EATON

**🅐🅐🅐 ▼▼ Econo Lodge M 🐾**
(937) 456-5959. **$40-$80, 3 day notice.** 6161 US Rt 127 N. I-70, exit 10 (US 127), just s. Ext corridors. **Pets:** Medium, other species. $10 daily fee/pet. Designated rooms, no service, supervision.
SAVE S6 ✕ 🔲 📖

## ELYRIA

**▼ ▼ Comfort Inn SH**
(440) 324-7676. **$59-$119.** 739 Leona St. I-80, exit 145, just n on SR 57, exit Midway Blvd. Int corridors. **Pets:** $8 daily fee/pet. Designated rooms, service with restrictions, supervision.
ASK S6 ✕ 🔲 📖

**▼ ▼ Super 8 Motel SH**
(440) 323-7488. **$49-$89.** 910 Lorain Blvd. I-80, exit 145, 0.5 mi s on SR 57. Int corridors. **Pets:** $10 one-time fee/pet. Designated rooms, service with restrictions, supervision.
ASK S6 ✕ 🔳 📖 🌊

## ENGLEWOOD

**▼▼▼▼ Holiday Inn-Dayton Northwest Airport SH**
(937) 832-1234. **$90-$115.** 10 Rockridge Rd. I-70, exit 29, just n. Int corridors. **Pets:** Accepted.
ASK S6 ✕ 🔳 🔲 📖 🍴 🌊

**▼▼ Red Roof Inn-Dayton (Englewood) M**
(937) 836-8339. **$45-$85.** 9325 N Main St. I-70, exit 29, just s. Ext corridors. **Pets:** Accepted.
ASK S6 ✕ 🔳 🔲 🌊

**▼▼ Super 8 Motel-Englewood M**
(937) 832-3350. **$40-$100.** 15 Rockridge Rd. I-70, exit 29, just n. Ext corridors. **Pets:** Medium. $10 daily fee/pet. Service with restrictions, supervision.
ASK S6 ✕ 🔲

## FAIRBORN

**🅐🅐🅐 ▼▼▼▼ Comfort Inn-Wright Patterson SH**
(937) 879-7666. **$59-$109.** 616 N Broad St. I-675, exit 24, 1.8 mi sw on SR 444. Int corridors. **Pets:** $75 deposit/room, $10 daily fee/pet. Service with restrictions, supervision.
SAVE S6 ✕ 🔳 🔲 📖 🌊

**🅐🅐🅐 ▼▼▼▼ Hawthorn Inn & Suites SH**
(937) 754-9109. **$99-$109, 3 day notice.** 730 E Xenia Dr. I-675, exit 22, just w. Int corridors. **Pets:** Medium, other species. $100 one-time fee/room. Service with restrictions, supervision.
SAVE S6 ✕ 🔳 🔳 🔲 📖

**🅐🅐🅐 ▼▼▼▼ Homewood Suites by
                 Hilton-Fairborn/Dayton SH**
(937) 429-0600. **$116-$161.** 2750 Presidential Dr. I-675, exit 17 (N Fairfield Rd), just w. Ext/int corridors. **Pets:** Accepted.
SAVE S6 ✕ 🔳 🔲 📖 🌊

**▼▼▼▼ Ramada Limited & Suites-Wright Patterson SH**
(937) 490-2000. **$68-$110, 30 day notice.** 2540 University Blvd. I-675, exit 15 (Colonel Glen Hwy), 1.5 mi e, then just s. Int corridors. **Pets:** Very small. $10 daily fee/pet. Service with restrictions, crate.
ASK S6 ✕ 🔳 🔲 📖 🌊

**▼▼▼ Red Roof Inn-Fairborn #7205 SH**
(937) 426-6116. **$55-$68.** 2580 Colonel Glenn Hwy. I-675, exit 17 (N Fairfield Rd), just w. Ext corridors. **Pets:** Accepted.
✕ 🔳 🔳 🔲

**▼▼▼ StudioPlus at Fairborn SH**
(937) 429-0140. **$80-$90.** 3131 Presidential Dr. I-675, exit 15 (Colonel Glen Hwy), 1.5 mi e, then just s. Int corridors. **Pets:** Accepted.
ASK ✕ 🔳 🔳 🔲 📖 🌊

## FAIRLAWN

**🅐🅐🅐 ▼▼ Akron Super 8 Motel SH**
(330) 666-8887. **$39-$79.** 79 Rothrock Rd. I-77, exit 137A, just e. Int corridors. **Pets:** $10 daily fee/pet. No service, crate.
SAVE S6 ✕ 🔳 📖

**▼▼ Motel 6 Akron North #2000 M**
(330) 666-0566. **$39-$55.** 99 Rothrock Rd. I-77, exit 137A, just e. Ext corridors. **Pets:** Accepted.
S6 ✕ 🔳

**▼▼ Quality Inn by Choice SH**
(330) 668-2700. **$55-$75.** 70 Rothrock Rd. I-77, exit 137A, just e. Ext/int corridors. **Pets:** Accepted.
ASK S6 ✕ 🔳 🔳 🔲 📖 🌊

**🅐🅐🅐 ▼▼▼▼ The Residence Inn by Marriott SH 🐾**
(330) 666-4811. **$109-$149.** 120 W Montrose Ave. I-77, exit 137B, just w. Ext corridors. **Pets:** Large, other species. $75 one-time fee/room. Service with restrictions.
SAVE S6 ✕ 🔲 📖 🌊 ✕

# FINDLAY

**Days Inn Findlay** M
(419) 423-7171. **$65-$76.** 1305 W Main Cross St. I-75, exit 157, just e. Int corridors. **Pets:** Other species. $10 daily fee/pet. Service with restrictions, supervision.

**Econo Lodge** M
(419) 422-0154. **$35-$75.** 316 Emma St. I-75, exit 157, just w. Ext corridors. **Pets:** $10 daily fee/pet. Service with restrictions.

**Hawthorn Suites-Findlay** SH
(419) 425-9696. **$69-$159.** 2355 Tiffin Ave. 3 mi e on US 224. Int corridors. **Pets:** Medium. $35 one-time fee/room. Service with restrictions, supervision.

**Quality Inn** M
(419) 423-4303. **$64-$94.** 1020 Interstate Ct. I-75, exit 159, just w. Ext corridors. **Pets:** Small. $10 deposit/pet. Service with restrictions, supervision.

**Red Roof Inn** M
(419) 424-0466. **$59-$99.** 1951 Broad Ave. I-75, exit 159, 0.5 mi e. Ext corridors. **Pets:** Accepted.

**Rodeway Inn** M ❖
(419) 424-1133. **$39-$52.** 1901 Broad Ave. I-75, exit 159, 0.5 mi e. Ext corridors. **Pets:** $10 one-time fee/pet. Service with restrictions, supervision.

**Super 8 Motel-Findlay** SH
(419) 422-8863. **$47-$55.** 1600 Fox St. I-75, exit 159, just e. Int corridors. **Pets:** Accepted.

# FOSTORIA

**Country Club Inn and Suites** M
(419) 435-6511. **$62-$70.** 737 Independence Rd. SR 12, 1 mi w of SR 23. Ext corridors. **Pets:** Small. $25 deposit/room. Designated rooms, service with restrictions.

# FREDERICKTOWN

**Heartland Country Resort** CA ❖
(419) 768-9300. **$100-$175, 7 day notice.** 3020 Township Rd 190. I-71, exit 151, 2 mi e on SR 95, 2 mi s on SR 314, then 1 mi e on SR 179. Ext corridors. **Pets:** Other species. $15 daily fee/room.

# FREMONT

**Comfort Inn & Suites** SH ❖
(419) 355-9300. **$86-$270.** 840 Sean Dr. I-80/90, exit 91, 2 mi s on SR 53. Int corridors. **Pets:** Other species. $15 one-time fee/pet. Service with restrictions, supervision.

**Holiday Inn-Fremont** SH
(419) 334-2682. **$95-$159.** 3422 Port Clinton Rd. I-80/90, exit 91, just s. Int corridors. **Pets:** Accepted.

# GALION

**Hometown Inn** M
(419) 468-9909. **$50-$150.** 172 N Portland Way. 1 mi w on SR 598, n of jct SR 309/61/19. Ext/int corridors. **Pets:** Other species. $10 daily fee/pet. Service with restrictions, supervision.

# GREEN

**Super 8 Motel** SH
(330) 899-9888. **$65-$90.** 1605 Corporate Woods Pkwy. I-77, exit 118, just w. **Pets:** Accepted.

# GREENVILLE

**Greenville Inn** SH
(937) 548-3613. **$60-$80, 10 day notice.** 851 E Martin. Jct US 36 and 127, 0.3 mi w on SR 571. Int corridors. **Pets:** $50 deposit/room. Service with restrictions, crate.

# HOLLAND

**Econo Lodge** M
(419) 866-6565. **$40-$55.** 1201 E Mall Dr. I-475, exit 8, just w on SR 2. Ext corridors. **Pets:** Medium, other species. $10 daily fee/pet. Service with restrictions, supervision.

**Extended StayAmerica** SH
(419) 861-1133. **$55-$65.** 6155 Trust Dr. I-475, exit 8, just e to Holland-Sylvania Rd, then just n. Int corridors. **Pets:** Accepted.

**Quality Inn Toledo Airport** M
(419) 867-1144. **$54-$129.** 1401 E Mall Dr. I-475, exit 8, just w on SR 2. Ext/int corridors. **Pets:** Large, other species. $10 daily fee/pet. No service, supervision.

**Red Roof Inn Toledo/Holland #7058** M
(419) 866-5512. **$45-$62.** 1214 Corporate Dr. I-475, exit 8, just e on Holland-Sylvania Rd, then just n to Trust Dr. Ext corridors. **Pets:** Accepted.

**Residence Inn by Marriott** SH
(419) 867-9555. **$66-$109.** 6101 Trust Dr. I-475, exit 8, just e to Holland-Sylvania Rd, then just n. Ext corridors. **Pets:** Accepted.

# HUBER HEIGHTS

**Holiday Inn Express Hotel & Suites** SH
(937) 235-2000. **$84-$104.** 5612 Merily Way. I-70, exit 36, just se on SR 202. Int corridors. **Pets:** Other species. $25 one-time fee/pet. Service with restrictions, supervision.

**Travelodge Dayton/Huber Heights** M
(937) 236-9361. **$50-$70.** 7911 Brandt Pike. I-70, exit 38, just s at SR 201. Ext/int corridors. **Pets:** Small, dogs only. $25 daily fee/pet. Designated rooms, service with restrictions, supervision.

# HURON

**Plantation Motel** M ❖
(419) 433-4790. **$42-$95, 3 day notice.** 2815 E Cleveland Rd. 3 mi e of town, on US 6. Ext corridors. **Pets:** Other species. $9 daily fee/pet. Service with restrictions, supervision.

# JACKSON

**Knights Inn** M
(740) 286-2135. **$42-$50.** 404 Chillicothe St. 0.7 mi n on US 35 business route. Ext corridors. **Pets:** Other species. $20 deposit/room.

**(AAA) ▼▼ Red Roof Inn M**
(740) 288-1200. **$63-$80.** 1000 Acy Ave. US 35, exit McCarty Ln, just nw. Int corridors. **Pets:** Medium. $25 deposit/room. Designated rooms, service with restrictions, supervision.
[SAVE] [SÒ] [✕] [ᶜᵛ] [🛢]

# JEFFERSONVILLE

**(AAA) ▼▼ AmeriHost Inn-Jeffersonville SH**
(740) 426-6400. **$59-$99.** 10160 Carr Rd NW. I-71, exit 69 (SR 41), just w. Int corridors. **Pets:** Accepted.
[SAVE] [SÒ] [✕] [ᶜᵛ] [🛢] [💻] [🏊]

# KENT

**▼▼ Days Inn-Akron Kent M**
(330) 677-9400. **$69-$85, 14 day notice.** 4422 Edson Rd. I-76, exit 33. Ext corridors. **Pets:** Accepted.
[ASK] [SÒ] [✕] [🍴] [ᶜᵛ] [🛢] [💻] [🏊]

**▼▼ Quality Inn & Suites SH**
(330) 678-0101. **$65-$99.** 4363 SR 43. I-76, exit 33. Ext corridors. **Pets:** Accepted.
[ASK] [SÒ] [✕] [🍴] [🛢] [💻] [🏊]

**▼▼ Super 8 Motel SH**
(330) 678-8817. **$50-$85, 7 day notice.** 4380 Edson Rd. I-76, exit 33. Int corridors. **Pets:** Accepted.
[ASK] [SÒ] [✕] [🍴] [🛢]

# LIMA

**▼▼▼ Holiday Inn Lima SH**
(419) 222-0004. **$99-$119.** 1920 Roschman Ave. I-75, exit 125A, just se. Int corridors. **Pets:** Accepted.
[ASK] [SÒ] [✕] [🍴] [ᶜᵛ] [🛢] [💻] [🍴] [🏊] [✕]

# LOGAN

**(AAA) ▼▼ AmeriHost Inn-Logan SH**
(740) 385-1700. **$69-$149.** 12819 SR 664. Jct US 33, just n. Int corridors. **Pets:** Small, other species. $10 daily fee/room. Designated rooms, service with restrictions.
[SAVE] [SÒ] [✕] [�ᴹ] [🍴] [ᶜᵛ] [🛢] [💻] [🏊]

**▼▼▼ Holiday Inn Express Hocking Hills SH**
(740) 385-7700. **$99-$159, 14 day notice.** 12916 Grey St. SR 664, just w to Lake Logan Rd, then just n. Int corridors. **Pets:** Small. Designated rooms, service with restrictions, supervision.
[ASK] [SÒ] [✕] [�ᴹ] [🍴] [ᶜᵛ] [🛢] [💻] [🏊]

# LOUDONVILLE

**▼▼ Little Brown Inn M**
(419) 994-5525. **$47-$74.** 940 S Market St. 1 mi s on SR 3. Int corridors. **Pets:** Small. $10 one-time fee/pet. Designated rooms, no service, supervision.
[ASK] [SÒ] [✕] [🛢]

# MANSFIELD

**▼▼ AmeriHost Inn Mansfield SH**
(419) 756-6670. **$49-$189.** 180 E Hanley Rd. I-71, exit 169, jct SR 13. Int corridors. **Pets:** $25 daily fee/pet. Service with restrictions, supervision.
[ASK] [SÒ] [✕] [🍴] [ᶜᵛ] [🛢] [💻] [🏊]

**▼▼▼ Baymont Inn & Suites Mansfield SH**
(419) 774-0005. **$85-$149.** 120 Stander Ave. I-71, exit 169. Int corridors. **Pets:** Medium. Service with restrictions.
[ASK] [✕] [�ᴹ] [🍴] [ᶜᵛ] [🛢] [💻] [🏊]

**▼▼ Comfort Inn North SH**
(419) 529-1000. **$65-$135.** 500 N Trimble Rd. Jct US 30. Int corridors. **Pets:** Accepted.
[ASK] [SÒ] [✕] [🍴] [🛢] [💻] [🏊] [✕]

**(AAA) ▼▼ Econo Lodge SH**
(419) 589-3333. **$44-$65.** 1017 Koogle Rd. I-71, exit 176, just e. Int corridors. **Pets:** Accepted.
[SAVE] [SÒ] [✕] [🛢]

**▼▼▼ Fairfield Inn by Marriott SH**
(419) 747-2200. **$80-$100.** 1065 N Lexington-Springmill Rd. Jct US 30, on south side. Int corridors. **Pets:** Accepted.
[ASK] [SÒ] [✕] [🍴] [ᶜᵛ] [🛢] [💻] [🏊]

**▼▼ Knights Inn M**
(419) 529-2100. **$50-$90.** 555 N Trimble Rd. Jct US 30. Ext corridors. **Pets:** Accepted.
[ASK] [SÒ] [✕] [🍴] [🛢] [💻]

**(AAA) ▼▼▼ Super 8 Motel SH**
(419) 756-8875. **$50-$90, 14 day notice.** 2425 Interstate Cir. I-71, exit 169. Int corridors. **Pets:** Accepted.
[SAVE] [SÒ] [✕] [🍴] [🛢] [💻]

**(AAA) ▼▼ Travelodge M**
(419) 756-7600. **$48-$95.** 90 W Hanley Rd. I-71, exit 169. Ext corridors. **Pets:** $10 one-time fee/pet. Service with restrictions, supervision.
[SAVE] [SÒ] [✕] [🍴] [🛢] [💻] [🏊]

# MARIETTA

**(AAA) ▼▼ Americas Best Value Inn M**
(740) 373-7373. **$47-$70.** 506 Pike St. I-77, exit 1. Ext corridors. **Pets:** Other species. $5 one-time fee/pet. Service with restrictions.
[SAVE] [SÒ] [✕] [ᶜᵛ] [🛢] [💻] [🏊]

**▼▼ Best Western Marietta M**
(740) 374-7211. **$55-$79.** 279 Muskingum Dr. I-77, exit 6, 3.5 mi sw on SR 821, then 1 mi s on SR 60. Ext corridors. **Pets:** Accepted.
[ASK] [SÒ] [✕] [🛢] [💻] [✕]

**(AAA) ▼▼▼ Econo Lodge M**
(740) 374-8481. **$45-$75.** 702 Pike St. I-77, exit 1, just e. Ext corridors. **Pets:** $7 daily fee/pet. No service, supervision.
[SAVE] [✕] [🛢] [💻]

**▼▼▼ The Lafayette Hotel LH**
(740) 373-5522. **$60-$115.** 101 Front St. Center. Int corridors. **Pets:** $100 deposit/room. Service with restrictions.
[ASK] [SÒ] [✕] [🛢] [💻] [🍴]

**▼▼ Super 8 Motel-Marietta SH**
(740) 374-8888. **$50-$51.** 46 Acme St. I-77, exit 1, just w. Int corridors. **Pets:** Other species. $5 daily fee/pet. Service with restrictions, supervision.
[ASK] [SÒ] [✕] [🛢]

# MARION

**▼▼ Comfort Inn by Choice Hotels SH**
(740) 389-5552. **$74-$94.** 256 James Way. Jct US 23 and SR 95, just w. Int corridors. **Pets:** Accepted.
[ASK] [SÒ] [✕] [🍴] [ᶜᵛ] [🛢] [💻] [🏊]

# MASSILLON

**▼▼▼ Hampton Inn-Canton/Massillon SH**
(330) 834-1144. **$79-$170.** 44 First St SW. Downtown. Int corridors. **Pets:** Accepted.
[ASK] [SÒ] [✕] [�ᴹ] [ᶜᵛ] [💻]

# MAUMEE

**(AAA) ▼▼ Arrowhead Super 8 Motel-Maumee/Toledo SH**
(419) 897-3800. **$49-$69.** 1390 Arrowhead Rd. I-475, exit 6, just e. Int corridors. **Pets:** Accepted.
[SAVE] [SÒ] [✕] [🍴] [ᶜᵛ] [🛢] [💻]

**Comfort Inn West Toledo/Maumee** SH
(419) 893-2800. **$69-$89.** 1426 S Reynolds Rd. I-80/90, exit 59, just s. Int corridors. **Pets:** Small. $10 daily fee/pet. Service with restrictions, supervision.
SAVE ⓈⒹ ✕ 🖥 💻 ⇴

**Days Inn-Toledo/Maumee** M
(419) 897-6900. **$39-$69.** 1704 Tollgate Dr. I-80/90, exit 59, just s. Ext corridors. **Pets:** Accepted.
SAVE ⓈⒹ ✕ ⎙ ⌨ 🖥 💻 ⇴

**Econo Lodge-Toledo/Maumee** M
(419) 893-9960. **$39-$79.** 150 Dussel Dr. I-80/90, exit 59, just s. Ext corridors. **Pets:** Other species. $10 deposit/pet. Service with restrictions, crate.
SAVE ⓈⒹ ✕ ⎙ 🖥 💻 ⇴

**Homewood Suites by Hilton-Toledo** SH
(419) 897-0980. **$109-$159, 14 day notice.** 1410 Arrowhead Rd. I-475, exit 6, just e. Int corridors. **Pets:** Accepted.
ASK ✕ ⌚Ⓜ ⎙ 🖥 💻 ⇴ ✕

**Red Roof Inn-Maumee #7046** M
(419) 893-0292. **$50-$72.** 1570 S Reynolds Rd. I-80/90, exit 59, just s. Ext/int corridors. **Pets:** Accepted.
✕ ⎙ ⌨ 🖥

# MENTOR

**Best Western Lawnfield Inn &**
**Suites** SH 🐾
(440) 205-7378. **$79-$149.** 8434 Mentor Ave. I-90, exit 195, 1.5 mi n to SR 20 (Mentor Ave) then just e. Int corridors. **Pets:** Medium. $20 one-time fee/pet. Service with restrictions, crate.
SAVE ⓈⒹ ✕ ⌚ⓂⓂ ⌨ 🖥 💻 ⇴

**Residence Inn by Marriott** SH
(440) 392-0800. **$89-$149.** 5660 Emerald Ct. Jct SR 2 and Heisley Rd, just s. Int corridors. **Pets:** Other species. $75 one-time fee/room. Service with restrictions.
ASK ⓈⒹ ✕ ⌨ 🖥 💻 ⇴ ✕

**Studio 6 #6019** M
(440) 946-0749. **$53-$67.** 7677 Reynolds Rd. Just s of SR 2 on SR 306. Ext corridors. **Pets:** Accepted.
✕ ⌚ⓂⓂ ⌨ 🖥 💻

**Super 8 Motel** SH
(440) 951-8558. **$40-$85.** 7325 Palisades Pkwy. On SR 306, just s of SR 2. Int corridors. **Pets:** Other species. $10 daily fee/room. Service with restrictions, supervision.
SAVE ⓈⒹ ✕ 🖥

# MIAMISBURG

**DoubleTree Guest Suites Dayton/Miamisburg** SH
(937) 436-2400. **$99-$109.** 300 Prestige Pl. I-75, exit 44, just se on SR 725, then just s. Int corridors. **Pets:** Accepted.
ⓈⒹ ✕ 🖥 💻 ❙❙ ⇴

**Holiday Inn-Dayton Mall** SH
(937) 434-8030. **$99-$105.** 31 Prestige Plaza Dr. I-75, exit 44, just e on SR 725, then just s. Int corridors. **Pets:** Small. $25 one-time fee/room. Service with restrictions, crate.
✕ ⎙ ⌨ 🖥 💻 ❙❙ ⇴ ✕

**Homewood Suites by Hilton-Dayton South** SH
(937) 432-0000. **$134-$154.** 3100 Contemporary Ln. I-75, exit 44, just e on SR 725, then just s. Int corridors. **Pets:** Accepted.
ASK ⓈⒹ ✕ ⎙ ⌨ 🖥 💻 ⇴

**Red Roof Inn-South #7006** SH
(937) 866-0705. **$51-$69.** 222 Byers Rd. I-75, exit 44, just w on SR 725. Ext corridors. **Pets:** Accepted.
✕ ⎙ ⌨ 🖥

**Residence Inn by Marriott-Dayton South** SH
(937) 434-7881. **$149-$179.** 155 Prestige Pl. I-75, exit 44, just e on SR 725, then just s. Ext corridors. **Pets:** Accepted.
ASK ⓈⒹ ✕ ⌨ 🖥 💻 ⇴ ✕

**Signature Inn Dayton South** SH
(937) 865-0077. **$49-$104.** 250 Byers Rd. I-75, exit 44, just w on SR 725. Int corridors. **Pets:** Accepted.
ASK ✕ ⎙ ⌨ 🖥 💻 ⇴

**Super 8 Miamisburg/South Dayton** SH
(937) 866-5500. **$64-$69.** 155 Monarch Ln. I-75, exit 44, 0.5 mi w on SR 725. Int corridors. **Pets:** Accepted.
ASK ⓈⒹ ✕ ⎙ ⌨ 🖥 💻

# MILAN

**Motel 6–4016** SH
(419) 499-8001. **$34-$144, 3 day notice.** 11406 US 250. I-80/90, exit 118, 1.5 mi n. Int corridors. **Pets:** Accepted.
ASK ⓈⒹ ✕ ⌨ ⇴

**Red Roof Inn** SH
(419) 499-4347. **$49-$149.** 11303 Rt 250/Milan Rd. I-80/90, exit 118, 0.5 mi n. Int corridors. **Pets:** Accepted.
ASK ⓈⒹ ✕ ⎙ ⌨ 🖥

**Super 8 Motel** SH
(419) 499-4671. **$49-$138.** 11313 Milan Rd. I-80/90, exit 118, 0.5 mi n on SR 250. Int corridors. **Pets:** Accepted.
ASK ⓈⒹ ✕ 🖥 ❙❙ ⇴

# MILLERSBURG

**Comfort Inn Millersburg** SH
(330) 674-7400. **$59-$139.** 1102 Glen Dr. SR 39, 0.5 mi s on S Clay. Int corridors. **Pets:** Small, other species. $15 daily fee/pet. Designated rooms, service with restrictions.
ASK ⓈⒹ ✕ ⌨ 🖥 💻 ⇴

# MONTPELIER

**Ramada Inn & Suites** SH
(419) 485-5555. **$81-$144, 3 day notice.** 13508 SR 15. I-80/90, exit 13, just s. Int corridors. **Pets:** Other species. Designated rooms, service with restrictions, crate.
ASK ⓈⒹ ✕ ⎙ 🖥 💻 ❙❙ ⇴ ✕

# MORAINE

**Holiday Inn Hotel & Suites Dayton South** SH
(937) 294-1471. **$86-$116.** 2455 Dryden Rd. I-75, exit 50A (Dryden Rd), just nw. Int corridors. **Pets:** Accepted.
ASK ⓈⒹ ✕ ⎙ ⌨ 🖥 💻 ❙❙ ⇴ ✕

**Super 8 Motel-Moraine** M
(937) 298-0380. **$39-$69.** 2450 Dryden Rd. I-75, exit 50A (Dryden Rd), just nw. Ext corridors. **Pets:** Small. $10 daily fee/pet. Designated rooms, no service, supervision.
SAVE ⓈⒹ ✕ 🖥 ⇴

# MOUNT GILEAD

**Knights Inn** M
(419) 946-6010. **$43-$58, 14 day notice.** 5898 SR 95. I-71, exit 151, 0.3 mi w. Ext corridors. **Pets:** Accepted.
ASK ⓈⒹ ✕ 🖥

# MOUNT VERNON

**Comfort Inn** SH
(740) 392-6886. **$70-$150, 7 day notice.** 150 Howard St. Jct SR 13; south of downtown. Int corridors. **Pets:** Accepted.
ASK ⓈⒹ ✕ 🖥 💻 ⇴ ✕

▼▼▼ **Holiday Inn Express** 🆂🅷 🐾
(740) 392-1900. **$84-$100.** 11555 Upper Gilchrist Rd. 3 mi e on US 36.
Int corridors. **Pets:** Medium, other species. Designated rooms, service with restrictions, supervision.
(ASK) (S🐾) (✕) (🄶🄼) (🄴) 🄴 🄳 🅿 ➿

# NAPOLEON

▼▼ ▼▼ **Best Western Napoleon Inn & Suites** 🆂🅷
(419) 599-0850. **$69-$84.** 1290 Independence Dr. From US 6/24, just se. Int corridors. **Pets:** Other species. $12 daily fee/pet. Service with restrictions, supervision.
(ASK) (S🐾) (✕) (🄿) (🄴) 🄴 🄳 🅿 ➿ (✕)

# NEWCOMERSTOWN

▼▼▼ **Hampton Inn** 🆂🅷 🐾
(740) 498-9800. **$69-$115.** 200 Morris Crossing. I-77, exit 65, 0.8 mi w. Int corridors. **Pets:** Dogs only. Designated rooms, no service, supervision.
(ASK) (S🐾) (✕) 🄴 🄳 🅿 ➿

# NEW PHILADELPHIA

▼▼▼ **Hampton Inn** 🆂🅷
(330) 339-7000. **$76-$95.** 1299 W High St. I-77, exit 81, just e. **Pets:** Small, dogs only. Service with restrictions, supervision.
(ASK) (S🐾) (✕) (🄶🄼) (🄴) 🄴 🄳 🅿 ➿ (✕)

▼ **Motel 6–254** 🄼
(330) 339-6446. **$35-$51.** 181 Bluebell Dr SW. I-77, exit 81, 0.4 mi e. Ext corridors. **Pets:** Accepted.
(S🐾) (✕) (🄴) ➿

# NEWTON FALLS

🅰🅰🅰 ▼▼▼ **Econo Lodge** 🄼
(330) 872-0988. **$39-$129.** 4248 SR 5. I-80, exit 209, just w. Ext corridors. **Pets:** Large. $10 daily fee/pet. Service with restrictions, crate.
(SAVE) (S🐾) (✕) 🄴

# NORTH CANTON

▼ ▼▼ **Super 8 Motel Canton North** 🄼
(330) 492-5030. **$39-$70.** 3950 Convenience Cir NW. I-77, exit 109 southbound, 0.3 mi e on Everhard, then 0.3 mi s on Whipple; exit 109A northbound, 0.3 mi s on Whipple. Ext corridors. **Pets:** Accepted.
(ASK) (S🐾) (✕) 🄴 🅿 ➿

# NORTH LIMA

▼ **Liberty Inn** 🄼
(330) 549-3988. **$50.** 10650 Market St. I-76, exit 232, 0.3 mi s on SR 7. Ext corridors. **Pets:** Accepted.
(ASK) (S🐾) (✕)

# NORTHWOOD

▼▼▼ **Comfort Inn South** 🆂🅷
(419) 666-2600. **$59-$150.** 2426 Oregon Rd. I-75, exit 198, just e; jct Wales and Oregon rds. Int corridors. **Pets:** Accepted.
(ASK) (S🐾) (✕) 🄴 🅿 (🍴) ➿

# NORWALK

▼▼ ▼▼ **Econo Lodge** 🄼
(419) 668-5656. **$49-$145.** 342 Milan Ave. 3 mi n on US 250; 6 mi s of I-80/90 (Ohio Tpke). Ext corridors. **Pets:** Small, dogs only. $50 deposit/ pet. Designated rooms, service with restrictions, supervision.
(ASK) (S🐾) (✕) 🄴 🅿 ➿

# OBERLIN

▼▼▼ **Oberlin Inn** 🄲🄸
(440) 775-1111. **$109-$189.** 7 N Main St. On SR 58; jct College and Main sts; center. Int corridors. **Pets:** Service with restrictions, supervision.
(ASK) (S🐾) (✕) 🄴 🅿 (🍴)

# OREGON

▼▼ ▼▼ **Comfort Inn East** 🆂🅷 🐾
(419) 691-8911. **$65-$95, 60 day notice.** 2930 Navarre Ave. I-280, exit 7, just n on access road, then 0.5 mi e on SR 2 (Navarre Ave). Int corridors. **Pets:** $15 one-time fee/room. Designated rooms, service with restrictions, supervision.
(ASK) (S🐾) (✕) (🄿) 🄴 🅿 ➿

▼▼ ▼▼ **Sleep Inn & Suites** 🆂🅷 🐾
(419) 697-7800. **$69-$99.** 1761 Meijer Cir. I-280, exit 6, just w. Int corridors. **Pets:** $15 one-time fee/room. Designated rooms, service with restrictions, supervision.
(ASK) (S🐾) (✕) (🄴) 🄴 🅿 ➿

# PERRYSBURG

🅰🅰🅰 ▼▼▼ **Baymont Inn & Suites Toledo-Perrysburg** 🆂🅷
(419) 872-0000. **$69-$129.** 1154 Professional Dr. I-75, exit 193, just w. Int corridors. **Pets:** Medium. Service with restrictions.
(SAVE) (✕) (🄿) (🄴) 🄴 🅿

🅰🅰🅰 ▼ **Economy Inn** 🄼
(419) 872-2902. **$45-$65.** 26054 N Dixie Hwy. I-475, exit 2, just s. Ext corridors. **Pets:** Small. $10 daily fee/pet. Designated rooms, service with restrictions, supervision.
(SAVE) (S🐾) (✕) 🄴

🅰🅰🅰 ▼▼▼ **Howard Johnson Inn Toledo South** 🄼
(419) 837-5245. **$39-$79.** 3555 Hanley Rd. I-80/90 (Ohio Tpke), exit 71 to I-280, exit 1B. Ext/int corridors. **Pets:** Other species. $10 daily fee/pet. Service with restrictions, supervision.
(SAVE) (S🐾) (✕) (🄿) 🄴 🅿 ➿

# PIQUA

🅰🅰🅰 ▼▼▼ **Comfort Inn-Piqua** 🆂🅷
(937) 778-8100. **$60-$125.** 987 E Ash St. I-75, exit 82, just w. Int corridors. **Pets:** Accepted.
(SAVE) (S🐾) (✕) (🄿) (🄴) 🄴 🅿 ➿

▼▼▼ **La Quinta Inn Piqua** 🆂🅷
(937) 615-0140. **$70-$89.** 950 E Ash St. I-75, exit 82, just w. Int corridors. **Pets:** Accepted.
(ASK) (S🐾) (✕) (🄴) 🄴 🅿 ➿

# POLAND

▼▼ **Red Roof Inn #7253** 🆂🅷
(330) 758-1999. **$46-$77.** 1051 Tiffany S. I-680, exit 11, just w. Int corridors. **Pets:** Accepted.
(✕) (🄿) (🄴) 🄴 🅿

▼▼▼ **Residence Inn by Marriott-Youngstown** 🆂🅷
(330) 726-1747. **$110-$170, 14 day notice.** 7396 Tiffany S. I-680, exit 11, just w. Int corridors. **Pets:** Accepted.
(ASK) (S🐾) (✕) (🄿) (🄴) 🄴 🄳 🅿 ➿ (✕)

# PORT CLINTON

▼▼ **Best Western Port Clinton** 🆂🅷
(419) 734-2274. **$49-$149.** 1734 E Perry St. 1.7 mi e on SR 163, w of jct SR 2. Int corridors. **Pets:** Accepted.
(ASK) (S🐾) (✕) 🅿 ➿

🅰🅰🅰 ▼▼▼ **Commodore Perry Inn & Suites** 🆂🅷 🐾
(419) 732-2645. **$49-$219.** 255 W Lakeshore Dr. Just n of the bridge. Int corridors. **Pets:** Medium. $20 one-time fee/pet. Crate.
(SAVE) (S🐾) (✕) 🄴 🅿 (🍴) ➿

▼▼ **Country Hearth Inn** 🄼
(419) 732-2111. **$45-$95.** 1815 E Perry St. 1.2 mi e on SR 163, w of jct SR 2. Ext/int corridors. **Pets:** Accepted.
(ASK) (S🐾) (✕) 🄴 🅿 ➿

💎💎 **Super 8** 🆂🄷
(419) 734-4446. **$49-$148.** 1704 E Perry St. 1.7 mi e on SR 163, w of jct SR 2. Int corridors. **Pets:** Small, dogs only. $50 deposit/pet. Designated rooms, no service, supervision.

(ASK) (S₆) (✕) (💻)

# PORTSMOUTH

💎💎 **Portsmouth Super 8 Motel** 🆂🄷
(740) 353-8880. **$48-$68.** 4266 US Rt 23 N. 5 mi n. Int corridors. **Pets:** Small, other species. $10 one-time fee/room. Service with restrictions, supervision.

(ASK) (S₆) (✕) (📷) (🖐) (🛏) (💻) (➿)

# RIO GRANDE

💎 **College Hill Motel** 🄼
(740) 245-5326. **$49-$99.** 10987 State Rt 588. US 35, exit Rio Grande. Ext corridors. **Pets:** Small, other species. $10 one-time fee/pet. Service with restrictions, crate.

(ASK) (S₆) (✕) (🛏)

# ST. CLAIRSVILLE

🔷 💎💎 **Americas Best Value Inn St.**
**Clairsville/Wheeling** 🄼 🐾
(740) 695-5038. **$280-$330.** 51260 National Rd. I-70, exit 218, 0.5 mi ne on US 40. Ext corridors. **Pets:** Other species. $10 one-time fee/room. Service with restrictions.

(SAVE) (S₆) (✕) (📷) (🛏) (💻) (➿)

💎💎 **Red Roof Inn** 🄼
(740) 695-4057. **$47-$79.** 68301 Red Roof Ln. I-70, exit 218, just n. Ext corridors. **Pets:** Accepted.

(✕) (🖐) (🛏)

# ST. MARYS

🔷 💎💎 **Americas Best Value Inn & Suites** 🆂🄷
(419) 394-2341. **$63-$99.** 1321 Celina Rd. SR 66/29, 0.8 mi w on SR 703. Ext corridors. **Pets:** Accepted.

(SAVE) (S₆) (✕) (🛏) (💻) (➿) (✕)

🔷 💎💎 **AmeriHost Inn-St. Marys** 🆂🄷
(419) 394-2710. **$74-$129.** 1410 Commerce Dr. Jct US 33 and SR 29, just s. Int corridors. **Pets:** Other species. $35 one-time fee/room. Designated rooms, service with restrictions, supervision.

(SAVE) (S₆) (✕) (📷) (🖐) (🛏) (💻) (➿)

# SANDUSKY

🔷 💎💎 **Best Budget Inn** 🄼
(419) 626-3610. **$49-$128.** 2027 Cleveland Rd. US 6, just e of Cedar Point Cswy. Ext/in: corridors. **Pets:** Medium, dogs only. $50 deposit/pet. Designated rooms, service with restrictions, supervision.

(SAVE) (S₆) (✕) (➿)

💎💎 **Clarion Inn Sandusky** 🆂🄷 🐾
(419) 625-6280. **$55-$189.** 1119 Sandusky Mall Blvd. On US 250, 1.5 mi n of SR 2. Int corridors. **Pets:** Medium. $25 daily fee/pet. Service with restrictions, supervision.

(ASK) (S₆) (✕) (📷) (🛏) (💻) (🍴) (➿) (✕)

💎💎 **Knights Inn Sandusky** 🄼
(419) 621-9000. **$38-$144, 3 day notice.** 2405 Cleveland Rd. US 6, 2 mi e of Cedar Point Cswy. Ext/int corridors. **Pets:** Other species. $25 deposit/room. Designated rooms, service with restrictions, crate.

(ASK) (✕) (🛏) (💻) (➿)

# SEVILLE

💎💎💎 **Hawthorn Suites Ltd** 🆂🄷 🐾
(330) 769-5025. **$89-$99, 7 day notice.** 5025 Park Ave W. SR 224, exit 2, just n. Int corridors. **Pets:** Medium. $75 one-time fee/room. Service with restrictions, supervision.

(ASK) (S₆) (✕) (🖐) (🛏) (💻) (➿)

💎💎 **Super 8 Motel-Seville** 🆂🄷
(330) 769-8880. **$60-$100.** 6116 Speedway Dr. Jct SR 224 and Lake Rd. Int corridors. **Pets:** Medium, other species. $30 deposit/room, $20 one-time fee/room. Service with restrictions, supervision.

(ASK) (S₆) (✕) (🖐M) (🖐) (🛏)

# SIDNEY

🔷 💎💎 **Comfort Inn** 🆂🄷
(937) 492-3001. **$90-$126.** 1959 W Michigan Ave. I-75, exit 92, just sw of SR 47. Int corridors. **Pets:** Accepted.

(SAVE) (S₆) (✕) (🛏) (💻) (➿)

💎💎 **Days Inn Sidney** 🄼
(937) 492-1104. **$55-$80, 7 day notice.** 420 Folkerth Ave. I-75, exit 92, just nw. Ext corridors. **Pets:** $5 daily fee/pet. Service with restrictions, supervision.

(ASK) (S₆) (✕) (🛏) (➿)

💎💎 **Econo Lodge** 🆂🄷
(937) 492-9164. **$59-$79.** 2009 W Michigan St. I-75, exit 92, just w on SR 47. Ext/int corridors. **Pets:** Small, dogs only. $25 deposit/room. Service with restrictions, supervision.

(ASK) (S₆) (✕) (🛏) (💻) (➿)

💎💎💎 **Holiday Inn** 🆂🄷
(937) 492-1131. **$79-$119, 3 day notice.** 400 Folkerth Ave. I-75, exit 92, just w. Int corridors. **Pets:** Small. Service with restrictions, crate.

(ASK) (S₆) (✕) (📷) (🖐) (🛏) (💻) (🍴) (➿)

# SPRINGFIELD

💎💎💎 **Holiday Inn South Springfield Ohio** 🆂🄷
(937) 323-8631. **$99-$104.** 383 E Leffel Ln. I-70, exit 54, just n, then e. Int corridors. **Pets:** Service with restrictions, supervision.

(ASK) (S₆) (✕) (🖐) (🛏) (💻) (🍴) (➿) (✕)

🔷 💎 **Knights Inn** 🄼
(937) 325-8721. **$37-$52.** 2207 W Main St. I-70, exit 52, 1.7 mi n on US 68, then just e on US 40. Ext corridors. **Pets:** Other species. $10 daily fee/pet. Service with restrictions, supervision.

(SAVE) (S₆) (✕) (🛏) (➿)

🔷 💎 **Ramada Limited** 🆂🄷
(937) 328-0123. **$49-$109.** 319 E Leffel Ln. I-70, exit 54, just n, then e. Int corridors. **Pets:** Accepted.

(SAVE) (S₆) (✕) (📷) (🛏) (💻) (➿)

🔷 💎💎 **Red Roof Inn** 🆂🄷
(937) 325-5356. **$64-$115.** 155 W Leffel Ln. I-70, exit 54, just n, then w. Int corridors. **Pets:** Medium, other species. No service, supervision.

(SAVE) (S₆) (✕) (🖐) (🛏) (💻) (➿)

# STRASBURG

🔷 💎💎💎 **Ramada Limited Dover/Strasburg** 🆂🄷
(330) 878-1400. **$65-$120.** 509 S Wooster Ave. I-77, exit 87, 0.4 mi n on US 250 and SR 21. Int corridors. **Pets:** $25 daily fee/room. Service with restrictions, supervision.

(SAVE) (S₆) (✕) (🖐M) (📷) (🖐) (🛏) (💻) (➿)

# STREETSBORO

💎💎 **Econo Lodge** 🆂🄷
(330) 626-5511. **$50-$110.** 9789 SR 14. I-80, exit 187, 0.5 mi s. Int corridors. **Pets:** Accepted.

(ASK) (S₆) (✕) (🛏) (💻)

💎💎 **Microtel Inn & Suites of Streetsboro** 🆂🄷 🐾
(330) 422-1234. **$58-$98.** 9371 SR 14. I-80, exit 187, 1.2 mi s. Int corridors. **Pets:** Small. $35 one-time fee/pet. Designated rooms, service with restrictions, supervision.

(ASK) (S₆) (✕) (🖐) (🛏) (💻) (➿)

**TownePlace Suites by Marriott** SH ❖
(330) 422-1855. **$69-$149.** 795 Mondial Pkwy. I-80, exit 187, 0.8 mi s.
Int corridors. **Pets:** Medium, other species. $75 one-time fee/room. Service
with restrictions.

ASK SÓ ✕ ❌ 💻 ⤳

## SWANTON

**Days Inn** SH
(419) 865-2002. **$69.** 10753 Airport Hwy. I-80/90, exit 3A, just s, then e.
Int corridors. **Pets:** Accepted.

ASK SÓ ✕ ❌ 💻

## TIFFIN

**Holiday Inn Express** SH
(419) 443-5100. **$79.** 78 Shaffer Park Dr. Just w of mall. Int corridors.
**Pets:** Accepted.

ASK SÓ ✕ ❌ 💻 ⤳

**Quality Inn** SH
(419) 447-6313. **$70-$116.** 1927 S SR 53. Jct US 224 and SR 53, 2 mi
sw. Ext/int corridors. **Pets:** Large. $15 daily fee/pet. Designated rooms,
service with restrictions, crate.

ASK SÓ ✕ 🔄 ❌ ❌ 💻 🍴 ⤳

## TOLEDO

**Comfort Inn-North** SH
(419) 476-0170. **$69-$160.** 445 E Alexis Rd. I-75, exit 210, 2 mi w on
SR 184; just e of jct US 24 and SR 184. Int corridors. **Pets:** Accepted.

SAVE SÓ ✕ 🔄 ❌ 💻

**Radisson Hotel Toledo** SH
(419) 241-3000. **$99-$155.** 101 N Summit St. Between Jefferson and
Monroe sts; downtown. Int corridors. **Pets:** Medium. Service with restrictions, supervision.

ASK SÓ ✕ 💻 🍴

**Red Roof Inn Toledo University #7196** M
(419) 536-0118. **$49-$65.** 3530 Executive Pkwy. I-475, exit 17, 0.5 mi s
on Secor Rd, then just e. Ext corridors. **Pets:** Accepted.

✕ 🔄 ❌ ❌

## TROY

**Fairfield Inn & Suites by Marriott** SH
(937) 332-1446. **$89-$159.** 83 Troy Town Dr. I-75, exit 74, just w. Int
corridors. **Pets:** Accepted.

ASK SÓ ✕ 🔄 ❌ ❌ 💻 ⤳

**Holiday Inn Express Hotel & Suites** SH
(937) 332-1700. **$81-$115.** 60 Troy Town Dr. I-75, exit 74, just w. Int
corridors. **Pets:** Small, other species. $25 one-time fee/pet. Designated
rooms, service with restrictions, supervision.

ASK SÓ ✕ 🔄 ❌ ❌ 💻 ⤳

**Residence Inn By Marriott** SH
(937) 440-9303. **$99-$175.** 87 Troy Town Dr. I-75, exit 74, just w. Int
corridors. **Pets:** Accepted.

ASK SÓ ✕ 🔄 ❌ ❌ 💻 ⤳ ✕

## UHRICHSVILLE

**Best Western Country Inn** M
(740) 922-0774. **$50-$70.** 111 McCauley Dr. US 250, exit McCauley Dr.
Ext corridors. **Pets:** $5 daily fee/room. Service with restrictions, crate.

SAVE SÓ ✕ 🔄 ❌ 💻

## UPPER SANDUSKY

**AmeriHost Inn-Upper Sandusky** SH
(419) 294-3919. **$63-$79.** 1726 E Wyandot Ave. Jct US 23 and 30. Int
corridors. **Pets:** Accepted.

ASK SÓ ✕ 🔄M 🔄 ❌ ❌ 💻 ⤳

## URBANA

**Econo Lodge Urbana** M
(937) 652-2188. **$58-$65.** 2551 S US Hwy 68. 1.3 mi s. Ext corridors.
**Pets:** $15 daily fee/pet. Service with restrictions, supervision.

ASK SÓ ✕ ❌ ⤳

## VANDALIA

**Super 8 Motel-Vandalia** M
(937) 898-7636. **$39-$89.** 550 E National Rd. I-75, exit 63, just w. Ext
corridors. **Pets:** Accepted.

SAVE SÓ ✕ 🔄 ❌ ⤳

**Travelodge Dayton Airport** M
(937) 898-8321. **$49-$89.** 75 Corporate Center Dr. Off National Rd. Ext
corridors. **Pets:** Accepted.

SAVE SÓ ✕ 🔄 ❌ 💻 ⤳

## VERMILION

**Holiday Inn Express** SH
(440) 967-8770. **$79-$169.** 2417 SR 60. Jct SR 2 and 60. Int corridors.
**Pets:** Medium, other species. $15 one-time fee/room. Service with restric-
tions, crate.

ASK SÓ ✕ 🔄 ❌ ❌ 💻 ⤳

**Motel Plaza** M
(440) 967-3191. **$65-$89, 3 day notice.** 4645 Liberty Ave. On US 6, 2
mi e of SR 60. Ext corridors. **Pets:** Small. $20 deposit/pet. No service,
supervision.

SAVE SÓ ✕ ❌ 💻

## WADSWORTH

**Legacy Inn** M
(330) 336-6671. **$42-$51, 3 day notice.** 810 High St. I-76, exit 9, just s.
Ext corridors. **Pets:** Medium. $30 one-time fee/room. Service with restric-
tions, crate.

SAVE SÓ ✕ ❌ ⤳

## WAPAKONETA

**Best Western Wapakoneta** SH
(419) 738-8181. **$69-$130.** 1510 Saturn Dr. I-75, exit 111, just w. Int
corridors. **Pets:** Accepted.

ASK SÓ ✕ 🔄 ❌ 💻 ⤳

**Super 8 Motel-Wapakoneta** SH
(419) 738-8810. **$55.** 1011 Lunar Dr. I-75, exit 111, just w. Ext/int
corridors. **Pets:** Accepted.

ASK ✕ ❌ 💻

**Travelodge** SH
(419) 739-9600. **$44-$60.** 413 Apollo Dr. I-75, exit 111, just w. Ext
corridors. **Pets:** Accepted.

ASK SÓ ✕ 💻

## WARREN

**Best Western** M
(330) 392-2515. **$47-$68, 14 day notice.** 777 Mahoning Ave. 0.3 mi n
of Courthouse Square. Ext corridors. **Pets:** Accepted.

SAVE SÓ ✕ 🔄 ❌ 💻 ⤳

**Comfort Inn** SH
(330) 393-1200. **$65-$100.** 136 N Park Ave. Downtown; east side of
Courthouse Square. Int corridors. **Pets:** Accepted.

SAVE SÓ ✕ ❌ 💻 🍴

# WAUSEON

**Best Western Del Mar**
(419) 335-1565. **$79-$120.** 8319 SR 108. I-80/90, exit 34, just s. Ext corridors. **Pets:** Other species. $15 one-time fee/room. Service with restrictions, supervision.

# WOOSTER

**Econo Lodge**
(330) 264-8883. **$59-$69.** 2137 E Lincoln Way. US 30, 3 mi e. Ext corridors. **Pets:** $10 daily fee/pet. Service with restrictions, supervision.

**The Wooster Inn**
(330) 263-2660. **$80-$225.** 801 E Wayne Ave. 0.5 mi e on Liberty St, 1 mi n on Beall Ave. Int corridors. **Pets:** Accepted.

# XENIA

**Holiday Inn-Xenia**
(937) 372-9921. **$89-$104.** 300 Xenia Towne Sq. On W Main St, 0.5 mi w. Int corridors. **Pets:** Accepted.

**Regency Inn**
(937) 372-9954. **$50-$70.** 600 Little Main St. 1 mi w. Ext corridors. **Pets:** Small. $10 daily fee/room. Service with restrictions, crate.

# ZANESVILLE

**AmeriHost Inn-Zanesville**
(740) 454-9332. **$79-$129.** 230 Scenic Crest Dr. I-70, exit 155, just s. Int corridors. **Pets:** Medium. $25 one-time fee/room. Service with restrictions, crate.

**Comfort Inn**
(740) 454-4144. **$69-$174.** 500 Monroe St. I-70, exit 155 westbound; exit 7th St eastbound, e on Elberon to light, just n on Underwood. Int corridors. **Pets:** Medium, other species. $10 one-time fee/room. Designated rooms, service with restrictions, supervision.

**Econo Lodge-Zanesville**
(740) 452-4511. **$69-$99.** 135 N 7th St. I-70, exit 155, on SR 60 via signs; downtown. Ext corridors. **Pets:** Small. $10 one-time fee/room. Designated rooms, service with restrictions, supervision.

**Holiday Inn Conference Center**
(740) 453-0771. **$72-$90.** 4645 E Pike. I-70, exit 160, on US 22 and 40. Int corridors. **Pets:** $20 one-time fee/room. Service with restrictions, supervision.

**Red Roof Inn**
(740) 453-6300. **$55-$107.** 4929 E Pike. I-70, exit 160, just s. Int corridors. **Pets:** Accepted.

**Super 8 Motel-Zanesville**
(740) 455-3124. **$39-$89.** 2440 National Rd. I-70, exit 152, just n. Int corridors. **Pets:** Medium. $10 daily fee/pet. Service with restrictions, supervision.

**Travelodge**
(740) 453-0611. **$50-$70.** 58 N 6th St. I-70, exit 155, on US 22 and SR 60 at Market St. Ext/int corridors. **Pets:** Accepted.

# OKLAHOMA

## CITY INDEX

## ALTUS

**Best Western Altus** SH
(580) 482-9300. **$69-$79.** 2804 N Main St. 2 mi n on US 283. Ext corridors. **Pets:** Large, other species. Service with restrictions.
SAVE 🔲 ✕ 🔲 💻 ⊠

## ARDMORE

**Best Western Inn** SH
(580) 223-7525. **$95-$110.** 6 Holiday Dr. I-35, exit 31A, just ne. Int corridors. **Pets:** Accepted.
SAVE 🔲 ✕ 🔲 💻 ～

**Holiday Inn** SH
(580) 223-7130. **$75-$99.** 2705 W Broadway. I-35, exit 31A, just e. Ext corridors. **Pets:** $20 one-time fee/room. Designated rooms, service with restrictions, supervision.
ASK ✕ 🔲 🔲 💻 🍴 ～ ⊠

**La Quinta Inn Ardmore** SH
(580) 223-7976. **$80-$85.** 2432 Veterans Blvd. I-35, exit 33, just e. Ext corridors. **Pets:** Other species. Service with restrictions, crate.
ASK 🔲 ✕ 🔲 🔲 💻 ～

**Microtel Inn & Suites** SH
(580) 224-2600. **$65-$75.** 1904 Cooper Dr. I-35, exit 32, just w. Int corridors. **Pets:** Accepted.
ASK 🔲 ✕ 🔲 🔲 🔲 💻

## BARTLESVILLE

**Holiday Inn** SH
(918) 333-8320. **$74-$78.** 1410 SE Washington Blvd. Just s of jct US 60 and 75. Int corridors. **Pets:** Accepted.
ASK 🔲 ✕ 🔲 💻 🍴 ～

**Super 8 Motel** M
(918) 335-1122. **$54-$59.** 211 SE Washington Blvd. 0.7 mi n of jct US 60 and 75. Ext/int corridors. **Pets:** Medium. Service with restrictions, supervision.
ASK 🔲 ✕ 🔲 💻

## BIG CABIN

**Big Cabin Super 8 Motel** M
(918) 783-5888. **$58-$68.** 30954 S Hwy 69. I-44, exit 283, just ne. Ext/int corridors. **Pets:** Other species. $20 deposit/room. Designated rooms, service with restrictions.
ASK 🔲 ✕ 🔲 ～

## BLACKWELL

**Comfort Inn** SH
(580) 363-7000. **$70.** 1201 N 44th St. I-35, exit 222, just ne. Int corridors. **Pets:** Small. $10 daily fee/pet. Designated rooms, service with restrictions, supervision.
SAVE ✕ 🔲 🔲 💻 ～

## CHICKASHA

**Holiday Inn Express Hotel & Suites** SH
(405) 224-8883. **$89.** 2610 S 4th St. I-44, exit 80, just se. Int corridors. **Pets:** Other species. $25 one-time fee/room. Service with restrictions, supervision.
ASK 🔲 ✕ 🔲 🔲 🔲 💻 ～

## CLINTON

**Days Inn** SH
(580) 323-5550. **$65, 7 day notice.** 1200 S 10th St. I-40, exit 65A, just n. Ext corridors. **Pets:** Small. $10 daily fee/pet. Crate.
ASK 🔲 ✕ 🔲 🔲 💻 🍴 ～

## DAVIS

**Microtel Inn & Suites-Treasure Valley Casino** SH
(580) 369-3223. **$58-$95.** Rt 1, Box 7C. I-35, exit 55. Int corridors. **Pets:** Accepted.
ASK ✕ 🔲 🔲 🔲 🔲 💻 ～ ⊠

## DUNCAN

**Chisholm Suite Hotel** SH
(580) 255-0551. **$72.** 1204 N Hwy 81. Center. Int corridors. **Pets:** Accepted.
ASK ✕ 🔲 🔲 💻 ～

## DURANT

**Holiday Inn Express Hotel & Suites** SH
(580) 924-8881. **$95-$140.** 2112 W Main St. Just e of jct US 75/69 and 70. Int corridors. **Pets:** Small, other species. $25 one-time fee/room. Designated rooms, service with restrictions, crate.
ASK 🔲 ✕ 🔲 🔲 🔲 💻 ～

## ELK CITY

**Holiday Inn** SH
(580) 225-6637. **$114-$199.** 101 Meadow Ridge Dr. I-40, exit 38, just sw. Ext/int corridors. **Pets:** Medium. Designated rooms, service with restrictions, supervision.
SAVE ✕ 🔲 🔲 💻 🍴 ～ ⊠

## ENID

**Comfort Inn** SH
(580) 234-1200. **$80-$100, 10 day notice.** 210 N Van Buren St. 0.7 mi n on US 81. Ext/int corridors. **Pets:** Accepted.
ASK 🔲 ✕ 🔲 💻 ～

## ERICK

**Comfort Inn** SH
(580) 526-8124. **$82-$109, 5 day notice.** 1001 N Sheb Wooley. I-40, exit 7, just nw. Ext corridors. **Pets:** Medium. $10 daily fee/pet. Designated rooms, service with restrictions, supervision.
ASK 🔲 ✕ 🔲 🔲 💻 ～

## FREDERICK

 Scottish Inns **M**
(580) 335-2129. **$60.** 1015 S Main St. 1 mi s. Ext corridors.
**Pets:** Accepted.

## GUYMON

▼▼ Ambassador Inn **SH**
(580) 338-5555. **$45-$60.** Hwy 64 N at 21st. 1.5 mi n on US 64 and SR 136. Ext corridors. **Pets:** Accepted.

 Guymon Super 8 **SH** ❀
(580) 338-0507. **$55-$99.** 1201 Hwy 54 E. Jct US 54 and 64. Int corridors. **Pets:** Other species. $5 daily fee/pet. Service with restrictions, supervision.

▲▲▲ ▼ Lodge U.S.A. **M**
(580) 338-5431. **$50.** 923 Hwy 54 E. Just s of jct US 64. Ext corridors.
**Pets:** Small. $8 one-time fee/room. Service with restrictions, supervision.

▼▼ Western Townsman Inn **SH**
(580) 338-6556. **$59-$79, 4 day notice.** 212 NE Hwy 54. 0.7 mi s of jct US 64. Ext corridors. **Pets:** Small. Designated rooms, service with restrictions, supervision.

## HENRYETTA

▲▲▲ ▼ Green Country Inn **M**
(918) 652-9988. **$42-$48.** 2004 Old Hwy 75 W. I-40, exit 237, just ne. Ext corridors. **Pets:** Small. $5 one-time fee/pet. Designated rooms, service with restrictions, supervision.

## HINTON

▼ Microtel Inn & Suites **SH**
(405) 542-6011. **Call for rates.** 4800 N Broadway. I-40, exit 101, just sw. Int corridors. **Pets:** Accepted.

## IDABEL

▼▼▼ Comfort Suites **SH**
(580) 286-9393. **$75-$85.** 400 SE Lincoln Blvd. Just s of jct US 70 and 259. Int corridors. **Pets:** Medium, other species. $15 daily fee/pet. No service, supervision.

## LAWTON

▼▼ Baymont Inn & Suites **SH**
(580) 353-5581. **$79-$89.** 1203 NW 40th St. I-44, exit 39A, 3.7 mi w. Int corridors. **Pets:** Small, other species. $25 deposit/room.

▲▲▲ ▼▼▼ Best Western Hotel & Convention Center **SH**
(580) 353-0200. **$84-$89.** 1125 E Gore Blvd. I-44, exit 37, just e. Ext/int corridors. **Pets:** Large. $40 one-time fee/pet. Designated rooms, service with restrictions, crate.

▼ Motel 6 Lawton #1412 **M**
(580) 355-9765. **$45-$55.** 202 SE Lee Blvd. I-44, exit 36 A/B, just w. Ext corridors. **Pets:** Accepted.

▼▼ Red Lion Hotel-Lawton **SH**
(580) 353-1682. **$79-$89.** 3134 NW Cache Rd. I-44, exit 39A, 2.5 mi w. Ext corridors. **Pets:** $15 one-time fee/room. Service with restrictions, supervision.

## MCALESTER

▼▼ Best Western Inn of McAlester **SH**
(918) 426-0115. **$70-$80.** 1215 George Nigh Expwy. 3 mi s on US 69. Ext corridors. **Pets:** Accepted.

▼▼▼ Holiday Inn Express Hotel & Suites **SH**
(918) 302-0001. **$91-$129.** 650 George Nigh Expwy. 1.2 mi s on US 69. Int corridors. **Pets:** Accepted.

▼ Super 8 Motel **M**
(918) 426-5400. **$49-$64.** 2400 S Main St. Just n of jct US 69. Ext corridors. **Pets:** Accepted.

## MIAMI

▲▲▲ ▼▼▼ Best Western Inn of Miami **SH** ❀
(918) 542-6681. **$59-$79.** 2225 E Steve Owens Blvd. I-44, exit 313, just w. Ext corridors. **Pets:** Small, other species. Service with restrictions, supervision.

## MUSKOGEE

▲▲▲ ▼▼▼ Days Inn of Muskogee **M**
(918) 683-3911. **$59-$69, 7 day notice.** 900 S 32nd St. 3 mi s on US 64 and 69. Ext corridors. **Pets:** Small. $5 daily fee/pet. Service with restrictions, supervision.

▼▼▼ La Quinta Inn & Suites Muskogee **SH**
(918) 687-9000. **Call for rates.** 3031 Military Blvd. Just se of jct US 62 and 69. Int corridors. **Pets:** Accepted.

---

# OKLAHOMA CITY METROPOLITAN AREA

## DEL CITY

▲▲▲ ▼▼▼ La Quinta Inn Oklahoma City East (Del City) **SH**
(405) 672-0067. **$75-$111.** 5501 Tinker Diagonal Rd. I-40, exit 156A (Sooner Rd), just nw. Ext/int corridors. **Pets:** Medium. Service with restrictions.

## EDMOND

▲▲▲ ▼▼▼ Best Western Edmond Inn & Suites **SH**
(405) 216-0300. **$84.** 2700 E 2nd St. I-35, exit 141, 1.1 mi w. Int corridors. **Pets:** Small. $10 one-time fee/pet. Service with restrictions, supervision.

▼▼ Ramada Plaza Hotel **SH**
(405) 341-3577. **$69-$79, 14 day notice.** 930 E 2nd St. I-35, exit 141, 2.3 mi w. Int corridors. **Pets:** Accepted.

# EL RENO

**Best Western Hensley's** 🆂🅷
(405) 262-6490. **$50-$70.** 2701 S Country Club Rd. I-40, exit 123, just s. Ext corridors. **Pets:** Small, dogs only. $20 deposit/room, $5 one-time fee/room. Service with restrictions, supervision.

# GUTHRIE

**Best Western Territorial Inn** 🆂🅷
(405) 282-8831. **$66-$79.** 2323 Territorial Tr. I-35, exit 157, just sw. Int corridors. **Pets:** Small, other species. Service with restrictions, supervision.

# MIDWEST CITY

**AmeriSuites (Midwest City/Tinker Air Force Base)** 🆂🅷
(405) 737-7777. **$99-$129.** 5701 Tinker Diagonal Rd. I-40, exit 156A (Sooner Rd), just n. Int corridors. **Pets:** Medium. $10 daily fee/pet. Designated rooms, service with restrictions, crate.

**Studio 6 #6003** Ⓜ
(405) 737-8851. **$47-$57.** 5801 Tinker Diagonal Rd. I-40, exit 156A (Sooner Rd), just ne. Ext corridors. **Pets:** Accepted.

# MOORE

**Best Western Green Tree Inn & Suites** 🆂🅷
(405) 912-8882. **$95-$105.** 1811 N Moore Ave. I-35, exit 118, just n on westbound frontage road. Int corridors. **Pets:** Small. $10 daily fee/pet. Service with restrictions, supervision.

**Microtel Inn & Suites** 🆂🅷
(405) 799-8181. **$50-$60.** 2400 S Service Rd. I-35, exit 116, just s on east service road. Int corridors. **Pets:** Medium, other species. $7 daily fee/pet. Service with restrictions, supervision.

# NORMAN

**La Quinta Inn & Suites Oklahoma City (Norman)** 🆂🅷
(405) 579-4000. **$91-$125.** 930 Ed Noble Dr. I-35, exit 108B (Lindsey), just nw. Int corridors. **Pets:** Medium. Service with restrictions.

**Quality Inn** Ⓜ
(405) 364-5554. **$95-$105.** 100 SW 26th Dr. I-35, exit 109 (Main St), just se. Ext corridors. **Pets:** Small. $5 daily fee/pet. Service with restrictions, supervision.

**The Residence Inn by Marriott** 🆂🅷
(405) 366-0900. **$95-$189.** 2681 Jefferson St. I-35, exit 108A, just se. Ext corridors. **Pets:** Accepted.

# OKLAHOMA CITY

**AmeriSuites (Oklahoma City/Airport)** 🆂🅷
(405) 682-3900. **$99-$109.** 1818 S Meridian Ave. I-40, exit 145 (Meridian Ave), 1 mi s. Int corridors. **Pets:** Accepted.

**AmeriSuites (Oklahoma City/Quail Springs)** 🆂🅷
(405) 749-1595. **$79-$129, 3 day notice.** 3201 W Memorial Rd. John Kilpatrick Tpke, exit May Ave, 0.4 mi w on north service road. Int corridors. **Pets:** Accepted.

**Baymont Inn** 🆂🅷
(405) 631-8661. **$73-$108.** 8315 I-35 S. I-35, exit 121A (82nd St), just sw. Ext corridors. **Pets:** Medium. Service with restrictions.

**Best Western Memorial Inn & Suites** 🆂🅷
(405) 286-5199. **$67-$105.** 1301 W Memorial Rd. Kilpatrick Tpke, exit Western Ave, just nw. Int corridors. **Pets:** Medium. $10 daily fee/pet. Service with restrictions, supervision.

**Best Western Saddleback Inn** 🅻🅷
(405) 947-7000. **$94-$114.** 4300 SW 3rd St. I-40, exit 145, just ne. Ext/int corridors. **Pets:** Accepted.

**Candlewood Suites Hotel** 🆂🅷
(405) 680-8770. **$85-$159.** 4400 River Park Dr. I-40, exit 145 (Meridian Ave), 1.1 mi s. Int corridors. **Pets:** Medium. $150 one-time fee/pet. Designated rooms, service with restrictions, supervision.

**Clarion Meridian Hotel and Convention Center** 🆂🅷
(405) 942-8511. **$68.** 737 S Meridian Ave. I-40, exit 145 (Meridian Ave), just s. Ext/int corridors. **Pets:** Other species. Designated rooms, service with restrictions, crate.

**Comfort Inn** 🆂🅷
(405) 943-4400. **$65-$75.** 4240 W I-40 Service Rd. I-40, exit 145 (Meridian Ave), just e on south frontage road. Ext/int corridors. **Pets:** Other species. No service, supervision.

**Comfort Inn at Founders Tower** 🆂🅷
(405) 810-1100. **$69-$149.** 5704 Mosteller Dr. 0.5 mi e of jct SR 74 and 3. Int corridors. **Pets:** Very small. Designated rooms, service with restrictions, supervision.

**Comfort Inn North** 🆂🅷
(405) 478-7282. **$60-$125.** 4625 NE 120th. I-35, exit 137 (122nd St), just sw. Int corridors. **Pets:** Other species. $10 daily fee/pet. Service with restrictions, crate.

**Courtyard by Marriott-Downtown Bricktown** 🆂🅷
(405) 232-2290. **$99-$149, 30 day notice.** 2 W Reno Ave. Gaylord and Reno aves; downtown. Int corridors. **Pets:** Small. $50 one-time fee/room. Designated rooms, service with restrictions, crate.

**Courtyard by Marriott-NW** 🆂🅷
(405) 848-0808. **$89-$239.** 1515 Northwest Expwy. I-44, exit 125C westbound; exit 125B eastbound, just e. Int corridors. **Pets:** Small. $75 one-time fee/room. Designated rooms, service with restrictions, supervision.

**Crowne Plaza Hotel** 🅻🅷 ✿
(405) 848-4811. **$79-$139, 7 day notice.** 2945 Northwest Expwy. 0.5 mi e of jct SR 74 and 3. Ext/int corridors. **Pets:** Small. $40 one-time fee/pet. Service with restrictions, supervision.

**Days Inn & Suites North** 🆂🅷
(405) 478-2554. **$52-$89.** 12013 N I-35 Service Rd. I-35, exit 137, just sw. Ext/int corridors. **Pets:** Accepted.

**(AAA) ▼▼▼ Days Inn West** SH
(405) 942-8294. **$50-$75.** 504 S Meridian Ave. I-40, exit 145 (Meridian Ave), just ne. Ext corridors. **Pets:** Other species. $10 daily fee/pet. Service with restrictions, crate.

SAVE ⑤ ⊠ 🖥 🖵 ⚤

**(AAA) ▼▼▼ Econo Lodge** SH
(405) 942-5955. **$47-$57.** 4601 SW 3rd. I-40, exit 145 (Meridian Ave), just nw. Ext corridors. **Pets:** $15 daily fee/room. Service with restrictions, supervision.

SAVE ⑤ ⊠ 🖵 ⚤

**▼▼▼ Embassy Suites** LH
(405) 682-6000. **$99-$179.** 1815 S Meridian Ave. I-40, exit 145 (Meridian Ave), 1 mi s. Int corridors. **Pets:** Large. $35 one-time fee/room. Service with restrictions, crate.

⊠ 🖉 🖥 🖵 🕪 ⚤ ⊠

**▼▼▼ Four Points by Sheraton Oklahoma City** SH
(405) 681-3500. **$90.** 6300 Terminal Dr. I-40, exit 145 (Meridian Ave), 4 mi s. Int corridors. **Pets:** Other species. $50 one-time fee/room. Service with restrictions.

A$K ⑤ ⊠ 🖳 🖥 🖵 🕪 ⚤

**▼▼▼ Holiday Inn Hotel & Suites** SH ❄
(405) 843-5558. **$92-$109.** 6200 N Robinson Ave. I-44, exit 127, just nw. Ext/int corridors. **Pets:** Medium, dogs only. $25 one-time fee/room. Service with restrictions, supervision.

A$K ⑤ ⊠ 🖳 🖥 🖵 🕪 ⚤

**(AAA) ▼▼ Howard Johnson Express Inn-Airport** M
(405) 943-9841. **$45-$65.** 400 S Meridian Ave. I-40, exit 145 (Meridian Ave), just n. Int corridors. **Pets:** Accepted.

SAVE ⑤ ⊠ 🖉 🖥 🖵 ⚤

**▼▼▼ La Quinta Inn & Suites Oklahoma City (Northwest Expressway)** SH
(405) 773-5575. **$97-$132.** 4829 Northwest Expwy. 1.9 mi w of jct SR 74 and 3. Int corridors. **Pets:** Medium. Service with restrictions.

A$K ⊠ 🖉 🖳 🖥 🖵 ⚤

**▼▼▼ La Quinta Inn and Suites-Quail Springs** SH
(405) 755-7000. **$89-$94.** 3003 W Memorial Rd. Kilpatrick Tpke, exit May Ave, just nw. Int corridors. **Pets:** Small. $50 one-time fee/room. Designated rooms, service with restrictions, supervision.

A$K ⑤ ⊠ 🖳 🖉 🖳 🖥 🖵 ⚤ ⊠

**(AAA) ▼▼▼ La Quinta Inn Oklahoma City (Airport)** SH
(405) 942-0040. **$69-$109.** 800 S Meridian Ave. I-40, exit 145 (Meridian Ave), just se. Ext/int corridors. **Pets:** Medium. Service with restrictions.

SAVE ⊠ 🖳 🖥 🖵 🕪 ⚤

**▼▼ Motel 6 Airport–116** M
(405) 946-6662. **$43-$53.** 820 S Meridian Ave. I-40, exit 145 (Meridian Ave), just s. Ext corridors. **Pets:** Accepted.

⑤ ⊠ 🖉 🖳 ⚤

**▼▼ Motel 6 West–1128** SH
(405) 947-6550. **$44-$57.** 4200 I-40 Service Rd. I-40, exit 145 (Meridian Ave), just e on south frontage road. Ext/int corridors. **Pets:** Accepted.

⑤ ⊠ 🖥 ⚤

**(AAA) ▼▼▼ Quality Inn** SH ❄
(405) 632-6666. **$70-$80.** 7800 CA Henderson Blvd. I-240, exit 2A, just s. Ext corridors. **Pets:** Small, dogs only. $10 one-time fee/room. Service with restrictions, supervision.

SAVE ⑤ ⊠ 🖉 🖳 🖥 🖵 ⚤

**(AAA) ▼▼▼ Quality Inn at Frontier City** SH
(405) 478-0400. **$45-$85.** 12001 N I-35 Service Rd. I-35, exit 137, just sw. Ext corridors. **Pets:** $7 daily fee/pet. Service with restrictions, supervision.

SAVE ⑤ ⊠ 🖳 🖵 ⚤

**(AAA) ▼▼▼ Ramada Limited** SH
(405) 948-8000. **$59-$139.** 2727 W I-44 Service Rd. I-44, exit 124, just n. Int corridors. **Pets:** Accepted.

SAVE ⑤ ⊠ 🖳 🖥 🖵 ⚤ ⊠

**▼▼▼ Renaissance Oklahoma City Hotel** LH
(405) 228-8000. **$109-$209.** 10 N Broadway Ave. Sheridan and Broadway aves; downtown. Int corridors. **Pets:** Accepted.

SAVE ⑤ ⊠ 🖳M 🖉 🖳 🖥 🖵 🕪 ⚤ ⊠

**▼▼▼ Residence Inn by Marriott-Oklahoma City West** SH ❄
(405) 942-4500. **$124-$149.** 4361 W Reno Ave. I-40, exit 145 (Meridian Ave), 0.3 mi n, then just e. Ext corridors. **Pets:** Other species. $75 one-time fee/pet. Service with restrictions, supervision.

A$K ⊠ 🖉 🖥 🖵 ⚤ ⊠

**▼▼▼ Residence Inn by Marriott South-Crossroads Mall** SH
(405) 634-9696. **$99-$159, 14 day notice.** 1111 E I-240 Service Rd. I-240, exit 4C eastbound, 0.4 mi nw; exit 5 westbound, 0.8 mi nw. Int corridors. **Pets:** Accepted.

A$K ⑤ ⊠ 🖳 🖥 🖵 ⚤

**(AAA) ▼▼▼ Sheraton Oklahoma City** LH ❄
(405) 235-2780. **$104-$249.** One N Broadway Ave. Sheridan and Broadway aves; downtown. Int corridors. **Pets:** Medium. Service with restrictions, crate.

SAVE ⊠ 🖉 🖳 🖥 🖵 🕪 ⚤

## PURCELL

**(AAA) ▼▼ Econo Lodge** M
(405) 527-5603. **$65-$75.** 2122 Hwy 74 S. I-35, exit 91, just e. Ext corridors. **Pets:** Small. $5 daily fee/pet. Service with restrictions, supervision.

SAVE ⊠ 🖉 🖥

## SHAWNEE

**▼▼ Motel 6–1236** M
(405) 275-5310. **$45-$61.** 4981 N Harrison. I-40, exit 186, just ne. Int corridors. **Pets:** Accepted.

⑤ ⊠ 🖉 🖳 ⚤

## YUKON

**(AAA) ▼▼▼ Best Western Inn & Suites Yukon** SH
(405) 265-2995. **$79-$89.** 11440 W I-40 Service Rd. I-40, exit 138, just sw. Int corridors. **Pets:** Other species. $25 deposit/room, $5 daily fee/room. Service with restrictions, supervision.

SAVE ⑤ ⊠ 🖉 🖳 🖥 🖵 ⚤

---

**END METROPOLITAN AREA**

# OKMULGEE

**Best Western Okmulgee** 🆂🅷
(918) 756-9200. **$73-$79.** 3499 N Wood Dr. Just n of jct US 75 and SR 56. Int corridors. **Pets:** Small. $50 deposit/pet. Service with restrictions, supervision.

# PRYOR

**Comfort Inn & Suites** 🆂🅷
(918) 476-6660. **$69-$105.** 307 Mid America Dr. 5 mi s on US 69. Int corridors. **Pets:** Dogs only. $10 daily fee/pet. Service with restrictions, supervision.

**Microtel Inn & Suites** 🆂🅷
(918) 476-4661. **$59-$70, 3 day notice.** 315 Mid America Dr. 5.1 mi s on US 69. Int corridors. **Pets:** $10 one-time fee/room. Service with restrictions, supervision.

# ROLAND

**Days Inn of Roland** 🆂🅷
(918) 427-1000. **$55-$70, 14 day notice.** 207 Cherokee Blvd. I-40, exit 325, just ne. Int corridors. **Pets:** Accepted.

# SALLISAW

**Best Western Blue Ribbon Inn** 🆂🅷
(918) 775-6294. **$69-$79.** 706 S Kerr Blvd (US 59). I-40, exit 308 (US 59), just n. Ext/int corridors. **Pets:** Accepted.

**Microtel Inn & Suites** 🆂🅷
(918) 774-0400. **$53-$93.** 710 S Kerr Blvd. I-40, exit 308 (US 59), just n. Int corridors. **Pets:** Small, dogs only. $10 one-time fee/pet. Service with restrictions, supervision.

# SAVANNA

**Candlelight Inn & Suites** 🆂🅷
(918) 548-3676. **$50-$75.** Hwy 69. 1.5 mi sw of jct US 69 and Indian Creek Tpke. Int corridors. **Pets:** Other species. $25 deposit/pet. Service with restrictions, supervision.

# SAYRE

**AmericInn Lodge & Suites of Sayre** 🆂🅷
(580) 928-2700. **$69-$140.** 2405 S El Camino Rd. I-40, exit 20, just n. Int corridors. **Pets:** Medium. $15 one-time fee/room. Service with restrictions, supervision.

# STILLWATER

**Best Western Stillwater** 🆂🅷
(405) 377-7010. **$70-$95.** 600 E McElroy. 1 mi n on US 177 (Perkins Rd). Int corridors. **Pets:** Accepted.

**Holiday Inn** 🆂🅷 🐾
(405) 372-0800. **$77.** 2515 W 6th Ave. 1.8 mi w on SR 51. Ext/int corridors. **Pets:** Other species. Supervision.

# TULSA METROPOLITAN AREA

# BROKEN ARROW

**Holiday Inn Tulsa South** 🆂🅷
(918) 258-7085. **$99.** 2600 N Aspen Ave. Just s of jct SR 51. Int corridors. **Pets:** Small. $25 one-time fee/room. Service with restrictions, supervision.

# CATOOSA

**Super 8 Motel** 🅼
(918) 266-7000. **$40-$55, 7 day notice.** 19250 Timbercrest Cir. I-44, exit 240A, just nw. Ext corridors. **Pets:** Accepted.

# CLAREMORE

**Claremore Motor Inn** 🅼
(918) 342-4545. **$39-$55.** 1709 N Lynn Riggs Blvd. 1.2 mi n on SR 66. Ext/int corridors. **Pets:** Accepted.

**Days Inn Claremore** 🆂🅷
(918) 343-3297. **$59-$85.** 1720 S Lynn Riggs. 1.6 mi s on SR 66. Int corridors. **Pets:** Accepted.

**Microtel Inn & Suites** 🆂🅷
(918) 343-2868. **$58.** 10600 E Mallard Lake Rd. 2.6 mi s on SR 66. Int corridors. **Pets:** Small, other species. $10 one-time fee/pet. Designated rooms, service with restrictions, supervision.

**Super 8 Motel** 🆂🅷
(918) 341-2323. **$59-$69.** 1100 E Will Rogers Blvd. I-44, exit 255, just w. Ext/int corridors. **Pets:** Small. $5 daily fee/pet. Designated rooms, service with restrictions, supervision.

**Travel Inn** 🅼
(918) 341-3254. **$45, 7 day notice.** 812 E Will Rogers Blvd. I-44, exit 255, 0.5 mi w. Ext corridors. **Pets:** Accepted.

# GLENPOOL

**Best Western Glenpool/Tulsa** 🆂🅷
(918) 322-5201. **$65-$75.** 14831 S Casper St. I-44, exit 224, 9.5 mi s on US 75. Ext corridors. **Pets:** Small. $50 deposit/pet. Service with restrictions, supervision.

# SAND SPRINGS

**Best Western Sand Springs Inn & Suites** 🆂🅷
(918) 245-4999. **$70-$75, 30 day notice.** 211 S Lake Dr. US 64 and 412, exit 81st W Ave, just sw. Ext/int corridors. **Pets:** Medium. $10 daily fee/room. Designated rooms, service with restrictions, supervision.

# TULSA

**Ambassador Hotel** 🆂🅷 🐾
(918) 587-8200. **$134-$290.** 1324 S Main St. 14th and Main sts. Int corridors. **Pets:** Medium. Service with restrictions, supervision.

**AmeriSuites (Tulsa/Hyde Park)** SH
(918) 491-4010. **$71-$109.** 7037 S Zurich Ave. I-44, exit 229 (Yale Ave/SR 66), 3 mi s to 71st St, then just e. Int corridors. **Pets:** Accepted.

ASK S✪ ✕ ⌖ ⟦⟧ 🛏 💻 ⇌

**Baymont Inn & Suites Tulsa** SH
(918) 488-8777. **$70-$80.** 4530 E Skelly Dr. I-44, exit 229 (Yale Ave/SR 66), just s, then w. Int corridors. **Pets:** Medium. Service with restrictions.

ASK ✕ ⌖ 🛏 💻 ⇌

**Best Western Trade Winds Central Inn** SH
(918) 749-5561. **$59-$79.** 3141 E Skelly Dr. I-44, exit 228 (Harvard Ave), on northwest frontage road. Ext/int corridors. **Pets:** Very small. $10 one-time fee/room. Service with restrictions, crate.

SAVE S✪ ✕ ⌖ 🛏 💻 ❘❘ ⇌

**Candlewood Suites** SH
(918) 294-9000. **$89-$109.** 10008 E 73rd St S. Just sw of jct 71st and 101st E Ave. Int corridors. **Pets:** Medium, other species. $50 one-time fee/pet. Service with restrictions, supervision.

ASK S✪ ✕ ⟦M⟧ ⌖ 🛏 💻

**Days Inn-Tulsa West** SH
(918) 446-1561. **$47-$53.** 5525 W Skelly Dr. I-44, exit 222B eastbound, just w on south service road; exit 222A westbound, just e on south service road. Ext/int corridors. **Pets:** Small. $25 daily fee/pet. Service with restrictions, supervision.

SAVE S✪ ✕ 🛏 ⇌

**DoubleTree Hotel At Warren Place** LH ❀
(918) 495-1000. **$155-$215.** 6110 S Yale Ave. I-44, exit 229 (Yale Ave/SR 66), 1.3 mi s. Int corridors. **Pets:** Medium, other species. $50 deposit/room. Service with restrictions, crate.

S✪ ✕ ⟦M⟧ ⌖ 🛏 💻 ❘❘ ⇌ ⊠

**Doubletree Hotel Downtown Tulsa** LH
(918) 587-8000. **$89-$189.** 616 W 7th St. 7th St and Houston. Int corridors. **Pets:** Medium, other species. $50 one-time fee/room. No service, crate.

✕ ⌖ 🛏 💻 ❘❘ ⇌ ⊠

**Fairfield Inn by Marriott-Tulsa/Woodland Hills** SH
(918) 252-7754. **$78-$98.** 9020 E 71st St. US 169, exit E 71st St, 1 mi w. Int corridors. **Pets:** Accepted.

ASK S✪ ✕ ⟦M⟧ 🛏 💻 ⇌

**Hampton Inn** SH
(918) 663-1000. **$79-$99, 3 day notice.** 3209 S 79th Ave E. I-44, exit 231 eastbound; exit 232 (Memorial Dr) westbound, just sw. Int corridors. **Pets:** Accepted.

ASK S✪ ✕ ⌖ ⟦M⟧ 🛏 💻 ⇌

**Holiday Inn Express** SH
(918) 459-5321. **$77-$97.** 9010 E 71st St. US 169, exit 71st St, 1 mi w. Int corridors. **Pets:** Accepted.

ASK S✪ ✕ ⌖ ⟦M⟧ 🛏 💻 ⇌

**Holiday Inn-International Airport** SH
(918) 437-7660. **$84.** 1010 N Garnett Rd. I-244, exit 14 (Garnett Rd), just n. Int corridors. **Pets:** Medium. $25 one-time fee/room. Service with restrictions, supervision.

ASK S✪ ✕ ⟦M⟧ ⌖ 🛏 💻 ❘❘ ⇌ ⊠

**Holiday Inn Select** SH
(918) 622-7000. **$149, 60 day notice.** 5000 E Skelly Dr. I-44, exit 229 (Yale Ave/SR 66); on south frontage road. Ext/int corridors. **Pets:** Small. $25 deposit/room, $25 one-time fee/room. Service with restrictions, crate.

ASK S✪ ✕ ⌖ 🛏 💻 ❘❘ ⇌ ⊠

**La Quinta Inn Tulsa (Airport)** SH
(918) 836-3931. **$65-$101.** 35 N Sheridan Rd. I-244, exit 11 (Sheridan Rd). Ext corridors. **Pets:** Medium. Service with restrictions.

ASK ✕ ⌖ 🛏 💻 ⇌

**La Quinta Inn Tulsa Central** SH
(918) 665-2630. **$69-$99.** 6030 S Skelly Dr. I-44, exit 230, just s. Int corridors. **Pets:** Medium, other species. Service with restrictions, supervision.

SAVE S✪ ✕ ⌖ 🛏 💻 ⇌

**La Quinta Inn Tulsa (East)** SH
(918) 665-0220. **$65-$105.** 10829 E 41st St. US 169, exit E 41st St. Ext corridors. **Pets:** Medium. Service with restrictions.

SAVE ✕ ⌖ 🛏 💻 ⇌

**La Quinta Inn Tulsa (South)** SH
(918) 254-1626. **$65-$105.** 12525 E 52nd St S. Broken Arrow Expwy (SR 51), exit 129th and 51st sts, just s. Ext corridors. **Pets:** Medium. Service with restrictions.

ASK ✕ ⌖ 🛏 💻 ⇌

**Microtel Inn & Suites** SH
(918) 234-9100. **$45-$65.** 16518 E Admiral Pl. I-44, exit 238 (161st Ave), just s. Int corridors. **Pets:** Small. $25 deposit/pet, $10 daily fee/pet. Designated rooms, service with restrictions, supervision.

ASK S✪ ✕ ⌖ ⟦M⟧ 🛏 💻

**Microtel Inn & Suites** SH
(918) 858-3775. **$52-$99.** 4531 E 21st St. Just w of 21st St and Yale Ave. Int corridors. **Pets:** Other species. $25 one-time fee/room. Service with restrictions, supervision.

ASK S✪ ✕ ⌖ 🛏 💻 ⇌

**Post Oak Lodge** SH
(918) 425-2112. **$95, 3 day notice.** 5323 W 31st N. 0.7 mi w of jct Apache/41st St. Int corridors. **Pets:** Accepted.

SAVE S✪ ✕ ❘❘ ⊠ ✈

**Red Roof Inn** M
(918) 622-6776. **$62-$79.** 4717 S Yale Ave. I-44, exit 229 (Yale Ave), just s. Ext corridors. **Pets:** Accepted.

ASK S✪ ✕ 🛏 ⇌

**Renaissance Tulsa Hotel & Convention Center** LH
(918) 307-2600. **$89-$249.** 6808 S 107th E Ave. Just ne of jct US 169 and 71st St. Int corridors. **Pets:** Service with restrictions, supervision.

SAVE ✕ ⟦M⟧ ⌖ 🛏 💻 ❘❘ ⇌ ⊠

**Residence Inn by Marriott** SH
(918) 250-4850. **$99-$199, 14 day notice.** 11025 E 73rd St. US 169, exit 71st St, just e. Int corridors. **Pets:** Accepted.

ASK S✪ ✕ 🛏 💻 ⇌ ⊠

**Rodeway Inn & Suites** SH
(918) 664-7241. **$80-$140.** 8181 E 41st St. 1.7 mi w of jct US 169. Ext corridors. **Pets:** Large, other species. $50 one-time fee/room. Service with restrictions, crate.

ASK ✕ ⌖ 🛏 💻 ⇌ ⊠

**Sheraton Tulsa Hotel** LH
(918) 627-5000. **$99.** 10918 E 41st St. Just e of US 169. Int corridors. **Pets:** Accepted.

ASK S✪ ✕ ⌖ ⟦⟧ 🛏 💻 ❘❘ ⇌ ⊠

**Sleep Inn & Suites Tulsa Central** SH
(918) 663-2777. **$64-$89.** 8021 E 33rd St S. I-44, exit 231 eastbound; exit 232 (Memorial Dr) westbound, just sw. Int corridors. **Pets:** Accepted.

ASK S✪ ✕ ⌖ ⟦⟧ 🛏 💻 ⇌ ⊠

**Staybridge Suites** SH
(918) 461-2100. **$89-$149.** 11111 E 73rd St. Just se of jct US 169 and 71st St. Int corridors. **Pets:** Small. $75 one-time fee/pet. Designated rooms, no service, crate.

ASK S✪ ✕ ⟦M⟧ ⌖ 🛏 💻 ⇌ ⊠

**AAA ◈◈ Super 8 Motel** SH
(918) 446-6000. **$42-$45.** 5811 S 49th West Ave. I-44, exit 222A, just e on south service road. Ext corridors. **Pets:** Accepted.

SAVE S⊘ ⊠ ▤ ⊃

**◈◈◈ Tulsa Hilton Southern Hills** LH
(918) 492-5000. **$79-$169.** 7902 S Lewis. I-44, exit 227, 3 mi s. Int corridors. **Pets:** Accepted.

⊠ ⊘ ⊛ ▤ ⊟ ¶ ⊃

## End Metropolitan Area

# WOODWARD

**AAA ◈◈ Northwest Inn** SH
(580) 256-7600. **$79-$89.** Hwy 270 S & 1st St. 1.4 mi s on US 183, 270, SR 3 and 34. Ext/int corridors. **Pets:** $10 one-time fee/room. Service with restrictions, supervision.

SAVE S⊘ ⊠ ▤ ⊟ ¶ ⊃

# OREGON

## ALBANY

### Best Western Albany Inn
(541) 928-6322. $55-$125. 315 Airport Rd SE. I-5, exit 234B southbound; exit 234 northbound, just w, then just s. Ext corridors. **Pets:** Other species. $10 daily fee/pet. Service with restrictions, supervision.

### Comfort Suites
(541) 928-2053. $67-$112. 100 Opal Ct NE. I-5, exit 234A southbound; exit 234 northbound, just e. Int corridors. **Pets:** $30 one-time fee/room. Service with restrictions, supervision.

### Days Inn & Suites
(541) 928-5050. $55-$79, 14 day notice. 1100 Price Rd SE. I-5, exit 233, just e, then just n. Int corridors. **Pets:** $10 one-time fee/pet. Designated rooms, service with restrictions, supervision.

### Econo Lodge
(541) 926-0170. $45-$77. 1212 SE Price Rd. I-5, exit 233, just e, then just n. Ext corridors. **Pets:** Accepted.

### Holiday Inn Express Hotel & Suites
(541) 928-8820. $59-$99. 105 Opal Ct NE. I-5, exit 234A southbound; exit 234 northbound, 0.4 mi e. Int corridors. **Pets:** Other species. $30 one-time fee/room. Service with restrictions, supervision.

### La Quinta Inn & Suites Albany
(541) 928-0921. $69-$130. 251 Airport Rd SE. I-5, exit 234B southbound; exit 234 northbound, just w. Int corridors. **Pets:** Other species. Service with restrictions, supervision.

### Motel 6 #4124
(541) 926-4233. $68-$74. 2735 E Pacific Blvd. I-5, exit 234B southbound; exit 234 northbound, 0.5 mi w. Ext corridors. **Pets:** Accepted.

### Phoenix Inn Suites-Albany
(541) 926-5696. $79-$109. 3410 Spicer Rd SE. I-5, exit 233, just e. Int corridors. **Pets:** Other species. $15 daily fee/pet. No service, supervision.

## ASHLAND

### Ashland Springs Hotel
(541) 488-1700. $79-$199. 212 E Main St. Corner of 1st St; center. Int corridors. **Pets:** Medium, other species. $30 one-time fee/room. Designated rooms, service with restrictions, supervision.

### Best Western Bard's Inn
(541) 482-0049. $80-$156. 132 N Main St. Just n on SR 99 (N Main St) from Downtown Plaza. Ext/int corridors. **Pets:** Accepted.

### Best Western Windsor Inn
(541) 488-2330. $79-$159. 2520 Ashland St. I-5, exit 14, just e on SR 66. Ext corridors. **Pets:** $15 daily fee/pet. Service with restrictions, supervision.

### Cedarwood Inn
(541) 488-2000. $59-$119, 3 day notice. 1801 Siskiyou Blvd. I-5, exit 11 northbound, 2.8 mi w; exit 14 southbound, just w on SR 66, 0.6 mi s on Tolman Creek Rd, then 0.6 mi w. Ext corridors. **Pets:** Accepted.

### Flagship Inn of Ashland
(541) 482-2641. $59-$119, 3 day notice. 1193 Siskiyou Blvd. I-5, exit 14, 1.3 mi w on SR 66, just n on SR 99 (Siskiyou Blvd). Ext corridors. **Pets:** Accepted.

### Knights Inn Motel
(541) 482-5111. $52-$98, 3 day notice. 2359 Hwy 66. I-5, exit 14, just w. Ext corridors. **Pets:** Other species. $10 daily fee/pet. Designated rooms, service with restrictions, supervision.

### La Quinta Inn & Suites Ashland
(541) 482-6932. $91-$159. 434 Valley View Rd. I-5, exit 19, just w. Int corridors. **Pets:** Other species. Designated rooms, service with restrictions, supervision.

### Plaza Inn & Suites At Ashland Creek
(541) 488-8900. $69-$179. 98 Central Ave. I-5, exit 19, 0.5 mi w, 1.9 mi s on SR 99 (N Main St), just e on Water St, then just n. Int corridors. **Pets:** Medium. $25 daily fee/room. Designated rooms, service with restrictions, supervision.

**△△△ ▽▽▽ Super 8 Motel-Ashland** SH
(541) 482-8887. **$65-$120.** 2350 Ashland St. I-5, exit 14, just w. Int corridors. **Pets:** Small, dogs only. $10 daily fee/pet. Service with restrictions, supervision.
SAVE [S]  [X]  [M]  [B]  [≈]

**△△△ ▽▽▽ Timbers Motel** M ☆
(541) 482-4242. **$44-$92, 3 day notice.** 1450 Ashland St. I-5, exit 14, 0.8 mi w. Ext corridors. **Pets:** Other species. Designated rooms, service with restrictions, crate.
SAVE [X]  [B]  [≈]

**△△△ ▽▽▽▽ Windmill Inn & Suites of Ashland** SH ☆
(541) 482-8310. **$89-$139.** 2525 Ashland St. I-5, exit 14, just e. Int corridors. **Pets:** Large, other species. Designated rooms, service with restrictions, supervision.
SAVE [S] [X] [M] [✏] [⌨] [B] [≈] [X]

## ASTORIA

**▽▽▽▽ Astoria Holiday Inn Express Hotel & Suites** SH
(503) 325-6222. **$89-$259.** 204 W Marine Dr. On US 30; west side of town. Int corridors. **Pets:** Other species. $15 daily fee/pet. Designated rooms, service with restrictions, supervision.
ASK [S] [X] [M] [✏] [⌨] [B] [≈] [X]

**△△△ ▽▽▽ Best Western Lincoln Inn** SH ☆
(503) 325-2205. **$79-$299.** 555 Hamburg Ave. On US 101/30; at east end of Young's Bay Bridge. Int corridors. **Pets:** Medium, dogs only. $10 daily fee/pet. Designated rooms, service with restrictions, supervision.
SAVE [S] [X] [B] [⌨] [≈] [X]

**▽▽▽ Clementine's Bed & Breakfast** BB
(503) 325-2005. **$80-$160, 7 day notice.** 847 Exchange St. At 8th and Exchange sts; in historic downtown. Int corridors. **Pets:** $15 one-time fee/room. Designated rooms, service with restrictions, supervision.
[X] [B] [⌨] [K] [Z]

**△△△ ▽▽▽ Crest Motel** M
(503) 325-3141. **$63-$139.** 5366 Leif Erickson Dr. 4 mi e of Astoria Bridge on US 30. Ext corridors. **Pets:** Other species. Service with restrictions, supervision.
SAVE [X] [B] [⌨] [K]

**△△△ ▽▽▽ Red Lion Inn Astoria** M
(503) 325-7373. **$72-$131.** 400 Industry St. Just w of Astoria Bridge on US 30, just n on Basin St (Caution: do not turn onto Astoria-Megler Bridge). Ext corridors. **Pets:** Large. $10 daily fee/room. Crate.
SAVE [S] [X] [✏] [B] [⌨] [K]

## BAKER CITY

**△△△ ▽▽▽▽ Best Western Sunridge Inn** SH ☆
(541) 523-6444. **$69-$77.** 1 Sunridge Ln. I-84, exit 304, just w. Int corridors. **Pets:** Medium, other species. $15 daily fee/room. Designated rooms, service with restrictions, supervision.
SAVE [S] [X] [M] [✏] [B] [⌨] [T1] [≈]

**△△△ ▽▽▽▽ Geiser Grand Hotel** SH ☆
(541) 523-1889. **$89-$109.** 1996 Main St. I-84, exit 304, 0.9 mi w on Campbell St, then 0.3 mi s; downtown. Int corridors. **Pets:** Other species. $75 deposit/room, $15 daily fee/pet. Service with restrictions, crate.
ASK [S] [X] [⌨] [T1]

## BANDON

**△△△ ▽▽▽ Bandon Inn (formerly Harbor View Inn)** M ☆
(541) 347-4417. **$69-$139.** 355 Hwy 101. Center. Ext corridors. **Pets:** Medium. $15 daily fee/pet. Designated rooms, service with restrictions, supervision.
SAVE [S] [X] [✏] [B] [⌨] [K]

**△△△ ▽▽▽ Best Western Inn at Face Rock** SH
(541) 347-9441. **$109-$274.** 3225 Beach Loop Dr. 1 mi s on US 101, 0.8 mi w on Seabird Rd, then just s. Ext corridors. **Pets:** $15 one-time fee/pet. Designated rooms, service with restrictions, supervision.
SAVE [S] [X] [✏] [⌨] [B] [⌨] [T1] [≈] [X] [K]

**△△△ ▽▽▽ Driftwood Motel** M
(541) 347-9022. **$65-$100.** 460 Hwy 1 1. On US 101; center. Ext corridors. **Pets:** Dogs only. $10 daily fee/pet. Designated rooms, no service, supervision.
SAVE [X] [B] [⌨] [K]

## BEND

**▽▽▽ Bend Riverside Motel Suites** SH
(541) 389-2363. **Call for rates.** 1565 NW Wall St. US 97, exit 137, jut s. Ext corridors. **Pets:** Medium. $25 daily fee/pet. Designated rooms, service with restrictions, supervision.
[X] [✏] [B] [⌨] [K]

**▽▽▽ Bend Super 8 Motel** SH
(541) 388-6888. **$65-$100, 24 day notice.** 1275 S Business Hwy 97. US 97, exit 139 (Reed Market Rd), just s; jct US 20 E, 3.5 mi s. Int corridors. **Pets:** Medium. $10 one-time fee/pet. No service, supervision.
ASK [S] [X] [B] [⌨] [≈]

**△△△ ▽▽▽ Best Western Inn & Suites of Bend** SH
(541) 382-1515. **$74-$129.** 721 NE 3rd St. On Business Rt US 97, just s of jct US 20. Ext corridors. **Pets:** $10 daily fee/pet. Designated rooms, service with restrictions, supervision.
SAVE [S] [X] [✏] [B] [≈]

**▽▽▽ Cricketwood Country Bed & Breakfast** BB
(541) 330-0747. **$95-$140, 7 day notice.** 63520 Cricketwood Rd. 3.8 mi se on Deschutes Market Rd, 0.5 mi e on Hamehook Rd, 0.5 mi on Repine Rd, then just n. Ext/int corridors. **Pets:** Dogs only. $10 daily fee/room. Designated rooms, no service.
[X] [B] [⌨]

**▽▽▽ Days Inn** SH ☆
(541) 383-3776. **$62-$94.** 849 NE 3rd St. US 97, just s of jct US 20. Ext corridors. **Pets:** $4 one-time fee/room. Supervision.
ASK [S] [X] [M] [✏] [⌨] [B] [⌨] [≈]

**△△△ ▽▽▽ Econo Lodge** SH
(541) 382-2211. **$39-$89.** 3705 N US Hwy 97 business loop. On US 97 business loop, 2 mi n. Ext corridors. **Pets:** Dogs only. $5 one-time fee/room. Designated rooms, supervision.
SAVE [S] [X] [B] [≈]

**△△△ ▽▽▽ Entrada Lodge** SH
(541) 382-4080. **$69-$129.** 19221 SW Century Dr. 5.7 mi w on Mt. Bachelor Rt via Division St/Colorado Av from jct US 20 W/97 N. Ext corridors. **Pets:** Accepted.
SAVE [S] [X] [B] [⌨] [≈]

**▽▽▽▽ Fairfield Inn & Suites by Marriott** SH
(541) 318-1747. **$79-$149.** 1626 NW Wall St. US 97, exit 137 (Revere Ave), just s; downtown. Int corridors. **Pets:** Other species. $75 one-time fee/room. Service with restrictions, crate.
ASK [S] [X] [M] [✏] [⌨] [B] [⌨] [≈] [X]

**△△△ ▽▽▽▽ Hampton Inn** SH
(541) 388-4114. **$79-$119.** 15 NE Butler Market Rd. US 97, exit 136, just n. Ext corridors. **Pets:** Medium. $10 daily fee/pet. Designated rooms, service with restrictions, supervision.
SAVE [S] [X] [B] [⌨] [≈]

**△△△ ▽▽▽▽ Holiday Inn Express Hotel & Suites** SH
(541) 317-8500. **$74-$179.** 20615 Grandview Dr. On US 97; north end of town. Int corridors. **Pets:** Other species. $10 one-time fee/room. Service with restrictions, supervision.
SAVE [S] [X] [M] [✏] [⌨] [B] [⌨] [≈] [X]

**AAA ▼▼▼ La Quinta Inn Bend SH**
(541) 388-2227. **$69-$129.** 61200 S Business Hwy 97. Jct US 20 E, 3 mi s. Int corridors. **Pets:** Accepted.
SAVE ☒ ⬚M 🅿 🖥 💻 ⟲

**AAA ▼▼▼ Plaza Motel M**
(541) 382-1621. **$55-$69.** 1430 NW Wall St. US 97, exit 137 (Revere Ave), just s; downtown. Ext corridors. **Pets:** Accepted.
SAVE ⬚ ☒ 🖥 💻

**AAA ▼▼▼ Quality Inn SH**
(541) 318-0848. **$59-$99.** 20600 Grandview Dr. On US 97; north end of town. Int corridors. **Pets:** Small. $10 daily fee/pet. Service with restrictions, supervision.
SAVE ⬚ ☒ ⬚M 🅿 ⬚ 🖥 💻 ⟲

**▼▼ Red Lion Inn/North SH**
(541) 382-7011. **$65-$105.** 1415 NE 3rd St. US 97, just n of jct US 20. Ext corridors. **Pets:** Accepted.
ASK ⬚ ☒ ⬚M 🅿 ⬚ 🖥 💻 🍴 ⟲

**AAA ▼▼▼ The Riverhouse Resort Hotel SH**
(541) 389-3111. **$95-$160.** 3075 N Business 97. US 97, exit 136 (Butler Market Rd) northbound, just n; exit 135B southbound. Ext/int corridors. **Pets:** Accepted.
SAVE ⬚ ☒ 🅿 ⬚ 🖥 💻 🍴 ⟲ ☒

**▼▼▼ Shilo Inn Suites Hotel Bend SH** 🐾
(541) 389-9600. **$89-$199.** 3105 O B Riley Rd. 1.5 mi n on US 97 from jct US 20 E. Ext corridors. **Pets:** $15 daily fee/pet. Designated rooms, service with restrictions, supervision.
ASK ⬚ ☒ 🅿 ⬚ 🖥 💻 🍴 ⟲ ☒

**▼▼ Sleep Inn of Bend SH**
(541) 330-0050. **$69-$109.** 600 NE Bellevue. On US 20 E, 2 mi e of jct US 97. Int corridors. **Pets:** Medium. $10 one-time fee/room. Service with restrictions, supervision.
ASK ⬚ ☒ ⬚M ⬚ 🖥 💻 ⟲

# BOARDMAN

**AAA ▼▼ Econo Lodge M**
(541) 481-2375. **$58-$89.** 105 SW Front St. I-84, exit 164, just s. Ext corridors. **Pets:** Other species. Designated rooms, service with restrictions, supervision.
SAVE ⬚ ☒ 🅿 🖥 💻 ⟲

# BROOKINGS

**AAA ▼▼▼ Best Western Beachfront Inn SH**
(541) 469-7779. **$114-$295.** 16008 Boat Basin Rd. Jct US 101, 0.6 mi w on Benham Ln. Ext corridors. **Pets:** Large. $10 daily fee/pet. Designated rooms, service with restrictions, supervision.
SAVE ☒ ⬚M 🅿 🖥 💻 ⟲

**AAA ▼▼▼ Westward Inn M**
(541) 469-7471. **$49-$89, 3 day notice.** 1026 Chetco Ave. On US 101; north end of town. Ext corridors. **Pets:** Medium, dogs only. $8 daily fee/pet. Designated rooms, service with restrictions, supervision.
SAVE ⬚ ☒ 🖥 ⬚

# BURNS

**AAA ▼▼▼ Americas Best Inn M**
(541) 573-1700. **$47-$74.** 999 Oregon Ave. 1 mi w on US 395/20 from jct SR 78. Ext/int corridors. **Pets:** Accepted.
SAVE ⬚ ☒ 🖥 💻 ⟲

**AAA ▼▼▼ Days Inn Burns M**
(541) 573-2047. **$53-$67.** 577 W Monroe St. Just w on US 395/20 from jct SR 78. Ext corridors. **Pets:** Other species. $5 daily fee/pet. Designated rooms, service with restrictions, supervision.
SAVE ⬚ ☒ 🖥 ⟲

**AAA ▼▼ Silver Spur Motel M**
(541) 573-2077. **$46-$51.** 789 N Broadway. US 395/20, at edge of town. Ext corridors. **Pets:** Large, other species. $5 daily fee/pet. Service with restrictions, crate.
SAVE ☒ 🖥 💻

# CANNON BEACH

**▼▼ Cannon Beach Ecola Creek Lodge M**
(503) 436-2776. **$52-$157, 3 day notice.** 208 5th St. 0.3 mi w of US 101 via north exit to Ecola State Park. Ext corridors. **Pets:** Accepted.
ASK ⬚ ☒ ⬚M 🖥 💻 ⬚

**▼▼▼ Hallmark Resort at Cannon Beach SH** 🐾
(503) 436-1566. **$79-$349, 3 day notice.** 1400 S Hemlock St. US 101, exit Sunset Blvd, just s. Ext corridors. **Pets:** $20 daily fee/pet. Designated rooms, supervision.
ASK ⬚ ☒ ⬚M 🅿 🖥 💻 ⟲ ☒ ⬚

**AAA ▼▼ Haystack Resort M** 🐾
(503) 436-1577. **$55-$249, 3 day notice.** 3339 S Hemlock St. US 101, exit Tolovana Park, just w. Ext corridors. **Pets:** Medium, dogs only. $10 daily fee/pet. Designated rooms, service with restrictions, supervision.
SAVE ⬚ ☒ 🖥 💻 ⟲ ⬚

**AAA ▼▼▼ Inn at Cannon Beach M** 🐾
(503) 436-9085. **$89-$239, 3 day notice.** 3215 S Hemlock St. US 101, exit Tolovana Park, just w, then just n. Ext corridors. **Pets:** $10 daily fee/pet. Designated rooms, service with restrictions, supervision.
SAVE ⬚ ☒ ⬚ 🖥 💻 ⬚

**AAA ▼▼▼ Ocean Lodge SH**
(503) 436-2241. **$179-$329, 7 day notice.** 2864 S Pacific. US 101, exit Tolovana Park, 1 mi s, then just w on Chisana. Ext/int corridors. **Pets:** Accepted.
SAVE ⬚ ☒ 🖥 💻

**AAA ▼▼▼ Surfsand Resort at Cannon Beach M** 🐾
(503) 436-2274. **$109-$339, 3 day notice.** Ocean Front & Gower. US 101, exit Cannon Beach (2nd exit); downtown. Ext corridors. **Pets:** Other species. $12 one-time fee/pet. Designated rooms, service with restrictions, supervision.
SAVE ⬚ ☒ 🅿 ⬚ 🖥 💻 🍴 ⟲ ☒ ⬚

**AAA ▼▼▼ Tolovana Inn CO** 🐾
(503) 436-2211. **$69-$379, 3 day notice.** 3400 S Hemlock St. 2 mi s off US 101 Beach Loop. Ext corridors. **Pets:** Medium, dogs only. $12 one-time fee/pet. Designated rooms, service with restrictions, supervision.
SAVE ⬚ ☒ ⬚ 🖥 💻 ⟲ ☒ ⬚

# CANYONVILLE

**AAA ▼▼▼ Best Western Canyonville Inn & Suites SH**
(541) 839-4200. **$69-$140.** 200 Creekside Rd. I-5, exit 99, just w. Int corridors. **Pets:** Small. $15 daily fee/pet. Designated rooms, service with restrictions, supervision.
SAVE ⬚ ☒ ⬚ 🖥 💻 ⟲

# CASCADE LOCKS

**AAA ▼▼ Best Western Columbia River Inn SH**
(541) 374-8777. **$69-$159.** 735 WaNaPa St. I-84, exit 44. Int corridors. **Pets:** Other species. $10 daily fee/pet. Designated rooms, service with restrictions, supervision.
SAVE ⬚ ☒ ⬚M 🅿 ⬚ 🖥 💻 ⟲

# CHEMULT

**AAA ▼▼▼ Dawson House Lodge BB**
(541) 365-2232. **$40-$105.** 109455 Hwy 97. US 97; center. Ext/int corridors. **Pets:** Small. $10 deposit/room. Service with restrictions, supervision.
SAVE ☒ 🖥 💻

# COOS BAY

**Best Western Holiday Motel** SH
(541) 269-5111. **$81-$109.** 411 N Bayshore Dr. Just n of downtown on US 101. Ext/int corridors. **Pets:** Small, dogs only. $10 daily fee/pet. Service with restrictions, supervision.

**Motel 6–1244** SH
(541) 267-7171. **$45-$73.** 1445 Bayshore Dr. 0.6 mi n of downtown on US 101. Ext corridors. **Pets:** Accepted.

**Red Lion Hotel Coos Bay** SH
(541) 267-4141. **$75-$92.** 1313 N Bayshore Dr. 0.5 mi n of downtown on US 101. Ext corridors. **Pets:** $10 daily fee/room. Service with restrictions.

# COQUILLE

**Myrtle Lane Motel** M
(541) 396-2102. **$46.** 787 N Central Blvd. SR 42, 0.4 mi n. Ext corridors. **Pets:** Accepted.

# CORVALLIS

**Best Western Grand Manor Inn** SH
(541) 758-8571. **$80-$110.** 925 NW Garfield. 1.5 mi n on 9th St; downtown. Int corridors. **Pets:** Accepted.

**Days Inn** SH
(541) 754-7474. **$52-$77.** 1113 NW 9th St. 1.3 mi n. Int corridors. **Pets:** Medium, other species. $10 daily fee/room. Designated rooms, service with restrictions, supervision.

**Holiday Inn Express On The River** SH
(541) 752-0800. **$79-$129.** 781 NE 2nd St. I-5, exit 228, 9.8 mi w on SR 34, then 0.4 mi nw. Int corridors. **Pets:** Accepted.

**Motel 6 #4243** SH
(541) 758-9125. **$55-$69.** 935 NW Garfield Ave. 1.5 mi n on 9th St. Int corridors. **Pets:** Accepted.

**Super 8 Motel** SH 🐾
(541) 758-8088. **$70-$90.** 407 NW 2nd St. US 20, just n of jct SR 34; downtown. Int corridors. **Pets:** Medium, other species. $25 deposit/room. Designated rooms, service with restrictions, supervision.

# COTTAGE GROVE

**Comfort Inn** SH
(541) 942-9747. **$69-$109, 7 day notice.** 845 Gateway Blvd. I-5, exit 174, just w. Ext/int corridors. **Pets:** Accepted.

**Holiday Inn Express** SH
(541) 942-1000. **$79-$99.** 1601 Gateway Blvd. I-5, exit 174, just w. Int corridors. **Pets:** Accepted.

**Village Green Resort** M 🐾
(541) 942-2491. **$69-$139.** 725 Row River Rd. I-5, exit 174, just e. Ext corridors. **Pets:** Designated rooms, service with restrictions, supervision.

# CRESWELL

**Best Western Creswell Inn** SH
(541) 895-3341. **$59-$149.** 345 E Oregon Ave. I-5, exit 182, just w. Ext corridors. **Pets:** Medium. $10 daily fee/pet. Service with restrictions, supervision.

# DALLAS

**Best Western Dallas Inn & Suites** SH
(503) 623-6000. **$80-$100.** 250 Orchard Dr. SR 223, just n. Int corridors. **Pets:** Accepted.

# THE DALLES

**Best Western River City Inn** SH
(541) 296-9107. **$64-$94.** 112 W 2nd St. I-84, exit 84 eastbound, just se; exit 85 westbound, 0.8 mi nw; at Liberty and W 2nd St; downtown. Ext/int corridors. **Pets:** Other species. $10 daily fee/pet. Designated rooms.

**Comfort Inn Columbia Gorge** SH
(541) 298-2800. **$70-$145.** 351 Lone Pine Dr. I-84, exit 87, just n. Int corridors. **Pets:** Small, other species. $10 daily fee/pet. Designated rooms, service with restrictions, supervision.

**Cousins Country Inn** SH 🐾
(541) 298-5161. **$74-$109.** 2114 W 6th. I-84, exit 83 eastbound, just n; exit 84 westbound, just nw on W 2nd St, just sw on Webber St, then just n. Ext corridors. **Pets:** Service with restrictions, supervision.

**Super 8 Motel** SH 🐾
(541) 296-6888. **$56-$89.** 609 Cherry Heights Rd. I-84, exit 84, just se. Int corridors. **Pets:** Large, other species. $10 daily fee/pet. Service with restrictions, supervision.

# DEPOE BAY

**Crown Pacific Inn** M
(541) 765-7773. **$50-$75.** 50 NE Bechill St. Center. Ext/int corridors. **Pets:** Medium. $10 one-time fee/room. Designated rooms, service with restrictions, supervision.

# ENTERPRISE

**Ponderosa Motel** M
(541) 426-3186. **$59-$69.** 102 E Greenwood St. Center. Ext corridors. **Pets:** Dogs only. $10 daily fee/pet. Supervision.

**The Wilderness Inn** M
(541) 426-4535. **$48-$68.** 301 W North St. Corner of NW 2nd. Ext corridors. **Pets:** Accepted.

# EUGENE

**Americas Best Value Inn** M
(541) 343-0730. **$44-$74.** 1140 W 6th Ave. I-5, exit 194B, 3 mi w on I-105, then just w on SR 99 N (6th Ave). Ext corridors. **Pets:** $5 daily fee/pet. Designated rooms, service with restrictions, supervision.

**Best Western Greentree Inn** SH 🐾
(541) 485-2727. **$84-$98.** 1759 Franklin Blvd. I-5, exit 194B southbound to I-105, then University of Oregon Rt; exit 192 northbound, 1.2 mi w. Ext/int corridors. **Pets:** $50 deposit/pet. Service with restrictions, supervision.

**(AAA)** ▼▼▼ **Best Western New Oregon Motel** SH ❖
(541) 683-3669. **$84-$98.** 1655 Franklin Blvd. I-5, exit 192 northbound, 1.3 mi w; exit 194B southbound to I-105, follow University of Oregon signs. Ext/int corridors. **Pets:** $50 deposit/pet. Service with restrictions, supervision.
SAVE 🗐 ✕ 🗐 🎮 🖥 ➤ ✕

**(AAA)** ▼▼▼ **The Campbell House, A City Inn** BB
(541) 343-1119. **$99-$349.** 252 Pearl St. Just n on High, just w on 4th, then just n; center. Int corridors. **Pets:** Accepted.
SAVE ✕ 🗐

**(AAA)** ▼ **Courtesy Inn** M
(541) 345-3391. **$50-$80.** 345 W 6th Ave. I-5, exit 194B, 2 mi w on I-105 (to end of freeway) to 7th Ave, just e to Lincoln, then just n; downtown. Ext corridors. **Pets:** Small, dogs only. $7 daily fee/pet. Designated rooms, service with restrictions, supervision.
SAVE 🗐 ✕ 🗐 🖥

**(AAA)** ▼▼▼ **Days Inn** SH
(541) 342-6383. **$69-$111.** 1859 Franklin Blvd. I-5, exit 192 northbound, 1 mi w; exit 194B southbound to I-105, follow signs to University of Oregon. Ext/int corridors. **Pets:** Other species. Designated rooms, service with restrictions, supervision.
SAVE 🗐 ✕ 🗐 🖥

▼▼▼ **Eugene/Springfield Residence Inn by Marriott** SH ❖
(541) 342-7171. **$99-$139.** 25 Club Rd. I-5, exit 194B, 1.3 mi w on I-105, exit 2 (Coburg Rd), just s, just w on Martin Luther King Jr Blvd (Centennial Blvd), then just se. Int corridors. **Pets:** Other species. $75 one-time fee/room. Service with restrictions, supervision.
ASK ✕ 🗐M 🎮 🗐 🖥 ➤ ✕

**(AAA)** ▼▼▼ **Express Inn & Suites** M
(541) 868-1520. **$45-$75, 3 day notice.** 990 W 6th Ave. I-5, exit 194B, 3 mi w on I-105, then just w on SR 99 N (6th Ave). Ext corridors. **Pets:** Accepted.
SAVE 🗐 ✕ 🗐

**(AAA)** ▼▼▼ **Franklin Inn** M
(541) 342-4804. **$69-$99, 3 day notice.** 1857 Franklin Blvd. I-5, exit 191 southbound; exit 192 northbound, just e, follow University of Oregon signs. Ex: corridors. **Pets:** Small, dogs only. $10 daily fee/pet. Designated rooms, service with restrictions, supervision.
SAVE 🗐 ✕ 🗐 🖥 ➤

▼▼▼ **Hilton Eugene** LH ❖
(541) 342-2000. **$129-$184.** 66 E 6th Ave. At 6th Ave and Oak St; center. Int corridors. **Pets:** Other species. $25 one-time fee/room. Service with restrictions, supervision.
ASK ✕ 🎮 🗐 🖥 🍴 ➤

**(AAA)** ▼▼▼ **La Quinta Inn & Suites Waterfront** SH
(541) 344-8335. **$69-$199.** 155 Day Island Rd. I-5, exit 194B, 1.3 mi w on I-105, exit 2 (Coburg Rd), go through Coburg Rd to Southwood Ln, just w, then 0.5 mi se on Country Club Rd; follow signs for Autzen Stadium. Int corridors. **Pets:** Large, other species. $50 deposit/room. Service with restrictions, supervision.
SAVE 🗐 ✕ 🎮 🗐 🖥 ➤

▼ **Motel 6-36** M
(541) 687-2395. **$47-$61.** 3690 Glenwood Dr. I-5, exit 191, just sw. Ext corridors. **Pets:** Accepted.
🗐 ✕ 🗐M 🎮 🗐 ➤

▼▼ **Red Lion Hotel Eugene** SH
(541) 342-5201. **$99-$109.** 205 Coburg Rd. I-5, exit 194B southbound, 1.3 mi w on I-105, exit 2 (Coburg Rd), then just n. Ext corridors. **Pets:** Accepted.
ASK 🗐 ✕ 🎮 🎮 🗐 🖥 🍴 ➤

▼▼▼ **Valley River Inn, a WestCoast Hotel** SH
(541) 743-1000. **$119-$200, 3 day notice.** 1000 Valley River Way. I-5, exit 194B southbound, 2.5 mi w on I-105, exit 1, follow Valley River Center signs, just s of mall. Int corridors. **Pets:** Other species. Designated rooms, service with restrictions, crate.
ASK 🗐 ✕ 🎮 🎮 🗐 🖥 🍴 ➤ ✕

# FLORENCE

**(AAA)** ▼ **Le Chateau Motel** SH
(541) 997-3481. **$54-$108.** 1084 Hwy 101 N. SR 126, just n. Ext corridors. **Pets:** Medium, other species. $18 one-time fee/room. Designated rooms, service with restrictions, supervision.
SAVE ✕ 🗐 🖥 ➤ ✕ 🎮

**(AAA)** ▼▼▼ **Oceanbreeze Motel** M
(541) 997-2642. **$49-$120.** 85165 Hwy 101 S. SR 126, 2 mi s; south end of Siuslaw Bridge. Ext corridors. **Pets:** Dogs only. $10 daily fee/pet. Service with restrictions, supervision.
SAVE 🗐 ✕ 🗐 🖥 🎮

**(AAA)** ▼ **Old Town Inn** M
(541) 997-7131. **$60-$93.** 170 Hwy 101. SR 126, 0.5 mi s. Ext corridors. **Pets:** Medium, other species. $10 one-time fee/pet. Designated rooms, service with restrictions, supervision.
SAVE 🗐 ✕ 🖥 🎮

**(AAA)** ▼ **Park Motel** M ❖
(541) 997-2634. **$51-$129.** 85034 Hwy 101 S. Jct SR 126 and US 101, 2.2 mi s. Ext corridors. **Pets:** Large, other species. $10 daily fee/pet. Service with restrictions, supervision.
SAVE 🗐 ✕ 🗐 🖥 🎮

# FOREST GROVE

▼▼ **Americas Best Value Inn & Suites** SH
(503) 357-9000. **$49-$69.** 3306 Pacific Ave. West end of town on SR 8. Int corridors. **Pets:** Accepted.
ASK 🗐 ✕ 🗐M 🗐 🖥 ➤

**(AAA)** ▼▼▼ **Best Western University Inn & Suites** SH
(503) 992-8888. **$79-$179.** 3933 Pacific Ave. East end of town on SR 8. Int corridors. **Pets:** Accepted.
SAVE 🗐 ✕ 🗐M 🎮 🗐 🖥 ➤ ✕

# GARIBALDI

**(AAA)** ▼▼▼ **Comfort Inn** SH
(503) 322-3338. **$59-$109.** 502 Garibaldi Ave. On US 101 at jct 5th St; center. Int corridors. **Pets:** Dogs only. $10 one-time fee/room. Designated rooms, service with restrictions, supervision.
SAVE 🗐 ✕ 🎮 🗐 🖥 ➤ ✕

# GEARHART

**(AAA)** ▼▼▼ **Gearhart By The Sea** CO
(503) 738-8331. **$88-$150, 3 day notice.** 1157 N Marion. 1 mi w off US 101 via City Center exit (Pacific Way). Ext corridors. **Pets:** $11 daily fee/pet. Designated rooms, service with restrictions, supervision.
SAVE 🗐 ✕ 🗐 🖥 ➤ 🎮

# GLENEDEN BEACH

**(AAA)** ▼▼▼ ▼▼▼ **Salishan Spa & Golf Resort** LH ❖
(541) 764-2371. **$99-$259, 3 day notice.** 7760 Hwy 101 N. Just e of US 101; center. Ext corridors. **Pets:** Other species. $25 one-time fee/pet. Service with restrictions, supervision.
SAVE ✕ 🎮 🎮 🗐 🖥 🍴 ➤ ✕ 🎮

# GLIDE

**(AAA)** ▼ **Illahee Inn** M
(541) 496-3338. **$75-$95.** 170 Bar L Ranch Rd. I-5, exit 124, 0.8 mi e, just n to SR 138, then e. Ext corridors. **Pets:** Medium. Service with restrictions.
SAVE ✕ 🗐 🖥 🍴

**(AAA) ▼▼▼ Steelhead Run B & B and Fine Art Gallery** BB
(541) 496-0563. **$65-$135, 7 day notice.** 23049 N Umpqua (Hwy 138). I-5, exit 124, 0.8 mi e, just n to SR 138, then 20.7 mi e; just e of MM 20. Ext/int corridors. **Pets:** Accepted.
SAVE ✕ 🏠 🖥 ✕

# GOLD BEACH

**(AAA) ▼▼ BREAKERS Gold Beach** M
(541) 247-6606. **$46-$146.** 29171 Ellensburg Ave. On US 101; south end of town. Ext corridors. **Pets:** Accepted.
SAVE S🔒 ✕ 🏠 🖥 🆇

**(AAA) ▼▼▼ Gold Beach Inn** M
(541) 247-7091. **$48-$189.** 29346 Ellensburg Ave. On US 101; center. Ext corridors. **Pets:** Accepted.
SAVE ✕ 🏠 🖥 🆇

**(AAA) ▼▼▼ Inn of the Beachcomber** M
(541) 247-6691. **$79-$189.** 29266 Ellensburg Ave. On US 101; south end of town. Ext/int corridors. **Pets:** Accepted.
SAVE S🔒 ✕ 🏠 🖥 ➿

**(AAA) ▼▼▼ Ireland's Rustic Lodges** CA
(541) 247-7718. **$54-$150.** 29330 Ellensburg Ave. On US 101; center. Ext corridors. **Pets:** Large. $10 daily fee/pet. Designated rooms, service with restrictions, supervision.
SAVE ✕ 🏠 🖥 🆇 ➿

**(AAA) ▼▼▼ Jot's Resort** M ☙
(541) 247-6676. **$60-$195, 3 day notice.** 94360 Wedderburn Loop. Just w of US 101, north end of bridge. Ext corridors. **Pets:** Other species. $15 daily fee/pet. Designated rooms, service with restrictions, supervision.
SAVE S🔒 ✕ 🕸 🏠 🖥 🍽 ➿ ✕ 🆇

**▼▼▼ Motel 6-4047** M
(541) 247-4533. **$80-$85.** 94433 Jerry's Flat Rd. Just e of jct US 101. Ext corridors. **Pets:** Accepted.
S🔒 ✕ 🏠 🖥 🆇

**(AAA) ▼▼▼ Sand 'n Sea Motel** M
(541) 247-6658. **$59-$139.** 29362 Ellensburg Ave. On US 101; center. Ext/int corridors. **Pets:** Other species. $5 daily fee/pet. Designated rooms, service with restrictions, supervision.
SAVE S🔒 ✕ 🆊 🏠 🖥 🆇

# GOVERNMENT CAMP

**(AAA) ▼▼▼▼ Mt. Hood Inn** SH
(503) 272-3205. **$99-$179.** 87450 E Government Camp. 0.5 mi w of center. Int corridors. **Pets:** Other species. $10 daily fee/pet. Service with restrictions, supervision.
SAVE S🔒 ✕ 🕸 🏠 🖥 🆇

# GRANTS PASS

**(AAA) ▼▼▼ Best Western Grants Pass Inn** SH
(541) 476-1117. **$70-$126.** 111 NE Agness Ave. I-5, exit 55, just w. Ext corridors. **Pets:** Other species. $10 one-time fee/room. Designated rooms, service with restrictions, supervision.
SAVE S🔒 ✕ 🆊 🆊 🏠 🖥 ➿

**(AAA) ▼▼▼ Best Western Inn at the Rogue** SH
(541) 582-2200. **$65-$125.** 8959 Rogue River Hwy. I-5, exit 48, just w. Int corridors. **Pets:** Other species. $20 daily fee/pet. Designated rooms, service with restrictions, supervision.
SAVE S🔒 ✕ 🏠 🖥 ➿

**(AAA) ▼▼▼ Comfort Inn** SH
(541) 479-8301. **$70-$114.** 1889 NE 6th St. I-5, exit 58, just s on SR 99. Int corridors. **Pets:** Accepted.
SAVE S🔒 ✕ 🏠 🖥 ➿

**(AAA) ▼▼▼ Holiday Inn Express** SH
(541) 471-6144. **$79-$119.** 105 NE Agness Ave. I-5, exit 55, just w. Int corridors. **Pets:** Large, other species. $10 daily fee/pet. Designated rooms, service with restrictions, supervision.
SAVE S🔒 ✕ 🆊 🏠 🖥

**(AAA) ▼▼ Knights Inn Motel** M ☙
(541) 479-5595. **$55-$90.** 104 SE 7th St. I-5, exit 58 southbound, 1.7 mi s on SR 99 to G St, 1 blk e, then just n; exit 55 northbound, 1.8 mi w on US 199 (Grants Pass Pkwy/Recwood Hwy), then just s. Ext corridors. **Pets:** Small, dogs only. $5 daily fee/pet. Designated rooms, service with restrictions, supervision.
SAVE S🔒 ✕ 🏠

**(AAA) ▼▼◆▼▼ La Quinta Inn & Suites Grants Pass** SH ☙
(541) 472-1808. **$75-$130.** 243 NE Morgan Ln. I-5, exit 58, 0.4 mi s on SR 99, just e on Hillcrest Dr to SR 99 northbound, then just n. Int corridors. **Pets:** Medium. Designated rooms, service with restrictions, supervision.
SAVE S🔒 ✕ 🆊 🆊 🏠 🖥 ➿

**▼▼ Motel 6-253** M
(541) 474-1331. **$45-$61.** 1800 NE 7th St. I-5, exit 58, 0.3 mi s on SR 99. Ext corridors. **Pets:** Accepted.
S🔒 ✕ 🆊 🆊 🏠 🖥

**(AAA) ▼▼▼ Redwood Motel** M ☙
(541) 476-0878. **$57-$250.** 815 NE 6th St. I-5, exit 58, 1.2 mi s on SR 99. Ext corridors. **Pets:** Small, dogs only. $10 daily fee/pet. Designated rooms, service with restrictions, supervision.
SAVE S🔒 ✕ 🆊 🆊 🏠 🖥 ➿

**(AAA) ▼▼▼ Riverside Inn Resort** SH
(541) 476-6873. **$99-$130.** 971 SE 6th St. I-5, exit 58, 2.5 mi s on SR 99. Ext corridors. **Pets:** Other species. $10 daily fee/pet. Designated rooms, service with restrictions, crate.
SAVE S🔒 ✕ 🆊 🏠 🖥 🍽 ➿ ✕

**◆ Shilo Inn** SH
(541) 479-8391. **$43-$103.** 1880 NW 6th St. I-5, exit 58, 0.4 mi s on SR 99. Int corridors. **Pets:** Accepted.
ASK S🔒 ✕ 🆊 🆊 🏠 🖥 ➿

**(AAA) ▼▼▼ Sunset Inn** M
(541) 479-3305. **$55-$115.** 1400 NW 6th St. I-5, exit 58, 0.6 mi s on SR 99. Ext corridors. **Pets:** Small. $10 deposit/pet. Designated rooms, service with restrictions, supervision.
SAVE S🔒 ✕ 🏠 🖥 ➿

**(AAA) ▼▼▼ Super 8 Motel-Grants Pass** M ☙
(541) 474-0888. **$55-$81.** 1949 NE 7th St. I-5, exit 58, 0.4 mi s on SR 99, just e on Hillcrest Dr to SR 99 northbound, then just n. Int corridors. **Pets:** Small. $25 deposit/pet. Service with restrictions, supervision.
SAVE S🔒 ✕ 🆊 🏠 ➿

**(AAA) ▼▼▼ Sweet Breeze Inn** M
(541) 471-4434. **$58-$110.** 1627 NE 6th St. I-5, exit 58, 0.5 mi s on SR 99. Ext/int corridors. **Pets:** Small, dogs only. $5 one-time fee/pet. Designated rooms, supervision.
SAVE S🔒 ✕ 🆊 🏠

**(AAA) ▼▼▼ Travelodge** M
(541) 479-6611. **$49-$74.** 1950 NW Vine St. I-5, exit 58, just s on SR 99. Ext corridors. **Pets:** Accepted.
SAVE ✕ 🆊 🏠 🖥 ➿

# HALSEY

**▼▼▼ Best Western Pioneer Lodge** M
(541) 369-2804. **$69-$72.** 33180 Hwy 228. I-5, exit 216, just e. Ext corridors. **Pets:** $5 daily fee/pet. Service with restrictions.
ASK S🔒 ✕ 🏠 🖥 🍽 ➿

# HERMISTON

**Oak Tree Inn** SH
(541) 567-2330. $63-$89. 1110 SE 4th St. 0.4 mi s on US 395, just w. Int corridors. **Pets:** Small. $5 daily fee/pet. Service with restrictions.

**Oxford Suites** SH ☀
(541) 564-8000. $85-$129. 1050 N 1st St. 0.3 mi n on US 395. Int corridors. **Pets:** Small, dogs only. $20 one-time fee/pet. Designated rooms, service with restrictions, supervision.

# HINES

**Best Western Rory & Ryan Inns** SH ☀
(541) 573-5050. $68-$105. 534 Hwy 20 N. On US 20 (Hines/Burns). Int corridors. **Pets:** Dogs only. $10 one-time fee/room. Designated rooms, service with restrictions, supervision.

# HOOD RIVER

**Best Western Hood River Inn** SH ☀
(541) 386-2200. $79-$159. 1108 E Marina Way. I-84, exit 64, just n, then just e. Int corridors. **Pets:** Medium, dogs only. $12 daily fee/room. Designated rooms, service with restrictions, supervision.

**Columbia Gorge Hotel** CI ☀
(541) 386-5566. $199-$399, 14 day notice. 4000 Westcliff Dr. I-84, exit 62, just w of overpass. Int corridors. **Pets:** Other species. $35 one-time fee/pet. Designated rooms, service with restrictions, supervision.

**Vagabond Lodge** M ☀
(541) 386-2992. $49-$85. 4070 Westcliff Dr. I-84, exit 62, just n, then just w. Ext corridors. **Pets:** Medium. $5 daily fee/pet, $8 one-time fee/pet. Designated rooms, service with restrictions, supervision.

# JACKSONVILLE

**The Stage Lodge** M
(541) 899-3953. $108-$195, 8 day notice. 830 N 5th St. On N 5th St (SR 238), 0.3 mi ne. Ext corridors. **Pets:** Accepted.

# JOHN DAY

**Best Western John Day Inn** M
(541) 575-1700. $78-$88. 315 W Main St. Just w on US 26 and 395. Ext corridors. **Pets:** Small. $10 daily fee/pet. Designated rooms, service with restrictions, supervision.

**Dreamers Lodge** M
(541) 575-0526. $49-$70. 144 N Canyon Blvd. Just n of jct US 26 and 395. Ext corridors. **Pets:** Dogs only. $5 one-time fee/pet. Service with restrictions, supervision.

# KEIZER

**Wittenberg Inn & Conference Center** SH
(503) 390-4733. $89-$99. 5188 Wittenberg Ln N. I-5, exit 260B southbound; exit 260 northbound, 1.5 mi w on Chemawa Rd and Lockhaven Dr, then just s on River Rd. Int corridors. **Pets:** $10 daily fee/pet. Service with restrictions, supervision.

# KLAMATH FALLS

**Best Western Klamath Inn** SH
(541) 882-1200. $50-$90. 4061 S 6th St. Just w on 6th St (SR 140) from jct SR 140 E/39 S and SR 39 N/US 97 business route. Ext corridors. **Pets:** $10 one-time fee/room. Service with restrictions, supervision.

**Golden West Motel** M ☀
(541) 882-1758. $38-$65. 6402 S 6th St. S 6th St (SR 140) at eastern edge of town. Ext corridors. **Pets:** Other species. Designated rooms, service with restrictions, supervision.

**Holiday Inn Express Hotel & Suites** SH
(541) 884-9999. $50-$95. 2500 S 6th St. 1.3 mi w on 6th St (SR 140) from jct SR 140 E/39 S and SR 39 N/US 97 business route. Int corridors. **Pets:** Small. $15 one-time fee/room. Designated rooms, service with restrictions, supervision.

**Majestic Inn & Suites** M
(541) 883-7771. $35-$81. 5543 S 6th St. 1 mi e on 6th St (SR 140) from jct SR 140 E/39 S and SR 39 N/US 97 business route. Ext corridors. **Pets:** Designated rooms, service with restrictions, supervision.

**Maverick Motel** M
(541) 882-6688. $39-$85. 1220 Main St. US 97 N to City Center exit, 0.3 mi e. Ext corridors. **Pets:** Service with restrictions, supervision.

**Motel 6-226** SH
(541) 884-2110. $45-$63. 5136 S 6th St. 0.5 mi e on 6th St E (SR 140) from jct SR 39/US 97 business route. Ext corridors. **Pets:** Accepted.

**Oregon Motel 8** M
(541) 883-3431. $54-$125. 5225 Hwy 97 N. On US 97; between MM 270 and 271; east side of highway. Ext corridors. **Pets:** Accepted.

**Quality Inn** SH
(541) 882-4666. $59-$99. 100 Main St. Just e of US 97, exit City Center. Ext corridors. **Pets:** Accepted.

**Red Lion Inn Klamath Falls** SH
(541) 882-8864. $69-$99. 3612 S 6th St. 0.3 mi w on 6th St (SR 140) from jct SR 140 E/39 S and SR 39 N/US 97 business route. Ext corridors. **Pets:** Other species. Supervision.

**The Running Y Ranch** SH
(541) 850-5500. $119-$219, 3 day notice. 5500 Running Y Rd. On 6th St (SR 140), 7.2 mi n from jct US 66 and SR 140. Int corridors. **Pets:** Accepted.

**Shilo Inn Klamath Falls** SH ☀
(541) 885-7980. $99-$145. 2500 Almond St. North end of US 97. Int corridors. **Pets:** $10 daily fee/pet. Service with restrictions, supervision.

**Super 8 Motel** SH ☀
(541) 884-8880. $62-$80, 10 day notice. 3805 Hwy 97. On US 97, 2 mi n. Int corridors. **Pets:** Other species. $25 deposit/room. Service with restrictions, supervision.

# LA GRANDE

**AAA** **WW** **Royal Motor Inn** **M**
(541) 963-4154. **$32-$41.** 1510 Adams Ave. I-84, exit La Grande on US 30, just n of jct SR 82; downtown. Ext corridors. **Pets:** Dogs only. $10 one-time fee/pet. Service with restrictions, supervision.

SAVE SO X ⏚ ⊟

# LAKEVIEW

**AAA** **WWW** **Best Western Skyline Motor Lodge** **SH**
(541) 947-2194. **$89-$149.** 414 N G St. Jct US 395 and SR 140. Ext corridors. **Pets:** Accepted.

SAVE SO X ⏚ ⊟ ⊠ ≋

# LA PINE

**WWWW** **Best Western Newberry Station** **SH**
(541) 536-5130. **$79-$129.** 16515 Reed Rd. North end of town, just off SR 97. Int corridors. **Pets:** Small, dogs only. $15 deposit/room, $10 one-time fee/room. Service with restrictions, supervision.

ASK SO X ⒨ ⏚ ⊟ ⊠ ≋

# LINCOLN CITY

**AAA** **WW** **Coho Inn** **M**
(541) 994-3684. **$62-$250.** 1635 NW Harbor Ave. US 101, exit N 17th St, just w. Ext corridors. **Pets:** Small. $10 daily fee/pet. Designated rooms, service with restrictions, supervision.

SAVE X ⊟ ⊠ ≋ ⊠ ₭

**AAA** **WW** **Crown Pacific Inn Express** **SH**
(541) 994-7559. **$70-$95.** 1070 SE 1st St. On US 101 near D River. Int corridors. **Pets:** Accepted.

SAVE SO X ⊟ ⊠ ₭

**AAA** **WW** **Lincoln City Inn** **SH**
(541) 996-4400. **$40-$90.** 1091 SE 1st St. On US 101 at D River. Int corridors. **Pets:** Accepted.

SAVE X ⒨ ⏚ ⊟ ⊠

**AAA** **WWW** **The O'dysius Hotel** **SH** 🐾
(541) 994-4121. **$155-$319.** 120 NW Inlet Ct. On US 101 at D River; center. Int corridors. **Pets:** Small. $10 daily fee/pet. Designated rooms, service with restrictions, supervision.

SAVE SO X ⏚ ⊟ ⊠ ≋ ⊠ ₭

# MADRAS

**AAA** **WW** **Best Western Madras Inn** **M**
(541) 475-6141. **$80-$115.** 12 SW 4th St. On US 97/26 southbound; downtown. Ext corridors. **Pets:** Other species. $10 daily fee/pet. Designated rooms, service with restrictions, supervision.

SAVE SO X ⒨ ⏚ ⊟ ⊠ ≋

**AAA** **WW** **Budget Inn** **M**
(541) 475-3831. **$55-$80.** 133 NE 5th St. On US 97/26 northbound; downtown. Ext corridors. **Pets:** Medium. $8 one-time fee/pet. Supervision.

SAVE SO X ⊟

# MCMINNVILLE

**WWW** **Red Lion Inn & Suites** **SH**
(503) 472-1500. **$97-$137, 30 day notice.** 2535 NE Cumulus Ave. Jct SR 99 W, 3.7 mi e on SR 18. Int corridors. **Pets:** Accepted.

ASK SO X ⒨ ⏚ ⊟ ⊠ ≋ ⊠

**AAA** **WW** **Safari Motor Inn** **M**
(503) 472-5187. **$69-$89.** 381 NE Hwy 99W. North end of SR 99 W. Ext corridors. **Pets:** Small. $10 daily fee/pet. Service with restrictions, supervision.

SAVE SO X ⏚ ⊟

# MEDFORD

**AAA** **WWWW** **Best Western Horizon Inn** **SH**
(541) 779-5085. **$71-$110.** 1154 E Barnett Rd. I-5, exit 27, just e. Ext corridors. **Pets:** Other species. $10 one-time fee/room. Service with restrictions, supervision.

SAVE SO X ⏚ ⒨ ⏚ ⊟ ⊠ ≋ ⊠

**AAA** **WW** **Cedar Lodge Motor Inn** **M**
(541) 773-7361. **$55-$72.** 518 N Riverside Ave. I-5, exit 27, 0.5 mi w on Barnett Rd, then 1.2 mi n on SR 99. Ext corridors. **Pets:** Medium. $5 one-time fee/pet. Designated rooms, service with restrictions, supervision.

SAVE SO X ⏚ ≋

**AAA** **WW** **Knights Inn** **M**
(541) 773-3676. **$48-$58.** 500 N Riverside Ave. I-5, exit 27, 0.4 mi w on Barnett Rd, then 1.2 mi n on SR 99. Ext corridors. **Pets:** Accepted.

SAVE SO X ⒨ ⏚ ⊟ ⊠ ≋

**AAA** **WWW** **Medford Inn and Suites** **SH**
(541) 773-8266. **$75-$120.** 1015 S Riverside Ave. I-5, exit 27, 0.4 mi w, then just n. Ext corridors. **Pets:** Accepted.

SAVE SO X ⏚ ⒨ ⏚ ⊟ ≋

**WW** **Motel 6-Medford North–739** **M**
(541) 779-0550. **$53-$65.** 2400 Biddle Rd. I-5, exit 30 northbound, just s; exit southbound, follow signs. Ext corridors. **Pets:** Accepted.

SO X ⒨ ⏚ ⊟ ≋

**WW** **Motel 6-Medford South–89** **M**
(541) 773-4290. **$45-$65.** 950 Alba Dr. I-5, exit 27, just e on Barnett Rd, then just n. Ext corridors. **Pets:** Accepted.

SO X ⒨ ⏚ ⊟ ≋

**AAA** **WWWW** **Red Lion Hotel Medford** **SH**
(541) 779-5811. **$69-$99.** 200 N Riverside Ave. I-5, exit 27, 0.4 mi w on Barnett Rd, then 1 mi n. Ext corridors. **Pets:** Other species. Designated rooms, service with restrictions.

SAVE SO X ⒨ ⏚ ⊟ ⊟ ⊟ ≋

**WW** **Shilo Inn Medford** **SH**
(541) 770-5151. **$63-$93.** 2111 Biddle Rd. I-5, exit 30 northbound, just s; exit southbound, follow signs for Biddle Rd, then just s. Int corridors. **Pets:** $10 daily fee/pet. Service with restrictions, supervision.

ASK SO X ⏚ ⊟

**AAA** **WWW** **Windmill Inn of Medford** **SH** 🐾
(541) 779-0050. **$75-$129.** 1950 Biddle Rd. I-5, exit 30 northbound, just s; exit southbound, follow signs for Biddle Rd, then just s. Int corridors. **Pets:** Other species. No service, supervision.

SAVE SO X ⒨ ⏚ ⊟ ≋ ⊠

# MYRTLE POINT

**AAA** **WW** **Myrtle Trees Motel** **M**
(541) 572-5811. **$52-$57.** 1010 8th St (Hwy 42). On SR 42, 0.5 mi e. Ext corridors. **Pets:** Very small, dogs only. $10 daily fee/pet. Designated rooms, service with restrictions, supervision.

SAVE X ⏚ ₭

# NEWBERG

**WW** **Shilo Inn Suites-Newberg** **SH** 🐾
(503) 537-0303. **$52-$103.** 501 Sitka Ave. On SR 99 W. Int corridors. **Pets:** $10 daily fee/pet. Service with restrictions, supervision.

ASK SO X ⒨ ⏚ ⊟ ≋

**WW** **Travelodge Suites** **SH**
(503) 537-5000. **$64.** 2816 Portland Rd. North end on SR 99 W; behind Finnigan's Restaurant. Int corridors. **Pets:** Medium. $10 daily fee/pet. Designated rooms, service with restrictions, supervision.

ASK SO X ⏚ ⊟ ≋ ⊠

# NEWPORT

**Best Western Agate Beach Inn** SH ❖
(541) 265-9411. **$74-$160.** 3019 N Coast Hwy. US 20, 1.5 mi n on US 101. Int corridors. **Pets:** $15 one-time fee/pet. Designated rooms, service with restrictions, supervision.
SAVE ⑤ ⊠ ⑦ 🛑 ▣ 🍴 ⊇ ⊠ 💺

**Econo Lodge** M
(541) 265-7723. **$40-$71.** 606 SW Coast Hwy 101. 0.5 mi s of US 20. Ext/int corridors. **Pets:** Service with restrictions, supervision.
SAVE ⑤ ⊠ ⑦ 🛑 💺

**Hallmark Resort** SH ❖
(541) 265-2600. **$69-$224.** 744 SW Elizabeth St. US 20, 0.7 mi s on US 101, just w on SW Bay St. Ext corridors. **Pets:** $8 daily fee/pet. Designated rooms, service with restrictions, supervision.
SAVE ⑤ ⊠ ⑤M ⑦ 💺 🛑 ▣ 🍴 ⊇ ⊠ 💺

**La Quinta Inn & Suites Newport** SH ❖
(541) 867-7727. **$66-$169.** 45 SE 32nd St. US 101, just s of Yaquina Bay Bridge. Int corridors. **Pets:** Other species. Designated rooms, service with restrictions, supervision.
SAVE ⑤ ⊠ ⑦ 💺 🛑 ▣ ⊇ ⊠

**Shilo Inn Oceanfront Resort** SH ❖
(541) 265-7701. **$85-$215.** 536 SW Elizabeth St. US 20, 0.5 mi s on US 101, just w on SW Falls St. Ext/int corridors. **Pets:** $10 daily fee/pet. Designated rooms, service with restrictions, supervision.
ASK ⑤ ⊠ ⑦ 🛑 ▣ 🍴 ⊇ 💺

**Val-U Inn** SH
(541) 265-6203. **$50-$100.** 531 SW Fall St. US 20, 0.5 mi s on US 101, just w. Int corridors. **Pets:** Accepted.
ASK ⑤ ⊠ 🛑 ▣ 💺

**Waves of Newport Motel and Vacation Rentals** M
(541) 265-4661. **$58-$113, 3 day notice.** 820 NW Coast St. US 101, 0.6 mi n from jct US 20, just w on NW 11th St, then just s. Ext corridors. **Pets:** Medium. $5 one-time fee/pet. Designated rooms, supervision.
SAVE ⊠ 🛑 ▣ 💺

**The Whaler Motel** M ❖
(541) 265-9261. **$85-$165.** 155 SW Elizabeth St. Just s on US 101 from jct US 20, just w on SW 2nd St. Ext corridors. **Pets:** Dogs only. $5 daily fee/pet. Designated rooms, service with restrictions, supervision.
SAVE ⑤ ⊠ ⑤M ⑦ 💺 🛑 ▣ ⊇ 💺

# NORTH BEND

**Comfort Inn** M
(541) 756-3191. **$69-$159.** 1503 Virginia Ave. 0.5 mi w of US 101. Ext/int corridors. **Pets:** Small, dogs only. $10 daily fee/pet. Service with restrictions, supervision.
SAVE ⑤ ⊠ ⑤M ⑦ 💺 🛑 ▣

# OAKLAND

**Best Western Rice Hill** M
(541) 849-3335. **$60-$90.** 621 John Long Rd. I-5, exit 148, just e. Ext corridors. **Pets:** Other species. $20 deposit/pet, $7 daily fee/pet. Service with restrictions.
SAVE ⑤ ⊠ 💺 🛑 ▣ ⊇ ⊠

# OAKRIDGE

**Best Western Oakridge Inn** M
(541) 782-2212. **$64-$89.** 47433 Hwy 58. West end of SR 58. Ext corridors. **Pets:** Medium, dogs only. $10 one-time fee/pet. Service with restrictions, supervision.
SAVE ⑤ ⊠ ⑤M ⑦ 💺 🛑 ▣ ⊇

# ONTARIO

**Creek House Bed & Breakfast Inn** BB
(541) 823-0717. **Call for rates.** 717 SW 2nd St. I-84, exit 376A, 0.8 mi w on Idaho Ave, then 0.4 mi s. Int corridors. **Pets:** Accepted.
⊠ 🛑 ▣ ☎

**Holiday Inn-Ontario, OR** SH ❖
(541) 889-8621. **$74-$84.** 1249 Tapadera Ave. I-84, exit 376B, just ne. Int corridors. **Pets:** Large, other species. $10 one-time fee/room. Designated rooms, service with restrictions, supervision.
SAVE ⑤ ⊠ ⑦ 💺 🛑 ▣ 🍴 ⊇

**Holiday Motel** SH ❖
(541) 889-9188. **$41-$48.** 615 E Idaho. I-84, exit 376A, just nw. Ext corridors. **Pets:** Other species. Designated rooms, service with restrictions, supervision.
SAVE ⊠ 🛑 🍴 ⊇

**Sleep Inn** SH
(541) 881-0007. **$69-$109.** 1221 SE First Ave. I-84, exit 376B, just se. Int corridors. **Pets:** Medium. $5 daily fee/pet. Designated rooms, service with restrictions, supervision.
SAVE ⑤ ⊠ ⑤M ⑦ 💺 🛑 ▣ ⊇

# PACIFIC CITY

**Inn at Cape Kiwanda** SH ❖
(503) 965-7001. **$109-$189.** 33105 Cape Kiwanda Dr. Just w on Pacific Ave, 1 mi n. Ext corridors. **Pets:** Other species. $20 daily fee/pet. Service with restrictions, supervision.
SAVE ⑤ ⊠ ⑤M 🛑 ▣ ⊠ 💺

**Pacific City Inn** M ❖
(503) 965-6464. **$61-$88, 3 day notice.** 35280 Brooten Rd. Center. Ext corridors. **Pets:** Dogs only. $20 daily fee/pet. Designated rooms, service with restrictions, supervision.
SAVE ⑤ ⊠ 🛑 ▣ 🍴 💺

# PENDLETON

**Best Western Pendleton Inn** SH
(541) 276-2135. **$70-$80.** 400 SE Nye Ave. I-84, exit 210, just se. Int corridors. **Pets:** Medium. $10 one-time fee/room. Service with restrictions, supervision.
SAVE ⊠ ⑤M 💺 🛑 ▣ ⊇

**Econo Lodge** M
(541) 276-8654. **$53-$59.** 620 SW Tutuilla Rd. I-84, exit 209, just s on US 395. Ext corridors. **Pets:** Small, dogs only. $7 daily fee/pet. Designated rooms, service with restrictions, supervision.
SAVE ⑤ ⊠ 🛑 ▣

**Holiday Inn Express** SH
(541) 966-6520. **$89-$165.** 600 SE Nye Ave. I-84, exit 210, just se. Int corridors. **Pets:** Dogs only. $10 daily fee/room. Designated rooms, service with restrictions, supervision.
SAVE ⑤ ⊠ 💺 🛑 ▣ ⊇

**Motel 6-349** M
(541) 276-3160. **$41-$55.** 325 SE Nye Ave. I-84, exit 210, just se. Ext corridors. **Pets:** Accepted.
⑤ ⊠ 🛑 ⊇

**Oxford Suites** SH ❖
(541) 276-6000. **$89-$179.** 2400 SW Court Pl. I-84, exit 207, just n, then 0.5 mi e on Cold Springs Junction. Int corridors. **Pets:** Other species. $15 one-time fee/room. Designated rooms.
ASK ⊠ ⑤M ⑦ 💺 🛑 ⊇ ⊠

**Red Lion Hotel Pendleton** SH
(541) 276-6111. **$78-$88.** 304 SE Nye Ave. I-84, exit 210, just s. Ext/int corridors. **Pets:** Accepted.
SAVE ⊠ ⑦ 💺 🛑 ▣ 🍴 ⊇ ⊠

**Super 8 Motel** SH
(541) 276-8881. **$62-$77.** 601 SE Nye Ave. I-84, exit 210, just se. Int corridors. **Pets:** Other species. $10 one-time fee/room. Service with restrictions, supervision.

ASK 🔊 ✕ 🖋 🖥 🏊

**Travelodge** M
(541) 276-7531. **$59-$125.** 411 SW Down Ave. I-84, exit 209, just w of town center on corner of SW 4th St; downtown. Ext corridors. **Pets:** Dogs only. $10 daily fee/room. Designated rooms, service with restrictions.

SAVE 🔊 ✕ 🖥 🖵

# PORTLAND METROPOLITAN AREA

## BEAVERTON

**Comfort Inn & Suites** SH
(503) 643-9100. **$59-$125.** 13455 SW Canyon Rd. SR 217, exit Canyon Rd (SR 8), 1 mi w. Int corridors. **Pets:** Medium, other species. $25 one-time fee/room. Service with restrictions, supervision.

ASK 🔊 ✕ 🖋 🖥 🖵 🏊 ✕

**Homestead Studio Suites Hotel-Beaverton** M
(503) 690-3600. **$63.** 875 SW 158th Ave. US 26, exit 65 westbound, just s on Cornell Rd, 1.1 mi se on 158th Ave; exit eastbound, just straight on feeder road, then same directions as westbound. Ext corridors. **Pets:** $25 daily fee/pet. Service with restrictions, supervision.

ASK 🔊 ✕ 🖋 🖥 🖵

**Homewood Suites By Hilton** SH 🐾
(503) 614-0900. **$139-$149.** 15525 NW Gateway Ct. US 26, exit 65, s on 158th Ave, then just e on Waterhouse Ave. Int corridors. **Pets:** Medium. $15 daily fee/pet. Designated rooms, service with restrictions, supervision.

ASK 🔊 ✕ 🖋 🖋 🖥 🖵 🏊

**Phoenix Inn Suites-Beaverton** SH
(503) 614-8100. **$79-$119.** 15402 NW Cornell Rd. US 26, exit 65, just n. Int corridors. **Pets:** Medium. $15 daily fee/pet. Designated rooms, service with restrictions, supervision.

SAVE 🔊 ✕ 🖋 🖋 🖥 🖵 🏊 ✕

**Shilo Inn–Portland/Beaverton** SH 🐾
(503) 297-2551. **$54-$130.** 9900 SW Canyon Rd. SR 217, exit Canyon Rd/Beaverton Hillsdale Hwy, take feeder road, 0.3 mi e to SR 8 (Canyon Rd), then 0.6 mi e. Int corridors. **Pets:** $10 daily fee/pet. Service with restrictions, supervision.

ASK 🔊 ✕ 🖋 🖋 🖥 🖵 🍴 🏊

## GLADSTONE

**Oxford Suites** SH
(503) 722-7777. **$95-$129.** 75 82nd Dr. I-205, exit 11, just w. Int corridors. **Pets:** Medium, other species. $10 one-time fee/pet. Service with restrictions, supervision.

ASK 🔊 ✕ 🖋 🖋 🖥 🖵 🏊 ✕

## GRESHAM

**Best Western Pony Soldier Inn** SH
(503) 665-1591. **$85-$103.** 1060 NE Cleveland Ave. I-84, exit 16, 2.7 mi s on NE 238th Dr, just w on Division St, then just n; I-205, exit 19, 5.5 mi e on Division St, then just n. Int corridors. **Pets:** Accepted.

SAVE 🔊 ✕ 🖥 🖵 🏊

**Days Inn & Suites** SH
(503) 465-1515. **$64-$89.** 24124 SE Stark St. I-84, exit 16, 1.5 mi s on NE 238th Dr/242nd, then just n. Int corridors. **Pets:** Small. $10 daily fee/pet. Designated rooms, service with restrictions, supervision.

SAVE 🔊 ✕ 🖋 🖥 🖵 🏊

**Quality Inn & Suites** SH
(503) 492-4000. **$60-$122.** 2323 NE 1 1st Ave. I-84, exit 13, just e. Int corridors. **Pets:** $10 one-time fee/pet. Service with restrictions.

SAVE 🔊 ✕ 🖋 🖋 🖥 🖵 🏊 ✕

**Sleep Inn-Portland Gresham** SH
(503) 618-8400. **$57-$100.** 2261 NE 1st Ave. I-84, exit 13, just s. Int corridors. **Pets:** Accepted.

ASK 🔊 ✕ 🖋 🖋 🖥 🖵 🏊

**Super 8 Motel** M 🐾
(503) 661-5100. **$57-$69.** 121 NE 18 1st Ave. I-84, exit 13, 1.4 mi s. Int corridors. **Pets:** Large, other species. $10 daily fee/pet. Service with restrictions, supervision.

SAVE 🔊 ✕ 🖋 🖥 🖵

## HILLSBORO

**The Dunes Motel** M
(503) 648-8991. **$47-$80.** 452 SE 10th Ave (SR 8). US 26, exit 62, 1 mi s on NW Cornelius Pass Rd, then 1.4 mi w on NE Cornell Rd. Int corridors. **Pets:** Medium, dogs only. $5 daily fee/pet. Service with restrictions, supervision.

SAVE 🔊 ✕ 🖥

**Extended Stay Deluxe** SH
(503) 439-0706. **$72.** 19311 NW Cornell Rd. US 26, exit 64, 0.5 mi s on 185th Ave, then 0.4 mi w. Int corridors. **Pets:** Service with restrictions, supervision.

ASK 🔊 ✕ 🖋 🖋 🖥 🖵 🏊

**Larkspur Landing Home Suite Hotel Hillsboro/Portland** SH 🐾
(503) 681-2121. **$169-$179.** 3133 NE Shute Rd. US 26, exit 61, 1.2 mi s. Int corridors. **Pets:** Medium. $10 daily fee/room, $75 one-time fee/room. Designated rooms, service with restrictions, crate.

SAVE 🔊 ✕ 🖋 🖋 🖥 🖵

**Red Lion Hotel Hillsboro** SH
(503) 648-3500. **$69-$139.** 3500 NE Cornell Rd. US 26, exit 62A, 1 mi s on Cornelius Pass Rd, then 2.5 mi w. Int corridors. **Pets:** Large, other species. $10 daily fee/room. Service with restrictions, supervision.

ASK ✕ 🖋 🖥 🖵 🍴 🏊 ✕

**Residence Inn by Marriott Portland West** SH
(503) 531-3200. **$99-$209.** 18855 NW Tanasbourne Dr. US 26, exit 64, just s. Ext/int corridors. **Pets:** Accepted.

ASK 🔊 ✕ 🖋 🖋 🖋 🖥 🖵 🏊 ✕

**TownePlace Suites by Marriott-Portland Hillsboro** SH
(503) 268-6000. **$59-$149.** 6550 NE Brighton St. US 26, exit 62A, 1 mi s on Cornelius Pass Rd, 0.7 mi w on Cornell Rd, just n on 229th Ave, then just w. Ext/int corridors. **Pets:** accepted.

ASK 🔊 ✕ 🖋 🖋 🖋 🖥 🖵 🏊 ✕

# KING CITY

**(AAA) ▼▼▼▼ Best Western Northwind Inn & Suites** SH
(503) 431-2100. **$84-$104, 5 day notice.** 16105 SW Pacific Hwy. I-5, exit 292, just nw on SR 217, exit SR 99W, then 2.5 mi s. Int corridors. **Pets:** Small. $10 daily fee/pet. Service with restrictions, supervision.
[SAVE] [S] [X] [&M] [刀] [点] [❚] [▣] [➳]

# LAKE OSWEGO

**(AAA) ▼▼▼▼ Crowne Plaza Hotel** SH
(503) 624-8400. **$69-$139.** 14811 Kruse Oaks Dr. I-5, exit 292B northbound; exit 292 southbound, just e. Int corridors. **Pets:** Accepted.
[SAVE] [X] [&M] [刀] [点] [❚] [▣] [➳]

**(AAA) ▼▼▼▼ Phoenix Inn Suites-Lake Oswego** SH
(503) 624-7400. **$79-$119.** 14905 SW Bangy Rd. I-5, exit 292 southbound, just e, then just s; exit 292B northbound, just s. Int corridors. **Pets:** Medium. $15 daily fee/pet. Designated rooms, service with restrictions, supervision.
[SAVE] [S] [X] [&M] [刀] [点] [❚] [▣] [➳] [X]

**▼▼▼▼ Residence Inn by Marriott-Portland South** SH ❖
(503) 684-2603. **$149-$209.** 15200 SW Bangy Rd. I-5, exit 292B northbound; exit 292 southbound, just e, then 0.3 mi s. Ext corridors. **Pets:** Other species. $75 one-time fee/room. Service with restrictions.
[ASK] [S] [X] [刀] [点] [❚] [▣] [➳] [X]

# MILWAUKIE

**(AAA) ▼▼▼ Econo Lodge Suites Inn** M
(503) 654-2222. **$59-$69.** 17330 SE McLoughlin Blvd. I-205, exit 9 (Oregon City/Gladstone), 2.3 mi n on SR 99E (McLoughlin Blvd). Ext corridors. **Pets:** Small, dogs only. $10 one-time fee/pet. Designated rooms, service with restrictions, supervision.
[SAVE] [S] [X] [刀] [❚] [▣] [➳]

# OREGON CITY

**(AAA) ▼▼▼▼ Rivershore Hotel** SH ❖
(503) 655-7141. **$79-$108.** 1900 Clackamette Dr. I-205, exit 9, just n. Int corridors. **Pets:** Other species. $5 daily fee/pet. Service with restrictions, supervision.
[SAVE] [S] [X] [刀] [点] [❚] [▣] [❚] [➳] [X]

# PORTLAND

**(AAA) ▼▼▼▼ 5th Avenue Suites Hotel** LH ❖
(503) 222-0001. **$134-$209.** 506 SW Washington St. At SW 5th Ave and SW Washington St. Int corridors. **Pets:** Other species. Service with restrictions, supervision.
[SAVE] [S] [X] [&M] [刀] [点] [▣] [❚] [X]

**(AAA) ▼▼▼ The Benson Hotel, a Coast Hotel** LH ❖
(503) 228-2000. **$129-$209.** 309 SW Broadway. At SW Broadway and Oak. Int corridors. **Pets:** $75 deposit/pet. Designated rooms, service with restrictions.
[SAVE] [S] [X] [&M] [刀] [点] [▣] [❚]

**▼▼▼▼ Best Western Inn at the Meadows** SH
(503) 286-9600. **$69-$99.** 1215 N Hayden Meadows Dr. I-5, exit 306B, just e. Int corridors. **Pets:** Accepted.
[ASK] [S] [X] [刀] [❚] [▣]

**(AAA) ▼▼▼▼ Best Western Pony Soldier Inn-Airport** SH
(503) 256-1504. **$115-$145.** 9901 NE Sandy Blvd. I-205, exit 23A, just e. Int corridors. **Pets:** Small. Designated rooms, service with restrictions, supervision.
[SAVE] [S] [X] [&M] [❚] [▣] [➳] [X]

**▼▼▼▼ Country Inn & Suites at Portland Airport** SH
(503) 255-2700. **$81-$97.** 7205 NE Alderwood Rd. I-205, exit 24A (Airport Way) northbound; exit 24 southbound, 1 mi w on Airport Way, just sw on NE 82nd Ave, then just w. Int corridors. **Pets:** Accepted.
[ASK] [S] [X] [&M] [刀] [点] [❚] [▣] [❚]

**(AAA) ▼▼▼ Days Inn-Portland North** SH ❖
(503) 289-1800. **$59-$68.** 9930 N Whitaker Rd. I-5, exit 306B, just e. Int corridors. **Pets:** Other species. $15 one-time fee/room. Service with restrictions.
[SAVE] [X] [刀] [点] [❚] [▣]

**▼▼▼▼ Four Points by Sheraton Portland Downtown** SH
(503) 221-0711. **$89-$109.** 50 SW Morrison St. At Morrison St and Naito Pkwy (formerly Front Ave). Int corridors. **Pets:** Accepted.
[ASK] [S] [X] [&M] [刀] [点] [❚] [▣] [❚]

**(AAA) ▼▼▼▼ The Heathman Hotel** SH
(503) 241-4100. **$149-$850.** 1001 SW Broadway. At SW Broadway and Salmon St. Int corridors. **Pets:** Medium. $25 daily fee/pet. Designated rooms, service with restrictions, supervision.
[SAVE] [X] [&M] [刀] [▣] [❚]

**(AAA) ▼▼▼▼ Hilton Portland & Executive Tower** LH
(503) 226-1611. **$89-$209.** 921 SW 6th Ave. I-405, exit 1B (6th Ave); at 6th Ave and Taylor St. Int corridors. **Pets:** Medium. $20 daily fee/pet. Service with restrictions, supervision.
[SAVE] [X] [刀] [❚] [▣] [❚] [➳] [X]

**(AAA) ▼▼▼ Hospitality Inn** SH ❖
(503) 244-6684. **$71-$109.** 10155 SW Capitol Hwy. I-5, exit 295 southbound; exit 294 northbound, just s. Int corridors. **Pets:** Dogs only. $10 daily fee/pet. Designated rooms, service with restrictions.
[SAVE] [S] [X] [刀] [点] [❚] [▣]

**(AAA) ▼▼▼ Hotel Lucia** SH ❖
(503) 225-1717. **$135-$185.** 400 SW Broadway. At SW Broadway and Stark St. Int corridors. **Pets:** $35 one-time fee/pet. Designated rooms, service with restrictions, crate.
[SAVE] [S] [X] [&M] [刀] [点] [▣] [❚]

**(AAA) ▼▼▼▼ Hotel Vintage Plaza** SH ❖
(503) 228-1212. **$129-$209.** 422 SW Broadway. At Broadway and Washington St. Int corridors. **Pets:** Other species. Service with restrictions, supervision.
[SAVE] [S] [X] [刀] [▣] [❚]

**(AAA) ▼▼▼▼ La Quinta Inn & Suites Portland Airport** SH
(503) 382-3820. **$79-$109.** 11207 NE Holman St. I-205, exit 24B northbound; exit 24 southbound, just e on Airport Way. Int corridors. **Pets:** Large, other species. Service with restrictions, supervision.
[SAVE] [S] [X] [&M] [刀] [点] [❚] [▣] [➳]

**(AAA) ▼▼▼ La Quinta Inn & Suites Portland (NW)** SH ❖
(503) 497-9044. **$76-$100.** 4319 NW Yeon. I-5, exit 302 B southbound, 2.5 mi w on US 30; I-5 to I-405, exit 3 (US 30) northbound, 2.5 mi w. Int corridors. **Pets:** Other species. Service with restrictions, supervision.
[SAVE] [S] [X] [刀] [点] [❚] [▣] [➳] [X]

**(AAA) ▼▼▼ La Quinta Inn Portland Lloyd Center/Convention Center** SH
(503) 233-7933. **$94-$99.** 431 NE Multnomah St. I-5, exit 302A, just e, then just s on Martin Luther King Blvd. Int corridors. **Pets:** Accepted.
[SAVE] [S] [X] [刀] [❚] [▣] [➳]

**(AAA) ▼▼▼ The Mark Spencer Hotel** SH ❖
(503) 224-3293. **$69-$129.** 409 SW 11th Ave. At SW Stark St and SW 11th Ave. Int corridors. **Pets:** Other species. $10 daily fee/pet. Designated rooms.
[SAVE] [S] [X] [❚] [▣]

**▼▼▼ Marriott City Center** 🔤
(503) 226-6300. **$169-$179.** 520 SW Broadway. At Washington St and SW Broadway. Int corridors. **Pets:** Accepted.
(ASK) ⊠ 🖉 🛋 🛢 🖃 🍴 ⊠

**▼▼ Motel 6 North Portland #4198** 🔤
(503) 247-3700. **$51-$61.** 1125 N Schmeer Rd. I-5, exit 306B, 0.4 mi s on N Whitaker Rd, then just e. Int corridors. **Pets:** Accepted.
🛢 ⊠ 🖉 🛋

**◈◈◈ ▼▼▼ Oxford Suites** 🔤
(503) 283-3030. **$89-$189, 7 day notice.** 12226 N Jantzen Dr. I-5, exit 308, just e on Hayden Island Dr. Int corridors. **Pets:** Small. $25 daily fee/pet. Service with restrictions, supervision.
(SAVE) 🛢 ⊠ 🛋 🖉 🛋 🛢 🖃 ⇔ ⊠

**◈◈◈ ▼▼▼ The Paramount Hotel, a Coast Hotel** 🔤
(503) 223-9900. **$109-$195.** 808 SW Taylor St. At SW 8th Ave and SW Taylor St. Int corridors. **Pets:** Medium. $250 deposit/pet, $50 one-time fee/room. Service with restrictions, supervision.
(SAVE) 🛢 ⊠ 🛋 🖉 🛋 🛢 🖃 🍴

**◈◈◈ ▼▼▼ Park Lane Suites** Ⓜ
(503) 226-6288. **$89-$159.** 809 SW King Ave. I-405, exit Couch/ Burnside St southbound, 0.5 mi w on Burnside St, then just s; exit Everett St northbound, 0.4 mi w on Glisan St, just s on NW 21st Ave, just w on Burnside St, then just s. Ext corridors. **Pets:** Accepted.
(SAVE) 🛢 ⊠ 🛋 🛢 🖃

**▼▼ The Portlander Inn** 🔤
(503) 345-0300. **$69.** 10350 N Vancouver Way. I-5, exit 307, follow signs for Marine Dr E, just ne, then 0.7 mi se. Int corridors. **Pets:** Accepted.
⊠ 🖉 🖃 🍴 ⊠

**◈◈◈ ▼▼▼ Quality Inn Portland Airport** 🔤
(503) 256-4111. **$74-$144.** 8247 NE Sandy Blvd. I-84, exit 5, 1.5 mi n on 82nd Ave; I-205, exit 23A southbound/23B northbound (US 30 business route/Sandy Blvd W), 1 mi w. Ext/int corridors. **Pets:** Accepted.
(SAVE) 🛢 ⊠ 🛢 🖃 ⇔

**◈◈◈ ▼▼▼ Red Lion Hotel on the River Jantzen Beach-Portland** 🔤
(503) 283-4466. **$69-$159.** 909 N Hayden Island Dr. I-5, exit 308, just e. Int corridors. **Pets:** Accepted.
(SAVE) 🛢 ⊠ 🛋 🖉 🛋 🛢 🖃 🍴 ⇔ ⊠

**▼▼▼ Red Lion Hotel Portland-Convention Center** 🔤
(503) 235-2100. **$79-$149.** 1021 NE Grand Ave. I-5, exit 302A, just e on Weidler, then just s on Martin Luther King Blvd. Int corridors. **Pets:** Small. $100 deposit/room, $10 daily fee/pet. Designated rooms, service with restrictions, supervision.
(ASK) 🛢 🖉 🛢 🖃 🍴

**▼▼▼ Red Lion Inn & Suites-Portland Airport** 🔤
(503) 252-6397. **$69-$99.** 5019 NE 102nd Ave. I-205, exit 23A, just e on NE Sandy Blvd. Int corridors. **Pets:** Accepted.
(ASK) 🛢 ⊠ 🖉 🛋 🛢 🖃 ⇔

**◈◈◈ ▼▼▼ Residence Inn by Marriott-Lloyd Center** 🔤 🐾
(503) 288-1400. **$159-$189.** 1710 NE Multnomah St. I-5, exit 302A, 0.8 mi e on Weidler St, then just s on 15th Ave; I-84, exit 1 (Lloyd Center) westbound, just n on 13th St, then just e. Ext corridors. **Pets:** Other species. $75 one-time fee/room. Service with restrictions, supervision.
(SAVE) 🛢 ⊠ 🛋 🖉 🛢 🖃 ⇔ ⊠

**▼▼▼ Residence Inn Portland Downtown at RiverPlace** 🔤 🐾
(503) 552-9500. **$89-$299.** 2115 SW River Pkwy. At SW Moody and SW River Pkwy; on the Willamette River Waterfront. Int corridors. **Pets:** Other species. $10 daily fee/pet.
(ASK) 🛢 ⊠ 🖉 🛋 🛢 🖃 ⇔ ⊠

**◈◈◈ ▼▼▼ RiverPlace Hotel** 🔤
(503) 228-3233. **$159-$289.** 1510 SW Harbor Way. At Naito Pkwy (formerly Front Ave) and SW Harbor Way. Int corridors. **Pets:** Accepted.
(SAVE) 🛢 ⊠ 🛋 🖉 🛋 🛢 🖃 🍴 ⊠

**◈◈◈ ▼▼▼ Sheraton Portland Airport Hotel** 🔤 🐾
(503) 281-2500. **$89-$186.** 8235 NE Airport Way. I-205, exit 24A northbound; exit 24 southbound, 1.5 mi w. Int corridors. **Pets:** Dogs only. $25 one-time fee/room. Service with restrictions, crate.
(SAVE) 🛢 ⊠ 🛋 🖉 🖃 🍴 ⇔ ⊠

**▼▼▼ Shilo Inn Rose Garden** 🔤
(503) 736-6300. **$89-$169.** 1506 NE 2nd Ave. I-5, exit 302A, just e, on NE Weidler, then just s. Int corridors. **Pets:** Accepted.
(ASK) 🛢 ⊠ 🛢 🖃

**▼▼▼ Staybridge Suites Portland-Airport** 🔤
(503) 262-8888. **$99-$204.** 11936 NE Glenn Widing Dr. I-205, exit 24B northbound; exit 24 southbound, just e. Int corridors. **Pets:** Medium, other species. $10 daily fee/pet, $25 one-time fee/pet. Service with restrictions, crate.
(ASK) 🛢 ⊠ 🛋 🖉 🛋 🛢 🖃 ⇔ ⊠

**◈◈◈ ▼▼ Travelodge Suites Portland** Ⓜ
(503) 788-9394. **$69-$89.** 7740 SE Powell Blvd. I-205, exit 19, 1 mi w. Ext/int corridors. **Pets:** Medium. $10 daily fee/pet. Service with restrictions, supervision.
(SAVE) 🛢 ⊠ 🛢 🖃

**◈◈◈ ▼▼▼▼ The Westin Portland** 🔤 🐾
(503) 294-9000. **$119-$199.** 750 SW Alder St. At Park Ave and SW Alder St. Int corridors. **Pets:** Service with restrictions.
(SAVE) 🛢 ⊠ 🛋 🖉 🛋 🛢 🖃 🍴

# TIGARD

**▼▼▼▼ Embassy Suites Hotel-Portland Washington Square** 🔤
(503) 644-4000. **$104-$170.** 9000 SW Washington Square Rd. SR 217, exit Progress/Scholls Ferry Rd, just e, then just s on Hall Blvd. Int corridors. **Pets:** Accepted.
(ASK) ⊠ 🛋 🖉 🛋 🛢 🖃 🍴 ⇔ ⊠

**▼▼ Homestead Studio Suites Hotel-Tigard/Lake Oswego** 🔤
(503) 670-0555. **$67.** 13009 SW 68th Pkwy. I-5, exit 293 (Haines), 0.5 mi s on SW 68th Ave; SR 217 S, exit 72nd Ave, just ne, just e on Hampton St, then just s. Ext corridors. **Pets:** $25 daily fee/pet. Service with restrictions, supervision.
(ASK) 🛢 ⊠ 🛋 🛢 🖃

**◈◈◈ ▼▼▼ Phoenix Inn Suites-Tigard** 🔤
(503) 624-9000. **$79-$119.** 9575 SW Locust. SR 217, exit Greenburg Rd, just e. Int corridors. **Pets:** Medium. $15 daily fee/pet. Designated rooms, service with restrictions, supervision.
(SAVE) 🛢 ⊠ 🛋 🖉 🛋 🛢 🖃 ⇔ ⊠

**▼▼ Shilo Inn-Tigard/Washington Square** 🔤 🐾
(503) 620-4320. **$52-$83.** 10830 SW Greenburg Rd. SR 217, exit Greenburg Rd, just w. Int corridors. **Pets:** $10 daily fee/pet. Designated rooms, service with restrictions, supervision.
(ASK) 🛢 ⊠ 🖉 🛋 🛢 🖃 ⊠

# TROUTDALE

**◈◈◈ ▼▼▼ Comfort Inn & Suites, Columbia Gorge West** 🔤
(503) 669-6500. **$59-$129.** 477 NW Phoenix Dr. I-84, exit 17. Int corridors. **Pets:** Small, other species. $10 daily fee/pet. Designated rooms, service with restrictions, supervision.
(SAVE) 🛢 ⊠ 🖉 🛢 🖃 ⇔

▼▼ ▼▼ **Holiday Inn Express-Portland East** 🅂🄷
(503) 492-2900. **$69-$79.** 1000 NW Graham Rd. I-84, exit 17, on north frontage road. Int corridors. **Pets:** Other species. $10 daily fee/room. Designated rooms, service with restrictions, supervision.

🄰🅂🄺 🅂🄳 ✖ 🕗 🛠 🛏 💻 ⊠

▼▼ **Motel 6-Portland Troutdale-407** 🄼
(503) 665-2254. **$37-$51.** 1610 NW Frontage Rd. I-84, exit 17, just s. Ext corridors. **Pets:** Accepted.

🅂🄳 ✖ 🗚 🕗 🛠 🛏 ⊅

## TUALATIN

▼▼▼ ▼▼▼ **Comfort Inn & Suites** 🅂🄷 🐾
(503) 612-9952. **$79-$179.** 7640 SW Warm Springs St. I-5, exit 289, w on Nyberg Rd; behind Fred Meyer. Int corridors. **Pets:** Medium. $10 daily fee/pet. Service with restrictions, supervision.

🅂🄰🅅🄴 🅂🄳 ✖ 🗚 🕗 🛠 🛏 ⊅

▼▼▼ ▼▼▼ **The Sweetbrier Inn & Suites** 🅂🄷
(503) 692-5800. **$69-$79.** 7125 SW Nyberg Rd. I-5, exit 289, just e. Ext/int corridors. **Pets:** Accepted.

🄰🅂🄺 🅂🄳 ✖ 🗚 🕗 🛠 🛏 💻 🍴 ⊅ ⊠

## WILSONVILLE

▼▼▼ ▼▼▼ **Best Western Willamette Inn** 🅂🄷
(503) 682-2288. **$74-$84.** 30800 SW Parkway Ave. I-5, exit 283, just e, then just s. Int corridors. **Pets:** Small. Designated rooms, service with restrictions, supervision.

🅂🄰🅅🄴 🅂🄳 ✖ 🗚 🛏 💻 ⊅ ⊠

▼▼▼ ▼▼▼ **Comfort Inn** 🅂🄷 🐾
(503) 682-9000. **$70-$120.** 8855 SW Citizens Dr. I-5, exit 283, just e, then just n on Town Center Loop W. Int corridors. **Pets:** $15 daily fee/room. Designated rooms, service with restrictions, supervision.

🅂🄰🅅🄴 🅂🄳 ✖ 🗚 🕗 🛠 🛏 💻 ⊅

▼▼▼▼ ▼▼▼▼ **Holiday Inn-Wilsonville** 🅂🄷
(503) 682-2211. **$89-$145.** 25425 SW 95th Ave. I-5, exit 286, just w. Int corridors. **Pets:** Other species. $15 one-time fee/room. Service with restrictions, supervision.

🄰🅂🄺 🅂🄳 ✖ 🗚 🕗 🛠 🛏 💻 🍴 ⊅

▼▼▼▼ ▼▼▼▼ **La Quinta Inn Wilsonville** 🅂🄷
(503) 682-3184. **$55-$90.** 8815 SW Sun Pl. I-5, exit 286, just e, then just n. Int corridors. **Pets:** Other species. Service with restrictions, supervision.

🅂🄰🅅🄴 🅂🄳 ✖ 🗚 🛏 💻 ⊅

▼▼▼▼ ▼▼▼▼ **Phoenix Inn Suites-Wilsonville** 🅂🄷
(503) 570-9700. **$79-$119.** 29769 SW Boones Ferry Rd. I-5, exit 283, just w. Int corridors. **Pets:** Medium. $15 daily fee/pet. Designated rooms, service with restrictions, supervision.

🅂🄰🅅🄴 🅂🄳 ✖ 🗚 🕗 🛠 🛏 💻 ⊅ ⊠

## WOOD VILLAGE

▼▼▼ ▼▼▼ **Portland/Troutdale Travelodge** 🅂🄷
(503) 666-6623. **$38-$69.** 23705 NE Sandy Blvd. I-84, exit 16, just n. Int corridors. **Pets:** Other species. $5 daily fee/pet. Service with restrictions, supervision.

🅂🄰🅅🄴 🅂🄳 ✖ 🗚 🛏 💻 🍴

---

# END METROPOLITAN AREA

---

## PORT ORFORD

▼▼▼ ▼▼ **Castaway by the Sea** 🄼
(541) 332-4502. **$55-$135, 3 day notice.** 545 W 5th St. Jct US 101, just w on Oregon St. Ext corridors. **Pets:** Accepted.

🅂🄰🅅🄴 ✖ 🛏 💻 🐾

▼▼▼ ▼▼ **Sea Crest Motel** 🄼 🐾
(541) 332-3040. **$50-$79.** 44 Hwy 101. On US 101, 1 mi s. Ext corridors. **Pets:** Medium. $5 daily fee/pet. Designated rooms, service with restrictions, supervision.

🅂🄰🅅🄴 ✖ 🛏 💻 🐾

## PRINEVILLE

▼▼▼ ▼▼▼ **Best Western Prineville Inn** 🅂🄷 🐾
(541) 447-8080. **$60-$81.** 1475 NE 3rd St. 1.4 mi e on US 26 from SR 126. Int corridors. **Pets:** Dogs only. $10 one-time fee/room. Service with restrictions, supervision.

🄰🅂🄺 🅂🄳 ✖ 🗚 🛏 💻 ⊅

▼▼▼ ▼▼▼ **Stafford Inn** 🅂🄷
(541) 447-7100. **$75-$85.** 1773 NE 3rd St. On US 26. Int corridors. **Pets:** $25 one-time fee/room. Service with restrictions, supervision.

🄰🅂🄺 🅂🄳 ✖ 🗚 🛏 💻 ⊅

## PROSPECT

▼▼ ▼▼ **Prospect Historical Hotel-Motel & Dinner House** 🄼 🐾
(541) 560-3664. **$55-$155.** 391 Mill Creek Dr. Jct SR 62, 0.3 mi s on 1st St (0.7 mi e of MM 43), just w. Ext/int corridors. **Pets:** Other species. Designated rooms, service with restrictions, supervision.

✖ 🛏 💻 🍴 ⊠

## REDMOND

▼▼▼ ▼▼▼ **Comfort Suites-Redmond Airport** 🅂🄷
(541) 504-8900. **$104-$174.** 2243 SW Yew Ave. US 97, just w. Int corridors. **Pets:** Accepted.

🄰🅂🄺 🅂🄳 ✖ 🗚 🛏 💻 ⊅

▼▼▼ ▼▼▼ **Eagle Crest Resort** 🅂🄷 🐾
(541) 923-2453. **$84-$157.** 1522 Cline Falls Rd. 5 mi w on SR 126, 1 mi s. Int corridors. **Pets:** Dogs only. $75 one-time fee/room. Designated rooms, service with restrictions, supervision.

🄰🅂🄺 ✖ 🗚 🕗 🛠 🛏 💻 🍴 ⊅ ⊠

▼▼▼ ▼▼ **Motel 6 Redmond-4076** 🅂🄷
(541) 923-2100. **$56-$69.** 2247 S Hwy 97. 1 mi s on US 97 from jct SR 126 W. Int corridors. **Pets:** Accepted.

🅂🄰🅅🄴 🅂🄳 ✖ 🗚 🕗 🛠 🛏

▼▼▼ ▼▼ **Redmond Inn** 🄼
(541) 548-1091. **$55-$70.** 1545 Hwy 97 S. 0.5 mi s on US 97 from jct SR 126 W. Ext corridors. **Pets:** Other species. $5 daily fee/pet. Service with restrictions, supervision.

🅂🄰🅅🄴 🅂🄳 ✖ 🛏 💻 ⊅

▼▼ ▼▼ **Redmond Super 8 Motel** 🅂🄷
(541) 548-8881. **$53-$90.** 3629 21st Pl SW. US 97, exit Yew Ave. Int corridors. **Pets:** Accepted.

🄰🅂🄺 🅂🄳 ✖ 🗚 🕗 🛠 ⊅

## REEDSPORT

▼▼▼ ▼▼ **Anchor Bay Inn** 🄼
(541) 271-2149. **$45-$77.** 1821 Winchester Ave (Hwy 101). On US 101, 0.8 mi s of jct SR 38. Ext corridors. **Pets:** Other species. $7 daily fee/pet. Designated rooms, service with restrictions, supervision.

🅂🄰🅅🄴 🅂🄳 ✖ 🛏 💻 ⊅ 🐾

**Best Western Salbasgeon Inn** M
(541) 271-4831. **$77-$99.** 1400 Hwy Ave 101 S. Just s on US 101 from jct SR 38. Ext corridors. **Pets:** Medium, dogs only. $15 daily fee/pet. Designated rooms, service with restrictions, supervision.

**Economy Inn** M
(541) 271-3671. **$59-$93.** 1593 Hwy 101. On US 101; center. Ext corridors. **Pets:** Small, dogs only. $5 one-time fee/pet. Designated rooms, service with restrictions, supervision.

**Salbasgeon Inn of the Umpqua** SH
(541) 271-2025. **$71-$145.** 45209 Hwy 38. Jct US 101, 7.3 mi e. Ext corridors. **Pets:** Accepted.

# ROCKAWAY BEACH

**Sea Treasures Inn** M
(503) 355-8220. **$50-$99.** 301 N Miller St. Jct 3rd Ave N; center. Ext corridors. **Pets:** Accepted.

**Silver Sands Motel** M
(503) 355-2206. **$100-$154.** 215 S Pacific St. US 101, exit S 2nd Ave, just w. Ext corridors. **Pets:** Dogs only. $10 one-time fee/room. Service with restrictions, supervision.

**Tradewinds Motel** M
(503) 355-2112. **$50-$135, 7 day notice.** 523 N Pacific St. Just w of US 101, off N 6th Ave. Ext corridors. **Pets:** Medium, dogs only. $15 daily fee/pet. Designated rooms, service with restrictions, supervision.

# ROSEBURG

**Best Western Douglas Inn** M
(541) 673-6625. **Call for rates.** 511 SE Stephens St. I-5, exit 124, 0.5 mi e, then just n; downtown. Ext corridors. **Pets:** Large, other species. $15 one-time fee/room. Designated rooms, service with restrictions, crate.

**Best Western Garden Villa Inn** M
(541) 672-1601. **$69-$99.** 760 NW Garden Valley Blvd. I-5, exit 125, just w. Ext corridors. **Pets:** Accepted.

**Holiday Inn Express** SH
(541) 673-7517. **$71-$104.** 375 W Harvard Blvd. I-5, exit 124, just e. Ext/int corridors. **Pets:** Other species. $5 daily fee/room. Designated rooms, service with restrictions, supervision.

**Howard Johnson Express Inn** M
(541) 673-5082. **$56-$89.** 978 NE Stephens St. I-5, exit 125, 0.6 mi e on Garden Valley Blvd, then 0.4 mi s. Ext corridors. **Pets:** Accepted.

**Quality Inn** SH
(541) 673-5561. **$69-$109.** 427 NW Garden Valley Blvd. I-5, exit 125, just e. Ext corridors. **Pets:** Accepted.

**Roseburg Travelodge** M
(541) 672-4836. **$67-$91.** 315 W Harvard Blvd. I-5, exit 124, just e. Ext corridors. **Pets:** Medium, other species. $10 daily fee/room. Designated rooms, service with restrictions, supervision.

**Shady Oaks Motel** M
(541) 672-2608. **$45-$65, 3 day notice.** 2954 Old Hwy 99 S. I-5, exit 120, 0.5 mi n. Ext corridors. **Pets:** Medium, dogs only. $8 daily fee/pet. Designated rooms, service with restrictions, supervision.

**Sleep Inn and Suites** SH
(541) 464-8338. **$54-$99.** 2855 NW Edenbower Blvd. I-5, exit 127, just n. Int corridors. **Pets:** Large. $10 one-time fee/room. Service with restrictions, crate.

**Super 8 Motel** SH
(541) 672-8880. **$53-$67.** 3200 NW Aviation Dr. I-5, exit 127, just ne. Int corridors. **Pets:** Large. $25 deposit/pet. Service with restrictions, supervision.

**Windmill Inn of Roseburg** SH
(541) 673-0901. **$86-$110.** 1450 NW Mulholland Dr. I-5, exit 125, just ne. Int corridors. **Pets:** Other species. Designated rooms, service with restrictions.

# ST. HELENS

**Best Western Oak Meadows Inn** SH
(503) 397-3000. **$79-$149.** 585 S Columbia River Hwy. South end of town on US 30. Int corridors. **Pets:** Medium, other species. $10 one-time fee/pet. Service with restrictions, supervision.

# SALEM

**Best Western Black Bear Inn** SH
(503) 581-1559. **$65-$96.** 1600 Motor Ct NE. I-5, exit 256, just e. Ext corridors. **Pets:** Cats only. $12 one-time fee/pet. Service with restrictions, supervision.

**Best Western Pacific Hwy Inn** SH
(503) 390-3200. **$75-$90.** 4646 Portland Rd NE. I-5, exit 258, just e. Ext corridors. **Pets:** Accepted.

**Holiday Inn Express** SH
(503) 391-7000. **$81-$108.** 890 Hawthorne Ave SE. I-5, exit 253, just w, then just n. Int corridors. **Pets:** Accepted.

**Motel 6–1343** M
(503) 371-8024. **$45-$57.** 1401 Hawthorne Ave NE. I-5, exit 256, just w, then just s. Ext corridors. **Pets:** Accepted.

**Phoenix Inn Suites-North Salem** SH
(503) 581-7004. **$79-$99.** 1590 Weston Ct NE. I-5, exit 256, just w, then just s. Int corridors. **Pets:** Medium. $15 daily fee/pet. Designated rooms, service with restrictions, supervision.

**Phoenix Inn Suites-South Salem** SH
(503) 588-9220. **$79-$99.** 4370 Commercial SE. I-5, exit 252, 1.5 mi w on Kuebler Rd, then 0.7 mi n. Int corridors. **Pets:** Medium. $15 daily fee/pet. Designated rooms, service with restrictions, supervision.

**Red Lion Hotel Salem** SI
(503) 370-7888. **$59-$129.** 3301 Market St NE. I-5, exit 256, just w. Int corridors. **Pets:** Medium. $10 daily fee/pet. Service with restrictions, crate.

▽▽▽▽ **Residence Inn by Marriott** 🏨
(503) 585-6500. **$75-$130.** 640 Hawthorne Ave SE. I-5, exit 253, just w, then n. Int corridors. **Pets:** Accepted.
A$K 🛏 ✕ 🗲M 🕸 🐾 🖥 💻 ⟿ ✕

▽▽ **Salem Inn** 🏨
(503) 588-0515. **$60-$94.** 1775 Freeway Ct NE. I-5, exit 256, just w. Int corridors. **Pets:** Other species. $50 deposit/room, $10 daily fee/pet. Service with restrictions, supervision.
A$K 🛏 ✕ 🗲M 🕸 🖥 💻 ⟿

▽▽ **Salem Super 8** 🏨 🐾
(503) 370-8888. **$54-$79.** 1288 Hawthorne Ave NE. I-5, exit 256, just w, then just s. Int corridors. **Pets:** Other species. $10 one-time fee/room. Designated rooms, service with restrictions, supervision.
A$K 🛏 ✕ 🗲M 🕸 🖥 ⟿

▲▲▲ ▽▽▽▽ **Shilo Inn Suites-Salem** 🏨 🐾
(503) 581-4001. **$73-$113.** 3304 Market St NE. I-5, exit 256, just w. Int corridors. **Pets:** Small. $10 daily fee/pet. Service with restrictions, supervision.
SAVE 🛏 ✕ 🖥 💻 ⟿ ✕

▲▲▲ ▽▽▽ **Travelodge Salem Capital** Ⓜ 🐾
(503) 581-2466. **$43-$54.** 1555 State St. I-5, exit 253, just w on SR 22/99 (Mission St), 0.6 mi n on Airport Rd SE, then 1 mi w. Ext corridors. **Pets:** Other species. $10 daily fee/room. Service with restrictions.
SAVE 🛏 ✕ 🕸 🖥 💻 ⟿

## SANDY

▽▽ **Best Western Sandy Inn** 🏨
(503) 668-7100. **$88-$125.** 37465 Hwy 26. West side of town. Int corridors. **Pets:** Medium, dogs only. $10 daily fee/pet. Service with restrictions, supervision.
A$K 🛏 ✕ 🗲M 🕸 🖥 💻 ⟿

## SEASIDE

▲▲▲ ▽▽▽ **Best Western Ocean View Resort** 🏨 🐾
(503) 738-3334. **$59-$289, 3 day notice.** 414 N Prom. US 101, exit 1st Ave, just w, just n on Necanicum Dr, then just w on 4th Ave. Ext/int corridors. **Pets:** $20 daily fee/pet. Designated rooms, service with restrictions, supervision.
SAVE 🛏 ✕ 🕸 🖥 💻 🍴 ⟿

▲▲▲ ▽▽▽ **Inn at Seaside** Ⓜ 🐾
(503) 738-9581. **$79-$189, 3 day notice.** 441 2nd Ave. US 101, exit 1st Ave, 0.4 mi w. Ext/int corridors. **Pets:** Other species. $10 daily fee/pet. Service with restrictions, crate.
SAVE 🛏 ✕ 🕸 🖥 💻 ⟿

▲▲▲ ▽▽▽ **Seashore Inn...on the Beach** Ⓜ
(503) 738-6368. **$69-$185.** 60 N Prom. US 101, exit 1st Ave, 0.4 mi w. Ext/int corridors. **Pets:** Small. $20 daily fee/room. Designated rooms.
SAVE 🛏 ✕ 🖥 💻 ⟿ 🐾

▲▲▲ ▽▽▽ **Sea Side Oceanfront Inn Bed & Breakfast Hotel** 🅱🅱
(503) 738-6403. **$95-$315, 5 day notice.** 581 S Prom. US 101, exit Ave G, 0.6 mi w, then just n. Int corridors. **Pets:** Medium. $35 one-time fee/pet. Designated rooms, service with restrictions, supervision.
SAVE ✕ 🖥 💻

## SHADY COVE

▲▲▲ ▽▽▽▽ **The Edgewater Inn on the Rogue River** Ⓜ 🐾
(541) 878-3171. **$67-$165.** 7800 Rogue River Dr. Off SR 62. Ext corridors. **Pets:** $7 daily fee/pet. Service with restrictions, supervision.
SAVE 🛏 ✕ 🕸 🖥 💻 ⟿ ✕

## SISTERS

▲▲▲ ▽▽▽▽ **Best Western Ponderosa Lodge** 🏨 🐾
(541) 549-1234. **$89-$219.** 500 Hwy 20 W. West end of town, just w on US 20 from jct SR 242. Ext corridors. **Pets:** Large. $15 one-time fee/room. Designated rooms, supervision.
SAVE 🛏 ✕ 🕸 🖥 💻 ⟿

▲▲▲ ▽▽▽ **Sisters Inn & RV Park** 🏨
(541) 549-7829. **$100-$105.** 540 Hwy 20 W. West end of town, just w on US 20 from jct SR 242. Ext corridors. **Pets:** Small, dogs only. $25 one-time fee/room. Designated rooms, service with restrictions, supervision.
SAVE 🛏 ✕ 🗲M 🕸 🖥 💻 ⟿

▽▽▽▽ **Sun Ranch Inn** 🅱🅱
(541) 549-0123. **$70-$150 (no credit cards).** 69013 Camp Polk Rd. East end of town, just w on US 20 from jct SR 126, 0.5 mi n on Locust Rd. Int corridors. **Pets:** Accepted.
A$K ✕ 🗲M 🕸 🖥 ⟿ ✕ ✕ ✕

## SPRINGFIELD

▲▲▲ ▽▽▽ **Best Western Grand Manor Inn** 🏨
(541) 726-4769. **$74-$125.** 971 Kruse Way. I-5, exit 195A, just e. Int corridors. **Pets:** Accepted.
SAVE 🛏 ✕ 🗲M 🕸 🕸 🖥 💻 ⟿

▽▽▽▽ **Comfort Suites Eugene/Springfield** 🏨
(541) 746-5359. **$89-$159.** 969 Kruse Way. I-5, exit 195A, just e. Int corridors. **Pets:** Medium, dogs only. $10 daily fee/pet. Designated rooms, service with restrictions, supervision.
A$K 🛏 ✕ 🕸 🕸 🖥 💻 ⟿

▲▲▲ ▽▽▽▽ **Holiday Inn Express** 🏨
(541) 746-8471. **$89-$129.** 3480 Hutton St. I-5, exit 195A, just e. Int corridors. **Pets:** Medium, dogs only. $10 daily fee/pet. Designated rooms, service with restrictions, supervision.
SAVE ✕ 🕸 🕸 🖥 💻 ⟿

▽▽▽ **Motel 6 #418** Ⓜ
(541) 741-1105. **$43-$57.** 3752 International Ct. I-5, exit 195A, just e, then just n on Gateway St. Ext corridors. **Pets:** Accepted.
🛏 ✕ 🗲M 🕸 ⟿

▲▲▲ ▽▽▽ **Quality Inn & Suites** Ⓜ 🐾
(541) 726-9266. **$70-$155.** 3550 Gateway St. I-5, exit 195A, just e, then just n. Int corridors. **Pets:** Small, dogs only. $5 one-time fee/pet. Service with restrictions, supervision.
SAVE 🛏 ✕ 🖥 💻 ⟿

▲▲▲ ▽▽▽ **Super 8 Motel** 🏨
(541) 746-1314. **$64-$89.** 3315 Gateway St. I-5, exit 195A, just e, then just s. Int corridors. **Pets:** Accepted.
SAVE 🛏 ✕ 🕸 🖥 💻

▲▲▲ ▽▽▽ **Village Inn** 🏨
(541) 747-4546. **$67.** 1875 Mohawk Blvd. I-5, exit 194A, 2.5 mi e, then just n. Ext corridors. **Pets:** Small. Designated rooms, service with restrictions, supervision.
SAVE ✕ 🖥 💻 🍴 ⟿

## SUMMER LAKE

▽▽▽ **Summer Lake Inn** 🅲🅸
(541) 943-3983. **$115-$240, 14 day notice.** 47531 Hwy 31. 10 mi s; between MM 81 and 82. Ext corridors. **Pets:** Dogs only. $10 one-time fee/pet. Service with restrictions, supervision.
✕ 🖥 💻 🍴 ✕ ✕

## SUNRIVER

▲▲▲ ▽▽▽▽ **Sunray Vacation Rentals** 🆅🅷 🐾
(541) 593-3225. **$125-$695, 30 day notice.** 56890 Venture Ln. 1 mi w on S Century Dr from jct US 97, then just e. Ext corridors. **Pets:** Other species. $75 deposit/room, $25 one-time fee/pet. Designated rooms.
SAVE ✕ 🖥 💻 ⟿ ✕

# SUTHERLIN

◆◆ Sutherlin Inn SH
(541) 459-6800. $54-$64. 1400 Hospitality Pl. I-5, exit 136, just se. Int corridors. Pets: Other species. $10 daily fee/pet. Service with restrictions, supervision.

⊗ 🛢 📖 💻

AAA ◆◆ Umpqua Regency Inn M
(541) 459-1424. $61-$79. 150 Myrtle St. I-5, exit 136, just e. Ext corridors. Pets: Accepted.

SAVE S�🐾 ⊗ 🛢 💻 ⇌

# SWEET HOME

AAA ◆◆ Sweet Home Inn M
(541) 367-5137. $59-$74. 805 Long St. Just e of jct US 20 and SR 228; just s on 10th Ave, just w. Ext corridors. Pets: Medium, dogs only. $10 one-time fee/pet. Service with restrictions, supervision.

SAVE S☐ ⊗ 🛢 💻

# TILLAMOOK

◆◆ Mar-Clair Inn M
(503) 842-7571. $66-$86. 11 Main Ave. US 101, just n of jct SR 6. Ext/int corridors. Pets: Small, dogs only. $10 one-time fee/pet. Service with restrictions, supervision.

⊗ 🛢 💻 ¶ ⇌ 🔏

AAA ◆◆ Shilo Inn SH 🐾
(503) 842-7971. $71-$133. 2515 Main Ave. 1 mi n on US 101. Int corridors. Pets: $10 daily fee/pet. Designated rooms, service with restrictions, supervision.

SAVE S☐ ⊠M ✈ 🛢 💻 ¶ ⇌ 🔏

# UMATILLA

AAA ◆◆ Desert River Inn SH
(541) 922-1000. $85. 705 Willamette Ave. I-82, exit 1 (US 730), 1.6 mi e, then 0.3 mi n. Int corridors. Pets: Other species. $10 daily fee/pet. Supervision.

SAVE S☐ ⊗ 🛢 💻 ¶ ⇌

# WALDPORT

AAA ◆ Alsea Manor Motel M 🐾
(541) 563-3249. $44-$84. 190 SW Hwy 101. SR 34, just s on US 101; downtown. Ext corridors. Pets: Other species. $5 daily fee/pet. Designated rooms, service with restrictions, supervision.

SAVE S☐ ⊗ 💻 🔏

# WARRENTON

◆◆ Shilo Inn Suites-Warrenton/Astoria SH 🐾
(503) 861-2181. $69-$209. 1609 E Harbor Dr. On US 26/101; near west end of Young's Bay Bridge. Int corridors. Pets: $15 daily fee/pet. Service with restrictions, supervision.

ASK S☐ ⊗ 🛢 💻 ¶ ⇌ ⊠

# WELCHES

AAA ◆◆◆ The Resort at the Mountain LH 🐾
(503) 622-3101. $99-$450, 3 day notice. 68010 E Fairway Ave. 0.8 mi s of US 26 on E Welches Rd. Ext corridors. Pets: Dogs only. $25 one-time fee/room. Designated rooms, service with restrictions, supervision.

SAVE S☐ ⊗ ✈ 🛢 💻 ¶ ⇌ ⊠

# WHEELER

◆ Wheeler on the Bay Lodge and Marina M
(503) 368-5858. $80-$145. 580 Marine Dr. On US 101; center. Ext corridors. Pets: Accepted.

ASK S☐ ⊗ 🛢 💻 ⊠ 🔏

# WINSTON

AAA ◆ Sweet Breeze Inn II M 🐾
(541) 679-2420. $55-$89, 3 day notice. 251 NE Main St. I-5, exit 119, 3 mi w. Ext corridors. Pets: Small, other species. $9 daily fee/pet. Designated rooms, service with restrictions, supervision.

SAVE S☐ ⊗ ✈ 🛢

# WOODBURN

AAA ◆◆◆ La Quinta Inn & Suites Woodburn SH
(503) 982-1727. $59-$139. 120 Arney Rd NE. I-5, exit 271, just w. Int corridors. Pets: Large, other species. Service with restrictions, supervision.

SAVE S☐ ⊗ ✈ 🛢 💻 ⇌

# YACHATS

AAA ◆◆◆ The Adobe Resort SH
(541) 547-3141. $75-$225. 1555 Hwy 101. 0.5 mi n. Int corridors. Pets: Accepted.

SAVE S☐ ⊗ ✈ 🛢 🛢 💻 ¶ ⇌ ⊠ 🔏

◆ The Dublin House M
(541) 547-3200. $39-$170. 251 W 7th St. US 101 at 7th St; downtown. Ext corridors. Pets: Medium, dogs only. $10 one-time fee/pet. Service with restrictions, supervision.

ASK S☐ ⊗ 🛢 💻 ⇌ 🔏

AAA ◆◆◆ Fireside Motel M 🐾
(541) 547-3636. $65-$140. 1881 Hwy 101 N. 0.6 mi n; just w of US 101. Ext corridors. Pets: Other species. $9 daily fee/pet. Designated rooms, service with restrictions, supervision.

SAVE S☐ ⊗ 🛢 💻 ⊠ 🔏

◆◆ Shamrock Lodgettes CA 🐾
(541) 547-3312. $59-$139, 3 day notice. 105 Hwy 101 S. On US 101, just s. Ext corridors. Pets: Other species. $10 daily fee/pet. Designated rooms, service with restrictions, supervision.

ASK S☐ ⊗ 🛢 💻 ⊠ 🔏

# PENNSYLVANIA

## CITY INDEX

## ABBOTTSTOWN

### 🔺 ▽▽▽ The Altland House 🅲🅸
(717) 259-9535. **$99-$150.** Center Square Rt 30. Jct SR 194. Int corridors. **Pets:** Accepted.
SAVE ⊠ 🔋 🍽

## ALLENTOWN

### 🔺 ▽▽ Allentown Howard Johnson Inn & Suites 🆂🅷
(610) 439-4000. **$49-$259.** 3220 Hamilton Blvd. I-78, exit 54 (Hamilton Blvd), 0.8 mi n. Int corridors. **Pets:** Accepted.
SAVE 🔋 ⊠ ⓜ 🔌 🎤 🔋 🖥 🛏

### 🔺 ▽▽ Allenwood Motel 🅼 🐾
(610) 395-3707. **$55-$125.** 1058 Hausman Rd. I-476, exit 56, 0.5 mi e on US 22, then 0.8 mi s on SR 309; I-78, exit 53 westbound; exit 51 eastbound, 1 mi n on SR 309, w on Tilghman St to light, then 0.8 mi n to dead end. Ext corridors. **Pets:** Medium. $10 daily fee/pet. Designated rooms, service with restrictions, supervision.
SAVE 🔋 ⊠ 🔋

### ▽▽▽ Crowne Plaza Hotel 🅻🅷
(610) 433-2221. **$99-$159.** 904 Hamilton Blvd. 9th St and Hamilton Blvd; downtown. Int corridors. **Pets:** Accepted.
ASK ⊠ 🔌 🎤 🔋 🖥 🍽 🛏

### ▽▽ Days Inn Conference Center 🆂🅷 🐾
(610) 395-3731. **$95-$150.** 1151 Bulldog Dr. I-476, exit 56, 0.5 mi e on US 22, then 0.6 mi n on SR 309 via Bulldog Dr access road. Ext/int corridors. **Pets:** Other species. $15 daily fee/room. Designated rooms, service with restrictions, crate.
ASK 🔋 ⊠ ⓜ 🔌 🎤 🔋 🖥 🍽 🛏 ⊠

### ▽▽▽ Four Points by Sheraton Hotel & Suites Lehigh Valley Airport 🆂🅷
(610) 266-1000. **$190-$210.** 3400 Airport Rd. On SR 987 N (Airport Rd), 0.5 mi n of jct US 22. Int corridors. **Pets:** Accepted.
⊠ ⓜ 🔌 🎤 🔋 🖥 🍽 🛏

### 🔺 ▽▽▽ Microtel Inn 🆂🅷
(610) 266-9070. **$35-$139.** 1880 Steelstone Rd. US 22, exit Airport Rd S. Int corridors. **Pets:** Accepted.
SAVE 🔋 ⊠ ⓜ 🔌 🎤 🔋 🖥

### 🔺 ▽▽▽ Quality Inn 🆂🅷
(610) 435-7880. **$40-$139.** 1715 Plaza Ln. US 22, exit 15th St, just n. Int corridors. **Pets:** Accepted.
SAVE 🔋 ⊠ 🎤 🔋

### ▽▽ Red Roof Inn #7110 🅼
(610) 264-5404. **$45-$86.** 1846 Catasauqua Rd. US 22, exit Airport Rd S, just s. Ext corridors. **Pets:** Accepted.
⊠ ⓜ 🎤 🔋 🔋

### ▽▽▽ Staybridge Suites Allentown-Airport 🆂🅷 🐾
(610) 443-5000. **$109-$269.** 1787-A Airport Rd. US 22, exit Airport Rd S, 0.3 mi s. Int corridors. **Pets:** Other species. $100 one-time fee/room. Service with restrictions, crate.
ASK 🔋 ⊠ ⓜ 🔌 🎤 🔋 🖥 🛏

### 🔺 ▽▽▽ Super 8 Motel 🅼
(610) 434-9550. **$49-$259.** 1033 Airport Rd. US 22, exit Airport Rd S, 1.1 mi s. Int corridors. **Pets:** Accepted.
SAVE 🔋 ⊠ ⓜ 🎤 🔋 🖥

## ALTOONA

### 🔺 ▽▽▽ Econo Lodge 🅼
(814) 944-3555. **$63.** 2906 Pleasant Valley Blvd. I-99/US 220, exit 32 (Frankstown Rd), 0.4 mi w, then 0.5 mi n. Ext corridors. **Pets:** Other species. Service with restrictions.
SAVE 🔋 ⊠ 🔋 🖥 🍽

### ▽▽ Motel 6 #1415 🅼
(814) 946-7601. **$45-$65.** 1500 Sterling St. I-99/US 220, exit 31 (Plank Rd), just w. Ext corridors. **Pets:** Accepted.
🔋 ⊠ ⓜ 🔋 🛏

**▼▼ ▼▼ Super 8 Motel Altoona 🅜**
(814) 942-5350. **$54-$60.** 3535 Fairway Dr. I-99/US 220, exit 32 (Frankstown Rd), just w. Int corridors. **Pets:** Medium. $6 daily fee/pet. Service with restrictions, supervision.
ⒶⓈⓀ Ⓢ ⓧ Ⓖⓜ 🅗

## BARKEYVILLE

**ⒶⒶⒶ ▼▼ ▼▼ Comfort Inn-Barkeyville 🅜 ❀**
(814) 786-7901. **$69-$120, 3 day notice.** 137 Gibb Rd. I-80, exit 29, just n on SR 8. Ext corridors. **Pets:** Medium. $10 one-time fee/room. Service with restrictions, supervision.
SAVE Ⓢ ⓧ 🅗 🖵

**▼▼ ▼▼ Super 8 Motel-Barkeyville 🅜**
(814) 786-8375. **$48-$69, 3 day notice.** 1010 Dholu Rd. I-80, exit 29, just n on SR 8. Int corridors. **Pets:** Other species. $5 daily fee/pet. Designated rooms, service with restrictions, supervision.
ⒶⓈⓀ Ⓢ ⓧ ⊘ 🅗

## BEDFORD

**ⒶⒶⒶ ▼▼▼▼ Best Western Bedford Inn 🆂🅷**
(814) 623-9006. **$69-$89.** 4517 Business Rt 220. I-70/76 (Pennsylvania Tpke), exit 146, 0.3 mi n. Ext/int corridors. **Pets:** Medium. $50 deposit/room, $10 one-time fee/room. Designated rooms, service with restrictions, supervision.
SAVE Ⓢ ⓧ ⊘ 🅗 🖵 ⑪ ⚊ ⓧ

**ⒶⒶⒶ ▼▼ Budget Host Inn 🅜**
(814) 623-8107. **$35-$85.** 4378 Business Rt 220. I-70/76 (Pennsylvania Tpke), exit 146, just n. Ext corridors. **Pets:** Small. $5 one-time fee/pet. Service with restrictions, supervision.
SAVE Ⓢ ⓧ 🅗 ⚊

**ⒶⒶⒶ ▼▼ Motel Town House 🅜**
(814) 623-5138. **$46-$56, 3 day notice.** 200 S Richard St. I-70/76 (Pennsylvania Tpke), exit 146, 2.5 mi s on US 220 business route. Ext corridors. **Pets:** Accepted.
SAVE Ⓢ ⓧ ⚊

**ⒶⒶⒶ ▼▼▼▼ Quality Inn Bedford 🆂🅷**
(814) 623-5188. **$70-$150.** 4407 Business Rt 220 N. I-70/76 (Pennsylvania Tpke), exit 146, just n. Ext/int corridors. **Pets:** Medium, other species. $50 deposit/pet, $10 daily fee/pet. Designated rooms, service with restrictions, crate.
SAVE Ⓢ ⓧ 🅗 🖵 ⑪ ⚊

**ⒶⒶⒶ ▼▼▼▼ Super 8 Motel 🅜**
(814) 623-5880. **$45-$55.** 4498 Business Rt 220. I-70/76 (Pennsylvania Tpke), exit 146, 0.3 mi n. Int corridors. **Pets:** $5 daily fee/pet. Supervision.
SAVE Ⓢ ⓧ 🅗

**ⒶⒶⒶ ▼▼▼▼ Travelodge 🅜 ❀**
(814) 623-7800. **$47-$116.** 4271 Business Rt 220. I-70/76 (Pennsylvania Tpke), exit 146, just s. Ext/int corridors. **Pets:** Other species. $7 daily fee/pet. Designated rooms, service with restrictions, supervision.
SAVE Ⓢ ⓧ 🅗 🖵

## BETHEL

**ⒶⒶⒶ ▼▼▼▼ Comfort Inn-Bethel/Midway 🆂🅷**
(717) 933-8888. **$72-$149.** 41 Diner Dr. I-78, exit 16, just w. Int corridors. **Pets:** Other species. $10 daily fee/pet. Designated rooms, service with restrictions, supervision.
SAVE Ⓢ ⓧ Ⓖⓜ ♿ 🅗 🖵 ⚊

## BETHLEHEM

**ⒶⒶⒶ ▼▼▼▼ Best Western Lehigh Valley Hotel & Conference Center 🆂🅷 ❀**
(610) 866-5800. **$69-$139, 3 day notice.** 300 Gateway Dr. US 22, exit Center St and SR 512. Ext/int corridors. **Pets:** Medium. $10 one-time fee/room. Designated rooms, service with restrictions, crate.
SAVE Ⓢ ⓧ Ⓖⓜ ⊘ 🅸 🅗 🖵 ⑪ ⚊

**▼▼▼▼ Comfort Inn 🆂🅷 ❀**
(610) 865-6300. **$79-$149, 7 day notice.** 3191 Highfield Dr. US 22, exit SR 191, just s. Ext/int corridors. **Pets:** Other species. $10 daily fee/pet. Service with restrictions, supervision.
ⒶⓈⓀ Ⓢ ⓧ ⊘ 🅗 🖵

**ⒶⒶⒶ ▼▼▼▼ Comfort Suites 🆂🅷**
(610) 882-9700. **$79-$159.** 120 W 3rd St. SR 378, exit 3rd St, W 3rd and Brodhead sts; center. Int corridors. **Pets:** $10 daily fee/room. Designated rooms, service with restrictions, supervision.
SAVE Ⓢ ⓧ ⊘ 🅗 🖵 ⑪

**ⒶⒶⒶ ▼▼▼▼ Historic Hotel Bethlehem 🅻🅷**
(610) 625-5000. **$164-$259.** 437 Main St. SR 378 S, exit 3 (City Center); downtown. Int corridors. **Pets:** Accepted.
SAVE Ⓢ ⓧ Ⓖⓜ 🅗 🖵

**▼▼▼▼ Residence Inn by Marriott 🆂🅷**
(610) 317-2662. **$169-$209.** 2180 Motel Dr. US 22, exit Airport Rd S, 0.8 mi se on Catasauqua Rd. Int corridors. **Pets:** Other species.
ⒶⓈⓀ Ⓢ ⓧ ⊘ 🅸 🅗 🖵 ⚊ ⓧ

## BLOOMSBURG

**ⒶⒶⒶ ▼▼ ▼▼ Econo Lodge at Bloomsburg 🆂🅷 ❀**
(570) 387-0490. **$65-$139, 3 day notice.** 189 Columbia Mall Dr. I-80, exit 232, just n on SR 42. Int corridors. **Pets:** $10 one-time fee/room. Designated rooms, service with restrictions, crate.
SAVE Ⓢ ⓧ ⊘ 🅗 🖵

**▼▼▼▼ The Inn at Turkey Hill 🅲🅸 ❀**
(570) 387-1500. **$110-$225.** 991 Central Rd. I-80, exit 236 eastbound; exit 236A westbound, just s. Ext/int corridors. **Pets:** Other species. $15 daily fee/room. Designated rooms, service with restrictions, supervision.
ⒶⓈⓀ Ⓢ ⓧ 🅗 🖵 ⑪

## BLUE MOUNTAIN

**ⒶⒶⒶ ▼▼ ▼▼ Kenmar Motel 🅜**
(717) 423-5915. **$65-$80.** 17788 Cumberland Hwy. I-76, exit 201, just e on SR 997 N. Ext corridors. **Pets:** Large, dogs only. $5 daily fee/pet. Designated rooms, service with restrictions, supervision.
SAVE Ⓢ ⓧ 🅗

## BOYERTOWN

**▼▼ Mel-Dor Motel 🅜**
(610) 367-2626. **$55-$65.** 5 Spring Garden Dr. SR 100, exit New Berlinville; 1 mi n of town. Ext corridors. **Pets:** Small, dogs only. $5 daily fee/pet. Service with restrictions, supervision.
ⓧ 🅗

## BRADFORD

**ⒶⒶⒶ ▼▼▼▼ Best Western Bradford Inn 🆂🅷**
(814) 362-4501. **$83-$88.** 100 Davis St S. US 219, exit Forman St southbound, just w to Davis St, then 0.3 mi s; exit Elm St northbound, just w. Ext/int corridors. **Pets:** $10 daily fee/pet. Service with restrictions, crate.
SAVE Ⓢ ⓧ ⑆ 🅗 🖵 ⑪ ⚊

▼▼▼ ▼▼▼ **Glendorn** 🆑 ❀
(814) 362-6511. **$495-$795, 30 day notice.** 1000 Glendorn Dr. SR 219, exit Forman St, just s on Mechanic St, 4.3 mi w on W Corydon. Ext/int corridors. **Pets:** Large, dogs only. $75 daily fee/pet. Designated rooms, service with restrictions, crate.

(A$K) (✕) 🏢 🖅 🖵 🍴 ⊋ (✕)

# BREEZEWOOD

⟨AAA⟩ ▼▼▼ **Breezewood Ramada Inn** 🆂🅷 ❀
(814) 735-4005. **$59-$72, 7 day notice.** 16620 Lincoln Hwy. I-76, exit 161, just e on US 30; I-70, exit 147, just e on US 30. Int corridors. **Pets:** Medium. $10 daily fee/room. Supervision.

(SAVE) (S🔘) (✕) 🏢 🖵 🍴 ⊋ (✕)

⟨AAA⟩ ▼▼▼ **Heritage Inn** Ⓜ
(814) 735-2200. **$59-$79.** 16550 Lincoln Hwy. I-76, exit 161, just w on US 30; I-70, exit 147, just e on US 30. Int corridors. **Pets:** Other species. $10 daily fee/pet. Designated rooms, service with restrictions, supervision.

(SAVE) (S🔘) (✕) (🖅) 🖵 ⊋

⟨AAA⟩ ▼▼ **Wiltshire Motel** Ⓜ
(814) 735-4361. **$41-$49.** 140 S Breezewood Rd. I-76, exit 161, just w on US 30; I-70, exit 147. Ext corridors. **Pets:** Small, dogs only. No service, supervision.

(SAVE) (✕) 🖵

# BROOKVILLE

⟨AAA⟩ ▼▼ **Budget Host Gold Eagle Inn** Ⓜ
(814) 849-7344. **$50-$80.** 250 W Main St. I-80, exit 78, 0.5 mi s on SR 36. Ext corridors. **Pets:** Service with restrictions, crate.

(SAVE) (✕) 🏢 🖵 🍴

⟨AAA⟩ ▼▼ **Holiday Inn Express** Ⓜ
(814) 849-8381. **$84-$89.** 235 Allegheny Blvd. I-80, exit 78, just s on SR 36. Int corridors. **Pets:** Accepted.

(SAVE) (✕) 🏢 🖵

⟨AAA⟩ ▼▼ **Super 8 Motel** Ⓜ
(814) 849-8840. **$49-$64.** 251 Allegheny Blvd. I-80, exit 78, just n on SR 36. Int corridors. **Pets:** $10 daily fee/pet. Service with restrictions, supervision.

(SAVE) (S🔘) (✕) 🏢

# CAMBRIDGE SPRINGS

▼▼ ▼▼ **The Riverside Inn** 🆑
(814) 398-4645. **$65-$170, 10 day notice.** 1 Fountain Ave. I-79, exit 154 northbound, 2.9 mi e on SR 198, then 8.4 mi n on US 19; exit 166 southbound, 2.4 mi e on US 6 N, then 7 mi s on SR 99. Int corridors. **Pets:** $25 one-time fee/pet. Crate.

(✕) 🏢 🍴 ⊋ (✕) (🅩)

# CARLISLE

▼▼▼ ▼ **Comfort Suites Hotel** 🆂🅷 ❀
(717) 960-1000. **$104-$179, 3 day notice.** 10 S Hanover St. Just s of the square; downtown. Int corridors. **Pets:** Medium. $10 daily fee/pet. Service with restrictions, crate.

(A$K) (S🔘) (✕) (🖅M) (🖅) 🏢 🖵 🍴

⟨AAA⟩ ▼▼▼ **Days Inn & Suites-Carlisle** 🆂🅷
(717) 258-4147. **$74-$150.** 101 Alexander Spring Rd. I-81, exit 45, just sw. Int corridors. **Pets:** $6 daily fee/room, $10 one-time fee/room. Designated rooms, service with restrictions, supervision.

(SAVE) (S🔘) (✕) (🖅M) (🖅) 🏢 🖵 ⊋

⟨AAA⟩ ▼▼ **Econo Lodge** Ⓜ
(717) 249-7775. **$54-$120.** 1460 Harrisburg Pike. I-81, exit 52 southbound; exit 52A northbound; I-76 (Pennsylvania Tpke), exit 226, 0.8 mi n. Ext corridors. **Pets:** Accepted.

(SAVE) (S🔘) (✕) 🏢 🖵

⟨AAA⟩ ▼▼▼ **Hampton Inn Carlisle** 🆂🅷
(717) 240-0200. **$69-$199.** 1164 Harrisburg Pike. I-76 (Pennsylvania Tpke), exit 226, just n; I-81, exit 52 (US 11) southbound; exit 52B northbound, 0.8 mi s. Int corridors. **Pets:** Medium. Service with restrictions, crate.

(SAVE) (✕) (🖅M) (🖅) 🏢 🖵 ⊋

⟨AAA⟩ ▼▼▼ **Holiday Inn Carlisle** 🆂🅷
(717) 245-2400. **$90-$158.** 1450 Harrisburg Pike. I-81, exit 52 southbound; exit 52A northbound, just se; I-76 (Pennsylvania Tpke), exit 226, 0.8 mi n. Int corridors. **Pets:** Medium, other species. $10 daily fee/room. Service with restrictions, supervision.

(SAVE) (S🔘) (✕) 🏢 🖵 🍴

⟨AAA⟩ ▼▼▼ **Hotel Carlisle** 🆂🅷
(717) 243-1717. **$99-$114.** 1700 Harrisburg Pike. I-81, exit 52 southbound; exit 52A northbound, 0.4 mi n; I-76 (Pennsylvania Tpke), exit 226, 1.2 mi n. Int corridors. **Pets:** Medium. $10 daily fee/pet. Designated rooms, service with restrictions, supervision.

(SAVE) (S🔘) (✕) 🏢 🖵 🍴 ⊋ (✕)

⟨AAA⟩ ▼▼▼ **Howard Johnson Inn** 🆂🅷
(717) 243-5411. **$37-$145, 3 day notice.** 1245 Harrisburg Pike. I-81, exit 52 (US 11) southbound; exit 52B northbound, 0.5 mi n; I-76 (Pennsylvania Tpke), exit 226, 0.8 mi n on US 11. Ext/int corridors. **Pets:** $10 daily fee/pet. Designated rooms, service with restrictions.

(SAVE) (S🔘) (✕) (🖅M) 🏢 🖵 🍴 ⊋

⟨AAA⟩ ▼▼▼▼ **Pheasant Field Bed & Breakfast** 🅱🅱 ❀
(717) 258-0717. **$100-$175, 3 day notice.** 150 Hickorytown Rd. I-76 (Pennsylvania Tpke), exit 226, 0.4 mi n on US 11, 2.3 mi se on S Middlesex Rd, 0.4 mi e on Ridge Dr, then just s (right turn). Ext/int corridors. **Pets:** Other species. $10 daily fee/room. Designated rooms, service with restrictions, supervision.

(SAVE) (✕) 🏢

⟨AAA⟩ ▼▼▼ **Quality Inn Carlisle** 🆂🅷
(717) 243-6000. **$69-$89.** 1255 Harrisburg Pike. I-81, exit 52 southbound; exit 52B northbound; I-76 (Pennsylvania Tpke), exit 226, 0.8 mi n. Int corridors. **Pets:** Small. $10 daily fee/room. Supervision.

(SAVE) (S🔘) (✕) (🖅) 🏢 🖵 ⊋

⟨AAA⟩ ▼▼▼ **Ramada Ltd** 🆂🅷
(717) 243-8585. **$70-$180.** 1252 Harrisburg Pike. I-81, exit 52 (US 11) southbound; exit 52B northbound; I-76 (Pennsylvania Tpke), exit 226, 1 mi n on US 11. Ext/int corridors. **Pets:** Other species. $10 daily fee/pet. Designated rooms, service with restrictions, crate.

(SAVE) (S🔘) (✕) (🖅) 🏢 🖵

⟨AAA⟩ ▼▼ **Rodeway Inn** Ⓜ
(717) 249-2800. **$45-$125, 3 day notice.** 1239 Harrisburg Pike. I-81, exit 52 (US 11) southbound; exit 52B northbound, 0.3 mi s; I-76 (Pennsylvania Tpke), exit 226, 0.8 mi s. Ext corridors. **Pets:** Other species. $8 daily fee/room. Service with restrictions, supervision.

(SAVE) (S🔘) (✕) 🏢 🖵 ⊋

⟨AAA⟩ ▼▼▼ **Sleep Inn Carlisle** 🆂🅷
(717) 249-8863. **$55-$155.** 5 E Garland Dr. I-81, exit 47 northbound, just ne; exit 47A southbound. Int corridors. **Pets:** Accepted.

(SAVE) (S🔘) (✕) (🖅M) (🖅) 🏢 🖵 ⊋

⟨AAA⟩ ▼▼ **Super 8 Motel/Carlisle South** Ⓜ
(717) 245-9898. **$50-$110.** 100 Alexander Spring Rd. I-81, exit 45, just se. Int corridors. **Pets:** Medium, other species. $8 daily fee/pet. Designated rooms, service with restrictions, supervision.

(SAVE) (S🔘) (✕) (🖅M) 🏢

⟨AAA⟩ ▼▼ **Super 8 Motel/North Carlisle** Ⓜ
(717) 249-7000. **$38-$135, 3 day notice.** 1800 Harrisburg Pike. I-81, exit 52A northbound; exit 52 (US 11) southbound, 0.5 mi n; I-76 (Pennsylvania Tpke), exit 226, 1.3 mi n. Ext/int corridors. **Pets:** Medium. $10 deposit/pet. Service with restrictions, supervision.

(SAVE) (S🔘) (✕) (🖅M) 🏢 ⊋

# CHAMBERSBURG

**Best Western Chambersburg** SH
(717) 262-4994. **$59-$169.** 211 Walker Rd. I-81, exit 16, just w on US 30, then just n. Int corridors. **Pets:** Accepted.

**Chambersburg Travelodge** M
(717) 264-4187. **$45-$99.** 565 Lincoln Way E. I-81, exit 16, 0.8 mi w on US 30. Ext corridors. **Pets:** Accepted.

**Comfort Inn-Chambersburg** SH
(717) 263-6655. **$69-$99.** 3301 Black Gap Rd. I-81, exit 20, just e, then just s on SR 997. Int corridors. **Pets:** Small. Designated rooms, no service, crate.

**Days Inn** SH
(717) 263-1288. **$60-$109.** 30 Falling Spring Rd. I-81, exit 16, just e on US 30. Int corridors. **Pets:** Medium, other species. $10 daily fee/pet. Designated rooms, service with restrictions, supervision.

**Econo Lodge** M
(717) 264-8005. **$57-$71.** 1110 Sheller Ave. I-81, exit 14, just w on SR 316. Int corridors. **Pets:** Other species. $10 one-time fee/pet. Service with restrictions, supervision.

**Red Carpet Inn** M
(717) 267-2323. **Call for rates.** 1175 Wayne Ave. I-81, exit 14, just e on SR 316. Ext corridors. **Pets:** Accepted.

# CLARION

**Holiday Inn** SH
(814) 226-8850. **$79-$139.** 45 Holiday Inn Rd. I-80, exit 62, 0.5 mi n on SR 68. Int corridors. **Pets:** Other species. $10 daily fee/room. Service with restrictions, supervision.

**Microtel Inn & Suites-Clarion** SH
(814) 227-2700. **$54-$74.** 151 Hotel Dr. I-80, exit 62, just n on SR 68, then just e. Int corridors. **Pets:** Small. $10 daily fee/pet. Designated rooms, service with restrictions, supervision.

**Quality Inn & Suites Clarion** M
(814) 226-8682. **$75-$90.** 24 United Dr. I-80, exit 62, just n on SR 68. Int corridors. **Pets:** Other species. $5 daily fee/pet. Designated rooms, service with restrictions, supervision.

**Super 8 Motel-Clarion** M
(814) 226-4550. **$50-$85.** 135 Hotel Rd. I-80, exit 62, just n on SR 68. Ext corridors. **Pets:** Other species. $10 one-time fee/pet. Designated rooms, service with restrictions, supervision.

# CLARKS SUMMIT

**Comfort Inn-Clarks Summit/Scranton** SH
(570) 586-9100. **$59-$159.** 811 Northern Blvd. I-81, exit 194 on US 6 and 11; I-476 (Pennsylvania Tpke), exit 131. Int corridors. **Pets:** Accepted.

**The Inn at Nichols Village** SH
(570) 587-1135. **$89-$220.** 1101 Northern Blvd. I-81, exit 194, just w; I-476 (Pennsylvania Tpke), exit 131, 0.5 mi w on US 6 and 11. Int corridors. **Pets:** Dogs only. $25 daily fee/room. Designated rooms, service with restrictions, crate.

**Ramada Plaza Hotel** SH
(570) 586-2730. **$89-$169.** 820 Northern Blvd. I-81, exit 194; I-476 (Pennsylvania Tpke), exit 131, 0.3 mi w on US 6 and 11. Int corridors. **Pets:** Medium. $20 daily fee/pet. Designated rooms, service with restrictions.

# CLEARFIELD

**Budget Inn** M
(814) 765-2639. **$38-$66.** 6321 Woodland Hwy (Rt 322 E). I-80, exit 120, 1.5 mi sw on SR 879, then 1.2 mi e. Ext/int corridors. **Pets:** $6 daily fee/pet. No service, supervision.

**Comfort Inn Clearfield** SH
(814) 768-6400. **$65-$89.** 1821 Industrial Park Rd. I-80, exit 120, just s. Int corridors. **Pets:** Other species. $15 daily fee/room. Service with restrictions, supervision.

**Super 8 Motel-Clearfield** M
(814) 768-7580. **$48-$81.** 14597 Clearfield/Shawville Hwy (Rt 879). I-80, exit 120, just s. Int corridors. **Pets:** Accepted.

# COOPERSBURG

**Econo Lodge** M
(610) 282-1212. **$59-$99.** 321 Rt 309 S. On SR 309; center. Ext corridors. **Pets:** Small. $10 daily fee/pet. Service with restrictions.

# DANVILLE

**Quality Inn & Suites Danville** M
(570) 275-5100. **$69-$179, 3 day notice.** 15 Valley West Rd. I-80, exit 224, just n on SR 54. Int corridors. **Pets:** Medium. $25 one-time fee/room. Designated rooms, service with restrictions, supervision.

# DICKSON CITY

**Days Inn Scranton** SH
(570) 383-9979. **$60-$110.** 1946 Scranton-Carbondale Hwy. I-81, exit 191A, 2 mi e on US 6; I-476 (Pennsylvania Tpke Northeast Extension), exit 131 (Clarks Summit), 4.5 mi e on US 6. Int corridors. **Pets:** Other species. $20 one-time fee/room. Service with restrictions.

**Residence Inn by Marriott-Scranton** SH
(570) 343-5121. **$80-$190, 14 day notice.** 947 Viewmont Dr. I-81, exit 190, just e, follow signs to Viewmont Dr. Int corridors. **Pets:** Accepted.

# DOUGLASSVILLE

**Econo Lodge** M
(610) 385-3016. **$79-$89.** 387 Ben Franklin Hwy (Rt 422) W. From Pottstown, 6 mi w on US 422; from Reading, 8 mi e on US 422. Ext corridors. **Pets:** $12 daily fee/pet. Service with restrictions, crate.

# DU BOIS

**Holiday Inn DuBois** SH
(814) 371-5100. **$75-$92.** 1896 Rich Hwy. I-80, exit 97, just s. Int corridors. **Pets:** Other species. Designated rooms, service with restrictions, supervision.

# DUNMORE

**(AAA) ▼▼▼ Days Inn** SH
(570) 348-6101. **$5C-$225.** 1226 O'Neill Hwy. I-81, exit 188, just n at SR 347. Int corridors. **Pets:** $5 daily fee/pet. Service with restrictions, supervision.

SAVE ⬛ ✕ 🔲 ⬛

**▼▼▼▼ Holiday Inn-Scranton East** SH
(570) 343-4771. **$69-$189.** 200 Tigue St. I-84/380, exit 1 (Tigue St), 0.3 mi e of jct I-81. Ext/int corridors. **Pets:** Medium, other species. $10 one-time fee/pet. Designated rooms, service with restrictions, crate.

ASK ⬛ ✕ 🔲 ⬛ ⬛ ⬛ 🍽 ⬛ ✕

**(AAA) ▼▼▼▼ Sleep Inn, Inn & Suites** SH
(570) 961-1116. **$72-$112.** 102 Monahan Ave. I-81, exit 188 (Throop), just e at SR 347 N (O'Neill Hwy), then just s. Int corridors. **Pets:** Medium. $10 daily fee/pet. Designated rooms, service with restrictions, supervision.

SAVE ⬛ ✕ ⬛ 🔲 ⬛ ⬛ ⬛

# EASTON

**▼▼ Comfort Inn** SH
(610) 253-0546. **$70-$150.** 2555 Nazareth Rd. US 22, exit 25th St, just e on N Service Rd. nt corridors. **Pets:** Accepted.

ASK ⬛ ✕ 🔲 ⬛

**▼▼▼▼ Easton Inn** SH
(610) 253-9131. **$69-$129.** 185 S 3rd St. I-78, exit 75, 1 mi n, follow signs; US 22, exit 4th St (SR 611), just e to 3rd St, then 0.5 mi s; downtown. Int corridors. **Pets:** Small. $25 one-time fee/room. Service with restrictions, supervision.

ASK ⬛ ✕ ⬛ ⬛ 🍽 ⬛

**▼▼▼▼ The Lafayette Inn** BB ❀
(610) 253-4500. **$110-$225.** 525 W Monroe St. US 22, exit 4th St (SR 611), just n on 3rd St, 0.3 mi ne on College Ave, then 0.3 mi n on Cattell St to jct Monroe St. Ext/int corridors. **Pets:** $20 daily fee/pet. Designated rooms, service with restrictions, supervision.

✕ ⬛ ⬛

# EBENSBURG

**▼▼▼▼ Comfort Inn** SH
(814) 472-6100. **$80-$135.** 111 Cook Rd. Jct US 219, just e on US 22. Int corridors. **Pets:** $25 deposit/pet, $8 daily fee/pet. Designated rooms, supervision.

ASK ⬛ ✕ ⬛ ⬛ ⬛ ⬛ 🌊

# ERIE

**(AAA) ▼▼▼▼ Best Western Erie Inn & Suites** SH
(814) 864-1812. **$52-$129.** 7820 Perry Hwy. I-90, exit 27, just n on SR 97. Int corridors. **Pets:** Medium. $10 daily fee/pet. Designated rooms, service with restrictions, supervision.

SAVE ⬛ ✕ ⬛ ⬛ ⬛ 🌊

**(AAA) ▼▼▼▼ Best Western Presque Isle Country Inn** SH
(814) 838-7647. **$46-$100.** 6467 Sterrettania Rd. I-90, exit 18, just s on SR 832. Int corridors. **Pets:** Accepted.

SAVE ⬛ ✕ ⬛ ⬛ ⬛ 🍽 🌊

**(AAA) ▼▼▼▼ Country Inn & Suites** SH
(814) 864-5810. **$54-$129.** 8040 Oliver Rd. I-90, exit 24, just s, then 0.5 mi w. Int corridors. **Pets:** Medium. $25 daily fee/pet. Designated rooms, service with restrictions, supervision.

SAVE ⬛ ✕ ⬛ ⬛ ⬛ ⬛

**▼▼ Days Inn** SH
(814) 868-8521. **$59-$129, 30 day notice.** 7415 Schultz Rd. I-90, exit 27, just n on SR 97. Int corridors. **Pets:** Other species. $5 daily fee/pet. Service with restrictions, crate.

ASK ⬛ ✕ ⬛ ⬛ 🌊

**▼▼▼▼ Hampton Inn Erie South** SH
(814) 866-6800. **$94-$159, 3 day notice.** 8050 Old Oliver Rd. I-90, exit 24, just s, then 0.5 mi w. Int corridors. **Pets:** Medium. $25 one-time fee/pet. Designated rooms, service with restrictions, supervision.

ASK ⬛ ✕ ⬛ ⬛ ⬛ ⬛ 🌊

**▼▼▼▼ Homewood Suites by Hilton** SH
(814) 866-8292. **$119-$209, 14 day notice.** 2084 Interchange Rd. I-79, exit 180, just e. Int corridors. **Pets:** Accepted.

ASK ⬛ ✕ ⬛ ⬛ 🌊

**▼▼ Microtel Inn-Erie** M
(814) 864-1010. **$52-$90.** 8100 Peach St. I-90, exit 24, just s. Int corridors. **Pets:** $10 daily fee/pet. Service with restrictions, supervision.

ASK ⬛ ✕ 🔲 ⬛ ⬛

**▼▼ Motel 6 #4020** M
(814) 864-4811. **$50-$100.** 7875 Peach St. I-90, exit 24, just n. Int corridors. **Pets:** Accepted.

✕ ⬛ 🌊

**▼▼ Red Roof Inn #7054** M
(814) 868-5246. **$46-$81.** 7865 Perry Hwy. I-90, exit 27, just n on SR 97. Ext/int corridors. **Pets:** Accepted.

✕ ⬛ ⬛

**▼▼ Residence Inn by Marriott** SH
(814) 864-2500. **$109-$299.** 8061 Peach St. I-90, exit 24, just s. Int corridors. **Pets:** Accepted.

ASK ⬛ ✕ 🔲 ⬛ ⬛ ⬛ 🌊 ✕

**▼▼ Super 8 Motel** SH
(814) 864-9200. **$50-$100.** 8040 Perry Hwy. I-90, exit 27, just s. Int corridors. **Pets:** Small. $5 daily fee/pet. Designated rooms, service with restrictions, supervision.

ASK ⬛ ✕ ⬛

# FAYETTEVILLE

**(AAA) ▼ Rite Spot Scottish Inn** M
(717) 352-2144. **$36-$71.** 5651 Lincoln Way E. On US 30, 1 mi w of jct SR 997. Ext corridors. **Pets:** Medium, other species. $7 daily fee/pet. Service with restrictions, supervision.

SAVE ⬛ ✕ ⬛ ⬛

# FOGELSVILLE

**▼▼▼▼ Comfort Inn Lehigh Valley-West** SH ❀
(610) 391-0344. **$80-$120.** 7625 Imperial Way. I-78, exit 49B (SR 100), just n. Int corridors. **Pets:** Medium, other species. $25 one-time fee/pet. Designated rooms, service with restrictions, crate.

ASK ⬛ ✕ 🔲 ⬛ ⬛

**▼▼▼▼ Glasbern** CI ❀
(610) 285-4723. **$160-$410, 7 day notice.** 2141 Packhouse Rd. I-78, exit 49B (SR 100), 0.3 mi n to 1st light, 0.3 mi w on Main St, 0.6 mi n on Church St, then 0.8 mi ne. Ext/int corridors. **Pets:** $25 daily fee/room. Designated rooms, service with restrictions, supervision.

ASK ⬛ ✕ ⬛ ⬛ ⬛ 🍽 🌊 ✕

**▼▼▼▼ Holiday Inn Conference Center** SH 🐾
(610) 391-1000. **$89-$169.** 7736 Adrienne Dr. I-78, exit 49A, 0.3 mi s on SR 100. Int corridors. **Pets:** $15 daily fee/room. Designated rooms, service with restrictions, crate.

ASK ⬛ ✕ ⬛ 🔲 ⬛ ⬛ ⬛ 🍽 🌊 ✕

**▼▼ Sleep Inn** SH
(610) 395-6603. **$59-$99.** 327 Star Rd. I-78, exit 49A, 0.3 mi s on SR 100, left at 1st traffic light, then immediate left on service road. Int corridors. **Pets:** Medium. $15 one-time fee/pet. Designated rooms, no service, supervision.

ASK ⬛ ✕ ⬛ 🔲 ⬛ ⬛ ⬛

# FRACKVILLE

### Econo Lodge M
(570) 874-3838. **$54-$109.** 501 S Middle St. I-81, exit 124B, 0.4 mi n on SR 61. Ext corridors. **Pets:** Accepted.

### Granny's Motel & Restaurant
(570) 874-0408. **$45-$52.** 115 W Coal St. I-81, exit 124B, 0.3 mi nw on SR 61, then 0.3 mi n on Altamont Blvd. Ext/int corridors. **Pets:** $5 one-time fee/room. Service with restrictions.

# FRANKLIN

### Franklin Super 8 Motel
(814) 432-2101. **$65.** 847 Allegheny Ave. 2 mi on SR 8. Int corridors. **Pets:** Accepted.

# GALETON

### Pine Log Motel M
(814) 435-6400. **$50-$65, 7 day notice.** 5156 US Rt 6 W. On US 6, 9 mi w. Ext corridors. **Pets:** Accepted.

# GETTYSBURG

### Americas Best Inn M
(717) 334-1188. **$50-$160.** 301 Steinwehr Ave. 1 mi s on US 15 business route, just s of jct SR 134. Ext/int corridors. **Pets:** Medium. $10 daily fee/pet. Designated rooms, service with restrictions, supervision.

### Gettysburg Travelodge M
(717) 334-1800. **$59-$165.** 613 Baltimore St. On SR 97 at US 15 business route. Ext/int corridors. **Pets:** Other species. Service with restrictions, supervision.

### Holiday Inn-Battlefield
(717) 334-6211. **$72-$196.** 516 Baltimore St. Jct US 15 business route and SR 97. Ext/int corridors. **Pets:** Other species. $10 one-time fee/room. Designated rooms, service with restrictions, supervision.

### Holiday Inn Express of Gettysburg M
(717) 337-1400. **$59-$117.** 869 York Rd. 1 mi e on US 30. Int corridors. **Pets:** Small. Designated rooms, no service, crate.

### Red Carpet Inn-Perfect Rest Motel M
(717) 334-1345. **$50-$139.** 2450 Emmitsburg Rd. 4.5 mi s on US 15 business route. Ext corridors. **Pets:** Medium, dogs only. $5 daily fee/pet. Designated rooms, service with restrictions, supervision.

# GIRARD

### The Green Roof Inn M
(814) 774-7072. **$55-$100.** 8790 Rt 18. I-90, exit 9, 1.9 mi s. Ext corridors. **Pets:** Other species. $10 daily fee/pet. Service with restrictions, supervision.

# GRANTVILLE

### Econo Lodge M
(717) 469-0631. **$45-$90.** 252 Bow Creek Rd. I-81, exit 80. Ext corridors. **Pets:** $6 daily fee/pet. Designated rooms, service with restrictions, supervision.

### Holiday Inn Harrisburg-Hershey Area, I-81
(717) 469-0661. **$99-$199.** 604 Station Rd. I-81, exit 80. Int corridors. **Pets:** Other species. $75 deposit/room. Service with restrictions, supervision.

# GREENCASTLE

### Comfort Inn
(717) 597-8164. **$70-$100.** 50 Pine Dr. I-81, exit 3, just s on US 11. Int corridors. **Pets:** Accepted.

# GROVE CITY

### Old Arbor Rose Bed & Breakfast
(724) 458-6425. **$75-$85, 4 day notice.** 114 W Main St. Just e. Int corridors. **Pets:** Accepted.

# HAMBURG

### Microtel Inn & Suites
(610) 562-4234. **$80-$125.** 50 Industrial Dr. I-78, exit 29B, 0.3 mi n on SR 61, then just e. Int corridors. **Pets:** Large, other species. $10 daily fee/pet. Service with restrictions, supervision.

# HANOVER

### Howard Johnson Inn M
(717) 646-1000. **$39-$119.** 1080 Carlisle St. 1.5 mi n on SR 94, just e. Ext corridors. **Pets:** Accepted.

# HARRISBURG

### Baymont Inn & Suites Harrisburg-Airport
(717) 939-8000. **$75-$135.** 990 Eisenhower Blvd. I-283, exit 2, just se; I-76 (Pennsylvania Tpke), exit 247, 1 mi n. Int corridors. **Pets:** Medium. Service with restrictions.

### Best Western Capital Plaza
(717) 545-9089. **$80-$85.** 150 Nationwide Dr. I-81, exit 69, just n. Ext/int corridors. **Pets:** Service with restrictions, supervision.

### Best Western Harrisburg/Hershey Hotel & Suites
(717) 652-7180. **$90-$165.** 300 N Mountain Rd. I-81, exit 72 southbound; exit 72B northbound. Int corridors. **Pets:** $10 daily fee/pet. Designated rooms, service with restrictions, supervision.

### Comfort Inn Harrisburg East
(717) 561-8100. **$89-$129, 3 day notice.** 4021 Union Deposit Rd. I-83, exit 48, just w. Int corridors. **Pets:** Medium, other species. $10 daily fee/pet. Service with restrictions, crate.

### Comfort Inn Harrisburg/Hershey
(717) 540-8400. **$69-$159.** 7744 Linglestown Rd. I-81, exit 77, 0.5 mi w. Int corridors. **Pets:** Other species. $10 daily fee/room. Designated rooms, service with restrictions.

### Comfort Inn-Riverfront
(717) 233-1611. **$89-$169.** 525 S Front St. I-83, exit 43, 0.5 mi n. Ext/int corridors. **Pets:** Accepted.

▼▼▼ Country Hearth Inn & Suites 🆂🅷
(717) 545-6944. **$69-$119.** 7965 Jonestown Rd. I-81, exit 77, just s. Int corridors. **Pets:** Accepted.
🆂❌🅱🏊

🅰🅰🅰 ▼▼▼▼ Crowne Plaza Harrisburg-Hershey 🅻🅷
(717) 234-5021. **$119-$210.** 23 S 2nd St. Jct Chestnut St; downtown. Int corridors. **Pets:** Accepted.
SAVE 🆂❌🅼🖍🅱🖥🍽🏊

▼▼ Greenlawn Motel Ⓜ
(717) 652-1530. **$69-$79, 3 day notice.** 7490 Allentown Blvd. W of jct SR 39 and US 22. Ext corridors. **Pets:** Accepted.
ASK ❌🅱

🅰🅰🅰 ▼▼▼▼ Holiday Inn Express Hotel & Suites 🆂🅷
(717) 657-2200. **$59-$199.** 5680 Allentown Blvd. I-81, exit 72, just s on N Mountain Rd, then just w on US 22. Int corridors. **Pets:** Medium. $10 one-time fee/room. Service with restrictions, supervision.
SAVE 🆂❌🅼🖍🅱🖥🏊

🅰🅰🅰 ▼▼▼▼ Holiday Inn Harrisburg East-Airport 🆂🅷
(717) 939-7841. **$113.** 4751 Lindle Rd. I-283, exit 2, just e. Int corridors. **Pets:** Medium, other species. $75 deposit/pet. No service, supervision.
SAVE 🆂❌🖍🅱🖥🍽🏊🐾

🅰🅰🅰 ▼▼▼ Howard Johnson Inn 🆂🅷 🐾
(717) 540-9100. **$49-$129.** 7930 Linglestown Rd. I-81, exit 77. Int corridors. **Pets:** Medium, other species. $10 one-time fee/room. Service with restrictions, crate.
SAVE 🆂❌🖍🅱🖥

🅰🅰🅰 ▼▼▼ Quality Inn 🆂🅷
(717) 540-9339. **$60-$160.** 200 N Mountain Rd. I-81, exit 72A northbound; exit 72 southbound. Int corridors. **Pets:** Service with restrictions, supervision.
SAVE 🆂❌🖍🅱🖥

▼▼▼ Red Roof Inn-North #7037 Ⓜ
(717) 657-1445. **$48-$79.** 400 Corporate Cir. I-81, exit 69, just n on Progress Ave. Ext/int corridors. **Pets:** Accepted.
❌🖍🖍🅱

▼▼▼ Red Roof Inn-South #7027 Ⓜ
(717) 939-1331. **$51-$86.** 950 Eisenhower Blvd. I-283, exit 2, just e. Ext/int corridors. **Pets:** Accepted.
❌🖍🖍🅱

▼▼▼ Residence Inn by Marriott Harrisburg-Hershey 🆂🅷
(717) 561-1900. **$179-$249.** 4480 Lewis Rd. US 322, exit Penhar Dr, just e. Ext corridors. **Pets:** $75 one-time fee/room. Service with restrictions, crate.
ASK 🆂❌🖍🅱🖥🏊🐾

🅰🅰🅰 ▼▼ Super 8 Motel-North Ⓜ
(717) 233-5891. **$65-$139.** 4125 N Front St. I-81, exit 66, 0.8 mi n. Ext corridors. **Pets:** Accepted.
SAVE 🆂❌🅱🍽🏊

🅰🅰🅰 ▼▼▼▼ Wyndham Harrisburg-Hershey 🅻🅷
(717) 564-5511. **$109-$119.** 4650 Lindle Rd. I-283, exit 2, just e. Int corridors. **Pets:** Accepted.
SAVE ❌🅼🖍🖍🅱🖥🍽🏊🐾

# HAZLETON

🅰🅰🅰 ▼▼▼ Best Western Genetti Lodge 🆂🅷
(570) 454-2494. **$79-$199.** 32nd & N Church St. I-80, exit 262, 6 mi s on SR 309. Ext/int corridors. **Pets:** Large. $10 daily fee/room. Service with restrictions, supervision.
SAVE 🆂❌🖍🅱🖥🏊

🅰🅰🅰 ▼▼ Hazleton Motor Inn Ⓜ
(570) 459-1451. **$35-$50.** 615 E Broad St. I-81, exit 143, 2 mi n on SR 924, then 1 mi s on SR 93. Int corridors. **Pets:** Other species. $5 daily fee/pet. Service with restrictions, supervision.
SAVE 🆂❌🅱

# HERSHEY

🅰🅰🅰 ▼▼▼▼ Best Western Inn-Hershey 🆂🅷
(717) 533-5665. **$89-$209.** US 422 & Sipe Ave. Jct US 322, just e. Ext/int corridors. **Pets:** Medium. $25 one-time fee/room. Designated rooms, service with restrictions, supervision.
SAVE 🆂❌🖍🅱🖥🏊

▼▼▼▼ Days Inn Hershey 🆂🅷 🐾
(717) 534-2162. **$99-$249.** 350 W Chocolate Ave. On US 422; center. Int corridors. **Pets:** Medium. $15 one-time fee/pet. Service with restrictions, supervision.
ASK 🆂❌🅼🖍🅱🖥🏊🐾

# HUMMELSTOWN

▼▼ Hershey Econo Lodge Ⓜ
(717) 533-2515. **$65-$155.** 115 Lucy Ave. Jct US 322, just e on US 422. Ext corridors. **Pets:** Medium, other species. $10 daily fee/pet. Designated rooms, service with restrictions.
ASK 🆂❌🖍🅱🖥

🅰🅰🅰 ▼▼▼▼ Holiday Inn Express 🆂🅷
(717) 583-0500. **$89-$219.** Just nw of jct US 322, 422 and SR 39 (Hershey Park Dr); just off Hershey Park Dr. Int corridors. **Pets:** Small, other species. $10 daily fee/pet. Designated rooms, service with restrictions, crate.
SAVE 🆂❌🖍🅱🖥🏊🐾

# HUNTINGDON

▼▼▼ Huntingdon Motor Inn Ⓜ
(814) 643-1133. **$50-$75.** Motor Inn Rd. On US 22 at SR 26. Ext corridors. **Pets:** Accepted.
❌🖍🅱🖥

# INDIANA

🅰🅰🅰 ▼▼▼▼ Best Western University Inn 🆂🅷
(724) 349-9620. **$69-$104.** 1545 Wayne Ave. US 422, exit Wayne Ave, 0.6 mi n. Int corridors. **Pets:** $5 daily fee/pet. Service with restrictions, supervision.
SAVE 🆂❌🅱🖥🏊

▼▼▼▼ Holiday Inn Holidome 🆂🅷
(724) 463-3561. **$119-$139.** 1395 Wayne Ave. US 422, exit Wayne Ave, 1 mi n. Ext/int corridors. **Pets:** Large, other species. $10 daily fee/pet. Service with restrictions, supervision.
ASK 🆂❌🖍🅱🖥🍽🏊🐾

# JOHNSTOWN

▼▼▼ Comfort Inn & Suites 🆂🅷
(814) 266-3678. **$85-$150.** 455 Theatre Dr. US 219, exit Elton (SR 756), just e. Int corridors. **Pets:** $15 daily fee/room. Designated rooms, service with restrictions, supervision.
ASK 🆂❌🅼🖍🅱🖥🏊

▼▼▼ Econo Lodge Ⓜ
(814) 536-1114. **$50-$149.** 430 Napoleon Pl. Jct SR 271 and 403; downtown. Int corridors. **Pets:** Large, other species. $10 deposit/room, $10 daily fee/room. Designated rooms, service with restrictions, supervision.
ASK 🆂❌🖍🖍🅱🖥

▼▼▼ Holiday Inn Downtown 🆂🅷
(814) 535-7777. **$99-$169.** 250 Market St. Corner of Market and Vine sts; downtown. Int corridors. **Pets:** Service with restrictions, supervision.
ASK 🆂❌🖍🅱🖥🍽🏊🐾

**▼▼ Holiday Inn Express Johnstown M**
(814) 266-8789. **$79-$89.** 1440 Scalp Ave. US 219, exit Windber (SR 56 E), just e. Int corridors. **Pets:** Accepted.
(ASK) (S♂) (X) (&M) (🗋) (&) (🖬) (💻)

**▼▼ Sleep Inn SH**
(814) 262-9292. **$65-$95.** 453 Theatre Dr. US 219, exit Elton (SR 756), just e. Int corridors. **Pets:** $15 daily fee/pet. Designated rooms, service with restrictions, supervision.
(ASK) (S♂) (X) (&M) (🗋) (&) (🖬) (💻)

**▲▲▲ ▼▼ Super 8 Motel Johnstown SH**
(814) 535-5600. **$52-$80, 3 day notice.** 627 Solomon Run Rd. US 219, exit Galleria Dr, just w. Int corridors. **Pets:** Other species. $7 daily fee/pet. Service with restrictions, supervision.
(SAVE) (S♂) (X) (&) (🖬)

# JONESTOWN

**▲▲▲ ▼▼ Days Inn Lebanon/Lickdale SH 🐾**
(717) 865-4064. **$99-$125, 3 day notice.** 3 Everest Ln. I-81, exit 90. Int corridors. **Pets:** Medium, other species. $10 one-time fee/room. Service with restrictions.
(SAVE) (S♂) (X) (&) (🖬) (💻)

**▼▼ Red Carpet Inn & Suites-Jonestown SH**
(717) 865-6600. **$48-$99.** 16 Marsenna Ln. I-81, exit 90, just w. Int corridors. **Pets:** Accepted.
(ASK) (S♂) (X) (🖬) (💻)

# KITTANNING

**▼▼▼ Comfort Inn SH**
(724) 543-5200. **$78.** 13 Hilltop Plaza. SR 28, exit 19A. Int corridors. **Pets:** Small. $15 one-time fee/pet. No service, supervision.
(ASK) (S♂) (X) (&) (🖬) (💻) (💦)

**▲▲▲ ▼▼▼▼ Quality Inn Royle SH**
(724) 543-1159. **$59-$95.** 405 Butler Rc. SR 28, exit US 422 W (Belmont). Ext/int corridors. **Pets:** Other species. $5 daily fee/pet. Designated rooms, service with restrictions, supervision.
(SAVE) (S♂) (X) (🗋) (🖬) (💻)

**▼▼ Rodeway Inn Kittanning M**
(724) 543-1100. **$55-$60.** US 422 E. E of jct Business Rt US 422, SR 66 and 28. Ext corridors. **Pets:** Other species. $5 daily fee/pet.
(ASK) (S♂) (X) (🖬) (💻)

# LAMAR

**▲▲▲ ▼▼ Comfort Inn of Lamar SH**
(570) 726-4901. **$85-$195, 14 day notice.** 31 Comfort Inn Ln. I-80, exit 173, just n on SR 64. Int corridors. **Pets:** Large, other species. $10 daily fee/pet. Designated rooms, service with restrictions, supervision.
(SAVE) (S♂) (X) (🖬) (💻) (💦)

---

## LAUREL HIGHLANDS AREA

# CHALK HILL

**▼▼▼▼ Historic Summit Inn LH**
(724) 438-8594. **$89-$276, 3 day notice.** On US 40; center. Int corridors. **Pets:** Medium. $15 daily fee/pet. Designated rooms, service with restrictions, supervision.
(ASK) (S♂) (X) (🖬) (💻) (🍴) (💦) (X)

**▲▲▲ ▼▼ The Lodge at Chalk Hill M**
(724) 438-8880. **$57-$100.** Just w. Ext corridors. **Pets:** Other species. $10 daily fee/pet. Designated rooms, service with restrictions, supervision.
(SAVE) (X) (🖬) (💻) (X)

# GREENSBURG

**▼▼▼ Comfort Inn Greensburg SH 🐾**
(724) 832-2600. **$84-$165.** 1129 E Pittsburgh St. I-76, exit 75, 5.6 mi on US 119 N, 4 mi e on US 30. Int corridors. **Pets:** $10 daily fee/pet. Designated rooms, service with restrictions, supervision.
(ASK) (S♂) (X) (🖬) (💻) (💦)

**▼▼▼ Four Points by Sheraton SH 🐾**
(724) 836-6060. **$129-$169.** 100 Sheraton Dr. I-76 (Pennsylvania Tpke), exit 75, 5.6 mi on US 119 N, 3 mi e on US 30, then just n. Int corridors. **Pets:** Medium. $10 daily fee/pet. Service with restrictions, crate.
(ASK) (S♂) (X) (&) (🖬) (💻) (🍴) (💦) (X)

**▼▼ Knights Inn-Greensburg SH**
(724) 836-7100. **$75.** 1215 S Main St. I-76 (Pennsylvania Tpke), exit 75, 4 mi s on US 119; just s of US 30. Ext corridors. **Pets:** Accepted.
(ASK) (S♂) (X) (🖬) (💻) (💦)

# LIGONIER

**▲▲▲ ▼▼▼▼ Lady of the Lake Bed & Breakfast BB**
(724) 238-6955. **$95-$135, 30 day notice.** 157 Rt 30 E. US 30 E, just w of jct SR 711; beside Idlewild Park. Ext/int corridors. **Pets:** Accepted.
(SAVE) (X) (🖬) (💻) (💦) (X) (🗋)

# NEW STANTON

**▲▲▲ ▼▼ Days Inn New Stanton SH**
(724) 925-3591. **$55-$99, 7 day notice.** 127 W Byers Ave. I-76, exit 75, 0.5 mi sw; I-70, exit 57B westbound; exit 57 eastbound. Int corridors. **Pets:** Medium. $100 deposit/room, $10 daily fee/pet. Service with restrictions, supervision.
(SAVE) (S♂) (X) (🗋) (🖬) (💻) (🍴) (💦)

**▲▲▲ ▼▼ Howard Johnson Inn M**
(724) 925-3511. **$45-$99 (no credit cards).** 112 W Byers Ave. I-76, exit 75, 0.5 mi sw; I-70, exit 57B westbound; exit 57 eastbound. Ext/int corridors. **Pets:** Other species. $7 daily fee/pet. Designated rooms, service with restrictions, supervision.
(SAVE) (S♂) (X) (🖬) (💻) (💦)

**▼▼ Quality Inn New Stanton SH**
(724) 925-6755. **$49-$79.** 110 N Main St/Byers Ave. I-76, exit 75, 0.5 mi se; I-70, exit 57B westbound; exit 57 eastbound, just ne. Int corridors. **Pets:** $10 daily fee/pet. Service with restrictions, supervision.
(ASK) (S♂) (X) (🖬) (💻) (💦)

**▼▼ Super 8 Motel-New Stanton M**
(724) 925-8915. **$52-$72.** 103 Bair Blvd. I-76, exit 75, 0.5 mi se; I-70, 57B westbound; exit 57 eastbound. Int corridors. **Pets:** Medium. $10 daily fee/pet. Designated rooms, service with restrictions, supervision.
(ASK) (S♂) (X) (🖬)

# SOMERSET

**▲▲▲ ▼▼▼▼ Best Western Executive Inn SH**
(814) 445-3996. **$55-$82.** 165 Water Works Rd. I-70/76 (Pennsylvania Tpke), exit 110, just e. Int corridors. **Pets:** Other species. $7 daily fee/pet. Designated rooms, service with restrictions, supervision.
(SAVE) (S♂) (X) (&) (🖬) (💻) (X)

**▼▼ Budget Host Inn M**
(814) 445-7988. **$45-$85, 7 day notice.** 799 N Center Ave. I-70/76 (Pennsylvania Tpke), exit 110, 0.3 mi s. Ext corridors. **Pets:** Small. $7 daily fee/pet. Designated rooms, no service, supervision.
(ASK) (S♂) (X) (🖬)

▼▼ **The Budget Inn** Ⓜ
(814) 443-6441. **$32-$75.** 736 N Center Ave. I-70/76 (Pennsylvania Tpke), exit 110, 0.4 mi s. Ext corridors. **Pets:** Accepted.

(A$K) (S⬦) (✕) (❚)

▼ **Days Inn-Somerset** Ⓜ
(814) 445-9200. **$49-$99 (no credit cards).** 220 Water Works Rd. I-70/76 (Pennsylvania Tpke), exit 110, just e. Ext corridors. **Pets:** Other species. $9 daily fee/pet. Service with restrictions, supervision.

(A$K) (S⬦) (✕) (❚)

(AAA) ▼ **Dollar Inn** Ⓜ
(814) 445-2977. **$37-$85.** 1146 N Center Ave. I-70/76 (Pennsylvania Tpke), exit 110, just e via Water Works Rd, then just n on SR 601, at top of hill. Ext corridors. **Pets:** $7 daily fee/pet. Designated rooms, service with restrictions, crate.

(SAVE) (S⬦) (✕) (❚)

▼▼ **Glades Pike Inn** BB
(814) 443-4978. **$65-$105, 3 day notice.** 2684 Glades Pike. I-70/76 (Pennsylvania Tpke), exit 110, 7.9 mi w on SR 31. Int corridors. **Pets:** $5 daily fee/pet. Service with restrictions, supervision.

(✕)

(AAA) ▼▼ **Holiday Inn** SH
(814) 445-9611. **$79-$104.** 202 Harmon St. I-70/76 (Pennsylvania Tpke), exit 110, just s. Int corridors. **Pets:** Small. $50 deposit/pet. Designated rooms, service with restrictions, supervision.

(SAVE) (S⬦) (✕) (🖉) (▣) (❚▣) (✕)

▼▼▼ **The Inn at Georgian Place** BB
(814) 443-1043. **$95-$185, 10 day notice.** 800 Georgian Place Dr. I-70/76 (Pennsylvania Tpke), exit 110, just e via Water Works Rd, then 0.5 mi n on SR 601. Int corridors. **Pets:** Medium. Service with restrictions, supervision.

(A$K) (S⬦) (✕) (❚▣)

▼ **Knights Inn** Ⓜ
(814) 445-8933. **$60-$65.** 585 Ramada Rd. I-70/76 (Pennsylvania Tpke), exit 110, just s. Ext corridors. **Pets:** Accepted.

(A$K) (S⬦) (✕) (❚) (▣) (≈)

(AAA) ▼▼▼ **Quality Inn Somerset** SH
(814) 443-4646. **$69-$120.** 215 Ramada Rd. I-70/76 (Pennsylvania Tpke), exit 110, just s. Int corridors. **Pets:** Accepted.

(SAVE) (S⬦) (✕) (❚) (▣) (❚▣) (≈) (✕)

▼▼ **Super 8 Motel** Ⓜ
(814) 445-8788. **$41-$107.** 125 Lewis Dr. I-70/76 (Pennsylvania Tpke), exit 110, just s. Int corridors. **Pets:** $10 one-time fee/pet. Service with restrictions, supervision.

(A$K) (S⬦) (✕) (❚) (▣)

# UNIONTOWN

▼▼▼ **Uniontown Holiday Inn** SH
(724) 437-2816. **$90-$139.** 700 W Main St. 1.8 mi w on US 40. Int corridors. **Pets:** Accepted.

(A$K) (S⬦) (✕) (🖉) (▣) (❚) (▣) (❚▣) (≈) (✕)

## END AREA

# LEBANON

▼▼▼ **Berry Patch Bed and Breakfast** BB
(717) 865-7219. **$115-$168, 14 day notice.** 115 Moore Rd. I-81, exit 90, 2.8 mi s on SR 72, 1 mi e on Jonestown Rd, 0.8 mi s on S Lancaster St, then just e. Ext/int corridors. **Pets:** Accepted.

(A$K) (S⬦) (✕)

(AAA) ▼▼▼ **Quality Inn-Lebanon Valley** SH
(717) 273-6771. **$89-$169.** 625 Quentin Rd. 0.5 mi s on SR 72. Ext/int corridors. **Pets:** Medium, other species. $5 daily fee/pet. Designated rooms, service with restrictions, supervision.

(SAVE) (S⬦) (✕) (👦M) (🖉) (🖉) (❚) (▣) (❚▣) (≈) (✕)

# LEWISBURG

(AAA) ▼▼▼ **Days Inn-Lewisburg** SH
(570) 523-1171. **$86-$103.** US Rt 15. 0.5 mi n of jct SR 45. Ext corridors. **Pets:** Other species. Service with restrictions.

(SAVE) (S⬦) (✕) (❚) (▣) (≈)

# LINCOLN FALLS

▼▼ **Morgan Century Farm** BB
(570) 924-4909. **$89-$129, 3 day notice.** Rt 154. In village. Ext/int corridors. **Pets:** Medium. $10 one-time fee/room. Designated rooms, service with restrictions, supervision.

(S⬦) (✕) (❚) (▣) (✏)

# LOCK HAVEN

▼▼ **Best Western-Lock Haven** SH
(570) 748-3297. **$79-$139.** 101 E Walnut St. Just w of jct US 220. Int corridors. **Pets:** Other species. $7 daily fee/pet. Service with restrictions.

(A$K) (S⬦) (✕) (🖉) (❚) (▣)

# MANSFIELD

(AAA) ▼▼▼ **Comfort Inn** SH
(570) 662-3000. **$69-$119.** 300 Gateway Dr. Jct US 6 and 15. Int corridors. **Pets:** Accepted.

(SAVE) (S⬦) (✕) (❚) (▣) (✕)

(AAA) ▼▼ **Mansfield Inn** Ⓜ
(570) 662-2136. **$55-$70, 3 day notice.** 26 S Main St. Jct US 6, just s on Business Rt 15; downtown. Ext corridors. **Pets:** $5 daily fee/pet. No service, supervision.

(SAVE) (S⬦) (✕) (❚) (▣)

(AAA) ▼ **West's Deluxe Motel** Ⓜ
(570) 659-5141. **$60-$80.** 2848 S Main St. SR 17, exit Covington and Canoe Camp, Business Rt 15/0.8 mi s on 660 W (Main St). Ext corridors. **Pets:** Accepted.

(SAVE) (S⬦) (✕) (❚) (▣) (≈)

# MARIENVILLE

▼▼ **Microtel Inn & Suites** SH 🐾
(814) 927-8300. **Call for rates.** 252 Cherry St. Center. Int corridors. **Pets:** Small. $10 daily fee/pet. Designated rooms, service with restrictions, supervision.

(✕) (🖉) (❚) (▣)

# MEADVILLE

▼ **Days Inn Conference Center** SH
(814) 337-4264. **$79-$129.** 18360 Conneaut Lake Rd. I-79, exit 147A, just e on US 322. Int corridors. **Pets:** Other species. $10 daily fee/pet. Service with restrictions, supervision.

(A$K) (S⬦) (✕) (❚) (▣) (❚▣) (≈)

▼▼ **Motel 6 #4019** Ⓜ
(814) 724-6366. **$60-$90.** 11237 Shaw Ave. I-79, exit 147A, just e on US 322. Int corridors. **Pets:** Accepted.

(A$K) (S⬦) (✕) (🖉)

▼▼ **Quality Inn** Ⓜ 🐾
(814) 333-8883. **$55-$137.** 17259 Conneaut Lake Rd. I-79, exit 147B, just w on US 322. Ext/int corridors. **Pets:** Other species. $10 one-time fee/pet. Designated rooms, service with restrictions, supervision.

(A$K) (S⬦) (✕) (❚) (▣)

# MECHANICSBURG

**AAA** **WWW** Comfort Inn Capital City **SH**
(717) 766-3700. **$80-$170.** 1012 Wesley Dr. I-76 (Pennsylvania Tpke), exit 236 (US 15), 1 mi n to Wesley Dr exit, then just w. Int corridors. **Pets:** Small, other species. $25 daily fee/pet. Service with restrictions, crate.
SAVE S X M 🔲 🖥 🎥

**WWW** Hampton Inn-Harrisburg West **SH**
(717) 691-1300. **$122-$142, 14 day notice.** 4950 Ritter Rd. I-76 (Pennsylvania Tpke), exit 236 (US 15), 1 mi n to Rossmoyne Rd exit. Int corridors. **Pets:** Other species. Designated rooms, service with restrictions, supervision.
ASK S X M 🔲 🖥 🎥 🚫

**WWW** Holiday Inn Harrisburg-West **SH**
(717) 697-0321. **$94-$134.** 5401 Carlisle Pike. Jct Carlisle Pike and US 11, just w. Ext corridors. **Pets:** Accepted.
ASK S X 🔲 🖥 🍴 🎥 🚫

# MERCER

**WWW** Colonial Inn Motel **M**
(324) 662-5600. **$35-$50.** 383 N Perry Hwy (US 19). I-80, exit 15, 3 mi n; I-79, exit 121, 4 mi w on SR 62 S, then 0.5 mi n on US 19. Ext corridors. **Pets:** Other species. $5 daily fee/pet. Service with restrictions, supervision.
ASK S X 🔲 🖥

**WWW** Howard Johnson Inn **SH**
(724) 748-3030. **$76-$79.** 835 Perry Hwy. I-80, exit 15, just n on US 19. Int corridors. **Pets:** Accepted.
ASK S X 🎥 🔲 🖥 🍴 🎥 🚫

# MIDDLETOWN

**WWW** Days Inn-Harrisburg Airport **SH**
(717) 939-4147. **$59-$109.** 800 S Eisenhower Blvd S. I-76 (Pennsylvania Tpke), exit 247, just n; I-283, exit 1B (Highspire). Ext corridors. **Pets:** Dogs only. $10 daily fee/pet. Service with restrictions, supervision.
ASK S X 🎥 🔲 🖥 🎥

# MIFFLINVILLE

**WW** Super 8 Motel **M**
(570) 759-6778. **$49-$90.** 450 3rd St. I-80, exit 242, just n on SR 339. Ext corridors. **Pets:** Dogs only. $10 one-time fee/room. Service with restrictions, crate.
ASK S X 🔲

# MORGANTOWN

**AAA** **WWW** Holiday Inn **SH**
(610) 286-3000. **$109-$149.** 6170 Morgantown Rd. I-76, exit 298, just s on SR 10. Int corridors. **Pets:** Medium, other species. $10 daily fee/pet. Designated rooms, service with restriction, supervision.
SAVE S X 🎥 🔲 🖥 🍴 🎥 🚫

# NEW CASTLE

**WWW** Comfort Inn-New Castle **M**
(724) 658-7700. **$59-$130.** 1740 New Butler Rd. Jct SR 65, 1 mi e on US 422, then 1 mi w on US 422 business route. Int corridors. **Pets:** Small. Designated rooms, no service, crate.
ASK S X 🔲 🖥

# NEW COLUMBIA

**AAA** **WWW** New Columbia Comfort Inn **SH**
(570) 568-8000. **$70-$130.** 330 Commerce Park Dr. I-80, exit 210A (US 15/New Columbia), just s. Int corridors. **Pets:** Other species.
SAVE S X M 🔲 🖥 🍴 🎥

# NEW CUMBERLAND

**AAA** **WWW** Days Inn Harrisburg South **SH** ✿
(717) 774-4156. **$69-$125, 3 day notice.** 353 Lewisberry Rd. I-83, exit 39A, just ne. Int corridors. **Pets:** Large. $15 daily fee/pet. Designated rooms, service with restrictions, supervision.
SAVE S X 🔲 🖥 🎥

**AAA** **WWW** Holiday Inn Hotel & Conference Center-Harrisburg **SH**
(717) 774-2721. **$99-$129.** 148 Sheraman Dr. I-83, exit 40A, just se. Int corridors. **Pets:** Small. $10 daily fee/pet. Designated rooms, service with restrictions, supervision.
SAVE X 🎥 🔲 🖥 🍴 🎥 🚫

# NORTH EAST

**AAA** **WWW** Super 8 Motel **M**
(814) 725-4567. **$49-$79.** 11021 Side Hill Rd. I-90, exit 41, just n on SR 89. Ext corridors. **Pets:** Dogs only. $5 one-time fee/room. No service, supervision.
SAVE S X

# PALMYRA

**AAA** **WWW** Red Carpet Inn & Suites **M**
(717) 838-5466. **$49-$129, 3 day notice.** 977 E Main St. Center. Ext corridors. **Pets:** Accepted.
SAVE S X 🔲 🖥 🎥

---

# PENNSYLVANIA DUTCH COUNTRY AREA

# ADAMSTOWN

**WWW** The Barnyard Inn B&B and Suites **BB** ✿
(717) 484-1111. **$85-$135, 10 day notice.** 2145 Old Lancaster Pike. 1 mi ne via Main St/Old Lancaster Pike; SR 272, just w on Willow St to Main St, 1 mi n bearing left at fork, then just n. Int corridors. **Pets:** Other species. $20 one-time fee/room. Designated rooms.
ASK X 🔲 🖥 🎥

# DENVER

**AAA** **WWW** Black Horse Lodge and Suites **SH**
(717) 336-7563. **$79-$179.** 2180 N Reading Rd. I-76 (Pennsylvania Tpke), exit 286, 1 mi w to SR 272, then 0.3 mi n. Ext/int corridors. **Pets:** Other species. Service with restrictions, supervision.
SAVE S X 🔲 🖥 🍴 🎥

**AAA** **WWW** Comfort Inn **SH**
(717) 336-4649. **$69-$159, 3 day notice.** 2017 N Reading Rd. I-76 (Pennsylvania Tpke), exit 286, 1 mi w to SR 272, then just s. Int corridors. **Pets:** Medium, dogs only. $10 daily fee/room. Designated rooms, service with restrictions, supervision.
SAVE S X 🎥 🔲 🖥

**AAA** **WWW** Holiday Inn-Lancaster County **SH**
(717) 336-7541. **$89-$179.** 1 Denver Rd. I-76 (Pennsylvania Tpke), exit 286, 1 mi w to SR 272, then just s. Int corridors. **Pets:** Small, other species. $10 daily fee/pet. Service with restrictions, supervision.
SAVE S X M 🎥 🔲 🖥 🍴 🎥

# EPHRATA

**AAA** ▼▼▼▼ **Historic Smithton Inn** BB
(717) 733-6094. **$95-$165, 14 day notice.** 900 W Main St. On US 322, just w of jct SR 272. Int corridors. **Pets:** Dogs only. Designated rooms, supervision.
SAVE ✕ 🖱 ✍

# GORDONVILLE

**AAA** ▼ **Motel 6-Lancaster #4174** M
(717) 687-3880. **$55-$100.** 2959 Lincoln Hwy E. On US 30; center. Int corridors. **Pets:** Accepted.
SAVE 🛎 ✕ 🖱 🖱

# LANCASTER

**AAA** ▼▼▼▼ **Best Western Eden Resort Inn & Suites** LH
(717) 569-6444. **$99-$189.** 222 Eden Rd. Jct US 30 (Lincoln Hwy) and SR 272 (Oregon Pike). Ext/int corridors. **Pets:** Medium, other species. $20 one-time fee/pet. Designated rooms, service with restrictions, crate.
SAVE 🛎 ✕ 🖱 📶 🖱 🖱 🖱 🖱 🖱 🖱

▼▼▼▼ **Hawthorn Inn & Suites** SH 🐾
(717) 290-7100. **$69-$139.** 2045 Lincoln Hwy E. Jct US 30 E and Lincoln Hwy. Int corridors. **Pets:** Medium, dogs only. $25 daily fee/pet. Service with restrictions, crate.
ASK 🛎 ✕ 📶 🖱 🖱 🖱

**AAA** ▼▼▼▼ **Holiday Inn Visitors Center** SH
(717) 299-2551. **$89-$109.** 521 Greenfield Rd. 3.3 mi e on US 30 (Lincoln Hwy), exit Greenfield Rd, just n. Ext/int corridors. **Pets:** Accepted.
SAVE 🛎 ✕ 📶 📶 🖱 🖱 🖱 🖱 🖱

▼▼ **Hotel Brunswick** LH
(717) 397-4800. **$60-$130.** 151 N Queen St. Center. Int corridors. **Pets:** Accepted.
ASK 🛎 ✕ 📶 🖱 🖱 🖱 🖱

▼▼▼▼ **Lancaster Host Resort & Conference Center** LH
(717) 299-5500. **$89-$169.** 2300 Lincoln Hwy E. On US 30 (Lincoln Hwy), 5 mi e. Int corridors. **Pets:** Medium, other species. $25 one-time fee/room. Designated rooms, service with restrictions, supervision.
ASK 🛎 ✕ 🖱 🖱 🖱 🖱 🖱 🖱

**AAA** ▼▼▼ **Lancaster Travelodge & Conference Center** SH
(717) 293-8400. **$59-$99.** 1492 Lititz Pike. US 30 (Lincoln Hwy), exit Lititz Pike (SR 501), just s. Ext corridors. **Pets:** Accepted.
SAVE 🛎 ✕ 🖱 🖱 🖱 🖱

# LITITZ

▼▼▼ **General Sutter Inn** CI 🐾
(717) 626-2115. **$87-$120.** 14 E Main St. Jct SR 501 and 772; downtown. Int corridors. **Pets:** Other species. $10 one-time fee/pet. Supervision.
✕ 🖱

# MANHEIM

**AAA** ▼ **Rodeway Inn** M
(717) 665-2755. **$48-$68.** 2931 Lebanon Rd. I-76 (Pennsylvania Tpke), exit 266, just s on SR 72. Ext corridors. **Pets:** Other species. $5 one-time fee/pet. Service with restrictions.
SAVE ✕ 🖱

# MOUNTVILLE

**AAA** ▼▼▼▼ **MainStay Suites** SH
(717) 285-2500. **$85-$200.** 314 Primrose Ln. US 30 (Lincoln Hwy), exit Mountville. Int corridors. **Pets:** Medium, other species. $100 deposit/room, $10 daily fee/pet. Service with restrictions, crate.
SAVE 🛎 ✕ 📶 📶 🖱 🖱 🖱 🖱

# STRASBURG

**AAA** ▼▼▼ **Carriage House Motor Inn** M
(717) 687-7651. **$49-$99.** 144 E Main St. 0.3 mi e on SR 896 and 741. Ext corridors. **Pets:** Accepted.
SAVE 🛎 ✕ 🖱

**AAA** ▼▼▼▼ **Netherlands Inn & Spa** SH
(717) 687-7691. **$99-$179.** One Historic Dr. 0.5 mi n on SR 896; 2.5 mi s of US 30 (Lincoln Hwy). Ext/int corridors. **Pets:** Accepted.
SAVE 🛎 ✕ 🖱 🖱 🖱 🖱 🖱

---

# PHILADELPHIA METROPOLITAN AREA

## AUDUBON

**AAA** ▼▼▼▼ **Homewood Suites by Hilton** SH 🐾
(610) 539-7300. **$179-$299.** 681 Shannondell Blvd. US 422, exit Trooper Rd, 1.2 mi n. Int corridors. **Pets:** Large, other species. $250 one-time fee/room.
SAVE 🛎 ✕ 📶 📶 🖱 🖱 🖱 🖱

## BENSALEM

**AAA** ▼▼▼▼ **Holiday Inn-Philadelphia Northeast** SH
(215) 638-1500. **$129-$159.** 3499 Street Rd. I-276 (Pennsylvania Tpke), exit 351, just s on US 1, then 0.3 mi e on SR 132. Ext/int corridors. **Pets:** Small, other species. $50 deposit/room. Service with restrictions, supervision.
SAVE 🛎 ✕ 📶 🖱 🖱 🖱 🖱

▼▼▼ **Sleep Inn & Suites-Bensalem** SH
(215) 244-2300. **$69-$189.** 3427 Street Rd. I-276 (Pennsylvania Tpke), exit 351, just s on US 1, then 0.3 mi e on SR 132. Int corridors. **Pets:** Medium. $20 daily fee/pet. Service with restrictions, supervision.
ASK 🛎 ✕ 📶 📶 🖱 🖱

## BERWYN

▼▼▼ **Residence Inn by Marriott** SH
(610) 640-9494. **$189-$199.** 600 W Swedesford Rd. US 202, exit Paoli/SR 252, 1 mi n. Ext corridors. **Pets:** Accepted.
✕ 📶 📶 🖱 🖱 🖱 🖱 🖱

## CHADDS FORD

**AAA** ▼▼▼▼ **Brandywine River Hotel** SH
(610) 388-1200. **$125-$169.** 1609 Baltimore Pike. Jct US 1 and SR 100, 2 mi w of US 202. Int corridors. **Pets:** Small, dogs only. $150 deposit/room, $20 daily fee/room. Designated rooms, service with restrictions, crate.
SAVE ✕ 📶 📶 🖱 🖱

## CONSHOHOCKEN

**AAA** ▼▼▼▼ **Residence Inn by Marriott**
**Philadelphia/Conshohocken** SH
(610) 828-8800. **$99-$289.** 191 Washington St. I-76 (Schuylkill Expwy), exit 332; I-476, exit 16 (SR 23), 0.3 mi over Fayette Bridge to Elm St, then just se along the river. Int corridors. **Pets:** Other species. $75 one-time fee/room.
SAVE ✕ 📶 📶 🖱 🖱 🖱 🖱

# DUBLIN

▼▼▼▼ **Stone Ridge Farm Bed & Breakfast** BB
(215) 249-9186. **$99-$225.** 956 Bypass Rd. SR 313, 1 mi w on Maple
Ave, then just s. Ext/int corridors. **Pets:** Accepted.
⊠ 🛇 📭 🕰 🐾

# EAST NORRITON

▼▼▼▼ **Summerfield Suites Hotel by Wyndham-Plymouth**
**Meeting East Norriton** SH
(610) 313-9990. **$119-$189.** 501 E Germantown Pike. I-476, exit 20;
I-276 (Pennsylvania Tpke), exit 333, 2.5 mi w. Int corridors.
**Pets:** Accepted.
A$K ⊠ 🕰 📭 🛇 📭 🐾

# ERWINNA

▼▼▼ **Golden Pheasant Inn** CI 🐾
(610) 294-9595. **$95-$175, 21 day notice.** 763 River Rd. SR 32, 0.5 mi
n of jct Dark Hollow Rd. Ext/int corridors. **Pets:** Medium, other species.
$20 daily fee/pet. Designated rooms, service with restrictions, crate.
⊠ 🛇 📭 ⫪ ⊠

# ESSINGTON

AAA ▼▼▼▼ **Comfort Inn Airport** SH
(610) 521-9800. **$89-$150.** 53 Industrial Hwy. I-95, exit 9A, 0.3 mi sw
on SR 291. Int corridors. **Pets:** Accepted.
SAVE S🛇 ⊠ 🕰 🛇 🛇 📭

AAA ▼▼▼▼ **Holiday Inn-Airport** LH 🐾
(610) 521-2400. **$105-$179.** 45 Industrial Hwy. I-95, exit 9A, 0.3 mi sw
on SR 291. Int corridors. **Pets:** Large. $25 one-time fee/pet. Designated
rooms, service with restrictions, supervision.
SAVE S🛇 ⊠ 🕰 🛇 📭 📭 ⫪ 🐾

▼▼▼ **Red Roof Inn-Airport #7119** M
(610) 521-5090. **$79-$104.** 49 Industrial Hwy. I-95, exit 9A, 0.3 mi sw
on SR 291. Ext corridors. **Pets:** Accepted.
⊠ 🕰 🛇 🛇 🛇

# EXTON

AAA ▼▼▼▼ **Holiday Inn Express** SH
(610) 524-9000. **$95.** 120 N Pottstown Pike. I-76 (Pennsylvania Tpke),
exit 312, 3 mi s at jct Business Rt US 30 and SR 100. Int corridors.
**Pets:** Accepted.
SAVE S🛇 ⊠ 🕰 🛇 🛇 📭 🐾

# HORSHAM

AAA ▼▼▼▼ **Days Inn-Horsham/Willow Grove** SH 🐾
(215) 674-2500. **$89-$129.** 245 Easton Rd. I-276 (Pennsylvania Tpke),
exit 343, 1 mi n. Int corridors. **Pets:** Other species. $10 daily fee/pet.
Service with restrictions, crate.
SAVE S🛇 🛇 🛇 🛇 📭

▼▼▼▼ **Homestead Studio Suites Hotel-Horsham/Willow**
**Grove** SH
(215) 956-9966. **$89-$99.** 537 Dresher Rd. I-276 (Pennsylvania Tpke),
exit 343, 1.5 mi n on SR 611 (Easton Rd), just w on Horsham Rd,
then 0.5 mi s. Int corridors. **Pets:** $25 daily fee/pet. Service with restric-
tions, supervision.
A$K S🛇 ⊠ 🕰 🛇 🛇 🛇 📭

▼▼▼▼ **Residence Inn by Marriott-Willow Grove** SH
(215) 443-7330. **$199-$239 (no credit cards).** 3 Walnut Grove Dr.
I-276 (Pennsylvania Tpke), exit 343, 1 mi n on SR 611 (Easton Rd),
then 1.3 mi w on Dresher Rd. Ext corridors. **Pets:** Accepted.
⊠ 🕰 🛇 🛇 🛇 📭 🐾 ⊠

# KING OF PRUSSIA

▼▼▼▼ **Homestead Studio Suites Hotel-King of**
**Prussia** SH
(610) 962-9000. **$90-$104.** 400 American Ave. I-76 (Pennsylvania
Tpke), exit 326 (Valley Forge); Schuylkill Expwy, exit 328A (Mall Blvd),
1.3 mi n on N Gulph Rd, then 1 mi ne on 1st Ave. Int corridors.
**Pets:** $25 daily fee/pet. Service with restrictions, supervision.
A$K S🛇 ⊠ 🕰 🛇 🛇 🛇 📭

AAA ▼▼▼▼ **MainStay Suites** SH
(484) 690-3000. **$134-$144.** 440 American Ave. I-76 (Pennsylvania
Tpke), exit 326 (Valley Forge); Schuylkill Expwy, exit 328A (Mall Blvd),
1.3 mi n on N Gulph Rd, 1 mi ne on 1st Ave, then just e. Int corridors.
**Pets:** Accepted.
SAVE S🛇 ⊠ 🛇 🛇 📭 📭

▼▼▼ **Motel 6 Philadelphia-King of Prussia #1280** SH
(610) 265-7200. **$65-$77.** 815 W DeKalb Pike. I-76 (Pennsylvania
Tpke), exit 326 (Valley Forge), 1.3 mi e to jct US 202 N and S Gulph
Rd; Schuylkill Expwy, exit 328A (US 202 N), just e. Int corridors.
**Pets:** Accepted.
S🛇 ⊠ 🛇 🐾

▼▼▼▼ **The Sheraton Park Ridge Hotel and Conference**
**Center** LH
(610) 337-1800. **$104-$229.** 480 N Gulph Rd. I-76 (Pennsylvania
Tpke), exit 327 (Valley Forge), 0.3 mi w. Int corridors. **Pets:** Accepted.
A$K S🛇 ⊠ 🕰 🛇 🛇 📭 ⫪ 🐾 ⊠

# KULPSVILLE

▼▼▼▼ **Best Western-The Inn at Towamencin** SH
(215) 368-3800. **$104-$114.** 1750 Sumneytown Pike. I-476, exit 31, just
e. Int corridors. **Pets:** Accepted.
A$K S🛇 ⊠ 🛇 🛇 🛇 ⫪ 🐾 ⊠

# LANGHORNE

▼▼▼▼ **Sheraton Bucks County Hotel** LH
(215) 547-4100. **$209-$399.** 400 Oxford Valley Rd. I-95, exit 46A
(Oxford Valley Rd), 0.8 mi e, exit off US 1 N. Int corridors.
**Pets:** Accepted.
⊠ 🕰 🛇 🛇 🛇 📭 ⫪ 🐾 ⊠

# LIONVILLE

AAA ▼▼▼▼ **Hampton Inn** SH 🐾
(610) 363-5555. **$99-$149.** 4 N Pottstown Pike. I-76 (Pennsylvania
Tpke), exit 312, 0.5 mi s; jct SR 113 and 100. Int corridors. **Pets:** Other
species. Service with restrictions, supervision.
SAVE S🛇 ⊠ 🕰 🛇 🛇 📭 🐾

▼▼▼▼ **Residence Inn by Marriott-Exton** SH
(610) 594-9705. **$90-$150, 14 day notice.** 10 N Pottstown Pike. I-76
(Pennsylvania Tpke), exit 312, 1 mi s on SR 100. Int corridors.
**Pets:** Accepted.
A$K S🛇 ⊠ 🛇 🛇 📭 🐾 ⊠

# MALVERN

▼▼▼▼ **Homestead Studio Suites Hotel-Malvern** SH
(610) 695-9200. **$74-$104.** 8 E Swedesford Rd. Just w of US 202 and
SR 29 N. Int corridors. **Pets:** $25 daily fee/pet. Service with restrictions,
supervision.
A$K S🛇 ⊠ 🛇 🛇 🛇 📭

AAA ▼▼▼▼ **Homewood Suites by Hilton** SH
(610) 296-3500. **$189-$239.** 12 E Swedesford Rd. US 202, exit SR 29,
follow signs. Int corridors. **Pets:** $50 one-time fee/pet. Service with restric-
tions, crate.
SAVE S🛇 ⊠ 🕰 🛇 🛇 🛇 📭 🐾

⚫⚫⚫ ▼▼▼▼ **Sheraton Great Valley Hotel** 🏨
(610) 524-5500. **$109-$219.** 707 Lancaster Pike. Jct US 202 and 30 E. Int corridors. **Pets:** Accepted.

⬛ ⬛ ⬛ ⬛ ⬛ ⬛ ⬛ ⬛ ⬛ ⬛

▼▼▼▼ **Staybridge Suites** 🅂🄷
(610) 296-4343. **$190-$230.** 20 Morehall Rd. Jct US 30 and SR 29, just nw. Ext/int corridors. **Pets:** Medium. $10 daily fee/room. Service with restrictions, supervision.

⬛ ⬛ ⬛ ⬛ ⬛ ⬛ ⬛ ⬛

## MONTGOMERYVILLE

▼▼ ▼▼ **Quality Inn Conference Center** 🅂🄷
(215) 699-8800. **$99-$119.** 969 Bethlehem Pike. I-276 (Pennsylvania Tpke), exit 339, 8 mi n on SR 309. Ext corridors. **Pets:** Accepted.

⬛ ⬛ ⬛ ⬛ ⬛ ⬛

▼▼▼▼ **Residence Inn by Marriott** 🅂🄷
(267) 468-0111. **$140-$170, 14 day notice.** 1110 Bethlehem Pike. I-276 (Pennsylvania Tpke), exit 339, 6.5 mi n on SR 309. Int corridors. **Pets:** Accepted.

⬛ ⬛ ⬛ ⬛ ⬛ ⬛ ⬛ ⬛ ⬛

## NEW HOPE

▼▼▼▼ **1870 Wedgwood Inn of New Hope** 🄱🄱 🐾
(215) 862-2570. **$95-$195, 10 day notice.** 111 W Bridge St (SR 179). 0.5 mi w of SR 32; downtown. Ext/int corridors. **Pets:** Medium, dogs only. $20 daily fee/pet. Service with restrictions, supervision.

⬛ ⬛ ⬛

▼▼▼▼ **Aaron Burr House Inn & Conference Center** 🄱🄱
(215) 862-2520. **$105-$230.** 80 W Bridge St (SR 179). 0.5 mi w of SR 32; at W Bridge and Chestnut sts. Int corridors. **Pets:** Medium, dogs only. $25 daily fee/pet. Service with restrictions, supervision.

⬛ ⬛ ⬛

⚫⚫⚫ ▼▼ ▼ **Best Western New Hope Inn** 🅂🄷
(215) 862-5221. **$81-$169.** 6426 Lower York Rd. 2 mi s on US 202, 1 mi w of jct SR 179. Ext corridors. **Pets:** Small, dogs only. $20 daily fee/room. Designated rooms, service with restrictions, supervision.

⬛ ⬛ ⬛ ⬛ ⬛ ⬛ ⬛ ⬛

⚫⚫⚫ ▼▼ **The New Hope Motel in the Woods** 🄼 🐾
(215) 862-2800. **$69-$149, 14 day notice.** 400 W Bridge St. 1 mi s on SR 179, e of jct US 202. Ext corridors. **Pets:** Medium, dogs only. $25 one-time fee/pet. Service with restrictions, supervision.

⬛ ⬛ ⬛ ⬛ ⬛

## PHILADELPHIA

⚫⚫⚫ ▼▼ ▼ **Best Western Center City Hotel** 🅂🄷
(215) 568-8300. **$129-$155.** 501 N 22nd St. Just n of Benjamin Franklin Pkwy. Int corridors. **Pets:** Medium, other species. $10 daily fee/pet. Designated rooms, service with restrictions, crate.

⬛ ⬛ ⬛ ⬛ ⬛ ⬛ ⬛ ⬛

⚫⚫⚫ ▼▼▼ **Best Western Independence Park Inn** 🅂🄷 🐾
(215) 922-4443. **$129-$249.** 235 Chestnut St. Between 2nd and 3rd sts. Int corridors. **Pets:** Small, other species. $50 one-time fee/room. Service with restrictions.

⬛ ⬛ ⬛ ⬛ ⬛ ⬛

▼▼▼▼ **The Doubletree Hotel Philadelphia** 🄻🄷
(215) 893-1600. **$179-$369.** 237 S Broad St. Jct Broad and Locust sts. Int corridors. **Pets:** Accepted.

⬛ ⬛ ⬛ ⬛ ⬛ ⬛ ⬛ ⬛ ⬛

▼▼ ▼▼ **Extended StayAmerica** 🅂🄷
(215) 492-6766. **$74-$109.** 9000 Tinicum Blvd. I-95, exit 12B (airport), just n on Essington Ave, then just w on Bartram Ave. Int corridors. **Pets:** Accepted.

⬛ ⬛ ⬛ ⬛ ⬛ ⬛

▼▼▼▼ **Four Points by Sheraton Philadelphia Airport** 🅂🄷
(215) 492-0400. **$189.** 4101 Island Ave. Jct I-95 and SR 291, exit 13 northbound; exit 15 southbound. Int corridors. **Pets:** Accepted.

⬛ ⬛ ⬛ ⬛ ⬛ ⬛ ⬛ ⬛

⚫⚫⚫ ▼▼▼▼ **Four Seasons Hotel Philadelphia** 🄻🄷 🌸
(215) 963-1500. **$355-$2700.** 1 Logan Square. Corner of 18th St and Benjamin Franklin Pkwy. Int corridors. **Pets:** Very small, dogs only. Designated rooms, service with restrictions, supervision.

⬛ ⬛ ⬛ ⬛ ⬛ ⬛ ⬛ ⬛ ⬛ ⬛

⚫⚫⚫ ▼▼▼▼ **Hampton Inn-Center City** 🄻🄷
(215) 665-9100. **$89-$229.** 1301 Race St. At 13th and Race sts. Int corridors. **Pets:** Small, dogs only. $100 deposit/room, $20 daily fee/room. Service with restrictions, supervision.

⬛ ⬛ ⬛ ⬛ ⬛ ⬛ ⬛ ⬛

▼▼▼▼ **Hampton Inn-Philadelphia Airport** 🅂🄷
(215) 966-1300. **$99-$170.** 8600 Bartram Ave. I-95, exit 12B (airport) southbound, bear right on exit ramp to light, just n; exit 10 northbound, follow SR 291 E to light, then 1 mi n. Int corridors. **Pets:** Accepted.

⬛ ⬛ ⬛ ⬛ ⬛ ⬛ ⬛ ⬛ ⬛ ⬛

⚫⚫⚫ ▼▼▼▼ **Loews Philadelphia Hotel** 🄻🄷 🌸
(215) 627-1200. **$159-$289.** 1200 Market St. Corner of 12th and Market sts. Int corridors. **Pets:** Other species. $35 one-time fee/room. Service with restrictions, supervision.

⬛ ⬛ ⬛ ⬛ ⬛ ⬛ ⬛ ⬛ ⬛ ⬛

⚫⚫⚫ ▼▼ ▼▼ **Park Hyatt Philadelphia at The Bellevue** 🄻🄷
(215) 893-1234. **$180-$315.** Broad & Walnut sts. Broad St; between Walnut and Locust sts. Int corridors. **Pets:** Accepted.

⬛ ⬛ ⬛ ⬛ ⬛ ⬛ ⬛ ⬛

⚫⚫⚫ ▼▼▼▼ **Philadelphia Airport Residence Inn** 🅂🄷
(215) 492-1611. **$139-$179.** 4630 Island Ave. I-95, exit 13 northbound; exit 15 southbound, 0.5 mi e; just e of SR 291. Ext/int corridors. **Pets:** Accepted.

⬛ ⬛ ⬛ ⬛ ⬛ ⬛ ⬛ ⬛ ⬛

⚫⚫⚫ ▼▼▼▼ **Philadelphia Downtown Marriott Hotel** 🄻🄷
(215) 625-2900. **$239-$269.** 1201 Market St. Between 12th and 13th sts. Int corridors. **Pets:** Accepted.

⬛ ⬛ ⬛ ⬛ ⬛ ⬛ ⬛ ⬛ ⬛ ⬛

⚫⚫⚫ ▼▼▼▼ **The Radisson Plaza-Warwick Hotel Philadelphia** 🄻🄷
(215) 735-6000. **$129-$349.** 1701 Locust St. Jct 17th and Locust sts. Int corridors. **Pets:** Dogs only. $50 one-time fee/room. Service with restrictions, supervision.

⬛ ⬛ ⬛ ⬛ ⬛ ⬛ ⬛ ⬛

▼▼▼▼ **Residence Inn by Marriott Philadelphia City Center** 🄻🄷
(215) 557-0005. **$239-$329.** 1 E Penn Square. Market and Juniper sts. Int corridors. **Pets:** Accepted.

⬛ ⬛ ⬛ ⬛ ⬛ ⬛ ⬛

⚫⚫⚫ ▼▼▼▼ **The Rittenhouse Hotel and Condominium Residences** 🄻🄷 🐾
(215) 546-9000. **$420-$460.** 210 W Rittenhouse Square. On Rittenhouse Square. Int corridors. **Pets:** Service with restrictions, supervision.

⬛ ⬛ ⬛ ⬛ ⬛ ⬛ ⬛ ⬛

▼▼▼▼ **The Ritz-Carlton Philadelphia** 🄻🄷
(215) 523-8000. **$279-$469.** Ten Avenue of the Arts. Chestnut and Broad sts. Int corridors. **Pets:** Accepted.

⬛ ⬛ ⬛ ⬛ ⬛

**▼▼▼▼ Sheraton Society Hill** 🏨
(215) 238-6000. **$289.** One Dock St. I-95, exit 20 (Historic District Center City), then 0.5 mi n on Delaware Ave to Dock St; at 2nd and Walnut sts. Int corridors. **Pets:** Accepted.
(ASK) ⊗ ✍ 🗲 🎬 📺 🍴 ⇌ ⊗

**▼▼▼▼ Sheraton Suites Philadelphia Airport** 🏨 ❦
(215) 365-6600. **$89-$189.** 4101 Island Ave. Jct I-95 and SR 291, exit 13 northbound; exit 15 southbound. Int corridors. **Pets:** Dogs only. Service with restrictions, supervision.
(ASK) 🔁 ⊗ ✍ 🎬 📺 🍴 ⇌ ⊗

**⟨AAA⟩ ▼▼▼▼ Sheraton University City** 🏨 ❦
(215) 387-8000. **$329.** 36th & Chestnut sts. I-76 (Pennsylvania Tpke), exit 345, 0.5 mi w. Int corridors. **Pets:** Medium, dogs only. Service with restrictions, supervision.
(SAVE) 🔁 ⊗ ♿ ✍ 🎬 📺 🍴 ⇌

**▼▼▼ ▼▼▼ Sofitel Philadelphia** 🏨 ❦
(215) 569-8300. **$199.** 120 S 17th St. Jct Sansom and 17th sts. Int corridors. **Pets:** Other species. Service with restrictions.
(ASK) 🔁 ⊗ ♿ ✍ 🎬 🍴

**⟨AAA⟩ ▼▼▼ ▼▼▼ The Westin Philadelphia** 🏨
(215) 563-1600. **$199-$309.** 99 S 17th St at Liberty Pl. On 17th St; between Market and Chestnut sts. Int corridors. **Pets:** Accepted.
(SAVE) ⊗ ✍ 🎬 📺 🍴 ⊗

**⟨AAA⟩ ▼▼▼▼ Wyndham Philadelphia at Franklin Plaza** 🏨
(215) 448-2000. **$99-$269.** 2 Franklin Plaza. Jct 17th and Race sts. Int corridors. **Pets:** Accepted.
(SAVE) ⊗ ✍ 🎬 📺 📺 🍴 ⇌ ⊗

## PLYMOUTH MEETING

**▼▼▼▼ Doubletree Guest Suites Plymouth Meeting** 🏨
(610) 834-8300. **$89-$249.** 640 W Germantown Pike. I-476, exit 20; I-276 (Pennsylvania Tpke), exit 333, just w on Plymouth Rd (Norristown), just e on Germantown Pike, then just e on Hickory Rd. Int corridors. **Pets:** Accepted.
⊗ ✍ 🎬 📺 🍴 ⇌ ⊗

## POTTSTOWN

**▼▼▼▼ Comfort Inn** 🆂🅷
(610) 326-5000. **$89-$122.** 99 Robinson St. SR 100, 1 mi n of jct US 422. Int corridors. **Pets:** Other species. $10 daily fee/room. Service with restrictions, crate.
(ASK) 🔁 ⊗ ♿ ✍ 🎬 🎬 📺 ⇌

**⟨AAA⟩ ▼▼▼ Days Inn** 🅼
(610) 970-1101. **$45-$69.** 29 High St. Just off SR 663, 0.5 mi e of jct SR 100. Ext corridors. **Pets:** Medium. $10 daily fee/room. No service, supervision.
(SAVE) 🔁 ⊗ 🎬

**▼▼▼ Motel 6** 🅼
(610) 819-1288. **$55-$70.** 78 Robinson St. Jct US 422, 1 mi n on SR 100, just w in Tri-County Business Campus. Int corridors. **Pets:** Other species. Service with restrictions, supervision.
🔁 ⊗ ♿ 🎬

**⟨AAA⟩ ▼▼▼ Quality Inn Pottstown** 🆂🅷
(610) 326-6700. **$74-$99.** 61 W King St. Just e of SR 100. Ext corridors. **Pets:** Accepted.
(SAVE) 🔁 ⊗ 🎬 📺 ⇌

## TREVOSE

**▼▼▼▼ Radisson Hotel of Philadelphia Northeast** 🏨
(215) 638-8300. **$139-$149.** 2400 Old Lincoln Hwy. I-276 (Pennsylvania Tpke), exit 351, 1 mi s on US 1; jct Roosevelt Blvd and Old Lincoln Hwy. Int corridors. **Pets:** Accepted.
(ASK) 🔁 ⊗ ♿ ✍ 🎬 🎬 📺 🍴 ⇌

**▼▼▼ Red Roof Inn #7185** 🅼
(215) 244-9422. **$62-$90.** 3100 Lincoln Hwy. I-276 (Pennsylvania Tpke), exit 351, 0.5 mi s on US   at US 132. Ext corridors. **Pets:** Accepted.
⊗ ♿ ✍ 🎬 🎬

## UPPER BLACK EDDY

**▼▼▼ ▼▼▼ The Bridgeton House on the Delaware** 🅱🅱 ❦
(610) 982-5856. **$139-$450, 14 day notice.** 1525 River Rd. On SR 32; center. Int corridors. **Pets:** Small, dogs only. $100 deposit/pet. Designated rooms, service with restrictions, supervision.
⊗ 🎬 📺 🍴 ⊗

## WEST CHESTER

**⟨AAA⟩ ▼▼▼ Microtel Inn & Suites** 🆂🅷
(610) 738-9111. **$70-$199.** 500 Willowbrook Ln. Just se of US 202, exit Matlack St. Int corridors. **Pets:** Accepted.
(SAVE) 🔁 ⊗ ♿ ✍ 🎬 🎬 📺

---

# END METROPOLITAN AREA

---

## PHILIPSBURG

**⟨AAA⟩ ▼▼ Main Liner Motel** 🅼
(814) 342-2004. **$39-$65.** 1896 Philipsburg Bigler (US 322 W) Hwy. 1 mi w of jct SR 53 N. Ext corridors. **Pets:** Small. $10 daily fee/pet. Designated rooms, service with restrictions, supervision.
(SAVE) 🔁 ⊗ 🎬

## PIGEON

**▼▼ The Forest Lodge & Campground** 🅼 ❦
(814) 927-8790. **$45-$60.** SR 66, 6 mi n of Marienville. Ext/int corridors. **Pets:** Other species. $6 daily fee/pet. Designated rooms, service with restrictions, supervision.
(ASK) 🔁 ⊗ 🎬 📺

## PINE GROVE

**▼▼ ▼▼ Comfort Inn** 🆂🅷
(570) 345-8031. **$63-$119.** SR 443. I-81, exit 100. Int corridors. **Pets:** Other species. $10 one-time fee/room. Designated rooms, service with restrictions, supervision.
(ASK) 🔁 ⊗ ♿ ✍ 🎬 📺 ⇌

**⟨AAA⟩ ▼▼ ▼▼ Econo Lodge** 🆂🅷
(570) 345-4099. **$55-$160.** 419 Suedberg Rd. I-81, exit 100, just e on SR 443. Ext/int corridors. **Pets:** Accepted.
(SAVE) 🔁 ⊗ ✍ 🎬 📺

# PITTSBURGH METROPOLITAN AREA

## BEAVER FALLS

**▼▼▼▼ Holiday Inn** SH
(724) 846-3700. **$114, 30 day notice.** 7195 Eastwood Rd. I-76 (Pennsylvania Tpke), exit 13, just n. Int corridors. **Pets:** Large, other species. $25 one-time fee/pet. Service with restrictions, supervision.

(ASK) (SÓ) (X) (k²) (H) (J) (YI) (☞) (X)

## BRIDGEVILLE

**▲▲▲ ▼ Knights Inn-Pittsburgh/Bridgeville** M
(412) 221-8110. **$43-$59.** 111 Hickory Grade Rd. I-79, exit 54 (SR 50). Ext corridors. **Pets:** Accepted.

(SAVE) (SÓ) (X) (J) (k²) (H) (J)

## BUTLER

**▼▼▼ Comfort Inn** SH
(724) 287-7177. **$69-$149.** 1 Comfort Ln. 4 mi s on SR 8. Int corridors. **Pets:** Medium. $10 daily fee/pet. Service with restrictions, supervision.

(ASK) (SÓ) (X) (k²) (H) (J) (☞)

**▼▼ Super 8 Motel** M
(724) 287-8888. **$60.** 138 Pittsburgh/SR 8. 2 mi s. Int corridors. **Pets:** Other species. $8 daily fee/pet. Service with restrictions, supervision.

(ASK) (SÓ) (X) (H)

## CANONSBURG

**▼▼ Super 8 Motel** M
(724) 873-8808. **$58-$69.** 8 Curry Ave. I-79, exit 45, follow signs. Int corridors. **Pets:** Medium. $10 daily fee/room. No service, crate.

(ASK) (SÓ) (X) (J) (H)

## CORAOPOLIS

**▼ Americas Best Value Inn-Pittsburgh Airport** M
(412) 604-2378. **$51-$56.** 8858 University Blvd. 0.5 mi n of Business Rt SR 60. Ext corridors. **Pets:** Accepted.

(ASK) (SÓ) (X) (H)

**▲▲▲ ▼▼▼ Crowne Plaza Hotel and Resort Pittsburgh International Airport** LH
(412) 262-2400. **$39-$149.** 1160 Thorn Run Rd. Business Rt SR 60, exit Thorn Run Rd. Int corridors. **Pets:** Small, other species. $20 deposit/pet. Service with restrictions, supervision.

(SAVE) (SÓ) (X) (J) (k²) (H) (J) (YI) (☞)

**▼▼▼ Embassy Suites-Pittsburgh International Airport** LH ✿
(412) 269-9070. **$99-$219.** 550 Cherrington Pkwy. Business Rt SR 60, exit Thorn Run Rd. Int corridors. **Pets:** Medium. $50 one-time fee/room. Service with restrictions, crate.

(ASK) (X) (kM) (J) (k²) (H) (J) (YI) (☞) (X)

**▼▼▼ Hampton Inn Airport-Pittsburgh** SH
(412) 264-0020. **$69-$109.** 8514 University Blvd. Business Rt SR 60, 0.5 mi n. Int corridors. **Pets:** Small. $10 one-time fee/room. Service with restrictions, supervision.

(X) (J) (H) (J)

**▲▲▲ ▼▼▼ Holiday Inn-Pittsburgh Airport** LH
(412) 262-3600. **$69-$129.** 8256 University Blvd. Business Rt SR 60, 1 mi n. Int corridors. **Pets:** Accepted.

(SAVE) (SÓ) (X) (kM) (J) (k²) (H) (J) (YI) (☞)

**▲▲▲ ▼▼▼ La Quinta Inn Pittsburgh (Airport)** SH
(412) 269-0400. **$85-$115.** 8507 University Blvd. 1 mi n of Business Rt SR 60. Int corridors. **Pets:** Medium. Service with restrictions.

(SAVE) (X) (kM) (J) (H) (J)

## CRANBERRY TOWNSHIP

**▲▲▲ ▼▼▼ AmeriSuites (Pittsburgh/Cranberry)** SH
(724) 779-7900. **$119-$139.** 136 Emeryville Dr. I-76 (Pennsylvania Tpke), exit 28; I-79, exit 76 northbound; exit 78 southbound, 0.3 mi s on US 19. Int corridors. **Pets:** Small. $10 daily fee/pet. Designated rooms, service with restrictions, supervision.

(SAVE) (SÓ) (X) (kM) (J) (k²) (H) (J) (☞)

**▼▼▼ Hampton Inn Cranberry** SH
(724) 776-1000. **$89-$104.** 210 Executive Dr. I-76 (Pennsylvania Tpke), exit 28, 0.5 mi n on US 19, then 0.3 mi w on Freedom Rd; I-79, exit 78 southbound, 0.5 mi w on Freedom Rd. Int corridors. **Pets:** Accepted.

(ASK) (SÓ) (X) (J) (k²) (H) (J) (☒)

**▼▼▼ Holiday Inn Express** SH
(724) 772-1000. **$89-$99.** 20003 Rt 19. I-76 (Pennsylvania Tpke), exit 28, jct US 19 and I-76 (Pennsylvania Tpke); I-79, exit 76 northbound; exit 78 southbound, just s. Int corridors. **Pets:** Large. $10 daily fee/pet. Service with restrictions, supervision.

(ASK) (X) (H) (J)

**▼▼ Red Roof Inn-Cranberry Township-Pittsburgh North #7079** M
(724) 776-5670. **$60-$79.** 20009 Rt 19. I-76 (Pennsylvania Tpke), exit 28; I-79, exit 76 northbound; exit 78 southbound. Ext corridors. **Pets:** Accepted.

(X) (J)

**▼▼▼ Residence Inn Cranberry** SH
(724) 779-1000. **$116.** 1308 Freedom Rd. I-76, exit 28, 0.5 mi n on US 19, then 0.3 mi w; I-79, exit 78 southbound, 0.5 mi w. Int corridors. **Pets:** Accepted.

(ASK) (X) (H) (J) (☞) (X)

## DELMONT

**▼▼ Super 8 Motel** M
(724) 468-4888. **$53-$57.** 180 Sheffield Dr. SR 66, just s of US 22. Int corridors. **Pets:** $5 daily fee/pet. Service with restrictions, supervision.

(ASK) (SÓ) (X) (kM) (H)

## GIBSONIA

**▼▼ Comfort Inn Gibsonia** M
(724) 444-8700. **$59-$159.** 5137 Rt 8. I-76 (Pennsylvania Tpke), exit 39, just n. Ext corridors. **Pets:** Other species. $10 daily fee/pet. Service with restrictions, supervision.

(ASK) (SÓ) (X) (k²) (H) (J)

## GREEN TREE

**▼▼▼ Hampton Inn Hotel Green Tree** SH
(412) 922-0100. **$85-$94 (no credit cards).** 555 Trumbull Dr. I-279, exit 4A to jct US 22 and 30, 1 mi nw via Mansfield Ave. Int corridors. **Pets:** Other species. Service with restrictions, supervision.

(ASK) (SÓ) (X) (J) (H) (J)

**▲▲▲ ▼▼▼ Holiday Inn-Green Tree** SH
(412) 922-8100. **$99.** 401 Holiday Dr. I-279, exit 4A to jct US 22 and 30, 1 mi nw via Mansfield Ave. Int corridors. **Pets:** Medium. Service with restrictions, supervision.

(SAVE) (SÓ) (X) (k²) (H) (J) (YI) (☞)

**▲▲▲ ▼▼▼ Quality Suites** SH
(412) 279-6300. **$109-$149.** 700 Mansfield Ave. I-279, exit 4A to jct US 22 and 30, 1.5 mi nw. Ext corridors. **Pets:** Accepted.

(SAVE) (SÓ) (X) (J) (H) (J) (☞) (X)

**(AAA) ▼▼▼ The Radisson Hotel Pittsburgh/Green Tree** 🄻
(412) 922-8400. **$99-$250.** 101 Radisson Dr. I-279, exit 4A to jct US 22 and 30, 1.1 mi nw via Mansfield Ave. Int corridors. **Pets:** Other species. $100 deposit/room. Service with restrictions, supervision.
[SAVE] [S🄳] [✕] [&M] [🄰] [&] [🄱] [🖵] [▯] [🍴] [⚓] [✕]

## HARMARVILLE

**▼ Days Inn Harmarville** 🄼
(412) 828-5400. **$57-$75.** 6 Landings Dr. I-76 (Pennsylvania Tpke), exit 48, just s on Freeport Rd. Ext corridors. **Pets:** Accepted.
[ASK] [S🄳] [✕] [🄱] [🖵]

## MARS

**▼▼ Comfort Inn Cranberry Township** 🅂🄷
(724) 772-2700. **$59-$95.** 924 Sheraton Dr. I-76 (Pennsylvania Tpke), exit 28; I-79, exit 76 northbound; exit 78 southbound, 0.5 mi s on US 19. Int corridors. **Pets:** Accepted.
[ASK] [S🄳] [✕] [🄰] [🄱] [🖵]

**▼ Motel 6 Pittsburgh North Cranberry #42** 🄼
(724) 776-4333. **$45-$59.** 19025 Perry Hwy. I-76 (Pennsylvania Tpke), exit 28, jct US 19; I-79, exit 76 northbound; exit 78 southbound on US 19. Ext corridors. **Pets:** Accepted.
[S🄳] [✕] [&] [🄱]

## MONACA

**▼▼▼ Holiday Inn Express Hotel & Suites-Center Township** 🅂🄷
(724) 728-5121. **$89-$99.** 105 Stone Quarry Rd. SR 60, exit 12, just n. Int corridors. **Pets:** Other species. $10 daily fee/pet. Service with restrictions, supervision.
[ASK] [✕] [🄱] [🖵] [⚓]

## MONROEVILLE

**▼▼ Comfort Inn Pittsburgh East** 🅂🄷
(412) 244-1600. **$79-$139.** 699 Rodi Rd. I-376, exit 11, just n. Int corridors. **Pets:** Accepted.
[ASK] [S🄳] [✕] [&] [🄱] [🖵] [🍴] [⚓] [✕]

**▼▼ Days Inn-Monroeville** 🄼
(412) 856-1610. **$42-$82.** 2727 Mosside Blvd. I-76 (Pennsylvania Tpke), exit 57; I-376, exit 14A, 1 mi s on SR 48. Ext corridors. **Pets:** Dogs only. $25 daily fee/room. Service with restrictions, supervision.
[ASK] [S🄳] [✕] [🄱]

**▼▼▼ Hampton Inn Monroeville/Pittsburgh** 🅂🄷
(412) 380-4000. **$114-$144.** 3000 Mosside Blvd. I-76 (Pennsylvania Tpke), exit 57; I-376, exit 14A, 0.3 mi s on SR 48. Int corridors. **Pets:** Accepted.
[ASK] [S🄳] [✕] [🄰] [&] [🄱] [🖵] [⚓]

**▼▼ Red Roof Inn-Monroeville #7174** 🄼
(412) 856-4738. **$54-$74.** 2729 Mosside Blvd. I-76 (Pennsylvania Tpke), exit 57; I-376, exit 14A, 0.8 mi s on SR 48. Ext corridors. **Pets:** Accepted.
[✕]

**▼▼ Super 8 Motel Pittsburgh/Monroeville** 🄼
(724) 733-8008. **$57-$65.** 1807 Rt 286. I-76 (Pennsylvania Tpke), exit 57; I-376, exit 14A, 2 mi e on US 22 E, then 2 mi e. **Pets:** $5 one-time fee/room. Supervision.
[ASK] [S🄳] [✕] [🄱]

## MOON RUN

**(AAA) ▼▼▼▼ AmeriSuites (Pittsburgh/Airport)** 🅂🄷
(412) 494-0202. **$139.** 6011 Campbells Run Rd. Jct US 22 and 30, exit Moon Run Rd, just w. Int corridors. **Pets:** Very small. $10 daily fee/pet. Service with restrictions, supervision.
[SAVE] [S🄳] [✕] [&M] [🄰] [&] [🄱] [🖵] [⚓]

**(AAA) ▼▼▼ Comfort Inn-Pittsburgh Airport** 🅂🄷
(412) 787-2600. **$60-$95.** 7011 Old Steubenville Pike. US 22 and 30, jct SR 60; 4 mi w of jct I-279 and 79. Ext/int corridors. **Pets:** Accepted.
[SAVE] [S🄳] [✕] [🄰] [🄱] [🖵] [🍴]

**▼▼▼ Comfort Suites** 🅂🄷
(412) 494-5750. **$79-$89.** 750 Aten Rd. SR 60, exit 2 (Montour Run Rd). Int corridors. **Pets:** Accepted.
[ASK] [S🄳] [✕] [&] [🄱] [🖵] [⚓]

**▼▼▼ MainStay Suites Pittsburgh Airport** 🅂🄷 🐾
(412) 490-7343. **$79-$90.** 1000 Park Lane Dr. SR 60, exit 2 (Montour Run Rd), just w on Cliff Mine Rd, then just s. Int corridors. **Pets:** Other species. $100 one-time fee/pet. Designated rooms.
[ASK] [S🄳] [✕] [&] [🄱] [🖵]

**▼▼ Motel 6 Pittsburgh #657** 🄼
(412) 922-9400. **$35-$45.** 211 Beecham Dr. I-79, exit 60A, just s on Steubenville Pike (SR 60), then e. Ext corridors. **Pets:** Accepted.
[S🄳] [✕] [&M] [&]

**(AAA) ▼▼▼ Pittsburgh Airport Marriott** 🄻
(412) 788-8800. **$109-$189.** 777 Aten Rd. SR 60, exit 2 (Montour Run Rd). Int corridors. **Pets:** Accepted.
[SAVE] [✕] [🄱] [🖵] [🍴] [⚓] [✕]

**▼ Red Roof Inn South Airport #7030** 🄼
(412) 787-7870. **$50-$69.** 6404 Steubenville Pike. I-79, exit 60A, 3.2 mi w on SR 60. Ext/int corridors. **Pets:** Accepted.
[✕] [🄰] [&] [🄱]

**▼▼▼ Residence Inn-Pittsburgh Airport** 🅂🄷
(412) 787-3300. **$149-$199.** 1500 Park Lane Dr. SR 60, exit 2 (Montour Run Rd), just w on Cliff Mine Dr to Summit Park Dr, just s to Park Lane Dr, then just e. Int corridors. **Pets:** Accepted.
[ASK] [S🄳] [✕] [&M] [🄰] [&] [🄱] [🖵] [⚓] [✕]

**▼▼ Sleep Inn Pittsburgh Airport** 🅂🄷
(412) 859-4000. **$74-$90.** 2500 Marketplace Blvd. SR 60, exit 2 (Montour Run Rd), 0.5 mi e, then 0.5 mi n. Int corridors. **Pets:** Small. $25 one-time fee/pet. Service with restrictions, supervision.
[ASK] [S🄳] [✕] [🄰] [&] [🖵] [⚓]

## NEW KENSINGTON

**▼▼ Clarion Hotel** 🅂🄷
(724) 335-9171. **$76-$99, 3 day notice.** 300 Tarentum Bridge Rd. SR 366, 1.5 mi s of SR 28, exit 14; at south end of Tarentum Bridge. Int corridors. **Pets:** Other species. Service with restrictions, supervision.
[ASK] [S🄳] [✕] [&] [🄱] [🖵] [🍴] [⚓]

## PITTSBURGH

**(AAA) ▼▼▼ Days Inn Pittsburgh** 🄼
(412) 531-8900. **$55-$120.** 1150 Banksville Rd. I-279, exit 5C northbound; exit 5A southbound, 0.5 mi s on US 19. Ext/int corridors. **Pets:** Accepted.
[SAVE] [✕] [&] [🄱] [🍴] [⚓]

**▼▼▼ Hilton Pittsburgh** 🄻
(412) 391-4600. **$99-$355.** 600 Commonwealth Pl. On Commonwealth Pl; in Gateway Center. Int corridors. **Pets:** Accepted.
[✕] [&M] [🄰] [&] [🄱] [🖵] [🍴]

**(AAA) ▼▼▼ Holiday Inn Pittsburgh North Hills** 🅂🄷
(412) 366-5200. **$79-$109.** 4859 McKnight Rd. I-279, exit 11, 7 mi n on US 19. Int corridors. **Pets:** Medium, other species. $25 one-time fee/room. Designated rooms, service with restrictions, crate.
[SAVE] [✕] [🄰] [&] [🄱] [🖵] [🍴] [⚓]

**▼▼▼ Omni William Penn Hotel** 🄻
(412) 281-7100. **$109-$219.** 530 William Penn Pl. Jct 6th St and William Penn Pl. Int corridors. **Pets:** Accepted.
[ASK] [S🄳] [✕] [&] [🄱] [🖵] [🍴]

**▼▼▼ Residence Inn by Marriott Pittsburgh-Oakland** 🆂🅷
(412) 621-2200. **$159-$229.** 3896 Bigelow Blvd. On SR 380. Int corridors. **Pets:** Accepted.

⊠ 🔑 📧 🖵 🏊 🔏

**▼▼▼ Sheraton Station Square Hotel** 🅻🅷
(412) 261-2000. **$239-$314.** 300 W Station Square St. I-376, exit Grant St, south end of Smithfield St Bridge. Int corridors. **Pets:** Accepted.

A$K ⊠ 🔑 📧 🖵 ¶¶ 🏊 🔏

**▼▼▼ The Westin Convention Center Pittsburgh** 🅻🅷 ❖
(412) 281-3700. **$89-$325.** 1000 Penn Ave. At Liberty Center; adjacent to convention center. Int corridors. **Pets:** Small. $50 one-time fee/room. Service with restrictions, supervision.

A$K 🆂🔟 ⊠ 🖉 📧 🖵 ¶¶ 🏊 🔏

**▼▼▼ Wyndham Garden Pittsburgh University Place** 🅻🅷
(412) 683-2040. **$109-$189.** 3454 Forbes Ave. Jct Forbes Ave and McKee Pl. Int corridors. **Pets:** Accepted.

A$K ⊠ 🔑 📧 🖵 ¶¶

# WASHINGTON

**AAA ▼▼ Ramada Inn** 🆂🅷
(724) 225-9750. **$69-$99.** 1170 W Chestnut St. I-70, exit 15, 0.5 mi e on US 40. Ext/int corridors. **Pets:** Small. $30 one-time fee/room. Designated rooms, service with restrictions, crate.

🆂🅰🆅🅴 🆂🔟 ⊠ 📧 🖵 ¶¶ 🏊

**▼▼ ▼▼ Red Roof Inn #7048** 🅼
(724) 228-5750. **$45-$55.** 1399 W Chestnut St. I-70, exit 15, just e on US 40. Ext/int corridors. **Pets:** Accepted.

⊠ 🔑 📧

# WEST MIFFLIN

**▼▼ ▼▼ Comfort Inn-West Mifflin** 🆂🅷
(412) 653-6600. **$70-$165.** 1340 Lebanon Church Rd. 0.6 mi e of jct SR 51. Int corridors. **Pets:** $10 daily fee/room. Designated rooms, service with restrictions, supervision.

A$K 🆂🔟 ⊠ 🔑 📧 🖵 🏊

**▼▼▼ Holiday Inn Express Hotel & Suites** 🆂🅷
(412) 469-1900. **$89-$129.** 3122 Lebanon Church Rd. 1.5 mi e of jct SR 51. Int corridors. **Pets:** Other species. $10 daily fee/pet. Service with restrictions, crate.

A$K 🆂🔟 ⊠ 📧 🖵

---

## END METROPOLITAN AREA

---

# PITTSTON

**AAA ▼▼ ▼▼ Knights Inn-Scranton/Pittston** 🅼
(570) 654-6020. **$40-$85.** 310 SR 315. I-81, exit 175 northbound, just s on SR 315; exit 175A southbound; I-476 (Northeast Extension Pennslyvania Tpke). exit 115. Ext corridors. **Pets:** Small. Service with restrictions, supervision.

🆂🅰🆅🅴 🆂🔟 ⊠ 📧

**AAA ▼▼ ▼▼ Super 8 Motel** 🆂🅷
(570) 654-3301. **$45-$150.** 307 Rt 315 Hwy. I-81, exit 48 northbound, just s on SR 315; exit 48A southbound and 37 (Northeast Pennsylvania Tpke). Int corridors. **Pets:** Medium, other species. $10 daily fee/pet. Designated rooms, service with restrictions, supervision.

🆂🅰🆅🅴 🆂🔟 ⊠ 🖉 🔑 📧

**▼▼ ▼▼ Victoria Inns and Suites** 🆂🅷
(570) 655-1234. **$89.** 400 SR 315. I-81, exit 175 northbound; exit 175B southbound; I-476 (Northeast Extension Pennsylvania Tpke), exit 115. Int corridors. **Pets:** Other species. Service with restrictions, supervision.

A$K 🆂🔟 ⊠ 📧 🖵 ¶¶

---

## POCONO MOUNTAINS AREA

---

# BLAKESLEE

**AAA ▼▼▼▼ Best Western Inn-Blakeslee/Pocono** 🆂🅷
(570) 646-6000. **$80-$185.** New Ventures Business Park. I-80, exit 284, just n. Int corridors. **Pets:** Medium. $50 deposit/room. Service with restrictions, supervision.

🆂🅰🆅🅴 🆂🔟 ⊠ ᴹ 🖉 🔑 🖵 🏊

**▼▼▼▼ Blue Berry Mountain Inn** 🅱🅱
(570) 646-7144. **$110, 30 day notice.** Thomas Rd. I-80, exit 284, 3 mi n on SR 115, just n on Thomas Rd, then to the end of Edmund Dr. Int corridors. **Pets:** Accepted.

A$K 🆂🔟 ⊠ 📧 🖵 🏊 🔏

# EAST STROUDSBURG

**AAA ▼▼▼▼ Budget Motel** 🆂🅷
(570) 424-5451. **$59-$95, 3 day notice.** I-80, exit 308. I-80, exit 308, just se on Greentree Rd. Ext/int corridors. **Pets:** Medium. Designated rooms, service with restrictions, crate.

🆂🅰🆅🅴 🆂🔟 ⊠ 📧 ¶¶

**▼▼ ▼▼ Super 8 Motel** 🅼
(570) 424-7411. **$60-$120.** 340 Greentree Dr. I-80, exit 308, just se. Int corridors. **Pets:** Accepted.

A$K 🆂🔟 ⊠ ᴹ 📧

# HAMLIN

**AAA ▼▼▼▼ Comfort Inn** 🆂🅷
(570) 689-4148. **$80-$150.** 117 Twin Rocks Rd. I-84, exit 17, just n on SR 191. Int corridors. **Pets:** Accepted.

🆂🅰🆅🅴 🆂🔟 ⊠ 📧 🖵

# LAKE HARMONY

**AAA ▼▼▼▼ Ramada Inn-Pocono** 🆂🅷
(570) 443-8471. **$75-$115.** I-80, exit 277, 0.5 mi e; I-476 (Northeast Extension Pennsylvania Tpke), exit 95 (Pocono). Int corridors. **Pets:** Accepted.

🆂🅰🆅🅴 🆂🔟 ⊠ 🖉 🔑 📧 🖵 ¶¶ 🏊 🔏

## MATAMORAS

▼▼▼ **Best Western Inn at Hunt's Landing** 🆂🅷 ❀
(570) 491-2400. **$79-$239.** 120 Rt 6 & 209. I-84, exit 53. Int corridors.
**Pets:** Other species. $10 daily fee/room. Designated rooms, service with
restrictions.

(ASK) 🆂 ✕ �I 🖥️ ⏻ ↼

## MILFORD

🅰🅰🅰 ▼▼▼ **Milford Motel** 🅼
(570) 296-6411. **$50-$95, 3 day notice.** 591 Rt 6 & 209. On US 6 and
209 N, 0.7 mi e. Ext corridors. **Pets:** Accepted.

(SAVE) 🆂 ✕ 🔌

🅰🅰🅰 ▼▼▼ **Red Carpet Inn-Milford** 🅼 ❀
(570) 296-9444. **$65-$115, 7 day notice.** 240 Rt 6. I-84, exit 46, just s.
Ext corridors. **Pets:** Small. $7 daily fee/pet. Designated rooms, no service,
supervision.

(SAVE) 🆂 ✕ 🔌

🅰🅰🅰 ▼ **Scottish Inns** 🅼
(570) 491-4414. **$50-$95.** 274 Rt 6 & 209. I-84, exit 53, 1 mi s. Ext
corridors. **Pets:** Accepted.

(SAVE) 🆂 ✕ 🔌 🖥️

---

# END AREA

---

## PUNXSUTAWNEY

▼ **Pantall Hotel** 🆂🅷
(814) 938-6600. **$59-$105.** 135 E Mahoning St. On US 119/SR 36;
downtown. Int corridors. **Pets:** Medium. Service with restrictions, supervision.

(ASK) 🆂 ✕ 🔌 ⏻

## READING

🅰🅰🅰 ▼▼▼▼ **Best Western Dutch Colony Inn & Suites** 🆂🅷
(610) 779-2345. **$88-$118.** 4635 Perkiomen Ave. US 422, 0.3 mi e of
jct US 422 business route. Ext/int corridors. **Pets:** Accepted.

(SAVE) 🆂 ✕ 🔌 🔌 🔌 🖥️ ⏻ ↼ ✕

🅰🅰🅰 ▼▼▼ **Quality Inn Airport** 🆂🅷
(610) 736-0400. **$55-$100.** 2017 Bernville Rd. US 222, exit SR 183, 2
mi s. Int corridors. **Pets:** Small, dogs only. $50 deposit/pet, $15 one-time
fee/pet. Designated rooms, service with restrictions, supervision.

(SAVE) 🆂 ✕ 🔌 🖥️

▼▼▼ **Wyndham Reading** 🅻🅷
(610) 372-3700. **$94-$139.** 100 N 5th St. 5th and Washington sts;
downtown. Int corridors. **Pets:** Accepted.

(ASK) ✕ 🔌 🔌 🔌 🔌 🖥️ ⏻

## ST. MARYS

▼▼▼ **Comfort Inn** 🆂🅷
(814) 834-2030. **$70-$90.** 195 Comfort Ln. SR 255, south end of town.
Int corridors. **Pets:** Accepted.

(ASK) 🆂 ✕ 🔌 🖥️ ↼

## SAYRE

▼▼▼ **Best Western Grand Victorian** 🆂🅷
(570) 888-7711. **$99-$179.** 255 Spring St. SR 17, exit 61, just s. Int
corridors. **Pets:** Small, other species. $25 one-time fee/room. Service with
restrictions, supervision.

(ASK) 🆂 ✕ 🔌 🖥️ ⏻ ↼ ✕

## SCRANTON

🅰🅰🅰 ▼▼▼▼ **Clarion Hotel** 🅻🅷
(570) 344-9811. **$79-$139, 30 day notice.** 300 Meadow Ave. I-81, exit
184, just w. Int corridors. **Pets:** $25 one-time fee/room. Service with
restrictions, crate.

(SAVE) 🆂 ✕ 🔌 🔌 🖥️ ⏻ ↼ ✕

## SELINSGROVE

🅰🅰🅰 ▼▼▼ **Comfort Inn** 🆂🅷
(570) 374-8880. **$69-$169.** 710 S US Hwy 11 & 15. Just n of jct US
522. Int corridors. **Pets:** Medium, other species. $25 daily fee/room. Des-
ignated rooms, service with restrictions, crate.

(SAVE) 🆂 ✕ 🔌 🖥️ ↼

## SHAMOKIN DAM

🅰🅰🅰 ▼▼▼▼ **Hampton Inn** 🆂🅷
(570) 743-2223. **$139-$169.** 3 Stettler Ave. US 11 and 15, 1 mi s of jct
SR 61. Int corridors. **Pets:** Medium. $25 one-time fee/room. Designated
rooms, service with restrictions, supervision.

(SAVE) 🆂 ✕ 🔌 🔌 🔌 🖥️ ↼

🅰🅰🅰 ▼▼▼ **Quality Inn & Suites** 🅼
(570) 743-1111. **$69-$169.** 2 Susquehanna Tr. US 11 and 15; just n of
jct SR 61. Ext corridors. **Pets:** Accepted.

(SAVE) 🆂 ✕ 🔌 🖥️ ↼

## SHARTLESVILLE

🅰🅰🅰 ▼▼ **Dutch Motel** 🅼
(610) 488-1479. **$40-$70.** 1 Motel Dr. I-78, exit 23, just nw. Ext corridors. **Pets:** Accepted.

(SAVE) 🆂 ✕ 🔌 🖥️

## SHICKSHINNY

▼▼ **The Blue Heron Bed & Breakfast** 🅱🅱
(570) 864-3305. **$60-$90 (no credit cards), 3 day notice.** 1270 Bethel
Hill Rd. Jct US 11, 6.2 mi n on SR 239, then 2 mi n on CR 4016
(Harveyville/Bethel Hill Rd). Int corridors. **Pets:** Accepted.

✕ 🔌

## SLIPPERY ROCK

▼ **Evening Star Motel** 🅼
(724) 794-3211. **$49.** 915 New Castle Rd. I-79, exit 105, 0.5 mi e on
SR 108. Ext corridors. **Pets:** Accepted.

(ASK) ✕ 🔌 🖥️

## SOUTH WILLIAMSPORT

🅰🅰🅰 ▼▼ **Quality Inn Williamsport** 🆂🅷
(570) 323-9801. **$79-$209.** 234 Montgomery Pike. 0.8 mi s on US 15.
Int corridors. **Pets:** $25 one-time fee/pet. Designated rooms, service with
restrictions, supervision.

(SAVE) 🆂 ✕ 🔌 🔌 🖥️ ↼

🅰🅰🅰 ▼▼ **Ridgemont Motel** 🅼
(570) 321-5300. **$39-$43.** 637 Rt 15 Hwy. 1.2 mi s on US 15. Ext
corridors. **Pets:** Accepted.

(SAVE) 🆂 ✕ 🔌

## STATE COLLEGE

▼▼ **The Autoport Motel & Restaurant Inc** 🆂🅷
(814) 237-7666. **$65-$89.** 1405 S Atherton St. US 322 business route,
1.4 mi e of jct SR 26. Ext/int corridors. **Pets:** $10 daily fee/pet. Desig-
nated rooms, service with restrictions, supervision.

(ASK) ✕ 🔌 🖥️ ⏻ ↼

**Comfort Suites** 🆂🅷
(814) 235-1900. **$79-$250, 14 day notice.** 132 Village Dr. SR 26, 1.1 mi on Business Rt US 322 W (Atherton St), just ne; center. Int corridors. **Pets:** Other species. $50 deposit/room, $20 daily fee/room. Designated rooms, service with restrictions, supervision.

**Days Inn Penn State** 🅻🅷
(814) 238-8454. **$93-$109, 30 day notice.** 240 S Pugh St. Just e of SR 26 northbound; 0.4 mi n of jct US 322 business route; downtown. Int corridors. **Pets:** Other species. $10 daily fee/pet. Supervision.

**Happy Valley Motor Inn** 🅼
(814) 234-1111. **$47-$130.** 1245 S Atherton St. 1.3 mi e on US 322 business route. Ext/int corridors. **Pets:** $20 one-time fee/room. Service with restrictions, supervision.

**Motel 6 State College** 🅼
(814) 234-1600. **$44-$66.** 1274 N Atherton St. US 322 business route, 1 mi w of jct SR 26. Int corridors. **Pets:** Accepted.

**Nittany Budget Motel** 🅼
(814) 238-0015. **$47-$51.** 2070 Cato Ave. SR 26, 2.6 mi s of jct US 322 business route. Ext corridors. **Pets:** Small, other species. $5 daily fee/pet. Supervision.

**Residence Inn by Marriott** 🆂🅷
(814) 235-6960. **$124-$169.** 1555 University Dr. US 322 business route, 1.5 mi e of jct SR 26. Int corridors. **Pets:** Accepted.

**Sleep Inn** 🆂🅷
(814) 235-1020. **$59-$150.** 111 Village Dr. US 322 business route, 1 mi w of jct SR 26. Int corridors. **Pets:** Medium. $25 one-time fee/pet. Service with restrictions, supervision.

**Super 8 State College** 🆂🅷
(814) 237-8005. **$54-$94.** 1663 N Atherton St. US 322 business route, 1.6 mi e of jct SR 26. Int corridors. **Pets:** $25 one-time fee/room. Designated rooms, service with restrictions, supervision.

## TOWANDA

**Towanda Motel & Restaurant** 🅼
(570) 265-2178. **$55-$80, 3 day notice.** 383 York Ave. 0.8 mi w on US 6. Ext corridors. **Pets:** Accepted.

## TOWN HILL

**Days Inn Breezewood** 🆂🅷
(814) 735-3860. **$53-$69.** 9648 Old Rt 126. I-70, exit 156, just n. Int corridors. **Pets:** Accepted.

## WARREN

**Holiday Inn of Warren** 🆂🅷
(814) 726-3000. **$94-$125.** 210 Ludlow St. Jct US 6, just n on Ludlow St (US 62 N). Int corridors. **Pets:** Accepted.

**Warren Super 8 Motel** 🆂🅷
(814) 723-8881. **$70-$74, 7 day notice.** 204 Struthers St. 1.5 mi w on US 6, exit Ludlow St, w on Allegheny, then s. Ext/int corridors. **Pets:** $25 deposit/room. Designated rooms, service with restrictions, supervision.

## WAYNESBORO

**Best Western of Waynesboro** 🅼
(717) 762-9113. **$75-$95, 3 day notice.** 239 W Main St. 0.5 mi w on SR 16. Ext corridors. **Pets:** Other species. $20 daily fee/pet. Designated rooms, service with restrictions, supervision.

## WAYNESBURG

**Comfort Inn** 🆂🅷
(724) 627-3700. **$69-$79.** 100 Comfort Ln. I-79, exit 14, just e. Int corridors. **Pets:** Accepted.

**Econo Lodge** 🅼
(724) 627-5544. **$47-$62.** 126 Miller Ln. I-79, exit 14, just w. Ext corridors. **Pets:** Service with restrictions, supervision.

**Super 8 Motel-Waynesburg** 🅼
(724) 627-8880. **$50-$55.** 100 Stanley Dr. I-79, exit 14, just w. Int corridors. **Pets:** Other species. Service with restrictions, supervision.

## WELLSBORO

**Coach Stop Inn** 🅼
(570) 724-5361. **$60-$90.** 4755 US Rt 6 W. On US 6, 12 mi w. Ext/int corridors. **Pets:** Small. $10 daily fee/pet. Service with restrictions, supervision.

**Penn Wells Lodge** 🅼
(570) 724-3463. **$50-$100.** 4 Main St. Just n on US 6 and SR 287. Ext/int corridors. **Pets:** Small. $20 daily fee/pet. Service with restrictions, supervision.

## WEST HAZLETON

**Comfort Inn Hazleton West Hazleton** 🆂🅷 🐾
(570) 455-9300. **$79-$149.** 58 SR 93. I-81, exit 145, 0.3 mi se; I-80, exit 256, 3.8 mi se. Int corridors. **Pets:** Other species. $5 daily fee/pet. Service with restrictions, crate.

## WEST MIDDLESEX

**Super 8 Motel-West Middlesex/Sharon** 🆂🅷
(724) 528-3888. **$54-$74.** 3369 New Castle Rd. I-80, exit 4B (SR 18), just s. Int corridors. **Pets:** Accepted.

## WHITE HAVEN

**Econo Lodge Inn & Suites** 🅼
(570) 443-0391. **$70-$100.** SR 940. I-80, exit 277 (Lake Harmony), 2.2 mi e; I-476, exit 95 (Pocono), 2 mi w. Ext corridors. **Pets:** Accepted.

## WILKES-BARRE

**Best Western Genetti Hotel & Conference Center** 🅻🅷
(570) 823-6152. **$99.** 77 E Market St. Market and Washington sts; downtown. Int corridors. **Pets:** Accepted.

**Econo Lodge** 🆂🅷 🐾
(570) 823-0600. **$55-$185.** 1075 Wilkes-Barre Township Blvd. I-81, exit 165 southbound; exit 165B northbound, on SR 309 business route. Int corridors. **Pets:** Large, other species. $10 daily fee/pet. Service with restrictions, supervision.

**AAA ◆◆ Holiday Inn SH ☼**
(570) 824-8901. **$94-$199.** 880 Kidder St. I-81, exit 170B to exit 1 (SR 309 S business route). Ext corridors. **Pets:** Medium, other species. $15 one-time fee/room. Service with restrictions, supervision.

SAVE S6 ⊠ &M 🔊 🖉 🔲 🔲 ⊣ 🌊

**AAA ◆◆◆ Host Inn Residential Suites SH ☼**
(570) 270-4678. **$129-$239.** 860 Kidder St. I-81, exit 170B to exit 1 off expressway, then 0.5 mi w. Int corridors. **Pets:** Other species. $15 one-time fee/pet. Designated rooms, service with restrictions, crate.

SAVE S6 ⊠ &M 🔊 🖉 🔲 🔲 ⊣

**◆◆ Red Roof Inn #7139 M**
(570) 829-6422. **$52-$66.** 1035 Hwy 315. I-81, exit 170B, jct SR 115, 0.7 mi w, exit 1 (SR 309 S business route) to SR 315, then just n. Ext corridors. **Pets:** Accepted.

⊠ 🔊 🖉 🔲

# WILLIAMSPORT

**AAA ◆◆ Best Western Williamsport Inn SH ☼**
(570) 326-1981. **$79-$129.** 1840 E 3rd St. I-180, exit 25 (Faxon St), just e; 1 mi w of W 3rd St. Ext corridors. **Pets:** Small. $15 one-time fee/pet. Service with restrictions, supervision.

SAVE S6 ⊠ 🔲 🔲 🔲 ⊣ ⊠

**AAA ◆◆ Genetti Hotel & Suites SH**
(570) 326-6600. **$71-$106, 7 day notice.** 200 W Fourth St. Jct William St; downtown. Int corridors. **Pets:** Large, other species. Service with restrictions, crate.

SAVE S6 ⊠ 🖉 🔲 🔲 🔲 ⊣

**◆◆◆ Holiday Inn Williamsport SH**
(570) 327-8231. **$114-$134.** 100 Pine St. Jct US 220 and SR 15 S; downtown. Int corridors. **Pets:** Small. $15 one-time fee/room. Designated rooms, service with restrictions, supervision.

ASK S6 ⊠ 🔲 🔲 🔲 ⊣

# WIND GAP

**AAA ◆◆ Travel Inn of Wind Gap M**
(610) 863-4146. **$50-$90.** 499 E Moorestown Rd. SR 512, e of jct SR 33, exit Bath/Wind Gap. Ext corridors. **Pets:** Medium. $10 one-time fee/pet. No service, supervision.

SAVE ⊠ 🔲

# WYOMISSING

**◆◆◆ Days Inn SH**
(610) 374-1500. **$59-$129.** 910 Woodland Rd. US 422 W, exit Papermill Rd, just e. Int corridors. **Pets:** Small, other species. $10 daily fee/pet. Designated rooms, service with restrictions, crate.

ASK S6 ⊠ &M 🔊 🖉 🔲 🔲

**◆◆ Econo Lodge SH**
(610) 378-5105. **$58-$88, 3 day notice.** 635 Spring St. Just off US 422, exit Papermill Rd. Int corridors. **Pets:** Accepted.

ASK S6 ⊠ 🔊 🔲 🔲

**◆◆◆ Homewood Suites-Reading/Wyomissing SH**
(610) 736-3100. **$164-$325.** 2801 Papermill Rd. US 422, exit Papermill Rd, 1.8 mi nw; US 222, exit Spring Ridge Rd. Int corridors. **Pets:** Medium. $75 one-time fee/pet. Service with restrictions, supervision.

ASK ⊠ &M 🔊 🖉 🔲 🔲 ⊣

**AAA ◆◆◆ The Inn at Reading SH**
(610) 372-7811. **$79-$103.** 1040 Park Rd. US 222, exit N Wyomissing Blvd, just n, then 0.3 mi e. Int corridors. **Pets:** Accepted.

SAVE S6 ⊠ 🔊 🔲 🔲 🔲 ⊣ ⊠

**◆◆◆ Sheraton Reading Hotel SH ☼**
(610) 376-3811. **$209-$219.** 1741 W Papermill Rd. US 422, exit Papermill Rd. Int corridors. **Pets:** Other species. $10 daily fee/room. Service with restrictions, supervision.

ASK S6 ⊠ 🔊 🖉 🔲 🔲 🔲 ⊣ ⊠

# WYSOX

**◆◆◆ Comfort Inn SH ☼**
(570) 265-5691. **$99-$125.** US 6. Center. Int corridors. **Pets:** Other species. $10 one-time fee/room. Service with restrictions, supervision.

ASK S6 ⊠ &M 🔊 🖉 🔲 🔲 ⊣

# YORK

**◆◆◆ Four Points by Sheraton Hotel and Suites SH**
(717) 846-4940. **$149-$159, 3 day notice.** 1650 Toronita St. I-83, exit 21A northbound; exit 21 southbound, just ne. Int corridors. **Pets:** Accepted.

ASK S6 ⊠ 🖉 🔲 🔲 🔲 ⊣

**◆◆◆ Holiday Inn Holidome & Conference Center SH**
(717) 846-9500. **$124.** 2000 Loucks Rd. I-83, exit 21B northbound, 2.5 mi w on US 30, then just n; exit 22 southbound, 0.5 mi s on SR 181, 2.2 mi w on US 30, then just n. Int corridors. **Pets:** Accepted.

ASK S6 ⊠ 🔊 🖉 🔲 🔲 ⊣ ⊠

**AAA ◆◆◆ Holiday Inn York I-83 & Rt 30 SH**
(717) 845-5671. **$90-$97.** 334 Arsenal Rd. I-83, exit 21A northbound; exit 21 southbound, just e on US 30. Ext corridors. **Pets:** Accepted.

SAVE S6 ⊠ 🔊 🖉 🔲 🔲 🔲 ⊣

**◆◆ Red Roof Inn #315 M**
(717) 843-8181. **$51-$81.** 125 Arsenal Rd. I-83, exit 21B Northbound, 0.3 mi w on US 30; exit 21 southbound, 0.5 mi s on SR 181 to US 30. Int corridors. **Pets:** Accepted.

⊠ 🖉 🔲

**◆◆ Super 8 Motel M**
(717) 852-8686. **$55-$90, 7 day notice.** 40 Arsenal Rd. I-83, exit 21B northbound, 0.3 mi w on US 30; exit 21 southbound, 0.5 mi s on SR 181 to US 30. Int corridors. **Pets:** Accepted.

ASK S6 ⊠ 🔲

# RHODE ISLAND

## CRANSTON

**Days Inn** M
(401) 942-4200. **$79-$109, 14 day notice.** 101 New London Ave. I-95, exit 14B to SR 37; exit 2B westbound, 0.5 mi ne. Ext corridors. **Pets:** Dogs only. $10 daily fee/pet. Designated rooms, service with restrictions, supervision.

## MIDDLETOWN

**The Bay Willows Inn** M
(401) 847-8400. **$39-$179, 7 day notice.** 1225 Aquidneck Ave. Jct SR 138 and 138A. Ext corridors. **Pets:** Accepted.

**Howard Johnson Inn-Newport** SH
(401) 849-2000. **$49-$244.** 351 W Main Rd. On SR 114, 0.3 mi s of jct SR 138. Int corridors. **Pets:** Other species. $10 daily fee/pet. Designated rooms, service with restrictions, supervision.

**Royal Plaza Hotel** M
(401) 846-3555. **$69-$199, 3 day notice.** 425 E Main Rd (Rt 138). Jct SR 138A. Int corridors. **Pets:** Service with restrictions.

**SeaView Inn** M
(401) 846-5000. **$59-$229, 7 day notice.** 240 Aquidneck Ave (SR 138A). Jct SR 214. Ext corridors. **Pets:** Accepted.

## NEWPORT

**Beech Tree Inn** BB
(401) 847-9794. **$99-$350, 15 day notice.** 34 Rhode Island Ave. Just e of SR 114; 0.8 mi s of jct SR 138. Int corridors. **Pets:** Service with restrictions.

**The Hotel Viking** LH
(401) 847-3300. **$139-$399, 7 day notice.** One Bellevue Ave. Corner of Kay St, Church and Bellevue Ave. Int corridors. **Pets:** Dogs only. Service with restrictions, supervision.

**Hyatt Regency Newport Hotel & Spa** LH
(401) 851-1234. **$99-$389, 3 day notice.** 1 Goat Island. 0.8 mi w of America's Cup Ave, follow signs to Goat Island. Int corridors. **Pets:** Accepted.

## NORTH KINGSTOWN

**Hamilton Village Inn** M
(401) 295-0700. **$79-$119, 7 day notice.** 642 Boston Neck Rd. SR 1A, 1.3 mi s of jct SR 102. Ext corridors. **Pets:** Other species. Designated rooms, service with restrictions, supervision.

## PORTSMOUTH

**Founder's Brook Motel & Suites** M
(401) 683-1244. **$59-$159, 3 day notice.** 314 Boyd's Ln. Jct SR 24, exit Mt. Hope Blvd, on SR 138. Ext corridors. **Pets:** Small, dogs only. $10 daily fee/pet. Designated rooms, service with restrictions, supervision.

## PROVIDENCE

**Marriott Providence Hotel** LH
(401) 272-2400. **$134-$206.** One Orms St. I-95, exit 23 to state offices. Int corridors. **Pets:** Other species. $50 one-time fee/pet. Service with restrictions, supervision.

**Providence Biltmore Hotel** LH
(401) 421-0700. **$249-$279.** 11 Dorrance St. I-95, exit 22A; downtown. Int corridors. **Pets:** Accepted.

**The Westin Providence** LH
(401) 598-8000. **$169-$419.** One W Exchange St. I-95, exit 22A; downtown. Int corridors. **Pets:** Medium, dogs only. Service with restrictions, supervision.

## WAKEFIELD

**The Kings' Rose Bed & Breakfast Inn** BB
(401) 783-5222. **$120-$170, 7 day notice.** 1747 Mooresfield Rd (SR 138). I-95, exit 3A, 11 mi e on SR 138; 3.3 mi w of US 1. Int corridors. **Pets:** Service with restrictions, supervision.

## WARWICK

**Crowne Plaza Hotel at the Crossings** LH
(401) 732-6000. **$139-$229.** 801 Greenwich Ave. I-95, exit 12A southbound; exit 12 northbound, 0.3 mi se on SR 5. Int corridors. **Pets:** Large, dogs only. $50 deposit/room. Service with restrictions, crate.

**Hampton Inn & Suites Providence-Warwick Airport** SH
(401) 739-8888. **$99-$179.** 2100 Post Rd. I-95, exit 13, e to US 1, then just n. Int corridors. **Pets:** Large. Service with restrictions.

**Holiday Inn Express Hotel & Suites** SH
(401) 736-5000. **$135-$159.** 901 Jefferson Blvd. I-95, exit 13, 0.4 mi on Airport Connector Rd, then exit Jefferson Blvd. Int corridors. **Pets:** $50 deposit/room. Designated rooms, service with restrictions, supervision.

**Homestead Studio Suites Hotel-Providence/Airport/Warwick** SH
(401) 732-6667. **$100.** 268 Metro Center Blvd. I-95, exit 12A, 0.4 mi e on SR 113, 0.4 mi n on SR 5, then 0.4 mi e. Int corridors. **Pets:** $25 daily fee/pet. Service with restrictions, supervision.

**Residence Inn by Marriott** SH
(401) 737-7100. **$79-$209.** 500 Kilvert St. I-95, exit 13 to Jefferson Blvd, 0.4 mi n, then 0.6 mi w. Ext corridors. **Pets:** Accepted.

**Sheraton Providence Airport Hotel** LH
(401) 738-4000. **$285.** 1850 Post Rd. I-95, exit 13, 0.6 mi n on US 1. Int corridors. **Pets:** Accepted.

# WESTERLY

**(AAA)** ▼ **The Pine Lodge** 🄲🄰
(401) 322-0333. **$63-$94.** 92 Old Post Rd. On US 1, 1.8 mi ne of jct SR 78. Ext corridors. **Pets:** Accepted.

[SAVE] [X] [■] [X]

# WOONSOCKET

▼▼▼ **Holiday Inn Express Hotel & Suites** 🆂🅷
(401) 769-5000. **$110-$140.** 194 Fortin Dr. I-295, exit 9 on SR 122, 3.5 mi n via SR 146/99/122. Int corridors. **Pets:** Other species. $10 daily fee/pet. Service with restrictions, crate.

[ASK] [S🐾] [X] [&M] [🖉] [👤] [■] [▣] [⊷]

# WYOMING

**(AAA)** ▼▼▼▼ **Stagecoach House Inn** 🅱🅱
(401) 539-9600. **$105-$199.** 1136 Main St (SR 138). I-95, exit 3B northbound, 0.7 mi nw; exit southbound, 0.4 mi now. Ext/int corridors. **Pets:** Large, dogs only. $20 daily fee/room. Designated rooms, service with restrictions, supervision.

[SAVE] [X] [🍴]

# SOUTH CAROLINA

## AIKEN

**▽ Days Inn-Downtown M**
(803) 649-5524. **$48-$60.** 1204 Richland Ave W. Jct US 1/78 and SR 19, 0.9 mi w on US 1/78. Ext corridors. **Pets:** Accepted.
[ASK] [S🄳] [✕] [🕜] [🖥] [≈]

**⦿ ▽▽ Econo Lodge M**
(803) 649-3968. **$40-$79.** 3560 Richland Ave W. Jct US 1/78 and SR 19, 2.6 mi w on US 1/78. Ext corridors. **Pets:** Accepted.
[SAVE] [S🄳] [✕] [🖥] [🖵] [≈]

**⦿ ▽▽ Quality Inn & Suites SH**
(803) 641-1100. **$60-$80.** 3608 Richland Ave W. Jct US 1/78 and SR 19, 2.9 mi w on US 1/78. Ext corridors. **Pets:** Large, other species. $10 daily fee/room. Service with restrictions, supervision.
[SAVE] [S🄳] [✕] [🕜] [🖥] [🖵] [≈]

**⦿ ▽▽ Ramada Limited SH**
(803) 648-6821. **$49-$64.** 1850 Richland Ave W. Jct US 1/78 and SR 19, 1.6 mi w on US 1/78. Ext corridors. **Pets:** $10 daily fee/pet. Service with restrictions, supervision.
[SAVE] [✕] [&] [🖥] [🖵] [≈]

**⦿ ▽▽ Sleep Inn SH**
(803) 644-9900. **$59-$89.** 1002 Monterey Dr. Jct US 78 and SR 302/19 (Whiskey Rd), 0.5 mi s on SR 19, then just e. Int corridors. **Pets:** $20 daily fee/pet. Service with restrictions, supervision.
[SAVE] [S🄳] [✕] [&M] [&] [🖥] [🖵] [≈]

**▽▽ Town & Country Inn BB ❖**
(803) 642-0270. **$80-$125.** 2340 Sizemore Cir. Jct US 78 and SR 302/19 (Whiskey Rd), 2.3 mi s on SR 19, then just w. Int corridors. **Pets:** Medium. $10 daily fee/pet. Service with restrictions, supervision.
[ASK] [S🄳] [✕] [≈] [🄭]

## ANDERSON

**▽◈◈ Country Inn & Suites SH ❖**
(864) 622-2200. **$79-$89.** 116 Interstate Blvd. I-85, exit 19B, just n, then just se. Int corridors. **Pets:** Small, other species. $25 daily fee/pet. Designated rooms, service with restrictions, supervision.
[ASK] [S🄳] [✕] [&M] [🕜] [&] [🖥] [🖵] [≈]

**▽▽ Days Inn M**
(864) 375-0375. **$69-$119.** 1007 Smith Mill Rd. I-85, exit 19A, just se. Ext corridors. **Pets:** Accepted.
[ASK] [S🄳] [✕] [&M] [🕜] [🖥] [🖵] [≈]

**⦿ ▽▽▽ Holiday Inn Express SH**
(864) 231-0231. **$75-$199.** 103 Anderson Business Park. I-85, exit 27, just s on SR 81. Int corridors. **Pets:** Small, dogs only. $25 one-time fee/room. Designated rooms, service with restrictions, supervision.
[SAVE] [✕] [&M] [🕜] [&] [🖥] [🖵] [≈]

**▽◈ La Quinta Inn Anderson SH**
(864) 225-3721. **$72-$91.** 3430 Clemson Blvd. I-85, exit 19A, 2.9 mi se on US 76/SR 28; exit 21 southbound, 2.6 mi s on US 178. Ext corridors. **Pets:** Medium. No service.
[ASK] [✕] [🕜] [&] [🖥] [🖵] [≈]

## BEAUFORT

**▽▽ Ramada Limited of Beaufort SH**
(843) 524-2144. **$59-$199.** 2001 Boundary St. Jct SR 170, 0.6 mi s on US 21. Ext corridors. **Pets:** Accepted.
[ASK] [S🄳] [✕] [🕜] [🖥] [🖵] [≈]

## BENNETTSVILLE

**⦿ ▽▽ Holiday Inn Express M ❖**
(843) 479-1700. **$69-$89.** 213 US Hwy 15 & 401 Bypass E. 0.6 mi s of center, just ne on US 15/401/SR 9. Ext corridors. **Pets:** $10 daily fee/room. Crate.
[SAVE] [S🄳] [✕] [🕜] [&] [🖥] [🖵] [≈]

## BLUFFTON

**▽▽▽ Comfort Suites of Bluffton SH ❖**
(843) 815-1700. **$90-$120.** 23 Towne Dr. I-95, exit 8 (US 278), 12.6 mi e on US 278; in Belfair Towne Village. Int corridors. **Pets:** Small, other species. $25 daily fee/pet. Designated rooms, service with restrictions, crate.
[ASK] [S🄳] [✕] [&M] [🕜] [&] [🖥] [🖵] [≈]

**▽▽▽ Holiday Inn Express Hotel & Suites SH**
(843) 757-2002. **$69-$129.** 35 Bluffton Rd. Jct William Hilton Pkwy (US 278/Bluffton Rd US 46), just se. Int corridors. **Pets:** Accepted.
[✕] [&M] [&] [🖥] [🖵] [≈]

## CAMDEN

**⦿ ▽▽ Colony Inn M**
(803) 432-5508. **$65-$75.** 2020 W DeKalb St. Jct US 521/1/601, 1.6 mi w on US 1/601. Ext/int corridors. **Pets:** Medium. Designated rooms, service with restrictions, supervision.
[SAVE] [S🄳] [✕] [🖥] [🖵] [🍴] [≈]

## CAYCE

**⦿ ▽▽ Riverside Inn M**
(803) 939-4688. **$55-$60.** 111 Knox Abbott Dr. US 21, just w of Congaree River Bridge. Ext corridors. **Pets:** $20 one-time fee/room. Service with restrictions, supervision.
[SAVE] [S🄳] [✕] [&] [🖥] [🖵] [≈] [✕]

# CHARLESTON METROPOLITAN AREA

## CHARLESTON

**Best Western Sweetgrass Inn** SH
(843) 571-6100. **$59-$189.** 1540 Savannah Hwy. US 17 S, 3.6 mi w of Ashley River Bridge; jct I-526 W (end) and US 17 N, 1.7 mi e. Ext corridors. **Pets:** Accepted.

**Charleston Place** LH ❖
(843) 722-4900. **$199-$499, 3 day notice.** 205 Meeting St. Between King and Meeting sts. Int corridors. **Pets:** $75 one-time fee/pet. Designated rooms, service with restrictions, supervision.

**Howard Johnson Riverfront** SH
(843) 722-4000. **$74-$149.** 250 Spring St. I-26, exit 221A (US 17 S), 1.2 mi sw; just e of Ashley River. Int corridors. **Pets:** Accepted.

**Residence Inn by Marriott** SH
(843) 571-7979. **$99-$239.** 90 Ripley Point Dr. US 17 S, just over Ashley River Bridge to Albermarle Rd, just s. Int corridors. **Pets:** Accepted.

**Town & Country Inn & Conference Center** SH
(843) 571-1000. **$79-$129.** 2008 Savannah Hwy. US 17 S, 3.5 mi nw of Ashley River Bridge; jct I-526 W (end) and US 17 N, just se. Ext corridors. **Pets:** $50 one-time fee/pet. Service with restrictions.

**Vendue Inn** CI
(843) 577-7970. **$155-$355, 3 day notice.** 19 Vendue Range. Off E Bay St, 1 blk from Waterfront Park; in historic district. Int corridors. **Pets:** Accepted.

## KIAWAH ISLAND

**Courtside Villas-Kiawah Island Golf Resort** CO
(843) 768-2121. **$117-$2700, 14 day notice.** 1 Town Center. 2 mi ne of main gate; in West Beach Village. Ext corridors. **Pets:** Dogs only. $25 daily fee/room. Designated rooms, service with restrictions, supervision.

**Fairway Oaks-Kiawah Island Golf Resort** CO
(843) 768-2121. **$117-$2700, 14 day notice.** 1 Town Center. 2 mi ne of main gate; in West Beach Village. Ext corridors. **Pets:** Dogs only. $25 daily fee/room. Designated rooms, service with restrictions, supervision.

**Mariners Watch Villas-Kiawah Island Golf Resort** CO
(843) 768-2121. **$117-$2700, 14 day notice.** 1 Town Center. 2 mi ne of main gate; in East Beach Village. Ext corridors. **Pets:** Dogs only. $25 daily fee/room. Designated rooms, service with restrictions, supervision.

**Parkside Villas-Kiawah Island Golf Resort** CO
(843) 768-2121. **$117-$2700, 14 day notice.** 1 Town Center. 2 mi ne of main gate; in East Beach Village. Ext corridors. **Pets:** Dogs only. $25 daily fee/room. Designated rooms, service with restrictions, supervision.

**Seascape Villas-Kiawah Island Golf Resort** CO
(843) 768-2121. **$117-$2700, 14 day notice.** 1 Town Center. 2 mi ne of main gate; in West Beach Village. Ext corridors. **Pets:** Dogs only. $25 daily fee/room. Designated rooms, service with restrictions, supervision.

**Shipwatch Villas-Kiawah Island Golf Resort** CO
(843) 768-2121. **$117-$2700, 14 day notice.** 1 Town Center. 2 mi ne of main gate; in West Beach Village. Ext corridors. **Pets:** Dogs only. $25 daily fee/room. Designated rooms, service with restrictions, supervision.

**Tennis Club Villas-Kiawah Island Golf Resort** CO
(843) 768-2121. **$117-$2700, 14 day notice.** 1 Town Center. 2 mi ne of main gate; in East Beach Village. Ext corridors. **Pets:** Dogs only. $25 daily fee/room. Designated rooms, service with restrictions, supervision.

**Turtle Cove Villas-Kiawah Island Golf Resort** CO
(843) 768-2121. **$117-$2700, 14 day notice.** 1 Town Center. 2 mi ne of main gate; in East Beach Village. Ext corridors. **Pets:** Dogs only. $25 daily fee/room. Designated rooms, service with restrictions, supervision.

**Turtle Point Villas-Kiawah Island Golf Resort** CO
(843) 768-2121. **$117-$2700, 14 day notice.** 1 Town Center. 2 mi ne of main gate; in East Beach Village. Ext corridors. **Pets:** Accepted.

**Wind Swept Villas-Kiawah Island Golf Resort** CO
(843) 768-2121. **$117-$2700, 14 day notice.** 1 Town Center. 2 mi ne of main gate; in East Beach Village. Ext corridors. **Pets:** Dogs only. $25 daily fee/room. Designated rooms, service with restrictions, supervision.

## MOUNT PLEASANT

**Comfort Inn East** SH
(843) 884-5853. **$49-$139.** 310 Hwy 17 (Johnnie Dodds Blvd). US 17, 0.7 mi n of Cooper River Bridge. Ext corridors. **Pets:** Medium, dogs only. $10 one-time fee/pet. Service with restrictions.

**Days Inn Patriots Point** M
(843) 881-1800. **$65-$205, 3 day notice.** 261 Johnnie Dodds Blvd. Just e of base of Cooper River Bridge. Ext corridors. **Pets:** Small, dogs only. $10 daily fee/pet. Designated rooms, service with restrictions, supervision.

**Hilton Charleston Harbor Resort & Marina** SH ❖
(843) 856-0028. **$99-$299.** 20 Patriots Point Rd. Base of Cooper River Bridge, 0.6 mi se on Coleman Blvd (SR 703), then 0.8 mi sw; past museum. Int corridors. **Pets:** Medium. $100 one-time fee/room. Service with restrictions.

**Homewood Suites by Hilton** SH
(843) 881-6950. **$99-$299, 7 day notice.** 1998 Riviera Dr. I-526, exit 32 (Georgetown/US 17 N), 1.4 mi ne on US 17, 1 mi se on Isle of Palms connector (SR 517), then just sw. Int corridors. **Pets:** Small. $75 one-time fee/room. Designated rooms, service with restrictions, supervision.

**MainStay Suites Mount Pleasant** SH
(843) 881-1722. **$59-$299.** 400 McGrath-Darby Blvd. Base of Cooper River Bridge, just ne on US 17, just n. Int corridors. **Pets:** Small, dogs only. $10 daily fee/pet. Designated rooms, service with restrictions.

**Red Roof Inn** M
(843) 884-1411. **$52-$84.** 301 Johnnie Dodds Blvd. Just e of base of Cooper River Bridge, on US 17 (Johnnie Dodds Blvd), then just s on McGrath-Darby Blvd. Ext corridors. **Pets:** Accepted.

▼▼▼ Residence Inn by Marriott SH ❖
(843) 881-1599. **$99-$189.** 1116 Isle of Palms Connector. I-526, exit 32 (Georgetown/US 17 N), 1.4 mi ne on US 17 to Isle of Palms connector (SR 517), then just se. Int corridors. **Pets:** Large. $75 one-time fee/room.

ASK S☐ ☒ ☖M ☐ ☐ ☒

▼▼ Sleep Inn Mt Pleasant SH
(843) 856-5000. **$49-$199.** 299 Wingo Way. Just e of base of Cooper River Bridge, then just n at McGrath-Darby Blvd. Int corridors. **Pets:** Accepted.

ASK S☐ ☒ ☖M ☐ ☐ ☐ ☐ ☒

# NORTH CHARLESTON

▲▲▲ ▼▼ Best Western Charleston Airport Hotel M
(843) 744-1621. **$59-$89.** 6099 Fain St. I-26, exit 211A (Aviation Ave), just w. Ext corridors. **Pets:** Accepted.

SAVE S☐ ☒ ☐ ☐ ☐ ☐ ☐ ☒

▼▼ Comfort Inn Coliseum M
(843) 554-6485. **$69-$89.** 5055 N Arco Ln. I-26, exit 213 westbound; exit 213A eastbound, just s, then n. Ext corridors. **Pets:** Accepted.

ASK S☐ ☒ ☐ ☐ ☐ ☒

▲▲▲ ▼ Country Hearth Inn & Suites M
(843) 572-2228. **$49-$74, 14 day notice.** 2311 Ashley Phosphate Rd. I-26, exit 209 (Ashley Phosphate Rd), just e. Ext corridors. **Pets:** Accepted.

SAVE S☐ ☒ ☐ ☒

▼▼ Homestead Studio Suites
Hotel-Charleston/Airport SH
(843) 740-3440. **$90-$540.** 5045 N Arco Ln. I-26, exit 213 westbound; exit 213A eastbound, just s, then n. Int corridors. **Pets:** $25 daily fee/pet. Service with restrictions, supervision.

ASK S☐ ☒ ☖M ☐ ☐ ☐ ☐ ☒

▼▼▼ La Quinta Inn Charleston SH
(843) 797-8181. **$72-$105.** 2499 La Quinta Ln. I-26, exit 209 (Ashley Phosphate Rd), just w. Ext corridors. **Pets:** Medium. Service with restrictions.

ASK ☒ ☐ ☐ ☐ ☒

▼ Motel 6 #642 M
(843) 572-6590. **$42-$55.** 2551 Ashley Phosphate Rd. I-26, exit 209 (Ashley Phosphate Rd), just w. Ext corridors. **Pets:** Accepted.

S☐ ☒ ☐ ☒

▲▲▲ ▼▼▼ Quality Suites Convention Center SH
(843) 747-7300. **$79-$269.** 5225 N Arco Ln. I-26, exit 213 westbound; exit 213A eastbound, just s, then n. Int corridors. **Pets:** Small. $35 one-time fee/room. Service with restrictions, crate.

SAVE S☐ ☒ ☐ ☐ ☐ ☒

▼▼ Red Roof Inn M
(843) 572-9100. **$53-$69.** 7480 Northwoods Blvd. I-26, exit 209 (Ashley Phosphate Rd), just e, then just n. Ext corridors. **Pets:** Accepted.

☒ ☐ ☐ ☐

▼▼▼ Residence Inn by Marriott SH
(843) 572-5757. **$146.** 7645 Northwoods Blvd. I-26, exit 209 (Ashley Phosphate Rd), just e, then n. Ext corridors. **Pets:** Other species. $75 one-time fee/room. Service with restrictions.

ASK S☐ ☒ ☐ ☐ ☐ ☐ ☒ ☒

▲▲▲ ▼▼▼ Residence Inn Charleston Airport SH ❖
(843) 266-3434. **$99-$199.** 5035 International Blvd. I-26, exit 213A eastbound, 0.4 mi s, then just w; exit westbound, 0.4 mi s, then just w; I-526, exit International Blvd, 0.8 mi e. Int corridors. **Pets:** Other species. $75 one-time fee/room. Service with restrictions, crate.

SAVE S☐ ☒ ☖M ☐ ☐ ☐ ☒ ☒

▲▲▲ ▼▼▼▼ Sheraton Hotel North Charleston Convention Center LH ❖
(843) 747-1900. **$89-$109.** 4770 Goer Dr. I-26, exit 213 westbound; exit 213B eastbound, just n. Int corridors. **Pets:** Medium, dogs only. $25 one-time fee/room. Designated rooms, service with restrictions, supervision.

SAVE S☐ ☒ ☐ ☐ ☐ ☐ ☒

▼▼ Sleep Inn Charleston North SH
(843) 572-8400. **$64-$119.** 7435 Northside Dr. I-26, exit 209 (Ashley Phosphate Rd), just w. Int corridors. **Pets:** Medium, other species. $10 daily fee/pet. Designated rooms, service with restrictions.

ASK S☐ ☒ ☐ ☐

▼▼ SuiteOne of Charleston SH
(843) 414-7000. **$59-$129.** 5035 N Arco Ln. I-26, exit 213 westbound; exit 213A eastbound, just s, then n. Ext corridors. **Pets:** Accepted.

ASK S☐ ☒ ☐ ☐ ☐

# SUMMERVILLE

▼▼▼ Country Inn & Suites SH
(843) 285-9000. **$79-$129.** 220 Holiday Dr. I-26, exit 199A, just w on US 17 alternate to Holiday Dr, then just n. Int corridors. **Pets:** Medium. $5 one-time fee/room. Service with restrictions, supervision.

ASK S☐ ☒ ☐ ☐ ☒

▲▲▲ ▼▼▼ Holiday Inn
Express-Charleston/Summerville SH ❖
(843) 875-3300. **$69-$99.** 120 Holiday Inn Dr. I-26, exit 199A, just w. Int corridors. **Pets:** Other species. Service with restrictions.

SAVE S☐ ☒ ☖M ☐ ☐ ☐ ☐ ☒

▲▲▲ ▼▼▼▼ Woodlands Resort & Inn CI ❖
(843) 875-2600. **$295-$850, 7 day notice.** 125 Parsons Rd. I-26, exit 199A, 2 mi s on US 17 alternate route, 1.5 mi w on W Richardson Ave (SR 165), then just s. Int corridors. **Pets:** Accepted.

SAVE S☐ ☒ ☐ ☐ ☒ ☒

---

# END METROPOLITAN AREA

---

# CHERAW

▲▲▲ ▼▼▼ Days Inn M
(843) 537-5554. **$45-$70.** 820 Market St. Jct US 52/1/SR 9. Ext corridors. **Pets:** Accepted.

SAVE S☐ ☒ ☐ ☐ ☒

▼▼ Jameson Inn M
(843) 537-5625. **$54-$104.** 885 Chesterfield Hwy. Jct US 1/52/SR 9, 1.6 mi w on SR 9. Ext corridors. **Pets:** Very small, other species. $10 daily fee/room. Service with restrictions, supervision.

ASK ☒ ☐ ☐ ☐ ☒

# CLEMSON

**Comfort Inn-Clemson** SH ❖
(864) 653-3600. **$89-$175.** 1305 Tiger Blvd. Jct US 76 and 123. Int corridors. **Pets:** Small. $10 daily fee/pet. Designated rooms, service with restrictions, supervision.

SAVE SM X 🐾 🚪 💻 ➿

**Ramada Inn of Clemson** SH
(864) 654-7501. **$69-$99.** 1310 Tiger Blvd. Jct US 76/123, just e. Int corridors. **Pets:** Accepted.

SAVE SM X 🐾 🚪 💻 🍴 ➿ ⊠

# CLINTON

**Comfort Inn** SH
(864) 833-5558. **$59-$89.** 105 Trade St. I-26, exit 52, just n; behind truck stop. Ext corridors. **Pets:** Small. $10 one-time fee/pet. Service with restrictions, supervision.

SAVE SM X 🐾 🚪 💻 ➿

**Days Inn** M
(864) 833-6600. **$55-$79.** 12374 Hwy 56 N. I-26, exit 52, just s. Ext corridors. **Pets:** Other species. $10 daily fee/pet. Service with restrictions, crate.

SAVE SM X 🚪 💻 ➿

# COLUMBIA

**AmeriSuites (Columbia/Northeast)** SH ❖
(803) 736-6666. **$89-$129.** 7525 Two Notch Rd. I-20, exit 74 (Two Notch Rd), just ne; I-77, exit 17 (Two Notch Rd), 0.5 mi sw. Int corridors. **Pets:** Small. $10 daily fee/pet. Designated rooms, service with restrictions, supervision.

SAVE SM X 🐾 🚪 💻 ➿

**Baymont Inn & Suites Columbia NE/Ft. Jackson Area** SH
(803) 736-6400. **$65-$79.** 1538 Horseshoe Dr. I-20, exit 74 (Two Notch Rd), just n; I-77, exit 17 (Two Notch Rd), 0.5 mi s. Int corridors. **Pets:** Medium. Service with restrictions.

SAVE X 🐾 🚪 💻 ➿

**Carolinian Hotel** SH
(803) 736-3000. **$109-$129.** 7510 Two Notch Rd. I-20, exit 74 (Two Notch Rd), just n; I-77, exit 17 (Two Notch Rd), 0.5 mi s. Int corridors. **Pets:** Accepted.

ASK SM X 🚪 💻 🍴 ➿ ⊠

**Chestnut Cottage Bed & Breakfast** BB
(803) 256-1718. **$95-$225, 14 day notice.** 1718 Hampton St. SR 12 (Taylor St), just s; between Henderson and Barnwell sts. Int corridors. **Pets:** Accepted.

ASK SM X 🚪 💻

**Columbiana Hotel and Conference Center** LH
(803) 731-0300. **$139-$165.** 2100 Bush River Rd. I-20, exit 63 (Bush River Rd), just e; I-26, exit 108 (Bush River Rd), 0.7 mi w. Int corridors. **Pets:** Medium, other species. $30 one-time fee/room. Designated rooms, service with restrictions, crate.

ASK SM X 🐾 🚪 💻 🍴 ➿ ⊠

**Days Inn** M
(803) 754-4408. **$49-$79.** 133 Plumbers Rd. I-20, exit 71 (Wilson Blvd), just n, then just e. Ext corridors. **Pets:** Small. $8 daily fee/pet. Designated rooms, service with restrictions, supervision.

ASK SM X 🚪 💻 ➿

**Days Inn** SH
(803) 798-5101. **$59-$99.** 911 Bush River Rd. I-26, exit 108 (Bush River Rd), just e. Int corridors. **Pets:** Accepted.

SAVE SM X 🐾 🚪 💻 ➿

**Microtel Inn** SH
(803) 736-3237. **$55-$70.** 1520 Barbara Dr. I-20, exit 74 (Two Notch Rd), just ne; I-77, exit 17 (Two Notch Rd), 0.5 mi sw. Int corridors. **Pets:** Medium. $7 daily fee/pet. Service with restrictions, supervision.

SAVE SM X 🐾 🚪

**Microtel Inn & Suites Harbison Area** SH
(803) 772-1914. **$59.** 411 Piney Grove Rd. I-26, exit 104 (Piney Grove Rd), just sw. Int corridors. **Pets:** Accepted.

ASK SM X 🐾 🚪 💻

**Motel 6 #1291** SH
(803) 736-3900. **$42-$53.** 7541 Nates Rd. I-20, exit 74 (Two Notch Rd), just n, then just e; I-77, exit 17 (Two Notch Rd), 0.5 mi s, then e. Int corridors. **Pets:** Accepted.

SM X 🐾 ➿

**Ramada Plaza Hotel** SH
(803) 736-5600. **$109.** 8105 Two Notch Rd. I-77, exit 17 (Two Notch Rd), just ne. Int corridors. **Pets:** Medium. $75 deposit/pet. Service with restrictions.

ASK SM X 🐾 🚪 💻 🍴 ➿ ⊠

**Red Roof Inn-West** M
(803) 798-9220. **$41-$54.** 10 Berryhill Rd. I-26, exit 106A westbound; exit 106 eastbound, just w. Ext corridors. **Pets:** Accepted.

X 🐾 🚪

**Residence Inn by Marriott** SH ❖
(803) 779-7000. **$99-$189.** 150 Stoneridge Dr. I-126, exit Greystone Blvd, just n, then just e. Ext corridors. **Pets:** Other species. $10 daily fee/room, $50 one-time fee/room. Service with restrictions.

ASK SM X 🐾 🚪 💻 ➿ ⊠

**Super 8** M
(803) 735-0008. **$49-$70.** 5719 Fairfield Rd. I-20, exit 70, just s. Ext corridors. **Pets:** Accepted.

SAVE SM X 🚪

**Super 8** SH
(803) 772-7275. **$55-$100.** 773 St Andrews Rd. I-26, exit 106A westbound; exit 106 eastbound, just w. Ext corridors. **Pets:** Small. $10 daily fee/pet. Service with restrictions, supervision.

ASK SM X 🚪 💻 ➿

**TownePlace Suites by Marriott** SH
(803) 781-9391. **$79-$109.** 350 Columbiana Dr. I-26, exit 103 (Harbison Blvd), just sw to Columbiana Dr, then 0.7 mi nw. Int corridors. **Pets:** Accepted.

ASK SM X 🐾 🚪 💻 ➿

# DUNCAN

**Jameson Inn** M
(864) 433-8405. **$54-$104.** 1546 E Main St. I-85, exit 63, 0.4 mi se on SR 290. Ext corridors. **Pets:** Very small, other species. $10 daily fee/room. Service with restrictions, supervision.

ASK X 🚪 💻 ➿

**Quality Inn** SH ❖
(864) 433-1333. **$55-$85.** 1391 E Main St. I-85, exit 63, just nw. Ext corridors. **Pets:** $15 daily fee/room. Service with restrictions.

ASK SM X 🚪 💻 ➿

# EASLEY

**Comfort Inn** SH ❖
(864) 859-7520. **$70-$75.** 5539 Calhoun Memorial Hwy. Jct US 123 and SR 93, just e on US 123. Ext corridors. **Pets:** Small, dogs only. $20 daily fee/pet. Designated rooms, service with restrictions, supervision.

SAVE SM X 🚪 💻 ➿

▼▼ **Jameson Inn** Ⓜ
(864) 306-9000. **$54-$104.** 211 Dayton School Rd. Jct US 123 and SR 93, 0.6 mi e on US 123; jct US 123 and SR 153, 1.4 mi w. Ext corridors. **Pets:** Very small, other species. $10 daily fee/room. Service with restrictions, supervision.

[ASK] [✕] [✂] [▤] [▣] [🌊]

## FLORENCE

🔶 ▼▼ **Comfort Inn** Ⓜ ✿
(843) 665-4558. **$50-$89.** 1916 W Lucas St. I-95, exit 164, just se. Ext/int corridors. **Pets:** $10 daily fee/pet. Service with restrictions, supervision.

[SAVE] [🔊] [✕] [▤] [▣] [🌊]

🔶 ▼ **Country Hearth Inn & Suites** Ⓜ
(843) 662-9421. **$45-$59.** 831 S Irby St. 1.3 mi s on US 301 and 52. Ext corridors. **Pets:** Accepted.

[SAVE] [🔊] [✕] [▤] [▣] [🍴] [🌊]

▼▼ **Days Inn Florence** Ⓜ
(843) 665-4444. **$53-$150.** 2111 W Lucas St. I-95, exit 164, 0.4 mi nw. Ext corridors. **Pets:** Medium, other species. Service with restrictions, supervision.

[ASK] [🔊] [✕] [▤] [🌊] [✕]

🔶 ▼▼ **Econo Lodge** Ⓜ
(843) 665-8558. **$60-$200.** 1811 W Lucas St. I-95, exit 164, just se. Ext corridors. **Pets:** Other species. $10 daily fee/room. Designated rooms, service with restrictions, supervision.

[SAVE] [🔊] [✕] [▤] [▣] [🌊]

🔶 ▼▼▼ **Holiday Inn Hotel & Suites** SH
(843) 665-4555. **$66-$85.** 1819 W Lucas St. I-95, exit 164, just se. Ext corridors. **Pets:** Accepted.

[SAVE] [🔊] [✕] [🛏] [🔊] [✂] [▤] [▣] [🍴] [🌊]

🔶 ▼▼▼ **Howard Johnson Express Inn & Suites** Ⓜ ✿
(843) 664-9494. **$95, 30 day notice.** 3821 Bancroft Rd. I-95, exit 157, just ne on US 76. Ext corridors. **Pets:** Medium, other species. $10 one-time fee/room. Service with restrictions, supervision.

[SAVE] [🔊] [✕] [✂] [▤] [▣] [🌊]

▼ **Motel 6 #1250** Ⓜ
(843) 667-6100. **$35-$47.** 1834 W Lucas St. I-95, exit 164, just sw. Ext corridors. **Pets:** Accepted.

[🔊] [✕] [✂] [🌊]

🔶 ▼▼▼ **Ramada Inn** SH
(843) 669-4241. **$67-$250.** 2038 W Lucas St. I-95, exit 164, just nw. Ext/int corridors. **Pets:** Medium, other species. $10 daily fee/pet. Designated rooms, service with restrictions, crate.

[SAVE] [🔊] [✕] [▤] [▣] [🌊] [✕]

▼▼ **Red Roof Inn** Ⓜ
(843) 678-9000. **$41-$55.** 2690 David McLeod Blvd. I-95, exit 160A, just e on service road. Ext corridors. **Pets:** Accepted.

[✕] [🔊M] [📄] [✂]

🔶 ▼▼▼ **Thunderbird Inn** Ⓜ
(843) 669-1611. **$45-$55.** 2004 W Lucas St. I-95, exit 164, just nw. Ext corridors. **Pets:** Accepted.

[SAVE] [🔊] [✕] [▤] [🍴] [🌊]

## GAFFNEY

▼▼ **Jameson Inn** Ⓜ
(864) 489-0240. **$54-$104.** 101 Stuard St. I-85, exit 92, 0.5 mi se on SR 11/W Floyd Baker Blvd. Ext corridors. **Pets:** Very small, other species. $10 daily fee/room. Service with restrictions, supervision.

[ASK] [✕] [✂] [▤] [▣] [🌊]

---

# THE GRAND STRAND AREA

## GEORGETOWN

🔶 ▼▼ **Americas Best Value Inn** Ⓜ
(843) 546-5191. **$59-$79.** 706 Church St. US 17, 0.7 mi se of jct US 17/17 alternate route/701. Ext corridors. **Pets:** Large. Designated rooms, service with restrictions, supervision.

[SAVE] [🔊] [✕] [📄] [▤] [▣] [🌊]

▼▼ **Jameson Inn Georgetown** Ⓜ
(843) 546-6090. **$54-$104.** 120 Church St. US 17, 1.2 mi se, jct US 17/17 alternate route/701; just w of ICW Bridge. Ext corridors. **Pets:** Very small, other species. $10 daily fee/room. Service with restrictions, supervision.

[ASK] [✕] [📄] [✂] [▤] [▣] [🌊]

▼▼▼▼ **Winyah Bay Inn Bed & Breakfast** BB
(843) 546-0464. **$95-$115, 3 day notice.** 3030 South Island Rd. 0.5 mi s of Sylvan L Rosen Bridge on US 17, 2 mi e. Ext/int corridors. **Pets:** $10 one-time fee/pet. Service with restrictions, crate.

[ASK] [✕] [▤] [▣] [🔖]

## LITTLE RIVER

▼▼▼▼ **Holiday Inn Hotel & Suites-North Myrtle Beach** SH ✿
(843) 281-9400. **$39-$219.** 722 Hwy 17. Jct SR 9/US 17, 1 mi e; at Coquina Harbor. Int corridors. **Pets:** Dogs only. $25 daily fee/room. Service with restrictions, supervision.

[ASK] [🔊] [✕] [▤] [▣] [🍴] [🌊]

## MYRTLE BEACH

🔶 ▼▼▼▼ **Compass Cove Oceanfront Resort** LH
(843) 448-8373. **$36-$186, 14 day notice.** 2311 S Ocean Blvd. Jct 24th Ave S. Ext corridors. **Pets:** Accepted.

[SAVE] [🔊] [✕] [📄] [▤] [▣] [🍴] [🌊] [✕]

🔶 ▼▼ **El Dorado Motel** Ⓜ
(843) 626-3559. **$39-$139, 7 day notice.** 2800 S Ocean Blvd. Jct 28th Ave S. Ext corridors. **Pets:** Small, dogs only. $25 one-time fee/pet. Service with restrictions, supervision.

[SAVE] [🔊] [✕] [▤] [▣] [🌊]

▼▼▼▼ **La Quinta Inn & Suites Myrtle Beach** SH
(843) 916-8801. **$71-$200.** 1561 21st Ave N. Jct US 17 Bypass, just se. Int corridors. **Pets:** Medium. Service with restrictions.

[ASK] [✕] [🔊M] [📄] [▤] [▣] [🌊]

🔶 ▼ **Mariner** Ⓜ ✿
(843) 449-5281. **$29-$149.** 7003 N Ocean Blvd. Jct 71st Ave N. Ext corridors. **Pets:** Dogs only. $9 daily fee/pet. Service with restrictions.

[SAVE] [🔊] [✕] [▤] [🌊]

▼▼ **Red Roof Inn & Suites** SH
(843) 626-4444. **$32-$103.** 2801 S Kings Hwy. Jct 28th Ave S and US 17 business route. Int corridors. **Pets:** Accepted.

[✕] [✂] [▤] [▣] [🌊]

**ⒶⒶⒶ ♦♦♦ Sea Mist Oceanfront Resort ⓛⓗ**
(843) 448-1551. **$32-$192, 14 day notice.** 1200 S Ocean Blvd. Jct
12th Ave S. Ext/int corridors. **Pets:** Accepted.
[SAVE] [✕] [🐾] [👤] [🛏] [🍴] [⇆] [✕]

**♦♦♦ Staybridge Suites-Fantasy Harbour ⓢⓗ ❖**
(843) 903-4000. **$69-$169.** 3163 Outlet Blvd. Jct US 17 Bypass, 0.7 mi
n on US 501, exit River Oaks Rd/George Bishop Pkwy, just w on
River Oaks Rd, then 0.4 mi s. Int corridors. **Pets:** Medium. $12 daily
fee/room. Service with restrictions, supervision.
[ASK] [🐾] [✕] [🐾] [👤] [🛏] [💻] [⇆] [✕]

**ⒶⒶⒶ ♦♦♦ Summer Wind Inn & Suites ⓜ**
(843) 946-6960. **$31-$159, 7 day notice.** 1903 S Ocean Blvd. Jct 19th
Ave S. Ext corridors. **Pets:** Small, dogs only. $10 daily fee/room. Service
with restrictions, supervision.
[SAVE] [🐾] [✕] [🛏] [⇆]

**ⒶⒶⒶ ♦♦ Super 8 Motel-Myrtle Beach ⓢⓗ**
(843) 293-6100. **$35-$199, 3 day notice.** 3450 Hwy 17 Bypass. Jct US
501/US 17 Bypass, 3.2 mi sw. Int corridors. **Pets:** Small, dogs only. $10
daily fee/pet. Service with restrictions, supervision.
[SAVE] [🐾] [✕] [🛏] [⇆]

# END AREA

## NORTH MYRTLE BEACH

**ⒶⒶⒶ ♦♦♦ Super 8 North Point ⓜ**
(843) 249-7339. **$59-$135, 4 day notice.** 1591 US 17 N. Jct SR 9, just
s. Ext corridors. **Pets:** Accepted.
[SAVE] [✕] [🛏] [⇆]

## PAWLEYS ISLAND

**♦♦♦ Best Western Hammock Inn ⓜ ❖**
(843) 237-4261. **$60-$110.** 7903 Ocean Hwy. 2.6 mi sw on US 17. Ext
corridors. **Pets:** Medium. Service with restrictions, supervision.
[ASK] [🐾] [✕] [🛏] [💻] [🍴] [⇆]

## GREENVILLE

**ⒶⒶⒶ ♦♦♦♦ AmeriSuites (Greenville/Haywood) ⓢⓗ**
(864) 232-3000. **$119.** 40 W Orchard Park Dr. I-385, exit 39 (Haywood
Rd), just n, then w. Int corridors. **Pets:** Small. $25 one-time fee/pet.
Designated rooms, service with restrictions, supervision.
[SAVE] [🐾] [✕] [🖥] [🛏] [💻] [⇆]

**♦♦♦♦ Crowne Plaza Hotel and Resort Greenville ⓛⓗ**
(864) 297-6300. **$103, 3 day notice.** 851 Congaree Rd. I-385, exit 37,
just s, then just nw. Int corridors. **Pets:** Medium. $50 one-time fee/room.
Service with restrictions, crate.
[ASK] [🐾] [✕] [🖥] [👤] [🛏] [💻] [🍴] [⇆] [✕]

**♦♦ Days Inn ⓢⓗ**
(864) 288-6900. **$53-$70.** 2756 Laurens Rd. I-85, exit 48B, just nw;
entry between auto dealership. Int corridors. **Pets:** Small. $10 daily
fee/pet. Service with restrictions, crate.
[ASK] [🐾] [✕] [🛏] [⇆]

**♦♦♦♦ Hawthorn Suites ⓢⓗ**
(864) 297-0099. **$79.** 48 McPrice Ct. I-385, exit 39 (Haywood Rd), just
n, just e on Orchard Park Rd, then just s. Ext corridors. **Pets:** Accepted.
[ASK] [🐾] [✕] [🐾] [🛏] [💻] [⇆] [✕]

**♦♦♦ Hilton Greenville ⓛⓗ**
(864) 232-4747. **$79-$319.** 45 W Orchard Park Dr. I-385, exit 39 (Haywood Rd), just n, then w. Int corridors. **Pets:** Small. $50 deposit/pet, $50
one-time fee/pet. Designated rooms, service with restrictions, supervision.
[✕] [🖥] [🐾] [👤] [🛏] [💻] [🍴] [⇆] [✕]

**♦♦♦ Holiday Inn Express Hotel & Suites ⓢⓗ**
(864) 213-9331. **$82-$100.** 2681 Dry Pocket Rd. I-85, exit 54 (Pelham
Rd), just nw, 0.3 mi ne on The Parkway to Parkway Rd, then 0.3 mi e.
Int corridors. **Pets:** Other species. $20 one-time fee/room. Service with
restrictions, crate.
[ASK] [🐾] [✕] [🐾] [🖥] [👤] [🛏] [💻] [⇆] [✕]

**♦♦♦ Holiday Inn Express Hotel & Suites-I-85/385 ⓢⓗ**
(864) 678-5555. **$89-$139.** 1036 Woodruff Rd. I-85, exit 51A, 0.5 mi ne;
US 385, exit 37, just sw on Roper Mountain Rd, then just se. Int
corridors. **Pets:** Accepted.
[ASK] [🐾] [✕] [🖥] [🐾] [👤] [💻] [⇆]

**♦♦♦ Holiday Inn I-85/Augusta Rd ⓢⓗ ❖**
(864) 277-8921. **$80-$120.** 4295 Augusta Rd. I-85, exit 46A, just s. Int
corridors. **Pets:** Large. $30 one-time fee/room. Service with restrictions,
supervision.
[ASK] [🐾] [✕] [🖥] [🐾] [👤] [🛏] [💻] [🍴] [⇆]

**♦♦ La Quinta Inn Greenville (Woodruff Rd.) ⓢⓗ**
(864) 297-3500. **$72-$85.** 31 Old Country Rd. I-85, exit 51A, just n on
SR 146; I-385, exit 35, just n. Ext/int corridors. **Pets:** Medium. Service
with restrictions.
[ASK] [✕] [🐾] [🛏] [💻] [⇆]

**♦♦♦ La Quinta Inns & Suites Greenville (Haywood) ⓢⓗ**
(864) 233-8018. **$81-$104.** 65 W Orchard Park Dr. I-385, exit 39 (Haywood Rd), just n, then w. Int corridors. **Pets:** Medium. Service with
restrictions.
[ASK] [✕] [🐾] [🖥] [🛏] [💻] [⇆] [✕]

**♦♦♦ MainStay Suites-Greenville ⓢⓗ ❖**
(864) 987-5566. **$64-$84.** 2671 Dry Pocket Rd. I-85, exit 54 (Pelham
Rd), just w to The Parkway, just n to Dry Pocket Rd, then 0.6 mi e. Int
corridors. **Pets:** Other species. $10 daily fee/pet. Service with restrictions,
crate.
[ASK] [🐾] [✕] [🐾] [🖥] [🛏] [💻] [⇆]

**♦♦ Microtel Inn & Suites ⓢⓗ**
(864) 297-3811. **$47-$67.** 1024 Woodruff Rd. I-85, exit 51A, 0.5 mi n on
SR 146. Int corridors. **Pets:** Other species. $35 one-time fee/room. Serv-
ice with restrictions, supervision.
[ASK] [🐾] [✕] [🖥] [🛏] [💻]

**ⒶⒶⒶ ♦♦♦♦ The Phoenix Greenville's Inn ⓢⓗ**
(864) 233-4651. **$70-$105, 3 day notice.** 246 N Pleasantburg Dr.
I-385, exit 40B, 0.6 mi s on SR 291. Ext corridors. **Pets:** Other species.
Service with restrictions, crate.
[SAVE] [🐾] [✕] [🐾] [🛏] [💻] [🍴] [⇆]

**ⒶⒶⒶ ♦♦♦ The Quality Inn Executive Center ⓜ 🐾**
(864) 271-0060. **$53-$68.** 540 N Pleasantburg Dr. I-385, exit 40B, just
s. Ext corridors. **Pets:** Large, other species. $15 one-time fee/room. Serv-
ice with restrictions.
[SAVE] [🐾] [✕] [🐾] [🛏] [💻] [⇆]

**♦♦ Red Roof Inn ⓜ**
(864) 297-4458. **$40-$60.** 2801 Laurens Rd. I-85, exit 48A, just s on
frontage road to dead end. Ext corridors. **Pets:** Accepted.
[✕] [🐾] [🛏]

**QQQ ▽▽▽ Sleep Inn Palmetto Expo Center 🕒 ❀**
(864) 240-2006. **$49-$99.** 231 N Pleasantburg Dr (SR 291). I-385, exit 40B, 0.6 mi s on SR 291. Int corridors. **Pets:** Large. $20 one-time fee/room. Service with restrictions, supervision.
[SAVE] [S�𝅓] [✕] [⚬M] [⚬] [⚬] [🛏] [▣]

# GREENWOOD

**▽ Days Inn 🕒**
(864) 223-1818. **$50.** 230 Birchtree Dr. Jct US 25/US 25 Bypass (SR 72 NE), just ne on US 25 Bypass (SR 72 NE), then just s. Int corridors. **Pets:** Accepted.
[ASK] [S�𝅓] [✕] [🛏] [▣]

# GREER

**▽▽ Super 8 Motel 🕒**
(864) 848-1626. **$50-$55, 30 day notice.** 1515 Hwy 101 S. I-85, exit 60, just nw. Int corridors. **Pets:** Accepted.
[ASK] [S�𝅓] [✕] [⚬M] [⚬] [🛏] [≈]

# HARDEEVILLE

**QQQ ▽▽▽ Comfort Inn 🕒**
(843) 784-2188. **$40-$76.** US 17 & I-95. I-95, exit 5 (US 17), just n. Ext/int corridors. **Pets:** Medium, other species. $10 one-time fee/pet. Supervision.
[SAVE] [S�𝅓] [✕] [🛏] [▣] [≈]

**QQQ ▽▽▽ Quality Inn & Suites 🅼 ❀**
(843) 784-7060. **$50-$200.** 19000 Whyte Hardee Blvd. I-95, exit 5 (US 17), just n. Ext corridors. **Pets:** Medium, other species. $10 daily fee/pet. Service with restrictions, supervision.
[SAVE] [S�𝅓] [✕] [⚬M] [⚬] [🛏] [▣]

**QQQ ▽▽▽ Sleep Inn Hardeeville 🕒**
(843) 784-7181. **$69-$109.** I-95 & US 17. I-95, exit 5 (US 17), just se. Int corridors. **Pets:** Medium. $10 daily fee/pet. Service with restrictions, supervision.
[SAVE] [S�𝅓] [✕] [⚬M] [⚬] [≈]

# HILTON HEAD ISLAND

**QQQ ▽▽▽ Comfort Inn 🕒**
(843) 842-6662. **$49-$179.** 2 Tanglewood Dr. Sea Pines Cir, 1.1 mi se on Pope Ave, just sw; at Coligny Plaza. Int corridors. **Pets:** Accepted.
[SAVE] [S☓] [✕] [⚬] [🛏] [▣] [🍽] [≈] [⊠]

**▽▽▽▽ Holiday Inn Express 🕒**
(843) 842-8888. **$60-$130.** 40 Waterside Dr. Sea Pines Cir, 0.7 mi se on Pope Rd, just e. Ext corridors. **Pets:** Medium, dogs only. $40 one-time fee/room. Service with restrictions, crate.
[ASK] [S☓] [✕] [⚬] [⚬] [🛏] [▣] [≈]

**▽ Motel 6–#1129 🅼**
(843) 785-2700. **$43-$61.** 830 William Hilton Pkwy. J Wilton Graves Bridge, 9 mi e on US 278 business route. Ext corridors. **Pets:** Accepted.
[S☓] [⚬] [⚬] [🛏] [▣] [≈]

**QQQ ▽▽▽▽ Quality Inn & Suites of Hilton Head Island 🕒**
(843) 681-3655. **$59-$139.** 200 Museum St. 3.3 mi e of J Wilton Graves Bridge on US 278 business route. Ext corridors. **Pets:** Medium. $10 daily fee/room, $25 one-time fee/room. Service with restrictions, crate.
[SAVE] [S☓] [✕] [⚬] [⚬] [🛏] [▣] [≈]

**▽▽▽ Red Roof Inn-Hilton Head 🅼**
(843) 686-6808. **$51-$91.** 5 Regency Pkwy. Over bridge, 9 mi e on US 278 business route; between Shipyard Plantation and Palmetto Dunes. Ext corridors. **Pets:** Accepted.
[✕] [⚬] [🛏] [≈]

# IRMO

**QQQ ▽▽▽▽ AmeriSuites (Columbia/I-26) 🕒**
(803) 407-1560. **$101.** 1130 Kinley Rd. I-26, exit 102B, just e, then n. Int corridors. **Pets:** Small, dogs only. $10 daily fee/pet. Designated rooms, service with restrictions, supervision.
[SAVE] [✕] [⚬M] [⚬] [⚬] [🛏] [▣] [≈]

**▽▽▽ Extended Stay Deluxe (Columbia/I-26) 🕒**
(803) 781-8590. **$79-$89.** 1170 Kinley Rd. I-26, exit 102B, just e, then n. Int corridors. **Pets:** $25 daily fee/pet. Service with restrictions, supervision.
[ASK] [S☓] [✕] [⚬M] [⚬] [⚬] [🛏] [▣] [≈]

# LANCASTER

**▽▽▽ Jameson Inn 🅼**
(803) 283-1188. **$54-$104.** 114 Commerce Blvd. Jct SR 9 Bypass and US 521, 1.3 mi w on SR 9 Bypass. Ext corridors. **Pets:** Very small, other species. $10 daily fee/room. Service with restrictions, supervision.
[ASK] [✕] [⚬M] [⚬] [⚬] [🛏] [▣] [≈]

# LANDRUM

**▽▽▽▽ The Red Horse Inn 🅲🅰 ❀**
(864) 909-1575. **$135-$250, 30 day notice.** 310 N Campbell Rd. Jct SR 14/414, 1.5 mi w on SR 414 to Campbell Rd, then 0.7 mi n. Ext corridors. **Pets:** Medium, dogs only. $25 one-time fee/pet. Designated rooms, service with restrictions, supervision.
[ASK] [S☓] [✕] [🛏] [▣] [⊠]

# LUGOFF

**▽▽ Best Western Camden West 🕒**
(803) 438-9441. **$69-$71.** 850 Hwy 1 S. I-20, exit 92 (US 601), 2.9 mi n. Ext corridors. **Pets:** Accepted.
[ASK] [S☓] [✕] [⚬] [🛏] [▣] [🍽] [≈]

**▽▽ Ramada Limited 🅼**
(803) 438-1807. **$69-$79.** 542 Hwy 601 S. I-20, exit 92 (US 601), just n. Ext corridors. **Pets:** Accepted.
[ASK] [S☓] [✕] [🛏] [▣] [≈]

# MANNING

**QQQ ▽▽▽ Best Western Palmetto Inn 🅼**
(803) 473-4021. **$45-$89, 5 day notice.** 2825 Paxville Hwy. I-95, exit 119 (SR 261), just se. Ext corridors. **Pets:** $5 one-time fee/pet. Designated rooms, service with restrictions.
[SAVE] [S☓] [✕] [🛏] [▣] [≈]

**▽▽ Comfort Inn 🅼**
(803) 473-7550. **$59-$89.** 3031 Paxville Hwy. I-95, exit 119 (SR 261), just se. Ext corridors. **Pets:** Other species. $9 one-time fee/room. Service with restrictions.
[ASK] [S☓] [✕] [⚬] [🛏] [▣] [≈]

**QQQ ▽ Econo Lodge 🅼**
(803) 473-2596. **$40-$50.** 6137 Alex Harvin Hwy. I-95, exit 115, just sw. Ext corridors. **Pets:** Other species. $10 daily fee/pet. Service with restrictions, supervision.
[SAVE] [S☓] [✕] [🛏] [≈]

**QQQ ▽▽▽▽ Ramada Limited 🅼**
(803) 473-5135. **$59-$135.** 2816 Paxville Hwy. I-95, exit 119 (SR 261), just se. Ext corridors. **Pets:** Accepted.
[SAVE] [S☓] [✕] [⚬] [🛏] [▣] [≈]

# NEWBERRY

**QQQ ▽▽▽ Best Western Newberry Inn 🅼**
(803) 276-5850. **$45-$70.** 11701 S Carolina Hwy 34. I-26, exit 74 (SR 34), just ne. Ext corridors. **Pets:** Small. $5 daily fee/pet. Service with restrictions, supervision.
[SAVE] [S☓] [✕] [🛏] [▣] [≈]

# ORANGEBURG

**AAA** ◆◆◆ **Comfort Inn & Suites** M ❖
(803) 531-9200. **$67-$126.** 3671 St Matthews Rd. I-26, exit 145A (US 601), just sw. Ext corridors. **Pets:** Other species. $10 one-time fee/room. Designated rooms, service with restrictions.
SAVE (S6) ✕ 🕸 🔅 🖶 🖵 🏊

**AAA** ◆◆◆ **Days Inn** M
(803) 534-0500. **$58-$86.** 3402 Five Chop Rd. I-26, exit 154B (US 301), just e. Ext corridors. **Pets:** Accepted.
SAVE (S6) ✕ 🔅 🖶 🖵 ❚❚ 🏊

◆◆◆ **Jameson Inn Orangeburg** M
(803) 534-1611. **$54-$104.** 2350 Chestnut St NE. I-26, exit 145A (US 601), 3.9 mi sw to jct US 601 and 21/178 Bypass, then 2 mi nw. Ext corridors. **Pets:** Very small, other species. $10 daily fee/room. Service with restrictions, supervision.
ASK ✕ 🔅 🖶 🖵 🏊

**AAA** ◆◆◆ **Orangeburg Days Inn** M
(803) 531-2590. **$50-$250.** 3691 St Matthews Rd. I-26, exit 145A (US 601), just sw. Ext corridors. **Pets:** Accepted.
SAVE (S6) ✕ 🖶 🖵 🏊

# PICKENS

◆◆◆ **The Schell Haus, A Resort Bed & Breakfast** BB
(864) 878-0078. **$90-$165, 7 day notice.** 117 Hiawatha Tr. Jct US 178/SR 11, 4.6 mi ne on SR 11, then just se; on southeast side of Table Rock State Park. Int corridors. **Pets:** Accepted.
ASK (S6) ✕ 🖵 🏊 📷

# POINT SOUTH

◆◆◆ **Holiday Inn Express Point South/Yemassee** SH
(843) 726-9400. **$89.** 138 Frampton Dr. I-95, exit 33 (US 17), just ne. Int corridors. **Pets:** Medium, other species. $10 one-time fee/room. No service, supervision.
ASK (S6) ✕ 🔅M 🔅 🖶 🖵 🏊

# RIDGELAND

**AAA** ◆◆◆◆ **Comfort Inn** SH
(843) 726-2121. **$72-$99.** Hwy 336 & I-95. I-95, exit 21, just nw. Ext/int corridors. **Pets:** Dogs only. $10 one-time fee/room. Service with restrictions, supervision.
SAVE (S6) ✕ 🕸 🖶 🖵 🏊

**AAA** ◆◆ **Days Inn Ridgeland** M
(843) 726-5553. **$55-$75.** 516 E Main St. I-95, exit 21, just nw. Ext corridors. **Pets:** Medium, other species. $7 daily fee/pet. Supervision.
SAVE (S6) ✕ 🖶 🖵

# ROCK HILL

**AAA** ◆◆◆ **Best Western Inn** SH
(803) 329-1330. **$65-$100.** 1106 N Anderson Rd. I-77, exit 82B (US 21), 0.4 mi sw to US 21 Bypass, then just s. Int corridors. **Pets:** Other species. $10 daily fee/room. Service with restrictions.
SAVE (S6) ✕ 🖶 🖵 ❚❚ 🏊

◆◆◆ **The Book & the Spindle** BB ❖
(803) 328-1913. **$95-$425, 14 day notice.** 626 Oakland Ave. I-77, exit 82B (US 21), 3.1 mi s; before Aiken. Int corridors. **Pets:** Small, other species. $10 deposit/room. Service with restrictions, crate.
✕ 🖶 🖵

◆◆◆ **Holiday Inn** SH
(803) 329-1122. **$69-$89.** 2640 N Cherry Rd. I-77, exit 82B (US 21), just ne. Int corridors. **Pets:** Accepted.
ASK (S6) ✕ 🔅M 🕸 🔅 🖶 🖵 ❚❚ 🏊

# ST. GEORGE

**AAA** ◆◆◆ **Comfort Inn** M ❖
(843) 563-4180. **$48-$60.** 139 Motel Dr. I-95, exit 77 (US 78), just e. Ext corridors. **Pets:** Other species. $10 one-time fee/pet. Service with restrictions, supervision.
SAVE (S6) ✕ 🖵 🏊

**AAA** ◆◆◆ **Country Hearth Inn & Suites** M
(843) 563-2277. **$35-$49.** 104 Interstate Dr. I-95, exit 77 (US 78), just w. Ext corridors. **Pets:** Accepted.
SAVE (S6) ✕ 🖵 🏊

**AAA** ◆ **Econo Lodge** M
(843) 563-4195. **$55-$75.** 5971 W Jim Bilton Blvd. I-95, exit 77 (US 78), just e. Ext corridors. **Pets:** Small. $5 daily fee/pet. Service with restrictions, supervision.
SAVE (S6) ✕ 🖶 🖵 🏊

◆◆◆ **Quality Inn-St. George** SH
(843) 563-4581. **$54-$69.** 6014 W Jim Bilton Blvd. I-95, exit 77 (US 78), just e. Ext corridors. **Pets:** Accepted.
ASK (S6) ✕ 🔅 🖶 🖵 🏊

# SANTEE

**AAA** ◆◆◆ **Howard Johnson Express Inn** M
(803) 854-3870. **$67-$77.** 9112 Old Hwy 6. I-95, exit 98 (SR 6), 0.4 mi se. Ext corridors. **Pets:** Small, dogs only. $10 one-time fee/room. Service with restrictions, crate.
SAVE (S6) ✕ 🖶 🖵 🏊

**AAA** ◆◆◆ **Super 8 Motel** M
(803) 854-3456. **$60-$75.** 9125 Old Hwy 6. I-95, exit 98 (SR 6), 0.4 mi se. Ext corridors. **Pets:** Small. $6 daily fee/pet. Designated rooms, service with restrictions.
SAVE (S6) ✕ 🖶 🖵 🏊

# SENECA

◆◆◆ **Jameson Inn** M
(864) 888-8300. **$54-$104.** 226 Hi-Tech Rd. Jct SR 28 and US 76/123, 0.9 mi w on US 76/123, just se. Ext corridors. **Pets:** Very small, other species. $10 daily fee/room. Service with restrictions, supervision.
ASK ✕ 🔅M 🕸 🔅 🖶 🖵 🏊

# SIMPSONVILLE

◆◆ **Days Inn** M
(864) 963-7701. **$64.** 45 Ray E Talley Ct. I-385, exit 27, just s, then just e. Ext corridors. **Pets:** Small. $10 daily fee/pet. Service with restrictions, supervision.
ASK (S6) ✕ 🖶 🖵 🏊

◆◆◆ **Holiday Inn Express-Simpsonville** SH
(864) 962-8500. **$59-$69.** 3821 Grandview Dr. I-385, exit 27, just s. Int corridors. **Pets:** Accepted.
ASK (S6) ✕ 🕸 🔅 🖶 🖵 🏊

**AAA** ◆ **Motel 6** SH
(864) 962-8484. **$42-$100.** 3706 Grandview Dr. I-385, exit 27, just s, then just w. Int corridors. **Pets:** Small. Service with restrictions, supervision.
SAVE (S6) ✕ 🔅M 🕸 🔅 🖶

# SPARTANBURG

◆◆◆ **Holiday Inn Express Hotel & Suites** SH
(864) 699-7777. **$89-$94.** 895 Spartan Blvd. I-26, exit 21B (US 29), just e to Blackstock Rd, then 0.7 mi n; adjacent to Westgate Mall. Int corridors. **Pets:** Accepted.
ASK ✕ 🔅M 🕸 🔅 🖶 🖵 🏊

# SUMMERTON

**(AAA) ▽▽▽ Days Inn of Summerton M**
(803) 485-2865. **$45-$89.** 18 Bluff Blvd. I-95, exit 108, just n. Ext corridors. **Pets:** Small. $5 daily fee/pet. Designated rooms, service with restrictions, supervision.
SAVE ⑤ⓧ 🖬 💻 ⌇

# SUMTER

**▽▽▽▽ Fairfield Inn by Marriott M**
(803) 469-9001. **$68-$89.** 2390 Broad St. On US 76/378, 0.7 mi w of jct US 76/378/521. Ext corridors. **Pets:** Medium. $50 one-time fee/room. Designated rooms, crate.
ASK ⑤ⓧ ⓜ 🍸 ⓢ 🖬 💻 ⌇

**(AAA) ▽▽▽ Ramada Inn SH**
(803) 775-2323. **$73-$89.** 226 N Washington St. US 76 business route/521, just n. Ext corridors. **Pets:** Accepted.
SAVE ⑤ⓧ 🍸 🖬 💻 🍴 ⌇ ⓧ

# TRAVELERS REST

**(AAA) ▽▽▽ Sleep Inn SH ✿**
(864) 834-7040. **$64-$89.** 110 Hawkins Rd. US 25, exit Hawkins Rd. Int corridors. **Pets:** Dogs only. $10 daily fee/room. Service with restrictions.
SAVE ⑤ⓧ ⓜ 🍸 ⓢ 🖬 ⌇

# TURBEVILLE

**(AAA) ▽ Days Inn M**
(843) 659-8060. **$45-$70.** Hwy 378. I-95, exit 135 (US 378), just e. Ext corridors. **Pets:** Small, other species. $10 daily fee/pet. Service with restrictions, crate.
SAVE ⑤ⓧ

**(AAA) ▽ Knights Inn-Turbeville M**
(843) 659-2175. **$45-$95.** 7840 Myrtle Beach Hwy. I-95, exit 135 (US 378), just e. Ext corridors. **Pets:** Other species. $10 one-time fee/room. Service with restrictions.
SAVE ⑤ⓧ 🖬 🍴

# WALTERBORO

**▽ Americas Best Value Inn M**
(843) 538-3948. **$39-$99.** 1577 Bells Hwy. I-95, exit 57 (SR 64), just se. Ext corridors. **Pets:** Other species. $10 daily fee/pet. Service with restrictions, supervision.
ASK ⑤ 🖬 ⌇

**(AAA) ▽▽▽ Best Western of Walterboro SH ✿**
(843) 538-3600. **$59-$89.** 1428 Sniders Hwy. I-95, exit 53 (SR 63), just e. Ext corridors. **Pets:** Small. $10 daily fee/pet. Designated rooms, service with restrictions, supervision.
SAVE ⑤ⓧ 🍸 💻 ⌇

**(AAA) ▽▽▽ Econo Lodge M**
(843) 538-3830. **$45-$89.** 1145 Sniders Hwy. I-95, exit 53 (SR 63), just e. Ext corridors. **Pets:** Other species. $10 daily fee/pet. Designated rooms, service with restrictions, supervision.
SAVE ⑤ⓧ 🖬 💻

**▽▽ Howard Johnson Express SH**
(843) 538-5473. **$45-$65, 14 day notice.** 1286 Sniders Hwy. I-95, exit 53 (SR 63), just e. Ext corridors. **Pets:** Accepted.
ASK ⑤ⓧ 🍸 ⓢ 💻 ⌇

**▽▽ Ramada Inn of Walterboro SH**
(843) 538-5403. **$60-$65.** 1245 Sniders Hwy. I-95, exit 53 (SR 63), just e. Ext corridors. **Pets:** Small. $10 daily fee/pet. Service with restrictions, supervision.
ASK ⑤ⓧ 🖬 💻 ⌇

**(AAA) ▽ Rice Planters Inn M**
(843) 538-8964. **$38.** I-95 & SR 63. I-95, exit 53 (SR 63), just e. Ext corridors. **Pets:** Other species. $6 daily fee/pet. Service with restrictions, supervision.
SAVE ⑤ⓧ ⌇

**(AAA) ▽ Royal Inn M**
(843) 538-2503. **$40-$60.** 1142 Sniders Hwy. I-95, exit 53 (SR 63), just e. Ext corridors. **Pets:** Medium. $10 daily fee/pet. Service with restrictions, supervision.
SAVE ⑤ⓧ

**(AAA) ▽▽▽ Super 8 Motel M**
(843) 538-5383. **$46-$65.** 1972 Bells Hwy. I-95, exit 57 (SR 64), just nw. Ext corridors. **Pets:** Medium. $5 daily fee/pet. Designated rooms, service with restrictions, supervision.
SAVE ⑤ⓧ 🖬 ⌇

# WINNSBORO

**▽▽ Days Inn M**
(803) 635-1447. **$50-$62.** 1894 US Hwy 321 Bypass. I-77, exit 34 (SR 34), 6.5 mi w, jct US 321/SR 34/213. Ext corridors. **Pets:** Small. $7 daily fee/pet. Designated rooms, service with restrictions, supervision.
ASK ⑤ⓧ 🍸 🖬 ⌇

**(AAA) ▽▽▽ Fairfield Motel M**
(803) 635-3458. **$35-$60.** 56 US 321 Bypass S. Jct SR 213/US 321 Bypass S, 1.8 mi n. Ext corridors. **Pets:** $5 daily fee/pet. Service with restrictions, supervision.
SAVE ⑤ⓧ 🖬 ⌇

# SOUTH DAKOTA

## CITY INDEX

## ABERDEEN

### ▼▼▼ Aberdeen East Super 8 Motel SH
(605) 229-5005. **$71-$170.** 2405 6th Ave SE. 1.8 mi e on US 12. Int corridors. **Pets:** $6 daily fee/pet. Service with restrictions, supervision.
ASK S⬦ ✕ ⬦M ⬦ ⬦ ⬦ ⬦ ✕

### ◆ ▼ Aberdeen North Super 8 Motel SH
(605) 226-2288. **$55-$136.** 770 NW Hwy 281. On US 281, 1.5 mi nw. Int corridors. **Pets:** Accepted.
ASK S⬦ ✕

### ▼▼ Aberdeen West Super 8 Motel SH
(605) 225-1711. **$61-$180.** 714 S Hwy 281. Jct US 12 and 281. Int corridors. **Pets:** Accepted.
ASK S⬦ ✕ ⬦

### ▼▼▼ Best Western Ramkota Hotel SH
(605) 229-4040. **$84-$119.** 1400 8th Ave NW. 1.5 mi nw on US 281. Ext/int corridors. **Pets:** Accepted.
ASK S⬦ ✕ ⬦M ⬦ ⬦ ⬦ ⬦ ⬦ ⬦ ✕

### ◆ ▼▼ Comfort Inn SH ❀
(605) 226-0097. **$65-$89.** 2923 6th Ave SE. 2 mi e on US 12. Int corridors. **Pets:** Medium. $30 deposit/room. Service with restrictions, crate.
SAVE S⬦ ✕ ⬦ ⬦ ⬦ ⬦ ✕

### ▼▼▼ Holiday Inn Express Hotel & Suites SH
(605) 725-4000. **$79-$135.** 3310 7th Ave SE. 2.1 mi e on US 12. Int corridors. **Pets:** Medium, dogs only. $15 daily fee/room. Service with restrictions, supervision.
ASK ✕ ⬦M ⬦ ⬦ ⬦ ⬦ ⬦ ✕

### ◆ ▼▼ Ramada Inn SH
(605) 225-3600. **$77-$87.** 2727 6th Ave SE. 2 mi e on US 12. Ext/int corridors. **Pets:** Other species.
SAVE S⬦ ✕ ⬦ ⬦ ⬦ ⬦

## BERESFORD

### ▼▼ Super 8 Motel SH
(605) 763-2001. **$58.** 1410 W Cedar. I-29, exit 47 (SR 46), just e. Int corridors. **Pets:** Accepted.
ASK S⬦ ✕ ⬦ ⬦ ⬦ ⬦ ✕

---

# BLACK HILLS AREA

## BELLE FOURCHE

### ▼ Ace Motel M
(605) 892-2612. **$38-$58.** 109 6th Ave. 0.5 mi n via US 85, just e; just s of US 212 Bypass. Ext corridors. **Pets:** Medium. $4 daily fee/pet. Designated rooms, service with restrictions, supervision.
✕ ⬦

## BLACK HAWK

### ▼▼ Black Hawk Super 8 SH
(605) 787-4844. **Call for rates.** 7900 Stagestop Rd. I-90, exit 48, just s. Int corridors. **Pets:** Accepted.
ASK ✕ ⬦ ⬦ ⬦ ⬦

## CUSTER

### ◆ ▼▼ Bavarian Inn Motel SH
(605) 673-2802. **$49-$119, 3 day notice.** 1000 N 5th St. 1 mi n on US 16 and 385. Ext/int corridors. **Pets:** Accepted.
SAVE S⬦ ✕ ⬦ ⬦ ⬦ ⬦ ✕

### ◆ ▼ Chief Motel M
(605) 673-2318. **$49-$93, 3 day notice.** 120 Mt. Rushmore Rd. Just w on US 16. Ext corridors. **Pets:** Small, dogs only. $10 daily fee/pet. Designated rooms, service with restrictions, supervision.
SAVE ✕ ⬦ ⬦ ⬦ ✕

### ◆ ▼▼ Rock Crest Lodge and Cabins CA ❀
(605) 673-4323. **$45-$84, 3 day notice.** 15 W Mt. Rushmore Rd. US 16, 0.5 mi w. Ext/int corridors. **Pets:** Medium, dogs only. $25 deposit/pet, $5 daily fee/pet. Designated rooms, service with restrictions, crate.
SAVE S⬦ ✕ ⬦ ⬦ ⬦ ✕

### ◆ ▼ Rocket Motel M
(605) 673-4401. **$36-$82.** 211 Mt. Rushmore Rd. On US 16; center. Ext corridors. **Pets:** $10 daily fee/room. Service with restrictions, supervision.
SAVE S⬦ ✕

### ▼ The Roost Resort CA
(605) 673-2326. **$46-$86, 10 day notice.** 12462 Hwy 16A. 2 mi e on US Alternate Rt 16. Ext corridors. **Pets:** Accepted.
S⬦ ✕ ⬦ ⬦

### ▼▼▼ State Game Lodge M
(605) 255-4541. **$90-$400, 15 day notice.** US 16A. On Alternate Rt 16, 14 mi e. Ext/int corridors. **Pets:** Accepted.
✕ ⬦ ⬦ ⬦

### ▼▼ Super 8 Custer SH
(605) 673-2200. **$55-$109.** 415 W Hwy 16. US 16, 0.8 mi w. Int corridors. **Pets:** Other species. $10 daily fee/pet. Designated rooms, service with restrictions, supervision.
ASK S⬦ ✕ ⬦ ⬦

# DEADWOOD

**(AAA) ◆◆◆ First Gold Hotel & Gaming** SH
(605) 578-9777. **$65-$299, 7 day notice.** 270 Main St. 0.7 mi n on US 85. Int corridors. **Pets:** Medium. $15 one-time fee/room. Designated rooms, service with restrictions, supervision.
[SAVE] [S6] [✕] [&*] [🖵] [¶]

# HILL CITY

**(AAA) ◆◆◆ Best Western Golden Spike Inn & Suites** SH ✿
(605) 574-2577. **$64-$143.** 106 Main St. Just n on US 16 and 385. Ext/int corridors. **Pets:** Medium. $10 one-time fee/pet. Designated rooms, service with restrictions, supervision.
[SAVE] [S6] [✕] [&*] [🖬] [🖵] [¶] [🛥] [✕]

**(AAA) ◆ Lantern Inn** M
(605) 574-2582. **$56-$120, 3 day notice.** 430 E Main St. On north side of town, on US 16 and 385. Ext corridors. **Pets:** Very small. $5 daily fee/pet. Designated rooms, supervision.
[SAVE] [S6] [✕] [🖬] [🛥]

**(AAA) ◆◆◆ The Lodge at Palmer Gulch** SH
(605) 574-2525. **$59-$250, 10 day notice.** 12620 SR 244. On SR 244, 5 mi w of Mt. Rushmore. Int corridors. **Pets:** Dogs only. $10 one-time fee/room. Designated rooms, service with restrictions, supervision.
[SAVE] [S6] [✕] [&*] [🖬] [🖵] [¶] [🛥] [✕]

# HOT SPRINGS

**(AAA) ◆◆◆ Americas Best Value Inn By The River** M
(605) 745-4292. **$40-$165.** 602 W River. On US 385; downtown. Ext corridors. **Pets:** Medium, other species. $10 daily fee/room. Designated rooms, service with restrictions, supervision.
[SAVE] [S6] [✕] [🖬] [🛥]

**(AAA) ◆◆◆ Best Western Sundowner Inn** SH ✿
(605) 745-7378. **$59-$119.** 737 S 6th St. 0.5 mi se off US 18 and 385. Int corridors. **Pets:** Medium. Designated rooms, service with restrictions, supervision.
[SAVE] [S6] [✕] [&M] [🖬] [🖵] [🛥] [✕]

**(AAA) ◆ Budget Host Hills Inn** M
(605) 745-3130. **$59-$144.** 640 S 6th St. 0.5 mi se off US 18 and 385. Ext corridors. **Pets:** Small. Designated rooms, service with restrictions, supervision.
[SAVE] [S6] [✕] [🖬] [🛥]

**(AAA) ◆◆ Hot Springs Super 8 Motel** SH
(605) 745-3888. **$47-$110.** 800 Mammoth St. US 18 Bypass. Int corridors. **Pets:** Medium, other species. $10 one-time fee/room. Service with restrictions, supervision.
[SAVE] [S6] [✕] [🖊] [🖬]

# KEYSTONE

**◆◆ The First Lady Inn** M
(605) 666-4990. **$59-$169.** 702 Hwy 16A. On US 16A; west side of town. Ext/int corridors. **Pets:** Accepted.
[ASK] [S6] [✕] [🖬] [🖵] [🛥]

**◆◆ Keystone/Mt Rushmore Super 8** SH
(605) 666-6666. **$59-$149.** 250 Winter St. On US 16A; downtown. Ext/int corridors. **Pets:** Accepted.
[ASK] [S6] [✕]

**◆◆◆ Mt. Rushmore's White House Resort** SH
(605) 666-4917. **$40-$100, 3 day notice.** 115 Swanzey St. Jct US 16A and SR 40. Ext/int corridors. **Pets:** Medium, dogs only. $10 daily fee/pet. Designated rooms, service with restrictions, crate.
[ASK] [S6] [✕] [&M] [&*] [🖬] [¶] [🛥]

**(AAA) ◆◆◆ Powder House Lodge** CA
(605) 666-4646. **$70-$250, 3 day notice.** 24125 Hwy 16A. On US 16A, 1.5 mi n. Ext corridors. **Pets:** Other species. $15 daily fee/pet. Service with restrictions, crate.
[SAVE] [🖬] [🖵] [¶] [🛥]

# LEAD

**(AAA) ◆◆◆◆ Spearfish Canyon Lodge** SH ✿
(605) 584-3435. **$89-$265, 5 day notice.** 10619 Roughlock Falls Rd. I-90, exit 14 (Spearfish Canyon), 13 mi s. Int corridors. **Pets:** $15 daily fee/pet. Service with restrictions, supervision.
[SAVE] [S6] [✕] [🖬] [🖵] [¶] [✕]

# RAPID CITY

**(AAA) ◆◆◆ Alex Johnson Hotel** SH
(605) 342-1210. **$79-$169.** 523 6th St. I-90, exit 57, s on I-190, then left at Omaha; downtown. Int corridors. **Pets:** Small. $25 one-time fee/room. Designated rooms, service with restrictions, supervision.
[SAVE] [S6] [✕] [🖊] [🖬] [🖵] [¶]

**(AAA) ◆◆◆ Americas Best Value Inn** SH
(605) 343-5434. **$40-$120.** 620 Howard St. I-90, exit 58, just nw of Haines Ave. Int corridors. **Pets:** Medium, dogs only. Designated rooms, service with restrictions, supervision.
[SAVE] [S6] [✕] [🖬] [🛥]

**◆◆◆ Best Western Ramkota Hotel** SH
(605) 343-8550. **$94-$154.** 2111 N LaCrosse St. I-90, exit 59 (LaCrosse St), just n. Ext/int corridors. **Pets:** Accepted.
[ASK] [S6] [✕] [&M] [🖊] [&*] [🖬] [🖵] [¶] [🛥] [✕]

**(AAA) ◆◆ Fair Value Inn** M
(605) 342-8118. **$40-$75.** 1607 LaCrosse St. I-90, exit 59 (LaCrosse St), 0.3 mi s. Ext corridors. **Pets:** Very small, dogs only. $20 deposit/pet. Designated rooms, service with restrictions, supervision.
[SAVE] [S6] [✕] [🖬]

**(AAA) ◆◆◆ Foothills Inn** SH ✿
(605) 348-5640. **$39-$139.** 1625 N LaCrosse St. I-90, exit 59 (LaCrosse St), just s. Int corridors. **Pets:** Medium. $20 daily fee/room. Designated rooms, service with restrictions, supervision.
[SAVE] [S6] [✕] [🖬] [🛥]

**(AAA) ◆◆◆ Gold Star Motel** M
(605) 341-7051. **$36-$68.** 801 E North. I-90, exit 60, 1.5 mi sw on I-90 business loop, 1.2 mi s, then just e, from exit 59 (LaCrosse St). Ext corridors. **Pets:** Medium, other species. $5 daily fee/pet. Service with restrictions, supervision.
[SAVE] [S6] [✕] [🖵]

**◆◆◆ Holiday Inn Express Hotel & Suites, I-90** SH
(605) 355-9090. **$84-$209.** 645 E Disk Dr. I-90, exit 59 (LaCrosse St), just ne. Int corridors. **Pets:** Accepted.
[ASK] [S6] [✕] [&M] [🖊] [&*] [🖬] [🖵] [🛥]

**◆◆ Holiday Inn Hotel & Suites I-90** SH
(605) 342-6400. **$94-$219.** 625 E Disk Dr. I-90, exit 59 (LaCrosse St), just ne. Ext/int corridors. **Pets:** Accepted.
[ASK] [S6] [✕] [🖬] [🖵] [🛥]

**(AAA) ◆◆◆ Holiday Inn-Rushmore Plaza** LH
(605) 348-4000. **$89-$149.** 505 N 5th St. I-90, exit 58, 1.3 mi s on Haines. Int corridors. **Pets:** Accepted.
[SAVE] [S6] [✕] [&M] [🖊] [&*] [🖬] [🖵] [¶] [🛥] [✕]

**(AAA) ◆◆◆ Microtel Inn & Suites** SH
(605) 348-2523. **$52-$120.** 1740 Rapp St. I-90, exit 59 (LaCrosse St), just se. Int corridors. **Pets:** Small, dogs only. $10 daily fee/pet. Designated rooms, service with restrictions, supervision.
[SAVE] [S6] [✕] [&M] [🖊] [&*] [🖬] [🖵] [🛥]

◆ Motel 6–352 **M**
(605) 343-3687. **$37-$75.** 620 E Latrobe St. I-90, exit 59 (LaCrosse St),
just se. Ext corridors. **Pets:** Accepted.

◆◆ Quality Inn **SH**
(605) 342-3322. **$49-$249.** 1902 LaCrosse St. I-90, exit 59 (LaCrosse
St), just s. Ext/int corridors. **Pets:** Accepted.

◆◆ Ramada Inn Gold Key **SH** ❀
(605) 342-1300. **$79-$229.** 1721 N LaCrosse St. I-90, exit 59
(LaCrosse St), just s. Int corridors. **Pets:** Medium. $10 daily fee/room.
Designated rooms, service with restrictions, supervision.

◆◆ Super 8 Motel-I-90 **SH**
(605) 348-8070. **$45-$175.** 2124 LaCrosse St. I-90, exit 59 (LaCrosse
St), just n. Int corridors. **Pets:** Medium, other species. $10 daily fee/pet.
Service with restrictions, crate.

⟨AAA⟩ ◆ Super 8 Motel-South **SH** ❀
(605) 342-4911. **$45-$105.** 2520 Tower Rd. 1.4 mi s on US 16, then
just e. Int corridors. **Pets:** Other species. $5 daily fee/pet. Service with
restrictions, supervision.

## ROCKERVILLE

◆ Rockerville Trading Post & Motel **M**
(605) 341-4880. **$55-$75, 3 day notice.** 13525 Main St. Center. Ext
corridors. **Pets:** Dogs only. $5 daily fee/room. Supervision.

## SPEARFISH

⟨AAA⟩ ◆◆◆ Best Western Black Hills Lodge **SH**
(605) 642-7795. **$65-$149, 30 day notice.** 540 E Jackson. I-90, exit 12,
just s. Ext/int corridors. **Pets:** Dogs only. $5 daily fee/pet. Designated
rooms, service with restrictions, supervision.

◆◆ Days Inn **SH** ❀
(605) 642-7101. **$60-$125.** 240 Ryan Rd. I-90, exit 10, 1.2 mi s. Ext/int
corridors. **Pets:** Other species. $10 daily fee/room. Service with restrictions,
supervision.

⟨AAA⟩ ◆◆◆ Holiday Inn Hotel & Convention
                Center **SH** ❀
(605) 642-4683. **$69-$279.** 305 N 27th St. I-90, exit 14 (Spearfish
Canyon), just n. Ext/int corridors. **Pets:** Other species. $100 deposit/
room, $25 one-time fee/room. Designated rooms, service with restrictions,
supervision.

⟨AAA⟩ ◆◆ Howard Johnson Express Inn **SH**
(605) 642-8105. **$45-$99.** 323 S 27th St. I-90, exit 14 (Spearfish Canyon), just s. Int corridors. **Pets:** Medium, other species. $10 daily fee/pet.
Designated rooms, service with restrictions, supervision.

⟨AAA⟩ ◆ Royal Rest Motel **M**
(605) 642-3842. **$30-$50.** 444 Main St. On US 14/85; downtown. Ext
corridors. **Pets:** Small. Service with restrictions, supervision.

◆◆ Travelodge of Spearfish **M** ❀
(605) 642-4676. **$40-$120.** 346 W Kansas St. Downtown off of Main St;
follow signs. Ext corridors. **Pets:** Other species. $10 daily fee/pet. Service
with restrictions, supervision.

## STURGIS

⟨AAA⟩ ◆◆◆ Best Western of Sturgis **SH**
(605) 347-3604. **$49-$109.** 2431 S Junction Ave. I-90, exit 32. Ext/int
corridors. **Pets:** Other species. Designated rooms, service with restrictions,
supervision.

⟨AAA⟩ ◆◆◆ Days Inn **SH**
(605) 347-3027. **$60-$90, 7 day notice.** 2630 Lazelle St. I-90, exit 30,
at jct US 14A. Ext/int corridors. **Pets:** Medium, other species. $10 daily
fee/pet. Designated rooms, service with restrictions, supervision.

⟨AAA⟩ ◆◆◆ Star Lite Motel **M**
(605) 347-2506. **$50-$75.** 2426 Junction Ave. I-90, exit 32, just n. Ext
corridors. **Pets:** Accepted.

---

## END AREA

---

## BRANDON

⟨AAA⟩ ◆◆◆ Comfort Inn **SH**
(605) 582-5777. **$69-$189.** 1105 N Splitrock Blvd. I-90, exit 406, just s.
Int corridors. **Pets:** Accepted.

## BROOKINGS

◆◆ Brookings Super 8 Motel **SH**
(605) 692-6920. **$52-$80.** 3034 Lefevre Dr. I-29, exit 132, just e. Int
corridors. **Pets:** Medium. $7 one-time fee/pet. Service with restrictions,
supervision.

⟨AAA⟩ ◆◆◆ Fairfield Inn & Suites **SH**
(605) 692-3500. **$63-$140.** 3000 Lefevre Dr. I-29, exit 132, just e. Int
corridors. **Pets:** Accepted.

◆◆◆ Holiday Inn Express Hotel & Suites **SH**
(605) 692-9060. **$95-$125.** 3020 Lefevre Dr. I-29, exit 132, just se. Int
corridors. **Pets:** $10 one-time fee/pet. Service with restrictions, supervision.

## BUFFALO

◆ Tipperary Lodge **M**
(605) 375-3721. **$51-$52.** 604 1st St W. 0.5 mi n on US 85, turn at
sign. Int corridors. **Pets:** Small, other species. Designated rooms, service
with restrictions, supervision.

## CANISTOTA

⟨AAA⟩ ◆◆◆ Best Western U-Bar Motel **M**
(605) 296-3466. **$60-$85.** 130 Ash St. I-90, exit 368, 6 mi s, follow
signs. Ext corridors. **Pets:** Very small, dogs only. Service with restrictions,
supervision.

# CHAMBERLAIN

**♦♦♦ ▼▼▼ AmericInn Lodge & Suites of Chamberlain** 🆂🅷
(605) 734-0985. **$60-$160.** 1981 E King St. I-90, exit 265, just e. Int corridors. **Pets:** Other species. $10 daily fee/pet. Service with restrictions, supervision.
📱 ⊠ 🅼 🖊 🛋 🖥 💻 🏊 ⊠

**♦♦♦ ▼ Bel Aire Motel** 🅼
(605) 734-5595. **$40-$64.** 312 E King St. On US 16 and I-90 business loop; downtown. Ext/int corridors. **Pets:** $5 daily fee/pet. Service with restrictions, supervision.
📱 🆂 ⊠ 🖥

**♦♦♦ ▼▼▼ Best Western Lee's Motor Inn** 🆂🅷
(605) 734-5575. **$50-$90.** 220 W King St. On US 17 and I-90 business loop; downtown. Ext/int corridors. **Pets:** Small, other species. No service, supervision.
📱 🆂 ⊠ 💻 🏊 ⊠

**♦♦♦ ▼▼▼▼ Cedar Shore Resort** 🄻🄷 🐾
(605) 734-6376. **$70-$150.** 1500 Shoreline Dr. I-90, exit 260, 2.5 mi e on Business Rt I-90, then 1 mi ne on Mickelson county road, follow signs. Int corridors **Pets:** Other species. $10 daily fee/room. Service with restrictions, supervision.
📱 🆂 ⊠ 🅼 🖊 🛋 🖥 💻 🏊 ⊠

**▼▼ ▼▼ Holiday Inn Express** 🆂🅷
(605) 734-5593. **$79-$149.** 100 W Hwy 16. I-90, exit 260, just n. Int corridors. **Pets:** Accepted.
🄰🅂🄺 🆂 ⊠ 🅼 🛋 💻

**♦♦♦ ▼ Lake Shore Motel** 🅼
(605) 234-5566. **$48-$85, 3 day notice.** 115 N River St. Just n of US 16 bridge (the northernmost bridge); just w of downtown. Ext corridors. **Pets:** $10 daily fee/room. Supervision.
📱 ⊠ 🖥

**♦♦♦ ▼▼▼ Oasis Inn** 🆂🅷
(605) 734-6061. **$51-$119.** 1100 E Hwy 16. I-90, exit 260, 0.4 mi e on US 16 and I-90 business loop. Ext/int corridors. **Pets:** Service with restrictions, supervision.
📱 🆂 ⊠ 🅼 🖊 🖥 💻 🏊

# DELL RAPIDS

**▼▼ ▼▼ Bilmar Inn & Suites** 🆂🅷
(605) 428-4288. **$53-$76.** 510 N Hwy 77. I-29, exit 98 (SR 115), 3 mi e, then just n. Int corridors. **Pets:** Medium, dogs only. $6 daily fee/pet. Designated rooms, service with restrictions, supervision.
🄰🅂🄺 🆂 ⊠ 🛋 🖥 💻

# DE SMET

**▼▼ ▼▼ De Smet Super 8** 🆂🅷
(605) 854-9388. **$62-$85.** 288 Hwy 14 E. US 14, just e. Int corridors. **Pets:** Accepted.
🄰🅂🄺 🆂 ⊠ 🛋 🖥 💻 🏊

# FAITH

**♦♦♦ ▼▼▼ Prairie Vista Inn** 🆂🅷
(605) 967-2343. **$67-$95.** Hwy 212 & E 1st. On US 212; at east city edge. Int corridors. **Pets:** Medium. $10 daily fee/pet. Designated rooms, service with restrictions, supervision.
📱 🆂 ⊠ 🛋 💻

# FAULKTON

**▼▼ ▼▼ Super 8 Motel** 🆂🅷
(605) 598-4567. **$50-$79.** 700 Main St. On US 212; center. Int corridors. **Pets:** Accepted.
🄰🅂🄺 🆂 ⊠ 🖥

# FLANDREAU

**♦♦♦ ▼▼▼▼ Royal River Casino & Hotel** 🆂🅷
(605) 997-3746. **$55-$199.** 607 S Veterans St. I-29, exit 114, 7 mi e, follow signs. Int corridors. **Pets:** Other species. $50 deposit/pet. Designated rooms, service with restrictions, supervision.
📱 🆂 ⊠ 🅼 🛋 🖥 💻 🍴 🏊

# FORT PIERRE

**▼▼ ▼▼ Fort Pierre Motel** 🅼
(605) 223-3111. **$52-$60, 3 day notice.** 211 S 1st Ave. On US 83, 1.2 mi s of jct US 14. Ext corridors. **Pets:** Accepted.
⊠ 🖥

# FREEMAN

**▼▼ ▼▼ Super 8 Motel** 🆂🅷
(605) 925-4888. **$47-$55.** 1019 S Hwy 81. On US 81, just s. Int corridors. **Pets:** Accepted.
🄰🅂🄺 ⊠ 🛋 🖥

# HURON

**▼▼ ▼▼ Best Western of Huron** 🆂🅷
(605) 352-2000. **$65-$95.** 2000 Dakota Ave. 1.3 mi s on SR 37. Ext/int corridors. **Pets:** Medium, dogs only. $10 daily fee/room. Service with restrictions, supervision.
🄰🅂🄺 🆂 ⊠ 🅼 🖊 🛋 🖥 💻 ⊠

**♦♦♦ ▼▼▼▼ Crossroads Hotel & Huron Event Center** 🄻🄷
(605) 352-3204. **$79-$105, 3 day notice.** 100 4th St. Just w of Dakota Ave; downtown. Int corridors. **Pets:** $15 daily fee/room. Supervision.
📱 🆂 ⊠ 🛋 🖥 💻 🍴 🏊 ⊠

**▼▼ ▼▼ Holiday Inn Express** 🆂🅷
(605) 352-6655. **$71-$114.** 100 21st St SW. 1.3 mi s on SR 37. Ext/int corridors. **Pets:** $25 one-time fee/room. Service with restrictions, supervision.
🄰🅂🄺 🆂 ⊠ 🅼 🖊 🛋 🖥 💻 ⊠

# INTERIOR

**♦♦♦ ▼ Badlands Budget Host Motel** 🅼
(605) 433-5335. **$41-$63.** 900 SD Hwy 377. Jct SR 44 and 377, 2 mi s of Badlands National Park. Ext corridors. **Pets:** Accepted.
📱 🆂 🖥 🏊 🅿

# KADOKA

**♦♦♦ ▼▼▼ Best Western H & H El Centro Motel** 🅼
(605) 837-2287. **$52-$135.** 105 E Hwy 16. 1.5 mi w on I-90 business route from exit 152, 1.3 mi e from exit 150. Ext corridors. **Pets:** Accepted.
📱 🆂 ⊠ 🖥 🍴 🏊 ⊠

**♦♦♦ ▼ West Motel** 🅼
(605) 837-2427. **$34-$70, 3 day notice.** 306 Hwy 16 W. I-90, exit 150, 1 mi e on I-90 business route. Ext corridors. **Pets:** Other species. $10 daily fee/room. Service with restrictions, supervision.
📱 ⊠ 🖥

# MADISON

**▼▼▼▼ AmericInn Lodge & Suites** 🆂🅷
(605) 256-3076. **$72-$109.** 504 10th St SE. SR 34, 0.5 mi se; south side of town. Int corridors. **Pets:** $25 one-time fee/pet. Designated rooms, supervision.
🄰🅂🄺 🆂 ⊠ 🅼 🛋 🖥 💻 🏊

# MITCHELL

**▼▼ ▼▼ AmericInn Lodge & Suites** 🆂🅷
(605) 996-9700. **$68-$100.** 1421 S Burr St. I-90, exit 332, just n. Int corridors. **Pets:** Accepted.
🄰🅂🄺 🆂 ⊠ 🅼 🛋 🖥 💻 🏊

**Hampton Inn** SH
(605) 995-1575. **$72-$122.** 1920 Highland Way. I-90, exit 332, just se. Int corridors. **Pets:** Dogs only. $20 daily fee/room. Service with restrictions, supervision.
[SAVE] [S] [X] [&M] [🐾] [🔥] [📞] [🖥] [🏊] [X]

**Holiday Inn** SH
(605) 996-6501. **$80-$159.** 1525 W Havens St. I-90, exit 330, 0.5 mi n. Ext/int corridors. **Pets:** Accepted.
[SAVE] [S] [X] [&M] [🐾] [🔥] [🖥] [🍴] [🏊] [X]

**Kelly Inn & Suites** SH
(605) 995-0500. **$69-$119.** 1010 Cabela Dr. I-90, exit 332, just sw. Ext/int corridors. **Pets:** Service with restrictions, supervision.
[SAVE] [S] [X] [🔥] [🔥] [📞] [🖥] [🏊] [X]

**Thunderbird Lodge** M
(605) 996-6645. **$45-$94.** 1601 S Burr St. I-90, exit 332, just n. Ext/int corridors. **Pets:** Large. $10 daily fee/room. Designated rooms, service with restrictions, supervision.
[SAVE] [S] [X] [&M] [📞] [🖥]

## MOBRIDGE

**Best Value Wrangler Inn** SH
(605) 845-3641. **$125.** 820 W Grand Crossing. 0.5 mi w on US 12. Ext/int corridors. **Pets:** Dogs only. Designated rooms, service with restrictions, supervision.
[SAVE] [S] [X] [📞] [🖥] [🍴] [🏊] [X]

**Grand River Casino & Resort** SH
(605) 845-7104. **$65-$70.** W Hwy 12. 4.5 mi w on US 12 and SR 20. Int corridors. **Pets:** Accepted.
[ASK] [S] [X] [&M] [🔥] [📞] [🖥] [🍴]

## MURDO

**Best Western Graham's** M
(605) 669-2441. **$59-$110.** 301 W 5th. On I-90 business loop, 0.5 mi w of jct US 83; I-90, exits 191 and 192. Ext corridors. **Pets:** Accepted.
[SAVE] [S] [X] [🖥] [🏊]

## NORTH SIOUX CITY

**Comfort Inn** SH
(605) 232-3366. **$60-$65.** 1311 River Dr. I-29, exit 2, just w. Int corridors. **Pets:** Medium. $10 one-time fee/pet. Service with restrictions, supervision.
[SAVE] [S] [X] [📞] [🖥] [🏊] [X]

**Hampton Inn** SH
(605) 232-9739. **$69-$110, 14 day notice.** 101 S Sodrac Dr. I-29, exit 2, just w. Int corridors. **Pets:** Medium. $20 one-time fee/room. Designated rooms, service with restrictions, supervision.
[ASK] [S] [X] [&M] [📞] [🖥] [🏊]

**Red Carpet Inn & Suites** SH
(605) 232-9600. **$35-$75.** 110 Sodrac Dr. I-29, exit 2, just w. Int corridors. **Pets:** Accepted.
[ASK] [S] [X] [🔥] [📞] [🖥]

**Super 8 Motel** SH
(605) 232-4716. **$44-$74.** 1300 River Dr. I-29, exit 2, just w. Int corridors. **Pets:** Accepted.
[ASK] [S] [X] [📞] [🖥]

## PICKSTOWN

**Fort Randall Inn** M
(605) 487-7801. **$60.** 116 US Hwy 18. On US 18/281; just e of the dam. Ext corridors. **Pets:** Other species. $10 daily fee/room. Service with restrictions.
[ASK] [S] [X] [📞]

## PIERRE

**Best Western Ramkota Hotel** SH
(605) 224-6877. **$93-$100.** 920 W Sioux Ave. 1 mi w on US 14/83. Ext/int corridors. **Pets:** Accepted.
[ASK] [S] [X] [&M] [🐾] [🔥] [📞] [🖥] [🍴] [🏊] [X]

**Comfort Inn** SH 🐾
(605) 224-0377. **$65-$109.** 410 W Sioux Ave. 0.3 mi w on US 14/83 and SR 34. Int corridors. **Pets:** Dogs only. $10 daily fee/pet. Designated rooms, service with restrictions, supervision.
[SAVE] [S] [X] [&M] [🔥] [📞] [🖥] [🏊]

**Governor's Inn** SH
(605) 224-4200. **$60-$125.** 700 W Sioux Ave. 0.8 mi w on US 14/83 and SR 34. Ext/int corridors. **Pets:** Other species. Service with restrictions, supervision.
[SAVE] [S] [X] [🐾] [🔥] [📞] [🖥] [🏊]

**Kelly Inn** SH
(605) 224-4140. **$59.** 713 W Sioux Ave. 0.8 mi w on US 14/83. Int corridors. **Pets:** Service with restrictions, supervision.
[ASK] [S] [X] [🔥] [📞] [🖥]

**Super 8 Motel** SH
(605) 224-1617. **$40-$75.** 320 W Sioux Ave. 0.3 mi w on US 14/83 and SR 34. Int corridors. **Pets:** $5 daily fee/pet. Service with restrictions, supervision.
[ASK] [S] [X] [🔥] [📞]

## PLANKINTON

**Super 8 Motel** SH
(605) 942-7722. **$44-$80.** 801 S Main St. I-90, exit 308, just n. Int corridors. **Pets:** Accepted.
[ASK] [S] [X]

## SIOUX FALLS

**Baymont Inn** SH
(605) 362-0835. **$74-$119.** 3200 Meadow Ave. I-29, exit 77 (41st St), just w, then just n. Int corridors. **Pets:** Accepted.
[ASK] [S] [X] [&M] [🐾] [🔥] [📞] [🖥] [🏊]

**Best Western Ramkota Hotel & Conference Center** LH
(605) 336-0650. **$89-$239.** 3200 W Maple. I-29, exit 81 (Airport/Russell St), just e. Ext/int corridors. **Pets:** Accepted.
[ASK] [S] [X] [&M] [🐾] [🔥] [📞] [🖥] [🍴] [🏊] [X]

**Clubhouse Hotel & Suites** SH
(605) 361-8700. **$129-$450, 7 day notice.** 2320 S Louise Ave. I-29, exit 78 (26th St), just e. Ext/int corridors. **Pets:** Accepted.
[ASK] [S] [X] [🔥] [📞] [🖥] [🏊]

**Comfort Inn by Choice Hotels South** SH
(605) 361-2822. **$64-$134.** 3216 S Carolyn Ave. I-29, exit 77 (41st St), just e, then n. Int corridors. **Pets:** Accepted.
[ASK] [S] [X] [🐾] [📞] [🖥] [🏊]

**Comfort Inn North** SH
(605) 331-4490. **$49-$129.** 5100 N Cliff Ave. I-90, exit 399 (Cliff Ave), 0.3 mi s. Int corridors. **Pets:** Accepted.
[SAVE] [S] [X] [&M] [🐾] [📞] [🖥] [🏊]

**Comfort Suites by Choice Hotels** SH
(605) 362-9711. **$74-$134.** 3208 S Carolyn Ave. I-29, exit 77 (41st St), just e, then n. Int corridors. **Pets:** Accepted.
[ASK] [S] [X] [🐾] [📞] [🖥] [🏊]

**Country Inn & Suites By Carlson** SH
(605) 373-0153. **$65-$92.** 200 E 8th St. Just e of Phillips Ave; downtown. Int corridors. **Pets:** $10 daily fee/room. Designated rooms, service with restrictions, supervision.
[ASK] [S] [X] [&M] [🐾] [🔥] [📞] [🖥] [🍴] [🏊]

**ⓐ ▽ Days Inn Airport** 🆂🅷
(605) 331-5959. **$60-$150.** 5001 N Cliff Ave. I-90, exit 399 (Cliff Ave), just s. Int corridors. **Pets:** Other species. $10 daily fee/room. Service with restrictions, supervision.
⟦SAVE⟧ ⟦S⟧ ⟦✕⟧ ⟦&M⟧ ⟦⟧ ⟦⟧ ⟦⟧ ⟦⟧

**ⓐ ▽ Days Inn-Empire** 🆂🅷
(605) 361-9240. **$65-$155.** 3401 Gateway Blvd. I-29, exit 77 (41st St), just w. Int corridors. **Pets:** Dogs only. $10 daily fee/pet. Service with restrictions, supervision.
⟦SAVE⟧ ⟦S⟧ ⟦✕⟧ ⟦⟧ ⟦⟧ ⟦⟧ ⟦⟧

**ⓐ ▽▽▽ Homewood Suites By Hilton** 🆂🅷 🐾
(605) 338-8585. **$89-$199.** 3620 W Avera Dr. I-229, exit 1C (Louise Ave), just s. Int corridors. **Pets:** Other species. $5 daily fee/pet, $15 one-time fee/room. Service with restrictions.
⟦SAVE⟧ ⟦S⟧ ⟦✕⟧ ⟦&⟧ ⟦&M⟧ ⟦⟧ ⟦⟧ ⟦⟧ ⟦⟧ ⟦⟧ ⟦⟧

**ⓐ ▽▽ Kelly Inn** 🆂🅷
(605) 338-6242. **$64-$79, 30 day notice.** 3101 W Russell St. I-29, exit 81 (Airport/Russell St), just e. Ext/int corridors. **Pets:** Service with restrictions, supervision.
⟦SAVE⟧ ⟦S⟧ ⟦✕⟧ ⟦⟧ ⟦⟧ ⟦⟧ ⟦⟧

**▽ Microtel Inn & Suites** 🆂🅷
(605) 361-7484. **$59-$75.** 2901 S Carolyn Ave. I-29, exit 77 (41st St), just e, then n. Int corridors. **Pets:** Medium, other species. $35 one-time fee/pet. Designated rooms, service with restrictions, supervision.
⟦ASK⟧ ⟦S⟧ ⟦✕⟧ ⟦&M⟧ ⟦⟧ ⟦⟧ ⟦⟧ ⟦⟧

**▽ Motel 6–0162** 🅼
(605) 336-7800. **$39-$55.** 3009 W Russell St. I-29, exit 81 (Airport/Russell St), just e. Ext corridors. **Pets:** Accepted.
⟦S⟧ ⟦✕⟧ ⟦&M⟧ ⟦⟧ ⟦⟧ ⟦⟧

**▽▽ Ramada Limited** 🆂🅷
(605) 330-0000. **$63-$78.** 407 S Lyons Ave. I-29, exit 79 (12th St), just e. Int corridors. **Pets:** Medium. $15 one-time fee/pet. Service with restrictions, supervision.
⟦ASK⟧ ⟦S⟧ ⟦✕⟧ ⟦&M⟧ ⟦⟧ ⟦⟧ ⟦⟧ ⟦⟧ ⟦⟧

**▽▽ Red Roof Inn** 🆂🅷
(605) 361-1864. **$52-$100.** 3500 S Gateway Blvd. I-29, exit 77 (41st St), just w. Int corridors. **Pets:** Accepted.
⟦ASK⟧ ⟦S⟧ ⟦✕⟧ ⟦⟧ ⟦⟧

**▽▽▽ Residence Inn by Marriott** 🆂🅷
(605) 361-2202. **$100-$215, 14 day notice.** 4509 W Empire Pl. I-29, exit 77 (41st St), 0.5 mi se. Int corridors. **Pets:** Accepted.
⟦ASK⟧ ⟦S⟧ ⟦✕⟧ ⟦&M⟧ ⟦⟧ ⟦⟧ ⟦⟧ ⟦⟧ ⟦⟧ ⟦⟧

**ⓐ ▽▽▽ Sheraton Sioux Falls Hotel** 🅻🅷
(605) 331-0100. **$99-$149.** 1211 N West Ave. I-29, exit 81 (Airport/Russell St), 1.3 mi e. Int corridors. **Pets:** Accepted.
⟦SAVE⟧ ⟦S⟧ ⟦✕⟧ ⟦&M⟧ ⟦⟧ ⟦⟧ ⟦⟧ ⟦⟧ ⟦🍽⟧ ⟦⟧ ⟦⟧

**ⓐ ▽▽ Sleep Inn Airport** 🆂🅷
(605) 339-3992. **$49-$99.** 1500 N Kiwanis Ave. I-29, exit 81 (Airport/Russell St), 0.7 mi e. Int corridors. **Pets:** Medium. $10 one-time fee/pet. Service with restrictions, supervision.
⟦SAVE⟧ ⟦S⟧ ⟦✕⟧ ⟦&M⟧ ⟦⟧ ⟦⟧ ⟦⟧ ⟦⟧ ⟦⟧

**▽▽▽ Staybridge Suites** 🆂🅷 🐾
(605) 361-2298. **$107-$179, 7 day notice.** 2505 S Carolyn Ave. I-29, exit 78, Just se. Int corridors. **Pets:** $75 one-time fee/room. Service with restrictions, supervision.
⟦ASK⟧ ⟦S⟧ ⟦✕⟧ ⟦&M⟧ ⟦⟧ ⟦⟧ ⟦⟧ ⟦⟧ ⟦⟧

**▽ Super 8/I-90/Airport East** 🆂🅷
(605) 339-9212. **$50-$90.** 4808 N Cliff Ave. I-90, exit 399 (Cliff Ave), 0.3 mi s. Int corridors. **Pets:** Accepted.
⟦ASK⟧ ⟦S⟧ ⟦✕⟧ ⟦⟧ ⟦⟧

**▽▽ Super 8 Motel-East** 🆂🅷
(605) 338-8881. **$57-$140.** 2616 E 10th St. I-229, exit 6, just e. Int corridors. **Pets:** Small. $5 one-time fee/pet. Designated rooms, service with restrictions, supervision.
⟦ASK⟧ ⟦S⟧ ⟦✕⟧ ⟦&M⟧ ⟦⟧ ⟦⟧ ⟦⟧ ⟦⟧

**▽▽▽ TownePlace Suites by Marriott** 🆂🅷
(605) 361-2626. **$69-$139.** 4545 W Homefield Dr. I-29, exit 78 (26th St), just w. Int corridors. **Pets:** Small. $75 one-time fee/room. Designated rooms, service with restrictions, supervision.
⟦ASK⟧ ⟦✕⟧ ⟦&M⟧ ⟦⟧ ⟦⟧ ⟦⟧ ⟦⟧ ⟦⟧ ⟦⟧

# VERMILLION

**ⓐ ▽▽ Comfort Inn** 🆂🅷
(605) 624-8333. **$70-$80.** 701 W Cherry St. I-29, exit 26 (SR 50), 7.5 mi w on Business Rt SR 50. Int corridors. **Pets:** $5 daily fee/pet. Service with restrictions, supervision.
⟦SAVE⟧ ⟦S⟧ ⟦✕⟧ ⟦⟧ ⟦⟧ ⟦⟧ ⟦⟧ ⟦⟧

**▽▽▽ Holiday Inn Express Hotel & Suites-Vermillion** 🆂🅷
(605) 624-7600. **$80-$200.** 1200 N Dakota St. I-29, exit 26, 7 mi w. Int corridors. **Pets:** Small, dogs only. $10 daily fee/pet. Designated rooms, service with restrictions, crate.
⟦ASK⟧ ⟦✕⟧ ⟦&M⟧ ⟦⟧ ⟦⟧ ⟦⟧ ⟦⟧ ⟦⟧

# WALL

**ⓐ ▽▽▽ Best Western Plains Motel** 🅼
(605) 279-2145. **$60-$165.** 712 Glenn St. I-90, exit 110, just n. Ext corridors. **Pets:** Other species. $10 daily fee/pet. Service with restrictions, supervision.
⟦SAVE⟧ ⟦S⟧ ⟦✕⟧ ⟦⟧ ⟦⟧ ⟦⟧ ⟦⟧

**▽▽ Days Inn** 🆂🅷
(605) 279-2000. **$55-$180.** 212 10th Ave. I-90, exit 110, just n, then just w. Int corridors. **Pets:** Medium. $10 one-time fee/room. Designated rooms, service with restrictions, crate.
⟦ASK⟧ ⟦S⟧ ⟦✕⟧ ⟦⟧

**ⓐ ▽▽▽ Econo Lodge** 🅼 🐾
(605) 279-2121. **$59-$109.** 804 Glenn St. I-90, exit 110, just n. Ext corridors. **Pets:** Medium, other species. $10 one-time fee/pet. Service with restrictions, supervision.
⟦SAVE⟧ ⟦S⟧ ⟦✕⟧ ⟦⟧ ⟦⟧ ⟦⟧

**ⓐ ▽ Sunshine Inn** 🅼
(605) 279-2178. **$48-$77.** 608 Main St. Downtown. Ext corridors. **Pets:** Other species. $5 one-time fee/room. Service with restrictions.
⟦SAVE⟧ ⟦S⟧ ⟦✕⟧

# WATERTOWN

**▽▽▽ Best Western Ramkota Hotel** 🆂🅷
(605) 886-8011. **$99-$124.** 1901 9th Ave SW. I-29, exit 177 (US 212), 4 mi w. Int corridors. **Pets:** Accepted.
⟦ASK⟧ ⟦S⟧ ⟦✕⟧ ⟦&M⟧ ⟦⟧ ⟦⟧ ⟦⟧ ⟦⟧ ⟦🍽⟧ ⟦⟧ ⟦⟧

**ⓐ ▽▽ Comfort Inn** 🆂🅷
(605) 886-3010. **$80.** 800 35th St Cir. I-29, exit 177 (US 212), just w. Ext/int corridors. **Pets:** $15 one-time fee/room. Service with restrictions, supervision.
⟦SAVE⟧ ⟦S⟧ ⟦✕⟧ ⟦&M⟧ ⟦⟧ ⟦⟧ ⟦⟧ ⟦⟧

**ⓐ ▽▽▽ Country Inn & Suites By Carlson** 🆂🅷 🐾
(605) 886-8900. **$80-$130.** 3400 8th Ave SE. I-29, exit 177 (US 212), just w. Int corridors. **Pets:** Medium. $20 one-time fee/room. Designated rooms, service with restrictions, supervision.
⟦SAVE⟧ ⟦S⟧ ⟦✕⟧ ⟦&M⟧ ⟦⟧ ⟦⟧ ⟦⟧ ⟦⟧

**ⓐ ▽▽ Days Inn** 🆂🅷
(605) 886-3500. **$55-$85, 14 day notice.** 2900 9th Ave SE. I-29, exit 177 (US 212), 0.5 mi w. Ext/int corridors. **Pets:** $10 one-time fee/room. Service with restrictions, supervision.
⟦SAVE⟧ ⟦S⟧ ⟦✕⟧ ⟦&M⟧ ⟦⟧ ⟦⟧ ⟦⟧ ⟦⟧ ⟦⟧

**Holiday Inn Express Hotel & Suites** 🆂🅷
(605) 882-3636. **$69-$169, 7 day notice.** 3900 9th Ave SE. I-29, exit 177 (US 212), just e. Int corridors. **Pets:** Other species. $10 daily fee/room. Service with restrictions, supervision.
🅰️🆂🅺 🆂🅾 ⊠ 🅺 🔒 🖵 🌊 ⊠

**Super 8 Motel-Watertown** 🆂🅷
(605) 882-1900. **$55-$89.** 503 14th Ave SE. On US 81, 0.3 mi s of jct US 212. Int corridors. **Pets:** Small. Designated rooms, no service, crate.
🅰️🆂🅺 🆂🅾 ⊠ 🔒 🖵 🌊

**Travelers Inn Motel** 🆂🅷 🐾
(605) 882-2243. **$51-$57.** 920 14th St SE. I-29, exit 177 (US 212), 1.5 mi w, then just s. Int corridors. **Pets:** Other species. $6 daily fee/pet. Designated rooms.
🆂🅰🆅🅴 🆂🅾 ⊠ 🅺 🔒 🖵

**Travel Host Motel** 🅼
(605) 886-6120. **$48-$55.** 1714 9th Ave SW. I-29, exit 177 (US 212), 4 mi w. Int corridors. **Pets:** Dogs only. $10 one-time fee/room. Designated rooms, no service, supervision.
🆂🅰🆅🅴 ⊠ 🔒

# WINNER

**Holiday Inn Express Hotel & Suites** 🆂🅷
(605) 842-2255. **$59-$129.** 1360 E Hwy 44. Just ne of jct US 18/183. Int corridors. **Pets:** Very small, dogs only. $50 deposit/pet, $25 daily fee/pet. Service with restrictions, crate.
🅰️🆂🅺 🆂🅾 ⊠ 🅶🅼 🍽 🅺 🔒 🖵 🌊

# YANKTON

**Best Western Kelly Inn-Yankton** 🆂🅷
(605) 665-2906. **$89-$119.** 1607 Hwy 50. On US 50, 1.8 mi e. Ext/int corridors. **Pets:** Service with restrictions, supervision.
🅰️🆂🅺 ⊠ 🅶🅼 🍽 🅺 🔒 🖵 🍴 🌊 ⊠

**Days Inn** 🆂🅷
(605) 665-8717. **$69.** 2410 Broadway. US 81, 1.7 mi n. Int corridors. **Pets:** Accepted.
🅰️🆂🅺 🆂🅾 ⊠ 🔒 🖵

**Lewis & Clark Resort** 🅼
(605) 665-2680. **$50-$229, 30 day notice.** 43496 Shore Dr. 4 mi w on SR 52; in Lewis and Clark State Park, turn into park, just w of Marina. Ext corridors. **Pets:** Other species. $25 deposit/pet, $5 daily fee/pet. Service with restrictions, supervision.
🆂🅰🆅🅴 ⊠ 🅺 🔒 🖵 🌊 ⊠ 🆉

# TENNESSEE

## ALCOA

**Family Inns of America** M
(865) 970-2006. **$46-$49.** 2450 Airport Hwy. US 129, just e. Ext corridors. **Pets:** Very small, dogs only. Service with restrictions, supervision.

**Holiday Inn Express Hotel & Suites** SH
(865) 981-9008. **$93-$128.** 130 Associates Blvd. US 129, just s. Int corridors. **Pets:** Accepted.

**Jameson Inn Alcoa** SH
(865) 984-6800. **$54-$104.** 206 Corporate Pl. US 129, just s. Int corridors. **Pets:** Very small, other species. $10 daily fee/room. Service with restrictions, supervision.

## ATHENS

**Days Inn-Athens** SH
(423) 745-5800. **$57-$65, 7 day notice.** 2541 Decatur Pike. I-75, exit 49. Ext corridors. **Pets:** Medium, other species. $5 daily fee/pet. Service with restrictions, crate.

**Ramada Inn** SH
(423) 745-1212. **$75-$95.** 115 CR 247. I-75, exit 52, just w. Ext corridors. **Pets:** Accepted.

## BRENTWOOD

**AmeriSuites (Nashville/Brentwood)** SH
(615) 661-9477. **$59-$109.** 202 Summit View Dr. I-65, exit 74A. Int corridors. **Pets:** Accepted.

**Baymont Inn & Suites** SH
(615) 376-4666. **$80-$90, 3 day notice.** 111 Penn Warren Dr. I-65, exit 74B, 1.5 mi w, then just s on West Park. Int corridors. **Pets:** Accepted.

**Candlewood Suites** SH
(615) 309-0600. **$63.** 5129 Virginia Way. I-65, exit 74B, 0.5 mi w, 0.5 mi s on Franklin Rd, 1.2 mi w on Marilyn Way, just s on Ward Cir, then just s. Int corridors. **Pets:** Medium. $150 one-time fee/room. Designated rooms, service with restrictions, supervision.

**MainStay Suites-Brentwood** SH
(615) 371-8477. **$87-$97.** 107 Brentwood Blvd. I-65, exit 74B, 1 mi w. Int corridors. **Pets:** Medium, other species. $50 one-time fee/room. Service with restrictions, supervision.

**Residence Inn Brentwood** SH ❀
(615) 371-0100. **$84-$124.** 206 Ward Cir. I-65, exit 74B, 0.3 mi s on Franklin Pike Cir (US 31 S), 0.5 mi w on Maryland Way. Ext/int corridors. **Pets:** Small, other species. $75 one-time fee/room. Service with restrictions, crate.

**Sleep Inn** SH
(615) 376-2122. **$70-$80.** 1611 Galleria Blvd. I-65, exit 69 northbound, 0.4 mi, then just n; exit 69W southbound, just n. Int corridors. **Pets:** $10 daily fee/room. Service with restrictions, supervision.

## BROWNSVILLE

**Comfort Inn** SH
(731) 772-4082. **$42-$82.** 2600 Anderson Ave. I-40, exit 56. Ext corridors. **Pets:** Accepted.

**Days Inn** SH
(731) 772-3297. **$42-$79.** 2530 Anderson Ave. I-40, exit 56. Ext corridors. **Pets:** Accepted.

**Obannons Inn** SH
(731) 772-4030. **$58.** 120 Sunny Hill Cove. I-40, exit 56. Int corridors. **Pets:** Accepted.

## BUCKSNORT

**Travel Inn** M
(931) 729-5450. **$36-$59.** 5032 Hwy 230 W. I-40, exit 152. Ext corridors. **Pets:** $10 deposit/pet. No service, supervision.

## BULLS GAP

**Best Western Executive Inn** SH
(423) 235-9111. **$54-$190, 14 day notice.** 50 Speedway Ln. I-81, exit 23. Int corridors. **Pets:** Small. $18 daily fee/pet. Designated rooms, service with restrictions, supervision.

**Super 8 Motel** M
(423) 235-4112. **$57-$95, 7 day notice.** 90 Speedway Ln. I-81, exit 23. Ext corridors. **Pets:** Medium. $10 daily fee/room. Designated rooms, service with restrictions, supervision.

# BUTLER

▼▼▼ Iron Mountain Inn B&B and Creekside Chalet 🅱🅱 ❀
(423) 768-2446. **$155-$300, 21 day notice.** 138 Moreland Dr. 1.6 mi w on Pine Orchard Rd from SR 67 at Stout Store, follow signs; 13 mi w on SR 67 from US 421 in Mountain City, follow sign at Stout Store area. Ext/int corridors. **Pets:** Medium, other species. $100 deposit/room. Designated rooms, no service, supervision.
Ⓐ🆂🅺 🆂💰 ☒ 🎁 💻

# CARYVILLE

🆔 ▼ Budget Host Inn 🎏
(423) 562-9595. **$25-$45.** 115 Woods Ave. I-75, exit 134, just w. Ext corridors. **Pets:** Very small. $12 one-time fee/pet. Service with restrictions, supervision.
🆂🅰🆅🅴 🆂💰 ☒

▼▼ Super 8 Motel of Caryville 🎏
(423) 562-8476. **$35-$65.** 200 John McGhee Blvd. I-75, exit 134, just e, then just s on CR 116. Ext corridors. **Pets:** Very small. $6 daily fee/pet. Designated rooms, service with restrictions, supervision.
Ⓐ🆂🅺 🆂💰 ☒ 🎵 🎁 🔄

# CENTERVILLE

▼▼ Days Inn 🆂🅷
(931) 729-5600. **$49-$59.** 634 David St. On SR 100, 3 mi w of jct SR 48. Int corridors. **Pets:** Accepted.
Ⓐ🆂🅺 🆂💰 ☒ 🎵 🎁 💻 🍽 🔄

# CHATTANOOGA

▼▼ Americas Best Inn-Hamilton Mall Area 🎏
(423) 894-5454. **$48-$90.** 7717 Lee Hwy. I-75, exit 7B northbound; exit 7 southbound. Ext corridors. **Pets:** Accepted.
☒ 🎵 🎁 💻 🔄

▼▼◆▼ Baymont Inn & Suites-Chattanooga 🆂🅷
(423) 821-1090. **$60-$110.** 3540 Cummings Hwy. I-24, exit 174, 0.4 mi s. Int corridors. **Pets:** Small. $50 deposit/pet. Designated rooms, service with restrictions, supervision.
Ⓐ🆂🅺 🆂💰 ☒ 🎁 💻 🔄

🆔 ▼▼ Best Western Heritage Inn 🆂🅷
(423) 899-3311. **$59-$99.** 7641 Lee Hwy. I-75, exit 7B northbound; exit 7 southbound. Ext corridors. **Pets:** Very small, other species. $10 daily fee/pet. Service with restrictions, crate.
🆂🅰🆅🅴 🆂💰 ☒ 🎁 💻 🍽 🔄

🆔 ▼▼ Best Western Royal Inn 🆂🅷
(423) 821-6840. **$60-$75.** 3644 Cummings Hwy. I-24, exit 174, 0.4 mi s. Ext corridors. **Pets:** Small. $10 daily fee/pet. Service with restrictions, supervision.
🆂🅰🆅🅴 🆂💰 ☒ 🎁 💻 🔄

🆔 ▼ Comfort Inn 🆂🅷
(423) 499-1993. **$60-$99.** 7620 Hamilton Park Dr. I-75, exit 7B northbound; exit southbound, just w to Lee Hwy, just s, then just e. Int corridors. **Pets:** Accepted.
🆂🅰🆅🅴 🆂💰 🎁 💻 🔄

🆔 ▼▼◆▼ Comfort Inn 🆂🅷
(423) 821-1499. **$49-$125, 30 day notice.** 3109 Parker Ln. I-24, exit 175, just s. Ext corridors. **Pets:** Other species. $5 daily fee/pet. Service with restrictions.
🆂🅰🆅🅴 🆂💰 ☒ 🎁 💻 🔄

▼▼ Days Inn Hamilton Place 🆂🅷
(423) 899-5151. **$59-$99.** 2341 Shallowford Village Dr. I-75, exit 5 (Shallowford Rd), just w, then just n. Int corridors. **Pets:** Accepted.
Ⓐ🆂🅺 🆂💰 ☒ 🎁 💻 🔄

🆔 ▼▼◆▼ Holiday Inn Chattanooga Choo-Choo 🅻🅷
(423) 266-5000. **$129-$149.** 1400 Market St. I-24, exit 178 (Broad St) eastbound, then E Main St; exit 178 (Market St) westbound, 0.5 mi n. Ext/int corridors. **Pets:** $25 one-time fee/room. Service with restrictions, supervision.
🆂🅰🆅🅴 🆂💰 ☒ 🎵 🎁 💻 🍽 🔄 ☒

🆔 ▼▼◆▼ La Quinta Inn Chattanooga 🆂🅷
(423) 855-0011. **$69-$83.** 7015 Shallowford Rd. I-75, exit 5 (Shallowford Rd), just w. Ext corridors. **Pets:** Medium. Service with restrictions.
🆂🅰🆅🅴 ☒ 🎵 🎁 💻 🔄

🆔 ▼▼◆▼ MainStay Suites-Chattanooga 🆂🅷
(423) 485-9424. **$53-$98.** 7030 Amin Dr. I-75, exit 5 (Shallowford Rd), just w, then s on Overnite Dr. Int corridors. **Pets:** Medium, other species. Designated rooms, service with restrictions, supervision.
🆂🅰🆅🅴 🆂💰 ☒ 🎁 💻

▼▼ Microtel Inn-Chattanooga 🆂🅷
(423) 510-0761. **$32-$60.** 7014 McCutcheon Rd. I-75, exit 5 (Shallowford Rd), just w, 0.3 mi n on Shallowford Village Dr, then just w. Int corridors. **Pets:** Small, other species. $10 daily fee/pet. Service with restrictions, supervision.
Ⓐ🆂🅺 🆂💰 ☒ 🎁

▼▼ Motel 6 Downtown 🆂🅷
(423) 265-7300. **$41-$100.** 2440 Williams St. I-24, exit 178 (Market St). Int corridors. **Pets:** Accepted.
🆂💰 ☒ 🎵 🎁 🎁

▼▼ Red Roof Inn-Chattanooga 🎏
(423) 899-0143. **$41-$66.** 7014 Shallowford Rd. I-75, exit 5 (Shallowford Rd), just w. Ext corridors. **Pets:** Accepted.
☒ 🎁

▼▼◆▼ Residence Inn by Marriott 🆂🅷
(423) 266-0600. **$114-$229.** 215 Chestnut St. US 27, exit 1C (4th St), just n. Int corridors. **Pets:** Accepted.
Ⓐ🆂🅺 🆂💰 ☒ 🆖 🎵 🎁 🎁 💻 🔄 ☒

▼▼◆▼ The Sheraton Read House Hotel 🅻🅷
(423) 266-4121. **$99-$500.** 827 Broad St. Us 27, exit 1A, just e. Int corridors. **Pets:** Accepted.
Ⓐ🆂🅺 🆂💰 ☒ 🎁 💻 🍽 🔄

▼▼◆▼ Staybridge Suites 🆂🅷 ❀
(423) 267-0900. **$139-$329.** 1300 Carter St. US 27, exit 1A, just e to Carter St, then 0.3 mi s. Int corridors. **Pets:** $75 one-time fee/room. Designated rooms, service with restrictions.
Ⓐ🆂🅺 ☒ 🆖 🎁 💻

▼▼ Super 8 Motel/Lookout Mountain 🆂🅷
(423) 821-8880. **$50-$130, 20 day notice.** 20 Birmingham Hwy. I-24, exit 174. Int corridors. **Pets:** Accepted.
Ⓐ🆂🅺 🆂💰 ☒ 🎁

# CLARKSVILLE

▼▼ Days Inn North 🆂🅷
(931) 552-1155. **$56-$66.** 130 Westfield Ct. I-24, exit 4, just s. Ext corridors. **Pets:** Accepted.
Ⓐ🆂🅺 🆂💰 ☒ 🆖 🎁 🔄

▼▼◆▼ Days Inn of Clarksville 🆂🅷
(931) 358-3194. **$50-$90.** 1100 Hwy 76 Connector Rd. I-24, exit 11. Ext corridors. **Pets:** Small. $8 daily fee/pet. Service with restrictions, supervision.
Ⓐ🆂🅺 🆂💰 ☒ 🎁 🔄

🆔 ▼▼◆▼ Holiday Inn-I-24 🆂🅷
(931) 648-4848. **$89-$99.** 3095 Wilma Rudolph Blvd. I-24, exit 4, just s. Ext corridors. **Pets:** Other species. $10 daily fee/room. Designated rooms, service with restrictions.
🆂🅰🆅🅴 🆂💰 ☒ 🆖 🎁 💻 🍽 🔄 ☒

▼▼ **Red Roof Inn** 🆂🅷
(931) 905-1555. **$49-$79.** 197 Holiday Dr. I-24, exit 4, just se. Ext corridors. **Pets:** Accepted.
🅰🆂🅺 🆂🅾 ⊠ 🅱 ⮐

## CLEVELAND

▼▼ **Comfort Inn** 🆂🅷
(423) 478-5265. **$50-$90.** 153 James Asbury Dr. I-75, exit 27, just w. Ext/int corridors. **Pets:** Accepted.
🅰🆂🅺 🆂🅾 ⊠ 🅱 🖵 ⮐

▼▼ **Douglas Inn & Suites** 🆂🅷
(423) 559-5579. **$60-$100.** 2600 Westside Dr NW. I-75, exit 25, just e. Ext/int corridors. **Pets:** Large. $10 daily fee/pet. Designated rooms, service with restrictions, supervision.
🅰🆂🅺 🆂🅾 ⊠ 🅱 🖵

🅐🅐🅐 ▼▼ **Econo Lodge of Cleveland** 🆂🅷
(423) 472-3281. **$45-$80.** 2655 Westside Dr NW. I-75, exit 25, just e. Ext corridors. **Pets:** $10 daily fee/pet. Service with restrictions, supervision.
🆂🅰🆅🅴 🆂🅾 ⊠ 🅱 🖵 ⮐

▼▼ **Hampton Inn-Cleveland** 🆂🅷
(423) 559-1001. **$79-$89.** 185 James Asbury Dr NW. I-75, exit 27. Ext corridors. **Pets:** Small. Designated rooms, no service, crate.
🅰🆂🅺 🆂🅾 ⊠ 🚿 🅱 🖵 ⮐

🅐🅐🅐 ▼▼▼ **Holiday Inn Mountain View** 🆂🅷
(423) 472-1500. **$63-$81.** 2400 Executive Park Dr. I-75, exit 25, just w. Ext/int corridors. **Pets:** Small. $25 one-time fee/room. Designated rooms, service with restrictions, supervision.
🆂🅰🆅🅴 🆂🅾 ⊠ 🅿 🅱 🖵 🍴 ⮐

▼▼ **Jameson Inn** 🆂🅷
(423) 614-5583. **$54-$104.** 360 Paul Huff Pkwy. I-75, exit 27, 1 mi e. Ext corridors. **Pets:** Very small, other species. $10 daily fee/room. Service with restrictions, supervision.
🅰🆂🅺 ⊠ 🅿 🚿 🅱 🖵 ⮐

▼▼ **Quality Inn Chalet** 🆂🅷
(423) 476-8511. **$65.** 2595 Georgetown Rd. I-75, exit 25, just e. Ext corridors. **Pets:** Accepted.
🅰🆂🅺 🆂🅾 ⊠ 🚿 🅱 🖵 🍴 ⮐

▼▼ **Ramada Limited** 🆂🅷
(423) 472-5566. **$69-$89, 7 day notice.** 156 James Asbury Dr. I-75, exit 27, just w. Ext corridors. **Pets:** Accepted.
🅰🆂🅺 🆂🅾 ⊠ 🚿 🅱 🖵 ⮐

🅐🅐🅐 ▼▼ **Super 8 Motel** 🆂🅷
(423) 476-5555. **$60-$75.** 163 Bernham Dr. I-75, exit 27, just w. Ext/int corridors. **Pets:** Accepted.
🆂🅰🆅🅴 🆂🅾 ⊠ 🚿 🅱 🖵 ⮐

## CLINTON

▼▼ **Clinton Inn** 🆂🅷
(865) 457-2311. **$44-$120, 3 day notice.** 720 Park Pl. I-75, exit 122, just w. Ext corridors. **Pets:** Medium. $10 daily fee/pet. Service with restrictions, supervision.
🅰🆂🅺 🆂🅾 ⊠ 🅶🅼 🅱 🖵 ⮐

▼▼ **Clinton Super 8 Motel** 🅼
(865) 457-0565. **$65-$125.** 2317 N Charles G Severs Blvd. I-75, exit 122, just w. Int corridors. **Pets:** Accepted.
🅰🆂🅺 🆂🅾 ⊠ 🅶🅼 🚿 🅱 🖵 ⮐

▼▼▼ **Holiday Inn Express Hotel & Suites** 🆂🅷
(865) 457-2233. **$80-$129, 7 day notice.** 141 Buffalo Rd. I-75, exit 122, just w. Ext corridors. **Pets:** Accepted.
🅰🆂🅺 🆂🅾 ⊠ 🅶🅼 🅱 🖵 ⮐

## COLUMBIA

🅐🅐🅐 ▼▼ **Americas Best Value Inn** 🆂🅷
(931) 381-1410. **$46-$56, 6 day notice.** 1548 Bear Creek Pike. I-65, exit 46, just w. Ext corridors. **Pets:** Other species. $5 daily fee/pet. Supervision.
🆂🅰🆅🅴 🆂🅾 ⊠ 🅱

▼▼ **Holiday Inn Express** 🆂🅷
(931) 380-1227. **$80-$99.** 1554 Bear Creek Pike. I-65, exit 46, just w. Ext corridors. **Pets:** Accepted.
🅰🆂🅺 🆂🅾 ⊠ 🅶🅼 🅱 🖵 ⮐

▼▼ **Jameson Inn** 🆂🅷
(931) 388-3326. **$77-$84.** 715 James M Campbell Blvd. 0.9 mi w jct SR 50 and US 31. Int corridors. **Pets:** Very small, other species. $10 daily fee/room. Service with restrictions, supervision.
🅰🆂🅺 ⊠ 🅱 🖵 ⮐

## COOKEVILLE

🅐🅐🅐 ▼▼ **Alpine Lodge & Suites** 🆂🅷
(931) 526-3333. **$38-$56.** 2021 E Spring St. I-40, exit 290, just s. Int corridors. **Pets:** Medium, other species. $5 daily fee/pet. Designated rooms, service with restrictions, supervision.
🆂🅰🆅🅴 ⊠ 🅿 🅱 🖵 ⮐

🅐🅐🅐 ▼▼▼ **Baymont Inn & Suites Cookeville** 🆂🅷
(931) 525-6668. **$69-$79.** 1151 S Jefferson Ave. I-40, exit 287, just s. Int corridors. **Pets:** Small, other species. Designated rooms, service with restrictions.
🆂🅰🆅🅴 🆂🅾 ⊠ 🅶🅼 🚿 🅱 🖵 ⮐

🅐🅐🅐 ▼▼▼ **Best Western Thunderbird Motel** 🆂🅷
(931) 526-7115. **$50-$55.** 900 S Jefferson Ave. I-40, exit 287, just n. Ext corridors. **Pets:** Other species. $5 daily fee/pet. Service with restrictions.
🆂🅰🆅🅴 🆂🅾 ⊠ 🅶🅼 🚿 🅱 🖵 ⮐

▼▼ **Country Hearth Inn & Suites** 🆂🅷 🐾
(931) 528-1040. **$45-$56.** 1100 S Jefferson Ave. I-40, exit 287. Ext corridors. **Pets:** Other species. $10 daily fee/pet. Designated rooms, service with restrictions, supervision.
🅰🆂🅺 🆂🅾 ⊠ 🅱 🖵 ⮐

🅐🅐🅐 ▼▼ **Days Inn** 🆂🅷 🐾
(931) 528-1511. **$57-$120.** 1296 S Walnut Ave. I-40, exit 287. Ext corridors. **Pets:** Medium. $10 one-time fee/pet. Designated rooms, service with restrictions, supervision.
🆂🅰🆅🅴 🆂🅾 ⊠ 🅱 🖵 ⮐

🅐🅐🅐 ▼▼▼ **Hampton Inn** 🆂🅷
(931) 520-1117. **$80-$115.** 1025 Interstate Dr. I-40, exit 287, 0.5 mi n. Ext corridors. **Pets:** Accepted.
🆂🅰🆅🅴 🆂🅾 ⊠ 🅶🅼 🅿 🚿 🅱 🖵 ⮐

▼▼ **Holiday Inn** 🆂🅷
(931) 526-7125. **$49-$99, 14 day notice.** 970 S Jefferson Ave. I-40, exit 287, just n. Ext/int corridors. **Pets:** Medium, other species. No service, supervision.
🅰🆂🅺 ⊠ 🅶🅼 🅱 🖵 🍴 ⮐

## CORNERSVILLE

🅐🅐🅐 ▼▼▼ **Econo Lodge** 🅼
(931) 293-2111. **$59-$69.** 3731 Pulaski Hwy. I-65, exit 22 at US 31A. Ext corridors. **Pets:** Accepted.
🆂🅰🆅🅴 🆂🅾 ⊠ 🖵 ⮐

## CROSSVILLE

🅐🅐🅐 ▼▼▼ **Ramada Inn** 🆂🅷 🐾
(931) 484-7581. **$60-$135.** 4083 Hwy 127 N. I-40, exit 317, just n. Ext corridors. **Pets:** Small. $10 daily fee/room. Designated rooms, service with restrictions, supervision.
🆂🅰🆅🅴 🆂🅾 ⊠ 🅱 🖵 ⮐

# CUMBERLAND GAP

### ▼▼ Ramada Inn of Cumberland Gap SH
(423) 869-3631. **$69-$179, 7 day notice.** Hwy 58. On US 58, just e of jct US 25 E. Int corridors. **Pets:** Other species. $25 one-time fee/room. Designated rooms, service with restrictions.

ASK SØ ✕ 🖬 💻 🍴 🏊

# DANDRIDGE

### ▲▲▲ ▼▼ Econo Lodge M
(865) 397-9437. **$50-$100.** 531 Patriot Dr. I-40, exit 417, just n. Ext corridors. **Pets:** Large, other species. $10 daily fee/pet, $50 one-time fee/pet. Designated rooms, service with restrictions, supervision.

SAVE SØ ✕ 🖬 💻

### ▲▲▲ ▼▼ Holiday Inn Express SH
(865) 397-1910. **$59-$69.** 119 Sharon Dr. I-40, exit 417, just s. Int corridors. **Pets:** Medium, other species. $25 one-time fee/room. Designated rooms, service with restrictions, crate.

SAVE SØ ✕ 🤚 🖬 💻 🏊

### ▼▼ Ramada SH
(865) 397-1200. **$40-$70.** 125 Sharon Dr. I-40, exit 417, just s. Int corridors. **Pets:** Accepted.

ASK SØ ✕ 🖫 🖬 💻 🏊

# DECHERD

### ▼▼ Jameson Inn SH
(931) 962-0130. **$54-$104.** 1838 Decherd Blvd. Jct Main St and SR 41A, just s. Ext corridors. **Pets:** Very small, other species. $10 daily fee/room. Service with restrictions, supervision.

ASK ✕ 🖬 💻 🏊

# DICKSON

### ▲▲▲ ▼▼▼ Best Western Executive Inn SH
(615) 446-0541. **$50-$60.** 2338 Hwy 46. I-40, exit 172, just n. Ext corridors. **Pets:** Medium, dogs only. $5 daily fee/pet. Designated rooms, service with restrictions, supervision.

SAVE SØ ✕ 🖬 💻 🏊

### ▲▲▲ ▼▼ Comfort Inn SH
(615) 441-5252. **$60-$70.** 1025 E Christi Rd. I-40, exit 172. Int corridors. **Pets:** Medium. $10 daily fee/pet. Designated rooms, service with restrictions, supervision.

SAVE SØ ✕ 🖬 💻 🏊

### ▲▲▲ ▼▼ Days Inn SH
(615) 740-7475. **$59.** 2415 Hwy 46 S. I-40, exit 172, just s. Ext corridors. **Pets:** $20 deposit/room. Designated rooms, service with restrictions, supervision.

SAVE SØ ✕ 🖬 🏊

### ▼▼ Holiday Inn SH
(615) 446-9081. **$76-$83.** 2420 Hwy 46 S. I-40, exit 172, just s. Ext corridors. **Pets:** Other species. $8 one-time fee/room. Designated rooms, supervision.

ASK SØ ✕ 🤚 🖬 💻 🍴 🏊

### ▼▼ Motel 6 #4226 SH
(615) 446-2423. **$39-$52.** 2325 Hwy 46 S. I-40, exit 172, just n. Ext corridors. **Pets:** Accepted.

ASK SØ ✕ 🤚 🖬 🏊

### ▲▲▲ ▼▼▼ Super 8 Motel SH
(615) 446-1923. **$49-$54.** 150 Suzanne Dr. I-40, exit 172, just n on SR 46, then just e. Int corridors. **Pets:** Accepted.

SAVE SØ ✕ 🖬 💻 🏊

# DYERSBURG

### ▼▼ Best Western Dyersburg SH
(731) 285-8601. **$65-$75.** 770 Hwy 51 Bypass W. I-155, exit 13, 0.5 mi s; jct of US 51 Bypass and SR 78. Ext corridors. **Pets:** Small. $10 daily fee/room. Service with restrictions, supervision.

ASK SØ ✕ 🤚 🖫 🖬 💻 🏊

### ▼▼ Comfort Inn SH
(731) 285-6951. **$59-$69.** 815 Reelfoot Dr. I-155, exit 13, just s. Ext corridors. **Pets:** Accepted.

ASK SØ ✕ 🖬 💻 🏊

### ▼▼ Executive Inn & Suites SH
(731) 287-0044. **$30-$40.** 2331 Lake Rd. I-155, exit 13, 0.5 mi s. Ext corridors. **Pets:** Accepted.

ASK SØ ✕ 🖬

### ▼▼▼ Hampton Inn SH
(731) 285-4778. **$69-$84.** 2750 Mall Loop Rd. I-155, exit 13, just s. Int corridors. **Pets:** Medium. Service with restrictions, supervision.

ASK SØ ✕ 🖫M 🤚 🖫 🖬 💻 🏊

# EAST RIDGE

### ▼▼ Americas Best Value Inn SH
(423) 894-6110. **$39-$59.** 639 Camp Jordan Pkwy. I-75, exit 1A (Ringgold Rd), 0.3 mi e. Ext/int corridors. **Pets:** Accepted.

ASK SØ ✕ 🖬 💻 🏊

### ▼▼▼ Howard Johnson Plaza Hotel SH
(423) 892-8100. **$49-$69.** 6700 Ringgold Rd. I-75, exit 1A (Ringgold Rd), just e. Int corridors. **Pets:** Other species. $15 one-time fee/pet. Designated rooms, no service.

ASK SØ ✕ 🖬 💻 🍴 🏊

### ▲▲▲ ▼▼ Ramada Limited SH 🐾
(423) 894-1860. **$54-$85.** 6650 Ringgold Rd. I-75, exit 1 (Ringgold Rd). Int corridors. **Pets:** Medium. $10 daily fee/pet. Service with restrictions, supervision.

SAVE SØ ✕ 💻 🏊

### ▼▼ Super 8 Motel M
(423) 894-6720. **Call for rates.** 6521 Ringgold Rd. I-75, exit 1B, just w. Ext corridors. **Pets:** Small. $10 one-time fee/pet. Designated rooms, service with restrictions, crate.

✕ 🖫 🖬 🏊

# ERWIN

### ▼▼▼ Holiday Inn Express SH
(423) 743-4100. **$69-$119.** 2002 Temple Hill Rd. I-26, exit 15, just e. Int corridors. **Pets:** Medium. $15 one-time fee/pet. Designated rooms, service with restrictions, supervision.

ASK SØ ✕ 🖫M 🤚 🖫 🖬 💻 🏊

# FAIRVIEW

### ▲▲▲ ▼▼ Deerfield Inn & Suites SH
(615) 799-4700. **$39-$69.** 1407 Hwy 96 N. I-40, exit 182. Ext corridors. **Pets:** Medium. $10 one-time fee/pet. Service with restrictions, supervision.

SAVE SØ ✕ 🖬 💻

# FAYETTEVILLE

### ▼▼ Best Western-Fayetteville Inn SH
(931) 433-0100. **$68-$71.** 3021 Thornton Taylor Pkwy. 0.7 mi e of US 431, on US 64 and 231 Bypass. Ext corridors. **Pets:** Other species. $10 one-time fee/pet. No service.

ASK SØ ✕ 🖬 💻 🍴 🏊

# FRANKLIN

**AAA ▼▼▼▼ AmeriSuites (Nashville/Cool Springs)** SH
(615) 771-8900. **$94.** 650 Bakers Bridge Ave. I-65, exit 69 (Galleria Blvd), 0.3 mi e on Moore's Ln to Carothers Pkwy, 0.5 mi s, then 0.3 mi w. Int corridors. **Pets:** Medium, other species. $15 daily fee/pet. Service with restrictions, crate.

SAVE S X M (⁂) (⌨) 🛏 💻 🏊

**AAA ▼▼▼ Baymont Inn & Suites Nashville-Franklin** M
(615) 791-7700. **$73-$94.** 4207 Franklin Commons Ct. I-65, exit 65, just e. Int corridors. **Pets:** Medium. Service with restrictions.

SAVE X (⌨) 🛏 💻 🏊

**AAA ▼▼▼ Best Western Franklin Inn** SH 🐾
(615) 790-0570. **$56-$89.** 1308 Murfreesboro Rd. I-65, exit 65, just w. Ext corridors. **Pets:** $10 one-time fee/room. Service with restrictions, supervision.

SAVE S X 🛏 💻 🏊

**AAA ▼▼▼▼ Comfort Inn** SH
(615) 791-6675. **$64-$130.** 4206 Franklin Commons Ct. I-65, exit 65, just e. Ext corridors. **Pets:** Very small. $10 one-time fee/pet. Designated rooms, service with restrictions, supervision.

SAVE S X M 💻 🏊

**AAA ▼▼▼▼ Days Inn** SH
(615) 790-1140. **$55-$85, 7 day notice.** 4217 S Carothers Rd. I-65, exit 65, just e. Ext corridors. **Pets:** Very small, dogs only. $10 daily fee/pet. No service, supervision.

SAVE S X (⌨) 🛏 💻 🏊

**▼▼▼▼ Holiday Inn Express Hotel & Suites** SH 🐾
(615) 591-6660. **$95-$159.** 4202 Franklin Commons Ct. I-65, exit 65, just e. Int corridors. **Pets:** Medium, other species. $25 daily fee/pet. Designated rooms, service with restrictions, supervision.

ASK S X 🛏 💻 🏊

**▼▼▼ Homestead Studio Suites Hotel-Nashville/Cool Springs/Brentwood** SH
(615) 771-7600. **$62-$72.** 680 Bakers Bridge Ave. I-65, exit 69 (Galleria Blvd), 0.3 mi e on Moore's Ln to Carothers Pkwy, 0.5 mi s, then 0.3 mi w. Ext corridors. **Pets:** $25 daily fee/pet. Service with restrictions, supervision.

ASK S X 🛏 💻

**▼▼◆▼ Namaste Acres Country Ranch Inn** BB
(615) 791-0333. **$95, 5 day notice.** 5436 Leipers Creek. SR 96, 5 mi w; SR 46, 6 mi sw, then 1.9 mi s. Ext/int corridors. **Pets:** Medium, dogs only. $10 one-time fee/room. No service, supervision.

X 🛏 💻 🏊

**AAA ▼▼▼▼ Ramada Limited & Suites** SH
(615) 791-4004. **$54-$129.** 6210 Hospitality Dr. I-65, exit 65, 0.5 mi e on US 96. Int corridors. **Pets:** Accepted.

SAVE S X M (⌨) 🛏 💻 🏊

# GALLATIN

**▼▼▼ Jameson Inn** SH
(615) 451-4494. **$54-$104.** 1001 Village Green Crossing. 2 mi s on US 31. Ext corridors. **Pets:** Very small, other species. $10 daily fee/room. Service with restrictions, supervision.

ASK X M (⁂) (⌨) 🛏 💻 🏊

# GATLINBURG

**AAA ▼▼▼▼ Cobbly Nob Rentals Inc** CA 🐾
(865) 436-5298. **$85-$250, 30 day notice.** 3722 E Parkway. On US 321, 10.3 mi n of jct US 441. Ext corridors. **Pets:** Small, dogs only. $200 deposit/pet. Designated rooms, no service, supervision.

SAVE X 🛏 💻 🏊

**▼▼▼▼ Econo Lodge Inn & Suites** M
(865) 436-7991. **Call for rates.** 135 Reagan Dr. US 441 traffic light 7. Ext/int corridors. **Pets:** Accepted.

X 🛏 💻 🏊

**AAA ▼▼◆▼ Greenbrier Valley Resorts at Cobbly Nob** CA 🐾
(865) 436-2015. **$90-$400, 30 day notice.** 3629 E Parkway. On US 321, 10.1 mi n of jct US 441. Ext corridors. **Pets:** Other species. $100 deposit/room, $10 daily fee/pet. Designated rooms, service with restrictions.

SAVE S X 🛏 💻 🏊

**AAA ▼▼◆▼ Holiday Inn SunSpree Resort** M 🐾
(865) 436-9201. **$59-$119.** 520 Historic Nature Tr. 0.4 mi e of jct US 441 at traffic light 8. Ext/int corridors. **Pets:** Medium, other species. $15 one-time fee/pet. Service with restrictions.

SAVE S X M (⁂) (⌨) 🛏 💻 🍴 🏊 X

**AAA ▼▼▼ Microtel Gatlinburg** SH
(865) 436-0107. **$45-$199, 3 day notice.** 211 Historic Nature Tr. Just e of US 441 at traffic light 8. Int corridors. **Pets:** Medium. $10 daily fee/pet. Designated rooms, service with restrictions, supervision.

SAVE S X M (⌨) 🛏 💻 🏊

**▼▼◆▼ The Park Vista Hotel** LH
(865) 436-9211. **$69-$129, 3 day notice.** 705 Cherokee Orchard Rd. 0.6 mi e of jct US 441 at traffic light 8. Int corridors. **Pets:** Accepted.

ASK S X M (⁂) (⌨) 🛏 💻 🍴 🏊 X

**▼ Terrace Motel** M
(865) 436-4965. **$55-$85, 7 day notice.** 396 Parkway. On US 441; between traffic lights 2 and 3. Ext corridors. **Pets:** Medium, dogs only. $5 daily fee/pet. Designated rooms, no service.

ASK S 🛏 🏊

# GREENEVILLE

**AAA ▼▼◆▼ Comfort Inn of Greeneville** SH 🐾
(423) 639-4185. **$73-$210.** 1790 E Andrew Johnson Hwy. US 11 E, 2.9 mi ne. Ext/int corridors. **Pets:** $10 daily fee/room. Designated rooms, service with restrictions, supervision.

SAVE S X 🛏 💻 🏊

**▼▼◆▼ Days Inn** M
(423) 639-2156. **$45-$190, 14 day notice.** 935 E Andrew Johnson Hwy. US 11 E Bypass, 2 mi ne. Ext corridors. **Pets:** Other species. $10 daily fee/pet. Designated rooms, service with restrictions, crate.

SAVE S X (⌨) 🏊

**▼▼◆▼ Jameson Inn** SH
(423) 638-7511. **$54-$104.** 3160 E Andrew Johnson Hwy. US 11 E Bypass, 3.6 mi ne. Int corridors. **Pets:** Very small, other species. $10 daily fee/room. Service with restrictions, supervision.

ASK X (⌨) 🛏 💻 🏊

# HARRIMAN

**AAA ▼▼▼ Best Western Sundancer Motor Lodge** M
(865) 882-6200. **$51-$70.** 120 Childs Rd. I-40, exit 347, just n. Ext corridors. **Pets:** Small. $10 one-time fee/pet. Service with restrictions, supervision.

SAVE S X 🛏 💻

**▼▼◆▼ Caney Creek Inn** SH
(865) 882-5340. **$60-$90.** 1845 S Roane St. I-40, exit 347, just s. Ext corridors. **Pets:** Other species. $25 one-time fee/room. No service, supervision.

ASK S X M (⌨) 🛏 💻 🏊

**AAA ▼▼▼ Super 8 Motel** M
(865) 882-6600. **$49-$60.** 1867 S Roane St. I-40, exit 347, 0.3 mi s on US 27/SR 61. Ext corridors. **Pets:** Small. $10 daily fee/pet. Designated rooms, service with restrictions, supervision.

SAVE S X 🛏 🏊

# HENDERSONVILLE

**AAA** ▼▼▼▼ **AmeriSuites**
**(Nashville/Hendersonville)** SH �✿
(615) 826-4301. **$89-$119.** 330 E Main St. US 31, 1 mi n. Int corridors.
**Pets:** Other species. Service with restrictions, supervision.
SAVE SO ✕ ᴸᴹ 🛢 ▭ ⌁

# HIXSON

▼▼▼ **Home Away Extended Stay Studios** SH
(423) 643-4663. **$69-$99.** 1949 North Point Blvd. Jct SR 153 and
Hixson Pike, just w. Ext corridors. **Pets:** Accepted.
ASK SO ✕ 🛢 ▭

# HURRICANE MILLS

**AAA** ▼▼▼ **Best Western of Hurricane Mills** M ✿
(931) 296-4251. **$80-$110.** 15542 Hwy 13 S. I-40, exit 143. Ext corridors. **Pets:** Small. $10 daily fee/pet. Service with restrictions, supervision.
SAVE SO ✕ 🗭 🛢 ▭ ⌁

**AAA** ▼▼▼▼ **Holiday Inn Express** SH
(931) 296-2999. **$68-$78.** 15368 Hwy 13 S. I-40, exit 143, just n. Int
corridors. **Pets:** Accepted.
SAVE SO ✕ 🗭 🛢 ▭ ⌁

# JACKSON

**AAA** ▼▼▼▼ **Baymont Inn & Suites Jackson** SH
(731) 664-1800. **$73-$94.** 2370 N Highland Ave. I-40, exit 82A. Int
corridors. **Pets:** Medium. Service with restrictions.
SAVE ✕ 🛢 ▭ ⌁

**AAA** ▼▼▼ **Best Western Inn & Suites** SH
(731) 664-3030. **$60-$190, 14 day notice.** 1936 Hwy 45 Bypass. I-40,
exit 80A, just s. Ext corridors. **Pets:** Small, dogs only. $10 daily fee/pet.
Designated rooms, service with restrictions, supervision.
SAVE SO ✕ 🦽 🛢 ▭ ⌁

▼▼▼ **Days Inn** SH
(731) 668-3444. **$43-$65, 14 day notice.** 1919 US 45 Bypass. I-40,
exit 80A, just s. Ext corridors. **Pets:** Medium, other species. $5 daily
fee/pet. Designated rooms, service with restrictions, supervision.
ASK SO ✕ 🛢 ⌁

▼▼▼ **Days Inn-West** SH
(731) 668-4840. **$43-$53.** 2239 Hollywood Dr. I-40, exit 79. Ext corridors. **Pets:** Medium. $5 daily fee/pet. Designated rooms, service with
restrictions, supervision.
ASK SO ✕ 🛢 ⌁

▼▼▼▼ **Doubletree Hotel Jackson** LH
(731) 664-6900. **$79-$129.** 1770 Hwy 45 Bypass. I-40, exit 80A, 0.5 mi
s. Int corridors. **Pets:** Accepted.
ASK SO ✕ 🗭 🛢 ▭ 🍴 ⌁

▼▼▼ **Hampton Inn-Jackson** SH
(731) 664-4312. **$59-$69.** 1890 Hwy 45 Bypass. I-40, exit 80A, just s.
Ext corridors. **Pets:** Small. $20 daily fee/pet. Designated rooms, no serv-
ice, crate.
ASK SO ✕ ᴸᴹ 🦽 🛢 ▭ ⌁

▼▼▼ **Jameson Inn** SH
(731) 660-8651. **$54-$104.** 1292 Vann Dr. I-40, exit 80B, 0.6 mi w. Int
corridors. **Pets:** Very small, other species. $10 daily fee/room. Service with
restrictions, supervision.
ASK ✕ 🛢 ▭ ⌁

# JELLICO

▼▼▼ **Days Inn** SH
(423) 784-7281. **$53-$80.** US 25 W. I-75, exit 160, just w. Ext corridors.
**Pets:** Accepted.
ASK SO ✕ ▭ 🍴 ⌁

# JOHNSON CITY

▼▼▼▼ **Best Western Johnson City Hotel & Conference
Center** SH ✿
(423) 282-2161. **$63-$96.** 2406 N Roan St. I-26, exit 35A westbound;
exit 35 eastbound, just n. Ext/int corridors. **Pets:** Small. $15 daily fee/
pet. Designated rooms, service with restrictions, crate.
ASK SO ✕ 🦽 🛢 ▭ 🍴 ⌁

▼▼▼ **Comfort Inn of Johnson City** SH
(423) 928-9600. **$65-$130.** 1900 S Roan St. I-26, exit 31, just w on US
321. Ext corridors. **Pets:** $10 one-time fee/pet.
ASK SO ✕ 🛢 ▭ ⌁

▼▼▼ **DoubleTree Hotel** SH
(423) 929-2000. **$79-$399, 7 day notice.** 211 Mockingbird Ln. I-26, exit
35 eastbound; exit 35B westbound, 0.6 mi e on N Roan. Int corridors.
**Pets:** Accepted.
ASK SO ✕ 🛢 ▭ 🍴 ⌁

**AAA** ▼▼▼ **Holiday Inn-Johnson City** SH
(423) 282-4611. **$86-$99.** 101 W Springbrook Dr. I-26, exit 35A westbound; exit 35 eastbound, just e on N Roan St, then just n. Int
corridors. **Pets:** Other species. $50 deposit/room. Supervision.
SAVE SO ✕ 🛢 ▭ ⌁

▼▼▼ **Jameson Inn** SH
(423) 282-0488. **$54-$104.** 119 Pinnacle Dr. I-26, exit 38, just w on CR
354, then just s. Ext corridors. **Pets:** Very small, other species. $10 daily
fee/room. Service with restrictions, supervision.
ASK ✕ 🦽 🛢 ▭ ⌁

▼▼▼ **Red Roof Inn-Johnson City** SH
(423) 282-3040. **$45-$63.** 210 Broyles Dr. I-26, exit 35B westbound;
exit 35 eastbound, just w on N Roan St. Ext corridors. **Pets:** Accepted.
✕ 🗭 🦽 🛢

▼▼▼ **Sleep Inn** SH
(423) 915-0081. **$62-$79.** 2020 Franklin Terrace Ct. I-26, exit 36, just w,
then just n, follow signs; must enter on Oakland Ave at the light. Int
corridors. **Pets:** Accepted.
ASK SO ✕ ᴸᴹ 🗭 🦽 🛢 ▭

# KINGSPORT

▼▼▼▼ **Jameson Inn** SH
(423) 230-0534. **$54-$104.** 3004 Bay Meadow Pl. I-181, exit 51 westbound; exit 51B eastbound, just n on SR 93. Int corridors. **Pets:** Very
small, other species. $10 daily fee/room. Service with restrictions, supervi-
sion.
ASK ✕ 🦽 🛢 ▭ ⌁

▼▼▼▼ **La Quinta Inn Kingsport** SH
(423) 323-0500. **$82-$115.** 10150 Airport Pkwy. I-81, exit 63, just e. Int
corridors. **Pets:** Medium. Service with restrictions.
ASK ✕ ᴸᴹ 🗭 🦽 🛢 ▭ ⌁

▼▼▼ **Sleep Inn** SH
(423) 279-1811. **$59-$75.** 200 Hospitality Pl. I-81, exit 63, just s. Int
corridors. **Pets:** Other species. Service with restrictions, crate.
ASK SO ✕ 🦽 🛢 ▭

# KINGSTON

**AAA** ▼▼▼ **Comfort Inn of Kingston** M
(865) 376-4965. **$60-$99.** 905 N Kentucky St. I-40, exit 352, 0.3 mi s.
Ext corridors. **Pets:** Medium. $10 daily fee/pet. Designated rooms, service
with restrictions, supervision.
SAVE SO ✕ 🛢 ▭

**AAA** ▼▼▼ **Days Inn** M
(865) 376-2069. **$60-$100.** 495 Gallaher Rd. I-40, exit 356, just n. Ext
corridors. **Pets:** Medium. $10 daily fee/pet. No service, supervision.
SAVE SO ✕ 🗭 🛢 ⌁

# KINGSTON SPRINGS

**Best Western Harpeth Inn** SH
(615) 952-3961. **$45-$85.** 116 Luy Ben Hills Rd. I-40, exit 188, just n. Ext corridors. **Pets:** Other species. $10 daily fee/pet. Service with restrictions, supervision.

# KNOXVILLE

**Candlewood Suites-Knoxville** SH
(865) 777-0400. **$79-$119.** 10206 Parkside Dr. I-40/75, exit 374 (Lovell Rd), 0.5 mi s, then 1 mi e. Int corridors. **Pets:** Medium. $150 one-time fee/room. Service with restrictions, supervision.

**The Clarion Inn** SH
(865) 687-8989. **$75-$109.** 5634 Merchant Center Blvd. I-75, exit 108 (Merchant Dr), just w, then just n. Int corridors. **Pets:** Accepted.

**ClubHouse Inn & Suites Knoxville** SH
(865) 531-1900. **$79-$149.** 208 Market Place Ln. I-40/75, exit 378 (Cedar Bluff Rd), just s to N Peters Rd, then just w. Int corridors. **Pets:** Medium, other species. $50 deposit/room. Service with restrictions, supervision.

**Crowne Plaza Knoxville** SH
(865) 522-2600. **$129-$159.** 401 W Summit Hill Dr. Corner of Walnut St; downtown. Int corridors. **Pets:** Accepted.

**Days Inn West** SH
(865) 966-5801. **$45-$90.** 326 Lovell Rd. I-40/75, exit 374, just s. Ext corridors. **Pets:** Medium. $10 daily fee/pet. Designated rooms, service with restrictions, supervision.

**Econo Lodge-North** SH
(865) 687-5680. **$45-$90.** 5505 Merchant Center Blvd. I-75, exit 108 (Merchant Dr), just w, then just n. Ext corridors. **Pets:** Accepted.

**Econo Lodge West** M
(865) 693-6061. **$45-$99.** 9240 Park West Blvd. I-40/75, exit 378 (Cedar Bluff Rd), just n to Park West Blvd, then just w. Ext corridors. **Pets:** Medium, dogs only. $10 daily fee/pet. Service with restrictions, supervision.

**Hampton Inn North** SH
(865) 689-1011. **$74-$124.** 117 Cedar Ln. I-75, exit 108 (Merchant Dr), just e. Ext corridors. **Pets:** Accepted.

**Holiday Inn-Central/Papermill Road** LH ❖
(865) 584-3911. **$84-$165.** 1315 Kirby Rd. I-40/75, exit 383 (Papermill Rd), 0.5 mi e. Int corridors. **Pets:** Medium, other species. $10 daily fee/pet. Service with restrictions, crate.

**Holiday Inn Select-Cedar Bluff** LH
(865) 693-1011. **$129-$159.** 304 Cedar Bluff Rd. I-40/75, exit 378 (Cedar Bluff Rd) eastbound; exit 378B westbound, just n to Executive Park Dr.. Int corridors. **Pets:** $50 one-time fee/room. Designated rooms, service with restrictions.

**Homewood Suites by Hilton** SH ❖
(865) 777-0375. **$119-$279, 3 day notice.** 10935 Turkey Dr. I-40, exit 374 (Lovell Rd), just s to Parkside Dr, then 0.5 mi n on Snow Goose. Int corridors. **Pets:** Medium, other species. $100 one-time fee/room. Service with restrictions.

**Jameson Inn of Knoxville** SH
(865) 531-7444. **$83-$89.** 209 Market Place Ln. I-40/75, exit 378 (Cedar Bluff Rd), just s to N Peters Rd, then just w. Int corridors. **Pets:** Very small, other species. $10 daily fee/room. Service with restrictions, supervision.

**La Quinta Inn Knoxville (West)** SH
(865) 690-9777. **$83-$105.** 258 Peters Rd N. I-40, exit 378 (Cedar Bluff Rd), just s, then just e. Ext corridors. **Pets:** Medium. Service with restrictions.

**Microtel** SH
(865) 531-8041. **$39-$75.** 309 N Peters Rd. I-40/75, exit 378 (Cedar Bluff Rd), just s, then just w. Int corridors. **Pets:** Accepted.

**Motel 6–1252** M
(865) 675-7200. **$41-$53.** 402 Lovell Rd. I-40/75, exit 374 (Lovell Rd), just s. Ext corridors. **Pets:** Accepted.

**Quality Inn North** SH
(865) 689-6600. **$49-$99.** 6712 Central Ave Pike. I-75, exit 110 (Callahan Dr), just e. Ext/int corridors. **Pets:** Medium, dogs only. $10 daily fee/pet. Designated rooms, service with restrictions, supervision.

**Ramada Limited-East** M
(865) 546-7271. **$60-$90.** 722 Brakebill Rd. I-40, exit 398 (Strawberry Plains), just n, then w. Ext corridors. **Pets:** Small. $10 daily fee/pet. Service with restrictions, supervision.

**Red Roof Inn-West** M
(865) 691-1664. **$50-$60.** 209 Advantage Pl. I-40/75, exit 378 (Cedar Bluff Rd), just s to N Peters Rd, then w. Ext corridors. **Pets:** Accepted.

**Super 8 East** M
(865) 524-0855. **$44-$89, 3 day notice.** 7585 Crosswood Blvd. I-40, exit 398 (Strawberry Plains), just n, then w. Ext corridors. **Pets:** Medium, other species. $10 daily fee/pet. Service with restrictions.

**Super 8 Motel-Knoxville** SH
(865) 584-8511. **$50-$80.** 6200 Papermill Rd. I-40/75, exit 383 (Papermill Rd), 0.3 mi e. Ext corridors. **Pets:** $6 one-time fee/room. Service with restrictions, supervision.

# LAKE CITY

**Days Inn** SH
(865) 426-2816. **$65-$85.** 221 Colonial Ln. I-75, exit 129, just w. Ext corridors. **Pets:** $10 daily fee/pet. Service with restrictions, supervision.

# LAWRENCEBURG

**Best Western Villa Inn** SH
(931) 762-4448. **$65-$85.** 2126 N Locust Ave. On US 43, 2.2 mi n of jct US 64. Ext corridors. **Pets:** Medium. $15 daily fee/pet. No service, supervision.

# LEBANON

**Americas Best Value Inn & Suites** SH
(615) 449-5781. **$37.** 822 S Cumberland St. I-40, exit 238. Ext corridors. **Pets:** Very small. $8 daily fee/pet. Service with restrictions, supervision.

**△△△ ♦♦♦ Best Western Executive Inn** SH
(615) 444-0505. **$59-$109.** 631 S Cumberland St. I-40, exit 238, 0.5 mi
n. Ext/int corridors. **Pets:** Accepted.
[SAVE] [S△] [✕] [₺M] [🛏] [🖵] [⊶]

**♦♦ Comfort Inn** SH
(615) 444-1001. **$49-$89.** 829 S Cumberland St. I-40, exit 238. Ext
corridors. **Pets:** Small, other species. $5 daily fee/room. Designated rooms,
service with restrictions, supervision.
[ASK] [S△] [✕] [🛏] [🖵] [⊶]

**♦♦ Days Inn** SH
(615) 444-5635. **$45-$65.** 914 Murfreesboro Rd. I-40, exit 238. Ext
corridors. **Pets:** $10 daily fee/pet. Service with restrictions, supervision.
[ASK] [S△] [✕] [🛏] [⊶]

**♦♦♦♦ Hampton Inn** SH
(615) 444-7400. **$69-$129.** 704 S Cumberland St. I-40, exit 238. Ext
corridors. **Pets:** Accepted.
[ASK] [✕] [₺M] [🖫] [🛏] [🖵] [⊶] [✕]

**♦♦ Super 8 Motel** SH
(615) 444-5637. **$45-$65.** 914 Murfreesboro Rd. I-40, exit 238. Ext
corridors. **Pets:** $10 daily fee/pet. Service with restrictions, supervision.
[ASK] [S△] [✕] [🛏] [⊶]

## LENOIR CITY

**△△△ ♦♦♦ Days Inn** SH
(865) 986-2011. **$75-$100.** 1110 Hwy 321 N. I-75, exit 81, just e. Ext
corridors. **Pets:** Very small. $10 daily fee/pet. Service with restrictions,
supervision.
[SAVE] [S△] [✕] [🛏] [⊶]

**△△△ ♦♦♦ Econo Lodge** SH
(865) 986-0295. **$52-$85.** 1211 Hwy 321 N. I-75, exit 81, just w. Ext
corridors. **Pets:** Large. $5 daily fee/pet. Service with restrictions, supervi-
sion.
[SAVE] [S△] [✕] [🖫] [🛏] [⊶]

## LEXINGTON

**♦♦ Econo Lodge** SH
(731) 968-0171. **$55-$60.** 732 W Church St. Jct of US 412 and SR
104, just w. Ext corridors. **Pets:** Accepted.
[ASK] [S△] [✕] [🛏] [⊶]

## LOUDON

**△△△ ♦♦♦ Americas Best Value Inn** M
(865) 458-5855. **$43-$69.** 15100 Hwy 72. I-75, exit 72, just w. Ext
corridors. **Pets:** Accepted.
[SAVE] [S△] [✕] [🛏] [⊶]

**♦♦ Super 8 Motel** SH
(865) 458-5669. **$55.** 12452 Hwy 72 N. I-75, exit 72, just e. Ext corri-
dors. **Pets:** $5 daily fee/room. Service with restrictions, supervision.
[ASK] [S△] [✕] [₺M] [🖫] [🖵] [⊶]

## MANCHESTER

**♦♦♦♦ Country Inn & Suites By Carlson** SH
(931) 728-7551. **$85.** 126 Expressway Dr. I-24, exit 114, just w. Int
corridors. **Pets:** Accepted.
[ASK] [S△] [✕] [₺M] [🖫] [🛏] [🖵] [⊶]

**△△△ ♦♦♦ Days Inn & Suites** SH
(931) 728-9530. **$60.** 2259 Hillsboro Blvd. I-24, exit 114, just w. Ext
corridors. **Pets:** Medium, dogs only. $10 daily fee/pet. Service with restric-
tions, supervision.
[S△] [✕] [🛏] [🖵] [⊶]

**♦♦ Economy Inn** M
(931) 728-6023. **$45-$75.** 890 Interstate Dr. I-24, exit 110, just n. Ext
corridors. **Pets:** Accepted.
[ASK] [S△] [✕] [🛏] [⊶]

**△△△ ♦♦♦ Ramada Inn** SH
(931) 728-0800. **$59-$94.** 2314 Hillsboro Blvd. I-24, exit 114, just n. Ext
corridors. **Pets:** Medium. $10 one-time fee/pet. Designated rooms, no serv-
ice, supervision.
[SAVE] [S△] [✕] [🛏] [🖵] [⊶]

**♦♦ Super 8 Motel** SH
(931) 728-9720. **Call for rates.** 2430 Hillsboro Blvd. I-24, exit 114, just
n. Ext corridors. **Pets:** Other species. $5 daily fee/pet. Service with restric-
tions, supervision.
[ASK] [✕] [🛏] [⊶]

## MCMINNVILLE

**△△△ ♦♦♦♦ Best Western Tree City Inn** SH
(931) 473-2159. **$74-$99.** 809 Sparta Hwy. Jct US 70 S Bypass and
Red Rd, 1 mi s, follow signs. Ext corridors. **Pets:** Medium, dogs only.
$10 one-time fee/room. Service with restrictions, supervision.
[SAVE] [S△] [✕] [🛏] [🖵] [⊶]

**△△△ ♦♦♦ McMinnville Inn** SH
(931) 473-7338. **$49-$79.** 2545 Sparta Hwy. I-24, exit 111, n on SR 55
to US 70 S Bypass. Ext corridors. **Pets:** Accepted.
[SAVE] [S△] [✕] [🛏] [🖵] [⊶]

---

# MEMPHIS METROPOLITAN AREA

## COLLIERVILLE

**♦♦ Comfort Inn** SH
(901) 853-1235. **$52-$105.** 1230 W Poplar Ave. 2.5 mi w on SR 57 and
US 72. Ext corridors. **Pets:** Accepted.
[ASK] [S△] [✕] [🖫] [🛏] [⊶]

**♦♦♦ Hampton Inn Collierville** SH
(901) 854-9400. **$89-$139.** 1280 W Poplar Ave. 0.9 mi w of jct CR 175
on US 72. Int corridors. **Pets:** Very small, dogs only. $10 daily fee/pet.
Service with restrictions, supervision.
[ASK] [S△] [✕] [₺M] [🖫] [♿] [🛏] [🖵] [⊶]

## CORDOVA

**△△△ ♦♦♦ Comfort Suites** SH
(901) 213-3600. **$69-$159.** 2427 N Germantown Pkwy. I-40, exit 16,
just s. Int corridors. **Pets:** Accepted.
[SAVE] [S△] [✕] [₺M] [🖫] [♿] [🛏] [🖵] [⊶]

**♦♦♦ Quality Suites-Wolfchase** SH
(901) 386-4600. **$70-$150.** 8166 Varnavas Dr. I-40, exit 16, 0.3 mi s on
Germantown Pkwy, then e. Int corridors. **Pets:** Accepted.
[ASK] [S△] [✕] [♿] [🛏] [🖵] [⊶]

# COVINGTON

**▼▼ Best Western Inn** SH
(901) 476-8561. **$55-$65.** 873 Hwy 51 N. 0.8 mi n of jct US 59 W. Ext corridors. **Pets:** Medium. $7 daily fee/pet. Designated rooms, service with restrictions, crate.
ASK Sᴅ ⊠ 🗇 🖶 ⮕ ⮕

**▼▼ Comfort Inn** SH
(901) 475-0380. **$71-$85.** 901 Hwy 51 N. 1 mi n of jct US 59. Ext corridors. **Pets:** Medium, other species. $10 daily fee/pet. Service with restrictions, crate.
ASK Sᴅ ⊠ 🖶 ⮕ ⮕

# GERMANTOWN

**▼▼ Comfort Inn & Suites-Germantown** SH 🐾
(901) 757-7800. **$79, 5 day notice.** 7787 Wolf River Blvd. I-40, exit 16, 5 mi s on Germantown Pkwy. Int corridors. **Pets:** Large, other species. Service with restrictions.
ASK Sᴅ ⊠ ᵃᴹ 🗇 🖶 ⮕ ⮕

**▼▼▼ Homewood Suites by Hilton-Germantown** SH
(901) 751-2500. **$114-$124.** 7855 Wolf River Blvd. I-40, exit 16, 5.8 mi s on CR 177 at jct Germantown Pkwy and Wolf River Blvd. Int corridors. **Pets:** Small. $50 one-time fee/room. Service with restrictions, crate.
ASK ⊠ 🗇 🖶 ⮕ ⮕

**▼▼▼ Residence Inn** SH
(901) 751-2500. **$94-$118.** 9314 Poplar Pike. I-240, exit 15 (Poplar Ave), 7 mi e. Int corridors. **Pets:** Accepted.
ASK Sᴅ ⊠ ᵃᴹ 🗇 🖶 ⮕ ⮕ ⊠

# LAKELAND

**▲▲▲ ▼▼▼ Super 8 Motel** SH
(901) 372-4575. **$55-$75.** 9779 Huff Puff Rd. I-40, exit 20. Ext corridors. **Pets:** Very small, dogs only. $10 daily fee/pet. Designated rooms, no service, supervision.
SAVE Sᴅ ⊠ 🖶 ⮕

# MEMPHIS

**▲▲▲ ▼▼▼▼ AmeriSuites (Memphis/Cordova)** SH
(901) 371-0010. **$109-$119.** 7905 Giacosa Pl. I-40, exit 16, just n on Germantown Rd, then just w. Int corridors. **Pets:** Accepted.
SAVE Sᴅ ⊠ ᵃᴹ 🗇 🖶 ⮕ ⮕

**▲▲▲ ▼▼▼▼ AmeriSuites (Memphis/Primacy Pkwy)** SH
(901) 680-9700. **$119-$179.** 1220 Primacy Pkwy. I-240, exit 15 (Poplar Ave), 0.3 mi e, s on Ridgeway, just w, then just s. Int corridors. **Pets:** Accepted.
SAVE Sᴅ ⊠ ᵃᴹ 🗇 🖶 ⮕ ⮕

**▲▲▲ ▼▼▼▼ Baymont Inn & Suites Memphis East** SH
(901) 377-2233. **$73-$94.** 6020 Shelby Oaks Dr. I-40, exit 12, just n. Int corridors. **Pets:** Medium. Service with restrictions.
SAVE ⊠ 🖶 ⮕ ⮕

**▼▼▼ Comfort Suites Thousand Oaks** SH
(901) 365-2575. **$79-$179.** 2575 Thousand Oaks Dr. I-240, exit 18. Int corridors. **Pets:** Accepted.
ASK Sᴅ ⊠ ᵃᴹ 🗇 🖶 ⮕ ⮕

**▼▼▼▼ Drury Inn & Suites-Memphis Northeast** SH
(901) 373-8200. **$75-$117.** 1556 Sycamore View. I-40, exit 12, just n. Int corridors. **Pets:** Accepted.
ASK ⊠ 🗇 🖶 ⮕ ⮕ ⊠

**▼▼▼ Extended Stay Deluxe** SH
(901) 380-1525. **$55-$65.** 2520 Horizon Lake Dr. I-40, exit 16B, just n, then just w. Int corridors. **Pets:** $25 daily fee/pet. Service with restrictions, supervision.
ASK Sᴅ ⊠ 🗇 🖶 ⮕ ⮕

**▲▲▲ ▼▼▼ Hampton Inn & Suites** SH
(901) 762-0056. **$299-$399.** 962 S Shady Grove Rd. I-240, exit 15 (Poplar Ave), 0.5 mi e. Int corridors. **Pets:** Small, dogs only. Service with restrictions, supervision.
SAVE Sᴅ ⊠ ᵃᴹ 🗇 🖶 ⮕

**▼▼▼ Hawthorn Suites** SH
(901) 682-1722. **$79-$139.** 1070 Ridge Lake Blvd. I-240, exit 15 (Poplar Ave), just e, then n under overpass. Int corridors. **Pets:** Accepted.
ASK Sᴅ ⊠ 🗇 🖶 ⮕ ⊠

**▼▼▼▼ Holiday Inn-University of Memphis** SH
(901) 678-8200. **$119-$149.** 3700 Central Ave. I-240 E, exit 20B, 1.7 mi w on Getwell Rd, 0.3 mi n on Park, 1 mi w on Goodlett, then just w; follow signs to university. Int corridors. **Pets:** Small. $50 one-time fee/room. No service, supervision.
ASK Sᴅ ⊠ ᵃᴹ 🗇 🖶 ⮕ 🍴

**▼▼▼ Homestead Studio Suites**
**Hotel-Memphis/Airport** SH
(901) 344-0010. **$65-$75.** 2541 Corporate Ave E. I-240, exit 23B (Airways Blvd S), just s to Democrat Rd, just w to Nonconnah Blvd, then 0.4 mi n to Corporate Ave, follow signs. Int corridors. **Pets:** $25 daily fee/pet. Service with restrictions, supervision.
ASK Sᴅ ⊠ ᵃᴹ 🗇 🖶

**▼▼▼ Homestead Studio Suites**
**Hotel-Memphis/Poplar** SH
(901) 767-5522. **$65-$75.** 6500 Poplar Ave. I-240, exit 15 (Poplar Ave), 1 mi e. Int corridors. **Pets:** $25 daily fee/pet. Service with restrictions, supervision.
ASK Sᴅ ⊠ ᵃᴹ 🗇 🖶

**▼▼▼ Homewood Suites** SH
(901) 763-0500. **$139-$179.** 5811 Poplar Ave. I-240, exit 15 (Poplar Ave). Ext/int corridors. **Pets:** Small, dogs only. $100 one-time fee/room. Service with restrictions.
ASK ⊠ 🖶 ⮕ ⮕

**▲▲▲ ▼▼▼ La Quinta Inn & Suites Memphis (Primacy**
**Parkway)** SH
(901) 374-0330. **$78-$105.** 1236 Primacy Pkwy. I-240, exit 15 (Poplar Ave), 0.3 mi e, s on Ridgeway, just w, then just s. Int corridors. **Pets:** Medium. Service with restrictions.
SAVE ⊠ ᵃᴹ 🗇 🖶 ⮕ ⮕

**▲▲▲ ▼▼▼ La Quinta Inn & Suites Sycamore**
**View-Memphis** SH
(901) 381-0044. **$160-$180.** 6069 Macon Cove. I-40, exit 12, just s. Int corridors. **Pets:** Medium. $50 deposit/room. Designated rooms, service with restrictions, supervision.
SAVE Sᴅ ⊠ ᵃᴹ 🗇 🖶 ⮕ ⮕

**▲▲▲ ▼▼▼ Marriott Residence Inn** SH
(901) 685-9595. **$89-$156.** 6141 Old Poplar Pike. I-240, exit 15 (Poplar Ave), 0.5 mi e. Ext/int corridors. **Pets:** Small. $75 one-time fee/room. Designated rooms, service with restrictions, supervision.
SAVE Sᴅ ⊠ ᵃᴹ 🗇 🖶 ⮕ ⮕

**▲▲▲ ▼▼▼ Quality Inn** SH
(901) 382-2323. **$59-$99, 7 day notice.** 6068 Macon Cove Rd. I-40, exit 12, just s. Ext corridors. **Pets:** Small. $10 daily fee/pet. Service with restrictions, supervision.
SAVE Sᴅ ⊠ ᵃᴹ 🖶 ⮕ ⮕

**▼▼ Quality Inn Airport/Graceland** SH
(901) 345-3344. **$50-$90.** 1581 E Brooks Rd. I-55, exit 5A (Brooks Rd), 0.3 mi e. Ext corridors. **Pets:** Accepted.
ASK Sᴅ ⊠ 🖶 ⮕

**▼ Red Roof Inn-East** SH
(901) 388-6111. **$47-$58.** 6055 Shelby Oaks Dr. I-40, exit 12, just n. Ext corridors. **Pets:** Accepted.
⊠ 🖶 ⮕

# MONTEAGLE

**▼▼▼▼ Best Western Smoke House Lodge** SH
(931) 924-2091. **$70-$95.** 850 W Main St. I-24, exit 134, just s. Ext corridors. **Pets:** Accepted.
⊠ 🖉 🖑 🚹 💻 🍽 ⇌ ⊠

# MORRISTOWN

**AAA ▼▼▼ Days Inn** M ❀
(423) 587-2200. **$49-$65.** 2512 E Andrew Johnson Hwy. I-81, exit 8, 6 mi n on US 25 E to exit 2B (Greenville-Morristown), then just w. Ext corridors. **Pets:** Very small, dogs only. $10 deposit/room. Designated rooms, service with restrictions, supervision.
SAVE 🗲 ⊠ 🖑 🚹 💻 ⇌

**▼▼▼▼ Holiday Inn Morristown Conference Center** SH
(423) 587-2400. **$85-$170.** 5435 S Davy Crockett Pkwy. I-81, exit 8, just n. Int corridors. **Pets:** Medium. $15 one-time fee/room. Service with restrictions, crate.
ASK 🗲 ⊠ 🚹 💻 🍽 ⇌

**▼▼▼▼ Lakeway Inn & Conference Center** SH
(423) 581-8700. **$56-$157.** 3304 W Andrew Johnson Hwy. 2.5 mi w on US 11 E. Ext corridors. **Pets:** Large, other species. $10 daily fee/pet. Designated rooms, service with restrictions.
ASK 🗲 ⊠ 🖉 🚹 💻 🍽 ⇌

**▼▼ Super 8 Motel** M
(423) 318-8888. **$45-$60.** 5400 S Davy Crockett Pkwy. I-81, exit 8, just n. Int corridors. **Pets:** $9 one-time fee/pet. Service with restrictions, supervision.
ASK 🗲 ⊠ 🖑 🖑 🚹 💻

# MOUNT JULIET

**AAA ▼▼▼ Microtel Inn & Suites** SH
(615) 773-3600. **$50-$85.** 1000 Hershel Dr. I-40, exit 226. Int corridors. **Pets:** Medium, dogs only. $25 one-time fee/room. No service, supervision.
SAVE 🗲 ⊠ 🚹 💻 ⇌

# MURFREESBORO

**AAA ▼▼▼ Best Western Chaffin Inn** SH
(615) 895-3818. **$59-$109.** 168 Chaffin Pl. I-24, exit 78B. Ext corridors. **Pets:** Other species. $12 daily fee/pet. Service with restrictions, crate.
SAVE 🗲 ⊠ 🚹 💻 ⇌

**▼▼▼▼ DoubleTree Hotel Murfreesboro** SH
(615) 895-5555. **$89-$169.** 1850 Old Fort Pkwy. I-24, exit 78B. Int corridors. **Pets:** Accepted.
ASK 🗲 ⊠ 🖉 🖑 🚹 💻 🍽 ⇌

**▼▼▼▼ Hampton Inn** SH ❀
(615) 896-1172. **$79-$159.** 2230 Armory Dr. I-24, exit 78B, just n. Ext corridors. **Pets:** Designated rooms, service with restrictions, crate.
ASK 🗲 ⊠ 🖑 🖉 🚹 💻 ⇌

**AAA ▼▼▼ Howard Johnson Express Inn** SH
(615) 896-5522. **$45-$99.** 2424 S Church St. I-24, exit 81A eastbound; exit 81 westbound. Int corridors. **Pets:** Small. $10 daily fee/pet. Service with restrictions, supervision.
SAVE 🗲 ⊠ 🚹 💻 🍽 ⇌

**AAA ▼▼▼▼ Quality Inn Murfreesboro** SH
(615) 890-1006. **$75-$99.** 2135 S Church St. I-24, exit 81 westbound; exit 81B eastbound. Int corridors. **Pets:** Other species. Service with restrictions, supervision.
SAVE 🗲 ⊠ 🖑 🚹 💻 ⇌

**AAA ▼▼▼ Ramada Limited** SH ❀
(615) 896-5080. **$60-$100.** 1855 S Church St. I-24, exit 81. Int corridors. **Pets:** Other species. $10 daily fee/pet. Service with restrictions, supervision.
SAVE 🗲 ⊠ 🚹 💻 ⇌

**AAA ▼▼▼ Vista Inn and Suites** SH
(615) 848-9030. **$49-$99.** 118 Westgate Blvd. I-24, exit 81A eastbound; exit 81 westbound. Int corridors. **Pets:** Small. $10 daily fee/pet. Service with restrictions, supervision.
SAVE 🗲 ⊠ 🚹 💻 ⇌

---

# NASHVILLE METROPOLITAN AREA

# ANTIOCH

**AAA ▼▼▼▼ Holiday Inn-The Crossings** SH ❀
(615) 731-2361. **$84-$104.** 201 Crossings Pl. I-24, exit 60, 0.5 mi e. Int corridors. **Pets:** Other species. Service with restrictions, crate.
SAVE 🗲 ⊠ 🖑 🖉 🖑 🚹 💻 🍽 ⇌

# GOODLETTSVILLE

**AAA ▼▼▼▼ Best Western Fairwinds Inn** SH ❀
(615) 851-1067. **$53-$99.** 100 Northcreek Blvd. I-65, exit 97 (Long Hollow Pike), 0.5 mi e. Ext corridors. **Pets:** Small. $10 daily fee/pet. Service with restrictions, supervision.
SAVE 🗲 ⊠ 🚹 💻 ⇌

**▼▼ Days Inn Business Place** SH
(615) 851-6600. **Call for rates.** 909 Conference Dr. I-65, exit 97, 0.5 mi e to Conference Dr, then 0.6 mi s. Ext corridors. **Pets:** Accepted.
⊠ 🖑 🚹 💻 ⇌

**AAA ▼▼▼▼ Holiday Inn Express Nashville North** SH
(615) 851-1891. **$89-$189.** 120 Cartwright St. I-65, exit 97 (Long Hollow Pike), just w. Int corridors. **Pets:** Accepted.
SAVE 🗲 ⊠ 🖑 🖉 🖑 🚹 💻 ⇌

**▼▼ Red Roof Inn-Nashville North** SH
(615) 859-2537. **$42-$54.** 110 Northgate Dr. I-65, exit 97 (Long Hollow Pike), 0.5 mi e. Ext corridors. **Pets:** Accepted.
⊠ 🖑 🖉

**AAA ▼▼▼ Rodeway Inn** M
(615) 859-1416. **$38-$50.** 650 Wade Cir. I-65, exit 96, just ne. Ext corridors. **Pets:** Medium, dogs only. $10 daily fee/pet. Designated rooms, service with restrictions, supervision.
SAVE 🗲 ⊠ 🚹 💻 ⇌

# HERMITAGE

**▼▼ Motel 6** SH
(615) 889-1060. **$55-$70.** 5768 Old Hickory Blvd. I-40, exit 221 westbound; exit 221B eastbound, just n. Ext corridors. **Pets:** Accepted.
ASK 🗲 ⊠ 🖑 🚹 💻 ⇌

# JOELTON

**▼▼ Days Inn** SH
(615) 876-3261. **$50-$65.** 201 Gifford Pl. I-24, exit 35, just s. Ext corridors. **Pets:** Small. Service with restrictions, supervision.
ASK 🗲 ⊠ ⇌

# NASHVILLE

**AAA ▼▼ Americas Best Value Inn** M
(615) 226-9805. **$50-$70.** 2403 Brick Church Pike. I-65, exit 87 (Trinity Ln), just nw. Ext corridors. **Pets:** Medium. $10 daily fee/pet. Designated rooms, service with restrictions, supervision.
SAVE 🗲 ⊠ 🚹

▼▼▼ **AmeriSuites (Nashville/Airport)** SH
(615) 493-5200. **$69-$129.** 721 Royal Pkwy. I-40, exit 216C (Donelson Pike). Int corridors. **Pets:** Accepted.
ASK SD ⊠ &M 🏢 🖵 ⇆

QQQ ▼▼▼ **AmeriSuites (Nashville/Opryland)** SH
(615) 872-0422. **$99-$108.** 220 Rudy's Circle Dr. I-40, exit 215B (Briley Pkwy), 6 mi ne to exit 11 (McGavock Pike), then 0.3 mi left. Int corridors. **Pets:** Small. $10 daily fee/pet. Service with restrictions, supervision.
SAVE SD ⊠ &M 🏢 🖵 ⇆

QQQ ▼▼▼ **Baymont Inn & Suites Nashville-Airport** SH
(615) 885-3100. **$78-$94.** 531 Donelson Pike. I-40, exit 216C (Donelson Pike), 0.3 mi n. Int corridors. **Pets:** Medium. Service with restrictions.
SAVE ⊠ 🏢 🖵 ⇆

▼▼▼ **Baymont Inn & Suites Nashville-West** SH
(615) 353-0700. **$75-$90.** 5612 Lenox Ave. I-40, exit 204. Int corridors. **Pets:** Other species. $25 deposit/room. Service with restrictions, supervision.
ASK SD ⊠ 🏢 🖵 ⇆

QQQ ▼▼▼ **Best Western Airport Inn** SH
(615) 889-9199. **$39-$85.** 701 Stewarts Ferry Pike. I-40, exit 219 (Stewarts Ferry Pike). Ext corridors. **Pets:** Accepted.
SAVE SD ⊠ 🏢 🖵 ⇆

QQQ ▼▼▼ **Best Western Music City Inn** SH
(615) 641-7721. **$59-$199.** 13010 Old Hickory Blvd. I-24, exit 62. Ext corridors. **Pets:** Accepted.
SAVE SD ⊠ 🏢 🖵 ⇆

QQQ ▼▼▼ **Best Western Music Row** SH
(615) 242-1631. **$59-$149.** 1407 Division St. I-40, exit 209B, just w. Int corridors. **Pets:** Small. $5 daily fee/pet. Service with restrictions.
SAVE SD ⊠ 🏢 🖵 ⇆

▼▼ **Capstone Inn-Nashville South** SH
(615) 834-7170. **$70-$100.** 341 Harding Pl. I-24, exit 56 (Harding Pl). Ext corridors. **Pets:** Accepted.
ASK ⊠ &M 🏢 🖵 ⇆

QQQ ▼▼▼ **ClubHouse Inn & Suites** SH
(615) 883-0500. **$62-$79.** 2435 Atrium Way. Briley Pkwy to exit 7 (Elm Hill Pike), just e. Int corridors. **Pets:** Accepted.
SAVE SD ⊠ 🏢 🖵 ⇆

QQQ ▼▼▼ **Comfort Inn Music City** SH
(615) 226-3300. **$69-$78.** 2407 Brick Church Pk. I-65, exit 87. Int corridors. **Pets:** Accepted.
SAVE SD ⊠ 🏢 🖵 ⇆

▼▼▼ **Comfort Inn Opryland** SH
(615) 889-0086. **$55-$99, 7 day notice.** 2516 Music Valley Dr. I-40, exit 215 (Briley Pkwy), 4 mi n; I-65, exit 90, exit McGavock Pike off Briley Pkwy. Int corridors. **Pets:** Small. $5 daily fee/pet. Service with restrictions, supervision.
ASK SD ⊠ 🖵 ⇆

QQQ ▼▼ **Days Inn Vanderbilt** SH
(615) 327-0922. **$75-$94.** 1800 West End Ave. I-40, exit 209A westbound; exit 209B eastbound, 0.5 mi w. Ext/int corridors. **Pets:** Small. $20 daily fee/pet. Designated rooms, service with restrictions, supervision.
SAVE ⊠ 🏢 🖵 ⇆

QQQ ▼▼▼ **Days Inn West** SH
(615) 356-9100. **$45-$88, 3 day notice.** 269 White Bridge Pk. I-40, exit 204, just s. Ext corridors. **Pets:** Accepted.
SAVE SD ⊠ 🏢

▼▼▼ **Drury Inn & Suites-Nashville Airport** SH
(615) 902-0400. **$80-$130.** 555 Donelson Pike. I-40, exit 216 (Donelson Pike). Int corridors. **Pets:** Accepted.
ASK ⊠ &M ☒ 🏢 🖵 ⇆

QQQ ▼▼▼ **Econo Lodge** M
(615) 262-9193. **$40-$75.** 110 Maplewood Trace. I-65, exit 90A, 0.5 mi s on Dickerson Pike; corner of Dickerson Pike and Maplewood Trace. Ext corridors. **Pets:** Medium. $8 daily fee/pet. Designated rooms, service with restrictions, supervision.
SAVE SD ⊠ 🏢 🖵 ⇆

QQQ ▼▼▼ **Embassy Suites** LH
(615) 871-0033. **$89-$149.** 10 Century Blvd. I-40, exit 215 (Briley Pkwy N), then exit 7 (Elm Hill Pike), 0.3 mi e to McGavock Pike, 0.3 mi s to Century Blvd, then 0.3 mi w. Int corridors. **Pets:** Accepted.
SAVE ⊠ &M ☒ 🏢 🖵 🍴 ⇆ ☒

QQQ ▼▼▼ **Fiddlers Inn** SH
(615) 885-1440. **$49-$109.** 2410 Music Valley Dr. I-40, exit 215B (Briley Pkwy), 4 mi n to exit 12 (McGavock Pike), then just w. Ext corridors. **Pets:** Accepted.
SAVE ⊠ 🏢 🖵 ⇆

▼▼▼ **GuestHouse International Inn & Suites** SH
(615) 885-4030. **$89-$119.** 2420 Music Valley Dr. Briley Pkwy, exit 12, 0.3 mi w, then 0.3 mi n. Int corridors. **Pets:** Accepted.
ASK SD ⊠ 🏢 🖵 ⇆

▼▼▼ **Hampton Inn & Suites at the University** SH
(615) 320-6060. **$99-$179.** 2330 Elliston Pl. 3.5 mi w. Int corridors. **Pets:** Accepted.
ASK SD ⊠ &M ⌀ ☒ 🏢 🖵 ⇆

QQQ ▼▼▼ **The Hermitage Hotel** LH 🐾
(615) 244-3121. **$189-$349.** 231 6th Ave N. Corner of Union St; center. Int corridors. **Pets:** Other species. $25 daily fee/pet. Crate.
SAVE ⊠ &M ☒ 🏢 🍴 ☒

QQQ ▼▼▼ **Holiday Inn Select Opryland/Airport** LH
(615) 883-9770. **$69-$119.** 2200 Elm Hill Pike. I-40, exit 215B (Briley Pkwy), 0.5 mi n. Int corridors. **Pets:** Accepted.
SAVE SD ⊠ &M ⌀ ☒ 🖵 🍴 ⇆ ☒

▼▼▼ **Homestead Studio Suites Hotel-Nashville/Airport** SH
(615) 316-9020. **$62-$72.** 727 McGavock Pike. I-40, exit 215B (Briley Pkwy), 1 mi n to exit 7 (Elm Hill Pike), then just e. Ext corridors. **Pets:** $25 daily fee/pet. Service with restrictions, supervision.
ASK SD ⊠ &M ⌀ ☒ 🏢 🖵

▼▼▼ **Homewood Suites by Hilton** SH
(615) 884-8111. **$89-$239.** 2640 Elm Hill Pike. I-40, exit 216C (Donelson Pike). Int corridors. **Pets:** Accepted.
ASK ⊠ &M ⌀ 🏢 🖵 ⇆

QQQ ▼▼▼ **Hotel Preston** LH 🐾
(615) 361-5900. **$79-$159, 3 day notice.** 733 Briley Pkwy. I-40, exit 215 (Briley Pkwy). Int corridors. **Pets:** Medium, other species. $50 deposit/room. Designated rooms, service with restrictions.
SAVE SD ⊠ ⌀ 🏢 🖵 🍴 ⇆

QQQ ▼▼▼ **La Quinta Inn Nashville (Airport)** M
(615) 885-3000. **$73-$89.** 2345 Atrium Way. I-40, exit 215B (Briley Pkwy), 1 mi n to exit 7 (Elm Hill Pike), e to Atrium Way, then 0.3 mi n. Int corridors. **Pets:** Medium. Service with restrictions.
SAVE ⊠ &M ⌀ 🖵 ⇆

QQQ ▼▼▼ **La Quinta Inn Nashville (South)** SH
(615) 834-6900. **$73-$90.** 4311 Sidco Dr. I-65, exit 78A. Ext corridors. **Pets:** Medium. Service with restrictions.
SAVE ⊠ &M 🏢 🖵 ⇆

**Loews Vanderbilt Hotel Nashville** 🏨 🐾
(615) 320-1700. **$145-$249.** 2100 West End Ave. I-40, exit 209 (Broadway), 1.3 mi w. Int corridors. **Pets:** Other species. Service with restrictions, supervision.

**Microtel Inn & Suites** 🄢
(615) 662-0004. **$54-$79.** 100 Coley Davis Ct. I-40, exit 196. Int corridors. **Pets:** Small. $10 daily fee/pet. Service with restrictions, supervision.

**Motel 6-156** 🄢
(615) 333-9933. **$35-$47.** 95 Wallace Rd. I-24, exit 56 (Harding Pl). Ext corridors. **Pets:** Accepted.

**Nashville Marriott at Vanderbilt University** 🄢
(615) 321-1300. **$139-$229.** 2555 West End Ave. I-40, exit 209B eastbound; exit 209A westbound, w on Broadway. Int corridors. **Pets:** Accepted.

**Pear Tree Inn by Drury-Nashville South** 🄢
(615) 834-4242. **$60-$90.** 343 Harding Pl. I-24, exit 56 (Harding Pl). Ext corridors. **Pets:** Accepted.

**The Quarters Motor Inn** 🄼
(615) 731-5990. **$49-$125.** 1100 Bell Rd. I-24, exit 59 (Bell Rd), just w. Ext corridors. **Pets:** Medium, other species. $25 deposit/pet. Designated rooms, no service, supervision.

**Radisson Hotel Nashville Airport** 🄢
(615) 889-9090. **$119-$149.** 1112 Airport Center Dr. I-40, exit 216C (Donelson Pike N). Int corridors. **Pets:** Medium. $50 deposit/room. Designated rooms, service with restrictions, supervision.

**Red Roof Inn** 🄢
(615) 889-0090. **$55-$95.** 2460 Music Valley Dr. I-40, exit 215B (Briley Pkwy), 4 mi n to exit 11 (McGavock Pike). Int corridors. **Pets:** Medium, other species. Service with restrictions, supervision.

**Red Roof Inn Airport** 🄼
(615) 872-0735. **$45-$55.** 510 Claridge Dr. I-40, exit 216C (Donelson Pike), 0.3 mi n. Ext corridors. **Pets:** Accepted.

**Red Roof Inn South** 🄢
(615) 832-0093. **$46-$66.** 4271 Sidco Dr. I-65, exit 78. Ext corridors. **Pets:** Accepted.

**Residence Inn** 🄢 🐾
(615) 889-8600. **$69-$124.** 2300 Elm Hill Pike. I-40, exit 215B (Briley Pkwy), 1.5 mi n. Ext corridors. **Pets:** Other species. $75 one-time fee/room. Service with restrictions.

**Select Hotel by Holiday Inn at Vanderbilt** 🄢
(615) 327-4707. **$89-$109.** 2613 West End Ave. I-40, exit 209B eastbound; exit 209A westbound, w on Broadway. Int corridors. **Pets:** Other species. $100 deposit/room, $50 one-time fee/room. Designated rooms, service with restrictions, crate.

**Sheraton Music City Hotel** 🏨 🐾
(615) 885-2200. **$99-$159.** 777 McGavock Pike. I-40, exit 215B (Briley Pkwy), 1 mi n to exit 7 (Elm Hill Pike), 0.5 mi e, then s. Int corridors. **Pets:** Other species. Service with restrictions, crate.

**Super 8 Motel-West** 🄢
(615) 356-6005. **$55-$80.** 6924 Charlotte Pike. I-40, exit 201. Ext corridors. **Pets:** Medium, dogs only. $10 daily fee/pet. Service with restrictions, supervision.

**Union Station-A Wyndham Historic Hotel** 🄢
(615) 726-1001. **$169-$179.** 1001 Broadway. I-40, exit 209A, just ne; corner of 10th Ave. Int corridors. **Pets:** Accepted.

## END METROPOLITAN AREA

# NEWPORT

**Best Western Newport Inn** 🄢
(423) 623-8713. **$49-$149.** 1015 Cosby Hwy. I-40, exit 435, just w. Ext corridors. **Pets:** Accepted.

**Comfort Inn** 🄢
(423) 623-5355. **$47-$129.** 1149 Smokey Mountain Ln. I-40, exit 432B. Int corridors. **Pets:** Accepted.

**Holiday Inn** 🄢
(423) 623-8622. **$58-$120.** 1010 Cosby Hwy. I-40, exit 435. Ext/int corridors. **Pets:** Accepted.

**Motel 6-4090** 🄼
(423) 623-1850. **$45-$75.** 255 Heritage Blvd. I-40, exit 435. Int corridors. **Pets:** Accepted.

**Relax Inn** 🄼
(423) 625-1521. **$55-$60, 3 day notice.** 1148 W Hwy 25-70. I-40, exit 432B. Ext corridors. **Pets:** $5 one-time fee/pet. Designated rooms, service with restrictions, supervision.

# OAK RIDGE

**Comfort Inn** 🄢
(865) 481-8200. **$76-$96.** 433 S Rutgers Ave. 0.9 mi se of SR 95 on SR 62. Int corridors. **Pets:** Medium. $10 daily fee/pet. Service with restrictions, supervision.

**DoubleTree Oak Ridge** 🄢
(865) 481-2468. **$79-$169, 3 day notice.** 215 S Illinois Ave. 0.3 mi se of SR 95 on SR 62. Int corridors. **Pets:** $25 one-time fee/room. Service with restrictions, supervision.

▼▼◆◆ **Jameson Inn** SH
(865) 483-6809. **$54-$104.** 216 S Rutgers Ave. Jct SR 95 and 62, 0.9 mi se on SR 62 tc Rutgers Ave, then 0.7 mi n. Int corridors. **Pets:** Very small, other species. $10 daily fee/room. Service with restrictions, supervision.

A$K ⊠ 🐾 ⟨& 🖥 💻 ≋

## ONEIDA

▼◆◆ **The Galloway Inn** M
(423) 569-8835. **$43.** 299 Galloway Dr. Jct SR 63, 3.3 mi n on US 27, just e. Ext corridors. **Pets:** Accepted.

A$K S🐾 ⊠ 🖥 💻

## OOLTEWAH

▼ **Super 8 Motel** M
(423) 238-5951. **$45-$49, 7 day notice.** 5111 Hunter Rd. I-75, exit 11, just w. Ext corridors. **Pets:** Accepted.

A$K S🐾 ⊠ 🖥 ≋

## PICKWICK DAM

▼◆◆◆ **Pickwick Landing State Resort Park Inn** LH
(731) 689-3135. **$59-$71.** 220 Playground Loop. Intersection of US 57 and SR 128. Ext/int corridors. **Pets:** $10 daily fee/pet. Designated rooms, service with restrictions, supervision.

⊠ 🖥 ⟨& 🖥 💻 🍴 ≋ ⊠

## PIGEON FORGE

◆◆◆ ▼◆◆◆ **Accommodations by Sunset Cottage** CA
(865) 429-8478. **$53-$750, 30 day notice.** 3630 S River Rd. Just e of jct US 441 at traffic light 8, just n. Ext corridors. **Pets:** Small. $100 deposit/pet, $25 one-time fee/pet. Designated rooms, no service, supervision.

SAVE ⊠ 🖥 💻

◆◆◆ ▼◆◆ **Americas Best Value Inn at Dollywood Lane** SH
(865) 429-0150. **$30-$170.** 202 Emert St. Just w of jct US 441; between traffic lights 7 and 8. Int corridors. **Pets:** Medium. $15 daily fee/pet. Designated rooms, service with restrictions, supervision.

SAVE S🐾 ⊠ ⟨& 🖥 ≋

◆◆◆ ▼◆◆ **Briarstone Inn** M
(865) 453-4225. **$27-$179.** 3626 Parkway. On US 441; between traffic lights 7 and 8. Ext corridors. **Pets:** Accepted.

SAVE ⊠ 🐾 🖥 💻 ≋

▼◆◆ **Holiday Inn Resort** SH
(865) 428-2700. **$49-$179.** 3230 Parkway. On US 441; between traffic lights 2 and 3. Int corridors. **Pets:** Accepted.

A$K S🐾 ⊠ 🐾 🖥 💻 🍴 ≋

▼◆ **Microtel Suites at Music Road** SH
(865) 453-1116. **$30-$119.** 2045 Parkway. On US 441, just s of traffic light 0. Int corridors. **Pets:** Other species. $25 one-time fee/pet. Designated rooms, service with restrictions.

A$K S🐾 ⊠ ⟨& 🖥 💻 ≋

◆◆◆ ▼◆◆ **Motel 6 #4021** SH
(865) 908-1244. **$29-$99.** 336 Henderson Chapel Rd. From jct US 441, just w at traffic light 1. Int corridors. **Pets:** Accepted.

SAVE ⊠ ⟨& 🖥 ≋

◆◆◆ ▼◆◆◆ **National Parks Resort Lodge** SH
(865) 453-4106. **$30-$120.** 2385 Parkway. On US 441 at traffic light 1. Int corridors. **Pets:** Large, other species. $20 deposit/room, $20 one-time fee/room. Designated rooms, service with restrictions, supervision.

SAVE ⊠ 🖥 💻 ≋

◆◆◆ ▼◆◆ **Rodeway Inn Mountain Sky** M
(865) 453-3530. **$29-$139.** 4236 Parkway. On US 441, at traffic light 10. Ext corridors. **Pets:** Small. $20 deposit/room. Designated rooms, service with restrictions.

SAVE ⊠ 🖥 💻 ≋

◆◆◆ ▼◆◆ **Smoky Shadows Motel & Conference Center** SH
(865) 453-7155. **$40-$150, 3 day notice.** 4215 Parkway. On US 441, just n of traffic light 10. Ext/int corridors. **Pets:** Small, dogs only. $10 daily fee/pet. Service with restrictions, crate.

SAVE S🐾 ⊠ 🖥 💻 ≋

◆◆◆ ▼◆◆◆ **Starr Crest Resort Cabin Rentals** VH
(865) 429-0156. **$175-$900, 30 day notice.** 1431 Upper Middle Creek Rd. I-40, exit 407 (SR 66) to US 441 S to town, n at light 8, then 1.5 mi e on Dollywood Ln. Ext corridors. **Pets:** Accepted.

SAVE S🐾 ⊠ 🖥 💻 ≋

## POWELL

▼◆ **Comfort Inn** M 🐾
(865) 938-5500. **$54-$109.** 323 E Emory Rd. I-75, exit 112. Ext corridors. **Pets:** Small. $10 daily fee/room. Service with restrictions, crate.

A$K S🐾 🖥 💻 ≋

## PULASKI

◆◆◆ ▼◆◆ **Super 8 Motel** SH 🐾
(931) 363-4501. **$42-$72.** 1-65 & Hwy 64, Exit 14 East. I-65, exit 14, just e. Ext corridors. **Pets:** Medium, other species. $5 daily fee/pet. Service with restrictions, supervision.

SAVE S🐾 ⊠ 🖥 ≋

## RICEVILLE

◆◆◆ ▼ **Rice Inn** M
(423) 462-2224. **$27-$35.** 3692 Hwy 11. I-75, exit 42, 1.5 mi e, then just n. Ext corridors. **Pets:** Accepted.

SAVE S🐾 ⊠ 🖥

## ROGERSVILLE

▼◆◆◆ **Holiday Inn Express** SH
(423) 272-1842. **$73-$83.** 7139 Hwy 11 W. Jct SR 66 and US 11, 0.5 mi sw. Int corridors. **Pets:** Accepted.

A$K S🐾 ⊠ ⟨& 🖥 ≋

## SELMER

▼◆ **Super 8 Motel-Selmer** SH
(731) 645-8880. **$50-$60.** 644 Mulberry Ave. Jct SR 64 and 45, just s on SR 45. Ext corridors. **Pets:** $25 deposit/room. Service with restrictions, supervision.

A$K S🐾 ⊠ ⟨& 🖥 ≋

## SEVIERVILLE

◆◆◆ ▼◆◆◆ **Best Western Dumplin Valley Inn** M 🐾
(865) 933-3467. **$38-$130.** 3426 Winfield Dunn Pkwy. I-40, exit 407, 0.4 mi s on SR 66. Ext corridors. **Pets:** Large. $10 daily fee/room. Designated rooms, service with restrictions, crate.

SAVE S🐾 ⊠ 🐾 🖥 💻 ≋

◆◆◆ ▼◆◆◆ **Comfort Inn Mountain River Suites** M
(865) 428-5519. **$49-$109.** 860 Winfield Dunn Pkwy. I-40, exit 407, 7 mi s on SR 66; 1.3 mi n of jct US 411. Ext corridors. **Pets:** Accepted.

SAVE S🐾 ⊠ 🐾 🖥 💻 ≋

**△△△ ▼▼▼▼ (Douglas Lake Resort) Mountain Top Resorts** CA
(865) 286-1150. **$75-$250, 30 day notice.** 2788 Windfall Estates Dr. I-40, exit 407 (66 S), 9 mi on SR 66, then n on 411 (Dolly Parton Pkwy) 7.2 mi, turn w on Hattie Branch Rd becomes Flat Creek Rd, 3 mi, then just w. Ext corridors. **Pets:** $25 one-time fee/room. Designated rooms.

SAVE S✓ ✕ 🛏 💻 ⊠

**▼▼▼▼ Holiday Inn Express Hotel & Suites** SH
(865) 933-9448. **$43-$150.** 2863 Winfield Dunn Pkwy. I-40, exit 407, 2.3 mi s on SR 66. Int corridors. **Pets:** Small, dogs only. $15 one-time fee/pet. Designated rooms, service with restrictions, crate.

ASK S✓ ✕ 🛏 ᴹ ⚲ 🕹 🛏 💻 ≋

**△△△ ▼▼▼▼ (Lone Branch Creek Resort) Mountain Top Resorts** CA
(865) 286-1150. **$75-$250, 30 day notice.** 2788 Windfall Estates Dr. I-40, exit 407 (SR 66 S), 9 mi on SR 66, then n on 411 (Dolly Parton Pkwy) 7.2 mi, turn w on Hattie Branch Rd, becomes Flat Creek Rd, continue 3 mi, then just w. Ext corridors. **Pets:** Medium. $45 one-time fee/room. Designated rooms, service with restrictions, crate.

SAVE S✓ ✕ 🛏 💻 ≋

## SMYRNA

**▼▼ Days Inn** M
(615) 355-6161. **$62-$100, 3 day notice.** 1300 Plaza Dr. I-24, exit 66B eastbound; exit 66 westbound, 2.5 mi ne. Ext corridors. **Pets:** Dogs only. $10 daily fee/pet. Service with restrictions, supervision.

ASK S✓ ✕ 🛏 💻 ≋

## SWEETWATER

**△△△ ▼▼ Comfort Inn** SH
(423) 337-6646. **$69.** 731 S Main St. On US 11, jct SR 68. Ext/int corridors. **Pets:** Medium. $5 daily fee/pet. Designated rooms, service with restrictions.

SAVE S✓ ✕ 🛏 💻 ≋

**△△△ ▼▼▼ Comfort Inn West** SH
(423) 337-3353. **$51-$119.** 249 Hwy 68. I-75, exit 60, just e. Ext/int corridors. **Pets:** Small. $5 daily fee/pet. Service with restrictions, supervision.

SAVE S✓ ✕ 🛏 💻 ≋

**▼▼ Days Inn** SH
(423) 337-4200. **$60-$69.** 229 Hwy 68. I-75, exit 60, just e. Ext corridors. **Pets:** Accepted.

ASK S✓ ✕ 🛏 💻 ≋

**△△△ ▼ Knights Inn** SH
(423) 337-9357. **$47-$90.** 207 Hwy 68. I-75, exit 60. Ext corridors. **Pets:** Accepted.

SAVE S✓ ✕ 🛏

**△△△ ▼▼▼▼ Quality Inn** SH
(423) 337-4900. **$77-$110.** 1116 Hwy 68. I-75, exit 60. Int corridors. **Pets:** $10 one-time fee/pet. Service with restrictions, supervision.

SAVE S✓ ✕ 🛏 💻 ≋

## TOWNSEND

**△△△ ▼▼▼▼ Comfort Inn** SH
(865) 448-9000. **$35-$169, 7 day notice.** 7824 E Lamar Alexander Pkwy. On US 321. Ext corridors. **Pets:** Small, dogs only. $20 daily fee/pet. Service with restrictions, supervision.

SAVE S✓ ✕ 🛏 💻 ≋

**△△△ ▼▼▼▼ Laurel Valley & Smoky Mountain Cabin Rentals** VH
(865) 448-6697. **$95-$389, 30 day notice.** 125 Townsend Park Rd. On US 321. Ext corridors. **Pets:** Medium. $50 one-time fee/room. Designated rooms, supervision.

SAVE ✕ 🛏 💻 ≋

**△△△ ▼▼▼▼ Valley View Lodge** SH
(865) 448-2237. **$47-$102.** 7726 E Lamar Alexander Pkwy. On US 321; center. Ext corridors. **Pets:** Small, dogs only. $10 one-time fee/pet. Service with restrictions, crate.

SAVE S✓ ✕ ⚲ 🛏 💻 ≋

## TULLAHOMA

**▼▼▼ Jameson Inn** SH
(931) 455-7891. **$54-$104.** 2113 N Jackson St. 3 mi n on SR 41A (N Jackson St). Ext corridors. **Pets:** Very small, other species. $10 daily fee/room. Service with restrictions, supervision.

ASK ✕ 🕹 🛏 💻 ≋

## VONORE

**▼▼▼▼ Grand Vista Hotel & Suites** SH
(423) 884-6200. **$80-$90.** 117 Grand Vista Dr. I-75, exit 172, 14 mi e. Int corridors. **Pets:** Accepted.

ASK S✓ ✕ ᴹ ⚲ 🕹 🛏 💻 ≋

## WHITE HOUSE

**▼▼ Holiday Inn Express** SH
(615) 672-7200. **$70-$80.** 354 Hester Ln. I-65, exit 108, just e. Ext corridors. **Pets:** Medium. $5 one-time fee/pet. Service with restrictions, supervision.

ASK ✕ ᴹ 🕹 🛏 💻 ≋

## WHITEVILLE

**▼▼ Super 8** SH
(731) 254-8884. **$45-$50.** 2040 Hwy 64. US 64 and SR 179. Ext corridors. **Pets:** Other species. $5 daily fee/pet. Service with restrictions, supervision.

ASK S✓ ✕ ᴹ 🕹 🛏

## WILDERSVILLE

**△△△ ▼▼▼ Best Western Crossroads Inn** SH
(731) 968-2532. **$50-$65.** 21045 Hwy 22 N. I-40, exit 108, just s. Ext corridors. **Pets:** Accepted.

SAVE S✓ ✕ 🛏 💻 ≋

# TEXAS

## CITY INDEX

## ABILENE

### ▼▼/▼▼ Antilley Inn M
(325) 695-3330. **$54-$59.** 6550 US Hwy 83. US 83/84, exit Antilley Rd. Ext corridors. **Pets:** Accepted.

(ASK) ⊠ 🛢 🖵 ⇒

### ◆◆◆ ▼▼/▼▼ Best Western Abilene Inn & Suites SH
(325) 672-5501. **$89-$109.** 350 I-20 W. I-20, exit 286C, just n. Int corridors. **Pets:** Small. $25 daily fee/pet. Designated rooms, service with restrictions, supervision.

(SAVE) (S♦) ⊠ 🛢 🖵 ⇒

### ◆◆◆ ◆▼/▼ Best Western Mall South SH
(325) 695-1262. **$75-$85.** 3950 Ridgemont Dr. US 83/84, exit Ridgemont Dr, just s. Ext corridors. **Pets:** Medium. $20 daily fee/pet. Designated rooms, service with restrictions, supervision.

(SAVE) (S♦) ⊠ 🛢 🖵 ⇒

### ◆◆◆ ▼▼/▼ Budget Host Colonial Inn M
(325) 677-2683. **$45-$60.** 3210 Pine St. Jct I-20 and US 83 business route, exit 286A. Ext/int corridors. **Pets:** Medium. $10 daily fee/pet. Designated rooms, service with restrictions, supervision.

(SAVE) (S♦) ⊠ 🛢 🖵 ⇒

### ◆◆◆ ▼▼/▼ Civic Plaza Hotel SH
(325) 676-0222. **$62-$99.** 505 Pine St. Downtown. Ext corridors. **Pets:** Accepted.

(SAVE) (S♦) ⊠ 🛢 🖵 ⊨ ⇒

### ◆◆◆ ▼▼/▼▼ Comfort Suites SH
(325) 795-8500. **$85-$140.** 3165 S Danville Dr. I-20, exit 279, s on US 83/84/277 to Southwest Dr, then just e. Int corridors. **Pets:** Medium, other species. $30 one-time fee/room. Service with restrictions, supervision.

(SAVE) (S♦) ⊠ 🛢 🖵 ⇒

### ▼▼/▼▼ Days Inn M
(325) 672-6433. **$59-$65, 7 day notice.** 1702 E Hwy 20. I-20, exit 288. Ext corridors. **Pets:** $10 deposit/pet, $10 one-time fee/pet.

(ASK) (S♦) ⊠ 🛢 🖵 ⇒

### ◆◆◆ ▼▼/▼▼ Econo Lodge M
(325) 673-5424. **$45.** 1633 W Stamford. S Frontage Rd off I-20 and US 80, exit 285 eastbound; exit 286A westbound. Ext corridors. **Pets:** Very small. $10 daily fee/pet. Service with restrictions, supervision.

(SAVE) (S♦) ⊠ 🛢 🖵 ⇒

### ▼▼/▼▼ Executive Inn M
(325) 677-2200. **$60-$70.** 1650 I-20 E. I-20, exit 288. Ext corridors. **Pets:** Other species. Service with restrictions, supervision.

(S♦) ⊠ 🛢 🖵 ⇒

### ◆◆◆ ▼▼/▼▼ La Quinta Inn Abilene SH
(325) 676-1676. **$82-$123.** 3501 W Lake Rd. I-20, exit 286C. Ext corridors. **Pets:** Medium. Service with restrictions.

(SAVE) ⊠ 🛢 🖵 ⇒

### ▼▼ Motel 6 Abilene #79 M
(325) 672-8462. **$37-$49.** 4951 W Stamford St. I-20, exit 282, on eastbound frontage road. Ext corridors. **Pets:** Accepted.

(S♦) ⊠ ⇒

▼▼ **Regency Inn & Suites** SH
(325) 695-7700. **$66-$74.** 3450 S Clack St. 5 mi sw on US 83/84, exit Southwest Dr. Int corridors. **Pets:** Other species. $15 one-time fee/pet. Service with restrictions, supervision.

(ASK) (S) (X) (&) (🔒) (💻) (🍴) (🏊)

▼▼ **Super 8 Motel** M
(325) 673-5251. **$55-$80.** 1525 E I-20. I-20, exit 288. Ext corridors. **Pets:** $8 daily fee/pet. Service with restrictions, crate.

(ASK) (S) (X) (🔒) (💻) (🏊)

# ALAMO

▼▼ **Super 8 Motel** SH
(956) 787-9444. **$50.** 714 N Alamo Rd. US 83, exit FM 907, just n. Ext corridors. **Pets:** Small. $10 daily fee/pet. Service with restrictions, supervision.

(ASK) (S) (X) (&) (🔒) (🏊)

# ALICE

▼ **Days Inn** SH
(361) 664-6616. **$60-$75.** 555 N Johnson St. On US 281 business route; n of jct US 281 (Bus) and Johnson St. Int corridors. **Pets:** Accepted.

(ASK) (S) (X) (🔒) (🏊)

# ALPINE

▲▲▲ ▼▼ **Oak Tree Inn** SH
(432) 837-5711. **$66-$75.** 2407 E Holland (Hwy 90/67). US 90, 2 mi e. Int corridors. **Pets:** Accepted.

(SAVE) (S) (X) (&M) (🔒) (&) (🔒) (💻)

▲▲▲ ▼▼▼ **Ramada Limited** SH
(432) 837-1100. **$90-$140.** 2800 W Hwy 90. On US 90, 2 mi n. Int corridors. **Pets:** Accepted.

(SAVE) (S) (X) (&M) (🔒) (🔒) (💻) (🏊)

# AMARILLO

▲▲▲ ▼▼▼ **Ambassador Hotel** LH
(806) 358-6161. **$109-$169.** 3100 I-40 W. I-40, exit 68, just w on north frontage road. Int corridors. **Pets:** Accepted.

(SAVE) (S) (X) (🔒) (🔒) (💻) (🍴) (🏊) (X)

▼▼▼▼ **Baymont Inn & Suites** SH
(806) 356-6800. **$89-$107.** 3411 I-40 W. I-40, exit 67, 0.3 mi e on south frontage road. **Pets:** Accepted.

(ASK) (S) (X) (🔒) (🔒) (💻) (🏊)

▲▲▲ ▼▼▼ **Best Western Amarillo Inn** SH
(806) 358-7861. **$69-$79.** 1610 Coulter Dr. I-40, exit 65 (Coulter Dr), 0.6 mi n. Ext/int corridors. **Pets:** Small, other species. $10 one-time fee/pet. Supervision.

(SAVE) (S) (X) (&) (🔒) (🔒) (💻) (🍴) (🏊)

▲▲▲ ▼▼▼ **Best Western Santa Fe** SH
(806) 372-1885. **$55-$100.** 4600 I-40 E. I-40, exit 73 (Eastern St) eastbound; exit 73 (Bolton St) westbound, U-turn on south frontage road. Int corridors. **Pets:** Accepted.

(SAVE) (S) (X) (🔒) (💻) (🏊)

▲▲▲ ▼▼▼ **Big Texan Motel** M
(806) 372-5000. **$65-$85, 3 day notice.** 7701 I-40 E. I-40, exit 75 (Lakeside Dr), 0.3 mi w on north frontage road. Ext corridors. **Pets:** Accepted.

(SAVE) (S) (X) (🔒) (🍴) (🏊)

▲▲▲ ▼▼ **Days Inn** SH
(806) 379-6255. **$59-$99.** 1701 I-40 E. I-40, exit 71 (Ross-Osage), just w on north frontage road. Int corridors. **Pets:** Other species. $25 one-time fee/pet. Service with restrictions, supervision.

(SAVE) (S) (X) (🔒) (🔒) (🔒) (💻) (🏊)

▲▲▲ ▼▼ **Days Inn** SH
(806) 359-9393. **$59-$109.** 2102 S Coulter Dr. I-40, exit 65 (Coulter Dr), just n. Ext corridors. **Pets:** Small. $15 daily fee/pet. Service with restrictions, supervision.

(SAVE) (S) (X) (&) (🔒) (🏊)

▼▼ **Days Inn South** SH
(806) 468-7100. **$55-$79, 7 day notice.** 8601 Canyon Dr. I-27, exit 116, just n on east service road. Int corridors. **Pets:** Accepted.

(ASK) (S) (X) (&) (🔒) (🏊)

▲▲▲ ▼▼▼ **Hampton Inn** SH
(806) 372-1425. **$64-$124.** 1700 I-40 E. I-40, exit 71 (Ross-Osage), just e on south frontage road. Int corridors. **Pets:** Other species. Service with restrictions, supervision.

(SAVE) (S) (X) (🔒) (🔒) (🔒) (💻) (🏊)

▼▼▼ **Holiday Inn-I-40** SH
(806) 372-8741. **$134.** 1911 I-40 at Ross-Osage. I-40, exit 71 (Ross-Osage), on north frontage road. Int corridors. **Pets:** Accepted.

(ASK) (S) (X) (🔒) (&) (🔒) (🔒) (💻) (🍴) (🏊)

▼▼▼ **La Quinta Inn Amarillo (East/Airport Area)** SH
(806) 373-7486. **$71-$121.** 1708 I-40 E. I-40, exit 71 (Ross-Osage), just e on south frontage road. Ext corridors. **Pets:** Medium. Service with restrictions.

(ASK) (X) (🔒) (🔒) (💻) (🏊)

▲▲▲ ▼▼▼▼ **La Quinta Inn Amarillo (West/Medical Center)** SH
(806) 352-6311. **$75-$112.** 2108 S Coulter Dr. I-40, exit 65 (Coulter Dr), just n. Ext corridors. **Pets:** Medium. Service with restrictions.

(SAVE) (X) (&M) (🔒) (🔒) (💻) (🏊)

▲▲▲ ▼▼▼ **Microtel Inn & Suites** SH
(806) 372-8373. **$59-$109.** 1501 S Ross St. I-40, exit 71 (Ross-Osage), just n. Int corridors. **Pets:** Small, dogs only. $10 one-time fee/pet. Designated rooms, service with restrictions, supervision.

(SAVE) (S) (X) (&M) (🔒) (&) (🔒) (💻) (🏊)

▼▼ **Motel 6 Amarillo East #409** M
(806) 374-6444. **$42-$55.** 3930 I-40 E. I-40, exit 72B, on eastbound frontage road. Ext corridors. **Pets:** Accepted.

(S) (X) (🏊)

▼▼ **Motel 6 Amarillo West #1146** M
(806) 359-7651. **$40-$54.** 6030 I-40 W. I-40, exit 66 (Bell St), just w, on north frontage road. Ext corridors. **Pets:** Accepted.

(S) (X) (&) (🏊)

▲▲▲ ▼▼▼▼ **Quality Inn & Suites** SH 🐾
(806) 335-1561. **$65-$80.** 1803 Lakeside Dr. I-40, exit 75 (Lakeside Dr), just n. Ext/int corridors. **Pets:** Medium. $10 daily fee/pet. Service with restrictions, supervision.

(SAVE) (S) (X) (&) (🔒) (💻) (🏊)

▲▲▲ ▼▼▼ **Quality Inn & Suites West** SH
(806) 358-7943. **$69-$109.** 6800 I-40 W. I-40, exit 66 (Bell St), 0.5 mi w on north frontage road. Ext corridors. **Pets:** Small. $20 one-time fee/pet. Service with restrictions, supervision.

(SAVE) (S) (X) (🔒) (💻) (🏊)

▲▲▲ ▼▼▼ **Quality Inn-East** SH
(806) 376-9993. **$50-$120.** 1515 I-40 E. I-40, exit 71 (Ross-Osage), just w on north frontage road. Ext corridors. **Pets:** Accepted.

(SAVE) (S) (X) (🔒) (🔒) (💻) (🏊)

▲▲▲ ▼▼▼ **Ramada Limited** SH
(806) 374-2020. **$54-$59.** 1620 I-40 E. I-40, exit 71 (Ross-Osage), just e on south frontage road. Ext corridors. **Pets:** Medium. $10 one-time fee/room. Designated rooms, service with restrictions, supervision.

(SAVE) (S) (X) (🔒) (💻) (🏊)

▼▼▼ **Residence Inn by Marriott** SH
(806) 354-2978. **$130-$160, 14 day notice.** 6700 I-40 W. I-40, exit 66 (Bell St), 0.5 mi w on north frontage road. Int corridors. **Pets:** Accepted.
(ASK) (S6) (×) (&M) (📶) (🐾) (🛏) (💻) (🏊) (⊠)

▼ ▼ **Ritz Airport Plaza Inn** SH
(806) 373-3303. **$40-$70, 3 day notice.** 7909 I-40 E. I-40, exit 75 (Lakeside Dr), just nw. Int corridors. **Pets:** Accepted.
(ASK) (S6) (×) (📶) (🛏) (💻) (🍴) (🏊)

(AAA) ▼ ▼ **Travelodge West** SH
(806) 353-3541. **$42-$65.** 2035 Paramount Blvd. I-40, exit 68A (Paramount Blvd), just s. Ext corridors. **Pets:** Small. $5 daily fee/room. Service with restrictions, supervision.
(SAVE) (S6) (×) (📶) (🛏) (💻) (🏊)

## ANGLETON

▼ ▼ **Best Western Angelton Inn** SH
(979) 849-5822. **$70.** 1809 N Velasco (Business Rt 288). 1.5 mi n of jct SR 35 and Business Rt SR 288, e of SR 288. Ext corridors. **Pets:** Accepted.
(ASK) (S6) (×) (🛏) (💻) (🏊)

## ARLINGTON

(AAA) ▼▼▼ **AmeriSuites (Dallas/Arlington)** SH
(817) 649-7676. **$99-$149.** 2380 E Rd to Six Flags St. I-30, exit 30 (SR 360), 0.5 mi sw. Int corridors. **Pets:** Small, other species. $10 daily fee/pet. Service with restrictions, crate.
(SAVE) (S6) (×) (📶) (🐾) (🛏) (💻) (🏊)

▼▼▼ **Arlington TownePlace Suites by Marriott** SH
(817) 861-8728. **$99-$109.** 1709 E Lamar Ave. 2 mi w of SR 360. Int corridors. **Pets:** Accepted.
(ASK) (×) (&M) (📶) (🐾) (🛏) (💻) (🏊)

(AAA) ▼ ▼ **Baymont Inn & Suites-Arlington** SH
(817) 633-2434. **$59-$69, 14 day notice.** 2401 Diplomacy Dr. I-30, exit 30 (SR 360), 0.5 mi s; off SR 360, exit Six Flags Dr northbound; exit Ave H/Lamar Blvd southbound, on southbound service road. Int corridors. **Pets:** Medium. $50 deposit/room. Service with restrictions, supervision.
(SAVE) (S6) (×) (&M) (📶) (🐾) (🛏) (💻) (🏊)

(AAA) ▼▼▼ **Country Inn & Suites By Carlson** SH
(817) 261-8900. **$64-$108.** 1075 Wet'N Wild Way. I-30, exit 28 (Collins St/FM 157), just e. Ext corridors. **Pets:** Small. $100 deposit/pet, $5 daily fee/pet. Designated rooms, service with restrictions, supervision.
(SAVE) (S6) (×) (&M) (📶) (🐾) (🛏) (💻) (🏊)

(AAA) ▼▼▼ **Days Inn Ballpark at Arlington/Six Flags** SH
(817) 261-8444. **$36-$89, 3 day notice.** 910 N Collins St. I-30, exit 28 (Collins St/FM 157), 1 mi s. Int corridors. **Pets:** Accepted.
(SAVE) (S6) (×) (🛏) (🏊)

▼▼▼ **Hawthorn Suites** SH
(817) 640-1188. **$55-$199.** 2401 Brookhollow Plaza Dr. I-30, exit 30 (SR 360), just n to Lamar Blvd, just w to Brookhollow Plaza Dr, then just n. Ext corridors. **Pets:** Accepted.
(ASK) (S6) (×) (📶) (🛏) (💻) (🏊) (⊠)

▼▼▼ **Homewood Suites by Hilton** SH
(817) 633-1594. **$109-$139, 14 day notice.** 2401 Rd to Six Flags St. I-30, exit 30 (SR 360), 0.5 mi sw. Int corridors. **Pets:** Accepted.
(ASK) (S6) (×) (&M) (📶) (🐾) (🛏) (💻) (🏊)

▼ ▼ **Howard Johnson Express Inn** SH
(817) 461-1122. **$40-$65.** 2001 E Copeland Rd. I-30, exit 30 (SR 360) westbound, just s to Six Flags Dr, just w to Copeland Rd, then 0.9 mi w; exit 29 (Ball Pkwy) eastbound. Int corridors. **Pets:** Medium. $10 daily fee/pet. Service with restrictions, crate.
(ASK) (S6) (×) (🛏) (💻) (🏊)

▼▼▼ **La Quinta Inn & Suites Dallas (Arlington South)** SH
(817) 467-7756. **$115-$125.** 4001 Scott's Legacy. I-20, exit 450 (Matlock Rd) on westbound service road. Int corridors. **Pets:** Medium. Service with restrictions.
(ASK) (×) (📶) (🛏) (💻) (🏊)

(AAA) ▼▼▼ **La Quinta Inn Dallas (Arlington Conference Center)** SH
(817) 640-4142. **$76-$104.** 825 N Watson Rd. I-30, exit 30 (SR 360), exit Six Flags Dr northbound; exit Ave H/Lamar Blvd southbound. Ext corridors. **Pets:** Medium. Service with restrictions.
(SAVE) (×) (📶) (🛏) (💻) (🏊) (⊠)

▼▼▼ **Marriott SpringHill Suites-Arlington** SH
(817) 860-2737. **$89-$119.** 1975 E Lamar Blvd. I-30, exit 29 (Ballpark Way), 0.4 mi n to Lamar Blvd, then just w. Int corridors. **Pets:** Accepted.
(ASK) (S6) (×) (&M) (📶) (🛏) (💻) (🏊) (⊠)

▼ ▼ **Microtel Inn** SH
(817) 557-8400. **$55-$70.** 1740 Oak Village Blvd. I-20, exit 449 (Cooper St) westbound; exit 449A (Cooper St) eastbound, just s. Int corridors. **Pets:** Accepted.
(ASK) (S6) (×) (🛏) (🏊)

▼ ▼ **Motel 6-122** SH
(817) 649-0147. **$39-$53.** 2626 E Randol Mill Rd. Jct SR 360 and Randol Mill Rd. Ext corridors. **Pets:** Accepted.
(S6) (×) (🏊)

(AAA) ▼▼▼ **Sleep Inn Main Gate-Six Flags** SH
(817) 649-1010. **$76-$110.** 750 Six Flags Dr. I-30, exit 30 (SR 360), 0.5 mi s. Int corridors. **Pets:** Small. $10 daily fee/pet. Designated rooms, service with restrictions, supervision.
(SAVE) (S6) (×) (📶) (🛏) (💻) (🏊)

▼ ▼ **Studio 6-South Arlington #6036** SH
(817) 465-8500. **$51-$61.** 1980 W Pleasant Ridge Rd. I-20, exit 449 (Cooper St), 0.3 mi n, then just w. Ext corridors. **Pets:** Accepted.
(S6) (×) (🐾) (🛏) (💻)

## AURORA

(AAA) ▼▼▼ **MD Resort Bed & Breakfast** BB 🐾
(817) 489-5150. **$89-$289, 14 day notice.** 601 Old Base Rd. 2 mi w of jct US 287 to Old Base Rd, 0.5 mi s. Ext/int corridors. **Pets:** Dogs only. $15 daily fee/pet. Designated rooms, no service, supervision.
(SAVE) (S6) (×) (🛏) (💻) (🏊) (⊠) (📷)

## AUSTIN

▼▼▼ **AmeriSuites (Austin/Airport)** SH
(512) 386-7600. **$99-$109.** 7601 Ben White Blvd. I-35, exit 230B (Ben White Blvd), 3.2 mi e. Int corridors. **Pets:** Medium, other species. $25 daily fee/room. Service with restrictions, supervision.
(ASK) (S6) (×) (📶) (🐾) (💻) (⊠)

(AAA) ▼▼◆ **AmeriSuites (Austin/Arboretum)** SH
(512) 231-8491. **$109-$119.** 3612 Tudor Blvd. Jct US 183 and SR 360, 1 blk e to Stonelake Blvd, 0.5 mi s to Tudor Blvd, then just e. Int corridors. **Pets:** Accepted.
(SAVE) (×) (&M) (📶) (🐾) (🛏) (💻) (🏊)

(AAA) ▼▼▼ **AmeriSuites (Austin/North Central)** SH
(512) 323-2121. **$89-$129.** 7522 N I-35. I-35, exit 240A, on west frontage road. Int corridors. **Pets:** Other species. $10 daily fee/room. Service with restrictions, crate.
(SAVE) (S6) (×) (&M) (📶) (🐾) (🛏) (💻) (🏊)

▼▼▼ **Austin Ambassador Hotel** SH
(512) 836-8520. **$122-$130.** 7800 I-35 N. I-35, exit 240A, on west frontage road at jct US 183. Int corridors. **Pets:** Other species. $50 one-time fee/room. Service with restrictions, crate.
(ASK) (S6) (×) (🐾) (🛏) (💻) (🍴) (🏊)

**▼▼▼ Austin Marriott at the Capitol** 🔡
(512) 478-1111. **$125-$199.** 701 E 11th St. I-35, exit 234B, 0.3 mi e. Int corridors. **Pets:** Accepted.
🔳 🔳 ✖ 🔲 🔳 🔳 🔳 🔳 ➔ ✖

**▲▲▲ ▼▼▼▼ Baymont Inn & Suites-Highland Mall** 🔢
(512) 452-9401. **$73-$83.** 7100 I-35 N. I-35, exit 239, on west frontage road. Ext corridors. **Pets:** Medium. Service with restrictions.
🔳 ✖ 🔲 🔳 🔳 ➔

**▼▼ Best Western Atrium North** 🔢
(512) 339-7311. **$65-$79, 7 day notice.** 7928 Gessner Dr. I-35, exit 240A, 0.4 mi w on Anderson Ln. Int corridors. **Pets:** Accepted.
🔳 🔳 ✖ 🔳 🔳 ➔

**▼▼ Best Western Seville Plaza Inn** 🔢
(512) 447-5511. **$59-$89.** 4323 I-35 S. I-35, exit 230A (Stassney Rd) southbound; exit 230 (Ben White Blvd) northbound. Int corridors. **Pets:** Medium. $20 one-time fee/room. Service with restrictions, supervision.
🔳 🔳 ✖ 🔲 🔳 🔳 🔳 ➔

**▼▼▼ Candlewood Suites Austin Northwest** 🔢
(512) 338-1611. **$79-$119.** 9701 Stonelake Blvd. Jct SR 360 (Capital of Texas Hwy) and Stonelake Blvd, just s. Int corridors. **Pets:** Accepted.
🔳 🔳 ✖ 🔳 🔲 🔳 🔳 🔳

**▼▼▼ Candlewood Suites-South** 🔢
(512) 444-8882. **$79-$120.** 4320 S I-35. I-35, exit 230 northbound; exit 230B southbound, on southbound frontage road. Int corridors. **Pets:** Accepted.
🔳 🔳 ✖ 🔳 🔲 🔳 🔳 🔳

**▲▲▲ ▼▼▼▼ Clarion Inn & Suites Conference Center** 🔢
(512) 444-0561. **$98-$159.** 2200 S I-35. I-35, exit 232A (Oltorf Blvd), on west side access road. Ext/int corridors. **Pets:** Medium, other species. $50 one-time fee/room. Designated rooms, service with restrictions, crate.
🔳 ✖ 🔲 🔳 🔳 🔳 🔳 ➔

**▼▼▼ Comfort Suites Airport** 🔢
(512) 386-6000. **$70, 30 day notice.** 7501 E Ben White Blvd. I-35, exit 230B (Ben White Blvd/SR 71), 3.6 mi e. Int corridors. **Pets:** Accepted.
🔳 🔳 ✖ 🔲 🔳 🔲 🔳 🔳

**▼▼▼ Crowne Plaza** 🔡
(512) 480-8181. **$169-$269.** 500 N I-35. I-35, exit 234B southbound; exit 234C northbound, on southbound frontage road. Int corridors. **Pets:** Small. $50 one-time fee/pet. Service with restrictions, supervision.
🔳 🔳 ✖ 🔳 🔲 🔳 🔳 🔳 🔳 ➔

**▲▲▲ ▼▼ Days Inn University-Downtown** 🅜
(512) 478-1631. **$57-$99.** 3105 N I-35. I-35, exit 236A at 32nd St from lower level. Ext corridors. **Pets:** Medium, other species. $10 one-time fee/room. Service with restrictions, supervision.
🔳 🔳 ✖ 🔳 🔳 ➔

**▼▼▼ DoubleTree Guest Suites-Austin** 🔡
(512) 478-7000. **$139-$199.** 303 W 15th St. Just nw of state capitol building. Int corridors. **Pets:** Dogs only. $25 one-time fee/room. Designated rooms, service with restrictions, supervision.
✖ 🔳 🔳 🔳 🔳 ➔ ✖

**▼▼▼ Doubletree Hotel Austin** 🔡
(512) 454-3737. **$99-$199.** 6505 I-35 N. I-35, exit 238A, on east frontage road. Int corridors. **Pets:** Accepted.
✖ 🔲 🔳 🔳 🔳 🔳 🔳 ➔

**▲▲▲ ▼▼▼▼ The Driskill** 🔡
(512) 474-5911. **$300-$330.** 604 Brazos St. Jct 6th St. Int corridors. **Pets:** Accepted.
🔳 ✖ 🔳 🔲 🔳

**▼▼▼ Drury Inn & Suites-Austin North** 🔢
(512) 467-9500. **$78-$130.** 6711 I-35 N. I-35, exit 238A, on east frontage road. Int corridors. **Pets:** Accepted.
🔳 ✖ 🔲 🔳 🔳 ➔

**▼▼▼ Drury Inn-Austin Highland Mall** 🔢
(512) 454-1144. **$72-$123.** 919 E Koenig Ln. I-35, exit 238A, on west frontage road. Int corridors. **Pets:** Accepted.
🔳 ✖ 🔳 ➔

**▼▼▼ Embassy Suites Hotel-Downtown** 🔡
(512) 469-9000. **$129-$269.** 300 S Congress Ave. Just s of Congress Ave Bridge. Int corridors. **Pets:** Accepted.
🔳 🔳 ✖ 🔳 🔲 🔳 🔳 🔳 🔳 ➔ ✖

**▲▲▲ ▼▼ Exel Inn Of Austin** 🔢
(512) 462-9201. **$43-$79.** 2711 I-35 S. I-35, exit 231 (Woodward Ave) southbound; exit 232A (Oltorf St) northbound, on northbound frontage road; just n of jct I-35 and US 290/SR 71. Int corridors. **Pets:** Small, other species. Designated rooms, service with restrictions, supervision.
🔳 🔳 ✖ 🔳 🔳 🔳

**▼▼▼ Extended StayAmerica Austin North Central** 🔢
(512) 339-6005. **$45-$75.** 8221 N I-35. I-35, exit 241, on east frontage road. Int corridors. **Pets:** $25 daily fee/pet. Service with restrictions, supervision.
🔳 🔳 ✖ 🔳 🔳 🔳 ➔

**▼▼▼ Extended StayAmerica (Austin/Northwest/Research Park)** 🔢
(512) 219-6500. **$45-$81.** 12424 Research Blvd. US 183, exit Oak Knoll, on eastbound frontage road. Int corridors. **Pets:** $25 daily fee/pet. Service with restrictions, supervision.
🔳 🔳 ✖ 🔳 🔳 🔳 🔳 ➔

**▼▼▼ Extended Stay Deluxe Austin-Arboretum-North** 🔢
(512) 833-0898. **$45-$85.** 2700 Gracy Farms Ln. 2 mi n of US 183 on Loop 1 (Mo-Pac Expwy), exit Burnet Rd (FM 1325). Int corridors. **Pets:** $25 daily fee/pet. Service with restrictions, supervision.
🔳 🔳 ✖ 🔳 🔳 🔳

**▼▼▼ Fairfield Inn & Suites Austin NW** 🔢
(512) 527-0734. **$94-$114.** 11201 N Mo-Pac Blvd. US 183 N, 1.5 mi n on Loop 1 (Mo-Pac Expwy) to Breaker exit, on east frontage road. Int corridors. **Pets:** Accepted.
🔳 🔳 ✖ 🔳 🔲 🔳 🔳 🔳 ➔ ✖

**▼▼▼ Four Seasons Hotel** 🔡 ✿
(512) 478-4500. **$315-$405.** 98 San Jacinto Blvd. Bordering Town Lake. Int corridors. **Pets:** Small, other species. Designated rooms, service with restrictions, supervision.
✖ 🔳 🔳 🔳 🔳 🔳 ➔ ✖

**▼▼▼ Hampton Inn Northwest** 🔢
(512) 349-9898. **$69-$109.** 3908 W Braker Ln. 1 mi n of US 183 on Loop 1 (Mo-Pac Expwy) to Braker Ln exit. Int corridors. **Pets:** Accepted.
🔳 🔳 ✖ 🔳 🔳 🔳 ➔

**▼▼▼ Hawthorn Suites Austin Central** 🔢
(512) 459-3335. **$69-$179.** 935 La Posada Dr. I-35, exit 238A, just off east frontage road. Ext corridors. **Pets:** Accepted.
🔳 🔳 ✖ 🔳 🔳 🔳 ➔

**▲▲▲ ▼▼▼ Hawthorn Suites Ltd-Austin-Bergstrom International Airport** 🔢
(512) 247-6166. **$79-$149.** 7800 E Riverside Dr. I-35, exit 230B (Ben White Blvd/SR 71), 3.2 mi e. Int corridors. **Pets:** Accepted.
🔳 🔳 ✖ 🔳 🔳 🔲 🔳 🔳 ➔ ✖

**▼▼▼ Holiday Inn Express Hotel & Suites** 🔢
(512) 251-9110. **$79-$109.** 14620 N I-35. I-35, exit 247, on west frontage road. Int corridors. **Pets:** Accepted.
🔳 🔳 ✖ 🔳 🔳 🔲 🔳 🔳

**▼▼▼▼ Holiday Inn Northwest/Arboretum** SH
(512) 343-0888. **$99.** 8901 Business Park Dr. Jct US 183 and Loop 1 (Mo-Pac Expwy), on southwest corner. Int corridors. **Pets:** Accepted.
[A$K] [SD] [✕] [⬚] [✆] [⬛] [▭] [⊞] [⇌]

**⬥⬥⬥ ▼▼▼▼ Holiday Inn-Town Lake** LH ✣
(512) 472-8211. **$109-$149.** 20 N I-35. I-35, exit 233. Int corridors. **Pets:** Medium. $100 deposit/pet, $25 one-time fee/pet. Designated rooms, service with restrictions.
[SAVE] [SD] [✕] [⬚] [✆] [⬛] [▭] [⊞] [⇌]

**▼▼ Homestead Studio Suites Hotel-Austin/Arboretum/South** SH
(512) 837-6677. **$41-$71.** 9100 Waterford Centre Blvd. US 183, exit Burnet Rd, on westbound frontage road. Ext corridors. **Pets:** $25 daily fee/pet. Service with restrictions, supervision.
[A$K] [SD] [✕] [✆] [⬛] [▭]

**▼▼▼▼ Homestead Studio Suites Hotel-Austin/Downtown/ Town Lake** SH
(512) 476-1818. **$55-$95.** 507 S 1st St. I-35, exit 234B southbound; exit 234A northbound, 1.3 mi w on Cesar Chavez/E 1st St, then 0.5 mi s. Int corridors. **Pets:** $25 daily fee/pet. Service with restrictions, supervision.
[A$K] [SD] [✕] [⬚] [✆] [⬛] [▭]

**▼▼▼▼ Homewood Suites by Hilton Arboretum NW** SH
(512) 349-9966. **$99-$179.** 10925 Stonelake Blvd. US 183 N to Loop 1 (Mo-Pac Expwy), 1.5 mi n to Braker Ln; on northwest corner. Int corridors. **Pets:** Medium. $75 one-time fee/room. Service with restrictions, crate.
[A$K] [SD] [✕] [⬚M] [⬚] [✆] [⬛] [▭] [⇌] [⊠]

**⬥⬥⬥ ▼▼▼ ▼▼▼ Hyatt Regency Austin** LH
(512) 477-1234. **$129-$209.** 208 Barton Springs Rd. At south end of Congress Bridge; on south bank of Town Lake. Int corridors. **Pets:** Accepted.
[SAVE] [✕] [⬚M] [⬚] [✆] [⬛] [▭] [⊞] [⇌] [⊠]

**⬥⬥⬥ ▼▼▼ ▼▼▼ La Quinta Inn & Suites** SH
(512) 246-2800. **$84-$105.** 150 Parker Dr. I-35, exit 250, on west frontage road. Int corridors. **Pets:** Medium. Service with restrictions.
[SAVE] [✕] [⬚M] [⬚] [✆] [⬛] [▭] [⇌]

**⬥⬥⬥ ▼▼▼ ▼▼▼ La Quinta Inn & Suites Austin (Airport)** SH
(512) 386-6800. **$76-$92.** 7625 E Ben White Blvd. I-35, exit 230B (Ben White Blvd/SR 71), 3.8 mi e. Int corridors. **Pets:** Medium. Service with restrictions.
[SAVE] [✕] [⬚M] [⬚] [✆] [⬛] [▭] [⇌]

**⬥⬥⬥ ▼▼▼ ▼▼▼ La Quinta Inn & Suites Austin (Mopac North)** SH
(512) 832-2121. **$87-$97.** 11901 N Mo-Pac Expwy. US 183, 2 mi n on Loop 1 (Mo-Pac Expwy) to Duval exit. Int corridors. **Pets:** Medium. Service with restrictions.
[SAVE] [✕] [⬚M] [⬚] [✆] [⬛] [▭] [⇌]

**▼▼▼▼ La Quinta Inn & Suites Austin (Southwest at Mopac)** SH
(512) 899-3000. **$108-$136.** 4424 S Loop 1 (Mo-Pac Expwy). Jct Loop 1 (Mo-Pac Expwy), US 290 and SR 71 E, on southbound frontage road. Int corridors. **Pets:** Medium. Service with restrictions.
[A$K] [✕] [⬚] [⬛] [▭] [⇌]

**▼▼▼▼ La Quinta Inn Austin (Capitol)** SH
(512) 476-1166. **$97-$115.** 300 E 11 St. Just e of state capitol building. Ext/int corridors. **Pets:** Medium. Service with restrictions.
[A$K] [✕] [⬚] [⬛] [▭] [⇌]

**⬥⬥⬥ ▼▼▼ ▼▼▼ La Quinta Inn Austin (Highland Mall)** SH
(512) 459-4381. **$73-$83.** 5812 I-35 N. I-35, exit 238A, on west frontage road. Ext corridors. **Pets:** Medium. Service with restrictions.
[SAVE] [✕] [⬚] [⬛] [▭] [⇌]

**⬥⬥⬥ ▼▼▼ ▼▼▼ La Quinta Inn Austin (I-35 South/Ben White)** SH
(512) 443-1774. **$62-$73.** 4200 I-35 S. I-35, exit 231 (St. Edwards/ Woodward Ave) southbound; exit 230 northbound, just s of jct I-35, US 290 and SR 71, on frontage road. Ext corridors. **Pets:** Medium. Service with restrictions.
[SAVE] [✕] [⬚M] [⬚] [⬛] [▭] [⇌]

**▼▼▼▼ La Quinta Inn Austin (Oltorf)** SH ✣
(512) 447-6661. **$79-$95.** 1603 E Oltorf Blvd. I-35, exit 232A (Oltorf Blvd), just s. Ext/int corridors. **Pets:** Medium. Service with restrictions.
[A$K] [✕] [⬚] [⬛] [▭] [⇌]

**⬥⬥⬥ ▼▼▼ ▼▼▼ The Mansion at Judge's Hill** SH ✣
(512) 495-1800. **$99-$395, 3 day notice.** 1900 Rio Grande. Jct Rio Grande and Martin Luther King Jr Blvd. Int corridors. **Pets:** Other species. Designated rooms.
[SAVE] [SD] [✕] [⊞]

**▼▼ Motel 6 Austin North-360** M
(512) 339-6161. **$39-$51.** 9420 N I-35. I-35, exit 241 (Rundberg St), just w. Ext corridors. **Pets:** Accepted.
[SD] [✕] [✆] [⇌]

**▼▼▼▼ Omni Austin Hotel & Suites** LH ✣
(512) 476-3700. **$149-$279.** 700 San Jacinto. 8th St and San Jacinto. Int corridors. **Pets:** Small. $50 one-time fee/room. Service with restrictions, crate.
[A$K] [SD] [✕] [⬚M] [⬚] [✆] [⬛] [▭] [⊞] [⇌] [⊠]

**⬥⬥⬥ ▼▼▼ ▼▼▼ Omni Austin Hotel Southpark** SH
(512) 448-2222. **$99-$199.** 4140 Governor's Row. I-35, exit 230B southbound; exit 230 northbound, on east frontage road. Int corridors. **Pets:** Small. $50 one-time fee/room.
[SAVE] [SD] [✕] [⬚M] [⬚] [✆] [⬛] [▭] [⇌] [⊠]

**▼▼▼▼ Park Plaza Austin** LH
(512) 451-5757. **$89-$159.** 6000 Middle Fiskville Rd. I-35, exit 238A, just off west frontage road. Int corridors. **Pets:** Accepted.
[✕] [⬚M] [⬚] [✆] [⬛] [▭] [⊞] [⇌]

**▼▼▼▼ Quality Inn Central** SH
(512) 452-4200. **$74-$84.** 909 E Koenig Ln. I-35, exit 238A, jct I-35 and US 290 on southwest corner. Ext corridors. **Pets:** Other species. $25 one-time fee/room. Service with restrictions, supervision.
[A$K] [SD] [✕] [⬛] [▭] [⇌]

**⬥⬥⬥ ▼▼▼ ▼▼▼ Ramada Inn Airport South** SH
(512) 447-0151. **$69-$89.** 1212 W Ben White Blvd. I-35, exit 231, 1 mi w to S First St exit, then 0.3 mi on north frontage road. Ext/int corridors. **Pets:** Accepted.
[SAVE] [SD] [✕] [⬛] [▭] [⊞] [⇌]

**▼▼▼▼ Ramada Limited Austin North** SH
(512) 836-0079. **$39-$110.** 9121 N I-35. I-35, exit 241 northbound; exit 240A southbound, on east frontage road. Int corridors. **Pets:** Medium. $10 daily fee/pet. Designated rooms, service with restrictions, supervision.
[A$K] [SD] [✕] [⬛] [▭] [⇌]

**▼▼▼ Red Lion Hotel Austin** SH
(512) 323-5466. **$69-$109.** 6121 I-35 N. I-35, exit 238A, on east frontage road. Int corridors. **Pets:** Accepted.
[A$K] [SD] [✕] [⬚] [⬛] [▭] [⊞] [⇌]

**▼▼▼▼ Red Roof Inn Austin North** M
(512) 835-2200. **$39-$52.** 8210 I-35 N. I-35, exit 241 northbound; exit 240A southbound, on west frontage road. Ext corridors. **Pets:** Accepted.
[✕] [⬚] [✆] [⊞] [⇌]

**▼▼▼▼ Red Roof Inn-Austin South** SH
(512) 448-0091. **$48-$59.** 4701 I-35 S. I-35, exit 230B (Ben White Blvd/SR 71) southbound; exit 229 (Stassney Rd) northbound, on northbound frontage road. Int corridors. **Pets:** Accepted.
[✕] [⬚M] [⬚] [✆] [⬛] [⇌]

**(AAA) ▼▼▼▼ Renaissance Austin Hotel** [LH] ❀
(512) 343-2626. **$139-$239.** 9721 Arboretum Blvd. Jct US 183 and Capital of Texas Hwy (SR 360); southwest corner. Int corridors. **Pets:** Other species. Service with restrictions, crate.

[SAVE] [S6] [✕] [&M] [🎜] [&'] [❒] [▣] [¶] [➔] [✕]

**▼▼▼▼ Residence Inn by Marriott Austin Airport/South** [SH]
(512) 912-1100. **$129-$159.** 4537 S I-35. I-35, exit 229 (Stassney Rd) southbound; exit 230 (Ben White Blvd/SR 71) northbound, on northbound frontage road. Int corridors. **Pets:** Small, other species. $50 one-time fee/room. Service with restrictions, supervision.

[ASK] [S6] [✕] [&'] [❒] [▣] [➔] [✕]

**▼▼▼▼ Residence Inn by Marriott-Austin North/Parmer Lane** [SH]
(512) 977-0544. **$159-$189.** 12401 N Lamar Blvd. I-35, exit 245, just w. Int corridors. **Pets:** Other species. $75 one-time fee/room. Service with restrictions.

[ASK] [S6] [✕] [&M] [🎜] [&'] [❒] [▣] [➔] [✕]

**(AAA) ▼▼▼ Rodeway Inn-University/Downtown** [M]
(512) 477-6395. **$59-$100.** 2900 I-35 N. I-35, exit 235B (University of Texas/LBJ Library) southbound; exit 236A (26th and 32nd sts) northbound; ne off lower level I-35, US 79 and SR 290. Ext corridors. **Pets:** Other species. $10 one-time fee/pet. Service with restrictions.

[SAVE] [S6] [✕] [&'] [❒] [▣] [➔]

**▼▼▼▼ Staybridge Suites Hotel** [SH]
(512) 349-0888. **$102-$169.** 10201 Stonelake Blvd. Jct US 183 and Capital of Texas Hwy (SR 360); northwest corner. Int corridors. **Pets:** Accepted.

[ASK] [S6] [✕] [&M] [🎜] [&'] [❒] [▣] [➔] [✕]

**▼▼ Studio 6-Austin Midtown #6033** [M]
(512) 458-5453. **$45-$57.** 937 Camino La Costa. I-35, exit 238A, on east frontage road. Ext corridors. **Pets:** Accepted.

[S6] [✕] [🎜] [&'] [❒] [▣]

**▼▼ Studio 6-Northwest #6032** [M]
(512) 258-3556. **$45-$57.** 11901 Pavillon Blvd. US 183, exit Oak Knoll westbound; exit Duval/Balcones Woods eastbound, on eastbound frontage road. Ext corridors. **Pets:** Accepted.

[S6] [✕] [🎜] [❒] [▣]

**▼▼▼ Summerfield Suites by Wyndham-Northwest Austin** [SH]
(512) 452-9391. **$99-$104.** 7685 Northcross Dr. Loop 1 (Mo-Pac Expwy), exit Anderson Rd, just e to Northcross Dr, then just s. Ext corridors. **Pets:** Accepted.

[ASK] [✕] [🎜] [❒] [▣] [➔]

**(AAA) ▼▼▼ Super 8 Austin North** [SH]
(512) 339-1300. **$52-$62.** 8128 N I-35. I-35, exit 241, on west frontage road. Int corridors. **Pets:** Small, other species. $75 deposit/room. Service with restrictions, supervision.

[SAVE] [S6] [✕] [🎜] [❒] [▣] [➔]

**(AAA) ▼▼▼ Super 8 Central** [M]
(512) 472-8331. **$50-$200.** 1201 N I-35. I-35, exit 234, at 12th St. Ext corridors. **Pets:** Accepted.

[SAVE] [✕] [&'] [❒] [➔]

**▼▼ The Woodward Hotel & Conference Center** [SH]
(512) 448-2444. **$59-$89.** 3401 I-35 S. I-35, exit 231 (Woodward St) southbound; exit 230 (Ben White Blvd/SR 71) northbound, on northbound frontage road. Ext/int corridors. **Pets:** Accepted.

[ASK] [S6] [✕] [🎜] [❒] [▣] [¶] [➔] [✕]

# BANDERA

**(AAA) ▼▼▼ Bandera Lodge Motel** [SH]
(830) 796-3093. **$75-$110, 7 day notice.** 700 Hwy 16 S. 1 mi s on SR 16; 7 mi s of jct SR 173. Ext corridors. **Pets:** Accepted.

[SAVE] [S6] [✕] [❒] [¶] [➔]

# BASTROP

**▼▼▼ Days Inn Bastrop** [SH]
(512) 321-1157. **$60-$75.** 4102 Hwy 71 E. On SR 71, 2 mi e of river at Loop 150 E. Ext corridors. **Pets:** Small. $25 one-time fee/pet. Designated rooms, service with restrictions, supervision.

[ASK] [S6] [✕] [&'] [❒] [▣] [➔]

**▼▼▼ Holiday Inn Express Hotel & Suites** [SH]
(512) 321-1900. **$59-$99.** 491 Agnes St. Jct SR 71/95, 2 mi w. Int corridors. **Pets:** Other species. $25 one-time fee/pet. Designated rooms, service with restrictions, supervision.

[ASK] [S6] [✕] [&M] [&'] [❒] [▣] [➔]

# BEAUMONT

**▼▼▼ Best Western Jefferson Inn** [SH]
(409) 842-0037. **$55-$65.** 1610 I-10 S. I-10, exit 851 (College St), westbound service road; I-10, exit s of jct US 90. Ext corridors. **Pets:** Other species. Service with restrictions, supervision.

[ASK] [S6] [✕] [🎜] [❒] [▣] [➔]

**▼▼▼ Days Inn Beaumont Inn** [SH]
(409) 898-8150. **$52-$59.** 2155 N 11th St. I-10, exit 853B (11th St), just n. Ext corridors. **Pets:** Other species. Service with restrictions.

[ASK] [S6] [✕] [❒] [▣] [➔]

**(AAA) ▼▼▼▼ Holiday Inn Beaumont Midtown** [SH]
(409) 892-2222. **$79.** 2095 N 11th St. I-10, exit 853B (11th St), just n. Int corridors. **Pets:** Accepted.

[SAVE] [S6] [✕] [&M] [🎜] [&'] [❒] [▣] [¶] [➔]

**(AAA) ▼▼▼▼ Holiday Inn Plaza** [LH]
(409) 842-5995. **$119.** 3950 I-10 S. I-10, exit 848 (Walden Rd), just n. Int corridors. **Pets:** Large, other species. $10 daily fee/room. Service with restrictions, crate.

[SAVE] [S6] [✕] [🎜] [&'] [❒] [▣] [¶] [➔] [✕]

**▼▼▼ Howard Johnson Express Inn & Suites** [SH]
(409) 832-0666. **$70-$120.** 2615 I-10 E. I-10, exit 853B (11th St). Ext corridors. **Pets:** Small. $20 daily fee/pet. Service with restrictions, supervision.

[ASK] [S6] [✕] [&M] [❒] [▣] [➔]

**▼▼▼▼ La Quinta Inn & Suites** [SH]
(409) 842-0002. **$89-$99.** 5820 Walden Rd. I-10, exit 848, just n. Int corridors. **Pets:** Small. $25 deposit/pet. Service with restrictions, supervision.

[ASK] [S6] [✕] [&M] [❒] [▣] [➔]

**▼▼▼ La Quinta Inn Beaumont (Midtown)** [SH]
(409) 838-9991. **$75-$85.** 220 I-10 N. I-10, exit 852B (Calder Ave) eastbound; exit 852A (Laurel Ave) westbound, on eastbound service road. Ext corridors. **Pets:** Medium. Service with restrictions.

[ASK] [✕] [🎜] [&'] [❒] [▣] [➔]

# BEDFORD

**▼▼▼ Courtyard by Marriott** [SH]
(817) 545-2202. **$59-$119.** 2201 W Airport Frwy. SR 121/183, exit Central Dr, just n to Plaza Dr. Int corridors. **Pets:** Accepted.

[ASK] [S6] [✕] [&M] [🎜] [&'] [❒] [▣] [¶] [➔]

**▼▼▼ La Quinta Inn Ft. Worth (Bedford/DFW Airport)** [SH]
(817) 267-5200. **$66-$76.** 1450 Airport Frwy. SR 121/183, 0.3 mi e of jct Bedford Rd/Forest Ridge Dr exit. Ext corridors. **Pets:** Medium. Service with restrictions.

[ASK] [✕] [🎜] [❒] [▣] [➔]

**▼▼ Super 8 Motel-Bedford** [SH]
(817) 545-8108. **$55-$59.** 1800 Airport Frwy. SR 183 at Bedford Rd, exit Forest Ridge Dr. Int corridors. **Pets:** Accepted.

[ASK] [S6] [✕] [&M] [&'] [❒]

# BEEVILLE

▼▼ ▼▼ **Atrium Inn** 🆂🅷
(361) 358-4000. **$45-$55.** 400 S US 181 Bypass. 0.3 mi s of jct US 59 and 181. Ext corridors. **Pets:** Accepted.
[ASK] [S🅾] [✕] [🛢] [🔊]

# BELTON

▲▲▲ ▼▼ ▼▼ **Budget Host Inn** 🆂🅷
(254) 939-0744. **$50-$75, 3 day notice.** 1520 S I-35. I-35, exit 292 southbound; exit 293A northbound. Ext corridors. **Pets:** Accepted.
[SAVE] [S🅾] [✕] [🛢] [🔊]

▼▼ ▼▼ **Ramada Limited** 🆂🅷
(254) 939-3745. **$65-$75.** 1102 E 2nd Ave. I-35, exit 294A southbound; exit 294B northbound. Ext corridors. **Pets:** Small. Service with restrictions, crate.
[ASK] [S🅾] [✕] [🛢] [🔊]

▼▼ ▼▼ **River Forest Inn** 🆂🅷
(254) 939-5711. **$55-$95.** 1414 E 6th Ave. I-35, exit 294B. Ext corridors. **Pets:** Very small, dogs only. $10 deposit/pet. No service, supervision.
[ASK] [S🅾] [✕] [🛢] [🔊]

# BENBROOK

▲▲▲ ▼▼▼▼ **Best Western Winscott Inn & Suites** 🆂🅷
(817) 249-0076. **$70-$195.** 590 Winscott Rd. I-20, exit 429B. Int corridors. **Pets:** Small. $10 daily fee/pet. Service with restrictions, supervision.
[SAVE] [S🅾] [✕] [🔑] [🛢] [🔊] [🔊]

▼▼ **Motel 6-4051** 🆂🅷
(817) 249-8885. **$52-$58.** 8601 Benbrook Blvd (Hwy 377 S). I-20, exit 429A, 0.7 mi s. Int corridors. **Pets:** Accepted.
[ASK] [✕] [🔊] [🔑] [🛢] [🔊]

# BIG SPRING

▲▲▲ ▼▼ ▼▼ **Best Western Plaza Inn** 🆂🅷
(432) 264-7086. **$59-$99.** 300 Tulane Ave. I-20, exit 179, just s. Ext corridors. **Pets:** Accepted.
[SAVE] [S🅾] [✕] [🔊] [🔑] [🛢] [🔊] [🔊]

▲▲▲ ▼▼ ▼▼ **Comfort Inn** 🅼
(432) 267-4553. **$55-$99.** 2900 E I-20. I-20, exit 179. Ext corridors. **Pets:** Accepted.
[SAVE] [✕] [🛢] [🔊] [🔊]

▲▲▲ ▼▼ ▼▼ **Super 8 Motel** 🅼
(432) 267-1601. **$60-$66, 3 day notice.** 700 W I-20. I-20, exit 177, just n. Ext corridors. **Pets:** Medium. $6 one-time fee/room. Service with restrictions, supervision.
[SAVE] [S🅾] [✕] [🔊] [🛢] [🔊] [🔊]

# BOERNE

▲▲▲ ▼▼ ▼▼ **Best Western Texas Country Inn** 🆂🅷
(830) 249-9791. **$72-$109.** 35150 I-10 W. I-10, exit 540 (SR 46), westbound access road. Ext corridors. **Pets:** Medium. $20 one-time fee/pet. Service with restrictions, supervision.
[SAVE] [S🅾] [✕] [🛢] [🔊] [🔊]

# BONHAM

▲▲▲ ▼▼ **5 Star Inn** 🅼 ❀
(903) 583-3121. **$45-$50.** 1515 Old Ector Rd. Jct SR 56 W and 121 S. Ext corridors. **Pets:** Large. $25 deposit/room. Designated rooms, service with restrictions, supervision.
[SAVE] [S🅾] [✕] [🛢] [🔊] [🔊]

# BORGER

▲▲▲ ▼▼▼▼ **Best Western Borger Inn** 🆂🅷
(806) 274-7050. **$70-$85.** 206 S Cedar. Jct SR 136 and 207, just n. Int corridors. **Pets:** Medium. $10 one-time fee/pet. Service with restrictions, supervision.
[SAVE] [S🅾] [✕] [🔑] [🛢] [🔊] [🔊]

# BOWIE

▲▲▲ ▼▼ ▼▼ **Days Inn** 🆂🅷
(940) 872-5426. **$50-$65, 7 day notice.** 2436 S US 287. Jct SR 59. Ext corridors. **Pets:** $5 daily fee/pet. Designated rooms, service with restrictions, supervision.
[SAVE] [S🅾] [✕] [🛢] [🔊]

▲▲▲ ▼▼ **Park's Inn** 🅼
(940) 872-1111. **$46-$60.** 708 W Wise St. 0.5 mi n of jct SR 59; downtown. Ext corridors. **Pets:** Other species. $5 daily fee/pet. Service with restrictions, supervision.
[SAVE] [S🅾] [✕] [🛢] [🔊]

# BRADY

▲▲▲ ▼▼ ▼▼ **Best Western Brady Inn** 🆂🅷
(325) 597-3997. **$85.** 2200 S Bridge St. 1.1 mi s on US 87/377. Ext corridors. **Pets:** Accepted.
[SAVE] [S🅾] [✕] [🛢] [🔊] [🔊]

▲▲▲ ▼▼ ▼▼ **Days Inn** 🅼
(325) 597-0789. **$49-$79, 5 day notice.** 2108 S Bridge St. 1 mi s on US 87/377 at US 190. Ext corridors. **Pets:** Accepted.
[SAVE] [S🅾] [✕] [🛢] [🔊] [🔊]

# BRENHAM

▼▼▼▼ **Comfort Suites** 🆂🅷
(979) 421-8100. **$69-$149.** 2350 S Day St. US 290, exit SR 36 S, just n on Business Rt SR 36. Int corridors. **Pets:** Accepted.
[ASK] [S🅾] [✕] [🛢] [🔊] [🔊]

# BROWNFIELD

▼▼ ▼▼ **Best Western Caprock Inn** 🆂🅷
(806) 637-9471. **$69.** 321 Lubbock Rd. Jct US 385 and 82, 2 blks n. Ext corridors. **Pets:** Accepted.
[ASK] [S🅾] [✕] [🔑] [🛢] [🔊]

# BROWNSVILLE

▼▼▼▼ **Hawthorn Suites** 🆂🅷
(956) 574-6900. **$89-$129.** 3759 North Expwy. US 77, exit McAllen Rd; on southbound access lane. Int corridors. **Pets:** Small, other species. $125 one-time fee/room. Service with restrictions, crate.
[ASK] [S🅾] [✕] [🔊] [🔊] [✕]

▲▲▲ ▼▼ ▼▼ **Red Roof Inn** 🅼
(956) 504-2300. **$49-$79.** 2377 North Expwy. US 83, exit FM 802, just s. Ext corridors. **Pets:** Small, other species. $75 deposit/room. Service with restrictions, supervision.
[SAVE] [S🅾] [✕] [🔑] [🛢] [🔊] [🔊]

▼▼▼▼ **Residence Inn by Marriott** 🆂🅷 ❀
(956) 350-8100. **$125-$154.** 3975 North Expwy. US 77 and 83, exit McAllen Rd. Int corridors. **Pets:** Medium. $75 one-time fee/pet. Service with restrictions, crate.
[ASK] [S🅾] [✕] [🔊] [🔑] [🛢] [🔊] [🔊] [✕]

# BROWNWOOD

▼▼ ▼▼ **Americas Best Value Inn** 🅼
(325) 646-3511. **$59-$79.** 410 E Commerce St. On US 67/84/377; just n of jct Main Ave. Ext corridors. **Pets:** Accepted.
[ASK] [S🅾] [✕] [🔑] [🛢] [🔊] [🔊]

**(AAA) ▼▼▼ Days Inn-Brownwood SH**
(325) 646-2551. **$59-$79.** 515 E Commerce St. On US 67/84/377, 0.4
mi n of jct Main Ave. Ext corridors. **Pets:** $15 one-time fee/room. Service
with restrictions.
[SAVE] [S6] [X] [8] [🔲] [🏊]

## BURLESON

**(AAA) ▼▼▼ Comfort Suites SH**
(817) 426-6666. **$79-$89.** 321 S Burleson Blvd. I-35W, exit 34 southbound, 2 mi s to exit 36, U-turn; exit 36 northbound, on northbound
access road. Int corridors. **Pets:** Small. $10 daily fee/pet. Designated
rooms, service with restrictions, supervision.
[SAVE] [S6] [X] [&M] [&] [8] [🔲] [🏊]

**(AAA) ▼▼▼ Days Inn SH**
(817) 447-1111. **$65.** 329 S Burleson Blvd. I-35W, exit 34 southbound,
2 mi s to exit 36, U-turn; exit 36 northbound, on northbound access
road. Ext corridors. **Pets:** Other species. $5 daily fee/pet.
[SAVE] [S6] [X] [8] [🏊]

## CANTON

**(AAA) ▼▼▼ Best Western Canton Inn SH**
(903) 567-6591. **$59-$79.** 2251 N Trade Days Blvd. Jct I-20 and SR 19,
exit 527. Ext corridors. **Pets:** Small. $5 daily fee/pet. Service with restric-
tions, crate.
[SAVE] [S6] [X] [8] [🔲] [🏊]

**▼▼ Super 8 Motel SH**
(903) 567-6567. **$52-$175, 3 day notice.** 17350 I-20. I-20, exit 527. Ext
corridors. **Pets:** $10 daily fee/pet. Service with restrictions, supervision.
[ASK] [S6] [X] [8] [🔲] [🏊]

## CANYON

**(AAA) ▼▼▼ Holiday Inn Express Hotel & Suites SH**
(806) 655-4445. **$79-$196.** 2901 4th Ave. I-27, exit 106, 2 mi w. Int
corridors. **Pets:** Other species. $10 one-time fee/room. Designated rooms,
service with restrictions, supervision.
[SAVE] [S6] [X] [&M] [&] [8] [🔲] [🏊]

## CEDAR PARK

**▼▼ Comfort Inn SH**
(512) 259-1810. **$70-$90.** 300 E Whitestone Blvd. I-35, exit 256, 8 mi w
on FM 1431. Int corridors. **Pets:** Other species. $10 daily fee/pet. No
service, supervision.
[ASK] [S6] [X] [&M] [&] [8] [🔲] [🏊]

## CENTER

**▼▼ Best Western Center Inn SH**
(936) 598-3384. **$51-$70.** 1005 Hurst St. On US 96, jct SR 87. Ext
corridors. **Pets:** Small. $10 daily fee/pet, $25 one-time fee/pet. Designated
rooms, service with restrictions, supervision.
[ASK] [S6] [X] [8] [🔲] [🏊]

## CHILDRESS

**(AAA) ▼▼ Best Western Childress M**
(940) 937-6353. **$74-$79, 14 day notice.** 1801 Ave F NW (Hwy 287).
On US 287, just s of jct US 62/83. Ext corridors. **Pets:** Medium, other
species. $35 daily fee/pet. Service with restrictions, supervision.
[SAVE] [S6] [X] [8] [🔲] [🏊]

**▼▼ Comfort Inn SH**
(940) 937-6363. **$79-$99.** 1804 Ave F NW (Hwy 287). On US 287, just
s of jct US 62/83. Ext corridors. **Pets:** $20 one-time fee/pet. No service,
supervision.
[ASK] [S6] [X] [&M] [📶] [8] [🔲] [🏊]

**(AAA) ▼▼▼ Days Inn SH**
(940) 937-0622. **$65-$75.** 2220 Ave F (Hwy 287). 1.8 mi w on US 287
from jct US 62/83. Int corridors. **Pets:** Accepted.
[SAVE] [S6] [X] [&] [8] [🏊]

**(AAA) ▼▼▼ Econo Lodge SH**
(940) 937-3695. **$48-$65.** 1612 Ave F NW, Hwy 287. On US 287, just
s of jct US 62/83. Ext corridors. **Pets:** Small, other species. $25 deposit/
pet, $10 daily fee/pet, $10 one-time fee/pet. Supervision.
[SAVE] [S6] [X] [🔲]

**(AAA) ▼▼▼ Super 8 Motel Childress M** 🐾
(940) 937-8825. **$65-$90.** 411 Ave F NE (Hwy 287 S). Jct US 83/287,
1.5 mi e. Ext corridors. **Pets:** Other species. $10 daily fee/pet. Designated
rooms, service with restrictions, supervision.
[SAVE] [S6] [X] [&] [8] [🔲] [🏊]

## CISCO

**▼▼ Best Western Inn Cisco M**
(254) 442-3735. **$69-$74.** 1898 Hwy 206 W. I-20, exit 330. Ext corridors. **Pets:** Accepted.
[ASK] [S6] [X] [8] [🔲] [🏊]

## CLARENDON

**▼▼▼ Best Western American Inn SH**
(806) 874-0160. **$80-$99.** 902 W 2nd St. Jct US 287 and SR 70. Int
corridors. **Pets:** Accepted.
[ASK] [X] [&M] [&] [8] [🔲] [🏊]

**(AAA) ▼▼▼ Western Skies Motel M**
(806) 874-3501. **$49-$99.** 800 W 2nd S. 0.5 mi nw on US 287 and SR
70. Ext corridors. **Pets:** $5 daily fee/pet. Designated rooms, service with
restrictions, supervision.
[SAVE] [S6] [X] [8] [🏊]

## CLAUDE

**(AAA) ▼▼ L A Motel M**
(806) 226-4981. **$35-$50, 5 day notice.** Hwy 287/200 E 1st St. 0.3 mi
s. Ext corridors. **Pets:** Medium. $5 one-time fee/pet. Designated rooms, no
service, supervision.
[SAVE] [S6] [X] [8] [🔲] [🍴]

## CLEBURNE

**▼▼ Budget Host Inn-Sagamar Inn M**
(817) 556-3631. **$75-$85.** 2107 N Main St. US 67, exit SR 174 (Main
St), just e. Ext corridors. **Pets:** Medium, dogs only. $10 daily fee/pet.
Service with restrictions, supervision.
[ASK] [S6] [X] [8] [🔲] [🏊]

**▼▼▼ Comfort Inn SH**
(817) 641-4702. **$85-$125.** 2117 N Main St. On SR 174, just s of jct US
67. Int corridors. **Pets:** Medium. $10 daily fee/room. Designated rooms,
service with restrictions, supervision.
[ASK] [S6] [X] [&M] [📶] [&] [8] [🔲] [🏊]

## CLUTE

**(AAA) ▼▼▼ Best Western Clute Inn & Suites SH**
(979) 388-0055. **$79-$139.** 900 Hwy 332. Just w of jct SR 288. Int
corridors. **Pets:** Very small. $15 daily fee/pet. Service with restrictions,
supervision.
[SAVE] [S6] [X] [&] [8] [🔲] [🏊]

**(AAA) ▼▼▼ La Quinta Inn Clute/Lake Jackson M**
(979) 265-7461. **$73-$83.** 1126 Hwy 332 W. On SR 288/332, just w of
jct Business Rt SR 288. Ext corridors. **Pets:** Medium. Service with
restrictions.
[SAVE] [X] [📶] [8] [🔲] [🏊]

**(AAA) ▼▼▼ Mainstay Suites Clute/Lake Jackson SH**
(979) 388-9300. **$99-$139.** 1003 W Hwy 332. Just w of jct SR 288. Int
corridors. **Pets:** Small. $100 deposit/room. Service with restrictions, super-
vision.
[SAVE] [X] [8] [🔲] [🏊]

# COLLEGE STATION

**▼▼ ◈◈ Clarion Hotel College Station** 🆂🅷
(979) 693-1736. **$59-$199.** 1503 S Texas Ave. 1.3 mi s of jct CR 60. Int corridors. **Pets:** Small. $25 one-time fee/pet. Service with restrictions.
Ⓐ🆂🅺 🆂🔟 ⊠ 🕮 🛢 🖵 🍽 ⊯

**▼▼▼▼ Hilton College Station and Conference Center** 🅻🅷
(979) 693-7500. **$99-$259.** 801 University Dr E. SR 6, exit University Dr, 1.1 mi w. Int corridors. **Pets:** Small. No service, crate.
⊠ 🆔 🛢 🖵 🍽 ⊯

**◈◈◈ ▼▼ Howard Johnson** 🆂🅷 🐾
(979) 693-6810. **$55-$140.** 3702 Hwy 6. SR 6 S, exit Rock Prairie Rd. Ext corridors. **Pets:** Medium. $10 daily fee/pet. Service with restrictions, crate.
🆂🅰🆅🅴 🆂🔟 ⊠ 🛢 🖵 ⊯

**◈◈◈ ▼▼▼▼ La Quinta Inn College Station** 🆂🅷
(979) 696-7777. **$74-$104.** 607 Texas Ave. Just s on jct SR 60/SR 6 business route to Live Oak St, then just e. Ext corridors. **Pets:** Medium. No service.
🆂🅰🆅🅴 ⊠ 🛢 🖵 ⊯

**◈◈◈ ▼▼ Manor House Inn** 🆂🅷
(979) 764-9540. **$65-$125, 3 day notice.** 2504 Texas Ave S. 2.4 mi s of jct SR 60. Ext corridors. **Pets:** $40 daily fee/pet. Designated rooms, service with restrictions, crate.
🆂🅰🆅🅴 🆂🔟 ⊠ 🛢 🖵 ⊯

**◈◈◈ ▼▼ Ramada Inn** 🆂🅷
(979) 693-9891. **$69-$125, 3 day notice.** 1502 Texas Ave S. 1.3 mi s of jct SR 60. Int corridors. **Pets:** Accepted.
🆂🅰🆅🅴 🆂🔟 ⊠ 🛢 🖵 🍽 ⊯

**▼▼▼▼ Super 8 Motel-College Station** 🅼
(979) 846-8800. **$70-$125.** 301 Texas Ave. Just n of jct SR 60. Int corridors. **Pets:** Accepted.
Ⓐ🆂🅺 🆂🔟 ⊠ 🎦 🆔 🆔

**▼▼▼▼ TownePlace Suites By Marriott** 🆂🅷 🐾
(979) 260-8500. **$89-$131.** 1300 E University Dr. SR 6, exit University Dr, 1 mi w. Ext corridors. **Pets:** Other species. $75 one-time fee/room. Service with restrictions.
⊠ 🎦 🆔 🛢 🖵 ⊯

# COLORADO CITY

**▼▼ ▼▼ Americas Best Value Inn** 🅼
(325) 728-5217. **$44-$52.** 2310 Hickory St. I-20, exit 216, just s. Ext/int corridors. **Pets:** Accepted.
Ⓐ🆂🅺 🆂🔟 ⊠ 🛢 🖵 ⊯

# COLUMBUS

**◈◈◈ ▼▼▼ Country Hearth Inn** 🆂🅷
(979) 732-6293. **$80-$150.** 2436 Hwy 71 S. I-10, exit 696 (SR 71). Ext corridors. **Pets:** Small, dogs only. $15 daily fee/room. Designated rooms, service with restrictions, supervision.
🆂🅰🆅🅴 ⊠ 🛢 🖵 ⊯

**◈◈◈ ▼▼▼▼ Holiday Inn Express Hotel & Suites** 🆂🅷
(979) 733-9300. **$89.** 4321 I-10. I-10, exit 696 (SR 71), just w on westbound service road. Int corridors. **Pets:** $10 one-time fee/pet. Service with restrictions, supervision.
🆂🅰🆅🅴 ⊠ 🎦 🆔 🖵 ⊯

# CONWAY

**◈◈◈ ▼▼ ▼▼ Budget Host S & S Motel** 🅼
(806) 537-5111. **$49-$50.** I-40 & SR 207. I-40, exit 96 (SR 207), 0.3 mi w on southbound access road. Ext corridors. **Pets:** Accepted.
🆂🅰🆅🅴 🆂🔟 ⊠ 🍽

# COPPERAS COVE

**▼▼▼▼ Howard Johnson Express Inn** 🆂🅷
(254) 547-2345. **$60-$80.** 302 W US 190. On US 190, jct Georgetown Rd, 0.4 mi w of jct US 190 and SR 116. Ext corridors. **Pets:** Accepted.
Ⓐ🆂🅺 🆂🔟 ⊠ 🛢 🖵 ⊯

# CORPUS CHRISTI

**◈◈◈ ▼▼▼▼ Best Western Garden Inn** 🅼
(361) 241-6675. **$74-$139.** 11217 I-37. I-37, exit 11B (Violet Rd), on southbound access road. Ext corridors. **Pets:** Other species. $5 daily fee/pet. Service with restrictions, supervision.
🆂🅰🆅🅴 ⊠ 🛢 🖵 ⊯ ⊠

**◈◈◈ ▼▼▼▼ Best Western Marina Grand Hotel** 🆂🅷
(361) 883-5111. **$79-$195.** 300 N Shoreline Dr. Center of downtown. Int corridors. **Pets:** Medium. $25 one-time fee/room. Designated rooms, service with restrictions, supervision.
🆂🅰🆅🅴 🆂🔟 ⊠ 🛢 🖵 ⊯

**▼▼▼▼ Christy Estate Suites** 🅲🅾
(361) 854-1091. **$109-$169.** 3942 Holly Rd. SR 358, exit Weber Rd, 0.5 mi s. Ext/int corridors. **Pets:** Small. $500 deposit/room, $45 one-time fee/room. Designated rooms, service with restrictions, crate.
Ⓐ🆂🅺 🆂🔟 ⊠ 🛢 🖵 ⊯

**◈◈◈ ▼▼ ◈◈ Clarion Hotel** 🆂🅷
(361) 883-6161. **$74-$120.** 5224 I-37 (Navigation Blvd). I-37, exit 3A (Navigation Blvd), on northbound access lane. Ext corridors. **Pets:** Small. $30 one-time fee/room. Designated rooms, service with restrictions, supervision.
🆂🅰🆅🅴 🆂🔟 ⊠ 🛢 🖵 ⊯

**▼▼ ▼▼ Days Inn-Airport** 🆂🅷
(361) 888-8599. **$40-$130.** 901 Navigation Blvd. I-37, exit 3A (Navigation Blvd), just w. Ext corridors. **Pets:** Small, dogs only. $15 daily fee/pet. Designated rooms, service with restrictions, supervision.
Ⓐ🆂🅺 🆂🔟 ⊠ 🎦 🛢 🖵 🍽 ⊯

**▼▼▼▼ Days Inn Corpus Christi South** 🆂🅷
(361) 854-0005. **$69-$189.** 2838 S Padre Island Dr. On SR 358 westbound access road, 0.4 mi w, exit Kostoryz Rd. Ext corridors. **Pets:** Accepted.
Ⓐ🆂🅺 🆂🔟 ⊠ 🛢 🖵 ⊯

**▼▼▼▼ Drury Inn-Corpus Christi** 🆂🅷
(361) 289-8200. **$77-$133.** 2021 N Padre Island Dr. I-37, exit SR 358, just se at Leopard St. Int corridors. **Pets:** Accepted.
⊠ 🎦 🛢 🖵 ⊯

**◈◈◈ ▼▼▼▼ Holiday Inn-Airport and Conference Center** 🅻🅷
(361) 289-5100. **$99.** 5549 Leopard St. Jct SR 358 and Leopard St, 5.5 mi w. Int corridors. **Pets:** Accepted.
🆂🅰🆅🅴 🆂🔟 ⊠ 🎦 🛢 🖵 🍽 ⊯

**▼▼▼▼ Holiday Inn-Emerald Beach** 🅻🅷
(361) 883-5731. **$130-$189.** 1102 S Shoreline Blvd. 1.5 mi s on bay from downtown marina. Ext/int corridors. **Pets:** Accepted.
Ⓐ🆂🅺 🆂🔟 ⊠ 🅲🅼 🎦 🆔 🛢 🖵 🍽 ⊯ ⊠

**▼▼▼▼ Homewood Suites by Hilton** 🆂🅷
(361) 854-1331. **$89-$149, 14 day notice.** 5202 Crosstown Expwy. I-37, exit SR 358 E (Greenwood), 0.6 mi e. Int corridors. **Pets:** Accepted.
Ⓐ🆂🅺 🆂🔟 ⊠ 🎦 🆔 🛢 🖵 ⊯ ⊠

**▼▼▼▼ La Quinta Inn Corpus Christi (North)** 🆂🅷
(361) 888-5721. **$69-$100.** 5155 I-37 N. I-37, exit 3A (Navigation Blvd), on southbound access road. Ext corridors. **Pets:** Medium. Service with restrictions.
Ⓐ🆂🅺 ⊠ 🎦 🛢 🖵 ⊯

**⟨AAA⟩ ◆◆◆ La Quinta Inn Corpus Christi (South) SH**
(361) 991-5730. **$104-$115.** 6225 S Padre Island Dr. SR 358 Expwy, exit Airline Rd. Ext corridors. **Pets:** Medium. Service with restrictions.
SAVE ⊠ 🐾 📶 💻 ⇌

**◆◆ Motel 6 #231 M**
(361) 289-9397. **$39-$53.** 845 Lantana St. I-37, exit 4B (Lantana St), on southbound access road. Ext corridors. **Pets:** Accepted.
🐾 ⊠ 🐾 ⇌

**◆◆ Motel 6 SPI Drive–413 SH**
(361) 991-8858. **$41-$57.** 8202 S Padre Island Dr. S Padre Island Dr at Paul Jones St. Ext corridors. **Pets:** Accepted.
🐾 ⊠ 🐾 ⇌

**⟨AAA⟩ ◆◆◆ Quality Inn Sandy Shores SH**
(361) 883-7456. **$59-$189, 3 day notice.** 3202 Surfside Blvd. 1 mi n on US 181; at north end of Harbor Bridge, exit Bridge St. Ext/int corridors. **Pets:** Small. $20 daily fee/pet. Service with restrictions, supervision.
SAVE 🐾 ⊠ 💻 ⇌

**⟨AAA⟩ ◆◆◆ Red Roof Inn Corpus Christi Airport M**
(361) 289-6925. **$42-$155.** 6301 I-37. I-37, exit 5 (Corn Products Rd), southbound access road. Ext corridors. **Pets:** Very small. $30 deposit/pet. Service with restrictions, supervision.
SAVE 🐾 ⊠ 🐾 📶 💻

**⟨AAA⟩ ◆◆◆ Surfside Condominium Apartments CO**
(361) 949-8128. **$130-$155, 3 day notice.** 15005 Windward Dr. Park Rd 22 on N Padre Island Dr, jct Whitecap Blvd, just e. Ext corridors. **Pets:** Medium. $15 daily fee/pet. Designated rooms, service with restrictions, crate.
SAVE 🐾 ⊠ 📶 💻 ⇌

## DALHART

**⟨AAA⟩ ◆◆◆ Best Western Nursanickel Motel SH**
(806) 244-5637. **$59-$79.** 102 Scott Ave (Hwy 87 S). Just s of jct US 54 and 87. Ext corridors. **Pets:** Small, dogs only. Service with restrictions, supervision.
SAVE 🐾 ⊠ 📶 💻 ⇌

**⟨AAA⟩ ◆◆ Budget Inn M**
(806) 244-4557. **$40-$69.** 415 Liberal St (Hwy 54). US 54, just e of US 87 and 385. Ext corridors. **Pets:** Accepted.
SAVE 🐾 ⊠ 📶

**⟨AAA⟩ ◆◆◆ Comfort Inn M**
(806) 249-8585. **$75-$120.** 1110 Hwy 54 E. 0.5 mi e of jct US 54 and 87. Ext corridors. **Pets:** Medium. Designated rooms, service with restrictions, supervision.
SAVE 🐾 ⊠ 📶 💻 ⇌

**◆◆◆ Holiday Inn Express SH**
(806) 249-1145. **$89-$149, 7 day notice.** 801 Liberal St (Hwy 54). 1 mi e of jct US 54 and 87. Int corridors. **Pets:** $250 one-time fee/room. Designated rooms, service with restrictions, supervision.
ASK ⊠ 📶 💻 ⇌

**⟨AAA⟩ ◆◆ Sands Motel M**
(806) 244-4568. **$30-$70.** 301 Liberal St (Hwy 54). On US 54, just e of US 87 and 385. Ext corridors. **Pets:** Small. Service with restrictions, supervision.
SAVE 🐾 ⊠ 📶 ⇌

**⟨AAA⟩ ◆◆ Super 8 Motel M**
(806) 249-8526. **$60-$65.** 403 Tanglewood Rd. Jct US 87/54, 0.5 mi e. Int corridors. **Pets:** Medium. $25 deposit/pet. Designated rooms, service with restrictions, supervision.
SAVE 🐾 ⊠ 📶

---

# DALLAS METROPOLITAN AREA

## ADDISON

**⟨AAA⟩ ◆◆◆ Comfort Inn Hotel by the Galleria SH**
(972) 701-0881. **$59-$89.** 14975 Landmark Blvd. Jct Belt Line Rd and Landmark Blvd, just s. Int corridors. **Pets:** Accepted.
SAVE 🐾 ⊠ 🐾M 📶 💻 ⇌

**◆◆◆ Comfort Suites by Choice Hotels SH**
(972) 503-6500. **$75-$80.** 4555 Belt Line Rd. Just ne of jct Midway and Belt Line rds. Int corridors. **Pets:** Accepted.
⊠ 🐾 🐾 📶 💻 ⇌

**◆◆◆ Homewood Suites by Hilton SH**
(972) 788-1342. **$89-$159.** 4451 Belt Line Rd. Just e of jct Belt Line and Midway rds. Ext/int corridors. **Pets:** Accepted.
ASK 🐾 ⊠ 🐾M 🐾 🐾 📶 💻 ⇌ 🐾

**◆◆◆ La Quinta Inn & Suites Dallas (Addison-Galleria Area) SH**
(972) 404-0004. **$95-$105.** 14925 Landmark Blvd. Jct Belt Line Rd and Landmark Blvd, just s. Int corridors. **Pets:** Medium. Service with restrictions.
ASK ⊠ 🐾M 🐾 🐾 📶 💻 ⇌

**◆◆◆ Summerfield Suites by Wyndham-Addison/North Dallas SH**
(972) 661-3113. **$95-$124.** 4900 Edwin Lewis Dr. Just n of jct Belt Line Rd and Quorum Dr to Edwin Lewis Dr, then just w. Ext/int corridors. **Pets:** Accepted.
ASK ⊠ 🐾M 🐾 📶 💻 ⇌ 🐾

## ALLEN

**⟨AAA⟩ ◆◆◆ AmeriHost Inn-Allen SH**
(972) 396-9494. **$84-$94.** 407 Central Expwy S. US 75, exit 33 (Bethany Dr). Int corridors. **Pets:** Medium, other species. $30 one-time fee/room. Service with restrictions, supervision.
SAVE 🐾 ⊠ 🐾 📶 💻 ⇌ 🐾

## CARROLLTON

**◆◆ Red Roof Inn-Carrollton M**
(972) 245-1700. **$39-$54.** 1720 S Broadway. I-35E, exit 442 (Valwood Pkwy), just ne. Ext corridors. **Pets:** Accepted.
⊠ 📶

## THE COLONY

**⟨AAA⟩ ◆◆◆ Comfort Suites SH**
(972) 668-5555. **$84-$90.** 4796 Memorial Dr. Just n of jct SR 121. Int corridors. **Pets:** Accepted.
SAVE 🐾 ⊠ 🐾M 📶 🐾 📶 💻 ⇌

## COMMERCE

**⟨AAA⟩ ◆◆◆ Holiday Inn Express Hotel & Suites SH**
(903) 886-4777. **$74-$94 (no credit cards).** 2207 Culver St. 0.9 mi e of jct SR 224, 24 and 50. Int corridors. **Pets:** Accepted.
SAVE 🐾 ⊠ 🐾M 🐾 📶 💻 ⇌

# DALLAS

**AAA ▼▼▼ AmeriSuites (Dallas/Near the Galleria) SH**
(972) 716-2001. **$89-$149.** 5229 Spring Valley Rd. Jct Dallas Pkwy, just e. Int corridors. **Pets:** Medium, other species. $10 daily fee/room. Service with restrictions, crate.
SAVE SÒ ✕ 🐾 ⌖ 🖬 📼 ➤

**AAA ▼▼▼ AmeriSuites (Dallas/Park Central) SH**
(972) 458-1224. **$119.** 12411 N Central Expwy. US 75, exit 8B (Coit Rd) northbound; exit 8 (Coit Rd), on southbound access road. Int corridors. **Pets:** Small. $10 daily fee/pet, $1.38 one-time fee/pet. Service with restrictions, supervision.
SAVE SÒ ✕ 🐾 ⌖ 🖬 📼 ➤

**▼▼▼ Baymont Inn & Suites SH**
(214) 350-5577. **$80.** 2370 W Northwest Hwy. I-35E, exit 436 Northwest Hwy (Loop 12), 0.8 mi e. Int corridors. **Pets:** Accepted.
ASK SÒ ✕ 🐾 ⌖ 🖬 📼 ➤

**AAA ▼▼ Best Western City Place Inn SH**
(214) 827-6080. **$59-$99.** 4150 N Central Expwy. US 75, exit 1B (Fitzhugh Ave) southbound; exit 2 (Fitzhugh Ave) northbound. Ext corridors. **Pets:** Small. $25 one-time fee/pet. Designated rooms, service with restrictions, supervision.
SAVE SÒ ✕ 🖬 📼 ➤

**▼▼ Best Western Dallas Telecom Area Suites SH**
(972) 669-0478. **$89-$149.** 13636 Goldmark Dr. US 75, exit 22 (Midpark Rd), just w. Ext/int corridors. **Pets:** Accepted.
ASK SÒ ✕ 🖬 📼 ➤

**▼▼▼ Candlewood Dallas Market Center SH**
(214) 631-3333. **$94-$189.** 7930 N Stemmons Frwy. I-35, exit 433B (Mockingbird Ln), just w. Int corridors. **Pets:** Small. $75 one-time fee/pet. Service with restrictions, crate.
ASK SÒ ✕ ⌖ 🖬 📼 ➤

**▼▼▼ Candlewood Suites-Dallas by the Galleria SH**
(972) 233-6888. **$79-$99.** 13939 Noel Rd. Jct Dallas Pkwy and Spring Valley, just e to Noel Rd, then just s. Int corridors. **Pets:** Accepted.
ASK SÒ ✕ 🐾M ⌖ 🖬 📼

**▼▼▼ Candlewood Suites Dallas North/Richardson SH**
(972) 669-9606. **$55-$75.** 12525 Greenville Ave. I-635, exit 18A (Greenville Ave), just n. Int corridors. **Pets:** Large. $75 one-time fee/pet. Service with restrictions.
ASK SÒ ✕ 🐾M ⌖ 🖬 📼

**▼▼▼ Comfort Inn & Suites Market Center SH**
(214) 461-2677. **$75-$140.** 7138 N Stemmons Frwy. I-35E, exit 433B (Mockingbird Ln) northbound; exit 432B (Commonwealth Dr) southbound, turn under freeway, 0.7 mi on north access road. Int corridors. **Pets:** Accepted.
ASK SÒ ✕ 🐾 ⌖ 🖬 📼

**▼▼▼ Country Inn & Suites Dallas Central SH**
(972) 907-9500. **$63-$81.** 13185 N Central Expwy. US 75 N, exit 22 (Midpark Rd). Int corridors. **Pets:** Accepted.
ASK SÒ ✕ 🐾 ⌖ 🖬 📼 ➤

**▼▼▼ Crowne Plaza Hotel and Resort Dallas Market Center LH ❀**
(214) 630-8500. **$99-$149.** 7050 Stemmons Frwy. I-35E, exit 433B northbound; exit 432B southbound. Int corridors. **Pets:** Other species. $25 one-time fee/pet. Service with restrictions, crate.
ASK SÒ ✕ ⌖ 🖬 📼 ⏹ ➤ ✕

**AAA ▼▼▼ Crowne Plaza Suites Hotel Dallas Park Central LH**
(972) 233-7600. **$139-$189.** 7800 Alpha Rd. I-635, exit 19C (Coit Rd) eastbound; exit 19B (Coit Rd) westbound, 0.3 mi nw of jct US 75. Int corridors. **Pets:** Small. $100 deposit/room, $25 one-time fee/room. Service with restrictions, crate.
SAVE SÒ ✕ ⌖ 🖬 📼 ⏹ ➤

**▼▼▼ Dallas Marriott Suites Market Center SH**
(214) 905-0050. **$89-$164.** 2493 N Stemmons Frwy. I-35E, exit 431 (Motor St). Int corridors. **Pets:** Accepted.
✕ 🐾M 🐾 ⌖ 🖬 📼 ⏹ ➤

**▼▼▼ Embassy Suites Dallas-Market Center LH**
(214) 630-5332. **$89-$239.** 2727 Stemmons Frwy. I-35E, exit 432A (Inwood Rd), just s. Int corridors. **Pets:** Small. $25 one-time fee/room. Service with restrictions.
ASK ✕ 🐾 ⌖ 🖬 📼 ⏹ ➤ ✕

**▼▼ Extended StayAmerica Dallas-North-Park Central SH**
(972) 671-7722. **$38-$59.** 9019 Vantage Point Rd. I-635, exit 18A (Greenville Ave), just sw. Ext corridors. **Pets:** $25 daily fee/pet. Service with restrictions, supervision.
ASK SÒ ✕ 🐾M ⌖ 🖬 📼

**▼▼ ▼▼ The Fairmont Dallas LH**
(214) 720-2020. **$149-$299.** 1717 N Akard St. Corner of Ross Ave and N Akard St. Int corridors. **Pets:** Small, other species. $25 daily fee/pet. Service with restrictions, supervision.
ASK SÒ ✕ 🐾M 🐾 ⌖ 🖬 ⏹ ➤

**▼▼ ▼▼ Holiday Inn Select Dallas Central LH**
(214) 373-6000. **$84-$109.** 10650 N Central Expwy. US 75, exit 6 (Walnut Hill Ln/Meadow Rd), 0.5 mi n on access road northbound. Int corridors. **Pets:** Accepted.
ASK ✕ 🐾 ⌖ 🖬 📼 ⏹ ➤

**▼▼ Homestead Studio Suites Hotel-Dallas/North Addison/Tollway SH**
(972) 447-1800. **$37-$68.** 17425 North Dallas Pkwy. North Dallas Tollway, exit Trinity Mills, just s of jct Trinity Mills and Dallas Pkwy, on southbound access road. Ext corridors. **Pets:** $25 daily fee/pet. Service with restrictions, supervision.
ASK SÒ ✕ ⌖ 🖬

**▼▼▼ Homestead Studio Suites Hotel-Dallas/Plano SH**
(972) 248-2233. **$51-$77.** 18470 N Dallas Pkwy. North Dallas Tollway, exit Frankford, just ne. Int corridors. **Pets:** $25 daily fee/pet. Service with restrictions, supervision.
ASK SÒ ✕ 🐾M 🐾 ⌖ 🖬 📼 ➤

**▼▼▼ Homewood Suites by Hilton SH**
(214) 819-9700. **$125.** 2747 N Stemmons Frwy. I-35E, exit 432A (Inwood Rd), just s. Int corridors. **Pets:** Accepted.
ASK SÒ ✕ ⌖ 🖬 📼 ➤

**▼▼▼ Homewood Suites by Hilton–I-635 SH**
(972) 437-6966. **$89-$149, 14 day notice.** 9169 Markville Dr. I-635, exit 18A (Greenville Ave S), just s, then just e. Int corridors. **Pets:** Accepted.
ASK SÒ ✕ ⌖ 🖬 📼 ➤ ✕

**▼▼▼ Hotel Crescent Court LH**
(214) 871-3200. **$365-$2500.** 400 Crescent Ct. Corner of Crescent Ct and McKinney Ave; uptown. Int corridors. **Pets:** Accepted.
✕ ⏹ ➤ ✕

**▼▼▼ Hotel Dallas Mockingbird SH**
(214) 634-8850. **$69-$109.** 1893 W Mockingbird Ln. I-35E, exit 433C (Mockingbird Ln), 0.8 mi e. Int corridors. **Pets:** Accepted.
SÒ ✕ 🐾 ⌖ 🖬 📼 ⏹ ➤ ✕

**▼▼▼ Hotel Lawrence SH**
(214) 761-9090. **$89-$119.** 302 S Houston St. I-35E, exit 428A (Commerce St), 0.8 mi to Griffin, just s to Jackson St, then just w. Int corridors. **Pets:** Accepted.
ASK SÒ ✕ ⏹

**AAA ▼▼ ▼▼ Hotel St. Germain CI ❀**
(214) 871-2516. **$290-$650, 7 day notice.** 2516 Maple Ave. Woodall Rogers Pkwy, exit Pearl St, 0.3 mi n. Int corridors. **Pets:** Small, dogs only. $50 daily fee/pet. Designated rooms, service with restrictions, supervision.
SAVE ✕ ⏹

**Hotel ZaZa** SH
(214) 468-8399. **$295-$395.** 2332 Leonard St. Jct Maple Ave/Routh St and McKinney Ave, northeast corner. Int corridors. **Pets:** Accepted.

**La Quinta Inn & Suites Dallas (North Central)** SH
(214) 361-8200. **$101-$111.** 10001 N Central Expwy. US 75, exit 6 (Walnut Hill Ln/Meadow Rd) northbound, 0.5 mi n to Meadow Rd, then U-turn under highway; exit 7 (Royal/Meadow Rd) southbound, 1 mi s on feeder. Int corridors. **Pets:** Medium. Service with restrictions.

**La Quinta Inn & Suites Dallas Northwest** SH
(214) 904-9955. **$69-$99.** 2380 W Northwest Hwy. I-35, exit 436 Northwest Hwy (Loop 12), 0.8 mi e. Int corridors. **Pets:** Small, other species. $50 deposit/pet. Service with restrictions, supervision.

**La Quinta Inn Dallas (City Place)** SH
(214) 821-4220. **$87-$104.** 4440 N Central Expwy. N off US 75, exit 2 (Henderson-Knox) northbound; exit 1B (Haskell/Blackburn) southbound. Ext corridors. **Pets:** Medium. Service with restrictions.

**La Quinta Inn Dallas (East)** SH
(214) 324-3731. **$69-$73.** 8303 E R L Thornton Frwy. I-30, exit 52A (Jim Miller Rd). Ext corridors. **Pets:** Medium. Service with restrictions.

**La Quinta Inn Dallas (Richardson)** SH
(972) 234-1016. **$65-$75.** 13685 N Central Expwy. US 75 N, exit 22 (Midpark Rd). Ext/int corridors. **Pets:** Medium. Service with restrictions.

**The Mansion On Turtle Creek** LH
(214) 559-2100. **$400-$2400.** 2821 Turtle Creek Blvd. 2 mi nw, entrance on Gillespie St, just e of jct Gillespie and Lawn sts. Int corridors. **Pets:** Accepted.

**The Melrose Hotel** SH
(214) 521-5151. **$285-$385.** 3015 Oak Lawn Ave. I-35E, exit 430, 0.8 mi n; entrance off Cedar Springs, just n. Int corridors. **Pets:** Accepted.

**Motel 6 #1479** M
(214) 388-8741. **$43-$55.** 8108 E R L Thornton. I-30, exit 52A (Jim Miller Rd). Ext corridors. **Pets:** Accepted.

**Motel 6 #1493** SH
(972) 506-8100. **$36-$52.** 10335 Gardner Rd. I-35E, exit 436, just sw of jct Northwest Hwy (Loop 12) and Spur 348; 0.8 mi w of I-35E and US 77. Ext corridors. **Pets:** Accepted.

**Motel 6–560** SH
(972) 620-2828. **$41-$53.** 2753 Forest Ln. I-635, exit 26 (Josey Ln) eastbound; exit 25 (Josey Ln) westbound, just s to Forest Ln, then just w. Ext corridors. **Pets:** Accepted.

**Motel 6 Forest Lane-South #1119** SH
(972) 484-9111. **$42-$55.** 2660 Forest Ln. I-635, exit 26 (Josey Ln) eastbound, 0.5 mi s to Forest Ln, then just w; exit 25 (Josey Ln) westbound, just s to Forest Ln, then just w. Ext corridors. **Pets:** Accepted.

**Quality Inn & Suites-North Dallas** SH
(972) 484-3330. **$76-$120.** 2421 Walnut Hill Ln. I-35E, exit 438 (Walnut Hill Ln). Int corridors. **Pets:** Accepted.

**Quality Inn Dallas Market Center** SH
(214) 747-9551. **$68-$129.** 1955 Market Center Blvd. I-35E, exit 430B (Market Center Blvd), 0.3 mi w. Ext corridors. **Pets:** Accepted.

**Radisson Hotel Central/Dallas** LH
(214) 750-6060. **$99-$139.** 6060 N Central Expwy. US 75, exit 3 (Mockingbird Ln), on northbound frontage road. Int corridors. **Pets:** Small. $50 one-time fee/room. Service with restrictions, supervision.

**Radisson Hotel Dallas Love Field** LH
(214) 630-7000. **$79-$99.** 1241 W Mockingbird Ln. I-35E, exit 433B, just nw of jct I-35E and W Mockingbird Ln. Int corridors. **Pets:** Accepted.

**Red Roof Inn-Market Center** M
(214) 638-5151. **$45-$55.** 1550 Empire Central Dr. I-35E, exit 434A (Empire Central Dr), 0.3 mi e. Ext corridors. **Pets:** Accepted.

**Renaissance Dallas Hotel** LH
(214) 631-2222. **$99-$229.** 2222 Stemmons Frwy. I-35E, exit 430B (Market Center Blvd), 0.3 mi nw on access road. Int corridors. **Pets:** Accepted.

**Residence Inn by Marriott at Dallas Central** SH
(214) 750-8220. **$116.** 10333 N Central Expwy. US 75, exit 6 (Walnut Hill Ln/Meadow Rd) northbound, 0.5 mi n to Meadow Rd, U-turn under highway; exit 7 (Royal/Meadow Rd) southbound, 1 mi s on access road. Ext corridors. **Pets:** Accepted.

**Residence Inn by Marriott-Dallas Market Center** SH
(214) 631-2472. **$129-$159.** 6950 N Stemmons Frwy. I-35E, exit 432B (Commonwealth Ln), 0.6 mi n on northbound frontage road. Ext/int corridors. **Pets:** Accepted.

**Residence Inn by Marriott-Dallas Park Central** SH
(972) 503-1333. **$119-$159, 30 day notice.** 7642 LBJ Frwy. I-635, exit 20 (Hillcrest), just e, on eastbound access road. Int corridors. **Pets:** Accepted.

**Sheraton Suites Market Center-Dallas** LH
(214) 747-3000. **$125, 3 day notice.** 2101 Stemmons Frwy. Nw off I-35E and US 77, exit 430B (Market Center Blvd). Int corridors. **Pets:** Accepted.

**SpringHill Suites Dallas Downtown/West End** SH
(214) 999-0500. **$159-$279.** 1907 N Lamar St. Between Corbin Ave and Munger St. Int corridors. **Pets:** Accepted.

**Staybridge Suites Dallas Near The Galleria** SH
(972) 391-0000. **$79-$149.** 7880 Alpha Rd. I-635, exit 19B (Coit Rd), 0.3 mi n, then just w. Int corridors. **Pets:** Medium. $125 one-time fee/pet. Service with restrictions, crate.

**Super 8 Motel** SH
(972) 572-1030. **$75.** 8541 S Hampton Rd. I-20, exit 465, 0.3 mi e to S Hampton Rd, then just s. Ext corridors. **Pets:** Accepted.

**The Westin City Center, Dallas** LH
(214) 979-9000. **$119-$169.** 650 N Pearl St. Between San Jacinto and Bryan St, 0.3 mi w of US 75 Central Expwy. Int corridors. **Pets:** Accepted.

▼▼ ▼▼ The Westin Galleria, Dallas 🄻🄷
(972) 934-9494. **$310, 3 day notice.** 13340 Dallas Pkwy. Just n of jct I-635 and N Dallas Pkwy. Int corridors. **Pets:** Accepted.

(ASK) 🆂🄳 ☒ 🄶M ⟨⟩ 🄴 🄳 🄳 ¶¶ ⟿

## DENTON

🄰🄰 ▼▼ ▼▼ Exel Inn of Denton 🅂🄷
(940) 383-1471. **$43-$79.** 4211 I-35E N. Jct US 380 and I-35, exit 469, just n. Int corridors. **Pets:** Small, other species. Designated rooms, service with restrictions, supervision.

(SAVE) 🆂🄳 ☒ 🄳 🄳 🄳 ⟿

▼▼▼ La Quinta Inn Denton 🅂🄷
(940) 387-5840. **$73-$86.** 700 Fort Worth Dr. I-35E, exit 465B (Fort Worth Dr), just n. Ext corridors. **Pets:** Medium. Service with restrictions.

(ASK) ☒ 🄶M ⟨⟩ 🄴 🄳 🄳 ⟿

▼▼ Motel 6 Denton #97 🄼
(940) 566-4798. **$43-$55.** 4125 I-35 N. I-35, exit 469. Ext corridors.
**Pets:** Accepted.

🆂🄳 ☒ 🄴 ⟿

▼▼ ▼▼ Quality Inn & Suites 🅂🄷
(940) 387-3511. **$69-$189.** 1500 Dallas Dr. 2 mi se of jct I-35E and US 77 business route, exit 464 westbound; exit 465A (Teasley Ln) eastbound, 0.4 mi n to Dallas Dr, then 0.5 mi e. Ext corridors.
**Pets:** Accepted.

(ASK) 🆂🄳 ☒ 🄳 🄳 🄳 ⟿

▼▼▼▼ Radisson Hotel Denton 🅂🄷 🐾
(940) 565-8499. **$69-$119.** 2211 I-35E N. Off I-35E and US 77, exit 466B (N Texas Blvd), 2.5 mi sw. Int corridors. **Pets:** Other species. Service with restrictions, crate.

(ASK) 🆂🄳 ☒ 🄳 🄳 ¶¶ ⟿

## DESOTO

▼▼ Red Roof Inn Dallas/DeSoto 🅂🄷
(972) 224-7100. **$45-$57.** 1401 N Beckley Ave. I-35E, exit 416, just s. Ext/int corridors. **Pets:** Accepted.

☒ ⟨⟩ 🄴 🄳

## DUNCANVILLE

▼▼ Motel 6–#1130 🅂🄷
(972) 296-0345. **$43-$55.** 202 Jellison Blvd. I-20, exit 462A (Duncanville Rd) eastbound; exit 462B (Main St) westbound, just s to Camp Wisdom, just w to Duncanville Rd, just n to Jellison Blvd, then just w. Ext/int corridors. **Pets:** Accepted.

🆂🄳 ☒ 🄴 🄳 ⟿

▼▼ ▼▼ Ramada Inn-Dallas Southwest 🅂🄷
(972) 298-8911. **$60-$76.** 711 E Camp Wisdom Rd. I-20, exit 463, 0.3 mi w of jct I-20 and Cockrell Hill Rd; 2 mi w of US 67. Ext/int corridors.
**Pets:** Medium. $25 one-time fee/pet. Service with restrictions, supervision.

(ASK) 🆂🄳 ☒ ⟨⟩ 🄳 🄳 ¶¶ ⟿

## FARMERS BRANCH

▼▼ ▼▼ Comfort Inn of North Dallas 🅂🄷
(972) 406-3030. **$49-$150.** 14040 Stemmons Frwy. I-35E, exit 442 (Valwood Pkwy). Int corridors. **Pets:** Accepted.

(ASK) 🆂🄳 ☒ ⟨⟩ 🄳 🄳 ⟿

🄰🄰 ▼▼ ▼▼ Days Inn-North Dallas 🅂🄷
(972) 488-0800. **$58-$68.** 13313 Stemmons Frwy. I-35E, exit 441 (Valley View Ln), on west side of frontage road. Int corridors. **Pets:** Very small, dogs only. $10 one-time fee/pet. Designated rooms, service with restrictions, supervision.

(SAVE) 🆂🄳 ☒ 🄴 🄳 ⟿

▼▼▼ Holiday Inn Select North Dallas 🅂🄷
(972) 243-3363. **$149-$189.** 2645 LBJ Frwy. I-635, exit 26 (Josey Ln) eastbound, just n; exit 25 westbound, 0.4 mi w. Int corridors.
**Pets:** Accepted.

(ASK) 🆂🄳 ☒ ⟨⟩ 🄴 🄳 🄳 ¶¶ ⟿ ☒

▼▼▼ La Quinta Inn Dallas (NW-Farmers Branch) 🅂🄷
(972) 620-7333. **$58-$68.** 13235 Stemmons Frwy N. I-35E, exit 441 (Valley View Ln), on southbound frontage road. Ext corridors.
**Pets:** Medium. Service with restrictions.

(ASK) ☒ ⟨⟩ 🄴 🄳 🄳 ⟿

🄰🄰 ▼▼▼▼ Omni Dallas Hotel Park West 🄻🄷
(972) 869-4300. **$99-$249.** 1590 LBJ Frwy. Nw off I-635, 1.5 mi w of jct I-35E, exit 29 (Luna Rd). Int corridors. **Pets:** Small. $50 one-time fee/ room. Service with restrictions, supervision.

(SAVE) 🆂🄳 ☒ ⟨⟩ 🄴 🄳 🄳 ¶¶ ⟿ ☒

## FRISCO

▼▼▼ Embassy Suites Dallas-Frisco Hotel & Conference
Center 🅂🄷 🐾
(972) 712-7200. **$119-$309.** 7600 John Q Hammons Dr. SR 121, exit Parkwood, just n. Int corridors. **Pets:** Medium. $25 daily fee/room. Designated rooms, service with restrictions, crate.

(ASK) ☒ 🄶M 🄴 🄳 🄳 ¶¶ ⟿ ☒

🄰🄰 ▼▼ ▼▼ The Westin Stonebriar Resort 🄻🄷
(972) 668-8000. **$119-$389.** 1549 Legacy Dr. 0.3 mi n of jct SR 121. Int corridors. **Pets:** Accepted.

(SAVE) 🆂🄳 ☒ 🄶M 🄴 🄳 🄳 ¶¶ ⟿ ☒

## GARLAND

🄰🄰 ▼▼ ▼▼ Best Western Lakeview Inn 🅂🄷
(972) 303-1601. **$65-$79.** 1635 E I-30 at Chaha Rd. I-30, exit 62 (Chaha Rd). Ext corridors. **Pets:** Accepted.

(SAVE) 🆂🄳 ☒ 🄴 🄳 🄳 ⟿

▼▼▼▼ Holiday Inn Select LBJ NE (Garland) 🅂🄷
(214) 341-5400. **$109.** 11350 LBJ Frwy. I-635, exit 13 (Jupiter/Kingsley rds), just sw. Int corridors. **Pets:** Accepted.

(ASK) 🆂🄳 ☒ 🄳 🄳 ¶¶ ⟿

🄰🄰 ▼▼▼▼ La Quinta Inn Dallas (Garland) 🅂🄷
(972) 271-7581. **$66-$76.** 12721 I-635. I-635, exit 11B, just nw. Ext/int corridors. **Pets:** Medium. Service with restrictions.

(SAVE) ☒ ⟨⟩ 🄳 🄳 ⟿

▼▼ ▼▼ Microtel Inn & Suites 🅂🄷
(972) 270-7200. **$59-$75.** 1901 Pendleton Dr. I-635, exit 11B, just n to Pendleton Dr, then just e. Int corridors. **Pets:** Accepted.

(ASK) 🆂🄳 ☒ 🄶M 🄴 🄳 🄳

▼▼ Motel 6–0620 🅂🄷
(972) 226-7140. **$41-$53.** 436 W I-30. I-30, exit 59 (Belt Line Rd). Ext corridors. **Pets:** Accepted.

🆂🄳 ☒ 🄴 ⟿

## GRAND PRAIRIE

▼▼▼ AmeriSuites (Dallas/Grand Prairie) 🅂🄷
(972) 988-6800. **$69-$85.** 1542 N Hwy 360. SR 360, exit J/K aves. Int corridors. **Pets:** Accepted.

(ASK) 🆂🄳 ☒ 🄶M 🄴 🄳 🄳 ⟿

▼▼▼▼ La Quinta Inn Dallas (Grand Prairie) 🅂🄷
(972) 641-3021. **$58-$72.** 1410 NW 19th St. I-30, exit 32, just e. Ext corridors. **Pets:** Medium. Service with restrictions.

(ASK) ☒ 🄶M ⟨⟩ 🄴 🄳 🄳 ⟿

▼▼ Motel 6–446 🅂🄷
(972) 642-9424. **$35-$48.** 406 E Palace Pkwy. I-30, exit 34 (Belt Line Rd), just n to Safari Pkwy, then 0.6 mi w. Ext corridors. **Pets:** Accepted.

🆂🄳 ☒ 🄴 🄳 🄳 ⟿

# GREENVILLE

**▼▼▼▼ Holiday Inn Express Hotel & Suites** SH
(903) 454-8680. **$104-$129, 3 day notice.** 2901 Mustang Crossing. I-30, exit 93A. Int corridors. **Pets:** Accepted.

ASK S⃝ ☒ &M &' ⊟ 🖵 ☲

# IRVING

**⊕ ▼▼▼▼ AmeriSuites (Dallas Las Colinas/Hidden Ridge)** SH
(972) 910-0302. **$75-$199.** 333 W John Carpenter Frwy. SR 114, exit Hidden Ridge. Int corridors. **Pets:** Accepted.

SAVE S⃝ ☒ &M ⊘ &' ⊟ 🖵 ☲

**⊕ ▼▼▼▼ AmeriSuites (Dallas Las Colinas/Walnut Hill)** SH
(972) 550-7400. **$49-$139.** 5455 Green Park Dr. SR 114, exit Walnut Hill Ln. Int corridors. **Pets:** Accepted.

SAVE S⃝ ☒ &M ⊘ &' ⊟ 🖵 ☲

**▼▼▼▼ Candlewood Dallas/Las Colinas** SH
(972) 714-9990. **$89.** 5300 Greenpark Dr. SR 114, exit Walnut Hill Ln, just s. Int corridors. **Pets:** Large, other species. $75 one-time fee/pet. Service with restrictions, crate.

ASK S⃝ ☒ &M ⊘ &' ⊟ 🖵

**⊕ ▼▼◆▼ Clarion Hotel DFW Airport South** LH
(972) 399-1010. **$109-$149.** 4440 W Airport Frwy. SR 183, exit Valley View Ln, on eastbound access road. Int corridors. **Pets:** Medium, other species. $10 one-time fee/pet. Service with restrictions, supervision.

SAVE S⃝ ☒ ⊘ &' ⊟ 🖵 ¶¶ ☲ ☒

**▼▼◆▼ Courtyard by Marriott-Dallas-Las Colinas** SH
(972) 550-8100. **$139-$179.** 1151 W Walnut Hill Ln. Nw off SR 114, 1.5 mi sw on Walnut Hill Ln, just w of jct MacArthur Blvd. Int corridors. **Pets:** Accepted.

ASK S⃝ ☒ ⊘ &' ⊟ 🖵 ¶¶ ☲

**▼▼ ▼▼ Days Inn DFW North** SH
(972) 621-8277. **$54.** 4325 W Hwy 114. SR 114, exit Belt Line Rd, on westbound service road. Ext corridors. **Pets:** Accepted.

ASK S⃝ ☒ ⊟ 🖵 ¶¶ ☲

**▼▼◆▼ Drury Inn & Suites-DFW Airport** SH
(972) 986-1200. **$80-$140.** 4210 W Airport Frwy. SR 183, exit Esters Rd, on southbound access road. Int corridors. **Pets:** Accepted.

ASK ☒ ⊘ ⊟ 🖵 ☲

**▼▼◆▼ Extended Stay Deluxe (Dallas-Las Colinas-Green Park Dr.)** SH
(972) 751-0808. **$64.** 5401 Green Park Dr. SR 114, exit Walnut Hill Ln, just s. Int corridors. **Pets:** $25 daily fee/pet. Service with restrictions, supervision.

ASK S⃝ ☒ &M ⊘ &' ⊟ 🖵 ☲

**⊕ ▼▼◆▼▼ Four Seasons Resort and Club** LH ✿
(972) 717-0700. **$350-$2000.** 4150 N MacArthur Blvd. Se off SR 114, 1.5 mi s of exit MacArthur Blvd. Int corridors. **Pets:** Very small. Designated rooms, service with restrictions, supervision.

SAVE ☒ &M ⊘ &' ⊟ 🖵 ¶¶ ☲ ☒

**▼▼◆▼ Hampton Inn-DFW Airport South** SH
(972) 986-3606. **$82-$141.** 4340 W Airport Frwy. SR 183, exit Valley View Ln, on southbound access road. Int corridors. **Pets:** Accepted.

ASK ☒ ⊘ &' ⊟ 🖵 ☲

**▼▼◆▼▼ Harvey Hotel-DFW Airport** LH
(972) 929-4500. **$89-$289.** 4545 W John Carpenter Frwy. Nw off SR 114, exit Esters Blvd. Int corridors. **Pets:** Accepted.

ASK S⃝ ☒ ⊘ ⊟ 🖵 ¶¶ ☲

**▼▼◆▼ Harvey Suites-DFW Airport** SH
(972) 929-4499. **$76-$109.** 4550 W John Carpenter Frwy. SR 114, exit Freeport Pkwy, on southbound service road. Int corridors. **Pets:** Medium. $25 one-time fee/room. Service with restrictions, crate.

ASK S⃝ ☒ &M ⊘ &' ⊟ 🖵 ☲

**◆▼ ▼▼ Homestead Studio Suites Hotel-Dallas/DFW Airport North** SH
(972) 929-3333. **$40-$59.** 7825 Heathrow Dr. SR 114, exit Esters Blvd, s to Plaza Dr, then just w. Int corridors. **Pets:** $25 daily fee/pet. Service with restrictions, supervision.

ASK S⃝ ☒ ⊟ 🖵

**◆▼ ▼▼ Homestead Studio Suites Hotel-Dallas/Las Colinas/ Carnaby St.** SH
(972) 756-0458. **$40-$59.** 5315 Carnaby St. SR 114, exit MacArthur Blvd, 0.5 mi s, then just e on Meadow Creek. Ext corridors. **Pets:** $25 daily fee/pet. Service with restrictions, supervision.

ASK S⃝ ☒ &' ⊟ 🖵

**▼▼◆▼ Homewood Suites by Hilton Las Colinas** SH
(972) 556-0665. **$149-$199.** 4300 Wingren Dr. Ne off SR 114, exit O'Connor Rd/Wingren Dr eastbound, just n to Las Colinas Blvd, 0.4 mi e to Rochelle Rd, then just s; exit Rochelle Rd westbound. Ext/int corridors. **Pets:** Small, other species. $75 one-time fee/room. Designated rooms, service with restrictions, supervision.

ASK S⃝ ☒ &M ⊟ 🖵 ☲ ☒

**▼▼◆▼ La Quinta Inn & Suites Dallas (DFW-Airport North)** SH
(972) 915-4022. **$76-$108.** 4850 W John Carpenter Frwy. SR 114, exit Freeport Pkwy, on eastbound service road. Int corridors. **Pets:** Medium. Service with restrictions.

ASK ☒ &M ⊘ &' ⊟ 🖵 ☲

**▼▼◆▼ La Quinta Inn & Suites Dallas DFW Airport South (Irving)** SH
(972) 252-6546. **$108-$118.** 4105 W Airport Frwy. 3 mi nw off SR 183, exit Esters Rd; on northbound access road. Int corridors. **Pets:** Medium. No service.

ASK ☒ &' ⊟ 🖵 ☲

**▼ Motel 6 #1274 DFW North** M
(972) 915-3993. **$45-$55.** 7800 Heathrow Dr. SR 114, exit Freeport Pkwy, just se. Int corridors. **Pets:** Accepted.

S⃝ ☒ &' ⊟ ☲

**▼▼◆▼ Omni Mandalay Hotel at Las Colinas** LH
(972) 556-0800. **$109-$249.** 221 E Las Colinas Blvd. Nw off SR 114, exit O'Connor Rd. Int corridors. **Pets:** Small. $50 one-time fee/pet. Service with restrictions, crate.

ASK S⃝ ☒ ⊘ &' ⊟ 🖵 ¶¶ ☲ ☒

**▼▼◆▼ Quality Inn & Suites DFW Airport North** SH
(972) 929-4008. **$59-$139.** 4100 W John Carpenter Frwy. SR 114, exit Esters Blvd, s to Reese St, then e. Ext corridors. **Pets:** Accepted.

ASK S⃝ ☒ ⊘ &' ⊟ 🖵

**▼ Red Roof Inn/DFW Airport North** M
(972) 929-0020. **$46-$64.** 8150 Esters Blvd. SR 114, exit Esters Blvd, just n. Ext corridors. **Pets:** Accepted.

☒ ⊘ &' ⊟ 🖵

**▼▼◆▼ Residence Inn by Marriott at Las Colinas** SH
(972) 580-7773. **$134, 14 day notice.** 950 W Walnut Hill Ln. SR 114, exit MacArthur Blvd, 0.5 mi s, then just e. Ext corridors. **Pets:** Small, other species. $75 one-time fee/room. Service with restrictions, supervision.

☒ &M ⊘ &' ⊟ 🖵 ☲ ☒

**▼▼◆▼ Residence Inn by Marriott-DFW/Irving** SH
(972) 871-1331. **$99-$199.** 8600 Esters Blvd. SR 114, exit Esters Blvd, 0.9 mi n. Int corridors. **Pets:** Accepted.

ASK S⃝ ☒ &M ⊘ &' ⊟ 🖵 ☲ ☒

◊◊◊◊ **Sheraton Grand Hotel** LH
(972) 929-8400. **$235-$255.** 4440 W John Carpenter Frwy. SR 114, exit Esters Blvd, just s. Int corridors. **Pets:** Accepted.

(ASK) (SO) (X) (&M) (D) (IS) (B) (DE) (TI) (2) (X)

◊◊◊ **Staybridge Suites Dallas-Las Colinas** SH
(972) 465-9400. **$145-$175.** 1201 Executive Cir. SR 114, exit Mac-Arthur Blvd, just s to W Walnut Hill Ln, then just w. Int corridors. **Pets:** Accepted.

(ASK) (SO) (X) (IS) (B) (DE) (2)

◊◊◊ **Summerfield Suites by Wyndham-Las Colinas** SH
(972) 831-0909. **$89-$159.** 5901 N MacArthur Blvd. SR 114, exit Mac-Arthur Blvd, jct MacArthur Blvd and SR 114, northwest corner. Ext/int corridors. **Pets:** Accepted.

(ASK) (X) (&M) (B) (DE) (2) (X)

◊◊ **Super 8 Motel DFW Airport North/Irving** SH
(214) 441-9000. **$50-$70.** 4770 W John Carpenter Frwy (SR 114). SR 114, exit Freeport Pkwy. Int corridors. **Pets:** Dogs only. $10 daily fee/pet. No service, crate.

(ASK) (SO) (X) (&M) (IS) (B) (DE)

## LEWISVILLE

◊◊ **Comfort Suites by Choice Hotels** SH
(972) 315-6464. **$80-$100.** 755A Vista Ridge Mall Dr. I-35E, exit 448A (Round Grove Rd), 0.5 mi s of jct I-35 and Round Grove Rd on southbound service road to Vista Ridge Mall Dr, then just w. Int corridors. **Pets:** Accepted.

(ASK) (SO) (X) (D) (IS) (B) (DE) (2)

◊◊◊ **Country Inn & Suites by Carlson** SH
(972) 315-6565. **$75-$95.** 755B E Vista Ridge Mall Dr. I-35E, exit 448A (Round Grove Rd), 0.5 mi s on service road to Vista Ridge Rd, then just w. Int corridors. **Pets:** Accepted.

(ASK) (SO) (X) (IS) (B) (DE) (2)

◊◊◊ **La Quinta Inn Dallas (Lewisville)** SH
(972) 221-7525. **$69-$79.** 1657 S Stemmons Frwy. I-35E, exit 449, just w. Ext corridors. **Pets:** Medium. Service with restrictions.

(ASK) (X) (&M) (D) (2)

◊ **Motel 6-1288** SH
(972) 436-5008. **$41-$53.** 1705 Lakepointe Dr. I-35E, exit 449, just n on access road. Int corridors. **Pets:** Accepted.

(ASK) (SO) (X) (D) (IS) (2)

◊◊◊ **Residence Inn by Marriott Dallas** SH
(972) 315-3777. **$119-$169, 14 day notice.** 755C Vista Ridge Mall Dr. I-35E, exit 448A, 0.5 mi s on service road; jct I-35 and Round Grove Rd to Vista Ridge Rd, just w. Int corridors. **Pets:** Accepted.

(ASK) (SO) (X) (&M) (D) (IS) (B) (DE) (2) (X)

◊◊ **Super 8-Lewisville/Dallas North/Airport** M
(972) 221-7511. **$40-$50.** 1305 S Stemmons Frwy. I-35E, exit 450, just sw. Ext corridors. **Pets:** Accepted.

(ASK) (SO) (X) (B) (DE) (2)

## MCKINNEY

◊◊ **Super 8 Motel-McKinney** SH
(972) 548-8880. **$76.** 910 N Central Expwy. US 75, exit 40A (Virginia/Louisiana sts), 0.5 mi n on northbound service road. Int corridors. **Pets:** Small. $10 daily fee/pet. No service, supervision.

(ASK) (X) (IS) (B) (2)

## MESQUITE

◊◊◊ **La Quinta Inn and Suites** SH
(972) 216-7460. **$79-$139.** 118 E Hwy 80. US 80 E, exit Belt Line Rd. Int corridors. **Pets:** Accepted.

(ASK) (SO) (X) (&M) (IS) (B) (DE) (2)

◊◊ **Super 8 Motel** SH
(972) 289-5481. **$48-$68.** 121 Grand Junction Blvd. I-635, exit 4 (Military Pkwy). Ext corridors. **Pets:** Accepted.

(SAVE) (SO) (X) (B) (DE) (2)

## MIDLOTHIAN

◊◊◊ **Best Western Midlothian Inn** SH
(972) 775-1891. **$64-$75.** 220 N Hwy 67. On US 67, just n of jct US 287. Ext corridors. **Pets:** Medium, other species. $10 daily fee/room. Service with restrictions, supervision.

(SAVE) (SO) (X) (B) (DE) (2)

## PLANO

◊◊◊◊ **AmeriSuites (Dallas/Plano)** SH 🐾
(972) 378-3997. **$99-$159.** 3100 Dallas Pkwy. Dallas Pkwy, exit Park Blvd northbound; exit Parker Blvd southbound, on northbound service road. Int corridors. **Pets:** Medium, other species. $10 daily fee/pet. Service with restrictions.

(SAVE) (SO) (X) (&M) (D) (IS) (B) (DE) (2)

◊◊◊ **Best Western Park Suites Hotel** SH
(972) 578-2243. **$72-$100.** 640 Park Blvd E. US 75, exit 29A northbound, just e; exit 29 southbound, 0.5 mi s on access road, just e on 15th St, then 0.5 mi n on access road. Int corridors. **Pets:** Other species. $50 one-time fee/room. Service with restrictions, supervision.

(ASK) (SO) (X) (&M) (D) (IS) (B) (DE) (2)

◊◊◊ **Candlewood Suites-Plano** SH
(972) 618-5446. **$69-$109.** 4701 Legacy Dr. Jct SR 289 (Preston Rd) and Legacy Dr, just e. Int corridors. **Pets:** Medium. $150 one-time fee/pet. Service with restrictions, supervision.

(ASK) (SO) (X) (IS) (B) (DE)

◊◊◊ **Extended Stay Deluxe (Dallas/Plano)** SH
(972) 378-9978. **$50-$77.** 2900 Dallas Pkwy. Dallas Pkwy, exit Park Blvd northbound; exit Parker Rd southbound, on northbound service road. Int corridors. **Pets:** $25 daily fee/pet. Service with restrictions, supervision.

(ASK) (SO) (X) (&M) (D) (IS) (B) (DE)

◊◊◊ **Hampton Inn Plano** SH
(972) 519-1000. **$69-$109.** 4901 Old Shepherd Pl. 0.4 mi n of jct SR 289 (Preston Rd) and W Plano Pkwy, just e. Int corridors. **Pets:** Accepted.

(ASK) (SO) (X) (D) (B) (DE) (2)

◊◊◊ **Holiday Inn Express Hotel & Suites Plano East** SH
(972) 881-1881. **$105-$205.** 700 Central Pkwy E. Just e of US 75; 0.3 mi ne of jct FM 544, exit 29A northbound; exit 29 southbound, 0.5 mi s on access road, just e on 15th St, then 0.5 mi n on access road. Int corridors. **Pets:** Accepted.

(ASK) (SO) (X) (D) (B) (DE) (2) (X)

◊◊◊ **Homestead Studio Suites Hotel-Dallas/Plano Parkway** SH
(972) 596-9966. **$53-$77.** 4709 W Plano Pkwy. Just n of jct Plano Pkwy and SR 289 (Preston Rd), then just e. Int corridors. **Pets:** $20 daily fee/pet. Service with restrictions, supervision.

(ASK) (SO) (X) (D) (IS) (B) (DE) (2)

◊◊◊ **Homewood Suites by Hilton** SH
(972) 758-8800. **$139.** 4705 Old Shepherd Pl. Jct Plano Pkwy and SR 289 (Preston Rd), 0.4 mi n, then just e. Int corridors. **Pets:** Small, other species. $75 one-time fee/room. Supervision.

(ASK) (SO) (X) (&M) (D) (IS) (B) (DE) (2) (X)

◊◊◊ **La Quinta Inn & Suites Dallas (West Plano)** SH
(972) 599-0700. **$71-$108.** 4800 W Plano Pkwy. Just n of jct SR 289 (Preston Rd), then just e. Int corridors. **Pets:** Medium. Service with restrictions.

(ASK) (X) (&M) (D) (IS) (B) (DE) (2)

**La Quinta Inn Dallas (Plano)** SH
(972) 423-1300. **$62-$79.** 1820 N Central Expwy. US 75, exit 29A (Park Blvd), northbound, just ne; exit 29 southbound, 0.5 mi s on access road, just e on 15th St, then just n on northbound access road. Ext corridors. **Pets:** Medium. Service with restrictions.

**Motel 6–1121** SH
(972) 578-1626. **$43-$55.** 2550 N Central Expwy. US 75, exit 29A (Park Blvd) northbound; exit 29 southbound, 1 mi n of jct Park Rd (SR 544), on east side of US 75. Ext/int corridors. **Pets:** Accepted.

**Red Roof Inn Dallas-Plano** SH
(972) 881-8191. **$42-$63.** 301 Ruisseau Dr. SR 75, exit 30 (Parker Rd), 0.5 mi w to Premier, then just n. Ext/int corridors. **Pets:** Accepted.

**Sleep Inn Plano** SH
(972) 867-1111. **$60-$72.** 4801 W Plano Pkwy. Just n of jct SR 289 (Preston Rd) and N Plano Pkwy, just e. Int corridors. **Pets:** Accepted.

**Southfork Hotel** SH
(972) 578-8555. **$89-$99.** 1600 N Central Expwy. US 75, exit 29A northbound; exit 29 southbound, on northbound access road. Int corridors. **Pets:** Accepted.

**Super 8 Motel-Plano** SH
(972) 423-8300. **$50.** 1704 N Central Expwy. US 75, exit 29A northbound, just e; exit 29 southbound, 0.5 mi s on access road, just e on 15th St, then just n on access road. Int corridors. **Pets:** Small. $10 daily fee/pet. Designated rooms, service with restrictions, supervision.

**TownePlace Suites by Marriott** SH
(972) 943-8200. **$57-$107.** 5005 Whitestone Ln. North Dallas Tollway, exit Spring Creek Pkwy, 1.9 mi e, just n on SR 289 (Preston Rd), to Whitestone Ln, then just w. Int corridors. **Pets:** Accepted.

## RICHARDSON

**Econo Lodge Inn & Suites** SH
(972) 470-9440. **$59-$65.** 2458 N Central Expwy. US 75, exit 27 northbound; exit 26 southbound, 0.8 mi n on access road. Int corridors. **Pets:** Accepted.

**Homestead Studio Suites Hotel-Dallas/Richardson** SH
(972) 479-0500. **$53-$77.** 901 E Campbell Rd. US 75, exit 26 (Campbell Rd), just e. Int corridors. **Pets:** $25 daily fee/pet. Service with restrictions, supervision.

**The Radisson Hotel Dallas North At Richardson** LH
(972) 644-4000. **$79-$159.** 1981 N Central Expwy. US 75, exit 26 (Campbell Rd), 1.8 mi n; jct SR 5. Int corridors. **Pets:** Other species. $50 one-time fee/room. Service with restrictions, supervision.

**Renaissance Dallas-Richardson Hotel** LH ❧
(972) 367-2000. **$98-$161.** 900 E Lookout Dr. US 75, exit 27A (Gallatin Pkwy/Renner Rd) northbound; exit 26 (Gallatin Pkwy/Campbell Rd) southbound, just e. Int corridors. **Pets:** Large. $50 deposit/room. Designated rooms, service with restrictions, supervision.

**Residence Inn by Marriott Richardson** SH
(972) 669-5888. **$69-$130.** 1040 Waterwood Dr. US 75, exit 26 (Campbell Rd), just e to Greenville Ave, 0.4 mi n to Glenville Rd, then just w. Int corridors. **Pets:** Accepted.

**The Richardson Hotel** LH
(972) 231-9600. **$89-$269.** 701 E Campbell Rd. US 75, exit 26 (Campbell Rd) southbound; exit northbound, on access road. Int corridors. **Pets:** Accepted.

## ROANOKE

**Comfort Suites Roanoke** SH
(817) 490-1455. **$70-$110.** 801 Byron Nelson Blvd/W Hwy 114 Bus. I-35, exit 70 (SR 114), 3.4 mi e, exit Rufe/Snow, then just se. Int corridors. **Pets:** Accepted.

**Speedway Sleep Inn & Suites** SH
(817) 491-3120. **$70-$90.** 13471 Raceway Dr. I-35, exit 70 (SR 114), just e, then just s. Int corridors. **Pets:** Accepted.

## TERRELL

**Americas Best Inn** M
(972) 563-2676. **$45-$65.** 309 I-20. Jct I-20 and SR 34, exit 501. Ext corridors. **Pets:** Accepted.

**Best Western Country Inn** SH
(972) 563-1521. **$50-$52.** 1604 Hwy 34 S. I-20, exit 501 (SR 34), just n. Ext corridors. **Pets:** Accepted.

---

# END METROPOLITAN AREA

## DECATUR

**Best Western Decatur Inn** M
(940) 627-5982. **$50-$75.** 1801 S Hwy 287. 0.6 mi s of jct Business Rt SR 380. Ext corridors. **Pets:** Accepted.

**Comfort Inn** SH
(940) 627-6919. **$69-$130.** 1709 S US 287. 0.6 mi s of jct Business Rt SR 380. Ext corridors. **Pets:** Small. $10 daily fee/pet. Service with restrictions, supervision.

## DEL RIO

**Best Western Inn of Del Rio** SH
(830) 775-7511. **$75.** 810 Veterans Blvd. 0.8 mi nw on US 90, 277 and 377. Ext corridors. **Pets:** Other species. $5 daily fee/pet. Service with restrictions, crate.

**Comfort Inn & Suites** SH
(830) 775-2933. **$59-$99.** 3616 Veterans Blvd. 3.2 mi nw on US 90. Ext/int corridors. **Pets:** Medium. $20 daily fee/pet. Service with restrictions, supervision.

**ⒶⒶⒶ ▼▼▼ Days Inn and Suites** 🅂🅷
(830) 775-0585. **$53-$76.** 3808 Veterans Blvd. 3.5 mi nw on US 90. Ext corridors. **Pets:** Other species. $5 daily fee/pet. Service with restrictions.
[SAVE] [S🔒] [✕] [🖥] [💻] [🏊]

**▼▼▼▼ La Quinta Inn Del Rio** 🅂🅷
(830) 775-7591. **$65-$75.** 2005 Veterans Blvd. 1.8 mi nw on US 90, 277 and 377. Ext/int corridors. **Pets:** Medium. Service with restrictions.
[ASK] [✕] [🖥] [🏊]

**▼ Motel 6 Del Rio #323** 🅂🅷
(830) 774-2115. **$37-$49.** 2115 Veterans Blvd. Jct US 90/277 and Garner Dr. Ext corridors. **Pets:** Accepted.
[S🔒] [✕] [🏊]

**ⒶⒶⒶ ▼▼▼▼ Ramada Inn** 🅂🅷 ❁
(830) 775-1511. **$89-$109.** 2101 Veterans Blvd. 1.8 mi nw on US 90, 277 and 377. Ext/int corridors. **Pets:** Small, other species. Designated rooms, service with restrictions, supervision.
[SAVE] [S🔒] [✕] [🖥] [💻] [🍴] [🏊] [✕]

# DONNA

**▼▼▼▼ Victoria Palms Express Inn & Suites** 🅂🅷
(956) 464-4656. **$64-$95.** 602 N Victoria Rd. US 83, exit Victoria Rd. Ext corridors. **Pets:** Very small, other species. $50 deposit/pet, $5 daily fee/pet. Designated rooms, service with restrictions, supervision.
[ASK] [S🔒] [✕] [🖥] [💻] [🍴] [🏊] [✕]

# DUMAS

**ⒶⒶⒶ ▼▼▼ Best Western Windsor Inn** 🅂🅷
(806) 935-9644. **$69-$89, 7 day notice.** 1701 S Dumas Ave. US 287, 2 mi s of US 87 and SR 152. Ext corridors. **Pets:** Small, dogs only. $20 deposit/pet, $10 daily fee/pet. Service with restrictions, supervision.
[SAVE] [S🔒] [✕] [🖥] [💻] [🏊] [✕]

**▼▼▼ Dumas Inn** Ⓜ
(806) 935-6441. **$52-$82, 3 day notice.** 1712 S Dumas Ave. US 287, 1.5 mi s from jct US 87 and SR 152. Ext/int corridors. **Pets:** Accepted.
[ASK] [S🔒] [✕] [🖥] [💻] [🏊]

**ⒶⒶⒶ ▼▼▼ Econo Lodge** 🅂🅷
(806) 935-9098. **$45-$75.** 1719 S Dumas Ave. US 287, 2 mi s of US 87 and SR 152. Int corridors. **Pets:** Accepted.
[SAVE] [S🔒] [✕]

**▼▼▼▼ Holiday Inn Express** 🅂🅷
(806) 935-4000. **$69-$99.** 1525 S Dumas Ave. US 87, 1.1 mi s of US 87 and SR 152. Int corridors. **Pets:** Other species. $15 one-time fee/room. Service with restrictions, supervision.
[ASK] [S🔒] [✕] [🖥] [💻] [🏊]

**▼▼▼ Super 8 Motel** Ⓜ
(806) 935-6222. **$79-$89.** 119 W 17th St. US 287, 2 mi s of jct US 87 and SR 152. Ext corridors. **Pets:** Accepted.
[ASK] [✕] [🖥] [💻]

# EAGLE PASS

**ⒶⒶⒶ ▼▼▼▼ Best Western** 🅂🅷
(830) 758-1234. **$90-$179.** 1923 Veterans Blvd. US 57, jct Loop 431 (US 277). Ext corridors. **Pets:** Accepted.
[SAVE] [✕] [🏊] [🖥] [💻] [🏊]

**ⒶⒶⒶ ▼▼▼▼ Holiday Inn Express Hotel & Suites** 🅂🅷
(830) 757-3050. **$84-$94, 10 day notice.** 2007 Veterans Blvd. 1.5 mi n on Loop 431 (US 277). Int corridors. **Pets:** Accepted.
[SAVE] [✕] [Ⓜ] [🖥] [💻] [🏊]

**▼▼▼▼ La Quinta Inn Eagle Pass** 🅂🅷
(830) 773-7000. **$62-$72.** 2525 E Main St. US 57 and 277 at Loop 431. Ext corridors. **Pets:** Medium. Service with restrictions, crate.
[ASK] [✕] [🏊] [🖥] [💻] [🏊]

**▼▼▼ Super 8 Motel** 🅂🅷
(830) 773-9531. **$49-$68.** 2150 N US Hwy 277. On US 277, 4 mi n. Ext corridors. **Pets:** Accepted.
[ASK] [S🔒] [✕] [🏊] [👁] [🖥] [💻] [🏊]

# EASTLAND

**▼▼▼ The Eastland** 🅱🅱
(254) 629-8397. **$70-$125.** 112 N Lamar St. I-20, exit 343, 1.7 mi n to Lamar St, then just e; downtown. Int corridors. **Pets:** Accepted.
[ASK] [✕] [🖥] [💻] [🏊]

**▼▼ Super 8 Motel & RV Park** Ⓜ
(254) 629-3336. **$69-$79.** 3900 I-20 E. I-20, exit 343, on north service road. Ext corridors. **Pets:** Small. $5 daily fee/pet. Designated rooms, service with restrictions, supervision.
[ASK] [S🔒] [✕] [🖥] [💻]

# EDINBURG

**ⒶⒶⒶ ▼▼▼ La Copa Inn & Suites** 🅂🅷
(956) 381-8888. **$49-$89.** 1210 E Canton Rd. US 281, exit Canton Rd, just off southbound access road. Ext corridors. **Pets:** Accepted.
[SAVE] [S🔒] [✕] [💻] [🏊]

**ⒶⒶⒶ ▼▼▼ Super 8 Motel** 🅂🅷
(956) 381-1688. **$54-$89.** 202 N Hwy 281. US 281, exit University Dr. Ext/int corridors. **Pets:** Accepted.
[SAVE] [S🔒] [✕] [👁] [🖥] [🏊]

# EL PASO

**ⒶⒶⒶ ▼▼▼▼ AmeriSuites (El Paso/Airport)** 🅂🅷
(915) 771-0022. **$134-$159, 5 day notice.** 6030 Gateway Blvd E. I-10, exit 24B (Geronimo Dr) eastbound; exit 24 westbound, 0.6 mi to Trowbridge, U-turn under interstate. Int corridors. **Pets:** Accepted.
[SAVE] [✕] [Ⓜ] [🏊] [👁] [🖥] [💻] [🏊]

**▼▼ Baymont Inn & Suites El Paso East** 🅂🅷
(915) 591-3300. **$81-$91.** 7944 Gateway Blvd E. I-10, exit 28B. Int corridors. **Pets:** Medium. No service.
[ASK] [✕] [Ⓜ] [💻] [🏊]

**ⒶⒶⒶ ▼▼▼ Baymont Inn & Suites El Paso West** 🅂🅷
(915) 585-2999. **$70-$80.** 7620 N Mesa St. I-10, exit 11 (Mesa St). Int corridors. **Pets:** Medium. Service with restrictions.
[SAVE] [✕] [🏊] [🖥] [💻] [🏊]

**▼▼ Best Western Airport Inn** 🅂🅷
(915) 779-7700. **$64.** 7144 Gateway Blvd E. I-10, exit 26 (Hawkins Blvd), on eastbound frontage road. Ext corridors. **Pets:** $10 daily fee/pet. Service with restrictions, supervision.
[S🔒] [✕] [🏊] [👁] [🖥] [💻] [🏊]

**▼▼ Best Western Sunland Park Inn** Ⓜ
(915) 587-4900. **$54-$89.** 1045 Sunland Park Dr. I-10, exit 13, just s. Ext corridors. **Pets:** Very small. $10 daily fee/pet. Designated rooms, service with restrictions, supervision.
[ASK] [S🔒] [✕] [🖥] [💻] [🏊]

**▼▼▼ Chase Suites by Woodfin** 🅂🅷 ❁
(915) 772-8000. **$109.** 6791 Montana Ave. I-10, exit 25 (Airway Blvd), 1 mi n, then just e. Ext corridors. **Pets:** Small, other species. $150 deposit/pet, $5 daily fee/pet. No service, supervision.
[ASK] [S🔒] [✕] [🖥] [💻] [🏊] [✕]

**▼▼▼ Comfort Inn Airport East** 🅂🅷
(915) 594-9111. **$84-$94.** 900 Yarbrough Dr. I-10, exit 28B. Ext corridors. **Pets:** Accepted.
[ASK] [S🔒] [✕] [🖥] [💻] [🏊]

**ⒶⒶⒶ ▼▼◆ Days Inn Ⓜ**
(915) 845-3500. **$60-$90, 3 day notice.** 5035 S Desert Blvd. I-10, exit 11 (Mesa St) eastbound; exit 9 (Redd) northbound, 1.5 mi e on eastbound service road. Ext corridors. **Pets:** Accepted.
SAVE ⓢ ✕ 🖥 🏊

**▼▼ Econo Lodge Ⓜ**
(915) 778-3311. **$55-$60.** 6363 Montana Ave. I-10, exit 24 (Geronimo St) westbound; exit 24B eastbound, 0.5 mi n on Geronimo St, 0.5 mi e. Ext corridors. **Pets:** Accepted.
ASK ⓢ ✕ 🖥 🖵 🏊

**▼▼▼ Hawthorn Inn & Suites SH**
(915) 778-6789. **$99-$109.** 6789 Boeing. 7 mi e on US 62 and 180 to Airway Blvd, then just n. Int corridors. **Pets:** Accepted.
✕ 🅜 🗐 🖥 🖵 🏊

**▼▼▼ Hilton El Paso Airport LH**
(915) 778-4241. **$85-$155.** 2027 Airway Blvd. I-10, exit 25 (Airway Blvd), 1.3 mi n. Int corridors. **Pets:** Accepted.
✕ 🗐 🖥 🖵 🍴 🏊 ✕

**ⒶⒶⒶ ▼▼▼ Holiday Inn-Airport SH 🐾**
(915) 778-6411. **$100-$135.** 6655 Gateway Blvd W. I-10, exit 25 (Airway Blvd). Ext/int corridors. **Pets:** Small, other species. $8 daily fee/pet, $25 one-time fee/pet. Service with restrictions, supervision.
SAVE ⓢ ✕ 🅜 🖥 🖵 🍴 🏊

**ⒶⒶⒶ ▼▼◆ Holiday Inn El Paso Sunland Park SH**
(915) 833-2900. **$90-$115.** 900 Sunland Park Dr. I-10, exit 13. Ext corridors. **Pets:** Medium, other species. $25 one-time fee/room. Service with restrictions, supervision.
SAVE ⓢ ✕ 🅜 🖥 🖵 🍴 🏊

**▼▼ Howard Johnson Inn SH**
(915) 591-9471. **$63-$75.** 8887 Gateway Blvd W. I-10, exit 26 (Hawkins Blvd). Int corridors. **Pets:** Service with restrictions, supervision.
ASK ⓢ ✕ 🖥 🖵 🍴 🏊

**▼▼ La Quinta Inn El Paso (Airport) Ⓜ**
(915) 778-9321. **$76-$86.** 6140 Gateway Blvd E. I-10, exit 24B (Geronimo Dr) eastbound; exit 24 westbound. Ext corridors. **Pets:** Medium. Service with restrictions.
ASK ✕ 🗐 🅜 🖥 🖵 🏊

**▼▼ La Quinta Inn El Paso (Cielo Vista) SH**
(915) 593-8400. **$72-$82.** 9125 Gateway Blvd W. I-10, exit 28B westbound; exit 27 eastbound. Ext corridors. **Pets:** Medium. Service with restrictions.
ASK ✕ 🗐 🅜 🖥 🖵 🏊

**▼▼ La Quinta Inn El Paso (Lomaland) SH**
(915) 591-2244. **$58-$72.** 11033 Gateway Blvd W. I-10, exit 29 eastbound; exit 30 westbound, 1 mi w. Ext corridors. **Pets:** Medium. Service with restrictions.
ASK ✕ 🅜 🗐 🅜 🖥 🖵 🏊

**ⒶⒶⒶ ▼▼▼ La Quinta Inn El Paso (West) Ⓜ**
(915) 833-2522. **$75-$85.** 7550 Remcon Cir. I-10, exit 11 (Mesa St). Ext corridors. **Pets:** Medium. Service with restrictions.
SAVE ✕ 🗐 🅜 🖥 🖵 🏊

**▼▼ Microtel Inn & Suites West Ⓜ**
(915) 584-2026. **$51-$65.** 6185 Desert Blvd S. I-10, exit 8 (Artcraft Rd/Paseo del Norte), on eastbound frontage road. Int corridors. **Pets:** Large, other species. $100 deposit/room. Designated rooms, service with restrictions, supervision.
ASK ⓢ ✕ 🅜 🖥 🖵

**▼▼ Microtel Inn & Suites SH**
(915) 772-3650. **$63-$88.** 2001 Airway Blvd. I-10, exit 25 (Airway Blvd), 1.3 mi n. Int corridors. **Pets:** Small, other species. $100 deposit/pet. Service with restrictions, crate.
ASK ✕ 🅜 🗐 🖥 🖵

**▼▼◆ Microtel Inn & Suites El Paso East SH**
(915) 858-1600. **$46-$66.** 12211 Gateway W at Don Haskins Rd. I-10, exit 34 (Joe Battle), on westbound frontage road. Int corridors. **Pets:** Small, other species. $100 deposit/room. Service with restrictions, supervision.
ASK ⓢ ✕ 🅜 🅜 🖥 🖵 🏊

**▼▼◆ Quality Inn & Suites SH**
(915) 772-3300. **$70-$80.** 6099 Montana Ave. I-10, exit 24 (Geronimo Dr) westbound; exit 24B (Geronimo Dr) eastbound, 0.5 mi n. Ext corridors. **Pets:** Accepted.
ASK ⓢ ✕ 🅜 🖥 🖵 🍴 🏊

**▼▼ Red Roof Inn West SH**
(915) 587-9977. **$46-$60.** 7530 Remcon Cir. I-10, exit 11 (Mesa St). Ext/int corridors. **Pets:** Accepted.
✕ 🅜 🗐 🅜 🖥 🏊

**▼▼▼ Residence Inn by Marriott El Paso SH**
(915) 771-0504. **$84-$189, 14 day notice.** 6355 Gateway Blvd W. I-10, exit 24B (Geronimo Dr) eastbound, n to Edgemere, then just e; exit 25 (Airway Blvd) westbound on westbound frontage road. Int corridors. **Pets:** Accepted.
ASK ⓢ ✕ 🅜 🖥 🖵 🏊 ✕

**▼▼ Sleep Inn by Choice Hotels SH**
(915) 585-7577. **$65-$85.** 953 Sunland Park Dr. I-10, exit 13. Int corridors. **Pets:** Accepted.
ASK ⓢ ✕ 🅜 🖥 🖵 🏊

**▼▼ Studio 6 El Paso #6001 SH**
(915) 594-8533. **$48-$58.** 11049 Gateway Blvd W. I-10, exit 29 eastbound; exit 30 westbound. Ext corridors. **Pets:** Accepted.
ⓢ ✕ 🅜 🖥 🖵 🏊

**▼▼ Travelodge Ⓜ**
(915) 833-2613. **$50-$90.** 7815 N Mesa St. I-10, exit 11 (Mesa St). Ext corridors. **Pets:** Accepted.
ASK ⓢ ✕ 🖥 🖵 🏊

# EULESS

**▼▼▼ La Quinta DFW Airport West-Euless SH**
(817) 540-0233. **$69-$79.** 1001 W Airport Frwy. SR 183, exit Industrial Blvd (FM 157). Ext corridors. **Pets:** Medium. Service with restrictions.
ASK ✕ 🗐 🖥 🖵 🏊

**▼▼ Microtel Inn and Suites SH**
(817) 545-1111. **$54-$74.** 901 W Airport Frwy. SR 183, exit Industrial Blvd (FM 157), just e. Int corridors. **Pets:** Small, dogs only. $25 one-time fee/room. Service with restrictions, supervision.
ASK ⓢ ✕ 🅜 🅜 🖥 🖵 🏊

**▼▼ Motel 6-Euless #1345 SH**
(817) 545-0141. **$37-$49.** 110 Airport Frwy. SR 183, exit Euless/Main St, on westbound access road. Ext corridors. **Pets:** Accepted.
ⓢ ✕ 🅜 🏊

# FORT DAVIS

**▼▼ Historical Prude Guest Ranch RA**
(432) 426-3202. **$80, 3 day notice.** 6 mi n Hwy 118. 4.5 mi n of jct SR 118 and 17. Ext corridors. **Pets:** Medium, other species. $10 one-time fee/pet. Designated rooms, service with restrictions, supervision.
ASK ⓢ ✕ 🖥 🍴 🏊 ✕ 🆆 🅩

# FORT STOCKTON

**ⒶⒶⒶ ▼▼▼ Atrium West Inn SH**
(432) 336-6666. **$70-$130.** 1305 N Hwy 285. I-10, exit 257, just s. Ext corridors. **Pets:** Small. $10 one-time fee/pet. Service with restrictions, supervision.
SAVE ⓢ ✕ 🖥 🖵 🏊 ✕

**▲▲▲ ▼▼▼ Best Western Swiss Clock Inn** 🆂🅷
(432) 336-8521. **$68.** 3201 W Dickinson Blvd. I-10, exit 256, 0.5 mi e.
Ext corridors. **Pets:** Medium, other species. $5 daily fee/room. Designated
rooms, service with restrictions, supervision.
🆂🅰🆅🅴 🆂🅾 ☒ 🕭 🖥 🖵 🍴 ≈

**▲▲▲ ▼▼▼ Comfort Inn of Fort Stockton** 🆂🅷
(432) 336-8531. **$69-$99.** 3200 W Dickinson Blvd. I-10, exit 256, just s.
Int corridors. **Pets:** Small. $5 daily fee/pet. Designated rooms, service with
restrictions, supervision.
🆂🅰🆅🅴 🆂🅾 ☒ 🕭 🖥 🖵 ≈

**▲▲▲ ▼▼▼ Days Inn** 🆂🅷
(432) 336-7500. **$49-$79.** 1408 N US Hwy 285. I-10, exit 257, just s.
Ext corridors. **Pets:** Small. Service with restrictions, supervision.
🆂🅰🆅🅴 🆂🅾 ☒ 🖉 🖥 ≈

**▼▼ ▼▼ Econo Lodge** 🅼
(432) 336-9711. **$37-$45.** 800 E Dickinson Blvd. I-10, exit 261, 1.3 mi w
on I-20 business route. Ext corridors. **Pets:** Accepted.
🅰🆂🅺 🆂🅾 ☒ 🖥 ≈

**▲▲▲ ▼▼▼▼ Holiday Inn Express** 🆂🅷
(432) 336-5955. **$63-$120.** 1308 N US Hwy 285. I-10, exit 257, just s.
Ext corridors. **Pets:** Medium. $25 one-time fee/pet. Designated rooms,
service with restrictions, crate.
🆂🅰🆅🅴 🆂🅾 ☒ 🖉 🖥 🖵 ≈

**▲▲▲ ▼▼ ▼▼ La Quinta Inn Fort Stockton** 🆂🅷
(432) 336-9781. **$63-$95.** 1537 N Hwy 285. I-10, exit 257. Ext corridors. **Pets:** Medium. Service with restrictions.
🆂🅰🆅🅴 ☒ 🖉 🖥 🖥 🖵 ≈

**▼▼ Motel 6 Fort Stockton #333** 🅼
(432) 336-9737. **$39-$51.** 3001 W Dickinson Blvd. I-10, exit 256, 0.5 mi
e. Ext corridors. **Pets:** Accepted.
🆂🅾 ☒ ≈

# FORT WORTH

**▲▲▲ ▼▼▼▼ AmeriSuites (Ft Worth/Cityview)** 🆂🅷
(817) 361-9797. **$109-$129.** 5900 Cityview Blvd. I-20, exit 431 (Bryant
Irvin Rd). Int corridors. **Pets:** Accepted.
🆂🅰🆅🅴 🆂🅾 ☒ 🖉🅼 🖉 🖉 🖥 🖵 ≈

**▼▼▼▼ The Ashton Hotel** 🆂🅷
(817) 332-0100. **$270-$790.** 610 Main St. Jct of 6th and Main sts;
center. Int corridors. **Pets:** Accepted.
☒ 🖉 🍴

**▼▼▼▼ Candlewood Suites** 🆂🅷
(817) 838-8229. **$99-$169.** 5201 Endicott Ave. I-820, exit 17B, just s.
Int corridors. **Pets:** Accepted.
🅰🆂🅺 🆂🅾 ☒ 🖉 🖥 🖵

**▼▼▼▼ Hampton Inn & Suites-FW Alliance Airport** 🆂🅷
(817) 439-0400. **$69-$129.** 13600 North Frwy. I-35W, exit 66 (Westport
Pkwy). Int corridors. **Pets:** Small, other species. $25 one-time fee/room.
Service with restrictions, crate.
🅰🆂🅺 🆂🅾 ☒ 🖉🅼 🖉 🖥 🖵 ≈

**▼▼▼▼ Holiday Inn Express Hotel & Suites-Fort Worth
West** 🆂🅷
(817) 560-4200. **$89.** 2730 Cherry Ln. I-30, exit 7A. Int corridors.
**Pets:** Accepted.
☒ 🖥 🖵 ≈

**▼▼▼▼ Holiday Inn Ft. Worth South & Conference
Center** 🆂🅷
(817) 293-3088. **$89-$199.** 100 Altamesa E Blvd. I-35, exit 44. Int
corridors. **Pets:** Accepted.
🅰🆂🅺 🆂🅾 ☒ 🖉 🖥 🖵 🍴 ≈

**▲▲▲ ▼▼▼▼ Holiday Inn North/Conference Center** 🆂🅷
(817) 625-9911. **$69-$75.** 2540 Meacham Blvd. I-35W, exit 56A. Int
corridors. **Pets:** Accepted.
🆂🅰🆅🅴 ☒ 🖉 🖥 🖥 🍴 ≈

**▼▼▼▼ Homestead Studio Suites Hotel-Fort Worth/Medical
Center** 🆂🅷
(817) 338-4808. **$53-$68.** 1601 River Run. I-30, exit 12 (University Dr),
just s. Ext corridors. **Pets:** $25 daily fee/pet. Service with restrictions,
supervision.
🅰🆂🅺 🆂🅾 ☒ 🖉 🖥 🖵

**▼▼▼▼ La Quinta Inn & Suites Fort Worth (North)** 🆂🅷
(817) 222-2888. **$99-$119.** 4700 North Frwy. I-35W, exit 56A, just n. Int
corridors. **Pets:** Medium. Service with restrictions.
🅰🆂🅺 ☒ 🖉 🖉 🖥 🖵 ≈

**▼▼▼▼ La Quinta Inn & Suites Fort Worth (Southwest)** 🆂🅷
(817) 370-2700. **$98-$114.** 4900 Bryant Irvin Rd. I-20, exit 431. Int
corridors. **Pets:** Medium. Service with restrictions.
🅰🆂🅺 ☒ 🖉🅼 🖉 🖉 🖥 🖵 ≈

**▲▲▲ ▼▼▼▼ La Quinta Inn Fort Worth (West/Medical
Center)** 🆂🅷
(817) 246-5511. **$69-$83.** 7888 I-30 W. I-30, exit 7A. Ext/int corridors.
**Pets:** Medium. Service with restrictions.
🆂🅰🆅🅴 ☒ 🖉 🖥 🖵 ≈

**▼▼ ▼▼ Microtel Inn & Suites** 🆂🅷
(817) 222-3740. **$59-$89.** 3740 Tanacross Dr. I-820, exit 17B (Beach
St), just s. Int corridors. **Pets:** Accepted.
🅰🆂🅺 🆂🅾 ☒ 🖉 🖥 🖥 🖵 ≈

**▼▼ Motel 6-#117** 🆂🅷
(817) 244-9740. **$35-$47.** 8701 I-30 W. I-30, exit 6, just s on Las
Vegas. Ext corridors. **Pets:** Accepted.
🆂🅾 ☒ 🖉 🖥 ≈

**▼▼ Motel 6 East-1341** 🆂🅷
(817) 834-7361. **$38-$49.** 1236 Oakland Blvd. I-30, exit 18. Ext corridors. **Pets:** Accepted.
🆂🅾 ☒ ≈

**▲▲▲ ▼▼▼▼ Radisson Plaza Hotel Fort Worth** 🅻🅷
(817) 870-2100. **$149-$179.** 815 Main St. Northeast corner of Main and
8th sts; center. Int corridors. **Pets:** Accepted.
🆂🅰🆅🅴 🆂🅾 ☒ 🖉🅼 🖉 🖉 🖥 🖥 🍴 ≈

**▲▲▲ ▼▼▼▼ ▼▼ The Renaissance Worthington Hotel** 🅻🅷
(817) 870-1000. **$137-$249.** 200 Main St. Northwest corner of 2nd and
Main sts. Int corridors. **Pets:** Accepted.
🆂🅰🆅🅴 🆂🅾 ☒ 🖉 🖉 🖥 🖥 🍴 ≈ 🆇

**▼▼▼▼ Residence Inn-Alliance Airport** 🆂🅷 🐾
(817) 750-7000. **$75-$149, 7 day notice.** 13400 North Frwy. I-35W, exit
66. Int corridors. **Pets:** $75 one-time fee/room. Service with restrictions,
crate.
🅰🆂🅺 🆂🅾 ☒ 🖉 🖥 🖥 🖵 ≈ 🆇

**▼▼▼▼ Residence Inn By Marriott Fort Worth-River
Plaza** 🆂🅷
(817) 870-1011. **$139.** 1701 S University Dr. I-30, exit 12 (University
Dr), 0.4 mi s. Ext corridors. **Pets:** Accepted.
🅰🆂🅺 🆂🅾 ☒ 🖉🅼 🖉 🖉 🖥 🖵 ≈ 🆇

**▼▼▼▼ TownePlace Suites by Marriott-Fort Worth** 🆂🅷
(817) 732-2224. **$109-$129.** 4200 International Plaza Dr. I-820, exit
433. Int corridors. **Pets:** Other species. $75 one-time fee/room. Service
with restrictions, crate.
🅰🆂🅺 ☒ 🖉 🖥 🖥 🖵

# FREDERICKSBURG

**▼▼▼▼ Best Western Fredericksburg SH**
(830) 992-2929. **$59-$159.** 314 E Highway St. Jct US 87 and 290, 6 blks s. Int corridors. **Pets:** Accepted.

ASK SÒ ✕ 🗒 ⊟ 🖵 ⇌

**◆◆◆ ▼▼▼ Budget Host Deluxe Inn M**
(830) 997-3344. **$40-$85.** 901 E Main St. US 290, 0.5 mi e. Ext corridors. **Pets:** Small, dogs only. $10 daily fee/pet. Designated rooms, service with restrictions, supervision.

SAVE ✕ ⊟ 🖵

**▼▼▼ Comfort Inn & Suites SH**
(830) 990-2552. **$89-$175.** 723 S Washington St. W on Main St, then left. Int corridors. **Pets:** Accepted.

ASK SÒ ✕ 🗒 ⊟ 🖵 ⇌

**◆◆◆ ▼▼▼ Dietzel Motel M** 🐾
(830) 997-3330. **$49-$89.** 1141 W US 290. 1 mi w on US 290 at US 87. Ext corridors. **Pets:** Other species. $7 daily fee/pet. Designated rooms, service with restrictions.

SAVE ✕

**◆◆◆ ▼▼▼◆ Fredericksburg Inn & Suites SH**
(830) 997-0202. **$79-$109.** 201 S Washington. US 290 and 87, 3 blks s. Ext corridors. **Pets:** Accepted.

SAVE SÒ ✕ ⊟ 🖵 ⇌

**▼▼ Frontier Inn & RV Park M**
(830) 997-4389. **$46-$110.** 1704 US Hwy 290 W. US 290, 1 mi w. Ext corridors. **Pets:** Other species. $5 daily fee/pet. No service.

ASK SÒ ✕ ⊟ 🖵

**▼▼▼ Holiday Inn Express SH**
(830) 990-4200. **$89-$149.** 1220 N Hwy 87. 1 mi w on US 290 at US 87. Int corridors. **Pets:** Small. $25 one-time fee/pet. Designated rooms, service with restrictions, supervision.

ASK SÒ ✕ ⓜ 🗒 ⊟ 🖵 ⇌

**▼▼▼▼ La Quinta Inn & Suites SH**
(830) 990-2899. **$95-$99.** 1465 E Main St. 1 mi e of downtown. Int corridors. **Pets:** Small, dogs only. Service with restrictions, supervision.

ASK SÒ ✕ ⓜ 🗒 ⊟ 🖵 ⇌

**◆◆◆ ▼▼▼◆ Quality Inn SH**
(830) 997-9811. **$72-$116.** 908 S Adams St. 0.8 mi sw on SR 16; 0.8 mi sw of jct US 87 and 290. Ext corridors. **Pets:** Medium. $15 daily fee/pet. Service with restrictions, crate.

SAVE SÒ ✕ ⊘ ⊟ 🖵 ⇌

**◆◆◆ ▼▼▼◆ Sunday House Inn & Suites SH**
(830) 997-4484. **$89-$110.** 501 E Main St. 0.4 mi e on US 290. Ext corridors. **Pets:** Very small. $10 daily fee/pet. Designated rooms, service with restrictions.

SAVE SÒ ✕ 🗒 ⊟ 🖵 ⇌

**◆◆◆ ▼▼ Sunset Inn M**
(830) 997-9581. **$45-$69.** 900 S Adams St. 0.8 mi sw of jct US 290 and SR 16. Ext corridors. **Pets:** Dogs only. Service with restrictions, supervision.

SAVE SÒ ✕ ⊟ 🖵 🍴

**◆◆◆ ▼▼▼ Super 8 Fredericksburg M**
(830) 997-6568. **$70-$90.** 514 E Main St. US 290, just e of jct US 87. Ext corridors. **Pets:** Small. $10 one-time fee/pet. Service with restrictions, supervision.

SAVE SÒ ✕ ⊟ 🖵 ⇌

# FRITCH

**▼▼ Lone Star Inn and Suites SH**
(806) 857-3191. **$40-$50.** 205 E Broadway. SR 136, in town. Ext corridors. **Pets:** Accepted.

ASK SÒ ✕ ⊟ 🖵

# FULTON

**◆◆◆ ▼▼▼▼ Best Western Inn by the Bay M** 🐾
(361) 729-8351. **$82-$99.** 3902 N Hwy 35. SR 35, 0.5 mi n of jct Business Rt SR 35 and FM 3063. Ext corridors. **Pets:** Other species. $10 daily fee/pet. Supervision.

SAVE SÒ ✕ ⊘ ⊟ 🖵 ⇌

# GAINESVILLE

**◆◆◆ ▼▼▼ Best Western Southwinds M** 🐾
(940) 665-7737. **$59-$169.** 2103 N I-35. I-35, exit 499 northbound, 1.4 mi n on access road to S Frontage Rd; exit 498B southbound. Ext corridors. **Pets:** Dogs only. $8 one-time fee/pet. Service with restrictions, crate.

SAVE SÒ ✕ ⊟ 🖵 ⇌

**◆◆◆ ▼▼ Budget Host Inn M**
(940) 665-2856. **$44.** 1900 N I-35. I-35, exit 499 northbound; exit 498B southbound. Ext corridors. **Pets:** Medium. $5 daily fee/pet. Service with restrictions, crate.

SAVE SÒ ✕ ⊟

**◆◆◆ ▼▼▼ Deluxe Inn/Super 8 SH**
(940) 665-5599. **$60.** 1936 I-35 N. I-35, exit 499 northbound, exit 498A southbound. Int corridors. **Pets:** Accepted.

SAVE SÒ ✕ ⇌

**◆◆◆ ▼▼▼ Ramada Limited SH**
(940) 665-8800. **$69-$129.** 600 Medal of Honor Blvd. I-35, exit 496B (California St). Ext corridors. **Pets:** $10 daily fee/pet. Service with restrictions, supervision.

SAVE SÒ ✕ ⊟ 🖵 ⇌

# GALVESTON

**▼▼▼ La Quinta Inn Galveston Seawall South SH**
(409) 763-1224. **$76-$146.** 1402 Seawall Blvd. Seawall Blvd at 14th St. Ext corridors. **Pets:** Medium. Service with restrictions.

ASK ✕ ⊘ 🗒 ⊟ 🖵 ⇌

# GEORGETOWN

**◆◆◆ ▼▼▼▼ La Quinta Inn Georgetown SH**
(512) 869-2541. **$69-$83.** 333 I-35 N. I-35, exit 264 northbound; exit 262 southbound; on west frontage road. Ext corridors. **Pets:** Medium. Service with restrictions.

SAVE ✕ 🗒 ⊟ 🖵 ⇌

# GEORGE WEST

**◆◆◆ ▼▼▼ Best Western George West Executive Inn SH**
(361) 449-3300. **$67, 5 day notice.** 208 N Nueces St. Just n of US 59 on SR 281. Ext corridors. **Pets:** Medium, other species. $50 deposit/pet. Designated rooms, service with restrictions, supervision.

SAVE SÒ ✕ 🗒 ⊟ 🖵 ⇌

# GIDDINGS

**◆◆◆ ▼▼▼ Ramada M**
(979) 542-9666. **$55-$80.** 4002 E Austin St. 2.5 mi e on US 290. Ext corridors. **Pets:** Medium, dogs only. $100 one-time fee/pet. Service with restrictions, crate.

SAVE SÒ ✕ ⊟ 🖵 ⇌

**◆◆◆ ▼▼▼ Super 8 Motel M**
(979) 542-5791. **$54-$64.** 3556 E Austin St. 2 mi e on US 290. Ext corridors. **Pets:** Accepted.

SAVE SÒ ✕ ⊟ 🖵 ⇌

# GLEN ROSE

**Best Western Dinosaur Valley Inn & Suites** SH
(254) 897-4818. **$110-$375.** 1311 NE Big Ben Tr. On US 67. Int corridors. **Pets:** Medium. $40 one-time fee/room. Service with restrictions, supervision.

# GRANBURY

**Comfort Inn** SH
(817) 573-2611. **$59-$119.** 1201 Plaza Dr N. 2 mi e on US 377 Bypass. Ext corridors. **Pets:** Other species. $10 daily fee/room.

**Plantation Inn on the Lake** SH
(817) 573-8846. **$65-$85.** 1451 E Pearl St. 0.3 mi w of Business Rt US 377 at US 377 Bypass. Ext/int corridors. **Pets:** Accepted.

# GRAPEVINE

**AmeriSuites (Dallas/DFW Airport North)** SH
(972) 691-1199. **$139-$159.** 2220 Grapevine Mills Cir W. SR 121 N, exit Bass Pro Dr. Int corridors. **Pets:** Accepted.

**Baymont Inn-Dallas-Ft Worth/Airport North** SH
(817) 329-9300. **$79-$159.** 301 Capital St. SR 114, exit Main St. Int corridors. **Pets:** Large, other species. $100 deposit/room. Service with restrictions, supervision.

**Embassy Suites Outdoor World** LH
(972) 724-2600. **$269.** 2401 Bass Pro Dr. US 121, exit Bass Pro Dr. Int corridors. **Pets:** Accepted.

**Homewood Suites by Hilton** SH
(972) 691-2427. **$149-$179, 14 day notice.** 2214 Grapevine Mills Cir W. SR 121 N, exit Bass Pro Dr. Int corridors. **Pets:** Accepted.

**Super 8 Motel-Grapevine** SH 🐾
(817) 329-7222. **$59-$110.** 250 E Hwy 114. SR 114, exit Main St. Int corridors. **Pets:** Medium. $5 daily fee/pet. Designated rooms, service with restrictions.

# GROOM

**Chalet Inn** M
(806) 248-7524. **$50-$60.** I-40 FM 2300. I-40, exit 113, just s. Ext corridors. **Pets:** Medium. $5 daily fee/pet. Designated rooms, service with restrictions, supervision.

# HARLINGEN

**Country Inn & Suites By Carlson** SH
(956) 428-0043. **$64-$125, 3 day notice.** 3825 S Expwy 83. US 83 and 77, exit Ed Carrey. Int corridors. **Pets:** Accepted.

**Howard Johnson Inn** SH
(956) 425-7070. **$57.** 6779 W Expwy 83. Jct US 77, 2.3 mi w on US 83, exit Stuart Place Rd. Ext corridors. **Pets:** Accepted.

**La Quinta Inn Harlingen** SH
(956) 428-6888. **$67-$83.** 1002 S Expwy 83. US 83 and 77, exit M St. Ext corridors. **Pets:** Medium. Service with restrictions.

**Ramada Limited** SH
(956) 425-1333. **$67-$77.** 4401 S Expwy 83. US 83 and 77, exit Ed Carey Dr. Ext corridors. **Pets:** Accepted.

**Super 8 Motel** SH
(956) 412-8867. **$60-$70.** 1115 S Expwy 83. US 83 and 77, exit M St, just n. Int corridors. **Pets:** Other species. $5 daily fee/pet. Service with restrictions, supervision.

# HEARNE

**Oak Tree Inn** SH
(979) 279-5599. **$60-$64.** 1051 N Market St. 0.6 mi n of jct US 79 and SR 6. Ext/int corridors. **Pets:** Medium. $10 one-time fee/pet. Service with restrictions, supervision.

# HENDERSON

**Best Western Inn of Henderson** SH
(903) 657-9561. **$74-$89.** 1500 Hwy 259 S. 2 mi s on US 259, 0.7 mi s of jct US 79 and 259 S. Ext/int corridors. **Pets:** Accepted.

# HEREFORD

**Best Western Red Carpet Inn** SH
(806) 364-0540. **$59-$75.** 830 W 1st St. Just w of jct US 385 and 60. Ext corridors. **Pets:** Medium. Service with restrictions, supervision.

**Holiday Inn Express** SH
(806) 364-3322. **$85-$120.** 1400 W 1st St. Jct US 385/60, just w. Int corridors. **Pets:** $20 one-time fee/room. Service with restrictions, supervision.

# HILLSBORO

**Best Western Hillsboro Inn** SH
(254) 582-8465. **$75-$80.** 307 I-35. I-35, exit 368A northbound; exit 368B southbound, just w. Ext corridors. **Pets:** Medium. $8 one-time fee/room. Service with restrictions, supervision.

**Days Inn Hillsboro** SH
(254) 582-3493. **$59-$63, 3 day notice.** 307 SE I-35. I-35, exit 368 A/B. Ext corridors. **Pets:** Small. $5 daily fee/pet. No service, supervision.

**Super 8** SH
(254) 580-0404. **Call for rates.** 1512 Hillview Dr. I-35, exit 368A northbound; 368 southbound, just e. Int corridors. **Pets:** Accepted.

# HONDO

**Hondo Executive Inn** M
(830) 426-2535. **$45-$95.** 102 E 19th St. On US 90 W. Ext corridors. **Pets:** $10 daily fee/pet. Service with restrictions, supervision.

**Regency Inn** M
(830) 426-3031. **$45-$85.** 401 Hwy 90 E. Jct SR 173. Ext corridors. **Pets:** Small, dogs only. $10 one-time fee/pet. Designated rooms, service with restrictions, supervision.

# HOUSTON METROPOLITAN AREA

## BAYTOWN

**ⒶⒶⒶ ▼▼▼ Baymont Inn & Suites Houston-Baytown** 🆂🅷
(281) 421-7300. **$73-$83.** 5215 I-10 E. I-10, exit 792 (Garth Rd). Int corridors. **Pets:** Medium. Service with restrictions.

🆂🅰🆅🅴 ☒ 🕐 🄳 🎫 💻 🏊

**▼▼▼ Comfort Suites Baytown** 🆂🅷
(281) 421-9764. **$99-$299.** 7209 Garth Rd. I-10, exit 792 (Garth Rd), just n. Int corridors. **Pets:** Accepted.

🄰🆂🅺 🆂🅰 ☒ 🅼 🄳 🎫 💻 🏊

**▼▼ Holiday Inn Express** 🆂🅷
(281) 421-7200. **$72.** 5222 I-10 E. I-10, exit 792 (Garth Rd). Int corridors. **Pets:** Small. $10 deposit/pet. Service with restrictions, supervision.

🄰🆂🅺 🆂🅰 ☒ 🅼 🕐 🄳 💻 🏊

**ⒶⒶⒶ ▼▼▼ La Quinta Inn Houston (Baytown)** 🅼
(281) 421-5566. **$73-$83.** 4911 I-10 E. I-10, exit 792 (Garth Rd). Ext corridors. **Pets:** Medium. Service with restrictions.

🆂🅰🆅🅴 ☒ 🕐 🎫 💻 🏊

**▼ Motel 6—1136** 🅼
(281) 576-5777. **$41-$51.** 8911 Hwy 146. I-10, exit 797 (SR 146). Ext corridors. **Pets:** Accepted.

🆂🅰 ☒ 🄳 🎫 🏊

## CONROE

**▼▼▼ Baymont Inn-Conroe** 🆂🅷
(936) 539-5100. **$64-$69, 30 day notice.** 1506 I-45 S. I-45, exit 85 (Gladstell St) northbound; exit 84 (Frazier St) southbound. Int corridors. **Pets:** Small. $10 daily fee/pet. Designated rooms, service with restrictions, crate.

🄰🆂🅺 🆂🅰 ☒ 🕐 🄳 🎫 💻 🏊

**▼▼▼ La Quinta Inn & Suites** 🆂🅷
(936) 228-0790. **$85-$95.** 4006 Sprayberry Ln. I-45, exit 91 (League Line Rd), just e. Int corridors. **Pets:** Small, dogs only. Designated rooms, service with restrictions, supervision.

🄰🆂🅺 🆂🅰 ☒ 🅼 🄳 🎫 💻 🏊

**▼ Motel 6 Conroe #385** 🅼
(936) 760-4003. **$39-$49.** 820 I-45 S. I-45, exit 85 (Gladstell Rd). Ext corridors. **Pets:** Accepted.

🆂🅰 ☒ 🏊

## DEER PARK

**▼▼ Best Western Deer Park Inn & Suites** 🆂🅷
(281) 476-5000. **$70-$78.** 1401 Center St. SR 225 (La Porte Rd), exit Center St, 0.9 mi s. Ext corridors. **Pets:** Accepted.

🄰🆂🅺 🆂🅰 ☒ 🄳 🎫 💻 🏊

## HOUSTON

**ⒶⒶⒶ ▼▼▼ Americas Best Value Inn** 🆂🅷
(281) 866-8686. **$59.** 609 FM 1960 W. I-45, exit 66 (FM 1960) southbound; exit 66A northbound, just w. Int corridors. **Pets:** Accepted.

🆂🅰🆅🅴 🆂🅰 ☒ 🄳 🎫 🏊

**▼▼▼ AmeriSuites (Houston Intercontinental Airport/Greenspoint)** 🆂🅷
(281) 820-6100. **$80-$100.** 300 Ronan Park Pl. Sam Houston Pkwy (Beltway 8), exit Imperial Valley westbound, 0.8 mi w on frontage road; exit Hardy Toll Rd eastbound, turn under parkway, 1.2 mi w on west frontage road. Int corridors. **Pets:** Accepted.

🄰🆂🅺 🆂🅰 ☒ 🅼 🄳 🎫 💻 🏊

**ⒶⒶⒶ ▼▼▼ Baymont Inn & Suites Houston Northwest** 🆂🅷
(713) 680-8282. **$73-$83.** 11130 Northwest Frwy. US 290 W, exit W 34th St, on southeast corner. Int corridors. **Pets:** Medium. No service.

🆂🅰🆅🅴 ☒ 🄳 🎫 💻 🏊

**ⒶⒶⒶ ▼▼▼ Baymont Inn & Suites Houston Southwest** 🆂🅷
(713) 784-3838. **$66-$76.** 6790 Southwest Frwy. US 59 (Southwest Frwy), exit Hillcroft St/W Park eastbound; exit Hillcroft St westbound. Int corridors. **Pets:** Medium. Service with restrictions.

🆂🅰🆅🅴 ☒ 🄳 🎫 💻 🏊

**▼▼▼ Best Western Houston Hotel & Suites Near the Galleria** 🆂🅷
(713) 688-2800. **$79.** 7625 Katy Fwy. -10, exit 762 westbound; exit 161B eastbound on eastbound frontage road. Int corridors. **Pets:** Accepted.

🄰🆂🅺 🆂🅰 ☒ 🅼 🄳 🎫 💻 🏊

**▼▼▼ Candlewood Suites Houston by the Galleria** 🆂🅷
(713) 839-9411. **$59-$104.** 4900 Loop Central Dr. I-610, exit 7 (Fournace Pl), on northbound frontage road. Int corridors. **Pets:** Accepted.

🄰🆂🅺 🆂🅰 ☒ 🄳 💻

**▼▼▼ Candlewood Suites-Houston-Clear Lake** 🆂🅷
(281) 461-3060. **$126-$130.** 2737 Bay Area Blvd. I-45, exit 26, 3.7 mi e. Int corridors. **Pets:** Accepted.

☒ 🄳 💻

**▼▼▼ Candlewood Suites-Town & Country** 🆂🅷
(713) 464-2677. **$87-$101.** 10503 Town & Country Way. I-10, exit 755 eastbound, 1.1 mi on frontage road to Town & Country Blvd, then 0.4 mi s; exit 756A westbound, U-turn under I-10, just e to Town & Country Blvd, then 0.4 mi s. Int corridors. **Pets:** Accepted.

🄰🆂🅺 🆂🅰 ☒ 🅼 🄳 🎫 💻

**▼▼▼ Candlewood Suites-Westchase** 🆂🅷
(713) 780-7881. **$65-$125.** 4033 W Sam Houston Pkwy S. Sam Houston Pkwy (Beltway 8), exit Westpark, southeast corner of Westpark and Sam Houston Pkwy (Beltway 8) on northbound frontage road. Int corridors. **Pets:** Accepted.

🄰🆂🅺 🆂🅰 ☒ 🅼 🄳 🎫 💻

**▼▼▼ Comfort Inn & Suites** 🆂🅷
(713) 623-4720. **$72-$119, 3 day notice.** 4020 Southwest Frwy. US 59, exit Weslayan St northbound; exit Eloe/Weslayan St southbound, on southbound frontage road. Ext corridors. **Pets:** Accepted.

🄰🆂🅺 🆂🅰 ☒ 🄳 🎫 💻 🏊

**ⒶⒶⒶ ▼▼▼ Comfort Inn Galleria/Westchase** 🆂🅷
(713) 783-1400. **$77-$97, 10 day notice.** 9041 Westheimer Rd. Just w of jct Fondren. Ext corridors. **Pets:** Other species. $25 one-time fee/pet. Service with restrictions, crate.

🆂🅰🆅🅴 🆂🅰 ☒ 🄳 💻 🏊

**ⒶⒶⒶ ▼▼▼ Comfort Suites** 🆂🅷
(281) 440-4448. **$79-$169.** 150 Overland Tr. I-45, exit 66 (FM 1960), on southbound frontage road. Int corridors. **Pets:** Small, other species. $25 one-time fee/pet. Service with restrictions, crate.

🆂🅰🆅🅴 🆂🅰 ☒ 🅼 🕐 🄳 🎫 💻 🏊

**ⒶⒶⒶ ▼▼▼ Comfort Suites-Galleria** 🆂🅷
(713) 787-0004. **$105-$200.** 6221 Richmond Ave. US 59, exit Hillcroft St, 1 mi n to Richmond Ave, then 0.6 mi e. Int corridors. **Pets:** Small. $50 one-time fee/room. Service with restrictions, crate.

🆂🅰🆅🅴 🆂🅰 ☒ 🄳 🎫 💻 🏊

**Courtyard by Marriott-Brookhollow** SH
(713) 688-7711. **$99-$129.** 2504 N Loop W. I-610, exit 13C (TC Jester), just nw. Int corridors. **Pets:** Accepted.

**Crowne Plaza Northwest Hotel** LH
(713) 462-9977. **$112.** 12801 Northwest Frwy. Nw on US 290, exit Hollister Rd, 0.7 mi e on south service road. Ext/int corridors. **Pets:** Small. $25 one-time fee/room. Service with restrictions, crate.

**Doubletree Guest Suites** LH
(713) 961-9000. **$99-$239.** 5353 Westheimer Rd. I-610, exit 8C (Westheimer Rd) northbound; exit 9A (San Felipe/Westheimer rds) southbound, 0.8 mi w. Int corridors. **Pets:** Accepted.

**Doubletree Hotel at Allen Center** LH
(713) 759-0202. **$89-$269.** 400 Dallas St. At Dallas and Bagby sts. Int corridors. **Pets:** Accepted.

**Drury Inn & Suites-Houston Hobby** SH
(713) 941-4300. **$70-$130.** 7902 Mosley Rd. I-45, exit 36 (Airport Blvd/College Rd) northbound, just w on Airport Blvd, then just n; exit southbound, follow frontage road to Mosley Rd. Int corridors. **Pets:** Accepted.

**Drury Inn & Suites-Houston Near Galleria** SH
(713) 963-0700. **$80-$120.** 1615 W Loop S. I-610, exit 9 (San Felipe Rd) northbound; exit 9A (San Felipe/Westheimer rds) southbound, on east service road. Int corridors. **Pets:** Accepted.

**Drury Inn & Suites-Houston West** SH
(281) 558-7007. **$70-$120.** 1000 N Hwy 6. I-10, exit 751 (Addicks/SR 6), just n on SR 6. Int corridors. **Pets:** Accepted.

**Executive Inn & Suites Houston/Hobby Airport** M
(713) 645-7666. **$47-$100.** 6711 Telephone Rd. I-610, exit 33, 2.1 mi s; 0.5 mi s of jct Telephone and Bellfort rds. Ext corridors. **Pets:** Medium. $8 daily fee/room. Designated rooms, service with restrictions, supervision.

**Extended Stay Deluxe-Houston-Med.Ctr-Reliant Pk.-Braeswood Blvd** SH
(713) 794-0800. **$51-$59.** 1301 S Braeswood Blvd. I-610, exit 1B, 1.5 mi n, just e. Int corridors. **Pets:** $25 daily fee/pet. Service with restrictions, supervision.

**Four Seasons Hotel Houston** LH
(713) 650-1300. **$325-$440.** 1300 Lamar St. Lamar and Austin sts. Int corridors. **Pets:** Accepted.

**Hilton Americas-Houston** LH
(713) 739-8000. **Call for rates.** 1600 Lamar. At George R Brown Convention Center; between Crawford and Avenida De Las Americas. Int corridors. **Pets:** Small. $50 deposit/pet. Service with restrictions.

**Hilton Houston Post Oak** LH
(713) 961-9300. **$109-$249.** 2001 Post Oak Blvd. I-610, exit 8C (Westheimer Rd) northbound, just w; exit 9A (San Felipe/Westheimer rds) southbound; between San Felipe and Westheimer rds. Int corridors. **Pets:** Medium. $75 deposit/room, $25 one-time fee/room. Service with restrictions, supervision.

**Holiday Inn Express Hotel & Suites-Intercontinental** SH
(281) 372-1000. **$89, 15 day notice.** 1330 N Sam Houston Pkwy. Off Sam Houston Pkwy (Beltway 8), exit Aldine Westfield eastbound, 0.8 mi e on service road; exit Hardy Toll Rd westbound, U-turn, then 1 mi e on service road. Int corridors. **Pets:** Small. $75 one-time fee/room. Service with restrictions.

**Holiday Inn Houston Intercontinental Airport** LH
(281) 449-2311. **$89-$169.** 15222 John F Kennedy Blvd. Jct N Sam Houston Pkwy (Beltway 8) E and John F Kennedy Blvd. Int corridors. **Pets:** Medium, other species. $125 deposit/room, $25 one-time fee/pet. Service with restrictions, crate.

**Holiday Inn Select-Greenway Plaza** SH
(713) 523-8448. **$69-$149.** 2712 Southwest Frwy. US 59, exit Kirby Dr. Int corridors. **Pets:** Accepted.

**Holiday Inn Select I-10** SH
(281) 558-5580. **$59-$159.** 14703 Park Row. I-10, exit 751 (Addicks Rd/SR 6), just n. Int corridors. **Pets:** Accepted.

**Homestead Studio Suites Hotel-Houston/Galleria Area** SH
(713) 960-9660. **$58-$86.** 2300 W Loop S. Loop 610, exit 9A (San Felipe/Westheimer rds) southbound; exit 9 (San Felipe Rd) northbound, on southbound frontage road. Int corridors. **Pets:** $25 daily fee/pet. Service with restrictions, supervision.

**Homestead Studio Suites Hotel-Houston/Willowbrook** SH
(281) 397-9922. **$43-$64.** 13223 Champions Center Dr. Jct SR 249 and FM 1960 W, 0.9 mi e to Champion Center Dr, just n to Champion Center Plaza, then just w. Ext corridors. **Pets:** $25 daily fee/pet. Service with restrictions, supervision.

**Homewood Suites by Hilton Intercontinental** SH
(281) 219-9100. **$119-$254.** 1340 N Sam Houston Pkwy E. Sam Houston Pkwy (Beltway 8), exit Aldine Westfield eastbound, 0.8 mi e on frontage road; exit Hardy Toll Rd westbound, U-turn, then 1 mi e on frontage road. Int corridors. **Pets:** Medium. $50 one-time fee/pet. Service with restrictions, supervision.

**Homewood Suites by Hilton-Westchase** SH
(713) 334-2424. **$114-$134, 14 day notice.** 2424 Rogerdale Rd. Sam Houston Pkwy (Beltway 8), exit Westheimer Rd, just w to Rogerdale Rd, then just n. Int corridors. **Pets:** Accepted.

**Homewood Suites by Hilton-Willowbrook** SH
(281) 955-5200. **$89-$189, 14 day notice.** 7655 W FM 1960. Just e of jct SR 249 and FM 1960. Int corridors. **Pets:** Accepted.

**Hotel Sofitel Houston** LH
(281) 445-9000. **$225-$245.** 425 N Sam Houston Pkwy E. Sam Houston Pkwy (Beltway 8), exit Imperial Valley Dr westbound; exit Hardy Toll Rd eastbound, on westbound frontage road. Int corridors. **Pets:** Service with restrictions, supervision.

**Houston Marriott Medical Center Hotel** LH
(713) 796-0080. **$89-$209.** 6580 Fannin St. I-610, exit 2 (Main St), 2.5 mi ne to Holcombe St, 0.3 mi e, then just n. Int corridors. **Pets:** Accepted.

**InterContinental Houston** LH
(713) 627-7600. **$199-$269.** 2222 W Loop S. I-610, exit 9 (San Felipe Rd) northbound; exit 9A (San Felipe/Westheimer rds) southbound. Int corridors. **Pets:** Accepted.

SAVE ⬛ ✕ ♿ 🚪 💻 ▯ ≈ ✕

**La Quinta Inn & Suites Houston (Bush Intercontinental Airport)** SH
(281) 219-2000. **$96-$116.** 15510 John F Kennedy Blvd. Sam Houston Pkwy (Beltway 8), exit John F Kennedy Blvd/Vickery, just n. Int corridors. **Pets:** Medium. Service with restrictions.

ASK ✕ ♿ ♿ 🚪 💻 ≈

**La Quinta Inn & Suites Houston (Galleria Area)** SH
(713) 355-3440. **$83-$132.** 1625 W Loop S. I-610, exit 9 (San Felipe Rd) northbound; exit 9A (San Felipe/Westheimer rds) southbound, on northbound service road. Int corridors. **Pets:** Medium. Service with restrictions.

ASK ✕ ♿ ♿ ♿ 🚪 💻 ≈

**La Quinta Inn & Suites Houston North Beltway** SH
(832) 554-5000. **$65-$75.** 10137 North Frwy. I-45, exit 59 (West Rd), on southbound frontage road. Int corridors. **Pets:** Small. $25 deposit/room. Service with restrictions, crate.

ASK ⬛ ✕ ♿ 🚪 💻 ≈

**La Quinta Inn & Suites Houston (Park 10)** SH
(281) 646-9200. **$76-$105.** 15225 Katy Frwy. I-10, exit 748 (Barker Cypress Rd) eastbound, 2.6 mi on eastbound service road; exit 751 (SR 6) westbound, just s to Grisby Rd, then 0.5 mi w. Int corridors. **Pets:** Medium. Service with restrictions.

ASK ✕ ♿ ♿ 🚪 💻 ≈

**La Quinta Inn Houston (Brookhollow)** M
(713) 688-2581. **$70-$80.** 11002 Northwest Frwy. Nw on US 290, exit Magnum Rd-Watonga Blvd. Ext corridors. **Pets:** Medium. No service.

ASK ✕ ♿ ♿ 🚪 💻 ≈

**La Quinta Inn Houston (Cyfair)** SH
(281) 469-4018. **$80-$90.** 13290 FM 1960 W. Just w of jct US 290 and FM 1960. Ext corridors. **Pets:** Medium. Service with restrictions.

SAVE ✕ ♿ ♿ 🚪 💻

**La Quinta Inn Houston (East)** SH
(713) 453-5425. **$76-$86.** 11999 East Frwy. I-10, exit 778A (Federal Rd) eastbound; exit 776B (Holland Ave) westbound, just n. Ext corridors. **Pets:** Medium. Service with restrictions.

ASK ✕ ♿ ♿ 🚪 💻

**La Quinta Inn Houston (Greenway Plaza)** SH
(713) 623-4750. **$69-$79.** 4015 Southwest Frwy. Sw off US 59 (Southwest Frwy), exit Weslayan. Ext/int corridors. **Pets:** Medium. Service with restrictions.

SAVE ✕ ♿ ♿ 🚪 💻 ≈

**La Quinta Inn Houston (Hobby Airport)** SH
(713) 941-0900. **$76-$86.** 9902 Gulf Frwy. I-45 S, exit 36 (Airport Blvd/College Rd), just s on southbound frontage road. Ext corridors. **Pets:** Medium. Service with restrictions.

SAVE ✕ ♿ ♿ 🚪 💻 ≈

**La Quinta Inn Houston (I-45 North)** SH
(281) 444-7500. **$69-$79.** 17111 North Frwy. I-45, exit 66, southbound service road, 0.4 mi s of jct FM 1960 and I-45. Ext corridors. **Pets:** Medium. Service with restrictions.

SAVE ✕ 🚪 💻 ≈

**La Quinta Inn Houston (Medical Center/Reliant Center)** SH
(713) 668-8082. **$80-$107.** 9911 Buffalo Speedway. I-610, exit 2 (Buffalo Speedway/S Main St), just s. Ext corridors. **Pets:** Medium. Service with restrictions.

SAVE ✕ ♿ 🚪 💻 ≈

**La Quinta Inn Houston (Wilcrest)** SH
(713) 932-0808. **$69-$79.** 11113 Katy Frwy. I-10, exit 754 (Kirkwood Dr) westbound; exit 755 (Wilcrest Rd) eastbound, on eastbound service road. Ext corridors. **Pets:** Medium. Service with restrictions.

SAVE ✕ ♿ 🚪 💻 ≈

**Marriott Houston Hobby Airport** LH
(713) 943-7979. **$79-$159, 30 day notice.** 9100 Gulf Frwy. I-45, exit 36 (Airport Blvd/College Rd) southbound; exit 38 (Monroe) northbound, on southbound frontage road. Int corridors. **Pets:** Accepted.

SAVE ⬛ ✕ ♿ ♿ 🚪 💻 ▯ ≈

**Motel 6-1401** M
(713) 334-9188. **$47-$57.** 2900 W Sam Houston Pkwy S. Sam Houston Pkwy (Beltway 8), exit Westheimer Rd. Int corridors. **Pets:** Accepted.

⬛ ✕ ♿ ♿ ≈

**Omni Houston Hotel** LH 🐾
(713) 871-8181. **$299-$319, 5 day notice.** Four Riverway. I-610, exit 10 (Woodway Dr), 0.3 mi w. Int corridors. **Pets:** Small. $50 one-time fee/room. Service with restrictions, supervision.

SAVE ⬛ ✕ ♿ 🚪 💻 ▯ ≈ ✕

**Omni Houston Westside** LH
(281) 558-8338. **$219.** 13210 Katy Frwy. I-10, exit 753A (Eldridge St), just n. Int corridors. **Pets:** Small. $50 one-time fee/room. Service with restrictions, supervision.

SAVE ⬛ ✕ ♿ 🚪 💻 ▯ ≈ ✕

**Ramada Limited/S.H. 249** SH
(281) 970-5000. **$60-$85.** 18836 Tomball Pkwy. SR 249, exit Grant, on northbound frontage road. Ext corridors. **Pets:** Accepted.

ASK ✕ 🚪 💻 ≈

**Ramada Plaza Hotel Near the Galleria** SH
(713) 688-2222. **$90-$109.** 7611 Katy Frwy. I-10, exit 762 (Silber Rd), on eastbound frontage road. Int corridors. **Pets:** Accepted.

ASK ⬛ ✕ 🚪 💻 ▯ ≈

**Red Roof Inn Hobby Airport** SH
(713) 943-3300. **$50-$55.** 9005 Airport Blvd. I-45, exit 36 (Airport Blvd/College Rd), just w. Int corridors. **Pets:** Accepted.

✕ ♿ ♿ 🚪 ≈

**Red Roof Inns** SH
(713) 939-0800. **$43-$67.** 12929 Northwest Frwy. US 290, exit Hollister and Tidwell rds, on eastbound service road. Ext/int corridors. **Pets:** Accepted.

✕ ♿ ♿ 🚪 ≈

**Red Roof Inns** M
(713) 785-9909. **$48-$66.** 2960 W Sam Houston Pkwy S. Sw Sam Houston Pkwy (Beltway 8), exit Westheimer Rd. Ext/int corridors. **Pets:** Accepted.

✕ ♿ 🚪 ≈

**Renaissance Houston Hotel Greenway Plaza** LH
(713) 629-1200. **$89-$209.** 6 Greenway Plaza E. US 59 (Southwest Frwy), exit Buffalo Speedway. Int corridors. **Pets:** Accepted.

SAVE ⬛ ✕ ♿ ♿ 🚪 💻 ▯ ≈ ✕

**Residence Inn by Marriott** SH
(832) 366-1000. **Call for rates (no credit cards).** 904 Dallas St. At Main St. Int corridors. **Pets:** Small, other species. $75 one-time fee/pet. Service with restrictions, supervision.

✕ ♿ 🚪 💻 ≈

▼▼▼ Residence Inn by Marriott Houston by the Galleria SH
(713) 840-9757. **$79-$289.** 2500 McCue. I-610, exit 8C (Westheimer Rd) northbound; exit 9A (San Felipe/Westheimer rds) southbound, just w to McCue, then just n. Ext/int corridors. **Pets:** Other species. $75 one-time fee/pet. Service with restrictions.

ASK SD X L H D C

▼▼▼ Residence Inn by Marriott Houston Westchase SH
(713) 974-5454. **$79-$139.** 9965 Westheimer Rd. Sam Houston Pkwy (Beltway 8), exit Westheimer Rd, 0.7 mi e to Elmside Dr, then just s. Int corridors. **Pets:** Accepted.

X L H D C X

▼▼▼ Residence Inn by Marriott-Medical Center/Reliant Park SH
(713) 660-7993. **$139-$299.** 7710 Main St. I-610, exit 2 (S Main St/Buffalo Speedway), 1.5 mi n. Ext corridors. **Pets:** Small. $75 one-time fee/room. Designated rooms, service with restrictions.

ASK SD X H D C X

AAA ▼▼▼ Residence Inn by Marriott-West University SH ✿
(713) 661-4660. **$89-$134.** 2939 Westpark Dr. US 59, exit Kirby Dr, just s, then just w. Int corridors. **Pets:** Other species. $75 one-time fee/room. Designated rooms, service with restrictions, crate.

SAVE SD X LN H D C X

▼▼▼ Residence Inn by Marriott Willowbrook SH
(832) 237-2002. **$109-$149, 14 day notice.** 7311 W Greens Rd. SR 249, exit Greens Rd, just e. Int corridors. **Pets:** Accepted.

ASK SD X L H D C X

▼▼▼ Residence Inn-Houston Clear Lake SH
(281) 486-2424. **$89-$162.** 525 Bay Area Blvd. I-45 S, exit 26 (Bay Area Blvd), 1.2 mi e. Ext/int corridors. **Pets:** Accepted.

ASK SD X L H D C

▼▼▼ Robin's Nest Bed & Breakfast Inn BB
(713) 528-5821. **$126-$175, 3 day notice.** 4104 Greeley St. US 59 (Southwest Frwy), exit Richmond Ave, just e, then just n. Ext/int corridors. **Pets:** Accepted.

ASK SD X H

AAA ▼▼▼▼ The St. Regis Hotel, Houston SH ✿
(713) 840-7600. **$450-$2500.** 1919 Briar Oaks Ln. I-610, exit 9A (San Felipe/Westheimer rds), 0.3 mi e. Int corridors. **Pets:** Medium, other species. Service with restrictions, supervision.

SAVE X L H D C X

AAA ▼▼▼ Sheraton North Houston Hotel LH
(281) 442-5100. **$75-$100.** 15700 John F Kennedy Blvd. Sam Houston Pkwy (Beltway 8), exit John F Kennedy Blvd, just n. Int corridors. **Pets:** Accepted.

SAVE SD X LM L H D C

▼▼▼ Sheraton Suites Houston Near The Galleria SH
(713) 586-2444. **$279-$379.** 2400 W Loop S. I-610, exit 9 (San Felipe Rd) northbound; exit 9A (San Felipe/Westheimer rds) southbound. Int corridors. **Pets:** Accepted.

ASK SD X L H D C

▼▼▼ Staybridge Suites Houston-Near The Galleria SH
(713) 355-8888. **$79-$299.** 5190 Hidalgo St. I-610, exit 9A (San Felipe/ Westheimer rds) southbound; exit 8C (Westheimer Rd) northbound, 0.4 mi w to Sage Rd, then just s. Int corridors. **Pets:** Accepted.

ASK SD X LM L H D C

▼▼ Studio 6 #6043 SH
(281) 579-6959. **$47-$60.** 1255 Hwy 6 N. I-10, exit 751 (Addicks Rd/SR 6), just n. Ext corridors. **Pets:** Accepted.

SD X L H D

▼▼ Studio 6-Cypress Station #6037 SH
(281) 580-2221. **$43-$63.** 220 Bammel-Westfield Rd. I-45, exit 66, southbound frontage road, then just w. Ext corridors. **Pets:** Accepted.

SD X L H D

▼▼ Studio 6-Houston Hobby South #6039 M
(281) 929-5400. **$47-$60.** 12700 Featherwood. I-45, exit 33 (Fuqua St) southbound, stay in right lane and cross over I-45, just e to Featherwood, then just s. Ext corridors. **Pets:** Accepted.

SD X L H D

▼▼ TownePlace Suites by Marriott-Central SH
(713) 690-4035. **$50-$95.** 12820 Northwest Frwy (US 290). US 290, exit Bingle/43rd St eastbound; exit Bingle/Pinemont/43rd St westbound, on westbound feeder. Int corridors. **Pets:** Accepted.

ASK SD X LM H D C X

▼▼ TownePlace Suites by Marriott-West SH
(281) 646-0058. **$50-$95.** 15155 Katy Frwy. I-10, exit 751, just s on SR 6 to Grisby Rd, then w. Int corridors. **Pets:** Accepted.

ASK SD X L H D C

▼▼▼ Uptown Hotel & Suites Galleria SH
(713) 681-5000. **$79-$109.** 7787 Katy Frwy. I-10, exit 762 (Antoine Dr) westbound; exit 761B (Antoine Dr) eastbound, on eastbound service road. Ext/int corridors. **Pets:** Accepted.

ASK SD X L L H D C H C

▼▼▼ The Warwick SH
(713) 526-1991. **$145-$175.** 5701 Main St. Jct Main and Ewing sts, just n of Herman Park. Int corridors. **Pets:** Accepted.

X LM L L H D C H C X

AAA ▼▼▼ ▼▼▼ The Westin Galleria, Houston LH
(713) 960-8100. **$309-$319.** 5060 W Alabama St. I-610, exit 8C (Westheimer Rd) norhtbound; exit 9A (San Felipe/Westheimer rds) southbound, 0.5 mi w on Westheimer Rd to Sage, just s, then just e. Int corridors. **Pets:** Accepted.

SAVE X LM L D C H C

AAA ▼▼▼ ▼▼▼ The Westin Oaks, Houston LH ✿
(713) 960-8100. **$309-$319.** 5011 Westheimer Rd. I-610, exit 8C (Westheimer Rd) northbound; exit 9A (San Felipe/Westheimer rds) southbound, just w. Int corridors. **Pets:** Medium, dogs only. Designated rooms, service with restrictions.

SAVE X L D C H C

# HUMBLE

▼▼ Fairfield Inn by Marriott SH
(281) 540-3311. **$75-$95.** 20525 Hwy 59. US 59, exit Townsen Rd, on southbound access road. Int corridors. **Pets:** Accepted.

ASK SD X LM H D C

# KATY

▼▼ Best Western-Houston West M
(281) 392-9800. **$59-$70.** 22455 I-10 (Katy Frwy). I-10, exit 743 (Grand Pkwy), just e on eastbound service road. Ext corridors. **Pets:** Medium. $10 daily fee/pet. Service with restrictions, crate.

ASK SD X H D C

# KINGWOOD

▼▼▼ Homewood Suites by Hilton at Kingwood Parc SH
(281) 358-5566. **$99-$179.** 23320 Hwy 59 N. US 59, exit Kingwood Dr, 1.4 mi n on northbound access road. Int corridors. **Pets:** Accepted.

ASK X LM L H D C X

# LA PORTE

▼▼ La Quinta Inn Houston (La Porte) SH
(281) 470-0760. **$72-$82.** 1105 Hwy 146 S. Jct SR 146, exit Fairmont Pkwy. Ext corridors. **Pets:** Medium. Service with restrictions.

ASK X D H D C

# NASSAU BAY

▼▼ Holiday Inn Houston/NASA **SH**
(281) 333-2500. **$81.** 1300 NASA Pkwy. I-45, exit 25 (NASA Rd One), 2.5 mi e. Ext/int corridors. **Pets:** Accepted.

(A$K) (S̲6) (✕) (🐾) (📧) (💻) (🍽) (🏊)

▼▼ Microtel Inn & Suites **SH**
(281) 335-0800. **$60.** 1620 NASA Rd One. I-45, exit 25 (NASA Rd One), 3 mi e. Int corridors. **Pets:** Accepted.

(S̲6) (✕) (🐾) (📧) (💻)

# SEABROOK

▼▼▼ Comfort Inn & Suites-NASA Clearlake **SH**
(281) 326-3301. **$69-$99.** 2901 NASA Pkwy. 1 mi w of jct W SR 146. Int corridors. **Pets:** Accepted.

(A$K) (S̲6) (✕) (📧) (💻) (🏊)

▼▼▼ La Quinta Inn & Suites #618 **SH**
(281) 326-7300. **$67-$149.** 3636 NASA Rd One. I-45, exit 25 (NASA Rd One), 6 mi e; SR 146, 2 mi w. Int corridors. **Pets:** Medium. Designated rooms, service with restrictions, supervision.

(A$K) (S̲6) (✕) (🐾) (📧) (💻) (🏊)

# STAFFORD

▲▲▲ ▼▼ La Quinta Inn Houston (Stafford/Sugarland) **SH**
(281) 240-2300. **$76-$86.** 12727 Southwest Frwy. US 59 eastbound service road, exit Corporate Dr southbound; exit Airport Blvd/Kirkwood Rd northbound. Int corridors. **Pets:** Medium. Service with restrictions.

(SAVE) (✕) (🐾) (📧) (💻) (🏊)

▼▼▼ Residence Inn by Marriott Houston/Sugar Land **SH**
(281) 277-0770. **$129.** 12703 Southwest Frwy. US 59, exit Corporate Dr southbound; exit Airport Blvd/Kirkwood Rd northbound. Int corridors. **Pets:** Medium, other species. $75 one-time fee/room. Service with restrictions, supervision.

(A$K) (S̲6) (✕) (🐾) (📧) (💻) (🏊) (✕)

▼▼ Studio 6 #6044 **M**
(281) 240-6900. **$43-$53.** 12827 Southwest. US 59, exit US 90 and SR 41 alternate route northbound, follow frontage road; exit US 90 southbound, first U-turn onto northbound frontage road. Ext corridors. **Pets:** Accepted.

(S̲6) (✕) (🐾) (📧) (💻)

# SUGAR LAND

▼▼▼ Drury Inn & Suites-Houston/Sugar Land **SH**
(281) 277-9700. **$75-$125.** 13770 Southwest Frwy. Sw on US 59, exit Dairy Ashford/Sugar Creek southbound; exit Dairy Ashford/Sugar Creek northbound, left under US 59. Int corridors. **Pets:** Accepted.

(A$K) (✕) (🐾) (🐾) (📧) (💻) (🏊)

# TOMBALL

▼▼ Holiday Inn Express **SH**
(281) 351-4114. **$76.** 1437 Keefer St. SR 249 and FM 2920; northeast corner. Ext corridors. **Pets:** Accepted.

(A$K) (S̲6) (✕) (📧) (💻) (🏊)

# WEBSTER

▼▼ Extended Stay Houston NASA-Bay Area Blvd **SH**
(281) 338-7711. **$55-$68.** 720 W Bay Area Blvd. I-45, exit 26 (Bay Area Blvd), just e. Int corridors. **Pets:** Small, other species. $25 daily fee/pet. Service with restrictions, supervision.

(A$K) (S̲6) (✕) (🐾) (🐾) (📧) (💻) (🏊)

# WINNIE

▲▲▲ ▼▼ Best Western Gulf Coast Inn **SH**
(409) 296-9292. **$54-$73.** 46318 I-10 E. I-10, exit 829, on eastbound frontage road. Ext corridors. **Pets:** Medium. $10 daily fee/pet. Service with restrictions, supervision.

(SAVE) (S̲6) (✕) (📧) (💻) (🏊)

▲▲▲ ▼▼ Winnie Inn & Suites **SH** 🐾
(409) 296-2947. **$55-$100.** 205 Spur 5, Hwy 124. I-10, exit 829, just s. Ext corridors. **Pets:** Dogs only. $10 one-time fee/room. Supervision.

(SAVE) (S̲6) (✕) (📧) (💻) (🏊)

# THE WOODLANDS

▼▼▼ Drury Inn & Suites-Houston/The Woodlands **SH**
(281) 362-7222. **$70-$120.** 28099 I-45 N. I-45, exit 76 southbound; exit 77 northbound, on west service road. Int corridors. **Pets:** Accepted.

(A$K) (✕) (🅰M) (🐾) (🐾) (📧) (💻) (🏊)

▼▼▼ Holiday Inn Express Hotel & Suites **SH**
(281) 681-8088. **$77.** 24888 I-45 N. I-45, exit 73 (Rayford/Sawdust Rd), on northbound access road. Int corridors. **Pets:** Small. $25 one-time fee/room. Service with restrictions, crate.

(A$K) (S̲6) (✕) (🐾) (📧) (💻) (🏊) (✕)

▲▲▲ ▼▼▼ La Quinta Inn Houston, The Woodlands North **SH**
(281) 367-7722. **$62-$76.** 28673 I-45 N. I-45, exit 78 southbound; exit 79 (SR 242) northbound, on southbound frontage road. Ext/int corridors. **Pets:** Medium. Service with restrictions.

(SAVE) (✕) (🐾) (📧) (💻) (🏊)

▼▼▼ Residence Inn by Marriott **SH**
(281) 292-3252. **$115-$160, 14 day notice.** 1040 Lake Front Cir. I-45, exit 78 southbound; exit 79 (SR 242) northbound, 0.8 mi s of jct I-45 and Research Forest Dr, just w. Int corridors. **Pets:** Accepted.

(A$K) (S̲6) (✕) (🐾) (📧) (💻) (🏊) (✕)

---

## END METROPOLITAN AREA

# HUNTSVILLE

▲▲▲ ▼▼▼▼ La Quinta Inn Huntsville **SH**
(936) 295-6454. **$76-$86.** 124 I-45 N. I-45, exit 116. Ext corridors. **Pets:** Medium. Service with restrictions.

(SAVE) (✕) (🐾) (📧) (💻) (🏊)

# HURST

▲▲▲ ▼▼▼▼ AmeriSuites (Ft Worth/Hurst) **SH**
(817) 577-3003. **$129-$169.** 1601 Hurst Town Center Dr. SR 183, exit Precinct Line Rd, just n to Thousand Oaks, then just w. Int corridors. **Pets:** Accepted.

(SAVE) (S̲6) (✕) (🅰M) (🐾) (🐾) (📧) (💻) (🏊)

# JACKSONVILLE

▼▼▼ Holiday Inn Express **SH**
(903) 589-8500. **$85-$90.** 1848 S Jackson. On US 69, 2 mi s of jct US 69 and 79. Int corridors. **Pets:** Small. $15 daily fee/pet. Service with restrictions, supervision.

(A$K) (S̲6) (✕) (🅰M) (📧) (💻) (🏊)

# JASPER

▲▲▲ ▼▼ Best Western Inn Of Jasper **SH**
(409) 384-7767. **$59-$69.** 205 W Gibson. US 190 and SR 63, 0.5 mi w of jct US 96. Ext corridors. **Pets:** Small. $10 daily fee/pet. Designated rooms, service with restrictions.

(SAVE) (S̲6) (✕) (📧) (💻)

**▼ Ramada Inn Jasper** SH
(409) 384-9021. **$51.** 239 E Gibson (US 190). US 190 and SR 63, just w of jct US 96. Ext corridors. **Pets:** Medium, dogs only. $25 one-time fee/pet. Service with restrictions, supervision.

ASK ⓢ ⊠ 🛏 💻 ⑪

## JUNCTION

**▼▼ Days Inn** SH
(325) 446-3730. **$66-$80.** 111 S Martinez St. I-10, exit 457, 0.3 mi s. Ext corridors. **Pets:** Medium, other species. $4 one-time fee/pet. Designated rooms, service with restrictions, supervision.

ASK ⓢ ⊠ 🛏 💻 ⌇

**▼ The Hills Motel** M
(325) 446-2567. **$40.** 1520 Main St. I-10, exit 456, 1.3 mi s on US 377. Ext corridors. **Pets:** Other species. Designated rooms, service with restrictions, supervision.

ASK ⓢ ⊠ 🛏 ⌇

**▲ ▼ Sun Valley Motel** M
(325) 446-2505. **$45-$50, 4 day notice.** 1611 Main St. I-10, exit 452, 1 mi s on US 377. Ext corridors. **Pets:** Other species. $5 daily fee/pet. Service with restrictions, supervision.

SAVE ⓢ ⊠ 🛏 ⌇

## KERRVILLE

**▲ ▼▼▼ Best Western Sunday House Inn** SH ❀
(830) 896-1313. **$75-$90.** 2124 Sidney Baker St. I-10, exit 508 (SR 16), just s. Ext corridors. **Pets:** Medium. $10 daily fee/pet. Designated rooms, service with restrictions.

SAVE ⓢ ⊠ 💻 ⑪ ⌇

**▲ ▼▼ Budget Inn** M
(830) 896-8200. **$45-$70.** 1804 Sidney Baker St. I-10, exit 508 (SR 16), 0.5 mi s on SR 16. Ext corridors. **Pets:** Small, dogs only. $5 daily fee/pet. Service with restrictions, supervision.

SAVE ⓢ ⊠ 🛏 ⌇

**▼▼▼ Days Inn of Kerrville** M
(830) 896-1000. **$69-$139.** 2000 Sidney Baker St. I-10, exit 508 (SR 16), 0.5 mi s. Ext/int corridors. **Pets:** Small. $10 daily fee/pet. Designated rooms, service with restrictions, supervision.

ASK ⓢ ⊠ 🐾 🛏 💻 ⌇

**▲ ▼▼ Econo Lodge of Kerrville** SH
(830) 896-1711. **$45-$149.** 2105 Sidney Baker St. I-10, exit 508 (SR 16), just s. Int corridors. **Pets:** Very small. $25 daily fee/pet. Designated rooms, service with restrictions, supervision.

SAVE ⓢ ⊠ 🛏 💻 ⌇

**▲ ▼▼▼ Y. O. Ranch Resort Hotel & Conference Center** LH
(830) 257-4440. **$89-$109.** 2033 Sidney Baker St. I-10, exit 508 (SR 16), 0.3 mi s. Ext/int corridors. **Pets:** Large. $50 deposit/room. Service with restrictions, supervision.

SAVE ⓢ ⊠ 🏊 🛏 💻 ⑪ ⌇ ⊠

## KILGORE

**▲ ▼▼▼ Best Western Inn of Kilgore** SH
(903) 986-1195. **$63.** 1411 N Hwy 259. I-20, exit 589, 3.9 mi s. Ext corridors. **Pets:** Accepted.

SAVE ⓢ ⊠ 🛏 💻 ⌇

## KILLEEN

**▲ ▼▼▼ Holiday Inn Express** SH
(254) 554-2727. **$85-$95.** 1602 E Central Texas Expwy. US 190, exit Trimmier Rd. Ext corridors. **Pets:** Medium, other species. Service with restrictions, supervision.

SAVE ⓢ ⊠ 🛏 💻

**▼▼▼▼ La Quinta Inn Killeen** SH
(254) 526-8331. **$79-$100.** 1112 S Fort Hood St. US 190, exit Fort Hood St, on westbound access road. Ext corridors. **Pets:** Medium. Service with restrictions.

ASK ⊠ 🏊 🛏 💻 ⌇

## KINGSVILLE

**▼▼ Quality Inn** SH
(361) 592-5251. **$55-$69.** 221 S Hwy 77 Bypass. On US 77, just s of jct SR 141. Ext corridors. **Pets:** Small, dogs only. $50 deposit/pet. Designated rooms, service with restrictions, crate.

ASK ⓢ ⊠ 🛏 💻 ⌇

**▼▼ Rodeway Inn** SH
(361) 595-5753. **Call for rates.** 3430 Hwy 77, S Bypass. 4.5 mi s on US 77. Ext corridors. **Pets:** Medium. $20 one-time fee/room. Supervision.

ASK ⊠ 🛏 💻 ⑪ ⌇

**▲▲▲ ▼▼ Super 8 Motel** M
(361) 592-6471. **$60-$80.** 105 S 77 Bypass. 0.8 mi e on US 77. Ext corridors. **Pets:** Large. $20 one-time fee/pet. No service, supervision.

SAVE ⓢ ⊠ 💻 ⌇

## LAJITAS

**▼▼▼▼ Lajitas The Ultimate Hideout** SH
(432) 424-5000. **$169-$850.** 1 Main St. Center. Ext/int corridors. **Pets:** Accepted.

ASK ⊠ 🛏 💻 ⑪ ⌇ ⊠

## LAKE JACKSON

**▼▼▼▼ Cherotel Brazosport Hotel & Conference Center** SH
(979) 297-1161. **$132-$161.** 925 Hwy 332. On SR 228/332, just w of jct Business Rt SR 288. Int corridors. **Pets:** Other species. $100 deposit/room. Service with restrictions, supervision.

ASK ⓢ ⊠ 🛏 💻 ⑪ ⌇

## LAMESA

**▼▼ Shiloh Inn** M
(806) 872-6721. **$46-$58, 3 day notice.** 1707 Lubbock Hwy. Jct US 87 and 180, 1 mi n. Ext corridors. **Pets:** Small, other species. $10 one-time fee/pet. Service with restrictions, supervision.

ASK ⓢ ⊠ 🛏 💻 ⑪ ⌇

## LAREDO

**▲▲▲ ▼▼▼ Days Inn & Suites** SH
(956) 724-8221. **$69-$139.** 7060 N San Bernardo Ave. I-35, exit 4 (San Bernardo Ave), just s on southbound access road. Ext/int corridors. **Pets:** Small. $10 daily fee/pet. Service with restrictions, supervision.

SAVE ⓢ ⊠ 🛏 💻 ⌇

**▲▲▲ ▼▼▼ Hampton Inn** SH
(956) 717-8888. **$104-$109.** 7903 San Dario. I-35, exit 4, on northbound access road. Int corridors. **Pets:** Accepted.

SAVE ⊠ ⓜ 🏊 🛏 💻 ⌇

**▲▲▲ ▼▼▼ La Quinta Inn Laredo (I-35)** SH
(956) 722-0511. **$94-$104.** 3610 Santa Ursula Ave. I-35, exit 2 (US 59). Ext corridors. **Pets:** Medium. Service with restrictions.

SAVE ⊠ 🛏 💻 ⌇

**▼▼ Motel 6 South-142** M
(956) 725-8187. **$45-$65.** 5310 San Bernardo Ave. I-35, exit 3B (Mann Rd). Ext corridors. **Pets:** Accepted.

ⓢ ⊠ ⓜ 🛏 ⌇

**▼▼ Red Roof Inn Laredo** M
(956) 712-0733. **$60-$75.** 1006 W Calton Rd. I-35, exit 3A, 0.3 mi w. Ext/int corridors. **Pets:** Accepted.

⊠ 🛏 ⌇

# LITTLEFIELD

**◆◆◆ ◆◆ Crescent Park Motel & Suites** **M**
(806) 385-4464. **$48.** 2000 Hall Ave. Jct US 84, just n on SR 385. Ext corridors. **Pets:** Accepted.
[SAVE] [S⭤] [✕] [🛏] [💻]

# LLANO

**◆◆◆ ◆◆ Best Western Llano** **SH**
(325) 247-4101. **$59-$86, 3 day notice.** 901 W Young St. 1 mi w on SR 71 and 29. Ext corridors. **Pets:** Accepted.
[SAVE] [S⭤] [✕] [🛏] [💻] [🏊]

**◆◆ Hill Country Suites** **SH**
(325) 247-1141. **$70-$90.** 609 Bessemer Ave. Jct SR 29 and 16/71, 2 blks s. Ext corridors. **Pets:** Accepted.
[ASK] [S⭤] [✕] [&M] [🐾] [⬧] [🛏] [💻] [🏊]

# LOCKHART

**◆◆ Plum Creek Inn** **M**
(512) 398-4911. **$69-$99.** 2001 Hwy 183 S. US 183 S, 1 mi s. Ext corridors. **Pets:** Accepted.
[ASK] [S⭤] [✕] [🛏] [💻] [🍴] [🏊]

# LONGVIEW

**◆◆◆ Best Western Inn & Conference Center** **SH**
(903) 758-0700. **$60.** 3119 Estes Pkwy. I-20, exit 595A, just n. Ext/int corridors. **Pets:** Accepted.
[ASK] [S⭤] [✕] [🛏] [💻] [🍴] [🏊]

**◆◆◆ Hampton Inn** **SH**
(903) 758-0959. **$76-$95.** 112 S Access Rd. I-20, exit 595A. Ext corridors. **Pets:** Accepted.
[SAVE] [S⭤] [✕] [&M] [🛏] [💻] [🏊]

**◆◆◆ ◆◆◆ La Quinta Inn Longview** **SH**
(903) 757-3663. **$65-$75.** 502 S Access Rd. I-20, exit 595. Ext corridors. **Pets:** Medium. Service with restrictions.
[SAVE] [✕] [🛏] [💻] [🏊]

**◆◆ Motel 6–158** **M**
(903) 758-5256. **$39-$49.** 110 S Access Rd. I-20, exit 595A. Ext corridors. **Pets:** Accepted.
[S⭤] [✕] [⬧]

# LUBBOCK

**◆◆◆ ◆◆◆ Best Western Lubbock Windsor Inn** **SH** ❀
(806) 762-8400. **$80-$160.** 5410 I-27. 3.5 mi s on I-27, exit 1B southbound; U-turn at exit 1A (50th St) northbound. Int corridors. **Pets:** $10 daily fee/room. Service with restrictions, supervision.
[SAVE] [S⭤] [✕] [♿] [🛏] [💻] [🏊]

**◆◆◆ ◆◆◆ Comfort Inn & Suites** **SH**
(806) 763-6500. **$70-$100.** 5828 I-27 S. I-27, exit 1B, just s. Int corridors. **Pets:** Small. $25 one-time fee/pet. No service, supervision.
[ASK] [S⭤] [✕] [⬧] [🛏] [💻] [🏊]

**◆◆◆ Econo Lodge** **SH**
(806) 747-3525. **$49-$99, 5 day notice.** 5401 Ave Q. I-27, exit 1A (US 84/Ave Q), 0.5 mi w. Ext/int corridors. **Pets:** Accepted.
[SAVE] [S⭤] [✕] [🛏] [🍴] [🏊]

**◆◆◆ ◆◆◆ Four Points Sheraton Hotel** **SH**
(806) 747-0171. **$81-$129.** 505 Ave Q. I-27, exit 4, 0.9 mi w to US 84 (Ave Q), then just s. Int corridors. **Pets:** Accepted.
[ASK] [S⭤] [✕] [🐾] [⬧] [🛏] [💻] [🍴] [🏊]

**◆◆◆ ◆◆◆ Holiday Inn Park Plaza** **SH**
(806) 797-3241. **$84-$139.** 3201 S Loop 289. 5 mi s on Loop 289, exit Indiana Ave, on south frontage road. Ext/int corridors. **Pets:** Accepted.
[ASK] [S⭤] [✕] [⬧] [🛏] [💻] [🍴] [🏊] [✕]

**◆◆ ◆◆◆ La Quinta Inn Lubbock** **SH**
(806) 763-9441. **$77-$113.** 601 Ave Q. 0.8 mi nw on US 84 (Ave Q). Ext corridors. **Pets:** Medium. Service with restrictions.
[ASK] [✕] [🐾] [⬧] [🛏] [💻] [🏊]

**◆◆ ◆◆◆ La Quinta Inn Lubbock (West/Medical Center)** **SH**
(806) 792-0065. **$90-$120.** 4115 Brownfield Hwy. 3.3 mi sw; 2.5 mi ne of Loop 289 on US 62 and 82. Int corridors. **Pets:** Medium. Service with restrictions.
[ASK] [✕] [🐾] [⬧] [🛏] [💻] [🏊]

**◆◆ ◆◆ Lubbock Super 8 Motel** **M**
(806) 762-8726. **$45-$95, 18 day notice.** 501 Ave Q. 1 mi nw on US 84. Ext corridors. **Pets:** $6 daily fee/pet. Service with restrictions.
[ASK] [S⭤] [✕] [🛏]

**◆◆ ◆◆ Ramada Inn and Conference Center** **SH**
(806) 745-2208. **$54-$99, 14 day notice.** 6624 I-27. 3.8 mi s on I-27 and US 87; just w of jct Loop 289, exit 1B southbound. Int corridors. **Pets:** Accepted.
[S⭤] [✕] [🛏] [💻] [🍴] [🏊] [✕]

**◆◆ ◆◆ Residence Inn by Marriott** **SH**
(806) 745-1963. **$109-$299.** 2551 S Loop 289. Loop 289, exit University, 3 mi s, south frontage road. Ext corridors. **Pets:** Accepted.
[ASK] [✕] [🐾] [⬧] [🛏] [💻] [🏊] [✕]

**◆◆ ◆◆ TownePlace Suites by Marriott** **SH**
(806) 799-6226. **$90-$170.** 5310 W Loop 289. W Loop 289, exit US 62/82 (Brownfield Rd), 0.5 mi s on west frontage road. Int corridors. **Pets:** Accepted.
[ASK] [S⭤] [✕] [&M] [🐾] [⬧] [🛏] [💻] [🏊]

# LUFKIN

**◆◆◆ ◆◆ Days Inn** **SH**
(936) 639-3301. **$55-$75.** 2130 S 1st St. 0.3 mi s of jct US 59 and Loop 287. Ext/int corridors. **Pets:** Small. $25 one-time fee/pet. Designated rooms, service with restrictions, supervision.
[SAVE] [S⭤] [✕] [🛏] [💻] [🏊]

**◆◆ ◆◆ La Quinta Inn Lufkin** **SH**
(936) 634-3351. **$73-$86.** 2119 S 1st St. US 59, exit Carriageway northbound, 0.3 mi s of jct S Loop 287 and US 59 business route. Ext corridors. **Pets:** Medium. Service with restrictions.
[ASK] [✕] [🐾] [🛏] [💻] [🏊]

# MADISONVILLE

**◆◆◆ ◆◆ Western Lodge** **M**
(936) 348-7654. **$45-$50.** 2007 E Main St. I-45, exit 142, 0.3 mi w. Ext corridors. **Pets:** Accepted.
[SAVE] [S⭤] [✕] [🛏] [🏊]

# MANSFIELD

**◆◆ ◆◆ Comfort Inn** **SH**
(817) 453-8848. **$70-$120.** 175 N Hwy 287. US 287 S, exit E Broad St. Int corridors. **Pets:** Accepted.
[ASK] [S⭤] [✕] [&M] [⬧] [🛏] [💻] [🏊]

# MARATHON

**◆◆ ◆◆ The Gage Hotel** **CI** ❀
(432) 386-4205. **$69-$350, 3 day notice.** Hwy 90. US 90; center. Ext/int corridors. **Pets:** Other species. $10 daily fee/pet. Service with restrictions, supervision.
[✕] [🛏] [💻] [🍴] [🏊]

# MARBLE FALLS

**◆◆◆ ◆◆◆ Best Western Marble Falls Inn** **SH**
(830) 693-5122. **$59-$119.** 1403 Hwy 281 N. 0.4 mi n of jct SR 281 and FM 1431. Ext/int corridors. **Pets:** Medium. $10 daily fee/pet. Designated rooms, service with restrictions, supervision.
[SAVE] [S⭤] [✕] [⬧] [🛏] [💻] [🏊]

**AAA ▼▼▼ Hill Country Inn** SH
(830) 693-3637. **$59-$125.** 1101 Hwy 281 N. Just n of jct SR 281 and FM 1431. Ext corridors. **Pets:** Accepted.
SAVE S✿ ✕ ⌧ ✆ ▦ ➔

## MARSHALL

**AAA ▼▼▼ Best Western Executive Inn** SH
(903) 935-0707. **$79-$99.** 5201 E End Blvd S. I-20, exit 617, 0.4 mi n on US 59. Ext corridors. **Pets:** Small. $10 daily fee/pet. Service with restrictions, supervision.
SAVE S✿ ✕ ✆ ▦ ➔

**▼▼▼ Holiday Inn Express Marshall** SH
(903) 935-7923. **$79-$99.** 4911 E End Blvd. I-20, exit 617, 0.5 mi n on US 59. Ext corridors. **Pets:** Other species. $30 one-time fee/pet. Service with restrictions.
ASK S✿ ✕ ♿ ✆ ▦ ➔

**AAA ▼▼▼ La Quinta Inn & East Texas Conference Center** SH
(903) 927-0009. **$69-$149.** 5301 E End Blvd S. I-20, exit 617, just n on US 59. Int corridors. **Pets:** Small. Designated rooms, service with restrictions, crate.
SAVE S✿ ✕ ♿ ✆ ▦ ➔

**▼ Motel 6 Marshall #422** M
(903) 935-4393. **$38-$50.** 300 I-20 E. I-20, exit 617, just e on access road. Ext corridors. **Pets:** Accepted.
S✿ ✕ ➔

## MCALLEN

**▼▼▼ Drury Inn-McAllen** SH
(956) 687-5100. **$80-$125.** 612 W Expwy 83. US 83, exit 2nd St, northwest frontage road. Int corridors. **Pets:** Accepted.
ASK ✕ ✆ ▦ ➔

**▼▼▼ Drury Suites-McAllen** SH
(956) 682-3222. **$83-$140.** 228 W Expwy 83. At US 83 and 6th St. Int corridors. **Pets:** Accepted.
ASK ✕ ♿ ✆ ▦ ➔

**▼▼▼ Hampton Inn-McAllen** SH
(956) 682-4900. **$80-$129.** 300 W Expwy 83. US 83, exit 2nd St, northwest frontage road. Int corridors. **Pets:** Accepted.
ASK ✕ ✆ ▦ ➔

**▼▼▼ La Quinta Inn McAllen** SH
(956) 687-1101. **$80.** 1100 S 10th St. 1.5 mi s on SR 336 (S 10th St); just n of jct US 83. Ext corridors. **Pets:** $25 deposit/room. Service with restrictions.
ASK ✕ ♿M ⌧ ♿ ✆ ▦ ➔

**▼ Motel 6 McAllen #212** M
(956) 687-3700. **$43-$55.** 700 Expwy 83 W. US 83, exit 2nd St, northwest frontage road. Ext corridors. **Pets:** Accepted.
S✿ ✕ ➔

**▼ Posada Ana Inn** SH
(956) 631-6700. **$65-$100.** 620 W Expwy 83. US 83, exit 2nd St, on northwest frontage road. Int corridors. **Pets:** Accepted.
ASK ✕ ▦

**▼▼▼ Residence Inn by Marriott** SH
(956) 994-8626. **$104.** 220 W Expwy 83. US 83, exit 2nd St, just w, then just n on 2nd St. Int corridors. **Pets:** Accepted.
ASK S✿ ✕ ✆ ▦ ➔ ✕

**▼▼▼ Super 8 Motel** SH
(956) 682-1190. **$59-$99.** 1420 E Jackson Ave. US 83, exit Jackson Ave/Sam Houston St, just s. Int corridors. **Pets:** Small. $10 one-time fee/pet. Service with restrictions, supervision.
ASK S✿ ✕ ✆ ➔

## MEMPHIS

**AAA ▼▼ Travelodge** M ❀
(806) 259-3583. **$39-$53, 5 day notice.** 1600 Boykin Dr. On US 287, 1.3 mi n of jct SR 256. Ext corridors. **Pets:** Small. $6 daily fee/pet, $6 one-time fee/pet. No service, supervision.
SAVE S✿ ✕ ✆ ⌶ ➔

## MIDLAND

**AAA ▼▼▼ Best Western Atrium Inn** SH
(432) 694-7774. **$89.** 3904 W Wall St. I-20, exit 134, 1 mi n on Midkiff Rd, 0.3 mi w on I-20 business route. Ext/int corridors. **Pets:** Accepted.
SAVE S✿ ✕ ⌧ ✆ ▦ ➔ ✕

**▼▼▼▼ Hilton Midland Plaza** LH
(432) 683-6131. **$79-$209, 3 day notice.** 117 W Wall St. Jct Wall and Loraine sts; downtown. Int corridors. **Pets:** Accepted.
✕ ♿M ⌧ ♿ ✆ ▦ ⌶ ➔ ✕

**▼▼▼ Holiday Inn** SH
(432) 697-3181. **$79-$89.** 4300 W Wall St. I-20, exit 134 (Midkiff Rd), 1 mi n to I-20 business loop, then 0.7 mi w. Ext/int corridors. **Pets:** Accepted.
ASK S✿ ✕ ✆ ▦ ⌶ ➔ ✕

**AAA ▼▼▼ La Quinta Inn Midland** SH
(432) 697-9900. **$71-$105.** 4130 W Wall St. I-20, exit 131, 0.9 mi n on SR 250 Loop to exit 1A; 1.2 mi e on I-20 business route. Ext corridors. **Pets:** Medium. Service with restrictions.
SAVE ✕ ⌧ ✆ ▦ ➔

**▼▼▼ Plaza Inn** SH
(432) 686-8733. **$73-$108.** 4108 N Big Spring St. I-20, exit 144, 6.1 mi on SR 250 Loop to SR 349 (Big Spring St), just s on SR 349. Ext corridors. **Pets:** Very small. $35 one-time fee/room. Service with restrictions, supervision.
ASK S✿ ✕ ⌧ ✆ ▦ ➔

**▼▼ Ramada Limited** SH
(432) 699-4144. **$62-$79.** 3100 W Wall St. 2 mi w on I-20 business loop. Int corridors. **Pets:** $7 daily fee/pet. Designated rooms, service with restrictions, supervision.
ASK S✿ ✕ ✆ ▦ ➔

## MINERAL WELLS

**AAA ▼▼▼ Best Western Clubhouse Inn & Suites** SH
(940) 325-2270. **$75-$159.** 4410 Hwy 180 E. Jct US 180 and SR 1195; in East Mineral Wells. Int corridors. **Pets:** $5 one-time fee/room. Service with restrictions, supervision.
SAVE S✿ ✕ ♿M ♿ ✆ ▦ ➔

## MISSION

**▼▼▼ Hawthorn Suites** SH ❀
(956) 519-9696. **$102-$108.** 3700 Plantation Grove Blvd. US 83, exit Sharyland Rd, 2.1 mi s to Plantation Grove Blvd. Ext corridors. **Pets:** Medium, other species. $25 one-time fee/room. Service with restrictions, crate.
ASK S✿ ✕ ▦ ➔

## MONAHANS

**▼▼ Best Western Colonial Inn** M
(432) 943-4345. **$63.** 702 W I-20. I-20, exit 80, just s. Ext/int corridors. **Pets:** Accepted.
ASK ✕ ⌧ ✆ ▦ ➔

## MOUNT PLEASANT

**AAA ▼▼▼ Best Western Mt. Pleasant Inn** SH
(903) 572-5051. **$80-$90.** 102 Burton St. I-30 and Business Rt US 271, exit 162. Ext corridors. **Pets:** Medium, dogs only. $10 one-time fee/pet. Service with restrictions, supervision.
SAVE S✿ ✕ ✆ ▦ ➔

**Comfort Inn** SH
(903) 577-7553. **$70-$110.** 2515 W Ferguson Rd. I-30, exit 160. Ext corridors. **Pets:** Small. $15 daily fee/room. Service with restrictions, supervision.
SAVE Sō ✕ ⟨⟩ ⊟ ⟐ ⛱

**Holiday Inn Express Hotel & Suites** SH
(903) 577-3800. **$75-$125.** 2306 Greenhill Rd. I-30, exit 162, just n. Int corridors. **Pets:** Accepted.
ASK Sō ✕ ⟨M⟩ ⟨⟩ ⊟ ⟐ ⛱

# MOUNT VERNON

**Super 8 Motel of Mount Vernon** SH ❀
(903) 588-2882. **$49-$69.** 401 W I-30. I-30, exit 146 (SR 37). Ext corridors. **Pets:** $5 daily fee/pet. Service with restrictions, supervision.
SAVE Sō ✕ ⟨⟩ ⊟ ⟐

# NACOGDOCHES

**La Quinta Inn Nacogdoches** SH
(936) 560-5453. **$62-$72.** 3215 South St. US 59, jct Loop 224 and US 59 business route, south of town. Ext corridors. **Pets:** Medium. Service with restrictions.
ASK ✕ ⟨⟩ ⊟ ⟐ ⛱

# NEDERLAND

**Best Western-Airport Inn** M
(409) 727-1631. **$54-$78.** 200 Memorial Hwy 69. US 69, 96 and 287, exit Nederland Ave. Ext corridors. **Pets:** Accepted.
✕ ⊟ ⟐ ⛱

# NEW BOSTON

**Best Western Inn of New Boston** SH
(903) 628-6999. **$64-$135.** 1024 N Center. I-30, exit 201, on westbound access road. Ext corridors. **Pets:** Large, other species. $25 daily fee/pet. Service with restrictions, crate.
SAVE Sō ✕ ⟨⟩ ⊟ ⟐ ⛱

# NORTH RICHLAND HILLS

**Benison Inn & Suites** SH
(817) 268-6879. **$59-$69.** 5151 Thaxton Pkwy. I-820, exit 21 (Holiday Ln), 0.5 mi w on north access road to Thaxton Pkwy, then just n. Int corridors. **Pets:** Accepted.
ASK Sō ✕ ⊟ ⟐ ⛱

**Studio 6 #6034** SH
(817) 788-6000. **$43-$53.** 7450 NE Loop 820. I-820, exit 21 (Holiday Ln), 0.4 mi e on south access road. Ext corridors. **Pets:** Accepted.
Sō ✕ ⟨⟩ ⟨⟩ ⊟ ⟐

# ODEM

**Days Inn-Odem** M
(361) 368-2166. **$49-$110, 3 day notice.** 1505 Voss Ave (US 77). US 77, 1 mi s of jct 631. Ext corridors. **Pets:** Accepted.
SAVE Sō ✕ ⊟ ⛱

# ODESSA

**Best Western Garden Oasis** SH
(432) 337-3006. **$78-$88 (no credit cards).** 110 W I-20. Jct I-20 and US 385, exit 116. Ext/int corridors. **Pets:** Accepted.
ASK Sō ✕ ⟨⟩ ⊟ ⟐ ⟨⟩ ⛱ ⟨✕⟩

**Days Inn** SH
(432) 335-8000. **$58.** 3075 E Business Loop 20. I-20, exit 121, 0.7 mi n on Loop 338, then 0.5 mi w. Int corridors. **Pets:** Small. $15 one-time fee/pet. Service with restrictions, supervision.
SAVE Sō ✕ ⊟ ⛱

**La Quinta Inn Odessa** SH
(432) 333-2820. **$75-$105.** 5001 E Business Loop I-20. I-20, exit 121, 0.8 mi n on Loop 338, then just w. Ext corridors. **Pets:** Medium. Service with restrictions.
ASK ✕ ⟨⟩ ⊟ ⟐ ⛱

**MCM Grande Hotel** SH
(432) 362-2311. **$75-$85.** 6201 E Business I-20. I-20, exit 121, 0.8 mi n on Loop 338, then 1 mi e. Ext/int corridors. **Pets:** Accepted.
ASK ✕ ⟨⟩ ⊟ ⟐ ⟨⟩ ⛱ ⟨✕⟩

**Motel 6 Odessa #439** M
(432) 333-4025. **$37-$47.** 200 E I-20 Service Rd. I-20, exit 116, on eastbound frontage road. Ext corridors. **Pets:** Accepted.
Sō ⛱

**Quality Inn & Suites** SH
(432) 333-3931. **$69-$199.** 3001 E Business I-20. I-20, exit 121, 0.7 mi n on Loop 338, then 0.5 mi w. Ext/int corridors. **Pets:** Accepted.
ASK Sō ✕ ⊟ ⟐ ⛱ ⟨✕⟩

# OZONA

**Americas Best Value Inn** M
(325) 392-2631. **$49-$59.** 820 11th St. I-10, exit 365 westbound to SR 163, 1 mi n; exit 363 eastbound to Loop 466, 2 mi e. Ext corridors. **Pets:** Small. $5 daily fee/pet. Service with restrictions, supervision.
SAVE Sō ✕

**Travelodge** M
(325) 392-2656. **$55-$60.** 8 11th St. I-10, exit 368 westbound, 2 mi w; exit 365 eastbound to Loop 466, 1 mi e. Ext corridors. **Pets:** Other species. $5 daily fee/pet, $5 one-time fee/pet. Service with restrictions, supervision.
SAVE Sō ✕ ⊟ ⟐ ⛱

# PALESTINE

**Best Western Palestine Inn** SH
(903) 723-4655. **$65-$75.** 1601 W Palestine Ave. Jct US 287/SR 19, 0.7 mi sw on US 79. Ext corridors. **Pets:** Accepted.
SAVE ✕ ⟨⟩ ⊟ ⟐ ⟨⟩

# PARIS

**Best Western Inn of Paris** SH
(903) 785-5566. **$54-$69.** 3755 NE Loop 286. Jct US 82 and E Loop 286, just n. Ext corridors. **Pets:** Medium. $10 daily fee/pet. Service with restrictions, supervision.
SAVE Sō ✕ ⟨⟩ ⟨⟩ ⊟ ⟐ ⛱

**Days Inn** SH
(903) 784-8164. **$65-$75, 10 day notice.** 2650 N Main. Ne Loop 286, exit US 271, just n. Ext corridors. **Pets:** Accepted.
SAVE Sō ✕ ⊟ ⟐ ⛱

**Holiday Inn** SH
(903) 785-5545. **$75.** 3560 NE Loop 286. E Loop 286, 0.3 mi n of jct US 82. Ext corridors. **Pets:** Accepted.
SAVE Sō ✕ ⟨⟩ ⟨⟩ ⊟ ⟐ ⟨⟩ ⛱

# PECOS

**Best Western Swiss Clock Inn** M
(432) 447-2215. **$69-$99.** 133 S Frontage Rd, I-20 W. I-20, exit 40, just e. Ext corridors. **Pets:** Small, dogs only. $10 one-time fee/pet. Designated rooms, service with restrictions, supervision.
SAVE Sō ✕ ⟨⟩ ⟨⟩ ⊟ ⟐ ⟨⟩ ⛱

**LAURA LODGE** M
(432) 445-4924. **$38-$55.** 1000 E Business 20. I-20, exit 42 (US 285), 1 mi nw to Business Rt I-20, then 0.5 mi e. Ext corridors. **Pets:** Medium. $15 daily fee/pet. Designated rooms, service with restrictions, supervision.
SAVE Sō ✕ ⊟ ⟐ ⛱

**(AAA) ▼▼▼ Oak Tree Inn** SH
(432) 447-0180. **$60-$79.** 22 N Frontage Rd. I-20, exit 42, just w on north access road. Int corridors. **Pets:** Small. $10 one-time fee/room. No service, supervision.
[SAVE] [S☉] [✕] [⟲] [⌂] [▯] [⌨]

## PHARR

**▼▼▼▼ Palace Inn & Suites** SH
(956) 702-3330. **$65-$70.** 1130 E Expwy 83. Jct US 83 Expwy, exit I Rd. Ext corridors. **Pets:** Accepted.
[ASK] [S☉] [✕] [⌂] [▯] [⌨] [⊃]

## PLAINVIEW

**▼▼ Best Western Conestoga** SH
(806) 293-9454. **$59-$69.** 600 N I-27. I-27, exit 49, just s of US 70, on eastbound access road. Ext corridors. **Pets:** Other species. $10 daily fee/pet. Service with restrictions.
[ASK] [S☉] [✕] [⟲] [▯] [⌨] [⊃]

**▼▼▼▼ Holiday Inn Express Hotel & Suites** SH
(806) 296-9900. **$90.** 4213 W 13th St. I-27, exit 49 northbound, just w to Mesa, then just n; exit 50 southbound, just s to 13th St, then just w. Int corridors. **Pets:** Accepted.
[ASK] [S☉] [✕] [⌂M] [⌂] [▯] [⌨] [⊃]

## PORTLAND

**(AAA) ▼▼▼▼ Comfort Inn** SH
(361) 643-2222. **$85-$139.** 1703 N Hwy 181. US 181 W access road, exit FM 3239 northbound; exit Lang St southbound. Ext corridors. **Pets:** Accepted.
[SAVE] [S☉] [✕] [▯] [⌨] [⊃] [✕]

## POST

**▼▼ Best Western Post Inn** SH
(806) 495-9933. **$81-$86.** 1011 N Broadway. 1 mi n on US 84. Int corridors. **Pets:** Accepted.
[ASK] [S☉] [✕] [⌂] [▯] [⌨] [⊃]

## RAYMONDVILLE

**(AAA) ▼▼▼ Americas Best Value Inn & Suites** SH ☙
(956) 689-5900. **$49-$69.** 450 S Expwy 77/I-69. Jct US 77 at FM 186, just s on southbound access road. Ext corridors. **Pets:** Other species. $25 deposit/room. Service with restrictions, supervision.
[SAVE] [S☉] [✕] [▯] [⌨] [⊃]

**▼▼ Best Western** SH ☙
(956) 689-4141. **$69-$119.** 118 N Expwy 77. US 77, jct FM 186 on southbound access road. Ext corridors. **Pets:** Small, other species. $10 daily fee/pet. Designated rooms, no service, supervision.
[ASK] [S☉] [✕] [▯] [⌨] [⊃]

## ROBSTOWN

**(AAA) ▼▼▼ Executive Inn** SH
(361) 387-9416. **$45-$70.** 620 Hwy 77 S. On US 77, 1 mi s. Ext corridors. **Pets:** Accepted.
[SAVE] [S☉] [✕] [▯] [⊃]

## ROCKPORT

**▼▼ Days Inn** M
(361) 729-6379. **$56-$150.** 1212 Laurel St @ Bus 35 Hwy. Jct Laurel St and Business Rt SR 35; center. Ext corridors. **Pets:** Medium, dogs only. $15 daily fee/pet. Service with restrictions, supervision.
[ASK] [S☉] [✕] [▯] [⊃]

**(AAA) ▼▼▼▼ Laguna Reef Hotel** CO
(361) 729-1742. **$85-$280.** 1021 Water St. 0.5 mi s, just e of Business Rt SR 35; entrance on S Austin St. Ext corridors. **Pets:** Accepted.
[SAVE] [S☉] [✕] [▯] [⌨] [⊃] [✕]

**(AAA) ▼▼▼▼ Sportsman's Manor** M
(361) 729-5331. **$59-$149.** 1075 N Fulton Beach Rd. 2.3 mi n on SR 35. Ext corridors. **Pets:** Accepted.
[SAVE] [S☉] [⊃]

**(AAA) ▼▼▼ The Village Inn** M
(361) 729-6370. **$48-$100.** 503 N Austin St. Just w of jct SR 35 and Business Rt SR 35. Ext corridors. **Pets:** Large. $10 daily fee/pet. Service with restrictions, crate.
[SAVE] [S☉] [✕] [▯] [⌨] [⊃]

## ROUND ROCK

**(AAA) ▼▼▼ Best Western Executive Inn** SH
(512) 255-3222. **$49-$79.** 1851 N I-35. I-35, exit 253 northbound; exit 253A U-turn southbound. Ext corridors. **Pets:** Service with restrictions.
[SAVE] [S☉] [✕] [⌂M] [⌂] [▯] [⌨] [⊃]

**▼▼▼ Candlewood Suites** SH
(512) 828-0899. **$55-$95.** 521 S I-35. I-35, exit 252A, just n on northbound frontage road. Int corridors. **Pets:** Other species. $25 one-time fee/pet. Service with restrictions, crate.
[ASK] [S☉] [✕] [⌂] [▯] [⌨]

**▼▼▼ Days Inn and Suites** SH
(512) 246-0055. **$54-$149.** 1802 S I-35. I-35, exit 251, just s. Ext/int corridors. **Pets:** Accepted.
[ASK] [S☉] [✕] [⌂] [▯] [⌨] [⊃]

**(AAA) ▼▼▼▼ La Quinta Inn Austin (Round Rock)** SH
(512) 255-6666. **$69-$83.** 2004 I-35 N. I-35, exit 254, on west frontage road. Int corridors. **Pets:** Medium. Service with restrictions.
[SAVE] [✕] [⟲] [▯] [⌨] [⊃]

**▼▼▼ Red Roof Inn** SH
(512) 310-1111. **$46-$66.** 1990 I-35 N. I-35, exit 254, on west frontage road. Int corridors. **Pets:** Accepted.
[✕] [⌂] [▯] [⊃]

**▼▼▼▼ Residence Inn by Marriott Austin Round Rock** SH
(512) 733-2400. **$139.** 2505 S I-35. I-35, exit 250 southbound; exit 251 northbound, on east frontage road. Int corridors. **Pets:** Other species. $75 one-time fee/room. Service with restrictions, crate.
[ASK] [S☉] [✕] [⌂M] [⟲] [⌂] [▯] [⌨] [⊃] [✕]

**▼▼▼▼ Staybridge Suites Austin-Round Rock** SH ☙
(512) 733-0942. **$79.** 520 I-35 S. I-35, exit 252B northbound; exit 252AB southbound, on west frontage road. Int corridors. **Pets:** Medium. $5 daily fee/room, $50 one-time fee/room. Service with restrictions, supervision.
[ASK] [S☉] [✕] [⌂M] [⟲] [⌂] [▯] [⌨] [⊃]

## SAN ANGELO

**(AAA) ▼▼▼ Americas Best Value Inn** M
(325) 653-1323. **$51-$70.** 1601 S Bryant Blvd. US 87 and 277 at Ave L. Ext/int corridors. **Pets:** Small, dogs only. $25 deposit/pet, $2 daily fee/pet. Service with restrictions, supervision.
[SAVE] [S☉] [✕] [▯] [⌨] [⊃]

**(AAA) ▼▼▼ Benchmark Comfort Inn** SH
(325) 944-2578. **$64-$84.** 2502 Loop 306. Loop 306, exit Knickerbocker Rd. Ext corridors. **Pets:** Service with restrictions, supervision.
[SAVE] [S☉] [✕] [▯] [⌨] [⊃]

**(AAA) ▼▼▼ Best Western San Angelo** SH
(325) 223-1273. **$69.** 3017 W Loop 306. Loop 306, exit College Hills Blvd, just s. Ext corridors. **Pets:** Small. $10 one-time fee/room. Designated rooms, service with restrictions, supervision.
[SAVE] [S☉] [✕] [⌂] [▯] [⌨] [⊃]

**(AAA) ▼▼▼ Days Inn San Angelo** SH
(325) 658-6594. **$55-$75.** 4613 S Jackson St. Jct US 87 and Jackson St. Ext corridors. **Pets:** Service with restrictions, supervision.
[SAVE] [✕] [▯] [⌨] [⍾] [⊃]

**▼▼▼ Hawthorn Inn & Suites** 〔SH〕
(325) 653-1500. **$92-$104.** 1355 Knickerbocker Rd. US 87 S, 1 mi w. Int corridors. **Pets:** Medium. $50 one-time fee/pet. Service with restrictions, crate.
〔ASK〕〔S6〕✕〔..〕🛏🖵🏊

**〔AAA〕 ▼▼▼ Howard Johnson San Angelo** 〔SH〕
(325) 653-2995. **$56-$65.** 415 W Beauregard. Just w on US 67 business route at US 87 southbound. Ext/int corridors. **Pets:** Small. Service with restrictions, supervision.
〔SAVE〕〔S6〕✕🛏🖵〔¶〕🏊

**▼▼▼ La Quinta Inn San Angelo (Conference Center)** 〔SH〕
(325) 949-0515. **$76-$108.** 2307 Loop 306. Loop 306, exit Knickerbocker Rd, just s. Ext corridors. **Pets:** Medium. Service with restrictions.
〔ASK〕✕🗁🛏🖵🏊

**▼▼▼ Motel 6 San Angelo #229** 〔M〕
(325) 658-8061. **$39-$51.** 311 N Bryant Blvd. Just n on US 87. Ext corridors. **Pets:** Accepted.
〔S6〕✕〔..〕🛏🖵🏊

**▼▼▼ Quality Inn & Suites** 〔SH〕
(325) 655-8000. **$89.** 333 Rio Concho Dr. US 87 to Concho Ave, 1 mi e. Ext/int corridors. **Pets:** Medium. Designated rooms, service with restrictions, crate.
〔ASK〕〔S6〕✕〔..〕🛏🖵🏊✕

**〔AAA〕 ▼▼▼▼ San Angelo Inn & Conference Center** 〔SH〕
(325) 658-2828. **$59-$119.** 441 Rio Concho Dr. US 87 to Concho Ave, 0.5 mi e; downtown. Int corridors. **Pets:** Medium, other species. $50 one-time fee/room. Service with restrictions.
〔SAVE〕〔S6〕✕🗁🛏🖵〔¶〕🏊

# SAN ANTONIO METROPOLITAN AREA

## ELMENDORF

**〔AAA〕 ▼▼▼ Comfort Inn & Suites Braunig Lake** 〔SH〕
(210) 633-1833. **$56-$90.** 13800 I-37 S. I-37, exit 130 (Donop, Southton Rd), on northbound access lane. Ext corridors. **Pets:** $5 daily fee/pet. Service with restrictions.
〔SAVE〕〔S6〕✕🛏🖵🏊

## FLORESVILLE

**▼▼▼▼ Best Western Floresville Inn** 〔SH〕
(830) 393-0443. **$64-$85.** 1720 S 10th St. US 181, just s of downtown. Ext corridors. **Pets:** Small. $10 daily fee/room. Service with restrictions, crate.
〔ASK〕〔S6〕✕🛏🖵🏊

## LEON VALLEY

**▼▼▼▼ Super 8 SeaWorld Area** 〔SH〕
(210) 520-0888. **$45-$99.** 5336 Wurzbach Rd. I-410, exit Bandera Rd, just n to Wurzbach Rd, then just w. Int corridors. **Pets:** Accepted.
〔ASK〕〔S6〕✕🛏🖵🏊

## LIVE OAK

**▼▼▼▼ La Quinta Inn San Antonio (I-35 North at Toepperwein)** 〔SH〕
(210) 657-5500. **$74-$100.** 12822 I-35 N. I-35, exit 170B (Toepperwein), on northbound access road. Ext/int corridors. **Pets:** Medium, other species. Service with restrictions.
〔ASK〕✕〔6M〕🛏🖵🏊

## NEW BRAUNFELS

**▼▼▼▼ Best Western Inn & Suites** 〔SH〕
(830) 625-7337. **$49-$149.** 1493 I-35 N. I-35, exit 190, on southbound access lane. Ext/int corridors. **Pets:** Small. $10 daily fee/pet. Service with restrictions, supervision.
〔ASK〕〔S6〕✕〔..〕🖵🏊

**▼▼▼ Executive Inn & Suites** 〔SH〕
(830) 625-3932. **$39-$199.** 808 Hwy 46 S. I-35, exit 189, 0.4 mi e. Ext corridors. **Pets:** Accepted.
〔ASK〕〔S6〕✕〔6M〕〔..〕🛏🖵🏊

**〔AAA〕 ▼▼▼▼ Holiday Inn** 〔SH〕
(830) 625-8017. **$69-$159.** 1051 I-35 E. I-35, exit 189, on southbound access road. Ext corridors. **Pets:** Large. $25 one-time fee/room. Service with restrictions, crate.
〔SAVE〕〔S6〕✕〔6M〕🛏🖵〔¶〕🏊

**▼▼▼▼ Quality Inn & Suites** 〔SH〕
(830) 643-9300. **$74-$400.** 1533 IH-35 N. I-35, exit 190, on southbound access lane. Int corridors. **Pets:** Medium, other species. $50 deposit/pet, $25 daily fee/pet. Service with restrictions, supervision.
〔ASK〕〔S6〕✕〔..〕🛏🖵🏊

**〔AAA〕 ▼▼▼ Rodeway Inn** 〔SH〕
(830) 629-6991. **$39-$129.** 1209 I-35 E. I-35, exit 189, on southbound access road. Ext corridors. **Pets:** Medium, other species. $20 one-time fee/pet. Service with restrictions, supervision.
〔SAVE〕〔S6〕✕🛏🖵🏊

**▼▼▼ Super 8 Motel-New Braunfels** 〔M〕
(830) 629-1155. **$44-$179.** 510 Hwy 46 S. I-35, exit 189 (SR 46), just e. Ext corridors. **Pets:** Medium. $10 daily fee/pet. Service with restrictions.
〔ASK〕〔S6〕✕🛏🖵🏊

## SAN ANTONIO

**〔AAA〕 ▼▼▼ Alamo Travelodge** 〔SH〕
(210) 222-1000. **$44-$109, 3 day notice.** 405 Broadway. US 281, exit Broadway, just s. Ext corridors. **Pets:** Accepted.
〔SAVE〕〔S6〕✕🛏🖵〔¶〕🏊

**▼▼▼▼ AmeriSuites (San Antonio/Airport)** 〔SH〕
(210) 930-2333. **$89-$159.** 7615 Jones Maltsberger Rd. US 281, exit Jones Maltsberger Rd, in Loop 410. Int corridors. **Pets:** Accepted.
〔ASK〕✕〔..〕🛏🖵🏊

**〔AAA〕 ▼▼▼▼ AmeriSuites (San Antonio/Northwest)** 〔SH〕
(210) 561-0099. **$59-$139.** 4325 AmeriSuites Dr. I-10, exit Wurzbach Rd, 0.5 mi on westbound frontage road. Int corridors. **Pets:** Accepted.
〔SAVE〕✕〔6M〕🗁〔..〕🛏🖵🏊

**〔AAA〕 ▼▼▼▼ AmeriSuites (San Antonio/Riverwalk)** 〔SH〕
(210) 227-6854. **$99-$169.** 601 S St. Mary's St. I-35, exit Durango St, 0.9 mi n. Int corridors. **Pets:** Small, other species. $10 daily fee/pet. Service with restrictions, supervision.
〔SAVE〕✕〔..〕🛏🖵🏊

**〔AAA〕 ▼▼▼▼ Arbor House Suites Bed & Breakfast** 〔BB〕
(210) 472-2005. **$125-$150, 7 day notice.** 109 Arciniega St. Just n of Durango St; near La Villita Historic District. Ext/int corridors. **Pets:** Medium, other species. No service, supervision.
〔SAVE〕〔S6〕✕🛏🖵

**▼▼▼▼ Best Western-Garden Inn** 〔SH〕
(210) 599-0999. **$89-$159.** 11939 N I-35. I-35, exit 170, on southbound access road, 0.5 mi s to Judson Rd exit. Ext corridors. **Pets:** Very small. $25 daily fee/pet. Service with restrictions, supervision.
〔ASK〕〔S6〕✕〔..〕🛏🖵🏊

▼▼▼ **Best Western Posada Ana Inn-San Antonio Airport** SH
(210) 342-1400. **$90-$140.** 8600 Jones Maltsberger Rd. I-410, exit 21A (Jones Maltsberger Rd), 0.5 mi s. Int corridors. **Pets:** Accepted.
ASK ✕ 🛏 💻 🌊

▼▼▼ **Best Western Posada Ana Inn San Antonio Medical Center** SH
(210) 561-9550. **$80-$134.** 9411 Wurzbach Rd. I-10 NW, exit 561 (Wurzbach Rd) on eastbound access road. Int corridors. **Pets:** Accepted.
ASK ✕ 🛏 💻 🌊

▼▼▼ **Brackenridge House B & B** BB
(210) 271-3442. **$110-$200, 14 day notice.** 230 Madison. Just s of S St. Marys St at Durango St. Ext/int corridors. **Pets:** Large, other species. Designated rooms, no service.
✕ 🛏 💻

▼▼▼ **Candlewood Suites Hotel** SH
(210) 615-0550. **$60-$80.** 9350 I-10 W. I-10 W, exit 561 (Wurzbach Rd), eastbound access road: between Wurzbach Rd and Callaghan. Int corridors. **Pets:** Other species. $75 one-time fee/room. Service with restrictions, supervision.
ASK ✕ ♿ 🛏 💻 🌊

AAA ▼▼▼ **Comfort Inn Sea World** SH
(210) 684-8606. **$69-$139.** 4 Piano Pl. I-410, exit Evers Rd westbound, U-turn; exit 14 Callahan/Babocks Rd eastbound. Ext corridors. **Pets:** Accepted.
SAVE ⑤D ✕ 🛏 💻 🌊

▼▼▼ **Courtyard by Marriott-Medical Center** SH
(210) 614-7100. **$94.** 8585 Marriott Dr. Off Fredericksburg Rd, 5 mi n, jct I-410. Int corridors. **Pets:** Small. $75 one-time fee/room. Supervision.
✕ ♿M ⌚ ♿ 🛏 💻 🌊

▼▼▼ **Crockett Hotel** LH
(210) 225-6500. **$155, 3 day notice.** 320 Bonham St. Center. Ext/int corridors. **Pets:** Accepted.
ASK ⑤D ✕ 🛏 💻 🍴 🌊

▼ ▼ **Days Inn Coliseum** SH
(210) 225-4040. **$43-$129, 3 day notice.** 3443 I-35 N. I-35, exit 160 (Splashtown), on southbound access road. Ext corridors. **Pets:** Medium. $25 one-time fee/pet. Designated rooms, service with restrictions, crate.
ASK ⑤D ✕ 🛏 💻 🌊

▼ ▼ **Days Inn-Downtown Laredo St** SH
(210) 271-3334. **$49-$139, 3 day notice.** 1500 I-35 S. I-10/35, exit 154 (Laredo St). Ext/int corridors. **Pets:** Medium. $25 one-time fee/pet. Designated rooms, service with restrictions, crate.
ASK ⑤D ✕ 🛏 💻 🌊

▼▼▼ **Drury Inn & Suites-San Antonio Airport** SH
(210) 308-8100. **$85-$145.** 95 NE Loop 410. I-410, exit 21A (Jones Maltsberger Rd), 1 8 mi w of airport. Int corridors. **Pets:** Accepted.
ASK ✕ ♿M ♿ 🛏 💻 🌊

▼▼▼ **Drury Inn & Suites-San Antonio North** SH
(210) 404-1600. **$90-$155.** 801 N FM 1604. On FM 1604, 0.4 mi w on US 281. Int corridors. **Pets:** Accepted.
ASK ✕ 🛏 💻 🌊

▼▼▼ **Drury Inn & Suites-San Antonio Northwest** SH
(210) 561-2510. **$81-$160.** 9806 I-10 W. I-10, exit Wurzbach Rd, on southeast corner. Int corridors. **Pets:** Accepted.
ASK ✕ 🛏 💻 🌊

▼▼▼ **Drury Inn-San Antonio Northeast** SH
(210) 654-1144. **$65-$130.** 8300 I-35 N. I-35, exit 165 (Walzem Rd), northbound access road. Ext/int corridors. **Pets:** Accepted.
ASK ✕ ♿M 🛏 💻 🌊

▼▼ **Econo Lodge Airport** M
(210) 247-4774. **$57-$74.** 2635 NE Loop 410. I-410, exit 25B (Perrin-Beitel Rd), on westbound access lane. Ext/int corridors. **Pets:** Accepted.
ASK ⑤D ✕ 🌊

▼▼ **Econo Lodge Inn** SH
(210) 224-5114. **$79-$110.** 13575 I-H 35 N. I-35, exit 161 (Binz-Engleman Rd), follow signs to I-35 S access road. Int corridors. **Pets:** Accepted.
ASK ⑤D ✕ 💻 🌊

▼▼ **Econo Lodge Lackland** M
(210) 645-1430. **Call for rates.** 6301 Old Hwy 90 W. US 90, exit Old US 90, 0.4 mi ne. Ext corridors. **Pets:** Medium, other species. $30 one-time fee/pet. Designated rooms, service with restrictions, supervision.
✕ 🛏 💻 🌊

▼▼ **Embassy Suites Hotel-Airport** LH
(210) 525-9999. **$139-$199.** 10110 Hwy 281 N. US 281, exit Jones Maltsberger Rd. Int corridors. **Pets:** Accepted.
✕ ⌚ 🛏 💻 🍴 🌊 ✕

AAA ▼▼▼ **Emily Morgan Hotel** LH 🐾
(210) 225-8486. **$119-$219.** 705 E Houston St. On Houston St, just n of Bonham St. Int corridors. **Pets:** Other species. Service with restrictions, supervision.
SAVE ⑤D ✕ ♿M ⌚ 💻 🍴 🌊 ✕

▼▼▼ **The Fairmount** SH
(210) 224-8800. **$199-$555.** 401 S Alamo St. Opposite convention center and Hemisfair Plaza. Ext/int corridors. **Pets:** Accepted.
ASK ⑤D ✕ 🛏 💻 🍴 🌊

▼▼▼ **Hampton Inn-San Antonio Airport** SH
(210) 366-1800. **$90-$160.** 8818 Jones Maltsberger Rd. I-410, exit 21B (Jones Maltsberger Rd), on westbound access road. Int corridors. **Pets:** Accepted.
ASK ✕ ⌚ 💻 🌊

AAA ▼▼▼ **Hampton Inn Six Flags Area** SH 🐾
(210) 561-9058. **$79-$109.** 11010 I-10 W. I-10, exit 560 westbound; exit 559 (Huebner Rd) eastbound. Int corridors. **Pets:** Medium, other species. $25 one-time fee/room. Service with restrictions, supervision.
SAVE ⑤D ✕ 🛏 💻 🌊

▼▼▼ **Hawthorn Suites Riverwalk** SH
(210) 527-1900. **$139-$179.** 830 N St. Mary's St. Just n of Navarro St. Int corridors. **Pets:** Accepted.
ASK ⑤D ✕ ♿ 🛏 💻 🌊

AAA ▼▼▼ **Holiday Inn-Downtown-Market Square** SH
(210) 225-3211. **$119-$169.** 318 W Durango St. I-35, exit Durango St, 2 blks e. Int corridors. **Pets:** Accepted.
SAVE ⑤D ✕ ♿M ♿ 🛏 💻 🍴 🌊 ✕

▼▼▼ **Holiday Inn Express-San Antonio Airport** SH
(210) 308-6700. **$90-$150.** 91 NE Loop 410. I-410, exit 21A (Jones Maltsberger Rd) eastbound; exit 20B westbound, on westbound access road; between San Pedro Ave and Jones Maltsberger Rd. Int corridors. **Pets:** Accepted.
ASK ✕ ♿M ♿ 🛏 💻 🌊

AAA ▼▼▼ **Holiday Inn Riverwalk** SH
(210) 224-2500. **$119-$199, 3 day notice.** 217 N St. Mary's St. Houston St, just s. Int corridors. **Pets:** Medium. $100 deposit/room, $25 one-time fee/room. Service with restrictions, supervision.
SAVE ⑤D ✕ 🛏 🍴 🌊

AAA ▼▼▼ **Holiday Inn Select** SH
(210) 349-9900. **$79-$189.** 77 NE Loop 410. I-410, exit 20B (McCullough St), on westbound access road. Int corridors. **Pets:** Small. $100 deposit/pet, $25 one-time fee/pet. Service with restrictions, supervision.
SAVE ⑤D ✕ ♿M ⌚ ♿ 🛏 💻 🍴 🌊

**▼▼ HomeGate Studios & Suites** 🆂🅷
(210) 342-4800. **$54-$89.** 11221 San Pedro Ave. I-410, exit US 281 (San Pedro Ave), 2.3 mi n on US 281, exit Nakoma, on west frontage road. Ext corridors. **Pets:** Accepted.
(A$K) 🛎 ☒ ❚ 🖵 🛋 ☒

**▼▼ Homestead Studio Suites Hotel-San Antonio/Airport** 🅼
(210) 491-9009. **$45-$75.** 1015 Central Pkwy S. I-410, exit US 281 (San Pedro Ave), 4 mi n on US 281, exit Bitters Rd, on northbound access road. Ext corridors. **Pets:** $25 daily fee/pet. Service with restrictions, supervision.
(A$K) 🛎 ☒ ❚ 🖵

**▼▼ Hotel Marquis Airport** 🆂🅷
(210) 653-9110. **$57-$89.** 2635 NE Loop 410. I-410, exit 25B (Perrin-Beitel Rd), on westbound access lane. Ext/int corridors. **Pets:** Accepted.
(A$K) 🛎 ☒ ❚ 🖵 🛋

**△△△ ▼▼ Howard Johnson Inn & Suites** 🆂🅷
(210) 675-9690. **$65-$79.** 6815 Hwy 90 W. I-410, exit US 90 to Military Dr, 0.5 mi e on westbound access road. Ext corridors. **Pets:** Small. $25 one-time fee/room. Service with restrictions, crate.
(SAVE) 🛎 ☒ ❚ 🖵 🛋

**▼▼ Inn on the River** 🅱🅱
(210) 225-6333. **$79-$119, 14 day notice.** 129 Woodward Pl. Just n of W Durango St. Ext/int corridors. **Pets:** Accepted.
(A$K) ☒ ❚ 🖵

**△△△ ▼▼ Knights Inn Windsor Park** 🅼
(210) 646-6336. **$70-$99.** 6370 I-35 N. I-410/35, exit 164A (Rittiman Rd), on northbound access road. Ext corridors. **Pets:** Accepted.
(SAVE) 🛎 ☒ ⊘ ❚ 🛋

**△△△ ▼▼▼ La Mansion del Rio** 🅻🅷
(210) 518-1000. **$219-$379, 3 day notice.** 112 College St. Just s on the Riverwalk. Ext/int corridors. **Pets:** Accepted.
(SAVE) ☒ ⊘ ❚ 🖵 🍴 🛋

**△△△ ▼▼▼ La Quinta Inn & Suites San Antonio (Convention Center)** 🆂🅷
(210) 222-9181. **$179-$189.** 303 Blum St. 0.5 mi ne. Ext/int corridors. **Pets:** Medium. Service with restrictions.
(SAVE) ☒ ❚ 🖵 🛋

**△△△ ▼▼▼ La Quinta Inn & Suites San Antonio Airport** 🆂🅷
(210) 342-3738. **$108-$119.** 850 Halm. I-410, exit US 281 S, southwest corner. Int corridors. **Pets:** Medium. Service with restrictions.
(SAVE) ☒ ❚ 🖵 🛋

**△△△ ▼▼▼ La Quinta Inn San Antonio-Downtown** 🆂🅷
(210) 212-5400. **$99-$139.** 100 W Durango Blvd. I-35, exit 155B (Durango Blvd), 3 blks e of jct E Flores St. Int corridors. **Pets:** Medium. Service with restrictions.
(SAVE) ☒ 🅼 ⊘ 🗡 ❚ 🖵 🛋

**▼▼▼ La Quinta Inn San Antonio (I-35 North @ Windsor Park Mall)** 🆂🅷
(210) 653-6619. **$79-$104.** 6410 I-35 N. I-35, exit 163B northbound, on I-35 northbound access road; between Rittiman and Eisenhauer rds; exit 164A (Rittiman Rd) southbound. Ext corridors. **Pets:** Medium. Service with restrictions.
(A$K) ☒ ❚ 🖵 🛋

**▼▼▼ La Quinta Inn San Antonio (Lackland)** 🆂🅷
(210) 674-3200. **$69-$100.** 6511 Military Dr W. Sw of jct US 90 and Military Dr W. Ext corridors. **Pets:** Medium. Service with restrictions.
(A$K) ☒ ❚ 🖵 🛋

**△△△ ▼▼▼ La Quinta Inn San Antonio (Market Square)** 🆂🅷
(210) 271-0001. **$79-$121.** 900 Dolorosa. I-10/35, exit Durango St, just n on Santa Rosa St, then just w on Nueva St. Ext corridors. **Pets:** Medium. Service with restrictions.
(SAVE) ☒ 🅼 ❚ 🖵 🛋

**△△△ ▼▼▼ La Quinta Inn San Antonio (SeaWorld/Ingram Park)** 🆂🅷
(210) 680-8883. **$73-$121.** 7134 NW Loop 410. I-410, exit 10 (Culebra Rd), on eastbound access road. Ext corridors. **Pets:** Medium. Service with restrictions.
(SAVE) ☒ ❚ 🖵 🛋

**▼▼▼ La Quinta Inn San Antonio (South Park)** 🆂🅷
(210) 922-2111. **$70-$121.** 7202 S Pan American Expwy. I-35, exit 150A (Military Dr) northbound; exit 150B southbound, southeast of jct I-35 and Military Dr SW. Ext corridors. **Pets:** Medium. Service with restrictions.
☒ 🅼 ❚ 🖵 🛋

**▼▼▼ La Quinta Inn San Antonio (Vance Jackson)** 🆂🅷
(210) 734-7931. **$69-$100.** 5922 I-10 W. I 10, exit 565B eastbound; exit 565C (Vance Jackson Rd) westbound, on eastbound access road. Ext corridors. **Pets:** Medium. Service with restrictions.
(A$K) ☒ ♿ ❚ 🖵 🛋

**▼▼▼ La Quinta Inn San Antonio (Wurzbach)** 🆂🅷
(210) 593-0338. **$74-$100.** 9542 I-10 W. -10, exit Wurzbach Rd, just e on eastbound access road. Ext corridors. **Pets:** Medium, other species. Service with restrictions.
(A$K) ☒ ❚ 🖵 🛋

**▼▼ ▼▼ Marriott Plaza San Antonio** 🅻🅷
(210) 229-1000. **$139-$289.** 555 S Alamo St. Opposite convention center and Hemisfair Plaza. Int corridors. **Pets:** Accepted.
(A$K) ☒ 🅼 ⊘ 🖵 🍴 🛋 ☒

**▼▼ ▼▼ Marriott Riverwalk** 🅻🅷
(210) 224-4555. **$344.** 711 E Riverwalk. Opposite convention center and Hemisfair Plaza. Int corridors. **Pets:** $25 one-time fee/room. Service with restrictions.
(A$K) 🛎 ☒ ⊘ 🗡 ❚ 🖵 🍴 🛋 ☒

**▼▼ Motel 6-1122** 🅼
(210) 225-1111. **$45-$61.** 211 N Pecos St. I-10/35, exit 155 B (Pecos St), on I-10 E/35 S access road. Ext corridors. **Pets:** Accepted.
🛎 ☒ 🗡 ❚ 🛋

**▼▼ Motel 6-134** 🅼
(210) 650-4419. **$35-$51.** 9503 I-35 N. -35, exit 167A (Randolf Blvd) southbound; exit 167 (Starlight Terrace) northbound. Ext corridors. **Pets:** Accepted.
🛎 ☒ 🛋

**▼▼ Motel 6-651** 🅼
(210) 673-9020. **$39-$61.** 2185 SW Loop 410. I-410, exit 7 (Marbach Rd), 0.7 mi w; on westbound access road. Ext corridors. **Pets:** Accepted.
🛎 ☒ ⊘ 🗡 ❚ 🛋

**▼▼ Motel 6 East #183** 🆂🅷
(210) 333-1850. **$35-$51.** 138 N WW White Rd. I-10, exit 580 (WW White Rd), just off westbound access road. Ext corridors. **Pets:** Accepted.
🛎 ☒ 🛋

**▼▼ ▼▼ Motel 6 Fort Sam Houston #1350** 🅼
(210) 661-8791. **$37-$55.** 5522 N Pan Am Expwy. I-35/410, exit 164 (Rittiman Rd), just s on northbound access lane; just off Goldfield St. Ext corridors. **Pets:** Accepted.
🛎 ☒ 🗡 🛋

▼▼ Motel 6 San Antonio #1188 **M**
(210) 653-8088. **$37-$51.** 4621 E Rittiman Rd. I-35, exit 164 (Rittiman Rd), on north side of Rittiman Rd. Ext corridors. **Pets:** Accepted.

▼▼ Pear Tree Inn San Antonio Airport **SH**
(210) 366-9300. **$75-$120.** 143 NE Loop 410. Loop 410 W, exit 21 (Jones Maltsberger Rd), on westbound access road; between Airport Blvd and Jones Maltsberger Rd. Int corridors. **Pets:** Accepted.

▼▼ Quality Inn & Suites **SH**
(210) 359-7200. **$45-$100.** 222 S WW White Rd. I-10, exit 580 (WW White Rd), 0.4 mi s. Ext corridors. **Pets:** Accepted.

▼▼▼ Quality Inn & Suites Coliseum **SH**
(210) 224-3030. **$59-$99.** 3817 I-35 N. I-35, exit 161 (Binz-Engleman Rd), follow signs to I-35 S access road northbound; exit Binz-Engleman Rd, continue southbound. Int corridors. **Pets:** Accepted.

◆◆◆ ▼▼▼▼ Quality Inn & Suites North Airport **SH**
(210) 545-5400. **$90-$120.** 1505 Bexar Crossing. US 281, exit 1604 (Anderson Loop), on southbound access lane. Int corridors. **Pets:** Small. $25 one-time fee/pet. Designated rooms, service with restrictions, supervision.

▼▼ Quality Inn Northwest **SH**
(210) 736-1900. **$49-$129.** 6023 NW I-10 W. I-10, exit 565B eastbound; exit 565C (Vance Jackson Rd) westbound, just n. Ext corridors. **Pets:** $25 one-time fee/pet. Service with restrictions, crate.

◆◆◆ ▼▼▼ Red Roof Inn Lackland **SH**
(210) 675-4120. **$48-$68.** 6861 Hwy 90 W. Northeast jct of US 90 and Military Dr W; access via Renwick St, off Military Dr, just n of jct US 90. Ext corridors. **Pets:** Small, other species. $75 deposit/room. Service with restrictions, supervision.

▼▼ Red Roof Inn-San Antonio Airport **SH**
(210) 340-4055. **$43-$64.** 333 Wolfe Rd. On southbound access road, just s of US 281 at Isom Rd. Ext/int corridors. **Pets:** Accepted.

▼▼▼▼ Red Roof Inn San Antonio (Downtown) **M**
(210) 229-9973. **$60-$95.** 1011 E Houston St. I-37, exit 141 northbound; exit 141B southbound. Int corridors. **Pets:** Accepted.

▼▼▼ Red Roof Inn San Antonio (NW-SeaWorld) **SH**
(210) 509-3434. **$42-$84.** 6880 NW Loop 410. I-410, exit 11 (Alamo Downs Pkwy), on eastbound access road. Ext/int corridors. **Pets:** Accepted.

▼▼▼▼ Residence Inn Alamo Plaza **SH**
(210) 212-5555. **$189.** 425 Bonham St. I-37/281, exit Commerce St, just w to Bowie St, then 4 blks n. Int corridors. **Pets:** Accepted.

▼▼▼ Residence Inn by Marriott San Antonio Downtown/ Market Square **SH** ❖
(210) 231-6000. **$99-$199.** 628 S Santa Rosa. I-10/35, exit Durango St, 0.5 mi e. Int corridors. **Pets:** Other species. $75 one-time fee/pet. Service with restrictions, crate.

▼▼▼▼ Residence Inn NW/Six Flags **SH**
(210) 561-9660. **$119-$159.** 4041 Bluemel Rd. I-10, exit Wurzbach Rd, 0.3 mi w on eastbound access road. Ext corridors. **Pets:** Accepted.

▼▼▼▼ Residence Inn San Antonio-Airport **SH**
(210) 805-8118. **$89-$109.** 1014 NE Loop 410. Loop 410, exit Broadway St, 0.4 mi e on access road. Ext corridors. **Pets:** Accepted.

▼▼▼ Rittiman Inn & Suites **SH**
(210) 657-0808. **$59-$99.** 6364 I-35 N. I-35, exit 163B (Rittiman Rd) northbound, on northbound access road; exit 164A (Rittiman Rd) southbound. Ext corridors. **Pets:** Accepted.

◆◆◆ ▼▼▼ Rodeway Inn Downtown **SH**
(210) 223-2951. **$59-$99.** 900 N Main Ave. I-35, exit San Pedro/Main aves; northeast corner. Ext corridors. **Pets:** Accepted.

◆◆◆ ▼▼▼ Rodeway Inn-Six Flags Fiesta **SH**
(210) 698-3991. **$39-$99.** 19793 I-10 W. I-10, exit 554 (Camp Bullis), on eastbound access road. Ext corridors. **Pets:** Small. $10 daily fee/ room. Service with restrictions, supervision.

▼▼▼▼ San Antonio Marriott Rivercenter **LH**
(210) 223-1000. **$344.** 101 Bowie St. Corner of Bowie and Commerce sts. Int corridors. **Pets:** $25 one-time fee/room. Service with restrictions.

◆◆◆ ▼▼▼▼ Sheraton Gunter **SH** ❖
(210) 227-3241. **$229-$294.** 205 E Houston St. Center. Int corridors. **Pets:** Small, dogs only. Designated rooms, service with restrictions, supervision.

▼▼▼ Staybridge Suites San Antonio-Airport **SH**
(210) 341-3220. **$110-$190.** 66 NE Loop 410. I-410, exit 20B (McCullough St), on eastbound access lane. Int corridors. **Pets:** Accepted.

▼▼▼ Staybridge Suites San Antonio NW-Colonnade **SH**
(210) 558-9009. **$98-$300.** 4320 Spectrum One. I-10 W, exit 560 (Wurzbach Rd), follow westbound access road through light, then just n. Int corridors. **Pets:** Accepted.

▼▼ Studio 6 #6046 **M**
(210) 691-0121. **$47-$63.** 11802 I-10 W. I-10, exit 558 (De Zavala Rd), 0.6 mi e on eastbound access road. Ext corridors. **Pets:** Accepted.

▼▼ Super 8 Motel Downtown North **M**
(210) 227-8888. **$48-$88, 7 day notice.** 3617 N PanAm Expwy. I-35, exit 160 (Splashtown), on southbound access road. Ext corridors. **Pets:** Accepted.

◆◆◆ ▼▼▼ Super 8 Motel on Roland **SH**
(210) 798-5500. **$55-$129.** 302 Roland Ave. I-10, exit 577 (Roland Ave) eastbound. Ext corridors. **Pets:** Other species. $10 daily fee/pet. Service with restrictions, supervision.

◆◆◆ ▼▼▼ Travelodge Lackland **SH**
(210) 645-1561. **$50-$125.** 120 Rustleaf Dr. Just off SW Military Dr; adjacent to Lackland AFB. Ext corridors. **Pets:** Very small. $10 daily fee/pet. Service with restrictions, supervision.

▼▼▼ Tropicano Riverwalk Hotel by Clarion **LH**
(210) 223-9461. **$99-$179, 3 day notice.** 110 Lexington Ave. 0.3 mi s of jct Lexington Ave and I-35. Int corridors. **Pets:** Accepted.

▼▼ ▼▼ The Westin Riverwalk 🇱🇭 ❀
(210) 224-6500. **$179-$339.** 420 W Market St. 2 blks w of Navarro St. Int corridors. **Pets:** Medium, dogs only. Service with restrictions, supervision.

(ASK) (S✗) ✗ (&M) (🖉) (&) (▯) (¶↑) (🛏) (✗)

## SEGUIN

▼▼▼▼ Holiday Inn Seguin 🆂🅷
(830) 372-0860. **$95-$130.** 2950 N 123 Bypass. I-10, exit 610 (SR 123). Ext corridors. **Pets:** Small. $25 deposit/room. Designated rooms, service with restrictions, supervision.

(ASK) (S✗) ✗ (🔧) (▯) (¶↑) (🛏)

▼▼ ▼▼ Super 8 Motel of Seguin 🆂🅷
(830) 379-6888. **$50-$120.** 1525 N Hwy 46. I-10, exit 607 (SR 46), on eastbound access road. Int corridors. **Pets:** Medium. $10 daily fee/pet. Service with restrictions, supervision.

(ASK) (S✗) ✗ (&) (▯) (🛏)

## UNIVERSAL CITY

🔺🔺🔺 ▼▼ ▼▼ Clarion Suites Hotel 🆂🅷
(210) 655-9491. **$79-$139.** 13101 E Loop, 1604 N. Loop 1604 at Pat Booker Rd; 0.8 mi e of I-35. Ext corridors. **Pets:** Medium. $25 one-time fee/room. Designated rooms, service with restrictions, crate.

(SAVE) (S✗) ✗ (&) (▯) (🛏)

---

# END METROPOLITAN AREA

---

## SANDERSON

🔺🔺🔺 ▼▼ Desert Air Motel 🅼
(432) 345-2572. **$36-$41.** 806 W Oak. 0.5 mi w on US 90, just e of jct US 285. Ext corridors. **Pets:** Accepted.

(SAVE) (S✗) (🔧)

## SAN MARCOS

▼▼ ▼▼ Best Western San Marcos 🆂🅷
(512) 754-7557. **$49-$119.** 917 I-35 N. I-35, exit 204B, on westside access road. Int corridors. **Pets:** Accepted.

(ASK) (S✗) ✗ (🔧) (▯) (🛏)

🔺🔺🔺 ▼▼ ▼▼ Days Inn 🆂🅷
(512) 353-5050. **$49-$125.** 1005 I-35 N. I-35, exit 205 northbound; exit 204B southbound, on southbound frontage road, jct SR 80. Ext corridors. **Pets:** Dogs only. $10 one-time fee/pet. Designated rooms, service with restrictions, crate.

(SAVE) (S✗) ✗ (🔧) (🛏)

🔺🔺🔺 ▼▼▼▼ La Quinta Inn San Marcos 🆂🅷
(512) 392-8800. **$69-$121.** 1619 I-35 N. I-35, exit 206 southbound, 0.5 mi s on west frontage road; exit northbound, 1 mi n to turnaround to west frontage road, then 1.5 mi s. Ext/int corridors. **Pets:** Medium. Service with restrictions.

(SAVE) (✗) (&M) (🖉) (&) (🔧) (▯) (🛏)

🔺🔺🔺 ▼▼▼▼ Ramada Limited 🆂🅷
(512) 395-8000. **$33-$170.** 1701 I-35 N. I-35, exit 206 southbound, 0.4 mi s on west frontage road; exit northbound, 1 mi n to turnaround for west frontage road, then 1.4 mi s. Ext corridors. **Pets:** Very small, dogs only. $10 daily fee/pet. No service, supervision.

(SAVE) (S✗) ✗ (▯) (🛏)

## SEALY

▼▼ ▼▼ Best Western Inn of Sealy 🆂🅷
(979) 885-3707. **$65.** 2107 Hwy 36 S. I-10, exit 720. Ext corridors. **Pets:** Accepted.

(S✗) ✗ (&) (▯) (🛏)

## SEGOVIA

🔺🔺🔺 ▼▼ ▼▼ Econo Lodge 🅼 ❀
(325) 446-2475. **$44-$69.** 311 S Segovia Access Rd. I-10, exit 465, on south access road. Ext corridors. **Pets:** $10 one-time fee/pet. Supervision.

(SAVE) (S✗) ✗ (▯) (🛏)

## SEMINOLE

🔺🔺🔺 ▼▼ ▼▼ Raymond Motor Inn 🅼
(432) 758-3653. **$40-$45.** 301 W Ave A. 0.3 mi w on US 62 and 180. Ext corridors. **Pets:** Other species. $5 daily fee/pet. Service with restrictions, supervision.

(SAVE) (S✗) ✗ (🔧) (▯)

🔺🔺🔺 ▼▼ ▼▼ Seminole Inn 🅼
(432) 758-9881. **$55-$59, 3 day notice.** 2200 Hobbs Hwy. 1.5 mi w on US 62 and 180. Ext corridors. **Pets:** Small. $5 one-time fee/pet. Service with restrictions, supervision.

(SAVE) (S✗) ✗ (🔧) (▯) (🛏)

## SHAMROCK

🔺🔺🔺 ▼▼ ▼▼ Econo Lodge 🅼
(806) 256-2111. **$45-$75.** 1006 E 12th St. I-40, exit 164 westbound; exit 161 or 163 eastbound, just e of US 83. Ext corridors. **Pets:** Small, other species. $5 daily fee/pet. Designated rooms, service with restrictions, supervision.

(SAVE) (S✗) ✗ (🔧) (▯) (🛏)

🔺🔺🔺 ▼▼ ▼▼ Irish Inn 🆂🅷
(806) 256-2106. **$57-$72.** 301 I-40 E. I-40, exit 163, 0.3 mi e on north service road. Ext/int corridors. **Pets:** Other species. $9 one-time fee/room. Designated rooms, service with restrictions, supervision.

(SAVE) (S✗) ✗ (🖉) (🔧) (▯) (¶↑) (🛏)

🔺🔺🔺 ▼▼ Western Motel 🅼
(806) 256-3244. **$49-$59.** 104 E 12th St. Business Rt I-40 and US 83. Ext corridors. **Pets:** Medium. $5 daily fee/pet. Service with restrictions, supervision.

(SAVE) (S✗) ✗ (¶↑)

## SHERMAN

▼▼▼▼ Comfort Suites of Sherman 🆂🅷
(903) 893-0499. **$76-$85, 10 day notice.** 2900 US Hwy 75 N. US 75, exit 63; 0.3 mi s of jct US 82. Int corridors. **Pets:** Accepted.

(ASK) (S✗) ✗ (&) (🔧) (▯) (🛏)

▼▼▼▼ La Quinta Inn & Suites Sherman/Denison 🆂🅷
(903) 870-1122. **$87-$104.** 2912 US 75 N. US 75, exit 63; just sw of jct US 82. Int corridors. **Pets:** Medium. Service with restrictions.

(ASK) (✗) (&) (🔧) (▯) (🛏)

▼▼▼▼ Quality Inn 🆂🅷
(903) 868-0555. **$80.** 3605 Hwy 75 S. US 75, exit 56. Int corridors. **Pets:** Other species. $20 one-time fee/room. Service with restrictions.

(ASK) (S✗) ✗ (🔧) (▯) (¶↑) (🛏)

## SMITHVILLE

▼▼ ▼▼ Pine Point Inn 🆂🅷
(512) 237-2040. **$60-$70.** 1503 Dorothy Nichols Ln. Jct SR 71 and Dorothy Nichols Ln. Ext corridors. **Pets:** $20 one-time fee/pet. Service with restrictions, supervision.

(ASK) (S✗) ✗ (🔧) (🛏)

## SNYDER

▼▼ ▼▼ Best Western Snyder Inn 🅼
(325) 574-2200. **$70.** 810 E Coliseum Dr. 1.5 mi w of US 84/80. Ext corridors. **Pets:** Accepted.

(ASK) (S✗) ✗ (🔧) (▯) (🛏)

**(AAA) ▼▼▼ Purple Sage Motel M**
(325) 573-5491. **$56-$74.** 1501 E Coliseum Dr. 1 mi w on US 180 from jct US 84. Ext corridors. **Pets:** Accepted.
SAVE Sô X 🕭 💻 ⫴

# SONORA

**(AAA) ▼ Americas Best Value Inn-Twin Oaks Motel M**
(325) 387-2551. **$45-$55, 7 day notice.** 1009 N Crockett Ave. I-10, exit 400 westbound; exit 399 eastbound, 0.5 mi e, then 0.3 mi s on US 277. Ext corridors. **Pets:** Accepted.
SAVE X 🕭

**▼▼◆ Comfort Inn of Sonora SH**
(325) 387-5800. **$73-$79.** 311 N Hwy 277. I-10, exit 400. Ext corridors. **Pets:** Accepted.
ASK Sô X ᴸM ⫴ 🕭 💻 ⫴

**(AAA) ▼▼ Days Inn M**
(325) 387-3516. **$62-$69.** 1312 N Service Rd. I-10, exit 400, just n. Ext corridors. **Pets:** Other species. $5 daily fee/pet. Service with restrictions, crate.
SAVE Sô X 🕭 💻 ⫴⫴ ⫴

**(AAA) ▼ Holiday Host Motel M**
(325) 387-2532. **$42-$50.** 127 Loop 467 (Hwy 290). Loop 467, exit 404 westbound, 3 mi w; exit 399 eastbound, 3 mi e. Ext corridors. **Pets:** Medium. $5 deposit/pet. No service, supervision.
SAVE X 🕭 ⫴

# SOUTH PADRE ISLAND

**(AAA) ▼▼▼ Americas Best Value Inn SH**
(956) 761-8500. **$35-$300, 3 day notice.** 3813 Padre Blvd. 2.6 mi n of Queen Isabella Cswy. Int corridors. **Pets:** Medium, other species. $25 daily fee/pet. Designated rooms, service with restrictions, supervision.
SAVE Sô X 🕭 ⫴

**(AAA) ▼▼▼ Best Western Fiesta Isles Hotel SH**
(956) 761-4913. **$39-$199, 3 day notice.** 5701 Padre Blvd. 3 mi n of Queen Isabella Cswy. Ext corridors. **Pets:** Accepted.
SAVE Sô X 🕭 💻 ⫴

**(AAA) ▼▼ Days Inn SH**
(956) 761-7831. **$39-$239, 3 day notice.** 3913 Padre Blvd. 2.6 mi n of Queen Isabella Cswy. Ext corridors. **Pets:** Accepted.
SAVE Sô X 🕭 ⫴

**▼▼◆▼ Howard Johnson Inn-Resort SH**
(956) 761-5658. **$49-$299, 3 day notice.** 1709 Padre Blvd. SR 100, 0.9 mi n at corner of W Palm St. Int corridors. **Pets:** Medium. $25 one-time fee/pet. Service with restrictions, supervision.
ASK Sô X ᴸM ᴸ 🕭 ⫴

**▼▼◆▼ La Copa Beach Resort SH**
(956) 761-6000. **$49-$299, 3 day notice.** 350 Padre Blvd. Just s of Queen Isabella Cswy. Int corridors. **Pets:** Small. $10 daily fee/pet. Service with restrictions, supervision.
ASK Sô X 🕭 💻 ⫴

**▼▼◆▼ La Quinta Inn and Suites South Padre Island SH**
(956) 772-7000. **$59-$300.** 7000 Padre Blvd. I-77, exit SR 100, over Queen Isabella Cswy, then 3 mi n. Int corridors. **Pets:** Accepted.
X ᴸM ᴸ 🕭 💻 ⫴ X

**(AAA) ▼▼▼ Ramada Limited SH**
(956) 761-4097. **$50-$300.** 4109 Padre Blvd. 2 mi n of Queen Isabella Cswy. Ext corridors. **Pets:** Small. $10 one-time fee/pet. Designated rooms, service with restrictions, supervision.
SAVE X 🕭 💻 ⫴

**▼▼ Super 8 Motel SH**
(956) 761-6300. **$49-$269.** 4205 Padre Blvd. 2.7 mi n of Queen Isabella Cswy. Ext corridors. **Pets:** Accepted.
ASK Sô X ᴸM ᴸ 🕭 💻 ⫴

**▼▼◆ The Tiki Condominium Hotel CO**
(956) 761-2694. **$79-$325, 3 day notice.** 6608 Padre Blvd. 3.8 mi n of Queen Isabella Cswy. Ext corridors. **Pets:** Accepted.
Sô X 🕭 💻 ⫴ X

**▼▼◆ Travelodge SH**
(956) 761-4744. **$35-$300, 3 day notice.** 6200 Padre Blvd. 3 mi n of Queen Isabella Cswy. Ext corridors. **Pets:** Medium. $10 daily fee/pet. No service, supervision.
ASK Sô X ᴸM 🕭 💻 ⫴

# STEPHENVILLE

**(AAA) ▼▼▼ Best Western Cross Timbers SH**
(254) 968-2114. **$70-$80.** 1625 W South Loop (US 377). 1.8 mi sw on US 377 bypass and US 67. Ext corridors. **Pets:** Very small. $50 deposit/room. Designated rooms, service with restrictions, supervision.
SAVE Sô X 🕭 💻 ⫴

**▼▼◆▼ Holiday Inn Stephenville SH**
(254) 968-5256. **$75-$80.** 2865 W Washington St. 1.5 mi s on US 377/167. Ext corridors. **Pets:** Accepted.
ASK X ᴼ 🕭 💻 ⫴⫴ ⫴

# SULPHUR SPRINGS

**▼▼◆▼ Best Western Trail Dust Inn SH**
(903) 885-7515. **$89-$119, 3 day notice.** 1521 Shannon Rd. Jct I-30 and Loop 301, exit 127. Ext/int corridors. **Pets:** Medium. $50 deposit/room. Designated rooms, service with restrictions, supervision.
ASK Sô X ᴸ 🕭 💻 ⫴

**(AAA) ▼▼◆▼ Comfort Suites SH**
(903) 438-0918. **$79-$94.** 1521 E Industrial Dr. I-30, exit 127, just n. Int corridors. **Pets:** Accepted.
SAVE Sô X ᴸM ᴸ 🕭 💻 ⫴

**▼▼◆▼ Days Inn Sulphur Springs SH**
(903) 885-0562. **$69-$79.** 1495 E Industrial Dr. I-30, exit 127. Ext/int corridors. **Pets:** Accepted.
ASK Sô X 🕭 💻 ⫴⫴ ⫴

# SWEETWATER

**(AAA) ▼▼◆ Comfort Inn SH**
(325) 235-5234. **$89-$125.** 216 SE Georgia Ave. I-20, exit 244. Ext corridors. **Pets:** Other species. $25 daily fee/pet. Service with restrictions, supervision.
SAVE Sô X ᴼ ᴸ 🕭 💻 ⫴

**(AAA) ▼▼◆ Holiday Inn SH**
(325) 236-6887. **$67-$169.** 500 NW Georgia St. I-20, exit 244, just w of jct SR 70 on north access road. Ext/int corridors. **Pets:** $25 one-time fee/room. Service with restrictions, crate.
SAVE Sô X 🕭 💻 ⫴⫴ ⫴

**(AAA) ▼▼◆ Ranch House Motel & Restaurant SH**
(325) 236-6341. **$49-$65.** 301 SW Georgia Ave. I-20, exit 244, just w of jct SR 70 on south access road. Ext/int corridors. **Pets:** Medium, other species. Designated rooms, service with restrictions, crate.
SAVE Sô X 🕭 💻 ⫴⫴ ⫴

# TEMPLE

**▼▼ Americas Best Value Inn M**
(254) 773-7221. **Call for rates.** 4001 S General Bruce Dr. I-35, exit 297 southbound; exit 299 northbound, on northbound access road. Ext corridors. **Pets:** Accepted.
X 🕭 💻

**▼▼ Howard Johnson Express Inn & Suites SH**
(254) 778-5521. **$64.** 1912 S 31st St. 0.4 mi ne of jct Loop 363, US 190 and SR 36. Ext corridors. **Pets:** Accepted.
ASK Sô X 🕭 💻

**(AAA) ▼▼▼▼ La Quinta Inn Temple** 🆂🅷
(254) 771-2980. **$68-$81.** 1604 W Barton Ave. SR 53, just e; jct I-35 and US 81, exit 301. Ext/int corridors. **Pets:** Medium. Service with restrictions.
🆂🅰🆅🅴 ⊠ 🛏 💻 ⚏

**▼ Motel 6–257** 🆂🅷
(254) 778-0272. **$35-$45.** 1100 N General Bruce Dr. I-35, exit 302 (Nugent Ave), just s on access road, follow signs. Ext corridors. **Pets:** Accepted.
🆂🅾 ⊠ ⚏

**(AAA) ▼▼▼ Super 8 Motel** 🆂🅷
(254) 778-0962. **$52-$70, 7 day notice.** 5505 S General Bruce Dr. I-35, exit 297 (Midway Dr). Ext corridors. **Pets:** Accepted.
🆂🅰🆅🅴 🆂🅾 ⊠ 🛏 💻 ⚏

## TERLINGUA

**(AAA) ▼▼▼ Big Bend Motor Inn** 🅼
(432) 371-2218. **$85-$90, 7 day notice.** 300 N Jim Wright Fwy. SR 118, 2 mi from entrance of Big Bend National Park. Ext corridors. **Pets:** Medium, dogs only. $5 daily fee/pet. Designated rooms, service with restrictions, supervision.
🆂🅰🆅🅴 ⊠ 🛏 💻

## TEXARKANA

**(AAA) ▼▼▼ Best Western Northgate Motor Lodge** 🆂🅷
(903) 793-6565. **$58-$69.** 400 W 53rd St. I-30, exit 223B, on northwest frontage road. Int corridors. **Pets:** Accepted.
🆂🅰🆅🅴 🆂🅾 ⊠ 🛏 💻 ⚏

**(AAA) ▼▼▼ Comfort Inn** 🆂🅷
(903) 792-6688. **$60-$120.** 5105 State Line Ave. I-30, exit 223A, just sw. Ext corridors. **Pets:** Accepted.
🆂🅰🆅🅴 🆂🅾 ⊠ 🛏 💻 ⚏

**(AAA) ▼▼▼▼ Four Points Hotel Sheraton Texarkana** 🆂🅷
(903) 792-3222. **$75-$140.** 5301 N State Line Ave. I-30, exit 223B. Int corridors. **Pets:** Accepted.
🆂🅰🆅🅴 🆂🅾 ⊠ 🅰🅼 🛏 💻 🍴 ⚏

**(AAA) ▼▼▼▼ Holiday Inn Express** 🆂🅷
(903) 792-3366. **$79.** 5401 N State Line Ave. I-30, exit 223B, 0.3 mi n on US 71. Int corridors. **Pets:** Accepted.
🆂🅰🆅🅴 🆂🅾 ⊠ 🛏 💻 ⚏

**(AAA) ▼▼▼▼ La Quinta Inn Texarkana** 🆂🅷
(903) 794-1900. **$68-$78.** 5201 State Line Ave. I-30, exit 223A, sw of jct US 59 and 71. Ext corridors. **Pets:** Medium. Service with restrictions.
🆂🅰🆅🅴 ⊠ 🛏 💻 ⚏

**▼ Motel 6–201** 🆂🅷
(903) 793-1413. **$41-$51.** 1924 Hampton Rd. I-30, exit 222 (Summerhill Rd). Ext corridors. **Pets:** Accepted.
🆂🅾 ⊠ 🖑 ⚏

## TEXAS CITY

**▼▼◆ La Quinta Inn Texas City** 🆂🅷
(409) 948-3101. **$71-$95.** 1121 Hwy 146 N. Jct SR 146 S and FM 1764, 5 mi se of I-45, exit 16 southbound; exit 15 northbound. Ext corridors. **Pets:** Medium. Service with restrictions.
🅰🆂🅺 ⊠ 🖉 🛏 💻 ⚏

## TULIA

**▼▼ Select Inn of Tulia** 🅼
(806) 995-3248. **$54-$64.** Rt 1, Box 60. I-27, exit 74. Ext corridors. **Pets:** Accepted.
🅰🆂🅺 ⊠ 🅰🅼 🛏 💻

## TYLER

**(AAA) ▼▼◆ Americas Best Value Inn & Suites** 🆂🅷
(903) 595-2681. **$58-$99.** 2828 W NW Loop 323. Jct US 69 N and Loop 323. Ext corridors. **Pets:** Accepted.
🆂🅰🆅🅴 🆂🅾 ⊠ 🛏 💻 ⚏

**▼▼◆ Candlewood Suites** 🆂🅷
(903) 509-4131. **$70-$85.** 315 Rieck Rd. 1.1 mi s of jct Loop 323 and US 69 (S Broadway) to Rieck Rd, just e. Int corridors. **Pets:** Accepted.
🅰🆂🅺 🆂🅾 ⊠ 🅰🅼 🖑 🛏 💻 ⚏

**▼▼◆ La Quinta Inn Tyler** 🆂🅷
(903) 561-2223. **$75-$90.** 1601 W SW Loop 323. 1 mi w of S US 69. Ext corridors. **Pets:** Medium. Service with restrictions.
🅰🆂🅺 ⊠ 🖉 🛏 💻 ⚏

**▼▼◆ Quality Hotel Conference Center** 🆂🅷
(903) 597-1301. **$69-$74.** 2843 W NW Loop 323. Just w of jct US 69. Int corridors. **Pets:** Other species. $25 deposit/room. Designated rooms, service with restrictions, supervision.
🅰🆂🅺 🆂🅾 ⊠ 🅰🅼 🖑 🛏 💻 🍴 ⚏

**(AAA) ▼▼◆ Ramada Tyler Conference Center** 🆂🅷
(903) 593-3600. **$125.** 3310 Troup Hwy. 0.3 mi n of jct E Loop 323 and SR 110. Ext corridors. **Pets:** Accepted.
🆂🅰🆅🅴 🆂🅾 ⊠ 🖑 🛏 💻 🍴 ⚏

**▼▼◆ Residence Inn by Marriott** 🆂🅷
(903) 595-5188. **$85-$135.** 3303 Troup Hwy. 0.3 mi n of jct E Loop 323 and SR 110. Ext corridors. **Pets:** Medium, other species. $75 one-time fee/pet. Service with restrictions, crate.
🅰🆂🅺 ⊠ 🖑 🛏 💻 ⚏ ⊠

## UVALDE

**▼▼ Holiday Inn** 🆂🅷
(830) 278-4511. **$76-$95.** 920 E Main St. 0.5 mi e on US 90. Ext corridors. **Pets:** Large, other species. Service with restrictions, supervision.
🅰🆂🅺 🆂🅾 ⊠ 🛏 💻 🍴 ⚏

## VAN HORN

**(AAA) ▼▼▼ Best Western American Inn** 🅼 🐾
(432) 283-2030. **$58-$95.** 1309 W Broadway. I-10, exit 138, 1 mi e. Ext corridors. **Pets:** Medium, other species. Designated rooms, service with restrictions, supervision.
🆂🅰🆅🅴 🆂🅾 ⊠ 🛏 💻 ⚏

**(AAA) ▼▼▼ Best Western Inn of Van Horn** 🅼 🐾
(432) 283-2410. **$49-$80.** 1705 W Broadway St. I-10, exit 138, 0.3 mi e, then 1 mi w on US 80. Ext corridors. **Pets:** Other species. $8 one-time fee/pet. Service with restrictions, supervision.
🆂🅰🆅🅴 🆂🅾 ⊠ 🛏 💻 ⚏

**(AAA) ▼▼ Budget Inn** 🅼
(432) 283-2019. **$30-$45.** 1303 W Broadway. I-10, exit 138, 0.7 mi e. Ext corridors. **Pets:** Accepted.
🆂🅰🆅🅴 🆂🅾 ⊠ 🛏

**(AAA) ▼▼▼ Days Inn** 🅼
(432) 283-1007. **$66-$99, 15 day notice.** 600 E Broadway St. I-10, exit 140B, just w. Ext corridors. **Pets:** Medium. $8 daily fee/pet. Service with restrictions, supervision.
🆂🅰🆅🅴 🆂🅾 ⊠ 🛏 💻 ⚏

**(AAA) ▼▼▼ Econo Lodge** 🆂🅷
(432) 283-2211. **$60-$95.** 1601 W Broadway St. I-10, exit 138, 0.5 mi e on Business Rt I-10. Ext corridors. **Pets:** Accepted.
🆂🅰🆅🅴 🆂🅾 ⊠ 🛏 💻 ⚏

**(AAA) ▼▼ Economy Inn** 🅼
(432) 283-2754. **$32-$55.** 1500 W Broadway St. I-10, exit 138, 0.5 mi e on US 80. Ext corridors. **Pets:** $3 one-time fee/pet. No service.
🆂🅰🆅🅴 🆂🅾 ⊠ 🛏

**▲▲▲ ▼▼▼▼ Holiday Inn Express SH**
(432) 283-7444. **$59-$109.** 1905 SW Frontage Rd. I-10, exit 138 (Golf Course Dr). Ext corridors. **Pets:** Small, other species. $10 one-time fee/pet. Service with restrictions, supervision.

**▼ Motel 6–4024 M**
(432) 283-2992. **$46.** 1805 W Broadway St. I-10, exit 138. Ext corridors. **Pets:** Accepted.

**▲▲▲ ▼▼▼ Ramada Limited SH ✿**
(432) 283-2780. **$76-$87.** 200 Golf Course Dr. I-10, exit 138 (Golf Course Dr). Ext/int corridors. **Pets:** Large, other species. $10 daily fee/pet. Designated rooms, supervision.

**▲▲▲ ▼▼▼ Van Horn Super 8 M**
(432) 283-2282. **$66-$99, 15 day notice.** 1807 E Service Rd. I-10, exit 138 (Golf Course Dr). Ext corridors. **Pets:** Medium. $8 daily fee/pet. Service with restrictions, supervision.

# VEGA

**▲▲▲ ▼▼▼ Best Western Country Inn M**
(806) 267-2131. **$59.** 1800 W Vega Blvd. 0.5 mi w on US 40 business loop. Ext corridors. **Pets:** Accepted.

# VERNON

**▼▼▼ Best Western Village Inn M**
(940) 552-5417. **$59-$74.** 1615 Expwy. US 287, exit Main St, just w. Ext/int corridors. **Pets:** Small, other species. Service with restrictions.

# VICTORIA

**▼▼▼ Holiday Inn Holidome SH**
(361) 575-0251. **$89.** 2705 E Houston Hwy (Business Rt 59). On Business Rt US 59, 2.5 mi ne. Ext/int corridors. **Pets:** $25 one-time fee/pet. Service with restrictions, supervision.

**▼▼ La Quinta Inn Victoria SH**
(361) 572-3585. **$69-$83.** 7603 N Navarro St (US 77 N). 4 mi n; at Loop 463. Ext corridors. **Pets:** Medium. Service with restrictions.

**▼▼ Motel 6 Victoria #225 M**
(361) 573-1273. **$41-$53.** 3716 Houston Hwy. On Business Rt US 59. Ext corridors. **Pets:** Accepted.

**▼▼ Quality Inn-Victoria SH**
(361) 578-2030. **$62-$81.** 3112 E Houston Hwy (Business Rt 59). On Business Rt US 59, 2 mi ne. Ext corridors. **Pets:** Accepted.

# WACO

**▲▲▲ ▼▼▼ Best Western Old Main Lodge SH**
(254) 753-0316. **$72-$115.** I-35 & 4th St. I-35 and US 81, exit 335A (4th-5th sts). Ext corridors. **Pets:** Small. Service with restrictions, supervision.

**▲▲▲ ▼▼▼ Days Inn SH ✿**
(254) 799-8585. **$59-$125.** 1504 I-35. I-35, exit 338B (Behrens Cir), just n. Ext corridors. **Pets:** Medium, dogs only. $10 daily fee/pet. Service with restrictions, supervision.

**▼▼▼▼ Hawthorn Suites SH**
(254) 799-9989. **$59-$179.** 1508 I-35 N. I-35, exit 338B southbound; exit 339 northbound, on southbound access road. Int corridors. **Pets:** Accepted.

**▼▼▼ Holiday Inn-Waco I-35 SH**
(254) 753-0261. **$69-$119, 3 day notice.** 1001 Martin Luther King Blvd. I-35, exit 335C (Lake Brazos Dr), just n. Int corridors. **Pets:** Other species. $100 deposit/room, $25 one-time fee/room. Service with restrictions.

**▼▼▼▼ La Quinta Inn Waco (University) SH**
(254) 752-9741. **$79-$100.** 1110 S 9th St. I-35, exit 334 (17th St) southbound; exit 334A (18th St) northbound. Ext corridors. **Pets:** Medium. Service with restrictions.

**▼▼▼▼ Residence Inn by Marriott SH**
(254) 714-1386. **$99-$199.** 501 S University Parks Dr. I-35, exit 335B, 0.3 mi w. Int corridors. **Pets:** Accepted.

**▼ Super 8 Motel-Waco SH**
(254) 754-1023. **$60-$100.** 1320 S Jack Kultgen Frwy. I-35, exit 334, just e. Int corridors. **Pets:** Accepted.

# WAXAHACHIE

**▲▲▲ ▼▼▼ Best Western Gingerbread Inn SH**
(972) 937-4202. **$62-$99.** 200 N I-35E. I-35E and US 287 business route, 1.8 mi s of jct US 287, exit 401B. Ext corridors. **Pets:** Accepted.

**▼▼▼ Super 8 Motel SH**
(972) 938-9088. **$65-$75.** 400 I-35E. I-35E, exit 401B. Int corridors. **Pets:** Accepted.

# WEATHERFORD

**▲▲▲ ▼▼▼ Best Western Santa Fe Inn SH**
(817) 594-7401. **$62-$73.** 1927 Santa Fe Dr. I-20, exit 409 (Clear Lake Rd/FM 2552), 0.3 mi nw. Ext corridors. **Pets:** Medium. $10 daily fee/pet. Service with restrictions, supervision.

**▼▼▼ Hampton Inn SH**
(817) 599-4800. **$90-$200.** 2524 S Main St. I-20, exit 408. Int corridors. **Pets:** Small. $10 daily fee/pet. Service with restrictions, supervision.

**▼▼▼▼ Holiday Inn Express Hotel & Suites SH**
(817) 599-3700. **$90-$200.** 2500 S Main St. I-20, exit 408. Ext/int corridors. **Pets:** Small. $10 daily fee/pet. No service, supervision.

**▼▼▼▼ La Quinta Inn & Suites SH**
(817) 594-4481. **$75, 3 day notice.** 1915 Wall St. I-20, exit 408, just se. Int corridors. **Pets:** Accepted.

**▼▼▼▼ Weatherford Comfort Suites SH**
(817) 599-3300. **$75-$150.** 210 Alford Dr. I-20, exit 408, just s on SR 171, then just w. Int corridors. **Pets:** Accepted.

# WEIMAR

**▲▲▲ ▼▼▼ Czech Inn M**
(979) 725-9788. **$60-$70.** 102 Townsend Ln. I-10, exit 682, just w on north access road. Int corridors. **Pets:** Small. $10 daily fee/room. Designated rooms, supervision.

# WELLINGTON

**◆ Cherokee Inn & Restaurant** 🅼
(806) 447-2508. **$34-$56.** 1105 Houston St. US 83, just n of jct FM 338. Ext corridors. **Pets:** Accepted.

(ASK) (S💰) (✕) (🍴)

# WESLACO

**(AAA) ◆◆◆◆ Best Western Palm Aire Hotel & Suites** 🆂🅷
(956) 969-2411. **$56-$111.** 415 S International Blvd. US 83, exit International Blvd. Ext corridors. **Pets:** Small. $50 deposit/pet. Service with restrictions, crate.

(SAVE) (S💰) (✕) (🐾) (🛎) (💻) (🍴) (🏊) (✕)

**◆◆◆ Super 8 Motel** 🆂🅷
(956) 969-9920. **$49-$64.** 1702 E Expwy 83. US 83, exit Airport Dr. Ext corridors. **Pets:** Other species. $10 daily fee/pet. Designated rooms, service with restrictions, supervision.

(ASK) (S💰) (✕) (🛎) (🏊)

# WEST COLUMBIA

**(AAA) ◆◆ Best Western Brazos Inn** 🆂🅷
(979) 345-2399. **$73.** 714 Columbia Dr (Hwy 36). Just w of jct Hwy 35. Ext corridors. **Pets:** Small. $10 daily fee/pet. Designated rooms, service with restrictions, supervision.

(SAVE) (S💰) (✕) (🛎) (💻) (🏊)

# WICHITA FALLS

**(AAA) ◆◆ Best Western Wichita Falls Inn** 🆂🅷
(940) 766-6881. **$70-$90, 7 day notice.** 1032 Central Frwy. I-44, exit 2, just w. Ext corridors. **Pets:** Small. $10 daily fee/pet. Service with restrictions, supervision.

(SAVE) (✕) (🛎) (💻) (🏊)

**◆◆◆ Comfort Inn & Suites** 🆂🅷
(940) 767-5653. **$65-$149.** 1740 Maurine St. US 287, exit Maurine St, just e. Ext/int corridors. **Pets:** $10 one-time fee/pet. Service with restrictions.

(ASK) (S💰) (✕) (♿M) (♿) (🛎) (💻) (🏊)

**◆◆◆ Hawthorn Suites Limited** 🆂🅷
(940) 692-7900. **$79-$149.** 1917 Elmwood Ave N. US 281 S, exit Southwest Pkwy (CR 319), 2.3 mi w to Kemp, 2 blks n to Elmwood Ave, then just e. Int corridors. **Pets:** Large. $100 one-time fee/room. Designated rooms, service with restrictions, crate.

(ASK) (S💰) (✕) (♿M) (🐾) (♿) (🛎) (💻) (🏊)

**◆◆◆◆ Holiday Inn Wichita Falls at The Falls** 🅻🅷
(940) 761-6000. **$99-$149.** 100 Central. I-287, exit 1C, on west side access road. Int corridors. **Pets:** Accepted.

(ASK) (S💰) (✕) (🛎) (💻) (🍴) (🏊)

**(AAA) ◆◆◆◆ La Quinta Inn Wichita Falls** 🆂🅷
(940) 322-6971. **$72-$92.** 1128 Central Frwy N. I-44, exit 2, just w. Ext corridors. **Pets:** Medium. Service with restrictions.

(SAVE) (✕) (🐾) (🛎) (💻) (🏊)

**◆ Motel 6 #130** 🅼
(940) 322-8817. **$43-$55.** 1812 Maurine St. I-44, exit 2, just e. Ext corridors. **Pets:** Accepted.

(S💰) (✕) (🐾) (♿) (🏊)

**◆◆◆ Quality Inn and Suites** 🅼
(940) 322-2477. **$64-$149.** 1750 Maurine St. I-44, exit 2, just e. Int corridors. **Pets:** $10 one-time fee/room. Service with restrictions.

(ASK) (S💰) (✕) (♿M) (♿) (🛎) (💻) (🏊)

**(AAA) ◆◆ Ramada Limited** 🅼
(940) 855-0085. **$48-$55.** 3209 Northwest Frwy. US 287, exit Beverly (CR 11), just w. Ext corridors. **Pets:** Accepted.

(SAVE) (S💰) (✕) (♿) (🛎) (💻) (🏊)

**(AAA) ◆◆ Towne Crest Inn** 🅼
(940) 322-1182. **$41.** 1601 8th St. US 287, exit Broad St/Business, w on 9th St, 1 blk n on Brook to 8th St, then just e. Ext corridors. **Pets:** Accepted.

(SAVE) (✕) (🛎) (💻)

# ZAPATA

**(AAA) ◆◆◆ Best Western Inn by the Lake** 🆂🅷
(956) 765-8403. **$80-$95.** Hwy 83 S. On US 83, 0.5 mi se. Ext corridors. **Pets:** Small. $12 one-time fee/pet. Service with restrictions, supervision.

(SAVE) (S💰) (✕) (🛎) (💻) (🏊)

# UTAH

## CITY INDEX

## BEAVER

### Best Western Butch Cassidy Inn M
(435) 438-2438. **$62-$100.** 161 S Main St. I-15, exit 109 or 112, just e. Ext corridors. **Pets:** Other species. $5 daily fee/pet. Service with restrictions, supervision.

### Best Western Paradise Inn M
(435) 438-2455. **$63-$79.** 1451 N 300 W. I-15, exit 112, just e; north end of town. Ext corridors. **Pets:** Small, other species. Designated rooms, service with restrictions, supervision.

### Country Inn M 🐾
(435) 438-2484. **$43-$60.** 1450 N 300 W. I-15, exit 112, 2 blks e. Ext corridors. **Pets:** $3 daily fee/pet. Service with restrictions, supervision.

### DeLano Motel M
(435) 438-2418. **$39-$45, 7 day notice.** 480 N Main St. I-15, exit 112, just e; north end of town. Ext corridors. **Pets:** Medium, dogs only. $5 daily fee/room. Service with restrictions, supervision.

### Motel 6 Beaver #4206 M
(435) 438-1666. **$43-$60.** 1345 N 400 W. I-15, exit 112, just se. Int corridors. **Pets:** Accepted.

### Quality Inn M
(435) 438-5426. **$55-$75.** 781 W 1800 S. I-15, exit 109, just w. Int corridors. **Pets:** Small, other species. Designated rooms, service with restrictions, supervision.

## BICKNELL

### Aquarius Motel and Restaurant M
(435) 425-3835. **$46-$53.** 240 W Main St. SR 24, 9 mi w of Capitol Reef National Park; downtown. Ext/int corridors. **Pets:** Other species. $5 daily fee/room. Service with restrictions, crate.

## BLANDING

### Best Western Gateway Inn M
(435) 678-2278. **$61-$89.** 88 E Center St. East side on US 191. Ext corridors. **Pets:** Accepted.

### Four Corners Inn M 🐾
(435) 678-3257. **$49-$67.** 131 E Center St. On US 191. Ext corridors. **Pets:** Other species. Service with restrictions, crate.

## BLUFF

### Kokopelli Inn M
(435) 672-2322. **$45-$55.** 160 E Main St. On US 191. Int corridors. **Pets:** Small. $13 daily fee/pet. Service with restrictions, supervision.

### Recapture Lodge M
(435) 672-2281. **$35-$60.** 220 E Main St. On US 191. Ext corridors. **Pets:** Other species. Service with restrictions, supervision.

## BOULDER

### Boulder Mountain Lodge M 🐾
(435) 335-7460. **$69-$168, 14 day notice.** 20 N Hwy 12. Jct SR 12 and Burr Tr. Ext/int corridors. **Pets:** $10 daily fee/pet. Designated rooms, service with restrictions, supervision.

## BRIGHAM CITY

### Crystal Inn M
(435) 723-0440. **$63-$99.** 480 Westland Dr. I-15 and 84, exit 362 (Logan and Brigham City), 1 mi e. Int corridors. **Pets:** Accepted.

### Howard Johnson Inn M
(435) 723-8511. **$51-$70.** 1167 S Main St. I-15 and 84, exit 362 (Logan and Brigham City), 2 mi e on US 89 and 91. Ext corridors. **Pets:** Medium. Service with restrictions, supervision.

## BRYCE

### Best Western Ruby's Inn SH
(435) 834-5341. **$55-$130.** UT Hwy 63. On SR 63, 1 mi s of SR 12, 1 mi n of Bryce Canyon National Park entrance. Ext/int corridors. **Pets:** $100 deposit/room. Service with restrictions, supervision.

### Bryce Canyon Resort M
(435) 834-5351. **$49-$149.** 13500 E Hwy 12. Jct of SR 12 and 63. Ext corridors. **Pets:** Accepted.

### Bryce View Lodge M
(435) 834-5180. **$60-$93.** SR 63. On SR 63, 1 mi s of SR 12; 1 mi n of Bryce Canyon National Park entrance. Ext corridors. **Pets:** $100 deposit/pet. Service with restrictions, supervision.

# CEDAR CITY

**▲▲▲ ▼▼▼▼ Best Value Inn M**
(435) 586-6557. **$34-$99.** 323 S Main St. Cross streets 300 S and Main sts; downtown. Ext corridors. **Pets:** Small. $7 daily fee/pet. Designated rooms, service with restrictions, supervision.
[SAVE] [S◐] [✕] [🛏] [💻] [🌊]

**▲▲▲ ▼▼▼ Cedar Rest Motel M**
(435) 586-9471. **$35-$75.** 479 S Main St. I-15, exit 59, just e. Ext corridors. **Pets:** Accepted.
[SAVE] [✕] [🛏]

**▼▼▼▼ Comfort Inn M**
(435) 586-2082. **$64-$125.** 250 N 1100 W. I-15, exit 59, just e. Ext corridors. **Pets:** Other species. Designated rooms, service with restrictions, crate.
[ASK] [S◐] [✕] [🗂] [🛏] [💻] [🌊]

**▲▲▲ ▼▼▼▼ Crystal Inn Cedar City SH**
(435) 586-8888. **$59-$99.** 1575 W 200 N. I-15, exit 59, just w. Ext/int corridors. **Pets:** Other species. $25 one-time fee/room. Service with restrictions, supervision.
[SAVE] [S◐] [✕] [🗂] [🛏] [💻] [🍽] [🌊] [✕]

**▲▲▲ ▼▼▼ Days Inn M**
(435) 867-8877. **$49-$94.** 1204 S Main St. I-15, exit 57, 0.4 mi e. Ext corridors. **Pets:** Small. $10 deposit/room, $10 daily fee/pet. Designated rooms, service with restrictions, supervision.
[SAVE] [S◐] [✕] [📶] [🛏] [🌊]

**▼▼▼ Holiday Inn Express Hotel & Suites M 🐾**
(435) 865-7799. **$89-$99.** 1555 S Old Hwy 91. I-15, exit 57, just e, then s. Int corridors. **Pets:** Large, other species. $10 daily fee/room. Designated rooms, service with restrictions, supervision.
[ASK] [S◐] [✕] [♿] [📶] [🛏] [💻] [🌊]

**▼▼▼ Ramada Limited M**
(435) 586-9916. **$59-$129.** 281 S Main St. I-15, exit 57, just e. Ext corridors. **Pets:** Small, dogs only. $7 daily fee/pet. Designated rooms, service with restrictions, supervision.
[ASK] [S◐] [✕] [🛏] [💻] [🌊]

**▲▲▲ ▼▼▼ Super 7 Motel M**
(435) 586-6566. **$35-$95.** 190 S Main St. I-15, exit 57, just e. Ext corridors. **Pets:** Accepted.
[SAVE] [S◐] [✕] [🛏]

**▼▼▼ Super 8 Motel M**
(435) 586-8880. **$53-$63.** 145 N 1550 W. I-15, exit 59, just w. Int corridors. **Pets:** Accepted.
[ASK] [S◐] [✕] [♿] [📶] [🛏]

**▲▲▲ ▼▼▼ Valu-Inn M**
(435) 586-9114. **$30-$90.** 344 S Main St. I-15, exit 57, just e. Ext corridors. **Pets:** Accepted.
[SAVE] [S◐] [✕] [🛏]

**▼▼▼ Willow Glen Inn BB**
(435) 586-3275. **$59-$195, 5 day notice.** 3308 N Bulldog Rd. I-15, exit 62, 1.5 mi sw via 3000 N. Ext corridors. **Pets:** Accepted.
[ASK] [✕] [🛏] [💻] [🍽] [🌊]

# CLEARFIELD

**▼▼▼ Travelers Inn of Clearfield M**
(801) 825-8000. **$54-$84.** 572 N Main St. I-15, exit 335, just w. Int corridors. **Pets:** Accepted.
[ASK] [S◐] [✕] [🗂] [📶] [🛏]

# COALVILLE

**▼▼▼▼ Best Western Holiday Hills M**
(435) 336-4444. **$79-$109.** 210 S 200 W. I-80, exit 162, just w. Int corridors. **Pets:** Other species. $15 daily fee/room. Designated rooms, service with restrictions, supervision.
[ASK] [S◐] [✕] [📶] [🛏] [💻] [🌊] [✕]

# DELTA

**▲▲▲ ▼▼▼▼ Best Western Motor Inn M**
(435) 864-3882. **$69-$80.** 527 E Topaz Blvd. US 6, at jct US 50. Ext corridors. **Pets:** Other species. $25 one-time fee/room. Designated rooms, supervision.
[SAVE] [S◐] [✕] [🗂] [🛏] [💻] [🌊]

# DUCK CREEK VILLAGE

**▼▼▼ Duck Creek Village Inn M**
(435) 682-2565. **$64-$74, 7 day notice.** Hwy 14. 30 mi e of Cedar City on SR 14; 10 mi w of US 89. Ext corridors. **Pets:** Accepted.
[ASK] [S◐] [✕] [🛏] [💻] [🍽] [♿] [🎿]

**▲▲▲ ▼▼▼ Pinewoods Resort M**
(435) 682-2512. **$125, 30 day notice.** 121 Duck Creek Ridge Rd. Just s of SR 14 via Cedar Mountain Rd, 31 mi e of Cedar City; in Cedar Mountain Village; 10 mi w of jct US 89. Ext/int corridors. **Pets:** Accepted.
[SAVE] [✕] [🛏] [💻] [🍽] [✕] [🎿]

# ESCALANTE

**▼▼▼ Rainbow Country Bed & Breakfast BB**
(435) 826-4567. **$55-$80, 3 day notice.** 586 E 300 S. Just off SR 12; south end of town. Int corridors. **Pets:** Service with restrictions, supervision.
[ASK] [S◐] [✕] [📺] [🎿]

# FILLMORE

**▲▲▲ ▼▼▼▼ Best Western Paradise Resort M**
(435) 743-6895. **$55-$79.** 905 N Main St. I-15, exit 167, just e. Ext corridors. **Pets:** Accepted.
[SAVE] [S◐] [✕] [🛏] [💻] [🍽] [🌊]

**▼▼▼▼ Inn at Apple Creek M**
(435) 743-4334. **$63-$100.** 940 S Hwy 99. I-15, exit 163, just e. Int corridors. **Pets:** Small. $6 daily fee/pet. Designated rooms, service with restrictions, supervision.
[ASK] [S◐] [✕] [♿] [🛏] [💻] [🌊]

# GARDEN CITY

**▼▼▼▼ Canyon Cove Inn M**
(435) 946-3565. **$69-$150, 99 day notice.** 315 W Logan (Hwy 89). On US 89, 3 blks w of downtown. Int corridors. **Pets:** $10 daily fee/room. Supervision.
[ASK] [S◐] [✕] [♿] [🛏] [🌊]

# GLENDALE

**▼▼▼ Historic Smith Hotel Bed & Breakfast BB**
(435) 648-2156. **$38-$80.** 295 N Main St. US 89; north end of town. Int corridors. **Pets:** Other species. $5 one-time fee/room. Service with restrictions.
[ASK] [S◐] [✕] [🎿] [🎿]

# GREEN RIVER

**▼▼▼▼ Holiday Inn Express M 🐾**
(435) 564-4439. **$59-$99.** 965 E Main. I-70, exit 160, 2.6 mi ne. Int corridors. **Pets:** $10 daily fee/room. Designated rooms, service with restrictions, supervision.
[ASK] [S◐] [✕] [♿] [🛏] [💻] [🌊]

◆ Motel 6 #289 **M**
(435) 564-3436. **$39-$57.** 946 E Main St. I-70, exit 160, 2.7 mi ne. Ext corridors. **Pets:** Accepted.

◆◆◆ Ramada Limited **M** ❀
(435) 564-8441. **$45-$74.** 1117 E Main St. I-70, exit 164, 1 mi nw. Ext/int corridors. **Pets:** Other species. $10 daily fee/pet. Service with restrictions, supervision.

◆◆◆ Super 8 Motel **M**
(435) 564-8888. **$49-$86.** 1248 E Main St. I-70, exit 160, 3.1 mi ne. Int corridors. **Pets:** Accepted.

# HATCH

◆◆ Riverside Resort & RV Park **M** ❀
(435) 735-4223. **$39-$85, 3 day notice.** 594 US Hwy 89. On US 89, 1 mi n. Ext corridors. **Pets:** Other species. $50 deposit/room, $5 daily fee/room. Designated rooms, service with restrictions, supervision.

# HEBER CITY

◆◆ National 9 High Country Inn **M**
(435) 654-0201. **$50-$75.** 1000 S Main St. On US 40 E; center. Ext corridors. **Pets:** Small. $10 daily fee/room. Designated rooms, service with restrictions, supervision.

◆◆ Swiss Alps Inn **M**
(435) 654-0722. **$70-$85.** 167 S Main St. On US 40; center. Ext corridors. **Pets:** Other species. Designated rooms, service with restrictions, supervision.

# HUNTSVILLE

◆◆ Jackson Fork Inn **BB**
(801) 745-0051. **$70-$140, 3 day notice.** 7345 E 900 S. On SR 39. Int corridors. **Pets:** Medium. $20 one-time fee/room. Supervision.

# HURRICANE

◆◆◆ Days Inn-Hurricane/Zion Park **M**
(435) 635-0500. **$35-$110.** 40 N 2600 W. West end of town. Int corridors. **Pets:** Accepted.

◆◆ Motel 6-4050 **M**
(435) 635-4010. **$42-$109.** 650 W State. Just w on SR 9. Ext corridors. **Pets:** Accepted.

◆◆ Super 8 **M**
(435) 635-0808. **$39-$110.** 65 S 700 W. Just s of SR 9. Ext corridors. **Pets:** Very small, dogs only. $10 daily fee/pet. Designated rooms, service with restrictions, crate.

◆◆ Travelodge **M**
(435) 635-4647. **$40-$109.** 280 W State. Just w on SR 9. Ext corridors. **Pets:** Very small, dogs only. $10 daily fee/pet. Designated rooms, service with restrictions, supervision.

# KANAB

◆◆ Aikens Lodge **M**
(435) 644-2625. **$33-$67.** 79 W Center St. On US 89. Ext corridors. **Pets:** Small, dogs only. $10 daily fee/pet. Designated rooms, supervision.

◆◆ Best Western Red Hills **M**
(435) 644-2675. **$55-$125.** 125 W Center St. Center. Ext/int corridors. **Pets:** Other species. $10 one-time fee/room.

◆◆ Bob-Bon Inn **M**
(435) 644-5094. **$36-$69, 3 day notice.** 236 Hwy 89 N. On US 89. Ext corridors. **Pets:** $10 one-time fee/pet. Designated rooms, service with restrictions, supervision.

◆◆ Clarion Hotel-Victorian Charm Inn **M** ❀
(435) 644-8660. **$79-$129.** 190 N Hwy 89. North end of town. Int corridors. **Pets:** Small, dogs only. $10 one-time fee/pet. Designated rooms, service with restrictions, supervision.

◆ Four Seasons Motel & Restaurant **M**
(435) 644-2635. **$49-$74.** 36 N 300 W.. Ext corridors. **Pets:** Other species. $6 daily fee/room. Designated rooms, service with restrictions, supervision.

◆ Holiday Inn Express **M**
(435) 644-8888. **$69-$119.** 815 E Hwy 89. On US 89, just e. Int corridors. **Pets:** Large. $10 daily fee/pet. Designated rooms, service with restrictions, supervision.

◆◆ Kanab Mission Inn **M**
(435) 644-5373. **$34-$99.** 386 E 300 S. E on US 89. Int corridors. **Pets:** Large, other species. $15 deposit/room. Service with restrictions, supervision.

◆◆ Parry Lodge **M**
(435) 644-2601. **$30-$80.** 89 E Center St. On US 89; corner of 100 E; center. Ext/int corridors. **Pets:** Medium. $5 daily fee/pet. Designated rooms, service with restrictions, supervision.

◆◆ Quail Park Lodge **M**
(435) 644-8700. **$43-$50.** 125 Hwy 89 N. On US 89. Ext corridors. **Pets:** Small, dogs only. $10 one-time fee/pet. Designated rooms, service with restrictions, supervision.

◆◆ Shilo Inn **SH** ❀
(435) 644-2562. **$45-$106.** 296 W 100 N. North of downtown on US 89. Int corridors. **Pets:** $10 daily fee/pet. Service with restrictions, supervision.

◆ Sun N Sand Motel **M**
(435) 644-5050. **$32-$42.** 347 S 100 E. Jct US 89 and 89A. Ext corridors. **Pets:** Medium, dogs only. $5 one-time fee/room. Designated rooms, service with restrictions, supervision.

◆◆ Super 8 **M**
(435) 644-5500. **$41-$78.** 70 S 200 W. Just s off US 89. Ext corridors. **Pets:** Other species. $6 daily fee/pet. Designated rooms, service with restrictions, supervision.

# LAKE POWELL

◆◆ Defiance House Lodge-Bullfrog Marina **M**
(435) 684-3000. **$62-$123, 3 day notice.** Bullfrog Marina. 70 mi s of Hanksville; 44 mi s off SR 95 on SR 276. Int corridors. **Pets:** Accepted.

# LAYTON

**Comfort Inn** M
(801) 544-5577. **$50-$85.** 877 N 400 W. I-15, exit 331, then e. Int corridors. **Pets:** Small, other species. $75 deposit/room. Service with restrictions, supervision.

**Hampton Inn** M
(801) 775-8800. **$99-$119.** 1700 Woodland Park Dr. I-15, exit 332, 0.3 mi se. Int corridors. **Pets:** Accepted.

**Holiday Inn Express** M
(801) 773-3773. **$89-$149.** 1695 Woodland Park Dr. I-15, exit 332, 0.3 mi se. Int corridors. **Pets:** Accepted.

**TownePlace Suites** M
(801) 779-2422. **$60-$119.** 1743 Woodland Park Dr. I-15, exit 331, 0.3 mi se. Int corridors. **Pets:** Accepted.

# LEHI

**Best Western Timpanogos Inn** M ❖
(801) 768-1400. **$59-$130.** 195 S 850 E. I-15, exit 279, southwest side. Int corridors. **Pets:** Other species. $10 one-time fee/room. Service with restrictions, supervision.

**Motel 6–1405** M
(801) 768-2668. **$41-$55.** 210 S 1200 E. I-15, exit 279, just e. Int corridors. **Pets:** Accepted.

**Super 8** M
(801) 766-8800. **$49-$89.** 125 S 850 E. I-15, exit 279, southwest side. Int corridors. **Pets:** Medium, other species. $50 deposit/room, $5 one-time fee/room. Designated rooms, service with restrictions, supervision.

# LOGAN

**Best Western Baugh Motel** M
(435) 752-5220. **$69-$139.** 153 S Main St. On US 89 and 91. Ext corridors. **Pets:** Accepted.

**Best Western Weston Inn** M
(435) 752-5700. **$60-$90.** 250 N Main St. On US 89 and 91; downtown. Ext corridors. **Pets:** Small, dogs only. $10 daily fee/pet. Designated rooms, service with restrictions, supervision.

**Logan Super 8** M
(435) 753-8883. **$50-$85.** 865 S Hwy 89 and 91. South end of town. Int corridors. **Pets:** $5 daily fee/pet. Service with restrictions, supervision.

**Ramada Limited** M
(435) 787-2060. **$63-$68.** 2002 S Hwy 89 and 91. South end of town. Int corridors. **Pets:** Other species. $50 deposit/pet. Service with restrictions, supervision.

# MANTI

**Manti Country Village** M
(435) 835-9300. **$59-$85.** 145 N Main St. On US 89. Ext corridors. **Pets:** Medium. $50 deposit/room. Designated rooms, service with restrictions, supervision.

# MARYSVALE

**Big Rock Candy Mountain Resort** M
(435) 326-2000. **$59-$99.** 4479 N Hwy 89. On US 89, 6 mi n. Ext corridors. **Pets:** Accepted.

# MEXICAN HAT

**San Juan Inn & Trading Post** M ❖
(435) 683-2220. **$74-$78.** Hwy 163 & San Juan River. On US 163. Ext corridors. **Pets:** Dogs only. $15 one-time fee/pet. Designated rooms, service with restrictions, supervision.

# MOAB

**Apache Motel** M
(435) 259-5727. **$35-$99.** 166 S 400 E. Just e off US 191. Ext corridors. **Pets:** Large, other species. Service with restrictions, supervision.

**Big Horn Lodge** SH
(435) 259-6171. **$34-$89.** 550 S Main St. South end of town. Ext corridors. **Pets:** Other species. $5 daily fee/pet. Designated rooms, service with restrictions, supervision.

**Bowen Motel** M
(435) 259-7132. **$35-$75.** 169 N Main St. Downtown. Ext corridors. **Pets:** Accepted.

**Cedar Breaks Condos** CO
(435) 259-5125. **$70-$145, 7 day notice.** 400 East & Center St. From jct Main and Center, just e, then just s. Ext corridors. **Pets:** $10 one-time fee/pet. Designated rooms, service with restrictions, supervision.

**Comfort Suites** M
(435) 259-5252. **$59-$149.** 800 S Main St.. Int corridors. **Pets:** Accepted.

**Days Inn** M ❖
(435) 259-4468. **$34-$88.** 426 N Main St.. Int corridors. **Pets:** $5 daily fee/pet. Designated rooms, service with restrictions, crate.

**The Gonzo Inn** M ❖
(435) 259-2515. **$81-$135.** 100 W 200 S. Downtown. Ext/int corridors. **Pets:** Other species. $25 daily fee/room. Service with restrictions.

**Kokopelli Lodge** M
(435) 259-7615. **$45-$69.** 72 S 100 E. From Main, just e on 100 S, then just n; downtown. Ext corridors. **Pets:** Medium, dogs only. $5 daily fee/pet. Service with restrictions, crate.

**La Quinta Inns Moab** M ❖
(435) 259-8700. **$55-$103.** 815 S Main St. South end of town. Int corridors. **Pets:** Large, other species. Service with restrictions, crate.

**Moab Valley Inn** M
(435) 259-4419. **$65-$120.** 711 S Main St. 1 mi s on US 191. Int corridors. **Pets:** Small. $10 daily fee/room. Designated rooms, service with restrictions, supervision.

**Motel 6 Moab #4119** M
(435) 259-6686. **$31-$110.** 1089 N Main St. North end of town; west side of street. Int corridors. **Pets:** Small. $20 one-time fee/pet. Designated rooms, service with restrictions, supervision.

**(AAA) ▼▼▼▼▼ Ramada of Downtown Moab M**
(435) 259-7141. **$45-$151.** 182 S Main St. Downtown. Ext/int corridors. **Pets:** Small. $20 one-time fee/pet. Designated rooms, service with restrictions, supervision.
[SAVE] [S] [X] [🖉] [🖬] [💻] [ᴎ] [≈]

**(AAA) ▼▼▼▼▼ Red Cliffs Adventure Lodge Cl**
(435) 259-2002. **$89-$270, 30 day notice.** Milepost 14 Hwy 128. 2 mi n to jct US 191 and SR 128, 14.5 mi e. Ext corridors. **Pets:** Large, dogs only. $20 daily fee/pet. Designated rooms, service with restrictions, supervision.
[SAVE] [S] [X] [🖬] [💻] [ᴎ] [≈] [⊠]

**(AAA) ▼▼▼ Red Stone Inn M ❀**
(435) 259-3500. **$55-$90.** 535 S Main St. Downtown. Ext/int corridors. **Pets:** Other species. $5 daily fee/pet. Designated rooms, service with restrictions, supervision.
[SAVE] [S] [X] [🖬] [💻]

**▼▼▼▼ River Canyon Lodge, An Extended Stay Inn & Suites M ❀**
(435) 259-8838. **$32-$135.** 71 W 200 N. Cross streets 100 W and 200 N; downtown. Int corridors. **Pets:** Small. $20 one-time fee/pet. Designated rooms, service with restrictions, supervision.
[SAVE] [S] [X] [🖉] [🖬] [💻] [≈]

**▼▼▼▼ Riverside Inn M**
(435) 259-8848. **$32-$90.** 988 N Main St. 1 mi n on US 191. Int corridors. **Pets:** Other species. $10 daily fee/room. Designated rooms, service with restrictions, crate.
[ASK] [S] [X] [🖉] [≈]

**(AAA) ▼▼ Silver Sage Inn M**
(435) 259-4420. **$34-$74.** 840 S Main St. South end of town on US 191. Int corridors. **Pets:** Large. $10 one-time fee/room. Service with restrictions.
[SAVE] [X] [🖬] [💻]

**▼▼ ▼▼ Sleep Inn M**
(435) 259-4655. **$39-$175, 14 day notice.** 1051 S Main St. South end of town. Int corridors. **Pets:** Accepted.
[ASK] [S] [X] [🖑] [🖉] [🖬] [💻] [≈]

**(AAA) ▼▼▼▼▼ Super 8 Motel, Moab M**
(435) 259-8868. **$33-$120.** 889 N Main St. US 191, 1 mi n. Int corridors. **Pets:** Small. $20 one-time fee/pet. Designated rooms, service with restrictions, supervision.
[SAVE] [S] [X] [🖉] [🖬] [≈]

**(AAA) ▼▼ ▼ The Virginian Motel M**
(435) 259-5951. **$39-$89.** 70 E 200 S. Just e of US 191. Ext corridors. **Pets:** Other species. $10 daily fee/pet. Service with restrictions, supervision.
[SAVE] [S] [X] [🖬] [🖬] [💻]

# MONTICELLO

**(AAA) ▼▼▼▼▼ Best Western Wayside Inn M**
(435) 587-2261. **$39-$98.** 197 E Central St. On US 491, just e of US 191. Ext corridors. **Pets:** Large. Service with restrictions, supervision.
[SAVE] [S] [X] [🖉] [🖬] [💻] [≈]

**▼▼▼▼ The Monticello Inn & Suites M**
(435) 587-2489. **$44-$62.** 649 N Main St. On US 194 N; end of town. Int corridors. **Pets:** Accepted.
[ASK] [S] [X] [🖬] [≈]

# MOUNT CARMEL JUNCTION

**(AAA) ▼▼ ▼ Golden Hills Motel M**
(435) 648-2268. **$41-$61.** 4473 S State St. US 89, jct SR 9. Ext/int corridors. **Pets:** Accepted.
[SAVE] [X] [🖬] [≈]

# NEPHI

**(AAA) ▼▼ ▼ Best Western Paradise Inn M**
(435) 623-0624. **$55-$85.** 1025 S Main St. I-15, exit 222, 0.5 mi n. Ext corridors. **Pets:** Accepted.
[SAVE] [X] [🖬] [💻] [≈]

**(AAA) ▼▼ ▼ Safari Motel M**
(435) 623-1071. **$42-$49.** 413 S Main St. I-15, exit 228, 3.2 mi w. Ext corridors. **Pets:** Other species. $3 daily fee/pet. Service with restrictions, supervision.
[SAVE] [S] [X] [🖬] [≈]

# OGDEN

**(AAA) ▼▼▼▼ Best Rest Inn M**
(801) 393-8644. **$55-$95.** 1206 W 2100 S. I-15, exit 343, just e. Ext corridors. **Pets:** Medium, dogs only. $20 deposit/room. Designated rooms, service with restrictions, supervision.
[SAVE] [X] [🖉] [🖬] [💻] [ᴎ] [≈]

**(AAA) ▼▼▼▼ Best Western High Country Inn M**
(801) 394-9474. **$59-$89.** 1335 W 12th St. I-15, exit 344 (12th St), then e. Ext corridors. **Pets:** Other species. Service with restrictions, crate.
[SAVE] [S] [X] [🖉] [🖑] [🖬] [💻] [ᴎ] [≈]

**▼▼▼▼ Comfort Suites of Ogden M**
(801) 621-2545. **$60-$155.** 2250 S 1200 W. I-15, exit 343E, just w. Int corridors. **Pets:** Accepted.
[ASK] [S] [X] [🖉] [🖑] [🖬] [💻] [ᴎ] [≈] [⊠]

**▼▼▼▼ Holiday Inn Express Hotel & Suites M**
(801) 392-5000. **$65-$155.** 2245 S 1200 W. I-15, exit 343, just e. Int corridors. **Pets:** Accepted.
[ASK] [S] [X] [🖉] [🖑] [🖬] [💻] [≈] [⊠]

**▼▼ Motel 6 Ogden #0111 M**
(801) 627-4560. **$39-$55.** 1455 Washington Blvd. Downtown. Int corridors. **Pets:** Accepted.
[S] [X] [🖬] [≈]

**▼▼ ▼▼ Red Roof Inn #7279 M**
(801) 627-2880. **$45-$69.** 1500 W Riverdale Rd. I-15, exit 343 southbound, just w; exit 342 northbound, just e. Ext/int corridors. **Pets:** Accepted.
[X] [🖑M] [🖑] [🖬] [≈]

**▼▼ ▼▼ Super 8 Motel M ❀**
(801) 731-7100. **$43-$63.** 1508 W 2100 S. I-15, exit 343, just w. Int corridors. **Pets:** $25 deposit/room. Service with restrictions, supervision.
[ASK] [S] [X] [🖉] [🖑] [💻]

**(AAA) ▼▼ ▼▼ Western Inn M**
(801) 731-6500. **$54-$68.** 1155 S 1700 W. I-15, exit 344, just w. Int corridors. **Pets:** Medium, other species. $10 daily fee/pet. Service with restrictions, supervision.
[SAVE] [S] [X] [🖉] [🖑] [🖬] [💻]

# OREM

**(AAA) ▼▼▼▼ La Quinta Inn & Suites Orem (University Parkway) M**
(801) 226-0440. **$75-$115.** 521 W University Pkwy. I-15, exit 269, 0.5 mi e. Int corridors. **Pets:** Medium. Service with restrictions.
[SAVE] [X] [🖑] [🖬] [💻] [≈]

**(AAA) ▼▼▼▼ La Quinta Inn Orem (North/Provo) M**
(801) 235-9555. **$49-$89.** 1100 W 780 N. I-15, exit 272, east side. Int corridors. **Pets:** Accepted.
[SAVE] [S] [X] [🖉] [🖬] [💻] [≈]

# PANGUITCH

**△△△ ▼▼▼ Bryce Way Motel M**
(435) 676-2400. **$25.** 429 N Main St. On US 89. Ext corridors.
**Pets:** Small. $4 one-time fee/room. Service with restrictions, crate.
`SAVE` `S6` `X` `8` `💻`

**△△△ ▼▼▼ Color Country Motel M 🐾**
(435) 676-2386. **$35-$62.** 526 N Main St. On US 89. Ext corridors.
**Pets:** Large, other species. $10 one-time fee/pet. Designated rooms, service with restrictions, supervision.
`SAVE` `X` `🏊`

**▼▼ Harold's Place Cabins CA 🐾**
(435) 676-2350. **$45-$75.** 3066 Hwy 12. 1 mi e off US 89 at jct SR 12; 17 mi w of Bryce Canyon. Ext corridors. **Pets:** Medium. $20 deposit/pet. Designated rooms, service with restrictions, supervision.
`ASK` `S6` `X` `💻` `🍴` `☎`

**▼▼ Harold's Place Inn M**
(435) 676-8886. **$45-$75.** 3068 Hwy 12. 0.5 mi e off US 89 at SR 12. Int corridors. **Pets:** Accepted.
`ASK` `S6` `X` `☎`

**△△△ ▼▼▼ Marianna Inn Motel M**
(435) 676-8844. **$30-$75.** 699 N Main St. On SR 89. Ext corridors.
**Pets:** $5 daily fee/pet. No service, supervision.
`SAVE` `S6` `X` `8` `💻`

**▼▼ Silverado Wild West "Movie Town" M**
(435) 676-8770. **$60-$89.** 3900 S Hwy 89. 0.3 mi n of jct SR 12 and 89, 5 mi s off Panguitch on US 89, then 17 mi w of Bryce Canyon. Ext corridors. **Pets:** Accepted.
`ASK` `S6` `X` `8` `🍴` `X`

# PARK CITY

**△△△ ▼▼▼▼ Best Western Landmark Inn M**
(435) 649-7300. **$69-$169.** 6560 N Landmark Dr. I-80, exit 145, at Kimball Junction. Int corridors. **Pets:** Medium, other species. $10 daily fee/pet. Designated rooms, service with restrictions, supervision.
`SAVE` `S6` `X` `&M` `🖏` `8` `💻` `🏊` `X`

**▼▼▼ Holiday Inn Express Hotel & Suites M**
(435) 658-1600. **$82-$229, 14 day notice.** 1501 W Ute Blvd. I-80, exit 145 (Kimball Juncton). Int corridors. **Pets:** Medium. $75 deposit/room. Service with restrictions, supervision.
`ASK` `S6` `X` `🖏` `🖏` `8` `💻` `🏊` `X`

**△△△ ▼▼▼▼ Park City Marriott LH**
(435) 649-2900. **$120-$350, 30 day notice.** 1895 Sidewinder Dr. Jct Park Ave, 0.6 mi ne on Kearns Blvd, just se; Prospector Square area. Int corridors. **Pets:** Accepted.
`SAVE` `S6` `X` `🖏` `🖏` `8` `💻` `🍴` `🏊` `X`

**▼▼▼▼ The Radisson Inn Park City SH**
(435) 649-5000. **$59-$269, 30 day notice.** 2121 Park Ave. I-80, exit 145 (Kimball Junction), 5.1 mi s; north end of town. Int corridors.
**Pets:** Accepted.
`ASK` `X` `🖏` `8` `💻` `🍴` `🏊` `X`

# PAROWAN

**△△△ ▼▼▼ Days Inn M**
(435) 477-3326. **$45-$99.** 625 W 200 S. I-15, exit 75, 1.5 mi e. Ext corridors. **Pets:** Small. $15 daily fee/pet. Designated rooms, service with restrictions, supervision.
`SAVE` `S6` `X` `8` `🏊` `X`

# PAYSON

**▼▼▼ Comfort Inn M**
(801) 465-4861. **$72-$99.** 830 N Main St. I-15, exit 250, just e. Int corridors. **Pets:** $20 deposit/room. Service with restrictions, supervision.
`ASK` `S6` `X` `🖏` `8` `💻` `🏊` `X`

# PRICE

**△△△ ▼▼◆ Budget Host Inn M**
(435) 637-2424. **$45-$59.** 145 N Carbonville Rd. US 6, exit 240, just e, then just n on 600 W. Ext corridors. **Pets:** Medium, dogs only. $10 daily fee/pet. Designated rooms, service with restrictions, supervision.
`SAVE` `S6` `X` `💻` `🏊`

**△△△ ▼▼◆ National 9-Price River Inn M 🐾**
(435) 637-7000. **$42-$60.** 641 W Price River Dr. US 6, exit 240, just w. Ext/int corridors. **Pets:** $5 daily fee/pet. Designated rooms, service with restrictions, supervision.
`SAVE` `S6` `X` `8` `💻`

# PROVO

**△△△ ▼▼▼ Days Inn M**
(801) 375-8600. **$59-$99, 7 day notice.** 1675 N 200 W. I-15, exit 269, 3.5 mi e on University Pkwy. Ext corridors. **Pets:** Other species. $5 one-time fee/room. Service with restrictions, crate.
`SAVE` `S6` `X` `🖏` `🖏` `8` `💻` `🏊`

**▼▼▼ Econo Lodge Provo Airport M**
(801) 373-0099. **$55-$70.** 1625 W Center St. I-15, exit 265A southbound; exit 265B northbound, 0.3 mi w. Ext corridors. **Pets:** $10 one-time fee/pet. Designated rooms, service with restrictions, supervision.
`ASK` `S6` `X` `8` `💻`

**▼▼▼ Hampton Inn M**
(801) 377-6396. **$65-$99.** 1511 S 40. I-15, exit 266, just e. Int corridors.
**Pets:** $20 one-time fee/room. Service with restrictions, supervision.
`ASK` `S6` `X` `🖏` `🖏` `8` `💻` `🏊`

**△△△ ▼▼▼ Provo Travelers Inn M**
(801) 373-8248. **$45-$70.** 469 W Center St. I-15, exit 265 southbound; exit 265A northbound. Ext corridors. **Pets:** Accepted.
`SAVE` `S6` `X` `8` `🏊`

**▼▼▼▼ Residence Inn by Marriott M**
(801) 374-1000. **$69-$149.** 252 W 2230 N. I-15, exit 269, 3.1 mi e via University Pkwy. Int corridors. **Pets:** Accepted.
`ASK` `S6` `X` `&M` `🖏` `🖏` `8` `💻` `🏊` `X`

**△△△ ▼▼▼ Sleep Inn M**
(801) 377-6597. **$50-$70.** 1505 S 40 E. I-15, exit 263, just e. Int corridors. **Pets:** Other species. $10 daily fee/pet. Service with restrictions, supervision.
`SAVE` `S6` `X` `🖏` `🖏` `8` `💻` `🏊` `X`

**△△△ ▼▼▼▼ Super 8 Provo BYU/Orem UVSC M 🐾**
(801) 374-6020. **$49-$109, 14 day notice.** 1555 N Canyon Rd. I-15, exit 269, 3.5 mi e. Ext/int corridors. **Pets:** Medium, other species. $10 daily fee/room. Service with restrictions, crate.
`SAVE` `S6` `X` `🖏` `8` `💻` `🏊`

# RICHFIELD

**△△△ ▼▼▼ AppleTree Inn M**
(435) 896-5481. **$35-$110.** 145 S Main St. I-70, exit 37 or 40; center of downtown. Ext corridors. **Pets:** Medium. $6 daily fee/room. Supervision.
`SAVE` `S6` `X` `🖏` `8` `💻` `🏊`

**▼▼◆ Best Western Richfield Inn M**
(435) 893-0100. **$59-$99.** 1275 N Main St. I-70, exit 40, just s. Int corridors. **Pets:** Accepted.
`ASK` `S6` `X` `🖏` `8` `💻`

**△△△ ▼▼▼ Budget Host Nights Inn M**
(435) 896-8228. **$36-$48.** 69 S Main St. I-70, exit 37 or 40; center of downtown. Ext corridors. **Pets:** Accepted.
`SAVE` `S6` `X` `8` `🏊`

**(AAA) ▼▼▼▼ Days Inn SH**
(435) 896-6476. **$60-$95.** 333 N Main St. I-70, exit 40, 1 mi s on US 89. Int corridors. **Pets:** Medium. $10 one-time fee/room. Designated rooms, service with restrictions, supervision.

SAVE S⌀ ✕ 🛏 🖵 ❓ ⊠

**(AAA) ▼ New West Motel M**
(435) 896-4076. **$38-$44.** 447 S Main St. I-70, exit 37 or 40; downtown. Ext corridors. **Pets:** Accepted.

SAVE S⌀ ✕ 🛏 🖉

**▼▼▼ Richfield Travelodge M**
(435) 896-9271. **$55-$70.** 647 S Main St. I-70, exit 37; south end of town. Int corridors. **Pets:** Accepted.

ASK S⌀ ✕ 🛏 🖵 ❓ ⊠

**(AAA) ▼▼▼ Romanico Inn M**
(435) 896-8471. **$33-$44.** 1170 S Cove View Rd. I-70, exit 37, 2 mi n. Ext corridors. **Pets:** Accepted.

SAVE ✕ 🛏

# ROOSEVELT

**(AAA) ▼▼▼ Frontier Motel M**
(435) 722-2201. **$50-$65.** 75 S 200 E. On US 40. Ext corridors. **Pets:** Small, dogs only. Service with restrictions, supervision.

SAVE S⌀ ✕ 🛏 ❓ ⊠

# ST. GEORGE

**▼▼▼▼ An Olde Penny Farthing Inn Bed & Breakfast BB**
(435) 673-7755. **$70-$145, 7 day notice.** 278 N 100 W. In historic district. Int corridors. **Pets:** Accepted.

✕ ❓ 🛏 🖉

**▼ Best Value Inn M**
(435) 673-4666. **$35-$99.** 60 W St. George Blvd. 1 blk w of Main St; downtown. Ext corridors. **Pets:** Medium, dogs only. $10 daily fee/room. Service with restrictions, supervision.

ASK S⌀ ✕ 🛏 🖵 ⊠

**▼▼ The Bluffs Inn & Suites M**
(435) 628-6699. **$42-$99.** 1140 S Bluff St. I-15, exit 6 (Bluff St), just w. Ext corridors. **Pets:** Accepted.

ASK S⌀ ✕ ❓ 🛏 🖵 ⊠

**▼▼▼ Budget Inn & Suites M**
(435) 673-6661. **$39-$166.** 1221 S Main St. I-15, exit 6 (Bluff St), just w. Ext corridors. **Pets:** Other species. $10 daily fee/room. Designated rooms, service with restrictions.

ASK S⌀ ✕ ❓ 🛏 🖵 ⊠ ⊠

**▼▼ Coronada Inn & Suites SH**
(435) 628-4436. **$39-$99, 3 day notice.** 559 E St. George Blvd. Downtown. Ext corridors. **Pets:** Small, other species. $20 deposit/pet. Service with restrictions, supervision.

ASK S⌀ ✕ 🛏 ⊠

**(AAA) ▼▼▼▼ Coyote Inn at Green Valley Resort & Spa SH**
(435) 628-8060. **$200-$300, 30 day notice.** 1871 W Canyon View Dr. Bluff and S Main sts, 4 mi sw via Hilton Dr to Tonaquint Dr, to Dixie Dr, then to Canyon View Dr. Ext corridors. **Pets:** Small. $500 deposit/room, $25 daily fee/room. Service with restrictions, crate.

SAVE ✕ ⚙M ❓ 🛏 🖵 ⊠ ⊠

**(AAA) ▼▼▼ Crystal Inn St. George SH**
(435) 688-7477. **$69-$119.** 1450 S Hilton Dr. I-15, exit 6 (Bluff St), just w. Int corridors. **Pets:** Accepted.

SAVE S⌀ ✕ 🛏 🖵 ❓ ⊠ ⊠

**(AAA) ▼▼▼ Econo Lodge M**
(435) 673-4861. **$40-$120.** 460 E St. George Blvd. I-15, exit 8, cross streets 500 E and St. George Blvd; downtown. Ext corridors. **Pets:** Small. $10 daily fee/pet. Service with restrictions, supervision.

SAVE ✕ 🖉 🛏 🖵 ⊠

**(AAA) ▼▼▼▼ Fairfield Inn by Marriott M**
(435) 673-6066. **$56-$84.** 1660 S Convention Center Dr. I-15, exit 6 (Bluff St), just e. Int corridors. **Pets:** Small, other species. $75 one-time fee/room. Service with restrictions, supervision.

SAVE S⌀ ✕ 🖉 ❓ 🛏 🖵 ⊠

**(AAA) ▼▼▼▼ GuestHouse International Inn & Suites M**
(435) 673-6161. **$49-$119.** 260 E St George Blvd. I-15, exit 8, 1.5 mi w. Ext corridors. **Pets:** Accepted.

SAVE S⌀ ✕ 🛏 🖵 ⊠

**(AAA) ▼▼▼▼ Howard Johnson Express Inn & Suites M**
(435) 628-8000. **$49-$149.** 1040 S Main St. I-15, exit 6 (Bluff St), just w, then just e. Ext corridors. **Pets:** Accepted.

SAVE S⌀ ✕ ❓ 🛏 🖵 ⊠

**(AAA) ▼▼▼▼ Red Cliffs Inn & Suites M**
(435) 673-3537. **$60-$139.** 912 Red Cliffs Dr. I-15, exit 10, just e. Ext/int corridors. **Pets:** Accepted.

SAVE S⌀ ✕ ❓ 🛏 🖵 ❓ ⊠

**▼▼▼ Seven Wives Inn BB**
(435) 628-3737. **$65-$200, 7 day notice.** 217 N 100 W. I-15, exit 8, 2.1 mi w, then n. Ext corridors. **Pets:** Large, other species. $25 one-time fee/pet. Designated rooms, service with restrictions, supervision.

ASK S⌀ ✕ ❓ 🛏 ⊠

**▼▼▼ Shuttle Lodge Inn M**
(435) 688-8383. **$59-$79.** 915 S Bluff St. I-15, exit 6 (Bluff St), just w. Int corridors. **Pets:** Accepted.

ASK S⌀ ✕ ⊠

**▼▼▼ Suntime Inn M**
(435) 673-6181. **$36-$99.** 420 E St. George Blvd. I-15, exit 8, cross streets 400 E and St. George Blvd; downtown. Ext corridors. **Pets:** Small. $10 daily fee/pet. Service with restrictions, supervision.

✕ 🛏 ⊠

# SALINA

**▼▼ Luxury Inn M**
(435) 529-1300. **$45-$59.** 1400 S State. I-70, exit 56, just n. Int corridors. **Pets:** Accepted.

ASK S⌀ ✕ ❓ 🛏 ⊠

**▼ Ranch Motel M**
(435) 529-7789. **$38-$52.** 80 N State St. On US 89; near town center. Ext/int corridors. **Pets:** Accepted.

ASK S⌀ ✕ 🛏

**(AAA) ▼▼▼ Scenic Hills Super 8 M**
(435) 529-7483. **$50-$62.** 75 E 1500 S. I-70, exit 53, just n. Ext corridors. **Pets:** Accepted.

SAVE S⌀ ✕ 🛏 ⊠

# SALT LAKE CITY METROPOLITAN AREA

## BOUNTIFUL

**♦♦♦ ▼▼▼▼ Country Inn & Suites M**
(801) 292-8100. **$77-$89.** 999 N 500 W. I-15, exit 317. Int corridors.
**Pets:** Medium, other species. $100 deposit/room. Service with restrictions, crate.

## COTTONWOOD HEIGHTS

**▼▼▼▼ Candlewood Suites Hotel M**
(801) 567-0111. **$77.** 6990 S Park Centre Dr. I-15, exit 297, 2.5 mi via 7200 S and Fort Union Blvd. Int corridors. **Pets:** Accepted.

**▼▼▼▼ Residence Inn by Marriott at The Cottonwoods M**
(801) 453-0430. **$169-$315.** 6425 S 3000 E. I-215 S, exit 6200 S, 0.3 mi se. Int corridors. **Pets:** Other species. $75 one-time fee/pet. Service with restrictions.

## DRAPER

**▼▼▼▼ Holiday Inn Express M ❖**
(801) 571-2511. **$89-$129.** 12033 S Factory Outlet Dr. I-15, exit 291, just n; on east side of interstate. **Pets:** Small, other species. $5 daily fee/pet. Service with restrictions, crate.

**▼▼ Ramada Limited M ❖**
(801) 571-1122. **$49-$89.** 12605 S Minuteman Dr. I-15, exit 291, 0.3 mi s on frontage road. Int corridors. **Pets:** Other species. $30 deposit/pet. Service with restrictions, crate.

## MIDVALE

**♦♦♦ ▼▼▼▼ Best Western Executive Inn M**
(801) 566-4141. **$69-$99.** 280 W 7200 S. I-15, exit 297, just e. Int corridors. **Pets:** Medium. $15 daily fee/room. Service with restrictions, supervision.

**♦♦♦ ▼▼▼▼ La Quinta Inn Salt Lake City (Midvale) M**
(801) 566-3291. **$71-$101.** 7231 S Catalpa St. I-15, exit 297, just e. Int corridors. **Pets:** Medium. Service with restrictions.

**▼▼ Motel 6 #476 M**
(801) 561-0058. **$45-$60.** 7263 S Catalpa Rd. I-15, exit 297, just e. Ext corridors. **Pets:** Accepted.

**♦♦♦ ▼▼▼▼ National 9 Discovery Inn M**
(801) 561-2256. **$55-$79.** 380 W 7200 S. I-15, exit 297, just e. Ext/int corridors. **Pets:** Medium. $25 deposit/pet, $6 daily fee/pet. Designated rooms, service with restrictions, supervision.

**▼▼ Super 8 M**
(801) 255-5559. **$59-$79.** 7048 S 900 E. I-15, exit 297, 1.5 mi e on 7200 S to 900 E. Int corridors. **Pets:** Accepted.

## MURRAY

**♦♦♦ ▼▼▼▼ Holiday Inn Express M**
(801) 268-2533. **$55-$75.** 4465 S Century Dr. I-15, exit 301, just w. Int corridors. **Pets:** Large, other species. $15 one-time fee/pet. Designated rooms, service with restrictions, supervision.

**▼▼ ▼▼ Studio 6 #6038 M**
(801) 685-2102. **$49-$61.** 975 E 6600 S. I-215, exit 9 on 900 E, 0.5 mi e. Ext corridors. **Pets:** Accepted.

## NORTH SALT LAKE

**♦♦♦ ▼▼▼▼ Best Western Cottontree Inn M**
(801) 292-7666. **$85-$109.** 1030 N 400 . I-15, exit 315, just e. Int corridors. **Pets:** Large. $50 deposit/room. Service with restrictions, supervision.

## SALT LAKE CITY

**▼▼▼▼ Airport Comfort Inn SH**
(801) 746-5200. **$74-$104.** 200 N Admiral Byrd Rd. I-80, exit 113, 0.8 mi n via 5600 W, Amelia Earhart  r, then s. Int corridors.
**Pets:** Accepted.

**▼▼ ▼▼ Alpine Executive Suites CO**
(801) 533-8184. **$99-$189, 10 day notice.** 164 S 900 E. Cross streets 200 S and 900 E. Int corridors. **Pets:** Accepted.

**▼▼▼▼ Armstrong Mansion Bed & Breakfast BB**
(801) 531-1333. **$99-$249, 7 day notice.** 667 E 100 S. Cross street 700 E. Int corridors. **Pets:** Accepted.

**▼▼▼▼ Best Western Airport Inn ⊟**
(801) 539-5005. **$70-$80, 30 day notice.** 5 N Admiral Byrd Rd. I-80, exit 113, 0.8 mi via 5600 W and Amelia Earhart Dr, then s. Int corridors. **Pets:** Accepted.

**♦♦♦ ▼▼▼▼ Best Western Garden Inn SH**
(801) 521-2930. **$69-$109.** 154 W 600 S. Between cross streets 100-200 W. Int corridors. **Pets:** Accepted.

**♦♦♦ ▼▼▼▼ Best Western Salt Lake Plaza LH**
(801) 521-0130. **$69-$129, 3 day notice.** 122 W S Temple Dr. W of Temple Square. Int corridors. **Pets:** Accepted.

**▼▼▼▼ Candlewood Suite Hotel ▲**
(801) 359-7500. **$90.** 2170 W N Temple. 3 mi w of Temple Square. Int corridors. **Pets:** Medium, other species. $75 one-time fee/room. Service with restrictions.

**♦♦♦ ▼▼▼▼ Chase Suite Hotel by Woodfin M**
(801) 532-5511. **$99-$129.** 765 E 400 S. Cross streets 700 E and 400 S. Ext corridors. **Pets:** Accepted.

**♦♦♦ ▼▼▼ City Creek Inn M**
(801) 533-9100. **$48-$77.** 230 W N Temple Dr. Cross street 200 W. Ext corridors. **Pets:** Accepted.

**▼▼▼▼ Days Inn-Salt Lake City Airport M**
(801) 539-8538. **$55-$110.** 1900 W N Temple. W of Temple 59, 2.5 mi. Int corridors. **Pets:** $5 daily fee/pet. Designated rooms, service with restrictions, supervision.

▼▼ **Econo Lodge Downtown** M
(801) 363-0062. **$64-$69.** 715 W N Temple. W from Temple Square, 1 mi. Ext corridors **Pets:** Small. $5 daily fee/pet. Service with restrictions, supervision.

A$K S♦ ✕ 🖥 💻 ➴

▼▼▼ **Hilton Salt Lake City Airport** LH
(801) 539-1515. **$79-$174.** 5151 Wiley Post Way. I-80, exit 114 westbound, 0.4 mi nw via Wright Brothers Dr and Wiley Post; exit 113 eastbound, 1.3 mi n via 5600 W, Amelia Earhart Dr then just s on Charles Lindbergh Dr. Int corridors. **Pets:** Large, other species. $25 deposit/pet, $25 one-time fee/pet. Designated rooms, service with restrictions, crate.

A$K S♦ ✕ 🖉 ✎ 🖥 💻 🍽 ➴ ✕

▲▲▲ ▼▼▼ ▼▼▼ **Hilton Salt Lake City Center** LH
(801) 328-2000. **$99-$249.** 255 S W Temple Dr. Just n of E 400 S; center. Int corridors. **Pets:** Accepted.

SAVE S♦ ✕ 🖉 ✎ 🖥 💻 🍽 ➴ ✕

▲▲▲ ▼▼▼ **Holiday Inn-Downtown** SH
(801) 359-8600. **$69-$129.** 999 S Main St. Cross streets 900 S and Main St. Int corridors. **Pets:** Medium. $35 one-time fee/room. Service with restrictions, supervision.

SAVE S♦ ✕ 🖉 ✎ 🖥 💻 🍽 ➴ ✕

▼▼ **Homestead Studio Suites Hotel-Salt Lake City/Sugar House** M
(801) 474-0771. **$71-$90.** 1220 E 2100 S. Cross streets 1300 E and 2100 S Sugarhouse. Ext corridors. **Pets:** $25 daily fee/pet. Service with restrictions, supervision.

A$K S♦ ✕ 🖉 ✎ 🖥 💻

▲▲▲ ▼▼▼ ▼▼▼ **Hotel Monaco** LH
(801) 595-0000. **$109-$209.** 15 W 200 South. Cross streets 200 S and Main St. Int corridors. **Pets:** Accepted.

SAVE S♦ ✕ 🖉 ✎ 💻 🍽 ✕

▲▲▲ ▼▼▼ **Howard Johnson Express Inn** M
(801) 521-3450. **$49-$79.** 121 N 300 W. At N Temple and 300 W. Ext/int corridors. **Pets:** Medium. $10 daily fee/pet. Designated rooms, service with restrictions, crate.

SAVE S♦ ✕ 🖉 🖥 💻 ➴

▲▲▲ ▼▼▼ **La Quinta Inn & Suites Salt Lake City (Airport)** SH
(801) 366-4444. **$90-$135.** 4905 W Wiley Post Way. I-80, exit 113 eastbound, 2 mi via 5600 W, Amelia Earhart Dr, just s on Lindbergh Dr, then just e; exit 114 westbound, 0.3 mi nw. Int corridors. **Pets:** Medium. Service with restrictions.

SAVE ✕ 🖉 ✎ 🖥 💻 ➴

▼▼ **Metropolitan Inn** M
(801) 531-7100. **$69-$129.** 524 SW Temple. Cross streets 500 S and W Temple. Ext corridors. **Pets:** Accepted.

A$K S♦ ✕ 🖉 🖥 💻 ➴

▼▼ **Microtel Inn & Suites** M
(801) 236-2800. **$49-$69.** 61 N Tommy Thompson Rd. I-80, exit 114 westbound, n on Wright Brothers Dr, e on Wiley Post Way; exit 113 eastbound, 2.4 mi ne via 5600 W, Amelia Earhart Dr, then s. Int corridors. **Pets:** Accepted.

✕ 🖉 ✎ 🖥 💻

▼▼▼ **Radisson Hotel Salt Lake City Downtown** LH
(801) 531-7500. **$179-$199.** 215 W South Temple. Opposite Delta Center. Int corridors. **Pets:** Accepted.

A$K ✕ 🖉 🖥 💻 🍽 ➴ ✕

▲▲▲ ▼▼▼ **Red Lion Hotel Salt Lake Downtown** LH
(801) 521-7373. **$179-$189.** 161 W 600 S. At W Temple and 600 S. Int corridors. **Pets:** Accepted.

SAVE S♦ ✕ 🖉 ✎ 🖥 💻 🍽 ➴ ✕

▼▼▼ **Residence Inn by Marriott-City Center** SH
(801) 355-3300. **$139-$289.** 285 W Broadway (300 S). Cross streets 300 W and Broadway (300 S). Int corridors. **Pets:** Medium. $75 one-time fee/room. Designated rooms, service with restrictions, crate.

A$K S♦ ✕ 🖉 ✎ 🖥 💻 ➴ ✕

▼▼▼ **Residence Inn by Marriott Salt Lake City Airport** SH
(801) 532-4101. **$121-$152.** 4883 W Douglas Corrigon Way. I-80, exit 114 westbound, via Wright Brothers Dr; exit 113 eastbound, via Amelia Earhart and Wright Brothers drs, then 2.6 mi se. Int corridors. **Pets:** Other species. $75 one-time fee/room. Service with restrictions, crate.

A$K S♦ ✕ 🖉M 🖉 ✎ 🖥 💻 ➴ ✕

▼▼▼ **Saltair Bed & Breakfast** BB
(801) 533-8184. **$79-$189, 10 day notice.** 164 S 900 E. Cross streets 900 E and 200 S. Ext/int corridors. **Pets:** Dogs only. $300 deposit/pet, $10 daily fee/pet. Designated rooms, service with restrictions, crate.

A$K S♦ ✕ 🖥 💻

▼▼▼ **Sheraton City Centre** LH
(801) 401-2000. **$129-$189.** 150 W 500 S. At 200 W and 500 S. Int corridors. **Pets:** Accepted.

A$K S♦ ✕ 🖉 ✎ 🖥 💻 🍽 ➴ ✕

▲▲▲ ▼▼▼ **Shilo Inn Hotel** LH ❀
(801) 521-9500. **$69-$155.** 206 S W Temple. Cross streets 200 S and W Temple. Int corridors. **Pets:** Small. $100 deposit/room, $25 daily fee/pet. Designated rooms, service with restrictions, supervision.

SAVE S♦ ✕ 🖉 ✎ 🖥 💻 🍽 ➴ ✕

▲▲▲ ▼▼▼ **The Skyline Inn** M
(801) 582-5350. **$59-$79.** 2475 E 1700 S. E off Foothill Dr. Ext corridors. **Pets:** Medium. $25 deposit/room. Service with restrictions.

SAVE S♦ ✕ 🖉 🖥 ➴

▼▼▼ **Super 8 Airport** M
(801) 533-8878. **$89-$129, 14 day notice.** 223 N Jimmy Doolittle Rd. I-80, exit 113, 0.7 mi ne via 5600 W, Amelia Earhart Dr and Admiral Byrd Rd, then e. Int corridors. **Pets:** Other species. $10 daily fee/pet. Designated rooms, service with restrictions, supervision.

A$K S♦ ✕ 🖉 🖥 💻 ➴

# SANDY

▲▲▲ ▼▼▼ **Best Western CottonTree Inn** M
(801) 523-8484. **$69-$129.** 10695 S Auto Mall Dr. I-15, exit 293 eastbound, 0.3 mi e. Int corridors. **Pets:** Medium, other species. Service with restrictions, supervision.

SAVE S♦ ✕ 🖉 ✎ 🖥 💻 ➴

▼▼▼ **Comfort Inn** M
(801) 255-4919. **$59-$80.** 8955 S 255 West. I-15, exit 295, just ne, follow signs. Int corridors. **Pets:** Other species. $10 daily fee/pet. Service with restrictions, supervision.

A$K S♦ ✕ 🖉 ✎ 🖥 💻 ➴

▼▼▼ **Comfort Suites Sandy** M ❀
(801) 495-1317. **$77-$80.** 10680 S Auto Mall Dr. I-15, exit 293 eastbound, 0.3 mi e. Int corridors. **Pets:** $10 daily fee/room. Service with restrictions, supervision.

A$K S♦ ✕ 🖉 🖥 💻 ➴

▼▼▼ **Residence Inn by Marriott** M ❀
(801) 561-5005. **$129-$229.** 270 W 10000 S. From Stare St, 0.3 mi w on 10000 S. Int corridors. **Pets:** Medium, other species. $75 one-time fee/room. Service with restrictions.

A$K S♦ ✕ 🖉 ✎ 🖥 💻 ➴ ✕

▼▼▼ **Sleep Inn** M
(801) 572-2020. **$49-$89.** 10676 S 300 W. I-15, exit 293 westbound, just w. Int corridors. **Pets:** Accepted.

A$K S♦ ✕ 🖥 💻 ➴

▼◆▼ Super 8 Motel South Jordan/Sandy **M**
(801) 553-8888. **$45-$75.** 10722 S 300 W. I-15, exit 293 westbound, just w. Int corridors. **Pets:** Accepted.

(ASK) (S6) (☒) (🗇) (&) (🔾) (🖃) (≈)

## SOUTH SALT LAKE

▼◆▼ Days Inn-Central **M**
(801) 486-8780. **$49-$99.** 315 W 3300 S. I-15, exit 303, Just e. Ext corridors. **Pets:** Small, other species. $30 deposit/pet. Service with restrictions, crate.

(ASK) (S6) (☒) (🗇) (🔾) (🖃) (≈) (☒)

▼◆▼ Ramada Limited Salt Lake City **M**
(801) 486-2400. **$69-$99.** 2455 S State St. Cross street Morris Ave. Int corridors. **Pets:** Medium. Service with restrictions, supervision.

(ASK) (S6) (☒) (🗇) (🔾) (🖃) (≈)

## TAYLORSVILLE

▼◆▼ Homestead Studio Suites Hotel-Salt Lake City/Mid Valley **M**
(801) 269-9292. **$54-$74.** 5683 S Redwood Rd. I-215, exit 13, 0.5 mi n. Ext corridors. **Pets:** $25 daily fee/pet. Service with restrictions, supervision.

(ASK) (S6) (☒) (🗇) (&) (🔾) (🖃)

## WEST VALLEY CITY

▼◆▼ Baymont Inn & Suites Salt Lake City-West Valley City **M**
(801) 886-1300. **$70-$80.** 2229 W City Center Ct. I-215, exit 18, just e. Int corridors. **Pets:** Medium. Service with restrictions.

(ASK) (☒) (🗇) (&) (🔾) (🖃) (≈)

◆◆◆ ▼◆▼ Country Inn & Suites By Carlson **M**
(801) 908-0311. **$79-$109.** 3422 S Decker Lake Dr. I-215, exit 18, 0.3 mi e. Int corridors. **Pets:** Medium. $10 deposit/room. Service with restrictions, supervision.

(SAVE) (S6) (☒) (🗇) (&) (🔾) (🖃) (≈)

▼◆▼ La Quinta Inn West Valley City (Salt Lake-West) **M**
(801) 954-9292. **$54-$94.** 3540 S 2200 W. I-215, exit 18; east side. Int corridors. **Pets:** Large, other species. Service with restrictions, supervision.

(ASK) (S6) (☒) (🗇) (&) (🔾) (🖃) (≈)

▼▼ Sleep Inn **M** 🐾
(801) 975-1888. **$49-$99.** 3440 S 2200 W. I-215, exit 18, just e. Int corridors. **Pets:** Medium, other species. Service with restrictions, supervision.

(ASK) (S6) (☒) (🗇) (&) (🔾) (🖃) (≈)

## WOODS CROSS

◆◆◆ ▼◆▼ Hampton Inn **M** 🐾
(801) 296-1211. **$74-$104, 5 day notice.** 2393 S 800 W. I-15, exit 315, just w of freeway. Int corridors. **Pets:** Large. $50 deposit/room. Service with restrictions, supervision.

(SAVE) (S6) (☒) (🗇) (&) (🔾) (🖃) (≈)

▼ Motel 6 #1205 **M**
(801) 298-0289. **$40-$53.** 2433 S 800 W. I-15, exit 315 westbound, just w. Ext corridors. **Pets:** Accepted.

(S6) (☒) (&) (🔾) (≈)

## END METROPOLITAN AREA

## SCIPIO

▼◆▼ Super 8 **M**
(435) 758-9188. **$55-$65.** 230 W 400 N. I-15, exit 188, just ne. Int corridors. **Pets:** Accepted.

(ASK) (S6) (☒) (&) (🔾) (🖃) (≈)

## SPANISH FORK

◆◆◆ ▼◆▼ Western Inn **M**
(801) 798-9400. **$50-$70.** 632 Kirby Ln. I-15, exit 258 southbound, 0.5 mi e; exit 257 northbound, 1 mi ne. Int corridors. **Pets:** Dogs only. $10 one-time fee/room. Service with restrictions, supervision.

(SAVE) (S6) (☒) (🔾)

## SPRINGDALE

◆◆◆ ▼◆▼ Best Western Zion Park Inn **M**
(435) 772-3200. **$70-$119.** 1215 Zion Park Blvd. 2 mi s of park entrance. Int corridors. **Pets:** Small. $25 one-time fee/room. Designated rooms, service with restrictions, supervision.

(SAVE) (S6) (☒) (🗇) (&) (🔾) (🖃) (🍴) (≈) (☒)

▼◆▼ Canyon Ranch Motel **M** 🐾
(435) 772-3357. **$49-$94.** 668 Zion Park Blvd. SR 9, just s of south gate to Zion National Park. Ext corridors. **Pets:** Dogs only. $10 one-time fee/pet. Supervision.

(☒) (🔾) (🖃) (≈)

◆◆◆ ▼◆▼ Driftwood Lodge **M**
(435) 772-3262. **$76-$110.** 1515 Zion Park Blvd. SR 9, 2 mi s of south gate to Zion National Park. Ext corridors. **Pets:** Other species. $10 one-time fee/room. Designated rooms, service with restrictions, supervision.

(SAVE) (S6) (☒) (🔾) (🖃) (🍴) (≈)

◆◆◆ ▼◆▼ Majestic View Lodge **SH**
(435) 772-0665. **$89-$209.** 2400 Zion Park Blvd. 3.5 mi s of park entrance. Ext corridors. **Pets:** Small, dogs only. $50 deposit/pet. Designated rooms, service with restrictions, supervision.

(SAVE) (☒) (🔾) (🖃) (🍴) (≈)

## SPRINGVILLE

◆◆◆ ▼◆▼ Best Western CottonTree Inn **M**
(801) 489-3641. **$64-$99, 7 day notice.** 1455 N 1750 W. I-15, exit 261, just e; just s of Provo. Int corridors. **Pets:** Other species. $10 one-time fee/room. Service with restrictions, crate.

(SAVE) (S6) (☒) (🗇) (&) (🔾) (🖃) (≈)

## TICABOO

▼◆▼ Ticaboo Resort **M**
(435) 788-2110. **$59-$189.** 84533 Hwy 276. Jct SR 95 and 276, 28 mi s. Int corridors. **Pets:** Accepted.

(ASK) (S6) (☒) (🍴) (≈)

## TORREY

▼◆▼ Cactus Hill Ranch Motel **M**
(435) 425-3578. **$48, 7 day notice.** 830 S 1000 E. 5 mi s of SR 24 at Teasdale; 5 mi w of SR 12, exit Teasdale; 13 mi w of Capitol Reef National Park, 2 mi se of town center. Ext corridors. **Pets:** Very small, dogs only. $10 one-time fee/pet. Designated rooms, service with restrictions, supervision.

(ASK) (S6) (☒) (🔾) (🖃)

▼◆▼ Comfort Inn at Capitol Reef/Torrey **M**
(435) 425-3866. **$49-$109.** 2424 E Hwy 24. On SR 24, 1.5 mi e of jct SR 12 and 24, 1.5 mi w of Capitol Rd. Ext corridors. **Pets:** Accepted.

(ASK) (S6) (☒) (&) (🔾)

▼▼ Rim Fock Inn **M**
(435) 425-3398. **$49-$79.** 2523 E Hwy 24. 2.5 mi e of jct SR 12 and 24; east end of town. Ext corridors. **Pets:** Accepted.
A$K S✿ ✕ 🐾 ▤ ¶

▼▼ Torrey/Capitol Reef-Econo Lodge **M**
(435) 425-3688. **$42-$85.** 600 E Hwy 24. On SR 24, 0.3 mi w of SR 12; 3.3 mi w of Capitol Reef National Park. Int corridors. **Pets:** Accepted.
A$K S✿ ✕ 🐾 ▤ 🏊

▲▲▲ ▼▼▼ Torrey Days Inn **M**
(435) 425-3111. **$55-$90.** 675 E Hwy 24. Jct SR 12 and 24. Int corridors. **Pets:** Very small, other species. $10 daily fee/room. Designated rooms, service with restrictions, supervision.
SAVE S✿ ✕ ▤ ▣ 🏊

▲▲▲ ▼▼▼ Wonderland Inn **M**
(435) 425-3775. **$40-$70.** 875 E Hwy 24. Jct SR 12 and 24; 3 mi w of Capitol Reef National Park. Ext corridors. **Pets:** $10 daily fee/room. Service with restrictions, supervision.
SAVE S✿ ✕ ▤ ¶ 🏊

# TREMONTON

▲▲▲ ▼ Sandman Motel **M**
(435) 257-7149. **$54-$60.** 585 W Main St. I-15/84 N, exit 376, 2.1 mi ne to 4-way stop, then 1.5 mi w; I-15 S, exit 381, 0.6 mi e to 4-way stop, s to Main St, then 0.5 mi e; I-84, exit 40, 1.5 mi e. Ext corridors. **Pets:** Accepted.
SAVE ✕

# TROPIC

▼ Bryce Pioneer Village **M**
(435) 679-8546. **$55-$85.** 80 S Main St. South end of town. Ext corridors. **Pets:** Medium, dogs only. $10 one-time fee/pet. Designated rooms, service with restrictions, supervision.
A$K ✕

# VERNAL

▼▼ Econo Lodge **M**
(435) 789-2000. **$54-$65.** 311 E Main St. On US 40. Ext corridors. **Pets:** Accepted.
A$K S✿ ✕ 🐾 ▤ ▣

▼▼ Rodeway Inn **M**
(435) 789-8172. **$60-$65.** 590 W Main St. US 40. Ext corridors. **Pets:** Other species. $5 daily fee/pet. Service with restrictions, crate.
A$K S✿ ✕ ▤ ▣

▼ Sage Motel & Restaurant **M**
(435) 789-1442. **$45-$65.** 54 W Main St. Center. Ext corridors. **Pets:** Other species. $5 one-time fee/room. Designated rooms, service with restrictions, supervision.
✕ ▤ ¶

# WELLINGTON

▼▼ National 9 Inn **M**
(435) 637-7980. **$42-$55.** 50 S 700. On US 6. Ext/int corridors. **Pets:** Medium. $25 deposit/pet, $5 daily fee/pet. Designated rooms, service with restrictions, supervision.
A$K S✿ ✕ ▤ ¶ 🏊

# WENDOVER

▲▲▲ ▼▼▼ Days Inn of Wendover **M**
(435) 665-2215. **$69-$160.** 685 E Wendover Blvd. I-80, exit 2. Int corridors. **Pets:** Accepted.
SAVE S✿ ✕ 🐾 🐾 ▤ 🏊

▼▼▼ Econo Lodge **M**
(435) 665-2226. **$59-$150.** 245 E Wendover Blvd. I-80, exit 2. Ext/int corridors. **Pets:** Small, other species. $5 daily fee/pet. Service with restrictions, supervision.
A$K S✿ ✕ ▤ 🏊

▼ Western Ridge Motel **M**
(435) 665-2211. **$35-$45.** 895 E Wendover Blvd. I-80, exit 2. Ext corridors. **Pets:** Small. $10 one-time fee/pet. Designated rooms, service with restrictions, supervision.
A$K S✿ ✕ ▤ 🏊

# VERMONT

## ALBURG

### ▼▼▼ Ransom Bay Inn BB
(802) 796-3399. **$85-$95.** 4 Center Bay Rd. 0.5 mi s on US 2, from jct SR 78. Int corridors. **Pets:** Accepted.

⊠ 🕅 🕿

## BARRE

### ❹❹❹ ▼▼▼ The Hollow Inn & Motel M ✿
(802) 479-9313. **$85-$150.** 278 S Main St. Jct US 302, 1 mi s on SR 14; I-89, exit 6, 4.3 mi e on SR 63, then 0.7 mi n on SR 14. Ext/int corridors. **Pets:** Small. $10 daily fee/pet, $10 one-time fee/pet. Service with restrictions, supervision.

SAVE 🖬 🖵 ➯ ⊠

## BENNINGTON

### ❹❹❹ ▼▼▼ Bennington Motor Inn M
(802) 442-5479. **$59-$130, 10 day notice.** 143 W Main St. Jct US 7, 0.4 mi w on SR 9. Ext corridors. **Pets:** Medium. $25 daily fee/pet. Designated rooms, service with restrictions, supervision.

SAVE 🔊 ⊠ 🖬 🖵

### ❹❹❹ ▼ Darling Kelly's Motel M
(802) 442-2322. **$48-$120, 3 day notice.** 357 US 7 S. Jct SR 9 and US 7, 1.2 mi s. Ext corridors. **Pets:** Dogs only. $8 daily fee/pet. No service, supervision.

SAVE 🔊 ⊠ 🖬 ➯

### ❹❹❹ ▼▼▼ Fife 'N Drum Motel M
(802) 442-4074. **$47-$112, 3 day notice.** 693 US Rt 7 S. Jct SR 9 and US 7, 1.6 mi s. Ext corridors. **Pets:** Medium, dogs only. $6 daily fee/pet. Service with restrictions, supervision.

SAVE 🔊 ⊠ 🖬 🖵 ➯ ⊠

### ❹❹❹ ▼ Harwood Hill Motel M
(802) 442-6278. **$48-$80, 3 day notice.** 864 Harwood Hill Rd (Historic Rt 7A). Jct SR 9, 1.2 mi n on US 7, then 1.7 mi n. Ext corridors. **Pets:** Medium, dogs only. $8 daily fee/room. Service with restrictions, crate.

SAVE 🔊 ⊠ 🖬 🖵

### ▼ Knotty Pine Motel M ✿
(802) 442-5487. **$54-$88.** 130 Northside Dr (SR 7A). Jct SR 9, 1.2 mi n on US 7, then just n on Historic SR 7A. Ext corridors. **Pets:** Designated rooms, service with restrictions, supervision.

⊠ 🖬 🖵 ➯

## BOLTON VALLEY

### ❹❹❹ ▼▼▼ Black Bear Inn CI ✿
(802) 434-2126. **$104-$300, 21 day notice.** 4010 Bolton Access Rd. I-89, exit 10 northbound, 6.2 mi w on US 2, then 4 mi n; exit 11 southbound, 8.4 mi e on US 2, then 4 mi n. Ext/int corridors. **Pets:** $20 daily fee/room. Designated rooms, service with restrictions, crate.

SAVE ⊠ 🖬 🖵 🍴 ➯

## BRANDON

### ❹❹❹ ▼▼▼ Brandon Motor Lodge M
(802) 247-9594. **$65-$125, 7 day notice.** 2095 Franklin St. 2 mi s on US 7. Ext corridors. **Pets:** Medium, dogs only. $5 daily fee/pet. Designated rooms, service with restrictions, supervision.

SAVE ⊠ 🖬 ➯ ⊠

### ▼▼▼ The Lilac Inn CI
(802) 247-5463. **$150-$295, 30 day notice.** 53 Park St. Just e on SR 73. Int corridors. **Pets:** Accepted.

A$K 🔊 ⊠ 🍴 🕿

### ▼▼ Maple Grove Dining Room & Cottages CA
(802) 247-6644. **$79-$129, 7 day notice.** 1246 Franklin St. Jct SR 73 and US 7, 1.2 mi s on US 7. Ext corridors. **Pets:** Dogs only. $10 daily fee/room. Supervision.

A$K 🔊 ⊠ 🖬 🖵 🍴 ➯ ⊠ 🕿

## BRATTLEBORO

### ▼▼▼ Colonial Motel & Spa SH
(802) 257-7733. **$79-$180.** 889 Putney Rd. I-91, exit 3, just e on SR 9, then 0.5 mi s on US 5. Ext corridors. **Pets:** Dogs only. $10 daily fee/room. Service with restrictions, supervision.

A$K 🔊 ⊠ 🖬 🖵 🍴 ➯ ⊠

### ❹❹❹ ▼▼ Econo Lodge M
(802) 254-2360. **$39-$129.** 515 Canal St. I-91, exit 1, 0.3 mi n on US 5. Ext corridors. **Pets:** Small, dogs only. $10 daily fee/pet. Designated rooms, service with restrictions, supervision.

SAVE 🔊 ⊠ 🖬 🖵 ➯

### ❹❹❹ ▼▼▼ Quality Inn & Suites SH
(802) 254-8701. **$69-$179.** 1380 Putney Rd. I-91, exit 3, 0.6 mi n on US 5. Int corridors. **Pets:** Small, dogs only. $50 one-time fee/room. Designated rooms, service with restrictions, supervision.

SAVE ⊠ 🕗 🖬 🖵 🍴 ➯ ⊠

### ❹❹❹ ▼▼▼ Super 8 Motel M
(802) 254-8889. **$50-$159.** 1043 Putney Rd. I-91, exit 3, just e on SR 9, then just s on US 5. Int corridors. **Pets:** Large. $20 one-time fee/room. Service with restrictions, supervision.

SAVE 🔊 ⊠ 🔊M 🖬

## CAVENDISH

### ❹❹❹ ▼▼▼▼ Clarion Hotel at Cavendish Pointe SH
(802) 226-7688. **$89-$299, 14 day notice.** 2940 SR 103. On SR 103, just n of jct SR 131. Int corridors. **Pets:** Other species. $20 daily fee/pet. Designated rooms, service with restrictions.

SAVE 🔊 ⊠ 🖬 🖵 🍴 ➯ ⊠

## CHITTENDEN

### ❹❹❹ ▼▼▼ The Mountain Top Inn & Resort CI
(802) 483-2311. **$130-$465, 21 day notice.** 195 Mountain Top Rd. Jct US 4, 1.8 mi n on Meadowlake Dr, 2.8 mi e on Chittenden Rd, then 2 mi n. Ext/int corridors. **Pets:** Accepted.

SAVE ⊠ 🖬 🖵 🍴 ➯ ⊠

# COLCHESTER

**▼▼▼ Days Inn SH**
(802) 655-0900. **$60-$175.** 124 College Pkwy. I-89, exit 15 northbound, just e on SR 15; exit 16 southbound, 1.1 mi s on US 7, then 1 mi e on SR 15. Int corridors. **Pets:** Dogs only. $50 deposit/room, $10 daily fee/pet. Designated rooms, service with restrictions, supervision.

(A$K) (S๑) (⊠) (&M) (🖨) (⊅)

**▼▼▼▼ Hampton Inn & Conference Center SH ❖**
(802) 655-6177. **$99-$169.** 42 Lower Mountain View Dr. I-89, exit 16, just n on US 7. Int corridors. **Pets:** $10 one-time fee/room. Designated rooms, service with restrictions, supervision.

(A$K) (S๑) (⊠) (&M) (🍳) (🐾) (🖨) (⊅)

**▼▼ Motel 6 #1407 SH**
(802) 654-6860. **$45-$67.** 74 S Park Dr. I-89, exit 16, just s on US 7. Int corridors. **Pets:** Accepted.

(S๑) (⊠) (🖨) (⊅)

# ESSEX JUNCTION

**▼▼▼▼ Handy Suites SH**
(802) 872-5200. **$74-$199.** 27 Susie Wilson Rd. I-89, exit 15 northbound, 2.1 mi e on SR 15, then 0.4 mi n. Int corridors. **Pets:** Accepted.

(A$K) (S๑) (⊠) (&M) (🖨) (🖵) (⊅)

**▲▲▲ ▼▼▼▼ The Inn at Essex SH ❖**
(802) 878-1100. **$119-$309, 7 day notice.** 70 Essex Way. SR 289, exit 10, 0.3 mi s. Int corridors. **Pets:** $300 deposit/room, $25 daily fee/pet. Designated rooms, service with restrictions.

(SAVE) (S๑) (⊠) (&M) (🐾) (🖨) (🖵) (🍴) (⊅) (⊠)

# FAIRLEE

**▲▲▲ ▼▼▼ Silver Maple Lodge & Cottages BB**
(802) 333-4326. **$69-$89, 14 day notice.** 520 US 5 S. I-91, exit 15, 0.5 mi s. Ext/int corridors. **Pets:** Other species. Designated rooms.

(SAVE) (S๑) (⊠) (🖨) (🖵) (🕿)

# FLETCHER

**▼▼▼▼ The Inn at Buck Hollow Farm BB ❖**
(802) 849-2400. **$78-$99, 14 day notice.** 2150 Buck Hollow Rd. 6.4 mi n of jct SR 104 via Buck Hollow Rd. Int corridors. **Pets:** $15 one-time fee/pet. Supervision.

(A$K) (⊠) (⊅) (⊠) (🕿)

# JAMAICA

**▲▲▲ ▼▼▼▼ Three Mountain Inn CI ❖**
(802) 874-4140. **$145-$345, 20 day notice.** 3732 Main St. On SR 30; center. Ext/int corridors. **Pets:** Dogs only. $25 daily fee/pet. Designated rooms, service with restrictions, supervision.

(SAVE) (⊠) (🍴) (⊅) (⊠)

# JEFFERSONVILLE

**▼▼▼ Deer Run Motor Inn M**
(802) 644-8866. **$85, 15 day notice.** 80 Deer Run Loop. 0.7 mi e on SR 15. Ext/int corridors. **Pets:** $10 daily fee/pet. Supervision.

(A$K) (S๑) (⊠) (🖨) (🖵) (⊅)

# KILLINGTON

**▲▲▲ ▼▼▼ Butternut on the Mountain SH**
(802) 422-2000. **$58-$205, 30 day notice.** 63 Weathervane Rd. Jct SR 100/US 4, 1.1 mi s on Killington Rd, then just e. Ext/int corridors. **Pets:** Accepted.

(SAVE) (S๑) (⊠) (🖨) (🖵) (⊅)

**▲▲▲ ▼▼▼▼ The Cascades Lodge SH**
(802) 422-3731. **$85-$239, 21 day notice.** 58 Old Mill Rd. 3.6 mi s on Killington Rd, from jct SR 100/US 4, then just e. Int corridors. **Pets:** Accepted.

(SAVE) (⊠) (🍳) (🖨) (🖵) (🍴) (⊅) (⊠)

**▲▲▲ ▼▼▼ Val Roc Motel M**
(802) 422-3881. **$65-$150, 14 day notice.** 8006 US 4. 5.9 mi e on US 4, from jct SR 100 N. Ext/int corridors. **Pets:** Accepted.

(SAVE) (S๑) (⊠) (🖨) (🖵) (⊅) (⊠)

# LUDLOW

**▲▲▲ ▼▼▼ Timber Inn Motel M**
(802) 228-8666. **$69-$199, 14 day notice.** 112 Rt 103 S. On SR 103 S, 1 mi e. Ext corridors. **Pets:** Large, dogs only. $15 daily fee/pet. Designated rooms, service with restrictions, crate.

(SAVE) (S๑) (⊠) (🖨) (🖵) (⊅) (⊠)

# MANCHESTER VILLAGE

**▼▼▼▼ The Village Country Inn CI**
(802) 362-1792. **$179-$345, 14 day notice.** 3835 Main St. On Historic SR 7A, 1 mi s of jct SR 11/30. Ext/int corridors. **Pets:** Small, dogs only. $40 one-time fee/pet. Designated rooms, service with restrictions, supervision.

(⊠) (🖨) (🖵) (🍴) (⊅)

# MENDON

**▼▼▼▼ Cortina Inn and Resort SH ❖**
(802) 773-3333. **$99-$229.** 103 US Rt 4. Jct SR 100 N, 3 mi w. Int corridors. **Pets:** Other species. $10 daily fee/pet. Designated rooms, service with restrictions, supervision.

(A$K) (S๑) (⊠) (🍳) (🖨) (🖵) (🍴) (⊅) (⊠)

**▲▲▲ ▼▼▼ Econo Lodge-Killington Area SH**
(802) 773-6644. **$65-$125, 7 day notice.** 51 US 4. Jct US 7, 5.3 mi e. Int corridors. **Pets:** $10 one-time fee/room. Designated rooms, service with restrictions, supervision.

(SAVE) (S๑) (⊠) (🖨) (🖵) (⊅)

**▼▼▼ Mendon Mountainview Lodge SH**
(802) 773-4311. **$52-$229, 7 day notice.** 78 US 4. On US 4, 6 mi e of jct US 7. Int corridors. **Pets:** Accepted.

(A$K) (S๑) (⊠) (🖨) (⊅) (⊠)

# MIDDLEBURY

**▲▲▲ ▼▼▼ The Middlebury Inn SH ❖**
(802) 388-4961. **$108-$395, 3 day notice.** 14 Court Square. On US 7; center. Ext/int corridors. **Pets:** Designated rooms, service with restrictions, crate.

(SAVE) (⊠) (🍳) (🍳) (🖨) (🖵) (🍴)

# NEWFANE

**▼▼▼ Four Columns Inn CI**
(802) 365-7713. **$175-$400, 14 day notice.** 21 West St. Just w of SR 30; center. Int corridors. **Pets:** Accepted.

(⊠) (🍴) (⊅)

# NORTH HERO

**▲▲▲ ▼▼▼ Shore Acres Inn SH**
(802) 372-8722. **$109-$199, 14 day notice.** 237 Shore Acres Dr. 1 mi s on US 2. Ext/int corridors. **Pets:** Dogs only. $15 daily fee/pet. Supervision.

(SAVE) (⊠) (🖨) (🍴) (⊠) (🕿)

# PERU

**▼▼▼ Johnny Seesaw's CI**
(802) 824-5533. **$80-$180, 14 day notice.** 3574 Vt Rt 11. 2.1 mi e on SR 11, from jct SR 30 S. Ext/int corridors. **Pets:** Accepted.

(🖨) (🍴) (⊅) (⊠)

# PUTNEY

**▼▼▼ The Putney Inn** 🆂🅷 ❀
(802) 387-5517. **$98-$178.** 57 Putney Landing Rd. I-91, exit 4, just e. Ext corridors. **Pets:** $10 daily fee/pet. Supervision.
✕ 🖃 🍴

# RUTLAND

**🅰🅰🅰 ▼▼▼▼ Holiday Inn Rutland/Killington** 🅻🅷
(802) 775-1911. **$135-$270.** 476 US Rt 7 S. 2.4 mi s on US 7, from US 4 W; 0.4 mi n, US 7 from US 4 E. Int corridors. **Pets:** Other species. $15 daily fee/pet. Service with restrictions.
🆂🅰🆅🅴 🆂🚳 ✕ 🅖🅜 ⊘ 🖥 🖃 🍴 ⇔ ✕

**🅰🅰🅰 ▼▼▼ Ramada Limited of Rutland** 🆂🅷
(802) 773-3361. **$69-$169.** 253 S Main St, US 7. 1.3 mi s on US 7, from US 4 W; 1.5 mi n on US 7, from US 4 E. Int corridors. **Pets:** Other species. $25 one-time fee/pet. Service with restrictions, supervision.
🆂🅰🆅🅴 🆂🚳 ✕ 🖥 🖃 ⇔

**🅰🅰🅰 ▼▼▼▼ Red Roof Inn Rutland-Killington** 🆂🅷
(802) 775-4303. **$69-$169.** 401 US Hwy 7 S. On US 7/4. Int corridors. **Pets:** Accepted.
🆂🅰🆅🅴 🆂🚳 ✕ 🖥 🖃 ⇔ ✕

**🅰🅰🅰 ▼▼ Rodeway Inn** 🅼
(802) 775-2575. **$47-$159, 5 day notice.** 138 N Main St. 0.5 mi n of jct US 4 E. Ext corridors. **Pets:** Small. $10 one-time fee/pet. Service with restrictions, supervision.
🆂🅰🆅🅴 🆂🚳 ✕ 🖥 🖃 ⇔

**🅰🅰🅰 ▼ Rodeway Inn** 🅼
(802) 773-9176. **$54-$109, 7 day notice.** 115 Woodstock Ave. Jct US 7, 0.5 mi e on US 4. Ext/int corridors. **Pets:** Small, dogs only. $10 daily fee/pet. Designated rooms, service with restrictions, supervision.
🆂🅰🆅🅴 🆂🚳 ✕ 🖥 ⇔

# ST. ALBANS

**▼▼▼ Comfort Inn & Suites** 🆂🅷
(802) 524-3300. **$79-$209.** 813 Fairfax Rd. I-89, exit 19, just w, then just s on SR 104. Int corridors. **Pets:** Other species. $50 deposit/room, $10 daily fee/pet. Designated rooms, service with restrictions, supervision.
🅰🆂🅺 🆂🚳 ✕ 🅖🅜 🖥 🖃 ⇔

**🅰🅰🅰 ▼▼ Econo Lodge** 🅼
(802) 524-5956. **$59-$109.** 287 S Main St. I-89, exit 19, 1 mi w to US 7, then 0.5 mi s. Ext/int corridors. **Pets:** Medium. $10 daily fee/pet. Designated rooms, service with restrictions.
🆂🅰🆅🅴 🆂🚳 ✕ 🖥 🖃

# ST. JOHNSBURY

**▼▼▼ Fairbanks Inn** 🅼 ❀
(802) 748-5666. **$80-$149.** 401 Western Ave. I-91, exit 21, 1 mi e on US 2. Ext corridors. **Pets:** Dogs only. $5 daily fee/pet. Service with restrictions, crate.
🅰🆂🅺 🆂🚳 ✕ 🖥 🖃 ⇔

**▼ O'Shea's Motel** 🅼
(802) 745-4500. **Call for rates.** 46 Vt, Rt 18. I-91, exit 1, 0.5 mi n. Ext corridors. **Pets:** Accepted.
✕ 🖃

# SHAFTSBURY

**▼ Governor's Rock Motel** 🅼
(802) 442-4734. **$59-$95, 7 day notice.** 4325 Rt 7A. 3.3 mi n on Historic SR 7A, from jct SR 67. Ext corridors. **Pets:** $10 one-time fee/room. Designated rooms, supervision.
🅰🆂🅺 🆂🚳 ✕ 🖥

**▼ Serenity Motel** 🅲🅰
(802) 442-6490. **$60-$80.** 4379 Rt 7A. 3.3 mi n on Historic SR 7A, from jct SR 67. Ext corridors. **Pets:** Large, other species. Service with restrictions, supervision.
✕ 🖥 🖃

# SOUTH BURLINGTON

**▼▼ Best Western Windjammer Inn & Conference Center** 🆂🅷 ❀
(802) 863-1125. **$104-$199.** 1076 Williston Rd. I-89, exit 14E, 0.3 mi e on US 2. Int corridors. **Pets:** $5 daily fee/pet. Designated rooms, service with restrictions, supervision.
🅰🆂🅺 🆂🚳 ✕ 🅖🅜 ⊘ 🅖 🖥 🖃 🍴 ⇔ ✕

**▼▼ Comfort Inn** 🆂🅷 ❀
(802) 865-3400. **$69-$189.** 1285 Williston Rd. I-89, exit 14E, 0.5 mi e on US 2. Int corridors. **Pets:** Other species. $10 one-time fee/room. Service with restrictions.
🅰🆂🅺 🆂🚳 ✕ 🅖🅜 ⊘ 🖥 🖃 ⇔

**🅰🅰🅰 ▼▼▼ Doubletree Hotel Burlington** 🆂🅷 ❀
(802) 658-0250. **$119-$239.** 1117 Williston Rd. I-89, exit 14E, just e on US 2. Int corridors. **Pets:** Other species. $50 deposit/room. Designated rooms, service with restrictions, supervision.
🆂🅰🆅🅴 ✕ 🅖🅜 ⊘ 🅖 🖥 🖃 🍴 ⇔

**🅰🅰🅰 ▼▼▼▼ Hawthorn Suites Hotel** 🆂🅷 ❀
(802) 860-1212. **$109-$245, 14 day notice.** 401 Dorset St. I-89, exit 14E, just e on US 2, then 0.8 mi s. Int corridors. **Pets:** Other species. $5 daily fee/room. Designated rooms.
🆂🅰🆅🅴 ✕ 🅖🅜 🅖 🖥 🖃 ⇔

**🅰🅰🅰 ▼▼▼▼ Holiday Inn Burlington** 🅻🅷
(802) 863-6363. **$129-$199.** 1068 Williston Rd. I-89, exit 14E, just e on US 2. Int corridors. **Pets:** $20 one-time fee/room. No service, supervision.
🆂🅰🆅🅴 🆂🚳 🅖🅜 ⊘ 🖥 🖃 ⇔

**🅰🅰🅰 ▼▼▼▼ MainStay Suites** 🆂🅷
(802) 846-1986. **$99-$189.** 1702 Shelburne Rd. I-89, exit 13 to US 7, then 1.5 mi s. Int corridors. **Pets:** Cats only. $25 one-time fee/room.
🆂🅰🆅🅴 🆂🚳 ✕ 🖥 🖃

**🅰🅰🅰 ▼▼▼▼ Sheraton Burlington Hotel & Conference Center** 🅻🅷
(802) 865-6600. **$129-$289.** 870 Williston Rd. I-89, exit 14W, just w on US 2. Int corridors. **Pets:** Accepted.
🆂🅰🆅🅴 🆂🚳 ✕ ⊘ 🖥 🖃 🍴 ⇔

**🅰🅰🅰 ▼▼▼▼ Smart Suites** 🆂🅷
(802) 860-9900. **$99-$189.** 1700 Shelburne Rd. I-89, exit 13 to US 7, then 1.5 mi s. Int corridors. **Pets:** Accepted.
🆂🅰🆅🅴 🆂🚳 ✕ 🖥 🖃

# SOUTH WOODSTOCK

**🅰🅰🅰 ▼▼▼ Kedron Valley Inn** 🅲🅸
(802) 457-1473. **$111-$250, 14 day notice.** Rt 106. Jct US 4, 5 mi s. Ext/int corridors. **Pets:** Other species. Designated rooms, supervision.
🆂🅰🆅🅴 ✕ 🖥 🖃 🍴 ✕ ☎

# SPRINGFIELD

**▼▼▼ The Hartness House** 🅲🅸
(802) 885-2115. **$99-$160, 7 day notice.** 30 Orchard St. 0.4 mi n on Summer St, bear left at old cemetery. Int corridors. **Pets:** Accepted.
🅰🆂🅺 ✕ 🖥 🍴 ⇔ ✕

**▼▼▼ Holiday Inn Express** 🆂🅸 ❀
(802) 885-4516. **$109-$189.** 818 Charlestown Rd. I-91, exit 7. Int corridors. **Pets:** Medium. $25 one-time fee/pet. Service with restrictions, supervision.
🅰🆂🅺 ✕ 🅖🅜 🅖 🖥 🖃 🍴 ⇔

# STOWE

**AAA** ▼▼▼ **1066 Ye Olde England Inne** **CI**
(802) 253-7558. **$89-$349, 15 day notice.** 433 Mountain Rd. 0.4 mi w on SR 108, from jct SR 100. Ext/int corridors. **Pets:** Large, other species. $10 daily fee/pet. Designated rooms, service with restrictions.
**SAVE** **S** **X** **&** **🔋** **📺** **🍴** **🏊** **X**

**AAA** ▼▼▼ **Andersen Lodge-An Austrian Inn** **CI**
(802) 253-7336. **$88-$198, 14 day notice.** 3430 Mountain Rd. 3.5 mi on SR 108, from jct SR 100. Int corridors. **Pets:** Medium. $10 one-time fee/pet. Designated rooms, service with restrictions, supervision.
**SAVE** **S** **X** **🔋** **🍴** **🏊** **X**

**AAA** ▼▼▼ **Commodores Inn** **LH**
(802) 253-7131. **$98-$198.** 823 S Main St. Jct SR 108, 0.8 mi s on SR 100. Int corridors. **Pets:** Other species. $10 one-time fee/room. Supervision.
**SAVE** **S** **X** **&** **🔋** **🍴** **🏊** **X**

▼▼▼ **Edson Hill Manor** **CI**
(802) 253-7371. **$159-$259, 15 day notice.** 1500 Edson Hill Rd. Jct SR 100, 3.5 mi w on SR 108, then 1.3 mi n. Ext/int corridors. **Pets:** Designated rooms, service with restrictions, supervision.
**X** **🍴** **🏊** **X**

▼▼ **Hob Knob Inn & Restaurant** **M**
(802) 253-8549. **$80-$240.** 2364 Mountain Rd. Jct SR 100, 2.5 mi w on SR 108. Ext/int corridors. **Pets:** $15 daily fee/pet. Designated rooms, service with restrictions, crate.
**ASK** **X** **🔋** **📺** **🍴** **🏊**

**AAA** ▼▼▼ **Honeywood Country Lodge** **M**
(802) 253-4124. **$79-$179, 15 day notice.** 4527 Mountain Rd. Jct SR 100, 4.5 mi w on SR 108. Ext corridors. **Pets:** Accepted.
**SAVE** **S** **X** **🔋** **📺** **🏊** **X**

**AAA** ▼▼▼ **Innsbruck Inn at Stowe** **M**
(802) 253-8582. **$74-$179, 15 day notice.** 4361 Mountain Rd. 4.5 mi w on SR 108, from jct SR 100. Ext/int corridors. **Pets:** Accepted.
**SAVE** **S** **X** **🔋** **📺** **🏊** **X**

**AAA** ▼▼▼▼ **The Mountain Road Resort at Stowe** **M**
(802) 253-4566. **$115-$260, 15 day notice.** 1007 Mountain Rd. 1 mi w on SR 108, from jct SR 100. Ext corridors. **Pets:** Medium, other species. $30 one-time fee/room. Supervision.
**SAVE** **S** **X** **🔋** **📺** **🏊** **X**

**AAA** ▼▼▼▼ **Ten Acres Lodge** **CI**
(802) 253-7638. **$89-$199, 14 day notice.** 14 Barrows Rd. Jct SR 100, 2.1 mi w on SR 108, then 0.5 mi s on Luce Hill Rd. Ext/int corridors. **Pets:** Designated rooms, service with restrictions, crate.
**SAVE** **X** **X**

**AAA** ▼▼▼▼ **Topnotch at Stowe Resort & Spa** **LH**
(802) 253-8585. **$245-$895, 14 day notice.** 4000 Mountain Rd. 4.2 mi w on SR 108, from jct SR 100. Ext/int corridors. **Pets:** Accepted.
**SAVE** **S** **X** **🔋** **📺** **🍴** **🏊** **X**

# WARREN

**AAA** ▼▼▼ **PowderHound Inn & Condominiums** **CO**
(802) 496-5100. **$84-$149, 14 day notice.** 203 Powderhound Rd. On SR 100, 0.3 mi s of jct Sugarbush Access Rd. Ext corridors. **Pets:** Other species. Designated rooms, supervision.
**SAVE** **X** **🔋** **📺** **🏊** **X**

# WEST BRATTLEBORO

▼ **Molly Stark Motel** **M** 🐾
(802) 254-2440. **$45-$85.** 829 Marlboro Rd. I-91, exit 2, 3.3 mi w on SR 9. Ext corridors. **Pets:** Large, dogs only. $5 daily fee/pet. Supervision.
**X** **🔋** **📺**

# WEST DOVER

▼▼▼ **Snow Goose Inn** **BB**
(802) 464-3984. **$115-$450, 14 day notice.** 259 Rt 100. 7.5 mi n on SR 100, from jct SR 9. Int corridors. **Pets:** Accepted.
**X** **🔋** **Z**

# WESTMORE

**AAA** ▼▼▼▼ **WilloughVale Inn on Lake Willoughby** **CI**
(802) 525-4123. **$85-$264, 14 day notice.** 793 VT Rt 5A. Just s on SR 5A, from jct SR 16. Ext/int corridors. **Pets:** Medium, dogs only. $20 daily fee/room. Service with restrictions, crate.
**SAVE** **S** **X** **🔋** **📺** **🍴** **X**

# WHITE RIVER JUNCTION

▼▼ **Comfort Inn** **SH**
(802) 295-3051. **$99-$199.** 56 Ralph Leehman Dr. I-91, exit 11, just e. Int corridors. **Pets:** Service with restrictions, supervision.
**ASK** **S** **X** **M** **🔋** **📺** **🏊**

▼▼ **Econo Lodge** **SH**
(802) 295-3015. **$69-$159.** 91 Ballardvale Dr. Jct I-89 and 91. Int corridors. **Pets:** Accepted.
**ASK** **S** **X** **🔋** **📺** **🏊** **X**

# WILLIAMSTOWN

▼▼ **Autumn Harvest Inn** **CI**
(802) 433-1355. **$89-$149, 14 day notice.** 118 Clark Rd. I-89, exit 5, 2.1 mi e on SR 64. Int corridors. **Pets:** Accepted.
**ASK** **X** **🍴** **X**

# WILLISTON

▼▼▼ **Residence Inn by Marriott** **SH** 🐾
(802) 878-2001. **$114-$239, 30 day notice.** 35 Hurricane Ln. I-89, exit 12, just s on SR 2A, then just e. Ext corridors. **Pets:** Other species. $75 one-time fee/room. Service with restrictions.
**ASK** **S** **X** **🔋** **📺** **🏊** **X**

▼▼▼ **TownePlace Suites by Marriott** **SH**
(802) 872-5900. **$99-$189.** 66 Zephyr Rd. I-89, exit 12, 1.1 mi n on SR 2A. Int corridors. **Pets:** Accepted.
**ASK** **S** **X** **M** **&** **🔋** **📺** **🏊**

# WOODSTOCK

**AAA** ▼ **Braeside Motel** **M**
(802) 457-1366. **$78-$118, 15 day notice.** 432 US 4 E (Woodstock Rd). 1 mi e. Ext corridors. **Pets:** Dogs only. $20 daily fee/pet. Designated rooms, service with restrictions, supervision.
**SAVE** **X** **🔋** **🏊**

▼▼▼ **The Winslow House** **BB**
(802) 457-1820. **$100-$175, 14 day notice.** 492 Woodstock Rd. 1.3 mi w on US 4. Int corridors. **Pets:** Accepted.
**ASK** **S** **X** **🔋**

# VIRGINIA

## ABINGDON

**Holiday Inn Express** SH
(276) 676-2829. **$76-$91.** 940 E Main St. I-81, exit 19 (US 11). Int corridors. **Pets:** Small, other species. $10 daily fee/room. Service with restrictions, crate.

**Quality Inn & Suites of Abingdon** SH
(276) 676-9090. **$80-$99.** 930 E Main St. I-81, exit 19 (US 11), just w. Int corridors. **Pets:** Accepted.

**Super 8 Motel of Abingdon** M
(276) 676-3329. **$55-$190.** 298 Towne Centre Dr. I-81, exit 17, just ne. Int corridors. **Pets:** $10 one-time fee/pet. Service with restrictions, supervision.

## ALTAVISTA

**Comfort Suites Hotel** SH
(434) 369-4000. **$77-$144.** 1558 Main St. US 29 business route, at jct US 29. Int corridors. **Pets:** Large, other species. $10 one-time fee/room. Designated rooms, service with restrictions, supervision.

## APPOMATTOX

**Super 8 Motel** M
(434) 352-2339. **$56-$66.** Rt 4, Box 100. US 460, just w of jct US 26. Int corridors. **Pets:** Accepted.

## BEDFORD

**Days Inn** SH
(540) 586-8286. **$42-$73.** 921 Blue Ridge Ave. Jct US 221, 1.5 mi w on US 460. Ext corridors. **Pets:** $7 daily fee/pet. Service with restrictions.

## BIG STONE GAP

**Country Inn Motel** M
(276) 523-0374. **$54.** 627 Gilley Ave. US 23, 1 mi w on US 23 business route and 58A. Ext corridors. **Pets:** $3 daily fee/pet. Service with restrictions, supervision.

## BLACKSBURG

**Comfort Inn** SH
(540) 951-1500. **$65-$100, 7 day notice.** 3705 S Main St. 3.5 mi s on US 460, jct US 460 Bypass. Int corridors. **Pets:** Service with restrictions, supervision.

## BRISTOL

**Econo Lodge** M
(276) 466-2112. **$69-$350.** 912 Commonwealth Ave. I-81, exit 3, 1.5 mi e. Ext corridors. **Pets:** Accepted.

**Holiday Inn Hotel & Suites** LH
(276) 466-4100. **$90-$99.** 3005 Linden Dr. I-81, exit 7, just w. Int corridors. **Pets:** Large. $10 daily fee/room. Designated rooms, service with restrictions, supervision.

**Knights Inn** M
(276) 591-5090. **$40.** 2221 Euclid Ave. I-81, exit 1, just e. Ext corridors. **Pets:** Small, dogs only. $10 daily fee/pet. Service with restrictions, supervision.

**La Quinta Inn Bristol** SH
(276) 669-9353. **$71-$115.** 1014 Old Airport Rd. I-81, exit 7, just e. Ext corridors. **Pets:** Medium. Service with restrictions.

**Microtel Inn & Suites** SH
(276) 669-8164. **$54-$74.** 131 Bristol Rd E. I-81, exit 7 northbound, just w; exit southbound, just e. Int corridors. **Pets:** Small. $10 one-time fee/pet. Designated rooms, service with restrictions, supervision.

**Motel 6 #4125** SH
(276) 466-6060. **$59-$200.** 21561 Clear Creek Rd. I-81, exit 7, 0.3 mi w. Int corridors. **Pets:** Accepted.

**Super 8 Motel** SH
(276) 466-8800. **$45-$289.** 2139 Lee Hwy. I-81, exit 5, just s. Int corridors. **Pets:** Accepted.

# BUENA VISTA

**Ⓐ ▼ Buena Vista Motel Ⓜ**
(540) 261-2138. **$40-$75.** 447 E 29th St. I-81, exit 188A, 4.3 mi e on US 60, then 0.4 mi w of Blue Ridge Pkwy. Ext corridors. **Pets:** Accepted.
Ⓢ Ⓢ Ⓧ Ⓗ Ⓟ

# BURKEVILLE

**Ⓐ ▼▼▼ Comfort Inn Burkeville Ⓢ ❀**
(434) 767-3750. **$75-$165.** 419 N Agnew St. On US 460, just e of jct US 360. Int corridors. **Pets:** Very small. $20 one-time fee/pet. Service with restrictions, supervision.
Ⓢ Ⓢ Ⓧ Ⓖ Ⓗ Ⓟ Ⓨ Ⓡ

# CAPE CHARLES

**Ⓐ ▼▼▼▼ Best Western Sunset Beach Resort Ⓢ**
(757) 331-1776. **$70-$140.** 32246 Lankford Hwy. US 13, just n of the Chesapeake Bay Bridge Tunnel. Ext corridors. **Pets:** Other species. $10 daily fee/pet. No service, supervision.
Ⓢ Ⓢ Ⓧ Ⓖ Ⓗ Ⓟ Ⓨ Ⓡ Ⓧ

# CHARLOTTESVILLE

**Ⓐ ▼▼▼▼ Comfort Inn Ⓢ ❀**
(434) 293-6188. **$69-$109.** 1807 Emmet St. Jct US 250 Bypass, just n on US 29. Int corridors. **Pets:** Other species. $10 daily fee/room. Designated rooms, service with restrictions, supervision.
Ⓢ Ⓢ Ⓧ Ⓩ Ⓖ Ⓗ Ⓟ Ⓡ

**Ⓐ ▼▼▼▼ Days Inn University Area Ⓢ**
(434) 293-9111. **$59-$190.** 1600 Emmet St. I-64, exit 118B (US 29), just n of jct US 250 Bypass. Ext corridors. **Pets:** Other species. $10 daily fee/pet. Service with restrictions, crate.
Ⓢ Ⓢ Ⓧ Ⓗ Ⓟ Ⓨ Ⓡ

**▼▼▼▼ Doubletree Hotel Charlottesville Ⓢ**
(434) 973-2121. **$84-$159.** 990 Hilton Heights Rd. I-64, exit 118B (US 29), 4 mi n of jct US 250 Bypass. Int corridors. **Pets:** Accepted.
Ⓐ Ⓢ Ⓧ Ⓩ Ⓖ Ⓗ Ⓟ Ⓨ Ⓡ Ⓧ

**ⒶⒶ ▼ Econo Lodge-University Ⓜ**
(434) 296-2104. **$52-$175.** 400 Emmet St. Jct US 250 Bypass, 1 mi s on US 29 business route. Ext corridors. **Pets:** Accepted.
Ⓢ Ⓢ Ⓧ Ⓩ Ⓗ Ⓟ Ⓡ

**▼▼▼ Holiday Inn-Monticello/Charlottesville Ⓛ ❀**
(434) 977-5100. **$90-$149.** 1200 5th St SW. I-64, exit 120, just n on SR 631. Int corridors. **Pets:** $15 daily fee/pet. Supervision.
Ⓐ Ⓢ Ⓧ Ⓩ Ⓗ Ⓟ Ⓡ

**ⒶⒶ ▼▼▼▼ Omni Charlottesville Hotel Ⓛ**
(434) 971-5500. **$124-$199.** 235 W Main St. I-64, exit 120, 2.3 mi n on SR 631; downtown. Int corridors. **Pets:** Small, dogs only. $50 one-time fee/room. Designated rooms, service with restrictions, crate.
Ⓢ Ⓢ Ⓧ Ⓗ Ⓟ Ⓨ Ⓡ Ⓧ

**ⒶⒶ ▼▼▼▼ Quality Inn-University Area Ⓢ**
(434) 971-3746. **$59-$190.** 1600 Emmet St. US 29 (Emmet St), just n of jct US 250 Bypass, just e on Holiday Dr. Ext corridors. **Pets:** Other species. $10 daily fee/pet. Service with restrictions, crate.
Ⓢ Ⓢ Ⓧ Ⓗ Ⓟ

**▼▼▼▼ Red Roof Inn of Charlottesville Ⓢ**
(434) 295-4333. **$74-$100.** 1309 W Main St. US 29 (Emmet St), 1 mi e on US 250 (University Ave). Int corridors. **Pets:** Accepted.
Ⓧ Ⓩ Ⓖ Ⓗ

**▼▼▼▼ Residence Inn by Marriott Ⓢ**
(434) 923-0300. **$94-$184.** 1111 Millmont St. I-64, exit 118B (US 29), 2.5 mi n on US 29/250 E, just s on Barracks Rd, then just se. Int corridors. **Pets:** $200 one-time fee/room. Service with restrictions, crate.
Ⓐ Ⓢ Ⓧ Ⓖ Ⓗ Ⓟ Ⓡ Ⓧ

**ⒶⒶ ▼▼▼ Sleep Inn & Suites Monticello Ⓢ**
(434) 244-9969. **$83-$119.** 1185 5th St. I-64, exit 120, just n. Int corridors. **Pets:** Other species. $10 daily fee/pet. Service with restrictions.
Ⓢ Ⓢ Ⓧ Ⓖ Ⓗ Ⓟ Ⓡ

**ⒶⒶ ▼▼▼ Super 8 Motel/Charlottesville Ⓢ**
(434) 973-0888. **$49-$109.** 390 Greenbrier Dr. US 29 (Emmet St), 1 mi n of US 250 Bypass. Int corridors. **Pets:** Accepted.
Ⓢ Ⓢ Ⓧ

# CHRISTIANSBURG

**ⒶⒶ ▼▼▼ Econo Lodge Ⓜ**
(540) 382-6161. **$44-$169.** 2430 Roanoke St. I-81, exit 118, just w on US 11/460. Ext corridors. **Pets:** Accepted.
Ⓢ Ⓢ Ⓧ Ⓖ Ⓗ Ⓟ Ⓡ

**▼▼▼ Quality Inn Ⓢ ❀**
(540) 382-2055. **$66-$79, 7 day notice.** 50 Hampton Blvd. I-81, exit 118C, just e. Ext corridors. **Pets:** Other species. $10 daily fee/room. Service with restrictions.
Ⓐ Ⓢ Ⓧ Ⓗ Ⓟ

**▼▼▼ Super 8 Motel-Christiansburg West Ⓢ**
(540) 382-5813. **$57-$62, 14 day notice.** 55 Laurel St NE. I-81, exit 118, 1 mi w on US 11/460, then 3.5 mi nw on US 460 Bypass; jct SR 114. Int corridors. **Pets:** Accepted.
Ⓢ Ⓧ Ⓗ

# CLARKSVILLE

**▼▼▼ Best Western On The Lake Ⓢ**
(434) 374-5023. **$69-$114, 3 day notice.** 103 Second St. Just n of US 58. Int corridors. **Pets:** Other species. $100 deposit/pet, $10 daily fee/pet, $20 one-time fee/pet. Designated rooms, service with restrictions.
Ⓐ Ⓢ Ⓧ Ⓖ Ⓗ Ⓟ Ⓡ

# COLLINSVILLE

**ⒶⒶ ▼▼▼ Knights Inn Ⓜ**
(276) 647-3716. **$60-$70.** 2357 Virginia Ave. Jct US 58, 3 mi n on US 220 business route. Ext corridors. **Pets:** Designated rooms, service with restrictions, supervision.
Ⓢ Ⓢ Ⓧ Ⓗ Ⓡ

**▼▼▼ Quality Inn-Dutch Inn Hotel and Convention Center Ⓢ**
(276) 647-3721. **$75-$300.** 2360 Virginia Ave. Jct US 58, 3 mi n on US 220 business route. Ext corridors. **Pets:** Accepted.
Ⓐ Ⓢ Ⓧ Ⓗ Ⓟ Ⓨ Ⓡ

# COVINGTON

**▼▼▼ Best Western Mountain View Ⓢ**
(540) 962-4951. **$98-$134.** 820 E Madison St. I-64, exit 16, just n. Ext corridors. **Pets:** Medium, other species. $12 one-time fee/room. Service with restrictions, supervision.
Ⓐ Ⓢ Ⓧ Ⓗ Ⓟ Ⓨ Ⓡ

**▼▼▼ Compare Inn & Suites Ⓢ**
(540) 962-2141. **$93-$105.** 203 Interstate Dr. I-64, exit 16, just sw. Int corridors. **Pets:** Large, other species. $12 one-time fee/room. Service with restrictions, supervision.
Ⓐ Ⓢ Ⓧ Ⓗ Ⓟ Ⓡ

# CULPEPER

**▼▼ Comfort Inn-Culpeper Ⓢ**
(540) 825-4900. **$79-$129.** 890 Willis Ln. 2 mi s on US 29 business route; jct US 29, then just e. Ext corridors. **Pets:** Small. $20 daily fee/pet. Designated rooms, no service, crate.
Ⓐ Ⓢ Ⓧ Ⓩ Ⓖ Ⓗ Ⓟ Ⓡ

# DAHLGREN

### ▼▼▼ Comfort Inn-Dahlgren 🆂🅷
(540) 663-3060. **$60-$82.** 4661 James Madison Pkwy. US 301; 2 mi s of entrance to US Navy Surface Weapons Center; 4 mi s of Potomac River Bridge. Int corridors. **Pets:** Small. $20 daily fee/pet. Designated rooms, no service, crate.

🅰🆂🅺 🆂🅳 ⊠ 🕭 🖉 🖉 🔋 🖵 🏊

# DALEVILLE

### ▼▼▼ Howard Johnson Express Inn 🆂🅷
(540) 992-1234. **$55-$92, 5 day notice.** 437 Roanoke Rd. I-81, exit 150B, just nw on US 220. Ext corridors. **Pets:** $15 one-time fee/room. Designated rooms, service with restrictions, supervision.

🅰🆂🅺 🆂🅳 ⊠ 🖉 🔋 🖵 🏊 ⊠

# DANVILLE

### ▼▼▼ Comfort Inn & Suites 🆂🅷
(434) 793-2000. **$84-$129.** 100 Tower Dr. US 58, just w of jct US 29 business route. Int corridors. **Pets:** Other species. $10 daily fee/room. Designated rooms, service with restrictions, supervision.

🅰🆂🅺 🆂🅳 ⊠ 🔋 🖵 🍴 🏊

---

# DISTRICT OF COLUMBIA METROPOLITAN AREA

# ALEXANDRIA

### ▼▼▼ Alexandria Hotel Pentagon South 🅻🅷
(703) 751-4510. **$149-$259.** 4641 Kenmore Ave. I-395, exit 4, 0.8 mi s of jct SR 7. Int corridors. **Pets:** Accepted.

🅰🆂🅺 🆂🅳 ⊠ 🖉 🖉 🔋 🖵 🍴 🏊

### 🅰🅰🅰 ▼▼▼ Embassy Suites-Alexandria-Old Town 🅻🅷 🐾
(703) 684-5900. **$149-$289.** 1900 Diagonal Rd. I-95/495, exit 176, 0.5 mi n on SR 241 N, then 0.5 mi e on SR 236. Int corridors. **Pets:** Medium. $25 daily fee/pet. Designated rooms, service with restrictions, crate.

🆂🅰🆅🅴 ⊠ 🖉 🖉 🔋 🖵 🍴 🏊 ⊠

### ▼▼ Hawthorn Suites LTD-Alexandria 🆂🅷
(703) 370-1000. **$99-$179.** 420 N Van Dorn St. I-395, exit 3A, 0.3 mi e on SR 236 to S Van Dorn St, then 0.5 mi n. Int corridors. **Pets:** Accepted.

🅰🆂🅺 🆂🅳 ⊠ 🖉 🖉 🔋 🖵 🏊

### ▼▼▼ Hilton Alexandria Old Town 🅻🅷
(703) 837-0440. **$149-$329.** 1767 King St. I-95/495, exit 176B, 0.5 mi n on SR 241, 0.5 mi e on SR 236, then just ne on Diagonal Rd. Int corridors. **Pets:** Accepted.

⊠ 🖉 🖉 🔋 🖵 🍴 🏊

### 🅰🅰🅰 ▼▼▼ Holiday Inn Hotel & Suites-Historic District Alexandria 🅻🅷
(703) 548-6300. **$159-$279.** 625 1st St. George Washington Memorial Pkwy; just e of jct 1st and Washington sts. Int corridors. **Pets:** Accepted.

🆂🅰🆅🅴 🆂🅳 ⊠ 🖉 🖉 🔋 🖵 🍴 🏊 ⊠

### 🅰🅰🅰 ▼▼▼ Holiday Inn Select-Old Town 🅻🅷
(703) 549-6080. **$209-$249.** 480 King St. On SR 7; between S Pitt and S Royal sts; just sw of City Hall. Int corridors. **Pets:** Accepted.

🆂🅰🆅🅴 🆂🅳 ⊠ 🖉 🖉 🖵 🍴 🏊 ⊠

### ▼▼ Homestead Studio Suites Hotel-Alexandria 🆂🅷
(703) 329-3399. **$114-$120.** 200 Bluestone Rd. I-95/495, exit 174 (Eisenhower Ave Connector), just n to Eisenhower Ave, then 1.2 mi e. Int corridors. **Pets:** $25 daily fee/pet. Service with restrictions, supervision.

🅰🆂🅺 🆂🅳 ⊠ 🖪🅼 🖉 🖉 🔋 🖵

### ▼▼ Innkeeper Danville North 🅼
(434) 836-1700. **$52-$58, 3 day notice.** 1030 Piney Forest Rd. US 29 N business route, 0.5 mi n of US 58. Ext corridors. **Pets:** Small. Service with restrictions, crate.

🅰🆂🅺 🆂🅳 ⊠ 🔋 🏊

### ▼▼ Ramada Inn Stratford 🆂🅷
(434) 793-2500. **$65-$128.** 2500 Riverside Dr. US 58, just e of jct US 29 business route. Ext corridors. **Pets:** Accepted.

🅰🆂🅺 🆂🅳 ⊠ 🖪🅼 🖉 🔋 🖵 🍴 🏊

### ▼ Super 8 Motel 🅼
(434) 799-5845. **$75-$200.** 2385 Riverside Dr. On US 58, just e of jct US 29 business route. Int corridors. **Pets:** Medium. $20 one-time fee/pet. Designated rooms, service with restrictions, supervision.

🅰🆂🅺 🆂🅳 ⊠ 🔋

### ▼▼ Red Roof Inn-Alexandria 🅼
(703) 960-5200. **$81-$99.** 5975 Richmond Hwy. I-95/495, exit 177A, 0.5 mi s on US 1. Ext corridors. **Pets:** Accepted.

⊠ 🖪🅼 🖉 🖉 🔋

### 🅰🅰🅰 ▼▼▼ Residence Inn by Marriott Alexandria-Old Town 🆂🅷
(703) 548-5474. **$139-$459.** 1456 Duke St. I-95/495, exit 176, 0.5 mi n on SR 241, then 0.7 mi e on SR 236. Int corridors. **Pets:** Medium. $150 one-time fee/pet. Service with restrictions, supervision.

🆂🅰🆅🅴 ⊠ 🆂🅳 🖪🅼 🖉 🖉 🔋 🖵 🏊

### 🅰🅰🅰 ▼▼▼ Sheraton Suites Alexandria 🅻🅷
(703) 836-4700. **$119-$279.** 801 N St Asaph St. Just e of Washington St. Int corridors. **Pets:** Accepted.

🆂🅰🆅🅴 ⊠ 🖉 🖉 🔋 🖵 🍴 🏊

### 🅰🅰🅰 ▼▼▼ Washington Suites-Alexandria 🆂🅷
(703) 370-9600. **$99-$229.** 100 S Reynolds St. I-395, exit 3A, 0.8 mi e on SR 236 E (Duke St), then just s; near a shopping center. Int corridors. **Pets:** Accepted.

🆂🅰🆅🅴 🆂🅳 ⊠ 🖪🅼 🖉 🖉 🔋 🖵 🍴 🏊

# ARLINGTON

### 🅰🅰🅰 ▼▼ The Arlington Residence Court a Clarion Collection 🅻🅷
(703) 524-4000. **$119-$199.** 1200 N Courthouse Rd. 1.5 mi sw of Theodore Roosevelt Bridge on US 50. Ext/int corridors. **Pets:** Accepted.

🆂🅰🆅🅴 🆂🅳 ⊠ 🖉 🖉 🔋 🖵 🍴 🏊

### 🅰🅰🅰 ▼▼▼ Best Western Washington Key Bridge 🆂🅷
(703) 522-0400. **$79-$189.** 1850 N Fort Myer Dr. I-66, exit 73, just sw of Key Bridge. Int corridors. **Pets:** Medium. $50 one-time fee/pet. Designated rooms, service with restrictions, crate.

🆂🅰🆅🅴 ⊠ 🔋 🖵 🏊

### 🅰🅰🅰 ▼▼▼ Residence Inn by Marriott-Pentagon City 🆂🅷
(703) 413-6630. **$129-$259.** 550 Army Navy Dr. I-395, exit 8C, just 1 mi s of 14th St Bridge. Int corridors. **Pets:** $8 daily fee/room, $200 one-time fee/room. Service with restrictions, supervision.

🆂🅰🆅🅴 🆂🅳 ⊠ 🖪🅼 🖉 🖉 🔋 🖵 🏊

▼▼ ▼▼ The Ritz-Carlton, Pentagon City 🏠
(703) 415-5000. **$299-$689.** 1250 S Hayes St. 1 mi s of 14th St Bridge.
Int corridors. **Pets:** Accepted.

(ASK) (S♦) (X) (L♦M) (♪) (L♦) (♦) (🍴) (🏊) (X)

▼▼▼▼ Sheraton Crystal City Hotel 🏠 🐾
(703) 486-1111. **$109-$329.** 1800 Jefferson Davis Hwy. I-395, exit 8C,
1.4 mi s of 14th St Bridge on US 1; hotel entrance corner of Eads St.
Int corridors. **Pets:** Medium, dogs only. Service with restrictions, supervision.

(ASK) (X) (♪) (L♦) (♦) (♦) (🍴) (🏊)

▼▼▼ Sheraton National Hotel 🏠
(703) 521-1900. **$89-$289.** 900 S Orme St. I-395, exit 8A, at jct SR 27
and 244; 1.3 mi s of 14th St Bridge. Int corridors. **Pets:** Accepted.

(ASK) (S♦) (X) (♦) (♦) (🍴) (🏊)

# ASHBURN

▼▼▼▼ Homewood Suites by Hilton-Dulles North 🖳 🐾
(703) 723-7500. **$89-$279.** 44620 Waxpool Rd. 1.7 mi w of Jct SR 28
and Waxpool Rd. Int corridors. **Pets:** Medium, other species. $25 daily
fee/room. Service with restrictions, crate.

(ASK) (X) (♦) (♦) (🏊)

# CHANTILLY

🅰🅰🅰 ▼▼▼▼ AmeriSuites (Dulles Airport
South/Chantilly) 🖳
(703) 961-8160. **$79-$219.** 4994 Westone Plaza Dr. I-66, exit 53, 2 mi
n on SR 28, just w on Westfields Blvd; 1.7 mi s of jct SR 28 and US
50. Int corridors. **Pets:** Accepted.

(SAVE) (X) (♪) (L♦) (♦) (♦) (🏊)

▼▼▼ Extended Stay Deluxe 🖳
(703) 263-7200. **$69-$135.** 4506 Brookfield Corporate Dr. I-66, exit 53,
3 mi n on SR 28; 1 mi s of jct SR 28 and US 50. Int corridors.
**Pets:** $25 daily fee/pet. Service with restrictions, supervision.

(ASK) (S♦) (X) (L♦M) (♪) (L♦) (♦) (♦) (🏊)

▼▼▼ Holiday Inn Select Chantilly-Dulles Expo
Center 🏠
(703) 815-6060. **$199-$350.** 4335 Chantilly Shopping Center. I-66, exit
53, 3 mi n on SR 28; 1 mi s of jct US 50 and SR 28. Int corridors.
**Pets:** Other species. $75 one-time fee/room. Service with restrictions, crate.

(ASK) (S♦) (X) (L♦M) (♪) (L♦) (♦) (♦) (🍴) (🏊)

▼▼▼ Staybridge Suites Hotel Chantilly/Dulles International
Airport 🖳 🐾
(703) 435-8090. **$19C-$495.** 3860 Centerview Dr. Jct SR 28, just e on
US 50. Int corridors. **Pets:** Small, other species. $150 one-time fee/room.
Designated rooms, crate.

(ASK) (S♦) (X) (L♦M) (♪) (L♦) (♦) (♦) (🏊)

▼▼▼ TownePlace Suites by Marriott-Chantilly 🖳
(703) 709-0453. **$125-$152.** 14036 Thunderbolt Pl. Jct SR 28, just e on
US 50. Int corridors. **Pets:** Accepted.

(ASK) (S♦) (X) (L♦) (♦) (♦) (🏊)

# DUMFRIES

🅰🅰🅰 ▼▼▼ Quality Inn 🖳
(703) 221-1141. **$69-$109.** 17133 Dumfries Rd. I-95, exit 152B, just w
on SR 234 N. Ext/int corridors. **Pets:** Medium. $10 daily fee/pet. Designated rooms, crate.

(SAVE) (S♦) (X) (♪) (♦) (♦) (🏊)

# FAIRFAX

▼▼ ▼ Candlewood Suites Fairfax-Washington, D.C. 🖳
(703) 359-4490. **Call for rates.** 11400 Random Hills Rd. I-66, exit 57A,
0.5 mi e on US 50, just s on Waples Mill Rd, then 0.4 mi w. Int
corridors. **Pets:** Accepted.

(X) (L♦M) (L♦) (♦) (♦)

🅰🅰🅰 ▼▼▼▼ Comfort Inn University Center 🖳
(703) 591-5900. **$79-$99.** 11180 Main St. I-66, exit 57A, 0.8 mi se on
US 50, 0.5 mi nw of jct US 29. Int corridors. **Pets:** Other species.
Service with restrictions.

(SAVE) (S♦) (X) (♦) (♦) (🍴) (🏊) (X)

▼▼ ▼▼ Homestead Studio Suites Hotel-Fair Oaks 🖳
(703) 273-3444. **$114-$124.** 12104 Monument Dr. I-66, exit 57B, 0.8 mi
w on US 50, 0.3 mi s on SR 620 (West Ox Rd), then just se. Ext
corridors. **Pets:** $25 daily fee/pet. Service with restrictions, supervision.

(ASK) (S♦) (X) (L♦M) (♪) (L♦) (♦) (♦)

▼▼ ▼▼ Homestead Studio Suites Hotel-Falls
Church/Merrifield 🖳
(703) 204-0088. **$124-$134.** 8281 Willow Oaks Corporate Dr. I-495, exit
50A, just w on US 50 to Gallows Rd, then just s. Ext corridors.
**Pets:** $25 daily fee/pet. Service with restrictions, supervision.

(ASK) (S♦) (X) (L♦M) (L♦) (♦) (♦)

▼▼▼▼ Residence Inn by Marriott-Fair Lakes 🖳
(703) 266-4900. **$99-$219.** 12815 Fair Lakes Pkwy. I-66, exit 55 (Fairfax County Pkwy N), just w. Int corridors. **Pets:** Accepted.

(ASK) (X) (L♦M) (♪) (L♦) (♦) (♦) (🏊) (X)

# FALLS CHURCH

▼▼▼▼ Fairfax-Merrifield Residence Inn by Marriott 🖳
(703) 573-5200. **$219-$299.** 8125 Gatehouse Rd. I-495, exit 50A, just
w to SR 640 N. Int corridors. **Pets:** $150 one-time fee/room.

(ASK) (X) (L♦M) (♪) (L♦) (♦) (♦) (🏊) (X)

▼▼▼▼ Homewood Suites by Hilton-Falls Church 🖳 🐾
(703) 560-6644. **$142-$246.** 8130 Porter Rd. I-495, exit 50A, just w to
SR 650; 0.4 mi n of SR 650. Int corridors. **Pets:** Medium, dogs only.
$100 one-time fee/room. Service with restrictions, crate.

(ASK) (S♦) (X) (♪) (L♦) (♦) (♦) (🏊)

▼▼▼▼ TownePlace Suites by Marriott-Falls Church 🖳
(703) 237-6172. **$109-$199.** 205 Hillwood Ave. I-495, exit 50B, 2.5 mi e
on US 50, 0.6 mi n on Annandale Rd, then e. Int corridors.
**Pets:** Accepted.

(ASK) (S♦) (X) (L♦M) (L♦) (♦) (♦)

# HERNDON

▼▼ ▼▼ Candlewood Suites Washington-Dulles Herndon 🖳
(703) 793-7100. **$179-$209.** 13845 Sunrise Valley Dr. SR 28, 0.4 mi e
on Frying Pan Rd, 0.6 mi nw. Int corridors. **Pets:** Accepted.

(ASK) (S♦) (X) (♦) (♦) (🏊)

▼▼▼▼ Hawthorn Suites Herndon 🖳
(703) 437-5000. **$99-$185.** 467 Herndon Pkwy. SR 267 (Dulles Toll
Rd), exit 11 (Fairfax County Pkwy). Int corridors. **Pets:** Accepted.

(ASK) (S♦) (X) (♪) (L♦) (♦) (♦) (🏊) (X)

🅰🅰🅰 ▼▼▼▼ Hilton Washington Dulles Airport 🏠
(703) 478-2900. **$89-$359, 3 day notice.** 13869 Park Center Rd. SR
267 (Dulles Toll Rd), exit 9, 3 mi s on SR 28; in a business park area.
Int corridors. **Pets:** Accepted.

(SAVE) (X) (♪) (L♦) (♦) (♦) (🍴) (🏊) (X)

▼▼▼▼ Homewood Suites by Hilton 🖳
(703) 793-1700. **$99-$350, 15 day notice.** 13460 Sunrise Valley Dr. SR
267 (Dulles Toll Rd), exit 10, 0.5 mi s on SR 657, then just w. Int
corridors. **Pets:** Medium. $150 one-time fee/room. Designated rooms, service with restrictions, crate.

(ASK) (S♦) (X) (L♦M) (♪) (L♦) (♦) (♦) (🏊)

🅰🅰🅰 ▼▼▼▼ Residence Inn by
Marriott-Herndon/Reston 🖳
(703) 435-0044. **$89-$289.** 315 Elden St. 0.5 mi e on SR 606. Int
corridors. **Pets:** $75 one-time fee/room. Service with restrictions, crate.

(SAVE) (X) (♪) (♦) (♦) (🏊) (X)

▼▼▼▼ **Staybridge Suites Herndon Dulles** SH
(703) 713-6800. **$85-$299.** 13700 Coppermine Rd. SR 267 (Dulles Toll Rd), exit 10, 0.7 mi s on Centreville Rd (SR 657), then 0.4 mi w. Ext corridors. **Pets:** Medium. $250 one-time fee/room. Service with restrictions, crate.

ASK 🔊 ✕ 🗲 🖪 🖵 🖘 ⊠

## LEESBURG

AAA ▼▼▼▼ **Best Western Leesburg Hotel & Conference Center** SH
(703) 777-9400. **$85-$125.** 726 E Market St. 0.5 mi e on SR 7 business route. Int corridors. **Pets:** Accepted.

SAVE 🔊 ✕ 🖪 🖵 🖘

▼▼▼ **Holiday Inn at Carradoc Hall** SH
(703) 771-9200. **$99-$139.** 1500 E Market St. 2 mi e on SR 7. Int corridors. **Pets:** Medium. $25 daily fee/room. Service with restrictions, supervision.

ASK 🔊 ✕ 🗲M 🗲 🖪 🖵 🍴 🖘

## LORTON

▼▼▼▼ **Comfort Inn Gunston Corner** SH
(703) 643-3100. **$89-$129.** 8180 Silverbrook Rd. I-95, exit 163, just w. Int corridors. **Pets:** Accepted.

ASK 🔊 ✕ 🗲 🗲 🖪 🖵 🖘 ⊠

## MANASSAS

AAA ▼▼▼ **Best Western Battlefield Inn** SH
(703) 361-8000. **$89-$175.** 10820 Balls Ford Rd. I-66, exit 47A westbound; exit 47 eastbound, just s on SR 234, then just w. Ext corridors. **Pets:** Medium, dogs only. $10 daily fee/pet. Service with restrictions, supervision.

SAVE 🔊 ✕ 🗲 🖪 🖵 🍴 🖘

▼▼▼ **Red Roof Inn-Manassas** M
(703) 335-9333. **$75-$90.** 10610 Automotive Dr. I-66, exit 47 eastbound; exit 47A westbound, just s on SR 234, then just e on Balls Ford Rd. Ext corridors. **Pets:** Accepted.

✕ 🗲 🗲 🖪

## MCLEAN

AAA ▼▼▼ **Best Western Tysons Westpark Hotel** LH
(703) 734-2800. **$79-$199.** 8401 Westpark Dr. I-495, exit 47A, 1.3 mi w on SR 7. Int corridors. **Pets:** Accepted.

SAVE 🔊 ✕ 🗲M 🗲 🗲 🖪 🖵 🖘 ⊠

AAA ▼▼▼▼ **Holiday Inn Tysons Corner** LH ❀
(703) 893-2100. **$99-$279.** 1960 Chain Bridge Rd. I-495, exit 46A, 0.5 mi s on SR 123, just nw on International Dr, then just sw on Greensboro Dr. Int corridors. **Pets:** Small. $40 one-time fee/room. Designated rooms, service with restrictions, crate.

SAVE 🔊 ✕ 🗲M 🗲 🖪 🖵 🍴 🖘 ⊠

▼▼▼▼ **Staybridge Suites-McLean/Tysons Corner** SH
(703) 448-5400. **$219-$399.** 6845 Old Dominion Dr. I-495, exit 46B, 2 mi n on SR 123, then 0.3 mi e on SR 309. Int corridors. **Pets:** Medium. $75 one-time fee/room. Designated rooms, service with restrictions, supervision.

ASK 🔊 ✕ 🗲M 🗲 🗲 🖪 🖵 🖘

## RESTON

▼▼▼ **Homestead Studio Suites Hotel-Reston** SH
(703) 707-9700. **$140-$145.** 12190 Sunset Hills Rd. SR 267 (Dulles Toll Rd), exit 12 (Reston Pkwy), just n, then just w. Ext corridors. **Pets:** $25 daily fee/pet. Service with restrictions, supervision.

ASK 🔊 ✕ 🗲 🖪 🖵

▼▼▼▼ **Sheraton Reston Hotel** SH
(703) 620-9000. **$75-$299.** 11810 Sunrise Valley Dr. SR 267 (Dulles Toll Rd), exit 12 (Reston Pkwy), just s. Int corridors. **Pets:** Accepted.

ASK 🔊 ✕ 🗲 🖪 🖵 🍴 🖘

## SPRINGFIELD

▼▼▼ **Comfort Inn Washington DC/Springfield** SH
(703) 922-9000. **$119-$149.** 6560 Loisdale Ct. I-95, exit 169A, just e on SR 644 E; jct I-395 and 495, 0.8 mi s. Int corridors. **Pets:** Accepted.

ASK 🔊 ✕ 🗲 🗲 🖪 🖵

▼▼▼ **Hampton Inn Washington DC/Springfield** SH
(703) 924-9444. **$129-$149.** 6550 Loisdale Ct. I-95, exit 169A, just e on SR 644 E; jct I-395 and 495, 0.8 mi s. nt corridors. **Pets:** Accepted.

ASK 🔊 ✕ 🗲M 🗲 🗲 🖪 🖵 🖘

▼▼▼ **Red Roof Inn Springfield** SH
(703) 644-5311. **$82-$97.** 6868 Springfield Blvd. I-95, exit 169B, just sw of SR 644; jct I-395 and 495, 0.8 mi s. Int corridors. **Pets:** Accepted.

✕ 🗲M 🗲 🖪

▼▼▼▼ **TownePlace Suites by Marriott Springfield** SH
(703) 569-8060. **$170-$200.** 6245 Brandon Ave. I-95, exit 169B, just nw of SR 644; jct I-395 and 495, 0.8 mi n. Int corridors. **Pets:** Accepted.

ASK ✕ 🗲M 🗲 🗲 🖪 🖵 🖘

## STERLING

AAA ▼▼▼▼ **AmeriSuites (Dulles Airport North/Sterling)** SH
(703) 444-3909. **$169-$229.** 21481 Ridgetop Cir. 1.8 mi e on SR 7 from jct SR 28. Int corridors. **Pets:** Small. $10 daily fee/pet. Designated rooms, service with restrictions, supervision.

SAVE 🔊 ✕ 🗲 🖪 🖵 🖘

▼▼▼ **Candlewood Suites Washington Dulles/Sterling** SH
(703) 674-2288. **$79-$209.** 45520 E Severn Way. Just e of SR 28; 1.7 mi n of jct 7 and 28. Int corridors. **Pets:** $75 one-time fee/room. Service with restrictions.

ASK 🔊 ✕ 🗲M 🗲 🖪 🖵

▼▼▼ **Hampton Inn-Dulles/Cascades** SH ❀
(703) 450-9595. **$79-$219.** 46331 McClellan Way. SR 28 N, 5 mi to exit 7E; SR 7 to Cascade Pkwy. Int corridors. **Pets:** Medium, other species. $10 daily fee/pet, $25 one-time fee/pet. Service with restrictions.

ASK 🔊 ✕ 🗲 🖪 🖵 ⊠

▼▼▼ **Hampton Inn Washington-Dulles Airport** SH
(703) 471-8300. **$79-$199.** 45440 Holiday Dr. SR 267 (Dulles Toll Rd), exit 9B, 1.8 mi n on SR 28, then just ne. Ext corridors. **Pets:** Accepted.

ASK 🔊 ✕ 🗲 🖪 🖵

AAA ▼▼▼▼ **Holiday Inn Washington Dulles International Airport** SH
(703) 471-7411. **$199-$285.** 1000 Sully Rd. SR 267 (Dulles Toll Rd), exit 9B, 1.8 mi n on SR 28. Ext/int corridors. **Pets:** Large, other species. $50 one-time fee/room. Service with restrictions, crate.

SAVE ✕ 🗲 🗲 🖪 🖵 🍴 🖘 ⊠

▼▼▼ **Homestead Studio Suites Hotel-Washington, DC-Sterling** SH
(703) 904-7575. **$115-$120.** 45350 Catalina Ct. SR 267 (Dulles Toll Rd), exit 9B, 0.8 mi n on SR 28, then just w on SR 606. Ext corridors. **Pets:** $25 daily fee/pet. Service with restrictions, supervision.

ASK 🔊 ✕ 🗲 🖪 🖵 ⊠

▼▼▼ **Suburban Extended Stay Hotel Washington-Dulles/Sterling** SH
(703) 674-2299. **Call for rates.** 45510 Severn Way. Just e of SR 28; 1.7 mi n of jct SR 7 and 28. Int corridors. **Pets:** Accepted.

✕ 🗲 🖪 🖵

▼▼▼▼ **TownePlace Suites by Marriott at Dulles Airport** 🆂🅷 ☀
(703) 707-2017. **$79-$189.** 22744 Holiday Park Dr. SR 267 (Dulles Toll Rd), exit 9B, 1.8 mi n on SR 28, then just ne. Int corridors. **Pets:** Other species. $75 one-time fee/room. Service with restrictions, crate.
🅰🆂🅺 🆂🔒 ⊠ 🕮 🔒 🅷 🔲 🔁

🔶🔶🔶 ▼▼▼▼ **TownePlace Suites by Marriott Sterling** 🆂🅷
(703) 421-1090. **$59-$209.** 21123 Whitfield Pl. US 7 to Cascades Pkwy, 0.5 mi n to Palisade Pkwy, just e, then 0.3 mi s. Int corridors. **Pets:** Large. $75 one-time fee/pet. Service with restrictions, crate.
🆂🅰🆅🅴 🆂🔒 ⊠ 🔒 🔒 🔲 🔁

## VIENNA

▼▼ ▼ **Homestead Studio Suites Hotel-Tysons Corner** 🆂🅷
(703) 356-6300. **$135-$145.** 8201 Old Courthouse Rd. I-495, exit 47A, 0.6 mi w on SR 7, then just s on Gallows Rd. Int corridors. **Pets:** $25 daily fee/pet. Service with restrictions, supervision.
🅰🆂🅺 🆂🔒 ⊠ 🔒🅼 🕮 🔒 🔲

▼▼▼▼ **Residence Inn by Marriott-Tysons Corner** 🆂🅷
(703) 893-0120. **$199-$299.** 8616 Westwood Center Dr. I-495, exit 47A, 1.9 mi w on SR 7, then just s. Ext corridors. **Pets:** Accepted.
🅰🆂🅺 🆂🔒 ⊠ 🔒 🔲 🔁 ⊠

▼▼▼▼ **Residence Inn by Marriott Tysons Corner Mall** 🆂🅷
(703) 917-0800. **$119-$269.** 8400 Old Courthouse Rd. I-495, exit 46A, 1.1 mi s on SR 123; 0.3 mi s of jct SR 7 and 123. Int corridors. **Pets:** Accepted.
🅰🆂🅺 🆂🔒 ⊠ 🔒🅼 🕮 🕮 🔒 🔲 🔁

▼▼▼▼ **Sheraton Premiere At Tysons Corner** 🅻🅷
(703) 448-1234. **$219-$229.** 8661 Leesburg Pike. SR 7, just e of jct SR 267 (Dulles Toll Rd). Int corridors. **Pets:** Accepted.
🅰🆂🅺 ⊠ 🕮 🕮 🔒 🔲 🍽 🔁 ⊠

## WOODBRIDGE

▼▼▼▼ **Potomac Mills Residence Inn by Marriott** 🆂🅷
(703) 490-4020. **$139-$199, 14 day notice.** 14301 Crossing Pl. I-95, exit 158B (Prince William Pkwy), 0.5 mi sw. Int corridors. **Pets:** Accepted.
🅰🆂🅺 🆂🔒 ⊠ 🔒🅼 🔒 🔒 🔲 🔁 ⊠

🔶🔶🔶 ▼▼▼▼ **Quality Inn at Potomac Mills** 🆂🅷
(703) 494-0300. **$65-$135.** 1109 Horner Rd. I-95, exit 161 southbound, 1.5 mi s on US 1, just n on SR 123, then just s; exit 160A northbound, 0.5 mi s on SR 123, then just s. Int corridors. **Pets:** Accepted.
🆂🅰🆅🅴 🆂🔒 ⊠ 🕮 🔒 🔲 🔁

---

## END METROPOLITAN AREA

---

## DUBLIN

▼▼ ▼▼ **Comfort Inn-Dublin** 🆂🅷
(540) 674-1100. **$52-$75.** 4424 Cleburne Blvd. I-81, exit 98, just e. Int corridors. **Pets:** $20 daily fee/room.
🅰🆂🅺 🆂🔒 ⊠ 🕮 🔒 🔲 🔁

## EMPORIA

🔶🔶🔶 ▼▼▼▼ **Best Western Emporia** 🆂🅷
(434) 634-3200. **$65-$85.** 1100 W Atlantic St. I-95, exit 11B, just w on US 58. Ext corridors. **Pets:** Other species. $10 daily fee/pet. Service with restrictions, supervision.
🆂🅰🆅🅴 🆂🔒 ⊠ 🕮 🔒 🔲 🔁

🔶🔶🔶 ▼▼ ▼ **Comfort Inn** 🆂🅷
(434) 348-3282. **$55-$70.** 1411 Skippers Rd. I-95, exit 8, just e on US 301. Ext corridors. **Pets:** Medium, other species. Service with restrictions, supervision.
🆂🅰🆅🅴 🆂🔒 ⊠ 🔒 🔲 🔁

🔶🔶🔶 ▼▼ ▼ **Days Inn-Emporia** 🆂🅷
(434) 634-9481. **$53-$70.** 921 W Atlantic St. I-95, exit 11B, just w on US 58. Ext corridors. **Pets:** Medium, other species. $8 one-time fee/room. Designated rooms, service with restrictions, supervision.
🆂🅰🆅🅴 🆂🔒 ⊠ 🔒 🔲 🔁

🔶🔶🔶 ▼▼ ▼ **Knights Inn** 🅼
(434) 535-8535. **$40-$60.** 3173 Sussex Dr. I-95, exit 17, 0.5 mi s on US 301. Ext corridors. **Pets:** Accepted.
🆂🅰🆅🅴 🆂🔒 ⊠ 🔒 🔁

## FANCY GAP

▼▼ ▼ **Doe Run Resorts, Inc** 🆂🅷
(276) 398-2212. **$107-$154, 7 day notice.** 27 Buck Hollar Rd. MM 189.2 on Blue Ridge Pkwy; 10 mi n from US 52 (parkway entrance). Ext corridors. **Pets:** Accepted.
🅰🆂🅺 🆂🔒 ⊠ 🔒 🔲 🍽 🔁 ⊠

## FARMVILLE

▼▼▼▼ **Comfort Inn-Farmville** 🆂🅷
(434) 392-8163. **$60-$135.** 2108 S Main St. Jct US 460 Bypass and US 15, exit Keysville. Int corridors. **Pets:** Small. $20 daily fee/pet. Designated rooms, no service, crate.
🅰🆂🅺 🆂🔒 ⊠ 🔒 🔲 🔁

▼▼ **Super 8 Motel** 🅼
(434) 392-8196. **$52-$65, 5 day notice.** 2012 S Main St. On US 15, just n of jct US 460. Int corridors. **Pets:** Accepted.
🅰🆂🅺 🆂🔒 ⊠ 🔒

## FREDERICKSBURG

🔶🔶🔶 ▼▼ ▼ **Best Western Central Plaza** 🅼
(540) 786-7404. **$70-$87.** 3000 Plank Rd. I-95, exit 130B on SR 3. Ext corridors. **Pets:** Accepted.
🆂🅰🆅🅴 🆂🔒 ⊠ 🔒🅼 🔒 🔲

🔶🔶🔶 ▼▼▼▼ **Best Western Fredericksburg** 🆂🅷
(540) 371-5050. **$67-$94, 7 day notice.** 2205 William St. I-95, exit 130A, 0.3 mi e on SR 3. Ext corridors. **Pets:** $9 daily fee/pet. Service with restrictions, supervision.
🆂🅰🆅🅴 🆂🔒 ⊠ 🔒🅼 🔒 🔲 🔁

🔶🔶🔶 ▼▼▼▼ **Dunning Mills Inn All Suites Hotel** 🅲🅾
(540) 373-1256. **$69-$89.** 2305-C Jefferson Davis Hwy. I-95, exit 126, 3 mi n on US 1. Ext corridors. **Pets:** Other species. $200 deposit/room, $5 daily fee/pet. Service with restrictions, crate.
🆂🅰🆅🅴 🆂🔒 ⊠ 🔒 🔲 🔁

🔶🔶🔶 ▼▼▼▼ **Hampton Inn** 🆂🅷 ☀
(540) 371-0330. **$79-$119.** 2310 William St. I-95, exit 130A on SR 3 E. Ext corridors. **Pets:** Other species. Designated rooms, service with restrictions.
🆂🅰🆅🅴 🆂🔒 ⊠ 🔒 🔲 🔁

🔶🔶🔶 ▼▼▼▼ **Holiday Inn-Fredericksburg North** 🆂🅷 ☀
(540) 371-5550. **$70-$105.** 564 Warrenton Rd. I-95, exit 133, just nw on US 17. Ext corridors. **Pets:** Medium. Service with restrictions, supervision.
🆂🅰🆅🅴 🆂🔒 ⊠ 🔒 🔲 🍽 🔁 ⊠

▼▼▼▼ **Holiday Inn Select Fredericksburg** 🎦
(540) 786-8321. **$109-$169.** 2801 Plank Rd. I-95, exit 130B on SR 3.
Int corridors. **Pets:** Small, dogs only. $75 one-time fee/room. Service with restrictions, supervision.

(ASK) (S🐾) (X) (&M) (🕸) (🛗) (🖥) (🖨) (¶¶) (🏊)

🐾🐾 ▼ **Howard Johnson Hotel** 🎦
(540) 898-1800. **$59-$99.** 5327 Jefferson Davis Hwy. I-95, exit 126. Int corridors. **Pets:** Other species. $10 daily fee/room. Service with restrictions, crate.

(SAVE) (S🐾) (X) (🛗) (🖥) (🖨) (🏊)

🐾🐾 ▼▼ **Quality Inn Fredericksburg** 🎦
(540) 373-0000. **$57-$80.** 543 Warrenton Rd. I-95, exit 133, just n on US 17. Ext corridors. **Pets:** Accepted.

(SAVE) (S🐾) (X) (🖨) (¶¶) (🏊)

🐾🐾 ▼▼▼ **Ramada Inn South** 🎦
(540) 898-1102. **$49-$114.** 5324 Jefferson Davis Hwy. I-95, exit 126, just n on US 1. Ext/int corridors. **Pets:** Accepted.

(SAVE) (S🐾) (X) (🖥) (🖨) (¶¶) (🏊) (X)

▼▼▼▼ **TownePlace Suites by Marriott** 🎦 🐾
(540) 891-0775. **$99-$169.** 4700 Market St. I-95, exit 126 southbound; exit 126A northbound, just n on US 1, then just e. Int corridors.
**Pets:** Medium. $200 deposit/pet, $10 daily fee/pet. Service with restrictions, supervision.

(ASK) (X) (🕸) (🛗) (🖥) (🖨) (🏊)

## FRONT ROYAL

🐾🐾 ▼ **Bluemont Inn** Ⓜ
(540) 635-9447. **$47-$195.** 1525 N Shenandoah Ave. I-66, exit 6, 1.8 mi s on US 340/522. Ext corridors. **Pets:** Supervision.

(SAVE) (S🐾) (X) (🖥) (🖨)

🐾🐾 ▼ **Budget Inn** Ⓜ
(540) 635-2196. **$39-$75.** 1122 N Royal Ave. I-66, exit 6, 2.2 mi s on US 340/522 and SR 55. Ext corridors. **Pets:** Medium, dogs only. $5 daily fee/pet. Designated rooms, service with restrictions, supervision.

(SAVE) (S🐾) (X) (🖥)

🐾🐾 ▼ **Relax Inn** Ⓜ
(540) 635-4101. **$50-$75.** 1801 Shenandoah Ave. I-66, exit 6, 1.5 mi s on US 340/522. Ext corridors. **Pets:** $5 daily fee/pet. Service with restrictions, supervision.

(SAVE) (S🐾) (X) (🖥) (🖨) (🏊)

🐾🐾 ▼▼ **Scottish Inn** Ⓜ
(540) 636-6168. **$45-$85.** 533 S Royal Ave. I-66, exit 6, 3.8 mi s on US 340, jct SR 55. Ext corridors. **Pets:** $5 one-time fee/pet. No service, supervision.

(SAVE) (S🐾) (X) (🖥) (🖨)

🐾🐾 ▼ **Twi-Lite Motel** Ⓜ
(540) 635-4148. **$45-$89, 3 day notice.** 53 W 14th St. I-66, exit 6, 2.3 mi s on US 340/522. Ext corridors. **Pets:** Accepted.

(SAVE) (S🐾) (X) (🖥) (🏊)

## GLADE SPRING

🐾🐾 ▼ **Swiss Inn Motel & Suites** Ⓜ
(276) 429-5191. **$45-$65.** 33361 Lee Hwy. I-81, exit 29, just e. Ext corridors. **Pets:** Very small, dogs only. $10 one-time fee/pet. Service with restrictions, supervision.

(SAVE) (S🐾) (X) (&M) (🖥)

## GREENVILLE

🐾🐾 ▼▼▼ **Budget Host-Historic Hessian House** 🎦
(540) 337-1231. **$35-$69.** 3554 Lee Jackson Hwy. I-81, exit 213, 0.3 mi e. Ext corridors. **Pets:** Medium. $6 daily fee/pet. Designated rooms, service with restrictions, crate.

(SAVE) (S🐾) (X) (🖥)

## GRUNDY

▼▼▼ **Comfort Inn** 🎦
(276) 935-5050. **$77-$155.** US 460 Main St. On US 460, 0.5 mi e. Int corridors. **Pets:** Accepted.

(ASK) (S🐾) (X) (&M) (🕸) (🛗) (🖥) (🖨)

# HAMPTON ROADS AREA

## CHESAPEAKE

▼▼▼▼ **Residence Inn by Marriott,**
  **Chesapeake-Greenbrier** 🎦 🐾
(757) 502-7300. **$139-$159.** 1500 Crossways Blvd. I-64, exit 289B (Greenbrier Pkwy), just s to Jarman Rd (at Crossways Center) to Crossways Blvd, then 6 mi n. Int corridors. **Pets:** Other species. $75 one-time fee/room.

(ASK) (S🐾) (X) (🕸) (🛗) (🖥) (🖨) (🏊) (X)

▼ **Super 8 Motel** Ⓜ 🐾
(757) 686-8888. **$58-$80.** 3216 Churchland Blvd. I-664, exit 9B, 1 mi s on SR 17. Int corridors. **Pets:** Other species. $6 daily fee/room. Designated rooms, service with restrictions, crate.

(ASK) (S🐾) (X) (&M) (🖥)

▼▼ **TownePlace Suites By Marriott** 🎦
(757) 523-5004. **$94-$139.** 2000 Old Greenbrier Rd. I-64, exit 289A (Greenbrier Pkwy), just n on Greenbrier Pkwy. Int corridors.
**Pets:** Accepted.

(ASK) (S🐾) (X) (&M) (🕸) (🛗) (🖥) (🖨) (🏊)

## GLOUCESTER

▼▼▼ **Comfort Inn Gloucester** 🎦
(804) 695-1900. **$79-$149.** 6639 Forest Hill Ave. US 17, just s. Int corridors. **Pets:** Medium, dogs only. $10 daily fee/pet. Service with restrictions, crate.

(ASK) (S🐾) (X) (🖥) (🖨) (🏊)

## HAMPTON

▼▼▼▼ **Candlewood Suites** 🎦
(757) 766-8976. **$59-$189.** 401 Butler Farm Rd. I-64, exit 261B (Hampton Roads Center Pkwy) eastbound; exit 262B (Magruder Blvd) westbound, then n. Int corridors. **Pets:** Accepted.

(ASK) (S🐾) (X) (&M) (🛗) (🖥) (🖨)

🐾🐾 ▼▼▼▼ **Clarion Hotel Hampton** 🎦 🐾
(757) 838-5011. **$99-$169.** 1809 W Mercury Blvd. I-64, exit 263B (Mercury Blvd), jct SR 58. Int corridors. **Pets:** Small, dogs only. $25 daily fee/pet. Designated rooms, service with restrictions, crate.

(SAVE) (S🐾) (X) (&M) (🕸) (🛗) (🖥) (🖨) (¶¶) (🏊)

▼▼▼▼ **Holiday Inn Hampton Hotel & Conference**
  **Center** 🎦
(757) 838-0200. **$79-$169.** 1815 W Mercury Blvd. I-64, exit 263B (Mercury Blvd) westbound; exit 263 eastbound. Ext/int corridors.
**Pets:** Accepted.

(ASK) (S🐾) (X) (&M) (🕸) (🛗) (🖥) (🖨) (¶¶) (🏊) (X)

🐾🐾 ▼▼▼▼ **La Quinta Inn Norfolk (Hampton)** 🎦
(757) 827-8680. **$81-$155.** 2138 W Mercury Blvd. I-64, exit 263 (Mercury Blvd), just s. Ext/int corridors. **Pets:** Medium. Service with restrictions.

(SAVE) (X) (&M) (🕸) (🛗) (🖥) (🖨) (🏊)

**Super 8 Motel** [M]
(757) 723-2888. **$59-$91.** 1330 Thomas St. I-64, 265B westbound; exit 265C eastbound. Int corridors. **Pets:** Accepted.

(ASK) [SD] [X] [H]

# NEWPORT NEWS

**Comfort Inn** [SH]
(757) 249-0200. **$129-$149.** 12330 Jefferson Ave. I-64, exit 255A, just s on Clarie Ln (mail parking lot). Int corridors. **Pets:** Large, other species. $10 daily fee/room. Designated rooms, service with restrictions, supervision.

(ASK) [SD] [X] [&M] [✍] [H] [◻] [➟]

**Days Inn** [SH]
(757) 874-0201. **$65-$85, 30 day notice.** 14747 Warwick Blvd. I-64, exit 250A (SR 105/Ft Eustis Blvd S), 2.5 mi to US 60 E (Warwick Blvd). Ext corridors. **Pets:** Other species. $10 daily fee/pet. Service with restrictions, supervision.

(SAVE) [SD] [X] [H] [◻] [➟]

**Days Inn-Oyster Point & Meeting Center** [SH]
(757) 873-6700. **$65-$139.** 11829 Fishing Point Dr. I-64, exit 255A, 2.5 mi s to Thimble Shoals Dr E, then 1 blk to property. Int corridors. **Pets:** Medium, other species. $15 daily fee/pet. Service with restrictions.

(SAVE) [SD] [X] [✍] [H] [◻] [➟]

**Host Inn** [M]
(757) 599-3303. **$49-$90.** 985 J Clyde Morris Blvd. I-64, exit 258B, 0.8 mi n. Ext corridors. **Pets:** Medium, dogs only. $10 daily fee/pet. Designated rooms, no service, supervision.

(SAVE) [X] [H] [◻]

**Omni Newport News Hotel** [LH]
(757) 873-6664. **$159.** 1000 Omni Blvd. I-64, exit 258A (US 17), just s to Oyster Point Rd. Int corridors. **Pets:** Accepted.

(ASK) [SD] [X] [&'] [H] [◻] [¶↑] [➟]

**Travelodge** [M] ❀
(757) 874-4100. **$65-$95.** 13700 Warwick Blvd. I-64, exit 255B, 1 mi w to Bland Blvd, 1 mi s to Warwick Blvd, then just n. Ext corridors. **Pets:** Other species. $5 daily fee/pet. No service, crate.

(SAVE) [SD] [X] [&M] [H] [◻]

# NORFOLK

**B & B @ Historic Page House Inn** [BB] ❀
(757) 625-5033. **$140-$225, 7 day notice.** 323 Fairfax Ave. I-264, exit 9, 1.4 mi n on Waterside Dr to Olney Rd, just w to Mowbray Arch, then just s; in Ghent historic district. Int corridors. **Pets:** Small, other species. $25 daily fee/pet. Service with restrictions, supervision.

(SAVE) [X] [H] [⊠]

**Quality Suites Lake Wright** [SH]
(757) 461-6251. **$109-$169.** 6280 Northampton Blvd. I-64, exit 282, just w on US 13. Int corridors. **Pets:** Other species. $35 one-time fee/room. Service with restrictions, supervision.

(SAVE) [SD] [X] [&M] [&'] [H] [◻] [¶↑] [➟]

**Radisson Hotel Norfolk** [SH]
(757) 627-5555. **$139-$182.** 700 Monticello Ave. Jct Brambleton Ave and St. Pauls Blvd; downtown. Int corridors. **Pets:** Accepted.

(SAVE) [SD] [X] [&M] [✍] [&'] [H] [◻] [¶↑] [➟]

**Residence Inn by Marriott Norfolk Airport** [SH]
(757) 333-3000. **$139-$164.** 1590 N Military Hwy. I-64, exit 281B (Military Hwy). Int corridors. **Pets:** Other species. $75 one-time fee/room. Service with restrictions, crate.

(ASK) [SD] [X] [&M] [✍] [&'] [H] [◻] [➟] [⊠]

**Sheraton Norfolk Waterside Hotel** [LH]
(757) 622-6664. **$99-$259.** 777 Waterside Dr. I-264 to Waterside Dr; downtown. Int corridors. **Pets:** Accepted.

(ASK) [SD] [X] [&M] [✍] [&'] [H] [◻] [¶↑] [➟]

**Sleep Inn Lake Wright** [SH]
(757) 461-1133. **$89-$149.** 6280 Northampton Blvd. I-64, exit 282, just w on US 13. Int corridors. **Pets:** Other species. $25 one-time fee/room. Service with restrictions, supervision.

(SAVE) [SD] [X] [&M] [&'] [H] [◻] [¶↑] [➟]

# PORTSMOUTH

**Holiday Inn-Olde Towne Portsmouth** [SH] ❀
(757) 393-2573. **$104-$149.** 8 Crawford Pkwy. Just nw from High St. Int corridors. **Pets:** $10 daily fee/pet. Service with restrictions, crate.

(SAVE) [SD] [X] [&'] [H] [◻] [¶↑] [➟]

# SUFFOLK

**Holiday Inn-Suffolk** [SH]
(757) 934-2311. **$80.** 2864 Pruden Blvd. US 460 at jct US 58 Bypass. Ext corridors. **Pets:** Accepted.

(ASK) [SD] [X] [✍] [H] [◻] [¶↑] [➟]

# VIRGINIA BEACH

**Best Western Beach Quarters Inn** [M] ❀
(757) 437-1200. **$29-$269, 3 day notice.** 300 Atlantic Ave. I-264, 1.2 mi s of terminus at Rudee Inlet. Ext corridors. **Pets:** Small, other species. $10 daily fee/pet. Designated rooms, service with restrictions, crate.

(SAVE) [SD] [X] [✍] [H] [◻] [➟]

**The Dolphin Inn** [SH]
(757) 491-1420. **$59-$329, 3 day notice.** 1705 Atlantic Ave. I-264, just s of terminus. Ext corridors. **Pets:** Accepted.

(SAVE) [SD] [X] [H] [◻] [➟]

**DoubleTree Hotel Virginia Beach** [SH]
(757) 422-8900. **$59-$219.** 1900 Pavilion Dr. I-264, exit 22 (Birdneck Rd). Int corridors. **Pets:** Medium. $25 one-time fee/pet. Designated rooms, service with restrictions, supervision.

(ASK) [SD] [X] [✍] [H] [◻] [¶↑] [➟]

**Holiday Inn-Executive Center** [LH]
(757) 499-4400. **$89-$189.** 5655 Greenwich Rd. I-64, exit 284B (Newtown Rd); jct I-64 and 264. Int corridors. **Pets:** Other species. Designated rooms, service with restrictions, crate.

[X] [&M] [✍] [&'] [H] [◻] [¶↑] [⊠]

**Holiday Inn Surfside Hotel & Suites** [SH]
(757) 491-6900. **$79-$229, 3 day notice.** 2607 Atlantic Ave. I-264, n of terminus; at Atlantic Ave and 26th St. Int corridors. **Pets:** Medium, other species. $40 one-time fee/pet. Designated rooms, service with restrictions, supervision.

(SAVE) [X] [&M] [✍] [H] [◻] [¶↑] [➟]

**La Quinta Inn Norfolk (Virginia Beach)** [SH]
(757) 497-6620. **$81-$175.** 192 Newtown Rd. I-64, exit 284B to I-264 (Virginia Beach-Norfolk Expwy), exit Newtown Rd S. Int corridors. **Pets:** Medium. Service with restrictions.

(SAVE) [X] [&M] [H] [◻] [➟]

**Ramada Plaza Resort Oceanfront** [LH]
(757) 428-7025. **$64-$247, 3 day notice.** Atlantic Ave & 57th St. I-264, 2.2 mi n of terminus. Int corridors. **Pets:** Dogs only. $25 daily fee/room. Designated rooms, service with restrictions, crate.

(SAVE) [SD] [X] [&M] [H] [◻] [➟] [⊠]

**Red Roof Inn VA Beach (Norfolk Airport)** [M] ❀
(757) 460-6700. **$46-$160, 3 day notice.** 5745 Northampton Blvd. I-64, exit 282, 1 mi n on US 13 (Northampton Blvd). Ext corridors. **Pets:** Small, dogs only. $10 one-time fee/room. Designated rooms, service with restrictions, supervision.

(SAVE) [SD] [X] [➟]

**WWWW Sheraton Oceanfront Hotel** SH
(757) 425-9000. **$79-$239, 3 day notice.** 3501 Atlantic Ave. I-264, 1 mi
n of terminus; jct 36th St. Int corridors. **Pets:** Accepted.

(ASK) (S6) (X) (&) (H) (I) (M) (≈) (X)

**WWWW TownePlace Suites By Marriott** SH
(757) 490-9367. **$94-$180.** 5757 Cleveland St. I-64, exit 284B to I-264
(Virginia Beach-Norfolk Expwy), exit Newtown Rd N. Int corridors.
**Pets:** Medium. $75 one-time fee/room. Service with restrictions.

(ASK) (X) (&M) (&) (H) (I) (≈)

# END AREA

# HARRISONBURG

**AAA WWWW Comfort Inn** SH
(540) 433-6066. **$75-$155.** 1440 E Market St. I-81, exit 247A, just e. Int
corridors. **Pets:** Other species. Service with restrictions, supervision.

(SAVE) (S6) (X) (⌒) (&) (H) (I) (≈)

**AAA WWW Days Inn Harrisonburg** SH
(540) 433-9353. **$65-$195.** 1131 Forest Hill Rd. I-81, exit 245, just e. Int
corridors. **Pets:** Accepted.

(SAVE) (S6) (X) (⌒) (H) (I) (≈)

**AAA WWWW Four Points by Sheraton** SH
(540) 433-2521. **$79-$139.** 1400 E Market St. I-81, exit 247A, just e on
US 33. Int corridors. **Pets:** Accepted.

(SAVE) (S6) (X) (⌒) (&) (H) (I) (M) (≈)

**AAA WWW Harrisonburg Econo Lodge** M
(540) 433-2576. **$45-$200.** 1703 E Market St. I-81, exit 247A, 0.5 mi e
on US 33. Ext/int corridors. **Pets:** Small. $10 daily fee/pet. Designated
rooms, service with restrictions, supervision.

(SAVE) (S6) (X) (H) (I) (≈)

**WWW Motel 6 Harrisonburg #1211** M
(540) 433-6939. **$45-$58.** 10 Linda Ln. I-81, exit 247A, just e on US 33.
Ext corridors. **Pets:** Accepted.

(S6) (X) (H) (≈)

**AAA WWW Ramada Inn** SH
(540) 434-9981. **$80-$95.** 1 Pleasant Valley Rd. I-81, exit 243, just w,
then just n on US 11. Ext corridors. **Pets:** Small, dogs only. $10 one-time
fee/room. Service with restrictions, supervision.

(SAVE) (S6) (X) (⌒) (H) (I) (≈)

**AAA WWW Super 8 Motel** M
(540) 433-8888. **$49-$199, 3 day notice.** 3330 S Main St. I-81, exit
243, just e, then just s on US 11. Int corridors. **Pets:** Small. $10 daily
fee/pet. Designated rooms, no service, supervision.

(SAVE) (S6) (X) (H)

**AAA WWWW The Village Inn** SH
(540) 434-7355. **$69-$74.** 4979 S Valley Pike. I-81, exit 240 southbound, 0.6 mi w on SR 257, then 1.5 mi n on US 11; exit 243
northbound, just w to US 11, then 1.7 mi s. Ext corridors. **Pets:** $9 daily
fee/pet. Service with restrictions, crate.

(SAVE) (X) (H) (I) (≈) (X)

# HILLSVILLE

**AAA WWWW Holiday Inn Express** SH
(276) 728-2120. **$74-$180, 7 day notice.** 85 Airport Rd. I-77, exit 14,
just w on US 58 and 221. Ext corridors. **Pets:** Small. $10 daily fee/pet.
Designated rooms, service with restrictions, supervision.

(SAVE) (S6) (X) (&M) (&) (H) (I) (≈)

**WWW Red Carpet Inn** M
(276) 728-9118. **$61-$130.** 2666 Old Galax Pike. I-77, exit 14, just n. Int
corridors. **Pets:** Accepted.

(ASK) (S6) (H) (I)

# HOPEWELL

**AAA WWW Candlewood Suites** SH
(804) 541-0200. **$99-$119.** 5113 Plaza Dr. I-295, exit 9B (SR 36), just
w; adjacent to Oak Lawn Plaza. Int corridors. **Pets:** Medium, other
species. $75 one-time fee/room. Service with restrictions, crate.

(SAVE) (S6) (X) (&) (H) (I)

**AAA WWW Econo Lodge** SH
(804) 541-4849. **$69-$99.** 4096 Oaklawn Blvd. I-295, exit 9A, just e. Int
corridors. **Pets:** Small. $10 one-time fee/room. Service with restrictions,
supervision.

(SAVE) (S6) (X) (&M) (&) (H) (I)

# HOT SPRINGS

**WW Roseloe Motel** M
(540) 839-5373. **$60-$80.** 590 US 220 N. 3 mi n. Ext corridors.
**Pets:** $10 one-time fee/pet. Service with restrictions, supervision.

(ASK) (S6) (X) (H) (I)

# HUDDLESTON

**WWW Mariners Landing** VH
(540) 297-4900. **$110-$415.** 1217 Graves Harbor Trail. On Smith
Mountain Lake; from Lake Retreat Rd, just w. Ext/int corridors.
**Pets:** Small, dogs only. $15 daily fee/pet. Designated rooms, service with
restrictions, supervision.

(X) (&M) (&) (H) (I) (M) (≈) (X)

# IRVINGTON

**AAA WWWW The Tides Inn** SH *
(804) 438-5000. **$159-$375, 7 day notice.** 480 King Carter Dr. 0.3 mi w
of CR 200. Ext/int corridors. **Pets:** Medium. $35 one-time fee/room. Des-
ignated rooms, service with restrictions, crate.

(SAVE) (S6) (X) (&M) (⌒) (&) (H) (I) (M) (≈) (X)

# KESWICK

**AAA WWWW Keswick Hall at Monticello** SH
(434) 979-3440. **$295-$795, 7 day notice.** 701 Club Dr. I-64, exit 129,
just n. Int corridors. **Pets:** Accepted.

(SAVE) (X) (&M) (&) (H) (M) (≈) (X)

# KEYSVILLE

**AAA WWW Sheldon's Motel** SH
(434) 736-8434. **$43-$75.** 1450 Four Locust Hwy. 1.3 mi n on US 15
and 360 business route. Ext corridors. **Pets:** Other species. Service with
restrictions, supervision.

(SAVE) (S6) (X) (H) (M)

# LAWRENCEVILLE

**WWWW Brunswick Mineral Springs B & B Circa
1785** BB *
(434) 848-4010. **$145, 5 day notice.** 14910 Western Mill Rd. 5 mi e on
US 58, 1 mi s on SR 712, then just e. Int corridors. **Pets:** Large, dogs
only. $25 one-time fee/pet. Designated rooms, no service, supervision.

(ASK) (S6) (X) (H) (I)

# LEXINGTON

◆◆◆◆ Best Western SH
(540) 458-3020. **$79-$210, 7 day notice.** 850 N Lee Hwy. I-64, exit 55, just s on US 11; I-81, exit 191, 1.6 mi w. Ext corridors. **Pets:** Accepted.

A$K SA X ⊘ 🖩 🖵

◆◆◆ ◆◆◆◆ Best Western Inn at Hunt Ridge SH
(540) 464-1500. **$59-$175, 7 day notice.** 25 Willow Spring Rd. I-64, exit 55, just n on US 11 to SR 39; I-81, exit 191, 0.6 mi w. Int corridors. **Pets:** Accepted.

SAVE SA X &M ⊘ 🕹 🖩 🖵 🍴 ➤

◆◆◆◆ Comfort Inn-Virginia Horse Center SH
(540) 463-7311. **$59-$155, 7 day notice.** 62 Comfort Way. I-64, exit 55, just s on US 11; I-81, exit 191, 0.6 mi w. Int corridors. **Pets:** Accepted.

A$K SA X 🖵 ➤

◆◆◆ ◆ ◆ Days Inn Keydet General SH
(540) 463-2143. **$55-$135.** 325 W Midland Tr. I-81, exit 188B, 4.5 mi on US 60 W; I-64, exit 50, 5 mi e on US 60. Ext/int corridors. **Pets:** Accepted.

SAVE SA X 🖩

◆◆ ◆ Econo Lodge M
(540) 463-7371. **$60-$125.** 65 Econo Ln. I-81, exit 191, just s on US 11. Ext corridors. **Pets:** Accepted.

A$K SA X 🖩 🖵

◆◆◆ ◆ ◆ Howard Johnson Inn SH
(540) 463-9181. **$65-$145.** 2836 N Lee Hwy. I-81, exit 195, just s on US 11. Int corridors. **Pets:** $10 daily fee/pet. Service with restrictions, supervision.

SAVE SA X ⊘ 🖩 🖵 ➤

◆◆ ◆ Ramada Inn Lexington SH
(540) 463-6400. **$51-$119.** 2814 N Lee Hwy. I-81, exit 195, just sw on US 11. Int corridors. **Pets:** Large, other species. $8 daily fee/pet. Service with restrictions, supervision.

A$K SA X ⊘ 🕹 🖩 🖵 ➤

◆◆ ◆ Super 8 Motel M
(540) 463-7858. **$67-$82, 7 day notice.** 1139 N Lee Hwy. I-64, exit 55, just n. Int corridors. **Pets:** Other species. Service with restrictions, supervision.

A$K SA X 🖩

# LURAY

◆◆◆ ◆◆◆◆ Best Western Intown of Luray SH
(540) 743-6511. **$65-$115.** 410 W Main St. 0.3 mi w on US 211 business route. Ext corridors. **Pets:** Accepted.

SAVE SA X 🖩 🖵 🍴 ➤

◆◆ ◆ Days Inn-Luray SH
(540) 743-4521. **$49-$109.** 138 Whispering Hill Rd. US 211 Bypass, 1.7 mi e of jct US 340. Ext corridors. **Pets:** Medium. $10 daily fee/pet. Designated rooms, service with restrictions, crate.

A$K SA X ➤ ⊗

# LYNCHBURG

◆◆◆ ◆ ◆ Best Western Lynchburg M
(434) 237-2986. **$76-$150.** 2815 Candlers Mountain Rd. Jct US 29 and 460. Ext corridors. **Pets:** $25 one-time fee/room. Service with restrictions.

SAVE SA X ⊘ 🖩 🖵 ➤

◆◆ ◆ Days Inn SH
(434) 847-8655. **$69-$89.** 3320 Candlers Mountain Rd. US 29, exit US 501, just e. Int corridors. **Pets:** Accepted.

A$K SA X 🖩 🖵 🍴 ➤

◆◆ ◆ Econo Lodge M
(434) 847-1045. **$60-$70.** 2400 Stadium Rd. US 29, exit 4 southbound; exit 6 northbound, just w on James St, then just n. Ext corridors. **Pets:** Very small, dogs only. $15 daily fee/pet. Designated rooms, service with restrictions.

SAVE SA X 🖩 🖵

◆◆◆◆ Holiday Inn Select SH
(434) 528-2500. **$99-$159.** 601 Main St. US 29 Expwy, exit 1 (Main St), just w; downtown. Int corridors. **Pets:** Accepted.

A$K SA X 🕹 🖩 🖵 🍴 ➤

◆◆◆ ◆◆◆◆ Quality Inn SH
(434) 847-9041. **$75-$90.** 3125 Albert Lankford Dr. US 29, exit 7, 2.5 mi s. Int corridors. **Pets:** Accepted.

SAVE SA X 🖩 🖵 🍴 ➤

# MARION

◆◆◆ ◆ ◆ Best Western-Marion SH
(276) 783-3193. **$69-$99, 30 day notice.** 1424 N Main St. I-81, exit 47, 0.3 mi s on US 11. Ext corridors. **Pets:** Medium, other species. $5 daily fee/pet. Designated rooms, service with restrictions, supervision.

SAVE SA X ⊘ 🕹 🖩 🖵 🍴 ➤

◆◆◆ ◆ Econo Lodge SH
(276) 783-6031. **$59-$89, 30 day notice.** 1424 N Main St. I-81, exit 47, 0.3 mi s on US 11. Ext corridors. **Pets:** Medium, other species. $5 daily fee/pet. Designated rooms, service with restrictions, supervision.

SAVE SA X ⊘ 🖩

# MARTINSVILLE

◆◆ ◆ Best Lodge M
(276) 647-3941. **$48-$55.** 1985 Virginia Ave. Jct US 58, 2.5 mi n on US 220 business route. Ext corridors. **Pets:** Small. $10 daily fee/pet. Designated rooms, service with restrictions, supervision.

A$K SA X 🖩 🖵

◆◆◆ ◆◆◆◆ Best Western Martinsville Inn SH
(276) 632-5611. **$79-$109.** US 220 Business Rt S. Jct US 58, 2.3 mi n. Ext corridors. **Pets:** Other species. Designated rooms, service with restrictions.

SAVE SA X 🖩 🖵 🍴 ➤

◆◆ ◆ Super 8 Motel M
(276) 666-8888. **$55-$65, 30 day notice.** 1044 N Memorial Blvd. Jct US 58, 1.5 mi n on US 220 business route. Int corridors. **Pets:** Accepted.

A$K SA X 🖩

# MAX MEADOWS

◆◆◆ ◆◆◆◆ Comfort Inn SH
(276) 637-4281. **$59-$79.** 2594 E Lee Hwy. I-77/81, exit 80, just w. Int corridors. **Pets:** Accepted.

SAVE SA X &M ⊘ 🖩 🖵 ➤

◆◆◆ ◆ ◆ Super 8 Motel SH
(276) 637-4141. **$50-$66.** 194 Ft Chiswell Rd. I-77/81, exit 80, just e. Ext corridors. **Pets:** Accepted.

SAVE SA X ⊘ 🖵

# MIDDLETOWN

◆◆◆ ◆ ◆ Super 8 Motel SH
(540) 868-1800. **$55-$155.** 2120 Relaince Rd. I-81, exit 302. Int corridors. **Pets:** Accepted.

SAVE SA X 🖩 ➤

# MINT SPRING

**▼▼ Days Inn-Staunton M**
(540) 337-3031. **$59-$119, 7 day notice.** 372 White Hill Rd. I-81, exit 217, just e on SR 654. Ext corridors. **Pets:** Small. $10 daily fee/pet. Designated rooms, service with restrictions, supervision.

ASK Sめ ✕ ♂ ♿ ♥ ▯ ⊃

# MOUNT JACKSON

**AAA ▼▼▼▼ Best Western-Shenandoah Valley SH**
(540) 477-2911. **$70-$130, 4 day notice.** 250 Conickville Rd. I-81, exit 273, just e. Ext corridors. **Pets:** Accepted.

SAVE Sめ ✕ ♥ ▯ ⑪ ⊃

**▼▼▼▼ The Widow Kip's BB ❖**
(540) 477-2400. **$90-$95, 5 day notice.** 355 Orchard Dr. I-81, exit 273, 1.5 mi s on US 11, just w on SR 263, then just sw on SR 698. Int corridors. **Pets:** Other species. $15 daily fee/pet. Designated rooms, service with restrictions, crate.

ASK Sめ ✕ ♥ ▯ ⊃

# NEW CHURCH

**▼▼▼▼ The Garden & The Sea Inn BB ❖**
(757) 824-0672. **$75-$205, 10 day notice.** 4188 Nelson Rd. US 13, 0.3 mi n, just w on CR 710 (Nelson Rd). Int corridors. **Pets:** Other species.

✕ ♥ ⑪ ⊃ ☎

# NEW MARKET

**AAA ▼ Budget Inn M**
(540) 740-3105. **$29-$69, 3 day notice.** 2192 Old Valley Pike. I-81, exit 264, 1 mi n on US 11. Ext corridors. **Pets:** Small. $5 one-time fee/pet. Designated rooms, no service, supervision.

SAVE Sめ ✕ ♥

**AAA ▼▼▼ Days Inn SH**
(540) 740-4100. **$40-$100, 10 day notice.** 9360 George Collins Pkwy. I-81, exit 264, just w on US 211. Ext corridors. **Pets:** Medium, dogs only. $10 daily fee/pet. Service with restrictions, supervision.

SAVE Sめ ✕ ▯ ⊃

# NORTON

**▼▼ Days Inn SH**
(276) 679-5340. **$40-$159.** 375 Wharton Ln. Jct US 58 and 23. Int corridors. **Pets:** Other species. $10 one-time fee/room. Service with restrictions, crate.

ASK Sめ ✕ ♂ ♿ ♥ ▯

# ONANCOCK

**AAA ▼▼▼ Spinning Wheel Bed & Breakfast BB ❖**
(757) 787-7311. **$70-$120, 10 day notice.** 31 North St. Just n of jct Market (SR 179) and North sts. Int corridors. **Pets:** Medium, dogs only. $10 daily fee/pet. Designated rooms, service with restrictions, supervision.

SAVE Sめ ✕ ♙ ☎

# PALMYRA

**▼▼▼▼ Inn 1831 and Restaurant BB**
(434) 589-1300. **$89-$195, 10 day notice.** Rt 2, Box 1390. On SR 640, 1.8 mi w of jct US 15. Ext/int corridors. **Pets:** $25 daily fee/pet. Service with restrictions, supervision.

ASK ✕ ▯ ⑪ ⊃ ✕ ☎

# PETERSBURG

**AAA ▼▼▼▼ Best Western-Steven Kent SH**
(804) 733-0600. **$49-$100.** 12205 S Crater Rd. I-95, exit 45, jct US 301. Ext/int corridors. **Pets:** Other species. $10 daily fee/pet. Designated rooms, service with restrictions, supervision.

SAVE Sめ ✕ ♂ ♥ ▯ ⑪ ⊃ ✕

**AAA ▼▼▼ Days Inn SH**
(804) 733-4400. **$59-$89.** 12208 S Crater Rd. I-95, exit 45, jct US 301. Ext corridors. **Pets:** Other species. $10 daily fee/pet. Designated rooms, service with restrictions, supervision.

SAVE Sめ ✕ ♥ ▯ ⊃

**AAA ▼▼▼ Econo Lodge-South SH**
(804) 862-2717. **$49-$99.** 16905 Parkdale Rd. I-95, exit 41, just e. Ext corridors. **Pets:** Accepted.

SAVE Sめ ✕ ♥ ▯ ⑪ ⊃

# PULASKI

**▼▼ Days Inn SH**
(540) 980-2230. **$50-$125.** 3063 Old Rt 100 Rd. I-81, exit 94, just e. Ext/int corridors. **Pets:** Accepted.

ASK Sめ ✕ ♥

# RADFORD

**AAA ▼▼▼▼ Best Western Radford Inn SH ❖**
(540) 639-3000. **$69-$109.** 1501 Tyler Ave. I-81, exit 109, 2.7 mi nw on SR 177. Int corridors. **Pets:** Medium, other species. $10 daily fee/room. Service with restrictions, supervision.

SAVE Sめ ✕ ♥ ▯ ⑪ ⊃ ✕

**▼▼▼ Super 8 Motel-Radford M**
(540) 731-9355. **$49-$60.** 1600 Tyler Ave. I-81, exit 109, just w. Int corridors. **Pets:** Other species. $15 one-time fee/room. No service, supervision.

ASK Sめ ✕ ♥

# RAPHINE

**▼▼ Days Inn-Shenandoah Valley M**
(540) 377-2604. **$59-$94.** 584 Oakland Cr. I-81, exit 205, just sw. Int corridors. **Pets:** Other species. $6 daily fee/pet. Supervision.

ASK Sめ ✕ ♥ ⊃

---

# RICHMOND METROPOLITAN AREA

# ASHLAND

**▼▼▼ Days Inn Ashland M**
(804) 798-4262. **$50-$90.** 806 England St. I-95, exit 92B, just w on SR 54. Ext corridors. **Pets:** Accepted.

✕ ♥ ⊃

**▼▼▼▼ The Henry Clay Inn CI**
(804) 798-3100. **$90-$165.** 114 N Railroad Ave. I-95, exit 92, 1.5 mi w on SR 54, then n. Ext/int corridors. **Pets:** Accepted.

ASK Sめ ✕ ♥ ▯

# CHESTER

**AAA ▼▼▼▼ AmeriSuites (Chester/River's Bend) SH ❖**
(804) 530-4600. **$109-$179.** 13148 Kingston Ave. I-295, exit 15B, just w; I-95, exit 61A 4.5 mi e; in River's Bend. Int corridors. **Pets:** Small. $10 daily fee/pet. Service with restrictions, supervision.

SAVE Sめ ✕ ♿ ♥ ▯ ⊃

# DOSWELL

**▲▲▲ ▼▼▼ Best Western-Kings Quarters** 🆂🅷
(804) 876-3321. **$59-$189, 3 day notice.** 16102 Theme Park Way. I-95, exit 98, just e on SR 30; entrance to theme park. Ext corridors. **Pets:** Small, other species. $25 deposit/pet. Service with restrictions, crate.
🆂🅰🆅🅴 🆂🔟 ✕ ⚙ 🚪 🖥 🍴 ➿ ✕

# GLEN ALLEN

**▲▲▲ ▼▼▼ AmeriSuites (Richmond/Innsbrook)** 🆂🅷
(804) 747-9644. **$99-$149.** 4100 Cox Rd. I-64, exit 178B, 0.5 mi e to Dominion Blvd, then just n. Int corridors. **Pets:** Accepted.
🆂🅰🆅🅴 🆂🔟 ✕ 🅼 ⚙ 🚪 🖥

**▼▼▼ Candlewood Suites Richmond-West** 🆂🅷
(804) 364-2000. **$94-$149.** 4120 Brookriver Dr. I-64, exit 178, just w on W Broad St. Int corridors. **Pets:** Medium, dogs only. $75 one-time fee/pet. Service with restrictions, crate.
🅰🆂🅺 🆂🔟 ✕ 🅼 ⚙ 🚪 🖥

**▼▼ Homestead Studio Suites**
**Hotel-Richmond/Innsbrook** 🅼
(804) 747-8898. **$70-$80.** 10961 W Broad St. I-64, exit 178B, just e on W Broad St, then just s on Cox Rd. Ext corridors. **Pets:** $25 daily fee/pet. Service with restrictions, supervision.
🅰🆂🅺 🆂🔟 ✕ 🚪 🖥

**▼▼▼ Homewood Suites by Hilton Richmond West**
**End-Innsbrook** 🆂🅷
(804) 217-8000. **$109-$159.** 4100 Innslake Dr. I-64, exit 178B, just e on W Broad St to Cox Rd, then just n. Int corridors. **Pets:** Accepted.
🅰🆂🅺 🆂🔟 ✕ 🅼 ⚙ 🚪 🖥 ➿

**▼▼▼ Residence Inn by Marriott** 🆂🅷
(804) 762-9852. **$144-$169.** 3940 Westerre Pkwy. I-64, exit 180, n on Gaskins Rd to W Broad St. Int corridors. **Pets:** Accepted.
🅰🆂🅺 🆂🔟 ✕ 🅼 ⚙ 🚪 🖥 ➿ ✕

# RICHMOND

**▲▲▲ ▼▼▼ AmeriSuites (Richmond/Arboretum)** 🆂🅷
(804) 560-1566. **$49-$129.** 201 Arboretum Pl. Jct Powhite Pkwy (US 76) and Midlothian Tpke (US 60), just w. Int corridors. **Pets:** Accepted.
🆂🅰🆅🅴 ✕ 🅼 ⚙ 🚪 🖥 ➿

**▼▼▼ Candlewood Suites** 🆂🅷
(804) 271-0016. **$85-$109.** 4301 Commerce Rd. I-95, exit 69, just n. Int corridors. **Pets:** Medium, other species. $50 one-time fee/room. Service with restrictions, crate.
🅰🆂🅺 🆂🔟 ✕ 🅼 ⚙ 🚪 🖥

**▲▲▲ ▼▼▼ Commonwealth Park Suites** 🆂🅷
(804) 343-7300. **$109-$169.** 901 Bank St. Jct 9th and Bank sts; across the green from the state capitol. Int corridors. **Pets:** Dogs only. $40 daily fee/room. Service with restrictions, crate.
🆂🅰🆅🅴 🆂🔟 ✕ ⚙ 🖥 🍴

**▼▼ Days Inn-Richmond West** 🆂🅷
(804) 282-3300. **$59-$159.** 2100 Dickens Rd. I-64, exit 183B westbound; exit 183 eastbound, 0.3 mi e on W Broad St, just n. Int corridors. **Pets:** Large, other species. $10 daily fee/pet. Designated rooms, service with restrictions, supervision.
🅰🆂🅺 🆂🔟 ✕ ⚙ 🚪 🖥 ➿

**▼▼ Holiday Inn-Richmond North** 🆂🅷
(804) 266-8753. **$79-$129.** 801 E Parham Rd. I-95, exit 83B. Int corridors. **Pets:** Accepted.
🅰🆂🅺 🆂🔟 ✕ 🅼 ⚙ 🎦 🚪 🖥 🍴 ➿

**▼▼▼ Homestead Studio Suites**
**Hotel-Richmond/Midlothian** 🆂🅷
(804) 272-1800. **$76-$81.** 241 Arboretum Pl. Jct Powhite Pkwy (US 76) and Midlothian Tpke (US 60), just w. Int corridors. **Pets:** $25 daily fee/pet. Service with restrictions, supervision.
🅰🆂🅺 🆂🔟 ✕ 🅼 ⚙ 🎦 🚪 🖥

**▲▲▲ ▼▼▼▼▼ The Jefferson Hotel** 🅻🅷 🐾
(804) 788-8000. **$285-$335.** 101 W Franklin St. Franklin and Adams sts; center. Int corridors. **Pets:** Other species. $40 daily fee/pet. Service with restrictions.
🆂🅰🆅🅴 🆂🔟 ✕ ⚙ 🎦 🚪 🍴 ➿

**▼▼▼ Omni Richmond Hotel** 🅻🅷
(804) 344-7000. **$215.** 100 S 12th St. I-95, exit 74A; I-195, exit Canal St. Int corridors. **Pets:** Accepted.
🅰🆂🅺 🆂🔟 ✕ ⚙ 🚪 🖥 🍴 ➿

**▲▲▲ ▼▼▼ Quality Inn West End** 🆂🅷
(804) 346-0000. **$79-$99.** 8008 W Broad St. I-64, exit 183C westbound; exit 183 eastbound, 1.5 mi w. Int corridors. **Pets:** Medium. $20 daily fee/room, $35 one-time fee/pet. Service with restrictions, supervision.
🆂🅰🆅🅴 🆂🔟 ✕ ⚙ 🚪 ➿

**▼▼▼ Radisson Hotel Historic Richmond** 🆂🅷
(804) 644-9871. **$90-$110.** 301 W Franklin St. Franklin St at Madison. Int corridors. **Pets:** Accepted.
✕ ⚙ 🚪 🖥 🍴 ➿

**▲▲▲ ▼▼▼ Sheraton Richmond West** 🅻🅷
(804) 285-2000. **$139-$189.** 6624 W Broad St. I-64, exit 183 eastbound; exit 183B westbound. Int corridors. **Pets:** Accepted.
🆂🅰🆅🅴 🆂🔟 ✕ 🅼 ⚙ 🎦 🚪 🖥 🍴 ➿ ✕

**▲▲▲ ▼▼▼ Wyndham Richmond Airport** 🆂🅷
(804) 226-4300. **$119-$129.** 4700 S Laburnum Ave. I-64, exit 195, 0.5 mi s. Int corridors. **Pets:** Accepted.
🆂🅰🆅🅴 ✕ ⚙ 🚪 🖥 🍴 ➿ ✕

# SANDSTON

**▲▲▲ ▼▼▼ Holiday Inn-Airport** 🆂🅷
(804) 222-6450. **$79-$169.** 5203 Williamsburg Rd. I-64, exit 195, 1.5 mi s to Williamsburg Rd, then just e. Ext/int corridors. **Pets:** Accepted.
🆂🅰🆅🅴 🆂🔟 ✕ ⚙ 🚪 🖥 🍴 ➿

**▼▼ Motel 6-Richmond Airport #435** 🅼
(804) 222-7600. **$41-$55.** 5704 Williamsburg Rd. I-64, exit 197A (Sandston-RIC Airport), just s to Williamsburg Rd, then just w. Ext corridors. **Pets:** Accepted.
🆂🔟 ✕ ⚙ ➿

---

**END METROPOLITAN AREA**

# ROANOKE

**AmeriSuites (Roanoke/Valley View Mall)** SH
(540) 366-4700. **$49-$129.** 5040 Valley View Blvd. I-581, exit 3E, just e, then just s via shopping center exit. Int corridors. **Pets:** Small. $10 daily fee/pet. Designated rooms, service with restrictions, supervision.

**Best Western Inn at Valley View** SH
(540) 362-2400. **$69-$139, 7 day notice.** 5050 Valley View Blvd. I-581, exit 3E, just e, then just s via shopping center exit. Int corridors. **Pets:** Accepted.

**Clarion Hotel Roanoke Airport** SH
(540) 362-4500. **$70-$75.** 3315 Ordway Dr. I-581, exit 3W, just w to Ordway Dr, then 0.6 mi n via service road. Int corridors. **Pets:** Medium. $35 one-time fee/room. Service with restrictions, crate.

**Comfort Inn Airport** SH
(540) 527-2020. **$74-$144.** 5070 Valley View Blvd. I-81, exit 143 to I-581, exit 3, e to Hershberger Rd. Int corridors. **Pets:** Accepted.

**Days Inn** SH
(540) 366-0341. **$54-$104.** 8118 Plantation Rd. I-81, exit 146, just e on SR 115. Ext/int corridors. **Pets:** Other species. $15 one-time fee/room. Service with restrictions, supervision.

**MainStay Suites Roanoke Airport** SH
(540) 527-3030. **$79-$180, 7 day notice.** 5080 Valley View Blvd. I-581, exit 3E, just n. Int corridors. **Pets:** Accepted.

**Ramada Inn Conference Center** SH
(540) 343-0121. **$49-$99.** 1927 Franklin Rd. Off US 220; US 220 business route exit northbound, Wonju St exit southbound. Ext corridors. **Pets:** Medium. $10 daily fee/pet. Service with restrictions, crate.

**Rodeway Inn-Civic Center** SH
(540) 981-9341. **$48-$125.** 526 Orange Ave NE. I-581, exit 4E, jct US 400 and 11, just n. Ext corridors. **Pets:** Accepted.

**Sleep Inn Tanglewood** SH
(540) 772-1500. **$69-$125.** 4045 Electric Rd. I-581/US 220, exit Franklin Rd/Salem, 0.7 mi n on SR 419. Int corridors. **Pets:** Accepted.

**Super 8 Motel** SH
(540) 563-8888. **$53-$73, 3 day notice.** 6616 Thirlane Rd. I-581, exit 25, s on SR 117 (Peters Creek Rd), then just w. Int corridors. **Pets:** Medium, other species. $10 daily fee/pet. Service with restrictions, supervision.

# ROCKY MOUNT

**Comfort Inn-Rocky Mount** M
(540) 489-4000. **$60-$130.** 1730 N Main St. 1.5 mi n on US 220 business route. Int corridors. **Pets:** Small. $20 daily fee/pet. Designated rooms, no service, crate.

**Franklin Motel** M
(540) 483-9962. **$45-$80, 7 day notice.** 20281 Virgil H Goode Hwy. 6.5 mi n on US 220. Ext corridors. **Pets:** Small, dogs only. $10 daily fee/pet. Designated rooms, service with restrictions, supervision.

# SALEM

**Blue Jay Budget Host Inn** M ❀
(540) 380-2080. **$32-$80, 3 day notice.** 5399 W Main St. I-81, exit 132, just e, then 0.3 mi n on US 11/460. Ext corridors. **Pets:** Medium. $7 daily fee/pet. Designated rooms, service with restrictions, supervision.

**Comfort Suites Inn at Ridgewood Farm** SH
(540) 375-4800. **$70-$175.** 2898 Keagy Rd. I-81, exit 141, 4.7 mi s on SR 419, then just w. Int corridors. **Pets:** Accepted.

**Econo Lodge-Roanoke/Salem** M
(540) 389-0280. **$44-$91.** 301 Wildwood Rd. I-81, exit 137, just e on SR 112. Ext corridors. **Pets:** Very small. $5 daily fee/pet. Service with restrictions, supervision.

**Holiday Inn Express** SH
(540) 986-1000. **$79-$125.** 1535 E Main St. I-81, exit 141, 2 mi s on SR 419, then just w on US 460. Ext/int corridors. **Pets:** Other species. $25 daily fee/pet. Service with restrictions.

**Quality Inn Roanoke/Salem** SH
(540) 562-1912. **$49-$120.** 179 Sheraton Dr. I-81, exit 141, 0.4 mi e on SR 419. Int corridors. **Pets:** Accepted.

# SOUTH BOSTON

**Holiday Inn-Express** SH
(434) 575-4000. **$89-$129.** 1074 Bill Tuck Hwy. Just e on US 58, from jct US 501. Int corridors. **Pets:** Accepted.

**Quality Inn Howard House** SH
(434) 572-4311. **$52-$129.** 2001 Seymour Dr. Jct US 58, 501 and 360, 1 mi e on US 360. Ext corridors. **Pets:** $10 one-time fee/room. Service with restrictions, supervision.

# SOUTH HILL

**Comfort Inn** SH
(434) 447-2600. **$56-$85.** 918 E Atlantic St. I-85, exit 12B, just w. Ext corridors. **Pets:** Accepted.

**Super 8 Motel** SH
(434) 447-2313. **$61-$136.** 250 Thompson St. I-85, exit 12A, just n. Int corridors. **Pets:** Medium. $10 daily fee/pet. Service with restrictions, supervision.

# STAFFORD

**Days Inn Aquia-Quantico** SH
(540) 659-0022. **$73-$89.** 2868 Jefferson Davis Hwy. I-95, exit 143A, jct US 1 and SR 610. Ext corridors. **Pets:** Medium, other species. $6 daily fee/pet. Designated rooms, service with restrictions, supervision.

**Holiday Inn Express** SH
(540) 657-5566. **$99-$129.** 28 Greenspring Dr. I-95, exit 143B, just w on Garrisonville Rd. Int corridors. **Pets:** Small, dogs only. $25 daily fee/pet. Service with restrictions, supervision.

# STAUNTON

**Best Western Staunton Inn** SH
(540) 885-1112. **$74-$125.** 92 Rowe Rd. I-81, exit 222, just e on US 250. Int corridors. **Pets:** Accepted.

**AAA ▼▼▼▼ Comfort Inn SH ❖**
(540) 886-5000. **$69-$129.** 1302 Richmond Ave. I-81, exit 222, just w on US 250. Int corridors. **Pets:** $10 daily fee/room. Designated rooms, service with restrictions, supervision.
SAVE S6 ✕ 🗗 🖥 🖵 ➽

**AAA ▼▼▼ Days Inn-Business Place SH ❖**
(540) 248-0888. **$39-$109, 30 day notice.** 273-D Bells Ln. I-81, exit 225, just w. Ext corridors. **Pets:** Other species. $10 daily fee/pet. Designated rooms, service with restrictions, supervision.
SAVE S6 ✕ 🖫 🖥 🖵 ➽

**AAA ▼▼▼ Econo Lodge Staunton SH**
(540) 885-5158. **$60-$90, 10 day notice.** 1031 Richmond Ave. I-81, exit 222, 0.7 mi w on US 250. Ext/int corridors. **Pets:** Medium. $10 daily fee/pet. Service with restrictions, supervision.
SAVE S6 ✕ 🖥 🖵

**▼▼ GuestHouse International Inn SH**
(540) 885-3117. **$52-$110.** 42 Sangers Ln. I-81, exit 222, just e on US 250. Ext corridors. **Pets:** $10 one-time fee/room. Designated rooms, service with restrictions, supervision.
✕ 🗗 🖫 🖥 🖵 ➽ ✕

**AAA ▼▼▼ Holiday Inn Golf & Conference
Center SH ❖**
(540) 248-6020. **$76-$169.** 152 Fairway Ln. I-81, exit 225, 0.3 mi w on SR 275 (Woodrow Wilson Pkwy). Int corridors. **Pets:** Large, other species. $15 one-time fee/pet. Designated rooms, service with restrictions, supervision.
SAVE S6 ✕ 🗗 🖥 🖵 🍽 ➽

**▼▼ Howard Johnson Express Inn SH**
(540) 886-5330. **$60-$90, 3 day notice.** 268 N Central Ave. I-81, exit 222, 2.2 mi w on SR 250 into downtown; between Pine and Baldwin sts. Ext corridors. **Pets:** $10 daily fee/pet. Service with restrictions, supervision.
✕ 🖫 🖥 🖵 ➽

**AAA ▼▼▼ Quality Inn-Conference Center SH ❖**
(540) 248-5111. **$45-$95, 30 day notice.** 96 Baker Ln. I-81, exit 225, just e on SR 275 (Woodrow Wilson Pkwy). Ext corridors. **Pets:** Large. $10 daily fee/pet. Designated rooms, service with restrictions, supervision.
SAVE S6 ✕ 🖥 🖵 🍽 ➽

**AAA ▼▼▼ Sleep Inn SH**
(540) 887-6500. **$74-$129, 7 day notice.** 222 Jefferson Hwy. I-81, exit 222, just e on US 250. Int corridors. **Pets:** Accepted.
SAVE S6 ✕ 🖫 🖥 🖵

**▼▼ Super 8 Motel M**
(540) 886-2888. **$45-$99, 3 day notice.** 1015 Richmond Rd. I-81, exit 222, 1.2 mi w on US 250. Int corridors. **Pets:** Accepted.
ASK S6 ✕ 🖥

## STEPHENS CITY

**AAA ▼▼▼▼ Comfort Inn-Stephens City SH**
(540) 869-6500. **$73-$150.** 167 Town Run Ln. I-81, exit 307, just se. Int corridors. **Pets:** Other species. $10 daily fee/pet. Service with restrictions, supervision.
SAVE S6 ✕ 🗗 🖥 🖵 ➽

## STONY CREEK

**AAA ▼▼▼▼ Hampton Inn-Stony Creek SH**
(434) 246-5500. **$79-$129.** 10476 Blue Star Hwy. I-95, exit 33, just s on SR 301. Int corridors. **Pets:** Medium, other species. $10 daily fee/pet. Service with restrictions, crate.
SAVE S6 ✕ 🖫M 🗗 🖫 🖥 🖵 ➽

**AAA ▼▼▼▼ Sleep Inn & Suites SH**
(434) 246-5100. **$60-$109.** 11019 Blue Star Hwy. I-95, exit 33, 0.3 mi s on SR 301. Int corridors. **Pets:** Medium, other species. $10 daily fee/pet. Service with restrictions, crate.
SAVE S6 ✕ 🗗 🖥 🖵 ➽

## STRASBURG

**AAA ▼▼▼▼ Hotel Strasburg CI**
(540) 465-9191. **$85-$120.** 213 S Holliday St. I-81, exit 298, 2.2 mi s on US 11, then just s. Int corridors. **Pets:** Medium, dogs only. $10 daily fee/pet. Service with restrictions, supervision.
SAVE S6 ✕ 🍽

## TAPPAHANNOCK

**▼▼ Super 8 Motel M**
(804) 443-3888. **$54-$75.** 1800 Tappahannock Blvd. SR 17 and 360. Int corridors. **Pets:** Small, other species. $6 daily fee/room. Designated rooms, service with restrictions, supervision.
ASK S6 ✕ 🖥

## THORNBURG

**▼▼▼ Quality Inn SH**
(540) 582-1097. **$59-$159.** 6409 Dan Bell Ln. I-95, exit 118 (SR 606), just w. Ext corridors. **Pets:** Accepted.
ASK S6 ✕ 🖫 🖥 🖵 ➽

## TROUTVILLE

**AAA ▼▼▼▼ Comfort Inn Troutville SH**
(540) 992-5600. **$64-$125.** 2545 Lee Hwy S. I-81, exit 150A, just s on US 11. Int corridors. **Pets:** Accepted.
SAVE S6 ✕ 🖥 🖵 ➽

**AAA ▼▼ Travelodge Roanoke North M**
(540) 992-6700. **$40-$95.** 2619 Lee Hwy S. I-81, exit 150A, just e, then just s on US 11. Ext corridors. **Pets:** Very small. $6 daily fee/pet. Service with restrictions, supervision.
SAVE S6 ✕ 🖥 🖵 ➽ ✕

## VERONA

**AAA ▼▼▼▼ Ramada Limited SH**
(540) 248-8981. **$39-$119, 3 day notice.** 70 Lodge Ln. I-81, exit 227, just w, then just n. Ext corridors. **Pets:** Small. $10 one-time fee/pet. Designated rooms, no service, supervision.
SAVE S6 ✕ 🗗 🖥 🖵 ➽

## WARRENTON

**AAA ▼▼▼▼ Comfort Inn SH ❖**
(540) 349-8900. **$89-$149.** 7379 Comfort Inn Dr. 1.5 mi n on US 15/29, on service road. Ext/int corridors. **Pets:** $10 one-time fee/pet. Designated rooms, service with restrictions, supervision.
SAVE S6 ✕ 🖥 🖵 ➽

**▼▼▼▼ Holiday Inn Express Hotel & Suites SH**
(540) 341-3461. **$85-$105.** 410 Holiday Ct. Off US 15/29 and 17, exit Meetze Rd (SR 643), just w, then 0.8 mi n on Walker Rd. Int corridors. **Pets:** Accepted.
ASK S6 ✕ 🖫M 🗗 🖫 🖥 🖵 ➽

## WARSAW

**▼▼▼▼ Best Western Warsaw SH**
(804) 333-1700. **$72-$155.** 4522 Richmond Rd. US 360, just w of town. Int corridors. **Pets:** Small, other species. $10 daily fee/pet. Service with restrictions, supervision.
ASK S6 ✕ 🖫 🖥 🖵 ➽

# WAYNESBORO

**Days Inn Waynesboro** SH
(540) 943-1101. **$49-$89.** 2060 Rosser Ave. I-64, exit 94, 0.5 mi n on US 340. Ext corridors. **Pets:** Other species. $10 daily fee/room. Service with restrictions, supervision.

**Quality Inn Waynesboro** SH
(540) 942-1171. **$68-$90.** 640 W Broad St. I-64, exit 96, 3 mi w on SR 624; jct US 250 and 340. Ext/int corridors. **Pets:** $10 daily fee/pet. Service with restrictions, crate.

**Super 8 Motel** SH
(540) 943-3888. **$54-$95, 7 day notice.** 2045 Rosser Ave. I-64, exit 94, n on US 340 to Lew DeWitt Blvd, then just w to Apple Tree Ln. Int corridors. **Pets:** Other species. $5 daily fee/pet. Designated rooms, service with restrictions, supervision.

---

# WILLIAMSBURG, JAMESTOWN & YORKTOWN AREA

## WILLIAMSBURG

**Best Western Colonial Capitol Inn** SH
(757) 253-1222. **$59-$119, 3 day notice.** 111 Penniman Rd. Just n of jct US 60/Richmond Rd and SR 5. Int corridors. **Pets:** Large, other species. $10 one-time fee/room. Service with restrictions.

**Best Western Patrick Henry Inn** SH
(757) 229-9540. **$59-$169, 3 day notice.** 249 E York St NW. E on US 60/Richmond Rd at jct SR 5 and 31; 1 blk from Colonial Williamsburg. Int corridors. **Pets:** Large, other species. $15 one-time fee/room. Service with restrictions.

**Best Western Williamsburg Westpark Hotel** SH
(757) 229-1134. **$39-$109.** 1600 Richmond Rd. Jct US 60/Richmond Rd and SR 612 (Ironbound Rd). Ext/int corridors. **Pets:** Accepted.

**Days Inn Colonial Downtown** SH
(757) 229-7600. **$69-$129.** 902 Richmond Rd. Just w of Colonial Williamsburg on US 60. Ext corridors. **Pets:** Small. $15 daily fee/pet. Service with restrictions, supervision.

**Four Points by Sheraton Hotel & Suites Williamsburg Historic District** SH
(757) 229-4100. **$59-$289.** 351 York St. US 60 E, 0.3 mi se of jct SR 5 and 31. Ext/int corridors. **Pets:** Medium, other species. $25 one-time fee/pet. Designated rooms, service with restrictions, crate.

**Holiday Inn Patriot** SH 🐾
(757) 565-2600. **$69-$129.** 3032 Richmond Rd. I-64, exit 234 (SR 199 E) to US 60, 2.5 mi e. Int corridors. **Pets:** Small. $10 daily fee/room. Designated rooms, service with restrictions.

**La Quinta Inn Williamsburg (Historic Area)** SH
(757) 253-1663. **$45-$135.** 119 Bypass Rd. US 60 Bypass Rd, 0.3 mi e of Richmond Rd. Ext corridors. **Pets:** Small, other species. Service with restrictions.

**Motel Rochambeau** M
(757) 229-2851. **$30-$56.** 929 Capitol Landing Rd. I-64, exit 238, 1 mi e on SR 143, then just w on SR 5. Ext corridors. **Pets:** Accepted.

**Quarterpath Inn** M
(757) 220-0960. **$39-$119, 3 day notice.** 620 York St. I-64, exit 242 (SR 199 W), 0.6 mi w to US 60 E, then just w. Ext corridors. **Pets:** Large. Service with restrictions.

**Ramada Inn 1776** SH
(757) 220-1776. **$55-$129.** 725 Bypass Rd. US 60 (Bypass Rd), 0.5 mi w of jct SR 132. Int corridors. **Pets:** Small. Designated rooms, no service, supervision.

**Red Roof Inn-Williamsburg** M
(757) 259-1948. **$32-$129.** 824 Capitol Landing Rd. I-64, exit 238, 0.9 mi se on SR 143, then just w on SR 5. Ext corridors. **Pets:** Accepted.

**Residence Inn by Marriott Williamsburg** SH
(757) 941-2000. **$99-$350.** 1648 Richmond Rd. US 60, just w of jct Bypass Rd. Int corridors. **Pets:** Accepted.

**Super 8 Motel-Historic** M
(757) 229-0500. **$30-$85.** 304 2nd St. I-642, exit 242 (SR 199 W), 0.6 mi w on SR 199 to SR 143, 1.6 mi w to SR 162, then just w. Ext corridors. **Pets:** Accepted.

## YORKTOWN

**Candlewood Suites-Yorktown** SH 🐾
(757) 952-1120. **$79-$129.** 329 Commonwealth Dr. I-64, exit 256B, just n, then just e. Int corridors. **Pets:** Small, other species. $75 one-time fee/pet. Service with restrictions, supervision.

**TownePlace Suites by Marriott** SH 🐾
(757) 874-8884. **$79-$129.** 200 Cybernetics Way. I-64, exit 256B, e to Kiln Creek Pkwy. Int corridors. **Pets:** Other species. $75 one-time fee/room. Service with restrictions.

---

# END AREA

---

## WINCHESTER

**Americas Best Value Inn** SH
(540) 662-2521. **$55-$85.** 2649 Valley Ave. I-81, exit 310, just w to US 11, then 2 mi n. Ext corridors. **Pets:** Accepted.

**Best Western Lee-Jackson Motor Inn** SH
(540) 662-4154. **$59-$84.** 711 Millwood Ave. I-81, exit 313B, just nw on US 50/522/17. Ext corridors. **Pets:** Medium. $5 daily fee/pet. Service with restrictions, supervision.

**⟠ ▼▼ Days Inn** SH
(540) 667-1200. **$50-$75.** 2951 Valley Ave. I-81, exit 310, just w, then 1.8 mi n on US 11. Ext corridors. **Pets:** Accepted.
[SAVE] [S∅] [✕] [🛏] [🍽] [☕]

**⟠ ▼▼▼ Holiday Inn Winchester** SH
(540) 667-3300. **$69-$89.** 1017 Millwood Pike. I-81, exit 313 northbound; exit 313A southbound, just se on US 50/17, at US 522. Ext/int corridors. **Pets:** Designated rooms, service with restrictions.
[SAVE] [S∅] [✕] [⟁] [🛏] [💻] [🍽] [☕]

**▼ Mohawk Motel** M
(540) 667-1410. **$51-$56.** 2754 Northwestern Pike. I-81, exit 317, 3 mi s on SR 37, then 1.7 mi w on US 50. Ext corridors. **Pets:** $10 daily fee/pet. Designated rooms, service with restrictions, supervision.
[ASK] [S∅] [✕]

**⟠ ▼▼ Red Roof Inn** SH
(540) 667-5000. **$58-$80.** 991 Millwood Pike. I-81, exit 313 northbound; exit 313A southbound, just se on US 50/17. Ext corridors. **Pets:** Accepted.
[SAVE] [S∅] [✕] [🛏] [💻]

**⟠ ▼▼ Super 8 Motel** SH ❀
(540) 665-4450. **$51-$62, 10 day notice.** 1077 Millwood Pike. I-81, exit 313 northbound; exit 313A southbound, 0.3 mi se on US 50/17. Int corridors. **Pets:** Other species. $7 one-time fee/pet. Service with restrictions, supervision.
[SAVE] [S∅] [✕] [🛏]

**⟠ ▼ Tourist City Motel** M
(540) 662-9011. **$38-$54, 5 day notice.** 214 Millwood Ave. I-81, exit 313 northbound; exit 313B southbound, 1 mi nw on US 50/522. Ext corridors. **Pets:** Medium. $5 one-time fee/pet. Designated rooms, service with restrictions, supervision.
[SAVE] [✕] [🛏]

**⟠ ▼▼▼ Travelodge of Winchester** SH
(540) 665-0685. **$64-$109.** 160 Front Royal Pike. I-81, exit 313 northbound; exit 313A southbound, just s on US 522. Int corridors. **Pets:** Small. $5 daily fee/pet. Service with restrictions.
[SAVE] [S∅] [✕] [⟁] [🛏] [💻] [☕]

## WOODSTOCK

**⟠ ▼ Budget Host Inn** M
(540) 459-4086. **$45-$52.** 1290 S Main St. I-81, exit 283, 0.8 mi se on SR 42, then 0.6 mi s on US 11. Ext corridors. **Pets:** Accepted.
[SAVE] [S∅] [✕] [🛏] [☕]

**⟠ ▼▼▼ Comfort Inn Shenandoah** SH
(540) 459-7600. **$69-$129.** 1011 Motel Dr. I-81, exit 283, just e. Int corridors. **Pets:** Accepted.
[SAVE] [S∅] [✕] [🛏] [💻] [☕]

## WYTHEVILLE

**⟠ ▼▼▼ Best Western Wytheville Inn** SH
(276) 228-7300. **$60-$160, 3 day notice.** 355 Nye Rd. I-77, exit 41, just e. Int corridors. **Pets:** Other species. Designated rooms, service with restrictions, supervision.
[SAVE] [S∅] [✕] [🛏] [💻] [☕]

**▼ Budget Host Inn/Interstate Inn** M
(276) 228-8618. **$45-$145.** 705 Chapman Rd. I-77/81, exit 73, just w. Ext corridors. **Pets:** Small, other species. $10 daily fee/pet. Service with restrictions, supervision.
[ASK] [S∅] [✕] [🛏]

**▼▼ Days Inn** SH
(276) 228-5500. **$55-$75.** 150 Malin Dr. I-81, exit 73, just w. Ext corridors. **Pets:** Medium. $5 daily fee/pet. Service with restrictions, supervision.
[ASK] [S∅] [✕] [⟁] [💻]

**⟠ ▼▼ Econo Lodge** M
(276) 228-5517. **$45-$150.** 1160 E Main St. I-81, exit 73, 0.8 mi w. Ext corridors. **Pets:** Accepted.
[SAVE] [S∅] [✕] [⟁] [🛏] [💻]

**▼▼ Holiday Inn** SH
(276) 228-5483. **$75-$105.** 1800 E Main St. I-77/81, exit 73, just w. Ext/int corridors. **Pets:** Accepted.
[ASK] [S∅] [✕] [⟁] [✑] [🛏] [💻] [🍽] [☕]

**⟠ ▼▼ Ramada Inn** SH ❀
(276) 228-6000. **$56-$72.** 955 Peppers Ferry Rd. I-77, exit 41, just e. Ext corridors. **Pets:** $10 daily fee/pet. Supervision.
[SAVE] [S∅] [✕] [🛏] [💻] [🍽] [☕]

**⟠ ▼ Red Carpet Inn** M
(276) 228-5525. **$45-$150, 7 day notice.** 280 Lithia Rd. I-77/81, exit 73, just w. Ext corridors. **Pets:** Very small. $10 daily fee/pet. Designated rooms, service with restrictions, supervision.
[SAVE] [S∅] [✕] [🛏]

**▼ Super 8 Motel** SH
(276) 228-6620. **$35-$95.** 130 Nye Cir. I-77, exit 41, just e. Ext corridors. **Pets:** Large, other species. $10 one-time fee/room. Service with restrictions, supervision.
[ASK] [S∅] [✕]

# WASHINGTON

## CITY INDEX

## ABERDEEN

### GuestHouse International Inn & Suites SH
(360) 537-7460. **$65-$279.** 701 E Heron St. Just e on US 12, cross street to Kansas St; downtown. Int corridors. **Pets:** Large. $50 deposit/room, $10 daily fee/pet. Service with restrictions, crate.

ASK SA X Z D H D A

### Olympic Inn M
(360) 533-4200. **$65-$85.** 616 W Heron St. 0.5 mi w; downtown. Ext corridors. **Pets:** Other species. $10 one-time fee/pet. Service with restrictions, supervision.

SAVE SA X H

### Red Lion Inn Aberdeen SH
(360) 532-5210. **$75-$90.** 521 W Wishkah. 0.5 mi w on US 101 N. Ext corridors. **Pets:** Medium. Service with restrictions, crate.

SAVE SA X M Z H D

## AIRWAY HEIGHTS

### Microtel Inn & Suites SH
(509) 242-1200. **$54-$79.** 1215 S Garfield Rd. I-90, exit 277 to SR 2, 4 mi w. Int corridors. **Pets:** Accepted.

ASK SA X Z D H D

## ANACORTES

### Anaco Inn SH
(360) 293-8833. **$59-$129, 3 day notice.** 905 20th St. Just s of downtown. Ext/int corridors. **Pets:** Small, other species. $25 one-time fee/pet. Designated rooms, service with restrictions, supervision.

SAVE X H D

### Anacortes Inn M
(360) 293-3153. **$65-$125.** 3006 Commercial Ave. Just s of downtown. Ext corridors. **Pets:** Accepted.

SAVE SA X H D A

### Cap Sante Inn M ❀
(360) 293-0602. **$62-$81.** 906 9th St. On 9th St, just e. Ext corridors. **Pets:** $10 daily fee/pet. Designated rooms, service with restrictions, supervision.

SAVE X H K

### Fidalgo Country Inn SH ❀
(360) 293-3494. **$94-$119.** 7645 SR 20. Jct Fidalgo Bay Rd. Ext/int corridors. **Pets:** Medium. $10 daily fee/pet. Designated rooms, service with restrictions.

SAVE SA X M Z H D A

### Islands Inn M
(360) 293-4644. **$69-$110.** 3401 Commercial Ave. Just s of downtown. Ext corridors. **Pets:** Accepted.

ASK SA X H D TI A

## ASHFORD

### Mountain Meadows Inn Bed & Breakfast BB
(360) 569-2788. **$99-$165, 14 day notice.** 28912 SR 706 E. West end of town. Ext/int corridors. **Pets:** Accepted.

X H D K W Z

## BELLINGHAM

### Best Western Lakeway Inn & Conference Center SH
(360) 671-1011. **$79-$149.** 714 Lakeway Dr. I-5, exit 253 (Lakeway Dr), just se. Int corridors. **Pets:** Small. $10 daily fee/room. Designated rooms, service with restrictions, crate.

SAVE SA X Z H D TI A X

### The Chrysalis Inn & Spa SH
(360) 756-1005. **$160-$299.** 804 10th St. I-5, exit 250, 1.3 mi nw on Old Fairhaven Pkwy, 0.6 mi n via 12th and 11th sts, just w on Taylor Ave, then just n. Int corridors. **Pets:** Small, dogs only. $50 one-time fee/room. Designated rooms, service with restrictions, supervision.

SAVE SA X H D TI

### Fairhaven Village Inn SH ❀
(360) 733-1311. **$119-$169.** 1200 10th St. I-5, exit 250, 1.5 mi w. Int corridors. **Pets:** Medium. $20 daily fee/pet. Designated rooms, service with restrictions, supervision.

SAVE X M Z D H D

### Holiday Inn Express-Bellingham SH ❀
(360) 671-4800. **$89-$112.** 4160 Guide Meridian St. I-5, exit 256A, 0.7 mi e. Int corridors. **Pets:** Medium, other species. $15 one-time fee/room. Designated rooms, service with restrictions, supervision.

SAVE SA X M Z D H D A

**AAA ◈◈◈ Hotel Bellwether SH** ❖
(360) 392-3100. **$139-$805, 3 day notice.** One Bellwether Way. I-5, exit 253 (Lakeway Dr), 0.9 mi nw via Lakeway Dr and E Holly St, just w on Bay St, 0.6 mi n on W Chestnut St, then just w. Int corridors. **Pets:** Medium, dogs only. $65 one-time fee/room. Designated rooms, service with restrictions, supervision.
SAVE S⦵ X ▆ ⦿ ⦻

**◈◈ Motel 6-44 M**
(360) 671-4494. **$45-$61.** 3701 Byron Ave. I-5, exit 252, just nw. Ext corridors. **Pets:** Accepted.
S⦵ X ⦿M ⛨ ⟆

**AAA ◈◈◈ Quality Inn Baron Suites SH** ❖
(360) 647-8000. **$90-$200.** 100 E Kellogg Rd. I-5, exit 256A, 1 mi ne via Guide Meridian St. Ext/int corridors. **Pets:** Large. $25 one-time fee/room. Designated rooms, service with restrictions, supervision.
SAVE S⦵ X ⦵ ⛨ ▆ ⟆

**AAA ◈◈ Travel House Inn SH**
(360) 671-4600. **$45-$89.** 3750 Meridian St. I-5, exit 256A, just w. Ext corridors. **Pets:** $6 daily fee/room. Designated rooms, service with restrictions, supervision.
SAVE S⦵ X ⛨ ⟆

**◈◈ Val-U Inn SH** ❖
(360) 671-9600. **$60-$85.** 805 Lakeway Dr. I-5, exit 253 (Lakeway Dr), just ne. Int corridors. **Pets:** Medium, dogs only. $5 daily fee/pet. Supervision.
ASK S⦵ X ⛨ ▆

# BLAINE

**◈ Anchor Inn Motel M**
(360) 332-5539. **$51-$73.** 250 Cedar St. I-5, exit 276, 0.6 mi sw via Peace Portal Dr. Ext corridors. **Pets:** Accepted.
ASK S⦵ X ⛨

**AAA ◈◈◈◈ Semiahmoo Resort SH**
(360) 318-2000. **$99-$219, 3 day notice.** 9565 Semiahmoo Pkwy. I-5, exit 270, 9.5 mi nw on Semiahmoo Spit. Int corridors. **Pets:** Medium, dogs only. $50 one-time fee/pet. Designated rooms, service with restrictions, supervision.
SAVE S⦵ X ⦵ ⛨ ▆ ⦿ ⟆ ⦻

# BUCKLEY

**AAA ◈◈◈ Mt View Inn SH**
(360) 829-1100. **$85-$95, 7 day notice.** 29405 SR 410 E. On SR 410 at SR 165. Int corridors. **Pets:** Small, dogs only. $20 one-time fee/pet. Service with restrictions supervision.
SAVE S⦵ X ⛨ ⟆

# BURLINGTON

**AAA ◈◈◈ Cocusa Motel SH** ❖
(360) 757-6044. **$62-$82.** 370 W Rio Vista. I-5, exit 230, just e. Ext corridors. **Pets:** $10 one-time fee/room. Designated rooms, service with restrictions, supervision.
SAVE X ⦵ ⛨ ▆ ⟆

# CASHMERE

**AAA ◈◈◈ Village Inn Motel M**
(509) 782-3522. **$54-$64, 7 day notice.** 229 Cottage Ave. On Business Rt US 2 and 97; downtown. Ext corridors. **Pets:** Small, dogs only. $10 daily fee/pet. Designated rooms, service with restrictions, supervision.
SAVE S⦵ X ⛨

# CASTLE ROCK

**AAA ◈◈◈ Timberland Inn & Suites M**
(360) 274-6002. **$75-$110.** 1271 Mount St. Helens Way. I-5, exit 49, just ne. Ext corridors. **Pets:** Medium. $10 daily fee/pet. Designated rooms, service with restrictions, supervision.
SAVE S⦵ X ⛨ ▆

# CENTRALIA

**◈◈ Motel 6-394 M**
(360) 330-2057. **$37-$51.** 1310 Belmont Ave. I-5, exit 82, 0.6 mi nw. Ext corridors. **Pets:** Accepted.
S⦵ X ⦵ ⛨ ⟆

# CHEHALIS

**AAA ◈◈◈◈ Best Western Park Place Inn & Suites SH**
(360) 748-4040. **$76-$96.** 201 SW Interstate Ave. I-5, exit 76, just se. Int corridors. **Pets:** Small, dogs only. $10 daily fee/pet. Designated rooms, service with restrictions, supervision.
SAVE S⦵ X ⦿M ⦵ ▆ ⟆

# CHELAN

**AAA ◈◈◈ Best Western Lakeside Lodge SH**
(509) 682-4396. **$79-$299, 7 day notice.** 2312 W Woodin Ave. West end of town. Ext corridors. **Pets:** Accepted.
SAVE S⦵ X ⦵ ⦵ ⛨ ▆ ⟆ ⦻

# CHEWELAH

**AAA ◈◈ Nordlig Motel M**
(509) 935-6704. **$56-$61.** W 101 Grant Ave. North edge of town on US 395. Ext corridors. **Pets:** Other species. $3 one-time fee/room. Service with restrictions, supervision.
SAVE S⦵ X ⛨

# CLE ELUM

**AAA ◈◈ Cle Elum Travelers Inn M** ❖
(509) 674-5535. **$49-$57.** 1001 E 1st St. I-90, exit 85, 1 mi w on SR 903. Ext/int corridors. **Pets:** Small. $5 daily fee/pet. Service with restrictions, supervision.
SAVE S⦵ X ⦵ ⛨

**◈◈ Timber Lodge Inn M** ❖
(509) 674-5966. **$60-$65.** 301 W 1st St. I-90, exit 84 eastbound, 1 mi ne; exit westbound, just w; downtown. Ext/int corridors. **Pets:** Other species. $15 one-time fee/pet. Service with restrictions, supervision.
ASK S⦵ X ⛨

# COLFAX

**◈◈◈ Best Western Wheatland Inn SH**
(509) 397-0397. **$59-$99.** 701 N Main. Downtown. Int corridors. **Pets:** $10 daily fee/pet. Service with restrictions, supervision.
ASK S⦵ X ⦿M ⦵ ⦵ ⛨ ▆ ⟆

# COLVILLE

**◈◈◈ Colville Comfort Inn SH**
(509) 684-2010. **$68-$200.** 166 NE Canning Dr. 1.5 mi n on US 395. Int corridors. **Pets:** Accepted.
ASK S⦵ X ⦿M ⦵ ⦵ ⛨ ▆ ⟆

# CONCRETE

**AAA ◈◈◈ Ovenell's Heritage Inn B&B and Log Cabins CA** ❖
(360) 853-8494. **$90-$125, 3 day notice.** 46276 Concrete Sauk Valley Rd. 0.5 mi w of downtown on SR 20, 3 mi se. Ext/int corridors. **Pets:** Dogs only. $15 daily fee/pet. Designated rooms, service with restrictions, supervision.
SAVE X ⛨ ▆ ⦻

# COUGAR

**◈ Lone Fir Resort M** ❖
(360) 238-5210. **$45-$85, 3 day notice.** 16806 Lewis River Rd. Center. Ext corridors. **Pets:** Large. $10 one-time fee/pet. Service with restrictions, supervision.
ASK X ⛨ ▆ ⟆ ⦻ ⦾

# COULEE DAM

### 🔷 💎💎 Coulee House Inn & Suites Ⓜ
(509) 633-1101. **$69-$149.** 110 Roosevelt Way. Just e of river bridge. Ext corridors. **Pets:** Other species. $15 daily fee/pet. Designated rooms, service with restrictions, supervision.

🆂🅰🆅🅴 🆂 ⊠ 🔋 💻 ⤳

# DAYTON

### 💎💎💎 The Weinhard Hotel 🆂🅷 🐾
(509) 382-4032. **$75-$150, 7 day notice.** 235 E Main St. Downtown. Int corridors. **Pets:** Dogs only. $20 one-time fee/pet. Supervision.

🅰🆂🅺 ⊠

# EAST WENATCHEE

### 💎💎💎 Cedars Inn, East Wenatchee 🆂🅷
(509) 886-8000. **$77-$82.** 80 Ninth St NE. Just e of SR 28. Int corridors. **Pets:** Accepted.

🅰🆂🅺 🆂 ⊠ 🔋 ⤳

# EATONVILLE

### 🔷 💎💎 Mill Village Motel Ⓜ
(360) 832-3200. **$80-$90.** 210 Center St E. Just e of jct SR 161; center. Ext corridors. **Pets:** Small. $10 one-time fee/pet. Service with restrictions, supervision.

🆂🅰🆅🅴 ⊠ 🔋 💻

# ELLENSBURG

### 🔷 💎💎💎 Best Western Lincoln Inn & Suites 🆂🅷 🐾
(509) 925-4244. **$79-$179.** 211 W Umptanum Rd. I-90, exit 109, just n, then just w. Int corridors. **Pets:** Medium, dogs only. $25 daily fee/pet. Service with restrictions, supervision.

🆂🅰🆅🅴 🆂 ⊠ 🔋 🗚 🔋 💻 ⤳

### 💎💎💎 Ellensburg Comfort Inn 🆂🅷 🐾
(509) 925-7037. **$81-$134.** 1722 Canyon Rd. I-90, exit 109. Int corridors. **Pets:** $10 daily fee/pet. Service with restrictions, supervision.

🅰🆂🅺 🆂 ⊠ 🔋 🔋 💻 ⤳

### 💎💎 Ellensburg Inn 🆂🅷
(509) 925-9801. **$62-$97.** 1700 Canyon Rd. I-90, exit 109, just n. Int corridors. **Pets:** Accepted.

🅰🆂🅺 🆂 ⊠ 🔋 🍽 ⤳

### 🔷 💎💎 I-90 Inn Motel Ⓜ
(509) 925-9844. **$58-$78.** 1390 Dollar Way Rd. I-90, exit 106, just n. Ext corridors. **Pets:** Medium, dogs only. $10 one-time fee/pet. Designated rooms, service with restrictions, supervision.

🆂🅰🆅🅴 🆂 ⊠ 🔋

### 💎💎 Nites Inn Ⓜ
(509) 962-9600. **$55-$70.** 1200 S Ruby. I-90, exit 109, 0.5 mi n. Ext corridors. **Pets:** Other species. $9 one-time fee/pet. Service with restrictions, supervision.

🅰🆂🅺 🆂 ⊠ 🔋 💻

# ELMA

### 💎💎 Microtel Inn & Suites-Elma 🆂🅷 🐾
(360) 482-6868. **Call for rates.** 800 E Main St. Just ne of jct US 12 and SR 8. Int corridors. **Pets:** Other species. Designated rooms, supervision.

⊠ 🔋 💻

# ENUMCLAW

### 🔷 💎💎 Park Center Hotel 🆂🅷
(360) 825-4490. **$80-$90.** 1000 Griffin Ave. Downtown. Ext corridors. **Pets:** $10 daily fee/pet. Designated rooms, service with restrictions, supervision.

🆂🅰🆅🅴 🆂 ⊠ 🔋 💻 🍽

# FERNDALE

### 💎💎 Ferndale Super 8 🆂🅷
(360) 384-8881. **$56-$74.** 5788 Barrett Ave. I-5, exit 262, just ne. Int corridors. **Pets:** Other species. $25 deposit/room. Designated rooms, service with restrictions, supervision.

🅰🆂🅺 🆂 ⊠ 🔋 🔋 🔋 ⤳

# FORKS

### 🔷 💎💎💎 Forks Motel Ⓜ
(360) 374-6243. **$54-$98, 5 day notice.** 351 US 101 (Forks Ave S). Just s. Ext corridors. **Pets:** Small. $10 deposit/pet. Service with restrictions.

🆂🅰🆅🅴 ⊠ 🔋 ⤳

### 💎💎 Manitou Lodge 🅱🅱 🐾
(360) 374-6295. **$90-$165, 14 day notice.** 813 Kilmer Rd. 7.7 mi sw on SR 110 (LaPush Rd), 0.7 mi w on Mora Rd, then 0.8 mi n. Ext/int corridors. **Pets:** Other species. $10 daily fee/room. Designated rooms, crate.

⊠ 🔋 💻 🗚 🗚 🔋

### 💎💎 Miller Tree Inn Bed & Breakfast 🅱🅱
(360) 374-6806. **$85-$185, 7 day notice.** 654 E Division St. 0.3 mi e of US 101 (S Forks Ave). Ext/int corridors. **Pets:** Other species. $10 daily fee/room. Designated rooms.

⊠ 🔋 💻 🗚 🔋

### 🔷 💎💎💎 Olympic Suites Inn Ⓜ
(360) 374-5400. **$59-$99.** 800 Olympic Dr. North end of town, just ne off US 101 (S Forks Ave). Ext corridors. **Pets:** Accepted.

🆂🅰🆅🅴 ⊠ 🔋 💻 🗚

### 💎💎 Pacific Inn Motel Ⓜ
(360) 374-9400. **$53-$72.** 352 US 101 (S Forks Ave). Just s. Ext corridors. **Pets:** Accepted.

🅰🆂🅺 ⊠ 🔋 💻

# GOLDENDALE

### 🔷 💎💎💎 Quality Inn & Suites Ⓜ
(509) 773-5881. **$69-$98.** 808 E Simcoe Dr. US 97, exit Simcoe Dr, just sw. Ext corridors. **Pets:** Accepted.

🆂🅰🆅🅴 🆂 ⊠ 🔋 💻 🍽 ⤳

# ILWACO

### 🔷 💎 Heidi's Inn Ⓜ
(360) 642-2387. **$48-$95, 7 day notice.** 126 Spruce St. Downtown. Ext corridors. **Pets:** Small, dogs only. $5 daily fee/pet. Designated rooms, service with restrictions, supervision.

🆂🅰🆅🅴 ⊠ 🔋 💻 🗚

# KALALOCH

### 🔷 💎💎💎 Kalaloch Lodge 🅲🅰
(360) 962-2271. **$92-$283, 3 day notice.** 157101 US 101. At MM 157. Ext/int corridors. **Pets:** $12.50 daily fee/pet. Designated rooms, service with restrictions, supervision.

🆂🅰🆅🅴 🆂 ⊠ 🔋 💻 🍽 🗚 🔋

# KALAMA

### 🔷 💎 Kalama River Inn Ⓜ
(360) 673-2855. **$45-$50.** 602 NE Frontage Rd. I-5, exit 30 northbound, 0.4 mi n; exit southbound, 0.4 mi s. Ext corridors. **Pets:** Small. $5 one-time fee/pet. Service with restrictions, supervision.

🆂🅰🆅🅴 🆂 ⊠ 🔋

# KELSO

**Best Western Aladdin** SH
(360) 425-9660. **$64-$99.** 310 Long Ave. I-5, exit 39, 1.1 mi w via Allen St and W Main St, then just n on 5th Ave. Int corridors. **Pets:** Medium, dogs only. $10 daily fee/pet. Designated rooms, service with restrictions, supervision.

**GuestHouse Inn & Suites** SH
(360) 414-5953. **$85-$185.** 501 Three Rivers Dr. I-5, exit 39, 0.3 mi w on Allen St, then 0.3 mi s. Int corridors. **Pets:** Other species. $10 daily fee/pet. Service with restrictions, supervision.

**Motel 6-43** M
(360) 425-3229. **$42-$61.** 106 Minor Rd. I-5, exit 39, 0.3 mi ne. Ext corridors. **Pets:** Accepted.

**Red Lion Hotel & Conference Center Kelso/Longview** SH
(360) 636-4400. **$89-$109.** 510 Kelso Dr. I-5, exit 39, 0.3 mi se. Int corridors. **Pets:** Medium, other species. $25 one-time fee/room. Service with restrictions, crate.

**Super 8 Motel** SH
(360) 423-8880. **$67-$93.** 250 Kelso Dr. I-5, exit 39, just se. Int corridors. **Pets:** Other species. $15 deposit/pet, $10 daily fee/pet. Service with restrictions, crate.

# KENNEWICK

**Best Western Kennewick Inn** SH
(509) 586-1332. **$80-$144.** 4001 W 27th Ave. I-82, exit 113 (US 395), 0.8 mi n. Int corridors. **Pets:** Large, other species. $10 one-time fee/room. Service with restrictions, supervision.

**Clover Island Inn** SH
(509) 586-0541. **$79-$109.** 435 Clover Island Dr. US 395, exit Port of Kennewick, 1 mi e on Columbia Dr, then just n. Int corridors. **Pets:** Other species. $25 one-time fee/pet. Service with restrictions.

**Comfort Inn** M
(509) 783-8396. **$69-$129.** 7801 W Quinault Ave. 0.5 mi s on Columbia Center Blvd from SR 240. Int corridors. **Pets:** Dogs only. $10 daily fee/pet. Service with restrictions, supervision.

**Days Inn Kennewick** SH
(509) 735-9511. **$59-$99.** 2811 W 2nd Ave. Jct US 395 and Clearwater Ave, just s, just w. Ext/int corridors. **Pets:** Medium. $10 one-time fee/room. Supervision.

**Econo Lodge** M
(509) 783-6191. **$78-$130.** 300 N Ely St #A. On US 395, jct Clearwater Ave. Ext corridors. **Pets:** Small, dogs only. $7 daily fee/pet. Designated rooms, service with restrictions, supervision.

**Fairfield Inn by Marriott** SH
(509) 783-2164. **$69-$79.** 7809 W Quinault Ave. 0.5 mi s on Columbia Center Blvd from SR 240. Int corridors. **Pets:** $10 daily fee/pet. Service with restrictions, supervision.

**Guesthouse International Suites** SH
(509) 735-2242. **$52-$62.** 5616 W Clearwater Ave. US 395, 1.9 mi w. Int corridors. **Pets:** $10 one-time fee/pet. Service with restrictions, supervision.

**Kennewick Super 8** SH
(509) 736-6888. **$58-$76.** 626 Columbia Center Blvd. 1.1 mi s of SR 240. Int corridors. **Pets:** $10 one-time fee/room. Service with restrictions, supervision.

**La Quinta Inn & Suites Kennewick** SH
(509) 736-3326. **$69-$109.** 4220 W 27th Pl. I-82, exit 113 (US 395), 0.8 mi n. Int corridors. **Pets:** Medium. Service with restrictions, supervision.

**Red Lion Hotel Columbia Center-Kennewick** SH
(509) 783-0611. **$89.** 1101 N Columbia Center Blvd. SR 240, 0.5 mi s. Int corridors. **Pets:** Large, other species. Service with restrictions, crate.

# LACEY

**Quality Inn & Suites** SH
(360) 493-1991. **$66-$96.** 120 College St SE. I-5, exit 109, just sw. Int corridors. **Pets:** Small. $15 daily fee/pet. Service with restrictions, supervision.

# LA CONNER

**La Conner Country Inn** SH
(360) 466-3101. **$94-$185.** 107 S 2nd St. 2nd and Morris sts; downtown. Ext/int corridors. **Pets:** Other species. $25 one-time fee/room. Designated rooms, service with restrictions, supervision.

# LANGLEY

**Island Tyme Bed & Breakfast** BB
(360) 221-5078. **$109-$195, 7 day notice.** 4940 S Bayview Rd. SR 525 at MM 15, just e on Marshview, 2.1 mi n. Int corridors. **Pets:** Accepted.

**Villa Isola Bed & Breakfast Inn** BB
(360) 221-5052. **$95-$150, 14 day notice.** 5489 Coles Rd. 5 mi w on SR 525 from Clinton ferry landing, 0.6 mi n. Ext/int corridors. **Pets:** $20 daily fee/room. Service with restrictions, supervision.

# LEAVENWORTH

**Alpine Rivers Inn** SH
(509) 548-8888. **$69, 7 day notice.** 1505 Alpensee Strasse St. East edge of town. Ext corridors. **Pets:** Medium. $10 one-time fee/pet. Designated rooms, service with restrictions, supervision.

**Bavarian Ritz Hotel** SH
(509) 548-5455. **$79-$249, 3 day notice.** 633 Front St. Center. Ext/int corridors. **Pets:** Dogs only. $10 daily fee/pet. Supervision.

**Der Ritterhof Motor Inn** SH
(509) 548-5845. **$81-$102, 3 day notice.** 190 US 2. 0.3 mi w. Ext corridors. **Pets:** Dogs only. $10 daily fee/pet. Service with restrictions.

▼ The Evergreen Inn **M** ❖
(509) 548-5515. **$79-$139, 14 day notice.** 1117 Front St. US 2, just s.
Ext corridors. **Pets:** Other species. $10 daily fee/room. Service with restrictions, supervision.
⊠ 🖶 🖳

▼▼ Howard Johnson Inn **M**
(509) 548-4326. **$59-$109.** 405 W US 2. West end of town. Ext corridors. **Pets:** Accepted.
🅰🆂🅺 🆂🖮 ⊠ 🖶 🖳 🌣

🅰🅰🅰 ▼▼◆ Obertal Inn **M**
(509) 548-5204. **$69-$139.** 922 Commercial St. Off US 2; center. Ext corridors. **Pets:** Other species. $15 daily fee/pet. Service with restrictions.
🆂🅰🆅🅴 🆂🖮 ⊠ 🖶 🖳

▼▼◆▼ Quality Inn & Suites **SH**
(509) 548-7992. **$69-$119.** 185 US 2. 0.3 mi w. Ext corridors.
**Pets:** Accepted.
🅰🆂🅺 🆂🖮 ⊠ 🅶🅼 🖉 🕭 🖶 🖳 🌣

▼▼ River's Edge Lodge **M** ❖
(509) 548-7612. **$69-$149.** 8401 US 2. 3.5 mi e. Ext corridors.
**Pets:** Other species. $10 daily fee/pet. Designated rooms, service with restrictions, supervision.
🅰🆂🅺 🆂🖮 ⊠ 🖶 🖳 🌣

# LIBERTY LAKE

▼▼◆▼ Comfort Inn Liberty Lake **SH**
(509) 340-3333. **$56-$87.** 2327 N Madson Rd. I-90, exit 296, 1 mi e on
Appleway, then just n. Int corridors. **Pets:** Accepted.
🅰🆂🅺 🆂🖮 ⊠ 🅶🅼 🖉 🕭 🖶 🖳 🌣 ⊠

# LONG BEACH

🅰🅰🅰 ▼▼◆ Anchorage Cottages **CA**
(360) 642-2351. **$70-$128, 14 day notice.** 2209 Boulevard N. Just w of
SR 103. Ext corridors. **Pets:** Accepted.
🆂🅰🆅🅴 ⊠ 🖶 🖳 🕭 🖉

🅰🅰🅰 ▼▼ The Breakers **CO** ❖
(360) 642-4414. **$68-$278, 5 day notice.** 26th & SR 103. North end of
downtown. Ext corridors. **Pets:** Dogs only. $10 daily fee/room. Designated rooms, supervision.
🆂🅰🆅🅴 🆂🖮 ⊠ 🖶 🖳 🌣 ⊠ 🕭

🅰🅰🅰 ▼▼ Edgewater Inn **SH**
(360) 642-2311. **$74-$124, 3 day notice.** 409 Sid Snyder Dr. Just w of
SR 103. Ext/int corridors. **Pets:** Large. $10 daily fee/pet. Designated rooms, service with restrictions, supervision.
🆂🅰🆅🅴 ⊠ 🕭 🖶 🖳 🍴 🕭

🅰🅰🅰 ▼▼ Our Place at the Beach **SH**
(360) 642-3793. **$46-$90.** 1309 South Blvd. Just w of SR 103 at south
end of town. Ext corridors. **Pets:** Large, other species. $5 daily fee/pet.
Service with restrictions, supervision.
🆂🅰🆅🅴 🆂🖮 ⊠ 🖶 🖳 🌣 🕭

🅰🅰🅰 ▼▼◆ Shaman Motel **SH**
(360) 642-3714. **$54-$99, 7 day notice.** 115 3rd St SW. Downtown. Ext
corridors. **Pets:** Other species. $6 daily fee/pet. Service with restrictions, supervision.
🆂🅰🆅🅴 ⊠ 🖶 🖳 🌣 🕭

🅰🅰🅰 ▼▼◆ Super 8 Motel **SH** ❖
(360) 642-8988. **$59-$139.** 500 Ocean Beach Blvd. On SR 103; downtown. Int corridors. **Pets:** Dogs only. $5 daily fee/pet. Service with restrictions, supervision.
🆂🅰🆅🅴 ⊠ 🅶🅼 🖉 🖶 🖳 🕭

# LONGVIEW

🅰🅰🅰 ▼▼◆ Hudson Manor Inn & Suites **M** ❖
(360) 425-1100. **$46-$70.** 1616 Hudson St. Downtown. Ext corridors.
**Pets:** Medium. $10 one-time fee/room. Service with restrictions, crate.
🆂🅰🆅🅴 ⊠ 🖶 🖳

🅰🅰🅰 ▼▼ Longview Travelodge **M**
(360) 423-6460. **$49-$65.** 838 15th Ave. Downtown; opposite Medical
Center. Ext corridors. **Pets:** Accepted.
🆂🅰🆅🅴 🆂🖮 ⊠ 🖶 🖳

▼▼◆▼ Ramada Limited Longview **SH**
(360) 414-1000. **$63-$176.** 723 7th Ave. I-5, exit 36, 3 mi w on SR 432.
Int corridors. **Pets:** Large, other species. $25 one-time fee/room. Service
with restrictions, supervision.
🅰🆂🅺 🆂🖮 ⊠ 🅶🅼 🖉 🕭 🖶 🖳 🌣

🅰🅰🅰 ▼▼ The Townhouse Motel **M** ❖
(360) 423-7200. **$44-$57, 3 day notice.** 744 Washington Way. Downtown. Ext corridors. **Pets:** Medium, dogs only. $7 daily fee/pet. Designated
rooms, service with restrictions, supervision.
🆂🅰🆅🅴 🆂🖮 ⊠ 🖶 🖳 🌣

# MOCLIPS

🅰🅰🅰 ▼▼▼ Ocean Crest Resort **SH** ❖
(360) 276-4465. **$41-$184.** 4651 SR 109 N. South edge of town. Ext
corridors. **Pets:** Other species. $18 daily fee/pet. Designated rooms, service with restrictions, supervision.
🆂🅰🆅🅴 🆂🖮 ⊠ 🕭 🖶 🖳 🍴 🌣 ⊠ 🖉

# MONTESANO

🅰🅰🅰 ▼▼◆ Monte Square Motel **M**
(360) 249-4424. **$49-$89.** 100 Brumfield Ave W. US 12, exit SR 107
(Montesano/Raymond), just nw. Ext corridors. **Pets:** Dogs only. $10
one-time fee/pet. Designated rooms, service with restrictions, supervision.
🆂🅰🆅🅴 🆂🖮 ⊠ 🅶🅼 🖶 🖳

# MORTON

🅰🅰🅰 ▼▼◆ The Seasons Motel **M**
(360) 496-6835. **$70-$90.** 200 Westlake Ave. On US 12, at jct SR 7.
Ext corridors. **Pets:** Small. $10 one-time fee/pet. Service with restrictions, supervision.
🆂🅰🆅🅴 ⊠ 🖶 🖳

# MOSES LAKE

▼▼◆▼ AmeriStay Inn & Suites **SH**
(509) 764-7500. **$85-$205.** 1157 N Stratford Rd. I-90, exit 179, 1 mi n
to SR 17, 2.8 mi nw to Stratford exit, just n, then just e. Int corridors.
**Pets:** Accepted.
🅰🆂🅺 🆂🖮 ⊠ 🅶🅼 🖉 🕭 🖶 🖳 🌣

🅰🅰🅰 ▼▼◆▼ Best Western Lake Inn **SH**
(509) 765-9211. **$55-$99.** 3000 Marina Dr. I-90, exit 176, just nw. Int
corridors. **Pets:** Accepted.
🆂🅰🆅🅴 🆂🖮 ⊠ 🅶🅼 🖉 🖶 🖳 🍴 🌣 ⊠

▼▼◆▼ Holiday Inn Express **SH**
(509) 766-2000. **$75-$120, 7 day notice.** 1745 E Kittleson. I-90, exit
179, just n. Int corridors. **Pets:** Accepted.
🅰🆂🅺 🆂🖮 ⊠ 🅶🅼 🕭 🖶 🖳 🌣

▼▼◆ Inn at Moses Lake **SH**
(509) 766-7000. **$65-$75.** 1741 E Kittleson. I-90, exit 179, just n. Int
corridors. **Pets:** Accepted.
🅰🆂🅺 🆂🖮 ⊠ 🖶

▼◆▼ Moses Lake Super 8 **SH** ❖
(509) 765-8886. **$60-$88, 10 day notice.** 449 Melva Ln. I-90, exit 176,
just n. Int corridors. **Pets:** $10 one-time fee/pet. Service with restrictions, supervision.
🅰🆂🅺 🆂🖮 ⊠ 🖶 🌣

▼▼ ▼▼ Shilo Inn Suites-Moses Lake **SH** ❖
(509) 765-9317. **$72-$117.** 1819 E Kittleson. I-90, exit 179, just n. Int corridors. **Pets:** $10 daily fee/pet. Service with restrictions, supervision.
[A$K] [S✚] [✕] [&M] [⟳] [⊟] [▣] [⟲] [⊠]

# MOUNT VERNON

▲▲▲ ▼▼ ▼▼ Best Western College Way Inn **SH**
(360) 424-4287. **$69-$93.** 300 W College Way. I-5, exit 227, just w. Ext corridors. **Pets:** $15 daily fee/room. Designated rooms, service with restrictions, supervision.
[SAVE] [S✚] [✕] [⟳] [⊟] [▣] [⟲]

▲▲▲ ▼▼ ▼▼ Best Western CottonTree Inn & Convention
Center **SH** ❖
(360) 428-5678. **$74-$109.** 2300 Market St. I-5, exit 227, 0.3 mi e on College Way, then 0.5 mi n on Riverside Dr. Int corridors. **Pets:** Dogs only. $25 one-time fee/room. Designated rooms, service with restrictions, supervision.
[SAVE] [S✚] [✕] [&M] [⟳] [⊟] [▣] [⟲]

▲▲▲ ▼▼ ▼▼ Comfort Inn-Mount Vernon **SH**
(360) 428-7020. **$70-$90.** 1910 Freeway Dr. I-5, exit 227, just w on College Way, then just n. Ext corridors. **Pets:** Medium. $10 daily fee/pet. Service with restrictions, supervision.
[SAVE] [S✚] [✕] [⊟] [▣] [⟲]

▲▲▲ ▼▼ Tulip Inn **M**
(360) 428-5969. **$60-$80.** 2200 Freeway Dr. I-5, exit 227, just w on College Way, then just n. Ext corridors. **Pets:** Other species. $10 one-time fee/pet. Designated rooms, service with restrictions, supervision.
[SAVE] [S✚] [✕] [⊟] [▣] [⟲]

# OAK HARBOR

▲▲▲ ▼▼ ▼▼ Acorn Motor Inn **SH**
(360) 675-6646. **$47-$109.** 31530 SR 20. On SR 20 at 300th Ave W (SE Barrington Dr). Int corridors. **Pets:** Other species. $10 daily fee/room. Designated rooms, service with restrictions, supervision.
[SAVE] [S✚] [✕] [⊟]

# OCEAN PARK

▲▲▲ ▼▼ Ocean Park Resort **M**
(360) 665-4585. **$69-$98, 10 day notice.** 25904 R St. Just e of SR 103; downtown. Ext corridors. **Pets:** Small, other species. $7 daily fee/pet. Designated rooms, service with restrictions, supervision.
[SAVE] [✕] [⊟] [▣] [⟲] [⊠] [🐾] [Ẑ]

# OCEAN SHORES

▲▲▲ ▼▼ ▼▼ The Grey Gull Resort **CO**
(360) 289-3381. **$120-$335, 3 day notice.** 651 Ocean Shores Blvd NW. Just s of Chance A La Mer Blvd. Ext corridors. **Pets:** Accepted.
[SAVE] [S✚] [✕] [⊟] [▣] [⟲] [🐾]

▲▲▲ ▼▼ ▼▼ The Nautilus **CO** ❖
(360) 289-2722. **$80-$160.** 835 Ocean Shores Blvd NW. 0.3 mi s of Chance A La Mer Blvd. Ext corridors. **Pets:** Dogs only. $20 one-time fee/pet. Service with restrictions, supervision.
[SAVE] [S✚] [✕] [⊟] [▣] [🐾]

▲▲▲ ▼▼▼▼ The Polynesian Condominium Resort **CO**
(360) 289-3361. **$99-$129.** 615 Ocean Shores Blvd NW. 0.3 mi s of Chance A La Mer Blvd. Ext/int corridors. **Pets:** Other species. $15 daily fee/pet. Service with restrictions, supervision.
[SAVE] [S✚] [✕] [⟳] [⊟] [▣] [⟲] [⊠] [🐾]

# OKANOGAN

▲▲▲ ▼▼ ▼▼ Ponderosa Motor Lodge **M**
(509) 422-0400. **$47-$52.** 1034 S 2nd Ave. 0.3 mi n on SR 215 from jct SR 20. Ext corridors. **Pets:** Accepted.
[SAVE] [S✚] [✕] [⊟] [▣] [⟲]

# OLYMPIA

▼▼▼▼ Ramada Governor House **SH**
(360) 352-7700. **$140.** 621 S Capitol Way. I-5, exit 105 (City Center) northbound; exit 105A southbound, 0.4 mi w on 14th Ave, then 0.6 mi n; downtown. Int corridors. **Pets:** $50 one-time fee/room. Service with restrictions, supervision.
[A$K] [S✚] [✕] [⟳] [⊟] [▣] [🍴] [⟲] [⊠]

▼▼▼▼ Red Lion Hotel Olympia **SH**
(360) 943-4000. **$100-$120.** 2300 Evergreen Park Dr SW. I-5, exit 104, 0.5 mi nw, via US 101 and Cooper Point Rd N exit. Int corridors. **Pets:** Small, other species. $25 one-time fee/room. Service with restrictions, crate.
[A$K] [S✚] [✕] [&M] [⟳] [&'] [⊟] [▣] [🍴] [⟲]

# OLYMPIC NATIONAL PARK

▲▲▲ ▼▼▼▼ Lake Crescent Lodge **SH**
(360) 928-3211. **$68-$211, 7 day notice.** 416 Lake Crescent Rd. 22 mi w of Port Angeles on US 101. Ext/int corridors. **Pets:** Accepted.
[SAVE] [✕] [⊟] [▣] [🍴] [⊠] [🐾] [🐾] [Ẑ]

◆ Log Cabin Resort **CA**
(360) 928-3325. **$53-$127, 7 day notice.** 3183 E Beach Rd. 3.3 mi nw of US 101 (MM 232). Ext corridors. **Pets:** Other species. $20 daily fee/pet. Designated rooms, service with restrictions, supervision.
[✕] [⊟] [▣] [🍴] [⊠] [🐾] [🐾] [Ẑ]

# OMAK

▲▲▲ ▼▼ Motel Nicholas **M**
(509) 826-4611. **$46.** 527 E Grape Ave. 0.8 mi n on SR 215 business route; 0.3 mi w of US 97, on north exit to Omak. Ext corridors. **Pets:** Accepted.
[SAVE] [S✚] [✕] [⊟] [▣]

▲▲▲ ▼▼▼▼ Omak Inn **SH**
(509) 826-3822. **$67-$77.** 912 Koala Dr. On US 97, just n of Riverside Dr. Int corridors. **Pets:** Small, dogs only. $25 one-time fee/pet. Designated rooms, service with restrictions, supervision.
[SAVE] [S✚] [✕] [&'] [⊟] [▣] [⟲]

▼▼ ▼▼ Rodeway Inn & Suites **M** ❖
(509) 826-0400. **$44-$69.** 122 N Main St. Downtown. Ext corridors. **Pets:** Medium. $10 daily fee/pet. Designated rooms, service with restrictions.
[A$K] [S✚] [✕] [&'] [⊟] [▣] [⟲]

# OTHELLO

▲▲▲ ▼▼▼▼ Best Western Lincoln Inn Othello **SH** ❖
(509) 488-5671. **$69-$139.** 1020 E Cedar St. Just off Main St at 10th and Cedar sts. Int corridors. **Pets:** Medium. $10 one-time fee/pet. Service with restrictions, supervision.
[SAVE] [S✚] [✕] [⊟] [▣] [⟲]

# PACIFIC BEACH

▲▲▲ ▼▼ ▼▼ Sandpiper Beach Resort **CO**
(360) 276-4580. **$65-$115.** 4159 SR 109. 1.8 mi s. Ext corridors. **Pets:** Other species. $13 daily fee/pet. Service with restrictions, supervision.
[SAVE] [✕] [⊟] [▣] [🐾] [🐾] [Ẑ]

# PACKWOOD

▼▼ Inn of Packwood **M**
(360) 494-5500. **$50-$70.** 13032 US 12. Center. Ext corridors. **Pets:** Accepted.
[A$K] [S✚] [✕] [⊟] [▣] [⟲]

# PASCO

**▼▼▼▼ AmeriSuites Pasco at TRAC** 🆂🇭
(509) 543-7000. **$85-$95.** 4525 Convention Pl. I-182, exit 9 (Rd 68), just n, then just e. Int corridors. **Pets:** Small, dogs only. $10 daily fee/pet. Designated rooms, service with restrictions, supervision.

(ASK) (S🖬) ☒ (&M) 🗂 🖱 🗄 🖳 ⊇�

**▼▼▼▼ Best Western Pasco Inn & Suites** 🆂🇭
(509) 543-7722. **$100-$110.** 2811 N 20th Ave. I-182, exit 12B, just n. Int corridors. **Pets:** Small. $10 one-time fee/room. Service with restrictions, supervision.

(ASK) (S🖬) ☒ (&M) 🗂 (&) 🖱 🖳 ⊇⊇ ⊠

**▲▲▲ ▼▼ Budget Inn** 🅼
(509) 546-2010. **$48-$55.** 1520 N Oregon St. I-182, exit 14A (SR 395 S). Ext corridors. **Pets:** Small. $20 deposit/pet. Service with restrictions, supervision.

(SAVE) (S🖬) ☒ 🖱 ⊇⊇

**▼▼ Red Lion Hotel Pasco** 🇱🇭
(509) 547-0701. **$109-$139.** 2525 N 20th Ave. I-182, exit 12B, just n. Int corridors. **Pets:** Accepted.

(ASK) ☒ (&M) 🗂 (&) 🖱 🖳 🍴 ⊇⊇

**▲▲▲ ▼▼▼ Sleep Inn** 🆂🇭
(509) 545-9554. **$65-$75.** 9930 Bedford St. I-182, exit 7, just ne. Int corridors. **Pets:** Medium. $15 daily fee/room. Designated rooms, service with restrictions, supervision.

(SAVE) (S🖬) ☒ (&M) 🗂 (&) 🖱 🖳 ⊇⊇

# PORT ANGELES

**▲▲▲ ▼ The Pond Motel** 🅼
(360) 452-8422. **$45-$85, 3 day notice.** 1425 W US 101. 2 mi w. Ext corridors. **Pets:** Accepted.

(SAVE) ☒ 🖱 🖳 (&) (⊠)

**▲▲▲ ▼▼▼ Portside Inn** 🆂🇭 🐾
(360) 452-4015. **$49-$129, 3 day notice.** 1510 E Front St. Front St at Alder, on east side. Ext corridors. **Pets:** Small. $5 daily fee/pet. Designated rooms, service with restrictions, supervision.

(SAVE) (S🖬) ☒ 🖱 🖳 ⊇⊇

**▲▲▲ ▼▼▼ Quality Inn-Uptown** 🔺
(360) 457-9434. **$79-$199.** 101 E 2nd St. At Laurel St, just w of US 101; on bluff. Ext corridors. **Pets:** Medium, dogs only. $10 daily fee/room. Designated rooms, service with restrictions, supervision.

(SAVE) (S🖬) ☒ 🖱 🖳 (&)

**▼▼▼ Red Lion Hotel Port Angeles** 🆂🇭
(360) 452-9215. **$89-$159.** 221 N Lincoln St. On US 101 westbound; at ferry landing. Ext/int corridors. **Pets:** Accepted.

(ASK) (S🖬) ☒ (&M) 🗂 (&) 🖱 🖳 🍴 ⊇⊇

**▲▲▲ ▼▼ Riviera Inn** 🅼
(360) 417-3955. **$39-$110.** 535 E Front St. On US 101 W; downtown. Ext corridors. **Pets:** Dogs only. $15 one-time fee/pet. Designated rooms, service with restrictions, supervision.

(SAVE) (S🖬) ☒ 🖱 (&)

**▼ Super 8 Motel** 🅼
(360) 452-8401. **$61-$106.** 2104 E 1st St. 1.8 mi e of downtown, just s of US 101. Int corridors. **Pets:** $15 deposit/room, $10 one-time fee/room. Designated rooms, service with restrictions, supervision.

(ASK) (S🖬) ☒ (&M)

---

# VANCOUVER

**▲▲▲ ▼▼▼ Comfort Inn** 🆂🇭
(360) 574-6000. **$66-$100.** 13207 NE 20th Ave. I-5, exit 7, just e; I-205, exit 36, just w. Int corridors. **Pets:** Accepted.

(SAVE) (S🖬) ☒ 🗂 🖱 🖳 ⊇⊇

**▼▼▼▼ Hilton Vancouver Washington and Vancouver Convention Center** 🇱🇭
(360) 993-4500. **$99-$189.** 301 W 6th St. I-5, exit 1C (Mill Plain Blvd) southbound, 0.3 mi w, then 0.3 mi s on W Columbia St; exit 1B northbound, 0.5 mi, follow signs to City Center/6th St. Int corridors. **Pets:** Medium. $50 one-time fee/room. Service with restrictions, crate.

(S🖬) ☒ (&M) 🗂 (&) 🖱 🖳 🍴 ⊇⊇

**▼▼▼ Homewood Suites by Hilton** 🆂🇭 🐾
(360) 750-1100. **$98-$161.** 701 SE Columbia Shores Blvd. SR 14, exit 1, just s. Ext/int corridors. **Pets:** Other species. $10 daily fee/pet, $25 one-time fee/room. Service with restrictions.

(ASK) (S🖬) ☒ (&) 🖱 🖳 ⊇⊇ (⊠)

**▲▲▲ ▼▼▼▼ Phoenix Inn Suites-Vancouver** 🆂🇭
(360) 891-9777. **$79-$129.** 12712 SE 2nd Cir. I-205, exit 28 (Mill Plain E), 0.8 mi e, then just n on SE 126th Ave. Int corridors. **Pets:** Medium. $15 daily fee/pet. Designated rooms, service with restrictions, supervision.

(SAVE) (S🖬) ☒ 🗂 (&) 🖱 🖳 ⊇⊇ (⊠)

**▼▼ Quality Inn & Conference Center** 🆂🇭 🐾
(360) 253-8900. **$63-$99.** 221 NE Chkalov Dr. I-205, exit 28 (Mill Plain E), just ne. Ext corridors. **Pets:** Medium, dogs only. $15 daily fee/pet. Service with restrictions.

(ASK) (S🖬) ☒ 🖱 🖳 ⊇⊇

**▲▲▲ ▼▼▼ Quality Inn & Suites** 🆂🇭
(360) 696-0516. **$59-$89.** 7001 NE Hwy 99. I-5, exit 4, 0.8 mi se. Int corridors. **Pets:** Accepted.

(SAVE) (S🖬) ☒ 🗂 🖱 🖳 ⊇⊇

**▼▼▼▼ Red Lion Hotel Vancouver @ the Quay** 🆂🇭
(360) 694-8341. **$59-$109.** 100 Columbia St. 0.5 mi s on dock at foot of Columbia St. Int corridors. **Pets:** Accepted.

(ASK) (S🖬) ☒ (&M) 🗂 (&) 🖱 🖳 🍴 ⊇⊇ (⊠)

**▼▼▼▼ Red Lion Inn at Salmon Creek** 🆂🇭
(360) 566-1100. **$89-$135.** 1500 NE 134th St. I-5, exit 7, just w; I-205, exit 36, 0.5 mi w. Int corridors. **Pets:** Large, other species. $25 one-time fee/room. Designated rooms, service with restrictions, supervision.

(ASK) (S🖬) ☒ (&M) (&) 🖱 🖳 ⊇⊇

**▼▼▼▼ Residence Inn Vancouver** 🆂🇭
(360) 253-4800. **$89-$169.** 8005 NE Parkway Dr. I-205, exit 30 (SR 500 W), 0.5 mi w to Thurston Way, just n to NE Parkway Dr, then just w. Ext corridors. **Pets:** Other species. $75 one-time fee/room.

(ASK) (S🖬) ☒ (&M) 🗂 🖱 🖳 ⊇⊇ (⊠)

**▼▼▼ Shilo Inn-Hazel Dell/Vancouver** 🆂🇭 🐾
(360) 573-0511. **$69-$103.** 13206 Hwy 99. I-5, exit 7, just e; I-205, exit 36, just w. Int corridors. **Pets:** $10 daily fee/pet. Service with restrictions, supervision.

(ASK) (S🖬) ☒ 🖱 🖳 ⊇⊇ (⊠)

**▲▲▲ ▼▼▼ Sleep Inn** 🆂🅷
(360) 254-0900. **$69-$89.** 9201 NE Vancouver Mall Dr. I-205, exit 30 (SR 500 W), 0.6 mi w to Thurston Way, just n to Vancouver Mall Dr, then 0.5 mi e; southeast edge of Westfield Shopping Center. Int corridors. **Pets:** Small, dogs only. $60 deposit/pet. Designated rooms, service with restrictions, supervision.
🆂🅰🆅 🆂🅾 ☒ 🅖🅜 ⟨⟩ ⟨⟩ 🔋 ⏻ �ほ

**▼▼▼▼ Staybridge Suites Vancouver-Portland** 🆂🅷
(360) 891-8282. **$79-$169.** 7301 NE 41st St. I-205, exit 30 (SR 500 W), 1.5 mi w to NE Andresen Rd, just n to NE 40th St, just e to NE 72nd St, just n to NE 41st St, then just e. Int corridors. **Pets:** Accepted.
🅰🆂🅺 🆂🅾 ☒ 🅖🅜 ⟨⟩ ⟨⟩ 🔋 ⏻ 🌾 ☒

## END METROPOLITAN AREA

## PORT TOWNSEND

**▲▲▲ ▼▼▼▼ Bishop Victorian Hotel** 🆂🅷
(360) 385-6122. **$109-$209, 3 day notice.** 714 Washington St. Corner of Washington and Quincy sts. Int corridors. **Pets:** Medium, dogs only. $15 daily fee/pet. Designated rooms, supervision.
🆂🅰🆅 ☒ 🔋 ⏻ 🅚

**▼▼▼▼ Harborside Inn** 🆂🅷
(360) 385-7909. **$70-$150.** 330 Benedict St. Just e of SR 20. Ext corridors. **Pets:** Dogs only. $5 daily fee/pet. Designated rooms, service with restrictions, supervision.
🅰🆂🅺 ☒ ⟨⟩ 🔋 ⏻ 🌾 🅚

**▲▲▲ ▼▼▼▼ Palace Hotel** 🆂🅷 ❖
(360) 385-0773. **$59-$289.** 1004 Water St. Downtown. Int corridors. **Pets:** $10 daily fee/pet. Supervision.
🆂🅰🆅 🆂🅾 ☒ 🔋 ⏻ 🅚

**▲▲▲ ▼▼▼▼ The Swan Hotel** 🅼
(360) 385-1718. **$89-$489, 3 day notice.** 216 Monroe St. Downtown. Ext corridors. **Pets:** Accepted.
🆂🅰🆅 ☒ 🔋 ⏻ 🅚

## PROSSER

**▼▼▼▼ Best Western Prosser Inn** 🆂🅷
(509) 786-7977. **$79-$109.** 225 Merlot Dr. I-82, exit 80, just s. Int corridors. **Pets:** Small, dogs only. $10 daily fee/pet. Supervision.
🅰🆂🅺 🆂🅾 ☒ ⟨⟩ 🔋 ⏻ 🌾

## PULLMAN

**▲▲▲ ▼▼▼▼ Hawthorn Inn & Suites** 🆂🅷 ❖
(509) 332-0928. **$79-$89.** 928 NW Olsen St. 1.6 mi e on SR 270 from US 195. Int corridors. **Pets:** $15 one-time fee/room. Designated rooms, supervision.
🆂🅰🆅 🆂🅾 ☒ 🅖🅜 ⟨⟩ ⟨⟩ 🔋 ⏻ 🌾 ☒

**▲▲▲ ▼▼▼▼ Holiday Inn Express Hotel & Suites** 🆂🅷 ❖
(509) 334-4437. **$94-$124.** SE 1190 Bishop Blvd. Jct US 195 business route, 0.5 mi s, 1 mi e on SR 270. Int corridors. **Pets:** Large, other species. Designated rooms, service with restrictions, crate.
🆂🅰🆅 🆂🅾 ☒ 🅖🅜 ⟨⟩ ⟨⟩ 🔋 ⏻ 🌾

**▼▼▼ ▼▼▼ Quality Inn Paradise Creek** 🆂🅷
(509) 332-0500. **$115-$135, 3 day notice.** 1400 SE Bishop Blvd. Jct US 195 business route, just s, 1 mi e on SR 270. Int corridors. **Pets:** Accepted.
🅰🆂🅺 🆂🅾 ☒ ⟨⟩ 🔋 ⏻ 🌾 ☒

## QUINAULT

**▲▲▲ ▼▼▼▼ Lake Quinault Lodge** 🆂🅷
(360) 288-2900. **$80-$199, 3 day notice.** 345 S Shore Rd. 2 mi off US 101. Ext/int corridors. **Pets:** Accepted.
🆂🅰🆅 🆂🅾 ☒ ⏻ 🍴 🌾 ☒ 🅚 🍴

## QUINCY

**▼▼ ▼▼ Traditional Inns** 🅼
(509) 787-3525. **$64-$67.** 500 F St SW. West end of town on SR 28. Ext corridors. **Pets:** Very small, dogs only. $5 daily fee/room. Service with restrictions, supervision.
🅰🆂🅺 🆂🅾 ☒ 🔋 ⏻

## REPUBLIC

**▲▲▲ ▼▼▼ Prospector Inn** 🆂🅷 ❖
(509) 775-3361. **$53-$110.** 979 S Clark Ave. Downtown. Int corridors. **Pets:** Other species. $12 daily fee/pet. Designated rooms, service with restrictions, supervision.
🆂🅰🆅 🆂🅾 ☒ 🔋 ⏻ ☒

## RICHLAND

**▲▲▲ ▼▼▼▼ Clarion Hotel & Conference Center** 🆂🅷
(509) 946-4121. **$54-$99.** 1515 George Washington Way. I-182, exit 5B, 2.5 mi n. Int corridors. **Pets:** Small, dogs only. $25 one-time fee/pet. Designated rooms, service with restrictions.
🆂🅰🆅 🆂🅾 ☒ 🅖🅜 ⟨⟩ ⟨⟩ 🔋 ⏻ 🍴 🌾 ☒

**▲▲▲ ▼▼▼▼ Days Inn** 🅼
(509) 943-4611. **$64.** 615 Jadwin Ave. I-182, exit 5B, 0.9 mi n; just w of SR 240 business route; downtown. Ext corridors. **Pets:** Medium, other species. $10 daily fee/room. No service, crate.
🆂🅰🆅 ☒ 🔋 ⏻

**▼▼▼▼ Holiday Inn Express Hotel & Suites** 🆂🅷
(509) 737-8000. **$90-$100.** 1970 Center Pkwy. Just s on Columbia Center Blvd from SR 240, just w. Int corridors. **Pets:** Accepted.
🅰🆂🅺 🆂🅾 ☒ 🅖🅜 ⟨⟩ ⟨⟩ 🔋 ⏻ 🌾

**▼▼▼▼ Red Lion Hotel Richland Hanford House** 🆂🅷
(509) 946-7611. **$89-$139.** 802 George Washington Way. I-182, exit 5B, 1.3 mi n on SR 240 business route. Ext/int corridors. **Pets:** Large, other species. $25 deposit/room. Service with restrictions.
🅰🆂🅺 🆂🅾 ☒ 🅖🅜 ⟨⟩ 🔋 ⏻ 🍴 🌾 ☒

**▼▼▼▼ Shilo Inn Hotel Richland Conference Center** 🆂🅷 ❖
(509) 946-4661. **$72-$213.** 50 Comstock St. I-182, exit 5B, 0.5 mi n. Ext corridors. **Pets:** $10 daily fee/pet. Service with restrictions, supervision.
🅰🆂🅺 🆂🅾 ☒ ⟨⟩ ⟨⟩ 🔋 ⏻ 🍴 🌾 ☒

## RIMROCK

**▼▼ Game Ridge Motel** 🅼
(509) 672-2212. **$70-$250, 7 day notice.** 27350 US Hwy 12. Downtown. Ext corridors. **Pets:** Accepted.
🅰🆂🅺 🆂🅾 ☒ 🔋 ⏻ ☒ 🅚 🍴

## RITZVILLE

**▲▲▲ ▼▼▼▼ Americas Best Value Inn-Colwell** 🅼 ❖
(509) 659-1620. **$44-$61.** 501 W 1st Ave. I-90, exit 220, 0.9 mi n; downtown. Ext corridors. **Pets:** Medium. $5 one-time fee/pet. Designated rooms, service with restrictions.
🆂🅰🆅 🆂🅾 ☒ 🔋 ⏻ 🌾

▼▼▼ Best Western Bronco Inn **SH**
(509) 659-5000. **$69-$129.** 105 W Galbreath Way. I-90, exit 221, go over overpass, take second left. Int corridors. **Pets:** Accepted.

(ASK) (SÃ) (X) (&M) (🐾) 🔒 💷 ⊒

▼▼ La Quinta Inn Ritzville **SH**
(509) 659-1007. **$39-$94.** 1513 Smitty's Blvd. I-90, exit 221, just n. Int corridors. **Pets:** Accepted.

(ASK) (SÃ) (X) (&M) (🐾) 🔒 💷 ⊒ (X)

▲▲▲ ▼▼ Top Hat Motel **M** 🐾
(509) 659-1100. **$42-$56.** 210 E 1st Ave. I-90, exit 221, 1 mi ne via Division St. Ext corridors. **Pets:** Dogs only. $4 one-time fee/room. Service with restrictions, supervision.

(SAVE) (SÃ) 🔒

# ROCHESTER

▲▲▲ ▼▼▼ Eagles Landing Hotel **SH**
(360) 273-8640. **Call for rates.** 12840 188th Ave SW. 3 mi w on US 12, 0.8 mi s on Anderson Rd, then just e. Int corridors. **Pets:** Small. $25 one-time fee/pet. Designated rooms, service with restrictions, supervision.

(SAVE) (X) 🔒 💷 ⊒

# SAN JUAN ISLANDS AREA

## DEER HARBOR

▼▼ Deer Harbor Inn **CI**
(360) 376-4110. **$125-$325, 14 day notice.** 33 Inn Ln. 7 mi sw of ferry landing; 3.5 mi sw of Westsound. Ext/int corridors. **Pets:** Accepted.

(X) 🔒 💷 (¶¶) (X) (☑)

## EASTSOUND

▼▼ Outlook Inn on Orcas Island **SH**
(360) 376-2200. **$54-$265, 7 day notice.** 171 Main St. In Eastsound; downtown. Ext/int corridors. **Pets:** Accepted.

(ASK) (SÃ) (X) 💷 (X)

## FRIDAY HARBOR

▲▲▲ ▼▼▼ Best Western Friday Harbor Suites **SH**
(360) 378-3031. **$89-$279, 7 day notice.** 680 Spring St. In Friday Harbor; 0.7 mi w of ferry dock. Int corridors. **Pets:** Small. $20 daily fee/pet. Designated rooms, service with restrictions, supervision.

(SAVE) (SÃ) (X) (&M) 🔒 💷 (¶¶) (X)

▲▲▲ ▼▼▼ The Friday Harbor Inn **SH**
(360) 378-4000. **$89-$189.** 410 Spring St. In Friday Habor; 0.5 mi w of ferry dock. Ext corridors. **Pets:** $15 one-time fee/room. Designated rooms, service with restrictions, supervision.

(SAVE) (X) (☜) 🔒 💷 ⊒ (X)

▼▼▼ Lakedale Resort **SH**
(360) 378-2350. **$145-$229, 30 day notice.** 4313 Roche Harbor Rd. 4 mi n of Friday Harbor via Tucker Ave. Ext/int corridors. **Pets:** Medium. $20 daily fee/room. Designated rooms, no service.

(ASK) (X) 🔒 💷 (X) (☑)

## LOPEZ ISLAND

▲▲▲ ▼▼ Lopez Islander Resort **SH**
(360) 468-2233. **$90-$143, 14 day notice.** 2864 Fisherman Bay Rd. From ferry landing, 4.8 mi s via Ferry Rd and Fisherman Bay Rd. Ext corridors. **Pets:** $20 one-time fee/pet. Designated rooms, service with restrictions, supervision.

(SAVE) (X) (☜) 🔒 💷 (¶¶) ⊒ (X) (☑)

# SEATTLE METROPOLITAN AREA

## AUBURN

▼▼ Travelodge Suites **SH**
(253) 833-7171. **$59-$99.** Nine 16th St NW. SR 167, exit 15th St NW, 0.8 mi e, then just n on A St NE. Int corridors. **Pets:** Accepted.

(ASK) (SÃ) (X) (&M) (☜) 🔒 💷

▼▼ Val-U Inn **SH**
(253) 735-9600. **$72-$104.** Nine 14th St NW. SR 167, exit 15th St NW, 0.8 mi e, just s on A St NE, then just w. Int corridors. **Pets:** Dogs only. $10 daily fee/pet. Service with restrictions, crate.

(ASK) (SÃ) (X) (☜) 🔒 💷

## BAINBRIDGE ISLAND

▲▲▲ ▼▼▼ Island Country Inn **M**
(206) 842-6861. **$99-$119.** 920 Hildebrand Ln NE. 0.8 mi n of ferry dock on SR 305, just w on High School Rd, then just s. Ext corridors. **Pets:** Accepted.

(SAVE) (SÃ) (X) (🐾) (☜) 🔒 💷 ⊒

## BELLEVUE

▲▲▲ ▼▼▼ ▼▼▼ Bellevue Club Hotel **SH** 🐾
(425) 454-4424. **$175-$1450.** 11200 SE 6th St. I-405, exit 12, 0.4 mi nw. Int corridors. **Pets:** Small, dogs only. $30 one-time fee/room. Service with restrictions.

(SAVE) (X) (&M) (🐾) (☜) 🔒 (¶¶) ⊒ (X)

▲▲▲ ▼▼▼ Days Inn Bellevue **SH**
(425) 643-6644. **$76-$89.** 3241 156th Ave SE. I-90, exit 11 westbound; exit 11A (156th Ave SE) eastbound, just ne. Ext corridors. **Pets:** Medium. $25 one-time fee/room. Service with restrictions, supervision.

(SAVE) (SÃ) (X) 🔒 💷

▼▼ Homestead Studio Suites Hotel-Bellevue/Factoria **M**
(425) 865-8680. **$90-$94.** 3700 132nd Ave SE. I-90, exit 11A westbound; exit 10B eastbound, 0.5 mi se. Ext corridors. **Pets:** $25 daily fee/pet. Service with restrictions, supervision.

(ASK) (SÃ) (X) (🐾) (☜) 🔒 💷

▼▼ Homestead Studio Suites Hotel-Redmond at Microsoft Headquarters Campus **M**
(425) 885-6675. **$52-$66.** 15805 NE 28th St. I-405, exit 14 (SR 520), 3.3 mi e to 148th Ave NE (south exit), just e on 24th St, just ne on Bel-Red Rd, just n on 156th Ave, then just e. Ext corridors. **Pets:** $25 daily fee/pet. Service with restrictions, supervision.

(ASK) (SÃ) (X) (🐾) (☜) 🔒 💷

▲▲▲ ▼▼ ▼▼ La Residence Suite Hotel **SH**
(425) 455-1475. **$105-$175.** 475 100th Ave SE. I-405, exit 13B, 0.9 mi w on NE 8th St, then just s. Int corridors. **Pets:** Accepted.

(SAVE) (SÃ) (X) 🔒 💷

**△△△ ▽▼▽▼ Larkspur Landing Home Suite Hotel**
**Bellevue/Seattle** 🆂🅷
(425) 373-1212. **$109-$219.** 15805 SE 37th St. I-90, exit 11 westbound;
exit 11A (150th Ave SE) eastbound, 0.9 mi se on south frontage road.
Int corridors. **Pets:** Medium. $10 daily fee/pet, $75 one-time fee/room.
Service with restrictions.
[SAVE] [🔊] [✕] [🖉] [🛏] [🖥] [🖨]

**▽▼▽▼ Red Lion Bellevue Inn** 🆂🅷
(425) 455-5240. **$89-$159.** 11211 Main St. I-405, exit 12, 0.4 mi n on
114th St. Int corridors. **Pets:** Accepted.
[ASK] [🔊] [✕] [🖉] [🛏] [🖥] [🖨] [🍴] [🏊]

**▽▼▽▼ Residence Inn by Marriott,**
**Bellevue-Redmond** 🆂🅷 🐾
(425) 882-1222. **$250-$350.** 14455 NE 29th Pl. I-405, exit 14 (SR 520),
2.3 mi e to 148th Ave NE (north exit), then just nw. Ext corridors.
**Pets:** Other species. $75 one-time fee/room. Service with restrictions,
supervision.
[ASK] [🔊] [✕] [🖉] [🛏] [🖥] [🏊] [✕]

**▽▼▽▼ Sheraton Bellevue-Seattle East Hotel** 🅻🅷 🐾
(425) 455-3330. **$79-$209.** 100 112th Ave NE. I-405, exit 12 northbound; exit 13 southbound, just s. Int corridors. **Pets:** Medium. $50
deposit/room. Service with restrictions.
[ASK] [🔊] [✕] [🔊M] [🖉] [🔧] [🛏] [🖥] [🍴] [🏊] [✕]

# BOTHELL

**△△△ ▽▼▽▼ Country Inn & Suites By Carlson** 🆂🅷
(425) 485-5557. **$99-$145.** 19333 N Creek Pkwy. I-405, exit 24, just e.
Int corridors. **Pets:** Accepted.
[SAVE] [🔊] [✕] [🖉] [🛏] [🖥] [🍴] [🏊]

**▽▼▽▼ Residence Inn by Marriott Seattle NE** 🆂🅷
(425) 485-3030. **$139-$199.** 11920 NE 195th St. I-405, exit 24, 0.4 mi
ne. Ext corridors. **Pets:** Accepted.
[ASK] [🔊] [✕] [🖉] [🛏] [🖥] [🏊] [✕]

# BREMERTON

**△△△ ▽▼▽▼ Flagship Inn** 🆂🅷
(360) 479-6566. **$69-$99.** 4320 Kitsap Way. 3.5 mi w of ferry terminal;
SR 3, exit Kitsap Way, 0.5 mi e. Int corridors. **Pets:** Very small, dogs
only. $6 daily fee/pet. Supervision.
[SAVE] [🔊] [✕] [🛏] [🖥] [🏊]

**△△△ ▽▼▽▼ Illahee Manor Bed & Breakfast** 🅱🅱 🐾
(360) 698-7555. **$115-$215, 10 day notice.** 6680 Illahee Rd NE. SR 3,
exit East Bremerton, 4.9 mi se on Wheaton Way (SR 303), 1.2 mi e
on McWilliams Rd, just n on East Blvd, 0.3 mi e on 3rd St, then just n.
Ext/int corridors. **Pets:** Medium, other species. $25 one-time fee/pet. Des-
ignated rooms, supervision.
[SAVE] [✕] [🛏] [🖥] [✏]

**△△△ ▽▼▽▼ Midway Inn** 🆂🅷
(360) 479-2909. **$69-$89.** 2909 Wheaton Way. SR 303, 2 mi n. Int
corridors. **Pets:** Small. $150 deposit/room, $15 daily fee/room. Designated
rooms, service with restrictions, supervision.
[SAVE] [🔊] [✕] [🛏] [🖥]

**▽▼▽▼ Super 8 Motel** 🆂🅷
(360) 377-8881. **$70-$88.** 5068 Kitsap Way. 4.2 mi w of ferry terminal;
SR 3, exit Kitsap Way, just ne. Int corridors. **Pets:** Other species. $15
deposit/room, $10 one-time fee/room. Service with restrictions, supervision.
[ASK] [🔊] [✕] [🔊M] [🛏]

# DUPONT

**▽▼▽▼ GuestHouse Inn & Suites** 🆂🅷 🐾
(253) 912-8900. **$89-$155.** 1609 McNeil St. I-5, exit 118, 0.6 mi w. Int
corridors. **Pets:** Other species. $10 daily fee/pet. Designated rooms, super-
vision.
[ASK] [🔊] [✕] [🔊M] [🖉] [🛏] [🖥] [🏊]

# EDMONDS

**△△△ ▽▼▽▼ Edmonds Harbor Inn & Suites** 🆂🅷 🐾
(425) 771-5021. **$99-$129.** 130 W Dayton St. Just s at Port of
Edmonds. Ext/int corridors. **Pets:** $10 one-time fee/pet. Designated
rooms, service with restrictions, supervision.
[SAVE] [🔊] [✕] [🖉] [🛏] [🖥]

**△△△ ▽▼ K & E Motor Inn** 🅼
(425) 778-2181. **$55-$75.** 23921 Hwy 99. I-5, exit 177, 1.3 mi w; just n
of jct SR 99 and 104. Ext corridors. **Pets:** Small. $10 daily fee/room.
Designated rooms, service with restrictions, supervision.
[SAVE] [🔊] [✕] [🛏]

**△△△ ▽▼▽▼ Travelodge Seattle/Edmonds** 🆂🅷
(425) 771-8008. **$59-$119.** 23825 Hwy 99. I-5, exit 177, 1 mi w on SR
104, exit at SR 99 (Everett-Lynnwood), then just n. Ext corridors.
**Pets:** Medium. $25 one-time fee/pet. Designated rooms, service with
restrictions, supervision.
[SAVE] [🔊] [✕] [🛏] [🖥]

# EVERETT

**△△△ ▽▼▽▼ Best Western Cascadia Inn** 🆂🅷
(425) 258-4141. **$64-$112.** 2800 Pacific Ave. I-5, exit 193 northbound;
exit 194 southbound, just w. Int corridors. **Pets:** Accepted.
[SAVE] [🔊] [✕] [🔧] [🛏] [🖥] [🏊]

**▽▼▽▼ Days Inn** 🆂🅷
(425) 355-1570. **$63-$99.** 1602 SE Everett Mall Way. I-5, exit 189
northbound, 0.5 mi w on SR 527, then 0.5 mi s; exit southbound, 0.7
mi s. Ext corridors. **Pets:** Medium, dogs only. $10 one-time fee/room.
Designated rooms, service with restrictions, supervision.
[ASK] [🔊] [✕] [🛏] [🖥] [🏊]

**△△△ ▽▼▽▼ Inn at Port Gardner** 🆂🅷
(425) 252-6779. **$109-$249.** 1700 W Marine View Dr. I-5, exit 193
northbound, 1.2 mi w on Pacific Ave, then 1.2 mi n; exit 194 southbound, 1.2 mi w on Everett Ave, then 1 mi n; in Everett Marina Village.
Int corridors. **Pets:** Small. $25 one-time fee/room. Service with restrictions,
supervision.
[SAVE] [🔊] [✕] [🛏] [🖥]

**▽▼▽▼ Quality Inn Hotel & Conference Center** 🆂🅷
(425) 337-2900. **$89-$114.** 101 A 128th St SE. I-5, exit 186, just e. Int
corridors. **Pets:** Accepted.
[ASK] [🔊] [✕] [🖉] [🛏] [🖥] [🍴] [🏊] [✕]

# FEDERAL WAY

**△△△ ▽▼▽▼ Federal Way Comfort Inn** 🆂🅷
(253) 529-0101. **$69-$169.** 31622 Pacific Hwy S. I-5, exit 143, 0.5 mi w
on 320th St, just n on 20th Ave, then just w on 316th Pl. Int corridors.
**Pets:** Other species. $25 one-time fee/pet. Designated rooms, service with
restrictions, supervision.
[SAVE] [✕] [🖉] [🔧] [🛏] [🖥] [🏊] [✕]

**▽▼ Federal Way Super 8** 🆂🅷
(253) 838-8808. **$63-$78, 7 day notice.** 1688 S 348th St. I-5, exit
142B, just w. Int corridors. **Pets:** Small. $10 daily fee/pet. Designated
rooms, service with restrictions, supervision.
[ASK] [🔊] [✕] [🛏]

**△△△ ▽▼▽▼ La Quinta Inn & Suites** 🆂🅷
(253) 529-4000. **$69-$119.** 32124 25th Ave S. I-5, exit 143, just sw. Int
corridors. **Pets:** Dogs only. Service with restrictions, supervision.
[SAVE] [🔊] [✕] [🛏] [🖥] [🍴] [🏊]

**△△△ ▽▼▽▼ Quality Inn & Suites** 🆂🅷
(253) 835-4141. **$59-$148.** 1400 S 348th St. I-5, exit 142B, 0.5 mi w.
Int corridors. **Pets:** Medium, dogs only. $25 one-time fee/pet. Designated
rooms, service with restrictions, supervision.
[SAVE] [🔊] [✕] [🔊M] [🖉] [🔧] [🛏] [🖥] [🏊]

# FIFE

**◆ Econo Lodge Inn & Suites** SH
(253) 922-9520. **$52-$62.** 3100 Pacific Hwy E. I-5, exit 136B northbound; exit 136 southbound, just nw. Ext corridors. **Pets:** Accepted.
ⒶⓈⓀ 🛏 ✕ 🖥 💻 ➿

**◆◆◆ ◆◆◆ Emerald Queen Hotel & Casino in Fife** SH
(253) 922-2000. **$69-$109.** 5700 Pacific & Hwy E Ave. I-5, exit 137, just ne. Int corridors. **Pets:** $25 one-time fee/room. Service with restrictions, supervision.
ⓈⒶⓋⒺ 🛏 ✕ &M 🏃 🖥 💻 ❚❙

**◆◆◆ ◆◆◆ Quality Inn** M
(253) 926-2301. **$75-$82.** 5601 Pacific Hwy E. I-5, exit 137, just ne. Ext corridors. **Pets:** Medium, other species. $15 one-time fee/pet. Designated rooms, service with restrictions, supervision.
ⓈⒶⓋⒺ 🛏 ✕ 🖥 💻

**◆◆◆ ◆◆◆ Ramada Limited** M ❀
(253) 926-1000. **$59-$110, 7 day notice.** 3501 Pacific Hwy E. I-5, exit 136B northbound; exit 136 southbound, just ne. Ext corridors. **Pets:** Small, dogs only. $15 daily fee/pet. No service, supervision.
ⓈⒶⓋⒺ ✕ 🖥 💻

**◆◆◆ ◆◆◆ Royal Coachman Inn** SH
(253) 922-2500. **$52-$85.** 5805 Pacific Hwy E. I-5, exit 137, just ne. Ext corridors. **Pets:** Small. $15 daily fee/pet. Designated rooms, service with restrictions, supervision.
ⓈⒶⓋⒺ 🛏 ✕ 🖥 💻

# GIG HARBOR

**◆◆◆ ◆◆◆ Best Western Wesley Inn** SH
(253) 858-9690. **$124-$250.** 6575 Kimball Dr. SR 16, exit City Center, just e on Pioneer Way, then 0.3 mi s. Int corridors. **Pets:** Accepted.
ⓈⒶⓋⒺ 🛏 ✕ &M 🏃 🖥 💻 ➿

**◆◆◆ ◆◆◆ The Inn at Gig Harbor** SH 🐾
(253) 858-1111. **$129-$199.** 3211 56th St NW. SR 16, exit Olympic Dr, just w, then 0.4 mi n. Int corridors. **Pets:** Other species. $25 one-time fee/room. Designated rooms, service with restrictions, supervision.
ⓈⒶⓋⒺ 🛏 ✕ &M 🏃 🖥 💻 ❚❙ ✕

# ISSAQUAH

**◆ Motel 6–295** M
(425) 392-8405. **$55-$75.** 1885 15th Pl NW. I-90, exit 15, 0.3 mi n on 17th Ave NW, then just w on NW Sammamish Rd. Ext corridors. **Pets:** Accepted.
🛏 ✕ 🏃 🖥 ➿

# KENT

**◆◆◆ ◆◆◆ Comfort Inn Kent** SH
(253) 872-2211. **$71-$139.** 22311 84th Ave S. SR 167, exit 84th Ave S, just n. Int corridors. **Pets:** Small, other species. $10 daily fee/pet. Supervision.
ⓈⒶⓋⒺ 🛏 ✕ 🖥 💻 ➿

**◆◆◆ ◆◆◆ Hawthorn Suites** SH
(253) 395-3800. **$79-$119.** 6329 S 212th St. I-5, exit 152, 2 mi se via Orilla Rd and 212th St. Ext corridors. **Pets:** Small. $150 one-time fee/room. Service with restrictions, crate.
ⒶⓈⓀ ✕ 🏃 🖥 💻 ➿ ✕

**◆◆◆ ◆◆◆ Kent-Ramada Inn** SH
(253) 520-6670. **$69-$99.** 25100 74th Ave S. I-5, exit 149, I-5, exit 149 southbound; exit 149A northbound, 2.5 mi se via Kent Des Moines Rd (SR 516) to 74th Ave. Int corridors. **Pets:** Accepted.
ⒶⓈⓀ 🛏 ✕ 🏃 🖥 💻 ➿ ✕

**◆◆◆ TownePlace Suites by Marriott-Seattle
Southcenter** SH ❀
(253) 796-6000. **$89-$129.** 18123 72nd Ave S. I-405, exit 1 (SR 181), 1.6 mi s on W Valley Hwy, just e on S 180th, then just s. Ext corridors. **Pets:** Other species. $10 daily fee/pet. Supervision.
ⒶⓈⓀ 🛏 ✕ &M 🏃 🖥 💻 ➿ ✕

**◆◆◆ Val-U Inn** SH
(253) 872-5525. **$64-$94.** 22420 84th Ave S. SR 167, exit 84th Ave S, just n. Int corridors. **Pets:** Accepted.
ⒶⓈⓀ 🛏 ✕ 🖥 💻

# KIRKLAND

**◆◆◆ ◆◆◆ Baymont Inn** SH
(425) 822-2300. **$84-$96.** 12223 NE 116th St. I-405, exit 20A northbound; exit 20 southbound, just e; in Totem Lake area. Ext corridors. **Pets:** Small, dogs only. $50 deposit/room. Designated rooms, service with restrictions, supervision.
ⓈⒶⓋⒺ 🛏 ✕ 🏃 🖥 💻 ➿

**◆◆◆ La Quinta Inn Seattle (Bellevue/Kirkland)** SH
(425) 828-6585. **$120-$165.** 10530 NE Northup Way. I-405, exit 14 (SR 520) via 108th Ave exit, s on 108th Ave, then just w. Int corridors. **Pets:** Medium. Service with restrictions.
ⒶⓈⓀ ✕ 🏃 🖥 💻 ➿

**◆ Motel 6–687** M
(425) 821-5618. **$55-$67.** 12010 120th Pl NE. I-405, exit 20B northbound; exit 20 southbound, just se. Ext corridors. **Pets:** Accepted.
🛏 ✕ 🏃 🖥 💻

**◆◆◆ ◆◆◆ ◆◆◆ The Woodmark Hotel on Lake
Washington** LH
(425) 822-3700. **$230-$1800.** 1200 Carillon Point. On Lake Washington Blvd, 1 mi n of SR 520. Int corridors. **Pets:** Accepted.
ⓈⒶⓋⒺ 🛏 ✕ 🏃 💻 ❚❙ ✕

# LAKEWOOD

**◆◆◆ ◆◆◆ Americas Best Value Inn** M ❀
(253) 589-8800. **$59-$85.** 4215 Sharondale St SW. I-5, exit 127 (S Tacoma Way), just w on SR 512, 0.8 m s on S Tacoma Way, then just w. Ext corridors. **Pets:** $20 one-time fee/pet. Designated rooms, service with restrictions, crate.
ⓈⒶⓋⒺ 🛏 ✕ 🏃 🖥 💻

**◆◆◆ ◆◆◆ Western Inn** SH
(253) 588-5241. **$65-$74.** 9920 S Tacoma Way. I-5, exit 127 (S Tacoma Way), 0.3 mi nw. Ext corridors. **Pets:** Accepted.
ⓈⒶⓋⒺ ✕ 🖥 💻

# LYNNWOOD

**◆◆◆ ◆◆◆ ◆◆◆ Best Western Alderwood** SH ❀
(425) 775-7600. **$89-$135.** 19332 36th Ave W. I-5, exit 181B northbound, just n on Poplar Way, just w on 196th St SW, then just n; exit 181 (SR 524 W) southbound, just nw. Int corridors. **Pets:** Small, dogs only. Service with restrictions.
ⓈⒶⓋⒺ 🛏 ✕ 🏃 🖥 💻 ➿

**◆◆◆ ◆◆◆ Embassy Suites Hotel Seattle North/Lynnwood** SH
(425) 775-2500. **$99-$194.** 20610 44th Ave W. I-5, exit 181A northbound, just se; exit 181 (SR 524 W) southbound, 0.5 w on 196th St SW, then 0.6 mi s. Int corridors. **Pets:** Small. $50 one-time fee/room. Designated rooms, service with restrictions, supervision.
ⒶⓈⓀ ✕ &M 🏃 🖥 💻 ❚❙ ➿ ✕

**◆◆◆ ◆◆◆ La Quinta Inn Lynnwood** SH ❀
(425) 775-7447. **$72-$109.** 4300 Alderwood Mall Blvd. I-5, exit 181A northbound, just w; exit 181 (SR 524 W) southbound, 0.5 mi w on 196th St SW, just s on 44th Ave SW, then just e. Int corridors. **Pets:** Small. Service with restrictions, supervision.
ⓈⒶⓋⒺ 🛏 ✕ 🖥 💻 ➿

▼▼▼ **Residence Inn by Marriott-Seattle North/Lynnwood** 🆂🅷
(425) 771-1100. **$99-$219.** 18200 Alderwood Mall Pkwy. I-5, exit 183 southbound, just w on 164th St SW, then 1.5 mi se on 28th St W; exit 182 northbound on SR 525, exit 1, then just s; just n of Alderwood Mall Shopping Center. Ext corridors. **Pets:** Large. $75 one-time fee/ room. Service with restrictions, crate.
A$K 🆂🅾 ⊠ 🕼 🕽 🕮 ⊇ ⊠

## MARYSVILLE

▲▲▲ ▼▼▼ **Village Inn & Suites** 🆂🅷
(360) 659-0005. **$64-$79.** 235 Beach Ave. I-5, exit 199, just se. Int corridors. **Pets:** Small. $15 daily fee/pet. No service, crate.
SAVE ⊠ 🕮 ⊇

## MONROE

▲▲▲ ▼▼▼ **Best Western Baron Inn** 🆂🅷
(360) 794-3111. **$83-$149.** 19233 US 2. West end of town. Int corridors. **Pets:** Large. $15 daily fee/room. No service, supervision.
SAVE 🆂🅾 ⊠ 🕼 🕽 🕮 ⊇

## MOUNTLAKE TERRACE

▼▼ ▼▼ **Studio 6 #6042** Ⓜ
(425) 771-3139. **$48-$71.** 6017 244th St SW. I-5, exit 177, just ne. Ext corridors. **Pets:** Accepted.
🆂🅾 ⊠ 🕼ᴹ 🕼 🕽 🕮 ⊇

## MUKILTEO

▼▼▼▼ **TownePlace Suites by Marriott-Mukilteo** 🆂🅷
(425) 551-5900. **$79-$129.** 8521 Mukilteo Speedway. Just se of jct 84th St SW and SR 525 (Mukilteo Speedway). Ext corridors. **Pets:** Medium. $10 daily fee/pet.
A$K 🆂🅾 ⊠ 🕼ᴹ 🕼 🕽 🕮 ⊇ ⊠

## POULSBO

▼▼▼▼ **Holiday Inn Express** 🆂🅷
(360) 697-4400. **$79-$149.** 19801 NE 7th. On SR 305. Int corridors. **Pets:** Small, other species. $10 daily fee/pet. Service with restrictions.
A$K 🆂🅾 ⊠ 🕼ᴹ 🕼 🕮 ⊇

▲▲▲ ▼▼▼▼ **Poulsbo Inn** 🆂🅷
(360) 779-3921. **$95-$130, 7 day notice.** 18680 SR 305. SR 3, 2.3 mi e. Ext corridors. **Pets:** Medium. $10 daily fee/pet. Designated rooms, service with restrictions, crate.
SAVE 🆂🅾 ⊠ 🕼ᴹ 🕼 🕽 🕮 ⊇ ⊠

## PUYALLUP

▲▲▲ ▼▼▼▼ **Best Western Park Plaza** 🆂🅷 ❀
(253) 848-1500. **$99-$124.** 620 S Hill Park Dr. SR 512, exit S Hill/ Eatonville, just w. Int corridors. **Pets:** Dogs only. $25 one-time fee/room. Service with restrictions, supervision.
SAVE 🆂🅾 ⊠ 🕼ᴹ 🕼 🕽 🕮 ⊇

▼▼ ▼▼ **Holiday Inn Express Hotel & Suites Puyallup** 🆂🅷
(253) 848-4900. **$129-$139.** 812 S Hill Park Dr. SR 512, exit S Hill/ Eatonville, just w. Int corridors. **Pets:** Small, dogs only. $50 one-time fee/pet. Service with restrictions, supervision.
A$K 🆂🅾 ⊠ 🕼 🕽 🕮 ⊇

## REDMOND

▲▲▲ ▼▼▼▼ **Residence Inn by Marriott Redmond Town Center** 🆂🅷
(425) 497-9226. **$199-$249.** 7575 164th Ave NE. I-405, exit 14 (SR 520), 5 mi e to W Lake Sammamish Pkwy, just n to Leary Way, just e to Bear Creek Pkwy, just s to NE 74th Ave, just w to 164th Ave NE, then just n; center. Int corridors. **Pets:** Accepted.
SAVE 🆂🅾 ⊠ 🕽 🕮 ⊇ ⊠

# RENTON

▲▲▲ ▼▼▼ **Americas Best Value Inn** 🆂🅷
(425) 251-9591. **$65-$79.** 3700 E Valley Rd. SR 167, exit E Valley Rd, just nw. Int corridors. **Pets:** Medium. $10 daily fee/pet. Designated rooms, no service, supervision.
SAVE 🆂🅾 ⊠ 🕽 🕮

▲▲▲ ▼▼▼ **Econo Lodge** Ⓜ
(425) 228-2858. **$50-$73.** 4710 Lake Washington Blvd NE. I-405, exit 7, just ne. Int corridors. **Pets:** Medium. $10 one-time fee/pet. Service with restrictions, supervision.
SAVE 🆂🅾 ⊠ 🕽 🕮 ⊇

▲▲▲ ▼▼▼▼ **Holiday Inn Select Seattle-Renton** 🆂🅷
(425) 226-7700. **$99-$159.** One S Grady Way. I-405, exit 2 (SR 167/ Rainier Ave), jct SR 167 N. Int corridors. **Pets:** Medium. $50 deposit/ room. Designated rooms, service with restrictions.
SAVE ⊠ 🕼 🕽 🕮 ⊇ 🍽 ⊇

# SEATAC

▲▲▲ ▼▼▼ **Clarion Hotel** 🆂🅷
(206) 242-0200. **$69-$170.** 3000 S 176th St. Just e of SR 99. Int corridors. **Pets:** Small. $20 daily fee/room. Service with restrictions, supervision.
SAVE 🆂🅾 ⊠ 🕼ᴹ 🕽 🕮 🍽 ⊇

▲▲▲ ▼▼▼ **Coast Gateway Hotel** 🆂🅷
(206) 248-8200. **$75-$135.** 18415 International Blvd. On SR 99. Int corridors. **Pets:** Large, other species. $100 deposit/room. Service with restrictions.
SAVE 🆂🅾 ⊠ 🕼ᴹ 🕼 🕽 🕮

▼▼▼▼ **Doubletree Hotel Seattle Airport** 🅻🅷
(206) 246-8600. **$89-$189.** 18740 International Blvd. On SR 99. Int corridors. **Pets:** Accepted.
⊠ 🕼 🕼 🕽 🕮 🍽 ⊇

▼▼▼▼ **Hilton Seattle Airport & Conference Center** 🅻🅷
(206) 244-4800. **$89-$209.** 17620 International Blvd. On SR 99. Int corridors. **Pets:** Small. $50 one-time fee/pet. Service with restrictions, supervision.
⊠ 🕼 🕼 🕽 🕮 🍽 ⊇ ⊠

▼▼▼▼ **Holiday Inn Express Hotel & Suites-Seattle Sea-Tac Airport** 🆂🅷
(206) 824-3200. **$80-$129.** 19621 International Blvd. On SR 99. Int corridors. **Pets:** Accepted.
A$K ⊠ 🕽 🕮

▲▲▲ ▼▼▼▼ **Holiday Inn Seattle SeaTac International Airport** 🅻🅷
(206) 248-1000. **$179-$222.** 17338 International Blvd. On SR 99. Int corridors. **Pets:** Accepted.
SAVE 🆂🅾 ⊠ 🕼ᴹ 🕼 🕽 🕮 🍽 ⊇

▲▲▲ ▼▼▼ **La Quinta Inn Seattle (Sea-Tac International)** 🆂🅷
(206) 241-5211. **$94-$144.** 2824 S 188th St. On SR 99. Int corridors. **Pets:** Medium. Service with restrictions.
SAVE ⊠ 🕼 🕽 🕮 ⊇

▼▼ **Motel 6–1332** Ⓜ
(206) 246-4101. **$47-$61.** 16500 International Blvd. On SR 99. Ext corridors. **Pets:** Accepted.
🆂🅾 ⊠ 🕼

▼▼ **Motel 6–736** Ⓜ
(206) 824-9902. **$45-$59.** 20651 Military Rd. I-5, exit 151, just se; 15 mi s of downtown. Ext corridors. **Pets:** Accepted.
🆂🅾 ⊠ 🕼 🕼 🕽 ⊇

▼ Motel 6–90 SH
(206) 241-1648. $45-$59. 18900 47th Ave S. I-5, exit 152, just sw. Int corridors. Pets: Accepted.
[icons]

▼▼ Quality Inn Seattle Airport SH
(206) 241-9292. $72-$82. 2900 S 192nd St. On SR 99. Int corridors. Pets: Accepted.
[icons]

▼▼▼ Red Lion Hotel Seattle Airport LH
(206) 246-5535. $89-$149. 18220 International Blvd. On SR 99. Int corridors. Pets: Accepted.
[icons]

▼▼ Red Roof Inn SH
(206) 248-0901. Call for rates. 16838 International Blvd. On SR 99. Int corridors. Pets: Accepted.
[icons]

▼▼ Super 8 Motel Sea-Tac SH ❀
(206) 433-8188. $64-$109. 3100 S 192nd St. Just e of SR 99. Int corridors. Pets: Other species. $25 deposit/room. Service with restrictions, supervision.
[icons]

# SEATTLE

AAA ▼▼ ▼▼ Alexis Hotel LH
(206) 624-4844. $175-$499. 1007 1st Ave. Corner of Madison St and 1st Ave. Int corridors. Pets: Accepted.
[icons]

AAA ▼▼▼ Aurora Seafair Inn M
(206) 524-3600. $75-$85. 9100 Aurora Ave N. I-5, exit 172, 1.5 mi w on N 85th St, then just n. Ext corridors. Pets: Small. $5 daily fee/pet. Service with restrictions, supervision.
[icons]

AAA ▼▼▼ Best Western Evergreen Inn & Suites SH ❀
(206) 361-3700. $85-$135. 13700 Aurora Ave N. I-5, exit 175, 1.1 mi w on NE 145th St, then 0.3 mi s. Int corridors. Pets: Large, other species. $10 daily fee/room. Designated rooms, service with restrictions, supervision.
[icons]

AAA ▼▼▼ Best Western Executive Inn/Seattle SH
(206) 448-9444. $134-$174. 200 Taylor Ave N. I-5, exit 166, 1 mi w; near Seattle Center; just w of SR 99. Int corridors. Pets: Medium. $35 one-time fee/room. Service with restrictions.
[icons]

AAA ▼▼▼ Best Western Loyal Inn SH
(206) 682-0200. $109-$139. 2301 8th Ave. Corner of 8th Ave and Denny Way. Int corridors. Pets: Accepted.
[icons]

▼▼▼ Crowne Plaza Seattle LH
(206) 464-1980. $99-$300. 1113 6th Ave. Corner of 6th Ave and Seneca St. Int corridors. Pets: Accepted.
[icons]

▼▼ Days Inn Town Center SH
(206) 448-3434. $89-$189. 2205 7th Ave. Between Bell and Blanchard sts. Int corridors. Pets: Accepted.
[icons]

▼▼ Executive Pacific Plaza Hotel SH
(206) 623-3900. $139-$199. 400 Spring St. Between 4th and 5th aves. Int corridors. Pets: Medium. Designated rooms, service with restrictions, crate.
[icons]

AAA ▼▼▼▼ The Fairmont Olympic Hotel LH
(206) 621-1700. $299-$429. 411 University St. Corner of 4th Ave and University St. Int corridors. Pets: Accepted.
[icons]

▼▼▼ Homewood Suites by Hilton-Seattle Downtown SH ❀
(206) 281-9393. $159-$219. 206 Western Ave W. I-5, exit 167 (Mercer St), 0.3 mi w, 0.5 mi s on Fairview Ave, 1.2 mi w on Denny Way, then just n. Int corridors. Pets: Medium, other species. $20 daily fee/room. Service with restrictions, supervision.
[icons]

AAA ▼▼▼ Hotel Max SH ❀
(206) 728-6299. $300-$350. 620 Stewart St. Corner of 7th Ave and Stewart St. Int corridors. Pets: Medium, other species. $250 deposit/room, $35 one-time fee/pet. Service with restrictions, supervision.
[icons]

AAA ▼▼▼ ▼▼ Hotel Monaco LH ❀
(206) 621-1770. $175-$309. 1101 4th Ave. Corner of 4th Ave and Spring St. Int corridors. Pets: Other species. Service with restrictions, crate.
[icons]

AAA ▼▼▼ ▼▼ Hotel Vintage Park LH ❀
(206) 624-8000. $135-$260. 1100 5th Ave. Corner of Spring St and 5th Ave. Int corridors. Pets: Other species. Service with restrictions, supervision.
[icons]

AAA ▼▼▼ La Quinta Inn & Suites Seattle Downtown SH
(206) 624-6820. $79-$159. 2224 8th Ave. Corner of 8th Ave and Blanchard St. Int corridors. Pets: Accepted.
[icons]

AAA ▼▼▼ Ramada Inn Seattle University District North SH
(206) 365-0700. $99-$119. 2140 N Northgate Way. I-5, exit 173, just nw. Ext corridors. Pets: Accepted.
[icons]

AAA ▼▼▼ Red Lion Hotel on Fifth Avenue-Seattle LH ❀
(206) 971-8000. $290. 1415 5th Ave. Between Pike and Union sts. Int corridors. Pets: Small, other species. $50 one-time fee/room.
[icons]

▼▼▼ Residence Inn Marriott Seattle Downtown/Lake Union SH
(206) 624-6000. $159-$249. 800 Fairview Ave N. I-5, exit 167 (Mercer St), south end of Lake Union. Int corridors. Pets: Large. $10 daily fee/pet.
[icons]

AAA ▼▼▼ ▼▼ Sheraton Seattle Hotel & Towers LH
(206) 621-9000. $149-$279. 1400 6th Ave. Corner of 6th Ave and Pike St. Int corridors. Pets: Accepted.
[icons]

AAA ▼▼▼ ▼▼ Sorrento Hotel SH ❀
(206) 622-6400. $305-$2900. 900 Madison St. I-5, exit Madison St, just e; at 9th Ave and Madison St. Int corridors. Pets: Supervision.
[icons]

AAA ▼▼▼ Travelodge by the Space Needle SH
(206) 441-7878. $89-$179. 200 6th Ave N. I-5, exit 167 (Mercer St), just n on Fairview Ave, just w via Valley and Broad sts, just s on 5th Ave, then just e on John St. Int corridors. Pets: Dogs only. $10 daily fee/room. Service with restrictions, supervision.
[icons]

▼▼▼▼ **University Inn** SH
(206) 632-5055. **$1C5-$135.** 4140 Roosevelt Way NE. I-5, exit 169, 0.5 mi e, then just s. Int corridors. **Pets:** Medium, dogs only. $20 daily fee/room. Designated rooms, service with restrictions, supervision.

[ASK] [S☭] [✕] [⊘] [🖥] [💻] [🍴] [⤳]

④④ ▼▼▼ ▼▼▼ **The Westin Seattle** LH
(206) 728-1000. **$129-$229.** 1900 5th Ave. Corner of 5th Ave and Stewart St. Int corridors. **Pets:** Accepted.

[SAVE] [S☭] [✕] [�& M] [⊘] [♿] [🖥] [💻] [🍴] [⤳]

▼▼▼ ▼▼▼ **W Seattle** LH ☙
(206) 264-6000. **$259-$479.** 1112 4th Ave. Corner of 4th Ave and Seneca St. Int corridors. **Pets:** Large, other species. $25 daily fee/room, $100 one-time fee/room. Service with restrictions, supervision.

[ASK] [✕] [💻] [🍴]

## SILVERDALE

▼▼ ▼▼ **Cimarron Motel** SH ☙
(360) 692-7777. **$77-$89.** 9734 NW Silverdale Way. SR 3, exit Newberry Hill Road, jus⁻ e, then 1.2 mi n. Int corridors. **Pets:** Small. $10 one-time fee/pet. Service with restrictions, supervision.

[ASK] [S☭] [✕] [🖥] [💻]

## SNOHOMISH

④④ ▼▼▼ ▼▼ **Inn At Snohomish** M
(360) 568-2208. **$65-$110.** 323 2nd St. East end of town. Ext corridors. **Pets:** $100 deposit/room. Crate.

[SAVE] [S☭] [✕] [🖥] [💻]

## TACOMA

▼▼▼ ▼▼▼ **La Quinta Inn & Suites Tacoma (Conference Center)** SH
(253) 383-0146. **$104-$144.** 1425 E 27th St. I-5, exit 135 southbound; exit 134 northbound, just n. Int corridors. **Pets:** Medium. Service with restrictions.

[ASK] [✕] [⊘] [🖥] [💻] [🍴] [⤳]

④④ ▼▼▼ ▼ **Sheraton Tacoma Hotel** LH ☙
(253) 572-3200. **$219.** 1320 Broadway Plaza. I-5, exit 133 (City Center) to I-705 N, exit A St, left on 11th St, then left; downtown. Int corridors. **Pets:** Medium. $250 deposit/pet. Service with restrictions, crate.

[SAVE] [S☭] [✕] [⊘] [🖥] [💻] [🍴]

▼▼ ▼▼ **Shilo Inn⁻Tacoma** SH ☙
(253) 475-4020. **$80-$110.** 7414 S Hosmer St. I-5, exit 129, just se. Int corridors. **Pets:** $10 daily fee/pet. Service with restrictions, supervision.

[ASK] [S☭] [✕] [♿] [🖥] [💻] [⤳] [✕]

## TUKWILA

④④ ▼▼▼ ▼▼ **Comfort Suites Tukwila** SH
(425) 227-7200. **$96-$139.** 7200 Fun Center Way. I-405, exit 1 (SR 181), just n on Interurban Ave, then just e. Int corridors. **Pets:** Small. $15 daily fee/pet. Designated rooms, service with restrictions, supervision.

[SAVE] [S☭] [✕] [�& M] [⊘] [♿] [🖥] [💻] [⤳] [✕]

▼▼ ▼▼ **Homestead Studio Suites Hotel-Sea-Tac Airport/Southcenter** M
(425) 235-7160. **$72.** 15635 W Valley Hwy. I-405, exit 1 (SR 181), just s. Ext corridors. **Pets:** $25 daily fee/pet. Service with restrictions, supervision.

[ASK] [S☭] [✕] [�& M] [⊘] [♿] [🖥] [💻]

▼▼▼ ▼▼ **Homewood Suites by Hilton** SH
(206) 433-8000. **$139-$159, 3 day notice.** 6955 Fort Dent Way. I-405, exit 1 (SR 181), just ne. Ext/int corridors. **Pets:** Medium. $20 daily fee/room. Designated rooms, service with restrictions, supervision.

[✕] [⊘] [🖥] [💻] [⤳] [✕]

④④ ▼▼▼ ▼▼ **Ramada Limited Sea-Tac Airport** SH
(206) 244-8800. **$80-$100.** 13900 Tukwila International Blvd. I-5, exit 158 southbound, 2 mi s; exit 154A (SR 518 W) northbound, 1 mi n on SR 99. Int corridors. **Pets:** Small. $15 daily fee/pet. Designated rooms, service with restrictions, supervision.

[SAVE] [S☭] [✕] [🖥] [💻]

▼▼▼ ▼▼ **Red Lion Hotel Seattle South** SH
(206) 762-0300. **$111.** 11244 Tukwila International Blvd. I-5, exit 158, 0.4 mi w on Boeing Access Rd, then 0.4 mi s. Int corridors. **Pets:** Accepted.

[ASK] [S☭] [✕] [🖥] [💻] [🍴] [⤳]

▼▼▼ ▼▼ **Residence Inn by Marriott-Seattle South** SH
(425) 226-5500. **$99-$209.** 16201 W Valley Hwy. I-405, exit 1 (SR 181), just s. Ext corridors. **Pets:** Small. $75 one-time fee/room. Service with restrictions, crate.

[ASK] [S☭] [✕] [�& M] [⊘] [♿] [🖥] [💻] [⤳] [✕]

## VASHON

▼▼ **The Swallow's Nest Guest Cottages** CA ☙
(206) 463-2646. **$85-$250.** 6030 SW 248th St. From north end Ferry Landing, 7.8 mi s on Vashon Hwy; from south end (Tahlequah) Ferry Landing, 5.8 mi n on Vashon Hwy, 1.4 mi e on Quartermaster Dr, 1.5 mi s on Dockton Rd, 0.4 mi s on 75th Ave, then 1 mi e. Ext corridors. **Pets:** Other species. $10 daily fee/pet. Designated rooms, service with restrictions, supervision.

[✕] [🖥] [💻] [✕]

---

# END METROPOLITAN AREA

## SEDRO-WOOLLEY

④④ ▼▼▼ ▼▼ **Three Rivers Inn** SH
(360) 855-2626. **$59-$79.** 210 Ball St. On SR 20, just w of jct SR 9 N. Ext corridors. **Pets:** Medium. $10 one-time fee/pet. Service with restrictions, supervision.

[SAVE] [S☭] [✕] [�& M] [🖥] [💻] [🍴] [⤳]

## SEQUIM

④④ ▼▼▼ ▼▼ **Econc Lodge** SH ☙
(360) 683-7113. **$67-$129.** 801 E Washington St. US 101, exit Sequim Ave, 0.4 mi n, then C.6 mi e; east end of downtown. Int corridors. **Pets:** Medium, other species. $10 daily fee/pet. Supervision.

[SAVE] [S☭] [✕] [⊘] [♿] [🖥] [💻]

④④ ▼▼▼ ▼▼ **Sequim West Inn** M
(360) 683-4144. **$69-$115.** 740 W Washington St. US 101, exit River Rd, 0.9 mi ne via River Rd and W Washington St. Ext corridors. **Pets:** Accepted.

[SAVE] [S☭] [✕] [🖥] [💻]

## SHELTON

▼▼ ▼▼ **Super 8 Motel of Shelton** SH
(360) 426-1654. **$59-$74, 3 day notice.** 2943 Northview Cir. US 101, exit Wallace-Kneeland Blvd, just se. Int corridors. **Pets:** Medium, dogs only. $15 daily fee/pet. Service with restrictions, supervision.

[S☭] [✕] [🖥] [💻]

# SKYKOMISH

### ⟨AAA⟩ ▼▼▼ SkyRiver Inn M ❖
(360) 677-2261. **$73-$110, 14 day notice.** 333 River Dr E. 16 mi w of Stevens Pass on US 2; south end of Skykomish River Bridge. Ext/int corridors. **Pets:** Other species. $5 one-time fee/pet.

⟨SAVE⟩ ⟨✕⟩ ⟨🛏⟩ ⟨💻⟩

# SNOQUALMIE PASS

### ▼▼ Summit Lodge at Snoqualmie Pass SH
(425) 434-6300. **$109-$299, 3 day notice.** 603 SR 906. I-90, exit 52 eastbound, 0.3 mi e; exit 53 westbound, 0.3 mi w. Int corridors. **Pets:** Medium, other species. $25 one-time fee/room. Designated rooms, service with restrictions, supervision.

⟨ASK⟩ ⟨SD⟩ ⟨✕⟩ ⟨🛏⟩ ⟨💻⟩ ⟨🍽⟩ ⟨➰⟩

# SOAP LAKE

### ▼▼▼ Notaras Lodge M
(509) 246-0462. **$65-$110.** 236 E Main Ave. Just w of SR 17. Ext corridors. **Pets:** Accepted.

⟨✕⟩ ⟨🛏⟩ ⟨💻⟩

# SOUTH BEND

### ⟨AAA⟩ ▼▼▼ The Russell House BB
(360) 875-6487. **$99-$250, 7 day notice.** 902 E Water St. 0.5 mi s on Harrison. Int corridors. **Pets:** Small, dogs only. $50 deposit/room, $25 daily fee/pet. Designated rooms, service with restrictions, supervision.

⟨SAVE⟩ ⟨✕⟩ ⟨🐾⟩

# SPOKANE

### ⟨AAA⟩ ▼▼▼ Apple Tree Inn M ❖
(509) 466-3020. **$45-$94.** 9508 N Division St. Jct US 2 and 395, just n. Ext/int corridors. **Pets:** Small, dogs only. $10 daily fee/room. Designated rooms, service with restrictions, supervision.

⟨SAVE⟩ ⟨SD⟩ ⟨✕⟩ ⟨🛏⟩ ⟨➰⟩

### ▼▼ Best Western Trade Winds North M ❖
(509) 326-5500. **$68-$88, 14 day notice.** 3033 N Division St. I-90, exit 281 (Division St), 2.3 mi n on US 2 and 395. Ext/int corridors. **Pets:** Medium. Service with restrictions, supervision.

⟨ASK⟩ ⟨SD⟩ ⟨✕⟩ ⟨🛏⟩ ⟨💻⟩ ⟨➰⟩

### ▼▼ Comfort Inn North SH
(509) 467-7111. **$49-$175.** 7111 N Division St. I-90, exit 281 (Division St), 4.6 mi n. Int corridors. **Pets:** Accepted.

⟨ASK⟩ ⟨SD⟩ ⟨✕⟩ ⟨💻⟩ ⟨➰⟩ ⟨✕⟩

### ⟨AAA⟩ ▼▼▼▼ The Davenport Hotel LH
(509) 455-8888. **$159-$189.** 10 S Post St. Downtown. Int corridors. **Pets:** Accepted.

⟨SAVE⟩ ⟨✕⟩ ⟨&M⟩ ⟨🗐⟩ ⟨&⟩ ⟨🛏⟩ ⟨🍽⟩ ⟨➰⟩ ⟨✕⟩

### ▼▼▼ Doubletree Hotel Spokane City Center LH
(509) 455-9600. **$89-$159, 3 day notice.** 322 N Spokane Falls Ct. I-90, exit 281 (Division St), just n; downtown. Int corridors. **Pets:** $25 one-time fee/room. Service with restrictions, supervision.

⟨ASK⟩ ⟨✕⟩ ⟨&⟩ ⟨🛏⟩ ⟨💻⟩ ⟨🍽⟩

### ▼▼ Econo Lodge SH
(509) 747-2011. **$39-$89.** 120 W 3rd Ave. I-90, exit 281 (Division St), just n, then just w on 2nd Ave. Ext corridors. **Pets:** Medium. $10 daily fee/pet. Service with restrictions, supervision.

⟨ASK⟩ ⟨SD⟩ ⟨✕⟩ ⟨🗐⟩ ⟨🛏⟩ ⟨💻⟩ ⟨🍽⟩ ⟨➰⟩

### ▼▼▼ Holiday Inn Spokane Airport SH
(509) 838-1170. **$89-$129.** 1616 S Windsor Dr. I-90, exit 277 westbound; exit 277B eastbound, just w on US 2, then just s. Int corridors. **Pets:** Medium. $50 deposit/room. Designated rooms, service with restrictions.

⟨ASK⟩ ⟨SD⟩ ⟨✕⟩ ⟨&M⟩ ⟨🗐⟩ ⟨&⟩ ⟨🛏⟩ ⟨💻⟩ ⟨🍽⟩ ⟨➰⟩

### ▼▼ Howard Johnson Inn SH
(509) 838-6630. **$59-$199.** 211 S Division St. I-90, exit 281 (Division St), just n. Int corridors. **Pets:** Accepted.

⟨ASK⟩ ⟨SD⟩ ⟨✕⟩ ⟨🗐⟩ ⟨🛏⟩ ⟨💻⟩

### ⟨AAA⟩ ▼▼▼ Madison Inn SH
(509) 474-4200. **$64-$69.** 15 W Rockwood Blvd. I-90, exit 281 (Division St) eastbound, just e to Cowley, 0.4 mi s, then just w; exit westbound, just n to 2nd Ave, just w to Browne St, 0.5 mi s to 9th Ave, then just e. Int corridors. **Pets:** Other species. $10 daily fee/room. Designated rooms, service with restrictions, supervision.

⟨SAVE⟩ ⟨SD⟩ ⟨✕⟩ ⟨&M⟩ ⟨🛏⟩ ⟨💻⟩

### ▼▼▼ Oxford Suites-Downtown Spokane SH
(509) 353-9000. **$99-$159.** 115 W North River Dr. I-90, exit 281 (Division St), 1 mi n, then just n. Int corridors. **Pets:** Accepted.

⟨ASK⟩ ⟨SD⟩ ⟨✕⟩ ⟨🗐⟩ ⟨&⟩ ⟨🛏⟩ ⟨💻⟩ ⟨➰⟩ ⟨✕⟩

### ▼▼▼ Quality Inn Oakwood SH
(509) 467-4900. **$89-$109.** 7919 N Division St. I-90, exit 281 (Division St), 6.5 mi n. Int corridors. **Pets:** Medium, other species. $20 one-time fee/room. Designated rooms, service with restrictions, supervision.

⟨ASK⟩ ⟨SD⟩ ⟨✕⟩ ⟨&M⟩ ⟨🗐⟩ ⟨&⟩ ⟨🛏⟩ ⟨💻⟩ ⟨➰⟩ ⟨✕⟩

### ▼▼▼ Ramada Inn Airport SH
(509) 838-5211. **$115-$125.** 8909 Airport Dr. I-90, exit 277B eastbound; exit 277 westbound, 3.4 mi n. Int corridors. **Pets:** Small, other species. $100 deposit/pet. Service with restrictions, supervision.

⟨ASK⟩ ⟨SD⟩ ⟨✕⟩ ⟨🗐⟩ ⟨🛏⟩ ⟨💻⟩ ⟨🍽⟩ ⟨➰⟩ ⟨✕⟩

### ⟨AAA⟩ ▼▼▼ Ramada Limited M ❖
(509) 838-8504. **$44-$69.** 123 S Post St. I-90, exit 280B (Lincoln St), just n to 1st Ave W, just e to Post St, then just s. Ext corridors. **Pets:** Very small. $25 one-time fee/pet. Designated rooms, service with restrictions, supervision.

⟨SAVE⟩ ⟨SD⟩ ⟨✕⟩ ⟨🗐⟩ ⟨🛏⟩ ⟨💻⟩

### ▼▼▼ Ramada Limited Suites SH
(509) 468-4201. **$69-$89.** 9601 N Newport Hwy. US 2 and 395, just n on US 2 (Newport Hwy). Int corridors. **Pets:** Medium. $25 one-time fee/pet. Service with restrictions, supervision.

⟨ASK⟩ ⟨SD⟩ ⟨✕⟩ ⟨&M⟩ ⟨🗐⟩ ⟨&⟩ ⟨🛏⟩ ⟨💻⟩ ⟨➰⟩

### ▼▼▼ Red Lion Hotel at the Park-Spokane LH
(509) 326-8000. **$85-$139.** 303 W North River Dr. I-90, exit 281 (Division St), 1.5 mi n on US 195, then just w. Int corridors. **Pets:** Large, other species. $10 one-time fee/room. Service with restrictions, supervision.

⟨ASK⟩ ⟨SD⟩ ⟨✕⟩ ⟨🗐⟩ ⟨&⟩ ⟨🛏⟩ ⟨💻⟩ ⟨🍽⟩ ⟨➰⟩ ⟨✕⟩

### ▼▼▼ Red Lion River Inn-Spokane SH
(509) 326-5577. **$72-$89.** N 700 Division St. I-90, exit 281 (Division St), 0.8 mi n; downtown. Int corridors. **Pets:** Accepted.

⟨ASK⟩ ⟨SD⟩ ⟨✕⟩ ⟨🛏⟩ ⟨💻⟩ ⟨🍽⟩ ⟨➰⟩ ⟨✕⟩

### ⟨AAA⟩ ▼▼ Shangri-La Motel M ❖
(509) 747-2066. **$41-$49.** 2922 W Government Way. I-90, exit 277A eastbound; exit 277 westbound, Garden Springs Rd to Sunset Blvd, 1 mi e to Government Way, then just n to Hartson. Ext corridors. **Pets:** Other species. $10 one-time fee/room. Supervision.

⟨SAVE⟩ ⟨SD⟩ ⟨✕⟩ ⟨🛏⟩ ⟨💻⟩

### ▼▼ Shilo Inn Hotel SH ❖
(509) 535-9000. **$70-$110.** 923 E 3rd Ave. I-90, exit 281 (Division St), just n to E 3rd Ave, then 0.7 mi e. Int corridors. **Pets:** $10 daily fee/pet. Service with restrictions, supervision.

⟨ASK⟩ ⟨SD⟩ ⟨✕⟩ ⟨&M⟩ ⟨🗐⟩ ⟨&⟩ ⟨🛏⟩ ⟨💻⟩ ⟨🍽⟩ ⟨➰⟩ ⟨✕⟩

### ⟨AAA⟩ ▼▼▼ Super 8 West SH
(509) 838-8800. **$59-$145.** 11102 W Westbow Blvd. I-90, exit 272 (Medical Lake), just s. Int corridors. **Pets:** Accepted.

⟨SAVE⟩ ⟨SD⟩ ⟨✕⟩ ⟨🛏⟩ ⟨💻⟩ ⟨➰⟩

▼▼ ▼▼ Travelodge SH ❀
(509) 623-9727. **$59-$139.** W 33 Spokane Falls Blvd. I-90, exit 281 (Division St), 0.5 mi n, then just w. Int corridors. **Pets:** Large, other species. $10 one-time fee/pet. Supervision.

ASK S✆ ✕ ⚹M 📁 🛏 ▣

▲▲ ▼▼ ▼▼ Travelodge Hotel SH
(509) 838-1471. **$63.** W 4301 Sunset Blvd. I-90, exit 277A eastbound, 1 mi n on Garder Springs Rd; exit 277 westbound, just n on Rustle St. Int corridors. **Pets:** Accepted.

SAVE ✕ ☕ 🍽 ➴ ⊠

▼▼▼▼ WestCoast Ridpath Hotel LH
(509) 838-2711. **$72-$87.** 515 W Sprague Ave. Downtown. Int corridors. **Pets:** Large, other species. $100 deposit/room. Crate.

ASK S✆ ✕ 🄟 ⚹M 🛏 ▣ ☕ 🍽

# SPOKANE VALLEY

▲▲ ▼▼ ▼▼ Best Western Pheasant Hill SH
(509) 926-7432. **$69-$129.** 12415 E Mission. I-90, exit 289, just se. Int corridors. **Pets:** Medium, dogs only. $10 daily fee/pet. Designated rooms, service with restrictions, crate.

SAVE S✆ ✕ ⚹M 📁 🛏 ▣ ➴

▲▲ ▼▼ ▼▼ Broadway Inn & Suites SH
(509) 535-7185. **$49-$169.** 6309 E Broadway. I-90, exit 286, just w. Ext/int corridors. **Pets:** Service with restrictions, supervision.

SAVE S✆ ✕ 🄟 🛏 ▣ ➴

▼▼ ▼▼ Comfort Inn Valley SH
(509) 924-3838. **$62-$109.** 905 N Sullivan Rd. I-90, exit 291B, just s. Int corridors. **Pets:** Accepted.

ASK S✆ ✕ 🛏 ▣ ➴

▼▼▼▼ Holiday Inn Express-Valley SH
(509) 927-7100. **$89-$169.** 9220 E Mission. I-90, exit 287, just s. Ext/int corridors. **Pets:** Accepted.

ASK S✆ ✕ ⚹M 🄟 ⚹ 🛏 ▣ ➴

▲▲ ▼▼▼▼ La Quinta Inn & Suites Spokane SH
(509) 893-0955. **$69-$129.** 3808 N Sullivan Rd. I-90, exit 291B, 1.3 mi n. Int corridors. **Pets:** Accepted.

SAVE S✆ ✕ ⚹M 📁 🛏 ▣ ➴

▲▲ ▼▼▼▼ Mirabeau Park Hotel and Convention Center SH
(509) 924-9000. **$79-$149.** 1100 N Sullivan Rd. I-90, exit 291B, just s. Int corridors. **Pets:** Accepted.

SAVE S✆ ✕ 🄟 ⚹ 🛏 ▣ 🍽 ➴ ⊠

▲▲ ▼▼▼▼ Oxford Suites Spokane Valley SH
(509) 847-1000. **$99-$119.** 15015 E Indiana Ave. I-90, exit 291A eastbound; exit 291B westbound, just nw. Int corridors. **Pets:** Small. $10 daily fee/pet. Service with restrictions, supervision.

SAVE S✆ ✕ ⚹M 🄟 ⚹ 🛏 ▣ ➴ ⊠

▼▼▼▼ Quality Inn Valley Suites SH
(509) 928-5218. **$68-$99, 3 day notice.** 8923 E Mission. I-90, exit 287. Int corridors. **Pets:** Medium, dogs only. $50 deposit/pet. Designated rooms, service with restrictions, supervision.

ASK S✆ ✕ 🄟 ⚹ 🛏 ▣ ➴ ⊠

▼▼▼▼ Residence Inn by Marriott SH ❀
(509) 892-9300. **$99-$109.** 15915 E Indiana. I-90, exit 291 westbound, just e; exit 291B eastbound, just n, then just e. Int corridors. **Pets:** Small. $75 one-time fee/room. Service with restrictions, supervision.

✕ ⚹M 🄟 ⚹ 🛏 ▣ ➴ ⊠

▼▼ ▼▼ Super 8 Motel SH
(509) 928-4888. **$58-$93.** N 2020 Argonne Rd. I-90, exit 287, just n. Int corridors. **Pets:** Accepted.

ASK S✆ ✕ 🛏 ▣ ➴ ⊠

# STEVENSON

▲▲ ▼▼▼▼ Skamania Lodge LH ❀
(509) 427-7700. **$169-$369, 5 day notice.** 1131 SW Skamania Lodge Way. 1 mi w on SR 14, just n on Rock Creek Dr, then just w. Int corridors. **Pets:** Other species. $50 one-time fee/room. Designated rooms, service with restrictions, crate.

SAVE S✆ ✕ 🄟 ⚹ 🛏 ▣ 🍽 ➴ ⊠

# SULTAN

▲▲ ▼▼ Dutch Cup Motel M
(360) 793-2215. **$55-$85.** 819 Main St. Jct US 2 and Main St. Ext corridors. **Pets:** Small, other species. $8 daily fee/room. Service with restrictions, supervision.

SAVE S✆ ✕ 🛏

# SUNNYSIDE

▼▼▼▼ Best Western Grape Vine Inn SH
(509) 839-6070. **Call for rates.** 1849 Quail Ln. I-82, exit 69, just n, then just w. Int corridors. **Pets:** Medium, dogs only. $25 one-time fee/pet. Service with restrictions, supervision.

✕ ⚹ 🛏 ▣ ➴

▲▲ ▼▼ Country Inn & Suites M ❀
(509) 837-7878. **$55-$65.** 408 Yakima Valley Hwy. Downtown. Ext corridors. **Pets:** Medium, other species. $10 daily fee/pet. Designated rooms, service with restrictions, supervision.

SAVE S✆ ✕ 🛏 ▣ ➴

▼▼ ▼▼ Rodeway Inn SH
(509) 837-5781. **$69-$89.** 3209 Picard Pl. I-82, exit 69, just n. Int corridors. **Pets:** Accepted.

ASK S✆ ✕ 🛏 ▣ ➴

# TOPPENISH

▲▲ ▼▼▼▼ Best Western Lincoln Inn SH
(509) 865-7444. **$69-$139.** 515 S Elm St. I-82, exit 50, 3.1 mi e. Int corridors. **Pets:** Accepted.

SAVE S✆ ✕ ⚹M 🛏 ▣ ➴

# TUMWATER

▲▲ ▼▼ ▼▼ Best Western Tumwater Inn SH
(360) 956-1235. **$70-$85.** 5188 Capitol Blvd. I-5, exit 102, just e. Int corridors. **Pets:** Medium. $10 daily fee/pet. Service with restrictions, supervision.

SAVE S✆ ✕ ⚹ 🛏 ▣ ⊠

▼▼▼▼ Comfort Inn and Conference Center SH
(360) 352-0691. **$79-$95.** 1620 74th Ave SW. I-5, exit 101, just se. Int corridors. **Pets:** Large, other species. $10 daily fee/pet. Service with restrictions, supervision.

ASK S✆ ✕ 🛏 ▣ ➴

▼▼▼▼ GuestHouse Inn & Suites SH
(360) 943-5040. **$71-$85.** 1600 74th Ave SW. I-5, exit 101, just se. Int corridors. **Pets:** Accepted.

ASK S✆ ✕ ⚹M 🄟 ⚹ 🛏 ▣ ➴

▼▼ Motel 6–77 M
(360) 754-7320. **$45-$55.** 400 W Lee St. I-5, exit 102, just e on Trosper Rd, just s on Capitol Blvd, then just w. Ext corridors. **Pets:** Accepted.

S✆ ✕ 🛏 ➴

# TWISP

▼▼ ▼▼ Idle-A-While Motel M 🐾
(509) 997-3222. **$64-$99.** 505 N SR 20. Just n of town. Ext corridors. **Pets:** Dogs only. $5 daily fee/pet. Service with restrictions, supervision.

ASK S✆ ✕ 🛏 ▣ ⊠

# UNION

**▼▼▼▼ Alderbrook Resort & Spa** 〓 ❀
(360) 898-2200. **$130-$400, 7 day notice.** 10 E Alderbrook Dr. On SR 106, just e of town. Ext/int corridors. **Pets:** Other species. $200 deposit/room, $20 daily fee/pet. Designated rooms, service with restrictions, supervision.
[ASK] [✕] [📠] [💻] [🍴] [🏊] [✕]

# UNION GAP

**▼▼▼▼ Best Western Ahtanum Inn** 〓
(509) 248-9700. **$109-$139.** 2408 Rudkin Rd. I-82, exit 36, just n. Int corridors. **Pets:** Accepted.
[ASK] [S6] [✕] [ᴹ] [📠] [💻] [🏊] [✕]

**▲▲▲ ▼▼ Quality Inn-Yakima Valley** 〓
(509) 248-6924. **$69-$129.** 12 E Valley Mall Blvd. I-82, exit 36, just s. Ext corridors. **Pets:** Small, dogs only. $10 daily fee/pet. Designated rooms, service with restrictions, crate.
[SAVE] [S6] [✕] [ᴹ] [⚙] [✦] [📠] [💻] [🏊]

**▼▼▼▼ Super 8 Motel Yakima** 〓
(509) 248-8880. **$68-$91.** 2605 Rudkin Rd. I-82, exit 36, just s. Int corridors. **Pets:** Other species. $25 one-time fee/room. Service with restrictions, supervision.
[ASK] [S6] [✕] [⚙] [🏊]

# WALLA WALLA

**▲▲▲ ▼▼▼▼ Best Western Walla Walla Suites Inn** 〓 ❀
(509) 525-4700. **$74-$129.** 7 E Oak St. US 12, exit 2nd Ave, just s. Int corridors. **Pets:** Dogs only. $10 daily fee/pet. Service with restrictions, supervision.
[SAVE] [S6] [✕] [ᴹ] [✦] [📠] [💻] [🏊]

**▲▲▲ ▼ Budget Inn** 🅼
(509) 529-4410. **$65-$95.** 305 N 2nd Ave. US 12, exit 2nd Ave, 0.3 mi s. Ext corridors. **Pets:** Medium. $5 one-time fee/pet. Service with restrictions, supervision.
[SAVE] [S6] [✕] [📠] [🏊]

**▲▲▲ ▼▼▼▼ Holiday Inn Express** 〓
(509) 525-6200. **$89-$139.** 1433 W Pine St. US 12, exit Pendleton/Prescott. Int corridors. **Pets:** Other species. $20 daily fee/pet. Service with restrictions, supervision.
[SAVE] [S6] [✕] [📠] [💻] [🏊] [✕]

**▼▼▼▼ Howard Johnson Express Inn** 〓
(509) 529-4360. **$89-$119, 30 day notice.** 325 E Main St. US 12, exit 2nd Ave, 0.5 mi s, then just e. Ext/int corridors. **Pets:** Accepted.
[✕] [📠] [💻] [🏊]

**▲▲▲ ▼▼▼▼ La Quinta Inn Walla Walla** 〓
(509) 525-2522. **$79-$119.** 520 N 2nd Ave. US 12, exit 2nd Ave, just s. Int corridors. **Pets:** Accepted.
[SAVE] [S6] [✕] [⚙] [📠] [💻] [🏊] [✕]

**▲▲▲ ▼▼▼▼ Marcus Whitman Hotel & Conference Center** 🅻🅷
(509) 525-2200. **$99-$174.** Six W Rose. Downtown. Int corridors. **Pets:** Accepted.
[SAVE] [S6] [✕] [📠] [💻] [🍴]

**▼▼ ▼▼ Walla Walla Super 8** 〓
(509) 525-8800. **$63-$93.** 2315 Eastgate St N. US 12, exit Wilbur Ave, just s. Int corridors. **Pets:** $10 one-time fee/room. Service with restrictions, supervision.
[ASK] [S6] [✕] [ᴹ] [⚙] [✦] [📠] [💻]

**▲▲▲ ▼▼ Walla Walla Travelodge** 🅼
(509) 529-4940. **$75-$95.** 421 E Main St. US 12, exit 2nd Ave, 0.5 mi s, then just e. Ext/int corridors. **Pets:** Medium. $7 daily fee/pet. Service with restrictions, supervision.
[SAVE] [S6] [✕] [📠] [💻] [🏊]

# WENATCHEE

**▼▼ Avenue Motel** 🅼
(509) 663-7161. **$45-$60.** 720 N Wenatchee Ave. On US 2 business loop; just nw of downtown. Ext/int corridors. **Pets:** Dogs only. $5 daily fee/pet. Designated rooms, service with restrictions, supervision.
[✕] [📠] [💻] [🏊]

**▲▲▲ ▼▼▼▼ Coast Wenatchee Center Hotel** 🅻🅷
(509) 662-1234. **$89-$135.** 201 N Wenatchee Ave. Downtown. Int corridors. **Pets:** Other species. $10 daily fee/room. Service with restrictions, supervision.
[SAVE] [S6] [✕] [✦] [📠] [💻] [🍴] [🏊]

**▼▼ ▼▼ Comfort Inn** 〓
(509) 662-1700. **$83-$96.** 815 N Wenatchee Ave. Downtown. Int corridors. **Pets:** Small. $10 daily fee/pet. Designated rooms, service with restrictions, supervision.
[ASK] [S6] [✕] [✦] [📠] [💻] [🏊]

**▼▼▼▼ Holiday Inn Express** 〓
(509) 663-6355. **$76-$129.** 1921 N Wenatchee Ave. Northwest side of town. Int corridors. **Pets:** Medium. Designated rooms, service with restrictions, supervision.
[ASK] [S6] [✕] [ᴹ] [⚙] [✦] [📠] [💻] [🏊]

**▲▲▲ ▼▼▼▼ La Quinta Inn & Suites Wenatchee** 〓 ❀
(509) 664-6565. **$79-$109.** 1905 N Wenatchee Ave. West end of town. Int corridors. **Pets:** Other species. Service with restrictions, crate.
[SAVE] [S6] [✕] [⚙] [✦] [📠] [💻] [🏊] [✕]

**▲▲▲ ▼▼▼▼ Red Lion Hotel Wenatchee** 🅻🅷
(509) 663-0711. **$72-$130.** 1225 N Wenatchee Ave. Just nw of downtown. Int corridors. **Pets:** Accepted.
[SAVE] [S6] [✕] [⚙] [📠] [💻] [🍴] [🏊]

**▲▲▲ ▼▼ Super 8** 〓
(509) 662-3443. **$79-$89.** 1401 N Miller St. 1.5 mi n on US 2. Int corridors. **Pets:** Other species. $10 daily fee/pet. Designated rooms, service with restrictions, supervision.
[SAVE] [S6] [✕] [📠] [🏊]

# WESTPORT

**▼▼ CoHo Motel** 🅼
(360) 268-0111. **$55-$80, 3 day notice.** 2501 N Nyhus. Just e of boat basin. Ext corridors. **Pets:** Very small, dogs only. $16 daily fee/pet. Designated rooms, service with restrictions, supervision.
[✕] [🐾]

**▼▼ Windjammer Motel** 🅼
(360) 268-9351. **$45-$90.** 461 E Pacific Ave. Downtown. Ext corridors. **Pets:** Accepted.
[✕] [📠] [💻] [🐾] [✉]

# WINTHROP

**▲▲▲ ▼▼▼▼ Best Western Cascade Inn** 〓 ❀
(509) 996-3100. **$69-$105, 3 day notice.** 960 SR 20. 1 mi e. Ext corridors. **Pets:** Medium, other species. $10 daily fee/room. Designated rooms, no service.
[SAVE] [S6] [✕] [📠] [💻] [🏊] [✕]

**▲▲▲ ▼▼▼▼ River Run Inn** 🅼
(509) 996-2173. **$65-$115, 10 day notice.** 27 Rader Rd. 0.5 mi w on SR 20. Ext corridors. **Pets:** $10 daily fee/pet. Service with restrictions, supervision.
[SAVE] [✕] [📠] [💻] [🏊]

**▲▲▲ ▼▼ ▼▼ Winthrop Inn** 🅼
(509) 996-2217. **$60-$110, 3 day notice.** 960 SR 20. 0.9 mi e. Int corridors. **Pets:** Medium, dogs only. $10 daily fee/pet. Service with restrictions, supervision.
[SAVE] [S6] [✕] [📠] [🏊] [✕]

# WOODLAND

**(AAA)** ▼▼▼ Best Western Woodland Inn & Suites **SH**
(360) 225-1000. **$100.** 1380 Atlantic Ave. I-5, exit 21, just ne. Int corridors. **Pets:** Small, dogs only. $12 one-time fee/pet. Service with restrictions, supervision.

[SAVE] [S&] [X] [🛏] [💻] [🏊]

**(AAA)** ▼▼ Econo Lodge **SH**
(360) 225-6548. **$55-$69, 14 day notice.** 1500 Atlantic Ave. I-5, exit 21, just ne. Ext corridors. **Pets:** $10 daily fee/pet. Service with restrictions, supervision.

[SAVE] [S&] [X] [🛏] [💻] [🏊]

**(AAA)** ▼▼▼ Lewis River Inn **M**
(360) 225-6257. **$60-$85.** 1100 Lewis River Rd. I-5, exit 21, just e. Ext corridors. **Pets:** Other species. $7 daily fee/pet. Designated rooms, service with restrictions, supervision.

[SAVE] [X] [🛏] [💻]

# YAKIMA

▼▼▼ Best Western Peppertree Yakima Inn **SH**
(509) 453-8898. **$85-$150.** 1614 N 1st St. I-82, exit 31, just s. Int corridors. **Pets:** Very small, dogs only. $10 daily fee/pet. Service with restrictions, supervision.

[ASK] [S&] [X] [&°] [🛏] [💻] [🏊]

**(AAA)** ▼▼▼ Cedars Suites Yakima Downtown **M**
(509) 452-8101. **$49-$89.** 1010 E A St. I-82, exit 33B eastbound; exit 33 westbound, just w to 9th St, just n to A St, then just e. Ext corridors. **Pets:** Small, dogs only. $50 deposit/pet, $10 daily fee/pet. Service with restrictions, supervision.

[SAVE] [S&] [X] [🛏]

▼▼ Clarion Hotel & Conference Center **SH**
(509) 248-7850. **$79-$109.** 1507 N 1st St. I-82, exit 31, 0.5 mi s. Int corridors. **Pets:** Medium. $5 daily fee/pet. Designated rooms, service with restrictions, crate.

[ASK] [S&] [X] [&M] [🐾] [&°] [🛏] [💻] [🍴] [🏊] [🐾]

**(AAA)** ▼▼▼ Comfort Suites **SH**
(509) 249-1900. **$79-$179.** 3702 Fruitvale Blvd. US 12, exit 40th Ave, just s. Int corridors. **Pets:** Accepted.

[SAVE] [S&] [X] [&M] [🐾] [&°] [🛏] [💻] [🏊]

▼▼▼ Holiday Inn Express Yakima **SH**
(509) 249-1000. **$75-$129.** 1001 E A St. I-82, exit 33B eastbound; exit 33 westbound, just w to 9th St, just n to A St, then just e. Int corridors. **Pets:** Small. $10 daily fee/room. Designated rooms, service with restrictions, supervision.

[ASK] [S&] [X] [&M] [🐾] [&°] [🛏] [💻] [🏊]

▼▼▼ Oxford Inn **SH**
(509) 457-4444. **$89.** 1603 E Yakima Ave. I-82, exit 33 westbound, just e; exit 33B eastbound. Int corridors. **Pets:** Small. $20 one-time fee/room. Designated rooms, service with restrictions, supervision.

[ASK] [S&] [X] [&M] [🐾] [&°] [🛏] [💻] [🏊] [🐾]

▼▼▼ Oxford Suites **SH** 🐾
(509) 457-9000. **$89-$159.** 1701 E Yakima Ave. I-82, exit 33 westbound; exit 33B eastbound. Int corridors. **Pets:** $20 one-time fee/room.

[ASK] [S&] [X] [&M] [&°] [🛏] [💻] [🏊] [🐾]

▼▼ Ramada Limited **M**
(509) 453-0391. **$49-$99.** 818 N 1st St. I-82, exit 31, 1.2 mi s. Ext corridors. **Pets:** Accepted.

[ASK] [S&] [X] [🐾] [&°] [🛏] [💻] [🏊]

▼▼▼▼ Red Lion Hotel Yakima Center **SH**
(509) 248-5900. **$88-$108.** 607 E Yakima Ave. I-82, exit 33 westbound; exit 33B eastbound, 0.8 mi w. Ext/int corridors. **Pets:** Accepted.

[ASK] [S&] [X] [🐾] [&°] [🛏] [💻] [🍴] [🏊]

▼▼▼▼ Red Lion Hotel Yakima Gateway **SH**
(509) 452-6511. **$83-$98.** 9 N 9th St. I-82, exit 33 westbound; exit 33B eastbound, just s. Int corridors. **Pets:** Medium. $5 daily fee/pet. Service with restrictions, supervision.

[ASK] [S&] [X] [&M] [🛏] [💻] [🍴] [🏊]

▼▼ Sun Country Inn **M**
(509) 248-5650. **$57-$68, 3 day notice.** 1700 N 1st St. I-82, exit 31, just s. Ext corridors. **Pets:** Other species. $7 daily fee/pet. Service with restrictions, supervision.

[ASK] [S&] [X] [🛏] [💻] [🏊]

# ZILLAH

▼▼▼ Comfort Inn **SH**
(509) 829-3399. **$89-$160.** 911 Vintage Valley Pkwy. I-82, exit 52, just n. Int corridors. **Pets:** Other species. $10 daily fee/pet. Supervision.

[ASK] [S&] [X] [&M] [🐾] [&°] [🛏] [💻] [🏊]

## CITY INDEX

# BARBOURSVILLE

### ♦♦♦♦ Comfort Inn by Choice Hotels SH
(304) 733-2122. **$75-$95.** 249 Mall Rd. I-64, exit 20, 0.4 mi n. Int corridors. **Pets:** Accepted.

# BECKLEY

### AAA ♦♦♦ Best Western Four Seasons Inn SH 🐾
(304) 252-0671. **$70-$99.** 1939 Harper Rd. I-64/77, exit 44, just e on SR 3. Ext/int corridors. **Pets:** Other species. $5 daily fee/pet. Service with restrictions.

### ♦♦♦ Comfort Inn SH 🐾
(304) 255-2161. **$65-$100.** 1909 Harper Rd. I-64/77, exit 44, 0.3 mi e on SR 3. Ext/int corridors. **Pets:** Other species. Service with restrictions.

### AAA ♦♦♦♦ Country Inn & Suites By Carlson SH
(304) 252-5100. **$86-$160.** 2120 Harper Rd. I-64/77, exit 44, just w on SR 3. Int corridors. **Pets:** Small. $25 one-time fee/pet. Designated rooms, service with restrictions, supervision.

### AAA ♦♦♦ Howard Johnson Express Inn SH
(304) 255-5900. **$70-$110.** 1907 Harper Rd. I-64/77, exit 44, 0.4 mi e on SR 3. Int corridors. **Pets:** Small, dogs only. $15 one-time fee/pet. Designated rooms, service with restrictions, supervision.

### AAA ♦♦♦ Microtel Inn SH
(304) 256-2000. **$50-$95.** 2130 Harper Rd. I-64/77, exit 44. Int corridors. **Pets:** Large, other species. $25 one-time fee/room. Service with restrictions.

### AAA ♦♦♦♦ Park Inn & Suites SH
(304) 255-9091. **$69-$99.** 134 Harper Park Dr. I-64/77, exit 44, just w on SR 3. Int corridors. **Pets:** Small. $10 one-time fee/pet. Designated rooms, service with restrictions, supervision.

### AAA ♦ Super 8 Motel SH
(304) 253-0802. **$59-$99.** 2014 Harper Rd. I-67/77, exit 44, just e. Int corridors. **Pets:** Small. $10 daily fee/room. Service with restrictions, supervision.

# BLUEFIELD

### AAA ♦♦♦ Econo Lodge M
(304) 327-8171. **$49-$175.** 3400 Cumberland Rd. I-77, exit 1, 3.8 mi nw via US 52/460, then 0.4 mi n on US 52. Ext corridors. **Pets:** Accepted.

### AAA ♦♦♦♦ Holiday Inn Bluefield-On The Hill SH
(304) 325-6170. **$86-$101.** 3350 Big Laurel Hwy. I-77, exit 1, 3.8 mi nw via US 52/460. Int corridors. **Pets:** Accepted.

# BRIDGEPORT

### AAA ♦♦♦♦ Holiday Inn Clarksburg-Bridgeport SH
(304) 842-5411. **$63-$79.** 100 Lodgeville Rd. I-79, exit 119, just e on US 50. Int corridors. **Pets:** Accepted.

### ♦♦ Knights Inn-Clarksburg M
(304) 842-7115. **$48-$80.** 1235 W Main St. I-79, exit 119, 0.3 mi e on US 50. Ext corridors. **Pets:** Accepted.

### ♦♦ Sleep Inn SH
(304) 842-1919. **$69.** 115 Tolley Dr. I-79, exit 119, just e on US 50. Int corridors. **Pets:** Other species. Supervision.

# BUCKHANNON

### AAA ♦♦♦ Main Street Inn SH
(304) 472-5000. **$60-$92.** 8 E Main St. Just e on Main St. Int corridors. **Pets:** Medium. $50 deposit/room. Service with restrictions, crate.

# CHARLESTON

### ♦♦♦ Charleston Comfort Suites SH 🐾
(304) 925-1171. **$88-$94.** 107 Alex Ln. I-77, exit 95, just s on SR 61. Int corridors. **Pets:** Medium, other species. Service with restrictions, supervision.

### ♦♦♦ Country Inn & Suites By Carlson SH 🐾
(304) 925-4300. **$88-$110.** 105 Alex Ln. I-77, exit 95, just s on SR 61. Int corridors. **Pets:** Other species. $10 daily fee/pet. Service with restrictions, crate.

### ♦♦ Days Inn Charleston East M
(304) 925-1010. **$57-$63.** 6400 MacCorkle Ave. I-77, exit 95, just s on SR 61. Int corridors. **Pets:** Accepted.

### ♦♦♦ Holiday Inn Express Civic Center SH
(304) 345-0600. **$90-$100.** 100 Civic Center Dr. I-64, exit 58B eastbound; exit 58C westbound, just s; downtown. Int corridors. **Pets:** Small. $25 one-time fee/room. Designated rooms, service with restrictions, supervision.

### AAA ♦♦♦ Knights Inn-Charleston East M
(304) 925-0451. **$47-$57.** 6401 MacCorkle Ave SE. I-77, exit 95, just s on SR 61. Ext corridors. **Pets:** Medium. $10 one-time fee/room. Service with restrictions, crate.

### ♦♦ Red Roof Inn-Kanawha City M
(304) 925-6953. **$47-$58.** 6305 SE MacCorkle Ave. I-77, exit 95, just s on SR 61. Ext corridors. **Pets:** Accepted.

# CROSS LANES

◆◆◆ ▼▼▼ Comfort Inn West Charleston SH ❖
(304) 776-8070. $77-$87. 102 Racer Dr. I-64, exit 47, just s. Int corridors. Pets: Large. $25 daily fee/room. Designated rooms, service with restrictions, supervision.

⟨SAVE⟩ ⟨S₀⟩ ⟨✕⟩ ⟨&⟩ ⟨❚⟩ ⟨▣⟩ ⟨➥⟩

# DAVIS

◆◆◆ ▼▼▼▼ Deerfield Village Resort-Canaan Valley CO
(304) 866-4698. $140-$320. Cortland Ln. 7 mi s on SR 32. Ext corridors. Pets: Other species. $50 one-time fee/pet. Designated rooms.

⟨SAVE⟩ ⟨✕⟩ ⟨❚⟩ ⟨▣⟩ ⟨¶⟩ ⟨➥⟩ ⟨⊠⟩ ⟨Ⅺ⟩

# DUNBAR

▼ Dunbar Super 8 Motel SH
(304) 768-6888. $61-$69, 15 day notice. 911 Dunbar Ave. I-64, exit 53, just w. Int corridors. Pets: Other species. Service with restrictions.

⟨ASK⟩ ⟨S₀⟩ ⟨✕⟩ ⟨❚⟩

# EDRAY

◆◆◆ ▼ ▼ Marlinton Motor Inn M ❖
(304) 799-4711. $70-$95. US 219 N. Center. Ext corridors. Pets: Other species. $10 daily fee/pet. Designated rooms, service with restrictions, crate.

⟨SAVE⟩ ⟨S₀⟩ ⟨✕⟩ ⟨❚⟩ ⟨▣⟩ ⟨¶⟩ ⟨➥⟩

# ELKINS

◆◆◆ ▼ Best Country Inn & Suites M
(304) 636-7711. $58-$120, 3 day notice. Route 219/250 S. 0.9 mi s of SR 219. Ext/int corridors. Pets: Other species. $5 one-time fee/room. Service with restrictions, crate.

⟨SAVE⟩ ⟨S₀⟩ ⟨✕⟩ ⟨❚⟩ ⟨▣⟩

◆◆◆ ▼▼▼▼ Cheat River Lodge & Inn CA
(304) 636-2301. $68-$83, 30 day notice. Rt 1, Box 115, Faulkner Rd. 4.8 mi e on US 33, then 1.5 mi ne. Ext corridors. Pets: Dogs only. $10 daily fee/pet. Service with restrictions, crate.

⟨SAVE⟩ ⟨✕⟩ ⟨❚⟩ ⟨▣⟩ ⟨¶⟩ ⟨⊠⟩

▼▼ Econo Lodge M
(304) 636-5311. $53-$75. US 33 E. 1 mi e. Ext/int corridors. Pets: Medium. $5 one-time fee/room. Designated rooms, service with restrictions, supervision.

⟨ASK⟩ ⟨S₀⟩ ⟨✕⟩ ⟨❚⟩ ⟨➥⟩

▼▼ Elkins Days Inn SH
(304) 637-4667. $65-$75. 1200 Harrison Ave. 1 mi w on US 33/250/SR 92; downtown; in an office building. Int corridors. Pets: Large, other species. $5 daily fee/pet. Service with restrictions, supervision.

⟨ASK⟩ ⟨S₀⟩ ⟨✕⟩ ⟨&M⟩ ⟨❚⟩ ⟨▣⟩ ⟨¶⟩

▼▼ Elkins Super 8 Motel SH
(304) 636-6500. $66-$76, 14 day notice. 350 Beverly Pike. 0.8 mi s on SR 219. Int corridors. Pets: Accepted.

⟨ASK⟩ ⟨S₀⟩ ⟨✕⟩ ⟨❚⟩

# FAIRMONT

◆◆◆ ▼▼▼▼ Holiday Inn Fairmont SH
(304) 366-5500. $63-$108. 930 E Grafton Rd. I-79, exit 137, just e. Int corridors. Pets: Other species. Designated rooms, service with restrictions, supervision.

⟨SAVE⟩ ⟨S₀⟩ ⟨✕⟩ ⟨&M⟩ ⟨⟳⟩ ⟨&⟩ ⟨❚⟩ ⟨▣⟩ ⟨¶⟩ ⟨➥⟩

▼▼ Red Roof Inn M
(304) 366-6800. $45-$59. 50 Middletown Rd. I-79, exit 132, 0.3 mi s on US 250, just w, then just s. Ext corridors. Pets: Accepted.

⟨✕⟩ ⟨⟳⟩

▼▼ Super 8 Motel SH
(304) 363-1488. $57-$79. 2208 Pleasant Valley Rd. I-79, exit 133, just e. Int corridors. Pets: Medium. Service with restrictions, crate.

⟨ASK⟩ ⟨S₀⟩ ⟨✕⟩ ⟨❚⟩

# FROST

▼▼▼ The Inn at Mountain Quest CI ❖
(304) 799-7267. $95-$165, 7 day notice. Rt 92 Frost. On SR 92, 0.4 mi n. Ext corridors. Pets: Large, other species. $20 deposit/room. Designated rooms, no service, supervision.

⟨ASK⟩ ⟨S₀⟩ ⟨✕⟩ ⟨¶⟩ ⟨⊠⟩

# HARPERS FERRY

▼▼▼▼ Quality Inn & Conference Center SH
(304) 535-6302. $70-$158. 4328 William L Wilson Frwy. 0.2 mi w on US 340. Int corridors. Pets: Accepted.

⟨ASK⟩ ⟨S₀⟩ ⟨✕⟩ ⟨&⟩ ⟨❚⟩ ⟨▣⟩ ⟨¶⟩ ⟨➥⟩

# HUNTINGTON

▼▼ Red Roof Inn SH
(304) 733-3737. $45-$65. 5190 US Rt 60 E. I-64, exit 15, just s. Ext corridors. Pets: Accepted.

⟨✕⟩ ⟨❚⟩

# HURRICANE

▼▼ Red Roof Inn M
(304) 757-6392. $45-$55. 500 Putnam Village Dr. I-64, exit 39, just n on SR 34, then just e. Ext corridors. Pets: Accepted.

⟨✕⟩ ⟨&⟩ ⟨❚⟩

# KEYSER

◆◆◆ ▼▼▼ Keyser Inn SH
(304) 788-0913. $57-$77. Rt 220 S. On US 220, 2.3 mi s. Int corridors. Pets: Medium. $20 one-time fee/room. Designated rooms, service with restrictions, supervision.

⟨SAVE⟩ ⟨S₀⟩ ⟨✕⟩ ⟨❚⟩ ⟨▣⟩

# LEWISBURG

◆◆◆ ▼▼▼ Brier Inn SH
(304) 645-7722. $59-$105. 540 N Jefferson St. I-64, exit 169, just s on US 219. Ext corridors. Pets: Other species. $10 daily fee/pet. Designated rooms, crate.

⟨SAVE⟩ ⟨S₀⟩ ⟨✕⟩ ⟨&⟩ ⟨❚⟩ ⟨▣⟩ ⟨¶⟩ ⟨➥⟩

◆◆◆ ▼▼▼ Relax Inn SH
(304) 645-2345. $55-$150, 3 day notice. 635 N Jefferson St. I-64, exit 169, 0.3 mi n on US 219. Ext corridors. Pets: Small. $10 daily fee/pet. Service with restrictions, supervision.

⟨SAVE⟩ ⟨S₀⟩ ⟨✕⟩ ⟨❚⟩ ⟨▣⟩

◆◆◆ ▼ Rodeway Inn M
(304) 645-7070. $30-$100. 107 W Fair St. I-64, exit 169, 3.1 mi s on US 219, then just e. Ext corridors. Pets: Accepted.

⟨SAVE⟩ ⟨S₀⟩ ⟨✕⟩ ⟨❚⟩ ⟨▣⟩

▼▼ Super 8 Motel SH
(304) 647-3188. $54-$60, 10 day notice. 550 N Jefferson St. I-64, exit 169, just s on US 219. Int corridors. Pets: Accepted.

⟨ASK⟩ ⟨S₀⟩ ⟨✕⟩ ⟨⟳⟩ ⟨❚⟩

# MARTINSBURG

▼▼ Days Inn Martinsburg SH
(304) 263-1800. $52-$64. 209 Viking Way. I-81, exit 13, just e on W King St (CR 15). Ext/int corridors. Pets: Small, dogs only. $10 one-time fee/room. No service, supervision.

⟨ASK⟩ ⟨S₀⟩ ⟨✕⟩ ⟨❚⟩

**Econo Lodge M**
(304) 274-2181. **$60-$63.** 5595 Hammonds Mill Rd. I-81, exit 20, just e. Ext/int corridors. **Pets:** Other species. Service with restrictions, supervision.

**Knights Inn-Martinsburg M**
(304) 267-2211. **$52-$85.** 1997 Edwin Miller Blvd. I-81, exit 16E, 0.4 mi e on SR 9. Ext corridors. **Pets:** Large, other species. $10 daily fee/pet. Designated rooms, service with restrictions.

**Quality Inn of Martinsburg SH**
(304) 263-8811. **$69-$99.** 94 McMillan Ct. I-81, exit 16E, just e. Ext/int corridors. **Pets:** Other species. $10 daily fee/pet. Service with restrictions, supervision.

**Relax Inn M**
(304) 263-0831. **$32-$59, 3 day notice.** 1022 Winchester Ave (US 11 N). I-81, exit 12, 0.3 mi e on SR 45, then just n. Ext corridors. **Pets:** Medium. $5 daily fee/pet. Service with restrictions, supervision.

**Super 8 Motel-Martinsburg SH**
(304) 263-0801. **Call for rates.** 2048 Edwin Miller Blvd. I-81, exit 16E, just e on SR 9. Int corridors. **Pets:** Medium, other species. $10 daily fee/pet. Service with restrictions, supervision.

## MINERAL WELLS

**AmeriHost Inn Parkersburg South at I-77 SH**
(304) 489-3111. **$60-$120.** 201 Hospitality Ln. I-77, exit 170, just w. Int corridors. **Pets:** Accepted.

**Microtel Inn SH**
(304) 489-3892. **$45-$57.** 104 Nickolette Rd. I-77, exit 170, just w. Int corridors. **Pets:** Dogs only. $10 daily fee/pet. Designated rooms, no service, supervision.

## MORGANTOWN

**Comfort Inn-Morgantown SH**
(304) 296-9364. **$55-$125.** 225 Comfort Inn Dr. I-68, exit 1, 0.3 mi n on US 119. Int corridors. **Pets:** Small. $20 daily fee/pet. Designated rooms, no service, crate.

**Friends Inn M**
(304) 599-4850. **$45-$75.** 452 Country Club Rd. I-79, exit 155, s on US 19 to SR 705, then e on University Ave. Ext corridors. **Pets:** Small. $5 daily fee/pet. Designated rooms, service with restrictions, supervision.

**Ramada Conference Center SH**
(304) 296-3431. **$60-$90.** 20 Scott Ave. I-68, exit 1, 0.3 mi n. Int corridors. **Pets:** Medium, other species. Service with restrictions, supervision.

## NITRO

**Econo Lodge M**
(304) 755-8341. **$48-$66.** 4115 1st Ave. I-64, exit 45, 0.8 mi e on SR 25. Ext corridors. **Pets:** $10 daily fee/pet. Designated rooms, service with restrictions, supervision.

## PARKERSBURG

**Holiday Inn Parkersburg SH**
(304) 485-6200. **$80-$116.** 225 Holiday Hills Dr. I-77, exit 176, just e. Int corridors. **Pets:** Medium. Service with restrictions, supervision.

**Red Carpet Inn M**
(304) 485-1851. **$40-$55.** 6333 Emerson Ave. I-77, exit 179, 0.4 mi sw on SR 68. Ext corridors. **Pets:** Dogs only. $5 daily fee/pet. Service with restrictions, supervision.

**Red Roof Inn M**
(304) 485-1741. **$52-$63.** 3714 E 7th St. I-77, exit 176, just w on US 50. Ext corridors. **Pets:** Other species. Service with restrictions, crate.

## PHILIPPI

**Philippi Lodging M**
(304) 457-5888. **$52-$83.** Rt 4, Box 155. 2.5 mi s on US 250. Int corridors. **Pets:** Accepted.

## PRINCETON

**Comfort Inn-Princeton SH**
(304) 487-6101. **$75-$80.** Ambrose Ln & US 460. I-77, exit 9, 0.3 mi w on US 460. Int corridors. **Pets:** Small. $20 daily fee/pet. Designated rooms, no service, crate.

**Days Inn SH**
(304) 425-8100. **$66-$85, 3 day notice.** 347 Meadowfield Ln. I-77, exit 9, 0.3 mi w on US 460, just s on Ambrose Ln, then just e. Ext corridors. **Pets:** Accepted.

**Holiday Inn Express Princeton SH**
(304) 425-8156. **$125-$136, 3 day notice.** 805 Oakvale Rd. I-77, exit 9, just w. Int corridors. **Pets:** $10 deposit/pet. Service with restrictions, supervision.

**Sleep Inn SH**
(304) 431-2800. **$75-$200.** 1015 Oakvale Rd. I-77, exit 9, just w on US 460, then just n via service road. Int corridors. **Pets:** Medium, other species. Service with restrictions, crate.

## RIPLEY

**Best Western McCoys Inn & Conference Center SH**
(304) 372-9122. **$80-$100.** 701 W Main St. I-77, exit 138, just e. Ext/int corridors. **Pets:** Other species. Designated rooms, service with restrictions, supervision.

**Ripley Super 8 Motel M**
(304) 372-8880. **$60-$70.** 102 Duke Dr. I-77, exit 138, just e on SR 33. Int corridors. **Pets:** Accepted.

## SNOWSHOE

**Inn at Snowshoe SH**
(304) 572-6520. **$89-$229, 21 day notice.** SR 66. 0.5 mi e on SR 66, from US 219 jct, follow signs. Int corridors. **Pets:** Accepted.

# SOUTH CHARLESTON

▼▼▼ **Ramada Plaza Hotel Charleston** SH
(304) 744-4641. **$72-$109.** 400 2nd Ave. I-64, exit 56, just nw. Int corridors. **Pets:** Accepted.

ASK S⊘ ✕ 🎲 🛏 🖵 🍽 ⇌

# STAR CITY

◈◈◈ ▼▼▼ **Econo Lodge-Coliseum** SH
(304) 599-8181. **$68.** 3506 Monongahela Blvd. I-79, exit 155, 1.4 mi s on US 119/SR 7. Ext corridors. **Pets:** Medium. Service with restrictions, supervision.

SAVE S⊘ ✕ 🛏 🖵

◈◈◈ ▼▼▼▼ **Quality Inn & Suites Morgantown** SH
(304) 599-1680. **$85-$170.** 1400 Saratoga Ave. I-79, exit 155, 1.7 mi s on US 119/SR 7. Ext corridors. **Pets:** Accepted.

SAVE S⊘ ✕ ♿ 🎲 🦽 🛏 🖵 ⇌

# SUMMERSVILLE

◈◈◈ ▼▼▼ **Best Western Summersville Lake Motor Lodge** SH
(304) 872-6900. **$70-$90.** 1203 S Broad St. US 19 and Broad St; 0.6 mi s of jct SR 39. Ext corridors. **Pets:** Small. $7 daily fee/pet. Designated rooms, service with restrictions, supervision.

SAVE S⊘ ✕ 🛏 🖵

◈◈◈ ▼▼◆▼ **Comfort Inn** SH
(304) 872-6500. **$65-$160, 30 day notice.** 903 Industrial Dr N. US 19, 1.9 mi n of jct SR 39. Int corridors. **Pets:** Small, other species. $10 daily fee/pet. Designated rooms, service with restrictions, supervision.

SAVE S⊘ ✕ 🎲 🛏 🖵 ⇌ ✕

◈◈◈ ▼▼▼ **Sleep Inn of Summersville** SH
(304) 872-4500. **$50-$150, 30 day notice.** 701 Professional Park Dr. US 19, 1.7 mi n of jct SR 39. Int corridors. **Pets:** Small, other species. $10 daily fee/pet. Designated rooms, service with restrictions, supervision.

SAVE S⊘ ✕ 🎲 🦽 🛏 🖵 ⇌

▼ **Super 8 Motel-Summersville** SH
(304) 872-4000. **$57.** 306 Merchants Walk. US 19, just n. Int corridors. **Pets:** $25 deposit/room. Service with restrictions, supervision.

ASK S⊘ ✕ 🛏

# TRIADELPHIA

◈◈◈ ▼▼◆▼ **Comfort Inn-Wheeling** SH
(304) 547-0610. **$59-$109.** I-70 & Dallas Pike. I-70, exit 11, just n. Int corridors. **Pets:** Small, dogs only. $10 daily fee/room. Designated rooms, service with restrictions, supervision.

SAVE S⊘ ✕ 🛏 🖵 ⇌

◈◈◈ ▼▼◆▼ **Holiday Inn Express Wheeling East** SH
(304) 547-1380. **$70-$119.** I-70, exit 11. Int corridors. **Pets:** Medium. $10 daily fee/pet. Service with restrictions, supervision.

SAVE S⊘ ✕ 🎲 🦽 🛏 🖵 ⇌

# WEIRTON

▼▼▼ **Holiday Inn** SH
(304) 723-5522. **$110-$149.** 350 Three Springs Dr. 4.5 mi e on US 22, exit Three Springs Dr. Int corridors. **Pets:** Large, other species. $50 one-time fee/room. Service with restrictions, supervision.

✕ 🎲 🦽 🛏 🖵 🍽 ⇌ ✕

# WESTON

◈◈◈ ▼▼◆▼ **Comfort Inn** SH
(304) 269-7000. **$55-$110.** 2906 US 33 E. I-79, exit 99, just e. Ext corridors. **Pets:** Accepted.

SAVE S⊘ ✕ 🎲 🦽 🛏 🖵 ⇌

▼▼◆▼ **Weston Super 8 Motel** SH
(304) 269-1086. **$59-$64, 10 day notice.** 100 Market Place Mall, Suite 12. I-79, exit 99, just e. Int corridors. **Pets:** Very small, other species. $10 one-time fee/pet. Service with restrictions, supervision.

ASK S⊘ ✕ 🦽 🛏

# WISCONSIN

## CITY INDEX

## ABBOTSFORD

### ▼▼ Sleep Inn SH 🐾
(715) 223-3337. **$70-$105.** 300 E Elderberry Rd. SR 29, exit 132 (SR 13), just se. Int corridors. **Pets:** $15 daily fee/room. Designated rooms, service with restrictions, supervision.

ASK S☉ ✕ 🕸 🛠 🍴 🖥 ➿

## ALGOMA

### ⬥⬥⬥ ▼ Algoma Beach Motel SH
(920) 487-2828. **$59-$299, 3 day notice.** 1500 Lake St. Jct SR 54, 0.4 mi s on SR 42. Ext/int corridors. **Pets:** Dogs only. $15 daily fee/pet. Designated rooms, supervision.

SAVE ✕ 🛠

### ▼ Scenic Shore Inn M 🐾
(920) 487-3214. **$45-$63, 3 day notice.** 2221 Lake St. Jct SR 54, 0.8 mi s on SR 42. Ext corridors. **Pets:** Small, dogs only. Service with restrictions, supervision.

✕ 🛠 🖥

## ANTIGO

### ▼▼ Super 8 Motel-Antigo SH
(715) 623-4188. **$70-$130.** 535 Century Ave. On US 45 at SR 64 E. Int corridors. **Pets:** Small. Designated rooms, no service, crate.

ASK S☉ ✕ 🕸 🛠 🍴 🖥 ➿ 🚫

## APPLETON

### ▼▼ Best Western Midway Hotel SH
(920) 731-4141. **$89-$149.** 3033 W College Ave. US 41, exit 137 (SR 125), 0.5 mi e. Int corridors. **Pets:** $10 daily fee/room. Designated rooms, service with restrictions, supervision.

ASK S☉ ✕ 🕸 🛠 🖥 🍴 ➿ 🚫

### ▼▼ Budgetel Inn Appleton M
(920) 734-6070. **$55-$70.** 3920 W College Ave. US 41, exit 137 (SR 125), just e. Ext/int corridors. **Pets:** Medium. Service with restrictions.

ASK ✕ 🛠 🖥 ➿

### ▼▼ Candlewood Suites SH
(920) 739-8000. **$79-$299.** 4525 W College Ave. Just w of US 41. Int corridors. **Pets:** Dogs only. $75 one-time fee/pet. Service with restrictions, crate.

ASK S☉ ✕ 🛠 🛠 🖥

### ▼▼▼ Comfort Suites Appleton Airport SH
(920) 730-3800. **$100-$199.** 3809 W Wisconsin Ave. US 41, exit 138 (Wisconsin Ave), just e. Int corridors. **Pets:** Other species. Service with restrictions, crate.

ASK S☉ ✕ 🕸 🛠 🖥 ➿ 🚫

### ⬥⬥⬥ ▼▼▼ Country Inn & Suites By Carlson SH
(920) 830-3240. **$79-$199.** 355 Fox River Dr. US 41, exit 137 (SR 125), just nw. Int corridors. **Pets:** Medium. Designated rooms, service with restrictions, crate.

SAVE S☉ ✕ 🛠 🛠 🖥 ➿ 🚫

### ⬥⬥⬥ ▼ Exel Inn of Appleton M
(920) 733-5551. **$48-$78.** 210 Westhill Blvd. US 41, exit 137 (SR 125), just e. Int corridors. **Pets:** Small, other species. Designated rooms, service with restrictions, supervision.

SAVE S☉ ✕ 🛠 🖥

### ▼▼ Fairfield Inn by Marriott SH
(920) 954-0202. **$70-$90.** 132 Mall Dr. US 41, exit 137 (SR 125), just nw. Int corridors. **Pets:** Accepted.

ASK S☉ ✕ 🕸 🛠 🖥 ➿

### ▼▼ Microtel Inn & Suites SH
(920) 997-3121. **$48-$116.** 321 Metro Dr. US 41, exit 137 (SR 125), just nw. Int corridors. **Pets:** Medium, other species. $10 daily fee/room. Designated rooms, service with restrictions, supervision.

✕ 🛠 🛠 🖥

### ▼▼ Residence Inn by Marriott SH
(920) 954-0570. **$110-$180, 14 day notice.** 310 Metro Dr. US 41, exit 137 (SR 125), just nw on Mall Dr. Int corridors. **Pets:** Accepted.

ASK S☉ ✕ 🕸 🛠 🛠 🖥 ➿ 🚫

### ⬥⬥⬥ ▼▼▼ Woodfield Suites Appleton SH
(920) 734-7777. **$92-$109.** 3730 W College Ave. US 41, exit 137 (SR 125), just e. Int corridors. **Pets:** Medium. Service with restrictions.

SAVE ✕ 🛠 🖥 ➿ 🚫

## ARCADIA

### ▼ RKD Motel M
(608) 323-3338. **$52-$62, 4 day notice.** 915 E Main St. On SR 95; 0.6 mi w of jct SR 93. Ext corridors. **Pets:** Accepted.

ASK ✕ 🛠 🖥

# ASHLAND

**Americinn of Ashland** SH
(715) 682-9950. **$99-$249.** 3009 Lake Shore Dr E. On US 2, 2.1 mi e of jct SR 13 S. Int corridors. **Pets:** Accepted.

**Ashland Motel** M
(715) 682-5503. **$69-$89.** 2300 W Lake Shore Dr. 1.8 mi w on US 2. Ext corridors. **Pets:** Small, dogs only. $5 daily fee/pet. Designated rooms, service with restrictions, supervision.

**Super 8 Motel** SH
(715) 682-9377. **$58-$140.** 1610 W Lake Shore Dr. On US 2 at 16th Ave. Int corridors. **Pets:** Accepted.

# BALDWIN

**Americinn of Baldwin** SH
(715) 684-5888. **$69-$139.** 500 Baldwin Plaza Dr. I-94, exit 19 (US 63), just ne. Int corridors. **Pets:** Accepted.

**Super 8 Motel** SH
(715) 684-2700. **$63-$98.** 2110 10th Ave. I-94, exit 19 (US 63), just se. Int corridors. **Pets:** Medium, other species. $10 one-time fee/pet. Service with restrictions, supervision.

# BARABOO

**Park Plaza Baraboo** SH
(608) 356-6422. **$58-$125.** 626 W Pine St. On US 12, 0.3 mi n of SR 33. Int corridors. **Pets:** Medium, other species. Designated rooms, service with restrictions, crate.

# BAYFIELD

**Old Rittenhouse Inn** CI
(715) 779-5111. **$109-$299, 10 day notice.** 301 Rittenhouse Ave. Just w on SR 13. Int corridors. **Pets:** Accepted.

# BEAVER DAM

**Americinn Lodge & Suites** SH
(920) 356-9000. **$85-$131.** 325 Seippel Blvd. US 151, exit 134 (CR B/Industrial Dr). Int corridors. **Pets:** Other species. $10 daily fee/room. Service with restrictions, supervision.

**Super 8 Motel** SH
(920) 887-8880. **$63-$77, 14 day notice.** 711 Park Ave. US 151, exit 132 (SR 33), just w. Int corridors. **Pets:** Large, other species. $50 deposit/pet. Designated rooms, service with restrictions, supervision.

# BELOIT

**Beloit Inn** SH
(608) 362-5500. **$89-$189.** 500 Pleasant St. Downtown. Int corridors. **Pets:** Accepted.

**Comfort Inn of Beloit** SH
(608) 362-2666. **$59-$89.** 2786 Milwaukee Rd. I-90, exit 185A, just w at jct I-43 and SR 81. Int corridors. **Pets:** Medium. $10 daily fee/room. Service with restrictions, supervision.

**Econo Lodge** M
(608) 364-4000. **$44-$56.** 2956 Milwaukee Rd. I-90, exit 185A, 0.3 mi w. Ext/int corridors. **Pets:** Medium. $6 daily fee/pet. Service with restrictions.

**Super 8 Motel** SH
(608) 365-8680. **$59-$79.** 3002 Milwaukee Rd. I-90, exit 185A, just sw at jct I-43 and SR 81. Int corridors. **Pets:** Accepted.

# BERLIN

**Best Western Countryside** M
(920) 361-4411. **$79-$99.** 227 Ripon Rd. On SR 49, at jct CR F. Int corridors. **Pets:** Small, dogs only. $10 daily fee/room. Designated rooms, service with restrictions, supervision.

# BLACK RIVER FALLS

**Best Western-Arrowhead Lodge & Suites** SH ❖
(715) 284-9471. **$60-$94.** 600 Oasis Rd. I-94, exit 116, jct SR 54. Int corridors. **Pets:** Other species. $10 daily fee/room. Service with restrictions, supervision.

**Days Inn** SH
(715) 284-4333. **$77-$99.** 919 Hwy 54 E. I-94, exit 116, just w. Int corridors. **Pets:** Accepted.

# BURLINGTON

**Americinn Lodge & Suites** SH
(262) 534-2125. **$79-$189.** 2059 S Browns Lake Rd. 3 mi n on SR 36 and 83, jct CR W. Int corridors. **Pets:** Very small, dogs only. $30 one-time fee/pet. Designated rooms, service with restrictions, supervision.

# CADOTT

**Countryside Motel** M
(715) 289-4000. **$48-$90.** 545 Lavorata Rd. SR 29, exit 91 (SR 27), just s. Int corridors. **Pets:** Small, dogs only. Designated rooms, service with restrictions, supervision.

# CAMP DOUGLAS

**K & K Motel** M
(608) 427-3100. **$60-$65.** 219 Hwy 12 & 16. I-90/94, exit 55, just s. Ext corridors. **Pets:** Accepted.

# CHILTON

**Best Western Stanton Inn** SH
(920) 849-3600. **$75-$159.** 1101 E Chestnut St. Jct US 151 and SR 32/57. Int corridors. **Pets:** Small. $50 deposit/pet. Service with restrictions, supervision.

# CHIPPEWA FALLS

**Americinn of Chippewa Falls** SH
(715) 723-5711. **$74-$124.** 11 W South Ave. 2 mi s on SR 124, access via CR J. Int corridors. **Pets:** Dogs only. Designated rooms, service with restrictions, supervision.

**Avalon Hotel & Conference Center** SH
(715) 723-2281. **$79-$109.** 1009 W Park Ave. Jct SR 124 and CR J. Ext/int corridors. **Pets:** Small. $10 daily fee/pet. Designated rooms, service with restrictions, crate.

## COLUMBUS

**Super 8 Motel-Columbus** SH
(920) 623-8800. **$64-$113.** 219 Industrial Dr. US 151, exit 118 (SR 16/60), just ne. Int corridors. **Pets:** Medium. $50 deposit/room, $10 one-time fee/room. Designated rooms, service with restrictions, supervision.

## CRIVITZ

**Shaffer Park Resort** M ❖
(715) 854-2186. **$49-$85, 14 day notice.** N 7217 Shaffer Rd. 5 mi w on CR W. Ext corridors. **Pets:** Medium, dogs only. $7 daily fee/pet. Service with restrictions, supervision.

## DE FOREST

**Holiday Inn Express** SH
(608) 846-8686. **$79-$139.** 7184 Morrisonville Rd. I-90/94, exit 126 (CR V), just e. Int corridors. **Pets:** $20 one-time fee/room. Designated rooms, service with restrictions, supervision.

## DELAVAN

**Comfort Suites** SH
(262) 740-1001. **$80-$110.** 313 Bauer Pkwy. I-43, exit 21 (SR 50), just w, just n, then just w. Int corridors. **Pets:** Accepted.

## DE PERE

**Kress Inn-A Clarion Collection** SH ❖
(920) 403-5100. **$81-$139.** 300 Grant St. US 41, exit 163 (Main St), 1 mi e, then just s on 3rd St. Int corridors. **Pets:** Medium, dogs only. Crate.

## DODGEVILLE

**Best Western Quiet House & Suites** SH
(608) 935-7739. **$89-$109.** 1130 N Johns St. On US 18, just e of jct SR 23. Int corridors. **Pets:** Other species. $15 daily fee/pet. Designated rooms, service with restrictions, supervision.

**Pine Ridge Motel** M ❖
(608) 935-3386. **$32-$69.** 405 CR YZ. On CR YZ, 0.5 mi e of jct SR 23. Ext corridors. **Pets:** Very small, dogs only. $20 deposit/pet. Designated rooms, service with restrictions, supervision.

**Super 8 Motel of Dodgeville** SH
(608) 935-3888. **$56-$90.** 1308 Johns St. Just n of US 18. Int corridors. **Pets:** $50 deposit/room. Supervision.

# DOOR COUNTY AREA

## FISH CREEK

**Julie's Park Cafe & Motel** M ❖
(920) 868-2999. **$41-$116, 10 day notice.** 4020 Hwy 42. On SR 42, 0.3 mi n. Ext corridors. **Pets:** Other species. $15 daily fee/pet. Service with restrictions, supervision.

## GILLS ROCK

**Harbor House Inn** BB ❖
(920) 854-5196. **$69-$199, 21 day notice.** 12666 SR 42. On SR 42; center. Ext/int corridors. **Pets:** $10 daily fee/pet. Service with restrictions, supervision.

**Maple Grove Motel** M
(920) 854-2587. **$60-$90.** 809 SR 42. On SR 42, 0.3 mi e; 1.5 mi w of car ferry. Ext corridors. **Pets:** Accepted.

## STURGEON BAY

**Super 8 Motel** SH ❖
(920) 743-9211. **$51-$104.** 409 Green Bay Rd. 1 mi s on Business Rt SR 42/57. Int corridors. **Pets:** Dogs only. $20 deposit/room, $5 daily fee/pet. Designated rooms, service with restrictions, supervision.

# END AREA

## EAGLE RIVER

**Best Western Derby Inn** SH
(715) 479-1600. **$70-$160, 3 day notice.** 1800 Hwy 45 N. On US 45, 1 mi n. Int corridors. **Pets:** Medium. $50 deposit/room. Designated rooms, service with restrictions, supervision.

**Days Inn** SH
(715) 479-5151. **$84-$105.** 844 Railroad St N. 0.5 mi n on US 45. Int corridors. **Pets:** Accepted.

## EAST TROY

**Country Inn & Suites by Carlson** SH
(262) 642-2100. **$80-$135.** 2921 O'Leary Ln. I-43, exit 36, at jct SR 120. Int corridors. **Pets:** Medium, dogs only. Designated rooms, service with restrictions, supervision.

## EAU CLAIRE

**AmericInn Motel & Suites** SH
(715) 874-4900. **$69-$159.** 6200 Texaco Dr. I-94, exit 59, jct US 12. Int corridors. **Pets:** $10 daily fee/pet. Supervision.

▼▼▼▼ **Best Western Trail Lodge Hotel & Suites** 🆂🅷
(715) 838-9989. **$79-$119.** 3340 Mondovi Rd. I-94, exit 65, just n. Int corridors. **Pets:** Accepted.
(A$K) 🛇 ⊠ 🔱 🔒 🛢 💻 ⊷ ⊠

▼▼ 🔷 **Best Western White House Inn** 🆂🅷
(715) 832-8356. **$76-$130.** 1828 S Hastings Way. On US 53; 1.3 mi n of jct US 12. Int corridors. **Pets:** $10 one-time fee/pet. Designated rooms, service with restrictions, supervision.
(A$K) 🛇 ⊠ 🗐 🔒 🛢 💻 ⊠

▼ 🔷 **Comfort Inn** 🆂🅷 🐾
(715) 833-9798. **$59-$109.** 3117 Craig Rd. I-94, exit 65, 1.3 mi n on SR 37; just s of jct US 12. Int corridors. **Pets:** Dogs only. $10 daily fee/pet. Designated rooms, service with restrictions, supervision.
(A$K) 🛇 ⊠ 🗐 🔒 🛢 💻

▼▼ 🔷 **Days Inn-West** 🆂🅷 🐾
(715) 874-5550. **$60-$110.** 6319 Truax Ln. I-94, exit 59, jct US 12. Int corridors. **Pets:** Large, other species. $10 one-time fee/pet. Designated rooms, service with restrictions, supervision.
(A$K) 🛇 ⊠ 🔱 🔒 🛢 💻 ⊷

▼▼ 🔷 **Econo Lodge** 🆂🅷
(715) 833-8818. **$55-$125.** 4608 Royal Dr. I-94, exit 68, just n on SR 93, just w on Golf Rd, then just s. Int corridors. **Pets:** Medium, dogs only. $7 daily fee/pet. Designated rooms, service with restrictions, supervision.
(A$K) 🛇 ⊠ 🔒 🛢 💻

🅐🅐🅐 ▼▼ **Exel Inn of Eau Claire** 🆂🅷
(715) 834-3193. **$49-$79.** 2305 Craig Rd. I-94, exit 65, 1.3 mi n on SR 37; just w of jct US 12. Int corridors. **Pets:** Small, other species. Designated rooms, service with restrictions, supervision.
(SAVE) 🛇 ⊠ 🔒 🛢 💻

▼▼ 🔷 **Grandstay Residential Suites** 🆂🅷
(715) 834-1700. **$94-$114.** 5310 Prill Rd. I-94, exit 70, 0.8 mi n on US 53. Int corridors. **Pets:** Small. $10 daily fee/pet. Designated rooms, service with restrictions, supervision.
(A$K) 🛇 ⊠ 🔱 🔒 🛢 💻 ⊷ ⊠

▼ 🔷 **Heartland Inn** 🆂🅷
(715) 839-7100. **$77-$97.** 4075 Commonwealth Ave. I-94, exit 70, 0.8 mi n on US 53, just w on CR AA (Golf Rd), then just s. Int corridors. **Pets:** Small. $10 daily fee/room. Designated rooms, service with restrictions, supervision.
(A$K) 🛇 ⊠ 🔒 🛢 💻 ⊷

▼ 🔷 ▼ **Holiday Inn Campus Area** 🆂🅷
(715) 835-2211. **$99-$129.** 2703 Craig Rd. I-94, exit 65, 1.3 mi n on SR 37; just w of jct US 12. Int corridors. **Pets:** Medium. $15 one-time fee/room. Designated rooms, no service, supervision.
(A$K) 🛇 ⊠ 🔱 🔒 🛢 💻 🍽 ⊷ ⊠

▼ 🔷 ▼ **The Plaza Hotel & Suites** 🅻🅷 🐾
(715) 834-3181. **$72-$200, 3 day notice.** 1202 W Clairemont Ave. I-94, exit 65, 1.3 mi n on SR 37; just w of jct US 12. Int corridors. **Pets:** $15 one-time fee/room. Designated rooms, service with restrictions, crate.
(A$K) 🛇 ⊠ 🗐 🔒 🛢 💻 🍽 ⊷ ⊠

▼ 🔷 ▼ **Ramada Convention Center** 🅻🅷
(715) 835-6121. **$82-$99.** 205 S Barstow St. Jct S Barstow and Gibson sts; downtown. Int corridors. **Pets:** Other species. $10 one-time fee/room. Designated rooms, service with restrictions.
⊠ 🔒 🛢 💻 🍽 ⊷

# EDGERTON

▼▼▼ 🔷 **Comfort Inn** 🆂🅷
(608) 884-2118. **$66-$150.** 11102 Goede Rd. I-90, exit 163, just e. Int corridors. **Pets:** Other species. $10 one-time fee/room. Service with restrictions, supervision.
(A$K) 🛇 ⊠ 🔱 🔒 🛢 💻 ⊷

# ELKHORN

▼ 🔷 ▼ **AmericInn Lodge & Suites** 🆂🅷
(262) 723-7799. **$69-$229.** 210 E Commerce Ct. I-43, exit 25, just s. Int corridors. **Pets:** Medium. $10 one-time fee/pet. Designated rooms, service with restrictions, crate.
(A$K) 🛇 ⊠ 🔱 🗐 🔒 🛢 💻 ⊷

# FITCHBURG

▼▼▼ 🔷 **Quality Inn & Suites** 🆂🅷
(608) 274-7200. **$90-$170.** 2969 Cahill Main. US 12/18, exit 260 (CR D/Fish Hatchery), 1.5 mi s at CR PD (McKee Rd). Int corridors. **Pets:** Accepted.
(A$K) 🛇 ⊠ 🗐 🔒 🛢 💻 ⊷ ⊠

# FOND DU LAC

▼▼ 🔷 **Baymont Inn & Suites-Fond du Lac** 🆂🅷
(920) 921-4000. **$65-$165.** 77 Holiday Ln. Sw of jct US 41 and 151. Int corridors. **Pets:** Accepted.
(A$K) 🛇 ⊠ 🔒 🛢 💻 ⊷ ⊠

▼▼ 🔷 **Econo Lodge of Fond du Lac** 🆂🅷
(920) 923-2020. **$54-$89.** 649 W Johnson St. On SR 23, 0.3 mi e jct of US 41. Int corridors. **Pets:** Designated rooms, service with restrictions, supervision.
(A$K) 🛇 ⊠ 🔒 🛢 ⊷

▼▼ 🔷 **Holiday Inn** 🆂🅷
(920) 923-1440. **$89-$200.** 625 W Rolling Meadows Dr. On US 151, just sw of jct US 41. Int corridors. **Pets:** Accepted.
(A$K) 🛇 ⊠ 🔱 🔒 🛢 💻 🍽 ⊷ ⊠

▼ 🔷 ▼ **Microtel Inn & Suites** 🆂🅷
(920) 929-4000. **$54-$104.** 920 S Military Rd. Jct US 41 and 151. Int corridors. **Pets:** Medium, other species. $10 daily fee/pet. Designated rooms, service with restrictions, supervision.
(A$K) 🛇 ⊠ 🔱 🔒 🛢 💻 ⊠

🅐🅐🅐 ▼ 🔷 ▼ **Ramada Plaza Hotel** 🅻🅷
(920) 923-3000. **$79-$269.** 1 N Main St. Downtown. Int corridors. **Pets:** Small, dogs only. $20 daily fee/room. Designated rooms, service with restrictions, supervision.
(SAVE) 🛇 ⊠ 🔒 🛢 💻 🍽 ⊷ ⊠

▼▼ 🔷 **Super 8 Motel-FOND DU LAC** 🆂🅷
(920) 922-1088. **$59-$120.** 391 N Pioneer Rd. US 41, exit SR 23, just n on east frontage road (CR VV). Int corridors. **Pets:** Medium, dogs only. $10 one-time fee/room. Designated rooms, service with restrictions, supervision.
(A$K) 🛇 ⊠ 🗐 🔒

# GRANTSBURG

🅐🅐🅐 ▼ **Wood River Motel** 🅼
(715) 463-2541. **$56-$105, 5 day notice.** 703 W SR 70. 1 mi w on SR 70. Ext corridors. **Pets:** Medium. Designated rooms, service with restrictions, supervision.
(SAVE) 🛇 ⊠ 🔱 🔒

# GREEN BAY

🅐🅐🅐 ▼ 🔷 **AmericInn** 🆂🅷
(920) 434-9790. **$75-$160, 30 day notice.** 2032 Velp Ave. US 41, exit 170, 0.3 mi w. Int corridors. **Pets:** Medium. $10 daily fee/pet. Designated rooms, service with restrictions, supervision.
(SAVE) 🛇 ⊠ 🔱 🗐 🔒 🛢 💻 ⊷

▼ 🔷 ▼ **Baymont Inn-Green Bay** 🆂🅷
(920) 494-7887. **$78-$159.** 2840 S Oneida St. US 41, exit 164 (Oneida St), just e. Int corridors. **Pets:** Medium. $25 deposit/room. Designated rooms, service with restrictions, supervision.
(A$K) 🛇 ⊠ 🔒 🛢 💻

**Bay Motel** M
(920) 494-3441. **$43-$75.** 1301 S Military Ave. US 41, exit 167 (Lombardi Ave), 0.4 mi e to Marlee, then 0.6 mi n. Ext corridors. **Pets:** Accepted.
SAVE | SÓ | ✕ | 🕯 | 🍴

**Comfort Inn by Choice Hotels** SH
(920) 498-2060. **$180, 30 day notice.** 2841 Ramada Way. US 41, exit 164 (Oneida St), just e. Int corridors. **Pets:** Accepted.
ASK | SÓ | ✕ | 🕐 | 🕯 | 🖭 | ≈

**Country Inn & Suites By Carlson** SH
(920) 336-6600. **$92-$159.** 2945 Allied St. US 41, exit 164 (Oneida St), just nw. Int corridors. **Pets:** Accepted.
ASK | SÓ | ✕ | 🕹 | 🕯 | 🖭 | ≈ | ✕

**Days Inn-Lambeau Field** SH
(920) 498-8088. **$59-$119.** 1978 Holmgren Way. US 41, exit 167 (Lombardi Ave), 1.4 mi e, then just s. Int corridors. **Pets:** Other species. Service with restrictions, supervision.
SAVE | SÓ | ✕ | 🕐 | 🕯 | 🖭 | ≈

**Exel Inn of Green Bay** SH
(920) 499-3599. **$49-$79.** 2870 Ramada Way. US 41, exit 164 (Oneida St), just e. Int corridors. **Pets:** Small, other species. Designated rooms, service with restrictions, supervision.
SAVE | SÓ | ✕ | 🕯 | 🖭

**Holiday Inn City Centre** LH
(920) 437-5900. **$89-$129.** 200 Main St. Downtown. Int corridors. **Pets:** Accepted.
ASK | SÓ | ✕ | 🕹 | 🖭 | 🍴 | ≈ | ✕

**Microtel Inn & Suites** SH
(920) 338-9000. **$66-$127.** 3031 Allied St. US 41, exit 164 (Oneida St), just sw. Int corridors. **Pets:** Accepted.
ASK | SÓ | ✕ | 🕐 | 🕹 | 🕯 | 🖭 | ≈

**Quality Inn & Suites** SH
(920) 437-8771. **$79-$109.** 321 S Washington St. On east side of Fox River, just s of Walnut St (SR 29); downtown. Int corridors. **Pets:** Accepted.
SAVE | SÓ | ✕ | 🕐 | 🕹 | 🕯 | 🖭 | ≈ | ✕

**Residence Inn by Marriott** SH
(920) 435-2222. **$89-$199.** 335 W St Joseph St. SR 172, exit Riverside Dr, 1.1 mi n on SR 57, then just e. Ext corridors. **Pets:** Accepted.
ASK | SÓ | ✕ | 🕯 | 🖭 | ≈ | ✕

**Super 8 Motel** SH
(920) 494-2042. **$64-$85, 21 day notice.** 2868 S Oneida St. US 41, exit 164 (Oneida St), just e. Int corridors. **Pets:** $25 deposit/room. Supervision.
SAVE | SÓ | ✕ | 🕐 | 🕯 | ✕

# HAYWARD

**AmericInn of Hayward** SH
(715) 634-2700. **$72-$149.** 15601 US Hwy 63. On US 63, just n of jct SR 77. Int corridors. **Pets:** Medium. $6 daily fee/pet. Designated rooms, service with restrictions, crate.
ASK | SÓ | ✕ | 🕹 | 🕯 | 🖭 | ≈

**Best Northern Pine Inn** SH
(715) 634-4959. **$45-$90.** 9966 N Hwy 27. On SR 27 S, 1.7 mi s of jct US 63. Ext/int corridors. **Pets:** Large, other species. $5 daily fee/pet. Service with restrictions, supervision.
SAVE | SÓ | ✕ | 🕯 | 🖭 | ≈ | ✕

**Comfort Suites** SH 🐾
(715) 634-0700. **$69-$170.** 15586 CR B. On CR B, 0.5 mi s of jct SR 27. Int corridors. **Pets:** $13 daily fee/room. Designated rooms, service with restrictions, supervision.
ASK | SÓ | ✕ | 🕮 | 🕹 | 🕯 | 🖭 | ≈ | ✕

**Hayward Inn & Suites** SH
(715) 634-4100. **$65-$150.** 10290 Hwy 27 S. On SR 27 S, 0.7 mi s of jct US 63. Int corridors. **Pets:** Other species. Designated rooms, service with restrictions, crate.
ASK | SÓ | ✕ | 🕯 | 🖭 | 🍴 | ≈

**Ross' Teal Lake Lodge and Teal Wing Golf Club** CA 🐾
(715) 462-3631. **$140-$350, 21 day notice.** 12425 N Ross Rd. On SR 77, 20 mi ne of jct US 63. Ext corridors. **Pets:** Large, other species. $10 daily fee/pet. Service with restrictions, supervision.
ASK | SÓ | ✕ | 🕯 | 🍴 | ≈ | ✕ | 🏌 | ✎

**Super 8 Motel** SH
(715) 634-2646. **$80-$120.** 10444 N SR 27. On SR 27, 0.3 mi s of jct US 63. Ext/int corridors. **Pets:** Service with restrictions, supervision.
ASK | SÓ | ✕ | ≈

# HILLSBORO

**Sleep Inn Hillsboro** SH 🐾
(608) 489-3000. **$65-$250.** 1234 Water Ave. On US 31; 0.5 mi n on Main St. Int corridors. **Pets:** Dogs only. $50 deposit/room, $50 one-time fee/pet. Designated rooms.
ASK | SÓ | ✕ | 🖭 | ≈

# HUDSON

**Comfort Inn** SH
(715) 386-6355. **$60-$95.** 811 Dominion Dr. I-94, exit 2 (CR F), 1 mi w on south frontage road (Crestview Dr). Int corridors. **Pets:** Medium. $50 deposit/pet, $5 daily fee/pet. Designated rooms, service with restrictions, supervision.
ASK | SÓ | ✕ | 🕯 | 🖭 | ≈

# HURLEY

**Days Inn of Hurley** SH
(715) 561-3500. **$75-$95.** 850 10th Ave N. Jct US 2 and 51, 0.4 mi s on US 51. Int corridors. **Pets:** Accepted.
SAVE | SÓ | ✕ | 🕯 | 🖭 | ≈ | ✕

# JANESVILLE

**Baymont Inn & Suites-Janesville** SH
(608) 758-4545. **$65-$95.** 616 Midland Rd. I-90, exit 175B (SR 11), just ne. Int corridors. **Pets:** Service with restrictions, crate.
✕ | 🕹 | 🕯 | 🖭 | ≈

**Best Western Janesville** SH
(608) 756-4511. **$75-$99.** 3900 Milton Ave. I-90, exit 171A (SR 26), just e. Int corridors. **Pets:** Accepted.
SAVE | SÓ | ✕ | 🕯 | 🖭 | 🍴 | ≈ | ✕

**Microtel Inn** SH
(608) 752-3121. **$56-$66.** 3121 Wellington Pl. I-90, exit 171C (US 14), just se. Int corridors. **Pets:** Other species. $10 one-time fee/room. Service with restrictions, crate.
ASK | ✕ | 🕮 | 🕐 | 🕹 | 🕯

**Ramada Inn** SH
(608) 756-2341. **$59-$69.** 3431 Milton Ave. I-90, exit 171A (SR 26), just sw. Int corridors. **Pets:** Medium. Service with restrictions, supervision.
SAVE | SÓ | ✕ | 🕯 | 🖭 | 🍴 | ≈ | ✕

**Select Inn** SH
(608) 754-0251. **$41-$80, 30 day notice.** 3520 Milton Ave. I-90, exit 171A (SR 26), just sw. Int corridors. **Pets:** $25 deposit/room, $5 daily fee/room. Designated rooms, service with restrictions, supervision.
SAVE | SÓ | ✕ | 🕹 | 🕯 | 🖭

# JEFFERSON

▼▼◆ **Rodeway Inn** Ⓜ
(920) 674-4404. **$55-$150.** 1456 S Ryan Ave. On SR 26, 1.2 mi s of jct US 18. Int corridors. **Pets:** Medium. $10 daily fee/pet. Designated rooms, service with restrictions, crate.

(ASK) Ⓢ ⊠ Ⓜ 🄰 ⓒ 🛏 🖵 🏊

# JOHNSON CREEK

◆◆ ▼▼ **Days Inn-Johnson Creek** 🆂🅷
(920) 699-8000. **$75-$90.** W4545 Linmar Ln. I-94, exit 267 (SR 26), just ne. Int corridors. **Pets:** Dogs only. $75 deposit/room. Service with restrictions, supervision.

(SAVE) Ⓢ ⊠ ⓒ 🛏 🖵 🏊 ⊠

# KAUKAUNA

▼▼ **Settle Inn** 🆂🅷
(920) 766-0088. **$65-$145.** 1201 Maloney Rd. US 41, exit 148, just e. Int corridors. **Pets:** Accepted.

(ASK) Ⓢ ⊠ 🛏 🖵 🏊

# KENOSHA

▼▼ **Best Western Harborside Inn & Kenosha Conference Center** 🆂🅷
(262) 658-3281. **$109-$185.** 5125 6th Ave. Just ne of jct SR 32 and 158; downtown. Int corridors. **Pets:** Small, other species. $25 one-time fee/pet. Designated rooms, service with restrictions, supervision.

(ASK) ⊠ 🄰 🛏 🖵 ⊠

▼▼◆ **Country Inn & Suites By Carlson** 🆂🅷
(262) 857-3680. **$92-$142.** 7011 122nd Ave. I-94, exit 344 (SR 50), just nw. Int corridors. **Pets:** Accepted.

(ASK) Ⓢ ⊠ Ⓜ 🄰 ⓒ 🛏 🖵 🏊 ⊠

# KEWAUNEE

▼▼◆ **The Historic Karsten Inn** 🆂🅷
(920) 388-3800. **$69-$129, 3 day notice.** 122 Ellis St. Center. Int corridors. **Pets:** Accepted.

(ASK) ⊠ 🖵

# LA CROSSE

◆◆ ▼▼▼ **Best Western-Midway Hotel Riverfront Resort** 🆂🅷 🐾
(608) 781-7000. **$89-$109.** 1835 Rose St. I-90, exit 3, 1 mi s on US 53. Int corridors. **Pets:** Small, dogs only. $25 one-time fee/pet. Service with restrictions, supervision.

(SAVE) Ⓢ ⊠ 🄰 🛏 🖵 🍽 🏊 ⊠

◆◆ ▼▼◆ **Days Inn Hotel & Conference Center** 🆂🅷 🐾
(608) 783-1000. **$54-$110.** 101 Sky Harbour Dr. I-90, exit 2, just sw; on French Island. Int corridors. **Pets:** Medium. $10 daily fee/pet. Designated rooms, service with restrictions, supervision.

(SAVE) Ⓢ ⊠ 🛏 🖵 🍽 🏊

◆◆ ▼▼ **Exel Inn of La Crosse** 🆂🅷
(608) 781-0400. **$49-$79.** 2150 Rose St. I-90, exit 3, 0.8 mi s on US 53. Int corridors. **Pets:** Small, other species. Designated rooms, service with restrictions, supervision.

(SAVE) Ⓢ ⊠ 🛏 🖵

▼▼▼ **Grandstay Residential Suites of La Crosse** 🆂🅷
(608) 796-1615. **$100-$159.** 525 Front St N. I-90, exit 3; downtown. Int corridors. **Pets:** Small. $20 daily fee/pet. Designated rooms, service with restrictions, crate.

(ASK) Ⓢ ⊠ ⓒ 🛏 🖵 🏊 ⊠

◆◆ ▼▼ **Guest House Motel** 🆂🅷
(608) 784-8840. **$60-$90.** 810 S 4th St. 0.5 mi s on US 14, 61 and SR 33. Int corridors. **Pets:** Accepted.

(SAVE) Ⓢ ⊠ 🛏 🍽 🏊

▲▲▲ ▼▼◆ **The Radisson Hotel La Crosse** 🅻🅷
(608) 784-6680. **$149-$179.** 200 Harborview Plaza. Just w of US 53; downtown. Int corridors. **Pets:** Accepted.

(SAVE) Ⓢ ⊠ 🄰 🛏 🖵 🍽 🏊 ⊠

# LADYSMITH

▼▼ **AmericInn Motel & Suites** 🆂🅷
(715) 532-6650. **$66-$108.** 800 W College Ave. On SR 27, 0.5 mi s of US 8. Int corridors. **Pets:** $10 daily fee/pet. Designated rooms, service with restrictions, supervision.

(ASK) ⊠ ⓒ 🛏 🖵 🏊

# LAKE DELTON

◆◆ ▼▼◆ **Motel 6** 🆂🅷
(608) 355-0700. **$49-$106.** E 10892 Fern Dell Rd. I-90/94, exit 92 (US 12), 0.3 mi s. Int corridors. **Pets:** Small, dogs only. $7 daily fee/pet. Service with restrictions, supervision.

(SAVE) Ⓢ ⊠ Ⓜ ⓒ 🛏 🖵

# LAND O'LAKES

▼▼ **Sunrise Lodge** 🄲🄰
(715) 547-3684. **$78-$102, 21 day notice.** 5894 W Shore Dr. 2 mi s on US 45, 2.8 mi e on CR E, then 1 mi n. Ext corridors. **Pets:** Other species. Service with restrictions.

🛏 🖵 🍽 ⊠ 🅩

# LODI

▼▼ **Best Western Countryside Inn** 🆂🅷
(608) 592-1450. **$55-$99.** W 9250 Prospect Dr. I-90/94/39, exit 119, just w. Int corridors. **Pets:** $20 one-time fee/pet. Designated rooms.

(ASK) Ⓢ ⊠ ⓒ 🛏 🖵 🏊 ⊠

▼▼ **Lodi Valley Suites** 🆂🅷
(608) 592-7331. **$40-$70.** 1440 N Hwy 113. On SR 113; 1.5 mi n of jct SR 60. Int corridors. **Pets:** Medium, dogs only. $5 daily fee/pet. Designated rooms, service with restrictions, supervision.

⊠ 🛏 🏊

# LUCK

◆◆ ▼▼◆ **Luck Country Inn** 🆂🅷
(715) 472-2000. **$60-$139.** 10 Robertson Rd. Jct SR 35 and 48. Int corridors. **Pets:** Small, dogs only. $50 deposit/room, $5 daily fee/pet. Designated rooms, service with restrictions, supervision.

(SAVE) Ⓢ ⊠ 🛏 🖵 🍽 🏊

# MADISON

▼▼▼ **Baymont Inn & Suites-Madison West** 🆂🅷
(608) 831-7711. **$89-$139.** 8102 Excelsior Dr. US 12 and 14, exit 253 (Old Sauk Rd), just nw. Int corridors. **Pets:** Accepted.

(ASK) ⊠ Ⓜ ⓒ 🛏 🖵 🏊 ⊠

◆◆ ▼▼◆ **Best Western East Towne Suites** 🆂🅷
(608) 244-2020. **$69-$169.** 4801 Annamark Dr. I-90/94, exit 135A, just sw on US 151. Int corridors. **Pets:** Other species. $25 deposit/room. Designated rooms, service with restrictions, crate.

(SAVE) ⊠ 🄰 🛏 🖵 🏊

◆◆ ▼▼◆ **Best Western West Towne Suites** 🆂🅷
(608) 833-4200. **$59-$149.** 650 Grand Canyon Dr. US 12 and 14, exit 255 (Gammon Rd), just e on Odana Rd, then just sw. Int corridors. **Pets:** Medium. $25 deposit/pet. Designated rooms, service with restrictions, supervision.

(SAVE) Ⓢ ⊠ 🛏 🖵

◆◆ ▼▼◆ **Clarion Suites Madison-Central** 🆂🅷
(608) 284-1234. **$89-$169, 3 day notice.** 2110 Rimrock Rd. US 12 and 18, exit 262 (Rimrock Rd), just nw. Int corridors. **Pets:** Accepted.

(SAVE) Ⓢ ⊠ ⓒ 🛏 🖵 🏊

**▼▼▼▼ Comfort Suites SH ❖**
(608) 836-3033. **$99-$260.** 1253 John Q Hammons Dr. US 12 and 14, exit 252 (Greenway Blvd), just sw. Int corridors. **Pets:** Service with restrictions.
A$K 🔊 ⊗ ♿ 🛄 💻 ➾ ⊠

**🅰🅰🅰 ▼▼▼▼ Crowne Plaza Hotel and Resort LH ❖**
(608) 244-4703. **$99-$209.** 4402 E Washington Ave. I-90/94, exit 135A, 0.4 mi w on US 151. Int corridors. **Pets:** Other species. $15 daily fee/pet. Designated rooms, service with restrictions, supervision.
SAVE 🔊 ⊗ 🎵 🛄 💻 🍴 ➾ ⊠

**🅰🅰🅰 ▼▼▼ Days Inn-Madison SH**
(608) 223-1800. **$72-$159, 15 day notice.** 4402 E Broadway Service Rd. US 12 and 18, exit 266 (US 51), just ne. Int corridors. **Pets:** $10 daily fee/pet. Service with restrictions, supervision.
SAVE 🔊 ⊗ ♿ 🛄 💻 ➾

**🅰🅰🅰 ▼▼▼ Econo Lodge of Madison SH**
(608) 241-4171. **$52-$99, 30 day notice.** 4726 E Washington Ave. I-90/94, exit 135A (US 151), just w. Int corridors. **Pets:** Other species. $10 daily fee/room. Service with restrictions, supervision.
SAVE 🔊 ⊗ ♿ 🛄 💻

**🅰🅰🅰 ▼▼▼ Exel Inn of Madison SH**
(608) 241-3861. **$49-$79.** 4202 E Towne Blvd. I-90/94, exit 135A (US 151), 0.5 mi w. Int corridors. **Pets:** Small, other species. Designated rooms, service with restrictions, supervision.
SAVE 🔊 ⊗ 🛄 💻

**🅰🅰🅰 ▼▼▼▼ GrandStay Residential Suites SH ❖**
(608) 241-2500. **$89-$119.** 5317 High Crossing Blvd. I-90/94, exit 135C (US 151), 0.5 mi e. Int corridors. **Pets:** Other species. $50 deposit/room. Designated rooms, service with restrictions, crate.
SAVE 🔊 ⊗ ♿M ♿ 🛄 💻 ➾ ⊠

**🅰🅰🅰 ▼▼▼▼ Holiday Inn Express-Madison SH**
(608) 255-7400. **$89-$129.** 722 John Nolen Dr. US 12 and 18, exit 263 (John Nolen Dr), just ne. Int corridors. **Pets:** Small, other species. Designated rooms, service with restrictions, supervision.
SAVE 🔊 ⊗ 🎵 ♿ 🛄 💻 ➾

**🅰🅰🅰 ▼▼▼▼ Holiday Inn Madison East SH ❖**
(608) 244-2481. **$79-$149.** 3841 E Washington Ave. I-90/94, exit 135A, 1 mi w on US 151. Int corridors. **Pets:** Other species. $15 daily fee/pet. Designated rooms, service with restrictions, supervision.
SAVE 🔊 ⊗ 🎵 ♿ 🛄 💻 🍴 ➾ ⊠

**🅰🅰🅰 ▼▼▼ La Quinta Inn & Suites SH**
(608) 245-0123. **$95-$129.** 5217 E Terrace Dr. US 151, exit 98B (American Pkwy), just sw. Int corridors. **Pets:** Medium. Service with restrictions.
SAVE ⊗ ♿M 🎵 ♿ 🛄 💻 ➾

**🅰🅰🅰 ▼▼▼ Madison Wingate Inn SH**
(608) 224-1500. **$79-$139.** 3510 Mill Pond Rd. I-90, exit 142B, just e on US 12 and 18, then w on south frontage road. Int corridors. **Pets:** Accepted.
SAVE 🔊 ⊗ ♿ 🛄 💻 ➾

**🅰🅰🅰 ▼▼▼ Microtel Inn & Suites SH**
(608) 242-9000. **$49-$69.** 2139 E Springs Dr. I-90/94, exit 135A, just s, then 0.5 mi e. Int corridors. **Pets:** Medium. $10 daily fee/room. Designated rooms, service with restrictions, supervision.
SAVE 🔊 ⊗ 🛄 💻

**▼▼▼ Red Roof Inn-Madison #7052 M**
(608) 241-1787. **$40-$69.** 4830 Hayes Rd. I-90/94, exit 135A, just sw on US 151. Ext corridors. **Pets:** Accepted.
⊗ 🎵 ♿

**▼▼▼▼ Residence Inn by Marriott SH**
(608) 244-5047. **$110-$170, 14 day notice.** 4862 Hayes Rd. I-90/94, exit 135A (US 151), just sw to Hayes Rd, then just ne. Int corridors. **Pets:** Accepted.
A$K 🔊 ⊗ 🎵 ♿ 🛄 💻 ➾ ⊠

**🅰🅰🅰 ▼▼▼ Select Inn SH**
(608) 249-1815. **$56-$99.** 4845 Hayes Rd. I-90/94, exit 135A, just sw on US 151. Int corridors. **Pets:** Other species. $25 deposit/pet. Service with restrictions, supervision.
SAVE 🔊 ⊗ ♿ 🛄 💻

**🅰🅰🅰 ▼▼▼▼ Staybridge Suites SH**
(608) 241-2300. **$109-$159.** 3301 City View Dr. I-90/94, exit 135C (US 151), just e on High Crossing Blvd. Int corridors. **Pets:** Accepted.
SAVE ⊗ 🎵 ♿ 🛄 💻 ➾

**▼▼▼▼ Super 8 Motel SH**
(608) 258-8882. **$55-$89.** 1602 W Beltline Hwy. US 12 and 18, exit 260B (CR D), just w on north frontage road. Int corridors. **Pets:** Medium. Designated rooms, service with restrictions, supervision.
A$K 🔊 ⊗ 🎵 ♿ 🛄 ➾

# MANITOWOC

**▼▼▼ Comfort Inn by Choice Hotels SH**
(920) 683-0220. **$49-$109, 7 day notice.** 2200 S 44th St. I-43, exit 149, just e. Int corridors. **Pets:** Accepted.
A$K 🔊 ⊗ 🛄 💻

**▼▼▼ Holiday Inn SH ❖**
(920) 682-6000. **$105-$159.** 4601 Calumet Ave. I-43, exit 149, just e. Int corridors. **Pets:** Large, other species. $100 deposit/room. Service with restrictions, crate.
A$K 🔊 ⊗ ♿ 🛄 💻 🍴 ➾ ⊠

# MARSHFIELD

**▼▼▼ Comfort Inn SH**
(715) 387-8691. **$70.** 114 E Upham St. On SR 97, 0.6 mi n of jct SR 13. Int corridors. **Pets:** $40 deposit/pet, $10 daily fee/pet. Designated rooms, supervision.
A$K 🔊 ⊗ 🎵 🛄 💻 ➾

**🅰🅰🅰 ▼▼▼▼ Holiday Inn & Conference Center SH**
(715) 486-1500. **$62-$89.** 750 S Central Ave. Jct SR 13 and 97, 0.5 mi s on SR 13. Int corridors. **Pets:** Accepted.
SAVE 🔊 ⊗ ♿M ♿ 🛄 💻 🍴 ➾ ⊠

**🅰🅰🅰 ▼▼ Park Motel M**
(715) 387-1741. **$39-$46.** 1806 S Roddis Ave. 1 mi s on SR 13. Ext corridors. **Pets:** Medium. $5 one-time fee/pet. Service with restrictions, supervision.
SAVE 🔊 ⊗ 🛄

# MAUSTON

**🅰🅰🅰 ▼▼▼▼ Country Inn By Carlson SH**
(608) 847-5959. **$81-$97.** 1001 SR 82. I-90/94, exit 69, just ne. Int corridors. **Pets:** Other species. $5 daily fee/room. Service with restrictions, crate.
SAVE 🔊 ⊗ 🛄 💻 ➾

**▼▼▼ Super 8 Motel M**
(608) 847-2300. **$55-$150.** 1001A Hwy 82. I-90/94, exit 69, just ne. Int corridors. **Pets:** Other species. $5 daily fee/room. Service with restrictions, supervision.
A$K 🔊 ⊗ 🛄 💻 ➾

# MEDFORD

**▼▼ Malibu Inn Motel M**
(715) 748-3995. **$56-$115.** 854 N 8th St. On SR 13, 0.6 mi n of jct SR 64. Int corridors. **Pets:** Accepted.
A$K 🔊 ⊗ 🛄 ➾

# MENOMONIE

**▼▼ AmericInn Lodge & Suites** 🅂🄷
(715) 235-4800. **Call for rates.** 1915 N Broadway. I-94, exit 41 (SR 25), just sw; behind Best Western. Int corridors. **Pets:** $10 one-time fee/pet. Service with restrictions, supervision.

🄰🅂🄺 🅂🄳 🅧 🄺 🄱 🄳 🔜

**🄰🄰🄰 ▼▼ Comfort Inn** 🅂🄷
(715) 233-1500. **$69-$129.** 1721 Plaza Dr NE. I-94, exit 45 (CR B), just sw. Int corridors. **Pets:** Accepted.

🅂🄰🅅🄴 🅂🄳 🅧 🄼 🄺 🄱 🄳 🔜

**▼▼▼ Country Inn & Suites** 🅂🄷
(715) 235-5664. **$109-$169.** 320 Oak Ave. I-94, exit 41 (SR 25), just se. Int corridors. **Pets:** Medium, dogs only. $15 daily fee/pet. Designated rooms, no service, supervision.

🄰🅂🄺 🅂🄳 🅧 🄺 🄱 🄳 🔜

**🄰🄰🄰 ▼ Menomonie Motel 6 #4109** 🅂🄷
(715) 235-6901. **$36-$65.** 2100 Stout St. I-94, exit 41 (SR 25), just se. Int corridors. **Pets:** Accepted.

🅂🄰🅅🄴 🅂🄳 🅧 🄺

**▼▼ Super 8 Motel-Menomonie** 🅂🄷
(715) 235-8889. **$49-$89.** 1622 N Broadway. I-94, exit 41 (SR 25), just s. Int corridors. **Pets:** Small. Designated rooms, no service, crate.

🄰🅂🄺 🅂🄳 🅧 🄺 🔜

# MERRILL

**🄰🄰🄰 ▼▼▼ AmericInn Lodge & Suites of Merrill** 🅂🄷 🐾
(715) 536-7979. **$79-$189.** 3300 E Main St. US 51, exit 208, 0.5 mi w on SR 64. Int corridors. **Pets:** Medium, other species. $10 daily fee/pet. Service with restrictions, supervision.

🅂🄰🅅🄴 🅂🄳 🅧 🄺 🄱 🄳 🔜

**🄰🄰🄰 ▼▼▼ Pine Ridge Inn** 🅂🄷
(715) 536-9526. **$49-$89.** 200 S Pine Ridge. I-39, exit 208, just w. Int corridors. **Pets:** Accepted.

🅂🄰🅅🄴 🅂🄳 🅧 🄱 🄳 🔜

**🄰🄰🄰 ▼▼▼ Super 8 Motel** 🅂🄷
(715) 536-6880. **$90-$100.** 3209 E Main St. I-39, exit 208, 0.5 mi w on SR 64. Int corridors. **Pets:** $5 daily fee/pet. Service with restrictions, supervision.

🅂🄰🅅🄴 🅂🄳 🅧 🄼 🄺 🄱 🄳 🔜 🅇

# MIDDLETON

**▼▼▼ Country Inn & Suites** 🅂🄷
(608) 831-6970. **$79-$199.** 2212 Deming Way. I-12/18, exit 252 (Greenway Blvd), just w. Int corridors. **Pets:** Accepted.

🄰🅂🄺 🅂🄳 🅧 🄺 🄱 🄳 🔜

**🄰🄰🄰 ▼▼▼▼ Marriott Madison West** 🄻🄷 🐾
(608) 831-2000. **$129-$179.** 1313 John Q Hammons Dr. US 12/14, exit 252 (Greenway Blvd), just w. Int corridors. **Pets:** Medium. $20 deposit/room. Service with restrictions, supervision.

🅂🄰🅅🄴 🅧 🄳 🄺 🄺 🄱 🄳 🍽 🔜 🅇

**▼▼▼▼ Residence Inn by Marriott-Madison West/Middleton** 🅂🄷
(608) 662-1100. **$107-$169.** 8400 Market St. US 12/14 (Beltline), exit 252 (Greenway Blvd), just w, then just n; in Greenway Station. Int corridors. **Pets:** Accepted.

🄰🅂🄺 🅂🄳 🅧 🄺 🄱 🄳 🔜

**🄰🄰🄰 ▼▼▼▼ Staybridge Suites by Holiday Inn** 🅂🄷 🐾
(608) 664-5888. **$129-$179.** 7790 Elmwood Ave. US 12/14, exit 251 (University Ave), just nw. Int corridors. **Pets:** Other species. $150 one-time fee/room. Supervision.

🅂🄰🅅🄴 🅧 🄼 🄺 🄱 🄳 🔜

# MILWAUKEE METROPOLITAN AREA

# BROOKFIELD

**🄰🄰🄰 ▼▼▼▼ Baymont Inn & Suites Milwaukee-Brookfield** 🅂🄷
(262) 782-9100. **$85-$121.** 20391 W Bluemound Rd. I-94, exit 297, just e on US 18. Int corridors. **Pets:** Medium. Service with restrictions.

🅂🄰🅅🄴 🅧 🄳 🄱 🄳

**🄰🄰🄰 ▼▼▼▼ Best Western Midway Hotel** 🅂🄷
(262) 786-9540. **$95-$149.** 1005 S Moorland Rd. I-94, exit 301A (Moorland Rd), just s. Int corridors. **Pets:** Large. $15 one-time fee/room. Service with restrictions, supervision.

🅂🄰🅅🄴 🅂🄳 🅧 🄳 🄺 🄱 🄳 🍽 🔜 🅇

**🄰🄰🄰 ▼▼▼▼ Country Inn & Suites Milwaukee West** 🄻🄷 🐾
(262) 782-1400. **$98-$170.** 1250 S Moorland Rd. I-94, exit 301A (Moorland Rd), just se. Int corridors. **Pets:** Medium, other species. $75 one-time fee/room. Service with restrictions, crate.

🅂🄰🅅🄴 🅂🄳 🅧 🄺 🄱 🄳 🍽 🔜 🅇

**▼▼ Homestead Studio Suites Hotel-Milwaukee/Brookfield** 🅂🄷
(262) 782-9300. **$52-$75.** 325 N Brookfield Rd. I-94, exit 297, 1.1 mi e on US 18, then just e. Int corridors. **Pets:** $25 daily fee/pet. Service with restrictions, supervision.

🄰🅂🄺 🅂🄳 🅧 🄺 🄺 🄱 🄳

**▼▼▼ Sheraton Milwaukee Brookfield** 🄻🄷
(262) 786-1100. **$209-$249.** 375 S Moorland Rd. I-94, exit 301B (Moorland Rd), just n. Int corridors. **Pets:** Accepted.

🄰🅂🄺 🅂🄳 🅧 🄺 🄱 🄳 🍽 🔜 🅇

**▼▼ TownePlace Suites by Marriott** 🅂🄷
(262) 784-8450. **$99-$159.** 600 N Calhoun Rd. I-94, exit 297 eastbound, 2.1 mi e on US 18; exit 301B (Moorland Rd)westbound, 1.5 mi n on, then 0.4 mi w on US 18. Int corridors. **Pets:** $100 one-time fee/room. Service with restrictions.

🄰🅂🄺 🅂🄳 🅧 🄺 🄱 🄳 🔜

# DELAFIELD

**▼▼ Baymont Inn & Suites Milwaukee-Delafield** 🅂🄷
(262) 646-8500. **$80-$125.** 2801 Hillside Dr. I-94, exit 287, just s on SR 83, then just e. Int corridors. **Pets:** Medium. Service with restrictions.

🄰🅂🄺 🅧 🄼 🄳 🄺 🄱 🄳 🔜

# GERMANTOWN

**▼▼▼ Holiday Inn Express Milwaukee NW-Germantown** 🅂🄷
(262) 255-1100. **$99-$139.** W 177 N9675 Riversbend Ln. US 41 and 45, exit CR Q (County Line Rd), then just w. Int corridors. **Pets:** Accepted.

🄰🅂🄺 🅂🄳 🅧 🄼 🄺 🄱 🄳 🔜 🅇

**🄰🄰🄰 ▼▼▼ Super 8 Motel-Germantown/Milwaukee** 🅂🄷 🐾
(262) 255-0880. **$72-$99.** N96 W17490 County Line Rd. US 41 and 45, exit CR Q (County Line Rd), then just w. Int corridors. **Pets:** $5 daily fee/pet. Service with restrictions, supervision.

🅂🄰🅅🄴 🅂🄳 🅧 🄺 🄱 🄳 🔜

# GLENDALE

**Baymont Inn Milwaukee-Glendale** SH
(414) 964-8484. **$76-$121.** 5110 N Port Washington Rd. I-43, exit 78A (Silver Spring Dr), 0.4 mi se. Int corridors. **Pets:** Medium. Service with restrictions.
SAVE ✕ 🛏 🖵

**Exel Inn of Milwaukee Northeast** SH
(414) 961-7272. **$62-$92.** 5485 N Port Washington Rd. I-43, exit 78A (Silver Spring Dr), just se. Int corridors. **Pets:** Small, other species. Designated rooms, service with restrictions, supervision.
SAVE 🛆 ✕ 🛏 🖵

**Residence Inn by Marriott** SH
(414) 352-0070. **$149-$199.** 7275 N Port Washington Rd. I-43, exit 80 (Good Hope Rd), just e. Ext corridors. **Pets:** Medium, other species. $75 one-time fee/room. Service with restrictions.
ASK 🛆 ✕ 🖋 🗝 🛏 🖵 🏊 ✕

**Woodfield Suites Milwaukee-Glendale** SH
(414) 962-6767. **$109-$145.** 5423 N Port Washington Rd. I-43, exit 78A (Silver Spring Dr), just se. Int corridors. **Pets:** Medium. Service with restrictions.
SAVE ✕ 🛆M 🖋 🗝 🛏 🖵 🏊 ✕

# HARTFORD

**Super 8 Motel-Hartford** SH
(262) 673-7431. **$50-$95.** 1539 E Sumner St. On SR 60, 1.1 mi e of center. Int corridors. **Pets:** Accepted.
ASK 🛆 ✕ 🛏

# JACKSON

**Comfort Inn & Suites of Jackson** SH
(262) 677-1133. **$70-$170.** W227 N16890 Tillie Lake Ct. Nw of jct US 45 and SR 60. Int corridors. **Pets:** Other species. $30 one-time fee/room. Designated rooms, service with restrictions, supervision.
ASK ✕ 🗝 🛏 🖵 🏊 ✕

# MEQUON

**Best Western Quiet House & Suites** SH
(262) 241-3677. **$86-$225.** 10330 N Port Washington Rd. I-43, exit 85 (Mequon Rd), just w on SR 167, then 1 mi s. Int corridors. **Pets:** Large. $15 daily fee/pet. Designated rooms, service with restrictions, supervision.
SAVE 🛆 ✕ 🛆M 🖋 🗝 🛏 🖵

**The Chalet Motel of Mequon** M 🐾
(262) 241-4510. **$69-$159.** 10401 N Port Washington Rd. I-43, exit 85 (Mequon Rd), just w on SR 167, then 1 mi s. Ext corridors. **Pets:** Other species. $10 daily fee/room. Designated rooms, service with restrictions, crate.
SAVE 🛆 ✕ 🛏 🖵 🍽

# MILWAUKEE

**AmeriSuites-Milwaukee Airport** SH
(414) 744-3600. **$80-$109.** 200 W Grange Ave. I-94, exit 318 (Airport), 1.1 mi e, just n on Howell Ave (SR 38), then just w. Int corridors. **Pets:** Accepted.
SAVE 🛆 ✕ 🖋 🛏 🖵

**AmeriSuites Milwaukee/West** SH
(414) 462-3500. **$80-$109.** 11777 W Silver Spring Dr. US 45, exit 46 (Silver Spring Dr), just w. Int corridors. **Pets:** Small. $10 daily fee/pet. Designated rooms, service with restrictions, supervision.
SAVE 🛆 ✕ 🛆M 🖋 🛏 🖵

**Baymont Inn & Suites Milwaukee NW** SH
(414) 535-1300. **$75-$121.** 5442 N Lovers Lane Rd. US 45, exit 46 (Silver Spring Dr), just se. Int corridors. **Pets:** Medium. Service with restrictions.
SAVE ✕ 🖋 🛏 🖵

**Best Western Inn Towne Hotel** SH
(414) 224-8400. **$59-$129.** 710 N Old World 3rd St. Corner of Wisconsin Ave and N Old World 3rd St. Int corridors. **Pets:** Medium. Designated rooms, service with restrictions.
SAVE ✕ 🗝 🛏 🖵 🍽

**Holiday Inn Hotel and Suites** SH
(414) 482-4444. **$109-$139.** 545 W Layton Ave. I-94, exit 317, 1.3 mi n. Int corridors. **Pets:** $25 one-time fee/pet. Designated rooms, service with restrictions, crate.
ASK 🛆 ✕ 🗝 🛏 🖵 🍽 🏊 ✕

**Hotel Metro-Milwaukee** SH 🐾
(414) 272-1937. **$179-$299.** 411 E Mason St. Corner of Mason and Milwaukee sts. Int corridors. **Pets:** Small. $25 daily fee/pet. Designated rooms, service with restrictions, supervision.
ASK 🛆 ✕ 🛆M 🖋 🗝 🖵 🍽 ✕

# OAK CREEK

**Baymont Inn & Suites Milwaukee-Airport** SH
(414) 762-2266. **$65-$113.** 7141 S 13th St. I-94, exit 320 (Rawson Ave), just se. Int corridors. **Pets:** Medium. Service with restrictions.
SAVE ✕ 🛏 🖵

**Comfort Suites Milwaukee Airport** SH
(414) 570-1111. **$99-$209.** 6362 S 13th St. I-94, exit 319 (College Ave), just e on CR 22, then just s. Int corridors. **Pets:** Small, other species. $5 daily fee/room. Service with restrictions, crate.
ASK 🛆 ✕ 🛆M 🖋 🗝 🛏 🖵 🏊 ✕

**Exel Inn of Milwaukee South** SH
(414) 764-1776. **$48-$82.** 1201 W College Ave. I-94, exit 319 (College Ave), just e. Int corridors. **Pets:** Small, other species. Designated rooms, service with restrictions, supervision.
SAVE 🛆 ✕ 🛏 🖵

**MainStay Suites Oak Creek** SH
(414) 571-8800. **$69-$329.** 1001 W College Ave. I-94, exit 319 (College Ave), just e. Int corridors. **Pets:** Medium. $100 one-time fee/room. Service with restrictions, crate.
ASK 🛆 ✕ 🗝 🛏 🖵

**Red Roof Inn-Milwaukee #7031** M
(414) 764-3500. **$45-$74.** 6360 S 13th St. I-94, exit 319 (College Ave), just e. Ext corridors. **Pets:** Accepted.
✕ 🖋 🛏

# OCONOMOWOC

**Olympia Resort & Conference Center** LH
(262) 369-4999. **$99-$199.** 1350 Royale Mile Rd. I-94, exit 282 (SR 67), 1 mi n. Int corridors. **Pets:** Small. $50 deposit/room, $10 daily fee/room. Service with restrictions, supervision.
SAVE 🛆 ✕ 🛏 🖵 🍽 🏊 ✕

# PORT WASHINGTON

**Holiday Inn Harborview** SH 🐾
(262) 284-9461. **$69-$199.** 135 E Grand Ave. On SR 33, waterfront of Lake Michigan; downtown. Int corridors. **Pets:** Medium, dogs only. $25 one-time fee/room. Designated rooms, service with restrictions, supervision.
SAVE 🛆 ✕ 🗝 🛏 🖵 🍽 🏊 ✕

# WAUKESHA

**Best Western Waukesha Grand** SH
(262) 524-9300. **$69-$119.** 2840 N Grandview Blvd. I-94, exit 293, just s on CR T. Int corridors. **Pets:** Accepted.
SAVE 🛆 ✕ 🛆M 🖋 🛏 🖵 🏊

**⚙ ▼▼ Select Inn** 🆂🅷
(262) 786-6015. **$45-$125.** 2510 Plaza Ct. I-94, exit 297, just w on CR JJ (Bluemound Rd). Int corridors. **Pets:** Medium. $25 deposit/room, $5 daily fee/room. Designated rooms, service with restrictions, supervision.
🆂🅰🆅🅴 ✖ 🅰 🅱 💻

## WAUWATOSA

**⚙ ▼▼ Exel Inn of Milwaukee West** 🆂🅷
(414) 257-0140. **$59-$89.** 115 N Mayfair Rd. I-94, exit 304B, just n on SR 100. Int corridors. **Pets:** Small, other species. Designated rooms, service with restrictions, supervision.
🆂🅰🆅🅴 🆂🅾 ✖ 🅱 💻

# END METROPOLITAN AREA

## MINERAL POINT

**▼▼▼ Comfort Inn** 🆂🅷
(608) 987-4747. **$50-$95.** 1345 Business Park Rd. On US 151; 0.6 mi n of jct SR 23 and 39. Int corridors. **Pets:** Accepted.
🅰🆂🅺 🆂🅾 ✖ 🅰 🅱 💻 🌊

## MINOCQUA

**⚙ ▼▼ AmericInn of Minocqua** 🆂🅷
(715) 356-3730. **$74-$189.** 700 Hwy 51. On US 51; downtown. Int corridors. **Pets:** Large, other species. $25 one-time fee/room. Designated rooms, service with restrictions, supervision.
🆂🅰🆅🅴 🆂🅾 ✖ 🅰 🅱 💻 🌊 ✖

**⚙ ▼▼ Comfort Inn-Minocqua** 🆂🅷
(715) 358-2588. **$59-$95.** 8729 US 51 N. On US 51 at SR 70 W. Int corridors. **Pets:** Small. $10 daily fee/room. Designated rooms, no service, crate.
🅰🆂🅺 🆂🅾 ✖ 🅱 💻 🌊

**⚙ ▼▼ Super 8 Motel** Ⓜ 🐾
(715) 356-9541. **$66-$91.** 8730 Hwy 51 N. On US 51 at SR 70 W. Ext/int corridors. **Pets:** $10 daily fee/room. Designated rooms, service with restrictions, supervision.
🆂🅰🆅🅴 ✖

## MONONA

**▼▼▼ AmericInn of Madison South/Monona** 🆂🅷 🐾
(608) 222-8601. **$84-$119.** 101 W Broadway. US 12 and 18, exit 265 (Monona Dr), just nw. Int corridors. **Pets:** Other species. $5 daily fee/room. Service with restrictions.
🅰🆂🅺 🆂🅾 ✖ 🅰 🅱 💻 🌊 ✖

## MONROE

**⚙ ▼▼ Gasthaus Motel** Ⓜ 🐾
(608) 328-8395. **$56-$64.** 685 30th St. 1.5 mi s on SR 69. Ext corridors. **Pets:** Other species. $10 daily fee/pet. Service with restrictions, crate.
🆂🅰🆅🅴 ✖ 🅰🅼 🅱 💻

## MOSINEE

**⚙ ▼▼ Comfort Inn** 🆂🅷 🐾
(715) 355-4449. **$54-$125.** 1510 County Hwy XX. I-39, exit 185 (Business Rt US 51), just se. Int corridors. **Pets:** Dogs only. $5 daily fee/room, $15 one-time fee/room. Designated rooms, service with restrictions.
🆂🅰🆅🅴 🆂🅾 ✖ 🔌 🅱 💻 🌊

## NEENAH

**▼▼▼▼ Holiday Inn Neenah Riverwalk** 🆂🅷
(920) 725-8441. **$99.** 123 E Wisconsin Ave. US 41, exit 132 (Main St), 2 mi e; downtown. Int corridors. **Pets:** Accepted.
🅰🆂🅺 ✖ 🔌 🅰 🅱 💻 🍴 🌊

## NEILLSVILLE

**▼▼ Super 8 Motel-Neillsville** 🆂🅷
(715) 743-8080. **$69-$99.** 1000 E Division St. US 10, jct Boon and Division St. Int corridors. **Pets:** Large. $10 daily fee/pet. Designated rooms, service with restrictions, supervision.
🅰🆂🅺 🆂🅾 ✖ 🅰 🅱 🌊

## NEW LISBON

**⚙ ▼▼ Edge O' the Wood Motel** Ⓜ
(608) 562-3705. **$30-$77.** W 7396 Frontage Rd. I-90/94, exit 61 (SR 80), just e. Ext corridors. **Pets:** Accepted.
🆂🅰🆅🅴 🆂🅾 ✖ 🅱 💻 🌊

**⚙ ▼▼ Travelodge of New Lisbon** 🆂🅷
(608) 562-5141. **$55-$110.** 1700 E Bridge St. I-90/94, exit 61 (SR 80), just ne. Int corridors. **Pets:** Accepted.
🆂🅰🆅🅴 🆂🅾 ✖ 🅰 🅱 💻 🌊

## NEW LONDON

**⚙ ▼ Americas Best Value Inn New London** 🆂🅷
(920) 982-5820. **$49-$90.** 1409 N Shawano St. US 45, exit US 54, just n. Int corridors. **Pets:** Dogs only. $8 daily fee/pet. Service with restrictions, crate.
🆂🅰🆅🅴 🆂🅾 ✖ 🅱 💻 🌊

**▼▼▼ AmericInn Lodge & Suites of New London** 🆂🅷
(920) 982-5700. **$69-$189.** 1404 N Shawano St. US 45, exit US 54, just n. Int corridors. **Pets:** Small, dogs only. $10 one-time fee/pet. Designated rooms, service with restrictions, supervision.
🅰🆂🅺 🆂🅾 ✖ 🅰🅼 🅰 🅱 💻 🌊

## NEW RICHMOND

**▼▼ AmericInn Motel & Suites** 🆂🅷
(715) 246-3993. **$62-$132.** 1020 S Knowles Ave. Just s on SR 65. Int corridors. **Pets:** Medium, dogs only. Service with restrictions, supervision.
🅰🆂🅺 🆂🅾 ✖ 🅰 🅱 💻 🌊 ✖

**▼▼ Super 8 Motel** 🆂🅷
(715) 246-7829. **$67-$95.** 1561 Dorset Ln. Just s on SR 65. Int corridors. **Pets:** Accepted.
🅰🆂🅺 🆂🅾 ✖ 🔌 🅱

## ONALASKA

**▼▼▼ Baymont Inn & Suites LaCrosse-Onalaska** 🆂🅷
(608) 783-7191. **$70-$189.** 3300 Kinney Coulee Rd N. I-90, exit 5, just ne. Int corridors. **Pets:** Medium, dogs only. $5 daily fee/pet. Designated rooms, service with restrictions, supervision.
🅰🆂🅺 🆂🅾 ✖ 🅰🅼 🔌 🅰 🅱 💻 🌊

**▼▼ Comfort Inn by Choice Hotels** 🆂🅷
(608) 781-7500. **$69-$144.** 1223 Crossing Meadows Dr. I-90, exit 4, just e on SR 157, then w on CR SS. Int corridors. **Pets:** Accepted.
🅰🆂🅺 🆂🅾 ✖ 🔌 🅱 💻 🌊

**▼▼▼ Holiday Inn Express** 🆂🅷
(608) 783-6555. **$84-$104.** 9409 Hwy 16. I-90, exit 5, 1 mi e. Int corridors. **Pets:** Other species. Service with restrictions, supervision.
🅰🆂🅺 ✖ 🅰 🅱 💻 🌊 ✖

**▼▼ Microtel Inn** 🆂🅷
(608) 783-0833. **$59-$69.** 3240 N Kinney Coulee Rd. I-90, exit 5, just ne. Int corridors. **Pets:** Other species. $5 daily fee/room. Service with restrictions, supervision.
🅰🆂🅺 ✖ 🅰 🅱

# OSCEOLA

**AAA ▼▼▼ River Valley Inn** SH
(715) 294-4060. **$94.** 1030 Cascade St. Just n on SR 35. Int corridors.
**Pets:** Small. $10 daily fee/pet. Service with restrictions, supervision.
SAVE S🐾 ✕ 🛏 💻 ➥

# OSHKOSH

**▼▼ Baymont Inn Oshkosh** SH
(920) 233-4190. **$59-$105.** 1950 Omro Rd. US 41, exit 119, jct SR 21.
Int corridors. **Pets:** Medium. Service with restrictions.
A$K ✕ 🗝 🛏 💻

**▼▼ Fairfield Inn by Marriott** SH
(920) 233-8504. **$60-$80.** 1800 S Koeller Rd. US 41, exit 117 (9th Ave),
0.8 mi s on east frontage road. Int corridors. **Pets:** Accepted.
A$K S🐾 ✕ 🗝 🛏 💻 ➥

**▼▼▼ Hawthorn Inn & Suites** SH
(920) 303-1133. **$89-$400.** 3105 S Washburn St. US 41, exit 116 (SR
44), just w, then just s. Int corridors. **Pets:** Medium, dogs only. $10 daily
fee/room. Designated rooms, service with restrictions, supervision.
A$K S🐾 ✕ 🖐M 🗝 🛏 💻 🍴 ➥

**AAA ▼▼▼ Holiday Inn Express Hotel & Suites** SH
(920) 303-1300. **$99-$165.** 2251 Westowne Ave. US 41, exit 119, 0.4
mi sw of jct SR 21. Int corridors. **Pets:** Dogs only. Designated rooms,
service with restrictions, crate.
SAVE ✕ 🖐M 🗝 🛏 💻 ➥ ✕

**AAA ▼ Oshkosh Travelodge** M 🐾
(920) 233-4300. **$38-$99.** 1015 S Washburn St. US 41, exit 117 (9th
Ave), just sw. Ext corridors. **Pets:** Large, other species. $10 one-time
fee/pet. Service with restrictions, supervision.
SAVE S🐾 ✕ 🛏 💻 ➥

**AAA ▼▼ Park Plaza Hotel & Convention Center** SH
(920) 231-5000. **$70-$160.** 1 N Main St. Downtown; on shore of Fox
River. Int corridors. **Pets:** Accepted.
SAVE S🐾 ✕ 🗝 🛏 💻 🍴 ➥ ✕

# PHILLIPS

**▼▼ Super 8 Motel** SH 🐾
(715) 339-2898. **$50-$80.** 726 S Lake Ave. 0.6 mi s on SR 13. Int
corridors. **Pets:** Other species. Supervision.
A$K S🐾 ✕

# PLATTEVILLE

**AAA ▼▼▼ Governor Dodge Hotel & Conference
Center** SH 🐾
(608) 348-2301. **$59-$69, 24 day notice.** 300 Business Hwy 151. Jct
US 151 and SR 80, just w. Int corridors. **Pets:** $10 deposit/pet. Service
with restrictions, crate.
SAVE S🐾 ✕ 🛏 💻 🍴 ➥

**▼▼ Mound View Inn** SH
(608) 348-9518. **$59-$74.** 1755 E Hwy 151. On US 151, exit 21, just w.
Int corridors. **Pets:** Medium, other species. $20 deposit/room. Service with
restrictions, supervision.
✕ 🗝 🛏 ✕

**AAA ▼▼ Super 8 Motel** SH
(608) 348-8800. **$58-$90.** 100 Hwy 80/81 S. Jct US 151 and SR 80. Int
corridors. **Pets:** Other species. $10 daily fee/pet.
SAVE S🐾 ✕ 🛏

# PLEASANT PRAIRIE

**AAA ▼▼▼ Baymont Inn Kenosha-Pleasant Prairie** SH
(262) 857-7911. **$71-$111.** 7540 118th Ave. I-94, exit 344 (SR 50), just
e. Int corridors. **Pets:** Medium. Service with restrictions.
SAVE ✕ 🗝 🛏 💻

**▼▼▼ Holiday Inn Express Hotel & Suites** SH
(262) 942-6000. **$79-$149.** 7887 94th Ave. I-94, exit 344 (SR 50), 1.5
mi e, then 0.3 mi s. Int corridors. **Pets:** Accepted.
A$K S🐾 ✕ 🖐M 🗝 🛏 💻 ➥ ✕

# PORTAGE

**▼▼ Super 8 Motel-Portage** SH
(608) 742-8330. **$49-$89.** 3000 New Pinery. I-39, exit 92, just s. Int
corridors. **Pets:** Small. Designated rooms, no service, crate.
A$K S🐾 ✕ 🗝 🛏 💻

# PRAIRIE DU CHIEN

**AAA ▼▼▼ Best Western Quiet House & Suites** SH
(608) 326-4777. **$80-$174.** US 18 and SR 35. On US 18, 1.9 mi e of jct
SR 27 N. Ext/int corridors. **Pets:** Accepted.
SAVE S🐾 ✕ 🛏 💻 ➥

**AAA ▼▼▼ Bridgeport Inn** SH
(608) 326-6082. **$67-$129.** Hwy 18, 35 & 60 S. On US 18, 2.2 mi e of
jct SR 27 N. Int corridors. **Pets:** Accepted.
SAVE S🐾 ✕ 🛏 ➥

**AAA ▼▼ Brisbois Motor Inn** M
(608) 326-8404. **$64-$114.** 533 N Marquette Rd. On SR 35 N, 0.5 mi n
of jct US 18/SR 35 S and 27 N. Ext/int corridors. **Pets:** Accepted.
SAVE ✕ 🛏 ➥

**AAA ▼▼▼ Country Inn & Suites By Carlson** SH
(608) 326-5700. **$79-$209.** 1801 Cabela's Dr. On SR 35; 2 mi n of jct
US 18/SR 35 S and 27 N. Int corridors. **Pets:** Accepted.
SAVE S🐾 ✕ 🗝 🛏 💻 🍴 ➥ ✕

**AAA ▼▼▼ Super 8 Motel-Prairie Du Chien** SH
(608) 326-8777. **$70-$90.** 1930 S Marquette Rd. On US 18, 1.9 mi e of
jct SR 27 N. Ext/int corridors. **Pets:** Accepted.
SAVE ✕ 🛏

# RACINE

**▼ Knights Inn** M
(262) 886-6667. **$43-$99.** 1149 Oakes Rd. I-94, exit 333, 4 mi e on SR
20. Ext corridors. **Pets:** Accepted.
A$K S🐾 ✕ 🗝 🛏 💻

**▼▼ Microtel Inn & Suites** SH
(262) 554-8855. **$65-$78, 14 day notice.** 5419 Durand Ave. On SR 11,
0.5 mi e of jct SR 31. Int corridors. **Pets:** Medium. $10 one-time fee/
room. Designated rooms, service with restrictions, crate.
A$K S🐾 ✕ 🖐M 🗝 🗝 🛏 💻

**▼▼▼ Racine Marriott Hotel** LH
(262) 886-6100. **$189.** 7111 Washington Ave. I-94, exit 333, 4 mi e on
SR 20. Int corridors. **Pets:** Accepted.
A$K S🐾 ✕ 🗝 🛏 💻 🍴 ➥ ✕

**AAA ▼▼▼ Super 8-Racine** SH
(262) 884-0486. **$55-$160.** 1150 Oakes Rd. I-94, exit 333, 4 mi e on
SR 20. Int corridors. **Pets:** Medium. $10 daily fee/pet. Designated rooms,
service with restrictions, supervision.
SAVE S🐾 ✕ 🗝 🛏

# REEDSBURG

**AAA ▼ Copper Springs Motel** M 🐾
(608) 524-4312. **$44-$68, 5 day notice.** E7278 Hwy 23 & 33. 2 mi e on
SR 23 and 33. Ext corridors. **Pets:** Other species. $10 one-time fee/pet.
Designated rooms, supervision.
SAVE 🛏 💻

# RHINELANDER

**▼▼ AmericInn of Rhinelander** SH
(715) 369-9600. **$64-$110.** 648 W Kemp St. On Business Rt US 8, 0.3 mi e of jct SR 47. Int corridors. **Pets:** Designated rooms, service with restrictions, crate.
ASK 🗲 ✕ 🐕 🚲 🛏 🖥 🏊 ✕

**▼▼ Best Western Claridge Motor Inn** SH
(715) 362-7100. **$85-$160.** 70 N Stevens St. On SR 17; center. Int corridors. **Pets:** Medium. $25 deposit/room, $10 daily fee/pet. Designated rooms, service with restrictions, supervision.
ASK 🗲 ✕ 🛏 🖥 🍴 🏊 ✕

**▲▲▲ ▼▼ Comfort Inn** SH
(715) 369-1100. **$69-$160.** 1490 Lincoln St. On Business Rt US 8, 2.6 mi e of jct SR 47. Int corridors. **Pets:** Accepted.
SAVE 🗲 ✕ 🛏 🖥 🏊 ✕

**▼ Holiday Acres Resort** SH
(715) 369-1500. **$63-$289, 15 day notice.** 4060 S Shore Dr. 4.5 mi e on Business Rt US 8, 2.3 mi n on W Lake George Rd. Ext/int corridors. **Pets:** Large, other species. $15 daily fee/pet. Designated rooms, service with restrictions, supervision.
ASK 🗲 ✕ 🛏 🖥 🍴 🏊 ✕

**▼▼ Holiday Inn Express** SH
(715) 369-3600. **$74-$174.** 668 W Kemp St. On Business Rt US 8, just e of jct SR 47. Int corridors. **Pets:** Other species. $25 one-time fee/room. Service with restrictions, supervision.
ASK 🗲 ✕ 🖥 🚲 🛏 🖥 🏊 ✕

# RICE LAKE

**▼▼ Microtel Inn & Suites** M
(715) 736-2010. **$50-$85.** 2771 Decker Dr. US 53, exit 140 (CR O), just ne. Int corridors. **Pets:** Accepted.
ASK 🗲 ✕ 🚲 🛏 🖥

# RICHLAND CENTER

**▼▼ Super 8 Motel-Richland Center** SH
(608) 647-8988. **$63-$110.** 100 Foundry Dr. 0.9 mi e on US 14. Int corridors. **Pets:** Accepted.
ASK 🗲 ✕ 🛏 🖥 🏊 ✕

# RIPON

**▼▼ AmericInn of Ripon** SH
(920) 748-7578. **$88-$138.** 1219 W Fond du Lac St. 1.8 mi w on SR 23. Int corridors. **Pets:** $10 one-time fee/room. Service with restrictions, crate.
ASK ✕ 🚲 🛏 🖥 🏊 ✕

# RIVER FALLS

**▼▼ Super 8 Motel** SH
(715) 425-8388. **$65-$120.** 1207 St. Croix St. On SR 65, 0.5 mi w jct SR 35. Int corridors. **Pets:** Accepted.
ASK 🗲 ✕ 🛏 🖥 🏊

# ST. GERMAIN

**▼ North Woods Rest Motel** M
(715) 479-8770. **$54, 3 day notice.** 8083 Hwy 70 E. On SR 70, 0.8 mi e. Ext corridors. **Pets:** Medium, dogs only. $5 daily fee/pet. Service with restrictions, supervision
✕ 🛏 🖥

# SHAWANO

**▼▼ Comfort Inn & Suites** SH
(715) 524-9090. **$69-$149.** W7393 River Bend Rd. SR 29, exit 225, just n on SR 22. Int corridors. **Pets:** $12 daily fee/pet. Designated rooms, no service, crate.
ASK 🗲 ✕ 🚲 🛏 🖥 🏊 ✕

**▼ Super 8 Motel-Shawano** SH
(715) 526-6688. **$49-$80.** 211 Waukechon St. 1.2 mi e on SR 29 business route; SR 29, exit 227, 1.8 mi n. then 1.1 mi w. Int corridors. **Pets:** Small. Designated rooms, no service, crate.
ASK 🗲 ✕ 🐕 🛏 🖥

# SHEBOYGAN

**▼▼ AmericInn of Sheboygan** SH
(920) 208-8130. **$79-$180.** 3664 S Taylor Dr. I-43, exit 123, just e. Int corridors. **Pets:** Accepted.
ASK 🗲 ✕ 🚲 🛏 🖥 🏊

**▼▼ Baymont Inn Sheboygan** SH
(920) 457-2321. **$66-$125.** 2932 Kohler Memorial Dr. I-43, exit 126, 1 mi e on SR 23. Int corridors. **Pets:** Medium. Service with restrictions.
ASK ✕ 🚲 🛏 🖥

**▼ Comfort Inn-Sheboygan** SH
(920) 457-7724. **$59-$119.** 4332 N 40th St. I-43, exit 128, 0.3 mi e on Business Rt SR 42. Int corridors. **Pets:** Small. Designated rooms, no service, crate.
ASK 🗲 ✕ 🐕 🛏 🖥 🏊

**▲▲▲ ▼ Super 8 Motel-Sheboygan** SH
(920) 458-8080. **$59-$79.** 3402 Wilgus Rd. I-43, exit 126, just ne. Int corridors. **Pets:** Accepted.
SAVE 🗲 ✕ 🛏 🖥

# SHELL LAKE

**▼▼ AmericInn of Shell Lake** SH
(715) 468-4494. **$69-$199.** 315 Hwy 63 S. US 53, exit CR B. Int corridors. **Pets:** Accepted.
ASK 🗲 ✕ 🚲 🛏 🖥 🏊 ✕

# SIREN

**▲▲▲ ▼▼▼ The Lodge at Crooked Lake** SH
(715) 349-2500. **$79-$139.** 24271 SR 35 N. On SR 35, 0.5 mi n of jct SR 70. Int corridors. **Pets:** Dogs only. $50 deposit/room, $10 daily fee/pet. Service with restrictions, supervision.
SAVE 🗲 ✕ 🚲 🛏 🖥 🍴 🏊 ✕

**▲▲▲ ▼ Pine Wood Motel** M
(715) 349-5225. **$40-$55.** 23862 Hwy 35 S. On SR 35, 0.3 mi s of jct SR 70 W and CR B E. Ext corridors. **Pets:** Small, dogs only. No service, supervision.
SAVE 🗲 ✕ 🛏

# SPARTA

**▲▲▲ ▼ Best Nights Inn** M
(608) 269-3066. **$32-$139.** 303 W Wisconsin St. I-90, exit 25 (SR 27), 0.5 mi n; exit 28 (SR 16), 1 mi w. Ext corridors. **Pets:** Large, other species. $7 daily fee/pet. Designated rooms, service with restrictions, crate.
SAVE 🗲 ✕ 🛏 🖥 🏊

**▼▼▼ Best Western Sparta Trail Lodge** SH
(608) 269-2664. **$74-$129.** 4445 Theatre Rd. I-90, exit 28 (US 16), just w. Int corridors. **Pets:** Other species. $20 one-time fee/pet. Service with restrictions, crate.
ASK 🗲 ✕ 🖥 🚲 🛏 🖥 🍴 🏊 ✕

**▲▲▲ ▼▼ Country Inn By Carlson** SH 🐾
(608) 269-3110. **$79-$153.** 737 Avon Rd. I-90, exit 25 (SR 27), just n. Int corridors. **Pets:** Medium, other species. $15 daily fee/pet. Service with restrictions, supervision.
SAVE 🗲 ✕ 🖥 🛏 🖥 🏊

**▼▼ Super 8 Sparta** SH
(608) 269-8489. **$80-$175.** 716 Avon Rd. I-90, exit 25 (SR 27), just n. Int corridors. **Pets:** Accepted.
ASK 🗲 ✕ 🛏 🖥

# SPOONER

**▼◆▼ Best Western American Heritage Inn** SH
(715) 635-9770. **$84-$129.** 101 Maple St. On SR 70 at US 63, 1 mi w of US 53. Int corridors. **Pets:** Accepted.

(ASK) 5⚬ ✕ 💻 ⪰ ⊠

**▲▲▲ ▼◆▼ Country House Motel & RV Park** M 🐾
(715) 635-8721. **$50-$110.** 717 S River St. On US 63, 0.5 mi s of jct SR 70. Ext/int corridors. **Pets:** Other species. $5 daily fee/pet. Designated rooms, service with restrictions, supervision.

(SAVE) ✕ 🖑M 🕖 🎇 🕒 💻 ⪰

# STEVENS POINT

**▼ Americas Best Value Inn** SH
(715) 341-8888. **$59-$79.** 247 N Division St. I-39, exit 161, 0.6 mi s on US 51 business route. Int corridors. **Pets:** Accepted.

(ASK) 5⚬ ✕ 🕒 💻

**▲▲▲ ▼◆▼ Baymont Inn & Suites Stevens Point** SH
(715) 344-1900. **$70-$105.** 4917 Main St. I-39, exit 158B (US 10), just w. Int corridors. **Pets:** Medium. Service with restrictions.

(SAVE) ✕ 🕖 🕒 💻 ⪰

**▼◆▼ Country Inn & Suites By Carlson** SH
(715) 345-7000. **$74-$139.** 301 Division St N. I-39, exit 161, on US 51 business route, 0.6 mi s. Int corridors. **Pets:** $25 one-time fee/room. Designated rooms, service with restrictions, supervision.

(ASK) 5⚬ ✕ 🎇 🕒 💻 ⪰

**▼ ▼ Fairfield Inn by Marriott** SH
(715) 342-9300. **$55-$90.** 5317 Hwy 10 E. I-39, exit 158 (US 10) at US 51. Int corridors. **Pets:** Accepted.

(ASK) ✕ 🕖 🎇 🕒 💻 ⪰

**▼◆▼ Holiday Inn Express** SH 🐾
(715) 344-0000. **$74-$119.** 1100 Amber Ave. I-39, exit 158 (US 10), 1 mi e. Int corridors. **Pets:** Other species. $25 one-time fee/room. No service.

(ASK) ✕ 🖑M 🎇 🕒 💻 ⪰

**▼ Point Motel** M
(715) 344-8312. **$42-$50.** 209 Division St. I-39, exit 161, 0.7 mi s. Ext corridors. **Pets:** Small. $6 daily fee/pet. Designated rooms, service with restrictions, supervision.

(ASK) 5⚬ ✕ 🕒 💻

# STURTEVANT

**▲▲▲ ▼ ▼ Grandview Inn** SH
(262) 886-0385. **$57-$87.** 910 S Sylvania Ave. I-94, exit 333 (SR 20), just s on west frontage road. Int corridors. **Pets:** Dogs only. Service with restrictions, supervision.

(SAVE) 5⚬ ✕ 🕒 💻 ⪰

**▲▲▲ ▼ ▼ Holiday Inn Express-Racine** SH
(262) 884-0200. **$74-$104.** 13339 Hospitality Ct. I-94, exit 333 (SR 20), just se. Int corridors. **Pets:** Small, other species. Designated rooms, service with restrictions, supervision.

(SAVE) 5⚬ ✕ 🖑M 🕖 🎇 🕒 💻 ⪰

# SUN PRAIRIE

**▲▲▲ ▼ ▼ AmeriHost Inn & Suites-Sun Prairie** SH
(608) 834-9889. **$69-$99.** 105 Business Park Dr. US 151, exit 103 (CR N), just n. Int corridors. **Pets:** Medium, dogs only. $10 daily fee/pet. Service with restrictions, supervision.

(SAVE) 5⚬ ✕ 🖑M 🎇 🕒 💻 ⪰

**▲▲▲ ▼ McGovern's Motel & Suites** M
(608) 837-7321. **$48-$81.** 820 W Main St. On US 151, exit 101, 1.2 mi ne. Ext/int corridors. **Pets:** Medium. $5 daily fee/pet. Designated rooms, service with restrictions, supervision.

(SAVE) 5⚬ ✕ 🕒 💻 🕕

# SUPERIOR

**▲▲▲ ▼ ▼ Barkers Island Inn** SH
(715) 392-7152. **$71-$212.** 300 Marina Dr. Just ne of US 2/53; on Barkers Island. Int corridors. **Pets:** Other species. $10 daily fee/pet. Designated rooms, service with restrictions, supervision.

(SAVE) 5⚬ ✕ 🕒 💻 🕕 ⪰ ⊠

**▼◆▼ Best Western Bay Walk Inn** SH
(715) 392-7600. **$59-$129.** 1405 Susquehanna Ave. Just e of US 2 on Belknap St. Int corridors. **Pets:** Small. Designated rooms, service with restrictions, supervision.

(ASK) 5⚬ ✕ 🕒 💻 ⪰ ⊠

**▲▲▲ ▼◆▼ Best Western Bridgeview Motor Inn** SH
(715) 392-8174. **$59-$149.** 415 Hammond Ave. 0.8 mi n at south end of Blatnik Bridge. Int corridors. **Pets:** Other species. Service with restrictions, supervision.

(SAVE) 5⚬ ✕ 🕒 💻 ⪰ ⊠

**▲▲▲ ▼◆▼ Days Inn-Superior/Bayfront** SH
(715) 392-4783. **$39-$159.** 110 Harborview Pkwy. Just n of jct US 2/53. Int corridors. **Pets:** Other species. $50 deposit/pet, $10 daily fee/pet. Designated rooms, service with restrictions, supervision.

(SAVE) 5⚬ ✕ 🎇 🕒 💻 🕕 ⪰ ⊠

**▼ Stockade Motel** M
(715) 398-3585. **$45-$75.** 1616 E 2nd St. On US 2/53, 2.8 mi se. Ext corridors. **Pets:** Accepted.

✕ 🕒 💻

**▲▲▲ ▼ Superior Inn** SH
(715) 394-7706. **$75-$130.** 525 Hammond Ave. 0.8 mi n at south end of Blatnik Bridge. Int corridors. **Pets:** Other species. Service with restrictions, supervision.

(SAVE) 5⚬ ✕ 🕒 💻 ⪰

# THORP

**▼◆▼ AmericInn Lodge & Suites** SH
(715) 669-5959. **$83-$144.** 203 1/2 W Hill St. US 29, exit 108 (SR 73), just nw. Int corridors. **Pets:** Small. $10 daily fee/pet. Designated rooms, service with restrictions, supervision.

✕ 🎇 🕒 💻 ⪰ ⊠

# TOMAH

**▼ ▼ Comfort Inn by Choice Hotels** SH
(608) 372-6600. **$60-$129.** 305 Wittig Rd. I-94, exit 143 (SR 21), just w. Int corridors. **Pets:** Accepted.

(ASK) 5⚬ ✕ 🕖 🕒 💻 ⪰

**▼◆▼ Cranberry Country Lodge Convention Center and Water Park** SH
(608) 374-2801. **$75-$200.** 319 Wittig Rd. I-94, exit 143 (SR 21), just w. Int corridors. **Pets:** Other species. $20 daily fee/pet. Service with restrictions, supervision.

(ASK) 5⚬ ✕ 🕒 💻 ⪰ ⊠

**▲▲▲ ▼ ▼ Econo Lodge** SH 🐾
(608) 372-9100. **$59-$141.** 2005 N Superior Ave. I-94, exit 143 (SR 21), just w. Ext/int corridors. **Pets:** Large, other species. $10 daily fee/pet. Service with restrictions.

(SAVE) 5⚬ ✕ 🕖 🕒 💻 ⪰

**▼◆▼ Holiday Inn** SH 🐾
(608) 372-3211. **$109-$114.** 1017 E McCoy Blvd. I-94, exit 143 (SR 21), just e. Int corridors. **Pets:** Other species. Supervision.

(ASK) 5⚬ ✕ 🎇 🕒 💻 🕕 ⪰ ⊠

**▲▲▲ ▼ ▼ Lark Inn** M 🐾
(608) 372-5981. **$59-$91.** 229 N Superior Ave. I-94, exit 143 (SR 21), 1.5 mi s on US 12; 1-90, exit 41, 2 mi n on US 12. Ext/int corridors. **Pets:** $7 daily fee/pet. Service with restrictions, supervision.

(SAVE) 5⚬ ✕ 🕒 💻

▼▼ ▼▼ **Microtel Inn & Suites** 🆂🅷
(608) 374-2050. **$49-$79.** 115 W Andres St. I-94, exit 143 (SR 21), just nw. Int corridors. **Pets:** Small. $10 daily fee/room. Service with restrictions, supervision.
🅰️$🄺 🆂🙆 ✕ 🔑 🛈 🖵

▼▼ ▼▼ **Super 8 Motel-Tomah** 🆂🅷
(608) 372-3901. **$49-$69.** 1008 E McCoy Blvd. I-94, exit 143 (SR 21), just e. Int corridors. **Pets:** Small. Designated rooms, no service, crate.
🅰️$🄺 🆂🙆 ✕ 🔑 🛈 🖵

# TOMAHAWK
▼▼▼▼ **Comfort Inn** 🆂🅷
(715) 453-8900. **$80-$130.** 1738 E Comfort Dr. US 51, exit 229. Int corridors. **Pets:** Other species. $25 one-time fee/room. Service with restrictions, supervision.
🅰️$🄺 🆂🙆 ✕ 🈁 🔑 🛈 🖵 🏊 ✖️

▼▼ ▼▼ **Super 8 Motel-Tomahawk** 🆂🅷
(715) 453-5210. **$45-$126.** 108 W Mohawk Dr. On US 51 business route, 0.6 mi n of downtown. Int corridors. **Pets:** $5 one-time fee/room. Designated rooms, service with restrictions, supervision.
🅰️$🄺 🆂🙆 🔑 🛈 🖵 🏊

# TWO RIVERS
▼▼▼ **Lighthouse Inn on the Lake** 🆂🅷
(920) 793-4524. **$90-$146.** 1515 Memorial Dr. 0.3 mi s on SR 42. Int corridors. **Pets:** Accepted.
🅰️$🄺 🆂🙆 ✕ 🛈 🖵 🍽 🏊 ✖️

▼▼▼ ▼▼ **Village Inn on the Lake** 🆰
(920) 794-8818. **$52-$110.** 3310 Memorial Dr. 2 mi s on SR 42. Ext/int corridors. **Pets:** Accepted.
🆂🅰️🆅🅴 🆂🙆 ✕ 🛈 🖵 🍽 🏊

# VERONA
▼▼ ▼▼ **Super 8 Motel-Verona** 🆂🅷 🐾
(608) 848-7829. **$64-$104, 7 day notice.** 131 Horizon Dr. US 18 and 151, exit 94 southbound; exit 89 northbound, just n. Int corridors. **Pets:** Other species. $13 daily fee/room. Service with restrictions, supervision.
🅰️$🄺 🆂🙆 ✕ 🛈 🏊

# WATERFORD
▼▼▼ ▼▼▼▼ **Baymont Inns & Suites-Waterford** 🆂🅷
(262) 534-4100. **$76-$151.** 750 Fox Ln. On SR 36, 1 mi s of jct SR 164. Int corridors. **Pets:** Medium, other species. Service with restrictions, supervision.
🆂🅰️🆅🅴 🆂🙆 ✕ 🔑 🛈 🖵 🏊

# WATERTOWN
▼▼ ▼▼ **Econo Lodge** 🆂🅷
(920) 261-9010. **$45-$130.** 700 E Main St. On SR 16 and 19. Int corridors. **Pets:** Accepted.
🅰️$🄺 🆂🙆 ✕

▼▼▼▼ **Holiday Inn Express** 🆂🅷
(920) 262-1910. **$72-$101.** 101 Aviation Way. On SR 26, 1.5 mi s of jct SR 19. Int corridors. **Pets:** Dogs only. $100 deposit/pet, $10 daily fee/pet. Designated rooms, service with restrictions, supervision.
🅰️$🄺 🆂🙆 ✕ 🔑 🛈 🖵 🏊 ✖️

▼▼ ▼▼ **Super 8 Motel** 🆂🅷
(920) 261-1188. **$73-$88.** 1730 S Church St. On SR 26, 1.5 mi s of jct SR 19. Int corridors. **Pets:** Dogs only. $75 deposit/room. Service with restrictions, supervision.
🅰️$🄺 🆂🙆 ✕ 🛈 🖵 🏊

# WAUPACA
▼▼▼ ▼▼▼▼ **Best Western Grand Seasons Hotel** 🆂🅷 🐾
(715) 258-9212. **$159-$179.** 110 Grand Seasons Dr. Jct US 10 and SR 54 W. Int corridors. **Pets:** Medium. $50 deposit/room. Designated rooms, supervision.
🆂🅰️🆅🅴 🆂🙆 ✕ 🕖 🔑 🛈 🖵 🏊 ✖️

▼▼▼▼ **Comfort Suites at Foxfire** 🆂🅷
(715) 942-0500. **$75-$165.** 199 Foxfire Dr. Jct US 10 and SR 54 W, 0.7 mi sw at Foxfire Dr. Int corridors. **Pets:** Small. $15 daily fee/room. Designated rooms, supervision.
🅰️$🄺 🆂🙆 ✕ 🛈 🖵 🍽 🏊 ✖️

# WAUPUN
▼▼ **Inn Town Motel** 🆰
(920) 324-4211. **$49-$71.** 27 S State St. US 151, exit 146 (SR 49), 1.3 mi w. Ext corridors. **Pets:** Small. $6 daily fee/pet. Service with restrictions, supervision.
🅰️$🄺 🆂🙆 ✕ 🛈 🖵

# WAUSAU
▼▼▼ ▼▼ **Baymont Inn-Wausau** 🆂🅷
(715) 842-0421. **$75-$111.** 1910 Stewart Ave. I-39, exit 192, just e. Int corridors. **Pets:** Medium. Service with restrictions.
🆂🅰️🆅🅴 ✕ 🕖 🛈 🖵 🏊

▼▼ ▼▼ **Best Western Midway Hotel** 🆂🅷
(715) 842-1616. **$105-$130, 3 day notice.** 2901 Martin Ave. I-39, exit 190 (CR NN), just sw. Int corridors. **Pets:** Medium. $20 daily fee/room. Designated rooms, service with restrictions, crate.
🅰️$🄺 🆂🙆 ✕ 🛈 🖵 🍽 🏊 ✖️

▼▼▼ ▼▼ ▼▼▼▼ **Days Inn-Wausau** 🆂🅷
(715) 355-5501. **$64-$89.** 4700 Rib Mountain Dr. I-39, exit 188, just e. Int corridors. **Pets:** $10 daily fee/pet. Designated rooms, service with restrictions, supervision.
🆂🅰️🆅🅴 ✕ 🛈 🖵 🏊

▼▼▼ ▼▼ ▼▼▼▼ **Exel Inn of Wausau** 🆰
(715) 842-0641. **$52-$82.** 116 S 17th Ave. I-39, exit 192, just e. Int corridors. **Pets:** Small, other species. Designated rooms, service with restrictions, supervision.
🆂🅰️🆅🅴 🆂🙆 ✕ 🛈 🖵

▼▼ ▼▼ **Rib Mountain Inn** 🆂🅷
(715) 848-2802. **$59-$209, 3 day notice.** 2900 Rib Mountain Way. I-39, exit 190 (CR NN), 1 mi w. Ext/int corridors. **Pets:** Accepted.
🅰️$🄺 🆂🙆 🛈 🖵 ✖️

▼▼▼ ▼▼ ▼▼▼▼ **Super 8 Motel** 🆂🅷
(715) 848-2888. **$70-$80.** 2006 Stewart Ave W. I-39, exit 192, just e. Int corridors. **Pets:** Medium, other species. $10 daily fee/pet. Designated rooms, service with restrictions, supervision.
🆂🅰️🆅🅴 🆂🙆 ✕ 🕖 🔑 🛈 🖵 🏊

# WAUTOMA
▼▼ ▼▼ **AmericInn** 🆂🅷
(920) 787-5050. **$68-$128.** W7696 SR 21/73. On SR 21 and 73, 1.2 mi e. Int corridors. **Pets:** Dogs only. $10 one-time fee/room. Service with restrictions, supervision.
🅰️$🄺 🆂🙆 ✕ 🅼 🔑 🛈 🖵 🏊

▼▼ ▼▼ **Super 8 Motel-Wautoma** 🆂🅷
(920) 787-4811. **$55-$83.** W7607 SR 21 and 73. On SR 21 and 73, 1.5 mi e. Int corridors. **Pets:** Other species. $10 one-time fee/pet. Service with restrictions, supervision.
🅰️$🄺 🆂🙆 ✕ 🛈 🏊

# WEST SALEM

### ◆◆ AmericInn SH
(608) 786-3340. **$73-$153.** 125 Buol Rd. I-90, exit 12, just sw on CR C. Int corridors. **Pets:** Accepted.

(ASK) (SD) (X) (GM) (B) (P) (≈) (X)

# WHITEWATER

### ◆◆◆ AmeriHost Inn & Suites SH
(262) 472-9400. **$59-$99.** 1355 W Main St. On US 12, 0.5 mi w of jct SR 59 W. Int corridors. **Pets:** Accepted.

(SAVE) (SD) (X) (GM) (②) (GM) (B) (P) (≈) (X)

### ◆◆ Super 8 Motel SH
(262) 473-8818. **$39-$199.** 917 E Milwaukee St. On US 12, just e of jct SR 59 E. Int corridors. **Pets:** Accepted.

(ASK) (SD) (X) (GM) (B)

# WINDSOR

### ◆◆◆ Days Inn SH
(608) 846-7473. **$51-$108.** 6311 Rostad Cir. I-90/94, exit 131 (SR 19). Int corridors. **Pets:** Accepted.

(SAVE) (SD) (X) (GM) (②) (B) (P) (≈) (X)

### ◆◆ Super 8 Motel-Windsor/North Madison SH
(608) 846-3971. **$63-$69.** 4506 Lake Cir. I-90/94, exit 131 (SR 19). Int corridors. **Pets:** Small, other species. $10 one-time fee/pet. Designated rooms, service with restrictions, supervision.

(ASK) (SD) (X) (B) (P)

# WISCONSIN DELLS

### ◆◆ America's Best Value Day's End Motel M
(608) 254-8171. **$34-$124, 3 day notice.** N 604 Hwy 12-16. I-90/94, exit 85 (US 12), 0.8 mi nw. Ext corridors. **Pets:** $7 daily fee/pet. Designated rooms, service with restrictions, crate.

(SAVE) (SD) (X) (B) (P) (≈) (X)

### ◆◆ Baker's Sunset Bay Resort SH ❀
(608) 254-8406. **$58-$147, 14 day notice.** 921 Canyon Rd. I-90/94, exit 92 (US 12), 0.5 mi w, right on E Adams St, right on Canyon Rd, then 0.8 mi on left. Ext/int corridors. **Pets:** Other species. $10 daily fee/pet. Service with restrictions.

(SAVE) (SD) (X) (B) (P) (≈) (X)

### ◆◆ Black Hawk Motel M ❀
(608) 254-7770. **$36-$135, 3 day notice.** 720 Race St. I-90/94, exit 87 (SR 13), 2 mi e on SR 13, 16 and 23. Ext corridors. **Pets:** Small, other species. $10 deposit/pet, $5 daily fee/pet. Service with restrictions, crate.

(SAVE) (SD) (X) (B) (P) (≈) (X)

### ◆ Bridge View Motel M
(608) 254-6114. **$49-$99, 3 day notice.** 1020 River Rd. Just n of SR 13; center. Ext corridors. **Pets:** Small, dogs only. $10 daily fee/pet. Designated rooms, service with restrictions, crate.

(ASK) (SD) (X) (B) (≈)

### ◆◆ Days Inn of Wisconsin Dells SH
(608) 254-6444. **$44-$139.** 944 Hwy 12 N. I-90/94, exit 87 (SR 13), 1 mi n at jct US 12 and SR 16. Int corridors. **Pets:** Medium, dogs only. $50 deposit/pet, $10 daily fee/pet. Service with restrictions, supervision.

(SAVE) (SD) (X) (B) (≈)

### ◆◆ Howard Johnson Hotel and Antiqua Bay Waterpark SH
(608) 254-8306. **$69-$185.** 655 Frontage Rd. I-90/94, exit 87 (SR 13), just e. Int corridors. **Pets:** Accepted.

(SAVE) (SD) (X) (②) (B) (P) (¶) (≈) (X)

### ◆◆ Super 8 Motel-Wisconsin Dells SH
(608) 254-6464. **$56-$165.** 800 CR H. I-90/94, exit 87 (SR 13), just e. Int corridors. **Pets:** $10 daily fee/room. Designated rooms, service with restrictions, supervision.

(SAVE) (X) (②) (P) (≈) (X)

# WISCONSIN RAPIDS

### ◆◆ Best Western Rapids Motor Inn SH
(715) 424-3211. **$68-$80.** 911 Huntington Ave. 0.5 mi s of jct SR 54 on SR 13. Int corridors. **Pets:** $5 one-time fee/pet. Service with restrictions, supervision.

(SAVE) (SD) (X) (B) (P) (≈)

### ◆◆ Hotel Mead LH
(715) 423-1500. **$115-$160.** 451 E Grand Ave. Just e of downtown. Int corridors. **Pets:** Medium, other species. $15 daily fee/pet. Designated rooms, service with restrictions, supervision.

(SAVE) (SD) (X) (②) (GM) (B) (P) (¶) (≈) (X)

### ◆◆◆ Sleep Inn & Suites SH
(715) 424-6800. **$67-$157.** 4221 8th St S. I-39, exit 136 (SR 73), 16.6 mi w; 3.5 mi n on SR 13. Int corridors. **Pets:** Medium, dogs only. $15 daily fee/pet. Designated rooms, service with restrictions, supervision.

(ASK) (SD) (X) (B) (P) (≈)

### ◆◆ Super 8 Motel SH
(715) 423-8080. **$53-$73.** 3410 8th St S. 1.9 mi s on SR 13 of jct SR 54 W. Int corridors. **Pets:** Accepted.

(SAVE) (SD) (X) (②) (B) (P)

# WITTENBERG

### ◆◆ Comfort Inn & Wilderness Conference Center SH
(715) 253-3755. **$59-$119.** W17267 Red Oak Ln. US 29, exit 198, just se. Int corridors. **Pets:** Small, dogs only. $20 one-time fee/room. Designated rooms, service with restrictions, supervision.

(ASK) (SD) (X) (GM) (②) (B) (P) (≈) (X)

# WYOMING

## CITY INDEX

## AFTON

**Hi Country Inn** M
(307) 885-3856. **$95-$100, 5 day notice.** 689 S Washington St (US Hwy 89). On US 89, 0.8 mi s. Ext corridors. **Pets:** Accepted.

**Lazy B Motel** M
(307) 885-3187. **$65-$75.** 219 Washington St (US Hwy 89). On US 89; center. Ext corridors. **Pets:** Other species. Designated rooms, service with restrictions, supervision.

## ALPINE

**Alpen Haus Resort Hotel** M
(307) 654-7545. **$60-$80.** 50 W Hwy 26. Jct US 26 and 89. Int corridors. **Pets:** Small. $10 daily fee/room. Designated rooms, service with restrictions, supervision.

**Best Western Flying Saddle Lodge** M
(307) 654-7561. **$79-$189.** 118878 Jct US 26 & 89. 0.5 mi e of jct US 26 and 89. Ext corridors. **Pets:** Accepted.

## BUFFALO

**Arrowhead Motel** M
(307) 684-9453. **$38-$55, 3 day notice.** 749 Fort St. Jct US 16/87/ Business Loop I-25, 0.6 mi w. Ext corridors. **Pets:** Small, dogs only. $7 daily fee/pet. Designated rooms, service with restrictions, supervision.

**Big Horn Motel** M
(307) 684-7822. **$47-$79, 3 day notice.** 209 N Main St, US Hwy 16. On US 16; downtown. Ext corridors. **Pets:** Dogs only. $100 deposit/ room. Designated rooms, service with restrictions, supervision.

**Canyon Motel** M
(307) 684-2957. **$34-$60.** 997 Fort St. Jct US 16/87/Business Loop I-25, 0.9 mi w on US 16. Ext corridors. **Pets:** Other species. $8 daily fee/pet. Service with restrictions, supervision.

**Comfort Inn** SH
(307) 684-9564. **$52-$150.** 65 Hwy 16 E. I-25, exit 299 (US 16), just e; I-90, exit 58, 1.3 mi w. Ext/int corridors. **Pets:** Other species. $5 daily fee/pet. Designated rooms, service with restrictions, supervision.

**Mountain View Cabins & Campground** CA
(307) 684-2881. **$40-$105, 7 day notice.** 585 Fort St. Jct US 16/87/ Business Loop I-25, 0.4 mi w on US 16. Ext corridors. **Pets:** Medium. $5 daily fee/pet. Designated rooms, service with restrictions, supervision.

**Rodeway Inn** M
(307) 684-2219. **$49-$109.** 333 E Hart St. I-25, exit 299 (US 16), just w. Ext corridors. **Pets:** Small. $10 daily fee/pet. Designated rooms, service with restrictions, supervision.

**Super 8 Motel of Buffalo** SH
(307) 684-2531. **$55-$130.** 655 E Hart St. I-25, exit 299 (US 16), just w; I-90, exit 58, 1.3 mi w. Int corridors. **Pets:** Large, other species. $8 daily fee/pet. Designated rooms, service with restrictions, supervision.

**WYO Motel** M
(307) 684-5505. **$33-$115.** 610 E Hart St. I-25, exit 299 (US 16), just w; I-90, exit 58, 1.3 mi w. Ext corridors. **Pets:** Medium. $5 daily fee/pet. Service with restrictions, supervision.

**Z-Bar Motel** CA
(307) 684-5535. **$40-$69.** 626 Fort St. Jct US 16/87/Business Loop I-25, 0.5 mi w on US 16. Ext corridors. **Pets:** Other species. $5 one-time fee/pet. Supervision.

## CASPER

**Best Western Ramkota** LH
(307) 266-6000. **$90-$95.** 800 N Poplar St. I-25, exit 188B, just e. Int corridors. **Pets:** Accepted.

**Days Inn Casper** SH
(307) 234-1159. **$89-$109.** 301 E 'E' St. I-25, exit 188A, just s. Int corridors. **Pets:** Service with restrictions, supervision.

**Holiday Inn** SH
(307) 235-2531. **$89-$93.** 300 W 'F' St. I-25, exit 188A, just e. Int corridors. **Pets:** Other species.

**Holiday Inn Express** SH
(307) 237-4200. **$99.** 4250 Legion Ln. I-25, exit 185, just w. Int corridors. **Pets:** Accepted.

**Parkway Plaza Hotel & Convention Centre** SH
(307) 235-1777. **$89-$119.** 123 W 'E' St. I-25, exit 188A, just w. Ext/int corridors. **Pets:** Accepted.

**Quality Inn & Suites** SH
(307) 266-2400. **$75-$125.** 821 N Poplar St. I-25, exit 188B, just e. Int corridors. **Pets:** Large, other species. $5 daily fee/room. Designated rooms, service with restrictions.

**The Royal Inn** M
(307) 234-3501. **$45-$50.** 440 E 'A' St. I-25, exit 188A (Center St), just s to 'A' St, then just e. Ext corridors. **Pets:** Small. $4 daily fee/pet. Designated rooms, service with restrictions, supervision.

[SAVE] [S&] [X] [🛏] [🖼]

**Skyler Inn** SH
(307) 232-5100. **$72-$99.** 111 S Wilson St. I-25, exit 186, 0.5 mi s to Yellowstone Hwy, then 1 mi w, jct 1st St. Int corridors. **Pets:** Small, dogs only. $25 one-time fee/pet. Service with restrictions, supervision.

[SAVE] [S&] [X] [🛏] [🖼]

**Super 8 Motel** SH ☼
(307) 266-3480. **$89-$99.** 3838 CY Ave. I-25, exit 188B, 1.7 mi w on S Poplar St (SR 220), then 1.8 mi n. Int corridors. **Pets:** Other species. Service with restrictions, supervision.

[ASK] [S&] [X] [🛏] [🖼]

# CHEYENNE

**Best Western Hitching Post Inn Resort & Conference Center** SH
(307) 638-3301. **$89-$250.** 1700 W Lincolnway. I-25, exit 9, 0.8 mi e. Ext/int corridors. **Pets:** Accepted.

[SAVE] [S&] [X] [&M] [📶] [🖢] [🛏] [🖼] [🍴] [🏊] [X]

**Cheyenne Super 8 Motel** M
(307) 635-8741. **$45-$85, 7 day notice.** 1900 W Lincolnway. I-25, exit 9, 0.7 mi e. Int corridors. **Pets:** Small. $6 daily fee/room. Service with restrictions, supervision.

[ASK] [S&] [X] [&M] [🖢] [🛏] [🖼]

**Comfort Inn of Cheyenne** SH
(307) 638-7202. **$59-$99.** 2245 Etchepare Dr. I-25, exit 7, just w. Int corridors. **Pets:** Accepted.

[SAVE] [S&] [X] [&M] [📶] [🛏] [🖼] [🏊]

**Days Inn Cheyenne** SH
(307) 778-8877. **$60-$85, 14 day notice.** 2360 W Lincolnway. I-25, exit 9, just e. Int corridors. **Pets:** Medium, other species. $10 one-time fee/room. Designated rooms, service with restrictions, crate.

[SAVE] [X] [📶] [🖢] [🛏] [🖼] [X]

**Express Inn** SH
(307) 632-7556. **$40-$75.** 2512 W Lincolnway. I-25, exit 9, just e. Int corridors. **Pets:** Accepted.

[SAVE] [X] [&M] [🛏] [🏊]

**Fleetwood Motel** M ☼
(307) 638-8908. **$47-$59, 30 day notice.** 3800 E Lincolnway. I-80, exit 364, 1.2 mi n on N College Dr (SR 212), then just w on I-80/US 30 business loop. Ext corridors. **Pets:** Medium. $5 daily fee/pet. Service with restrictions, supervision.

[SAVE] [S&] [X] [🛏] [🏊]

**Holiday Inn Cheyenne Dream in the West** SH
(307) 638-4466. **$99-$209.** 204 W Fox Farm Rd. I-80, exit 362, just s. Int corridors. **Pets:** $25 one-time fee/room. Service with restrictions, supervision.

[SAVE] [S&] [X] [&M] [🖢] [🛏] [🖼] [🍴] [🏊] [X]

**La Quinta Inn Cheyenne** SH
(307) 632-7117. **$79-$129.** 2410 W Lincolnway. I-25, exit 9, just e. Int corridors. **Pets:** Medium. Service with restrictions.

[SAVE] [X] [&M] [📶] [🛏] [🖼] [🏊]

**Nagle Warren Mansion B & B** BB
(307) 637-3333. **$118-$168, 3 day notice.** 222 E 17th St. I-80, exit 362, 1.2 mi n on I-25 business loop/US 85/87 business route, then just e; jct House St; downtown. Int corridors. **Pets:** Medium. $20 daily fee/room. Designated rooms.

[SAVE] [X] [🖢] [X]

**Oak Tree Inn** SH
(307) 778-6620. **$70-$150.** 1625 Stillwater. 1.2 mi e of jct Dell Range Blvd and Yellowstone Rd, 0.4 mi s. Ext/int corridors. **Pets:** Small. $10 one-time fee/pet. Service with restrictions, supervision.

[SAVE] [S&] [X] [🛏] [🍴]

**The Plains Hotel** SH ☼
(307) 638-3311. **$89-$349.** 1600 Central Ave. I-80, exit 362, 1 mi n on I-180/I-25 business loop/US 85/87 business route, then just w on I-80 business loop/US 30; downtown. Int corridors. **Pets:** Medium. $25 one-time fee/room. Service with restrictions, supervision.

[ASK] [X] [&M] [🛏] [🖼] [🍴]

**Porch Swing Bed & Breakfast** BB ☼
(307) 778-7182. **$85.** 502 E 24th St. I-80, exit 362, 1.8 mi n on I-25 business loop/US 85/87 business route, then just e; downtown. Int corridors. **Pets:** Large, other species. Service with restrictions, supervision.

[X] [AC]

**Windy Hills Guest House** BB ☼
(307) 632-6423. **$99-$200, 7 day notice.** 393 Happy Jack Rd. I-25, exit 10B, 22 mi w on SR 210 (Happy Jack Rd), then 1 mi s on private gravel road. Ext corridors. **Pets:** Other species. $50 deposit/pet. Designated rooms, no service, crate.

[ASK] [S&] [X] [🛏] [🖼] [X] [AC]

# CHUGWATER

**Super 8 Motel-Chugwater** EH
(307) 422-3248. **$46-$76.** 100 Buffalo Dr. I-25, exit 54, just ne. Int corridors. **Pets:** Medium. $10 daily fee/pet. Designated rooms, service with restrictions, supervision.

[ASK] [S&] [X] [🍴] [🏊]

# CODY

**Beartooth Inn of Cody** SH
(307) 527-5505. **$59-$159.** 2513 Greybull Hwy. 1.5 mi e on US 14/16/20. Ext/int corridors. **Pets:** Medium, dogs only. Designated rooms, service with restrictions, supervision.

[SAVE] [S&] [X] [🛏] [🖼] [X]

**Best Western Sunset Motor Inn** SH
(307) 587-4265. **$59-$155.** 1601 8th St. 1.8 mi w on US 14/16/20. Ext corridors. **Pets:** Medium, dogs only. $25 one-time fee/pet. Designated rooms, service with restrictions, crate.

[SAVE] [S&] [X] [📶] [🛏] [🖼] [🍴] [🏊] [X]

**Big Bear Motel** M ☼
(307) 587-3117. **$44-$84.** 139 W Yellowstone Ave. 2 mi w on US 14/16/20, from city center. Ext corridors. **Pets:** Other species. $10 daily fee/pet. Designated rooms, supervision.

[SAVE] [X] [🛏] [🖼] [🏊] [🐾]

**Cody Motor Lodge** 🅰 ☼
(307) 527-6291. **$55-$115.** 1455 Sheridan Ave. Just w on US 14/16/20 and SR 120. Int corridors. **Pets:** Other species. Designated rooms, service with restrictions, supervision.

[SAVE] [S&] [X]

**Green Gables Inn** M
(307) 587-6886. **$54-$108.** 1636 Central Ave. Just e on US 14/16/20 and SR 120. Ext corridors. **Pets:** Dogs only. $25 deposit/room. Service with restrictions, supervision.

[SAVE] [S&] [X] [X]

**Skyline Motor Inn** M
(307) 587-4201. **$42-$76.** 1919 17th St. 0.8 mi e on US 14/16/20 and SR 120. Ext corridors. **Pets:** Accepted.

[SAVE] [X]

ⓐⓐⓐ ▼▼▼ **Sunrise Motor Inn** Ⓜ
(307) 587-5566. **$44-$145.** 1407 8th St. 0.8 mi w on US 14/16/20. Ext corridors. **Pets:** Medium. $10 one-time fee/room. Service with restrictions, supervision.
(SAVE) Ⓢⓓ ⓧ ⓩ ⓘ ⓐ

## DOUGLAS

ⓐⓐⓐ ▼▼▼ **Best Western Douglas Inn & Conference Center** 🅢🅗 ☙
(307) 358-9790. **$79-$99.** 1450 Riverbend Dr. I-25, exit 140, 0.8 mi e. Int corridors. **Pets:** Large, other species. $15 one-time fee/room. Designated rooms, service with restrictions, supervision.
(SAVE) Ⓢⓓ ⓧ ⓛⓜ ⓩ ⓘ ⓘ ⓘ ⓘ ⓐ ⓧ

ⓐⓐⓐ ▼▼▼▼ **Holiday Inn Express Hotel & Suites** 🅢🅗
(307) 358-4500. **$79-$109.** 900 W Yellowstone Hwy. I-25, exit 140, 0.5 mi e. Int corridors. **Pets:** Small. $20 daily fee/pet. Designated rooms, service with restrictions, supervision.
(SAVE) Ⓢⓓ ⓧ ⓛⓜ ⓩ ⓔ ⓘ ⓘ ⓐ

## DUBOIS

▼▼ **Bald Mountain Inn** Ⓜ
(307) 455-2844. **$52-$80, 3 day notice.** 1349 W Ramshorn St. 1.6 mi w on US 26 and 287. Ext corridors. **Pets:** Dogs only. $7 daily fee/pet. Supervision.
(ASK) Ⓢⓓ ⓧ ⓘ ⓘ ⓧ Ⓚ

ⓐⓐⓐ ▼ **Branding Iron Inn** Ⓒⓐ ☙
(307) 455-2893. **$40-$90.** 401 W Ramshorn St. 0.3 mi w on US 26 and 287. Ext corridors. **Pets:** Other species. $5 one-time fee/room. Supervision.
(SAVE) Ⓢⓓ ⓧ ⓘ ⓘ Ⓚ

▼ **Chinook Winds Mt. Lodge** Ⓜ
(307) 455-2987. **$45-$75.** 640 S First St. 0.8 mi e on US 26 and 287; center. Ext corridors. **Pets:** Accepted.
(ASK) Ⓢⓓ ⓧ ⓘ ⓘ ⓧ Ⓚ

▼ **Riverside Inn & Campground** Ⓜ
(307) 455-2337. **$45-$54.** 5810 US Hwy 26. 3 mi e on US 26 and 287. Ext corridors. **Pets:** Medium, dogs only. $5 daily fee/pet. Designated rooms, supervision.
Ⓢⓓ ⓧ ⓘ ⓘ ⓘ ⓧ Ⓚ Ⓦ Ⓩ

ⓐⓐⓐ ▼▼▼ **Stagecoach Motor Inn** 🅢🅗 ☙
(307) 455-2303. **$48-$80.** 103 Ramshorn St. On US 26 and 287; center. Ext corridors. **Pets:** Medium, dogs only. $10 daily fee/pet. Designated rooms, no service, supervision.
(SAVE) ⓧ ⓔ ⓘ ⓘ ⓘ ⓐ ⓧ Ⓚ

## EVANSTON

▼▼◆ **Comfort Inn** 🅢🅗
(307) 789-7799. **$79-$109.** 1931 Harrison Dr. I-80, exit 3 (Harrison Dr), just n. Int corridors. **Pets:** Accepted.
(ASK) Ⓢⓓ ⓧ ⓔ ⓘ ⓘ ⓘ

ⓐⓐⓐ ▼▼▼ **Days Inn** 🅢🅗
(307) 789-0783. **$63-$99.** 1983 Harrison Dr. I-80, exit 3, just n. Int corridors. **Pets:** $10 daily fee/pet. Designated rooms, no service, supervision.
(SAVE) Ⓢⓓ ⓧ ⓘ ⓘ ⓘ ⓐ

ⓐⓐⓐ ▼ **Prairie Inn** Ⓜ
(307) 789-2920. **$55-$70.** 264 Bear River Dr. I-80, exit 6, 0.3 mi n. Ext/int corridors. **Pets:** Small. $6 daily fee/pet. Designated rooms, service with restrictions, supervision.
(SAVE) ⓧ ⓘ

## EVANSVILLE

▼▼ **Comfort Inn by Choice Hotels-Casper** 🅢🅗
(307) 235-3038. **$85-$105.** 480 Lathrop Rd. I-25, exit 185, just e. Int corridors. **Pets:** Accepted.
(ASK) Ⓢⓓ ⓧ ⓛⓜ ⓩ ⓔ ⓘ ⓘ ⓐ

▼◆▼ **Super 8 East Casper** 🅢🅗 ☙
(307) 237-8100. **$99-$119.** 269 Miracle Dr. I-25, exit 185, just e. Int corridors. **Pets:** Service with restrictions, supervision.
(ASK) Ⓢⓓ ⓧ ⓔ ⓘ ⓘ ⓐ

## GILLETTE

ⓐⓐⓐ ▼◆▼ **Best Western Tower West Lodge** 🅢🅗
(307) 686-2210. **$54-$199.** 109 N US Hwy 14-16. I-90, exit 124, just n. Int corridors. **Pets:** Medium, other species. $15 daily fee/pet. Designated rooms, service with restrictions, supervision.
(SAVE) Ⓢⓓ ⓧ ⓔ ⓘ ⓘ ⓘ ⓘ ⓐ ⓧ

ⓐⓐⓐ ▼ **Budget Inn Express** Ⓜ
(307) 686-1989. **$39-$99.** 2011 Rodgers Dr. I-90, exit 124, just n. Int corridors. **Pets:** $5 daily fee/pet. Designated rooms, service with restrictions, supervision.
(SAVE) Ⓢⓓ ⓧ ⓘ ⓐ

▼▼ **Clarion Hotel & Convention Center** 🅢🅗
(307) 686-3000. **$77-$153.** 2009 S Douglas Hwy 59. I-90, exit 126, just se. Ext/int corridors. **Pets:** Accepted.
(ASK) Ⓢⓓ ⓧ ⓩ ⓘ ⓘ ⓘ ⓐ ⓧ

▼◆▼ **Comfort Inn & Suites of Gillette** 🅢🅗
(307) 685-2223. **$89-$209.** 1607 W 2nd Ave. I-90, exit 124, just ne. Int corridors. **Pets:** Accepted.
(ASK) Ⓢⓓ ⓧ ⓛⓜ ⓔ ⓘ ⓘ ⓐ

▼▼▼ **Holiday Inn Express Hotel & Suites** 🅢🅗
(307) 686-9576. **$89-$189.** 1908 Cliff Davis Dr. I-90, exit 126. Int corridors. **Pets:** Accepted.
(ASK) ⓧ ⓛⓜ ⓩ ⓔ ⓘ ⓘ ⓐ ⓧ

## GLENROCK

▼ **All American Inn** Ⓜ
(307) 436-2772. **$42-$57.** 500 W Aspen. I-25, exit 165, 2.2 mi n. Ext corridors. **Pets:** Accepted.
(ASK) Ⓢⓓ ⓧ ⓘ

## GRAND TETON NATIONAL PARK

ⓐⓐⓐ ▼◆▼ **Flagg Ranch Resort** 🄻🄷
(307) 543-2861. **$155-$170, 7 day notice.** US 89 and 191; 2 mi s of Yellowstone National Park south entrance; 5 mi n of Grand Teton National park north entrance. Ext corridors. **Pets:** $10 daily fee/pet. Service with restrictions, crate.
(SAVE) ⓧ ⓛⓜ ⓩ ⓔ ⓘ ⓘ ⓘ ⓧ Ⓚ Ⓦ

▼▼▼ **Jackson Lake Lodge** 🄻🄷
(307) 543-2811. **$141-$575, 7 day notice.** 5 mi nw of Moran at jct US 89 and 287. Ext/int corridors. **Pets:** $10 daily fee/room. Designated rooms, service with restrictions.
ⓧ ⓛⓜ ⓩ ⓔ ⓘ ⓘ ⓘ ⓐ ⓧ Ⓚ Ⓦ

▼▼ **Signal Mountain Lodge** 🅢🅗 ☙
(307) 543-2831. **$99-$280, 7 day notice.** Teton Park Rd, 2 mi s of US 89, 191 and 287. Ext corridors. **Pets:** Other species. $10 daily fee/room. Designated rooms, service with restrictions, crate.
ⓧ ⓘ ⓘ ⓘ ⓧ Ⓚ Ⓦ

ⓐⓐⓐ ▼▼▼ **Togwotee Mountain Lodge** Ⓒⓐ
(307) 543-2847. **$109-$209, 7 day notice.** 16.5 mi e of Moran at jct US 26 and 287. Ext/int corridors. **Pets:** Other species. $20 one-time fee/pet. Designated rooms, crate.
(SAVE) Ⓢⓓ ⓧ ⓘ ⓘ ⓘ ⓧ

# GREEN RIVER

**Coachman Inn Motel** M
(307) 875-3681. **$62-$72.** 470 E Flaming Gorge Way. I-80, exit 91, just w on I-80 business loop. Ext corridors. **Pets:** Accepted.

**Oak Tree Inn** SH
(307) 875-3500. **$63-$77.** 1170 W Flaming Gorge Way. I-80, exit 89, just s. Ext/int corridors. **Pets:** Medium. $5 daily fee/pet. Service with restrictions, supervision.

# GUERNSEY

**The Bunkhouse Motel** M
(307) 836-2356. **$52-$60, 7 day notice.** 350 W Whalen. On US 26; center. Ext corridors. **Pets:** $10 daily fee/pet. Designated rooms, service with restrictions, supervision.

# JACKSON

**49'er Inn and Suites (Quality Inn and Suites)** SH
(307) 733-7550. **$64-$209, 14 day notice.** 330 W Pearl St. Just w and just s of town square. Ext/int corridors. **Pets:** Service with restrictions, supervision.

**Antler Inn** SH
(307) 733-2535. **$82-$160.** 43 W Pearl St. Just s of town square. Ext/int corridors. **Pets:** Dogs only. Service with restrictions, supervision.

**Cowboy Village Resort** CA
(307) 733-3121. **$80-$225.** 120 S Flat Creek Dr. 0.3 mi w on Broadway to Flat Creek Dr, just s; downtown. Ext corridors. **Pets:** Service with restrictions, supervision.

**Elk Country Inn** M
(307) 733-2364. **$60-$156.** 480 W Pearl St. Just w, then just s of town square. Ext/int corridors. **Pets:** Other species. Designated rooms, service with restrictions, supervision.

**Jackson Hole Lodge** SH
(307) 733-2992. **$79-$124, 15 day notice.** 420 W Broadway. 0.3 mi w on US 26/89/191. Ext corridors. **Pets:** Medium. $50 deposit/room. Designated rooms, no service, supervision.

**Painted Buffalo Inn** SH
(307) 733-4340. **$69-$159.** 400 W Broadway. Just w of town square. Ext corridors. **Pets:** Large, other species. $15 one-time fee/room. Service with restrictions, supervision.

**Snow King Resort** LH
(307) 733-5200. **$150-$750.** 400 E Snow King Ave. Just se of town square. Ext/int corridors. **Pets:** Accepted.

**Virginian Lodge** SH
(307) 733-2792. **$55-$195.** 750 W Broadway. Just w. Ext/int corridors. **Pets:** Large. $10 daily fee/room. Designated rooms, service with restrictions, supervision.

# LANDER

**Budget Host Pronghorn Lodge** SH
(307) 332-3940. **$78-$125, 14 day notice.** 150 E Main St. Just n of jct US 287 and SR 789. Ext corridors. **Pets:** Accepted.

**Holiday Lodge** M
(307) 332-2511. **$50-$65.** 210 McFarlane Dr. Just e of jct US 287 and SR 789. Ext corridors. **Pets:** Dogs only. $10 daily fee/pet. Designated rooms, service with restrictions, supervision.

**Silver Spur Motel** M
(307) 332-5189. **$45-$60.** 1240 W Main St. 1.5 mi n on US 287. Ext corridors. **Pets:** $100 deposit/room, $10 daily fee/room. Service with restrictions, supervision.

# LARAMIE

**1st Inn Gold** SH
(307) 742-3721. **$54-$70.** 421 Boswell. I-80, exit 313, just n on US 287. Ext/int corridors. **Pets:** Accepted.

**Days Inn** SH
(307) 745-5678. **$79-$120.** 1368 McCue St. I-80, exit 310, just e. Int corridors. **Pets:** Medium. $15 daily fee/pet. Designated rooms, service with restrictions, supervision.

**Gas Lite Inn Motel** M
(307) 742-6616. **$46-$66.** 960 N 3rd St. I-80, exit 313, 1.6 mi n on US 287; downtown. Ext corridors. **Pets:** Other species. $5 daily fee/pet. Service with restrictions, supervision.

**Howard Johnson Inn** SH
(307) 742-8371. **$79-$110, 7 day notice.** 1555 Snowy Range Rd. I-80, exit 311, just s. Ext corridors. **Pets:** Accepted.

**Sunset Inn** M
(307) 742-3741. **$45-$75.** 1104 S 3rd St. I-80, exit 313, just n on US 287. Ext corridors. **Pets:** Medium, other species. $100 deposit/room. Designated rooms, service with restrictions, supervision.

**Travelodge Downtown** M
(307) 742-6671. **$55-$95.** 165 N 3rd St. I-80, exit 313, 1 mi n on US 287; downtown. Ext corridors. **Pets:** Other species. $50 deposit/pet. Designated rooms, service with restrictions, supervision.

# LUSK

**Town House Motel, LLC** M
(307) 334-2376. **$44-$60.** 525 S Main St. Just n of jct US 20/85. Ext corridors. **Pets:** Other species. $5 daily fee/room. Service with restrictions.

# NEWCASTLE

**Auto Inn Motel** M
(307) 746-2734. **$48-$69.** 2503 W Main St. West end of town on US 16. Ext corridors. **Pets:** $6 daily fee/pet. Designated rooms, no service, crate.

**Pines Motel** M
(307) 746-4334. **$55-$140.** 248 E Wentworth St. Just e from Summit St (US Business Rt 16); downtown. Ext corridors. **Pets:** Accepted.

**(AAA) ▼ Sage Motel M**
(307) 746-2724. **$44-$68, 3 day notice.** 1227 S Summit Ave. 0.3 mi s of jct US 16 on US 85, just w. Ext corridors. **Pets:** Small, other species. $5 daily fee/pet. Designated rooms, service with restrictions, supervision.
[SAVE] [S🐾] [✕] [🖥] [💻]

# PAINTER

**▼ Hunter Peak Ranch RA**
(307) 587-3711. **$130, 90 day notice.** 4027 Crandall Rd. SR 296, 5 mi s of US 212; 40 mi n of SR 120. Ext corridors. **Pets:** Dogs only. $15 daily fee/pet. Designated rooms, supervision.
[✕] [🖥] [💻] [🍴] [✕] [🎿] [🏊] [🎾]

# PINEDALE

**(AAA) ▼▼ Best Western Pinedale Inn SH**
(307) 367-6869. **$80-$150.** 850 W Pine St. 0.5 mi n on US 191. Int corridors. **Pets:** Designated rooms, service with restrictions, supervision.
[SAVE] [S🐾] [✕] [🖥] [💻] [🏊]

**▼▼ Lakeside Lodge Resort & Marina CA**
(307) 367-2221. **$75-$159, 3 day notice.** 99 Forest Rd 111. 5 mi ne from US 191; on Fremont Lake. Ext corridors. **Pets:** Dogs only. Supervision.
[✕] [🖥] [💻] [🍴] [✕] [🎿] [🎾]

**▼▼ The Lodge at Pinedale SH**
(307) 367-8800. **$59-$109.** 1054 W Pine St. 0.7 mi n on US 191. Int corridors. **Pets:** Medium. $10 daily fee/pet. Designated rooms.
[✕] [🖥] [🏊]

**(AAA) ▼ Sun Dance Motel M**
(307) 367-4336. **$55-$140.** 148 E Pine St. US 191; city center. Ext corridors. **Pets:** Other species. $5 daily fee/pet. Service with restrictions, supervision.
[SAVE] [S🐾] [✕] [🖥] [💻] [🎿]

# POWELL

**(AAA) ▼▼ Kings Inn M**
(307) 754-5117. **$58-$77.** 777 E 2nd St. 0.3 mi e on US 14A. Ext corridors. **Pets:** Accepted.
[SAVE] [S🐾] [✕] [🖥] [💻] [🏊]

**(AAA) ▼ Park Motel M**
(307) 754-2233. **$55-$100.** 737 E 2nd St. 0.4 mi e on US 14A. Ext corridors. **Pets:** Small, dogs only. $5 daily fee/pet. Designated rooms, no service, supervision.
[SAVE] [✕] [🖥]

# RAWLINS

**(AAA) ▼▼ Best Western CottonTree Inn SH**
(307) 324-2737. **$89-$129, 14 day notice.** 2221 W Spruce St. I-80, exit 211, just n. Ext/int corridors. **Pets:** Other species. $10 daily fee/room. Designated rooms, service with restrictions, supervision.
[SAVE] [S🐾] [✕] [🖥] [💻] [🍴] [🏊] [✕]

**(AAA) ▼▼ Quality Inn SH**
(307) 324-2783. **$74-$94.** 1801 E Cedar. I-80, exit 215, just w of jct US 287. Int corridors. **Pets:** Accepted.
[SAVE] [S🐾] [✕] [🖥] [💻] [🍴] [🏊]

# RIVERTON

**▼▼ Days Inn SH**
(307) 856-9677. **$52-$89.** 909 W Main St. 0.5 mi nw on US 26. Ext corridors. **Pets:** $10 daily fee/pet. Service with restrictions, supervision.
[ASK] [S🐾] [✕] [♿] [🖥]

**(AAA) ▼▼▼ Holiday Inn Convention Center SH** 🐾
(307) 856-8100. **$69-$119.** 900 E Sunset Dr. 0.8 mi ne on US 26/SR 789. Int corridors. **Pets:** Other species. $20 one-time fee/room. Designated rooms, service with restrictions, crate.
[SAVE] [S🐾] [✕] [♿M] [🖥] [💻] [🍴] [🏊]

**▼ Paintbrush Motel M**
(307) 856-9238. **$52-$56.** 1550 N Federal Blvd. 1.3 mi ne on US 26/SR 789. Ext corridors. **Pets:** Medium, dogs only. $10 one-time fee/pet. Designated rooms, service with restrictions, supervision.
[ASK] [✕] [🖥] [💻]

**▼ Super 8 Motel SH**
(307) 857-2400. **$50-$80.** 1040 N Federal Blvd. 1 mi ne on US 26/SR 789. Int corridors. **Pets:** Other species. $5 daily fee/pet. Service with restrictions, supervision.
[ASK] [S🐾] [✕] [🖥]

# ROCK SPRINGS

**▼▼▼ Comfort Inn SH** 🐾
(307) 382-9490. **$79-$89.** 1670 Sunset Dr. I-80, exit 102 (Dewar Dr), 0.3 mi s, then just w. Ext corridors. **Pets:** Other species. $10 one-time fee/pet. Designated rooms, supervision.
[ASK] [S🐾] [✕] [♿] [🖥] [💻] [🏊] [✕]

**▼▼ Econo Lodge SH**
(307) 382-4217. **$50-$95.** 1635 Elk St. I-80, exit 104 (Elk St), just n. Ext corridors. **Pets:** Accepted.
[ASK] [S🐾] [✕] [🖥] [💻] [🏊]

**▼▼▼ Holiday Inn SH**
(307) 382-9200. **$99-$125.** 1675 Sunset Dr. I-80, exit 102 (Dewar Dr), 0.3 mi sw. Ext/int corridors. **Pets:** Other species. $10 daily fee/room. Designated rooms, service with restrictions, crate.
[ASK] [S🐾] [✕] [🚗] [♿] [🖥] [💻] [🍴] [✕]

**▼▼▼ La Quinta Inn SH**
(307) 362-1770. **$109-$159.** 2717 Dewar Dr. I-80, exit 102 (Dewar Dr), just n. Int corridors. **Pets:** Other species. Designated rooms, service with restrictions, supervision.
[ASK] [S🐾] [✕] [🚗] [🖥] [💻] [🏊]

**▼ Motel 6–#395 M**
(307) 362-1850. **$43-$58.** 2615 Commercial Way. I-80, exit 102 (Dewar Dr), n to Foothills Blvd, then just e. Ext corridors. **Pets:** Accepted.
[S🐾] [✕] [♿] [🖥] [🏊]

**(AAA) ▼ Springs Motel M**
(307) 362-6683. **$55-$62.** 1525 9th St. I-80, exit 107, 0.3 mi w. Ext corridors. **Pets:** Accepted.
[SAVE] [S🐾] [✕]

# SARATOGA

**▼ Hacienda Motel M**
(307) 326-5751. **$59-$79.** 1500 S First St. 0.5 mi s on SR 130. Int corridors. **Pets:** $5 daily fee/pet. Designated rooms, service with restrictions, supervision.
[ASK] [S🐾] [✕] [🖥]

# SHERIDAN

**(AAA) ▼ Americas Best Value Inn M** 🐾
(307) 672-9757. **$49-$88.** 580 E 5th St. I-90, exit 23, 0.4 mi w. Ext corridors. **Pets:** Other species. $50 deposit/room. Designated rooms, service with restrictions, supervision.
[SAVE] [✕] [🖥]

**(AAA) ▼▼▼ Best Western Sheridan Center SH**
(307) 674-7421. **$74-$129.** 612 N Main St. I-90, exit 20, 1.7 mi s. Ext/int corridors. **Pets:** Small. $20 one-time fee/room. Designated rooms, no service, supervision.
[SAVE] [✕] [🚗] [🖥] [💻] [🍴] [🏊]

**(AAA) ▼ Budget Host Inn M**
(307) 674-7496. **$59-$79.** 2007 N Main St. I-90, exit 20, 0.7 mi s; on I-90 business loop. Ext corridors. **Pets:** Accepted.
[SAVE] [S🐾] [✕] [🖥] [💻]

**AAA ▼▼▼ Holiday Inn Atrium & Convention Center SH** ✿
(307) 672-8931. **$109-$139.** 1809 Sugarland Dr. I-90, exit 25, 0.3 mi nw. Int corridors. **Pets:** Other species. $50 deposit/room. Service with restrictions, supervision.
SAVE 🔊 ⊠ 🖉 🖉 🛢 🖵 🍴 🌊 ⊠

**AAA ▼▼▼ Mill Inn M** ✿
(307) 672-6401. **$55-$120.** 2161 Coffeen Ave. I-90, exit 25, 0.3 mi w. Ext/int corridors. **Pets:** Medium. $15 daily fee/room. Service with restrictions, crate.
SAVE 🔊 ⊠ 🛢 🖵

# SUNDANCE

**AAA ▼▼▼ Best Western Inn at Sundance SH**
(307) 283-2800. **$51-$121.** 2719 E Cleveland Ave. I-90, exit 189, just n, then just w on I-90 business loop. Int corridors. **Pets:** Other species. $10 daily fee/pet. Supervision.
SAVE 🔊 ⊠ 🛢 🖵 🌊

**AAA ▼▼ Budget Host Arrowhead Motel M**
(307) 283-3307. **$39-$69.** 214 Cleveland Ave. I-90 business loop and US 14. Ext corridors. **Pets:** Dogs only. $20 deposit/room. Service with restrictions, supervision.
SAVE ⊠

**AAA ▼▼▼ Rodeway Sundance Mountain Inn M**
(307) 283-3737. **$49-$149.** 26 SR 585. I-90, exit 187, 0.4 mi n. Ext corridors. **Pets:** Small. $10 daily fee/pet. Designated rooms, service with restrictions, supervision.
SAVE 🔊 ⊠ 🛢 🖵 🌊

# TETON VILLAGE

**▼▼▼ ▼▼▼ Four Seasons Resort Jackson Hole LH** ✿
(307) 732-5000. **$165-$4000, 30 day notice.** 7680 Granite Loop Rd. Located at the base of Jackson Hole Mountain Resort. Int corridors. **Pets:** Small, other species. Service with restrictions, supervision.
⊠ 🕭 🖉 🖉 🛢 🖵 🍴 🌊 ⊠

# THERMOPOLIS

**▼▼▼ Holiday Inn of the Waters SH**
(307) 864-3131. **$85-$139.** 115 E Park St. In Hot Springs State Park. Ext/int corridors. **Pets:** Accepted.
ASK ⊠ 🖉 🖉 🖵 🍴 🌊 ⊠

**▼▼ Hot Springs Super 8 SH**
(307) 864-5515. **$54-$119.** Lane 5, Hwy 20 S. On US 20, just se. Int corridors. **Pets:** Accepted.
ASK 🔊 ⊠ 🕭 🖉 🖉 🛢 🖵 🌊

# TORRINGTON

**▼▼ Holiday Inn Express Hotel & Suites SH**
(307) 532-7600. **$68-$124.** 1700 E Valley Rd. US 85, e on US 26. Int corridors. **Pets:** $15 one-time fee/pet. Designated rooms, service with restrictions, supervision.
ASK 🔊 ⊠ 🕭 🖉 🖉 🛢 🖵 🌊 ⊠

**▼▼ Kings Inn SH**
(307) 532-4011. **$56-$67.** 1555 Main St. Just s of jct US 26/85. Int corridors. **Pets:** Accepted.
ASK 🔊 ⊠ 🛢 🖵 🍴 🌊

**▼▼ Maverick Motel M**
(307) 532-4064. **$42-$46.** 4577 US Hwy 26/85. 1.7 mi w on US 26/85. Ext corridors. **Pets:** $5 one-time fee/pet. Service with restrictions, supervision.
⊠ 🛢 🖵

# UCROSS

**AAA ▼▼▼ The Ranch at Ucross RA**
(307) 737-2281. **$199-$299, 3 day notice.** 2673 US Hwy 14 E. Jct US 14/16, 0.5 mi w on US 14. Ext/int corridors. **Pets:** Accepted.
SAVE ⊠ 🍴 🌊 ⊠ 🕅

# WAPITI

**AAA ▼▼ Green Creek Inn M**
(307) 587-5004. **$40-$75.** 2908 Yellowstone Hwy. 2.8 mi w on US 14/16/20. Ext corridors. **Pets:** Accepted.
SAVE 🔊 ⊠ 🕿

**▼▼ Yellowstone Valley Inn SH**
(307) 587-3961. **$59-$169, 21 day notice.** 3324 Yellowstone Park Hwy. 3.3 mi w on US 14/16/20. Ext corridors. **Pets:** Accepted.
ASK 🔊 ⊠ 🛢 🖵 🍴 🌊 ⊠ 🕿

# WHEATLAND

**AAA ▼▼▼ Best Western Torchlite Motor Inn SH**
(307) 322-4070. **$50-$95.** 1809 N 16th St. I-25, exit 78, just e; 1.5 mi n on US 87/I-25 business loop (16th St). Ext corridors. **Pets:** Other species. $5 one-time fee/pet. Service with restrictions, supervision.
SAVE 🔊 ⊠ 🛢 🖵 🌊

# WORLAND

**▼▼ 🔷 Days Inn M** ✿
(307) 347-4251. **$70-$130.** 500 N 10th St. 0.5 mi n on US 20. Ext corridors. **Pets:** Small. $5 daily fee/pet. Designated rooms, service with restrictions, supervision.
ASK ⊠ 🛢 🖵

# YELLOWSTONE NATIONAL PARK

**AAA ▼▼▼ Elephant Head Lodge CA** ✿
(307) 587-3980. **$117-$150, 30 day notice.** 1170 Yellowstone Hwy. 11.7 mi e of Yellowstone National Park East Gate on US 14/16/20. Ext corridors. **Pets:** Other species. Service with restrictions.
SAVE 🔊 ⊠ 🛢 🖵 🍴 ⊠ 🕅 🕅 🕿

# Canada

# ALBERTA

## CITY INDEX

## ATHABASCA

**▼▼▼▼ Best Western Athabasca Inn** SH
(780) 675-2294. **$99-$109.** 5211 41st Ave. 1 km s on Hwy 2. Int corridors. **Pets:** Accepted.
ASK S X 🖥 💻 ⊺⊺

## BANFF

**▼▼ Banff Rocky Mountain Resort** CO
(403) 762-5531. **$160-$440, 3 day notice.** 1029 Banff Ave. Banff Ave and Tunnel Mountain Rd; just s of Trans-Canada Hwy 1. Ext corridors. **Pets:** Accepted.
ASK S X 🖥 💻 ⊺⊺ ⇌ ✕ ✗

**CAA ▼▼ Best Western Siding 29 Lodge** SH
(403) 762-5575. **$99-$305.** 453 Marten St. 1.3 km ne off Banff Ave. Int corridors. **Pets:** Other species. Service with restrictions, supervision.
SAVE S X 🖥 💻 ⇌

**CAA ▼▼ Castle Mountain Chalets** CA
(403) 762-3868. **$145-$335, 14 day notice.** 32 km w on Trans-Canada Hwy 1, jct Castle, 1 km ne on Hwy 1A (Bow Valley Pkwy). Ext corridors. **Pets:** Accepted.
SAVE X ⟲ 🖥 💻 ✕ ✗ ✆

**CAA ▼▼ ▼▼ The Fairmont Banff Springs** LH
(403) 762-2211. **$233-$593, 3 day notice.** 405 Spray Ave. Just s on Banff Ave over the bridge, 0.5 km e. Int corridors. **Pets:** $25 daily fee/room. Designated rooms, service with restrictions.
SAVE X ⟲ 🖥 💻 ⊺⊺ ⇌ ✕

**▼▼ Johnston Canyon Resort** CA
(403) 762-2971. **$116-$284.** Hwy 1A. 24 km nw on Hwy 1A (Bow Valley Pkwy). Ext corridors. **Pets:** Other species. $10 daily fee/room. Service with restrictions, supervision.
X 🖥 💻 ⊺⊺ ✕ ✗ ✆

**CAA ▼▼▼ Red Carpet Inn** SH
(403) 762-4184. **$69-$179.** 425 Banff Ave. 1 km ne. Ext/int corridors. **Pets:** Accepted.
SAVE S X 🖥 💻

## BROOKS

**▼▼▼ Best Western Brooks Inn** SH
(403) 363-0080. **$99-$149, 30 day notice.** 115 Fifteenth Ave W. Just s off Trans-Canada Hwy 1. Ext/int corridors. **Pets:** Accepted.
ASK S X 🖥 💻 ⇌ ✗

**▼▼ The Douglas Country Inn** 3B
(403) 362-2873. **$80.** Hwy 873, 6.5 km n of jct Trans-Canada Hwy 1. Int corridors. **Pets:** Accepted.
X 🄿 ✆

**▼▼ Heritage Inn** SH
(403) 362-6666. **$97-$99.** 1217 2nd St W. Trans-Canada Hwy 1, exit Hwy 873, 0.8 km s. Int corridors. **Pets:** Accepted.
ASK S X 🖥 💻 ⊺⊺ ✗

**▼▼▼ Holiday Inn Express Hotel & Suites Brooks** SH
(403) 362-7440. **$121-$139.** 1307 2nd S W. Trans-Canada Hwy 1, exit Hwy 873, just s. Int corridors. **Pets:** Accepted.
X 🄿 🖥 💻 ⇌

**▼▼ Travelodge Brooks** SH
(403) 362-8000. **$90-$135.** 1240 Cassils Rd E. Trans-Canada Hwy 1, 0.3 km sw on SR 542, exit E Brooks. Ext/int corridors. **Pets:** Accepted.
ASK S X ⟲M 🖥 💻

---

# CALGARY METROPOLITAN AREA

## AIRDRIE

**CAA ▼▼▼▼ Ramada Inn & Suites** SH
(403) 945-1288. **$114-$289.** 191 Eastlake. Hwy 2, exit E Airdrie, 0.8 km e on Hwy 587 E. Int corridors. **Pets:** Large, other species. $13 daily fee/room. Service with restrictions, supervision.
SAVE S X ⟲M ⟲ 🖥 💻 ⊺⊺ ⇌

**▼▼ Super 8 Motel-Airdrie** SH 🐾
(403) 948-4188. **$74-$90.** 815 E Lake Blvd. Hwy 2, exit E Airdrie, 0.8 km e on Hwy 587 E. Int corridors. **Pets:** Medium, other species. $15 one-time fee/room. Service with restrictions, supervision.
ASK S X 🖥 💻

## CALGARY

**▼▼▼ 5 Calgary Downtown Suites** LH 🐾
(403) 263-0520. **$159-$210.** 618 5th Ave SW. Corner of 5th Ave SW and 5th St SW. Int corridors. **Pets:** Other species. $10 daily fee/pet. Service with restrictions, crate.
ASK S X 🖥 💻 ⊺⊺ ⇌ ✗

**CAA ▼▼▼▼ Best Western Hospitality Inn** SH 🐾
(403) 278-5050. **$129-$209, 5 day notice.** 135 Southland Dr SE. On Hwy 2A (MacLeod Tr); corner of Southland Dr. Int corridors. **Pets:** Medium. Designated rooms, service with restrictions, supervision.
SAVE S X 🖥 💻 ⊺⊺ ⇌ ✗

**▼▼ Best Western Village Park Inn** SH
(403) 289-0241. **$99-$189.** 1804 Crowchild Tr NW. Just ne of jct Trans-Canada Hwy 1 and Crowchild Tr. Int corridors. **Pets:** Accepted.
ASK S X 🄿 🖥 💻 ⊺⊺ ⇌

**▼▼▼▼ Blackfoot Inn 🅂🄷 ❖**
(403) 252-2253. **$99-$235, 60 day notice.** 5940 Blackfoot Tr SE. At 58th Ave SE; access to property from 58th Ave only. Int corridors. **Pets:** Other species. Designated rooms, service with restrictions, crate.

🄰🅂🄺 🅂🄳 ⊠ 🄺 💻 🍴 🌊 ⊠

**🄒🄐 ▼▼▼▼ Calgary Marriott Hotel 🄻🄷**
(403) 266-7331. **$119-$299.** 110 9th Ave SE. Jct 9th Ave and Centre St; attached to Telus Convention Centre. Int corridors. **Pets:** Other species.

🅂🄰🅅🄴 🅂🄳 ⊠ 🄺 🄺 🄷 💻 🍴 🌊 ⊠

**🄒🄐 ▼▼▼▼ Calgary Westways Guest House 🄱🄱 ❖**
(403) 229-1758. **$85-$150, 7 day notice.** 216 25th Ave SW. 1.7 km s on Hwy 2A (MacLeod Tr S), 0.5 km w. Int corridors. **Pets:** Other species. $8 daily fee/pet.

🅂🄰🅅🄴 🅂🄳 ⊠

**🄒🄐 ▼▼ ▼▼ Carriage House Inn 🅂🄷 ❖**
(403) 253-1101. **$95-$135, 3 day notice.** 9030 MacLeod Tr S. On Hwy 2A (MacLeod Tr); corner of 90th Ave SW. Int corridors. **Pets:** Other species. $10 one-time fee/pet. Service with restrictions.

🅂🄰🅅🄴 🅂🄳 ⊠ 🄺 💻 🍴 🌊 ⊠

**▼▼▼▼ Coast Plaza Hotel & Conference Centre 🄻🄷 ❖**
(403) 248-8888. **$169.** 1316 33rd St NE. Just s of jct 16th Ave (Trans-Canada Hwy 1) and 36th St NE, just w on 12th Ave NE. Int corridors. **Pets:** Other species. $25 one-time fee/room. Designated rooms, service with restrictions, supervision.

🄰🅂🄺 🅂🄳 ⊠ 🄼 🄺 🄺 💻 🍴 🌊 ⊠

**▼▼▼▼ Days Inn Calgary Airport 🅂🄷**
(403) 250-3297. **$100-$125.** 2799 Sunridge Way NE. Barlow Tr, just e of Sunridge Way NE. Int corridors. **Pets:** Medium, dogs only. $10 one-time fee/pet. Designated rooms, service with restrictions, crate.

🄰🅂🄺 🅂🄳 ⊠ 🄼 💻 🌊 ⊠

**🄒🄐 ▼▼ ▼▼ Days Inn Calgary South 🅂🄷 ❖**
(403) 243-5531. **$79-$169.** 3828 MacLeod Tr S. Corner of MacLeod Tr and 38th Ave SE. Int corridors. **Pets:** Other species. $10 daily fee/pet. Service with restrictions, supervision.

🅂🄰🅅🄴 🅂🄳 ⊠ 🄺 💻 🌊 ⊠

**▼▼▼▼ Delta Bow Valley 🄻🄷 ❖**
(403) 266-1980. **$206-$296.** 209 4th Ave SE. 1st St SE and 4th Ave SE. Int corridors. **Pets:** $35 one-time fee/pet. Service with restrictions.

🄰🅂🄺 🅂🄳 ⊠ 🄺 🍴 🌊 ⊠

**▼▼▼▼ Delta Calgary Airport 🄻🄷 ❖**
(403) 291-2600. **$125-$242.** 2001 Airport Rd NE. At Calgary International Airport. Int corridors. **Pets:** Large. $35 one-time fee/room. Service with restrictions, supervision.

⊠ 🄺 💻 🍴 🌊 ⊠

**🄒🄐 ▼▼ ▼▼ Econo Lodge South 🄼**
(403) 252-4401. **$89-$119.** 7505 MacLeod Tr S. Corner of MacLeod Tr and 75th Ave. Ext/int corridors. **Pets:** Medium. $10 daily fee/room. Designated rooms, service with restrictions, supervision.

🅂🄰🅅🄴 🅂🄳 ⊠ 🄺 💻 🌊 ⊠

**▼▼▼▼ Executive Royal Inn North Calgary 🅂🄷**
(403) 291-2003. **$110-$165.** 2828 23rd St NE. 27th Ave NE and Barlow Tr. Int corridors. **Pets:** Accepted.

🄰🅂🄺 🅂🄳 ⊠ 🄼 🄺 💻 🍴 ⊠

**▼▼▼▼ The Fairmont Palliser 🄻🄷**
(403) 262-1234. **$239-$399.** 133 9th Ave SW. 9th Ave SW and 1st St SW. Int corridors. **Pets:** Accepted.

🄰🅂🄺 🅂🄳 ⊠ 💻 🍴 🌊 ⊠

**🄒🄐 ▼▼▼▼ Greenwood Inn Hotels 🅂🄷**
(403) 250-8855. **$119-$159.** 3515 26th St NE. From Barlow Tr N, just e on 32nd Ave NE, then just n. Int corridors. **Pets:** Other species. $10 daily fee/room. Service with restrictions, supervision.

🅂🄰🅅🄴 🅂🄳 ⊠ 🄺 🄺 💻 🍴 🌊 ⊠

**🄒🄐 ▼▼▼▼ Holiday Inn Calgary-Airport 🅂🄷**
(403) 230-1999. **$99-$199.** 1250 McKinnon Dr NE. 1 km e of jct Hwy 2 (Deerfoot Tr) and 16th Ave NE (Trans-Canada Hwy 1). Int corridors. **Pets:** Small. $10 daily fee/pet. Designated rooms, service with restrictions, supervision.

🅂🄰🅅🄴 🅂🄳 ⊠ 🄺 💻 🍴 🌊

**🄒🄐 ▼▼▼▼ Holiday Inn Express Calgary-University 🅂🄷**
(403) 289-6600. **$110-$220.** 2227 Banff Tr NW. 16th Ave (Trans-Canada Hwy 1) and Banff Tr NW. Int corridors. **Pets:** Other species. Designated rooms, service with restrictions, supervision.

🅂🄰🅅🄴 ⊠ 🄼 🄺 🄺 💻

**🄒🄐 ▼▼▼▼ Holiday Inn Express Hotel & Suites Calgary Downtown 🅂🄷**
(403) 269-8262. **$149-$289.** 1020 8th Ave SW. 8th Ave at 10th St SW. Int corridors. **Pets:** Accepted.

🅂🄰🅅🄴 🅂🄳 ⊠ 🄺 💻

**▼▼▼▼ Holiday Inn Express Hotel & Suites Calgary-South 🅂🄷**
(403) 225-3000. **$127-$199.** 12025 Lake Fraser Dr SE (MacLeod Tr S). Hwy 2 (Deerfoot Tr), exit Anderson Rd w, then just s on MacLeod Tr. Int corridors. **Pets:** Accepted.

🄰🅂🄺 🅂🄳 ⊠ 🄺 💻 🌊 ⊠

**🄒🄐 ▼▼▼▼ Hotel Arts 🅂🄷**
(403) 266-4611. **$119-$349.** 119 12th Ave SW. At 1st St SW; centre. Int corridors. **Pets:** Accepted.

🅂🄰🅅🄴 ⊠ 🄼 🄺 🄺 💻 🍴 🌊

**▼▼ ▼▼ International Hotel of Calgary 🄻🄷**
(403) 265-9600. **$229-$259.** 220 4th Ave SW. Corner of 4th Ave and 2nd St SW. Int corridors. **Pets:** Accepted.

🄰🅂🄺 🅂🄳 ⊠ 🄺 💻 🍴 🌊 ⊠

**▼▼▼▼ Marriott Residence Inn-Calgary Airport 🅂🄷**
(403) 735-3336. **$129-$219, 10 day notice.** 2622 39th Ave NE. Corner of Barlow Tr and 39th Ave NE. Int corridors. **Pets:** Small, other species. $100 one-time fee/pet. Service with restrictions.

🄰🅂🄺 ⊠ 🄼 🄺 🄺 💻 🌊 ⊠

**🄒🄐 ▼▼ ▼▼ Quality Inn University 🅂🄷**
(403) 289-1973. **$80-$169.** 2359 Banff Tr NW. Just n of jct Trans-Canada Hwy 1 and Crowchild Tr. Ext/int corridors. **Pets:** Medium. $10 daily fee/pet. Designated rooms, service with restrictions, supervision.

🅂🄰🅅🄴 🅂🄳 ⊠ 🄺 💻 🍴 🌊

**▼▼▼▼ Radisson Hotel Calgary Airport 🅂🄷**
(403) 291-4666. **$149-$249.** 2120 16th Ave NE. 0.5 km e of jct 16th Ave NE (Trans-Canada Hwy 1) and Hwy 2 (Deerfoot Tr). Int corridors. **Pets:** Accepted.

🄰🅂🄺 🅂🄳 ⊠ 🄼 🄺 💻 🍴 🌊

**▼▼▼▼ Sandman Hotel Downtown Calgary 🄻🄷**
(403) 237-8626. **$129-$200.** 888 7th Ave SW. Corner of 7th Ave SW and 8th St SW. Int corridors. **Pets:** Medium. $10 daily fee/room. Designated rooms, service with restrictions, supervision.

🄰🅂🄺 🅂🄳 ⊠ 🄺 💻 🍴 🌊

**▼▼▼▼ Sandman Hotel Suites & Spa Calgary Airport 🅂🄷**
(403) 219-2475. **$109-$169.** 25 Hopewell Way NE. Just n of jct Barlow Tr and McKnight Blvd. Int corridors. **Pets:** Medium. $10 one-time fee/room. Service with restrictions, supervision.

🄰🅂🄺 🅂🄳 ⊠ 🄺 💻 🍴 🌊 ⊠

**▼▼▼▼ Sheraton Cavalier Hotel 🄻🄷**
(403) 291-0107. **$269, 3 day notice.** 2620 32nd Ave NE. Barlow Tr at 32nd Ave NE. Int corridors. **Pets:** Accepted.

🄰🅂🄺 ⊠ 💻 🍴 🌊 ⊠

(CAA) ▼▼▼ ▼▼▼ Sheraton Suites Calgary Eau Claire LH
(403) 266-7200. **$165-$474.** 255 Barclay Parade SW. At 3rd St SW and 2nd Ave SW. Int corridors. **Pets:** Accepted.

SAVE 🔽 ✕ 🔾 🛏 💳 🍴 🏊 🐾

(CAA) ▼▼▼ Super 8 Motel Calgary Airport SH
(403) 291-9888. **$70-$200.** 3030 Barlow Tr NE. Corner of 32nd Ave and Barlow Tr NE. Int corridors. **Pets:** Small, dogs only. $20 daily fee/pet. Service with restrictions, supervision.

SAVE 🔽 ✕ 🛏

▼▼▼ Travelodge Hotel Calgary Airport SH 🐾
(403) 291-1260. **$97-$149.** 2750 Sunridge Blvd NE. Just se of jct 32nd Ave NE and Barlow Tr NE. Int corridors. **Pets:** Large, other species. Service with restrictions, crate.

ASK 🔽 ✕ 🛏 💳 🍴 🏊

▼▼▼ Travelodge Hotel Calgary Macleod Trail SH 🐾
(403) 253-7070. **$90-$159.** 9206 MacLeod Tr S. On Hwy 2 (Deerfoot Tr) at 90th Ave SW. Int corridors. **Pets:** Large, other species. $15 one-time fee/room. Designated rooms, service with restrictions, crate.

ASK 🔽 ✕ 🛏 💳 🍴 🏊

(CAA) ▼▼▼ ▼▼▼ The Westin Calgary LH 🐾
(403) 266-1611. **$115-$329.** 320 4th Ave SW. Corner of 4th Ave SW and 3rd St. Int corridors. **Pets:** Medium, other species. Service with restrictions, crate.

SAVE 🔽 ✕ 🔾 🛏 💳 🍴 🏊 🐾

(CAA) ▼▼▼ ▼▼▼ Wingate Inn SH 🐾
(403) 514-0099. **$99-$259.** 400 Midpark Way. Hwy 2A (MacLeod Tr), 0.5 km e on Sun Valley, 0.3 km n on Midpark Way, then just s. Int corridors. **Pets:** Other species. $25 daily fee/room. Service with restrictions, supervision.

SAVE 🔽 ✕ 🔾 🛏 💳 🏊 🐾

## COCHRANE

▼▼▼ Best Western Harvest Country Inn SH
(403) 932-1410. **$89-$169.** 11 West Side Dr. Hwy 1A, 1 km sw on Hwy 22. Ext/int corridors. **Pets:** Small, dogs only. $10 daily fee/pet. Designated rooms, supervision.

✕ 🛏 💳

▼▼ ▼▼ Bow River Inn M
(403) 932-7900. **$69-$109.** 3 West Side Dr. Hwy 1A, 1 km sw on Hwy 22. Ext corridors. **Pets:** Accepted.

ASK 🔽 ✕ 🛏 💳

▼▼▼ Super 8 Motel-Cochrane SH
(403) 932-6355. **$100-$170, 14 day notice.** 10 West Side Dr. Hwy 1A, 1 km sw on Hwy 22. Int corridors. **Pets:** Accepted.

ASK 🔽 ✕ 🛏 💳 🏊 🐾

## OKOTOKS

(CAA) ▼▼▼ ▼▼▼ Best Western Okotoks Lodge SH 🐾
(403) 938-7400. **$119-$129.** 22 Southridge Dr. Hwy 2, exit 2A, 4 km s to Southridge Dr. Int corridors. **Pets:** Medium, other species. $5 daily fee/pet. Designated rooms, service with restrictions, supervision.

SAVE 🔽 ✕ 🛏 💳

## STRATHMORE

▼▼ ▼▼ Best Western Strathmore Inn SH
(403) 934-5777. **$85-$169.** 550 Hwy 1. Trans-Canada Hwy 1, jct SR 817; centre. Int corridors. **Pets:** $10 one-time fee/room. Designated rooms, no service, supervision.

ASK 🔽 ✕ 🛏 💳 🏊

▼▼ ▼▼ Super 8 Motel SH
(403) 934-1808. **$82-$126.** 450 Westlake Rd. Just n on SR 817. Ext/int corridors. **Pets:** Accepted.

ASK 🔽 ✕ 🛏 💳

▼▼ ▼▼ Travelodge Strathmore SH
(403) 901-0000. **$89-$129.** 350 Ridge Rd. Just n of Trans-Canada Hwy 1; at Ridge Rd. Int corridors. **Pets:** Accepted.

ASK 🔽 ✕ 🛏 💳 🏊 🐾

## CAMROSE

▼▼ ▼▼ Norsemen Inn SH
(780) 672-9171. **$79-$179.** 6505 48th Ave. Hwy 13 (48th Ave) at 65th St; west end of town. Int corridors. **Pets:** Accepted.

ASK ✕ 🛏 💳 🍴

▼▼ ▼▼ The Travellers Inn M
(780) 672-3377. **$62-$100.** 6216 48th Ave. Hwy 13 E (48th Ave) at 62nd St. Ext corridors. **Pets:** Medium. $10 daily fee/pet. Service with restrictions, crate.

ASK 🔽 ✕ 🛏 💳

## CANMORE

(CAA) ▼▼ ▼▼ Banff Boundary Lodge CO
(403) 678-9555. **$99-$269, 3 day notice.** 1000 Harvie Heights Rd. Just e of Banff National Park east gate, parallel to Trans-Canada Hwy 1, exit Harvie Heights Rd. Ext corridors. **Pets:** Accepted.

SAVE 🔽 ✕ 🛏 💳 🏕

(CAA) ▼▼ ▼▼ Canadian Rockies Chalets CO
(403) 678-3799. **$99-$279, 3 day notice.** 1206 Bow Valley Tr. 5.8 km e of Banff National Park east gate on Hwy 1A (Bow Valley Tr); Trans-Canada Hwy 1, exit Canmore. Ext corridors. **Pets:** Medium. $30 one-time fee/room. Service with restrictions, supervision.

SAVE 🔽 ✕ 🛏 💳 🏕

▼▼ ▼▼ Canmore Inn & Suites SH
(403) 609-4656. **$79-$240.** 1402 Bow Valley Tr. 5.6 km e of Banff National Park east gate on Hwy 1A (Bow Valley Tr); Trans-Canada Hwy 1, exit Canmore. Int corridors. **Pets:** Medium. $15 daily fee/pet. Designated rooms, service with restrictions.

ASK 🔽 ✕ 🛏 💳 🏊 🐾

▼▼ ▼▼ Mystic Springs Chalets & Hot Pools CO 🐾
(403) 609-0333. **$185-$335, 5 day notice.** 140 Kananaskis Way. Trans-Canada Hwy 1, exit Three Sisters Pkwy, 3 km w to Kananaskis Way. Ext corridors. **Pets:** Other species. $20 daily fee/pet. Designated rooms, service with restrictions.

ASK 🔽 ✕ 🛏 💳 🏊 🐾

▼▼ ▼▼ Radisson Hotel & Conference Centre SH
(403) 678-3625. **$119-$279.** 511 Bow Valley Tr. Trans-Canada Hwy 1, exit Canmore; 6 km e of Banff National Park east gate on Hwy 1A (Bow Valley Tr). Ext/int corridors. **Pets:** $10 daily fee/room. Service with restrictions, crate.

ASK 🔽 ✕ 🛏 💳 🍴 🏊 🐾

(CAA) ▼▼▼ ▼▼▼ Residence Inn by Marriott Canmore SH
(403) 678-3400. **$149-$279.** 91 Three Sisters Dr. Trans-Canada Hwy 1, exit Three Sisters Pkwy, then 4 km n. Int corridors. **Pets:** Accepted.

SAVE 🔽 ✕ 🔾 🍴 🛏 💳 🏊 🐾

ⒶⒶ 💎💎 Rocky Mountain Ski Lodge Ⓜ
(403) 678-5445. **$55-$205.** 1711 Bow Valley Tr. Trans-Canada Hwy 1, exit Canmore; 4.8 km e of Banff National Park east gate on Hwy 1A (Bow Valley Tr). Ext corridors. **Pets:** Medium. $5 daily fee/room. Designated rooms, service with restrictions, supervision.

ⓈⒶⓋⒺ Ⓢ Ⓧ 🚹 🖰 🔀

ⒶⒶ 💎💎 Rundle Mountain Lodge Ⓜ 🐾
(403) 678-5322. **$69-$125, 7 day notice.** 1723 Bow Valley Tr. Trans-Canada Hwy 1, exit Canmore; 4.8 km e of Banff National Park east gate on Hwy 1A (Bow Valley Tr). Ext corridors. **Pets:** Other species. $7 daily fee/pet. Designated rooms, service with restrictions, supervision.

ⓈⒶⓋⒺ Ⓢ Ⓧ 🚹 🖰 ⇆

ⒶⒶ 💎 Rundle Ridge Chalets ⒸⒶ 🐾
(403) 678-5387. **$34-$215.** 1100 Harvie Heights Rd. Trans-Canada Hwy 1, exit Harvie Heights Rd; 1 km e of Banff National Park east gate. Ext corridors. **Pets:** $10 daily fee/pet. Designated rooms, service with restrictions, supervision.

ⓈⒶⓋⒺ Ⓧ 🚹 🔀 Ⓚ ⿻

💎 The Stockade Log Cabins ⒸⒶ
(403) 678-5212. **$78-$225.** 1050 Harvie Heights Rd. Trans-Canada Hwy 1, exit Harvie Heights Rd; 1 km e of Banff National Park east gate. Ext corridors. **Pets:** Accepted.

ⒶⓈⓀ Ⓢ Ⓧ 🚹 🖰 Ⓚ ⿻

ⒶⒶ 💎💎 Windtower Lodge & Suites ⒸⓄ
(403) 609-6600. **$89-$399, 3 day notice.** 160 Kananaskis Way. Trans-Canada Hwy 1, exit 1A (Bow Valley Tr), 1 km w, then n at Montane Dr. Int corridors. **Pets:** Other species. $15 one-time fee/pet. Designated rooms, service with restrictions, supervision.

ⓈⒶⓋⒺ Ⓢ Ⓧ 🚹 🖰 Ⓨ Ⓚ

## CLAIRMONT

💎💎💎 Ramada Inn & Suites ⓈⒽ
(780) 814-7448. **Call for rates.** 7201 99 St. Jct Hwy 43 and 2, just n. Int corridors. **Pets:** Accepted.

Ⓧ 🚹 🖰

## CLARESHOLM

💎💎 Bluebird Motel Ⓜ
(403) 625-3395. **$64-$72.** 5505 1st St W. 0.5 km n on Hwy 2. Ext corridors. **Pets:** Accepted.

ⒶⓈⓀ Ⓢ Ⓧ 🚹 🖰

## DEAD MAN'S FLATS

ⒶⒶ 💎 Pigeon Mountain Motel Ⓜ
(403) 678-5756. **$75-$120, 4 day notice.** 250 1st Ave. On Trans-Canada Hwy 1. Ext corridors. **Pets:** Accepted.

ⓈⒶⓋⒺ Ⓢ Ⓧ 🚹 🖰 Ⓚ

## DRAYTON VALLEY

💎💎 Lakeview Inns & Suites ⓈⒽ
(780) 542-3200. **$121-$155.** 4302 50th St. Hwy 22, exit Drayton Valley, 0.4 km n. Int corridors. **Pets:** Very small. $10 daily fee/pet. Designated rooms, service with restrictions, supervision.

ⒶⓈⓀ Ⓢ Ⓧ 🚹 🖰 🍽 🔀

## DRUMHELLER

💎💎 Best Western Jurassic Inn ⓈⒽ
(403) 823-7700. **$99-$139, 30 day notice.** 1103 Hwy 9 S. Hwy 9, se access to town. Ext/int corridors. **Pets:** Accepted.

ⒶⓈⓀ Ⓢ Ⓧ 🚹 🖰 🍽 ⇆

ⒶⒶ 💎💎💎 Inn at Heartwood Manor ⒸⒾ
(403) 823-6495. **$79-$260.** 320 N Railway Ave E. Just e of Hwy 9; downtown. Int corridors. **Pets:** Accepted.

ⓈⒶⓋⒺ Ⓧ 🚹 🖰

💎💎 Super 8 Motel ⓈⒽ
(403) 823-8887. **$109-$209.** 600-680 2nd St SE. Off Hwy 9. Ext/int corridors. **Pets:** Other species. $10 daily fee/pet. Designated rooms, service with restrictions, supervision.

ⒶⓈⓀ Ⓢ Ⓧ 🚹 🖰 ⇆ 🔀

---

## EDMONTON METROPOLITAN AREA

## EDMONTON

💎💎 Alberta Place Suite Hotel ⒸⓄ
(780) 423-1565. **$87-$140.** 10049 103rd St. Just s of Jasper Ave. Int corridors. **Pets:** $10 daily fee/pet. Designated rooms, service with restrictions, crate.

ⒶⓈⓀ Ⓢ Ⓧ 🚹 🖰 🍽 ⇆

💎 Argyll Plaza Hotel ⓈⒽ
(780) 438-5876. **$64-$129.** 9933 63rd Ave. 63rd Ave at 99th St. Int corridors. **Pets:** Medium, other species. $10 daily fee/pet. Designated rooms, service with restrictions, crate.

ⒶⓈⓀ Ⓢ Ⓧ 🚹 🖰 🍽

ⒶⒶ 💎💎 Best Western Cedar Park Inn ⓈⒽ
(780) 434-7411. **$119-$169, 3 day notice.** 5116 Gateway Blvd. Hwy 2 (Gateway Blvd) at 51st Ave. Int corridors. **Pets:** Accepted.

ⓈⒶⓋⒺ Ⓢ Ⓧ 🚹 🖰 🍽 ⇆

ⒶⒶ 💎💎 Chateau Louis Hotel & Conference Centre ⓈⒽ
(780) 452-7770. **$109-$199.** 11727 Kingsway. On Kingsway and 117th St. Int corridors. **Pets:** Accepted.

ⓈⒶⓋⒺ Ⓢ Ⓧ Ⓜ 🏊 🏌 🚹 🖰 🍽

ⒶⒶ 💎💎 Comfort Inn & Suites Downtown Edmonton ⓈⒽ
(780) 423-5611. **$79-$89.** 10425 100th Ave. Corner of 100th Ave; centre. Int corridors. **Pets:** Medium, other species. $10 daily fee/pet. Designated rooms, service with restrictions.

ⓈⒶⓋⒺ Ⓢ Ⓧ 🚹 🖰 🍽

ⒶⒶ 💎💎 Comfort Inn West ⓈⒽ 🐾
(780) 484-4415. **$89-$129.** 17610 100th Ave. At 176th St. Int corridors. **Pets:** Medium, dogs only. $10 daily fee/room. Service with restrictions, supervision.

ⓈⒶⓋⒺ Ⓢ Ⓧ 🚹 🖰 🍽

💎💎💎 Courtyard by Marriott Edmonton ⓁⒽ
(780) 423-9999. **$95.** One Thornton Ct. Just s of Jasper Ave at Thornton Ct and 99th St. Int corridors. **Pets:** Small. $75 one-time fee/pet. Designated rooms, service with restrictions, supervision.

ⒶⓈⓀ Ⓧ Ⓜ 🏊 🚹 🖰 🍽

💎💎💎 Crowne Plaza Edmonton-Chateau Lacombe ⓁⒽ
(780) 428-6611. **$139-$169.** 10111 Bellamy Hill. Jct 101st St, MacDonald Dr and Bellamy Hill. Int corridors. **Pets:** Accepted.

ⒶⓈⓀ Ⓢ Ⓧ Ⓜ 🚹 🍽

💎💎💎💎 Delta Edmonton Centre Suite Hotel ⓁⒽ
(780) 429-3900. **$170.** 10222 102nd St. At 102nd St at 103rd Ave. Int corridors. **Pets:** Accepted.

ⒶⓈⓀ Ⓢ Ⓧ 🏊 🏌 🖰 🍽 🔀

💎💎💎 Delta Edmonton South Hotel and Conference Centre ⓁⒽ
(780) 434-6415. **$111-$115.** 4404 Gateway Blvd. Jct Calgary Tr (Hwy 2) and Whitemud Dr. Int corridors. **Pets:** Accepted.

Ⓢ Ⓧ 🚹 🖰 🍽 ⇆

▼▼ **Executive Royal Inn West Edmonton** 🆂🅷
(780) 484-6000. **$128-$235.** 10010 178th St. Corner of 178th St and 100th Ave. Int corridors. **Pets:** Accepted.

🅰🆂🅺 🆂🅾 ✖ 🄷 ▣ 🍴 ⊠

🆀🅰 ▼▼▼ **The Fairmont Hotel Macdonald** 🅻🅷
(780) 424-5181. **$179-$299.** 10065 100th St. Just s of Jasper Ave. Int corridors. **Pets:** Accepted.

🆂🄰🆅🄴 🆂🅾 ✖ 🄻🄼 ▣ 🍴 ⤳ ⊠

🆀🅰 ▼▼▼▼ **Four Points by Sheraton Edmonton South** 🅻🅷 🐾
(780) 465-7931. **$95-$155.** 7230 Argyll Rd. Hwy 2 (Gateway Blvd), 3.7 km e at 63rd Ave (turns into Argyll Rd); at 75th St. Int corridors. **Pets:** Other species. $10 one-time fee/pet. Designated rooms, service with restrictions, supervision.

🆂🄰🆅🄴 🆂🅾 ✖ 🄷 ▣ 🍴 ⤳

🆀🅰 ▼▼▼▼ **Greenwood Hotel & Suites** 🆂🅷
(780) 431-1100. **$99-$199.** 4485 Gateway Blvd. Hwy 2 (Gateway Blvd), just n of Whitemud Dr. Int corridors. **Pets:** Service with restrictions, crate.

🆂🄰🆅🄴 🆂🅾 ✖ 🄻🄼 🖉 🄲 🄷 ▣ 🍴 ⤳ ⊠

🆀🅰 ▼▼▼▼ **Holiday Inn Convention Centre (S.E. Edmonton)** 🆂🅷
(780) 468-5400. **$109-$129.** 4520 76th Ave. Hwy 14, just s via 50th St exit, then just e. Int corridors. **Pets:** Small, dogs only. $15 daily fee/room. Supervision.

🆂🄰🆅🄴 🆂🅾 ✖ 🖉 🄷 ▣ 🍴 ⤳ ⊠

▼▼◆ **Holiday Inn Edmonton-The Palace** 🆂🅷
(780) 438-1222. **$119-$129, 14 day notice.** 4235 Gateway Blvd. Just s of Whitemud Dr. Int corridors. **Pets:** Other species. $10 daily fee/pet. Designated rooms, service with restrictions.

🅰🆂🅺 🆂🅾 ✖ 🄷 ▣ 🍴

🆀🅰 ▼▼▼ **Holiday Inn Express Edmonton-Downtown** 🆂🅷 🐾
(780) 423-2450. **$99.** 10010 104th St. Corner of 100th Ave; centre. Int corridors. **Pets:** Large. $25 one-time fee/room. Designated rooms, service with restrictions, crate.

🆂🄰🆅🄴 ✖ 🄷 ▣ ⤳ ⊠

🆀🅰 ▼▼▼ **Mayfield Inn & Suites at West Edmonton** 🅻🅷
(780) 484-0821. **$129-$199.** 16615 109th Ave. 1.6 km n of jct Hwy 2 (Gateway Blvd) and 16A on Mayfield Rd. Int corridors. **Pets:** Accepted.

🆂🄰🆅🄴 🆂🅾 ✖ 🄷 ▣ 🍴 ⤳

▼▼◆ **Metterra Hotel on Whyte** 🆂🅷
(780) 465-8150. **$190-$330.** 10454 82nd Ave (Whyte Ave). Just e of 105th St. Int corridors. **Pets:** Accepted.

🅰🆂🅺 🆂🅾 ✖ ▣

🆀🅰 ▼▼ **Rosslyn Inn & Suites** 🆂🅷 🐾
(780) 476-6241. **$79-$121.** 13620 97 St. Hwy 16 (Yellowhead Hwy), 2 km n at 97th St. Int corridors. **Pets:** Medium. $10 daily fee/room. Designated rooms, service with restrictions, crate.

🆂🄰🆅🄴 ✖ 🄷 ▣ 🍴

▼▼ **Signature Suite Hotel Edmonton House** 🄲🅾
(780) 420-4000. **$119-$220.** 10205 100th Ave. Just se of jct 102nd St and 100th Ave. Int corridors. **Pets:** Accepted.

🅰🆂🅺 🆂🅾 ✖ 🄷 ▣ 🍴 ⤳ ⊠

🆀🅰 ▼▼▼ **Super 8 Hotel** 🆂🅷
(780) 433-8688. **$89-$249.** 3610 Gateway Blvd. Jct 36th Ave. Int corridors. **Pets:** Medium. $15 daily fee/room. Designated rooms, service with restrictions, crate.

🆂🄰🆅🄴 🆂🅾 ✖ 🄻🄼 🄷 ▣ ⤳

▼▼▼ **The Sutton Place Hotel, Edmonton** 🅻🅷
(780) 428-7111. **$172-$222.** 10235 101st St. 102nd Ave at 101st St. Int corridors. **Pets:** Small. $20 one-time fee/room. Service with restrictions, supervision.

🅰🆂🅺 🆂🅾 ✖ 🄷 ▣ 🍴 ⤳ ⊠

🆀🅰 ▼▼▼ **Travelodge Beverly Crest** 🆂🅷 🐾
(780) 474-0456. **$69-$79.** 3414 118th Ave. 8 km e of Capilano Dr, 1 km s from W Hwy 16 (Yellowhead Tr) on Victoria Tr exit. Int corridors. **Pets:** Small. Service with restrictions, supervision.

🆂🄰🆅🄴 ✖ ▣ 🍴

▼▼▼ **Travelodge Edmonton South** 🆂🅷 🐾
(780) 436-9770. **$79-$115.** 10320 45th Ave S. Jct Calgary Tr (Hwy 2) and 45th Ave, just n of Whitemud Dr. Int corridors. **Pets:** Large. Designated rooms, service with restrictions, supervision.

🅰🆂🅺 🆂🅾 ✖ 🄷 ▣ ⤳

▼▼▼ **Travelodge Edmonton West** 🆂🅷
(780) 483-6031. **$104-$129.** 18320 Stony Plain Rd. Hwy 16A (Stony Plain Rd) at 184 St. Int corridors. **Pets:** Medium. $25 deposit/room. Designated rooms, service with restrictions, supervision.

🅰🆂🅺 🆂🅾 ✖ 🄷 ▣ 🍴 ⤳ ⊠

▼▼▼ **The Varscona Hotel** 🆂🅷
(780) 434-6111. **$170-$290.** 8208 106th St. Corner of 82nd Ave (Whyte Ave) and 106th St. Int corridors. **Pets:** Accepted.

🅰🆂🅺 🆂🅾 ✖ ▣ 🍴

▼▼▼ **The Westin Edmonton** 🅻🅷 🐾
(780) 426-3636. **$105-$145.** 10135 100th St. 101st Ave at 100th St. Int corridors. **Pets:** Service with restrictions, crate.

🅰🆂🅺 🆂🅾 ✖ 🖉 ▣ 🍴 ⤳ ⊠

🆀🅰 ▼▼▼ **Wingate Inn Edmonton West** 🆂🅷
(780) 443-1000. **$129-$189.** 18220 100th Ave. 100th Ave at 182nd St. Int corridors. **Pets:** Dogs only. $15 daily fee/pet. Designated rooms, service with restrictions, supervision.

🆂🄰🆅🄴 🆂🅾 ✖ 🄻🄼 🄷 ▣ ⤳ ⊠

## LEDUC

▼▼ **Edmonton International Airport-Super 8 Motel** 🆂🅷
(780) 986-8898. **$90.** 8004 Sparrow Crescent. Hwy 2, exit N Business Section. Int corridors. **Pets:** Accepted.

🅰🆂🅺 🆂🅾 ✖ 🄷 ▣

▼▼▼ **Executive Royal Inn Hotel & Conference Centre** 🆂🅷
(780) 986-1840. **$95.** 8450 Sparrow Dr. Hwy 2, 1 km e. Int corridors. **Pets:** $20 one-time fee/pet. Designated rooms, service with restrictions, supervision.

🅰🆂🅺 🆂🅾 ✖ 🄻🄼 🄷 ▣ 🍴

## NISKU

🆀🅰 ▼▼▼ **Holiday Inn Express Edmonton Int'l Airport** 🆂🅷
(780) 955-1000. **$108-$162.** 1102 4th St. Hwy 2, exit Edmonton International Airport/Nisku Business Park (10th Ave), 0.8 km e. Int corridors. **Pets:** Other species. $10 one-time fee/pet. Designated rooms, service with restrictions, crate.

🆂🄰🆅🄴 🆂🅾 ✖ 🄻🄼 🖉 🄲 🄷 ▣

🆀🅰 ▼▼▼ **Nisku Inn & Conference Centre-Edmonton Airport** 🆂🅷
(780) 955-7744. **$95-$149.** 1101 4th St. Hwy 2, exit Edmonton International Airport/Nisku Business Park (10th Ave), 0.5 km e. Int corridors. **Pets:** Large. $20 daily fee/pet. Service with restrictions.

🆂🄰🆅🄴 ✖ 🄻🄼 🄷 ▣ 🍴 ⤳

## SHERWOOD PARK

⟨AA⟩ ▼▼ **Franklin's Inn** 🆂🅷
(780) 467-1234. **$75-$85.** 2016 Sherwood Dr. At Granada Blvd. Int corridors. **Pets:** Accepted.
🆂🅰🆅🅴 ⊠ 🛏 🖥 🍴

⟨AA⟩ ▼▼ **Ramada Limited-Edmonton East/Sherwood Park** 🆂🅷 🌺
(780) 467-6727. **$129-$149.** 30 Broadway Blvd. Hwy 14, 1.5 km e on Baseline Rd, 0.4 km n on Broadmoor Blvd; Hwy 16, exit Broadmoor Blvd, 2.5 km s. Int corridors. **Pets:** Medium. $15 daily fee/pet. Designated rooms, service with restrictions, supervision.
🆂🅰🆅🅴 🆂🄳 ⊠ 🛗 🛏 🖥

⟨AA⟩ ▼▼ **Roadking Inns** 🆂🅷 🌺
(780) 464-1000. **$89-$119.** 26 Strathmoor Dr. Just sw of Hwy 16, exit Broadmoor Blvd. Int corridors. **Pets:** $100 deposit/room. Designated rooms, service with restrictions, supervision.
🆂🅰🆅🅴 🆂🄳 ⊠ 🛏 🖥 🍴

## SPRUCE GROVE

▼▼ **Royal Inn Express Hotel** 🆂🅷 🌺
(780) 962-6050. **$82-$105.** 20 Westgrove Dr. I-16A, just n. Int corridors. **Pets:** Small, dogs only. $10 daily fee/pet. Designated rooms, service with restrictions, supervision.
🅰🆂🄺 🆂🄳 ⊠ 🛏 🖥

## STONY PLAIN

▼▼▼ **Ramada Inn & Suites** 🆂🅷
(780) 963-0222. **$67-$110.** 3301 43rd Ave. Hwy 16A, exit Dunmore Rd, just s. Ext/int corridors. **Pets:** Other species. $4 daily fee/pet. Designated rooms, service with restrictions, supervision.
🅰🆂🄺 🆂🄳 ⊠ 🛏 🖥 🍴 🞭

▼ **Stony Convention Inn** 🆂🅷
(780) 963-3444. **$66-$84.** 4620 48th St. Hwy 16A, exit Stony Plain Rd, 0.8 km s on SR 779. Int corridors. **Pets:** $10 daily fee/pet. Designated rooms, service with restrictions, supervision.
🅰🆂🄺 🆂🄳 ⊠ 🛏 🖥 🍴

---

# END METROPOLITAN AREA

---

## EDSON

▼▼▼ **Best Western High Road Inn** 🆂🅷
(780) 712-2378. **$109-$199.** 300 52nd St. On 2nd Ave; centre. Int corridors. **Pets:** $10 daily fee/pet. Designated rooms, service with restrictions, supervision.
⊠ 🛏 🖥 🍴 🞭 🞭

⟨AA⟩ ▼▼ **Guest House Inn & Suites** 🅼
(780) 723-4486. **$82-$98.** 4411 4th Ave. 1 km e on Hwy 16. Ext/int corridors. **Pets:** Accepted.
🆂🅰🆅🅴 🆂🄳 ⊠ 🛏 🖥 🍴 🞭

▼▼ **Super 8 Motel** 🆂🅷
(780) 723-2500. **$90-$110.** 4300 2nd Ave. 1.1 km e on Hwy 16. Int corridors. **Pets:** Accepted.
🅰🆂🄺 ⊠ 🛏 🖥

## FORT MACLEOD

▼ **Fort Motel** 🅼
(403) 553-3606. **$40-$55.** 451 Main St. Centre. Ext corridors. **Pets:** Accepted.
🅰🆂🄺 🆂🄳 ⊠ 🛏 🖥

⟨AA⟩ ▼ **Sunset Motel** 🅼
(403) 553-4448. **$46-$64.** 104 Hwy 3W. 1 km w on Hwy 2 and 3. Ext corridors. **Pets:** Accepted.
🆂🅰🆅🅴 🆂🄳 ⊠ 🛏 🖥

## FORT MCMURRAY

⟨AA⟩ ▼▼▼ **Quality Hotel & Conference Centre Fort McMurray** 🆂🅷
(780) 791-7200. **$119-$179.** 424 Gregoire Dr. Hwy 63, 1 km e at Gregoire Dr. Int corridors. **Pets:** Accepted.
🆂🅰🆅🅴 🆂🄳 ⊠ 🛏 🖥 🍴 🞭

## GRANDE PRAIRIE

▼▼▼▼ **Best Western Grande Prairie Hotel & Suites** 🆂🅷
(780) 402-2378. **$139-$149.** 10745 117th Ave. Corner of Hwy 43 and 117th Ave. Int corridors. **Pets:** Accepted.
🅰🆂🄺 🆂🄳 ⊠ 🞭 🛏 🖥 🍴 🞭

⟨AA⟩ ▼▼▼ **Pomeroy Inn & Suites** 🆂🅷
(780) 831-2999. **$119-$129.** 11710 102nd St. 102nd St at 117th Ave. Int corridors. **Pets:** Other species. $20 daily fee/room. Designated rooms, service with restrictions, supervision.
🆂🅰🆅🅴 🆂🄳 ⊠ 🛏 🖥 🞭 🞭

⟨AA⟩ ▼▼ **Quality Hotel & Conference Centre Grande Prairie** 🆂🅷
(780) 539-6000. **$94.** 11201 100th Ave. 2.9 km w on Hwy 2. Int corridors. **Pets:** Accepted.
🆂🅰🆅🅴 ⊠ 🛏 🖥 🍴

▼▼▼ **Service Plus Inns and Suites** 🆂🅷
(780) 538-3900. **$119-$129.** 10810 107th A Ave. 2.2 km w on Hwy 2, just n. Int corridors. **Pets:** Accepted.
🅰🆂🄺 🆂🄳 ⊠ 🞭 🛏 🖥 🞭 🞭

▼▼ **Stanford Inn** 🆂🅷
(780) 539-5678. **$90-$100.** 11401 100th Ave. 2.8 km w on Hwy 2. Ext/int corridors. **Pets:** Accepted.
🅰🆂🄺 🆂🄳 ⊠ 🛏 🖥 🍴 🞭

▼▼ **Super 8 Motel** 🆂🅷
(780) 532-8288. **Call for rates.** 10050 116 Ave. 102nd St at 117th Ave. Int corridors. **Pets:** Accepted.
⊠ 🛏 🖥 🞭 🞭

## HIGH RIVER

▼▼ **Heritage Inn** 🆂🅷
(403) 652-3834. **$97-$99.** 1104 11th Ave SE. Trans-Canada Hwy 2, exit 23, 2 km w of Hwy 2. Int corridors. **Pets:** Large. $10 daily fee/pet. Designated rooms, service with restrictions, supervision.
🅰🆂🄺 🆂🄳 ⊠ 🛏 🖥 🍴 🞭

▼▼▼ **Super 8 Motel** 🆂🅷
(403) 652-4448. **$100-$160.** 1601 13th Ave SE. Trans-Canada Hwy 2, exit High River, just w. Int corridors. **Pets:** Medium. $10 daily fee/pet. Service with restrictions, supervision.
🅰🆂🄺 🆂🄳 ⊠ 🛗 🞭 🛏 🖥 🞭 🞭

## HINTON

▼▼ **Best Western White Wolf Inn** 🆂🅷
(780) 865-7777. **$129-$139, 5 day notice.** 828 Carmichael Ln. At west end of town; just off Hwy 16. Ext corridors. **Pets:** Accepted.
🅰🆂🄺 🆂🄳 ⊠ 🛏 🖥

⟨AA⟩ ▼▼ **Days Inn** 🆂🅷
(780) 817-1960. **$139-$179.** 358 Smith St. 2.3 km e on Hwy 16. Int corridors. **Pets:** Other species. $10 daily fee/room. Service with restrictions, supervision.
🆂🅰🆅🅴 ⊠ 🛏 🖥

▼▼▼ **Lakeview Inns & Suites** SH
(780) 865-2575. **$94-$149.** 500 Smith St. 17 km e on Hwy 16. Ext/int corridors. **Pets:** Accepted.

ASK ⊠ 🛄 💻

# JASPER

CAA ▼▼▼ **Amethyst Lodge** SH
(780) 852-3394. **$89-$270.** 200 Connaught Dr. 0.5 km e. Ext/int corridors. **Pets:** Other species. $10 daily fee/room. Designated rooms, service with restrictions, crate.

SAVE 🔊 ⊠ 💻 🍴

▼▼▼▼ **The Fairmont Jasper Park Lodge** LH
(780) 852-3301. **$199-$579, 3 day notice.** Lodge Rd. 4.8 km ne via Hwy 16; 3.2 km se off highway via Maligne Rd, follow signs for lodge. Ext corridors. **Pets:** Accepted.

ASK 🔊 ⊠ 🐾 🛄 💻 🍴 🏊 ⊠ 🎾

CAA ▼▼▼ **Jasper Inn Alpine Resort** SH ❀
(780) 852-4461. **$95-$282, 3 day notice.** 98 Geikie St. 1.2 km ne; at Geikie and Bonhomme sts. Ext/int corridors. **Pets:** Other species. $10 one-time fee/room. Designated rooms, service with restrictions.

SAVE ⊠ 🛄 💻 🍴 🏊 ⊠ 🎾

CAA ▼▼▼▼ **Lobstick Lodge** SH
(780) 852-4431. **$107-$237.** 94 Geikie St. 1.2 km ne at Geikie and Juniper sts. Int corridors. **Pets:** Other species. $10 daily fee/room. Designated rooms, service with restrictions, crate.

SAVE 🔊 ⊠ 🛄 💻 🍴 ⊠ 🎾

CAA ▼▼▼ **Maligne Lodge** M
(780) 852-3143. **$86-$473.** 900 Connaught. 1 km sw. Ext/int corridors. **Pets:** Accepted.

SAVE 🔊 ⊠ 🛄 💻 🍴 🏊

CAA ▼▼▼ **Marmot Lodge** M
(780) 852-4471. **$99-$231.** 86 Connaught Dr. 1.6 km ne. Ext corridors. **Pets:** Other species. $10 daily fee/room. Designated rooms, service with restrictions, crate.

SAVE 🔊 ⊠ 🛄 💻 🍴 🏊

▼▼ **Patricia Lake Bungalows** CA
(780) 852-3560. **$59-$270, 7 day notice.** Pyramid Lake Rd. 4.8 km nw via Pyramid Lake Rd. Ext corridors. **Pets:** Medium, dogs only. $10 daily fee/pet. Designated rooms, service with restrictions, supervision.

⊠ 🛄 ⊠ 🎾 🐾

CAA ▼▼▼ **Pyramid Lake Resort** SH
(780) 852-4900. **$125-$399, 3 day notice.** Pyramid Lake Rd. Jct Connaught Dr and Cedar St, 6 km nw via Pyramid Lake Rd. Ext corridors. **Pets:** Medium. $25 daily fee/room. Designated rooms, service with restrictions, supervision.

SAVE 🔊 ⊠ 🛄 💻 🍴 ⊠ 🎾

CAA ▼▼▼ **The Sawridge Inn and Conference Centre** SH ❀
(780) 852-5111. **$115-$295, 3 day notice.** 82 Connaught Dr. 1.7 km e. Int corridors. **Pets:** Small, dogs only. $20 one-time fee/room. Designated rooms, service with restrictions, supervision.

SAVE 🔊 ⊠ 🔆 🛄 💻 🏊 ⊠

CAA ▼▼▼ **Sunwapta Falls Resort** M
(780) 852-4852. **$79-$368.** Hwy 93. 55 km s on Icefields Pkwy (Hwy 93). Ext corridors. **Pets:** Accepted.

SAVE ⊠ 🛄 💻 🍴 ⊠ 🎾 🐾

CAA ▼▼▼ **Tonquin Inn** M
(780) 852-4987. **$93-$398.** 100 Juniper St. Corner of Juniper and Geikre sts. Ext/int corridors. **Pets:** Accepted.

SAVE 🔊 ⊠ 🛄 💻 🍴 🏊

# KANANASKIS

▼▼▼ **Delta Lodge at Kananaskis** LH ❀
(403) 591-7711. **$129-$279, 3 day notice.** Kanasaskis Village. Trans-Canada Hwy 1, 23.5 km s on Hwy 40 (Kananaskis Tr), then 3 km on Kananaskis Village access road, follow signs. Int corridors. **Pets:** Medium. $85 one-time fee/pet. Designated rooms, service with restrictions, supervision.

ASK 🔊 ⊠ 🐾 🛄 💻 🍴 🏊 ⊠

# LAKE LOUISE

CAA ▼▼▼▼ **The Fairmont Chateau Lake Louise** LH
(403) 522-3511. **$199-$989, 3 day notice.** 111 Lake Louise Dr. 3 km up the hill from the village. Int corridors. **Pets:** Accepted.

SAVE 🔊 ⊠ 💻 🍴 🏊 ⊠

▼▼ **Lake Louise Inn** SH
(403) 522-3791. **$98-$251.** 210 Village Rd. Just w of 4-way stop. Ext/int corridors. **Pets:** $100 deposit/pet. Designated rooms, service with restrictions, supervision.

ASK 🔊 ⊠ 🛄 💻 🍴 🏊 ⊠

# LETHBRIDGE

▼▼▼ **Comfort Inn** SH
(403) 320-8874. **$94-$130.** 3226 Fairway Plaza Rd S. Southeast end of city; Mayor Magrath Dr, exit n at Scenic Dr. Int corridors. **Pets:** Other species. $10 daily fee/pet. Service with restrictions, supervision.

ASK 🔊 ⊠ 🛄 💻 🏊

CAA ▼▼▼ **Days Inn Lethbridge** SH
(403) 327-6000. **$84-$94.** 100 3rd Ave S. Corner of 3rd Ave and Scenic Dr; centre. Ext/int corridors. **Pets:** Medium. Designated rooms, service with restrictions, supervision.

SAVE 🔊 ⊠ 🛄 💻 🏊

CAA ▼▼▼ **Econo Lodge & Suites Lethbridge** M
(403) 328-5591. **$70-$100.** 1124 Mayor Magrath Dr S. Hwy 3, 4 or 5, exit Mayor Magrath Dr S. Ext corridors. **Pets:** Small. $10 one-time fee/room. Designated rooms, service with restrictions, supervision.

SAVE 🔊 ⊠ 🛄

▼▼▼ **Holiday Inn Express Hotel & Suites Lethbridge** SH
(403) 394-9292. **$135-$225.** 120 Stafford Dr S. Hwy 3, exit Stafford Dr, just s; downtown. Int corridors. **Pets:** Small. $35 daily fee/room. Designated rooms, service with restrictions, supervision.

ASK 🔊 ⊠ 🛄 💻 ⊠

CAA ▼▼▼ **Lethbridge Lodge Hotel and Conference Centre** LH
(403) 328-1123. **$110-$180.** 320 Scenic Dr. Scenic Dr at 4th Ave S; centre. Int corridors. **Pets:** Accepted.

SAVE 🔊 ⊠ 🛄 💻 🍴 🏊

▼▼▼ **Ramada Hotel & Suites** LH
(403) 380-5050. **Call for rates.** 2375 Mayor Magrath Dr S. 4.5 km se on Hwy 4 and 5, exit Mayor Magrath Dr S. Int corridors. **Pets:** Dogs only. $10 one-time fee/pet. Designated rooms, service with restrictions, crate.

ASK 🔊 ⊠ 🛄 💻 🍴 🏊 ⊠

▼▼ **South Country Inn** SH
(403) 380-6677. **$70-$125.** 2225 Mayor Magrath Dr. 4.5 km se on Hwy 4 and 5, exit Mayor Magrath Dr, then just w. Int corridors. **Pets:** Accepted.

⊠ 🛄

CAA ▼▼ **Thriftlodge** M
(403) 328-4436. **$50-$70.** 1142 Mayor Magrath Dr S. 4 km se on Hwy 4 and 5, exit Mayor Magrath Dr S. Ext corridors. **Pets:** Medium. $7 daily fee/room. Designated rooms, service with restrictions, supervision.

SAVE 🔊 ⊠ 🛄 🏊

# LLOYDMINSTER

**Best Western Wayside Inn & Suites** SH
(780) 875-4404. **$123-$265.** 5411 44th St. 0.8 km w on Hwy 16 from jct Hwy 17. Int corridors. **Pets:** Accepted.
(ASK) (S6) (X) (8) (P) (T) (z)

**Tropical Inn** SH
(780) 875-7000. **$98-$254.** 5621 44th St. Jct Hwy 16 and 17, 1 km w. Int corridors. **Pets:** Accepted.
(SAVE) (S6) (X) (8) (P) (T) (z) (X)

# MEDICINE HAT

**Best Western Inn** SH
(403) 527-3700. **$99-$269.** 722 Redcliff Dr. On Trans-Canada Hwy 1; 0.4 km w of jct Hwy 3, access 7th Ave SW. Ext/int corridors. **Pets:** Accepted.
(ASK) (S6) (X) (LM) (8) (P) (z) (X)

**Imperial Inn** M
(403) 527-8811. **$79-$100.** 3282 13th Ave SE. 3.6 km se; just n off Trans-Canada Hwy 1. Ext/int corridors. **Pets:** Other species. $10 daily fee/room. Designated rooms, service with restrictions, supervision.
(SAVE) (S6) (X) (8) (P) (T) (z) (X)

**Medicine Hat Lodge Hotel Casino Convention Centre Health Spa & Indoor** LH
(403) 529-2222. **$103-$131.** 1051 Ross Glen Dr SE. East end approach to city on Trans-Canada Hwy 1, at jct Dunmore Rd. Int corridors. **Pets:** Other species. $10 daily fee/room. Designated rooms, service with restrictions, supervision.
(ASK) (S6) (X) (8) (P) (T) (z) (X)

**Motel 6-Medicine Hat** SH
(403) 524-1749. **$70-$76.** 20 Strochon Ct SE. Trans-Canada Hwy 1, exit Dunmore Rd, just sw. Int corridors. **Pets:** Small. Service with restrictions, crate.
(S6) (X) (LM) (L) (8)

**Ranchmen Motel** M
(403) 527-2263. **$57-$67.** 535 16th St SW. Trans-Canada Hwy 1 at 16th St SW. Ext corridors. **Pets:** Very small, dogs only. $5 daily fee/pet. Designated rooms, service with restrictions, supervision.
(X) (8) (P)

**Super 8 Motel** SH
(403) 528-8888. **$76-$89.** 1280 Trans-Canada Way SE. Trans-Canada Hwy 1 at 13 Ave SE; just n off Trans-Canada Hwy 1. Ext/int corridors. **Pets:** Other species. $5 daily fee/pet. Designated rooms, service with restrictions, supervision.
(ASK) (S6) (X) (8) (P) (z)

**Travelodge Hotel Medicine Hat** SH
(403) 527-2275. **$115-$125.** 1100 Redcliff Dr SW. 2.8 km sw on Trans-Canada Hwy 1 at jct Hwy 3. Ext/int corridors. **Pets:** Small. $10 one-time fee/pet. Designated rooms, service with restrictions, supervision.
(SAVE) (S6) (X) (8) (P) (T) (z) (X)

# PEACE RIVER

**Travellers Motor Hotel** M
(780) 624-3621. **$67-$99.** 9510 100th St. Just s off Hwy 2 S, exit town centre. Ext/int corridors. **Pets:** Accepted.
(ASK) (S6) (X) (8) (P) (T)

# PINCHER CREEK

**Heritage Inn** SH
(403) 627-5000. **$92-$100.** 919 Waterton Ave (Hwy 6). SR 3, 4.7 km s on SR 6. Int corridors. **Pets:** Medium, other species. $10 daily fee/room. Designated rooms, service with restrictions, supervision.
(ASK) (S6) (X) (8) (P) (T)

# RED DEER

**Capri Hotel Trade & Convention Centre** LH
(403) 346-2091. **$95-$148.** 3310 50th Ave. 2 km n on Hwy 2A (Gaetz Ave). Int corridors. **Pets:** Accepted.
(SAVE) (S6) (X) (8) (P) (T) (z) (X)

**Comfort Inn & Suites** SH
(403) 348-0025. **$99-$139.** 6846 66th St. Hwy 2, exit Hwy 2A (Gaetz Ave), just n, then 0.5 km w. Int corridors. **Pets:** Accepted.
(SAVE) (S6) (X) (LM) (L) (8) (P) (z) (X)

**Holiday Inn 67 Street** SH
(403) 342-6567. **$94-$99.** 6500 67th St. 3.2 km nw, 0.8 km e of Hwy 2, exit 67th St. Int corridors. **Pets:** Small. $15 daily fee/pet. Designated rooms, service with restrictions, crate.
(SAVE) (X) (8) (P) (T) (z) (X)

**Holiday Inn Express Red Deer** SH
(403) 343-2112. **$109-$129.** 2803 50th Ave. 1.8 km e on Hwy 2A (Gaetz Ave). Int corridors. **Pets:** Medium. $15 daily fee/room. Designated rooms, supervision.
(SAVE) (S6) (X) (8) (P) (z) (X)

**Sandman Hotel Red Deer** SH 🐾
(403) 343-7400. **$105-$199.** 2818 Gaetz Ave. 1.6 km n on Hwy 2A (Gaetz Ave). Int corridors. **Pets:** Medium, other species. $10 daily fee/room. Service with restrictions, crate.
(X) (LM) (8) (P) (T) (z)

**Service Plus Inns and Suites** SH
(403) 342-4445. **$99-$199.** 6853 66th St. Hwy 2, exit 67th St, just e. Int corridors. **Pets:** Small. $15 daily fee/room. Designated rooms, service with restrictions, supervision.
(SAVE) (S6) (X) (8) (P) (T) (z) (X)

**Stanford Inn** SH
(403) 347-5551. **$75-$80, 24 day notice.** 4707 Ross St. Centre; just e of Hwy 2A (Gaetz Ave). Int corridors. **Pets:** Accepted.
(ASK) (S6) (X) (8) (P) (T)

# ROCKY MOUNTAIN HOUSE

**Chinook Inn** M
(403) 845-2833. **$65-$75.** 5321 59th Ave. 1.3 km w on Hwy 11, then s. Int corridors. **Pets:** $10 daily fee/pet. Crate.
(SAVE) (S6) (X) (8) (P)

**Holiday Inn Express Rocky Mountain House** SH
(403) 845-2871. **$89-$99.** 4715 45th St. Just nw of jct 47th Ave and 45th St. Int corridors. **Pets:** $10 one-time fee/room. Service with restrictions, supervision.
(SAVE) (S6) (X) (8) (P)

**Super 8 Motel** SH
(403) 846-0088. **$89-$189.** 4406 41st Ave. Just off Hwy 11 at east end of town. Int corridors. **Pets:** Accepted.
(ASK) (S6) (X) (8) (P) (z) (X)

# TABER

**Heritage Inn** SH
(403) 223-4424. **$88.** 4830 46th Ave. 1 km e of jct Hwy 3 and 36 S, on Hwy 3. Int corridors. **Pets:** Medium, other species. $10 daily fee/room. Service with restrictions, supervision.
(ASK) (S6) (X) (8) (P) (T) (X)

# WATERTON PARK

**Bayshore Inn** M
(403) 859-2211. **$104-$225, 3 day notice.** 111 Waterton Ave. Centre. Ext corridors. **Pets:** Other species. $20 one-time fee/room. Designated rooms, service with restrictions.
(SAVE) (S6) (X) (8) (P) (T) (K)

▼▼▼ **Waterton Lakes Lodge** 🔲
(403) 859-2150. **$114-$219, 3 day notice.** 101 Clematis Ave. Centre.
Ext/int corridors. **Pets:** Accepted.
(ASK) (S₀) (✕) (♿) (⛽) (📱) (📺) (🍴) (🏊) (✕)

## WETASKIWIN

▼▼ **Best Western Wayside Inn** 🔲
(780) 352-6681. **$89-$119.** 4103 56 St. Just n of Hwy 13 W, on Hwy
2A. Int corridors. **Pets:** Large, other species. $100 deposit/room. Desig-
nated rooms, service with restrictions, supervision.
(ASK) (S₀) (✕) (📺) (🍴)

▼▼ **Super 8 Motel** 🔲
(780) 361-3808. **$89-$109.** 3820 56th St. On Hwy 2A, just s of jct Hwy
13 W. Ext/int corridors. **Pets:** Small. $50 deposit/room. Designated rooms,
service with restrictions, supervision.
(ASK) (S₀) (✕) (♿) (📱)

## WHITECOURT

CAA ▼▼▼ **Quality Inn** 🔲
(780) 778-5477. **$65-$95.** 5420 49th Ave. On Hwy 43, 0.5 km e of Hwy
32. Int corridors. **Pets:** Other species. Designated rooms, service with
restrictions, supervision.
(SAVE) (S₀) (✕) (📱) (📺) (🍴) (✕)

▼▼ **Super 8 Motel** 🔲
(780) 778-8908. **$119-$185, 4 day notice.** 4121 Kepler St. On Hwy 43,
just e of Hwy 32. Int corridors. **Pets:** Medium. $20 one-time fee/room.
Designated rooms, service with restrictions, supervision.
(ASK) (S₀) (✕) (📱) (📺)

# BRITISH COLUMBIA

## CITY INDEX

## 100 MILE HOUSE

### ▼▼ ▼▼ 100 Mile House Super 8 M
(250) 395-8888. $88-$98, 4 day notice. 989 Alder Ave. 1 km s on Hwy 97. Ext corridors. Pets: Accepted.

[S0] [X] [H] [P]

### ▼▼ ▼▼ Ramada Limited M
(250) 395-2777. $85-$139. 917 Alder Ave. 1 km s on Hwy 97. Int corridors. Pets: Other species. $10 one-time fee/pet. Designated rooms, service with restrictions.

[ASK] [S0] [X] [H] [P]

### ▼▼ ▼▼ Red Coach Inn SH ❖
(250) 395-2266. $68-$80. 170 Cariboo Hwy N. On Hwy 97, on the north end of town. Ext/int corridors. Pets: Other species. $6 daily fee/room. Designated rooms.

[ASK] [S0] [X] [GM] [H] [P] [YI] [≈]

## 108 MILE HOUSE

### CAA ▼▼ ▼▼ 108 Resort & Conference Centre SH
(250) 791-5211. $72-$125. 4816 Telqua Dr. From Hwy 97, 1.6 km nw on access road, follow signs. Ext corridors. Pets: Medium. $10 one-time fee/pet. Designated rooms, service with restrictions, supervision.

[SAVE] [S0] [X] [GM] [H] [P] [YI] [≈] [X]

## ABBOTSFORD

### CAA ▼▼ ▼▼ Best Western Bakerview Inn M
(604) 859-1341. $89-$109. 1821 Sumas Way. Trans-Canada Hwy 1, exit 92 (Town Centre), just n on Hwy 11. Ext corridors. Pets: Large, other species. $50 deposit/room. Service with restrictions, supervision.

[SAVE] [S0] [X] [H] [P] [YI] [≈]

### ▼▼▼▼ Coast Abbotsford Hotel & Suites SH
(604) 853-1880. $160-$195. 2020 Sumas Way. Trans-Canada Hwy 1, exit 92 (Town Centre), just n on Hwy 11. Int corridors. Pets: Accepted.

[ASK] [S0] [X] [H] [P] [YI] [≈]

### CAA ▼▼▼▼ Comfort Inn SH
(604) 859-6211. $59-$149. 2073 Clearbrook Rd. Trans-Canada Hwy 1, exit 87 (Clearbrook Rd). Ext/int corridors. Pets: Medium. $10 daily fee/pet. Service with restrictions, crate.

[SAVE] [S0] [X] [GM] [H] [P] [YI] [≈] [X]

### ▼▼ ▼▼ Ramada Plaza & Conference Centre-Abbotsford SH
(604) 870-1050. $129. 36035 N Parallel Rd. Trans-Canada Hwy 1, exit 95 (Whatcom Rd). Int corridors. Pets: Accepted.

[ASK] [S0] [X] [GM] [⌖] [H] [P] [YI] [≈] [X]

### CAA ▼▼▼ Super 8 Motel Abbotsford M ❖
(604) 853-1141. $79-$129. 1881 Sumas Way. Trans-Canada Hwy 1, exit 92 (Town Centre), just n on Hwy 11. Ext corridors. Pets: Medium. $10 daily fee/pet. Designated rooms, service with restrictions, supervision.

[SAVE] [S0] [X] [H] [P]

## BLUE RIVER

### CAA ▼▼ ▼▼ Glacier Mountain Lodge M ❖
(250) 673-2393. $79-$109. 869 Shell Rd. On Hwy 5 (Yellowhead Hwy) at Shell Rd, follow signs. Int corridors. Pets: Medium. $10 daily fee/room. Designated rooms, service with restrictions, supervision.

[SAVE] [S0] [X] [H]

### ▼▼▼▼ Mike Wiegele Helicopter Skiing Resort CA
(250) 673-8381. $85-$195. 1 Harrwood Dr. On Hwy 5 (Yellowhead Hwy) at Harrwood Dr, follow signs. Ext corridors. Pets: Other species. $30 daily fee/pet. Designated rooms, service with restrictions, supervision.

[ASK] [S0] [X] [H] [P] [X]

## BOWEN ISLAND

### ▼▼ ▼▼ Wildwood Lane Cottages CA
(604) 947-2253. $150-$175, 14 day notice. 1291 Adams Rd. From ferry terminal, 5.6 km w on Grafton Rd, then 1 km n. Ext corridors. Pets: $20 daily fee/pet. No service, supervision.

[X] [H] [P] [X]

## CACHE CREEK

### CAA ▼▼ ▼▼ Bonaparte Motel M ❖
(250) 457-9693. $50-$100. 1395 Hwy 97 N. 1 km n of jct Trans-Canada Hwy 1. Ext corridors. Pets: Other species. $10 daily fee/pet. Designated rooms, no service, supervision.

[SAVE] [S0] [X] [H] [≈]

## CAMPBELL RIVER

### CAA ▼▼▼▼ Anchor Inn & Suites SH
(250) 286-1131. $109-$289. 261 Island Hwy. On Island Hwy 19A, 2 km s. Int corridors. Pets: Small. $6 daily fee/pet. Designated rooms, service with restrictions, supervision.

[SAVE] [S0] [X] [H] [P] [YI] [≈] [X]

### CAA ▼▼▼▼ Best Western Austrian Chalet M
(250) 923-4231. $111-$169. 462 S Island Hwy. 3.2 km s on Island Hwy 19A. Ext/int corridors. Pets: Medium, other species. $6 daily fee/pet. Designated rooms, service with restrictions, supervision.

[SAVE] [S0] [X] [H] [P] [≈] [X] [X]

**Campbell River Lodge Fishing & Adventure Resort** M
(250) 287-7446. **$74-$99, 3 day notice.** 1760 N Island Hwy. On Island Hwy 19A, 2 km nw of downtown; just e from Hwy 19 and 28. Ext/int corridors. **Pets:** Medium. $8 daily fee/pet. Designated rooms, service with restrictions, supervision.

**Campbell River Super 8** M
(250) 286-6622. **$72-$96.** 340 S Island Hwy. 3 km s on Island Hwy 19A. Int corridors. **Pets:** Accepted.

**Town Centre Inn** M
(250) 287-8866. **$69-$89.** 1500 Dogwood St. Follow Island Hwy 19A through town, watch for signs, just e on Dogwood St; corner of 16th Ave. Ext corridors. **Pets:** Accepted.

## CASTLEGAR

**Quality Inn Castlegar** M
(250) 365-2177. **$70-$100.** 1935 Columbia Ave. Jct Hwy 3A and 3B, just s. Ext/int corridors. **Pets:** $5 daily fee/pet. Service with restrictions, supervision.

**Super 8 Motel-Castlegar** SH
(250) 365-2700. **$89-$179.** 651 18th St. Hwy 3, exit city centre. Int corridors. **Pets:** $10 daily fee/pet. Service with restrictions, supervision.

## CHASE

**Chase Country Inn Motel** M
(250) 679-3333. **$59-$95, 3 day notice.** 576 Coburn St. Trans-Canada Hwy 1 and Coburn St. Ext corridors. **Pets:** Large. $5 daily fee/pet. Service with restrictions, supervision.

**Quaaout Resort & Conference Centre** SH
(250) 679-3090. **$70-$180.** Trans-Canada Hwy 1, exit Squilax Bridge, 2.5 km w on Little Shuswap Rd. Int corridors. **Pets:** Other species. $10 daily fee/pet. Designated rooms, service with restrictions.

## CHEMAINUS

**Best Western Chemainus Festival Inn** SH
(250) 246-4181. **$99-$219.** 9573 Chemainus Rd. Trans-Canada Hwy 1, exit Henry Rd, 1.4 km e. Int corridors. **Pets:** Accepted.

## CHILLIWACK

**Best Western Rainbow Country Inn** SH
(604) 795-3828. **$86-$129.** 43971 Industrial Way. Trans-Canada Hwy 1, exit 116 (Lickman Rd). Int corridors. **Pets:** Accepted.

**Chilliwack Travelodge** SH
(604) 792-4240. **$77-$105.** 45466 Yale Rd W. Trans-Canada Hwy 1, exit 119, just n. Int corridors. **Pets:** Small. $10 daily fee/room. Designated rooms, service with restrictions, supervision.

**Comfort Inn** M
(604) 858-0636. **$90-$129.** 45405 Luckakuck Way. Trans-Canada Hwy 1, exit 119, s on Vedder Rd, then 1 km w. Int corridors. **Pets:** Medium, other species. $5 daily fee/room. Designated rooms, service with restrictions, supervision.

## CHRISTINA LAKE

**New Horizon Motel** M
(250) 447-9312. **$79-$310, 15 day notice.** 2037 Hwy 3. Just e. Ext corridors. **Pets:** Small, other species. $10 daily fee/pet. Designated rooms, service with restrictions, supervision.

## CLEARWATER

**Clearwater Lodge** SH
(250) 674-3080. **$123-$145.** 331 Eden Rd. Jct Clearwater Valley Rd and Hwy 5 (Yellowhead Hwy). Ext/int corridors. **Pets:** Accepted.

**Clearwater Valley Resort** CA
(250) 674-3909. **$50-$110.** 373 Clearwater Valley Rd. Jct Hwy 5 (Yellowhead Hwy) and Clearwater Valley Rd. Ext corridors. **Pets:** Large, dogs only. $5 daily fee/pet. Service with restrictions, supervision.

**Jasper Way Inn Motel on beautiful Dutch Lake** M
(250) 674-3345. **$56-$95.** 57 E Old N Thompson Hwy. 1 km w on Old N Thompson Hwy, just off Hwy 5 (Yellowhead Hwy). Ext corridors. **Pets:** Accepted.

## COURTENAY

**The Coast Westerly Hotel** SH
(250) 338-7741. **$129-$239.** 1590 Cliffe Ave. Corner of Cliffe Ave and Island Hwy 19A N. Int corridors. **Pets:** Large. $10 daily fee/pet. Service with restrictions, supervision.

**Kingfisher Oceanside Resort & Spa** SH
(250) 338-1323. **$125-$165, 7 day notice.** 4330 S Island Hwy. 6 km s on Island Hwy 19A S, watch for signs. Ext corridors. **Pets:** Accepted.

**Travelodge Courtenay** M
(350) 334-4491. **$83-$125.** 2605 Cliffe Ave. 1.2 km s on Island Hwy 19A S. Ext corridors. **Pets:** $5 deposit/pet. Designated rooms, service with restrictions, supervision.

## CRANBROOK

**Heritage Inn** SH
(250) 489-4301. **$82-$105.** 803 Cranbrook St N. Hwy 3 and 95; centre. Int corridors. **Pets:** Accepted.

**Model A Inn** M
(250) 489-4600. **$75-$129.** 1908 Cranbrook St N. 2.5 km n on Hwy 3 and 95. Ext corridors. **Pets:** Accepted.

**St. Eugene Mission Resort** LH
(250) 420-2000. **$99-$129.** 7731 Mission Rd. Hwy 3, exit Kimberley/Airport (Hwy 95A) to Mission Rd, 4.5 km n. Int corridors. **Pets:** Accepted.

**Super 8 Motel** SH
(250) 489-8028. **$90-$115.** 2370 Cranbrook St N. Just w of jct Hwy 93 and 95; corner of 30th Ave. Int corridors. **Pets:** Accepted.

## CRESTON

**Downtowner Motor Inn** SH
(250) 428-2238. **$45-$62.** 1218 Canyon St. Corner of 12th Ave N. Int corridors. **Pets:** $4 daily fee/pet.

(CAA) 🔷🔷🔷 **Skimmerhorn Inn** **M**
(250) 428-4009. **$70-$96.** 2711 Hwy 3. On Hwy 3, 0.8 km e. Ext corridors. **Pets:** Medium, dogs only. $5 daily fee/pet. Service with restrictions, supervision.
[SAVE] [X] [■] [■] [≈]

(CAA) 🔷 **Sunset Motel** **M** 🐾
(250) 428-2229. **$64-$84.** 2705 Canyon St, Hwy 3 E. 1 km e on Hwy 3. Ext corridors. **Pets:** Small, other species. $5 deposit/pet. Service with restrictions, supervision.
[SAVE] [S6] [X] [■] [■] [≈]

## DAWSON CREEK

(CAA) 🔷🔷🔷 **Dawson Creek Super 8** **SH**
(250) 782-8899. **$95-$200.** 1440 Alaska Ave. Just s of jct Hart Hwy 97 S and Alaska Hwy 97 N. Int corridors. **Pets:** Accepted.
[SAVE] [S6] [X] [■] [■] [†1]

## DUNCAN

(CAA) 🔷🔷🔷 **Best Western Cowichan Valley Inn** **SH**
(250) 748-2722. **$101-$165.** 6474 Trans-Canada Hwy 1. 3 km n. Int corridors. **Pets:** Other species. Designated rooms, service with restrictions, supervision.
[SAVE] [S6] [X] [■] [■] [†1] [≈]

🔷 **Falcon Nest Motel** **M** 🐾
(250) 748-8188. **$58-$85.** 5867 Trans-Canada Hwy 1. 1.5 km n. Ext corridors. **Pets:** Medium, dogs only. $7 daily fee/pet. Designated rooms, service with restrictions, supervision.
[ASK] [X] [■] [■] [≈]

🔷🔷🔷 **Travelodge Silver Bridge Inn Duncan** **SH**
(250) 748-4311. **$99-$139.** 140 Trans-Canada Hwy 1. Just n of the Silver Bridge. Ext corridors. **Pets:** Other species. $10 daily fee/room. Designated rooms.
[ASK] [S6] [X] [■] [■] [†1]

## ENDERBY

(CAA) 🔷🔷🔷 **Howard Johnson Inn Fortunes Landing** **M**
(250) 838-6825. **$79-$109.** 1510 George St. 1 km n on Hwy 97A. Ext corridors. **Pets:** Other species. S5 daily fee/pet. Service with restrictions, supervision.
[SAVE] [S6] [X] [■] [■] [†1] [≈]

## FERNIE

(CAA) 🔷🔷🔷🔷 **Best Western Fernie Mountain Lodge** **SH**
(250) 423-5500. **$122-$332.** 1622 7th Ave. Hwy 3, exit 7th Ave, on Hwy 3; east end of Fernie. Int corridors. **Pets:** Accepted.
[SAVE] [S6] [X] [■] [■] [†1] [≈]

🔷 **Fernie Log Inn** **M**
(250) 423-6222. **$65-$85, 7 day notice.** 141 Commerce Rd. 1.8 km e on Hwy 3. Ext corridors. **Pets:** $10 daily fee/pet. Service with restrictions, crate.
[ASK] [S6] [X] [■] [■] [†1] [🐾]

(CAA) 🔷🔷🔷 **Park Place Lodge** **SH**
(250) 423-6871. **$104-$234.** 742 Hwy 3. At 7th St. Int corridors. **Pets:** Medium, other species. Designated rooms, service with restrictions, supervision.
[SAVE] [S6] [X] [■] [■] [†1] [≈] [X]

(CAA) 🔷🔷🔷🔷 **Stanford Inn** **CO**
(250) 423-5000. **$109-$159.** 100 Riverside Way. Hwy 3, 2 km w. Ext/int corridors. **Pets:** Accepted.
[SAVE] [S6] [X] [■] [■] [†1] [≈] [X]

🔷🔷 **Super 8 Motel-Fernie** **SH**
(250) 423-6788. **$72-$96.** 2021 Hwy 3. 1.5 km w. Int corridors. **Pets:** Accepted.
[ASK] [S6] [X] [■]

## FORT ST. JOHN

(CAA) 🔷🔷 **Best Western Coachman Inn** **SH**
(250) 787-0651. **$100.** 8540 Alaska Rd. 2 km s on Hwy 97. Int corridors. **Pets:** Medium. $15 one-time fee/pet. Designated rooms, service with restrictions, supervision.
[SAVE] [S6] [X] [■] [■] [†1] [X]

(CAA) 🔷 **Econo Lodge** **SH**
(250) 787-8475. **$90-$95, 14 day notice.** 10419 Alaska Rd. 0.5 km n on Hwy 97. Int corridors. **Pets:** Accepted.
[SAVE] [S6] [X] [■]

🔷🔷🔷 **Quality Inn Northern Grand** **LH** 🐾
(250) 787-0521. **$118-$149.** 9830 100th Ave. Centre. Int corridors. **Pets:** $12 one-time fee/room. Designated rooms, supervision.
[ASK] [S6] [X] [■] [■] [†1] [≈] [X]

🔷🔷 **Ramada Limited** **SH**
(250) 787-0779. **$105-$123.** 10103 98th Ave. Corner of 100th Ave; centre of downtown. Int corridors. **Pets:** Small. $10 daily fee/room. Designated rooms, service with restrictions, supervision.
[ASK] [S6] [X] [LM] [🐾] [■] [■] [†1]

🔷🔷🔷 **Super 8 Motel-Fort St. John** **SH**
(250) 785-7588. **$109-$275, 7 day notice.** 9500 Alaska Hwy. Just s on Hwy 97 (Alaska Hwy). Int corridors. **Pets:** Accepted.
[ASK] [S6] [X] [LM] [🐾] [■] [■] [†1] [≈] [X]

## FORT STEELE

🔷🔷 **Bull River Guest Ranch** **RA**
(250) 429-3760. **$125-$145, 14 day notice.** Hwy 95, 21.9 km se of town on Ft Steele-Wardner Rd, 12 km ne on gravel road, follow signs; Hwy 3 W, 41 km e of Cranbrook, use Ft Steele Rd. Ext corridors. **Pets:** Accepted.
[ASK] [X] [■] [■] [X] [🐾] [W] [🐾]

## GIBSONS

(CAA) 🔷🔷🔷 **Cedars Inn Hotel & Convention Centre** **M**
(604) 886-3008. **$96-$136.** 895 Gibsons Way. Hwy 101 and Shaw Rd; 6 km n from ferry terminal. Ext/int corridors. **Pets:** $15 daily fee/pet. Designated rooms, service with restrictions, crate.
[SAVE] [S6] [X] [■] [■] [†1] [≈] [X]

## GOLD BRIDGE

🔷🔷🔷 **Morrow Chalets** **CA**
(250) 238-2462. **$200-$300, 30 day notice.** 8 km n from the Tyaughton Lake turnoff, follow signs. Ext corridors. **Pets:** Accepted.
[ASK] [S6] [X] [■] [🐾]

🔷🔷 **Tyax Mountain Lake Resort** **SH**
(250) 238-2221. **$134-$168, 30 day notice.** Tyaughton Lake Rd. 8 km n from the Tyaughton Lake turnoff, follow signs. Int corridors. **Pets:** Accepted.
[ASK] [S6] [X] [■] [†1] [X] [🐾]

## GOLDEN

(CAA) 🔷🔷🔷🔷 **Best Western Mountain View Inn** **SH**
(250) 344-2333. **$109-$189.** 1024 11th St N. On Trans-Canada Hwy 1, south service road; 0.7 km w of jct Hwy 95 and Trans-Canada Hwy 1. Int corridors. **Pets:** Other species. $20 daily fee/pet. Designated rooms, service with restrictions, supervision.
[SAVE] [S6] [X] [■] [■] [≈]

🔷 **Golden Gate Motel** **M**
(250) 344-2252. **$45-$70.** 1408 Golden View Rd. On Trans-Canada Hwy 1, 1.5 km e of jct Hwy 95. Ext corridors. **Pets:** Accepted.
[ASK] [S6] [X] [■]

**▼▼ Golden Rim Motor Inn M**
(250) 344-2216. **$69-$120.** 1416 Golden View Rd. 1.5 km e on Trans-Canada Hwy 1 from jct Hwy 95. Ext corridors. **Pets:** Accepted.
[ASK] [S$] [✕] [🖴] [▣] [♨] [🛁] [✕]

**(CAA) ▼▼▼ Hillside Lodge & Chalets CA**
(250) 344-7281. **$118-$145, 5 day notice.** 1740 Seward Frontage Rd. 15 km w on Hwy 1, follow signs n off highway. Ext corridors. **Pets:** Accepted.
[SAVE] [✕] [🖴] [▣] [✕] [K] [Z]

**(CAA) ▼ Rondo Motel M**
(250) 344-5295. **$75-$92.** 824 Park Dr. Jct Trans-Canada Hwy 1 and 95, 2 km s on 10th Ave, just w on Park Dr; downtown. Ext corridors. **Pets:** $5 daily fee/pet. Designated rooms, service with restrictions, supervision.
[SAVE] [S$] [✕] [🖴]

# GULF ISLANDS NATIONAL PARK RESERVE AREA

## PENDER ISLAND

**(CAA) ▼▼▼ Poets Cove Resort & Spa SH**
(250) 629-2100. **$219-$307.** 9801 Spalding Rd, South Pender Island. From Otter Bay Ferry Terminal, follow signs to South Pender Island 16 km s; Otter Bay Rd to Bidwell Harbour Rd to Canal Rd. Ext/int corridors. **Pets:** Accepted.
[SAVE] [S$] [✕] [&M] [🖴] [▣] [♨] [🛁] [✕]

## QUADRA ISLAND

**▼▼ Taku Resort M**
(250) 285-3031. **$89-$280, 15 day notice.** 616 Taku Rd. From Campbell River ferry terminal, 6.6 km n on West Rd, then just e on Heriot Bay Rd, follow signs to Heriot Bay. Ext corridors. **Pets:** $10 daily fee/pet. Designated rooms, service with restrictions, supervision.
[✕] [🖴] [▣] [✕] [K]

## SALTSPRING ISLAND

**▼▼ Harbour House SH**
(250) 537-5571. **$59-$335.** 121 Upper Ganges Rd. 1 km n on Lower Ganges Rd, then just e, towards Long Harbour ferry terminal. Ext/int corridors. **Pets:** Accepted.
[ASK] [S$] [✕] [&M] [&] [▣] [♨] [K]

**▼▼ Seabreeze Inne M**
(250) 537-4145. **$69-$195, 3 day notice.** 101 Bittancourt Rd. From Ganges township, 1 km s on Fulford-Ganges Rd. Ext corridors. **Pets:** Accepted.
[ASK] [S$] [✕] [🖴] [▣] [✕] [K]

## SATURNA

**▼▼ Saturna Lodge CI**
(250) 539-2254. **$120-$195, 14 day notice.** 130 Payne Rd. From BC ferry terminal, just s on Narvaez Bay Rd, then just e, follow signs. Int corridors. **Pets:** Accepted.
[✕] [♨] [K] [W] [Z]

# END AREA

## HARRISON HOT SPRINGS

**(CAA) ▼▼▼ Harrison Hot Springs Resort & Spa LH ❧**
(604) 796-2244. **$129-$399, 3 day notice.** 100 Esplanade Ave. Just w; on lakefront. Int corridors. **Pets:** Dogs only. Designated rooms, service with restrictions, supervision.
[SAVE] [✕] [🖴] [▣] [♨] [🛁] [✕]

## HOPE

**(CAA) ▼▼ Alpine Motel M**
(604) 869-9931. **$70-$95.** 505 Old Hope-Princeton Way. Trans-Canada Hwy 1, exit 173 westbound; exit 170 eastbound, just n from lights. Ext corridors. **Pets:** Small. $100 deposit/room, $10 daily fee/room. No service, supervision.
[SAVE] [S$] [✕] [🖴] [▣]

**(CAA) ▼ Best Continental Motel M**
(604) 869-9726. **$55-$85.** 860 Fraser Ave. Trans-Canada Hwy 1, exit 170 to downtown; at Fort St. Ext corridors. **Pets:** Small, dogs only. $6 daily fee/pet. Service with restrictions, supervision.
[SAVE] [S$] [✕] [▣]

**(CAA) ▼▼ Inn Towne Motel M**
(604) 869-7276. **$65-$110.** 510 Trans-Canada Hwy. Trans-Canada Hwy 1, exit 170, 1 km n to downtown. Ext corridors. **Pets:** Accepted.
[SAVE] [S$] [✕] [🖴] [🛁]

**(CAA) ▼▼ Quality Inn M**
(604) 869-9951. **$73-$104.** 350 Old Hope-Princeton Way. Trans-Canada Hwy 1, exit 173 westbound; exit 170 eastbound, just n from lights. Int corridors. **Pets:** Medium. $2 one-time fee/pet. Service with restrictions, supervision.
[SAVE] [S$] [✕] [&M] [🖴] [▣] [🛁]

## INVERMERE

**(CAA) ▼▼ Best Western Invermere Inn SH**
(250) 342-9246. **$99-$159.** 1310 7th Ave. 3 km w of Hwy 93 and 95 at Invermere exit; centre. Int corridors. **Pets:** Accepted.
[SAVE] [✕] [🖴] [▣] [♨]

**▼▼ Invermere Super 8 SH**
(250) 342-8888. **$85-$100.** 8888 Arrow Rd. On Hwy 95. Int corridors. **Pets:** Accepted.
[S$] [✕] [🖴] [♨]

## GRAND FORKS

**▼▼ Ramada Limited M**
(250) 442-2127. **$89-$109.** 2729 Central Ave. West end of town on Hwy 3. Ext corridors. **Pets:** Dogs only. $10 daily fee/pet. Service with restrictions, supervision.
[ASK] [S$] [✕] [🖴] [▣] [♨] [🛁]

**(CAA) ▼ Western Traveller Motel M**
(250) 442-5566. **$59-$129.** 1591 Central Ave. West end of town on Hwy 3. Ext corridors. **Pets:** Medium, dogs only. $100 deposit/room, $7 daily fee/pet. Designated rooms, service with restrictions, supervision.
[SAVE] [S$] [✕] [🖴] [▣]

# KAMLOOPS

### ⓐ 🔷🔷 Accent Inns Ⓜ ❀
(250) 374-8877. **$89-$149.** 1325 Columbia St W. Trans-Canada Hwy 1, exit 369 (Columbia St) eastbound at Notre Dame Dr; exit 370 (Summit Dr) westbound at Notre Dame Dr. Ext corridors. **Pets:** Other species. $10 daily fee/room. Service with restrictions.
🆂 🆂 ✕ 🔳 💻 🍴 ⮂ ✕

### 🔷🔷 Days Inn 🅢🅗 ❀
(250) 374-5911. **$99-$119.** 1285 Trans-Canada Hwy W. Trans-Canada Hwy 1, exit 368 (Hillside Ave), just s. Int corridors. **Pets:** Large, other species. $15 daily fee/pet. Designated rooms, service with restrictions, supervision.
🅐🅢🅚 ✕ 🔳 💻 🍴 ⮂

### ⓐ 🔷🔷 Econo Lodge Inn & Suites Ⓜ
(250) 372-8533. **$65-$89.** 1773 Trans-Canada Hwy E. 2.4 km e on Trans-Canada Hwy 1, south side of service access road. Ext corridors. **Pets:** Accepted.
🆂 🆂 ✕ 🔳 💻 ⮂

### ⓐ 🔷 Grandview Motel Ⓜ ❀
(250) 372-1312. **$55-$99.** 463 Grandview Terr. Trans-Canada Hwy 1, exit 369 (Columbia St) eastbound, 2 km n; exit 370 (Summit Dr) westbound to Columbia St via City Centre. Ext corridors. **Pets:** Medium. $5 daily fee/pet. Designated rooms, service with restrictions, supervision.
🆂 🆂 ✕ 🔳 💻 ⮂

### ⓐ 🔷🔷 Hampton Inn 🅢🅗
(250) 571-7897. **$99-$250.** 1245 Rogers Way. Trans-Canada Hwy 1, exit 368 (Hillside Ave), just s via Hillside Way. Int corridors. **Pets:** Large, dogs only. $20 daily fee/pet. Designated rooms, service with restrictions, supervision.
🆂 🆂 ✕ 🅼 🔳 💻 ⮂ ✕

### 🔷 Hospitality Inn Ⓜ
(250) 374-4164. **$55-$89.** 500 W Columbia St. Trans-Canada Hwy 1, exit 369 (Columbia St) eastbound, 2 km n; exit 370 (Summit Dr) westbound to Columbia St via City Centre. Ext corridors. **Pets:** Large. $15 daily fee/pet. Service with restrictions.
🅐🅢🅚 🆂 ✕ 🔳 💻 🍴 ⮂

### ⓐ 🔷🔷 Kamloops Super 8 Motel Ⓜ
(250) 374-8688. **$64-$97.** 1521 Hugh Allan Dr. Trans-Canada Hwy 1, exit 367 (Pacific Way). Int corridors. **Pets:** Accepted.
🆂 🆂 ✕ 🅼

### ⓐ 🔷🔷 Ramada Inn-Kamloops 🅢🅗
(250) 374-0358. **$69-$109.** 555 W Columbia St. Trans-Canada Hwy 1, exit 369 (Columbia St) eastbound, 2 km n; exit 370 (Summit Dr) westbound to Columbia St via City Centre. Int corridors. **Pets:** Accepted.
🆂 🆂 ✕ 🔳 💻 🍴 ⮂ ✕

### 🔷 Ranchland Motel Ⓜ
(250) 828-8787. **$45-$75.** 2357 Trans-Canada Hwy E. 4.5 km e on Trans-Canada Hwy 1, exit River Rd, then just w along service access road. Ext corridors. **Pets:** Small, dogs only. $8 daily fee/pet. Designated rooms, service with restrictions, supervision.
🆂 ✕ 🔳 💻

### ⓐ 🔷🔷 Scott's Inn & Restaurant Ⓜ
(250) 372-8221. **$59-$99.** 551 11th Ave. Trans-Canada Hwy 1, exit 369 (Columbia St) eastbound, 5 km n; exit City Centre westbound, 1.6 km s on Columbia St. Ext corridors. **Pets:** Small. $6 daily fee/pet. Service with restrictions, supervision.
🆂 🆂 ✕ 🔳 💻 🍴 ⮂

# KELOWNA

### ⓐ 🔷🔷 Accent Inns 🅢🅗 ❀
(250) 862-8888. **$99-$159.** 1140 Harvey Ave. Corner of Hwy 97 N (Harvey Ave) and Gordon Dr. Ext corridors. **Pets:** Medium, other species. $10 daily fee/room. Designated rooms, service with restrictions, supervision.
🆂 🆂 ✕ 🔳 💻 🍴 ⮂ ✕

### ⓐ 🔷🔷🔷 Best Western Inn-Kelowna 🅢🅗 ❀
(250) 860-1212. **$115-$269.** 2402 Hwy 97 N. 1 km s of jct Hwy 33 and 97 N (Harvey Ave); corner of Leckie Rd. Ext/int corridors. **Pets:** Small. $25 daily fee/pet. Designated rooms, service with restrictions, crate.
🆂 🆂 ✕ 🅸 🔳 💻 🍴 ⮂ ✕

### ⓐ 🔷🔷 Comfort Inn Kelowna-Westside 🅢🅗 ❀
(250) 769-2355. **$76-$143.** 1655 Westgate Rd. Jct Hwy 97 (Harvey Ave) and Bartley Rd, s to Ross Rd. Int corridors. **Pets:** Medium, other species. $10 daily fee/pet. Designated rooms, service with restrictions, supervision.
🆂 🆂 ✕ 🔳 💻 🍴 ⮂

### 🔷🔷🔷 The Grand Okanagan Lakefront Resort & Conference Centre 🅛🅗
(250) 763-4500. **$155-$539.** 1310 Water St. Hwy 97 (Harvey Ave), 1 km w. Int corridors. **Pets:** Accepted.
🅐🅢🅚 🆂 ✕ 🅼 🔳 💻 🍴 ⮂ ✕

### ⓐ 🔷🔷 The Royal Anne Hotel 🅢🅗
(250) 763-2277. **$89-$189.** 348 Bernard Ave. Corner of Pandosy and Bernard Ave; downtown. Int corridors. **Pets:** Small. $10 daily fee/pet. Designated rooms, service with restrictions, supervision.
🆂 🆂 ✕ 💻

### 🔷 Town & Country Motel Ⓜ
(250) 860-7121. **$83-$129.** 2629 Hwy 97 N. 0.5 km n on Hwy 97 N (Harvey Ave) from jct Hwy 33. Ext corridors. **Pets:** Accepted.
🅐🅢🅚 ✕ 🅸 🔳 💻 ⮂

### 🔷🔷 Vineyard Inn Ⓜ
(250) 860-5703. **$69-$169.** 2486 Hwy 97 N. Southwest corner of jct Hwy 97 (Harvey Ave) and 33. Ext corridors. **Pets:** Small, dogs only. $5 daily fee/room. Service with restrictions, supervision.
🅐🅢🅚 🆂 ✕ 🔳 💻 ⮂ ✕

# KIMBERLEY

### ⓐ 🔷🔷🔷 Trickle Creek Residence Inn by Marriott 🅢🅗
(250) 427-5175. **$104-$380, 14 day notice.** 500 Stemwinder Dr. Hwy 95A, 3.1 km w on Ross St, follow signs for Alpine Village, then just e. Int corridors. **Pets:** Accepted.
🆂 🆂 ✕ 🔽 🅸 🔳 💻 🍴 ⮂ ✕

# LOGAN LAKE

### 🔷 Logan Lake Lodge Ⓜ ❀
(250) 523-9466. **$65-$69, 7 day notice.** 111 Chartrand Ave. Centre at Meadow Creek Rd and Chartrand Cresent. Int corridors. **Pets:** Other species. $15 one-time fee/room. Supervision.
🅐🅢🅚 🆂 ✕ 🔳 💻 🍴 🅰

# LUND

### 🔷 The Historic Lund Hotel 🅢🅗
(604) 414-0474. **Call for rates (no credit cards).** 1436 Hwy 101. End of Hwy 101; on the Sunshine Coast. Ext/int corridors. **Pets:** Small. $10 daily fee/room. Designated rooms, service with restrictions, supervision.
✕ 💻 🍴

# MADEIRA PARK

### 🔷🔷🔷 Sunshine Coast Resort 🅒🅞 ❀
(604) 883-9177. **$70-$275, 21 day notice.** 12695 Sunshine Coast (Hwy 101). Just n of Madeira Park Rd, follow signs. Ext/int corridors. **Pets:** Other species. $20 daily fee/pet. Supervision.
✕ 🅼 🅸 🔳 💻 ✕ 🅰

# MANNING PARK

▼▼ **Manning Park Resort** 🅂🄷
(250) 840-8822. **$94-$155, 14 day notice.** Hwy 3. Crowsnest Hwy 3; midway between Hope and Princeton. Ext/int corridors. **Pets:** Accepted.

🄰🅂🄺 🅂🐾 ☒ 🔌 🖵 🍴 ⌘ ☒ 🄰🄲

# MCBRIDE

🄰🄰 ▼▼ **North Country Lodge** 🄼
(250) 569-0001. **$79-$109.** 868 Frontage Rd N. Just w of village main exit, on Hwy 16 north service road. Ext corridors. **Pets:** Accepted.

🅂🄰🅅🄴 🅂🐾 ☒ 🔌 🖵 🍴

# MERRITT

🄰🄰 ▼▼▼ **Best Western Nicola Inn** 🅂🄷
(250) 378-4253. **$85-$119.** 4025 Walters St. Hwy 5, exit 290, 1 km w. Ext corridors. **Pets:** Accepted.

🅂🄰🅅🄴 🅂🐾 ☒ 🔌 🖵 🍴 ⌘

▼▼ **Ramada Limited** 🄼
(250) 378-3567. **$80-$110.** 3571 Voght St. Hwy 5, exit 290, just w. Ext corridors. **Pets:** Other species. $5 daily fee/pet. Designated rooms, service with restrictions, supervision.

🄰🅂🄺 🅂🐾 ☒ 🔌 🖵 ⌘ ☒

🄰🄰 ▼▼ **Super 8 Motel** 🄼
(250) 378-9422. **$75-$105.** 3561 Voght St. Hwy 5, exit 290, just w. Ext corridors. **Pets:** Accepted.

🅂🄰🅅🄴 🅂🐾 ☒ 🔌 🖵 🍴 ⌘

# NAKUSP

🄰🄰 ▼▼ **The Selkirk Inn** 🅂🄷
(250) 265-3666. **$45-$79.** 210 W 6th Ave. Just n. Int corridors. **Pets:** Small. $20 deposit/room, $8 daily fee/pet. Designated rooms, service with restrictions, supervision.

🅂🄰🅅🄴 ☒ 🔌 🖵

# NANAIMO

🄰🄰 ▼▼ **Best Western Dorchester Hotel** 🅂🄷 🐾
(250) 754-6835. **$72-$108.** 70 Church St. Trans-Canada Hwy 1 to Comox Rd; follow signs downtown. Int corridors. **Pets:** Medium. $20 daily fee/pet. Designated rooms, service with restrictions, crate.

🅂🄰🅅🄴 🅂🐾 ☒ 🔌 🖵 🍴

🄰🄰 ▼▼ **Best Western Northgate Inn** 🅂🄷 🐾
(250) 390-2222. **$79-$119.** 6450 Metral Dr. Hwy 19A (Island Hwy), just w on Aulds Rd, then just s. Int corridors. **Pets:** Other species. $20 daily fee/pet. Designated rooms.

🅂🄰🅅🄴 ☒ 🔌 🖵 🍴 ☒

▼▼ **Days Inn Nanaimo Harbourview** 🅂🄷
(250) 754-8171. **$89-$119.** 809 Island Hwy S. On Island Hwy 1, 2 km s. Int corridors. **Pets:** Large, dogs only. $10 daily fee/pet. Designated rooms, service with restrictions, supervision.

🄰🅂🄺 🅂🐾 ☒ 🔌 🖵 🍴 ⌘

🄰🄰 ▼▼▼ **Inn on Long Lake** 🅂🄷 🐾
(250) 758-1144. **$109-$169.** 4700 Island Hwy N. 5 km n on Hwy 19A (Island Hwy) from Departure Bay ferry terminal. Ext corridors. **Pets:** Other species. $20 one-time fee/pet. Supervision.

🅂🄰🅅🄴 ☒ 🅂🄼 🔌 🖵 ☒

🄰🄰 ▼▼ **Travelodge Nanaimo** 🄼
(250) 754-6355. **$84-$109.** 96 Terminal Ave N. Jct Terminal Ave and Island Hwy 19A. Int corridors. **Pets:** Medium. $10 one-time fee/pet. Designated rooms, service with restrictions, supervision.

🅂🄰🅅🄴 🅂🐾 ☒ 🔌 🖵

# NANOOSE BAY

▼▼ **Fairwinds Schooner Cove Hotel & Marina** 🅂🄷 🐾
(250) 468-7691. **$69-$179.** 3521 Dolphin Dr. Island Hwy 1, 8.5 km se, follow signs via Powderpoint Rd (which becomes Fairwinds Dr). Int corridors. **Pets:** Medium. $10 daily fee/room. Designated rooms, service with restrictions, supervision.

🄰🅂🄺 🅂🐾 ☒ 🅂🄼 🖵 🍴 ⌘ ☒ 🄰🄲

# NARAMATA

▼▼ **The Village Motel** 🄼
(250) 496-5535. **$60-$147, 14 day notice.** 244 Robinson Dr. 14 km n on Naramata Rd from Penticton. Ext corridors. **Pets:** Accepted.

🅂🐾 ☒ 🔌 🖵 🄰🄲 🄲

# NELSON

🄰🄰 ▼▼▼ **Best Western Baker Street Inn & Convention Centre** 🅂🄷
(250) 352-3525. **$119-$139.** 153 Baker St. Jct of Hwy 6 and 3A. Int corridors. **Pets:** Other species. $10 one-time fee/room. Designated rooms, service with restrictions, supervision.

🅂🄰🅅🄴 🅂🐾 ☒ 🅂🄼 🔌 🖵 🍴

# NEW DENVER

▼▼ **Sweet Dreams Guesthouse** 🄲🄸
(250) 358-2415. **$80-$95, 7 day notice.** 702 Eldorado St. 0.4 km w of Hwy 6 on Slocan Ave. Int corridors. **Pets:** Accepted.

🄰🅂🄺 🅂🐾 ☒ 🍴 🄰🄲 🄿🅅 🄲

# PARKSVILLE

🄰🄰 ▼▼▼ **Quality Resort Bayside** 🅂🄷
(250) 248-8333. **$109-$259.** 240 Dogwood St. Island Hwy 19, exit 51 (Parksville/Coombs), 2 km e, then 1 km n on Hwy 19A. Int corridors. **Pets:** Medium, dogs only. $15 daily fee/pet. Designated rooms, service with restrictions, supervision.

🅂🄰🅅🄴 🅂🐾 ☒ 🅂🄼 🖵 🍴 ⌘ ☒

▼ **Skylite Motel** 🄼
(250) 248-4271. **$62-$129.** 459 E Island Hwy. Island Hwy 19, exit 46 (Parksville), 3.5 km n on Hwy 19A. Ext corridors. **Pets:** Accepted.

🄰🅂🄺 🅂🐾 ☒ 🔌 🄰🄲

🄰🄰 ▼▼▼ **Tigh-Na-Mara Seaside Spa Resort & Conference Center** 🄻🄷 🐾
(250) 248-2072. **$129-$329.** 1155 Resort Dr. Island Hwy 19, exit 46 (Parksville), 2 km n on Hwy 19A. Ext corridors. **Pets:** Other species. $25 one-time fee/room. Designated rooms, service with restrictions, supervision.

🅂🄰🅅🄴 🅂🐾 ☒ 🔌 🖵 🍴 ⌘ ☒ 🄰🄲

▼▼ **Travelodge Parksville** 🅂🄷
(250) 248-2232. **$99-$199.** 424 W Island Hwy. Island Hwy 19, exit 51 (Parksville/Coombs), 2 km e, then just n on Hwy 19A. Int corridors. **Pets:** Other species. $10 daily fee/pet. Designated rooms, supervision.

🄰🅂🄺 🅂🐾 ☒ 🅂🄼 🖵 ⌘

🄰🄰 ▼▼ **V.I.P. Motel** 🄼 🐾
(250) 248-3244. **$89-$129, 7 day notice.** 414 W Island Hwy. Island Hwy 19, exit 51 (Parksville/Coombs), 2 km e, then just n on Hwy 19A. Ext corridors. **Pets:** $10 daily fee/pet. Service with restrictions, supervision.

🅂🄰🅅🄴 🅂🐾 ☒ 🔌 🖵 🄰🄲

# PARSON

▼▼ **Timber Inn-Chalets & Restaurant** 🅂🄷
(250) 348-2228. **$75-$95, 30 day notice.** 3483 Hwy 95. Just off Hwy 95; 34 km s of Golden. Ext/int corridors. **Pets:** Accepted.

☒ 🔌 🖵 🍴 ☒ 🄰🄲 🄿🅅 🄲

# PEMBERTON

Ⓐ ◆◆◆◆ **Pemberton Valley Lodge** 🆂🄷 🐾
(604) 894-2000. **$169-$329.** 1490 Portage Rd. Just e on Hwy 99 from Pioneer Junction. Int corridors. **Pets:** $20 one-time fee/pet. Designated rooms, supervision.

🆂🅰🆅🅴 💲🗙 🖥 💻 🏊

# PENTICTON

◆◆ ◆◆ **Best Western Inn at Penticton** 🆂🄷
(250) 493-0311. **$89-$169.** 3180 Skaha Lake Rd. 4 km s. Ext corridors. **Pets:** Accepted.

🄰🅂🄺 💲🗙 🖥 💻 🍴 🏊

◆◆ ◆◆ **Days Inn Penticton** 🆂🄷
(250) 493-6616. **$99-$199, 7 day notice.** 152 Riverside Dr. Hwy 97, just n. Ext/int corridors. **Pets:** Accepted.

🄰🅂🄺 💲🗙 🖥 💻 🍴 🏊

Ⓐ ◆◆ ◆◆ **Golden Sands Resort Motel** 🄲🄾
(250) 492-4210. **$70-$295, 21 day notice.** 1028 Lakeshore Dr W. Riverside Dr and Lakeshore Dr W. Ext corridors. **Pets:** Small, dogs only. $10 daily fee/pet. Designated rooms, service with restrictions, supervision.

🆂🅰🆅🅴 💲🗙 🖥 💻 🏊

Ⓐ ◆◆◆◆ **Penticton Lakeside Resort, Convention Centre & Casino** 🄻🄷 🐾
(250) 493-8221. **$155-$275, 7 day notice.** 21 Lakeshore Dr W. Main St at Lakeshore Dr W. Int corridors. **Pets:** $10 daily fee/room. Designated rooms, service with restrictions, supervision.

🆂🅰🆅🅴 💲🗙 🖥 💻 🍴 🏊 🚫

Ⓐ ◆◆ **Penticton Slumber Lodge** 🄼
(250) 492-4008. **$68-$198, 7 day notice.** 274 Lakeshore Dr W. Corner of Lakeshore Dr and Winnipeg St; Hwy 97, n on Riverside, 1.5 km n. Ext corridors. **Pets:** Dogs only. $100 deposit/pet, $10 daily fee/pet. Designated rooms, service with restrictions, supervision.

🆂🅰🆅🅴 🗙 📶 🖥 💻 🏊

◆◆ ◆◆ **Penticton Travelodge** 🆂🄷
(250) 492-0225. **$69-$199.** 950 Westminster Ave W. Hwy 97 (Eckhart Ave), just ne. Ext/int corridors. **Pets:** Small. $10 daily fee/pet. Service with restrictions, supervision.

🄰🅂🄺 💲🗙 🖥 💻 🍴 🏊 🚫

Ⓐ ◆◆◆◆ **Ramada Inn & Suites** 🆂🄷
(250) 492-8926. **$89-$249.** 1050 Eckhardt Ave W. 1.2 km w on Hwy 97. Ext corridors. **Pets:** Accepted.

🆂🅰🆅🅴 💲🗙 📶 🗂 🖥 💻 🍴 🚫

Ⓐ ◆◆ **Spanish Villa Resort** 🄼
(250) 492-2922. **$68-$198, 7 day notice.** 890 Lakeshore Dr W. Corner of Power St and Lakeshore Dr W. Ext corridors. **Pets:** Large, dogs only. $100 deposit/pet, $10 daily fee/pet. Designated rooms, service with restrictions, supervision.

🆂🅰🆅🅴 🗙 🖥 💻 🏊

◆◆ ◆◆ **Super 8 Motel Penticton** 🄼
(250) 492-3829. **$80-$130.** 1706 Main St. Jct Main St and Industrial. Ext/int corridors. **Pets:** Accepted.

🄰🅂🄺 💲🗙 🖥 💻 🏊

# PORT ALBERNI

Ⓐ ◆◆◆◆ **Best Western Barclay Hotel** 🆂🄷
(250) 724-7171. **$109-$159, 14 day notice.** 4277 Stamp Ave. Johnston Rd (Hwy 4), just s on Gertrude St. Int corridors. **Pets:** Small, other species. $20 daily fee/room. Designated rooms, service with restrictions, supervision.

🆂🅰🆅🅴 💲🗙 📶 🖥 💻 🍴 🚫

◆◆◆◆ **Hospitality Inn** 🆂🄷 🐾
(250) 723-8111. **$120-$159.** 3835 Redford St. 3.2 km sw of jct Hwy 4 via City Centre/Port Alberni South Rt. Int corridors. **Pets:** Large, other species. $10 daily fee/pet. Designated rooms, service with restrictions, supervision.

🄰🅂🄺 💲🗙 🖥 💻 🍴

Ⓐ ◆◆ **Riverside Motel** 🄼
(250) 724-9916. **$69-$87.** 5065 Roger St. Johnston Rd (Hwy 4), just s on Gertrude St, then just w. Ext corridors. **Pets:** Accepted.

🆂🅰🆅🅴 💲🗙 🖥 💻 🐾

# PORT HARDY

◆◆ **Airport Inn** 🆂🄷
(250) 949-9434. **$70-$120.** 4030 Byng Rd. Hwy 19, 5 km ne, follow signs. Int corridors. **Pets:** Accepted.

🗙 🖥 💻 🍴 🐾

◆◆ ◆◆ **Glen Lyon Inn** 🆂🄷
(250) 949-7115. **$85-$140, 3 day notice.** 6435 Hardy Bay Rd. Hwy 19, 1.5 km n, follow signs. Ext corridors. **Pets:** Medium. $10 daily fee/room. Designated rooms, service with restrictions, supervision.

🗙 🖥 💻 🍴 🐾

# POWELL RIVER

◆◆◆◆ **Powell River Town Centre Hotel** 🆂🄷
(604) 485-3000. **$144-$180.** 4660 Joyce Ave. 0.8 km e on Duncan St (BC ferry terminal), then 1 km n. Int corridors. **Pets:** Accepted.

🄰🅂🄺 💲🗙 📶 💻 🍴

# PRINCE GEORGE

Ⓐ ◆◆ ◆◆ **P.G. Hi-Way Motel** 🄼
(250) 564-6869. **$65-$70.** 1737 20th Ave. Jct Hwy 97, 1.2 km e on Trans-Canada Hwy 16 (Yellowhead Hwy). Ext corridors. **Pets:** Small. $10 daily fee/pet. Designated rooms, no service, supervision.

🆂🅰🆅🅴 💲🗙 🖥 💻

# PRINCE RUPERT

Ⓐ ◆◆ **Aleeda Motel** 🄼
(250) 627-1367. **$55-$85.** 900 3rd Ave W. Corner of 3rd Ave W and 8th St. Int corridors. **Pets:** $5 daily fee/pet. Designated rooms, service with restrictions.

🆂🅰🆅🅴 💲🗙 🖥 💻 🐾

◆◆ ◆◆ **The Coast Prince Rupert Hotel** 🆂🄷 🐾
(250) 624-6711. **Call for rates.** 118 6th St. Between 1st and 2nd aves W. Int corridors. **Pets:** Designated rooms, service with restrictions, supervision.

🗙 📶 💻 🍴

◆◆ ◆◆ **Howard Johnson Highliner Plaza Hotel** 🆂🄷 🐾
(250) 624-9060. **$69-$159.** 815 1st Ave W. Corner of 1st Ave W and 7th St; downtown. Int corridors. **Pets:** Medium. $15 daily fee/pet. Designated rooms, service with restrictions, supervision.

🄰🅂🄺 💲🗙 🖥 💻 🍴 🐾

# PRINCETON

Ⓐ ◆◆◆◆ **Best Western Princeton Inn** 🄼
(250) 295-3537. **$80-$119.** 169 Hwy 3. On Hwy 3. Ext corridors. **Pets:** Medium. $10 daily fee/pet. Designated rooms, service with restrictions, supervision.

🆂🅰🆅🅴 💲🗙 🖥 💻 🏊

Ⓐ ◆◆ **Villager Inn** 🄼 🐾
(250) 295-6996. **$59-$129.** 244 4th St. Just off Hwy 3. Ext corridors. **Pets:** Small, other species. $20 deposit/pet. Service with restrictions, supervision.

🆂🅰🆅🅴 💲🗙 🖥 💻 🏊

# QUALICUM BEACH

**Old Dutch Inn (By The Sea)** SH
(250) 752-6914. **$79-$109.** 2690 Island Hwy W. Hwy 19, exit 60 (Qualicum Beach/Port Alberni), 4 km on Memorial Ave at jct Hwy 19A. Int corridors. **Pets:** Accepted.

**Qualicum Heritage Inn** SH
(250) 752-9262. **$89-$119.** 427 College Rd. Hwy 19, exit 60 (Qualicum Beach/Port Alberni), 4 km e on Memorial Ave, then 1 km s on Island Hwy 19A. Int corridors. **Pets:** Accepted.

# QUESNEL

**Talisman Inn** M
(250) 992-7247. **$65-$81.** 753 Front St. Hwy 97, 1 km n of Carson Ave. Int corridors. **Pets:** Accepted.

# RADIUM HOT SPRINGS

**Chalet Europe** M
(250) 347-9305. **$79-$179, 7 day notice.** 5063 Madsen Rd. Hwy 93 and 95, just e, 1 km off Hwy 93 up the hill. Ext corridors. **Pets:** Dogs only. $10 daily fee/room. Designated rooms, supervision.

**Lido Motel** M
(250) 347-9533. **$45-$75, 3 day notice.** 4876 McKay St. Hwy 93 and 95 S, Stanley St W to Main St W, then s. Ext corridors. **Pets:** Other species. $5 daily fee/pet. Supervision.

**Sunrise Suites Motel** CO
(250) 347-0008. **$70-$175, 7 day notice.** 7369 Prospector Ave. Hwy 93 and 95, 0.7 km n on Hwy 95, just sw. Ext corridors. **Pets:** Accepted.

**Sunset Motel** M
(250) 347-0021. **$55-$120.** 4883 McKay St. Hwy 93 and 95 S, w to service road (Main St), just s. Ext corridors. **Pets:** Accepted.

# REVELSTOKE

**Best Western Wayside Inn** SH
(250) 837-6161. **$89-$169.** 1901 LaForme Blvd. North side of Trans-Canada Hwy 1, at intersection nearest east end of Columbia River Bridge. Ext/int corridors. **Pets:** Large, other species. Designated rooms, service with restrictions, supervision.

**The Coast Hillcrest Resort Hotel** LH
(250) 837-3322. **$125-$235.** 2100 Oak Dr. 4.3 km e on Trans-Canada Hwy 1, 0.9 km sw. Int corridors. **Pets:** Large, other species. $15 daily fee/room. Designated rooms, service with restrictions, supervision.

**Monashee Lodge** M
(250) 837-6778. **$59-$85.** 1601 3rd St W. South side of Trans-Canada Hwy 1, just e of Columbia River Bridge at Victoria Rd, then just se on Wright Ave. Ext corridors. **Pets:** Small, other species. $5 one-time fee/room. Designated rooms, service with restrictions, crate.

**Regent Inn** SH
(250) 837-2107. **$129-$139.** 112 1st St E. 2 km s from Trans-Canada Hwy 1 at Victoria Rd; downtown. Int corridors. **Pets:** Accepted.

**Swiss Chalet Motel** M
(250) 837-4650. **$54-$99.** 1101 Victoria Rd. 1 km s from Trans-Canada Hwy 1. Ext corridors. **Pets:** Small. $5 daily fee/pet. Designated rooms, service with restrictions, supervision.

# ROSSLAND

**Thriftlodge Rossland** M
(250) 362-7364. **$74-$89, 3 day notice.** 1199 Nancy Green Hwy. 1 km w on Hwy 3B, jct Hwy 22. Ext corridors. **Pets:** Other species. $7 daily fee/room. Designated rooms, service with restrictions, supervision.

# SALMON ARM

**Holiday Inn Express Hotel & Suites Salmon Arm** SH
(250) 832-7711. **$119-$299.** 1090 22nd St NE. 0.5 mi on Trans-Canada Hwy 1. Int corridors. **Pets:** Accepted.

**Super 8 Motel** SH
(250) 832-8812. **$75-$130.** 2901 10th Ave NE. 1 km e on Trans-Canada Hwy 1. Int corridors. **Pets:** Small, dogs only. $10 daily fee/pet. Designated rooms, no service, supervision.

# SECHELT

**Driftwood Inn** M
(604) 885-5811. **$99-$169.** 5454 Trail Ave. Follow Sunshine Coast Hwy 101, just w of city centre. Ext/int corridors. **Pets:** Accepted.

# SICAMOUS

**Sicamous Super 8 Motel** SH
(250) 836-4988. **$60-$150.** 1120 Riverside Ave. Trans-Canada Hwy 1, s on Hwy 97A, just w on Main St to traffic circle, then just s. Ext corridors. **Pets:** Medium. $7 daily fee/pet. No service, supervision.

# SILVERTON

**William Hunter Cabins** CA
(250) 358-2844. **$85-$108, 10 day notice.** 303 Lake Ave. Centre. Ext corridors. **Pets:** No service, supervision.

# SMITHERS

**Aspen Motor Inn** M
(250) 847-4551. **$89-$98.** 4628 Yellowhead Hwy. 1.5 km w on Hwy 16 (Yellowhead Hwy). Ext corridors. **Pets:** Small, other species. $7 daily fee/pet. Designated rooms, service with restrictions, supervision.

# SQUAMISH

**Sea To Sky Hotel** SH
(604) 898-4874. **$89-$159.** 40330 Tantalus Way. 4.5 km n on Hwy 99 at Garibaldi Way. Int corridors. **Pets:** Small. $15 one-time fee/pet. Designated rooms, service with restrictions, supervision.

# SUMMERLAND

**Summerland Motel** M
(250) 494-4444. **$66-$199, 10 day notice.** 2107 Tait St. 5 km s on Hwy 97. Ext corridors. **Pets:** Accepted.

## SUN PEAKS

ⓐ ▼▼ ▼▼ **Delta Sun Peaks Resort** 🄻🄷 ❀
(250) 578-6000. **$89-$269, 7 day notice.** 3240 Village Way. Hwy 5, 31 km ne on Todd Mountain Rd, follow signs to village. Int corridors. **Pets:** $35 one-time fee/room. Designated rooms, service with restrictions.
🆂🅰🆅🅴 ⊠ 🄼 🄳 🄳 🄳 🄼 🅇

## TERRACE

ⓐ ▼▼▼▼ **Best Western Terrace Inn** 🅂🄷 ❀
(250) 635-0083. **$81-$120.** 4553 Greig Ave. Hwy 16, just e on Greig Ave, follow City Centre signs. Int corridors. **Pets:** Large, other species. $10 one-time fee/room. Supervision.
🆂🅰🆅🅴 🅂🄳 ⊠ 🄳 🄳 🄼

## TOFINO

ⓐ ▼▼▼▼ **Best Western Tin Wis Resort Lodge** 🅂🄷
(250) 725-4445. **$119-$355.** 1119 Pacific Rim Hwy. 3.5 km s on Hwy 4. Ext corridors. **Pets:** Accepted.
🆂🅰🆅🅴 🅂🄳 ⊠ 🄼 🄳 🄳 🄳 🄼 🅇

▼▼▼ **Long Beach Lodge Resort** 🅂🄷 ❀
(250) 725-2442. **$169-$529, 7 day notice.** 1441 Pacific Rim Hwy. 7.5 km s on Hwy 4. Ext/int corridors. **Pets:** $50 one-time fee/room. Designated rooms, service with restrictions, supervision.
🄰🅂🄺 ⊠ 🄳 🄳 🄳 🅇

ⓐ ▼▼▼▼ **Wickaninnish Inn** 🅂🄷 ❀
(250) 725-3100. **$260-$1500, 7 day notice.** Osprey Ln at Chesterman Beach. 4.3 km e on Hwy 4. Int corridors. **Pets:** $40 daily fee/pet. Designated rooms, service with restrictions, crate.
🆂🅰🆅🅴 ⊠ 🄼 🄳 🄳 🄳 🅇 🅇

## VALEMOUNT

ⓐ ▼▼ ▼▼ **Canoe Mountain Lodge** 🅂🄷 ❀
(250) 566-9171. **$78-$124, 10 day notice.** 1465 5th Ave. Just e of Hwy 5 (Yellowhead Hwy). Int corridors. **Pets:** Medium. $10 daily fee/room. Designated rooms, service with restrictions, supervision.
🆂🅰🆅🅴 🅂🄳 ⊠ 🄳 🄳

ⓐ ▼▼ ▼▼ **Chalet Continental Motel** 🅂🄷 ❀
(250) 566-9787. **$79-$129.** 1450 5th Ave. Just e, off Hwy 5 (Yellowhead Hwy). Int corridors. **Pets:** Medium, dogs only. $10 daily fee/pet. Designated rooms, service with restrictions, supervision.
🆂🅰🆅🅴 🅂🄳 ⊠ 🄳 🄳 🄳 🅇

ⓐ ▼▼ ▼▼ **Holiday Inn Hotel & Suites Valemount** 🅂🄷
(250) 566-0086. **$89-$175.** 1950 Hwy 5 S. 1.5 km s on Hwy 5 (Yellowhead Hwy). Int corridors. **Pets:** Other species. $35 one-time fee/room. Service with restrictions, supervision.
🆂🅰🆅🅴 🅂🄳 ⊠ 🄼 🄼 🄳 🄳 🄳 🄳 🅇

---

# VANCOUVER METROPOLITAN AREA

## ALDERGROVE

ⓐ ▼▼▼▼ **Best Western Country Meadows** 🅂🄷
(604) 856-9880. **$79-$119.** 3070 264th St. Trans-Canada Hwy 1, exit 73 (264th St/Aldergrove), 5 km s on 264th St (Hwy 13). Int corridors. **Pets:** $10 daily fee/pet. Designated rooms, service with restrictions, supervision.
🆂🅰🆅🅴 🅂🄳 ⊠ 🄼 🄳 🄳 🄳

## BURNABY

ⓐ ▼▼▼ **Accent Inns** 🄼 ❀
(604) 473-5000. **$109-$149.** 3777 Henning Dr. Trans-Canada Hwy 1, exit 28 (Grandview Hwy), just n on Boundary Rd. Ext corridors. **Pets:** Small, other species. $15 daily fee/room. Service with restrictions, supervision.
🆂🅰🆅🅴 🅂🄳 ⊠ 🄼 🄼 🄳 🄳 🄳 🅇

ⓐ ▼▼▼ **Best Western Kings Inn and Conference Centre** 🅂🄷
(604) 438-1383. **$109-$189.** 5411 Kingsway. Trans-Canada Hwy 1, exit 29 (Willingdon Ave), 3 km s to Kingsway, then 2 km e. Ext corridors. **Pets:** Small. $15 daily fee/pet. Service with restrictions, supervision.
🆂🅰🆅🅴 🅂🄳 ⊠ 🄳 🄳 🄳 🄳

ⓐ ▼▼▼▼ **Hilton Vancouver Metrotown** 🄻🄷
(604) 438-1200. **$140-$229.** 6083 McKay Ave. Trans-Canada Hwy 1, exit 29 (Willingdon Ave), 3 km s to Kingsway, then just e. Int corridors. **Pets:** Accepted.
🆂🅰🆅🅴 ⊠ 🄼 🄼 🄳 🄳 🄳 🄳

▼▼▼ **Lake City Motor Inn** 🄼
(604) 294-5331. **$89-$109.** 5415 Lougheed Hwy. Trans-Canada Hwy 1, exit 29 (Willington Ave), just n, 1 km e on Lougheed Hwy, just n on Springer Ave, then just e on Broadway. Ext corridors. **Pets:** Accepted.
⊠ 🄳 🄳

## COQUITLAM

ⓐ ▼▼▼▼ **Best Western Coquitlam Inn Convention Centre** 🅂🄷
(604) 931-9011. **$149-$169.** 319 North Rd. Trans-Canada Hwy 1, exit 37 (Cariboo Rd/Gaglardi Way), 2 km e on Lougheed Hwy (Hwy 7), then just s. Ext/int corridors. **Pets:** Accepted.
🆂🅰🆅🅴 🅂🄳 ⊠ 🄳 🄳 🄳 🄳 🅇

▼▼▼ **Ramada Inn Coquitlam** 🅂🄷
(604) 931-4433. **$89-$159.** 631 Lougheed Hwy. Trans-Canada Hwy 1, exit 37 (Gaglardi Way) eastbound, 3.5 km e on Lougheed Hwy (Hwy 7); exit 44 (Coquitlam) westbound, then 3 km w on Lougheed Hwy (Hwy 7). Ext/int corridors. **Pets:** Small, other species. $30 one-time fee/room. Designated rooms, service with restrictions.
🄰🅂🄺 🅂🄳 ⊠ 🄼 🄳 🄳 🄳 🄳

## DELTA

▼▼▼ **The Coast Tsawwassen Inn** 🅂🄷 ❀
(604) 943-8221. **$99-$149.** 1665 56th St. Hwy 99, exit 28 (Tsawwassen Ferries), 8 km w on Hwy 17; 5 km from the BC ferry terminal. Int corridors. **Pets:** Small. $10 daily fee/pet. Supervision.
🄰🅂🄺 🅂🄳 ⊠ 🄼 🄳 🄳 🄳 🅇

▼▼▼ **River Run Cottages** 🄱🄱
(604) 946-7778. **$129-$210, 21 day notice.** 4551 River Rd W. Hwy 17, 2.5 km n on Ladner Trunk Rd (becomes 47A St, then becomes River Rd W). Ext corridors. **Pets:** Medium, dogs only. $20 daily fee/pet. Designated rooms, supervision.
🄰🅂🄺 🅂🄳 ⊠ 🄳 🄳 🅇 🄼 🄶

## LANGLEY

ⓐ ▼▼ **Best Value Westward Inn** 🄼
(604) 534-9238. **$65-$83.** 19650 Fraser Hwy. Trans-Canada Hwy 1, exit 58 (200th St), 5 km s, 1 km w on Hwy 10, then just w. Ext corridors. **Pets:** Other species. $4 daily fee/pet. Service with restrictions, supervision.
🆂🅰🆅🅴 ⊠ 🄳 🄳

(AA) ▼▼▼▼ **Best Western Langley Inn** SH
(604) 530-9311. **$99-$119.** 5978 Glover Rd. Trans-Canada Hwy 1, exit 66 (232nd St), 6 km s, follow signs. Int corridors. **Pets:** Accepted.
SAVE SO X TI

(AA) ▼▼▼▼ **Coast Hotel & Convention Centre** SH 🐾
(604) 530-1500. **$124-$179.** 20393 Fraser Hwy. Trans-Canada Hwy 1, exit 58 (200th St), 6.3 km s on 200th St, then just w. Int corridors. **Pets:** $15 daily fee/room. Designated rooms, service with restrictions, supervision.
SAVE SO X GM TI

(AA) ▼▼▼ **Holiday Inn Express Hotel & Suites Langley** SH
(604) 882-2000. **$109-$191.** 8750 204th St. Trans-Canada Hwy 1, exit 58 (200th St), just e on 88th Ave. Int corridors. **Pets:** Medium. $10 daily fee/pet. Designated rooms, service with restrictions, supervision.
SAVE SO X GM 🏊 🗙

▼▼ **Sandman Hotel Langley** SH
(604) 888-7263. **$130-$150.** 8855 202nd St. Trans-Canada Hwy 1, exit 58 (200th St), just e on 88th Ave. Int corridors. **Pets:** $10 daily fee/room. Designated rooms, service with restrictions, supervision.
ASK SO X TI

▼▼ **Sleep Inn Langley** M
(604) 514-3111. **$80-$110.** 6722 Glover Rd. Trans-Canada Hwy 1, exit 66 (232nd St), 4 km s on Glover Rd, follow signs. Int corridors. **Pets:** Accepted.
ASK SO X

(AA) ▼▼▼ **Travelodge-Langley City** M
(604) 533-4431. **$69-$99.** 21653 Fraser Hwy. Trans-Canada Hwy 1, exit 66 (232nd St), 6 km s, 1 km se on Langley Bypass, then 1.5 km e to 216 St. Ext corridors. **Pets:** $10 daily fee/pet. Designated rooms, service with restrictions, crate.
SAVE SO X

# MAPLE RIDGE

(AA) ▼▼▼▼ **Best Western Maple Ridge** SH
(604) 463-5111. **$89-$139.** 21735 Lougheed Hwy. 2 km w on Lougheed Hwy (Hwy 7). Ext corridors. **Pets:** Accepted.
SAVE SO X TI

(AA) ▼▼▼ **Travelodge Maple Ridge** M
(604) 467-1511. **$85-$99.** 21650 Lougheed Hwy. 2 km w on Lougheed Hwy (Hwy 7). Int corridors. **Pets:** Accepted.
SAVE SO X 🗙

# MISSION

(AA) ▼▼▼ **Best Western Mission City Lodge** SH
(604) 820-5500. **$80-$120.** 32281 Lougheed Hwy. Just w of Hwy 11, corner of Lougheed Hwy (Hwy 7) and Hurd St. Int corridors. **Pets:** $10 daily fee/pet. Designated rooms, service with restrictions, supervision.
SAVE SO X GM 🗙 🏊 🗙

# NORTH VANCOUVER

(AA) ▼▼▼▼ **Holiday Inn Hotel & Suites North Vancouver** LH 🐾
(604) 985-3111. **$109-$189.** 700 Old Lillooet Rd. Trans-Canada Hwy 1, exit 22 (Mt Seymour Pkwy), follow signs. Int corridors. **Pets:** Small, dogs only. $20 daily fee/pet. Designated rooms, service with restrictions, supervision.
SAVE SO X GM 🏊 🗙

▼ **Lionsgate Travelodge** M
(604) 985-5311. **$55-$200.** 2060 Marine Dr. Trans-Canada Hwy 1, exit 14 (Capilano Rd), 1.5 km s, then just w; from north end of Lions Gate Bridge, just e. Ext corridors. **Pets:** Medium. $25 one-time fee/room. Designated rooms, service with restrictions, supervision.
ASK SO X 🏊

▼▼ **Lonsdale Quay Hotel** SH 🐾
(604) 986-6111. **$115-$350.** 123 Carrie Cates Ct. Trans-Canada Hwy 1, exit 18 (Lonsdale Ave), 2.5 km s. Int corridors. **Pets:** Medium. $25 one-time fee/room. Designated rooms, service with restrictions, supervision.
ASK SO X GM TI

(AA) ▼▼▼ **Ramada Inn Vancouver Northshore** M
(604) 987-4461. **$79-$139.** 1800 Capilano Rd. Trans-Canada Hwy 1, exit 14 (Capilano Rd), 1.5 km s; from north end of Lions Gate Bridge, 1 km e on Marine Dr, then just n. Ext corridors. **Pets:** Medium. Designated rooms, service with restrictions, supervision.
SAVE SO X GM 🏊

# RICHMOND

(AA) ▼▼▼ **Accent Inns** SH
(604) 273-3311. **$89-$149.** 10551 St. Edwards Dr. Hwy 99, exit 39 (Bridgeport/Airport) northbound to St. Edwards Dr; exit 39A (Richmond/Airport) southbound. Ext corridors. **Pets:** Medium. $15 daily fee/room. Designated rooms, service with restrictions, crate.
SAVE SO X GM 🗙 TI

(AA) ▼▼▼ **Best Western Abercorn Inn** SH 🐾
(604) 270-7576. **$85-$159.** 9260 Bridgeport Rd. Hwy 99, exit 39 (Bridgeport/Airport) northbound; exit 39A (Richmond/Airport) southbound. Int corridors. **Pets:** Medium. $15 daily fee/pet. Designated rooms, service with restrictions, supervision.
SAVE SO X GM TI

(AA) ▼▼▼ **Best Western Richmond Hotel & Convention Center** LH 🐾
(604) 273-7878. **$109-$169.** 7551 Westminster Hwy. Corner of Minoru Rd and Westminster Hwy. Int corridors. **Pets:** $15 daily fee/room, $30 one-time fee/room. Service with restrictions, crate.
SAVE SO X GM TI 🏊 🗙

(AA) ▼▼▼ **Comfort Inn Vancouver Airport** SH
(604) 278-5161. **$99-$199.** 3031 #3 Rd. Hwy 99, exit 39 (Bridgeport/Airport) northbound; exit 39A (Richmond/Airport) southbound. Int corridors. **Pets:** Accepted.
SAVE SO X TI 🏊

(AA) ▼▼▼▼ **Delta Vancouver Airport** LH 🐾
(604) 278-1241. **$169-$209.** 3500 Cessna Dr. Corner of Russ Baker Way and Cessna Dr; near the Moray Bridge. Int corridors. **Pets:** Medium. $35 one-time fee/room. Designated rooms, service with restrictions, supervision.
SAVE SO X GM 🗙 TI 🏊 🗙

(AA) ▼▼▼ ▼▼▼ **The Fairmont Vancouver Airport** LH 🐾
(604) 207-5200. **$239-$309.** 3111 Grant McConachie Way. In Vancouver International Airport. Int corridors. **Pets:** Small, other species. $25 daily fee/room. Designated rooms, service with restrictions, supervision.
SAVE SO X GM 🗙 TI 🏊 🗙

▼▼▼ **Holiday Inn Express Vancouver-Airport** SH
(604) 273-8080. **$99-$159.** 9351 Bridgeport Rd. Hwy 99, exit 39 (Bridgeport/Airport) northbound; exit 39A (Richmond/Airport) southbound. Int corridors. **Pets:** $10 daily fee/room. Designated rooms, service with restrictions, supervision.
ASK SO X GM

▼▼▼ **Holiday Inn International Vancouver Airport** SH
(604) 821-1818. **$109-$169.** 10720 Cambie Rd. Hwy 99, exit 39 (Bridgeport/Airport) northbound to St. Edwards Dr; exit 39A (Richmond/Airport) southbound, then e. Int corridors. **Pets:** Small. $100 daily fee/pet. Designated rooms, service with restrictions, supervision.
ASK SO X GM TI

(AA) ▼▼▼ **La Quinta Inn Vancouver Airport** SH
(604) 276-2711. **$89-$129.** 8640 Alexandra Rd. No. 3 Rd, just e on Alderbridge Way, just n on Kwantlen St. Int corridors. **Pets:** Small. $50 deposit/room. Designated rooms, service with restrictions, supervision.
SAVE SO X GM TI 🏊

**Sandman Hotel Vancouver Airport** SH
(604) 303-8888. **$139-$169.** 3233 St. Edwards Dr. Hwy 99, exit 39 (Bridgeport/Airport) northbound to St. Edwards Dr; exit 39A (Richmond/Airport) southbound. Int corridors. **Pets:** $10 daily fee/pet. Designated rooms, crate.

ASK Sⓓ ✕ ⓕM 🖥 💻 ¶¶ ➔

**Vancouver Airport Marriott** SH
(604) 276-2112. **$105-$189.** 7571 Westminster Hwy. Corner of Minoru Rd and Westminster Hwy. Int corridors. **Pets:** Accepted.

SAVE Sⓓ ✕ ⓕM 🖥 💻 ¶¶ ➔

## SURREY

**Aston Pacific Inn Resort & Conference Ctr** SH
(604) 535-1432. **$117-$144.** 1160 King George Hwy. Hwy 99, exit 2B southbound; exit 2 northbound, just n. Int corridors. **Pets:** $25 daily fee/room. Designated rooms, service with restrictions, crate.

SAVE Sⓓ ✕ ⓕM 💻 ¶¶ ➔ ✕

**Days Hotel-Surrey** SH ✿
(604) 588-9511. **$89-$107.** 9850 King George Hwy. Jct Fraser Hwy (Hwy 1A) and Hwy 99A (King George Hwy). Int corridors. **Pets:** Large. $10 daily fee/pet. Service with restrictions, crate.

SAVE Sⓓ ✕ ⓕM 📶 🖥 💻 ¶¶ ➔

**Ramada Hotel & Suites Surrey/Guildford** SH
(604) 930-4700. **$79-$99.** 10410 158th St. Trans-Canada Hwy 1, exit 50 (160th St), just w on 104th Ave. Int corridors. **Pets:** Large, other species. $10 daily fee/pet.

ASK Sⓓ ✕ ⓕM 📶 🖥 💻 ¶¶ ➔

**Ramada Limited Surrey-Langley** SH
(604) 576-8388. **$89-$139.** 19225 Hwy 10. Trans-Canada Hwy 1, exit 58, 5 km s on 200th St, then 2 km w on Rt 10; corner of 192nd St and Rt 10. Int corridors. **Pets:** Other species. $10 daily fee/pet. Service with restrictions, crate.

ASK Sⓓ ✕ ⓕM 📶 🖥 💻 ¶¶ ➔

## VANCOUVER

**2400 Motel** M ✿
(604) 434-2464. **$55-$125.** 2400 Kingsway. 7.2 km se on Hwy 1A and 99A (Kingsway and 33rd Ave). Ext corridors. **Pets:** Other species. $5 daily fee/pet. Designated rooms, service with restrictions, crate.

✕ 🖥 Ⓚ

**Best Western Chateau Granville** SH
(604) 669-7070. **$119-$229.** 1100 Granville St. Between Davie and Helmcken sts. Int corridors. **Pets:** Small, dogs only. $25 one-time fee/pet. Designated rooms, service with restrictions, supervision.

SAVE Sⓓ ✕ ⓕM 🖥 💻 ¶¶

**Best Western Downtown Vancouver** SH ✿
(604) 669-9888. **$99-$219.** 718 Drake St. Corner of Drake and Granville sts. Int corridors. **Pets:** Small, other species. $20 one-time fee/pet. Designated rooms, supervision.

SAVE Sⓓ ✕ ⓕM 🖥 💻 ¶¶ ✕

**Best Western Sands** SH ✿
(604) 682-1831. **$129-$239.** 1755 Davie St. Between Bidwell and Denman sts. Int corridors. **Pets:** Large, other species. $10 daily fee/pet. Designated rooms, service with restrictions, supervision.

SAVE Sⓓ ✕ 🖥 💻 ¶¶

**Bosmans Hotel** M
(604) 682-3171. **$119-$129.** 1060 Howe St. Between Nelson and Helmcken sts. Int corridors. **Pets:** Medium, other species. Service with restrictions, supervision.

SAVE Sⓓ ✕ ¶¶ ➔

**Comfort Inn Downtown** SH
(604) 605-4333. **$72-$229.** 654 Nelson St. Between Granville and Seymour sts. Int corridors. **Pets:** Accepted.

ASK Sⓓ ✕ 💻

**Crowne Plaza Vancouver-Hotel Georgia** LH
(604) 682-5566. **$129-$239.** 801 W Georgia St. Between Howe and Hornby sts. Int corridors. **Pets:** Accepted.

SAVE Sⓓ ✕ ⓕM 💻 ¶¶

**Delta Vancouver Suites** SH ✿
(604) 689-8188. **$159-$269.** 550 W Hastings St. Between Seymour and Richards sts; entrance in alley way. Int corridors. **Pets:** Medium, other species. $35 one-time fee/pet. Service with restrictions.

SAVE ✕ ⓕM 💻 ¶¶ ➔ ✕

**The Fairmont Hotel Vancouver** LH ✿
(604) 684-3131. **$239-$389.** 900 W Georgia St. Corner of Burrard at W Georgia St; enter from Hornby St. Int corridors. **Pets:** Other species. $25 daily fee/room. Service with restrictions, supervision.

SAVE Sⓓ ✕ ⓕM 💻 ¶¶ ➔ ✕

**The Fairmont Waterfront** LH ✿
(604) 691-1991. **$219-$369.** 900 Canada Place Way. Howe St at Cordova St. Int corridors. **Pets:** Medium. $25 one-time fee/room. Designated rooms.

SAVE Sⓓ ✕ ⓕM 💻 ¶¶ ➔ ✕

**Four Seasons Hotel Vancouver** LH ✿
(604) 689-9333. **$260-$2500.** 791 W Georgia St. Between Howe and W Georgia sts. Int corridors. **Pets:** Small. Designated rooms, service with restrictions, supervision.

SAVE ✕ 📶 ¶¶ ➔ ✕

**The Georgian Court Hotel** SH ✿
(604) 682-5555. **$115-$260.** 773 Beatty St. Between Georgia and Robson sts. Int corridors. **Pets:** $20 one-time fee/room. Service with restrictions, supervision.

ASK Sⓓ ✕ ⓕM 💻 ¶¶ ✕

**Granville Island Hotel** SH
(604) 683-7373. **$160-$250.** 1253 Johnston St. Granville Island; below the bridge, follow signs. Int corridors. **Pets:** Other species. $25 daily fee/pet. Designated rooms, service with restrictions, supervision.

SAVE Sⓓ ✕ ⓕM 💻 ¶¶ ✕

**Holiday Inn Express Vancouver** SH ✿
(604) 254-1000. **$79-$209.** 2889 E Hastings St. Between Renfrew and Kaslo sts. Int corridors. **Pets:** Medium. $15 daily fee/pet. Service with restrictions, supervision.

SAVE Sⓓ ✕ ⓕM 🖥 💻

**Holiday Inn Hotel & Suites
Vancouver-Downtown** LH
(604) 684-2151. **$109-$299.** 1110 Howe St. Between Helmcken and Davie sts. Int corridors. **Pets:** Service with restrictions, supervision.

SAVE Sⓓ ✕ ⓕM 🖥 💻 ¶¶ ➔

**Holiday Inn Vancouver-Centre (Broadway)** SH
(604) 879-0511. **$119-$199.** 711 W Broadway. Between Heather and Willow sts. Int corridors. **Pets:** $15 one-time fee/room. Designated rooms, service with restrictions, supervision.

ASK Sⓓ ✕ ⓕM 🖥 💻 ¶¶ ➔

**Hotel Le Soleil** SH ✿
(604) 632-3000. **$335-$465.** 567 Hornby St. Between Dunsmuir and Pender sts. Int corridors. **Pets:** $75 one-time fee/room. Service with restrictions, crate.

SAVE Sⓓ ✕ ⓕM 💻 ¶¶

**Howard Johnson Hotel** SH
(604) 688-8701. **$89-$169.** 1176 Granville St. Between Davie and Helmcken sts. Int corridors. **Pets:** Accepted.

SAVE Sⓓ ✕ 🖥 💻 ¶¶

**The London Guard Motel** M
(604) 430-4646. **$49-$100.** 2227 Kingsway. 6.8 km se on Hwy 1A and 99A (Kingsway and Nanaimo St). Ext corridors. **Pets:** Accepted.

✕ 🖥 Ⓚ

◎◎ ▼▼ ▼▼ **Metropolitan Hotel** 🆂🅷 ❄️
(604) 687-1122. **$189-$399.** 645 Howe St. Between Georgia and Dunsmuir sts. Int corridors. **Pets:** Medium, other species. Service with restrictions, crate.
🆂🅰🆅🅴 🆂🖥 ⊠ ✦M 📶 💻 🍴 🛥 ⊠

◎◎ ▼▼▼▼ **Pacific Palisades Hotel** 🅻🅷 ❄️
(604) 688-0461. **$139-$390.** 1277 Robson St. Between Jervis and Bute sts. Int corridors. **Pets:** Other species. Service with restrictions, supervision.
🆂🅰🆅🅴 🆂🖥 ⊠ ✦M 📶 🔒 💻 🍴 🛥 ⊠

◎◎ ▼▼▼▼▼ **Pan Pacific Vancouver** 🅻🅷 ❄️
(604) 662-8111. **$390-$590.** 300-999 Canada Place. Motor entrance off Burrard St. Int corridors. **Pets:** Small. $30 daily fee/room. Service with restrictions, supervision.
🆂🅰🆅🅴 🆂🖥 ⊠ ✦M 🔒 💻 🍴 🛥 ⊠

▼▼ ▼▼ **Quality Hotel Downtown-The Inn at False**
        **Creek** 🆂🅷 ❄️
(604) 682-0229. **$89-$189.** 1335 Howe St. Between Drake and Pacific sts. Int corridors. **Pets:** Small. $15 daily fee/pet. Designated rooms, service with restrictions, supervision.
🅰🆂🅺 🆂🖥 ⊠ ✦M 🔒 🔒 💻 🍴 🛥

◎◎ ▼▼ ▼▼ **Ramada Inn & Suites Downtown Vancouver** 🆂🅷
(604) 685-1111. **$99-$219.** 1221 Granville St. Between Davie and Drake sts. Int corridors. **Pets:** Other species. $20 daily fee/pet. Service with restrictions, crate.
🆂🅰🆅🅴 🆂🖥 ⊠ 🔒 💻 🍴

◎◎ ▼▼▼ **Ramada Limited Downtown Vancouver** 🆂🅷
(604) 488-1088. **$124-$199.** 435 W Pender St. Between Homer and Richards sts. Int corridors. **Pets:** Accepted.
🆂🅰🆅🅴 🆂🖥 ✦M 🔒 💻

◎◎ ▼▼▼▼ **Renaissance Vancouver Hotel**
        **Harbourside** 🅻🅷
(604) 689-9211. **$129-$209.** 1133 W Hastings St. Between Bute and Thurlow sts. Int corridors. **Pets:** Accepted.
🆂🅰🆅🅴 🆂🖥 ⊠ ✦M 💻 🍴 🛥 ⊠

◎◎ ▼▼▼▼ **Residence Inn by Marriott Vancouver** 🆂🅷
(604) 688-1234. **$139-$299.** 1234 Hornby St. Between Drake and Davie sts. Int corridors. **Pets:** Medium. $75 one-time fee/pet.
🆂🅰🆅🅴 🆂🖥 ⊠ ✦M 🔒 💻 🍴 🛥

▼▼▼▼ **Sandman Hotel Downtown Vancouver** 🆂🅷
(604) 681-2211. **$90-$190.** 180 W Georgia St. Between Cambie and Beatty sts. Int corridors. **Pets:** $5 daily fee/pet. Designated rooms, service with restrictions, supervision.
🅰🆂🅺 🆂🖥 ⊠ 💻 🍴 🛥

◎◎ ▼▼▼▼ **Sheraton Vancouver Wall Centre**
        **Hotel** 🅻🅷 ❄️
(604) 331-1000. **$169-$429.** 1088 Burrard St. Between Helmcken and Nelson sts. Int corridors. **Pets:** Medium. $60 one-time fee/pet. Service with restrictions, supervision.
🆂🅰🆅🅴 🆂🖥 ⊠ ✦M 👁 💻 🍴 🛥 ⊠

◎◎ ▼▼▼▼▼ **The Sutton Place Hotel** 🅻🅷 ❄️
(604) 682-5511. **$191-$478, 3 day notice.** 845 Burrard St. Between Smithe and Robson sts. Int corridors. **Pets:** Other species. $150 one-time fee/room. Designated rooms, service with restrictions, supervision.
🆂🅰🆅🅴 🆂🖥 ⊠ ✦M 📶 💻 🍴 🛥 ⊠

▼▼ ▼▼ **Sylvia Hotel** 🆂🅷 ❄️
(604) 681-9321. **$85-$275.** 1154 Gilford St. Beach Ave and Gilford St; across from English Bay. Int corridors. **Pets:** Service with restrictions, supervision.
⊠ 🔒 🍴 🎯

◎◎ ▼▼▼▼ **Vancouver Marriott Pinnacle**
        **Downtown** 🅻🅷
(604) 684-1128. **$129-$299.** 1128 W Hastings St. Between Thurlow and Bute sts. Int corridors. **Pets:** Medium. $30 one-time fee/room. Service with restrictions, supervision.
🆂🅰🆅🅴 ⊠ ✦M 💻 🍴 🛥 ⊠

◎◎ ▼▼▼▼ **The Westin Bayshore Resort &**
        **Marina** 🅻🅷 ❄️
(604) 682-3377. **$130-$460.** 1601 Bayshore Dr. W Georgia and Cardero sts. Int corridors. **Pets:** Small, dogs only. Service with restrictions, supervision.
🆂🅰🆅🅴 🆂🖥 ⊠ ✦M 📶 💻 🍴 🛥 ⊠

◎◎ ▼▼▼▼ **The Westin Grand, Vancouver** 🅻🅷
(604) 602-1999. **$379-$529.** 433 Robson St. Between Homer and Richards sts. Int corridors. **Pets:** Accepted.
🆂🅰🆅🅴 🆂🖥 ⊠ ✦M 💻 🍴 🛥 ⊠

# WHITE ROCK

◎◎ ▼▼▼ **Ocean Promenade Hotel** 🆂🅷
(604) 542-0102. **$139-$489.** 15611 Marine Dr. Hwy 99, exit 2B southbound; exit 2 (White Rock/8th Ave) northbound, 2 km w. Ext/int corridors. **Pets:** Accepted.
🆂🅰🆅🅴 🆂🖥 ⊠ ✦M 🔒 💻

---

# END METROPOLITAN AREA

---

# VERNON

◎◎ ▼▼▼ **Best Western Vernon Lodge & Conference**
        **Centre** 🆂🅷 ❄️
(250) 545-3385. **$99-$136.** 3914 32nd St. 1.5 km n on Hwy 97 (32nd St). Int corridors. **Pets:** $15 daily fee/room. Designated rooms, service with restrictions, supervision.
🆂🅰🆅🅴 🆂🖥 ⊠ ✦M 🔒 💻 🍴 🛥

◎◎ ▼▼▼▼ **Holiday Inn Express Hotel & Suites**
        **Vernon** 🆂🅷
(250) 550-7777. **$104-$134.** 4716 34th St. Hwy 97 (32nd St) northbound at 48th Ave. Int corridors. **Pets:** Dogs only. $20 one-time fee/pet. Designated rooms, service with restrictions, supervision.
🆂🅰🆅🅴 🆂🖥 ⊠ 🔒 💻 🛥

◎◎ ▼▼▼ **Tiki Village Motor Inn** 🅼 ❄️
(250) 503-5566. **$79-$155.** 2408 34th St. Jct Hwy 97 (32nd St) and 6 (25th Ave), just w. Ext corridors. **Pets:** Medium, dogs only. $10 one-time fee/pet. Designated rooms, supervision.
🆂🅰🆅🅴 🆂🖥 ⊠ 🔒 💻 🍴 🛥 ⊠

▼▼▼ **Vernon Travelodge** 🆂🅷
(250) 545-2161. **$69-$95.** 3000 28th Ave. Hwy 97 (32nd St), just e on 28th Ave; near Polson Park. Ext corridors. **Pets:** Accepted.
🅰🆂🅺 🆂🖥 ⊠ 🔒 💻 🛥

# VICTORIA METROPOLITAN AREA

## MALAHAT

### 🐾 ▼▼▼ ▼▼ The Aerie Resort [CI]
(250) 743-7115. **$195-$775, 7 day notice.** 600 Ebadora Ln. 32 km n of Victoria off Trans-Canada Hwy 1, use Spectacle Lake turn off, follow signs. Int corridors. **Pets:** Small, dogs only. $25 daily fee/pet. Designated rooms, service with restrictions, supervision.

[SAVE] [✕] [▭] [¶¶] [⇌] [⊠]

### ▼▼ Malahat Bungalows Motel [M]
(250) 478-3011. **$62-$150, 3 day notice.** Trans-Canada Hwy 1, 26 km n of Victoria. Ext corridors. **Pets:** Medium, other species. $10 daily fee/pet. Service with restrictions, supervision.

[✕] [📞] [⚓] [☑]

## SAANICHTON

### 🐾 ▼▼ Quality Inn Waddling Dog [SH] ❖
(250) 652-1146. **$85-$145.** 2476 Mt Newton Crossroad. Corner of Hwy 17 and Mt Newton Crossroad. Int corridors. **Pets:** Dogs only. $10 daily fee/pet. Service with restrictions, supervision.

[SAVE] [🔊] [✕] [▭] [¶¶]

### 🐾 ▼▼ Victoria Airport Super 8 [SH]
(250) 652-6888. **$77-$115.** 2477 Mt Newton Crossroad. Just e of Hwy 17. Int corridors. **Pets:** Other species. $10 one-time fee/pet. Service with restrictions, supervision.

[SAVE] [🔊] [✕] [ᶜᴹ] [▭]

## SIDNEY

### ▼▼▼ Best Western Emerald Isle Motor Inn [SH]
(250) 656-4441. **$1¯9-$179.** 2306 Beacon Ave. Hwy 17, exit Sidney, just e. Int corridors. **Pets:** Accepted.

[ASK] [🔊] [✕] [ᶜᴹ] [📞] [▭] [¶¶]

### ▼▼▼ The Cedarwood Inn & Suites [SH]
(250) 656-5551. **$€9-$139.** 9522 Lochside Dr. Hwy 17, just e on McTavish Rd, then 1.4 km n. Ext corridors. **Pets:** Other species. $15 daily fee/pet. Designated rooms, service with restrictions.

[ASK] [🔊] [✕] [📞] [▭] [ᴷᶜ]

### ▼▼▼ Miraloma on the Cove [SH] ❖
(250) 656-6622. **$119-$339, 7 day notice.** 2326 Harbour Rd. Beacon Ave, 2 km n on Resthaven Dr, then 1 km e. Int corridors. **Pets:** Small, other species. $25 one-time fee/room. Service with restrictions, supervision.

[ASK] [🔊] [✕] [ᶜᴹ] [☑] [📞] [▭] [⊠] [ᴷᶜ]

### 🐾 ▼▼ Victoria Airport Travelodge Sidney [SH]
(250) 656-1176. **$99-$215.** 2280 Beacon Ave. Just e of Hwy 17, exit Sidney. Int corridors. **Pets:** Other species. $10 daily fee/room. Designated rooms, service with restrictions, supervision.

[SAVE] [🔊] [✕] [ᶜᴹ] [☑] [📞] [▭] [⇌]

## SOOKE

### ▼▼ Ocean Wilderness Inn & Spa [BB]
(250) 646-2116. **$95-$175, 7 day notice.** 9171 W Coast Rd. 14 km w on Hwy 14. Ext/int corridors. **Pets:** Dogs only. $15 daily fee/pet. Service with restrictions, supervision.

[ASK] [🔊] [✕] [📞] [ᴷᶜ] [ᴾᵂ] [☑]

### 🐾 ▼▼▼ Sooke Harbour House [SH] ❖
(250) 642-3421. **$275-$575, 15 day notice.** 1528 Whiffen Spit Rd. 2 km w on Hwy 14. Ext/int corridors. **Pets:** Other species. $30 daily fee/pet. Service with restrictions. crate.

[SAVE] [✕] [ᶜᴹ] [☑] [📞] [▭] [¶¶] [ᴷᶜ] [ᴾᵂ]

## VICTORIA

### 🐾 ▼▼▼ Abigail's Hotel [BB] ❖
(250) 388-5363. **$139-$450, 7 day notice.** 906 McClure St. Blanshard St (Hwy 17), just e on Fairfield Rd, then just n on Vancouver St. Int corridors. **Pets:** Dogs only. $25 one-time fee/room. Designated rooms, service with restrictions, crate.

[SAVE] [🔊] [✕] [📞] [▭]

### 🐾 ▼▼ Accent Inns [SH] ❖
(250) 475-7500. **$89-$159.** 3233 Maple St. 3 km n on Blanshard St (Hwy 17); corner of Blanchard St and Cloverdale Ave. Ext corridors. **Pets:** Small, other species. $15 daily fee/room. Designated rooms, service with restrictions, supervision.

[SAVE] [🔊] [✕] [ᶜᴹ] [📞] [▭] [¶¶]

### 🐾 ▼▼▼ Admiral Inn [M] ❖
(250) 388-6267. **$89-$249.** 257 Belleville St. Corner of Belleville and Quebec sts. Ext corridors. **Pets:** $10 daily fee/room. Service with restrictions, supervision.

[SAVE] [🔊] [✕] [📞] [▭]

### 🐾 ▼▼▼ Best Western Carlton Plaza Hotel [SH] ❖
(250) 388-5513. **$89-$249.** 642 Johnson St. Between Douglas and Broad sts. Int corridors. **Pets:** $10 daily fee/room. Service with restrictions, supervision.

[SAVE] [🔊] [✕] [ᶜᴹ] [📞] [▭] [¶¶]

### 🐾 ▼▼ Blue Ridge Inns [SH]
(250) 388-4345. **$69-$119.** 3110 Douglas St. Between Finlayson St and Speed Ave. Ext corridors. **Pets:** Other species. $10 daily fee/room. Service with restrictions, supervision.

[SAVE] [🔊] [✕] [📞] [▭] [¶¶] [⇌] [ᴷᶜ]

### ▼▼▼ Chateau Victoria Hotel and Suites [LH] ❖
(250) 382-4221. **$84-$299.** 740 Burdett Ave. Between Douglas St and Fairfield Rd. Int corridors. **Pets:** Dogs only. $15 daily fee/pet. Designated rooms, service with restrictions, supervision.

[ASK] [✕] [📞] [▭] [¶¶] [⇌]

### 🐾 ▼▼▼ Comfort Inn & Suites [M] ❖
(250) 388-7861. **$89-$279.** 101 Island Hwy. Douglas St, 5 km w on Gorge Rd, then just s on Admirals Rd. Ext/int corridors. **Pets:** Small, dogs only. $15 daily fee/pet. Service with restrictions, supervision.

[SAVE] [🔊] [✕] [📞] [▭]

### 🐾 ▼▼ Crystal Court Motel [M]
(250) 384-0551. **$69-$135.** 701 Belleville St. Between Douglas and Blanshard sts. Ext corridors. **Pets:** Service with restrictions, crate.

[SAVE] [🔊] [✕] [📞] [ᴷᶜ]

### 🐾 ▼▼▼ Days Inn on the Harbour [SH] ❖
(250) 386-3451. **$83-$223.** 427 Belleville St. Between Oswego and Menzies sts; entrance on Quebec St. Int corridors. **Pets:** $10 daily fee/room. Designated rooms, service with restrictions.

[SAVE] [✕] [📞] [▭] [¶¶] [⇌] [ᴷᶜ]

### 🐾 ▼▼▼ ▼▼ Delta Victoria Ocean Pointe Resort & Spa [LH]
(250) 360-2999. **$109-$379.** 45 Songhees Rd. Just w of Johnson St Bridge, Esquimalt at Tyee rds. Int corridors. **Pets:** Accepted.

[SAVE] [🔊] [✕] [ᶜᴹ] [📞] [▭] [¶¶] [⇌] [⊠]

### 🐾 ▼▼▼ Executive House Hotel [SH] ❖
(250) 388-5111. **$85-$195.** 777 Douglas St. Between Blanshard and Douglas sts; downtown. Int corridors. **Pets:** Other species. $15 daily fee/pet.

[SAVE] [🔊] [✕] [📞] [▭] [¶¶] [⊠] [ᴷᶜ]

**⊕ ▼▼▼ The Fairmont Empress** 🄻🄷
(250) 384-8111. **$159-$579.** 721 Government St. Between Belleville and Humboldt sts. Int corridors. **Pets:** Small. $25 one-time fee/pet. Supervision.
🅢🄰🆅 🆂🄳 ⊠ 🄲🄼 ⬭ 💻 🍴 ⇌ ⊠ 🐾

**⊕ ▼▼▼▼ Harbour Towers Hotel & Suites** 🄻🄷 🐾
(250) 385-2405. **$94-$414.** 345 Quebec St. Between Oswego and Pendray sts. Int corridors. **Pets:** Medium. $15 daily fee/room. Designated rooms, service with restrictions, supervision.
🅢🄰🆅 🆂🄳 ⊠ 🄲🄼 🐾 🖥 💻 🍴 ⇌ ⊠ 🐾

**⊕ ▼▼▼▼ Hotel Grand Pacific** 🄻🄷 🐾
(250) 386-0450. **$129-$319.** 463 Belleville St. Between Oswego and Menzies sts. Int corridors. **Pets:** Small. $60 one-time fee/room. Designated rooms, service with restrictions, supervision.
🅢🄰🆅 🆂🄳 ⊠ 🄲🄼 ⬭ 🖥 💻 🍴 ⇌ ⊠

**▼▼▼ Howard Johnson Hotel & Suites** 🆂🄷 🐾
(250) 704-4656. **$109-$199.** 4670 Elk Lake Dr. Hwy 17, just w on Royal Oak Dr, then just n. Ext/int corridors. **Pets:** Other species. $15 daily fee/room, $30 one-time fee/room. Designated rooms, service with restrictions, supervision.
🄰🅂🄺 🆂🄳 ⊠ 🄲🄼 🐾 🖥 💻 🍴 ⇌

**⊕ ▼▼▼ Howard Johnson Hotel-City Centre** 🆂🄷 🐾
(250) 382-2151. **$59-$189.** 310 Gorge Rd E. From Douglas St, 1.4 km w; between Jutland St and Washington Ave. Int corridors. **Pets:** Small, dogs only. $150 deposit/room, $15 one-time fee/pet. Designated rooms, service with restrictions, supervision.
🅢🄰🆅 🆂🄳 ⊠ 🖥 💻 🍴 ⇌

**⊕ ▼▼▼▼ The Magnolia Hotel & Spa** 🆂🄷 🐾
(250) 381-0999. **$169-$315.** 623 Courtney St. Corner of Courtney and Gordon sts. Int corridors. **Pets:** Small. $60 one-time fee/room. Service with restrictions, crate.
🅢🄰🆅 🆂🄳 ⊠ 🄲🄼 💻 🍴 ⊠

**⊕ ▼▼▼▼ Marriott Victoria Inner Harbour** 🄻🄷
(250) 480-3800. **$149-$309.** 728 Humboldt St. Between Blanshard and Douglas sts. Int corridors. **Pets:** Small. $50 one-time fee/room. Service with restrictions, supervision.
🅢🄰🆅 ⊠ 🄲🄼 🐾 💻 🍴 ⇌ ⊠

**⊕ ▼▼▼ Oxford Castle Inn** 🄼
(250) 388-6431. **$70-$158.** 133 Gorge Rd E. Douglas St, 2 km w. Int corridors. **Pets:** Accepted.
🅢🄰🆅 🆂🄳 ⊠ 🖥 💻 ⇌ 🐾

**⊕ ▼▼▼▼ Prior House B&B Inn** 🄱🄱
(250) 592-8847. **$129-$299,** 14 day notice. 620 St. Charles St. Blanshard St (Hwy 17), 2 km e on Fort St, then just s. Int corridors. **Pets:** Medium, dogs only. $25 one-time fee/room. Designated rooms, service with restrictions, supervision.
🅢🄰🆅 🆂🄳 ⊠ 🖥 💻 🐾 🉐

**⊕ ▼▼▼ Robin Hood Motel** 🄼
(250) 388-4302. **$57-$99.** 136 Gorge Rd E. Douglas St, 2.4 km w. Ext corridors. **Pets:** Dogs only. $5 daily fee/pet. Designated rooms, service with restrictions, supervision.
🅢🄰🆅 🆂🄳 ⊠ 🖥 💻 🐾

**⊕ ▼▼▼▼ Travelodge Victoria** 🆂🄷
(250) 388-6611. **$65-$175.** 229 Gorge Rd E. From Douglas St, 2 km w on Gorge Rd E; at Washington Ave. Ext corridors. **Pets:** Medium. $10 daily fee/pet. Service with restrictions.
🅢🄰🆅 🆂🄳 ⊠ 💻 🍴 ⇌

**⊕ ▼▼▼▼ Westin Bear Mountain Victoria Resort & Spa** 🆂🄷 🐾
(250) 391-7160. **$129-$339.** 1999 Country Club Way. Trans-Canada Hwy 1, exit 14 (Highlands), 1.7 km n on Millstream Rd, then 3 km ne on Bear Mountain Pkwy, follow signs. Int corridors. **Pets:** Small. $60 one-time fee/room. Designated rooms, supervision.
🅢🄰🆅 🆂🄳 ⊠ 🄲🄼 🖥 💻 🍴 ⇌ ⊠

---

## END METROPOLITAN AREA

## WESTBANK

**⊕ ▼▼▼▼ Holiday Inn Westbank (Kelowna)** 🆂🄷
(250) 768-8879. **$77-$131,** 7 day notice. 2569 Dobbin Rd. Hwy 97 (Dobbin Rd) and Herbert Rd. Int corridors. **Pets:** Other species. $10 daily fee/pet. Service with restrictions, crate.
🅢🄰🆅 🆂🄳 ⊠ 🄲🄼 🖥 💻 🍴 ⇌

## WHISTLER

**⊕ ▼▼▼ Best Western Listel Whistler Hotel** 🆂🄷
(604) 932-1133. **$99-$449,** 14 day notice. 4121 Village Green. Hwy 99, just e on Village Gate Blvd, then follow Whistler Way. Int corridors. **Pets:** Medium, other species. $25 daily fee/pet. Designated rooms, service with restrictions, supervision.
🅢🄰🆅 🆂🄳 ⊠ 🖥 💻 🍴 ⇌

**▼▼▼ Crystal Lodge** 🆂🄷 🐾
(604) 932-2221. **$153-$1125,** 30 day notice. 4154 Village Green. Hwy 99, just e on Village Gate Blvd, then follow Whistler Way. Int corridors. **Pets:** Dogs only. $20 daily fee/pet. Service with restrictions, supervision.
🄰🅂🄺 🆂🄳 ⊠ 🄲🄼 🖥 🖥 💻 🍴 ⇌ ⊠

**⊕ ▼▼▼ Delta Whistler Village Suites** 🆂🄷
(604) 905-3987. **$95-$585.** 4308 Main St. Hwy 99, just e on Village Gate Blvd, just n on Northlands Blvd, then just e. Int corridors. **Pets:** Accepted.
🅢🄰🆅 🆂🄳 ⊠ 🄲🄼 🖥 💻 🍴 ⇌ ⊠

**⊕ ▼▼ Edgewater Lodge** 🄼
(604) 932-0688. **$125-$320,** 14 day notice. 8030 Alpine Way. 4 km n of Whistler Village via Hwy 99, e on Alpine Way. Ext corridors. **Pets:** Accepted.
🅢🄰🆅 🆂🄳 ⊠ 🍴 🐾

**⊕ ▼▼▼ ▼▼▼ The Fairmont Chateau Whistler** 🄻🄷 🐾
(604) 938-8000. **$161-$999,** 30 day notice. 4599 Chateau Blvd. Hwy 99, 1 km e on Lorimer Rd (Upper Village), then just w on Blackcomb Way. Int corridors. **Pets:** $50 daily fee/room. Service with restrictions, supervision.
🅢🄰🆅 ⊠ 🄲🄼 🐾 💻 🍴 ⇌ ⊠

**⊕ ▼▼▼ ▼▼▼ Four Seasons Resort Whistler** 🄻🄷
(604) 935-3400. **$245-$3900.** 4591 Blackcomb Way. Hwy 99, 1 km e on Lorimer Rd (Upper Village). Int corridors. **Pets:** Accepted.
🅢🄰🆅 ⊠ 🄲🄼 🖥 💻 🍴 ⇌ ⊠

◆◆◆◆ **Hilton Whistler Resort & Spa** 🄻🄷
(604) 932-1982. **$133-$699.** 4050 Whistler Way. Hwy 99, just e on Village Gate Blvd, then follow Whistler Way. Int corridors. **Pets:** $15 daily fee/pet. Designated rooms, service with restrictions, crate.
(ASK) (S⚫️) ✕ (&M) (🐾) 🖥 💻 🍴 🏊 ✕

◆◆◆ **Pan Pacific Whistler Village Centre** 🅂🄷
(604) 966-5500. **$179-$1209.** 4299 Blackcomb Way. Hwy 99, just e on Village Gate Blvd. Int corridors. **Pets:** Accepted.
(ASK) (S⚫️) ✕ (&M) 🖥 💻 🏊 ✕

◆◆◆ **Residence Inn by Marriott** 🄲🄾 🐾
(604) 905-3400. **$129-$899, 30 day notice.** 4899 Painted Cliff Rd. Hwy 99, 1 km e on Lorimer Rd (Upper Village), just se on Blackcomb Way, then just w, follow road all the way to the end. Int corridors. **Pets:** $25 daily fee/pet. Service with restrictions, supervision.
(ASK) (S⚫️) ✕ 🖥 💻 🏊 ✕

🄰🄰 ◆◆◆◆ **Summit Lodge & Spa** 🅂🄷
(604) 932-2778. **$129-$550, 30 day notice.** 4359 Main St. Hwy 99, just n on Village Gate Blvd, just w on Northlands Blvd. Int corridors. **Pets:** Accepted.
(SAVE) (S⚫️) ✕ (&M) 🖥 💻 🍴 🏊 ✕

🄰🄰 ◆◆◆◆ **Sundial Boutique Hotel** 🅂🄷
(604) 932-2321. **$199-$849, 45 day notice.** 4340 Sundial Crescent. Hwy 99, just e on Village Gate Blvd, then just s on Blackcomb Way. Int corridors. **Pets:** Accepted.
(SAVE) ✕ (&M) 🖥 💻

◆◆ **Tantalus Resort Lodge** 🄲🄾
(604) 932-4146. **$139-$799, 14 day notice.** 4200 Whistler Way. Hwy 99, just e on Village Gate Blvd, then follow Whistler Way to the end. Int corridors. **Pets:** Accepted.
(ASK) (S⚫️) ✕ 🖥 💻 🏊 ✕ (🐾)

🄰🄰 ◆◆◆◆ **The Westin Resort & Spa** 🄻🄷 🐾
(604) 905-5000. **$149-$899, 3 day notice.** 4090 Whistler Way. Hwy 99, just e on Village Gate Blvd, then s. Int corridors. **Pets:** Medium, dogs only. Supervision.
(SAVE) (S⚫️) ✕ (&M) 🖥 💻 🍴 🏊 ✕

# WILLIAMS LAKE

◆◆ **Drummond Lodge Motel** 🄼
(250) 392-5334. **$76-$1117.** 1405 Cariboo Hwy. 1 km s on Hwy 97. Ext corridors. **Pets:** Accepted.
✕ 🖥 💻

🄰🄰 ◆◆ **Williams Lake Super 8 Motel** 🄼
(250) 398-8884. **$80-$86, 5 day notice.** 1712 Broadway Ave S. 2 km s on Hwy 97. Int corridors. **Pets:** Other species. $7 daily fee/pet. Designated rooms, no service, supervision.
(SAVE) (S⚫️) ✕ (&M) 🖥 💻

# MANITOBA

## BEAUSEJOUR

### ▼▼ Super 8 SH
(204) 268-9050. **$85-$95.** 1055 Park Ave. Jct Hwy 44, 12 and 302. Int corridors. **Pets:** Other species. $8 daily fee/pet. Designated rooms, service with restrictions, supervision.

## BOISSEVAIN

### ▼▼ Canadian Wilderness Inn SH
(204) 534-7155. **$68-$98.** 306 Mountain Ave. Centre. Int corridors. **Pets:** Small, dogs only. $5 daily fee/pet. Designated rooms, supervision.

## BRANDON

### ⒶⒶ ▼▼▼ Canad Inns-Brandon SH
(204) 727-1422. **$168.** 1125 18th St. On Hwy 10 (18th St) at jct Brandon Ave. **Pets:** Accepted.

### ▼▼ Comfort Inn SH
(204) 727-6232. **$85-$130.** 925 Middleton Ave. Northside Trans-Canada Hwy 1 service road; between Hwy 10 N and 10 S; just e of McDonald's Restaurant. Int corridors. **Pets:** Accepted.

### ⒶⒶ ▼▼▼ Days Inn SH
(204) 727-3600. **$94-$104.** 2130 Currie Blvd. Jct Trans-Canada Hwy 1, 8 km s on Hwy 10 S (18th St). Int corridors. **Pets:** Other species. $10 daily fee/pet. Service with restrictions, supervision.

### ⒶⒶ ▼ Rodeway Inn Motel SH
(204) 728-7230. **$59-$64.** 300 18th St N. On Hwy 10 S, 3.2 km s of Trans-Canada Hwy 1. Ext/int corridors. **Pets:** Accepted.

### ▼▼ Royal Oak Inn & Suites SH
(204) 728-5775. **$121-$138.** 3130 Victoria Ave. 5 km s of Trans-Canada Hwy 1; 1.4 km w of jct Hwy 10 (18th St) and 1A (Victoria Ave). Int corridors. **Pets:** Medium, other species. $10 daily fee/room. Designated rooms, service with restrictions.

### ▼▼ Super 8 Motel Brandon SH 🐾
(204) 729-8024. **$90-$125.** 1570 Highland Ave. On Trans-Canada Hwy 1, south service road, just e of Hwy 10 (18th St). Int corridors. **Pets:** Medium. $20 one-time fee/room. Designated rooms, service with restrictions, supervision.

### ▼▼▼ Victoria Inn SH
(204) 725-1532. **$86-$165.** 3550 Victoria Ave. 5 km s of Trans-Canada Hwy 1; 1.8 km w of jct Hwy 10 (18th St) and 1A (Victoria Ave). Int corridors. **Pets:** Accepted.

## CHURCHILL

### ▼▼ Polar Inn & Suites M
(204) 675-8878. **$135-$200.** 153 Kelsey Blvd. Centre. Int corridors. **Pets:** Crate.

### ▼▼ The Tundra Inn SH
(204) 675-8831. **$105-$195.** 34 Franklin St. Centre. Int corridors. **Pets:** Accepted.

## DAUPHIN

### ▼▼ Canway Inn & Suites SH
(204) 638-5102. **$74-$110.** 1601 Main St S. 2.4 km s on Hwy 5A and 10A (Main St). Ext/int corridors. **Pets:** Accepted.

## FLIN FLON

### ▼▼ Victoria Inn North SH
(204) 687-7555. **$75.** 160 Hwy 10A. Jct Hwy 10 and 10A, 1 km nw (eastern approach to city). Int corridors. **Pets:** Accepted.

## HECLA

### ▼▼ Solmundson Gesta Hus BB
(204) 279-2088. **$55-$80.** On Hwy 8; in Hecla Village. Int corridors. **Pets:** Medium, other species. Supervision.

## NEEPAWA

### ▼▼ Bay Hill Inns & Suites M
(204) 476-8888. **$80-$85.** 160 Main St W. Hwy 16, just w of jct Rt 5. Int corridors. **Pets:** Accepted.

## THE PAS

### ▼▼ Kikiwak Inn SH
(204) 623-1800. **Call for rates.** Hwy 10 N. On Hwy 10, 0.6 km n. Int corridors. **Pets:** Accepted.

### ▼▼ Super 8 SH
(204) 623-1888. **$80-$110.** 1717 Gordon Ave. At southern approach to town. Int corridors. **Pets:** Small, other species. Service with restrictions, supervision.

### ⒶⒶ ▼ Wescana Inn SH
(204) 623-5446. **$95.** 439 Fischer Ave. On Hwy 10; centre. Ext/int corridors. **Pets:** Other species. No service, supervision.

## PORTAGE LA PRAIRIE

### ▼▼ Super 8 M
(204) 857-8883. **$72-$84.** 1.5 km w on Trans-Canada Hwy 1A. Int corridors. **Pets:** Accepted.

### ▼ Westgate Inn Motel M
(204) 239-5200. **$55-$57.** 1010 Saskatchewan Ave E. 1 km e on Trans-Canada Hwy 1A. Ext corridors. **Pets:** Accepted.

## RUSSELL

▼▼ **The Russell Inn Hotel & Conference Centre** 🆂🅷 ❖
(204) 773-2186. **$90-$104, 14 day notice.** Hwy 16 Russell. 1.2 km se on Hwy 16 and 83. Ext/int corridors. **Pets:** Medium, other species. Service with restrictions, supervision.

(A$K) 🆂 ⊠ 🖥 🖵 ⏶ ⏴ ⊠

## STEINBACH

▼▼ **Days Inn** 🆂🅷
(204) 320-9200. **$76-$81.** 75 Hwy 12 N. Jct Trans-Canada Hwy 1 and 12, 20 km s. Int corridors. **Pets:** Accepted.

(A$K) 🆂 ⊠ 🗄 🖥 🖵 ⏴

## THOMPSON

▼▼▼ **Country Inn & Suites By Carlson** 🆂🅷
(204) 778-8879. **$108.** 70 Thompson Dr N. Just w of Hwy 6. Int corridors. **Pets:** Accepted.

(A$K) 🆂 ⊠ 🖥 🖵 ⏴ ⊠

## WINKLER

▼▼ **Heartland Resort & Conference Centre** 🆂🅷
(204) 325-4381. **$99-$149.** 851 Main St N. Main St and Hwy 14; centre. Int corridors. **Pets:** Accepted.

(A$K) 🆂 ⊠ 🗄 🖥 🖵 ⏶ ⊠

# WINNIPEG METROPOLITAN AREA

## WINNIPEG

🆀🅰 ▼▼▼ **Canad Inns Polo Park** 🆂🅷
(204) 775-8791. **$149.** 1405 St. Matthews Ave. Just e of St James St. Int corridors. **Pets:** Medium. $25 daily fee/room. Designated rooms, supervision.

(SAVE) 🆂 ⊠ 🗄 🖥 🖵 ⏶ ⏴ ⊠

🆀🅰 ▼ **Carlton Inn** 🆂🅷
(204) 942-0881. **$84-$94.** 220 Carlton St. Just s off Metro Rt 85 (Portage Ave). Int corridors. **Pets:** Other species. Service with restrictions.

(SAVE) 🆂 ⊠ 🖥 🖵 ⏶ ⏴

▼▼ **Clarion Hotel & Suites** 🆂🅷 ❖
(204) 774-5110. **$129-$229.** 1445 Portage Ave. Jct Empress St. Int corridors. **Pets:** Medium, other species. $15 daily fee/room. Designated rooms, service with restrictions, crate.

(A$K) 🆂 ⊠ 🖥 🖵 ⏶ ⏴ ⊠

▼▼ **Comfort Inn Airport** 🆂🅷
(204) 783-5627. **$89-$130.** 1770 Sargent Ave. At Sargent Ave and King Edward St. Int corridors. **Pets:** Large, other species. $5 daily fee/room. Designated rooms, service with restrictions, supervision.

(A$K) 🆂 ⊠ 🗄 🖥 🖵

🆀🅰 ▼▼ **Comfort Inn South** 🆂🅷
(204) 269-7390. **$89-$130.** 3109 Pembina Hwy. Just n of jct Perimeter Hwy 100 and 75. Int corridors. **Pets:** Medium. $10 daily fee/room. Designated rooms, service with restrictions, supervision.

(SAVE) 🆂 ⊠ 🖥 🖵

▼▼ **Country Inn & Suites By Carlson** 🆂🅷
(204) 783-6900. **$95-$105.** 730 King Edward St. Just s of jct Wellington Ave. Int corridors. **Fets:** Accepted.

(A$K) 🆂 ⊠ 🗄 🖥 🖵

▼ **Dakota Motor Hotel** 🆂🅷
(204) 256-4315. **$69-$79, 3 day notice.** 1105 St. Mary's Rd. At Dunkirk Dr; jct Metro Rt 52 and 62. Int corridors. **Pets:** Accepted.

(A$K) 🆂 ⊠ 🖥 🖵 ⏶

🆀🅰 ▼▼ **Days Inn** 🆂🅷
(204) 586-8525. **$119-$129.** 550 McPhillips St. Just n of Logan Ave. Int corridors. **Pets:** Accepted.

(SAVE) 🆂 ⊠ 🖥 🖵 ⏶ ⏴

🆀🅰 ▼▼▼ **Delta Winnipeg** 🅻🅷 ❖
(204) 942-0551. **$89-$199.** 350 St. Mary Ave. At Hargrave St. Int corridors. **Pets:** Medium, other species. $35 daily fee/room. Service with restrictions, crate.

(SAVE) 🆂 ⊠ 🗄 🖥 🖵 ⏶ ⏴ ⊠

▼▼▼ **The Fairmont Winnipeg** 🅻🅷 ❖
(204) 957-1350. **$99-$1400.** 2 Lombard Pl. Just e of corner Portage Ave and Main St. Int corridors. **Pets:** $25 daily fee/pet.

(A$K) 🆂 ⊠ ✎ 🖥 🖵 ⏶ ⏴ ⊠

🆀🅰 ▼▼▼ **Greenwood Inn** 🆂🅷
(204) 775-9889. **$159-$279.** 1715 Wellington Ave. Wellington Ave at Century St. Int corridors. **Pets:** Other species. Designated rooms, service with restrictions, supervision.

(SAVE) 🆂 ⊠ 🗄 🖥 🖵 ⏶ ⏴ ⊠

🆀🅰 ▼▼▼ **Holiday Inn Winnipeg-South** 🆂🅷
(204) 452-4747. **$120-$140.** 1330 Pembina Hwy. At McGillivray Blvd. Int corridors. **Pets:** Other species. Designated rooms, service with restrictions, supervision.

(SAVE) 🆂 ⊠ 🖥 🖵 ⏶ ⏴ ⊠

▼▼▼ **Place Louis Riel All-Suite Hotel** 🅻🅷 ❖
(204) 947-6961. **$90-$150.** 190 Smith St. At St. Mary Ave. Int corridors. **Pets:** Other species. $10 daily fee/room. Designated rooms, supervision.

(A$K) 🆂 ⊠ 🅼 🖥 🖵 ⏶ ⊠

▼▼▼ **Radisson Hotel Winnipeg Downtown** 🅻🅷
(204) 956-0410. **$89-$124.** 288 Portage Ave. At Smith St. Int corridors. **Pets:** Accepted.

(A$K) 🆂 ⊠ 🖥 🖵 ⏶ ⏴ ⊠

▼▼▼ **Ramada Marlborough Hotel** 🆂🅷
(204) 942-6411. **$89.** 331 Smith St. Just n off Metro Rt 85 (Portage Ave). Int corridors. **Pets:** Other species. $10 one-time fee/pet. Designated rooms, service with restrictions, supervision.

(A$K) 🆂 ⊠ 🖥 🖵 ⏶ ⏴ ⊠

▼▼ **Super 8** 🆂🅷 ❖
(204) 269-8888. **$89-$99.** 1714 Pembina Hwy. 1 km n of jct Bishop Grandin Blvd. Int corridors. **Pets:** Other species. $10 daily fee/room. Service with restrictions, supervision.

🆂 ⊠ 🖥 🖵 ⏶ ⊠

🆀🅰 ▼▼ **Travelodge** 🆂🅷 ❖
(204) 255-6000. **$83-$93.** 20 Alpine Ave. Just e of jct Fermor Ave and St. Anne's Rd. Int corridors. **Pets:** Medium, other species. $6 daily fee/room. Designated rooms, service with restrictions, supervision.

(SAVE) 🆂 ⊠ 🖥 🖵 ⏶ ⏴ ⊠

🆀🅰 ▼▼▼ **Victoria Inn Hotel & Convention Centre** 🆂🅷
(204) 786-4801. **$89.** 1808 Wellington Ave. At Berry St. Int corridors. **Pets:** Other species. $10 one-time fee/room. Service with restrictions, crate.

(SAVE) ⊠ 🗄 🖥 🖵 ⏶ ⏴ ⊠

🆀🅰 ▼▼▼ **Viscount Gort Hotel** 🆂🅷
(204) 775-0451. **$83-$119.** 1670 Portage Ave. Portage Ave at Rt 90. Int corridors. **Pets:** Accepted.

(SAVE) ⊠ 🖥 🖵 ⏶ ⏴ ⊠

🆀🅰 ▼▼▼ **York The Hotel** 🅻🅷
(204) 942-5300. **$95-$159.** 161 Donald St. At York Ave. Int corridors. **Pets:** Accepted.

(SAVE) 🆂 ⊠ 🖥 🖵 ⏶ ⏴ ⊠

# NEW BRUNSWICK

## CITY INDEX

## BATHURST

### ▼▼ Atlantic Host Hotel SH
(506) 548-3335. **$92-$120.** 1450 Vanier Blvd. Rt 11, exit 310 (Vanier Blvd). Int corridors. **Pets:** Small. $50 deposit/pet. Designated rooms, no service, supervision.

(ASK) ⊠ 🖼 🍽 🏊 🚫

### ▼▼ Comfort Inn SH
(506) 547-8000. **$82-$112.** 1170 St Peter's Ave. 3.4 km n on Rt 134 (St Peter's Ave). Int corridors. **Pets:** Accepted.

(ASK) 🛏 ⊠ 🖼

### ▼▼ Danny's Inn & Conference Centre SH
(506) 546-6621. **$71-$99.** Rt 11, exit 310 (Vanier Blvd) northbound to Rt 134 (St Peter's Ave), 4 km n; exit 318 southbound to Rt 134 (St Peter's Ave), 3.8 km s. Ext/int corridors. **Pets:** Accepted.

🛏 ⊠ 🖼 🖼 🍽 🏊 🚫

### ▼▼ Lakeview Inn & Suites SH
(506) 548-4949. **$94.** 777 St Peter's Ave. 3 km n on Rt 134 (St Peter's Ave). Int corridors. **Pets:** Small, dogs only. $8 daily fee/room. Designated rooms, service with restrictions, supervision.

(ASK) 🛏 ⊠ 🖼M 🖼 🖼

### ▼▼ Le Chateau Bathurst SH
(506) 546-6691. **$96-$110.** 80 Main St. On Rt 134 (St Peter's Ave) and Rt 7; centre. Ext/int corridors. **Pets:** Medium. $10 one-time fee/room. Designated rooms, service with restrictions, supervision.

⊠ 🖼 🍽 🏊 🚫

## BOUCTOUCHE

### ▼▼▼ Les Chalets Chebooktoosk CA
(506) 743-1999. **$80-$185, 7 day notice.** 23 Acadie St. 1 km e on Rt 134; centre. Ext corridors. **Pets:** Other species. Supervision.

⊠ 🖼 🖼 🐾

## CAMPBELLTON

### ▼▼ Comfort Inn SH
(506) 753-4121. **$91-$110.** 111 Val D'amour Rd. Hwy 11, exit 415, 1 km e on Sugarloaf St W. Ext/int corridors. **Pets:** Other species. Service with restrictions.

(ASK) 🛏 ⊠ 🖼 🖼

### CAA ▼▼ Howard Johnson SH
(506) 753-4133. **$95-$115, 3 day notice.** 157 Water St. Hwy 134; in City Centre Complex. Int corridors. **Pets:** Accepted.

(SAVE) ⊠ 🖼 🖼 🍽

## CARAQUET

### ▼▼▼ Super 8 Motel SH
(506) 727-0888. **$89-$154.** 9 Carrefour Ave. Just e of jct Rt 11 and St Pierre Blvd E. Int corridors. **Pets:** Small. Service with restrictions, supervision.

(ASK) 🛏 ⊠ 🖼M 🖼 🖼 🍽 🏊 🚫

## CHANCE HARBOUR

### CAA ▼▼▼ The Mariner's Inn ◼I
(506) 659-2619. **$119-$140, 3 day notice.** 32 Mawhinney Cove Rd. Hwy 1, exit 96, 9 km s on Rt 790; 30 km w of Saint John. Int corridors. **Pets:** Very small, dogs only. $10 daily fee/pet. Designated rooms, service with restrictions, supervision.

(SAVE) ⊠ 🖼 🖼 🍽

## COCAGNE

### ▼▼ Cocagne Motel M
(506) 576-6657. **$50-$90.** Rt 11, exit 15, 1 km n on Rt 535. Ext corridors. **Pets:** Accepted.

🖼 🐾

## DALHOUSIE

### ▼▼▼ Best Western Manoir Adelaide SH
(506) 684-5681. **$119.** 385 Adelaide St. Centre. Int corridors. **Pets:** Very small, dogs only. $75 deposit/pet. Designated rooms, service with restrictions, supervision.

(ASK) 🛏 ⊠ 🖼 🖼 🍽

## EDMUNDSTON

### CAA ▼▼▼ Chateau Edmundston Hotel & Suites SH
(506) 739-7321. **$100-$138, 7 day notice.** 100 Rice St. 1.6 km sw off Trans-Canada Hwy 2, exit 18 (Hebert Blvd), just w on Church Rd. Int corridors. **Pets:** Very small. Designated rooms, service with restrictions, supervision.

(SAVE) 🛏 ⊠ 🖼 🍽 🏊

### ▼▼ Comfort Inn SH
(506) 739-8361. **$80-$160.** 5 Bateman Ave. Trans-Canada Hwy 2, exit 18 (Hebert Blvd). Int corridors. **Pets:** Other species. Service with restrictions, crate.

(ASK) 🛏 ⊠ 🖼 🖼

### ▼▼▼ Days Inn Edmundston 🖼
(506) 263-0000. **$95-$159.** 10 rue Mathieu. 8 km e on Trans-Canada Hwy 2, exit 26. Int corridors. **Pets:** Accepted.

(ASK) 🛏 ⊠ 🖼 🖼

## FREDERICTON

### ▼▼ Auberge Wandlyn Inn SH
(506) 462-4444. **$100-$140.** 958 Prospect St. Rt 8, exit 3 (Hanwell Rd) eastbound; exit 5 (Smythe St) westbound. Ext/int corridors. **Pets:** Small. $300 deposit/room. Designated rooms, service with restrictions, supervision.

(ASK) 🛏 ⊠ 🖼 🖼 🍽 🏊

### ▼▼ City Motel SH
(506) 450-9900. **$95-$115.** 1216 Regent St. Trans-Canada Hwy 2, exit 285A and B eastbound; exit 285B westbound, 3.3 km n on Rt 101 (Regent St). Int corridors. **Pets:** Accepted.

(ASK) 🛏 ⊠

### ▼▼ Comfort Inn SH 🐾
(506) 453-0800. **$100-$199.** 797 Prospect St. Rt 8, exit 3 (Hanwell Rd) eastbound; exit 5 (Smythe St) westbound. Int corridors. **Pets:** Other species. Designated rooms.

(ASK) 🛏 ⊠ 🖼 🖼

(AA) ▼▼▼ **Crowne Plaza Fredericton Lord Beaverbrook** [LH]
(506) 455-3371. **$99-$169.** 659 Queen St. Centre. Int corridors. **Pets:** Large. $15 one-time fee/pet. Designated rooms, service with restrictions, crate.
[SAVE] [Sᴅ] [✕] [▭] [¶] [⇌] [✕]

▼▼▼▼ **Delta Fredericton** [LH]
(506) 457-7000. **$244-$319, 30 day notice.** 225 Woodstock Rd. 1.6 km n on Rt 102; downtown. Int corridors. **Pets:** Accepted.
[ASK] [Sᴅ] [✕] [&ᴹ] [▤] [▭] [¶] [⇌] [✕]

▼▼▼▼ **Holiday Inn Fredericton** [SH]
(506) 363-5111. **$129-$159.** 35 Mactaquac Rd (Hwy 102). Trans-Canada Hwy 2, exit 258 eastbound, 11 km e; exit 294 westbound, 30 km w. Ext/int corridors. **Pets:** Accepted.
[ASK] [✕] [&ᴹ] [▤] [▭] [¶] [⇌] [✕]

▼▼▼ **Lakeview Inn & Suites-Fredericton** [SH]
(506) 459-0035. **$105-$117.** 665 Prospect St. Rt 8, exit 3 (Hanwell Rd) eastbound; exit 5 (Smythe St) westbound. Int corridors. **Pets:** Accepted.
[ASK] [Sᴅ] [✕] [▭]

▼▼▼▼ **Ramada Hotel Fredericton** [SH] ❧
(506) 460-5500. **$99-$149, 30 day notice.** 480 Riverside Dr. On Rt 105 at the north end of Princess Margaret Bridge. Int corridors. **Pets:** Designated rooms, service with restrictions, supervision.
[ASK] [Sᴅ] [✕] [▤] [▭] [⇌] [✕]

## GRAND FALLS

▼▼▼ **Auberge Pres-du-Lac Inn** [SH]
(506) 473-1300. **$85-$120.** 10039 Rt 144. Trans-Canada Hwy 2, exit 75, just w. Ext/int corridors. **Pets:** Small. Designated rooms, service with restrictions, supervision.
[Sᴅ] [✕] [&ᴹ] [▤] [▭] [¶] [⇌] [✕]

▼▼ **Hill Top Motel & Restaurant** [SH]
(506) 473-2684. **$60-$92.** 131 Madawaska Rd. Trans-Canada Hwy 2, exit 75, 2.4 km se. Ext corridors. **Pets:** Accepted.
[ASK] [Sᴅ] [✕] [▤] [¶]

## MIRAMICHI

▼▼▼ **Comfort Inn** [SH] ❧
(506) 622-1215. **$87-$135, 7 day notice.** 201 Edward St. 1 km w on Rt 8. Int corridors. **Pets:** Medium. Designated rooms, service with restrictions, supervision.
[ASK] [Sᴅ] [✕] [▤] [▭]

▼▼ **Lakeview Inn & Suites** [SH]
(506) 627-1999. **$90-$109, 7 day notice.** 333 King George Hwy. 1.8 km w on Rt 8. Int corridors. **Pets:** Medium, other species. $50 deposit/room. Designated rooms, service with restrictions, crate.
[ASK] [Sᴅ] [✕] [▤] [▭]

▼▼▼▼ **Rodd Miramichi River-A Rodd Signature Hotel** [SH]
(506) 773-3111. **$105-$203.** 1809 Water St. Hwy 11, exit 120, 0.6 km e. Int corridors. **Pets:** Other species. $10 one-time fee/room. Designated rooms, supervision.
[ASK] [Sᴅ] [✕] [&ᴹ] [♿] [▤] [▭] [¶] [≋]

## MONCTON

(AA) ▼▼▼ **Beacon Light Motel** [M]
(506) 384-1734. **$85-$105.** 1062 Mountain Rd. Trans-Canada Hwy 2, exit 454 (Mapleton Rd), 2.8 km to Rt 126 (Mountain Rd), then just s. Ext/int corridors. **Pets:** Accepted.
[SAVE] [✕] [▤] [▭] [¶] [⇌]

▼▼▼▼ **Best Western Moncton** [SH]
(506) 388-0888. **$120-$165.** 300 Lewisville Rd. Trans-Canada Hwy 2, exit 459A eastbound, s on Rt 115 to Lewisville Rd, then left; exit 467A westbound, 8 km w on Hwy 15, exit 10. Int corridors. **Pets:** Accepted.
[ASK] [Sᴅ] [✕] [&ᴹ] [♿] [▤] [▭] [≋]

▼▼ **Coastal Inn Champlain** [SH]
(506) 857-9686. **$109-$119.** 502 Kennedy St. At Paul St; opposite Champlain Place Shopping Centre. Ext/int corridors. **Pets:** Accepted.
[ASK] [Sᴅ] [✕] [▤] [▭] [¶] [⇌]

▼▼ **Colonial Inns** [SH]
(506) 382-3395. **$90.** 42 Highfield St. 1 blk n of Main St; centre. Ext/int corridors. **Pets:** Accepted.
[✕] [▤] [¶] [⇌] [✕]

▼▼ **Comfort Inn** [SH]
(506) 384-3175. **$85-$195.** 2495 Mountain Rd. Trans-Canada Hwy 2, exit 450. Int corridors. **Pets:** Accepted.
[ASK] [Sᴅ] [✕] [▤] [▭]

(AA) ▼▼▼ **Comfort Inn** [SH] ❧
(506) 859-6868. **$98-$295.** 20 Maplewood Dr. Trans-Canada Hwy 2, exit 459A onto Hwy 115 S, left on Rt 134 E (Lewisville Rd). Int corridors. **Pets:** Medium, other species. Service with restrictions, supervision.
[SAVE] [Sᴅ] [✕] [▤] [▭]

▼▼▼ **Country Inn & Suites By Carlson** [SH]
(506) 852-7000. **$130-$170.** 2475 Mountain Rd. Trans-Canada Hwy 2, exit 450. Int corridors. **Pets:** Accepted.
[ASK] [Sᴅ] [✕] [▤] [▭]

(AA) ▼▼▼▼ **Crowne Plaza Moncton Downtown** [LH]
(506) 854-6340. **$99-$169.** 1005 Main St. Highfield and Main sts; downtown. Int corridors. **Pets:** $10 one-time fee/room. Designated rooms, service with restrictions, supervision.
[SAVE] [Sᴅ] [✕] [▤] [▭] [¶] [⇌]

▼▼▼▼ **Delta Beausejour** [LH]
(506) 854-4344. **$129-$199.** 750 Main St. Main and Bacon sts; centre of downtown. Int corridors. **Pets:** Accepted.
[✕] [▤] [¶] [⇌] [✕]

(AA) ▼▼▼ **Holiday Inn Express Hotel & Suites Moncton** [SH] ❧
(506) 384-1050. **$120-$170.** 2515 Mountain Rd. Trans-Canada Hwy 2, exit 450. Ext/int corridors. **Pets:** Medium, other species. $100 deposit/room. Designated rooms, service with restrictions, crate.
[SAVE] [Sᴅ] [✕] [&ᴹ] [⊘] [▭] [¶] [⇌] [✕]

▼▼▼ **Rodd Park House Inn** [SH]
(506) 382-1664. **$80-$176.** 434 Main St. 1 km e on Rt 106. Ext/int corridors. **Pets:** Accepted.
[ASK] [Sᴅ] [✕] [▭] [¶] [⇌]

## ROTHESAY

▼▼▼ **Shadow Lawn Inn** [CI]
(506) 847-7539. **$119-$195, 3 day notice.** 3180 Rothesay Rd. Hwy 1, exit 137B eastbound; exit 137A westbound, follow signs for Rothesay Rd and Rt 100, 1.6 km left on Old Hampton Rd (Rt 100), then left on Rt 100. Int corridors. **Pets:** Accepted.
[ASK] [✕] [▤] [▭] [¶]

## SACKVILLE

▼▼ **Coastal Inn Sackville** [SH]
(506) 536-0000. **$99-$105.** 15 Wright St. Trans-Canada Hwy 2, exit 504. Int corridors. **Pets:** Designated rooms, no service, supervision.
[ASK] [Sᴅ] [✕]

(AA) ▼▼▼ **Marshlands Inn** [CI]
(506) 536-0170. **$75-$180.** 55 Bridge St. On Hwy 106; centre. Int corridors. **Pets:** Accepted.
[SAVE] [✕] [¶] [♫]

# ST. ANDREWS

**▼▼▼ The Fairmont Algonquin** 🔲
(506) 529-8823. **$129-$399, 3 day notice.** 184 Adolphus St. Off Hwy 127. Int corridors. **Pets:** Accepted.

(ASK) (✕) (🔋) (💻) (🍴) (🌊) (✕)

**▼▼▼ St. Andrews Cottages** 🔲
(506) 529-8555. **$79-$139, 3 day notice.** 3907 Rt 127. On Hwy 127, 2.5 km n. Ext corridors. **Pets:** Accepted.

(✕) (🔋) (🌊) (🅰️)

(CAA) **▼▼▼ The Windsor House of St. Andrews** 🔲
(506) 529-3330. **$125-$300, 14 day notice.** 132 Water St. Centre. Int corridors. **Pets:** Other species.

(SAVE) (S🔒) (✕) (🍴) (🅰️)

# SAINT JOHN

**▼▼ Coastal Inn Fort Howe Hotel** 🔲
(506) 657-7320. **$105-$119.** 10 Portland St at Main St. 1 km w on Hwy 1; north end Chesley Dr, exit 121 eastbound off Harbour Bridge; exit 123 westbound. Int corridors. **Pets:** Accepted.

(ASK) (S🔒) (✕) (🔋) (💻) (🍴) (🌊)

**▼ Colonial Inns** 🔲
(506) 652-3000. **$84-$90.** 175 City Rd. Adjacent to Hwy 1, exit 123. Ext/int corridors. **Pets:** Accepted.

(ASK) (✕) (🔋) (🍴) (🌊)

**▼▼ Comfort Inn** 🔲
(506) 674-1873. **$121-$144.** 1155 Fairville Blvd. Hwy 1, exit 117 westbound; exit 119 eastbound, turn left. Int corridors. **Pets:** Accepted.

(ASK) (S🔒) (✕) (💻)

**▼▼ Country Inn & Suites** 🔲
(506) 635-0400. **$104-$124.** 1011 Fairville Blvd. Hwy 1, exit 119B eastbound, left on Catherwood Dr, left at lights; exit 119A westbound. Int corridors. **Pets:** Other species. $15 one-time fee/room. Service with restrictions, crate.

(ASK) (S🔒) (✕) (🔋) (💻)

**▼▼▼ Delta Brunswick** 🔲
(506) 648-1981. **$119-$149.** 39 King St. Centre of downtown; in Brunswick Square Mall. Int corridors. **Pets:** Accepted.

(ASK) (S🔒) (✕) (🔆M) (🅰️) (💻) (🍴) (🌊) (✕)

**▼▼▼ Hilton Saint John** 🔲
(506) 693-8484. **$122.** One Market Square. Hwy 1, exit 122 at Market Square. Int corridors. **Pets:** Accepted.

(✕) (💻) (🍴) (🌊) (✕)

(CAA) **▼▼▼ Inn on the Cove and Spa** 🔲
(506) 672-7799. **$95-$225, 7 day notice.** 1371 Sand Cove Rd. Hwy 1, exit 119, right to Sand Cove Rd, then 2 km w. Int corridors. **Pets:** Medium, dogs only. $35 one-time fee/pet. Designated rooms, service with restrictions, supervision.

(SAVE) (S🔒) (✕) (🔆M) (💻) (🍴) (🅰️)

**▼ Regent Motel** 🔲
(506) 672-8273. **$55-$70, 3 day notice.** 2121 Ocean West Way. Hwy 1, exit 112 eastbound, 2.4 km e on Rt 100; exit 114 westbound onto exit 96W, 0.5 km w on Rt 100. Ext corridors. **Pets:** Accepted.

(✕) (🔋) (🅰️) (🅰️)

# ST. STEPHEN

**▼ St. Stephen Inn** 🔲
(506) 466-1814. **$60-$90.** 99 King St. On Hwy 1; centre. Ext/int corridors. **Pets:** Accepted.

(ASK) (S🔒) (✕) (🍴)

# SHEDIAC

**▼▼▼ Gaudet Chalets & Motel** 🔲
(506) 533-8877. **$65-$119, 30 day notice.** 14 Belleview Heights. On Rt 133, 2.4 km w of Rt 15, exit 37. Ext corridors. **Pets:** Accepted.

(✕) (🔋) (💻)

# ST-LEONARD

(CAA) **▼▼▼ Daigle's Motel** 🔲
(506) 423-6351. **$78-$99.** 68 rue DuPont. Hwy 17, 1 km s of Trans-Canada Hwy 2, exit 58. Ext corridors. **Pets:** Accepted.

(SAVE) (S🔒) (✕) (🍴) (🌊)

# SUSSEX

(CAA) **▼ All Seasons Inn** 🔲
(506) 433-2220. **$75-$140.** 1015 Main St. Hwy 1, exit 192 eastbound; exit 198 westbound, left towards Sussex Corner; centre. Ext corridors. **Pets:** $10 daily fee/pet. Service with restrictions, supervision.

(SAVE) (S🔒) (✕) (💻) (🍴)

**▼▼ Fairway Inn** 🔲
(506) 433-3470. **$92-$155.** 216 Roachville Rd. Hwy 1, exit 193. Ext/int corridors. **Pets:** Small. $10 daily fee/pet. Designated rooms, service with restrictions, supervision.

(ASK) (S🔒) (✕) (💻) (🍴) (🌊)

**▼▼ Pine Cone Motel** 🔲
(506) 433-3958. **$65-$75.** 12808 Rt 114. Hwy 1, exit 198, 2 km e on Hwy 114 towards Penobsquis. Ext corridors. **Pets:** Accepted.

(ASK) (✕) (🅰️)

# WOODSTOCK

**▼▼ Econo Lodge** 🔲
(506) 328-8876. **$89-$139.** 168 Rt 555. Trans-Canada Hwy 2, exit 188 (Houlton Rd). Ext/int corridors. **Pets:** Accepted.

(ASK) (S🔒) (✕) (💻) (🍴) (🌊)

**▼▼ Howard Johnson Inn** 🔲
(506) 328-3315. **$100-$110.** Trans-Canada Hwy 2, exit 188 (Houlton Rd). Ext/int corridors. **Pets:** Accepted.

(ASK) (S🔒) (✕) (💻) (🍴) (🌊) (✕)

**▼ Stiles Motel Hill View** 🔲
(506) 328-6671. **$85-$105, 3 day notice.** 827 Main St. Trans-Canada Hwy 2, exit 185 eastbound, 2.5 km e; exit 188 (Houlton Rd) westbound, 5.5 km via Rt 555 and 103 (Main St). Ext corridors. **Pets:** Accepted.

(ASK) (S🔒) (✕) (🍴)

# YOUNGS COVE ROAD

(CAA) **▼ McCready's Motel** 🔲
(506) 362-2916. **$54-$60, 3 day notice.** 10995 Rt 10. Trans-Canada Hwy 2, exit 365, just w. Ext corridors. **Pets:** Accepted.

(SAVE) (🍴) (🅰️) (🅰️)

# NEWFOUNDLAND AND LABRADOR

## CHANNEL-PORT-AUX-BASQUES

**St. Christopher's Hotel** SH
(709) 695-7034. **$75-$105.** 146 Caribou Rd. Trans-Canada Hwy 1, exit Port Aux Basques (downtown), follow signs 2 km. Int corridors. **Pets:** Other species. Designated rooms, service with restrictions, supervision.
ASK ☒ ✕ 🛏 💻 ⑴

## CLARENVILLE

**Restland Motel** SH
(709) 466-7636. **$74-$82.** 262 Memorial Dr. Centre. Ext/int corridors. **Pets:** Accepted.
ASK ☒ ✕ 🛏 ⑴ ⒦

**St. Jude Hotel** SH
(709) 466-1717. **$95-$113.** 249 Trans-Canada Hwy. On Trans-Canada Hwy 1; centre. Int corridors. **Pets:** Accepted.
ASK ☒ ✕ 🛏 💻 ⑴

## CORNER BROOK

**Comfort Inn** SH ❀
(709) 639-1980. **$104-$116.** 41 Maple Valley Rd. Trans-Canada Hwy 1, exit 5 eastbound; exit 6 westbound, via Confederation Ave. Int corridors. **Pets:** Service with restrictions, supervision.
✕ 💻 ⑴

**Glynmill Inn** SH
(709) 634-5181. **$119-$128, 7 day notice.** 1B Cobb Ln. Centre. Int corridors. **Pets:** Accepted.
ASK ☒ ✕ 🛏 💻 ⑴

**Holiday Inn Corner Brook** LH
(709) 634-5381. **$100-$109.** 48 West St. Centre. Int corridors. **Pets:** Other species. Service with restrictions, supervision.
✕ 🛏 💻 ⑴ ⇆

**Mamateek Inn** SH
(709) 639-8901. **$99-$109, 30 day notice.** Maple Valley Rd. Trans-Canada Hwy 1, exit 5 eastbound; exit 6 westbound via Confederation Ave. Int corridors. **Pets:** Accepted.
ASK ☒ ✕ ⑴

## COW HEAD

**Shallow Bay Motel & Cabins** SH
(709) 243-2471. **$85-$105.** Hwy 430, 4 km w towards the ocean, follow signs. Ext/int corridors. **Pets:** Small, other species. Designated rooms, service with restrictions, crate.
ASK ✕ 🛏 💻 ⑴ ⇆ ⒦

## GANDER

**Albatross Hotel** SH
(709) 256-3956. **$88-$89.** On Trans-Canada Hwy 1. Ext/int corridors. **Pets:** Other species. Service with restrictions.
ASK ✕ 🛏 💻 ⑴

**Comfort Inn** SH
(709) 256-3535. **$109-$119.** 112 Trans-Canada Hwy 1. Centre. Ext/int corridors. **Pets:** Accepted.
ASK ☒ ✕ 🛏 💻 ⑴

**Hotel Gander** SH
(709) 256-3931. **$79-$99, 30 day notice.** 100 Trans-Canada Hwy 1. Centre. Int corridors. **Pets:** Accepted.
ASK ☒ ✕ 🛏 💻 ⑴ ⇆

**Sinbad's Hotel & Suites** SH
(709) 651-2678. **$88.** Bennett Dr. Centre. Ext corridors. **Pets:** Other species. Service with restrictions, supervision.
ASK ☒ ✕ 🛏 💻 ⑴

## GRAND FALLS-WINDSOR

**Mount Peyton Hotel** SH
(709) 489-2251. **$85.** 214 Lincoln Rd. 1 km ne on Trans-Canada Hwy 1. Ext/int corridors. **Pets:** Accepted.
ASK ☒ ✕ 🛏 💻 ⑴

## LABRADOR CITY

**Carol Inn** SH
(709) 944-7736. **$65-$85.** 215 Drake Ave. Centre. Int corridors. **Pets:** Accepted.
ASK ☒ ✕ 🛏 💻 ⑴

## L'ANSE AU CLAIR

**Northern Light Inn** SH
(709) 931-2332. **$75-$150.** Rt 510. On Rt 510; centre. Int corridors. **Pets:** Accepted.
ASK ☒ ✕ 🛏 ⑴

## ST. JOHN'S

CAA **Best Western Travellers Inn** SH
(709) 722-5540. **$89-$149.** 199 Kenmount Rd. Jct of Pippy Place Rd. Ext/int corridors. **Pets:** Medium, other species. $50 deposit/pet. Service with restrictions, supervision.
SAVE ☒ ✕ 🛏 💻 ⑴ ⇆ ⒦

**Capital Hotel** SH
(709) 738-4480. **$125-$129.** 196 Kenmount Rd. Jct Pippy Place Rd. Int corridors. **Pets:** Accepted.
ASK ✕ 🛏 💻 ⑴

CAA **Comfort Inn Airport** SH
(709) 753-3500. **$89-$149.** 106 Airport Rd. Trans-Canada Hwy 1, exit 47A, 0.7 km n on Rt 40 (Portugal Cove Rd); 0.5 km s of airport. Int corridors. **Pets:** $35 one-time fee/room. Service with restrictions, supervision.
SAVE ☒ ✕ 🛏 💻 ⑴

**Delta St. John's Hotel and Conference Centre** LH
(709) 739-6404. **$135-$155, 30 day notice.** 120 New Gower St. Centre. Int corridors. **Pets:** Accepted.
ASK ☒ ✕ ⒨ ⒦ 💻 ⑴ ⇆ ⊠

**The Fairmont Newfoundland** LH
(709) 726-4980. **$151-$322.** Cavendish Square. Centre. Int corridors. **Pets:** Medium, dogs only. $25 one-time fee/room. Designated rooms, supervision.
ASK ✕ 💻 ⑴ ⇆ ⊠

**Holiday Inn St. John's-Govt Centre** LH
(709) 722-0506. **$154-$172.** 180 Portugal Cove Rd. Trans-Canada Hwy 1, exit 47A, 1.4 km s. Ext/int corridors. **Pets:** Accepted.
✕ ⒨ ⒦ 💻 ⑴ ⇆

## STEPHENVILLE

**Holiday Inn Stephenville** SH
(709) 643-6666. **$148-$158.** 44 Queen St. Centre. Int corridors. **Pets:** Accepted.
ASK ☒ ✕ 💻 ⑴

# NORTHWEST TERRITORIES

## YELLOWKNIFE

▼▼▼ **Fraser Tower Suite Hotel** 🅛🅗
(867) 873-8700. **$145-$195.** 5303 52nd St. Corner of 52nd St and 53rd Ave. Int corridors. **Pets:** $10 daily fee/room. Service with restrictions, supervision.
☒ 🖪 🖵 🎦

▼▼ **Yellowknife Super 8 Motel** 🅜 🐾
(867) 669-8888. **$134-$179.** 308 Old Airport Rd. 2 km s on Franklin, 1 km w; in WalMart Plaza. Int corridors. **Pets:** Large. $25 one-time fee/room. Designated rooms, service with restrictions.
🅐🅢🅚 🆂🆅 ☒ 🖪 🖵

## CITY INDEX

## AMHERST

**▼▼ Auberge Wandlyn Inn** SH
(902) 667-3331. **$125-$135.** Victoria St. Trans-Canada Hwy 104, exit 3, 1 km w. Ext/int corridors. **Pets:** Accepted.

ASK ✕ 📱 💻 🍴 ➷

**▼▼ Comfort Inn** SH
(902) 667-0404. **$122-$160, 7 day notice.** 143 Albion St S. Trans-Canada Hwy 104, exit 4, 1.5 km n on Rt 2. Int corridors. **Pets:** Accepted.

ASK 🔒 ✕ 💻

**▼▼▼ Super 8 Motel** SH 🐾
(902) 660-8888. **$89-$139, 14 day notice.** 40 Lord Amherst Dr. Trans-Canada Hwy 104, exit 4. Int corridors. **Pets:** Medium. $10 daily fee/room. Service with restrictions, supervision.

## ANNAPOLIS ROYAL

**▼▼ Annapolis Royal Inn** M
(902) 532-2323. **$89-$150, 30 day notice.** 1 km w on Hwy 1. Ext corridors. **Pets:** Accepted.

ASK 🔒 ✕ 💻

**▼▼ Champlain Motel** M
(902) 532-5473. **$105-$125, 30 day notice.** RR 2. 4.2 km w on Hwy 1. Ext corridors. **Pets:** Accepted.

ASK 🔒 ✕ 📱 💻 ➷

**▼▼▼ The King George Inn** BB 🐾
(902) 532-5286. **$99-$189.** 548 Upper St George St. Centre. Int corridors. **Pets:** Accepted

ASK 🔒 ✕ 🖼

## ANTIGONISH

**CAA ▼▼ Maritime Inn Antigonish** SH
(902) 863-4001. **$99-$139.** 158 Main St. Centre. Ext/int corridors. **Pets:** Other species. Designated rooms, service with restrictions, supervision.

SAVE ✕ 💻 🍴

## AULD'S COVE

**CAA ▼▼▼ The Cove Motel & Restaurant/Gift Shop** M 🐾
(902) 747-2700. **$95-$115.** 227 Auld's Cove. 1 km n off Trans-Canada Hwy 104; 3 km w of Canso Cswy. Ext corridors. **Pets:** Medium. Designated rooms, service with restrictions, crate.

SAVE ✕ 📱 💻 🍴 🖼

## BADDECK

**▼▼ The Ceilidh Country Lodge** M
(902) 295-3500. **$89-$129, 3 day notice.** 357 Shore Rd. Trans-Canada Hwy 105, exit 8, 1.6 km e on Rt 205 (Shore Rd). Ext/int corridors. **Pets:** Accepted.

✕ 📱 💻

**CAA ▼▼▼▼ Inverary Resort** SH
(902) 295-3500. **$109-$189, 3 day notice.** 368 Shore Rd. Trans-Canada Hwy 105, exit 8, 1.6 km e on Rt 205 (Shore Rd). Ext/int corridors. **Pets:** $20 daily fee/pet. Designated rooms, service with restrictions, supervision.

SAVE ✕ 📱 💻 🍴 ➷ 🖼

**▼▼▼ McIntyre's Housekeeping Cottages** CA
(902) 295-1133. **$68-$350, 4 day notice.** 8908 Hwy 105. Trans-Canada Hwy 105, 5 km w. Ext corridors. **Pets:** $8 daily fee/pet. Service with restrictions, crate.

✕ 📱 💻 🖼

**CAA ▼▼▼ Silver Dart Lodge & MacNeil House** SH
(902) 295-2340. **$89-$159, 3 day notice.** 257 Hwy 205. Trans-Canada Hwy 105, exit 8, 1 km e on Rt 205 (Shore Rd). Ext/int corridors. **Pets:** Small. $15 daily fee/pet. Designated rooms, service with restrictions, crate.

SAVE ✕ 📱 💻 🍴 ➷ 🖼

## BLACK POINT

**▼▼ Grand View Motel and Cottages** M
(902) 857-9776. **$75-$93, 30 day notice.** 8414 Hwy 3. Hwy 103, exit 5 westbound, 2 km s to Rt 3, then 15 km w; exit 6 eastbound to Rt 3, then 9 km e. Ext corridors. **Pets:** Medium. $25 one-time fee/room. Designated rooms, service with restrictions, supervision.

🔒 ✕ 📱 🎫 🖼

## BRIDGETOWN

**▼▼ Bridgetown Motor Inn** SH
(902) 665-4403. **$72-$82.** 396 Granville St. Hwy 101, exit 20, 1 km w on Rt 1. Ext corridors. **Pets:** Accepted.

✕ ➷

## BRIDGEWATER

**▼▼ Auberge Wandlyn Inn** SH
(902) 543-7131. **$93-$120.** 50 North St. 1 km e on Hwy 325; Hwy 103, exit 12 to North St. Int corridors. **Pets:** Other species. Designated rooms, service with restrictions, supervision.

ASK 🔒 ✕ 📱 💻 🍴 ➷

**▼▼ Bridgewater Bogan Villa Inn** SH
(902) 543-8171. **$75-$95.** 35 High St. Hwy 103, exit 13, just e. Int corridors. **Pets:** Service with restrictions.

ASK 🔒 ✕ 💻 🍴 ➷

**▼▼ Comfort Inn** SH 🐾
(902) 543-1498. **$80-$160.** 49 North St. Hwy 103, exit 12, 1.7 km s on Rt 10. Int corridors. **Pets:** Other species. Service with restrictions, supervision.

ASK 🔒 ✕ 📱 📱 💻

## CHESTER

**▼ Windjammer Motel** M
(902) 275-3567. **$55-$80.** 4070 Rt 3. 1 km w. Ext corridors. **Pets:** Other species. Supervision.

🔒 ✕ 📱 🍴

# CHETICAMP

**▽▽ Cabot Trail Sea & Golf Chalets** CA
(902) 224-1777. **$129-$169, 7 day notice.** 71 Fraser Doucet Ln. Centre. Ext corridors. **Pets:** Medium, dogs only. $15 daily fee/pet. Service with restrictions, crate.
⊠ 🏢 ▣ ⊠ ✆

**▽▽ Laurie's Motor Inn** SH
(902) 224-2400. **$80-$149.** 15456 Laurie Rd. 1 km n, 7.2 km sw of West Gate Cape Breton Highlands National Park on Cabot Tr. Ext/int corridors. **Pets:** Large. Service with restrictions, crate.
(ASK) 🆂 ⊠ 🏢 ▣ 🍽

**CAA ▽ Parkview Motel, Dining Room & Lounge** M
(902) 224-3232. **$79-$109.** 16546 Cabot Tr. 7.2 km n at West Gate Cape Breton Highlands National Park. Ext corridors. **Pets:** Accepted.
(SAVE) ⊠ 🏢 ▣ 🍽 ✆

# CHURCH POINT

**▽▽ Le Manoir Samson Inn** M
(902) 769-2526. **$85-$125.** 1768 Rt 1. On Hwy 1; centre. Ext corridors. **Pets:** Accepted.
(ASK) ⊠ 🏢 🎟

# DARTMOUTH

**CAA ▽▽ Comfort Inn** SH
(902) 463-9900. **$125-$165.** 456 Windmill Rd. Hwy 111, exit Shannon Park. Int corridors. **Pets:** Accepted.
(SAVE) 🆂 ⊠ ▣

**▽▽ Country Inn & Suites By Carlson** SH
(902) 465-4000. **$90-$160.** 101 Yorkshire Ave Ext. Hwy 111, exit Princess Margaret Blvd. Int corridors. **Pets:** Accepted.
(ASK) 🆂 ⊠ 🏢 ▣

**CAA ▽▽▽ Holiday Inn Halifax-Harbourview** LH
(902) 463-1100. **$119-$189.** 99 Wyse Rd. Adjacent to Angus L MacDonald Bridge. Int corridors. **Pets:** $25 one-time fee/room. Designated rooms, service with restrictions, supervision.
(SAVE) 🆂 ⊠ 🏢 ▣ 🍽 🏊

**CAA ▽▽▽ Park Place Hotel & Conference Centre Ramada Plaza** LH
(902) 468-8888. **$110-$145.** 240 Brownlow Ave. From Murray Mackay Bridge, 1.2 km n on Hwy 111, exit 3 (Burnside Dr). Int corridors. **Pets:** Small. $50 deposit/room. Designated rooms, service with restrictions, supervision.
(SAVE) 🆂 ⊠ 🅼 ▣ 🍽 🏊 ⊠

**CAA ▽▽ Quality Inn Halifax/Dartmouth** SH
(902) 469-5850. **$100-$180.** 313 Prince Albert Rd. Hwy 111, exit 6A, 1 blk s. Int corridors. **Pets:** Accepted.
(SAVE) 🆂 ⊠ 🏢 ▣ 🍽

# DIGBY

**CAA ▽▽ Admiral Digby Inn** SH
(902) 245-2531. **$75-$250.** 441 Shore Rd. Hwy 101, exit 26, 2.5 km n, follow St John Ferry signs, 5 km w on Victoria Rd, then 1 km e of ferry terminal. Ext corridors. **Pets:** Small. Supervision.
(SAVE) 🆂 ⊠ 🏢 ▣ 🍽 🏊

# HALIFAX

**▽▽▽ Airport Hotel Halifax** SH
(902) 873-3000. **$110-$120.** 60 Sky Blvd. Hwy 102, exit 6. Int corridors. **Pets:** Designated rooms, service with restrictions.
⊠ 🏢 ▣ 🍽 🏊 ⊠

**CAA ▽▽ ▽▽ Casino Nova Scotia Hotel** LH
(902) 421-1700. **$109-$179.** 1919 Upper Water St. Adjacent to historic properties and Casino Nova Scotia. Int corridors. **Pets:** Accepted.
(SAVE) ⊠ 🅼 🅿 🏢 ▣ 🍽 🏊 ⊠

**▽▽ Chebucto Inn** SH
(902) 453-4330. **$75-$145.** 6151 Lady Hammond Rd. Jct Hwy 111 and Rt 2 (Bedford Hwy), 0.7 km e. Ext corridors. **Pets:** Accepted.
⊠ 🍽

**CAA ▽▽▽▽ Citadel Halifax Hotel** LH
(902) 422-1391. **$219-$299.** 1960 Brunswick St. Between Cogswell and Duke sts. Int corridors. **Pets:** Accepted.
(SAVE) 🆂 ⊠ 🏢 ▣ 🍽 🏊 ⊠

**CAA ▽▽▽▽ Delta Barrington** LH
(902) 429-7410. **$85-$192.** 1875 Barrington St. Between Cogswell and Duke sts. Int corridors. **Pets:** Accepted.
(SAVE) 🆂 ⊠ ▣ 🍽 🏊 ⊠

**CAA ▽▽▽▽ Delta Halifax** LH
(902) 425-6700. **$85-$192.** 1990 Barrington St. Corner of Cogswell and Barrington sts. Int corridors. **Pets:** Accepted.
(SAVE) 🆂 ⊠ ▣ 🍽 🏊 ⊠

**CAA ▽▽▽ Econo Lodge & Suites** SH
(902) 443-0303. **$74-$169.** 560 Bedford Hwy. On Rt 2 (Bedford Hwy), 9.6 km w. Int corridors. **Pets:** $10 one-time fee/pet. Designated rooms, service with restrictions, supervision.
(SAVE) 🆂 ⊠ 🅼 🏢 ▣ 🍽 🏊

**▽▽▽ Esquire Motel** M
(902) 835-3367. **$60-$90.** 771 Bedford Hwy. Hwy 102, exit 4A, 5.3 km e on Rt 2 (Bedford Hwy). Ext corridors. **Pets:** Service with restrictions, supervision.
(ASK) 🆂 ⊠ 🏢 ▣ 🏊 🅺

**CAA ▽▽▽ Holiday Inn Express Halifax/Bedford** SH 🐾
(902) 445-1100. **$109-$129, 14 day notice.** 133 Kearney Lake Rd. Hwy 102, exit 2. Int corridors. **Pets:** Medium. $25 one-time fee/room. Designated rooms, service with restrictions, supervision.
(SAVE) 🆂 ⊠ 🅼 🅺 🏢 ▣ 🏊

**CAA ▽▽▽▽ Holiday Inn Select Halifax-Centre** LH
(902) 423-1161. **$149-$209.** 1980 Robie St. Jct Quinpool St. Int corridors. **Pets:** Service with restrictions, supervision.
(SAVE) 🆂 ⊠ 🏢 ▣ 🍽 🏊 ⊠

**▽▽▽ Lakeview Inn & Suites** SH 🐾
(902) 450-3020. **$135-$375.** 98 Chain Lake Dr. Hwy 102, exit 2A eastbound; Hwy 103, exit 2. Int corridors. **Pets:** Medium. $100 deposit/room. Service with restrictions, crate.
(ASK) 🆂 ⊠ 🅼 🏢 ▣ 🏊

**CAA ▽▽▽ The Lord Nelson Hotel & Suites** LH
(902) 423-6331. **$109-$229.** 1515 S Park St. Corner of Park St and Spring Garden Rd; centre. Int corridors. **Pets:** Service with restrictions, supervision.
(SAVE) 🆂 ⊠ 🏢 ▣ 🍽

**CAA ▽▽▽▽ The Prince George Hotel** LH
(902) 425-1986. **$145-$205.** 1725 Market St. Between Prince and Carmichael sts. Int corridors. **Pets:** Other species. Supervision.
(SAVE) ⊠ 🅼 ▣ 🍽 ⊠

**▽▽▽▽ Residence Inn by Marriott** SH 🐾
(902) 422-0493. **$139-$179.** 1599 Grafton St. Corner of Sackville St. Int corridors. **Pets:** $75 one-time fee/room. Service with restrictions, crate.
⊠ 🅼 🅺 🏢 ▣

**▽▽ Travelers Motel** M
(902) 835-3394. **$55-$82.** 773 Bedford Hwy. Hwy 102, exit 4A, 5.3 km e on Rt 2 (Bedford Hwy). Ext corridors. **Pets:** Accepted.
🆂 ⊠ 🅺

**CAA ▽▽▽▽ The Westin Nova Scotian** LH
(902) 421-1000. **$199-$275.** 1181 Hollis St. Between Barrington and Lower Water sts. Int corridors. **Pets:** Accepted.
(SAVE) 🆂 ⊠ 🅼 ▣ 🍽 🏊 ⊠

# INGONISH BEACH

▼▼▼▼ Keltic Lodge 🄻🄷
(902) 285-2880. **$129-$374, 3 day notice.** Middle Head Peninsula. Inside the Cape Breton Highlands National Park; off Cabot Tr main highway. Ext/int corridors. **Pets:** Designated rooms, service with restrictions, supervision.

(ASK) ⊠ 🔋 💻 ⍭ ⤳ ⊠

# KEMPTVILLE

▼▼▼ Trout Point Lodge 🄲🄸
(902) 749-7629. **$90-$315, 21 day notice.** 289 Trout Point Rd. 11 km e on Rt 203, 3.5 km n on gravel entry road. Ext corridors. **Pets:** Accepted.

(ASK) 🆂 ⊠ ⍭ ⊠ 🄺 🅆 ☑

# KENTVILLE

▼▼ Auberge Wandlyn Inn 🅂🄷
(902) 678-8311. **$110-$125.** 7270 Hwy 1. Hwy 101, exit 14. Ext/int corridors. **Pets:** Accepted.

(ASK) ⊠ 🔋 💻 ⍭ ⤳

CAA ▼ Sun Valley Motel 🄼
(902) 678-7368. **$55-$90.** 905 Park St. Hwy 101, exit 14, 0.8 km e on Rt 1. Ext corridors. **Pets:** Accepted.

(SAVE) 🆂 ⊠ 🔋 💻 🄺 ☑

# LISCOMB

▼▼▼ Liscombe Lodge 🅂🄷
(902) 779-2307. **$145, 3 day notice.** RR 1, 2884 Hwy 7. On Hwy 7. Ext/int corridors. **Pets:** Accepted.

(ASK) ⊠ 🔋 🄼 🄴 🔋 💻 ⍭ ⤳ ⊠

# LUNENBURG

CAA ▼▼▼ Boscawen Inn 🄲🄸
(902) 634-3325. **$85-$205, 3 day notice.** 150 Cumberland St. Centre. Int corridors. **Pets:** Accepted.

(SAVE) ⊠ ⍭ 🄺

▼▼ The Homeport Motel 🄼
(902) 634-8234. **$99-$109, 3 day notice.** 167 Victoria Rd. 1 km w on Rt 3. Ext corridors. **Pets:** Accepted.

(ASK) ⊠ 🔋 💻

CAA ▼▼▼ Lunenburg Arms Hotel 🅂🄷 🐾
(902) 640-4040. **$109-$249, 7 day notice.** 94 Pelham St. Corner of Pelham and Duke sts; centre. Int corridors. **Pets:** Large, other species. Supervision.

(SAVE) ⊠ 🄼 🄴 💻 ⍭

# MAHONE BAY

▼▼▼ Bayview Pines Country Inn 🄱🄱
(902) 624-9970. **$85-$150, 5 day notice.** 678 Oakland Rd. Hwy 103, exit 10, 2 km w on Rt 3 to Kecly's Landing, 6 km e of Mahone Bay. Ext/int corridors. **Pets:** Small, dogs only. Designated rooms, no service, supervision.

⊠ 🔋 💻 🄺 ☑

# MAVILLETTE

▼ Cape View Motel & Cottages 🄼
(902) 645-2258. **$70-$80.** Rt 1, 32 km ne of Yarmouth; centre. Ext corridors. **Pets:** Service with restrictions, supervision.

🆂 ⊠ 🔋 🄺 ☑

# MIDDLETON

▼▼▼ Mid-Valley Motel 🅂🄷
(902) 825-3433. **$80-$105.** 121 Main St. 1 km w on Rt 1; Hwy 101, exit 18. Ext corridors. **Pets:** Accepted.

⊠ 🔋 ⍭ ⤳

# NEW GLASGOW

▼▼ ▼▼ Comfort Inn 🅂🄷
(902) 755-6450. **$110-$159.** 740 Westville Rd. On Hwy 289, just e of jct Trans-Canada Hwy 104, exit 23. Int corridors. **Pets:** Medium. Service with restrictions, supervision.

(ASK) 🆂 ⊠ 🔋 💻

▼▼ Country Inn & Suites By Carlson 🅂🄷
(902) 928-1333. **$93-$154.** 700 Westville Rd. On Hwy 289, just e of jct Trans-Canada Hwy 104, exit 23. Int corridors. **Pets:** Accepted.

(ASK) 🆂 ⊠ 🔋 💻

# NEW HARBOUR

▼▼▼▼ Lonely Rock Seaside Bungalows 🄲🄰
(902) 387-2668. **$100-$230, 14 day notice.** 150 New Harbour Rd. Rt 316, 0.7 km s. Ext corridors. **Pets:** Dogs only. No service, crate.

⊠ 🔋 💻 ⊠ 🄺 ☑

# NORTH SYDNEY

CAA ▼▼▼▼ Best Western North Star Inn 🅂🄷
(902) 794-8581. **$95-$150.** 39 Forrest St. Trans-Canada Hwy 105, exit 21; at ferry terminal. Int corridors. **Pets:** Accepted.

(SAVE) 🆂 ⊠ 🄼 🄴 💻 ⍭ ⤳

CAA ▼▼▼ Clansman Motel 🅂🄷 🐾
(902) 794-7226. **$89-$125.** 9 Baird St. Hwy 125, exit 2, just e on King St. Ext/int corridors. **Pets:** Large, other species. Designated rooms, service with restrictions.

(SAVE) 🆂 ⊠ 🔋 💻 ⍭ ⤳

# PARRSBORO

▼▼▼ The Sunshine Inn 🄼 🐾
(902) 254-3135. **$76-$96.** 3.2 km n on Rt 2. Ext corridors. **Pets:** $10 one-time fee/pet. Designated rooms, service with restrictions, supervision.

🆂 ⊠ 🔋 ⊠ ☑

# PICTOU

▼▼▼ Willow House Inn 🄱🄱
(902) 485-5740. **$55-$80.** 11 Willow St. Corner of Willow and Church sts; centre. Int corridors. **Pets:** Accepted.

⊠ ☑

# PORT DUFFERIN

▼▼ Marquis of Dufferin Seaside Inn 🄼
(902) 654-2696. **$60-$94.** 25658 Hwy 7, RR 1. On Hwy 7. Ext corridors. **Pets:** Medium, other species. $10 one-time fee/pet. Service with restrictions, supervision.

⊠ ⍭ ⊠ 🄺 ☑

# PORT HASTINGS

CAA ▼ Cape Breton Causeway Inn 🅂🄷
(902) 625-0460. **$65-$110.** E of Canso Cswy on Trans-Canada Hwy 105 rotary; entrance through north side of church. Ext/int corridors. **Pets:** Accepted.

(SAVE) 🆂 ⊠ 🔋 💻 ⍭

▼▼▼ Econo Lodge MacPuffin 🄼
(902) 625-0621. **$84-$119.** 373 Hwy 4. 1.6 km n on Hwy 4; 1.6 km s of Canso Cswy. Ext corridors. **Pets:** Other species. Service with restrictions, crate.

(ASK) 🆂 ⊠ 💻 ⤳

# PORT HAWKESBURY

CAA ▼▼▼ Maritime Inn Port Hawkesbury 🅂🄷
(902) 625-0320. **$98-$149.** 717 Reeves St. 6.4 km e of Canso Cswy on Hwy 4. Ext/int corridors. **Pets:** Accepted.

(SAVE) ⊠ 🔋 💻 ⍭ ⤳

# SCOTSBURN

▼▼▼▼▼ Stonehame Lodge & Chalets 🅒🅐 ❀
(902) 485-3468. **$75-$205.** RR 3. Rt 256, 12 km w of Pictou via Rt 376, last 2 km on gravel entry road. Ext corridors. **Pets:** Large, other species. Service with restrictions, supervision.

🅰🆂🅺 🆂🔟 ⊠ 🖥 🖵 ⤳ ⊠ 🅺

# SHELBURNE

🅐🅐 ▼▼▼ Mackenzie's Motel, Cottages, and Suites 🅜
(902) 875-2842. **$75-$85.** 260 Water St. Hwy 103, exit 26, 1.5 km e on Rt 3. Ext corridors. **Pets:** Accepted.

🆂🅰🆅🅴 ⊠ 🖥 🖵 ⤳

# SMITHS COVE

▼▼ Hedley House Inn By The Sea 🅜
(902) 245-5841. **$69-$189.** RR 1. Hwy 101, exit 25 eastbound; exit 24 westbound. Ext corridors. **Pets:** Accepted.

🆂🔟 ⊠ 🖥 🖵 🍽 🅺 🕿

🅐🅐 ▼▼▼ Mountain Gap Inn 🆂🅷
(902) 245-5841. **$99-$142, 3 day notice.** 217 Hwy 1, Smiths Cove. Hwy 101, exit 25 eastbound; exit 24 westbound. Ext corridors. **Pets:** Accepted.

🆂🅰🆅🅴 ⊠ 🖥 🖵 🍽 ⤳ ⊠

# SYDNEY

🅐🅐 ▼▼▼▼ Cambridge Suites Hotel 🅛🅷
(902) 562-6500. **$109-$165.** 380 Esplanade. Hwy 4, 5 km e of jct Hwy 125, exit 6E; downtown. Int corridors. **Pets:** Accepted.

🆂🅰🆅🅴 🆂🔟 ⊠ 🖥 🖵 🍽

▼▼ Comfort Inn 🆂🅷 ❀
(902) 562-0200. **$103-$179.** 368 Kings Rd. Hwy 4, 3.5 km e of jct Hwy 125, exit 6E. Int corridors. **Pets:** Service with restrictions, supervision.

🅰🆂🅺 🆂🔟 ⊠ 🖵

🅐🅐 ▼▼▼ Days Inn Sydney 🆂🅷
(902) 539-6750. **$119.** 480 Kings Rd. Hwy 4, 2.8 km e of jct Hwy 125, exit 6E. Int corridors. **Pets:** Accepted.

🆂🅰🆅🅴 🆂🔟 ⊠ 🖥 🖵 ⤳ ⊠

▼▼▼ Delta Sydney 🅛🅷
(902) 562-7500. **$139-$189.** 300 Esplanade. Hwy 4, 5.5 km e of jct Hwy 125, exit 6E; downtown. Int corridors. **Pets:** Accepted.

🅰🆂🅺 🆂🔟 ⊠ 🖥 🖵 🍽 ⤳ ⊠

▼▼ Quality Inn Sydney 🆂🅷
(902) 539-8101. **$101-$142.** 560 Kings Rd. Hwy 4, 3.3 km e of jct Hwy 125. Int corridors. **Pets:** Accepted.

🅰🆂🅺 🆂🔟 ⊠ 🅲 🖵 🍽 ⤳

# SYDNEY MINES

▼▼▼ Gowrie House Country Inn 🅒🅘
(902) 544-1050. **$99-$295, 3 day notice.** 840 Shore Rd. Hwy 105, exit 21E, 3 km n on Rt 305. Ext/int corridors. **Pets:** Accepted.

⊠ 🖥 🖵 🍽

# TRURO

▼▼ Comfort Inn 🆂🅷
(902) 893-0330. **$108-$131.** 12 Meadow Dr. Hwy 102, exit 14. Int corridors. **Pets:** Accepted.

🅰🆂🅺 🆂🔟 ⊠ 🖥 🖵

▼▼ Howard Johnson Hotel and Convention Centre 🆂🅷
(902) 895-1651. **$108-$118.** 437 Prince St. Centre. Ext/int corridors. **Pets:** Accepted.

🅰🆂🅺 🆂🔟 ⊠ 🖥 🖵 🍽 ⤳

🅐🅐 ▼ The Palliser Motel 🅜 ⬱
(902) 893-8951. **$69-$79.** 103/104 Tidal Bore Rd. Hwy 102, exit 14. Ext corridors. **Pets:** Medium. Designated rooms, service with restrictions, supervision.

🆂🅰🆅🅴 ⊠ 🍽 🕿

▼▼▼ Super 8 Motel 🆂🅷
(902) 895-8884. **$95-$159.** 85 Treaty T. Hwy 102, exit 13A. Int corridors. **Pets:** Medium, dogs only. $10 daily fee/pet. Service with restrictions, supervision.

⊠ 🆂🅼 🅲 🖥 🖵 ⤳

# WESTERN SHORE

🅐🅐 ▼▼▼▼ Oak Island Resort, Spa and Convention Centre 🆂🅷
(902) 627-2600. **$99-$159.** 36 Treasure Dr. Hwy 103, exit 9 or 10, follow signs on Rt 3; 10 km e o Mahone Bay. Int corridors. **Pets:** Accepted.

🆂🅰🆅🅴 ⊠ 🆂🅼 🅲 🖥 🖵 🍽 ⤳ ⊠

# WHITE POINT

▼▼ White Point Beach Resort 🆂🅷
(902) 354-2711. **$100-$190, 3 day notice.** 75 White Point Rd 2. Hwy 103, exit 20A, 9 km w on Rt 3. Ext/int corridors. **Pets:** Other species. Designated rooms.

⊠ 🖥 🖵 🍽 ⤳ ⊠

# YARMOUTH

🅐🅐 ▼▼▼ Best Western Mermaid 🅜
(902) 742-7821. **$79-$180.** 545 Main S. Corner of Main St and Starrs Rd. Ext corridors. **Pets:** Designated rooms, service with restrictions.

🆂🅰🆅🅴 🆂🔟 ⊠ 🖥 🖵 ⤳ 🅺

🅐🅐 ▼▼▼ Capri Motel 🅜
(902) 742-7168. **$59-$150.** 8-12 Herbert St. Corner of Herbert and Main sts. Ext corridors. **Pets:** Service with restrictions.

🆂🅰🆅🅴 🆂🔟 ⊠ 🖥 🖵

▼▼▼ Comfort Inn 🆂🅷 ❀
(902) 742-1119. **$95-$195.** 96 Starrs Rd. Jct Hwy 101 E and Hwy 3. Int corridors. **Pets:** Designated rooms, service with restrictions.

🅰🆂🅺 🆂🔟 ⊠ 🖵

🅐🅐 ▼ Lakelawn Motel 🅜
(902) 742-3588. **$79-$99.** 641 Main St. 1 km n on Hwy 1. Ext/int corridors. **Pets:** Small, dogs only. Designated rooms, service with restrictions, supervision.

🆂🅰🆅🅴 ⊠ 🅺 🕿

▼▼ Rodd Colony Harbour Inn 🆂🅷
(902) 742-9194. **$90-$145.** 6 Forest St. At ferry terminal. Int corridors. **Pets:** Other species. Service with restrictions, crate.

🅰🆂🅺 🆂🔟 ⊠ 🖥 🖵 🍽 🅺

▼▼▼ Rodd Grand Yarmouth – Rodd Signature Hotel 🅛🅷
(902) 742-2446. **$127-$223.** 417 Main St. Near centre of downtown. Int corridors. **Pets:** Accepted.

🅰🆂🅺 🆂🔟 ⊠ 🖥 🖵 🍽 ⤳ ⊠

▼ Voyageur Motel 🅜
(902) 742-7157. **$69-$179.** 4.8 km ne on Hwy 1. Ext corridors. **Pets:** Accepted.

⊠ 🖥 🅺

# ONTARIO

## AJAX

### ▼▼ ▼▼ Super 8 Motel-Ajax SH
(905) 428-6884. **$99-$129.** 210 Westney Rd S. Jct Bayly St from Hwy 401, exit Westney Rd, 1 km s. Int corridors. **Pets:** Accepted.
(A$K) (S🐾) ⊠ 💷 🏊

## ALGONQUIN PROVINCIAL PARK

### ▼▼▼ Killarney Lodge CA
(705) 633-5551. **$278-$558, 3 day notice.** Hwy 60-Lake of Two Rivers-Algonquin. On Hwy 60; 33 km into park from west gate; 23 km from east gate. Ext corridors. **Pets:** Dogs only. $300 deposit/room, $25 daily fee/room. Designated rooms, crate.
(🍴) ⊠ (X̶) (�iW) (☎)

## ARNPRIOR

### ▼▼ Country Squire Motel M
(613) 623-6556. **$65-$89.** 111 Staye Court Dr. Hwy 17, exit White Lake Rd N. Ext corridors. **Pets:** Medium, dogs only. $10 one-time fee/pet. Service with restrictions, supervision.
(A$K) (S🐾) ⊠ 🛢 (X̶)

## AURORA

### CAA ▼▼ ▼▼ Howard Johnson Hotel Aurora SH 🐾
(905) 727-1312. **$89-$135.** 15520 Yonge St. 0.5 km n of Wellington St. Int corridors. **Pets:** Small, other species. $15 one-time fee/room. Designated rooms, supervision.
(SAVE) (S🐾) ⊠ 🛢 💷 (🍴)

## BANCROFT

### CAA ▼▼ ▼▼ Best Western Sword Motor Inn M
(613) 332-2474. **$113-$149.** 146 Hastings St. On Hwy 62 N; centre. Ext/int corridors. **Pets:** Small. $10 one-time fee/pet. Designated rooms, service with restrictions, supervision.
(SAVE) (S🐾) ⊠ 🛢 💷 (🍴) 🏊 (X̶)

## BARRIE

### CAA ▼▼ ▼▼ Comfort Inn SH
(705) 722-3600. **$93-$120.** 75 Hart Dr. Hwy 400, exit 96A E (Dunlop St). Int corridors. **Pets:** Medium, other species. Service with restrictions, supervision.
(SAVE) (S🐾) ⊠ 🛢 💷

### ▼▼ ▼▼ Days Inn Barrie SH
(705) 733-8989. **$99-$150.** 60 Bryne Dr. Hwy 400, exit 94 (Essa Rd), just s, then just e. Int corridors. **Pets:** Other species. $10 daily fee/room. Designated rooms, service with restrictions, supervision.
(A$K) (S🐾) ⊠ 🛢 💷 🏊

### CAA ▼▼ ▼▼ Holiday Inn Barrie-Hotel & Conference Centre SH
(705) 728-6191. **$139-$189.** 20 Fairview Rd. Hwy 400, exit 94 (Essa Rd), just e. Int corridors. **Pets:** Designated rooms, service with restrictions, supervision.
(SAVE) (S🐾) ⊠ (🛢M) 🛢 💷 (🍴) 🏊 (X̶)

### CAA ▼▼ ▼▼ Holiday Inn Express Hotel & Suites Barrie SH
(705) 725-1002. **$129-$180.** 506 Bryne Dr. Hwy 400, exit 90 (Molson Park Dr), just sw. Int corridors. **Pets:** Medium. $15 one-time fee/pet. Service with restrictions, supervision.
(SAVE) (S🐾) ⊠ 🛢 💷 🏊

### ▼▼ ▼▼ Travelodge Barrie SH
(705) 734-9500. **$99-$139.** 55 Hart Dr. Hwy 400, exit 96A E (Dunlop St). Int corridors. **Pets:** Other species. Service with restrictions, supervision.
⊠ 🛢 💷 (🍴) 🏊

## BARRY'S BAY

### ▼▼ Mountain View Motel M 🐾
(613) 756-2757. **$60-$94, 7 day notice.** 18508 Hwy 60 E. On Hwy 60, 4 km e. Ext corridors. **Pets:** Other species. No service, supervision.
⊠ 🛢 💷

## BAYFIELD

### CAA ▼▼▼ ▼▼▼ The Little Inn of Bayfield CI 🐾
(519) 565-2611. **$192-$325, 4 day notice.** 26 Main St. Hwy 21, exit Main St, jct Catherine St. Int corridors. **Pets:** Medium. $50 daily fee/room. Designated rooms, service with restrictions, supervision.
(SAVE) (S🐾) ⊠ 💷 (🍴)

### ▼▼ The Martha Ritz House CI
(519) 565-2325. **$125, 4 day notice.** 27 Main St. Hwy 21, exit Main St, jct Catherine St. Int corridors. **Pets:** Accepted.
(A$K) (S🐾) (🍴) (iW) (☎)

## BELLEVILLE

### CAA ▼▼ ▼▼ Best Western Belleville SH
(613) 969-1112. **$113-$143.** 387 N Front St. Hwy 401, exit 543A, 0.5 km s on Hwy 62 (N Front St). Int corridors. **Pets:** Large, other species. Designated rooms, service with restrictions, supervision.
(SAVE) (S🐾) ⊠ 🛢 💷 🏊

### ▼▼ ▼▼ Comfort Inn SH
(613) 966-7703. **$109-$123.** 200 N Park St. Hwy 401, exit 543A, 1 km s on Hwy 62 (N Front St). Int corridors. **Pets:** Accepted.
⊠ 🛢 💷

▼▼▼ **Ramada Inn on the Bay** SH ❀
(613) 968-3411. **$159-$194, 3 day notice.** 11 Bay Bridge Rd. Hwy 2, 0.5 km s. Int corridors. **Pets:** Medium, other species. Designated rooms, service with restrictions, crate.
ASK SO X ☐ ☐ ☐ ☐ X

# BLIND RIVER

▼ **Lakeview Inn** M
(705) 356-0800. **$77-$84, 3 day notice.** 143 Causley St. On Hwy 17, just e of Hwy 557. Ext corridors. **Pets:** Accepted.
ASK SO X ☐ ☐

▼ **Old Mill Motel** M
(705) 356-2274. **$64-$78.** Hwy 17 & Woodward St. Centre. Ext corridors. **Pets:** Accepted.
ASK SO X ☐

# BRACEBRIDGE

CAA ▼▼▼ **Travelodge Bracebridge** M
(705) 645-2235. **$99-$179.** 320 Taylor Rd. Hwy 11, exit 189 (Hwy 42/Taylor Rd), 1 km w. Ext corridors. **Pets:** Medium. $10 daily fee/room. Service with restrictions, supervision.
SAVE SO X ☐ ☐ ☐ X

# BRAMPTON

▼▼ **Comfort Inn** SH
(905) 452-0600. **$111-$119.** 5 Rutherford Rd S. Hwy 401, exit Hwy 410 N, 11 km to Hwy 7 E (Queen St), then 1 km w. Int corridors. **Pets:** Service with restrictions, supervision.
ASK SO X ☐ ☐

▼▼ **Motel 6 #1902** SH
(905) 451-3313. **$73-$85.** 160 Steelwell Rd. Hwy 410, exit Steeles Ave E, s on Tomken, then just w. Int corridors. **Pets:** Accepted.
SO X

# BRANTFORD

▼▼ **Comfort Inn** SH
(519) 753-3100. **$119-$159.** 58 King George Rd. Just s of jct Hwy 403 and 24. Int corridors. **Pets:** Other species. Service with restrictions, supervision.
ASK SO X ☐ ☐ ☐

▼▼ **Days Inn** SH
(519) 759-2700. **$79-$109.** 460 Fairview Dr. Hwy 403, exit Wayne Gretzky Pkwy, 0.8 km n. Int corridors. **Pets:** Other species. $15 one-time fee/room. Service with restrictions, supervision.
ASK SO X ☐ ☐ ☐

▼▼▼ **Holiday Inn Brantford** SH
(519) 758-9999. **$106-$115.** 664 Colborne St. Hwy 403, exit Wayne Gretzky Pkwy, 2 km s to Colborne St, then just w. Int corridors. **Pets:** Accepted.
ASK SO X ☐ ☐ ☐ X

# BRIGHTON

▼ **Presquile Beach Motel** M
(613) 475-1010. **$59-$99.** 243 Main St W. Hwy 401, exit 509, 4 km s on Hwy 30, then 2 km w on Hwy 2. Ext corridors. **Pets:** Other species. Supervision.
X ☐ X

# BROCKVILLE

CAA ▼▼▼ **Comfort Inn** SH ❀
(613) 345-0042. **$119-$159.** 7777 Kent Blvd. Hwy 401, exit 696, just nw. Int corridors. **Pets:** Other species. $5 daily fee/pet. Service with restrictions, crate.
SAVE SO X ☐ ☐

▼ **Travelodge** SH
(613) 345-3900. **$60-$199.** 7789 Kent Blvd. Hwy 401, exit 696, just nw. Int corridors. **Pets:** Service with restrictions, supervision.
ASK SO X ☐ ☐

# BURLINGTON

CAA ▼▼▼ **Burlington on the Lake Travelodge Hotel** SH ❀
(905) 681-0762. **$137-$164.** 2020 Lakeshore Rd. Jct Brant. Int corridors. **Pets:** Large. $10 daily fee/room. Designated rooms, service with restrictions, supervision.
SAVE SO X ☐ ☐ ☐ ☐ X

CAA ▼▼▼ **Comfort Inn** SH ❀
(905) 639-1700. **$79-$139.** 3290 S Service Rd. QEW, exit Walker's Line Rd westbound, just s to Harvester Rd, then just w; exit Guelph Line Rd eastbound, just s to Harvester Rd, then just e. Int corridors. **Pets:** Large. Service with restrictions, supervision.
SAVE X ☐ ☐

▼▼ **Motel 6 Canada #1900** SH
(905) 331-1955. **$63-$80.** 4345 N Service Rd. QEW, exit Walker's Line Rd N to N Service Rd. Int corridors. **Pets:** Accepted.
SO X ☐

▼▼▼ **Travelodge Burlington** SH
(905) 639-9290. **$99-$139.** 950 Walker's Line Rd. QEW, exit Walker's Line Rd, just s. Int corridors. **Pets:** Large. Service with restrictions, crate.
ASK SO X ☐ ☐ X

# CAMBRIDGE

CAA ▼▼▼ **Comfort Inn** SH ❀
(519) 658-1100. **$99-$149.** 220 Holiday Inn Dr. Hwy 401, exit 282, just n to Groh Ave. Int corridors. **Pets:** Other species. Service with restrictions, supervision.
SAVE SO X ☐ ☐ X

CAA ▼▼▼▼ **Langdon Hall Country House Hotel & Spa** CI ❀
(519) 740-2100. **$259-$329, 7 day notice.** 1 Langdon Dr. Hwy 401, exit 275 to Homer Watson Blvd (Fountain St), 1 km s to Blair Rd, then follow signs 1 km to Langdon Dr. Ext/int corridors. **Pets:** Designated rooms.
SAVE X ☐ ☐ ☐ ☐ X

CAA ▼▼▼ **Super 8 Motel-Cambridge** SH
(519) 622-1070. **$89-$109, 30 day notice.** 650 Hespeler Rd. Hwy 401, exit 282, 1 km s. Int corridors. **Pets:** Dogs only. $10 daily fee/pet. Service with restrictions, supervision.
SAVE SO X ☐ ☐ ☐ X

▼▼ **Travelodge Cambridge** SH
(519) 622-1180. **$75-$150.** 605 Hespeler Rd. Hwy 401, exit 282, 1 km s. Int corridors. **Pets:** Accepted.
ASK SO X ☐ ☐ ☐

# CHAPLEAU

▼ **Riverside Motel** M
(705) 864-0440. **$68-$98.** 116 Cherry St. Corner of Grey and Cherry sts. Ext corridors. **Pets:** Accepted.
ASK SO X ☐ ☐ X

# CHATHAM

▼▼ **Comfort Inn** SH
(519) 352-5500. **$95-$113.** 1100 Richmond St. Hwy 401, exit 81 (Bloomfield Rd), 5 km n. Int corridors. **Pets:** Accepted.
ASK SO X ☐ ☐

# CHATSWORTH

▼▼ ▼▼ Key Mctel Ⓜ
(519) 794-2350. **$70-$80.** 317051 Hwy 6/10. On Hwy 6 and 10. Ext/int corridors. **Pets:** Accepted.

⊠ 🛢 ➳ ⊠

# COBOURG

Ⓐ ▼▼▼▼ Best Western Cobourg Inn and Convention Centre 🆂🅷
(905) 372-2105. **$128-$160.** 930 Burnham St. Hwy 401, exit 472 (Burnham St S). Int corridors. **Pets:** Medium, dogs only. Service with restrictions, supervision.

🆂🅰🆅🅴 🆂🛢 ⊠ 🛢 ➴ 🍴 ➳

▼▼ ▼▼ Comfort Inn 🆂🅷
(905) 372-7007. **$99-$150.** 121 Densmore Rd. Hwy 401, exit 474, just se. Int corridors. **Pets:** Accepted.

🅰🆂🅺 🆂🛢 ⊠ 🛢 ➴

# CORNWALL

Ⓐ ▼▼▼▼ Best Western Parkway Inn & Conference Centre 🆂🅷
(613) 932-0451. **$129-$199.** 1515 Vincent Massey Dr. Hwy 401, exit 789 (Brookdale Ave), 2.8 km s, then just w. Int corridors. **Pets:** Medium. Designated rooms, service with restrictions.

🆂🅰🆅🅴 🆂🛢 ⊠ ➴ 🍴 ➳

Ⓐ ▼▼ ▼▼ Comfort Inn-Cornwall 🆂🅷
(613) 937-0111. **$91-$185.** 1625 Vincent Massey Dr. Hwy 401, exit 789 (Brookdale Ave), 2.8 km s, then 0.7 km w. Int corridors. **Pets:** Large, other species. $20 one-time fee/room. Designated rooms, service with restrictions, crate.

🆂🅰🆅🅴 🆂🛢 ⊠ 🛢 ➴ ➳

Ⓐ ▼▼ Econo Lodge 🆂🅷
(613) 936-1996. **$78-$93.** 1142 Brookdale Ave. Hwy 401, exit 789 (Brookdale Ave), 3 km s. Ext/int corridors. **Pets:** Small. $10 daily fee/pet. Service with restrictions, supervision.

🆂🅰🆅🅴 🆂🛢 ⊠ 🛢

Ⓐ ▼▼▼▼ Ramada Inn & Conference Centre 🆂🅷 ❀
(613) 933-8000. **$95-$149.** 805 Brookdale Ave. Hwy 401, exit 789 (Brookdale Ave), 4 km s. Int corridors. **Pets:** Small. $10 one-time fee/room. Designated rooms, service with restrictions, supervision.

🆂🅰🆅🅴 🆂🛢 ⊠ 🛢 ➴ 🍴 ➳ ⊠

# DRYDEN

Ⓐ ▼▼▼▼ Best Western Motor Inn 🆂🅷
(807) 223-3201. **$93-$105.** 349 Government St. On Hwy 17. Ext/int corridors. **Pets:** Accepted.

🆂🅰🆅🅴 🆂🛢 ⊠ 🛢 ➴ 🍴 ➳ ⊠

▼▼ ▼▼ Comfort Inn Ⓜ
(807) 223-3893. **$109-$143.** 522 Government St. On Hwy 17. Int corridors. **Pets:** Large, other species. Designated rooms, service with restrictions, supervision.

🅰🆂🅺 🆂🛢 ⊠ 🛢 ➴

Ⓐ ▼▼▼▼ Holiday Inn Express Dryden 🆂🅷
(807) 223-3000. **$99-$119.** 585 Government St. On Hwy 17. Int corridors. **Pets:** Accepted.

🆂🅰🆅🅴 🆂🛢 ⊠ 🛢 ➴ ➳

# ELLIOT LAKE

▼▼ Dunlop Lake Lodge 🆂🅷
(705) 848-8090. **$65-$75.** 74 Dunlop Lake Rd. Hwy 17, 38.8 km n on Hwy 108, 0.8 km w, follow signs. Int corridors. **Pets:** Accepted.

🅰🆂🅺 🆂🛢 ⊠ ➴ 🍴 ⊠ 🐾

# FONTHILL

▼▼ Hipwell's Motel Ⓜ
(905) 892-3588. **$52-$80.** 299 Reg Rd 20 W. 1.6 km w; centre. Ext corridors. **Pets:** Accepted.

🅰🆂🅺 🆂🛢 ⊠ 🛢 ➴

# FORT FRANCES

▼▼ ▼▼ Super 8 🆂🅷 ❀
(807) 274-4945. **$88-$138.** 810 Kings Hwy. On Hwy 11. Int corridors. **Pets:** Other species. Designated rooms, service with restrictions, crate.

🅰🆂🅺 🆂🛢 ⊠ 🛢 ➴ ➳

# GANANOQUE

Ⓐ ▼▼ Travelodge 1000 Islands Ⓜ
(613) 382-4282. **$49-$299.** 555 King St E. Hwy 401, exit 647 eastbound; exit 648 westbound, 1.5 km w on Hwy 2 (King St). Ext corridors. **Pets:** Accepted.

🆂🅰🆅🅴 🆂🛢 ⊠ 🛢 ➴ 🍴 ➳

▼▼▼▼ Trinity House Inn 🅲🅸
(613) 382-8383. **$90-$225, 7 day notice.** 90 Stone St S. Corner of Pine St; centre. Int corridors. **Pets:** Accepted.

⊠ 🛢 ➴ 🍴 🆉

# GRIMSBY

Ⓐ ▼▼▼▼ Super 8 Motel-Grimsby 🆂🅷
(905) 309-8800. **$89-$129, 3 day notice.** 11 Windward Dr. QEW, exit 74 (Casablanca N). Int corridors. **Pets:** Accepted.

🆂🅰🆅🅴 🆂🛢 ⊠ 🛢 ➴ ➳

# GUELPH

▼▼ ▼▼ Comfort Inn Guelph 🆂🅷
(519) 763-1900. **$110-$142.** 480 Silvercreek Pkwy. Jct Hwy 6 and 7. Int corridors. **Pets:** Medium. Service with restrictions, supervision.

🅰🆂🅺 🆂🛢 ⊠ 🛢 ➴

Ⓐ ▼▼▼▼ Holiday Inn Guelph 🅻🅷 ❀
(519) 836-0231. **$125-$179.** 601 Scottsdale Dr. Jct Hwy 6 N and Stone Rd E; 8 km n of jct Hwy 401. Int corridors. **Pets:** Other species. Service with restrictions, crate.

🆂🅰🆅🅴 🆂🛢 ⊠ 🛢 ➴ 🍴 ➳ ⊠

Ⓐ ▼▼ ▼▼ Ramada Hotel & Conference Centre 🆂🅷
(519) 836-1240. **$160.** 716 Gordon St. Jct Gordon St and Stone Rd; 8 km n of Hwy 401 via Brock Rd. Int corridors. **Pets:** Other species. Designated rooms, service with restrictions, supervision.

🆂🅰🆅🅴 ⊠ 🛢 ➴ 🍴 ➳

# HALIBURTON

▼▼ Lakeview Motel Ⓜ
(705) 457-1027. **$85-$160, 5 day notice.** 4951 CR 21. Jct Hwy 118, 2.5 km w on CR 21. Ext corridors. **Pets:** Medium. $8 daily fee/pet. Designated rooms, service with restrictions, crate.

🅰🆂🅺 ⊠ 🛢 ➴ 🍴 ➳

# HAMILTON

Ⓐ ▼▼ ▼▼ Knights Inn at Clappison Corners Ⓜ ❀
(905) 689-6615. **$89-$119.** 15 Hwy 5 W. Jct Hwy 5 and 6. Ext/int corridors. **Pets:** Dogs only. $25 one-time fee/room.

🆂🅰🆅🅴 🆂🛢 ⊠ 🛢 ➴

Ⓐ ▼▼▼▼ Sheraton Hamilton 🅻🅷 ❀
(905) 529-5515. **$119-$129.** 116 King St W. On Hwy 6 and 8 westbound; downtown. Int corridors. **Pets:** Other species. Service with restrictions, supervision.

🆂🅰🆅🅴 ⊠ �🅼 🛢 ➴ 🍴 ➳ ⊠

▼▼▼▼ Staybridge Suites 🆂🅷 🐾
(905) 577-9000. **$153-$261.** 118 Market St. Hwy 403, exit King St, then e across from Jackson Square, jct Caroline. Int corridors. **Pets:** Medium, other species. $95 one-time fee/room. Service with restrictions, supervision.

[X] [🅗] [📺] [🏊]

# HANOVER

🄰🄰 ▼▼▼▼ The Victorian Manor Bed & Breakfast 🅱🅱
(519) 364-1117. **$80-$100.** 500 9th Ave. Just n of 10th St. Int corridors. **Pets:** Accepted.

[SAVE] [🅢] [X] [🖀]

# HAWKESBURY

▼▼▼ Best Western L'Heritage 🆂🅷
(613) 632-5941. **$96-$140.** 1575 Tupper St. Jct Hwy 34, 3 km e on Hwy 17. Int corridors. **Pets:** Accepted.

[ASK] [🅢] [X] [🅗] [📺] [🍽]

# HUNTSVILLE

▼▼ Comfort Inn 🆂🅷
(705) 789-1701. **$110-$170.** 86 King William St. Jct Hwy 60. Int corridors. **Pets:** Other species. Designated rooms, service with restrictions, supervision.

[ASK] [🅢] [X] [🅗] [📺]

▼ Tulip Inn 🅜 🐾
(705) 789-4001. **$65-$120, 3 day notice.** 211 Arrowhead Park Rd. Hwy 11, exit 226 (Muskoka Rd 3), follow signs for Arrowhead Park. Ext corridors. **Pets:** Service with restrictions, supervision.

[ASK] [🅢] [X] [🅗] [📺]

# INGERSOLL

▼▼▼▼ Travelodge Ingersoll 🆂🅷
(519) 425-1100. **$91-$120.** 20 Samnah Crescent. Hwy 401, exit 216 (Culloden Rd). Int corridors. **Pets:** Accepted.

[ASK] [🅢] [X] [🅗] [📺] [🏊]

# KAPUSKASING

▼▼ Comfort Inn 🆂🅷
(705) 335-8583. **$99-$104, 14 day notice.** 172 Government Rd E. Hwy 11, corner of Brunelle Rd. Int corridors. **Pets:** Accepted.

[ASK] [🅢] [X] [🅗] [📺]

# KENORA

▼▼ Best Western Lakeside Inn & Conference Centre 🆂🅷
(807) 468-5521. **$112-$135, 7 day notice.** 470 First Ave S. Centre. Int corridors. **Pets:** Small, other species. Designated rooms, service with restrictions, supervision.

[🅢] [X] [🅗] [📺] [🍽] [🏊]

▼▼ Comfort Inn 🅜 🐾
(807) 468-8845. **$94-$114.** 1230 Hwy 17 E. 1.5 km e. Int corridors. **Pets:** Other species. Service with restrictions, crate.

[ASK] [🅢] [X] [🅗] [📺]

▼◆▼ Days Inn 🆂🅷
(807) 468-2003. **$93-$102.** 920 Hwy 17 E. On Hwy 17, 1 km e. Ext/int corridors. **Pets:** Accepted.

[ASK] [🅢] [X] [🅗] [📺] [🍽] [🏊] [🗙]

🄰🄰 ▼▼ Kenora Travelodge 🆂🅷
(807) 468-3155. **$99-$139.** 800 Hwy 17 E. 1 km e. Int corridors. **Pets:** Designated rooms, service with restrictions, supervision.

[SAVE] [🅢] [X] [🅗] [📺] [🍽] [🏊] [🗙]

# KILLALOE

▼◆▼ Annie's Inn 🅱🅱
(613) 757-0950. **$65-$85 (no credit cards), 7 day notice.** 67 Roche St. Hwy 60, exit Maple St, 1 blk to Roche St, then w; driveway entrance is at the end of the street. Int corridors. **Pets:** Accepted.

[ASK] [🅢] [X] [🅗] [🖀]

# KINGSTON

▼▼ Comfort Inn 🆂🅷 🐾
(613) 549-5550. **$99-$169.** 1454 Princess St. Hwy 401, exit 613 (Sydenham Rd), 4 km se. Int corridors. **Pets:** Other species. Service with restrictions, supervision.

[ASK] [🅢] [X] [🅗] [📺]

🄰🄰 ▼◆▼ Comfort Inn 🆂🅷 🐾
(613) 546-9500. **$89-$169.** 55 Warne Crescent. Hwy 401, exit 617 (Division St), 0.3 km s to Dalton Ave. Int corridors. **Pets:** Service with restrictions, crate.

[SAVE] [🅢] [X] [🅗] [📺]

🄰🄰 ▼ The Executive Inn & Suites 🅜
(613) 549-1620. **$69-$139, 3 day notice.** 794 Hwy 2 E. Hwy 401, exit 623, 8 km s, then 2 km e. Ext corridors. **Pets:** Accepted.

[SAVE] [🅢] [X] [🅗] [📺] [🏊]

🄰🄰 ▼▼▼ Holiday Inn Kingston-Waterfront 🆂🅷
(613) 549-8400. **$159-$259.** 2 Princess St. Corner of Ontario St; centre of downtown. Int corridors. **Pets:** Designated rooms, service with restrictions, supervision.

[SAVE] [🅢] [X] [🅜] [🄴] [🅗] [📺] [🍽] [🏊] [🗙]

🄰🄰 ▼▼ Howard Johnson Confederation Place Hotel 🆂🅷 🐾
(613) 549-6300. **$139-$239.** 237 Ontario St. Centre of downtown. Int corridors. **Pets:** Other species. $15 daily fee/pet. Designated rooms, supervision.

[SAVE] [🅢] [X] [🅗] [📺] [🍽] [🏊]

▼▼ Super 8 Motel 🆂🅷
(613) 542-7395. **$45-$159.** 720 Princess St. Centre. Int corridors. **Pets:** Accepted.

[ASK] [🅢] [X] [🅗]

# KIRKLAND LAKE

▼▼ Comfort Inn 🆂🅷
(705) 567-4909. **$75-$175.** 455 Government Rd W. Rt 66, just w of centre. Int corridors. **Pets:** Accepted.

[ASK] [🅢] [X] [🅗] [📺]

# KITCHENER

▼▼▼ Delta Kitchener 🄻🅷
(519) 744-4141. **$89-$169.** 105 King St E. Corner of King and Benton sts; downtown. Int corridors. **Pets:** Accepted.

[ASK] [🅢] [X] [🅗] [📺] [🍽] [🏊] [🗙]

▼▼ The Howard Johnson Hotel 🆂🅷
(519) 893-1234. **$79-$99.** 1333 Weber St E. Hwy 401, exit 278, 6.4 km w on Hwy 8, exit Weber St W. Ext/int corridors. **Pets:** Accepted.

[ASK] [🅢] [X] [🅗] [📺] [🍽] [🏊]

▼▼ Mornington Crescent B&B 🅱🅱
(519) 743-4557. **$85-$120.** 11 Sunbridge Crescent. Hwy 86 N, exit University E, 1 km to Bridge St S, 0.5 km s to Bridal Tr, then just e. Int corridors. **Pets:** Other species. Supervision.

[X] [🅗] [📺] [🏊] [🖀]

🄰🄰 ▼▼▼▼ Radisson Hotel Kitchener 🆂🅷
(519) 894-9500. **$99-$149.** 2960 King St E. Hwy 401, exit 278, 6 km w on Hwy 8, exit Weber St. Int corridors. **Pets:** Service with restrictions, crate.

[SAVE] [🅢] [X] [🅗] [📺] [🍽] [🏊]

▼▼▼▼ **Walper Terrace Hotel** SH
(519) 745-4321. **$108-$134.** 1 King St W. Corner of King and Queen sts; downtown. Int corridors. **Pets:** Accepted.

A$K S⊘ ☒ 🖥 🖵 ⑪

# LEAMINGTON

▼▼ **Comfort Inn** SH ☙
(519) 326-9071. **$85-$130.** 279 Erie St S. Just s of jct Talbot and Erie sts; on direct route to Point Pelee National Park. Int corridors. **Pets:** $10 one-time fee/room. Designated rooms, service with restrictions, supervision.

A$K S⊘ ☒ 🖥 🖵

◑ ▼▼▼▼ **Ramada Leamington** SH
(519) 325-0260. **$99-$369, 3 day notice.** 201 Erie St N. 1 km n of Talbot St. Int corridors. **Pets:** Small, dogs only. $15 daily fee/pet. Designated rooms, service with restrictions, supervision.

SAVE ☒ 🖉 🖥 🖵 ⌦ ☒

◑ ▼ **Sun Parlor Motel** M
(519) 326-6131. **$55-$85, 7 day notice.** 135 Talbot St W. 1 km w of Erie St. Ext corridors. **Pets:** Dogs only. $10 daily fee/pet. Designated rooms, service with restrictions, supervision.

SAVE S⊘ ☒ 🖥

# LISTOWEL

◑ ▼▼▼ **Country Inn Motel** M
(519) 291-1580. **$89-$175.** RR 1 Hwy 23 N-8500 Rd 164. On Hwy 23 N, 3.5 km n of Main St. Ext/int corridors. **Pets:** Medium. Designated rooms, service with restrictions, supervision.

SAVE S⊘ ☒ 🖥 🖵 ☒

# LONDON

▼▼▼▼ **Airport Inn & Suites** SH
(519) 457-1200. **$92-$99.** 2230 Dundas St E. Hwy 401, exit Airport Rd, 7.7 km n; corner of Airport Rd and Dundas St E. Int corridors. **Pets:** Accepted.

A$K S⊘ ☒ 🖥 🖵

◑ ▼▼▼ **Best Western Lamplighter Inn & Conference Centre** SH
(519) 681-7151. **$169-$179.** 591 Wellington Rd S. 3.7 km n off Hwy 401, exit 186 (Wellington Rd). Int corridors. **Pets:** Medium, other species. $10 daily fee/pet. Designated rooms, service with restrictions, supervision.

SAVE S⊘ ☒ 🖥 🖵 ⑪ ⌦ ☒

▼▼ **Comfort Inn** SH
(519) 685-9300. **$80-$150.** 1156 Wellington Rd. Hwy 401, exit 186B (Wellington Rd), just n. Int corridors. **Pets:** Accepted.

A$K S⊘ ☒ 🖥 🖵

▼▼ **Days Inn London** SH ☙
(519) 681-1240. **$75-$145.** 1100 Wellington Rd S. Hwy 401, exit 186B (Wellington Rd), 1.5 km n. Int corridors. **Pets:** Large, other species. Service with restrictions, crate.

A$K ☒ 🖥 🖵 ⑪ ⌦

◑ ▼▼▼ **Delta London Armouries** LH ☙
(519) 679-6111. **$109-$169.** 325 Dundas St. On Hwy 2. Int corridors. **Pets:** Other species. $35 one-time fee/room. Service with restrictions.

SAVE S⊘ ☒ 🖉 🖥 🖵 ⌦ ☒

◑ ▼▼▼ **Holiday Inn Hotel & Suites-London** SH
(519) 680-0077. **$119-$159.** 864 Exeter Rd. Hwy 401, exit 186 (Wellington Rd) westbound; exit 186B (Wellington Rd) eastbound. Int corridors. **Pets:** Service with restrictions, supervision.

SAVE S⊘ ☒ 🖉 🖥 🖵 ⑪ ⌦

◑ ▼▼ **Quality Suites** SH
(519) 680-1024. **$119-$189.** 1120 Dearness Dr. Hwy 401, exit 186B (Wellington Rd), 1.6 km n. Int corridors. **Pets:** Small, other species. Designated rooms, service with restrictions, supervision.

SAVE S⊘ ☒ 🖥 🖵

▼▼▼▼ **Residence Inn by Marriott London** SH ☙
(519) 433-7222. **$149-$219.** 383 Colborne St. Jct King St. Int corridors. **Pets:** Other species. $75 one-time fee/room. Service with restrictions.

A$K S⊘ ☒ 🖉 🖥 🖵 ☒

◑ ▼▼▼▼ **StationPark All Suite Hotel** LH ☙
(519) 642-4444. **$174-$179.** 242 Pall Mall St. Hwy 401, exit 186B (Wellington Rd), 9 km n to Pall Mall St. Int corridors. **Pets:** Large. $100 deposit/room. Designated rooms, service with restrictions.

SAVE S⊘ ☒ 🖵 ⑪ ☒

# MARATHON

◑ ▼ **Peninsula Inn** M
(807) 229-0651. **$85-$95.** On Hwy 17, 2.4 km w of jct Hwy 626. Ext corridors. **Pets:** Small. $10 one-time fee/pet. Designated rooms, service with restrictions, supervision.

SAVE ☒ 🖥 ⑪

# MASSEY

◑ ▼ **Mohawk Motel Canada** M
(705) 865-2722. **$69-$165.** 335 Sable St. Centre. Ext/int corridors. **Pets:** Medium. $8 daily fee/room. Designated rooms, service with restrictions, supervision.

SAVE ☒ 🖥 🖵

# MCKELLAR

◑ ▼▼▼▼ **The Inn at Manitou** SH
(705) 389-2171. **$285-$465, 30 day notice.** 81 The Inn Rd. Hwy 124, exit McKellar Centre Rd, 8 km s, follow signs. Ext corridors. **Pets:** Accepted.

SAVE ☒ 🖥 ⑪ ⌦ ☒

# MIDLAND

▼▼ **Comfort Inn** SH
(705) 526-2090. **$99-$174.** 980 King St. Jct King St and Hwy 12. Int corridors. **Pets:** Service with restrictions, supervision.

A$K S⊘ ☒ 🖥 🖵

# MINDEMOYA

▼ **Mindemoya Motel** M
(705) 377-4779. **$79-$107, 3 day notice.** 6375 Hwy 542. In Mindemoya; 1 km w of jct Hwy 551 and 542. Ext corridors. **Pets:** Accepted.

A$K S⊘ ☒ 🖥 🖵

# MISSISSAUGA

▼▼ **Ambler Airport Hotel** SH
(905) 624-9500. **$75-$109.** 5599 Ambler Dr. Hwy 401, exit 346 (S Dixie Rd), w on Aerowood Dr, then just n. Int corridors. **Pets:** Small. $10 one-time fee/room. Designated rooms, service with restrictions, supervision.

A$K S⊘ ☒ 🖥 🖵 ⑪ ⌦

◑ ▼▼▼▼ **Best Western Admiral Hotel & Suites @ Conference Centre-Mississauga Airport** SH
(905) 795-1011. **$109-$249.** 40 Admiral Blvd. Hwy 401, exit Hwy 10 (Hurontario St), 1.5 km n; just s of Derry Rd. Int corridors. **Pets:** Accepted.

SAVE S⊘ ☒ 🖥 🖵 ⌦ ☒

◑ ▼▼▼ **Comfort Inn Airport West** SH
(905) 624-6900. **$94-$124.** 1500 Matheson Blvd. Hwy 401, exit Dixie Rd, then s. Int corridors. **Pets:** Accepted.

SAVE ☒ 🖥 🖵 ⑪

ⓐ ▼▼▼▼ **Delta Meadowvale Resort and Conference Centre** LH ❀
(905) 821-1981. **$89-$189.** 6750 Mississauga Rd. Hwy 401 W, exit 336 (Mississauga Rd), just s. Int corridors. **Pets:** Medium. $35 one-time fee/room. Service with restrictions.
SAVE Ⓢ ⊠ 🅱 💷 �🍴 ⤳ ⊠

ⓐ ▼▼▼▼ **Delta Toronto Airport West** LH ❀
(905) 624-1144. **$99-$199.** 5444 Dixie Rd. 1 km s of jct Hwy 401 and Dixie Rd. Int corridors. **Pets:** Large, other species. $35 one-time fee/pet. Designated rooms, service with restrictions, crate.
SAVE Ⓢ ⊠ 🅱 💷 ⍾ ⤳ ⊠

▼▼▼▼ **Four Points by Sheraton, Mississauga/Meadowvale** LH
(905) 858-2424. **$89-$159.** 2501 Argentia Rd. Sw of Hwy 401 and Mississauga Rd; corner of Derry and Argentia rds. Int corridors. **Pets:** Accepted.
ASK Ⓢ ⊠ 🅱 💷 ⍾ ⤳ ⊠

ⓐ ▼▼▼▼ **Holiday Inn Toronto-Mississauga** LH
(905) 855-2000. **$109-$149.** 2125 N Sheridan Way. QEW, exit Erin Mills Pkwy. Int corridors. **Pets:** Medium, other species. $25 one-time fee/room. Service with restrictions, supervision.
SAVE Ⓢ ⊠ 🅼 🄲 🅱 💷 ⍾ ⤳

ⓐ ▼▼▼▼ **Holiday Inn Toronto-West** SH
(905) 890-5700. **$119-$165.** 100 Britannia Rd E. Hwy 401, exit Hwy 10 S (Hurontario St). Int corridors. **Pets:** Service with restrictions, crate.
SAVE Ⓢ ⊠ 🅱 💷 ⍾ ⤳

▼▼ **Motel 6 #1910** SH
(905) 814-1664. **$71-$81.** 2935 Argentia Rd. Hwy 401, exit 333 (Winston Churchill Blvd), just s. Int corridors. **Pets:** Accepted.
Ⓢ ⊠ 🅼 🄲 ⤳

ⓐ ▼▼▼▼ **Novotel Hotel Mississauga** LH ❀
(905) 896-1000. **$119-$139.** 3670 Hurontario St. On Hwy 10 at Burnhamthorpe Rd; Hwy 401, exit Hwy 10 S (Hurontario St), 5 km. Int corridors. **Pets:** Large, other species. Service with restrictions, crate.
SAVE Ⓢ ⊠ 🅱 💷 ⍾ ⤳ ⊠

▼▼▼▼ **Residence Inn by Marriott** SH
(905) 567-2577. **$145-$229.** 7005 Century Ave. Hwy 401, exit Erin Mills Pkwy/Mississauga Rd, s to Argentia Rd. Int corridors. **Pets:** Medium. $75 one-time fee/room. Service with restrictions, crate.
ASK Ⓢ ⊠ 🅼 🄲 🅱 💷 ⤳

ⓐ ▼▼▼▼ **Sandalwood Suites Hotel Toronto Airport** SH
(905) 238-9600. **$99-$189.** 5050 Orbitor Dr. Jct Eglinton Ave and Renforth Dr, 2.3 km w on Eglinton Ave. Int corridors. **Pets:** Medium. $8 daily fee/pet. Designated rooms, service with restrictions, crate.
SAVE Ⓢ ⊠ 🅱 💷

ⓐ ▼▼▼ ▼▼▼ **Sheraton Gateway Hotel In Toronto International Airport** LH ❀
(905) 672-7000. **$99-$349, 14 day notice.** In Lester B. Pearson International Airport. Int corridors. **Pets:** Large. Service with restrictions, supervision.
SAVE Ⓢ ⊠ 🅼 💷 ⍾ ⤳ ⊠

▼▼▼ ▼▼ **Studio 6 Mississauga #190** M
(905) 502-8897. **$83-$110.** 60 Brittannia Rd E. Hwy 401, exit Hwy 10 (Hurontario St). Int corridors. **Pets:** Accepted.
Ⓢ ⊠ 🄲 🅱 💷

▼▼▼▼ **Toronto Airport Hilton** LH
(905) 677-9900. **$109-$279.** 5875 Airport Rd. Hwy 401, exit Dixon Rd, 3.5 km w; 1 km from Lester B. Pearson International Airport. Int corridors. **Pets:** Accepted.
ASK Ⓢ ⊠ 💷 ⍾ ⤳

## MONETVILLE

▼▼▼ ▼▼ **Memquisit Lodge** CA
(705) 898-2355. **$87-$95, 90 day notice.** 506 Memquisit Rd. 20.8 km ne on west arm of Lake Nipissing, on Hwy 64 and Memquisit Lodge Rd; 36.8 km sw off Hwy 17, on Hwy 64 Ext corridors. **Pets:** Accepted.
🅱 💷 ⍾ ⊠ 🄺 ⤳

## MORRISBURG

ⓐ ▼▼▼ **The McIntosh Country Inn & Conference Centre** SH
(613) 543-3788. **$79-$129.** 12495 Hwy 2 E. Hwy 401, exit 750, 2 km s on Rt 31, then 1 km e. Int corridors. **Pets:** Medium. $20 one-time fee/pet. Designated rooms, service with restrictions, crate.
SAVE Ⓢ ⊠ 🅱 💷 ⍾ ⤳ ⊠

## NEWMARKET

ⓐ ▼▼▼ **Comfort Inn** SH
(905) 895-3355. **$95-$135.** 1230 Journey's End Cir. Hwy 404, exit 51 (Davis Dr). Int corridors. **Pets:** Other species. Service with restrictions, supervision.
ASK Ⓢ ⊠ 🅱 💷

---

# NIAGARA FALLS METROPOLITAN AREA

## FORT ERIE

ⓐ ▼▼ ▼▼ **Comfort Inn** SH
(905) 871-8500. **$110-$135.** 1 Hospitality Dr. QEW, exit 2 (Berti St) westbound; exit 1B (Concession Rd S) eastbound. Int corridors. **Pets:** Accepted.
SAVE Ⓢ ⊠ 🅱 💷

## LINCOLN

ⓐ ▼▼ ▼▼ **Best Western Beacon Harbourside Resort & Conference Centre** SH
(905) 562-4155. **$89-$199.** 2793 Beacon Blvd. QEW, exit 57. Int corridors. **Pets:** Accepted.
SAVE Ⓢ ⊠ 💷 ⍾ ⤳ ⊠

## NIAGARA FALLS

ⓐ ▼▼ ▼▼ **Best Western Fallsview** SH
(905) 356-0551. **$79-$299, 3 day notice.** 6289 Fallsview Blvd. Jct Niagara River Pkwy, just n on Murray St. Ext/int corridors. **Pets:** Accepted.
SAVE Ⓢ ⊠ 💷 ⍾ ⤳

ⓐ ▼▼ ▼▼ **Camelot Inn** M
(905) 354-3754. **$50-$225.** 5640 Stanley Ave. Just n of Hwy 20; just s of Hwy 420. Ext corridors. **Pets:** Medium. $10 daily fee/room. Service with restrictions.
SAVE Ⓢ ⊠ 🅱 ⤳ 🅩

ⓐ ▼▼ ▼▼ **Flamingo Thriftlodge** M
(905) 356-4646. **$54-$179.** 7701 Lundy's Ln. QEW, exit Hwy 20, 3.4 km w. Ext corridors. **Pets:** Accepted.
SAVE Ⓢ ⊠ 🅱 ⤳

▼▼ **Hilltop Hotel** M
(905) 374-7777. **$58-$199.** 4955 Clifton Hill. Just s of jct Victoria Ave. Int corridors. **Pets:** Accepted.
ASK Ⓢ

ⓐ ▼▼ ▼▼ **The Niagara Falls Plaza Hotel** LH
(905) 353-1010. **$60-$210.** 5807 Ferry St. Jct Main and Ferry sts, just s. Int corridors. **Pets:** Accepted.
SAVE Ⓢ ⊠ 🄲 🅱 💷 ⍾ ⤳

▼▼▼ ▼▼▼ **Niagara Fallsview Casino Resort** 🄻🄷
(905) 358-3255. **$189-$399, 3 day notice.** 6380 Fallsview Blvd. Jct Murray St. Int corridors. **Pets:** Accepted.
(A̲S̲K̲) 🆂 ⊠ 🔋 ▣ 🍴 ➤ ⊠

(AA) ▼ **Niagara Parkway Court Motel** 🄼
(905) 295-3331. **$49-$149.** 3708 Main St (Niagara River Pkwy S). 2.5 km s of the falls. Ext corridors. **Pets:** Small. $10 one-time fee/pet. Designated rooms, service with restrictions, supervision.
(S̲A̲V̲E̲) 🆂 ⊠ 🔋 ▣

(AA) ▼▼▼ **Peninsula Inn & Resort** 🅂🄷
(905) 354-8812. **$59-$199.** 7373 Niagara Square Dr. QEW, exit McLeod Rd, just w. Int corridors. **Pets:** Small, other species. $10 daily fee/pet. Designated rooms, service with restrictions, crate.
(S̲A̲V̲E̲) 🆂 ⊠ 🔋 🔋 ▣ 🍴 ➤ ⊠

(AA) ▼▼▼ ▼▼▼ **Sheraton Fallsview Hotel & Conference Centre** 🄻🄷 🐾
(905) 374-1077. **$99-$499.** 6755 Fallsview Blvd. Near Konica Minolta Tower. Int corridors. **Pets:** Medium, dogs only. $25 one-time fee/pet. Designated rooms, service with restrictions, supervision.
(S̲A̲V̲E̲) 🆂 ⊠ 🔋 🔋 ▣ 🍴 ➤ ⊠

(AA) ▼▼▼ ▼▼▼ **Sheraton on the Falls** 🄻🄷
(905) 374-4445. **$99-$999.** 5875 Falls Ave. Entrance to Rainbow Bridge on Hwy 20. Int corridors. **Pets:** Accepted.
(S̲A̲V̲E̲) 🆂 ⊠ 🔋 ▣ 🍴 ➤

(AA) ▼ ▼ **Stanley Motor Inn** 🄼
(905) 358-9238. **$60-$150.** 6220 Stanley Ave. 2 blks from the falls; w of Skylon Tower. Ext/int corridors. **Pets:** Small, dogs only. $10 daily fee/pet. Service with restrictions, crate.
(S̲A̲V̲E̲) ⊠ 🔋 ➤ 🅩

(AA) ▼ **Thriftlodge Clifton Hill** 🄼
(905) 357-4330. **$49-$329.** 4945 Clifton Hill. Just s on jct Victoria Ave. Ext corridors. **Pets:** Medium. Service with restrictions, supervision.
(S̲A̲V̲E̲) 🆂 ⊠ 🔋 ▣

## NIAGARA-ON-THE-LAKE

▼▼▼ ▼▼▼ **Harbour House Hotel** 🅂🄷 🐾
(905) 468-4683. **$199-$370, 10 day notice.** 85 Melville St. Jct Ricardo St. Int corridors. **Pets:** Dogs only. $25 daily fee/room. Designated rooms, service with restrictions, supervision.
(A̲S̲K̲) 🆂 ⊠ ▣

(AA) ▼▼▼ ▼▼▼ **The Oban Inn and Spa** 🄲🄸
(905) 468-2165. **$150-$325.** 160 Front St. Jct Gate. Ext/int corridors. **Pets:** Accepted.
(S̲A̲V̲E̲) ⊠ 🍴

(AA) ▼▼▼ ▼▼▼ **The Pillar and Post Inn, Spa & Conference Center** 🅂🄷 🐾
(905) 468-3246. **$175-$365.** 6 Picton St. Jct Picton and King sts; 14.4 km e of jct QEW and Hwy 55, via Hwy 55. Ext/int corridors. **Pets:** Other species. $35 daily fee/pet. Designated rooms, supervision.
(S̲A̲V̲E̲) 🆂 ⊠ 🔋 🍴 ➤ ⊠

(AA) ▼▼▼ ▼▼▼ **The Pillar & Post Inn Spa & Conference Centre** 🄲🄸
(905) 468-2123. **$175-$365.** 48 John St. Just n on Hwy 55 (Mississauga St), just e; 13 mi from QEW. Ext/int corridors. **Pets:** Accepted.
(S̲A̲V̲E̲) 🆂 ⊠ 🔋 🍴 ➤ ⊠

(AA) ▼▼▼ ▼▼▼ **Queen's Landing Inn & Conference Resort** 🅂🄷
(905) 468-2195. **$175-$365.** 155 Byron St. Just n on King St, just e. Int corridors. **Pets:** Small, other species. $100 daily fee/pet. Supervision.
(S̲A̲V̲E̲) 🆂 ⊠ 🍴 ➤ ⊠

## ST. CATHARINES

(AA) ▼▼▼ ▼▼▼ **Comfort Inn** 🅂🄷
(905) 687-8890. **$99-$159.** 2 Dunlop Dr. QEW, exit 46 (Lake St); between Lake and Geneva sts. Int corridors. **Pets:** Designated rooms, service with restrictions, supervision.
(S̲A̲V̲E̲) 🆂 ⊠ 🔋 🔋 🍴

(AA) ▼▼▼ ▼▼▼ **Holiday Inn St. Catharines/Niagara** 🅂🄷
(905) 934-8000. **$129-$299.** 2 N Service Rd. QEW, exit 46 (Lake St), just e. Int corridors. **Pets:** $15 daily fee/pet. Designated rooms, supervision.
(S̲A̲V̲E̲) 🆂 ⊠ 🔋 ▣ 🍴 ➤ ⊠

(AA) ▼▼▼ ▼▼▼ **Howard Johnson Hotel & Conference Centre** 🅂🄷
(905) 934-5400. **$89-$289.** 89 Meadowvale Dr. QEW, exit 46 (Lake St). Int corridors. **Pets:** Medium. $10 one-time fee/room. Designated rooms, service with restrictions, supervision.
(S̲A̲V̲E̲) 🆂 ⊠ 🔋 ▣ 🍴 ➤ ⊠

(AA) ▼▼▼ ▼▼▼ **Quality Hotel Parkway Convention Centre** 🄻🄷
(905) 688-2324. **$99-$309.** 327 Ontario St. QEW, exit 47 (Ontario St), 0.8 km s. Int corridors. **Pets:** Accepted.
(S̲A̲V̲E̲) ⊠ 🔋 ▣ 🍴 ➤ ⊠

(AA) ▼▼▼ ▼▼▼ **The Travelodge St. Catharines** 🄼
(905) 688-1646. **$89-$139.** 420 Ontario St. QEW, exit 47 (Ontario St). Ext corridors. **Pets:** $10 one-time fee/room. Service with restrictions, crate.
(S̲A̲V̲E̲) 🆂 ⊠ 🔋 ▣ 🍴 ➤

## THOROLD

▼▼▼ ▼▼▼ **Four Points by Sheraton St. Catharines** 🄻🄷
(905) 984-8484. **$99-$199.** 3530 Schmon Pkwy. Hwy 406, exit St. David's Rd W. Int corridors. **Pets:** $10 daily fee/room. Designated rooms, service with restrictions, crate.
(A̲S̲K̲) 🆂 ⊠ 🔋 🔋 ▣ 🍴 ➤ ⊠

## NORTH BAY

(AA) ▼▼▼ ▼▼▼ **Best Western North Bay** 🅂🄷
(705) 474-5800. **$89-$199.** 700 Lakeshore Dr. Hwy 11, exit Lakeshore Dr, 4 km n on Hwy 11B. Int corridors. **Pets:** Large, other species. Service with restrictions, crate.
(S̲A̲V̲E̲) 🆂 ⊠ 🔋 ▣ 🍴 ➤ ⊠

(AA) ▼▼▼ ▼▼▼ **Clarion Resort Pinewood Park** 🅂🄷
(705) 472-0810. **$129-$160.** 201 Pinewood Park Dr. Hwy 11, exit Lakeshore Dr, immediately turn s on Pinewood Park Dr, then 0.7 km. Int corridors. **Pets:** Service with restrictions, crate.
(S̲A̲V̲E̲) 🆂 ⊠ 🔋 ▣ 🍴 ➤ ⊠

**❤❤ Comfort Inn** 🆂🅷
(705) 494-9444. **$82-$117.** 676 Lakeshore Dr. Hwy 11B, exit Lakeshore Dr; 4 km n of jct Hwy 11. Int corridors. **Pets:** Accepted.
🅰🆂🅺 🆂🔯 ⊠ 🎴 🖵

**❤❤ Comfort Inn-Airport** 🆂🅷
(705) 476-5400. **$95-$144.** 1200 O'Brien St. 3 km e on Hwy 11 and 17 Bypass; at O'Brien St exit. Int corridors. **Pets:** Other species. Designated rooms, service with restrictions, supervision.
🅰🆂🅺 🆂🔯 ⊠ 🎴 🖵

**❤❤ Super 8** 🆂🅷
(705) 495-4551. **$79-$89.** 570 Lakeshore Dr. Hwy 11, exit Lakeshore Dr, 4.5 km n on Hwy 11B. Int corridors. **Pets:** Medium, other species. Service with restrictions, supervision.
🅰🆂🅺 🆂🔯 ⊠ 🔖 🎴

**❤❤ Travelodge-Airport** 🆂🅷 🐾
(705) 495-1133. **$99-$159.** 1525 Seymour St. Jct Hwy 11, 17 and Seymour St. Int corridors. **Pets:** Large, other species. Service with restrictions, supervision.
🅰🆂🅺 🆂🔯 ⊠ 🎴 🖵 🏊

## OAKVILLE

**❤❤❤ Holiday Inn Oakville-Centre** 🆂🅷
(905) 842-5000. **$169-$189.** 590 Argus Rd. QEW, exit Trafalgar Rd, then s. Int corridors. **Pets:** Accepted.
🅰🆂🅺 🆂🔯 ⊠ 🎴 🖵 🍽 🏊 🏌

**Ⓐ ❤❤❤❤ Quality Hotel & Suites-Oakville** 🆂🅷
(905) 847-6667. **$109-$139.** 754 Bronte Rd. QEW, exit 111 (Bronte Rd/Hwy 25), 0.4 km s. Int corridors. **Pets:** $50 one-time fee/pet. Service with restrictions, crate.
🆂🅰🆅🅴 🆂🔯 ⊠ 🎴 🖵 🍽 🏊 🏌

**❤❤❤ Ramada Inn and Convention Centre Oakville** 🆂🅷
(905) 845-7561. **$89-$149.** 360 Oakville Place Dr. QEW, exit Trafalgar Rd, just n. Int corridors. **Pets:** Accepted.
🅰🆂🅺 🆂🔯 ⊠ 🎴 🖵 🍽 🏊 🏌

## ORILLIA

**❤❤ Comfort Inn** 🆂🅷
(705) 327-7744. **$108-$135.** 75 Progress Dr. Hwy 11 N, exit Hwy 12, s on Memorial Ave; corner of Progress D and Memorial Ave. Int corridors. **Pets:** Accepted.
🅰🆂🅺 🆂🔯 ⊠ 🎴 🖵

**Ⓐ ❤❤ Econo Lodge** 🆂🅷
(705) 326-3554. **$79-$109.** 265 Memoria Ave. 0.5 km n of Hwy 12. Int corridors. **Pets:** Accepted.
🆂🅰🆅🅴 🆂🔯 ⊠ 🎴 🖵

## OSHAWA

**❤❤ Comfort Inn** 🆂🅷
(905) 434-5000. **$89-$139.** 605 Bloor St W. Hwy 401, exit 416 (Park Rd), s to Bloor St, then 0.8 km w. Int corridors. **Pets:** Accepted.
🅰🆂🅺 🆂🔯 ⊠ 🎴 🖵

**Ⓐ ❤❤❤❤ Holiday Inn Oshawa** 🆂🅷
(905) 576-5101. **$129-$179.** 1011 Bloor St E. Hwy 401, exit 419 (Harmony Rd). Int corridors. **Pets:** $15 daily fee/pet. Designated rooms, service with restrictions, crate.
🆂🅰🆅🅴 🆂🔯 ⊠ 🎴 🖵 🍽 🏊 🏌

**❤❤❤ Oshawa Travelodge** 🆂🅷 🐾
(905) 436-9500. **$99-$129.** 940 Champlain Ave. Hwy 401, exit 412 (Thickson Rd N). Int corridors. **Pets:** Large. $25 daily fee/room. Service with restrictions, supervision.
🅰🆂🅺 🆂🔯 ⊠ 🎴 🖵 🏊

---

# OTTAWA METROPOLITAN AREA

## OTTAWA

**Ⓐ ❤❤❤ Adam's Airport Inn** 🆂🅷
(613) 738-3838. **$94-$99.** 2721 Bank St. Jct Hunt Club Rd and Bank St, 1 km s. Int corridors. **Pets:** Accepted.
🆂🅰🆅🅴 🆂🔯 ⊠ 🎴 🖵

**❤❤❤ Best Western Barons Hotel & Conference Centre** 🆂🅷
(613) 828-2741. **$129-$265.** 3700 Richmond Rd. Hwy 417, exit 130, 2 km s. Int corridors. **Pets:** Accepted.
🆂🅰🆅🅴 🆂🔯 ⊠ 🔖 🎴 🖵 🍽 🏊 🏌

**❤❤❤ Bostonian Executive Suites** 🆂🅷 🐾
(613) 594-5757. **$159-$189.** 341 MacLaren St. Between Bank and O'Connor sts. Int corridors. **Pets:** Large, other species. $50 daily fee/room, $150 one-time fee/room. Designated rooms, service with restrictions, crate.
🅰🆂🅺 🆂🔯 ⊠ 🎴 🖵

**Ⓐ ❤❤❤❤ Brookstreet Resort** 🅻🅷 🐾
(613) 271-1800. **$139-$349.** 525 Legget Dr. Hwy 417, exit 138 (March Rd), 3.7 km n, just e on Solandt Dr to Legget Dr, then just n. Int corridors. **Pets:** Small. $25 daily fee/pet. Service with restrictions, supervision.
🆂🅰🆅🅴 ⊠ 🖵 🍽 🏊 🏌

**Ⓐ ❤❤❤ Cartier Place Suite Hotel** 🆂🅷
(613) 236-5000. **$109-$229.** 180 Cooper St. Between Elgin and Cartier sts. Int corridors. **Pets:** Accepted.
🆂🅰🆅🅴 🆂🔯 ⊠ 🎴 🖵 🍽 🏊 🏌

**Ⓐ ❤❤❤ Comfort Inn** 🆂🅷
(613) 744-2900. **$99-$129.** 1252 Michael St. Hwy 417, exit 115 (St. Laurent Blvd), just ne. Int corridors. **Pets:** Medium, other species. Designated rooms, service with restrictions, crate.
🆂🅰🆅🅴 🆂🔯 ⊠ 🎴 🖵

**Ⓐ ❤❤❤ Comfort Inn Ottawa West** 🆂🅷 🐾
(613) 592-2200. **$122-$127.** 222 Hearst Way. Hwy 417, exit 138 (Eagleson Rd), 0.6 km s, then 0.3 km w on Katimavik Rd. Int corridors. **Pets:** Other species. Designated rooms, service with restrictions, supervision.
🆂🅰🆅🅴 🆂🔯 ⊠ 🎴 🖵

**Ⓐ ❤❤❤ Days Inn-Downtown (Ottawa)** 🆂🅷
(613) 789-5555. **$99-$139.** 319 Rideau St. Between Nelson St and King Edward Ave. Ext/int corridors. **Pets:** Designated rooms, service with restrictions, supervision.
🆂🅰🆅🅴 🆂🔯 ⊠ 🎴 🖵 🍽

**❤❤❤ The Days Inn Ottawa West** 🆂🅷
(613) 726-1717. **$99-$135.** 350 Moodie Dr. Hwy 417, exit 134, 1.5 km s. Int corridors. **Pets:** $20 daily fee/room. Designated rooms, service with restrictions, supervision.
🅰🆂🅺 🆂🔯 ⊠ 🎴 🖵 🍽

ⒸⒶ ▼▼▼ **Delta Ottawa Hotel and Suites** 🅛🅗
(613) 238-6000. $129-$229. 361 Queen St. Corner of Lyon St. Int
corridors. **Pets:** Accepted.

[SAVE] [✕] [🛏] [▦] [¶] [➳] [✕]

ⒸⒶ ▼ **Econo Lodge-Ottawa East** 🅜
(613) 745-1531. $85-$99. 2098 Montreal Rd. Hwy 417, exit 113, 2.5 km
e on Hwy 174 to Montreal Rd W exit. Ext corridors. **Pets:** Large. $10
daily fee/pet. Service with restrictions, crate.

[SAVE] [S🛏] [✕] [🛏] [▦]

ⒸⒶ ▼▼ ▼▼ **Extended Stay Deluxe Ottawa Downtown** 🅢🅗
(613) 236-7500. $119-$179. 141 Cooper St. Between Elgin and Cartier
sts. Int corridors. **Pets:** Accepted.

[SAVE] [S🛏] [✕] [🛏] [▦] [¶] [✕]

ⒸⒶ ▼▼▼ ▼▼▼ **Fairmont Chateau Laurier** 🅛🅗
(613) 241-1414. $169-$399. 1 Rideau St. Just e of Parliament buildings. Int corridors. **Pets:** Small. Service with restrictions, supervision.

[SAVE] [S🛏] [✕] [🛏M] [🛏] [▦] [¶] [➳] [✕]

ⒸⒶ ▼▼▼ ▼▼▼ **Holiday Inn Hotel & Suites** 🅢🅗 ✥
(613) 238-1331. $129. 111 Cooper St. Corner of Cartier St. Int corri-
dors. **Pets:** Large, other species.

[SAVE] [✕] [🅢] [🛏] [▦] [¶]

ⒸⒶ ▼▼▼ ▼▼▼ **Les Suites Hotel Ottawa** 🅛🅗 ✥
(613) 232-2000. $169-$209. 130 Besserer St. Between Nicholas and
Waller sts. Int corridors. **Pets:** Other species. $25 one-time fee/room.
Service with restrictions.

[SAVE] [S🛏] [✕] [🛏M] [🛏] [▦] [¶] [➳] [✕]

▼▼▼ ▼▼▼ **Lord Elgin Hotel** 🅛🅗
(613) 235-3333. $129-$169. 100 Elgin St. Between Laurier Ave and
Slater St. Int corridors. **Pets:** Designated rooms, service with restrictions,
crate.

[ASK] [S🛏] [✕] [🅢] [🛏] [▦] [¶] [➳] [✕]

ⒸⒶ ▼▼▼ ▼▼▼ **Novotel Ottawa Hotel** 🅛🅗
(613) 230-3033. $139-$199. 33 Nicholas St. Corner of Daly Ave. Int
corridors. **Pets:** Accepted.

[SAVE] [S🛏] [✕] [▦] [¶] [➳] [✕]

ⒸⒶ ▼▼▼ ▼▼▼ **Ottawa Marriott** 🅛🅗
(613) 238-1122. $120-$206. 100 Kent St. Corner of Queen St. Int
corridors. **Pets:** Service with restrictions, supervision.

[SAVE] [S🛏] [✕] [🛏] [▦] [¶] [➳] [✕]

ⒸⒶ ▼▼ ▼▼ **Quality Hotel Ottawa, Downtown** 🅢🅗 ✥
(613) 789-7511. $129-$155. 290 Rideau St. Corner of King Edward
Ave. Int corridors. **Pets:** Medium. Service with restrictions, supervision.

[SAVE] [S🛏] [✕] [🛏] [▦] [¶]

ⒸⒶ ▼▼ ▼▼ **Radisson Hotel Ottawa Parliament Hill** 🅢🅗
(613) 236-1133. $129-$179. 402 Queen St. Corner of Bay and Queen
sts. Int corridors. **Pets:** Service with restrictions.

[SAVE] [S🛏] [✕] [🛏] [▦] [¶]

▼▼▼ ▼▼▼ **Residence Inn by Marriott** 🅢🅗
(613) 231-2020. $129-$299. 161 Laurier Ave W. Corner of Elgin St. Int
corridors. **Pets:** Accepted.

[ASK] [S🛏] [✕] [🛏] [▦] [➳] [✕]

▼▼ ▼▼ **Rideau Heights Motor Inn** 🅜
(613) 226-4152. $89-$109. 72 Rideau Heights Dr. Prince of Wales Dr,
0.5 km n of Hunt Club Rd. Ext corridors. **Pets:** Small, other species. $20
daily fee/pet. Designated rooms, service with restrictions, supervision.

[ASK] [S🛏] [✕] [🛏] [▦]

ⒸⒶ ▼▼▼ ▼▼▼ **Sheraton Ottawa Hotel** 🅛🅗 ✥
(613) 238-1500. $149-$260. 150 Albert St. Corner of O'Connor St. Int
corridors. **Pets:** Small, dogs only. Designated rooms, service with restrictions, supervision.

[SAVE] [S🛏] [✕] [🛏] [▦] [¶] [➳]

ⒸⒶ ▼▼▼ ▼▼▼ **Southway Inn of Ottawa** 🅢🅗
(613) 737-0811. $128-$148, 3 day notice. 2431 Bank St. On Hwy 31,
corner of Hunt Club Rd. Int corridors. **Pets:** $30 daily fee/pet. Designated
rooms, service with restrictions, supervision.

[SAVE] [S🛏] [✕] [🛏] [▦] [¶] [➳] [✕]

ⒸⒶ ▼▼▼ ▼▼▼ **Travelodge Hotel & Convention Centre** 🅢🅗
(613) 722-7600. $109-$189. 1376 Carling Ave. Just e of jct Kirkwood
Ave. Int corridors. **Pets:** Service with restrictions, supervision.

[SAVE] [S🛏] [✕] [🛏] [▦] [¶] [✕]

ⒸⒶ ▼▼ ▼▼ **Travelodge Ottawa East** 🅢🅗 ✥
(613) 745-1133. $99-$149. 1486 Innes Rd. Hwy 417, exit 112 (Innes
Rd), just e. Int corridors. **Pets:** Other species. Designated rooms, service
with restrictions, supervision.

[SAVE] [S🛏] [✕] [🛏] [▦] [¶] [➳]

ⒸⒶ ▼▼ ▼▼ **Webb's Motel** 🅜
(613) 728-1881. $95-$100. 1705 Carling Ave. Hwy 417, exit 126, 0.5
km n on Maitland Ave, then 0.5 km e. Ext/int corridors. **Pets:** Accepted.

[SAVE] [✕] [🛏]

▼▼▼ ▼▼▼ **The Westin Ottawa** 🅛🅗
(613) 560-7000. $169-$305. 11 Colonel By Dr. Corner of Rideau St. Int
corridors. **Pets:** Accepted.

[✕] [🔒] [🅢] [🛏] [▦] [¶] [➳] [✕]

# END METROPOLITAN AREA

## OWEN SOUND

▼▼ ▼▼ **Comfort Inn** 🅢🅗
(519) 371-5500. $99-$170. 955 9th Ave E. Jct Hwy 6, 10, 21 and 26.
Int corridors. **Pets:** Accepted.

[ASK] [S🛏] [✕] [🛏] [▦]

ⒸⒶ ▼▼▼ ▼▼▼ **Days Inn Hotel and Convention
Centre** 🅢🅗 ✥
(519) 376-1551. $79-$199. 950 6th St E. Jct Hwy 6 and 10. Int corridors. **Pets:** Other species. $20 daily fee/pet. Service with restrictions.

[SAVE] [S🛏] [✕] [🛏] [▦] [¶] [➳] [✕]

▼▼ **Owen Sound Inn** 🅢🅗
(519) 371-3011. $55-$150. 485 9th Ave E. Jct Hwy 6, 10, 26 and 21;
follow Hwy 6 and 10 1 km s. Int corridors. **Pets:** Accepted.

[ASK] [S🛏] [✕] [🛏]

▼▼ **Travelodge** 🅢🅗
(519) 371-9297. $119-$148, 15 day notice. 880 10th St E. Jct Hwy 6,
10, 21 and 26. Int corridors. **Pets:** Accepted.

[ASK] [S🛏] [✕] [🛏] [▦]

## PARRY SOUND

▼▼ ▼▼ **Comfort Inn** 🅢🅗
(705) 746-6221. $103-$166. 120 Bowes St. Hwy 69, exit 224 (Bowes
St), just w. Int corridors. **Pets:** Other species. Designated rooms, service
with restrictions, supervision.

[ASK] [S🛏] [✕] [🛏] [▦]

▼▼▼ **Georgian Inn & Suites** SH
(705) 746-5837. **$90-$179.** 48 Joseph St. Hwy 69, exit Parry Sound Dr, 2 km w; at northern approach to city. Ext/int corridors. **Pets:** Accepted.

ASK SÒ ⊠ 🛏 💻 🍽 ➤

▼▼ **Log Cabin Inn** M
(705) 746-7122. **$89-$150, 3 day notice.** RR 2 (Little Beaver Rd). Hwy 69, exit 220 (Hunter Dr), 1.9 km w on Oastler Park Dr, then 1.2 km s. Ext corridors. **Pets:** Accepted.

⊠ 💻 🍽 ⊠ ℳ

▼▼ **Resort Tapatoo** SH
(705) 378-2208. **$88-$193, 30 day notice.** Otter Lake Rd. Hwy 69, exit 217. 6.2 km sw. Ext/int corridors. **Pets:** Accepted.

ASK SÒ ⊠ 🛏 💻 🍽 ➤ ⊠

## PEMBROKE

▼▼ **Best Western Pembroke Inn & Conference**
            **Centre** SH
(613) 735-0131. **$130-$150.** One International Dr. Jct Hwy 17 and 41. Int corridors. **Pets:** Small. $10 daily fee/room. Designated rooms, service with restrictions, supervision.

ASK SÒ ⊠ 🛏 💻 🍽 ➤ ⊠

▼ **Colonial Fireside Inn** M
(613) 732-3623. **$70-$85.** 1350 Pembroke St W. Jct Hwy 17, 5 km n on Forest Lea Rd, just e. Ext corridors. **Pets:** Small. Service with restrictions, supervision.

⊠ 🛏 💻 ➤

▼▼ **Comfort Inn** SH
(613) 735-1057. **$92-$149.** 959 Pembroke St E. 1.6 km e on Old Hwy 17. Int corridors. **Pets:** Accepted.

ASK SÒ ⊠ 🛏 💻

## PETAWAWA

CAA ▼▼▼ **Thriftlodge Petawawa** SH 🐾
(613) 687-4686. **$99-$169.** 3520 Petawawa Blvd. Hwy 17, exit Paquette Rd, 2.4 km e, then just s. Int corridors. **Pets:** Other species. $10 daily fee/room. Service with restrictions, supervision.

SAVE SÒ ⊠ 🛏 💻

## PETERBOROUGH

▼▼ **King Bethune House, Guest House & Spa** BB 🐾
(705) 743-4101. **$149-$299, 14 day notice.** 270 King St. From Charlotte and George St (clock tower), 1 blk s on George St to King St, then just w. Int corridors. **Pets:** Other species. $25 daily fee/pet. No service, supervision.

⊠ 🛏 💻

CAA ▼▼▼ **Quality Inn** SH
(705) 748-6801. **$115-$135, 7 day notice.** 1074 Lansdowne St W. 3 km from jct Hwy 115 and Bypass. Int corridors. **Pets:** Small. Designated rooms, service with restrictions, supervision.

SAVE SÒ ⊠ 🛏 💻

## PICKERING

▼▼ **Comfort Inn** SH
(905) 831-6200. **$95-$165.** 533 Kingston Rd. Hwy 401, exit 394 N (White's Rd) to Hwy 2, 0.5 km w. Int corridors. **Pets:** Accepted.

ASK SÒ ⊠ 🛏 💻

## PLANTAGENET

▼▼ **Motel de Champlain** M
(613) 673-5220. **$70-$110.** 5999 Hwy 17. Jct CR 9. Ext/int corridors. **Pets:** Accepted.

ASK SÒ ⊠ 🛏 🍽

## PORT HOPE

CAA ▼▼▼ **Comfort Inn** SH 🐾
(905) 885-7000. **$105-$195.** Hwy 401 & 28. Hwy 401, exit 464, just n. Int corridors. **Pets:** Small. Designated rooms, service with restrictions, supervision.

SAVE SÒ ⊠ 🛏 💻

## PROVIDENCE BAY

CAA ▼ **Huron Sands Motel** M
(705) 377-4616. **$79-$109, 3 day notice.** 5216 Hwy 551. In Providence Bay; on Hwy 551, 27.2 km w of South Baymouth via 10th Side Rd, follow signs; centre. Ext corridors. **Pets:** Other species. $10 one-time fee/room. Service with restrictions, supervision.

SAVE ⊠ 🍽 ☎

## RENFREW

CAA ▼▼▼ **Best Western-Renfrew Inn and Conference**
            **Centre** SH
(613) 432-8109. **$99-$130.** 760 Gibbons Rd. Hwy 17, exit O'Brien Rd. Int corridors. **Pets:** Other species. $10 daily fee/room. Service with restrictions, supervision.

SAVE SÒ ⊠ 🛏 💻 🍽 ➤ ⊠

▼▼ **The Rocky Mountain House** M
(613) 432-5801. **$69-$149.** 409 Stewart St N. Jct Bruce St. Ext corridors. **Pets:** Accepted.

ASK SÒ ⊠ 🛏 💻 🍽

## ROSSPORT

▼▼ **The Willows Inn Bed & Breakfast** BB
(807) 824-3389. **$75-$130, 5 day notice.** 1 Main St. Centre. Int corridors. **Pets:** Accepted.

SÒ ⊠ ℳ

## ST. THOMAS

CAA ▼▼▼ **Comfort Inn** SH
(519) 633-4082. **$119-$159.** 100 Centennial Ave. 6.5 km e on Hwy 3. Int corridors. **Pets:** Accepted.

SAVE SÒ ⊠ 🛏 💻

## SARNIA

CAA ▼▼▼▼ **Best Western Guildwood Inn and Conference**
            **Centre** SH
(519) 337-7577. **$125-$141.** 1400 Venetian Blvd. 1 km e of Bluewater Bridge. Ext/int corridors. **Pets:** Accepted.

SAVE SÒ ⊠ 🛏 💻 🍽 ➤

▼▼▼ **Holiday Inn Sarnia-Point Edward** SH
(519) 336-4130. **$110-$200.** 1498 Venetian Blvd. E of Bluewater Bridge. Int corridors. **Pets:** Accepted.

⊠ 🛏 💻 🍽 ➤ ⊠

▼▼ **Super 8 Motel-Sarnia** SH
(519) 337-3767. **$79-$99.** 420 Christina St N. Between Exmouth and London rds. Ext/int corridors. **Pets:** Accepted.

ASK ⊠ ⊆M 🛏 💻

## SAULT STE. MARIE

▼ **Adams Motel** M
(705) 254-4345. **$59-$99.** 647 Great Northern Rd. 4.4 km n on Hwy 17B. Ext corridors. **Pets:** Accepted.

ASK SÒ ⊠ 🛏 💻

CAA ▼▼▼▼ **Algoma's Water Tower Inn** SH
(705) 949-8111. **$119-$189.** 360 Great Northern Rd. Jct Hwy 17 and Second Line. Int corridors. **Pets:** Designated rooms, service with restrictions, supervision.

SAVE SÒ ⊠ ♿ 🛏 💻 🍽 ➤ ⊠

**◆ Ambassador Motel M**
(705) 759-6199. **$64-$99.** 1275 Great Northern Rd. 6.4 km n on Hwy 17. Ext corridors. **Pets:** Accepted.

⊠ 🖥 💻 ⇒ ⊠

**(CAA) ◆ Bel-Air Motel M**
(705) 945-7950. **$55-$99.** 398 Pim St. 2 km n on Hwy 17B. Ext corridors. **Pets:** $5 daily fee/pet. Designated rooms, no service.

SAVE S🖥 ⊠ 🖥 💻

**(CAA) ◆ Catalina Motel M**
(705) 945-9260. **$92-$114.** 259 Great Northern Rd. 3.2 km n on Hwy 17B. Ext corridors. **Pets:** Accepted.

SAVE S🖥 ⊠ 🖥 💻

**◆◆ Comfort Inn SH**
(705) 759-8000. **$96-$141.** 333 Great Northern Rd. 3.6 km n on Hwy 17B. Ext/int corridors. **Pets:** Large. $5 daily fee/pet. Service with restrictions, supervision.

ASK S🖥 ⊠ 🖥 💻

**◆◆ Glenview Cottages CA ❖**
(705) 759-3436. **$99-$150, 5 day notice.** 2611 Great Northern Rd. 9.6 km n on Hwy 17. Ext corridors. **Pets:** $5 daily fee/room. Designated rooms, crate.

ASK ⊠ 🖥 💻 ⇒ ⊠

**(CAA) ◆◆◆ Holiday Inn Sault Ste.**
**Marie-Waterfront SH ❖**
(705) 949-0611. **$119-$189.** 208 St. Marys River Dr. On the waterfront. Int corridors. **Pets:** Other species. Designated rooms, service with restrictions, crate.

SAVE S🖥 ⊠ 🖥 💻 ⵏ ⇒ ⊠

**◆ Holiday Motel M**
(705) 759-8608. **$50-$75.** 435 Trunk Rd. Jct Hwy 17 and 17B, just e. Ext corridors. **Pets:** Large. Service with restrictions, supervision.

⊠ 🖥 💻

**(CAA) ◆ Northlander Motel M**
(705) 254-6452. **$50-$85.** 243 Great Northern Rd. 3 km n on Hwy 17B. Ext corridors. **Pets:** Large. Service with restrictions, supervision.

SAVE S🖥 ⊠ 🖥 💻

**◆ Satelite Motel M**
(705) 759-2897. **$55-$95.** 248 Great Northern Rd. 3 km n on Hwy 17B. Ext corridors. **Pets:** Other species. $5 daily fee/room. Service with restrictions.

⊠ 🖥 💻

**(CAA) ◆ Skyline Motel M**
(705) 942-1240. **$60-$85.** 232 Great Northern Rd. 3 km n on Hwy 17B. Ext corridors. **Pets:** Very small, dogs only. $10 one-time fee/room. Designated rooms, service with restrictions, supervision.

SAVE S🖥 ⊠ 🖥 💻

**◆◆ Sleep Inn SH**
(705) 253-7533. **$79-$137.** 727 Bay St. Between East and Church sts; downtown. Int corridors. **Pets:** Accepted.

ASK S🖥 ⊠ 🖥 💻 ⊠

**(CAA) ◆◆◆ Super 8 SH**
(705) 254-6441. **$60-$130.** 184 Great Northern Rd. 2 km n on Hwy 17B. Int corridors. **Pets:** Large. $15 one-time fee/room. Service with restrictions, supervision.

SAVE S🖥 ⊠ 🖥 💻

**(CAA) ◆◆◆ Travelodge SH**
(705) 759-1400. **$109-$130, 45 day notice.** 332 Bay St. Opposite Station Mall. Int corridors. **Pets:** Small. Designated rooms, service with restrictions, supervision.

SAVE S🖥 ⊠ 🖥 💻 ⵏ

**◆◆ Villa Inn Motel M**
(705) 942-2424. **$49-$79.** 724 Great Northern Rd. 4.6 km n on Hwy 17B. Ext corridors. **Pets:** Accepted.

⊠ 🖥 💻

# SIMCOE

**◆◆ Comfort Inn SH**
(519) 426-2611. **$159-$169.** 85 Queensway E. 0.5 km e on Hwy 3. Int corridors. **Pets:** Other species. Designated rooms, service with restrictions, supervision.

ASK S🖥 ⊠ 🖥 💻

**◆◆ Travelodge Simcoe SH ❖**
(519) 426-4751. **$115.** 385 Queensway W (Hwy 3). 1 km w. Ext/int corridors. **Pets:** $10 daily fee/pet. Service with restrictions, supervision.

ASK S🖥 ⊠ 🖥 💻 ⇒ ⊠

# SMITHS FALLS

**◆◆ Best Western Colonel By Inn SH**
(613) 284-0001. **$69-$160.** 88 Lombard St. 1.2 km s on Hwy 15. Ext/int corridors. **Pets:** Accepted.

ASK S🖥 ⊠ 🖥 💻 ⵏ ⇒

**◆ Roger's Motel M**
(613) 283-5200. **$55-$85.** 178 Lombard St. 1.6 km s on Hwy 15. Ext corridors. **Pets:** Accepted.

ASK S🖥 ⊠ 🖥

# SOUTH BAYMOUTH

**◆ Huron Motor Lodge SH**
(705) 859-3131. **$75-$99.** 24 Water St N. In South Baymouth; centre; opposite ferry terminal dock. Ext corridors. **Pets:** $10 daily fee/pet. Designated rooms, supervision.

S🖥 ⊠ 🖥 ⇒ ⵝ 📠

# STRATFORD

**◆◆◆ Arden Park Hotel SH**
(519) 275-2936. **$129-$225.** 552 Ontario St. Jct Romeo St. Int corridors. **Pets:** Small, dogs only. Designated rooms, service with restrictions, supervision.

⊠ 🖥 💻 ⵏ ⇒

# SUDBURY

**(CAA) ◆◆ Best Western Downtown Sudbury**
**Centre-Ville SH**
(705) 673-7801. **$100-$110.** 151 Larch St. Centre. Int corridors. **Pets:** Other species. $25 one-time fee/pet. No service.

SAVE S🖥 ⊠ 💻

**◆◆ Comfort Inn SH**
(705) 522-1101. **$88-$145.** 2171 Regent St S. 5 km s on Hwy 46. Int corridors. **Pets:** Other species. Designated rooms, service with restrictions, supervision.

ASK S🖥 ⊠ 🖥 💻

**◆◆ Comfort Inn SH**
(705) 560-4502. **$90-$175.** 440 Second Ave N. Kingsway Hwy at Second Ave. Int corridors. **Pets:** Medium. Designated rooms, service with restrictions, supervision.

ASK S🖥 ⊠ 🖥M 🖥 💻

**◆◆ Days Inn Sudbury SH**
(705) 674-7517. **$120-$135.** 117 Elm St. Centre of downtown. Int corridors. **Pets:** Small. $10 daily fee/pet. Designated rooms, service with restrictions, supervision.

ASK S🖥 ⊠ 🖥 💻 ⵏ ⇒

◈ ▽▽▽▽ **Holiday Inn Hotel Sudbury** SH
(705) 522-3000. **$99-$205.** 1696 Regent St S. Hwy 69 (Regent St), just n of Paris St. Ext/int corridors. **Pets:** Medium. $25 daily fee/pet. Designated rooms, service with restrictions, supervision.
SAVE ⬛ ✕ ✎ 🛏 🖵 ⑪ 🏊 ⊠

◈ ▽▽ ▽▽ **Quality Inn & Conference Centre** SH
(705) 675-1273. **$89-$165.** 390 Elgin St S. Jct Kingsway Hwy and Paris St, 0.5 km s, just e. Int corridors. **Pets:** Medium. Designated rooms, service with restrictions, supervision.
SAVE ⬛ ✕ 🛏 🖵 ⑪ 🏊 ⊠

▽▽▽▽ **Radisson Hotel, Sudbury** SH
(705) 675-1123. **$110-$160.** 85 St. Anne Rd. Jct St. Anne Rd and Notre Dame Ave; downtown. Int corridors. **Pets:** Accepted.
ASK ⬛ ✕ 🛏 🖵 ⑪ 🏊

▽▽ **Travelodge Hotel Sudbury** SH ❀
(705) 522-1100. **$109-$159.** 1401 Paris St. 1.5 km n of jct Hwy 69 (Regent St). Int corridors. **Pets:** Large, other species. Designated rooms, service with restrictions, crate.
ASK ⬛ ✕ 🛏 🖵 ⑪ 🏊

## THESSALON

◈ ▽▽ **Carolyn Beach Motor Inn** M ❀
(705) 842-3330. **$79-$109.** 1 Lakeside Dr. Just w on Hwy 17; jct Hwy 17B. Ext corridors. **Pets:** $10 daily fee/pet. Service with restrictions, supervision.
SAVE ✕ 🛏 🖵 ⑪ ⊠

## THUNDER BAY

◈ ▽▽ ▽ **Best Western Crossroads Motor Inn** SH
(807) 577-4241. **$105-$114.** 655 W Arthur St. Jct Hwy 61, 17 and 11, just e. Int corridors. **Pets:** Medium, other species. $15 one-time fee/room. Designated rooms, service with restrictions, supervision.
SAVE ⬛ ✕ 🛏 🖵

◈ ▽▽ ▽ **Best Western Nor'Wester Resort Hotel** SH
(807) 473-9123. **$132-$162, 30 day notice.** 2080 Hwy 61. 9.2 km sw of jct Hwy 11, 17 and 61, exit Loch Lomond Rd. Int corridors. **Pets:** Medium. $20 one-time fee/pet. Service with restrictions, crate.
SAVE ⬛ ✕ 🛏 🖵 ⑪ 🏊 ⊠

▽▽ ▽▽ **Comfort Inn** M
(807) 475-3155. **$122-$152.** 660 W Arthur St. Jct Hwy 11, 17 and 61, just e. Int corridors. **Pets:** Accepted.
ASK ⬛ ✕ 🛏 🖵

◈ ▽▽ ▽ **Super 8 Motel** SH
(807) 344-2612. **$79-$85.** 439 Memorial Ave. Jct Hwy 11, 17 and Harbour Expwy, 3 km e on Harbour Expwy, 2 km n. Int corridors. **Pets:** Other species. $10 one-time fee/room. Designated rooms, service with restrictions, supervision.
SAVE ⬛ ✕ 🛏

▽▽ ▽ **Victoria Inn** SH
(807) 577-8481. **$105-$110.** 555 W Arthur St. 0.8 km e of jct Hwy 11B, 17B and 61 (western access to town). Int corridors. **Pets:** Other species. $10 daily fee/room. Service with restrictions, supervision.
ASK ⬛ ✕ 🛏 🖵 ⑪ 🏊 ⊠

## TILLSONBURG

◈ ▽▽ ▽ **Super 8 Motel-Tillsonburg** SH
(519) 842-7366. **$98-$129.** 92 Simcoe St. Hwy 19, just e. Int corridors. **Pets:** Other species. $10 daily fee/pet. Service with restrictions, crate.
SAVE ⬛ ✕ 🛏 🖵 ⑪

## TIMMINS

▽▽ ▽ **Comfort Inn** SH
(705) 264-9474. **$105, 30 day notice.** 939 Algonquin Blvd E. Hwy 101, 0.5 km e of Hwy 655. Int corridors. **Pets:** Accepted.
ASK ⬛ ✕ 🛏 🖵

## TOBERMORY

▽ **Coach House Inn** M
(519) 596-2361. **$59-$102.** 7189 Hwy 6. Hwy 6, 2 km s of ferry docks. Ext corridors. **Pets:** Accepted.
✕ 🛏 🏊 ⊠ ☎

---

# TORONTO METROPOLITAN AREA

## MARKHAM

◈ ▽▽▽▽ **Comfort Inn** SH
(905) 477-6077. **$108-$113.** 8330 Woodbine Ave. Hwy 401, exit 375, 9 km n; Hwy 404, exit Hwy 7, just e, then s. Int corridors. **Pets:** Accepted.
SAVE ⬛ ✕ 🛏 🖵 🏊 ⊠

◈ ▽▽▽▽ **Howard Johnson Hotel Toronto-Markham** SH
(905) 479-5000. **$99-$139.** 555 Cochrane Dr. Hwy 404 N, exit Hwy 7 E to E Valhalla Dr. Int corridors. **Pets:** Accepted.
ASK ⬛ ✕ 🛏 🖵 ⑪ 🏊 ⊠

◈ ▽▽▽▽ **Radisson Hotel Toronto-Markham** LH ❀
(905) 477-2010. **$109-$149.** 50 E Valhalla Dr. Hwy 404, exit Hwy 7, then e. Int corridors. **Pets:** Medium, other species. $25 one-time fee/room. Service with restrictions, crate.
SAVE ⬛ ✕ 🛏 🖵 ⑪ 🏊 ⊠

▽▽▽▽ **Residence Inn by Marriott** SH
(905) 707-7933. **$139-$169.** 55 Minthorn Blvd. Directly s of jct Hwy 7 and Leslie St. Int corridors. **Pets:** Accepted.
ASK ⬛ ✕ ✎ 🛏 🖵 🏊

▽▽▽▽ **Staybridge Suites Toronto-Markham** SH
(905) 771-9333. **$139-$209, 6 day notice.** 355 S Park Rd. Jct Hwy 404 and 7, w on Hwy 7, then e. Int corridors. **Pets:** Accepted.
ASK ⬛ ✕ ✎ 🛏 🖵 🏊

## RICHMOND HILL

◈ ▽▽▽▽ **Best Western Parkway Hotel Toronto North** SH
(905) 881-2600. **$105-$129.** 600 Hwy 7 E. Jct Hwy 401 and Don Valley Pkwy (Hwy 404), exit 375 via Don Valley Pkwy (Hwy 404), 8 km n to jct Hwy 7, then 1 km w. Int corridors. **Pets:** Accepted.
SAVE ⬛ ✕ 🛏 🖵 🏊 ⊠

## TORONTO

◈ ▽▽ ▽▽ **Cambridge Suites Hotel** LH
(416) 368-1990. **$199-$209.** 15 Richmond St E. Just e of Yonge St. Int corridors. **Pets:** Accepted.
SAVE ✕ ✎ 🛏 🖵 ⑪ ⊠

▽▽ ▽ **Carlingview Airport Inn** SH
(416) 675-3303. **$89-$169.** 221 Carlingview Dr. QEW, exit Hwy 427 N to Dixon Rd E, 1 km to Carlingview Dr, then just s. Ext/int corridors. **Pets:** Accepted.
ASK ⬛ ✕ 🛏 🖵 ⑪

▼▼▼▼ **Cawthra Square Inn** BB
(416) 966-0013. **$139-$319, 14 day notice.** 10 Cawthra Square. Directly w of Jarvis St. Int corridors. **Pets:** Accepted.
A$K S⚇ ⊠

▼▼ **Comfort Inn** SH ❖
(416) 736-4700. **$89-$149.** 66 Norfinch Dr. Hwy 400, exit Finch Ave E, just n. Int corridors **Pets:** Medium. Designated rooms, service with restrictions, supervision.
A$K S⚇ ⊠ ▤ ▦

CAA ▼▼▼▼ **Crowne Plaza Toronto Don Valley** LH ❖
(416) 449-4111. **$129-$219.** 1250 Eglinton Ave E. Don Valley Pkwy, exit 375 (Wynford Dr); jct Don Valley Pkwy and Eglinton Ave E. Int corridors. **Pets:** Medium. $20 daily fee/room. Designated rooms, service with restrictions, supervision.
SAVE ⊠ ⟨⟩ ▤ ▦ ¶¶ ⇌ ⊠

CAA ▼▼ **Days Hotel & Conference Centre-Toronto Downtown** LH
(416) 977-6655. **$90-$179.** 30 Carlton St. Adjacent to Maple Leaf Gardens. Int corridors. **Pets:** Accepted.
SAVE S⚇ ⊠ ▤ ▦ ¶¶ ⇌

CAA ▼▼ **Days Inn Toronto West Lakeshore** SH
(416) 532-9900. **$89-$149.** 14 Roncesvalles Ave. Jct King and Queen sts W and The Queensway. Int corridors. **Pets:** Accepted.
SAVE S⚇ ⊠ ▤ ▦

CAA ▼▼▼▼ **Delta Chelsea Hotel** LH ❖
(416) 595-1975. **$97-$205.** 33 Gerrard St W. Just w of Yonge St; just s of College St. Int corridors. **Pets:** Medium. $35 one-time fee/room. Service with restrictions, crate.
SAVE S⚇ ⊠ ▤ ▦ ¶¶ ⇌ ⊠

▼▼▼▼ **Delta Toronto East** LH
(416) 299-1500. **$139-$199.** 2035 Kennedy Rd. Just ne of jct Hwy 401 and Kennedy Rd, exit 379. Int corridors. **Pets:** Accepted.
⊠ ▤ ▦ ¶¶ ⇌ ⊠

CAA ▼▼▼▼ **DoubleTree International Plaza Hotel Toronto Airport** LH
(416) 244-1711. **$109-$259.** 655 Dixon Rd. Jct Hwy 27 N, just w of jct Hwy 401. Int corridors. **Pets:** Small. Service with restrictions, supervision.
SAVE ⊠ ⟨⟩ ▤ ▦ ¶¶ ⇌ ⊠

CAA ▼▼▼▼ **The Fairmont Royal York** LH
(416) 368-2511. **$170-$314.** 100 Front St W. QEW/Gardiner Expwy, exit n on York or Bay sts; entrance on Wellington St. Int corridors. **Pets:** Accepted.
SAVE S⚇ ⊠ ⟨M ▤ ▦ ¶¶ ⇌ ⊠

CAA ▼▼▼▼ **Four Seasons Hotel** LH ❖
(416) 964-0411. **$350-$570.** 21 Avenue Rd. Corner of Avenue Rd and Cumberland Ave. Int corridors. **Pets:** Small. Service with restrictions, supervision.
SAVE ⊠ ▤ ▦ ¶¶ ⇌ ⊠

▼▼▼▼ **Gloucester Square Inns of Toronto** BB
(416) 966-0013. **$139-$319, 14 day notice.** 512-514 Jarvis St. Jct Gloucester. Int corridors. **Pets:** Accepted.
A$K S⚇ ⊠

▼▼▼▼ **Hilton Toronto** LH
(416) 869-3456. **$149-$349, 3 day notice.** 145 Richmond St W. Jct University Ave. Int corridors. **Pets:** Accepted.
A$K ⊠ ⟨⟩ ▤ ▦ ¶¶ ⇌ ⊠

CAA ▼▼▼▼ **Holiday Inn Express Toronto Downtown** SH
(416) 367-5555. **$129-$199.** 111 Lombard St. West side of Jarvis St; between Adelaide and Richmond sts; 1 km n off Gardiner Expwy at Jarvis St exit. Int corridors. **Pets:** Medium. Service with restrictions, supervision.
SAVE S⚇ ⊠ ▤ ▦

CAA ▼▼▼▼ **Holiday Inn Toronto Midtown** SH
(416) 968-0010. **$139-$199.** 280 Bloor St W. Just w of St. George. Int corridors. **Pets:** Small. $25 daily fee/pet. Service with restrictions, supervision.
SAVE S⚇ ⊠ ▤ ▦ ¶¶

CAA ▼▼▼▼ **Holiday Inn Toronto On King (Downtown)** LH ❖
(416) 599-4000. **$199-$289.** 370 King St W. Between Spadina Ave and Peter St. Int corridors. **Pets:** Other species. Designated rooms, no service.
SAVE S⚇ ⊠ ⟨⟩ ▤ ▦ ¶¶ ⇌ ⊠

▼▼▼▼ **Hotel Le Germain** SH
(416) 345-9500. **$225-$395.** 30 Mercer St. Between John St and Blue Jays Way. Int corridors. **Pets:** Accepted.
⊠ ▤ ▦ ¶¶

CAA ▼▼▼▼ **InterContinental Toronto** LH ❖
(416) 960-5200. **$225-$2000, 3 day notice.** 220 Bloor St W. Just w of Avenue Rd. Int corridors. **Pets:** Medium. $50 one-time fee/room. Designated rooms, service with restrictions, supervision.
SAVE S⚇ ⊠ ▤ ▦ ¶¶ ⇌ ⊠

▼▼▼▼ **Le Royal Meridien King Edward Hotel** LH ❖
(416) 863-3131. **$200-$400.** 37 King St E. Just e of Yonge St. Int corridors. **Pets:** Small, other species.
A$K ⊠

CAA ▼▼▼▼ **Metropolitan Hotel** LH ❖
(416) 977-5000. **$139-$269.** 108 Chestnut St. Just s of Dundas St. Int corridors. **Pets:** Medium, other species. $10 daily fee/room, $25 one-time fee/room. Designated rooms, service with restrictions, supervision.
SAVE S⚇ ⊠ ▤ ▦ ¶¶ ⇌ ⊠

▼▼▼ **Montecassino Hotel & Suites** SH
(416) 630-8100. **$99-$119.** 3710 Chesswood Dr. On Chesswood Dr at Sheppard Ave. Int corridors. **Pets:** Small. Designated rooms, service with restrictions, supervision.
A$K S⚇ ⊠ ▤ ▦ ¶¶

CAA ▼▼▼▼ **Novotel Toronto Centre** LH ❖
(416) 367-8900. **$149-$229.** 45 The Esplanade. Just ne of Gardiner Expwy via Yonge St. Int corridors. **Pets:** Other species. Service with restrictions.
SAVE ⊠ ▤ ▦ ⇌ ⊠

CAA ▼▼▼ **Novotel Toronto North York** LH
(416) 733-2929. **$139-$144.** 3 Park Home Ave. Hwy 401, exit Yonge St, 1 km n, then just w. Int corridors. **Pets:** Accepted.
SAVE ⊠ ▤ ▦ ¶¶ ⇌

CAA ▼▼▼ **Quality Hotel & Suites Toronto Airport East** SH
(416) 240-9090. **$129-$159.** 2180 Islington Ave. Hwy 401, exit 356. Int corridors. **Pets:** $15 daily fee/pet. Designated rooms, service with restrictions, supervision.
SAVE S⚇ ⊠ ▤ ▦ ¶¶

CAA ▼▼▼▼ **Quality Suites Toronto Airport** LH
(416) 674-8442. **$97-$159.** 262 Carlingview Dr. 1 km w of jct Hwy 27 N and Dixon Rd. Int corridors. **Pets:** Accepted.
SAVE S⚇ ⊠ ▤ ▦ ¶¶

CAA ▼▼▼▼ **Radisson Hotel Toronto East** LH
(416) 493-7000. **$119-$159.** 55 Hallcrown Pl. Hwy 401, exit Victoria Park N to Consumers Rd, then w. Int corridors. **Pets:** Designated rooms, service with restrictions, crate.
SAVE ⊠ ⟨M ⟨⟩ ▤ ▦ ¶¶ ⇌

CAA ▼▼▼▼ **Radisson Suite Hotel Toronto Airport** LH
(416) 242-7400. **$129-$189.** 640 Dixon Rd. Just e of jct Hwy 27; 0.3 km w of jct Hwy 401. Int corridors. **Pets:** Service with restrictions, crate.
SAVE S⚇ ⊠ ▦ ¶¶

Ⓐ ▼▼▼▼ **Ramada Hotel Toronto Airport** 🄻🄷
(416) 621-2121. **$109-$129.** 2 Holiday Dr. Hwy 427, exit Holiday Dr southbound; exit Burnhamthorpe Rd northbound. Int corridors. **Pets:** Other species. $10 daily fee/room. Designated rooms, service with restrictions, supervision.
🅂🄰🄴 🆂🄳 ☒ 🄴 💻 🍴 ⇒ ☒

Ⓐ ▼▼▼▼ **Ramada Hotel-Toronto Centre** 🄻🄷
(416) 493-9000. **$99-$115.** 185 Yorkland Blvd. Just s of Sheppard Ave. Int corridors. **Pets:** Accepted.
🅂🄰🄴 🆂🄳 ☒ 🄴 💻 🍴 ⇒

Ⓐ ▼▼▼ ▼▼▼ **Renaissance Toronto Airport Hotel** 🄻🄷
(416) 675-6100. **$119-$249.** 801 Dixon Rd. Jct Hwy 27 N and Dixon Rd. Int corridors. **Pets:** Accepted.
🅂🄰🄴 ☒ 🄴🄼 🄰 🄴 🄴 💻 🍴 ⇒

▼▼▼ ▼▼▼ **Residence Inn by Marriott Toronto Airport** 🅂🄷
(416) 798-2900. **$119-$315.** 17 Reading Ct. Just w of jct Hwy 27 and Dixon Rd. Int corridors. **Pets:** Accepted.
🄰🅂🄺 🆂🄳 ☒ 🄴 💻 ⇒ ☒

Ⓐ ▼▼▼ ▼▼▼ **The Sheraton Centre Toronto Hotel** 🄻🄷
(416) 361-1000. **$320-$389, 3 day notice.** 123 Queen St W. Opposite Toronto Civic Centre and City Hall. Int corridors. **Pets:** Accepted.
🅂🄰🄴 ☒ 🄴🄼 🄴 💻 🍴 ⇒ ☒

Ⓐ ▼▼▼ ▼▼▼ **SoHo Metropolitan Hotel** 🅂🄷 ☙
(416) 599-8800. **$385-$725.** 318 Wellington St W. Jct Blue Jays Way. Int corridors. **Pets:** Small, dogs only. Service with restrictions, crate.
🅂🄰🄴 ☒ 🄴 💻 🍴 ⇒ ☒

Ⓐ ▼▼▼ ▼▼▼ **The Sutton Place Hotel** 🄻🄷
(416) 924-9221. **$149-$400.** 955 Bay St. Jct Wellesley St. Int corridors. **Pets:** Accepted.
🅂🄰🄴 ☒ 🄴 💻 🍴 ⇒ ☒

▼▼▼ ▼▼▼ **Toronto Airport Marriott Hotel** 🄻🄷
(416) 674-9400. **$109-$259.** 901 Dixon Rd. Corner of Dixon Rd and Carlingview Dr. Int corridors. **Pets:** Accepted.
🄰🅂🄺 ☒ 🄴🄼 🄴 💻 🍴 ⇒ ☒

▼▼▼ ▼▼▼ **Toronto Marriott Downtown Eaton Centre** 🄻🄷
(416) 597-9200. **$169-$299.** 525 Bay St. Just s of Dundas St. Int corridors. **Pets:** Accepted.
🄰🅂🄺 ☒ 🄴🄼 🄴 💻 🍴 ⇒ ☒

Ⓐ ▼▼▼ ▼▼▼ **Travelodge Hotel Toronto Airport (Dixon Road)** 🅂🄷
(416) 674-2222. **$99-$169.** 925 Dixon Rd. Corner of Carlingview Dr and Dixon Rd. Int corridors. **Pets:** $25 one-time fee/room. Designated rooms, service with restrictions, supervision.
🅂🄰🄴 🆂🄳 ☒ 🄴 💻 🍴 ⇒ ☒

▼▼▼ ▼▼▼ **Travelodge Toronto East** 🅂🄷 ☙
(416) 299-9500. **$99-$119.** 20 Milner Business Ct. Jct Hwy 401 and Markham Rd, just n on Markham Rd. In corridors. **Pets:** Large. Service with restrictions, supervision.
🄰🅂🄺 🆂🄳 ☒ 🄴 💻 🍴 ⇒

Ⓐ ▼▼▼ ▼▼▼ **The Westin Harbour Castle** 🄻🄷 ☙
(416) 869-1600. **$149-$329.** One Harbour Sq. At the foot of Bay St; on shore of Lake Ontario. Int corridors. **Pets:** Medium, dogs only. Service with restrictions, supervision.
🅂🄰🄴 🆂🄳 ☒ 💻 🍴 ⇒ ☒

▼▼▼ ▼▼▼ **Windsor Arms Hotel** 🅂🄷 ☙
(416) 971-9666. **$275-$2000.** 18 St. Thomas St. Jct Bloor St. Int corridors. **Pets:** Medium. Supervision.
🄰🅂🄺 ☒ 🍴 ⇒ ☒

Ⓐ ▼▼▼ ▼▼▼ **Wyndham Bristol Place-Toronto Airport** 🄻🄷
(416) 675-9444. **$125-$215.** 950 Dixon Rd. 3 km w of jct Hwy 401. Int corridors. **Pets:** Accepted.
🅂🄰🄴 ☒ 🄰 🄴 💻 🍴 ⇒

---

## END METROPOLITAN AREA

## TRENTON

▼▼▼ ▼▼ **Comfort Inn** 🅂🄷
(613) 965-6660. **$109-$139.** 68 Monogram Pl. Hwy 401, exit 526 (Glen Miller Rd S). Int corridors. **Pets:** Accepted.
🄰🅂🄺 🆂🄳 ☒ 🄴🄼 🄴 💻

Ⓐ ▼▼▼ ▼▼ **Holiday Inn Trenton** 🅂🄷
(613) 394-4855. **$102-$125.** 99 Glen Miller Rd. Hwy 401, exit 526 (Glen Miller Rd S). Int corridors. **Pets:** Other species. $5 daily fee/pet. Designated rooms, service with restrictions, supervision.
🅂🄰🄴 🆂🄳 ☒ 🄴 💻 🍴 ⇒ ☒

## TWEED

▼▼ **Park Place Motel** 🄼
(613) 478-3134. **$60.** 43 Victoria St. Hwy 37, 0.5 km s of centre. Ext corridors. **Pets:** Other species. Service with restrictions.
🄰🅂🄺 ☒ 🄴 💻

## WALLACEBURG

▼▼ **Super 8 Motel** 🅂🄷
(519) 627-0781. **$69-$99.** 76 McNaughton Ave. On Hwy 40 (McNaughton Ave), south side of town. Int corridors. **Pets:** Accepted.
☒ 🄴

## WASAGA BEACH

▼▼ **Kingsbridge Inn** 🄼
(705) 429-6364. **$60-$200.** 268 Main St. Hwy 92, just n. Ext corridors. **Pets:** Accepted.
☒ 🄴 💻 ⇒ ☒ 🄌

## WATERLOO

▼▼ ▼▼ **Comfort Inn** 🅂🄷
(519) 747-9400. **$109-$159.** 190 Weber St N. East side off Weber St; 0.3 km s of Hwy 86. Int corridors. **Pets:** Other species. Service with restrictions, supervision.
🄰🅂🄺 🆂🄳 ☒ 🄴 💻 🍴

▼▼▼ ▼▼ **Les Diplomates B&B (Executive Guest House)** 🄱🄱
(519) 725-3184. **$116-$156.** 100 Blythwood Rd. Hwy 85 N, exit King St, s to Columbia, w to Hazel St, then e. Ext/int corridors. **Pets:** Medium. $18 daily fee/pet. Designated rooms, service with restrictions, supervision.
🄰🅂🄺 🆂🄳 ☒ 🄴 💻

▼▼▼ ▼▼ **The Waterloo Inn & Conference Centre** 🅂🄷
(519) 884-0220. **$149-$199.** 475 King St N. 3 km n on King St, jct Hwy 85. Int corridors. **Pets:** Large, cats only. $15 daily fee/pet. Designated rooms, service with restrictions, supervision.
🄰🅂🄺 🆂🄳 ☒ 🄴 💻 🍴 ⇒ ☒

# WAWA

### ◈ Kinniwabi Pines Motel/Cottages M
(705) 856-7302. **$68-$89.** 106 Hwy 17. Hwy 17, 5.3 km s of jct Hwy 101. Ext corridors. **Pets:** Accepted.

⊠ 🖃 🖃 ⊠ 🖾

### ◈ Parkway Motel M
(705) 856-7020. **$65-$85.** 120 Hwy 17. Hwy 17, 4 km s of jct Hwy 101. Ext corridors. **Pets:** Other species. $10 daily fee/room. Service with restrictions, supervision.

⊠ 🖃 🖃 🖾

### ◈ Sportsman's Motel M
(705) 856-2272. **$80-$90.** 45 Mission Rd. Hwy 101, 2.4 km e of jct Hwy 17. Ext corridors. **Pets:** Accepted.

⊠ 🖃 🖃 🖾

### Ⓐ ◈ Wawa Northern Lights Motel & Chalets M
(705) 856-1900. **$79-$109.** 237 Hwy 17. On Hwy 17, 8 km n of jct Hwy 101. Ext corridors. **Pets:** Other species. Service with restrictions, supervision.

SAVE ⊠ 🖃 🖃 🖾 🖾

# WHITBY

### ◈◈ Motel 6 #1907 SH
(905) 665-8883. **$73-$91.** 165 Consumers Dr. Hwy 401, exit 410 (Brock St/Hwy 12), just ne. Int corridors. **Pets:** Accepted.

🖾 ⊠ 🖾 🖃

### Ⓐ ◈◈ Quality Suites SH
(905) 432-8800. **$149-$219.** 1700 Champlain Ave. Hwy 401, exit 412 (Thickson Rd), 0.5 km n to Champlain Ave, then 1 km e. Int corridors. **Pets:** Accepted.

SAVE 🖾 ⊠ 🖃 🖃

### ◈◈◈ Residence Inn by Marriott SH ❖
(905) 444-9756. **$139-$229, 7 day notice.** 160 Consumers Dr. Hwy 401, exit 410 (Brock St/Hwy 12). Int corridors. **Pets:** $75 one-time fee/room. Service with restrictions, crate.

ASK 🖾 ⊠ 🖾 🖾 🖃 🖃 🖾

# WHITEFISH FALLS

### ◈◈◈ The Island Lodge ⒸⒶ
(705) 285-4343. **$140.** In Whitefish Falls; parking and dock, just w of Hwy 6 (phone for boat at Espanola or Little Current). Ext corridors. **Pets:** Large, other species. $20 daily fee/pet.

🖃 🖃 🖾 ⊠ 🖾 🖾 🖾

# WINDSOR

### ◈◈ Comfort Inn SH
(519) 966-7800. **$108-$159.** 2955 Dougall Ave. 5.3 km s on Hwy 3B, off Hwy 401 via Detroit-Windsor Tunnel exit. Int corridors. **Pets:** Medium, other species. $10 daily fee/pet. Designated rooms, service with restrictions, supervision.

ASK 🖾 ⊠ 🖃 🖃

### ◈◈ Comfort Inn SH
(519) 972-1331. **$95-$165.** 2765 Huron Church Rd. West side of Huron Church Rd; 0.8 km s of EC Row Expwy. Int corridors. **Pets:** Medium. $10 daily fee/room. Service with restrictions, supervision.

ASK 🖾 ⊠ 🖃 🖃 🖾

### ◈◈◈ Hampton Inn and Suites SH ❖
(519) 972-0770. **$139-$169.** 1840 Huron Church Rd. 1.5 km n of EC Row Expwy. Int corridors. **Pets:** Large. $20 one-time fee/pet. Designated rooms, service with restrictions, supervision.

ASK 🖾 ⊠ 🖃 🖃 🖾

### ◈◈◈ Hilton Windsor LH
(519) 973-5555. **$129-$199.** 277 Riverside Dr W. 1 km w of Detroit-Windsor Tunnel; 1 km e of Ambassador Bridge; downtown. Int corridors. **Pets:** $50 one-time fee/room. Service with restrictions, crate.

ASK 🖾 ⊠ 🖾 🖾

### Ⓐ ◈◈◈ Holiday Inn Select Windsor (Ambassador Bridge) LH ❖
(519) 966-1200. **$126.** 1855 Huron Church Rd. Jct Huron Church and Malden rds; 1.5 km n of EC Row Expwy. Int corridors. **Pets:** Other species. Service with restrictions.

SAVE 🖾 ⊠ 🖃 🖃 🖾 🖾 🖾

### Ⓐ ◈◈◈ Ivy Rose Motor Inn Ltd. M
(519) 966-1700. **$69-$150.** 2885 Howard Ave. 4.8 km s of downtown; just n of Devonshire Shopping Mall. Ext corridors. **Pets:** Accepted.

SAVE 🖾 ⊠ 🖃 🖾 🖾

### Ⓐ ◈◈◈ Quality Suites Windsor SH ❖
(519) 977-9707. **$129-$249.** 250 Dougall Ave. Jct Dougall Ave and Chatham St; downtown. Int corridors. **Pets:** Other species. $50 one-time fee/room. Service with restrictions, supervision.

SAVE 🖾 ⊠ 🖾 🖃 🖃 🖾

### ◈◈◈ Radisson Riverfront Hotel LH ❖
(519) 977-9777. **$119-$189.** 333 Riverside Dr W. 1 km w of Detroit-Windsor Tunnel; 1 km e of Ambassador Bridge. Int corridors. **Pets:** Other species. $50 one-time fee/room. Service with restrictions, supervision.

ASK 🖾 ⊠ 🖃 🖃 🖾 🖾 🖾

### ◈◈◈ Royal Marquis Hotel SH
(519) 966-1900. **$100-$120, 7 day notice.** 590 Grand Marais Rd E. Just n of Devonshire Mall and EC Row Expwy. Int corridors. **Pets:** Accepted.

⊠ 🖃 🖃 🖾 🖾 🖾

### Ⓐ ◈◈◈ Travelodge Windsor Ambassador Bridge SH
(519) 972-1100. **$88-$185.** 2330 Huron Church Rd. N of EC Row Expwy. Int corridors. **Pets:** $25 deposit/room. Designated rooms, service with restrictions, supervision.

SAVE 🖾 ⊠ 🖃 🖃 🖾 🖾

# WOODSTOCK

### Ⓐ ◈◈◈ Quality Hotel and Suites SH
(519) 537-5586. **$89-$199.** 580 Bruin Blvd. Hwy 401, exit 232, just n; w of Hwy 59. Int corridors. **Pets:** Service with restrictions, supervision.

SAVE 🖾 ⊠ 🖃 🖃 🖾 🖾 🖾

### ◈◈ Super 8 Motel SH
(519) 421-4588. **$76-$93.** 560 Norwich Ave. Jct Hwy 401 and 59, exit 232, just n. Int corridors. **Pets:** Accepted.

ASK 🖾 ⊠ 🖃 🖃

# WYOMING

### ◈◈ Country View Motel and RV Camping Resort M
(519) 845-3394. **$59-$94.** 4569 London Line. Hwy 402, exit 25, 1 km s on Hwy 21 to Hwy 22, then just e. Ext corridors. **Pets:** Small. $20 one-time fee/pet. Designated rooms, service with restrictions, supervision.

⊠ 🖃 🖾 🖾

# PRINCE EDWARD ISLAND

## CAVENDISH

**▽▽▽▽ Bay Vista Motor Inn** Ⓜ
(902) 963-2225. **$53-$97.** 9517 Cavendish Rd. Jct Rt 13, 4.8 km w on Rt 6. Ext corridors. **Pets:** Small. Service with restrictions, supervision.
⊠ 🛢 ⇌ ☎

**▽▽▽▽ Cavendish Bosom Buddies Cottages** Ⓒ🄰
(902) 963-3449. **$80-$280, 14 day notice.** RR 1. Jct Rt 6 and 13, 0.6 km e on Rt 6. Ext corridors. **Pets:** Large, other species. Supervision.
(ASK) ⊠ 🛢 ⬛ 🄺 ☎

**Ⓒ🄰 ▽▽▽▽ Cavendish Maples Cottages** Ⓒ🄰
(902) 963-2818. **$70-$280, 30 day notice.** Jct Rt 6 and 13, 2.5 km w on Rt 6. Ext corridors. **Pets:** Accepted.
(SAVE) ⊠ 🛢 ⬛ ⇌ ⊠ ☎

## CHARLOTTETOWN

**Ⓒ🄰 ▽▽▽ Best Western Charlottetown** 🆂🅷
(902) 892-2461. **$112-$174.** 238 Grafton St. Centre. Int corridors. **Pets:** Designated rooms, service with restrictions, supervision.
(SAVE) 🆂🄾 ⊠ 🅶🄼 📶 🄺 🛢 ⬛ 🍴 ⇌ ⊠

**▽▽▽ Comfort Inn** 🆂🅷 🐾
(902) 566-4424. **$105-$165.** 112 Trans-Canada Hwy 1. Trans-Canada Hwy 1, 4.5 km w. Int corridors. **Pets:** Other species. Service with restrictions, supervision.
(ASK) 🆂🄾 ⊠ ⬛

**▽▽▽▽ Delta Prince Edward** 🄻🅷
(902) 566-2222. **$129-$289.** 18 Queen St. At Water and Queen sts. Int corridors. **Pets:** Accepted.
(ASK) 🆂🄾 ⊠ 🛢 ⬛ 🍴 ⇌ ⊠

**▽▽▽▽ Econo Lodge** Ⓜ 🐾
(902) 368-1110. **$89-$189.** 20 Lower Malpeque Rd. Jct Trans-Canada Hwy 1 and Lower Malpeque Rd, 4.5 km w. Ext/int corridors. **Pets:** Medium, other species. Service with restrictions, supervision.
(ASK) 🆂🄾 ⊠ 🛢 ⬛ ⇌

**Ⓒ🄰 ▽▽▽▽ Holiday Inn Express Hotel & Suites Charlottetown** 🆂🅷 🐾
(902) 892-1201. **$94-$262.** 200 Trans-Canada Hwy. On Trans-Canada Hwy 1, 4.8 km w. Int corridors. **Pets:** Other species.
(SAVE) 🆂🄾 ⊠ 🅶🄼 🄺 🛢 ⬛ ⇌

**▽▽▽▽ Quality Inn on the Hill** 🆂🅷
(902) 894-8572. **$119-$259.** 150 Euston St. Just e of University Ave. Int corridors. **Pets:** Accepted.
(ASK) 🆂🄾 ⊠ 🛢 ⬛ 🍴

**▽▽▽▽ Rodd Charlottetown-A Rodd Signature Hotel** 🆂🅷
(902) 894-7371. **$106-$244.** 75 Kent St. Corner of Kent and Pownal sts. Int corridors. **Pets:** Other species. $10 one-time fee/room. Designated rooms, supervision.
(ASK) 🆂🄾 ⊠ 🛢 ⬛ 🍴 ⇌ ⊠

**▽▽▽▽ Rodd Confederation Inn & Suites** Ⓜ
(902) 892-2481. **$74-$154.** Trans-Canada Hwy 1. On Trans-Canada Hwy 1, 4 km w. Ext/int corridors. **Pets:** Other species. $10 one-time fee/room. Designated rooms, supervision.
(ASK) 🆂🄾 ⊠ 🛢 ⬛ 🍴 ⇌

**▽▽▽▽ Rodd Royalty Inn** 🆂🅷
(902) 894-8566. **$92-$180.** Intersection Hwy 1 & 2. 4 km w on Trans-Canada Hwy 1. Ext/int corridors. **Pets:** Medium. Designated rooms, service with restrictions.
(ASK) 🆂🄾 ⊠ 🛢 ⬛ 🍴 ⇌

## CORNWALL

**▽▽▽ Sunny King Motel** Ⓜ
(902) 566-2209. **$49-$116, 3 day notice.** On Hwy 1; centre. Ext corridors. **Pets:** Accepted.
(ASK) 🆂🄾 ⊠ 🛢 ⬛ ⇌ 🄺

## MAYFIELD

**▽▽▽▽ Cavendish Gateway Resort by Clarion Collection** Ⓜ
(902) 963-2213. **$89-$179.** Rt 13. On Rt 13, 6 km w of Cavendish; centre. Ext/int corridors. **Pets:** Small, dogs only. Service with restrictions, supervision.
(ASK) 🆂🄾 ⊠ 🛢 ⬛ ⇌

## NORTH RUSTICO

**▽▽▽ St. Lawrence Motel** Ⓜ
(902) 963-2053. **$45-$149, 14 day notice.** 351 Gulf Shore Rd. On RR 2. Ext corridors. **Pets:** Accepted.
⊠ 🛢 ⬛ 🄺 ☎

## RICHMOND

**▽▽▽▽ Caernarvon Cottages, B&B and Gardens** Ⓒ🄰
(902) 854-3418. **$100, 30 day notice.** 4697 Hwy 12, RR 1. Jct Hwy 2 and Rt 131, 10 km e. Ext/int corridors. **Pets:** Accepted.
🛢 ⬛ 🄺

## ROSENEATH

**▽▽▽▽ Rodd Brudenell River-A Rodd Signature Resort** 🄻🅷
(902) 652-2332. **$127-$239, 3 day notice.** Jct Rt 4 and 3, 5.5 km e on Rt 3. Ext/int corridors. **Pets:** Accepted.
(ASK) 🆂🄾 ⊠ 🛢 ⬛ 🍴 ⇌ ⊠

## ST. PETERS

**▽▽▽▽ Greenwich Gate Lodge** Ⓜ
(902) 961-3496. **$79-$119, 7 day notice.** Rt 2. Jct Rt 2 and 16; centre. Ext corridors. **Pets:** Accepted.
(ASK) 🆂🄾 ⊠ 🛢 ⬛

**Ⓒ🄰 ▽▽▽▽ The Inn at St. Peters** 🄲🄸
(902) 961-2135. **$315-$390, 7 day notice.** 1668 Greenwich Rd. Jct Rt 16 and 313, 1 km w on Rt 313. Ext corridors. **Pets:** Service with restrictions.
(SAVE) 🆂🄾 ⊠ 🅶🄼 🛢 ⬛ 🍴

## SUMMERSIDE

**▽▽▽ Econo Lodge** 🆂🅷
(902) 436-9100. **$85-$125.** 80 All Weather Hwy. Jct Hwy 1A and 2, 5 km w on Hwy 2. Int corridors. **Pets:** Dogs only. Designated rooms, service with restrictions, supervision.
(ASK) 🆂🄾 ⊠ 🛢 ⬛ 🍴 ⇌

**Ⓒ🄰 ▽▽▽ Quality Inn Garden of the Gulf** Ⓜ
(902) 436-2295. **$84-$189.** 618 Water St. 1.6 km e on Hwy 11. Ext/int corridors. **Pets:** Designated rooms, service with restrictions.
(SAVE) 🆂🄾 ⊠ 🛢 ⬛ ⇌

## WOODSTOCK

**▽▽▽ Rodd Mill River Resort** 🆂🅷
(902) 859-3555. **$89-$207, 3 day notice.** Rt 180. On Rt 136, just e of jct Rt 2. Int corridors. **Pets:** Accepted.
(ASK) 🆂🄾 ⊠ 🛢 ⬛ 🍴 ⇌ ⊠

# QUEBEC

## ALMA

 Comfort Inn SH
(418) 668-9221. **$86-$106, 30 day notice.** 870 ave du Pont S. On Hwy 169; centre of town. Int corridors. **Pets:** Accepted.

(ASK) (S) (X) (T)

Hotel Motel Les Cascades M
(418) 662-6547. **$60-$150.** 140 ave du Pont N. On Hwy 169, just n of bridge; centre. Ext/int corridors. **Pets:** Accepted.

(ASK) (S) (X) (T) (D) (I)

## BAIE-COMEAU

Comfort Inn SH
(418) 589-8252. **$111-$129.** 745 boul Lafleche. On Rt 138. Int corridors. **Pets:** Service with restrictions, crate.

(ASK) (S) (X) (T) (D)

Hotel Le Manoir SH
(418) 296-3391. **$99.** 8 ave Cabot. Rt 138, 4.4 km e, follow signs. Int corridors. **Pets:** Accepted.

(ASK) (S) (X) (D) (I) (X)

## BERTHIERVILLE

Days Inn Berthierville SH
(450) 836-1621. **$89-$165.** 760 rue Gadoury. Hwy 40, exit 144. Ext/int corridors. **Pets:** Designated rooms, service with restrictions, supervision.

(ASK) (S) (X) (T) (D)

## BROMONT

Hotel Le Menhir SH
(450) 534-3790. **$98-$195.** 125 boul Bromont. Hwy 10, exit 78, 2.7 km s. Ext/int corridors. **Pets:** $15 daily fee/pet. Service with restrictions, supervision.

(X) (T) (D) (I) (D)

## CARLETON-SAINT-OMER

Hostellerie Baie Bleue M
(418) 364-3355. **$73-$181.** 482 boul Perron. On Hwy 132. Ext corridors. **Pets:** Very small. Service with restrictions, supervision.

(X) (T) (D) (I) (D) (X) (AC)

## CHICOUTIMI

Comfort Inn SH
(418) 693-8686. **$85-$112.** 1595 boul Talbot. Jct Rt 170, 2.8 km n. Int corridors. **Pets:** Accepted.

(ASK) (S) (X) (T) (D)

Hotel La Sagueneenne SH ᵖ
(418) 545-8326. **$109-$162.** 250 des Sagueneens. Just w of jct Rt 175 (boul Talbot). Int corridors. **Pets:** Small. $200 deposit/room. Service with restrictions, crate.

(ASK) (S) (X) (M) (L) (T) (D) (I) (D) (X)

## COWANSVILLE

Days Inn-Cowansville SH
(450) 263-7331. **$67-$105.** 111 place Jean-Jacques Bertrand. Hwy 10, exit 68, 15.9 km s on Rt 139. Int corridors. **Pets:** $15 one-time fee/room. Service with restrictions, supervision.

(ASK) (S) (X) (T) (D) (I)

## DRUMMONDVILLE

(CAA) Best Western Hotel Universel SH
(819) 478-4971. **$99-$409.** 915 rue Hains. Hwy 20, exit 177, 0.3 km s on boul St-Joseph, then just e. Int corridors. **Pets:** Medium. $15 daily fee/room. Service with restrictions, supervision.

(SAVE) (S) (X) (T) (D) (I) (D)

Comfort Inn SH
(819) 477-4000. **$91-$115.** 1055 rue Hains. Hwy 20, exit 177, 0.5 km s on boul St-Joseph, then just w. Int corridors. **Pets:** Designated rooms, service with restrictions, supervision.

(ASK) (S) (X) (T) (D)

Quality Suites SH
(819) 472-2700. **$110-$160.** 2125 rue Canadien. Hwy 20, exit 175, just s. Int corridors. **Pets:** $100 deposit/room. Designated rooms, supervision.

(ASK) (S) (X) (T) (D) (D)

## GATINEAU

(CAA) Clarion Hotel & Conference Center SH
(819) 568-5252. **$109-$122.** 111 rue Bellehumeur. Hwy 50, exit 139, 1.6 km se on boul Maloney ouest (Hwy 148), then just sw. Int corridors. **Pets:** Accepted.

(SAVE) (S) (X) (T) (D) (I) (D) (X)

(CAA) Comfort Inn Gatineau SH
(819) 243-6010. **$106-$155.** 630 boul La Gappe. Hwy 50, exit 140, 2 km e. Int corridors. **Pets:** Other species. Designated rooms, service with restrictions, supervision.

(SAVE) (S) (X) (D)

(CAA) Four Points by Sheraton & Conference Centre Gatineau-Ottawa LH
(819) 778-6111. **$99-$195.** 35 rue Laurier. Corner of rue Victoria, across from Canadian Museum of Civilization; in Hull sector. Int corridors. **Pets:** Medium. Service with restrictions, crate.

(SAVE) (S) (X) (T) (D) (I) (D)

(CAA) Holiday Inn Plaza La Chaudiere Gatineau-Ottawa LH ᵖ
(819) 778-3880. **$100-$130.** 2 rue Montcalm. 0.8 km w of Portage Bridge at Rt 148 and rue Montcalm; in Hull sector. Int corridors. **Pets:** $35 one-time fee/room. Service with restrictions, supervision.

(SAVE) (S) (X) (T) (D) (I) (D) (X)

## GRENVILLE-SUR-LA-ROUGE

Ⓐ ▼▼▼▼ Hotel du Lac Carling 🄻🄷
(450) 533-9211. **$225-$250, 15 day notice.** 2255 Rt 327 nord. 5 km n.
Int corridors. **Pets:** Accepted.

(SAVE) 🆂🄳 🗙 🄱 🖃 🍴 🏊 🛇

## LAC-BROME (KNOWLTON)

▼▼▼▼ Auberge Knowlton 🄲🄸
(450) 242-6886. **$110-$120.** 286 chemin Knowlton. Corner of Hwy 104
and Rt 243; centre. Int corridors. **Pets:** Service with restrictions, supervision.

🗙 🍴 🄀

## LA MALBAIE

Ⓐ ▼▼▼▼ Fairmont Le Manoir Richelieu 🄻🄷
(418) 665-3703. **$143-$251.** 181 rue Richelieu. On Rt 362, 4.1 km w of
jct Rt 138. Int corridors. **Pets:** Small. $25 daily fee/pet. Service with
restrictions, supervision.

(SAVE) 🆂🄳 🗙 🄱 🖃 🍴 🏊 🛇

## LA POCATIERE

▼▼ ▼▼ Motel Le Pocatois 🄼
(418) 856-1688. **$63-$90.** 235 Rt 132. Hwy 20, exit 439, 0.8 km s.
Ext/int corridors. **Pets:** Accepted.

🗙 🄱 🍴

## LENNOXVILLE

Ⓐ ▼ La Paysanne Motel & Hotel 🄼
(819) 569-5585. **$77-$97.** 42 rue Queen. On Rt 143. Ext/int corridors.
**Pets:** Accepted.

(SAVE) 🆂🄳 🗙 🄱 🍴 🏊

## L'ISLET

▼▼▼▼ Auberge La Paysanne 🄲🄾
(418) 247-7276. **$70-$120.** 497 des Pionniers est. On Rt 132, 4.2 km e,
jct Rt 285; centre. Ext corridors. **Pets:** Accepted.

🆂🄳 🗙 🄱 🖃 🄀

## LOUISEVILLE

▼▼▼▼ Gite du Carrefour et Maison historique J.L.L.
   Hamelin 🄱🄱
(819) 228-4932. **$75-$85 (no credit cards), 15 day notice.** 11 ave
St-Laurent ouest. On Rt 138; Hwy 40, exit 174 westbound; exit 166
eastbound; centre. Int corridors. **Pets:** No service, supervision.

🗙 🄀 🅦 🚷

## MARIA

▼▼ ▼▼ Hotel Honguedo 🅂🄷
(418) 759-3488. **$84-$147.** 548 boul Perron. On Rt 132, in town centre.
Ext/int corridors. **Pets:** Accepted.

(A$K) 🆂🄳 🗙 🄱 🖃 🍴 🏊

## MATANE

Ⓐ ▼ Motel La Marina 🄼
(418) 562-3234. **$52-$77.** 1032 ave du Phare ouest. On Rt 132. Ext
corridors. **Pets:** Dogs only. No service, supervision.

(SAVE) 🗙 🄱 🖃 🄀

## MONTEBELLO

Ⓐ ▼▼▼▼ Fairmont Le Chateau Montebello 🄻🄷 🐾
(819) 423-6341. **$189-$289, 3 day notice.** 392 rue Notre-Dame. On Rt
148. Int corridors. **Pets:** $35 daily fee/pet. Service with restrictions, crate.

(SAVE) 🗙 🄱 🖃 🍴 🏊 🛇

## MONTMAGNY

▼▼▼▼ Manoir des Erables 🄲🄸
(418) 248-0100. **$89-$160, 10 day notice.** 220 boul Tache est (Rt 132).
Hwy 20, exit 376, 2.2 km e on Rt 228, 1.5 km e. Ext/int corridors.
**Pets:** Small, other species. $15 daily fee/pet. Designated rooms, service
with restrictions, crate.

🗙 🖃 🍴 🏊 🛇

---

# MONTREAL METROPOLITAN AREA

## BOUCHERVILLE

▼▼ ▼▼ Comfort Inn 🄼
(450) 641-2880. **$120-$165.** 96 boul de Mortagne. Hwy 20, exit 92, just
n. Int corridors. **Pets:** Very small. Designated rooms, service with restrictions, supervision.

(A$K) 🆂🄳 🗙 🖃

## BROSSARD

▼▼ ▼▼ Comfort Inn 🅂🄷
(450) 678-9350. **$96-$105.** 7863 boul Taschereau. Rt 134, 1.5 km w of
Hwy 10, exit boul Taschereau ouest. Int corridors. **Pets:** Medium. $10
daily fee/pet. Designated rooms, service with restrictions, supervision.

(A$K) 🆂🄳 🗙 🄱

## DORVAL

▼▼ ▼▼ Comfort Inn Dorval 🅂🄷
(514) 636-3391. **$121-$147.** 340 ave Michel-Jasmin. Hwy 520, exit 2
eastbound; exit 1 westbound, 0.3 km along service road to ave Marshall, follow to ave Michel-Jasmin. Int corridors. **Pets:** Accepted.

(A$K) 🆂🄳 🗙 🄱 🖃

Ⓐ ▼▼▼▼ Hampton Inn & Suites 🅂🄷
(514) 633-8243. **$150-$190.** 1900 route Transcanadienne (Hwy 40).
Hwy 40, exit 55, 0.8 km e of boul Sources on south side service road.
Int corridors. **Pets:** Designated rooms, service with restrictions, supervision.

(SAVE) 🆂🄳 🗙 🅕🄼 🄱 🖃 🏊

Ⓐ ▼▼▼ Travelodge Dorval Airport 🅂🄷 🐾
(514) 631-4537. **$104-$225.** 1010 chemin Herron. Hwy 20, exit 54
westbound, just s on boul Fenelon to ave Dumont, follow to chemin
Herron; exit 56 eastbound, 1.7 km along service road. Int corridors.
**Pets:** Other species. $40 deposit/pet. Designated rooms, service with
restrictions, crate.

(SAVE) 🆂🄳 🗙 🄱 🖃 🛇

## LAVAL

▼▼ ▼▼ Comfort Inn 🅂🄷
(450) 686-0600. **$113-$124.** 2055 Autoroute des Laurentides. Hwy 15,
exit 8 (boul St-Martin), e on boul St-Martin, 0.7 km n on boul Le
Corbusier, then w on boul Tessier. Int corridors. **Pets:** Medium. Designated rooms, service with restrictions, supervision.

(A$K) 🗙 🄱 🍴

▼▼ ▼▼ Econo Lodge 🅂🄷
(450) 681-6411. **$89-$135.** 1981 boul Cure-Labelle. Hwy 15, exit 8
(boul St-Martin) northbound; exit 10 southbound, 2 km w on boul
St-Martin ouest, then 0.5 km n. Ext/int corridors. **Pets:** Designated
rooms, service with restrictions, supervision.

(A$K) 🆂🄳 🗙 🄱 🖃 🏊

**Hampton Inn & Suites-Laval** SH
(450) 687-0010. **$114-$154.** 1961 boul Cure-Labelle. Hwy 15, exit 8 (boul St-Martin) northbound; exit 10 southbound, 2 km w on boul St-Martin ouest, then just n. Int corridors. **Pets:** Very small, dogs only. Service with restrictions, supervision.

ASK SAVE X 🖥 🖥 🐾

CAA  **Quality Suites Laval** SH
(450) 686-6777. **$128-$161.** 2035 Autoroute des Laurentides. Hwy 15, exit 8 (boul St-Martin), 0.7 km n on boul Le Corbusier, w on boul Tessier. Int corridors. **Pets:** Medium. Designated rooms, service with restrictions, supervision.

SAVE SAVE X 🖥 🖥

 **Sheraton Laval Hotel** LH 🐾
(450) 687-2440. **$130.** 2440 Autoroute des Laurentides. Hwy 15, exit 10. Int corridors. **Pets:** Small. Service with restrictions, supervision.

ASK SAVE X 🖥 🖥 🍴 🐾 🖾

# LONGUEUIL

**Days Inn Longueuil** SH
(450) 677-8911. **$84-$103, 3 day notice.** 2800 boul Marie-Victorin. Hwy 20/Rt 132, exit 15 eastbound, follow signs for boul Marie-Victorin est; exit 90 westbound from Pont-Tunnel Louis-Hippolyte-Lafontaine. Int corridors. **Pets:** Small. Service with restrictions.

ASK SAVE X 🖥 🍴

# MONTREAL

CAA **Chateau Versailles Hotel** SH 🐾
(514) 933-3611. **$194-$254.** 1659 rue Sherbrooke ouest. Corner rue St-Mathieu. Int corridors. **Pets:** Other species. $20 daily fee/room. Designated rooms, service with restrictions, crate.

SAVE SAVE X 🖥

CAA **Delta Montreal** LH 🐾
(514) 286-1986. **$139-$289.** 475 ave President-Kennedy. Corner rue City Councillors. Int corridors. **Pets:** Medium. $35 one-time fee/room. Designated rooms, service with restrictions, crate.

SAVE SAVE X 🖥 🖥 🍴 🐾 🖾

CAA **Fairmont The Queen Elizabeth** LH
(514) 861-3511. **$149-$299.** 900 boul Rene-Levesque ouest. Between rue University and Mansfield. Int corridors. **Pets:** Accepted.

SAVE X 🔣 🖥 🍴 🐾 🖾

CAA **Four Points by Sheraton Montreal Centre-Ville** LH
(514) 842-3961. **$139-$235.** 475 rue Sherbrooke ouest. Between rue Durocher and Aylmer. Int corridors. **Pets:** Service with restrictions, supervision.

SAVE SAVE X 🖥 🖥 🍴

CAA **Hilton Montreal Bonaventure** LH
(514) 878-2332. **$149-$299.** 900 rue de La Gauchetiere W, Ste 10750. Corner of Mansfield and de la Gauchetiere. Int corridors. **Pets:** Designated rooms, service with restrictions, supervision.

SAVE X 🖥 🖥 🍴 🐾

CAA **Holiday Inn Express Hotel & Suites** SH
(514) 448-7100. **$144-$399.** 155 boul Rene-Levesque est. Corner de Bullion. Int corridors. **Pets:** Medium. $100 one-time fee/room. Service with restrictions, crate.

SAVE SAVE X 🖥 🖥

**Holiday Inn Montreal-Midtown** LH
(514) 842-6111. **$109-$154.** 420 rue Sherbrooke ouest. Between rue Bleury and City Councillors. Int corridors. **Pets:** Small. $35 one-time fee/room. Designated rooms, service with restrictions, supervision.

ASK SAVE X 🖥 🖥 🍴 🐾 🖾

**Hotel Gault** SH
(514) 904-1616. **$199-$749.** 449 rue Ste-Helene. Just s of rue Notre-Dame. Int corridors. **Pets:** Medium. $20 daily fee/pet. Service with restrictions, crate.

X 🖥 🖥

**Hotel Godin** SH 🐾
(514) 843-6000. **$225-$300.** 10 rue Sherbrooke ouest. Corner of boul St-Laurent. Int corridors. **Pets:** Large. $50 one-time fee/pet. Service with restrictions, supervision.

ASK X 🖥 🖥 🍴

CAA **Hotel InterContinental Montreal** LH
(514) 987-9900. **$360-$540.** 360 rue St-Antoine ouest. Corner of rue St-Pierre. Int corridors. **Pets:** Accepted.

SAVE SAVE X 🖥 🖥 🍴 🐾 🖾

CAA **Hotel La Tour Centre-Ville** CO
(514) 866-8861. **$88-$128.** 400 boul Rene-Levesque ouest. Corner of rue de Bleury. Int corridors. **Pets:** Very small. Service with restrictions, supervision.

SAVE X 🖥 🖥 🍴 🐾

**Hotel Le Germain** SH 🐾
(514) 849-2050. **$230-$330.** 2050 rue Mansfield. Just n of ave President-Kennedy. Int corridors. **Pets:** Medium. $30 daily fee/room. Service with restrictions, supervision.

X 🖥 🖥 🍴

**Hotel Le St-James** SH
(514) 841-3111. **$400-$5000.** 355 rue St-Jacques ouest. Corner of rue St-Pierre. Int corridors. **Pets:** Accepted.

ASK X 🍴

**Hotel Lord Berri** SH
(514) 845-9236. **$129-$165.** 1199 rue Berri. Between boul Rene-Levesque and rue Ste-Catherine. Int corridors. **Pets:** Accepted.

ASK SAVE X 🖥 🖥 🍴

**Hotel Omni Mont-Royal** LH
(514) 284-1110. **$249-$359.** 1050 rue Sherbrooke ouest. Corner of rue Peel. Int corridors. **Pets:** Accepted.

ASK X 🖉 🖥 🍴 🐾 🖾

CAA **Hotel Travelodge Montreal Centre** SH
(514) 874-9090. **$99-$149.** 50 boul Rene-Levesque ouest. Between rue Clark and St-Urbain. Int corridors. **Pets:** Other species. $10 daily fee/pet. Service with restrictions, crate.

SAVE SAVE X 🖥 🖥 🍴

CAA **L'Appartement Hotel** CO
(514) 284-3634. **$139-$400.** 455 rue Sherbrooke ouest. Corner of rue Durocher. Int corridors. **Pets:** Accepted.

SAVE SAVE X 🖥 🖥 🐾

**La Presidence Appartements De Luxe** CO
(514) 842-9988. **$159-$249.** 505 rue Sherbrooke est. Between rue Berri and St-Hubert. Int corridors. **Pets:** Small. $30 one-time fee/pet. Service with restrictions, supervision.

ASK SAVE X 🖥 🖥 🍴 🐾 🖾

CAA **Le Centre Sheraton** LH
(514) 878-2000. **$325-$395.** 1201 boul Rene-Levesque ouest. Between rue Drummond and Stanley. Int corridors. **Pets:** Accepted.

SAVE SAVE X 🔣 🖥 🖥 🍴 🐾 🖾

CAA **Le Meridien Versailles-Montreal** SH 🐾
(514) 933-8111. **$179-$239.** 1808 rue Sherbrooke ouest. Corner of rue St-Mathieu. Int corridors. **Pets:** Other species. $20 daily fee/room. Service with restrictions, crate.

SAVE SAVE X 🖥 🖥 🍴

(CAA) ▼▼▼ ▼▼▼ **Le Saint-Sulpice Hotel Montreal** SH ❖
(514) 288-1000. **$169-$469.** 414 rue St-Sulpice. Just n of rue St-Paul.
Int corridors. **Pets:** Large, other species. $40 one-time fee/room.

SAVE  ✕  🛏  🖵  ¶  ✕

(CAA) ▼▼▼ **Le Square Phillips Hotel & Suites** SH
(514) 393-1193. **$133-$187.** 1193 Place Phillips. Between rue Ste-
Catherine and boul Rene-Levesque. Int corridors. **Pets:** Designated
rooms, service with restrictions, supervision.

SAVE  ⓢ  ✕  🛏  🖵  ¶  ➷

(CAA) ▼▼▼ ▼▼▼ **Loews Hotel Vogue** LH ❖
(514) 285-5555. **$152-$428.** 1425 rue de la Montagne. Between rue
Ste-Catherine and boul de Maisonneuve. Int corridors. **Pets:** Large.
Designated rooms, service with restrictions, supervision.

SAVE  ⓢ  ✕  🛏  🖵

(CAA) ▼▼▼ **Marriott Residence Inn-Montreal**
**Downtown** SH
(514) 982-6064. **$155-$450.** 2045 rue Peel. Between rue Sherbrooke
and boul de Maisonneuve. Int corridors. **Pets:** Medium. $100 one-time
fee/room. Service with restrictions, crate.

SAVE  ⓢ  ✕  🛏  🖵  ➷

(CAA) ▼▼▼ **Novotel Montreal Centre** LH ❖
(514) 861-6000. **$119-$189.** 1180 rue de la Montagne. Between rue
Ste-Catherine and boul Rene-Levesque. **Pets:** Other species. Service with restrictions.

SAVE  ⓢ  ✕  🛏  ¶

(CAA) ▼▼▼ **Plaza Hotel Centre-Ville Montreal** LH
(514) 842-8581. **$149-$229.** 505 rue Sherbrooke est. Between rue Berri
and St-Hubert. Int corridors. **Pets:** Small. $30 one-time fee/room. Service
with restrictions, supervision.

SAVE  ⓢ  ✕  🛏  ¶  ➷  ✕

(CAA) ▼▼ **Quality Hotel Downtown Montreal** SH
(514) 849-1413. **$99-$169.** 3440 ave du Parc. Between rue Sherbrooke
and Milton. Int corridors. **Pets:** Other species. $25 one-time fee/pet. Des-
ignated rooms, service with restrictions, supervision.

SAVE  ⓢ  ✕  🛏  🖵  ¶

(CAA) ▼▼▼ **Residence Inn by Marriott Montreal**
**Westmount** SH
(514) 935-9224. **$105-$189.** 2170 ave Lincoln. Just e of rue Atwater. Int
corridors. **Pets:** Accepted.

SAVE  ⓢ  ✕  ⌖M  🛏  🖵  ➷

▼▼▼ ▼▼▼ **The Ritz-Carlton, Montreal** LH
(514) 842-4212. **$147-$199.** 1228 rue Sherbrooke ouest. Corner de la
Montagne. Int corridors. **Pets:** Accepted.

✕  ¶  ✕

(CAA) ▼▼▼ **Sofitel Montreal** SH ❖
(514) 285-9000. **$195-$530.** 1155 rue Sherbrooke ouest. Corner of rue
Stanley. Int corridors. **Pets:** Other species. No service.

SAVE  ⓢ  ✕  🛏  ¶  ✕

▼▼▼ **XIX siecle Hotel Montreal** SH
(514) 985-0019. **$145-$275.** 262 rue St-Jacques ouest. Between rue
St-Jean and rue St-Pierre. Int corridors. **Pets:** Accepted.

ASK  ⓢ  ✕  🛏  ¶

# POINTE-CLAIRE

(CAA) ▼▼ ▼▼ **Comfort Inn** SH
(514) 697-6210. **$99-$228.** 700 boul St-Jean. Hwy 40, exit 52, 0.3 km
s. Int corridors. **Pets:** Designated rooms, service with restrictions, supervision.

SAVE  ⓢ  ✕  🛏  🖵

(CAA) ▼▼▼▼ **Quality Suites Montreal Aeroport,**
**Pointe-Claire** SH ❖
(514) 426-5060. **$99-$169, 30 day notice.** 6300 Rt Transcanadienne.
Hwy 40, exit 52 eastbound, south side service road; westbound, follow
signs for boul St-Jean sud and Hwy 40 est to access south side
service road. Int corridors. **Pets:** Designated rooms, service with restrictions, supervision.

SAVE  ⓢ  ✕  ⌖M  🛏  🖵  ¶

# ROSEMERE

▼▼▼ ▼▼ **Hotel Le Rivage** SH
(450) 437-2171. **$79-$249.** 125 boul LaBelle. Hwy 15, exit 19, 1.4 km e
on Rt 344, then 0.5 km s. Int corridors. **Pets:** Accepted.

✕  🛏  🖵  ➷

# ST-LAURENT

(CAA) ▼▼▼▼ **Four Points by Sheraton Montreal Airport** LH
(514) 344-1999. **$119-$169.** 6600 Cote-de-Liesse. Hwy 520, exit 5
eastbound on south side service road; exit westbound to rue Ness,
follow signs for rue Hickmore and Hwy 520 E. Int corridors.
**Pets:** Accepted.

SAVE  ⓢ  ✕  ⌖  🛏  🖵  ¶  ➷  ✕

▼▼▼ ▼▼ **Holiday Inn Montreal-Airport** SH
(514) 739-3391. **$108-$169.** 6500 Cote-de-Liesse. Hwy 520, exit 5
eastbound on south side service road; exit westbound to rue Ness,
follow signs for rue Hickmore and Hwy 520 E. Ext/int corridors.
**Pets:** Large, other species. $35 one-time fee/room. Service with restrictions,
crate.

ASK  ✕  ⌖M  🛏  🖵  ¶  ➷  ✕

▼▼▼ ▼▼ **Quality Hotel Dorval** SH
(514) 731-7821. **$176.** 7700 Cote-de-Liesse. Hwy 520, exit 4 east-
bound on south side service road; exit Montee-de-Liesse westbound.
Int corridors. **Pets:** Accepted.

ASK  ✕  🛏  🖵  ¶  ➷  ✕

(CAA) ▼▼▼ ▼▼ **Ramada Montreal Airport Hotel** SH
(514) 733-8818. **$129-$169, 7 day notice.** 7300 Cote-de-Liesse. Hwy
520, exit 4 eastbound on south side service road; exit Montee-de-
Liesse westbound. Int corridors. **Pets:** Service with restrictions, supervision.

SAVE  ⓢ  ✕  🛏  🖵  ¶  ➷

# VAUDREUIL-DORION

(CAA) ▼▼▼ ▼▼ **Chateau Vaudreuil Suites Hotel** LH
(450) 455-0955. **$189-$495.** 21700 Trans-Canada Hwy 40. Hwy 40,
exit 36 westbound; exit 35 eastbound. Int corridors. **Pets:** Accepted.

SAVE  ⓢ  ✕  🛏  🖵  ¶  ➷  ✕

---

## END METROPOLITAN AREA

---

# MONT-TREMBLANT

(CAA) ▼▼▼ ▼▼ **Hotel Quintessence** SH
(819) 425-3400. **$289-$1739, 7 day notice.** 3004 chemin de la
Chapelle. Hwy 117 N, exit 119 (Montee Ryan), 10 km e to Mont-
Tremblant Resort centre. Int corridors. **Pets:** Accepted.

SAVE  ✕  🖵  ¶  ➷  ✕

(CAA) ▼▼▼ ▼▼ **Le Grand Lodge Mont-Tremblant** SH
(819) 425-2734. **$100-$550, 8 day notice.** 2396 rue Labelle. Jct Hwy
117 and 327, 1.5 km s. Int corridors. **Pets:** Accepted.

SAVE  ⓢ  ✕  🛏  🖵  ¶  ➷  ✕

# NEW RICHMOND

**▼▼▼▼ Hotel Le Francis** 🅼
(418) 392-4485. **$76-$130.** 210 chemin Pardiac. Just s of Rt 132. Ext/int corridors. **Pets:** Accepted.

Ⓐ⑃ Ⓢ⑥ ⊠ ⎘ 🔲 ⑪ ⇔ ⌧

# NORTH HATLEY

Ⓒ🅐 ▼▼▼▼ **Auberge Hatley, Relais &**
**Chateaux** 🅲🅸 🐾
(819) 842-2451. **$290-$690, 20 day notice.** 325 Virgin Hill Rd. Hwy 55, exit 29, 11 km e on Rt 108. Int corridors. **Pets:** Medium. $30 daily fee/room.

🆂🅰🆅🅴 ⊠ ⑪ ⇔ ⌧

# PASPEBIAC

▼▼▼▼ **Auberge du Parc Inn** 🆂🅷
(418) 752-3355. **$79-$165.** 68 boul Gerard D Levesque ouest. On Rt 132; centre. Ext corridors. **Pets:** Accepted.

⊠ ⑪ ⇔ ⌧ 🅺

# PERCE

▼ **Au Pic de l'Aurore** 🅲🅰
(418) 782-2151. **$59-$145.** 1 Rt 132. 2 km e from village. Ext corridors. **Pets:** Medium. $50 deposit/pet, $25 one-time fee/pet. Designated rooms, service with restrictions, supervision.

⊠ ⎘ 🔲 🅺

▼▼▼▼ **Hotel La Normandie** 🆂🅷
(418) 782-2112. **$79-$239.** 221 Rt 132 ouest. Centre. Int corridors. **Pets:** Medium. $50 one-time fee/room. Designated rooms, service with restrictions, crate.

⊠ ⎘ 🔲 ⑪ 🅺

**▼▼▼▼ Hotel/Motel Le Mirage** 🅼
(418) 782-5151. **$71-$158.** 288 Rt 132 ouest. On Rt 132. Ext corridors. **Pets:** Small, dogs only.

⌧ ⎘ ⑪ ⇔

**▼▼ Hotel Motel Manoir de Perce** 🆂🅷
(418) 782-2022. **$65-$168.** 212 Rt 132. Centre. Ext/int corridors. **Pets:** $25 one-time fee/room. No service, supervision.

🆂⑥ ⊠ ⎘ ⑪

# PLESSISVILLE

▼▼▼ **Motel A la Claire Fontaine** 🅼
(819) 362-6388. **$50-$75.** 2165 rue St-Calixte. Rt 165, 1 km e on Rt 116, follow signs. Ext corridors. **Pets:** Very small. Designated rooms, service with restrictions, supervision.

Ⓐ⑃ ⊠ ⎘ ⑪

# PORTNEUF

▼▼ **Hotel Le Portneuvois** 🆂🅷
(418) 286-6400. **$100-$110.** 101 rue Simeon-Delisle. Hwy 40, exit 261, then 0.5 km s on rue Provencher. Int corridors. **Pets:** Accepted.

Ⓐ⑃ 🆂⑥ ⊠ ⎘ 🔲

---

# QUEBEC METROPOLITAN AREA

# BEAUPRE

▼▼▼▼ **Auberge La Camarine** 🅲🅸
(418) 827-5703. **$105.** 10947 boul Ste-Anne. On Hwy 138, 1.5 km w of jct Hwy 360. Int corridors. **Pets:** Accepted.

Ⓐ⑃ ⊠ ⎘ 🔲 ⑪

Ⓒ🅐 ▼▼▼▼ **Hotel Chateau Mont-Sainte-Anne** 🅻🅷 🐾
(418) 827-5211. **$119-$266, 7 day notice.** 500 boul du Beau-Pre'. Hwy 360, 3.7 km ne from jct Hwy 138. Int corridors. **Pets:** Dogs only. $20 daily fee/room. Designated rooms, service with restrictions, supervision.

🆂🅰🆅🅴 ⊠ ⎘ 🔲 ⑪ ⇔ ⌧

Ⓒ🅐 ▼▼▼▼ **Hotel Val des Neiges** 🅻🅷
(418) 827-5711. **$99-$179.** 201 rue Val-des-Neiges. Just off Hwy 360. Int corridors. **Pets:** Small. $20 daily fee/room. Designated rooms, service with restrictions, supervision.

🆂🅰🆅🅴 🆂⑥ ⊠ ⎘ 🔲 ⑪ ⇔ ⌧

# L'ANCIENNE-LORETTE

▼▼▼ **Comfort Inn** 🆂🅷
(418) 872-5900. **$100-$140.** 1255 boul Duplessis. Jct boul Duplessis and Wilfrid-Hamel (Hwy 138). Int corridors. **Pets:** Accepted.

Ⓐ⑃ 🆂⑥ ⊠ ⎘ 🔲

# LEVIS

▼▼▼ **Comfort Inn** 🆂🅷
(418) 835-5605. **$97-$165.** 10 du Vallon est. Hwy 20, exit 325S eastbound; exit 325 westbound. Int corridors. **Pets:** Small. $50 deposit/room. Designated rooms, service with restrictions, supervision.

Ⓐ⑃ 🆂⑥ ⊠ ⎘ 🔲

▼▼▼ **Hotel Motel Bernieres** 🆂🅷
(418) 831-3119. **$75-$132.** 535 rue Arena. Hwy 20, exit 311, just sw; in St-Nicolas sector. Ext/int corridors. **Pets:** Cats only. Crate.

Ⓐ⑃ 🆂⑥ ⊠ ⎘ 🔲 ⑪

# QUEBEC

▼▼ **Appartements La Pergola** 🅲🅾
(418) 681-1428. **$65-$120, 15 day notice.** 405 boul Rene-Levesque ouest. Between aves Moncton and des Erables. Int corridors. **Pets:** Accepted.

Ⓐ⑃ 🆂⑥ ⎘ 🔲

Ⓒ🅐 ▼▼▼▼ **Auberge Saint-Antoine** 🆂🅷
(418) 692-2211. **$149-$299.** 8 rue St-Antoine. Corner of rue Dalhousie. Int corridors. **Pets:** Small, dogs only. $150 one-time fee/pet. Service with restrictions, supervision.

🆂🅰🆅🅴 ⊠ ⎘ 🔲 ⑪

▼▼ **Comfort Inn** 🆂🅷 🐾
(418) 666-1226. **$75-$180.** 240 boul Ste-Anne. Hwy 440, exit Francois-de-Laval. Int corridors. **Pets:** Large. Service with restrictions, supervision.

Ⓐ⑃ 🆂⑥ ⊠ ⎘ 🔲

▼▼ **Comfort Inn de l'Aeroport** 🆂🅷
(418) 872-5038. **$90-$140.** 7320 boul Wilfrid-Hamel. Hwy 138, 1.5 km w of boul Duplessis. Int corridors. **Pets:** Medium. Designated rooms, service with restrictions, supervision.

Ⓐ⑃ 🆂⑥ ⊠ ⎘ 🔲

Ⓒ🅐 ▼▼▼▼ **Delta Quebec** 🅻🅷
(418) 647-1717. **$219-$309.** 690 boul Rene-Levesque est. Just w of boul Honore-Mercier. Int corridors. **Pets:** Medium. $35 one-time fee/room. Designated rooms, service with restrictions, supervision.

🆂🅰🆅🅴 🆂⑥ ⊠ ⎘ 🔲 ⑪ ⇔ ⌧

**▼▼ ▼▼ Gite du Vieux-Bourg** 🅱🅱
(418) 661-0116. **$75-$105, 15 day notice.** 492 ave Royale. Hwy 440, exit Francois-de-Laval, just n, then 0.5 km e; in Beauport sector. Int corridors. **Pets:** Accepted.

🄰🅂🄺 ⊠ ⤳

**ⓐ ▼▼▼ ▼▼ Hilton Quebec** 🅛🅗
(418) 647-2411. **$125-$299.** 1100 boul Rene-Levesque est. Corner of ave Honore-Mercier. Int corridors. **Pets:** Small. $25 one-time fee/room. Designated rooms, service with restrictions, supervision.

🆂🅰🆅🅴 🆂🗖 ⊠ 🛅 🖵 🍴 ⤳ ⊠

**▼▼▼▼ Hotel Clarion Quebec** 🅛🅗
(418) 653-4901. **$89-$299.** 3125 boul Hochelaga. Hwy 73, exit 136 (Hochelaga ouest); in Ste-Foy sector. Int corridors. **Pets:** Accepted.

🄰🅂🄺 🆂🗖 ⊠ 🛅 🖵 🍴 ⤳ ⊠

**▼▼▼▼ Hotel Gouverneur Quebec-Sainte-Foy** 🅛🅗
(418) 651-3030. **$99-$250.** 3030 boul Laurier. Corner rue Lavigerie; in Ste-Foy sector. Ext/int corridors. **Pets:** Accepted.

🄰🅂🄺 ⊠ 🛅 🖵 🍴 ⤳

**ⓐ ▼▼▼ Hotel Quality Suites Quebec** 🅂🅗
(418) 622-4244. **$115-$185.** 1600 rue Bouvier. Hwy 40, exit 312N (Pierre-Bertrand nord), 2 km w of jct Rt 358. Int corridors. **Pets:** Other species. Service with restrictions, supervision.

🆂🅰🆅🅴 🆂🗖 ⊠ 🛅 🖵

**ⓐ ▼▼▼ Hotel Universel** 🅂🅗
(418) 653-5250. **$96-$146.** 2300 chemin Ste-Foy. Hwy 73, exit 137, 2.3 km e on chemin des Quatre-Bourgeois; in Ste-Foy sector. Ext/int corridors. **Pets:** Accepted.

🆂🅰🆅🅴 🆂🗖 ⊠ 🛅 🖵 🍴 ⤳

**ⓐ ▼▼▼ L'Hotel du Vieux Quebec** 🅂🅗 🐾
(418) 692-1850. **$99-$259.** 1190 rue St-Jean. Corner of rue de l'Hotel-Dieu. Int corridors. **Pets:** Other species. $10 daily fee/room. Designated rooms, service with restrictions, supervision.

🆂🅰🆅🅴 ⊠ 🛅 🍴

**ⓐ ▼▼▼ Loews Le Concorde** 🅛🅗 🐾
(418) 647-2222. **$134-$390.** 1225 Cours du General-de-Montcalm. Corner of Grande Allee est. Int corridors. **Pets:** Other species. Service with restrictions, supervision.

🆂🅰🆅🅴 🆂🗖 ⊠ 🛅 🖵 🍴 ⤳ ⊠

**▼▼ Motel Oncle Sam** 🅜
(418) 872-1488. **$45-$119.** 7025 boul Wilfrid-Hamel. On Hwy 138 at jct boul Duplessis; in Ste-Foy sector. Ext corridors. **Pets:** Designated rooms, service with restrictions, supervision.

⊠ 🛅 🖵 ⤳

## ST-FERREOL-LES-NEIGES

**ⓐ ▼▼▼ Chalets Montmorency Condominiums** 🄲🄾
(418) 826-2600. **$89-$129.** 1768 ave Royale. On Hwy 360. Ext corridors. **Pets:** Dogs only. $25 daily fee/pet. No service, supervision.

🆂🅰🆅🅴 🆂🗖 ⊠ 🛅 🖵 ⤳ ⊠

**▼▼▼ Chalets-Village Mont-Sainte-Anne** 🄲🄰
(418) 826-3331. **$895-$9250 (weekly).** 1815 boul Les Neiges. On north side of Hwy 360; village center. Ext corridors. **Pets:** Other species. $100 one-time fee/room. Designated rooms, no service.

🛅 🖵 ⊠

---

## END METROPOLITAN AREA

## RIMOUSKI

**▼▼ ▼▼ Comfort Inn** 🅂🅗
(418) 724-2500. **$99-$140.** 455 boul St-Germain ouest. On Rt 132. Int corridors. **Pets:** Designated rooms, no service, supervision.

🄰🅂🄺 🆂🗖 ⊠ 🛅 🖵

## RIVIERE-DU-LOUP

**ⓐ ▼▼▼ Comfort Inn** 🅂🅗
(418) 867-4162. **$100-$170.** 85 boul Cartier. Hwy 20, exit 507, just sw; Hwy 185, exit 96 (Fraserville). Int corridors. **Pets:** Other species. Designated rooms.

🆂🅰🆅🅴 🆂🗖 ⊠ 🛅 🖵

## ROBERVAL

**ⓐ ▼▼▼▼ Hotel Chateau Roberval** 🅛🅗
(418) 275-7511. **$79-$149.** 1225 boul Marcotte. On Hwy 169; centre. Int corridors. **Pets:** Accepted.

🆂🅰🆅🅴 ⊠ 🛅 🖵 🍴 ⤳

## ROUYN-NORANDA

**▼▼ ▼▼ Comfort Inn** 🅂🅗
(819) 797-1313. **$73-$84.** 1295 rue Lariviere. On Rt 117, 4 km s from town centre. Int corridors. **Pets:** Accepted.

🄰🅂🄺 🆂🗖 ⊠ 🛅 🖵

## SALABERRY-DE-VALLEYFIELD

**▼▼▼▼ Hotel Plaza Valleyfield** 🅛🅗
(450) 373-1990. **$85.** 40 ave du Centenaire. Corner of rue St-Laurent; centre. Int corridors. **Pets:** Accepted.

🄰🅂🄺 🆂🗖 ⊠ 🛅 🖵 🍴 ⤳ ⊠

## SHAWINIGAN

**▼▼ ▼▼ Auberge Escapade Inn** 🅂🅗
(819) 539-6911. **$77-$150.** 3383 rue Garnier. Hwy 55, exit 217, then 0.5 km n on Rt 351. Ext/int corridors. **Pets:** Accepted.

⊠ 🛅 🍴

**ⓐ ▼▼▼ Auberge Gouverneur & Centre de Congres Shawinigan** 🅂🅗
(819) 537-6000. **$150-$175.** 1100 Promenade-du-St-Maurice. Hwy 55 N, exit 211, 4.4 km n on Hwy 153, follow signs. Int corridors. **Pets:** Small. Crate.

🆂🅰🆅🅴 🆂🗖 ⊠ 🛅 🖵 🍴 ⤳ ⊠

**▼▼▼▼ Comfort Inn & Suites** 🅂🅗
(819) 536-2000. **$72-$145.** 500 boul du Capitaine. Hwy 55 N, exit 211, 4.4 km n on Hwy 153, then 2 km s on Rt 157. Int corridors. **Pets:** Accepted.

🄰🅂🄺 🆂🗖 ⊠ 🛅 🖵

## SHERBROOKE

**▼▼ ▼▼ Comfort Inn** 🅂🅗
(819) 564-4400. **$86-$108.** 4295 boul Bourque. Hwy 410, exit 4, 1.5 km w on Rt 112. Ext/int corridors. **Pets:** Small. Designated rooms, service with restrictions, supervision.

🄰🅂🄺 🆂🗖 ⊠ 🛅 🖵

**ⓐ ▼▼▼▼ Delta Sherbrooke Hotel and Conference Centre** 🅛🅗
(819) 822-1989. **$105-$155.** 2685 rue King ouest. Hwy 410, exit 4E, 1 km e on Rt 112. Int corridors. **Pets:** Accepted.

🆂🅰🆅🅴 ⊠ 🛅 🖵 🍴 ⤳ ⊠

# ST-ANTOINE-DE-TILLY

▼▼▼▼ Manoir de Tilly CI
(418) 886-2407. **$129-$276, 3 day notice.** 3854 chemin de Tilly. Jct Hwy 20, exit 291, 8.5 km n on Rt 273; centre. Int corridors. **Pets:** Accepted.

Ⓢ◎ ⊠ ⬛ ▦ ⑪

# STE-ANNE-DE-BEAUPRE

Ⓐ ▼▼▼ Manoir Ste-Anne M
(418) 827-8383. **$65-$105, 3 day notice.** 9776 boul Ste-Anne. On Hwy 138. Ext corridors. **Pets:** Small. $10 one-time fee/pet. Service with restrictions, supervision.

SAVE ⊠ ⬛ ▦

# STE-ANNE-DES-MONTS

Ⓐ ▼▼▼ Motel Beaurivage M
(418) 763-2291. **$55-$160.** 245 1ere ave ouest. Just off Rt 132. Ext/int corridors. **Pets:** Accepted.

SAVE ⊠ ⬛ ⑪ ℀

# STE-MARTHE

▼▼▼▼ Auberge des Gallant CI
(450) 459-4241. **$125-$275, 14 day notice.** 1171 chemin St-Henri. 8.5 km w on chemin St-Henri from Hwy 201. Int corridors. **Pets:** Accepted.

⊠ ▦ ⑪ ⇒ ⊠

# ST-FAUSTIN-LAC-CARRE

▼▼ Motel sur la Colline M
(819) 688-2102. **$60-$105, 15 day notice.** 357 Rt 117. On Rt 117, 4 km n of exit for city. Ext/int corridors. **Pets:** Large. $15 daily fee/pet. Designated rooms, service with restrictions, supervision.

ⒶSK Ⓢ◎ ⊠ ⬛ ▦ ⇒

# ST-FELICIEN

▼▼▼▼ Hotel du Jardin LH
(418) 679-8422. **$100-$190.** 1400 boul du Jardin. On Hwy 167. Int corridors. **Pets:** Small. Service with restrictions, crate.

ⒶSK ⊠ ⬛ ▦ ⑪ ⇒ ⊠

# ST-HONORE

▼▼ Motel Jasper M
(418) 497-2322. **$64-$72.** 657 Rt 185. On Rt 185. Ext corridors. **Pets:** Accepted.

ⒶSK Ⓢ◎ ⊠ ⑪

# ST-HYACINTHE

▼▼▼▼ Hotel des Seigneurs Saint-Hyacinthe LH
(450) 774-3810. **$89-$199.** 1200 rue Johnson. Hwy 20, exit 130S, just e on Gauvin St from boul Laframboise. Int corridors. **Pets:** Medium. Designated rooms, service with restrictions, supervision.

ⒶSK Ⓢ◎ ⊠ ⬛ ▦ ⑪ ⇒ ⊠

# ST-JEAN-PORT-JOLI

▼▼▼▼ Auberge du Faubourg M
(418) 598-6455. **$89-$105, 10 day notice.** 280 ave de Gaspe ouest (Rt 132). 2.4 km w on Rt 132 from jct Rt 204; Hwy 20, exit 414. Ext corridors. **Pets:** Small, other species. $15 daily fee/pet. Designated rooms, service with restrictions, crate.

ⒶSK ⊠ ⬛ ▦ ⑪ ⇒ ⊠ ℀

# ST-JEAN-SUR-RICHELIEU

Ⓐ ▼▼▼ Comfort Inn SH
(450) 359-4466. **$95-$149.** 700 rue Gadbois. Hwy 35, exit 9, e on rue Pierre-Caisse. Int corridors. **Pets:** $25 deposit/room. Service with restrictions, supervision.

SAVE Ⓢ◎ ⊠ ⬛ ⇒

▼▼▼▼ Hotel Relais Gouverneur St-Jean-sur-Richelieu SH
(450) 348-7376. **$85-$89, 30 day notice.** 725 boul du Seminaire nord. Hwy 35, exit 7. Int corridors. **Pets:** Accepted.

ⒶSK ⊠ ⬛ ▦ ⑪ ⇒

# ST-LIBOIRE

▼▼ Econo Lodge SH
(450) 793-4444. **$87-$117.** 110 Rang Charlotte. Hwy 20, exit 147, just s. Int corridors. **Pets:** Accepted.

ⒶSK Ⓢ◎ ⊠ ⬛ ▦ ⑪ ⇒

# THETFORD MINES

▼▼ Comfort Inn SH ❀
(418) 338-0171. **$110-$113 (no credit cards).** 123 boul Frontenac ouest. On Rt 112. Int corridors. **Pets:** Other species. Service with restrictions, crate.

ⒶSK Ⓢ◎ ⊠ ⬛

# TROIS-RIVIERES

▼▼ Comfort Inn SH
(819) 371-3566. **$94-$100.** 6255 rue Corbeil. Hwy 55, exit 183 (boul Jean XXIII); 2 km n of Laviolette Bridge, then 0.5 km e. Int corridors. **Pets:** Accepted.

ⒶSK Ⓢ◎ ⊠ ⬛ ▦

Ⓐ ▼▼▼ Days Inn SH
(819) 377-4444. **$90-$160.** 3155 boul Saint-Jean. Hwy 55, exit 183 (boul Jean XXIII), 0.5 km w, then 0.4 km n. Int corridors. **Pets:** Medium. $10 daily fee/pet. Service with restrictions, supervision.

SAVE Ⓢ◎ ⊠ ⬛ ▦

▼▼▼▼ Delta Trois-Rivieres Hotel and Conference Center LH
(819) 376-1991. **$95-$105.** 1620 rue Notre-Dame. Corner of rue St-Roch; centre. Int corridors. **Pets:** Accepted.

ⒶSK Ⓢ◎ ⊠ ▦ ⑪ ⇒ ⊠

Ⓐ ▼▼▼ Hotel Du Roy Trois-Rivieres SH
(819) 379-3232. **$75-$125.** 3600 boul Gene H Kruger. On Hwy 138, 2 km e of Pont Laviolette and jct Hwy 55. Ext/int corridors. **Pets:** $50 deposit/room. Designated rooms, service with restrictions, supervision.

SAVE Ⓢ◎ ⊠ ⬛ ▦ ⑪ ⇒

# VAL-D'OR

▼▼ Comfort Inn SH
(819) 825-9360. **$89-$101.** 1665 3ieme ave. In town centre. Int corridors. **Pets:** Accepted.

ⒶSK Ⓢ◎ ⊠ ⬛ ▦

▼▼▼▼ Hotel Forestel LH
(819) 825-5660. **$80-$120.** 1001 3ieme ave est. On Rt 117. Int corridors. **Pets:** Accepted.

ⒶSK Ⓢ◎ ⊠ ⬛ ▦ ⑪

▼▼ Hotel-Motel Prelude SH
(819) 825-0090. **$74-$81.** 1159 3ieme ave. On Rt 117 N; in town centre. Ext/int corridors. **Pets:** Accepted.

ⒶSK Ⓢ◎ ⊠ ⬛ ▦

▼▼▼▼ Motel L'Escale Hotel Suite SH
(819) 824-2711. **$98-$128.** 1100 rue L'Escale. In town centre. Ext/int corridors. **Pets:** Accepted.

⊠ ⬛ ⑪

# SASKATCHEWAN

## CARONPORT

▼▼ ▼▼ The Pilgrim Inn ⏚
(306) 756-5002. **$70-$77.** Hwy 1 W. Jct Main Access; on Trans-Canada Hwy 1. Int corridors. **Pets:** Other species. $100 deposit/room. Designated rooms, service with restrictions.

## ESTEVAN

Ⓒ ▼▼▼▼ Perfect Inns & Suites ⏚
(306) 634-8585. **$84-$185.** 134 2nd Ave. Just n of jct Hwy 39 E and 2nd Ave. Int corridors. **Pets:** Accepted.

## FOAM LAKE

▼▼ La Vista Motel Ⓜ
(306) 272-3341. **$66-$75, 30 day notice.** Jct Hwy 16 & 310. On Hwy 16. Int corridors. **Pets:** Medium. Designated rooms, service with restrictions, supervision.

## KINDERSLEY

Ⓒ ▼▼ Best Western Westridge Inn ⏚
(306) 463-4687. **$85-$90, 7 day notice.** 100 12th Ave NW. Jct of Hwy 7 and 21. Ext/int corridors. **Pets:** Very small. Designated rooms, service with restrictions, supervision.

## MOOSE JAW

▼▼ ▼▼ Comfort Inn ⏚
(306) 692-2100. **$87.** 155 Thatcher Dr W. Just w of jct Main St. Int corridors. **Pets:** Accepted.

▼▼ ▼▼ Days Inn ⏚
(306) 691-5777. **$92.** 1720 Main St N. From jct Trans-Canada Hwy 1, just s. Int corridors. **Pets:** Medium. $10 daily fee/pet. Service with restrictions, crate.

▼▼ ▼▼ Heritage Inn ⏚
(306) 693-7550. **$100-$105.** 1590 Main St N. 1.5 km s of jct Trans-Canada Hwy 1 and 2; access from Hwy 2 via Thatcher Dr. Int corridors. **Pets:** Accepted.

Ⓒ ▼▼ ▼▼ Prairie Oasis Motel Ⓜ
(306) 693-8888. **$84.** 955 Thatcher Dr E. Just s of jct Trans-Canada Hwy 1 and Thatcher Dr E. Ext corridors. **Pets:** Accepted.

▼▼ ▼▼ Super 8 Motel-Moose Jaw Ⓜ
(306) 692-8888. **$80-$95.** 1706 Main St N. 1.5 km s of jct Trans-Canada Hwy 1; access from Hwy 2 via Thatcher Dr. Int corridors. **Pets:** Other species. $50 one-time fee/room. Designated rooms, service with restrictions, supervision.

## NORTH BATTLEFORD

▼▼ Super 8 Motel ⏚
(306) 446-8888. **$74-$89.** 1006 Hwy 16 Bypass. 0.5 km nw of jct Hwy 16. Int corridors. **Pets:** Accepted.

▼▼ ▼▼ Tropical Inn ⏚
(306) 446-4700. **$75-$90.** 1001 Hwy 16 Bypass. Corner of Battleford Rd and Hwy 16 Bypass. Int corridors. **Pets:** Accepted.

## PRINCE ALBERT

▼▼ ▼▼ Comfort Inn ⏚
(306) 763-4466. **$100-$127.** 3863 2nd Ave W. 2.3 km s at jct Hwy 2 and Marquis Rd. Int corridors. **Pets:** Accepted.

▼▼ ▼▼ Super 8 ⏚
(306) 953-0088. **$78.** 4444 2nd Ave W. Just s of jct Hwy 2 and Marquis Rd. Int corridors. **Pets:** Accepted.

◆ ▼▼ Travelodge Prince Albert ⏚
(306) 764-6441. **$75-$125.** 3551 2nd Ave W. 2.2 km s at jct Hwy 2 and Marquis Rd. Ext/int corridors. **Pets:** Accepted.

## REGINA

▼▼ ▼▼ Comfort Inn ⏚
(306) 789-5522. **$91-$106.** 3221 E Eastgate Dr. Trans-Canada Hwy 1, 2 km e of Ring Rd; at eastern approach to Regina. Int corridors. **Pets:** Accepted.

▼▼ ▼▼ Country Inn & Suites By Carlson ⏚
(306) 789-9117. **$90-$120, 3 day notice.** 3321 Eastgate Bay. Trans-Canada Hwy 1, 2 km e of Ring Rd, at eastern approach to city. Int corridors. **Pets:** Medium, other species. Designated rooms, service with restrictions, supervision.

▼▼ ▼▼ Days Inn ⏚
(306) 522-3297. **$87.** 3875 Eastgate Dr. Trans-Canada Hwy 1, exit Prince of Wales Dr, at eastern approach to city. Int corridors. **Pets:** Accepted.

▼▼▼▼ Delta Regina ⒧
(306) 525-5255. **$120.** 1919 Saskatchewan Dr. At Rose St; centre. Int corridors. **Pets:** $35 daily fee/pet. Service with restrictions, crate.

▼▼ Howard Johnson ⏚
(306) 584-8800. **$120-$141.** 4255 Albert St S. 1.25 km n of jct Trans-Canada Hwy 1 and Albert St (Hwy 6). Ext/int corridors. **Pets:** Accepted.

▼▼▼▼ Quality Hotel ⏚
(306) 569-4656. **$89-$105.** 1717 Victoria Ave. Just e of Broad St; downtown. Int corridors. **Pets:** Accepted.

**Radisson Plaza Hotel Saskatchewan** LH
(306) 522-7691. **$118-$153.** 2125 Victoria Ave. Victoria Ave at Scarth St; centre. Int corridors. **Pets:** $35 one-time fee/room. Service with restrictions, crate.

SAVE S$ X &M ∎ ▦ ☂ ⊠

**Ramada Hotel & Convention Centre** LH
(306) 569-1666. **$149.** 1818 Victoria Ave. Victoria Ave and Broad St; centre of downtown. Int corridors. **Pets:** Accepted.

A$K S$ X ∎ ▦ ☂ ⊠

**Regina Inn Hotel & Conference Centre** LH
(306) 525-6767. **$99-$109.** 1975 Broad St. Jct Victoria Ave; centre of downtown. Int corridors. **Pets:** Accepted.

SAVE X ∎ ▦ ☂

**Regina Super 8** SH
(306) 789-8833. **$74-$84, 14 day notice.** 2730 Victoria Ave E. Trans-Canada Hwy 1, 1.6 km e of Ring Rd; at eastern approach to Regina. Int corridors. **Pets:** Other species. $10 daily fee/room. Service with restrictions.

A$K S$ X &M ∎ ▦

**Sandman Hotel Suites and Spa** SH
(306) 757-2444. **$109-$144.** 1800 Victoria Ave E. Just e of Ring Rd; at eastern approach to city. Int corridors. **Pets:** Accepted.

X &' ∎ ▦ ☂ ⊇

**Travelodge Regina East** SH
(306) 565-0455. **$80-$109.** 1110 Victoria Ave E. Trans-Canada Hwy 1, just w of Ring Rd, at eastern approach to city. Int corridors. **Pets:** Accepted.

SAVE S$ X ∎ ▦ ⊇

# SASKATOON

**Best Western Inn & Suites** SH
(306) 244-5552. **$84-$90.** 1715 Idylwyld Dr N. 2.6 km n on Hwy 11 (Idylwyld Dr). Ext/int corridors. **Pets:** Medium. Designated rooms, service with restrictions, supervision.

A$K S$ X ∎ ▦ ☂ ⊠

**Colonial Square Motel & Suites** SH 🐾
(306) 343-1676. **$79.** 1301 8th St E. Just w of Cumberland St. Ext/int corridors. **Pets:** Small. $5 daily fee/room. Service with restrictions, supervision.

SAVE X ∎ ▦

**Comfort Inn** SH
(306) 934-1122. **$80-$110.** 2155 Northridge Dr. 3 km n; just ne of jct Hwy 11 (Idylwyld Dr) and Circle Dr. Int corridors. **Pets:** Accepted.

A$K S$ X &M ∎ ▦

**Country Inn & Suites By Carlson** SH
(306) 934-3900. **$90.** 617 Cynthia St. Just w of jct Hwy 11 (Idylwyld Dr) and Circle Dr. Int corridors. **Pets:** Accepted.

A$K S$ X &M ∎ ▦

**Delta Bessborough** LH
(306) 244-5521. **$114-$234.** 601 Spadina Crescent E. At 21st St E; centre of downtown. Int corridors. **Pets:** Accepted.

A$K S$ X ∎ ▦ ☂ ⊇ ⊠

**Heritage Inn** SH
(306) 665-8121. **$90-$92.** 102 Cardinal Crescent. Jct Circle and Airport drs. Int corridors. **Pets:** Other species. $10 daily fee/room. Service with restrictions, supervision.

A$K S$ X ∎ ▦ ☂ ⊇

**Holiday Inn Express Hotel & Suites Saskatoon** SH
(306) 384-8844. **$99-$159.** 315 Idylwyld Dr N. Jct 25th St W. Int corridors. **Pets:** Very small, other species. $10 daily fee/room. Designated rooms, service with restrictions, crate.

A$K X &M ∎ ▦ ⊇

**Radisson Hotel Saskatoon** SH
(306) 665-3322. **$114-$149.** 405 20th St E. At 4th Ave S; centre. Int corridors. **Pets:** Small, other species. $25 one-time fee/room. Service with restrictions, supervision.

A$K S$ X &M ∎ ▦ ☂ ⊇ ⊠

**Ramada Hotel & Golf Dome** LH 🐾
(306) 665-6500. **$116, 3 day notice.** 806 Idylwyld Dr N. 4 km s of jct Circle Dr. Int corridors. **Pets:** Other species. $10 one-time fee/pet. Designated rooms, service with restrictions, crate.

A$K S$ X ∎ ▦ ☂ ⊇

**Sandman Hotel** LH
(306) 477-4844. **$89-$117.** 310 Circle Dr W. Jct Ave C N. Int corridors. **Pets:** Accepted.

A$K S$ X ∎ ▦ ☂ ⊇

**Saskatoon Inn Hotel & Conference Centre** LH 🐾
(306) 242-1440. **$139-$169.** 2002 Airport Dr. Jct Circle and Airport drs. Int corridors. **Pets:** Large, other species. Service with restrictions.

SAVE S$ X ∎ ▦ ☂ ⊇

**Saskatoon Travelodge Hotel** SH
(306) 242-8881. **$130.** 106 Circle Dr W. 3 km n, then just w of jct Hwy 11 (Idylwyld Dr). Int corridors. **Pets:** Accepted.

SAVE X ∎ ▦ ☂ ⊇ ⊠

**Sheraton Cavalier** SH
(306) 652-6770. **$199.** 612 Spadina Crescent E. At 21st St E; centre of downtown. Int corridors. **Pets:** Accepted.

A$K S$ X ∎ ▦ ☂ ⊇ ⊠

**Super 8** SH
(306) 384-8989. **$85-$93.** 706 Circle Dr E. 2 km e of jct Hwy 11 (Idylwyld Dr). Ext/int corridors. **Pets:** $5 one-time fee/room. Service with restrictions, supervision.

X ∎ ▦

**Thriftlodge** M
(306) 244-2191. **$76-$96.** 1825 Idylwyld Dr N. Just s of Circle Dr N. Ext corridors. **Pets:** Small, dogs only. $10 one-time fee/pet. Designated rooms, service with restrictions, supervision.

SAVE S$ X ∎ ▦

# SHAUNAVON

**Hidden Hilten Motel** M
(306) 297-4166. **$55-$70.** 352 5th St W. 0.5 km e from jct Hwy 13 and 37, just n. Ext corridors. **Pets:** Accepted.

A$K S$ X ∎ ▦

# SWIFT CURRENT

**Comfort Inn** SH
(306) 778-3994. **$90-$112.** 1510 S Service Rd E. Trans-Canada Hwy 1, just w of 22nd Ave NE. Int corridors. **Pets:** Accepted.

A$K S$ X ∎ ▦

**Green Hectares Bed & Breakfast** BB 🐾
(306) 773-7632. **$65-$105 (no credit cards).** Waker Rd. Trans-Canada Hwy 1, exit 22nd Ave NE, just n to Waker Rd, 0.5 km e, follow signs. Ext/int corridors. **Pets:** Other species. $10 daily fee/pet. Designated rooms, crate.

X ∎ ▦ ⊠

**Rodeway Inn Motel** SH
(306) 773-4664. **$65-$72.** 1200 S Service Rd E. Trans-Canada Hwy 1, just w of 22nd Ave NE. Ext/int corridors. **Pets:** Small. Designated rooms, service with restrictions, supervision.

SAVE S$ X ∎ ☂

Ⓐ ◆ **Safari Inn Motel M**
(306) 773-4608. **$57-$62.** 810 S Service Rd E. 1 km w of jct Hwy 1 and
4. Ext corridors. **Pets:** Small. $10 daily fee/pet. Designated rooms, service
with restrictions, supervision.
〔SAVE〕 ✕ 🛏 ▣

◆◆ **Super 8 Motel SH**
(306) 778-6088. **$82-$150, 30 day notice.** 405 N Service Rd E. Just e
of Central Ave. Int corridors. **Pets:** Medium. $5 daily fee/pet. Designated
rooms, service with restrictions, supervision.
〔ASK〕 〔S〕 ✕ 🛏 ▣ ⇌

◆◆ **Swift Current Travelodge M**
(306) 773-3101. **$75-$95.** Trans-Canada Hwy 1 E. Just e of Central
Ave, on North Service Rd. Ext corridors. **Pets:** Accepted.
〔ASK〕 〔S〕 ✕ 🛏 ▣ ⇌

Ⓐ ◆ **Westwind Motel M**
(306) 773-1441. **$50-$68.** 155 N Service Rd W. Trans-Canada Hwy 1,
0.5 km w of Central Ave. Ext corridors. **Pets:** Small, dogs only. Designated rooms, service with restrictions, supervision.
〔SAVE〕 ✕ 🛏 ⑪ ⇌

# WEYBURN

Ⓐ ◆◆ **Perfect Inns & Suites M**
(306) 842-2691. **$65-$85.** 238 Sims Ave. 0.5 km w of jct Hwy 35 and
39. Ext/int corridors. **Pets:** Accepted.
〔SAVE〕 ✕ 🛏 ▣

# YORKTON

◆◆ **Comfort Inn & Suites SH**
(306) 783-0333. **$78-$154.** 22 Dracup Ave. Just w of jct Hwy 9, 10 and
16 (Yellowhead Hwy). Int corridors. **Pets:** Accepted.
〔ASK〕 〔S〕 ✕ 🛏 ▣ ⇌

◆ **Howard Johnson Inn SH** 🐾
(306) 783-6581. **$68-$90.** 207 Broadway St E. Jct Hwy 9, 10 and 16
(Yellowhead Hwy). Ext/int corridors. **Pets:** Designated rooms, service
with restrictions, supervision.
〔ASK〕 〔S〕 ✕ 🛏 ▣ ⑪ ⇌

# YUKON TERRITORY

## DAWSON CITY

◆ **Bonanza Gold Motel** Ⓜ
(867) 993-6789. **$69-$189.** 2.4 km s on Hwy 2. Ext corridors.
**Pets:** Accepted.
⊠ ⌨ 🖥 💻 🍽 🅺

◆◆ **Klondike Kate's Cabins** Ⓒ🄰
(867) 993-6527. **$85-$135.** 1103 3rd Ave & King St. Downtown.
**Pets:** Other species. $20 one-time fee/room.
🄰🅂🄺 ⊠ ⌨ 🖥 💻 🍽 🅺

🄐🄐 ◆◆ **Westmark Inn Dawson City** Ⓜ
(867) 993-5542. **$149.** 5th St & Harper. At 5th and Harper sts; downtown. Ext/int corridors. **Pets:** Accepted.
🅂🄰🆅🄴 ⊠ 💻 🍽 🅺

## HAINES JUNCTION

🄐🄐 ◆◆ **Alcan Motor Inn** Ⓜ
(867) 634-2371. **$90-$120.** Jct of Alaska and Haines hwys (1 and 3). Ext corridors. **Pets:** Accepted.
🅂🄰🆅🄴 ⊠ 🖥 💻

## WHITEHORSE

🄐🄐 ◆◆ **High Country Inn** 🆂🄷 🐾
(867) 667-4471. **$99-$199, 3 day notice.** 4051 4th Ave. 0.6 km e of Main St. Int corridors. **Pets:** Other species. $15 one-time fee/pet. Designated rooms, service with restrictions, supervision.
🅂🄰🆅🄴 🅂🄾 ⊠ 🖥 💻 🍽

🄐🄐 ◆ **The Town and Mountain Hotel** 🆂🄷
(867) 668-7644. **$69-$119.** 401 Main St. Downtown. Int corridors.
**Pets:** Other species. $10 daily fee/pet. Designated rooms, service with restrictions.
🅂🄰🆅🄴 🅂🄾 ⊠ 🖥 💻 🍽 🅺

🄐🄐 ◆◆ **Westmark Whitehorse Hotel & Conference Centre** 🆂🄷
(867) 393-9700. **$129.** 201 Wood St. At 2nd Ave; centre. Int corridors.
**Pets:** Medium. Designated rooms, service with restrictions, crate.
🅂🄰🆅🄴 ⊠ 🅼 🕜 ⌨ 🖥 💻 🍽 🅺

# CAMPGROUNDS

## United States
## Canada

# UNITED STATES

## Alabama

**CHILDERSBURG** — DESOTO CAVERNS PARK CAMPGROUND. (256) 378-7252. **4P $22-$23, XP $2-$3.** 5181 DeSoto Caverns Pkwy, 35044. On SR 76, 5 mi e.

**PELHAM** — BIRMINGHAM SOUTH CAMPGROUND. (205) 664-8832. **2P $31, XP $2.** 222 Hwy 33, 35124. I-65, exit 242, 0.5 mi w on CR 52, then 0.3 mi n.

## Alaska

**ANCHORAGE** — ANCHORAGE RV PARK 🆎 (907) 338-7275. **2P $32-$45, XP $2-$14.** 1200 N Muldoon Rd, 99506. SR 1, exit Muldoon Rd N, 0.5 mi nw.

## Arizona

**AMADO** — DEANZA TRAILS RV RESORT. (520) 398-8628. **2P $30, XP $5.** 2869 E Frontage Rd, 85645. I-19, exit 48, just e, then 1.6 mi s.

**APACHE JUNCTION** — SUPERSTITION SUNRISE LUXURY RV RESORT. (480) 986-4524. **2P $20-$35, XP $5. (no credit cards).** 702 S Meridian Rd, 85220. US 60, exit 193 (Signal Butte Rd), 0.4 mi n to Southern, 1 mi e, then 0.5 mi n.

**BENSON** — BUTTERFIELD RV RESORT. (520) 586-4400. **2P $22-$25, XP $2.** 251 S Ocotillo Ave, 85602. I-10, exit 304 (Ocotillo Ave), 0.6 mi s.

**BENSON** — COCHISE TERRACE RV RESORT. (520) 586-0600. **2P $19-$24, XP $2.** 1030 S Barrel Cactus Ridge, 85602. I-10, exit 302, 1 mi s on SR 90, then just w.

**BENSON** — PATO BLANCO LAKES RV PARK. (520) 586-8966. **2P $16-$32, XP $2.** 635 E Pearl St, 85602. I-10, exit 306, just s, 0.7 mi w on Frontage Rd, then 0.4 mi n on County Rd.

**BENSON** — SAN PEDRO TERRITORY MOBILE HOME & RV RESORT. (520) 586-9546. **2P $18-$22, XP $2.** 1110 S Hwy 80, Box 1, 85602. I-10, exit 304 (Ocotillo Ave), 0.5 mi s, 1 mi e on 4th St, then 1.3 mi se.

**CAMP VERDE** — DISTANT DRUMS RV RESORT. (928) 554-8000. **2P $30-$35, XP $5.** 583 W Middle Verde Rd, 86322. I-17, exit 289, just sw.

**CASA GRANDE** — FIESTA GRANDE-RV RESORT 🆎 (520) 836-7222. **2P $31, XP $2.** 1511 E Florence Blvd, 85222. I-10, exit 194, 2 mi w.

**CASA GRANDE** — PALM CREEK GOLF AND RV RESORT. (520) 421-7000. **Call for rates.** 1110 N Henness Rd, 85222. I-10, exit 194, 1 mi w, then just n.

**FORT MCDOWELL** — EAGLE VIEW RV RESORT AT FT MCDOWELL 🆎 (480) 836-5310. **4P $32, XP $10.** 9605 N Ft McDowell Rd, 85264. Jct Shea Blvd, 2 mi ne on SR 89, 0.5 mi se.

**HUACHUCA CITY** — TOMBSTONE TERRITORIES RV PARK 🆎 (520) 457-2584. **2P $28-$30, XP $1.** 2111 E Hwy 82, 85616. Jct SR 90, 7.7 mi e on SR 82; between MM 59 and 60.

**MESA** — GOOD LIFE RV RESORT 🆎 (480) 832-4990. **2P $25-$35, XP $3.** 3403 E Main St, 85213. US 60, exit 184 (Val Vista Dr), 2 mi n, then just w. Small pets allowed.

**MESA** — MESA SPIRIT RV RESORT 🆎 (480) 832-1770. **2P $18-$45, XP $4.** 3020 E Main St, 85213. US 60, exit 184 (Val Vista Dr), 2 mi n to Main St, then 0.8 mi w.

**MESA** — VALLE DEL ORO RV RESORT. (480) 984-1146. **Call for rates. (no credit cards).** 1452 S Ellsworth Rd, 85208. US 60, exit 191, just n. Small pets allowed.

**PICACHO** — PICACHO PEAK RV RESORT 🆎 (520) 466-7841. **2P $25, XP $2.** 17065 E Peak Ln, 85241. I-10, exit 219, 1.3 mi s on frontage road. (PO Box 1100, RED ROCK, 85245).

**SHOW LOW** — VOYAGER AT JUNIPER RIDGE 🆎 (928) 532-3456. **2P $20-$35, XP $2.** 1993 Juniper Ridge Resort, 85901. Jct US 60, 7.3 mi n on SR 77 to White Mountain Lake Rd, then 3 mi e.

**SIERRA VISTA** — PUEBLO DEL SOL RV RESORT. (520) 378-0213. **2P $33, XP $5.** 3400 Resort Dr, 85650. Jct SR 90, 4 mi s on SR 92, just e on Canyon de Flores.

**SUN CITY/SUN CITY WEST** — PARADISE RV RESORT. (623) 977-0344. **2P $27-$29, XP $2-$3.** 10950 W Union Hills Dr, 85373. Loop 101, 3.8 mi w. Small pets allowed.

**TONOPAH** — SADDLE MOUNTAIN RV PARK. (623) 386-3892. **2P $23, XP $2.** 3607 N 411th Ave, 85354. I-10, exit 94, 0.5 mi s.

**TUCSON** — BEAUDRY RV RESORT. (520) 239-1300. **2P $20-$60.** 5151 S Country Club, 85706. I-10, exit 264B (Palo Verde and Irvington), just n to Irvington, 0.5 mi w, then just s.

**TUCSON** — VOYAGER RV RESORT 🍁 (520) 574-5000. **Call for rates.** 8701 S Kolb Rd, 85706. I-10, exit 270, 0.7 mi s.

**YUMA** — BONITA MESA RV RESORT. (928) 342-2999. **2P $30, XP $3. (no credit cards).** 9400 N Frontage Rd, 85365. I-8, exit 12 (Fortuna Rd), just n, then 1.6 mi w.

**YUMA** — COCOPAH RV & GOLF RESORT. (928) 343-9300. **Call for rates.** 6800 Strand Ave, 85364. I-8, exit Winterhaven/4th Ave, 0.5 mi s on 4th Ave, 2.4 mi w on 1st St, just s on Ave C, 1.4 mi w on Riverside, then 0.9 mi nw.

**YUMA** — SUN VISTA RV RESORT 🍁 (928) 726-8920. **2P $40, XP $3.** 7201 E 32nd St (Business 8), 85365. I-8, exit 7 (Araby Rd), just s, then 0.5 mi e. Small pets allowed.

**YUMA** — WESTWIND RV & GOLF RESORT. (928) 342-2992. **Call for rates.** 9797 E 32nd St, 85365. I-8, exit 12 (Fortuna Rd) on south side, 1 mi w. Small pets allowed.

# California

**AGUANGA** — OUTDOOR RESORTS RANCHO CALIFORNIA. (951) 767-0848. **Call for rates.** 45525 Hwy 79 S, 92536. SR 371, just se.

**BAKERSFIELD** — BAKERSFIELD PALMS RV RESORT 🍁 (661) 366-6700. **2P $26-$28, XP $2.** 250 Fairfax Rd, 93307. SR 99, exit SR 58, 6 mi e, exit Fairfax Rd, then 0.5 mi n.

**BIG BEAR LAKE** — BIG BEAR SHORES RV RESORT & YACHT CLUB. (909) 866-4151. **6P $54-$120.** 40751 North Shore Ln, 92315. SR 18, 5 mi e of the dam on SR 38 (North Shore Dr), 1.2 mi se. (PO Box 1572).

**BUELLTON** — FLYING FLAGS RV PARK & CAMPGROUND 🍁 (805) 688-3716. **2P $20-$44, XP $3.** 180 Ave of the Flags, 93427. Just w of US 101, exit SR 246.

**CASTAIC** — VALENCIA TRAVEL VILLAGE 🍁 (661) 257-3333. **6P $43-$55, XP $2.** 27946 Henry Mayo Rd, 91384. I-5, exit SR 126, 1.3 mi w.

**CATHEDRAL CITY** — OUTDOOR RESORTS/PALM SPRINGS. (760) 324-4005. **6P $35-$65.** 69-411 Ramon Rd, 92234. I-10, exit Date Palm Dr, 2.2 mi s, then 0.5 mi e.

**CHULA VISTA** — CHULA VISTA RV RESORT. (619) 422-0111. **4P $42-$64, XP $3.** 460 Sandpiper Way, 91910. I-5, exit J St/Marina Pkwy, 4 mi w, then 0.5 mi n. Small pets allowed.

**CHULA VISTA** — SAN DIEGO METRO KOA. (619) 427-3601. **2P $30-$85, XP $4.** 111 N 2nd Ave, 91910. I-5, exit E St, 1 mi e to 2nd Ave, then 1 mi n; I-805, exit E St, 1 mi w, then just n.

**COLOMA** — COLOMA RESORT. (530) 621-2267. **6P $31-$35, XP $4-$12.** 6921 Mt Murphy Rd, 95613. E off SR 49 on Mt. Murphy Rd; on South Fork of the American River. (PO Box 516).

**DEL LOMA** — DEL LOMA RV PARK & CAMPGROUND. (530) 623-2834. **$22, XP $2.** Rt 1, Box 54, 96101. US 229, southwest Del Loma.

**DESERT HOT SPRINGS** — SKY VALLEY RESORT. (760) 329-2909. **2P $38-$40, XP $5.** 74-711 Dillon Rd, 92241. I-10, exit Palm Dr, 3.3 mi n, then 8.5 mi e.

**EL CENTRO** — DESERT TRAILS RV PARK. (760) 352-7275. **2P $26-$33, XP $3.** 225 Wake Ave, 92243. I-8, exit 4th St, just s, then just e. Small pets allowed.

**EL CENTRO** — SUNBEAM LAKE RV RESORT. (760) 352-7154. **Call for rates.** 1716 W Sunbeam Lake Dr, 92243. I-8, exit Drew Rd, 0.5 mi n, then 8 mi w of SR 86.

**GARBERVILLE** — BENBOW VALLEY RV RESORT & GOLF COURSE 🍁 (707) 923-2777. **2P $29-$50, XP $4.** 7000 Benbow Dr, 95542. US 101, exit Benbow Dr, just e.

**GROVELAND** — YOSEMITE LAKES CAMPGROUND AND RESORT 🍁 (209) 962-0121. **$35-$38, XP $5.** 31191 Hardin Flat Rd, 95321. 18 mi e on SR 120, 5 mi w of Yosemite National Park's SR 120 Gate/Entrance.

**HEMET** — GOLDEN VILLAGE PALMS RV RESORT 🍁 (951) 925-2518. **2P $40-$57, XP $5-$10.** 3600 W Florida Ave, 92545. SR 79 N (San Jacinto St), 3 mi w. Small pets allowed.

**INDIO** — INDIAN WELLS RV PARK. (760) 347-0895. **2P $34-$37, XP $2-$3.** 47-340 Jefferson St, 92201. I-10, exit Jefferson St, 3 mi s.

**INDIO** — OUTDOOR RESORTS-MOTORCOACH RESORT & SPA. (760) 775-7255. **Call for rates.** 80-394 48th Ave, 92201. I-10, exit Jefferson St, 3.5 mi s, then just e.

**NEWPORT BEACH** — NEWPORT DUNES WATERFRONT RV RESORT. (949) 729-3863. **6P $35-$200.** 1131 Back Bay Dr, 92660. SR 73, exit Jamboree Rd southbound, 3 mi s, then just n on SR 1; exit Bison Ave northbound, just w to MacArthur Blvd, 2.5 mi s to SR 1, then 1.5 mi n.

**NILAND** — FOUNTAIN OF YOUTH SPA. (760) 354-1340. **2P $21-$33, XP $2.** 10249 Coachella Canal Rd, 92257. 14 mi nw on SR 111, then 2.3 mi ne on Hot Mineral Spa Rd.

**ORANGE** — ORANGELAND RECREATION VEHICLE PARK (AAA) (714) 633-0414. **8P $55-$70, XP $2.** 1600 W Struck Ave, 92867. SR 57, exit Katella Ave, 0.5 mi e, then just s.

**PISMO BEACH** — PACIFIC DUNES RANCH RV PARK. (805) 489-7787. **6P $28-$40, XP $5.** 1205 Silver Spur Pl, 93445. In Oceano; SR 1, exit 22nd St, 0.3 mi s, then 0.4 mi w.

**PISMO BEACH** — PISMO COAST VILLAGE RV RESORT. (805) 773-1811. **6P $34-$47, XP $2.** 165 S Dolliver St, 93449. 0.5 mi s on SR 1.

**PLYMOUTH** — FAR HORIZONS 49'ER VILLAGE (AAA) (209) 245-6981. **4P $36-$62, XP $5.** 18265 Hwy 49, 95669. On SR 49, 0.3 mi s.

**SAN DIEGO** — CAMPLAND ON THE BAY. (858) 581-4260. **4P $43-$245, XP $5.** 2211 Pacific Beach Dr, 92109. I-5, exit Grand Ave northbound, 1 mi w to Olney, then 0.3 mi s; exit Balboa/Garnet southbound, s on Mission Bay Dr to Grand Ave, then 1 mi w to Olney.

**SAN DIMAS** — EAST SHORE RV PARK (AAA) (909) 599-8355. **2P $37-$44, XP $2.** 1440 Camper View Rd, 91773. I-10, exit Fairplex Dr, 0.6 mi n, 0.6 mi w on Via Verde, then 0.6 mi n; in Frank G Bonelli Regional Park.

**SAN JUAN BAUTISTA** — BETABEL RV RESORT (AAA) (831) 623-2202. **Call for rates.** 9664 Betabel Rd, 95045. US 101, exit Betabel Rd, just w. Small pets allowed.

**SANTA BARBARA** — EL CAPITAN CANYON. (805) 685-3887. **$115-$345.** 11560 Calle Real, 93117. 20 mi nw on north side of US 101 at El Capitan State Beach.

**SHAVER LAKE** — CAMP EDISON. (559) 841-3134. **Call for rates.** 42696 Tollhouse Rd, 93664. Just ne; lakeside. (PO Box 600).

**TEMECULA** — PECHANGA RV RESORT (AAA) (951) 303-2658. **$32-$37.** 45000 Pechanga Pkwy, 92592. I-15, exit SR 79 S, 1 mi e, then 2 mi s.

**TEMECULA** — VAIL LAKE RESORT. (951) 303-0173. **6P $25-$55, XP $5.** 38000 Hwy 79 S, 92592. I-15, exit SR 79 S, 9 mi se.

**WEAVERVILLE** — TRINITY LAKE RESORTS AT PINEWOOD COVE RV PARK & CAMPGROUND. (530) 286-2201. **2P $18-$34, XP $3-$10.** 45110 State Hwy 3, 96091. 14 mi ne of town.

**WINTERHAVEN** — RIVER'S EDGE RV RESORT. (760) 572-5105. **2P $25, XP $2.** 2299 Winterhaven Dr, 92283. I-8, exit first Winterhaven eastbound; exit Winterhaven Dr westbound, 0.5 mi e on frontage road. Small pets allowed.

# Colorado

**FORT COLLINS** — HERON LAKE RV PARK. (970) 484-9880. **2P $30-$48, XP $2.** 1910 N Taft Hill Rd, 80524. I-25, exit 269B, 6 mi w to Taft Hill, then 2.2 mi n.

**GOLDEN** — DAKOTA RIDGE RV PARK. (303) 279-1625. **2P $37, XP $4.** 17800 W Colfax Ave, 80401. I-70, exit 262 (W Colfax Ave), 1.8 mi w on US 40.

**GRAND LAKE** — WINDING RIVER RESORT. (970) 627-3215. **2P $27-$34, XP $4.** 1447 Country Road 49, 80447. 1.5 mi ne on US 34 to CR 491, then 1.5 mi w. (PO Box 629).

**LOVELAND** — JOHNSON'S CORNER RV RETREAT. (970) 669-8400. **2P $25-$32, XP $3.** 3618 SE Frontage Rd, 80537. I-25, exit 254, 0.3 mi se; adjacent to the Great Colorado Marketplace. Small pets allowed.

# Florida

**ARCADIA** — TOBY'S RV RESORT. (863) 494-1744. **2P $25-$37, XP $2.** 3550 NE Hwy 70, 34266. On SR 70, 2.7 mi e.

**BRADENTON** — ENCORE RV RESORT-SARASOTA NORTH. (941) 745-2600. **Call for rates.** 800 Kay Rd NE, 34212. I-75, exit 220 southbound; exit 220B northbound, 0.6 mi w on SR 64, then 0.8 mi n on 60th Court St.

**BRADENTON** — HORSESHOE COVE RV RESORT. (941) 758-5335. **2P $27-$42, XP $3.** 5100 60th St E, 34203. I-75, exit 217 southbound; exit 217B northbound, 1.7 mi w on SR 70, then just n on Caruso Rd.

**BRADENTON** — SARASOTA BAY RV PARK (AAA) (941) 794-1200. **$30-$40, XP $2.** 10777 Cortez Rd W, 34210. Jct US 41 business route, 5.8 mi w on SR 684.

**BUSHNELL** — BLUEBERRY HILL RV PARK. (352) 793-4112. **Call for rates. (no credit cards).** 6233 CR 609, 33513. I-75, exit 314, just e on SR 48, then just s. Small pets allowed. 🏔 🚐 ⊠

**CHOKOLOSKEE** — OUTDOOR RESORTS OF AMERICA OF CHOKOLOSKEE. (239) 695-2881. **Call for rates.** 100-159 CR 29 S, 34138. On CR 29; center. (PO Box 39). 🏔 🚐 ⊠

**CRYSTAL RIVER** — ENCORE SUPERPARK CRYSTAL RIVER. (352) 795-3774. **Call for rates.** 11419 W Fort Island Tr, 34429. Jct US 19, 4.5 mi w on SR 44 W. 🚐 ⊠

**CRYSTAL RIVER** — ROCK CRUSHER CANYON RV PARK. (352) 795-3870. **2P $15-$28, XP $2.** 275 S Rock Crusher Rd, 34429. 1.5 mi s of SR 44. 🚐 ⊠

**DAVENPORT** — DEER CREEK RV RESORT. (863) 424-2839. **2P $40-$45.** 42749 Hwy 27, 33837. I-4, exit 55, 1 mi se. 🆂🅳 🚐 ⊠

**DAVENPORT** — FORT SUMMIT KOA 🗛🗛🗛 (863) 424-1880. **2P $37-$59, XP $4-$5.** 2525 Frontage Rd, 33837. Jct US 27 and I-4, exit 55, on frontage road; behind Best Western. 🆂🅳 🚐 ⊠

**DEBARY** — HIGH BANKS MARINA & CAMP RESORT. (386) 668-4491. **2P $30-$40, XP $5.** 488 W High Banks Rd, 32713. 2.7 mi w of US 17-92. 🚐 ⊠

**DESTIN** — DESTIN RV BEACH RESORT. (850) 837-3529. **2P $55-$69, XP $4.** 362 Miramar Beach Dr, 32550. 4.1 mi e of SR 293 (Mid-Bay Bridge), just s. 🏔 🚐

**FORT MYERS BEACH** — GULF WATERS RV RESORT 🗛🗛🗛 (239) 437-5888. **2P $38-$65.** 11301 Summerlin Square Rd, 33931. 2.4 mi ne of jct Matanzas Pass Bridge, 0.8 mi ne on Pine Ridge Rd, just w. 🏔 🚐 ⊠

**FORT MYERS BEACH** — INDIAN CREEK PARK RV RESORT 🗛🗛🗛 (239) 466-6060. **2P $22-$45, XP $4.** 17340 San Carlos Blvd, 33931. 2.4 mi ne of jct Matanzas Pass Bridge. 🏔 🚐 ⊠

**FORT MYERS** — SIESTA BAY RV RESORT 🗛🗛🗛 (239) 466-8988. **$22-$46, XP $4.** 19333 Summerlin Rd, 33908. 1.6 mi w of jct US 41 on Gladiolus Dr, 4.8 mi s on Summerlin Rd (CR 869). 🏔 🚐 ⊠

**JACKSONVILLE** — FLAMINGO LAKE RV RESORT 🗛🗛🗛 (904) 766-0672. **$35, XP $3.** 3640 Newcomb Rd, 32218. I-295, exit 32, just nw on SR 115. Small pets allowed. 🏔 🚐 ⊠

**JENNINGS** — JENNINGS OUTDOOR RESORT CAMPGROUND. (386) 938-3321. **2P $22-$28, XP $2.** 2039 Hamilton Ave, 32053. I-75, exit 467, just w on SR 143. 🚐 ⊠

**JENSEN BEACH** — NETTLES ISLAND. (772) 229-1300. **$36-$62.** 9803 S Ocean Dr, 34957. On SR A1A, 2.3 mi n of jct SR 732 (Jensen Beach Cswy); on S Hutchinson Island. 🏔 🚐 ⊠

**KISSIMMEE** — OUTDOOR RESORTS AT ORLANDO. (863) 424-1259. **$30.** On US 192, 1 mi e of jct US 27; jct I-4, exit 64B, 6.3 mi w. (9000 W US 192, CLERMONT, 34711). Small pets allowed. 🚐 ⊠

**KISSIMMEE** — TROPICAL PALMS RESORT. (407) 396-4595. **Call for rates.** 2650 Holiday Tr, 34746. I-4, exit 64A, 1.5 mi e on US 192, then 0.8 mi s. 🚐 ⊠

**LA BELLE** — WHISPER CREEK RV RESORT. (863) 675-6888. **2P $30. (no credit cards).** 1980 Hickory Dr, 33935. On SR 29, 1.8 mi n of jct SR 80. 🚐 ⊠

**LAKE BUENA VISTA** — DISNEY'S FORT WILDERNESS RESORT & CAMPGROUND 🗛🗛🗛 (407) 824-2900. **2P $39-$92, XP $2.** 4510 N Fort Wilderness Tr, 32830-1000. On US 192; in Walt Disney World. (PO Box 10,000). 🚐 ⊠

**LAKELAND** — LAKELAND RV RESORT. (863) 687-6146. **2P $36-$38, XP $3.** 900 Old Combee Rd, 33805. I-4, exit 33 eastbound, 1 mi ne on SR 33, then just w; exit 38 westbound, 5 mi sw on SF 33, then just nw. 🚐 ⊠

**LAKELAND** — SANLAN RANCH CAMPGROUND 🗛🗛🗛 (863) 665-1726. **2P $22-$50, XP $3-$5.** 3929 US 98 S, 33813. I-4, exit 32, 8.7 mi s on US 98; just s of SR 570. 🚐 ⊠

**LEESBURG** — HOLIDAY TRAVEL RESORT 🗛🗛🗛 (352) 787-5151. **4P $29-$32, XP $3-$5.** 28229 CR 33, 34748. 3.5 mi s via US 27, 0.5 mi w. 🚐 ⊠

**MELBOURNE BEACH** — OUTDOOR RESORTS MELBOURNE BEACH LUXURY RV RESORT. (321) 724-2600. **Call for rates.** 214 Horizon Ln, 32951. 2.5 mi s. 🏔 🚐 ⊠

**MIMS** — SEASONS IN THE SUN MOTOR COACH RESORT. (321) 385-0440. **Call for rates.** 2400 Seasons In The Sun Blvd, 32754. I-95, exit 223, 0.5 mi w on SR 46. 🏔 🚐 ⊠

**NOKOMIS** — ENCORE RESORT-SARASOTA SOUTH. (941) 488-9674. **Call for rates.** 1070 Laurel Rd E, 34275. I-75, exit 195, 2.6 mi w. 🚐 ⊠

**OCALA** — OCALA-SILVER SPRINGS KOA. (352) 237-2138. **Call for rates.** 3200 SW 38th Ave, 34474. I-75, exit 350, just w on SR 200, just n on SW 38th Ct, then 0.5 mi e. 🚐 ⊠

**OKEECHOBEE** — OKEECHOBEE KOA RESORT & GOLF COURSE. (863) 763-0231. **2P $34-$75, XP $4-$6.** 4276 Hwy US 441 S, 34974. On US 98 and 441, 3 mi s of jct SR 70; 0.3 mi n of Lake Okeechobee and jct SR 78.

**OLD TOWN** — YELLOW JACKET CAMPGROUND. (352) 542-8365. **2P $24-$35, XP $6-$10.** 55 SE 503 Ave, 32680. 10.7 mi s on SR 349, then 1.2 mi on dirt road.

**ORMOND BEACH** — ENCORE SUPERPARK-DAYTONA BEACH NORTH ⚠ (386) 672-3045. **2P $30-$40, XP $5.** 1701 N US 1, 32174. I-95, exit 273, 0.5 mi nw.

**PANAMA CITY BEACH** — EMERALD COAST RV BEACH RESORT ⚠ (850) 235-0924. **2P $39-$55, XP $3.** 1957 Allison Ave, 32407. US 98/98A and Allison Ave, 1.5 mi w of Hathaway Bridge.

**PORT CHARLOTTE** — ENCORE RV RESORT-PORT CHARLOTTE. (941) 624-4511. **Call for rates.** 3737 El Jobean Rd, 33953. On SR 776, 4.6 mi w of jct US 41.

**PORT CHARLOTTE** — RIVERSIDE RV RESORT & CAMPGROUND ⚠ (863) 993-2111. **4P $29-$44, XP $2.** 9770 SW CR 769, 34269. I-75, exit 170, 4.5 mi ne on CR 769 (Kings Hwy).

**REDDICK** — ENCORE RV PARK-OCALA. (352) 591-1723. **Call for rates.** 16905 NW CR 225, 32686. I-75, exit 368, just w on CR 318, then 0.8 mi s.

**RIVER RANCH** — RIVER RANCH RV RESORT ⚠ (863) 692-1116. **4P $40-$50, XP $2.** 30529 River Ranch Blvd, 33867. 3.5 mi s of SR 60; 25 mi e of US 27; 23 mi w of Florida Tpke and US 441; just w of the Kissimmee River.

**ROCKLEDGE** — SPACE COAST RV RESORT. (321) 636-2873. **2P $35-$40, XP $3.** 820 Barnes Blvd, 32955. I-95, exit 195 (Fiske Blvd), 0.3 mi se, 2 mi w of US 1 on SR 502. Small pets allowed.

**SARASOTA** — SUN-N-FUN RV RESORT ⚠ (941) 371-2505. **$27-$62.** 7125 Fruitville Rd, 34240. I-75, exit 210, 1.2 mi e on SR 780.

**SEBASTIAN** — ENCORE RV PARK-VERO BEACH. (772) 589-7828. **Call for rates.** I-95, exit 156, just e on CR 512. (9455 108th Ave, VERO BEACH, 32967-3154).

**SEBRING** — BUTTONWOOD BAY RV RESORT ⚠ (863) 655-1122. **2P $23-$39, XP $4.** 10001 US 27 S, 33876. 1.5 mi s of SR 98. Small pets allowed.

**SILVER SPRINGS** — COLBY WOODS RV RESORT. (352) 625-1122. **Call for rates. (no credit cards).** 10613 E Hwy 40, 34488. On SR 40, 4.5 mi e of Silver Springs attraction.

**SILVER SPRINGS** — THE SPRINGS RV RESORT. (352) 236-5250. **2P $25, XP $3.** 2950 NE 52nd Ct, 34488. On SR 40, 0.5 mi w of Silver Springs attraction, 0.5 mi n.

**ST. PETERSBURG** — ST. PETERSBURG-MADEIRA BEACH RESORT KOA. (727) 392-2233. **2P $37-$55, XP $4-$6.** 5400 95th St N, 33708. Jct 38th Ave N, 1.4 mi n on Tyrone/Bay Pines Blvd (Alternate Rt US 19), 0.5 mi e.

**SUMTERVILLE** — SHADY BROOK GOLF & RV RESORT. (352) 568-2244. **Call for rates.** 178 N US 301, 33585. I-75, exit 321, 2.5 mi e on CR 470, then 0.7 mi n. (PO Box 130).

**TITUSVILLE** — THE GREAT OUTDOORS RV & GOLF RESORT. (321) 269-5004. **2P $35-$55, XP $3.** 125 Plantation Dr, 32780. I-95, exit 215, 0.5 mi w on SR 50, 1.8 mi s on paved entrance road. Small pets allowed.

**UMATILLA** — OLDE MILL STREAM RV RESORT ⚠ (352) 669-3141. **2P $18-$29, XP $3.** 1000 N Central Ave, 32784. 0.8 mi n on SR 19. Small pets allowed.

# Georgia

**PINE MOUNTAIN** — PINE MOUNTAIN CAMPGROUND. (706) 663-4329. **2P $20-$35, XP $2.** 8804 Hamilton Rd, 31822. I-185, exit 42, 8 mi s on US 27.

**STONE MOUNTAIN** — STONE MOUNTAIN PARK CAMPGROUND. (770) 498-5710. **Call for rates.** Stone Mountain Park, 30086. On east side of Stone Mountain; in Stone Mountain Memorial Park. (PO Box 778). Small pets allowed.

# Idaho

**CASCADE** — ARROWHEAD R.V. PARK ON THE RIVER ⚠ (208) 382-4534. **2P $25-$27, XP $2.** 955 S Hwy 55, 83611. South end of town. (PO Box 337).

**COEUR D'ALENE** — BLACKWELL ISLAND RV RESORT. (208) 665-1300. **2P $33-$44, XP $2.** 800 S Marina Dr, 83814. I-90, exit 12, 1.5 mi s on US 95.

**KAMIAH** — LEWIS-CLARK RESORT RV PARK. (208) 935-2556. **Call for rates.** 1.5 mi e on US 12. (Rt 1, Box 17X, 83536).

**PINEHURST** — KELLOGG/SILVER VALLEY KOA. (208) 682-3612. **2P $18-$37, XP $3.** 801 N Division St, 83850. I-90, exit 45, just s. (PO Box 949).

**WHITE BIRD** — SWIFTWATER RV PARK & STORE. (208) 839-2700. **2P $20-$22, XP $3.** HC 01, Box 24, 83554. Just n of Milepost 222, exit Hammer Creek Recreational area, 0.8 mi nw. (PO Box 150).

# Illinois

**LEE CENTER** — O'CONNELL'S YOGI BEAR JELLYSTONE PARK (815) 857-3860. **2P $30-$49, XP $10-$12.** 970 Greenwing Rd, 61310. I-39, exit 87 (US 30), 12.8 mi w to CR 1955 E, then 3.3 mi se, follow signs. (PO Box 200, AMBOY).

**MILLBROOK** — YOGI BEAR'S JELLYSTONE PARK CAMP RESORT (630) 553-5172. **Call for rates.** 8574 Millbrook Rd, 60536. 1.5 mi n of jct SR 71. (PO Box 306).

# Indiana

**CRAWFORDSVILLE** — CRAWFORDSVILLE KOA. (765) 362-4190. **Call for rates.** 1600 Lafayette Rd, 47933. I-74, exit 34, 2 mi s on US 231.

**FREMONT** — YOGI BEAR'S JELLYSTONE PARK CAMP RESORT (260) 833-1114. **5P $32-$49, XP $5-$7.** 140 Ln, 201 Barton Lake, 46737-9652. I-69, exit 157 southbound; exit 154 northbound, 3 mi w on SR 120, then 0.5 mi n on CR 300 W; Toll Rd, exit 144 to SR 120.

**GRANGER** — SOUTH BEND EAST KOA. (574) 277-1335. **2P $18-$45, XP $3-$10.** 50707 Princess Way, 46530. I-80/90, exit 83, 2.3 mi ne on SR 23.

**MONTICELLO** — INDIANA BEACH CAMP RESORT. (574) 583-8306. **8P $19-$30, XP $3.** 5224 E Indiana Beach Rd, 47960. 0.5 mi w on US 24, 3.3 mi n on W Shafer Dr (6th St).

**PIERCETON** — YOGI BEAR'S JELLYSTONE PARK CAMP-RESORT. (574) 594-2124. **5P $33-$50, XP $5.** 1916 N 850 E, 46562. US 30, 4.3 mi n on SR 13, 1.3 mi e on CR 200.

**SANTA CLAUS** — LAKE RUDOLPH CAMPGROUND & RV RESORT. (812) 937-4458. **8P $20-$42.** 78 N Holiday Blvd, 47579. I-64, exit 63, 7.9 mi s on SR 162. (PO Box 98).

# Louisiana

**CARENCRO** — BAYOU WILDERNESS RV RESORT. (337) 896-0598. **4P $27-$33, XP $5.** 201 St Clair Rd, 70520. I-49, exit 2, 2.5 mi e on SR 98, then 1 mi n on Wilderness Tr.

**HAMMOND** — NEW ORLEANS-HAMMOND KOA KAMP-GROUND. (985) 542-8094. **$24-$26.** 14154 Club Deluxe Rd, 70403. I-12 to I-55 S, exit 28, 1 blk n, then 0.7 mi w.

**KINDER** — COUSHATTA CASINO RV RESORT. (337) 738-1200. **6P $17-$22.** 777 Pow Wow Pkwy, 70648. N of jct US 190 and 165, 4.5 mi on US 165. (PO Box 1240).

**ROBERT** — YOGI BEAR'S JELLYSTONE PARK CAMP-RESORT. (985) 542-1507. **5P $24-$50, XP $9-$11.** 46049 SR 445 N, 70455. I-12, exit 47, 3 mi n. (PO Box 519).

**SCOTT** — KOA KAMPGROUND OF LAFAYETTE. (337) 235-2739. **2P $32-$42, XP $3-$4.** 537 Apollo Rd, 70583. I-10, exit 97, 0.5 mi s. Small pets allowed.

**SLIDELL** — KOA-NEW ORLEANS-EAST. (985) 643-3850. **Call for rates.** 56009 Hwy 433, 70461. I-10, exit 263, 0.8 mi e.

**VIDALIA** — RIVER VIEW RV PARK  (318) 336-1400. **2P $23-$32, XP $2.** 100 River View Pkwy, 71373. Jct US 65/84, 0.8 mi s on SR 131.

# Maine

**CASCO** — POINT SEBAGO RESORT. (207) 655-3821. **4P $25-$72, XP $5-$10.** 261 Point Sebago Rd, 04015. Jct SR 121, 3.7 mi n on US 302, then 1 mi w, follow signs.

**DAMARISCOTTA** — LAKE PEMAQUID, INC. (207) 563-5202. **4P $24-$42, XP $10.** Twin Cove Ln, 04543. 0.8 mi n on US 1 business route, 2 mi e on Biscay Rd, then 0.3 mi n on Egypt Rd. (PO Box 967).

**NORTH WATERFORD** — PAPOOSE POND RESORT & CAMP-GROUND. (207) 583-4470. **6P $20-$61, XP $3-$6.** 700 Norway Rd, 04088. 1.9 mi w on SR 118 from jct SR 37; from Norway, 10 mi w on SR 118.

**OLD ORCHARD BEACH** — POWDER HORN FAMILY CAMP-ING RESORT. (207) 934-4733. **2P $33-$57, XP $3-$7.** 48 Cascade Rd, 04064. 1 mi w on SR 98; jct US 1, 1.8 mi e on SR 98. (PO Box 366).

**OLD ORCHARD BEACH** — WILD ACRES FAMILY CAMPING RESORT. (207) 934-2535. **2P $24-$55, XP $3-$8.** 179 Saco Ave, 04064. I-95 (Maine Tpke), exit 36, 3 mi e on I-195 and SR 5.

**SCARBOROUGH** — BAYLEY'S CAMPING RESORT ⏺ (207) 883-6043. **2P $23-$55, XP $5-$12.** 275 Pine Point Rd, 04074. Jct US 1, 2 mi e via SR 9 (Pine Point Rd), watch for sign.

**WELLS** — WELLS BEACH RESORT CAMPGROUND ⏺ (207) 646-7570. **2P $41-$65, XP $7.** 1000 Post Rd (US 1), 04090-4109. Jct SR 109 and 9, 1.3 mi s on US 1.

# Maryland

**ABINGDON** — BAR HARBOR RV PARK & MARINA ⏺ (410) 679-0880. **2P $37-$42, XP $4.** 4228 Birch Ave, 21009. I-95, exit 80, 1.5 mi s on SR 543, 1.7 mi w on US 40, 0.7 mi s on Long Bar Harbor Rd, then 0.5 mi e on E Baker Ave.

**BERLIN** — FRONTIER TOWN CAMPGROUND. (410) 641-0880. **2P $25-$72, XP $5-$10.** 8428 Stephen Decatur Hwy, 21811. Jct SR 50, 4 mi s on SR 611. (PO Box 691, OCEAN CITY, 21843).

**COLLEGE PARK** — CHERRY HILL PARK ⏺ (301) 937-7116. **2P $50-$65, XP $5.** 9800 Cherry Hill Rd, 20740. I-95, exit 29B, 1 mi w on SR 212 (Powder Mill Rd), then 1 mi s; I-495, exit 25, just s to Cherry Hill Rd, then 1 mi nw.

**FLINTSTONE** — HIDDEN SPRINGS CAMPGROUND. (814) 767-9676, off season (301) 478-2282. **$24-$28, XP $2.** I-68, exit 50 to Rocky Gap State Park, 3.5 mi n on Pleasant Valley Rd. (PO Box 190, 21530).

**FREELAND** — MORRIS MEADOWS RECREATION FARM. (410) 329-6636. **Call for rates.** 1523 Freeland Rd, 21053. I-83, exit 36 (SR 439), w to jct SR 45, 1 mi n, then 3 mi w, follow signs.

**WILLIAMSPORT** — YOGI BEAR'S JELLYSTONE PARK CAMP RESORT HAGERSTOWN. (301) 223-7117. **2P $20-$49, XP $2-$6.** 16519 Lappans Rd, 21795. I-81, exit 1, 1.2 mi e on SR 68.

# Massachusetts

**BRIMFIELD** — QUINEBAUG COVE CAMPGROUND. (413) 245-9525. **4P $22-$35, XP $3-$6.** 49 E Brimfield-Holland Rd, 01010. I-84, exit 3B, 3.8 mi w on US 20, then 0.3 mi s.

**FOXBORO** — NORMANDY FARMS CAMPGROUND. (508) 543-7600. **2P $20-$62, XP $5-$10.** 72 West St, 02035. I-495, exit 14A, 1 mi n on US 1, then 1.3 mi e on Thurston and West sts.

**OAKHAM** — PINE ACRES FAMILY CAMPING RESORT. (508) 882-9509. **2P $22-$49, XP $5-$15.** 203 Bechan Rd, 01068. Jct SR 122, 2 mi sw on SR 148, then just s via Spencer Rd.

**SAVOY** — SHADY PINES CAMPGROUND. (413) 743-2694. **Call for rates.** 547 Loop Rd, 01256. On SR 8A and 116, 3.1 mi se.

# Michigan

**BAY VIEW** — PETOSKEY KOA RV & CABIN RESORT. (231) 347-0005. **2P $26-$59, XP $3-$5.** 1800 N US 31, 49770. US 31, 1 mi n of SR 119.

**DECATUR** — TIMBER TRAILS RV PARK. (269) 423-7311. **$25-$27, XP $1.** 84981 47 1/2 St, 49045. 1.9 mi sw on SR 51, 0.8 mi n.

**PORT HURON** — PORT HURON KOA KAMPGROUND. (810) 987-4070. **2P $24-$62, XP $3-$4.** 5111 Lapeer Rd, 48074. I-94, exit 262, 8 mi n on Wadhams Rd, then 0.3 mi e; I-69, exit 196, 0.4 mi n on Wadhams Rd, then 0.3 mi e.

# Minnesota

**CALEDONIA** — DUNROMIN' PARK. (507) 724-2514. **Call for rates.** 12757 Dunromin Dr, 55921. 2.8 mi s on SR 76 S from jct SR 44, 0.5 mi e.

**CASS LAKE** — STONY POINT RESORT, TRAILER PARK CAMPGROUNDS ⏺ (218) 335-6311. **2P $20-$30, XP $2.** 5510 US 2 NW, 56633. On US 2, 2 mi e of jct SR 371. (PO Box 518).

**COKATO** — COKATO LAKE CAMPING & RV RESORT. (320) 286-5779. **Call for rates.** 2945 CR 4 SW, 55321. 2.8 mi n of jct SR 12.

**DETROIT LAKES** — FOREST HILLS GOLF & RV RESORT ⏺ (218) 439-6033. **Call for rates.** 22931 185th St, 56501-7910. 3.5 mi w on US 10.

**HINCKLEY** — GRAND CASINO HINCKLEY RV RESORT. (320) 384-4703. **$13-$19.** 1326 Fire Monument Rd, 55037. I-35, exit 183, 1 mi e on SR 48.

**PARK RAPIDS** — BREEZE CAMPING & RV RESORT ON EAGLE LAKE. (218) 732-5888. **2P $30-$34, XP $3.** 25824 CR 89, 56470. 9 mi n on US 71 from jct SR 34.

**PARK RAPIDS** — VAGABOND VILLAGE CAMPGROUND. (218) 732-5234. **Call for rates. (no credit cards).** 23801 Green Pines Rd, 56470. 2 mi e on SR 34, 5.7 mi n on CR 4, just w on CR 40, then 0.5 mi w via signs.

**PRIOR LAKE** — DAKOTAH MEADOWS RV PARK AND CAMP-GROUND 🛲 (952) 445-8800. **$20-$29.** 2341 Park Pl, 55372. Off CR 83.

**RICHMOND** — EL RANCHO MANANA CAMPGROUND & RIDING STABLE 🛲 (320) 597-2740. **5P $14-$40, XP $1-$2.** 27302 C Ranch Rd, 56368. 4 mi n on CR 9 from jct SR 23 and 24, 2 mi ne on Manana and Ranch rds; 9 mi s of jct I-94, exit 153, via CR 9.

**WALKER** — SHORES OF LEECH LAKE CAMPGROUND & MARINA. (218) 547-1819. **Call for rates.** 6166 Morriss Point Rd, 56484. 2.8 mi nw on SR 371 and 200 from jct SR 34, 0.5 mi e on gravel road, follow signs.

# Mississippi

**MERIDIAN** — MERIDIAN EAST/TOOMSUBA KOA. (601) 632-1684. **2P $22-$52, XP $2-$3.** 3953 KOA Campground Rd, 39364. I-20/59, exit 165, 1.5 mi s, follow signs.

**OCEAN SPRINGS** — CAMP JOURNEY'S END. (228) 875-2100. **2P $28-$32, XP $2-$3.** 7501 Hwy 57, 39565. I-10, exit 57, 0.5 mi n.

**PICAYUNE** — SUN ROAMERS RV RESORT. (601) 798-5818. **2P $26-$31, XP $3.** 41 Mississippi Pines Blvd, 39466. I-59, exit 4, 0.8 mi e on SR 43 s, then 0.5 mi s on Stafford Rd.

# Missouri

**BRANSON** — THE WILDERNESS AT SILVER DOLLAR CITY LOG CABINS AND RV'S. (417) 338-8189. **2P $26-$29, XP $2.** 5125 SR 265, 65616. 0.5 mi s of jct SR 76.

**EUREKA** — YOGI BEAR'S JELLYSTONE PARK CAMP-RESORT. (636) 938-5925. **Call for rates.** 5300 Fox Creek Rd, 63069. I-44, exit 261, 0.5 mi w. (PO Box 626, 63025).

# Montana

**MISSOULA** — JELLYSTONE RV RESORT. (406) 543-9400. **2P $24-$31, XP $4.** 9900 Jellystone Ave, 59808. I-90, exit 96 (west side entry), 0.9 mi n.

**POLSON** — POLSON/FLATHEAD LAKE KOA. (406) 883-2151. **Call for rates.** 200 Irvine Flats Rd, 59860. 1 mi n on US 93, 0.3 mi w.

**WEST GLACIER** — WEST GLACIER KOA. (406) 387-5341. **2P $21-$45, XP $4-$5.** 355 Halfmoon Flats Rd, 59936. 2.5 mi w on US 2, 1 mi s. (PO Box 215).

# Nebraska

**NORTH PLATTE** — HOLIDAY PARK 🛲 (308) 534-2265. **2P $15-$30, XP $1-$2.** 601 Halligan Dr, 69101. I-80, exit 177, just n on US 83, immediate right turn on frontage road (Halligan Dr), then 0.5 mi e.

# Nevada

**BOULDER CITY** — BOULDER OAKS RV RESORT. (702) 294-4425. **Call for rates.** 1010 Industrial Rd, 89005. Just w of US 93.

**LAS VEGAS** — OASIS LAS VEGAS RV RESORT. (702) 260-2020. **4P $35-$43, XP $1.** 2711 W Windmill Ln, 89123. I-15, exit 33 (Blue Diamond Rd), 0.5 mi e to Las Vegas Blvd, then 0.5 mi s. Small pets allowed.

**MESQUITE** — DESERT SKIES RV RESORT. (928) 347-6000. **$40, XP $5.** 350 E Hwy 91, 89024. I-15, exit 122, 1.5 mi ne via Hillside Dr. (PO Box 3780).

**MINDEN** — CARSON VALLEY RV RESORT & CASINO. (775) 782-9711. **Call for rates.** 1639 US 395 N, 89423. Center.

**MINDEN** — SILVER CITY RV RESORT 🛲 (775) 267-3359. **2P $26-$33, XP $4.** 3165 US 395, 89423. 6 mi s of Carson City; 3 mi s of jct US 50 W.

**PAHRUMP** — SEIBT DESERT RETREAT LUXURY RV PARK 🛲 (775) 751-1174. **4P $30-$80, XP $10.** 301 W Leslie St, 89060. 10 mi n of SR 160 and 372, jct SR 160.

**PAHRUMP** — TERRIBLE'S LAKESIDE CASINO & RV RESORT 🛲 (775) 751-7770. **Call for rates.** 5870 S Homestead Rd, 89048. SR 160, 3.5 mi s.

**RENO** — KOA AT THE RENO HILTON. (775) 789-2147. **2P $24-$99, XP $3-$5.** 2500 E 2nd St, 89595. US 395, exit Mill St, just e.

**SPARKS** — RIVERS EDGE RV PARK ⟨AAA⟩ (775) 358-8533. **Call for rates.** 1405 S Rock Blvd, 89431. I-80, exit Rock Blvd S; US 395, exit SR 66 (Mill St).

**VERDI** — GOLD RANCH CASINO & RV RESORT. (775) 345-8880. **$33-$36.** 320 Gold Ranch Rd, 89439. I-80, exit 2. (PO Box 160).

**ZEPHYR COVE** — ZEPHYR COVE RESORT CAMPGROUND ⟨AAA⟩ (775) 589-4907. **$26-$53.** 760 Hwy 50, 89448. US 50, 4 mi n of state line. (PO Box 830).

# New Hampshire

**BARRINGTON** — AYERS LAKE FARM CAMPGROUND ⟨AAA⟩ (603) 335-1110, off season (603) 332-5940. **4P $30-$40, XP $2-$5. (no credit cards).** 557 US 202, 03825. Spaulding Tpke, exit 13, 4.5 mi w.

**BARRINGTON** — BARRINGTON SHORES CAMPGROUND ⟨AAA⟩ (603) 664-9333. **5P $35-$42, XP $3-$12.** 70 Hall Rd, 03825. Jct SR 125 and US 4, 2.5 mi w on US 4, then 3 mi n.

**CHICHESTER** — HILLCREST CAMPGROUND. (603) 798-5124. **Call for rates.** 78 Dover Rd, 03234. I-93, exit 15, 8 mi e on SR 4; jct SR 28 and 4, 2 mi w on SR 4.

**FREEDOM** — DANFORTH BAY CAMPING RESORT ⟨AAA⟩ (603) 539-2069. **Call for rates.** 196 Shawtown Rd, 03836. Jct SR 25/153, 1 mi n on SR 153, 3 mi w on Ossipee Lake Rd.

**GLEN** — GLEN ELLIS FAMILY CAMPGROUND. (603) 383-4567. **$24-$28, XP $3-$5.** US 302, 03838. 0.3 mi w of jct SR 16. (PO Box 397).

**HAMPTON FALLS** — WAKEDA CAMPGROUND LLC ⟨AAA⟩ (603) 772-5274. **2P $25-$60, XP $5.** 294 Exeter Rd (SR 88), 03844. SR 88, 3.8 mi w of jct US 1.

**LACONIA** — PAUGUS BAY CAMPGROUND. (603) 366-4757. **4P $25-$37, XP $3-$6. (no credit cards).** 96 Hilliard Rd, 03246. Jct US 3 and SR 11B, 0.5 mi n on US 3, then w. Small pets allowed.

**MEREDITH** — CLEARWATER CAMPGROUND ⟨AAA⟩ (603) 279-7761. **Call for rates.** 26 Campground Rd (SR 104), 03253. I-93, exit 23, 3 mi e.

**MEREDITH** — MEREDITH WOODS 4 SEASON CAMPING AREA ⟨AAA⟩ (603) 279-5449. **Call for rates.** 551 SR 104, 03253. I-93, exit 23, 3 mi e. (26 Campground Rd).

**MILTON** — MI-TE-JO LAKESIDE FAMILY CAMPGROUND ⟨AAA⟩ (603) 652-9022. **2P $29-$40, XP $5-$8. (no credit cards).** 111 Mi-Te Jo Rd, 03851. SR 16, exit 17 northbound, 0.8 mi e on SR 75, 3.3 mi n on SR 125, then 1 mi e on Townhouse Rd; exit southbound, 3.3 mi on SR 125, 1 mi e on Townhouse Rd. (PO Box 830).

**NEW HAMPTON** — TWIN TAMARACK FAMILY CAMPING & RV RESORT ⟨AAA⟩ (603) 279-4387. **2P $32-$36, XP $1-$8.** 41 Twin Tamarack Rd, 03256. I-93, exit 23, 2.5 mi e on SR 104.

**RAYMOND** — PINE ACRES FAMILY CAMPGROUND ⟨AAA⟩ (603) 895-2519. **Call for rates.** 74 Freetown Rd, 03077. On SR 107, just n of jct SR 102; SR 101, exit 5, 0.5 mi s.

**SOUTH WEARE** — COLD SPRINGS CAMP RESORT. (603) 529-2528. **2P $42-$46, XP $3-$7.** 62 Barnard Hill Rd, 03281. On jct SR 77/149, 1.5 mi se, 0.3 mi n on sign posted road; 10 mi nw of jct SR 114/101. (22 Wildlife Dr).

**TAMWORTH** — CHOCORUA CAMPING VILLAGE ⟨AAA⟩ (603) 323-8536. **2P $22-$45, XP $6-$8.** 893 White Mountain Hwy, 03817. SR 16, 2.5 mi n of jct SR 25. (PO Box 484, CHOCORUA).

**TWIN MOUNTAIN** — TWIN MOUNTAIN KOA KAMPGROUND ⟨AAA⟩ (603) 846-5559. **2P $25-$149, XP $2-$12.** 372 SR 115, 03595. Jct US 302, 2.1 mi n on US 3, then 0.8 mi ne. (PO Box 148).

**WOODSTOCK** — BROKEN BRANCH KOA. (603) 745-8008. **2P $29-$36, XP $3-$8.** 1002 Eastside Rd (SR 175), 03293. I-93, exit 31, 2 mi s, follow signs. (PO Box 6).

# New Jersey

**CAPE MAY COURT HOUSE** — BIG TIMBER LAKE CAMPING RESORT ⟨AAA⟩ (609) 465-4456. **4P $36-$54, XP $3-$7.** 116 Swainton Goshen Rd, 08210. Garden State Pkwy, exit 13 southbound, 0.5 mi w on paved road, 1 mi s on US 9, then 1 mi w (CR 646). (PO Box 366).

**CAPE MAY** — BEACHCOMBER CAMPING RESORT. (609) 886-6035. **2P $23-$56, XP $3-$5.** 462 Seashore Rd, 08204. Garden State Pkwy, exit 4A (SR 47 N), w to 3rd traffic light, then 1 mi s; Railroad Ave and Seashore Rd.

**CAPE MAY** — **CAPE ISLAND CAMPGROUND** ⬟ (609) 884-5777. **4P $44-$50, XP $5.** 709 Rt 9, 08204. Garden State Pkwy, exit 0 (US 9), 1.5 mi n on SR 109 and US 9.

**CAPE MAY** — **HOLLY SHORES BEST HOLIDAY TRAV-L-PARK** ⬟ (609) 886-1234. **Call for rates.** 491 US 9, 08204. Garden State Pkwy, exit 4A (SR 47 N) to 2nd traffic light, 1 mi s. Small pets allowed.

**CAPE MAY** — **SEASHORE CAMPSITES INC** ⬟ (609) 884-4010. **4P $24-$44, XP $3-$5.** 720 Seashore Rd, 08204. Garden State Pkwy, exit 4A (SR 47 N), 1 mi n to CR 626, then 2.7 mi s.

**OCEAN VIEW** — **OCEAN VIEW RESORT CAMPGROUND** ⬟ (609) 624-1675. **4P $39-$58, XP $5.** 2555 Rt 9, 08230. US 9, 0.8 mi nw of Garden State Pkwy, exit 17 southbound; exit northbound, use service area turnaround. (PO Box 607).

# New Mexico

**ALBUQUERQUE** — **ALBUQUERQUE KOA-CENTRAL.** (505) 296-2729. **2P $25-$47, XP $3-$5.** 12400 Skyline Rd NE, 87123. I-40, exit 166, just s, then left.

**ALBUQUERQUE** — **AMERICAN RV PARK** ⬟ (505) 831-3545. **$28-$45, XP $3.** 13500 Central Ave SW, 87121. I-40, exit 149, just s, then w.

**DEMING** — **A LITTLE VINEYARD RV PARK** ⬟ (505) 546-3560. **2P $19-$21, XP $2.** 2901 E Pine St, 88030. I-10, exit 85, 1 mi w.

**GALLUP** — **USA RV PARK** ⬟ (505) 863-5021. **2P $27-$29.** 2925 W Hwy 66, 87301. I-40, exit 16, 1 mi e.

**LAS CRUCES** — **HACIENDA RV RESORT** ⬟ (505) 528-5800. **2P $30-$40, XP $2.** 740 Stern Dr, 88005. I-10, exit 140, just e. (PO Box 1479, MESILLA, 88046-1479).

**RIO RANCHO** — **STAGECOACH STOP RV RESORT.** (505) 867-1000. **2P $28-$36, XP $2.** 3650 SR 528, 87144. I-25, exit 242, w to SR 528, then 0.5 mi s.

**SILVER CITY** — **SILVER CITY KOA.** (505) 388-3351. **4P $17-$33, XP $2-$3.** 11824 E Hwy 180, 88022. 4.9 mi e on US 180 and SR 90.

# New York

**BATH** — **HICKORY HILL CAMPING RESORT** ⬟ (607) 776-4345. **2P $35-$44, XP $3.** 7531 CR 13, 14810. SR 17, exit 38, 1 mi n on SR 54, then at fork, 2 mi n on Haverling St.

**DEWITTVILLE** — **CHAUTAUQUA HEIGHTS CAMPING RESORT CAMPGROUND.** (716) 386-3804. **4P $25-$35, XP $4-$8.** 5652 Thumb Rd, 14728. I-86, exit 10 westbound, 5 mi on CR 430 W; I-90, exit 60 to Mayville, 2.4 mi on CR 430 E, just e.

**GARDINER** — **YOGI BEAR'S JELLYSTONE PARK CAMP-RESORTS AT LAZY RIVER.** (845) 255-5193. **Call for rates.** 50 Bevier Rd, 12525. 1.5 mi w on US 44 and SR 55, 0.8 mi se on Albany Post and Bevier rds, follow signs.

**GARRATTSVILLE** — **YOGI BEAR'S JELLYSTONE PARK AT CRYSTAL LAKE.** (607) 965-8265. **4P $18-$53, XP $3-$10.** 111 E Turtle Lake Rd, 13342. Jct SR 80, 6.2 mi s on CR 16, 0.7 mi n on CR 51, then 1.1 mi w on CR 17.

**GREENFIELD PARK** — **SKYWAY CAMPING RESORT.** (845) 647-5747. **Call for rates.** 99 Mountaindale Rd, 12435. Jct US 209 and SR 52, 5.2 mi w on SR 52, then 1.1 mi sw.

**GREENFIELD PARK** — **YOGI BEAR'S JELLYSTONE PARK CAMP-RESORT AT BIRCHWOOD ACRES.** (845) 434-4743. **4P $29-$59, XP $6-$12.** 85 Martinfeld Rd, 12789. Jct US 209 and SR 52, 8 mi w on SR 52, then 0.5 mi s. (PO Box 482, WOODRIDGE).

**LAKE GEORGE** — **LAKE GEORGE ESCAPE.** (518) 623-3207. **2P $21-$51, XP $6.** 175 E Schroon River Rd, 12845. I-87, exit 23, 0.4 mi e on Diamond Point Rd, then 0.8 mi n. (PO Box 431).

**OLD FORGE** — **OLD FORGE CAMPING RESORT.** (315) 369-6011. **2P $23-$39, XP $2-$4.** 3347 SR 28, 13420. 1 mi n of town. (PO Box 51).

**PLATTEKILL** — **NEWBURGH/NEW YORK CITY NORTH KOA** ⬟ (845) 564-2836. **2P $30-$53, XP $5.** 119 Freetown Hwy, 12568. 1.5 mi n on SR 32, 3 mi s of jct US 44 and SR 55, 0.5 mi e, follow signs.

**PULASKI** — **BRENNAN BEACH RV PARK** ⬟ (315) 298-2242. **Call for rates.** 80 Brennan Beach, 13142. I-81, exit 36, 4 mi w on SR 13, 1 mi n on SR 3.

**QUEENSBURY** — **LAKE GEORGE RV PARK.** (518) 792-3775. **2P $40-$65, XP $7.** I-87 (New York State Thruway), exit 20, 0.5 mi n on US 9, then 0.4 mi e. (74 SR 149, LAKE GEORGE, 12845).

**QUEENSBURY** — **LEDGEVIEW VILLAGE RV PARK.** (518) 798-6621. **$31-$38, XP $5-$10.** 321 SR 149, 12845. I-87 (New York State Thruway), exit 20, 0.5 mi n on US 9, then 1.5 mi e.

**VERONA** — THE VILLAGES AT TURNING STONE. (315) 361-7275. **4P $25-$48, XP $5.** 5065 SR 365, 13478. I-90, exit 33, 1.3 mi w. (PO Box 126).

**SHELBY** — SHELBY/MANSFIELD KOA. (419) 347-1392. **2P $29-$57.** 6787 Baker 47, 44875-9103. 4 mi nw on SR 39, then 4.5 mi n, follow signs.

## North Carolina

**BOONE** — KOA-BOONE. (828) 264-7250. **2P $27-$35, XP $2-$4.** 123 Harmony Mt Ln, 28607. Jct US 221 and 421, 3 mi n on SR 194, 1 mi w on Ray Brown Rd.

**CANDLER** — KOA ASHEVILLE WEST. (828) 665-7015. **2P $25-$45, XP $3-$7.** 309 Wiggins Rd, 28715. I-40, exit 37, just s, 0.5 mi w on US 19/23, then 0.3 mi n.

**CASHIERS** — SINGING WATERS CAMPING RESORT ⁴⁴⁴ (828) 293-5872. **2P $25-$32, XP $2-$5.** Jct US 64, 10 mi n on SR 107, then 1 mi e. (1006 Trout Creek Rd, TUCKASEGEE, 28783). Small pets allowed.

**CEDAR MOUNTAIN** — BLACK FOREST CAMPING RESORT. (828) 884-2267. **$22-$28, XP $2-$4.** 100 Summer Rd, 28718. On US 276, 12.6 mi s of Brevard. (PO Box 709).

**CHEROKEE** — CHEROKEE GREAT SMOKIES KOA. (828) 497-9711. **2P $25-$65, XP $5.** 4 mi n on Big Cove Rd. (92 KOA Campground Rd, 28719).

## North Dakota

**BISMARCK** — BISMARCK KOA. (701) 222-2662. **2P $20-$32, XP $3.** 3720 Centennial Rd, 58503-8001. I-94, exit 161 (Centennial Rd), 1 mi n.

## Ohio

**AURORA** — JELLYSTONE PARK CAMP RESORT ⁴⁴⁴ (330) 562-9100. **2P $30-$52, XP $3-$8.** 3392 SR 82, 44255. 4 mi e.

**BROOKVILLE** — DAYTON TALL TIMBERS RESORT KOA. (937) 833-3888. **Call for rates.** 7796 Wellbaum Rd, 45309. 0.5 mi n on SR 49; jct I-70, exit 24, 0.5 mi w on Pleasant Plain Rd, then 0.3 mi s.

**GENEVA-ON-THE-LAKE** — INDIAN CREEK CAMPING & RESORT. (440) 466-8191. **2P $30-$39, XP $3-$5.** 4710 Lake Rd E, 44041-9459. 2 mi e on SR 531.

## Oregon

**ASHLAND** — HOWARD PRAIRIE LAKE RESORT ⁴⁴⁴ (541) 482-1979. **2P $23-$25, XP $5.** 3249 Hyatt Prairie Rd, 97520. I-5, exit 14, 0.7 mi e on SR 66, 17 mi e on Dead Indian Memorial Rd, then 3.4 mi s.

**BEND** — CROWN VILLA RV RESORT. (541) 388-1131, off season (541) 382-1636. **Call for rates.** 60801 Brosterhous Rd, 97702. Business Rt US 97, 1 mi e on Murphy Rd, then just s.

**CANNON BEACH** — RV RESORT AT CANNON BEACH ⁴⁴⁴ (503) 436-2231. **2P $25-$36, XP $3.** 340 Elk Creek Rd, 97110. US 101, exit Sunset Blvd. (PO Box 1037).

**EUGENE** — PREMIER RV RESORT OF EUGENE. (541) 686-3152. **2P $30-$40, XP $3.** 33022 Van Duyn Rd, 97408. I-5, exit 199, just e, then 0.4 mi s; n of town at Coburg exit.

**LEBANON** — PREMIER RV RESORT AT MALLARD CREEK GOLF COURSE. (541) 259-0070. **2P $41, XP $3.** 31958 Bellinger Scale Rd, 97355. I-5, exit 228, 5.6 mi e on SR 34 (follow south and east truck route), 1.3 mi s on Denny School Rd, 2.2 mi e on Airport Dr, 4.6 mi s on US 20, 1.1 mi ne on Waterloo Rd, just e on Berlin Rd, then 0.4 mi n.

**NETARTS** — NETARTS BAY RV PARK & MARINA. (503) 842-7774. **Call for rates.** 2260 Bilyeu, 97143. Just w. (PO Box 218). Small pets allowed.

**NEWPORT** — OUTDOOR RESORTS PACIFIC SHORES MOTOR-COACH RESORT. (541) 265-3750. **Call for rates.** 6225 N Coast Hwy 101, 97365. On US 101, 3.4 mi n.

**SALEM** — PHOENIX RV PARK. (503) 581-2497. **2P $30, XP $2.** 4130 Silverton Rd NE, 97305. I-5, exit 256, 0.3 mi e on Market, 1 mi n on Lancaster, then just e.

**SALEM** — SALEM PREMIER RV RESORT. (503) 364-7714. **2P $29-$41, XP $3.** 4700 Salem-Dallas Hwy 22, 97304. I-5, exit 260A (Salem Pkwy), follow signs to city center, 3 mi sw to Commercial St NE, then 1.4 mi s to Marion St; 4.7 mi sw from Marion St Bridge via SR 22; 4.3 mi e of jct SR 22 and 99 W.

**SISTERS** — SISTERS INN & RV PARK ⁴⁴⁴ (541) 549-7275. **4P $30, XP $5.** 540 Hwy 20 W, 97759. On US 20, 0.3 mi w. (PO Box 938).

**SISTERS** — SISTERS/BEND KOA. (541) 549-3021. **2P $20-$40, XP $2-$9.** 67667 Hwy 20 W, 97701. On US 20, 3.5 mi e. 🏊 ➷ ⊠

**WARM SPRINGS** — KAHNEETA HIGH DESERT RESORT & CASINO RV PARK. (541) 553-1112. **10P $38, XP $8.** 6823 Hwy 8, 97761. 11 mi ne off US 26 on Warm Springs Indian Reservation. (PO Box 1240). 🏊 🎿 ➷ ⊠

**WARRENTON** — ASTORIA/WARRENTON/SEASIDE KOA ⒶⒶⒶ (503) 861-2606. **2P $23-$152, XP $4-$5.** 1100 NW Ridge Rd, 97121. 4.6 mi nw of jct US 101, follow signs to Fort Stevens State Park. ➷ ⊠

**WELCHES** — MT. HOOD VILLAGE VACATION COTTAGES & RV RESORT. (503) 622-4011. **6P $23-$41.** 65000 E Hwy 26, 97067. On US 26, 2 mi w. 🏊 ➷ ⊠

**WILSONVILLE** — PHEASANT RIDGE RV RESORT ⒶⒶⒶ (503) 682-7829. **2P $31-$35, XP $1.** 8275 SW Elligsen Rd, 97070. I-5, exit 286, just e. Small pets allowed. 🎿 ➷ ⊠

# Pennsylvania

**BAKERSVILLE** — PIONEER PARK CAMPGROUND. (814) 445-6348. **2P $20-$31, XP $3.** Just e on SR 31, 0.5 mi s via signs. (273 Trent Rd, SOMERSET, 15501). ➷ ⊠

**BEDFORD** — FRIENDSHIP VILLAGE CAMPGROUND ⒶⒶⒶ (814) 623-1677. **4P $25-$31, XP $2.** 348 Friendship Village Rd, 15522. 1.3 mi w on US 30 from jct US 220, 0.5 mi n via signs. ➷ ⊠

**BELLEFONTE** — BELLEFONTE/STATE COLLEGE KOA ⒶⒶⒶ (814) 355-7912. **2P $22-$45, XP $2-$5.** 2481 Jacksonville Rd, 16823. I-80, exit 161, 2 mi ne on SR 26. ➷ ⊠

**BOWMANSVILLE** — LAKE IN WOOD CAMPGROUND. (717) 445-5525. **6P $29-$50, XP $6.** 576 Yellow Hill Rd, 17555. SR 23, 4.5 mi n on SR 625, 1 mi ne on Oaklyn Dr, then 1.5 mi e, follow signs. ➷ ⊠

**BOWMANSVILLE** — OAK CREEK CAMPGROUNDS ⒶⒶⒶ (717) 445-6161. **4P $25-$41, XP $6.** 400 E Maple Grove Rd, 17507. From SR 625, 1.5 mi e. (PO Box 128). 🏊 ➷ ⊠

**BOWMANSVILLE** — SUN VALLEY CAMPGROUND. (717) 445-6262. **4P $28-$42, XP $6.** 451 E Maple Grove Rd, 17507. From SR 625, 1.9 mi e. (PO Box 129). ➷ ⊠

**BUTLER** — SMITH GROVE CAMPGROUND ⒶⒶⒶ (724) 285-3600. **4P $21-$24, XP $2-$4. (no credit cards).** 1085 Herman Rd, 16002. SR 8, e on SR 422 to Bonnie Brook Rd, follows signs s to Herman Rd, 2 mi w. ➷ ⊠

**CLAY** — STARLITE CAMPING RESORT. (717) 733-9655. **2P $34, XP $1-$5.** 1500 Furnace Hill Rd, 17578. US 322, 1.1 mi n on Clay Rd, 2.4 mi ne, follow signs. ➷ ⊠

**COOKSBURG** — KALYUMET CAMPGROUND ⒶⒶⒶ (814) 744-9622. **4P $22-$30, XP $5.** I-80, exit 62, 2 mi e on SR 68 E to light at Clarion Courthouse, go straight for 9.5 mi. (8630 Miola Rd, LUCINDA, 16235). Small pets allowed. ➷ ⊠

**ELVERSON** — WARWICK WOODS FAMILY CAMPING RESORT ⒶⒶⒶ (610) 286-9655. **2P $30-$40, XP $3-$6.** 401 Trythall Rd, 19520. I-76 (Pennsylvania Tpke), exit 298 eastbound, 1 mi s on SR 10. then 7.5 mi e on SR 23 to sign at Trythall Rd; exit 312 westbound, 8.5 mi n on SR 100, then 5 mi w on SR 23. (PO Box 280, ST. PETERS, 19470). ➷ ⊠

**ERIE** — ERIE KOA KAMPGROUNDS. (814) 476-7706. **2P $33-$75, XP $3-$6.** I-90, exit 18, 1.3 mi s on SR 832, then 0.8 mi e; I-79, exit 174, 1.5 mi w. (6645 West Rd, MCKEAN, 16426). ➷ ⊠

**FARMINGTON** — BENNER'S MEADOW RUN CAMPING & CABINS. (724) 329-4097. **2P $27-$34, XP $3-$8.** 315 Nelson Rd, 15437. 2.5 mi n of US 40, follow signs. Small pets allowed. ➷ ⊠

**GARDNERS** — MOUNTAIN CREEK CAMPGROUND ⒶⒶⒶ (717) 486-7681. **Call for rates.** 349 Pine Grove Rd, 17324. 2 mi w of SR 34, follow signs. ➷ ⊠

**GETTYSBURG** — DRUMMER BOY CAMPING RESORT ⒶⒶⒶ (717) 334-3277. **$29-$42, XP $2-$5.** 1300 Hanover Rd, 17325. 2 mi e on SR 116 at US 15 Bypass, exit Hanover Rd. ➷ ⊠

**GETTYSBURG** — GETTYSBURG CAMPGROUND ⒶⒶⒶ (717) 334-3304. **4P $29-$36, XP $3-$6.** 2030 Fairfield Rd, 17325. 3 mi w on SR 116 W. ➷ ⊠

**GETTYSBURG** — GETTYSBURG KOA KAMPGROUND ⒶⒶⒶ (717) 642-5713. **2P $20-$53, XP $3-$6.** 20 Knox Rd, 17325. 3 mi w on US 30, 3 mi s on Knoxlyn Rd, follow signs. ➷ ⊠

**GETTYSBURG** — GRANITE HILL CAMPING RESORT ⒶⒶⒶ (717) 642-8749. **2P $24-$44, XP $2-$8.** 3340 Fairfield Rd, 17325. 5.8 mi w on SR 116. ➷ ⊠

**GETTYSBURG** — ROUND TOP CAMPGROUND. (717) 334-9565. **Call for rates.** 180 Knight Rd, 17325. 3 mi s on SR 134 at US 15. ➷ ⊠

**HARRISVILLE** — KOZY REST KAMPGROUND ⬤ (724) 735-2417. **2P $20-$25, XP $2-$4.** 449 Campground Rd, 16038. Jct SR 8, 0.3 mi e on SR 58, 2 mi n on SR 4014.

**HERSHEY** — HERSHEY HIGHMEADOW CAMPGROUND. (717) 534-8999. **4P $27-$42, XP $4.** 1200 Matlack Rd, 17036. 0.5 mi n on SR 39 W from jct US 322 and 422. (PO Box 866, 17033).

**HOLTWOOD** — MUDDY RUN RECREATION PARK. (717) 284-5850. **6P $20-$25, XP $3.** 172 Bethesda Church Rd W, 17532. 1.8 mi ne on SR 372.

**HONEY BROOK** — BRANDYWINE MEADOWS FAMILY CAMPGROUND ⬤ (610) 273-9753. **2P $25-$50, XP $2-$5.** 449 Icedale Rd, 19344. 3 mi e on US 322, 1.3 mi se, follow signs.

**JONESTOWN** — JONESTOWN KOA. (717) 865-2526. **2P $26-$28, XP $2-$4.** 145 Old Rt 22, 17038. 2 mi e on US 22 from jct SR 72, 0.5 mi s; I-81, exit 90, 5 mi se; I-78, exit 6, 5 mi w, follow signs. (PO Box 867).

**KNOX** — WOLFS CAMPING RESORT ⬤ (814) 797-1103. **2P $23-$33, XP $3-$5.** 308 Timberwolf Run, 16232. I-80, exit 53.

**LANCASTER** — OLD MILL STREAM CAMPGROUND. (717) 299-2314. **4P $29-$36, XP $3.** 2249 Lincoln Hwy E, 17602. 5 mi e on US 30.

**LENHARTSVILLE** — ROBIN HILL CAMPING RESORT. (610) 756-6117. **Call for rates.** 149 Robin Hill Rd, 19534. I-78, exit 40 (Krumsville) or exit 35 (Lenhartsville), follow signs for 3 mi.

**LICKDALE** — LICKDALE CAMPGROUND. (717) 865-6411. **4P $21-$29, XP $5.** 11 Lickdale Rd, 17038. I-81, exit 90, just e.

**LIVERPOOL** — FERRY BOAT CAMPSITES ⬤ (717) 444-3200. **4P $19-$37, XP $2-$3.** 32 Ferry Ln, 17045. 2 mi s on US 11/15.

**MANHEIM** — PINCH POND FAMILY CAMPGROUND & RV PARK ⬤ (717) 665-7640. **6P $29-$37, XP $4-$7.** 3075 Pinch Rd, 17545. I-76 (Pennsylvania Tpke), exit 266, 1 mi s on SR 72, 0.5 mi w on Cider Press Rd, then 1 mi n.

**MANSFIELD** — BUCKTAIL CAMPING RESORT. (570) 662-2923, off season (610) 489-3737. **4P $18-$45, XP $7-$10.** 130 Bucktail Rd, 16933. US 15, 2nd Mansfield exit (Rt 6), 0.3 mi e on US 6, 1.5 mi n on Lambs Creek Rd, then 1 mi w.

**MARSHALLS CREEK** — OTTER LAKE CAMP RESORT. (570) 223-0123. **2P $32-$51, XP $3-$5.** I-80, exit 309, 3 mi n on US 209, just n on SR 402, then 7 mi w on Marshalls Creek Rd. (PO Box 850, 18335).

**MEADVILLE** — BROOKDALE FAMILY CAMPGROUND. (814) 789-3251. **4P $24-$37, XP $3-$5.** 25164 State Hwy 27, 16335. On SR 27, 8 mi e.

**MERCERSBURG** — SAUNDEROSA PARK INC. (717) 328-2216. **4P $24-$28, XP $1-$2.** 5909 Little Cove Rd, 17236. 4.8 mi w on SR 16, 2.5 mi s on SR 456.

**MERCER** — JUNCTION 19-80 CAMPGROUND. (724) 748-4174. **Call for rates. (no credit cards).** 1266 Old Mercer Rd, 16137. I-80, exit 15, 0.3 mi s on US 19, follow signs.

**MERCER** — MERCER-GROVE CITY KOA. (724) 748-3160. **2P $30-$65, XP $3-$5.** 1337 Butler Pike, 16137. I-79, exit 113, 3 mi n on SR 258, follow signs.

**MERCER** — ROCKY SPRINGS CAMPGROUND. (724) 662-4415. **4P $19-$24, XP $2. (no credit cards).** 84 Rocky Spring Rd, Rt 318, 16137. I-80, exit 15 westbound, 2 mi n on US 19 to Butler St (SR 318), then 4.5 mi w; exit eastbound, jct I-80 and exit 4A (SR 318), 6.5 mi ne.

**MILL RUN** — YOGI BEAR'S JELLYSTONE PARK CAMP RESORT. (724) 455-2929. **4P $20-$48, XP $2-$6.** 839 Mill Run Rd, 15464. Just s on SR 381. (PO Box 91).

**NEW COLUMBIA** — NITTANY MOUNTAIN CAMPGROUND ⬤ (570) 568-5541. **4P $24-$37, XP $1-$5.** 2751 Millers Bottom Rd, 17856. I-80, exit 210A, 0.5 mi s on US 15, 4.5 mi w on New Columbia Rd, then 0.4 mi nw.

**NEW HOLLAND** — SPRING GULCH RESORT. (717) 354-3100. **Call for rates.** 475 Lynch Rd, 17557. Jct SR 23 and 897, 4 mi s on SR 897.

**NORTHUMBERLAND** — YOGI-ON-THE-RIVER. (570) 473-8021. **Call for rates.** 213 Yogi Blvd, 17857. I-80, exit 224, 2 mi e on SR 54, 8 mi s on US 11; 2.5 mi n on US 11.

**PINE GROVE** — PINE GROVE KOA AT TWIN GROVE PARK ⬤ (717) 865-4602. **4P $20-$120, XP $10.** 1445 Suedburg Rd, 17963. I-81, exit 100, 5 mi w on SR 443.

**PORTERSVILLE** — BEAR RUN CAMPGROUND ⬤ (724) 368-3564. **2P $24-$27, XP $3-$5.** 184 Badger Hill Rd, 16051. I-79, exit 96, 0.8 mi n on SR 488.

**PORTLAND** — DRIFTSTONE ON THE DELAWARE ⏺ (570) 897-6859. **$28-$39, XP $3-$5.** 4 mi s from jct SR 611 and Portland Bridge. (2731 River Rd, MOUNT BETHEL, 18343).

**QUARRYVILLE** — YOGI BEAR'S JELLYSTONE PARK. (717) 786-3458. **Call for rates.** 340 Blackburn Rd, 17566. 2.7 mi s on US 222, 1.5 mi se, follow signs.

**ROBESONIA** — ADVENTURE BOUND CAMPING RESORTS-EAGLES PEAK. (610) 589-4800. **4P $26-$46, XP $2-$10.** 397 Eagles Peak Rd, 19551. 2 4 mi s on SR 419 from jct US 422, 2.3 mi e, follow signs.

**ROSE POINT** — COOPER'S LAKE. (724) 368-8710. **Call for rates.** 205 Currie Rd, 16057. I-79, exit 99, 0.8 mi w on US 422, then 1 mi n.

**SANDY LAKE** — GODDARD PARK VACATION LAND CAMP-GROUND. (724) 253-4645. **Call for rates.** 867 Georgetown Rd, 16145. I-79, exit 130, 0.3 mi w on SR 358, then 3.5 mi n, follow signs.

**SHARTLESVILLE** — APPALACHIAN CAMPSITES. (610) 488-6319. **Call for rates.** 60 Motel Dr, 19554. I-78, exit 23, 0.5 mi w on service road (entrance just past motel). (PO Box 27, ALLENTOWN).

**SHARTLESVILLE** — MOUNTAIN SPRINGS CAMPING RESORT INC & ARENA ⏺ (610) 488-6859. **4P $27-$35, XP $3-$5.** 3450 Mountain Rd, 19554. I-78, exit 23, 1 mi n. (PO Box 365).

**SIGEL** — CAMPERS PARADISE CAMPGROUNDS, CABINS, LODGE OUTPOST. (814) 752-2393. **2P $21, XP $4.** 37 Steele Dr, 15860. On SR 949 N, 3 mi n of SR 36.

**STRASBURG** — WHITE OAK CAMPGROUND ⏺ (717) 687-6207. **4P $22-$28, XP $3.** 3156 White Oak Rd, 17566. 3.7 mi s of Centre Square on S Decatur St/May Post Office Rd, then 0.3 mi e. (PO Box 90, 17579).

**UPPER BLACK EDDY** — COLONIAL WOODS FAMILY CAMP-ING RESORT. (610) 847-5808. **$28-$34, XP $4-$6.** 545 Lonely Cottage Dr, 18972. 1.5 mi e on Marienstein Rd from jct SR 611, then 1 mi n, follow signs.

**WATERFORD** — SPARROW POND FAMILY CAMPGROUND AND RECREATION FACILITY. (814) 796-6777. **$20-$45, XP $2-$5.** 11103 Route 19 N, 16441. I-90, exit 24, 10 mi s on US 19 (Peach St).

# South Carolina

**HILTON HEAD ISLAND** — HILTON HEAD HARBOR RV RESORT & MARINA. (843) 681-3256. **4P $38-$48, XP $2.** 43 Jenkins Rd, 29926. 0.9 mi se of Intracoastal Waterway Bridge off US 278, 0.4 mi n, follow signs.

**HILTON HEAD ISLAND** — OUTDOOR RESORTS' MOTOR-COACH RESORT ⏺ (843) 785-7699. **4P $42-$48, XP $2.** 133 Arrow Rd, 29928. 5.6 mi e on Cross Island Pkwy (US 278 toll), then just w.

**NORTH MYRTLE BEACH** — MYRTLE BEACH RV RESORT. (843) 249-1484. **5P $22-$33. (no credit cards).** 5400 Little River Neck Rd, 29582. US 17, exit Cherry Grove, just e to SR 9, just n to Little River Neck Rd, then 2.6 mi e.

# South Dakota

**CHAMBERLAIN** — CEDAR SHORE CAMPGROUND ⏺ (605) 734-5273, off season (605) 734-6376. **$12-$27.** 1500 Shoreline Dr, 57365. I-90, exit 260, 2.5 mi e on US 16 and I-90 business loop, then 1 mi ne on Mickelson country road, follow signs. (PO Box 308, 57325).

**DEADWOOD** — WHISTLER GULCH CAMPGROUND & RV PARK. (605) 578-2092. **$20-$35.** 235 Cliff, 57732. 0.7 mi s on US 85.

**HILL CITY** — RAFTER J BAR RANCH CAMPGROUND ⏺ (605) 574-2527. **2P $21-$39, XP $3.** 12325 Rafter J Rd, 57745. 3.3 mi s on US 16 and 385 at SR 87/244. (PO Box 128).

**INTERIOR** — BADLANDS WHITE RIVER KOA ⏺ (605) 433-5337. **2P $22-$30, XP $2-$3.** 20720 SD Hwy 44, 57750. On SR 44, 4 mi e from jct SR 377.

**MITCHELL** — RIVERSIDE KOA. (605) 996-1131. **2P $27-$30, XP $3.** 41244 SD Hwy 38, 57301-7800. I-90, exit 335, 0.5 mi n, then 0.3 mi w.

**NORTH SIOUX CITY** — SIOUX CITY NORTH KOA. (605) 232-4519. **2P $30-$38, XP $3.** 601 Streeter Dr, 57049. I-29, exit 2 northbound, 1 mi n on west service road; exit 4 southbound, 1 mi s on west service road.

**SIOUX FALLS** — YOGI BEAR CAMP RESORT. (605) 332-2233. **Call for rates.** 26014 478th Ave, 57005. I-90, exit 402, just n.

# Tennessee

**EAST RIDGE** — BEST HOLIDAY TRAV-L-PARK/CHATTANOOGA. (706) 891-9766. **2P $20-$30, XP $2.** 1709 Mack Smith Rd, 37412. I-75, exit 1 southbound; exit 1B northbound, 0.3 mi w, then 1 mi s.

**EAST RIDGE** — SHIPP'S RV CENTER & CAMPGROUND. (423) 892-8275. **Call for rates.** 6728 Ringgold Rd, 37412. I-75, exit 1, 0.3 mi e.

**GATLINBURG** — OUTDOOR RESORTS OF GATLINBURG. (865) 436-5861. **Call for rates.** 11.5 mi e on US 321 N. (4229 Parkway E, 37738).

**NASHVILLE** — NASHVILLE JELLYSTONE PARK ⏚ (615) 889-4225. **2P $21-$45, XP $4.** 2572 Music Valley Dr, 37214-1096. I-40, exit 215 (Briley Pkwy N), 6 mi to exit 12 (Music Valley Dr), follow signs.

**PIGEON FORGE** — CLABOUGH'S CAMPGROUND. (865) 428-1951. **4P $26-$30, XP $2.** 405 Wear's Valley Rd, 37863. 0.7 mi w of jct US 441 at traffic light 3.

**PIGEON FORGE** — RIVEREDGE RV PARK. (865) 453-5813. **2P $23-$33, XP $4.** 4220 Huskey St, 37863. Just off US 441 at traffic light 10.

**TOWNSEND** — LITTLE RIVER VILLAGE CAMPGROUND ⏚ (865) 448-2241. **2P $15-$42, XP $2-$4.** 8533 State Hwy 73, 37882. On SR 73, 0.4 mi w of entrance to Great Smoky Mountain National Park.

# Texas

**ABILENE** — KOA-ABILENE. (325) 672-3681. **2P $26-$34, XP $2-$3.** 4851 W Stamford St, 79603. I-20, exit 282 (Shirley Rd), 0.5 mi w of US 83-277, follow signs.

**AMARILLO** — AMARILLO RV RANCH ⏚ (806) 373-4962. **2P $25-$32.** 1414 Sunrise Dr, 79104. I-40, exit 74 (Whitaker Rd), 0.3 mi w on north frontage road.

**AMARILLO** — FORT AMARILLO RV RESORT. (806) 331-1700. **2P $30-$40, XP $2.** 10101 Amarillo Blvd W, 79124. I-40, exit 64 westbound, 0.3 mi n on Soncy to Amarillo Blvd, then 1 mi w; exit 62B eastbound, 0.7 mi e.

**AUSTIN** — AUSTIN LONE STAR RV RESORT. (512) 444-6322. **$25-$45.** 7009 I-35 S, 78744. I-35, exit 226B/227 (Slaughter/S Congress aves) southbound; exit 228/229 (Wm Cannon Dr) northbound, on northbound Frontage Rd.

**BEAUMONT** — GULF COAST RV RESORT. (409) 842-2285. **2P $30, XP $3-$5.** 5175 Brooks Rd, 77705. I-10, exit 846 westbound; exit 845 eastbound, follow blue signs.

**BOERNE** — ALAMO FIESTA RV RESORT ⏚ (830) 249-4700. **2P $30, XP $2.** 33000 IH-10 W, 78006. I-10, exit 543, 1 mi w on westbound access road. Small pets allowed.

**DONNA** — VICTORIA PALMS RESORT. (956) 464-7801. **Call for rates.** 602 E Victoria Rd, 78537. Just s of jct US 83. Small pets allowed.

**GOODLETT** — OLD TOWNE COTTON GIN RV PARK. (940) 674-2477. **Call for rates.** 230 Market St, 79252. US 287, 1 blk e; in town.

**KERRVILLE** — GUADALUPE RIVER RV RESORT. (830) 367-5676. **Call for rates.** 2605 Junction Hwy, 78028. I-10, exit 505 (Harper Rd), 2.5 mi s, then 2.5 mi w on SR 27.

**KERRVILLE** — KERRVILLE KOA. (830) 895-1665. **Call for rates.** 2400 Goat Creek Rd, 78028. I-10, exit 501, 1.5 mi s on FM 1338.

**LA FERIA** — LA FERIA RV PARK. (956) 797-1043. **Call for rates. (no credit cards).** 300 E Expwy 83, 78559. 0.3 mi e of jct US 83 and FM 506, on S Frontage Rd. Small pets allowed.

**LUBBOCK** — LUBBOCK KOA. (806) 762-8653. **Call for rates.** 5502 CR 6300, 79416. 2.5 mi nw of Loop 289 on US 84.

**LUBBOCK** — LUBBOCK RV PARK ⏚ (806) 747-2366. **2P $22-$26, XP $1-$2.** 4811 N I-27, 79403. I-27, exit 9, 2 mi n of Loop 289. (PO Box 597).

**MERCEDES** — PARADISE SOUTH. (956) 565-2044. **2P $28-$30, XP $5.** 8000 Paradise S, 78570. On Mile 2 W Rd, just n of US 83.

**MONTGOMERY** — HAVENS LANDING RV RESORT ⏚ (936) 582-1200. **2P $31, XP $3.** 19785 Hwy 105 W, 77356. I-45, exit 87, 13 mi w.

**SAN ANTONIO** — ADMIRALTY RV RESORT ⏚ (210) 647-7878. **2P $32-$36, XP $3.** 1485 N Ellison Dr, 78251. Jct Loop 1604 and SR 151, 1.3 mi nw on SR 151 to Military Dr, just w to Ellison Dr, then 0.7 mi n.

**SAN ANTONIO** — ALAMO KOA KAMPGROUND. (210) 224-9296. **2P $22-$32, XP $3.** 602 Gembler Rd, 78219. I-35, exit Coliseum, 0.5 mi s, then 0.8 mi e; I-10, exit WW White Rd, 0.3 mi n, then 1 mi w.

**SAN ANTONIO** — BLAZING STAR LUXURY RV RESORT ⚹⚹⚹
(210) 680-7827. **2P $32-$45, XP $4.** 1120 W Loop 1604 N, 78251. Just s of Military Hwy.

**SAN BENITO** — FUN-N-SUN RV RESORT. (956) 399-5125. **Call for rates.** 1400 Zillock Rd, 78586. 4 mi nw from US 83 and 77, exit Paso Real Rd, 0.4 mi s.

**SOUTH PADRE ISLAND** — LONG ISLAND VILLAGE. (956) 943-6449. **$40-$45.** 900 S Garcia St, 78597. On SR 100, turn right before crossing causeway. (PO Box 695, PORT ISABEL, 78578).

**UVALDE** — QUAIL SPRINGS RV PARK. (830) 278-8182. **2P $23-$25, XP $3.** 2727 E Main St, 78801. 2.2 mi e on US 90.

**WESLACO** — PINE TO PALM RESORT PARK. (956) 968-5760. **$20, XP $2. (no credit cards).** 802 International Blvd, 78596. FM 1015, 0.8 mi s of jct US 83, just s of jct Business Rt US 83.

**WICHITA FALLS** — WICHITA FALLS RV PARK ⚹⚹⚹ (940) 723-1532. **2P $23-$25, XP $2.** 2944 Seymour Hwy (Business 277 S), 76301. I-44, exit 1A, 1.2 mi s.

## Utah

**BRYCE** — RUBY'S INN CAMPGROUND TRAILER PARK ⚹⚹⚹ (435) 834-5301, off season (435) 834-5341. **Call for rates.** 1230 S Hwy 63, 84764. On SR 63, 1 mi n of Bryce Canyon Park entrance. (PO Box 640022).

**FRUIT HEIGHTS** — CHERRY HILL CAMPING RESORT ⚹⚹⚹ (801) 451-5379. **2P $26-$32, XP $2.** 1325 S Main St, 84037. I-15 N, exit 326, 1.5 mi n via US 89 and 273, follow signs; I-15 S, exit 331, 2 mi se via 2nd N and Main sts, follow signs.

**MOAB** — MOAB KOA CAMPGROUND ⚹⚹⚹ (435) 259-6682. **2P $21-$60, XP $4.** 3225 S Hwy 191, 84532. 4 mi s; e off US 191.

**MOAB** — MOAB VALLEY RV & RESORT. (435) 259-4469. **2P $19-$67, XP $5.** 1773 N Hwy 191, 84532. 2 mi n, just s of Colorado River Bridge. Small pets allowed.

**RICHFIELD** — RICHFIELD KOA. (435) 896-6674. **2P $20-$30, XP $2-$3.** 600 W 600 S, 84701. 6 blks w of US 89 (Main St); I-70, exit 40 southbound, 2.5 mi via Main St; exit 37 northbound, 1.5 mi via 1200 S and 400 W.

**ST. GEORGE** — MCARTHUR'S TEMPLE VIEW RV RESORT ⚹⚹⚹ (435) 673-6400. **2P $24-$35, XP $2.** 975 S Main St, 84770. I-15, exit 6 (Bluff St), 0.5 mi w, then just n. Small pets allowed.

**ST. GEORGE** — SETTLERS RV PARK ⚹⚹⚹ (435) 628-1624. **$22-$28, XP $2.** 1333 E 100 South, 84790. E of I-15, exit 8, right on River Rd. Small pets allowed.

**VIRGIN** — ZION RIVER RESORT RV PARK & CAMPGROUND ⚹⚹⚹ (435) 635-8594. **4P $30-$45, XP $3.** 730 E Hwy 9, 84779. I-15, exit 16 (SR 16) northbound, 22 mi ne; exit 27 southbound, 12 mie ne. (PO Box 790219).

## Virginia

**BIG ISLAND** — WILDWOOD CAMPGROUND. (434) 299-5228. **Call for rates.** SR 130, 1.3 mi e from jct Blue Ridge Pkwy, 14 mi w of SR 29. (6252 Elon Rd, MONROE, 24574).

**CHARLOTTESVILLE** — CHARLOTTESVILLE KOA. (434) 296-9881. **2P $23-$33, XP $2-$5.** 3825 Red Hill Rd, 22903. US 29 (s of I-64), 4.2 mi e on CR 708; SR 20, 1.4 mi w on CR 708.

**CHERITON** — CHERRYSTONE FAMILY CAMPING RESORT ⚹⚹⚹ (757) 331-3063. **2P $17-$51, XP $4-$12.** 1511 Townfields Dr, 23316. 1.5 mi w on SR 680 from jct US 13. (PO Box 545).

**DOSWELL** — PARAMOUNT KINGS DOMINION CAMPGROUND ⚹⚹⚹ (804) 876-5355. **Call for rates.** 10061 Kings Dominion Blvd, 23047. I-95, exit 98, 1 mi e on SR 30; adjacent to theme park.

**FRONT ROYAL** — FRONT ROYAL RV CAMPGROUND. (540) 635-2741. **2P $30-$65, XP $2-$5.** 585 KOA Dr, 22630. I-66, exit 6 or 13, entrance is 2 mi s of town on US 340 S. (PO Box 274).

**LURAY** — THE COUNTRY WAYE CAMPGROUND ⚹⚹⚹ (540) 743-7222. **2P $24-$39, XP $3-$5.** 3402 Kimball Rd, 22835. Jct US 211, 2 mi n on US 340, then 0.3 mi e on SR 658.

**LURAY** — YOGI BEAR'S JELLYSTONE PARK ⚹⚹⚹ (540) 743-4002. **2P $35-$55, XP $3-$6.** 2250 Hwy 211 E, 22835. On US 211, 3 mi e. (PO Box 191).

**MADISON** — SHENANDOAH HILLS CAMPGROUND ⚹⚹⚹ (540) 948-4186. **2P $21-$35, XP $2-$5.** 110 Campground Ln, 22727. 2 mi s on US 29.

**MEADOWS OF DAN** — MEADOWS OF DAN CAMPGROUND ⚹⚹⚹ (276) 952-2292. **2P $18-$24, XP $2.** 2182 JEB Stuart Hwy, 24120. US 58, just w of Blue Ridge Pkwy.

**MINT SPRING** — WALNUT HILLS CAMPGROUND. (540) 337-3920. **2P $26-$34, XP $3.** I-81, exit 217, 0.7 mi w to US 11, 1.5 mi s, then 1.2 mi e on SR 655. (484 Walnut Hills Rd, STAUNTON, 24401).

**NATURAL BRIDGE** — NATURAL BRIDGE KOA KAMP-
GROUND ⒶⒶⒶ (540) 291-2770. **2P $22-$54, XP $3-$4.** 214 Kildeer Ln,
24578. I-81, exit 180 northbound; exit 180B southbound, just nw on US 11.
(PO Box 148).

**URBANNA** — BETHPAGE CAMP RESORT. (804) 758-4349.
**4P $30-$45, XP $4.** 679 Brown's Ln, 23175. 1 mi n of town on CR 602.
(PO Box 178).

**VIRGINIA BEACH** — HOLIDAY TRAV-L-PARK ⒶⒶⒶ (757) 425-
0249. **6P $20-$48, XP $5.** 1075 General Booth Blvd, 23451. I-264 terminus
to Pacific Ave, 2.5 mi s.

**VIRGINIA BEACH** — OUTDOOR RESORTS/VIRGINIA BEACH.
(757) 721-2020. **Call for rates.** 3665 S Sandpiper Rd, 23456. I-264 terminus to Pacific Ave, 2 mi s to Rudee Inlet Bridge/General Booth Blvd, 5.6 mi
s to Princess Anne Rd, 0.8 mi e to Sandbridge Rd, 5.5 mi e to Sandpiper
Rd, then 3.5 mi s.

**VIRGINIA BEACH** — VIRGINIA BEACH KOA ⒶⒶⒶ (757) 428-
1444. **Call for rates.** 1240 General Booth Blvd, 23451. I-264 terminus to
Pacific Ave/General Booth Blvd, 2 mi s.

# Washington

**BURLINGTON** — BURLINGTON KOA. (360) 724-5511. **2P $21-
$37, XP $3-$4.** 6397 N Green Rd, 98233. I-5, exit 232, 3.5 mi n on Old US
99.

**CLARKSTON** — GRANITE LAKE RV RESORT. (509) 751-1635.
**$20-$33, XP $3.** 306 Granite Lake Dr, 99403. Just w of Snake River Bridge
on US 12, just n on 5th St.

**COULEE CITY** — SUN LAKES PARK RESORT. (509) 632-5291.
**Call for rates.** 34228 Park Lake Rd NE, 99115. US 2, 4 mi s on SR 17.

**EPHRATA** — STARS AND STRIPES RV PARK & DRIVING RANGE.
(509) 787-1062. **Call for rates.** 5707 US 28 W, 98823. 5 mi w.

**LYNDEN** — LYNDEN KOA. (360) 354-4772. **Call for rates.** 8717 Line
Rd, 98264. 1.7 mi n of downtown on SR 539 (Guide Meridian Rd), 3 mi e
on SR 546 (E Badger Rd), then 0.5 mi s.

**OAK HARBOR** — NORTH WHIDBEY RV PARK. (360) 675-9597.
**Call for rates.** 565 W Cornet Bay Rd, 98277. On SR 20, 1 mi s of Decep-
tion Pass Bridge, 8 mi n of Oak Harbor.

**PORT ANGELES** — PORT ANGELES/SEQUIM KOA. (360) 457-
5916. **Call for rates.** 80 O'Brien Rd & US 101 E, 98362. 7 mi e on US
101; 8 mi w of Sequim on US 101; just e of US 101, MM 255.

**SPOKANE VALLEY** — SPOKANE KOA. (509) 924-4722. **Call for
rates.** I-90, exit 293, 1.5 mi n. (3025 N Barker Rd, 99027).

**SPOKANE** — ALDERWOOD RV RESORT. (509) 467-5320. **Call for
rates.** 14007 N Newport Hwy, 99021. I-90, exit 287, 8 mi n to SR 206, then
1.5 mi w.

**SPOKANE** — YOGI BEAR'S CAMP RESORT. (509) 747-9415. **Call
for rates.** 7520 S Thomas Mallen Rd, 99004. I-90, exit 272, 2 mi s.

# West Virginia

**HARPERS FERRY** — HARPERS FERRY/WASHINGTON D.C. NW
KOA ⒶⒶⒶ (304) 535-6895. **2P $24-$35, XP $4-$5.** 343 Campground Rd,
25425. 1 mi sw on US 340 from Shenandoah River Bridge, 0.3 mi s, follow signs.

**MILTON** — FOX FIRE CAMPING RESORT. (304) 743-5622. **4P $27-
$35, XP $3. (no credit cards).** US 60, 25541. I-64, exit 28, 0.3 mi s, then
2.7 mi w. (Rt 2, Box 655).

# Wisconsin

**BAGLEY** — YOGI BEAR'S JELLYSTONE PARK CAMP RESORT.
(608) 996-2201. **4P $20-$40, XP $6.** 11354 CR X, 53801. 1.3 mi n.

**ELKHART LAKE** — PLYMOUTH ROCK CAMPING RESORT.
(920) 892-4252. **Call for rates.** N7271 Lando St, 53073. 3 mi s on SR 67,
4 mi n of Plymouth. (PO Box 445, 53020).

**FORT ATKINSON** — JELLYSTONE PARK OF FORT ATKINSON.
(920) 568-4100. **4P $24-$34, XP $5-$9.** N 551 Wishing Well Dr, 53538. 5
mi s on SR 26 from jct US 12, 0.8 mi w on Koshkonong Lake Rd, then just
s. Small pets allowed.

**FREMONT** — YOGI BEAR'S JELLYSTONE PARK CAMP RESORT.
(920) 446-3420. **Call for rates.** E 6506 Hwy 110, 54940. On SR 110 N, 1.5
mi w. (PO Box 497).

**WARRENS** — YOGI BEAR'S JELLYSTONE PARK CAMP RESORT.
(608) 378-4977. **Call for rates.** 1500 Jellystone Park Dr, 54666. I-94, exit
135, 0.5 mi e.

**WISCONSIN DELLS** — YOGI BEAR'S JELLYSTONE PARK
CAMP-RESORT ⒶⒶⒶ (608) 254-2568. **4P $19-$99, XP $5-$10.** I-90/94,
exit 89 eastbound; exit 92 westbound, follow signs. (PO Box 510, 53965).

# CANADA

## Alberta

**CALGARY** — PINE CREEK R.V. CAMPGROUND. (403) 256-3002. **2P $27-$34, XP $2.** 3.1 km s on Hwy 2A from Hwy 22X overpass. (PO Box 174, DE WINTON, T0L 0X0).

**EDMONTON** — GLOWING EMBERS TRAVEL CENTRE & RV PARK (780) 962-8100. **4P $28-$32, XP $1.** 26309 Hwy 16A, T7X 5A6. 3 km w of city limits; 1.8 km sw from Devon exit (Hwy 60 S), follow signs.

**HINTON** — HINTON/JASPER KOA (780) 865-5062, off season (403) 288-8351. **2P $20-$38, XP $3-$5.** Hwy 16, T9B 1X3. On Hwy 16, 4 km w. (4720 Vegas Rd NW, CALGARY, T3A 1W3).

**OKOTOKS** — COUNTRY LANE RV PARK (403) 995-2330. **Call for rates.** E on Hwy 7 and 2A: jct Hwys 2, 7 and 2A. (PO Box 1530, T1S 1B4).

**PINE LAKE** — LEISURE CAMPGROUNDS. (403) 886-4705. **Call for rates.** On Hwy 42, 2.6 km e off Hwy 2. (PO Box 68, T0M 1S0).

**SUNDRE** — TALL TIMBER LEISURE PARK. (403) 638-3555. **Call for rates.** 1 km e of Centre St on Main Ave E (Hwy 27 E). (PO Box 210, T0M 1X0).

## British Columbia

**BURNABY** — BURNABY CARIBOO R.V. PARK (604) 420-1722. **2P $30-$45, XP $3-$5.** 8765 Cariboo Pl, V3N 4T2. Trans-Canada Hwy 1, exit 37 (Cariboo Rd), follow signs.

**CAMPBELL RIVER** — RIPPLE ROCK RV PARK. (250) 287-7108. **2P $25-$33, XP $3.** 15011 Browns Bay Rd, V9H 1N9. Jct Hwy 19A, 28 and 19, 19 km n on Hwy 19, then 4.5 km e.

**FAIRMONT HOT SPRINGS** — FAIRMONT HOT SPRINGS RV PARK. (250) 345-6033. **$22-$41.** 1.6 km e off Hwy 93 and 95; adjacent to Fairmont Hot Springs Resort. (PO Box 10, V0B 1L0).

**MALAHAT** — VICTORIA WEST KOA. (250) 478-3332. **2P $30-$33, XP $4-$6.** On Trans-Canada Hwy 1 (Malahat Dr), 25.6 km n of Victoria. (PO Box 103).

**OLIVER** — DESERT GEM RV RESORT (250) 498-5544. **2P $17-$31, XP $5.** 34037 Hwy 97, V0H 1T0. 1 km s from 342nd Ave. (PO Box 400).

**SURREY** — PEACE ARCH RV PARK. (604) 594-7009. **2P $23-$30, XP $3.** 14601 40th Ave, V3S 0L2. Hwy 99, exit 10, follow signs.

**WHISTLER** — RIVERSIDE RV RESORT AND CAMPGROUND. (604) 905-5533. **Call for rates.** 8018 Mons Rd, V0N 1B8. From Hwy 99 (Whistler Village), exit Blackcomb Way, 1.5 km n, follow signs. Small pets allowed.

## New Brunswick

**WOODSTOCK** — YOGI BEAR'S JELLYSTONE PARK AT KOZY ACRES. (506) 328-6287. **5P $30-$38, XP $5-$6.** Trans-Canada Hwy 2, exit 191 (Beardsley Rd). (PO Box 9004, E7M 6B5).

## Nova Scotia

**BADDECK** — BADDECK-CABOT TRAIL CAMPGROUND & GOOD SAM PARK (902) 295-2288. **4P $22-$30, XP $3-$4.** 9584 Trans-Canada Hwy 105, B0E 1B0. 8 km w. (PO Box 417).

## Ontario

**AMHERSTBURG** — YOGI BEAR JELLYSTONE PARK CAMP RESORTS. (519) 736-3201. **Call for rates.** 4610 County Rd 18, RR 1, N9V 2Y7. 4 km e on Pike Rd (Simco St).

**BRADFORD** — YOGI BEAR'S JELLYSTONE PARK & CAMP-RESORT (905) 775-1377. **2P $32-$43, XP $6-$8.** 3666 Simcoe Rd 88, L3Z 2A4. Hwy 400, exit 64B, jct Hwy 400 and Simcoe Rd 88. (RR 1, 3666 Simcoe Rd 88). Small pets allowed.

**FOREST** — OUR PONDEROSA FAMILY CAMPGROUND & GOLF RESORT. (519) 786-2031. **$35-$44.** 9338 W Ipperwash Rd, N0N 1J0. 3 km n on W Ipperwash Rd from jct CR 7. (RR 2).

**KINCARDINE** — FISHERMAN'S COVE TENT & TRAILER PARK LTD. (519) 395-2757. **$30-$36, XP $3-$4.** 13 Southline Ave, N2Z 2X5. Jct Hwy 21 and 9, 17.7 km e to Kinloss, then 3 km s; follow signs. (RR 4).

**KITCHENER** — BINGEMANS. (519) 744-1002. **6P $30-$45, XP $6.** 425 Bingemans Centre Dr, N2B 3X7. 5.6 km n on Hwy 7, 1.6 km e of jct Hwy 7 and Conestoga Pkwy (Hwy 86).

**NIAGARA FALLS** — CAMPARK RESORTS (CAA) (905) 358-3873. **2P $33-$42, XP $3-$5.** 9387 Lundy's Ln, L2E 6S4. 6.3 km w of falls on Hwy 20.

**NIAGARA FALLS** — NIAGARA FALLS KOA KAMPGROUND. (905) 356-2267. **2P $38-$75, XP $5-$8.** 8625 Lundy's Ln, L2H 1H5. 5.6 km w on Hwy 20.

**SAUBLE BEACH** — CARSON'S CAMP LTD. (519) 422-1143. **2P $26-$38, XP $3-$7. (no credit cards).** 110 Southampton Pkwy, N0H 2G0. 1 km s on CR 13. (Rt 1).

**SAUBLE BEACH** — WOODLAND PARK. (519) 422-1161. **2P $30-$50, XP $3-$10.** 47 Sauble Falls Pkwy, RR 1, N0H 2G0. 1 km n on CR 13.

# Québec

**LEVIS** — KOA-QUEBEC CITY. (418) 831-1813. **2P $29-$39, XP $3-$5.** 684 chemin Olivier, G7A 2N6. Hwy 20, exit 311, 1.5 km w, northside service road; in St-Nicolas sector.

**ST-LIBOIRE** — CAMPING PLAGE LA LIBERTE. (450) 793-2716. **$23-$26, XP $5.** 129 Rang Charlotte, J0H 1R0. Hwy 20, exit 147, 0.5 km s.

**ST-MATHIEU-DE-BELOEIL** — CAMPING ALOUETTE (CAA) (450) 464-1661. **2P $27-$36, XP $3.** 3449 de l'Industrie, J3G 4S5. Hwy 20, exit 105; follow signs.

**STE-SABINE** — CAMPING CARAVELLE. (450) 293-7637. **2P $23-$29, XP $2. (no credit cards).** 180 Rang de la Gare, J0J 2B0. Jct Rt 104, 4.7 km s on Rt 235, then 0.8 km w on Rang de la Gare; 6 km s of Farnham.